UNIVERSITY CASEBOOK SERIES®

HART AND WECHSLER'S

THE FEDERAL COURTS AND THE FEDERAL SYSTEM

EIGHTH EDITION

WILLIAM BAUDE
Harry Kalven, Jr. Professor of Law
University of Chicago Law School

JACK GOLDSMITH
Learned Hand Professor of Law
Harvard Law School

JOHN F. MANNING
Harvard University Provost
Dane Professor of Law
Harvard Law School

JAMES E. PFANDER
Owen L. Coon Professor of Law
Northwestern University Pritzker School of Law

AMANDA L. TYLER
Shannon Cecil Turner Professor of Law
University of California, Berkeley School of Law

FOUNDATION
PRESS

University Casebook Series is a trademark registered in the U.S. Patent and Trademark Office.

© 1953, 1973, 1988, 1996, 2003 FOUNDATION PRESS
© 2009 By THOMSON REUTERS/FOUNDATION PRESS
© 2015 LEG, Inc. d/b/a West Academic
© 2025 LEG, Inc. d/b/a West Academic
   860 Blue Gentian Road, Suite 350
   Eagan, MN 55121
   1-877-888-1330

Published in the United States of America

ISBN: 978-1-68467-897-6

We dedicate this edition to Richard H. Fallon, Jr., whose brilliant mind, extraordinary scholarship, and gentle ways have influenced this field and his many students so profoundly.

PREFACE TO THE EIGHTH EDITION

I

In this Eighth Edition we have tried above all to carry on the great intellectual and scholarly tradition bequeathed to us by the authors of the First Edition, Henry Hart and Herbert Wechsler, and sustained by successive editors. As in previous editions, we have kept up with developments in the Supreme Court, provided relevant background, and called attention to important scholarship.

We have also worked hard to make this edition as user-friendly and teachable as possible. In a number of places, we have prefaced leading cases with brief introductory notes, to explain to students how cases and materials that they are about to read fit into an emerging historical or doctrinal picture. We have trimmed and in some instances eliminated discussions of old cases of decreasing relevance. The Notes continue to probe the most challenging problems that lawyers, judges, and lawmakers confront.

We have continued the policy of recent editions of relegating to footnotes material that we have included in the book primarily for those interested in pursuing further research.

As part of our commitment to continuity, we have retained the core structure of the previous edition and have retained most (but not all) of the principal cases. We have omitted, however, what in the Seventh Edition were Chapters XII and XIII. We have moved large amounts of material from both chapters to other chapters (primarily Chapters VIII and XI, respectively). And we have changed the title and content of Chapter III. Drawing on material in prior editions, it now analyzes the Supreme Court's docket as a whole, including expanded coverage on certiorari and other elements of the Supreme Court's appellate jurisdiction and the use of extraordinary writs. It also contains new treatment of the Court's emergency orders.

II

Beyond our elimination of two chapters and the expansion of Chapter III, developments since the publication of the Seventh Edition have occasioned several significant changes in our selection and organization of materials. Harkening back to earlier editions, we have included excerpts from the Federalist Papers in Chapter I, and added excerpts from essays penned by Brutus to which the Federalist Papers were responding. Significant evolution in the law of standing and ripeness has led to the inclusion of many new principal cases in Chapter II, including Clapper v. Amnesty International (2013), California v. Texas (2021), TransUnion v. Ramirez (2021), and Susan B. Anthony List v. Driehaus (2014), as well as extensively revised notes including more emphasis on the issues of causation and redressability. New principal cases in the expanded Chapter III include Singleton v. Commissioner of Internal Revenue (1978), Ex parte Bollman (1807), Ex parte Republic of

Peru (1943), and several opinions in connection with emergency orders. Chapter IV adds Ex parte Yerger (1868), United States v. Klein (1871), Patchak v. Zinke (2018), Oil States Energy v. Greene's Energy Group (2018), and Haywood v. Drown (2009). Chapter V now includes NAACP v. Alabama ex rel. Patterson (1958) as a principal case. United States v. Hudson & Goodwin (1812) is moved from Chapter VII to Chapter VI, which also now has Grupo Mexicano de Desarrollo, S.A. v. Alliance Bond Fund, Inc. (1999) as a principal case. Chapter VII adds three principal cases: O'Melveny & Myers v. Federal Deposit Insurance Corp. (2008), Hernández v. Mesa (2020), and Sosa v. Alvarez-Machain (2008). Chapter VIII's now-unified discussion of subject matter jurisdiction contains several new principal cases on the nature of jurisdiction, and on the scope of admiralty jurisdiction. Chapter IX updates the treatment of federal equity in light of Whole Woman's Health v. Jackson (2021) and Armstrong v. Exceptional Child Center, Inc. (2015), which are both now principal cases, and includes new material on universal injunctions and tribal sovereign immunity as well as other new principal cases. Chapter X reorganizes the material on judicial federalism and adds a new principal case on the Anti-Injunction Act. We have also undertaken revisions in Chapter XI's habeas corpus materials on executive detention, reorganizing the materials and adding discussion of, among other things, the mass incarceration of Japanese Americans during World War II. In Chapter XI, we also have updated the coverage of collateral habeas corpus review in light of extensive recent developments, added Montgomery v. Louisiana (2016) as a principal case, and incorporated discussion of the relationship between habeas corpus and 42 U.S.C. § 1983 that was previously in Chapter XII. Other, smaller changes occur throughout the book.

In making these and other revisions, we have benefited immeasurably from comments and suggestions by a number of colleagues and friends. Our thanks go to Rachel Bayefsky, A.J. Bellia, Erwin Chemerinsky, Brad Clark, Brian Fitzpatrick, Willy Fletcher, Kellen Funk, Myriam Gilles, Vicki Jackson, Genevieve Lakier, Leah Litman, Bruce Markell, Henry Monaghan, Richard Re, Elizabeth Reese, Alex Reinert, Stephen Sachs, Randall Schmidt, Thomas Schmidt, Joanna Schwartz, Catherine Struve, Carlos Vázquez, Steve Vladeck, Howard Wasserman, Larry Yackle, and Ernest Young.

III

No two instructors using this book are likely to select the same materials for study, but all must make choices in compiling their syllabi. We therefore offer some brief comments about the possible contents of a three- or four-(or more) credit course. Chapter I provides important background reading, but none of us devotes class time to discussion of its contents. In three-or four-credit courses, each of us teaches some of Chapter II, primarily in the section on standing, but we also rely on exposure to issues of justiciability in courses on Civil Procedure,

Constitutional Law, and Administrative Law. Each of us teaches some aspects of Chapter III, typically Section 2 on the Supreme Court's original jurisdiction and/or Section 4 on the Court's Emergency Docket. We all teach substantial portions of Chapter IV, involving congressional control of judicial jurisdiction. (Section 2, relating to non-judicial federal tribunals, is challenging and important, but some find it does not fit in its entirety in a three-credit course.) We often cover Sections 1 and 2 of Chapter V (Supreme Court review of state court judgments); dip into Chapters VI (discussing at least the Erie decision), VII (federal common law), VIII (subject matter jurisdiction), and X (dealing with limitations on federal jurisdiction or its exercise); and assign much of Chapter IX (suits against federal and state governments and their officials). Chapter XI on habeas corpus may either be taught as a unit or divided by focusing on collateral federal review of state court decisions in conjunction with Chapter V, on direct review.

In four-credit courses (or for those with the even greater luxury of five or six credits), the opportunity exists to delve more deeply into each of these topics, including the portion of Chapter XI on executive detention and the war on terrorism.

IV

Although every chapter is the product of extensive review and comment among the five authors, primary responsibility is divided among us as follows:

Baude	Chapters II, VIII (§§ 5, 6)
Goldsmith	Chapters III, VI, VII
Manning	Chapter IV
Pfander	Chapters VIII (§§ 1–4; 7–8), IX, X
Tyler	Chapters I, V, XI

V

A few notes on form and related matters: In many instances, we adhere not to the Bluebook but largely to the style of previous editions.[1] With respect to principal cases and quotations in our Notes, no indication of omitted footnotes or citations is normally given; those footnotes that have been retained carry their original numbers. All other omissions, whether of a few words, a paragraph, or several pages, are indicated by spaced asterisks.

Several of the authors of this and prior editions took part in various ways as counsel or amici curiae in some of the cases in this book. As in

---

[1] For example, we do not use first names of authors, unless necessary to avoid confusion; we do not italicize case names (or case "nicknames") in either text or footnotes, and we do not indicate that certiorari was denied except in the few instances where it has special relevance. We have, however, decided at long last in this edition to discontinue adherence in our own text to the British practice of putting inside a quote only that punctuation that is part of the quote.

prior editions, we concluded that it would constitute an excess of caution to advert, in each case, to such participation. We believe that our editorial process has fairly guarded us against resulting bias (or undue leaning over backwards).

VI

We are grateful to a number of our present and former students for their research and for invaluable assistance in connection with this edition: Madilyn Abbe, Samy Abdelsalam, Andrew Albright, Areeb Asif, Gabriel Blacklock, Gene Chang, Djenab Conde, Melissa Cordial, John Czubek, Addison Eisley, Lana El-Farra, Thomas Gergely, Matthew Gluck, Connie Gong, Wesley Hardin, Will Horvath, Yeju Hwang, Tom Koenig, Erin Kramer, Sophie Li, James Marmaduke, Lydia McVeigh, Levi Moneyhun, Rachel Mucha, Chris Nardi, Chloe Pan, Joseph Partain, Sarah Patrick, Matt Phillips, Akhil Rajasekar, Samuel Goldman Reiss, Quinten Rimolde, Jonathan Rosenthal, Georgios Sarris, Brandon Stras, Mark Thomas, Jordan Varberg, and Jeremiah Vroegop. Many other students helped us in other ways over the years that we prepared this edition, and we thank them as well. Our thanks go also to Jane Brock, Jennifer McBride, Deema Qashat, and Thea Rood for their splendid administrative assistance, and to the Library Reference Staff at our home institutions for their help on a number of difficult problems.

VII

This Eighth Edition marks a new chapter in the history of this book, as we add new editors and honor those who have come before us. Since publication of the last edition, both Daniel Meltzer (in 2015) and David Shapiro (in 2019) have passed away. Dan served as an editor of this book from the Third through the Seventh Editions, and David served as an editor of this book from its Second through its Seventh Editions. Further, in 2022, Richard Fallon retired as an editor of the book, having served in that role from the Fourth through the Seventh Editions. The new editors who joined the book in 2016 (Jack Goldsmith and Amanda Tyler) and 2022 (William Baude and James Pfander) have prepared this edition humbled by the shoes into which they have stepped.

W.P.B.
J.G.
J.F.M.
J.E.P.
A.L.T.

July 2024

SUMMARY OF CONTENTS

TABLE OF CONTENTS

TABLE OF CASES

The principal cases are in bold type.

TABLE OF AUTHORITIES

THE CONSTITUTION OF THE UNITED STATES OF AMERICA

We the people of the United States, in order to form a more perfect union, establish justice, insure domestic tranquility, provide for the common defense, promote the general welfare, and secure the blessings of liberty to ourselves and our posterity, do ordain and establish this Constitution for the United States of America.

Article I

Section 1. All legislative powers herein granted shall be vested in a Congress of the United States, which shall consist of a Senate and House of Representatives.

Section 2. [1] The House of Representatives shall be composed of members chosen every second year by the people of the several states, and the electors in each state shall have the qualifications requisite for electors of the most numerous branch of the state legislature.

[2] No person shall be a Representative who shall not have attained to the age of twenty five years, and been seven years a citizen of the United States, and who shall not, when elected, be an inhabitant of that state in which he shall be chosen.

[3] Representatives and direct taxes shall be apportioned among the several states which may be included within this union, according to their respective numbers, which shall be determined by adding to the whole number of free persons, including those bound to service for a term of years, and excluding Indians not taxed, three fifths of all other Persons. The actual Enumeration shall be made within three years after the first meeting of the Congress of the United States, and within every subsequent term of ten years, in such manner as they shall by law direct. The number of Representatives shall not exceed one for every thirty thousand, but each state shall have at least one Representative; and until such enumeration shall be made, the state of New Hampshire shall be entitled to chuse three, Massachusetts eight, Rhode Island and Providence Plantations one, Connecticut five, New York six, New Jersey four, Pennsylvania eight, Delaware one, Maryland six, Virginia ten, North Carolina five, South Carolina five, and Georgia three.

[4] When vacancies happen in the Representation from any state, the executive authority thereof shall issue writs of election to fill such vacancies.

[5] The House of Representatives shall choose their speaker and other officers; and shall have the sole power of impeachment.

Section 3. [1] The Senate of the United States shall be composed of two Senators from each state, chosen by the legislature thereof, for six years; and each Senator shall have one vote.

[2] Immediately after they shall be assembled in consequence of the first election, they shall be divided as equally as may be into three classes. The seats of the Senators of the first class shall be vacated at the expiration of the second year, of the second class at the expiration of the fourth year, and the third class at the expiration of the sixth year, so that one third may be chosen every second year; and if vacancies happen by resignation, or otherwise, during the recess of the legislature of any state, the executive thereof may make temporary appointments until the next meeting of the legislature, which shall then fill such vacancies.

[3] No person shall be a Senator who shall not have attained to the age of thirty years, and been nine years a citizen of the United States and who shall not, when elected, be an inhabitant of that state for which he shall be chosen.

[4] The Vice President of the United States shall be President of the Senate, but shall have no vote, unless they be equally divided.

[5] The Senate shall choose their other officers, and also a President pro tempore, in the absence of the Vice President, or when he shall exercise the office of President of the United States.

[6] The Senate shall have the sole power to try all impeachments. When sitting for that purpose, they shall be on oath or affirmation. When the President of the United States is tried, the Chief Justice shall preside: And no person shall be convicted without the concurrence of two thirds of the members present.

[7] Judgment in cases of impeachment shall not extend further than to removal from office, and disqualification to hold and enjoy any office of honor, trust or profit under the United States: but the party convicted shall nevertheless be liable and subject to indictment, trial, judgment and punishment, according to law.

Section 4. [1] The times, places and manner of holding elections for Senators and Representatives, shall be prescribed in each state by the legislature thereof; but the Congress may at any time by law make or alter such regulations, except as to the places of choosing Senators.

[2] The Congress shall assemble at least once in every year, and such meeting shall be on the first Monday in December, unless they shall by law appoint a different day.

Section 5. [1] Each House shall be the judge of the elections, returns and qualifications of its own members, and a majority of each shall constitute a quorum to do business; but a smaller number may adjourn from day to day, and may be authorized to compel the attendance of absent members, in such manner, and under such penalties as each House may provide.

[2] Each House may determine the rules of its proceedings, punish its members for disorderly behavior, and, with the concurrence of two thirds, expel a member.

[3] Each House shall keep a journal of its proceedings, and from time to time publish the same, excepting such parts as may in their judgment require secrecy; and the yeas and nays of the members of either House on any question shall, at the desire of one fifth of those present, be entered on the journal.

[4] Neither House, during the session of Congress, shall, without the consent of the other, adjourn for more than three days, nor to any other place than that in which the two Houses shall be sitting.

Section 6. [1] The Senators and Representatives shall receive a compensation for their services, to be ascertained by law, and paid out of the treasury of the United States. They shall in all cases, except treason, felony and breach of the peace, be privileged from arrest during their attendance at the session of their respective Houses, and in going to and returning from the same; and for any speech or debate in either House, they shall not be questioned in any other place.

[2] No Senator or Representative shall, during the time for which he was elected, be appointed to any civil office under the authority of the United States, which shall have been created, or the emoluments whereof shall have been increased during such time: and no person holding any office under the United States, shall be a member of either House during his continuance in office.

Section 7. [1] All bills for raising revenue shall originate in the House of Representatives; but the Senate may propose or concur with amendments as on other Bills.

[2] Every bill which shall have passed the House of Representatives and the Senate, shall, before it become a law, be presented to the President of the United States; if he approve he shall sign it, but if not he shall return it, with his objections to that House in which it shall have originated, who shall enter the objections at large on their journal, and proceed to reconsider it. If after such reconsideration two thirds of that House shall agree to pass the bill, it shall be sent, together with the objections, to the other House, by which it shall likewise be reconsidered, and if approved by two thirds of that House, it shall become a law. But in all such cases the votes of both Houses shall be determined by yeas and nays, and the names of the persons voting for and against the bill shall be entered on the journal of each House respectively. If any bill shall not be returned by the President within ten days (Sundays excepted) after it shall have been presented to him, the same shall be a law, in like manner as if he had signed it, unless the Congress by their adjournment prevent its return, in which case it shall not be a law.

[3] Every order, resolution, or vote to which the concurrence of the Senate and House of Representatives may be necessary (except on a question of adjournment) shall be presented to the President of the United States; and before the same shall take effect, shall be approved by him, or being disapproved by him, shall be repassed by two thirds of the Senate and House of Representatives, according to the rules and limitations prescribed in the case of a bill.

Section 8. [1] The Congress shall have power to lay and collect taxes, duties, imposts and excises, to pay the debts and provide for the common defense and general welfare of the United States; but all duties, imposts and excises shall be uniform throughout the United States;

[2] To borrow money on the credit of the United States;

[3] To regulate commerce with foreign nations, and among the several states, and with the Indian tribes;

[4] To establish a uniform rule of naturalization, and uniform laws on the subject of bankruptcies throughout the United States;

[5] To coin money, regulate the value thereof, and of foreign coin, and fix the standard of weights and measures;

[6] To provide for the punishment of counterfeiting the securities and current coin of the United States;

[7] To establish post offices and post roads;

[8] To promote the progress of science and useful arts, by securing for limited times to authors and inventors the exclusive right to their respective writings and discoveries;

[9] To constitute tribunals inferior to the Supreme Court;

[10] To define and punish piracies and felonies committed on the high seas, and offenses against the law of nations;

[11] To declare war, grant letters of marque and reprisal, and make rules concerning captures on land and water;

[12] To raise and support armies, but no appropriation of money to that use shall be for a longer term than two years;

[13] To provide and maintain a navy;

[14] To make rules for the government and regulation of the land and naval forces;

[15] To provide for calling forth the militia to execute the laws of the union, suppress insurrections and repel invasions;

[16] To provide for organizing, arming, and disciplining, the militia, and for governing such part of them as may be employed in the service of the United States, reserving to the states respectively, the appointment of the officers, and the authority of training the militia according to the discipline prescribed by Congress;

[17] To exercise exclusive legislation in all cases whatsoever, over such District (not exceeding ten miles square) as may, by cession of particular states, and the acceptance of Congress, become the seat of the government of the United States, and to exercise like authority over all places purchased by the consent of the legislature of the state in which the same shall be, for the erection of forts, magazines, arsenals, dockyards, and other needful buildings;—And

[18] To make all laws which shall be necessary and proper for carrying into execution the foregoing powers, and all other powers vested by this Constitution in the government of the United States, or in any department or officer thereof.

Section 9. [1] The migration or importation of such persons as any of the states now existing shall think proper to admit, shall not be prohibited by the Congress prior to the year one thousand eight hundred and eight, but a tax or duty may be imposed on such importation, not exceeding ten dollars for each person.

[2] The privilege of the writ of habeas corpus shall not be suspended, unless when in cases of rebellion or invasion the public safety may require it.

[3] No bill of attainder or ex post facto Law shall be passed.

[4] No capitation, or other direct, tax shall be laid, unless in proportion to the census or enumeration herein before directed to be taken.

[5] No tax or duty shall be laid on articles exported from any state.

[6] No preference shall be given by any regulation of commerce or revenue to the ports of one state over those of another: nor shall vessels bound to, or from, one state, be obliged to enter, clear or pay duties in another.

[7] No money shall be drawn from the treasury, but in consequence of appropriations made by law; and a regular statement and account of receipts and expenditures of all public money shall be published from time to time.

[8] No title of nobility shall be granted by the United States: and no person holding any office of profit or trust under them, shall, without the consent of the Congress, accept of any present, emolument, office, or title, of any kind whatever, from any king, prince, or foreign state.

Section 10. [1] No state shall enter into any treaty, alliance, or confederation; grant letters of marque and reprisal; coin money; emit bills of credit; make anything but gold and silver coin a tender in payment of debts; pass any bill of attainder, ex post facto law, or law impairing the obligation of contracts, or grant any title of nobility.

[2] No state shall, without the consent of the Congress, lay any imposts or duties on imports or exports, except what may be absolutely

necessary for executing it's inspection laws: and the net produce of all duties and imposts, laid by any state on imports or exports, shall be for the use of the treasury of the United States; and all such laws shall be subject to the revision and control of the Congress.

[3] No state shall, without the consent of Congress, lay any duty of tonnage, keep troops, or ships of war in time of peace, enter into any agreement or compact with another state, or with a foreign power, or engage in war, unless actually invaded, or in such imminent danger as will not admit of delay.

Article II

Section 1. [1] The executive power shall be vested in a President of the United States of America. He shall hold his office during the term of four years, and, together with the Vice President, chosen for the same term, be elected, as follows:

[2] Each state shall appoint, in such manner as the Legislature thereof may direct, a number of electors, equal to the whole number of Senators and Representatives to which the State may be entitled in the Congress: but no Senator or Representative, or person holding an office of trust or profit under the United States, shall be appointed an elector.

[3] The electors shall meet in their respective states, and vote by ballot for two persons, of whom one at least shall not be an inhabitant of the same state with themselves. And they shall make a list of all the persons voted for, and of the number of votes for each; which list they shall sign and certify, and transmit sealed to the seat of the government of the United States, directed to the President of the Senate. The President of the Senate shall, in the presence of the Senate and House of Representatives, open all the certificates, and the votes shall then be counted. The person having the greatest number of votes shall be the President, if such number be a majority of the whole number of electors appointed; and if there be more than one who have such majority, and have an equal number of votes, then the House of Representatives shall immediately choose by ballot one of them for President; and if no person have a majority, then from the five highest on the list the said House shall in like manner choose the President. But in choosing the President, the votes shall be taken by States, the representation from each state having one vote; A quorum for this purpose shall consist of a member or members from two thirds of the states, and a majority of all the states shall be necessary to a choice. In every case, after the choice of the President, the person having the greatest number of votes of the electors shall be the Vice President. But if there should remain two or more who have equal votes, the Senate shall choose from them by ballot the Vice President.

[4] The Congress may determine the time of choosing the electors, and the day on which they shall give their votes; which day shall be the same throughout the United States.

[5] No person except a natural born citizen, or a citizen of the United States, at the time of the adoption of this Constitution, shall be eligible to the office of President; neither shall any person be eligible to that office who shall not have attained to the age of thirty five years, and been fourteen Years a resident within the United States.

[6] In case of the removal of the President from office, or of his death, resignation, or inability to discharge the powers and duties of the said office, the same shall devolve on the Vice President, and the Congress may by law provide for the case of removal, death, resignation or inability, both of the President and Vice President, declaring what officer shall then act as President, and such officer shall act accordingly, until the disability be removed, or a President shall be elected.

[7] The President shall, at stated times, receive for his services, a compensation, which shall neither be increased nor diminished during the period for which he shall have been elected, and he shall not receive within that period any other emolument from the United States, or any of them.

[8] Before he enter on the execution of his office, he shall take the following oath or affirmation:—'I do solemnly swear (or affirm) that I will faithfully execute the office of President of the United States, and will to the best of my ability, preserve, protect and defend the Constitution of the United States.'

Section 2. [1] The President shall be commander in chief of the Army and Navy of the United States, and of the militia of the several states, when called into the actual service of the United States; he may require the opinion, in writing, of the principal officer in each of the executive departments, upon any subject relating to the duties of their respective offices, and he shall have power to grant reprieves and pardons for offenses against the United States, except in cases of impeachment.

[2] He shall have power, by and with the advice and consent of the Senate, to make treaties, provided two thirds of the Senators present concur; and he shall nominate, and by and with the advice and consent of the Senate, shall appoint ambassadors, other public ministers and consuls, judges of the Supreme Court, and all other officers of the United States, whose appointments are not herein otherwise provided for, and which shall be established by law: but the Congress may by law vest the appointment of such inferior officers, as they think proper, in the President alone, in the courts of law, or in the heads of departments.

[3] The President shall have power to fill up all vacancies that may happen during the recess of the Senate, by granting commissions which shall expire at the end of their next session.

Section 3. He shall from time to time give to the Congress information of the state of the union, and recommend to their consideration such measures as he shall judge necessary and expedient;

he may, on extraordinary occasions, convene both Houses, or either of them, and in case of disagreement between them, with respect to the time of adjournment, he may adjourn them to such time as he shall think proper; he shall receive ambassadors and other public ministers; he shall take care that the laws be faithfully executed, and shall commission all the officers of the United States.

Section 4. The President, Vice President and all civil officers of the United States, shall be removed from office on impeachment for, and conviction of, treason, bribery, or other high crimes and misdemeanors.

Article III

Section 1. The judicial power of the United States, shall be vested in one Supreme Court, and in such inferior courts as the Congress may from time to time ordain and establish. The judges, both of the supreme and inferior courts, shall hold their offices during good behaviour, and shall, at stated times, receive for their services, a compensation, which shall not be diminished during their continuance in office.

Section 2. [1] The judicial power shall extend to all cases, in law and equity, arising under this Constitution, the laws of the United States, and treaties made, or which shall be made, under their authority;—to all cases affecting ambassadors, other public ministers and consuls;—to all cases of admiralty and maritime jurisdiction;—to controversies to which the United States shall be a party;—to controversies between two or more states;—between a state and citizens of another state;—between citizens of different states;—between citizens of the same state claiming lands under grants of different states, and between a state, or the citizens thereof, and foreign states, citizens or subjects.

[2] In all cases affecting ambassadors, other public ministers and consuls, and those in which a state shall be party, the Supreme Court shall have original jurisdiction. In all the other cases before mentioned, the Supreme Court shall have appellate jurisdiction, both as to law and fact, with such exceptions, and under such regulations as the Congress shall make.

[3] The trial of all crimes, except in cases of impeachment, shall be by jury; and such trial shall be held in the state where the said crimes shall have been committed; but when not committed within any state, the trial shall be at such place or places as the Congress may by law have directed.

Section 3. [1] Treason against the United States, shall consist only in levying war against them, or in adhering to their enemies, giving them aid and comfort. No person shall be convicted of treason unless on the testimony of two witnesses to the same overt act, or on confession in open court.

[2] The Congress shall have power to declare the punishment of treason, but no attainder of treason shall work corruption of blood, or forfeiture except during the life of the person attainted.

Article IV

Section 1. Full faith and credit shall be given in each state to the public acts, records, and judicial proceedings of every other state. And the Congress may by general laws prescribe the manner in which such acts, records, and proceedings shall be proved, and the effect thereof.

Section 2. [1] The citizens of each state shall be entitled to all privileges and immunities of citizens in the several states.

[2] A person charged in any state with treason, felony, or other crime, who shall flee from justice, and be found in another state, shall on demand of the executive authority of the state from which he fled, be delivered up, to be removed to the state having jurisdiction of the crime.

[3] No person held to service or labor in one state, under the laws thereof, escaping into another, shall, in consequence of any law or regulation therein, be discharged from such service or labor, but shall be delivered up on claim of the party to whom such service or labor may be due.

Section 3. [1] New states may be admitted by the Congress into this union; but no new states shall be formed or erected within the jurisdiction of any other state; nor any state be formed by the junction of two or more states, or parts of states, without the consent of the legislatures of the states concerned as well as of the Congress.

[2] The Congress shall have power to dispose of and make all needful rules and regulations respecting the territory or other property belonging to the United States; and nothing in this Constitution shall be so construed as to prejudice any claims of the United States, or of any particular state.

Section 4. The United States shall guarantee to every state in this union a republican form of government, and shall protect each of them against invasion; and on application of the legislature, or of the executive (when the legislature cannot be convened) against domestic violence.

Article V

The Congress, whenever two thirds of both houses shall deem it necessary, shall propose amendments to this Constitution, or, on the application of the legislatures of two thirds of the several states, shall call a convention for proposing amendments, which, in either case, shall be valid to all intents and purposes, as part of this Constitution, when ratified by the legislatures of three fourths of the several states, or by conventions in three fourths thereof, as the one or the other mode of ratification may be proposed by the Congress; provided that no amendment which may be made prior to the year one thousand eight hundred and eight shall in any manner affect the first and fourth clauses in the ninth section of the first article; and that no state, without its consent, shall be deprived of its equal suffrage in the Senate.

Article VI

[1] All debts contracted and engagements entered into, before the adoption of this Constitution, shall be as valid against the United States under this Constitution, as under the Confederation.

[2] This Constitution, and the laws of the United States which shall be made in pursuance thereof; and all treaties made, or which shall be made, under the authority of the United States, shall be the supreme law of the land; and the judges in every state shall be bound thereby, anything in the Constitution or laws of any State to the contrary notwithstanding.

[3] The Senators and Representatives before mentioned, and the members of the several state legislatures, and all executive and judicial officers, both of the United States and of the several states, shall be bound by oath or affirmation, to support this Constitution; but no religious test shall ever be required as a qualification to any office or public trust under the United States.

Article VII

The ratification of the conventions of nine states, shall be sufficient for the establishment of this Constitution between the states so ratifying the same.

ARTICLES IN ADDITION TO, AND AMENDMENT OF, THE CONSTITUTION OF THE UNITED STATES OF AMERICA, PROPOSED BY CONGRESS, AND RATIFIED BY THE LEGISLATURES OF THE SEVERAL STATES PURSUANT TO THE FIFTH ARTICLE OF THE ORIGINAL CONSTITUTION.

Amendment I [1791]

Congress shall make no law respecting an establishment of religion, or prohibiting the free exercise thereof; or abridging the freedom of speech, or of the press; or the right of the people peaceably to assemble, and to petition the government for a redress of grievances.

Amendment II [1791]

A well regulated militia, being necessary to the security of a free state, the right of the people to keep and bear arms, shall not be infringed.

Amendment III [1791]

No soldier shall, in time of peace be quartered in any house, without the consent of the owner, nor in time of war, but in a manner to be prescribed by law.

Amendment IV [1791]

The right of the people to be secure in their persons, houses, papers, and effects, against unreasonable searches and seizures, shall not be violated, and no warrants shall issue, but upon probable cause, supported by oath or affirmation, and particularly describing the place to be searched, and the persons or things to be seized.

Amendment V [1791]

No person shall be held to answer for a capital, or otherwise infamous crime, unless on a presentment or indictment of a grand jury, except in cases arising in the land or naval forces, or in the militia, when in actual service in time of war or public danger; nor shall any person be subject for the same offense to be twice put in jeopardy of life or limb; nor shall be compelled in any criminal case to be a witness against himself, nor be deprived of life, liberty, or property, without due process of law; nor shall private property be taken for public use, without just compensation.

Amendment VI [1791]

In all criminal prosecutions, the accused shall enjoy the right to a speedy and public trial, by an impartial jury of the state and district wherein the crime shall have been committed, which district shall have been previously ascertained by law, and to be informed of the nature and cause of the accusation; to be confronted with the witnesses against him; to have compulsory process for obtaining witnesses in his favor, and to have the assistance of counsel for his defense.

Amendment VII [1791]

In suits at common law, where the value in controversy shall exceed twenty dollars, the right of trial by jury shall be preserved, and no fact tried by a jury, shall be otherwise reexamined in any court of the United States, than according to the rules of the common law.

Amendment VIII [1791]

Excessive bail shall not be required, nor excessive fines imposed, nor cruel and unusual punishments inflicted.

Amendment IX [1791]

The enumeration in the Constitution, of certain rights, shall not be construed to deny or disparage others retained by the people.

Amendment X [1791]

The powers not delegated to the United States by the Constitution, nor prohibited by it to the states, are reserved to the states respectively, or to the people.

Amendment XI [1798]

The judicial power of the United States shall not be construed to extend to any suit in law or equity, commenced or prosecuted against one of the United States by citizens of another state, or by citizens or subjects of any foreign state.

Amendment XII [1804]

The electors shall meet in their respective states and vote by ballot for President and Vice-President, one of whom, at least, shall not be an inhabitant of the same state with themselves; they shall name in their ballots the person voted for as President, and in distinct ballots the person voted for as Vice-President, and they shall make distinct lists of all persons voted for as President, and of all persons voted for as Vice-President, and of the number of votes for each, which lists they shall sign and certify, and transmit sealed to the seat of the government of the United States, directed to the President of the Senate;—The President of the Senate shall, in the presence of the Senate and House of Representatives, open all the certificates and the votes shall then be counted;—the person having the greatest number of votes for President, shall be the President, if such number be a majority of the whole number of electors appointed; and if no person have such majority, then from the persons having the highest numbers not exceeding three on the list of those voted for as President, the House of Representatives shall choose immediately, by ballot, the President. But in choosing the President, the votes shall be taken by states, the representation from each state having one vote; a quorum for this purpose shall consist of a member or members from two-thirds of the states, and a majority of all the states shall be necessary to a choice. And if the House of Representatives shall not choose a President whenever the right of choice shall devolve upon them, before the fourth day of March next following, then the Vice-President shall act as President, as in the case of the death or other constitutional disability of the President. The person having the greatest number of votes as Vice-President, shall be the Vice-President, if such number be a majority of the whole number of electors appointed, and if no person have a majority, then from the two highest numbers on the list, the Senate shall choose the Vice-President; a quorum for the purpose shall consist of two-thirds of the whole number of Senators, and a majority of the whole number shall be necessary to a choice. But no person constitutionally ineligible to the office of President shall be eligible to that of Vice-President of the United States.

Amendment XIII [1865]

Section 1. Neither slavery nor involuntary servitude, except as a punishment for crime whereof the party shall have been duly convicted, shall exist within the United States, or any place subject to their jurisdiction.

Section 2. Congress shall have power to enforce this article by appropriate legislation.

Amendment XIV [1868]

Section 1. All persons born or naturalized in the United States, and subject to the jurisdiction thereof, are citizens of the United States and of the state wherein they reside. No state shall make or enforce any law which shall abridge the privileges or immunities of citizens of the United States; nor shall any state deprive any person of life, liberty, or property, without due process of law; nor deny to any person within its jurisdiction the equal protection of the laws.

Section 2. Representatives shall be apportioned among the several states according to their respective numbers, counting the whole number of persons in each state, excluding Indians not taxed. But when the right to vote at any election for the choice of electors for President and Vice President of the United States, Representatives in Congress, the executive and judicial officers of a state, or the members of the legislature thereof, is denied to any of the male inhabitants of such state, being twenty-one years of age, and citizens of the United States, or in any way abridged, except for participation in rebellion, or other crime, the basis of representation therein shall be reduced in the proportion which the number of such male citizens shall bear to the whole number of male citizens twenty-one years of age in such state.

Section 3. No person shall be a Senator or Representative in Congress, or elector of President and Vice President, or hold any office, civil or military, under the United States, or under any state, who, having previously taken an oath, as a member of Congress, or as an officer of the United States, or as a member of any state legislature, or as an executive or judicial officer of any state, to support the Constitution of the United States, shall have engaged in insurrection or rebellion against the same, or given aid or comfort to the enemies thereof. But Congress may by a vote of two-thirds of each House, remove such disability.

Section 4. The validity of the public debt of the United States, authorized by law, including debts incurred for payment of pensions and bounties for services in suppressing insurrection or rebellion, shall not be questioned. But neither the United States nor any state shall assume or pay any debt or obligation incurred in aid of insurrection or rebellion against the United States, or any claim for the loss or emancipation of any slave; but all such debts, obligations and claims shall be held illegal and void.

Section 5. The Congress shall have power to enforce, by appropriate legislation, the provisions of this article.

Amendment XV [1870]

Section 1. The right of citizens of the United States to vote shall not be denied or abridged by the United States or by any state on account of race, color, or previous condition of servitude.

Section 2. The Congress shall have power to enforce this article by appropriate legislation.

Amendment XVI [1913]

The Congress shall have power to lay and collect taxes on incomes, from whatever source derived, without apportionment among the several states, and without regard to any census of enumeration.

Amendment XVII [1913]

[1] The Senate of the United States shall be composed of two Senators from each state, elected by the people thereof, for six years; and each Senator shall have one vote. The electors in each state shall have the qualifications requisite for electors of the most numerous branch of the state legislatures.

[2] When vacancies happen in the representation of any state in the Senate, the executive authority of such state shall issue writs of election to fill such vacancies: Provided, that the legislature of any state may empower the executive thereof to make temporary appointments until the people fill the vacancies by election as the legislature may direct.

[3] This amendment shall not be so construed as to affect the election or term of any Senator chosen before it becomes valid as part of the Constitution.

Amendment XVIII [1919]

Section 1. After one year from the ratification of this article the manufacture, sale, or transportation of intoxicating liquors within, the importation thereof into, or the exportation thereof from the United States and all territory subject to the jurisdiction thereof for beverage purposes is hereby prohibited.

Section 2. The Congress and the several states shall have concurrent power to enforce this article by appropriate legislation.

Section 3. This article shall be inoperative unless it shall have been ratified as an amendment to the Constitution by the legislatures of the several states, as provided in the Constitution, within seven years from the date of the submission hereof to the states by the Congress.

Amendment XIX [1920]

[1] The right of citizens of the United States to vote shall not be denied or abridged by the United States or by any state on account of sex.

[2] Congress shall have power to enforce this article by appropriate legislation.

Amendment XX [1933]

Section 1. The terms of the President and Vice President shall end at noon on the 20th day of January, and the terms of Senators and Representatives at noon on the 3d day of January, of the years in which such terms would have ended if this article had not been ratified; and the terms of their successors shall then begin.

Section 2. The Congress shall assemble at least once in every year, and such meeting shall begin at noon on the 3d day of January, unless they shall by law appoint a different day.

Section 3. If, at the time fixed for the beginning of the term of the President, the President elect shall have died, the Vice President elect shall become President. If a President shall not have been chosen before the time fixed for the beginning of his term, or if the President elect shall have failed to qualify, then the Vice President elect shall act as President until a President shall have qualified; and the Congress may by law provide for the case wherein neither a President elect nor a Vice President elect shall have qualified, declaring who shall then act as President, or the manner in which one who is to act shall be selected, and such person shall act accordingly until a President or Vice President shall have qualified.

Section 4. The Congress may by law provide for the case of the death of any of the persons from whom the House of Representatives may choose a President whenever the right of choice shall have devolved upon them, and for the case of the death of any of the persons from whom the Senate may choose a Vice President whenever the right of choice shall have devolved upon them.

Section 5. Sections 1 and 2 shall take effect on the 15th day of October following the ratification of this article.

Section 6. This article shall be inoperative unless it shall have been ratified as an amendment to the Constitution by the legislatures of three-fourths of the several states within seven years from the date of its submission.

Amendment XXI [1933]

Section 1. The eighteenth article of amendment to the Constitution of the United States is hereby repealed.

Section 2. The transportation or importation into any state, territory, or possession of the United States for delivery or use therein of intoxicating liquors, in violation of the laws thereof, is hereby prohibited.

Section 3. This article shall be inoperative unless it shall have been ratified as an amendment to the Constitution by conventions in the several states, as provided in the Constitution, within seven years from the date of the submission hereof to the states by the Congress.

Amendment XXII [1951]

Section 1. No person shall be elected to the office of the President more than twice, and no person who has held the office of President, or acted as President, for more than two years of a term to which some other person was elected President shall be elected to the office of the President more than once. But this article shall not apply to any person holding the office of President when this article was proposed by the Congress, and shall not prevent any person who may be holding the office of President, or acting as President, during the term within which this article becomes operative from holding the office of President or acting as President during the remainder of such term.

Section 2. This article shall be inoperative unless it shall have been ratified as an amendment to the Constitution by the legislatures of three-fourths of the several states within seven years from the date of its submission to the states by the Congress.

Amendment XXIII [1961]

Section 1. The District constituting the seat of government of the United States shall appoint in such manner as the Congress may direct:

A number of electors of President and Vice President equal to the whole number of Senators and Representatives in Congress to which the District would be entitled if it were a state, but in no event more than the least populous state; they shall be in addition to those appointed by the states, but they shall be considered, for the purposes of the election of President and Vice President, to be electors appointed by a state; and they shall meet in the District and perform such duties as provided by the twelfth article of amendment.

Section 2. The Congress shall have power to enforce this article by appropriate legislation.

Amendment XXIV [1964]

Section 1. The right of citizens of the United States to vote in any primary or other election for President or Vice President, for electors for President or Vice President, or for Senator or Representative in Congress, shall not be denied or abridged by the United States or any state by reason of failure to pay any poll tax or other tax.

Section 2. The Congress shall have power to enforce this article by appropriate legislation.

Amendment XXV [1967]

Section 1. In case of the removal of the President from office or of his death or resignation, the Vice President shall become President.

Section 2. Whenever there is a vacancy in the office of the Vice President, the President shall nominate a Vice President who shall take office upon confirmation by a majority vote of both Houses of Congress.

Section 3. Whenever the President transmits to the President pro tempore of the Senate and the Speaker of the House of Representatives his written declaration that he is unable to discharge the powers and duties of his office, and until he transmits to them a written declaration to the contrary, such powers and duties shall be discharged by the Vice President as Acting President.

Section 4. Whenever the Vice President and a majority of either the principal officers of the executive departments or of such other body as Congress may by law provide, transmit to the President pro tempore of the Senate and the Speaker of the House of Representatives their written declaration that the President is unable to discharge the powers and duties of his office, the Vice President shall immediately assume the powers and duties of the office as Acting President.

Thereafter, when the President transmits to the President pro tempore of the Senate and the Speaker of the House of Representatives his written declaration that no inability exists, he shall resume the powers and duties of his office unless the Vice President and a majority of either the principal officers of the executive department or of such other body as Congress may by law provide, transmit within four days to the President pro tempore of the Senate and the Speaker of the House of Representatives their written declaration that the President is unable to discharge the powers and duties of his office. Thereupon Congress shall decide the issue, assembling within forty-eight hours for that purpose if not in session. If the Congress, within twenty-one days after receipt of the latter written declaration, or, if Congress is not in session, within twenty-one days after Congress is required to assemble, determines by two-thirds vote of both Houses that the President is unable to discharge the powers and duties of his office, the Vice President shall continue to discharge the same as Acting President; otherwise, the President shall resume the powers and duties of his office.

Amendment XXVI [1971]

Section 1. The right of citizens of the United States, who are 18 years of age or older, to vote, shall not be denied or abridged by the United States or any state on account of age.

Section 2. The Congress shall have the power to enforce this article by appropriate legislation.

Amendment XXVII [1992]

No law varying the compensation for the services of the Senators and Representatives shall take effect until an election of Representatives shall have intervened.

UNIVERSITY CASEBOOK SERIES®

HART AND WECHSLER'S

THE FEDERAL COURTS AND THE FEDERAL SYSTEM

EIGHTH EDITION

CHAPTER I

THE DEVELOPMENT AND STRUCTURE OF THE FEDERAL JUDICIAL SYSTEM

INTRODUCTORY NOTE: THE JUDICIARY ARTICLE IN THE CONSTITUTIONAL CONVENTION AND THE RATIFICATION DEBATES

Article III, the judiciary article of the Constitution, emerged from the Convention that met in Philadelphia during the summer of 1787.[1] In the words of a leading scholar, however, to "one who is especially interested in the judiciary, there is surprisingly little on the subject to be found in the records of the convention."[2] For most of the delegates, the judiciary was a secondary or even a tertiary concern. To understand the Convention's deliberations about Article III, attention to context is therefore vital.

---

[1]   Farrand, The Records of the Federal Convention 20–23 (1911) (hereinafter cited as Farrand), is the basic document for the study of the Convention. Three volumes were published in 1911; a fourth, published in 1937, has been revised and expanded. Hutson, Supplement to Max Farrand's Records of the Federal Convention of 1787 (1987).

Secondary sources include Farrand, The Framing of the Constitution of the United States (1913) (hereinafter cited as Farrand, Framing); Warren, The Making of the Constitution 3–54 (1937 ed.); Goebel, History of the Supreme Court of the United States: Antecedents and Beginnings to 1801, at 196–250 (1971); McDonald, Novus Ordo Seclorum: The Intellectual Origins of the Constitution (1985); Rakove, Original Meanings: Politics and Ideas in the Making of the Constitution (1996); Amar, America's Constitution: A Biography (2006); Stewart, The Summer of 1787: The Men Who Invented the Constitution (2007); and Gienapp, The Second Creation: Fixing the American Constitution in the Founding Era (2018).

Professors Kurland and Lerner have assembled a five-volume anthology, The Founders' Constitution (1987), which presents views expressed on constitutional problems before, during, and after the Convention, through 1835. The volumes are keyed to the provisions of the Constitution and the first twelve amendments.

One of the most important sources for the Convention debates is James Madison's Notes on the 1787 Constitutional Convention. Bilder, Madison's Hand: Revising the Constitutional Convention (2015), reveals that Madison's revisions to his notes over the course of the decades that followed the Convention were far more extensive than scholars have previously recognized. By comparing the version of Madison's notes first published in 1840 to earlier sources and using technology to date Madison's many revisions, Bilder shows the evolution of Madison's thinking on many important issues debated at the Convention while calling into question the reliability of his description of the debates regarding certain topics. For discussion emphasizing the significance of Bilder's findings and probing the conclusions she draws, consult Rakove, *A Biography of Madison's Notes of Debates*, 31 Const.Comment. 317 (2016).

[2]   Farrand, Framing, note 1, *supra*, at 154.

A. Background of the Convention

On the whole, the period from the end of the Revolution to the ratification of the Constitution was one of economic growth.[3] Nonetheless, a downturn in the middle of the 1780s caused significant dislocations, especially for debtors. For this among other reasons, "the Critical Period," as it has been called,[4] was a time of frustration, tension, and anxiety.[5]

By all accounts, the prevailing structure of "national" government, the Articles of Confederation, had proved inadequate to the challenges confronting the new nation. The Articles provided no executive branch and no established system of courts. Each state had equal representation in Congress, and the concurrence of nine was needed for most important matters, including the appropriation of money. To levy a tariff required unanimous consent, which was never forthcoming. Perhaps the most basic problem, however, was that Congress lacked mechanisms to enforce its mandates. It could pass resolutions and make recommendations, but it had to rely on the states to implement them. The states proved increasingly unwilling to do so.

Efforts to enforce the Treaty of Paris with Great Britain illustrated the difficulty. The treaty guaranteed the integrity of some of the private debts owed to British subjects, provided for post-war return of certain British property interests acquired before the war, and limited private causes of action against British subjects arising out of legitimate war activities. Yet nearly all the states enacted statutes that violated these and other provisions of the treaty. Even when states formally allowed suits by aliens, the cherished right to trial by jury often functioned as an instrument of nullification, as it sometimes did in other debtor-creditor actions.[6]

Under the circumstances, the nation suffered a series of embarrassments in foreign affairs. In addition, the need for a national power to tax and to regulate commerce was increasingly obvious. By 1787 "[a]lmost every political leader in the country, including most of the later opponents of the Constitution, wanted something done to strengthen the Articles of Confederation."[7]

Related to the problems stemming from national weakness, but possessing a dynamic of their own, were anxieties about emerging political currents in the state legislatures and elsewhere.[8] By the 1780s, a burgeoning commercialism had broadly expanded networks of credit and debt, and resentments accumulated around debtor-creditor relations, including those

---

[3] See generally Wood, The Creation of the American Republic, 1776–1787, at 393–96 (1969); Jensen, The New Nation: A History of the United States During the Articles of Confederation, 1781–1789, at 256, 339–40, 423–24 (1950).

[4] The label apparently originated with Fiske, The Critical Period of American History, 1783–89 (1883).

[5] See generally Wood, note 3, *supra*, at 393–467.

[6] See Holt, *"To Establish Justice": Politics, The Judiciary Act of 1789, and the Invention of the Federal Courts*, 1989 Duke L.J. 1421, 1427–58.

[7] Wood, Empire of Liberty: A History of the Early Republic, 1789–1815, at 15 (2009).

[8] See *id.* 15–20; Holton, Unruly Americans and the Origins of the Constitution 21–123 (2007).

between the states—most of which had borrowed heavily during the Revolution—and their debt holders. At least six states responded by authorizing paper money, which was widely expected to yield inflation.[9] Some feared that it would spawn a broad-based financial instability. In the state legislatures, movements were afoot to pass debtor relief laws. In Massachusetts, Shays' Rebellion—a revolt of western debtors—broke out.[10]

To many of those who came to be called Federalists, "a rage for paper money, for an abolition of debts,"[11] and similar proposals reflected not only bad policy, but also a form of political immorality—a breach of honor, if not of natural right, and one that threatened to produce both financial and political turmoil.[12] From this perspective, a new, national constitution was necessary to restore a regime of virtuous government—or, failing that, a scheme that would protect individual rights and the public good by ensuring that faction would be checked by faction[13] and ambition set against ambition.[14]

When the Constitutional Convention met in Philadelphia with a charge to amend the Articles of Confederation, it agreed immediately to ignore the limits on its mandate and instead to draft an entirely new Constitution.[15]

---

[9] See, *e.g.*, Reisman, *Money, Credit, and Federalist Political Economy*, in Beeman, Botein, & Carter, Beyond Confederation: Origins of the Constitution and American National Identity 128, 150–51 (1987); Jensen, note 3, *supra*, at 313–26.

[10] To some, Shays' Rebellion revealed the need for a much stronger national government. For example, referencing the events, George Washington wrote to James Madison, "What stronger evidence can be given of the want of energy in our governments than these disorders?" Letter from George Washington to James Madison (Nov. 5, 1786), in 4 The Papers of George Washington 331, 332 (Abbot & Twohig eds. 1995).

[11] The Federalist, No. 10 (Madison).

[12] See Wood, note 7, *supra*, at 15–20.

[13] See The Federalist, No. 10 (Madison).

[14] See The Federalist, No. 51 (Madison).

[15] For an overview of the continuing influence of the Articles on constitutional meaning and a detailed comparison of the provisions of the Articles and the Constitution, consult Maggs, *A Concise Guide to the Articles of Confederation as a Source for Determining the Original Meaning of the Constitution*, 85 Geo.Wash.L.Rev. 397 (2017). See also Rakove, *The Legacy of the Articles of Confederation*, 12 Publius 45 (1982) (appraising the failings and contributions of the Articles). *Cf.* Maggs, *A Guide and Index for Finding Evidence of the Original Meaning of the U.S. Constitution in Early State Constitutions and Declarations of Rights*, 98 N.C.L.Rev. 779 (2020) (exploring how existing state constitutions may have influenced the drafting of the federal Constitution).

On the relationships among formal legality and illegality, popular sovereignty, and the theory of political legitimacy reflected in the framing and ratification of the Constitution, and on the implications of the implicit constitutional theory of the founding for subsequent American constitutional history, see Ackerman, 1 We the People: Foundations (1991); Ackerman & Katyal, *Our Unconventional Founding*, 62 U.Chi.L.Rev. 475 (1995); Amar, *Philadelphia Revisited: Amending the Constitution Outside Article V*, 55 U.Chi.L.Rev. 1043 (1988); Amar, *The Consent of the Governed: Constitutional Amendment Outside Article V*, 94 Colum.L.Rev. 457 (1994); Rakove, *The Super-Legality of the Constitution, or, A Federalist Critique of Bruce Ackerman's Neo-Federalism*, 108 Yale L.J. 1931 (1999). Professor Ackerman generally sees the founders as breaking sharply with existing legal forms, in the name of higher law or "We the People," whereas Professors Amar and Rakove assert the availability of legal justifications for the course of action followed at the Convention and after. In a provocative assessment, Klarman, The Framers' Coup: The Making of the United States Constitution (2017), describes the Convention and decision to move beyond the Articles as effectively an undemocratic coup. For probing analysis, consult Fried, *The Cunning of Reason: Michael Klarman's The Framers' Coup*, 116 Mich.L.Rev. 981 (2018); Finkelman, *The Nefarious Intentions of the Framers?*, 84 U.Chi.L.Rev. 2139 (2017). Ellis, The Quartet: Orchestrating the Second American Revolution, 1783–1789

With the agenda thus framed, the central questions involved the extent to which a new Constitution should create and empower a truly national government to replace the existing confederation. At one pole stood the nationalists.[16] At the other were those who preferred more minor departures from the existing confederated structure, with authority concentrated in the sovereign states and delegated to a federal government by the states for limited purposes only.[17]

As historical studies of "republican" ideology[18] have emphasized, this division tended to correlate with, and at least partly reflected, a more profound disagreement about the foundations of legitimate government. The nationalists—or "Federalists," as they came to be called—generally favored centralized institutions in which enlightened representatives would be at least partly insulated from, and reasonably asked to rise above, the play of passions and factional interests that often characterized local politics. By contrast, those wishing to retain the central significance of more local institutions tended to be suspicious of political and economic elites and supportive of democratic egalitarianism.[19]

Against this backdrop, perhaps the most crucial decision of the Constitutional Convention was that a federal government should be established with powers to act directly on individuals, not just on the member states. The most important implementing decisions were those defining the powers of the national government, allocating representation among the states, distributing responsibilities between the national legislature and the national executive, and providing for the supremacy of federal law. Almost without exception, decisions regarding the judiciary were ancillary, and reflected settlements and divisions concerning more deeply controversial issues.

(2015), details the roles that Washington, Hamilton, Madison, and Jay played in the transition from the Articles of Confederation to the Constitution, giving special attention to Washington's influence as chair of the Constitutional Convention.

[16]   Crosskey, Politics and the Constitution in the History of the United States (1953), makes especially strong claims about the nationalism of the Constitution that emerged from the Convention. On the general dismissal of Crosskey's work by a later generation of historians, see Beeman, *Introduction*, in Beeman, Botein, & Carter, note 9, *supra*, at 6–8. But see McConnell, The President Who Would Not Be King: Executive Power under the Constitution (2005) (relying on Crosskey's observations regarding the adoption of royal prerogative powers by Congress in exploring more generally the division of prerogative powers in the Constitution).

[17]   Middlekauff, The Glorious Cause: The American Revolution, 1763–1789 (2005).

[18]   The pathbreaking works are Bailyn, The Ideological Origins of the American Revolution (1967); Wood, note 3, *supra*; and Pocock, The Machiavellian Moment: Florentine Political Thought and the Atlantic Republican Tradition (1975). For valuable overviews, see Appleby, Liberalism and Republicanism in the Historical Imagination (1992); Kloppenberg, The Virtues of Liberalism (1998); and Rodgers, *Republicanism: The Career of a Concept*, 79 J.Am.Hist. 11 (1992).

[19]   See generally Wood, note 3, *supra*, at 393–615; Wood, note 7, *supra*; Ellis, Founding Brothers: The Revolutionary Generation (2001). For a more skeptical survey, see Holton, note 8, *supra*, at 162–98. Recent scholarship stresses the importance of studying the constitutional vision advanced by Federalists in the period between 1787 and 1800—the Constitution's "formative years"—during which time the Federalist constitutional ideology predominated before fading thereafter. For an overview of how such studies may alter assessments of the founding period and discussion of how many aspects of constitutional meaning remained contested then, see *Symposium: The Federalist Constitution*, 89 Fordham L.Rev. 1669 (2021).

B. The Convention

The Convention's main decisions concerning the federal courts may be grouped under six headings:

First, that there should be a federal judicial power operating, like the legislative and executive powers, upon both states and individuals;

Second, that the power should be vested in a Supreme Court and in such inferior federal courts as Congress might establish;

Third, that the federal judiciary should be as "independent as the lot of humanity will admit"[20];

Fourth, that its power should be judicial only but should include the power to pass upon the constitutionality of both state and federal legislation;

Fifth, that the power should extend to nine specified classes of cases; and

Sixth, that in certain cases the Supreme Court should have original jurisdiction and in the remainder "appellate Jurisdiction, both as to Law and Fact, with such Exceptions, and under such Regulations as the Congress shall make." U.S. Const. Art. III, Sec. 2.

To understand the judicial structure chosen at the Convention, however, one must have a general picture of the way the Convention worked. Its deliberations divided into three main phases.

The settlement of general principles (May 30 to July 26). Although the Convention was scheduled to convene on May 14, a quorum did not arrive until May 25, and the Convention did not begin its substantive business until four days later. On May 29, Governor Edmund Randolph of Virginia presented fifteen resolutions, variously referred to as the "Virginia Plan" or the "Randolph Plan," that as amended and expanded ultimately became the Constitution of the United States.[21]

Jointly drafted by the Virginia delegation, but with Madison exerting a heavy influence,[22] the Randolph Plan called for a national government consisting of legislative, executive, and judicial branches. It provided national legislative authority "in all cases to which the separate States are incompetent, or in which the harmony of the United States may be interrupted by the exercise of individual Legislation"; and it conferred a legislative veto over state legislation. The national legislature was to consist of two houses, each apportioned according to the states' free population or their contributions to the national treasury. The Randolph Plan contemplated a national executive and a judiciary "to consist of one or more supreme tribunals, and of inferior tribunals to be chosen by the National Legislature."[23]

---

[20]   Article XXIX of the Declaration of Rights of the Massachusetts Constitution of 1780.

[21]   1 Farrand, note 1, *supra*, at 20–23.

[22]   See Banning, The Sacred Fire of Liberty: James Madison and the Founding of the Federal Republic 111–37 (1995).

[23]   1 Farrand, note 1, *supra*, at 21–22.

On May 30, the Convention resolved itself into a Committee of the Whole to begin serious deliberation of Randolph's resolutions. On the same day, Charles Pinckney of South Carolina proposed a draft constitution that was also referred to the committee.[24] As discussed and amended through two weeks of debate, the Randolph Plan provided the substance of the first report of the Committee of the Whole to the Convention on June 13.

Randolph's plan had a distinctly nationalist thrust, and, unsurprisingly, it precipitated a counterproposal (by William Paterson of New Jersey),[25] which would have retained the existing unicameral Congress, with each state continuing to possess an equal vote. Even the Paterson Plan, however, would have created a national executive and a national judiciary. During this period, Alexander Hamilton of New York presented the fourth and last of the complete plans before the Convention.[26] As a final contribution to the mix, the Convention probably had before it a draft, of a judiciary article only, in the handwriting of John Blair of Virginia.[27]

But it was the Randolph Plan, and to a lesser extent the Paterson alternative, on which the delegates principally focused. Upon the introduction of the Paterson Plan, both it and the Randolph Plan were returned to the Committee of the Whole. Following four days of debate, the Committee voted on June 19, seven states to three with Maryland divided,[28] to adhere to its original report of the Randolph resolutions.

There followed the second major round of debate, in the Convention proper. At the outset, progress stalled for nearly a month, as—amid threats that delegates from the small states would pull out—the Convention wrestled with the divisive issue of proportional versus equal representation of the states. Finally, on July 16, the delegates reached a compromise under which representation would be proportional in the House but equal in the Senate. The delegates resolved remaining disagreements, frequently by compromise, over the next ten days.

The elaboration of detail (July 27 to September 10).[29] The Convention adjourned from July 27 to August 6 while a Committee of Detail comprised of five members elected by the delegates, prepared the first definite draft of the Constitution.[30] The Committee built upon the votes of the Convention adopting or modifying Randolph's Virginia Plan, but it drew also on the other plans that had been submitted, on the provisions of various state constitutions, and on a report drafted in 1781 by a committee of the Continental Congress that had sought to revise the Articles of Confederation. The Committee's work proved "arguably the most creative period of constitutional drafting of the entire summer."[31] During this time, the group

---

[24]   3 *id.* 595–609 (Appendix D).

[25]   1 *id.* 242–45; 3 *id.* 611–16 (Appendix E).

[26]   1 *id.* 291–93; 3 *id.* 617–30 (Appendix F).

[27]   Blair's draft was later found in the papers of George Mason. 2 *id.* 432–33.

[28]   1 *id.* 313, 322.

[29]   This phase is described in Farrand, Framing, note 1, *supra,* at 124–75, and Warren, note 1, *supra,* at 368–685.

[30]   2 Farrand, note 1, *supra,* at 177–89.

[31]   Ewald, *The Committee of Detail,* 28 Const.Comment. 197, 201 (2012).

worked through many aspects of the Constitution's federal structure and established many of the core components of legislative, executive, and judicial power. Among other things, the Committee drafted the first detailed provisions for the jurisdiction of the federal courts. The resulting report of the Committee of Detail introduced the third major round of debate, during which the Convention finally came to agreement on all remaining problems of general principle.

Final settlement and polishing (September 10 to 17).[32] Toward the end of the Convention, the delegates elected "a Committee of five to revise the style of and arrange the articles agreed to by the House * * *."[33] The Committee on Style, which made more than stylistic changes, reported to the Convention on September 12.[34] There ensued a final review, which produced minor amendments and culminated in the signing of the engrossed Constitution on Monday, September 17.

C.   The Judiciary Article

1.   A Federal Judicial Power

On the first day of substantive debate (May 30), the Committee of the Whole accepted Randolph's resolution "that a national government ought to be established consisting of a supreme Legislative, Judiciary, and Executive."[35] Again on June 4, Madison records in his notes, the first clause of Randolph's ninth resolution—"Resolved that a national Judiciary be established"—passed unanimously.[36] Without discussion or further question, the delegates thereby agreed to a substantial innovation in American experience. The Articles of Confederation had declared Congress the "last resort on appeal, in all disputes and differences * * * between two or more States concerning boundary, jurisdiction, or any other cause whatever * * *." Under this umbrella, the Articles provided that upon a petition from a complaining state, disputes over borders should be resolved by what were effectively *ad hoc* tribunals.[37] In addition, the Articles of

---

[32]   For this final phase, see Farrand, Framing, note 1, *supra*, at 176–95, and Warren, note 1, *supra*, at 686–721.

[33]   2 Farrand, note 1, *supra*, at 547.

[34]   2 Farrand, note 1, *supra*, at 590–603. For details on the pro-nationalist membership of the committee, see Gienapp, note 1, *supra*, at 58. For an explication of the significant changes made by the Committee on Style, as well as Gouverneur Morris's role on the committee, consult Treanor, *The Case of the Dishonest Scrivener: Gouverneur Morris and the Creation of the Federalist Constitution*, 120 Mich.L.Rev. 1 (2021). Treanor argues that in altering the vesting language of Article III, Morris sought to provide a textual basis for his view that favored mandating the creation of inferior federal courts while downplaying the Madisonian Compromise. Treanor further posits that Morris altered the wording of the Supremacy Clause in order to provide a textual anchor for the practice of judicial review. For a skeptical analysis of both assertions, consult Schwartz, *Framing the Framer: A Commentary on Treanor's Gouverneur Morris as "Dishonest Scrivener"*, 120 Mich.L.Rev. Online 51 (2022) (downplaying the importance of the relevant changes made by the Committee of Style and claiming that language supporting Morris's vision of the federal courts had already been embraced by the delegates).

[35]   Connecticut alone opposed, with New York divided. 1 Farrand, note 1, *supra*, at 30–32.

[36]   Madison's Journal 108 (Scott ed. 1895). See also 1 Farrand, note 1, *supra*, at 104.

[37]   Articles of Confederation, Art. IX, para. 2. The Articles of Confederation provided a cumbersome machinery for resolving such disputes, under which the disputing states selected judges by joint consent. If judges could not be agreed upon by the relevant States, the Articles stipulated that Congress should select three candidates from each state, after which the

Confederation vested Congress with the power to "appoint[ ]" state courts for the trial of "piracies and felonies on the high seas,"[38] which Congress exercised in 1781.[39] Finally, the Articles of Confederation granted authority to Congress to "establish[ ] courts; for receiving and determining finally appeals in all cases of captures,"[40] which Congress had already done in 1780.[41] But what was now proposed at the Convention was much more than a specialized tribunal. It was a national judicial power joined with executive and legislative powers as part of a national government.

The Convention's unhesitating initial agreement about the need for a national judiciary was only a prelude to serious disagreements about the kinds of tribunals that should exercise the judicial power and about the scope

---

disputing states would alternate to strike names until they reached a quorum of no less than five judges. The Articles also provided that any judgment of the court would be final. Once selected, the commission's "judgment and sentence" would be "final and decisive," binding even on states refusing to participate, and all proceedings were to be "lodged among the acts of Congress." The Articles established the same regime for any controversies pertaining to "the private right of soil claimed under different grants of two or more States." *Id.* para. 3.

The only case ever to proceed to judgment under the border dispute provision involved a contest between Connecticut and Pennsylvania over territory on the banks of the Susquehanna River. In 1775, prior to the enactment of the Articles, the Congress appointed a special committee, which recommended the terms of an armistice to govern until the dispute could be settled. When the two states appointed a court in 1782 by joint consent, it sat for forty-two days in Trenton, New Jersey, then rendered a unanimous judgment against Connecticut. Although Connecticut acquiesced, individual Connecticut settlers were unwilling to cede their lands, and uncertainty persisted. Carson, The Supreme Court of the United States 67–74 (1891).

[38]   Articles of Confederation, Art. IX, para. 1.

[39]   19 Journals of the Continental Congress 354–56 (1781). In all such cases, any appeal was to be to Congress, or such person or persons as Congress should appoint. All the states but New York complied, and even New York ultimately appears to have come into partial compliance. See Carson, note 37, *supra*, at 45.

[40]   Articles of Confederation, Art. IX, para. 1. The Articles prohibited members of Congress from serving as judges on said courts.

[41]   The first appeal from a state tribunal came up in August of 1776, and Congress appointed a special committee to hear it. The practice of appointing special committees continued until January, 1777, when Congress established a five-member Standing Committee. Then, in January, 1780, Congress resolved "that a Court be established for trial of all appeals from the Courts of Admiralty in these United States, in cases of capture, to consist of three Judges appointed and commissioned by Congress * * *." See Carson, note 37, *supra*, at 41–64.

Although this was the first national court, it lacked several necessary powers in its authorizing provisions, including those of fining and imprisoning for contempt and disobedience and directing that the state admiralty courts should execute its decrees. *Id.* 56. Indeed, the court was never really independent of its creator. In the case of the brig "Lusanna," involving a delicate question of national power arising out of conflict between a New Hampshire statute and the act of Congress creating the Court of Appeals, Congress ordered that all proceedings upon the sentence of the court be stayed and attempted to determine the dispute itself. Congress never took any final action in the case, but it defeated a motion stating that it was improper for Congress in any manner to reverse or control the court's decision. In December 1784, business had dwindled; the court had cleared its docket; and after a few more occasional sessions, the court ceased to function on May 16, 1787. *Id.* 58–60.

Nonetheless, "at least 118 admiralty cases were disposed of by the congressional committees and the Court of Appeals, and the idea became well fixed that cases of admiralty and maritime jurisdiction pertained to federal jurisdiction." Hockett, The Constitutional History of the United States 33 (1939). Congress subsequently directed that the court's records and proceedings be housed in the new Supreme Court's office. Act of May 8, 1792, ch. 36, § 12, 1 Stat. 275, 279 (1792). The Supreme Court, in turn, treated the decrees of the federal appellate tribunals that had existed under the Articles as binding in later proceedings in the new federal courts. See United States v. Peters, 5 Cranch. (9 U.S.) 115 (1809); Treacy, *The Olmstead Case, 1778–1809*, 10 West.Pol.Q. 675, 685–86 (1957).

of the jurisdiction that these tribunals should possess. Nonetheless, the unanimity bespoke a general understanding that an efficacious government requires courts.

2. The Tribunals Exercising the Power

The Convention next proceeded swiftly to vote on June 4 that the judicial branch should "consist of one supreme tribunal, and of one or more inferior tribunals."[42] The vote, reiterated on June 5, reflected an uncontroversial agreement, never to be reconsidered, that there should be one Supreme Court.[43] The decision concerning inferior federal courts proved less stable.[44]

On June 5, after an inconclusive discussion about where the power to appoint inferior tribunals should lie, Rutledge moved to reconsider the provision for their establishment at all. He urged that "the State Tribunals might and ought to be left in all cases to decide in the first instance the right of appeal to the supreme national tribunal being sufficient to secure the national rights & uniformity of Judgmts: that it was making an unnecessary encroachment on the jurisdiction of the States, and creating unnecessary obstacles to their adoption of the new system."[45] Sherman, supporting him, dwelled on the expense of an additional set of courts.[46]

Madison strongly opposed the motion. He argued that "unless inferior tribunals were dispersed throughout the Republic with *final* jurisdiction in *many* cases, appeals would be multiplied to a most oppressive degree."[47] Besides, he maintained, "an appeal would not in many cases be a remedy." "What was to be done after improper Verdicts in State tribunals obtained under the biassed directions of a dependent Judge, or the local prejudices of an undirected jury? To remand the cause for a new trial would answer no purpose. To order a new trial at the supreme bar would oblige the parties to bring up their witnesses, tho' ever so distant from the seat of the Court. An effective Judiciary establishment commensurate to the legislative authority, was essential."[48] Wilson and Dickinson spoke in the same vein, with the former emphasizing the special need for an admiralty jurisdiction.[49]

Despite these appeals, Rutledge's motion to strike out "inferior tribunals" carried, five states to four with two divided.[50] This, however, was not the end of the matter. Picking up on a suggestion by Dickinson, Wilson and Madison moved a compromise resolution, which provided that "the

---

[42] 1 Farrand, note 1, *supra*, at 104–05 (June 4), 119 (June 5).

[43] All the plans submitted to the Convention provided for a Supreme Court. See *id.* 21, 244, 292; 2 *id.* 432; 3 *id.* 600.

[44] Although the Randolph and Pinckney plans called for mandatory establishment of inferior federal courts, the Paterson plan did not provide for any such courts at all. Hamilton's plan empowered Congress to create them if it so chose. John Blair's plan provided only for lower courts of admiralty. See 3 *id.* 593–94 (Randolph); *id.* 600 (Pinckney); *id.* 612 (Paterson); *id.* 618 (Hamilton); 2 *id.* 432 (Blair).

[45] 1 *id.* 124.

[46] *Id.* 125.

[47] *Id.* 124.

[48] *Id.*

[49] *Id.* 124 (Wilson), 125 (Dickinson).

[50] *Id.* 125.

National Legislature [should] be empowered" to "institute"—the verb recorded in Madison's notes[51]—or "appoint"—the word in the Convention Journal[52] and another set of contemporary notes[53]—"inferior tribunals." According to Madison, he and Wilson "observed that there was a distinction between establishing such tribunals absolutely, and giving a discretion to the Legislature to establish or not establish them."[54]

Pierce Butler objected even to this compromise proposal: "The people will not bear such innovations. The States will revolt at such encroachments."[55] Despite this protest, the delegates agreed to "the Madisonian Compromise," as it has come to be called: eight states in favor, two against, with one divided.[56]

Renewed opposition to a system of inferior federal courts arose when the report of the Committee of the Whole came before the Convention on July 18. But it was milder, with Sherman saying that he "was willing to give the power to the Legislature but wished them to make use of the State Tribunals whenever it could be done with safety to the general interest." This time the vote accepting the compromise was unanimous,[57] and the decision stood without further question.[58] The Committee of Detail reported a draft prescribing that the judicial power "shall be vested in one Supreme Court, and in such inferior Courts as shall, when necessary, from time to time, be constituted by the Legislature of the United States."[59] The Committee of Style further altered the language to its current form.

---

[51]   *Id.*

[52]   *Id.* 118.

[53]   *Id.* 127 (Yates).

[54]   *Id.* 125.

[55]   *Id.*

[56]   *Id.* 124–25 (June 5). Professor Collins sees a puzzle in the sequence of the Convention's actions on June 4–5: Why, within so short a span, did the Convention swing from unanimous approval of constitutionally-mandated lower federal courts, to preclusion of lower federal courts altogether, to approval of a compromise apparently authorizing Congress to "appoint" or "establish" lower federal courts? See Collins, *Article III Cases, State Court Duties, and the Madisonian Compromise*, 1995 Wisc.L.Rev. 39, 116–19. During the interval between the vote to approve mandatory federal courts and adoption of Rutledge's motion to reconsider, the Convention voted to delete the provision of the Randolph Plan that the national judiciary should be elected by the national legislature and to leave open for the time being the question of judicial selection. Emphasizing this background, Collins speculates that Rutledge's motion to reconsider may have been motivated by the intervening debate on the selection of the federal judiciary; if the power did not lie with the legislature, the Convention might have considered it too dangerous to be vested elsewhere.

A related suggestion ascribes significance to the contested wording of Madison's and Wilson's compromise resolution: if the congressional power was one to "appoint" inferior tribunals, this formulation may hark back to the practice under the Articles of Confederation by which Congress "appointed" existing state courts, rather than creating independent federal courts, to conduct certain forms of judicial business. See Goebel, note 1, *supra*, at 211–12. On the subsequent alteration of the language to its final form, see *infra*.

[57]   2 Farrand, note 1, *supra*, at 45–46 (July 18).

[58]   In the debate on the report of the Committee of Detail, a motion, recorded only in the Journal, was made and seconded to give the inferior federal courts only an appellate jurisdiction over decisions of state courts, but the motion was withdrawn. *Id.* 424 (August 27).

[59]   *Id.* 186. According to Pfander, *Federal Supremacy, State Court Inferiority, and the Constitutionality of Jurisdiction-Stripping Legislation*, 101 Nw.U.L.Rev. 191 (2007), a full understanding of the significance of the report of the Committee of Detail requires attention not only to the judiciary article, but also to the provision of Article I, § 8, cl. 9, authorizing Congress

3. Separation and Independence of the Judicial Power

a. Appointment of Judges

The method of appointing federal judges occasioned significant controversy. The Randolph Plan called for appointment by the legislature. Madison objected that many legislators would be incompetent to assess judicial qualifications and proposed appointment by the "less numerous & more select" Senate.[60] The Committee of the Whole agreed to Madison's suggested amendment on June 13. The Convention adhered to this decision on July 21, when it rejected another proposal by Madison, who now feared that senatorial appointment would confer too much power on the states, and instead urged appointment by the national executive, with or without the approval of the Senate.[61] In the closing days of the Convention, the delegates reopened the issue yet again and finally resolved, as part of a general settlement on appointments, in favor of appointment by the executive with the advice and consent of the Senate.[62]

b. Tenure and Salary

The provisions protecting the tenure and salary of judges received almost complete assent.[63] The Committee of the Whole first accepted language barring increase as well as diminution in salary during tenure in office,[64] but the prohibition against increases was rejected in the subsequent debate in the Convention and again in the debate on the report of the Committee of Detail.[65] Rejection rested largely on the practical ground that the cost of living might rise.

The lone assault on the principle of tenure during good behavior occurred in the debate on the report of the Committee of Detail, when Dickinson of Delaware, seconded by Gerry and Sherman, moved that the

---

"[t]o constitute Tribunals inferior to the supreme Court." Pfander maintains that when Articles I and III are read in conjunction, the import of the report of the Committee of Detail was that "Congress could proceed either by appointing state courts to serve as tribunals under Article I (as Sherman hoped), or by creating new federal courts under Article III (as Madison hoped)." Insofar as Congress fails to vest federal courts with jurisdiction to rule on federal claims, Pfander maintains, state courts should be regarded as having been constituted as "Tribunals inferior to the supreme Court." Compare Calabresi & Lawson, *The Unitary Executive, Jurisdiction Stripping, and the Hamdan Opinions: A Textualist Response to Justice Scalia*, 107 Colum.L.Rev. 1002, 1034 (2007) (contending in the eighteenth century the term "court" had a broader meaning than "tribunal").

[60] 1 Farrand, note 1, *supra*, at 233 (June 13).

[61] Hamilton advanced the first proposal for appointment by the President with the concurrence of the Senate on June 5. Motions for executive appointment alone, or executive appointment subject to Senate approval, were defeated on several occasions thereafter. See *id.* 128, 224, 232–33; 2 *id.* 80–83; Warren, note 1, *supra*, at 327–29.

[62] The draft reported by the Committee of Detail retained appointment by the Senate. 2 Farrand, note 1, *supra*, at 132, 155, 169, 183. The final compromise was worked out between August 25 and September 7. See *id.* 498, 538–40; Warren, note 1, *supra*, at 639–42. For Hamilton's comments on the matter, see The Federalist, Nos. 76, 77.

[63] All four of the principal plans provided that the judges should hold office during good behavior, and the Randolph, Pinckney, and Paterson plans forbade either a decrease or an increase in salary during continuance in office.

[64] 1 Farrand, note 1, *supra*, at 121.

[65] 2 *id.* 44–45, 429–30; Warren, note 1, *supra*, at 532–34. See also Rosenn, *The Constitutional Guaranty Against Diminution of Judicial Compensation*, 24 UCLA L.Rev. 308, 311–18 (1976).

judges "may be removed by the Executive on the application by the Senate and House of Representatives." The motion drew strong opposition, however, and only Connecticut ultimately supported it.[66]

c.   Extra-Judicial Functions

Randolph's eighth resolution proposed to create a council of revision composed of "the Executive and a convenient number of the National Judiciary" with authority, first, "to examine every act of the National Legislature before it shall operate," and, second, to review every negative exercised by the National Legislature upon an act of a state legislature, pursuant to a power proposed in the sixth resolution, before it "shall be final." The dissent of the council was to "amount to a rejection, unless the Act of the National Legislature be again passed, or that of a particular Legislature be again negatived by [blank] of the members of each branch."[67]

In an early vote of 8–2, the Committee of the Whole rejected this plan to mingle executive and judicial functions and substituted a purely executive veto of national legislation.[68] Madison and Wilson renewed the proposal for a council of revision on three subsequent occasions, but the Convention defeated it each time.[69]

Madison and Wilson believed judicial participation in a council of revision would have furnished a necessary check upon legislative aggrandizement and provided an assurance of wiser laws. Gerry and King concisely stated the arguments that prevailed against it:

"Mr. Gerry doubts whether the Judiciary ought to form a part of [the council of revision], as they will have a sufficient check agst. encroachments on their own department by their exposition of the laws, which involved a power of deciding on their Constitutionality. In some States the Judges had actually set aside laws as being agst. the Constitution. This was done too

---

[66]   2 Farrand, note 1, *supra*, at 428–29; Warren, note 1, *supra*, at 532. For an extensive analysis of the problems of tenure and removal in the Constitution, see Berger, Impeachment: The Constitutional Problems (1973). Prakash & Smith, *How to Remove a Federal Judge*, 116 Yale L.J. 72 (2006), challenges the traditional assumption that Article III permits the removal of a judge only by impeachment. The authors argue that Article III should be read, in light of established English and colonial practice, to embody standards of "good Behaviour" under which various public and private officers could be removed from office pursuant to the judgment of an ordinary court. According to them, the "good Behaviour" standard is "more general and less severe" than that of "high Crimes and Misdemeanors." But see Redish, *Response: Good Behavior, Judicial Independence, and the Foundations of American Constitutionalism*, 116 Yale L.J. 139 (2006) (defending the traditional position by arguing that the interpretation urged by Prakash & Smith is not linguistically necessary, is incompatible with the commitment to strong judicial independence reflected in the overall constitutional structure, and finds little support in post-ratification evidence); Pfander, *Removing Federal Judges*, 74 U.Chi.L.Rev. 1227 (2007) (arguing that the Constitution's provision for a judicial tenure in office rules out any removal mechanism not specified by the Constitution).

[67]   1 Farrand, note 1, *supra*, at 21.

[68]   *Id*. 97–104, 108–10 (June 4).

[69]   The Committee of the Whole adhered to the rejection, 8–3, on June 6. *Id*. 138–40 (June 6). The Convention did likewise in the later debate on the report of the Committee of the Whole, this time 4–3, with two states divided. 2 *id*. 73–80 (July 21). Madison and Wilson made their final attempt in the debate on the report of the Committee of Detail, but their proposal, which this time took a somewhat different form, again failed. *Id*. 298 (August 15).

with general approbation. It was quite foreign from the nature of ye. office to make them judges of the policy of public measures."

King added "that the Judges ought to be able to expound the law as it should come before them, free from the bias of having participated in its formation."[70]

The last important reference to extra-judicial functions occurred near the close of the Convention, when Dr. Johnson moved to extend the judicial power to cases arising under the Constitution of the United States, as well as under its laws and treaties.[71] Madison, responding, "doubted whether it was not going too far to extend the jurisdiction of the Court generally to cases arising Under the Constitution, & whether it ought not to be limited to cases of a Judiciary Nature. The right of expounding the Constitution in cases not of this nature ought not to be given to that Department." Madison's concern notwithstanding, "The motion of Docr. Johnson was agreed to [without opposition]: it being generally supposed that the jurisdiction given was constructively limited to cases of a Judiciary nature."[72]

4. The Power to Declare Statutes Unconstitutional

At no time did the Constitutional Convention systematically discuss the availability or scope of judicial review, but the subject drew recurrent mention in debates over related issues. As in Madison's comment on Dr. Johnson's motion, the existence of a power of judicial review appears to have been taken for granted by most if not all delegates.[73] The point became perhaps most explicit in a debate over the proposed congressional negative of state laws, during which the delegates appear to have accepted the existence of a power in the federal courts to invalidate unconstitutional state laws. The crux of the controversy turned on whether this was a sufficient safeguard.[74] Resolution came through acceptance of Luther Martin's

---

[70] 1 *id*. 97–98, 109 (June 4).

[71] Two other plans for using judges non-judicially never came to a vote. The first was a suggestion advanced by Ellsworth and elaborated by Gouverneur Morris to make the Chief Justice a member of the projected Privy Council of the President. See Warren, note 1, *supra*, at 643–50. The second was a proposal by Charles Pinckney that "Each branch of the Legislature, as well as the Supreme Executive shall have authority to require the opinions of the supreme Judicial Court upon important questions of law, and upon solemn occasions." 2 Farrand, note 1, *supra*, at 340–41 (August 20). The Committee of Detail never reported Pinckney's proposal out.

[72] 2 Farrand, note 1, *supra*, at 430 (August 27). On whether the limitation of judicial authority to cases of a judiciary nature clearly precluded advisory opinions, see Chap. II, Sec. 1, *infra*.

[73] Berger, Congress v. The Supreme Court (1969), marshals the supporting evidence. Snowiss, Judicial Review and the Law of the Constitution 40 (1990), which deals much more broadly with shifting historical understandings concerning the Constitution's nature and judicial enforceability, concludes that "[t]here was more support than opposition for judicial authority over legislation in the convention, and this was probably an accurate reflection of the strength of the contending sides outside the convention." For historical discussions on the origins of judicial review prior to the Convention, see Bilder, The Transatlantic Constitution: Colonial Legal Culture and the Empire (2005); Smith, Appeals to the Privy Council from the American Plantations (1950); and Wood, note 3, *supra*, at 453–63.

[74] Wilson summarized the proponents' case: "The power of self-defence had been urged as necessary for the State Governments—It was equally necessary for the General Government. The firmness of Judges is not of itself sufficient. Something further is requisite—It will be better to prevent the passage of an improper law, than to declare it void when passed." 2 Farrand, note 1, *supra*, at 391 (August 23).

proposal of the Supremacy Clause, which strengthened the judicial check by express statement of the parallel power and responsibility of state judges.[75]

Both sides in the debates over the proposal for a council of revision of acts of the national legislature similarly recognized the existence of a judicial safeguard against unconstitutional federal laws. On at least eight other occasions, speakers substantially echoed Gerry's statement presupposing a power of judicial review, already quoted.[76]

The only note of challenge came in the fourth and last debate on the proposal when Mercer, a recently arrived delegate, speaking in support of the alternative plan of judicial participation in the veto, said that he "disapproved of the Doctrine that the Judges as expositors of the Constitution should have authority to declare a law void." Dickinson then observed that he was impressed with Mr. Mercer's remark and "thought no such power ought to exist" but "[h]e was at the same time at a loss what expedient to substitute." Gouverneur Morris at once said that he could not agree that the judiciary "should be bound to say that a direct violation of the Constitution was law," and there the discussion ended.[77]

Meanwhile, the Convention approved the final version of the Supremacy Clause.[78] The Convention's matter-of-course approval of the express grant of

---

[75] *Id.* 27–29. See also *id.* 390–91. The proposal of a legislative negative, first advanced and vigorously supported throughout by Madison, was embodied in Randolph's sixth resolution, which authorized a negative only of state laws "contravening in the opinion of the National Legislature the articles of Union." 1 *id.* 21. The Committee of the Whole initially approved the proposal in this form on May 31 without debate or dissent. *Id.* 54. The Committee first discussed the plan on June 8, when the Committee rejected Charles Pinckney's motion to extend the negative to "all laws which they shd. judge to be improper." *Id.* 164, 171. Rumblings of opposition then appeared and culminated in a debate in the Convention on July 17, when the delegates rejected the plan. 2 *id.* 21–22.

Madison, in support of a negative power, urged that states "can pass laws which will accomplish their injurious objects before they can be repealed by the Genl Legislre, or be set aside by the National Tribunals." Sherman and Gouverneur Morris, in opposition, relied upon the courts to set aside unconstitutional laws, with Sherman saying that the proposal "involves a wrong principle, to wit, that a law of a State contrary to the articles of the Union, would if not negatived, be valid & operative." None doubted the judicial power. For a discussion of the relationship between the Supremacy Clause, Madison's "federal negative," and the controversial pre-Revolution practice of Parliamentary nullification of legislation by the colonies, see LaCroix, The Ideological Origins of American Federalism (2010).

[76] See Rufus King, 1 Farrand, note 1, *supra*, at 109 (June 4); Wilson, 2 *id.* 73 (July 21); Madison, *id.* 74 (July 21), 92–93 (July 23); Martin, *id.* 76 (July 21); Mason, *id.* 78 (July 21); Pinckney, *id.* 298 (August 15); G. Morris, *id.* 299 (August 15). See also Williamson, *id.* 376 (August 22). *Cf.* Snowiss, note 73, *supra*, at 39–40: "It was not always clear, however, whether speakers endorsing judicial review were supporting a general power over legislation or one limited to defense of the courts' constitutional sphere. Gerry's observation was immediately preceded by the remark that the judiciary 'will have a sufficient check against encroachments on their own department * * *.'"

[77] 2 Farrand, note 1, *supra*, at 298–99 (August 15).

[78] Luther Martin moved adoption of the Supremacy Clause on July 17, just one day after the Convention voted to give the states equal suffrage in the Senate. For a discussion of the possible significance of this timing, consult Clark, *Constitutional Compromise and the Supremacy Clause*, 83 Notre Dame L.Rev. 1421 (2008).

In its original form, the clause referred only to "Legislative acts of the U. S. made by virtue & in pursuance of the articles of Union" and to treaties, declaring them to be the supreme law only "of the respective States." 2 Farrand, note 1, *supra*, at 28–29 (July 17). On August 23, the Convention amended the clause without debate to declare expressly the supremacy of "This Constitution & the laws of the U. S. made in pursuance thereof." *Id.* 389. The Committee on jurisdiction in cases arising under the Constitution gives further indication that some form of judicial review was contemplated.[79]

There was no exchange of views, even indirectly, concerning appropriate judicial methodology in constitutional interpretation.[80]

5. The Scope of Jurisdiction

As initially formulated, the Randolph Plan contemplated apparently mandatory federal jurisdiction of "all piracies & felonies on the high seas, captures from an enemy; cases in which foreigners or citizens of other States applying to such jurisdictions may be interested, or which respect the collection of the National revenue; impeachments of any National officers, and questions which may involve the national peace and harmony."[81] When the Committee of the Whole first discussed this subject on June 12 and 13, however, Randolph concluded that it was "the business of a sub-committee to detail" the jurisdiction. He "therefore moved to obliterate such parts of the resolve so as only to establish the principle, to wit, *that the jurisdiction of the national judiciary shall extend to all cases of national revenue, impeachment of national officers, and questions which involve the national peace or harmony.*" The Committee agreed to this proposal by unanimous vote.[82]

In considering the report of the Committee of the Whole on July 18, the Convention again confined itself to general principle. But "[s]everal criticisms having been made on the definition [of jurisdiction]; it was proposed by Mr. Madison so to alter as to read thus—'that the jurisdiction shall extend to all cases arising under the Natl. laws: And to such other questions as may involve the Natl. peace & harmony.' which was agreed to [without opposition]."[83]

With only this general direction, the Committee of Detail took the lead in defining the categories to which the federal judicial power would extend. The nine heads of federal jurisdiction that eventually emerged in Article III, § 2 can be grouped in various ways. Thematically, for example, the jurisdictional categories appear to contemplate federal judicial power to promote four central purposes: (i) to protect and enforce federal authority

---

Style's final draft declared the Constitution, laws and treaties to be "the supreme law of the land" and not just "of the respective states." *Id.* 603.

[79]   See text at note 73, *supra.*

[80]   Several prominent scholars have argued that it was widely understood during the 1780s and 1790s that judicial nullification should occur only in cases of plain unconstitutionality. See, *e.g.,* Snowiss, note 73, *supra,* at 13–44; Kramer, *Putting the Politics Back into the Political Safeguards of Federalism,* 100 Colum.L.Rev. 215, 240 (2000); Wood, *The Origins of Judicial Review Revisited, or How the Marshall Court Made More out of Less,* 56 Wash. & Lee L.Rev. 787, 798–99 (1999). Kramer has argued separately that many in the founding generation subscribed to a "departmental" theory of constitutional interpretation, under which each branch of government would decide for itself how to construe the Constitution in discharging its responsibilities. See Kramer, The People Themselves: Popular Constitutionalism and Judicial Review (2004). According to the departmental theory, disputes among the branches would need to be resolved politically, with ultimate responsibility residing in "the people themselves."

[81]   1 Farrand, note 1, *supra,* at 22. All of the plans respecting the judiciary that were put before the Convention specified various definite heads of federal jurisdiction.

[82]   *Id.* 238 (June 13, Yates's notes). See also *id.* 220 (June 12), 223–24, 232 (June 13).

[83]   2 *id.* 46 (July 18).

(jurisdiction of federal question cases and cases to which the United States is a party); (ii) to resolve disputes relating to foreign affairs (jurisdiction of suits affecting foreign envoys, admiralty cases, cases arising under treaties, and suits involving foreign nations); (iii) to provide an interstate umpire (suits between states or involving their conflicting land grants); and (iv) to furnish an impartial tribunal where state court bias was feared (party-based cases involving citizens of different states, a state and a non-citizen, or an alien).

On the face of the text, however, a linguistically striking divide exists between the first three and the last six jurisdictional categories. For the first three categories, which are defined mostly if not exclusively by subject matter,[84] Article III, § 2 provides that the judicial power shall extend to "all Cases." By contrast, in the last six categories, which are defined primarily by reference to the status of the parties, the "all" disappears, and the judicial power is extended to "Controversies," not "Cases."

The shift in language seems sufficiently sharp to require explanation. Yet no recorded discussion occurred in the Committee of the Whole or on the floor of the Convention. Partly as a result, whether the change of language marks a distinction of constitutional intent—especially with reference to Congress's power over the jurisdiction of the federal courts—is much controverted and explored more fully in later Chapters.[85]

Regardless of its intended significance, the linguistic division provides a useful framework for examining the scope of federal jurisdiction authorized, if not required, by Article III.

a.   Jurisdiction Based Primarily on Subject Matter: The First Three Headings

(i)   Cases Arising Under the Constitution, Laws, and Treaties of the United States. Faithful to the vote of July 18, the Committee of Detail placed at the head of its list of subjects of jurisdiction "all cases arising under laws passed by the Legislature of the United States."[86] Except for the change in wording by the Committee of Style, this provision was accepted and incorporated into the Constitution without further question or discussion.[87]

But the provision for jurisdiction of cases "arising under [federal] laws" was not left standing alone. As already noted, in a general discussion of the

---

[84]   The jurisdiction for the first and third of these categories, involving "all Cases * * * arising under" the Constitution, laws, and treaties of the United States and "all Cases of admiralty and maritime Jurisdiction," is based unequivocally on subject matter. By contrast, the second category of "all Cases affecting Ambassadors, other public Ministers and Consuls" arguably straddles the distinction between subject-matter-based and party-based jurisdiction.

[85]   For discussion of the possible significance of the distinction for Congress's power to define and limit federal jurisdiction in the various categories of cases, see Chap. IV, Sec. 1, *infra*.

[86]   2 Farrand, note 1, *supra*, at 186 (August 6). The clause had antecedents, partial or complete, in all of the judiciary plans: Randolph: cases "which respect the collection of the National revenue," 1 *id*. 22; Pinckney: "all cases arising under the laws of the United States," 3 *id*. 600; Paterson: all cases "which may arise on any of the Acts for regulation of trade, or the collection of the federal Revenue," 1 *id*. 244; Hamilton: "all causes in which the revenues of the general Government * * * are concerned," with power in the legislature "to institute Courts in each State for the determination of all matters of general concern," *id*. *292*; Blair: "all cases in law and equity arising under * * * the laws of the United States," 2 *id*. 432.

[87]   2 *id*. 600 (committee report), 628 (September 15, entire Article approved).

judiciary article as crafted by the Committee of Detail, Dr. Johnson moved to insert an express provision for jurisdiction of cases under "this Constitution," and the motion carried without opposition.[88] Immediately thereafter, according to Madison's notes, Rutledge moved to extend the jurisdictional category to encompass cases involving "treaties made or which shall be made" under the authority of the United States. The vote to adopt the motion was again unanimous.[89]

(ii) Cases Affecting Ambassadors, Other Public Ministers, or Consuls. Under the Articles of Confederation, the United States could give no assurance of legal protection to the representatives of foreign countries living in the United States. "The Convention was convinced that if foreign officials were either to seek justice at law or be subjected to its penalties, it should be at the hand of the national government."[90] The Committee of Detail reported out the present clause, which passed without dispute, and, again without dispute, the delegates included such cases within the Supreme Court's original jurisdiction.[91]

(iii) Admiralty and Maritime Cases. The inclusion of admiralty and maritime jurisdiction in the report of the Committee of Detail went unchallenged.[92] The principal commerce of the period was, of course, maritime; and as Wilson pointed out on the floor, it was in the admiralty jurisdiction that disputes with foreigners were most likely to arise.[93] In addition, maritime law had been administered by British vice-admiralty rather than colonial courts before the war,[94] and state courts had therefore not been accustomed to exercising general maritime jurisdiction. Following

---

[88] See note 710, *supra*, and accompanying text. Among the plans presented to the Convention, only the Blair plan had included such a provision. 2 Farrand, note 1, *supra*, at 432.

[89] 2 Farrand, note 1, *supra*, at 431 (August 27). This amendment could be viewed as implementing the Convention's earlier determination that federal judicial power should extend to "questions which involve the national peace and harmony." Earlier, Randolph made clear that this language was intended to include questions of "the security of foreigners where treaties are in their favor." 1 *id.* 238 (June 13). Nevertheless, the Committee of Detail omitted any express reference to treaties, perhaps because of the provisions giving jurisdiction when foreigners were parties.

By all indications, the Convention regarded federal judicial power to enforce treaties as possessing vital importance. All the other plans except Pinckney's contemplated a similar jurisdiction. Paterson: appellate jurisdiction where construction of a treaty was involved, 1 *id.* 244; Hamilton: where "citizens of foreign nations are concerned," *id.* 292; Blair: cases arising under a treaty, 2 *id.* 432. In addition, the Convention at one time had extended the proposed negative on state laws, upon motion by Benjamin Franklin, to include laws contravening "any treaties subsisting under the authority of the Union." 1 *id.* 54 (May 31).

[90] Frank, *Historical Bases of the Federal Judicial System*, 13 Law & Contemp.Prob. 3, 14 (1948). All the plans contemplated such a jurisdiction. The Paterson plan gave the Supreme Court appellate jurisdiction in cases "touching the rights of ambassadors," as well as in cases "in which foreigners may be interested." 1 Farrand, note 1, *supra*, at 244. The Pinckney plan gave the Court original jurisdiction in cases "affecting Ambassadors & other public Ministers." 3 *id.* 600. The Blair plan added consuls, in substantially the language of the present grant. 2 *id.* 432. The Randolph and Hamilton plans provided generally for jurisdiction where foreigners were concerned. 1 *id.* 22, 292.

[91] 2 Farrand, note 1, *supra*, at 186, 431.

[92] *Id.* 186. See The Federalist No. 80 (Hamilton): "The most bigoted idolizers of state authority, have not thus far shown a disposition to deny the National Judiciary the cognizances of maritime causes."

[93] 1 Farrand, note 1, *supra*, at 124 (June 5).

[94] See Benedict on Admiralty § 61 (7th ed.rev.2007).

the break with England, some states established courts with general admiralty jurisdiction, but others did not.[95] Further, experience during the Revolution with state court adjudication of prize cases had shown the need for a federal tribunal.[96]

b. Jurisdiction Based on Party Status: The Remaining Categories

(i) **United States a Party.** Under the Articles of Confederation, the United States had to go into state courts for enforcement of its laws and collection of its claims.[97] Of the five plans before the Convention, however, only Blair's included a general grant of jurisdiction in cases to which the United States was a party.[98] The other plans and the initial report of the Committee of Detail possibly omitted the clause because the problem was thought to be addressed through jurisdiction over cases arising under federal law. Regardless, responding to a motion by Charles Pinckney, the committee later specially recommended, on August 22, that jurisdiction be given in controversies "between the United States and an individual State or the United States and an individual person."[99] Madison and Gouverneur Morris introduced the provision as it stands via motion on the floor on August 27, apparently influenced by this recommendation. Soon after, on the same day, it was moved that "in cases in which the United States shall be a Party the jurisdiction shall be original or appellate as the Legislature may direct," but the motion failed,[100] with the result that the jurisdiction of the Supreme Court was made appellate only.

(ii) **Two or More States.** Border disputes had plagued the new states.[101] In a speech introducing his resolutions, Randolph said: "Are we not on the eve of war, which is only prevented by the hopes from the convention"?[102] Though not specifically mentioned, a jurisdiction in

---

[95]   See *id.* §§ 83–89.

[96]   See note 41, *supra.*

[97]   Thus, even treason against the United States had to be tried in state courts under state law. In 1781, Congress recommended that the state legislatures pass laws punishing infractions of the law of nations, and erect courts or clothe existing courts with authority to decide what constituted such an offense. Where an official of the United States Post Office was guilty of misdemeanor in office, Congress could only prescribe penalties and let the Postmaster General bring an action in debt in a state court to recover them. In settling accounts of the military and in recovering debts from individuals, Congress recommended that the state legislatures pass laws empowering Congress's agents to bring such actions in state courts. Carson, note 37, *supra,* at 83–86.

[98]   2 Farrand, note 1, *supra,* at 432. One version of the Paterson plan included a resolution that "provision ought to be made for hearing and deciding upon all disputes arising between the United States and an individual State respecting territory." 3 *id.* 611.

[99]   2 *id.* 367 (August 22). This report was distributed to the members, *id.* 376, but seems not to have been acted upon. For Pinckney's earlier motion, see *id.* 342 (August 20).

[100]   *Id.* 424–25, 430.

[101]   See note 37, *supra.*

[102]   1 Farrand, note 1, *supra,* at 26 (May 29). Others expressed similar views. When the Convention was close to complete impasse, Gerry appealed to the members to keep trying. Without a Union, "We should be without an Umpire to decide controversies and must be at the mercy of events." *Id.* 515 (July 2). And Sherman listed a national power to prevent internal disputes and resorts to force as one of the four basic objects of a Union. *Id.* 133 (June 6).

controversies between states could be viewed as implicit in Randolph's "national peace and harmony" provision.

The Committee of Detail's report qualified its proposed grant of jurisdiction to the Supreme Court in "controversies between two or more States" with an exception for "such as shall regard Territory or Jurisdiction." For these disputes, the Committee retained an analogue to the cumbersome machinery of the Articles of Confederation, which the Senate was charged with implementing.[103] On the floor, Rutledge moved to strike these provisions, saying that they were "necessary under the Confederation, but will be rendered unnecessary by the National Judiciary now to be established." Some expressed concerns that "[t]he Judges might be connected with the States being parties." But the motion to strike carried eight states to two, with only North Carolina and Georgia dissenting.[104]

(iii) A State and Citizens of Another State. The grant of jurisdiction in controversies between a state and citizens of another state had no specific forerunner in any of the five plans before the Convention.[105] The clause first appears in a marginal note in Rutledge's handwriting on Randolph's draft for the Committee of Detail,[106] and that committee reported it out in its present form.[107] No discussion of the clause occurred, but concern about prejudice seems a likely explanation.[108]

(iv) Citizens of Different States. The grant of diversity jurisdiction aroused bitter opposition in the ratification debates, and the controversy has continued intermittently ever since.[109] The clause passed without question in the Convention, and thus without clarification of its purposes.[110]

Randolph's initial plan provided for jurisdiction in "cases in which foreigners or citizens of other States applying to such jurisdictions may be interested,"[111] in contrast with Paterson's, Hamilton's, and Blair's, which protected only foreigners, and Pinckney's, which had no provision against bias. When the Committee of the Whole first considered Randolph's proposal on June 12, it voted to give jurisdiction in "cases in which foreigners or

---

[103] See the proposed Art. IX, Sec. 3, 2 Farrand, note 1, *supra*, at 183–84. The provision seems to have originated in Randolph's draft in the Committee of Detail. *Id.* 144.

[104] *Id.* 400–01 (August 24).

[105] Randolph's original resolution, detailed in Paragraph 5(b)(iv), *infra*, and in 1 Farrand, note 1, *supra*, at 22, would not have guarded against the possibility of antagonism when a state was suing in the courts of another state. Further, if Hamilton was right in The Federalist, No. 81, that the Convention did not contemplate that a state could be sued by a citizen of another state without its consent (at least on causes of action not based on federal law), it would have been of no assistance to an out-of-state citizen as plaintiff.

[106] 2 Farrand, note 1, *supra*, at 147.

[107] *Id.* 186.

[108] For discussion of whether the provision allowed for suits to proceed against nonconsenting states, see Chap. IX, Sec. 2, *infra*.

[109] The problem is more fully treated in Chap. VIII, Sec. 5, *infra*.

[110] Of possible relevance to the subsequent doctrine of Swift v. Tyson, 41 U.S. (16 Pet.) 1 (1842), explored in Chap. VI, Sec. 2, *infra*, one proposal would have granted jurisdiction in any case "which may arise * * * on the Law of Nations or general commercial or maritime Laws." The provision was found in a draft in Wilson's handwriting among the records of the Committee of Detail, which was derived from the Paterson plan and therefore provided only for appellate jurisdiction. 2 Farrand, note 1, *supra*, at 157.

[111] 1 *id.* 22. See also note 105, *supra*.

citizens of two distinct States of the Union" may be interested.[112] This specification reappeared in its present form in the report of the Committee of Detail, and the Convention accepted it without challenge on August 27.[113]

(v) Citizens of the Same State, Claiming Lands Under Grants of Different States. The Committee of Detail proposed the same mode of settling these controversies as for controversies over territory or jurisdiction between the states themselves, and the delegates voted to strike both proposals by the same vote.[114] Sherman's motion to insert the present provision during the later debate passed unanimously.[115]

(vi) States, or Citizens Thereof, and Foreign States, Citizens or Subjects. All the plans except Pinckney's provided for jurisdiction where foreigners were interested,[116] and the need for a grant going beyond cases involving treaties and foreign representatives seems to have aroused no dispute. The clause came out of the Committee of Detail in its present form.[117]

6.   Jurisdiction of the Supreme Court

a.   Original Jurisdiction

The Randolph Plan, which required the establishment of lower federal courts, made no provision for an original jurisdiction of the Supreme Court, but all other plans did.[118] Once it had been decided that the creation of inferior courts should be at the discretion of Congress, the Supreme Court's original jurisdiction took on new importance as the only assured means of access to a federal tribunal. In the Committee of Detail, one draft of the Constitution in Randolph's handwriting gave the Supreme Court original jurisdiction in cases of impeachment and such other cases as the legislature might prescribe.[119] A later draft in Wilson's handwriting, and the draft submitted to the Convention, provided for original jurisdiction in cases of impeachment, in cases affecting ambassadors and other public ministers and consuls, and in cases in which a state was a party. This grant, however, was subject to a general power in the legislature to assign this jurisdiction, except for a trial of the President, to inferior federal courts.[120] The delegates struck

---

[112]   1 Farrand, note 1, *supra*, at 22, 211.

[113]   2 *id.* 431–32. Mask & MacMahon, *The Revolutionary War Prize Cases and the Origins of Diversity Jurisdiction*, 63 Buff.L.Rev. 477 (2015), argues that the experience of the Continental Congress in entertaining appeals from state tribunals in prize cases, note 37, *supra*, persuaded influential Framers of the importance of national courts free of geographic bias. According to the authors, their findings "rehabilitate[ ] the view that geographic bias was a driving force behind the grant of diversity jurisdiction." *Id.* 547.

[114]   See note 104, *supra*, and accompanying text.

[115]   2 Farrand, note 1, *supra*, at 431–32 (August 27).

[116]   See note 89, *supra*.

[117]   2 Farrand, note 1, *supra*, at 186.

[118]   Paterson's plan, contemplating primarily an appellate jurisdiction from state courts, provided for original jurisdiction in cases of impeachment. 1 *id.* 244. Pinckney's gave original jurisdiction in impeachment and in cases affecting ambassadors and other public ministers, see 3 *id.* 600; Hamilton's, in cases of captures, see 1 *id.* 292; and Blair's, "in all cases affecting ambassadors, other public ministers and consuls, and those in which a State shall be a party, and suits between persons claiming lands under grants of different states," 2 *id.* 432–33.

[119]   2 *id.* 147.

[120]   *Id.* 173, 186–87.

the provision for impeachments and the legislative power of assignment on the floor.[121]

b.   Appellate Jurisdiction

The decisions as to the scope of the Supreme Court's original jurisdiction settled that the balance of its jurisdiction should be appellate.[122]

The important provision that the appellate jurisdiction should be subject to exceptions and regulations by Congress appeared in none of the plans.[123] It emerged for the first time in the report of the Committee of Detail and, remarkably, provoked no discussion on the floor of the Convention at the time of its acceptance. There are few clues even to the thinking of the Committee of Detail.[124]

Discussions on the floor of the Convention do speak, however, to another question that would later occasion bitter political controversy. In debates about whether lower federal courts should be constitutionally mandatory or prohibited, it was universally assumed that the Supreme Court would have jurisdiction to review the decisions of state courts on matters of federal concern.[125] Indeed, it was the staunchest partisans of state authority who most insistently urged the appropriateness of this method of protecting federal interests.

The provision that the jurisdiction should extend to both law and fact was added on the floor of the Convention.[126] Gouverneur Morris asked if the appellate jurisdiction extended to matters of fact as well as law, and Wilson said he thought that was the intention of the Committee of Detail. Dickinson then moved to add the words "both as to law and fact," and his motion passed unanimously.[127]

The phrase "and fact" opened the Constitution to the charge that the Supreme Court was authorized to re-examine jury verdicts.[128] The charge

---

[121] See *id.* 423–24, 430–31 (August 27). The resulting Constitution assigns the trial of impeachments to the Senate. See U.S. Const., Art. I, Sec. 3, cl. 6 (providing the "Senate shall have the sole Power to try all Impeachments").

[122] 1 Farrand, note 1, *supra*, at 243–44; 2 *id.* 433.

[123] All the plans appear to have made the appellate jurisdiction a constitutional requirement, and Blair's even went to the point of prescribing a constitutional jurisdictional amount.

[124] The Exceptions Clause is foreshadowed in Randolph's draft for the committee and then appears in a later draft in Wilson's handwriting in substantially the form in which the committee reported it. 2 *id.* 147, 173, 186. Madison's comments on the potential for oppressive or ineffectual appeals might shed some light on the impetus for the Exceptions Clause. See text accompanying notes 46–47, *supra*. For an argument that the clause has its origins in the legal system of Scotland—where Wilson was born and partly educated—see Pfander & Birk, *Article III and the Scottish Judiciary*, 124 Harv.L.Rev. 1613, 1671–84 (2011).

[125] See text accompanying notes 44–59, *supra*.

[126] Paterson's plan included a similar provision. 1 Farrand, note 1, *supra*, at 243. Blair's plan gave jurisdiction as to law only, except in cases of equity and admiralty. 2 *id.* 433. But the point was not touched on in the report of the Committee of Detail.

[127] 2 *id.* 431 (August 27). One reason the proposal met with no controversy may have been because English law permitted the review of both law and fact on appeal before courts of equity in certain circumstances. See Baker, Introduction to English Legal History (5th ed.2019); I Holdsworth, A History of English Law: The Judicial System 438 (1922 ed.).

[128] According to Ritz, Rewriting the History of the Judiciary Act of 1789, at 6 (Holt & LaRue eds. 1990), for the framing generation "there was no clear distinction between the

was made even as to criminal cases, where the right of trial by jury was guaranteed, but more especially as to civil cases, where it was not.[129] The protests bore fruit in the Seventh Amendment, which not only established the right of trial by jury in civil cases, but also provided that "no fact tried by a jury, shall be otherwise re-examined in any Court of the United States, than according to the rules of the common law."

D. The Ratification Debates and Proposals for Amendment

The judiciary article, which had aroused only relatively minor disagreement in the Convention, became a center of controversy in the ratification debates. The conventions of six of the initially ratifying states suggested amendments, and all of these but South Carolina wanted changes in Article III.[130] At least 19 of the 103 amendments proposed by these six states related to the judiciary or judicial proceedings.[131] According to Charles Warren, "The principal Amendments which were regarded as necessary, relative to the Judiciary, were: (a) an express provision guaranteeing jury trials in civil as well as criminal cases; (b) the confinement of appellate power to questions of law, and not of fact; (c) the elimination of any Federal Courts of first instance, or, at all events, the restriction of such original Federal jurisdiction to a Supreme Court with very limited original jurisdiction; (d)

---

functions of an 'appellate' court and a 'trial' court," since appellate courts routinely retried entire cases. "Distinctness and hierarchy did not characterize the [then familiar] court structures, and 'superior' usually meant only that a reviewing court had more judges sitting on it." *Id.*

[129] Of the five plans, only Blair's referred to trial by jury. While contemplating the trial of crimes in state courts, it required the use of juries. Blair's plan said nothing of civil cases. 2 Farrand, note 1, *supra*, at 433.

The provision in Article III for trial of crimes by jury first appears in a draft for the Committee of Detail in Wilson's handwriting, *id.* 173, and the Committee included the provision in its report, *id.* 187. The delegates then amended the provision to provide for the venue of trial for crimes not committed in any state and approved it unanimously on August 28. *Id.* 438.

On September 12, while the report of the Committee of Style was being printed, Williamson "observed to the House that no provision was yet made for juries in Civil cases and suggested the necessity of it." Gorham said it was impossible "to discriminate equity cases from those in which juries are proper," and added that the "Representatives of the people may be safely trusted in this matter." Gerry supported Williamson. Mason said he saw the difficulty of specifying jury cases, but, broadening the discussion, said that a bill of rights "would give great quiet to the people." Gerry and Mason moved that a committee be appointed to prepare such a bill. Sherman thought the state bills of rights sufficient, and repeated Gorham's points about juries. The Convention voted down the motion unanimously. *Id.* 587–88.

[130] Rhode Island's belated convention in 1790 also proposed amendments to Article III. Ames, Proposed Amendments to the Constitution, 1789–1889, at 310 (1897).

For a comprehensive and illuminating examination of the ratification debates, see Maier, Ratification: The People Debate The Constitution, 1787–1788 (2010). Older but still useful works on the ratification process, and especially on the character of anti-federalist opinion, include Main, The Anti-Federalists: Critics of the Constitution, 1781–1788 (1961); Mason, The States Rights Debate: Antifederalism and the Constitution (1964); Kenyon, The Anti-Federalists (1966); Rutland, The Ordeal of the Constitution: The Anti-Federalists and the Ratification Struggle of 1787–1788 (1966); Goebel, note 1, *supra*, at 251–91; Storing, The Complete Anti-Federalist (1981); and Wood, note 3, *supra*. On the debate over the judiciary during the ratification process, see Clinton, *A Mandatory View of Federal Court Jurisdiction: A Guided Quest for the Original Understanding of Article III*, 132 U.Pa.L.Rev. 741, 797–829 (1984).

[131] Ames, note 130, *supra*, at 307–10.

the elimination of all jurisdiction based on diverse citizenship and status as a foreigner."[132]

Ames lists 173 amendments proposed in the first session of the first Congress, although this figure includes many repetitions. Of the total, 48 were primarily concerned with courts and court proceedings; most had to do with trial by jury and various rights of defendants in criminal proceedings.[133] The Fourth, Fifth, Sixth, Seventh, and Eighth Amendments respond to the central concerns.

Of the remaining proposals, the most drastic, originating in the Virginia convention and offered only in the Senate, would have substantially redrafted Article III, altering not only the structure of the courts but the scope and conception of the judicial power.[134] Virginia's measure also challenged the power of Congress to establish inferior federal courts, building off the motion advanced three times in the House by Representative Tucker of South Carolina to limit the power to the establishment of courts of admiralty.[135] Tucker likewise moved to abolish the diversity jurisdiction, as did Virginia's plan introduced in the Senate.[136] Other proposals would have increased amount-in-controversy requirements in diversity cases. These too failed. Finally, the House approved a proposal to exclude appeals to the Supreme Court "where the value in controversy shall not amount to one thousand dollars," but it failed in the Senate.[137]

EXCERPTS FROM THE FEDERALIST PAPERS AND BRUTUS

As the ratification debates waged on, various authors penned commentary both supportive of ratification and critical of the draft Constitution. Alexander Hamilton, John Jay, and James Madison wrote the eighty-five Federalist papers, which provide the most influential contemporaneous exposition of the Constitution and its underlying premises.[1] References to the courts and the judiciary are woven throughout the arguments supporting the new Constitution. Five of the papers (Nos. 78

---

[132] Warren, *New Light on the History of the Federal Judiciary Act of 1789*, 37 Harv.L.Rev. 49, 56 (1923).

[133] Ames, note 130, *supra*, at 310–21 (Nos. 135–38, 140, 142–43, 169–76, 183–86, 188–89, 213–14, 221–24, 226–27, 254–55, 258, 292–94, 297).

[134] *Id.* at 320 (No. 284); Senate Journal, 1st Cong., 1st Sess., p. 126–27.

[135] Ames, note 130, *supra*, at 314 (No. 201), 315 (No. 208), 317 (No. 237); 1 Annals of Congress 791 (Aug. 18, 1789), 807 (Aug. 22, 1789).

[136] Ames, note 130, *supra*, at 315 (No. 209); 1 Annals of Congress 791 (Aug. 18, 1789).

[137] Ames, note 130, *supra*, at 316 (No. 225, drawn from Nos. 141, 181, 182); Senate Journal, 1st Cong., 1st Sess., p. 130.

[1] Noting that the Federalist Papers had little circulation outside of New York, scholars have questioned their influence on the outcome of state ratification debates and surrounding public understandings of the Constitution. See, *e.g.*, Kramer, *Madison's Audience*, 112 Harv.L.Rev. 611, 664–65 (1999). Yet the influence of the Papers on subsequent interpreters can hardly be doubted, nor can the insight that they offer into the understandings of their influential authors, Jay, Hamilton, and Madison. For a revealing window into how contemporary debates over analogous provisions played out among the public during the ratification of the Massachusetts Constitution of 1780, consult The Popular Sources of Political Authority: Documents on the Massachusetts Constitution of 1780 (Handlin & Handlin eds. 1966).

to 82), all authored by Hamilton, deal directly with the judiciary and build upon his assessment in No. 22 that "the defects of the confederation" encompassed "the want of a judiciary power." "Laws are a dead letter," Hamilton there concluded, "without courts to expound and define their true meaning and operation." Nos. 78 and 80 are particularly illuminating with respect to issues of federal judicial power and the judicial role. Excerpts of each follow below.

No. 78, Hamilton

WE PROCEED now to an examination of the judiciary department of the proposed government. * * *

According to the plan of the convention, all judges who may be appointed by the United States are to hold their offices DURING GOOD BEHAVIOR * * *. The standard of good behavior for the continuance in office of the judicial magistracy, is certainly one of the most valuable of the modern improvements in the practice of government. In a monarchy it is an excellent barrier to the despotism of the prince; in a republic it is a no less excellent barrier to the encroachments and oppressions of the representative body. And it is the best expedient which can be devised in any government, to secure a steady, upright, and impartial administration of the laws.

Whoever attentively considers the different departments of power must perceive, that, in a government in which they are separated from each other, the judiciary, from the nature of its functions, will always be the least dangerous to the political rights of the Constitution; because it will be least in a capacity to annoy or injure them. The Executive not only dispenses the honors, but holds the sword of the community. The legislature not only commands the purse, but prescribes the rules by which the duties and rights of every citizen are to be regulated. The judiciary, on the contrary, has no influence over either the sword or the purse; no direction either of the strength or of the wealth of the society; and can take no active resolution whatever. It may truly be said to have neither FORCE nor WILL, but merely judgment; and must ultimately depend upon the aid of the executive arm even for the efficacy of its judgments.

This simple view of the matter suggests several important consequences. It proves incontestably, that the judiciary is beyond comparison the weakest of the three departments of power*; that it can never attack with success either of the other two; and that all possible care is requisite to enable it to defend itself against their attacks. It equally proves, that though individual oppression may now and then proceed from the courts of justice, the general liberty of the people can never be endangered from that quarter; I mean so long as the judiciary remains truly distinct from both the legislature and the Executive. For I agree, that "there is no liberty, if the power of judging be not separated from the legislative and executive powers."** * * *

---

* [Ed.] Here, Hamilton cited Montesquieu, I Spirit of Laws 186.

** [Ed.] Here, Hamilton quoted Montesquieu, note *, *supra*, at 181.

The complete independence of the courts of justice is peculiarly essential in a limited Constitution. By a limited Constitution, I understand one which contains certain specified exceptions to the legislative authority; such, for instance, as that it shall pass no bills of attainder, no ex-post-facto laws, and the like. Limitations of this kind can be preserved in practice no other way than through the medium of courts of justice, whose duty it must be to declare all acts contrary to the manifest tenor of the Constitution void. Without this, all the reservations of particular rights or privileges would amount to nothing.

Some perplexity respecting the rights of the courts to pronounce legislative acts void, because contrary to the Constitution, has arisen from an imagination that the doctrine would imply a superiority of the judiciary to the legislative power. It is urged that the authority which can declare the acts of another void, must necessarily be superior to the one whose acts may be declared void. * * *

There is no position which depends on clearer principles, than that every act of a delegated authority, contrary to the tenor of the commission under which it is exercised, is void. No legislative act, therefore, contrary to the Constitution, can be valid. * * *

If it be said that the legislative body are themselves the constitutional judges of their own powers, and that the construction they put upon them is conclusive upon the other departments, it may be answered, that this cannot be the natural presumption, where it is not to be collected from any particular provisions in the Constitution. It is not otherwise to be supposed, that the Constitution could intend to enable the representatives of the people to substitute their WILL to that of their constituents. It is far more rational to suppose, that the courts were designed to be an intermediate body between the people and the legislature, in order, among other things, to keep the latter within the limits assigned to their authority. The interpretation of the laws is the proper and peculiar province of the courts. A constitution is, in fact, and must be regarded by the judges, as a fundamental law. It therefore belongs to them to ascertain its meaning, as well as the meaning of any particular act proceeding from the legislative body. If there should happen to be an irreconcilable variance between the two, that which has the superior obligation and validity ought, of course, to be preferred; or, in other words, the Constitution ought to be preferred to the statute, the intention of the people to the intention of their agents.

Nor does this conclusion by any means suppose a superiority of the judicial to the legislative power. It only supposes that the power of the people is superior to both; and that where the will of the legislature, declared in its statutes, stands in opposition to that of the people, declared in the Constitution, the judges ought to be governed by the latter rather than the former. * * *

If, then, the courts of justice are to be considered as the bulwarks of a limited Constitution against legislative encroachments, this consideration will afford a strong argument for the permanent tenure of judicial offices, since nothing will contribute so much as this to that independent spirit in the judges which must be essential to the faithful performance of so arduous a duty.

* * * [I]t is easy to see, that it would require an uncommon portion of fortitude in the judges to do their duty as faithful guardians of the Constitution, where legislative invasions of it had been instigated by the major voice of the community. * * *

That inflexible and uniform adherence to the rights of the Constitution, and of individuals, which we perceive to be indispensable in the courts of justice, can certainly not be expected from judges who hold their offices by a temporary commission. Periodical appointments, however regulated, or by whomsoever made, would, in some way or other, be fatal to their necessary independence. * * *

PUBLIUS.

No. 80, Hamilton

To JUDGE with accuracy of the proper extent of the federal judicature, it will be necessary to consider, in the first place, what are its proper objects.

It seems scarcely to admit of controversy, that the judiciary authority of the Union ought to extend to these several descriptions of cases: 1st, to all those which arise out of the laws of the United States, passed in pursuance of their just and constitutional powers of legislation; 2d, to all those which concern the execution of the provisions expressly contained in the articles of Union; 3d, to all those in which the United States are a party; 4th, to all those which involve the PEACE of the CONFEDERACY, whether they relate to the intercourse between the United States and foreign nations, or to that between the States themselves; 5th, to all those which originate on the high seas, and are of admiralty or maritime jurisdiction; and, lastly, to all those in which the State tribunals cannot be supposed to be impartial and unbiased.

The first point depends upon this obvious consideration, that there ought always to be a constitutional method of giving efficacy to constitutional provisions. What, for instance, would avail restrictions on the authority of the State legislatures, without some constitutional mode of enforcing the observance of them? The States, by the plan of the convention, are prohibited from doing a variety of things, some of which are incompatible with the interests of the Union, and others with the principles of good government. * * * No man of sense will believe, that such prohibitions would be scrupulously regarded, without some effectual power in the government to restrain or correct the infractions of them. This power must either be a direct negative on the State laws, or an authority in the federal courts to overrule such as might be in manifest contravention of the articles of Union. There is no third course that I can imagine. * * *

* * * If there are such things as political axioms, the propriety of the judicial power of a government being coextensive with its legislative, may be ranked among the number. The mere necessity of uniformity in the interpretation of the national laws, decides the question. Thirteen independent courts of final jurisdiction over the same causes, arising upon the same laws, is a hydra in government, from which nothing but contradiction and confusion can proceed.

* * * Controversies between the nation and its members or citizens, can only be properly referred to the national tribunals. Any other plan would be contrary to reason, to precedent, and to decorum.

The fourth point rests on this plain proposition, that the peace of the WHOLE ought not to be left at the disposal of a PART. The Union will undoubtedly be answerable to foreign powers for the conduct of its members. And the responsibility for an injury ought ever to be accompanied with the faculty of preventing it. As the denial or perversion of justice by the sentences of courts, as well as in any other manner, is with reason classed among the just causes of war, it will follow that the federal judiciary ought to have cognizance of all causes in which the citizens of other countries are concerned. This is not less essential to the preservation of the public faith, than to the security of the public tranquillity. A distinction may perhaps be imagined between cases arising upon treaties and the laws of nations and those which may stand merely on the footing of the municipal law. The former kind may be supposed proper for the federal jurisdiction, the latter for that of the States. But it is at least problematical, whether an unjust sentence against a foreigner, where the subject of controversy was wholly relative to the lex loci, would not, if unredressed, be an aggression upon his sovereign, as well as one which violated the stipulations of a treaty or the general law of nations. And a still greater objection to the distinction would result from the immense difficulty, if not impossibility, of a practical discrimination between the cases of one complexion and those of the other. So great a proportion of the cases in which foreigners are parties, involve national questions, that it is by far most safe and most expedient to refer all those in which they are concerned to the national tribunals.

The power of determining causes between two States, between one State and the citizens of another, and between the citizens of different States, is perhaps not less essential to the peace of the Union than that which has been just examined. * * *

A method of terminating territorial disputes between the States, under the authority of the federal head, was not unattended to, even in the imperfect system by which they have been hitherto held together. But there are many other sources, besides interfering claims of boundary, from which bickerings and animosities may spring up among the members of the Union. * * * Whatever practices may have a tendency to disturb the harmony between the States, are proper objects of federal superintendence and control.

It may be esteemed the basis of the Union, that "the citizens of each State shall be entitled to all the privileges and immunities of citizens of the several States." And if it be a just principle that every government OUGHT TO POSSESS THE MEANS OF EXECUTING ITS OWN PROVISIONS BY ITS OWN AUTHORITY, it will follow, that in order to the inviolable maintenance of that equality of privileges and immunities to which the citizens of the Union will be entitled, the national judiciary ought to preside in all cases in which one State or its citizens are opposed to another State or its citizens. To secure the full effect of so fundamental a provision against all evasion and subterfuge, it is necessary that its construction should be committed to that tribunal which, having no local attachments, will be likely to be impartial between the different States and their citizens, and which, owing its official existence to the Union, will never be likely to feel any bias inauspicious to the principles on which it is founded.

* * * The most bigoted idolizers of State authority have not thus far shown a disposition to deny the national judiciary the cognizances of maritime causes. These so generally depend on the laws of nations, and so commonly affect the rights of foreigners, that they fall within the considerations which are relative to the public peace. * * *

The reasonableness of the agency of the national courts in cases in which the State tribunals cannot be supposed to be impartial, speaks for itself. No man ought certainly to be a judge in his own cause, or in any cause in respect to which he has the least interest or bias. This principle has no inconsiderable weight in designating the federal courts as the proper tribunals for the determination of controversies between different States and their citizens. And it ought to have the same operation in regard to some cases between citizens of the same State. Claims to land under grants of different States, founded upon adverse pretensions of boundary, are of this description. The courts of neither of the granting States could be expected to be unbiased. * * *

From this review of the particular powers of the federal judiciary, as marked out in the Constitution, it appears that they are all conformable to the principles which ought to have governed the structure of that department, and which were necessary to the perfection of the system. If some partial inconveniences should appear to be connected with the incorporation of any of them into the plan, it ought to be recollected that the national legislature will have ample authority to make such EXCEPTIONS, and to prescribe such regulations as will be calculated to obviate or remove these inconveniences. * * *

PUBLIUS.

In No. 81, Hamilton continued his defense of the proposed federal judiciary and responded to critics who argued that it would enjoy unchecked power. To that end, he posited that "the supposed danger of judiciary encroachments on the legislative authority, which has been upon many occasions reiterated, is in reality a phantom. Particular misconstructions and contraventions of the will of the legislature may now and then happen; but they can never be so extensive as to amount to an inconvenience, or in any sensible degree to affect the order of the political system." Hamilton likewise contended that the legislative "power of instituting impeachments * * * is alone a complete security."

Federalist No. 81 also defends the importance of inferior federal courts, building upon arguments made in No. 80 regarding potential biases that state courts may have in adjudicating federal causes. To that end, Hamilton observed in No. 81 that "State judges, holding their offices during pleasure, or from year to year, will be too little independent to be relied upon for an inflexible execution of the national laws."

These and other Federalist papers came in response to critiques of the proposed Constitution advanced by opponents in various publications, including a series of essays published under the pseudonym Brutus. Brutus recognized the need for a stronger union, but like another opposition publication, The Federal Farmer, raised concerns that the new federal government would subsume the states.[2] Brutus also raised concerns over the proposed new national judiciary.

In No. 11, Brutus contended that the federal judiciary "will operate to a total subversion of the state judiciaries, if not, to the legislative authority of the states." More generally, he feared, the new national judiciary likely would "give such a meaning to the constitution in all cases where it can possibly be done, as will enlarge the sphere of their own authority" at the expense of the states. In No. 14, Brutus took pains to emphasize that trial by jury would be preserved in the state courts, echoing the common complaint that the Constitution provided for no such jury right in the inferior federal courts.[3] Brutus's final paper on the judiciary follows below.

No. 15, Brutus

* * * [T]he supreme court under this constitution would be exalted above all other power in the government, and subject to no controul. * * * I question whether the world ever saw, in any period of it, a court of justice invested with such immense powers, and yet placed in a situation so little responsible. Certain it is, that in England, and in the several states, where we have been taught to believe, the courts of law are put upon the most prudent establishment, they are on a very different footing.

The judges in England, it is true, hold their offices during their good behaviour, but then their determinations are subject to correction by the house of lords; and their power is by no means so extensive as that of the proposed supreme court of the union.—I believe they in no instance assume the authority to set aside an act of parliament under the idea that it is inconsistent with their constitution. They consider themselves bound to decide according to the existing laws of the land, and never undertake to

---

[2]   Scholars have suggested that Brutus was likely Melancton Smith or an associate. See The Anti-Federalist Writings of the Melancton Smith Circle xi–xxxii (Zuckert & Webb eds. 2009). Others have suggested Smith may have written the Letters from the Federal Farmer. See Webking, *Melancton Smith and the Letters from the Federal Farmer*, 44 Wlm. & Mary Q. 510 (1987). Wood, *The Authorship of the Letters from the Federal Farmer*, 31 Wlm. & Mary Q. 299 (1974), disputes the suggestion that Richard Henry Lee authored the Federal Farmer letters and doubts authorship of the letters can be proven. Zuckert & Webb, *supra*, believe Smith wrote one, but not both, of the publications and "lean toward *Brutus*." For his part, Smith, an abolitionist and prominent Anti-Federalist in New York, ultimately supported ratification and voted in favor of the Constitution.

[3]   In No. 13, Brutus also raised concerns that Article III's jurisdictional provisions "subject[ ] a state to answer in a court of law, to the suit of an individual," a prospect deemed "humiliating and degrading to a government, and, what I believe, the supreme authority of no state ever submitted to." No. 13 also specifically feared that Article III would permit individuals to sue for the "recovery of the debts [states] have contracted in effecting the revolution."

controul them by adjudging that they are inconsistent with the constitution—much less are they vested with the power of giving an *equitable* construction to the constitution.

* * * But the judges under this constitution will controul the legislature, for the supreme court are authorised in the last resort, to determine what is the extent of the powers of the Congress; they are to give the constitution an explanation, and there is no power above them to set aside their judgment. * * *

I do not object to the judges holding their commissions during good behaviour. * * * [But t]here is no power above them, to controul any of their decisions. There is no authority that can remove them, and they cannot be controuled by the laws of the legislature. In short, they are independent of the people, of the legislature, and of every power under heaven. Men placed in this situation will generally soon feel themselves independent of heaven itself. * * *

1st. There is no power above them that can correct their errors or controul their decisions—The adjudications of this court are final and irreversible, for there is no court above them to which appeals can lie, either in error or on the merits.—In this respect it differs from the courts in England, for there the house of lords is the highest court, to whom appeals, in error, are carried from the highest of the courts of law.

2d. They cannot be removed from office or suffer a dimunition of their salaries, for any error in judgement or want of capacity. * * *

The only clause in the constitution which provides for the removal of the judges from office, is that which declares, that "the president, vice-president, and all civil officers of the United States, shall be removed from office, on impeachment for, and conviction of treason, bribery, or other high crimes and misdemeanors." By this paragraph, civil officers, in which the judges are included, are removable only for crimes. Treason and bribery are named, and the rest are included under the general terms of high crimes and misdemeanors.—Errors in judgement, or want of capacity to discharge the duties of the office, can never be supposed to be included in these words, *high crimes and misdemeanors.* * * *

3d. The power of this court is in many cases superior to that of the legislature. * * * [T]his court will be authorised to decide upon the meaning of the constitution, and that, not only according to the natural and ob[vious] meaning of the words, but also according to the spirit and intention of it. In the exercise of this power they will not be subordinate to, but above the legislature. For all the departments of this government will receive their powers, so far as they are expressed in the constitution, from the people immediately, who are the source of power. * * * [T]he judicial hold their powers independently of the legislature, as the legislature do of the judicial.—The supreme court then have a right, independent of the legislature, to give a construction to the constitution and every part of it, and there is no power provided in this system to correct their construction or do it away. If, therefore, the legislature pass any laws, inconsistent with the sense the judges put upon the constitution, they will declare it void; and

therefore in this respect their power is superior to that of the legislature.
* * *

I have, in the course of my observation on this constitution, affirmed and endeavored to shew, that it was calculated to abolish entirely the state governments, and to melt down the states into one entire government, for every purpose as well internal and local, as external and national. * * *

Perhaps nothing could have been better conceived to facilitate the abolition of the state governments than the constitution of the judicial. They will be able to extend the limits of the general government gradually, and by insensible degrees, and to accommodate themselves to the temper of the people. Their decisions on the meaning of the constitution will commonly take place in cases which arise between individuals, with which the public will not be generally acquainted; one adjudication will form a precedent to the next, and this to a following one. * * * In this situation, the general legislature, might pass one law after another, extending the general and abridging the state jurisdictions, and to sanction their proceedings would have a course of decisions of the judicial to whom the constitution has committed the power of explaining the constitution.—If the states remonstrated, the constitutional mode of deciding upon the validity of the law, is with the supreme court, and neither people, nor state legislatures, nor the general legislature can remove them or reverse their decrees.

Had the construction of the constitution been left with the legislature, they would have explained it at their peril; if they exceed their powers, or sought to find, in the spirit of the constitution, more than was expressed in the letter, the people from whom they derived their power could remove them, and do themselves right; and indeed I can see no other remedy that the people can have against their rulers for encroachments of this nature. A constitution is a compact of a people with their rulers; if the rulers break the compact, the people have a right and ought to remove them and do themselves justice; but in order to enable them to do this with the greater facility, those whom the people chuse at stated periods, should have the power in the last resort to determine the sense of the compact; if they determine contrary to the understanding of the people, an appeal will lie to the people at the period when the rulers are to be elected, and they will have it in their power to remedy the evil; but when this power is lodged in the hands of men independent of the people, and of their representatives, and who are not, constitutionally, accountable for their opinions, no way is left to controul them but *with a high hand and an outstretched arm*.

NOTE ON THE ORGANIZATION AND DEVELOPMENT OF THE FEDERAL JUDICIAL SYSTEM

A.   The First Judiciary Act

The judiciary article of the Constitution was not self-executing, and the first Congress therefore faced the task of structuring a court system and, within limits established by the Constitution, of defining its jurisdiction. The controversies that had flared during the ratification debates made it clear that the definition of federal jurisdiction was freighted with political ramifications.

The Judiciary Act of 1789,[1] the twentieth statute enacted by the first Congress, responded to multiple pressures.[2] The Act is of interest today along at least two dimensions. First, the 1789 Act reflects the beginning of an organic development. It is impossible to understand the current judicial structure without a basic awareness of the foundations from which it evolved.[3] Second, the first Judiciary Act is widely viewed as an indicator of the original understanding of Article III and, in particular, of Congress's constitutional obligations concerning the vesting of federal jurisdiction.[4]

1. Court Organization

a. The Supreme Court

The first section of the 1789 Act provided that "the supreme court of the United States shall consist of a chief justice and five associate justices." It called for two sessions annually at the seat of government, with one commencing the first Monday of February and the other the first Monday of August.

b. The Circuit and District Courts

The "transcendent achievement"[5] of the First Judiciary Act lay in its exercise of the constitutional option to establish a system of federal trial courts.[6] Nonetheless, the original statutory scheme seems a curious one today. The Act provided for two tiers of trial courts: district courts, each with its own district judge, and circuit courts, without judges of their own. The circuit courts, which were to hold two sessions a year in each district within

---

[1]   Act of Sept. 24, 1789, 1 Stat. 73.

[2]   On the 1789 Act, see, *e.g.*, Goebel, History of the Supreme Court of the United States: Antecedents and Beginnings to 1801, at 457–508 (1971); Ritz, Rewriting the History of the Judiciary Act of 1789 (Holt & LaRue eds. 1990); Amar, *The Two-Tiered Structure of the Judiciary Act of 1789*, 138 U.Pa.L.Rev. 1499 (1990); Holt, *"To Establish Justice": Politics, the Judiciary Act of 1789, and the Invention of the Federal Courts*, 1989 Duke L.J. 1421; Clinton, *A Mandatory View of Federal Court Jurisdiction: Early Implementation of and Departures from the Constitutional Plan*, 86 Colum.L.Rev. 1515 (1986); Casto, *The First Congress's Understanding of Its Authority over the Federal Courts' Jurisdiction*, 26 B.C.L.Rev. 1101 (1985); Warren, *New Light on the History of the Federal Judiciary Act of 1789*, 37 Harv.L.Rev. 49 (1923); and Collins, *The Federal Courts, the First Congress, and the Non-Settlement of 1789*, 91 Va.L.Rev. 1515 (2005).

[3]   Still perhaps the most valuable source on the sequence of federal judiciary acts is Frankfurter & Landis, The Business of the Supreme Court (1928). For a useful summary, see Bator, *Judicial System, Federal*, 3 Encyclopedia of The American Constitution 1068–75 (1986). For a brief but valuable description of the historical development of the jurisdiction of the lower federal courts, see Frankfurter, *Distribution of Judicial Power Between United States and State Courts*, 13 Cornell L.Q. 499, 507–15 (1928).

[4]   Scholars have long debated how much influence the 1789 Act should wield on modern debates over the judicial power; these debates often are subsumed within larger debates over the importance of original meaning. For exploration of how and why these debates matter, see generally Chap. IV, *infra*.

[5]   Frankfurter & Landis, note 3, *supra*, at 4.

[6]   See Frank, *Historical Bases of the Federal Judicial System*, 13 Law & Contemp.Prob. 3, 9–11 (1948).

the circuit, were to be staffed by one district judge and two Supreme Court Justices sitting on circuit.

The Act divided the eleven states then in the Union into thirteen districts with boundaries corresponding to state lines, except that the parts of Massachusetts and Virginia that later became Maine and Kentucky were made into separate districts. The Act thus established a precedent, still almost invariably observed, against the crossing of state lines in setting the boundaries of federal judicial districts. Its provisions grouped eleven of the thirteen districts into three circuits, with special provision made for the remote Maine and Kentucky districts.[7]

2.   Jurisdiction of the District and Circuit Courts

The Act provided that the jurisdiction of the district courts would be entirely original, partly exclusive of the state courts and partly concurrent.[8]

The circuit courts also had an important original jurisdiction, as well as authority to review on writ of error final decisions of the district courts in civil cases in which the matter in controversy exceeded $50, and, on appeal, final decrees in admiralty and maritime cases in which the matter in controversy exceeded $300.

The original jurisdiction of both sets of courts can usefully be considered together, as the jurisdiction of the Supreme Court will be below, under the nine jurisdictional headings of Article III.

a.   Jurisdiction Based Primarily on Subject Matter

(i)   Cases Arising Under the Constitution, Laws, and Treaties of the United States. In the sphere of private civil litigation, the 1789 Act, curiously, did not invoke the grant of judicial power over cases arising under the Constitution or laws of the United States to provide for general federal question jurisdiction.[9] Congress gave the district courts, however, "exclusive original cognizance of all seizures on land, or other waters than as aforesaid, made, and of all suits for penalties and forfeitures incurred, under the laws of the United States."[10]

The Act vested the circuit courts with "exclusive cognizance of all crimes and offences cognizable under the authority of the United States," subject to

---

[7]   The district courts in those two districts were authorized to sit also as circuit courts, a device afterward used repeatedly in outlying areas.

[8]   For a discussion of exclusive federal jurisdiction, see Chap. IV, Sec. 3, *infra*.

[9]   Moore, *Trimming the Least Dangerous Branch: The Anti-Federalists and the Implementation of Article III*, 56 Tulsa L.Rev. 1 (2020), argues that the Judiciary Act's failure to grant sweeping federal question jurisdiction to the district courts resulted from the influence of Anti-Federalists. See also Casto, *An Orthodox View of the Two-Tier Analysis of Congressional Control over Federal Jurisdiction*, 7 Const.Comment. 89, 97 (1990) (stating that the 1789 Act "completely excluded a number of federal question cases from original and appellate federal jurisdiction"). For further discussion, see pp. 37–38, *infra*.

The development of later statutory grants of "arising under" jurisdiction is traced in Chap. VIII, *infra*.

[10]   § 9, 1 Stat. 73, 77. Subsequent acts provided for a host of specialized grants of jurisdiction over federal questions. For example, in the Patent Act of 1793, Congress granted the federal circuit courts exclusive jurisdiction over actions for patent infringement, see Act of Feb. 21, 1793, ch. 11, § 5, 1 Stat. 318, 322, and in 1819, it granted the same courts jurisdiction over all actions "arising under" the patent laws, see Act of Feb. 15, 1819, ch. 19, 3 Stat. 481, 481.

a concurrent jurisdiction of the district courts to try certain minor criminal offenses.[11]

The only reference to suits arising under treaties came in a provision conferring district court jurisdiction, concurrent with the state courts or the circuit courts, of "all causes where an alien sues for a tort only in violation of * * * a treaty of the United States."[12]

(ii) Cases Affecting Ambassadors, Other Public Ministers, and Consuls. Suits affecting ambassadors came within the original jurisdiction of the Supreme Court.[13] But the Act conferred district court jurisdiction, exclusive of the state courts, of all suits against consuls and vice-consuls (except criminal cases triable in the circuit courts).[14]

(iii) Admiralty Jurisdiction. In terms that in substance survive today, the 1789 Act gave the district courts "exclusive original cognizance of all civil causes of admiralty and maritime jurisdiction, * * * saving to suitors, in all cases, the right of a common law remedy, where the common law is competent to give it."[15] This grant included jurisdiction of "all seizures under laws of impost, navigation or trade of the United States, where the seizures are made, on waters which are navigable from the sea by vessels of ten or more tons burthen, within their respective districts as well as upon the high seas."[16]

b.   Jurisdiction Based on Party Status

(i)   United States a Party. The Act did not in terms contemplate the possibility of suits against the United States.

In addition to the jurisdiction for civil and criminal enforcement actions by the United States arising under federal law, discussed above, the 1789 Act gave the circuit courts concurrent jurisdiction with the state courts of all civil suits at common law or in equity in which "the United States are plaintiffs, or petitioners" and the matter in dispute exceeded five hundred dollars.[17] The district courts were given jurisdiction, similarly concurrent, "of all suits at common law where the United States sue, and the matter in dispute amounts * * * to the sum or value of one hundred dollars."[18]

(ii) Diversity Jurisdiction. Although the Act invoked the constitutional grant of judicial power in cases of diverse citizenship, it did so by providing jurisdiction to the circuit courts only in controversies "between a citizen of the State where the suit is brought, and a citizen of another

---

[11]   § 11, 1 Stat. 73, 78–79.

[12]   § 9, 1 Stat. 73, 77. For discussion, see Chap. VII, pp. 949–970, *infra.*

[13]   See p. 36, *infra.*

[14]   § 9, 1 Stat. 73, 77.

[15]   *Id.* For the current provision, see 28 U.S.C. § 1333; see also Chap. VIII, Sec. 6, *infra.*

[16]   Lee, *Article IX, Article III, and the First Congress: The Original Constitutional Plan for the Federal Courts,* 1787–1792, 89 Fordham L.Rev. 1895 (2021), observes that "the federal courts were originally established, in significant part, to reduce tensions with foreign governments by subordinating states' conflicting interests and protecting foreigners and providing them favorable forums for resolving maritime and commercial disputes with Americans." *Id.* 1896.

[17]   § 11, 1 Stat. 73, 78.

[18]   § 9, 1 Stat. 73, 77.

State."[19] Strawbridge v. Curtiss, 7 U.S. (3 Cranch) 267 (1806), p. 1077, *infra*, soon construed this language to require "complete diversity" when there are multiple parties on one or more sides of a case. In addition, to prevent defendants from being summoned long distances to defend small claims, the Act limited jurisdiction to cases in which the matter in dispute exceeded five hundred dollars. State courts enjoyed concurrent jurisdiction over all such cases.[20]

The Act vested the circuit courts with additional jurisdiction, also concurrent with the state courts, in all suits of a civil nature at common law or equity where an alien was a party when more than five hundred dollars was in dispute.[21] As noted above, the 1789 Act also gave the district courts jurisdiction, concurrent with the circuit and state courts, "of all causes where an alien sues for a tort only in violation of the law of nations or a treaty of the United States."[22]

These party-based grants of jurisdiction were qualified by the "assignee clause," framed to avoid collusive assignments to create jurisdiction, which with various changes survived until 1948. Under its terms, no district or circuit court had "cognizance of any suit to recover the contents of any promissory note or other chose in action in favour of any assignee, unless a suit might have been prosecuted in such court * * * if no assignment had been made, except in cases of foreign bills of exchange."[23]

The Act also originated the policy, which has endured ever since, of authorizing the removal to a federal court, before trial, of certain proceedings begun in the state courts.[24] The statute provided for removal to a circuit court, subject to the jurisdictional amount requirement of five hundred dollars. The privilege of removing was given to three classes of parties: (i) a defendant who was an alien; (ii) a defendant who was a citizen of another state, when sued by a plaintiff who was a citizen of the state where suit was brought; and (iii) either party, where title to land was in dispute, if one party claimed under a grant from another state and the other party claimed under a grant of the state in which the suit was brought.

3. Jurisdiction of the Supreme Court

a. Original Jurisdiction[25]

Possibly not foreseeing the later-established doctrine that the original jurisdiction of the Supreme Court derives directly from the Constitution, the framers of the First Judiciary Act provided for the Court's original

---

[19] § 11, 1 Stat. 73, 78. The Act provided that the district courts in the Districts of Kentucky and Maine would "have jurisdiction of all other causes, except of appeals and writs of error, hereinafter made cognizable in a circuit court." § 10, 1 Stat. 73, 77–78.

[20] For the development of the diversity jurisdiction, see Chap. VIII, Sec. 5, *infra*.

[21] § 11, 1 Stat. 73, 78.

[22] § 9, 1 Stat. 73, 77. The successor provision is 28 U.S.C. § 1350. See Chap. VII, Sec. 1, pp. 949–970, *infra*.

[23] § 11, 1 Stat. 73, 79. For discussion, see Sheldon v. Sill, 49 U.S. (8 How.) 441 (1859), p. 406, *infra*. The successor provision is 28 U.S.C. § 1359.

[24] § 12, 1 Stat. 73, 79. For the later history of the removal provisions, see Chap. VIII, Sec. 8, *infra*.

[25] See generally Chap. III, Sec. 2, *infra*.

jurisdiction in terms that are nearly, but not exactly, coextensive with the constitutional grant. Under the 1789 Act, the original jurisdiction included:[26]

(1) "all controversies of a civil nature, where a state is a party, except between a state and its citizens;" and

(2)(a) "all such jurisdiction * * * as a court of law can have or exercise consistently with the law of nations" of suits "against ambassadors, or other public ministers, or their domestics, or domestic servants"; and

(b) "all suits brought by ambassadors, or other public ministers, or in which a consul, or vice consul, shall be a party."[27]

The Act distinguished, as have all later acts, between instances in which this original jurisdiction was exclusive of other courts and those in which it was not. The jurisdiction was exclusive in the cases in clause (1), above, except suits "between a state and citizens of other states, or aliens," and in all the cases in clause (2)(a).

b. Appellate Jurisdiction[28]

The 1789 Act did not provide for Supreme Court as-of-right appellate review of all decisions of the lower federal courts. Final judgments or decrees of the circuit courts in civil cases were reviewable on writ of error only if "the matter in dispute exceed[ed] the sum or value of two thousand dollars, exclusive of costs."[29] There was no provision for review of federal criminal cases.[30] The Act did, however, confer on the Supreme Court a habeas corpus jurisdiction, which the Court later classified as appellate, through which it could review federal decisions resulting in detentions.[31]

With respect to state court decisions, § 25 provided for Supreme Court review of final judgments or decrees "in the highest court of law or equity of a State in which a decision in the suit could be had," in three classes of cases:

(1) "* * * where is drawn in question the validity of a treaty or statute of, or an authority exercised under the United States, and the decision is against their validity;" or

(2) "* * * where is drawn in question the validity of a statute of, or an authority exercised under any State, on the ground of their being repugnant to the constitution, treaties or laws of the United States, and the decision is in favour of such their validity;" or

(3) "* * * where is drawn in question the construction of any clause of the constitution, or of a treaty, or statute of, or commission held under the

---

[26] § 13, 1 Stat. 73, 80–81.

[27] The jurisdiction conferred by clause 2 was therefore framed in terms of party status, rather than echoing the broader constitutional language authorizing jurisdiction in all cases "*affecting* Ambassadors, other public Ministers and Consuls" (emphasis added).

[28] See Chap. V, Sec. 1, *infra*.

[29] § 22, 1 Stat. 73, 84.

[30] Once the potential existed for ties on the circuit courts, see p. 38, *infra*, the Supreme Court reviewed a number of federal criminal cases over which it would not otherwise have enjoyed appellate jurisdiction. See Nash & Collins, *The Certificate of Division and the Early Supreme Court*, 94 S.Calif.L.Rev. 733 (2021) (documenting that the Court reviewed 44 such cases during the tenure of Chief Justices Marshall and Taney).

[31] See Chap. III, Sec. 3, *infra*.

United States, and the decision is against the title, right, privilege or exemption specially set up or claimed" thereunder.[32]

In all cases within the Court's appellate jurisdiction, review occurred by "writ of error." This limitation "eliminate[d] all possibility of a second trial of the facts, by jury or otherwise," in the Supreme Court.[33]

4. The Overall Scope of Federal Jurisdiction Under the First Judiciary Act

When the respective jurisdictions of district and circuit courts and the Supreme Court are viewed together, the 1789 Act fell short of vesting federal jurisdiction in "all Cases" in which Article III would have permitted jurisdiction based primarily on subject matter.

(i) In the category of cases arising under federal law, Congress provided no general federal question jurisdiction in the lower federal courts. Nor, under § 25, did the Supreme Court's appellate jurisdiction extend to cases originating in the state courts in which the federal claim was *upheld*. Further, habeas corpus aside, the Supreme Court lacked appellate jurisdiction over federal criminal cases.

(ii) In the category of cases affecting foreign envoys, § 13 conferred original Supreme Court jurisdiction over a broad category of suits to which denominated officials, and in some cases their servants, were *parties*. It did not, however, extend to all suits by which ambassadors, other public ministers, and consuls might be "affect[ed]."

(iii) In the category of admiralty and maritime jurisdiction, § 9 gave the federal courts exclusive jurisdiction in admiralty, but saved "to suitors, in all cases, the right of a common law remedy." In practice, this provision has meant that claims that can be enforced in a federal court in admiralty can typically also be enforced in a state court *in personam* action.

With respect to Article III's authorizations of jurisdiction based on party status, the 1789 Act did not provide in its terms for suits against the United States. By contrast, the Act did authorize jurisdiction of a variety of civil suits to which states were parties, "except between a state and its citizens," without expressly limiting the grant to cases in which the states were plaintiffs or petitioners. The diversity jurisdiction included a significant amount-in-controversy limitation and was construed by the Supreme Court as limited to cases of "complete diversity" in cases involving multiple parties.

Taking stock of the drafting of the Act and its resulting terms, Warren observes that the Act's "final form * * * and its subsequent history cannot be properly understood, unless it is realized that it was a compromise measure, so framed as to secure the votes of those who, while willing to see the experiment of a Federal Constitution tried, were insistent that the Federal Courts should be given the minimum powers and jurisdiction." Although the

---

[32]   For the later development, see Chap. V, Sec. 1, *infra*.

[33]   Ritz, note 2, *supra*, at 88.

Act's final provisions "completely satisfied no one," Warren concludes that
"they pleased the Anti-Federalists more than the Federalists."[34]

The scope of the Act's jurisdictional provisions and limitations continues
to be much controverted, as does the question of the first Congress's
understanding of the scope of its constitutional obligation, if any, to vest
federal jurisdiction in various classes of cases. For further discussion, see
Chap. IV, Sec. 1, and Chap. IX, Sec. 2, *infra.*

B.   The Years Before the Civil War

The period before the Civil War witnessed the emergence of two
enduring patterns in the judicial history of the United States. The first
involved the relative stability of the structure of courts established by the
First Judiciary Act—at least at its base in the district courts and its apex in
the Supreme Court.[35] The circuit courts quickly emerged as a weak spot, due
to their lack of any judges of their own and the inordinate burden that circuit
riding cast upon Supreme Court Justices. Congress reduced the burden in
1793 by requiring only one Justice per circuit court;[36] but the reduction came
at the cost of establishing a two-judge court, which created a problem of split
decisions.

A second emerging pattern concerned the incremental adjustment of
federal jurisdiction to reflect shifting political currents and, in particular,
preferences for greater or lesser national authority vis-a-vis the states. The
famous Law of the Midnight Judges,[37] enacted by a lame duck Federalist
Congress after the Federalist party had lost control of both Congress and the
Presidency in the elections of 1800,[38] furnishes an egregious example. The
new Act, which aimed in part to protect the nationalist values of the outgoing
administration, gave the district and circuit courts, taken together, a
jurisdiction almost coextensive with the constitutional authorization. The
Act also abolished circuit riding by Supreme Court Justices and provided
instead that five of the circuit courts would each have a bench of three circuit
judges and that the sixth (the western circuit) would have a single circuit

[34]   Warren, note 2, *supra*, at 53. Warren notes that Attorney General Edmund Randolph,
a Federalist, "submitted a voluminous report recommending many radical changes" to the Act
as early as December 1790, and consistent "efforts were made by the Federalists" in the ensuing
ten years "to amend the Act by broadening the scope of the Federal Judiciary." *Id.* 54. In
assessing the Act ten years after its passage, Hamilton called it "inadequate to its object."
Hamilton, 8 The Works of Alexander Hamilton 278 (Lodge ed. 1904). Hand-in-hand with the
Judiciary Act came the first of two Process Acts, which declined to adopt uniform rules for the
operation of the federal courts and instead instructed federal courts to follow many of the
practices of the state courts in which they sat. Act of Sept. 29, 1789, ch. 21, 1 Stat. 93 (repealed
1792); Act of May 8, 1792, ch. 36, 1 Stat. 275 (repealed 1872).

[35]   For a detailed account of the administration and business of the district and circuit
courts under the First Judiciary Act from 1789 to 1801, see Henderson, Courts for a New Nation
(1971); see also Goebel, note 2, *supra*, at 552–661. For details of President Washington's judicial
nominees, see Arnold, *Judicial Politics Under President Washington*, 38 Ariz.L.Rev. 473 (1996).

[36]   Act of March 2, 1793, 1 Stat. 333. For discussions of contemporary criticisms of the
circuit riding obligation, see Frankfurter & Landis, note 3, *supra*, at 14–30; 1 Warren, The
Supreme Court in United States History 85–90 (1926).

[37]   Act of February 13, 1801, 2 Stat. 89. See generally Surrency, *The Judiciary Act of 1801*,
2 Am.J.Legal Hist. 53 (1958); Turner, *The Midnight Judges*, 109 U.Pa.L.Rev. 494 (1961);
Turner, *Federalist Policy and the Judiciary Act of 1801*, 22 Wm. & Mary Q. 3 (1965).

[38]   For further discussion, see Wood, Empire of Liberty: A History of the Early Republic,
1789–1815, at 400–32 (2009), and pp. 68–87, *infra.*

judge. The new judges, appointed by President Adams and confirmed by the outgoing Senate, were all Federalists.

The incoming Jeffersonians, their anger heightened by the behavior of some of the new judges, repealed the act and abolished the judgeships.[39] For the most part, the new Act of April 29, 1802,[40] prescribed a return to the *status quo ante*. Although the repeal raised serious constitutional questions, none of the ousted judges appears to have pressed a challenge in the courts, and the Supreme Court, in Stuart v. Laird, rejected a constitutional objection to the requirement that Supreme Court Justices resume acting as circuit judges.[41]

Among its innovations, the 1802 Act authorized the circuit courts, in cases where the judges were divided, to certify questions to the Supreme Court.[42] In addition to its old jurisdiction to entertain a writ of error, the Supreme Court was empowered to hear appeals from the circuit courts in equity, admiralty, and prize cases where the amount in dispute exceeded $2,000.

In the wake of the 1802 Act, however, the circuit courts grew more and more rickety. Although Congress remained attached to circuit riding as a means of keeping Supreme Court Justices in touch with the people, the burgeoning number of judicial districts put increasing strains on the system. To allow for circuit court sessions in each district, the Act had reduced the number of Supreme Court sessions to one a year and authorized the holding of the circuit court by a single district judge. As the country grew, however, the Justices increasingly invoked the privilege of non-attendance in remote districts. Correspondingly, circuit court review of district court decisions became increasingly futile.

In 1807 Congress created a seventh circuit to meet the needs of Kentucky, Tennessee, and Ohio.[43] This action automatically triggered the appointment of a sixth associate Justice for the new circuit. With the size of the Supreme Court tied to the circuit system, Congress proved unable to agree upon similar action for later-entering states for more than twenty years. As a result, these states remained outside the circuit system. In 1837, Congress re-divided the country into nine circuits and increased the membership of the Supreme Court to nine.[44] California (joined soon after by

---

[39]   Act of March 8, 1802, 2 Stat. 132. See Frankfurter & Landis, note 3, *supra*, at 24–30; 1 Warren, note 36, *supra*, at 184–230.

[40]   2 Stat. 156, as amended by the Act of March 3, 1803, 2 Stat. 244.

[41]   5 U.S. (1 Cranch) 299 (1803). For a provocative study of the location of Stuart v. Laird in the constitutional politics surrounding the 1800 presidential election and its aftermath, see Ackerman, The Failure of the Founding Fathers: Jefferson, Marshall, and the Rise of Presidential Democracy (2005).

[42]   The Act made certification optional in civil and mandatory in criminal cases. Professor White reports that in the early nineteenth century, the Justices sometimes deliberately created divisions when riding circuit, to permit Supreme Court review on certificate of decisions that otherwise were not reviewable. See White, III–IV History of the Supreme Court of the United States: The Marshall Court and Cultural Change, 1815–35, at 173–74 (1988).

[43]   Act of Feb. 24, 1807, 2 Stat. 420, amended by the Act of March 22, 1808, 2 Stat. 477, and the Act of Feb. 4, 1809, 2 Stat. 516.

[44]   Act of March 3, 1837, 5 Stat. 176.

Oregon) became a tenth circuit in 1855;[45] and in 1863 Congress briefly added a tenth Justice to the Supreme Court,[46] before shortly reorganizing the districts into nine circuits[47] and reducing the number of Justices.[48]

Meanwhile, a series of collisions between federal and state authority led Congress to extend federal jurisdiction to meet threats to federal interests. New England's resistance to the War of 1812 led Congress to provide for removal of suits against federal officers and others enforcing customs duties from state to federal court.[49] Similarly, the "Force Bill" of 1833[50] responded to South Carolina's threats of nullification by authorizing removal of suits and prosecutions based on acts done under federal customs laws[51] and conferring federal habeas corpus jurisdiction in cases of confinement "for any act done, or omitted to be done, in pursuance of a law of the United States."[52] The advent of the Civil War occasioned further removal acts.[53] It also witnessed President Lincoln persuade Congress to abolish the Circuit Court in the District of Columbia, which Lincoln believed to be staffed by judges disloyal to the Union cause; Lincoln in turn appointed loyalists to the newly-established Supreme Court of the District of Columbia.[54]

C. Reconstruction

Reconstruction Congresses complemented the profound changes in constitutional structure wrought by the Civil War amendments with a compendious series of statutes extending the jurisdiction of the federal courts and expanding federal causes of action.[55] The relevant statutes included what is now 42 U.S.C. § 1983.[56] Notably, in 1867, Congress authorized federal courts to issue writs of habeas corpus on behalf of persons detained by state authorities in violation of the Constitution, laws, and treaties of the United States.[57] In addition, the various civil rights acts included jurisdictional grants. Congress also enacted at least twelve pieces of removal legislation during the Reconstruction era.[58] Most sweepingly, the

---

[45]   Act of March 2, 1855, 10 Stat. 631.

[46]   Act of March 3, 1863, 12 Stat. 794, amended by the Act of Feb. 19, 1864, 13 Stat. 4.

[47]   Act of July 23, 1866, § 2, 14 Stat. 209.

[48]   In 1866, Congress reduced the number of Justices to seven, *id.*, § 1, to keep President Johnson from filling vacancies; but three years later Congress restored the number to nine, Act of April 10, 1869, 16 Stat. 44, where it has remained ever since.

[49]   See Act of Feb. 4, 1815, § 8, 3 Stat. 195, 198.

[50]   Act of March 2, 1833, 4 Stat. 632.

[51]   For general discussion of removal, see Chap. VIII, Sec. 8, *infra.*

[52]   For discussion of the habeas corpus provisions, see p. 1467 *infra.*

[53]   See Hart & Wechsler's The Federal Courts and the Federal System 853–854 n.6 (Fallon, Manning, Meltzer & Shapiro eds. 7th ed.2015).

[54]   Act of Mar. 3, 1863, ch. 91, 12 Stat. 762. Lincoln was responding at least in part to the issuance of a writ of habeas corpus by one of the Circuit Court judges ordering release of an underage soldier. See McGuire, An Anecdotal History of the United States District Court for the District of Columbia, 1801–1976, at 43 (1976).

[55]   For useful overviews, see Kutler, Judicial Power and Reconstruction Politics (1968); Wiecek, *The Reconstruction of the Federal Judicial Power,* 1863–1875, 13 Am.J.Leg.Hist. 333 (1969).

[56]   Act of Apr. 20, 1871, ch. 22, 17 Stat. 13.

[57]   See Act of Feb. 5, 1867, ch. 28, § 1, 14 Stat. 385. See generally Chap. XI, Sec. 3, *infra.*

[58]   See Kutler, note 55, *supra,* at 147.

Judiciary Act of 1875 conferred on the federal judiciary a general jurisdiction over all civil cases "arising under" federal law, subject only to an amount-in-controversy requirement.[59] With the enactment of this statute, the Supreme Court later observed, "the lower federal courts * * * 'became the primary and powerful reliances for vindicating every right given by the Constitution, the laws, and treaties of the United States.' "[60]

D. Structural Reforms

The surge in federal judicial business in the years following the Civil War and Reconstruction created untenable strains on the federal judicial structure. Congress enacted a minor reform in 1869, when it finally provided for the permanent appointment of circuit judges and authorized one judge for each of the nine circuits.[61] At the same time, it reduced the circuit-riding duty of the Supreme Court Justices to attendance at one term every two years in each district of the circuit to which the Justice was assigned.

Nonetheless, docket pressures continued to mount. Growth in the Supreme Court's caseload resulted both from an increased population and from congressional additions to the Court's jurisdiction, including civil rights,[62] habeas corpus,[63] and patent and copyright[64] cases. In 1875, Congress restricted the Court's appellate jurisdiction by increasing the jurisdictional amount to $5,000.[65] Yet even this restriction was partially offset by further enlargements in the years immediately following.[66] By 1890, the number of cases on the Court's docket was nearly three times as large as in 1870.[67]

In the lower federal courts, which were the principal feeders of the stream, similar conditions prevailed. In 1873, there were 29,013 cases pending in the circuit and district courts, including 5,108 bankruptcy cases. By 1880, the total had increased to 38,045, even though the repeal of the Bankruptcy Act had eliminated the inward flow of bankruptcy cases. The year 1890 saw a further upward surge to 54,194 filings.[68]

---

[59]   See pp. 1025–1026, *infra.*

[60]   Steffel v. Thompson, 415 U.S. 452, 464 (1974) (quoting Frankfurter & Landis, note 3, *supra,* at 65).

[61]   Act of April 10, 1869, 16 Stat. 44.

[62]   Act of April 9, 1866, § 10, 14 Stat. 27, 29; Act of April 20, 1871, 17 Stat. 13.

[63]   Act of Feb. 5, 1867, § 1, 14 Stat. 385, 386. Congress abolished appeals to the Supreme Court under this law by the Act of March 27, 1868, § 2, 15 Stat. 44, see Ex parte McCardle, 74 U.S. (7 Wall.) 506 (1869), p. 407, *infra,* but restored them by the Act of March 3, 1885, 23 Stat. 437.

[64]   Act of Feb. 18, 1861, 12 Stat. 130.

[65]   Act of Feb. 16, 1875, § 3, 18 Stat. 315.

[66]   To the matters reviewable without regard to the amount in controversy, Congress added more civil rights cases by the Act of March 1, 1875, § 5, 18 Stat. 335, 337, and jurisdictional questions by the Act of Feb. 25, 1889, 25 Stat. 693. In 1889, Congress provided for the time that writs of error would be permitted in cases of capital crime. Act of Feb. 6, 1889, § 6, 25 Stat. 655, 656.

[67]   The figures in this paragraph come from Frankfurter & Landis, note 3, *supra,* at 60.

[68]   *Id.*

Congress finally responded with the Judiciary Acts of 1887–1888, which put a series of curbs on access to the lower federal courts.[69] Two years later, Congress fundamentally reshaped the federal judicial system and substantially established the framework of the contemporary system when it enacted the Evarts Act (the Circuit Court of Appeals Act of 1891).[70] The Act, which finally absolved the Justices of the Supreme Court of their obligation to "ride circuit," established circuit courts of appeals, consisting of three judges each, for each of the nine existing circuits. The legislation also created an additional circuit judgeship in each circuit, thus providing two circuit judges in all the circuits except the second, which, having received an additional judge in 1887,[71] now had three. The Evarts Act provided for the third place on court of appeals' panels ordinarily to be filled by a district judge, but Supreme Court Justices also remained eligible to sit.[72]

With respect to the Supreme Court's appellate jurisdiction, the Evarts Act introduced the then revolutionary, but now familiar, principle of discretionary review of federal judgments on writ of certiorari.[73] The Act also made circuit court of appeals' decisions "final" in diversity litigation, in suits under the revenue and patent laws, in criminal prosecutions, and in admiralty suits. In such cases, however, the Supreme Court, "by certiorari or otherwise," was authorized, regardless of the amount in controversy, to order the judgment brought before it for review. Despite this innovation, the Act continued to permit Supreme Court review as of right in important classes of cases, subject in general to a jurisdictional amount requirement of

---

[69] See Act of March 3, 1887, 24 Stat. 552, corrected by Act of Aug. 13, 1888, 25 Stat. 433. The specific restrictions of jurisdiction that the Act introduced were each relatively minor, but they had considerable aggregate effect:

(1) The Act raised the jurisdictional amount to $2,000.

(2) The privilege of removal was withdrawn from plaintiffs and confined to defendants; in diversity cases it was confined to nonresident defendants.

(3) Specific language made clear that the general removal jurisdiction did not extend to any cases except those that might have been brought originally in a federal court.

(4) No longer was venue proper in any district in which the defendant "shall be found," but only in the district of which the defendant was an "inhabitant," with an option in diversity cases of the district of either the plaintiff's or the defendant's residence.

(5) Banking associations were no longer allowed to sue in federal courts merely on the ground that they were incorporated under the laws of the United States.

(6) The Act broadened the assignee clause limiting diversity jurisdiction.

These restrictions of the 1887 act, however, were partly offset by the Tucker Act, 24 Stat. 505, which the President signed into law on the same day. See pp. 1343–1344, *infra*.

[70] Act of March 3, 1891, 26 Stat. 826. For the view that the Evarts Act was one of a package of post-Reconstruction measures by which the Republican Party attempted to expand federal power as a means of promoting national economic development—and thereby helped to lay the foundation for the Lochner era—see Gilman, *How Political Parties Can Use the Courts to Advance Their Agendas: Federal Courts in the United States, 1875–1891*, 96 Am.Pol.Sci.Rev. 511 (2002).

[71] Act of March 3, 1887, 24 Stat. 492.

[72] In deference to the traditionalists, the Act did not abolish the old circuit courts, although it took away their appellate jurisdiction over the district courts. For another twenty years there remained two sets of federal trial courts. The Judicial Code of 1911 finally abolished the Circuit Courts. See Act of March 3, 1911, 36 Stat. 1087.

[73] The Evarts Act did not alter the prevailing scheme of review of state court judgments by writ of error.

$1,000. In addition, as remains true today, a circuit court of appeals was authorized to "certify to the Supreme Court * * * any questions or propositions of law concerning which it desires the instruction of that court for its proper decision."[74]

The principle of discretionary review also served as an important feature of the structurally significant Act of December 23, 1914.[75] Animated at least partly by hostility to state court decisions invalidating legislation under the Due Process Clause,[76] Congress expanded the Supreme Court's appellate jurisdiction to encompass, for the first time, cases in which a state court rendered a decision favorable to a claim of federal right. To protect the Court from further docket overload, the statute provided for review of such cases by writ of certiorari. Congress further expanded the scope of discretionary Supreme Court review in the Judges' Bill, enacted in 1925,[77] which was drafted by a committee of Supreme Court Justices. Since then, the principle of review at the Court's discretion has become ever more dominant until, today, mandatory appellate jurisdiction has entirely disappeared in cases originating in state courts and has virtually disappeared in federal cases.[78]

E.   Political Responses to Federal Jurisdiction and Judicial Administration: The Lochner Era and Beyond

In the late nineteenth and early twentieth centuries, during the Lochner era, the federal courts began to engage in broader and potentially more intrusive scrutiny of state and federal legislation than ever before. The substantive constitutional theory underlying judicial review of economic legislation occasioned controversy from the outset, and critics viewed federal injunctions against the enforcement of state law as a special irritant in the structure of American federalism.

Congress responded with a number of jurisdictional enactments. In 1910, Congress provided that federal interlocutory injunctions against the enforcement of state statutes on constitutional grounds could be issued only by special, three-judge district courts, with direct appeal as of right to the Supreme Court.[79]

The Johnson Act, passed in 1934, sharply circumscribed the district courts' jurisdiction to issue injunctions interfering with state regulation of public utilities whenever "a plain, speedy, and efficient remedy may be had at law or in equity in the courts of" the state.[80] The Tax Injunction Act of 1937 similarly forbade federal injunctions against "the assessment, levy, or

---

[74]   For additional discussion of certification, see Chap. III, Sec. 1.

[75]   Act of Dec. 23, 1914, 38 Stat. 790.

[76]   See Frankfurter & Landis, note 3, *supra*, at 187–98.

[77]   Act of Feb. 13, 1925, 43 Stat. 936. See generally Frankfurter & Landis, note 3, *supra*, at 255–94; Mason, William Howard Taft: Chief Justice 88–120 (1964). For a critical history of the Judges' Act's genesis and enactment, see Hartnett, *Questioning Certiorari: Some Reflections Seventy-Five Years After the Judges' Bill*, 100 Colum.L.Rev. 1643, 1660–1704 (2000).

[78]   On review of state court decisions, see Chap. V, Sec. 1, *infra*.

[79]   36 Stat. 557. For a discussion of this statute and its subsequent history, see Chap. X Sec. 2.

[80]   48 Stat. 775, now codified at 28 U.S.C. § 1342. See Chap. X, Sec. 1, *infra*.

collection of any tax imposed by or pursuant to the laws of any State" as long as "a plain, speedy, and efficient remedy may be had at law or in equity in the courts of such State."[81]

Another congressional enactment of the same era, the Norris-LaGuardia Act of 1932,[82] sought to protect unions and their right to strike by narrowly restricting the authority of the federal courts to issue injunctions in "a case involving or growing out of a labor dispute." The Act further provided that "yellow-dog" contracts under which employees promised not to join a labor union "shall not be enforceable in any court of the United States," despite then-existing Supreme Court precedent holding that state legislation similarly limiting employers' remedies violated the Due Process Clause.[83]

In 1937, after decisions of the Supreme Court in 1934–1936 had invalidated important portions of the New Deal program[84] and raised apprehensions concerning the remainder, President Franklin D. Roosevelt sought to salvage the situation by "packing" the federal courts and especially the Supreme Court with New Deal sympathizers.[85] The plan that he submitted to Congress[86] would have authorized the President to appoint one additional judge to the federal courts, including the Supreme Court, for any federal judge who had served 10 years and who, after reaching the age of 70, did not retire or resign.[87]

But the Court-packing proposal, which the President initially defended on the dubious ground that it was needed to keep the Supreme Court abreast of its work,[88] aroused widespread opposition as an attack on the independence of the federal judiciary and the principle of judicial review.[89]

---

[81]   50 Stat. 738, now codified at 28 U.S.C. § 1341. See pp. 1418–1419, *infra*.

[82]   47 Stat. 70, now codified at 29 U.S.C. §§ 101–115.

[83]   For discussion, see Chap. IV, Sec. 1, pp. 455–457, *infra*.

[84]   See, *e.g.*, Panama Refining Co. v. Ryan, 293 U.S. 388 (1935); Railroad Retirement Board v. Alton R. Co., 295 U.S. 330 (1935); A.L.A. Schechter Poultry Corp. v. United States, 295 U.S. 495 (1935); United States v. Butler, 297 U.S. 1 (1936); Carter v. Carter Coal Co., 298 U.S. 238 (1936).

[85]   Before settling on this plan, the Administration canvassed other possible measures, including restrictions on the courts' jurisdiction and substantive constitutional amendments. See Leuchtenburg, *The Origins of Franklin D. Roosevelt's "Court-Packing" Plan*, 1966 Sup.Ct.Rev. 347. See also Burns, Roosevelt: The Lion and the Fox ch. 15 (1956).

[86]   S. 1392, 75th Cong., 1st Sess. (1937), printed in Sen.Rep. No. 711, 75th Cong., 1st Sess. (1937) (Reorganization of the Federal Judiciary).

[87]   Not more than 50 additional judges were to be so appointed, and the membership of the Supreme Court was to be limited to 15. The proposal would have allowed President Roosevelt to add six Justices to the Supreme Court if none of the sitting members over 70 had stepped down.

[88]   See the President's Message to Congress of February 5, 1937, printed in Sen.Rep. No. 711, note 86, *supra*, at 25–27. Subsequently the President became much more forthright in justifying his plan on the ground that the Court's decisions posed an obstacle to the New Deal. See generally Burns, note 85, *supra*. See also 6 The Public Papers and Addresses of Franklin D. Roosevelt lxv (1941): "I made one major mistake when I first presented the plan. I did not place enough emphasis upon the real mischief—the kind of decisions which, as a studied and continued policy, had been coming down from the Supreme Court. I soon corrected that mistake—in the speeches which I later made about the plan."

[89]   The suggestion that the plan was justified by the needs of judicial administration was strongly rebutted by Chief Justice Hughes, speaking also for Justices Brandeis and Van Devanter, in a letter to Senator Wheeler, which stated that the Court was abreast of its work

The Senate Judiciary Committee reported the plan adversely in June, 1937,[90] and in late July the Senate allowed it to die.[91] In the meantime, the Supreme Court upheld the constitutionality of a number of regulatory statutes,[92] Justice Van Devanter retired, and the Lochner era came to an end. Scholars continue to debate whether the Court-packing scheme, Roosevelt's overwhelming victory in the 1936 election, or related political pressures influenced Justice Roberts's "switch in time," which provided the critical fifth vote to uphold New Deal legislation.[93] (Congress did adopt legislation in 1937 that, among other things, called for three-judge panels in cases seeking injunctive relief against the execution of federal laws, which remained in place until 1976.[94])

After only a brief respite from the vortex of controversy, the substance of federal judicial action again began to occasion proposals to curb federal jurisdiction during the years of the Warren Court.[95] Congress did not, however, enact any of the relevant proposals.

F.   Further Reforms

The defeat of the Court-packing plan left the basic organization of the federal court system in the form established by the Evarts Act and the Judges' Bill of 1925.[96] The Judicial Code of 1948 (the present codification of the organization and business of the federal courts) retained that structure while making a number of important but interstitial changes.

---

and that the appointment of additional Justices would impair the Court's effectiveness. See Sen.Rep. No. 711, note 86, *supra*, at 38–40 (quoting the letter).

[90]   Sen.Rep. No. 711, note 86, *supra*.

[91]   See Burns, note 85, *supra*, at 306–09.

[92]   See, in particular, West Coast Hotel Co. v. Parrish, 300 U.S. 379 (1937); NLRB v. Jones & Laughlin Steel Corp., 301 U.S. 1 (1937).

[93]   Contemporaneous discussions almost invariably attributed the Court's apparent turnaround to political pressures, including the Court-packing plan. Later, however, Justice Frankfurter reported having received a memo from Justice Roberts that detailed the sequence of events and established that Roberts had cast his crucial votes in the West Coast Hotel and Jones & Laughlin cases, note 92, *supra*, before the President's announcement of his Court-packing proposal. See Frankfurter, *Mr. Justice Roberts*, 104 U.Pa.L.Rev. 311 (1955). *Cf.* Ariens, *A Thrice-Told Tale, or Felix the Cat*, 107 Harv.L.Rev. 620 (1994) (doubting Frankfurter's claims). Notwithstanding the Roberts memo, some historians have continued to maintain that political factors including the 1936 election—even if not the Court-packing plan in particular—provide the best explanation for Justice Roberts's 1937 votes to uphold key New Deal legislation. See, *e.g.*, Leuchtenburg, The Supreme Court Reborn: The Constitutional Revolution in the Age of Roosevelt (1995). Revisionist works that attribute the "switch in time" less to immediate political pressure than to gradually unfolding changes in constitutional doctrine and prevailing jurisprudential assumptions include Cushman, Rethinking the New Deal: The Structure of a Constitutional Revolution (1998), and White, The Constitution and the New Deal (2000). For an outstanding review of the scholarly debate between those who attribute the turn-around to "external" political or "internal" legal forces, and a search for common ground, see Kalman, *The Constitution, the Supreme Court, and the New Deal*, 110 Am.Hist.Rev. 1052 (2005).

[94]   See Act of Aug. 24, 1937, ch. 754, 50 Stat. 751; Act of Aug. 12, 1976, Pub.L.No. 94–381, 90 Stat. 1119. For background on the 1937 legislative changes, see Cushman, *The Judicial Reforms of 1937*, 61 Wm. & Mary L.Rev. 995 (2020).

[95]   For discussion, see Chap. IV, Sec. 1, *infra*. For a broader discussion of the relation of Warren Court decisionmaking to surrounding political currents, see Powe, The Warren Court and American Politics (2000).

[96]   Congress created the present Tenth Circuit in 1929. Act of Feb. 28, 1929, 45 Stat. 1346.

Since the 1948 recodification, the major legislative changes in the federal judicial system have included:

1.   Elimination in 1980 of the amount-in-controversy requirement in federal question cases brought under 28 U.S.C. § 1331.[97]

2.   Increases in the amount-in-controversy requirement in diversity cases under 28 U.S.C. § 1332 from $3,000 to $10,000 in 1958,[98] from $10,000 to $50,000 in 1988,[99] and then to $75,000 in 1996.[100]

3.   Legislation adopted in 1958 redefining corporate citizenship[101] and permitting certain interlocutory appeals to the courts of appeals from the district courts.[102]

4.   The virtual elimination of the requirement that certain cases be heard before a district court of three judges, with a right of direct appeal to the Supreme Court.[103] The story of the rise and fall of this requirement is told in Chap. X, Sec. 4(A), p. 1417, *infra*.

5.   Elimination of several other provisions for direct appeal to the Supreme Court of federal district court decisions.[104]

6.   Division of the Fifth Circuit into a new Fifth Circuit (Louisiana, Mississippi, and Texas) and a new Eleventh Circuit (Alabama, Florida, and Georgia).[105]

7.   Numerous changes in the character and scope of the specialized federal courts, including the creation of a new Court of Appeals for the Federal Circuit. These changes are described in Parts G and H of this Note.

8.   Elimination of the Supreme Court's mandatory appellate jurisdiction in the general jurisdictional statutes governing review of state and lower federal court judgments and substitution of discretionary review by writ of certiorari. The major amendments are described at pp. 617–619, *infra*.

---

[97]   Act of Dec. 1, 1980, 94 Stat. 2369.

[98]   Act of July 25, 1958, 72 Stat. 415.

[99]   Act of Nov. 19, 1988, 102 Stat. 4642, 4646.

[100]   See the Federal Courts Improvement Act of 1996, 110 Stat. 3847. The Judicial Improvements Act of 1990, 104 Stat. 5089, besides creating 85 new judgeships (11 at the appellate level and 74 at the district court level) (§§ 201–206, 104 Stat. 5098–5104), required that each district court formulate a plan to reduce the cost and delay of civil litigation (§ 103, 104 Stat. 5090, adding §§ 471–482 to Title 28).

[101]   Act of July 25, 1958, 72 Stat. 415 (amending 28 U.S.C. § 1332 to provide that a corporation shall be considered a citizen of both its state of incorporation and the state in which it maintains its principal place of business).

[102]   Act of Sept. 2, 1958, 72 Stat. 1770 (amending 28 U.S.C. § 1292 to permit district courts to certify questions for interlocutory appeal).

[103]   Act of Aug. 12, 1976, 90 Stat. 1119.

[104]   See, *e.g.*, Omnibus Crime Control Act of 1970, 18 U.S.C. § 3731, as amended by Act of Jan. 2, 1971, § 14(a), 84 Stat. 1890; Act of Dec. 21, 1974, 88 Stat. 1708–09 (amending the Expediting Act).

[105]   Act of Oct. 14, 1980, 94 Stat. 1994.

G. Specialized Courts Under Article III

For the most part, the Article III courts have been courts of broad-based, although not "general," jurisdiction,[106] and many have viewed the diversity of the federal docket as a large asset in attracting able lawyers to the bench and achieving cross-pollination among different areas of the law.[107] There are important exceptions to the norm of relatively general jurisdiction, however, as well as continuing debate about whether the benefits of specialization (with respect to at least some subject matters) outweigh the drawbacks.[108]

1. The Court of International Trade

In 1926, the old Board of General Appraisers, which had been established to hear appeals from decisions of customs collectors, received formal status as a specialized court with the name of the United States Customs Court.[109] Congress vested the court with Article III status in 1956[110] and in 1980 redesignated it the United States Court of International Trade.[111]

2. The Court of Appeals for the Federal Circuit

In 1982, Congress created the United States Court of Appeals for the Federal Circuit.[112] This court has exclusive jurisdiction to hear appeals from (1) the Court of Federal Claims,[113] (2) the Federal Merit System Protection Board, (3) agency boards of contract appeals under the Contract Disputes Act of 1978, (4) the Court of International Trade, (5) the Patent Office in patent and trademark cases,[114] (6) the district courts in certain actions in

---

[106] By contrast, there are a number of specialized Article I courts—a concept discussed in Part H of this Note—created by Congress exercising Article I power and that are staffed by judges who lack the tenure and salary protection provided by Article III.

[107] See, *e.g.*, Posner, The Federal Courts: Challenge and Reform 249–50 (rev. ed.1996).

[108] With *id.*, compare Bator, *The Judicial Universe of Judge Richard Posner*, 52 U.Chi.L.Rev. 1146, 1154–56 (1985) (advocating "increase[d] specialization at the court of appeals level" and arguing that specialization would "attract more real lawyers and fewer pseudo-politicians" to the bench and would subject them to the "kind of intellectual discipline that comes from having to demonstrate detailed substantive mastery over a field").

[109] Act of May 28, 1926, 44 Stat. 669. See also Act of June 17, 1930, § 518, 46 Stat. 590, 737; Act of Oct. 10, 1940, 54 Stat. 1101; Act of June 2, 1970, § 110, 84 Stat. 274, 278.

[110] Act of July 14, 1956, 70 Stat. 532.

[111] Act of Oct. 10, 1980, 94 Stat. 1727. The provisions governing its organization are collected in Chapter 11 of the Judicial Code and the jurisdictional provisions in Chapter 95.

[112] The Federal Courts Improvement Act of 1982, § 127, 96 Stat. 25, 37–38. The jurisdictional provision appears in the Judicial Code at 28 U.S.C. § 1295.

[113] For further discussion of the Court of Federal Claims and its history, see Chap. II, Sec. 2, pp. 109–110, and Chap. IX, Sec. 5, pp. 1343–1344, *infra*.

[114] Items (4) and (5) embrace the jurisdiction of the former Court of Customs and Patent Appeals. The Court of Customs Appeals was established in 1909 as the second of the specialized federal courts with nationwide jurisdiction to hear appeals from the Board of General Appraisers—appeals that were then swamping some of the regular courts. Act of Aug. 5, 1909, § 29, 36 Stat. 11, 105. The court continued to hear these appeals after the board became the Customs Court in 1926, and in 1929 Congress gave the court the jurisdiction over appeals from the Patent Office that had been vested in the Court of Appeals of the District of Columbia. Act of March 2, 1929, 45 Stat. 1475. See also Act of June 17, 1930, § 646, 46 Stat. 590, 762; Act of Dec. 24, 1970, § 143, 84 Stat. 1542, 1558. Congress designated the Court of Customs and Patent Appeals an Article III court in 1958, see 72 Stat. 848, and the Supreme Court recognized the validity of that designation in Glidden Co. v. Zdanok, 370 U.S. 530 (1962).

which district court jurisdiction was based in whole or in part on the "Little Tucker Act" (28 U.S.C. § 1346(a)(2)), involving claims against the United States that, *inter alia*, neither exceed $10,000 nor sound in tort, and (7) the district courts in all patent cases in which district court jurisdiction was based in whole or in part on 28 U.S.C. § 1338.[115]

3.   Special Courts with Non-Specialist Judges

In addition to creating specialized courts whose judges are nominated by the President and confirmed by the Senate to do those courts' specialized business, Congress has from time to time constituted tribunals with specialized jurisdiction but staffed with Article III judges drawn from the regular district courts and courts of appeals. Past examples include an Emergency Court of Appeals with exclusive jurisdiction to entertain challenges to orders and regulations issued under the Emergency Price Control Act of 1942[116] and a Temporary Emergency Court of Appeals, created by the 1971 amendments to the Economic Stabilization Act of 1970,[117] to hear all appeals from district court decisions arising under the Act or its implementing regulations.

A contemporary example is the Foreign Intelligence Surveillance Court (FISC), established by Congress in 1978. The FISC consists of eleven Article III judges assigned by the Chief Justice and rules on applications seeking approval for electronic surveillance and certain physical searches relating to suspected foreign intelligence agents and international terrorists within the United States.[118] Appeals are reviewable by the Foreign Intelligence Surveillance Court of Review, made up of three Article III judges, also selected by the Chief Justice.

In response to leaked reports of U.S. intelligence-gathering practices, Congress adopted some proposals recommended by a presidentially-

---

[115]   See Christianson v. Colt Industries Operating Corp., 486 U.S. 800 (1988) (deciding whether a federal action arises under the patent or antitrust laws, which in turn determines whether the Federal Circuit or the regional court of appeals has appellate jurisdiction); United States v. Hohri, 482 U.S. 64 (1987) (resolving ambiguity in 1982 Act by holding that Federal Circuit has exclusive jurisdiction over "mixed cases" involving claims under both the Little Tucker Act and the Federal Tort Claims Act).

Assessments of the performance of the Federal Circuit have tended to be mixed, with friendly commentary emphasizing its contribution to doctrinal consistency and critics questioning the substantive quality of its decisions, especially with respect to patent law. See, *e.g.*, Dreyfuss, *In Search of Institutional Identity: The Federal Circuit Comes of Age*, 23 Berkeley Technology L.J. 787, 788–92 (2008). Gugliuzza, *Rethinking Federal Circuit Jurisdiction*, 100 Geo.L.J. 1437 (2012), maintains that the narrowness of the Federal Circuit's non-patent jurisdiction adversely affects both its development of patent law and its performance in non-patent-law cases and calls for a major reshaping of the court's non-patent jurisdiction. Narechania, *Certiorari, Universality, and A Patent Puzzle*, 116 U.Mich.L.Rev. 1345 (2018), argues that the Supreme Court reviews the Federal Circuit's patent decisions at a high rate to ensure that any "patent exceptionalism" is warranted, often rejecting patent law-specific rules in favor of transsubstantive rules. For discussion of a variety of issues involving the nature of the Federal Circuit and its performance, see *Symposium: The Federal Circuit as an Institution*, 43 Loy.L.A.L.Rev. 749 (2010).

[116]   Act of Jan. 29, 1942, 56 Stat. 23. See pp. 471–475, *infra*.

[117]   Act of Dec. 22, 1971, 85 Stat. 743.

[118]   See 50 U.S.C. § 1803. The FISC also carries out certain programmatic functions under § 702. See *id.* § 1881a. In April 2024, Congress reauthorized § 702 for two additional years. See Reforming Intelligence and Securing America Act, Pub.L.No. 118–49 (2024).

appointed review group in the USA FREEDOM Act of 2015. The Act established procedures for the appointment of amici to appear before the FISC in cases involving "a novel or significant interpretation of the law" or where otherwise appropriate. The Act also provides for the certification of questions of law to higher courts and the declassification of significant FISC decisions, orders, and opinions.[119]

Another specialized court is the Alien Terrorist Removal Court, which Congress established in 1996. The court consists of five Article III judges chosen by the Chief Justice and determines whether to grant applications by the Attorney General for removal of suspected alien terrorists, first in a private, *ex parte* review by one judge, and then, upon a finding of probable cause, in an open, public hearing before the Removal Court.[120]

H. Non-Article III Courts and Adjudicators

Although this Note has so far focused on the Article III federal courts, Congress, from the very first, has asserted a power to organize tribunals under Article I. Judges of these Article I tribunals lack the Article III guarantees of tenure during good behavior and non-reduction in salary, but the tribunals' functions are often indistinguishable from those of the Article III courts.

Almost no one disputes the highly general principle that Article III imposes some limits on Congress's authority to vest judicial power in non-Article III federal tribunals, but there is much less consensus or certainty concerning precisely what those limits are. The relevant doctrine and its perplexities are explored in Chap. IV, Sec. 2, *infra*.

For present purposes, it will be useful to distinguish three broad categories: (i) congressionally-created courts, (ii) administrative agencies, and (iii) non-Article III adjudicators appointed by and subject to the supervision of Article III judges.

1. Congressionally-Created Non-Article III Courts

There are a host of courts established under Congress's legislative powers under Article I. Typically, such courts are charged with adjudicating disputes involving specialized subject matters or with exercising jurisdiction in discrete geographical enclaves, such as the federal territories. They are characteristically constituted as "courts" and are seldom assigned significant executive or legislative functions.[121]

a. The Courts of the District of Columbia

The organization of the District of Columbia compelled the establishment of tribunals to perform the functions of local courts as well as of ordinary federal courts. From the beginning, the District has had inferior

---

[119] See Uniting and Strengthening America by Fulfilling Rights and Ensuring Effective Discipline over Monitoring (USA FREEDOM) Act of 2015, Pub.L.No. 114–23, 129 Stat. 268 (2015), codified at 50 U.S.C. § 1861.

[120] See 8 U.S.C. §§ 1532–1537.

[121] For further generalizations about the characteristic nature of legislative courts, as well as some qualifications, see Chap. IV, Sec. 2, pp. 498–501, *infra*.

courts with distinctively local jurisdiction.[122] From 1863 to 1893, this judicial system was headed by a Supreme Court of the District of Columbia, which was comparable both to a federal circuit court and to a state supreme court. In 1893, Congress established the Court of Appeals of the District of Columbia as a superior tribunal corresponding to the new circuit courts of appeals.[123] Both of these appellate tribunals had a local as well as a federal jurisdiction. But by successive steps, the former District supreme court was given the title and status of a district court of the United States, and the former court of appeals became a United States Court of Appeals.[124]

In 1970 the District of Columbia Court Reorganization Act[125] ended the system of combining federal and local jurisdictions in the courts of the District. Under this Act, the United States District Court for the District of Columbia and the United States Court of Appeals for the District of Columbia Circuit exercise only the jurisdiction exercised by other federal district courts and circuit courts of appeals. The Act transferred the remaining local jurisdiction to two non-Article III courts. The highest local court continues to be the District of Columbia Court of Appeals,[126] an appellate tribunal whose judgments are reviewable by the Supreme Court under 28 U.S.C. § 1257(b) as if they were rendered by the highest court of a state. The Superior Court of the District of Columbia is now the trial court of general jurisdiction,[127] analogous to a state trial court. The judges of both these local courts serve for 15-year terms.[128]

b. The Territorial and Related Courts

The statutes organizing each of the territories have likewise had to make provision for courts of local as well as federal jurisdiction. Today the Commonwealth of Puerto Rico has a system of local courts, headed by the Supreme Court of Puerto Rico;[129] decisions of the latter are reviewed by the United States Supreme Court much as state court judgments are.[130] In addition, a United States District Court for the District of Puerto Rico, exercising federal jurisdiction, sits in the commonwealth. Its decisions are reviewable in the United States Court of Appeals for the First Circuit.[131]

Guam, the Virgin Islands, and the Northern Mariana Islands all have courts, designated as "district courts" but organized under Article I, that

---

[122] For an overview of the history, see Bloch & Ginsburg, *Celebrating the 200th Anniversary of the Federal Courts of the District of Columbia*, 90 Geo.L.J. 549 (2002).

[123] Act of Feb. 9, 1893, 27 Stat. 434. For the history of this court and of the old District supreme court, see O'Donoghue v. United States, 289 U.S. 516, 548–49 (1933).

[124] For the present provisions, see 28 U.S.C. §§ 41, 43 (court of appeals), and §§ 88, 132 (district court).

[125] Act of July 29, 1970, 84 Stat. 473.

[126] D.C.Code §§ 11–701 *et seq.*

[127] *Id.* §§ 11–901 *et seq.*

[128] *Id.* § 11–1502. For discussion of the constitutional status of the courts of the District of Columbia, see Palmore v. United States, 411 U.S. 389 (1973).

[129] See Puerto Rico Constitution Art. V, superseding 48 U.S.C. § 861.

[130] 28 U.S.C. § 1258.

[131] *Id.* § 41. This district court is constituted among the regular district courts by Chapter 5 of the Judicial Code, *id.* §§ 119, 132. Its judges have life tenure by virtue of the Act of September 12, 1966, 80 Stat. 764, amending 28 U.S.C. § 134(a).

exercise both local and federal jurisdiction.[132] The judgments of the district courts of the Virgin Islands and those of Guam and the Northern Mariana Islands are reviewable by the Third and Ninth Circuits respectively.[133] These territories also have local inferior courts.

c.   The Tax Court

Until 1969 the United States Tax Court, which hears taxpayer petitions contesting deficiency determinations, was an independent agency in the Executive Branch. Congress then declared it to be a "court."[134] Decisions of the Tax Court are reviewed by the courts of appeals "in the same manner and to the same extent as decisions of the district courts in civil actions tried without a jury."[135]

d.   The Court of Federal Claims

The story of the establishment of the Court of Claims by statutes of 1855, 1863, and 1866, and its replacement in 1982 by the United States Claims Court, which was itself retitled the United States Court of Federal Claims a decade later, is summarized in Chap. II, Sec. 2.[136] The decisions of the Court of Federal Claims are reviewed by the Article III Court of Appeals for the Federal Circuit.[137]

e.   The Court of Veterans Appeals

In 1988 Congress created the Court of Appeals for Veterans Claims, with exclusive jurisdiction to review decisions of the Board of Veterans' Appeals. Decisions of the Court of Appeals for Veterans Claims are reviewable by the Article III Court of Appeals for the Federal Circuit.[138]

f.   Military Courts

Throughout American history, Congress has provided a separate set of military courts with jurisdiction over offenses arising from military

---

[132]   See 48 U.S.C. §§ 1611–1614 (Virgin Islands), 1424 (Guam), 1821–1824 (Northern Mariana Islands).

The Supreme Court held in Nguyen v. United States, 539 U.S. 69 (2003), that judges of the non-Article III district courts are ineligible to sit on federal courts of appeals under 28 U.S.C. § 292(a), which provides that "[t]he chief judge of a circuit may designate and assign one or more district judges within the circuit to sit upon the court of appeals * * * whenever the business of that court so requires."

[133]   See 28 U.S.C. §§ 1291, 1294(3), 1294(4); 48 U.S.C. § 1821(a).

[134]   Act of Dec. 30, 1969, § 951, 83 Stat. 487, 730, amending 26 U.S.C. § 7441. Tax Court judges are appointed for 15-year terms. 26 U.S.C. § 7443(e). In response to the decision in Kuretski v. Commissioner, 755 F.3d 929, 932 (D.C.Cir.2014), ruling that "the Tax Court * * * exercises Executive authority as part of the Executive Branch," Congress amended various provisions governing the Tax Court and added the following language to the court's chartering provision: "The Tax Court is not an agency of, and shall be independent of, the executive branch of the Government." See Protecting Americans from Tax Hikes Act of 2015, Pub.L.No. 114–113, 129 Stat. 2242, codified at 26 U.S.C. § 7441.

[135]   26 U.S.C. § 7482(a)(1). For discussion and defense of this non-deferential standard of review despite the Tax Court's expertise, see Lederman, *(Un)appealing Deference to the Tax Court*, 63 Duke L.J. 1835 (2014).

[136]   See also Glidden Co. v. Zdanok, 370 U.S. 530 (1962). See also note 113, *supra*.

[137]   See 28 U.S.C. § 1295(a)(3). Under the 1982 statute, Court of Federal Claims judges are appointed for 15-year terms. 28 U.S.C. § 172(a).

[138]   See 38 U.S.C. §§ 7104, 7251–7256, 7292.

service.[139] In addition, Congress and the President have from time to time established special military courts or "commissions" to dispense justice in areas subject to martial law or military occupation and to try alleged illegal combatants under the laws of war. The use of such special military courts or commissions is discussed in Chap. IV, Sec. 2, *infra*.

The more regularized and enduring system of military courts exercising jurisdiction over the service-related offenses of American service members comprises three tiers. At the trial level, the least serious form of court-martial may be presided over by a commissioned officer, but trials of more serious offenses usually require a military judge—a position that has formally existed only since 1968—as presiding officer.[140] The trial-level judges do not serve for fixed terms and perform judicial duties only when assigned to do so by the Judge Advocate General of the service of which they are members.[141]

At the first appellate tier are Courts of Criminal Appeals for each of the services. The appellate judges may be either military officers or civilians. They do not serve for fixed terms and are assigned by the appropriate Judge Advocate General.[142]

At the top of the system sits a five-member, all-civilian Court of Appeals for the Armed Forces (CAAF), the judges of which are appointed by the President, with the advice and consent of the Senate, to 15-year terms.[143] The decisions of the CAAF are subject to review on certiorari by the Supreme Court of the United States.[144]

2. Administrative Agencies

Administrative agencies frequently adjudicate rights and obligations under their organic statutes.[145] In classic regimes of agency adjudication, ultimate adjudicative authority resides in "the agency" or its head. Agencies characteristically differ from legislative courts along several dimensions,[146]

---

[139] "The very first Congress continued the court-martial system as it then operated. And from that day to this one, Congress has maintained courts-martial in all their essentials to resolve criminal charges against service members." Ortiz v. United States, 585 U.S. 427, 439 (2018) (citations omitted). For an earlier discussion of military justice and its relation to Article III, see Note, *Military Justice and Article III*, 103 Harv.L.Rev. 1909 (1990).

[140] See Art. 26, Uniform Code of Military Justice ("UCMJ"), 10 U.S.C. § 826.

[141] As of 2022, there were over 180 judges certified to preside at various types of courts-martial. See Department of the Air Force Report on the State of Military Justice for Fiscal Year 2022 (2022), https://jsc.defense.gov/Annual-Reports/.

[142] See Art. 66, UCMJ, 10 U.S.C. § 866.

[143] Arts. 67, 142, UCMJ, 10 U.S.C. §§ 867, 941, 942.

[144] See 28 U.S.C. § 1259. There is also a limited opportunity to test the judgments of military courts in federal habeas corpus actions.

The Supreme Court reaffirmed its jurisdiction to review the CAAF's decisions in Ortiz v. United States, 585 U.S. 427 (2018), holding that "the judicial character and constitutional pedigree of the court-martial system enable this Court, in exercising appellate jurisdiction, to review the decisions of the court sitting at its apex." *Id.* 435. It does not matter, the Court observed, that the CAAF lacks Article III judges, for the appellate jurisdiction "covers more than the decisions of Article III courts." *Id.* 429 (noting that the Court reviews decisions of state courts, territorial courts, and the District of Columbia courts).

[145] This discussion encompasses commissions as well, although they sometimes embody distinct characteristics from the classic agency model with a Cabinet member head.

[146] The differences are explored in Chap. IV, Sec. 2, *infra*.

perhaps the most important of which is that agencies frequently perform a mix of functions, including rulemaking and enforcement as well as adjudication. In the modern agency, initial adjudication is typically performed by an "administrative law judge" or "administrative judge," who enjoys some insulation from pressure by officials performing other functions, but nonetheless is an employee of the agency.[147]

Although administrative adjudication is often overlooked in portrayals of the "judicial" system, by 2017 the federal government employed almost 1,931 officials denominated as "administrative law judges,"[148] as well as a further group of so-called "administrative judges" or "presiding officers" that numbered roughly 3370 in 2002.[149] More recently, the Bureau of Labor Statistics reported that the federal government employed 3,010 "Administrative Law Judges, Adjudicators, and Hearing Officers" as of May 2022.[150] The number of cases resolved by such officials each year is staggering. The Social Security Administration alone employed 1,235 administrative law judges and disposed of 451,046 cases via hearing in fiscal year 2021, with another 350,137 cases pending at year's end[151]—a caseload larger than the civil docket of all Article III courts combined.

The adjudicative decisions of federal administrative agencies are generally reviewable in the Article III courts—often directly by the courts of

---

[147] For a discussion of important differences between administrative law judges ("ALJs") and administrative judges ("AJs"), including the procedures by which they are appointed, the protections that they enjoy from removal, and their roles within agencies, see Barnett, *Against Administrative Judges*, 49 U.C. Davis L.Rev. 1643 (2016) (arguing ALJs are superior to AJs because of their higher likelihood of impartiality and greater insulation from agency pressures).

In Lucia v. SEC, 585 U.S. 237 (2018), the Supreme Court held that ALJs presiding over enforcement actions in the Securities and Exchange Commission (SEC) are not merely employees, but "Officers of the United States," a class of government officials subject to the Appointments Clause. See Art. II, § 2, cl. 2. Accordingly, the Court held the appointment of SEC ALJs by SEC staff, rather than the by the SEC's Commissioners themselves, ran afoul of that Clause. Relying on Freytag v. Commissioner, 501 U.S. 868 (1991), which reached the same conclusion with respect to special trial judges of the United States Tax Court, the Court emphasized the extensive powers that the SEC ALJs exercise and the potential for their decisions to become final where the Commission declines to review them. See also Buckley v. Valeo, 424 U.S. 1 (1976) (per curiam) (defining officers for Appointments Clause purposes as exercising "significant authority"). The holding in Lucia raises important questions, including how many other ALJs and possibly AJs may fall under its purview depending on how they are appointed. Lucia may also have ramifications for how ALJs and AJs may be removed by agency heads, a matter the Court declined to address in Lucia. See also United States v. Arthrex, Inc., 594 U.S. 1 (2021) (deeming Administrative Patent Judges to be inferior officers for purposes of the Appointments Clause and holding their decisions therefore must be subject to direct review by a principal officer). These developments have the potential to introduce extensive changes to the status of, and appointment and removal processes governing, both ALJs and AJs.

[148] Office of Personnel Management, Administrative Law Judges: ALJs by Agency, https://www.opm.gov/services-for-agencies/administrative-law-judges/#url=By-Agency.

[149] See Limon, The Federal Administrative Judiciary: Then and Now: A Decade of Change, 1992–2002, at 4–5 (2002) (published by the Office of Administrative Law Judges in the Office of Personnel Management). Although a current figure is hard to come by, in 1989 administrative judges rendered decisions in roughly 350,000 on-the-record adjudications per year. See Verkuil, *Reflections upon the Federal Administrative Judiciary*, 39 UCLA L.Rev. 1341, 1345–46 (1992).

[150] This figure excludes Arbitrators, Mediators, and Conciliators. Bureau of Labor Statistics, 23–1021 Administrative Law Judges, Adjudicators, and Hearing Officers May 2022, https://www.bls.gov/oes/2022/may/oes231021.htm.

[151] Social Security Office of Retirement and Disability Policy, Annual Statistical Supplement, 2022, Table 2.F9, https://www.ssa.gov/policy/docs/statcomps/supplement/2022/2f8-2f11.html.

appeals, but in some instances by the district courts.[152] According to at least one commentator, this relationship between agencies and the Article III courts demonstrates that traditional thought about the federal judicial system has lagged behind the reality: Reconceptualization is needed to account for a fourth tier of federal adjudication (beneath the federal district courts, the courts of appeals, and the Supreme Court). See Resnik, *Rereading "The Federal Courts": Revising the Domain of Federal Courts Jurisprudence at the End of the Twentieth Century*, 47 Vand.L.Rev. 1021 (1994). For further consideration of administrative adjudication and constitutional limits on its permissibility, see Chap. IV, Sec. 2, *infra*.

3. Non-Article III Adjudicators Appointed by and Subject to the Supervision of Article III Judges

a. Magistrate Judges

The Federal Magistrates Act of 1968, 82 Stat. 1107, as amended, 28 U.S.C. §§ 631 *et seq.*, created the position of "magistrate," which was subsequently retitled as "magistrate judge."[153] Magistrate judges are appointed by the federal district judges, in such numbers as the Judicial Conference of the United States may determine. They may be appointed on a full-time basis for an eight-year term, or on a part-time basis for a four-year term. Magistrate judges were initially given (a) the powers previously exercised by United States commissioners (*e.g.*, issuing warrants, conducting probable cause and other preliminary hearings in criminal cases), (b) jurisdiction to try "minor offenses," and (c) "such additional duties as are not inconsistent with the Constitution and laws" and as might be established at the district court level, including service as special masters in civil cases, assistance in discovery or other pretrial proceedings, and preliminary review of applications for post-conviction relief.[154]

Congress further expanded the role of magistrates in the Federal Magistrate Act of 1979,[155] which authorized magistrates to hear, determine, and enter final judgment in both jury and nonjury civil cases if all parties consent. Magistrate judges may also try criminal misdemeanor cases if the defendant consents. Aggrieved parties may appeal to the court of appeals. 28 U.S.C. § 636(c)(3).

In 2022, there were 562 full-time and 25 part-time magistrate judges, supplemented by 96 retired magistrate judges who had been temporarily recalled to service and two clerks of court who doubled as magistrate judges.[156] Altogether these officials disposed of more than one million judicial matters in 2022 alone.[157] For more discussion of the kinds of matters handled

---

[152] In Axon Enterprise, Inc. v. Federal Trade Commission, 598 U.S. 175 (2023), the Supreme Court held that challenges to the constitutionality of the appointment and retention structure for ALJs in the SEC and Federal Trade commission could proceed directly in federal district court and need not be brought in the first instance within the commission adjudication framework.

[153] See the Judicial Improvements Act of 1990, § 321, 104 Stat. 5089, 5117.

[154] 28 U.S.C. § 636, 82 Stat. 1107, 1113.

[155] 93 Stat. 643, amending 28 U.S.C. §§ 604, 631, 633–636, 1915(b), and 18 U.S.C. § 3401.

[156] Administrative Office of the U.S. Courts, 2022 Judicial Business, Table 12.

[157] *Id.*, Table S-17.

by magistrate judges, see p. 57, *infra*. For discussion of the statutory and especially constitutional issues that the role of magistrate judges presents, see *Note on Magistrate Judges*, p. 546, *infra*.[158]

b. Bankruptcy Courts

Until enactment of the Bankruptcy Reform Act of 1978, the district courts acted as bankruptcy courts. Proceedings were generally conducted before court-appointed referees; the district court could at any time withdraw the case from the referee; and the referee's final order was appealable to the district court. In the 1978 Act, Congress created a "court of record known as the United States Bankruptcy Court" as "an adjunct to the district court" for each district. The law provided that the judges of the new courts would be appointed by the President and confirmed by the Senate to serve 14-year terms; they were removable by the judicial councils of the circuits; and their salaries were not protected against diminution.

The Supreme Court invalidated the system of bankruptcy courts created by this statute in Northern Pipeline Construction Co. v. Marathon Pipe Line Co., 458 U.S. 50 (1982), p. 501, *infra*. After considerable delay and controversy, in 1984, Congress changed the system once again. Under the revised law, bankruptcy judges are appointed as officers of the district courts for a term of fourteen years; appointments are made by the courts of appeals for the districts within their respective circuits, and the judges in each district "constitute a unit of the district court to be known as the bankruptcy court for that district." 28 U.S.C. §§ 151, 152. As of September 30, 2022, there were 345 authorized and funded bankruptcy judgeships, 35 of which were vacant. In addition, 27 retired judges had been called to temporary service.[159]

Issues involving the constitutionally permissible functions of bankruptcy judges have arisen recurrently in the decades since the Northern Pipeline case. For discussion of the relevant decisions and surrounding uncertainties, see Chap. IV, Sec. 2, *infra*.

I. Additional Components in the United States Judicial System: State and Tribal Courts

From the beginning, the constitutional framework contemplated that state courts would play an important role in adjudicating federal matters. Indeed, under the 1789 Judiciary Act, state courts resolved a host of federal questions, only some of which were eligible for the Supreme Court review on appeal. See pp. 36–37, *supra*. It remains the case today that courts in all fifty states decide a range of federal issues within their dockets. Meanwhile, state court caseloads dramatically eclipse those of the federal courts. By way of example, in 2021, courts in the 42 states able to provide publishable data witnessed the filing of 52.9 million cases.[160] Statistics from 41 states with publishable data from that same year report the filing of 2.9 million criminal

---

[158] See also *Symposium: Magistrate Judges and the Transformation of the Federal Judiciary*, 16 Nev.L.J. 775 (2016).

[159] Administrative Office of the U.S. Courts, 2022 Judicial Business, Table 11.

[160] National Center for State Courts, Court Statistics Project, 2021 Caseload Highlights. The same courts witnessed a 28% drop in incoming cases from 2019 to 2020 due to the COVID-19 pandemic. *Id.*

felony cases alone.[161] As is explored in Chapter V, however, in recent Terms, the Supreme Court has reviewed only a handful of cases on appeal from state courts, leaving a host of federal questions resolved exclusively by the state courts.

Collectively in turn, "[t]here are approximately 400 Tribal justice systems" in the United States,[162] which together exercise jurisdiction over millions of acres of Indian Country throughout the United States.[163] In so doing, tribal courts sometimes rule on claims sounding in federal law, such as the Indian Civil Rights Act of 1968.[164] Like state courts, tribal courts may be specialized courts or courts of general jurisdiction. They may also embrace conflict resolution models born out of Native American traditions, such as the Navajo Nation's Peacemaking Program. Some tribal court systems may handle only a handful of cases a year; by comparison, the courts of the Navajo Nation, making up eleven districts, handle over 100,000 cases per year.[165]

J. The Article III Courts Today

The Federal Judicial Branch today, "while tiny in comparison to the Executive Branch, is nevertheless a large and complex institution, with an annual budget exceeding $7 billion and more than 32,000 employees." *Ayestas v. Davis*, 584 U.S. 28, 39 (2018) (citing Administrative Office of the U.S. Courts, The Judiciary FY 2018 Congressional Budget Summary Revised 9–10 (June 2017)).

1. The District Courts

Chapter 5 of the Judicial Code of 1948 (Title 28, U.S. Code) codified the statutes establishing the district courts. It now provides for 94 district courts: 92 for the fifty states, and one each for the District of Columbia and Puerto Rico.

Each state has at least one district court. The more populous states are divided into two, three, or four districts. Many districts are in turn divided into divisions. On September 30, 2022, there were 677 authorized district

---

[161] *Id.*

[162] Tribal Court Systems, U.S. Department of the Interior, Indian Affairs, https://www.bia.gov/CFRCourts/tribal-justice-support-directorate. In 2023, there were 574 federally recognized Native American tribal nations in the United States. See United States Department of the Interior, Bureau of Indian Affairs, Frequently Asked Questions (2023).

[163] Federal law defines "Indian country" in 18 U.S.C. § 1151. Tribal court jurisdiction is exclusive, subject to certain caveats, over matters involving tribal members that take place on tribal land. See Williams v. Lee, 358 U.S. 217 (1959) (holding that Arizona courts could not exercise jurisdiction over lawsuit brought against member of Navajo Nation over dispute that arose on the Navajo Reservation). More generally, one prominent handbook states that the core principle of federal Indian law is that "apart from alienating tribal land and treating with foreign nations, Indian tribes retain their original inherent sovereign authority over all persons, property, and events within Indian country unless Congress clearly and unambiguously acts to limit the exercise of that power." 1 Cohen's Handbook of Federal Indian Law § 7.02 (2023).

[164] 82 Stat. 77, 25 U.S.C. § 1301 *et seq.* The Act provides for "habeas corpus as the exclusive means for federal-court review of tribal criminal proceedings." Santa Clara Pueblo v. Martinez, 436 U.S. 49, 67 (1978).

[165] Fletcher, Federal Indian Law 280 (2016); Becker and Spruhan, *Navajo Nation Judiciary* (2002), reprinted in Richland & Deer, Introduction to Tribal Legal Studies 125–28 (3d ed.2016).

judgeships. In addition, 407 senior district judges continued to hear cases following their retirement from full-time status.[166]

The current business of the district courts (as well as of other federal courts) is described in detail by the Director of the Administrative Office of the United States Courts in the Annual Reports of the Director: Judicial Business of the United States Courts.[167] Although nothing ages more quickly than statistics, this and the following subsections of this Part attempt to give a summary picture of the work of the Article III courts.

In the 2022 fiscal year, the district courts docketed 274,771 civil and 68,482 criminal cases, for a total of 343,253.[168] (By contrast, parties filed 375,870 civil and criminal cases in 2013, 313,615 in 2001, 281,864 in 1994, 296,318 in 1986, 127,280 in 1970, and 89,091 in 1960.) In addition, the district courts received 383,810 bankruptcy petitions, a stark drop from the 2013 figure of 1,107,699.[169]

In the 2022 fiscal year, on the civil side, 105,212 came within the diversity jurisdiction and 131,131 within the federal question jurisdiction (including admiralty).[170] The United States appeared as a plaintiff in 2,839 civil cases and as a defendant in 35,589 actions.[171]

Two factors are crucial in permitting the federal district courts to handle the current volume of business. First, most cases never come to trial. Of the 308,326 civil cases terminated in the district courts in 2022, trials occurred in only 3,502 (of which 1,363 were before a jury).[172] On the criminal side, federal cases terminated in 2022 involved 71,954 defendants.[173] The federal courts dismissed cases involving 5,901 defendants; 64,384 other defendants pleaded guilty.[174] (Of those whose cases actually went to trial, 290 were acquitted, and 1,379 were convicted.)[175]

Second, a growing volume of business is handled by magistrate judges. In 2022, magistrate judges disposed of 332,667 civil matters and received 246,886 references (mostly involving motions, hearings, and conferences) in criminal felony cases.[176] These figures include final dispositions of 19,785 civil cases with the consent of the parties (in comparison with 12,024 in 2001, 7,835 in 1994, and 4,960 in 1986), 283 of which involved a trial.[177]

---

[166] Administrative Office of the U.S. Courts, 2022 Judicial Business, Table 10.

[167] These reports are available on-line at https://www.uscourts.gov/statistics-reports/us-district-courts-judicial-business-2022.

[168] Administrative Office of the U.S. Courts, 2022 Judicial Business, Table JCI. Certain years have witnessed a dramatic climb in civil filings due to a rise in multidistrict litigation cases, such as the year 2019–2020, when total civil filings totaled 470,581, inclusive of over 200,000 filings related to a single defendant in multidistrict litigation cases. Administrative Office of the U.S. Courts, 2020 Judicial Business, Analysis & Tables.

[169] Administrative Office of the U.S. Courts, 2022 Judicial Business, Table JCI.

[170] *Id.*, Table 4.

[171] *Id.*

[172] *Id.*, Table 3.

[173] *Id.*, Table D-4.

[174] *Id.*

[175] *Id.*

[176] *Id.*, Table S-17.

[177] *Id.*, Table M-5.

By most if not all accounts, the federal district courts are seriously overtaxed by their current caseloads, and thoughtful and much discussed reform proposals have emerged, *inter alia*, from the American Law Institute in 1969;[178] from the Federal Courts Study Committee, appointed by the Chief Justice at the direction of Congress, in 1990;[179] and from the Committee on Long Range Planning of the Judicial Conference of the United States in 1995.[180] The leading studies have all recommended substantial curtailments in the diversity jurisdiction, but Congress has not agreed.[181] To the contrary, in recent decades, Congress has expanded diversity jurisdiction in certain respects.[182]

One obvious response to the problem of growing federal caseloads would be to increase substantially the number of federal judges. Although this mode of reform has not wanted for champions, the Committee on Long Range Planning of the Judicial Conference discouraged the idea and the Federal Courts Study Committee rejected it in strong terms, regarding the preservation of elite status as crucial to maintaining the quality of the federal bench.[183] The Committee also argued that an expanded federal bench would increase the difficulties of coordination: more district judges would

---

[178] See American Law Institute, Study of the Division of Jurisdiction Between State and Federal Courts (1969). For appraisals, see Wright, *Restructuring Federal Jurisdiction: The American Law Institute Proposals*, 26 Wash. & Lee L.Rev. 185 (1969); Currie, *The Federal Courts and the American Law Institute*, 36 U.Chi.L.Rev. 1, 268 (1969).

[179] Report of the Federal Courts Study Committee (1990). The Committee recommended, among other things: (1) substantial reduction of the diversity jurisdiction, (2) vesting of nearly exclusive tax jurisdiction in the Article I Tax Court (coupled with the creation of an Article III appellate division of that court), (3) creation of a new Article I Court of Disability Claims, and (4) reliance on non-judicial, or at least non-Article III, fora for resolving some disputes. For comment, see, *e.g.*, *Symposium, The Federal Court Docket: Issues and Solutions*, 22 Conn.L.Rev. 615 (1990).

[180] See Long Range Plan for the Federal Courts, as approved by the Judicial Conference of the United States (1995) (reprinted in 166 F.R.D. 49 (1995)).

[181] For an iconoclastic examination of the federal judicial docket and of the role of the federal courts in the American legal system, see Resnik, *Building the Federal Judiciary (Literally and Legally): The Monuments of Chief Justices Taft, Warren, and Rehnquist*, 87 Ind.L.J. 823 (2012). Professor Resnik emphasizes that although the size of the federal docket has continued to grow, the rate of increase has flattened in recent decades, as a result, among other factors, of jurisdictional doctrines developed by the Supreme Court and congressional legislation. For an elaboration of these points and a broader discussion of how the federal courts constitute American lawyers' " 'common intellectual heritage,' " consult Resnik, *Revising Our "Common Intellectual Heritage": Federal and State Courts in Our Federal System*, 91 Notre Dame L.Rev. 1831 (2016) (quoting Meltzer, *The Judiciary's Bicentennial*, 56 U.Chi.L.Rev. 423, 427 (1989)).

[182] See, *e.g.*, Class Action Fairness Act of 2005, Pub. L. No. 109–2, § 2(a)(3)–(4), 119 Stat. 4 (codified in scattered sections of 28 U.S.C.).

[183] See Report, note 179, *supra*. The Committee wrote: "The independence secured to federal judges by Article III is compatible with responsible and efficient performance of judicial duties only if federal judges are carefully selected from a pool of competent and eager applicants and only if they are sufficiently few in number to feel a personal stake in the consequences of their actions." Were the judiciary greatly enlarged, "[t]he process of presidential nomination and senatorial confirmation would become pro forma * * *, [and] a sufficient number of highly qualified applicants could not be found unless the salaries of federal judges were greatly increased * * *." *Id.* at 7.

generate more appeals, and more appeals would heighten the obstacles to maintaining uniformity both within and among the circuits.[184]

2.   The Courts of Appeals

Chapter 3 of the Judicial Code of 1948 changed the name of the former circuit courts of appeals to the United States Courts of Appeals and codified the provisions establishing them. There are currently thirteen judicial circuits: eleven in the various states; one for the District of Columbia; and one for the Federal Circuit, which has a nationwide but specialized jurisdiction and is located in the District of Columbia and other places as the court may direct by rule. The number of judges per circuit ranges from six (on the First Circuit) to 29 (on the Ninth Circuit). 28 U.S.C. § 44(a). As of September 30, 2022, legislation authorized 179 judgeships on the courts of appeals, and there were an additional 113 senior judges.[185]

The principal business of the courts of appeals consists of review of the district courts, including the district courts in the territories.[186] The most important provision governing appeals from the district courts is 28 U.S.C. § 1291, which provides for jurisdiction of appeals from those courts' "final decisions." This limitation aims to avoid excessive appeals, especially of issues that may be mooted by settlement or by the ultimate outcome after trial.

The Supreme Court has given this statutory limitation a pragmatic construction, allowing litigants to appeal decisions in certain circumstances.[187] In addition, Congress has authorized appeals of interlocutory decisions in a number of situations. See, *e.g.*, 28 U.S.C. § 1292(a)(1) (involving orders "granting, continuing, modifying, refusing or dissolving injunctions, or refusing to dissolve or modify injunctions"); *id.* § 1292(b) (permitting an appeal where the district judge in a civil action concludes an order "involves a controlling question of law as to which there is substantial ground for difference of opinion" and immediate appeal "may materially advance the ultimate termination of the litigation"); see also Fed.R.Civ.P. 23(f) (permitting interlocutory appeal of class certification decisions).[188] Even then, the court of appeals has discretion to accept or reject the appeal, and permission for such appeals is difficult to obtain.

---

[184]   The Report posited that the total number of judgeships (then at 750) should not exceed 1000—a view shared by Judge Newman, among others. See Newman, *1,000 Judges—The Limit for an Effective Federal Judiciary*, 76 Judicature 187 (1993).

[185]   Administrative Office of the U.S. Courts, Judicial Business 2022, Table 10.

[186]   For a comprehensive survey and analysis of this topic see 15, 15A & 16, Wright, Miller & Cooper, Federal Practice and Procedure.

[187]   For example, the "collateral order doctrine" allows an appeal of matters that are "separable from, and collateral to" the merits of the main proceeding, "too important to be denied review," and "too independent of the case itself to require that appellate consideration be deferred until the whole case is adjudicated." Cohen v. Beneficial Industrial Loan Corp., 337 U.S. 541, 546 (1949).

[188]   See also Fed.R.Civ.P.54(b) (permitting district court to "direct entry of a final judgment as to one or more, but fewer than all, claims or parties" if "the court expressly determines that there is no just reason for delay").

A last resort for a litigant seeking appellate review is the All Writs Act, 28 U.S.C. § 1651, which authorizes extraordinary writs including those of prohibition and mandamus.[189]

Finally, some statutes limit or prohibit the appeal even of final judgments. See, *e.g.*, 28 U.S.C. § 2253(c) (habeas corpus), p. 1551, *infra*; 28 U.S.C. § 1447(d) (remand orders).

Cases in the courts of appeals are normally heard and determined by panels of three judges, but each court may, by vote of a majority of the judges in regular active service, order a hearing or rehearing by the court en banc. 28 U.S.C. § 46(c).[190] Rehearings en banc are rare; original hearings en banc are even rarer.[191] A number of circuits, however, have specified that panel decisions may be overruled only by the full bench sitting en banc.[192]

The number of appeals filed in the courts of appeals rose from 3,899 in 1960, to 11,662 in 1970, to 34,292 in 1986, to 48,322 in 1994, to 66,618 in 2006, before falling to 56,475 in 2013, and 41,839 in 2022.[193] As the volume of appeals grew, many courts of appeals altered their traditional procedures.[194] Most circuits have sharply restricted opportunities for oral argument,[195] and the proportion of cases decided without any opinion, or by

---

[189] In such cases, the standard of review imposed by the Supreme Court is a restrictive one: in referring to the availability of mandamus, the Court has said that "[o]nly exceptional circumstances amounting to a judicial 'usurpation of power' will justify the invocation of [such an] extraordinary remedy." Will v. United States, 389 U.S. 90 (1967).

[190] A court en banc consists of all circuit judges in regular active service, except that (a) a senior circuit judge who sat on the decision being reviewed is also eligible to participate, and (b) circuits with more than fifteen active judges—currently the fifth, sixth and ninth—may prescribe by rule the number of members required to perform en banc functions.

[191] En banc courts were responsible for only a little more than 0.15% of decisions rendered on the merits by the courts of appeals in the year ending September 30, 2022. (That year, of the 28,504 cases decided on the merits after either oral argument or submission on briefs, en banc courts only reheard 43.) See Administrative Office of the U.S. Courts, 2022 Judicial Business, Table B-10. Stein, *Uniformity in the Federal Courts: A Proposal for Increasing the Use of En Banc Appellate Review*, 54 U.Pitt.L.Rev. 805, 808–19 (1993), provides interesting historical background.

[192] See, *e.g.*, Bonner v. City of Prichard, 661 F.2d 1206, 1209–11 (11th Cir.1981); United States v. Fatico, 603 F.2d 1053, 1058 (2d Cir.1979). For examples of some of the difficulties that have arisen in the en banc process, see 16A Wright, Miller, Cooper & Gressman, Federal Practice and Procedure § 3981.

[193] Administrative Office of the U.S. Courts, 2013 Judicial Business, Table 1; Administrative Office of the U.S. Courts, 2022 Judicial Business, Analysis & Tables B. Filings by pro se litigants accounted for just shy of half of new filings in 2020–2021. Administrative Office of the U.S. Courts, 2021 Judicial Business, Table B-9. For scholarly analysis of appellate caseloads, see, *e.g.*, Levy, *Judging Justice on Appeal*, 123 Yale L.J. 2386 (2014); Richman & Reynolds, Injustice on Appeal: The United States Court of Appeals Crisis (2013). Levy, *The Promise of Senior Judges*, 115 Nw.U.L.Rev. 1227 (2021), notes that over the last fifty years, the average number of cases filed per judgeship has more than doubled despite the addition of nearly sixty judges during that same period.

[194] See generally Richman & Reynolds, note 193, *supra*, at 83–127. Apart from more formal changes, one commentator, who examined the flood of immigration appeals following reforms passed in the wake of the September 11, 2001, terrorist attacks, has argued that increased caseload pressure leads to lower rates of reversal of district courts. See Huang, *Lightened Scrutiny*, 124 Harv.L.Rev. 1109 (2011).

[195] In the year ending September 30, 2022, the percentage of decisions on the merits rendered without oral argument ranged from 52% in the D.C. Circuit to 89% in the Fourth Circuit. The nationwide percentage stood at 79%. See Administrative Office of the U.S. Courts, 2013 Judicial Business, Table B-10.

per curiam opinion, has increased.[196] Of the 28,504 cases (including those consolidated with other cases) decided on the merits during the year ending September 30, 2022 (by courts of appeals other than the Court of Appeals for the Federal Circuit), only 3,424—roughly 12%—resulted in signed, published opinions.[197] Although most circuits once had rules, adopted at the urging of the Judicial Conference of the United States, that restricted the citation of their "unpublished" opinions and orders as precedents, this practice attracted significant criticism,[198] and gradually the circuits began to reverse themselves. The heated debate generated by the practice has been mooted, at least for now, by the Supreme Court's adoption in 2006 of a new Federal Rule of Appellate Procedure 32.1, under which "[a] court may not prohibit or restrict the citation of federal judicial opinions" designated as "unpublished" or "the like" that are "issued on or after January 1, 2007." The problem of congestion in the courts of appeals has also led to increased reliance on "central" legal staffs.[199]

As with the district courts, crowded appellate dockets have prompted a number of calls for reform, including proposals to replace appeal as of right with a system of discretionary review.[200] Also generating reform pressures

---

[196] See Administrative Office of the U.S. Courts, 2022 Judicial Business, Table B-12. For a study of the case management systems through which different circuits determine which cases will receive oral argument, which dispositions will initially be drafted by staff attorneys rather than judges, and which opinions will be unpublished, see Levy, *The Mechanics of Federal Appeals: Uniformity and Case Management in the Circuit Courts*, 61 Duke L.J. 315 (2011) (finding a nearly pervasive lack of formal transparency and considerable variation among the circuits).

[197] Administrative Office of the U.S. Courts, 2022 Judicial Business, Table B-12. As one mark of change over time, Judge Posner has reported that of all "contested terminations"—terminations after hearing or submission—74% were disposed of by written, signed opinions in 1960. Posner, The Federal Courts: Crisis and Reform 69–70 (1985).

[198] Critics raised serious questions about the desirability and even the constitutionality of such rules. See, *e.g.*, Carrington, Meador & Rosenberg, Justice on Appeal 36–41 (1976); Reynolds & Richman, *An Evaluation of Limited Publication in the United States Courts of Appeals: The Price of Reform*, 48 U.Chi.L.Rev. 573 (1981). See also Pether, *Inequitable Injunctions: The Scandal of Private Judging in the U.S. Courts*, 56 Stan.L.Rev. 1435 (2004). But see Martineau, *Restrictions on Publication and Citation of Judicial Opinions: A Reassessment*, 28 U.Mich.J.L.Ref. 119 (1994) (summarizing and answering objections to rules restricting publication of judicial opinions and citation of unpublished opinions).

In a decision subsequently vacated on mootness grounds, a panel of the Eighth Circuit held that a rule denying precedential effect to "unpublished" opinions violates Article III. See Anastasoff v. United States, 223 F.3d 898, vacated, 235 F.3d 1054 (8th Cir.2000) (en banc). The panel opinion had concluded that the doctrine of precedent was implicit in the original understanding of "the judicial power" and it embraced unpublished as well as published opinions. The panel emphasized that the issue was whether all opinions "ought to have precedential effect, whether published or not." For the opposing view that a prohibition against the citation of unpublished opinions does not violate Article III, see Hart v. Massanari, 266 F.3d 1155 (9th Cir.2001).

[199] For a comprehensive account of this and related developments in one circuit, see Hellman, Restructuring Justice: The Innovations of the Ninth Circuit and the Future of the Federal Courts (1990); Oakley, *The Screening of Appeals: The Ninth Circuit's Experience in the Eighties and Innovations for the Nineties*, 1991 B.Y.U.L.Rev. 859.

[200] See, *e.g.*, Federal Judicial Center, Structural and Other Alternatives for the Federal Courts of Appeals: Report to the United States Congress and the Judicial Conference of the United States (1993), which included as alternative proposals creation of a writ system that would have introduced discretionary review at the appeals court level and what it described as a "two-track" appellate review structure, under which many cases would be summarily disposed of at the Track One stage. For a critical survey of other reform proposals, see Baker, *Imagining the Alternative Futures of the U.S. Courts of Appeals*, 28 Ga.L.Rev. 913 (1994).

in recent decades have been the size of the Ninth Circuit and a worry by some
that it has grown bureaucratically unwieldy.[201]

3. The Supreme Court

The Supreme Court maintains an original and an appellate docket.[202]
Original cases are few, but characteristically laborious and prolonged. Cases
that are fully heard are invariably referred to a master, whose findings the
Court then determines whether to accept.[203] The staple of the Court's docket
is appellate cases, virtually all of which come within the discretionary
certiorari jurisdiction.

The number of cases filed annually in the Court has risen over time,
though it has fallen in recent years. During the 2020 Term, the Court
docketed 5,307 cases (in comparison with 3,419 in the 1970, 4,174 in the
1980, 5,502 in the 1990, 7,852 in the 2000, and 7,857 in the 2010 Terms). The
total cases docketed fell even further to 4,159 in the 2022 Term. Of the total
cases docketed in the 2020 Term, two came within the Court's original
jurisdiction.[204]

Although the number of docketed cases has climbed quite steadily, the
number of cases actually reviewed by the Court has dropped over the same
period. The Court granted review in just 74 cases in the 2020 Term,[205] in
comparison with 170 in the 1970, 185 in the 1980, 144 in the 1990, 101 in
the 2000, and 91 in the 2010 Terms. That number dropped even lower to 62
in the 2022 Term. Some of the decline in the more recent figures reflects
Congress's virtual abolition of the Court's mandatory appellate jurisdiction
in 1988. But other factors appear to have played a role. For a provocative,
though dated, analysis, see Hellman, *The Shrunken Docket of the Rehnquist
Court*, 1996 Sup.Ct.Rev. 403. For a more recent analysis, see Owens &
Simon, *Explaining the Supreme Court's Shrinking Docket*, 53 Wm. & Mary
L.Rev. 1219 (2012).[206] Recent years have also witnessed an uptick in the

---

[201] In response to concerns such as these and to congressional proposals to split the Ninth
Circuit, in 1997 Congress established a Commission on Structural Alternatives for the Federal
Courts of Appeals. 111 Stat. 2440, 2491. The Commission called for the Circuit to be
restructured into three regional divisions, but did not recommend it be split. Commission on
Structural Alternatives for the Federal Courts of Appeals: Final Report 40–45 (1998). The
Commission did, however, recommend that any Circuit with more than 15 judges should be
authorized to restructure itself into adjudicative divisions. Congress took no action on the
proposals advanced by the Commission, and debate about dividing or restructuring the Ninth
Circuit continues to this day.

[202] The Court's original jurisdiction is discussed in Chap. III, Sec. 2, *infra*. The
development of the provisions for review of state court decisions is described in Chap. V, Sec. 1,
infra.

[203] See generally Note on Procedure in Original Actions, Chap. III, p. 350, *infra*.

[204] These numbers are drawn from the Journal of the Supreme Court for the relevant
Term. See Statistics, J.S.Ct.U.S., Oct. Term 2022, at II; Statistics, J.S.Ct.U.S., Oct. Term 2020,
at II; Statistics, J.S.Ct.U.S., Oct. Term 2010, at II; Statistics, J.S.Ct.U.S., Oct. Term 2000, at II;
Statistics, J.S.Ct.U.S., Oct. Term 1990, at II; Statistics, J.S.Ct.U.S., Oct. Term 1980, at II;
Statistics, J.S.Ct.U.S., Oct. Term 1970, at 2.

[205] The cases granted review figures are drawn from the Journal of the Supreme Court
and represent the sum of cases in which the Court granted a petition for certiorari, granted an
appeal, and set a case falling within its original jurisdiction for oral argument after a prior grant
of a motion for leave to file a bill of complaint.

[206] An empirical study of 93,000 certiorari petitions filed between the 2001 Supreme Court
Term and the start of the 2015 Term found that factors influencing the probability of a petition

Court issuing opinions through its emergency docket—that is, in conjunction with awarding or reversing the issuance of emergency relief in cases making their way through the lower courts.[207]

Especially during the years when the Court was producing well in excess of 100 written dispositions per year, a variety of proposals emerged to lighten the Justices' workload. Perhaps the most recurring suggestion called for the development of a national court of appeals, subordinate to the Supreme Court, but with jurisdiction to review decisions of the existing circuit courts of appeals.[208] None of the proposals to create a national court of appeals has come to a vote in Congress. More recently, following the 2020 election, a presidential commission studied various proposals for Supreme Court reform in a host of areas but ultimately made no significant recommendations for reform.[209]

---

being granted include whether the federal government supports a grant, the attorneys involved, and the lower court that rendered the decision. See Feldman & Kappner, *Finding Certainty in Cert: An Empirical Analysis of the Factors Involved in Supreme Court Certiorari Decisions from 2001–2015*, 61 Vill.L.Rev. 795 (2017).

[207] For a detailed and critical analysis of this trend, consult Vladeck, The Shadow Docket: How the Supreme Court Uses Stealth Rulings to Amass Power and Undermine the Republic (2023). See also Chap. III, Sec. 4, *infra*.

[208] See, *e.g.*, Federal Judicial Center, Report of the Study Group on the Caseload of the Supreme Court (1972) (proposing elimination of the Court's obligatory review jurisdiction and creation of a new national court of appeals with the authority, inter alia, to screen cases for the Supreme Court's docket). This proposal by the so-called Freund Committee met a predominantly critical response. See, *e.g.*, Warren, *Let's Not Weaken The Supreme Court*, 60 A.B.A.J. 677 (1974); Black, *The National Court of Appeals: An Unwise Proposal*, 83 Yale L.J. 883 (1974). For a defense, see Freund, *Why We Need the National Court of Appeals*, 59 A.B.A.J. 247 (1973). Nevertheless, variations have subsequently appeared in a report by the Commission on Revision of the Federal Court Appellate System, Structure and Internal Procedures: Recommendations for Change (1975) (reprinted in 67 F.R.D. 195 (1975)), and as part of a comprehensive package of reform proposals by the Federal Courts Study Committee, which proposed a 5-year pilot project authorizing the Supreme Court to refer intercircuit conflicts to a court of appeals for an en banc, nationally binding decision. Report of the Federal Courts Study Committee 125–29 (1990). *Cf.* George & Guthrie, *"The Threes": Re-Imagining Supreme Court Decisionmaking*, 61 Vand.L.Rev. 1825 (2008) (advocating statutory reform to allow the Supreme Court to sit in panels of three (with or without en banc review) and thereby expand the number of cases that the Court can hear).

[209] See Final Report, Presidential Commission on the Supreme Court of the United States (2021).

CHAPTER II

THE NATURE OF THE FEDERAL JUDICIAL FUNCTION: CASES AND CONTROVERSIES

1. INTRODUCTION AND HISTORICAL CONTEXT

This chapter examines questions of justiciability—a cluster of related issues that define the scope of federal judicial power through categories such as standing, ripeness, mootness, and the political question doctrine. These categories deal respectively with questions such as who constitutes a proper plaintiff to invoke federal judicial power (standing); when is a matter sufficiently immediate and concrete to justify judicial consideration (ripeness); what should a court do when a crucial element of a live dispute goes away during the adjudication process (mootness); and what sorts of legal disputes, if any, does the Constitution mark off for exclusive resolution by branches other than the judiciary (political question doctrine). Viewed together, these doctrines help define the role of the federal courts in our constitutional structure— a goal that entails not only identifying the judicial function but also understanding how it relates to the powers of the coordinate branches.

Needless to say, there is no intrinsically correct or universally accepted idea of appropriate judicial power. The Constitution, moreover, says little about the matter. The document has no Standing, Ripeness, Mootness, or Political Question Clause. Although Article III vests in the federal courts "the judicial Power" and grants jurisdiction to exercise it in various "cases" or "controversies," it nowhere defines those terms. The Philadelphia Convention and the thirteen state ratifying conventions do not offer much guidance either. Nevertheless, these open-ended terms both reflect and embody legal traditions, practices, and understandings that help define the role of Article III courts.

Because the operative terms of Article III are so open-ended, this chapter begins with the historical context in which "the judicial Power" first came to be understood. In reading the materials that follow, consider the following questions. First, to what extent should one assume that those who adopted the Constitution—all of whom were raised in the English legal tradition—understood technical legal terms (such as "judicial Power" or "case") in their common-law English sense?[1] Second,

---

[1]   The Court has frequently stated that legal concepts informed the understanding of technical legal terms used in drafting the Constitution. See, *e.g.*, Ex parte Grossman, 267 U.S.

to what extent is constitutional meaning revealed by practical constructions given to the document by those officials who were charged with implementing it?[2] Third, to what extent, if any, should original understanding and early practice guide the interpretation of Article III's language more than two centuries later?[3]

Starting from the premise that the early historical context supplies at least a relevant data point for understanding, refining, and critiquing some of the constitutional traditions that have taken shape around "the judicial Power," this Section begins by exploring practical controversies that gave rise to certain established conceptions of federal judicial power.

INTRODUCTORY NOTE

This discussion of judicial power begins with President Washington's efforts to ascertain the legal rights and duties of the United States in relation to those involved in the late-eighteenth-century European hostilities that had spilled into North America. Secretary of State Jefferson propounded the following questions to the Court. Today, the prohibition against the Court's issuing "advisory opinions" is taken for granted. It is an uncontroversial and central element of our understanding of federal judicial power. In reading the materials below, consider to what extent the conventional tools of legal

---

87, 110 (1925); Myers v. United States, 272 U.S. 52, 118 (1926); United States v. Wilson, 32 U.S. (7 Pet.) 150, 160 (1833) (Marshall, C.J.). The Court has also recognized, however, that in many respects the American constitutional structure deviates from and is incompatible with English premises about government, making certain English common law traditions inapposite to aspects of the U.S. Constitution. See, *e.g.*, Grosjean v. American Press Co., 297 U.S. 233, 248–49 (1936); Belknap v. Schild, 161 U.S. 10, 15 (1896); Fleming v. Page, 50 U.S. (9 How.) 603, 618 (1850).

[2] See Knowlton v. Moore, 178 U.S. 41, 56 (1900) (crediting early practical constructions of the Constitution by public officials because "all questions which related to the Constitution and its adoption must have been, at that early date, vividly impressed in their minds"). See also, *e.g.*, Wisconsin v. Pelican Ins. Co., 127 U.S. 265, 297 (1888); The Laura, 114 U.S. 411, 416 (1885); Cohens v. Virginia, 19 U.S. (6 Wheat.) 264, 420 (1821). Some early Supreme Court cases treated the political branches' practical constructions as conclusively settling the Constitution's meaning. See Stuart v. Laird, 5 U.S. (1 Cranch) 299, 309 (1803) (upholding statutorily required circuit riding by Supreme Court Justices); United States v. Hudson & Goodwin, 11 U.S. (7 Cranch) 32 (1812), p. 747, *infra* (rejection of federal common law crimes). For further discussion see Powell, *The Original Understanding of Original Intent*, 98 Harv.L.Rev. 885, 935–44 (1985); Nelson, *Stare Decisis and Demonstrably Erroneous Precedents*, 87 Va.L.Rev. 1, 9–21 (2001); Baude, *Constitutional Liquidation*, 71 Stan.L.Rev. 1 (2019).

[3] See, *e.g.*, Brest, *The Misconceived Quest for the Original Understanding*, 60 B.U.L.Rev. 204, 225 (1980) (arguing that the reliance on original meaning violates Lockean premises because our present society "did not adopt the Constitution, and those who did are dead and gone"); Strauss, *Common Law Constitutional Interpretation*, 63 U.Chi.L.Rev. 877, 880 (1996) ("Following a written constitution means accepting the judgments of people who lived centuries ago in a society that was very different from ours."); but see Scalia, *Originalism: The Lesser Evil*, 57 U.Cin.L.Rev. 849 (1989) (arguing that originalism better fits the practice of judicial review, theoretically and practically, than nonoriginalism); Baude, *Is Originalism Our Law?*, 115 Colum.L.Rev. 2349, 2408 (2015) ("The original meaning of the Constitution continues to control precisely because we the living continue to treat it as law and use the legal institutions it makes, and we do so in official continuity with the document's past. So the decisions of the dead still govern, but only because we the living, for reasons of our own, receive them as law."); Sachs, *Originalism as a Theory of Legal Change*, 38 Harv. J.L. & Pub.Pol'y 817, 838 (2015) (arguing that "[o]ur law is still the Founders' law, as it's been lawfully changed.").

interpretation dictated the result that is taken as a given today. In other words, how much is the embedded understanding a matter of historical contingency?

Correspondence of the Justices (1793)[1]

Letter from Thomas Jefferson, Secretary of State, to Chief Justice Jay and Associate Justices:

Philadelphia, July 18, 1793.

Gentlemen:

The war which has taken place among the powers of Europe produces frequent transactions within our ports and limits, on which questions arise of considerable difficulty, and of greater importance to the peace of the United States. These questions depend for their solution on the construction of our treaties, on the laws of nature and nations, and on the laws of the land, and are often presented under circumstances *which do not give a cognizance of them to the tribunals of the country.* Yet their decision is so little analogous to the ordinary functions of the executive, as to occasion much embarrassment and difficulty to them. The President therefore would be much relieved if he found himself free to refer questions of this description to the opinions of the judges of the Supreme Court of the United States, whose knowledge of the subject would secure us against errors dangerous to the peace of the United States, and their authority insure the respect of all parties. He has therefore asked the attendance of such of the judges as could be collected in time for the occasion, to know, in the first place, their opinion, whether the public may, with propriety, be availed of their *advice on these questions?* And if they may, to present, for their advice, the abstract questions which have already occurred, or may soon occur, from which they will themselves strike out such as any circumstances might, in their opinion, forbid them to pronounce on. I have the honour to be with sentiments of the most perfect respect, gentlemen,

----

Your most obedient and humble servant,

Thos. Jefferson.

Anticipating that the Justices would proffer the requested "advice," the President's Cabinet agreed to address no fewer than twenty-nine

----

[1] The letters are respectively taken from 3 Correspondence and Public Papers of John Jay 486–89 (Johnston ed. 1891) and 15 The Papers of Alexander Hamilton 111 n.1 (H. Syrett ed. 1969), and the questions from 10 Sparks, Writings of Washington 542–45 (1836).

specific questions to the Court. It is unclear whether those questions were appended to Jefferson's letter, but the Justices were surely aware of the questions' "general content." Jay, Most Humble Servants: The Advisory Role of Early Judges 136–37 (1997). The following are some of the questions prepared by the President and his Cabinet for submission to the Justices:

"1. Do the treaties between the United States and France give to France or her citizens a *right*, when at war with a power with whom the United States are at peace, to fit out originally in and from the ports of the United States vessels armed for war, with or without commission?

"2. If they give such a *right*, does it extend to all manner of armed vessels, or to particular kinds only? If the latter, to what kinds does it extend?

"3. Do they give to France or her citizens, in the case supposed, a right to refit or arm anew vessels, which, before their coming within any port of the United States, were armed for war, with or without commission?

"4. If they give such a right, does it extend to all manner of armed vessels, or to particular kinds only? If the latter, to what kinds does it extend? Does it include an *augmentation* of force, or does it only extend to replacing the vessel *in statu quo*? * * *

"17. Do the laws of neutrality, considered as aforesaid, authorize the United States to permit France, her subjects, or citizens, the sale within their ports of prizes made of the subjects or property of a power at war with France, before they have been carried into some port of France and there condemned, refusing the like privilege to her enemy?

"18. Do those laws authorize the United States to permit to France the erection of courts within their territory and jurisdiction for the trial and condemnation of prizes, refusing that privilege to a power at war with France? * * *

"20. To what distance, by the laws and usages of nations, may the United States exercise the right of prohibiting the hostilities of foreign powers at war with each other within rivers, bays, and arms of the sea, and upon the sea along the coasts of the United States?

"22. What are the articles, by name, to be prohibited to both or either party? * * *

"25. May we, within our own ports, sell ships to both parties, prepared merely for merchandise? May they be pierced for guns? * * *

"29. May an armed vessel belonging to any of the belligerent powers follow *immediately* merchant vessels, enemies, departing from our ports, for the purpose of making prizes of them? If not, how long ought the former to remain, after the latter have sailed? And what shall be considered as the place of departure from which the time is to be counted? And how are the facts to be ascertained?"

On July 20, 1793, Chief Justice Jay and the Associate Justices wrote to President Washington expressing their wish to postpone the answer to Jefferson's letter until the sitting of the Court. On August 8, 1793, they wrote to the President as follows:

"Sir:

"We have considered the previous question stated in a letter written to us by your direction by the Secretary of State on the 18th of last month. The lines of separation drawn by the Constitution between the three departments of the government—their being in certain respects checks upon each other—and our being judges of a court in the last resort—are considerations which afford strong arguments against the propriety of our extrajudicially deciding the questions alluded to; especially as the power given by the Constitution to the President of calling on the heads of departments for opinions, seems to have been *purposely* as well as expressly limited to the *executive* departments."

NOTE ON ADVISORY OPINIONS

(1) Foundations. The prohibition against advisory opinions has been termed "the oldest and most consistent thread in the federal law of justiciability." Wright & Kane, Law of Federal Courts 65–66 (7th ed.2011). But how clear was the Justices' decision from the Constitution's language and history?[1] The English judicial practice with which early Americans were familiar had long permitted the Crown to solicit advisory opinions from judges. See Jay, Most Humble Servants: The Advisory Role of Early Judges 3 (1997). As Professor Jay further notes, neither the constitutional text nor the discussions at the Constitutional Convention reflected any clear prohibition against advisory opinions. Consider, also, whether the position taken in the Correspondence accords with early American practice.

In 1790, Chief Justice Jay and a minority of the Justices were said to have sent a letter to President Washington advising him of their view that circuit riding was unconstitutional. See 4 Am.Jur. & L.Mag. 293 (1830). But see Wheeler, note 1, *supra*, at 148 (suggesting that the letter was never sent). Chief Justice Jay himself regularly gave informal legal advice to the Washington Administration. Jay, *supra*. Some of the advice pertained to sensitive questions of foreign affairs, including the international law ramifications of a potential British request to cross over American soil to attack Spain during the Nootka Sound crisis of 1790. At Alexander Hamilton's initiation, moreover, Chief Justice Jay prepared a draft of the Neutrality Proclamation declaring the Nation to be impartial toward the belligerent powers, and he advised the national government to commence criminal prosecutions of those who violated the proclamation. Well after the Correspondence of the Justices, Chief Justice Ellsworth gave an opinion to Senator Trumbull on an aspect of the Jay Treaty and another to Secretary of

---

[1]   For an illuminating discussion of the Correspondence of the Justices, see Wheeler, *Extrajudicial Activities of the Early Supreme Court*, 1973 Sup.Ct.Rev. 123, 144–58.

State Pickering on the legality of the Sedition Act. See Casto, The Supreme
Court in the Early Republic: The Chief Justiceships of John Jay and Oliver
Ellsworth 71–72, 74–75, 97–98, 148–49 (1995). These informal practices
suggest another side to the question addressed by the Correspondence.[2]

Does the separation of powers justify the now well-settled rejection of
judicial power to give advisory opinions? In the Correspondence, the Justices
generally invoked the "lines of separation" among the branches and the
background understanding that each branch would serve as a check on the
others. After invoking separation-of-powers considerations more generally,
the Justices added that "the power given by the Constitution to the President
of calling on the heads of departments for opinions, seems to have been
purposely as well as expressly limited to the *executive* departments." See p.
4, *supra.* In other words, the Justices apparently believed that the Opinion
Clause of Article II—which provides that the President "may require the
Opinion, in writing, of the principal Officer in each of the executive
Departments, upon any Subject relating to the Duties of their respective
Offices" (U.S. Const. Art. II, § 2, cl. 1)—carried a negative implication that
the President could not ask *judges* for such opinions. Is that general
inference from the constitutional structure sufficient to justify deviation
from the specific expectations that early Americans likely held about judicial
power, given the longstanding tradition of English judges' issuing advisory
opinions? Compare Amar, *Some Opinions on the Opinion Clause*, 82
Va.L.Rev. 847 (1996) (arguing that the Opinion Clause meant to distinguish
the President from the Crown, *inter alia*, by precluding the former from
treating the other branches as his or her subordinates).

Perhaps due to these historical complexities, Felix Frankfurter
defended the prohibition against advisory opinions based on the policies
implicit in Article III, rather than on historical pedigree. Frankfurter,
Advisory Opinions, 1 Encyc. of the Social Sciences 475, 476 (1937). What are
these policies? Perhaps the prohibition serves the interest, discussed below,
in making federal judicial power available only to resolve concrete disputes
based on private rights. See p. 92, *infra.* Or it might serve the interest, also
discussed below, in ensuring that cases and controversies satisfy the
"functional requisites" of effective adjudication. See p. 94, *infra.* To what
extent could the Court address objections to advisory opinions by restricting
itself to giving advisory rulings on definite states of fact, real or assumed? If
the Justices had answered questions like those presented to them by

---

[2]   Based on the historical precedents, Professor Casto would minimize the significance of
the Correspondence. He thus argues that "the early Justices clearly believed that they had a
discretionary power" to furnish advisory opinions for the executive branch and that "[t]he only
absolute rule that can be teased out of their 1793 letter to President Washington, is that the
President is not empowered to require the federal judiciary to provide an advisory opinion."
Casto, *The Early Supreme Court Justices' Most Significant Opinion*, 29 Ohio Northern U.L.Rev.
173, 201 (2002). Professor Jay argues that the Correspondence reflected idiosyncratic
considerations, such as the desire of the Justices, who wished to be relieved of circuit riding
responsibilities, to avoid entanglement in a potentially divisive political controversy. Jay, *supra*,
at 149–70. But see Pushaw, *Why the Supreme Court Never Gets Any "Dear John" Letters:
Advisory Opinions in Historical Perspective*, 87 Geo.L.J. 473 (1998) (book review) (arguing that
the Correspondence of the Justices is best explained by constitutional considerations unrelated
to the immediate political context).

Jefferson, would the Court's prestige, and the acceptability of its decisions, have been enhanced or diminished?[3]

(2) Identifying Advisory Opinions. How does one distinguish a forbidden advisory opinion from, on the one hand, the adjudication of a proper "case" or "controversy," and, on the other hand, permissible nonjudicial pronouncements by the Justices in books, articles, lectures, and the like? Consider how the idea of "advisory opinions" bears on the following questions:

(a) Would a purely prospective decision, which did not apply a newly propounded rule of decision to the parties in the case, constitute an advisory opinion forbidden by Article III?[4] The question of prospectivity typically has arisen when a ruling of the Court overrules a past decision or departs significantly from settled understandings and establishes rights and obligations not previously recognized in our history. Until fairly recently, the Court's tradition had been to give even novel rulings full retroactivity—applying them not only to the case before it but also to other cases pending on direct review. Perhaps because of the pathbreaking character of many of its criminal procedure rulings, the Warren Court broke with that tradition in criminal cases. In Linkletter v. Walker, 381 U.S. 618 (1965), the Court held that the rule in Mapp v. Ohio, 367 U.S. 643 (1961), though applied to the case in which it was announced, would not be applied in collateral review of a final state court conviction. In so doing, moreover, Linkletter suggested in dictum that nothing in Article III precluded even a "purely prospective" decision. The next year, in Johnson v. New Jersey, 384 U.S. 719 (1966), the Court asserted power to make rules of criminal procedure nonretroactive, by which it meant that the new rule would be applied in the case before it but otherwise would not apply in cases pending on direct review. In civil cases, too, the Court also gestured toward very expansive judicial discretion to announce new rules prospectively. See Chevron Oil Co. v. Huson, 404 U.S. 97, 107 (1971); England v. Louisiana St. Bd. of Med. Examiners, 375 U.S. 411, 422 (1964).

In that same period, the Court also began to voice some concerns about pure prospectivity, stating in Stovall v. Denno, 388 U.S. 293, 301 (1967), that

---

[3] Historical scholarship argues that the prohibition against advisory opinions in American founding-era practice was in fact part of a global phenomenon throughout the anglophone world in the late eighteenth century, including in England and British India. Burset, *Advisory Opinions and the Problem of Legal Authority*, 74 Vand.L.Rev. 621 (2021). According to Burset, the refusal to issue advisory opinions was a judicial response to a contemporary global dispute about the nature of common law authority, and had little to do with the specifics of the American Constitution. If this is so, does it imply that the prohibition on advisory opinions may be less deeply rooted than the conventional wisdom has it? Or the opposite?

[4] For general discussion of questions concerning the retroactivity or prospectivity of judicial decisions, see McGinnis & Rappaport, *An Originalist Approach to Prospective Overruling*, 99 Notre Dame L.Rev. 425 (2023); Beswick, *Retroactive Adjudication*, 130 Yale L.J. 276 (2020); Fallon & Meltzer, *New Law, Non-Retroactivity, and Constitutional Remedies*, 104 Harv.L.Rev. 1731 (1991); Beytagh, *Ten Years of Non-retroactivity: A Critique and a Proposal*, 61 Va.L.Rev. 1557 (1975); Mishkin, *Foreword: The High Court, The Great Writ, and the Due Process of Time and Law*, 79 Harv.L.Rev. 56 (1965); Schwartz, *Retroactivity, Reliability, and Due Process: A Response to Professor Mishkin*, 33 U.Chi.L.Rev. 719 (1966); Note, 71 Yale L.J. 907 (1962).

"[s]ound policies of decision-making, rooted in the command of Article III of the Constitution that we resolve issues solely in cases or controversies, * * * militate against" pure prospectivity. More recently, the Court expressly reconsidered its authority to make rules of criminal procedure nonretroactive to cases pending on direct review. In Griffith v. Kentucky, 479 U.S. 314, 322–23 (1987), the Court wrote: "[F]ailure to apply a newly declared constitutional rule to criminal cases pending on direct review violates basic norms of constitutional adjudication. * * * [A]fter we have decided a new rule in the case selected, the integrity of judicial review requires that we apply that rule to all similar cases pending on direct review." (Although the Court continues to insist upon the presumptive nonretroactivity of new rules on collateral review of final state court convictions, its decision to do so rests squarely upon the special characteristics of the habeas remedy. See Chap. XI, Sec. 3, *infra*.) The Court has also drawn back from any suggestion in civil cases that pure prospectivity is appropriate. See, *e.g.*, American Trucking Ass'ns, Inc. v. Smith, 496 U.S. 167 (1990); James B. Beam Distilling Co. v. Georgia, 501 U.S. 529 (1991); Harper v. Virginia Dep't of Taxation, 509 U.S. 86 (1993); Reynoldsville Casket Co. v. Hyde, 514 U.S. 749 (1995); Ryder v. United States, 515 U.S. 177 (1995). In Harper, the Court explained that even in civil cases, non-retroactive decisionmaking is a legislative function, and that such decisionmaking denies equal treatment to similarly situated litigants.

Despite all of these developments, the Court has never squarely held that purely prospective judicial decisionmaking would violate Article III. Would a purely prospective ruling violate the prohibition against advisory opinions? When a court first identifies a constitutional violation, then denies relief under harmless error, qualified immunity, or analogous doctrines, has it rendered a constitutionally impermissible advisory opinion? See Teague v. Lane, 489 U.S. 288, 318 (1989) (Stevens, J., concurring in part and concurring in the judgment); Fallon & Meltzer, note 3, *supra*, at 1798–1800. On qualified immunity, see pp. 1311–1328, *infra*.[5]

(b) When a court renders alternative holdings, has it violated constitutional norms? Settled practice surely suggests not, but why not? Consider the relevance of the following factors: (i) a concretely framed dispute, (ii) adverse parties, (iii) adversarial presentation of competing arguments, (iv) res judicata and stare decisis effects in subsequent judicial actions; and (v) conclusiveness of the determination for other branches of government.

(c) In Steel Co. v. Citizens for a Better Environment, 523 U.S. 83 (1998), p. 979, *infra*, Justice Scalia's opinion for the Court invoked the specter of an "advisory opinion" in holding that federal courts must resolve questions of subject matter jurisdiction—in this case standing—at the threshold. Under the rubric of "hypothetical jurisdiction," several courts of

---

[5]   For an argument that many non-retroactivity issues should be analyzed as involving the necessity or appropriateness of particular judicial remedies for constitutional violations, see Fallon & Meltzer, *supra*. For criticism of that position, see Roosevelt, *A Little Theory is a Dangerous Thing: The Myth of Adjudicative Retroactivity*, 31 Conn.L.Rev. 1075 (1999); Liebman & Ryan, *"Some Effectual Power": The Quantity and Quality of Decisionmaking Required of Article III Courts*, 98 Colum.L.Rev. 696 (1998).

appeals had found "it proper to proceed immediately to the merits question, despite jurisdictional objections, at least where (1) the merits question is more readily resolved, and (2) the prevailing party on the merits would be the same as the prevailing party were jurisdiction denied." Justice Scalia reasoned, however, that "[h]ypothetical jurisdiction produces nothing more than a hypothetical judgment—which comes to the same thing as an advisory opinion." When the decision of a question conclusively resolves a lawsuit, in what sense could a judicial opinion deciding that question count as "advisory"?[6]

(d)   Despite the general acceptance of the view that advisory opinions fall without "the judicial Power of the United States," see Wright & Kane, Paragraph (1), *supra*, individual Justices have engaged in extrajudicial expression of their legal views on innumerable occasions. For later examples, see: Opinion given by Justice Johnson, with the approval of other members of the Court, to President Monroe, in 1 Warren, The Supreme Court in United States History 596–97 (1937 ed.); Letter of Chief Justice Hughes to Senator Wheeler, Chairman of the Senate Judiciary Committee, concerning President Roosevelt's proposals for reorganizing the Supreme Court, Sen.Rep. No. 711, 75th Cong., 1st Sess. (1937), at 38–40; Letter of Chief Justice Taney to Secretary of the Treasury Chase concerning the 1862 tax levied upon the salaries of federal judges, in Tyler, Memoir of Roger B. Taney 432–34 (1872). In recent years, sitting Justices have published numerous books, articles, and lectures commenting on legal issues.[7] Does this practice contradict the view that advisory opinions are constitutionally prohibited?

(e)   Is it possible to specify necessary or sufficient conditions for identifying advisory opinions that lie outside Article III judicial power? According to Lee, *Deconstitutionalizing Justiciability: The Example of Mootness*, 105 Harv.L.Rev. 603, 644–45 (1992), the Supreme Court has used the term "advisory opinion" to embrace "[a]ny judgment subject to review by a co-equal branch of government," "[a]dvice to a coequal branch of government prior to the other branch's contemplated action," "Supreme Court review of any state judgment for which there is or may be an adequate and independent state ground," "[a]ny opinion, or portion thereof, not truly necessary to the disposition of the case at bar (that is, dicta)," and "[a]ny decision on the merits of a case that is moot or unripe or in which one of the parties lacks standing." Lee concludes that "only the first two of these usages denote a constitutional bar. The other three usages are a function of judicial discretion."

(3) Declaratory Judgments. The Federal Declaratory Judgment Act of 1934, 48 Stat. 955, provides that federal courts "may declare the rights and legal relations of any interested party seeking such declaration" in "a case of actual controversy." For the present provisions, see 28 U.S.C. §§ 2201–2202.

---

[6]   For a case that seems to qualify Steel Co., see Sinochem Int. Co. Ltd. v. Malaysia Int. Shipping Corp., 549 U.S. 422 (2007) (holding that a district court may dismiss a case on forum non conveniens grounds without first determining whether it has subject matter jurisdiction and noting that a forum non conveniens determination is not "on the merits").

[7]   For a comprehensive review and compilation of informal comments through 1962, see Westin, *Out-of-Court Commentary by United States Supreme Court Justices, 1790–1962: Of Free Speech and Judicial Lockjaw*, 62 Colum.L.Rev. 633 (1962).

Prior to the Act's adoption, there had been some division of authority on the question whether declaratory judgments constitute advisory opinions. Compare Willing v. Chicago Auditorium Ass'n, 277 U.S. 274, 289 (1928) (holding that federal courts lacked jurisdiction to resolve a lessee's doubts about its rights under a lease and that a request for "simply a declaratory judgment" lies "beyond the power conferred upon the federal judiciary"), with Nashville, C. & St. L. Ry. v. Wallace, 288 U.S. 249 (1933) (finding jurisdiction to review a state court declaratory judgment action on the ground that it had all of the elements of a bill of injunction except a request for a coercive decree and a claim of irreparable injury, neither of which was essential to the existence of a "case" or "controversy" in an Article III sense).

The Court put the question to rest when it unanimously upheld the Declaratory Judgment Act's constitutionality in Aetna Life Ins. Co. v. Haworth, 300 U.S. 227 (1937). Aetna had brought the action to secure a declaration that four policies held by the defendant had lapsed for nonpayment of premiums, and that the company's only obligation was to pay $45 on the insured's death as extended insurance on one policy. The complaint asserted that the defendant claimed to be totally and permanently disabled, in which event all of the policies would be in full force, and two of them would oblige the company presently to pay disability benefits. The complaint added that the defendant, while making this claim repeatedly against the insurer, had failed to institute any action in which the company could prove its falsity. The complaint pointed to the danger posed by the possible disappearance, illness, or death of witnesses, and to the necessity meanwhile of maintaining reserves against the policies in excess of $20,000.[8]

Writing for the Court, Chief Justice Hughes said:

"* * * The Declaratory Judgment Act of 1934, in its limitation to 'cases of actual controversy,' manifestly has regard to the constitutional provision and is operative only in respect to controversies which are such in the constitutional sense. The word 'actual' is one of emphasis rather than of definition. Thus the operation of the Declaratory Judgment Act is procedural only. In providing remedies and defining procedure in relation to cases and controversies in the constitutional sense the Congress is acting within its delegated power over the jurisdiction of the federal courts which the Congress is authorized to establish. * * * Exercising this control of practice and procedure the Congress is not confined to traditional forms or traditional remedies. * * *

"There is here a dispute between parties who face each other in an adversary proceeding. The dispute relates to legal rights and obligations arising from the contracts of insurance. The dispute is definite and concrete, not hypothetical or abstract. * * * It calls, not for an advisory opinion upon a hypothetical basis, but for an adjudication of present right upon established facts. * * *

---

8   Bray, *Preventive Adjudication*, 77 U.Chi.L.Rev. 1275 (2010), contends that such actions are appropriate when the administrative and error costs of anticipatory litigation are outweighed by the benefits of legal clarification, as he concludes is true in cases involving legal status (such as citizenship) and clouds on title. Is this use of cost-benefit analysis judicially manageable? Consistent with the text of the statute?

"If the insured had brought suit to recover the disability benefits currently payable under two of the policies there would have been no question that the controversy was of a justiciable nature, whether or not the amount involved would have permitted its determination in a federal court. * * * [T]he character of the controversy and of the issue to be determined is essentially the same whether it is presented by the insured or by the insurer."

Would it be safe to say that an actual controversy always exists if either party could maintain an action for coercive relief?[9]

(4) Advisory Opinions by State Courts. Article III's prohibition against advisory opinions by federal courts does not extend to state courts, a number of which are authorized to render such opinions.[10] For example, part 2, ch. 3, art. 2 of the constitution of Massachusetts (1780) provides: "Each branch of the legislature, as well as the governor or the council, shall have authority to require the opinions of the justices of the supreme judicial court, upon important questions of law, and upon solemn occasions."[11] There are variants of this provision in the constitutions of Colorado, Florida, Maine, Michigan, New Hampshire, Rhode Island, and South Dakota. In three states— Alabama, Delaware, and Oklahoma—advisory opinions are authorized, in certain circumstances, by statute. "Ten other states have rejected or abandoned the practice." Hershkoff, *State Courts and the "Passive Virtues": Rethinking the Judicial Function*, 114 Harv.L.Rev. 1833, 1840 n.68 (2001). According to Professor Hershkoff, advisory opinions perform a useful dialogic function within state constitutional regimes by "allow[ing] state courts to articulate constitutional principles, while effectively 'remanding' disputes back to the other branches" for a considered response. Her judgment rests

---

[9] In MedImmune, Inc. v. Genentech, Inc., 549 U.S. 118 (2007), the Supreme Court suggested that the capacity to request coercive relief may not be necessary, as long as the Court's opinion resolves the plaintiff's *potential* liability. There, a patent licensee (Medimmune) received a demand letter from the patent holder (Genentech) stating that its patent covered Synagis, a drug manufactured by Medimmune. Medimmune paid royalties under protest and brought a declaratory judgment action seeking to establish that the patent was invalid and did not apply. Although Medimmune's payment of royalties meant that it had no "reasonable apprehension" of liability, the Court held that the suit constituted a proper declaratory judgment action. If Medimmune had declined to pay, and Genentech had successfully sued for patent infringement, Medimmune could have been liable for treble damages and attorney's fees and could have been enjoined from selling Synagis, which accounted for eighty percent of its sales. Invoking the principle that plaintiffs who wish to challenge the validity of state criminal statutes need not first violate those statutes in order to have actionable controversies under the Declaratory Judgment Act or Article III, the Court rejected the idea that a plaintiff must "risk treble damages and the loss of 80 percent of its business, before seeking a declaration of its actively contested legal rights." Justice Thomas dissented, arguing that for so long as a patent licensee continued to pay royalties, neither the licensor nor the licensee had a justiciable controversy with the other concerning the patent's scope or validity.

[10] For discussion of the evolving use of advisory opinions versus other forms of adjudication in European constitutional practice, see Gardbaum, *The Myth and the Reality of American Constitutional Exceptionalism*, 107 Mich.L.Rev. 391, 411–16 (2008). See also Jackson & Tushnet, Comparative Constitutional Law, Chap. 6 (3d ed.2014).

[11] See Farina, *Supreme Judicial Court Advisory Opinions: Two Centuries of Interbranch Dialogue*, in The History of the Law in Massachusetts: The Supreme Judicial Court 1692–1992, at 353 (Osgood ed. 1992) (giving a generally favorable assessment of advisory opinion practice in Massachusetts); see also, *e.g.*, In re Opinions of the Justices to the Senate, 440 Mass. 1201 (2004) (concluding that a pending bill providing for same-sex civil unions, but not same-sex marriages, violated the state constitution).

partly on an assumption about the nature of state constitutional practice: "[A]dvisory opinions suit the conditional nature of all state constitutional decisions, which are easily amended and frequently experimental in approach."

If a state court renders an advisory opinion on a question of federal law, that opinion may significantly affect the operations of state government. How may federal interests be protected in such a case? See pp. 208–209, *infra*.

INTRODUCTORY NOTE ON MARBURY V. MADISON

Typically, one thinks of the case that follows—Marbury v. Madison—as establishing conclusively the federal courts' authority to invalidate Acts of Congress as unconstitutional. It did that, to be sure. But Chief Justice Marshall's opinion for the Court also grappled with another question that is taken as a given today: judicial authority to judge the legality of actions by the officer of a coordinate branch and to direct that officer to comply with federal law. In wrestling with both issues—judicial review and mandamus—the Court in Marbury necessarily articulated a vision of the role of the federal judiciary in our system of separation of powers. Perhaps because of Marbury's canonical status, scholars today offer competing views of what vision the Court, in fact, articulated. In reading the case, try to identify theory of judicial power on which the Court justifies its role in assessing the legality of both statutes and executive action.

Marbury v. Madison
5 U.S. (1 Cranch) 137 (1803).
On Petition for Mandamus.

■ * * * [T]he following opinion of the Court was delivered by the CHIEF JUSTICE:

Opinion of the Court.

At the last term on the affidavits then read and filed with the clerk, a rule was granted in this case, requiring the secretary of state to show cause why a *mandamus* should not issue, directing him to deliver to William Marbury his commission as a justice of the peace for the county of Washington, in the district of Columbia.

No cause has been shown, and the present motion is for a *mandamus*. The peculiar delicacy of this case, the novelty of some of its circumstances, and the real difficulty attending the points which occur in it, require a complete exposition of the principles on which the opinion to be given by the court is founded. * * *

In the order in which the court has viewed this subject, the following questions have been considered and decided.

1st. Has the applicant a right to the commission he demands?

2dly. If he has a right, and that right has been violated, do the laws of his country afford him a remedy?

3dly. If they do afford him a remedy, is it a *mandamus* issuing from this court?

The first object of inquiry is,

1st. Has the applicant a right to the commission he demands?

His right originates in an act of congress passed in February 1801, concerning the district of Columbia.

[The statute authorizes the appointment of justices of the peace, "to continue in office for five years."] * * *

In order to determine whether [Marbury] is entitled to this commission, it becomes necessary to enquire whether he has been appointed to the office. For if he has been appointed, the law continues him in office for five years, and he is entitled to the possession of those evidences of office, which, being completed, became his property.

[The Court then discussed the constitutional and statutory provisions governing the appointment of Officers of the United States. As relevant here, the Appointments Clause, U.S. Const. Art. II, § 2, cl. 2, provides that the President "shall nominate, and by and with the Advice and Consent of the Senate, shall appoint * * * Officers of the United States." Under Article 2, § 3, the President "shall commission all the officers of the United States." Finally, the statute establishing the Department of State provided that the Secretary of State must affix the seal of the United States to "all civil commissions" after the President signed them.]

Some point of time must be taken when the power of the executive over an officer, not removable at his will, must cease. That point of time must be when the constitutional power of appointment has been exercised. And this power has been exercised when the last act, required from the person possessing the power, has been performed. This last act is the signature of the commission. * * *

The signature is a warrant for [the Secretary of State's] affixing the great seal to the commission; and the great seal is only to be affixed to an instrument which is complete. It attests, by an act supposed to be of public notoriety, the verity of the Presidential signature. * * *

[The Court then rejected the argument] that the transmission of the commission, and the acceptance thereof, might be deemed necessary to complete the right of the plaintiff.

* * * The appointment is the sole act of the President * * *. A commission is transmitted to a person already appointed; not to a person to be appointed or not, as the letter enclosing the commission should

happen to get into the post-office and reach him in safety, or to miscarry.
* * *

If the transmission of a commission be not considered as necessary to give validity to an appointment; still less is its acceptance. * * *

Mr. Marbury, then, since his commission was signed by the President, and sealed by the secretary of state, was appointed; and as the law creating the office, gave the officer a right to hold for five years, independent of the executive, the appointment was not revocable; but vested in the officer legal rights, which are protected by the laws of this country.

To withhold his commission, therefore, is an act deemed by the court not warranted by law, but violative of a vested legal right.

This brings us to the second enquiry; which is,

2dly. If he has a right, and the right has been violated, do the laws of the country afford him a remedy?

The very essence of civil liberty consists in the right of every individual to claim the protection of the laws, whenever he receives an injury. One of the first duties of government is to afford that protection. In Great Britain the king himself is sued in the respectful form of a petition, and he never fails to comply with the judgment of his court. * * *

The government of the United States has been emphatically termed a government of laws and not of men. It will certainly cease to deserve this high appellation, if the laws furnish no remedy for the violation of a vested legal right.

If this obloquy is to be cast on the jurisprudence of our country, it must arise from the peculiar character of the case.

[In concluding that our jurisprudence did not merit that "obloquy," the Court first found that Marbury's case was not "one of *damnum absque injuria*; a loss without an injury."]

This description of cases never has been considered, and it is believed never can be considered, as comprehending offices of trust, of honor or of profit. The office of justice of peace in the district of Columbia * * * has been created by special act of congress, and has been secured, so far as the laws can give security to the person appointed to fill it, for five years. It is not then on account of the worthlessness of the thing pursued, that the injured party can be alleged to be without remedy.

Is it in the nature of the transaction? Is the act of delivering or withholding a commission to be considered a mere political act, belonging to the executive department alone, for the performance of which, entire confidence is placed by our constitution in the supreme executive; and for any misconduct concerning which the injured individual has no remedy.

That there be such cases is not to be questioned; but that every act of duty, to be performed in any of the great departments of government, constitutes such a case, is not to be admitted. * * *

* * * [T]he question, whether the legality of an act of the head of a department be examinable in a court of justice or not, must always depend on the nature of that act.

If some acts be examinable, and others not, there must be some rule of law to guide the court in the exercise of its jurisdiction. * * *

By the Constitution of the United States, the President is invested with certain important political powers, in the exercise of which he is to use his own discretion, and is accountable only to his country in his political character, and to his conscience. To aid him in the performance of these duties, he is authorized to appoint certain officers, who act by his authority and in conformity with his orders.

In such cases, their acts are his acts; and whatever opinion may be entertained of the manner in which executive discretion may be used, still there exists, and can exist, no power to control that discretion. The subjects are political: they respect the nation, not individual rights, and being entrusted to the executive, the decision of the executive is conclusive. * * *

But when the legislature proceeds to impose on that officer other duties; when he is directed peremptorily to perform certain acts; when the rights of individuals are dependent on the performance of those acts; he is so far the officer of the law; is amenable to the laws for his conduct; and cannot at his discretion sport away the vested rights of others.

The conclusion from this reasoning is that, where the heads of departments are the political or confidential agents of the executive, merely to execute the will of the President, or rather to act in cases in which the executive possesses a constitutional or legal discretion, nothing can be more perfectly clear than that their acts are only politically examinable. But where a specific duty is assigned by law, and individual rights depend upon the performance of that duty, it seems equally clear that the individual who considers himself injured, has the right to resort to the laws of his country for a remedy. * * *

[Mr. Marbury's right having been established,] it remains to be inquired whether,

3dly. He is entitled to the remedy for which he applies. This depends on,

1st. The nature of the writ applied for; and,

2dly. The power of this court.

1st. The nature of the writ. * * *

* * * [T]o render the *mandamus* a proper remedy, the officer to whom it is to be directed, must be one to whom, on legal principles, such writ

may be directed; and the person applying for it must be without any other specific and legal remedy.

1st. With respect to the officer to whom it would be directed. The intimate political relation subsisting between the president of the United States and the heads of departments, necessarily renders any legal investigation of the acts of one of those high officers peculiarly irksome, as well as delicate; and excites some hesitation with respect to the propriety of entering into such investigation. Impressions are often received without much reflection or examination and it is not wonderful that in such a case as this the assertion, by an individual, of his legal claims in a court of justice, to which claims it is the duty of that court to attend, should at first view be considered by some, as an attempt to intrude into the cabinet, and to intermeddle with the prerogatives of the executive.

It is scarcely necessary for the court to disclaim all pretensions to such a jurisdiction. An extravagance, so absurd and excessive, could not have been entertained for a moment. The province of the court is, solely, to decide on the rights of individuals, not to inquire how the executive, or executive officers, perform duties in which they have a discretion. Questions in their nature political, or which are, by the constitution and laws, submitted to the executive, can never be made in this court.

But, if this be not such a question; if, so far from being an intrusion into the secrets of the cabinet, it respects a paper which, according to law, is upon record, and to a copy of which the law gives a right, on the payment of ten cents; if it be no intermeddling with a subject over which the executive can be considered as having exercised any control; what is there in the exalted station of the officer, which shall bar a citizen from asserting, in a court of justice, his legal rights, or shall forbid a court to listen to the claim, or to issue a *mandamus*, directing the performance of a duty, not depending on executive discretion, but on particular acts of congress, and the general principles of law?

If one of the heads of departments commits any illegal act, under colour of his office, by which an individual sustains an injury, it cannot be pretended that his office alone exempts him from being sued in the ordinary mode of proceeding, and being compelled to obey the judgment of the law. How, then, can his office exempt him from this particular mode of deciding on the legality of his conduct, if the case be such a case as would, were any other individual the party complained of, authorize the process?

It is not by the office of the person to whom the writ is directed, but the nature of the thing to be done, that the propriety or impropriety of issuing a *mandamus* is to be determined. Where the head of a department acts in a case, in which executive discretion is to be exercised; in which he is the mere organ of executive will; it is again repeated, that any application to a court to control, in any respect, his conduct would be rejected without hesitation.

But where he is directed by law to do a certain act affecting the absolute rights of individuals, in the performance of which he is not placed under the particular direction of the president, and the performance of which the president cannot lawfully forbid, and therefore is never presumed to have forbidden; as for example, to record a commission, or a patent for land, which has received all the legal solemnities; or to give a copy of such record; in such cases, it is not perceived on what ground the courts of the country are further excused from the duty of giving judgment that right be done to an injured individual, than if the same services were to be performed by a person not the head of a department. * * *

This, then, is a plain case for a *mandamus*, either to deliver the commission, or a copy of it from the record; and it only remains to be inquired,

Whether it can issue from this court.

The act to establish the judicial courts of the United States authorizes the supreme court, "to issue writs of *mandamus*, in cases warranted by the principles and usages of law, to any courts appointed or persons holding office, under the authority of the United States."

The secretary of state being a person holding an office under the authority of the United States, is precisely within the letter of the description; and if this court is not authorized to issue a writ of *mandamus* to such an officer, it must be because the law is unconstitutional, and therefore, absolutely incapable of conferring the authority, and assigning the duties which its words purport to confer and assign.

The constitution vests the whole judicial power of the United States in one supreme court, and such inferior courts as congress shall, from time to time, ordain and establish. This power is expressly extended to all cases arising under the laws of the United States; and, consequently, in some form, may be exercised over the present case; because the right claimed is given by a law of the United States.

In the distribution of this power it is declared, that "the supreme court shall have original jurisdiction in all cases affecting ambassadors, other public ministers and consuls, and those in which a state shall be a party. In all other cases, the supreme court shall have appellate jurisdiction."

It has been insisted, at the bar, that as the original grant of jurisdiction, to the supreme and inferior courts, is general, and the clause, assigning original jurisdiction to the supreme court, contains no negative or restrictive words, the power remains to the legislature, to assign original jurisdiction to that court in other cases than those specified in the article which has been recited; provided those cases belong to the judicial power of the United States.

If it had been intended to leave it in the discretion of the legislature to apportion the judicial power between the supreme and inferior courts according to the will of that body, it would certainly have been useless to have proceeded further than to have defined the judicial power, and the tribunals in which it should be vested. The subsequent part of the section is mere surplusage, is entirely without meaning, if such is to be the construction. If congress remains at liberty to give this court appellate jurisdiction where the constitution has declared their jurisdiction shall be original; and original jurisdiction where the constitution has declared it shall be appellate; the distribution of jurisdiction, made in the constitution, is form without substance.

Affirmative words are often, in their operation, negative of other objects than those affirmed; and in this case, a negative or exclusive sense must be given to them, or they have no operation at all.

It cannot be presumed that any clause in the constitution is intended to be without effect; and therefore, such a construction is inadmissible, unless the words require it.

If the solicitude of the convention, respecting our peace with foreign powers, induced a provision that the supreme court should take original jurisdiction in cases which might be supposed to affect them; yet the clause would have proceeded no further than to provide for such cases, if no further restriction on the powers of congress had been intended. That they should have appellate jurisdiction in all other cases, with such exceptions as congress might make, is no restriction; unless the words be deemed exclusive of original jurisdiction.

When an instrument organizing fundamentally a judicial system, divides it into one supreme, and so many inferior courts as the legislature may ordain and establish; then enumerates its powers, and proceeds so far to distribute them, as to define the jurisdiction of the supreme court, by declaring the cases in which it shall take original jurisdiction, and that in others it shall take appellate jurisdiction; the plain import of the words seems to be, that in one class of cases its jurisdiction is original, and not appellate; in the other it is appellate, and not original. If any other construction would render the clause inoperative, that is an additional reason for rejecting such other construction, and for adhering to their obvious meaning.

To enable this court then to issue a *mandamus*, it must be shown to be an exercise of appellate jurisdiction, or to be necessary to enable them to exercise appellate jurisdiction. * * *

It is the essential criterion of appellate jurisdiction, that it revises and corrects the proceedings in a cause already instituted, and does not create that cause. Although, therefore, a *mandamus* may be directed to courts, yet to issue such a writ to an officer for the delivery of a paper, is in effect the same as to sustain an original action for that paper, and, therefore, seems not to belong to appellate, but to original jurisdiction.

Neither is it necessary in such a case as this, to enable the court to exercise its appellate jurisdiction.

The authority, therefore, given to the supreme court by the act establishing the judicial courts of the United States, to issue writs of *mandamus* to public officers, appears not to be warranted by the constitution; and it becomes necessary to inquire whether a jurisdiction so conferred can be exercised.

The question, whether an act, repugnant to the constitution, can become the law of the land, is a question deeply interesting to the United States; but, happily, not of an intricacy proportioned to its interest. It seems only necessary to recognize certain principles, supposed to have been long and well established, to decide it.

That the people have an original right to establish, for their future government, such principles, as in their opinion, shall most conduce to their own happiness is the basis on which the whole American fabric has been erected. The exercise of this original right is a very great exertion; nor can it, nor ought it, to be frequently repeated. The principles, therefore, so established, are deemed fundamental. And as the authority from which they proceed is supreme, and can seldom act, they are designed to be permanent.

This original and supreme will organizes the government, and assigns to different departments their respective powers. It may either stop here, or establish certain limits not to be transcended by those departments.

The government of the United States is of the latter description. The powers of the legislature are defined and limited; and that those limits may not be mistaken, or forgotten, the constitution is written. To what purpose are powers limited, and to what purpose is that limitation committed to writing, if these limits may, at any time, be passed by those intended to be restrained? The distinction between a government with limited and unlimited powers is abolished, if those limits do not confine the persons on whom they are imposed, and if acts prohibited and acts allowed, are of equal obligation. It is a proposition too plain to be contested, that the constitution controls any legislative act repugnant to it; or, that the legislature may alter the constitution by an ordinary act.

Between these alternatives, there is no middle ground. The constitution is either a superior paramount law, unchangeable by ordinary means, or it is on a level with ordinary legislative acts, and, like other acts, is alterable when the legislature shall please to alter it.

If the former part of the alternative be true, then a legislative act, contrary to the constitution, is not law: if the latter part be true, then written constitutions are absurd attempts, on the part of the people, to limit a power in its own nature, illimitable.

Certainly all those who have framed written constitutions contemplate them as forming the fundamental and paramount law of the nation, and, consequently, the theory of every such government must be, that an act of the legislature, repugnant to the constitution, is void.

This theory is essentially attached to a written constitution, and is consequently, to be considered, by this court, as one of the fundamental principles of our society. It is not therefore to be lost sight of, in the further consideration of this subject.

If an act of the legislature, repugnant to the constitution, is void, does it, notwithstanding its invalidity, bind the courts, and oblige them to give it effect? Or, in other words, though it be not law, does it constitute a rule as operative as if it was a law? This would be to overthrow in fact what was established in theory; and would seem, at first view, an absurdity too gross to be insisted on. It shall, however, receive a more attentive consideration.

It is emphatically the province and duty of the judicial department to say what the law is. Those who apply the rule to particular cases, must of necessity expound and interpret that rule. If two laws conflict with each other, the courts must decide on the operation of each.

So if a law be in opposition to the constitution; if both the law and the constitution apply to a particular case, so that the court must either decide that case conformably to the law, disregarding the constitution; or conformably to the constitution, disregarding the law; the court must determine which of these conflicting rules governs the case. This is of the very essence of judicial duty.

If then the courts are to regard the constitution, and the constitution is superior to any ordinary act of the legislature, the constitution, and not such ordinary act, must govern the case to which they both apply.

Those then who controvert the principle that the constitution is to be considered, in court, as a paramount law, are reduced to the necessity of maintaining that courts must close their eyes on the constitution, and see only the law.

This doctrine would subvert the very foundation of all written constitutions. It would declare that an act which, according to the principles and theory of our government, is entirely void, is yet, in practice, completely obligatory. It would declare that if the legislature shall do what is expressly forbidden, such act, notwithstanding the express prohibition, is in reality effectual. It would be giving to the legislature a practical and real omnipotence, with the same breath which professes to restrict their powers within narrow limits. It is prescribing limits, and declaring that those limits may be passed at pleasure.

That it thus reduces to nothing, what we have deemed the greatest improvement on political institutions, a written constitution, would of itself be sufficient, in America, where written constitutions have been viewed with so much reverence, for rejecting the construction. But the peculiar expressions of the constitution of the United States furnish additional arguments in favour of its rejection.

The judicial power of the United States is extended to all cases arising under the constitution.

Could it be the intention of those who gave this power, to say that in using it the constitution should not be looked into? That a case arising under the constitution should be decided, without examining the instrument under which it arises?

This is too extravagant to be maintained.

In some cases then, the constitution must be looked into by the judges. And if they can open it at all, what part of it are they forbidden to read or to obey?

There are many other parts of the constitution which serve to illustrate this subject.

It is declared, that "no tax or duty shall be laid on articles exported from any state." Suppose, a duty on the export of cotton, of tobacco, or of flour; and a suit instituted to recover it. Ought judgment to be rendered in such a case? ought the judges to close their eyes on the constitution, and only see the law?

The constitution declares "that no bill of attainder or *ex post facto* law shall be passed."

If, however, such a bill should be passed, and a person should be prosecuted under it; must the court condemn to death those victims whom the constitution endeavors to preserve?

"No person," says the constitution, "shall be convicted of treason unless on the testimony of two witnesses to the same overt act, or on confession in open court."

Here the language of the constitution is addressed especially to the courts. It prescribes, directly for them, a rule of evidence not to be departed from. If the legislature should change that rule, and declare *one* witness, or a confession *out* of court, sufficient for conviction, must the constitutional principle yield to the legislative act?

From these, and many other selections which might be made, it is apparent, that the framers of the constitution contemplated that instrument as a rule for the government of courts, as well as of the legislature.

Why otherwise does it direct the judges to take an oath to support it? This oath certainly applies in an especial manner, to their conduct in their official character. How immoral to impose it on them, if they were to be used as the instruments, and the knowing instruments, for violating what they swear to support!

The oath of office, too, imposed by the legislature, is completely demonstrative of the legislative opinion on this subject. It is in these words: "I do solemnly swear that I will administer justice without respect to persons, and do equal right to the poor and to the rich; and that I will faithfully and impartially discharge all the duties incumbent on me as ___, according to the best of my abilities and understanding, agreeably to *the constitution* and laws of the United States."

Why does a judge swear to discharge his duties agreeably to the constitution of the United States, if that constitution forms no rule for his government? if it is closed upon him, and cannot be inspected by him?

If such be the real state of things, this is worse than solemn mockery. To prescribe, or to take this oath, becomes equally a crime.

It is also not entirely unworthy of observation, that in declaring what shall be the *supreme* law of the land, the *constitution* itself is first mentioned; and not the laws of the United States, generally, but those only which shall be made in *pursuance* of the constitution, have that rank.

Thus, the particular phraseology of the constitution of the United States confirms and strengthens the principle, supposed to be essential to all written constitutions, that a law repugnant to the constitution is void; and that *courts*, as well as other departments, are bound by that instrument.

The rule must be discharged.

NOTE ON MARBURY V. MADISON

(1) Historical Background.[1] Control of the national government passed from Federalist to Republican hands for the first time in the national elections of 1800. The lines of political division were sharp. The Federalists generally favored a strong national government, a sound currency, and domestic and foreign policies promoting mercantile interests. The Republicans, by contrast, were the party of states' rights and political and economic democracy.

Before the Republican Thomas Jefferson assumed office as President, the outgoing Federalists took a variety of measures to preserve their party's influence through the life-tenured federal judiciary. First, President John Adams appointed his Secretary of State, John Marshall, as Chief Justice of the United States, and the Senate quickly confirmed him. Marshall, while continuing to serve as Secretary of State, took office as Chief Justice on February 4, 1801. Second, a new Circuit Court Act of February 13, 1801, relieved Supreme Court Justices of their circuit-riding duties and created sixteen new circuit court judgeships. With only two weeks remaining in his

---

[1] For contrasting views of Marshall's opinion, compare Van Alstyne, *A Critical Guide to Marbury v. Madison*, 1969 Duke L.J. 1, with Haggard, *Marbury v. Madison: A Concurring/ Dissenting Opinion*, 10 J. Law & Pol. 543 (1994). For additional historical background, see Ackerman, The Failure of the Founding Fathers: Jefferson, Marshall, and the Rise of Presidential Democracy (2005); Simon, What Kind of Nation: Thomas Jefferson, John Marshall, and the Epic Struggle to Create a United States (2002); Haskins & Johnson, Foundations of Power: John Marshall, 1801–15 (1981); Ellis, The Jeffersonian Crisis: Courts and Politics in the Young Republic (1971); McCloskey, The American Supreme Court 36–44 (1960).

term, Adams hurried to nominate Federalists to the newly created positions, and the Senate confirmed the "midnight judges" with equal alacrity. Finally, on February 27, Congress enacted legislation authorizing the President to appoint justices of the peace for the District of Columbia. Adams nominated forty-two justices on March 2, and the Senate confirmed them on March 3, the day before the conclusion of Adams's term. Adams signed the commissions, and John Marshall, as Secretary of State, affixed the great seal of the United States. Nonetheless, some of the commissions, including that of William Marbury, were not delivered before Adams's term expired, and the new President refused to honor those appointments.

While Marbury's suit was pending in the Supreme Court, the newly installed Republicans worked on a number of fronts to frustrate the outgoing Federalists' designs for the federal judiciary. Congress repealed the Circuit Court Act of 1801 and abolished the sixteen judgeships that it had created. By statute, Congress also abolished the Supreme Court's previously scheduled June and December Terms and provided that there be only one Term, in February. As a result, the Supreme Court did not meet at all in 1802. Having received Marbury's petition in December 1801, it could not hear his case until February 1803. Even more menacingly, the Jeffersonians embarked on a program of judicial impeachments. Early in 1802, the House voted articles of impeachment against the Federalist district judge John Pickering of New Hampshire, who apparently was burdened by mental infirmity and an alcohol problem. On the day after Pickering's conviction by the Senate in March 1804, the House impeached Supreme Court Justice Samuel Chase. The case against Chase failed in the Senate. Had it succeeded, the impeachment of John Marshall was widely expected to follow.

In this charged political climate, it seems doubtful, at least, that James Madison, Thomas Jefferson's Secretary of State, would have obeyed a judicial order to deliver Marbury's commission as a justice of the peace. Might this consideration have influenced Marshall's decision of the case?[2] In light of his involvement in the events leading up to the case, should Marshall have recused himself?

(2) A Political Masterstroke? The Marbury opinion is widely regarded as a political masterstroke. Marshall seized the occasion to uphold the

---

[2]   Commentators have overwhelmingly thought that Marshall's decision was motivated by political considerations. See Pfander, *Marbury, Original Jurisdiction, and the Supreme Court's Revisory Powers*, 101 Colum.L.Rev. 1515, 1515–18 (2001) (summarizing views and collecting citations). Among the corroborating evidence is the Court's decision the week after Marbury in Stuart v. Laird, 5 U.S. (1 Cranch) 299 (1803), declining to consider the constitutionality of the Repeal Act of 1802, which abolished the sixteen circuit court judgeships created by the Circuit Court Act of 1801. See, *e.g.*, Alfange, *Marbury v. Madison and Original Understandings of Judicial Review: In Defense of Traditional Wisdom*, 1993 Sup.Ct.Rev. 329, 362–68, 409–10 (treating Stuart v. Laird as strongly probative of the Court's awareness of the political sensitivity of its situation and its willingness to shape its decisions accordingly). See also Ackerman, note 1, *supra*, at 163–98 (discussing the relationship between the Marbury and Stuart decisions). For the contrary view that Marshall's Marbury opinion was essentially innocent of political motivation, see Clinton, Marbury v. Madison and Judicial Review 79–138 (1989).

institution of judicial review,[3] but he did so in the course of reaching a judgment that his political opponents could neither defy nor protest.[4]

Is it ironic if Marbury, which authorizes the courts to hold some issues outside the bounds of permissible political decisionmaking, was itself a political decision? See generally Fallon, *Marbury and the Constitutional Mind: A Bicentennial Essay on the Wages of Doctrinal Tension*, 91 Calif.L.Rev. 1 (2003). Does the answer depend on sorting out various possible senses of "political" and determining in which sense, if any, Marbury should be so characterized?

(3) Marbury's Jurisdictional Holdings. Marbury ultimately holds that the Supreme Court lacked jurisdiction to decide the case before it.

The jurisdictional analysis proceeds in two steps. First, Marshall concludes that § 13 of the 1789 Judiciary Act—which authorized the Court "to issue * * * writs of mandamus, in cases warranted by the principles and usages of law, to any courts appointed, or persons holding office, under the authority of the United States," 1 Stat. 73, 81—confers original Supreme Court jurisdiction in actions for mandamus. Some believe that Marshall misread § 13. Professor Amar, for example, argues that "the mandamus clause is best read as simply giving the Court remedial authority—for both original and appellate cases after jurisdiction * * * has been independently established." Amar, *Marbury, Section 13, and the Original Jurisdiction of the Supreme Court*, 56 U.Chi.L.Rev. 443, 456 (1989). See also Van Alstyne, note 1, *supra*, at 15. In contrast, Professor Pfander contends that "supreme" courts traditionally possessed a supervisory authority over lower courts and governmental officers, exercised through writs of mandamus and prohibition, and that against this background "section 13 appears to confer precisely the sort of freestanding power on the Court that Marshall

---

[3] The issue, however, was "by no means new," according to Currie, *The Constitution in the Supreme Court: The Powers of the Federal Courts, 1801–1835*, 49 U.Chi.L.Rev. 646, 655–56 (1982): "The Supreme Court itself had measured a state law against a state constitution in Cooper v. Telfair, 4 U.S. (4 Dall.) 14 (1800), and had struck down another under the Supremacy Clause in Ware v. Hylton, 3 U.S. (3 Dall.) 199 (1796); in both cases the power of judicial review was expressly affirmed. Even acts of Congress had been struck down by federal circuit courts [as in Hayburn's Case, 2 U.S. (2 Dall.) 409 (1792), p. 101, *infra*], and the Supreme Court, while purporting to reserve the question of its power to do so, had reviewed the constitutionality of a federal statute in Hylton v. United States, 3 U.S. (3 Dall.) 171 (1796). Justice James Iredell had explicitly asserted this power both in Chisholm v. Georgia, 2 U.S. (2 Dall.) 419 (1793), and in Calder v. Bull, 3 U.S. (3 Dall.) 386 (1798), and Chase had acknowledged it in Cooper. * * * Yet though Marshall's principal arguments echoed those of Hamilton [in Federalist No. 78,] he made no mention of any of this material, writing as if the question had never arisen before." In a detailed study of early case law, Treanor, *Judicial Review Before Marbury*, 58 Stan.L.Rev. 455 (2005), concludes that judicial review was exercised by state and federal courts in more than thirty cases before Marbury. On the understanding of the Convention, see Chap. I, pp. 1–22, *supra*. See also Klarman, *How Great Were the "Great" Marshall Court Decisions?*, 87 Va.L.Rev. 1111, 1114–15 (2001) (observing that judicial review "became far less controversial" during the period between the Convention and the decision in Marbury).

[4] For a detailed critical review of Marshall's opinion, culminating in the conclusion that "[j]ust about everything in Marbury is wrong," see Paulsen, *Marbury's Wrongness*, 20 Const.Comm. 343, 343 (2003). For a defense of Marbury on nearly every point, including a rejection of the claim that the opinion was "disingenuously manipulative * * * in order to create an occasion for the exercise of judicial review," see Treanor, *The Story of Marbury v. Madison: Judicial Authority and Political Struggle*, in Federal Courts Stories (Jackson & Resnik eds. 2010), at 29.

attributed to it in Marbury." Pfander, note 2, *supra*, at 1535. Should the Court have adopted Amar's construction under the principle favoring interpretations that render statutes constitutional?[5]

Second, Marshall concludes that the second paragraph of Article III, § 2 restricts the permissible scope of the Supreme Court's original jurisdiction to "cases affecting Ambassadors, other public Ministers and Consuls, and those in which a State shall be a Party." According to Van Alstyne, *supra* note 1, at 31, this clause "readily supports the interpretation that the Court's original jurisdiction may not be *reduced* by Congress, but that it may be supplemented" *Cf.* Amar, *supra*, at 469–76 (arguing that the Court's original jurisdiction was limited partly to spare parties from the burden of traveling to the seat of government to litigate their disputes). For further discussion of the Supreme Court's original jurisdiction, see Chap. III, *infra*.[6]

(4) Marbury's Arguments for Judicial Review. Consider the arguments Marshall offers to support the power of judicial review and whether those arguments are persuasive.

A common criticism is developed in Bickel, The Least Dangerous Branch 2–14 (1962). Everyone accepted the proposition that the Constitution was binding on the national government. Dispute centered on the quite separate proposition that the courts were authorized to enforce their interpretations of the Constitution against the conflicting interpretations of Congress and the President. Marshall's arguments prove the first, undisputed proposition, but furnish no support for the second. In sum, Marshall's arguments beg the only question really in issue.

In support of this criticism, note that there are issues on which, without further inquiry, courts accept a formally correct determination of the legislative or executive branches—*e.g.*, a statement that a certain statute has in fact been enacted in accordance with the prescribed procedure or an executive determination that a certain government is the established government of a country. See Sec. 6, *infra* (discussing "political questions"). Would it not be possible for courts, in all cases, similarly to accept the determination of Congress and the President (or in the case of a veto, of a

---

[5]   For discussion of that principle, see pp. 98–101, *infra*.

[6]   With the Supreme Court lacking jurisdiction in Marbury v. Madison, would any other court have had jurisdiction to entertain Marbury's claim? A state court could not have issued mandamus relief against a federal official, see McClung v. Silliman, 19 U.S. (6 Wheat.) 598 (1821), and the 1789 Judiciary Act failed to vest the lower federal courts with mandamus jurisdiction, see McIntire v. Wood, 11 U.S. (7 Cranch) 504 (1813). In Kendall v. United States ex rel. Stokes, 37 U.S. (12 Pet.) 524 (1838), the Supreme Court held that the Circuit Court for the District of Columbia, which had been established by a special act, was uniquely authorized to issue writs of mandamus in original actions against federal officials. Based on Kendall, Bloch, *The Marbury Mystery: Why Did William Marbury Sue in the Supreme Court?*, 18 Const.Comment. 607 (2002), concludes unequivocally that the Circuit Court would have had jurisdiction had Marbury chosen to file there. Professor Bloch further speculates that Marbury may have deliberately bypassed the Circuit Court in order to permit John Marshall to issue the precise rulings about Supreme Court jurisdiction and judicial review for which Marbury v. Madison is famous. Compare Fallon, Paragraph (2), *supra*, at 52 n.271 (deeming it "highly doubtful that the [Supreme] Court, in the politically charged atmosphere of 1803, would have upheld the authority of the D.C. courts to order mandamus relief for William Marbury against James Madison").

super majority of Congress) that a statute is duly authorized by the Constitution?

On the other hand, does Congress in voting to enact a bill, or the President in approving it, typically make or purport to make such a determination? With respect to the validity of the statute as applied in particular situations, how could they?[7]

(5) Judicial Supremacy in Historical Perspective. Conventional wisdom now treats the federal judiciary as "supreme in the exposition of the law of the Constitution" and traces that premise back to Marbury itself. Cooper v. Aaron, 358 U.S. 1, 18 (1958). See also, *e.g.*, United States v. Morrison, 529 U.S. 598, 616 n.7 (2000); United States v. Nixon, 418 U.S. 683, 703 (1974). Modern historical studies, however, have suggested that the present conventional wisdom may reflect an ahistorical understanding of Marbury and of the intellectual and legal context that preceded it. Some historians contend, in particular, that the founding generation initially distinguished between fundamental or constitutional law (embodying the basic terms of the social compact) and ordinary law (interpreted and enforced by courts through ordinary means). See, *e.g.*, Snowiss, Judicial Review and the Law of the Constitution 13–89 (1990); Wood, *The Origins of Judicial Review Revisited, or How the Marshall Court Made More Out of Less*, 56 Wash. & Lee L.Rev. 787, 796–99 (1999). Under this conception of judicial review, moreover, courts and commentators of the time apparently thought it proper for courts to invalidate legislation on constitutional grounds only in cases of such relatively clear legislative or executive overreaching that little or no "interpretation" was required.[8] According to Snowiss, "Marshall's key innovations [to that set of understandings] did not come in Marbury," in which he said little about *how* the Constitution should be interpreted, but in opinions of the 1810s and 1820s in which he subjected the Constitution to "rules of statutory interpretation" and "transformed explicit fundamental law, different in kind from ordinary law, into supreme written law, different only in degree" and enforceable by the courts in all cases.[9]

In a similar vein, Professor Kramer argues that when viewed in proper historical context, Marbury represented the application of an earlier, modest understanding of judicial review rather than a bold articulation of the idea of judicial supremacy. See Kramer, The People Themselves: Popular Constitutionalism and Judicial Review 93–127 (2004). Kramer notes that judicial review arose against a backdrop of popular constitutionalism—the

---

[7] For an attempt to "provide a clear and persuasive derivation of Marbury's conclusion from the constitutional text," see Harrison, *The Constitutional Origins and Implications of Judicial Review*, 84 Va.L.Rev. 333 (1998). See also Prakash & Yoo, *The Origins of Judicial Review*, 70 U.Chi.L.Rev. 887 (2003) (arguing that the Constitution's text, structure, and history all support the practice of judicial review).

[8] With respect to the circumstances under which courts would hold statutes unconstitutional, see also Alfange, note 2, *supra*, at 342–49 (noting the expectation of the founding generation that judicial invalidation of statutes would occur only in cases of clear mistake); Casto, *James Iredell and the American Origins of Judicial Review*, 27 Conn.L.Rev. 329, 341–48 (1995) (same); Klarman, note 3, *supra*, at 1120–21.

[9] For a more traditional account of the development of judicial review, in which the distinction between fundamental and ordinary law is not emphasized, see Corwin, *The Establishment of Judicial Review*, 9 Mich.L.Rev. 102–25, 283–316 (1910–11).

notion, inherited from British constitutional theory, that ultimate responsibility for the enforcement of constitutional law lay with the community through political action, protest, and even revolution. From this starting point, Kramer maintains that many early Americans embraced a "departmental" theory of judicial review under which Congress and the President, no less than the judiciary, had an obligation to decide for themselves how the duties imposed by the Constitution constrained their authority. On that view, the interpretations by one branch—such as the judiciary—did not necessarily bind the others; ultimately, "the people themselves" would have to resolve conflicts among the branches about the Constitution's meaning through popular action.[10] Kramer contends that Marbury, properly understood, is consistent with departmentalism rather than the judicial supremacy with which many now associate it.

These historical accounts, of course, have not gone unchallenged.[11] But even if historians such as Snowiss, Wood, and Kramer are correct in their understanding of Marbury and its historical context, is the modern conception of Marbury too well entrenched to reconsider?[12]

―――――――――――

NOTE ON MARBURY V. MADISON AND THE FUNCTION OF ADJUDICATION

(1) Marbury and Judicial Power. Marbury is often quoted for the observation that "[i]t is emphatically the province and duty of the judicial department to say what the law is." But how far does the law declaration power extend? Imagine that Marbury, although wishing to take office as justice of the peace, had no interest in litigating Madison's refusal to deliver his commission. Given the tenor of Chief Justice Marshall's opinion, could a concerned citizen of the District of Columbia have brought suit to establish that Madison acted unlawfully and to compel him to deliver Marbury's commission (assuming that Congress had vested appropriate jurisdiction in

―――――――――――

[10]   For a sweeping historical account of both the Court's role as a catalyst of political debate and the influence of public opinion on the development of constitutional doctrine, see Friedman, The Will of the People: How Public Opinion Has Influenced the Supreme Court and Shaped the Meaning of the Constitution (2009).

[11]   For other interventions, see, *e.g.*, Hamburger, Law and Judicial Duty (2008) (arguing that what we now think of as judicial review was merely an aspect of a more general common law judicial duty to decide in accordance with the law of the land and to respect the hierarchical character of law by treating inferior law as void when it conflicted with superior law); Bilder, *The Corporate Origins of Judicial Review*, 116 Yale L.J. 502 (2006) (arguing that judicial review originated in the common law practice of invalidating corporate charters that were "repugnant" to the law of nations and that the seamless adaptation of that practice to the context of judicial review leaves us little useful founding-era evidence about questions such as "departmentalism" or the standard of review in constitutional cases); Treanor, note 3, *supra*, at 458 (arguing that in pre-Marbury cases, "the standard of review varied with subject matter" and that courts were especially aggressive in rebuffing threats to judicial power and in invalidating state statutes).

[12]   See, *e.g.*, White, *The Constitutional Journey of Marbury v. Madison*, 89 Va.L.Rev. 1463 (2003) (tracing historically evolving interpretations of Marbury); Whittington & Rinderle, *Making a Mountain out of a Molehill? Marbury and the Construction of the Constitutional Canon*, 39 Hastings Const.L.Q. 823 (2012) (arguing that while courts and commentators cited Marbury for various purposes in the nineteenth century, the case attained its status as the cornerstone of judicial review nearer the turn of the twentieth century).

a federal court)? What if it were instead a concerned citizen living in Boston who—like many others—felt aggrieved that Madison, as an officer of the United States, had failed to comply with the law? Should it matter whether Congress explicitly authorized such suits?

(2) Dispute Resolution Model. Chief Justice Marshall's opinion in Marbury treats the law declaration power as incidental to the resolution of a concrete dispute occasioned by Marbury's claim to a "private right" to take possession of the office. Marshall emphasizes this recurrent theme, moreover, in ways that seem obviously calculated to make two aspects of his decision more palatable: first, the assertion of judicial authority to grant affirmative relief against a senior political officer of the executive branch; and, second, the claimed authority to invalidate an Act of Congress. The Court, in Marshall's view, had the authority to impose in those ways on the coordinate branches because doing so was an unavoidable consequence of its obligations to adjudicate Marbury's claim of right.

In response to the charge that the relief requested against Secretary of State Madison would "intrude into the cabinet, and * * * intermeddle with the prerogatives of the executive," Marshall parried that "[t]he province of the court is, solely, to decide on the rights of individuals." While the Court could "never" resolve "political" questions that the Constitution or laws assigned to the executive's "discretion," the fact that Madison occupied public office did not "exempt[ ] him from being sued in the ordinary mode of proceeding." On this view, the suit did not rest upon the notion that the Court's special function was to bring public officials into conformity with the rule of law. On the contrary, the Court granted the requested relief to vindicate Marbury's private right, just as it could if the defendant had been a private citizen.

Marshall's discussion of the authority to engage in judicial review similarly assumed that the Court had no choice but to interpret and apply the Constitution when presented with a proper case requiring decision. Hence, in deeming it "emphatically the province and duty of the judicial department to say what the law is," Marshall took pains to elaborate in the very next sentence that "[t]hose who apply the rule to particular cases, must of necessity expound and interpret that rule."

This "dispute resolution" model—under which the Court treats its law declaration power as incidental to its responsibility to resolve concrete disputes—recurs in several related aspects of the Court's justiciability case law. First, to avoid intrusion upon the prerogatives of the other branches, leading cases affirm that courts should eschew any role as a general overseer of government conduct; that is, the federal judiciary's function is not to vindicate abstract interests in the government's compliance with the rule of law. See, *e.g.*, FEC v. Akins, 524 U.S. 11, 23–24 (1998); Lujan v. Defenders of Wildlife, 504 U.S. 555, 573–74 (1992), p. 166, *infra*. Second, justiciable "cases" should be restricted to disputes in which a defendant's violation of a legal duty has caused a distinct and palpable injury to a concrete, legally protected interest of the plaintiff. See, *e.g.*, Allen v. Wright, 468 U.S. 737 (1984); Warth v. Seldin, 422 U.S. 490 (1975). These themes are taken up in detail in Sections 3, 4, and 5 of this Chapter.

(3) Law Declaration Model. In the past half century, a competing account of the courts has found considerable support in the commentary and also, albeit less than completely, in several aspects of the law of justiciability. Rather than treating law declaration as an incidental function of resolving concrete claims of individual right, the "law declaration" account of the judicial function presupposes that federal courts (and especially the Supreme Court) have a special function of enforcing the rule of law, independent of the task of resolving concrete disputes over individual rights.[1] This approach questions the importance of requiring that the plaintiff have a personal stake in the outcome of a lawsuit; in its purest form, it would permit any citizen to bring a "public action" to challenge allegedly unlawful government conduct. Under this view, the judiciary should be recognized not as a mere settler of disputes, but rather as an institution with a distinctive capacity to declare and explicate norms that transcend individual controversies.[2]

At least three historical phenomena have contributed to the emergence of the law declaration model. First, the vast increase in the modern administrative state has created diffuse rights shared by large groups and new legal relationships that are hard to capture in traditional, private law terms. At the same time, a need has arisen for judicial control of administrative power.[3] Encouraged by statutes authorizing judicial review of administrative action, leading administrative law decisions gradually departed from the dispute resolution model and accorded "standing" to persons asserting interests not protected at common law in order to represent the "public interest" in statutory enforcement. See, *e.g.*, FCC v. Sanders Bros. Radio Station, 309 U.S. 470 (1940); Scripps-Howard Radio, Inc. v. FCC, 316 U.S. 4 (1942). For further discussion, see p. 127, *infra*.

Second, the substantive expansion of constitutional rights, especially under the Warren Court in the 1960s, has broadened the conception of legally cognizable interests. For example, the widely shared interests of voters in challenging a malapportioned legislative district, see Baker v. Carr, 369 U.S. 186 (1962), p. 306, *infra*, or of public school pupils in challenging school prayer, see School Dist. v. Schempp, 374 U.S. 203 (1963), differ markedly from the liberty and economic interests recognized at common law.

---

[1]   Support for the law declaration approach, particularly in constitutional adjudication, is found by some commentators in Marbury itself. See, *e.g.*, Monaghan, *Constitutional Adjudication: The Who and When*, 82 Yale L.J. 1363 (1973); Fallon, *Marbury and the Constitutional Mind: A Bicentennial Essay on the Wages of Doctrinal Tension*, 91 Calif.L.Rev. 1 (2003).

[2]   For a range of commentary elaborating aspects of this approach, see, *e.g.*, Pushaw, *Article III's Case/Controversy Distinction and the Dual Functions of Federal Courts*, 69 Notre Dame L.Rev. 447 (1994); Bandes, *The Idea of a Case*, 42 Stan.L.Rev. 227 (1990); Sunstein, *Standing and the Privatization of Public Law*, 88 Colum.L.Rev. 1432 (1988); Chayes, *Foreword: Public Law Litigation and the Burger Court*, 96 Harv.L.Rev. 4 (1982); Dworkin, Taking Rights Seriously 131–49 (1977); Fiss, *Foreword: The Forms of Justice*, 93 Harv.L.Rev. 1 (1979); Vining, Legal Identity: The Coming of Age of Public Law (1978); Tushnet, *The New Law of Standing: A Plea for Abandonment*, 62 Cornell L.Rev. 663 (1977); Chayes, *The Role of the Judge in Public Law Litigation*, 89 Harv.L.Rev. 1281 (1976); Jaffe, *The Citizen as Litigant in Public Actions: The Non-Hohfeldian or Ideological Plaintiff*, 116 U.Pa.L.Rev. 1033 (1968).

[3]   See generally Jaffe, *Standing to Secure Judicial Review: Public Actions*, 74 Harv.L.Rev. 1265, 1282–84 (1961); Stewart, *The Reformation of American Administrative Law*, 88 Harv.L.Rev. 1667, 1674–81 (1975).

Third, one contemporary notion of constitutional rights treats them not merely as shields against governmental coercion, but as swords authorizing the award of affirmative relief to redress injury to constitutionally protected interests. That understanding, the origins of which can be traced in part to the landmark decision in Ex parte Young, 209 U.S. 123 (1908), p. 1184, *infra*, also finds expression in the institutional reform litigation following Brown v. Board of Education, 347 U.S. 483 (1954). After the recognition of such rights as those to school desegregation, courts inevitably found themselves awarding remedies of a kind difficult to square with at least some of the premises of the private rights or dispute resolution model.

(4) Overlap of the Approaches. No two stylized and oversimplified models can capture the full historical or functional complexity of the role of the federal judiciary. School desegregation cases, for example, have their origin in individual grievances that seemingly require the reshaping of institutions. But such cases resolve questions about the structure of legal and social institutions that far transcend the context of any individual's claimed deprivation of private right. The devices of the class action, like other techniques for broadening the scope of litigation, frequently also meld the two functional models, and many of the tensions about the proper role of the courts have been felt in the resulting cases and doctrines.[4]

The distinction between the dispute resolution and law declaration models blurs, moreover, because the law declaration model, sensibly construed, cannot be understood to license judicial review at the behest of any would-be litigant on the basis of any hypothesized set of facts or indeed no facts whatsoever. For there to be a constitutionally justiciable case under the public rights approach, at least "the functional requisites of effective adjudication" must be satisfied. Fallon, *Of Justiciability, Remedies, and Public Law Litigation: Notes on the Jurisprudence of Lyons*, 59 N.Y.U.L.Rev. 1, 51 (1984). These requisites cannot be reduced to a determinate list, but involve such considerations as: (a) the importance of a concrete set of facts to permit the accurate formulation of the legal issue to be decided and the limits of the ruling ultimately issued and (b) adversary presentation as an aid to the accurate determination of factual and legal issues. In the end, disputes about the comparative merits of the competing models are not so much about the appropriate formula for deciding cases as about one's foundational views with respect to the proper role of the federal judiciary.

(5) The Supreme Court and the Models. The Supreme Court has never explicitly rejected the dispute resolution model. Indeed, its formal pronouncements have been consistently to the contrary. There are, however, some holdings that may be seen as reflecting, though not in explicit terms, a

---

[4]   For further discussion of such complex litigation, compare, *e.g.*, Fuller, *The Forms and Limits of Adjudication*, 92 Harv.L.Rev. 353 (1978) (arguing that adjudication is not well adapted to resolve "polycentric" disputes, which he claims have too many interdependent aspects to yield to rational, properly judicial solution), with Sabel & Simon, *Destabilization Rights: How Public Law Litigation Succeeds*, 117 Harv.L.Rev. 1015, 1019 (2004) (arguing that institutional reform remedies have become more successful as they have moved from "from command-and-control injunctive regulation toward experimentalist intervention" that combines "more flexible and provisional norms with procedures for ongoing stakeholder participation and measured accountability").

shift in conception of the judicial role. See, *e.g.*, the developments discussed in the *Note on Mootness in Class Actions*, p. 263, *infra*, and discussion of the The Special Problem of First Amendment Overbreadth, p. 241, *infra*. See also Fallon & Meltzer, *New Law, Non-Retroactivity, and Constitutional Remedies*, 104 Harv.L.Rev. 1731, 1779–1800 (1991) (citing, *inter alia*, harmless error practice, the practice of providing alternative grounds for decision, and the exception to mootness doctrine for cases "capable of repetition, yet evading review" in support of the conclusion that "there exists a substantial body of case law, rising almost to the level of a general tradition, in which adjudication * * * functions more as a vehicle for the pronouncement of norms than for the resolution of particular disputes").

In a bolder argument, Professor Monaghan maintains that the Supreme Court now substantially embraces the law declaration model as the dominant approach to its own jurisdiction. First, in addition to noting some of the examples cited in the previous paragraph, Professor Monaghan argues that the Court's special rules governing review of official immunity decisions (see pp. 1326–1327, *infra*) and its qualification of the statutory "final judgment" rule of 28 U.S.C. § 1257 (see pp. 712–725, *infra*) show that the Court will often find a way around jurisdictional constraints that would otherwise limit its ability to review important propositions of law. Second, he catalogues a broad array of "agenda control" devices—making limited grants of certiorari, reformulating questions presented, injecting new questions into cases, appointing amici to defend positions abandoned by the litigants, and strategically accepting or rejecting party stipulations, waivers, or concessions. Based on these phenomena, he concludes that the Court has defined "its current place in our constitutional order" in a way that establishes "a 'final say' default position." Monaghan, *On Avoiding Avoidance, Agenda Control, and Related Matters*, 112 Colum.L.Rev. 665 (2012). To the extent that these innovations deviate from the assumptions about justiciability that govern the lower courts, does the Court have an obligation to specify some basis in the text or history of Article III for treating its own jurisdiction differently? Do the practices identified by Professor Monaghan raise concerns about judicial self-aggrandizement? *Cf.* Vermeule, *The Judicial Power in the State (and Federal) Courts*, 2000 Sup.Ct.Rev. 357, 361 (discussing "cognitive pressures that cause judges to press judicial prerogatives to implausible extremes").[5]

(6) Discretion, Prudence, and the Judicial Function. Does the power of judicial review upheld in Marbury carry with it a correlative duty to decide any claims of unconstitutionality in a properly presented case, or is there some measure of discretion to abstain from rendering such decisions? In Cohens v. Virginia, 19 U.S. (6 Wheat.) 264, 404 (1821), Chief Justice Marshall said: "It is most true that this Court will not take jurisdiction if it should not: but it is equally true, that it must take jurisdiction, if it should. * * * We have no more right to decline the exercise of jurisdiction which is

---

[5]   For contrasting views on whether the federal courts should have discretion to reframe the issues by the parties, compare Frost, *The Limits of Advocacy*, 59 Duke L.J. 447 (2009) (arguing that such judicial discretion avoids potential distortions of law by the parties), with Lawson, *Stipulating the Law*, 109 Mich.L.Rev. 1191 (2011) (arguing that allowing the parties to structure the case promotes judicial restraint and minimalism).

given, than to usurp that which is not given. The one or the other would be treason to the constitution."

Shapiro, *Jurisdiction and Discretion*, 60 N.Y.U.L.Rev. 543 (1985), argues (in discussing a wide range of traditional and contemporary doctrines, including equitable discretion, abstention doctrines, prudential components of justiciability doctrines, forum non conveniens, and others) that Marshall's dictum cannot be taken at face value: On many issues, courts have exercised a "principled discretion" in refusing to exercise jurisdiction seemingly granted by Congress. The discretion of which Shapiro approves is not ad hoc, but rather constitutes a fine-tuning of legislative enactments in accordance with criteria that are openly applied and that are "drawn from the relevant statutory * * * grant of jurisdiction or from the tradition within which the grant arose." Compare Redish, The Federal Courts in the Political Order: Judicial Jurisdiction and American Political Theory 47–74 (1991) (arguing that federal judicial jurisdiction is mandatory and that failure to exercise jurisdiction conferred is an illegitimate usurpation of Congress's lawmaking power).

Beyond the "principled discretion" defended by Professor Shapiro, is there a further judicial power to decline to exercise jurisdiction on a more ad hoc basis, for what might loosely be termed "prudential" reasons?[6]

According to Fallon, note 1, *supra*, at 16–20, a prudential tradition in constitutional adjudication can be traced back to Marbury itself: "In Marbury, the Court reached the only prudent conclusion: It could not, indeed must not, issue a quixotic order to Madison to deliver Marbury's commission." Moreover, Fallon writes, "[e]ven if the face of prudence is typically one of judicial self-abnegation, there may be occasions when prudence counsels an otherwise constitutionally dubious assertion of judicial power. In Marbury itself, for example, the Court arguably invented a non-existent statutory jurisdiction in order to be able to hold * * * that Congress had overstepped constitutional bounds" thereby established what the Justices believed to be a functionally desirable tradition of judicial review. For a classic defense of judicial "prudence" in deciding jurisdictional questions, see Bickel, The Least Dangerous Branch (1962).

(7) Marbury and Constitutional Avoidance. Is the power of judicial review so fraught that federal courts should exercise it only when truly necessary to resolve the case before it? This is the logic behind the so-called doctrine of constitutional avoidance. See, *e.g.*, Department of Commerce v. United States House of Representatives, 525 U.S. 316, 343 (1999) (" 'If there is one doctrine more deeply rooted than any other in the process of constitutional adjudication, it is that we ought not to pass on questions of constitutionality * * * unless such adjudication is unavoidable.' ") (quoting Spector Motor Service v. McLaughlin, 323 U.S. 101, 105 (1944)).

The nearly canonical citation for the avoidance doctrine is Justice Brandeis's concurring opinion in Ashwander v. Tennessee Valley Authority,

---

[6] For further discussion, see Paragraph (5), pp. 207–208, *infra*.

297 U.S. 288, 345–48 (1936).[7] Although his famous opinion included among the avoidance devices a number of the justiciability doctrines discussed below (doctrines we now think of as the prohibition of feigned cases and the requirements of ripeness and standing),[8] Justice Brandeis also identified several avoidance devices that the Court had applied "to cases confessedly within its own jurisdiction." First, Justice Brandeis noted that " 'the Court will not formulate a rule of constitutional law broader than is required by the precise facts to which it is to be applied' " (quoting Liverpool, N.Y. & Phila. Steamship Co. v. Emigration Commissioners, 113 U.S. 33, 39 (1885)). Second, he emphasized that federal courts "will not pass upon a constitutional question although properly presented by the record, if there is also present some other ground upon which the case may be disposed of." Third, and perhaps most important in modern terms, he invoked avoidance in matters of statutory interpretation: " 'When the validity of an act of the Congress is drawn in question, and even if a serious doubt of constitutionality is raised, it is a cardinal principle that this Court will first ascertain whether a construction of the statute is fairly possible by which the question may be avoided' " (quoting Crowell v. Benson, 285 U.S. 22, 62 (1932)). How closely do these principles follow from the approach to constitutional adjudication articulated by Chief Justice Marshall in Marbury?

(a) Breadth of Decision. The principle that the Court should not "formulate a rule of constitutional law broader than is required by the precise facts" necessarily includes a judgmental element, involving the appropriate specification of the applicable rule of decision. What rationale supports this principle? Would it *always* be sound practice for the Court to decide cases on the narrowest possible grounds?[9]

---

[7] The majority opinion in Ashwander considered on the merits and rejected a constitutional challenge to the existence and authority of the Tennessee Valley Authority. Concurring, Justice Brandeis argued that the Court should have avoided the constitutional issues, principally on equitable grounds.

[8] Although such doctrines of justiciability might sometimes result in the avoidance of constitutional questions, those doctrines are not framed to serve that purpose directly. Could they legitimately be adapted to such ends? In his famous "passive virtues" argument, Professor Bickel suggests that the Court might properly rely, at times, on a result-oriented approach to justiciability as a way to achieve avoidance. Bickel, Paragraph (6), *supra*, at 127 (1969). According to Bickel, this technique of constitutional avoidance is necessary to reconcile the Court's role as the ultimate enforcer of constitutional "principle" with competing demands of "prudence" and expediency that counsel the Court sometimes to avoid constitutional decisions that aroused political constituencies would be unwilling to accept. In contrast, Gunther, *The Subtle Vices of the "Passive Virtues"—A Comment on Principle and Expediency in Judicial Review*, 64 Colum.L.Rev. 1 (1964), argues that Bickel's proposed approach tends "to blur the fact that jurisdiction under our system is rooted in Article III, that it is not a domain solely within the Court's keeping." He adds that in cases within the Court's jurisdiction, proper avoidance techniques "are devices which go to the choice of the ground of decision of a case, not devices which avoid decision on the merits, not devices which 'decline to exercise' the jurisdiction to decide."

[9] Sunstein, One Case at a Time: Judicial Minimalism on the Supreme Court (1999), argues that a minimalist approach to judicial decision making tends "to make judicial errors less frequent and (above all) less damaging" and to maximize the space for the operation of political democracy. Sunstein acknowledges, however, that sometimes broad clear rules are necessary or at least desirable to avoid chilling the exercise of constitutional freedoms and to facilitate advance planning.

(b) Last Resort Rule. The principle that the Court should avoid ruling on constitutional issues "if there is also present some other ground on which the case may be disposed of" has been termed the "last resort" rule. Kloppenberg, *Avoiding Constitutional Questions*, 35 B.C.L.Rev. 1003, 1004 (1994). This rule continues to be much invoked when a party claiming relief on federal constitutional grounds also asserts a right to relief under a federal statute or regulations or on state law grounds. See, *e.g.*, Department of Commerce v. U.S. House of Representatives, 525 U.S. 316 (1999); United States v. Locke, 471 U.S. 84, 93 (1985).

In some contexts, however, the Court has taken a different approach, one that is more consistent with the law declaration model. See, *e.g.*, United States v. Leon, 468 U.S. 897, 925–26 (1984) (determining first whether a search violated the Fourth Amendment and then asking whether reasonable reliance on a warrant would negate the remedy of the exclusionary rule despite the unconstitutional search). Consider, in particular, the Court's approach to the "qualified immunity" doctrine, which provides that governmental officials who are sued in their personal capacities typically are immune from suits for money damages under federal law unless they violated "clearly established" federal rights. See generally Chap. IX, Sec. 3, *infra*. In ruling on qualified immunity defenses, the Court has stated that lower courts have discretion to decide initially whether the plaintiff has stated a valid constitutional claim and then to determine whether the plaintiff's rights were clearly established for purposes of qualified immunity. See Pearson v. Callahan, 555 U.S. 223 (2009) pp. 1326–1327, *infra*. Although acknowledging circumstances that would warrant addressing those issues in the opposite order (for example, "cases in which it is plain that the constitutional right is not clearly established but far from obvious whether there is in fact such a right"), the Court noted that deciding the underlying constitutional question first may "promote[ ] the development of constitutional precedent," which "is especially valuable with respect to questions that do not frequently arise in cases in which a qualified immunity defense is unavailable." Is there a general constitutional interest in achieving judicial articulation of legal norms that may outweigh the interest in avoiding "unnecessary" decisions of constitutional law?[10]

(c) The Canon of Avoidance. Among the avoidance rules offered by Justice Brandeis, the most important and controversial is the last: "When the validity of an act of the Congress is drawn in question, and even if a serious doubt of constitutionality is raised, it is a cardinal principle that this Court will first ascertain whether a construction of the statute is fairly possible by which the question may be avoided." In tracing the history of this principle, commentators have noted a slide from what might be termed an "unconstitutionality" to a "doubts" canon of statutory interpretation. Nagle, *Delaware & Hudson Revisited*, 72 Notre Dame L.Rev. 1495, 1495–97 (1997). See also Nelson, *Avoiding Constitutional Questions Versus Avoiding*

---

[10]   See also Katyal, *Judges as Advicegivers*, 50 Stan.L.Rev. 1709 (1998); Mikva, *Why Judges Should Not Be Advicegivers: A Response to Professor Neal Katyal*, 50 Stan.L.Rev. 1825 (1998); Healy, *The Rise of Unnecessary Constitutional Rulings*, 83 N.C.L.Rev. 847 (2005); Kamin, *An Article III Defense of Merits-First Decisionmaking in Civil Rights Litigation: The Continued Viability of Saucier v. Katz*, 16 Geo.Mason L.Rev. 53 (2008).

Unconstitutionality, 128 Harv.L.Rev.F. 331 (2015); Kelley, *Avoiding Constitutional Questions as a Three-Branch Problem*, 86 Cornell L.Rev. 831 (2001); Vermeule, *Saving Constructions*, 85 Geo.L.J. 1945 (1997). Under the unconstitutionality approach, which was commonly practiced during the nineteenth century, the courts adopted an alternative interpretation only after first deciding that the preferred interpretation would render the statute unconstitutional. See Nagle, *supra*. Modern avoidance, which can be traced back to United States v. Delaware & Hudson Co., 213 U.S. 366, 407–08 (1909), rejects the unconstitutionality approach on the ground that the former practice still required an unnecessary constitutional ruling. Instead, the Court now holds that "where an otherwise acceptable construction of a statute would raise constitutional problems, the Court will construe the statute to avoid such problems unless such construction is plainly contrary to the intent of Congress." Edward J. DeBartolo Corp. v. Florida Gulf Coast Bldg. and Constr. Trades Council, 485 U.S. 568, 575 (1988).

How closely is the modern canon tied to Marbury's premises that judicial review is justified because (and, thus, presumably only when) necessary to resolve a case? The Court has suggested that, in the interest of judicial restraint, the modern canon seeks "to minimize disagreement between the branches by preserving congressional enactments that might otherwise founder on constitutional objections." Almendarez-Torres v. United States, 523 U.S. 224, 238 (1998). A second prominent rationale rests on an empirical assumption that the canon respects Congress's presumed intent not "to press ahead into dangerous constitutional thickets in the absence of firm evidence that it courted those perils." Public Citizen v. United States Dep't of Justice, 491 U.S. 440, 466 (1989). A third rationale argues that the modern avoidance canon represents a "resistance norm" disfavoring interpretations of statutes that press close to the border of actual unconstitutionality. See Young, *Constitutional Avoidance, Resistance Norms, and the Preservation of Judicial Review*, 78 Tex.L.Rev. 1549, 1585 (2000). See also Eskridge & Frickey, *Quasi-Constitutional Law: Clear Statement Rules as Constitutional Lawmaking*, 45 Vand.L.Rev. 593 (1992) (presenting a related justification); Stephenson, *The Price of Public Action: Constitutional Doctrine and the Judicial Manipulation of Enactment Costs*, 118 Yale L.J. 2 (2008) (same); Sunstein, *Interpreting Statutes in the Regulatory State*, 103 Harv.L.Rev. 405, 468–69 (1989) (same).[11]

Although the Court has stated that the modern avoidance canon "has so long been applied by this Court that it is beyond debate," Edward J. DeBartolo Corp., *supra*, the canon has in fact become the subject of growing

---

[11] The avoidance canon sometimes overlaps with other precepts of statutory interpretation, including "clear statement" rules under which the Court will not read federal statutes to preclude all judicial review of administrative action, see Chap. IV, pp. 461–462, *infra*, or to impose duties or liabilities on the states, see Chap. IX, p. 1234, *infra*, in the absence of clear statutory statements mandating that effect. For contrasting views on the legitimacy of clear statement rules generally, compare, *e.g.*, Manning, *Clear Statement Rules and the Constitution*, 110 Colum.L.Rev. 339 (2010) (arguing that clear statement rules impermissibly abstract constitutional values from the limits placed upon them by the constitutional text), with Sunstein, *Nondelegation Canons*, 67 U.Chi.L.Rev. 315 (2000) (suggesting that such canons merely require Congress to take responsibility for decisions that push against accepted constitutional values).

debate and criticism. Some have argued that the doctrine contradicts, rather than implements, principles of judicial restraint. First, Professor Schauer has maintained that "it is by no means clear that a strained interpretation of a federal statute that avoids a constitutional question is any less a judicial intrusion than the judicial invalidation on constitutional grounds of a less strained interpretation of the same statute." Schauer, *Ashwander Revisited*, 1995 Sup.Ct.Rev. 71, 74. Accordingly, Schauer concludes that the canon permits judges to use disingenuous interpretations of statutes "to substitute their judgment for that of Congress" without assuming responsibility for rendering a constitutional holding.[12] Second, because the modern avoidance canon is triggered by mere constitutional doubt rather than a finding of actual unconstitutionality, its effect is "to enlarge the already vast reach of constitutional prohibition beyond even the most extravagant modern interpretation of the Constitution—to create a judge-made 'penumbra' that has much the same prohibitory effect as * * * [the already extravagantly interpreted] Constitution itself." Posner, *Statutory Interpretation—In the Classroom and in the Courtroom*, 50 U.Chi.L.Rev. 800, 816 (1983). Third, when the Court practices avoidance in reviewing an agency's interpretation of its own organic act, see, *e.g.*, Edward J. DeBartolo Corp., *supra*, the Court's reliance on the canon may devalue the executive's own responsibility to determine the constitutionality of action that it undertakes pursuant to authority delegated by Congress. See Kelley, *supra*.

The Court has frequently emphasized that the canon is "not a license for the judiciary to rewrite language enacted by the legislature," United States v. Monsanto, 491 U.S. 600, 611 (1989) (internal quotations omitted), and that in no case should a court "press statutory construction to the point of disingenuous evasion even to avoid a constitutional question." United States v. Locke, 471 U.S. 84, 96 (1985) (internal quotations omitted). But does that premise correspond to the reality of the cases? Compare Ullman v. United States, 350 U.S. 422, 433 (1956) (emphasizing that "the Court has stated that words may be strained 'in the candid service of avoiding a serious constitutional doubt' ").

Divisions among the Justices about whether a construction is sufficiently plausible to trigger the avoidance canon are not infrequent. See, *e.g.*, Jennings v. Rodriguez, 583 U.S. 281 (2018) (dividing, 5–3, over whether three immigration provisions could plausibly be read to require periodic bond hearings for long-term detainees); see also Katyal & Schmidt, *Active Avoidance: The Modern Supreme Court and Legal Change,* 128 Harv.L.Rev. 2109 (2015) (arguing that recent decisions invoking the avoidance doctrine have engaged in "constitutional adventurism of a uniquely pernicious sort"

---

[12]   Professor Mashaw suggests that the strategic misconstruction of a statute may intrude upon legislative supremacy more severely than would the decision to strike down an unconstitutional statute. See Mashaw, Greed, Chaos, and Governance: Using Public Choice To Improve Public Law 105 (1997). According to Mashaw, if the Court invalidates a statute, that course of action returns matters to the pre-statutory status quo. To fill the policy vacuum created by such a judicial ruling, the legislature must go back to the drawing board in a process that requires the House, the Senate, and the President to bargain afresh. If, however, the Court relies on avoidance to misread a statute, the resultant misinterpretation will remain in place if any one of those three actors prefers it to the likely outcome of corrective legislation.

by announcing new rules of constitutional law and relying on them as a predicate for substantially rewriting statutes).

---

2. ISSUES OF PARTIES, THE REQUIREMENT OF FINALITY, AND THE PROHIBITION AGAINST FEIGNED AND COLLUSIVE SUITS

INTRODUCTORY NOTE

Helping to define the appropriate scope of an Article III "case" or "controversy" are a set of technical requirements that include the Court's insistence that federal courts have the capacity to enter final judgments and its prohibition against the parties' colluding to invoke federal jurisdiction, not to resolve a genuine dispute but to secure a judicial ruling on a subject of interest to one or more of the litigants. In reading the following materials, consider how readily one can derive these doctrines from the standard constitutional materials and how readily one can subject the doctrines to principled limits.

Hayburn's Case
2 U.S. (2 Dall.) 408 (1792).
On Petition for Mandamus.

This was a motion for a *mandamus* to be directed to the *Circuit Court* for the district of *Pennsylvania*, commanding the said court to proceed in a certain petition of *Wm. Hayburn*, who had applied to be put on the pension list of the *United States*, as an invalid pensioner.

[The Invalid Pensions Act of 1792,* which provided financial assistance to injured veterans of the Revolutionary War, charged the federal circuit courts with entertaining petitions from would-be pensioners. The courts were to receive evidence of the petitioners' military service, their war injuries, their resulting disabilities, and the proportion of their monthly pay corresponding to those disabilities. If the court found that a petitioner qualified for a pension, it was directed to submit the petitioner's name, as well as a recommended sum, to the Secretary of War. The statute directed the Secretary to place any applicant certified by a circuit court on the pension list, except that, in cases of suspected "imposition or mistake," the Secretary was to withhold the suspected petitioner's name and so report to Congress.]

---

* [Ed.] Act of March 23, 1792, ch. 11, 1 Stat. 243 (1792) (repealed in part and amended by Act of Feb. 28, 1793, ch. 17, 1 Stat. 324 (1793)).

The Attorney General (Randolph) who made the motion for the *mandamus*, having premised that it was done *ex officio*, without an application from any particular person, but with a view to procure the execution of an act of Congress, particularly interesting to a meritorious and unfortunate class of citizens, THE COURT declared that they entertained great doubt upon his right, under such circumstances, and in a case of this kind, to proceed *ex officio*; and directed him to state the principles on which he attempted to support the right. The Attorney General, accordingly, entered into an elaborate description of the powers and duties of his office:—

But the COURT being divided in opinion on that question, the motion, made *ex officio*, was not allowed.

The Attorney General then changed the ground of his interposition, declaring it to be at the instance, and on behalf of Hayburn, a party interested; and he entered into the merits of the case, upon the act of Congress, and the refusal of the Judges to carry it into effect.

The COURT observed, that they would hold the motion under advisement, until the next term; but no decision was ever pronounced, as the Legislature, at an intermediate session, provided, in another way, for the relief of the pensioners.

[The following was added by the reporter as a footnote to the above report:]

As the reasons assigned by the Judges, for declining to execute the first act of Congress, involve a great Constitutional question, it will not be thought improper to subjoin them, in illustration of Hayburn's case.

▪ The Circuit Court for the district of New York (consisting of JAY, CHIEF JUSTICE, CUSHING, JUSTICE, and DUANE, DISTRICT JUDGE) * * * were * * * unanimously, of opinion and agreed.

"That by the Constitution of the United States, the government thereof is divided into *three* distinct and independent branches, and that it is the duty of each to abstain from, and to oppose, encroachments on either.

"That neither the *Legislative* nor the *Executive* branches, can constitutionally assign to the *Judicial* any duties, but such as are properly judicial, and to be performed in a judicial manner.

"That the duties assigned to the Circuit courts, by this act, are not of that description, and that the act itself does not appear to contemplate them as such; in as much as it subjects the decisions of these courts, made pursuant to those duties, first to the consideration and suspension of the Secretary [of] War, and then to the revision of the Legislature; whereas by the Constitution, neither the Secretary [of] War, nor any other Executive officer, nor even the Legislature, are authorized to sit as a court of errors on the judicial acts or opinions of this court.

"As, therefore, the business assigned to this court, by the act, is not judicial, nor directed to be performed judicially, the act can only be considered as appointing commissioners for the purposes mentioned in it, by *official* instead of *personal* descriptions.

"That the Judges of this court regard themselves as being the commissioners designated by the act, and therefore as being at liberty to accept or decline that office.

"That as the objects of this act are exceedingly benevolent, and do real honor to the humanity and justice of Congress; and as the Judges desire to manifest, on all proper occasions, and in every proper manner, their high respect for the National Legislature, they will execute this act in the capacity of commissioners. * * *"

■ The Circuit court for the district of Pennsylvania, (consisting of WILSON, and BLAIR, JUSTICES, and PETERS, DISTRICT JUDGE) made the following representation, in a joint letter to the President of the United States, on the 18th of April, 1792.

"* * * It is a principle important to freedom, that in government, the *judicial* should be distinct from, and independent of, the legislative department. To this important principle the people of the United States, in forming their Constitution, have manifested the highest regard. * * *

"Upon due consideration, we have been unanimously of opinion, that, under this act, the Circuit court held for the Pennsylvania district could not proceed;

"1st. Because the business directed by this act is not of a judicial nature. It forms no part of the power vested by the Constitution in the courts of the United States; the Circuit court must, consequently, have proceeded *without* constitutional authority.

"2d. Because, if, upon that business, the court had proceeded, its *judgments* (for its *opinions* are its judgments) might, under the same act, have been revised and controuled by the legislature, and by an officer in the executive department. Such revision and controul we deemed radically inconsistent with the independence of that judicial power which is vested in the courts; and, consequently, with that important principle which is so strictly observed by the Constitution of the United States. * * *"

■ The Circuit court for the district of North Carolina, (consisting of IREDELL, JUSTICE, and SITGREAVES, DISTRICT JUDGE) made the following representation in a joint letter to the President of the United States, on the 8th of June, 1792. * * *

"1. That the Legislative, Executive, and Judicial departments, are each formed in a separate and independent manner; and that the ultimate basis of each is the Constitution only, within the limits of which each department can alone justify any act of authority.

"2. That the Legislature, among other important powers, unquestionably possess that of establishing courts in such a manner as to their wisdom shall appear best, limited by the terms of the constitution only; and to whatever extent that power may be exercised, or however severe the duty they may think proper to require, the Judges, when appointed in virtue of any such establishment, owe implicit and unreserved obedience to it.

"3. That at the same time such courts cannot be warranted, as we conceive, by virtue of that part of the Constitution delegating *Judicial power*, for the exercise of which any act of the legislature is provided, in exercising (even under the authority of another act) any power not in its nature *judicial*, or, if *judicial*, not provided for upon the terms the Constitution requires.

"4. That whatever doubt may be suggested, whether the power in question is properly of a judicial nature, yet inasmuch as the decision of the court is not made final, but may be at least suspended in its operation by the Secretary [of] War, if he shall have cause to suspect imposition or mistake; this subjects the decision of the court to a mode of revision which we consider to be unwarranted by the Constitution; for, though Congress may certainly establish, in instances not yet provided for, courts of appellate jurisdiction, yet such courts must consist of judges appointed in the manner the Constitution requires, and holding their offices by no other tenure than that of their good behaviour, by which tenure the office of Secretary [of] War is not held. And we beg leave to add, with all due deference, that no decision of any court of the United States can, under any circumstances, in our opinion, agreeable to the Constitution, be liable to a reversion [sic], or even suspension, by the Legislature itself, in whom no judicial power of any kind appears to be vested, but the important one relative to impeachments. * * *"

[The judges then indicated that they were of the opinion that they could not regard the Act as appointing them commissioners for the purpose of its execution, since the Act appeared to confer power on the circuit courts and not on the judges personally.]

* * * [W]e have had some doubts as to the propriety of giving an opinion in a case which has not yet come regularly and judicially before us. None can be more sensible than we are of the necessity of judges being, in general, extremely cautious in not intimating an opinion, in any case, extra-judicially, because we well know how liable the best minds are, notwithstanding their utmost care, to a bias, which may arise from a preconceived opinion * * *: [B]ut in the present instance, as many unfortunate and meritorious individuals * * * may suffer great distress, even by a short delay, * * * we determined at all events to make our sentiments known as early as possible, considering this as a case which must be deemed an exception to the general rule, upon every principle of humanity and justice * * *.

NOTE ON HAYBURN'S CASE

(1) Jurisdictional Basis. Jurisdiction in the mandamus proceeding in the Supreme Court was no doubt premised on the statute later held unconstitutional in Marbury v. Madison. Is this case distinguishable? See Ex parte Peru, 318 U.S. 574 (1943), and materials in Chap. III, pp. 358–365, *infra*.

(2) The Ex Officio Action by the Attorney General. Why did three Justices conclude that the Attorney General could not proceed *ex officio*? Was the problem that the Attorney General lacked a personal stake or interest in the outcome? Surely the Attorney General can enforce both the criminal law and federal regulatory statutes. See Hartnett, *The Standing of the United States: How Criminal Prosecutions Show That Standing Doctrine is Looking for Answers in All the Wrong Places*, 97 Mich.L.Rev. 2239 (1999). Was the Attorney General's problem in Hayburn's Case merely a lack of statutory authorization to sue? For suggestions to that effect, see Bloch, *The Early Role of the Attorney General in Our Constitutional Scheme: In the Beginning There Was Pragmatism*, 1989 Duke L.J. 561, 608–18; Marcus & Teir, *Hayburn's Case: A Misinterpretation of Precedent*, 1988 Wis.L.Rev. 527, 540–41.

In Pasadena City Bd. of Educ. v. Spangler, 427 U.S. 424 (1976), high school students and their parents brought an action seeking injunctive relief from allegedly unconstitutional segregation in the Pasadena schools. The United States intervened as a party plaintiff pursuant to 42 U.S.C. § 2000h–2, which provides that upon such intervention, "the United States shall be entitled to the same relief as if it had instituted the action." By the time the case reached the Supreme Court, all the student plaintiffs had graduated. The Court held that the continued presence of the United States was authorized by the statute, and that the case was therefore not moot. On the other hand, in United States v. Texas, 565 U.S. 74 (2021), the United States attempted to proceed in equity as a plaintiff against the state of Texas to enjoin the operation of the State's abortion regulation, SB8, as contrary to the Fourteenth Amendment. See p. 1221, *infra*. After the Fifth Circuit concluded that private plaintiffs in a separate case lacked the ability to challenge the statute, it stayed the United States's enforcement action. The Supreme Court granted certiorari, but then dismissed certiorari as improvidently granted.

(3) Advisory Opinion? The Supreme Court never pronounced a judgment on the motion for mandamus in Hayburn's Case, and the opinions of the Justices on the merits emerge only through the reporter's footnote, which includes an opinion of the Circuit Court for the District of New York and letters from the Circuit Courts for the Districts of Pennsylvania and North Carolina to President Washington. Were the latter two communications, at least, advisory opinions? How can the issuance of these letters be reconciled with the formal position taken in the Correspondence of the Justices, p. 67, *supra*? Note that the letter from Justice Iredell and Judge Sitgreaves for the

Circuit Court of North Carolina explicitly acknowledges that it is deviating from the general rule against extrajudicial statements.

Apart from the advisory opinion question about the letters themselves, note that a broader theme also links the Correspondence of the Justices and the substance of the opinions expressed in the reporter's footnote in Hayburn's Case: Judicial independence requires that the Article III courts not be subject to requisition by Congress or the executive to act as subordinates to those two branches in the performance of their characteristic functions.[1]

(4) Intragovernmental Litigation. In Hayburn's Case, the original parties in the Supreme Court were the Attorney General and the Circuit Court for the District of Pennsylvania. Does the idea of a "case" entirely between the government and its own officials smack too much of the government's litigating with itself?

In United States v. Nixon, 418 U.S. 683 (1974), enforcement of a subpoena against the President was sought by the Watergate Special Prosecutor, who was appointed—and also (under specified conditions) removable—by the Attorney General, an official directly answerable to the President within the executive branch. In finding the action justiciable, the Court relied heavily on the fact that the Attorney General had promulgated a regulation providing that the Special Prosecutor would not be removed except for "extraordinary improprieties." Although the Attorney General could revoke the regulation, it had the force of law as long as it remained in effect. Because the President could not, therefore, control the litigation decisions of the Special Prosecutor, the Court found that the action to enforce the subpoena possessed the requisite adverseness. How important was what the Court described as "the uniqueness of the setting in which the conflict arises"—the need to devise some efficacious way for the executive branch to conduct a criminal investigation of alleged wrongdoing that potentially involved the President himself?[2] For discussion of potential pathologies of intragovernmental litigation, see Kelley, *The Constitutional Dilemma of Litigation Under the Independent Counsel System*, 83 Minn.L.Rev. 1197 (1999).

---

[1] See also Pfander, *Judicial Compensation and the Definition of Judicial Power in the Early Republic*, 107 Mich.L.Rev. 1 (2008), which argues that in the Correspondence of the Justices, p. 67, *supra*, and in Hayburn's Case, the Justices may have reacted in part against efforts by the political branches to add significant, but uncompensated, duties to what the Justices regarded as an already heavy workload and burdensome circuit riding responsibilities.

[2] The Court has also deemed justiciable certain actions between an independent agency, whose principal officers are insulated by statute from presidential removal, and executive agencies, whose officers the President may remove at will. See United States v. ICC, 337 U.S. 426 (1949) (action by the United States, as shipper, to set aside reparations order of ICC, an independent agency); United States ex rel. Chapman v. FPC, 345 U.S. 153 (1953) (action by Secretary of Interior challenging authority of the FPC, an independent agency, to grant license). See generally Herz, *United States v. United States: When Can the Federal Government Sue Itself?*, 32 Wm. & Mary L.Rev. 893 (1991).

NOTE ON HAYBURN'S CASE AND THE PROBLEM OF REVISION OF JUDICIAL JUDGMENTS

Among the concerns in the opinions of the Justices and the district judges in Hayburn's Case was the possibility of "revision" of a judicial judgment by the executive or legislative branch. Similar concerns have been said to raise issues about the existence of a justiciable case or controversy under Article III in other cases.

A.   Executive Revision

(1) Doctrinal Foundations. Why did the judges in the circuit courts in Hayburn's Case think that the existence of an executive power of revision was fatal to the exercise of "judicial power"? Note that the statutory scheme made short-run practical sense. The judges were in a better position than the Secretary of War to appraise the personal good faith of claimants and the extent of their disability, which was the job they were given to do, but the Secretary was in a better position to check the official military records. Did the objection to executive revision rest simply on judicial dignity and a desire to keep face, or on more fundamental concerns about the integrity of the judicial process?[1]

(a)   Pursuant to the treaty of 1819 between the United States and Spain, Congress directed the judge of the territorial court, and later of the district court, in Florida to "receive, examine and adjudge" claims for losses suffered by certain Spanish citizens through operations of the American army in Florida. The judge was to report decisions in favor of the claimants, together with the supporting evidence, to the Secretary of the Treasury, who, if satisfied that the awards were just and within the provisions of the treaty, was to authorize payment. 3 Stat. 768, 6 *id.* 569, 9 *id.* 788. In United States v. Ferreira, 54 U.S. (13 How.) 40 (1851), the Supreme Court dismissed an appeal by the United States from an award by the district judge "for want of jurisdiction." The Court said that the judge was not acting judicially, but as a commissioner—a non-Article III administrative official charged with adjusting claims against the United States. See Chap. IV, Sec. 2, *infra.* It noted but did not decide the question whether the judge could be appointed in that capacity by statute rather than by the President with the advice and consent of the Senate.

(b)   In Chicago & Southern Air Lines v. Waterman S.S. Corp., 333 U.S. 103 (1948), the Supreme Court considered the reviewability of an order of the Civil Aeronautics Board allocating an overseas air route. Under the Civil Aeronautics Act, the Board's orders were submitted to the President for approval before publication.

In a 5–4 decision, the Court held that the order was not subject to judicial review. On one hand, the courts could not review the orders after they were approved by the President because such orders "embody

---

[1]   See Baude, *The Judgment Power*, 96 Geo.L.J. 1807 (2008) (arguing that "the judicial power is the power to issue binding judgments" and that the separate opinions in Hayburn's Case reflect this principle of "judgment supremacy"). For historical discussion, see Tushnet, *Dual Office Holding and the Constitution: A View from Hayburn's Case*, in Origins of the Federal Judiciary: Essays on the Judiciary Act of 1789, at 196 (Marcus ed. 1992).

Presidential discretion as to political matters beyond the competence of the courts to adjudicate."

On the other hand, the Court rejected an approach proposed by the court of appeals, in which after the courts had reviewed the order, the case should be resubmitted to the President so "that his power to disapprove would apply after as well as before the court acts," thus "interposing judicial review between the action by the Board and that by the President." In rejecting this approach, the Court said:

"But if the President may completely disregard the judgment of the court, it would be only because it is one the courts were not authorized to render. Judgments, within the powers vested in courts by the Judiciary Article of the Constitution, may not lawfully be revised, overturned or refused faith and credit by another Department of Government.

"To revise or review an administrative decision which has only the force of a recommendation to the President would be to render an advisory opinion in its most obnoxious form—advice that the President has not asked, tendered at the demand of a private litigant, on a subject concededly within the President's exclusive, ultimate control. This Court early and wisely determined that it would not give advisory opinions even when asked by the Chief Executive. It has also been the firm and unvarying practice of Constitutional Courts to render no judgments not binding and conclusive on the parties and none that are subject to later review or alteration by administrative action."

(2) A Contemporary Application: Extradition Proceedings. To effect an extradition under 18 U.S.C. § 3184, the government must file a complaint with "any justice or judge of the United States, or any magistrate," or with any judge of a state court of general jurisdiction, who then conducts a hearing. Upon a finding of probable cause that the accused has committed an extraditable crime, the presiding judge certifies this finding to the Secretary of State, who then determines whether to deliver the accused to the country seeking extradition. Although the Supreme Court has not addressed the question, the courts of appeals thus far have rejected Hayburn's Case objections to this procedure, reasoning that judges in extradition proceedings act as extradition officers in their individual rather than judicial capacities. See, *e.g.*, Lopez-Smith v. Hood, 121 F.3d 1322, 1327 (9th Cir.1997); Lo Duca v. United States, 93 F.3d 1100 (2d Cir.1996).[2] Is it relevant that § 3184, although permitting the Secretary of State to exercise a power analogous to clemency in cases found to satisfy the statutory requirements, does not allow the Secretary to "revise" a finding that the statutory requirements of extradition have not been satisfied?

B. Legislative Revision

(1) The Problem Defined. Recall that in Hayburn's Case, the Pension Act provided that, if the Secretary of War found that the circuit court's determination was mistaken, the Secretary would withhold the pensioner

---

[2]   For criticism of this position, see generally Parry, *The Lost History of International Extradition Litigation*, 43 Va.J.Int'l L. 93 (2002) (attacking the purported historical foundations for the view that the judicial role in extradition proceedings falls outside Article III).

from the pension rolls and report the case to Congress. Was Congress's power to revise the decision of the judges open to the same objections as the Secretary's power to do so? What if the Secretary had been directed to put all names certified by the courts on the pension roll, and Congress had simply retained power to refuse to pay any particular pension by virtue of its power over appropriations? Unsurprisingly, the issue of congressional revision of final judicial judgments has arisen many times in history, most commonly when Congress determines whether to appropriate money to pay judgments against the United States. Consider the examples follow.

(2) Claims Against the United States. Article I, § 9, clause 7 of the Constitution provides that "[n]o Money shall be drawn from the Treasury, but in Consequence of Appropriations made by Law." Because the payment of any judgment against the United States thus requires a specific or general appropriation by Congress, suits against the United States present especially complex issues involving legislative revision of judicial judgments. Many of the Supreme Court's encounters with those issues have been further complicated by Congress's recurrent use of non-Article III tribunals—whose judges lack life tenure and whose powers are not subject to Article III justiciability doctrines—either to adjudicate or to recommend to Congress whether to pay claims against the United States. The Court has assumed these arrangements are valid. (Issues involving non-Article III courts are discussed in Chap. IV, Sec. 2, *infra*.) But when Congress provides for review of the decisions of non-Article III tribunals by Article III courts, Article III justiciability rules apply to the appeal, and the Court has had to determine whether its own judgment might be subject to impermissible legislative revision. What follows is a brief history of Congress's approach to funding judgments against the United States and the Court's reaction to any resultant prospect of legislative revisions of federal judicial judgments.

(a)   Before 1855, no general statute waived the sovereign immunity of the United States on claims for money, and a claimant's only recourse was to petition Congress for a private act. In order to relieve the burden posed by the need to consider numerous private acts, Congress in 1855 established a non-Article III Court of Claims with authority to "hear and determine" most types of money claims not sounding in tort. Initially, this court embodied its decisions not in judgments but in reports to Congress and drafts of private bills requiring congressional action. In 1863, Congress enacted new legislation to permit the Court of Claims to render judgments, but the statutory scheme continued to provide that "no money shall be paid out of the Treasury for any claim passed on by the Court of Claims till after an appropriation therefor shall have been estimated for by the Secretary of the Treasury." In Gordon v. United States, 69 U.S. 561 (1865), the Court construed this provision as authorizing executive revision of judgments against the United States and, accordingly, held that Supreme Court review of Court of Claims judgments was barred by Article III.[3] Congress responded by amending the statute once again, omitting the "objectionable section," and

---

[3]   The Court did not question the authority of Congress to vest non-judicial functions in the non-Article III Court of Claims. As a result, the only issue in Gordon was whether the Supreme Court could review Court of Claims decisions.

the Court upheld its own jurisdiction to entertain appeals from decisions of the Court of Claims in United States v. Jones, 119 U.S. 477 (1886). (Note the assumption that Supreme Court review of a "judicial" decision by a "legislative court" was an exercise of "appellate jurisdiction" within the meaning of Article III. See pp. 545–546, *infra*.)[4]

(b)   From 1956 to 1977, Congress provided that judgments of $100,000 or less were to be paid by the General Accounting Office; judgments in excess of that amount were to be certified by the Secretary of the Treasury to Congress for consideration. The effect of that provision on the justiciability of money claims against the United States in Article III courts was considered by the Supreme Court on two occasions:

(i)   Glidden Co. v. Zdanok, 370 U.S. 530 (1962), the Court's opinion dealt with two consolidated cases, one addressing the Article III status of the former Court of Claims. In determining that the Court of Claims could constitutionally exercise Article III power, Justice Harlan's plurality opinion concluded that claims against the United States were justiciable even when they exceeded $100,000.[5] In so doing, he referred to a study (46 Harv.L.Rev. 677, 685–86 n.63 (1933)) that discovered only 15 instances in 70 years when Congress had refused to pay a judgment. "This historical record," he said, "surely more favorable to prevailing parties than that obtaining in private litigation, may well make us doubt whether the capacity to enforce a judgment is always indispensable for the exercise of judicial power." Justice Harlan noted that a similar insecurity marked the Court's ability to execute monetary judgments awarded by it in suits between states, given "the Court's recognition of judicial impotence to compel a levy of taxes or otherwise by process to enforce [such an] award." He thus concluded that "[i]f this Court may rely on the good faith of state governments or other public bodies to respond to its judgments, there seems to be no sound reason why the Court of Claims may not rely on the good faith of the United States."

Does Justice Harlan's reasoning effectively sanction the issuance of advisory opinions? If Congress has no binding legal obligation to comply with money judgments in excess of $100,000, in what way does a Court of Claims judgment for such a sum change the legal status quo? Certainly, Congress could appropriate the money to satisfy a claim with or without a Court of Claims' judgment finding liability.[6]

---

[4]   On the history of the Court of Claims, see generally Richardson, History, Jurisdiction and Practice of the Court of Claims (2d ed.1885); Cowen, Section I: 1855–1887, in Cowen et al., The United States Court of Claims: A History 1–34 (1978). The United States Court of Federal Claims (an Article I court), along with the Court of Appeals for the Federal Circuit (an Article III court), has succeeded to the jurisdiction of the Court of Claims. For further discussion, see Symposium, *Proceedings of the 15th Judicial Conference Celebrating the 20th Anniversary of the United States Court of Federal Claims*, 71 Geo.Wash.L.Rev. 529 (2003).

[5]   In 1953, Congress "declared" the Court of Claims "to be a court established under article III," 67 Stat. 226, codified at 28 U.S.C. § 171. Glidden upheld this characterization. In 1982, this Court of Claims was replaced with a non-Article III Court of Federal Claims, 96 Stat. 25.

[6]   For discussion of the relationship early in United States history between federal jurisdiction and Congress's appropriations power, see Pfander & Hunt, *Public Wrongs and Private Bills: Indemnification and Government Accountability in the Early Republic*, 85 N.Y.U.L.Rev. 1862, 1920–22 (2010).

(ii)   The Regional Rail Reorganization cases, Blanchette v. Connecticut General Ins. Corp., 419 U.S. 102 (1974), involved a challenge to the constitutionality of amendments to the Bankruptcy Act enacted after eight northeastern railroads had filed for reorganization. The amendments required creditors and shareholders of the railroads to exchange their interests for stock and debt in Conrail (a government-created but private, for-profit corporation) and also required the railroads to continue operating until the exchange occurred. The Court held that the previously discussed remedy in the Court of Claims remained available to compensate for any deficiency in the value of the Conrail securities and for losses incurred by reason of the mandatory continued operation. Justice Brennan, for the Court, relied on the above-quoted language in Glidden to answer the contention that this remedy was inadequate. Justice Douglas's dissent, joined on this issue by Justice Stewart, argued that while Congress ordinarily pays judgments over $100,000 as a matter of routine, "this is an exceptional case, involving the possibility of judgments in the billions of dollars."

(c)   In 1977, Congress eliminated the dollar amount limitation in the statute. The current version, 31 U.S.C. § 1304, provides generally for payment by the Secretary of the Treasury of final judgments, awards, and compromise settlements against the United States.

(d)   As long as Congress makes lump sum appropriations, whether for judgments already entered or to be entered, particular judgments can be questioned only by means of an additional, separate legislative act. In the instances mentioned in the Harvard Law Review study cited by Justice Harlan in Glidden, such a special act was the means actually used. Given its constitutional responsibility for appropriations, could Congress always defeat a particular judgment against the United States by the adoption of later legislation forbidding its payment, or might such legislation itself be unconstitutional?

(e)   Many cases have upheld statutes limiting the binding effect of judgments in favor of the United States. See, e.g., Cherokee Nation v. United States, 270 U.S. 476 (1926) (waiving effect of res judicata with respect to a former judgment concerning interest on a judgment in favor of the Cherokee Nation); Pope v. United States, 323 U.S. 1 (1944) (upholding a statute directing the Court of Claims to rehear a claim after adverse judgment for the claimant and to give judgment according to a different principle of proof); United States v. Sioux Nation of Indians, 448 U.S. 371 (1980) (upholding a statute providing for de novo review, by the Court of Claims, of Native Americans' claims against the United States without regard to defenses of res judicata or collateral estoppel based on a prior Court of Claims proceeding). Similarly, if the United States, acting through Congress, has permissibly defined a public right on which an injunctive decree rests, the Court has held that Congress has the authority to modify that public right going forward. See Pennsylvania v. Wheeling & Belmont Bridge Co., 59 U.S. (18 How.) 421 (1855) (sustaining a statute that declared a bridge not to be an obstruction to navigation, even though the Supreme Court had previously enjoined the bridge's maintenance on grounds of such obstruction), pp. 486–487, *infra*.[7]

(3) Other Legislative Revision of Final Judgments. In Plaut v. Spendthrift Farm, Inc., 514 U.S. 211 (1995), the Supreme Court ruled that a federal statute directing federal courts to reopen final judgments in private lawsuits violated Article III and the separation of powers. The original action between the parties, involving allegations of securities fraud, was dismissed with prejudice after the Supreme Court held in Lampf, Pleva, Lipkind, Prupis & Petigrow v. Gilbertson, 501 U.S. 350, 364 (1991), that the suit was time-barred. The decision in the Lampf case surprised many litigants by establishing a shorter limitations period than most courts had previously applied, and Congress responded by enacting legislation that authorized reinstatement of certain actions dismissed as time-barred under Lampf. Relying on the congressional enactment, the plaintiffs moved to reopen their lawsuit. But the Supreme Court held that Congress had infringed the judicial power. In an opinion for six Justices, Justice Scalia concluded that the Framers, having "lived among the ruins of a system of intermingled legislative and judicial powers," wished to insulate final judicial judgments—those by the highest courts possessing jurisdiction or lower court decisions from which the time for appeal has expired—from legislative revision. The Court distinguished from the case before it those in which Congress (a) had changed the applicable law while a case was pending but prior to entry of a final judgment, see pp. 453–454, *infra* (discussing Robertson v. Seattle Audubon Soc., 503 U.S. 429 (1992)), (b) had waived the res judicata effect of a prior judgment in favor of the government, or (c) had annulled judgments rendered by legislative (rather than Article III) courts. Justice Breyer filed a concurring opinion. Justice Stevens, joined by Justice Ginsburg, dissented.

In the absence of a final judgment dismissing a lawsuit, the Court in Plaut did not question Congress's power to enact laws establishing the retroactive liability of one private party to another or to authorize suits that otherwise would be time-barred. What purposes are served by attaching so much significance to the form of a final judgment of an Article III court?

(4) Changes of Law and Orders Mandating Ongoing Relief. The Court distinguished both Plaut and Hayburn's Case in Miller v. French, 530 U.S. 327 (2000), which sharply differentiated judgments in suits for damages from judgments providing ongoing injunctive relief. The Prison Litigation Reform Act of 1995, 110 Stat. 1321 (1996), provides in part that "in any civil action with respect to prison conditions, a defendant * * * shall be entitled to the immediate termination of any prospective relief if the relief was approved or granted in the absence of a finding by the court that the relief * * * extends no further than necessary to correct the violation of the Federal right, and is the least intrusive means necessary to correct the violation of the Federal right." 18 U.S.C. § 3626(b)(2). A further provision of the PLRA, § 3626(e)(2),

---

7   In an article tracing the history and constitutional implications of the idea of "public rights," Professor Nelson notes the traditional understanding that such rights—like the right to unobstructed use of navigable waterways—were "held in common by the public at large" and "belong[ed] to the body politic." Nelson, *Adjudication in the Political Branches*, 107 Colum.L.Rev. 559, 562 (2007). Should that understanding affect Congress's ability to waive judgments based on public rights claims?

establishes that a motion to terminate injunctive relief in prison cases "shall operate as a stay" of any previously entered remedial order beginning 30 days after the filing of the motion (extendable up to 90 days for "good cause"). Assuming without holding that § 3626(b)(2) establishes a substantively valid standard for the termination of injunctive remedies, Miller held that the "automatic stay" provision of § 3626(e)(2) does not infringe the judicial role under the separation of powers.

Speaking on this point for seven Justices, Justice O'Connor's opinion began by holding that the "automatic stay" provision was mandatory. Then, for a majority of five, she concluded that nothing in Plaut or Hayburn's Case restricted "Congress' authority to alter the prospective effect of previously entered injunctions." Rather, past cases established that where Congress validly alters the substantive law on which an injunction was predicated, entitlement to the injunction lapses without Congress's having impermissibly revised a "final" judgment: "The provision of prospective relief is subject to the continuing supervisory jurisdiction of the court, and therefore may be altered according to subsequent changes in the law."

Justice Souter, joined by Justice Ginsburg, concurred in the part of the Court's opinion construing the statute, but dissented from the disposition. He would have remanded the case to the district court to determine whether the "automatic stay" provision gave the court too little time to determine whether the extant injunction remained valid under the changed substantive standard. If so, he saw "a serious question"—which he thought should be decided by the district court in the first instance—"whether Congress has in practical terms assumed the judicial function." The majority, too, left open whether the time limit would be constitutionally valid, "particularly in a complex case," but treated the question as one of due process, not separation of powers, and thus as "not before [the Court]." (Justice Breyer, joined by Justice Stevens, dissented on statutory grounds.)

Does the Court's reasoning leave any doubt about the constitutional validity of § 3626(b)(2), the underlying PLRA provision that provides for termination of injunctive orders not found to be narrowly tailored to correct proven constitutional violations?

C. Judicial Revision

(1) Res Judicata Effect and the Judicial Function. Judicial judgments are obviously subject to judicial revision until they become "final" following the completion of appellate review or the expiration of the period for appeal. After the judgments of Article III courts have become final, mustn't they have at least some res judicata effect in order to avoid being forbidden advisory opinions? See Shapiro, Preclusion in Civil Actions 14 (2001). The Supreme Court has seldom had to consider how much res judicata effect is necessary.

INTRODUCTORY NOTE ON ADVERSARINESS

Are there reasons apart from the concerns about executive and legislative revision just discussed that the functions assigned to the circuit courts in Hayburn's Case might have been considered nonjudicial? A proper Article III "case" or "controversy" requires least two parties who are genuinely adverse to each other. Does this requirement post a difficulty in making a "case" out of an application by a private person for a grant by the government of money or other tangible property or an intangible permission?

Consider how the Court later confronted this problem in the context of naturalization petitions.

Tutun v. United States

270 U.S. 568 (1926).
On Certificates from the United States Courts of Appeals
for the First and Second Circuits.

■ MR. JUSTICE BRANDEIS delivered the opinion of the Court.

These cases present, by certificate, the question whether the Circuit Courts of Appeals have jurisdiction to review a decree or order of a federal District Court denying the petition of an alien to be admitted to citizenship in the United States. * * *

The function of admitting to citizenship has been conferred exclusively upon courts continuously since the foundation of our government. See Act of March 26, 1790, c. 3, 1 Stat. 103. * * * The constitutionality of this exercise of jurisdiction has never been questioned. If the proceeding were not a case or controversy within the meaning of article 3, § 2, this delegation of power upon the courts would have been invalid. Hayburn's Case, 2 Dall. 409 [(1792)]; United States v. Ferreira, 13 How. 40 [(1851)]; Muskrat v. United States, 219 U.S. 346 [(1911)]. * * * Whenever the law provides a remedy enforceable in the courts according to the regular course of legal procedure, and that remedy is pursued, there arises a case within the meaning of the Constitution, whether the subject of the litigation be property or status. A petition for naturalization is clearly a proceeding of that character.

The petitioner's claim is one arising under the Constitution and laws of the United States. The claim is presented to the court in such a form that the judicial power is capable of acting upon it. The proceeding is instituted and is conducted throughout according to the regular course of judicial procedure. The United States is always a possible adverse party. By section 11 of the Naturalization Act the full rights of a litigant are expressly reserved to it. Its contentions are submitted to the court for adjudication. Section 9 provides that every final hearing must be held in open court, that upon such hearing the applicant and witnesses shall be examined under oath before the court and in its presence, and that every final order must be made under the hand of the court and shall be entered in full upon the record. The judgment entered, like other judgments of a court of record, is accepted as complete evidence of its own validity unless set aside. * * *

The opportunity to become a citizen of the United States is said to be merely a privilege, and not a right. It is true that the Constitution does not confer upon aliens the right to naturalization. But it authorizes Congress to establish a uniform rule therefor. Article 1, § 8, cl. 4. The opportunity having been conferred by the Naturalization Act, there is a statutory right in the alien to submit his petition and evidence to a court, to have that tribunal pass upon them, and, if the requisite facts are established, to receive the certificate. * * * In passing upon the application the court exercises judicial judgment. It does not confer or withhold a favor.

[The Court went on to address an issue of statutory appellate jurisdiction.]

To the questions asked in the two cases, we answer that the Circuit Court of Appeals has jurisdiction to review by appeal the order or decree of the District Court denying the petition to be admitted to citizenship in the United States.

NOTE ON TUTUN AND ADVERSARINESS

(1) **Tutun's Logic.** Can Tutun's reasoning be reconciled with the separate opinions in Hayburn's Case, p. 101, *supra*? After Tutun, would Hayburn's Case remain a bar to Congress's charging an Article III court with routine determinations of eligibility for disability benefits under the Social Security Act? Certainly, the United States is always a possible adverse party in such proceedings. Hayburn's Case, however, seems to reject rather decisively Congress's effort to enlist federal courts to act as administrative agencies by applying law to fact outside the context of a concrete dispute between adverse parties. Is there way to understand Tutun that does not contradict that premise?

The Court in Tutun relied in part on practice dating back to the founding. What role should such a consideration play in constitutional adjudication? Compare Ex parte Quirin, 317 U.S. 1, 41–42 (1942) (a legislative construction of the Constitution "which has been followed since the founding of our government * * * is entitled to the greatest respect"); The Laura, 114 U.S. 411, 416 (1885) ("[T]he practice [under federal legislation] and acquiescence under it, 'commencing with the organization of the judicial system, affords an irresistible answer, and has, indeed" fixed the construction.' ") (quoting Stuart v. Laird, 5 U.S. (1 Cranch) 299, 308 (1803)). See also Baude, *Constitutional Liquidation*, 71 Stan.L.Rev. 1 (2019); Young, *Our Prescriptive Judicial Power: Constitutive and Entrenchment Effects of Historical Practice in Federal Courts Law*, 58 Wm. & Mary L.Rev. 535 (2016)

When, if ever, should a deep historical pedigree sustain a practice if the Court would otherwise find it unconstitutional?

(2) Questioning the Adversariness Requirement. In a comprehensive article, Pfander & Birk, *Article III Judicial Power, the Adverse-Party Requirement, and Non-Contentious Jurisdiction,* 124 Yale L.J. 1346 (2015), seek to revise long-settled assumptions that Article III jurisdiction requires adverse parties in all cases. The authors trace a history of "non-contentious" jurisdiction from Roman times through the English Court of Chancery sitting in Westminster to colonial and early American courts that had sundry powers to rule on ex parte or otherwise uncontested petitions to establish or register legal rights or interests. According to the authors, historical or modern residues of that tradition can be seen not only in naturalization proceedings (as in Tutun), but also, *inter alia,* in uncontested prize and salvage cases in admiralty, appointments of bankruptcy trustees, issuances of warrants, entries of default judgments, class action settlements, and consent decrees. In the authors' view, Article III requires adverse parties in "controversies," but not necessarily in all "cases," some of which can be non-contentious. "The lesson of Hayburn's Case," they write, "is not that the federal courts lack power to hear ex parte proceedings, but that they can act only where their decision will have a binding, legally determinative effect." Seeking to distill normative lessons from historical practice, Pfander & Birk conclude: "[W]hile no adverse party need appear in non-contentious proceedings, federal courts should exercise jurisdiction only if the party invoking federal power has a concrete interest in the recognition of a legal claim. * * * The courts also should exercise non-contentious jurisdiction only where they have been called upon to employ judicial judgment in the application of law to the facts and only where their decisions will enjoy the finality long viewed as essential to the federal judicial role. The courts must be especially mindful of the potential for cases heard on the non-contentious side of their dockets to affect the rights of absent parties, and due process will continue to require that third parties receive notice of, and an opportunity to participate in, matters that concern them."

Pfander & Birk are unquestionably correct that federal courts routinely act on ex parte motions and render uncontested rulings in a number of contexts. As the authors acknowledge, many of these rulings come in proceedings that are potentially contested (as in Tutun) or are ancillary to the resolution of live disputes (as, for example, in the appointment of bankruptcy trustees). That said, their study generates an important question: Is there a large enough residual category to warrant the development of forward-looking principles—such as those that they propose—to identify, limit, and structure exercises of "non-contentious jurisdiction" under Article III?

Woolhandler, *Adverse Interests and Article III,* 111 Nw.U.L.Rev. 1025 (2017), answers in the negative. According to Professor Woolhandler, the examples adduced by Pfander and Birk show at most that Article III does not require adverse *arguments* in every case; the authors fail to refute the more fundamental proposition that Article III jurisdiction always requires parties with adverse *interests.* Pfander & Birk, *Adverse Interests and Article*

III: A Reply, 111 Nw.U.L.Rev. 1067 (2017), retort that Woolhandler adopts a conceptualization of Article III's requirements that emerged only in the late nineteenth century and that she offers no theory adequate to explain earlier discussion of and practice involving non-contentious jurisdiction. Pfander has expanded further on these and other arguments in a book, Pfander, Cases Without Controversies: Uncontested Adjudication in Article III Courts (2021).

(3) "Genuine" Adversariness. Even if parties to a lawsuit have nominally adverse interests, they cannot obtain a judgment from an Article III court if one party controls or dominates the other party's conduct of the litigation. In reading the case below and the material that follows, consider how consistent the Court has been in enforcing the resulting principle against "feigned" or "collusive" lawsuits. Does the pattern of enforcement and nonenforcement reveal anything about the interests that principle is meant to serve?

United States v. Johnson

319 U.S. 302 (1943).
Appeal from the District Court of the United States
for the Northern District of Indiana.

■ PER CURIAM. One Roach, a tenant of residential property belonging to appellee, brought this suit in the district court alleging that the property was within a "defense rental area" established by the Price Administrator pursuant to §§ 2(b) and 302(d) of the Emergency Price Control Act of 1942; that the Administrator had promulgated Maximum Rent Regulation No. 8 for the area; and that the rent paid by Roach and collected by appellee was in excess of the maximum fixed by the regulation. The complaint demanded judgment for treble damages and reasonable attorney's fees, as prescribed by § 205(e) of the Act. The United States, intervening pursuant to 28 U.S.C. § 401, filed a brief in support of the constitutionality of the Act, which appellee had challenged by motion to dismiss. The district court dismissed the complaint on the ground—as appears from its opinion and judgment—that the Act and the promulgation of the regulation under it were unconstitutional because Congress by the Act had unconstitutionally delegated legislative power to the Administrator.

Before entry of the order dismissing the complaint, the Government moved to reopen the case on the ground that it was collusive and did not involve a real case or controversy. This motion was denied. The Government brings the case here on appeal, and assigns as error both the ruling of the district court on the constitutionality of the Act, and its refusal to reopen and dismiss the case as collusive. * * *

The affidavit of the plaintiff, submitted by the Government on its motion to dismiss the suit as collusive, shows without contradiction that he brought the present proceeding in a fictitious name; that it was instituted as a "friendly suit" at appellee's request; that the plaintiff did not employ, pay, or even meet, the attorney who appeared of record in his behalf; that he had no knowledge who paid the $15 filing fee in the district court, but was assured by appellee that as plaintiff he would incur no expense in bringing the suit; that he did not read the complaint which was filed in his name as plaintiff; that in his conferences with the appellee and appellee's attorney of record, nothing was said concerning treble damages and he had no knowledge of the amount of the judgment prayed until he read of it in a local newspaper.

Appellee's counter-affidavit did not deny these allegations. It admitted that appellee's attorney had undertaken to procure an attorney to represent the plaintiff and had assured the plaintiff that his presence in court during the trial of the cause would not be necessary. It appears from the district court's opinion that no brief was filed on the plaintiff's behalf in that court.

The Government does not contend that, as a result of this cooperation of the two original parties to the litigation, any false or fictitious state of facts was submitted to the court. But it does insist that the affidavits disclose the absence of a genuine adversary issue between the parties, without which a court may not safely proceed to judgment, especially when it assumes the grave responsibility of passing upon the constitutional validity of legislative action. Even in a litigation where only private rights are involved, the judgment will not be allowed to stand where one of the parties has dominated the conduct of the suit by payment of the fees of both.

Here an important public interest is at stake—the validity of an Act of Congress having far-reaching effects on the public welfare in one of the most critical periods in the history of the country. That interest has been adjudicated in a proceeding in which the plaintiff has had no active participation, over which he has exercised no control, and the expense of which he has not borne. He has been only nominally represented by counsel who was selected by appellee's counsel and whom he has never seen. Such a suit is collusive because it is not in any real sense adversary. It does not assume the "honest and actual antagonistic assertion of rights" to be adjudicated—a safeguard essential to the integrity of the judicial process, and one which we have held to be indispensable to adjudication of constitutional questions by this Court. Chicago & G.T. Ry. Co. v. Wellman, 143 U.S. 339, 345 [(1892)]. Whenever in the course of litigation such a defect in the proceedings is brought to the court's attention, it may set aside any adjudication thus procured and dismiss the cause without entering judgment on the merits. It is the court's duty to do so where, as here, the public interest has been placed at hazard by the amenities of parties to a suit conducted under the domination of only one of them. The district court should have granted the Government's motion to dismiss the suit as collusive. We accordingly vacate the judgment below with instructions to the district court to dismiss the cause on that ground alone. * * *

So ordered.

Judgment vacated with directions.

NOTE ON FEIGNED AND COLLUSIVE CASES

(1) Collusive Litigation. In principle it is easy to see why an important constitutional issue should not be determined in a proceeding in which one nominal party has dominated the conduct of the other. But why didn't the government's intervention in the Johnson case, pursuant to what is now 28 U.S.C. § 2403, cure the difficulty?

(2) Background to the Johnson Case. The Supreme Court's current approach to feigned and collusive litigation reflects an apparent departure from some of its early precedents.

(a) In at least two early cases, the Court reached the merits despite evidence that the controversy was feigned or collusive. See Hylton v. United States, 3 U.S. (3 Dall.) 171 (1796);[1] Fletcher v. Peck, 10 U.S. (6 Cranch) 87 (1810).[2] Indeed, according to Bloch, *The Early Role of the Attorney General in Our Constitutional Scheme: In the Beginning There Was Pragmatism*, 1989 Duke L.J. 561, 612, "[f]eigned and contrived suits were reasonably common * * * [the 1790s], and appear to have raised no red flags." Does this history suggest any parallels to the conventional wisdom about advisory opinions? See pp. 69–76, *supra*. Isn't it predictable that it would sometimes—perhaps often—take the institutions responsible for implementing the Constitution a long period of time to come to rest on how to understand certain elements of a highly complex constitutional structure?[3]

(b) Compare Lord v. Veazie, 49 U.S. (8 How.) 251 (1850), in which Veazie had executed a deed to Lord warranting that he had certain rights claimed by third persons, and an action on the covenant by Lord against Veazie "was docketed by consent." The circuit court "gave judgment for the defendant *pro forma*, at the request of the parties, in order that the judgment and question might be brought before" the Supreme Court. On a third person's motion, the Court dismissed the case, saying that the judgment

---

[1]   Hylton was an apparently contrived suit to settle the constitutionality of a federal tax, in which the Supreme Court overlooked a number of potential obstacles to justiciability, among them that the government had evidently paid Hylton's lawyers. See Currie, *The Constitution in the Supreme Court: 1789–1801*, 48 U.Chi.L.Rev. 819, 854 (1981).

[2]   See 1 Warren, The Supreme Court in United States History 392–99 (rev.ed.1926). But *cf.* Fletcher, 10 U.S. (6 Cranch) at 147–48 (Johnson, J., dissenting) (noting that although the case "bear[s] strong evidence" of being "feigned," "[m]y confidence * * * in the respectable gentlemen who have been engaged by the parties, has induced me to abandon my scruples, in the belief that they would never consent to impose a mere feigned case upon this court").

[3]   At least some of the Constitution's architects expected as much. See, *e.g.*, The Federalist No. 37 (Madison) ("All new laws, though penned with the greatest technical skill and passed on the fullest and most mature deliberation, are considered as more or less obscure and equivocal, until their meaning be liquidated and ascertained by a series of particular discussions and adjudications.").

below was a nullity upon which no writ of error would lie, and that "the whole proceeding was in contempt of the court, and highly reprehensible." What accounts for the change in the Court's attitude?[4]

(3) Test Cases. Does the rule against collusive cases defeat the planning of a test case by the parties to a real controversy? See Evers v. Dwyer, 358 U.S. 202 (1958), in which the plaintiff (who was a Black man) boarded a bus once, refused to obey an order to sit in the rear, got off, and brought a class action for a declaratory judgment against the enforced segregation. The Court held the action justiciable despite findings by the district court that the plaintiff had ridden a city bus on only that one occasion, for the purpose of instituting the litigation.[5] See also Havens Realty Corp. v. Coleman, 455 U.S. 363 (1982), discussed pp. 181–182, *infra*, in which the Court upheld the standing of a "testers" who "without an intent to rent or purchase a home or apartment, pose as renters or purchasers for the purpose of collecting evidence of unlawful steering practices."

(4) Test Cases Framed by Congress: The Muskrat Case. Is it constitutionally objectionable for Congress to frame a case for judicial resolution or to provide specifically for decision of a case by an Article III court?

In the puzzling case of Muskrat v. United States, 219 U.S. 346 (1911), the Court refused to entertain a suit that Congress had specifically authorized. In 1902, Congress had provided for the transfer of Cherokee property from tribal to private ownership. Every citizen of the Cherokee Nation as of September 1, 1902, was entitled to be enrolled and, upon enrollment, to receive an allotment equal in value to 110 acres of the average allottable lands of the tribe (plus a proportionate share of any tribal funds on deposit in the U.S. Treasury and, presumably, of any land remaining after the allotments). In 1906, Congress extended the time for completion of the roll by permitting enrollment of minor children living on March 4, 1906. At the same time, it imposed new restraints on alienation by the original allottees. The Secretaries of the Interior and of the Treasury were charged with implementation of various aspects of these statutes.

In 1907, Congress authorized certain named original allottees—David Muskrat, Levi Gritts, and two others—to bring suit against the United States in the Court of Claims, with a right of appeal by either party to the Supreme Court, "to determine the validity of any acts of Congress" passed after the 1902 act that purported to diminish their rights as allottees. Attorney's fees for plaintiffs, if they prevailed, were to be paid by the

---

[4]   For a discussion of Veazie, as well as a more general discussion of the "feigned issue," including changes in both equity practice and substantive law, see Sachs, *The Feigned Issue in the Federal System*, *available at* https://ssrn.com/abstract=1032682. For an argument that the problem in Veazie was the use of a manufactured dispute to prejudice an unrepresented third party, see Pfander, *Standing, Litigable Interests, and Article III's Case-or-Controversy Requirement*, 65 UCLA L.Rev. 170, 178, 192 (2018).

[5]   See also Bankamerica Corp. v. United States, 462 U.S. 122, 124 (1983) (deciding an issue of federal antitrust law after noting that the proceedings before it were "companion test cases" brought by the United States against ten corporations and five individuals). *Cf.* Buchanan v. Warley, 245 U.S. 60 (1917) (reaching the merits without discussion of justiciability in a challenge to a segregated housing law that had every appearance of a test case); Martin v. Hunter's Lessee, 14 U.S. (1 Wheat.) 304 (1816), p. 620, *infra*.

Treasury out of tribal funds. Pursuant to this statute, Muskrat and other allottees brought suit in the Court of Claims, challenging the 1906 act on the ground that it deprived them of property without due process of law. The Court of Claims rejected this contention, and the case came to the Supreme Court on appeal. The Court ordered the suit dismissed for want of jurisdiction:

"The right to declare a law unconstitutional arises because an act of Congress relied upon by one or the other of such parties in determining their rights is in conflict with the fundamental law. The exercise of this, the most important and delicate duty of this court, is not given to it as a body with revisory power over the action of Congress, but because the rights of the litigants in justiciable controversies require the court to choose between the fundamental law and a law purporting to be enacted within constitutional authority, but in fact beyond the power delegated to the legislative branch of the government. This attempt to obtain a judicial declaration of the validity of the act of Congress is not presented in a 'case' or 'controversy,' to which, under the Constitution of the United States, the judicial power alone extends. It is true the United States is made a defendant to this action, but it has no interest adverse to the claimants. The object is not to assert a property right as against the government, or to demand compensation for alleged wrongs because of action upon its part. The whole purpose of the law is to determine the constitutional validity of this class of legislation, in a suit not arising between parties concerning a property right necessarily involved in the decision in question, but in a proceeding against the government in its sovereign capacity, and concerning which the only judgment required is to settle the doubtful character of the legislation in question. Such judgment will not conclude private parties, when actual litigation brings to the court the question of the constitutionality of such legislation. In a legal sense the judgment could not be executed, and amounts in fact to no more than an expression of opinion upon the validity of the acts in question."

Why didn't Muskrat present a justiciable controversy? Assuming the plaintiffs had a plausible due process claim, whom should they have sued?[6] Was the Court's decision influenced by doubts that a request for a declaratory judgment, without more, was a sufficient basis for the invocation of judicial power? See pp. 73–75, *supra*. If so, Muskrat would lack contemporary significance. Yet the Supreme Court regularly cites the decision as authority for the meaning of Article III. See, *e.g.*, Students for Fair Admissions v. Harvard, 600 U.S. 181, 199 (2023); Whole Woman's Health v. Jackson, 595 U.S. 30, 39 (2021); TransUnion LLC v. Ramirez, 594

---

[6] The following year the Court decided the same substantive issues in a different case, which sought an injunction against federal officials to prevent them from carrying out their duties under the 1906 statute. Gritts v. Fisher, 224 U.S. 640 (1912). The Court in Muskrat briefly mentioned these pending suits. 219 U.S. at 362 ("Nor can it make any difference that the petitioners had brought suits in the supreme court of the District of Columbia to enjoin the Secretary of the Interior from carrying into effect the legislation subsequent to the act of July 1, 1902, which suits were pending when the jurisdictional act here involved was passed. The latter act must depend upon its own terms and be judged by the authority which it undertakes to confer.").

U.S. 413, 426 (2021); Steel Co. v. Citizens for a Better Environment, 523 U.S. 83, 101 (1998); Raines v. Byrd, 521 U.S. 811, 819 (1997).

(5) Parties in Agreement. If one party agrees with the position of the other, does that necessarily preclude the presence of a case or controversy?

(a) In Moore v. Charlotte-Mecklenburg Bd. of Educ., 402 U.S. 47 (1971), "confronted with the anomaly that both litigants desire precisely the same result, namely, a holding that the anti-busing statute is constitutional," the Court held that "[t]here is, therefore, no case or controversy within the meaning of Art. III of the Constitution."[7]

How does Moore square with the accepted judicial practice of entering consent decrees, resulting from a negotiated settlement among the parties, that are invested with the force of law? See, *e.g.*, New Hampshire v. Maine, 426 U.S. 363 (1976). See generally Morley, *Consent of the Governed or Consent of the Government? The Problems with Consent Decrees in Government-Defendant Cases*, 16 U.Pa.J.Const.L. 637 (2014); Morley, *Non-Contentious Jurisdiction and Consent Decrees*, 19 U.Pa.J.Const.L.Online 1 (2016); Schwarzschild, *Public Law by Private Bargain: Title VII Decrees and the Fairness of Negotiated Institutional Reform*, 1984 Duke L.J. 887, 902–03.[8] Of granting uncontested naturalization decrees? See Tutun v. United States, 270 U.S. 568 (1926) p. 114, *supra*. Of expunging convictions? For an illuminating discussion of issues raised by practices such as these, see Resnik, *Whose Judgment? Vacating Judgments, Preferences for Settlement, and the Role of Adjudication at the Close of the Twentieth Century*, 41 UCLA L.Rev. 1471 (1994).

(b) Issues arising from agreement among the parties have frequently drawn notice in cases involving the government. Government counsel who becomes convinced that the other side deserves to prevail can settle a case before judgment or, if the government is seeking review, withdraw the

---

[7] As authority, the Court cited Muskrat v. United States, Paragraph (4), *supra*. Did the Court cite Muskrat fairly?

[8] The threat of "collusion" in framing consent decrees may be particularly acute in mass tort litigation. See, *e.g.*, Coffee, *Class Wars: The Dilemma of the Mass Tort Class Action*, 95 Colum.L.Rev. 1343 (1995), arguing that corporate defendants often prefer to be sued in class actions (in order to establish an upper limit on liability, for example), and sometimes collude with accommodating plaintiffs' attorneys to arrange for such suits to be filed—and then settled on favorable terms—by nominal plaintiffs.

The Supreme Court addressed related issues concerning Federal Rule of Civil Procedure 23 in Amchem Products, Inc. v. Windsor, 521 U.S. 591 (1997). After holding that the existence of a settlement agreement was "relevant to class certification," the Court ruled that requirements of Rule 23 "designed to protect absentees by blocking unwarranted or overbroad class definition * * * demand undiluted, even heightened, attention in the settlement context," since there is no opportunity for the court "to adjust the class, informed by proceedings as they unfold." See also Ortiz v. Fibreboard Corp., 527 U.S. 815 (1999) (applying the heightened scrutiny of settlement classes and refusing to certify a settlement class under Rule 23(b)(3)).

The Class Action Fairness Act of 2005 sought to address some of the concerns about collusion. See Pub.L.No. 109–2, 109th Cong., 1st Sess., 119 Stat. 4 (2005). For example, the Act requires that appropriate state and federal officials receive notice and an opportunity to comment on proposed class settlements. See 28 U.S.C. § 1715. See also S.Rep. No. 14, 109th Cong., 1st Sess. 35 (2005), as reprinted in 2005 U.S.C.C.A.N. 3, 34 (arguing that the notice required by § 1715 "will * * * deter collusion between class counsel and defendants to craft settlements that do not benefit the injured parties"). For further discussion of the Act, see Chap. VIII, Sec. 4, *infra*.

appeal or other petition. When the government has prevailed below, the problem becomes stickier; in a number of such instances the Solicitor General has confessed error in the judgment and asked the Supreme Court to vacate or reverse. These confessions have historically been accepted by the Court in many cases, but not without complication or controversy: The Court has sometimes recited that it accepts a confession of error "upon an independent examination of the record." See, *e.g.*, Pope v. United States, 392 U.S. 651 (1968); Rosengart v. Laird, 405 U.S. 908 (1972). In some cases dissenting Justices have objected to accepting confessions of error, for instance where the Court did not independently examine the record, or where the confession of error is incomplete. without independent review of the record. See, *e.g.*, Nunez v. United States, 554 U.S. 911 (2008) (Scalia, J., dissenting); Lawrence v. Chater, 516 U.S. 163, 176–92 (1996) (Scalia, J., dissenting); Mariscal v. United States, 449 U.S. 405 (1981) (Rehnquist, J., dissenting); Watts v. United States, 422 U.S. 1032, 1032 (1975) (Burger, C.J., dissenting); Casey v. United States, 343 U.S. 808, 808 (1952) (Douglas, J., dissenting). And in Grzegorczyk v. United States, 142 S. Ct. 2580 (2022), the Court refused to accept a confession of error by the government, with five justices stating that because the lower court's decision was correct, "this Court has no appropriate legal basis to vacate the * * * judgment." *Id.* 2580 (Statement of Justice Kavanaugh, joined by Chief Justice Roberts, Justice Thomas, Justice Alito, and Justice Barrett). Those justices further stated that because the President has broad power to grant pardons and commutations, "the Executive Branch therefore has no need to enlist the judiciary, or to ask the Judiciary to depart from standard practices and procedure." A four-justice dissent (by Justice Sotomayor, joined by Justices Breyer, Kagan, and Gorsuch) disagreed with this approach and complained that "the Court appears to be quietly constricting its GVR practice."

(c)   What are the justiciability implications of the executive's decision to enforce a statute whose constitutionality it will not defend? In United States v. Windsor, 570 U.S. 744 (2013), the plaintiff, who had entered a lawful same-sex marriage, challenged the constitutionality of § 3 of the Defense of Marriage Act (DOMA), 110 Stat. 2419, which excluded partners in a same-sex marriage from the definition of "spouse" for federal law purposes. This provision rendered Windsor ineligible for the "surviving spouse" exclusion from the federal estate tax. Windsor paid $363,053 in federal estate taxes under protest and filed suit in federal district court challenging DOMA and seeking a refund.

While the case was pending, the President instructed the Department of Justice not to defend the constitutionality of § 3 of DOMA. He simultaneously directed the executive branch to continue to enforce § 3 and thus to refuse to provide the refund. The President's directive made clear that this approach was designed to "recogniz[e] the judiciary as the final arbiter" of constitutionality. The House committee that advises the Speaker of the House on legal matters—the Bipartisan Legal Advisory Group (BLAG)—intervened in the district court to defend the statute's constitutionality.

The district court found § 3 unconstitutional and ordered the Treasury to refund the plaintiff's estate tax payments. Although the United States agreed with the merits of the district court's decision, it refused to comply with the judgment and appealed to the Second Circuit. After the Second Circuit affirmed, the United States sought review in the Supreme Court.

In an opinion by Justice Kennedy (joined by Justices Ginsburg, Breyer, Sotomayor, and Kagan), the Court found that a justiciable controversy existed between Windsor and the United States. The Court reasoned that whatever commonality the parties had concerning the law, the government's continued enforcement of § 3 meant that Windsor's "injury (failure to obtain a refund allegedly required by law) was concrete, persisting, and unredressed." The United States continued to have a justiciable interest in the suit as well; however much the government might welcome a ruling that § 3 is unconstitutional, such a ruling would inflict injury upon it by requiring a refund of several hundred thousand dollars in taxes.

In the Court's view, the parties' agreement that DOMA was unconstitutional implicated only the "prudential limits" that the judiciary has traditionally placed on the exercise of its own power. See pp. 95–96, *supra*, & pp. 207–208, *infra*. Thus, the Court needed only to assure itself that the case presented the concrete adverseness necessary to ensure sharp presentation of the issues. Here, the fact that the attorneys for BLAG presented "a substantial argument" for DOMA's constitutionality fully addressed "the 'prudential concerns' that might otherwise counsel against hearing" a case in this unusual posture.[9] The Court added that a failure to address the question presented would leave the district courts in "94 districts throughout the Nation * * * without precedential guidance not only in tax refund suits but also in cases involving the whole of DOMA's sweep involving over 1,000 federal statutes and a myriad of federal regulations." Finally, Justice Kennedy's opinion emphasized that "if the Executive's agreement with a plaintiff that a law is unconstitutional is enough to preclude judicial review, then the Supreme Court's primary role in determining the constitutionality of a law that has inflicted real injury on a plaintiff * * * would become only secondary to the President's."

In a dissent joined by Chief Justice Roberts and Justice Thomas, Justice Scalia wrote that "[i]n the more than two centuries that this Court has existed * * *, we have never suggested that we have the power to decide a question when every party agrees with both its nominal opponent *and the court below* on that question's answer." In Justice Scalia's view, the matter should not have come before the judiciary in this posture, and the proper course for the government was to decline to enforce a statute that it regarded as unconstitutional. He concluded by stressing that Justice Kennedy's concern about preserving the Court's law declaration function conflicted with

---

9   Having determined that the suit between Windsor and the United States satisfied constitutional and prudential requirements for standings, the Court found it unnecessary to determine whether BLAG would have standing in its own right. Because Justice Scalia and Alito found that there was no justiciable controversy between Windsor and the United States, both found it necessary to address the question whether BLAG had standing to oppose Windsor on appeal. For discussion, see pp. 217–218, *infra*.

the founders' vision of the Court as a dispute resolver and reflected an ahistorical "desire to place this Court at the center of the Nation's life."

---

3. SOME PROBLEMS OF STANDING TO SUE

A. PLAINTIFFS' STANDING

INTRODUCTORY NOTE

Standing is one of the key components of the modern definition of the judicial power to decide "cases" or "controversies." Standing doctrine rations the exercise of judicial power by determining *who* is entitled to invoke the power of the federal courts to decide cases. In particular, under modern Supreme Court doctrine, a plaintiff wishing to sue in federal court must be able to identify a concrete injury (a) that he or she has sustained, (b) that the defendant has caused, and (c) that a properly framed judicial decree can redress. Despite the clarity with which the Court articulates the elements of standing, the Constitution contains no Standing Clause. Nor does any one specific standing doctrine run deep in our history. Among the many questions raised by the following materials are these: What structural, functional, and other arguments might justify the Court's current doctrine? How much do conventional rationales for standing doctrine help us evaluate how to apply the doctrine in particular cases?

Frothingham v. Mellon
262 U.S. 447 (1923).
Appeal from the Court of Appeals of the District of Columbia.

■ MR. JUSTICE SUTHERLAND delivered the opinion of the Court.

[The case was an appeal of a request by Harriet Frothingham for an injunction against the enforcement of a federal statute: the Maternity Act, 42 Stat. 224 (1921), which provided federal spending "to reduce maternal and infant mortality and protect the health of mothers and infants." It was decided along with a similarly unsuccessful suit filed by the state of Massachusetts in the Supreme Court's original jurisdiction, discussed at p. 212, *infra*.]

[T]his plaintiff alleges * * * that she is a taxpayer of the United States; and her contention, though not clear, seems to be that the effect of the appropriations complained of will be to increase the burden of future taxation and thereby take her property without due process of law. The right of a taxpayer to enjoin the execution of a federal appropriation act, on the ground that it is invalid and will result in taxation for illegal purposes, has never been passed upon by this court. * * * [The taxpayer's] interest in the moneys of the treasury—partly realized from taxation and partly from other sources—is shared with millions of others, is comparatively minute and indeterminable, and the effect upon future taxation, of any payment out of the funds, so remote, fluctuating and uncertain, that no basis is afforded for an appeal to the preventive powers of a court of equity.

The administration of any statute, likely to produce additional taxation to be imposed upon a vast number of taxpayers, the extent of whose several liability is indefinite and constantly changing, is essentially a matter of public and not of individual concern. If one taxpayer may champion and litigate such a cause, then every other taxpayer may do the same, not only in respect of the statute here under review, but also in respect of every other appropriation act and statute whose administration requires the outlay of public money, and whose validity may be questioned. The bare suggestion of such a result, with its attendant inconveniences, goes far to sustain the conclusion which we have reached, that a suit of this character cannot be maintained. * * *

The functions of government under our system are apportioned. To the legislative department has been committed the duty of making laws, to the executive the duty of executing them, and to the judiciary the duty of interpreting and applying them in cases properly brought before the courts. * * * We have no power per se to review and annul acts of Congress on the ground that they are unconstitutional. That question may be considered only when the justification for some direct injury suffered or threatened, presenting a justiciable issue, is made to rest upon such an act. Then the power exercised is that of ascertaining and declaring the law applicable to the controversy. It amounts to little more than the negative power to disregard an unconstitutional enactment, which otherwise would stand in the way of the enforcement of a legal right. The party who invokes the power must be able to show, not only that the statute is invalid, but that he has sustained or is immediately in danger of sustaining some direct injury as the result of its enforcement, and not merely that he suffers in some indefinite way in common with people generally. If a case for preventive relief be presented, the court enjoins, in effect, not the execution of the statute, but the acts of the official, the statute notwithstanding. Here the parties plaintiff have no such case. Looking through forms of words to the substance of their complaint, it is merely that officials of the executive department of the government are executing and will execute an act of Congress asserted to be unconstitutional; and this we are asked to prevent. To do so would be, not to decide a judicial controversy, but to assume a position of authority over the governmental acts of another and coequal department, an authority which plainly we do not possess. * * *

NOTE ON THE DEVELOPMENT OF STANDING DOCTRINE

(1) The Modern Origins of Standing Doctrine. Although one can identify at least some apparent precursors to modern standing doctrine in cases such as Frothingham, "[t]he word '*standing*' * * * does not appear to have been commonly used until the middle of * * * [the twentieth] century." Vining, Legal Identity: The Coming of Age of Public Law 55 (1978).[1] The absence of such discussion should perhaps come as little surprise. Traditionally, most litigants had challenged official action on the ground that it unlawfully invaded legal interests plainly recognized at common law, such as contract and property rights, and they made such challenges through well-established forms in common law and equity. See Stewart, *The Reformation of American Administrative Law*, 88 Harv.L.Rev. 1667, 1717–18, 1723–24 (1975); Bellia, *Article III and the Cause of Action*, 89 Iowa L.Rev. 777, 817–18 (2004).[2]

During the twentieth century, courts became self-conscious about the concept of standing only after developments in the legal culture subjected the traditional model to unfamiliar strains. One of these strains came from transformations in the nature of legal rights: the advent of the administrative state brought the enactment of statutes to protect interests, unprotected at common law, that were shared by large numbers of people.[3] Shortly thereafter, courts also increasingly recognized substantive constitutional rights, such as voting rights and rights to educational equality, that were broadly shared and that were not associated with the kind of liberty or property interests protected by the common law. A second development was the transformation in the nature of procedures and remedies in federal courts. See Baude & Bray, *Proper Parties, Proper Relief*, 137 Harv.L.Rev. 153, 153–54 (2023). The distinctive technical forms of the common law and equity were merged into a single capacious and flexible civil action. And injunctions on issues of public law, especially pre-enforcement injunctions brought as a substitute for defensive litigation, became more routine. Taken together, these transformations caused courts to confront many lawsuits that were quite distant from the traditional common law model. Such lawsuits naturally raised the question of whether the separation of powers imposed any limits on the federal courts' role to oversee these transformations.

(2) Other Early Cases. There were other cases in the first half of the twentieth century that, like Frothingham, denied judicial review because the

---

[1]   On the history of standing as a concept, see Winter, *The Metaphor of Standing and the Problem of Self-Governance*, 40 Stan.L.Rev. 1371, 1418–25 (1988).

[2]   At times, the prerogative writs or other forms of action seem to have permitted suit by litigants not asserting traditional common law interests. See pp. 200–201, *infra*. For the intriguing suggestion that the legal system's earlier focus on common law causes of action and prerogative writs would provide a more workable framework than contemporary standing law's emphasis on injury in fact, see Mashaw, *Rethinking Judicial Review of Administrative Action: A Nineteenth Century Perspective*, 32 Cardozo L.Rev. 2241 (2011). Professor Mashaw adds that Congress should have the authority to supplement these nineteenth century sources with fresh statutory causes of action. For further discussion of this possibility, see pp. 166–210, *infra*.

[3]   See generally Sunstein, *Standing and the Privatization of Public Law*, 88 Colum.L.Rev. 1432 (1988).

plaintiffs lacked what we would now call "standing." Consider these examples and ask what principles emerge from them.

(a)   In Fairchild v. Hughes, 258 U.S. 128 (1922), a citizen of New York sought an injunction against the U.S. Secretary of State and Attorney General declaring that the recently-ratified Nineteenth Amendment was void. The Court refused his claim, writing that Fairchild's "alleged interest in the question submitted is not such as to afford a basis for this proceeding. * * * In form it is a bill in equity; but it is not a case, within the meaning of section 2 of article 3 of the Constitution, which confers judicial power on the federal courts." The Court emphasized that the plaintiff had no claim that the Amendment would directly affect his individual or private rights. "Plaintiff has only the right, possessed by every citizen, to require that the government be administered according to law and that the public moneys be not wasted. Obviously this general right does not entitle a private citizen to institute in the federal courts a suit to secure by indirection a determination whether a statute, if passed, or a constitutional amendment, about to be adopted, will be valid."[4]

(b)   In Ex parte Levitt, 302 U.S. 633 (1937), a member of the Supreme Court bar moved to have the appointment of Justice Hugo Black declared null and void under Article I, Section 6, Clause 2 of the Constitution. The Court rejected it, citing Mellon and Fairchild, among other cases: "The motion papers disclose no interest upon the part of the petitioner other than that of a citizen and a member of the bar of this Court. That is insufficient. It is an established principle that to entitle a private individual to invoke the judicial power to determine the validity of executive or legislative action he must show that he has sustained, or is immediately in danger of sustaining, a direct injury as the result of that action and it is not sufficient that he has merely a general interest common to all members of the public."

(c)   In Tileston v. Ullman, 318 U.S. 44 (1943), a Connecticut doctor sought a declaratory judgment in state court that the state's ban on contraception was unconstitutional. The Supreme Court declined to hear his appeal on standing grounds: "We are of the opinion that the proceedings in the state courts present no constitutional question which appellant has standing to assert. The sole constitutional attack upon the statutes under the Fourteenth Amendment is confined to their deprivation of life—obviously not appellant's but his patients'. There is no allegation or proof that appellant's life is in danger. His patients are not parties to this proceeding and there is no basis on which we can say that he has standing to secure an adjudication of his patients' constitutional right to life, which they do not assert in their own behalf." For more modern cases on standing to assert the rights of others in federal court, see pp. 227–229, *infra*.

All of these early cases concluded that the plaintiffs lacked the injury or interest necessary to invoke federal jurisdiction. How much do they tell us

---

[4]   The Court did reach and reject the Nineteenth Amendment challenge in another case decided the same day, Leser v. Garnett, 268 U.S. 130 (1922), where the plaintiffs had exercised their statutory rights under Maryland law to challenge a voter's registration as invalid. For the context of this litigation, see Siegel, *She the People: The Nineteenth Amendment, Sex Equality, Federalism, and the Family*, 115 Harv.L.Rev. 947, 1003–06 (2002).

about what kind of injury or interest is necessary, and what kind would be sufficient?

NOTE ON TAXPAYER STANDING

(1) One specific line of standing cases that grew out of Frothingham considers whether a taxpayer has standing to challenge expenditures from the public fisc. In Frothingham the Court answered no, concluding that the plaintiff's "interest in the moneys of the [federal] treasury" was "comparatively minute and indeterminable" and that "the effect upon future taxation of any payment out of" federal funds was "remote, fluctuating and uncertain."

(2) In Flast v. Cohen, 392 U.S. 83 (1968), a suit by federal taxpayers alleging that a federal statute violated the Establishment Clause by providing financial support for educational programs in religious schools, the Court distinguished Frothingham and upheld standing. Emphasizing that standing turns on "whether the dispute sought to be adjudicated will be presented in an adversary context and in a form historically viewed as capable of judicial resolution," Chief Justice Warren concluded that Frothingham did not erect "an absolute bar" to federal taxpayer standing. Rather, the problem at hand entailed "determining the circumstances under which a federal taxpayer will be deemed to have [the requisite] personal stake and interest" to satisfy those criteria. In a case in which standing rested upon the plaintiff's status (*e.g.*, as taxpayer), the Court reasoned that part of its task was "to determine whether there was a logical nexus between the status asserted and the claim sought to be adjudicated." The Court continued: "The nexus demanded of federal taxpayers has two aspects to it. First, the taxpayer must establish a logical link between that status and the type of legislative enactment attacked. * * * Secondly, the taxpayer must establish a nexus between that status and the precise nature of the constitutional infringement alleged."

On the facts, the Court found both nexus requirements to be satisfied. It perceived a link between taxpayer status and the alleged "unconstitutionality only of exercises of congressional power under the taxing and spending clause of Art. I, § 8 of the Constitution." With respect to the second nexus, the Court found that the Establishment Clause at least partly resulted from concern that "the taxing and spending power would be used to favor one religion over another or to support religion in general." The Court thus distinguished Frothingham as involving no allegation that Congress "had breached a specific limitation upon its taxing and spending power."

Dissenting, Justice Harlan argued that "the Court's standard for the determination of standing," which focused on whether the plaintiff had the requisite personal stake in the outcome, was "entirely unrelated" to its double nexus test for whether this standard was satisfied. "I am quite unable to understand how, if a taxpayer believes that a given public expenditure is unconstitutional, and if he seeks to vindicate that belief in a federal court, his interest in the suit can be said necessarily to vary according to [the nature of the spending program that he attacks or] the constitutional provision under which he states his claim."

Justice Harlan was correct, wasn't he, about the transparent artificiality of Flast's double-nexus test for taxpayer standing? How is that artificiality to be explained? Surely, Flast fits uneasily, at best, with the traditional, dispute resolution model of standing that underlay Frothingham. The concurring opinions in Flast disagreed about how to reconcile it with Frothingham. Justice Douglas wrote that it would "be the part of wisdom, as I see the problem, to be rid of Frothingham here and now." Justice Stewart and Justice Fortas, however, each thought that the Establishment Clause created a special distinction from the general rule against taxpayer standing. Justice Stewart argued that the Establishment Clause, unlike Article I, created "a personal constitutional right not to be taxed for the support of a religious institution," which meant that the plaintiffs "have a clear stake as taxpayers in assuring that they not be compelled to contribute" to an establishment. Flast v. Cohen, *supra*, 392 U.S. at 107 (Stewart, J., concurring). And Justice Fortas emphasized that "[t]he status of taxpayer should not be accepted as a launching pad for an attack upon any target other than legislation affecting the Establishment Clause." *Id.* at 116 (Fortas, J., concurring).

(3) In the years following Flast v. Cohen, it became clear that Flast would not expand to other forms of federal citizen and taxpayer standing. Nor did it even fully settle the scope of taxpayer standing under the Establishment Clause itself. In Valley Forge Christian College v. Americans United for Separation of Church and State, Inc., 454 U.S. 464 (1982), plaintiffs challenged an *executive* decision to transfer surplus property worth $577,500 to a religious institution.[1] The Court ruled that the taxpayer plaintiffs failed the first prong of Flast's test—permitting challenges only to "exercises of congressional power under the taxing and spending clause"—for two reasons: first, "the source of their complaint is not a congressional action, but a decision by HEW to transfer a parcel of federal property"; second, the authorizing statute was "an * * * exercise of Congress's power under the Property Clause, Art. IV, § 3, cl. 2," rather than under the Taxing and Spending Clause. In dissent, Justice Brennan rejected the Court's distinction of Flast as unconvincing.

(4) The Roberts Court has divided over the continuing reach of Flast v. Cohen and over whether it remains—or should remain—good law. In Hein v. Freedom from Religion Foundation, Inc., 551 U.S. 587 (2007), a plurality read Flast narrowly. The President, by executive order, had created a White House office and several centers within federal agencies to ensure that faith-based community groups would be eligible to apply for federal funding for activities that were not inherently religious. Suing as taxpayers, the

---

[1]   On Valley Forge, see Nichol, *Standing on the Constitution: The Supreme Court and Valley Forge*, 61 N.C.L.Rev. 798 (1983). For earlier commentary on taxpayer standing, see Bittker, *The Case of the Fictitious Taxpayer: The Federal Taxpayer's Suit Twenty Years After Flast v. Cohen*, 36 U.Chi.L.Rev. 364 (1969); Davis, *The Case of the Real Taxpayer: A Reply to Professor Bittker*, 36 U.Chi.L.Rev. 375 (1969).

respondents challenged a number of executive actions that, they said, violated the Establishment Clause by expending public funds to promote religious community groups over secular ones. The plurality opinion by Justice Alito, joined by Chief Justice Roberts and Justice Kennedy, held Flast distinguishable on the ground that the expenditures at issue were not made pursuant to any specific Act of Congress, as in Flast, but rather occurred under general appropriations to the Executive Branch.

Concurring in the judgment, Justice Scalia (joined by Justice Thomas) argued that Flast ultimately rested on the principle, indefensible in his view, that "Psychic Injury," rather than "Wallet Injury," sufficed to establish standing. Arguing that efforts to distinguish Flast had been arbitrary and unconvincing, he maintained that the precedent's lack of a logical theoretical underpinning should lead it to be overruled. Justice Souter's dissent (joined by Justices Stevens, Ginsburg, and Breyer) agreed that efforts to distinguish Flast were unconvincing and contended that the respondents sought "not to 'extend' Flast, but merely to apply it. When executive agencies spend identifiable sums of tax money for religious purposes, no less than when Congress authorizes the same thing, taxpayers suffer injury."

(5) In Arizona Christian School Tuition Org. v. Winn, 563 U.S. 125 (2011), the Court again divided over Flast's meaning. Under Arizona law, taxpayers earn tax credits for money they contribute to "school tuition organizations" (STOs) that fund scholarships for children attending private schools, including sectarian ones. Arizona taxpayers challenged the state statute, arguing that it violates the Establishment Clause. In an opinion by Justice Kennedy, a closely divided Court held that the plaintiffs could not "take advantage of Flast's narrow exception to the general rule against taxpayer standing." In particular, the Court noted that Flast had relied on James Madison's influential Memorial and Remonstrance Against Religious Assessments (1785), which had objected to public funding for religion on the ground that it "would coerce [taxpayers into] a form of religious devotion in violation of conscience." Since the STO program consisted entirely of voluntary contributions by taxpayers, the Court reasoned that, in contrast with the expenditures challenged in Flast, the program did not forcibly extract money from religious dissenters.

In dissent, Justice Kagan, joined by Justices Ginsburg, Breyer, and Sotomayor, argued that the Court's position was unsupported by precedent or fiscal reality. In particular, she emphasized that the Court had resolved five cases involving state tax expenditures (the use of tax relief rather than direct expenditures to achieve public purposes) but had not once questioned Flast's applicability. In addition, she maintained that "targeted tax breaks" are economically no different from a direct appropriation because each requires the diversion of tax revenues to support religion. As Justice Kagan elaborated, "Suppose a State desires to reward Jews—by, say, $500 per year—for their religious devotion. Should the nature of the taxpayers' concern vary if the State allows Jews to claim the aid on their tax returns in lieu of receiving an annual stipend?" Justice Kagan would have reaffirmed Flast and upheld standing in Winn. In an opinion concurring in the Court's opinion, Justices Scalia and Thomas again urged that Flast be overruled.

(6) Has the Court engaged in a "stealth" overruling of Flast by drawing thin, and sometimes arbitrary, distinctions that essentially limit Flast to its facts? See, *e.g.*, Friedman, *The Wages of Stealth Overruling (With Particular Attention to Miranda v. Arizona)*, 99 Geo.L.J. 1, 9–11, 34–36, 47–49 (2010); Sherry, *The Four Pillars of Constitutional Doctrine*, 32 Cardozo L.Rev. 969, 977–81 (2011). Or, has the narrowing of Flast saved it? See Re, *Narrowing Precedent in the Supreme Court*, 114 Colum.L.Rev. 1861, 1894–95 (2014) ("Having been narrowed down to its core, *Flast* may at last have achieved a secure status in precedent."). Rather than a change in approach to standing doctrine, does the narrowing of Flast instead suggest a shift in the Court's approach to the underlying First Amendment issues? If so, what does that suggest about the Court's overall approach to standing?

(7) Finally, consider how the arguments for or against *federal* taxpayer standing apply to *state* or *municipal* taxpayers.

Frothingham distinguished earlier cases endorsing municipal taxpayer standing, such as Crampton v. Zabriskie, 101 U.S. 601, 609 (1879), arguing that "The interest of a taxpayer of a municipality in the application of its moneys is direct and immediate," and that "the reasons which support the extension of the equitable remedy to a single taxpayer in such cases are based upon the peculiar relation of the corporate taxpayer to the corporation, which is not without some resemblance to that subsisting between stockholder and private corporation." Subsequent cases such as Everson v. Board of Education, 330 U.S. 1 (1947), continued to allow municipal taxpayer suits.

Although municipal taxpayer standing doctrine is well settled, the Court has not applied it without reservation. In Doremus v. Board of Education, 342 U.S. 429 (1952), the Court refused to recognize a (state and) municipal taxpayer's standing to challenge a state statute requiring teachers to read five verses of the Old Testament, without comment, at the beginning of each school day. The plaintiffs had nowhere alleged that reading the verses would add to school costs. On review from the state supreme court, the Court's 6–3 decision reasoned: "The taxpayer's action can meet [the case-or-controversy] test * * * only when it is a good-faith pocketbook action. It is apparent that the grievance which it is sought to litigate here is not a direct dollars-and-cents injury but is a religious difference. If appellants established the requisite special injury necessary to a taxpayer's case or controversy, it would not matter that their dominant inducement to action was more religious than mercenary. It is not a question of motivation but of possession of the requisite financial interest that is, or is threatened to be, injured by the unconstitutional conduct."

Doremus also rejected state taxpayer standing, noting that absent "direct pecuniary injury, * * * what the [Frothingham] Court said of a federal statute is equally true when a state Act is assailed." The Court has repeatedly upheld that line of demarcation. See, *e.g.*, DaimlerChrysler Corp. v. Cuno, 547 U.S. 332, 345 (2006); ASARCO Inc. v. Kadish, 490 U.S. 605, 613–14 (1989) (plurality opinion). Is it obvious that a municipal taxpayer's stake in the constitutionality of a local expenditure or tax subsidy is more particularized or less conjectural than a state taxpayer's stake in a comparable state policy? In light of the modern regulatory power of municipalities, is Frothingham's analogy to the stockholder of a private corporation still valid?

INTRODUCTORY NOTE ON MODERN STANDING DOCTRINE

The Supreme Court's modern standing doctrine has generally hardened into requiring the plaintiff to make three related but separate showings: an injury in fact, traceability of the injury to the challenged action; and the redressability of that injury by a favorable ruling and appropriate remedy. In reading the cases and notes that follow, consider the operation of these standing requirements as well as the functions that they serve.

Clapper v. Amnesty International
568 U.S. 398 (2013).
Appeal from the Court of Appeals of the Second Circuit.

■ JUSTICE ALITO delivered the opinion of the Court.

Section 702 of the Foreign Intelligence Surveillance Act of 1978 allows the Attorney General and the Director of National Intelligence to acquire foreign intelligence information by jointly authorizing the surveillance of individuals who are not "United States persons" and are reasonably believed to be located outside the United States. Before doing so, the Attorney General and the Director of National Intelligence normally must obtain the Foreign Intelligence Surveillance Court's approval. Respondents are United States persons whose work, they allege, requires them to engage in sensitive international communications with individuals who they believe are likely targets of surveillance under § 1881a. Respondents seek a declaration that § 1881a is unconstitutional, as well as an injunction against § 1881a-authorized surveillance. The question before us is whether respondents have Article III standing to seek this prospective relief.

Respondents assert that they can establish injury in fact because there is an objectively reasonable likelihood that their communications will be acquired under § 1881a at some point in the future. But respondents' theory of future injury is too speculative to satisfy the well-established requirement that threatened injury must be "certainly impending." *E.g.*, Whitmore v. Arkansas, 495 U.S. 149, 158 (1990). And even if respondents could demonstrate that the threatened injury is certainly impending, they still would not be able to establish that this injury is fairly traceable to § 1881a. As an alternative argument, respondents contend that they are suffering present injury because the risk of § 1881a-authorized surveillance already has forced them to take costly and burdensome measures to protect the confidentiality of their international communications. But respondents cannot manufacture standing by choosing to make expenditures based on hypothetical future harm that is not certainly impending. We therefore hold that respondents lack Article III standing. * * *

II

Article III of the Constitution limits federal courts' jurisdiction to certain "Cases" and "Controversies." As we have explained, "[n]o principle is more fundamental to the judiciary's proper role in our system of government than the constitutional limitation of federal-court jurisdiction to actual cases or controversies." DaimlerChrysler Corp. v. Cuno, 547 U.S. 332, 341 (2006) (internal quotation marks omitted). * * *

The law of Article III standing, which is built on separation-of-powers principles, serves to prevent the judicial process from being used to usurp the powers of the political branches. In keeping with the purpose of this doctrine, "[o]ur standing inquiry has been especially rigorous when reaching the merits of the dispute would force us to decide whether an action taken by one of the other two branches of the Federal Government was unconstitutional." Raines [v. Byrd, 521 U.S. 811,] 819–820 [(1997)]. "Relaxation of standing requirements is directly related to the expansion of judicial power," United States v. Richardson, 418 U.S. 166, 188 (1974) (Powell, J., concurring), and we have often found a lack of standing in cases in which the Judiciary has been requested to review actions of the political branches in the fields of intelligence gathering and foreign affairs, see, *e.g.*, Richardson, *supra*, at 167–170 (plaintiff lacked standing to challenge the constitutionality of a statute permitting the Central Intelligence Agency to account for its expenditures solely on the certificate of the CIA Director); Schlesinger [v. Reservists Comm. to Stop the War, 418 U.S. 208,] 209–211 [(1974)] (plaintiffs lacked standing to challenge the Armed Forces Reserve membership of Members of Congress); Laird v. Tatum, 408 U.S. 1, 11–16 (1972) (plaintiffs lacked standing to challenge an Army intelligence-gathering program).

To establish Article III standing, an injury must be "concrete, particularized, and actual or imminent; fairly traceable to the challenged action; and redressable by a favorable ruling." Monsanto Co. v. Geertson Seed Farms, 561 U.S. 139, [150] (2010). "Although imminence is concededly a somewhat elastic concept, it cannot be stretched beyond its purpose, which is to ensure that the alleged injury is not too speculative for Article III purposes—that the injury is certainly impending." [Lujan v. Defenders of Wildlife, 504 U.S. 555,] 565, n. 2 [(1992)]. Thus, we have repeatedly reiterated that "threatened injury must be certainly impending to constitute injury in fact," and that "[a]llegations of possible future injury" are not sufficient. Whitmore, 495 U.S., at 158.

III

A

Respondents assert that they can establish injury in fact that is fairly traceable to § 1881a because there is an objectively reasonable likelihood that their communications with their foreign contacts will be intercepted under § 1881a at some point in the future. This argument fails. * * * As discussed below, respondents' theory of standing, which relies on a highly attenuated chain of possibilities, does not satisfy the requirement that threatened injury must be certainly impending. Moreover, even if respondents could demonstrate injury in fact, the second link in the above-described chain of contingencies—which amounts to mere speculation about whether surveillance would be under § 1881a or some other authority—shows that respondents cannot satisfy the requirement that any injury in fact must be fairly traceable to § 1881a.

First, it is speculative whether the Government will imminently target communications to which respondents are parties. * * *

[R]espondents have no actual knowledge of the Government's § 1881a targeting practices. Instead, respondents merely speculate and make assumptions about whether their communications with their foreign contacts will be acquired under § 1881a. For example, journalist Christopher Hedges states: "I have no choice but to assume that any of my international communications may be subject to government surveillance, and I have to make decisions . . . in light of that assumption." * * * "The party invoking federal jurisdiction bears the burden of establishing" standing—and, at the summary judgment stage, such a party "can no longer rest on . . . 'mere allegations,' but must 'set forth' by affidavit or other evidence 'specific facts.'" Defenders of Wildlife, 504 U.S., at 561. Respondents, however, have set forth no specific facts demonstrating that the communications of their foreign contacts will be targeted. Moreover, because § 1881a at most authorizes—but does not mandate or direct—the surveillance that respondents fear, respondents' allegations are necessarily conjectural. See United Presbyterian Church in U.S.A. v. Reagan, 738 F.2d 1375, 1380 (C.A.D.C.1984) (Scalia, J.); [Amnesty International v. Clapper,] 667 F.3d [163,] 187 [(2011)] (opinion of Raggi, J., [dissenting, below, from denial of rehearing en banc]). Simply put, respondents can only speculate as to how the Attorney General and the Director of National Intelligence will exercise their discretion in determining which communications to target.

Second, even if respondents could demonstrate that the targeting of their foreign contacts is imminent, respondents can only speculate as to whether the Government will seek to use § 1881a-authorized surveillance (rather than other methods) to do so. The Government has numerous other methods of conducting surveillance, none of which is challenged here. * * * Even if respondents could demonstrate that their foreign contacts will imminently be targeted—indeed, even if they could show that interception of their own communications will imminently occur—they would still need to show that their injury is fairly traceable to § 1881a. But, because respondents can only speculate as to whether any (asserted) interception would be under § 1881a or some other authority, they cannot satisfy the "fairly traceable" requirement.

Third, even if respondents could show that the Government will seek the Foreign Intelligence Surveillance Court's authorization to acquire the communications of respondents' foreign contacts under § 1881a, respondents can only speculate as to whether that court will authorize such surveillance. * * *

Fourth, even if the Government were to obtain the Foreign Intelligence Surveillance Court's approval to target respondents' foreign contacts under § 1881a, it is unclear whether the Government would succeed in acquiring the communications of respondents' foreign contacts. And fifth, even if the Government were to conduct surveillance of respondents' foreign contacts, respondents can only speculate as to whether their own communications with their foreign contacts would be incidentally acquired.

In sum, respondents' speculative chain of possibilities does not establish that injury based on potential future surveillance is certainly impending or is fairly traceable to § 1881a.[5]

B

Respondents' alternative argument—namely, that they can establish standing based on the measures that they have undertaken to avoid § 1881a-authorized surveillance—fares no better. Respondents assert that they are suffering ongoing injuries that are fairly traceable to § 1881a because the risk of surveillance under § 1881a requires them to take costly and burdensome measures to protect the confidentiality of their communications. Respondents claim, for instance, that the threat of surveillance sometimes compels them to avoid certain e-mail and phone conversations, to "tal[k] in generalities rather than specifics," or to travel so that they can have in-person conversations. Tr. of Oral Arg. 38. * * *

[R]espondents cannot manufacture standing merely by inflicting harm on themselves based on their fears of hypothetical future harm that is not certainly impending. Any ongoing injuries that respondents are suffering are not fairly traceable to § 1881a.

* * * [A]llowing respondents to bring this action based on costs they incurred in response to a speculative threat would be tantamount to

---

[5]   Our cases do not uniformly require plaintiffs to demonstrate that it is literally certain that the harms they identify will come about. In some instances, we have found standing based on a "substantial risk" that the harm will occur, which may prompt plaintiffs to reasonably incur costs to mitigate or avoid that harm. Monsanto Co. v. Geertson Seed Farms, 561 U.S. 139 (2010). But to the extent that the "substantial risk" standard is relevant and is distinct from the "clearly impending" requirement, respondents fall short of even that standard, in light of the attenuated chain of inferences necessary to find harm here. * * *

accepting a repackaged version of respondents' first failed theory of standing. * * *

IV

* * *

B

Respondents also suggest that they should be held to have standing because otherwise the constitutionality of § 1881a could not be challenged. It would be wrong, they maintain, to "insulate the government's surveillance activities from meaningful judicial review." Brief for Respondents 60. Respondents' suggestion is both legally and factually incorrect. First, " '[t]he assumption that if respondents have no standing to sue, no one would have standing, is not a reason to find standing.' " Valley Forge Christian College [v. Americans United for Separation of Church and State, Inc.,] 454 U.S. [464,] 489 [(1982)]; Schlesinger, 418 U.S., at 227; see also Richardson, 418 U.S., at 179; Raines, 521 U.S., at 835 (Souter, J., joined by Ginsburg, J., concurring in judgment).

Second, our holding today by no means insulates § 1881a from judicial review. * * *

[I]f the Government intends to use or disclose information obtained or derived from a § 1881a acquisition in judicial or administrative proceedings, it must provide advance notice of its intent, and the affected person may challenge the lawfulness of the acquisition. §§ 1806(c), 1806(e), 1881e(a) (2006 ed. and Supp. V). Thus, if the Government were to prosecute one of respondent-attorney's foreign clients using § 1881a-authorized surveillance, the Government would be required to make a disclosure. Although the foreign client might not have a viable Fourth Amendment claim, see, e.g., United States v. Verdugo-Urquidez, 494 U.S. 259, 261 (1990), it is possible that the monitoring of the target's conversations with his or her attorney would provide grounds for a claim of standing on the part of the attorney. Such an attorney would certainly have a stronger evidentiary basis for establishing standing than do respondents in the present case. In such a situation, unlike in the present case, it would at least be clear that the Government had acquired the foreign client's communications using § 1881a-authorized surveillance.

Finally, any electronic communications service provider that the Government directs to assist in § 1881a surveillance may challenge the lawfulness of that directive before the FISC. § 1881a(h)(4), (6). * * *

* * *

We hold that respondents lack Article III standing because they cannot demonstrate that the future injury they purportedly fear is certainly impending and because they cannot manufacture standing by incurring costs in anticipation of non-imminent harm. We therefore reverse the judgment of the Second Circuit and remand the case for further proceedings consistent with this opinion.

It is so ordered.

■ JUSTICE BREYER, with whom JUSTICE GINSBURG, JUSTICE SOTOMAYOR, and JUSTICE KAGAN join, dissenting.

The plaintiffs' standing depends upon the likelihood that the Government, acting under the authority of 50 U.S.C. § 1881a (2006 ed., Supp. V), will harm them by intercepting at least some of their private, foreign, telephone, or e-mail conversations. In my view, this harm is not "speculative." Indeed it is as likely to take place as are most future events that commonsense inference and ordinary knowledge of human nature tell us will happen. This Court has often found the occurrence of similar future events sufficiently certain to support standing. * * *

I

* * * No one here denies that the Government's interception of a private telephone or e-mail conversation amounts to an injury that is "concrete and particularized." Moreover, the plaintiffs, respondents here, seek as relief a judgment declaring unconstitutional (and enjoining enforcement of) a statutory provision authorizing those interceptions; and, such a judgment would redress the injury by preventing it. Thus, the basic question is whether the injury, *i.e.*, the interception, is "actual or imminent." * * *

III

Several considerations, based upon the record along with commonsense inferences, convince me that there is a very high likelihood that Government, acting under the authority of § 1881a, will intercept at least some of the communications just described. First, the plaintiffs have engaged, and continue to engage, in electronic communications of a kind that the 2008 amendment, but not the prior Act, authorizes the Government to intercept. These communications include discussions with family members of those detained at Guantanamo, friends and acquaintances of those persons, and investigators, experts and others with knowledge of circumstances related to terrorist activities. * * *

Second, the plaintiffs have a strong motive to engage in, and the Government has a strong motive to listen to, conversations of the kind described. A lawyer representing a client normally seeks to learn the circumstances surrounding the crime (or the civil wrong) of which the client is accused. * * *

At the same time, the Government has a strong motive to conduct surveillance of conversations that contain material of this kind. The Government, after all, seeks to learn as much as it can reasonably learn about suspected terrorists (such as those detained at Guantanamo), as well as about their contacts and activities, along with those of friends and family members. * * *

Third, the Government's past behavior shows that it has sought, and hence will in all likelihood continue to seek, information about alleged terrorists and detainees through means that include surveillance of electronic communications. * * *

Fourth, the Government has the capacity to conduct electronic surveillance of the kind at issue. * * *

Of course, to exercise this capacity the Government must have intelligence court authorization. But the Government rarely files requests that fail to meet the statutory criteria. * * *

The upshot is that (1) similarity of content, (2) strong motives, (3) prior behavior, and (4) capacity all point to a very strong likelihood that the Government will intercept at least some of the plaintiffs' communications, including some that the 2008 amendment, § 1881a, but not the pre-2008 Act, authorizes the Government to intercept.

* * * One can, of course, always imagine some special circumstance that negates a virtual likelihood, no matter how strong. But the same is true about most, if not all, ordinary inferences about future events. Perhaps, despite pouring rain, the streets will remain dry (due to the presence of a special chemical). But ordinarily a party that seeks to defeat a strong natural inference must bear the burden of showing that some such special circumstance exists. And no one has suggested any such special circumstance here.

Consequently, we need only assume that the Government is doing its job (to find out about, and combat, terrorism) in order to conclude that there is a high probability that the Government will intercept at least some electronic communication to which at least some of the plaintiffs are parties. The majority is wrong when it describes the harm threatened plaintiffs as "speculative."

IV

A

The majority more plausibly says that the plaintiffs have failed to show that the threatened harm is "certainly impending." But, as the majority appears to concede, certainty is not, and never has been, the touchstone of standing. The future is inherently uncertain. Yet federal courts frequently entertain actions for injunctions and for declaratory relief aimed at preventing future activities that are reasonably likely or highly likely, but not absolutely certain, to take place. And that degree of certainty is all that is needed to support standing here. * * *

B

1

* * * Moreover, courts have often found probabilistic injuries sufficient to support standing. * * *

How could the law be otherwise? Suppose that a federal court faced a claim by homeowners that (allegedly) unlawful dam-building practices created a high risk that their homes would be flooded. Would the court deny them standing on the ground that the risk of flood was only 60, rather than 90, percent?

Would federal courts deny standing to a plaintiff in a diversity action who claims an anticipatory breach of contract where the future breach depends on probabilities? The defendant, say, has threatened to load wheat onto a ship bound for India despite a promise to send the wheat to the United States. No one can know for certain that this will happen. Perhaps the defendant will change his mind; perhaps the ship will turn and head for the United States. Yet, despite the uncertainty, the Constitution does not prohibit a federal court from hearing such a claim.

Would federal courts deny standing to a plaintiff who seeks to enjoin as a nuisance the building of a nearby pond which, the plaintiff believes, will very likely, but not inevitably, overflow his land?

Neither do ordinary declaratory judgment actions always involve the degree of certainty upon which the Court insists here. * * *

4

* * * As our case law demonstrates, what the Constitution requires is something more akin to "reasonable probability" or "high probability." The use of some such standard is all that is necessary here to ensure the actual concrete injury that the Constitution demands. * * *

NOTE ON INJURY IN FACT

(1) Injury in Fact: General Principles. As Clapper makes plain, the Court has for many years relied on concrete and personalized injury as a test of Article III standing. The Court's cases have articulated a range of purposes served by the injury-in-fact requirement: (a) ensuring the stakes and the limits of any resulting ruling are well understood;[1] (b) limiting the judicial process to litigants who will be energetic adversaries;[2] (c) assigning the right to sue to those most immediately affected by a government policy in order to ensure that their interests will be adequately represented;[3] (d) protecting democratic prerogatives by ensuring both that the judicial process is invoked only when necessary and that generalized grievances widely shared by the

---

[1] See, *e.g.*, Valley Forge Christian College v. Americans United for Separation of Church and State, Inc., 454 U.S. 464, 475–79 (1982); Schlesinger v. Reservists Committee to Stop the War, 418 U.S. 208, 222 (1974).

[2] See, *e.g.*, Flast v. Cohen, 392 U.S. 83, 101 (1968); Baker v. Carr, 369 U.S. 186, 204 (1962).

[3] See, *e.g.*, Diamond v. Charles, 476 U.S. 54, 62 (1986); Sierra Club v. Morton, 405 U.S. 727, 740 (1972). See also Brilmayer, *The Jurisprudence of Article III: Perspectives on the "Case or Controversy" Requirement*, 93 Harv.L.Rev. 297, 302 (1979).

public are vindicated through the political process;[4] and (e) preserving the constitutional powers of the executive—including the law enforcement authority prescribed by Article II—from unnecessary interference by federal court adjudication.[5] Consider whether the lines drawn by the cases that follow correspond well to these asserted purposes.

(a) In Sierra Club v. Morton, 405 U.S. 727 (1972), the Sierra Club sued the United States Forest Service, claiming that its approval of the development of a ski resort in the Sequoia National Forest violated federal statutes and regulations. Alleging that it had "a special interest in the conservation and sound maintenance of the national parks, game refuges, and forests of the country" and that the project would adversely affect the aesthetics and ecology of the area, the Club claimed to be "adversely affected or aggrieved" under § 10 of the Administrative Procedure Act (APA), 5 U.S.C. § 702.[6]

The Court ruled that the plaintiff lacked standing because it had not alleged that it would suffer "injury in fact" from the challenged action. Although acknowledging that the Court allows organizations to litigate as representatives of their members (if some members themselves would have standing to sue),[7] the Court emphasized that "[n]owhere * * * did the Club state that its members use [the area in question] for any purpose, much less that they use it in any way that would be significantly affected by the proposed actions of the [defendants]." The Court termed the requirement of injury a "rough attempt to put the decision as to whether review will be sought in the hands of those who have a direct stake in the outcome." Justice Stewart added for the Court that the goals of the injury-in-fact requirement would be "undermined" if organizations were permitted to sue under the APA merely to "vindicate their own value preferences through the judicial process."

Justice Blackmun (joined by Justice Brennan) dissented, calling for "an imaginative expansion of our traditional concepts of standing in order to enable an organization such as the Sierra Club, possessed, as it is, of

---

[4] See, *e.g.*, Lujan v. Defenders of Wildlife, 504 U.S. 555, 576 (1992); Lewis v. Casey, 518 U.S. 343, 357 (1996).

[5] See, *e.g.*, Laird v. Tatum, 408 U.S. 1, 15 (1972).

[6] That section provides: "A person suffering legal wrong because of agency action, or adversely affected or aggrieved by agency action within the meaning of a relevant statute, is entitled to judicial review thereof." For further discussion of the APA and judicial review of agency action, see pp. 1341–1342, *infra*.

[7] See Hunt v. Washington State Apple Advertising Comm'n, 432 U.S. 333, 343 (1977) (holding "that an association has standing to bring suit on behalf of its members when: (a) its members would otherwise have standing to sue in their own right; (b) the interests it seeks to protect are germane to the organization's purpose; and (c) neither the claim asserted nor the relief requested requires the participation of individual members in the lawsuit"); see also Students for Fair Admissions v. Harvard, 600 U.S. 181, 199–201 (2023) (applying and reaffirming Hunt). Does Hunt's broad endorsement of associational standing make an end run around the procedural protections that Fed.R.Civ.P. 23 imposes on plaintiffs seeking to represent those whose claims present common questions of law and fact against the same defendant? For a decision reaffirming Hunt in the face of such an objection, see International Union, UAW v. Brock, 477 U.S. 274 (1986); for criticisms of associational standing on this and other grounds, see Food & Drug Administration v. Alliance for Hippocratic Medicine, 602 U.S. 367, 399–405 (2024) (Thomas, J., concurring); Morley & Hessick, *Against Associational Standing*, 91 U.Chi.L.Rev. (forthcoming 2024).

pertinent, *bona fide* and well-recognized attributes and purposes in the area of the environment, to litigate environmental issues."[8] Would it be proper for the Court to make ad hoc judgments about the litigating capacity of particular parties? Do the courts do so, in effect, when deciding whether to certify class actions under Federal Rule of Civil Procedure 23? Did the Sierra Club's incentives or capacity to litigate depend on whether some members used the relevant part of the national forest?

(b)   United States v. Richardson, 418 U.S. 166 (1974), held, 5–4, that the plaintiff lacked standing to litigate whether the CIA was violating Article I, § 9, cl. 7 (requiring "a regular Statement and Account of the Receipts and Expenditures of all public Money") by accounting for its expenditures, in accordance with a federal statute, "solely on the certificate of the Director." Chief Justice Burger wrote: "The respondent's claim is that without detailed information on CIA expenditures—and hence its activities—he cannot intelligently follow the actions of Congress or the Executive, nor can he properly fulfill his obligations as a member of the electorate in voting for candidates seeking national office."

"This is surely [a] * * * generalized grievance * * * since the impact on him is plainly undifferentiated and 'common to all members of the public.' While we can hardly dispute that this respondent has a genuine interest in the use of funds and that his interest may be prompted by his status as a taxpayer, he has not alleged that, as a taxpayer, he is in danger of suffering any concrete injury as a result of the operation of the statute."

The Chief Justice continued: "It can be argued that if respondent is not permitted to litigate this issue, no one can do so. In a very real sense, the absence of any particular individual or class to litigate these claims gives support to the argument that the subject matter is committed to the surveillance of Congress, and ultimately to the political process. * * * Slow, cumbersome, and unresponsive though the traditional electoral process may be thought at times, our system provides for changing members of the political branches when dissatisfied citizens convince a sufficient number of their fellow electors that elected representatives are delinquent in performing duties committed to them."

Justice Powell elaborated on this theme in his concurring opinion:

"[R]epeated and essentially head-on confrontations between the life-tenured branch and the representative branches of government will not, in the long run, be beneficial to either. The public confidence essential to the former and the vitality critical to the latter may well erode if we do not exercise self-restraint in the utilization of our power to negative the actions of the other branches. * * * The irreplaceable value of the power [of judicial review] * * * lies in the protection it has afforded the constitutional rights and liberties of individual citizens and minority groups against oppressive or discriminatory government action. It is this role, not some amorphous general supervision of the operations of government, that has maintained

---

8   Justice Douglas also dissented; he would have upheld standing "in the name of the inanimate object about to be despoiled, defaced, or invaded by roads and bulldozers and where injury is the subject of public outrage."

public esteem for the federal courts and has permitted the peaceful coexistence of the countermajoritarian implications of judicial review and the democratic principles upon which our Federal Government in the final analysis rests."

Does the fact that a grievance is widely shared ensure that the political branches will respond to it—or that, if they do not, the grievance must not be very serious? Should the lack of any other or better plaintiff count in favor of upholding a litigant's standing?[9]

(c)   In Heckler v. Mathews, 465 U.S. 728 (1984), Congress had provided larger benefit awards under the Social Security Act to certain women than to similarly situated men. A severability clause provided that if the provision in question were found to deny equal protection, men and women alike should receive the smaller amount. Despite the unavailability of any material compensation for the male plaintiff, the Court upheld his standing to challenge the unequal treatment. Because he asserted "the right to receive 'benefits * * * distributed according to classifications which do not without sufficient justification differentiate * * * solely on the basis of sex,' and not a substantive right to any particular amount of benefits, [plaintiff's] standing does not depend on his ability to obtain increased Social Security payments. * * * [D]iscrimination itself, by perpetuating 'archaic and stereotypic notions' or by stigmatizing members of the disfavored group as 'innately inferior,' * * * can cause serious noneconomic injuries."

(d)   In Allen v. Wright, 468 U.S. 737 (1984), parents of Black children attending public schools brought a nationwide class action against the Internal Revenue Service to require it to do more to deny tax-exempt status to racially discriminatory private schools, which were alleged to make it harder to integrate the public schools. Among other injuries,[10] the plaintiffs invoked "the stigmatizing injury often caused by racial discrimination." The Court held this injury inadequate for standing. It acknowledged Heckler v. Mathews' holding that "this sort of noneconomic injury is one of the most serious consequences of discriminatory government action and is sufficient in some circumstances to support standing," but concluded that "such injury accords a basis for standing only to 'those persons who are personally denied equal treatment' by the challenged discriminatory conduct."

Allowing federal courts to hear broader claims of stigmatic injury, the Court concluded, would allow standing to "extend nationwide to all members of the particular racial groups against which the Government was alleged to be discriminating by its grant of a tax exemption to a racially discriminatory school, regardless of the location of that school. * * * A black person in Hawaii could challenge the grant of a tax exemption to a racially discriminatory school in Maine. Recognition of standing in such circumstances would transform the federal courts into 'no more than a vehicle for the vindication of the value interests of concerned bystanders.'

---

[9]   See Meltzer, *Deterring Constitutional Violations by Law Enforcement Officials: Plaintiffs and Defendants as Private Attorneys General*, 88 Colum.L.Rev. 247, 297–306 (1988); Re, *Relative Standing*, 102 Geo.L.J. 1191 (2014).

[10]   Allen also addressed and rejected the possibility of standing from the indirect effect on public school integration, discussed at p. 157, *infra*.

United States v. SCRAP, 412 U.S. 669, 687 (1973). Constitutional limits on the role of the federal courts preclude such a transformation."

Is the Court's treatment of the alleged injuries in Mathews and Allen v. Wright consistent?[11] What is the theory of stigmatic harm that would justify the distinction the Court tried to draw?

(e)   Trump v. Hawaii, 583 U.S. 941 (2018), upheld the standing of three U.S. citizens or permanent residents to challenge a presidential proclamation that restricted entry into the United States by nationals of six predominantly Muslim countries. In doing so, the Court declined to decide whether injury to a "claimed dignitary interest" in being free from religious establishments and the designation of a "disfavored faith" sufficed for standing. The individual plaintiffs had alleged adequate injury in the "real-world effect that the Proclamation has had in keeping them separated from certain relatives who seek to enter the country."[12]

(f)   Uzuegbunam v. Preczewski, 592 U.S. 279 (2021), held that a plaintiff satisfied the requirements for standing by seeking nominal damages for a past deprivation of free speech rights (specifically, to engage in religious proselytization on the campus of a public college) even in the absence of allegations of quantifiable economic harm. In an opinion by Justice Thomas, the Court held, 8–1, that the plaintiff had alleged an injury in fact, caused by the defendants, and that nominal damages would redress his injury. Justice Thomas's opinion relied heavily on English and American common law, which he said allowed suits seeking nominal damages based on the premise that *"every* legal injury necessarily causes damage," even when "there was no apparent continuing or threatened injury for nominal damages to redress." "By permitting plaintiffs to pursue nominal damages whenever they suffered a personal legal injury, the common law avoided the oddity of

---

[11]   For a critical analysis of the treatment of stigma in Mathews, Allen v. Wright, and other cases, see Healy, *Stigmatic Harm and Standing*, 92 Iowa L.Rev. 417 (2007).

[12]   In other cases under the Establishment Clause challenging governmental displays of crèches, crosses, and the Ten Commandments, the Supreme Court has often ruled on the merits, typically without discussion of standing. For example, in American Legion v. American Humanist Ass'n, 588 U.S. 29 (2019), which rejected a challenge to the display of a cross as a war memorial, the majority took no notice of any standing issue. But Justice Gorsuch, in an opinion concurring in the judgment that Justice Thomas joined, would have dismissed on standing grounds. More broadly, he would have rejected "the plaintiffs' 'offended observer' theory of standing" and also would have held the implied recognition of standing in a number of prior religious display cases to be error. According to Justice Gorsuch, the plausibility of the "offended observer" theory depends on a mistaken test of substantive constitutional validity, under which displays of religious symbols are unconstitutional if a "reasonable observer" would perceive them as "endorsing" religion. Justice Ginsburg's dissenting opinion, which Justice Sotomayor joined, described "Justice Gorsuch's 'no standing' opinion [as] startling in view of the many religious-display cases this Court has resolved on the merits." She also suggested that it would have intolerable consequences.

In Kennedy v. Bremerton Sch. Dist., 597 U.S. 507 (2022), Justice Gorsuch wrote an opinion for the Court officially announcing "that this Court long ago abandoned Lemon [v. Kurtzman, 403 U.S. 602 (1971),] and its endorsement test offshoot," and that "In place of Lemon and the endorsement test, this Court has instructed that the Establishment Clause must be interpreted by 'reference to historical practices and understandings.' " The Court did not discuss standing. But does its treatment of the substance of the Establishment Clause have implications for the standing of offended observers of religious displays?

privileging small-dollar economic rights over important, but not easily quantifiable, nonpecuniary rights," he wrote.

Chief Justice Roberts dissented. He maintained that the Court's reliance on English common law was inapt, since English courts were not subject to the constraints of Article III. He further argued that the American common law cases clearly established only that plaintiffs could sue for nominal damages as a form of relief against ongoing or threatened future harms. Viewing the issue through a more contemporary lens, the Chief Justice also thought allowance of nominal damages for purely past injuries irreconcilable with "modern justiciability principles" that do not permit standing to challenge every invasion of a statutorily conferred right and that authorize suit only when judicial relief will "compensat[e] the plaintiff for a past loss" or prevent "an ongoing or future harm."

For discussion of the impact of Uzuegbunam v. Preczewski on mootness doctrine, see p. 252, *infra*.

(2) Injury in Fact: Probabilistic or Uncertain Harms. The Court has said that injury in fact must be concrete, imminent, and not speculative—a point it emphasized in Clapper when it rejected the "speculative chain of possibilities," which, in the Court's view, failed to show that an injury from future surveillance was "certainly impending." Yet, in many instances, the injury that litigation seeks to prevent may reflect merely a probability of harm. The Court has taken varying positions on whether and when a plaintiff can predicate Article III standing on the objective probability of sustaining harm and the reasonable concerns flowing from such a probability.

(a) In City of Los Angeles v. Lyons, 461 U.S. 95 (1983), a Black man brought a civil rights action against the city and certain of its police officers in federal district court, claiming that he had been unconstitutionally subjected to a "chokehold" after being stopped for a traffic violation. He alleged that pursuant to official authorization, chokeholds were routinely applied in situations where they were not warranted and that many people had suffered injury as a consequence. (Between 1975 until the Supreme Court's decision, sixteen people, twelve of whom were Black, had died as a result of LAPD police chokeholds.) Lyons sought both damages and declaratory and injunctive relief. The district court granted a preliminary injunction against the use of chokeholds "under circumstances which do not threaten death or serious bodily injury"—an injunction that was to continue in effect until an improved training and reporting program had been approved by the court. The court of appeals affirmed.

The Supreme Court reversed on the ground that Lyons lacked "standing to seek the injunction requested" because he had not demonstrated that "he was likely to suffer future injury from the use of the chokeholds by police officers." Noting that only the question of an injunctive remedy was before it and that the damages claim could be severed on remand, the Court concluded that the fact that "Lyons may have been illegally choked by the police on October 6, 1976 * * * does nothing to establish a real and immediate threat that he would again be stopped for a traffic violation, or for any other offense,

by an officer or officers who would illegally choke him into unconsciousness
without any provocation or resistance on his part." The Court stated that it
was "no more than speculation to assert either that Lyons himself will again
be involved in one of those unfortunate instances, or that he will be arrested
in the future and provoke the use of a chokehold by resisting arrest,
attempting to escape, or threatening deadly force or serious bodily injury."

Justice Marshall, for four dissenters, objected, *inter alia*, that the
majority's approach "immunizes from prospective equitable relief any policy
that authorizes persistent deprivations of constitutional rights as long as no
individual can establish with substantial certainty that he will be injured, or
injured again, in the future." The dissent argued that "[g]iven the necessarily
preliminary nature of its inquiry, there was no way for the District Court to
know the precise contours of the City's policy or to ascertain the risk that
Lyons, who had alleged that the policy was being applied in a discriminatory
manner, might again be subjected to a chokehold. But in view of the Court's
conclusion that the unprovoked choking of Lyons was pursuant to a City
policy, Lyons has satisfied the usual basis for injunctive relief, that there
exists some cognizable danger of recurrent violation." The dissent further
observed that five people were killed by LAPD chokeholds during a period
where the district court's preliminary injunction was stayed, and that "the
risk of serious injuries and deaths to other citizens also supported the
decision to grant a preliminary injunction."[13]

(b)   In Summers v. Earth Island Institute, Inc., 555 U.S. 488 (2009), the
Court, 5–4, rejected efforts by environmental organizations to base standing
on the "statistical probability that some of their members" would suffer
harms by virtue of the U.S. Forest Service's pervasive application of
challenged regulations to sites throughout a park system frequented by the
organizations' members. The Forest Service Decision Making and Appeals
Reform Act, 16 U.S.C. § 1612, afforded interested parties the right to notice
and comment and to an appellate process concerning certain land and
resource management plans implemented by the Forest Service. The
plaintiffs sought to enjoin the enforcement of Forest Service regulations that
excluded fire-rehabilitation activities and salvage-timber sales of a certain
size from those procedures. Consistent with the requirements of Sierra Club
v. Morton, pp. 141–142, *supra*, a member of one of the plaintiff groups had
filed an affidavit stating that he had visited and intended again to visit the
site of a particular salvage-timber sale that the challenged regulations
exempted from the Act's procedures. Because the litigation concerning that
site had been settled, however, the plaintiff groups could not rely on that
injury to sustain injunctive relief. Nor, said the Court, could the plaintiff
organizations establish the requisite concrete, particularized injury by
relying on the affidavit of another member who simply averred that he has

---

[13]   The dissent framed this inquiry as a question about equitable entitlement to relief,
rather than about standing for purely future injuries, because of Lyons's unquestioned standing
to seek damages for the past injury. The majority, by contrast, also rejected the argument that
Lyons's standing to seek damages for past injury was relevant to his standing for injunctive
relief. See p. 160, *infra*, for further discussion.

visited many National Forests and plans to visit (unnamed) National Forests in the future.

In a dissent joined by Justices Stevens, Souter, and Ginsburg, Justice Breyer argued that given the sweep of the Forest Service's policy and the vast membership of the plaintiff organizations, establishing the requisite injury in this case should not necessarily depend on whether any identifiable individual member of the plaintiff organizations had alleged a sufficiently concrete injury. In particular, he contended that the government's application of the challenged regulations to thousands of projects in the future sufficed to establish a realistic threat of injury to the plaintiffs' many thousands of members who, according to uncontested allegations in the complaint, have used and intend to use the National Forests to which the regulations apply. The majority responded that "[t]his novel approach to the law of organizational standing would make a mockery of our prior cases, which have required plaintiff-organizations to make specific allegations establishing that at least one identified member had suffered or would suffer harm."

Does Summers' rejection of standing ultimately turn on issues of probabilities or uncertainty, on issues of organizational standing (see p. 141, note 7, *supra*), or both?

(c)   In contrast to Summers, in Monsanto Co. v. Geertson Seed Farms, 561 U.S. 139 (2010), the Court held that conventional alfalfa growers had standing to challenge the Secretary of Agriculture's deregulation of genetically-engineered alfalfa, given the "reasonable probability" that such action would result in cross-contamination of conventional and organic alfalfa with the altered gene. This risk of cross-contamination concretely injured the conventional growers in at least two ways. First, in order to continue marketing their product to consumers "who wish to buy non-genetically-engineered alfalfa, [the growers] would have to conduct testing to find out whether and to what extent their crops have been contaminated." Second, "the risk of gene flow [from genetically altered to conventional alfalfa] will cause them to take certain measures to minimize the likelihood of potential contamination and to ensure an adequate supply of non-genetically-engineered alfalfa" for customers who insist on such crops. The Court found these harms sufficed to confer standing, even if the growers' crops were not actually infected.

Why does the reasonable probability of an injury suffice to confer standing here if it did not in the Summers case? Does the difference flow from the costly precautions that the plaintiffs in Monsanto had to take to avoid those concerns—a harm that was certain and not merely probabilistic?

(d)   In Trump v. New York, 592 U.S. 125 (2020), also discussed p. 288, *infra*, the Court found that the plaintiffs lacked standing to challenge a memorandum directing the Secretary of Commerce to provide information that would facilitate the President's exclusion of "aliens without lawful status" from the population base used in apportioning the states' representation in Congress and disbursing certain federal funds. Emphasizing uncertainty concerning the number of "aliens without lawful status" that the Secretary would be able to identify and that the President would be able to exclude from his tally, the Court held that the plaintiffs had not established a "substantial risk" of either reduced representation or diminished funding. Justice Breyer, joined by Justices Sotomayor and Kagan, dissented. He argued that despite uncertainties as to precise numbers, "the memorandum presents the 'substantial risk' that our precedents require."[14]

(e) Most recently, in Whole Woman's Health v. Jackson, 595 U.S. 30 (2021), the Supreme Court concluded that abortion providers lacked standing to sue a private individual, Mark Lee Dickson, who might have filed state lawsuits against them under the Texas abortion statute S. B. 8. The Court relied on sworn statements by Dickson that he did not intend to sue the plaintiffs under S. B. 8, and concluded that the plaintiffs had not established an injury traceable to his conduct. It apparently rejected (without explanation) the plaintiffs' arguments that those disavowals were too limited and conditional to eliminate their risk of injury. This portion of the decision was not contested by the dissenting justices. For additional discussion of Whole Woman's Health, see pp. 1211–1224, *infra*.

(f) Is there a difference between uncertainty that comes from the inherently speculative nature of the future and uncertainty that comes from a lack of sufficient evidence? In Clapper, was there any significance to the fact that the classified nature of the program at issue limited the plaintiffs' ability and the government's willingness to present evidence bearing on likelihood? For perspectives on the challenges posed by such litigation, see, *e.g.*, Michelman, *Who Can Sue over Government Surveillance?*, 57 UCLA L.Rev. 71 (2009); Rubenfeld, *The End of Privacy*, 61 Stan.L.Rev. 101, 138 (2008).

(g) The Court's cases seem to vary in their willingness to treat uncertain harms as a basis for granting standing. Is there anything at play other than the Court's own rough judgment about how realistic the threat of a contingent harm might be for the plaintiff in question? Despite the Court's stated reluctance to allow standing for "speculative" events, should it recognize standing for low probability events if their realization would produce catastrophic consequences? Compare the discussion of Massachusetts v. EPA, 549 U.S. 497 (2007), pp. 212–214, *infra*. See also Nash, *Standing's Expected Value*, 111 Mich.L.Rev. 1283 (2013).

In a systematic examination of probabilistic standing, Professors Bradley and Young argue that "courts and commentators tend to ask too much of standing doctrine in probabilistic cases." Bradley & Young, *Standing and Probabilistic Injury*, 122 Mich.L.Rev. 1557 (2024). The authors argue that it is important to distinguish between: (1) uncertainty about who is *subject* to a challenged action (as in Clapper), (2) uncertainty about whether those subject to an action will be *harmed* (as in Monsanto), and (3) uncertainty about the *causation and redressability* of the injury. (Causation

---

[14] The Commerce Department subsequently announced a delay in its reporting of even preliminary census data until after the end of the Trump administration, and the Biden administration revoked the challenged memorandum.

and redressability are addressed pp. 156–166, *infra*.) They therefore see cases such as Clapper and Monsanto as addressing fundamentally different questions. The authors also argue that questions of probabilistic harm cannot be solved through the brute force of the injury in fact test, but rather should be redirected to questions of institutional competence (such as the role of Congress in establishing standing)[15] and to the law of remedies and the doctrines of ripeness and mootness. In studying each of these doctrines, consider whether they are any more suited to provide stable, predictable, coherent answers to questions of probabilistic standing.

California v. Texas

593 U.S. 659 (2021).
Appeal from the Court of Appeals of Fifth Circuit.

■ JUSTICE BREYER delivered the opinion of the Court.

As originally enacted in 2010, the Patient Protection and Affordable Care Act required most Americans to obtain minimum essential health insurance coverage. The Act also imposed a monetary penalty, scaled according to income, upon individuals who failed to do so. In 2017, Congress effectively nullified the penalty by setting its amount at $0. See Tax Cuts and Jobs Act of 2017, Pub.L. 115–97, § 11081, 131 Stat. 2092 (codified in 26 U.S.C. § 5000A(c)).

Texas and 17 other States brought this lawsuit against the United States and federal officials. They were later joined by two individuals (Neill Hurley and John Nantz). The plaintiffs claim that without the penalty the Act's minimum essential coverage requirement is unconstitutional. Specifically, they say neither the Commerce Clause nor the Tax Clause (nor any other enumerated power) grants Congress the power to enact it. See U.S. Const., Art. I, § 8. They also argue that the minimum essential coverage requirement is not severable from the rest of the Act. Hence, they believe the Act as a whole is invalid. We do not reach these questions of the Act's validity, however, for Texas and the other plaintiffs in this suit lack the standing necessary to raise them.

* * *

II

We proceed no further than standing. The Constitution gives federal courts the power to adjudicate only genuine "Cases" and "Controversies." Art. III, § 2. That power includes the requirement that litigants have standing. A plaintiff has standing only if he can "allege personal injury fairly traceable to the defendant's allegedly unlawful conduct and likely to be redressed by the requested relief." DaimlerChrysler Corp. v. Cuno, 547 U.S. 332, 342 (2006) (internal quotation marks omitted); see also

---

[15] The Court's decision in TransUnion v. Ramirez, 594 U.S. 413 (2021), p. 187, *infra*, confronts the question of Congress's power to recognize standing in cases of future injury.

Lujan v. Defenders of Wildlife, 504 U.S. 555, 560–561 (1992). Neither the individual nor the state plaintiffs have shown that the injury they will suffer or have suffered is "fairly traceable" to the "allegedly unlawful conduct" of which they complain.

A

We begin with the two individual plaintiffs. They claim a particularized individual harm in the form of payments they have made and will make each month to carry the minimum essential coverage that § 5000A(a) requires. The individual plaintiffs point to the statutory language, which, they say, commands them to buy health insurance. But even if we assume that this pocketbook injury satisfies the injury element of Article III standing, the plaintiffs nevertheless fail to satisfy the traceability requirement.

Their problem lies in the fact that the statutory provision, while it tells them to obtain that coverage, has no means of enforcement. With the penalty zeroed out, the IRS can no longer seek a penalty from those who fail to comply. Because of this, there is no possible Government action that is causally connected to the plaintiffs' injury—the costs of purchasing health insurance. Or to put the matter conversely, that injury is not "fairly traceable" to any "allegedly unlawful conduct" of which the plaintiffs complain. Allen v. Wright, 468 U.S. 737, 751 (1984). They have not pointed to any way in which the defendants, the Commissioner of Internal Revenue and the Secretary of Health and Human Services, will act to enforce § 5000A(a). They have not shown how any other federal employees could do so either. In a word, they have not shown that any kind of Government action or conduct has caused or will cause the injury they attribute to § 5000A(a). * * *

* * * [O]ur cases have consistently spoken of the need to assert an injury that is the result of a statute's actual or threatened *enforcement*, whether today or in the future. * * *

* * * Here, there is no action—actual or threatened—whatsoever. There is only the statute's textually unenforceable language.

To consider the matter from the point of view of another standing requirement, namely, redressability, makes clear that the statutory language alone is not sufficient. To determine whether an injury is redressable, a court will consider the relationship between "the judicial relief requested" and the "injury" suffered. Allen, 468 U.S., at 753, n.19. The plaintiffs here sought injunctive relief and a declaratory judgment. The injunctive relief, however, concerned the Act's other provisions that they say are inseverable from the minimum essential coverage requirement. The relief they sought in respect to the only provision they attack as unconstitutional—the minimum essential coverage provision—is declaratory relief, namely, a judicial statement that the provision they attacked is unconstitutional.

Remedies, however, ordinarily "operate with respect to specific parties." Murphy v. National Collegiate Athletic Ass'n, 584 U.S. [453, 489] (2018) (Thomas, J., concurring). In the absence of any specific party, they do not simply operate "on legal rules in the abstract." *Ibid.*; see also [Frothingham v.] Mellon, 262 U.S. [447,] 488 ("If a case for preventive relief be presented, the court enjoins, in effect, not the execution of the statute, but the acts of the official, the statute notwithstanding").

This suit makes clear why that is so. The Declaratory Judgment Act, 28 U.S.C. § 2201, alone does not provide a court with jurisdiction. See Skelly Oil Co. v. Phillips Petroleum Co., 339 U.S. 667, 671–672 (1950); R. Fallon, J. Manning, D. Meltzer, & D. Shapiro, Hart and Wechsler's The Federal Courts and the Federal System 841 (7th ed.2015) (that Act does "not confe[r] jurisdiction over declaratory actions when the underlying dispute could not otherwise be heard in federal court"). Instead, just like suits for every other type of remedy, declaratory-judgment actions must satisfy Article III's case-or-controversy requirement. * * * Thus, to satisfy Article III standing, we must look elsewhere to find a remedy that will redress the individual plaintiffs' injuries.

What is that relief? The plaintiffs did not obtain damages. Nor, as we just said, did the plaintiffs obtain an injunction in respect to the provision they attack as unconstitutional. But, more than that: How could they have sought any such injunction? The provision is unenforceable. There is no one, and nothing, to enjoin. They cannot enjoin the Secretary of Health and Human Services, because he has no power to enforce § 5000A(a) against them. And they do not claim that they might enjoin Congress. In these circumstances, injunctive relief could amount to no more than a declaration that the statutory provision they attack is unconstitutional, *i.e.*, a declaratory judgment. But once again, that is the very kind of relief that cannot alone supply jurisdiction otherwise absent.

The matter is not simply technical. To find standing here to attack an unenforceable statutory provision would allow a federal court to issue what would amount to "an advisory opinion without the possibility of any judicial relief." Los Angeles v. Lyons, 461 U.S. 95, 129 (1983) (Marshall, J., dissenting); see also Steel Co. v. Citizens for Better Environment, 523 U.S. 83, 107 (1998) (to have standing, a plaintiff must seek "an acceptable Article III remedy" that will "redress a cognizable Article III injury"). It would threaten to grant unelected judges a general authority to conduct oversight of decisions of the elected branches of Government. See United States v. Richardson, 418 U.S. 166, 188 (1974) (Powell, J., concurring). Article III guards against federal courts assuming this kind of jurisdiction. * * *

B

Next, we turn to the state plaintiffs. We conclude that Texas and the other state plaintiffs have similarly failed to show that they have alleged an "injury fairly traceable to the defendant's allegedly *unlawful* conduct."

Cuno, 547 U.S. at 342 (emphasis added). They claim two kinds of
pocketbook injuries. First, they allege an indirect injury in the form of
the increased use of (and therefore cost to) state-operated medical
insurance programs. Second, they claim a direct injury resulting from a
variety of increased administrative and related expenses required, they
say, by the minimum essential coverage provision, along with other
provisions of the Act that, they add, are inextricably " 'interwoven' " with
it.

1

First, the state plaintiffs claim that the minimum essential coverage
provision has led state residents subject to it to enroll in state-operated
or state-sponsored insurance programs such as Medicaid, the Children's
Health Insurance Program (CHIP), and health insurance programs for
state employees. The state plaintiffs say they must pay a share of the
costs of serving those new enrollees. As with the individual plaintiffs, the
States also have failed to show how this injury is directly traceable to any
actual or possible unlawful Government conduct in enforcing § 5000A(a).
Cf. Clapper v. Amnesty Int'l USA, 568 U.S. 398, 414, n.5 (2013)
("plaintiffs bear the burden of . . . showing that the defendant's *actual
action* has caused the substantial risk of harm" (emphasis added)). That
alone is enough to show that they, like the individual plaintiffs, lack
Article III standing. * * *

2

The state plaintiffs add that § 5000A(a)'s minimum essential
coverage provision also causes them to incur additional costs directly.
They point to the costs of providing beneficiaries of state health plans
with information about their health insurance coverage, as well as the
cost of furnishing the IRS with that related information.

The problem with these claims, however, is that other provisions of
Act, not the minimum essential coverage provision, impose these other
requirements. Nothing in the text of these form provisions suggests that
they would not operate without § 5000A(a). * * * To show that the
minimum essential coverage requirement is unconstitutional would not
show that enforcement of any of these other provisions violates the
Constitution. The state plaintiffs do not claim the contrary. The
Government's conduct in question is therefore not "fairly traceable" to
enforcement of the "allegedly unlawful" provision of which the plaintiffs
complain—§ 5000A(a). Allen, 468 U.S., at 751. * * *

* * *

For these reasons, we conclude that the plaintiffs in this suit failed
to show a concrete, particularized injury fairly traceable to the
defendants' conduct in enforcing the specific statutory provision they
attack as unconstitutional. They have failed to show that they have
standing to attack as unconstitutional the Act's minimum essential
coverage provision. Therefore, we reverse the Fifth Circuit's judgment in

respect to standing, vacate the judgment, and remand the cases with instructions to dismiss.

It is so ordered.

■ [The concurring opinion of JUSTICE THOMAS is omitted.]

■ JUSTICE ALITO, with whom JUSTICE GORSUCH joins, dissenting.

Today's decision is the third installment in our epic Affordable Care Act trilogy, and it follows the same pattern as installments one and two. In all three episodes, with the Affordable Care Act facing a serious threat, the Court has pulled off an improbable rescue. * * *

Now, in the trilogy's third episode, the Court is presented with the daunting problem of a "tax" that does not tax. Can the taxing power, which saved the day in the first episode, sustain such a curious creature? In 2017, Congress reduced the "tax" imposed on Americans who failed to abide by the individual mandate to $0. With that move, the slender reed that supported the decision in NFIB was seemingly cut down, but once again the Court has found a way to protect the ACA. Instead of defending the constitutionality of the individual mandate, the Court simply ducks the issue and holds that none of the Act's challengers, including the 18 States that think the Act saddles them with huge financial costs, is entitled to sue.

Can this be correct? The ACA imposes many burdensome obligations on States in their capacity as employers, and the 18 States in question collectively have more than a million employees. Even $1 in harm is enough to support standing. Yet no State has standing? * * *

In this suit, as I will explain, Texas and the other state plaintiffs have standing, and now that the "tax" imposed by the individual mandate is set at $0, the mandate cannot be sustained under the taxing power. As a result, it is clearly unconstitutional, and to the extent that the provisions of the ACA that burden the States are inextricably linked to the individual mandate, they too are unenforceable. * * *

* * *

II

* * * While the individual plaintiffs' claim to standing raises a novel question, the States have standing for reasons that are straightforward and meritorious. The Court's contrary holding is based on a fundamental distortion of our standing jurisprudence.

A

The governing rules are well-settled. To establish Article III standing, a plaintiff must show: (1) "an injury in fact"; (2) that this injury "is fairly traceable to the challenged conduct of the defendant"; and (3) that the injury "is likely to be redressed by a favorable judicial decision." Spokeo, Inc. v. Robins, 578 U. S. 330, 338 (2016).

In the present suit, there is no material dispute that the States have satisfied two of these requirements. First, there is no question that the States have demonstrated an injury in fact. * * * A financial or so-called "pocketbook" injury constitutes injury in fact, and even a small pocketbook injury—like the loss of $1—is enough. Here, the States have offered plenty of evidence that they incur substantial expenses in order to comply with obligations imposed by the ACA.

There is likewise no material dispute that these financial injuries could be redressed by a favorable judgment. The District Court declared the entire ACA unenforceable, and that judgment, if sustained, would spare the States from the costs of complying with the ACA's provisions. So too would a more modest judgment limited to only those ACA provisions that directly burden the States.

The standing dispute in this suit thus turns on traceability. But once this requirement is properly understood, it is apparent that it too is met.

Our cases explain that traceability requires "a causal connection between the injury and *the conduct complained of.*" Lujan, 504 U.S., at 560 (emphasis added). In other words, the injury has to be " 'fairly traceable to *the challenged action of the defendant.*' " *Ibid.* (emphasis added). We have repeatedly and consistently described the traceability inquiry this way. * * *

The States have clearly shown that they suffer concrete and particularized financial injuries that are traceable to conduct of the Federal Government. The ACA saddles them with expensive and burdensome obligations, and those obligations are enforced by the Federal Government. That is sufficient to establish standing. * * *

Consider what the state plaintiffs have shown with respect to the ACA reporting requirements codified at 26 U.S.C. §§ 6055 and 6056. * * * The States plainly have demonstrated standing to seek relief from these burdensome reporting obligations.

Start with injury in fact. The States have offered undisputed evidence documenting the ongoing financial costs of complying with these reporting requirements. * * *

Now turn to traceability. Are these financial injuries "fairly traceable to the challenged conduct"? Hollingsworth [v. Perry], 570 U.S. [693,] 704 [(2013)]. The answer is clearly yes. The reporting requirements in §§ 6055 and 6056 are enforceable by the Federal Government, and noncompliance may result in heavy penalties. * * * These penalties can amount to at least $280 per infraction, and they can quickly run up into the millions of dollars.

That leaves redressability, which asks whether the requested relief is likely to redress the party's injury. Steel Co. v. Citizens for Better Environment, 523 U.S. 83, 103 (1998). Looking to the relief the District Court in fact granted makes it obvious that the States' injuries in the form of ongoing reporting expenses are redressable. The District Court entered a judgment that, among other things, declared the reporting requirements in §§ 6055 and 6056 unenforceable. With that judgment in hand, the States would be freed from the obligation to expend funds to comply with those requirements—redressing their financial injury prospectively. * * *

B

The Court largely ignores the theory of standing outlined above. It devotes most of its attention to two other theories, and when it does address the relevant injuries, its arguments are deeply flawed.

The Court's primary argument rests on a patent distortion of the traceability prong of our established test for standing. Partially quoting a line in Allen, the Court demands a showing that the "*Government's conduct* in question is . . . 'fairly traceable' to enforcement of *the 'allegedly unlawful' provision of which the plaintiffs complain—§ 5000A(a)*." This is a flat-out misstatement of the law and what the Court wrote in Allen. What Allen actually requires is a "personal injury fairly traceable to *the defendant's allegedly unlawful conduct*," [468 U.S.,] at 751 (emphasis added). And what this statement means is that the plaintiff's "injury" must be traceable to the defendant's conduct, and that conduct must be "allegedly unlawful." "Allegedly unlawful" means that the plaintiff must allege that the conduct is unlawful. (The States allege that the challenged enforcement actions are unlawful using a traditional legal argument.) But a plaintiff's standing (and thus the court's Article III jurisdiction) does not require a demonstration that the defendant's conduct is in fact unlawful. That is a merits issue. * * *

C

The Court's distortion of the traceability requirement is bad enough in itself, but there is more. After imposing an obstacle that the States should not have to surmount to establish standing, the Court turns around and refuses to consider whether the States have cleared that obstacle. It's as if the Court told the States: "In order to bring your case in federal court, you have to pay a filing fee of $100,000, but we will not give you a chance to pay that money."

The Court says that the States cannot establish standing unless they show that their injuries are traceable to the individual mandate, and the States claim that their injuries are indeed traceable to the mandate. Their argument proceeds in two steps. First, they contend that the individual mandate is unconstitutional because it does not fall within any power granted to Congress by the Constitution. Second, they argue that costly obligations imposed on them by other provisions of the ACA cannot be severed from the mandate. If both steps of the States' argument that the challenged enforcement actions are unlawful are correct, it follows that the Government cannot lawfully enforce those obligations against the States. * * *

D

The Court has no real response to the arguments set out above, so it falls back on the claim that the States forfeited those arguments * * *

* * *

I would hold that the States have demonstrated standing to seek relief from the ACA provisions that burden them and that they claim are inseparable from the individual mandate. * * *

NOTE ON CAUSATION AND REDRESSABILITY

As both Clapper v. Amnesty International and especially California v. Texas recognize, Article III requires more than merely a cognizable injury. Rather, the injury must be (i) "fairly traceable" in a causal sense to the challenged action and (ii) redressable by the relief sought.[1] The way the Court has specified these two requirements in its case law is critically important to the functioning of modern standing doctrine, but not always intuitive.

(1) Redressability, Causation, and the Actions of Third Parties.

(a) Linda R.S. v. Richard D., 410 U.S. 614 (1973), was a class action, brought by the mother of a child born out of wedlock, against state officials whose policy was to bring non-support prosecutions against only the fathers of children born in wedlock. Asserting that the policy violated the Equal Protection Clause, the complaint sought an injunction requiring prosecution of the fathers of out-of-wedlock children who failed to pay required child support. Justice Marshall's opinion for the Court found no standing: "[I]n the unique context of a challenge to a criminal statute, appellant has failed to allege a sufficient nexus between her injury and the government action which she attacks to justify judicial intervention. * * * [T]he requested relief * * * would result only in the jailing of the child's father. The prospect that prosecution will, at least in the future, result in payment of support can, at best, be termed only speculative." The opinion also rested on the proposition that "in American jurisprudence at least, a private citizen lacks a judicially cognizable interest in the prosecution or nonprosecution of another." Since the suit was brought as a class action, is the result of prosecuting non-supporting fathers any more speculative than the general theory that the criminal law deters? See also Simon v. Eastern Ky. Welfare Rights Organization, 426 U.S. 26 (1976) (deeming it "purely speculative" whether the IRS' abandonment of a requirement that nonprofit hospitals provide services to indigent patients in order to receive favorable tax treatment caused "the denial of access to hospital services" complained of by the plaintiffs).

---

[1] For critical commentary on the Court's early development of the "causation" and "redressability" requirements, see Chayes, *Foreword: Public Law Litigation and the Burger Court*, 96 Harv.L.Rev. 4, 17–19 (1982); Nichol, *Causation as a Standing Requirement: The Unprincipled Use of Judicial Restraint*, 69 Ky.L.Rev. 185 (1981); Tushnet, *The New Law of Standing: A Plea for Abandonment*, 62 Cornell L.Rev. 663, 680–88 (1977).

(b)   In Allen v. Wright, 468 U.S. 737 (1984), in addition to their stigma-based injury (discussed p. 143, *supra*), the challengers alleged "that the federal tax exemptions to racially discriminatory private schools in their communities impair[ed] their ability to have their public schools desegregated." The Court readily agreed that this theory alleged an injury in fact—"their children's diminished ability to receive an education in a racially integrated school"—but concluded that this injury was "not fairly traceable to the government conduct respondents challenge as unlawful."

In particular, the Court concluded that the "line of causation" from "the IRS's grant of tax exemptions to some racially discriminatory schools" to "desegregation of respondents' schools is attenuated at best." It elaborated: "The diminished ability of respondents' children to receive a desegregated education would be fairly traceable to unlawful IRS grants of tax exemptions only if there were enough racially discriminatory private schools receiving tax exemptions in respondents' communities for withdrawal of those exemptions to make an appreciable difference in public school integration. * * * It is, first, uncertain how many racially discriminatory private schools are in fact receiving tax exemptions. Moreover, it is entirely speculative * * * whether withdrawal of a tax exemption from any particular school would lead the school to change its policies. It is just as speculative whether any given parent of a child attending such a private school would decide to transfer the child to public school as a result of any changes in educational or financial policy made by the private school once it was threatened with loss of tax-exempt status. It is also pure speculation whether, in a particular community, a large enough number of the numerous relevant school officials and parents would reach decisions that collectively would have a significant impact on the racial composition of the public schools. The links in the chain of causation between the challenged Government conduct and the asserted injury are far too weak for the chain as a whole to sustain respondents' standing."

Is the problem in Allen that the Court genuinely doubted whether government tax incentives in fact affect behavior on the margin? (Wouldn't that be contrary to the basic premises of economics?) Or is it more likely that the Court discerned a special separation of powers principle that made it especially reluctant to allow one person to sue based on the government's failure to enforce the law against another? Fallon, *The Linkage Between Justiciability and Remedies—And Their Connections to Substantive Rights*, 92 Va.L.Rev. 633 (2006), argues that the Court treats a particular set of remedies—injunctions directing executive officials to enforce the law against third parties (as in Allen v. Wright, *supra*, and Linda R.S. v. Richard D., *supra*)—as especially problematic, though not as categorically forbidden, and that this consideration has influenced the Court's development and application of the causation and redressability requirements.

(c)   In Department of Commerce v. New York, 588 U.S. 752 (2019), the Court ruled that some plaintiff states and possibly other parties had standing to challenge the citizenship question in the 2020 census questionnaire. In an opinion by Chief Justice Roberts, the Court upheld standing based on the prediction that the "citizenship question would result in noncitizen households responding to the census at lower rates than other groups, which in turn would cause them to be undercounted and lead to" such harms to the states as "los[ing] out on federal funds that are distributed on the basis of state population." For a Court that was unanimous on this point, the Chief Justice reasoned: "The Government invokes our steady refusal to 'endorse standing theories that rest on speculation about the decisions of independent actors,' Clapper v. Amnesty Int'l USA, 568 U.S. 398, 414 (2013), particularly speculation about future unlawful conduct, Los Angeles v. Lyons, 461 U.S. 95, 105 (1983). But * * * evidence at trial established that noncitizen households have historically responded to the census at lower rates than other groups, and the District Court did not clearly err in crediting the Census Bureau's theory that the discrepancy is likely attributable at least in part to noncitizens' reluctance to answer a citizenship question. Respondents' theory of standing thus does not rest on mere speculation about the decisions of third parties; it relies instead on the predictable effect of Government action on the decisions of third parties." Compare Allen v. Wright, *supra*, and Simon v. Eastern Ky. Welfare Rights Org., *supra*, both denying standing on the ground that anticipated harm resulting from actions by third parties was too speculative to support standing.

(d)   In United States v. Texas, 599 U.S. 670 (2023), the Court returned to these issues to reject another claim of standing, this time Texas and Louisiana's assertion of standing to challenge the executive branch's prioritization of certain categories of arrests in enforcing immigration policy. The states claimed that by not making more arrests, the federal government was imposing costs on the state, forcing them to incarcerate or provide social services to those that the government was declining to arrest. The Court rejected this claim of standing, relying heavily and extensively on "[t]he leading precedent" of Linda R.S. v. Richard D., p. 156, *supra*. According to the Court, this case shielded some set of "challenges to the Executive Branch's exercise of enforcement discretion over whether to arrest or prosecute," The Court grounded this principle more generally in "precedents and longstanding historical practice" as well as a range of other "good reasons," such as the scope of Article II, judicial manageability, foreign policy concerns, and more.

Notwithstanding its heavy reliance on Linda R.S., it is not clear whether the majority decided the case on the basis of redressability and traceability, or instead on the basis of lack of injury. In discussing the monetary costs imposed on the states, for example, the Court wrote: "Monetary costs are of course an injury. But this Court has 'also stressed that the alleged injury must be legally and judicially cognizable.' " (quoting Raines v. Byrd, 521 U.S. 811, 819 (1997)). It explained that this " 'requires, among other things,' that the 'dispute is traditionally thought to be capable of resolution through the judicial process'—in other words, that the asserted injury is traditionally redressable in federal court" (quoting Raines, 521 U.S. at 819), and emphasized that this would be assessed on the basis of "history and tradition." In later parts of its analysis, the Court relied heavily on substantive arguments in favor of executive discretion, seeming to blend its standing analysis with the merits.

By contrast, concurring in the judgment (and joined by two colleagues), Justice Gorsuch argued more specifically that "[t]he problem here is redressability." The redressability problem that Justice Gorsuch saw, however, was also quite distinct from the Linda R.S. principle, and involved his substantive skepticism about the reach of various federal remedies. Most notably, Justice Gorsuch questioned the power of federal courts to vacate agency rules under the Administrative Procedure Act, on the basis of the statute's text, history, and structure, as well as background principles of judicial power. Finally he argued that even if such a remedy was authorized by the APA, "faithful application of [equitable] principles suggests that an extraordinary remedy like vacatur would demand truly extraordinary circumstances to justify it" (citing and quoting Bray & Miller, *Getting Into Equity*, 97 Notre Dame L.Rev. 1763, 1797 (2022) ("[I]n equity it all connects—the broader and deeper the remedy the plaintiff wants, the stronger the plaintiff's story needs to be.")).[2]

The scope of the majority's holding in United States v. Texas is somewhat unclear. After establishing broad principles of executive discretion, the Court also listed a series of cases that might be justiciable nonetheless: "selective-prosecution claims under the Equal Protection Clause"; cases where Congress had specifically authorized judicial review; cases where "the Executive Branch wholly abandoned its statutory responsibilities"; cases where the executive also granted legal benefits or legal status; and "policies governing the continued detention of noncitizens who have already been arrested." Does United States v. Texas establish a broad principle of judicial restraint, or does it approximate a case-specific judgment on the merits that will affect few other cases?

(2) Redefining the Injury? Determining whether an injury is redressable depends, centrally, on how the injury is defined in the first place. Doesn't this give the Court strong incentive, in some cases, to redefine the relevant injury in order to reach a preferred outcome on the question of redressability?

(a) For instance, in Heckler v. Mathews, 465 U.S. 728 (1984), discussed at p. 143, *supra*, the severability clause of a facially discriminatory benefits statute might seem to make it impossible for a court to redress the discrimination imposed by the statute. But by redefining the injury as one of discrimination rather than simply entitlement to benefits, the Court found an injury that could be redressed.

(b) Similarly, Regents of the University of California v. Bakke, 438 U.S. 265 (1978), granted standing to a white plaintiff to challenge the defendant's operation of a special admissions program for minority applicants to medical school. Some amici argued that the plaintiff lacked standing because he had not shown that his asserted injury—exclusion from medical school—would be redressed by a favorable decision, since he might not have been admitted even absent any preference for minority applicants.

---

[2] The following year in Corner Post v. Board of Governors of the Federal Reserve, 144 S.Ct. 2440 (2024), Justice Kavanaugh wrote a concurring opinion providing an extensive defense of the remedy of vacatur, relying heavily on the scholarship of Professor Sohoni. See Sohoni, *The Past and Future of Universal Vacatur*, 133 Yale L.J. 2305 (2024); Sohoni, *The Power To Vacate a Rule*, 88 Geo.Wash.L.Rev. 1121 (2020).

In a portion of his opinion endorsed by four other Justices, Justice Powell affirmed Bakke's standing, arguing that relief would redress the injury Bakke had suffered by having been deprived, simply because of his race, of the chance to *compete* for every place in the entering class. See also Northeastern Florida Chapter of the Associated General Contractors of America v. City of Jacksonville, 508 U.S. 656 (1993) (taking a similar approach in an action by a non-minority bidder on municipal contracts who wished to challenge a municipal ordinance that set aside 10% of city contracts for "minority business enterprises").[3]

In light of Mathews and Bakke, consider Sunstein, *Standing and the Privatization of Public Law*, 88 Colum.L.Rev. 1432, 1464–69 (1988): "The central problem [is] how to characterize the relevant injury. [In Simon,] for example, the plaintiffs might have characterized their injury as an impairment of the opportunity to obtain medical services under a regime undistorted by unlawful tax incentives. In Allen, the plaintiffs themselves argued that their injury should be characterized as the deprivation of an opportunity to undergo desegregation in school systems unaffected by unlawful tax deductions. Thus recharacterized, the injuries are not speculative at all." To what extent could the standing difficulties in Simon, Allen, and many of the other cases discussed in this Note be resolved by recharacterization?

(3) The Relationship Between Standing and Remedies. Although inquiries into causation and redressability often overlap, they do not inevitably do so. Because of distinctive concerns about redressability, a plaintiff may have standing to seek some forms of relief but not others. This point was emphasized sharply by Los Angeles v. Lyons, 461 U.S. 95 (1983) (discussed at pp. 145–146, *supra*), where the Court held that the plaintiff who was assumed to have standing to pursue a claim for *damages* for an unprovoked illegal chokehold *in the past* did not have standing to seek *equitable relief* against such chokeholds *in the future*. The district court had held, and the parties agreed, that the damages claim could be severed from the claim for equitable relief, and the Court proceeded on the assumption that Lyons would have standing to pursue his damages remedy on remand. The Court concluded, however, that he was required to establish standing for each element of relief he sought, and that the equitable relief he requested would not redress the harms he alleged. The fact that "Lyons may have been illegally choked by the police on October 6, 1976, while presumably affording Lyons standing to claim damages," the Court explained, "does

---

[3]   In Texas v. Lesage, 528 U.S. 18 (1999) (per curiam), the Court held that a rejected applicant challenging an affirmative action program could not recover damages where the defendant proved that it would have made the same decision to exclude the applicant even in the absence of an affirmative action program. Under these circumstances, the Court said, "there is no cognizable injury warranting relief." If the injury grounding standing in Bakke and Associated General Contractors is "the denial of equal treatment" rather than "the ultimate inability to obtain the benefit," why will that injury support injunctive but not damages relief? See Bhagwat, *Injury Without Harm: Texas v. Lesage and the Strange World of Article III Injuries*, 28 Hastings Const.L.Q. 445 (2001). See also Boddie, *The Sins of Innocence,* 68 Vand.L.Rev. 297 (2015) (arguing that presumed injuries to white plaintiffs seeking to enjoin affirmative action programs rely on racialized conceptions of innocence and make standing both a product and an instrument of racial inequality).

nothing to establish a real and immediate threat that he would again be stopped for a traffic violation, or for any other offense, by an officer or officers who would illegally choke him into unconsciousness without any provocation or resistance on his part." Because the requested relief would therefore not redress Lyons' alleged injury, the Court found that he was "no more entitled to an injunction than any other citizen of Los Angeles."[4]

Disputing this proposition was the centerpiece of Justice Marshall's dissent (joined by three other Justices). The dissent charged that "by fragmenting a single claim into multiple claims for particular types of relief and requiring a separate showing of standing for each form of relief, the decision today departs from this Court's traditional conception of standing and of the remedial powers of the federal courts." The dissent argued that the purpose of the standing requirement was to ensure that the litigants have a "personal stake" sufficient to guarantee "adversary presentation" of the legal issues, and that because Lyons's damages claim rested on the same core constitutional question, there was no Article III problem adjudicating his claim for equitable relief.

As a more practical matter, the dissent also argued that it would be difficult and anomalous to fully consider remedial issues at the threshold standing stage. "[S]ince the merger of law and equity," the dissent argued, "[t]he federal practice has been to reserve consideration of the appropriate relief until after a determination of the merits, not to foreclose certain forms of relief by a ruling on the pleadings." Emphasizing the "broad discretion to grant appropriate equitable relief to protect a party who has been injured by unlawful conduct," the dissent warned that "it will rarely be easy to decide with any certainty at the outset of a lawsuit that no equitable relief would be appropriate under any conceivable set of facts that he might establish in support of his claim."

The Court has repeated the rule that a plaintiff must have standing to seek each form of relief several times after Lyons. See, *e.g.*, Friends of the Earth Inc. v. Laidlaw Environmental Services (TOC), Inc., 528 U.S. 167, 185 (2000) (holding that "a plaintiff must demonstrate standing separately for each form of relief sought"); Lewis v. Casey, 518 U.S. 343, 358, n.6 (1996) ("[S]tanding is not dispensed in gross."). Town of Chester v. Laroe Estates, Inc., 581 U.S. 433 (2017), also applied the principle that plaintiffs must separately demonstrate standing for all forms of relief when they seek to intervene as of right under Fed.R.Civ.P. 24(a)(2) and seek relief not requested by the plaintiffs. But, if taken to its full logic, isn't Justice Marshall right that it would require courts to consider all factors relevant to the exercise of equitable relief, which can be quite contextual, at the very earliest stage of litigation? What is more, since the Court has held that standing is jurisdictional and cannot be waived, might it even have to consider these issues without adequate adversary presentation? Is that not

---

4   For earlier decisions resting on similar reasoning to Lyons, see, *e.g.*, Rizzo v. Goode, 423 U.S. 362 (1976); O'Shea v. Littleton, 414 U.S. 488 (1974) (discussed pp. 280–282, *infra*); Golden v. Zwickler, 394 U.S. 103 (1969).

the opposite of the kind of prudent judicial decisionmaking that standing doctrine is supposed to promote?

(4) Recent Applications of the Causation and Redressability Principles.

(a)   In Haaland v. Brackeen, 599 U.S. 255 (2023), the Court rejected a set of challenges to the constitutionality of the Indian Child Welfare Act on redressability grounds. Most importantly, it rejected a claim by a group of individual non-Native American plaintiffs who argued that the Act violated equal protection principles by treating them less favorably than Native American parents seeking to adopt or foster a Native American child. The Court agreed that "[t]he racial discrimination [these plaintiffs] allege counts as an Article III injury," but it held that they "have not shown that this injury is 'likely' to be 'redressed by judicial relief.'" (quoting TransUnion LLC v. Ramirez, 594 U.S. 413, 423 (2021)). The plaintiffs sought relief (an injunction and a declaratory judgment) against various federal parties, but "enjoining the federal parties would not remedy the alleged injury, because state courts apply the placement preferences, and state agencies carry out the court-ordered placements."

The Court acknowledged the plaintiffs' argument that "state courts are likely to defer to a federal court's interpretation of federal law" and thus that "winning this case would solve their problems." But this possibility still did not satisfy the redressability prong. "[R]edressability requires that the court be able to afford relief *through the exercise of its power*, not through the persuasive or even awe-inspiring effect of the opinion *explaining* the exercise of its power" (quoting Franklin v. Massachusetts, 505 U. S. 788, 825 (1992) (Scalia, J., concurring in part and concurring in judgment) (emphasis in original)). This meant that redressability draws a hard line between judicial judgments and judicial opinions: "It is a federal court's judgment, not its opinion, that remedies an injury; thus it is the judgment, not the opinion, that demonstrates redressability. The individual petitioners can hope for nothing more than an opinion, so they cannot satisfy Article III."

(b)   The Court's divergent standing decisions in two challenges to the Biden administration's proposed student-loan forgiveness plan further illustrate the complicated interplay between causation and redressability principles. In Department of Education v. Brown, 600 U.S. 551 (2023), the Court unanimously found that two individual plaintiffs lacked standing to sue. The plaintiffs' argument, in brief, was that they had been injured because their loans had not been covered, or not covered adequately, by the administration's chosen plan. But had the administration been forced to use a different statutory authority to pursue loan relief, it would have been required to use more elaborate administrative procedures, and the result of that process might have benefited the plaintiffs.

The Court expressed doubts about the plaintiffs' injury and about its redressability, but concluded that "the deficiencies of respondents' claim are clearest with respect to traceability." The two possible statutory authorities for student-loan relief were independent from another. Thus, "the Department's decision to give *other* people relief under a *different* statutory scheme did not cause respondents not to obtain the benefits they want. The cause of their supposed injury is far more pedestrian than that: The Department has simply *chosen* not to give them the relief they want."

Meanwhile, the same day, a 6–3 majority did uphold standing to challenge the program by a different plaintiff: the state of Missouri, which was one of the plaintiffs in a case captioned Biden v. Nebraska, 143 S.Ct. 2355 (2023). Missouri's standing came from the economic effect that student-loan relief would have on the Missouri Higher Education Loan Authority (MOHELA), depriving it of servicing fees it otherwise would have earned had the loans continued. It was accepted on all sides that MOHELA would have had standing to sue if it chose, and the Justices disagreed about whether the state of Missouri could be the one to sue instead. For discussion of that issue, see p. 215, *infra*.

(c) In Food & Drug Administration v. Alliance for Hippocratic Medicine, 602 U.S. 367 (2024), the Court unanimously rejected the standing of a group of doctors to challenge the FDA's relaxation of restrictions on the abortion drug mifepristone. The doctors did not themselves take or prescribe mifepristone, but rather argued that the FDA's actions injured them indirectly, because it would cause more patients to have complications from the drug, and those patients would be more likely to seek treatment from the plaintiffs. After noting its general skepticism of standing for unregulated parties that "challenge[ ] the government's unlawful regulation (or lack of regulation) of *someone else*," (see Paragraph (1), *supra*), the Court rejected the doctors' theories of standing. The Court concluded that the connection between the FDA's actions and any potential burden on the doctors who would have to treat women who took mifepristone was "too speculative or otherwise too attenuated." As a more general matter, it cautioned, "[a]llowing doctors or other healthcare providers to challenge general safety regulations as unlawfully lax would be an unprecedented and limitless approach and would allow doctors to sue in federal court to challenge almost any policy affecting public health."

(d) In Murthy v. Missouri, 144 S.Ct. 1972 (2024), the Court rejected the standing of a group of plaintiffs who sought to enjoin government officials from pressuring social media companies to remove certain kinds of speech. In a 6–3 decision, written by Justice Barrett, the Court held that all of the plaintiffs lacked standing. In doing so, it emphasized two principles discussed above: that standing must be shown with particularity for each claim of relief against each defendant, not "at a high level of generality" and not "by treating the defendants, plaintiffs, and platforms each as a unified whole" (see Paragraph (3), *supra*); and also that standing is much more difficult to show when the plaintiffs' claim to relief turn on the future behavior of third parties (see Paragraph (1), *supra*). Taken together, these principles left the Court unconvinced that the plaintiffs had shown with specificity that the social media companies' policies had been caused by the government officials, or that the policies would change going forward if an injunction required the officials to stop jawboning the companies. Justice Alito wrote a dissent (joined by Justice Thomas and Justice Gorsuch) zeroing in on the speech of one plaintiff—Jill Hines—who they believed had made a sufficient showing of redressability and causation as to her posts on Facebook.

(5) The Political Valence of Standing. Considering the historical development of standing doctrine in the early twentieth century, Professor Sunstein argues that "the principal early architects of * * * standing limits were Justices Brandeis and Frankfurter," whose aim in so doing "was to insulate progressive New Deal legislation from frequent judicial attack." Sunstein, *What's Standing After Lujan? Of Citizen Suits, "Injuries," and Article III*, 91 Mich.L.Rev. 163, 179 (1992). See also Pushaw, *Justiciability and Separation of Powers: A Neo-Federalist Approach*, 81 Cornell L.Rev. 394, 458–63 (1996). Based on an empirical study of more than 1,500 standing cases decided between 1921 and 2006, Ho and Ross conclude that attributing the rise of standing doctrine to the progressive goals of Justices Brandeis and Frankfurter misstates the history. See Ho & Ross, *Did Liberal Justices Invent the Standing Doctrine? An Empirical Study of the Evolution of Standing*, 1921–2006, 62 Stan.L.Rev. 591 (2010). In particular, they argue that the early standing cases (1921–1930) had no political valence; many were unanimous or at least included some of the conservative Justices associated with the Lochner era and, later, with the Court's resistance to the New Deal. During the New Deal, however, Ho and Ross's study finds that the doctrine shifted, and that voting blocs substantiate the liberal reliance on standing to insulate administrative agencies from judicial review. After 1950, the valence of standing doctrine shifted again, as it became more associated with conservative efforts to insulate government action from public interest challenges—as evidenced by cases ranging from Allen v. Wright, p. 143, *supra*, and Los Angeles v. Lyons, p. 145, *supra*, to Clapper v. Amnesty International, p. 133, *supra*.

The political valence of standing may be shifting again, however. More than a decade ago Professor Elliott argued that standing limitations were increasingly filtering out not merely progressive interest group litigation, but also litigation by conservative interest groups seeking to challenge laws dealing with same-sex marriage, health care reform, and stem cell research. Elliott, *Standing Lessons: What We Can Learn When Conservative Plaintiffs Lose Under Article III Standing Doctrine*, 87 Ind.L.J. 551 (2012). And more recently Professor Re has also explored "the possibility of a broader standing realignment, in which the legal Left becomes jurisdictionally hawkish." *Does the Discourse on 303 Creative Portend a Standing Realignment?*, 99 Notre Dame L.Rev. Reflection 67 (2023). As Professor Re notes, California v. Texas, United States v. Texas, and Biden v. Nebraska, are all consistent with that hypothesis.

(6) Are Standing Requirements Judicially Manageable? In light of the cases discussed thus far in this section, consider the following contentions about the objectivity, determinacy, and efficacy of standing requirements:[5]

---

[5]   Some commentators suggest that the Court uses standing to pursue unarticulated strategic aims unrelated to the doctrine's stated goals. See, *e.g.*, Staudt, *Modeling Standing*, 79 N.Y.U.L.Rev. 612 (2004); Pierce, *Is Standing Law or Politics?*, 77 N.C.L.Rev. 1741, 1742–43 (1999); Varat, *Variable Justiciability and the Duke Power Case*, 58 Tex.L.Rev. 273 (1980). In a

(i)   "In classifying some harms as injuries in fact and other harms as purely ideological, courts must inevitably rely on some standard that is normatively laden and independent of facts. * * * When blacks challenge a grant or tax deductions to segregated schools, they believe that the grant is an injury in fact, not that it is purely ideological. When an environmentalist complains about the destruction of a pristine area, he believes that the loss of that area is indeed an injury to him. When we deny these claims, we are making a judgment based not on any fact, but instead on an inquiry into what should count as a judicially cognizable injury." Sunstein, note 2, *supra*, at 188–90.

(ii)   "The factors relevant to the case determination exist on a continuum, and the Court must unavoidably make choices about where on the continuum a line should be drawn. * * * The Court must make distinctions of degree, not of kind." Bandes, *The Idea of a Case*, 42 Stan.L.Rev. 227, 264 (1990).

(iii)   "One way of describing the Court's mistake in standing cases is to say that it has tried to formulate standing principles at too high a level of generality. Lawyers and judges usually try to formulate principles at as high a level of generality as the nature of the material will permit, but there is a limit on the generality of any given principle. That limit is passed when too many bad results are obtained by following the principle, or when the principle is too often evaded by subterfuge." Fletcher, *The Structure of Standing*, 98 Yale L.J. 221, 290 (1988).

Do those criticisms seem well grounded? Assuming a lack of a tight connection between the lines drawn in particular standing cases and the background goals articulated in those cases, might the Court's approach still plausibly promote a sound conception of the limits on Article III power? The Court has consistently made clear that an abstract interest in the government's "proper application of the Constitution and laws" cannot alone justify Article III standing. Lujan v. Defenders of Wildlife, 504 U.S. 555, 573–74 (1992). See also, *e.g.*, Schlesinger v. Reservists Committee to Stop the War, 418 U.S. 208, 217 (1974); Valley Forge Christian College v. Americans United for Separation of Church and State, Inc., 454 U.S. 464, 475–79 (1982). As one of the first modern standing cases, Fairchild v. Hughes, p. 128, *supra*, put it, the judicial power cannot be invoked to vindicate "the [general] right, possessed by every citizen, to require that the government be administered according to law." Might the Court's modern cases be understood as a crude, imperfect way of trying to fulfill that broad purpose, namely, to filter out plaintiffs who really wish only to vindicate the rule of law?

Finally, consider the following alternative framework: Judge (formerly Professor) Fletcher has argued that the standing inquiry should focus on the *meaning* of the particular constitutional or statutory provision relied upon

---

survey of standing doctrine under the Roberts Court, Fallon, *The Fragmentation of Standing*, 93 Tex.L.Rev. 1061 (2015), identifies a series of patterns to the Court's standing decisions which "frequently exhibit an implicit normative logic" and enable predictions of future outcomes, but require scholars and judges to look behind the Court's words to "the kinds of facts that actually drive decisions in practice." Professor Fallon suggests that his "doctrinal Realist credo affords a note of hope, not despair" for those seeking ordered consistency among leading decisions.

and on the question whether such provision should be construed to grant the plaintiff a right to sue. See Fletcher, *The Structure of Standing*, 98 Yale L.J. 221 (1988). See also Warth v. Seldin, 422 U.S. 490, 500 (1975) (suggesting that the standing question "is whether the constitutional or statutory provision on which the claim rests properly can be understood as granting persons in the plaintiff's position a right to judicial relief"). Does this approach solve some of the apparent anomalies in the case law? Would a shift to an approach inquiring whether particular constitutional or statutory provisions create rights in plaintiffs that are supposed to be judicially enforceable prove more reliable or administrable than the present framework? More principled? Or would many of the same disputes about plaintiffs' standing recur, recast as arguments about which specific constitutional rights plaintiffs do and do not have?

INTRODUCTORY NOTE ON CONGRESSIONAL POWER TO REGULATE STANDING

If standing reflects an irreducible constitutional minimum that authorizes judges to measure the existence of injury in fact, causation, and redressability against a constitutional ideal of what constitutes a "case" or "controversy," then the availability of standing may not depend upon the way Congress defines new rights of action. If, however, standing turns on the articulation of a *legal* injury, then Congress has greater leeway to define injuries and chains of causation that will create standing where none would otherwise exist. In the materials that follow, consider (i) where Congress derives its authority to create novel forms of standing and (ii) where the judiciary derives its authority to displace Acts of Congress that give particular classes of plaintiffs the right to sue.

Lujan v. Defenders of Wildlife
504 U.S. 555 (1992).
Certiorari to the United States Court of Appeals for the Eighth Circuit.

■ JUSTICE SCALIA delivered the opinion of the Court with respect to Parts I, II, III-A, and IV, and an opinion with respect to Part III-B, in which THE CHIEF JUSTICE, JUSTICE WHITE, and JUSTICE THOMAS join.

* * *

I

The E[ndangered] S[pecies] A[ct], 87 Stat. 884, as amended, 16 U.S.C. § 1531 *et seq.*, seeks to protect species of animals against threats to their continuing existence caused by man. * * * Section 7(a)(2) of the Act * * * provides, in pertinent part:

"Each Federal agency shall, in consultation with and with the assistance of the Secretary [of the Interior], insure that any action authorized, funded, or carried out by such agency . . . is not likely to jeopardize the continued existence of any endangered species or threatened species or result in the destruction or adverse modification of habitat of such species which is determined by the Secretary, after consultation as appropriate with affected States, to be critical." 16 U.S.C. § 1536(a)(2).

In 1978, the Fish and Wildlife Service (FWS) and the National Marine Fisheries Service (NMFS), on behalf of the Secretary of the Interior and the Secretary of Commerce respectively, promulgated a joint regulation stating that the obligations imposed by § 7(a)(2) extend to actions taken in foreign nations. * * * [In 1986, the Interior Department promulgated a "revised joint regulation, reinterpreting § 7(a)(2) to require consultation only for actions taken in the United States or on the high seas."]

Shortly thereafter, respondents, organizations dedicated to wildlife conservation and other environmental causes, filed this action against the Secretary of the Interior, seeking a declaratory judgment that the new regulation is in error as to the geographic scope of § 7(a)(2) and an injunction requiring the Secretary to promulgate a new regulation restoring the initial interpretation. The District Court granted the Secretary's motion to dismiss for lack of standing. The Court of Appeals for the Eighth Circuit reversed by a divided vote. On remand, the Secretary moved for summary judgment on the standing issue, and respondents moved for summary judgment on the merits. The District Court denied the Secretary's motion, on the ground that the Eighth Circuit had already determined the standing question in this case; it granted respondents' merits motion, and ordered the Secretary to publish a revised regulation. The Eighth Circuit affirmed. We granted certiorari.

II

* * * Over the years, our cases have established that the irreducible constitutional minimum of standing contains three elements. First, the plaintiff must have suffered an "injury in fact"—an invasion of a legally protected interest which is (a) concrete and particularized, [see Allen v. Wright, 468 U.S. 737,] 756 [(1984)]; and (b) "actual or imminent, not 'conjectural' or 'hypothetical.'" Whitmore [v. Arkansas, 495 U.S. 149,] 155 [(1990)] (quoting Los Angeles v. Lyons, 461 U.S. 95, 102 (1983)). Second, there must be a causal connection between the injury and the conduct complained of—the injury has to be "fairly . . . trace[able] to the challenged action of the defendant, and not . . . th[e] result [of] the independent action of some third party not before the court." Simon v. Eastern Ky. Welfare Rights Organization, 426 U.S. 26, 41–42 (1976). Third, it must be "likely," as opposed to merely "speculative," that the injury will be "redressed by a favorable decision." Id., at 38, 43.

The party invoking federal jurisdiction bears the burden of establishing these elements. * * * [O]n a motion to dismiss we "presum[e] that general allegations embrace those specific facts that are necessary to support the claim." [Lujan v.] National Wildlife Federation, [497 U.S. 871,] 889 [(1990)]. In response to a summary judgment motion, however, the plaintiff can no longer rest on such "mere allegations," but must "set forth" by affidavit or other evidence "specific facts," Fed.R.Civ.Proc. 56(e), which for purposes of the summary judgment motion will be taken to be true. And at the final stage, those facts (if controverted) must be "supported adequately by the evidence adduced at trial."

When the suit is one challenging the legality of government action or inaction, the nature and extent of facts that must be averred (at the summary judgment stage) or proved (at the trial stage) in order to establish standing depends considerably upon whether the plaintiff is himself an object of the action (or forgone action) at issue. If he is, there is ordinarily little question that the action or inaction has caused him injury, and that a judgment preventing or requiring the action will redress it. When, however, as in this case, a plaintiff's asserted injury arises from the government's allegedly unlawful regulation (or lack of regulation) of *someone else*, much more is needed. In that circumstance, causation and redressability ordinarily hinge on the response of the regulated (or regulable) third party to the government action or inaction—and perhaps on the response of others as well. The existence of one or more of the essential elements of standing "depends on the unfettered choices made by independent actors not before the courts and whose exercise of broad and legitimate discretion the courts cannot presume either to control or to predict," ASARCO Inc. v. Kadish, 490 U.S. 605, 615 (1989) (opinion of Kennedy, J.); and it becomes the burden of the plaintiff to adduce facts showing that those choices have been or will be made in such manner as to produce causation and permit redressability of injury. Thus, when the plaintiff is not himself the object of the government action or inaction he challenges, standing is not precluded, but it is ordinarily "substantially more difficult" to establish. Allen, *supra*, 468 U.S., at 758.

III

We think the Court of Appeals failed to apply the foregoing principles in denying the Secretary's motion for summary judgment. Respondents had not made the requisite demonstration of (at least) injury and redressability.

A

Respondents' claim to injury is that the lack of consultation with respect to certain funded activities abroad "increas[es] the rate of extinction of endangered and threatened species." Of course, the desire to use or observe an animal species, even for purely esthetic purposes, is undeniably a cognizable interest for purpose of standing. See, *e.g.*, Sierra Club v. Morton, 405 U.S. [727,] 734 [(1972)]. "But the 'injury in fact' test requires more than an injury to a cognizable interest. It requires that the party seeking review be himself among the injured." *Id.*, at 734–735. To survive the Secretary's summary judgment motion, respondents had to submit affidavits or other evidence showing, through specific facts, not only that listed species were in fact being threatened by funded activities abroad, but also that one or more of respondents' members would thereby be "directly" affected apart from their " 'special interest' in th[e] subject." *Id.*, at 735, 739. * * *

With respect to this aspect of the case, the Court of Appeals focused on the affidavits of two Defenders' members—Joyce Kelly and Amy Skilbred. Ms. Kelly stated that she traveled to Egypt in 1986 and "observed the traditional habitat of the endangered nile crocodile there and intend[s] to do so again, and hope[s] to observe the crocodile directly," and that she "will suffer harm in fact as the result of [the] American . . . role . . . in overseeing the rehabilitation of the Aswan High Dam on the Nile . . . and [in] develop[ing] . . . Egypt's . . . Master Water Plan." Ms. Skilbred averred that she traveled to Sri Lanka in 1981 and "observed th[e] habitat" of "endangered species such as the Asian elephant and the leopard" at what is now the site of the Mahaweli project funded by the Agency for International Development (AID), although she "was unable to see any of the endangered species"; "this development project," she continued, "will seriously reduce endangered, threatened, and endemic species habitat including areas that I visited . . . [, which] may severely shorten the future of these species"; that threat, she concluded, harmed her because she "intend[s] to return to Sri Lanka in the future and hope[s] to be more fortunate in spotting at least the endangered elephant and leopard." When Ms. Skilbred was asked at a subsequent deposition if and when she had any plans to return to Sri Lanka, she * * * confessed that she had no current plans * * *.

We shall assume for the sake of argument that these affidavits contain facts showing that certain agency-funded projects threaten listed species—though that is questionable. They plainly contain no facts, however, showing how damage to the species will produce "imminent" injury to Mses. Kelly and Skilbred. That the women "had visited" the areas of the projects before the projects commenced proves nothing. * * * And the affiants' profession of an "inten[t]" to return to the places they had visited before—* * * without any description of concrete plans, or indeed even any specification of *when* the some day will be—do not support a finding of the "actual or imminent" injury that our cases require.

Besides relying upon the Kelly and Skilbred affidavits, respondents propose a series of novel standing theories. The first, inelegantly styled "ecosystem nexus," proposes that any person who uses *any part* of a "contiguous ecosystem" adversely affected by a funded activity has standing even if the activity is located a great distance away. This approach, as the Court of Appeals correctly observed, is inconsistent with our opinion in National Wildlife Federation, which held that a plaintiff claiming injury from environmental damage must use the area affected by the challenged activity and not an area roughly "in the vicinity" of it. 497 U.S., at 887–889. It makes no difference that the general-purpose section of the ESA states that the Act was intended in part "to provide a means whereby the ecosystems upon which endangered species and threatened species depend may be conserved," 16 U.S.C. § 1531(b). To say that the Act protects ecosystems is not to say that the Act creates (if it were possible) rights of action in persons who have not been injured in fact, that is, persons who use portions of an ecosystem not perceptibly affected by the unlawful action in question.

Respondents' other theories are called, alas, the "animal nexus" approach, whereby anyone who has an interest in studying or seeing the endangered animals anywhere on the globe has standing; and the "vocational nexus" approach, under which anyone with a professional interest in such animals can sue. Under these theories, anyone who goes to see Asian elephants in the Bronx Zoo, and anyone who is a keeper of Asian elephants in the Bronx Zoo, has standing to sue because the Director of the Agency for International Development (AID) did not consult with the Secretary regarding the AID-funded project in Sri Lanka. This is beyond all reason. * * * It is clear that the person who observes or works with a particular animal threatened by a federal decision is facing perceptible harm, since the very subject of his interest will no longer exist. It is even plausible—though it goes to the outermost limit of plausibility—to think that a person who observes or works with animals of a particular species in the very area of the world where that species is threatened by a federal decision is facing such harm, since some animals that might have been the subject of his interest will no longer exist, see Japan Whaling Assn. v. American Cetacean Society, 478 U.S. 221, 231, n.4 (1986). It goes beyond the limit, however, and into pure speculation and fantasy, to say that anyone who observes or works with an endangered species, anywhere in the world, is appreciably harmed by a single project affecting some portion of that species with which he has no more specific connection.

B

Besides failing to show injury, respondents failed to demonstrate redressability. Instead of attacking the separate decisions to fund particular projects allegedly causing them harm, respondents chose to challenge a more generalized level of Government action (rules regarding consultation) * * *. * * *

* * * Since the agencies funding the projects were not parties to the case, the District Court could accord relief only against the Secretary: He could be ordered to revise his regulation to require consultation for foreign projects. But this would not remedy respondents' alleged injury unless the funding agencies were bound by the Secretary's regulation, which is very much an open question. * * * When the Secretary promulgated the regulation at issue here, he thought it was binding on the agencies. The Solicitor General, however, has repudiated that

position here, and the agencies themselves apparently deny the Secretary's authority. * * *

* * * The short of the matter is that redress of the only injury in fact respondents complain of requires action (termination of funding until consultation) by the individual funding agencies; and any relief the District Court could have provided in this suit against the Secretary was not likely to produce that action.

A further impediment to redressability is the fact that the agencies generally supply only a fraction of the funding for a foreign project. AID, for example, has provided less than 10% of the funding for the Mahaweli project. Respondents have produced nothing to indicate that the projects they have named will either be suspended, or do less harm to listed species, if that fraction is eliminated. As in Simon, 426 U.S., at 43–44, it is entirely conjectural whether the nonagency activity that affects respondents will be altered or affected by the agency activity they seek to achieve. There is no standing.

IV

The Court of Appeals found that respondents had standing for an additional reason: because they had suffered a "procedural injury." The so-called "citizen-suit" provision of the ESA provides, in pertinent part, that "any person may commence a civil suit on his own behalf (A) to enjoin any person, including the United States and any other governmental instrumentality or agency . . . who is alleged to be in violation of any provision of this chapter." 16 U.S.C. § 1540(g). The court held that, because § 7(a)(2) requires interagency consultation, the citizen-suit provision creates a "procedural righ[t]" to consultation in all "persons"—so that *anyone* can file suit in federal court to challenge the Secretary's (or presumably any other official's) failure to follow the assertedly correct consultative procedure, notwithstanding his or her inability to allege any discrete injury flowing from that failure. To understand the remarkable nature of this holding one must be clear about what it does *not* rest upon: This is not a case where plaintiffs are seeking to enforce a procedural requirement the disregard of which could impair a separate concrete interest of theirs (*e.g.*, the procedural requirement for a hearing prior to denial of their license application, or the procedural requirement for an environmental impact statement before a federal facility is constructed next door to them).[7] Nor is it simply

---

[7]   There is this much truth to the assertion that "procedural rights" are special: The person who has been accorded a procedural right to protect his concrete interests can assert that right without meeting all the normal standards for redressability and immediacy. Thus, under our case law, one living adjacent to the site for proposed construction of a federally licensed dam has standing to challenge the licensing agency's failure to prepare an environmental impact statement, even though he cannot establish with any certainty that the statement will cause the license to be withheld or altered, and even though the dam will not be completed for many years. (That is why we do not rely, in the present case, upon the Government's argument that, *even if* the other agencies were obliged to consult with the Secretary, they might not have followed his advice.) What respondents' "procedural rights" argument seeks, however, is quite

a case where concrete injury has been suffered by many persons, as in mass fraud or mass tort situations. Nor, finally, is it the unusual case in which Congress has created a concrete private interest in the outcome of a suit against a private party for the government's benefit, by providing a cash bounty for the victorious plaintiff. Rather, the court held that the injury-in-fact requirement had been satisfied by congressional conferral upon *all* persons of an abstract, self-contained, noninstrumental "right" to have the Executive observe the procedures required by law. We reject this view.

We have consistently held that a plaintiff raising only a generally available grievance about government—claiming only harm to his and every citizen's interest in proper application of the Constitution and laws, and seeking relief that no more directly and tangibly benefits him than it does the public at large—does not state an Article III case or controversy. * * *

To be sure, our generalized-grievance cases have typically involved Government violation of procedures assertedly ordained by the Constitution rather than the Congress. But there is absolutely no basis for making the Article III inquiry turn on the source of the asserted right. Whether the courts were to act on their own, or at the invitation of Congress, in ignoring the concrete injury requirement described in our cases, they would be discarding a principle fundamental to the separate and distinct constitutional role of the Third Branch—one of the essential elements that identifies those "Cases" and "Controversies" that are the business of the courts rather than of the political branches. "The province of the court," as Chief Justice Marshall said in Marbury v. Madison, 5 U.S. (1 Cranch) 137, 170 (1803), "is, solely, to decide on the rights of individuals." Vindicating the *public* interest (including the public interest in Government observance of the Constitution and laws) is the function of Congress and the Chief Executive. The question presented here is whether the public interest in proper administration of the laws (specifically, in agencies' observance of a particular, statutorily prescribed procedure) can be converted into an individual right by a statute that denominates it as such, and that permits all citizens (or, for that matter, a subclass of citizens who suffer no distinctive concrete harm) to sue. If the concrete injury requirement has the separation-of-powers significance we have always said, the answer must be obvious: To permit Congress to convert the undifferentiated public interest in executive officers' compliance with the law into an "individual right" vindicable in the courts is to permit Congress to transfer from the President to the courts the Chief Executive's most important constitutional duty, to "take Care that the Laws be faithfully executed," Art. II, § 3. It would enable the courts, with the permission of Congress, "to assume a position of authority over the governmental acts of another

different from this: standing for persons who have no concrete interests affected—persons who live (and propose to live) at the other end of the country from the dam.

and co-equal department," Frothingham v. Mellon, 262 U.S. [447,] 489 [(1923)], and to become "'virtually continuing monitors of the wisdom and soundness of Executive action.'" Allen, [468 U.S.,] at 760 (quoting Laird v. Tatum, 408 U.S. 1, 15 (1972)). We have always rejected that vision of our role * * *.

Nothing in this contradicts the principle that "[t]he ... injury required by Art. III may exist solely by virtue of 'statutes creating legal rights, the invasion of which creates standing.'" Warth [v. Seldin,] 422 U.S. [490,] 500 [(1975)] (quoting Linda R. S. v. Richard D., 410 U.S. 614, 617, n.3 (1973)). Both of the cases used by Linda R. S. as an illustration of that principle involved Congress' elevating to the status of legally cognizable injuries concrete, *de facto* injuries that were previously inadequate in law (namely, injury to an individual's personal interest in living in a racially integrated community, see Trafficante v. Metropolitan Life Ins. Co., 409 U.S. 205, 208–212 (1972), and injury to a company's interest in marketing its product free from competition, see Hardin v. Kentucky Utilities Co., 390 U.S. 1, 6 (1968)). As we said in Sierra Club, "[Statutory] broadening [of] the categories of injury that may be alleged in support of standing is a different matter from abandoning the requirement that the party seeking review must himself have suffered an injury." 405 U.S., at 738. Whether or not the principle set forth in Warth can be extended beyond that distinction, it is clear that in suits against the Government, at least, the concrete injury requirement must remain. * * *

It is so ordered.

■ JUSTICE KENNEDY, with whom JUSTICE SOUTER joins, concurring in part and concurring in the judgment.

Although I agree with the essential parts of the Court's analysis, I write separately to make several observations.

I agree with the Court's conclusion in Part III-A that, on the record before us, respondents have failed to demonstrate that they themselves are "among the injured." Sierra Club v. Morton, 405 U.S. 727, 735 (1972). * * *

While it may seem trivial to require that Mses. Kelly and Skilbred acquire airline tickets to the project sites or announce a date certain upon which they will return, this is not a case where it is reasonable to assume that the affiants will be using the sites on a regular basis, nor do the affiants claim to have visited the sites since the projects commenced. With respect to the Court's discussion of respondents' "ecosystem nexus," "animal nexus," and "vocational nexus" theories, I agree that on this record respondents' showing is insufficient to establish standing on any of these bases. I am not willing to foreclose the possibility, however, that in different circumstances a nexus theory similar to those proffered here might support a claim to standing.

In light of the conclusion that respondents have not demonstrated a concrete injury here sufficient to support standing under our precedents, I would not reach the issue of redressability that is discussed by the plurality in Part III-B.

I also join Part IV of the Court's opinion with the following observations. As Government programs and policies become more complex and far reaching, we must be sensitive to the articulation of new rights of action that do not have clear analogs in our common-law tradition. Modern litigation has progressed far from the paradigm of Marbury suing Madison to get his commission, Marbury v. Madison, 5 U.S. (1 Cranch) 137 (1803), or Ogden seeking an injunction to halt Gibbons' steamboat operations, Gibbons v. Ogden, 22 U.S. (9 Wheat.) 1 (1824). In my view, Congress has the power to define injuries and articulate chains of causation that will give rise to a case or controversy where none existed before, and I do not read the Court's opinion to suggest a contrary view. In exercising this power, however, Congress must at the very least identify the injury it seeks to vindicate and relate the injury to the class of persons entitled to bring suit. The citizen-suit provision of the Endangered Species Act does not meet these minimal requirements, because while the statute purports to confer a right on "any person ... to enjoin ... the United States and any other governmental instrumentality or agency ... who is alleged to be in violation of any provision of this chapter," it does not of its own force establish that there is an injury in "any person" by virtue of any "violation." 16 U.S.C. § 1540(g)(1)(A).

The Court's holding that there is an outer limit to the power of Congress to confer rights of action is a direct and necessary consequence of the case and controversy limitations found in Article III. I agree that it would exceed those limitations if, at the behest of Congress and in the absence of any showing of concrete injury, we were to entertain citizen suits to vindicate the public's nonconcrete interest in the proper administration of the laws. While it does not matter how many persons have been injured by the challenged action, the party bringing suit must show that the action injures him in a concrete and personal way. This requirement is not just an empty formality. It preserves the vitality of the adversarial process by assuring both that the parties before the court have an actual, as opposed to professed, stake in the outcome, and that "the legal questions presented ... will be resolved, not in the rarified atmosphere of a debating society, but in a concrete factual context conducive to a realistic appreciation of the consequences of judicial action." Valley Forge Christian College v. Americans United for Separation of Church and State, Inc., 454 U.S. 464, 472 (1982). In addition, the requirement of concrete injury confines the Judicial Branch to its proper, limited role in the constitutional framework of Government.

An independent judiciary is held to account through its open proceedings and its reasoned judgments. In this process it is essential for the public to know what persons or groups are invoking the judicial power, the reasons that they have brought suit, and whether their claims are vindicated or denied. The concrete injury requirement helps assure that there can be an answer to these questions; and, as the Court's opinion is careful to show, that is part of the constitutional design. * * *

■ JUSTICE STEVENS, concurring in the judgment.

[Justice Stevens concurred in the judgment on the ground that he did not believe that § 7(a)(2) of the Endangered Species Act of 1973 (ESA), 16 U.S.C. § 1536(a)(2), required consultation about projects in foreign countries. He believed, however, that respondents had established their standing to sue. First, he contended that "injury to an individual's interest in studying or enjoying a species and its natural habitat occurs when someone (whether it be the Government or a private party) takes action that harms that species and habitat." Accordingly, the affidavits sufficed to survive summary judgment even though they did not specify a date for the plaintiffs' return to the habitats. Justice Stevens also rejected the plurality's conclusions about redressability on two grounds. First, he argued that the Court "must presume that if [we] hold[ ] that § 7(a)(2) requires consultation, all affected agencies would abide by that interpretation and engage in the requisite consultations." Second, he argued that the Court should credit Congress' judgment that consultation would affect the allocation of funds. And despite the varying levels of federal aid to different foreign projects, he argued that "it is not mere speculation to think that foreign governments, when faced with the threatened withdrawal of United States assistance, will modify their projects to mitigate the harm to endangered species."]

■ JUSTICE BLACKMUN, with whom JUSTICE O'CONNOR joins, dissenting.

I part company with the Court in this case in two respects. First, I believe that respondents have raised genuine issues of fact—sufficient to survive summary judgment—both as to injury and as to redressability. Second, I question the Court's breadth of language in rejecting standing for "procedural" injuries. I fear the Court seeks to impose fresh limitations on the constitutional authority of Congress to allow citizen suits in the federal courts for injuries deemed "procedural" in nature. I dissent.

I

* * *

A

To survive petitioner's motion for summary judgment on standing, respondents * * * need show only a "genuine issue" of material fact as to standing. Fed.R.Civ.Proc. 56(c). This is not a heavy burden. A "genuine issue" exists so long as "the evidence is such that a reasonable jury could return a verdict for the nonmoving party [respondents]." Anderson v. Liberty Lobby, Inc., 477 U.S. 242, 248 (1986). * * *

1

* * * I think a reasonable finder of fact could conclude from the information in the affidavits and deposition testimony that either Kelly or Skilbred will soon return to the project sites, thereby satisfying the "actual or imminent" injury standard. * * *

By requiring a "description of concrete plans" or "specification of *when* the some day [for a return visit] will be," the Court, in my view, demands what is likely an empty formality. No substantial barriers prevent Kelly or Skilbred from simply purchasing plane tickets to return to the Aswan and Mahaweli projects. This case differs from other cases in which the imminence of harm turned largely on the affirmative actions of third parties beyond a plaintiff's control. * * *

I fear the Court's demand for detailed descriptions of future conduct will do little to weed out those who are genuinely harmed from those who are not. More likely, it will resurrect a code-pleading formalism in federal court summary judgment practice, as federal courts, newly doubting their jurisdiction, will demand more and more particularized showings of future harm. * * *

2

The Court also concludes that injury is lacking, because respondents' allegations of "ecosystem nexus" failed to demonstrate sufficient proximity to the site of the environmental harm. To support that conclusion, the Court mischaracterizes our decision in Lujan v. National Wildlife Federation as establishing a general rule that "a plaintiff claiming injury from environmental damage must use the area affected by the challenged activity." In National Wildlife Federation, the Court required specific geographical proximity because of the particular type of harm alleged in that case: harm to the plaintiff's visual enjoyment of nature from mining activities. One cannot suffer from the sight of a ruined landscape without being close enough to see the sites actually being mined. Many environmental injuries, however, cause harm distant from the area immediately affected by the challenged action. * * *

The Court also rejects respondents' claim of vocational or professional injury. The Court says that it is "beyond all reason" that a zoo "keeper" of Asian elephants would have standing to contest his Government's participation in the eradication of all the Asian elephants in another part of the world. I am unable to see how the distant location of the destruction *necessarily* (for purposes of ruling at summary judgment) mitigates the harm to the elephant keeper. If there is no more access to a future supply of the animal that sustains a keeper's livelihood, surely there is harm. * * *

B

A plurality of the Court suggests that respondents have not demonstrated redressability * * *: The plurality identifies two obstacles. The first is that the "action agencies" * * * cannot be required to undertake consultation with petitioner Secretary, because they are not directly bound as parties to the suit and are otherwise not indirectly bound by being subject to petitioner Secretary's regulation. Petitioner, however, officially and publicly has taken the position that his regulations regarding consultation under § 7 of the Act are binding on action agencies. 50 CFR § 402.14(a) (1991). And he has previously taken the same position in this very litigation * * *. I cannot agree with the plurality that the Secretary (or the Solicitor General) is now free, for the convenience of this appeal, to disavow his prior public and litigation positions. * * *

The second redressability obstacle relied on by the plurality is that "the [action] agencies generally supply only a fraction of the funding for a foreign project." What this Court might "generally" take to be true does not eliminate the existence of a genuine issue of fact to withstand summary judgment. Even if the action agencies supply only a fraction of the funding for a particular foreign project, it remains at least a question for the finder of fact whether threatened withdrawal of that fraction would affect foreign government conduct sufficiently to avoid harm to listed species. * * *

* * * [T]he relevant inquiry is not, as the plurality suggests, what will happen if AID or other agencies stop funding projects, but what will happen if AID or other agencies comply with the consultation requirement for projects abroad. Respondents filed suit to require consultation, not a termination of funding. Respondents have raised at least a genuine issue of fact that the projects harm endangered species and that the actions of AID and other United States agencies can mitigate that harm. * * *

II

The Court concludes that any "procedural injury" suffered by respondents is insufficient to confer standing. It rejects the view that the "injury-in-fact requirement . . . [is] satisfied by congressional conferral upon *all* persons of an abstract, self-contained, noninstrumental 'right' to have the Executive observe the procedures required by law." Whatever the Court might mean with that very broad language, it cannot be saying that "procedural injuries" *as a class* are necessarily insufficient for purposes of Article III standing.

Most governmental conduct can be classified as "procedural." * * * When the Government, for example, "procedurally" issues a pollution permit, those affected by the permittee's pollutants are not without standing to sue. Only later cases will tell just what the Court means by its intimation that "procedural" injuries are not constitutionally cognizable injuries. In the meantime, I have the greatest of sympathy for the courts across the country that will struggle to understand the Court's standardless exposition of this concept today.

The Court expresses concern that allowing judicial enforcement of "agencies' observance of a particular, statutorily prescribed procedure" would "transfer from the President to the courts the Chief Executive's most important constitutional duty, to 'take Care that the Laws be faithfully executed,' Art. II, § 3." In fact, the principal effect of foreclosing judicial enforcement of such procedures is to transfer power into the hands of the Executive at the expense—not of the courts—but of Congress, from which that power originates and emanates.

Under the Court's anachronistically formal view of the separation of powers, Congress legislates pure, substantive mandates and has no business structuring the procedural manner in which the Executive implements these mandates. To be sure, in the ordinary course, Congress does legislate in black-and-white terms of affirmative commands or negative prohibitions on the conduct of officers of the Executive Branch. In complex regulatory areas, however, Congress often legislates, as it were, in procedural shades of gray. That is, it sets forth substantive policy goals and provides for their attainment by requiring Executive Branch officials to follow certain procedures, for example, in the form of reporting, consultation, and certification requirements. * * *

The consultation requirement of § 7 of the Endangered Species Act is a[n] * * * action-forcing statute. Consultation is designed as an integral check on federal agency action, ensuring that such action does not go forward without full consideration of its effects on listed species. Once consultation is initiated, the Secretary is under a duty to provide to the action agency "a written statement setting forth the Secretary's opinion, and a summary of the information on which the opinion is based, detailing how the agency action affects the species or its critical habitat." 16 U.S.C. § 1536(b)(3)(A). The Secretary is also obligated to suggest "reasonable and prudent alternatives" to prevent jeopardy to listed species. *Ibid.* The action agency must undertake as well its own "biological assessment for the purpose of identifying any endangered species or threatened species" likely to be affected by agency action. § 1536(c)(1). After the initiation of consultation, the action agency "shall not make any irreversible or irretrievable commitment of resources" which would foreclose the "formulation or implementation of any reasonable and prudent alternative measures" to avoid jeopardizing listed species. § 1536(d). These action-forcing procedures are "designed to protect some threatened concrete interest," of persons who observe and work with endangered or threatened species. That is why I am mystified by the Court's unsupported conclusion that "[t]his is not a case where plaintiffs are seeking to enforce a procedural requirement the disregard of which could impair a separate concrete interest of theirs." * * *

To prevent Congress from conferring standing for "procedural injuries" is [for Justice Scalia] another way of saying that Congress may not delegate to the courts authority deemed "executive" in nature. * * *

Here Congress seeks not to delegate "executive" power but only to strengthen the procedures it has legislatively mandated. * * *

It is to be hoped that over time the Court will acknowledge that some classes of procedural duties are so enmeshed with the prevention of a substantive, concrete harm that an individual plaintiff may be able to demonstrate a sufficient likelihood of injury just through the breach of that procedural duty. For example, in the context of the NEPA requirement of environmental-impact statements, this Court has acknowledged "it is now well settled that NEPA itself does not mandate particular results [and] simply prescribes the necessary process," but *"these procedures are almost certain to affect the agency's substantive decision."* Robertson v. Methow Valley Citizens Council, 490 U.S. [332,] 350 [(1989)] (emphasis added). * * *

In short, determining "injury" for Article III standing purposes is a fact-specific inquiry. * * * There may be factual circumstances in which a congressionally imposed procedural requirement is so insubstantially connected to the prevention of a substantive harm that it cannot be said to work any conceivable injury to an individual litigant. But, as a general matter, the courts owe substantial deference to Congress' substantive purpose in imposing a certain procedural requirement. In all events, * * * [t]here is no room for a *per se* rule or presumption excluding injuries labeled "procedural" in nature.

III

In conclusion, I cannot join the Court on what amounts to a slash-and-burn expedition through the law of environmental standing. In my view, "[t]he very essence of civil liberty certainly consists in the right of every individual to claim the protection of the laws, whenever he receives an injury." Marbury v. Madison, 1 Cranch 137, 163 (1803).

I dissent.

NOTE ON LUJAN AND ITS AFTERMATH

(1) Prior Congressional Grants of Standing. With the possible exceptions of the Court's cryptic opinion in Muskrat v. United States, 219 U.S. 346 (1911), p. 120, *supra*, and its unexplained summary affirmance in McClure v. Reagan, 454 U.S. 1025 (1981),[1] Lujan represents the first time that the Court clearly refused to apply an Act of Congress on the ground that it unconstitutionally conferred standing upon someone who did not meet the

---

[1]   Despite a relevant congressional authorization to sue, McClure v. Carter, 513 F.Supp. 265 (D.Idaho 1981), summarily affirmed *sub nom*. McClure v. Reagan, 454 U.S. 1025 (1981), the Court denied Senator McClure standing to challenge the appointment of former Congressman Mikva to the United States Court of Appeals for the D.C. Circuit as a violation of the Emoluments Clause. See U.S. Const. Art. I, § 6, cl. 2 (prohibiting the appointment of any Senator or Representative to any federal office whose emoluments were increased during the time for which the Senator or Representative was elected). For further discussion of congressional standing, see pp. 215–221, *supra*.

requisite injury requirements.[2] Indeed, prior Court opinions suggested that the determination about who possessed a judicially cognizable right to sue ultimately lay within congressional control. See Warth v. Seldin, 422 U.S. 490, 500–01 (1975) (dictum) (stating that "[t]he actual or threatened injury required by Art. III may exist solely by virtue of 'statutes creating legal rights, the invasion of which creates standing' "); Sierra Club v. Morton, 405 U.S. 727, 732 n.3 (1972) ("[W]here a dispute is otherwise justiciable, the question whether the litigant is a 'proper party to request an adjudication of a particular issue,' is one within the power of Congress to determine.").

As Justice Harlan noted in his influential separate opinion in Flast v. Cohen, 392 U.S. 83, 120 (1968), administrative law decisions of the 1940s had recognized significant congressional power to confer standing where none otherwise would have existed. In the absence of an authorizing statute, standing to challenge administrative action had generally depended on the coercive infringement of a liberty or property interest recognized at common law. See Sunstein, *Standing and the Privatization of Public Law*, 88 Colum.L.Rev. 1432 (1988). In effect, this common law approach to standing meant that the targets of regulatory action, but not the intended beneficiaries of regulatory statutes, possessed standing to sue. In a series of pathbreaking decisions, however, the Supreme Court held that Congress could authorize standing to protect the "public interest" in statutory enforcement. Consider the following pre-Lujan examples.

(a) Competitors' Standing. The evolution of competitors' standing provides the paradigmatic example of Congress's recognized power to create standing where none previously existed. The traditional rule was that the proprietor of a business lacks standing to object to the government's support of competing activities, because the common law does not recognize an interest in freedom from competition. See Tennessee Elec. Power Co. v. Tennessee Valley Auth., 306 U.S. 118, 137–38 (1939) (power companies that sell electricity lack standing to enjoin the TVA's competing operations, which are alleged to be unconstitutional); see also Alabama Power Co. v. Ickes, 302 U.S. 464 (1938). A major shift occurred in FCC v. Sanders Bros. Radio Station, 309 U.S. 470 (1940), where a radio station sought judicial review of the FCC's award of a broadcast license to a competitor. Section 402(b) of the Communications Act allowed an appeal "by any * * * person aggrieved or whose interests are adversely affected by a decision of the Commission granting or refusing any such application." The complainant argued that the Act created a legal interest in freedom from competition, which required consideration by the FCC of the economic impact of the award on existing licensees. The Court rejected this argument on the merits, but upheld the complainant's standing to protect the public interest: "Congress * * * may have been of opinion that one likely to be financially injured by the issue of

---

[2]   For critical discussion of Lujan, see Sunstein, *What's Standing After Lujan? Of Citizen Suits, "Injuries," and Article III*, 91 Mich.L.Rev. 163 (1992); Pierce, *Lujan v. Defenders of Wildlife: Standing as a Judicially Imposed Limit on Legislative Power*, 42 Duke L.J. 1170 (1993); and Nichol, *Justice Scalia, Standing, and Public Law Litigation*, 42 Duke L.J. 1141 (1993). For more favorable commentary, see Breger, *Defending Defenders: Remarks on Nichol and Pierce*, 42 Duke L.J. 1202 (1993); Roberts, *Article III Limits on Statutory Standing*, 42 Duke L.J. 1219 (1993).

a license would be the only person having a sufficient interest to bring to the attention of the appellate court errors of law in the action of the Commission in granting the license. It is within the power of Congress to confer such standing to prosecute an appeal." See also Scripps-Howard Radio, Inc. v. FCC, 316 U.S. 4, 14 (1942) (under Sanders, "these private litigants have standing only as representatives of the public interest"). Even if injury to the plaintiff's competitive position did not count as an injury to a legally protected interest, does the economic impact on the aggrieved party seem like concrete and personalized injury in fact, as that concept has come to be understood? For a thoughtful historical analysis suggesting that the competitor standing cases reflected—and, at the time, were generally understood by the legal community to reflect—the Court's view that Congress could authorize those without *any* private legal interest to sue on the public's behalf, see Magill, *Standing for the Public: A Lost History*, 95 Va.L.Rev. 1131 (2009).

(b) Civil Rights Enforcement. In Trafficante v. Metropolitan Life Ins. Co., 409 U.S. 205 (1972), a white and a Black tenant were held to have standing under § 810 of the Civil Rights Act of 1968, 42 U.S.C. § 3610, to seek injunctive relief and damages from their landlord for discriminating against non-white rental applicants. Section 810(d) of the Act provides that a "person aggrieved" may bring suit in federal court "to enforce rights granted or protected" by the Act. Section 810(a) defines "person aggrieved" to mean one "who claims to have been injured by a discriminatory housing practice." The plaintiffs here claimed damages for (1) lost social benefits of living in an integrated community, (2) lost business and professional advantages, and (3) embarrassment and economic injury from being "stigmatized" as residents of a "white ghetto."

Justice Douglas, for a unanimous Court, held that the statute "showed 'a congressional intention to define standing as broadly as is permitted by Article III * * *' insofar as tenants of the same housing unit * * * are concerned." The opinion further inferred from the Civil Rights Act's structure that, in achieving compliance, "the main generating force must be private suits in which * * * the complainants act not only on their own behalf but also 'as private attorneys general in vindicating a policy that Congress considered to be of the highest priority.' "

Justice White, joined by Justices Blackmun and Powell, concurred in the opinion of the Court but wrote specially to note: "Absent the Civil Rights Act of 1968, I would have great difficulty in concluding that petitioners' complaint in this case presented a case or controversy within the jurisdiction of the District Court under Article III of the Constitution. But with that statute purporting to give all those who are authorized to complain to the agency the right also to sue in court, I would sustain the statute insofar as it extends standing to those in the position of the petitioners in this case."

In Havens Realty Corp. v. Coleman, 455 U.S. 363, 372–74 (1982), the Court held that a Black "tester"—who posed as a renter or purchaser of housing to collect evidence of racial steering practices—had standing to seek equitable and monetary relief against private parties under § 804 of the Fair Housing Act of 1968, 42 U.S.C. § 3604. The Court reasoned that the Act conferred on the tester an enforceable legal right not to be denied, because of racial steering, truthful information about the availability of housing. (A white tester, to whom the defendant had given truthful information, was held to lack standing under this theory.)

Even if the plaintiffs in Trafficante can be said to have sustained concrete and personalized injury within the meaning of today's cases, can the testers in Havens be understood as having an interest beyond gathering evidence of illegal conduct to help ensure enforcement of the law?

(2) From Lujan to TransUnion. Lujan generated much uncertainty about Congress's authority to define judicially cognizable injuries that will provide Article III standing. Two subsequent cases seemed to confirm such authority, while two others seemed to anticipate a much narrower congressional role.

(a) In Federal Election Commission v. Akins, 524 U.S. 11 (1998), the Court held that a group of voters had standing to challenge a determination by the Federal Election Commission (FEC) that the American Israel Public Affairs Committee (AIPAC) is not a "political committee" within the meaning of the Federal Election Campaign Act of 1971, 2 U.S.C. § 431(4) (FECA). Based on that determination, the FEC "ha[d] refused to require AIPAC to make disclosures regarding its membership, contributions, and expenditures that FECA would otherwise require." As a group of voters whose views often contradicted those of AIPAC, respondents had filed a complaint with the FEC arguing that AIPAC was a "political committee" within the meaning of the Act and asking the FEC to order AIPAC to make the disclosures required of such a committee under the Act. When the FEC dismissed the complaint on the ground that AIPAC was an advocacy organization rather than a political committee, respondents filed an action in federal court seeking review.

In an opinion by Justice Breyer, the Court held that the respondent-voters had standing to challenge the FEC's decision: "Congress has specifically provided in FECA that 'any person who believes a violation of this Act . . . has occurred, may file a complaint with the Commission.' § 437g(a)(1). It has added that 'any party aggrieved by an order of the Commission dismissing a complaint filed by such party . . . may file a petition' in district court seeking review of that dismissal. § 437g(8)(A)." The Court reasoned that the statute was intended "to cast the standing net broadly—beyond the common-law interests and substantive statutory rights upon which 'prudential' standing traditionally rested." Finding, in particular, that Congress had sought "to protect voters such as respondents from suffering the kind of injury here at issue," the Court rejected contentions that Congress lacked power to authorize such an action:

"The 'injury in fact' that respondents have suffered consists of their inability to obtain information—lists of AIPAC donors (who are, according to AIPAC, its members), and campaign-related contributions and expenditures—that, on respondents' view of the law, the statute requires that AIPAC make public. There is no reason to doubt their claim that the information would help them (and others to whom they would communicate it) to evaluate candidates for public office, especially candidates who received assistance from AIPAC, and to evaluate the role that AIPAC's financial assistance might play in a specific election. Respondents' injury consequently seems concrete and particular."

Rejecting an analogy to the Court's prior decision in United States v. Richardson, 418 U.S. 166 (1974), p. 142, *supra*, the Court concluded that the present pursuit of information differed importantly from Richardson's efforts to ascertain the CIA's budget by virtue of the Accounts Clause, U.S. Const. Art. I, § 9, cl. 7 ("[A] regular Statement and Account of the Receipts and Expenditures of all public Money shall be published from time to time."). First, the plaintiff in Richardson had sued in his capacity as a taxpayer, and the Court found no "logical nexus" (as required by Flast v. Cohen, 392 U.S. 863 (1968), p. 129, *supra*) between his status as a taxpayer and the government's failure to provide a detailed statement of account. Second, even if Richardson had asserted a particular interest in such information as a voter, Justice Breyer noted, "the Court would * * * have had to consider whether 'the Framers . . . ever imagined that the *general directives* [of the Constitution] . . . would be subject to enforcement by an individual citizen.'" That determination, Justice Breyer added, "would have rested in significant part upon the Court's view of the Accounts Clause."

The Court then considered but rejected the FEC's contention that Akins presented "a generalized grievance." Justice Breyer first observed: "Whether styled as a constitutional or prudential limit on standing, the Court has sometimes determined that where large numbers of Americans suffer alike, the political process, rather than the judicial process, may provide the more appropriate remedy for a widely shared grievance." But the generalized grievance concern "invariably appears in cases where the harm at issue is not only widely shared, but is also of an abstract and indefinite nature—for example, harm to the 'common concern for obedience to law'" (quoting L. Singer & Sons v. Union Pacific R. Co., 311 U.S. 295, 303 (1940)). Acknowledging that abstractness often corresponds with an injury being widely shared, Justice Breyer explained that "their association is not invariable, and where a harm is concrete, though widely shared, the Court has found 'injury in fact.'"

Justice Breyer added: "This conclusion seems particularly obvious where (to use a hypothetical example) large numbers of individuals suffer the same common-law injury (say, a widespread mass tort), or where large numbers of voters suffer interference with voting rights conferred by law. We conclude that similarly, the informational injury at issue here, directly related to voting, the most basic of political rights, is sufficiently concrete and specific such that the fact that it is widely shared does not deprive Congress of constitutional power to authorize its vindication in the federal courts."

In dissent, Justice Scalia argued that the analogy to Richardson was closer than the Court recognized, and, indeed, that "the aggrievement there was more direct, since the Government already had the information in its possession, whereas here the respondents seek enforcement action that will bring information within the Government's possession and then require the information to be made public." He also contested the Court's analysis of the generalized grievance prohibition, noting that "if concrete generalized grievances (like concrete particularized grievances) are OK, and abstract generalized grievances (like abstract particularized grievances) are bad[,] * * * one must wonder why we ever developed the superfluous distinction between generalized and particularized grievances at all." He argued that even if many people suffer the same type of harm—*e.g.*, interference with the right to vote or a personal injury—each has still suffered "a particularized and differentiated harm." In contrast, he reasoned, a generalized grievance is "undifferentiated": "the * * * harm caused to Mr. Akins by the allegedly unlawful failure of FECA is precisely the same as the harm caused to everyone else: unavailability of a description of AIPAC's activities." Invoking concerns about intrusion upon the President's prerogative to "take Care that the Laws be faithfully executed," Justice Scalia concluded by observing that "[i]f today's decision is correct, it is within the power of Congress to authorize any interested person to manage (through the courts) the Executive's enforcement of any law that includes a requirement for the filing and public availability of a piece of paper."

Consider the following possible ways to understand the conjunction of Akins with Lujan: (a) an injury sufficient for purposes of Article III may exist simply by virtue of the invasion of a legal right created by Congress; (b) Congress has the power, by statute, to transform into cognizable injuries concrete harms that had been "previously inadequate in law," Lujan, p. 166, *supra*; or (c) whatever else one might say about Congress's authority to create judicially cognizable injuries, the inability to procure information to which Congress has created a right itself constitutes a concrete injury that gives rise to Article III standing.[3]

(b)   In Massachusetts v. EPA, 549 U.S. 497 (2007), the Court upheld the standing of a state to challenge a refusal by the EPA to issue regulations governing greenhouse gas emissions by new motor vehicles. In an opinion joined by four other Justices, Justice Stevens reasoned that Congress had authorized "this type of challenge to EPA action." In so holding, he emphasized that the Clean Air Act not only required the EPA to prescribe emissions standards in specified circumstances (42 U.S.C. § 7521(a)(1)), but also conferred upon parties the "procedural right" to challenge the EPA's denial of their petition to promulgate such standards (*id.* § 7607(b)(1)). Quoting Lujan v. Defenders of Wildlife, 504 U.S. 555, 572 n.7 (1992), Justice Stevens added that "a litigant to whom Congress has 'accorded a procedural right to protect his interests' * * * 'can assert that right without meeting all the normal standards for redressability and immediacy.' When a litigant is vested with a procedural right, that litigant has standing if there is some possibility that the requested relief will prompt the injury-causing party to reconsider the decision that allegedly harmed the litigant." The Court further noted that "[g]iven [the existence of a statutorily conferred]

---

[3]   By itself, congressional power to confer "informational standing" is of large importance. See Sunstein, *Informational Regulation and Informational Standing: Akins and Beyond*, 147 U.Pa.L.Rev. 613 (1999). (To underscore the point, consider who, under Justice Scalia's view, could bring suit under the Freedom of Information Act?)

procedural right and Massachusetts' stake in protecting its quasi-sovereign interests," which set it apart from ordinary litigants, "the Commonwealth is entitled to special solicitude in our standing analysis." Dissenting, Chief Justice Roberts, joined by Justices Scalia, Thomas, and Alito, argued that the state had alleged no threat of imminent or particularized injury.

Given the importance that the Court's opinion attached to the statutory right to sue, one might have read Massachusetts v. EPA to signal further tension with Lujan. But the case also came to be understood as depending importantly on the "special solicitude" for a state plaintiff protecting its quasi-sovereign interests. This aspect of the case is discussed further at pp. 212–214, *infra*.

(c)   In Summers v. Earth Island Institute, Inc., 555 U.S. 488 (2009), also discussed at p. 146, *supra*, a 5–4 Court rebuffed efforts by environmental organizations to base standing on the statistical probability that at least some of their members would suffer harms from the U.S. Forest Service's application of challenged regulations to parklands frequented by the organizations' members. The Court then discussed congressional authority to create standing when it turned to the organizations' alleged "procedural injury"—"namely, that they have been denied the ability to file comments on some Forest Service actions and will continue to be so denied." The Court responded that "deprivation of a procedural right without some concrete interest that is affected by the deprivation—a procedural right *in vacuo*—is insufficient to create Article III standing." Quoting footnote 7 of Lujan, the Court reaffirmed that "Only a 'person who has been accorded a procedural right to protect *his concrete interests* can assert that right without meeting all the normal standards for redressability and immediacy.' " The Court then seemed to deny congressional authority over injury in fact: "It makes no difference that the procedural right has been accorded by Congress. That can loosen the strictures of the redressability prong of our standing inquiry * * * Unlike redressability, however, the requirement of injury in fact is a hard floor of Article III jurisdiction that cannot be removed by statute."

Justice Kennedy, however (whose vote was necessary to the majority) wrote that "[t]his case would present different considerations if Congress had sought to provide redress for a concrete injury 'giv[ing] rise to a case or controversy where none existed before' " (quoting Lujan, 504 U.S., 580 (Kennedy, J., concurring in part and concurring in the judgment)). Summers thus seemed to reaffirm Lujan. But as with Lujan, reconciling Justice Kennedy's concurring opinion with the language of the majority opinion he joined in full has presented courts and scholars with some difficulty.[4]

(d)   In Spokeo, Inc. v. Robins, 578 U.S. 330 (2016), the Court again reaffirmed the framework that it had developed in Lujan to define

---

[4]   Judge Posner has argued that as a general matter "casting the essential fifth vote for the 'majority' opinion while also writing a separate opinion qualifying the Court's opinion is bad practice because it leaves the reader uncertain whether the majority opinion or the concurring opinion should be regarded as the best predictor of how the Court would decide a similar case in the future," and that doing so reflects the Court's "disregard [of] the consequences of its decisions for the lower courts that have to apply them." Posner, *Foreword: A Political Court*, 119 Harv.L.Rev. 31, 95 (2005).

congressional authority to confer standing, but divided 6–2 over how to apply that framework. The Fair Credit Reporting Act requires consumer reporting agencies to "follow reasonable procedures to assure maximum possible accuracy of" consumer reports and provides that " '[a]ny person who willfully fails to comply with any requirement [of the Act] with respect to any [individual] is liable to that [individual].' " Robins brought suit under the Act against Spokeo, a "people search engine" that maintained an inaccurate report about him on its website. In evaluating Robins's standing, the Court, in an opinion by Justice Alito, reaffirmed that "a bare procedural violation, divorced from any concrete harm," would not satisfy the Article III injury requirement "without [harm to] some concrete interest that is affected by the deprivation." The question thus became "whether the particular procedural violations alleged in this case entail a degree of risk sufficient to meet" the requirements of Article III. According to Robins, Spokeo falsely reported, *inter alia*, that he was in his fifties, had a graduate degree, and was economically well off, when in fact he was out of work and seeking employment. Robins maintained that Spokeo's report damaged his employment prospects by making him appear overqualified for jobs that he might have obtained otherwise.

In appraising that claim Justice Alito emphasized that Article III requires plaintiffs to allege injuries that are both "particularized" and "concrete," which he defined as meaning " 'real, and not 'abstract.' " He also acknowledged Lujan's recognition that "Congress may 'elevat[e] to the status of legally cognizable injuries concrete, de facto injuries that were previously inadequate in law.' " Against this background, Justice Alito concluded that Robins had alleged an injury particularized to him, but noted that "not all inaccuracies cause harm or present any material risk of harm." As an example, the majority offered the dissemination of an incorrect zip code, which it thought unlikely to "work any concrete harm." The lower court, the majority found, had focused its standing analysis exclusively on the requirement of particularized injury and thus failed to analyze "whether the particular procedural violations alleged in this case"—which the plaintiff said resulted in the publication of misinformation about him—"entail a degree of risk sufficient to meet the concreteness requirement." Accordingly, the Court vacated and remanded for further proceedings without deciding whether Robins "adequately alleged an injury in fact."[5]

---

[5]   Three years after Spokeo, the Court decided (8–1) to vacate a lower court decision finding Article III standing under the Stored Communications Act, 18 U.S.C. § 2701 *et seq.*, raising "substantial questions about whether any of the named plaintiffs has standing to sue in light of our decision in Spokeo," and remanding the case to the Ninth Circuit. Frank v. Gaos, 596 U.S. 485. 488 (2019). Justice Thomas alone was confident that there was standing. And in Thole v. U.S. Bank N.A., 590 U.S. 538 (2020), the Court held, 5–4, that retired participants in the Bank's defined-benefit retirement plan lacked standing to challenge alleged mismanagement of the plan, despite a provision of the Employee Retirement Income Security Act (ERISA) authorizing suits by plan beneficiaries. Because the plaintiffs had been paid all benefits due in the past, and were "legally and contractually entitled to receive * * * [fixed] monthly payments for the rest of their lives," they had suffered no cognizable injury, the Court reasoned. Absent a concrete injury, the statute's attempted conferral of a right to sue failed to satisfy Article III. Justice Sotomayor, joined by Justices Ginsburg, Breyer, and Kagan, dissented. She argued that "[b]ecause ERISA requires that retirement-plan assets be held in trust," beneficiaries had "equitable interests" in the plan's assets—analogous to those

Justice Thomas, who joined the Court's opinion, also concurred separately. Justice Ginsburg, joined by Justice Sotomayor, dissented. Although Justice Ginsburg "agree[d] with much of the Court's opinion," she would have affirmed the lower court's decision to uphold standing without a remand, based on the allegation in Robins's complaint that "Spokeo's misinformation 'cause[s] actual harm to [his] employment prospects.' "

The principal significance of Spokeo appeared to lie in the affirmation in the majority opinion—which six Justices joined and with which the dissenting Justices registered no express disagreement—that "Congress' role in identifying and elevating intangible harms does not mean that a plaintiff automatically satisfies the injury-in-fact requirement whenever a statute grants a person a statutory right and purports to authorize that person to sue to vindicate that right."[6] The question remaining is how to identify the relevant limitations on Congress's authority in this regard.

(e) Five years later, the Court returned to the Fair Credit Reporting Act in the next principal case, TransUnion LLC v. Ramirez, 594 U.S. 413 (2021).

TransUnion LLC v. Ramirez

594 U.S. 413 (2021).
Certiorari to the United States Court of Appeals for the Ninth Circuit.

■ JUSTICE KAVANAUGH delivered the opinion of the Court.

[The case grew out of a product marketed by TransUnion to alert its customers when consumers on whom it maintained files had names matching those of people on a U.S. government list of terrorists, drug traffickers, and other serious criminals with whom it is generally unlawful to transact business. In determining which individuals to flag as "potential match[es]" with names on the government list, TransUnion initially conducted no investigation beyond a comparison of first and last names. After a series of events that began with a rebuffed attempt to buy a car because his name was on a "terrorist list," the plaintiff Sergio Ramirez, relying on a Fair Credit Reporting Act provision that creates a cause of action for "any consumer" whose rights under the Act are violated, brought a class action lawsuit alleging (among other things) that TransUnion "failed to follow reasonable procedures to ensure the

---

recognized by the traditional law of trusts—the alleged harms to which constituted actionable injuries.

   6   The scholarly reaction to Spokeo was largely critical. For three noteworthy examples, see Hessick, *Standing and Contracts*, 89 Geo.Wash.L.Rev. 298 (2021) (arguing that Spokeo's logic renders many traditionally enforceable contracts unenforceable in federal court); Bennett, *The Paradox of Exclusive State-Court Jurisdiction over Federal Claims*, 105 Minn.L.Rev. 1211 (2021) (arguing that Spokeo's reasoning leads to the illogical conclusion that many federal claims are enforceable only in state court); Bayefsky, *Constitutional Injury and Tangibility*, 59 Wm. & Mary L.Rev. 2285 (2018) (criticizing Spokeo's focus on concreteness and tangibility). See also Baude, *Standing in the Shadow of Congress*, 2016 Sup.Ct.Rev. 197 (2017) (arguing that Justice Thomas's concurring opinion, and the Ninth Circuit decision under review in Spokeo, provided the better approach).

accuracy of information in his credit file" in violation of 15 U.S.C. § 1681e(b), invoking FCRA's private cause of action for actual and statutory damages, § 1681n(a). A jury awarded the class as a whole more than $60 million.]

To have Article III standing to sue in federal court, plaintiffs must demonstrate, among other things, that they suffered a concrete harm. No concrete harm, no standing. Central to assessing concreteness is whether the asserted harm has a "close relationship" to a harm traditionally recognized as providing a basis for a lawsuit in American courts—such as physical harm, monetary harm, or various intangible harms including (as relevant here) reputational harm. Spokeo, Inc. v. Robins, 578 U.S. 330, 340–341 (2016).

In this case, a class of 8,185 individuals sued TransUnion, a credit reporting agency, in federal court under the Fair Credit Reporting Act. The plaintiffs claimed that TransUnion failed to use reasonable procedures to ensure the accuracy of their credit files, as maintained internally by TransUnion. For 1,853 of the class members, TransUnion provided misleading credit reports to third-party businesses. We conclude that those 1,853 class members have demonstrated concrete reputational harm and thus have Article III standing to sue on the reasonable-procedures claim. The internal credit files of the other 6,332 class members were not provided to third-party businesses during the relevant time period. We conclude that those 6,332 class members have not demonstrated concrete harm and thus lack Article III standing to sue on the reasonable-procedures claim. * * *

II

The question in this case is whether the 8,185 class members have Article III standing as to their three claims. * * *

A

* * * Article III confines the federal judicial power to the resolution of "Cases" and "Controversies." For there to be a case or controversy under Article III, the plaintiff must have a " 'personal stake' " in the case—in other words, standing. Raines [v. Byrd], 521 U.S. [811,] 819 [(1997)]. To demonstrate their personal stake, plaintiffs must be able to sufficiently answer the question: " 'What's it to you?' " Scalia, *The Doctrine of Standing as an Essential Element of the Separation of Powers*, 17 Suffolk U.L.Rev. 881, 882 (1983).

To answer that question in a way sufficient to establish standing, a plaintiff must show (i) that he suffered an injury in fact that is concrete, particularized, and actual or imminent; (ii) that the injury was likely caused by the defendant; and (iii) that the injury would likely be redressed by judicial relief. Lujan v. Defenders of Wildlife, 504 U.S. 555, 560–561 (1992). If "the plaintiff does not claim to have suffered an injury that the defendant caused and the court can remedy, there is no case or controversy for the federal court to resolve." Casillas v. Madison Avenue Assocs., Inc., 926 F.3d 329, 333 (CA7 2019) (Barrett, J.).

Requiring a plaintiff to demonstrate a concrete and particularized injury caused by the defendant and redressable by the court ensures that federal courts decide only "the rights of individuals," Marbury v. Madison, 1 Cranch 137, 170, 5 U.S. 137 (1803), and that federal courts exercise "their proper function in a limited and separated government," Roberts, *Article III Limits on Statutory Standing*, 42 Duke L.J. 1219, 1224 (1993). Under Article III, federal courts do not adjudicate hypothetical or abstract disputes. Federal courts do not possess a roving commission to publicly opine on every legal question. Federal courts do not exercise general legal oversight of the Legislative and Executive Branches, or of private entities. And federal courts do not issue advisory opinions. As Madison explained in Philadelphia, federal courts instead decide only matters "of a Judiciary Nature." 2 Records of the Federal Convention of 1787, p. 430 (M. Farrand ed. 1966).

In sum, under Article III, a federal court may resolve only "a real controversy with real impact on real persons." American Legion v. American Humanist Assn., 588 U.S. [29, 87] (2019) (Gorsuch, J., concurring in the judgment).

B

The question in this case focuses on the Article III requirement that the plaintiff's injury in fact be "concrete"—that is, "real, and not abstract." Spokeo, Inc. v. Robins, 578 U.S. 330, 340 (2016) (internal quotation marks omitted).

What makes a harm concrete for purposes of Article III? As a general matter, the Court has explained that "history and tradition offer a meaningful guide to the types of cases that Article III empowers federal courts to consider." Sprint Communications Co. v. APCC Services, Inc., 554 U.S. 269, 274 (2008); see also Steel Co. v. Citizens for Better Environment, 523 U.S. 83, 102 (1998). And with respect to the concrete-harm requirement in particular, this Court's opinion in Spokeo v. Robins indicated that courts should assess whether the alleged injury to the plaintiff has a "close relationship" to a harm "traditionally" recognized as providing a basis for a lawsuit in American courts. 578 U.S., at 341. That inquiry asks whether plaintiffs have identified a close historical or common-law analogue for their asserted injury. Spokeo does not require an exact duplicate in American history and tradition. But Spokeo is not an open-ended invitation for federal courts to loosen Article III based on contemporary, evolving beliefs about what kinds of suits should be heard in federal courts.

As Spokeo explained, certain harms readily qualify as concrete injuries under Article III. The most obvious are traditional tangible harms, such as physical harms and monetary harms. If a defendant has caused physical or monetary injury to the plaintiff, the plaintiff has suffered a concrete injury in fact under Article III.

Various intangible harms can also be concrete. Chief among them are injuries with a close relationship to harms traditionally recognized as providing a basis for lawsuits in American courts. *Id.*, at 340–341. Those include, for example, reputational harms, disclosure of private information, and intrusion upon seclusion. See, *e.g.*, Meese v. Keene, 481 U.S. 465, 473 (1987) (reputational harms); Davis v. Federal Election Comm'n, 554 U.S. 724, 733 (2008) (disclosure of private information); see also Gadelhak v. AT&T Services, Inc., 950 F.3d 458, 462 (CA7 2020) (Barrett, J.) (intrusion upon seclusion). And those traditional harms may also include harms specified by the Constitution itself. See, *e.g.*, Spokeo, 578 U. S., at 340 (citing Pleasant Grove City v. Summum, 555 U.S. 460 (2009) (abridgment of free speech), and Church of Lukumi Babalu Aye, Inc. v. Hialeah, 508 U.S. 520 (1993) (infringement of free exercise)).

In determining whether a harm is sufficiently concrete to qualify as an injury in fact, the Court in Spokeo said that Congress's views may be "instructive." 578 U.S., at 341. Courts must afford due respect to Congress's decision to impose a statutory prohibition or obligation on a defendant, and to grant a plaintiff a cause of action to sue over the defendant's violation of that statutory prohibition or obligation. See *id.*, at 340–341. In that way, Congress may "elevate to the status of legally cognizable injuries concrete, de facto injuries that were previously inadequate in law." *Id.*, at 341 (alterations and internal quotation marks omitted); see Lujan, 504 U.S. at 562–563, 578. But even though "Congress may 'elevate' harms that 'exist' in the real world before Congress recognized them to actionable legal status, it may not simply enact an injury into existence, using its lawmaking power to transform something that is not remotely harmful into something that is." Hagy v. Demers & Adams, 882 F.3d 616, 622 (CA6 2018) (Sutton, J.) (citing Spokeo, 578 U.S., at 341). * * *

For standing purposes, therefore, an important difference exists between (i) a plaintiff's statutory cause of action to sue a defendant over the defendant's violation of federal law, and (ii) a plaintiff's suffering concrete harm because of the defendant's violation of federal law. Congress may enact legal prohibitions and obligations. And Congress may create causes of action for plaintiffs to sue defendants who violate those legal prohibitions or obligations. But under Article III, an injury in law is not an injury in fact. Only those plaintiffs who have been concretely harmed by a defendant's statutory violation may sue that private defendant over that violation in federal court. * * *

To appreciate how the Article III "concrete harm" principle operates in practice, consider two different hypothetical plaintiffs. Suppose first that a Maine citizen's land is polluted by a nearby factory. She sues the company, alleging that it violated a federal environmental law and damaged her property. Suppose also that a second plaintiff in Hawaii files a federal lawsuit alleging that the same company in Maine violated that same environmental law by polluting land in Maine. The violation did not personally harm the plaintiff in Hawaii.

Even if Congress affords both hypothetical plaintiffs a cause of action (with statutory damages available) to sue over the defendant's legal violation, Article III standing doctrine sharply distinguishes between those two scenarios. The first lawsuit may of course proceed in federal court because the plaintiff has suffered concrete harm to her property. But the second lawsuit may not proceed because that plaintiff has not suffered any physical, monetary, or cognizable intangible harm traditionally recognized as providing a basis for a lawsuit in American courts. An uninjured plaintiff who sues in those circumstances is, by definition, not seeking to remedy any harm to herself but instead is merely seeking to ensure a defendant's "compliance with regulatory law" (and, of course, to obtain some money via the statutory damages). Spokeo, 578 U.S., at 345 (Thomas, J., concurring) (internal quotation marks omitted); see Steel Co., 523 U.S., at 106–107. Those are not grounds for Article III standing.

As those examples illustrate, if the law of Article III did not require plaintiffs to demonstrate a "concrete harm," Congress could authorize virtually any citizen to bring a statutory damages suit against virtually any defendant who violated virtually any federal law. Such an expansive understanding of Article III would flout constitutional text, history, and precedent. In our view, the public interest that private entities comply with the law cannot "be converted into an individual right by a statute that denominates it as such, and that permits all citizens (or, for that matter, a subclass of citizens who suffer no distinctive concrete harm) to sue." Lujan, 504 U.S., at 576–577.[2]

A regime where Congress could freely authorize unharmed plaintiffs to sue defendants who violate federal law not only would violate Article III but also would infringe on the Executive Branch's Article II authority. We accept the "displacement of the democratically elected branches when necessary to decide an actual case." Roberts, 42 Duke L.J., at 1230. But otherwise, the choice of how to prioritize and how aggressively to pursue legal actions against defendants who violate the law falls within the discretion of the Executive Branch, not within the purview of private plaintiffs (and their attorneys). Private plaintiffs are not accountable to the people and are not charged with pursuing the public interest in

---

[2]   A plaintiff must show that the injury is not only concrete but also particularized. But if there were no concrete-harm requirement, the requirement of a particularized injury would do little or nothing to constrain Congress from freely creating causes of action for vast classes of unharmed plaintiffs to sue any defendants who violate any federal law. (Congress might, for example, provide that everyone has an individual right to clean air and can sue any defendant who violates any air-pollution law.) That is one reason why the Court has been careful to emphasize that concreteness and particularization are separate requirements. See Spokeo, 578 U.S., at 339–340; see generally Bayefsky, *Constitutional Injury and Tangibility*, 59 Wm. & Mary L.Rev. 2285, 2298–2300, 2368 (2018).

enforcing a defendant's general compliance with regulatory law. See Lujan, 504 U.S., at 577.

In sum, the concrete-harm requirement is essential to the Constitution's separation of powers. To be sure, the concrete-harm requirement can be difficult to apply in some cases. Some advocate that the concrete-harm requirement be ditched altogether, on the theory that it would be more efficient or convenient to simply say that a statutory violation and a cause of action suffice to afford a plaintiff standing. But as the Court has often stated, "the fact that a given law or procedure is efficient, convenient, and useful in facilitating functions of government, standing alone, will not save it if it is contrary to the Constitution." [INS v.] Chadha, 462 U.S. [919], 944 [(1983)]. So it is here.[3]

III

We now apply those fundamental standing principles to this lawsuit. We must determine whether the 8,185 class members have standing to sue TransUnion for its alleged violations of the Fair Credit Reporting Act. The plaintiffs argue that TransUnion failed to comply with statutory obligations (i) to follow reasonable procedures to ensure the accuracy of credit files so that the files would not include OFAC alerts labeling the plaintiffs as potential terrorists; and (ii) to provide a consumer, upon request, with his or her complete credit file, including a summary of rights. * * *

A

We first address the plaintiffs' claim that TransUnion failed to "follow reasonable procedures to assure maximum possible accuracy" of the plaintiffs' credit files maintained by TransUnion. 15 U.S.C. § 1681e(b). In particular, the plaintiffs argue that TransUnion did not do enough to ensure that OFAC alerts labeling them as potential terrorists were not included in their credit files. * * *

1

Start with the 1,853 class members (including the named plaintiff Ramirez) whose reports were disseminated to third-party businesses.

---

[3] The lead dissent [by Justice Thomas] would reject the core standing principle that a plaintiff must always have suffered a concrete harm, and would cast aside decades of precedent articulating that requirement, such as Spokeo, Summers, and Lujan. As we see it, the dissent's theory would largely outsource Article III to Congress. As we understand the dissent's theory, a suit seeking to enforce "general compliance with regulatory law" would not suffice for Article III standing because such a suit seeks to vindicate a duty owed to the whole community. Spokeo, 578 U.S., at 345 (Thomas, J., concurring). But under the dissent's theory, so long as Congress frames a defendant's obligation to comply with regulatory law as an obligation owed to individuals, any suit to vindicate that obligation suddenly suffices for Article III. Suppose, for example, that Congress passes a law purporting to give all American citizens an individual right to clean air and clean water, as well as a cause of action to sue and recover $100 in damages from any business that violates any pollution law anywhere in the United States. The dissent apparently would find standing in such a case. We respectfully disagree. In our view, unharmed plaintiffs who seek to sue under such a law are still doing no more than enforcing general compliance with regulatory law. And under Article III and this Court's precedents, Congress may not authorize plaintiffs who have not suffered concrete harms to sue in federal court simply to enforce general compliance with regulatory law.

The plaintiffs argue that the publication to a third party of a credit report bearing a misleading OFAC alert injures the subject of the report. The plaintiffs contend that this injury bears a "close relationship" to a harm traditionally recognized as providing a basis for a lawsuit in American courts—namely, the reputational harm associated with the tort of defamation. Spokeo, Inc. v. Robins, 578 U.S. 330, 341 (2016).

We agree with the plaintiffs. Under longstanding American law, a person is injured when a defamatory statement "that would subject him to hatred, contempt, or ridicule" is published to a third party. Milkovich v. Lorain Journal Co., 497 U.S. 1, 13 (1990) (internal quotation marks omitted). TransUnion provided third parties with credit reports containing OFAC alerts that labeled the class members as potential terrorists, drug traffickers, or serious criminals. The 1,853 class members therefore suffered a harm with a "close relationship" to the harm associated with the tort of defamation. We have no trouble concluding that the 1,853 class members suffered a concrete harm that qualifies as an injury in fact. * * *

2

The remaining 6,332 class members are a different story. To be sure, their credit files, which were maintained by TransUnion, contained misleading OFAC alerts. But the parties stipulated that TransUnion did not provide those plaintiffs' credit information to any potential creditors during the class period from January 2011 to July 2011. Given the absence of dissemination, we must determine whether the 6,332 class members suffered some other concrete harm for purposes of Article III.

The initial question is whether the mere existence of a misleading OFAC alert in a consumer's internal credit file at TransUnion constitutes a concrete injury. As Judge Tatel phrased it in a similar context, "if inaccurate information falls into" a consumer's credit file, "does it make a sound?" Owner-Operator Independent Drivers Assn., Inc. v. United States Dept. of Transp., 879 F.3d 339, 344 (CADC 2018).

Writing the opinion for the D.C. Circuit in Owner-Operator, Judge Tatel answered no. Publication is "essential to liability" in a suit for defamation. Restatement of Torts § 577, Comment a, at 192. And there is "no historical or common-law analog where the mere existence of inaccurate information, absent dissemination, amounts to concrete injury." Owner-Operator, 879 F.3d at 344–345. * * *

The standing inquiry in this case thus distinguishes between (i) credit files that consumer reporting agencies maintain internally and (ii) the consumer credit reports that consumer reporting agencies disseminate to third-party creditors. The mere presence of an inaccuracy in an internal credit file, if it is not disclosed to a third party, causes no concrete harm. In cases such as these where allegedly inaccurate or misleading information sits in a company database, the plaintiffs' harm is roughly the same, legally speaking, as if someone wrote a defamatory letter and then stored it in her desk drawer. A letter that is not sent does not harm anyone, no matter how insulting the letter is. So too here.

Because the plaintiffs cannot demonstrate that the misleading information in the internal credit files itself constitutes a concrete harm, the plaintiffs advance a separate argument based on an asserted risk of future harm. They say that the 6,332 class members suffered a concrete injury for Article III purposes because the existence of misleading OFAC alerts in their internal credit files exposed them to a material risk that the information would be disseminated in the future to third parties and thereby cause them harm. The plaintiffs rely on language from Spokeo where the Court said that "the risk of real harm" (or as the Court otherwise stated, a "material risk of harm") can sometimes "satisfy the requirement of concreteness." 578 U. S., at 341–342 (citing Clapper v. Amnesty Int'l USA, 568 U.S. 398 (2013)). * * *

TransUnion advances a persuasive argument that in a suit for damages, the mere risk of future harm, standing alone, cannot qualify as a concrete harm—at least unless the exposure to the risk of future harm itself causes a *separate* concrete harm. TransUnion contends that if an individual is exposed to a risk of future harm, time will eventually reveal whether the risk materializes in the form of actual harm. If the risk of future harm materializes and the individual suffers a concrete harm, then the harm itself, and not the pre-existing risk, will constitute a basis for the person's injury and for damages. If the risk of future harm does not materialize, then the individual cannot establish a concrete harm sufficient for standing, according to TransUnion.

Consider an example. Suppose that a woman drives home from work a quarter mile ahead of a reckless driver who is dangerously swerving across lanes. The reckless driver has exposed the woman to a risk of future harm, but the risk does not materialize and the woman makes it home safely. As counsel for TransUnion stated, that would ordinarily be cause for celebration, not a lawsuit. But if the reckless driver crashes into the woman's car, the situation would be different, and (assuming a cause of action) the woman could sue the driver for damages. * * *

In sum, the 6,332 class members whose internal TransUnion credit files were not disseminated to third-party businesses did not suffer a concrete harm. By contrast, the 1,853 class members (including Ramirez) whose credit reports were disseminated to third-party businesses during the class period suffered a concrete harm. * * *

* * *

* * * We reverse the judgment of the U.S. Court of Appeals for the Ninth Circuit and remand the case for further proceedings consistent with this opinion. * * *

It is so ordered.

■ JUSTICE THOMAS, with whom JUSTICE BREYER, JUSTICE SOTOMAYOR, and JUSTICE KAGAN join, dissenting.

TransUnion generated credit reports that erroneously flagged many law-abiding people as potential terrorists and drug traffickers. In doing so, TransUnion violated several provisions of the Fair Credit Reporting Act (FCRA) that entitle consumers to accuracy in credit-reporting procedures; to receive information in their credit files; and to receive a summary of their rights. Yet despite Congress' judgment that such misdeeds deserve redress, the majority decides that TransUnion's actions are so insignificant that the Constitution prohibits consumers from vindicating their rights in federal court. The Constitution does no such thing. * * *

II

A

Article III vests "[t]he judicial Power of the United States" in this Court "and in such inferior Courts as the Congress may from time to time ordain and establish." § 1. This power "shall extend to all Cases, in Law and Equity, arising under this Constitution, the Laws of the United States, and Treaties made, or which shall be made, under their Authority." § 2 (emphasis added). When a federal court has jurisdiction over a case or controversy, it has a "virtually unflagging obligation" to exercise it. Colorado River Water Conservation Dist. v. United States, 424 U.S. 800, 817 (1976).

The mere filing of a complaint in federal court, however, does not a case (or controversy) make. Article III "does not extend the judicial power to every violation of the constitution" or federal law "which may possibly take place." Cohens v. Virginia, 6 Wheat. 264, 405 (1821). Rather, the power extends only "to 'a case in law or equity,' in which a right, under such law, is asserted." *Ibid.* (emphasis added).

Key to the scope of the judicial power, then, is whether an individual asserts his or her own rights. At the time of the founding, whether a court possessed judicial power over an action with no showing of actual damages depended on whether the plaintiff sought to enforce a right held privately by an individual or a duty owed broadly to the community. See Spokeo, Inc. v. Robins, 578 U.S. 330, 344–346 (2016) (Thomas, J., concurring). Where an individual sought to sue someone for a violation of his private rights, such as trespass on his land, the plaintiff needed only to allege the violation. See Entick v. Carrington, 2 Wils. K.B. 275, 291, 95 Eng.Rep. 807, 817 (K.B. 1765). Courts typically did not require any showing of actual damage. But where an individual sued based on the violation of a duty owed broadly to the whole community, such as the overgrazing of public lands, courts required "not only injuria [legal injury] but also damnum [damage]." Spokeo, 578 U.S., at 346 (Thomas, J., concurring) (citing Robert Marys's Case, 9 Co.Rep. 111b, 112b, 77 Eng.Rep. 895, 898–899 (K.B. 1613); brackets in original).

This distinction mattered not only for traditional common-law rights, but also for newly created statutory ones. The First Congress enacted a law defining copyrights and gave copyright holders the right to sue infringing persons in order to recover statutory damages, even if the holder "could not show monetary loss." Muransky v. Godiva Chocolatier, Inc., 979 F.3d 917, 972 (CA11 2020) (Jordan, J., dissenting) (citing Act of May 31, 1790, § 2, 1 Stat. 124–125). In the patent context, a defendant challenged an infringement suit brought under a similar law. Along the lines of what TransUnion argues here, the infringer contended that "the making of a machine cannot be an offence, because no action lies, except for actual damage, and there can be no actual damages, or even a rule for damages, for an infringement by making a machine." Whittemore v. Cutter, 29 F.Cas. 1120, 1121 (No. 17,600) (CC Mass.1813). Riding circuit, Justice Story rejected that theory, noting that the plaintiff could sue in federal court merely by alleging a violation of a private right: "[W]here the law gives an action for a particular act, the doing of that act imports of itself a damage to the party" because "[e]very violation of a right imports some damage." *Ibid.*[2]

* * * In light of this history, tradition, and common practice, our test should be clear: So long as a "statute fixes a minimum of recovery . . ., there would seem to be no doubt of the right of one who establishes a technical ground of action to recover this minimum sum without any specific showing of loss." T. Cooley, Law of Torts *271.[3] While the Court today discusses the supposed failure to show "injury in fact," courts for centuries held that injury in law to a private right was enough to create a case or controversy.

B

Here, each class member established a violation of his or her private rights. * * *

C

* * * A statute that creates a public right plus a citizen-suit cause of action is insufficient by itself to establish standing. See Lujan, 504 U.S., at 576. A statute that creates a private right and a cause of action, however, does gives plaintiffs an adequate interest in vindicating their private rights in federal court. * * *

---

[2]   The "public rights" terminology has been used to refer to two different concepts. In one context, these rights are " 'take[n] from the public' "—like the right to make, use, or sell an invention—and " 'bestow[ed] . . . upon the' " individual, like a "decision to grant a public franchise." Oil States Energy Services, LLC v. Greene's Energy Group, LLC, 584 U. S. [325, 334] (2018). Disputes with the Government over these rights generally can be resolved "outside of an Article III court." *Id.*, at [337]. Here, in contrast, the term "public rights" refers to duties owed collectively to the community. For example, Congress owes a duty to all Americans to legislate within its constitutional confines. But not every single American can sue over Congress' failure to do so. Only individuals who, at a minimum, establish harm beyond the mere violation of that constitutional duty can sue.

[3]   Etymology is also a helpful guide. The word "injury" stems from the Latin "injuria," which combines "in" (expressing negation) and "jus" (right, law, justice). See Barnhart Dictionary of Etymology 529 (1988).

* * * Never before has this Court declared that legal injury is *inherently* insufficient to support standing. And never before has this Court declared that legislatures are constitutionally precluded from creating legal rights enforceable in federal court if those rights deviate too far from their common-law roots. According to the majority, courts alone have the power to sift and weigh harms to decide whether they merit the Federal Judiciary's attention. In the name of protecting the separation of powers, this Court has relieved the legislature of its power to create and define rights.

III

Even assuming that this Court should be in the business of second-guessing private rights, this is a rather odd case to say that Congress went too far. TransUnion's misconduct here is exactly the sort of thing that has long merited legal redress. * * *

* * * [E]ven setting aside everything already mentioned—the Constitution's text, history, precedent, financial harm, libel, the risk of publication, and actual disclosure to a third party—one need only tap into common sense to know that receiving a letter identifying you as a potential drug trafficker or terrorist is harmful. All the more so when the information comes in the context of a credit report, the entire purpose of which is to demonstrate that a person can be trusted.

And if this sort of confusing and frustrating communication is insufficient to establish a real injury, one wonders what could rise to that level. If, instead of falsely identifying Ramirez as a potential drug trafficker or terrorist, TransUnion had flagged him as a "potential" child molester, would that alone still be insufficient to open the courthouse doors? What about falsely labeling a person a racist? Including a slur on the report? Or what about openly reducing a person's credit score by several points because of his race? If none of these constitutes an injury in fact, how can that possibly square with our past cases indicating that the inability to "observe an animal species, even for purely esthetic purposes, . . . undeniably" is? Lujan, 504 U.S., at 562. Had the class members claimed an aesthetic interest in viewing an accurate report, would this case have come out differently?

And if some of these examples do cause sufficiently "concrete" and "real"—though "intangible"—harms, how do we go about picking and choosing which ones do and which do not? I see no way to engage in this "inescapably value-laden" inquiry without it "devolv[ing] into [pure] policy judgment." Sierra v. Hallandale Beach, 996 F.3d 1110, 1129 (CA11 2021) (Newsom, J., concurring). Weighing the harms caused by specific facts and choosing remedies seems to me like a much better fit for legislatures and juries than for this Court.

Finally, it is not just the harm that is reminiscent of a constitutional case or controversy. So too is the remedy. Although statutory damages are not necessarily a proxy for unjust enrichment, they have a similar flavor in this case. TransUnion violated consumers' rights in order to create and sell a product to its clients. Reckless handling of consumer information and bungled responses to requests for information served a means to an end. And the end was financial gain. "TransUnion could not confirm that a single OFAC alert sold to its customers was accurate." 951 F.3d, at 1021, n.4. Yet thanks to this Court, it may well be in a position to keep much of its ill-gotten gains.[9]

* * *

Ultimately, the majority seems to pose to the reader a single rhetorical question: Who could possibly think that a person is harmed when he requests and is sent an incomplete credit report, or is sent a suspicious notice informing him that he may be a designated drug trafficker or terrorist, or is not sent anything informing him of how to remove this inaccurate red flag? The answer is, of course, legion: Congress, the President, the jury, the District Court, the Ninth Circuit, and four Members of this Court.

I respectfully dissent.

■ JUSTICE KAGAN, with whom JUSTICE BREYER and JUSTICE SOTOMAYOR join, dissenting.

* * * The Court here transforms standing law from a doctrine of judicial modesty into a tool of judicial aggrandizement. It holds, for the first time, that a specific class of plaintiffs whom Congress allowed to bring a lawsuit cannot do so under Article III. I join Justice Thomas's dissent, which explains why the majority's decision is so mistaken. * * *

I add a few words about the majority's view of the risks of harm to the plaintiffs. In addressing the claim that TransUnion failed to maintain accurate credit files, the majority argues that the "risk of dissemination" of the plaintiffs' credit information to third parties is "too speculative." But why is it so speculative that a company in the business of selling credit reports to third parties will in fact sell a credit report to a third party? * * * I sign up with Justice Thomas: "[O]ne need only tap into common sense to know that receiving a letter identifying you as a potential drug trafficker or terrorist is harmful."

I differ with Justice Thomas on just one matter, unlikely to make much difference in practice. In his view, any "violation of an individual right" created by Congress gives rise to Article III standing. But in Spokeo, this Court held that "Article III requires a concrete injury even

---

[9]   Today's decision might actually be a pyrrhic victory for TransUnion. The Court does not prohibit Congress from creating statutory rights for consumers; it simply holds that federal courts lack jurisdiction to hear some of these cases. That combination may leave state courts—which "are not bound by the limitations of a case or controversy or other federal rules of justiciability even when they address issues of federal law," ASARCO Inc. v. Kadish, 490 U.S. 605, 617 (1989)—as the sole forum for such cases, with defendants unable to seek removal to federal court. See also Bennett, *The Paradox of Exclusive State-Court Jurisdiction Over Federal Claims*, 105 Minn.L.Rev. 1211 (2021). By declaring that federal courts lack jurisdiction, the Court has thus ensured that state courts will exercise exclusive jurisdiction over these sorts of class actions.

in the context of a statutory violation." 578 U.S., at 341. I continue to adhere to that view, but think it should lead to the same result as Justice Thomas's approach in all but highly unusual cases. As *Spokeo* recognized, "Congress is well positioned to identify [both tangible and] intangible harms" meeting Article III standards. *Ibid.* Article III requires for concreteness only a "real harm" (that is, a harm that "actually exist[s]") or a "risk of real harm." *Ibid.* And as today's decision definitively proves, Congress is better suited than courts to determine when something causes a harm or risk of harm in the real world. For that reason, courts should give deference to those congressional judgments. Overriding an authorization to sue is appropriate when but only when Congress could not reasonably have thought that a suit will contribute to compensating or preventing the harm at issue. Subject to that qualification, I join Justice Thomas's dissent in full.

NOTE ON CONGRESSIONAL POWER TO CONFER STANDING TO SUE AFTER TRANSUNION

(1) What Rights? After TransUnion, what legally created rights can support standing to sue in federal court?

(a) The Role of the Common Law. The Fair Credit Reporting Act itself gives individuals the right not to have false credit reports about them, regardless of whether they are "disclosed to a third party" versus "sit[ting] in a company database," as TransUnion put it. The Court's imposition of a constitutional distinction between those two classes of plaintiffs does not come from a statute or congressional decision. So where does it come from? The Court points to the common law of defamation, which did draw such a distinction. Is that a suggestion that Article III constitutionalizes the common law, even when Congress creates new statutes designed to depart from the common law? Or is the Court pointing to the common law in order to support a judicial policy decision?

(b) Intangible Harms. Despite its insistence that a violation of a statutory right must be "concrete" to support standing, TransUnion also recognizes that "intangible" harms can nonetheless be concrete. Yet how can a harm be both intangible and concrete? See generally Bayefsky, *Constitutional Injury and Tangibility*, 59 Wm. & Mary L.Rev. 2285 (2018). The Court's examples of cognizable intangible harms are those with a close analogy to a common law right or "specified by the Constitution itself." Does this suggest that no new intangible harms can be recognized and made enforceable by Congress? What about modern privacy statutes that go well beyond the common law rights of privacy? What about statutes banning private racial discrimination or other forms of private discrimination in contexts that were long permitted by the common law? What about statutes such as the Religious Freedom Restoration Act, which recognize a right to be free from substantial burdens on one's religious exercise well beyond what the Court has understood the Constitution itself to require? See

Chemerinsky, *What's Standing After TransUnion LLC v. Ramirez*, 96
N.Y.U.L.Rev. Online 269, 283–84 (2021).

(c) Property Interests. A trespass or other injury to an individual's
private property would seem to be a rock-solid example of a cognizable injury
in fact, foundational to the common law. The Court in TransUnion does not
disagree—distinguishing (in n.3, *supra*) between a federal pollution statute
that purports to create individual rights for distant citizens and one that
protects the property rights of nearby individuals. Are there limits to
Congress's ability to create or recognize *property* interests? If Congress
creates and recognizes new individual property rights in airways or
waterways, would that allow it to enforce environmental rights that would
otherwise be non-concrete? What if Congress had given every American
citizen a 0.0000003% property interest in federally endangered species—
would that federal property right have allowed citizens to sue to enforce the
Endangered Species Act despite the ruling in Lujan? If not, what
distinguishes property rights that are constitutionally cognizable from ones
that are not?

**(2) The (Contested) Historical Understanding of the Judicial
Power.** Both the majority opinion and the lead dissent in TransUnion advert
in some respects to perceived founding-era purposes or original legal
understandings. If history is relevant to this inquiry, how much significance
should be attached to the conclusions of legal scholarship suggesting that the
treatment of injury in fact as a constitutional requirement contradicts the
historical understanding of judicial power, both at the founding era and as
that idea later unfolded?[1]

Most commentators, while not agreeing in all respects, have found that
English judicial practice at the time of the founding permitted so-called
"strangers" (*i.e.*, private litigants with no personalized injury) to file various
prerogative writs to test the legality of the exercise of public authority. See,
e.g., Berger, *Standing to Sue in Public Actions: Is It a Constitutional
Requirement?*, 78 Yale L.J. 816 (1969); Sunstein, *What's Standing After
Lujan? Of Citizen Suits, "Injuries," and Article III*, 91 Mich.L.Rev. 163, 171–
73 (1992); Winter, *The Metaphor of Standing and the Problem of Self-
Governance*, 40 Stan.L.Rev. 1371, 1396–99 (1988). For example, such
litigants could seek writs of prohibition or certiorari in the courts at
Westminster to challenge action in excess of jurisdiction by other courts
(such as ecclesiastical tribunals) or by local administrative tribunals.
English law prior to the founding also authorized informers' actions, which

---

[1]   In his influential separate opinion in Coleman v. Miller, 307 U.S. 433, 460 (1939),
Justice Frankfurter wrote: "Judicial power could come into play only in matters that were the
traditional concern of the courts at Westminster and only if they arose in ways that to the expert
feel of lawyers constituted 'Cases' or 'Controversies.'" That idea has framed subsequent
analysis, even in cases widely regarded to take a generous view of Article III power. See, *e.g.*,
Federal Election Commission v. Akins, 524 U.S. 11, 24 (1998); Flast v. Cohen, 392 U.S. 83, 101
(1968). But see Pfander, *Standing, Litigable Interests, and Article III's Case-or-Controversy
Requirement*, 65 UCLA L.Rev. 170 (2018) (questioning the Westminster paradigm in light of
early assignment to Article III courts of "noncontentious" cases arising under federal law,
including naturalization petitions, and arguing that eighteenth-century Scottish practice
provides a better model for understanding early American analogues to modern standing
doctrine).

gave strangers financial inducements to prosecute unlawful conduct, and relators' actions, which allowed private parties to bring actions against public authorities in the name of the Attorney General. See Berger, *supra*, at 816–26.[2] Although this view of the history has come under some challenge,[3] it is fair to say, at the very least, that the English common law background in the founding era does not reliably supply a basis for the Court's modern position that concrete and personalized injury is a prerequisite to invoking "the judicial Power."

In a highly influential book published in 1965, Professor Jaffe wrote that despite some initial "doubts and misgivings," "the public action has become broadly established in this country in a large and continually increasing majority of jurisdictions." Jaffe, Judicial Control of Administrative Action 467 (1965). In particular, the "very considerable weight of [state court] authority" came over time to support "the citizen-mandamus suit," and taxpayer's injunction actions "have become even more acclimated in this country than the citizen's mandamus." *Id.* 468–70. Winter, *supra*, similarly maintains that, until the twentieth century, courts did not view injury in fact either as part of the case or controversy requirement or as a prerequisite for seeking review of official action, but instead granted relief whenever a plaintiff asserted a right for which one of the forms of action afforded a remedy.[4]

---

[2]   Berger further noted that strangers could bring writs of quo warranto to prosecute those who usurped the franchise, and that, while the evidence is less clear, they apparently could also file writs of mandamus "to compel action by one who was under a duty to act." Berger, *supra*, at 823–25.

Professor Jaffe believed that the English history was somewhat less conclusive. See Jaffe, *Standing to Secure Judicial Review: Public Actions*, 74 Harv.L.Rev. 1265, 1269–75, 1308 (1961). But he found, at minimum, that "in prerogative proceedings in the King's Bench the character of the relator was often obscure or unstated" and that "[a] number of notable statements [in the eighteenth century English case law] expressed the King's general concern for legality, and in the writ of prohibition, at least, there is overt authority for allowing anyone to initiate the proceeding."

[3]   One commentator has argued that the actual practice of the courts at Westminster offers only scant evidence to support the proposition that parties without any personal interest could bring prerogative writs. See Clanton, *Standing and the English Prerogative Writs: The Original Understanding*, 63 Brook.L.Rev. 1001 (1997).

[4]   Pfander, note 6, *supra*, argues that Congresses and courts of the early republic distinguished between "controversies," which required parties with concretely adverse interests, and "cases," which could encompass noncontentious federal business that involved no injury, such as petitions for naturalization. According to Pfander, that practice mirrored features of Scots law, in which distinctive limitations—not unlike the statutory qualifications sometimes attached to modern citizen-suit provisions—applied to public actions involving broadly shared injuries. He argues, however, that a more historically accurate account of standing would accord Congress broader powers to confer jurisdiction in the absence of modern notions of injury in fact, "especially where Congress has taken [alternative] steps to protect the government's enforcement primacy and the defendant's interest in the avoidance of duplicative litigation." Pfander expands further on these and other arguments in his book, Pfander, Cases Without Controversies: Uncontested Adjudication in Article III Courts (2021). But see Bellia, *Article III and the Cause of Action*, 89 Iowa L.Rev. 777, 855 (2004) (arguing that modern standing doctrine "attempt[s] to generalize * * * in constitutional terms" certain limits on the reach of judicial power that were embedded in historic forms of action but then were eliminated by the merger of law and equity); Young, *Standing, Equity, and Injury in Fact*, 97 Notre Dame L.Rev. 1885, 1888 (2022) ("To the extent that Court's standing jurisprudence defines Article III's requirements in line with traditional practice, longstanding practice in equity may provide a firmer ground for injury in fact than does traditional practice on the law side of the house.").

Professors Woolhandler and Nelson, however, suggest that although early American courts did not speak in the terms employed by modern standing doctrine, they nonetheless determined proper parties by distinguishing "public rights" (those belonging to the public as a whole, such as free passage on waterways and public highways or the interests protected by penal laws) from "private rights" (those held by particular individuals, such as the common law rights to property or bodily integrity). Woolhandler & Nelson, *Does History Defeat Standing Doctrine?*, 102 Mich.L.Rev. 689, 691, 693–705 (2004). On that view of early American common law practice, a private individual could not vindicate public rights unless suffering special damage not shared by the public at large. Moreover, although relevant federal case law from the early days of the Republic is sparse and mixed, at least some of it suggests that the Supreme Court subscribed to that distinction.[5] This is essentially the view adopted by Justice Thomas's dissent in TransUnion.[6]

Insofar as historical understandings—whether from the founding era or subsequent periods—inform modern standing doctrine, how can one make sense of the foregoing history? If TransUnion rests on a claim of constitutional authority to invalidate Acts of Congress granting standing in the absence of concrete and particularized injury, should any significant indeterminacy in the evidence of original meaning and early constitutional practice tip the balance in favor of Congress? See generally Manning, *Foreword: The Means of Constitutional Power*, 128 Harv.L.Rev. 1 (2014) (arguing that, by virtue of the Necessary and Proper Clause, Congress should have the final say on the means of implementing federal powers—including the judicial power—where evidence of constitutional meaning is unclear). Or, given the now-long line of precedents treating injury in fact as a constitutional requirement of an Article III case or controversy, does stare decisis counsel against abandoning that requirement unless the historical record convincingly shows that the precedents misread Article III?

In general, consider the potential difficulties inherent in translating historical evidence from English and state contexts into the distinctive context of federal judicial power under the United States Constitution. For example, the prerogative writs "were conceived of as public proceedings brought in the King's name" and, "in their origin and until the middle of the nineteenth century, were used primarily to control authorities below the

---

[5]   For example, Professors Woolhandler and Nelson argue that while jurisdictional statutes sharply limited the availability of federal mandamus jurisdiction until well into the twentieth century, the small number of federal court opinions that did address mandamus in the nineteenth century (including Marbury) assumed that private relators must allege private injury. They also note that various nineteenth century cases involving the Supreme Court's original jurisdiction seemed to adopt the private injury requirement. While acknowledging that the First Congress passed statutes authorizing qui tam actions, which permitted litigants (informers) with no personal interest to sue for penalties that were to be shared between the sovereign and the informer, Woolhandler and Nelson maintain that such actions constitute, at most, a limited exception to the nation's dominant judicial tradition. See Woolhandler & Nelson, *supra*, at 707, 713–17, 724–31.

When the evidence of relevant practice is sparse, how does one determine which practices should count as the exception and which as the rule?

[6]   In addition to Woolhandler & Nelson, *supra*, Justice Thomas has relied on Hessick, *Standing, Injury in Fact, and Private Rights*, 93 Cornell L.Rev. 275 (2008) in support of his view.

level of the central government." Jaffe, *Judicial Control, supra,* at 462. Does this context cast doubt on the relevance of English practice, without more, to understanding an American constitutional structure predicated on quite different assumptions about sovereignty and the allocation of powers? How much weight should one give to the state court practice when the design of the federal government so frequently deviates from state structural premises, including state structural premises about the judiciary?

(3) Standing, Injury, and the Separation of Powers. Congress has often given the Attorney General or other federal officials power to bring suit for the purpose of enforcing laws that do not benefit the agency or officials empowered to sue. See, *e.g.,* § 301 of the Voting Rights Act Amendments of 1975, 52 U.S.C. § 10701; Title VII of the Civil Rights Act of 1964, §§ 706–07, as amended, 42 U.S.C. §§ 2000e–5 to 2000e–6. Hartnett, *The Standing of the United States: How Criminal Prosecutions Show That Standing Doctrine is Looking for Answers in All the Wrong Places,* 97 Mich.L.Rev. 2239, 2255–58 (1999), argues that the recognized standing of the United States to bring criminal suits demonstrates that personal injury to the party initiating a case is not a requirement for Article III standing. If that is correct, should Congress have equal power to use the device of suits by *private* attorneys general?[7] Does the Necessary and Proper Clause give Congress the power to decide how the federal laws it enacts should be implemented? Or do separation of powers considerations distinguish private from public enforcement actions, as even the dissent in TransUnion argued?

TransUnion expressly declares that limitations on the standing of private parties are also supported by Article II's assignment of executive power and could interfere with the President's constitutionally assigned responsibility to "take Care that the Laws be faithfully executed."[8] In earlier cases such as Lujan and Akins, Justice Scalia repeatedly emphasized that point in questioning statutory authorizations of private standing either to compel enforcement actions by the executive or to enforce what he regarded as public rights. See also Scalia, *The Doctrine of Standing as an Essential Element of the Separation of Powers,* 17 Suffolk U.L.Rev. 881 (1983); Roberts, *Article III Limits on Statutory Standing,* 42 Duke L.J. 1219, 1230 (1993); Grove, *Standing as an Article II Nondelegation Doctrine,* 11 U.Pa.J.Const.L.

---

[7]   Compare Fallon, *Of Justiciability, Remedies, and Public Law Litigation: Notes on the Jurisprudence of Lyons,* 59 N.Y.U.L.Rev. 1, 30–35, 54–56 (1984), with Krent & Shenkman, *Of Citizen Suits and Citizen Sunstein,* 91 Mich.L.Rev. 1793 (1993).

[8]   Some scholars have argued that the Take Care Clause imposes a duty but does not create a power. See, *e.g.,* May, *Presidential Defiance of "Unconstitutional" Laws: Reviving the Royal Prerogative,* 21 Hastings Const.LQ. 865, 873–74 (1994); Tiefer, *The Constitutionality of Independent Officers as Checks on Abuses of Executive Power,* 63 B.U.L.Rev. 59, 90 (1983). Others believe that it provides the President with significant authority to oversee the Executive Branch's interpretations of law. See, *e.g.,* Paulsen, *The Most Dangerous Branch: Executive Power To Say What the Law Is,* 83 Geo.L.J. 217, 261–62 (1994). Professor Sunstein finds it "clear" from both "its text and history" that "the Take Care Clause confers both a duty and a power." Sunstein, Paragraph (2), *supra,* at 212–13; see also Goldsmith & Manning, *The Protean Take Care Clause,* 164 U.Pa.L.Rev. 1835, 1836, 1838 (2016) (observing that "the functions that the Court ascribes to the Take Care Clause are often in unacknowledged tension with one another" and that "[t]hrough a long and varied course of interpretation, however, the Court has read that vague but modest language, in the alternative, either as a source of vast presidential power or as a sharp limitation on the powers of both the President and the other branches of government").

781 (2009); Sierra v. City of Hallandale Beach, Fla., 996 F.3d 1110, 1132–39 (11th Cir.2021) (Newsom, J., concurring).

How persuasive is this view? Consider first cases of standing to sue the government—generally the executive branch—because of disagreement with its implementation of federal law. Professor Sunstein argues that even though the Take Care Clause gives the President some oversight authority over the bureaucracy's implementation of the law, it also "imposes on the President both a responsibility to be faithful to the law and an obligation to enforce the law as it has been enacted." Sunstein, Paragraph (2), *supra*, at 212–13. See also Siegel, *A Theory of Justiciability*, 86 Tex.L.Rev. 73, 100 (2007). Accordingly, he believes that when a plaintiff "establishes that an agency has enforced the law in an unlawful way," the President has violated the Take Care Clause, and judicial enforcement does no violence to presidential authority.

If the Take Care Clause establishes some presidential superintendence over the bureaucracy's legal decisionmaking, is Sunstein correct to assume that the Take Care Clause has been violated every time a court concludes that an agency acts unlawfully? A great deal of modern law hinges on the proposition that reasonable people can differ about the best answer to a legal interpretive question.[9] The idea is captured by Justice Jackson's famous aphorism about the Supreme Court: "We are not final because we are infallible, but we are infallible only because we are final." Brown v. Allen, 344 U.S. 443, 540 (1953) (Jackson, J., concurring in the result), p. 1558, *infra*. Under this idea, the mere fact that a reviewing court disagrees with the executive's legal interpretation does not mean that that interpretation violates the President's duty under the Take Care Clause. In Loper Bright Enterprises v. Raimondo, however, 144 S.Ct. 2244 (2024), the Supreme Court rejected this approach in the context of judicial review under the Administrative Procedure Act, stating that "even if some judges might (or might not) consider the statute ambiguous, there is a best reading all the same * * *. It therefore makes no sense to speak of a 'permissible' interpretation that is not the one the court, after applying all relevant interpretive tools, concludes is best. In the business of statutory interpretation, if it is not the best, it is not permissible."[10] How does Loper Bright bear on Sunstein's assumptions about the Take Care Clause?

Now consider cases such as TransUnion and Spokeo, where the executive is not a party to the case. Is the Article II argument stronger or weaker in such a context? Professor Sunstein argues: "In TransUnion itself, Article II could not possibly be relevant. The case involved a suit between private parties! If Congress authorizes Private Citizen A to sue Private

---

[9]   See, *e.g.*, Sawyer v. Smith, 497 U.S. 227, 234 (1990) (application of the bar against applying "new law" on federal habeas review of state court convictions depends on whether "reasonable" people could differ about the law when a state court conviction became final); Anderson v. Creighton, 483 U.S. 635, 640 (1987) (qualified immunity is available unless right is "sufficiently clear that a reasonable official would understand that what he [or she] is doing violates that right").

[10]   Loper Bright therefore overruled the case of Chevron U.S.A., Inc. v. Natural Resources Defense Council, Inc., 467 U.S. 837, 844 (1984), which had established a regime of deference to agency interpretations of statutory ambiguities. For further discussion, see pp. 492–493, *infra*.

Citizen B in federal court, there might be an Article III issue, depending on what A is suing B for, and depending on the right conception of Article III. But it would require an adventurous understanding of Article II to think that the authority of the Executive is at stake or in danger." Sunstein, *Injury in Fact, Transformed*, 2021 Sup.Ct.Rev. 349, 367 n.99. In contrast, Judge Newsom argues that the Article II problem is that "at its core, the 'executive power' entailed the authority to bring legal actions on behalf of the community for remedies that accrued to the public generally." Sierra v. City of Hallandale Beach, Fla., 996 F.3d 1110, 1134 (11th Cir.2021) (Newsom, J., concurring) (citing Prakash, *The Essential Meaning of Executive Power*, 2003 U.Ill.L.Rev. 701, 743–52 (2003).[11] Judge Newsom explains: "Under this view, Congress has broad authority to grant a private plaintiff a cause of action, so long as it empowers him only to vindicate his own rights and to seek remedies that will accrue to him personally. But Congress may not give to anyone but the President and his subordinates a right to sue on behalf of the community and seek a remedy that accrues to the public—paradigmatically (but by no means exclusively) criminal punishment or a fine." Judge Newsom's argument, if accepted, would provide an Article II basis for standing in suits for statutory damages between private parties.

This being said, the enforcement of *constitutional* limits on standing to sue a *private* party may itself be something of a novelty. Professor Schmidt observes: "Until 2020, the Supreme Court had *never* dismissed for lack of Article III standing a private party's claim against another private party on the ground that the injury alleged was inadequate." Schmidt, *Standing Between Private Parties*, 2024 Wisc.L.Rev. 1, 8. Schmidt argues that Article III standing doctrine should be inapplicable in such contexts. See also *Case Comment: TransUnion LLC v. Ramirez*, 135 Harv.L.Rev. 333, 339 (2021); Hessick, *The Separation-of-Powers Theory of Standing*, 95 N.C.L.Rev. 673, 675–76 (2017).

(4) Qui Tam Actions. The False Claims Act (FCA), a federal statute with antecedents nearly as old as the republic itself, authorizes private citizens— called "relators"—to bring "qui tam" actions on behalf of the United States seeking civil penalties and damages payable to the Treasury against "any person" who procured payment on a false claim against the United States. When a qui tam action succeeds, the relator receives a percentage of the money payable to the government. Although divided on other issues, the Court held without dissent in Vermont Agency of Natural Resources v. United States ex rel. Stevens, 529 U.S. 765 (2000), that a relator has Article III standing. Justice Scalia's majority opinion first rejected the suggestion that a relator's interest in recovering a bounty for successful prosecution could support standing. Where no previous injury existed, "an interest that is merely a 'byproduct' of the suit itself" did not satisfy the injury requirement. But the opinion then concluded that the relator, as the assignee of the Government's claim, "has standing to assert the injury in fact suffered

---

[11]   If Judge Newsom's argument requires the assumption that Congress cannot regulate the executive's enforcement discretion, there are substantial criticisms of that assumption. See, *e.g.*, Price, *Enforcement Discretion and Executive Duty*, 67 Vand.L.Rev. 671, 711–16 (2014). For other skepticism of the Article II basis for standing, see Litman, *Taking Care of Federal Law*, 101 Va.L.Rev. 1289, 1340–56 (2015).

by the assignor." The Court pronounced itself "confirmed in this conclusion by the long tradition of qui tam actions in England and the American Colonies." Justice Scalia termed the historical practice "particularly relevant * * * since * * * Article III's restriction of the judicial power to 'Cases' and 'Controversies' is properly understood to mean 'cases and controversies of the sort traditionally amenable to * * * the judicial process.' "[12]

With the standing question thus resolved, Justice Scalia dropped a footnote: "In so concluding, we express no view on the question whether qui tam suits violate Article II, in particular the Appointments Clause of § 2 and the 'Take Care' Clause of § 3." In support of this reservation he quoted Steel Co. v. Citizens for a Better Environment, 523 U.S. 83, 102 (1998), for the proposition that " '[O]ur standing jurisprudence, * * * though it may sometimes have an impact on Presidential powers, derives from Article III and not Article II.' "[13] Is this reservation consistent with TransUnion's statement that "A regime where Congress could freely authorize unharmed plaintiffs to sue defendants who violate federal law not only would violate Article III but also would infringe on the Executive Branch's Article II authority"? If not, how should the Article II objections be resolved?

In United States ex rel. Polansky v. Executive Health Resources, Inc., 559 U.S. 419 (2023), a case about the scope of government control of a qui tam suit under the False Claims Act, Justice Thomas's dissent on the statutory question also expressed his view that "there is good reason to suspect that Article II does not permit private relators to represent the United States' interests in FCA suits."[14] Justice Kavanaugh, joined by

---

[12]   In Sprint Communications Co. v. APCC Services, Inc., 554 U.S. 269 (2008), the Court appeared to extend Vermont Agency. In Sprint, pay telephone operators assigned to a litigation service numerous small claims against long-distance carriers for nonpayment of fees owed to the operators for certain types of pay telephone calls. The litigation service received a periodic fee for its services rather than a percentage of the recovery it collected as assignee of the claims. Any actual sums recovered went straight to the operators themselves. Relying in significant part on its understanding of "history and tradition," the Court determined, 5–4, that such a suit fit among "the types of cases that Article III empowers federal courts to consider," even though the assignee lacked a "personal stake" in the outcome of the litigation. The Court added that the assignee's economic interest as a litigation service provider assured that it would litigate with the concrete adverseness required by Article III. Notably, all nine Justices agreed that standing would exist if a small portion of the assigned claim itself, perhaps even "a dollar or two," had been reserved to the assignee. Given the majority's and dissent's apparent agreement on the sufficiency of even a small personal stake in a lawsuit, why didn't the statutory damages in TransUnion—well more than a "dollar or two"—suffice for Article III?

[13]   Justice Ginsburg concurred in the judgment only. Justice Stevens, joined by Justice Souter, dissented on other grounds.

[14]   Justice Thomas also noted that "The potential inconsistency of qui tam suits with Article II has been noticed for decades," citing Riley v. St. Luke's Episcopal Hospital, 252 F.3d 749, 758–75 (CA5 2001) (en banc) (Smith, J., dissenting); Blanch, Note, *The Constitutionality of the False Claims Act's Qui Tam Provision*, 16 Harv.J.L. & Pub.Pol'y 701, 736–67 (1993); *Constitutionality of the Qui Tam Provisions of the False Claims Act*, 13 Op. OLC 207, 221–24, 228–32 (1989). For arguments on the other side, see, *e.g.*, Caminker, *The Constitutionality of Qui Tam Actions*, 99 Yale L.J. 341, 354–80 (1989) (arguing that qui tam actions do not violate Article II); Shane, *Returning Separation-of-Powers Analysis to Its Normative Roots: The Constitutionality of Qui Tam Actions and Other Private Suits to Enforce Civil Fines*, 30 Envtl.L.Rep. 11081 (2000) (same); Craig, *Will Separation of Powers Challenges "Take Care" of Environmental Citizen Suits? Article II, Injury-in-Fact, Private "Enforcers," and Lessons from Qui Tam Litigation*, 72 U.Colo.L.Rev. 93 (2001) (same); Beck, *Qui Tam Litigation Against Government Officials: Constitutional Implications of A Neglected History*, 93 N.D.L.Rev. 1235, 1310–16 (2018) (same); see also Pfander & Joffroy, *Public Law Litigation in Eighteenth Century*

Justice Barrett, joined the majority opinion but noted their "agree[ment] with Justice Thomas that there are substantial arguments that the *qui tam* device is inconsistent with Article II."

The assignment in Vermont Agency involved a "proprietary" or financial interest of the United States. Could Congress also confer standing by providing for the assignment of a more paradigmatically "sovereign" interest, such as that in enforcing the criminal law? See Lee, Comment, *The Standing of Qui Tam Relators Under the False Claims Act*, 57 U.Chi.L.Rev. 543, 551 (1990) (arguing not); Gilles, *Representational Standing: U.S. ex rel. Stevens and the Future of Public Law Litigation*, 89 Calif.L.Rev. 315, 341–45 (2001) (same). Similarly, even Justice Thomas's dissent in *Polansky, supra,* noted that under his view of Article II one might need to distinguish between a relator's suit for his own, assigned, interest and the United States's interest in the suit. One analysis suggests that applying the distinction between private and public rights (described p. 202, *supra*) resolves these questions. It would allow a qui tam statute to assign proprietary or financial interests without offending Article II or Article III, because these rights can be made private, while forbidding the assignment of more sovereign interests in enforcing the law, because these are quintessentially public. See Leitner, *The Private Rights Model of Qui Tam*, 76 Fla.L.Rev. 865 (2024).

(5) The Validity of "Prudential" Standing. How does the Court's emphasis on constitutional limitations on *Congress's* power to determine who has standing affect, if at all, *judge-made* doctrines concerning standing? Recall the Court has long exercised judicial authority to apply prudential limitations on its power to hear cases that otherwise satisfy Article III case or controversy requirements. See pp. 95–96, *supra*. For example, two frequently invoked aspects of standing doctrine—the bars against raising generalized grievances and asserting the legal rights of third parties—have often been described as prudential, rather than constitutional elements of standing doctrine. See, *e.g.*, Warth v. Seldin, 422 U.S. 490, 499–500 (1975); see also pp. 183–184, *supra*, & p. 228, *infra*. On that basis, such limitations might be understood to fit within a wide array of traditional doctrines of judicial self-governance, such as equitable discretion, abstention, and forum non conveniens—and, thus, to be appropriate qualifications upon a general judicial obligation to hear cases within a federal court's jurisdiction. See Shapiro, *Jurisdiction and Discretion*, 60 N.Y.U.L.Rev. 543 (1985). In Lexmark Int'l, Inc. v. Static Control Components, Inc., 572 U.S. 118 (2014), however, the Court called into question the continuing validity of prudential standing doctrine.

At issue in Lexmark was whether the plaintiff fell within the "zone of interests" protected by the Lanham Act—a test that had previously been described as a doctrine of prudential standing. See, *e.g.*, Allen v. Wright, 468 U.S. 737, 751 (1984); Valley Forge Christian College v. Americans United for Separation of Church & State, Inc., 454 U.S. 464, 475 (1982). In a unanimous

---

America: Diffuse Law Enforcement for a Partisan World, 92 Fordham L.Rev. 469 (2023) (describing the success of anti-slavery groups, such as the Quakers, in securing and enforcing federal legislation in the 1790s that authorized private individuals to enforce public law against American sailors and vessels engaged in the international trade in enslaved people).

opinion by Justice Scalia, the Court approached the case by broadly questioning the entire genre of prudential standing. The Court acknowledged that it had in "[i]n recent decades * * * adverted to a 'prudential' branch of standing, a doctrine not derived from Article III and * * * encompassing (we have said) at least three broad principles: [1] the general prohibition on a litigant's raising another person's legal rights, [2] the rule barring adjudication of generalized grievances more appropriately addressed in the representative branches, and [3] the requirement that a plaintiff's complaint fall within the zone of interests protected by the law invoked." But it suggested that a barrier to standing that is " 'prudential,' rather than constitutional * * * is in some tension with * * * the principle that a "federal court's obligation to hear and decide cases within its jurisdiction is virtually unflagging."

While the Court expressed uncertainty about the proper status of category [1], third-party standing,[15] it rejected the idea of "prudential standing" doctrines in categories [2] or [3]. As to category [2], the Court observed that after cases such as Lujan, its "reluctance to entertain generalized grievances" had been understood to come from "constitutional reasons, not 'prudential' ones." As to category [3], the one actually at issue in the case, the Court recharacterized the zone-of-interests question as one of statutory interpretation—an inquiry that turns on the scope of the right of action established by the statute, and indeed is neither a standing issue nor a jurisdictional issue at all.

One might read Lexmark as the Court's attempt to formalize previously-judge-made standing doctrines by grounding them, as much as possible, in the interpretation of written law—either statutory interpretation in the case of the zone-of-interests test, or constitutional interpretation in the case of generalized grievances. But an unyielding rejection of prudential standing doctrine would potentially have further-reaching implications, not only for third-party standing, considered pp. 221–244, *infra*, but also for abstention doctrines, explored in Chapter X, and many more elements of judicial discretion.

(6) Standing in State Courts. State courts have concurrent jurisdiction over most issues of federal law and they are not bound by limits on *federal* jurisdiction, as is explored in Chapter IV. For instance, many state courts have their own more permissive doctrines of standing and some even issue advisory opinions. The Court has recognized this principle in many cases. See, *e.g.*, ASARCO Inc. v. Kadish, 490 U.S. 605, 617 (1989) ("We have recognized often that the constraints of Article III do not apply to state courts, and accordingly the state courts are not bound by the limitations of a case or controversy or other federal rules of justiciability even when they address issues of federal law, as when they are called upon to interpret the Constitution or, in this case, a federal statute.").[16]

---

[15] See pp. 228–229, *infra*, for discussion of the "prudential" status of third-party standing.

[16] There is also a long-settled converse assumption that a plaintiff suing in federal court on a state law claim must satisfy federal standing rules. For a challenge to that assumption as applied to diversity cases not raising federal questions, see Hessick, *Cases, Controversies, and Diversity,* 109 Nw.L.Rev. 57 (2015).

ASARCO recognized an important corollary, however, which is that a state court decision where plaintiffs lacked Article III standing could sometimes itself become the basis for Article III standing when seeking review in the U.S. Supreme Court. ASARCO held that "[w]hen a state court has issued a judgment in a case where plaintiffs in the original action had no standing to sue under the principles governing the federal courts, we may exercise our jurisdiction on certiorari if the judgment of the state court causes direct, specific, and concrete injury to the parties who petition for our review, where the requisites of a case or controversy are also met." In ASARCO, state taxpayers and an association of public school teachers challenged a state statute governing mineral leases on state school lands as void under federal law. Some of the private leaseholders intervened as defendants. The state supreme court found the statute invalid and remanded for entry of a declaratory judgment and consideration of injunctive relief. On certiorari, the Supreme Court held that it had power to review the judgment. Justice Kennedy's opinion (for four Justices) first concluded that in a federal court action, the plaintiffs would lack standing. Even accepting the plaintiffs' premise that the state's issuance of mineral leases in violation of federal law had cost state school trust funds millions of dollars, the Court deemed it "pure speculation" whether the relief sought would result in tax reductions for the plaintiff-taxpayers or pay increases for the plaintiff-teachers. Accordingly, the plaintiff-respondents would not have had standing to bring their action in federal district court in the first instance. Nevertheless, Justice Kennedy (here speaking for a majority of six) ruled that given the way the proceedings had unfolded, the Supreme Court could review the state court decision, which had proceeded to final judgment under the state's more liberal standing rules. Because the state court judgment invalidated mineral leases held by the private leaseholders who had petitioned for certiorari, it had produced "the kind of injury [to them] cognizable in this Court on review from the state courts."[17]

Consider the interaction of the longstanding principles of state court standing with the constitutional principle set forth by Lujan and TransUnion. Because Lujan and TransUnion do not deny Congress's Article I power to create new rights distinct from the common law, and because Article III does not limit the jurisdiction of the state courts, it would seem that important federal statutory rights are now enforceable exclusively in state courts. And what is more, these nationally-established federal rights will be enforceable in some state courts but not others, depending on the particulars of state law. As Professor Bennett puts it: "This is a paradox. The classic model assumes that federal law should be decided mainly in federal court, or at least that federal courts have an important role to play in the adjudication of federal claims. So how can there be a federal right, duly created by Congress, the remedy for which lies exclusively in (some) state courts?" Bennett, *The Paradox of Exclusive Jurisdiction Over Federal Claims*, 105 Minn.L.Rev. 1211, 1212 (2021). Justice Thomas made this point, citing Bennett, in his dissent in TransUnion.

---

[17]   Chief Justice Rehnquist, joined by Justice Scalia, dissented in relevant part.

What is the constitutional logic of this arrangement? Or is this, as Professor Bennett suggests, an "unintended consequence" of the doctrine culminating in TransUnion? *Id.* 1213. Or, as a third possibility, should the principles of TransUnion in fact restrict the state courts as well as the federal courts, overturning the often-recognized principle described in ASARCO? Judge Newsom has argued that if standing limitations are grounded in Article II instead of Article III, "these Article II limitations would apply to all actions arising under federal law regardless of whether they were brought in federal or state court." Sierra v. City of Hallandale Beach, Fla., 996 F.3d 1110, 1138 (11th Cir.2021). For an earlier argument that state courts should be required to adhere to Article III standing doctrine, see Fletcher, *The "Case or Controversy" Requirement in State Court Adjudication of Federal Questions*, 78 Calif.L.Rev. 263 (1990).

NOTE ON THE STANDING OF STATES AND LEGISLATORS

(1) Introductory Note. Although the majority of the Court's standing doctrine has been developed in the context of private plaintiffs, the Court has also had to address the standing of "public" plaintiffs, such as states or legislators. Though public plaintiffs present different considerations from each other, each provides a valuable case study in the general concept of the judicial role and the ability of standing doctrine to advance that concept. In reading the materials that follow, consider whether this area of standing doctrine, in fact, presents special considerations, and if so whether those considerations should make courts more or less reluctant to entertain such suits.

(2) State Standing. States can bring suit in a number of different capacities—and sometimes in more than one capacity in a single litigation— which can affect the state's standing to sue in federal court.

(a) States as the Real Party in Interest. Many cases establish that states can bring suit in federal court to enforce their own concrete interests, such as in boundaries, *e.g.*, New Jersey v. New York, 523 U.S. 767 (1998),[1] in water rights, *e.g.*, Kansas v. Colorado, 533 U.S. 1 (2001), and even in some cases in their "specific tax revenues," Wyoming v. Oklahoma, 502 U.S. 437 (1992).[2] Many of the notable precedents in this area involve state lawsuits against other states, which also implicate special access to the Supreme Court's original jurisdiction (see Chap. III) and special ability to overcome the potential defense of sovereign immunity (see Chap. IX).

Although a state may sue to vindicate its own property rights, it has no standing to sue either another state or a private party when it is merely

---

[1]   Chief Justice Taney's dissent in Rhode Island v. Massachusetts, 37 U.S. (12 Pet.) 657, 753 (1838), argued that such cases were not justiciable if they concerned "sovereignty and jurisdiction" rather than "property in the soil of the territory in controversy." But the prevailing view is that these interstate disputes, though not justiciable at common law, were made justiciable by the Constitution, see, *e.g.*, Hans v. Louisiana, 134 U.S. 1, 15 (1890).

[2]   This it not to say that a state can sue whenever its own tax revenues are negatively affected by another state's policies. See Pennsylvania v. New Jersey, 426 U.S. 660 (1976) (per curiam).

sponsoring the claims of a small number of individual citizens. Thus, in New Hampshire v. Louisiana, 108 U.S. 76 (1883), the plaintiff states sued on defaulted bonds, as assignees for collection only, on behalf of certain of their citizens. The Court held the real parties in interest were the private citizens, whose claims against Louisiana were barred by state sovereign immunity. But in South Dakota v. North Carolina, 192 U.S. 286 (1904), South Dakota, having learned a lesson from the decision in New Hampshire v. Louisiana, acquired absolute title (by gift from an individual) to defaulted North Carolina bonds and was able to obtain judgment on them.[3]

(b) States as Parens Patriae. Thus, the more complicated situations arise when the state attempts to sue on behalf of the well-being of its citizens generally, often called a suit *parens patriae* (literally translated as parent of the country). The early *parens patriae* decisions appeared to rest on two premises. First, a state not complaining of injury to its own property could not sue merely because its citizens were injured by the actions of another state, see Louisiana v. Texas, 176 U.S. 1 (1900), or by actions of private persons, see Oklahoma v. Atchison, Topeka and Santa Fe Ry. Co., 220 U.S. 277 (1911). Second, suits were permitted to challenge physical intrusions into the plaintiff state that harmed state citizens. Missouri v. Illinois, 180 U.S. 208 (1901); Georgia v. Tennessee Copper Co., 206 U.S. 230 (1907).

Beginning in the 1920s, a series of decisions extended *parens patriae* standing to situations in which the harm to the plaintiff state's citizens did not arise from physical intrusion but rather from regulations adopted within the defendant state. See, *e.g.*, Pennsylvania v. West Virginia, 262 U.S. 553 (1923) (enjoining enforcement of a West Virginia statute designed to limit the export of natural gas); Maryland v. Louisiana, 451 U.S. 725 (1981) (permitting eight states to challenge the constitutionality of a Louisiana tax on the "first use" of previously untaxed natural gas coming into the state, a tax whose incidence fell on many customers in the plaintiff states). This more liberal attitude to standing was also extended to suits against private defendants, see Georgia v. Pennsylvania R.R., 324 U.S. 439 (1945) (challenging a rate-fixing conspiracy), and culminating in the broad language in Alfred L. Snapp & Son, Inc. v. Puerto Rico ex rel. Barez, 458 U.S. 592 (1982), upholding a district court action by Puerto Rico, as *parens patriae*, against apple growers in eastern states who allegedly had illegally preferred Jamaican over Puerto Rican temporary workers. The Court also stated that in determining whether a state may sue as *parens patriae* to redress injury to its citizens' health and welfare, "[o]ne helpful indication * * * is whether the injury is one that the State, if it could, would likely attempt to address through its sovereign lawmaking powers."

(c) Suits Against the Federal Government. This broad scope of state standing, especially as parens patriae, has faced special limitations and challenges when states wish to sue the federal government.

---

[3]   See generally Siegel, *Congress's Power to Authorize Suits Against States*, 68 Geo.Wash.L.Rev. 44, 100 (1999) (reading the two decisions as indicating that "what matters is whether the plaintiff has a proper interest that entitles it to bring the suit, not whether plaintiff has an appropriate motive").

(i)   In Massachusetts v. Mellon, 262 U.S. 447 (1923), decided in the
same opinion as Frothingham v. Mellon, p. 125, *supra*, the Court
unanimously held that Massachusetts lacked standing to sue the Secretary
of the Treasury on a claim that a federal grant program exceeded Congress's
Article I powers and thus violated the Tenth Amendment. The Court
reasoned that the state's claim, if brought on its own behalf, involved "not
rights of person or property, not rights of dominion over physical domain, not
quasi-sovereign rights actually invaded or threatened, but abstract
questions of political power, of sovereignty, of government." As for a suit
representing the state's citizens, the Court said that "[w]e need not go so far
as to say that a State may never intervene by suit to protect its citizens
against any form of enforcement of unconstitutional acts of Congress; but we
are clear that the right to do so does not arise here. * * * While the State,
under some circumstances, may sue [as *parens patriae*] for the protection of
its citizens, it is no part of its duty or power to enforce their rights in respect
of their relations with the Federal Government. In that field it is the United
States, and not the State, which represents them as *parens patriae*."

(ii)   More recently, however, in Massachusetts v. EPA, 549 U.S. 497
(2007), the Court recognized a state's standing to sue to require the federal
government to comply with a federal statute, suggesting as well that a state's
standing is broader than that of a private citizen.

Along   with   private   organizations   and   other   governments,
Massachusetts challenged the EPA's determinations that (i) it did not have
regulatory authority over greenhouse gas emissions and (ii) it would not
exercise that regulatory authority in any event. Without deciding whether
any of the other plaintiffs had standing, Justice Stevens's majority opinion
concluded that Massachusetts had adequately alleged that global warming
could cause rising sea levels that would threaten the considerable coastal
land owned by the state and that the relief sought would reduce the risk of
harm to Massachusetts.

Rejecting arguments that the injury was too remote, and causation and
redressability were too uncertain, the Court emphasized two special factors
supporting standing. One was a statutory provision, 42 U.S.C. § 7606(b)(1),
that authorized the filing of "[a] petition for review of * * * final action taken"
by EPA. The other was the fact that Massachusetts was a state. The Court
stated that "States are not normal litigants for the purposes of invoking
federal jurisdiction" and characterized Massachusetts' interests as quasi-
sovereign because it had surrendered its powers to "invade Rhode island to
force reductions in greenhouse gas emotions" or to "negotiate an emissions
treaty with China or India" by entering the union. "Given that procedural
right and Massachusetts' stake in protecting its quasi-sovereign interests,
the Commonwealth is entitled to special solicitude in our standing analysis."

Chief Justice Roberts, joined by Justices Scalia, Thomas, and Alito
dissented, arguing that "[g]lobal warming is a phenomenon 'harmful to
humanity at large,' and the redress petitioners seek is focused no more on
them than on the public generally—it is literally to change the atmosphere
of the world." The Chief Justice also maintained that "[p]etitioners are never
able to trace their alleged injuries * * * to the fractional amount of global

emissions that might have been limited with EPA standards" and that "given events elsewhere in the world * * * the Court never explains" why the injury resulting from its alleged, impending loss of land would be redressed by such standards. The Chief Justice concluded: "The good news is that the Court's 'special solicitude' for Massachusetts limits the future applicability of the diluted standing requirements applied in this case. The bad news is that the Court's self-professed relaxation of * * * Article III requirements has caused us to transgress 'the proper—and properly limited—role of the courts in a democratic society' " (quoting Allen v. Wright, 468 U.S. 737, 750 (1984)).

It is difficult to ascertain how much the majority's decision turned on the proposition that a state is not bound by the standing rules that apply to private plaintiffs. But given the Court's other precedents about uncertainty, injuries, causation and redressability, and given that the Court's subsequent holdings about the limited power of Congress over Article III standing, mustn't "special solicitude" have been doing some work?

As a practical matter, lawsuits by states against the federal government became commonplace in the period after Massachusetts v. EPA—more than 250 such suits have been filed since that decision, against Presidents from both major political parties.[4] It is far from clear, however, how much the specific doctrinal holding of state standing has contributed to this. Professors Baude and Bray write: "The decision in Massachusetts v. EPA contributed to this dynamic, but it is not the only thing that did, and perhaps not even the most important thing that did. Other causes discussed include the rising sophistication and resources of state solicitors general, ideological polarization in Congress, changes in the preliminary injunction, the rise of the national injunction, and a trend toward major executive actions being taken with only an attenuated claim of legislative authorization. Whatever the precise accumulation of causes, however, Massachusetts v. EPA is a key part of the story because it allowed suits by states that would never have been considered cognizable under previous standing law." Baude & Bray, *Proper Parties, Proper Relief*, 137 Harv.L.Rev. 153, 165 (2023). Professor Crocker, however, expresses stronger doubt about the significance of "special solicitude." Surveying all of the federal appellate decisions after Massachusetts v. EPA she concludes: "there does not appear to exist even a single circuit-court case where special solicitude made a definitive and dispositive difference in providing state standing." Crocker, *Not-So-Special Solicitude*, 109 Minn.L.Rev. (forthcoming 2024).

Insofar as the decision did herald a relaxation of standing for states (at least when suing in a quasi-sovereign capacity), does it make sense? Professor Massey thinks so, *inter alia*, because such an approach creates a further level of accountability for the federal executive, at the behest of discrete polities of the union. Massey, *Of Sovereignty, States, and Standing*, 61 Fla.L.Rev. 249 (2009). Professors Freeman and Vermeule disagree, contending that the states have greater ability to mobilize congressional power vis-a-vis agencies than do private litigants. They suggest that the majority may have included that statement in order to secure Justice

---

[4]   See State Lawsuits Database, https://attorneysgeneral.org/list-of-lawsuits-1980-present/.

Kennedy's vote, but that it is hard to square with the faith, expressed by the other members of the majority in other decisions, in the political safeguards of federalism. See Freeman & Vermeule, *Massachusetts v. EPA: From Politics to Expertise*, 2007 Sup.Ct.Rev. 51, 67–71. Likewise, Professors Woolhandler and Collins suggest that states should face and historically have faced a *heightened* standard for standing. Woolhandler & Collins, *Reining in State Standing*, 94 N.D. L.Rev. 2015, 2024 (2019).[5]

(iii) In 2023, a majority of the court addressed the topic of special solicitude for state standing for the first time since Massachusetts v. EPA.[6] In United States v. Texas, 599 U.S. 670 (2023), the Court held that the states of Texas and Louisiana did not have standing to challenge the executive branch's prioritization of certain immigration arrests. As discussed p. 158, *supra*, much of the Court's reasoning turned on its application of the holding of Linda R.S. v. Richard D., 410 U.S. 614, 619 (1973) that "a citizen lacks standing to contest the policies of the prosecuting authority when he himself is neither prosecuted nor threatened with prosecution." But in the course of extending that principle to a state lawsuit, the Court also discussed state standing.

In one footnote, the Court wrote: "Also, the plaintiffs here are States, and federal courts must remain mindful of bedrock Article III constraints in cases brought by States against an executive agency or officer. To be sure, States sometimes have standing to sue the United States or an executive agency or officer. But in our system of dual federal and state sovereignty, federal policies frequently generate indirect effects on state revenues or state spending. And when a State asserts, for example, that a federal law has produced only those kinds of indirect effects, the State's claim for standing can become more attenuated."

And in a second footnote that directly addressed the relevance of Massachusetts v. EPA, the Court wrote: "As part of their argument for standing, the States also point to Massachusetts v. EPA, 549 U. S. 497, 127

---

[5] See also Davis, *The New Public Standing*, 71 Stan.L.Rev. 1229 (2019); Young, *State Standing and Cooperative Federalism*, 94 Notre Dame L.Rev. 1893 (2019); Grove, *When Can a State Sue the United States?*, 101 Cornell L.Rev. 851 (2016); Hessick & Marshall, *State Standing to Constrain the President*, 21 Chap.L.Rev. 83, 107–08 (2018); Mank, *Should States Have Greater Standing Rights Than Ordinary Citizens?: Massachusetts v. EPA's New Standing Test for States*, 49 Wm. & Mary L.Rev. 1701 (2008).

[6] Before 2023, the Court had decided five other cases relevant to state standing. California v. Texas, 593 U.S. 659 (2021), p. 149, *supra*, and Trump v. New York, 592 U.S. 125 (2020), denied standing; Department of Commerce v. New York, 588 U.S. 752 (2019), granted standing. None of these decisions mentioned or seemed to apply special solicitude to the state's standing. In addition, the Supreme Court affirmed by an equally divided Court in United States v. Texas, 579 U.S. 547 (2016), a case in which the Fifth Circuit had affirmed a universal injunction against the Obama administration's program of Deferred Action for Parents of Americans and Lawful Permanent Residents, known as "DAPA." Finally, the Court affirmed state standing by an equally divided vote in American Electric Power v. Connecticut, 564 U.S. 410 (2011) (and then reversed unanimously on the merits). It said the following about Connecticut's standing in that case: "Four members of the Court would hold that at least some plaintiffs have Article III standing under Massachusetts, which permitted a State to challenge EPA's refusal to regulate greenhouse gas emissions, and, further, that no other threshold obstacle bars review. Four members of the Court, adhering to a dissenting opinion in Massachusetts, or regarding that decision as distinguishable, would hold that none of the plaintiffs have Article III standing. We therefore affirm, by an equally divided Court, the Second Circuit's exercise of jurisdiction and proceed to the merits."

(2007). Putting aside any disagreements that some may have with Massachusetts v. EPA, that decision does not control this case. The issue there involved a challenge to the denial of a statutorily authorized petition for rulemaking, not a challenge to an exercise of the Executive's enforcement discretion. *Id.*, at 520, 526; see also *id.*, at 527 (noting that there are 'key differences between a denial of a petition for rulemaking and an agency's decision not to initiate an enforcement action' and that 'an agency's refusal to initiate enforcement proceedings is not ordinarily subject to judicial review')."

Two separate opinions were more direct in rejecting the notion of special solicitude. In a concurring opinion joined by Justices Barrett and Thomas, Justice Gorsuch wrote: "In Massachusetts v. EPA, the Court chose to overlook [standing principles] in part because it thought the State's claim of standing deserved 'special solicitude.' *Id.*, at 520. I have doubts about that move. Before Massachusetts v. EPA, the notion that States enjoy relaxed standing rules 'ha[d] no basis in our jurisprudence.' *Id.*, at 536 (Roberts, C.J., dissenting). Nor has 'special solicitude' played a meaningful role in this Court's decisions in the years since. Even so, it's hard not to wonder why the Court says nothing about 'special solicitude' in this case. And it's hard not to think, too, that lower courts should just leave that idea on the shelf in future ones." And in a dissenting opinion, Justice Alito argued that "The obvious parallel to the case before us is Massachusetts v. EPA," and he observed that "the majority's footnote on Massachusetts raises more questions about Massachusetts itself—most importantly, has this monumental decision been quietly interred?

(iv) Also in 2023, the Court held, 6–3, that the state of Missouri had standing to challenge a student-loan forgiveness plan proposed by the Biden administration, in a case captioned Biden v. Nebraska, 143 S.Ct. 2355 (2023). As discussed at p. 163, *supra*, the Court concluded that the plan would cause economic losses to the Missouri Higher Education Loan Authority (MOHELA). It further concluded that "[t]he plan's harm to MOHELA is also a harm to Missouri" because "MOHELA is a 'public instrumentality' of the State." By contrast, the dissenting opinion by Justice Kagan argued that because MOHELA was financially and legally independent, with statutory power to sue and be sued, it was the proper party, not Missouri. What is the nature of the dissent's objection to MOHELA's standing? Is it a problem of "third-party standing," (see pp. 221–244, *infra*) as the dissent seemed to suggest? Is it a problem of traceability and redressability, (see pp. 156–164, *supra*) because even relief to MOHELA will have no effect on the state of Missouri itself? Or is it a distinct issue of state standing which entities and persons should be seen as a part of the state? For further discussion of MOHELA and standing, see Baude & Bray, *Proper Parties, Proper Relief,* 137 Harv.L.Rev. 153, 184–86 (2023).

(3) Actions by Legislators. Another specialized area of standing doctrine involves actions by legislators challenging intrusions upon their prerogatives. These cases present two related considerations. First, the Court must articulate what type of injury to a legislator's vote is legally actionable. Second, the Court must determine precisely what types of actions inflict such injuries. Consider whether the Court's handling of those questions in the following cases reflect a discernible theory of separation of powers.

(a) In Coleman v. Miller, 307 U.S. 433 (1939), a bare majority of the Court held that Kansas state legislators who had voted against ratification of the Child Labor Amendment had standing to seek review of a state court's refusal to enjoin state officials from certifying that Kansas had ratified the amendment. One of the grounds of suit was that the amendment had been approved in the state senate only by virtue of the vote of the lieutenant-governor, as presiding officer, to break a tie, and that under the federal Constitution such a vote was ineffectual. The Court recognized not only the standing of state senators to raise this issue, in protection of their official vote, but also the standing of both state senators and representatives to urge that the ratification was invalid because a previous rejection by Kansas was final, and because the proposed amendment, having been outstanding for what was claimed to be more than a reasonable time, was no longer susceptible of ratification. In so holding, the Court reasoned: "[T]he plaintiffs include twenty senators, whose votes against ratification have been overridden and virtually held for naught although if they are right in their contentions their votes would have been sufficient to defeat ratification. We think that these senators have a plain, direct and adequate interest in maintaining the effectiveness of their votes."

(b) In Raines v. Byrd, 521 U.S. 811 (1997), the Court rejected the standing of six present and former members of the House and Senate to challenge the constitutionality of the Line Item Veto Act, which authorized the President to "cancel" certain spending and tax benefit measures after signing them into law. The Act specifically authorized suit for declaratory and injunctive relief by "[a]ny Member of Congress or any individual adversely affected." Plaintiffs brought suit the day after the Act took effect, claiming that the statute " 'dilute[d] their Article I voting power.' " The Court noted that "our standing inquiry has been especially rigorous when reaching the merits of the dispute would force us to decide whether an action taken by one of the other two branches of the Federal Government was unconstitutional." The Court then concluded that plaintiffs based their claim of standing on a "type of institutional injury"—"a loss of political power"— and did "not claim that they have been deprived of something to which they *personally* are entitled—such as their seats as members of Congress after their constituents had elected *them*" (emphasis in original). The Court distinguished Coleman as standing "at most * * * for the proposition that legislators whose votes would have been sufficient to defeat (or enact) a specific legislative act have standing to sue if that legislative action goes into effect (or does not go into effect), on the ground that their votes have been completely nullified." Although plaintiffs alleged that the Line Item Veto Act diluted the significance of their votes for bills subject to presidential cancellation, there was a "vast difference" between the "level of vote nullification" in this case and that in Coleman.[7]

---

[7]   Justice Souter, joined by Justice Ginsburg, concurred in the judgment that the plaintiffs lacked standing. Justice Stevens, dissenting, would have sustained standing and

Is the majority's attempted distinction of "personal" and "institutional" injuries convincing? If not, is the degree of difference in the "institutional" injuries in the two cases sufficient to support the divergent results, or has Coleman effectively been limited to its facts?

(c) The issue of congressional standing arose again in Windsor v. United States, 570 U.S. 744 (2013), which considered the constitutionality of the Defense of Marriage Act's exclusion of same-sex married couples from the definition of "spouses" for purposes of federal law. As discussed at pp. 123–125, *supra*, the President directed the Attorney General not to defend the Act's constitutionality but also directed the executive branch to continue to enforce the Act in order to give Congress an opportunity to defend its validity. Pursuant to the rules of the House, the Speaker consulted with the Bipartisan Legal Advisory Group (BLAG) to discuss the proper course of action. By a 3–2 party line vote, BLAG in 2011 recommended that the Speaker direct the House General Counsel to intervene in Windsor to defend DOMA's constitutionality. After the Supreme Court had granted certiorari, the House itself passed a resolution "authoriz[ing] [BLAG] * * * to defend [DOMA's] constitutionality * * * including in the case of Windsor v. United States."

Because the Court found that there remained a justiciable controversy between Windsor and the United States, it declined to reach the question whether BLAG had standing. The dissenting Justices, however, not only reached the question but also disagreed about its resolution. Justice Alito concluded that BLAG had standing because the House, which authorized BLAG to represent it, suffered a concrete, justiciable injury. Justice Alito noted that when the executive declined to defend the legislative veto in INS v. Chadha, 462 U.S. 919 (1983), the Court held that the House and Senate had standing to defend the statute authorizing such a veto. Justice Alito reasoned that just as invalidation of the legislative veto injured Congress's institutional power, so too did the refusal to defend DOMA. "[B]ecause legislating is Congress' central function," he wrote, "any impairment of that function is a more grievous injury than the impairment of a procedural add-on." Justice Alito distinguished Raines v. Byrd, *supra*, in part, on the ground that the six individual Members of Congress who sought to challenge the Line Item Veto Act neither had the institutional backing of the House nor the status of pivotal actors whose votes would have altered legislative outcomes absent the challenged procedure.

In an opinion joined by Chief Justice Roberts and Justice Thomas, Justice Scalia rejected Justice Alito's analysis of congressional standing. Because DOMA, unlike the legislative veto, did not regulate Congress's institutional authority as such, he argued that Justice Alito's position would permit Congress to "hale the Executive before the courts not only to vindicate its own institutional powers to act, but to correct a perceived inadequacy in the execution of its laws." This approach, he added, would permit Congress to "pop immediately into Court" not only when "the President refuses to implement a statute he believes to be unconstitutional," but also when he or

---

invalidated the Act on the merits. Justice Breyer, who also dissented, argued that the case was not distinguishable from Coleman.

she "implements a law in a manner that is not to Congress' liking." Such matters, in Justice Scalia's view, have long been properly "left for political resolution" between Congress and the President.[8]

(d)   In Hollingsworth v. Perry, 570 U.S. 693 (2013), decided the same day as Windsor, the Court held that the official proponents of a state ballot initiative prohibiting same-sex marriage lacked standing to defend its constitutionality in federal court. The question of standing had arisen because regularly appointed state officials had declined to defend the statute's constitutionality below. On a certified question from the Ninth Circuit, the California Supreme Court held that as a matter of California law, proponents of a ballot initiative have authority to defend the initiative's constitutionality when state officials do not do so, and the Ninth Circuit accordingly found standing. But in an opinion by Chief Justice Roberts, joined by Justices Scalia, Breyer, Ginsburg, and Kagan, the Supreme Court reversed. The Court acknowledged that the state has a "cognizable interest" in defending Proposition 8 and that it may vindicate that interest by "designat[ing] agents to represent it in federal court." The Court found, however, that despite the California Supreme Court's ruling, the proponents were not acting as agents of the state. The Court stressed that under the Restatement of Agency, an agent owes a fiduciary duty to a principal, and the principal must be able to control the agent—elements wholly lacking in the proponents' relationship to the California government. Nor did the proponents take an oath of office or receive attorney's fees from the state. The Court stressed that whatever state law might say, "standing in federal court is a question of federal law," and that states cannot "issu[e] to private parties who otherwise lack standing a ticket to the federal courthouse."

Justice Kennedy, joined by Justices Thomas, Alito, and Sotomayor dissented. The dissent stressed that California law gave the proponent of an initiative "authority to appear in court and assert the State's interest in defending an enacted initiative," at least when public officials would not do so. Justice Kennedy added that nothing in Article III requires a state "to

---

[8]   For an argument that a single House should have standing to go to court to enforce its own subpoenas but not to defend legislation against constitutional attack, see Grove & Devins, *Congress's (Limited) Power to Defend Itself in Court*, 99 Cornell L.Rev. 571 (2014).

Compare Nash, *A Functional Theory of Congressional Standing*, 114 Mich.L.Rev. 339 (2015) (arguing that congressional standing should be based on a broader view of injury than mere vote nullification and should extend to injuries involving Congress's "constitutional functions" such as impediments to information gathering and certain diminishments of bargaining power). For further discussions of congressional standing, see Campbell, *Executive Action and Nonaction*, 95 N.C.L.Rev. 553 (2017) (arguing that Congress should have standing to challenge presidential failures to enforce the law when "congressional votes resulting in the passage of a law have been completely nullified"); Sant'Ambrogio, *Legislative Exhaustion*, 58 Wm. & Mary L.Rev. 1253 (2017) (coining the term "Legislative Exhaustion" to describe the argument that Congress ought to have standing only when it lacks nonjudicial methods of resolving a dispute with the executive branch, as when the President declines to enforce federal law based on constitutional objections); Grove, *Standing Outside of Article III*, 162 U.Pa.L.Rev. 1311 (2014) (identifying Article I and Article II as well as Article III limits on the standing of Congress and the executive branch); Jackson, *Congressional Standing to Sue: The Role of Courts and Congress in U.S. Constitutional Democracy*, 93 Ind.L.J. 845 (2018) (canvasing competing considerations and concluding that, although there should be no categorical preclusion of congressional standing, "most controversies between the branches are best addressed through political mechanisms").

comply with the Restatement of Agency or with this Court's view of how a state should * * * structure its government." He further reasoned that because the purpose of a ballot initiative was to establish a lawmaking process that "does not depend upon state officials," the Court's insistence upon the presence of state officials or others answerable to them would undermine the initiative process. "A prime purpose of justiciability is to ensure vigorous advocacy," the dissent concluded, "yet the Court insists upon litigation conducted by state officials whose preference is to lose the case."

(e)   In an opinion by Justice Ginsburg (joined by Justices Kennedy, Breyer, Sotomayor, and Kagan), the Court in Arizona State Legislature v. Arizona Independent Redistricting Comm'n, 576 U.S. 787 (2015) ("AIRC"), held that the Arizona State Legislature had standing to challenge a state ballot initiative that transferred to an independent commission the legislature's previous authority to redistrict Arizona's seats in the U.S. House of Representatives. The state legislature argued, *inter alia*, that this shift violated the Elections Clause, U.S. Const. art. I, § 4, cl. 1, which gives "the Legislature" of each state the power to prescribe the "Time, Places and Manner" of federal legislative elections. Although ultimately rejecting that claim on the merits, the Court found that the suit asserted a concrete and legally cognizable injury caused by the initiative's alleged infringement of the legislature's constitutionally assigned role.

The Court distinguished Raines v. Byrd, *supra*, on the ground that, in that case, "six *individual Members* of Congress" challenged the Line Item Veto Act and that neither the House nor the Senate had authorized suit by those Members. In contrast, the Arizona Legislature in AIRC sued as "an institutional plaintiff asserting an institutional injury, and * * * commenced this action after authorizing votes in both of its chambers." Quoting Coleman, *supra*, the Court in AIRC further noted that the challenged Arizona initiative would " 'completely nullif[y]' " the legislature's votes on federal redistricting. This consideration, said the Court, made the injury analogous to that of the twenty state senators who had been granted standing in Coleman to argue that their votes against ratifying a constitutional amendment were nullified, in violation of Article V, by the lieutenant governor's tie-breaking vote in favor.

Dissenting in AIRC, Justice Scalia (joined by Justice Thomas) contended that the traditional Anglo-American conception of "cases" or "controversies" does not "include suits between units of government regarding their legitimate powers." Even if such a suit was sufficiently "concrete" to permit effective adjudication, Justice Scalia concluded that the "separation of powers" precludes federal adjudication of interbranch disputes unless necessary to redress some resultant "concrete harm" to "a private party." Limiting the judicial power in this way, he added, "keeps us minding our own business." While acknowledging that Coleman seemed at odds with his position, Justice Scalia viewed that decision as an outlier whose true holding was far from clear.[9]

---

[9]   Grove, *Government Standing and the Fallacy of Institutional Injury*, 167 U.Pa.L.Rev. 611 (2019), also maintains that Coleman should not be followed. According to her, Coleman relied on "a now outdated rule of appellate standing" that permitted Supreme Court review of

Would the Court's approach in AIRC justify congressional standing if Congress itself (or even a particular House) authorized members to sue to vindicate an alleged "institutional injury" to Congress? Justice Ginsburg's opinion reserved that question, noting that "a suit between Congress and the President would raise separation-of-powers concerns absent here." Justice Scalia replied that if the Framers would have disfavored congressional standing, they presumably would have been "*all the more averse* to unprecedented judicial meddling by federal courts with the branches of their state governments." How should the Court sort out such competing contentions about implied limits on federal judicial power?

(f)   In Virginia House of Delegates v. Bethune-Hill, 587 U.S. 658 (2019), the Court held, 5–4, that the Virginia House of Delegates lacked standing to appeal from a lower court ruling that a state redistricting plan (adopted by the state House and Senate) constituted a forbidden racial gerrymander. The issue arose when the Virginia Attorney General, after defending the plan in the lower court, decided not to pursue an appeal, and the state House, which had previously participated as an intervenor, sought Supreme Court review. Justice Ginsburg's opinion, in which Justices Thomas, Sotomayor, Kagan, and Gorsuch joined, first ruled that the House lacked authority under Virginia law to represent the state's interests. Though Virginia could have "designated the House to represent its interests," it had not done so. Justice Ginsburg's opinion then held that a single house of a bicameral legislature suffered no sufficiently distinctive injury from the invalidation of a state law, including a districting statute, to support standing. In so ruling, the Court distinguished Sixty-seventh Minnesota State Senate v. Beens, 406 U.S. 187 (1972) (per curiam), which allowed the Minnesota Senate to challenge a lower court ruling in a malapportionment case that reduced the Senate's size from 67 to 35. "Cutting the size of the legislative chamber in half would necessarily alter its day-to-day operations" in a way that a mere change in district lines and membership would not, she reasoned: "[T]he House as an institution has no cognizable interest in the identity of its members."

Justice Alito's dissenting opinion deemed it unnecessary to "address the [majority's] first" holding that "Virginia law does not authorize the House to defend the invalidated redistricting plan on behalf of the Commonwealth." In his view, it was "obvious" that the Virginia House, like "any group consisting of members who must work together to achieve the group's aims has a keen[, constitutionally cognizable] interest in the identity of its members [and] in how its members are selected." Accordingly, he thought it decisive that "neither the Court nor the Virginia Solicitor General has provided any support for the proposition that Virginia law bars the House from defending, in its own right, the constitutionality of a districting plan."

---

state court decisions of federal claims that a federal district court could not have entertained. Professor Grove argues more broadly that claims of standing predicated on "institutional injuries" are incompatible with a constitutional design that allocates rights to individuals, not institutions, and relies on individuals to assert their own rights. She would allow only narrow exceptions to permit government bodies to perform functions that they could not perform without resort to a court, such as imposing sanctions (including for contempt of legislative bodies).

The majority and dissenting opinions appear ultimately to agree that state law is capable of controlling whether one branch of a bicameral legislature has standing to defend a state districting plan—either as a representative of the state or, according to the dissent, in its own right. To the extent that state law is controlling, which side should bear the burden of establishing a state-law authorization or prohibition?

B. STANDING TO ASSERT THE RIGHTS OF OTHERS AND RELATED ISSUES INVOLVING "FACIAL CHALLENGES" TO STATUTES

INTRODUCTORY NOTE

The standing issues considered thus far have involved whether a party may invoke the jurisdiction of an Article III court at all. In some cases, however, a further question may arise concerning whether parties with Article III standing—including, in some cases, criminal defendants—may rely on the rights of third parties as a basis for their claims to relief. The next principal case and the materials that immediately follow it address the issues presented when one party tries to assert the rights of others or seeks to establish what is often referred to as "third-party" or "*jus tertii*" standing.

Subsequent principal cases then take up the questions whether, and if so under what circumstances, a party may challenge a statute on the ground that it is unconstitutional "on its face." Although parties can always argue that statutes are unconstitutional as applied to them, the standards governing facial challenges are complex and often controverted. Among the central questions to be considered are why this is so and what the pertinent standards for the availability of facial challenges ought to be.

Craig v. Boren
429 U.S. 190 (1976).
Appeal from the District Court for the Western District of Oklahoma.

■ JUSTICE BRENNAN delivered the opinion of the Court.

[Oklahoma law prohibited the sale of a low-alcohol, 3.2% beer to males under the age of 21 and to females under the age of 18. On the merits, the question was whether this gender-based disparity violated the Equal Protection Clause. Suit was initially brought by two named plaintiffs—Craig, a male between the ages of 18 and 21, and a licensed vendor of 3.2% beer. After the Supreme Court noted probable jurisdiction to review a decision upholding the statutory scheme, Craig turned 21, and his challenge became nonjusticiable under the mootness doctrine, discussed in Sec. 4, *infra*.] The question thus arises whether appellant Whitener, the beer vendor, who has a live controversy against enforcement of the statute, may rely upon the equal protection objections of males 18–20 years of age to establish her claim of unconstitutionality of the age-sex differential. We conclude that she may.

Initially, it should be noted that, despite having had the opportunity to do so, appellees never raised before the District Court any objection to Whitener's reliance upon the claimed unequal treatment of 18–20-year-old males as the premise of her equal protection challenge to Oklahoma's 3.2% beer law. Indeed, at oral argument Oklahoma acknowledged that appellees always "presumed" that the vendor, subject to sanctions and loss of license for violation of the statute, was a proper party in interest to object to the enforcement of the sex-based regulatory provision. While such a concession certainly would not be controlling upon the reach of this Court's constitutional authority to exercise jurisdiction under Art. III, our decisions have settled that limitations on a litigant's assertion of *jus tertii* are not constitutionally mandated, but rather stem from a salutary "rule of self-restraint" designed to minimize unwarranted intervention into controversies where the applicable constitutional questions are ill-defined and speculative. See, *e.g.*, Barrows v. Jackson, 346 U.S. 249, 255, 257 (1953). These prudential objectives, thought to be enhanced by restrictions on third-party standing, cannot be furthered here, where the lower court already has entertained the relevant constitutional challenge and the parties have sought—or at least have never resisted—an authoritative constitutional determination. In such circumstances, a decision by us to forgo consideration of the constitutional merits in order to await the initiation of a new challenge to the statute by injured third parties would be impermissibly to foster repetitive and time-consuming litigation under the guise of caution and prudence. Moreover, insofar as the applicable constitutional questions have been and continue to be presented vigorously and "cogently," Holden v. Hardy, 169 U.S. 366, 397 (1898), the denial of *jus tertii* standing in deference to a direct class suit can serve no functional purpose. * * *

In any event, we conclude that appellant Whitener has established independently her claim to assert *jus tertii* standing. The operation of [the challenged statutory provisions] plainly has inflicted "injury in fact" upon appellant sufficient to guarantee her "concrete adverseness," Baker v. Carr, 369 U.S. 186, 204 (1962), and to satisfy the constitutionally based standing requirements imposed by Art. III. The legal duties created by the statutory sections under challenge are addressed directly to vendors such as appellant. She is obliged either to heed the statutory discrimination, thereby incurring a direct economic injury through the constriction of her buyers' market, or to disobey the statutory command and suffer, in the words of Oklahoma's Assistant Attorney General, "sanctions and perhaps loss of license." This Court repeatedly has recognized that such injuries establish the threshold requirements of a "case or controversy" mandated by Art. III. See, *e.g.*, Singleton v. Wulff, [428 U.S. 106,] 113 [(1976)] (doctors who receive payments for their abortion services are "classically adverse" to government as payer); Barrows v. Jackson, *supra*, at 255–256.

As a vendor with standing to challenge the lawfulness of [applicable Oklahoma statutes], appellant Whitener is entitled to assert those concomitant rights of third parties that would be "diluted or adversely affected" should her constitutional challenge fail and the statutes remain in force. Griswold v. Connecticut, 381 U.S. 479, 481 (1965); see Note, *Standing to Assert Constitutional Jus Tertii*, 88 Harv.L.Rev. 423, 432 (1974). Otherwise, the threatened imposition of governmental sanctions might deter appellant Whitener and other similarly situated vendors from selling 3.2% beer to young males, thereby ensuring that "enforcement of the challenged restriction against the [vendor] would result indirectly in the violation of third parties' rights." Warth v. Seldin, 422 U.S. 490, 510 (1975). Accordingly, vendors and those in like positions have been uniformly permitted to resist efforts at restricting their operations by acting as advocates of the rights of third parties who seek access to their market or function. See, *e.g.*, Eisenstadt v. Baird, 405 U.S. 438 (1972).[4]

Indeed, the *jus tertii* question raised here is answered by our disposition of a like argument in Eisenstadt v. Baird, *supra*. There, as here, a state statute imposed legal duties and disabilities upon the claimant, who was convicted of distributing a package of contraceptive foam to a third party.[5] Since the statute was directed at Baird and penalized his conduct, the Court did not hesitate—again as here—to conclude that the "case or controversy" requirement of Art. III was satisfied. In considering Baird's constitutional objections, the Court fully recognized his standing to defend the privacy interests of third parties. Deemed crucial to the decision to permit *jus tertii* standing was the recognition of "the impact of the litigation on the third-party interests."

---

[4]   The standing question presented here is not answered by the principle stated in United States v. Raines, 362 U.S. 17, 21 (1960), that "one to whom application of a statute is constitutional will not be heard to attack the statute on the ground that impliedly it might also be taken as applying to other persons or other situations in which its application might be unconstitutional." In Raines, the Court refused to permit certain public officials of Georgia to defend against application of the Civil Rights Act to their official conduct on the ground that the statute also might be construed to encompass the "purely private actions" of others. The Raines rule remains germane in such a setting, where the interests of the litigant and the rights of the proposed third parties are in no way mutually interdependent. Thus, a successful suit against Raines did not threaten to impair or diminish the independent private rights of others, and consequently, consideration of those third-party rights properly was deferred until another day.

[5]   The fact that Baird chose to disobey the legal duty imposed upon him by the Massachusetts anticontraception statute, resulting in his criminal conviction, does not distinguish the standing inquiry from that pertaining to the anticipatory attack in this case. In both Eisenstadt and here, the challenged statutes compel *jus tertii* claimants either to cease their proscribed activities or to suffer appropriate sanctions. The existence of Art. III "injury in fact" and the structure of the claimant's relationship to the third parties are not altered by the litigative posture of the suit. * * *

Id., at 445. Just as the defeat of Baird's suit and the "[e]nforcement of the Massachusetts statute will materially impair the ability of single persons to obtain contraceptives," *id.*, at 446, so too the failure of Whitener to prevail in this suit and the continued enforcement of [the challenged statutes] will "materially impair the ability of" males 18–20 years of age to purchase 3.2% beer despite their classification by an overt gender-based criterion. Similarly, just as the Massachusetts law in Eisenstadt "prohibit[ed], not use, but distribution," and consequently the least awkward challenger was one in Baird's position who was subject to that proscription, the law challenged here explicitly regulates the sale rather than use of 3.2% beer, thus leaving a vendor as the obvious claimant.

We therefore hold that Whitener has standing to raise relevant equal protection challenges to Oklahoma's gender-based law. * * *

[The Court went on to hold the statute unconstitutional.]

■ CHIEF JUSTICE BURGER, dissenting.

* * * I cannot agree that appellant Whitener has standing arising from her status as a saloon-keeper to assert the constitutional rights of her customers. In this Court "a litigant may only assert his own constitutional rights or immunities." United States v. Raines, 362 U.S. 17, 22 (1960). There are a few, but strictly limited exceptions to that rule; despite the most creative efforts, this case fits within none of them.

This is not * * * Barrows v. Jackson, 346 U.S. 249 (1953) [which permitted the seller of property to challenge the validity of a covenant barring the sale of that property to non-whites by asserting the equal protection rights of racial minorities], for there is here no barrier whatever to Oklahoma males 18–20 years of age asserting, in an appropriate forum, any constitutional rights they may claim to purchase 3.2% beer. Craig's successful litigation of this very issue was prevented only by the advent of his 21st birthday. There is thus no danger of interminable dilution of those rights if appellant Whitener is not permitted to litigate them here.

Nor is this controlled by Griswold v. Connecticut, 381 U.S. 479 (1965), [in which a doctor was allowed to assert the constitutional rights of his patients]. It borders on the ludicrous to draw a parallel between a vendor of beer and the intimate professional physician-patient relationship which undergirded relaxation of standing rules in that case.

Even in Eisenstadt, the Court carefully limited its recognition of third-party standing to cases in which the relationship between the claimant and the relevant third party "was not simply the fortuitous connection between a vendor and potential vendees, but the relationship between one who acted to protect the rights of a minority and the minority itself." 405 U.S., at 445. This is plainly not the case here.

In sum, permitting a vendor to assert the constitutional rights of vendees whenever those rights are arguably infringed introduces a new concept of constitutional standing to which I cannot subscribe. * * **

NOTE ON ASSERTING THE RIGHTS OF OTHERS

(1) *Jus Tertii* Doctrine.

(a) In Craig v. Boren, the appellant Whitener was threatened with criminal prosecution if she sold low alcohol beer in violation of an Oklahoma statute and, thus, concededly satisfied the Article III requirement of injury in fact. The only standing question was whether Whitener could argue that the statute under which she was threatened with prosecution violated the equal protection rights of 18-to-20-year-old males—a question often described as one of third-party standing.

(b) For purposes of analytical clarity, it may help to restrict the label of third-party standing or *jus tertii* to cases in which litigants claim that the application of a law against them will also harm the very third parties whose rights the litigants seek to raise. If observed, this conceptual limitation permits a distinction between the doctrine governing *jus tertii* standing and that applicable to overbreadth challenges, discussed at pp. 241–244, *infra*: "The most common example of * * * an [overbreadth] attack arises under the first amendment, when a litigant whose speech may not itself be constitutionally protected claims that the relevant statute must be struck down because it could be applied to restrict speech that cannot constitutionally be burdened. Thus, overbreadth attacks involve both the application of the challenged law to the claimant and a different, hypothetical application of the law to third parties. Quite different from this sort of third party claim is an assertion of jus tertii—a litigant's claim that a single application of a law both injures him and impinges upon the constitutional rights of third persons." Note, *Standing to Assert Constitutional Jus Tertii*, 88 Harv.L.Rev. 423, 423–24 (1974).

(2) The Traditional View. The traditional rule, from which Craig and the precedents that it relied on deviated, was that parties to a lawsuit could only assert their own rights or immunities.

(a) In Tileston v. Ullman, 318 U.S. 44 (1943) (per curiam), the Connecticut Supreme Court had rejected, on the merits, a physician's constitutional challenge to the application to him of a state statute prohibiting the use or distribution of contraceptives. The Supreme Court dismissed his appeal on the ground that the only constitutional attack on the statute—that it worked a deprivation of liberty without due process—was

---

    *   [Ed.] The concurring opinions of Justices Powell, Stevens, Blackmun, and Stewart and the dissenting opinion of Justice Rehnquist—none of which addressed standing issues—are omitted.

based on the rights not of the physician but of his patients, which he had no
standing to assert.[1]

(b)   McGowan v. Maryland, 366 U.S. 420 (1961), involved a prosecution
of department store employees for Sunday sales in violation of the state's
"Blue Laws." The Court denied the defendants' standing to assert their
customers' First Amendment right to free exercise of religion: "[A]ppellants
* * * allege only economic injury to themselves; they do not allege any
infringement of their own religious freedoms due to Sunday closing. * * *
Those persons whose religious rights are allegedly impaired by the statutes
are not without effective ways to assert these rights. *Cf.* NAACP v. Alabama,
357 U.S. 449, 459–460 (1958); Barrows v. Jackson, 346 U.S. 249, 257 (1953).
Appellants present no weighty countervailing policies here to cause an
exception to our general principles."[2]

(c)   Notwithstanding this traditional view, there were important
exceptions, most notably Pierce v. Society of the Sisters, 268 U.S. 510 (1925).
In Pierce, the Court allowed a private school (an Oregon corporation) to
challenge the state's compulsory education law, on the grounds that it
burdened the Fourteenth Amendment "liberty of parents and guardians to
direct the upbringing and education of children under their control." The
Court addressed the problem of third-party standing in two different
passages. In one, concerning the rights of corporations, it wrote: "Appellees
are corporations, and therefore, it is said, they cannot claim for themselves
the liberty which the Fourteenth Amendment guarantees. Accepted in the
proper sense, this is true. But they have business and property for which
they claim protection. These are threatened with destruction through the
unwarranted compulsion which appellants are exercising over present and
prospective patrons of their schools."

The Court also addressed the issue in the following passage: "Generally,
it is entirely true, as urged by counsel, that no person in any business has
such an interest in possible customers as to enable him to restrain exercise
of proper power of the state upon the ground that he will be deprived of
patronage. But the injunctions here sought are not against the exercise of
any proper power. Appellees asked protection against arbitrary,
unreasonable, and unlawful interference with their patrons and the
consequent destruction of their business and property. Their interest is clear
and immediate, within the rule approved in * * * many * * * cases where

---

[1]   Although Tileston is often cited as holding that a litigant may not assert the rights of
third persons, some have read the case more narrowly, as resting on the absence of any injury
to the doctor himself: he failed to allege that the statute injured him economically, and the risk
of a criminal prosecution was insufficiently ripe to constitute redressable injury. See Bickel, The
Least Dangerous Branch 143–45 (1962); Scott, *Standing in the Supreme Court—A Functional
Analysis*, 86 Harv.L.Rev. 645, 649 n.14 (1973). On this view, the case stands merely for the
proposition that a party not personally injured may not start a lawsuit solely to alleviate harm
to others.

[2]   In a companion case to McGowan involving Orthodox Jewish merchants, the Court
rejected the free exercise challenge on the merits. See Braunfeld v. Brown, 366 U.S. 599 (1961).

injunctions have issued to protect business enterprises against interference with the freedom of patrons or customers."[3]

(3) Doctrinal Evolution. After Craig v. Boren the Court became somewhat more willing to permit assertions of third-party rights upon finding (i) some sort of "relationship" between the litigants seeking third-party standing and those whose rights they want to assert and (ii) some sort of impediment to third parties' effective assertion of their own rights through litigation. Consider the following cases:

(a) In United States Dept. of Labor v. Triplett, 494 U.S. 715 (1990), a state court disciplined an attorney for receiving prohibited contingent fees from claimants under the Federal Black Lung Benefits Act. The Court concluded that he had standing to assert the due process rights of his clients to challenge that part of the act. After reciting the principle that "Ordinarily, of course, a litigant must assert his own legal rights and interests, and cannot rest his claim to relief on the legal rights or interests of third parties," the Court concluded that nonetheless, when "enforcement of a restriction against the litigant prevents a third party from entering into a relationship with the litigant (typically a contractual relationship), to which relationship the third party has a legal entitlement (typically a constitutional entitlement), third-party standing has been held to exist."[4]

(b) In Powers v. Ohio, 499 U.S. 400 (1991), a criminal defendant (who was white) wished to challenge the prosecution's use of peremptory challenges to prevent Black jurors from serving on his jury, as violating Batson v. Kentucky, 476 U.S. 79 (1989). Again, the Court acknowledged the traditional principle, but held that there was a close relationship between the defendant and the excluded jurors, because "[v]oir dire permits a party to establish a relation, if not a bond of trust, with the jurors. This relation continues throughout the entire trial and may in some cases extend to the sentencing as well." The Court also held that there were "considerable practical barriers to suit by the excluded juror," and emphasized at length that invidious race discrimination placed the integrity and legitimacy of the proceedings in great doubt. Justice Scalia, joined by Chief Justice Rehnquist, dissented.

(c) In Kowalski v. Tesmer, 543 U.S. 125 (2004), however, the Court denied third-party standing. The Kowalski plaintiffs were lawyers who sought to challenge provisions of Michigan law that made the appointment of appellate counsel discretionary, rather than a matter of right (as before), for indigent state defendants who pleaded guilty or nolo contendere. In an opinion by Chief Justice Rehnquist, the Court assumed that the plaintiffs had suffered an injury in fact, based on the likelihood of lost revenues, but refused to accord them third-party standing to assert the rights of indigent

---

[3]   Notably, Prince is also an early example of a "universal" injunction, preventing enforcement of the law against anyone anywhere in the state of Oregon. Universal injunctions are discussed in Chapter IX, Section 5, *infra*.

[4]   A concurring opinion by Justice Marshall questioned whether the Court needed to address the standing of the attorney, as the respondent who had prevailed in state court, in light of the Court's decision in ASARCO v. Kadish, 490 U.S. 605 (1989), discussed p. 209, *supra*.

defendants.[5] Writing for a 6–3 majority, Chief Justice Rehnquist reasoned that "[t]he attorneys before us do not have a 'close relationship' with their alleged clients; indeed, they have no relationship at all." Nor had the attorneys "demonstrated that there is a 'hindrance' to the indigents' advancing their own constitutional rights." That "hypothesis" was disproved, the Court said, by the success of pro se defendants in asserting their rights in Michigan's appellate courts: "While we agree that an attorney would be valuable to a criminal defendant challenging the constitutionality of the scheme, we do not think that the lack of an attorney here is the type of hindrance necessary to allow another to assert the indigent defendants' rights."

Justice Ginsburg, joined by Justices Stevens and Souter, dissented. She noted that "the Court has found an adequate 'relation' between litigants alleging third-party standing and those whose rights they seek to assert when nothing more than a buyer-seller connection was at stake," and she emphasized the difficulties confronting "indigent and poorly educated defendants" attempting to present constitutional claims in a pro se appeal.

Do Kowalski, Powers and Triplett adopt a consistent standard for the relationship and impediment needed to find third-party standing? How tethered are the Court's standing determinations to the underlying merits of the claims being asserted?

(4)   The Current Status of Third Party Standing.

(a)   It was established well before Craig—by authorities that Craig cited—that the rule against third-party standing is a discretionary and waivable "rule of self-restraint," not a mandate of Article III. But in Lexmark Int'l, Inc. v. Static Control Components, Inc., 572 U.S. 118 (2014), also discussed pp. 207–208, *supra,* a unanimous Court noted "some tension" between prudential standing doctrine and the "principle that a federal court's obligation to hear and decide cases within its jurisdiction is virtually unflagging." The Court concluded that other categories of prudential standing should be better understood as principles of Article III constitutional standing, or as principles of statutory interpretation. But the Court declined to decide the "proper place in the standing firmament" for third party standing. The Court wrote: "The limitations on third-party standing are harder to classify; we have observed that third-party standing is 'closely related to the question whether a person in the litigant's position will have a right of action on the claim,' Department of Labor v. Triplett, 494 U.S. 715, 721, n.* * (1990), but most of our cases have not framed the inquiry in that way. See, *e.g.,* Kowalski v. Tesmer, 543 U.S. 125, 128–129 (2004) (suggesting it is an element of "prudential standing"). This case does not present any issue of third-party standing, and consideration of that doctrine's proper place in the standing firmament can await another day." Is third party standing the one remaining form of prudential standing doctrine?

---

[5]   In another case decided during the same term brought by an indigent defendant himself, Halbert v. Michigan, 545 U.S. 605 (2005), the Court held that the Michigan law did violate the defendant's due process rights.

If so, how can it be squared with Lexmark and the concerns expressed in that opinion? If not, what kind of doctrine is it?

(b) In Trump v. Hawaii, 585 U.S. 667 (2018), also discussed p. 144, *supra*, the Court allowed a group of individuals to challenge a presidential proclamation as discriminating on the basis of religion. The Court recognized the individual's standing because of "the alleged real-world effect that the Proclamation has had in keeping them separated from certain relatives who seek to enter the country," finding that "a person's interest in being united with his relatives is sufficiently concrete and particularized to form the basis of an Article III injury in fact."

The government raised a third-party standing objection, because "the Proclamation [did] not apply to any of the plaintiffs, and the only persons subject to it—aliens abroad—have no rights under the [Establishment] Clause." Trump Reply Br. 4. But the Court recharacterized this argument as a claim about the merits, rather than justiciability, and then declined to reach it: "The Government responds that plaintiffs' Establishment Clause claims are not justiciable because the Clause does not give them a legally protected interest in the admission of particular foreign nationals. But that argument—which depends upon the scope of plaintiffs' Establishment Clause rights—concerns the merits rather than the justiciability of plaintiffs' claims."

(c) Still, many justices continue to treat third-party standing as a prudential standing doctrine. Take the sharply-divided opinions in June Medical Services LLC v. Russo, 591 U.S. 299 (2020), which invalidated a Louisiana statute that required any doctor who performs abortions to have admitting privileges at a nearby hospital. In allowing abortion doctors to assert the rights of their patients, Justice Breyer's plurality opinion for four Justices—with which the Chief Justice agreed with regard to standing—interwove several strands of argument: (1) the rule against third-party standing is prudential and therefore waivable; (2) the state had waived its objection in the lower courts; and (3) in any event, the Court "generally permitted plaintiffs to assert third-party rights where the 'enforcement of the challenged restriction against the litigant would result directly in the violation of third parties' rights'," as reflected in prior cases that had "permitted abortion providers to invoke the rights of their actual or potential patients."

Justice Alito, joined in relevant part by Justices Thomas and Gorsuch, disagreed about waiver on factual grounds, and disputed the claim of a close relationship between the parties. He also disputed the inability of women seeking abortions to assert their own rights. Besides joining much of Justice Alito's opinion, Justice Thomas dissented separately to argue that the Court lacked subject matter jurisdiction on the basis that third-party standing was incompatible with historical understandings of Article III. Does this suggest that the prudential standing status of third-party standing remains well-established?[6]

---

[6]   Most recently, in Dobbs v. Jackson Women's Health Organization, 597 U.S. 215 (2022), which overruled Roe v. Wade, 410 U.S. 113 (1973), and Planned Parenthood v. Casey, 505 U.S.

(5) Attempted Re-Conceptualizations.

(a)   Professors Monaghan and Sedler have argued forcefully that many of the cases viewed by the Court as involving assertions of third-party rights would be better conceptualized as presenting first-party claims. See Sedler, *The Assertion of Constitutional Jus Tertii: A Substantive Approach*, 70 Calif.L.Rev. 1308, 1329 (1982); Monaghan, *Third Party Standing*, 84 Colum.L.Rev. 277, 299 (1984). According to Monaghan, "a litigant asserts his own rights (not those of a third person) when he seeks to void restrictions that directly impair his freedom to interact with a third person who himself could not be legally prevented from engaging in the interaction."

In support of his view, Professor Monaghan suggests that the "first party" approach is preferable because it eliminates "unanalyzed and ungrounded notions of judicial 'discretion.'" 84 Colum.L.Rev. at 278–79. A further asserted benefit of Monaghan's approach is that it supplies a straightforward answer to some troubling questions of judicial power, such as the source of a federal court's authority to provide relief to which a party has no personal "right."

Consider, however, whether judicial power to provide remedies to parties with no personal right to relief, as a means of ensuring that the rights of others are not harmed, has not been implicitly recognized by such well-established doctrines as the First Amendment overbreadth doctrine, see pp. 241–242, *infra*, and the exclusionary rule. The Supreme Court has concluded that the Fourth Amendment's exclusionary rule does not prevent or redress any harm to the criminal defendant who invokes it, but instead simply helps to protect the citizenry at large by generally deterring constitutional violations. See, *e.g.*, United States v. Calandra, 414 U.S. 338, 353–54 (1974); Herring v. United States, 555 U.S. 135, 141–44 (2009). On this view, isn't the criminal defendant, in moving to suppress evidence, given standing to claim a remedy whose purpose is to safeguard the rights of others?[7]

(b)   Building on a suggestion by Professor Monaghan,[8] Professor Fallon goes even farther in recharacterizing some purportedly third-party rights as first-party rights. See Fallon, *As-Applied and Facial Challenges and Third-Party Standing*, 113 Harv.L.Rev. 1321, 1331–32 (2000). He argues that under the presuppositions of Marbury v. Madison, everyone has a *personal* constitutional right not to be sanctioned except pursuant to a constitutionally valid rule of law.[9] In Craig v. Boren, for example, the beer

---

833 (1992), the Court's majority opinion (written by Justice Alito) stated: "The Court's abortion cases * * * have ignored the Court's third-party standing doctrine," citing the dissents in June Medical and other cases. Insofar as it may arise in future cases, does Dobbs then cast doubt on the third-party standing reasoning of June Medical?

   [7]   See generally Meltzer, *Deterring Constitutional Violations by Law Enforcement Officials: Plaintiffs and Defendants as Private Attorneys General*, 88 Colum.L.Rev. 247 (1988); Monaghan, *supra*, at 279–82, 310–15.

   [8]   See Monaghan, *Overbreadth*, 1981 Sup.Ct.Rev. 1, 3; see also Monaghan, *Harmless Error and the Valid Rule Requirement*, 1989 Sup.Ct.Rev. 195.

   [9]   For criticism of Fallon's argument, see Adler, *Rights, Rules, and the Structure of Constitutional Adjudication: A Response to Professor Fallon*, 113 Harv.L.Rev. 1371 (2000). Adler argues that all constitutional rights are rights against rules; that it is a mistake to think of litigants as having "personal" rights in the sense assumed by Fallon's argument; and that Fallon

vendor had a personal right not to be punished criminally for violating the constitutionally invalid Oklahoma statute that she challenged in the Supreme Court. See also Bond v. United States, 564 U.S. 211 (2011) (Ginsburg, J., concurring) (joining a Court opinion that permitted a criminal defendant to attack a statute on the ground that it exceeded congressional authority under Article I and the Tenth Amendment and explaining that "Bond, like any other defendant, has a personal right not to be convicted under a constitutionally invalid law").

If the premise is granted that everyone has a personal right not to be sanctioned under a constitutionally invalid rule of law, Fallon maintains, then all actual and potential *defendants* in legal enforcement proceedings are entitled (once the Article III requirement of injury-in-fact is satisfied) to challenge the constitutional validity of the rules of law invoked against them; in other words, distinctions between first- and third-party standing do not arise in cases involving actual or possible defendants, for all are asserting personal rights not to be sanctioned under invalid statutes.[10] Questions of prudence and judicial administration aside, would it have been a constitutionally tolerable situation in Craig for the plaintiff beer vendor to have been jailed for violating a statute that was constitutionally invalid under the Equal Protection Clause and would have been held to be such in a case involving a different challenger?

(c) Professors Bradley and Young argue that much of the perceived incoherence of third-party standing comes from attempting to capture several distinct legal issues into a single unitary principle. Bradley & Young, *Unpacking Third-Party Standing*, 131 Yale L.J. 1 (2021). Instead, they argue, the analysis should "unpack" the doctrine by way of two sets of distinctions. First, it should distinguish litigants who fall within the "zone of interests" of a substantive right and who are really litigating their own rights from true third-party claims. Second, it should distinguish various kinds of third parties: the directly regulated, the collaterally injured, and representatives. In particular, regulated parties should always be able to assert third-party standing when enforcement of the law against them will violate the rights of third parties. Finally, Bradley and Young challenge the "valid rule" argument made by Fallon, *supra*, as over- and underinclusive.

---

particularly errs in assuming that there is a well-grounded personal right not to be sanctioned except pursuant to a constitutionally valid rule of law.

[10] Although Professor Fallon attempts to fit many third-party standing claims into a first-party mold, his view does not wholly eliminate the category of third-party standing (as Professor Monaghan's appears to do). According to Fallon, it is only actual and potential defendants who enjoy a Marbury-based entitlement to challenge the validity of rules invoked against them; questions remain about whether and to what extent *plaintiffs* who face no threat of legal coercion—such as the lawyer plaintiffs in Kowalski v. Tesmer, Paragraph (3), *supra*—should be able to assert third-party rights. In addition, some defendants may plausibly claim entitlements to assert rights best conceptualized as those of third-parties—for example, in Powers v. Ohio, Paragraph (3), *supra*.

Yazoo & Mississippi Valley R. R.
v. Jackson Vinegar Co.

226 U.S. 217 (1912).

Appeal from the Circuit Court of Hinds County, Mississippi.

■ MR. JUSTICE VAN DEVANTER delivered the opinion of the Court.

This was an action to recover damages from a railway company for the partial loss of a shipment of vinegar carried over the company's line from one point to another in the state of Mississippi. * * * The position of the railway company, unsuccessfully taken in the state court and now renewed, is that the Mississippi statute providing for the penalty is repugnant to the due process of law and equal protection clauses of the 14th Amendment to the Constitution of the United States. The statute reads:

> "Railroads, corporations, and individuals engaged as common carriers in this state are required to settle all claims for lost or damaged freight which has been lost or damaged between two given points on the same line or system, within sixty days from the filing of written notice of the loss or damage with the agent at the point of destination * * *. A common carrier failing to settle such claims as herein required shall be liable to the consignee for $25 damages in each case, in addition to actual damages, all of which may be recovered in the same suit: Provided that this section shall only apply when the amount claimed is $200 or less." Laws 1908, 205, chap. 196.

The facts showing the application made of the statute are these: The plaintiff gave notice of its claim in the manner prescribed, placing its damages at $4.76, and, upon the railway company's failure to settle within sixty days, sued to recover that sum and the statutory penalty. Upon the trial the damages were assessed at the sum stated in the notice, and judgment was given therefor, with the penalty. Thus, the claim presented in advance of the suit, and which the railway company failed to settle within the time allotted, was fully sustained.

As applied to such a case, we think the statute is not repugnant to either the due process of law or the equal protection clause of the Constitution, but, on the contrary, merely provides a reasonable incentive for the prompt settlement, without suit, of just demands of a class admitting of special legislative treatment.

Although seemingly conceding this much, counsel for the railway company urge that the statute is not confined to cases like the present, but equally penalizes the failure to accede to an excessive or extravagant claim; in other words, that it contemplates the assessment of the penalty in every case where the claim presented is not settled within the time allotted, regardless of whether, or how much, the recovery falls short of the amount claimed. But it is not open to the railway company to complain on that score. It has not been penalized for failing to accede to an excessive or extravagant claim, but for failing to make reasonably prompt settlement of a claim which, upon due inquiry, has been pronounced just in every respect. Of course, the argument to sustain the contention is that, if the statute embraces cases such as are supposed, it is void as to them, and, if so void, is void *in toto*. But this court must deal with the case in hand, and not with imaginary ones. It suffices, therefore, to hold that, as applied to cases like the present, the statute is valid. How the state court may apply it to other cases, whether its general words may be treated as more or less restrained, and how far parts of it may be sustained if others fail, are matters upon which we need not speculate now.

The judgment is accordingly affirmed.

NOTE ON AS-APPLIED AND FACIAL CHALLENGES AND THE PROBLEM OF SEVERABILITY

(1) As-Applied Versus Facial Challenges. Judges and scholars have traditionally distinguished between two types of challenges to statutes—as-applied challenges and facial challenges. As a first approximation, a party presenting an as-applied challenge argues that a statute cannot be applied to her because its application would violate her personal constitutional rights. By contrast, a party making a facial challenge seeks to have a statute declared unconstitutional in all possible applications. Although these concepts may seem straightforward, they have generated substantial controversy and debate, and the line between them is not always clear.

(2) Underlying Policies. Is the Yazoo approach, which generally precludes consideration of a statute's constitutionality as applied to the facts of other cases, a sound one? Consider Fallon, *Making Sense of Overbreadth*, 100 Yale L.J. 853, 860–61 (1991): "The Yazoo rule is harsh and in some ways counterintuitive. The challenged statute imposed pressure on railroads to settle even frivolous cases. The Court, in prescribing the approach that it did, bypassed a clear opportunity to consider the permissibility of the statutory policy and, if it found injustice, to end it."

According to Professor Fallon, at least three policy reasons support the Yazoo approach. First, if the defendant's conduct may constitutionally be forbidden, the defendant has no personal right to escape punishment, at least as long as a statute's valid applications are severable from its invalid application. Second, to permit adjudication to turn on hypothetical disputes would give too abstract a flavor to constitutional litigation. Third, it is a fundamental premise of constitutional federalism that state courts may provide narrowing constructions of state statutes, and state courts should therefore be given the opportunity to do so.

Alternatively, might the Yazoo approach be grounded in the separation of powers? Recall the Court's statements in Frothingham v. Mellon, 262 U.S. 447 (1923), p. 125, *supra*, that courts "have no power per se to review and annul acts of Congress on the ground that they are unconstitutional," that judicial review "amounts to little more than the negative power to disregard an unconstitutional enactment, which otherwise would stand in the way of the enforcement of a legal right"; and that "the court enjoins, in effect, not the execution of the statute, but the acts of the official, the statute notwithstanding." On this conception of judicial review, would all challenges inherently be as-applied challenges focused on the facts of the particular case?

(3) Severability. The Yazoo approach depends on the premise that statutes are typically "separable" or "severable," and that invalid applications can somehow be severed from valid applications without invalidating the statute as a whole—a premise that is deeply rooted in American constitutional law.[1] Sometimes the severability question is whether a linguistically identifiable part of a statute can survive after another part has been found invalid—whether, for example, a statute prohibiting the sale of "lewd or obscene" materials can be enforced against sellers of "obscene" materials if a prohibition against materials that are merely "lewd" violates the First Amendment. In other instances, as in Yazoo, the question will be whether a statutory provision that does not on its face reflect divisible linguistic units—such as a requirement that railroads must settle "all claims"—can nonetheless be severed into valid and invalid elements, or whether valid applications can be separated from invalid ones.[2] According to conventional understandings, a "presumption" of statutory severability applies. See Dorf, *Facial Challenges to State and Federal Statutes*, 46 Stan.L.Rev. 235, 250 (1994); Monaghan, *Overbreadth*, 1981 Sup.Ct.Rev. 1, 6–7.

Challenging the conventional view, Fallon, *Fact and Fiction About Facial Challenges,* 99 Calif.L.Rev. 915 (2011), argues that the ascription to Yazoo of a nearly categorical presumption of severability "leaves open the question of how Yazoo related to such cases as the nearly contemporaneous Lochner v. New York, [198 U.S. 45 (1905),] which upheld a facial challenge to a law regulating the hours of employment of bakery workers under the

---

[1] The classic study of severability is Stern, *Separability and Separability Clauses in the Supreme Court*, 51 Harv.L.Rev. 76 (1937); two useful more recent discussions are Nagle, *Severability*, 72 N.C.L.Rev. 203 (1993); Baude, *Severability First Principles*, 109 Va. L.Rev. 1 (2023).

[2] Fallon, *As-Applied and Facial Challenges and Third-Party Standing*, 113 Harv.L.Rev. 1321, 1331–33 (2000), maintains that the Court's frequent refusals to adjudicate facial challenges involves an implicit assumption that statutory rules are reducible to what might be characterized as statutory "sub-rules." In a case such as Yazoo, he suggests, the Court assumes that the statutory requirement that the railroad settle "all claims" should be viewed as potentially encompassing multiple sub-rules, including the sub-rule "(i) settle all valid and non-exorbitant claims," as well as possible further sub-rules such as "(ii) settle all frivolous and excessive claims." If the statute is viewed as comprising a number of sub-rules, it becomes comprehensible that sub-rule (i) could survive even if sub-rule (ii) were constitutionally invalid and had to be severed.

Professor Fallon emphasizes, however, that a statute's full meaning is not always obvious. For example, one of the open questions in Yazoo was whether the statute should be "specified," in Fallon's terms, as applying to frivolous and excessive claims at all. According to Fallon, recognition that a statute can be separated into separately specified sub-rules, some of which are valid even if others are not, is necessary to explain why courts, in cases such as Yazoo, can postpone questions about whether a statute might apply to cases not currently before the Court and about whether it would be constitutional as so applied.

same Due Process Clause that was involved in Yazoo. In Lochner, the Court made no suggestion that the possibility of statutory severing limited the challenger to asserting as-applied claims." According to Fallon, a general presumption of severability would make it impossible for courts ever to hold a statute irrational or otherwise invalid because it is too broadly written, but "Yazoo is easily distinguishable from cases that have held statutes irrationally overinclusive * * * because in Yazoo, unlike those cases, there was an obvious surgical cure [that would remove the problem of irrational overbreadth] if severing turned out to be necessary in a future case. Even if the challenged statute was invalid as applied to cases involving frivolous, excessive, or disputable claims for damages, it could have been so severed as to remain enforceable in cases involving admittedly valid claims, such as the one before the Court." If a truly general presumption of severability applied, what would be the point of asking whether a *statute*—as opposed to an *application* of a statute—was rationally related to a legitimate state interest, or narrowly tailored to a compelling state interest, or satisfied a similar test of constitutional validity?

(4)　Deference to State Interpretations. Although federal courts apply a presumption of severability, questions about the meaning and thus the severability of state statutes are primarily questions of state law.[3]

(a)　In Dorchy v. Kansas, 264 U.S. 286 (1924), a criminal defendant sought review of his conviction under § 19 of the Court of Industrial Relations Act of Kansas, which he claimed was an unconstitutional restriction of the right to strike. Pending the decision of this case, the Supreme Court held in another case that other provisions of the statute (providing for compulsory arbitration of labor disputes) violated the federal Constitution as there applied. After pointing out that it would be unnecessary to consider Dorchy's objections to § 19 if that section were inseverable from the arbitration provisions, it vacated the state court's judgment and remanded the case for a determination of that question:

"Whether § 19 is so interwoven with the system held invalid that the section cannot stand alone, is a question of interpretation and of legislative intent. * * * The task of determining the intention of the state legislature in this respect, like the usual function of interpreting a state statute, rests primarily upon the state court. Its decision as to the severability of a provision is conclusive upon this Court. * * * In cases coming from the state courts, this Court, in the absence of a controlling state decision, may, in passing upon the claim under the federal law, decide, also, the question of severability. But it is not obliged to do so. The situation may be such as to make it appropriate to leave the determination of the question to the state court. We think that course should be followed in this case."[4]

---

[3]　For one survey of each state's severability doctrine, see Dorf, *Facial Challenges to State and Federal Statutes*, 46 Stan.L.Rev. 235, 295–304 (1994).

[4]　Similarly, in Fox Film Corp. v. Muller, 296 U.S. 207 (1935), p. 651, *infra*, the question of severability of a contract in state court was treated as a question of state law, such that it could provide an adequate and independent ground insulating the state court's judgment from Supreme Court review.

(b)   The Court has continued to emphasize that states should be given a chance to sever unconstitutional parts of their statutes to save them from complete invalidation. The issue has been especially prominent in abortion litigation. In Leavitt v. Jane L., 518 U.S. 137 (1996), the Tenth Circuit found a Utah restriction on abortions before 20 weeks gestational age to be unconstitutional; it then concluded that another section of the statute restricting abortions after 20 weeks was inseverable from the unconstitutional section. The Supreme Court summarily reversed without oral argument. It emphasized that "[s]everability is of course a matter of state law," and that in this case the Utah legislature had enacted an explicit severability provision and other language making clear that it would prefer each provision of the law to stand even if others were declared unconstitutional. Under Utah law as the Court understood it, the Tenth Circuit had plainly erred in finding the law inseverable.

Similarly, in Ayotte v. Planned Parenthood of Northern New England, 546 U.S. 320 (2006), the Court reviewed a lower federal court judgment facially invalidating a state statute that barred minors from having abortions in the absence of parental notification or judicial authorization unless "necessary to prevent the minor's death." Agreeing with the lower court that the Constitution required further exceptions for non-life-threatening health emergencies, the majority opinion said that "[a]fter finding an application or portion of a statute unconstitutional, we must next ask: Would the legislature have preferred what is left of its statute to no statute at all?" Though the Court did not refer to the specifics of state law as it had in Leavitt, it again emphasized that the lower court had been too quick to deny the possibility that the New Hampshire legislature would have preferred to avoid complete facial invalidation of the statute, and remanded for further proceedings.

(c)   But in Whole Woman's Health v. Hellerstedt, 579 U.S. 582 (2016), the Court took a more skeptical approach to the severability of a state statute. On the merits the Court ruled, 5–3, that the district court had correctly upheld a facial challenge (which the Fifth Circuit subsequently rejected) to two provisions of Texas law that the Court found to constitute undue burdens on abortion rights. The Court ruled the provisions facially invalid despite a severability clause providing that "every provision, section, subsection, sentence, clause, phrase, or word in this Act, and every application of the provision [sic] in this Act, are severable from each other." The clause further directed that if "any application of any provision * * * is found by a court to be invalid, the remaining applications of that provision to all other persons and circumstances shall be severed and may not be affected."

Writing for the Court, Justice Breyer reasoned that the challenged provisions "vastly increase the obstacles confronting women seeking abortions in Texas without providing any benefit to women's health capable of withstanding any meaningful scrutiny" and are therefore "unconstitutional on their face." He continued: "Including a severability provision in the law does not change that conclusion. Severability clauses, it is true, do express the enacting legislature's preference for a narrow judicial remedy. As a general matter, we attempt to honor that preference. But our cases have never required us to proceed application by conceivable application when confronted with a facially unconstitutional statutory provision. * * * Indeed, if a severability clause could impose such a requirement on courts, legislatures would easily be able to insulate unconstitutional statutes from most facial review. * * * We reject Texas' invitation to pave the way for legislatures to immunize their statutes from facial review."

Justice Alito, joined by Chief Justice Roberts and Justice Thomas, dissented: "Federal courts have no authority to carpet-bomb state laws, knocking out provisions that are perfectly consistent with federal law, just because it would be too much bother to separate them from unconstitutional provisions. * * * By forgoing severability, the Court strikes down numerous provisions that could not plausibly impose an undue burden. For example, * * * [c]enters must maintain fire alarm and emergency communications systems, and eliminate '[h]azards that might lead to slipping, falling, electrical shock, burns, poisoning, or other trauma'. [The enforcement of these and other unexceptionable provisions is now] * * * enjoined. * * * If the Court is unwilling to undertake the careful severability analysis required, * * * [t]he proper course would be to remand to the lower courts."

Should Whole Women's Health be read to reject or modify the assumption that state law determines the severability of state statutes, possibly on the ground that federal law determines facial invalidity and that total invalidation (rather than separation) is sometimes a necessary remedy, also as a matter of federal law? If so, would Yazoo & Mississippi Valley R.R. v. Jackson Vinegar Co., come out differently today? Or should Whole Women's Health be read as a one-off, perhaps motivated by special concerns around the legislative restriction of abortion rights?[5]

(5) Severability of Federal Statutes. The severability of a federal statute is, of course, a purely federal issue. Although many federal statutes contain severability clauses directing that the judicial invalidation of one provision should not preclude enforcement of others, even in the absence of such clauses the Supreme Court generally presumes that invalid statutory applications should be severed and the remainder of a statute enforced whenever possible.

(a) In United States v. Jackson, 390 U.S. 570 (1968), the district court had dismissed a federal kidnaping indictment after holding unconstitutional the statute's death penalty provision. The Supreme Court agreed that the death penalty could not be imposed, but ruled that the kidnaping charge was nonetheless valid: "Unless it is evident that the legislature would not have enacted those provisions which are within its power, independently of that which is not, the invalid part may be dropped if what is left is fully operative

---

[5]   In Dobbs v. Jackson Women's Health Organization, 597 U.S. 215 (2022), the Court's majority opinion (written by Justice Alito) stated: "The Court's abortion cases * * * have flouted the ordinary rules on the severability of unconstitutional provisions." (citing Whole Woman's Health v. Hellerstedt, 579 U.S. 582, 623–26 (2016), and *id.* 644–45 (Alito, J., dissenting). As noted at pp. 229–230, note 6, *supra,* the Court made similar comments about other doctrines including third-party standing.

as a law." Though the statute at issue had no severability clause, the Court
remarked that "the ultimate determination of severability will rarely turn
on the presence or absence of such a clause."[6]

Exactly what is the question of legislative intent that the Court asks in
severability cases? Can it be resolved on the basis of a statute's text, or does
it inevitably require an assessment of legislative purposes and legislative
history—one that adherents of textualist theories of statutory interpretation
would ordinarily resist?

(b) In several recent cases, some Justices (including adherents of
textualism) have found the presumption of severability to be rebutted and
found major statutes to be inseverable.

(i)   In National Federation of Independent Business v. Sebelius, 567
U.S. 519 (2012), the Court held that a provision of the Patient Protection and
Affordable Care Act violated principles of constitutional federalism by
coercively requiring states to dramatically expand their Medicaid coverage
or potentially forfeit all Medicaid funds. But that problem could be
adequately remedied, Chief Justice Roberts held (writing for a plurality only
on this point), by barring any cut-offs of pre-existing funds that were
unconnected with the challenged expansion mandate. This limitation was
supported, he argued, by a severability clause in the chapter of the U.S. Code
in which the provision authorizing funds cutoffs was codified.

In a joint dissenting opinion, Justices Scalia, Kennedy, Thomas, and
Alito concluded that two major provisions of the Act—the Medicaid extension
and a mandate to otherwise uninsured individuals to purchase health
insurance—were both unconstitutional. (The majority had held the latter to
be valid under the Taxing and Spending Clause.) Having so determined, the
joint opinion would have held the Act inseverable and therefore invalid in its
entirety. According to the dissent, severability is improper unless "Congress
would have enacted" the otherwise valid provisions of a partially invalidated
law "standing alone." A number of the Act's otherwise unchallenged "major
provisions" were inseparable because they could not "operate as Congress
intended without the Individual Mandate and Medicaid Expansion." With
respect to a number of "minor provisions"—including such matters as break
times at work for nursing mothers and taxes on tanning booths and some
medical devices—the dissenting Justices quoted a statement by the Senate
majority leader in support of the conclusion that "[o]ften, a minor provision
will be the price paid for support of a major provision. So, if the major
provision were unconstitutional, Congress would not have passed the minor
one." According to the four dissenting Justices, "[a]n automatic or too cursory
severance of statutory provisions risks 'rewrit[ing] a statute'" and
"impos[ing] on the Nation, by the Court's decree, its own new statutory
regime" in contravention of the separation of powers.

(ii)   In Murphy v. NCAA, 584 U.S. 453 (2018), a majority of the Justices
followed the approach of the NFIB v. Sebelius dissent by refusing to sever

---

[6]   Accord, Buckley v. Valeo, 424 U.S. 1, 108 (1976); Regan v. Time, Inc., 468 U.S. 641, 653
(1984) (plurality opinion) (severability "is largely a question of legislative intent, but the
presumption is in favor of severability").

and uphold what they regarded as secondary statutory provisions after invalidating a central one. The Court ruled that the Professional and Amateur Sports Protection Act unconstitutionally commandeered state legislatures by forbidding them to authorize gambling on sporting events. Having done so, the majority declined to sever provisions that would have (a) prohibited the States from themselves sponsoring or advertising sports gambling schemes and (b) barred private actors from operating gambling schemes pursuant to state law. Writing for a 6–3 majority, Justice Alito reasoned that if Congress had known that states could authorize gambling by private entities, it would not have "wanted" to bar state lotteries, which "were thought more benign" than private gambling, nor to prohibit only those private gambling operations that the states had authorized. Justice Ginsburg's dissenting opinion, which Justice Sotomayor joined in whole and Justice Breyer joined in part, complained that "[t]he Court wields an axe to cut down [the challenged statute] instead of using a scalpel to trim [it]."[7]

(iii) Barr v. American Ass'n of Political Consultants, 591 U.S. 610 (2020), however, saw several Justices turn away from the Murphy approach. The case involved the Telephone Consumer Protection Act of 1991, which generally prohibits robocalls to cell phones but, following a 2015 amendment, excepted robocalls made to collect debts owed to or guaranteed by the United States. In a challenge brought by plaintiffs who wished to make political robocalls, six Justices—though without a majority opinion—concluded that the statute discriminated impermissibly on the basis of content. Again without a majority opinion, seven Justices agreed that the appropriate judicial response was to sever the provision that exempted robocalls involving debts owed to or guaranteed by the government.

Justice Kavanaugh, writing for himself, Justice Alito, and Chief Justice Roberts, proposed abandoning the search for hypothetical congressional intent to rebut the presumption of severability. After acknowledging that "some of the Court's cases declare that courts should sever" a statute's unconstitutional provisions "unless 'the statute created in its absence is one that Congress would not have enacted,'" Justice Kavanaugh immediately asserted that "this formulation often leads to an analytical dead end * * * because courts are not well equipped to imaginatively reconstruct a prior Congress's hypothetical intent." Justice Kavanaugh therefore endorsed "a strong presumption of severability" as a better, more workable alternative.

Justice Gorsuch, joined by Justice Thomas, dissented from the severability holding, accusing the majority of "rewrit[ing] the law." He would have wholly enjoined the prohibition on robocalls, and concluded: "[I]f this is what modern 'severability doctrine' has become, it seems to me all the more reason to reconsider our course."

(c) As noted above, some Justices have expressed dissatisfaction with current severability doctrine and the nature of the inquiry it requires. What are the alternatives? One might begin by considering the respective

---

[7]   Justice Thomas joined the opinion in Murphy but wrote a concurring opinion suggesting that the Court's approach to severability needed to be completely overhauled. See Paragraph 5(c), *infra*.

attractions of two polar alternatives: (i) never sever and (ii) always sever. For a close approximation of (i), see Campbell, *Severability of Statutes*, 62 Hastings L.J. 1495 (2011), arguing that severability doctrine should be abolished, with the effect that any statute with even a single invalid application would be deemed invalid in its entirety. In an approximation of (ii), Walsh, *Partial Unconstitutionality*, 85 N.Y.U.L.Rev. 738 (2010), argues that early courts declined to enforce statutory provisions insofar as they were "repugnant" to the Constitution, but did not frame the further "severability" question of whether a partially unconstitutional statute could survive. Professor Walsh argues for a return to the earlier approach, under which courts would enforce all partially (un)constitutional federal statutes to the extent of their constitutional validity unless Congress had enacted a non-severability clause or other fallback law. Between these polar alternatives, is there any coherent and otherwise satisfactory middle position that would not require some kind of inquiry into what Congress intended or whether it would have enacted particular provisions if it had known that others would be invalidated?

Justice Thomas and Justice Gorsuch have endorsed something like Professor Walsh's approach in several concurring opinions. See Murphy v. NCAA, 584 U.S. 453, 486–91 (2018) (Thomas, J., concurring); Seila Law v. CFPB, 591 U.S. 197, 251–61 (2020) (Thomas. J., joined by Gorsuch J., concurring in part and dissenting in part); United States v. Arthrex, Inc., 594 U.S. 1, 27–35 (2021) (Gorsuch, J., concurring in part and dissenting in part), though at times even those two Justices have disagreed about what that approach entails in particular cases. Compare Collins v. Yellen, 594 U.S. 220, 261–71 (2021) (Thomas, J., concurring), with *id.* 271–83 (Gorsuch, J., concurring in part); see Baude, *Severability First Principles*, 109 Va.L.Rev. 1, 26–32, 37–41 (2023).[8]

(d) Severability is not itself a remedy, because courts do not act on statutes in the abstract, but severability issues are often *relevant* to issues of redressability, and therefore to standing. In addition to cases such as Yazoo, this was apparent in California v. Texas, 593 U.S. 659 (2021), p. 149, *supra*. In that case one theory of standing for the state of Texas was based on its assertion (following the NFIB dissent) that the entire Affordable Care Act was inseverable. The entanglement of severability and remedial issues has also arisen in several recent separation of powers cases such as Seila Law v. CFPB, 591 U.S. 197 (2020), Collins v. Yellen, 594 U.S. 220 (2021), and United States v. Arthrex, 594 U.S. 1 (2021). In each case, a majority of the Court has found the statutory arrangements for an executive branch official to violate separation of powers principles, prompting further questions about (i) how those unconstitutional statutory arrangements relate to the plaintiff, and thus (ii) what remedy the plaintiff ought to be awarded. If one believes that the unconstitutional portions of those statutes are generally severable, then it is possible that no remedy is due. But this

---

[8] For additional modern scholarship, see Harrison, *Severability, Remedies, and Constitutional Adjudication*, 83 Geo.Wash.L.Rev. 56 (2014); Fish, *Severability as Conditionality*, 64 Emory L.J. 1293 (2015); Manheim, *Beyond Severability*, 101 Iowa L.Rev. 1833 (2016); and Mitchell, *The Writ-of-Erasure Fallacy*, 104 Va.L.Rev. 933 (2018).

might in turn lead one to question whether standing in these cases is consistent with Yazoo. See Baude, *Severability First Principles*, *supra*, at 58–59.

(6) The Special Problem of First Amendment Overbreadth. A special doctrine of First Amendment "overbreadth" allows a speaker to argue that even if his own speech or conduct is not protected by the First Amendment, a statute "punishes so much protected speech that it cannot be applied to anyone, including him." United States v. Hansen, 599 U.S. 762, 769 (2023). "In the First Amendment context * * * a law may be invalidated as overbroad if a substantial number of its applications are unconstitutional, judged in relation to the statute's plainly legitimate sweep." United States v. Stevens, 559 U.S. 460, 473 (2010).

As the Court has acknowledged, the doctrine "is unusual. For one thing, litigants typically lack standing to assert the constitutional rights of third parties. For another, litigants mounting a facial challenge to a statute normally 'must establish that no set of circumstances exists under which the [statute] would be valid.' United States v. Salerno, 481 U.S. 739, 745 (1987). Breaking from both of these rules, the overbreadth doctrine instructs a court to hold a statute facially unconstitutional even though it has lawful applications, and even at the behest of someone to whom the statute can be lawfully applied." Hansen, 599 U.S. at 769; see also Moody v. NetChoice, 144 S.Ct. 2383, 2397 (2024) ("To provide breathing room for free expression, we have substituted a less demanding though still rigorous standard.").

This doctrine, usually traced to Thornhill v. Alabama, 310 U.S. 88 (1940), appears to reflect at least three assumptions. First, as stated in Gooding v. Wilson, 405 U.S. 518, 521 (1972), constitutionally protected speech possesses "transcendent value to all society" and therefore merits special protection. Second, if overbroad restrictions on speech could not be challenged on their face, persons whose expression is constitutionally protected might be chilled from exercising their rights for fear of criminal sanctions. Third, regulations of speech that fail to establish clear standards are likely to be enforced in invidiously discriminatory ways. See, *e.g.*, City of Lakewood v. Plain Dealer Pub. Co., 486 U.S. 750, 757–69 (1988). Are these assumptions well-founded? If so, can they and/or should they be limited to the freedom of speech?

The Supreme Court continues to invoke the overbreadth doctrine in facially invalidating statutes under the First Amendment, including more recently in Americans for Prosperity v. Bonta, 594 U.S. 595 (2021), which invalidated state disclosure requirements for charities, and Iancu v. Brunetti, 588 U.S. 388, 398 (2019), which invalidated a ban on registering "immoral or scandalous" trademarks.[9] At the same time, the Court has called overbreadth "strong medicine that is not to be casually employed." Hansen, 599 U.S. at 770. Thus, the Court has said that "[t]o justify facial invalidation, a law's unconstitutional applications must be realistic, not fanciful, and their

---

[9]   Two other notable overbreadth findings in the past few decades include United States v. Stevens, 559 U.S. 460 (2010), in which the Court invalidated a ban on depictions of animal cruelty, and Reno v. ACLU, 521 U.S. 844 (1997), which invalidated restrictions on the online distribution of indecent and offensive materials to minors.

number must be substantially disproportionate to the statute's lawful sweep. In the absence of a lopsided ratio, courts must handle unconstitutional applications as they usually do—case-by-case."[10]

Justice Thomas has repeatedly criticized the entire enterprise of First Amendment overbreadth. He has argued that "the overbreadth doctrine lacks any basis in the Constitution's text, violates the usual standard for facial challenges, and contravenes traditional standing principles." United States v. Sineneng-Smith, 590 U.S. 371, 383 (2020) (Thomas, J., concurring); see also Americans for Prosperity v. Bonta, 594 U.S. 595, 620–92 (2021) (Thomas, J., concurring). He has also questioned overbreadth on separation-of-powers grounds, analogizing judicial applications of overbreadth to the rejected proposal to create a "federal council of revision": "When courts apply the facial overbreadth doctrine, they function in a manner strikingly similar to the federal council of revision that the Framers rejected. The doctrine contemplates that courts can declare laws unconstitutional in the abstract without the law ever being applied against any individual in an unconstitutional manner. Along the way, courts must examine the sum total of the law's application to people who are not parties to any proceeding; courts then weigh the law's various applications to determine if any unconstitutional applications outweigh the law's constitutional sweep or might 'chill' protected speech. That is nothing short of a society-wide policy determination of the sort that legislatures perform." United States v. Hansen, 599 U.S. 762, 791 (2023) (Thomas, J., concurring). How many other doctrines of judicial review might be subject to similar critique, and could Justice Thomas intend to jettison all of them?[11]

(7) Overbreadth Beyond the First Amendment? Are the considerations supporting First Amendment overbreadth doctrine any less forceful when applied to statutes whose overbreadth violates other fundamental rights? In United States v. Salerno, 481 U.S. 739, 746 (1987), the Supreme Court confronted arguments that the Bail Reform Act of 1984, which establishes a mandatory scheme of pretrial detention for certain arrestees, violated the guarantees of substantive due process and the Excessive Bail Clause of the Eighth Amendment. In rejecting both challenges, Chief Justice Rehnquist wrote: "A facial challenge to a legislative Act is, of course, the most difficult challenge to mount successfully, since the challenger must establish that no set of circumstances exists under which the Act would be valid. The fact that the Bail Reform Act might operate unconstitutionally under some conceivable set of circumstances is insufficient to render it wholly invalid, since we have not recognized an

---

[10] For scholarly treatments of overbreadth doctrine, see Fallon, *As-Applied and Facial Challenges and Third-Party Standing*, 113 Harv.L.Rev. 1321, 1359–64 (2001); Alexander, *Is There an Overbreadth Doctrine*, 22 San Diego L.Rev. 541, 553–54 (1985); Monaghan, *Overbreadth*, 1981 Sup.Ct.Rev. 1.

[11] In Moody v. NetChoice, 144 S.Ct. 2383 (2024), Justice Thomas wrote a concurrence in the judgment further expanding on his objections to the overbreadth doctrine, arguing that the adjudication of facial challenges was categorically unconstitutional. Justice Thomas argued that facial challenges do not comply with Article III standing requirements and intrude upon the powers of the political branches and the states, and concluded that "holding a statute unconstitutional as applied to nonparties is not simply disfavored—it exceeds the authority granted to federal courts."

'overbreadth' doctrine outside the limited context of the First Amendment."
See also Schall v. Martin, 467 U.S. 253, 269 n.18 (1984). Although Justices
Brennan, Marshall, and Stevens dissented on the merits in Salerno, none of
the dissenting Justices challenged the Court's framing of the rules governing
the availability of facial challenges outside the First Amendment.

The Salerno standard is not impossible to satisfy in all cases. For
example, a statute that has an unconstitutional motivation is presumably
invalid under all "conceivable * * * circumstances." In other cases, however,
the Salerno formulation's meaning may be less than pellucid. Consider, for
example, how the Salerno formulation would apply to a statutory
classification such as that in Craig v. Boren, 429 U.S. 190 (1976), p. 221,
supra, under which young men who wished to buy low alcohol beer were
disadvantaged relative to young women. If there are any circumstances
under which a particular young man might be more prone to drive
dangerously as a result of drinking low alcohol beer than would most young
women, should a facial challenge fail under the Salerno standard? If not, why
not?

Despite the strength of the Salerno formulation, the Court has
sustained facial challenges across a range of doctrinal contexts. For instance,
City of Los Angeles v. Patel, 576 U.S. 409 (2015), upheld a facial challenge
under the Fourth Amendment to a provision compelling hotel operators to
keep records containing specified information about their guests and to make
those records available to police on demand. A number of cases have upheld
facial challenges on the basis of vagueness. See, *e.g.*, City of Chicago v.
Morales, 527 U.S. 41 (1999); Johnson v. United States, 576 U.S. 591 (2015);
Sessions v. Dimaya, 584 U.S. 148 (2018). The Court has also sometimes
sustained facial challenges in the enumerated-powers context, such as
United States v. Lopez, 514 U.S. 549 (1995), which held that a federal statute
prohibiting guns near schools exceeded Congress's authority under the
Commerce Clause, and Shelby County v. Holder, 570 U.S. 529 (2013), which
held that the provisions of the Voting Rights Act that required certain
jurisdictions to seek prior clearance from the Department of Justice before
changing their voting procedures exceeded Congress's authority under the
Fourteenth and Fifteenth Amendments.

Are these cases exceptions or anomalies, or do they countenance a
rethinking of the conventional wisdom that successful facial challenges are
rare outside of First Amendment cases, and of Salerno's description of the
normally applicable standard? See Fallon, *Fact and Fiction About Facial
Challenges,* 99 Calif.L.Rev. 915 (2011), for an argument to this effect. For
further efforts to clarify issues involving facial challenges and non-First
Amendment overbreadth, see Isserles, *Overcoming Overbreadth: Facial
Challenges and the Valid Rule Requirement,* 48 Am.U.L.Rev. 359 (1998);
Fallon, note 7, *supra*; Gans, *Strategic Facial Challenges,* 85 B.U.L.Rev. 1333
(2005); Hartnett, *Modest Hope for a Modest Roberts Court: Deference, Facial
Challenges, and the Comparative Competence of Courts,* 59 S.M.U.L.Rev.
1735 (2006); Rosenkranz, *The Subjects of the Constitution,* 62 Stan.L.Rev.
1209 (2010); Meier, *Facial Challenges and the Separation of Powers,* 83

Ind.L.J. 1557 (2010); Harrison, *Power, Duty, and Facial Invalidity*, 16 U.Pa.J.Const.L. 501 (2013).

---

4. MOOTNESS

INTRODUCTORY NOTE

If the requisite injury exists at the outset of a lawsuit, must it persist throughout the life of the litigation? Settled Supreme Court case law suggests that a live controversy must exist throughout. In reading the materials that follow, consider where the mootness doctrine originates, whether its essential elements mirror or deviate from those of standing, and how answers to those questions affect one's view of the choice between the dispute resolution and law declaration models of judicial authority discussed above. See pp. 92–94, *supra*.

DeFunis v. Odegaard

416 U.S. 312 (1974).
Certiorari to the Supreme Court of Washington.

■ PER CURIAM.

In 1971 the petitioner Marco DeFunis, Jr., applied for admission as a first-year student at the University of Washington Law School, a state-operated institution. The size of the incoming first-year class was to be limited to 150 persons, and the Law School received some 1,600 applications for these 150 places. DeFunis was eventually notified that he had been denied admission. He thereupon commenced this suit in a Washington trial court, contending that the procedures and criteria employed by the Law School Admissions Committee invidiously discriminated against him on account of his race in violation of the Equal Protection Clause of the Fourteenth Amendment to the United States Constitution.

DeFunis brought the suit on behalf of himself alone, and not as the representative of any class, against the various respondents, who are officers, faculty members, and members of the Board of Regents of the University of Washington. He asked the trial court to issue a mandatory injunction commanding the respondents to admit him as a member of the first-year class entering in September 1971, on the ground that the Law School admissions policy had resulted in the unconstitutional denial of his application for admission. The trial court agreed with his claim and granted the requested relief. DeFunis was, accordingly, admitted to the Law School and began his legal studies there in the fall of 1971. On appeal, the Washington Supreme Court reversed the judgment of the trial court and held that the Law School admissions policy did not violate the Constitution. By this time DeFunis was in his second year at the Law School.

He then petitioned this Court for a writ of certiorari, and Mr. Justice Douglas, as Circuit Justice, stayed the judgment of the Washington Supreme Court pending the "final disposition of the case by this Court." By virtue of this stay, DeFunis has remained in law school, and was in the first term of his third and final year when this Court first considered his certiorari petition in the fall of 1973. Because of our concern that DeFunis' third-year standing in the Law School might have rendered this case moot, we requested the parties to brief the question of mootness before we acted on the petition. In response, both sides contended that the case was not moot. The respondents indicated that, if the decision of the Washington Supreme Court were permitted to stand, the petitioner could complete the term for which he was then enrolled but would have to apply to the faculty for permission to continue in the school before he could register for another term.[2]

We granted the petition for certiorari on November 19, 1973. The case was in due course orally argued on February 26, 1974.

In response to questions raised from the bench during the oral argument, counsel for the petitioner has informed the Court that DeFunis has now registered "for his final quarter in law school." Counsel for the respondents have made clear that the Law School will not in any way seek to abrogate this registration. In light of DeFunis' recent registration for the last quarter of his final law school year, and the Law School's assurance that his registration is fully effective, the insistent question again arises whether this case is not moot, and to that question we now turn.

The starting point for analysis is the familiar proposition that "federal courts are without power to decide questions that cannot affect the rights of litigants in the case before them." North Carolina v. Rice, 404 U.S. 244, 246 (1971). The inability of the federal judiciary "to review moot cases derives from the requirement of Art. III of the Constitution under which the exercise of judicial power depends upon the existence of a case or controversy." Liner v. Jafco, Inc., 375 U.S. 301, 306 n.3 (1964). Although as a matter of Washington state law it appears that this case would be saved from mootness by "the great public interest in the continuing issues raised by this appeal," the fact remains that under Art. III "[e]ven in cases arising in the state courts, the question of mootness is a federal one which a federal court must resolve before it assumes jurisdiction." North Carolina v. Rice, *supra*, at 246.

---

[2]   By contrast, in their response to the petition for certiorari, the respondents had stated that DeFunis "will complete his third year [of law school] and be awarded his J.D. degree at the end of the 1973–74 academic year regardless of the outcome of this appeal."

The respondents have represented that, without regard to the ultimate resolution of the issues in this case, DeFunis will remain a student in the Law School for the duration of any term in which he has already enrolled. Since he has now registered for his final term, it is evident that he will be given an opportunity to complete all academic and other requirements for graduation, and, if he does so, will receive his diploma regardless of any decision this Court might reach on the merits of this case. In short, all parties agree that DeFunis is now entitled to complete his legal studies at the University of Washington and to receive his degree from that institution. A determination by this Court of the legal issues tendered by the parties is no longer necessary to compel that result, and could not serve to prevent it. DeFunis did not cast his suit as a class action, and the only remedy he requested was an injunction commanding his admission to the Law School. He was not only accorded that remedy, but he now has also been irrevocably admitted to the final term of the final year of the Law School course. The controversy between the parties has thus clearly ceased to be "definite and concrete" and no longer "touch[es] the legal relations of parties having adverse legal interests." Aetna Life Ins. Co. v. Haworth, 300 U.S. 227, 240–241 (1937).

It matters not that these circumstances partially stem from a policy decision on the part of the respondent Law School authorities. The respondents, through their counsel, the Attorney General of the State, have professionally represented that in no event will the status of DeFunis now be affected by any view this Court might express on the merits of this controversy. And it has been the settled practice of the Court, in contexts no less significant, fully to accept representations such as these as parameters for decision. See Gerende v. Election Board, 341 U.S. 56 (1951).

There is a line of decisions in this Court standing for the proposition that the "voluntary cessation of allegedly illegal conduct does not deprive the tribunal of power to hear and determine the case, *i.e.*, does not make the case moot." United States v. W.T. Grant Co., 345 U.S. 629, 632 (1953); United States v. Trans-Missouri Freight Assn., 166 U.S. 290, 308–310 (1897). These decisions and the doctrine they reflect would be quite relevant if the question of mootness here had arisen by reason of a unilateral change in the *admissions procedures* of the Law School. For it was the admissions procedures that were the target of this litigation, and a voluntary cessation of the admissions practices complained of could make this case moot only if it could be said with assurance "that 'there is no reasonable expectation that the wrong will be repeated.'" United States v. W.T. Grant Co., *supra*, at 633. Otherwise, "[t]he defendant is free to return to his old ways," *id.*, at 632, and this fact would be enough to prevent mootness because of the "public interest in having the legality of the practices settled." *Ibid.* But mootness in the present case depends not at all upon a "voluntary cessation" of the admissions practices that were the subject of this litigation. It depends, instead, upon the simple fact that DeFunis is now in the final quarter of the final year of his course of study, and the settled and unchallenged policy of the Law School to permit him to complete the term for which he is now enrolled.

It might also be suggested that this case presents a question that is "capable of repetition, yet evading review," Southern Pacific Terminal Co. v. ICC, 219 U.S. 498, 515 (1911); Roe v. Wade, 410 U.S. 113, 125 (1973), and is thus amenable to federal adjudication even though it might otherwise be considered moot. But DeFunis will never again be required to run the gantlet of the Law School's admission process, and so the question is certainly not "capable of repetition" so far as he is concerned. Moreover, just because this particular case did not reach the Court until the eve of the petitioner's graduation from law school, it hardly follows that the issue he raises will in the future evade review. If the admissions procedures of the Law School remain unchanged, there is no reason to suppose that a subsequent case attacking those procedures will not come with relative speed to this Court, now that the Supreme Court of Washington has spoken. This case, therefore, in no way presents the exceptional situation in which the Southern Pacific Terminal doctrine might permit a departure from "[t]he usual rule in federal cases * * * that an actual controversy must exist at all stages of appellate or certiorari review, and not simply at the date the action is initiated." Roe v. Wade, *supra*, at 125; United States v. Munsingwear, Inc., 340 U.S. 36 (1950).

Because the petitioner will complete his law school studies at the end of the term for which he has now registered regardless of any decision this Court might reach on the merits of this litigation, we conclude that the Court cannot, consistently with the limitations of Art. III of the Constitution, consider the substantive constitutional issues tendered by the parties.[5] Accordingly, the judgment of the Supreme Court of Washington is vacated, and the cause is remanded for such proceedings as by that court may be deemed appropriate.

It is so ordered.

■ MR. JUSTICE DOUGLAS, dissenting.

I agree with MR. JUSTICE BRENNAN that this case is not moot, and because of the significance of the issues raised I think it is important to reach the merits. * * *

■ MR. JUSTICE BRENNAN, with whom MR. JUSTICE DOUGLAS, MR. JUSTICE WHITE, and MR. JUSTICE MARSHALL concur, dissenting.

I respectfully dissent. Many weeks of the school term remain, and petitioner may not receive his degree despite respondents' assurances that petitioner will be allowed to complete this term's schooling

---

[5] It is suggested in dissent that "[a]ny number of unexpected events—illness, economic necessity, even academic failure—might prevent his graduation at the end of the term." "But such speculative contingencies afford no basis for our passing on the substantive issues [the petitioner] would have us decide," Hall v. Beals, 396 U.S. 45, 49 (1969), in the absence of "evidence that this is a prospect of 'immediacy and reality.' " Golden v. Zwickler, 394 U.S. 103, 109 (1969).

regardless of our decision. Any number of unexpected events—illness, economic necessity, even academic failure—might prevent his graduation at the end of the term. Were that misfortune to befall, and were petitioner required to register for yet another term, the prospect that he would again face the hurdle of the admissions policy is real, not fanciful; for respondents warn that "Mr. DeFunis would have to take some appropriate action to request continued admission for the remainder of his law school education, and *some discretionary action by the University on such request would have to be taken.*" (Emphasis supplied). Thus, respondents' assurances have not dissipated the possibility that petitioner might once again have to run the gantlet of the University's allegedly unlawful admissions policy. The Court therefore proceeds on an erroneous premise in resting its mootness holding on a supposed inability to render any judgment that may affect one way or the other petitioner's completion of his law studies. For surely if we were to reverse the Washington Supreme Court, we could insure that, if for some reason petitioner did not graduate this spring, he would be entitled to re-enrollment at a later time on the same basis as others who have not faced the hurdle of the University's allegedly unlawful admissions policy.

In these circumstances, and because the University's position implies no concession that its admissions policy is unlawful, this controversy falls squarely within the Court's long line of decisions holding that the "[m]ere voluntary cessation of allegedly illegal conduct does not moot a case." United States v. Phosphate Export Assn., 393 U.S. 199, 203 (1968). Since respondents' voluntary representation to this Court is only that they will permit petitioner to complete this term's studies, respondents have not borne the "heavy burden," [*id.*], at 203, of demonstrating that there was not even a "mere possibility" that petitioner would once again be subject to the challenged admissions policy. United States v. W.T. Grant Co., *supra*, at 633. On the contrary, respondents have positioned themselves so as to be "free to return to [their] old ways." *Id.*, at 632.

I can thus find no justification for the Court's straining to rid itself of this dispute. While we must be vigilant to require that litigants maintain a personal stake in the outcome of a controversy to assure that "the questions will be framed with the necessary specificity, that the issues will be contested with the necessary adverseness and that the litigation will be pursued with the necessary vigor to assure that the constitutional challenge will be made in a form traditionally thought to be capable of judicial resolution," Flast v. Cohen, 392 U.S. 83, 106 (1968), there is no want of an adversary contest in this case. Indeed, the Court concedes that, if petitioner has lost his stake in this controversy, he did so only when he registered for the spring term. But petitioner took that action only after the case had been fully litigated in the state courts, briefs had been filed in this Court, and oral argument had been heard. The case is thus ripe for decision on a fully developed factual record with sharply defined and fully canvassed legal issues. *Cf.* Sibron v. New York, 392 U.S. 40, 57 (1968).

Moreover, in endeavoring to dispose of this case as moot, the Court clearly disserves the public interest. The constitutional issues which are avoided today concern vast numbers of people, organizations, and colleges and universities, as evidenced by the filing of twenty-six *amicus curiae* briefs. Few constitutional questions in recent history have stirred as much debate, and they will not disappear. * * * Because avoidance of repetitious litigation serves the public interest, that inevitability counsels against mootness determinations, as here, not compelled by the record. Although the Court should, of course, avoid unnecessary decisions of constitutional questions, we should not transform principles of avoidance of constitutional decisions into devices for sidestepping resolution of difficult cases. *Cf.* Cohens v. Virginia, 6 Wheat. 264, 404–405 (1821) (Marshall, C.J.). * * *

NOTE ON MOOTNESS: ITS RATIONALE AND APPLICATIONS

(1) The Relation of Mootness and Standing. In an influential article, Professor Monaghan characterized mootness as "the doctrine of standing set in a time frame: The requisite personal interest that must exist at the commencement of the litigation (standing) must continue through its existence (mootness)." Monaghan, *Constitutional Adjudication: The Who and When*, 82 Yale L.J. 1363, 1384 (1973). After quoting that formulation on two previous occasions,[1] the Court later rejected it in Friends of the Earth v. Laidlaw Environmental Services (TOC), Inc., 528 U.S. 167, 190 (2000).

The case arose when Friends of the Earth sued under the citizen suit provision of the Clean Water Act to enjoin a violation of the environmental laws and to secure a civil penalty payable to the government. After the defendant's violations ceased subsequent to the filing of suit, the Court of Appeals held the case moot; it reasoned that all elements of Article III standing must persist throughout litigation and that the only remedy available once the defendant's violations had stopped—civil penalties payable to the government—would not redress any injury to the plaintiff. In an opinion by Justice Ginsburg, the Court reversed, holding that "the Court of Appeals confused mootness with standing." Justice Ginsburg described this confusion as "understandable, given this Court's repeated statements that the doctrine of mootness can be described as 'the doctrine of standing set in a time frame'" (citing cases that had quoted Professor Monaghan's formulation). But "[c]areful reflection on the long-recognized exceptions to mootness," such as that allowing adjudication of issues capable of repetition yet evading review, revealed that "there are circumstances in which the prospect that a defendant will engage in (or resume) harmful conduct may be too speculative to support standing, but not too speculative to overcome

---

[1]   Arizonans for Official English v. Arizona, 520 U.S. 43, 68 n.22 (1997); U.S. Parole Comm'n v. Geraghty, 445 U.S. 388, 397 (1980).

mootness. * * * Standing doctrine functions to ensure, among other things, that the scarce resources of the federal courts are devoted to those disputes in which the parties have a concrete stake. In contrast, by the time mootness is an issue, the case has been brought and litigated, often (as here) for years. To abandon the case at an advanced stage may prove more wasteful than frugal. This argument from sunk costs does not license courts to retain jurisdiction over cases in which one or both of the parties plainly lacks a continuing interest * * * [but it] surely highlights an important difference between the two doctrines."

Justice Scalia, joined by Justice Thomas, dissented on the ground that the plaintiffs never had standing. Assuming arguendo that standing existed, he did "not disagree" with the Court's conclusion as to mootness on the facts of the case, but was "troubled by the Court's too-hasty retreat from our characterization of mootness as 'the doctrine of standing set in a time frame.'" In his view, that conception correctly emphasized that "[b]ecause the requirement of a continuing case or controversy derives from the Constitution * * * it may not be avoided when inconvenient * * * or, as the Court suggests, to save 'sunk costs.'"[2]

In addition to the "sunk costs" cited by Justice Ginsburg, consider the following reasons for treating mootness doctrine differently from standing: (i) an actual course of conduct, even if past, continues to frame litigation in a factual context and thereby focus judicial decisionmaking; (ii) the unlawful causation of a past injury deprives a defendant of any moral entitlement to freedom from judicial intervention; (iii) since a defendant who has caused wrongful conduct would otherwise remain free to repeat it, a judicial decision forbidding such conduct is not an advisory opinion in any objectionable sense; and (iv) there is an important public interest in protecting the legal system against manipulation by parties, especially those prone to involvement in repeat litigation, who might contrive to moot cases that otherwise would be likely to produce unfavorable precedents.

In reading more about the specific doctrines that distinguish mootness from standing (Paragraphs (2) and (3), *infra*), consider what they imply about the legal nature of mootness doctrine (discussed in Paragraph (4), *infra*) and whether other new exceptions to mootness doctrine might be justified (for example, Paragraph (5), *infra*).

(2) Voluntary Cessation. As noted in DeFunis, a long line of cases holds that an action for an injunction, or other judgment with continuing force, does not become moot merely because the conduct immediately complained of has terminated, if there is a sufficient possibility of a recurrence that would be barred by a proper decree.[3] But the Court has given mixed signals concerning how likely recurrence needs to be for this exception to mootness

---

[2]   For earlier discussions of the relation of standing and mootness doctrines, see Chemerinsky, *A Unified Approach to Justiciability*, 22 Conn.L.Rev. 677 (1990); Fallon, *Of Justiciability, Remedies, and Public Law Litigation: Notes on the Jurisprudence of Lyons*, 59 N.Y.U.L.Rev. 1, 24–30 (1984).

[3]   See, *e.g.*, United States v. Concentrated Phosphate Export Ass'n, 393 U.S. 199, 202–04 (1968); United States v. W.T. Grant Co., 345 U.S. 629 (1953); United States v. Trans-Missouri Freight Ass'n, 166 U.S. 290, 307–09 (1897).

doctrine to apply. See, *e.g.*, the various formulations quoted in the majority and dissenting opinions in DeFunis and in the cases that follow.

(a)   According to Iron Arrow Honor Society v. Heckler, 464 U.S. 67, 72 (1983) (per curiam), a case mooted by the voluntary act of a non-party, "[d]efendants face a heavy burden to establish mootness" in voluntary cessation cases "because otherwise they would be 'free to return to [their] old ways' after the threat of a lawsuit had passed" (quoting United States v. W.T. Grant Co., 345 U.S. 629, 632 (1953)).

(b)   In Vitek v. Jones, 445 U.S. 480 (1980), a prisoner brought a federal court action challenging (on procedural grounds) his transfer from a prison to a mental hospital. While the case was pending, he was retransferred to prison, placed in the psychiatric ward, paroled on condition that he accept psychiatric treatment at a V.A. hospital, and subsequently returned to prison for violation of parole. The Court, by 5–4, agreed with both parties that the case was not moot, stating that against the background of Jones's mental illness, it was not "absolutely clear" that the challenged wrong would not recur. Justice Stewart, for three dissenters, argued that the case was moot because there was "no demonstrated probability" of recurrence.

(c)   In City of Erie v. Pap's A.M., 529 U.S. 277 (2000), the state court enjoined the enforcement of the city's anti-nudity ordinance. But the nude dancing establishment that brought the challenge had closed by the time the case reached the Supreme Court and the proprietor submitted an affidavit attesting that he did not intend to resume business. By a vote of 7–2, the Court held the case not moot. Writing for the majority, Justice O'Connor reasoned that "this is not a run of the mill voluntary cessation case." The majority noted, *inter alia*, that the city suffered "an ongoing injury because it [was] barred from enforcing" its public nudity prohibitions; Pap's was "still incorporated" and "could again decide to operate a nude dancing establishment in Erie"; Pap's failed to raise the mootness issue in its brief in opposition to the petition for certiorari, even though the nude dancing establishment was already closed; and the "interest in preventing litigants from attempting to manipulate the Court's jurisdiction to insulate a favorable decision from review further counsels against a finding of mootness."

(d)   New York State Rifle & Pistol Ass'n, Inc. v. City of New York, 590 U.S. 336 (2020), arose when the petitioners sought declaratory and injunctive relief from a New York City ordinance that barred possessors of licenses to keep handguns in their homes from transporting their weapons anywhere besides seven firing ranges within the City. The challengers' complaint maintained that the Second Amendment requires "unrestricted access to gun ranges and shooting events." After two lower courts upheld the ordinance and the Supreme Court granted certiorari, the New York Legislature enacted legislation abrogating any local regulation that prevented the holders of "premises licenses" from transporting their guns "directly to or from" an authorized range, competition, or second home. Nearly contemporaneously, the City amended its regulation to conform to the new state law.

The Supreme Court vacated the lower court's decision upholding the original New York ordinance in a brief *per curiam* opinion that held the petitioners' claim to declaratory and injunctive relief to be moot. Following the changes in New York State and City law, the Court reasoned, "petitioners may now transport firearms to a second home or shooting range outside the city, which is the precise relief that [they] requested." The Court then declined to consider whether mootness might be averted based on a request for damages that the petitioners raised for the first time in the Supreme Court. Instead, it remanded the case for the lower courts to consider whether the petitioners "may still add a claim for damages in this lawsuit."

Justice Alito dissented, joined by Justice Gorsuch in full and Justice Thomas in part. He maintained that New York's newly enacted rule continued to burden the petitioners' asserted right of "unrestricted access" to gun ranges by limiting them to traveling "directly" to and from their homes. Accordingly, he reasoned, they had not received the complete relief that they sought, and their claim to injunctive relief therefore was not moot. Justice Alito concluded that the petitioners' claim to damages relief also sufficed to save the case from mootness. Reaching the merits, he found that the amended New York ordinance violated the Second Amendment.

Under these circumstances, how should the Court have responded to New York's deliberate efforts to render the case moot?

(e) Uzuegbunam v. Preczewski, 592 U.S. 279 (2021), also discussed at p. 144, *supra*, held that a suit for nominal damages sufficed to avoid mootness in a case in which the plaintiff challenged the enforcement against him of the policies of a public college that (he claimed) violated his free speech rights. By the time the case reached the Supreme Court, the plaintiff was no longer a student at the college and the college had withdrawn the rules from which he had initially sought injunctive, as well as nominal monetary, relief. In an opinion by Justice Thomas, the Court held that the plaintiff's claim to nominal damages sufficed for standing and thus forestalled any mootness objection to the adjudication of his claim on the merits that might have arisen otherwise. Chief Justice Roberts dissented on the ground that the plaintiff's suit for damages failed to satisfy the "redressability" requirement of standing doctrine and that the case was therefore moot.

Does Uzuegbunam v. Preczewski deprive mootness doctrine of any continuing force in barring adjudication of the substantive merits of a constitutional claim in any case in which the plaintiff seeks nominal damages as well as injunctive relief from a past constitutional violation? Chief Justice Roberts suggested that the effect of the decision might "admit of a sweeping exception: Where a plaintiff asks only for a dollar, the defendant should be able to end the case by giving him a dollar, without the court needing to pass on the merits of the plaintiff's claims. Although we recently reserved the question whether a defendant can moot a case by depositing the full amount requested by the plaintiff, Campbell-Ewald Co. v. Gomez, 577 U.S. 153, 166 (2016), our cases have long suggested that he can, see, *e.g.*, California v. San Pablo & Tulare R. Co., 149 U.S. 308, 313–314 (1893)." Would the "exception" contemplated by the Chief Justice, which

Justice Kavanaugh also endorsed in a concurring opinion, be a desirable one? For discussion of the Campbell-Ewald case, see p. 267, note 2, *infra*.

(f)   West Virginia v. EPA, 597 U.S. 697 (2022), found jurisdiction to review the legality of the Clean Power Plan, despite a lower court ruling and change in agency position that meant that the plan was unlikely to be enforced in the future. In doing so, the Court emphasized the difference between standing and mootness analysis. Though the government framed its argument in standing terms, the Court responded: "It is the doctrine of *mootness*, not standing, that addresses whether 'an intervening circumstance [has] deprive[d] the plaintiff of a personal stake in the outcome of the lawsuit' " (emphasis in original, quoting Genesis HealthCare Corp. v. Symczyk, 569 U.S. 66, 72 (2013)).

The mootness label meant that the government bore a "heavy" burden of proving that it was " 'absolutely clear that the allegedly wrongful behavior could not reasonably be expected to recur' " (quoting Parents Involved in Community Schools v. Seattle School Dist. No. 1, 551 U.S. 701, 719 (2007)). Because the government still maintained that the Clean Power Plan had been legal, and did not disavow similar using legal arguments to support rulemaking in the future, it failed to meet its burden.

Justice Kagan (joined by Justices Breyer and Sotomayor) dissented on the merits, and also described the Court's opinion as "really an advisory opinion." But she conceded that "[t]he Court may be right that [exercising jurisdiction] does not violate Article III mootness rules (which are notoriously strict)." West Virginia v. EPA thus continued to emphasize the distinction between mootness and standing discussed in Paragraph (1).

(g)   Finally, in Federal Bureau of Investigation v. Fikre, 601 U.S. 234 (2024), the Court again refused to dismiss a case as moot. The plaintiff, a Muslim man and U.S. citizen, challenged the government's decision to place him on "the No Fly List," which he alleged violated his due process rights and was unconstitutionally discriminatory. After he filed his lawsuit, the government removed him from the No Fly List without explanation, and argued that this mooted the case. The Court unanimously disagreed. Writing that "[t]he Constitution deals with substance, not strategies," the Court emphasized the heavy burden needed to prove voluntary cessation, and that it "holds for governmental defendants no less than private ones." Because the government had provided insufficient reason to believe that it might not again put Fikre back on the list in the future, the Court deemed the case not moot.

(3)   Capable of Repetition, Yet Evading Review.

(a)   In addition to the "voluntary cessation" decisions are cases, also discussed in DeFunis, in which the alleged wrong has ceased but the wrong is capable of repetition, yet evading review.[4] Consider, for example, Federal

---

[4]   See, *e.g.*, Globe Newspaper Co. v. Superior Court, 457 U.S. 596 (1982) (order excluding press and public from certain portions of rape trial had expired with the completion of the trial); Nebraska Press Ass'n v. Stuart, 427 U.S. 539 (1976) (short-term judicial orders restricting press coverage of criminal proceedings had expired prior to Supreme Court review); Moore v. Ogilvie, 394 U.S. 814 (1969) (challenge to signature requirement on nominating petitions; election had occurred before Supreme Court review); Carroll v. President and Com'rs of Princess Anne, 393

Election Commission v. Wisconsin Right to Life, Inc. ("WRTL"), 551 U.S. 449 (2007). During the 2004 election cycle, respondents filed suit challenging the constitutionality, as applied to them, of a provision of a federal prohibition on running advertisements that referred by name to a candidate for federal office within 30 days of a primary election. Despite the passing of the 2004 election, the Court held (in an opinion by Chief Justice Roberts) that the case was not moot because (1) it would have been unreasonable to expect the respondents' challenge to make its way through the courts within a single election cycle and (2) similar issues were likely to arise between the parties in the future.[5]

The requisite degree of likelihood is unclear. The Court has spoken of a "reasonable expectation" or "demonstrated probability" that the controversy would recur and insisted that a "mere physical or theoretical possibility" was insufficient. See, e.g., Murphy v. Hunt, 455 U.S. 478, 482 (1982). Yet in Southern Pac. Term. Co. v. ICC, 219 U.S. 498 (1911), where the Commission had issued a short-term cease-and-desist order that had expired, there was no showing that the Commission proposed to issue similar short-term orders in the future. And in Roe v. Wade, 410 U.S. 113, 124–25 (1973), a challenge to an abortion statute was held not moot even though the woman who had initiated the action was no longer pregnant. "Pregnancy," the Court said, "often comes more than once to the same woman * * * [and] truly could be 'capable of repetition, yet evading review.' "[6] Cf. Honig v. Doe, 484 U.S. 305, 318–19 n.6 (1988) (finding, over two dissenting votes, that a "reasonable expectation" of recurrence may suffice to avoid mootness, even if there is no "demonstrated probability" of recurring, challengeable action).

Two cases applying the exception are explored below:

(b)   In Kingdomware Technologies, Inc. v. United States, 579 U.S. 162 (2016), a business owned by a service-disabled veteran challenged the Government's failure to award it short-term contracts pursuant to a narrow interpretation of a statute mandating preferences for service-disabled or other veteran-owned businesses. The contracts whose award Kingdomware Technologies sought to challenge were performed in less than two years, well before the Supreme court heard the case and so, the Court acknowledged, "no live controversy in the ordinary sense remains."

The Court nonetheless applied the capable of repetition yet evading review exception, concluding that two years was a period "too short to complete judicial review of the lawfulness of the procurement," and that in light of past practice, Kingdomware had "shown a reasonable likelihood that it would be awarded a future contract if its interpretation" prevailed. "Thus, we have jurisdiction because the same legal issue in this case is likely to

---

U.S. 175 (1968) (ten-day injunction restraining white supremacist organization from holding public rallies had expired two years before).

[5]   The Court has stressed for some time that, in the absence of a class action, the relevant question turns on the possibility of recurrence with respect to the complaining party specifically. See Weinstein v. Bradford, 423 U.S. 147, 149 (1975); Murphy v. Hunt, 455 U.S. 478, 482 (1982).

[6]   Since Roe was brought as a class action (a fact the Court ignored in its mootness analysis), the mootness question would presumably not be difficult today. See *Note on Mootness in Class Actions*, p. 263, *infra*.

recur in future controversies between the same parties in circumstances where the period of contract performance is too short to allow full judicial review before performance is complete."

(c) By contrast, the Court held the exception inapplicable in United States v. Sanchez-Gomez, 584 U.S. 381 (2018), a case challenging the practice of routinely shackling criminal defendants during pretrial proceedings. While the defendants' appeals were pending on appeal, their charges were each resolved through dismissal or guilty plea. The Supreme Court agreed that "the challenged action is in its duration too short to be fully litigated prior to its cessation or expiration," but it denied that there was a "reasonable expectation that the same complaining party will be subjected to the same action again," even though the defendants said they were likely to be arrested and shackled again for similar crimes. Instead, the Court said, quoting O'Shea v. Littleton, 414 U.S. 488, 497 (1974), "[w]e have * * * assumed that litigants will conduct their activities within the law and so avoid prosecution and conviction as well as exposure to the challenged course of conduct."

Notably, the defendants argued that in this case that the assumption was unwarranted, because criminal immigration offenses implicated by the case had notably high rates of recidivism, and indeed two of the defendants already *had* reentered the country, been reapprehended, and been charged with new offenses. Nonetheless, the Court held the case moot, emphasizing that "Sanchez-Gomez and Patricio-Guzman * * * are able—and indeed required by law—to refrain from further criminal conduct. Their personal incentives to return to the United States, plus the elevated rate of recidivism associated with illegal entry offenses, do not amount to an inability to obey the law."

(4) Foundations of Mootness Doctrine. The Court in DeFunis viewed the mootness doctrine as a function of the Article III case or controversy requirement. The Court apparently made this link explicit for the first time in 1964, in Liner v. Jafco, Inc., 375 U.S. 301, 306 n.3 (1964): "Our lack of jurisdiction to review moot cases derives from the requirement of Article III of the Constitution under which the exercise of judicial power depends upon the existence of a case or controversy."

Concurring in Honig v. Doe, 484 U.S. 305, 330 (1988), Chief Justice Rehnquist conceded that "our recent cases have taken that position" but argued that the Court had erred; mootness doctrine, he contended, is rooted in policy judgments, not "forced upon us by the case or controversy requirement of Art. III itself." The Chief Justice rested his position partly on history; he thought it "very doubtful that the earliest case I have found discussing mootness, Mills v. Green, 159 U.S. 651 (1895), was premised on constitutional constraints; Justice Gray's opinion in that case nowhere mentions Art. III." Chief Justice Rehnquist also maintained that the recognized exceptions to mootness doctrine for cases involving voluntary cessation of challenged conduct and for acts "capable of repetition, yet evading review," see Paragraphs (3) and (4), *supra*, could not be justified if Article III barred the adjudication of moot cases.

By contrast, Justice Scalia had "little doubt that the Court [in Mills v. Green] believed the [mootness] doctrine called into question the Court's power and not merely its prudence, for (in an opinion by the same Justice who wrote Mills) it had said two years earlier: '[T]he Court is not *empowered* to decide moot questions. * * * No stipulation of the parties or counsel * * * can enlarge the *power*, or affect the duty, of the court in this regard.' California v. San Pablo & Tulare R. Co., 149 U.S. 308, 314 (1893) (Gray, J.)" (emphasis added by Justice Scalia).

What is the better way to understand mootness? Doesn't Chief Justice Rehnquist have a point that the mootness exceptions suggest a pragmatic approach, inconsistent with the Court's current approach to interpreting Article III in standing cases? Doesn't the Court's treatment of cases that are capable of repetition, yet evading review suggest a kind of justiciability by necessity where there may otherwise be no way to obtain review of an important issue? Contrast this approach with that of United States v. Richardson, 418 U.S. 166 (1974), discussed at p. 142, *supra*, denying standing to challenge the constitutionality of official conduct under the Accounts Clause, despite recognizing the probability that "if respondent is not permitted to litigate this issue, no one can do so."

Professor Lee has argued that although there might be statutory, doctrinal, or prudential impediments to the adjudication of moot cases, they remain "cases" within the meaning of Article III. Lee, *Deconstitutionalizing Justiciability: The Example of Mootness*, 105 Harv.L.Rev. 603 (1992). Meanwhile, Professor Hall has argued that the Court has long treated post-filing events that moot the *issue* underlying the claim as a jurisdictional bar negating a case or controversy, while treating events that merely moot the plaintiff's *personal stake* in the matter as a prudential limitation on the exercise of judicial power. Hall, *The Partially Prudential Doctrine of Mootness*, 77 Geo.Wash.L.Rev. 562 (2009). Finally, Professor Lindley argues that mootness doctrine is entirely constitutional, and that the voluntary cessation and capable-of-repetition-yet-evading-review "exceptions" are in fact applications of ordinary Article III principles about the likelihood of future injury drawn from practical experience. Lindley, *The Constitutional Model of Mootness*, 48 B.Y.U. L.Rev. 2151 (2023).

(5) Mootness in the Supreme Court.

(a) Should special considerations apply to events that take place after the Supreme Court has selected a case for discretionary review and granted certiorari? This was Chief Justice Rehnquist's position in Honig v. Doe, 484 U.S. 305, 331–32 (1988), where he argued in a concurrence that "unique resources—the time spent preparing to decide the case by reading briefs, hearing oral argument, and conferring—are squandered in every case in which it becomes apparent after the decisional process is underway that we may not reach the question presented. To me the unique and valuable ability of this Court to decide a case—we are, at present, the only Art. III court which can decide a federal question in such a way as to bind all other courts— is a sufficient reason either to abandon the doctrine of mootness altogether in cases which this Court has decided to review, or at least to relax the doctrine * * *."

Perhaps Chief Justice Rehnquist's concerns would be even more acute today, when the Supreme Court takes even fewer cases. See Chap. III, *infra*. In addition to his concerns about wasted resources, the Justices might worry about strategic behavior on behalf of the parties. A respondent who wins a victory that is unlikely to be upheld upon Supreme Court review might play the odds that the Supreme Court will not grant certiorari, but in the unlikely event that the Supreme Court does grant certiorari, the respondent could then abandon their position and moot the case, avoiding an adverse nationwide precedent.

Formally, the Court has never endorsed such an exception.[7] But in some cases the Court seems especially reluctant to find a case moot once it has taken jurisdiction.

(b) In addition to Pap's A.M. and New York City Rifle & Pistol Association discussed at Paragraph (2), *supra,* consider these additional examples:

(i)   In Pacific Bell Telephone Co. v. Linkline Communications, Inc., 555 U.S. 438 (2009), after the Supreme Court granted review of a Ninth Circuit decision in which the plaintiffs had prevailed, the plaintiffs conceded in the Supreme Court that they now agreed with the defendants on the question presented. At the same time, they asked the Court to vacate the court of appeals decision in their favor and to remand the case to the district court in order to seek relief on a different antitrust theory from the one on which they had prevailed in the court of appeals. Even though the parties were no longer adverse on the question presented, the Court concluded that the case was not moot because the parties still sought different outcomes and because there remained some ambiguity in the plaintiffs' position. Because amici continued to defend the plaintiffs' now-abandoned position, the Court had no difficulty concluding that it should proceed to the merits. Consider the Court's unabashedly pragmatic arguments for proceeding to the question on which it had originally granted certiorari:

"Plaintiffs defended the Court of Appeals' decision at the certiorari stage, and the parties have invested a substantial amount of time, effort, and resources in briefing and arguing the merits of this case. In the absence of a decision from this Court on the merits, the Court of Appeals' decision would presumably remain binding precedent in the Ninth Circuit, and the Circuit conflict we granted certiorari to resolve would persist. Two amici have submitted briefs defending the Court of Appeals' decision on the merits, and we granted the motion of one of those amici to participate in oral argument. We think it appropriate to proceed to address the question presented."

(ii) In Knox v. SEIU, 567 U.S. 298 (2012), a group of non-members filed a class action against a public-sector labor union objecting to the use of state-mandated agency fees for political purposes. The Ninth Circuit rejected the challenge, but after the Supreme Court granted certiorari, the union offered a full refund to all members of the class, and argued that the case had become moot.

---

[7]   For an endorsement of Chief Justice Rehnquist's position, see Nichol, *Moot Cases, Chief Justice Rehnquist, and the Supreme Court*, 22 U.Conn.L.Rev. 703 (1990).

The Supreme Court refused to find mootness, noting that: "Such postcertiorari maneuvers designed to insulate a decision from review by this Court must be viewed with a critical eye." After noting uncertainty about whether the "voluntary cessation" doctrine applied because the plaintiffs had not sought any prospective relief, the Court concluded that the SEIU's offer of a full refund was arguably inadequate because of a dispute about the nature of the notice it would provide to members of the class. This was enough to save the case from mootness.

(iii) And in Moore v. Harper, 600 U.S. 1 (2023), the Court decided a case on certiorari from the Supreme Court of North Carolina, even though the Supreme Court of North Carolina had reconsidered crucial parts of its earlier decision while the case was pending before the U.S. Supreme Court. In brief: the North Carolina Supreme Court had concluded that the North Carolina General Assembly had violated the state constitution in gerrymandering districts for federal congressional elections and had ordered the maps to be redrawn. It had both written a precedential opinion and entered a judgment to that effect ("Harper I") and litigation about the proper remedy continued in the state courts. The U.S. Supreme Court then granted certiorari to decide whether the North Carolina Supreme Court's decision violated Article I, § 4's Elections Clause. While that part of the case was pending before the U.S. Supreme Court, the North Carolina Supreme Court issued an additional decision on the remedial issues ("Harper II") and then (after a change in membership on the North Carolina Supreme Court) granted a petition for rehearing that both eliminated its remedial decision and "overruled" its original gerrymandering decision, which was on review at the U.S. Supreme Court.

The Supreme Court decided that the case was not moot, noting that the court below had not tried to and could not disturb the *judgment* in Harper I, even as it overruled the *precedent*: "In other words, although partisan gerrymandering claims are no longer viable under the North Carolina Constitution, the North Carolina Supreme Court has done nothing to alter the effect of the judgment in Harper I enjoining the use of the 2021 maps. As a result, the legislative defendants' path to complete relief runs through this Court." Justice Thomas, joined on this point by Justice Alito and Justice Gorsuch, dissented, arguing that the distinction on which the Court relied lacked any substance: "our jurisdiction requires a case, and this case is over no matter what becomes of the empty husk of Harper I's interlocutory judgment."

(c) If one concludes that in each of these cases, the Court has reached to find the cases justiciable so as to avoid wasted resources and avoid rewarding strategic behavior, what ought one to conclude about mootness doctrine? Is it evidence that the doctrine is ultimately a pragmatic one? Does it suggest that Chief Justice Rehnquist's view ought to be forthrightly adopted, rather than employed on the sly? Or should the Court simply be more willing to dismiss these cases as moot and wait for the relevant issues to reoccur?

(6) Mootness and the Merits. In Chafin v. Chafin, 568 U.S. 165 (2013), Chief Justice Roberts's opinion for the Court admonished lower courts not to hold a case moot because the claim at issue reflected a low probability of success on the merits, or because the judgment was unlikely to be executed if the plaintiff prevailed. The case involved an international child custody battle. Lynn Chafin, a citizen of the United Kingdom, filed an action against Jeffrey Chafin seeking the return of her daughter to Scotland under the Hague Convention on the Civil Aspects of International Child Abduction and U.S. legislation implementing the Convention. Pursuant to an order of the district court, Lynn Chafin returned to Scotland with the child. Jeffrey Chafin appealed to the Eleventh Circuit, which held that an appeal under the Convention is moot once the child has been returned to a foreign country.

The Supreme Court reversed. Lynn Chafin argued that the case was moot because the district court lacked authority under the Convention, and had no inherent equitable powers, to order the return of the child if the court of appeals reversed. The Court held that this argument's dependence on the proper interpretation of the Convention confused the question of mootness with that of the merits, adding that Jeffrey Chafin's claim "cannot be dismissed as so implausible that it is insufficient to preserve jurisdiction." The Court also rejected the contention that the case was moot because Scottish courts would "ignore" any district court order to return the child to the United States. "A re-return order," said the Court, "may not result in the return of [the child] to the United States, just as an order that an insolvent defendant pay $100 million may not make the plaintiff rich." Whatever the "potential difficulties in enforcement," the Court found that Jeffrey Chafin retained a sufficiently "concrete" interest in the case to defeat mootness.

NOTE ON THE DISPOSITION OF MOOTED CASES

When a case becomes moot on appeal, the disposition of the case depends on both the nature of the case and the events that have led to mootness. The technical questions about the treatment of mooted cases implicate much broader questions about the nature of precedent and the role of federal courts in declaring the law.

(1) The Munsingwear Principle.

(a)   As United States v. Munsingwear, Inc., 340 U.S. 36, 39–40 (1950) described it: "The established practice of the Court in dealing with a civil case from a court in the federal system which has become moot while on its way here or pending our decision on the merits is to reverse or vacate the judgment below and remand with a direction to dismiss." The Court explained that the purpose of that practice was to "clear[ ] the path for future relitigation of the issues between the parties and eliminate[ ] a judgment, review of which was prevented through happenstance. When that procedure is followed, the rights of all parties are preserved; none is prejudiced by a decision which in the statutory scheme was only preliminary."

This discussion was arguably dicta in Munsingwear itself, because the United States government had not asked to vacate the moot judgment while it was on appeal. Because the United States had "slept on its rights" it remained bound by the moot judgment, which was res judicata as to another claim in the same case.

But what is more important is the principle for which Munsingwear came to stand: Civil cases that—through happenstance, conduct not attributable to the parties, or the unilateral action of the prevailing party in the lower court—become moot either (i) on appeal, (ii) during the pendency of a petition for certiorari, or (iii) after the grant of such a petition but prior to decision by the Supreme Court, should be vacated.

(b)   The death of a criminal defendant ordinarily moots the defendant's case on direct or collateral review. See, *e.g.*, Singer v. United States, 323 U.S. 338, 346 (1945). In federal criminal cases, the Supreme Court held for a time that death while a certiorari petition was pending abated "not only the appeal but also all proceedings had in the prosecution from its inception," thus requiring dismissal of the indictment. Durham v. United States, 401 U.S. 481, 483 (1971). But in Dove v. United States, 423 U.S. 325 (1976), the Court overruled this holding without explanation and dismissed a petition for a writ of certiorari on learning of petitioner's death.[1] Does any good reason support the disparity in the Court's practices concerning civil and criminal cases?

(2)   The Bancorp Decision.

(a)   In United States Bancorp Mortgage Co. v. Bonner Mall Partnership, 513 U.S. 18 (1994), the Supreme Court granted certiorari to resolve a question under the Bankruptcy Code, and the parties thereafter reached a settlement that mooted the case. Relying on Munsingwear, *supra*, Bancorp, the losing party in the court of appeals, asked the Supreme Court to vacate the judgment below as well as dismissing the writ. Bonner opposed the motion. Following briefing and argument, the Court, in an opinion by Justice Scalia, unanimously announced an important limit to the Munsingwear principle and ruled that "mootness by reason of settlement does not [ordinarily] justify vacatur of a judgment under review."

Justice Scalia began by rejecting an argument that, when a case becomes moot, a federal court loses jurisdiction to take any action, including entry of a vacatur order. Although mootness nullifies jurisdiction to pronounce on the merits, the court retains authority to take such ancillary action, including vacatur and the award of costs, as justice may require.

It then turned to the question of when vacatur was appropriate. Conceding that its prior practice, before and after Munsingwear, had not been completely consistent or well-reasoned, the Court explained that it would newly restate the relevant principles "in the light shed by adversary presentation." First, whether to vacate was a question of justice and equitable principles. Second, while such principles generally support vacatur when one party has lost the opportunity to seek review of an adverse judgment as the result of happenstance, the "voluntary forfeiture of review" through settlement ordinarily shifts the balance of equities. "[T]he party seeking relief from the status quo of the appellate judgment [must]

---

[1]   Dove was a case before the Supreme Court on direct review; the procedure was later followed on collateral review as well. Warden v. Palermo, 431 U.S. 911 (1977).

demonstrate * * * equitable entitlement to the extraordinary remedy of vacatur." Third, the Court also considered "the public interest," as with all forms of equitable relief. "Judicial precedents are presumptively correct and valuable to the legal community as a whole. They are not merely the property of private litigants and should stand unless a court concludes that the public interest would be served by vacatur."

Some litigants, of course, will settle their disputes without much personal concern about the vacatur issue. But the Bancorp decision is of concern to litigants likely to be involved in a number of similar disputes, who have a keen interest not only in the outcome of any particular case, but also in the preclusive or precedential effects of any judicial resolution. Isn't the Court right that there would be something unseemly about letting repeat players "buy up" judgments that they dislike by settling cases pending on appeal and seeking vacatur?[2]

(b)　In Alvarez v. Smith, 558 U.S. 87 (2009), the Court made clear that the Bancorp exception to vacatur would not apply if the circumstances demonstrated that the parties had not arranged their affairs to render the case moot. In Alvarez, the plaintiffs (six individuals) had brought a due process challenge to the procedures used under Illinois law to seize property used to facilitate a drug crime and had prevailed on their claims in the Seventh Circuit. The Supreme Court, however, found that the case was moot. The plaintiffs had sought only injunctive and declaratory relief. By the time the case reached the Supreme Court, the plaintiffs had agreed on the disposition of the forfeited property. The agreements were reached not in the federal court lawsuit then before the Court, but rather in the state court actions whose procedures the federal case challenged. In an opinion by Justice Breyer, the Court held that the federal case was moot because the dispute over the validity of the Illinois law was no longer embedded in any actual controversy about the plaintiffs' particular legal rights.

Although the case had been mooted by the settlement of the state proceedings that underlay the federal challenge, the Court concluded that Bancorp did not govern. First, the Court found it significant that the parties did not settle the federal case itself; rather, "[t]he six individual cases proceeded through a different court system without any procedural link to the federal case before us." Second, the plaintiffs had not raised their federal claims in the state forfeiture cases themselves. Third, "[t]he disparate dates at which plaintiffs' forfeiture proceedings terminated—11, 14, 27, and 40 months after the seizures—indicate that the [state] did not coordinate the resolution of plaintiffs' state court cases, either with each other or with plaintiffs' federal civil rights case." Accordingly, the Court concluded that the presence of this federal case played no role at all in producing the state court terminations and followed its ordinary practice of vacating the judgment of the court of appeals. Justice Stevens dissented.

---

[2]　For illuminating discussions, see, *e.g.*, Fisch, *The Vanishing Precedent: Eduardo Meets Vacatur*, 70 Notre Dame L.Rev. 325 (1994); Resnik, *Whose Judgment? Vacating Judgments, Preferences for Settlement, and the Role of Adjudication at the Close of the Twentieth Century*, 41 UCLA L.Rev. 1471 (1994).

Given the difficulty of identifying the motives underlying the settlement of a case, does a bright-line rule precluding vacatur in cases of settlement make more sense than Alvarez's fact-bound inquiry into whether the settlement was driven by a desire to vacate the lower court judgment?

(c)   In Camreta v. Greene, 563 U.S. 692 (2011), which is further discussed at pp. 1324–1325, *infra*, the Court addressed the appropriateness of a Munsingwear order in a qualified immunity case in which the lower court had ruled both on the merits and on grounds of qualified immunity. As discussed at p. 1326, *infra*, Pearson v. Callahan, 555 U.S. 223 (2009) had held that in order to "promote[ ] the development of constitutional precedent," federal courts in constitutional tort actions have discretion to reach the merits of a constitutional claim before deciding whether the defendants are entitled to qualified immunity on the ground that the asserted rights were not "clearly established." In Camreta, the Court held that when a lower court applying Pearson ruled against a state official on the merits but for the official on qualified immunity grounds, the official could, at least in some circumstances, seek certiorari despite having prevailed in the court below. Of interest here, because Camreta became moot while the defendants' case was pending before the Supreme Court, the Court issued a Munsingwear order vacating the court of appeals' adverse merits decision. In so doing, the Court rejected the argument that vacatur was inappropriate in this context because it would undermine Pearson's goal of giving the court of appeals discretion to resolve constitutional questions for future cases. The Court reasoned that because "a constitutional ruling in a qualified immunity case is a legally consequential decision" that entitles even a prevailing defendant to Supreme Court review, the normal rule of vacatur should apply when "happenstance prevents that review from occurring."

(3)   Modern Controversy. In Acheson Hotels v. Laufer, 601 U.S. 1 (2023), the Supreme Court had granted certiorari to resolve a disagreement about standing to sue under the Americans with Disabilities Act. While the case was pending, it then decided to dismiss a case as moot after the plaintiff had voluntarily dismissed her case in the district court, as well as many other pending ADA cases she had in other courts. (This decision followed ethical allegations against, and the ultimate suspension of, the plaintiff's lawyer.) The Court invoked its "well settled" practice under Munsingwear and vacated the judgment below.

Justice Jackson concurred in the judgment of vacatur "on the basis of * * * precedent," and wrote separately to express her objections to the established practice.[3]

First, Justice Jackson argued that decisions to vacate were equitable in nature, and therefore must always be made on a case-by-case basis: "automatic vacatur plainly flouts the requirement of an individualized,

---

[3]   Justice Jackson had more briefly raised similar issues in Chapman v. Doe ex rel Rothert, 143 S.Ct. 857 (2023). For a substantial analysis and critique of current trends in vacatur practice, see Tucker & Risch, *Canceling Appellate Precedent*, 76 Fla.L.Rev. 175 (2024).

circumstance-driven fairness evaluation, which * * * is the hallmark of an equitable remedy."

Second, Justice Jackson argued that "automatic vacatur is flatly inconsistent with our common-law tradition of case-by-case adjudication, which assumes that judicial decisions are valuable and should not be cast aside lightly." Emphasizing the coequal duty of lower court judges "to say what the law is" (quoting *Marbury v. Madison*, 1 Cranch (5 U.S.) 137, 177 (1803), Justice Jackson continued: "Every federal case fades to black at some point, yet in our common-law system of case-by-case adjudication, the rulings that Article III judges have issued in those cases remain good law."

Thus, in Justice Jackson's view, vacatur was appropriate only in unusual situations where leaving the decision intact produced a special hardship for the appellant—such as the original facts of Munsingwear, or where a litigant was deliberately manipulating the Court's jurisdiction.

(4) Mootness and State Court Litigation. In DeFunis, after concluding that the action was moot, the Supreme Court vacated the judgment and remanded "for such proceedings [in the state supreme court] as * * * may be deemed appropriate." In ASARCO Inc. v. Kadish, 490 U.S. 605, 621 n.1 (1989), discussed p. 209, *supra*, the Court noted its decision in DeFunis to vacate and remand for further proceedings in state court, but said that its more recent practice has been to dismiss cases that become moot on review from the state courts, leaving undisturbed the state court judgment (citing Kansas Gas & Elec. Co. v. State Corp. Comm'n of Kansas, 481 U.S. 1044 (1987); Times-Picayune Pub. Corp. v. Schulingkamp, 420 U.S. 985 (1975)).

If a state court holds moot a case involving a federal question, is Supreme Court review precluded? In Liner v. Jafco, Inc., 375 U.S. 301 (1964), a state court enjoined picketing in a labor dispute, despite a contention that its jurisdiction was federally preempted. Pending decision on appeal, construction at the site was completed, and the state appellate court held that the case had become moot (though it also expressed an opinion on the merits). The Supreme Court unanimously held, per Justice Brennan, that "in this case the question of mootness is itself a question of federal law upon which we must pronounce final judgment." In holding the case not moot, the Court cited an indemnity bond requiring payment if the injunction was "wrongfully" sued out, but also relied on the frustration of federal policy that might result if the state court's ruling on the preemption claim were immunized from review. See also, *e.g.*, Gannett Co., Inc. v. DePasquale, 443 U.S. 368 (1979).

Is mootness always a "federal" question, or only when the state court's view of mootness is broader than that under federal law?

NOTE ON MOOTNESS IN CLASS ACTIONS

(1) The Geraghty Case. The leading case on mootness in class actions is United States Parole Commission v. Geraghty, 445 U.S. 388 (1980), in which a federal prisoner who was refused parole filed a class action challenging the applicable parole guidelines. The district court declined to certify a class action and granted summary judgment for the defendants on all the claims. Geraghty then appealed the denial of class certification, but before any briefs were filed in the court of appeals, he was released from prison for reasons unrelated to the lawsuit. Despite Geraghty's release, the U.S. Court of Appeals for the Third Circuit found the dispute not moot, reversed the judgment of the district court, and remanded for further proceedings. The Supreme Court, 5–4, agreed that Geraghty's appeal of the denial of class certification was not moot. Writing for the majority, Justice Blackmun concluded that a review of prior decisions demonstrated the "flexible character of the Art. III mootness doctrine. As has been noted in the past, Art. III justiciability is 'not a legal concept with a fixed content or susceptible of scientific verification.' Poe v. Ullman, 367 U.S. 497, 508 (1961) (plurality opinion)."

Justice Blackmun continued: "A plaintiff who brings a class action presents two separate issues for judicial resolution. One is the claim on the merits; the other is the claim that he is entitled to represent a class. * * *

"In order to achieve the primary benefits of class suits, the Federal Rules of Civil Procedure give the proposed class representative the right to have a class certified if the requirements of the rules are met. This 'right' is more analogous to the private attorney general concept than to the type of interest traditionally thought to satisfy the 'personal stake' requirement.

"* * * [T]he purpose of the 'personal stake' requirement is to assure that the case is in a form capable of judicial resolution. The imperatives of a dispute capable of judicial resolution are sharply presented issues in a concrete factual setting and self-interested parties vigorously advocating opposing positions. * * * We conclude that these elements can exist with respect to the class certification issue notwithstanding the fact that the named plaintiff's claim on the merits has expired. * * * In Sosna v. Iowa, [419 U.S. 393 (1975),] it was recognized that a named plaintiff whose claim on the merits expires *after* class certification may still adequately represent the class. Implicit in that decision was the determination that vigorous advocacy can be assured through means other than the traditional requirement of a 'personal stake in the outcome.' * * *

"We therefore hold that an action brought on behalf of a class does not become moot upon expiration of the named plaintiff's substantive claim, even though class certification has been denied. The proposed representative retains a 'personal stake' in obtaining class certification sufficient to assure that Art. III values are not undermined. If the appeal results in reversal of the class certification denial, and a class subsequently is properly certified, the merits of the class claim then may be adjudicated pursuant to the holding in Sosna.

"Our holding is limited to the appeal of the denial of the class certification motion. A named plaintiff whose claim expires may not continue to press the appeal on the merits until a class has been properly certified. * * * If, on appeal, it is determined that class certification properly was denied, the claim on the merits must be dismissed as moot. * * *"

Justice Powell wrote a sharp dissent, joined by Chief Justice Burger and Justices Stewart and Rehnquist, protesting both the Court's pronouncement "that mootness is a 'flexible' doctrine which may be adapted as we see fit to 'nontraditional' forms of litigation" and its holding "that the named plaintiff has a right 'analogous to the private attorney general concept' to appeal the denial of class certification even when his personal claim for relief is moot."

Justice Powell wrote: "Art. III contains no exception for class actions. Thus, we have held that a putative class representative who alleges no individual injury 'may not seek relief on behalf of himself or any other member of the class.' O'Shea v. Littleton, 414 U.S. 488, 494 (1974). Only after a class has been certified in accordance with Rule 23 can it 'acquir[e] a legal status separate from the interest asserted by [the named plaintiff].' Sosna v. Iowa, *supra*, 419 U.S. at 399 (1975)."

He continued: "The Court splits the class aspects of this action into two separate 'claims': (i) that the action may be maintained by respondent on behalf of a class, and (ii) that the class is entitled to relief on the merits. Since no class has been certified, the Court concedes that the claim on the merits is moot. But respondent is said to have a personal stake in his 'procedural claim' despite his lack of a stake in the merits.

"The Court makes no effort to identify any injury to respondent that may be redressed by, or any benefit to respondent that may accrue from, a favorable ruling on the certification question. Instead, respondent's 'personal stake' is said to derive from two factors having nothing to do with concrete injury or stake in the outcome. First, the Court finds that the Federal Rules of Civil Procedure create a 'right,' 'analogous to the private attorney general concept,' to have a class certified. Second, the Court thinks that the case retains the 'imperatives of a dispute capable of judicial resolution' * * *.

"The Court's reliance on some new 'right' inherent in Rule 23 is misplaced. We have held that even Congress may not confer federal court jurisdiction when Art. III does not. * * * Far less so may a rule of procedure which 'shall not be construed to extend * * * the jurisdiction of the United States district courts.' Fed.R.Civ.Proc. 82. Moreover, the 'private attorney general concept' cannot supply the personal stake necessary to satisfy Art. III. It serves only to permit litigation by a party who has a stake of his own but otherwise might be barred by prudential standing rules. * * *

"Although we have refused steadfastly to countenance the 'public action,' the Court's redefinition of the personal stake requirement leaves no principled basis for that practice."[1]

(2) Evolution of Mootness Doctrine in Class Actions. Though Geraghty is the most important decision governing mootness in the class action context, its approach fits comfortably with that of cases decided both before and after it.

---

[1]   For forceful criticism of the Geraghty majority's reliance on a Rule 23 right to seek class certification (but a defense of the decision on other grounds), see Greenstein, *Bridging the Mootness Gap in Federal Court Class Actions*, 35 Stan.L.Rev. 897, 907–08 (1983). Does the Court's reliance on the rule raise a question under the Rules Enabling Act? See Chap. VI, Sec. 1, *infra*.

(a) In Sosna v. Iowa, 419 U.S. 393 (1975), the Court announced that certification as a class action could save litigation from mootness when thereafter the named plaintiff no longer had an individual claim. The Court, however, appeared to require that the controversy (over a state durational residency requirement for obtaining a divorce) be within the "capable of repetition, yet evading review" category (not for the named plaintiff but for the remaining members of the class).

(b) Franks v. Bowman Transp. Co., 424 U.S. 747 (1976), was a class action in which the sole issue before the Supreme Court was a demand for retroactive seniority in employment and in which the plaintiff, the only named representative of the class, had been lawfully discharged by the employer after certification. In holding the case not moot, the Court, which was unanimous on this point, said: "[N]othing in our Sosna * * * [or other] opinions holds or even intimates that the fact the named plaintiff no longer has a personal stake in the outcome of a certified class action renders the class action moot unless there remains an issue 'capable of repetition, yet evading review.' * * * Given a properly certified class action, Sosna contemplates that mootness turns on whether, in the specific circumstances of the given case at the time it is before this Court, an adversary relationship sufficient to [ensure that the 'concrete adverseness which sharpens the presentation of issues'] exists. In this case, that adversary relationship obviously obtained as to unnamed class members * * *."

How significant was it that other members of the class in the Franks case were "individually named in the record" and actively sought relief?

(c) In Gerstein v. Pugh, 420 U.S. 103 (1975), a putative class action challenging pretrial detention procedures was held by a unanimous Court not to be moot even though the named plaintiffs had evidently been tried before the district court certified the class. The Court said: "Such a showing [that the case was not moot as to all named plaintiffs at the time of certification] ordinarily would be required to avoid mootness under Sosna. But this case is a suitable exception to that requirement. * * * It is by no means certain that any given individual, named as plaintiff, would be in pretrial custody long enough for a district judge to certify the class. Moreover, in this case the constant existence of a class of persons suffering deprivation is certain. The attorney representing the named respondents [plaintiffs] is a public defender, and we can safely assume that he has other clients with a continuing live interest in the case."

(d) Genesis Healthcare Corp. v. Symczyk, 569 U.S. 66 (2013), emphasizes the filing of a motion for certification as the pivotal moment in determining whether a collective action becomes moot when the named plaintiff's claim is mooted. There, the plaintiff sued under the Fair Labor Standards Act (FLSA), 29 U.S.C. § 201 et seq., on the ground that the employer illegally deducted thirty minutes for an unpaid lunch break each day, even when the employee performed compensable work during that time. Under the FLSA, a plaintiff may file an action individually and on behalf of "other employees similarly situated." 29 U.S.C. § 216(b). Before Symczyk moved for "conditional certification," Genesis Healthcare tendered a settlement offer that purported to satisfy the full amount of the plaintiff's individual claim. Because the lower courts had held that this tender mooted the plaintiff's individual claim (even though she did not accept the offer), and a majority of the Justices thought the plaintiff had failed to preserve a challenge to that finding, the Court, in an opinion by Justice Thomas, accepted the premise that her claim was moot.[2] Given that premise, the Court held that the plaintiff could not maintain the collective action on behalf of other similarly situated employees under the FLSA. The Court emphasized that Geraghty had "explicitly limited its holding to cases in which the named plaintiff's claim remains live at the time the district court denies class certification." The plaintiff in Genesis Healthcare, however, had not even moved for conditional certification under § 216(b) when her claim became moot.[3]

(e) Geraghty and Genesis Healthcare make clear that filing a motion for certification defines the moment after which a plaintiff may maintain a putative class action even though his or her individual claim has become moot. Did the Court draw the proper line? What constitutional or prudential interests would have been served by holding, as Justice Powell would have in Geraghty, that the named plaintiff may continue to represent the class only if formal certification has taken place before the individual claim has become moot? After all, a class may be certified without any real contest between the parties, since certification sometimes works to the advantage of both sides. Even after certification, moreover, other members of the class

---

[2] In dissent, Justice Kagan (joined by Justices Ginsburg, Breyer, and Sotomayor) argued that the mootness of the individual claim was properly before the Court, and that the employer's tender of a settlement offer could not moot the individual claim if the plaintiff did not accept it.

The Court adopted the theory of Justice Kagan's dissent in Genesis Healthcare in Campbell-Ewald Co. v. Gomez, 577 U.S. 153 (2016). Gomez filed a class action complaint in which he alleged that the defendant violated his rights under the Telephone Consumer Protection Act by sending him unauthorized text messages and sought $1,500 in damages, the maximum that he could recover under the Act. Campbell-Ewald made a settlement offer of the full amount, which Gomez refused. Campbell-Ewald then argued that its offer had mooted the case. Writing for five Justices, Justice Ginsburg held that "[u]nder basic principles of contract law" the "unaccepted offer" was "a legal nullity, with no operative effect" and that both parties thus "retained the same stake in the litigation they had at the outset." In a potentially important passage at the end of her opinion, however, Justice Ginsburg reserved the question "whether the result would be different if a defendant deposits the full amount of the plaintiff's individual claim in an account payable to the plaintiff, and the court then enters judgment for the plaintiff in that amount." Is there any reason why a defendant who wished to forestall a class action by offering to pay the named plaintiff's claim prior to class certification would not make such a deposit? (If not, has Justice Ginsburg suggested that the defendant may moot any such class action simply by taking one additional step with respect to the named plaintiff?) Justice Thomas concurred on the ground that the defendant had not satisfied the common law standard for a "tender" of complete relief, which required an admission of liability. Chief Justice Roberts, joined by Justices Scalia and Alito, dissented.

Again emphasizing the significance of Rule 23, United States v. Sanchez-Gomez, 584 U.S. 381 (2018), unanimously held that the rationale of Gerstein and Geraghty did not extend to challenges, raised on motions in criminal actions, to a United States Marshals Service policy of shackling in-custody defendants for some court appearances. Although the court of appeals had viewed the challenges by four defendants as a "functional class action," the Court found all of the individual cases to be moot on appeal in the absence of any formal mechanism for class certification.

[3] The Court also emphasized that the premise of cases such as Geraghty and Sosna was that "a putative class acquires an independent legal status once it is certified under [Fed.R.Civ.P.] 23." In contrast, certification under the FLSA procedure merely resulted in sending notice to employees, who could then become parties by filing written consent with the court.

may be able to opt out (see Fed.R.Civ.P. 23(c)(2)), or to challenge the adequacy of representation and thus the binding effect of the judgment in a collateral proceeding (see Hansberry v. Lee, 311 U.S. 32 (1940)). Conversely, what interests, if any, are served by insisting, as Genesis Healthcare seems to, that the motion for certification be filed before the individual claim becomes moot? Will the Court's position prevent strategic litigation behavior or merely ensure that plaintiffs move for class certification when they file their complaints?

(3) Possible Significance of a Plaintiff with a Personal Stake. The constitutional argument for nonjusticiability in a case such as Geraghty centers on the lack of an ongoing dispute involving the class member before the court. Whether or not that argument is accepted, does the absence of a named plaintiff with a stake in the outcome invoke prudential considerations favoring a refusal to adjudicate? Consider whether the central goal of the class action—more vigorous and effective enforcement of group rights—requires that the litigation be prosecuted by a representative of the group who continues to share its concerns or whether it suffices that members of the group not themselves before the court have an ongoing dispute. See Deposit Guar. Nat'l Bank v. Roper, 445 U.S. 326, 342–44 (1980) (Stevens, J., concurring). See also Shapiro, *Class Actions: The Class as Party and Client*, 73 Notre Dame L.Rev. 913 (1998). Indeed, in some instances, insistence that class counsel have an identifiable client with an ongoing interest may lead only to the naming of a class representative with little or no knowledge of the case who will play no role in the course of the litigation. Does it follow that such insistence is always and necessarily a sterile formalism? For discussion of the role of lawyers in class litigation, see, for example, Hay & Rosenberg, *"Sweetheart" and "Blackmail" Settlements in Class Actions: Reality and Remedy*, 75 Notre Dame L.Rev. 1377 (2000); Rhode, *Class Conflicts in Class Actions*, 34 Stan.L.Rev. 1183 (1982).

(4) State Class Action Doctrine and Mootness on Appeal. Richardson v. Ramirez, 418 U.S. 24 (1974), was a state court action against state election officials challenging a law disenfranchising convicted felons. The Supreme Court concluded that the state courts had treated the case as a class action and that, as such, it presented a justiciable controversy; even though the named plaintiffs had received all the relief that they sought, there was a continuing dispute involving "the unnamed members of the classes represented below by petitioner and respondents." The Court observed that if the suit had been brought in federal court, there "would be serious doubt as to whether it could have proceeded as a class action * * *. But California is at liberty to prescribe its own rules for class actions." (Quite apart from any remaining differences between state court versus federal court class actions, would there still be "serious doubt" after Franks v. Bowman Transp. Co., 424 U.S. 747 (1976), p. 266, *supra*, if the suit had commenced in federal court?) The Court saw strong practical arguments militating against a holding of mootness, especially the fact that were the state judgment for the plaintiffs allowed to stand, the defendant officials would be "permanently bound by [the state court's] conclusion on a matter of federal constitutional law"—a conclusion that the U.S. Supreme Court went on to reverse. *Cf.* ASARCO Inc. v. Kadish, 490 U.S. 605 (1989), p. 209, *supra.*

(5) Implications for Standing Doctrine? Should Geraghty's recognition that mootness is a "flexible" doctrine and its characterization of justiciability doctrine more generally as "not a legal concept with a fixed content" have any implications for standing and ripeness, either generally or in class action cases? For example, would and should the Court uphold standing in a class action—perhaps alleging raced-based targeting of motorists for traffic stops—in which no individual plaintiff could establish the requisite likelihood of individual injury but in which the practice, if proved to exist, would be certain to affect at least some members of the plaintiff class? To date, the indications from the Court are negative. See *Preliminary Note on Ripeness, Paragraph (3) ("Institutional Reform Litigation"),* p. 280, *infra.* If Geraghty is accepted, is this an intellectually tenable position? Compare Meltzer, *Deterring Constitutional Violations by Law Enforcement Officials: Plaintiffs and Defendants as Private Attorneys General,* 88 Colum.L.Rev. 247, 301–03 (1988) (discussing implications of modern mootness doctrine for justiciability doctrine generally).

---

5. RIPENESS

INTRODUCTORY NOTE

Understood as a temporal aspect of justiciability, the ripeness doctrine seeks to prevent the adjudication in federal court of disputes that remain too ill-defined for proper judicial resolution. The classic example of a ripeness concern involves the plaintiff who wishes to challenge the validity of a governmental policy that has not yet been enforced against him or her and may never be. In the pages that follow, consider in what ways ripeness differs from the law of standing.

United Public Workers v. Mitchell

330 U.S. 75 (1947).
Appeal from the District Court for the District of Columbia.

■ MR. JUSTICE REED delivered the opinion of the Court.

[The appellant federal employees and their union sought declaratory and injunctive relief from a provision of the Hatch Act and an implementing civil service rule that forbade executive officers and employees to "take any active part in political management or in political campaigns." This prohibition was claimed to violate the First, Fifth, Ninth, and Tenth Amendments to the Constitution.]

* * * It is alleged that the individuals desire to engage in acts of political management and in political campaigns. Their purposes are as stated in the excerpt from the complaint set out in the margin.[11] From the affidavits it is plain, and we so assume, that these activities will be carried on completely outside of the hours of employment. * * *

None of the appellants, except George P. Poole, has violated the provisions of the Hatch Act. They wish to act contrary to its provisions and those of * * * the Civil Service Rules and desire a declaration of the legally permissible limits of regulation. Defendants moved to dismiss the complaint for lack of a justiciable case or controversy. The [three-judge] District Court determined that each of these individual appellants had an interest in their claimed privilege of engaging in political activities, sufficient to give them a right to maintain this suit. The District Court further determined that the questioned provision of the Hatch Act was valid and * * * accordingly dismissed the complaint and granted summary judgment to defendants. * * *

Second. At the threshold of consideration, we are called upon to decide whether the complaint states a controversy cognizable in this Court. We defer consideration of the cause of action of Mr. Poole until section *Three* of this opinion. The other individual employees have elaborated the grounds of their objection in individual affidavits for use in the hearing on the summary judgment. We select as an example one that contains the essential averments of all the others and print below the portions with significance in this suit.[18] Nothing similar to the fourth

---

[11] "In discharge of their duties of citizenship, of their right to vote, and in exercise of their constitutional rights of freedom of speech, of the press, of assembly, and the right to engage in political activity, the individual plaintiffs desire to engage in the following acts: write for publication letters and articles in support of candidates for office; be connected editorially with publications which are identified with the legislative program of UFWA [former name of the present union appellant] and candidates who support it; solicit votes, aid in getting out voters, act as accredited checker, watcher, or challenger; transport voters to and from the polls without compensation therefor; participate in and help in organizing political parades; initiate petitions, and canvass for the signatures of others on such petitions; serve as party ward committeeman or other party official; and perform any and all acts not prohibited by any provision of law other than the second sentence of Section 9(a) and Section 15 of the Hatch Act, which constitute taking an active part in political management and political campaigns."

[18] "At this time, when the fate of the entire world is in the balance, I believe it is not only proper but an obligation for all citizens to participate actively in the making of the vital political decisions on which the success of the war and the permanence of the peace to follow so largely depend. For the purpose of participating in the making of these decisions it is my earnest desire to engage actively in political management and political campaigns. I wish to engage in such activity upon my own time, as a private citizen.

"I wish to engage in such activities on behalf of those candidates for public office who I believe will best serve the needs of this country and with the object of persuading others of the correctness of my judgments and of electing the candidates of my choice. This objective I wish to pursue by all proper means such as engaging in discussion, by speeches to conventions, rallies and other assemblages, by publicizing my views in letters and articles for publication in newspapers and other periodicals, by aiding in the campaign of candidates for political office by posting banners and posters in public places, by distributing leaflets, by 'ringing doorbells', by addressing campaign literature, and by doing any and all acts of like character reasonably designed to assist in the election of candidates I favor.

"I desire to engage in these activities freely, openly, and without concealment. However, I understand that the second sentence of Section 9(a) of the Hatch Act and the Rules of the C.S.C. provide that if I engage in this activity, the Civil Service Commission will order that I be

paragraph of the printed affidavit is contained in the other affidavits. The assumed controversy between affiant and the Civil Service Commission as to affiant's right to act as watcher at the polls on November 2, 1943, had long been moot when this complaint was filed. We do not therefore treat this allegation separately. The affidavits, it will be noticed, follow the generality of purpose expressed by the complaint. They declare a desire to act contrary to the rule against political activity but not that the rule has been violated. In this respect, we think they differ from the type of threat adjudicated in Railway Mail Association v. Corsi, 326 U.S. 88 [(1945)]. In that case, the refusal to admit an applicant to membership in a labor union on account of race was involved. Admission had been refused. Definite action had also been taken in Hill v. Florida, 325 U.S. 538 [(1945)]. In the Hill case an injunction had been sought and allowed against Hill and the union forbidding Hill from acting as the business agent of the union and the union from further functioning as a union until it complied with the state law. The threats which menaced the affiants of these affidavits in the case now being considered are closer to a general threat by officials to enforce those laws which they are charged to administer than they are to the direct threat of punishment against a named organization for a completed act that made the Mail Association and the Hill cases justiciable.

As is well known, the federal courts established pursuant to Article III of the Constitution do not render advisory opinions. For adjudication of constitutional issues, "concrete legal issues, presented in actual cases, not abstractions" are requisite. This is as true of declaratory judgments as any other field. These appellants seem clearly to seek advisory opinions upon broad claims of rights protected by the First, Fifth, Ninth and Tenth Amendments to the Constitution. As these appellants are classified employees, they have a right superior to the generality of citizens, compare Fairchild v. Hughes, 258 U.S. 126 [(1922)], but the facts of their personal interest in their civil rights, of the general threat of possible interference with those rights by the Civil Service Commission under its rules, if specified things are done by appellants, does not make a justiciable case or controversy. Appellants want to engage in "political management and political campaigns," to persuade others to follow

---

dismissed from federal employment. Such deprivation of my job in the federal government would be a source of immediate and serious financial loss and other injury to me.

"At the last Congressional election I was very much interested in the outcome of the campaign and offered to help the party of my choice by being a watcher at the polls. I obtained a watcher's certificate but I was advised that there might be some question of my right to use the certificate and retain my federal employment. Therefore, on November 1, 1943, the day before the election, I called the regional office of the Civil Service Commission in Philadelphia and spoke to a person who gave his name as * * *. Mr. * * * stated that if I used my watcher's certificate, the Civil Service Commission would see that I was dismissed from my job at the * * * for violation of the Hatch Act. I, therefore, did not use the certificate as I had intended.

"I believe that Congress may not constitutionally abridge my right to engage in the political activities mentioned above. However, unless the courts prevent the Civil Service Commission from enforcing this unconstitutional law, I will be unable freely to exercise my rights as a citizen." [Identifying words omitted.]

appellants' views by discussion, speeches, articles and other acts reasonably designed to secure the selection of appellants' political choices. Such generality of objection is really an attack on the political expediency of the Hatch Act, not the presentation of legal issues. It is beyond the competence of courts to render such a decision.

The power of courts, and ultimately of this Court to pass upon the constitutionality of acts of Congress arises only when the interests of litigants require the use of this judicial authority for their protection against actual interference. A hypothetical threat is not enough. We can only speculate as to the kinds of political activity the appellants desire to engage in or as to the contents of their proposed public statements or the circumstances of their publication. It would not accord with judicial responsibility to adjudge, in a matter involving constitutionality, between the freedom of the individual and the requirements of public order except when definite rights appear upon the one side and definite prejudicial interferences upon the other.

The Constitution allots the nation's judicial power to the federal courts. Unless these courts respect the limits of that unique authority, they intrude upon powers vested in the legislative or executive branches. * * * Should the courts seek to expand their power so as to bring under their jurisdiction ill-defined controversies over constitutional issues, they would become the organ of political theories. Such abuse of judicial power would properly meet rebuke and restriction from other branches. * * * No threat of interference by the Commission with rights of these appellants appears beyond that implied by the existence of the law and the regulations. * * * These reasons lead us to conclude that the determination of the trial court, that the individual appellants, other than Poole, could maintain this action, was erroneous.

Third. The appellant Poole does present by the complaint and affidavit matters appropriate for judicial determination. The affidavits filed by appellees confirm that Poole has been charged by the Commission with political activity and a proposed order for his removal from his position adopted subject to his right under Commission procedure to reply to the charges and to present further evidence in refutation. We proceed to consider the controversy over constitutional power at issue between Poole and the Commission as defined by the charge and preliminary finding upon one side and the admissions of Poole's affidavit upon the other. Our determination is limited to those facts. This proceeding so limited meets the requirements of defined rights and a definite threat to interfere with a possessor of the menaced rights by a penalty for an act done in violation of the claimed restraint.

Because we conclude hereinafter that the prohibition of § 9 of the Hatch Act and Civil Service Rule 1, * * * are valid, it is unnecessary to consider, as this is a declaratory judgment action, whether or not this appellant sufficiently alleges that an irreparable injury to him would result from his removal from his position. Nor need we inquire whether or not a court of equity would enforce by injunction any judgment declaring rights. Since Poole admits that he violated the rule against political activity and that removal from office is therefore mandatory under the act, there is no question as to the exhaustion of administrative remedies. * * * Under such circumstances, we see no reason why a declaratory judgment action, even though constitutional issues are involved, does not lie. * * *

[The Court held that Poole had violated the Act, and that the Act as applied to him was valid.

■ [MR. JUSTICE FRANKFURTER delivered a concurring opinion dealing with a point of appellate procedure.

■ [MR. JUSTICE BLACK delivered a dissenting opinion, expressing the view that all the complaints stated a case or controversy, and that the Act as applied in all the cases was invalid.]

■ MR. JUSTICE DOUGLAS, dissenting in part.

I disagree with the Court on two of the four matters decided.

First. There are twelve individual appellants here asking for an adjudication of their rights. The Court passes on the claim of only one of them, Poole. It declines to pass on the claims of the other eleven on the ground that they do not present justiciable cases or controversies. With this conclusion I cannot agree. * * *

The declaratory judgment procedure is designed "to declare rights and other legal relations of any interested party * * * whether or not further relief is or could be prayed." Judicial Code, § 274d, 28 U.S.C. § 400. The fact that equity would not restrain a wrongful removal of an office holder but would leave the complainant to his legal remedies is, therefore, immaterial. A judgment which, without more, adjudicates the status of a person is permissible under the Declaratory Judgment Act. Perkins v. Elg, 307 U.S. 325, 349, 350 [(1939)]. * * * The right to hold an office or public position against such threats is a common example of its use. Borchard, Declaratory Judgments (2d ed.), pp. 858 *et seq.* Declaratory relief is the singular remedy available here to preserve the status quo while the constitutional rights of these appellants to make these utterances and to engage in these activities are determined. The threat against them is real not fanciful, immediate not remote. The case is therefore an actual not a hypothetical one. And the present case seems to me to be a good example of a situation where uncertainty, peril, and insecurity result from imminent and immediate threats to asserted rights.

Since the Court does not reach the constitutionality of the claims of these eleven individual appellants, a discussion of them would seem to be premature. * * *

Abbott Laboratories v. Gardner

387 U.S. 136 (1967).

Certiorari to the United States Court of Appeals for the Third Circuit.

■ MR. JUSTICE HARLAN delivered the opinion of the Court.

In 1962 Congress amended the Federal Food, Drug, and Cosmetic Act * * * to require manufacturers of prescription drugs to print the "established name" of the drug "prominently and in type at least half as large as that used thereon for any proprietary [or brand] name * * *" on labels and other printed material * * *. The underlying purpose of the 1962 amendment was to bring to the attention of doctors and patients the fact that many of the drugs sold under familiar trade names are actually identical to drugs sold under their "established" or less familiar trade names at significantly lower prices. The Commissioner of Food and Drugs, exercising authority delegated to him by the Secretary, * * * promulgated [a regulation providing] * * *:

> "If the label or labeling of a prescription drug bears a proprietary name or designation for the drug or any ingredient thereof, the established name, if such there be, corresponding to such proprietary name or designation, shall accompany each appearance of such proprietary name or designation."

A similar rule was made applicable to advertisements for prescription drugs * * *.

The present action was brought by a group of 37 individual drug manufacturers and by the Pharmaceutical Manufacturers Association, of which all the petitioner companies are members, and which includes manufacturers of more than 90% of the Nation's supply of prescription drugs. They challenged the regulations on the ground that the Commissioner exceeded his authority under the statute by promulgating an order requiring labels, advertisements, and other printed matter relating to prescription drugs to designate the established name of the particular drug involved every time its trade name is used anywhere in such material.

The District Court, on cross motions for summary judgment, granted the declaratory and injunctive relief sought, finding that the statute did not sweep so broadly as to permit the Commissioner's "every time" interpretation. * * * The Court of Appeals for the Third Circuit reversed without reaching the merits of the case. * * * [T]he Court of Appeals held [*inter alia*] that no "actual case or controversy" existed * * *.

I.

[Congress did not] * * * intend to forbid pre-enforcement review of this sort of regulation promulgated by the Commissioner. * * * [Based on applicable precedents], only upon a showing of "clear and convincing evidence" of a contrary legislative intent should the courts restrict access

to judicial review [quoting Rusk v. Cort, 369 U.S. 367, 379–80 (1962)].
* * *

Given this standard, we are wholly unpersuaded that the statutory scheme in the food and drug area excludes this type of action. * * *

II.

A further inquiry must, however, be made. The injunctive and declaratory judgment remedies are discretionary, and courts traditionally have been reluctant to apply them to administrative determinations unless these arise in the context of a controversy "ripe" for judicial resolution. Without undertaking to survey the intricacies of the ripeness doctrine it is fair to say that its basic rationale is to prevent the courts, through avoidance of premature adjudication, from entangling themselves in abstract disagreements over administrative policies, and also to protect the agencies from judicial interference until an administrative decision has been formalized and its effects felt in a concrete way by the challenging parties. The problem is best seen in a twofold aspect, requiring us to evaluate both the fitness of the issues for judicial decision and the hardship to the parties of withholding court consideration.

As to the former factor, we believe the issues presented are appropriate for judicial resolution at this time. First, all parties agree that the issue tendered is a purely legal one: whether the statute was properly construed by the Commissioner to require the established name of the drug to be used *every time* the proprietary name is employed. Both sides moved for summary judgment in the District Court, and no claim is made here that further administrative proceedings are contemplated. It is suggested that the justification for this rule might vary with different circumstances, and that the expertise of the Commissioner is relevant to passing upon the validity of the regulation. This of course is true, but the suggestion overlooks the fact that both sides have approached this case as one purely of congressional intent, and that the Government made no effort to justify the regulation in factual terms.

Second, the regulations in issue we find to be "final agency action" within the meaning of § 10 of the Administrative Procedure Act, 5 U.S.C. § 704, as construed in judicial decisions. * * *

This is also a case in which the impact of the regulations upon the petitioners is sufficiently direct and immediate as to render the issue appropriate for judicial review at this stage. These regulations purport to give an authoritative interpretation of a statutory provision that has a direct effect on the day-to-day business of all prescription drug companies; its promulgation puts petitioners in a dilemma that it was the very purpose of the Declaratory Judgment Act to ameliorate. As the District Court found on the basis of uncontested allegations, "Either they must comply with the every time requirement and incur the costs of changing over their promotional material and labeling or they must follow their present course and risk prosecution." The regulations are clear-cut, and were made effective immediately upon publication; as noted earlier the agency's counsel represented to the District Court that immediate compliance with their terms was expected. If petitioners wish to comply they must change all their labels, advertisements, and promotional materials; they must destroy stocks of printed matter; and they must invest heavily in new printing type and new supplies. The alternative to compliance—continued use of material which they believe in good faith meets the statutory requirements, but which clearly does not meet the regulation of the Commissioner—may be even more costly. That course would risk serious criminal and civil penalties for the unlawful distribution of "misbranded" drugs.

It is relevant at this juncture to recognize that petitioners deal in a sensitive industry, in which public confidence in their drug products is especially important. To require them to challenge these regulations only as a defense to an action brought by the Government might harm them severely and unnecessarily. Where the legal issue presented is fit for judicial resolution, and where a regulation requires an immediate and significant change in the plaintiffs' conduct of their affairs with serious penalties attached to noncompliance, access to the courts under the Administrative Procedure Act and the Declaratory Judgment Act must be permitted, absent a statutory bar or some other unusual circumstance, neither of which appears here. * * *

[The Court also upheld pre-enforcement review of an administrative regulation in the companion cases of Gardner v. Toilet Goods Ass'n, 387 U.S. 167 (1967), but reached a different conclusion as to ripeness in Toilet Goods Ass'n, Inc. v. Gardner, 387 U.S. 158 (1967), discussed p. 277, *infra*.*

■ [MR. JUSTICE FORTAS, joined by CHIEF JUSTICE WARREN and JUSTICE CLARK, concurred in the judgment in Toilet Goods Ass'n v. Gardner, but dissented from the decisions finding the controversies in Abbott Laboratories and Gardner v. Toilet Goods Ass'n ripe for review.]

* * * Those challenging the regulations have a remedy and there are no special reasons to relieve them of the necessity of deferring their challenge to the regulations until enforcement is undertaken. In this way, and only in this way, will the administrative process have an opportunity to function—to iron out differences, to accommodate special problems, to grant exemptions, etc. The courts do not and should not pass on these complex problems in the abstract and the general—because these regulations peculiarly depend for their quality and substance upon the facts of particular situations. We should confine ourselves—as our jurisprudence dictates—to actual, specific, particularized cases and controversies, in substance as well as in technical analysis.

---

    *   [Ed.] Justice Brennan did not take part in any of the three cases. Justice Douglas dissented in Toilet Goods Association v. Gardner.

PRELIMINARY NOTE ON "RIPENESS"

(1) The Nature of Ripeness. Why did the Court hold that the plaintiffs in United Public Workers v. Mitchell (except for Poole) had failed to present a justiciable controversy? The Court refers to the impermissibility of advisory opinions, but would a decision on the merits have been "advisory"? The rights of the parties would have been determined, and the judgment would have had res judicata effect in any subsequent litigation between them.

Was the problem, then, that there was no threat of "actual interference" by the defendants with any constitutional rights of the plaintiffs? Inquiries into the presence or absence of actual threats are by no means unfamiliar in ripeness cases, but doesn't this focus substantially replicate the standing inquiry?

By contrast, there is a real issue in United Public Workers v. Mitchell about whether the dispute was too "ill-defined" to be appropriate for judicial resolution until further developments had more sharply framed the issues for decision. If ripeness doctrine has a distinctive role or focus, mustn't this be it?

(2) The Abbott Labs Test. Abbott Laboratories is invariably cited as the leading case on the ripeness of challenges to federal administrative regulations, and its two-part test is often applied in cases involving constitutional attacks on state and federal statutes. How do the two parts of its test relate to each other? If a court first determines that "the issues tendered are appropriate for judicial resolution," may it still deem the case unripe if there would be no substantial "hardship to the parties if judicial relief is denied at that stage"?

(a) A companion case to Abbott Laboratories, Toilet Goods Ass'n, Inc. v. Gardner, 387 U.S. 158 (1967), involved a pre-enforcement challenge to a regulation that required manufacturers of color additives to give "free access" to inspectors from the Food and Drug Administration; if access were denied, the regulation authorized the Commissioner to suspend the certification needed for manufacturers to market their products. With Justice Harlan again writing for the majority, the Court concluded that "the legal issue as presently framed" was "not appropriate for judicial resolution." The Court reasoned that "[t]he regulation serves notice only that the Commissioner *may* under certain circumstances order inspection of certain facilities and data, and that further certification of additives *may* be refused to those who decline to permit a duly authorized inspection until they have complied in that regard." In the face of such uncertainty about the circumstances in which the Commissioner would order inspections, the Court concluded that awaiting application of the regulation would place judicial review "on a much surer footing." The Court also found that the regulation would not "be felt immediately by [manufacturers] in conducting their day-to-day affairs" because they were already under a "statutory duty to permit reasonable inspections" and because the only consequence of refusing to admit an inspector was "a suspension of certification services," which the manufacturers could promptly challenge before the agency.

(b) In Lujan v. National Wildlife Federation, 497 U.S. 871 (1990), the Court held that the Interior Department's "land withdrawal review program" was not "agency action" or "final agency action" within the meaning of the APA and thus was not "ripe" for review. A "wholesale" attack on an administrative program, wrote Justice Scalia for the majority, was inappropriate: "Under the terms of the APA, [plaintiff] must direct its attack against some particular 'agency action' that causes it harm. * * * [Absent a statutory provision permitting judicial review of broad regulations or policies], a regulation is not ordinarily considered the type of agency action 'ripe' for judicial review under the APA until the scope of the controversy has been reduced to more manageable proportions, and its factual components fleshed out, by some concrete action applying the regulation to the claimant's situation in a fashion that harms or threatens to harm him. (The major exception, of course [citing Abbott Laboratories, *supra*, and Toilet Goods, *supra*], is a substantive rule which as a practical matter requires the plaintiff to adjust his conduct immediately. Such agency action is 'ripe' for review at once, whether or not explicit statutory review apart from the APA is provided.)"

How would Lujan's standard for determining ripeness deal with a regulation that does not require anything of the party seeking review, or of anyone else, but that causes others to change their conduct toward that party? What of a case in which nothing more will be learned by waiting for the regulation to be applied in a particular case?

(c) A stringent conception of ripeness was also at work in Reno v. Catholic Social Services, Inc., 509 U.S. 43 (1993), which involved disputes under the Immigration Reform and Control Act of 1986—legislation that permitted certain undocumented aliens to apply for and obtain authorization to reside permanently in the United States. In two class actions, undocumented aliens challenged as unduly restrictive certain INS regulations interpreting the Act. In an opinion by Justice Souter, the Court ruled, *sua sponte*, that the challenges were not ripe, stressing that the regulations imposed no penalty upon class members, but merely limited the availability of a benefit. Emphasizing that class members might have their applications for adjustment of status denied because they failed to meet eligibility criteria unrelated to the challenged regulations, the Court ruled that plaintiffs would have a ripe claim only if their application were denied *because* of the challenged regulations. If and when that occurred, plaintiffs could obtain adequate judicial review on appeal of a deportation order, as provided by the Act.

The Court recognized that in some instances applications from aliens had been excluded from the formal review process altogether on grounds of facial ineligibility: In such cases no further judicial review was available under the Act, and some exclusions may have been based on the challenged regulations. The Court ruled that in such circumstances challenges to the regulations would be ripe, but it remanded the case because the record did not reveal whether any class members had been rejected on that basis.

The majority did not suggest that the legal issues relating to the regulations' validity were not appropriate for judicial resolution. Justice Stevens's dissenting opinion, joined by Justices White and Blackmun, argued forcefully that legal uncertainty alone caused considerable hardship to the plaintiffs—a continued need to live in a "shadow" status.[1] Is the Court's differential treatment of regulated parties (who, under Abbott Laboratories, will often and perhaps typically be able to obtain immediate review of regulations) and regulatory beneficiaries (who, under this decision, will frequently be able to obtain review of regulations only after the benefit is denied) justifiable?

(d) Mashaw, *Improving the Environment of Agency Rulemaking: An Essay on Management, Games, and Accountability*, 57 Law & Contemp.Probs. 185, 235–36 (1994), argues that Abbott Labs has made pre-enforcement review of administrative regulations "the norm" in suits by regulated parties. Professor Mashaw believes that such pre-enforcement review (i) creates incentives for the targets of regulation to litigate immediately rather than attempt to develop technologies needed to comply with regulations while maintaining economic viability; (ii) invites "the invocation of a laundry list of potential frailties in a rule's substantive content or procedural regularity," rather than a focused challenge to particular applications; (iii) deprives agencies of an enforcement record on which to defend a rule as applied, confronts courts with increased uncertainties, and thereby increases the likelihood of judicial invalidation; and (iv) as a result, promotes "defensive" rulemaking or avoidance of rulemaking altogether. Mashaw traces these difficulties not only to Abbott Labs, but also to a variety of statutes making specific agencies' rules immediately appealable. He sees the need for a context-sensitive legislative solution, rather than a blanket prohibition of—or even a presumption against—pre-enforcement review.[2]

(e) Is the Abbott Labs approach to ripeness more or less appropriate in constitutional challenges to statutes than in challenges to administrative regulations? In his opinion in the Food, Drug, and Cosmetic Act cases, Justice Fortas suggested that at least some constitutional attacks might be entertained under a less restrictive standard than otherwise applied. He also said: "Where personal status or liberties are involved, the courts may well insist upon a considerable ease of challenging administrative orders or regulations."

---

[1] Justice O'Connor concurred in the judgment, though disagreeing with much of the ripeness analysis.

[2] For further skepticism of Abbott Labs' blessing of pre-enforcement review, see Bagley, *The Puzzling Presumption of Reviewability*, 127 Harv.L.Rev. 1285, 1337–39 (2014). The costs and benefits of anticipatory adjudication are interestingly modeled in Landes & Posner, *The Economics of Anticipatory Adjudication*, 23 J.Leg.Stud. 683 (1994). For general discussions of the issue of ripeness in administrative law, see Jaffe, Judicial Control of Administrative Action 395–417 (1965); 2 Pierce & Hickman, Administrative Law Treatise, Chap. 17 (7th ed. 2024); Vining, *Direct Judicial Review and the Doctrine of Ripeness in Administrative Law*, 69 Mich.L.Rev. 1443 (1971).

(3) Institutional Reform Litigation.

(a)   A different kind of ripeness problem arose in O'Shea v. Littleton, 414 U.S. 488 (1974), where a group of nineteen citizens of Cairo, Illinois alleged a longstanding pattern of discrimination against African-Americans by various government officials, including the city's police commissioner, the state's attorney for Alexander County, and a magistrate (O'Shea) and judge (Spomer) of the county court. In particular, they alleged an effort to deter participation in an economic boycott of city merchants believed to engage in race discrimination. The plaintiffs alleged, *inter alia*, that the magistrate and judge set bond in criminal cases and imposed sentences on a discriminatory basis. The complaint cited examples of unlawful conduct committed against named plaintiffs by the state's attorney and his investigator, but contained only general allegations against the magistrate and judge. The plaintiffs sought to bring the case as a class action and requested injunctive (but no damages) relief.

In a 6–3 decision (in relevant part),[3] the Supreme Court held that there was no Article III case or controversy as to the magistrate and judge. To have standing to seek injunctive relief the plaintiffs had to show that they were likely to sustain a future injury:

"But here the prospect of future injury rests on the likelihood that respondents will again be arrested for and charged with violations of the criminal law and will again be subjected to bond proceedings, trial, or sentencing before petitioners. Important to this assessment is the absence of allegations that any relevant criminal statute of the State of Illinois is unconstitutional on its face or as applied or that respondents have been or will be improperly charged with violating criminal law. If the statutes that might possibly be enforced against respondents are valid laws, and if charges under these statutes are not improvidently made or pressed, the question becomes whether any perceived threat to respondents is sufficiently real and immediate to show an existing controversy simply because they anticipate violating lawful criminal statutes and being tried for their offenses, in which event they may appear before petitioners and, if they do, will be affected by the allegedly illegal conduct charged. Apparently, the proposition is that *if* respondents proceed to violate an unchallenged law and *if* they are charged, held to answer, and tried in any proceedings before petitioners, they will be subjected to the discriminatory practices that petitioners are alleged to have followed. But it seems to us that attempting to anticipate whether and when these respondents will be charged with crime and will be made to appear before either petitioner takes us into the area of speculation and conjecture. * * * We assume that respondents will conduct their activities within the law and so avoid prosecution and conviction as well as exposure to the challenged course of conduct said to be followed by petitioners."

Justice Douglas, joined by Justice Brennan and Justice Marshall, wrote a strongly worded dissent: "What has been alleged here is not only wrongs

---

[3]   In a subsequent portion of the opinion joined by only five Justices (not including Justice Blackmun) the Court also held that "even if were inclined to consider the complaint as presenting an existing case or controversy, we would firmly disagree * * * that an adequate basis for equitable relief against petitioners had been stated."

done to named plaintiffs, but a recurring pattern of wrongs which establishes, if proved, that the legal regime under control of the whites in Cairo, Illinois, is used over and over again to keep the blacks from exercising First Amendment rights, to discriminate against them, to keep from the blacks the protection of the law in their lawful activities, to weight the scales of justice repeatedly on the side of white prejudices and against black protests, fears, and suffering. This is a more pervasive scheme for suppression of blacks and their civil rights than I have ever seen. It may not survive a trial. But if this case does not present a "case or controversy" involving the named plaintiffs, then that concept has been so watered down as to be no longer recognizable. This will please the white superstructure, but it does violence to the conception of evenhanded justice envisioned by the Constitution."

Unlike earlier ripeness cases such as United Public Workers v. Mitchell or Abbott Labs, O'Shea did not challenge any statute or regulation, but rather a pattern of past events (and their implication for the future) formed the basis of the complaint and the prayer for equitable relief. Second, in a case such as O'Shea, in which the matters complained of consist of official practices in law enforcement, it is especially difficult to identify the individuals who are likely to be harmed by those practices in the future. Third, such cases may also involve requests for "structural relief"—for the shaping of a decree designed to modify significantly the way in which an arm of government (or, in some instances, a private institution) conducts its affairs. The Court's evident reluctance to become enmeshed in disputes of this kind, especially when state institutions are at the bar, has been expressed, in part, in terms of justiciability doctrines.[4]

(b) The injunction sought in O'Shea was designed to effectuate a significant change in the practices of a local government. Judicial efforts to reform or restructure governmental institutions seem imperative in at least some instances, but undoubtedly place great if not excessive demands on the practical competence of courts, and sometimes may even prove dysfunctional.[5]

---

[4] For another important example, building on O'Shea, see Los Angeles v. Lyons, 461 U.S. 95 (1983), which held that a Black man who had subjected to an illegal chokehold by the police did not have standing to see equitable relief against such chokeholds in the future (though he could seek damages for his past injury). As in O'Shea, the Court deemed it speculative that the police would improperly arrest Lyons in the future, even though they had done it in the past. Lyons is discussed in more detail pp. 145, 160, *supra*. See also Rizzo v. Goode, 423 U.S. 362 (1976), in which the Supreme Court, partly on grounds of nonjusticiability, set aside a lower court order requiring Philadelphia police authorities to institute comprehensive civilian complaint procedures in accordance with specified guidelines. The order was based on some 19 instances in one year in which the police were found to have violated citizens' constitutional rights. The majority, per Justice Rehnquist, said that the considerations expressed in O'Shea "apply here with even more force, for the individual [plaintiffs'] claim to 'real and immediate' injury rests not upon what the named [defendants] might do to them in the future—such as set a bond on the basis of race—but upon what one of a small, unnamed minority of policemen might do to them in the future because of that unknown policeman's perception of departmental disciplinary procedures."

[5] For analysis of the issues raised by institutional or structural reform litigation, see, *e.g.*, Feeley & Rubin, Judicial Policy Making and the Modern State: How the Courts Reformed America's Prisons (1998); Rosenberg, The Hollow Hope: Can Courts Bring About Social Change? (1991); Sandler & Schoenbrod, Democracy by Decree: What Happens When Courts Run

Is it appropriate for the Supreme Court to employ justiciability doctrines as a means of shielding the federal courts from the hazards of institutional reform litigation? See generally Fallon, *The Linkage Between Justiciability and Remedies—And Their Connections to Substantive Rights*, 92 Va.L.Rev. 633 (2006) (arguing that concerns about "unacceptable" and occasionally "necessary" remedies pervasively influence the formulation and application of justiciability doctrines). Justiciability questions are generally resolved at the outset of litigation. By contrast, framing the central question as involving the law of remedies would allow a balancing of affected public and private interests upon a full record. Why has the Supreme Court rejected this approach? Is it significant that the doctrine of "remedial discretion" makes it difficult for appellate courts to set aside lower courts' remedial decrees and that a Supreme Court that is skeptical of institutional reform litigation—and possibly of the good judgment of lower federal courts—can exercise more effective appellate control through the blunter instrument of justiciability doctrine? See Fallon, *Of Justiciability, Remedies, and Public Law Litigation: Notes on the Jurisprudence of Lyons*, 59 N.Y.U.L.Rev. 1, 39–43 (1984).

(c)   While decisions like O'Shea, and Los Angeles v. Lyons, 461 U.S. 95 (1983), discussed pp. 145, 160, *supra*, make institutional reform litigation harder to bring, they do not make it impossible. Patel, *Jumping Hurdles to Sue the Police*, 104 Minn.L.Rev. 2257 (2020), describes the doctrinal barriers posed by these cases and then shows how some major structural reform lawsuits against the police have successfully navigated those barriers. Focusing especially on Lyons, Professor Patel describes the Court's Article III doctrine as posing "three barriers to structural reform injunctions: the repeated harm, speculative harm, and innocence barriers." The first two barriers are evident in the Court's treatment of the relationship between past police misconduct and the likelihood of future misconduct, which work together to "block[ ] many prospective police abuse cases for lack of a case or controversy." The "innocence barrier" is evident in the Court's assumptions that the arrest, bond, and sentencing practices challenged in Lyons and O'Shea would only be imposed on those who violated valid laws. "Subsequent courts have interpreted this reasoning as requiring plaintiffs to be blameless in provoking officers in order to have standing to enforce injunctions against police."

That being said, Patel provides detailed discussion of several structural reform lawsuits that have successfully navigated these barriers. For example, in Floyd v. City of New York, a challenge to the New York City

---

Government (2003); Chayes, *Foreword: Public Law Litigation and the Burger Court*, 96 Harv.L.Rev. 4 (1982); Eisenberg & Yeazell, *The Ordinary and the Extraordinary in Institutional Litigation*, 93 Harv.L.Rev. 465 (1980); Fletcher, *The Discretionary Constitution: Institutional Remedies and Judicial Legitimacy*, 91 Yale L.J. 635 (1982); Friedman, *When Rights Encounter Reality: Enforcing Federal Remedies*, 65 S.Calif.L.Rev. 735 (1992); Jeffries & Rutherglen, *Structural Reform Revisited*, 95 S.Calif.L.Rev. 1387 (2007); Mishkin, *Federal Courts as State Reformers*, 35 Wash. & Lee L.Rev. 949 (1978); Nagel, *Separation of Powers and the Scope of Federal Equitable Remedies*, 30 Stan.L.Rev. 661 (1978); Sabel & Simon, *Destabilization Rights: How Public Law Litigation Succeeds*, 117 Harv.L.Rev. 1015, 1019 (2004); Schlanger, *Civil Rights Injunctions Over Time: A Case Study of Jail and Prison Court Orders*, 81 N.Y.U.L.Rev. 550 (2006).

Police Department's "stop and frisk" policy, the plaintiffs provided evidence of millions of police stops, "of which at least 60,000 were unconstitutional (thirty facially unconstitutional stops a day)." They also offered a plaintiff who provided evidence that he had repeatedly been stopped while engaged in innocent conduct, rather than violating the law. This kind of evidence, Patel argues, overcame the barriers described above.

In light of this experience, how might the plaintiffs in O'Shea and Lyons have redrawn their complaints to give them the best possible chance for surviving a motion to dismiss for lack of standing and lack of ripeness?

(d)   In both O'Shea and Lyons, in addition to the Court's holdings about Article III justiciability, the decisions made separate determinations that principles of "equity" precluded awarding relief. In O'Shea, the Court wrote that the justiciability problems "obviously shade into those determining whether the complaint states a sound basis for equitable relief; and even if we were inclined to consider the complaint as presenting an existing case or controversy, we would firmly disagree with the Court of Appeals that an adequate basis for equitable relief against petitioners had been stated." The Court pointed to federalism concerns and the longstanding presumption against enjoining criminal prosecutions, both of which were reflected in Younger v. Harris, 401 U.S. 37 (1971) and other precedents discussed in Chapter X, *infra*. It also expressed a broader concern that the injunction sought would be "intrusive and unworkable" because it would require extensive federal supervision of state institutions.

In Lyons, the Court also held that even "if it be assumed that [Lyons's] pending damages suit affords him Article III standing to seek an injunction," his claim failed to satisfy "the preconditions for equitable relief." In analysis similar to O'Shea, which it cited, the Court expressed concerns about the federalism, comity, the availability of alternative remedies, and the speculativeness of Lyons's future injury.

The nature and source of equitable discretion in federal courts is a rich and complicated question, discussed in Chapter VI, sec. 3(b), *infra*, and Chapter IX, sec. 2, 5, *infra*, among other places. How does it relate to the doctrine of justiciability and their underlying values? Does it provide an independent basis for limiting the role of the federal judiciary, over and above doctrines of standing, mootness, and ripeness, and so on? Or should it instead be incorporated into standing doctrine, perhaps through the "redressability" prong of the modern standing test? See "The Relationship Between Standing and Remedies," pp. 160–162, *supra*.

Susan B. Anthony List v. Driehaus

573 U.S. 149 (2014).
Certiorari to the United States Court of Appeals for the Sixth Circuit.

■ JUSTICE THOMAS delivered the opinion of the Court.

[The petitioners were two advocacy groups that challenged the constitutionality of an Ohio statute that made it a crime for any person to "[m]ake a false statement concerning the voting record of a candidate or public official," or to "[p]ost, publish, circulate, distribute, or otherwise disseminate a false statement concerning a candidate, either knowing the same to be false or with reckless disregard of whether it was false or not" "during the course of any campaign for nomination or election to public office or office of a political party." Any private person could file a complaint requiring a probable cause hearing before the Ohio Elections Commission.

Susan B. Anthony List (SBA), a pro-life organization, had criticized members of Congress who voted for the Affordable Care Act as supporting "taxpayer-funded abortion." Driehaus, one of the subjects of the criticism, had filed a complaint, but then withdrew it after losing re-election in 2010. A second group, Coalition Opposed to Additional Spending and Taxes (COAST), alleged that it intended to make a similar statement criticizing Driehaus, but refrained from doing so because of the proceedings against SBA.

Both groups alleged that they wish to make similar statements in the future, and sought declaratory and injunctive relief against the enforcement of Ohio's law. The district court dismissed the case for lack of standing and lack of ripeness, and the Sixth Circuit affirmed on ripeness grounds.]

III

A

Article III of the Constitution limits the jurisdiction of federal courts to "Cases" and "Controversies." U.S. Const., Art. III, § 2. The doctrine of standing gives meaning to these constitutional limits by "identify[ing] those disputes which are appropriately resolved through the judicial process."[5] Lujan v. Defenders of Wildlife, 504 U.S. 555, 560 (1992). * * * To establish Article III standing, a plaintiff must show (1) an "injury in fact," (2) a sufficient "causal connection between the injury and the conduct complained of," and (3) a "likel[ihood]" that the injury "will be redressed by a favorable decision." Lujan, *supra*, at 560–561 (internal quotation marks omitted).

This case concerns the injury-in-fact requirement, which helps to ensure that the plaintiff has a "personal stake in the outcome of the controversy." Warth v. Seldin, 422 U.S. 490, 498 (1975). An injury sufficient to satisfy Article III must be "concrete and particularized" and "actual or imminent, not 'conjectural' or 'hypothetical.'" Lujan, *supra*, at 560. An allegation of future injury may suffice if the threatened injury is "certainly impending," or there is a "'substantial risk' that the harm will

---

[5] The doctrines of standing and ripeness "originate" from the same Article III limitation. DaimlerChrysler Corp. v. Cuno, 547 U.S. 332, 335 (2006). As the parties acknowledge, the Article III standing and ripeness issues in this case "boil down to the same question." MedImmune, Inc. v. Genentech, Inc., 549 U.S. 118, 128, n.8 (2007). Consistent with our practice in cases like Virginia v. American Booksellers Assn., Inc., 484 U.S. 383, 392 (1988), and Babbitt v. Farm Workers, 442 U.S. 289, 299, n.11 (1979), we use the term "standing" in this opinion.

occur." Clapper [v. Amnesty Int'l USA], 568 U.S. [398, 414], n.5 [(2013)].
* * *

B

One recurring issue in our cases is determining when the threatened enforcement of a law creates an Article III injury. When an individual is subject to such a threat, an actual arrest, prosecution, or other enforcement action is not a prerequisite to challenging the law. See Steffel v. Thompson, 415 U.S. 452, 459 (1974) ("[I]t is not necessary that petitioner first expose himself to actual arrest or prosecution to be entitled to challenge a statute that he claims deters the exercise of his constitutional rights"); see also MedImmune, Inc. v. Genentech, Inc., 549 U.S. 118, 128–129 (2007) ("[W]here threatened action by government is concerned, we do not require a plaintiff to expose himself to liability before bringing suit to challenge the basis for the threat"). Instead, we have permitted pre-enforcement review under circumstances that render the threatened enforcement sufficiently imminent. Specifically, we have held that a plaintiff satisfies the injury-in-fact requirement where he alleges "an intention to engage in a course of conduct arguably affected with a constitutional interest, but proscribed by a statute, and there exists a credible threat of prosecution thereunder." Babbitt v. Farm Workers, 442 U.S. 289, 298 (1979). * * *

IV

Here, SBA and COAST contend that the threat of enforcement of the false statement statute amounts to an Article III injury in fact. We agree: Petitioners have alleged a credible threat of enforcement.

A

First, petitioners have alleged "an intention to engage in a course of conduct arguably affected with a constitutional interest." *Ibid.* Both petitioners have pleaded specific statements they intend to make in future election cycles. SBA has already stated that representatives who voted for the ACA supported "taxpayer-funded abortion," and it has alleged an "inten[t] to engage in substantially similar activity in the future." COAST has alleged that it previously intended to disseminate materials criticizing a vote for the ACA as a vote "to fund abortions with tax dollars," and that it "desires to make the same or similar statements about other federal candidates who voted for [the ACA]." Because petitioners' intended future conduct concerns political speech, it is certainly "affected with a constitutional interest." Babbitt, *supra*, at 298.

B

Next, petitioners' intended future conduct is "arguably . . . proscribed by [the] statute" they wish to challenge. Babbitt, *supra*, at 298. The Ohio false statement law sweeps broadly, and covers the subject matter of petitioners' intended speech. * * * And, a Commission panel here already found probable cause to believe that SBA violated the statute when it stated that Driehaus had supported "taxpayer-funded abortion"—the same sort of statement petitioners plan to disseminate in the future. Under these circumstances, we have no difficulty concluding that petitioners' intended speech is "arguably proscribed" by the law. * * *

Respondents, echoing the Sixth Circuit, contend that SBA's fears of enforcement are misplaced because SBA has not said it "plans to lie or recklessly disregard the veracity of its speech." [Brief for Respondents] 15. The Sixth Circuit reasoned that because SBA "can only be liable for making a statement 'knowing' it is false," SBA's insistence that its speech is factually true "makes the possibility of prosecution for uttering such statements exceedingly slim."

The Sixth Circuit misses the point. SBA's insistence that the allegations in its press release were true did not prevent the Commission panel from finding probable cause to believe that SBA had violated the law the first time around. And, there is every reason to think that similar speech in the future will result in similar proceedings, notwithstanding SBA's belief in the truth of its allegations. Nothing in this Court's decisions requires a plaintiff who wishes to challenge the constitutionality of a law to confess that he will in fact violate that law.

C

Finally, the threat of future enforcement of the false statement statute is substantial. Most obviously, there is a history of past enforcement here: SBA was the subject of a complaint in a recent election cycle. We have observed that past enforcement against the same conduct is good evidence that the threat of enforcement is not "chimerical." Steffel, 415 U.S., at 459. Here, the threat is even more substantial given that the Commission panel actually found probable cause to believe that SBA's speech violated the false statement statute. * * *

The credibility of that threat is bolstered by the fact that authority to file a complaint with the Commission is not limited to a prosecutor or an agency. Instead, the false statement statute allows "any person" with knowledge of the purported violation to file a complaint. Because the universe of potential complainants is not restricted to state officials who are constrained by explicit guidelines or ethical obligations, there is a real risk of complaints from, for example, political opponents. And petitioners, who intend to criticize candidates for political office, are easy targets.

Finally, Commission proceedings are not a rare occurrence. Petitioners inform us that the Commission "handles about 20 to 80 false statement complaints per year," and respondents do not deny that the Commission frequently fields complaints alleging violations of the false statement statute. Moreover, respondents have not disavowed enforcement if petitioners make similar statements in the future. * * * On these facts, the prospect of future enforcement is far from "imaginary or speculative." Babbitt, *supra*, at 298. * * *

That conclusion holds true as to both SBA and COAST. Respondents, relying on Younger v. Harris, 401 U.S. 37 (1971), appear to suggest that COAST lacks standing because it refrained from actually disseminating its planned speech in order to avoid Commission proceedings of its own. In Younger, the plaintiff had been indicted for distributing leaflets in violation of the California Criminal Syndicalism Act. When he challenged the constitutionality of the law in federal court, several other plaintiffs intervened, arguing that their own speech was inhibited by Harris' prosecution. The Court concluded that only the plaintiff had standing because the intervenors "d[id] not claim that they ha[d] ever been threatened with prosecution, that a prosecution [wa]s likely, or even that a prosecution [wa]s remotely possible." 401 U.S., at 42.

That is not this case. Unlike the intervenors in Younger, COAST has alleged an intent to engage in the same speech that was the subject of a prior enforcement proceeding. Also unlike the intervenors in Younger, who had never been threatened with prosecution, COAST has been the subject of Commission proceedings in the past. See, *e.g.*, COAST Candidates PAC v. Ohio Elections Comm'n, 543 Fed.Appx. 490 (CA6 2013). COAST is far more akin to the plaintiff in Steffel, who was not arrested alongside his handbilling companion but was nevertheless threatened with prosecution for similar speech. 415 U.S., at 459.

In sum, we find that both SBA and COAST have alleged a credible threat of enforcement.

V

In concluding that petitioners' claims were not justiciable, the Sixth Circuit separately considered two other factors: whether the factual record was sufficiently developed, and whether hardship to the parties would result if judicial relief is denied at this stage in the proceedings. 525 Fed.Appx., at 419. Respondents contend that these "prudential ripeness" factors confirm that the claims at issue are nonjusticiable. But we have already concluded that petitioners have alleged a sufficient Article III injury. To the extent respondents would have us deem petitioners' claims nonjusticiable "on grounds that are 'prudential,' rather than constitutional," "[t]hat request is in some tension with our recent reaffirmation of the principle that a federal court's obligation to hear and decide' cases within its jurisdiction is virtually unflagging." Lexmark Int'l, Inc. v. Static Control Components, Inc., 572 U.S. 118, 126 (2014).

In any event, we need not resolve the continuing vitality of the prudential ripeness doctrine in this case because the "fitness" and "hardship" factors are easily satisfied here. First, petitioners' challenge to the Ohio false statement statute presents an issue that is "purely legal, and will not be clarified by further factual development." Thomas v. Union Carbide Agricultural Products Co., 473 U.S. 568, 581 (1985). And denying prompt judicial review would impose a substantial hardship on petitioners, forcing them to choose between refraining from core political speech on the one hand, or engaging in that speech and risking costly Commission proceedings and criminal prosecution on the other.

* * *

Petitioners in this case have demonstrated an injury in fact sufficient for Article III standing. We accordingly reverse the judgment of the United States Court of Appeals for the Sixth Circuit and remand the case for further proceedings consistent with this opinion, including a determination whether the remaining Article III standing requirements are met.

It is so ordered.

NOTE ON THE NATURE OF "RIPENESS" AFTER SBA LIST

(1) The Validity of Prudential Ripeness. Relying on Lexmark v. Static Control Components, discussed at p. 207, *supra*, SBA List expressed some skepticism about "the continuing vitality of the prudential ripeness doctrine." Is there any good response to that skepticism? Once a Court has concluded that a plaintiff faces an imminent threat of harm that would be redressed by the remedy he seeks—*i.e.*, has standing—what justification could there be for withholding relief because judicial review would be difficult or because of inadequate hardship to the parties?

On the other hand, does the possibility of the continuing vitality of third-party standing doctrine, suggest that Lexmark cannot be read for all it is worth? If third-party standing doctrine might survive Lexmark, why not prudential ripeness?

(2) Ripeness or Standing?

(a) Consider again Professor Monaghan's discussion of "standing set in a time frame," Monaghan, *Constitutional Adjudication: The Who and When*, 82 Yale L.J. 1363, 1384 (1973), discussed above in connection with mootness, at p. 249, *supra*. While the Court has rejected the equation of *mootness* and standing, the decision in SBA List seems to embrace the equation of *ripeness* and standing. Why would ripeness be equated to standing when mootness is not so viewed? Other than (perhaps) the "prudential ripeness" factors, can every ripeness case be rewritten as a standing case, and every standing case be rewritten as a ripeness case?

(b) Trump v. New York, 592 U.S. 125 (2020), also discussed at p. 147 *supra*, held that a challenge to a presidential memorandum directing the Secretary of Commerce to take steps facilitating the President's intended exclusion of undocumented immigrants from the population count used to apportion congressional representation and disburse certain federal funds was not justiciable. There were too many contingencies, the Court reasoned in a per curiam opinion, involving how many undocumented immigrants the Secretary might identify and the President might exclude, as well as what adverse effects the plaintiff states might suffer. The Court characterized its conclusion in both standing and ripeness terms simultaneously: "At the end of the day, the standing and ripeness inquiries both lead to the conclusion that judicial resolution of this dispute is premature." Justice Breyer, joined by Justices Sotomayor and Kagan, dissented with respect to justiciability and would have ruled that relevant statutes required the counting of all persons without regard to immigration status. President Trump's term expired before the Commerce Department produced the data required to implement the exclusion policy, and President Biden issued an executive order revoking the memorandum in January 2021. See Exec. Order No. 13986, 86 Fed.Reg. 7015 (Jan. 20, 2021).

(3) Ripeness and Uncertainty. By framing the issue as one of standing, the Court in SBA List had to address a question of uncertain future harm. Quoting Clapper v. Amnesty International, 568 U.S. 398 (2013), the Court stated that: "An allegation of future injury may suffice if the threatened injury is 'certainly impending,' or there is a " 'substantial risk" that the harm will occur.' " And applying this test to the specific problem of pre-enforcement review—an injunction seeking to prevent the enforcement of a disputed law—the Court wrote: "we have permitted pre-enforcement review under circumstances that render the threatened enforcement sufficiently imminent."

Does the Court's resolution of this issue shed light on the general issue of standing for uncertain future injuries, which is discussed above at pp. 145–149, *infra*, and is its resolution consistent with the other cases discussed there? Aside from standing, the availability of pre-enforcement review against the government presents distinct doctrinal issues which are discussed in Chapter IX, *infra*.

(4) Ripeness and the Merits. Finally, consider the way disputes about ripeness overlap with disputes about the scope of the underlying substantive rights at issue.

(a) First Amendment Overbreadth Challenges. Adler v. Board of Education, 342 U.S. 485 (1952), was a state court action challenging New York statutes that required the dismissal of public school teachers who advocated the "doctrine that any government in the United States should be overthrown or overturned by force or violence" or who belonged to any organization so advocating. After the issuance of implementing rules, but before any enforcement actions or even the publication of a list of organizations deemed subversive, the plaintiffs sued to enjoin enforcement. The New York Court of Appeals rejected the suit, and the Supreme Court affirmed.

Justice Minton, for the Court, held that the statute and the rules did not deprive teachers of any constitutional right. Justice Douglas, joined by Justice Black, dissented on the merits. Justice Frankfurter alone perceived a ripeness problem: "The allegations in the present action fall short of those found insufficient in the Mitchell case. These teachers do not allege that they have engaged in proscribed conduct or that they have any intention to do so. * * * They do not assert that they are threatened with action under the law, or that steps are imminent whereby they would incur the hazard of punishment for conduct innocent at the time, or under standards too vague to satisfy due process of law. * * * Since we rightly refused in the Mitchell case to hear government employees whose conduct was much more intimately affected by the law there attacked than are the claims of plaintiffs here, this suit is wanting in the necessary basis for our review."

Consider the discussion of Adler in Scharpf, *Judicial Review and the Political Question: A Functional Analysis*, 75 Yale L.J. 517, 532 (1966): "For [Justice Minton, writing for the majority], the statute was clearly constitutional because it in no way deprived teachers of their freedoms of speech and association—it merely put before them the choice of either exercising these freedoms or continuing their employment in the public school system which, after all, was not a right but merely a privilege. * * * For [Justices Black and Douglas, dissenting,] the statute was clearly unconstitutional because it penalized teachers for the exercise of their 'absolute' freedoms of speech and association. The conclusion seems inevitable that Justice Frankfurter alone advocated avoidance because he alone defined the substantive issues in terms of a close balance between the equally legitimate interests of society in its self-preservation and of the teachers in their freedom of thought, inquiry and expression. Thus, in order to strike this balance in the particular case, Frankfurter would have had to know much more about the actual practices of enforcement and the degree of surveillance to which the teachers would be subjected than the bare text of an unenforced statute permitted him to know."

How much is the Supreme Court's very different approach to the justiciability of the claims in SBA List explained by its different substantive view about the likely unconstitutionality and overbreadth of the statute under the First Amendment?

(b) Takings Claims. In Williamson Cty. Regional Planning Comm'n v. Hamilton Bank of Johnson City, 473 U.S. 172 (1985), the Supreme Court held that a Fifth Amendment takings claim challenging various zoning regulations, was not ripe because the plaintiff had failed to institute an inverse condemnation action under state law and had not applied for potentially available variances. That decision could be viewed as a holding, on the merits, that no taking should be imputed to the defendant until these steps had been taken. See Nichol, *Ripeness and the Constitution*, 54 U.Chi.L.Rev. 153, 167 (1987) (stating that "the takings clause demands a showing by the challenger that the regulating authority has foreclosed all economically viable options").[1]

The effect of Williamson's first holding, that a just compensation claim is not ripe until a claimant has sought compensation through available state procedures, was to require much takings litigation to take place in state court rather than federal court. Moreover, additional decisions such as San Remo Hotel, L.P. v. City and County of San Francisco, 545 U.S. 323 (2005), frequently made it impossible to return to federal court after the state court litigation, because of preclusion principles.

---

[1]   See also Yee v. City of Escondido, 503 U.S. 519 (1992); Pennell v. City of San Jose, 485 U.S. 1 (1988).

In Knick v. Township of Scott, 588 U.S. 180 (2019), the Court, 5–4, overruled Williamson County's first holding as based on a substantive misinterpretation of the Takings Clause. Under a proper interpretation, the Court ruled in an opinion by Chief Justice Roberts, a property owner suffers a constitutional violation as soon as "the government takes his property without just compensation, and therefore may bring his claim in federal court under § 1983 at that time." The requirement that the plaintiff pursue compensation in state court first constituted an impermissible requirement to exhaust state remedies that is incompatible with § 1983, the Chief Justice reasoned. The Court did not question Williamson County's alternative holding that a takings claim is not ripe if a property owner could still pursue opportunities for administrative relief (such as seeking a variance from a zoning ordinance).[2]

Dissenting, Justice Kagan defended the aspect of Williamson County that the Court overruled as "rooted in" a correct "understanding of the Fifth Amendment's Takings Clause stretching back to the late 1800s." Like the Chief Justice, Justice Kagan appeared to view Williamson County's reference to ripeness as inseparable from its conclusions about the scope of the Taking Clause's substantive guarantee.

6. POLITICAL QUESTIONS

Among the most controversial elements of justiciability, the political question doctrine comes into play only in a case that otherwise has a proper plaintiff with a live claim. Despite the presence of all of the other elements of an Article III case or controversy, the Court forbears on the ground that something about the subject matter of the case makes it inappropriate for judicial resolution. Sometimes, this conclusion entails a determination that the constitutional text, read in context, assigns resolution of the controversy to a branch of government other than the federal judiciary. Other times, the determination of a political question touches on pragmatic or prudential questions about the appropriateness of judicial intervention. Which factors predominate in the case that follows?

---

[2]   In Pakdel v. City and County of San Francisco, 594 U.S. 474 (2021), the Court unanimously clarified that this remaining requirement did *not* require a property to owner to "compl[y] with administrative processes in obtaining [the government's] decision." For instance, in that case the property owners had not applied for an exemption in a timely fashion and so the agency could no longer consider granting it. All that was required was clarity that the government was not going to change its mind, so their claim was ripe.

Nixon v. United States

506 U.S. 224 (1993).

Certiorari to the United States Court of Appeals for the District of Columbia Circuit.

■ CHIEF JUSTICE REHNQUIST delivered the opinion of the Court.

Petitioner Walter L. Nixon, Jr., asks this court to decide whether Senate Rule XI, which allows a committee of Senators to hear evidence against an individual who has been impeached and to report that evidence to the full Senate, violates the Impeachment Trial Clause, Art. I, § 3, cl. 6. That Clause provides that the "Senate shall have the sole Power to try all Impeachments." But before we reach the merits of such a claim, we must decide whether it is "justiciable," that is, whether it is a claim that may be resolved by the courts. We conclude that it is not.

Nixon, a former Chief Judge of the United States District Court for the Southern District of Mississippi, was convicted by a jury of two counts of making false statements before a federal grand jury and sentenced to prison. The grand jury investigation stemmed from reports that Nixon had accepted a gratuity from a Mississippi businessman in exchange for asking a local district attorney to halt the prosecution of the businessman's son. Because Nixon refused to resign from his office as a United States District Judge, he continued to collect his judicial salary while serving out his prison sentence.

On May 10, 1989, the House of Representatives adopted three articles of impeachment for high crimes and misdemeanors. The first two articles charged Nixon with giving false testimony before the grand jury and the third article charged him with bringing disrepute on the Federal Judiciary.

After the House presented the articles to the Senate, the Senate voted to invoke its own Impeachment Rule XI, under which the presiding officer appoints a committee of Senators to "receive evidence and take testimony." The Senate committee held four days of hearings, during which 10 witnesses, including Nixon, testified. Pursuant to Rule XI, the committee presented the full Senate with a complete transcript of the proceeding and a report stating the uncontested facts and summarizing the evidence on the contested facts. Nixon and the House impeachment managers submitted extensive final briefs to the full Senate and delivered arguments from the Senate floor during the three hours set aside for oral argument in front of that body. Nixon himself gave a personal appeal, and several Senators posed questions directly to both parties. The Senate voted by more than the constitutionally required two-thirds majority to convict Nixon on the first two articles. The presiding officer then entered judgment removing Nixon from his office as United States District Judge.

Nixon thereafter commenced the present suit, arguing that Senate Rule XI violates the constitutional grant of authority to the Senate to "try" all impeachments because it prohibits the whole Senate from taking part in the evidentiary hearings. See Art. I, § 3, cl. 6. Nixon sought a declaratory judgment that his impeachment conviction was void and that his judicial salary and privileges should be reinstated. The District Court held that his claim was nonjusticiable, and the Court of Appeals for the District of Columbia Circuit agreed.

A controversy is nonjusticiable—*i.e.*, involves a political question—where there is "a textually demonstrable constitutional commitment of the issue to a coordinate political department; or a lack of judicially discoverable and manageable standards for resolving it. . . ." Baker v. Carr, 369 U.S. 186, 217 (1962). But the Courts must, in the first instance, interpret the text in question and determine whether and to what extent the issue is textually committed. See *ibid*; Powell v. McCormack, 395 U.S. 486 (1969). As the discussion that follows makes clear, the concept of a textual commitment to a coordinate political department is not completely separate from the concept of a lack of judicially discoverable and manageable standards for resolving it; the lack of judicially manageable standards may strengthen the conclusion that there is a textually demonstrable commitment to a coordinate branch.

In this case, we must examine Art. I, § 3, cl. 6, to determine the scope of authority conferred upon the Senate by the Framers regarding impeachment. It provides:

> "The Senate shall have the sole Power to try all Impeachments. When sitting for the Purpose, they shall be on Oath or Affirmation. When the President of the United States is tried, the Chief Justice shall preside: And no Person shall be convicted without the Concurrence of two thirds of the Members present."

The language and structure of this Clause are revealing. The first sentence is a grant of authority to the Senate, and the word "sole" indicates that this authority is reposed in the Senate and nowhere else. The next two sentences specify requirements to which the Senate proceedings shall conform: the Senate shall be on oath or affirmation, a two-thirds vote is required to convict, and when the President is tried the Chief Justice shall preside.

Petitioner argues that the word "try" in the first sentence imposes by implication an additional requirement on the Senate in that the proceedings must be in the nature of a judicial trial. From there petitioner goes on to argue that this limitation precludes the Senate from delegating to a select committee the task of hearing the testimony of witnesses, as was done pursuant to Senate Rule XI. " '[T]ry' means more than simply 'vote on' or 'review' or 'judge.' In 1787 and today, trying a case means hearing the evidence, not scanning a cold record." Petitioner concludes from this that courts may review whether or not the Senate "tried" him before convicting him.

There are several difficulties with this position which lead us ultimately to reject it. The word "try," both in 1787 and later, has considerably broader meanings than those to which petitioner would limit it. Older dictionaries define try as "[t]o examine" or "[t]o examine as a judge." See 2 S. Johnson, A Dictionary of the English Language (1785). In more modern usages the term has various meanings. For example, try can mean "to examine or investigate judicially," "to conduct the trial of," or "to put to the test by experiment, investigation, or trial." Webster's Third New International Dictionary 2457 (1971). Petitioner submits that "try," as contained in T. Sheridan, Dictionary of the English Language (1796), means "to examine as a judge; to bring before a judicial tribunal." Based on the variety of definitions, however, we cannot say that the Framers used the word "try" as an implied limitation on the method by which the Senate might proceed in trying impeachments. "As a rule the Constitution speaks in general terms, leaving Congress to deal with subsidiary matters of detail as the public interests and changing conditions may require . . . ." Dillon v. Gloss, 256 U.S. 368, 376 (1921).

The conclusion that the use of the word "try" in the first sentence of the Impeachment Trial Clause lacks sufficient precision to afford any judicially manageable standard of review of the Senate's actions is fortified by the existence of the three very specific requirements that the Constitution does impose on the Senate when trying impeachments: the members must be under oath, a two-thirds vote is required to convict, and the Chief Justice presides when the President is tried. These limitations are quite precise, and their nature suggests that the Framers did not intend to impose additional limitations on the form of the Senate proceedings by the use of the word "try" in the first sentence.

Petitioner devotes only two pages in his brief to negating the significance of the word "sole" in the first sentence of Clause 6. As noted above, that sentence provides that "[t]he Senate shall have the sole Power to try all Impeachments." We think that the word "sole" is of considerable significance. Indeed, the word "sole" appears only one other time in the Constitution—with respect to the House of Representatives' "*sole* Power of Impeachment." Art. I, § 2, cl. 5 (emphasis added). The common sense meaning of the word "sole" is that the Senate alone shall have authority to determine whether an individual should be acquitted or convicted. The dictionary definition bears this out. "Sole" is defined as "having no companion," "solitary," "being the only one," and "functioning . . . independently and without assistance or interference." Webster's Third New International Dictionary 2168 (1971). If the courts may review the actions of the Senate in order to determine whether that body "tried" an impeached official, it is difficult to see how the Senate would be "functioning . . . independently and without assistance or interference." * * *

The history and contemporary understanding of the impeachment provisions support our reading of the constitutional language. The parties do not offer evidence of a single word in the history of the Constitutional Convention or in contemporary commentary that even alludes to the possibility of judicial review in the context of the impeachment powers. This silence is quite meaningful in light of the several explicit references to the availability of judicial review as a check on the Legislature's power with respect to bills of attainder, *ex post facto* laws, and statutes. See The Federalist No. 78, p. 524 (J. Cooke ed. 1961) ("Limitations . . . can be preserved in practice no other way than through the medium of the courts of justice.").

The Framers labored over the question of where the impeachment power should lie. Significantly, in at least two considered scenarios the power was placed with the Federal Judiciary. Indeed, Madison and the Committee of Detail proposed that the Supreme Court should have the power to determine impeachments. Despite these proposals, the Convention ultimately decided that the Senate would have "the sole Power to Try all Impeachments." Art. I § 3, cl. 6. According to Alexander Hamilton, the Senate was the "most fit depository of this important trust" because its members are representatives of the people. See The Federalist No. 65, p. 440 (J. Cooke ed. 1961). The Supreme Court was not the proper body because the Framers "doubted whether the members of that tribunal would, at all times, be endowed with so eminent a portion of fortitude as would be called for in the execution of so difficult a task" or whether the Court "would possess the degree of credit and authority" to carry out its judgment if it conflicted with the accusation brought by the Legislature—the people's representative. See *id.*, at 441. In addition, the Framers believed the Court was too small in number: "The awful discretion, which a court of impeachments must necessarily have, to doom to honor or to infamy the most confidential and the most distinguished characters of the community, forbids the commitment of the trust to a small number of persons." *Id.*, at 441–442.

There are two additional reasons why the Judiciary, and the Supreme Court in particular, were not chosen to have any role in impeachments. First, the Framers recognized that most likely there would be two sets of proceedings for individuals who commit impeachable offenses—the impeachment trial and a separate criminal trial. In fact, the Constitution explicitly provides for two separate proceedings. See Art. I, § 3, cl. 7. The Framers deliberately separated the two forums to avoid raising the specter of bias and to ensure independent judgments:

> "Would it be proper that the persons, who had disposed of his fame and his most valuable rights as a citizen in one trial, should in another trial, for the same offence, be also the disposers of his life and his fortune? Would there not be the greatest reason to apprehend, that error in the first sentence would be the parent of error in the second sentence? That the strong bias of one decision would be apt to overrule the influence of any new lights, which might be brought to vary the

complexion of another decision?" The Federalist No. 65, p. 442
(J. Cooke ed. 1961).

Certainly judicial review of the Senate's "trial" would introduce the same
risk of bias as would participation in the trial itself.

Second, judicial review would be inconsistent with the Framers'
insistence that our system be one of checks and balances. In our
constitutional system, impeachment was designed to be the *only* check
on the Judicial Branch by the Legislature. * * * Judicial involvement in
impeachment proceedings, even if only for purposes of judicial review, is
counterintuitive because it would eviscerate the "important
constitutional check" placed on the Judiciary by the Framers. See *id.*, No.
81, p. 545. Nixon's argument would place final reviewing authority with
respect to impeachments in the hands of the same body that the
impeachment process is meant to regulate.

Nevertheless, Nixon argues that judicial review is necessary in order
to place a check on the Legislature. Nixon fears that if the Senate is given
unreviewable authority to interpret the Impeachment Trial Clause, there
is a grave risk that the Senate will usurp judicial power. The Framers
anticipated this objection and created two constitutional safeguards to
keep the Senate in check. The first safeguard is that the whole of the
impeachment power is divided between the two legislative bodies, with
the House given the right to accuse and the Senate given the right to
judge. *Id.*, No. 66, p. 446. This split of authority "avoids the inconvenience
of making the same persons both accusers and judges; and guards
against the danger of persecution from the prevalency of a factious spirit
in either of those branches." The second safeguard is the two-thirds
supermajority vote requirement. Hamilton explained that "[a]s the
concurrence of two-thirds of the senate will be requisite to a
condemnation, the security to innocence, from this additional
circumstance, will be as complete as itself can desire." *Ibid.*

In addition to the textual commitment argument, we are persuaded
that the lack of finality and the difficulty of fashioning relief counsel
against justiciability. See Baker v. Carr, 369 U.S., at 210. We agree with
the Court of Appeals that opening the door of judicial review to the
procedures used by the Senate in trying impeachments would "expose the
political life of the country to months, or perhaps years, of chaos." This
lack of finality would manifest itself most dramatically if the President
were impeached. The legitimacy of any successor, and hence his
effectiveness, would be impaired severely, not merely while the judicial
process was running its course, but during any retrial that a differently
constituted Senate might conduct if its first judgment of conviction were
invalidated. Equally uncertain is the question of what relief a court may
give other than simply setting aside the judgment of conviction. Could it
order the reinstatement of a convicted federal judge, or order Congress
to create an additional judgeship if the seat had been filled in the
interim?

Petitioner finally contends that a holding of nonjusticiability cannot be reconciled with our opinion in Powell v. McCormack, [*supra*]. The relevant issue in Powell was whether courts could review the House of Representatives' conclusion that Powell was "unqualified" to sit as a Member because he had been accused of misappropriating public funds and abusing the process of the New York courts. We stated that the question of justiciability turned on whether the Constitution committed authority to the House to judge its members' qualifications, and if so, the extent of that commitment. 395 U.S. at 519, 521. Article I, § 5 provides that "Each House shall be the Judge of the Elections, Returns and Qualifications of its own Members." In turn, Art. I, § 2 specifies three requirements for membership in the House: The candidate must be at least 25 years of age, a citizen of the United States for no less than seven years, and an inhabitant of the State he is chosen to represent. We held that, in light of the three requirements specified in the Constitution, the word "qualifications"—of which the House was to be the Judge—was of a precise, limited nature. *Id.*, at 522.

Our conclusion in Powell was based on the fixed meaning of "[q]ualifications" set forth in Art. I, § 2. The claim by the House that its power to "be the Judge of the Elections, Returns and Qualifications of its own Members" was a textual commitment of unreviewable authority was defeated by the existence of this separate provision specifying the only qualifications which might be imposed for House membership. The decision as to whether a member satisfied these qualifications *was* placed with the House, but the decision as to what these qualifications consisted of was not.

In the case before us, there is no separate provision of the Constitution which could be defeated by allowing the Senate final authority to determine the meaning of the word "try" in the Impeachment Trial Clause. We agree with Nixon that courts possess power to review either legislative or executive action that transgresses identifiable textual limits. As we have made clear, "whether the action of [either the Legislative or Executive Branch] exceeds whatever authority has been committed, is itself a delicate exercise in constitutional interpretation, and is a responsibility of this Court as ultimate interpreter of the Constitution." Baker v. Carr, *supra*, 369 U.S., at 211; accord, Powell, *supra*, 395 U.S., at 521. But we conclude, after exercising that delicate responsibility, that the word "try" in the Impeachment Clause does not provide an identifiable textual limit on the authority which is committed to the Senate.

For the foregoing reasons, the judgment of the Court of Appeals is

Affirmed.

■ JUSTICE WHITE, with whom JUSTICE BLACKMUN joins, concurring in the judgment.*

---

* [Ed.] The concurring opinion of Justice Stevens is omitted.

Petitioner contends that the method by which the Senate convicted him on two articles of impeachment violates Art. I, § 3, cl. 6 of the Constitution, which mandates that the Senate "try" impeachments. The Court is of the view that the Constitution forbids us even to consider his contention. I find no such prohibition and would therefore reach the merits of the claim. I concur in the judgment because the Senate fulfilled its constitutional obligation to "try" petitioner.

I

It should be said at the outset that, as a practical matter, it will likely make little difference whether the Court's or my view controls this case. This is so because the Senate has very wide discretion in specifying impeachment trial procedures and because it is extremely unlikely that the Senate would abuse its discretion and insist on a procedure that could not be deemed a trial by reasonable judges. Even taking a wholly practical approach, I would prefer not to announce unreviewable discretion in the Senate to ignore completely the constitutional direction to "try" impeachment cases. When asked at oral argument whether that direction would be satisfied if, after a House vote to impeach, the Senate, without any procedure whatsoever, unanimously found the accused guilty of being "a bad guy," counsel for the United States answered that the Government's theory "leads me to answer that question yes." Especially in light of this advice from the Solicitor General, I would not issue an invitation to the Senate to find an excuse, in the name of other pressing business, to be dismissive of its critical role in the impeachment process.

Practicalities aside, however, since the meaning of a constitutional provision is at issue, my disagreement with the Court should be stated.

II

The majority states that the question raised in this case meets two of the criteria for political questions set out in Baker, [*supra*]. It concludes first that there is "a textually demonstrable constitutional commitment of the issue to a coordinate political department." It also finds that the question cannot be resolved for "a lack of judicially discoverable and manageable standards."

Of course the issue in the political question doctrine is *not* whether the Constitutional text commits exclusive responsibility for a particular governmental function to one of the political branches. There are numerous instances of this sort of textual commitment, *e.g.*, Art. I, § 8, and it is not thought that disputes implicating these provisions are nonjusticiable. Rather, the issue is whether the Constitution has given one of the political branches final responsibility for interpreting the scope and nature of such a power. * * *

A

The majority finds a clear textual commitment in the Constitution's use of the word "sole" in the phrase "the Senate shall have the sole Power to try all impeachments." Art. I, § 3, cl. 6. It attributes "considerable significance" to the fact that this term appears in only one other passage in the Constitution. * * *

In disagreeing with the Court, I note that the Solicitor General stated at oral argument that "[w]e don't rest our submission on sole power to try." The Government was well advised in this respect. The significance of the Constitution's use of the term "sole" lies not in the infrequency with which the term appears, but in the fact that it appears exactly twice, in parallel provisions concerning impeachment. That the word "sole" is found only in the House and Senate Impeachment Clauses demonstrates that its purpose is to emphasize the distinct role of each in the impeachment process. As the majority notes, the Framers, following English practice, were very much concerned to separate the prosecutorial from the adjudicative aspects of impeachment. Giving each House "sole" power with respect to its role in impeachments effected this division of labor. While the majority is thus right to interpret the term "sole" to indicate that the Senate ought to "functio[n] independently and without assistance or interference," it wrongly identifies the judiciary, rather than the House, as the source of potential interference with which the Framers were concerned when they employed the term "sole."

Even if the Impeachment Trial Clause is read without regard to its companion clause, the Court's willingness to abandon its obligation to review the constitutionality of legislative acts merely on the strength of the word "sole" is perplexing. Consider, by comparison, the treatment of Art. I, § 1, which grants "All legislative powers" to the House and Senate. As used in that context "all" is nearly synonymous with "sole"—both connote entire and exclusive authority. Yet the Court has never thought it would unduly interfere with the operation of the Legislative Branch to entertain difficult and important questions as to the extent of the legislative power. * * *

The historical evidence reveals above all else that the Framers were deeply concerned about placing in any branch the "awful discretion, which a court of impeachments must necessarily have." The Federalist No. 65, p. 441 (J. Cooke ed. 1961). Viewed against this history, the discord between the majority's position and the basic principles of checks and balances underlying the Constitution's separation of powers is clear. In essence, the majority suggests that the Framers conferred upon Congress a potential tool of legislative dominance yet at the same time rendered Congress' exercise of that power one of the very few areas of legislative authority immune from any judicial review. While the majority rejects petitioner's justiciability argument as espousing a view "inconsistent with the Framers' insistence that our system be one of checks and balances," it is the Court's finding of nonjusticiability that truly upsets the Framers' careful design. In a truly balanced system, impeachments tried by the Senate would serve as a means of controlling the largely unaccountable judiciary, even as judicial review would ensure that the

Senate adhered to a minimal set of procedural standards in conducting impeachment trials.

B

The majority also contends that the term "try" does not present a judicially manageable standard. It notes that in 1787, as today, the word "try" may refer to an inquiry in the nature of a judicial proceeding, or, more generally, to experimentation or investigation. * * *

Th[e] argument * * * that one simply cannot ascertain the sense of "try" which the Framers employed and hence cannot undertake judicial review, is clearly untenable. To begin with, one would intuitively expect that, in defining the power of a political body to conduct an inquiry into official wrongdoing, the Framers used "try" in its legal sense. That intuition is borne out by reflection on the alternatives. The third clause of Art. I, § 3 cannot seriously be read to mean that the Senate shall "attempt" or "experiment with" impeachments. It is equally implausible to say that the Senate is charged with "investigating" impeachments given that this description would substantially overlap with the House of Representatives' "sole" power to draw up articles of impeachment. Art. I, § 2, cl. 5. That these alternatives are not realistic possibilities is finally evidenced by the use of "tried" in the third sentence of the Impeachment Trial Clause ("[w]hen the President of the United States is tried . . ."), and by Art. III, § 2, cl. 3 ("[t]he Trial of all Crimes, except in Cases of Impeachment . . .").

The other variant of the majority position focuses not on which sense of "try" is employed in the Impeachment Trial Clause, but on whether the legal sense of that term creates a judicially manageable standard. The majority concludes that the term provides no "identifiable textual limit." Yet, as the Government itself conceded at oral argument, the term "try" is hardly so elusive as the majority would have it. Were the Senate, for example, to adopt the practice of automatically entering a judgment of conviction whenever articles of impeachment were delivered from the House, it is quite clear that the Senate will have failed to "try" impeachments. Indeed in this respect, "try" presents no greater, and perhaps fewer, interpretive difficulties than some other constitutional standards that have been found amenable to familiar techniques of judicial construction, including, for example, "Commerce . . . among the several States," Art. I, § 8, cl. 3, and "due process of law." Amdt. 5.[3]

---

[3]   The majority's *in terrorem* argument against justiciability—that judicial review of impeachments might cause national disruption and that the courts would be unable to fashion effective relief—merits only brief attention. In the typical instance, court review of impeachments would no more render the political system dysfunctional than has this litigation. Moreover, the same capacity for disruption was noted and rejected as a basis for not hearing Powell, [*supra*], at 549. The relief granted for unconstitutional impeachment trials would presumably be similar to the relief granted to other unfairly tried public employee-litigants. Finally, as applied to the special case of the President, the majority's argument merely points out that, were the Senate to convict the President without any kind of a trial, a constitutional crisis might well result. It hardly follows that the Court ought to refrain from upholding the Constitution in all impeachment cases. Nor does it follow that, in cases of Presidential

III

The majority's conclusion that "try" is incapable of meaningful judicial construction is not without irony. One might think that if any class of concepts would fall within the definitional abilities of the judiciary, it would be that class having to do with procedural justice. Examination of the remaining question—whether proceedings in accordance with Senate Rule XI are compatible with the Impeachment Trial Clause—confirms this intuition.

Petitioner bears the rather substantial burden of demonstrating that, simply by employing the word "try," the Constitution prohibits the Senate from relying on a factfinding committee. It is clear that the Framers were familiar with English impeachment practice and with that of the States employing a variant of the English model at the time of the Constitutional Convention. Hence there is little doubt that the term "try" as used in Art. I, § 3, cl. 6 meant that the Senate should conduct its proceedings in a manner somewhat resembling a judicial proceeding. Indeed, it is safe to assume that Senate trials were to follow the practice in England and the States, which contemplated a formal hearing on the charges, at which the accused would be represented by counsel, evidence would be presented, and the accused would have the opportunity to be heard.

Petitioner argues, however, that because committees were not used in state impeachment trials prior to the Convention, the word "try" cannot be interpreted to permit their use. It is, however, a substantial leap to infer from the absence of a particular device of parliamentary procedure that its use has been forever barred by the Constitution. And there is textual and historical evidence that undermines the inference sought to be drawn in this case. * * *

[That] evidence reveals that the Impeachment Trial Clause was not meant to bind the hands of the Senate beyond establishing a set of minimal procedures. Without identifying the exact contours of these procedures, it is sufficient to say that the Senate's use of a factfinding committee under Rule XI is entirely compatible with the Constitution's command that the Senate "try all impeachments." Petitioner's challenge to his conviction must therefore fail.

IV

Petitioner has not asked the Court to conduct his impeachment trial; he has asked instead that it determine whether his impeachment was tried by the Senate. The majority refuses to reach this determination out of a laudable respect for the authority of the legislature. Regrettably, this concern is manifested in a manner that does needless violence to the

---

impeachment, the Justices ought to abandon their Constitutional responsibilities because the Senate has precipitated a crisis.

Constitution.[4] The deference that is owed can be found in the Constitution itself, which provides the Senate ample discretion to determine how best to try impeachments.

■ JUSTICE SOUTER, concurring in the judgment.

I agree with the Court that this case presents a nonjusticiable political question. Because my analysis differs somewhat from the Court's, however, I concur in its judgment by this separate opinion.

As we cautioned in Baker v. Carr, [*supra*, at] 210–211, "the 'political question' label" tends "to obscure the need for case-by-case inquiry." The need for such close examination is nevertheless clear from our precedents, which demonstrate that the functional nature of the political question doctrine requires analysis of "the precise facts and posture of the particular case," and precludes "resolution by any semantic cataloguing," *id.*, at 217. * * *

Whatever considerations feature most prominently in a particular case, the political question doctrine is "essentially a function of the separation of powers," *ibid.*, existing to restrain courts "from inappropriate interference in the business of the other branches of Government," United States v. Munoz-Flores, 495 U.S. 385, 394 (1990), and deriving in large part from prudential concerns about the respect we owe the political departments. See Goldwater v. Carter, 444 U.S. 996, 1000 (1979) (Powell, J., concurring in the judgment); A. Bickel, The Least Dangerous Branch 125–126 (2d ed.1986); Finkelstein, Judicial Self-Limitation, 37 Harv.L.Rev. 338, 344–345 (1924). Not all interference is inappropriate or disrespectful, however, and application of the doctrine ultimately turns, as Learned Hand put it, on "how importunately the occasion demands an answer." L. Hand, The Bill of Rights 15 (1958).

This occasion does not demand an answer. The Impeachment Trial Clause commits to the Senate "the sole Power to try all Impeachments," subject to three procedural requirements: the Senate shall be on oath or affirmation; the Chief Justice shall preside when the President is tried;

---

[4] Although our views might well produce identical results in most cases, the same objection may be raised against the prudential version of the political question doctrine presented by Justice Souter. According to the prudential view, judicial determination of whether the Senate has conducted an impeachment trial would interfere unacceptably with the Senate's work and should be avoided except where necessitated by the threat of grave harm to the constitutional order. As articulated, this position is missing its premise: no explanation is offered as to why it would show disrespect or cause disruption or embarrassment to review the action of the Senate in this case as opposed to, say, the enactment of legislation under the Commerce Clause. * * *

In any event, the prudential view cannot achieve its stated purpose. The judgment it wishes to avoid—and the attendant disrespect and embarrassment—will inevitably be cast because the courts still will be required to distinguish cases on their merits. Justice Souter states that the Court ought not to entertain petitioner's constitutional claim because "[i]t seems fair to conclude," that the Senate tried him. In other words, on the basis of a preliminary determination that the Senate has acted within the "broad boundaries" of the Impeachment Trial Clause, it is concluded that we must refrain from making that determination. At best, this approach offers only the illusion of deference and respect by substituting impressionistic assessment for constitutional analysis.

and conviction shall be upon the concurrence of two-thirds of the Members present. U.S. Const., Art. I, § 3, cl. 6. It seems fair to conclude that the Clause contemplates that the Senate may determine, within broad boundaries, such subsidiary issues as the procedures for receipt and consideration of evidence necessary to satisfy its duty to "try" impeachments. Other significant considerations confirm a conclusion that this case presents a nonjusticiable political question: the "unusual need for unquestioning adherence to a political decision already made," as well as "the potentiality of embarrassment from multifarious pronouncements by various departments on one question." Baker, *supra*, 369 U.S., at 217. As the Court observes, judicial review of an impeachment trial would under the best of circumstances entail significant disruption of government.

One can, nevertheless, envision different and unusual circumstances that might justify a more searching review of impeachment proceedings. If the Senate were to act in a manner seriously threatening the integrity of its results, convicting, say, upon a coin-toss, or upon a summary determination that an officer of the United States was simply "a bad guy," (White, J., concurring in the judgment), judicial interference might well be appropriate. In such circumstances, the Senate's action might be so far beyond the scope of its constitutional authority, and the consequent impact on the Republic so great, as to merit a judicial response despite the prudential concerns that would ordinarily counsel silence. "The political question doctrine, a tool for maintenance of governmental order, will not be so applied as to promote only disorder." Baker, *supra*, at 215.

NOTE ON POLITICAL QUESTIONS

(1) Political Questions and the Judicial Function. What, exactly, did the Supreme Court mean in dismissing Nixon's lawsuit as raising a "political question"? Nixon's standing was not in question. He presented a live controversy, which was neither moot nor unripe, and there was no lack of adverse parties. How does the political question relate to Marbury v. Madison, p. 76, *supra*, and its assertions that it is "the province and duty of the judicial department to say what the law is" and that for every violation of a vested right there should be a legal remedy?[1]

Note that in Marbury, Chief Justice Marshall suggested that questions should be deemed "political," and therefore not subject to judicial review, if non-judicial officials possessed "discretion." Does the political question doctrine refer only to questions that are "political" in this sense? If so, a judicial holding that a suit was governed by the political question doctrine would amount to a decision that no "legal" rights of the plaintiff had been

---

[1] For an argument that the political question doctrine cannot be reconciled with the judicial function as it has descended from Marbury and should therefore be abandoned, see Redish, *Judicial Review and the "Political Question,"* 79 Nw.U.L.Rev. 1031 (1985).

violated—that the challenged action lay within the legal discretion of the officials who took it.

To some extent, competing views of the political question doctrine mirror debates about whether doctrines such as standing or ripeness, in fact, represent implicit judgments about the merits of the underlying legal disputes or, instead, more purely reflect inferences about the reach of Article III power. Hence, one prominent conception—the "classical" position—maintains that political question decisions, properly understood, consist of a series of interpretations of the substantive meaning of particular clauses of the Constitution. The leading exponent of that position, Herbert Wechsler, thus wrote: "[A]ll the [political question] doctrine can defensibly imply is that the courts are called upon to judge whether the Constitution has committed to another agency of government the autonomous determination of the issue raised, a finding that itself requires an interpretation. * * * [T]he only proper judgment that may lead to an abstention from decision is that the Constitution has committed the determination of the issue to another agency of government than the courts. Difficult as it may be to make that judgment wisely, whatever factors may be rightly weighed in situations where the answer is not clear, what is involved is in itself an act of constitutional interpretation, to be made and judged by standards that should govern the interpretive process generally. That, I submit, is *toto caelo* different from a broad [judicial] discretion to abstain or intervene." See Wechsler, Principles, Politics and Fundamental Law 11–14 (1961).

A competing theory—the "prudential" position—is associated with Alexander Bickel, who argued that the political question doctrine, in fact, appropriately reflects prudential concerns about the exercise of judicial power. Bickel wrote: "[O]nly by means of a play on words can the broad discretion that the courts have in fact exercised be turned into an act of constitutional interpretation governed by the general standards of the interpretive process. The political-question doctrine simply resists being domesticated in this fashion. There is * * * something different about it, in kind not in degree; something greatly more flexible, something of prudence, not construction and not principle. And it is something that cannot exist within the four corners of Marbury v. Madison. * * *

"Such is the foundation, in both intellect and instinct, of the political-question doctrine: the Court's sense of lack of capacity, compounded in unequal parts of (a) the strangeness of the issue and its intractability to principled resolution; (b) the sheer momentousness of it, which tends to unbalance judicial judgment; (c) the anxiety, not so much that the judicial judgment will be ignored, as that perhaps it should but will not be; (d) finally ('in a mature democracy'), the inner vulnerability, the self-doubt of an institution which is electorally irresponsible and has no earth to draw strength from." Bickel, The Least Dangerous Branch 125–26, 184 (1962).

In Bickel's view, a fundamental problem of American constitutionalism lies in the necessity to reconcile adherence to principle, on which the legitimacy of judicial review depends, with the demands of sensible, prudent governance. He thought he found the key in a distinction between judicial judgments on the merits, which he argued must be unyieldingly principled, and determinations of justiciability, which he thought could and should turn largely on prudential concerns. Are both the Wechsler and Bickel positions reflected in the various opinions in Nixon? Properly so?[2]

Another significant position, advanced by Professor Henkin, is that the political question doctrine is "an unnecessary, deceptive packaging of several established doctrines" whose "proper content" relates to such matters as the obligation of the courts to "accept decisions by the political branches within their constitutional authority" and the ability of the courts to "refuse some (or all) remedies for want of equity." Henkin, *Is There a Political Question Doctrine?*, 85 Yale L.J. 597, 622–23 (1976).

(2) Historical and Doctrinal Foundations. Two more recent studies attempt to trace the history and doctrinal basis of the political question doctrine in the Supreme Court.[3]

Grove, *The Lost History of the Political Question Doctrine*, 90 N.Y.U.L.Rev. 1908 (2015), argues that the modern political question doctrine is a twentieth-century invention. Under the "traditional" doctrine that applied throughout the nineteenth century, Professor Grove writes, "political questions were *factual* determinations made by the political branches that courts treated as conclusive in the course of resolving cases." Based on Professor Grove's evidence, the line between law and fact does not appear sharp, and she acknowledges that the Court breached it, at least in dictum, in Luther v. Borden, 48 U.S. (7 How.) 1 (1849), discussed at p. 315, *infra*. Nevertheless, she maintains, the traditional doctrine was not jurisdictional: the Court exercised its jurisdiction to apply the determination of another branch. According to Professor Grove, the modern, jurisdictional doctrine had its first flowering in 1912, in Pacific States Tel. & Tel. Co. v. Oregon, 223 U.S. 118 (1912), p. 315, *infra* but even the reasoning of that decision was arguably limited to the Guarantee Clause. After gaining traction in some plurality opinions, the modern, general, jurisdictional doctrine emerged only in 1962 in Baker v. Carr, 369 U.S. 186 (1962), p. 306, *infra*. Professor Grove attributes the rise of the modern doctrine largely to casebook authors in the "legal process" school, beginning with then-Professor Felix Frankfurter and later including Henry Hart and Herbert Wechsler, who, she writes, sought more generally to limit the range of properly judicial authority with jurisdictional doctrines that they ascribed to Article III. In Professor Grove's view, the modern political question doctrine is vulnerable to criticism both

---

[2]   Compare Brown, *When Political Questions Affect Individual Rights: The Other Nixon v. United States*, 1993 Sup.Ct.Rev. 125, 126 which argues that the Court should not invoke the political question doctrine to foreclose judicial review of a separation-of-powers question implicating individual rights.

[3]   For other accounts of the political question doctrine, see, *e.g.*, Fallon, *Political Questions and the Ultra Vires Conundrum*, 87 U.Chi.L.Rev. 1481 (2020); Paulsen, *The Constitutional Power to Interpret International Law*, 118 Yale L.J. 1762, 1817–1823 (2009); Choper, *The Political Question Doctrine: Suggested Criteria*, 54 Duke L.J. 1457 (2005); Field, *The Doctrine of Political Questions in the Federal Courts*, 8 Minn.L.Rev 485 (1924); Finkelstein, *Further Notes on Judicial Self-Limitation*, 39 Harv.L.Rev. 338 (1924); Seidman, *The Secret Life of the Political Question Doctrine*, 37 J. Marshall L.Rev. 441 (2004); Tushnet, *Law and Prudence in the Law of Justiciability: The Transformation of the Political Question Doctrine*, 80 N.C.L.Rev. 1203 (2002); Scharpf, *Judicial Review and the Political Question: A Functional Analysis*, 75 Yale L.J. 517 (1966); Weston, *Political Questions*, 38 Harv.L.Rev. 296 (1925).

because it lacks historical foundations and because it gives the Supreme
Court too much power, not too little: by reserving "for itself the power to
decide which institution decides any constitutional question * * * the Court
has most often used its modern political question cases * * * as a vehicle to
assert its supremacy over various areas of constitutional law."

Harrison, *The Political Question Doctrines*, 67 Am.U.L.Rev. 457 (2017)
also argues that a core of the political question doctrine is a principle of "non-
judicial finality," particularly in three situations: those involving
sovereignty, those involving the process of enacting laws or constitutional
amendments, and those involving the Constitution's textual commitment of
a judging power to a house of Congress (as in Nixon). Professor Harrison
believes that the holdings of the Supreme Court's political question cases
remain consistent with this view today. In addition, Professor Harrison
suggests that a lesser branch of the political question doctrine limits judicial
remedies that would excessively direct executive discretion, as in Gilligan v.
Morgan, 413 U.S. 1 (1973). And he argues emphatically that the Supreme
Court has never actually held that the political question doctrine is a limit
on the jurisdiction of Article III courts.

Are Professor Grove's and Professor Harrison's assessments ultimately
compatible? How do they relate to the views of Bickel, Wechsler, and
Henkin?

(3) Baker v. Carr.

(a) A leading modern political question case is Baker v. Carr, 369 U.S.
186 (1962), which the Court applied in Nixon. Baker presented the question
whether an equal protection challenge to the apportionment of the
Tennessee legislature raised a nonjusticiable political question. At the time
the suit was brought, representation in both houses of the legislature was
based on an apportionment scheme adopted in 1901. Since then, population
shifts had resulted in gross imbalances in the number of voters in various
districts, with the result that even a substantial majority of the state's voters
might fail to elect a majority in the legislature. In Colegrove v. Green, 328
U.S. 549 (1946), a narrowly divided Supreme Court had concluded that a
challenge to congressional districting in Illinois presented a nonjusticiable
political question. Districting questions, the Court reasoned, were questions
of political power and thus "not meet for judicial determination."[4]
Analogously, the Court noted, "[v]iolation of the great guaranty of a
republican form of government in States cannot be challenged in the courts."
In Baker, the Court effectively overruled Coleman and rejected the relevance
of the Guarantee Clause. Instead, the Court focused on the Equal Protection
Clause. "Judicial standards under the Equal Protection Clause," Justice
Brennan wrote, "are well developed and familiar."[5]

---

[4]   In several cases, however, the Supreme Court had upheld judicial challenges to alleged
racial discrimination in the drawing of election districts and in the organization of state political
parties. See, *e.g.*, Gomillion v. Lightfoot, 364 U.S. 339 (1960) (drawing of political boundaries to
disenfranchise Black voters); Terry v. Adams, 345 U.S. 461 (1953) (discrimination by political
party); Smith v. Allwright, 321 U.S. 649 (1944) (same).

[5]   Compare Reynolds v. Sims, 377 U.S. 533 (1964) (adopting the "one person, one vote"
formula).

In a dissenting opinion joined by Justice Harlan, Justice Frankfurter charged that Baker presented "a Guarantee Clause claim masquerading under a different label." In his view, the Equal Protection Clause provided no clearer standards for apportioning electoral power than did the Guarantee Clause. For a court to enter the dispute without such standards would embroil the judicial process in politics and threaten judicial legitimacy. Justice Harlan, in a separate dissenting opinion also joined by Justice Frankfurter, argued that Tennessee's apportionment scheme offended no applicable constitutional standard and that the plaintiffs had therefore failed to state a valid claim on the merits. Were the dissenting opinions of Justice Frankfurter and Harlan, each joined by the other, mutually consistent?

Baker v. Carr is notable, among other things, for its canvas of prior political question decisions. The Court began by identifying entire subject areas in which challenges to congressional or executive authority had sometimes been thought to raise non-justiciable political questions: foreign relations, questions involving dates of duration of hostilities, the formal validity of legislative enactments, the status of the Native American tribes, and questions about whether a republican form of government exists in the states. But the categorical divides were misleading, the Court concluded. "Much of the confusion results from the capacity of the 'political question' label to obscure the need for case-by-case inquiry." From its survey, the Court distilled a list of governing criteria:

"Prominent on the surface of any case held to involve a political question is found a textually demonstrable constitutional commitment of the issue to a coordinate political department; or a lack of judicially discoverable and manageable standards for resolving it; or the impossibility of deciding without an initial policy determination of a kind clearly for nonjudicial discretion; or the impossibility of a court's undertaking independent resolution without expressing lack of the respect due coordinate branches of government; or an unusual need for unquestioning adherence to a political decision already made; or the potentiality of embarrassment from multifarious pronouncements by various departments on one question."

These criteria are frequently cited, as they were in Nixon v. United States, but the division over their applicability in that case was by no means unusual. No single criterion seems to control, and some appear to reflect the classical position ("textually demonstrable commitment," "lack of judicially discoverable or manageable standards") while others have a more prudential or functional feel to them (e.g., "an unusual need for unquestioning adherence to a political decision already made" and "the potentiality of embarrassment from multifarious pronouncements by various departments on one question").

(b) Textually Demonstrable Commitment to Another Branch. The Nixon majority found a "textually demonstrable constitutional commitment of the issue" presented "to a coordinate political department"—but only after conducting an inquiry into the "history and contemporary understanding of the impeachment provisions." Are those contextual considerations always necessary to make sense of the textual commitment factor?[6]

The notion of textual commitment may connote two distinct ideas. First, textual commitment, within the formulation of Marbury v. Madison, may serve as shorthand for describing the textual assignment of some significant element of "discretion" to another branch. On that view, even if the Impeachment Clause commits to the Senate "discretion" to decide how to "try" an impeachment, could the Senate's textually committed discretion plausibly be treated as constitutionally unbounded? (Recall Justice Souter's coin-toss example.) Second, textual commitment could suggest a constitutional assignment of exclusive interpretive authority to a branch other than the judiciary. On that view, the Nixon Court would have to accept the Senate's understanding of "try" as conclusive, even if the Court thinks it means something else.[7] Under both versions of textual commitment—the "discretion theory" and the "interpretive authority theory"—the Court's application of the political question doctrine still requires an interpretation of the underlying constitutional provision to determine where the relevant discretion or interpretive authority is vested. Does that process itself satisfy Marbury's requirement that the judiciary "say what the law is" in resolving cases or controversies? Compare Baker, *supra*, at 64: "Deciding whether a matter has in any measure been committed by the Constitution to another branch of government, or whether the action of that branch exceeds whatever authority has been committed, is itself a delicate exercise in constitutional interpretation, and is a responsibility of this Court as ultimate interpreter of the Constitution."

Compare Powell v. McCormack, 395 U.S. 486 (1969), which presented the question whether an unbounded discretion was conferred on the House of Representatives by Art. I, § 5, which provides that "Each House shall be the Judge of the * * * Qualifications of its own Members." At issue was whether Adam Clayton Powell, Jr. was constitutionally entitled to take the seat in the House of Representatives to which he had been elected. It was conceded that he met the age, citizenship, and residence requirements of Art. I, § 2, but he had been denied his seat by a House resolution on the basis of findings by a Select Committee that he "had asserted an unwarranted privilege and immunity from the processes of the courts of New York; that he had wrongfully diverted House funds for the use of others and himself; and that he had made false reports on expenditures of foreign currency to the Committee on House Administration." Together with some voters in his district, Powell sued for a declaration that his exclusion was unconstitutional (and for back salary).

---

[6]   Bradley & Morrison, *Historical Gloss and the Separation of Powers*, 126 Harv.L.Rev. 411, 429–30 (2012), argues that finding "a textually demonstrable constitutional commitment of [an] issue to a coordinate political department" often depends on an assessment of historical practice. For example, they explain, historical practice largely accounts for the constitutional principle that the Article II power to "receive Ambassadors" (U.S. Const. Art. II, § 3) also confers upon the President exclusive power to recognize foreign governments.

[7]   For discussion of the two different approaches to textual commitment, see, *e.g.*, Redish, note 1, *supra*, at 1039–43; Seidman, note 3, *supra*, at 444–59.

Chief Justice Warren, for the Court, held that the claim did not present a political question. After a lengthy historical examination, he concluded that the provision of Art. I, § 5, is "at most a 'textually demonstrable commitment' to Congress to judge only the qualifications expressly set forth in the Constitution."

In light of Powell, was Justice White correct that the Court in Nixon should have examined more carefully the constitutional bounds on the Senate's power? If courts always had to inquire into whether other branches had acted within the bounds of their constitutionally permissible discretion, wouldn't every political question argument collapse (as Professor Wechsler contends it should) into an argument on the merits about how the Constitution should be applied to a particular, challenged action by a non-judicial official?

(c) Judicially Manageable Standards. The Nixon Court observed that "the lack of judicially manageable standards may strengthen the conclusion that there is a textually demonstrable commitment to a coordinate branch." The Court relied heavily on this prong in Rucho v. Common Cause, 588 U.S. 684 (2019). Rucho involved two consolidated cases brought to challenge partisan redistricting schemes that significantly diluted the equality of votes so as to enhance the incumbent interests of the party in control of the state legislature—in one case, the Democrats, and in the other, the Republicans. Voters challenged the indisputably intentional partisan gerrymanders based on claims sounding the First Amendment, Equal Protection, the Elections Clause, and Article I, § 2. Writing for a 5–4 majority, the Chief Justice framed the issue as "whether such claims are claims of *legal* right, resolvable according to *legal* principles, or political questions that must find their resolution elsewhere."[8] The Chief Justice continued to explain that if the courts review such matters, it is "vital" that they do so "only in accord with especially clear standards" so as to avoid the risk of " 'assuming political, not legal, responsibility for a process that often produces ill will and distrust' " (citations omitted).

Unlike other constitutional constraints on districting that the Court had ruled justiciable in the past (such as the rules against malapportionment or racial gerrymandering, see p. 242, *supra*[9]), a political gerrymandering claim created an insurmountable line-drawing problem. The Court stressed that "[t]here are no legal standards discernible in the Constitution for making such judgments, let alone limited and precise standards that are clear, manageable, and politically neutral." Ultimately, the majority rejected the plaintiffs' request for what it deemed "an unprecedented expansion of judicial power" and viewed the matter better left to the political branches.

---

[8] Prior to Rucho, the Justices had effectively punted on whether judicially manageable standards could be developed for addressing partisan gerrymandering, with multiple Justices questioning the ability of the Court to do so. See Gill v. Whitford, 585 U.S. 48 (2018); Vieth v. Jubelirer, 541 U.S. 267 (2004); Davis v. Bandemer, 478 U.S. 109 (1986).

[9] Compare Rogers v. Lodge, 458 U.S. 613 (1982) (holding racial gerrymandering claim justiciable). But see Alexander v. South Carolina State Conference of the NAACP, 144 S.Ct. 1221, 1253–58 (2024) (Thomas, J., concurring in the part and concurring in the judgment in part) (arguing that racial gerrymandering claims should also be held nonjusticiable).

This being said, at various points, the Chief Justice evinced a skeptical view of the underlying merits, writing that "[t]o hold that legislators cannot take partisan interests into account when drawing district lines would essentially countermand the Framers' decision to entrust districting to political entities." The Chief Justice added, "[t]he only provision in the Constitution that specifically addresses [partisan gerrymandering] assigns it to the political branches."[10]

Writing for the four dissenting Justices, Justice Kagan declared that "[f]or the first time ever, this Court refuses to remedy a constitutional violation because it thinks the task beyond judicial capabilities." She continued, "[i]n the face of grievous harm to democratic governance and flagrant infringements on constitutional rights—in the face of escalating partisan manipulation whose compatibility with this nation's values and law no one defends—the majority declares that it can't provide a remedy because it can't find a manageable legal standard to apply." But, she argued, what the majority "says can't be done *has* been done." Pointing to numerous "detailed, thorough, [and] painstaking" lower court decisions that had chosen and implemented models for ascertaining when gerrymandering goes constitutionally too far, Justice Kagan asserted that the issue fell squarely within the judiciary's competence. She concluded by arguing that, if anything, "the need for judicial review is at its most urgent in cases like these."

Who is right in Rucho? Are the majority's arguments that (1) no manageable standards can be ascertained and that (2) there may be no merit to the underlying claims contradictory, or complementary?

(d) Respect for Coordinate Branches. A further consideration cited by Baker is "the impossibility of a court's undertaking independent resolution without expressing lack of the respect due coordinate branches of government." Is this criterion too conclusory to do independent work in identifying a political question?

In United States v. Munoz-Flores, 495 U.S. 385 (1990), the Court considered on the merits a challenge to the validity of a provision of the Victims of Crime Act requiring those convicted of federal crimes to pay a special assessment to a Crime Victims Fund established by that Act. Munoz-Flores contended that the provision had originated in the Senate and therefore violated the requirement of the Origination Clause of the Constitution (Art. I, § 7, cl. 1) that "all Bills for raising Revenue shall originate in the House of Representatives." The Court rejected the position of the United States that the case presented a nonjusticiable political question. With respect to the suggestion that invalidation of a law on Origination Clause grounds would evidence a "lack of respect" for the House that passed the bill, the Court said: "[D]isrespect, in the sense the Government uses the term, cannot be sufficient to create a political question.

---

[10]   In Alexander v. South Carolina State Conference of the NAACP, 144 S.Ct. 1221 (2024), a racial gerrymandering case, the first paragraph of the opinion of the Court by Justice Alito states: "claims that a map is unconstitutional because it was drawn to achieve a partisan end are not justiciable in federal court. Thus, as far as the Federal Constitution is concerned, a legislature may pursue partisan ends when it engages in redistricting."

If it were, *every* judicial resolution of a constitutional challenge to a congressional enactment would be impermissible. * * * Nor do the House's incentives to safeguard its origination prerogative obviate the need for judicial review. * * * [T]he fact that one institution of government has mechanisms available to guard against incursions into its power by other governmental institutions does not require that the judiciary remove itself from the controversy by labeling the issue a political question."

The Court then rejected the government's argument that judicial intervention was inappropriate since the case did not involve a question of individual rights. The argument, the Court said, is "simply irrelevant to the political question doctrine. * * * Furthermore, * * * [p]rovisions for separation of powers within the Legislative Branch are * * * *not* different in kind from provisions concerning relations between the branches: both sets of provisions safeguard liberty."[11]

On the merits, the Court held that, even if the bill did not originate in the House, it did not violate the Origination Clause because a statute that does not raise revenue to support government generally, but rather creates and raises revenue to support a particular program, is not a "Bill for raising Revenue."

Justice Stevens, joined by Justice O'Connor, concurred on the ground that a bill that passes both Houses and is signed by the President becomes law even if it originated unconstitutionally. Justice Scalia, also concurring, argued that any enacted law that bears an attestation that it originated in the House (as this law did) should "establish[ ] that fact as officially and authoritatively as it establishes the fact that its recited text was adopted by both Houses." Although neither concurring opinion rested in terms on the political question doctrine, both interpreted and applied the constitutional text in a manner that immunizes from judicial review certain actions of the legislature even when those actions violate the Constitution.

(e) Speaking with One Voice. In his concurring opinion in Nixon, Justice Souter noted that "significant considerations" suggested "the 'unusual need for unquestioning adherence to a political decision already made,' as well as 'the potentiality of embarrassment from multifarious pronouncements by various departments on one question' " (quoting Baker v. Carr). He added, however, that such considerations might not carry the day "[i]f the Senate were to act in a manner seriously threatening the integrity of its results, convicting, say, upon a coin toss."

Consider Black, Impeachment: A Handbook 61–62 (1974): "If the Supreme Court [were] to order reinstatement of an impeached and convicted president, there would be, to say the least, a very grave and quite legitimate

---

[11] Compare Choper, Judicial Review and the National Political Process (1980), which contends that questions involving the proper relationship of Congress to the President (as well as questions involving the proper relationship between the states and the federal government) should be nonjusticiable. Professor Choper maintains that the political process is capable of protecting the relevant interests and that the courts should preserve their institutional capital for the protection of individual rights. See also Choper, note 3, *supra* (proposing functional criteria to guide application of the political question doctrine based on notions of comparative judicial competence).

doubt whether that decree had any title to being obeyed, or whether it was [as] widely outside judicial jurisdiction as would be a judicial order to Congress to increase the penalty for counterfeiting. To cite the most frightening consequence, our military commanders would have to decide for themselves which president they were bound to obey, the reinstated one or his successor. * * * It would be most unfortunate if the notion got about that the Senate's verdict was somewhat tentative. * * * No senator should be encouraged to think he can shift to any court responsibility for an unpalatable or unpopular decision."[12]

Do functional concerns about the role of the judiciary in our constitutional scheme explain these grounds for forbearance? If so, from what source does this understanding of the judicial role derive?

(4) Constitutional Challenges to Statutes. Zivotofsky v. Clinton, 566 U.S. 189 (2012), suggests that the Court may be especially reluctant to find a political question where the question at issue is whether an Act of Congress is unconstitutional. Zivotofsky presented a question involving the constitutionality of § 214(d) of the Foreign Relations Authorization Act, Fiscal Year 2003, 116 Stat. 1350, which provides that an American citizen born in Jerusalem may list Israel as his or her place of birth on a U.S. Passport. Given the contested status of that city, State Department policy had long provided that American citizens born in Jerusalem could list Jerusalem, but not Israel or Jordan, as their place of birth. Born in Jerusalem to American parents, Zivotofsky (through his parents) sued the Secretary of State under the statute, seeking to enjoin her to designate Israel as the place of birth on his passport. The court of appeals held that Zivotofsky's complaint presented a political question because the Constitution assigns the executive unreviewable discretion to recognize foreign sovereigns and because the State Department's determination fell within that power.

After describing the political question doctrine as a "narrow exception" to its presumptive duty to hear cases within its jurisdiction, the Supreme Court reversed. The Court focused only on the first two Baker factors—textual commitment of the question to a coordinate branch and the absence of judicially manageable standards. The Court reasoned that Zivotofsky's invocation of an Act of Congress made both of those criteria harder to establish. First, the Court argued that whether or not the President has exclusive authority to recognize foreign governments and thus to make appropriate designations on U.S. Passports, "there is, of course, no exclusive commitment to the Executive of the power to determine the constitutionality of a statute." The judiciary, the Court made clear, must properly resolve any conflicts between Congress and the President over the contested allocation of power over passports.

Second, the Court suggested that if it had been asked to determine the political status of Jerusalem in the absence of a statute, it would have lacked

---

12   Compare Berger, Impeachment: The Constitutional Problems 103–21 (1973) (arguing, primarily in the context of non-presidential impeachment proceedings, that the scope and content of the terms "other high Crimes and Misdemeanors" in Art. II, § 4, is a question of law subject to judicial review).

judicially manageable standards to do so. But the problem "dissipate[d] * * * when the issue is recognized to be the more focused one of the [statute's] constitutionality." In arguing that the contested power lay exclusively with the President, the executive branch relied on the constitutional text, longstanding executive practice, congressional acquiescence in that practice, and judicial precedent. Zivotofsky, by contrast, contended that the power to designate a citizen's place of birth fell squarely within Congress's authority over immigration and foreign commerce, and that Congress had traditionally exercised extensive control over the form and content of passports. Relying on passages from the Federalist Papers, moreover, Zivotofsky argued that the recognition power is not exclusively executive and that, even if it were, designating a citizen's place of birth does not intrude on that power. After cataloguing (but not resolving) these competing arguments, the Court concluded that Zivotofsky's claims "sound in familiar principles of constitutional interpretation" and, while difficult, did not leave the Court without manageable standards.[13]

Justice Sotomayor, joined in part by Justice Breyer, concurred in the judgment. She criticized the Court for failing to consider whether its assertion of jurisdiction would impinge on Baker's prudential factors, such as the need for the government to speak with one voice. She added that, in her view, the political question doctrine could, under proper circumstances, apply to a constitutional challenge to a statute. Finally, she noted that the Court should not have held that the case presented judicially manageable standards simply because the parties made textual, structural, and historical arguments—something that the parties in Nixon v. United States, p. 292, *supra*, had also done. She argued that when "parties' textual, structural, and historical evidence is inapposite or wholly unilluminating, rendering judicial decision no more than guesswork, a case relying on the ordinary kinds of arguments offered to courts might well still present justiciability concerns." Justice Breyer also dissented. Invoking the prudential Baker factors, he concluded that "this case is unusual both in its minimal need for judicial intervention and in its more serious risk that intervention will bring about 'embarrassment,' show lack of 'respect' for the other branches, and potentially disrupt sound foreign policy decisionmaking."

(5) The Political Question Doctrine Beyond the Supreme Court.

(a) In light of the certiorari statute and related legal rules, see Chapter III, *infra*, the Supreme Court has near complete control over its own docket. If it merely wishes to avoid opining on a "political" question, it can simply decline to hear the case. So an important function of the political question doctrine is to forbid the *lower federal courts* from deciding such questions either.

In that light, consider Bradley & Posner, *The Real Political Question Doctrine*, 75 Stan. L.Rev. 1031 (2023), which surveys 1200 cases in the lower

---

[13] Three years later, the case came before the Court on the merits, and a 6–3 majority held that the statute was unconstitutional as applied to passports. Zivotofsky v. Kerry, 576 U.S. 1 (2015). Justice Thomas, who concurred on that point, would have severed and upheld the application of the statute to consular reports of birth abroad.

federal courts over a 60-year period after Baker v. Carr. The authors conclude that the lower court practice is significantly different from scholarly assumptions based on Supreme Court case law in five respects: the doctrine is used much more often, it is heavily focused on foreign affairs, it often applies in non-constitutional cases, it is more prudential rather than more formalistic, and it does not necessarily permanently foreclose judicial review. The authors note that the difference between the doctrine's implementation in the lower federal courts and in the Supreme Court may reflect the very different nature of those courts' dockets. But to the extent that the differences do reflect legal disagreements, should these findings be taken as an implicit criticism of the Supreme Court's too-limited and too-formalistic use of the doctrine, or as evidence that the lower courts have not been following the law?

(b)   Does the federal political question doctrine apply in *state* courts? If the political question doctrine is understood to come from Article III itself, then presumably it would only limit the jurisdiction of Article III courts. In a concurring opinion in Goldwater v. Carter, 444 U.S. 996, 1005 n.2 (1979), Justice Rehnquist wrote: "This Court, of course, may not prohibit state courts from deciding political questions, any more than it may prohibit them from deciding questions that are moot, *Doremus v. Board of Education,* 342 U.S. 429, 434 (1952), so long as they do not trench upon exclusively federal questions of foreign policy. *Zschernig v. Miller*, 389 U.S. 429, 441 (1968)."[14]

On the other hand, to the extent that the political question doctrine is understood to reflect interpretations of the substance of other parts of the Constitution (for instance, of Article I, § 3, in Nixon, or of the Fourteenth Amendment, in Rucho) the Supreme Court's interpretations of the Constitution would presumably be binding on state courts, see Cooper v. Aaron, 358 U.S. 1, 18–19 (1958). This seems to follow from Professor Wechsler's view of the doctrine (Paragraph (1), *supra*) and has been argued by many other scholars since. See Dodson, *Article III and the Political Question Doctrine*, 116 Nw.U.L.Rev. 681, 715–35 (2021); Harrison, *supra*, at 493; Bradley & Posner, *supra*, at 1088.

NOTE ON SPECIFIC SUBJECT MATTER AREAS IMPLICATING THE POLITICAL QUESTION DOCTRINE

(1)   The Political Question Doctrine as Applied. The political question doctrine plays a recurring role in several subject matter areas. Even within these areas, relatively fine distinctions often seem to separate cases treated as nonjusticiable from cases adjudicated on the merits. When engaging in judicial review in an area potentially governed by the political question doctrine, the Court frequently does not even address the doctrine's

---

[14]   Of course, state constitutional law could still contain its own political question doctrine that constrained that state's courts. See Stern, *Don't Answer That: Revisiting the Political Question Doctrine in State Courts*, 21 U.Pa.J.Const.L. 153 (2018). Alternatively, as Rucho observed, "state statutes and state constitutions can provide standards and guidance for state courts to apply." 588 U.S. at 719.

applicability. See generally Barkow, *More Supreme Than Court? The Fall of the Political Question Doctrine and the Rise of Judicial Supremacy*, 102 Colum.L.Rev. 237 (2002). Do the diverse results in the subject matter areas discussed below suggest that the political question doctrine cannot be applied in a principled manner? Or does the variance merely suggest that the inquiry is fine-grained enough to produce different results in cases that have superficial similarities but that ultimately involve important differences in terms of textual commitment, judicially manageable standards, or relevant practical considerations?

(2) The Guarantee Clause. The leading early case on the political question doctrine, Luther v. Borden, 48 U.S. (7 How.) 1 (1849), involved Article IV, § 4, which provides that "[t]he United States shall guarantee to every State in the Union a Republican Form of Government." The case grew "out of the unfortunate political differences which agitated the people of Rhode Island in 1841 and 1842." Despite popular unrest with a "charter" government elected under a state constitution that predated the American Revolution, incumbent officials thwarted reform, and the "Dorr Rebellion" broke out. As an aspect of that rebellion, Dorr was elected governor under the purported authority of a new constitution adopted outside established legal forms. But his effort to take power by force was repulsed, and the charter government implemented martial law. The charter government did, finally, call a constitutional convention, and a new constitution was peaceably introduced in May of 1843.

Meantime, however, Borden and other state officers broke into the house of Luther, a Dorr supporter. When Luther sued for trespass, the forced entry was admitted. The claim turned on whether the defendants were lawfully authorized to enter. This, the plaintiff maintained, depended on whether the charter government was indeed, as the defendants asserted and the plaintiff denied, the lawfully constituted, "republican" government of Rhode Island at the time of the entry. Rejecting the plaintiff's demand that it inquire into the charter government's lawful authority under the Guarantee Clause, the lower court entered judgment for the defendants, and the Supreme Court affirmed.

In an opinion by Chief Justice Taney, the Supreme Court offered several reasons for holding the issue nonjusticiable, including the practical difficulties that would ensue if judicial challenges to the lawful authority of state governments were invited. The Court's holding was that the question presented was one for congressional, not judicial, resolution: "Congress must necessarily decide what government is established in the state before it can determine whether it is republican or not. And when the senators and representatives of a state are admitted into the councils of the Union, the authority of the government under which they are appointed, as well as its republican character, is recognized by the proper constitutional authority. And its decision is binding on every other department of government, and could not be questioned in a judicial tribunal."

Since the Luther decision, the Supreme Court has never expressly found a Guarantee Clause claim to present a justiciable question, and indeed on several occasions has held such claims to be nonjusticiable. *E.g.*, Pacific

States Tel. & Tel. Co. v. Oregon, 223 U.S. 118 (1912) (holding the question whether state laws enacted by initiative and referendum procedures were consistent with "republican" government to be nonjusticiable). Other decisions, however, are more ambiguous in their import. *E.g.*, Texas v. White, 74 U.S. (7 Wall.) 700 (1868) (a state engaged in rebellion against the Union in violation of the Constitution was depriving its citizens of a republican form of government);[1] Coyle v. Smith, 221 U.S. 559 (1911) (holding that Congress could not rely on the Guarantee Clause—or any other provision—as a basis for conditioning the entry of a state into the Union on the state's agreement to locate its capital in a particular city for at least a decade).[2] Is there a good reason why all Guarantee Clause claims should be deemed political questions? Is the Guarantee Clause any less definite than the Equal Protection Clause to which the Baker Court shifted its analysis of reapportionment? See generally Symposium, *Guaranteeing a Republican Form of Government*, 65 Colo.L.Rev. 709 (1994). See also Williams, *The "Guarantee" Clause*, 132 Harv.L.Rev. 602 (2018) (maintaining that the "guarantee" language echoed eighteenth-century treaty formulations that would not have been judicially enforceable and concluding that "available evidence regarding the [Guarantee Clause's] original meaning strongly supports" treating disputes under the provision as nonjusticiable).

(3) Constitutional Amendments. In Coleman v. Miller, 307 U.S. 433 (1939), the Court "affirmed" a judgment of the Supreme Court of Kansas refusing to restrain the Kansas Secretary of State from certifying that Kansas had ratified the Child Labor Amendment. Chief Justice Hughes, in an opinion for three Justices, said (a) that the question whether Kansas, once having rejected the amendment, could later ratify it was a question that Congress had the ultimate authority to decide, and (b) that while ratification of a proposed amendment must occur within a "reasonable time" after promulgation of the proposal, decision of that question was "essentially political and not justiciable. * * * In determining whether a question falls within that category [of political questions], the appropriateness under our system of government of attributing finality to the action of the political departments and also the lack of satisfactory criteria for a judicial determination are dominant considerations."

Justice Black, in an opinion for four Justices, said that "Congress has sole and complete control over the amending process, subject to no judicial

---

[1]   The Court in White went on to say that it did not need to determine whether every step taken by Congress to restore the state government after the rebellion complied with the Guarantee Clause, because the power to effectuate that clause was "primarily" a legislative power. 74 U.S. at 730.

[2]   See generally Shapiro, Federalism: A Dialogue 21–22, 60–61, 110–13 (1995); Merritt, *The Guarantee Clause and State Autonomy: Federalism for a Third Century*, 88 Colum.L.Rev. 1 (1988); Bonfield, *The Guarantee Clause of Article IV, Section 4: A Study in Constitutional Desuetude*, 46 Minn.L.Rev. 513 (1962). Professor Shapiro contends that in New York v. United States, 505 U.S. 144 (1992), which held that Congress may not require states to adopt legislation providing nuclear waste disposal, the Court implied that the Guarantee Clause was relevant to its decision. See Shapiro, *supra*, at 68 n.46 (also citing lower court cases relying on the Guarantee Clause).

review," and thus no opinion should be expressed even on the question whether ratification must take place within a reasonable time.[3]

Can Coleman be reconciled with the Court's earlier decision in Hawke v. Smith, 253 U.S. 221 (1920)? In that case, the Court reviewed the constitutionality of a provision of the Ohio Constitution requiring that the state legislature's ratification of a federal constitutional amendment be subject to a popular referendum in the state. The Court held that Ohio's referendum provision contradicts the procedures for adopting constitutional amendments prescribed by Article V of the United States Constitution. Article V provides that when two-thirds of each House of Congress propose a federal constitutional amendment, that amendment shall be considered part of the Constitution "when ratified by the Legislatures of three-fourths of the several states." Finding the language of Article V to be "plain," the Court held that "the method of ratification is the exercise of a national power specifically granted by the Constitution" and that it "is not the function of courts or legislative bodies, national or state, to alter the method which the Constitution has fixed." This conclusion left only the question of what constitutes the "Legislatures * * * of the several States." The Court then concluded that this term excluded any role for state referenda in the Article V process.

Does the difference between Coleman and Hawke come down to the fact that the Court in Hawke read Article V to speak unambiguously to the question of state ratification procedure, whereas the questions in Coleman lacked "satisfactory criteria for a judicial determination"? If correct, does that conclusion suggest that the political question doctrine tracks the merits, at least in some important instances? For an argument that in practice the political question doctrine does just that and is not actually a prudential rule of restraint (save, arguably, in the Guarantee Clause context), see Henkin, *Is There a Political Question Doctrine?*, 85 Yale L.J. 597 (1976).

(4) External Relations. In its survey of political question cases in Baker v. Carr, the Court observed that "[t]here are sweeping statements to the effect that all questions touching foreign relations are political questions," but then rejected this conclusion. "Our cases in this field seem invariably to show a discriminating analysis of the particular question posed, in terms of the history of its management by the political branches, of its susceptibility to judicial handling in light of its nature and posture in the specific case, and of the possible consequences of judicial action."[4]

---

[3] Compare Professor Dellinger's argument for a substantially expanded judicial role in reviewing amending process issues, *The Legitimacy of Constitutional Change: Rethinking the Amendment Process*, 97 Harv.L.Rev. 386 (1983); Professor Tribe's reply, *A Constitution We Are Amending: In Defense of a Restrained Judicial Role*, 97 Harv.L.Rev. 433 (1983); and Professor Dellinger's response, *Constitutional Politics: A Rejoinder*, 97 Harv.L.Rev. 446 (1983).

[4] On the justiciability of foreign affairs issues, see generally Ely, War and Responsibility: Constitutional Lessons of Vietnam and Its Aftermath 55–58 (1993); Franck, Political Questions/Judicial Answers: Does the Rule of Law Apply to Foreign Affairs? (1992); Tigar, *Judicial Power, the "Political Question Doctrine," and Foreign Relations*, 17 UCLA L.Rev. 1135 (1970); Champlin & Schwarz, *Political Question Doctrine and the Allocation of Foreign Affairs Power*, 13 Hofstra L.Rev. 215 (1985).

(a)   In Goldwater v. Carter, 444 U.S. 996 (1979), the Court, summarily and without opinion, vacated a lower court judgment holding, on the merits, that the President had authority to terminate a mutual defense treaty with Taiwan without the approval of either two-thirds of the Senate or a majority of both Houses of Congress. Justice Rehnquist, in an opinion for four Justices, concurred in the judgment. He argued that since the Constitution speaks only of the ratification of treaties, and not of their termination, the question of the President's power unilaterally to terminate a treaty is a political one. "[In] light of [the] fact that different termination procedures may be appropriate for different treaties, the [case] 'must surely be controlled by political standards' " (quoting Dyer v. Blair, 390 F.Supp. 1291, 1302 (N.D.Ill.1975)). Justice Rehnquist also emphasized that the question involved the politically sensitive area of foreign affairs and that, especially in this field, judicial intervention in "a dispute between coequal branches of our Government, each of which has resources available to protect and assert its interests," was inappropriate.

Justice Powell, in a concurring opinion, disagreed with the view that the question was a political one; he argued that the case was not ripe—that prudential considerations militated against judicial involvement in a quarrel between the other two branches until and unless those branches were more at loggerheads than was indicated by the record before the Court.

Justice Brennan, who dissented, would have affirmed on the merits. Although the political question doctrine bars judicial review of some executive decisions in the field of foreign policy, he argued that "the doctrine does not pertain when a court is faced with the *antecedent* question whether a particular branch has been constitutionally designated as the repository of political decisionmaking power." After addressing that antecedent question, he concluded that the Court should decide the question of presidential authority to terminate a treaty.[5]

(b)   In Japan Whaling Ass'n v. American Cetacean Society, 478 U.S. 221 (1986), the Court (unanimously on this point) rejected the government's argument that it should not review a decision of the Secretary of Commerce refusing to certify that Japan's whaling practices diminished the effectiveness of an international conservation program. "[U]nder the Constitution," the Court said, "one of the judiciary's characteristic roles is to interpret statutes, and we cannot shirk this responsibility merely because our decision may have significant political overtones" bearing on American relations with Japan.

When, if ever, could the political question doctrine be properly invoked in a statutory interpretation case? *Cf.* Chicago & S. Air Lines v. Waterman S.S. Corp., 333 U.S. 103, 111 (1948).

(c)   The Court has long shown reluctance to entertain challenges to the President's military judgment. In Martin v. Mott, 25 U.S. (12 Wheat.) 19 (1827), the Court refused to review the legality of the President Madison's

---

[5]   Justice Marshall concurred in the result. Justices White and Blackmun, dissenting from the summary disposition, would have "set the case for oral argument and give[n] it the plenary consideration it so obviously deserves."

decision to call the New York militia into the active service of the United States during the War of 1812. Article I, § 8, clause 15 of the Constitution authorizes Congress "[t]o provide for calling forth the Militia to execute the Laws of the Union, suppress Insurrections and repel Invasions." Pursuant to that authority, Congress enacted the Militia Act of 1792, 1 Stat. 264, 264, stating "that whenever the United States shall be invaded, or be in imminent danger of invasion from any foreign nation or Indian tribe, it shall be lawful for the President of the United States to call forth such number of the militia of the State or States most convenient to the place of danger, or scene of action, as he may judge necessary to repel such invasion, and to issue his order for that purpose to such officer or officers of the militia as he shall think proper."

A court martial had convicted Jacob Mott for refusing to enter into the service of the United States pursuant to an order calling up the New York militia in 1812. After refusing to pay the fine imposed by court martial, Mott was sentenced to a year in prison. Mott then challenged the order calling him into service, in relevant part, on the ground that President Madison had not made findings of the statutory conditions for calling the militia into service. In rejecting Mott's objection, the Court concluded that the Constitution and the statute confided the determination of such exigencies to the President's judgment alone. In his opinion for the Court, Justice Story wrote:

"The power thus confided by Congress to the President, is, doubtless, of a very high and delicate nature. * * * It is, in its terms, a limited power, confined to cases of actual invasion, or of imminent danger of invasion. If it be a limited power, the question arises, by whom is the exigency to be judged of and decided? * * * We are all of opinion, that the authority to decide whether the exigency has arisen, belongs exclusively to the President, and that his decision is conclusive upon all other persons. We think that this construction necessarily results from the nature of the power itself, and from the manifest object contemplated by the act of Congress. The power itself is to be exercised upon sudden emergencies, upon great occasions of state, and under circumstances which may be vital to the existence of the Union. A prompt and unhesitating obedience to orders is indispensable to the complete attainment of the object. * * * Besides, in many instances, the evidence upon which the President might decide that there is imminent danger of invasion, might be of a nature not constituting strict technical proof, or the disclosure of the evidence might reveal important secrets of state, which the public interest, and even safety, might imperiously demand to be kept in concealment.

"* * * [The President] is necessarily constituted the judge of the existence of the exigency in the first instance, and is bound to act according to his belief of the facts. * * * The law does not provide for any appeal from the judgment of the President * * *. Whenever a statute gives a discretionary power to any person, to be exercised by him upon his own opinion of certain facts, it is a sound rule of construction, that the statute constitutes him the sole and exclusive judge of the existence of those facts. * * *

"* * * When the President exercises an authority confided to him by law, the presumption is, that it is exercised in pursuance of law. * * * It is not necessary to aver, that the act which he may rightfully do, was so done. If the fact of the existence of the exigency were averred, it would be traversable, and of course might be passed upon by a jury; and thus the legality of the orders of the President would depend, not on his own judgment of the facts, but upon the finding of those facts upon the proofs submitted to a jury."

Does Martin v. Mott merely represent a judgment that the Militia Act gave the President unreviewable power to determine the appropriateness of calling the militia into service, or does Justice Story's opinion reflect a broader functional assessment of the permissibility of judicial review of the President's military judgment? See Baker v. Carr, p. 306, *supra* (describing Martin v. Mott as a political question case).[6]

During the late 1960s and early 1970s, a number of suits were brought attacking the legality of the Vietnam War and related executive actions in the absence of a formal declaration of war. The Supreme Court never gave plenary consideration to the justiciability of any of these challenges, though in one case it summarily affirmed a three-judge court's holding of nonjusticiability,[7] and in another it summarily denied leave to file an original complaint.[8] But several lower courts did pass on this question and invariably held all or a substantial part of the issues raised to be nonjusticiable.[9] Factors cited included the lack of manageable standards, commitment of final authority to other branches of the federal government, and the difficulty of gaining access to and determining the relevant facts. Several commentators urged, however, that at least some of the challenges

---

[6] Note that an earlier version of legislation granting the President the authority to call up the militia passed by the Second Congress, gave the President the power to call forth such militia "as he may judge necessary to repel [an] invasion" or "sufficient to suppress [an] insurrection." Insurrection Act of 1792, ch. 28, § 1, 1 Stat. 264 (repealed 1795). The Act, however, also required the President to seek certification from a judge before calling forth the militia in certain circumstances. *Id.* § 2. (providing that a judge need "notif[y] to the President" that "the laws of the United States shall be opposed, or the execution thereof obstructed, in any state, by combinations too powerful to be suppressed by the ordinary course of judicial proceedings, or by the powers vested in the marshals by this act"). Under the auspices of the 1792 Act, "President Washington sent troops to put down the Whiskey Rebellion only after receiving certification from * * * Supreme Court Justice [James Wilson] that the situation was dire enough to warrant such a dramatic response." Tyler, *Assessing the Role of History in the Federal Courts Canon: A Word of Caution*, 90 Notre Dame L.Rev. 1739 (2015). What, if any, gloss does this framework put on the Court's approach in Martin v. Mott? More generally, what do the 1792 Act's terms suggest (at least from an originalist perspective) about the judicial capacity to review questions relating to war and other kinds of emergencies?

[7] Atlee v. Richardson, 411 U.S. 911 (1973). Justices Douglas, Brennan, and Stewart would have noted probable jurisdiction.

[8] Massachusetts v. Laird, 400 U.S. 886 (1970). Justices Harlan, Stewart, and Douglas dissented; Justice Douglas, in a separate opinion, considered the justiciability issue at some length. In several other cases involving similar challenges, there were dissents from decisions denying certiorari. *E.g.*, Mora v. McNamara, 389 U.S. 934 (1967); Da Costa v. Laird, 405 U.S. 979 (1972).

[9] *E.g.*, Mitchell v. Laird, 488 F.2d 611 (D.C.Cir.1973); Orlando v. Laird, 443 F.2d 1039 (2d Cir.1971); Massachusetts v. Laird, 451 F.2d 26 (1st Cir.1971). In Orlando, the court held that there was a manageable standard "imposing on the Congress a duty of mutual participation in the prosecution of war," but that the question of "[t]he form which congressional authorization should take is one of policy, committed to the discretion of Congress and outside the power and competency of the judiciary."

presented justiciable issues concerning the scope of executive power. See, e.g., Henkin, Paragraph (3), *supra*, at 623–24.[10]

If American actions in Vietnam and Cambodia had been held to violate the Constitution, what consequences would have flowed from the decision? Do problems of judicial enforcement and confrontation with other branches loom larger in a case challenging executive actions in Vietnam than in a case such as Powell?[11] Have challenges to more recent military actions confirmed the lesson of the Vietnam-era cases or left the door open for reconsideration?[12]

Despite concerns about confronting the President on questions of military judgment in a time of armed conflict, the Court has also, at times, shown a willingness to do just that. The Court, of course, famously ordered the federal government to relinquish control over steel mills seized during the Korean Conflict, notwithstanding President Truman's executive order specifically finding that seizure of the mills in the face of an impending labor strike was essential to the Nation's military efforts. See Youngstown Sheet & Tube Co. v. Sawyer, 343 U.S. 579 (1952). Justice Black's opinion for the Court held that the power to seize the mills did not lie within the President's Article II commander-in-chief power (§ 2, cl. 1) or within the more general

---

[10] For echoes of the Vietnam decisions, see Crockett v. Reagan, 720 F.2d 1355 (D.C.Cir.1983), and Sanchez-Espinoza v. Reagan, 770 F.2d 202 (D.C.Cir.1985), holding nonjusticiable challenges to the Reagan Administration's activities in El Salvador and Nicaragua.

[11] Some earlier cases suggest that, at least in some contexts, the presence of a political question cannot rest on the asserted absence of judicially manageable standards for determining the existence of a "war." See, e.g., Fleming v. Mohawk Wrecking Co., 331 U.S. 111, 115 (1947) (determining whether after the cessation of hostilities in World War II, the President retained authority to redistribute functions within the executive branch under the First War Powers Act, whose authorization expired six months after "the termination of the war"); Prize Cases, 67 U.S. 635, 669 (1863) (holding that despite the absence of a congressional declaration of war, the Civil War constituted a "war" for purposes of determining the question whether a right to prize exists); Bas v. Tingy, 4 U.S. (4 Dall.) 37 (1800) (determining whether hostilities between the United States and France constituted "war" for purposes of the law of capture). See also note 39, *supra*.

[12] In challenges to post-Vietnam era conflicts, lower court decisions have relied on various justiciability doctrines to avoid passing on the legality of military actions undertaken by the executive. See, e.g., Dellums v. Bush, 752 F.Supp. 1141 (D.D.C.1990) (holding that a suit challenging the constitutional authority of the first Bush administration to launch the Gulf War without congressional authorization was unripe because Congress had not acted with respect to the issue); Campbell v. Clinton, 203 F.3d 19, 25 (D.C.Cir.2000) (holding that members of Congress lacked standing to challenge whether the Clinton administration's intervention in Kosovo violated the War Powers Resolution); Doe v. Bush, 323 F.3d 133, 140–41 (1st Cir.2003) (holding unripe a suit seeking to enjoin second Bush administration from launching war against Iraq without a declaration of war by Congress). These actions have expressed a variety of views on the political question doctrine. In Dellums, the district court declined to hold that the political question doctrine precluded review of a challenge to the President's launching a war without a congressional declaration of war, reasoning that the Supreme Court had in many contexts determined whether the country was at war and that it would be inappropriate for the judiciary to disregard "the clause granting to the Congress, and to it alone, the authority 'to declare war.'" Compare also, e.g., Campbell v. Clinton, *supra*, at 25 (Silberman, J., concurring) (arguing in connection with challenge to Kosovo intervention that no judicially manageable standards are available to determine applicability of War Powers Resolution and what counts as "war" under the Constitution), with *id.* 37 (Tatel, J., concurring) (concluding that historical practice and precedent provides judicially manageable standard to determine what counts as a "war" in a constitutional sense and to apply the less exacting statutory trigger for the War Powers Resolution).

grant of "the executive Power" (§ 1, cl. 1), but rather fell squarely within Congress's Article I authority to enact laws "necessary and proper" to carry into execution its other powers (§ 8, cl. 18), presumably including the power (as Justice Jackson noted in his concurrence) to "raise and support Armies" and to "provide and maintain a Navy" (§ 8, cls. 12–13). Justice Black noted that whatever the scope of the President's authority as commander-in-chief in theaters of war, "we cannot with faithfulness to our constitutional system hold that the Commander in Chief of the Armed Forces has the ultimate power as such to take possession of private property in order to keep labor disputes from stopping production." Given Justice Jackson's observation, in concurrence, that "what our forefathers * * * envision[ed] [about executive war powers], or would have envisioned had they foreseen modern conditions, must be divined from materials almost as enigmatic as the dreams Joseph was called upon to interpret for Pharaoh," how did the Justices derive judicially manageable standards for drawing the necessary lines?[13] Even though the government argued that the power to seize the mills was committed to the President by virtue of the commander-in-chief power, none of the Justices found it controversial to determine the scope of that commitment. Although the government did not raise the political question doctrine in Youngstown, how different are the factors that the Court handled easily in that case from the factors that come into play in classic political question doctrine cases?

(d) In reviewing military judgments that implicate individual rights, the Court has frequently (and, sometimes, infamously) given significant deference to the political branches' decisions. See, *e.g.*, Hirabayashi v. United States, 320 U.S. 81 (1943) (holding that an executive order imposing a curfew on Japanese Americans during World War II did not result from an unconstitutional delegation of legislative power or violate the equal protection component of the Due Process Clause and noting that "[w]here, as they did here, the conditions call for the exercise of judgment and discretion and for the choice of means by those branches of the Government on which the Constitution has placed the responsibility of warmaking, it is not for any court to sit in review of the wisdom of their action or substitute its judgment for theirs"); Korematsu v. United States, 323 U.S. 214 (1944) (reviewing legality of the mass incarceration of Japanese Americans during World War II and relying on Hirabayashi for the conclusion that " 'we cannot reject as unfounded the judgment of the military authorities and of Congress' " that resulted in the challenged evacuation order that led to Korematsu's detention under the auspices of Executive Order 9066); Rostker v. Goldberg, 453 U.S. 57 (1981) (rejecting a challenge under the equal protection component of the Due Process Clause to the application of the Military Selective Service Act to males only and noting that "perhaps in no other area has the Court accorded Congress greater deference" than in cases involving

---

[13]   For an in-depth historical study of the President's war powers, see Barron & Lederman, *The Commander in Chief at the Lowest Ebb—A Constitutional History*, 121 Harv.L.Rev. 941 (2008); Barron & Lederman, *The Commander in Chief at the Lowest Ebb—Framing the Problem, Doctrine, and Original Understanding*, 121 Harv.L.Rev. 689 (2008). For a contrasting view, see Yoo, *The Continuation of Politics by Other Means: The Original Understanding of War Powers*, 84 Calif.L.Rev. 167 (1999).

"Congress' authority over national defense and military affairs"). Is the political question doctrine just the ultimate exhibition of deference—of complete deference—by the courts to the political branches?[14]

Should a textually demonstrable commitment of power to Congress or the President under a power-conferring provision of the Constitution ever preclude judicial review of an alleged violation of individual rights under another provision of the Constitution? What would have been the result in the Nixon case if Nixon had alleged a due process or equal protection violation involving race-based discrimination? Choper, *The Political Question Doctrine: Suggested Criteria*, 54 Duke L.J. 1457 (2005), contends that allegations of individual rights violations should never be deemed to present political questions.[15]

(5) Political Questions and Political Cases. The mere fact that a case has political stakes or has generated political controversy clearly does not render it nonjusticiable under the political question doctrine. "The doctrine of which we treat is one of 'political questions,' not one of 'political cases.'" Baker v. Carr, 369 U.S. 186, 217 (1962).

The Court's willingness to decide cases charged with political consequences was dramatically manifest in two decisions arising from the 2000 presidential election in the state of Florida, Bush v. Palm Beach County Canvassing Board, 531 U.S. 70 (2000) (per curiam), and Bush v. Gore, 531 U.S. 98 (2000) (per curiam), the latter of which reversed a decision of the Florida Supreme Court ordering a manual recount of ballots that had failed to register any presidential choice in a machine count. The Court ruled that a hand recount in which election officials were directed only to attempt to discern "the will of the voter" would lead to counting disparities and violate the Due Process and Equal Protection Clauses. Apart from the obvious political ramifications, there were colorable arguments, raised in amicus curiae briefs, that the cases involved political questions in the technical sense.[16] In particular, amici argued that the Twelfth Amendment commits to Congress the question whether a state's electors have been chosen in accord with the constitutionally specified requirements of Article II. Nonetheless, the Court opinions did not refer to the political question

---

[14] Emphasizing the distinction between deference and complete abdication, however, Professor Tyler writes: "[T]he Court has reiterated that even when the war power is at its zenith, its exercise does not stand immune from judicial review, particularly in cases dealing with the consequences of war. And when the war power is abused in this context, the courts have interposed respectfully to remind the political branches that exercises of the war power are not without restrictions." Tyler, *Is Suspension A Political Question?*, 59 Stan.L.Rev. 333, 407 (2006)

[15] In Hamdi v. Rumsfeld, 542 U.S. 507, 578 (2004), Justice Scalia, joined by Justice Stevens and with the endorsement of Justice Thomas, asserted in dissent that if Congress were to suspend the writ of habeas corpus, any challenge to its action would present a political question under the Suspension Clause, Article I, § 9, cl. 2. For a contrasting view, see Tyler, *Is Suspension a Political Question?*, note 14, *supra*. For further discussion, see Chap. XI, Sec. 2, *infra*.

[16] See also Barkow, *More Supreme Than Court? The Fall of the Political Question Doctrine and the Rise of Judicial Supremacy*, 102 Colum.L.Rev. 237, 273–300 (2002); Chemerinsky, *Bush v. Gore Was Not Justiciable*, 76 Notre Dame L.Rev. 1093, 1105–09 (2001); Tribe, *Hsub v. Erog and Its Disguises: Freeing Bush v. Gore From Its Hall of Mirrors*, 115 Harv.L.Rev. 170, 276–87 (2001).

doctrine in either decision, and the concurring and dissenting opinions in
Bush v. Gore dealt with the doctrine only glancingly.

(a)   Commentators on Bush v. Gore argued that the Court that decided
it—much more than its predecessors—held a Court-centered view of
constitutionalism and regarded itself as central and indispensable in
ensuring the correctness and legitimacy of constitutional decisions. *See, e.g.*,
Barkow, note 16, *supra* (characterizing Bush v. Gore and the relative decline
of the political question doctrine as reflecting the modern Court's assumption
that it alone has the competency to identify constitutional meaning); Tribe,
note 16, *supra*, at 288 (citing, *inter alia*, Bush v. Gore as evidence that "[t]he
Court's self-confidence in matters constitutional is matched only by its
disdain for the meaningful participation of other actors in constitutional
debate"); Kramer, *Foreword: We The Court*, 115 Harv.L.Rev. 4, 153, 158
(2001) (terming Bush v. Gore an "emblematic" decision of the Rehnquist
Court and "the capstone of [its] campaign to control all things
constitutional").

(b)   In a partial inversion of Professor Bickel's famous argument that
courts should avoid decision of certain momentous issues for prudential
reasons (see Note on Political Questions, Paragraph (1), *supra*), Posner,
Breaking the Deadlock: The 2000 Election, the Constitution, and the Courts
143 (2001), suggests that there were compelling "pragmatic" reasons for the
Court to accept jurisdiction and to resolve Bush v. Gore as it did: If Gore
emerged victorious in the Florida recount, Florida's legislature was prepared
to appoint an alternate slate of electors pledged to Bush. Because of a
predictable split between the Republican-controlled House and the
Democrat-controlled Senate, "there was a real and disturbing *potential* for
disorder and temporary paralysis," and "[w]hatever Congress did would have
been regarded as the product of raw politics, with no tincture of justice." The
circumstances, Judge Posner argues, called for a "a reverse political
questions doctrine. Political considerations in a broad, nonpartisan sense
will sometimes counsel the Court to abstain, but sometimes to intervene."[17]

---

[17]   For a critique of this argument based within the same "pragmatic" framework that
Posner advocates, see Farnsworth, *"To Do a Great Right, Do a Little Wrong": A User's Guide to
Judicial Lawlessness*, 86 Minn.L.Rev. 227 (2001).

CHAPTER III

THE SUPREME COURT'S DOCKET

INTRODUCTION

Article III confers original and appellate jurisdiction on the Supreme Court, and Congress has enacted jurisdictional statutes with respect to both. Parties invoke the Court's jurisdiction through many different submissions (petitions, appeals, motions) and the Court responds through various orders, judgments, decrees, and opinions. Together, all matters brought to the Court's attention and assigned docket numbers by the clerk comprise the Court's docket. The way in which the Court resolves or disposes of matters on its docket will vary in accordance with the nature of the proceeding.

The most prominent element of the Court's docket consists of those matters on which the Court grants plenary review in appeals from state or federal court decisions, or in original jurisdiction cases. The Court typically sets plenary matters for full briefing and argument and renders a reasoned opinion disposing of the issues presented. Yet this "merits" docket, which typically consists of fewer than one hundred cases each year, is a tiny fraction of the Court's docket. The largest component of the Court's docket is devoted to its thousands of decisions each year whether to grant review by certiorari or appeal in its appellate jurisdiction, or to grant leave to file a bill of complaint in its original jurisdiction. These important decisions appear on an Order List or on a list of Miscellaneous Orders issued by the Court, and are unsigned and almost always announced without reasoning.[1] Also appearing on the Order list or a Miscellaneous List are various summary dispositions, dispositions for extraordinary or emergency relief, and dispositions on relatively mundane matters, such as briefing schedules, denials of requests for rehearing, and attorney discipline decisions.

This Chapter examines the most important elements of the Court's docket in four parts. Part I analyzes how the Court manages its appellate jurisdiction docket. Part II assesses how it manages its original jurisdiction docket and also considers fundamental issues raised by Article III's conferral of original jurisdiction on the Court. Part III examines the Court's issuance of extraordinary writs. Part IV studies the Court's emergency docket.

---

[1] The Court issues regularly scheduled lists of orders on each Monday (or, if Monday is a holiday, the next business day) after the justices hold a private conference.

1. THE APPELLATE JURISDICTION OF THE SUPREME COURT

Article III provides that in all cases within "the judicial Power" not allocated to the Supreme Court's original jurisdiction, "the supreme Court shall have appellate Jurisdiction, both as to Law and Fact, with such Exceptions, and under such Regulations as the Congress shall make." Since the Judiciary Act of 1789, Congress has by statute provided only for a fraction of this appellate jurisdiction. The appellate jurisdiction of the Supreme Court is examined throughout the book—most notably, in Chapter IV's discussion of Congress's power to limit the Supreme Court's appellate jurisdiction, and in Chapter V's discussion of Supreme Court review of state court decisions. This Section focuses on the growth of Supreme Court control over its appellate docket, the significance of that control, and the policies that inform that control.

NOTE ON THE HISTORY OF SUPREME COURT DISCRETION IN ITS STATUTORY APPELLATE JURISDICTION

This Note sketches the statutory development of the Supreme Court's appellate jurisdiction with special emphasis on how Congress and the Court transformed the Court's appellate docket from one that from 1789 until 1891 was entirely mandatory into one that today is almost entirely discretionary.[1]

(1) 1789–1891. The original structure of federal courts established by the Judiciary Act of 1789 had at its base two levels of trials courts—district courts, which had an original jurisdiction, and circuit courts, which had both original jurisdiction and authority to review on writ of error certain district court decisions. The 1789 Act authorized the Court to review final judgments or decrees from the highest state courts by a writ of error in cases that denied the validity of a federal claim or defense; and as modified by an 1803 statute, it authorized the Supreme Court to review by writ of error or appeal certain federal circuit court civil cases.[2] This basic scheme lasted for more than a century, with changes only of detail. Throughout the period, the Court lacked discretion to pick and choose appellate cases: its appellate jurisdiction was entirely mandatory.[3] It was in the context of this jurisdictional scheme that Chief Justice Marshall famously stated, "We have no more right to decline

---

[1]   For more detailed treatment of this evolution, see Frankfurter & Landis, The Business of the Supreme Court: A Study in the Federal Judicial System (1928); Watts, *Constraining Certiorari Using Administrative Law Principles*, 160 U.Pa.L.Rev. 1, 7–18 (2011); Hartnett, *Questioning Certiorari: Some Reflections Seventy-Five Years After the Judges' Bill*, 100 Colum.L.Rev. 1643, 1649–1713 (2000).

[2]   Judiciary Act of 1789, §§ 22, 25, as modified, Act of March 3, 1803.

[3]   Both a writ of error and an appeal issued as of right. A writ of error allowed a litigant to challenge a final judgment issued by a lower court only as to questions of law. An appeal allowed a litigant to challenge a final judgment issued by a lower court on both questions of law and fact but was (beginning with the Act of March 3, 1803) permitted only in admiralty and equity cases.

the exercise of jurisdiction which is given, than to usurp that which is not given." Cohens v. Virginia, 19 U.S. 264, 404 (1821).

(2) The Evarts Act of 1891. With the massive growth of federal constitutional and statutory law after the Civil War, two problems emerged in federal court appellate jurisdiction. The circuit courts, which consisted of a district court judge and one or two Supreme Court justices, proved ill-equipped to perform their growing appellate duties. And the Supreme Court's caseload grew dramatically, as did its backlog. By 1890, "it took three and a half years between the time a case was first docketed in the Supreme Court and the time it was orally argued before the justices." Rehnquist, The Supreme Court 236 (2001).

Congress addressed these problems in 1891 in the Evarts Act.[4] That statute created the circuit courts of appeals with their own judges, interposed these courts between the Supreme Court and the circuit and district courts, and stripped the extant circuit courts of their appellate jurisdiction. It also gave the Supreme Court mandatory appellate jurisdiction over specified circuit court decisions, and declared other such decisions—diversity cases, suits under the revenue and patent laws, criminal cases, and admiralty suits—to be "final." The Supreme Court could nonetheless review such final decisions through two mechanisms. First, the Evarts Act authorized the courts of appeals to certify to the Supreme Court "any questions or propositions of law concerning which it desires the instruction of that court for its proper decision."[5] Second, it empowered the Supreme Court to review final decisions "by certiorari or otherwise, * * * as if it had been carried by appeal or writ of error to the Supreme Court."[6]

This latter provision, for the first time, gave the Supreme Court plenary discretion over a component of its appellate docket.[7] It "marked an innovation in the concept of federal appellate jurisdiction, for it meant that

---

[4] Act of Mar. 3, 1891, ch. 517, 26 Stat. 826. The House Report to the Evarts Act recounted the following statistics. In 1860, the Court had 310 cases on its docket and decided 91 of them. In 1870, it had 636 cases on its docket and disposed of 280. In 1880, the Court had 1,202 cases on its docket and decided 365. In 1886, it had 1,396 cases on its docket and decided 451. At the time of the Evarts Act, there were 1,381 cases on the Court's docket and the Court was "over three years (about three years and two months) behind its work." H.R.Rep. No. 50–942, at 3 (1888).

[5] Certification to the Supreme Court originated in an 1802 statute that provided for certification to the Supreme Court of "any question" on which "opinions of the judges [of a federal circuit court] shall be opposed," and added that a certified question "shall, by the [Supreme Court], be finally decided." 2 Stat. 159–161 (1802). For the background to this statute, and a history of certification to the Supreme Court prior to the Evarts Act, see Moore & Vestal, *Present and Potential Role of Certification in Federal Appellate Procedure*, 35 Va.L.Rev. 1, 10–14 (1949).

[6] The Evarts Act altered the Court's appellate jurisdiction over circuit or district court decisions in other ways as well but did not alter the prevailing scheme of review of state court judgments by writ of error.

[7] The Court prior to 1891 sometimes issued the common law writ of certiorari pursuant to the "all writs" provision in § 14 of the Judiciary Act of 1789. At common law, certiorari was used primarily to transfer records to a superior court or to remove a criminal case before trial; but it was also used by a superior court, in its discretion, to secure judicial review of an inferior tribunal. Oaks, *The "Original" Writ of Habeas Corpus in the Supreme Court*, 1962 Sup.Ct.Rev. 153, 182–83. The common law writ of certiorari, however, "was never issued as freely in federal courts as it had been in England," and prior to the Evarts Act the Supreme Court did not deploy it as a discretionary means to review the judgment of an inferior court. *Id.* 183–84. See also United States v. Young, 94 U.S. 258, 259–60 (1876).

even when a case met constitutional and statutory jurisdictional requirements, the Court could decline to exercise its power to decide it if the case did not meet certain standards formulated by the Court itself." Leiman, *The Rule of Four*, 57 Colum.L.Rev. 975, 979 (1957). The Court developed its own criteria for exercising this discretion, see p. 331, *infra*.

(3) The 1914 Act. A 1914 statute expanded the Supreme Court's appellate jurisdiction over state court judgments—which had been limited to cases where the state court denied a federal claim or defense—to include cases in which the state court upheld a federal claim or defense.[8] Congress tempered the impact of this expansion by empowering the Court to review such cases by discretionary writs of certiorari.[9]

(4) The Judges' Bill of 1925 and the Growth of Discretionary Appellate Jurisdiction. Despite the reforms of 1891 and 1914, the Supreme Court's caseload continued to grow in step with the growth in the economy and in public law after the Civil War. Its mandatory appellate docket thus remained large, and its backlog persisted. Congress addressed the problem in 1925 by giving the Court significantly more discretion over its appellate docket. The Judiciary Act of 1925, ch. 229, 43 Stat. 936, is known as the "Judges' Bill," since it was drafted and supported by several Supreme Court Justices under the leadership of Chief Justice Taft. Taft argued to Congress, and Congress appeared to accept, that the Court's role should not be to correct lower-court errors, but rather to pass upon "constitutional questions and other important questions of law for the public benefit." Jurisdiction of Circuit Courts of Appeals and United States Supreme Court: Hearing on H.R. 10479 Before H.Comm. on the Judiciary, 67th Cong. 2 (1922).

The Act achieved these goals by significantly expanding the Court's certiorari jurisdiction. First, it limited the Court's mandatory appellate review of state court judgments to those that invalidated a treaty or Act of Congress or upheld a state statute attacked on federal grounds. All other state court judgments were subject to review by writ of certiorari. Second, it limited the Court's mandatory review of circuit court of appeals decisions to cases "where is drawn in question the validity of a statute of any State, on the ground of its being repugnant to the Constitution, treaties, or laws of the United States, and the decision is against its validity"; and even then, obligatory review was "restricted to an examination and decision of the Federal questions presented" and could be sought only by the party relying on the state law. In all other situations the Supreme Court could pass on courts of appeals decisions only by certiorari or certification. The Act also contracted the area of direct Supreme Court review of the district courts,

---

[8]   Act of Dec. 23, 1914, ch. 2, 38 Stat. 790. For further discussion of the significance of the 1914 Act, see pp. 617–618, *infra*.

[9]   Congress extended the principle of discretionary review to cases under (among others) the Trademark Act of 1905, ch. 592, Section 18, 33 Stat. 724, 729, all bankruptcy cases, Act of Jan. 28, 1915, ch. 22, Section 4, 38 Stat. 803, 804, and, most significantly, cases under the Federal Employers' Liability Act, ch. 448, Section 3, 39 Stat. 726, 727 (1916). The 1916 law also gave the Court discretionary control via writ of certiorari over some other cases that denied federal claims. *Id.* § 2. For the details and uncertainties about the scope of the 1916 statute, see Frankfurter & Landis, note 1, *supra*, at 211–16; Hartnett, note 1, *supra*, at 1657–60.

eliminating the categories of cases in which the Evarts Act preserved direct review and shifting appellate jurisdiction to the circuit courts of appeals.

(5) The Supreme Court Expands Discretion over Mandatory Appeals. With regard to the remaining tranche of mandatory appeals, the Court expanded its practice of dismissing appeals on the ground that they did not present a substantial federal question.[10] The practice had its roots in decisions prior to the Judges' Bill. See, *e.g.*, Zucht v. King, 260 U.S. 174, 176 (1922) (Court must "decline jurisdiction whenever it appears that the constitutional question presented is not * * * substantial in character."); New Orleans v. New Orleans Waterworks Co., 142 U.S. 79, 87 (1891) (dismissing a frivolous claim "wholly without foundation"); see generally Ulman & Spears, *Dismissed for Want of a Substantial Federal Question,* 20 B.U.L.Rev. 501, 506–16 (1940). To facilitate insubstantiality determinations without time-consuming oral argument, the Court in 1928 required each appellant to file a jurisdictional statement "particularly disclosing the basis on which it is contended this court has jurisdiction to review on appeal,"[11] and in 1936 required the jurisdictional statement to include "the grounds upon which it is contended the questions involved are substantial."[12]

The Court initially limited jurisdictional dismissals for want of a substantial federal question to inherently frivolous federal claims or federal claims foreclosed by prior decisions. But in the 1930s, it began to dismiss non-frivolous claims based on their relative importance and other non-merits discretionary factors that were similar to those that governed petitions for certiorari. See Griswold, *Equal Justice Under Law,* 33 Wash. & Lee L.Rev. 813, 820–21 (1976); Ulman & Spears, *supra,* at 528–30, 529 n.135. The Court typically announced these insubstantiality rulings in a per curiam decision that provided little if any reasoning. While the dismissals were styled as "jurisdictional," they were (in contrast to denials of petitions for certiorari) treated as rulings on the merits entitled to stare decisis effect. See Hicks v. Miranda, 422 U.S. 332, 343–44 (1975); compare Washington v. Confederated Bands & Tribes of Yakima Indian Nation, 439 U.S. 463, 477 n.20 (1979) (noting that while summary dismissals are "rulings on the merits" they do not "have the same precedential value here as does an opinion of this Court after briefing and oral argument on the merits").

This practice was consistent with mandatory statutory appellate jurisdiction to the extent that the Court was simply deciding appeals on the merits without plenary briefing and oral argument. Hicks, 422 U.S. at 343–44. But several Justices have commented that the Court's standards for appeals were akin to its standards for certiorari. See, *e.g.*, Hogge v. Johnson, 526 F.2d 833, 836 (4th Cir.1975) (Clark, J., concurring) (former Justice Clark stating that when he was on the Court, "appeals from state court decisions received treatment similar to that accorded petitions for certiorari"); 31 A.L.I.Proc. 1, 6 (1954) (Chief Justice Warren stating that "[i]t is only accurate to a degree to say that our jurisdiction in cases on appeal is obligatory as

---

[10]   The Court also sometimes affirmed appeals, typically without significant explanation, from both state and federal courts.

[11]   Sup.Ct.R. 12, 275 U.S. 603 (1928).

[12]   Sup.Ct.R. 12, 297 U.S. 733 (1936).

distinguished from discretionary on certiorari"). And many commentators criticized the Court for defying Congress's command of a statutory appeal as of right by dismissing appeals due to discretionary factors other than the merits. See, *e.g.*, Wechsler, *The Appellate Jurisdiction of the Supreme Court: Reflections on the Law and the Logistics of Direct Review*, 34 Wash. & Lee L.Rev. 1043, 1061 (1977); Griswold, *supra*, at 821–24.[13] The practice was also criticized on the ground that the Court's per curiam dismissals for insubstantiality provided too little guidance to lower courts and were treated as precedents by the Supreme Court inconsistently and opportunistically. See, *e.g.*, Griswold, *supra*, at 821–23.

(6) 1988: Virtual Elimination of the Supreme Court's Mandatory Appellate Jurisdiction. Congress was less concerned with these criticisms of the Court's discretionary practices related to its mandatory appellate docket than it was by the Court's relentlessly growing caseload on that docket. Between 1925 and 1988, as the Court's caseload continued to swell, Congress in fits and starts continued to expand the Court's discretionary control of its appellate docket via certiorari. Then, in 1988, in the Supreme Court Case Selections Act, Congress with broad support and little controversy abolished almost all of the Supreme Court's mandatory appellate jurisdiction.[14] The Act amended 28 U.S.C. § 1254 to make all cases in the court of appeals reviewable only by writ of certiorari, and amended 28 U.S.C. § 1257 to make all state court judgments raising federal questions reviewable only by writ of certiorari. The few appeals as of right that remain today are from orders granting or denying injunctive relief by three-judge district courts as specified in 28 U.S.C. § 1253.[15]

---

[13]   The Court has also asserted discretion to refuse to answer questions certified by the courts of appeals pursuant to 28 U.S.C. § 1254(2), see, *e.g.*, Wisniewski v. United States, 353 U.S. 901, 902 (1957), even though the statute purports to mandate certification jurisdiction, see Moore & Vestal, note 5, *supra*, at 42. The Court rarely considers certified questions, and courts of appeals today, perhaps unsurprisingly, rarely certify. On certification, see generally Tyler, *Setting the Supreme Court's Agenda: Is There a Place for Certification?*, 78 Geo.Wash.L.Rev. 1310 (2010); Nielson, *The Death of the Supreme Court's Certified Question Jurisdiction*, 59 Cath.U.L.Rev. 483 (2010).

[14]   The Act passed Congress by voice votes. It also had the blessing of all nine Justices. In response to an invitation of members of Congress who sponsored the predecessor to the 1988 Act, the Justices in 1982 wrote a letter expressing their "complete support for the proposals * * * substantially to eliminate the Supreme Court's mandatory jurisdiction." The main reason was that mandatory appeals required the Court to "devote a great deal of its limited time and resources on cases which do *not*, in Chief Justice Taft's words, 'involve principles, the application of which are of wide public importance or governmental interest, and which should be authoritatively declared by the final court.' " H.R.Rep. No. 100–660, at 2, 27 (1988), 1988 4 U.S.C.C.A.N. (102 Stat. 662) 767–81.

[15]   Several statutes contemplate adjudication in three-judge district courts. See, *e.g.*, 28 U.S.C. § 2284(a) (requiring a three-judge district court "when an action is filed challenging the constitutionality of the apportionment of congressional districts or the apportionment of any statewide legislative body"); 18 U.S.C. § 3626(a)(3)(B) (providing that a prisoner release order in civil actions concerning prison conditions can be entered only by a three-judge district court).

The Court continues to dispose summarily of most of the few remaining appeals on its docket. Of the four appeals filed in October Term 2022, for example, the Court noted probable jurisdiction in one, dismissed one as moot, and dismissed two for want of jurisdiction. See Journal of the Supreme Court of the United States, October Term, 2022, iii.

INTRODUCTORY NOTE ON THE CONSIDERATION AND DISPOSITION OF PETITIONS FOR CERTIORARI

The statutes establishing the Court's appellate review by certiorari say nothing explicit about how the Court should exercise its discretion. The Court has developed its own rules and practices.

(1) The Criteria for Certiorari. Supreme Court Rule 10 states the "considerations" that govern the Court's discretionary review on writ of certiorari. It provides that a petition for a writ of certiorari "will be granted only for compelling reasons," and then lists a number of factors that, "although neither controlling nor fully measuring the Court's discretion, indicate the character of the reasons the Court considers:

"(a) a United States court of appeals has entered a decision in conflict with the decision of another United States court of appeals on the same important matter; has decided an important federal question in a way that conflicts with a decision by a state court of last resort; or has so far departed from the accepted and usual course of judicial proceedings, or sanctioned such a departure by a lower court, as to call for an exercise of this Court's supervisory power;

"(b) a state court of last resort has decided an important federal question in a way that conflicts with the decision of another state court of last resort or of a United States court of appeals;

"(c) a state court or a United States court of appeals has decided an important question of federal law that has not been, but should be, settled by this Court, or has decided an important federal question in a way that conflicts with relevant decisions of this Court."

The Rule concludes: "A petition for a writ of certiorari is rarely granted when the asserted error consists of erroneous factual findings or the misapplication of a properly stated rule of law."

Professor Perry argues that Rule 10 "is really not much help," since "[w]ith the exception of specifying certain types of conflicts," the Court has "essentially defined certworthiness tautologically; that is, that which makes a case important enough to be certworthy is a case that we consider to be important enough to be certworthy." Perry, Deciding to Decide: Agenda Setting in the United States Supreme Court 33–34 (1991). Empirical studies conclude that a clear conflict of authority between lower courts is the most salient factor informing a grant of certiorari, but identify other salient factors, including the identity of the advocates, "importance" understood in various ways, exogenous historical events, and egregiously erroneous lower court decisions. See Narechania, *Certiorari in the Roberts Court*, 67 St. Louis U.L.J. 587 (2023); Narechania, *Certiorari in Important Cases*, 122 Colum.L.Rev. 923 (2022); Nielson & Stancil, *Gaming Certiorari*, 170 U.Pa.L.Rev. 1129 (2022); Heise, Wells & Chutkow, *Does Docket Size Matter? Revisiting Empirical Accounts of the Supreme Court's Incredibly Shrinking*

Docket, 95 Notre Dame L.Rev. 1565 (2020); Lazarus, *Docket Capture at the High Court*, 119 Yale L.J. Online 89 (2009).[1]

(2) The Number of Petitions Filed and Granted. In recent years, between five and seven thousand cases have been docketed in the Supreme Court each Term. Only a handful of these cases have fallen within the Supreme Court's original jurisdiction or its much-reduced obligatory appellate jurisdiction. Almost all of the remainder are petitions for certiorari under 28 U.S.C. § 1254(1) or § 1257. Of these petitions, approximately two-thirds are filed *"in forma pauperis,"* in which the Court waives costs and printing requirements on the basis of a showing of indigence. (These *"ifp"* petitions are filed primarily by state and federal prisoners.) The remaining third or so have been petitions in which costs are paid by the parties.

Below is a chart of the Court's grant rate since 1970.[2] While many factors inform the trends reflected in these numbers, the impact of the 1988 statute that made the Court's appellate jurisdiction almost entirely discretionary stands out.

	1970	1980	1990	2000	2010	2020
Paid/Original Cases						
Cases docketed	1588	2224	1988	1955	1558	1830
Review granted	129 (8.1%)	168 (7.6%)	117 (5.9%)	87 (4.5%)	77 (4.9%)	71 (3.9%)
IFP Cases						
Cases docketed	1831	1950	3514	5897	6299	3477
Review granted	41 (2.2%)	17 (0.9%)	27 (0.8%)	14 (0.2%)	14 (0.2%)	3 (0.1%)

---

[1]   Professors Nielson and Stancil survey the literature and conclude that "[a]ll else equal, a petition for certiorari review is *less likely* to be granted if one or more of the following criteria are satisfied: the petition is based on frivolous claims; there are '[t]hreshold' jurisdictional concerns or the fear that '[i]ntervening circumstances [may] have arisen since the lower court's decision that may moot the case'; the lower court opinion is 'fact-bound'; there are '[g]aps in the appellate record that may make the facts unclear'; the lower court opinion is unpublished; the decision below is not final; the lower court opinion offers alternative grounds; the lower court holds that a claim has been waived or, for whatever reason, the lower court did not decide the issue; the conflict in the lower courts is based on a decision that has been discredited or no longer has authority; or the conflict is not well presented." Nielson & Stancil, *supra*, at 1140–41 (citations omitted).

[2]   The numbers are drawn from the Journal of the Supreme Court of the United States for the Terms in question. Following the Journal's conventions, the "Paid and Original Cases" include the paid cases on certiorari and appeal, and original jurisdiction cases, respectively. The combined "Review granted" figures are the sum of the number of cases where the Court granted a petition for certiorari, granted an appeal, or set a case for oral argument after a prior grant of motion for leave to file a bill of complaint in its original jurisdiction. The figures exclude summary reversals and cases for which the Court granted, vacated, and remanded a decision.

Combined

Cases docketed	3419	4174	5502	7852	7857	5307
Review granted	170 (5.0%)	185 (4.4%)	144 (2.6%)	101 (1.3%)	91 (1.2%)	74 (1.4%)

In the 2021, Term the Court received 4900 petitions and granted 76 cases for review (1.6%). In the 2022 Term, the Court received 4159 petitions and granted 62 cases for review (1.5%). For examination of the reasons for the Court's shrinking docket beyond the impact of the 1988 reform, see Lane, *A Separation-of-Powers Approach to the Supreme Court's Shrinking Caseload*, 10 J.L. & Cts. 1 (2022); Heise, Wells & Chutkow, *supra*; Owens & Simon, *Explaining the Supreme Court's Shrinking Docket*, 53 Wm. & Mary L.Rev. 1219 (2012).

(3) The Processing of Petitions. The burden of considering certiorari petitions is lightened by the work of the Justices' law clerks, who prepare memoranda summarizing the petitions and recommending dispositions. Most of the Justices use "pool memos" prepared by a clerk of one of the Justices and distributed to the others in the group. The majority of petitions are not discussed by the Justices in the conference in which they make their decisions. Rather, the Justices only consider the petitions on a "discuss list" prepared by the Chief Justice that includes cases that the Justices decide, often based on pool memoranda, that they want to consider at conference. Shapiro et al., Supreme Court Practice ch. 5 (11th ed.2019); Rehnquist, The Supreme Court 233–35 (2001). The Court has suggested that only 3% or so of all petitions are included on the discuss list. See Supreme Court, Statement of the Court Regarding the Code of Conduct 11 (Nov. 13, 2023) ("Roughly 97 percent of [certiorari petitions] may be and are denied at a preliminary stage, without joint discussion among the Justices, as lacking any reasonable prospect of certiorari review."). Petitions not on the discuss list are automatically denied. Shapiro et al., *supra*, ch. 5.

Despite these time-saving devices, the exercise of discretion is clearly a burden. Over the years, the extent of the burden, the quality of the exercise of the Court's discretion, and the desirability of change have been vigorously debated.[3]

---

[3] These issues were well canvassed in testimony before the Presidential Commission on the Supreme Court of the United States. See, in particular, the testimony of the Supreme Court Practitioners' Committee, Michael Dreeben, Deepak Gupta, and Richard Lazarus. Presidential Commission on the Supreme Court of the United States, Comments, at https://www.regulations. gov/document/PCSCOTUS-2021-0001-0003/comment.

Singleton v. Commissioner of Internal Revenue

439 U.S. 940 (1978).
Petition for Certiorari to the United States Court of Appeals for the Fifth Circuit.

The petition for a writ of certiorari is denied.

■ MR. JUSTICE BLACKMUN, with whom MR. JUSTICE MARSHALL and MR. JUSTICE POWELL join, dissenting.

The issue in this federal income tax case is whether a cash distribution that petitioner husband (hereafter petitioner) received in 1965 with respect to his shares in Capital Southwest Corporation (CSW) was taxable to him as a dividend, as the United States Court of Appeals for the Fifth Circuit held, or whether that distribution was a return of capital and therefore not taxable, as the Tax Court held. I regard the issue as of sufficient importance in the administration of the income tax laws to justify review here, and I dissent from the Court's failure to grant certiorari. * * *

I hope that the Court's decision to pass this case by is not due to a natural reluctance to take on another complicated tax case that is devoid of glamour and emotion and that would be remindful of the recent struggles, upon argument and reargument, in United States v. Foster Lumber Co., 429 U.S. 32 (1976), and Laing v. United States, 423 U.S. 161 (1976).

■ Opinion of MR. JUSTICE STEVENS respecting the denial of a petition for writ of certiorari.

What is the significance of this Court's denial of certiorari? That question is asked again and again; it is a question that is likely to arise whenever a dissenting opinion argues that certiorari should have been granted. Almost 30 years ago Mr. Justice Frankfurter provided us with an answer to that question that should be read again and again.

> "This Court now declines to review the decision of the Maryland Court of Appeals. The sole significance of such denial of a petition for writ of certiorari need not be elucidated to those versed in the Court's procedures. It simply means that fewer than four members of the Court deemed it desirable to review a decision of the lower court as a matter 'of sound judicial discretion.' [quoting then Supreme Court Rule 38, paragraph 5]. A variety of considerations underlie denials of the writ, and as to the same petition different reasons may lead different Justices to the same result. This is especially true of petitions for review on writ of certiorari to a State court. Narrowly technical reasons may lead to denials. Review may be sought too late; the judgment of the lower court may not be final; it may not be the judgment of a State court of last resort; the decision may be supportable as a matter of State law, not subject to review by this Court, even though the State court also passed on issues of federal law. A decision may satisfy all these

technical requirements and yet may commend itself for review to fewer than four members of the Court. Pertinent considerations of judicial policy here come into play. A case may raise an important question but the record may be cloudy. It may be desirable to have different aspects of an issue further illumined by the lower courts. Wise adjudication has its own time for ripening.

"Since there are these conflicting and, to the uninformed, even confusing reasons for denying petitions for certiorari, it has been suggested from time to time that the Court indicate its reasons for denial. Practical considerations preclude. In order that the Court may be enabled to discharge its indispensable duties, Congress has placed the control of the Court's business, in effect, within the Court's discretion. * * * If the Court is to do its work it would not be feasible to give reasons, however brief, for refusing to take these cases. The time that would be required is prohibitive, apart from the fact as already indicated that different reasons not infrequently move different members of the Court in concluding that a particular case at a particular time makes review undesirable. It becomes relevant here to note that failure to record a dissent from a denial of a petition for writ of certiorari in nowise implies that only the member of the Court who notes his dissent thought the petition should be granted.

"Inasmuch, therefore, as all that a denial of a petition for a writ of certiorari means is that fewer than four members of the Court thought it should be granted, this Court has rigorously insisted that such a denial carries with it no implication whatever regarding the Court's views on the merits of a case which it has declined to review. The Court has said this again and again; again and again the admonition has to be repeated." Opinion respecting the denial of the petition for writ of certiorari in Maryland v. Baltimore Radio Show, 338 U.S. 912, 917–919 (1950).

When those words were written, Mr. Justice Frankfurter and his colleagues were too busy to spend their scarce time writing dissents from denials of certiorari. Such opinions were almost nonexistent. It was then obvious that if there was no need to explain the Court's action in denying the writ, there was even less reason for individual expressions of opinion about why certiorari should have been granted in particular cases.

Times have changed. Although the workload of the Court has dramatically increased since Mr. Justice Frankfurter's day, most present Members of the Court frequently file written dissents from certiorari denials. It is appropriate to ask whether the new practice serves any important goals or contributes to the strength of the institution.

One characteristic of all opinions dissenting from the denial of certiorari is manifest. They are totally unnecessary. They are examples of the purest form of dicta, since they have even less legal significance than the orders of the entire Court which, as Mr. Justice Frankfurter reiterated again and again, have no precedential significance at all.

Another attribute of these opinions is that they are potentially misleading. Since the Court provides no explanation of the reasons for denying certiorari, the dissenter's arguments in favor of a grant are not answered and therefore typically appear to be more persuasive than most other opinions. Moreover, since they often omit any reference to valid reasons for denying certiorari, they tend to imply that the Court has been unfaithful to its responsibilities or has implicitly reached a decision on the merits when, in fact, there is no basis for such an inference.

In this case, for example, the dissenting opinion suggests that the Court may have refused to grant certiorari because the case is "devoid of glamour and emotion." I am puzzled by this suggestion because I have never witnessed any indication that any of my colleagues has ever considered "glamour and emotion" as a relevant consideration in the exercise of his discretion or in his analysis of the law. With respect to the Court's action in this case, the absence of any conflict among the Circuits is plainly a sufficient reason for denying certiorari. Moreover, in allocating the Court's scarce resources, I consider it entirely appropriate to disfavor complicated cases which turn largely on unique facts. A series of decisions by the courts of appeals may well provide more meaningful guidance to the bar than an isolated or premature opinion of this Court. As Mr. Justice Frankfurter reminded us, "wise adjudication has its own time for ripening."

Admittedly these dissenting opinions may have some beneficial effects. Occasionally a written statement of reasons for granting certiorari is more persuasive than the Justice's oral contribution to the Conference. For that reason the written document sometimes persuades other Justices to change their votes and a case is granted that would otherwise have been denied. That effect, however, merely justifies the writing and circulating of these memoranda within the Court; it does not explain why a dissent which has not accomplished its primary mission should be published.

It can be argued that publishing these dissents enhances the public's understanding of the work of the Court. But because they are so seldom answered, these opinions may also give rise to misunderstanding or incorrect impressions about how the Court actually works. Moreover, the selected bits of information which they reveal tend to compromise the otherwise secret deliberations in our Conferences. There are those who believe that these Conferences should be conducted entirely in public or, at the very least, that the votes on all Conference matters should be publicly recorded. The traditional view, which I happen to share, is that confidentiality makes a valuable contribution to the full and frank exchange of views during the decisional process; such confidentiality is especially valuable in the exercise of the kind of discretion that must be employed in processing the thousands of certiorari petitions that are reviewed each year. In my judgment, the importance of preserving the tradition of confidentiality outweighs the minimal educational value of these opinions.

In all events, these are the reasons why I have thus far resisted the temptation to publish opinions dissenting from denials of certiorari.

NOTE ON THE SUPREME COURT'S CERTIORARI POLICY

(1) The Rule of Four. As Justice Stevens's opinion in Singleton suggests, the Court by unwritten custom grants a petition for certiorari if four Justices vote to grant the writ.[1] Congress probably "had the rule of four in mind when it approved the Judges Bill [in 1925]." Leiman, *The Rule of Four*, 57 Colum.L.Rev. 975, 985 (1957). The testifying Justices frequently mentioned the so-called "rule of four" when defending the fairness of the certiorari process. *Id.* 981, 985–86.

"The rule of four is a device by which a minority of the Court can impose on the majority a question that the majority does not think it appropriate to address." Kurland & Hutchinson, *The Business of the Supreme Court, O.T. 1982*, 50 U.Chi.L.Rev 628, 645 (1983). But what, exactly, does it mean for the majority to have to consider the question? In Leiman's view, it means only that the vote of four would commit all nine to a more extended look at the case; it would not commit anyone to a vote on the merits if a majority were convinced, after briefing and oral argument, that the writ should be dismissed as improvidently granted. (Five Justices can vote to dismiss certiorari as improvidently granted.[2]) Justice Stevens articulated a similar view in New York v. Uplinger, 467 U.S. 246 (1984). In that case, the majority after oral argument dismissed a writ of certiorari as improvidently granted because of the ambiguity of the state court opinion below and the possibility that it rested on state law. Four dissenters said that the merits of the decision below were "properly before us and should be addressed." The majority did not discuss the significance of the rule of four, but Justice Stevens, concurring, did:

"As long as we adhere to the Rule of Four, four Justices have the power to require that a case be briefed, argued, and considered at a postargument conference. Why, then, should they not also have the power to command that its merits be decided by the Court? * * * It might be suggested that [under the rule of four] the case must be decided unless there has been an

---

[1]   For an examination of this and other unwritten customs that have a significant impact on the Court's decision-making, see Bressman, *The Rise and Fall of the Self-Regulatory Court*, 101 Tex.L.Rev. 1 (2022).

[2]   For explanation and analysis of the Court's practice of dismissing writs of certiorari as improvidently granted, see Solimine & Gely, *The Supreme Court and the Sophisticated Use of DIGs*, 18 Sup.Ct.Econ.Rev. 155 (2010); Solimine & Gely, *The Supreme Court and the DIG: An Empirical and Institutional Analysis*, 2005 Wis.L.Rev. 1421 (2005).

intervening development that justifies a dismissal. * * * I am now persuaded, however, that there is *always* an important intervening development that may be decisive. The Members of the Court have always considered a case more carefully after full briefing and argument on the merits than they could at the time of the certiorari conference, when almost 100 petitions must be considered each week. * * * [T]he Rule of Four is a valuable, though not immutable, device for deciding when a case must be argued, but its force is largely spent once the case has been heard. At that point, a more fully informed majority of the Court must decide whether some countervailing principle outweighs the interest in judicial economy in deciding the case."

But other Justices appear to believe that the rule of four implies that any dismissal of a case as improvidently granted after oral argument must be based on reasons beyond the ones that led the majority of Justices not to vote to grant certiorari in the first place. See Ferguson v. Moore-McCormack Lines, Inc., 352 U.S. 521, 559 (1957) (Harlan, J., concurring and dissenting) (arguing that "due adherence to [the rule of four] requires that once certiorari has been granted a case should be disposed of on the premise that it is properly here, in the absence of considerations appearing which were not manifest or fully apprehended at the time certiorari was granted.").

For an examination of how the rule of four might induce strategic behavior by the Justices, lower courts, and litigants, see Nielson & Stancil, *Gaming Certiorari*, 170 U.Pa.L.Rev. 1129 (2022); Revesz & Karlan, *Nonmajority Rules and the Supreme Court*, 136 U.Pa.L.Rev. 1067 (1988).

(2) The Significance of a Denial of Certiorari. Justice Frankfurter in the Baltimore Radio Show Case, quoted by Justice Stevens in Singleton, stated the orthodox view that a denial of certiorari "carries with it no implication whatever regarding the Court's views on the merits of a case which it has declined to review." Compare Justice Jackson's statement about denials of certiorari in his concurrence in Brown v. Allen, 344 U.S. 443, 543 (1953):

"I agree that, as *stare decisis*, denial of certiorari should be given no significance whatever. It creates no precedent and approves no statement of principle entitled to weight in any other case. But, for the case in which certiorari is denied, its minimum meaning is that this Court allows the judgment below to stand with whatever consequences it may have upon the litigants involved under the doctrine of *res judicata* as applied either by state or federal courts. A civil or criminal judgment usually becomes *res judicata* in the sense that it is binding and conclusive even if new facts are discovered and even if a new theory of law were thought up, except for some provision for granting a new trial, which usually is discretionary with the trial court and limited in time."

To test these claims, consider the fate of the constitutional right to same-sex marriage prior to the Supreme Court's ruling upholding that right in Obergefell v. Hodges, 576 U.S. 644 (2015). Before Obergefell, thirty-seven states had legalized same-sex marriage—eleven through democratic processes, eight through state court interpretations of state constitutions, and eighteen by virtue of lower federal court rulings invalidating or enjoining same-sex marriage bans under the U.S. Constitution. States sought Supreme Court review from many of these lower federal court rulings, but the Court in the two years prior to Obergefell denied petitions for certiorari every time. "Those refusals then allowed the lower-court rulings to go into effect, clearing the way for same-sex partners to marry in those states." Vladeck, The Shadow Docket: How the Supreme Court Uses Stealth Rulings to Amass Power and Undermine the Republic 62 (2023); see generally Blackman & Wasserman, *The Process of Marriage Equality*, 43 Hastings Const.L.Q. 243 (2016) (comprehensive analysis of the role of the Court's certiorari denials, in combination with its stays and denials of stays of lower court rulings, to the spread of marriage equality). Professor Vladeck draws general lessons:

"[E]ven if denials of certiorari are not 'precedential,' there are circumstances in which they can still have enormous practical impact. Sometimes, they send implicit messages both to lower courts and to policymakers about the justices' lack of appetite for particular issues, or their unwillingness to set aside lower-court judgments even on questions they have never considered. In other cases, where the lower-court ruling at issue blocked the enforcement of a state or federal law or policy, a denial of certiorari preserves that status quo; the policy remains blocked even if the reasons why the lower court froze it have not received the Supreme Court's explicit imprimatur. In general, although denials of certiorari therefore cannot be cited as proof of the Supreme Court's views on any particular issue, they regularly produce significant substantive effects by changing the status quo on the ground." Vladeck, *supra*, at 64.

Consistent with this view, Professor Linzer observed a tendency on the part of lower courts to rely on denials of certiorari as indicating the Supreme Court's view on the merits in cases "in which the Court had denied certiorari despite the great importance and controversial nature of an earlier lower court holding or series of holdings identical to the one being made by the current lower court; cases in which the Supreme Court had remanded a case to a lower court and then had denied certiorari after the lower court had made fact findings or legal holdings on the remand; and cases involving limited grants of certiorari." Linzer, *The Meaning of Certiorari Denials*, 79 Colum.L.Rev. 1227, 1278 (1979).

(3) Publicly Announced Dissents from Denials of Certiorari. The Court announces denials of certiorari on an "Order List" that simply lists the petitions denied without comment. Occasionally, however, individual Justices will append statements or opinions, including dissents, to particular denials of certiorari.

As Justice Stevens indicated in Singleton, the practice of noting dissents to denials of certiorari, and of writing opinions in support of such dissents, became increasingly common in in the 1970s. The practice has continued to the present. Some such dissents are noted without any comment. Some argue that certiorari should have been granted without taking a view on the merits. And some dissents argue the merits of the case. Linzer, Paragraph (2), *supra*, at 1267–73, places dissents on the merits from denials of certiorari into three general categories: those that concern "what the dissenter perceives as a miscarriage of justice in the particular case"; " 'irredentist' dissents" that state disagreement with clear precedent; and dissents that address "unresolved points of law" where the dissenters "set forth their views on how the issues should be resolved."

Are such dissents of value in informing the bar and the public of possible directions the law may take, and of areas of interest to particular Justices? If the decision to accept or reject a petition is a judicial act, is the expression of dissent any more "unnecessary" (as Justice Stevens put it) than a dissent from any other judicial act? Is the problem with such dissents that in the absence of a defender like Justice Stevens, the majority's unexplained denial is too easy a target?

The Justices also sometimes append statements "respecting the denial of certiorari" to comment on matters related to a case. An unusual example occurred in McClinton v. United States, 143 S.Ct. 2400 (2023), where the Court denied a certiorari petition that raised the question whether prosecutors can introduce information about conduct for which a defendant was acquitted in the sentencing phase for a related crime. Three Justices attached opinions to the denial in connection with the Sentencing Commission's announcement that it would soon address the acquitted-conduct issue. Justice Sotomayor raised concerns about acquitted-conduct sentencing and warned that "[if] the Commission does not act expeditiously or chooses not to act, * * * this Court may need to take up the constitutional issues presented." Justice Kavanaugh, in a statement joined by Justices Gorsuch and Barrett, noted that acquitted-conduct sentencing "raises important questions" and added that the Court should "wait for the Sentencing Commission's determination before" deciding whether to grant certiorari on the issue. Justice Alito, concurring in the denial, laid out "countervailing arguments" in favor of acquitted-conduct sentencing. He also noted that "no one should misinterpret my colleagues' statements as an effort to persuade the Sentencing Commission to alter its longstanding decision that acquitted conduct may be taken into account at sentencing." But weren't some of the Justices' statements trying to influence the Sentencing Commission? If so, were they an appropriate use of the Court's certiorari discretion?

(4) Question Selection. The Court in its certiorari jurisdiction focuses on particular questions, not the entire case. Rule 14.1(a) requires a petition for certiorari to present "questions" for review, and states that "[o]nly the questions set out in the petition, or fairly included therein, will be considered by the Court." The Court has said that because it receives many thousands of petitions each year and has "the capacity to decide only a small fraction of these cases on the merits," it "forces the parties to focus on the questions the Court has viewed as particularly important, thus enabling us to make efficient use of our resources." Yee v. Escondido, 503 U.S. 519, 536 (1992).

Within three years of the 1925 Judges' Bill that significantly expanded the Court's discretionary certiorari jurisdiction, the Court asserted the authority to limit grants of certiorari, in its discretion, to particular questions rather than to every issue in the case. See Olmstead v. United States, 276 U.S. 609, 609–10 (1928) (granting three petitions but "limiting their consideration" to a single question "whether the use of evidence of private telephone conversations * * * intercepted by means of wire tapping, is a violation of the Fourth and Fifth Amendments"). It later asserted the authority to order the parties to address a question not raised in the certiorari petition. For some famous examples, see Citizens United v. Fed. Election Comm'n, 557 U.S. 932 (2009) (ordering parties after argument to brief for reargument the question, "should the Court overrule [*inter alia*] * * * Austin v. Michigan Chamber of Commerce, 494 U.S. 652 (1990) * * *?"); Furman v. Georgia, 403 U.S. 952 (1971) (adding the question, "Does the imposition and carrying out of the death penalty in [these cases] constitute cruel and unusual punishment in violation of the Eighth and Fourteenth Amendments?"); Gideon v. Wainwright, 372 U.S. 335, 338 (1963) (noting that the Court added the question, "Should this Court's holding in Betts v. Brady, 316 U.S. 455 [(1942)], be reconsidered?").

The selection of questions for review amplifies the Court's agenda-setting power in its certiorari jurisdiction.[3] This discretionary power, Chief Justice Warren stated, permits the Court "to achieve control of its docket" and "to establish our national priorities in constitutional and legal matters." *Retired Chief Justice Warren Attacks, Chief Justice Burger Defends Freund Study Group's Composition and Proposal*, 59 A.B.A.J. 721, 728 (1973). For a defense of the long-settled practice, see Bice, *The Limited Grant of Certiorari and the Justification for Judicial Review*, 1975 Wis.L.Rev. 343 (1975). For criticism on the grounds that the practice is in tension with the case or controversy requirement, thrusts the Court into politics, and is not supported by the relevant jurisdictional statutes, see Hartnett, *Questioning Certiorari: Some Reflections Seventy-Five Years After the Judges' Bill*, 100 Colum.L.Rev. 1643, 1705–07 (2000); Johnson, *The Origins of Supreme Court Question Selection*, 122 Colum.L.Rev. 793 (2022); Johnson, *The Active Vices*, 74 Ala.L.Rev. 917 (2023).

(5) Summary Reversals. The Supreme Court occasionally grants certiorari and summarily reverses a case on the merits based only on the papers that seek review. When the Court's docket featured a good number of mandatory appeals, it tended to summarily reverse (or affirm) cases in clear conflict (or agreement) with controlling Supreme Court precedent. See Chen, *Summary Dispositions as Precedent*, 61 Wm. & Mary L.Rev. 691, 701 (2020). Chen notes that as the Court's certiorari docket grew during Chief Justice Warren's tenure, the Court developed the frequent practice of granting a petition for certiorari and, without additional briefing or oral argument, reversing the case on the merits with no more than a citation or two of explanation. This practice on the certiorari side of the docket was more controversial because the Court did not need to resolve the case, and because its reversals often seemed to extend the law without explanation or guidance. Bickel & Wellington, *Legislative Purpose and the Judicial Process: The Lincoln Mills Case*, 71 Harv.L.Rev. 1, 3 (1957), for example, argued that the

---

[3]   So too does its practice of appointing *amici* to defend lower court judgments in cases where the party that prevailed in the lower court declines for various reasons to defend its judgment. For a description and criticism of this practice, see Monaghan, *On Avoiding Avoidance, Agenda Control, and Related Matters*, 112 Colum.L.Rev. 665, 680, 691–93 (2012); Goldman, Note, *Should the Supreme Court Stop Inviting Amici Curiae to Defend Abandoned Lower Court Decisions?*, 63 Stan.L.Rev. 907 (2011).

Court announced "results accompanied by little or no effort to support them in reason" based on per curiam orders that "fail to build the bridge between the authorities they cite and the results they decree." See generally Brown, *The Supreme Court, 1957 Term—Foreword: Process of Law*, 72 Harv.L.Rev. 77 (1958).

Today, the Court typically provides a reasoned per curiam opinion when it summarily reverses.[4] Yet the practice is only lightly institutionalized. Rule 16.1 says that an "appropriate order" after consideration of the certiorari documents "may be a summary disposition on the merits." And recall that Rule 10 says that certiorari petitions will be granted "only for compelling reasons" and indicates (with emphasis added) that "certiorari is *rarely* granted when the asserted error consists of erroneous factual findings or the misapplication of a properly stated rule of law," which implies that it is sometimes granted in these circumstances. See, *e.g.*, Presley v. Georgia, 558 U.S. 209, 209–13 (2010) (per curiam) (summarily reversing because court below "contravened this Court's clear precedents"); Wearry v. Cain, 577 U.S. 385, 395 (2016) (per curiam) (noting that "the Court has not shied away from summarily deciding fact-intensive cases where, as here, lower courts have egregiously misapplied settled law"). The dominant rationale for such reversals is that they permit the Supreme Court with a relatively small expenditure of resources to discipline lower state and federal courts that defy clear Supreme Court precedent. See Baude, *Foreword: The Supreme Court's Shadow Docket*, 9 N.Y.U.J.L. & Lib. 1, 43–49 (2015); see also Hartnett, note 4, *supra*, at 597–606.

The Roberts Court has issued approximately six summary reversals per year on average.[5] These decisions have focused primarily on a handful of subject matter areas: federal habeas corpus more than anything else, followed by qualified immunity, and then state habeas corpus, and the Federal Arbitration Act. See Chen, *supra*, at 707; Hartnett, note 4, *supra*, at 594–95; Baude, *supra*, at 43–45. In the federal habeas corpus and qualified immunity contexts, moreover, the state and federal governments win much more often than they lose. See Chen, *supra*, at 707–09; Hartnett, note 4, *supra*, at 594–96. What explains these patterns? How likely is it that of the

---

[4] The votes needed for a summary reversal at the Court are unclear. Justices Alito and Breyer are reported to have said that a summary reversal requires six votes. Weiss, *Breyer Explains Reason for Late-Night Opinions, Comments on Once Secret Summary Reversal Custom*, ABA J. (Oct. 18, 2021), And yet the Court has summarily reversed, by a vote of 5–4, see, *e.g.*, Am. Tradition P'ship, Inc. v. Bullock, 567 U.S. 516 (2012). Professor Hartnett notes: "It does appear * * * that a summary reversal will not be entered over the dissent of four who call for full briefing and argument. That is, if as many as four dissent on the merits, or as many as four would deny certiorari (or some combination thereof), five may summarily reverse. But if four call for full briefing and argument, it seems that they can insist on it. There does not appear to be a case in which four who wanted full briefing and argument were refused; such a refusal would seem to be inconsistent with the Rule of Four." Hartnett, *Summary Reversals in the Roberts Court*, 38 Cardozo L.Rev. 591, 614–15 (2016).

[5] This figure is based on Chen, *supra*, at 706, from October Term (OT) 2005 through OT 2018, and on SCOTUSblog's Stat Packs for OT 2019–OT 2021. These figures exclude the species of summary orders that grant certiorari petitions, vacate the judgment below, and remand the case to the lower court (so-called "GVRs"), typically in light of some intervening decision or a change in law. This practice, another element of the Court's extraordinary discretion over its certiorari docket, is analyzed and critiqued in Bruhl, *The Supreme Court's Controversial GVRs— And an Alternative*, 107 Mich.L.Rev. 711 (2009).

thousands of certiorari petitions the Court receives, plain error by recalcitrant lower courts warrants a higher rate of reversal predominantly in these ways in these types of cases?

If the proper criterion for summary reversal is a manifest and grievous error in a case that plainly does not require full briefing and argument, should the Court summarily reverse only when unanimous? Doesn't a dissent from a summary reversal undermine its justification? Is even a unanimous summary reversal unfair to the losing party unless an opportunity is afforded for briefing on the merits? See Brown, *supra*, at 94–95 (suggesting this). Would a requirement of such briefing "undermine the power of the message sent by summary reversal"? Hartnett, note 4, *supra*, at 614.

Summary reversals are difficult to assess because it is often unclear whether the Court is exercising its discretion based on a principled need for hierarchical control or on a special interest in some issues more than others. The lack of guiding criteria for summary reversal, combined with the extremely limited process provided before summary reversal, has led some commentators to question the soundness of the practice. See, *e.g.*, Chen, *supra*, at 710–19; Baude, *supra*, at 52–55.

(6) Certiorari Before Judgment. The Court has the authority to grant certiorari following a federal district court decision, but before the federal court of appeals renders judgment, if the case is formally pending "in" the court of appeals, which typically means that the case is docketed there. See 28 U.S.C. § 1254(1); see also 28 U.S.C. § 2101(e). The Court purports to exercise its discretion to grant certiorari before judgment in cases that it deems of extraordinary public importance and in need of swift resolution. See Sup.Ct.R. 11 (certiorari before judgment "will be granted only upon a showing that the case is of such imperative public importance as to justify deviation from normal appellate practice and to require immediate determination in this Court"); see also Department of Commerce v. New York, 588 U.S. 752 (2019) (granting the writ before judgment in February 2019 in a case challenging the legality of a question in the decennial census "because the case involved an issue of imperative public importance, and the census questionnaire needed to be finalized for printing by the end of June 2019").

In the two decades after the 1988 Amendments expanding the Court's certiorari jurisdiction, the Court granted certiorari before judgment three times. But in the three years from February 2019 through January 2022, the Court granted certiorari before judgment fourteen times, six of which resulted in plenary review. See Vladeck, *The Rise of Certiorari Before Judgment, SCOTUSblog* (Jan. 25, 2022). Professor Vladeck speculates that the sharp uptick reflects the Court's rapidly changing composition, possible hostility toward certain circuits, or broader pressures, reflected mostly on the Court's emergency docket (discussed in Section 4, *infra*), "to act at the outset of most major contemporary legal disputes." Vladeck argues that the Court should explain its certiorari before judgment practice, since "if courts of appeals can be bypassed even in cases that aren't of both the utmost national importance and temporal urgency, then it would certainly help if the parties—and, even more importantly, the lower courts—were clued in."

(7) The Consequences of Agenda Control. It is hard to overstate the significance of the Supreme Court's near-complete control over its appellate docket. The Court today does not passively accept and decide cases presented to it, as it did during its first century. Rather, it determines in its discretion, and by its own conception of importance, what cases to take and what issues to address, and when and how to do so, often irrespective of the wishes of the parties.

(a) Justice Black correctly believed that "whoever has the power to decide what cases will appear has the power of the Court." Black, My Father: A Remembrance 187 (1975). The Court's increasing control of its docket has been central to its enhanced role in American life in the last century for at least two reasons. First, and most obviously, agenda control allows the Court to focus on and develop legal issues that it cares about, and to delay considering or ignore other issues. See Vladeck, Paragraph (2), *supra*, at 52 ("A Court with more time on its hands, and with more of an ability to decide which cases to hear and to not hear, is necessarily better situated for pursuing long-term substantive goals than one that is limited to simply reacting to each case as it comes in."). And second, agenda control fosters legal change on the topics the Court cares about by allowing the justices— through denials of certiorari or other summary process—to "hand down decisions opening new frontiers in constitutional law without fearing that such rulings would inundate them with follow-on cases." *Id.* 53. In this sense, the Court's plenary docket control can be seen as akin to other legal doctrines analyzed in this book that lower the costs to the Supreme Court of legal change—for example, injunctions (as opposed to damages), see, *e.g.*, pp. 1190–1191, *infra*, and certain nonretroactivity rules, see pp. 585, note 15 and 1320, *infra*.

Hartnett, Paragraph (4), *supra*, offers the example of the incorporation doctrine. It is no accident, he suggests, that the Court began to incorporate the many protections of the Bill of Rights in the Fourteenth Amendment soon after the Judges' Bill of 1925. He says that the Supreme Court might not have "incorporated the Fourth, Fifth, Sixth, and Eighth Amendments if it were obliged to review every state judgment that upheld a criminal conviction or sentence over a defendant's objection based on one of these amendments." *Id.* 1732. See also Vladeck, Paragraph (2), *supra*, at 51–52 (arguing, more broadly, but for similar reasons, that the "rise of the Court's discretion over its docket coincided with the birth of what's generally viewed as 'modern' constitutional law" that repudiated "the aggressive judicial protection of economic rights" and instead focused on "more protection of the rights of defendants in both federal and state criminal proceedings, as well as toward the prohibition of discrimination against members of 'discrete and insular' minority groups"). In recent years, the Court's agenda-setting power has been apparent, for example, in its grants of petitions for certiorari in cases the Court deemed important but that did not grow out of a split of lower-court authority. See, *e.g.*, Dobbs v. Jackson Women's Health Organization, 597 U.S. 215 (2022) (overruling Roe v. Wade, 410 U.S. 113

(1973)); West Virginia v. EPA, 597 U.S. 697 (2022) (invigorating the major questions doctrine).

(b) Is plenary docket control consistent with the Marbury paradigm that judicial review is an incident of the Court's obligation to adjudicate a claim of right? Hartnett, Paragraph (4), *supra*, at 1717, argues that because "[a] court that can simply refuse to hear a case can no longer credibly say that it had to decide it," the shift to a discretionary docket "calls into question the exercise of judicial review by the Supreme Court." Relatedly, Professor Monaghan argues that the Court's aggressive exercise of docket control to shape and resolve the issues "puts pressure on * * * the adversary system model and the dispute resolution model," and indicates that the Court sees its essential role "as law declaration, not dispute resolution." Monaghan, *On Avoiding Avoidance, Agenda Control, and Related Matters*, 112 Colum.L.Rev. 665, 680, 690 (2012). Is this right? Monaghan maintains that the Court's agenda control is "troublesome because it * * * allows the Court to alter the very disputes that are presented to it for resolution." But he also notes that "quite arguably, it also allows the Court, which operates at the intersection between law and politics, to accommodate more readily the manifold pressures on it—such as law development and the play of 'politics,' grandly conceived—as well as the inescapable human dimensions present in any system of adjudication." *Id*. 681.

(c) Justice Brennan claimed that the Court's "screening function is second to none in importance." Brennan, *The National Court of Appeals: Another Dissent*, 40 U.Chi.L.Rev. 473, 477 (1973). And yet this crucial exercise of judicial power is unguided by law and takes place almost entirely behind closed doors, with the public seeing only an announcement by the Court of cases granted and denied, very occasionally accompanied by a statement or dissent from one or a few justices. Professor Narechania argues that this opacity about such important decisions makes it hard for future litigants to predict the Court's actions and deprives the public and Congress of an opportunity to review and respond to the Court's decisional principles. Narechania, *Certiorari in Important Cases*, 122 Colum.L.Rev. 923, 987–89 (2022).

Should the Court give reasons for its many thousand review decisions each year? Professor Narechania argues that it should. But doing so would expend extraordinary resources. And since the explanations would surely be curt at best, the practice might provide little useful information, and indeed in the aggregate might produce more confusion or uncertainty than the current practice. If the problem is that the justices and their law clerks lack the resources to explain thousands of review decisions each year, should the Court create an office of staff attorneys to assist with the processing of and justification for certiorari decisions? See Written Statement of Richard Lazarus, Presidential Commission on the Supreme Court of the United States (2021) (proposing this). Should Congress establish a national court of appeals to screen out unworthy petitions? See Federal Judicial Center, Report of the Study Group on the Case Load of the Supreme Court 47 (1972) (proposing this). What about simply requiring the justices to disclose their votes to review or not review a case? See Watts, *Constraining Certiorari*

Using Administrative Law Principles, 160 U.Pa.L.Rev. 1 (2011) (proposing this). Given that there are many reasons to grant or deny, and that many petitions are obviously uncertworthy, would that vote disclosure reveal meaningful information?

---

2. THE ORIGINAL JURISDICTION OF THE SUPREME COURT

Marbury v. Madison

5 U.S. (1 Cranch) 137 (1803).
On Petition for Mandamus.

[See pp. 76–86, *supra*.]

NOTE ON THE POWER OF CONGRESS TO REGULATE THE ORIGINAL JURISDICTION OF THE SUPREME COURT

(1) The Constitutional and Statutory Grants. Article III, Sec. 2, cl. 2 declares: "In all Cases affecting Ambassadors, other public Ministers and Consuls, and those in which a State shall be Party, the supreme Court shall have original Jurisdiction." The Supreme Court has repeatedly said that exercise of this jurisdiction does not require enabling action by Congress. See, *e.g.*, California v. Arizona, 440 U.S. 59, 65 (1979). Nevertheless, beginning with the provision at issue in Marbury, § 13 of the Judiciary Act of 1789, Congress has specified the Court's original jurisdiction. The current provision, 28 U.S.C. § 1251, reads:

> (a) The Supreme Court shall have original and exclusive jurisdiction of all controversies between two or more States.
>
> (b) The Supreme Court shall have original but not exclusive jurisdiction of:
>
> > (1) All actions or proceedings to which ambassadors, other public ministers, consuls, or vice consuls of foreign states are parties;
> >
> > (2) All controversies between the United States and a State;
> >
> > (3) All actions or proceedings by a State against the citizens of another State or against aliens.

The congressional grants of jurisdiction, taken collectively from 1789 to the present, have given rise to three central questions. First, may Congress *expand* the original jurisdiction by assigning to it cases beyond those described in Article III, Sec. 2, cl. 2? Second, may Congress *contract* the original jurisdiction by excluding from it cases that are described in Article III, Sec. 2, cl. 2? Third, may Congress prescribe that the Supreme Court's original jurisdiction is concurrent with the jurisdiction of state and/or lower federal courts, thereby contracting its mandatory scope? This Note discusses each of these three questions.

(2) Congressional Expansion of the Original Jurisdiction. Marbury's statutory ruling, that § 13 purported to vest the Supreme Court with a general, original jurisdiction in mandamus actions, was controversial. See pp. 88–89, *supra*. No less controversial was its constitutional ruling that § 13 was invalid in that situation because it purported to confer original jurisdiction over a case other than one of those described by Article III, Sec. 2, cl. 2.

To understand the controversy over the constitutional holding, consider that a primary reason for the Court's original jurisdiction is that the exercise of jurisdiction over another sovereign (here, over one of the states, or, in the case of the foreign-envoy jurisdiction, over cases affecting a sovereign) is so sensitive that only the court of greatest dignity—the Supreme Court—should exercise it. Indeed, the Constitution itself established the Supreme Court and this original jurisdiction. These rationales can explain why Article III might bar Congress from depriving states or foreign envoys of an original hearing before the Supreme Court. See, *e.g.*, Ames v. Kansas ex rel. Johnston, 111 U.S. 449, 464 (1884). But why should Article III preclude Congress from giving other litigants direct access to the Court? To protect the Court from a crushing burden imposed by an irresponsible Congress? To protect litigants far from Washington from a possibly inconvenient forum?

(3) Congressional Restriction of the Original Jurisdiction. Consider now the opposite situation, in which Congress purports to contract the scope of original jurisdiction set forth in Article III, Sec. II, cl. 2. The question is not merely hypothetical. Today 28 U.S.C. § 1251, like its predecessor in the First Judiciary Act, falls short of the constitutional grant. For example, § 1251 does not include cases *affecting* foreign envoys but to which they are not parties,[1] nor does it include disputes between a state and a foreign nation.

(a) Elimination of Jurisdiction Altogether. Doubts that Congress may limit the constitutional grant were expressed in California v. Arizona, 440 U.S. 59 (1979), an original action by California against Arizona and the United States to quiet title to land. One question presented was whether the Supreme Court's exercise of original jurisdiction was barred by 28 U.S.C. §§ 1346(f), 2409a(a), which together had the effect of (i) waiving the United States' sovereign immunity, rendering it liable to a quiet title action, but (ii) conferring on the federal district courts *exclusive* jurisdiction over actions falling within the scope of the waiver. The Court refused to read the exclusivity provision as purporting to divest the Supreme Court of original jurisdiction, interpreting it instead merely to bar state court jurisdiction. Any other construction, the Court said, would raise constitutional difficulties: although Congress need not waive the United States' immunity from suit, once it had done so, it was far from clear that Congress could

---

[1]   Compare United States v. Ortega, 24 U.S. (11 Wheat.) 467, 468–69 (1826), holding that an indictment for "offering violence" to a public minister was not a case "affecting" the minister.

"withdraw the constitutional jurisdiction of this Court over such suits." The Framers, the Court said, seemed to wish to "[match] the dignity of the parties"—States and the envoys of foreign nations—"to the status of the Court," and "[e]limination of this Court's original jurisdiction would require those sovereign parties to go to another court, in derogation of this constitutional purpose."[2]

(b) Remedial or Procedural Limitations on the Exercise of Jurisdiction. The Supreme Court has not decided whether, or to what extent, the constitutional concern expressed in California v. Arizona extends to congressional efforts to regulate, for example, the procedures followed or the remedies available in original action. But individual Justices have suggested that Article III sharply restricts congressional power.

In Kansas v. Colorado, 556 U.S. 98 (2009), a suit between two states heard in the Supreme Court's original jurisdiction, Kansas, the prevailing party, sought to have the costs of its expert witness fees awarded against Colorado. A federal statute, 28 U.S.C. § 1821(b), authorizes the award of $40/day as witness fees for proceedings in "any court of the United States." Kansas, in seeking more than $40/day for its expert witnesses, argued first that the statute does not apply to an original action in the Supreme Court, and second that Congress lacked the constitutional power to limit the Court's ultimate authority to set its own procedures for original actions.

In an opinion by Justice Alito, the Court found it unnecessary to address either the statutory or the constitutional issue. "[A]ssuming for the sake of argument that the matter is left entirely to [its] discretion," the Court decided to apply the limitations found in § 1821(b) on the ground that "the best approach is to have a uniform rule that applies in all federal cases." Chief Justice Roberts, joined by Justice Souter, wrote a concurrence to address the constitutional question. Noting that Article III, Sec. 2, authorizes Congress to make "Exceptions" and "Regulations" concerning the Court's appellate jurisdiction but says no such thing about its original jurisdiction, the Chief Justice wrote that "[i]t is accordingly our responsibility to determine matters related to our original jurisdiction,

---

[2]   See also South Carolina v. Katzenbach, 383 U.S. 301 (1966), in which the state filed suit in the Supreme Court against Attorney General Katzenbach (a New Jersey citizen), seeking to enjoin enforcement of various provisions of the Voting Rights Act of 1965. In deciding the case, the Court did not mention § 14(b) of the Act, which provided that only the District Court for the District of Columbia "shall have jurisdiction to issue * * * any restraining order or temporary or permanent injunction" against enforcement of the Act. Justice Black, in dissent, stated that he thought § 14(b) was unconstitutional insofar as it purported to restrict the Supreme Court's original jurisdiction.

For an argument that Congress has some power to limit the Supreme Court's original jurisdiction, see Amar, *Marbury, Section 13, and the Original Jurisdiction of the Supreme Court*, 56 U.Chi.L.Rev. 443, 478–88 (1989). This conclusion flows from Amar's general view, described at pp. 429–431, *infra*, that the nine heads of jurisdiction defined in Article III, Sec. 2, cl. 1 fall into two tiers: a first tier (comprising admiralty and federal question cases and cases affecting foreign envoys) based on subject matter and over which federal jurisdiction is mandatory; and a second tier (comprising the remaining six heads of jurisdiction) based on party status and over which federal jurisdiction is optional. Because controversies to which a state is a party fall within the optional second tier, Amar argues, Congress need not confer federal court jurisdiction over them, notwithstanding their inclusion in the Original Jurisdiction Clause. For critical discussion of this argument, see Meltzer, *The History and Structure of Article III*, 138 U.Pa.L.Rev. 1569, 1602–08 (1990).

including the availability and amount of witness fees." He agreed that the statutory rate was reasonable but stressed that "the choice is ours."[3]

Can it be that no congressional regulation of procedure or remedies can have effect of its own force in original actions in the Supreme Court, and that the statutory rule will be followed only if, as the Chief Justice suggested in Kansas v. Colorado, the Court chooses in its discretion to do so? Consider statutes providing that all "process issuing from a court of the United States shall be under the seal of the court and signed by the clerk thereof" (28 U.S.C. § 1691), or that certified copies of the Journals of the Senate and the House of Representatives "shall be received in evidence with the same effect as the originals would have" (28 U.S.C. § 1736). Does Article III permit the Supreme Court to decide each of these matters on its own, reaching an independent resolution?

(4) Concurrent Jurisdiction. Ever since § 13 of the Judiciary Act of 1789 provided that the Supreme Court shall have "original, *but not exclusive* jurisdiction" over certain cases involving ambassadors, other public ministers, and consuls, Congress has claimed the authority to make the Court's original jurisdiction concurrent with the jurisdiction of the lower federal courts or of state courts. Relatedly, despite dicta in Marbury that the original and the appellate jurisdictions are mutually exclusive, Chief Justice Marshall's opinion for the Court in Cohens v. Virginia, 19 U.S. (6 Wheat.) 264, 395–401 (1821), held in the alternative that Congress may grant appellate jurisdiction over cases falling within the Court's original jurisdiction.

Today, § 1251(a) makes the Supreme Court's original jurisdiction exclusive only for controversies between states. Section 1251(b) makes the remainder of the Court's original jurisdiction concurrent. But § 1251(b) does not itself confer concurrent jurisdiction on any other court; instead, it simply permits the operation of any jurisdiction otherwise granted. In Ames v. Kansas ex rel. Johnston, 111 U.S. 449 (1884), the Court put to rest any doubts about the constitutionality of concurrent jurisdiction, leaning heavily on the understanding of the First Congress and on an unbroken line of judicial authority. The opinion also stressed the inconvenience to the parties that would arise if the Supreme Court had to hear every small claim involving a state or a foreign envoy; an obvious additional concern, though not stated explicitly, was the potential burden on the Court itself.

---

[3]   A similar question was raised in South Carolina v. Regan, 465 U.S. 367 (1984), where the state sought to enjoin, as a violation of its Tenth Amendment rights, federal income taxation of the interest on certain state-issued bonds. A federal statute, 26 U.S.C. § 7421(a), bars injunctions in suits in any court challenging the assessment or collection of any federal tax. The Court did not address § 7421(a)'s applicability to original actions in the Supreme Court, finding instead that the statute did not apply when an aggrieved party, like South Carolina, lacks an alternative forum for litigating a tax's validity. Justice O'Connor, concurring in the judgment, disagreed with that reading of § 7421(a), but agreed that the statute did not bar South Carolina's action; to rule otherwise would raise the "grave" question "whether Congress constitutionally can impose remedial limitations so jurisdictional in nature that they effectively withdraw the original jurisdiction of this Court."

For discussion of whether statutory restrictions on the exercise of federal habeas corpus jurisdiction apply to the Supreme Court when entertaining "original" writs of habeas corpus, see p. 362, *infra*.

A case falling within the Court's concurrent jurisdiction but filed in lower federal court, or filed in state court but turning on a federal question, is subject to Supreme Court review. But the Supreme Court has not doubted the validity of concurrent jurisdiction even when there is no prospect of such review—for example, when a state brings an action raising only state law issues against a citizen of another state. See Plaquemines Tropical Fruit Co. v. Henderson, 170 U.S. 511, 520–21 (1898). When the plaintiff is a state or a foreign envoy, might that result be rationalized on the basis that the "right" to file suit in the Supreme Court is a waivable privilege of the sovereign, and that the privilege was waived by filing the suit within a state court's concurrent jurisdiction?

NOTE ON PROCEDURE IN ORIGINAL ACTIONS

Supreme Court Rule 17.3 states that "[t]he initial pleading [in an original action] shall be preceded by a motion for leave to file." The Court often disposes of major jurisdictional issues when ruling on the motion for leave to file. Although four votes suffice to grant a writ of certiorari, a majority seems to be needed to grant a motion for leave to file. Oklahoma ex rel. Williamson v. Woodring, 309 U.S. 623 (1940) (motion denied by evenly divided Court). From 1961–1993, 50 of the 102 motions for leave to file were denied, generally without opinion. See McKusick, *Discretionary Gatekeeping: The Supreme Court's Management of Its Original Jurisdiction Docket Since 1961*, 45 Me.L.Rev. 185, 188–90 (1993).

Although the Seventh Amendment applies to trials at common law in the Supreme Court (as 28 U.S.C. § 1872 recognizes), no jury trial seems to have been held since the eighteenth century, as original cases have usually been equitable in character.[1] Invariably, the Court appoints a special master to take evidence and prepare findings of fact, which, though in theory only advisory, the Court regularly accepts. See United States v. Raddatz, 447 U.S. 667, 683 n.11 (1980). But *cf.* Maryland v. Louisiana, 451 U.S. 725, 765 (1981) (Rehnquist, J., dissenting) (referring to the "appellate-type review which this Court necessarily gives to [a special master's] findings and recommendations"). See generally Shapiro et al., Supreme Court Practice ch. 10 (11th ed.2019).

INTRODUCTORY NOTE ON THE SUPREME COURT'S POWER TO DECLINE TO EXERCISE ORIGINAL JURISDICTION

In cases that fall within the Supreme Court's original jurisdiction, what is the scope of the Court's power to decline to hear the case? Does it matter whether the denial occurs in the Court's statutory concurrent jurisdiction

---

[1]   See Georgia v. Brailsford, 3 U.S. (3 Dall.) 1 (1794). A study of Brailsford found that the jury in that case was a "special jury" of merchants, who could provide expertise and insight about mercantile custom. See Shelfer, Note, *Special Juries in the Supreme Court*, 123 Yale L.J. 208 (2013).

under § 1251(b), which would relegate a litigant to an alternative forum, or in its statutory exclusive jurisdiction under § 1251(a), which denies the litigant any forum to pursue its claim?

Nebraska v. Colorado

577 U.S. 1211 (2016).
On Motion for Leave to File a Bill of Complaint.

The motion for leave to file bill of complaint denied.

■ JUSTICE THOMAS, with whom JUSTICE ALITO joins, dissenting from the denial of motion for leave to file complaint.

Federal law does not, on its face, give this Court discretion to decline to decide cases within its original jurisdiction. Yet the Court has long exercised such discretion, and does so again today in denying, without explanation, Nebraska and Oklahoma's motion for leave to file a complaint against Colorado. I would not dispose of the complaint so hastily. Because our discretionary approach to exercising our original jurisdiction is questionable, and because the plaintiff States have made a reasonable case that this dispute falls within our original and exclusive jurisdiction, I would grant the plaintiff States leave to file their complaint.

I

The Constitution provides that "[i]n all Cases . . . in which a State shall be [a] Party, the supreme Court shall have original Jurisdiction." Art. III, § 2, cl. 2. In accordance with Article III, Congress has long provided by statute that this Court "shall have original and exclusive jurisdiction of all controversies between two or more States." 28 U.S.C. § 1251(a).

Federal law is unambiguous: If there is a controversy between two States, this Court—and only this Court—has jurisdiction over it. Nothing in § 1251(a) suggests that the Court can opt to decline jurisdiction over such a controversy. Context confirms that § 1251(a) confers no such discretion. When Congress has chosen to give this Court discretion over its merits docket, it has done so clearly. Compare § 1251(a) (the Court "shall have" jurisdiction over controversies between States) with § 1254(1) (cases in the courts of appeals "may be reviewed" by this Court by writ of certiorari) and § 1257(a) (final judgments of state courts "may be reviewed" by this Court by writ of certiorari).

The Court's lack of discretion is confirmed by the fact that, unlike other matters within our original jurisdiction, our jurisdiction over controversies between States is exclusive. Compare § 1251(a) with § 1251(b) (the Court "shall have original but not exclusive jurisdiction" of other cases over which Article III gives this Court original jurisdiction). If this Court does not exercise jurisdiction over a controversy between two States, then the complaining State has no judicial forum in which to seek relief. When presented with such a controversy, "[w]e have no more right to decline the exercise of jurisdiction which is given, than to usurp that which is not given." Cohens v. Virginia, 6 Wheat. 264, 404 (1821) (Marshall, C. J.).

Nonetheless, the Court has exercised discretion and declined to hear cases that fall within the terms of its original jurisdiction. See, *e.g.*, United States v. Nevada, 412 U.S. 534, 537–540 (1973) (per curiam) (controversy between United States and individual States); Ohio v. Wyandotte Chemicals Corp., 401 U.S. 493, 500–505 (1971) (action by a State against citizens of other States). The Court has even exercised this discretion to decline cases where, as here, the dispute is between two States and thus falls within our *exclusive* jurisdiction. See, *e.g.*, Arizona v. New Mexico, 425 U.S. 794, 796–798 (1976) (per curiam). The Court has concluded that its original jurisdiction is "obligatory only in appropriate cases" and has favored a "sparing use" of that jurisdiction. Illinois v. Milwaukee, 406 U.S. 91, 93–94 (1972). The Court's reasons for transforming its mandatory, original jurisdiction into discretionary jurisdiction have been rooted in policy considerations. The Court has, for example, cited its purported lack of "special competence in dealing with" many interstate disputes and emphasized its modern role "as an appellate tribunal." Wyandotte Chemicals Corp., 401 U.S., at 498. * * *

Because our discretionary approach appears to be at odds with the statutory text, it bears reconsideration. Moreover, the "reasons" we have given to support the discretionary approach are policy judgments that are in conflict with the policy choices that Congress made in the statutory text specifying the Court's original jurisdiction. * * *

NOTE ON THE ORIGINAL JURISDICTION AS AN INAPPROPRIATE FORUM

(1) Actions Within the Supreme Court's Concurrent Original Jurisdiction. For 150 years, the Supreme Court "never refused to permit the filing of a complaint in a case falling within its original jurisdiction." Texas v. California, 141 S.Ct. 1469, 1470 (2021) (Alito, J., joined by Thomas, J., dissenting). It first did so in Massachusetts v. Missouri, 308 U.S. 1 (1939). There, Massachusetts sought declaratory and injunctive relief to protect an alleged exclusive right to exact taxes from trusts administered by Missouri trustees. On the assumption that the claim was against Missouri citizens, and therefore within the Court's concurrent original jurisdiction, the Court, in an opinion by Chief Justice Hughes, ruled that "the invocation of our jurisdiction must fail." The Court worried that accepting jurisdiction over state tax enforcement claims would be unduly burdensome and interfere with its consideration of more important matters. And it maintained, citing *forum non conveniens* decisions, that courts can "properly withhold the exercise of the jurisdiction conferred * * * where there is no want of another suitable forum." The Court denied leave to file a complaint after stating that Massachusetts could enforce its tax claims against Missouri citizens in Missouri state or federal district courts.

The Court expanded on this rationale for declining original jurisdiction in suits under § 1251(b) in Ohio v. Wyandotte Chemicals Corp., 401 U.S. 493 (1971). There, Ohio sued chemical companies from other states alleged to be responsible for pollution of Lake Erie, seeking compensatory and injunctive relief. Justice Harlan's opinion for the Court acknowledged the "time-honored maxim of the Anglo-American common-law tradition that a court possessed of jurisdiction generally must exercise it. Cohens v. Virginia, 6 Wheat. 264, 404 (1821). Nevertheless, although it may initially have been contemplated that this Court would always exercise its original jurisdiction when properly called upon to do so, * * * changes in the American legal system and the development of American society have rendered untenable, as a practical matter, the view that this Court must stand willing to adjudicate all or most legal disputes that may arise between one State and a citizen or citizens of another * * *." States have increasingly been drawn into legal disputes with noncitizens, often "bottomed on local law" as to which the Supreme Court has no special competence; "[t]his Court's paramount responsibilities to the national system lie almost without exception in the domain of federal law," but nothing in the complaint suggested that it raised important questions of federal law. He added that the Court is "structured to perform as an appellate tribunal, ill-equipped for the task of factfinding and so forced, in original cases, awkwardly to play the role of factfinder without actually presiding over the introduction of evidence." Thus, he concluded that the Court may properly exercise discretion to decline to hear a case not merely or primarily to protect the Court from vexatious or unfamiliar tasks, but also, and primarily, to preserve the Court's capacity as an appellate tribunal resolving matters of federal law. He noted that exercising this power of declination would not require a state to bring suit in the courts of another state, given the prevalence of long-arm statutes under which a state like Ohio could sue the defendants in its own courts.[1]

It is unclear whether these decisions read the phrase "shall have original" jurisdiction in Article III and § 1251(b) implicitly to confer the discretion exercised, or whether they maintain that policy concerns trump these texts. See Shapiro, *Jurisdiction and Discretion*, 60 N.Y.U.L.Rev. 543 (1985) (canvassing several instances of the Court claiming discretion in exercising otherwise seemingly mandatory federal jurisdiction). Do Article

---

[1]   The Court followed Wyandotte the next year in declining to exercise original jurisdiction over, and remitting to federal district courts, an interstate pollution case, Illinois v. City of Milwaukee, 406 U.S. 91 (1972), and a case in which 18 states sought to bring antitrust claims against automobile manufacturers and their trade association, Washington v. General Motors Corp., 406 U.S. 109 (1972). The following year, in United States v. Nevada, 412 U.S. 534 (1973), the Court applied the Wyandotte doctrine to a suit by the United States that involved a dispute over the waters of the Truckee River, noting, *inter alia*, that its jurisdiction over the case was not exclusive and that private users of the disputed waters could participate in a district court litigation but could not intervene in an original action in the Supreme Court. Recognizing that the United States could not sue California in an action against Nevada in the Nevada district court, the Court characterized the controversy between the United States and California as "remote" and capable of resolution in separate actions in lower federal courts in California.

III and § 1251(b) support Justice Harlan's judgment in Wyandotte that the Court's "paramount responsibilities" are to enforce federal law in an appellate capacity? What "changes in the American legal system and the development of American society" might justify this view? Are they the same changes that led the Court, through statutory revision and its own devices, to conceive its role on its appellate docket as primarily one of resolving federal law questions of national importance? See pp. 328–330, *supra*.

(2) Actions Within the Supreme Court's Exclusive Original Jurisdiction. The Court took the more significant step of refusing to exercise its exclusive original jurisdiction under § 1251(a) for the first time in Arizona v. New Mexico, 425 U.S. 794 (1976). There the Court denied Arizona's motion for leave to file a bill of complaint seeking relief from a New Mexico tax on the ground that a pending state court action by three Arizona utilities against New Mexico raised the same constitutional issues as the bill of complaint and was an appropriate forum for resolving the issues.

As Justice Thomas notes in his dissent in Nebraska v. Colorado, this interpretation of § 1251(a) means that "the complaining State has no judicial forum in which to seek relief," since the Court's original jurisdiction in this instance is exclusive.[2] Does a State's lack of any forum to pursue its claim matter if other parties can pursue the claim in another court?[3] Or does this argument turn a central rationale for original jurisdiction—to match the dignity of the parties to the status of the court, see California v. Arizona, p. 347, *supra*—on its head by denying a State the ability to make its legal case in any court?

Although §§ 1251(a) and 1251(b) both provide that the Court "shall have original * * * jurisdiction," Justice Thomas appears to limit his argument for mandatory jurisdiction to § 1251(a) when he says that the "lack of discretion [under § 1251(a)] is confirmed by the fact that, unlike other matters within our original jurisdiction, our jurisdiction over controversies between States is exclusive."[4] See also Shapiro, Paragraph (1), *supra*, at 576 (generally

---

[2]   After the Court denied the State's motion to file a bill of complaint in Louisiana v. Missouri, 488 U.S. 990 (1988), it rejected Louisiana's subsequent effort to file a third-party complaint against Mississippi in a pending federal district court suit raising the same boundary dispute issues on the ground that § 1251(a)'s "uncompromising language" of exclusivity "necessarily denies jurisdiction * * * to any other federal court." Mississippi v. Louisiana, 506 U.S. 73, 77–78 (1992). (The Court later granted Louisiana's renewed motion for leave to file a bill of complaint and decided the merits. Louisiana v. Missouri, 516 U.S. 22 (1995).). A grant of exclusive federal jurisdiction also typically preempts state court jurisdiction. *Cf.* Franchise Tax Bd. v. Hyatt, 587 U.S. 230, 245 (2019) (noting "inability of one State to hale another into its courts without the latter's consent" due to state sovereign immunity).

[3]   In Nebraska v. Colorado, the parties opposing review argued that the issue presented in the bill could be resolved in a suit by non-sovereign parties in federal district court. Since the Court denied the bill without explanation, it is impossible to know how much, if at all, this factor influenced its decision.

[4]   In three cases subsequent to Nebraska v. Colorado, Justices Thomas and Alito dissented from denials of leave to file under § 1251(a). See Texas v. California, 141 S.Ct. 1469 (2021) (Alito, J., joined by Thomas, J., dissenting); Texas v. Pennsylvania, 141 S.Ct. 1230 (2020) (statement by Alito, J., joined by Thomas, J.); Arizona v. California, 140 S.Ct. 684 (2020) (Thomas, J., joined by Alito, J., dissenting). But they did not dissent from a denial of leave to file in a subsequent § 1251(b) case, Arizona v. Sackler, 140 S.Ct. 812 (2019), even though the State seeking review had argued for obligatory review based on the dissent in Nebraska v. Colorado.

supportive of principled discretion in mandatory jurisdiction contexts, but arguing that the "grant of exclusive jurisdiction to resolve certain controversies" in § 1251(a) "should be read as depriving the court of discretion to determine that it is an inappropriate forum"). If the argument for mandatory review turns on the text of § 1251(a), shouldn't original jurisdiction under § 1251(b) also be mandatory even if the parties have another available forum?

3. EXTRAORDINARY WRITS IN THE SUPREME COURT

The writ of mandamus sought in Marbury was one of several "extraordinary" writs—others include prohibition, common-law certiorari, quo warranto, and habeas corpus—that have been available in federal courts since the founding.[1] Sections 13 and 14 of the Judiciary Act of 1789 authorized federal courts to issue these writs with various conditions.

These writs continue to be available in federal court today, but, as explained below, the language of the relevant statutory authorizations is different. They enable the Supreme Court to perform important supervisory functions over lower courts but raise complex statutory and constitutional interpretive questions.

Ex parte Bollman

8 U.S. (4 Cranch) 75 (1807).
Motion for Leave to File Petition for a Writ of Habeas Corpus.

[Petitioners Bollman and Swartwout were arrested by military officials in Louisiana in connection with Aaron Burr's alleged western conspiracy, transported to the east coast, and eventually charged with treason before the federal circuit court in the District of Columbia.* The court found probable cause, denied bail, and ordered petitioners

---

[1]   A writ of mandamus is an order to a lower court or official directing the performance of a duty. See, *e.g.*, Marbury v. Madison, 5 U.S. (1 Cranch) 137 (1803), p. 76, *supra*. A writ of prohibition is an order to a lower court to cease adjudication for lack of jurisdiction. See, *e.g.*, United States v. Peters, 3 U.S. 121 (1795). A writ of common-law certiorari compels a lower court to produce its record to a superior court for review. See, *e.g.*, Degge v. Hitchcock, 229 U.S. 162 (1913). The writ of quo warranto requires a person or entity to demonstrate the public authority on which it acts. See, *e.g.* Newman v. United States ex rel. Frizzell, 238 U.S. 537 (1915). A writ of habeas corpus requires the production of a prisoner before a court and is explained further in Chapter XI, *infra*.

*   [Ed.] Bollman and Swartwout were transferred from Louisiana to Washington D.C., where they were originally detained in military custody without a warrant. It was only after counsel for the two prisoners moved for their discharge from military custody via a motion for habeas corpus, and after it became apparent that the House of Representatives likely would not pass a proposed suspension of the writ that the Senate had passed, that the government charged the two with treason before the federal circuit court in the District of Columbia. For details, see Tyler, Habeas Corpus in Wartime: From the Tower of London to Guantanamo Bay 145–54 (2017).

committed to prison pending trial. Petitioners then filed a petition for a writ of habeas in the Supreme Court.]

■ MARSHALL, CH. J. delivered the opinion of the court, as follows:

* * * Courts which originate in the common law possess a jurisdiction which must be regulated by their common law, until some statute shall change their established principles; but courts which are created by written law, and whose jurisdiction is defined by written law, cannot transcend that jurisdiction. * * * [F]or the meaning of the term *habeas corpus*, resort may unquestionably be had to the common law; but the power to award the writ by any of the courts of the United States, must be given by written law. * * *

The inquiry therefore on this motion will be, whether by any statute, compatible with the constitution of the United States, the power to award a writ of *habeas corpus*, in such a case as that of Erick Bollman and Samuel Swartwout, has been given to this court.

The 14th section of the judicial act has been considered as containing a substantive grant of this power.

It is in these words: "That all the before mentioned courts of the United States shall have power to issue writs of *scire facias, habeas corpus*, and all other writs, not specially provided for by statute, which may be necessary for the exercise of their respective jurisdictions, and agreeable to the principles and usages of law. And that either of the justices of the supreme court, as well as judges of the district courts, shall have power to grant writs of *habeas corpus*, for the purpose of an inquiry into the cause of commitment. *Provided*, that writs of *habeas corpus* shall in no case extend to prisoners in gaol, unless where they are in custody under or by colour of the authority of the United States, or are committed for trial before some court of the same, or are necessary to be brought into court to testify."

The only doubt of which this section can be susceptible is, whether the restrictive words of the first sentence limit the power to the award of such writs of *habeas corpus* as are necessary to enable the courts of the United States to exercise their respective jurisdictions in some cause which they are capable of finally deciding. * * *

It may be worthy of remark, that this act was passed by the first congress of the United States, sitting under a constitution which had declared "that the privilege of the writ of *habeas corpus* should not be suspended, unless when, in cases of rebellion or invasion, the public safety might require it." [U.S. Const., Art. I, Sec. 9.]

Acting under the immediate influence of this injunction, they must have felt, with peculiar force, the obligation of providing efficient means by which this great constitutional privilege should receive life and activity; for if the means be not in existence, the privilege itself would be lost, although no law for its suspension should be enacted. Under the impression of this obligation, they give, to all the courts, the power of awarding writs of *habeas corpus*.

[The Court went on to reject the argument that § 14 authorized issuance of the writ only as an exercise of jurisdiction otherwise conferred. It read the phrase "which may be necessary for the exercise of their respective jurisdictions" to apply to "all *other* writs," not habeas corpus. (Emphasis added). It read the standalone authority in the next sentence to "grant writs of *habeas corpus*, for the purpose of an inquiry into the cause of commitment" as implicitly vesting the authority in courts. The Court reasoned that "congress could never intend to give a power of this kind to one of the judges of this court, which is refused to all of them when assembled," adding that it "would be strange if the judge, sitting on the bench, should be unable to hear a motion for this writ where it might be openly made, and openly discussed, and might yet retire to his chamber, and in private receive and decide upon the motion."]

If the act of congress gives this court the power to award a writ of *habeas corpus* in the present case, it remains to inquire whether that act be compatible with the constitution.

In the *mandamus* case, Marbury v. Madison, it was decided that this court would not exercise original jurisdiction except so far as that jurisdiction was given by the constitution. But so far as that case has distinguished between original and appellate jurisdiction, that which the court is now asked to exercise is clearly *appellate*. It is the revision of a decision of an inferior court, by which a citizen has been committed to jail.

It has been demonstrated at the bar, that the question brought forward on a *habeas corpus*, is always distinct from that which is involved in the cause itself. The question whether the individual shall be imprisoned is always distinct from the question whether he shall be convicted or acquitted of the charge on which he is to be tried, and therefore these questions are separated, and may be decided in different courts.

The decision that the individual shall be imprisoned must always precede the application for a writ of *habeas corpus*, and this writ must always be for the purpose of revising that decision, and therefore appellate in its nature. * * *

If at any time the public safety should require the suspension of the powers vested by this act in the courts of the United States, it is for the legislature to say so.

That question depends on political considerations, on which the legislature is to decide. Until the legislative will be expressed, this court can only see its duty, and must obey the laws.

The motion, therefore, must be granted.*

■ JOHNSON, J., dissenting. * * *

Ex parte Republic of Peru

318 U.S. 578 (1943).
On Motion for Leave to File Petition for a Writ of Prohibition
and/or a Writ of Mandamus.

■ MR. CHIEF JUSTICE STONE delivered the opinion of the Court.

[On March 30, 1942, a Cuban corporation filed a libel in a federal district court in Louisiana against the Ucayali for its failure to carry cargo from a Peruvian port to New York. The petitioner, a foreign sovereign, procured the release of the vessel by filing a surety release bond, and, after seeking extensions, filed various motions asserting its foreign sovereign immunity and disclaiming any waiver of this defense. Petitioner also sought recognition by the State Department of its immunity claim. On June 29, the United States Attorney communicated the State Department's formal recognition to the court and suggested and prayed that court recognize and give full effect to the ship's immunity. On July 1, petitioner moved for release of the vessel and dismissal of the suit. The district court denied the motion on the ground that petitioner had waived its immunity by applying for extensions of time within which to answer, and by taking the deposition of the master. Instead of seeking relief from the court of appeals on direct review, petitioner filed in the Supreme Court a motion for leave to file for a writ of prohibition or of mandamus. The petition asked this Court to prohibit respondent, the federal district court judge, from further exercise of jurisdiction over the proceeding *in rem*, and to direct the district judge to enter an order declaring the vessel immune from suit.]

The first question for our consideration is that of our jurisdiction. Section 13 of the Judiciary Act of 1789 conferred upon this Court "power to issue writs of prohibition to the district courts, when proceeding as courts of admiralty and maritime jurisdiction, and writs of mandamus, in cases warranted by the principles and usages of law, to any courts appointed, or persons holding office, under the authority of the United States." And § 14 provided that this Court and other federal courts "shall have power to issue writs of scire facias, habeas corpus, and all other writs not specially provided for by statute, which may be necessary for the exercise of their respective jurisdictions, and agreeable to the principles and usages of law." These provisions have in substance been carried over into * * * the Judicial Code * * *.

---

*   [Ed.] In a later opinion written by Chief Justice Marshall, the Court ruled that the petitioners must be released due to lack of sufficient evidence of treason as defined in Article III. Ex parte Bollman, 8 U.S. (4 Cranch) 125 (1807).

The jurisdiction of this Court as defined in Article III, § 2 of the Constitution is either "original" or "appellate." Suits brought in the district courts of the United States, not of such character as to be within the original jurisdiction of this Court under the Constitution, are cognizable by it only in the exercise of its appellate jurisdiction. Hence its statutory authority to issue writs of prohibition or mandamus to district courts can be constitutionally exercised only insofar as such writs are in aid of its appellate jurisdiction. Marbury v. Madison, 1 Cranch 137, 173–180 [(1803)].

Under the statutory provisions, the jurisdiction of this Court to issue common-law writs in aid of its appellate jurisdiction has been consistently sustained. The historic use of writs of prohibition and mandamus directed by an appellate to an inferior court has been to exert the revisory appellate power over the inferior court. The writs thus afford an expeditious and effective means of confining the inferior court to a lawful exercise of its prescribed jurisdiction, or of compelling it to exercise its authority when it is its duty to do so. Such has been the office of the writs when directed by this Court to district courts, both before the Judiciary Act of 1925,[1] and since.[2] In all these cases (cited in notes 1 and 2), the appellate, not the original, jurisdiction of this Court was invoked and exercised.[3]

The common law writs, like equitable remedies, may be granted or withheld in the sound discretion of the Court, and are usually denied where other adequate remedy is available. And ever since the [1925 Judges Bill] vested in the circuit courts of appeals appellate jurisdiction on direct appeal from the district courts, this Court, in the exercise of its discretion, has in appropriate circumstances declined to issue the writ to a district court, but without prejudice to an application to the circuit court of appeals, which likewise has power under § 262 of the Judicial Code to issue the writ.

After a full review of the traditional use of the common law writs by this Court, and in issuing a writ of mandamus, in aid of its appellate jurisdiction, to compel a district judge to issue a bench warrant in conformity to statutory requirements, this Court declared in Ex parte United States, 287 U.S. 241, 248–249 [(1932)]: "The rule deducible from the later decisions, and which we now affirm, is that this court has full power in its discretion to issue the writ of mandamus to a federal district court, although the case be one in respect of which direct appellate jurisdiction is vested in the circuit court of appeals—this Court having

---

[1]   [Citing numerous cases.]

[2]   Ex parte United States, 287 U.S. 241 [(1932)]; Maryland v. Soper (No. 1), 270 U.S. 9, 27–28 [(1926)]; Maryland v. Soper (No. 2), 270 U.S. 36 [(1926)]; Maryland v. Soper (No. 3), 270 U.S. 44 [(1926)]; Colorado v. Symes, 286 U.S. 510 [(1932)]; McCullough v. Cosgrave, 309 U.S. 634 [(1940)]; Ex parte Kawato, 317 U.S. 69 [(1942)]; see Los Angeles Brush Corp v. James, 272 U.S. 701 [(1027)].

[3]   See particularly the discussion in Maryland v. Soper (No. 1), 270 U.S. 9, 28–30, and in Ex parte United States, 287 U.S. 241. Compare Ex parte Siebold, 100 U.S. 371 [(1879)]. * * *

ultimate discretionary jurisdiction by certiorari—but that such power will be exercised only where a question of public importance is involved, or where the question is of such a nature that it is peculiarly appropriate that such action by this Court should be taken. In other words, application for the writ ordinarily must be made to the intermediate appellate court, and made to this Court as the court of ultimate review only in such exceptional cases."[4]

We conclude that we have jurisdiction to issue the writ as prayed. And we think that—unless the sovereign immunity has been waived—the case is one of such public importance and exceptional character as to call for the exercise of our discretion to issue the writ rather than to relegate the Republic of Peru to the circuit court of appeals, from which it might be necessary to bring the case to this Court again by certiorari. The case involves the dignity and rights of a friendly sovereign state, claims against which are normally presented and settled in the course of the conduct of foreign affairs by the President and by the Department of State. When the Secretary elects, as he may and as he appears to have done in this case, to settle claims against the vessel by diplomatic negotiations between the two countries rather than by continued litigation in the courts, it is of public importance that the action of the political arm of the Government taken within its appropriate sphere be promptly recognized, and that the delay and inconvenience of a prolonged litigation be avoided by prompt termination of the proceedings in the district court. If the Republic of Peru has not waived its immunity, we think that there are persuasive grounds for exercising our jurisdiction to issue the writ in this case and at this time without requiring petitioner to apply to the circuit court of appeals * * *.

[The Court proceeded to find that Peru had not waived its immunity.]

The motion for leave to file is granted. We assume that, in view of this opinion, formal issuance of the writ will be unnecessary * * *.

---

[4]   The suggestion that the Judiciary Act of 1925 [p. 328, *supra*] was intended to curtail the jurisdiction previously exercised by this Court in granting such writs to the district courts finds no support in the history or language of the Act. [The four Justices who testified about the Act revealed that its] great purpose * * * was to curtail the Court's obligatory jurisdiction by substituting, for the appeal as of right, discretionary review by certiorari in many classes of cases. In all the oral and written submissions by members of this Court, and in the reports of the committees of Congress which recommended adoption of the bill, there is not a single suggestion that the Act would withdraw or limit the Court's existing jurisdiction to direct the common-law writs to the district courts when, in the exercise of its discretion, it deemed such a remedy appropriate. The changes in existing law proposed to be made by the Act were set forth with painstaking detail. It is hardly conceivable that the justices of this Court, fully familiar with its practice, would have left unexpressed an intention—had such intention really existed—to curtail drastically a jurisdiction which the Court had exercised under statutory authority from the beginning of its history. Ex parte United States, and most of the other cases cited in note 2, *supra*, were decided at a time when members of the Court's committee responsible for the 1925 Act were still members of the Court. The Court's unanimous concurrence in the existence of its jurisdiction in the cases subsequent to the 1925 Act establishes a practice which would be beyond explanation if there had been any thought that any provision of the Act had placed such a restriction on the Court's jurisdiction to issue the writs. * * *

■ MR. JUSTICE ROBERTS concurs in the result. * * *

■ MR. JUSTICE FRANKFURTER, dissenting.

* * * [The majority and I agree] that this Court "can exercise no appellate jurisdiction, except in the cases, and in the manner and form, defined and prescribed by Congress." Had this case arisen under the Evarts Act [of 1891, see p. 327, *supra*], appeal could have been taken from the district court, since its jurisdiction was in issue, directly to this Court without going to the Circuit Court of Appeals. And since the case would have been within the immediate appellate jurisdiction of this Court, §§ 13 and 14 of the first Judiciary Act would have authorized this Court to issue an appropriate writ to prevent frustration of its appellate power, or have enabled it to accelerate its own undoubted reviewing authority where, under very exceptional circumstances, actual and not undefined interests of justice so required.

The power to issue these auxiliary writs is not a qualification or even a loose construction of the strict limits, defined by the Constitution and the Congress, within which this Court must move in reviewing decisions of lower courts. There have been occasional, but not many, deviations from the true doctrine in employing these auxiliary writs as incidental to the right granted by Congress to this Court to review litigation, in aid of which it may become necessary to issue a facilitating writ. The issuance of such a writ is, in effect, an anticipatory review of a case that can in due course come here directly. When the Act of 1891 established the intermediate courts of appeals and gave to them a considerable part of the appellate jurisdiction formerly exercised by the Supreme Court, the philosophy and practice of federal appellate jurisdiction came under careful scrutiny. This Court uniformly and without dissent held that it was without power to issue a writ of mandamus in a case in which it did not otherwise have appellate jurisdiction. In re Massachusetts, 197 U.S. 482 [(1905)], and In re Glaser, 198 U.S. 171 [(1905)]. In these cases, rules were discharged because, under the Circuit Courts of Appeals Act, appeals could not be brought directly to the Supreme Court but would have to go to the Circuit Court of Appeals, and only thereafter could they come here, if at all, through certiorari. But review could be brought directly to this Court of cases in which the jurisdiction of the district court was in issue, and therefore writs of "prohibition or mandamus or certiorari as ancillary thereto," In re Massachusetts, *supra,* at 488, were available. Cases which came here directly, prior to the Judiciary Act of February 13, 1925, to review the jurisdiction of the district courts, whether on appeal or through the informal procedure of auxiliary writs, are therefore not relevant precedents for the present case. * * *

[The dissent then argued that the Judiciary Act of 1925 removed the basis for issuance of an ancillary writ directly to a district court, save in the special situations in which direct review was authorized. (Compare the present provision for direct review in 28 U.S.C. § 1253.) It cited the general purpose of the Act to remove "[t]he needless clog on the Court's proper business," in particular, by restricting appellate jurisdiction over the district courts.]

Finally, it is urged that practice since the Judiciary Act of 1925 sanctions the present assumption of jurisdiction. [Justice Frankfurter here sought to distinguish the cases in note 2, *supra*, mainly on the ground that none of them involved a case in which a matter had not yet been, but could be, reviewed by the court of appeals.]

Had the Court jurisdiction, this case would furnish no occasion for its exercise. On whatever technical basis of jurisdiction the availability of these writs may have been founded, their use has been reserved for very special circumstances. * * *

No palpable exigency either of national or international import is made manifest for seeking this extraordinary relief here. * * *

To remit a controversy like this to the circuit court of appeals where it properly belongs is not to be indifferent to claims of importance but to be uncompromising in safeguarding the conditions which alone will enable this Court to discharge well the duties entrusted exclusively to us. * * *

Mr. Justice Reed is of the opinion that this Court has jurisdiction to grant the writ requested, Ex parte United States, 287 U.S. 241, but concurs in this dissent on the ground that application for the writ sought should have been made first to the Circuit Court of Appeals.

NOTE ON EXTRAORDINARY WRITS IN THE SUPREME COURT

(1) Statutory Authorization for Extraordinary Writs. Article III directly confers the original jurisdiction on the Supreme Court, see U.S. Const. art. III, § 2, cl. 2. Thus, the Court would likely need no statutory authorization in any situation if the issuance of an extraordinary writ would constitute an exercise of original jurisdiction. See Oaks, *The "Original" Writ of Habeas Corpus in the Supreme Court*, 1962 Sup.Ct.Rev. 153, 156–59 (discussing possibilities).

The situation is different for the Court's appellate jurisdiction. Article III Sec. 2, cl. 2 gives the Supreme Court appellate jurisdiction "with such Exceptions, and under such Regulations as the Congress shall make." In Durousseau v. United States, 10 U.S. (6 Cranch) 307 (1810), the Court construed the Judiciary Act of 1789 as impliedly withdrawing the Supreme Court's appellate jurisdiction in every situation in which jurisdiction was not expressly conferred. (For greater discussion, see Chap. IV, Sec. 1.) As a result, the Court's power to issue an extraordinary writ as an exercise of appellate jurisdiction must as a general matter be found in some affirmative statutory grant.

But should this conclusion apply to the writ of habeas corpus? The writ at issue in Bollman, the writ of habeas corpus *ad subjiciendum*, requires the respondent, ordinarily a government official, to appear in court to justify the legality of the detention of the individual who petitions for the writ.[1] Habeas corpus had a long history as an important protection of liberty in England. Its importance was recognized in the Constitution's Suspension Clause, Article I, Section 9, which provides that the "Privilege of the Writ of Habeas Corpus shall not be suspended, unless when in Cases of Rebellion or Invasion the public Safety may require it."

Bollman held that "the power to award the writ [of habeas corpus] by any of the courts of the United States, must be given by written law," and added that Congress, acting under the "immediate influence" of the Suspension Clause, gave the power to award writs of habeas corpus to all federal courts. This conclusion has been criticized on the ground that it makes the existence of Suspension Clause protections dependent upon congressional grace. See, *e.g.*, Freedman, *Just Because John Marshall Said It Doesn't Make It So: Ex parte Bollman and the Illusory Prohibition on the Federal Writ of Habeas Corpus for State Prisoners in the Judiciary Act of 1789*, 51 Ala.L.Rev. 531 (2000). The Court later effectively rejected this aspect of Bollman in Boumediene v. Bush, 553 U.S. 723 (2008), which held that the Suspension Clause confers a right to habeas corpus in some circumstances, even in the absence of statutory authorization. For more discussion of these issues, see Chap. IV, pp. 464–471, and Chap. XI, Sec. 1, *infra*.

(2) Extraordinary Writs and Article III: Appellate Versus Original Jurisdiction. The Supreme Court's authority to issue an extraordinary writ can also depend on whether the writ is an exercise of the Court's Article III original or appellate jurisdiction. The issuance of an extraordinary writ in a case that otherwise falls within the original jurisdiction—one affecting a foreign envoy or in which a state is a party—raises little difficulty. But as Marbury v. Madison famously held, Congress may not authorize the Supreme Court to issue a writ, as an exercise of original jurisdiction, in a case beyond the scope of Article III's grant of original jurisdiction.

Bollman establishes an important qualification to this holding. Bollman might have been seen as an exercise of original jurisdiction since petitioner was seeking the writ of habeas corpus in the first instance from the Supreme Court, and since the Court lacked statutory authority for direct review of the district court's confinement decision (through, for example, a writ or error or appeal). The Court circumvented this difficulty in two steps. It first ruled that Section 14 did not limit the Supreme Court's authority to issue the writ only as an auxiliary to jurisdiction otherwise conferred upon them, but rather authorized an independent action in habeas corpus. And then it distinguished Marbury's constitutional holding by ruling that the issuance

---

[1]   The writ of habeas corpus *ad subjiciendum*, sometimes known as the "Great writ," was one of "various writs of *habeas corpus*" at common law that required a custodian to produce a prisoner before a court. Ex parte Bollman, 8 U.S. (4 Cranch) 75, 95–97 (1807). The others were the writ of habeas corpus *ad respondendum*, which (among other things) required production for a new trial; the writ of habeas corpus *ad satisfaciendum*, which required production to execute a judgment; and the writ of habeas corpus *ad testificandum*, which required production for testimony. *Id.* 97–98.

of the writ of habeas corpus implicated the Court's Article III appellate jurisdiction because it involved a "revision of a decision of an inferior court."

These rulings would prove vital to the subsequent availability of the writ of habeas corpus. In Ex parte Yerger, 75 U.S. (8 Wall.) 85 (1868), where a circuit court had granted and thereafter dismissed the writ sought by a military prisoner, the Supreme Court ruled that its consideration of a petition for a writ of habeas corpus under the jurisdiction provided in § 14 was an exercise of Article III appellate jurisdiction—despite congressional repeal of the statute that had authorized an ordinary appeal from the denial of the writ by lower courts.[2] Felker v. Turpin, 518 U.S. 651 (1996), similarly upheld the Court's power to issue a writ to review a lower federal court decision, notwithstanding a statutory provision that the decision below "shall not be appealable and shall not be the subject of a petition for * * * writ of certiorari." 28 U.S.C. § 2244(b)(3)(E). For more on the relationship of these line of cases to Congress's power to regulate the appellate jurisdiction of the Supreme Court, see pp. 425–427, *infra*, and to the Suspension Clause, see p. 1577, *infra*.

(3) The Background to and Limits of Ex parte Peru. In contrast to its treatment of the writ of habeas corpus, the Supreme Court at one time believed that it lacked authority to issue mandamus in a case over which it lacked direct statutory appellate jurisdiction. See In re Glaser, 198 U.S. 171, 173 (1905); In re Massachusetts, 197 U.S. 482, 488 (1905). Ex parte United States, 287 U.S. 241 (1932), cast doubt on this view. There the U.S. government sought a writ of mandamus to compel the district court to issue a bench warrant upon an indictment. The Judges Bill of 1925 had eliminated the Supreme Court's direct review over the district court and shifted appellate review to the intermediate circuit courts of appeals. The Court ruled that this change did not affect its power to issue a writ of mandamus to the district court because, "even if the appellate jurisdiction of this court could not in any view be immediately and directly invoked, the issue of the writ may rest upon the ultimate power which we have to review the case itself by certiorari to the circuit court of appeals in which such immediate and direct appellate jurisdiction is lodged." *Id.* 246.

Ex parte Peru sided with the latter decision and held that the Court could issue a writ of mandamus or prohibition even though the court of appeals, not the Supreme Court, had direct appellate review from the district court. What is the basis for this conclusion? Does it rest on an interpretation of the 1925 Judges Bill? See Ex parte Peru, *supra*, at n. 4. Does the Court apply §§ 13 or 14 of the Judiciary Act of 1789, or both? Note that § 13 authorizes the Supreme Court to issue writs of prohibition to the district courts in admiralty and maritime cases, and writs of mandamus to the district courts in "cases warranted by the principles and usages of law"; and that § 14 authorizes "all other writs," but only if they "may be necessary for the exercise of their respective jurisdictions, and agreeable to the principles and usages of law." And recall that Ex parte Peru states (with emphasis

---

[2]　See also Ex parte Siebold, 100 U.S. (10 Otto) 371 (1879). But see Ex parte Barry, 43 U.S. (2 How.) 65 (1844) (no appellate jurisdiction to issue writ to test confinement by a private party in a child custody case).

added) that "[u]nder *the statutory provisions*, the jurisdiction of this Court to issue common-law writs in aid of its appellate jurisdiction has been consistently sustained," but declined to provide further details. By "in aid of its appellate jurisdiction," did the Court mean statutory appellate jurisdiction or Article III appellate jurisdiction? Compare Pfander, *Jurisdiction-Stripping and the Supreme Court's Power to Supervise Inferior Tribunals*, 78 Tex.L.Rev. 1433, 1496, 1496 n.290 (2000) (arguing that it refers to Article III appellate jurisdiction), with Ex parte Peru, *supra* (framing the Court's "full power" to issue the writ in the context of "th[e] Court having ultimate discretionary jurisdiction by certiorari").

Wolfson, *Extraordinary Writs in the Supreme Court Since Ex parte Peru*, 51 Colum.L.Rev. 977, 991 (1951), argues as follows: "In Ex parte *Peru*, doubtless as a result of Mr. Justice Frankfurter's scholarly dissent, the Supreme Court was compelled to articulate the criteria delimiting its power. When that was done, the Court found that, with respect to cases coming from the federal courts, its power was practically limitless. Thus, the inquiry into power, which had plagued the judiciary since the establishment of the Republic, was answered, and the conflict moved into the area of discretion." Convincing? Would the Court in Ex parte Peru have issued the requested writs if Congress had cut off all statutory appellate review to the Supreme Court (as opposed to placing intermediate federal appellate review between the district court and the Supreme Court)? Compare Ex parte Yerger and Felker v. Turpin, Paragraph (2), *supra*, which held that the Court could issue a writ of habeas corpus to a lower court over which the Court lacked any potential statutory appellate jurisdiction.

(4) Contemporary Statutory Authority for the Issuance of Extraordinary Writs. Five years after Ex parte Peru, the 1948 revision of the Judicial Code repealed the successor provision to § 13 of the Judiciary Act of 1789. Congress combined the free-standing writ of mandamus that had been available in § 13 with the "all * * * writs" authority of § 14 into a statute, the contemporary All Writs Act, that today reads: "The Supreme Court and all courts established by Act of Congress may issue all writs necessary or appropriate in aid of their respective jurisdictions and agreeable to the usages and principles of law." 28 U.S.C. § 1651(a). The Reviser's Note stated that "[t]he special provisions of [the successor to § 13], with reference to writs of prohibition and mandamus, admiralty courts and other courts and officers of the United States were omitted as unnecessary in view of the revised section."[3] Thus, at present the only statutory authority for the

---

[3]   The 1948 Revision of the Judicial Code, which is today reflected in Title 28 of the U.S. Code, originally aimed to reorganize and consolidate disparate provisions on jurisdiction, venue, and procedure for federal courts, but ended up making changes to the law in these areas. The Chief Reviewer of the 1948 revision explained that changes that were "substantive in nature * * * were carefully outlined in the Reviser's Notes," and that "no changes of law or policy w[ere to] be presumed from changes of language in revision unless an intent to make such changes is clearly expressed." Barron, *The Judicial Code 1948 Revision*, 8 F.R.D. 439, 441, 445 (1948). The Supreme Court subsequently made clear that it would not view alterations to the 1948 revision as effecting a substantive change unless the change was specified in the Revisers' Notes. See, *e.g.*, John R. Sand & Gravel Co. v. United States, 552 U.S. 130, 136 (2008) (no substantive change to the Court of Federal Claim's jurisdictional statute because there was no "suggestion in the Reviser's Notes or anywhere else that Congress intended to change the prior meaning"); Fourco Glass Co. v. Transmirra Prods. Corp., 353 U.S. 222, 227 (1957) (alteration to the statute

issuance of extraordinary writs other than habeas corpus (which is specifically authorized today in 28 U.S.C. § 2241(a)) is 28 U.S.C. § 1651(a).

The impact of the 1948 revision on the availability of mandamus relief in the Supreme Court is unsettled. Judge Magruder argued that the statute "withdraw[s] from the Supreme Court its special appellate power to supervise proceedings in the lower federal courts by means of the writ of mandamus," such that "all federal courts, including the Supreme Court, are now limited to the issuance of 'all writs necessary or appropriate in aid of their respective jurisdictions.'" In re Josephson, 218 F.2d 174, 179 (1st Cir.1954). Judge Friendly, by contrast, maintained that it "hard to believe, in the absence of better evidence than the Reviser's Note, that Congress meant to curtail a power the Supreme Court had possessed for 159 years." United States v. Weinstein, 452 F.2d 704, 711 (2d Cir.1971).[4]

(5) The Chandler Decision. The Supreme Court addressed some of the issues in this Note, albeit inconclusively, in Chandler v. Judicial Council of the Tenth Circuit of the United States, 398 U.S. 74 (1970). In that case, the Tenth Circuit Judicial Council issued an order that found District Judge Chandler "unable or unwilling" to discharge his duties, and then reassigned cases pending before and barred any new assignments to him. Judge Chandler asked the Supreme Court for leave to file a petition for writs of mandamus or prohibition, arguing that the Council's orders were illegal.

The Court declined to issue the writ because certain (unspecified) avenues of relief on the merits "may yet be open to Judge Chandler." But along the way it questioned whether Article III permitted it to issue the writ. The Court noted that "[i]f the challenged action of the Judicial Council was a judicial act or decision by a judicial tribunal, then perhaps it could be reviewed by this Court without doing violence to the constitutional requirement that such review be appellate." But the Court worried that the Council order was instead an "administrative action not reviewable in this Court." Justice Harlan's concurrence, by contrast, argued that the Court could issue the writ as an exercise of its Article III appellate jurisdiction because the orders of the Council were an exercise of judicial power, not administrative power. Consider how the interpretation of Article III in Marbury and Bollman support the notion that a writ of mandamus or prohibition issued in review of a judicial act falls within the Court's Article III appellate jurisdiction, but such a writ in connection with an

---

governing venue in patent infringement cases effected no change in the law because "the Revisers' Notes do not express any substantive change"). For commentary on the significance of the 1948 Revisions, see Listwa, *Comment, Uncovering the Codifier's Canon: How Codification Informs Interpretation*, 127 Yale L.J. 464 (2017); Sisk, *Lifting the Blindfold from Lady Justice: Allowing Judges to See the Structure in the Judicial Code*, 62 Fla.L.Rev. 457 (2010).

[4]   Professor Pfander sides with Judge Friendly as part of a more ambitious argument that the Constitution's reference in Article III to the "Supreme" Court, and in Articles I and III to Congress's control over "inferior" courts, understood in historical context, supports a "Supreme" Court power—which Congress may not eliminate—to supervise the "inferior" courts via extraordinary writs. Pfander, Paragraph (3), *supra*, at 1435, 1451–59. Professor Hartnett, in *Not the King's Bench*, 20 Const.Comment. 283 (2003), disagrees. He argues that an indefeasible Supreme Court authority to issue extraordinary writs is hard to square with Bollman and Marbury, both of which treated habeas as subject to congressional control, and with Congress's power to regulate the Court's appellate jurisdiction "[i]n all other Cases" not allocated to its original jurisdiction, see Art. III, § 2.

administrative decision, even by a group of judges, might not. Could Congress provide for direct Supreme Court review of an NLRB decision in an unfair labor practice proceeding? And if the Supreme Court could review directly a decision of the NLRB, could it also review directly a determination made not by a five-member federal agency, but by a single federal official? If so, why couldn't the Supreme Court review Secretary of State Madison's "adjudication" that Marbury was not entitled to his commission? For further discussion of these questions, see the analysis of Ortiz v. United States, 585 U.S. 427 (2018), p. 369, *infra*.

Justice Harlan concurred in the Court's denial of the writ on discretionary grounds but wrote separately to argue (among other things) that the modern All Writs Act, 28 U.S.C. § 1651, provided authority for the Court to entertain the petition in this case. He acknowledged that prior Supreme Court invocations of § 1651(a) to issue a writ "in aid of [its jurisdiction]" involved cases over which the Court would later have statutory jurisdiction to review. By contrast, here the Judicial Council's action affected "hundreds of cases over which the Court has appellate * * * jurisdiction," and the orders reassigning cases "constitute a usurpation of power that cannot adequately be remedied on final review of those cases by certiorari or appeal in this Court." Justice Harlan concluded that the application of § 1651(a) in such circumstances, while lacking direct precedent, seemed "in line with the history of that statute and consistent with the manner in which it has been interpreted both here and in the lower courts."

(6) Writs Issued in Connection with the Decisions of State Courts. Does the Supreme Court have the same authority to issue an extraordinary writ with regard to a case pending in a state court, if the case presents a federal issue that is potentially reviewable by the Supreme Court? (Section 13 of the Judiciary Act of 1789 permitted writs to be issued only to "courts appointed * * * under the authority of the United States," but the authority granted by 28 U.S.C. § 1651(a) lacks that restriction.) Is it relevant that State courts are not Article III courts and yet Supreme Court review of state court decisions is not thought to be an exercise of original jurisdiction? The only decisions on this issue concern cases where the Court had already exercised appellate jurisdiction over the merits, and, without discussion of jurisdiction, subsequently granted leave to file a petition for a writ of mandamus ordering the state court to conform its decision to the Supreme Court's mandate. See Bucolo v. Adkins, 424 U.S. 641 (1976); Deen v. Hickman, 358 U.S. 57 (1958); General Atomic Co. v. Felter, 436 U.S. 493 (1978). If the Court does not possess this power, how, if at all, may it enforce its appellate decisions reversing state courts on issues of federal law?

(7) Military Courts. After World War II, the Supreme Court received more than a hundred petitions for writs of habeas corpus, by or on behalf of persons convicted by or held for trial before various American or international military tribunals abroad. See Fairman, *Some New Problems of the Constitution Following the Flag*, 1 Stan.L.Rev. 587, 591 (1949). Such cases, not involving foreign envoys or a state, did not fall within the Court's Article III original jurisdiction. And in almost none of these cases was relief first sought in a lower federal court.[5] Could they be entertained on the theory that the Court could exercise its Article III appellate jurisdiction to entertain what was, in substance, an appeal not from a federal or state court but from an American or multinational military tribunal?

The Court used jurisdictional and discretionary mechanisms to avoid this question, but came closest to addressing it in Hirota v. MacArthur, 338 U.S. 197 (1948). There, a group of Japanese who had been convicted by the International Military Tribunal of the Far East, including former Premier Hirota, filed motions for leave to file original petitions of habeas corpus. The per curiam order denying leave to file first stated that the tribunal sentencing the petitioners was "not a tribunal of the United States," but rather was established by General Douglas MacArthur as "the agent of the Allied Powers" that were occupying Japan. The Court then said, without further explanation, that "[u]nder the foregoing circumstances the courts of the United States have no power or authority to review, to affirm, set aside or annul the judgments and sentences imposed on these petitioners * * *."[6]

A similar issue about the Supreme Court's jurisdiction to review a criminal conviction before a military tribunal is raised by 28 U.S.C. § 1259. That provision authorizes direct Supreme Court review (on writ of certiorari) of decisions of the United States Court of Appeals for the Armed Forces (CAAF). The CAAF is a "court of record" that reviews decisions of the four

---

[5]   An exception was Ex parte Quirin, 317 U.S. 1 (1942), p. 554, *infra,* involving the trial of German saboteurs by a domestic military commission appointed by President Roosevelt. During argument in the Supreme Court on a motion for leave to file petitions for habeas corpus, counsel perfected appeals in the court of appeals from the district court's denial of the writ and petitioned for certiorari before judgment. The Supreme Court denied permission to file the habeas petitions but granted the petitions for certiorari.

In re Yamashita, 327 U.S. 1 (1946), like Quirin, did not involve direct Supreme Court review of military tribunals. There, a Japanese general on trial for war crimes before an American military tribunal in the Philippines sought leave to file petitions for writs of habeas corpus and prohibition in the Supreme Court. The Court stayed the case, 326 U.S. 693 (1945), pending receipt of a petition for certiorari from a decision of the Supreme Court of the Philippines that had denied similar relief. Subsequently the Court denied certiorari and leave to file, opining that Yamashita was not entitled to relief on the merits. In dictum, Chief Justice Stone, citing Ex parte Vallandigham, 68 U.S. (1 Wall.) 243 (1863), stated that the decisions of military tribunals authorized by Congress are not subject to Supreme Court review.

[6]   In Hirota's immediate wake, the D.C. Circuit read the decision broadly to suggest a barrier to the exercise of judicial power not by the Supreme Court in particular but by American courts generally and relied on that reading in dismissing a habeas petition filed by a German businessman convicted by a military tribunal and detained in Germany. See Flick v. Johnson, 174 F.2d 983 (D.C.Cir.1949). Distinguishing its own decision in Eisentrager v. Forrestal, 174 F.2d 961 (D.C.Cir.1949), upholding jurisdiction over petitions from aliens detained abroad, the court of appeals said that Flick was held by an "international court" and, relying on Hirota, ruled that no American court has power to review the conviction. For discussion, see Huq, *The Hirota Gambit,* 63 N.Y.U. Ann.Surv.Am.L. 63 (2007); Vladeck, *Deconstructing Hirota: Habeas Corpus, Citizenship, and Article III,* 95 Geo.L.J. 1497, 1526–27 (2007).

In Munaf v. Geren, 553 U.S. 674 (2008), the Supreme Court distinguished Hirota in upholding the jurisdiction of a District Court to entertain a petition on behalf of an American citizen held by the multinational forces in Iraq. Chief Justice Roberts's opinion for a unanimous Court described Hirota as a "slip of a case" that could not "bear the weight the government" placed on it. The Court distinguished Hirota on two grounds: first, the government had argued that General MacArthur did not serve under U.S. Authority, whereas here the government conceded that the petitioner was in the direct physical custody of American forces that were subject to control by the President and the Defense Department; and second, unlike the petitioners in Hirota, Munaf was an American citizen. Do those distinctions properly tip the scales in favor of federal court jurisdiction?

appellate courts for the armed services, which, in turn, review decisions by trial-level courts martial. The CAAF is not an Article III court, however, because its members lack tenure and salary protections. Rather, it is located within the Executive branch. (On non-Article III courts, see Chap. IV, Sec. 2, *infra*.)

In Ortiz v. United States, 585 U.S. 427 (2018), the Court held that Article III permits direct Supreme Court review of the decisions of the CAAF. In an opinion by Justice Kagan, the Court acknowledged that review of CAAF decisions cannot rest on its original jurisdiction because the CAAF does not resolve cases that affect ambassadors, public ministers or consuls, or that involve a State party, as Article III, § 2, cl. 2, requires. But the Court ruled that such review is an exercise of appellate jurisdiction because it involves a federal question and satisfies (in Marbury's words) the "essential criterion of appellate jurisdiction" since "it revises and corrects the proceedings in a cause already instituted, and does not create that cause."

The Court rejected an argument by an amicus, and seconded in a dissent by Justice Alito, joined by Justice Gorsuch, that courts located in the Executive branch are akin to Secretary of State James Madison, over whose decision the Court in Marbury held it lacked appellate jurisdiction. In contrast with Madison, the CAAF's "essential character" is "judicial" and therefore is similar to the other non-Article III courts—state courts, territorial courts and District of Columbia courts—over which the Court has long exercised appellate jurisdiction. This is so, the Court explained, because of the manifold similarities between modern military and civilian courts, including "virtually the same" procedural protections and basic jurisdictional structure, and the applicability of res judicata and the Double Jeopardy Clause to its judgments. The Court distinguished Ex parte Vallandigham, 68 U.S. (1 Wall.) 243 (1863), which held that neither § 14 of the First Judiciary Act nor Article III permitted the Supreme Court to entertain a petition for a writ of certiorari directly from a military commission that had convicted a prisoner of disloyalty during the Civil War. In contrast with the CAAF, that commission lacked "judicial character" because it was created and controlled entirely by a Union general and thus was "more an adjunct to a general than a real court." The Court noted that in upholding Article III appellate jurisdiction over CAAF decisions, "we say nothing about whether we could exercise appellate jurisdiction over cases from other adjudicative bodies in the Executive Branch, including those in administrative agencies."

What are Ortiz's implications for the Supreme Court's appellate jurisdiction over other types of military courts? Does Ortiz provide a clearer rationale for Hirota, since the International Military Tribunal of the Far East, similar to the commission in Vallandigham but unlike the CAAF, was "set up by General MacArthur as the agent of the Allied Powers" and was a far cry from ordinary civilian courts? What if General MacArthur had established a formal appellate court of military lawyers independent of his command to review Tribunal decisions? What light does Ortiz shed on the questions in paragraph (5) about the direct reviewability in the Supreme Court of the decisions of administrative agencies? For further discussion of Ortiz, see pp. 545–546, *infra*.

(8) Supreme Court Practice. Supreme Court Rule 20.1 states that issuance of extraordinary writs under § 1651(a) "is not a matter of right, but of discretion sparingly exercised," and adds that "[t]o justify the granting of any such writ, the petition must show that the writ will be in aid of the Court's appellate jurisdiction, that exceptional circumstances warrant the exercise of the Court's discretionary powers, and that adequate relief cannot be obtained in any other form or from any other court." See also Ex parte Peru, *supra* (noting that a petition for a writ of mandamus to a district court "ordinarily must be made to the intermediate appellate court"). Rule 20.4(a), which governs issuance of the writ of habeas corpus, similarly states that to obtain relief, "the petitioner must show that exceptional circumstances warrant the exercise of the Court's discretionary powers, and that adequate relief cannot be obtained in any other form or from any other court," and adds that this writ "is rarely granted."

The Court has not issued a writ of mandamus or a writ of habeas corpus in many decades.[7] Yet it would be wrong to conclude that extraordinary writ practice in the Court has grown irrelevant. As the next Section makes clear, the Court issues extraordinary writs of injunction under the All Writs Act somewhat more regularly. And requests for petitions of mandamus often work in tandem with requests for other emergency relief to permit the Court to influence or supervise lower court proceedings at a relatively early stage. In Mountain Valley Pipeline, LLC v. Wilderness Society, 144 S.Ct. 42 (2023), a pipeline company filed an emergency request with the Court to vacate court of appeals' orders granting stays of federal agency action concerning construction of a natural gas pipeline pending judicial review. Alternatively, the company asked the Court to issue a writ of mandamus to vacate the stays. (The underlying argument was that the court of appeals clearly lacked subject matter jurisdiction over the case.). The Court vacated the stay and added: "Although the Court does not reach applicant's suggestion that it treat the application as a petition for a writ of mandamus at this time, that determination is without prejudice to further consideration in light of subsequent developments." By including this language, the Court tipped off its view of the proceedings, and sent a message to the courts below, without actually issuing the writ.

One reason why the Court rarely grants an extraordinary writ is that the very high bar to issuing such writs directly to a district court means that most litigants seek extraordinary relief first in the court of appeals, which the Court can then supervise via a writ of certiorari. This happened in In re United States, 583 U.S. 29, 29–31 (2017), where the plaintiffs challenged the Trump Administration's rescission of the Deferred Action for Childhood Arrivals ("DACA") immigration program. After the district court ordered the Department of Homeland Security to "complete" the administrative record, the government sought but was denied a writ of mandamus from the Ninth Circuit Court of Appeals. The government then submitted to the Supreme

---

[7]   The last case in which the Court formally granted a writ of mandamus was United States v. Haley, 371 U.S. 18 (1962), though the Court later maintained the practice of intimating that it will issue the writ unless the lower court complies, without formally granting a petition. See, *e.g.*, General Atomic Co. v. Felter, 436 U.S. 493 (1978). The last case in which the Court formally granted a writ of habeas corpus was Ex parte Grossman, 267 U.S. 87 (1925).

Court "a petition for a writ of mandamus to the District Court, or, in the alternative, for a writ of certiorari to the Court of Appeals." The Court granted the petition for a writ of certiorari, vacated the order of the court of appeals, and remanded the case with instructions. It thus accomplished via writ of certiorari basically what it could have accomplished by issuing a writ of mandamus, thereby securing "adequate relief * * * in [another] form" that precluded extraordinary relief under Rule 20.1.

---

4. THE SUPREME COURT'S EMERGENCY DOCKET

The Supreme Court's docket consists primarily of cases that have been adjudicated extensively, often over several years, by more than one lower federal or state court. This is typically true, for example, of the relatively few merits cases to which the Court gives plenary review each year, and of the vast majority of the cases for which it denies review in its discretion. But as supervisory writs and the Court's power to grant certiorari before judgment in the federal courts of appeals make clear, the Court has statutory and constitutional authority to intervene in a case long before proceedings below run their full course. Another example, and arguably the most consequential, is the Court's authority to issue emergency relief in a case in the midst of adjudication in courts below.

INTRODUCTORY NOTE ON EMERGENCY RELIEF IN THE SUPREME COURT

The law governing emergency relief in the Supreme Court seeks to balance the presumptive need for orderly appellate process with the occasional need for the Court to intervene early in a case, depending on the equities, to establish what legal arrangement should prevail during the potentially multi-year course of the litigation, including full appellate review. The most common emergency applications ask a Justice or the Court to grant or vacate a stay of a lower court judgment or order pending appeal, or to issue or vacate a writ of injunction against a party pending appeal. The Court's decision on any such application can take place in a matter of days or weeks after the application is filed, and typically comes with limited briefing, no oral argument, and in the form of an unsigned order with no reasoning or, occasionally, with cursory reasoning. Despite this truncated process and the limited explanation for decision, the Court's ruling on an application for emergency relief can be momentous. The Court's order, for example, may be its final say regarding whether the government can go through with a particular action.[1]

---

[1]   For example, in Trump v. Sierra Club, 140 S.Ct. 1 (2019), the Court in July 2019 stayed a lower court injunction of a Trump administration order to reallocate funds for the construction of a wall at the border. The stay persisted throughout lower court litigation until the Biden

To obtain emergency relief in the Supreme Court an applicant ordinarily must first seek it from appropriate courts below. Sup.Ct.R. 20.1 (petition for an extraordinary writ of injunction must show "that adequate relief cannot be obtained in any other form or from any other court"); 23.3 ("Except in the most extraordinary circumstances, an application for a stay will not be entertained unless the relief requested was first sought in the appropriate court or courts below or from a judge or judges thereof."). An application for emergency relief in the Supreme Court is initially presented to the Justice responsible for the Circuit from which the case arises. Sup.Ct.R. 22.3, 23.1; 28 U.S.C. § 2101(f). That Justice can grant or deny the application or refer it to the full Court.[2] When a single Justice grants or denies relief, that Justice can (but need not) issue an in-chambers opinion explaining the decision.[3] "[T]he practice in recent years appears to be that non-trivial stay applications received by a Circuit Justice are referred to the full Court for consideration as a matter of course." McFadden & Kapoor, *The Precedential Effects of the Supreme Court's Emergency Stays*, 44 Harv.J.L. & Pub.Pol'y 827, 836 (2021).[4] But in-chambers opinions remain important sources of precedential authority.

Ohio Citizens for Responsible Energy, Inc. v. Nuclear Regulatory Commission

479 U.S. 1312 (1986).
On Application for Stay.

■ JUSTICE SCALIA, CIRCUIT JUSTICE.

Ohio Citizens for Responsible Energy, Inc., has filed with me as Circuit Justice for the Sixth Circuit an "Application to Stay Mandate of United States Court of Appeals for the Sixth Circuit Pending Certiorari," seeking an order under 28 U.S.C. § 2101(f) staying the full-power operation of the Perry Nuclear Power Plant located near Cleveland, Ohio. The order sought would remain in effect until the Court of Appeals for the Sixth Circuit issues its final decision in the pending suit filed by the applicant against the Nuclear Regulatory Commission, and, should the

---

administration came into office, withdrew the order, and ceased all litigation concerning it. The Trump administration was therefore able to spend money for construction of the border wall for a year and a half without any definitive ruling on the legality of the practice. See also p. 386, note 4, *infra*.

[2] If a Justice denies an application, the party may "renew it to any other Justice," though that course "is not favored" unless the denial was "without prejudice." Sup.Ct.R. 22.4. "The general policy is to refer the renewed application to the full Court for action unless time does not permit * * *." Shapiro et al., Supreme Court Practice ch. 17.2 (11th ed.2019).

[3] In-chambers opinions sometimes state that the Circuit Justice has attempted to anticipate and reflect the views of the entire Court, see, *e.g.*, Holtzman v. Schlesinger, 414 U.S. 1304, 1313 (1973) (Marshall, J., in chambers), but such opinions are of course a less reliable indication of the Court's views than an opinion for the Court.

[4] The most recent in-chambers opinion is Navarro v. United States, 144 S.Ct. 771 (2024) (Roberts, C.J., in chambers). The next-most-recent one was issued a decade earlier. See Teva Pharms. USA, Inc. v. Sandoz, Inc., 572 U.S. 1301 (2014) (Roberts, C.J., in chambers).

applicant be unsuccessful in that suit, until disposition of a petition for writ of certiorari in this Court.

The application must be denied. Section 2101(f) provides: "In any case in which the *final* judgment or decree of any court is subject to review by the Supreme Court on writ of certiorari, the execution and enforcement of *such* judgment or decree may be stayed for a reasonable time to enable the party aggrieved to obtain a writ of certiorari from the Supreme Court." (Emphasis added.) It is clear from this language that, even though certiorari review of interlocutory orders of federal courts is available, see 28 U.S.C. §§ 1254(1) and 1292, it is only the execution or enforcement of *final* orders that is stayable under § 2101(f). In this case, the only extant order which, if stayed, could conceivably affect the full-power operation of the Perry plant, is the Sixth Circuit's order of December 23, 1986, lifting the stay of full-power operation that it imposed on November 13, 1986. That order, however—like the stay itself—is interlocutory.

What the applicant would require in order to achieve the substantive relief that it seeks is an original writ of injunction, pursuant to the All Writs Act, 28 U.S.C. § 1651(a), and this Court's [former] Rule 44.1, against full-power operation of the powerplant. A Circuit Justice's issuance of such a writ—which, unlike a § 2101(f) stay, does not simply suspend judicial alteration of the status quo but grants judicial intervention that has been withheld by lower courts—demands a significantly higher justification than that described in the § 2101(f) stay cases cited by the applicant, *e.g.*, Rostker v. Goldberg, 448 U.S. 1306, 1308 (1980) (Brennan, J., in chambers). The Circuit Justice's injunctive power is to be used " 'sparingly and only in the most critical and exigent circumstances,' " Fishman v. Schaffer, 429 U.S. 1325, 1326 (1976) (Marshall, J., in chambers) (quoting Williams v. Rhodes, 89 S.Ct. 1, 2 (1968) (Stewart, J., in chambers)), and only where the legal rights at issue are "indisputably clear," Communist Party of Indiana v. Whitcomb, 409 U.S. 1235 (1972) (Rehnquist, J., in chambers). Moreover, the applicant must demonstrate that the injunctive relief is "necessary or appropriate in aid of [the Court's] jurisdictio[n]." 28 U.S.C. § 1651(a). I will not consider counsel to have asked for such extraordinary relief where, as here, he has neither specifically requested it nor addressed the peculiar requirements for its issuance.

The application for stay is denied.

Maryland v. King

567 U.S. 1301 (2012).
On Application for Stay.

■ CHIEF JUSTICE ROBERTS, CIRCUIT JUSTICE.

Maryland's DNA Collection Act, Md.Pub.Saf.Code Ann. § 2–501 *et seq.*, authorizes law enforcement officials to collect DNA samples from individuals charged with but not yet convicted of certain crimes, mainly violent crimes and first-degree burglary. In 2009, police arrested Alonzo Jay King, Jr., for first-degree assault. When personnel at the booking facility collected his DNA, they found it matched DNA evidence from a rape committed in 2003. Relying on the match, the State charged and successfully convicted King of, among other things, first degree rape. A divided Maryland Court of Appeals overturned King's conviction, holding the collection of his DNA violated the Fourth Amendment because his expectation of privacy outweighed the State's interests. Maryland now applies for a stay of that judgment pending this Court's disposition of its petition for a writ of certiorari.

To warrant that relief, Maryland must demonstrate (1) "a reasonable probability" that this Court will grant certiorari, (2) "a fair prospect" that the Court will then reverse the decision below, and (3) "a likelihood that irreparable harm [will] result from the denial of a stay." Conkright v. Frommert, 556 U.S. 1401, 1402 (2009) (Ginsburg, J., in chambers) (internal quotation marks omitted).

To begin, there is a reasonable probability this Court will grant certiorari. Maryland's decision conflicts with decisions of the U.S. Courts of Appeals for the Third and Ninth Circuits as well as the Virginia Supreme Court, which have upheld statutes similar to Maryland's DNA Collection Act.

The split implicates an important feature of day-to-day law enforcement practice in approximately half the States and the Federal Government. See 114 Stat. 2728, as amended, 42 U.S.C. § 14135a(a)(1)(A) (authorizing the Attorney General to "collect DNA samples from individuals who are arrested, facing charges, or convicted"). Indeed, the decision below has direct effects beyond Maryland: Because the DNA samples Maryland collects may otherwise be eligible for the Federal Bureau of Investigation's national DNA database, the decision renders the database less effective for other States and the Federal Government. These factors make it reasonably probable that the Court will grant certiorari to resolve the split on the question presented. In addition, given the considered analysis of courts on the other side of the split, there is a fair prospect that this Court will reverse the decision below.

Finally, the decision below subjects Maryland to ongoing irreparable harm. "[A]ny time a State is enjoined by a court from effectuating statutes enacted by representatives of its people, it suffers a form of irreparable injury." New Motor Vehicle Bd. of Cal. v. Orrin W. Fox Co., 434 U.S. 1345, 1351 (1977) (Rehnquist, J., in chambers). Here there is, in addition, an ongoing and concrete harm to Maryland's law enforcement and public safety interests. According to Maryland, from 2009—the year Maryland began collecting samples from arrestees—to 2011, "matches from arrestee swabs [from Maryland] have resulted in 58 criminal prosecutions." Collecting DNA from individuals arrested for violent felonies provides a valuable tool for investigating unsolved crimes and thereby helping to remove violent offenders from the general population. Crimes for which DNA evidence is implicated tend to be serious, and serious crimes cause serious injuries. That Maryland may not employ a duly enacted statute to help prevent these injuries constitutes irreparable harm.

King responds that Maryland's eight-week delay in applying for a stay undermines its allegation of irreparable harm. In addition, he points out that of the 10,666 samples Maryland seized last year, only 4,327 of them were eligible for entry into the federal database and only 19 led to an arrest (of which fewer than half led to a conviction). These are sound points. Nonetheless, in the absence of a stay, Maryland would be disabled from employing a valuable law enforcement tool for several months—a tool used widely throughout the country and one that has been upheld by two Courts of Appeals and another state high court.

Accordingly, the judgment and mandate below are hereby stayed pending the disposition of the petition for a writ of certiorari. Should the petition for a writ of certiorari be denied, this stay shall terminate automatically. In the event the petition for a writ of certiorari is granted, the stay shall terminate upon the issuance of the mandate of this Court.

It is so ordered.

NOTE ON EMERGENCY STAYS IN THE SUPREME COURT

(1) Stays v. Injunctions. The most common emergency applications ask a Justice or the Court to grant or vacate a stay of a lower court judgment or order pending appeal, or to issue or vacate a writ of injunction against a party pending appeal. While the issuance of a stay is a form of equitable relief with "some functional overlap with an injunction, particularly a preliminary one," Nken v. Holder, 556 U.S. 418, 428 (2009), an injunction and a stay operate differently and serve different purposes. An injunction "directs the conduct of a party, and does so with the backing of [the court's] full coercive powers. * * * By contrast, instead of directing the conduct of a particular actor, a stay operates upon the judicial proceeding itself * * * either by halting or postponing some portion of the proceeding, or by temporarily divesting an order of enforceability. A stay pending appeal certainly has some functional overlap with an injunction, particularly a preliminary one. Both can have the practical effect of preventing some action before the legality of that action has been conclusively determined. But a stay achieves this result by temporarily suspending the source of authority to act—the order or judgment in question—not by directing an actor's conduct." *Id.* 428–29.[1]

(2) The Legal Basis for a Stay. There are two primary legal bases for the Supreme Court to issue a stay. First, 28 U.S.C. § 2101(f) provides that "[i]n any case in which the final judgment or decree of any court is subject to review by the Supreme Court on writ of certiorari," a Supreme Court Justice may grant a stay of the "execution and enforcement of [the] judgment or decree" for "a reasonable time to enable the party aggrieved to obtain a writ of certiorari from the Supreme Court." Second, the All Writs Act, 28 U.S.C. § 1651(a), authorizes the Court to issue a stay. See Nken, 556 U.S. at 426. The All Writs Act provides broader authority than § 2101(f) to the extent that it permits the Court to stay lower court interlocutory orders or decrees, and not just final judgments or decrees, and it applies to stays pending appeal to the Supreme Court (as opposed to just certiorari). But a stay under the Act must be "in aid of" the Court's jurisdiction and "agreeable to the usages and principles of law." Although these two sources of law have different scopes and limitations, Ohio Citizens is a rare emergency order opinion that attends to these differences.

(3) Test for a Stay. " 'A stay is not a matter of right,' " but "is instead 'an exercise of judicial discretion,' and 'the propriety of its issue is dependent upon the circumstances of the particular case.' " Nken, 556 U.S. at 433 (quoting Virginian Ry. Co. v. United States, 272 U.S. 658, 672–73 (1926)). Although the Court is not always consistent on the criteria that govern the exercise of this discretion, Maryland v. King states the standard three-part test that an applicant typically must satisfy to prevail: (1) "a reasonable probability" that the Supreme Court will grant certiorari, (2) "a fair prospect" that the Court will reverse the lower court's decision, and (3) "a likelihood that irreparable harm will result from the denial of a stay." See also Hollingsworth v. Perry, 558 U.S. 183, 190 (2010) (per curiam); Ind. State Police Pension Tr. v. Chrysler LLC, 556 U.S. 960, 960 (2009) (per curiam). In addition, "[i]n close cases the Circuit Justice or the Court will balance the equities and weigh the relative harms to the applicant and to the respondent." Hollingsworth, 558 U.S. at 190; compare Trump v. Int'l Refugee Assistance Project, 582 U.S. 571, 580 (2017) (before issuing a stay, " '[i]t is ultimately necessary . . . to balance the equities—to explore the relative

---

[1]   In an oft-quoted formulation, Nken v. Holder, 556 U.S. 418, 429 (2009), stated that a "stay 'simply suspend[s] judicial alteration of the *status quo.*' " (quoting Ohio Citizens for Responsible Energy, Inc. v. NRC, 479 U.S. 1312, 1313 (1986) (Scalia, J., in chambers)) (emphasis added). But as Justice Barrett has noted, the Court's stay jurisprudence provides "no settled way of defining 'the status quo.' " United States v. Texas, 144 S.Ct. 797, 798 n.2 (2024). In the context of emergency relief in the Supreme Court concerning a challenge to a new law, for example, it is unsettled whether the "status quo" to be preserved by a stay is the situation before the law is enacted, after the law is enacted but before judicial review, or the situation after one or both of the lower courts have ruled. See Labrador v. Poe, 144 S.Ct. 921, 930 (2024) (Kavanaugh, J., concurring in the grant of stay) (noting that each of these conceptions of the status quo "is defensible, but there is no sound or principled reason to pick one over another as a rule to apply in all cases involving new laws").

harms to applicant and respondent, as well as the interests of the public at large'") (citation omitted).[2]

Since Chief Justice Roberts did not balance the equities in Maryland v. King, should one assume that he concluded that the case for a stay was not close due to the likelihood of success and irreparable harm inquiries?

INTRODUCTORY NOTE ON EMERGENCY INJUNCTIVE RELIEF IN THE SUPREME COURT

The next principal decision considers an application for injunctive relief rather than an application for a stay.

Tandon v. Newsom

593 U.S. 61 (2021).
On Application for Injunctive Relief.

[On October 13, 2020, ten plaintiffs sued the Governor of California and other state officials in federal district court, alleging that California's restrictions related to the COVID-19 pandemic, including a ban on religious gatherings in private homes, violated the Free Exercise Clause of the First Amendment and other constitutional provisions. Plaintiffs sought injunctive relief, which the district court on February 5, 2021,

----

[2]   The factors for a stay when emergency relief is sought in the Supreme Court are a variation of the standard four-part test for stays issued by lower courts. That test is: "(1) whether the stay applicant has made a strong showing that he is likely to succeed on the merits; (2) whether the applicant will be irreparably injured absent a stay; (3) whether issuance of the stay will substantially injure the other parties interested in the proceeding; and (4) where the public interest lies." Nken v. Holder, 556 U.S. 418, 434 (2009). The "first two factors of the traditional standard are the most critical." *Id. The* test for a stay in the Supreme Court appears to differ from this test in at least two important respects. First, the Court asks, in addition to the likelihood of success factor, whether there is "a reasonable probability" that the Court will grant certiorari. Second, the Court weighs the equities only in close cases. See generally Pedro, *Stays,* 106 Calif.L.Rev. 869, 887–88 (2018). Another at least nominal difference is the applicant in the Supreme Court must demonstrate "a fair prospect" rather than a "strong showing" of success on the merits, though it is hard to tell in practice whether the choice of terminology makes a difference. See Labrador v. Poe, 144 S.Ct. 921, 929 n.2 (2024) (Kavanaugh, J., concurring in the grant of stay) (doubting that there is any "meaningful difference" between these formulations).

In Ohio v. Environmental Protection Agency, 144 S.Ct. 2040 (2024), a case in which applicants sought to stay an EPA ozone regulation issued pursuant to the Clean Air Act, the Court, citing Nken, stated that it would "apply the same 'sound * * * principles' as other federal courts," and then applied a version of the Nken four-part test that construed the merits inquiry as "likel[ihood] of success" rather than (as in Nken) a "strong showing" of likelihood of success. Ohio v. EPA was an unusual case because the Court delayed consideration of the stay application pending oral argument on the stay request and finally granted the stay over eight months after the application's filing based entirely on the Court's assessment of the merits. See *id.* 2052 (noting that the Court had "received and reviewed over 400 pages of briefing and a voluminous record, held over an hour of oral argument on the applications, and engaged in months of postargument deliberations"). In this non-standard context, where the Court (after extensive deliberation of a stay application) focused on the merits, it is perhaps unsurprising that the Court did not consider the relevance of a grant of certiorari and believed that the relevant test on the merits was likelihood of success rather than just a strong showing of likelihood of success.

denied on the ground that the restrictions were lawful. Plaintiffs asked the Ninth Circuit Court of Appeals to enter an injunction pending appeal, which it denied on March 30, for basically the same reason. Plaintiffs then applied to the Supreme Court for an emergency writ of injunction against the enforcement of the California law on April 2. After receiving California's response in opposition on April 8, the Court issued the following order and opinion the next day.]

■ PER CURIAM.

The application for injunctive relief presented to Justice Kagan and by her referred to the Court is granted pending disposition of the appeal in the United States Court of Appeals for the Ninth Circuit and disposition of the petition for a writ of certiorari, if such writ is timely sought. Should the petition for a writ of certiorari be denied, this order shall terminate automatically. In the event the petition for a writ of certiorari is granted, the order shall terminate upon the sending down of the judgment of this Court.

* * *

The Ninth Circuit's failure to grant an injunction pending appeal was erroneous. This Court's decisions have made the following points clear.

First, government regulations are not neutral and generally applicable, and therefore trigger strict scrutiny under the Free Exercise Clause, whenever they treat *any* comparable secular activity more favorably than religious exercise. Roman Catholic Diocese of Brooklyn v. Cuomo, 592 U.S. 14 (2020) (per curiam). It is no answer that a State treats some comparable secular businesses or other activities as poorly as or even less favorably than the religious exercise at issue. *Id.*, at 29 (Kavanaugh, J., concurring).

Second, whether two activities are comparable for purposes of the Free Exercise Clause must be judged against the asserted government interest that justifies the regulation at issue. *Id.*, at 17–18 (per curiam) (describing secular activities treated more favorably than religious worship that either "have contributed to the spread of COVID-19" or "could" have presented similar risks). Comparability is concerned with the risks various activities pose, not the reasons why people gather. *Id.*, at 21–25 (Gorsuch, J., concurring).

Third, the government has the burden to establish that the challenged law satisfies strict scrutiny. To do so in this context, it must do more than assert that certain risk factors "are always present in worship, or always absent from the other secular activities" the government may allow. South Bay United Pentecostal Church v. Newsom, 141 S.Ct. 716, 718 (2021) (statement of Gorsuch, J.); *id.*, at 717 (Barrett, J., concurring). Instead, narrow tailoring requires the government to show that measures less restrictive of the First Amendment activity could not address its interest in reducing the spread of COVID. Where the government permits other activities to proceed with precautions, it must show that the religious exercise at issue is more dangerous than those activities even when the same precautions are applied. Otherwise, precautions that suffice for other activities suffice for religious exercise too. Roman Catholic Diocese, *supra*; South Bay, 141 S.Ct., at 719 (statement of Gorsuch, J.)

Fourth, even if the government withdraws or modifies a COVID restriction in the course of litigation, that does not necessarily moot the case. And so long as a case is not moot, litigants otherwise entitled to emergency injunctive relief remain entitled to such relief where the applicants "remain under a constant threat" that government officials will use their power to reinstate the challenged restrictions. Roman Catholic Diocese, 592 U.S., at 20.

These principles dictated the outcome in this case, as they did in Gateway City Church v. Newsom, 141 S.Ct. 1460 (2021). First, California treats some comparable secular activities more favorably than at-home religious exercise, permitting hair salons, retail stores, personal care services, movie theaters, private suites at sporting events and concerts, and indoor restaurants to bring together more than three households at a time. Second, the Ninth Circuit did not conclude that those activities pose a lesser risk of transmission than *applicants'* proposed religious exercise at home. The Ninth Circuit erroneously rejected these comparators simply because this Court's previous decisions involved public buildings as opposed to private buildings. Third, instead of requiring the State to explain why it could not safely permit at-home worshipers to gather in larger numbers while using precautions used in secular activities, the Ninth Circuit erroneously declared that such measures might not "translate readily" to the home. The State cannot "assume the worst when people go to worship but assume the best when people go to work." Roberts v. Neace, 958 F.3d 409, 414 (6th Cir.2020) (per curiam). And fourth, although California officials changed the challenged policy shortly after this application was filed, the previous restrictions remain in place until April 15th, and officials with a track record of "moving the goalposts" retain authority to reinstate those heightened restrictions at any time. South Bay, 141 S.Ct., at 720 (statement of Gorsuch, J.).

Applicants are likely to succeed on the merits of their free exercise claim; they are irreparably harmed by the loss of free exercise rights "for even minimal periods of time"; and the State has not shown that "public health would be imperiled" by employing less restrictive measures. Roman Catholic Diocese, 592 U.S., at 19. Accordingly, applicants are entitled to an injunction pending appeal.

This is the fifth time the Court has summarily rejected the Ninth Circuit's analysis of California's COVID restrictions on religious exercise. It is unsurprising that such litigants are entitled to relief. California's Blueprint System contains myriad exceptions and accommodations for comparable activities, thus requiring the application of strict scrutiny. And historically, strict scrutiny requires the State to further "interests of the highest order" by means "narrowly tailored in pursuit of those interests." Church of Lukumi Babalu Aye, Inc. v. Hialeah, 508 U.S. 520, 546 (1993) (internal quotation marks omitted). That standard "is not watered down"; it "really means what it says." *Ibid.* (quotation altered).

■ THE CHIEF JUSTICE would deny the application.

■ JUSTICE KAGAN, with whom JUSTICE BREYER and JUSTICE SOTOMAYOR join, dissenting.

I would deny the application largely for the reasons stated in South Bay United Pentecostal Church v. Newsom, 141 S.Ct. 716 (2021) (Kagan, J., dissenting). The First Amendment requires that a State treat religious conduct as well as the State treats comparable secular conduct. Sometimes finding the right secular analogue may raise hard questions. But not today. California limits religious gatherings in homes to three households. If the State also limits all secular gatherings in homes to three households, it has complied with the First Amendment. And the State does exactly that: It has adopted a blanket restriction on at-home gatherings of all kinds, religious and secular alike. California need not, as the per curiam insists, treat at-home religious gatherings the same as hardware stores and hair salons—and thus unlike at-home secular gatherings, the obvious comparator here. As the per curiam's reliance on separate opinions and unreasoned orders signals, the law does not require that the State equally treat apples and watermelons. * * *

NOTE ON EMERGENCY WRITS OF INJUNCTION IN THE SUPREME COURT

(1) Legal Basis and Test. The All Writs Act, 28 U.S.C. § 1651(a), is the legal basis for the Court to issue a writ of injunction. The test for an injunction is on the surface similar to the test for a stay. The applicants must demonstrate likelihood of success on the merits, irreparable injury absent the injunction, favorable balance of equities, and that the injunction is in the public interest. See Winter v. Nat. Res. Def. Council, Inc., 555 U.S. 7, 20 (2008); see also Nken, 556 U.S. at 434 ("There is substantial overlap between [stay factors and] factors governing preliminary injunctions; not because the two are one and the same, but because similar concerns arise whenever a court order may allow or disallow anticipated action before the legality of that action has been conclusively determined"); note 2, *supra.*

But as Ohio Citizens and many other in-chambers opinions make clear, the standard for obtaining an emergency writ of injunction has often been harder to satisfy. See also Respect Maine PAC v. McKee, 562 U.S. 996, 996 (2010) (citing Ohio Citizens for proposition that an emergency injunction "demands a significantly higher justification" than a stay) (internal quotations omitted). Because the Justice or Court is asked at a preliminary stage to issue coercive affirmative relief against a party that was withheld by lower courts, individual Justices have often said or suggested, as in Ohio Citizens, that the legal rights at issue should be "indisputably clear" before injunctive relief will issue. See, *e.g.*, Chrysafis v. Marks, 141 S.Ct. 2482, 2483 (2021) (Breyer, J., joined by Sotomayor and Kagan, JJ., dissenting from grant of application for injunctive relief); Calvary Chapel Dayton Valley v. Sisolak, 140 S.Ct. 2603 (2020) (Alito, J., joined by Thomas and Kavanaugh, JJ., dissenting from denial of application for injunctive relief); South Bay United Pentecostal Church v. Newsom, 140 S.Ct. 1613 (2020) (Roberts, C.J., concurring in denial of application for injunctive relief). These are some of the reasons why the Court has traditionally issued emergency writs of injunction very rarely.

The Court in recent years has not always required a heightened showing for issuing emergency writs of injunction. In Tandon, for example, the Court issued an emergency writ of injunction against California's pandemic-related limit on religious gatherings in private homes based primarily on a straight-up assessment of the merits, without requiring any heightened justification for such relief. Far from demanding that the legal rights at issue be "indisputably clear," the Court appeared to premise the injunction on a novel theory of the Free Exercise Clause, citing other emergency relief orders and concurring opinions in such orders, that invalidates a facially neutral government regulation if it treats any secular activities more favorably than comparable religious activities. See Vladeck, *The Most-Favored Right: COVID, the Supreme Court, and the (New) Free Exercise Clause*, 15 N.Y.U J.L. & Lib. 699, 733–35 (2022). And it did so with only cursory consideration of injunctive relief factors beyond success on the merits. This different approach to emergency writs of injunction came primarily in a spate of such injunctions in religious liberty cases at the height of the COVID-19 pandemic, from November 2020 through April 2021. See Vladeck, Written Testimony, Case Selection and Review at the Supreme Court, Presidential Commission on the Supreme Court of the United States 6 (2021) (reporting that "Tandon was the sixth emergency writ of injunction issued by the Court since November 2020—after it hadn't issued *one* since 2015, and had only issued *four* since Chief Justice Roberts's 2005 confirmation").[1]

(2) The Relevance of Certworthiness. The certworthiness of the underlying issue in dispute is an element of the test for emergency application for stay in the Supreme Court. However, as Tandon suggests, certworthiness has not appeared in the Court's test for an emergency application for a writ of injunction. Is the difference justified, especially since, for reasons stated in Ohio Citizens, writs of injunctions should be harder to get than a stay?

Justice Barrett offered an answer in an opinion concurring in the denial of application for injunctive relief in Does 1–3 v. Mills, 142 S.Ct. 17 (2021). In that case, lower federal courts had denied injunctive relief from Maine's

---

[1] For other cases in recent years where the Court granted emergency relief without showing that the underlying issues were indisputably clear, see Whole Woman's Health v. Jackson, 595 U.S. 40 (2021); Roman Catholic Diocese of Brooklyn v. Cuomo, 592 U.S. 14, 15–21 (2020) (per curiam); Wheaton Coll. v. Burwell, 573 U.S. 958, 958–59 (2014).

requirement that all workers in licensed healthcare facilities be vaccinated against the coronavirus. Plaintiffs then sought emergency injunctive relief in the Supreme Court pending certiorari, which the Court without explanation denied. In her concurrence, joined by Justice Kavanaugh, Justice Barrett wrote:

"When this Court is asked to grant extraordinary relief, it considers, among other things, whether the applicant " 'is likely to succeed on the merits.' " Nken v. Holder, 556 U.S. 418, 434 (2009). I understand this factor to encompass not only an assessment of the underlying merits but also a discretionary judgment about whether the Court should grant review in the case. See, *e.g.*, Hollingsworth v. Perry, 558 U.S. 183, 190 (2010) (per curiam); *cf.* Supreme Court Rule 10. Were the standard otherwise, applicants could use the emergency docket to force the Court to give a merits preview in cases that it would be unlikely to take—and to do so on a short fuse without benefit of full briefing and oral argument. In my view, this discretionary consideration counsels against a grant of extraordinary relief in this case, which is the first to address the questions presented."

Justice Barrett suggests that in ruling on requests for emergency injunctive relief, the Court should consider certworthiness as a component of the likelihood of relief on the merits because the Court should not otherwise tip its hand on the merits in an emergency posture.[2] A certworthiness inquiry is clearly relevant for a *stay* sought and issued under 28 U.S.C. § 2101(f), which is designed "to enable the party aggrieved to obtain a writ of certiorari from the Supreme Court." But is it relevant to the issuance of an emergency writ of injunction pursuant to the All Writs Act, which has no such language? See Lawrence ex rel. Lawrence v. Chater, 516 U.S. 163, 168 (1996) (per curiam) (suggesting that under "the All Writs Act standard, * * * relief is granted only upon a showing that a grant of certiorari and eventual reversal are probable") (citing Heckler v. Lopez, 463 U.S. 1328, 1330 (1983) (Rehnquist, J., in chambers).[3] Note that Justice Barrett cited cases (like Hollingsworth) involving stays, and that at least some other Justices appear to look to certworthiness before issuing an emergency *stay* under the All Writs Act.[4] Why shouldn't they do the same for emergency writs of injunction under the Act?

---

[2]   In Labrador v. Poe, 144 S.Ct. 921 (2024), Justice Barrett joined Justice Kavanaugh's concurrence in the grant of a stay, which stated: "Of course, the certworthiness factor is, by definition, only a partial cure [for avoiding consideration of the merits on requests for emergency relief]. * * * Although emphasizing that factor reduces the number of emergency applications involving new laws where we have to assess the merits, some of the most significant and difficult emergency applications will readily clear the certworthiness bar. And in those cases, we may still have to assess likelihood of success on the merits." *Id.* at 931.

[3]   Note, *The Role of Certiorari in Emergency Relief*, 137 Harv.L.Rev. 1951 (2024), argues that certworthiness should be a prerequisite for the Court to issue injunctive relief under the All Writs Act because (i) the "in aid of jurisdiction" prong of the Act limits such relief to instances in which the Court plans to exercise jurisdiction, and (ii) the requirement that a writ be "agreeable to the usages and principles of law" means that it must be "designed to achieve the rational ends of law," which in turn precludes the Court from giving a merits preview in cases that it would be unlikely to take through the vehicle of injunctive relief without benefit of full briefing and oral argument (citing Price v. Johnston, 334 U.S. 266, 282 (1948)).

[4]   See, *e.g.*, Little v. Reclaim Idaho, 140 S.Ct. 2616, 2616 (2020) (staying district court preliminary injunctions); *id.* 2616–18 (Roberts, C.J., joined by Alito, Gorsuch, and Kavanaugh,

Justice Barrett's opinion was widely viewed as a response to criticisms that the Court during the COVID-19 pandemic had been issuing emergency injunctive relief too readily, especially in cases of first impression. See, *e.g.*, Pickup & Templin, *Emergency-Docket Experiments*, 98 Notre Dame L.Rev. Reflection 1, 3 (2022). Is the introduction of certworthiness a functional substitute for an "indisputably clear" merits claim in the calculus for emergency injunctive relief? Or is Justice Barrett suggesting the Court should not issue emergency injunctive relief to correct non-certworthy errors by courts below? Or, combining the two ideas, is she suggesting that the Court should not engage in error correction with emergency writs of injunction absent an error at least as egregious as would warrant summary reversal?

For analysis of Does 1–3 v. Mills, see Pickup & Templin, *supra*, at 15–18; Bressman, *The Rise and Fall of the Self-Regulatory Court*, 101 Tex.L.Rev. 1, 55–56 (2022); p. 398 & note 19, *infra*.

Danco Laboratories, LLC v. Alliance for Hippocratic Medicine

143 S.Ct. 1075 (2023).
On Application for Stay.

[In 2000, the Food and Drug Administration ("FDA") approved a branded version of the drug mifepristone, with conditions, for use to terminate early pregnancy. In 2019, it approved a generic version of the drug. And in 2016 and 2021 it modified the drug's approved conditions. In November 2022, medical groups opposed to abortion sued the FDA in federal district court in Texas to challenge these and related actions and sought a preliminary injunction ordering the FDA to suspend its actions since 2000. The district court on April 7, 2023 ruled that the FDA actions were arbitrary and capricious and contrary to the Comstock Act, and entered what it called a "stay" of all of the FDA actions. The FDA and the drug's manufacturer, Danco Laboratories, asked the Fifth Circuit for a stay of the district court order. On April 12, a Fifth Circuit panel granted the stay with respect to the FDA's original 2000 approval but denied it with respect to its other actions. On April 14, the FDA and Danco asked the Supreme Court to stay the district court order in its entirety. One week later, on April 21, the Supreme Court issued the following ruling.]

The applications for stays presented to Justice Alito and by him referred to the Court are granted. The April 7, 2023 order of the United States District Court for the Northern District of Texas, is stayed pending disposition of the appeal in the United States Court of Appeals

----

JJ., concurring in the grant of stay) (applying traditional test for a stay, including reasonable probability of granting certiorari); see also CBS, Inc. v. Davis, 510 U.S. 1315, 1318 (1994) (Blackmun, J., in chambers); Coleman v. Paccar, Inc., 424 U.S. 1301, 1303–04 (1976) (Rehnquist, J., in chambers) (certworthiness a relevant criterion in application under All Writs Act to vacate a stay).

for the Fifth Circuit and disposition of a petition for a writ of certiorari, if such a writ is timely sought. Should certiorari be denied, this stay shall terminate automatically. In the event certiorari is granted, the stay shall terminate upon the sending down of the judgment of this Court.

■ JUSTICE THOMAS would deny the applications for stays.

■ JUSTICE ALITO, dissenting from grant of applications for stays.

In recent cases, this Court has been lambasted for staying a District Court order "based on the scanty review this Court gives matters on its shadow docket," Merrill v. Milligan, 142 S.Ct. 879, 883 (2022) (Kagan, J., dissenting). In another, we were criticized for ruling on a stay application while "barely bother[ing] to explain [our] conclusion," a disposition that was labeled as "emblematic of too much of this Court's shadow-docket decisionmaking—which every day becomes more unreasoned." Whole Woman's Health v. Jackson, 141 S.Ct. 2494, 2500 (2021) (Kagan, J., dissenting from denial of application for injunctive relief). And in a third case in which a stay was granted, we were condemned for not exhibiting the "restraint" that was supposedly exercised in the past and for not "resisting" the Government's effort to "shortcut" normal process. Barr v. East Bay Sanctuary Covenant, 140 S.Ct. 3, 6 (2019) (Sotomayor, J., dissenting). *Cf.* Does 1–3 v. Mills, 142 S.Ct. 17, 18 (2021) (Barrett, J., concurring in denial of application for injunctive relief) (warning that the Court should not act "on a short fuse without benefit of full briefing and oral argument" in a case that is "first to address the questions presented").

I did not agree with these criticisms at the time, but if they were warranted in the cases in which they were made, they are emphatically true here. As narrowed by the Court of Appeals, the stay that would apply if we failed to broaden it would not remove mifepristone from the market. It would simply restore the circumstances that existed (and that the Government defended) from 2000 to 2016 under three Presidential administrations. In addition, because the applicants' Fifth Circuit appeal has been put on a fast track, with oral argument scheduled to take place in 26 days, there is reason to believe that they would get the relief they now seek—from either the Court of Appeals or this Court—in the near future if their arguments on the merits are persuasive. * * *

[The] applicants' argument on irreparable harm is largely reduced to the claim that Danco could not continue to market mifepristone because the drug would be mislabeled and that distribution could not resume until Danco jumped through a series of regulatory steps that would be largely perfunctory under present circumstances. That would not take place, however, unless the FDA elected to use its enforcement discretion to stop Danco, and the applicants' papers do not provide any reason to believe the FDA would make that choice. The FDA has previously invoked enforcement discretion to permit the distribution of mifepristone in a way that the regulations then in force prohibited, and here, the Government has not dispelled legitimate doubts that it would even obey an unfavorable order in these cases, much less that it would choose to take enforcement actions to which it has strong objections.

For these reasons, I would deny the stay applications. Contrary to the impression that may be held by many, that disposition would not express any view on the merits of the question whether the FDA acted lawfully in any of its actions regarding mifepristone. Rather, it would simply refuse to take a step that has not been shown as necessary to avoid the threat of any real harm during the presumably short period at issue.

NOTE ON EMERGENCY RELIEF IN OPERATION

(1) Universal Injunctions. To understand how emergency relief works in practice, consider a federal district court that stays the federal government from enforcing a statute or regulation with respect to nonparties in other districts and circuits—a so-called "universal injunction."[1] District courts have issued such orders to halt major initiatives by presidents of both parties. Unsurprisingly, a significant number of applications for (and grants of) emergency applications for stays in the Supreme Court have come in response to such universal injunctions.

If neither the court of appeals nor the Supreme Court stays a universal injunction, it can take a long time, often years, before the court of appeals and then the Supreme Court can review the district court decision. In the interim the government might be wrongly disabled from implementing one of its programs based on the views of a single judge that might turn out to be wrong.[2] Yet if a court of appeals or the Supreme Court issues a stay but the court with final disposition ultimately rules that the government

---

[1]   When a lower federal court or the Supreme Court suspends the effect of agency action pursuant to 5 U.S.C. § 705 (authorizing the court reviewing agency action to "issue all necessary and appropriate process to postpone the effective date of an agency action"), it typically issues what it calls a "stay" rather than an "injunction" of agency action even though the practical effect of such relief is essentially equivalent to a preliminary injunction. This is what the district court did in Danco Laboratories, for example. Compare West Virginia v. E.P.A., 577 U.S. 1126 (2016) (staying Environmental Protection Agency's Carbon Pollution Emission Guidelines pending disposition of the petition for review in the court of appeals). See also Nken, 556 U.S. at 428 (reviewing a lower court's denial of a stay of a removal order by the Board of Immigration Appeals pending judicial review and noting that "a stay operates upon the judicial proceeding itself * * * either by halting or postponing some portion of the proceeding, or by temporarily divesting an order of enforceability"). For an argument that § 705 authorizes reviewing courts to choose between staying agency action or enjoining agencies, and that the Supreme Court should adhere to its traditional heightened standard for issuing injunctive relief either way, see Note, *Halting Administrative Action in the Supreme Court*, 137 Harv.L.Rev. 2016 (2024).

[2]   Consider Biden v. Texas, 597 U.S. 785 (2022). That case began when the Biden administration terminated the Trump administration's Remain-in-Mexico policy on June 1, 2021. After Missouri and Texas sued the administration in a federal court in Texas, the district court in August 2021 issued a universal injunction effectively barring the Biden administration from repealing the policy. Texas v. Biden, 554 F.Supp.3d 818, 857 (N.D.Tex.2021). Eleven days later, the Supreme Court declined to stay the district court's injunction. Biden v. Texas, 142 S.Ct. 926 (2021). The administration lost its appeal at the Fifth Circuit, all the while complying with the injunction. After full briefing and oral argument, the Supreme Court in late June 2022 reversed and remanded. Biden v. Texas, 597 U.S. 785 (2022). The district court's universal injunction thus delayed the Biden administration's lawful termination of the Remain-in-Mexico policy for almost a year.

program is unlawful, the government will have implemented an illegal program perhaps for many years.[3] See generally Labrador v. Poe, 144 S.Ct. 921, 929 (2024) (Kavanaugh, J., concurring in the grant of stay) (describing these tradeoffs in detail, and noting that "the interim status of the law—that is, whether the law is enforceable during the several years while the parties wait for a final merits ruling—itself raises a separate question of extraordinary significance to the parties and the American people * * * [that] this Court often must address when deciding emergency applications involving new laws"). These same basic tradeoffs arise in other contexts, including when the Supreme Court is asked to enjoin a government program that the courts below declined to enjoin; or when it is asked to lift a stay of a district court injunction issued by the court of appeals; or when these applications come in the context of a state program.

This is a central problem that the test for an emergency stay seeks to sort out: which baseline—an operational government program or an enjoined one—will prevail during lengthy litigation to test the program's legality. See Nken, 556 U.S. at 421, 427 (noting that "if a court takes the time it needs" to decide an appeal, its "decision may in some cases come too late for the party seeking review" and describing the issue as a "conflict between considered review and effective relief"). The answer to this question in an emergency posture has large consequences during the pendency of the litigation and often is the last word on whether the government can implement a program.[4]

Which values does the test for an emergency stay try to accommodate in resolving this tradeoff: Fairness to the parties? Good governance? Judicial efficiency? Legal accuracy? All of these things? How well, and how reliably, does it accommodate these values?

Consider each element of the test for an emergency stay.

(a) Certiorari. The first question the Court asks in analyzing a request for an emergency stay—whether there is "a reasonable probability" that it will grant certiorari—can be hard to answer since no firm rules bind

---

[3]   See, *e.g.*, Allen v. Milligan, 599 U.S. 1 (2023) (ruling that Alabama's congressional districting plan likely violated § 2 of the Voting Rights Act almost a year and a half after the Supreme Court had stayed a three-judge district court's injunction of the plan, thereby permitting the plan that it later deemed likely illegal to be used in an intervening election); compare Murthy v. Missouri, 144 S.Ct. 7 (2023) (Alito, J., dissenting from grant of application for stay) (criticizing Supreme Court's unreasoned October 2023 stay of court of appeals injunction preventing federal officials from coercing social-media platforms into censoring content in part on the ground that the stay permits allegedly unlawful speech restrictions to continue "until the Court completes its review of this case, an event that may not occur until late in the spring of next year").

[4]   In addition to the example, p. 371, note 1, *supra*, consider two emergency orders issued on January 13, 2022. The Court stayed, pending full appellate review, a federal district court's order granting a preliminary injunction against the Centers for Medicare and Medicaid Services' vaccination mandate for health-care workers at federally funded facilities, Biden v. Missouri, 595 U.S. 87 (2022) (per curiam), and it stayed, pending full appellate review, an Occupational Safety and Health Administration (OSHA) emergency rule imposing a vaccine-or-test mandate on businesses with more than 100 employees, Nat'l Fed. Indep. Bus. v. Dep't of Labor, 595 U.S. 109 (2022) (per curiam). Both emergency rulings were in effect final rulings. As a result of the stay, the vaccine mandate remained in effect for a year and a half, until the Biden administration withdrew it and ended the case. And the Biden administration withdrew the OSHA emergency rule rather than litigate its validity in light of the Supreme Court's brief assessment of the merits in that emergency relief decision.

the Court in deciding this question. Compare Brennan, *The National Court of Appeals: Another Dissent*, 40 U.Chi.L.Rev. 473 (1973) ("I subscribe completely to the observation of the late Mr. Justice Harlan that 'Frequently the question whether a case is "certworthy" is more a matter of "feel" than of precisely ascertainable rules.' "). A circuit split is a prominent reason for granting certiorari, see p. 331, *supra*, and is often cited by justices as a ground in support of a stay, see, *e.g.*, Labrador v. Poe, 144 S.Ct. 921, 925 (2024) (Gorsuch, J., concurring in the grant of stay) (citing a circuit split as grounds for certworthiness in stay context); compare Barnes v. Ahlman, 140 S.Ct. 2620, 2623 (2020) (Sotomayor, J., dissenting from the grant of stay); (grounding dissent from grant of stay in part on fact that there was no "certworthy circuit split"). Yet circuit splits are often not present in requests for emergency relief, especially when they stem from recent changes in the law. See, *e.g.*, Moyle v. United States, 144 S.Ct. 540 (2024) (staying preliminary injunction by federal district court of new Idaho law prohibiting abortions unless needed to protect the life of the mother on which there was no conflict of lower court authority); Barr v. East Bay Sanctuary Covenant, 140 S.Ct. 3 (2019) (granting stay of universal injunction of Department of Justice rule barring certain migrants from entering United States even though there was no conflict of lower court authority).

When the emergency application is before the Court, is the issue simply whether four Justices will in fact vote to grant certiorari, for whatever reason? How is the Court supposed to assess certworthiness when it is examining a district court injunction before plenary review by the court of appeals? See Francois v. Wilkinson, 141 S.Ct. 652, 655 n.* (2021) (Sotomayor, J., dissenting from the denial of application for stay) (noting that the certworthiness inquiry "is complicated in cases such as this one where there is not yet a decision by the court of appeals, which often informs whether a case presents substantial questions of law").

(b) Success on the Merits. The second consideration tends to be the most consequential one in an emergency application, since the Court will not grant a stay unless the applicant shows at least a fair prospect of success on the merits, and since success on the merits often appears to be the Court's major concern. From one perspective, it makes little sense to permit a district court judge (or a court of appeals panel) to put a government program on ice (or to allow it to operate) for years if the Supreme Court is fairly confident that the controlling lower court decision is wrong. But from another perspective, the Court is interrupting normal appellate process and ruling on this merits question with great speed, sparse briefing, truncated process and deliberation, and usually without the benefit of extensive reasoning by courts below. It thus might well get the answer wrong in its intervention in normal appellate process. Which perspective should predominate? Should the answer to this question turn on how thoroughly (or not) the lower courts have assessed the merits issue? For a thorough examination of these and related issues, see Labrador v. Poe, 144 S.Ct. 921, 928–34 (2024) (Kavanaugh, J., concurring in grant of stay).

In Ohio v. Environmental Protection Agency, 144 S.Ct. 2040 (2024), the Court granted an application to stay an EPA ozone regulation issued under the Clean Air Act based entirely on its assessment of "the merits and the question who is likely to prevail at the end of this litigation." The Court did so, it explained, because both parties had "strong arguments" about the other stay factors considered below, namely, "the harms they face[d] and equities involved." Unlike the typical context for a stay application, the Court decided Ohio v. EPA after oral argument and extensive deliberation. See *id.* 2052, see also p. 377, note 2, *supra*. In this context, is deciding on emergency relief based entirely on the likelihood of success on the merits more justified than in the typically rushed case in which the process is more truncated?

(c) Irreparable Harm. The third consideration concerns the "likelihood that irreparable harm will result from the denial of a stay." Maryland v. King, 567 U.S. 1301, 1302 (2012), p. 374, *supra*. A party suffers an irreparable injury when there is no "possibility that adequate compensatory or other corrective relief will be available at a later date." Sampson v. Murray, 415 U.S. 61, 90 (1974) (internal quotations omitted). In general, the loss of constitutional rights is deemed an irreparable injury. See, *e.g.*, Roman Cath. Diocese of Brooklyn v. Cuomo, 592 U.S. 14, 19 (2020) (per curiam) (concluding in the context of an application for injunctive relief that a New York executive order barring congregants from attending a church service constitutes irreparable injury because "[t]he loss of First Amendment freedoms, for even minimal periods of time, unquestionably constitutes irreparable injury" (quoting Elrod v. Burns, 427 U.S. 347, 373 (1976) (plurality opinion))). The rule in Maryland v. King—that the government as applicant for emergency relief suffers irreparable injury whenever its statutes (or regulations) are enjoined—appears now to be followed by most of the Justices.[5] The satisfaction of the irreparable harm prong in any case where the government seeks emergency relief from an injunction of one of its programs is an important reason why, in such instances, the Court's analysis of the merits predominates.[6] See Vladeck, *The Solicitor General and the Shadow Docket*, 133 Harv.L.Rev. 123, 155–56 (2019).

---

[5]   See Abbott v. Perez, 585 U.S. 579, 602 n.17 (2018); see also Republican Party of Pa. v. Degraffenreid, 141 S.Ct. 732, 733 (2021) (Thomas, J., dissenting from denial of certiorari) (quoting and relying on Maryland v. King in assessing appropriateness of stay); Little v. Reclaim Idaho, 140 S.Ct. 2616, 2617 (2020) (Roberts, C.J., joined by Alito, Gorsuch, and Kavanaugh, JJ., concurring in grant of stay) (citing Abbott for the proposition that "the State is likely to suffer irreparable harm absent a stay" because "the preliminary injunction disables Idaho from vindicating its sovereign interest in the enforcement of initiative requirements that are likely consistent with the First Amendment"). But see, *e.g.*, Food & Drug Admin. v. Am. Coll. of Obstetricians & Gynecologists, 141 S.Ct. 578, 584 (2021) (Sotomayor, J., joined by Kagan, J., dissenting from grant of stay) (stating that government's "sweeping" argument that "all injunctions against a government inherently cause irreparable harm" is not supported by precedent).

[6]   The presumption that the government suffers irreparable injury whenever its statutes or regulations are enjoined originated in a series of in-chambers opinions by Chief Justice Rehnquist. In addition to New Motor Vehicle Bd. of California v. Orrin W. Fox Co., 434 U.S. 1345, 1351–52 (1977) (Rehnquist, J., in chambers), see, *e.g.*, Bowen v. Kendrick, 483 U.S. 1304, 1304–05 (1987) (Rehnquist, C.J., in chambers); Walters v. Nat'l Ass'n of Radiation Survivors, 468 U.S. 1323, 1324 (1984) (Rehnquist, J., in chambers). According to Rehnquist, the special treatment for government-enjoined programs is an outgrowth of the view that state and federal laws are "presumptively constitutional," New Motor Vehicle Bd., *supra*, at 1352 (state statute); Bowen, *supra*, at 1304 (noting the "presumption of constitutionality which attaches to every Act of Congress") (quoting Walters). Rehnquist noted in Bowen that "[i]t has been the unvarying practice of this Court so long as I have been a Member of it to note probable jurisdiction and

(d) The Equities. The last consideration—balancing the equities to the parties and public in a "close case"—is perhaps the most elusive. What counts as a close case? How exactly is the Court supposed to balance the various equities?

For an illustration of the difficulties, consider the Court's order vacating a stay of a district court order that vacated on a nationwide basis the Center for Disease Control's COVID-era eviction moratorium. See Alabama Ass'n of Realtors v. Dep't of Health & Hum. Servs., 594 U.S. 758 (2021) (per curiam).[7] After determining that the applicants—realtor associations and rental property managers—had a very strong chance of prevailing on the merits due to an absence of legal authority for the moratorium, the Court ruled that the "equities do not justify depriving the applicants of the District Court's judgment in their favor."[8] The Court believed that the moratorium put the applicants and "millions of [other] landlords across the country," including many of modest means, "at risk of irreparable harm by depriving them of rent payments with no guarantee of eventual recovery." At the same time, the Court believed that the Government had diminished interests since the stay had given it time to distribute rental-assistance funds. The Court acknowledged the public's "strong interest in combating the spread of the COVID-19 Delta variant," but, underscoring the primacy of the merits, it stated: "[O]ur system does not permit agencies to act unlawfully even in

---

decide on the merits all cases in which a single district judge declares an Act of Congress unconstitutional." *Id.* 1304. These formulations entail that the reviewability prong, too, is always satisfied when a government program is enjoined for reasons of unconstitutionality. The Court has not yet expressly adopted that conclusion, however. For criticism of the Rehnquist view, see Laycock & Hasen, Modern American Remedies: Cases and Materials 397 (5th ed.2019) (the Rehnquist view "makes it unnecessary to consider the likelihood and magnitude of [any] actual injuries; it substitutes an abstract injury to sovereignty that requires no proof and that may be given substantial weight in the balancing process").

7   The Court in Alabama Ass'n of Realtors did not make clear how the test for vacating a stay differs from the test for granting a stay, and the full Court has never done so. An influential in-chambers formulation, often cited in separate opinions in subsequent emergency orders cases, is Coleman v. Paccar, Inc., 424 U.S. 1301, 1304 (1976) (Rehnquist, J., in chambers), which suggested that "a Circuit Justice has jurisdiction to vacate a stay where it appears that the rights of the parties to a case pending in the court of appeals, which case could and very likely would be reviewed here upon final disposition in the court of appeals, may be seriously and irreparably injured by the stay, and the Circuit Justice is of the opinion that the court of appeals is demonstrably wrong in its application of accepted standards in deciding to issue the stay." See also Planned Parenthood of Greater Texas Surgical Health Servs. v. Abbott, 571 U.S. 1061 (2013) (Scalia, J., concurring in denial of application to vacate stay) ("We may not vacate a stay entered by a court of appeals unless that court clearly and " 'demonstrably' " erred in its application of " 'accepted standards' '' " (quoting Western Airlines, Inc. v. Teamsters, 480 U.S. 1301, 1305 (1987) (O'Connor, J., in chambers) (quoting Coleman v. Paccar Inc., 424 U.S. 1301, 1304 (1976) (Rehnquist, J., in chambers)))). Justice Breyer in dissent in Alabama Ass'n of Realtors drew on these formulations. 594 U.S. 758, 766–67 (2021) (Breyer, J., dissenting). See also Raysor v. DeSantis, 140 S.Ct. 2600, 2602–03 (2020) (Sotomayor, J., dissenting from denial of application to vacate stay) (relying on the three Coleman factors for analysis of whether to vacate lower court's stay).

8   The Court had earlier denied an application to vacate a district court's stay of its own order granting relief against an earlier iteration of the eviction moratorium. See Alabama Ass'n of Realtors v. Dep't of Health & Hum. Servs., 141 S.Ct. 2320 (2021). Justice Kavanaugh, who provided the fifth vote against granting relief, concurred to explain that while he agreed that the moratorium was unlawful, the equities nonetheless favored keeping the stay in place for the few remaining weeks before it expired in order to "allow for additional and more orderly distribution of the congressionally appropriated rental assistance funds." *Id.* 2321 (Kavanaugh, J., concurring).

pursuit of desirable ends." *Cf.* Youngstown Sheet & Tube Co. v. Sawyer, 343 U.S. 579, 582, 585–86 (1952) (concluding that even the Government's belief that its action "was necessary to avert a national catastrophe" could not overcome a lack of congressional authorization).

Justice Breyer, joined by Justices Kagan and Sotomayor, dissented. After challenging the Court's assessment of the merits, Justice Breyer argued that "the balance of equities strongly favors leaving the stay in place." The applicants' loss of rental income was attenuated, he maintained, by the moratorium order's directive that tenants have an obligation to make "as close to the full rent payment" as possible. And this acknowledged injury to the applicants, he argued, paled in comparison with the massive harms from vacating the stay, which included what the CDC described as a strong "likelihood of mass evictions nationwide" with public-health consequences that would be "difficult to reverse."

How should the Court, in an emergency posture, compare the financial harms to applicants against the harms of increased COVID-19 exposure for evicted tenants, and how should these harms, however they cash out, be considered in relation to the applicants' likelihood of success on the merits?[9] The Court's stay jurisprudence provides no concrete guidance. Compare Hilton v. Braunskill, 481 U.S. 770, 777 (1987) ("Since the traditional stay factors contemplate individualized judgments in each case, the formula cannot be reduced to a set of rigid rules."). The problem is exacerbated by the fact that the Court rarely explains in any detail how it applies the stay factors. Most often it simply announces its conclusion in an order with no analysis, as in Danco Laboratories.

(2) Election Cases. In Purcell v. Gonzales, 549 U.S. 1 (2006) (per curiam), the Supreme Court vacated a court of appeals injunction that "just weeks before an election" had barred Arizona from enforcing its voter identification requirements. The Court explained that the injunction was inappropriate because it could "result in voter confusion and consequent incentive to remain away from the polls," and because it failed to provide Arizona election officials with "clear guidance." *Id.* 4–5. This decision gave rise to "the Purcell principle," see Hasen, *Reining in the Purcell Principle*, 43 Fla.St.U.L.Rev. 427 (2016) (coining the phrase), which in a nutshell holds that "lower federal courts should ordinarily not alter the election rules on the eve of an election,"

---

[9]   In Nat'l Fed. Indep. Bus. v. Occupational Safety & Health Admin., 595 U.S. 109 (2022) (per curiam), which stayed OSHA's emergency rule imposing a vaccine-or-test mandate on certain businesses, the Court faced a similar tradeoff but appeared to disclaim any role for balancing. After discussing the merits of the OSHA rule, the Court stated that "[t]he equities do not justify withholding interim relief." Then, after noting that applicants claimed that the OSHA mandate would result in "billions of dollars in unrecoverable compliance costs and [ ] cause hundreds of thousands of employees to leave their jobs," while the federal government claimed that the mandate would "save over 6,500 lives and prevent hundreds of thousands of hospitalizations," the Court stated: "It is not our role to weigh such tradeoffs. In our system of government, that is the responsibility of those chosen by the people through democratic processes." For criticisms of this opinion, see Vladeck, *Emergency Relief During Emergencies*, 102 B.U.L.Rev. 1787, 1789–90 (2022); Baude, *Balancing the Equities in the Vaccine Mandate Case*, Volokh Conspiracy (Jan. 14, 2022); Re, *Did the Supreme Court Overrule Equity?*, Re's Judicata (Jan. 14, 2022).

Republican Nat'l Comm. v. Democratic Nat'l Comm., 589 U.S. 423, 424 (2020) (per curiam).

It is an understatement to say that the Supreme Court "has not yet had occasion to fully spell out all of [the] contours" of the Purcell principle. Merrill v. Milligan, 142 S.Ct. 879, 881 (2022) (Kavanaugh, J., concurring in grant of applications for stays) (order staying district court injunctions and granting certiorari before judgment in one case and noting probable jurisdiction in another). Beyond Purcell's emphasis on avoiding voter confusion and election official uncertainty, the Court has not clarified the rationale for the principle.

Nor, relatedly, has it made clear the principle's relationship to the traditional criteria for emergency relief. "Some of [the] Court's opinions, including Purcell itself, could be read to imply that the principle is absolute and that a district court may *never* enjoin a State's election laws in the period close to an election." *Id*. 881 (Kavanaugh, J., concurring in grant of applications for stays); compare Republican Nat'l Comm., 589 U.S. at 424 ("This Court has repeatedly emphasized that lower federal courts should ordinarily not alter the election rules on the eve of an election."). In Merrill, Justice Kavanaugh, joined by Justice Alito, argued that Purcell is a "refinement" of "ordinary stay principles for the election context" that could be "overcome even with respect to an injunction issued close to an election if a plaintiff establishes at least the following: (i) the underlying merits are entirely clearcut in favor of the plaintiff; (ii) the plaintiff would suffer irreparable harm absent the injunction; (iii) the plaintiff has not unduly delayed bringing the complaint to court; and (iv) the changes in question are at least feasible before the election without significant cost, confusion, or hardship." Merrill, 142 S.Ct. at 881 (Kavanaugh, J., concurring in grant of applications for stays); compare Democratic Nat'l Comm. v. Wisconsin State Legislature, 141 S.Ct. 28, 42 (2020) (Kagan, J., dissenting from denial of application to vacate stay) ("[C]ourts must consider all relevant factors, not just the calendar."). See generally Hasen, *supra*, at 440–44 (arguing that even though elections raise special factors for emergency relief, all of the traditional emergency criteria should be applied in resolving such issues).

Another unsettled issue under the Purcell principle is precisely when an election is too close for courts to intervene with emergency relief. Merrill is illustrative. The Court there granted a stay of a three-judge District Court order that had enjoined Alabama's congressional districting plan, and ordered Alabama to redraw its congressional districts, a tad over two months before primary elections (via absentee voting) began, and nine months before the general election. Justice Kavanaugh in his concurring opinion stated that the Purcell principle applies in "the period close to an election" or when the "election is close at hand,"142 S.Ct. at 880–81, which he said was satisfied in Merrill. Justice Kagan in dissent maintained that the principle applies to changes in election rules "at the eleventh hour" or "just weeks before an election," *id*. 888 (internal quotation marks and citation omitted), which she argued was not the case in Merrill. Professor Vladeck argues that the uncertainty in the trigger for Purcell invites "the very subjective decision-making from judges that [Purcell] claimed it was trying to eliminate."

Vladeck, The Shadow Docket: How the Supreme Court Uses Stealth Rulings to Amass Power and Undermine the Republic 206 (2023).

But if the traditional criteria should be applied to determine emergency relief in election law cases, won't the appropriate temporal trigger depend a lot on the election law issue at stake? Compare Merrill, 142 S.Ct. at 881 n.1 (Kavanaugh, J., concurring in grant of applications for stays) ("How close to an election is too close may depend in part on the nature of the election law at issue, and how easily the State could make the change without undue collateral effects. Changes that require complex or disruptive implementation must be ordered earlier than changes that are easy to implement.") with Democratic Nat'l Comm., 141 S.Ct. at 42 (Kagan, J., dissenting) ("Last-minute changes to election processes may baffle and discourage voters; and when that is likely, a court has strong reason to stay its hand. But not every such change poses that danger.").

(3) Capital Cases. Requests for emergency relief in the Supreme Court often arise in cases involving capital punishment, especially as the date of execution approaches. The Court will typically be asked to vacate a stay issued by a lower court or to stay the execution if the lower courts do not. As a general matter, the Court applies the same emergency orders principles in death penalty cases as in other cases. See, *e.g.*, Hill v. McDonough, 547 U.S. 573, 584 (2006); Shapiro et al., Supreme Court Practice ch. 18.2 (11th ed.2019) ("Stays in capital cases are governed by the same general principles applicable to other stays, including consideration of irreparable harm in the absence of a stay."). However, the Court applies a laches principle to last-minute requests for emergency relief. See, *e.g.*, Hill, 547 U.S. at 584 ("A court considering a stay must also apply a strong equitable presumption against the grant of a stay where a claim could have been brought at such a time as to allow consideration of the merits without requiring entry of a stay.") (internal quotations omitted); see also Nance v. Ward, 597 U.S. 159, 174 (2022); Bucklew v. Precythe, 587 U.S. 119, 149–51 (2019).[10]

One issue that has special salience in the capital punishment context arises from the fact that it takes four votes for the Court to grant certiorari but five votes to grant a stay of execution. It is thus possible that four Justices would vote to grant certiorari but the capital defendant would be executed before the Court's consideration of the merits because none of the other five Justices voted to stay the execution. To address this issue, the Court appears to have adopted the practice of a "courtesy fifth," whereby "a Justice who does not believe that either certiorari or a stay is warranted will nonetheless vote to issue a stay if four other Justices have voted to grant certiorari, thus preserving the Court's jurisdiction." Presidential Commission on the Supreme Court of the United States, Final Report 214–15 (2021). The best evidence for this practice is that, at least during the Roberts Court, "there has not been a grant of certiorari coupled with a denial

---

[10]   The Court also frequently vacates lower court stays of executions, often in the form of unreasoned orders. For criticism of the practice and its influence on lower federal courts, see Barber v. Ivey, 143 S.Ct. 2545 (2023) (Sotomayor, J., dissenting from the denial of application for stay). See also Green, *A Cruel and Unusual Docket, The Supreme Court's Harsh New Standard for Last Minute Stays of Execution*, 16 Harv.L. & Pol'y.Rev. 623, 654–56 (2022).

of a stay, nor an order denying a stay and reciting that four Justices would have granted certiorari." Shapiro et al., Supreme Court Practice, ch. 18.8 (11th ed.2019).

Sometimes, but not always, a Justice will provide a courtesy fifth to allow other Justices more time to consider whether to vote to grant certiorari. Compare Arthur v. Dunn, 580 U.S. 977 (2016) (Statement of Roberts, C.J.) (voting to grant a stay "as a courtesy," even though he believed the application did not satisfy the Court's stay criteria, in order to afford the four Justices who voted for a stay "the opportunity to more fully consider the suitability of this case for review"), with Dunn v. Price, 139 S.Ct. 1312 (2019) (Breyer, J., dissenting from grant of application to vacate stay) (noting that the Court vacated a stay of execution over four dissents and rejected Justice Breyer's request for a one-day delay so the Court could deliberate on the matter at Conference). Four votes to grant a stay unaccompanied by four votes to grant certiorari, however, do not appear to trigger a courtesy fifth. See, *e.g.*, McGehee v. Hutchinson, 581 U.S. 933 (2017); see generally Freedman, *No Execution If Four Justices Object*, 43 Hofstra L.Rev. 639, 651 n.50 (2015) ("[T]here are dozens of cases * * * denying stays over four dissents * * *.").

(4) Administrative Stays. An administrative stay temporarily stays a lower court order while the Court deliberates whether to stay definitively that order pending appeal. See, *e.g.*, United States v. Texas, 144 S.Ct. 797, 799 (2024) (Barrett, J., concurring in denial of applications to vacate stay) ("[A]n administrative stay is supposed to be a short-lived prelude to the main event: a ruling on the motion for a stay pending appeal."); June Medical Services, L.L.C. v. Gee, 139 S.Ct. 661 (2019) (issuing an administrative stay of the mandate of the court of appeals during the period when the Court was considering an application for a stay of the mandate pending a petition for certiorari, on the ground that "the filings regarding the application for a stay in this matter were not completed until earlier today and the Justices need time to review these filings").

The Court has never clarified the legal basis for an administrative stay, but Justice Barrett has plausibly suggested that it is a combination of the All Writs Act, 28 U. S. C. § 1651, and the Court's inherent authority. United States v. Texas, *supra,* at 798 n.1 (Barrett, J., concurring in denial of applications to vacate stay) (citing Bayefsky, *Administrative Stays: Power and Procedure*, 97 Notre Dame L.Rev. 1941, 1960–64 (2022)). The Court has also never clarified the standard for issuing an administrative stay. Justice Barrett has explained that, in contrast to the traditional stay factors, "[a]dministrative stays do not typically reflect the court's consideration of the merits of the stay application," but rather usually aim (among other considerations) to "minimize harm while an appellate court deliberates," and "reflect[ ] a first-blush judgment about the relative consequences of staying the lower court judgment versus allowing it go to into effect." *Id.* 798. But see United States v. Texas, 142 S.Ct. 14, 17 (2021) (Sotomayor, J., concurring in part and dissenting in part) (dissenting from Court's refusal to issue an administrative stay of lower court ruling in part due to consideration of the merits).[11]

For a comprehensive assessment of administrative stays, see Bayefsky, *supra.*

(5) The Precedential Effect of Emergency Orders. The Supreme Court typically does not issue emergency relief unless it concludes that the applicant has a fair prospect or likelihood of success on the merits. How should the Supreme Court's assessment of the merits of the case in an emergency posture guide the Court and lower courts when they consider the merits of the same dispute or of disputes raising similar issues?[12] The Court in Tandon, for example, issued an emergency writ of injunction against California's COVID-19-related limit on religious gatherings in private homes in reliance on what Justice Kagan in dissent described as "separate opinions and unreasoned orders" from the Court's prior emergency relief decisions.[13] And the Court near the end of its opinion reprimanded the Ninth Circuit for not following the Court's prior emergency orders related to California's COVID-19 restrictions.[14] When and to what extent should emergency orders have precedential value?

---

[11]   United States v. Texas involved an application on March 4, 2024, to the Supreme Court to vacate an administrative stay that the Court of Appeals for the Fifth Circuit on March 2, 2024, had placed on a federal district court injunction of a Texas law that criminalized unlawful entry into the country and authorized state officials to issue state deportation orders. When the Court denied the application on March 19, the "temporary" court of appeals administrative stay had been in place for more than two weeks. Should the Supreme Court be in the business of reviewing abusively long administrative stays issued by lower courts? See United States v. Texas, 144 S.Ct. 797, 799–800 (2024) (Barrett, J., concurring in denial of applications to vacate stay) (considering it "unwise to invite emergency litigation in this Court about whether a court of appeals abused its discretion" in issuing an administrative stay but noting that "[t]he time may come, in this case or another, when this Court is forced to conclude that an administrative stay has effectively become a stay pending appeal and review it accordingly").

[12]   As Justice Alito notes in his dissent in Danco Laboratories, a denial of emergency relief, at least without further explanation, implies nothing necessarily about the Court's views on the merits, since, among other reasons, the Court might deny relief because the applicant did not suffer irreparable harm. See Ruckelshaus v. Monsanto Co., 463 U.S. 1315, 1317 (1983) (Blackmun, J., in chambers) ("An applicant's likelihood of success on the merits need not be considered, * * * if the applicant fails to show irreparable injury from the denial of the stay").

[13]   Three cases seemed most relevant. The Court in Roman Catholic Diocese of Brooklyn v. Cuomo, 592 U.S. 14 (2020) (per curiam) granted emergency injunctive relief from a New York Executive Order restricting attendance at religious services during the COVID-19 pandemic. The Court's per curiam opinion announced what appeared to be a new test under the Free Exercise Clause in a five-paragraph discussion of applicants' likelihood of success on the merits; brief concurring opinions by Justices Gorsuch and Kavanaugh elaborated on the issue. The Court in South Bay United Pentecostal Church v. Newsom, 141 S.Ct. 716 (2021), granted in part a request for emergency injunctive relief from a California restriction on attendance at religious services during the pandemic with no opinion for the Court. Chief Justice Roberts filed a brief concurring opinion, Justice Gorsuch (joined by Justices Thomas and Alito) filed a statement that argued that the injunction in full was required under Roman Catholic Diocese, Justice Barrett (joined by Justice Kavanaugh) filed a concurrence that mostly agreed with Justice Gorsuch, and Justice Kagan (joined by Justices Breyer and Sotomayor), in dissent, distinguished Roman Catholic Diocese. And in Gateway City Church v. Newsom, 141 S.Ct. 1460 (2021), the Court without opinion enjoined a California County's capacity limit on indoor worship services, stating that the "outcome is clearly dictated by this Court's decision in South Bay United Pentecostal Church"—a "decision" that, as noted above, was an order without explanation by the Court.

[14]   The Court has also treated emergency orders as precedential in response to requests for emergency relief by granting certiorari (including certiorari before judgment), vacating a

(a) Supreme Court. Because an emergency order issued by the Supreme Court is not itself "a ruling on the merits," Merrill v. Milligan, 142 S.Ct. 879, 879 (2022) (Kavanaugh, J., concurring in grant of applications for stays), the Court is not bound by an earlier grant of emergency relief when it later considers the merits of the same case. See, *e.g.*, Ritter v. Migliori, 142 S.Ct. 1824, 1824 (2022) (Alito, J., dissenting from the denial of the application for stay) (noting that, "as is almost always the case when we decide whether to grant emergency relief, I do not rule out the possibility that further briefing and argument might convince me that my current view [of the merits] is unfounded").

Nonetheless, the Court usually reaches the same conclusion if it reaches the merits that it did at the emergency relief stage. See McFadden & Kapoor, *The Precedential Effects of the Supreme Court's Emergency Stays*, 44 Harv.J.L. & Pub.Pol'y 827, 871 (2021). But see Allen v. Milligan, 599 U.S. 1 (2023) (ruling against the successful applicant for an emergency stay on the merits and affirming original lower court order calling for redrawing of congressional districting maps after intervening election in which they were used); Biden v. Texas, 597 U.S. 785 (2022) (reversing a universal injunction that the Court had approximately a year earlier declined to stay). Does this mean that the Court is good at predicting the merits at the emergency stage, or that its views and predictions at the emergency stage shape how it will view the case when it reaches the merits? See Bray, Written Testimony, Case Selection and Review at the Supreme Court, Presidential Commission on the Supreme Court of the United States 14–15 (2021) (suggesting the latter).

The Court also frequently cites emergency orders, including ones without opinions, and concurring and dissenting opinions accompanying such orders, and in-chambers opinions accompanying a single-Justice order, in deciding requests for emergency relief in different cases. Is this practice sound? What is the alternative? Compare the Court's practice of treating its summary dismissals of appeals as rulings on the merits entitled to stare decisis effect, albeit not the same effect as a ruling on the merits following plenary review. See p. 329, *supra*. And compare its occasional practice of citing dicta and concurring or dissenting opinions from prior cases that it finds persuasive.

(b) Lower Federal Courts. What should the impact of a Supreme Court emergency stay order be on lower federal courts considering the same issue at stake in the emergency order? In U.S. Dep't of Homeland Sec. v. New York, 140 S.Ct. 599 (2020), the Court in an unsigned order stayed lower court injunctions of the Trump administration's rule defining which aliens are ineligible for admission into the United States or for lawful permanent resident status on the ground that they are likely to become "public charges." When the Fourth Circuit Court of Appeals reviewed a preliminary injunction raising the same issue, Judge Wilkinson for the majority reasoned that while

---

district court order, and remanding the case for further consideration in light of an earlier emergency order (a GVR), including ones without any reasoning for the Court. See, *e.g.*, Gish v. Newsom, 141 S.Ct. 1290 (2021) (issuing GVR in a case seeking emergency relief from California COVID restriction in light of South Bay United Pentecostal Church v. Newsom, 141 S.Ct. 716 (2021)).

the court of appeals may "have the technical authority to hold that, notwithstanding the Supreme Court's view, the plaintiffs are likely after all to succeed on the merits of their challenge[,] * * * every maxim of prudence suggests that we should decline to take the aggressive step of ruling that the plaintiffs here are in fact likely to succeed on the merits right upon the heels of the Supreme Court's stay order necessarily concluding that they were unlikely to do so" absent "powerful evidence that the Supreme Court's stay was erroneously issued." CASA de Md., Inc. v. Trump, 971 F.3d 220, 229–30 (4th Cir.2020). In dissent, Judge King said, "assigning such significance to perfunctory stay orders is problematic" because the Court's orders are so rushed, and because giving deference to the Court's assessment of the likelihood of success in emergency relief would obviate the need "for an intermediate appellate court to even consider the merits of an appeal in which the Court has granted a stay." *Id.* 281 n.16. Who is right? Compare Labrador v. Poe, 144 S.Ct. 921, 933–34 (2024) (Kavanaugh, J., concurring in grant of stay) ("[A] written opinion by this Court assessing likelihood of success on the merits at a preliminary stage can create a lock-in effect because of the opinion's potential vertical precedential effect (de jure or de facto), which can thereby predetermine the case's outcome in the proceedings in the lower courts and hamper percolation across other lower courts on the underlying merits question.").[15]

McFadden & Kapoor, Paragraph (5)(a), *supra*, at 832, argue that the answer depends on how confident the lower court is that "a majority of the Supreme Court has expressed a view on the merits of the stay applicant's case." If the lower court can be so confident, the authors maintain, the Court's decision "should be considered authoritative" and "treated by lower courts much as other per curiam opinions and summary dispositions are treated." *Id.* 853, 872.[16] The Court in Tandon seemed to adopt something like this view. But is it right?[17] Per curiam opinions (at least ones in non-emergency contexts) and summary dispositions (such as a summary reversal) generally reflect a view about the merits of the case, and their precedential force, though weak, might be justified by that fact. See Hicks v.

---

[15]   In Ohio v. Environmental Protection Agency, 144 S.Ct. 2040 (2024), the Court granted an emergency application to stay an EPA ozone regulation over eight months after the application was filed, following oral argument and "months of postargument deliberations," *id.* 2052. Is it open to the lower courts on remand to reach a different assessment of the legal merits because the Court's analysis occurred in an "emergency" posture?

[16]   McFadden & Kapoor summarize their full account of the precedential impact of stay orders as follows: "[D]ecisions to deny a stay have no precedential value. Nor do decisions to grant a stay issued by a single Justice without an explanatory opinion. In-chambers opinions can be quite useful as persuasive authority, as can concurrences, dissents, and statements respecting stay decisions. When the full Supreme Court grants a stay application, lower courts should accord that decision great weight, unless there is compelling reason not to do so. This is true even if the stay grant features little legal reasoning, and may well be true even when there is no reasoning. Of course, any discussion of the merits of a question increases the confidence with which a lower court can act. But a statement by the full Court about the movant's likelihood of success on the merits ought not to be simply ignored or cast aside." McFadden & Kapoor, Paragraph (5)(a), *supra*, at 882. For an empirical analysis of how emergency orders are invoked as precedent by lower courts, see Badas, Justus & Li, *Assessing the Influence of Supreme Court's Shadow Docket in the Judicial Hierarchy*, 43 Just.Sys.J. 609 (2022).

[17]   For arguments that it is not, see Bressman, *The Rise and Fall of the Self-Regulatory Court*, 101 Tex.L.Rev. 1, 56–57 (2022); Vladeck, *The Most-Favored Right: COVID, the Supreme Court, and the (New) Free Exercise Clause*, 15 N.Y.U J.L. & Lib. 699, 734 (2022).

Miranda, 422 U.S. 332, 344–45 (1975). By contrast, the Court's ruling in an emergency posture is not a ruling on the merits. It is instead a tentative judgment about the likely outcome of the merits that is subject to revision and very often is accompanied by no explanation.

The precedential impact of emergency orders may depend on one's theory of vertical stare decisis. Professor Re outlines (among others) three models of stare decisis: (1) an authority model, under which "the holdings of Supreme Court majority opinions are [constitutive of] legal correctness" and which "calls for lower courts to treat the Court's majority holdings as law in much the way that a statute is law"; (2) a prediction model, which "holds that lower courts should do what they imagine that higher courts would do if faced with the same case" and "views higher court precedent not as constitutively correct, but rather as evidence of how higher courts would rule"; and (3) a "signals model," in which Justices make statements "in their official, adjudicatory capacities"—including in summary orders, separate opinions, and dicta—that do not establish conventional precedent, but nonetheless have "precedential force * * * subordinate to conventional precedent" because they "indicate some aspect of how lower courts should decide cases." Re, *Narrowing Supreme Court Precedent from Below*, 104 Geo.L.J. 921, 936, 940, 942–43 (2016). Although it is hard to see how a tentative assessment of the merits in the context of a stay should constitute a precedent under an authority model, should it do so in a weak sense under the other two models?

(6) Criticisms of the Emergency Orders Docket. The Court's rulings on its emergency docket, sometimes referred to as its "shadow docket," have come under withering criticism in recent years.[18] As Justice Alito's dissent in Danco Laboratories makes plain, some of these criticisms have come from within the Court. See also Louisiana v. American Rivers, 142 S.Ct. 1347, 1349 (2022) (Kagan, J., dissenting). In a nutshell, the critics charge that the Court has granted emergency relief much more frequently than in the past with much greater consequence for the scope of individual rights and governmental power than in the past, in ways that are sometimes politically tilted. It has done this, the critics maintain, in a procedurally impoverished context characterized by very limited briefing (including limited amicus briefing), no oral argument, rushed deliberations, and orders that often contain no majority explanation for the decision or, at best, a cursory per curiam analysis, but which are nonetheless treated sometimes as binding precedents. According to critics, the convergence of these decisions' haste and import undermines the public's understanding of them and its confidence in the Court as an institution guided by law. See, *e.g.*, Baude, note 18, *supra*; Pickup & Templin, *Emergency-Docket Experiments*, 98 Notre Dame L.Rev. Reflection 1 (2022); Presidential Commission on the Supreme Court of the United States, Final Report 204–08 (2021); Vladeck, Paragraph (2), *supra*;

---

[18] Professor Baude coined the phrase "shadow docket" to refer to the entire "range of orders and summary decisions that defy its normal procedural regularity," including emergency orders, summary reversals, denials of certiorari, and the like. Baude, *Foreword: The Supreme Court's Shadow Docket*, 9 N.Y.U.J.L. & Lib. 1, 1 (2015). The phrase is now used in many different ways, including as a descriptor for the emergency orders docket.

Vladeck, Paragraph (1)(c), *supra*; Pierce, *The Supreme Court Should Eliminate Its Lawless Shadow Docket*, 74 Admin.L.Rev. 1 (2022).

There is no doubt that the Court's emergency orders docket has grown significantly in recent years. See Goelzhauser, *The Applications Docket*, 58 Ga.L.Rev. 97, 135–36 (2023) (finding that applications for stays and preliminary injunctions increased significantly from 2016–2021). But there is no single explanation for why it has done so. Part of the explanation is a sharp rise in universal injunctions and other orders by district courts that threaten to shut down government programs for years and thus lead government lawyers to seek emergency stays of such orders from the Court much more frequently. Other explanations include the rise of novel emergency orders during the COVID-19 pandemic; the growth of voting rights litigation which invites emergency intervention near elections; the Trump administration's reinvigoration of the federal death penalty, which raised many novel emergency orders issues; changes in the application of tests for emergency relief noted above; and the changing composition of the Court in recent years. The increase in emergency orders requests and grants due to these and other exogenous factors, in turn, might have changed the Court's attitude toward the propriety of issuing such relief, and might have led litigants to seek emergency relief more frequently. See Baude, *Reflections of a Supreme Court Commissioner*, 106 Minn.L.Rev. 2631, 2650 (2022); Vladeck, Written Testimony, Case Selection and Review at the Supreme Court, Presidential Commission on the Supreme Court of the United States 11–17 (2021).

Stepping back from the current controversies, Professor Baude maintains that everyone agrees that the Supreme Court "should have the power to act in a very quick, and thereby less procedurally elaborate, fashion in certain cases[,]" but says because "it is hard to lay down a clear rule defining that class of cases, * * * it is likely that the Court must be vested with substantial discretion over emergency rulings," at which point "objections to the Court's emergency procedures are likely to reduce to objections to the Court's decisions." Baude, *Reflections*, *supra*, at 2649. Compare Das, Epstein & Gulati, *Deep in the Shadows?: The Facts About the Emergency Docket*, 109 Va.L.Rev. Online 73 (2023) (concluding, based on empirical study of the Court's docket for October Term 2021, that the ideological patterns on the emergency orders docket are consonant with the ideological patterns on the merits docket).

The Court, or individual Justices, have recently taken steps that appear to address some of the criticisms of its emergency orders docket and to be more circumspect in issuing emergency relief. Justice Barrett's concurrence in Does 1–3 v. Mills, 142 S.Ct. 17 (2021), is widely seen to be an example.[19] The Court has increasingly explained its dispositions of stays and preliminary injunctions in recent terms. See Goelzhauser, *supra*, at 152. It has also provided more process in response to some emergency order

---

[19] Note, *The Role of Certiorari in Emergency Relief*, 137 Harv.L.Rev. 1951 (2024), reports that while applicants in the year before Does 1–3 secured seven emergency injunctions, the fifty-four applicants seeking injunctive relief after Does 1–3 and through March 18, 2024, were all denied such relief.

applications by, for example, transferring the application to its merits docket for plenary review, see, *e.g.*, Biden v. Nebraska, 143 S.Ct. 477 (2022); Dep't of Education v. Brown, 143 S.Ct. 541 (2022); United States v. Texas, 142 S.Ct. 14 (2021), or by entertaining oral argument on certain especially important emergency applications, see Order in Pending Case, U.S. Steel Corp. v. EPA (Dec. 20, 2023) (No.23A384); Nat'l Fed'n of Indep. Bus. v. Dep't of Labor, 595 U.S. 109 (2022) (per curiam); Biden v. Missouri, 595 U.S. 87 (2022) (per curiam). See also Labrador v. Poe, 144 S.Ct. 921, 933 (2024) (Kavanaugh, J., concurring in the grant of stay) (noting that the Court in responding to important emergency order requests "should use as many tools as feasible and appropriate to make the most informed and best decision," including "taking more time (if available), ordering supplemental briefing, * * * inviting amicus briefs[,] * * * oral argument or * * * certiorari before judgment"). For analysis of this trend, see Pickup and Templin, *supra*. The Court has also made the filings in every emergency docket case available online, which assists in understanding emergency orders, since many such orders are unexplained. And it has given guidance about filing amicus briefs in connection with emergency applications. See Sup.Ct.R. 37.4.

Congress has significant authority to regulate the emergency orders docket which, as noted above, is authorized by federal statute. The scope of Congress's control over jurisdiction, procedure, and remedies on the Supreme Court's appellate docket is examined in Chapter IV.

CHAPTER IV

CONGRESSIONAL CONTROL OF THE DISTRIBUTION OF JUDICIAL POWER AMONG STATE AND FEDERAL TRIBUNALS

In our dual federal system, much of the adjudication occurring in the United States takes place in state courts. A great deal of it turns on questions of state common law—ordinary cases of contracts, property, and torts—as well as state statutory, constitutional, and regulatory law. But in light of the Madisonian Compromise (see pp. 9–10, *supra*) and the Supremacy Clause's directive that "the Judges in every State shall be bound [by federal law]," state courts also have broad power and responsibility for the disposition of claims that turn on federal law. Other than the fundamental requirements of due process, however, no provision of the U.S. Constitution specifies the particulars of how state courts—or other state tribunals—must be structured. Questions of state court judicial selection, tenure, and salary protection are matters of state law, and the structural protections afforded state judges vary considerably across the nation.

At the federal government level, a range of tribunals exercise adjudicative authority. Federal courts exercise "[t]he judicial Power of the United States," U.S. Const. Art. III, § 1, which extends to "Cases" or "Controversies" that lie within one of the nine heads of jurisdiction specified in Article III, § 2. Sometimes these cases involve the adjudication of federal questions "arising under this Constitution" and "the Laws of the United States," and other times they may involve the disposition of state law matters (see Erie R.R. Co. v. Tompkins, 304 U.S. 64 (1938), p. 760, *infra*). Article III, § 1, requires federal judges exercising "[t]he judicial Power of the United States" to have life tenure and salary protection. As explored below, Congress has broad authority to compose and regulate the jurisdiction of these Article III courts. In addition, pursuant to Congress's substantive grants of authority in Article I (and in Article IV, Sec. 3, relating to the governance of territories), as well as the Necessary and Proper Clause, Congress has assigned at least the initial adjudication of some claims to non-Article III tribunals whose officers lack the tenure and salary protections afforded to the Article III judiciary. These tribunals include military courts, territorial courts,

courts in the District of Columbia, administrative agencies, and bankruptcy courts.

This chapter examines Congress's authority to allocate responsibility for adjudication among these state and federal entities and the constitutional limits on that authority.

1. CONGRESSIONAL REGULATION OF FEDERAL JURISDICTION

INTRODUCTORY NOTE ON CONGRESSIONAL POWER OVER THE JURISDICTION OF THE ARTICLE III COURTS

This section considers the scope and limits of Congress's authority to confer less than the full measure of Article III jurisdiction on lower federal courts and to make exceptions to the jurisdiction conferred by Article III upon the Supreme Court.

(1) Sources of Congressional Power.

(a) The Vesting Clause. Article III, § 1 vests "[t]he judicial Power of the United States" in "one supreme Court, and in such inferior Courts *as the Congress may from time to time ordain and establish*" (emphasis added). Read against the backdrop of the Madisonian Compromise (see pp. 9–10, *supra*), the Vesting Clause of Article III has long been understood to authorize but not obligate Congress to "ordain and establish" federal tribunals "inferior" to the Supreme Court and to permit Congress to establish lower federal courts with jurisdiction more limited than the Constitution would allow.

(b) The Exceptions Clause. Article III, § 2, cl. 2 specifies that the appellate jurisdiction of the Supreme Court shall be subject to "such Exceptions, and under such Regulations as the Congress shall make."

(2) Historical Context. Development of the law of federal courts has been path dependent, and the Court has often noted that the precise meaning of Article III's open-ended provisions may become settled by constitutional practice.[1] Beginning with the Judiciary Act of 1789, Congress has never vested the federal courts with the entire scope of "[t]he judicial Power of the

---

[1] See, *e.g.*, Ex parte Quirin, 317 U.S. 1, 41–42 (1942) (stating that a legislative "construction of the Constitution which has been followed since the founding of our Government * * * is entitled to the greatest respect"); Tutun v. United States, 270 U.S. 568, 576 (1926) (upholding an exercise of jurisdiction that "has been conferred exclusively upon courts continuously since the foundation of our government" and "has never been questioned"); The Laura, 114 U.S. 411, 416 (1885) ("[T]he practice [under federal legislation] and acquiescence under it, 'commencing with the organization of the judicial system, affords an irresistible answer, and has indeed fixed the construction.'" (quoting Stuart v. Laird, 5 U.S. (1 Cranch) 299, 309 (1803))).

United States" to which Article III extends. A partial list of historical exclusions includes the following:

(a) Jurisdiction of the Lower Federal Courts.

(i)   Federal Question Cases.[2] The First Judiciary Act did not provide for any general federal question jurisdiction in civil cases "arising under" the Constitution, laws, or treaties of the United States. Federal question cases that did not fall within one of the small number of specialized grants of jurisdiction to lower federal courts had to be litigated in state court, subject to Supreme Court review, which was available only if the state court ruled against a "title, right, privilege, or exemption" asserted under federal law.[3] Only in 1875 did Congress provide an enduring grant of general federal question jurisdiction, now found in 28 U.S.C. § 1331. From 1875 to 1980, the federal question statute included an amount-in-controversy requirement.

Even today, § 1331 confers jurisdiction only when the federal question appears on the face of the plaintiff's well-pleaded complaint. See *Louisville & Nashville R.R. Co. v. Mottley*, 211 U.S. 149 (1908), pp. 1024–1025, *infra*. Thus, for example, cases raising federal defenses, although they arise under federal law within the meaning of Article III, generally may not be litigated in the lower federal courts. See generally pp. 1025–1030, *infra*.

(ii) Diversity Jurisdiction.[4] Beginning in 1789, lower federal courts have had jurisdiction to hear many types of diversity cases. But the general statutory grant, as construed by the Supreme Court, has always required "complete diversity" when there are multiple parties on one or more sides of a case, see *Strawbridge v. Curtiss*, 7 U.S. (3 Cranch) 267 (1806), p. 1077, *infra*—a requirement not imposed by Article III. The diversity statute has always had an amount-in-controversy requirement, which today is $75,000. 28 U.S.C. § 1332(a). Finally, in-state defendants are prohibited from removing cases filed in state court, even when the other requisites of diversity jurisdiction are met. *Id*. § 1441(b)(2).

(b) Supreme Court Jurisdiction. From 1789–1914, the Supreme Court could review only those state court decisions that denied a claim of federal right; state court decisions upholding federal claims were thus excluded from the Court's appellate jurisdiction. See Chap. V, Sec. 1, *infra*. Nor, until 1891, did the Supreme Court possess statutory authority to review most decisions of lower federal courts in criminal cases.

(3) The "Parity" Question. The text of Article III, as noted, gives Congress apparent discretion to refrain from vesting the full scope of potential Article III jurisdiction in the inferior federal courts as well as express power to make exceptions to the Supreme Court's appellate jurisdiction, informed by assessments of the relative competency and capacity of state courts to adjudicate federal rights and responsibilities.

---

[2]   The statutory history is discussed more fully in Chapter VIII, Sec. 1, *infra*.

[3]   See pp. 616–617, *infra* (discussing Section 25 of the Judiciary Act of 1789, 1 Stat. 73, 86).

[4]   The statutory history is discussed more fully in Chapter XIII, Sec. 1, *infra*.

Putting to one side general assessments of the relative quality of federal and state judges,[5] are there systemic or structural reasons to expect that state courts will be less hospitable than their federal counterparts to federal rights? In an influential article that has framed much of the ensuing "parity" debate, Professor Neuborne argued that federal judges, unlike the judges in all but a handful of states, enjoy life tenure and are therefore more insulated from majoritarian pressures. See Neuborne, *The Myth of Parity*, 90 Harv.L.Rev. 1105 (1977). In a similar vein, commentators have focused on concerns relating to the selection of state court judges and, in particular, reliance by many states on elections to select members of their highest courts.[6] Although some have pointed out that early efforts to embrace election of state judges reflected the stated assumption that elections would strengthen judicial independence,[7] many now believe that state judicial elections have become more "politicized,"[8] with interest groups becoming more active in judicial campaigns and candidates' advertisements increasingly stressing not only qualifications but also positions.[9] These

---

[5]   See, *e.g.*, Posner, The Federal Courts: Challenge and Reform 216 (2d ed.1996) (arguing that there is a widely held view among the practicing bar that federal judges are "on average (an important qualification), of higher quality").

[6]   A recent study of the selection methods for state supreme court justices found that 38 states use some form of electoral process, with seven relying on contested partisan elections, 14 staging nonpartisan contested elections, and 16 using some form of merit selection that involves unopposed retention elections after gubernatorial appointment. Brennan Ctr. for Justice, Judicial Selection: An Interactive Map, https://brennancenter.org/judicial-selection-map (last visited July 28, 2023). On state selection methods, see Am. Judicature Soc'y, Judicial Selection in the States: Appellate and General Jurisdiction Courts (2013). Methods for lower state courts differ, with merit selection used less often than for state supreme courts. See generally Schotland, *New Challenges to States' Judicial Selection*, 95 Geo.L.J. 1077, 1084–86 (2007).

[7]   See Shugerman, The People's Courts (2012) (describing some of the cited justifications in the nineteenth century for embracing judicial elections).

[8]   See Pozen, *The Irony of Judicial Elections*, 108 Colum.L.Rev. 265 (2008). The Supreme Court has enforced First Amendment constraints on state efforts to regulate judicial elections but has also acknowledged that states have some latitude to adopt properly tailored regulations designed to preserve the integrity of the judicial selection process. In Republican Party of Minnesota v. White, 536 U.S. 765 (2002), the Court held that a canon of judicial conduct prohibiting "a candidate for judicial office," not currently a judge, from "announc[ing] his or her views on disputed legal or political issues" violated the First Amendment. In Williams-Yulee v. Florida Bar, 575 U.S. 433 (2015), however, the Court rejected a First Amendment challenge to Florida's ban on the solicitation of campaign funds by candidates for state judicial office. Distancing the Court from its earlier decision in White, Chief Justice Roberts's opinion for the Court in Williams-Yulee applied strict scrutiny and held (a) that Florida has a compelling governmental interest in preserving public confidence in the neutrality of the state's judicial officers and (b) that the state's limit on personal solicitation is narrowly tailored to that interest.

[9]   See generally Sample, Skaggs, Blitzer & Casey, The New Politics of Judicial Elections 2000–2009 (Brennan Center for Justice; Charles Hall ed. 2010), *available at* http://www. brennancenter.org/sites/default/files/legacy/JAS-NPJE-Decade-ONLINE.pdf; Running for Judge: The Rising Political, Financial, and Legal Stakes of Judicial Elections (Streb ed. 2007); Brown, *Political Judges and Popular Justice: A Conservative Victory or a Conservative Dilemma?*, 49 Wm. & Mary L.Rev. 1543, 1552–53 (2008).

Defenders of partisan elections contend that non-partisan elections provide insufficient information to promote accountability; that retention elections, lacking opponents and partisan affiliation, generate little voter knowledge or interest and little turnover; and that because politics inevitably plays a key role in judicial selection, even under merit-based systems, those systems have little to recommend themselves over elections. More broadly, defenders of elections contend that making judges accountable through partisan elections is appropriate given the broad policymaking discretion that they possess.

developments have fueled concerns by many that judicial elections undermine actual and perceived judicial impartiality.[10]

Is it possible to test whether structural or cultural differences between state and federal courts undermine the presumption of parity on which the Madisonian Compromise was built? Some studies have tried, examining whether state courts are as protective of federal rights as are federal courts.[11] In a 1988 review of the reported studies, however, Professor Chemerinsky concluded that the methodological difficulties confronting inquiries of this kind—including differences in the types and difficulty of federal questions characteristically raised in state and federal court, and the problem that state trial courts frequently fail to write opinions—are so daunting that "[a]lthough parity is an empirical question, no empirical answer seems possible." Chemerinsky, *Parity Reconsidered: Defining a Role for the Federal Judiciary*, 36 UCLA L.Rev. 233, 273 (1988).[12]

Even if one could identify reasons for concluding that federal courts are more protective of federal rights than are state courts, should that conclusion inform judicial assessments of congressional decisions to withhold or strip jurisdiction in particular areas? Professors Hart and Bator argue that parity

---

[10]　For a forceful expression of such concerns, see Croley, *The Majoritarian Difficulty: Elective Judiciaries and the Rule of Law*, 62 U.Chi.L.Rev. 689 (1995); Carrington, *Judicial Independence and Democratic Accountability in Highest State Courts*, 61 Law & Contemp.Probs. 79 (1998) (arguing that selection processes for states' highest courts have become increasingly politicized and canvassing possible correctives); Frost & Lindquist, *Countering the Majoritarian Difficulty*, 96 Va.L.Rev. 719 (2010) (urging heightened review of elected (rather than appointed) state court judges by the Supreme Court, as well as by lower federal courts exercising habeas corpus jurisdiction).

A number of studies (most of which have focused on criminal sentencing in capital and other cases) have found evidence that an impending election has an effect on the behavior of sitting judges. See Gordon & Huber, *Accountability and Coercion: Is Justice Blind When It Runs for Office?*, 48 Am.J.Pol.Sci. 247 (2004); Hall, *Electoral Politics and Strategic Voting in State Supreme Courts*, 54 J.Pol. 427 (1992); Brace & Boyea, *State Public Opinion, the Death Penalty, and the Practice of Electing Judges*, 52 Am.J.Pol.Sci. 360 (2008). See also, *e.g.*, Gordon & Huber, *The Effect of Electoral Competitiveness on Incumbent Behavior*, 2 Q.J.Pol.Sci. 107 (2007); Pinello, The Impact of Judicial Selection Method on State-Supreme-Court Policy (1995). For a contrasting view, see Blume & Eisenberg, *Judicial Politics, Death Penalty Appeals, and Case Selection*, 72 S.C.L.Rev. 465 (1999) (showing no significant effect of selection methods).

[11]　Solimine & Walker, *Constitutional Litigation in Federal and State Courts: An Empirical Analysis of Judicial Parity*, 10 Hastings Const.L.Q. 213 (1983), for example, compared the decisions of federal district courts and state appellate courts concerning selected constitutional issues, finding that federal courts upheld the constitutional claim in 41% of the cases within their sample, while state courts did so in only 32% of the cases. Although this difference was "statistically significant," the authors viewed it as "unimportant," interpreting the data as showing that state courts exhibit no clear reluctance to uphold federal claims that a federal district court would uphold. Focusing on one discrete area of law, Gerry, *Parity Revisited: An Empirical Comparison of State and Lower Federal Court Interpretations of Nollan v. California Coastal Commission*, 23 Harv.J.L. & Pub.Pol'y 233 (1999), examined all reported cases applying a Supreme Court decision involving a claim of an unconstitutional taking— Nollan v. California Coastal Comm'n, 483 U.S. 825 (1987)—from 1987–1997 and concluded that "[t]he aggregate findings are startling in their similarity." Another studied LGBTQ+ rights claims and concluded that they generally fared better in state courts; although the state court victories almost invariably rested on state law grounds, the author argued that the experience raises doubts about the thesis that federal courts are generally more protective of civil rights. Rubenstein, *The Myth of Superiority*, 16 Const.Comment. 599 (1999).

[12]　For general discussion, see Symposium, *Fair and Independent Courts: A Conference on the State of the Judiciary*, 95 Geo.L.J. 895 (2007), and 137 Daedalus No. 4 (2008) (articles concerning judicial independence).

is a constitutional concept that rests on the Madisonian Compromise and the structure of Article III: since Congress need not create any lower federal courts, state courts must be regarded as enjoying constitutional parity with the lower federal courts. See Bator, *The State Courts and Federal Constitutional Litigation*, 22 Wm. & Mary L.Rev. 605 (1981); Hart, *The Power of Congress to Limit the Jurisdiction of Federal Courts: An Exercise in Dialectic*, 66 Harv.L.Rev. 1362 (1953) (hereinafter cited as "Hart, *Dialogue*").

(4) Framing the Question. In addressing questions about the basic scope of congressional authority to regulate federal jurisdictions, a central issue is whether and to what extent Congress has authority to strip jurisdiction because it disagrees with the way that federal courts (especially the Supreme Court) handle particular substantive issues and/or because it sees federal courts as overstepping their proper role in a constitutional democracy.

Sheldon v. Sill

49 U.S. (8 How.) 441 (1850).
Appeal from the Circuit Court for the District of Michigan.

■ MR. JUSTICE GRIER delivered the opinion of the Court.

The only question which it will be necessary to notice in this case is, whether the Circuit Court had jurisdiction.

[Sill, a New York citizen, sued Sheldon, a Michigan citizen, to recover on a bond and mortgage that had been assigned to Sill by Hastings, also a Michigan citizen. Sheldon's answer contended that the statutory grant of diversity jurisdiction did not reach a case like this one in which diverse citizenship exists only because of the assignment of rights to the plaintiff.]

The eleventh section of the Judiciary Act, which defines the jurisdiction of the Circuit Courts, restrains them from taking "cognizance of any suit to recover the contents of any promissory note or other chose in action, in favor of an assignee, unless a suit might have been prosecuted in such court to recover the contents, if no assignment had been made, except in cases of foreign bills of exchange."

The third article of the Constitution declares that "the judicial power of the United States shall be vested in one Supreme Court, and such inferior courts as the Congress may, from time to time, ordain and establish." The second section of the same article enumerates the cases and controversies of which the judicial power shall have cognizance, and, among others, it specifies "controversies between citizens of different States."

It has been alleged, that this restriction of the Judiciary Act, with regard to assignees of choses in action, is in conflict with this provision of the Constitution, and therefore void.

It must be admitted, that if the Constitution had ordained and established the inferior courts, and distributed to them their respective powers, they could not be restricted or divested by Congress. But as it has made no such distribution, one of two consequences must result,— either that each inferior court created by Congress must exercise all the judicial powers not given to the Supreme Court, or that Congress, having the power to establish the courts, must define their respective jurisdictions. The first of these inferences has never been asserted, and could not be defended with any show of reason, and if not, the latter would seem to follow as a necessary consequence. And it would seem to follow, also, that, having a right to prescribe, Congress may withhold from any court of its creation jurisdiction of any of the enumerated controversies. Courts created by statute can have no jurisdiction but such as the statute confers. * * *

The Constitution has defined the limits of the judicial power of the United States, but has not prescribed how much of it shall be exercised by the Circuit Court; consequently, the statute which does prescribe the limits of their jurisdiction, cannot be in conflict with the Constitution, unless it confers powers not enumerated therein.

Such has been the doctrine held by this court since its first establishment. To enumerate all the cases in which it has been either directly advanced or tacitly assumed would be tedious and unnecessary.

In the case of Turner v. Bank of North America, 4 Dall. 10 [(1799)], [another case involving diversity created only by assignment,] * * * the court said,—"The political truth is, that the disposal of the judicial power (except in a few specified instances) belongs to Congress: and Congress is not bound to enlarge the jurisdiction of the Federal courts to every subject, in every form which the Constitution might warrant." This decision was made in 1799; since that time, the same doctrine has been frequently asserted by this court * * *.

[Finding that Sill was an assignee of a "chose in action" within the meaning of the statute, the Court held that jurisdiction was lacking.] * * *

The judgment of the Circuit Court must therefore be reversed, for want of jurisdiction.

Ex parte McCardle

74 U.S. (7 Wall.) 506 (1869).
Appeal from the Circuit Court for the Southern District of Mississippi.

[On February 5, 1867, Congress enacted legislation authorizing federal judges "to grant writs of habeas corpus in all cases where any person may be restrained of his or her liberty in violation of the constitution, or of any treaty or law of the United States." The Act's principal purpose was to establish federal habeas corpus jurisdiction to review detentions of persons held under *state and local authority*—especially newly freed African-Americans, their supporters, and federal officials, all of whom were subjected to harassment and baseless arrests in southern states. (Habeas jurisdiction to review detention under *federal* authority had existed since 1789.) Among its provisions, the 1867 Act authorized a right of appeal from decisions of the circuit courts to the Supreme Court of the United States.

[McCardle, the editor of the *Vicksburg Times* in Mississippi, was arrested by federal military authorities acting pursuant to the Military Reconstruction Act, enacted in March of 1867. The charges against him, based solely on editorials published in his newspaper, included disturbing the peace, libel, incitement to insurrection, and impeding reconstruction. While his trial before a military commission was pending, McCardle filed a habeas corpus petition in the federal Circuit Court for the Southern District of Mississippi. He contended that it was unconstitutional to try him before a military tribunal rather than an Article III court—a contention to which the Court's decision in Ex parte Milligan, 71 U.S. (4 Wall.) 2 (1867), p. 553, *infra*, though not conclusive, gave some support. McCardle also contended more broadly that the provisions of the Military Reconstruction Act, placing ten states under military jurisdiction, were unconstitutional. The Supreme Court ruled that two prior challenges to the Act were not fit for judicial resolution,[*] but McCardle's case did not pose the same barriers to adjudication on the merits.

[After the circuit court denied the petition, McCardle appealed to the Supreme Court. Following oral argument there but before the case was decided, Congress, over the President's veto, passed the Act of March 27, 1868, ch. 34, § 2, 15 Stat. 44, which provided: "* * * That so much of the act approved [February 5, 1867], entitled 'An act to amend "An act to establish the judicial courts of the United States," approved [September 24, 1789],' as authorizes an appeal from the judgment of the circuit court to the Supreme Court of the United States, or the exercise of any such jurisdiction by said Supreme Court on appeals which have been or may hereafter be taken, be, and the same is, hereby repealed."]

The attention of the court was directed to this statute at the last term, but counsel having expressed a desire to be heard in argument upon its effect, and the Chief Justice being detained from his place here, by his duties in the Court of Impeachment, the cause was continued under advisement. Argument was now heard upon the effect of the repealing act. * * *

■ THE CHIEF JUSTICE [CHASE] delivered the opinion of the Court.

---

[*]   [Ed.] See Mississippi v. Johnson, 71 U.S. (4 Wall.) 475, 501 (1867); Georgia v. Stanton, 73 U.S. (6 Wall.) 50, 76–77 (1867).

The first question necessarily is that of jurisdiction; for, if the act of March, 1868, takes away the jurisdiction defined by the act of February, 1867, it is useless, if not improper, to enter into any discussion of other questions.

It is quite true, as was argued by the counsel for the petitioner, that the appellate jurisdiction of this court is not derived from acts of Congress. It is, strictly speaking, conferred by the Constitution. But it is conferred "with such exceptions and under such regulations as Congress shall make."

It is unnecessary to consider whether, if Congress had made no exceptions and no regulations, this court might not have exercised general appellate jurisdiction under rules prescribed by itself. For among the earliest acts of the first Congress, at its first session, was the act of September 24th, 1789, to establish the judicial courts of the United States. That act provided for the organization of this court, and prescribed regulations for the exercise of its jurisdiction.

The source of that jurisdiction, and the limitations of it by the Constitution and by statute, have been on several occasions subjects of consideration here. In the case of Durousseau v. The United States,[12] particularly, the whole matter was carefully examined, and the court held, that while "the appellate powers of this court are not given by the judicial act, but are given by the Constitution," they are, nevertheless, "limited and regulated by that act, and by such other acts as have been passed on the subject." The court said, further, that the judicial act was an exercise of the power given by the Constitution to Congress "of making exceptions to the appellate jurisdiction of the Supreme Court." "They have described affirmatively," said the court, "its jurisdiction, and this affirmative description has been understood to imply a negation of the exercise of such appellate power as is not comprehended within it."

The principle that the affirmation of appellate jurisdiction implies the negation of all such jurisdiction not affirmed having been thus established, it was an almost necessary consequence that acts of Congress, providing for the exercise of jurisdiction, should come to be spoken of as acts granting jurisdiction, and not as acts making exceptions to the constitutional grant of it.

The exception to appellate jurisdiction in the case before us, however, is not an inference from the affirmation of other appellate jurisdiction. It is made in terms. The provision of the act of 1867, affirming the appellate jurisdiction of this court in cases of *habeas corpus* is expressly repealed. It is hardly possible to imagine a plainer instance of positive exception.

We are not at liberty to inquire into the motives of the legislature. We can only examine into its power under the Constitution; and the

---

[12]   6 Cranch, 312 [(1810)].

power to make exceptions to the appellate jurisdiction of this court is given by express words.

What, then, is the effect of the repealing act upon the case before us? We cannot doubt as to this. Without jurisdiction the court cannot proceed at all in any cause. Jurisdiction is power to declare the law, and when it ceases to exist, the only function remaining to the court is that of announcing the fact and dismissing the cause. And this is not less clear upon authority than upon principle. * * *

It is quite clear, therefore, that this court cannot proceed to pronounce judgment in this case, for it has no longer jurisdiction of the appeal; and judicial duty is not less fitly performed by declining ungranted jurisdiction than in exercising firmly that which the Constitution and the laws confer.

Counsel seem to have supposed, if effect be given to the repealing act in question, that the whole appellate power of the court, in cases of *habeas corpus*, is denied. But this is an error. The act of 1868 does not except from that jurisdiction any cases but appeals from Circuit Courts under the act of 1867. It does not affect the jurisdiction which was previously exercised.[17]

The appeal of the petitioner in this case must be dismissed for want of jurisdiction.

NOTE ON THE GENERAL POWER OF CONGRESS TO LIMIT THE JURISDICTION OF THE FEDERAL COURTS, IN PARTICULAR THE LOWER FEDERAL COURTS

(1) Putting Sheldon and McCardle Together. Sheldon v. Sill and Ex parte McCardle define the conventional view concerning congressional authority to control and limit the jurisdiction of the inferior federal courts and the Supreme Court. Sheldon makes clear that Congress's discretion to "ordain and establish" the inferior courts encompasses power to vest less than the full measure of available Article III jurisdiction in those courts. Similarly, McCardle articulates a broad conception of Article III, § 2's Exceptions Clause, emphasizing that the Court is "not at liberty to inquire into the motives of the legislature" and that "the power to make exceptions to the appellate jurisdiction of this court is given by express words." As the following discussion explores, however, these strong formulations of congressional authority have not gone unchallenged by judges and scholars advancing textual, structural, and historical arguments for the position that federal jurisdiction should be considered mandatory, at least in some respects.

(2) Mandatory Theories of Article III: Justice Story's Views. In the Judiciary Act of 1789, Congress rejected the view that Article III requires it

---

[17]   Ex parte McCardle, 6 Wallace, 324 [(1867)].

to vest federal courts with the full scope of federal judicial power. See pp. 37–38, *supra*; see also Casto, *The First Congress's Understanding of Its Authority over the Federal Courts' Jurisdiction*, 26 B.C.L.Rev. 1101 (1985); Warren, *New Light on the History of the Federal Judiciary Act of 1789*, 37 Harv.L.Rev. 49 (1923). Notwithstanding this history and decisions such as Sheldon and McCardle, various theories over the centuries have argued for a constitutional requirement of federal court jurisdiction in at least some cases. Nearly all of these theories build on dictum in Justice Story's opinion for the Court in Martin v. Hunter's Lessee, 14 U.S. (1 Wheat.) 304 (1816). Although Justice Story's exposition was complex and arguably internally contradictory, it provides the foundation of many of the theories of mandatory federal jurisdiction discussed in this Note.

In Martin v. Hunter's Lessee, Justice Story wrote:

"* * * The language of [Article III] throughout is manifestly designed to be mandatory upon the legislature. * * * The judicial power of the United States *shall be vested* (not may be vested) in one supreme court, and in such inferior courts as congress may, from time to time, ordain and establish. Could congress have lawfully refused to create a supreme court, or to vest in it the constitutional jurisdiction? * * *

"If, then, it is a duty of congress to vest the judicial power of the United States, it is a duty to vest the *whole judicial power*. The language, if imperative as to one part, is imperative as to all. If it were otherwise, this anomaly would exist, that congress might successively refuse to vest the jurisdiction in any one class of cases enumerated in the constitution, and thereby defeat the jurisdiction as to all; for the constitution has not singled out any class on which congress are bound to act in preference to others.

"The next consideration is as to the courts in which the judicial power shall be vested. It is manifest, that a supreme court must be established; but whether it be equally obligatory to establish inferior courts, is a question of some difficulty. If congress may lawfully omit to establish inferior courts, it might follow, that in some of the enumerated cases the judicial power could nowhere exist. * * * [I]f in any of the cases enumerated in the constitution, the state courts did not then possess jurisdiction, the appellate jurisdiction of the supreme court * * * could not reach those cases, and, consequently, the injunction of the constitution, that the judicial power *'shall be vested'*, would be disobeyed. It would seem, therefore, to follow, that congress are bound to create some inferior courts, in which to vest all that jurisdiction which, under the constitution, is *exclusively* vested in the United States, and of which the supreme court cannot take original cognizance. They might establish one or more inferior courts; they might parcel out the jurisdiction among such courts from time to time at their own pleasure. But the power of the United States should be, at all times, vested either in an original or appellate form, in some courts created under its authority.

"This construction will be fortified by an attentive examination of the second section of the third article. The words are 'the judicial power *shall extend*,' &c. Much minute and elaborate criticism has been employed upon these words. It has been argued that they are equivalent to the words 'may

extend,' and that 'extend' means to widen to new cases not before within the
scope of the power. For the reasons which have been already stated, we are
of opinion that the words are used in an imperative sense. * * *"

A few pages later, Justice Story continued his analysis of Article III:

"[T]here are two classes of cases enumerated in the constitution,
between which a distinction seems to be drawn. The first class includes cases
arising under the constitution, laws, and treaties of the United States; cases
affecting ambassadors, other public ministers and consuls, and cases of
admiralty and maritime jurisdiction. In this class the expression is, and that
the judicial power shall extend to *all cases*; but in the subsequent part of the
clause which embraces all the other cases of national cognizance, and forms
the second class, the word '*all*' is dropped seemingly *ex industria*. Here the
judicial authority is to extend to controversies (not to *all* controversies) to
which the United States shall be a party, &c. From this difference of
phraseology, perhaps, a difference of constitutional intention may, with
propriety, be inferred. * * * [I]t is not very difficult to find a reason sufficient
to support the apparent change of intention. In respect to the first class, it
may well have been the intention of the framers of the constitution
imperatively to extend the judicial power either in an original form or
appellate form to *all cases;* and in the latter class to leave it to congress to
qualify the jurisdiction, original or appellate, in such manner as public policy
might dictate.

"The vital importance of all the cases enumerated in the first class to
the national sovereignty, might warrant such a distinction. * * * All these
cases, then, enter into the national policy, affect the national rights, and may
compromit the national sovereignty. * * *

"A different policy might well be adopted in reference to the second class
of cases; for although it might be fit that the judicial power should extend to
all controversies to which the United States should be a party, yet this power
might not have been imperatively given, least it should imply a right to take
cognizance of original suits brought against the United States as defendants
in their own courts. It might not have been deemed proper to submit the
sovereignty of the United States, against their own will, to judicial
cognizance, either to enforce rights or to prevent wrongs; and as to the other
cases of the second class, they might well be left to be exercised under the
exceptions and regulations which congress might, in their wisdom, choose to
apply. It is also worthy of remark, that congress seem, in a good degree, in
* * * [the Judiciary Act of 1789] to have adopted this distinction. In the first
class of cases, the jurisdiction is not limited except by the subject matter; in
the second, it is made materially to depend upon the value in controversy."

Note the three different positions suggested in these excerpts. First,
Justice Story argues that Congress must vest all of the judicial power "either
in an original or appellate form" in some federal court. Second, he argues
that if any cases described in Article III are beyond the jurisdiction of the
state courts, and thus cannot be reviewed by the Supreme Court on appeal
from a state court, Congress must vest jurisdiction over them in the inferior

federal courts, so that they can be heard in some federal court.[1] (His argument rests on the premise that such cases fall outside the Supreme Court's own original jurisdiction, which is limited to cases in which a state is a party and those affecting foreign envoys.) Third, he appears to limit any congressional obligation to the first three categories of cases described in Article III, as to which the Constitution uses the adjective "all."

Are Justice Story's positions consistent with the compromises struck at the Philadelphia Convention or the practical constructions of Article III by the early Congresses first responsible for implementing it? Would Justice Story have dissented in the Sheldon and McCardle cases? Whatever his view might have been of Congress's duty in those cases, White v. Fenner, 1 Mason 520, 29 F.Cas. 1015 (C.C.D.R.I.1818) (No. 17,547), in which Story sat as a circuit justice, dismissed a diversity suit excluded from the statutory grant. Although pronouncing it "somewhat singular, that the jurisdiction actually conferred on the courts of the United States should have stopped so far short of the constitutional extent," Justice Story wrote that the "court has no jurisdiction, which is not given by some statute." Is it possible that Justice Story meant the dicta in Martin to provide a basis only for appealing to Congress?

The Fenner decision notwithstanding, mandatory federal jurisdiction positions articulated by Justice Story in Martin have had modern echoes, which are explored below.

(3) Congressional Power to Exclude Cases from the Lower Federal Courts: The Orthodox View. Sheldon v. Sill defines the orthodox view that Congress has wide discretion to define and limit the jurisdiction of the lower federal courts. As the history of the Madisonian Compromise confirms, the language in the Vesting Clause of Article III referring to "such inferior courts *as the Congress may from time to time ordain and establish*" (emphasis added) contemplates that Congress may—but is not required to—"ordain and establish" inferior federal courts in which to vest the judicial power of the United States.

From that starting point, the Court in Sheldon inferred that the greater congressional power to refrain from establishing inferior federal courts includes the lesser power of establishing such courts while vesting them with less than the full measure of jurisdiction specified in the categories of cases and controversies enumerated in Article III, § 2. Does it follow, however, that the greater power necessarily includes the lesser? Could one read the Vesting Clause to mean that Congress has the power to refrain from creating lower federal courts, but that if it chooses to "ordain and establish" such courts, all of the judicial power of the United States "shall be vested" in those courts along with the Supreme Court? What other arguments might suggest that Congress has less than full discretion to shape lower court discretion?

---

[1] In this connection, see Collins, *The Federal Courts, the First Congress, and the Non-Settlement of 1789*, 91 Va.L.Rev. 1515, 1560 (2005) (maintaining that debates over the Judiciary Act of 1789 reflected widely shared assumptions of state court incapacity to entertain certain federal claims, but not necessarily the further conclusion that Congress was obliged to create federal courts in which such cases could be heard).

Consider, in this regard, the role history plays in justifying Sheldon's holding. Although Sheldon did not rely on the Madisonian Compromise, Professor Bator argues that it would "make nonsense of" that compromise to hold that "the only power to be exercised is the all-or-nothing power to decide whether *none* or *all* of the cases to which the federal judicial power extends need the haven of a lower federal court." Bator, *Congressional Power over the Jurisdiction of the Federal Courts*, 27 Vill.L.Rev. 1030, 1031 (1982).[2] Is that right?[3] Does Professor Bator give too much weight to the Convention history leading to the Madisonian Compromise, which was not known to those who ratified the Constitution?[4]

Consider another source of historical meaning—this one relating to the history of Article III's implementation over time and expressly relied on by the Court in Sheldon. Madison influentially argued that "the science of government has yet been able to discriminate and define, with sufficient certainty * * * the legislative, executive, and judiciary [powers]" and that "[a]ll new laws, though penned with the greatest technical skill and passed on the fullest and most mature deliberation, are considered as more or less obscure and equivocal, until their meaning be liquidated and ascertained by a series of particular discussions and adjudications."[5] In U.S. constitutional practice, that idea has found expression, in part, in established doctrine that the Court will credit the practical construction of constitutional provisions by those charged with implementing the particular provisions, particularly when the constructions originated close to the provision's adoption and then withstood the test of time.[6] The Court has applied this doctrine many times

---

[2] But see Goebel, History of the Supreme Court of the United States: Antecedents and Beginnings to 1801, at 246–47 (1971) (arguing that Congress must create lower federal courts and vest them with the full possible jurisdiction). See also Dow, *Is the "Arising Under" Jurisdictional Grant in Article III Self-Executing?*, 25 Wm. & Mary Bill Rts.J. 1, 10 (2016) (arguing that Professor Bator's argument is "perfectly question-begging" and that "such evidence as there is of original intent on this question reveals that the Framers themselves did not believe Congress would enjoy the power Bator" ascribed to the Madisonian Compromise).

[3] Compare Engdahl, *Intrinsic Limits of Congress' Power Regarding the Judicial Branch*, 1999 B.Y.U.L.Rev. 75 (arguing, based on debates at the Constitutional Convention, that Congress's power to limit the jurisdiction of the federal courts rests on the Necessary and Proper Clause, not Article III, and that total exclusions of categories of cases cannot be justified).

[4] The Philadelphia Convention adopted a rule of secrecy concerning their proceedings, see Charles Warren, The Making of the Constitution 134–39 (1928), and Madison's Notes were not published until 1840, long after the Constitution's adoption. See Kesavan & Paulsen, *The Interpretive Force of the Constitution's Secret Drafting History*, 91 Geo.L.J. 1113, 1115 (2003). Although a number of the delegates to the Philadelphia Convention served as delegates to the ratifying conventions as well and, at times, injected their understandings of the Convention into the proceedings, see Warren, *supra*, at 792–93, one cannot reliably assume that knowledge of the Madisonian Compromise informed, much less formed the basis of, the ratifiers' votes on Article III. For a critique of reliance on the Philadelphia Convention in constitutional interpretation, see Manning, *The Role of the Philadelphia Convention in Constitutional Adjudication*, 80 Geo.Wash.L.Rev. 1753 (2012).

[5] The Federalist, No. 37 (Madison).

[6] The Court, for example, gives weight to early legislative constructions of the Constitution, in part, because such interpretations may capture nuances and shared understandings that can become lost over time. See Knowlton v. Moore, 178 U.S. 41, 56 (1900) (noting that early legislators "must have had a keen appreciation of the influences which had shaped the Constitution and the restrictions which it embodied, since all questions which related to the Constitution and its adoption must have been, at that early date, vividly impressed on their minds"). Perhaps reflecting the further value of having a settled meaning, the Court also places weight on practical constructions that have withstood the test of time. See,

in cases defining the contours of the separation of powers. In particular, beginning in the earliest days of the Constitution, the Court has frequently relied on this idea in defining the scope of the spare and often indeterminate text of Article III.[7]

The Court in Sheldon expressly invoked this idea, noting that as early as 1799, Turner v. Bank of North America, 4 U.S. (4 Dall.) 8, 10 (1799), had made clear that "the disposal of the judicial power (except in a few specified instances) belongs to congress. * * * [C]ongress is not bound * * * to enlarge the jurisdiction of the federal Courts, to every subject, in every form, which the constitution might warrant." That decision, in turn, reflected Congress's already well-established practice of vesting less than the full measure of available jurisdiction in the inferior courts—a practice that continues to this day. As noted above, see p. 403, *supra*, the First Judiciary Act did not, for example, provide for general federal question jurisdiction in civil cases "arising under" the Constitution, laws, or treaties of the United States, and the general statutory grant of diversity jurisdiction has always had an amount-in-controversy requirement and, as construed by the Supreme Court, has always required "complete diversity" when there are multiple parties on one or more sides of a case.[8]

Does this history provide a firmer basis than the Madisonian Compromise for Sheldon's conclusion that Congress has discretion to vest in the inferior federal courts less than the full measure of judicial power identified Article III, § 2?

---

e.g., Myers v. United States, 272 U.S. 52, 175 (1926) (noting that "a contemporaneous legislative exposition of the Constitution, when the founders of our government and framers of our Constitution were actively participating in public affairs, acquiesced in for a long term of years, fixes the construction to be given its provisions"); Ex parte Grossman, 267 U.S. 87, 118–19 (1923) (holding that "long practice under the pardoning power and acquiescence in it strongly sustains the construction it is based on"). For discussions of the tradition of "liquidating" the meaning of the Constitution, see, *e.g.*, Baude, *Constitutional Liquidation*, 71 Stan.L.Rev. 1 (2019); Nelson, *Originalism and Interpretive Conventions*, 70 U.Chi.L.Rev. 519, 525–29 (2003); Powell, *The Original Understanding of Original Intent*, 98 Harv.L.Rev. 885, 910, 940–41 (1985).

[7]   See, *e.g.*, Stuart v. Laird, 5 U.S. (1 Cranch) 299, 309 (1803) ("[I]t is sufficient to observe, that practice and acquiescence under [the custom of Justices riding circuit] for a period of several years, commencing with the organization of the judicial system, affords an irresistible answer, and has indeed fixed the construction."); United States v. Hudson & Goodwin, 11 U.S. (7 Cranch) 32, 32 (1812) (rejecting the federal courts' previously asserted authority to craft a federal common law of crimes, reasoning in part that "the general acquiescence of legal men shews the prevalence of opinion in favor of the negative of the proposition"); Martin v. Hunter's Lessee, 14 U.S. (1 Wheat.) 304, 352 (1816) (affirming the Supreme Court's authority to review state court judgments in part because of the "weight of contemporaneous exposition by all parties, this acquiescence of enlightened state courts, and these judicial decisions of the supreme court through so long a period"); Cohens v. Virginia, 19 U.S. (6 Wheat.) 264, 420 (1819) ("A contemporaneous exposition of the constitution * * * is the judiciary act itself. We know that in the Congress which passed that act were many eminent members of the Convention which formed the constitution."); Tutun v. United States, 270 U.S. 568, 576 (1926) (upholding a statutory grant of naturalization power to the federal courts on the ground that it "has been conferred exclusively upon courts continuously since the foundation of our government").

[8]   The statutory history of federal question and diversity jurisdiction is discussed more fully in Chapter XIII, *infra*.

(4) Modern Echoes of the Story Position. Although the Court has repeatedly reaffirmed the principle articulated in Sheldon,[9] echoes of Justice Story's mandatory jurisdiction theory persist to the present. Recall that each of the three variants of the Story position assumes that Article III is satisfied so long as a case falls within *either* the lower federal courts' jurisdiction or the Supreme Court's appellate jurisdiction over state court decisions. Some have inferred from that proposition that Article III, properly understood, in fact requires Congress to vest certain jurisdiction over certain classes of cases in the lower federal courts, at least if it has made exceptions to the Supreme Court's appellate jurisdiction.[10]

Professor Clinton, for example, has embraced something akin to Story's first position, contending that "Congress [must] allocate to the federal judiciary as a whole each and every type of case or controversy" within the scope of Article III, "excluding, possibly, only those cases that Congress deemed to be so trivial that they would pose an unnecessary burden." Clinton, *A Mandatory View of Federal Court Jurisdiction: A Guided Quest for the Original Understanding of Article III*, 132 U.Pa.L.Rev. 741, 749–50 (1984).[11] Professor Clinton, however, is hard-pressed to explain the gaps left in federal jurisdiction by the Judiciary Act of 1789, see pp. 37–38, *supra*, notably with respect to diversity cases.

Indeed, given other constitutional limitations, it is difficult to see how the Story position embraced by Clinton would operate in diversity cases. After Sheldon v. Sill, certain cases falling within the constitutional definition—but outside the statutory definition—of diversity would have to be adjudicated, in the first instance, in state courts. Under the first position attributed to Justice Story—that some federal court must have jurisdiction to review every case within the federal judicial power—it would follow that the Supreme Court must have jurisdiction to review final decisions of state courts in such cases. The Supreme Court, however, has never exercised jurisdiction to review a state court decision, governed entirely by non-federal law, solely on the basis that the parties are diverse. (Indeed, in light of the decision in Erie R.R. Co. v. Tompkins, 304 U.S. 64 (1938), p. 760, *infra,* how could the Court second-guess a state supreme court on an issue of state law?) If the Supreme Court cannot review state court decisions based on diversity, would Clinton's view oblige Congress to vest essentially the full scope of diversity jurisdiction in the lower federal courts, eliminating, for example, the statutory requirement of complete diversity? Apart from requiring a

---

[9]   See, *e.g.,* Palmore v. United States, 411 U.S. 389, 401 (1973); Kline v. Burke Construction Co., 260 U.S. 226, 234 (1922); Case of the Sewing Machine Co., 85 U.S. 553, 577 (1873).

[10]   In his three-volume treatise on the Constitution, Professor Crosskey argued "[t]he meaning of this requirement—that 'the judicial power *shall* extend to' all of these 'Cases,' including those described in the enumeration as 'Controversies'—is that the power in question 'shall extend to' *all the questions* of law and fact of which these cases consist." 1 Crosskey, Politics and the Constitution in the History of the United States 615 (1953).

[11]   See also Clinton, *A Mandatory View of Federal Court Jurisdiction: Early Implementation of and Departures from the Constitutional Plan*, 86 Colum.L.Rev. 1515 (1986). Clinton's view is challenged, based on a study of the First Judiciary Act, in Casto, *The First Congress's Understanding of Its Authority over the Federal Courts' Jurisdiction*, 26 B.C.L.Rev. 1101 (1985).

striking expansion of diversity jurisdiction, could such an obligation be squared with the Madisonian Compromise?

What about federal question cases? In theory, so long as suit can be filed in state court and the Supreme Court has the power to review, the allocation of jurisdiction squares with the thrust of Justice Story's views, subject to two qualifications.

The first qualification builds on Justice Story's assumption, which is hotly contested, that the Constitution may preclude state courts from exercising jurisdiction in at least some cases that fall within Article III. (Possible examples are federal criminal cases and suits seeking specific relief against federal officials. See pp. 575–585, *infra*.) A case outside state court jurisdiction can make its way into the federal judiciary (aside from the few cases within the Supreme Court's original jurisdiction) only by way of original jurisdiction in the lower federal courts. Accordingly, Justice Story argued that in such cases Congress must vest jurisdiction in the lower federal courts.[12] But that position is in tension with the Madisonian Compromise and the language of Article III, both of which reflected the understanding that the decision whether to create lower federal courts should be a matter for discretionary decision by Congress.

The second qualification arises from changes in the Supreme Court's jurisdiction. When Justice Story wrote, the Court's jurisdiction to review state court decisions was mandatory. Since 1914, that jurisdiction has been discretionary, and in recent years the Court has rarely decided more than a handful of the several thousand cases from the state courts in which review is sought. Is certiorari jurisdiction, especially when exercised so rarely, a sufficient "vesting" of the federal judicial power in the federal judiciary?[13]

(5) Internal and External Restraints. Consider the statement in Sheldon v. Sill that a statute defining the jurisdiction of the lower federal courts "cannot be in conflict with the Constitution, unless it confers powers not enumerated therein." That statement presumably refers only to a conflict with Article III—what commentators sometimes call "internal restraints" on Congress's power to define federal court jurisdiction.

But consider a statute that removed federal jurisdiction over claims brought by plaintiffs who were of a particular race, or gender, or religion. Even if such a statute does not violate Article III, it would surely run afoul of "external" restrictions imposed by other constitutional provisions, such as the equal protection component of the Fifth Amendment's Due Process Clause.

---

[12]   For one version of this argument, see Redish & Woods, *Congressional Power to Control the Jurisdiction of Lower Federal Courts: A Critical Review and a New Synthesis*, 124 U.Pa.L.Rev. 45 (1975).

[13]   Eisenberg, *Congressional Authority to Restrict Lower Federal Court Jurisdiction*, 83 Yale L.J. 498, 513, 516 (1974), asserts that the federal judiciary was intended to be able to hear all cases within its jurisdiction under Article III. According to Eisenberg, since the Supreme Court no longer has the capacity to review all cases originating in the state courts, he contends that it is "no longer reasonable to assert that Congress may simply abolish the lower federal courts." Eisenberg concludes that "[t]he power to curtail [federal court jurisdiction] is limited to prudent steps which help avoid case overloads."

What other "external" limits might restrain Congress's authority over the jurisdiction of the federal courts? For example, would any provision of the Constitution besides Article III bar Congress from withdrawing federal district court jurisdiction over a particular category of federal questions, such as challenges to prayer in public schools? Professor Tribe has argued that to single out a particular category of constitutional claims, like challenges to school prayer, for exclusion from the federal courts imposes an impermissible burden on the underlying constitutional right being asserted.[14] But how convincing is Tribe's premise—that it is an unconstitutional "burden" to send a case to a state court—in light of the Madisonian Compromise?

Does your sense about the "parity" of federal and state courts shape your view of these questions or of how to understand the historical record?[15] Consider the fact that, in the founding era, "in the vast majority of states—covering a full 85% of the population by 1790—state judges enjoyed the same tenure as federal judges: life with good behavior." Fitzpatrick, *The Constitutionality of Federal Jurisdiction-Stripping Legislation and the History of State Judicial Selection and Tenure*, 98 Va.L.Rev. 839, 857 (2012). Do the changes since 1789 in state judicial selection methods and the character of state judicial elections call into question arguments, based on the Madisonian Compromise, that state courts must be viewed as on a par with federal courts for purposes of Article III? See pp. 403–406, *supra*. Is there an argument that the Reconstruction Amendments, although directed at the states rather than at Congress, have relevantly altered the constitutional framework?[16] For further consideration of potential limits on Congress's power to strip jurisdiction over particular subject matter areas, see pp. 431–433, *infra*.

INTRODUCTORY NOTE ON EX PARTE YERGER

Later the same year that the Supreme Court decided Ex parte McCardle, 74 U.S. (7 Wall.) 506 (1869), p. 407, *supra*, another Mississippian detained by the military, one Yerger, sought a writ of habeas corpus in federal court on grounds similar to those raised by McCardle. After the circuit court denied the writ, Yerger followed the suggestion in the penultimate paragraph of the McCardle opinion and filed in the Supreme Court an application for an original writ of habeas corpus, as authorized by

---

[14]   See Tribe, *Jurisdictional Gerrymandering: Zoning Disfavored Rights Out of the Federal Courts*, 16 Harv.C.R.-C.L.L.Rev. 129, 141–43 (1981).

[15]   Gunther, *Congressional Power to Curtail Federal Court Jurisdiction: An Opinionated Guide to the Ongoing Debate*, 36 Stan.L.Rev. 895, 918 (1984), argues that "[i]f one accepts that the article III compromise gave Congress the power to decide how to channel federal issues as between federal and state courts, assigning some classes of cases to the state courts does not 'discriminate against,' or 'burden,' or 'prejudice' the rights involved in those cases." Does Gunther's conclusion require adherence to a strong presumption of parity? What if that presumption is empirically unfounded?

[16]   See generally Fallon, *Reflections on the Hart and Wechsler Paradigm*, 47 Vand.L.Rev. 953, 980–83 (1994), arguing that the Civil War Amendments reflected a conception of federalism different from that embodied in the original Constitution generally, and possibly Article III specifically, and claiming that Federal Courts scholars should attend more self-consciously to resulting problems of "intertemporal synthesis."

Section 14 of the Judiciary Act of 1789, 1 Stat. 81–82. In the opinion that follows, the Court addressed the question whether it had jurisdiction to entertain Yerger's application.

Ex parte Yerger

75 U.S. (8 Wall.) 85 (1869).
On motion and petition for writs of *habeas corpus* and *certiorari*.

■ THE CHIEF JUSTICE [CHASE] delivered the opinion of the Court.

* * * The general question of jurisdiction in this case resolves itself necessarily into two other questions:

1.　Has the court jurisdiction, in a case like the present, to inquire into the cause of detention, alleged to be unlawful, and to give relief, if the detention be found to be in fact unlawful, by the writ of *habeas corpus*, under the Judiciary Act of 1789?

2.　If, under that act, the court possessed this jurisdiction, has it been taken away by the second section of the act of March, 27, 1868, repealing so much of the act of February 5, 1867, as authorizes appeals from Circuit Courts to the Supreme Court? * * *

The great writ of *habeas corpus* has been for centuries esteemed the best and only sufficient defence of personal freedom.

In England, after a long struggle, it was firmly guaranteed by the famous Habeas Corpus Act of May 27, 1679, "for the better securing of the liberty of the subject," which, as Blackstone says, "is frequently considered as another Magna Charta."

It was brought to America by the colonists, and claimed as among the immemorial rights descended to them from their ancestors.

Naturally, therefore, when the confederated colonies became united States, * * * this great writ found prominent sanction in the Constitution. That sanction is in these words: "The privilege of the writ of *habeas corpus* shall not be suspended unless when in cases of rebellion or invasion the public safety may require it."

The terms of this provision necessarily imply judicial action. In England, all the higher courts were open to applicants for the writ, and it is hardly supposable that, under the new government, founded on more liberal ideas and principles, any court would be, intentionally, closed to them.

* * * [T]he act of September 24, 1789, * * * in the 14th section, * * * enact[ed], "that all the beforementioned courts of the United States shall have power to issue writs of *scire facias, habeas corpus*, and all other writs, not specially provided by statute, which may be necessary for the exercise of their respective jurisdictions, and agreeable to the principles and usages of law." In the same section, it was further provided "that either of the Justices of the Supreme Court, as well as Judges of the District Courts, shall have power to grant writs of *habeas corpus* for the purpose of an inquiry into the cause of commitment; provided that writs of *habeas corpus* shall in no case extend to prisoners in jail, unless they are in custody, under, or by color of the authority of the United States, or are committed for trial before some court of the same, or are necessary to be brought into court to testify."

That this court is one of the courts to which the power to issue writs of *habeas corpus* is expressly given by the terms of this section has never been questioned. * * *

* * * [T]he general spirit and genius of our institutions has tended to the widening and enlarging of the *habeas corpus* jurisdiction of the courts and judges of the United States; and this tendency, except in one recent instance, has been constant and uniform; and it is in the light of it that we must determine the true meaning of the Constitution and the law in respect to the appellate jurisdiction of this court. We are not at liberty to except from it any cases not plainly excepted by law * * *.

It seems to be a necessary consequence that if the appellate jurisdiction of *habeas corpus* extends to any case, it extends to this. * * * We agree that [the appellate jurisdiction] is given subject to exception and regulation by Congress; but it is too plain for argument that the denial to this court of appellate jurisdiction in this class of cases must greatly weaken the efficacy of the writ, deprive the citizen in many cases of its benefits, and seriously hinder the establishment of that uniformity in deciding upon questions of personal rights which can only be attained through appellate jurisdiction, exercised upon the decisions of courts of original jurisdiction. In the particular class of cases, * * * it is evident that the imprisoned citizen, however unlawful his imprisonment may be in fact, is wholly without remedy unless it be found in the appellate jurisdiction of this court.

These considerations forbid any construction giving to doubtful words the effect of withholding or abridging this jurisdiction. They would strongly persuade against the denial of the jurisdiction even were the reasons for affirming it less cogent than they are.

We are obliged to hold, therefore, that in all cases where a Circuit Court of the United States has, in the exercise of its original jurisdiction, caused a prisoner to be brought before it, and has, after inquiring into the cause of detention, remanded him to the custody from which he was taken, this court, in the exercise of its appellate jurisdiction, may, by the writ of *habeas corpus*, aided by the writ of *certiorari*, revise the decision of the Circuit Court, and if it be found unwarranted by law, relieve the prisoner from the unlawful restraint to which he has been remanded.

This conclusion brings us to the inquiry whether the 2d section of the act of March 27th, 1868, takes away or affects the appellate jurisdiction of this court under the Constitution and the acts of Congress prior to 1867. * * *

[In the 1867 Act,] Congress * * * extend[ed] the original jurisdiction by *habeas corpus* * * * to all cases of restraint of liberty in violation of the Constitution, treaties, or laws of the United States. This act authorized appeals to this court from judgments of the Circuit Court, but did not repeal any previous act conferring jurisdiction by *habeas corpus*, unless by implication. * * *

The effect of the [1868 repealing act] act was to oust the court of its jurisdiction of the particular case then before it on appeal, and it is not to be doubted that such was the effect intended. * * *

It was, doubtless, within the constitutional discretion of Congress to determine whether such an [imperious public] exigency existed; but it is not to be presumed that an act, passed under such circumstances, was intended to have any further effect than that plainly apparent from its terms. * * *

The words of the repealing section are, "that *so much* of the act approved February 5th, 1867, as *authorizes* an appeal from the judgment of the Circuit Court to the Supreme Court of the United States, or the exercise of any such jurisdiction by said Supreme Court on appeals which have been, or may be hereafter taken, be, and the same is hereby repealed."

These words are not of doubtful interpretation. They repeal only so much of the act of 1867 as authorized appeals, or the exercise of appellate jurisdiction by this court. They affected only appeals and appellate jurisdiction authorized by that act. They do not purport to touch the appellate jurisdiction conferred by the Constitution, or to except from it any cases not excepted by the act of 1789. * * *

[The Court next rejected the argument that the 1867 Act repealed the habeas corpus provisions of the 1789 Act.] If it repealed the act of 1789, it did so by implication * * *.

Repeals by implication are not favored. They are seldom admitted except on the ground of repugnancy; and never, we think, when the former act can stand together with the new act. * * * [T]he provision of a new and more convenient mode of its exercise does not necessarily take away the old; and that this effect was not intended is indicated by the fact that the authority conferred by the new act is expressly declared to be "in addition" to the authority conferred by the former acts. Addition is not substitution. * * *

The argument having been confined, by direction of the court, to the question of jurisdiction, this opinion is limited to that question. The jurisdiction of the court to issue the writ prayed for is affirmed.*

---

*   [Ed.] After the Supreme Court upheld its jurisdiction to entertain Yerger's application under the 1789 Act, Congress considered a bill that would have stripped the Supreme Court of

NOTE ON CONGRESSIONAL POWER OVER THE SUPREME COURT'S APPELLATE JURISDICTION

(1) History. Article III's provision that Congress may create "Exceptions" to the Supreme Court's appellate jurisdiction was added to the Constitutional Convention's working draft by the Committee of Detail. Its purposes and possible limits were not discussed on the floor of the Convention. See p. 21, *supra*.[1]

(2) Can "Exceptions" Swallow the Rule? Congress's power to limit the Supreme Court's appellate jurisdiction is presumably subject to the same "external" limits as is the power to define the lower courts' jurisdiction. (Recall in this regard McCardle's broad statement: "We are not at liberty to inquire into the motives of the legislature.") But does Article III impose any "internal" limits on Congress's authority to create "exceptions"?[2]

In his influential *Dialogue*, 66 Harv.L.Rev. at 1364–65, Professor Hart offered the following exchange:

"Q. * * * The *McCardle* case says that the appellate jurisdiction of the Supreme Court is entirely within Congressional control.

"A. You read the *McCardle* case for all it might be worth rather than the least it has to be worth, don't you?

"Q. No, I read it in terms of the language of the Constitution and the antecedent theory that the Court articulated in explaining its decision. This

---

all appellate jurisdiction over habeas corpus petitions. See 2 Ackerman, We The People: Transformations 243 (1998). In a later form, the bill purported to bar the Court from questioning the constitutional validity of Reconstruction. See *id*. Because the government transferred Yerger from military custody to the local civil authority and the proposed legislation never became law, the Court never adjudicated the merits of challenges to military Reconstruction. See *id*. 243–44; see also Fairman, History of the Supreme Court of the United States: Reconstruction and Reunion, 1864–88, Part One, at 589 (1971).

[1] Glashausser, *A Return to Form for the Exceptions Clause*, 51 B.C.L.Rev. 1383 (2010), argues that the first draft of what became the Exceptions Clause sought only to permit Congress to transfer cases from the Court's appellate to its original jurisdiction, an objective that was obscured by revisions that culminated in the current language.

[2] Pfander, *Jurisdiction-Stripping and the Supreme Court's Power to Supervise Inferior Tribunals*, 78 Tex.L.Rev. 1433 (2000), argues that Congress may not restrict Supreme Court oversight of the lower federal courts so as to undermine the constitutional premise that they must be "inferior" to the Supreme Court. He argues that historically, supervisory authority was available through "discretionary writs, such as mandamus, habeas corpus, and prohibition" and hence need not be provided by a formal appeal. Does this view give too little significance to the Exceptions Clause? In a subsequent article, Pfander & Birk, *Article III and the Scottish Judiciary*, 124 Harv.L.Rev. 1613 (2011), contend that the example of the Scottish judiciary supports the view that the Constitution requires a single Supreme Court with supervisory authority over inferior courts. Further, Birk, *The Common-Law Exceptions Clause: Congressional Control of Supreme Court Appellate Jurisdiction in Light of British Precedent*, 63 Vill.L.Rev. 189 (2018), concludes that historically when Parliament made "exceptions" or "exemptions" to the jurisdiction of English and Scottish "supreme courts" at common law, it did not divest the courts of power to correct major interpretive errors, denials of due process, or transgressions of jurisdictional limits. Consistent with that history, Birk infers that the Founders' understanding of the power granted Congress by the Exceptions Clause would not readily have accommodated exceptions denying the Supreme Court of the United States power to exercise such supervisory authority over inferior courts.

seems to me to lead inevitably to the same result, whatever jurisdiction is denied to the Court.

"A. You would treat the Constitution, then, as authorizing exceptions which engulf the rule, even to the point of eliminating the appellate jurisdiction altogether? How preposterous!

"Q. If you think an 'exception' implies some residuum of jurisdiction, Congress could meet that test by excluding everything but patent cases. This is so absurd, and it is so impossible to lay down any measure of a necessary reservation, that it seems to me the language of the Constitution must be taken as vesting plenary control in Congress.

"A. It's not impossible for me to lay down a measure. The measure is simply that the exceptions must not be such as will destroy the essential role of the Supreme Court in the constitutional plan. * * *

"Q. The measure seems pretty indeterminate to me.

"A. Ask yourself whether it is any more so than the tests which the Court has evolved to meet other hard situations. But whatever the difficulties of the test, they are less, are they not, than the difficulties of reading the Constitution as authorizing its own destruction?"

This last statement is assumed to reflect Hart's own view. How convincing is the structural argument that authority to make "exceptions" cannot swallow the rule, thereby negating the essential role of the Court? On one level, the argument resembles the Court's holdings in statutory cases that an agency's delegated authority to "modify" the terms of a statute should not be read to authorize "basic and fundamental changes in the scheme" prescribed by the statute. See MCI Telecomms. Corp. v. AT&T Co., 512 U.S. 218, 225 (1994). See also Biden v. Nebraska, 143 S.Ct. 2355, 2368–70 (2023) (relying on MCI). At the same time, because Hart's approach offers no clear metric for deciding when "exceptions" would swallow the rule and thus compromise the Court's "essential role," see Redish, *Congressional Power to Regulate Supreme Court Jurisdiction Under the Exceptions Clause: An Internal and External Examination*, 27 Vill.L.Rev. 900, 902 (1982), would efforts to apply that test trigger the Court's reluctance to enforce constitutional criteria that entail matters of degree and thus lack judicially manageable standards? See, *e.g.*, Rucho v. Common Cause, 588 U.S. 684 (2019) (holding that the Court had failed to derive "judicially manageable standards" for partisan gerrymandering claims); Whitman v. Am. Trucking Ass'ns, 531 U.S. 457, 474–75 (2001) (holding that the Court has " 'almost never felt qualified to second-guess' " Congress's judgment about the " 'degree' " of policymaking discretion the latter may delegate to an agency) (quoting Mistretta v. United States, 488 U.S. 361, 416 (1989) (Scalia, J., dissenting)).

In an effort to give definition to Hart's "essential role" theory, Professor Ratner argues that, to be constitutionally valid, "exceptions" to the Court's appellate jurisdiction must not "negate" the Court's "essential constitutional functions of maintaining the uniformity and supremacy of federal law." Ratner, *Congressional Power over the Appellate Jurisdiction of the Supreme Court*, 109 U.Pa.L.Rev. 157, 201–02 (1960). "[L]egislation that precludes

Supreme Court review in every case involving a particular subject is an unconstitutional encroachment," he concludes. See also Ratner, *Majoritarian Constraints on Judicial Review: Congressional Control of Supreme Court Jurisdiction*, 27 Vill.L.Rev. 929 (1982).[3]

Consider the extent to which historic practice squares with Professor Ratner's elaboration of the "essential functions" thesis. With respect to maintaining the uniform application of federal law, recall the significant gaps in Supreme Court jurisdiction left by the Judiciary Act of 1789—both the lack of jurisdiction to review state court decisions *upholding* claims of federal right and the lack of a general jurisdiction to review federal criminal cases.[4] With respect to maintaining the supremacy of federal law, is any scope left for the exceptions power when state conduct is asserted to violate federal law? In light of difficulties such as these, Professor Gunther suggests that essential functions arguments confuse "the familiar with the necessary, the desirable with the constitutionally mandated." Gunther, *Congressional Power to Curtail Federal Court Jurisdiction: An Opinionated Guide to the Ongoing Debate*, 36 Stan.L.Rev. 895, 905 (1984).

Indeed, Frost, *Overvaluing Uniformity*, 94 Va.L.Rev. 1567 (2008), finds little evidence that the founders were concerned with promoting uniformity, contends that the Supreme Court may never have had (and today surely lacks) the capacity to maintain uniformity, and argues that the benefits of uniformity have been greatly exaggerated. Grove, *Article III in the Political Branches*, 90 Notre Dame L.Rev. 1835 (2015), shows that, at least since McCardle, Congress and the President have fairly consistently rejected proposals under the Exceptions Clause to strip Supreme Court jurisdiction over specific subject areas. Professor Grove argues, however, that the political branches' decisions *not* to enact legislation may shed little light on the validity of jurisdiction stripping because it is difficult to know whether

---

[3]   For further elaboration of Hart's view, see Monaghan, *Jurisdiction Stripping Circa 2020: What the Dialogue (Still) Has to Teach Us*, 69 Duke L.J. 1 (2020). Monaghan proposes that the Court should "excise subject-matter limitations on its appellate jurisdiction when a substantial, undefended purpose of such jurisdiction-stripping legislation is to limit the Court's ability to consider a properly preserved constitutional claim." He grounds this conclusion in "Marbury v. Madison's emphasis on limited government and rule-of-law principles," arguing that "the line of our constitutional development" has given the Court a "unique and essential role in maintaining the idea of the limited government contemplated by the written 1789 Constitution." Responding to Monaghan, Sprigman, *Congress's Article III Power and the Process of Constitutional Change*, 95 N.Y.U.L.Rev. 1778 (2020), argues that Congress's explicit and extensive "Article III power" over federal court jurisdiction enables it, in effect, to "prescribe, by ordinary legislation, constitutional rules in areas where the meaning of the Constitution is unsettled" or even to "displace otherwise settled constitutional rules by ordinary legislation." Thus, "the real barriers to Congress's exercise of its power * * * are not constitutional but rather political and prudential." Which of these positions better aligns with the text of Article III and the subsequent history?

[4]   See pp. 36–37, *supra*. *Cf.* Felker v. Turpin, 518 U.S. 651, 667 (1996) (Souter, J., joined by Stevens and Breyer, JJ., concurring) (terming it an "open" question whether a statute limiting the Supreme Court's appellate jurisdiction would be unconstitutional if, in practice, it stopped the Court from reviewing "divergent interpretations" of a federal statute). For the view that the Exceptions Clause responded to significant concerns that the grant of appellate jurisdiction would authorize the Court to revisit jury verdicts and that the clause thus provided robust constitutional authority to limit appellate review, see Lee, *Article IX, Article III, and the First Congress: The Original Constitutional Plan for the Federal Courts, 1787–1792*, 89 Fordham L.Rev. 1895, 1935–36 (2021).

and to what extent such decisions reflect political rather than constitutional judgments about jurisdiction stripping. If constitutional text and history are as inconclusive as Frost and Grove suggest, would the judicial branch ever be justified in displacing a legislative judgment to strip Supreme Court jurisdiction? Does Hart's "essential role" thesis, as elaborated by Ratner, ask the Court to enforce a high-level constitutional purpose—uniformity and supremacy—that lacks textual or historical grounding? If understood as a judicially enforceable norm, does the "essential functions" thesis overlook the possibility that the Constitution, through Article III's Exceptions Clause, vests in Congress the authority to determine what aspects of the Court's appellate jurisdiction are essential to its constitutional role?[5]

Hart's view failed to persuade his collaborator, Professor Wechsler, who thought it "antithetical to the plan of the Constitution for the courts—which was quite simply that the Congress would decide from time to time how far the federal judicial institution should be used within the limits of the federal judicial power; or, stated differently, how far judicial jurisdiction should be left to the state courts, bound as they are by the [Supremacy Clause]. Federal courts, including the Supreme Court, do not pass on constitutional questions because there is a special function vested in them to enforce the Constitution or police the other agencies of the government. They do so rather for the reason that they must decide a litigated issue that is otherwise within their jurisdiction and in doing so must give effect to the supreme law of the land. That is, at least, what Marbury v. Madison was all about." Wechsler, *The Courts and the Constitution*, 65 Colum.L.Rev. 1001, 1005–06 (1965).[6]

(3) McCardle v. Yerger. The McCardle decision arose in a period of deep constitutional and political controversy. (Indeed, isn't that likely to be true when legislation limiting federal jurisdiction is not merely proposed but actually enacted?) The case appeared to require the Supreme Court to resolve the vital question of the constitutionality of the Military

---

[5]   Does the sparse history of jurisdiction stripping suggest that such a choice poses little practical risk to the Court's essential functions, however defined? Professor Grove contends that political actors in a competitive political system have long-term incentives to maintain an independent judiciary that can check the opposition party when it becomes dominant, and that the hurdles erected by Article I's bicameralism and presentment requirements generally allow the minority faction to block attempts by the majority to strip jurisdiction. Grove, *The Structural Safeguards of Federal Jurisdiction*, 124 Harv.L.Rev. 869 (2011). In a subsequent article, she argues that the President and the Department of Justice also have strong incentives to oppose jurisdiction-stripping bills. See Grove, *The Article II Safeguards of Federal Jurisdiction*, 112 Colum.L.Rev. 250 (2012). For further elaboration of this theme, see Grove, *The Origins (and Fragility) of Judicial Independence*, 71 Vand.L.Rev. 465 (2018), which argues that central conventions of judicial independence are historically contingent rather than structurally compelled. See also Bradley & Siegel, *Historical Gloss, Constitutional Conventions, and the Judicial Separation of Powers*, 105 Geo.L.J. 255 (2017) (arguing that uncodified conventions about judicial independence considerations have influenced the political defeat or rejection of important jurisdiction-stripping proposals in the past century).

[6]   The McCardle decision gave effect to a statute withdrawing jurisdiction over a case after the Supreme Court had obtained jurisdiction. Compare Hamdan v. Rumsfeld, 548 U.S. 557 (2006), p. 557, *infra*, where Congress enacted a statute limiting lower federal court jurisdiction over a habeas corpus action by an alien detained at Guantanamo Bay after the Supreme Court had granted certiorari. The majority held that the statute did not withdraw jurisdiction over the pending case; in dissent, Justice Scalia contested the majority's statutory construction and, in rejecting the argument that removing jurisdiction over a pending case posed a constitutional problem, contended that the Exceptions Clause "explicitly permits" Congress to do just that.

Reconstruction Act of 1867's authorization of criminal trials before military commissions. A decision might also reach broader issues concerning the legality of that Act, which had displaced Southern governments with military rule. Rumors swirled that the Court would uphold McCardle's appeal.

Some of the language in McCardle suggests few if any limits on Congress's power to make exceptions to the appellate jurisdiction, and many have viewed the Court as having caved in to the political dominance of the congressional Republicans, who had not only passed the Repealer Act over a presidential veto but also impeached and nearly convicted President Johnson, and who saw a fellow Republican capture the Presidency with Grant's election in 1868.[7]

On the other hand, the Court's penultimate paragraph, reaching out in dictum to deny that all aspects of its jurisdiction had been withdrawn, could be viewed as a significant qualification to any broad reading of the Exceptions Clause as well as a notable assertion of power vis-à-vis Congress. The Republicans who passed the Repealer Act undoubtedly expected to block the Court from ruling on McCardle's case and would have been surprised that the Act left someone like McCardle free to reach the Supreme Court by filing an original writ of habeas corpus under § 14 of the First Judiciary Act.

And just months after deciding McCardle, the Court, in another opinion authored by Chief Justice Chase, upheld its § 14 jurisdiction in Yerger. Although Yerger does not contradict McCardle, aspects of the decision—especially its emphasis on the role of appellate jurisdiction in providing for uniformity of federal law along with its account of the importance of the writ of habeas corpus, and of not lightly diminishing its availability—are in considerable tension with a broad reading of McCardle. McCardle and Yerger together can be seen to reflect a Court struggling over how to reconcile Congress's seemingly broad authority under the Exceptions Clause and the judiciary's important role in protecting individual rights in habeas cases.

(4) The Contemporary Significance of Yerger. In Felker v. Turpin, 518 U.S. 651 (1996), the Court relied on Yerger to avoid potential constitutional questions about congressional restriction of the Supreme Court's appellate jurisdiction. Under the provision at issue in Felker, 28 U.S.C. § 2244(b), a state prisoner may file a second or successive habeas petition in federal district court only after having obtained, from the court of appeals, a "gatekeeping" determination that the petition satisfies stringent statutory criteria. Section 2244(b) also declares that decisions by the courts of appeals in this gatekeeping capacity "shall not be appealable and shall not be the subject of a petition for rehearing or for a writ of certiorari."

---

[7]   For discussion of McCardle's political context, see Fairman, History of the Supreme Court of the United States: Reconstruction and Reunion, 1864–88, Part One, ch. X (1971); Friedman, *The History of the Countermajoritarian Difficulty, Part II: Reconstruction's Political Court*, 91 Geo.L.J. 1, 25–38 (2002); Meltzer, *The Story of Ex parte McCardle: The Power of Congress to Limit the Supreme Court's Appellate Jurisdiction*, in Federal Courts Stories (Jackson & Resnik eds. 2010); Van Alstyne, *A Critical Guide to Ex parte McCardle*, 15 Ariz.L.Rev. 229 (1973).

The court of appeals denied Felker, a state prisoner, authorization to file a successive petition. He then filed in the Supreme Court a document styled "Petition for Writ of Habeas Corpus, for Appellate or Certiorari Review * * *, and for Stay of Execution." The Court held unanimously that the Act's preclusion of certiorari review of the court of appeals' gatekeeping decisions did not offend Article III, § 2. But the Court reached that conclusion only after having interpreted § 2244(b) as not withdrawing the Court's authority to entertain original habeas petitions under 28 U.S.C. § 2241 (the successor provision in this respect to § 14 of the First Judiciary Act). It read § 2244(b) in this way because, "for reasons similar to those stated in Yerger," implied repeals of the Supreme Court's appellate jurisdiction are disfavored.[8] See Tyler, *Continuity, Coherence, and the Canons*, 99 Nw.U.L.Rev. 1389, 1443–47 (2005) (Felker is best explained by "stare decisis and the canon against implied repeals").

This conclusion, Felker said, "obviates" the need to address petitioner's constitutional challenge to Congress's authority to strip the Court's appellate jurisdiction. But was the Court, in relying on Yerger's presumption against implied jurisdictional repeals, nonetheless enforcing a vague constitutional value by, in effect, rewriting a statute? Was the Court clearer in Felker about how the presumption against implied repeals served underlying constitutional values?

(5) Uncertainty and Its Consequences. Professor Bator contends that for Congress to withdraw the Supreme Court's appellate jurisdiction would "violate the spirit of the Constitution, even if it would not violate its letter * * * because the structure contemplated by the instrument makes sense * * * only on the premise that there would be a federal Supreme Court with the power to pronounce uniform and authoritative rules of federal law."[9] Bator, *Congressional Power over the Jurisdiction of the Federal Courts*, 27 Vill.L.Rev. 1030, 1039 (1982). Others, including some strong supporters of broad judicial protection of individual rights, view the power to withdraw jurisdiction as an important political counterweight whose existence gives

---

[8]   The Court also held that § 2244(b)'s stringent requirements for the authorization of successive petitions in the district courts, whether or not they formally limited the Court's power to issue writs of habeas corpus under § 2241, should "inform our authority to grant such relief as well" and were well within the permissible range of congressional judgments. Finding that the petitioner failed to satisfy those requirements, "let alone" the requirements of Supreme Court Rule 20.4(a) that there must be "exceptional circumstances" justifying issuance of original writs, the Court dismissed Felker's petition. Concurring, Justice Stevens (joined by Justices Souter and Breyer) described the Court's response "to the argument that [§ 2244(b)] has deprived this Court of appellate jurisdiction in violation of Article III, § 2" as "incomplete," and noted additional statutes that might authorize Supreme Court review of a gatekeeping decision, including the All Writs Act (28 U.S.C. § 1651) and 28 U.S.C. § 1254(2), which authorizes a court of appeals to certify a question for the Court's review. Justice Souter's separate concurring opinion (joined by Justices Stevens and Breyer) reserved the question that would be presented if the courts of appeals "adopted divergent interpretations of the gatekeeper standard" and in practice "statutory avenues other than certiorari for reviewing a gatekeeping determination were closed."

[9]   In contrast, Huq, *The Constitutional Law of Agenda Control*, 104 Calif.L.Rev. 1401, 1435–36 (2016), argues that, "in the absence of a definitive statement to the contrary from the Court, it would seem that the text of Article III to [sic] vests the legislature with tolerably broad authority to determine which constitutional questions of national import end up on the judiciary's agenda."

legitimacy to judicial review. See, *e.g.*, Black, *The Presidency and Congress*, 32 Wash. & Lee L.Rev. 841, 846 (1975). Of course, the political branches can exercise some control over the Court in other ways—by selecting new Justices or by changing the size of the Court (which has happened seven times over the years, see Orth, *How Many Judges Does It Take to Make a Supreme Court?*, 19 Const.Comment. 681 (2002)). Is jurisdiction stripping, or at least the threat of jurisdiction stripping, an appropriate means for the people's representatives to seek accountability from Justices with life tenure? Does the answer to this question depend upon one's view of the appropriate role of the courts in exercising the power of judicial review?[10] Is it perhaps politically healthy that the limits of congressional power over Supreme Court appellate jurisdiction have never been completely clarified?

NOTE ON CONGRESSIONAL POWER TO WITHDRAW ALL FEDERAL JURISDICTION

(1) Framing the Issue. Would *simultaneous* restrictions on Supreme Court and lower federal court jurisdiction over matters that remain subject to adjudication in state court raise distinctive issues under Article III? Such limits have been accepted historically with respect to diversity cases, for example, but debate has swirled around the cases arising under federal law, and the Supreme Court appears never to have addressed directly the issues thus presented.

(2) Constitutional Arguments. As noted at pp. 410–413, *supra*, Justice Story argued that denial of all federal jurisdiction to hear cases within Article III would offend the Constitution. If understood to apply to every case falling within the federal judicial power, Justice Story's argument is hard to square with the Judiciary Act of 1789—which is frequently viewed as a repository of insight into the original understanding of Article III—and with historical practice surrounding the diversity jurisdiction. See pp. 416–417, *supra*.

In modern times, some more limited versions of Story's argument—that Article III requires the vesting of federal jurisdiction in either original or federal appellate form in *some*, but not all, categories of cases—have been put forward.

(a) Professor Sager has argued that the Constitution requires either original or appellate federal jurisdiction over *constitutional* claims. See

---

[10]   Consider, in this regard, the argument of proponents of "popular constitutionalism" that constitutional understanding should be less concentrated in the courts and informed more broadly by the views of officials in other branches of government and of the people. See, *e.g.*, Kramer, The People Themselves: Popular Constitutionalism and Judicial Review 246–48 (2004); Tushnet, Taking the Constitution Away from the Courts (1999). Kramer views Reconstruction as a high point in popular constitutionalism: the Supreme Court, after it had issued rulings that were deeply unpopular with the Republicans who dominated Congress, was "threatened with 'annihilation' in Congress, and on important matters it was forced to back down in various ways—including both jurisdiction stripping and court packing, to which it meekly submitted." Kramer, *The Supreme Court 2000 Term—Foreword: We the Court*, 115 Harv.L.Rev. 4, 117–18 (2001).

Sager, *The Supreme Court, 1980 Term—Foreword: Constitutional Limitations on Congress' Authority to Regulate the Jurisdiction of the Federal Courts*, 95 Harv.L.Rev. 17 (1981). He rests largely on the premise that these cases present the largest constitutional interest in adjudication by a judge with the safeguards from political influence established by Article III. How firmly is this appeal to "history and logic" anchored in the constitutional text?[1]

(b) Professor Amar has argued that Article III requires vesting either original or appellate federal jurisdiction in three of the nine categories of cases listed in Article III, § 2. See, *e.g.*, Amar, *A Neo-Federalist View of Article III: Separating the Two Tiers of Federal Jurisdiction*, 65 B.U.L.Rev. 205 (1985); Amar, *The Two-Tiered Structure of the Judiciary Act of 1789*, 138 U.Pa.L.Rev. 1499 (1990); Amar, *Reports of My Death Are Greatly Exaggerated: A Reply*, 138 U.Pa.L.Rev. 1651 (1990). Following Justice Story, Amar stresses the language of Article III, § 1 directing that the "judicial Power *shall* be vested" (emphasis added), but relies even more heavily on the selective use of the word "all" in Article III, § 2. With respect to the first three of the nine listed categories—federal question cases, cases affecting foreign envoys, and admiralty cases—Article III, § 2 says that the judicial power shall extend to "*all* Cases." With respect to the remaining six categories, Article III omits "all" and says simply that the judicial power shall extend to the denominated categories of "Controversies." According to Amar, Article III thus establishes two "tiers" of federal jurisdiction: a first tier, comprising the first three categories, in which federal jurisdiction (in either original or appellate form) is mandatory in "all Cases"; and a second tier, consisting of the remaining six categories, in which the decision whether to vest federal jurisdiction is a matter for Congress to decide.

This interpretation leaves a role for congressional discretion, as contemplated by the Madisonian Compromise, about whether to create lower federal courts, for even in their absence, the Supreme Court's exercise of appellate jurisdiction would satisfy Article III's mandate. The two-tier thesis also recognizes Congress's power to create "exceptions" to the Supreme Court's appellate jurisdiction even within Amar's first tier; exceptions are permissible wherever there is original jurisdiction in the lower federal courts. But what Congress may not do, Amar contends, is exercise its power to deny *both* Supreme Court and lower federal court jurisdiction with respect to the same class of cases within the mandatory first tier.[2]

---

[1] For criticism, see Redish, *Constitutional Limitations on Congressional Power to Control Federal Jurisdiction: A Reaction to Professor Sager*, 77 Nw.U.L.Rev. 143 (1982).

[2] Consider whether the following regime comports with Amar's thesis. In Santa Clara Pueblo v. Martinez, 436 U.S. 49 (1978), the Court held that federal courts possess no jurisdiction over suits to enforce the federal Indian Civil Rights Act, 25 U.S.C. §§ 1301–1303, the express purpose of which is to "protect individual Indians from arbitrary and unjust actions of tribal governments" by imposing "limitations on an Indian tribe in the exercise of its powers of self-government." S.Rep. No. 841, 90th Cong., 1st Sess. 6 (1967). Enforcement actions, although they arise under federal law, can be filed only in tribal courts, see Worthen, *Shedding New Light on an Old Debate: A Federal Indian Law Perspective on Congressional Authority to Limit Federal Question Jurisdiction*, 75 Minn.L.Rev. 65, 90–91 (1990), and there is no possibility of Supreme Court review.

Amar buttresses his reading of Article III with a wide range of supporting arguments.

(i)   At the Convention, all of the central drafts of the judiciary article, in describing the cases to which the federal judicial power would extend, referred to "all" actions arising under federal law but omitted "all" in listing other cases.

(ii) Despite some gaps, the Judiciary Act of 1789 was reasonably consistent with the two-tier thesis.

(iii) Language said to support the two-tier thesis appears not only in Martin v. Hunter's Lessee but also in other early Supreme Court opinions.[3]

(iv) The theory ensures adjudication by federal judges, whose tenure and salary are protected, in the cases of most profound national consequence.

Each of these arguments by Amar is skeptically probed in Meltzer, *The History and Structure of Article III*, 138 U.Pa.L.Rev. 1569 (1990), which contends:

(i)   As to use of the word "all," some evidence suggests that the founding generation understood the word "cases"—in contrast to the word "controversies"—to include criminal as well as civil actions, and the word "all" might have been used to emphasize that both were encompassed.[4] (But why would the drafters have needed to use "all" to underscore the breadth of the word "cases"? If the contrast was known to eighteenth century lawyers, wouldn't the disparate use of "cases" and "controversies" have sufficed?) What is more, Meltzer argues, there is virtually no support in either the Convention's records or the ratification debates for Amar's understanding.

(ii) The fit between Amar's thesis and the Judiciary Act of 1789 is not as close as Amar suggests, especially insofar as Section 25 of that Act allowed review of federal questions decided by the state courts only when the decision was adverse to a claim of federal right.[5] (See Chap. V, Sec. 1, *infra*.)

---

[3]   Amar cites American Ins. Co. v. 356 Bales of Cotton, 26 U.S. (1 Pet.) 511, 545 (1828); Osborn v. Bank of the United States, 22 U.S. (9 Wheat.) 738, 821–22 (1824); Cohens v. Virginia, 19 U.S. (6 Wheat.) 264, 378 (1821). See Amar, *Two-Tiered Structure*, p. 429, *supra*, at 1513 n.37. See also The Moses Taylor, 71 U.S. (4 Wall.) 411, 428–29 (1866); Stevenson v. Fain, 195 U.S. 165, 167 (1904).

[4]   Harrison, *The Power of Congress to Limit the Jurisdiction of Federal Courts and the Text of Article III*, 64 U.Chi.L.Rev. 203 (1997), offers a sustained textual critique of Amar's thesis. For a response, see Pushaw, *Congressional Power Over Federal Court Jurisdiction: A Defense of the Neo-Federalist Interpretation of Article III*, 1997 BYU L.Rev. 847.

[5]   Amar contends that in fact Section 25 covered all federal questions, because whenever one party claimed a federal right, the other party could claim a federal immunity (*e.g.*, that the other party lacked a federal right). In response, Meltzer acknowledges that some twentieth century cases seemed to take that view, but he points to Marshall and Taney Court decisions dismissing appeals for want of jurisdiction when the state court had upheld federal rights. More recently, Professor Woolhandler advanced a middle ground, finding that the Court was more likely to accept the expansive view in cases involving the scope of federal statutes. She states that "no one seems to have thought review was available when [in 1911] the New York Court of Appeals struck down the state workers' compensation statute on federal constitutional grounds"—the decision that motivated Congress in 1914 to eliminate the restriction on Supreme Court review of state court decisions against the claimed federal right. Woolhandler, *Power, Rights, and Section 25*, 86 Notre Dame L.Rev. 1241, 1286 (2011). Finally, Professor Walsh identifies yet another potentially significant gap in Section 25's coverage, arguing that the text of Section 25, read in its historical context, does not reach criminal cases. See Walsh, *In the*

(iii) Meltzer views early Supreme Court dicta as much less probative than Amar suggests.

(iv) Amar's first mandatory tier does not reach a number of cases for which one could argue that mandatory federal jurisdiction would be important to the union.

(v) Meltzer also notes that "Charles Black, the dean of structural constitutional interpretation, has argued that congressional power to control federal court jurisdiction 'is the rock on which rests the legitimacy of the judicial work in a democracy.' " (quoting Black, p. 428, *supra*, at 846).

Judge Fletcher offers a distinct challenge to Amar's interpretation of the significance of the use of the word "all." Noting that "all" also appears in the clause defining the Supreme Court's original jurisdiction as embracing cases involving foreign envoys and those in which a state is a party, Fletcher contends that Article III's use of "all authorizes, but does not require, Congress to confer exclusive jurisdiction on the federal courts" over the cases in Amar's first tier (and to confer exclusive jurisdiction on the Supreme Court in cases affecting foreign envoys or those in which a state is a party). See Fletcher, *Congressional Power Over the Jurisdiction of Federal Courts: The Meaning of the Word "All" in Article III*, 59 Duke L.J. 929, 934 (2010). He asserts that his interpretation is consistent with Article III's text and with the Judiciary Acts of 1789 and 1801, and is somewhat, though not perfectly, consistent with Hamilton's views in Federalist No. 82 and with Justice Story's opinion in Martin v. Hunter's Lessee.

How does one make sense of the conflicting array of textual, historical, and policy evidence arrayed in the debate over two-tiered jurisdiction? Does the conflicting history and the lack of a clear purposive account of the disparity overcome that presumption? Or, put another way, is it too late in the day to reconsider the evident judgment reflected in the Judiciary Act of 1789 and subsequent jurisdictional statutes? Does the contrasting textual and early historical evidence cast doubt on whether originalism can adequately resolve this question? For an argument that the complexity and indeterminacy of the evidence suggests that the Court should eschew originalism in determining the scope of congressional jurisdiction-stripping authority, see Fallon, *Jurisdiction-Stripping Reconsidered*, 96 Va.L.Rev. 1043 (2010).

INTRODUCTORY NOTE ON JURISDICTION STRIPPING DIRECTED AT SUBSTANTIVE ENDS

Do special considerations govern the question of jurisdiction stripping when Congress restricts jurisdiction based on an evident dissatisfaction with the way the federal courts are deciding cases or, to put the point more

---

Beginning There Was None: Supreme Court Review of State Criminal Prosecutions, 90 Notre Dame L.Rev. 1867 (2015). How heavy is Professor Walsh's burden of persuasion, given that Chief Justice Marshall's opinion for the Court in Cohens v. Virginia, 19 U.S. (6 Wheat.) 264 (1821), expressed a contrary view about Section 25?

strongly, with an evident purpose to achieve certain substantive outcomes? This set of issues has existed since early in the Republic. "In the Marshall Court years, especially during the 1820's, those who perceived a tendency towards centralization in the Court's decisions proposed repealing section 25 of the 1789 Judiciary Act, which authorized Supreme Court review of certain state court judgments." Gunther, *Congressional Power to Curtail Federal Court Jurisdiction: An Opinionated Guide to the Ongoing Debate*, 36 Stan.L.Rev. 895, 896–97 (1984).

Legislative proposals to strip jurisdiction have arisen from time to time, though they have almost all invariably failed to pass into law. In the late 1950s and 1960s, members of Congress introduced bills to curb federal jurisdiction to review the admissibility of confessions in state criminal cases,[1] state legislative apportionments,[2] and legislation regulating or restricting subversive activities.[3] Beginning in the early 1970s, a number of bills sought to limit federal court jurisdiction to order busing to remedy school segregation.[4] In the 1980s, two efforts to limit jurisdiction concerned abortion and school prayer.[5] In 2004, the House of Representatives passed bills that would have eliminated federal jurisdiction over challenges to the Defense of Marriage Act and to recitations of the Pledge of Allegiance.[6]

In only one context has Congress actually enacted proposed legislation stripping the federal courts of jurisdiction with respect to a particular substantive area. In the wake of the terrorist attacks of September 11, 2001, the Detainee Treatment Act of 2005,[7] as amended by the Military Commissions Act of 2006,[8] prohibited federal (and state) courts from entertaining habeas corpus and all other actions by alien enemy combatant detainees or those awaiting determination of such status. (As explored in detail in Chapter XI, habeas corpus is a traditional form of relief the purpose of which is to permit the courts to determine if the petitioner's detention is lawful, and if not, in a classic case, to order that the petitioner be released from custody.) In the Acts, Congress substituted for habeas corpus a limited judicial review procedure in the D.C. Circuit. In Boumediene v. Bush, 553

---

[1]   See, *e.g.*, S. 917, 90th Cong., 2d Sess. (1968).

[2]   See, *e.g.*, H.R. 11926, 88th Cong., 2d Sess. (1964) (eliminating federal district court jurisdiction; one of more than fifty bills introduced in 1964 to restrict jurisdiction in reapportionment cases). See generally McKay, *Court, Congress, and Reapportionment*, 63 Mich.L.Rev. 255 (1964).

[3]   See, *e.g.*, the Jenner bill, S. 2646, 85th Cong., 1st Sess. (1957) (eliminating Supreme Court jurisdiction in cases relating to functions or practices of a congressional committee or state laws relating to subversive activities or to admission to the practice of law). For discussion of court-curbing proposals during the Warren era, see Ross, *Attacks on the Warren Court by State Officials: A Case Study of Why Court-Curbing Movements Fail*, 50 Buff.L.Rev. 483 (2002).

[4]   See, *e.g.*, Student Transportation Moratorium Act of 1972, S. 3388, 92d Cong., 2d Sess.; H.R. 13916, 92d Cong., 2d Sess.; Equal Educational Opportunities Act of 1972, S. 3395, 92d Cong., 2d Sess.; H.R. 13915, 92d Cong., 2d Sess.

[5]   See, *e.g.*, H.R. 326, 97th Cong., 1st Sess. (1981) (school prayer); H.R. 865, 97th Cong., 1st Sess. (1981) (school prayer); H.R. 867, 97th Cong., 1st Sess. (1981) (abortion).

[6]   For discussion of these and other proposals, see Norton, *Reshaping Federal Jurisdiction: Congress's Latest Challenge to Judicial Review*, 41 Wake Forest L.Rev. 1003 (2006).

[7]   119 Stat. 2739, codified at 10 U.S.C. § 801 note.

[8]   120 Stat. 2600.

U.S. 723 (2008), pp. 1507–1526, *infra*, the Supreme Court held the legislation to be an unconstitutional restriction of the guarantee of the privilege of habeas corpus contained in the "Suspension Clause" of Article I, Sec. 9. See pp. 1514, 1518, *infra*.

In recent decades, renewed interest in jurisdiction stripping has taken shape. A growing body of constitutional scholarship has posited, to differing degrees and by varying means, that the federal courts should step back from a posture of judicial supremacy in their exposition of the Constitution, leaving the people with greater responsibility to set the scope and content of constitutional powers, rights, and immunities.[9] Other recent scholarship has tied the aims of popular constitutionalism to jurisdiction stripping, proposing that the withdrawal of jurisdiction over constitutional issues provides a legitimate and effective way for the people to have voice in determining constitutional meaning.[10] Does a more thoroughgoing effort to strip jurisdiction from the federal courts or, in some cases, all courts over constitutional questions pose different questions from targeted efforts to strip jurisdiction over particular issues for which Congress disagrees with the courts' decisions on the merits?

A.   Prescribing a Rule of Decision

The next principal case, United States v. Klein, 80 U.S. (13 Wall.) 128 (1871), was the first Supreme Court case to invalidate a statutory limitation on federal court power framed in jurisdictional terms. Unfortunately, the

---

[9]   See, *e.g.*, Parker, "Here the People Rule": A Popular Constitutionalist Manifesto (1994); Tushnet, Taking the Constitution Away from the Courts (1999); Waldron, The Dignity of Legislation (1999); Bowie & Renan, *The Separation-of-Powers Counterrevolution*, 131 Yale.L.J. 2020 (2022); Post & Siegel, *Equal Protection by Law: Federal Antidiscrimination Legislation After Morrison and Kimel*, 110 Yale L.J. 441 (2000); Post & Siegel, *Protecting the Constitution from the People: Juricentric Restrictions on Section Five Power*, 78 Ind.L.J. 1 (2003). A strong competing strain of scholarship has defended Marbury-style judicial review, with the judiciary exercising the traditional power to say what the law is. See, *e.g.*, Chemerinsky, *In Defense of Judicial Review: A Reply to Professor Kramer*, 92 Calif.L.Rev. 1013 (2004); Fallon, *The Core of an Uneasy Case for Judicial Review*, 121 Harv.L.Rev. 1693 (2008); Siegel, *The Institutional Case for Judicial Review*, 97 Iowa L.Rev. 1147 (2012).

[10]   See, *e.g.*, Doerfler & Moyn, *Democratizing the Supreme Court*, 109 Calif.L.Rev. 1703 (2021); Sprigman, *Congress's Article III Power and the Process of Constitutional Change*, 95 N.Y.U.L.Rev. 1778 (2020). For an argument questioning the practical utility of jurisdiction stripping, see Epps & Trammell, *The False Promise of Jurisdiction Stripping*, 123 Colum.L.Rev. 2077 (2023).

In 2021, President Biden established a Presidential Commission on the Supreme Court of the United States to consider the "role and operation of the Supreme Court in our constitutional system" and to analyze arguments "for and against Supreme Court reform." See Presidential Commission on the Supreme Court of the United States, Final Report i (2021) (https://www. whitehouse.gov/wp-content/uploads/2021/12/SCOTUS-Report-Final-12.8.21-1.pdf). Declining to take a position on prominent jurisdiction-stripping proposals and noting disagreement among Commission members, the Commission's Final Report observed that withdrawing Supreme Court jurisdiction over particular issues—such as the validity of a wealth tax or abortion legislation—would risk creating disuniformity in the definition of federal rights or might effectively leave the determination of such rights to a single lower court (given the availability of nationwide injunctions). See *id.* 159, 161–62. The Report added that solely stripping Supreme Court jurisdiction (as opposed to also stripping jurisdiction from lower courts, federal and state) would do relatively little to enhance democratic participation in rights definition. See *id.* 160. Finally, the Report concluded that jurisdiction-stripping legislation "would likely trigger constitutional challenges," some of which the Court might deem meritorious. *Id.* 169. The likelihood of success of such challenges, it added, would diminish if Congress left open alternative avenues of judicial review, but would then raise the concerns noted above. See *id.*

Court's opinion raises more questions than it answers and can be read to support a wide range of holdings.[11] In reading Chief Justice Chase's opinion for the Court, consider whether the decision has more to do with efforts by Congress to tell a court *how* to decide—and in particular, to tell a court to decide in a way that conflicts with the Constitution—than *whether* the court may exercise jurisdiction to decide. The case that follows—Patchak v. Zinke, 583 U.S. 244 (2018)—offers some additional insight into Klein but, in part because of divisions among the Court, still leaves many open questions regarding the extent to which Article III limits Congress's power to regulate federal jurisdiction as a means to particular substantive legal ends.

———

United States v. Klein

80 U.S. (7 Wall.) 128 (1871).
Appeal from the United States Court of Claims.

[During the Civil War, federal agents, acting pursuant to wartime legislation, seized and sold a large quantity of cotton that belonged to a Southerner named Wilson. The Abandoned or Captured Property Act of March 12, 1863, 12 Stat. 820, provided that the proceeds of the sale of captured or abandoned property would be placed in the U.S. Treasury and that parties from whom property had been seized could, within two years of the suppression of the rebellion, file a claim for the net proceeds from the relevant sale in the Court of Claims, provided that parties could prove that they had "never given any aid or comfort to the present rebellion." Earlier legislation had authorized the President "by proclamation, to extend to persons who may have participated in the existing rebellion * * * pardon and amnesty, with such exceptions and at such time and on such conditions as he may deem expedient for the public welfare." Act of July 17, 1862, 12 Stat. 589, 592. On December 8, 1863, President Lincoln issued his Amnesty Proclamation pursuant to that legislation and his Article II pardon power, granting pardons to a class of persons who had engaged in the rebellion provided that they took a specific loyalty oath. Several other proclamations of pardon followed over the next five years.

[After Wilson's death, Klein, the administrator of his estate, prevailed in an action in the Court of Claims, which awarded the considerable sum of $125,300 for the loss of Wilson's cotton. In the earlier case of United States v. Padelford, 76 U.S. (11 Wall.) 531 (1870), the Supreme Court held that one who, like Wilson, had received a presidential pardon must be treated as loyal for purposes of the Constitution. The Court of Claims' ultimate judgment reaffirming the award for Wilson seemed consistent with Padelford, although it was not

---

[11] For a useful overview of the case and its context, see Tyler, *The Story of Klein: The Scope of Congress's Authority to Shape the Jurisdiction of the Federal Courts*, in Federal Courts Stories 87 (Jackson & Resnik eds. 2010).

cited. While an appeal by the United States from the judgment for Wilson's estate was pending, Congress passed a bill providing that no pardon should be admissible as proof of loyalty and, further, that acceptance of a pardon without an express disclaimer of guilt constituted "conclusive evidence" of the claimant's *disloyalty*. Act of July 12, 1870, 16 Stat. 230, 235. The statute further provided that, with respect to any pending appeal in which a claimant had prevailed based on a proffer other than affirmative proof of loyalty, "the Supreme Court shall, on appeal, have no further jurisdiction of the cause, and shall dismiss the same for want of jurisdiction." *Id*. Senator Edmunds, in response to a question whether this provision would simply require dismissal of the appeal (leaving the lower court judgment intact), said: "No; * * * we say they shall dismiss the case out of court for want of jurisdiction; not dismiss the appeal, but dismiss the case—everything." Cong.Globe, 41st Cong., 2d Sess. 3824 (1870). Consistent with that view, the statute provided that, in any case based upon a pardon, "the jurisdiction of court * * * shall cease, and the court shall forthwith dismiss the suit." 16 Stat. 235. On behalf of Wilson's estate, Klein challenged the constitutionality of the 1870 legislation.]

■ THE CHIEF JUSTICE [CHASE] delivered the opinion of the court.

* * * [T]he provision in question was introduced as a proviso to the clause in the general appropriation bill, appropriating a sum of money for the payment of judgments of the Court of Claims, and became a part of the act, with perhaps little consideration in either House of Congress.

This proviso declares in substance that no pardon, acceptance, oath, or other act performed in pursuance, or as a condition of pardon, shall be admissible in evidence in support of any claim against the United States in the Court of Claims, or to establish the right of any claimant to bring suit in that court; nor, if already put in evidence, shall be used or considered on behalf of the claimant, by said court, or by the appellate court on appeal. Proof of loyalty is required to be made according to the provisions of certain statutes, irrespective of the effect of any executive proclamation, pardon, or amnesty, or act of oblivion; and when judgment has been already rendered on other proof of loyalty, the Supreme Court, on appeal, shall have no further jurisdiction of the cause, and shall dismiss the same for want of jurisdiction. It is further provided that whenever any pardon, granted to any suitor in the Court of Claims, for the proceeds of captured and abandoned property, shall recite in substance that the person pardoned took part in the late rebellion, or was guilty of any act of rebellion or disloyalty, and shall have been accepted in writing without express disclaimer and protestation against the fact so recited, such pardon or acceptance shall be taken as conclusive evidence in the Court of Claims, and on appeal, that the claimant did give aid to the rebellion; and on proof of such pardon, or acceptance, which proof may be made summarily on motion or otherwise, the jurisdiction of the court shall cease, and the suit shall be forthwith dismissed.

The substance of this enactment is that an acceptance of a pardon, without disclaimer, shall be conclusive evidence of the acts pardoned, but shall be null and void as evidence of the rights conferred by it, both in the Court of Claims and in this court on appeal.

It was urged in argument that the right to sue the government in the Court of Claims is a matter of favor; but this seems not entirely accurate. * * *

[As constituted at the time,] [t]he Court of Claims is * * * one of those inferior courts which Congress authorizes, and has jurisdiction of contracts between the government and the citizen, from which appeal regularly lies to this court.

Undoubtedly the legislature has complete control over the organization and existence of that court and may confer or withhold the right of appeal from its decisions. And if this act did nothing more, it would be our duty to give it effect. If it simply denied the right of appeal in a particular class of cases, there could be no doubt that it must be regarded as an exercise of the power of Congress to make 'such exceptions from the appellate jurisdiction' as should seem to it expedient.

But the language of the proviso shows plainly that it does not intend to withhold appellate jurisdiction except as a means to an end. Its great and controlling purpose is to deny to pardons granted by the President the effect which this court had adjudged them to have. The proviso declares that pardons shall not be considered by this court on appeal. We had already decided that it was our duty to consider them and give them effect, in cases like the present, as equivalent to proof of loyalty. It provides that whenever it shall appear that any judgment of the Court of Claims shall have been founded on such pardons, without other proof of loyalty, the Supreme Court shall have no further jurisdiction of the case and shall dismiss the same for want of jurisdiction. The proviso further declares that every pardon granted to any suitor in the Court of Claims and reciting that the person pardoned has been guilty of any act of rebellion or disloyalty, shall, if accepted in writing without disclaimer of the fact recited, be taken as conclusive evidence in that court and on appeal, of the act recited; and on proof of pardon or acceptance, summarily made on motion or otherwise, the jurisdiction of the court shall cease and the suit shall be forthwith dismissed.

It is evident from this statement that the denial of jurisdiction to this court, as well as to the Court of Claims, is founded solely on the application of a rule of decision, in causes pending, prescribed by Congress. The court has jurisdiction of the cause to a given point; but when it ascertains that a certain state of things exists, its jurisdiction is to cease and it is required to dismiss the cause for want of jurisdiction.

It seems to us that this is not an exercise of the acknowledged power of Congress to make exceptions and prescribe regulations to the appellate power.

The court is required to ascertain the existence of certain facts and thereupon to declare that its jurisdiction on appeal has ceased, by dismissing the bill. What is this but to prescribe a rule for the decision of a cause in a particular way? In the case before us, the Court of Claims has rendered judgment for the claimant and an appeal has been taken to this court. We are directed to dismiss the appeal, if we find that the judgment must be affirmed, because of a pardon granted to the intestate of the claimants. Can we do so without allowing one party to the controversy to decide it in its own favor? Can we do so without allowing that the legislature may prescribe rules of decision to the Judicial Department of the government in cases pending before it?

We think not; and thus thinking, we do not at all question what was decided in the case of Pennsylvania v. Wheeling Bridge Company[, 59 U.S. (18 How.) 421 (1855)]. In that case, after a decree in this court that the bridge, in the then state of the law, was a nuisance and must be abated as such, Congress passed an act legalizing the structure and making it a post-road; and the court, on a motion for process to enforce the decree, held that the bridge had ceased to be a nuisance by the exercise of the constitutional powers of Congress, and denied the motion. No arbitrary rule of decision was prescribed in that case, but the court was left to apply its ordinary rules to the new circumstances created by the act. In the case before us no new circumstances have been created by legislation. But the court is forbidden to give the effect to evidence which, in its own judgment, such evidence should have, and is directed to give it an effect precisely contrary.

We must think that Congress has inadvertently passed the limit which separates the legislative from the judicial power.

It is of vital importance that these powers be kept distinct. The Constitution provides that the judicial power of the United States shall be vested in one Supreme Court and such inferior courts as the Congress shall from time to time ordain and establish. The same instrument, in the last clause of the same article, provides that in all cases other than those of original jurisdiction, 'the Supreme Court shall have appellate jurisdiction both as to law and fact, with such exceptions and under such regulations as the Congress shall make.'

Congress has already provided that the Supreme Court shall have jurisdiction of the judgments of the Court of Claims on appeal. Can it prescribe a rule in conformity with which the court must deny to itself the jurisdiction thus conferred, because and only because its decision, in accordance with settled law, must be adverse to the government and favorable to the suitor? This question seems to us to answer itself.

The rule prescribed is also liable to just exception as impairing the effect of a pardon, and thus infringing the constitutional power of the Executive.

It is the intention of the Constitution that each of the great co-ordinate departments of the government—the Legislative, the Executive, and the Judicial—shall be, in its sphere, independent of the others. To the executive alone is intrusted the power of pardon; and it is granted without limit. Pardon includes amnesty. It blots out the offence pardoned and removes all its penal consequences. It may be granted on conditions. In these particular pardons, that no doubt might exist as to their character, restoration of property was expressly pledged, and the pardon was granted on condition that the person who availed himself of it should take and keep a prescribed oath.

Now it is clear that the legislature cannot change the effect of such a pardon any more than the executive can change a law. Yet this is attempted by the provision under consideration. The court is required to receive special pardons as evidence of guilt and to treat them as null and void. It is required to disregard pardons granted by proclamation on condition, though the condition has been fulfilled, and to deny them their legal effect. This certainly impairs the executive authority and directs the court to be instrumental to that end.

We think it unnecessary to enlarge. The simplest statement is the best. * * *

■ [The dissenting opinion of JUSTICE MILLER, joined by JUSTICE BRADLEY, is omitted.]

Patchak v. Zinke

583 U.S. 244 (2018).
Certiorari to the United States Court of Appeals for the District of Columbia Circuit.

[The Match-E-Be-Nash-She-Wish Band of Pottawatomi Indians wanted to build a casino in Wayland Township, Michigan, on land known as the Bradley property. The Secretary of the Interior granted the Band's request to take the property into trust for these purposes under the Indian Reorganization Act, 25 U.S.C. § 5108. When Patchak sued to challenge the Secretary's authority, the government argued that sovereign immunity barred the suit and that Patchak lacked standing. In Match-E-Be-Nash-She-Wish Band of Pottawatomi Indians v. Patchak, 567 U.S. 209 (2012) (Patchak I), the Court rejected these claims, ruled that "Patchak's suit may proceed," and remanded the case for further proceedings. While the case was before the District Court, Congress enacted the Gun Lake Trust Land Reaffirmation Act ("Gun Lake Act"), Pub.L.No. 113–179, 128 Stat. 1913:

SEC. 2. REAFFIRMATION OF INDIAN TRUST LAND.

(a) IN GENERAL.—The land taken into trust by the United States for the benefit of the Match-E-Be-Nash-She-Wish Band of Pottawatomi Indians and described in the final Notice of

Determination of the Department of the Interior (70 Fed. Reg. 25596 (May 13, 2005)) is reaffirmed as trust land, and the actions of the Secretary of the Interior in taking that land into trust are ratified and confirmed.

(b) NO CLAIMS.—Notwithstanding any other provision of law, an action (including an action pending in a Federal court as of the date of enactment of this Act) relating to the land described in subsection (a) shall not be filed or maintained in a Federal court and shall be promptly dismissed.

[The District Court subsequently dismissed Patchak's suit on the basis of § 2(b) of the Gun Lake Act. The D.C. Circuit affirmed. The Supreme Court "granted certiorari to review whether § 2(b) violates Article III of the Constitution."]

■ JUSTICE THOMAS announced the judgment of the Court and delivered an opinion, in which JUSTICE BREYER, JUSTICE ALITO, and JUSTICE KAGAN join.

* * *

II

A

* * * The separation of powers, among other things, prevents Congress from exercising the judicial power. See Plaut v. Spendthrift Farm, Inc., 514 U.S. 211, 218 (1995). One way that Congress can cross the line from legislative power to judicial power is by "usurp[ing] a court's power to interpret and apply the law to the [circumstances] before it." Bank Markazi v. Peterson, 136 S.Ct. 1310, 1323 (2016). The simplest example would be a statute that says, "In Smith v. Jones, Smith wins." See id., at 1323, n.17. At the same time, the legislative power is the power to make law, and Congress can make laws that apply retroactively to pending lawsuits, even when it effectively ensures that one side wins. See id., at 1324–1327.

To distinguish between permissible exercises of the legislative power and impermissible infringements of the judicial power, this Court's precedents establish the following rule: Congress violates Article III when it "compel[s] . . . findings or results under old law." [Robertson v.] Seattle Audubon [Soc., 503 U.S. 429,] 438 [(1992)]. But Congress does not violate Article III when it "changes the law." Plaut, *supra*, at 218.

B

Section 2(b) changes the law. Specifically, it strips federal courts of jurisdiction over actions "relating to" the Bradley Property. Before the Gun Lake Act, federal courts had jurisdiction to hear these actions. See 28 U.S.C. § 1331. Now they do not. This kind of legal change is well within Congress' authority and does not violate Article III.

1

Section 2(b) * * * uses jurisdictional language. It states that an "action" relating to the Bradley Property "shall not be filed or maintained in a Federal court." It imposes jurisdictional consequences: Actions relating to the Bradley Property "shall be promptly dismissed." See Ex parte McCardle, 7 Wall. 506, 514 (1869) ("[W]hen [jurisdiction] ceases to exist, the only function remaining to the court is that of announcing the fact and dismissing the cause"). Section 2(b) has no exceptions. And it applies "[n]otwithstanding any other provision of law," including the general grant of federal-question jurisdiction, 28 U.S.C. § 1331. Although § 2(b) does not use the word "jurisdiction," this Court does not require jurisdictional statutes to "incant magic words." Sebelius v. Auburn Regional Medical Center, 568 U.S. 145, 153 (2013). Indeed, § 2(b) uses language similar to other statutes that this Court has deemed jurisdictional. * * *

* * * Because § 2(b) addresses "a court's competence to adjudicate a particular category of cases," Wachovia Bank, N.A. v. Schmidt, 546 U.S. 303, 316 (2006), it is best read as a jurisdiction-stripping statute.

2

Statutes that strip jurisdiction "chang[e] the law" for the purpose of Article III, Plaut, supra, at 218, just as much as other exercises of Congress' legislative authority. Article I permits Congress "[t]o constitute Tribunals inferior to the supreme Court," § 8, and Article III vests the judicial power "in one supreme Court, and in such inferior Courts as the Congress may from time to time ordain and establish," § 1. These provisions reflect the so-called Madisonian Compromise, which resolved the Framers' disagreement about creating lower federal courts by leaving that decision to Congress. Congress' greater power to create lower federal courts includes its lesser power to "limit the jurisdiction of those Courts." United States v. Hudson, 7 Cranch 32, 33 (1812); accord, Lockerty v. Phillips, 319 U.S. 182, 187 (1943). So long as Congress does not violate other constitutional provisions, its "control over the jurisdiction of the federal courts" is "plenary." Trainmen v. Toledo, P. & W.R. Co., 321 U.S. 50, 63–64 (1944). Thus, when Congress strips federal courts of jurisdiction, it exercises a valid legislative power no less than when it lays taxes, coins money, declares war, or invokes any other power that the Constitution grants it.

Indeed, this Court has held that Congress generally does not violate Article III when it strips federal jurisdiction over a class of cases. [The opinion here recounts the circumstances of Ex parte McCardle, 74 U.S. 506 (1866).][4]

---

[4]   The dissent appears to disagree with McCardle, questions the motives of the unanimous Court that decided it, asserts that it is "inconsistent" with Klein, and distinguishes it on the ground that the statute there "did not foreclose all avenues of judicial review." But the core holding of McCardle—that Congress does not exercise the judicial power when it strips jurisdiction over a class of cases—has never been questioned, has been repeatedly reaffirmed,

This Court has reaffirmed these principles on many occasions. Congress generally does not infringe the judicial power when it strips jurisdiction because, with limited exceptions, a congressional grant of jurisdiction is a *prerequisite* to the exercise of judicial power. See Steel Co. v. Citizens for Better Environment, 523 U.S. 83, 94–95 (1998); Cary v. Curtis, 3 How. 236, 245 (1845). Congress' power over federal jurisdiction is "an essential ingredient of separation and equilibration of powers, restraining the courts from acting at certain times, and even restraining them from acting permanently regarding certain subjects." Steel Co., *supra*, at 101. * * *

III

Patchak does not dispute Congress' power to withdraw jurisdiction from the federal courts. He instead raises two arguments why § 2(b) violates Article III, even if it strips jurisdiction. First, relying on United States v. Klein, 13 Wall. 128 (1872), Patchak argues that § 2(b) flatly directs federal courts to dismiss lawsuits without allowing them to interpret or apply any new law. Second, relying on Plaut, 514 U.S. 211, Patchak argues that § 2(b) attempts to interfere with this Court's decision in Patchak I—specifically, its conclusion that his suit "may proceed," 567 U.S., at 212. We reject both arguments.

A

Section 2(b) does not flatly direct federal courts to dismiss lawsuits under old law. It creates new law for suits relating to the Bradley Property, and the District Court interpreted and applied that new law in Patchak's suit. Section 2(b)'s "relating to" standard effectively guaranteed that Patchak's suit would be dismissed. But "a statute does not impinge on judicial power when it directs courts to apply a new legal standard to undisputed facts." Bank Markazi, 136 S.Ct., at 1325. * * *

Patchak argues that the last four words of § 2(b)—"shall be promptly dismissed"—direct courts to reach a particular outcome. But a statute does not violate Article III merely because it uses mandatory language. See Seattle Audubon, 503 U.S., at 439. Instead of directing outcomes, the mandatory language in § 2(b) "simply imposes the consequences" of a court's determination that it lacks jurisdiction because a suit relates to

---

and was reaffirmed in Klein itself. See [United States v. Klein,] 13 Wall. [128], at 145 [(1872)] ("[T]here could be no doubt" that Congress can "den[y] the right of appeal in a particular class of cases"). And if there is any inconsistency between the two, this Court has said that it is Klein—not McCardle—that "cannot [be] take[n] . . . 'at face value.'" Bank Markazi, *supra*, at 228. Moreover, it is true that McCardle emphasized that the statute there did not withdraw "the whole appellate power of the court, *in cases of habeas corpus*." But McCardle's reservation, this Court later explained, was responding to a potential problem under the Suspension Clause, not a potential problem under Article III. See Ex parte Yerger, 8 Wall. 85, 102–103 (1869) ("We agree that [jurisdiction] is given subject to exception and regulation by Congress; but it is too plain for argument that the denial to this court of appellate jurisdiction in this class of cases must greatly weaken the efficacy of the writ"); *id.*, at 96 ("It would have been . . . a remarkable anomaly if this court . . . had been denied, under a constitution which absolutely prohibits suspension of the writ, except under extraordinary exigencies, that power in cases of alleged unlawful restraint").

the Bradley Property. Miller v. French, 530 U.S. 327, 349 (2000); see McCardle, 7 Wall., at 514.

Patchak compares § 2(b) to the statute this Court held unconstitutional in Klein. * * *

This Court has since explained that "the statute in Klein infringed the judicial power, not because it left too little for courts to do, but because it attempted to direct the result without altering the legal standards governing the effect of a pardon—standards Congress was powerless to prescribe." Bank Markazi, *supra*, at 1324. Congress had no authority to declare that pardons are not evidence of loyalty, so it could not achieve the same result by stripping jurisdiction whenever claimants cited pardons as evidence of loyalty. See Klein, 13 Wall., at 147–148. Nor could Congress confer jurisdiction to a federal court but then strip jurisdiction from that same court once the court concluded that a pardoned claimant should prevail under the statute. See *id.*, at 146–147.

* * * Section 2(b) does not attempt to exercise a power that the Constitution vests in another branch. And unlike the selective jurisdiction-stripping statute in Klein, § 2(b) strips jurisdiction over every suit relating to the Bradley Property. Indeed, Klein itself explained that statutes that do "nothing more" than strip jurisdiction over "a particular class of cases" are constitutional. *Id*, at 145. That is precisely what § 2(b) does.

B

Section 2(b) does not unconstitutionally interfere with this Court's decision in Patchak I. Article III, this Court explained in Plaut, prohibits Congress from "retroactively commanding the federal courts to reopen final judgments." 514 U.S., at 219. But Patchak I did not finally conclude Patchak's case. When this Court said that his suit "may proceed," 567 U.S., at 212, it meant that the Secretary's preliminary defenses lacked merit and that Patchak could return to the District Court for further proceedings. It did not mean that Congress was powerless to change the law that governs his case. As this Court emphasized in Plaut, Article III does not prohibit Congress from enacting new laws that apply to pending civil cases. See 514 U.S., at 226–227. When a new law clearly governs pending cases, Article III does not prevent courts from applying it because "each court, at every level, must 'decide according to existing laws.'" *Ibid.* (quoting United States v. Schooner Peggy, 1 Cranch 103, 109 (1801)). This principle applies equally to statutes that strip jurisdiction. See Landgraf v. USI Film Products, 511 U.S. 244, 274 (1994). * * * [B]ecause Patchak's suit is not final, applying § 2(b) here does not offend Article III.

Of course, we recognize that the Gun Lake Act was a response to this Court's decision in Patchak I. The text of the Act, after all, cites both the administrative decision and the property at issue in that case. See §§ 2(a)(b). And we understand why Patchak would view the Gun Lake

Act as unfair. By all accounts, the Band exercised its political influence to persuade Congress to enact a narrow jurisdiction-stripping provision that effectively ends all lawsuits threatening its casino, including Patchak's.

But the question in this case is "[n]ot favoritism, nor even corruption, but power." Plaut, *supra*, at 228; see also McCardle, 7 Wall., at 514 ("We are not at liberty to inquire into the motives of the legislature. We can only examine into its power under the Constitution"). Under this Court's precedents, Congress has the power to "apply newly enacted, outcome-altering legislation in pending civil cases," Bank Markazi, 136 S.Ct., at 1325, even when the legislation "govern[s] one or a very small number of specific subjects," *id.*, at 1328. For example, this Court has upheld narrow statutes that identified specific cases by caption and docket number in their text. See *id.*, at 1326–1327; Seattle Audubon, 503 U.S., at 440. * * * If these targeted statutes did not cross the line from legislative to judicial power, then § 2(b) does not either.

IV

The dissent offers a different theory for why § 2(b) violates Article III. A statute impermissibly exercises the judicial power, the dissent contends, when it "targets" a particular suit and "manipulates" jurisdiction to direct the outcome, "practical[ly] operat[es]" to affect only one suit, and announces a legal standard that does not "imply some measure of generality" or "preserv[e] . . . an adjudicative role for the courts."

We doubt that the constitutional line separating the legislative and judicial powers turns on factors such as a court's doubts about Congress' unexpressed motives, the number of "cases [that] were pending when the provision was enacted," or the time left on the statute of limitations. But even if it did, we disagree with the dissent's characterization of § 2(b). Nothing on the face of § 2(b) is limited to Patchak's case, or even to his challenge under the Indian Reorganization Act. Instead, the text extends to all suits "relating to" the Bradley Property. Thus, § 2(b) survives even under the dissent's theory: It "prospectively govern[s] an open-ended class of disputes," and its "relating to" standard "preserv[es] . . . an adjudicative role for the courts". * * * [T]his Court's precedents *encourage* Congress to draft jurisdictional statutes in this manner.

* * *

We conclude that § 2(b) of the Gun Lake Act does not violate Article III of the Constitution. The judgment of the Court of Appeals is, therefore, affirmed.

It is so ordered.

■ JUSTICE BREYER, concurring.

The statutory context makes clear that this is not simply a case in which Congress has said, "In Smith v. Jones, Smith wins." In 2005, the

Secretary of the Interior announced her decision to take the Bradley Property into trust for an Indian Tribe, the Match-E-Be-Nash-She-Wish Band of Pottawatomi Indians. See 70 Fed.Reg. 25596 (2005). The petitioner brought suit, claiming that the Secretary lacked the statutory authority to do so.

Congress then enacted the law here at issue. * * * The first part "reaffirm[s]," "ratifie[s]," and "confirm[s]" the Secretary's "actions in taking" the Bradley Property "into trust," as well as the status of the Bradley Property "as trust land." § 2(a). The second part says that actions "relating to" the Bradley Property "shall not be filed or maintained in a Federal court and shall be promptly dismissed." § 2(b). Read together, Congress first made certain that federal statutes gave the Secretary the authority to take the Bradley Property into trust, and second tried to dot all the i's by adding that federal courts shall not hear cases challenging the land's trust status. The second part, the jurisdictional part, perhaps gilds the lily, perhaps simplifies judicial decisionmaking (the judge need only determine whether a lawsuit relates to the Bradley Property), but, read in context, it does no more than provide an alternative legal standard for courts to apply that seeks the same real-world result as does the first part: The Bradley Property shall remain in trust.

The petitioner does not argue that Congress acted unconstitutionally by ratifying the Secretary's actions and the land's trust status, and I am aware of no substantial argument to that effect. See United States v. Heinszen & Co., 206 U.S. 370, 382–383, 387 (1907) (Congress may retroactively ratify Government action that was unauthorized when taken). The jurisdictional part of the statute therefore need not be read to do more than eliminate the cost of litigating a lawsuit that will inevitably uphold the land's trust status.

This case is consequently unlike United States v. Klein, 13 Wall. 128 (1872), where this Court held unconstitutional a congressional effort to use its jurisdictional authority to reach a result (involving the pardon power) that it could not constitutionally reach directly. *Id.*, at 146. And the plurality, in today's opinion, carefully distinguishes from the case before us other circumstances where Congress' use of its jurisdictional power could prove constitutionally objectionable. Here Congress has used its jurisdictional power to supplement, without altering, action that no one has challenged as unconstitutional. Under these circumstances, I find its use of that power unobjectionable. And, on this understanding, I join the plurality's opinion.

■ JUSTICE GINSBURG, with whom JUSTICE SOTOMAYOR joins, concurring in the judgment.

What Congress grants, it may retract. That is undoubtedly true of the Legislature's authority to forgo or retain the Government's sovereign immunity from suit. The Court need venture no further to decide this case.

[Justice Ginsburg proceeded to argue that in the Gun Lake Act, "Congress acted effectively to displace the [Administrative Procedure Act's] waiver of immunity for suits against the United States" with respect to suits related to the Bradley Property.]

■ JUSTICE SOTOMAYOR, concurring in the judgment.

I agree with the dissent that Congress may not achieve through jurisdiction stripping what it cannot permissibly achieve outright, namely, directing entry of judgment for a particular party. I also agree that an Act that merely deprives federal courts of jurisdiction over a single proceeding is not enough to be considered a change in the law and that any statute that portends to do so should be viewed with great skepticism. I differ with the dissent's ultimate conclusion only because, as Justice GINSBURG explains, the Gun Lake Trust Land Reaffirmation Act (Gun Lake Act) should not be read to strip the federal courts of jurisdiction but rather to restore the Federal Government's sovereign immunity. * * *

■ CHIEF JUSTICE ROBERTS, with whom JUSTICE KENNEDY and JUSTICE GORSUCH join, dissenting.

Two Terms ago, this Court unanimously agreed that Congress could not pass a law directing that, in the hypothetical pending case of Smith v. Jones, "Smith wins." Bank Markazi v. Peterson, 136 S.Ct. 1310, 1323, n.17 (2016). Today, the plurality refuses to enforce even that limited principle in the face of a very real statute that dictates the disposition of a single pending case. Contrary to the plurality, I would not cede unqualified authority to the Legislature to decide the outcome of such a case. Article III of the Constitution vests that responsibility in the Judiciary alone.

I

A

* * * The Framers' decision to establish a judiciary "truly distinct from both the legislature and the executive," The Federalist No. 78, p. 466 (C. Rossiter ed. 1961) (A. Hamilton), was born of their experience with legislatures "extending the sphere of [their] activity and drawing all power into [their] impetuous vortex," id., No. 48, at 309 (J. Madison). Throughout the 17th and 18th centuries, colonial legislatures routinely functioned as courts of equity, "grant[ing] exemptions from standing law, prescrib[ing] the law to be applied to particular controversies, and even decid[ing] the merits of cases." Manning, *Response, Deriving Rules of Statutory Interpretation from the Constitution,* 101 Colum.L.Rev. 1648, 1662 (2001). In Virginia, for instance, Thomas Jefferson lamented that the assembly had, "in many instances, decided rights which should have been left to judiciary controversy." Notes on the State of Virginia 120 (W. Peden ed. 1982). And in Pennsylvania, the Council of Censors—a body charged with ensuring compliance with the state constitution—denounced the state assembly's practice of "extending their deliberations

to the cases of individuals" in order to ease the "hardships which will always arise from the operation of general laws." Report of the Committee of the Pennsylvania Council of Censors 38, 43 (F. Bailey ed. 1784). * * *

Given the "disarray" produced by this "system of legislative equity," the Framers resolved to take the innovative step of creating an independent judiciary. Plaut v. Spendthrift Farm, Inc., 514 U.S. 211, 221 (1995). They recognized that such a structural limitation on the power of the legislative and executive branches was necessary to secure individual freedom. * * *

The Constitution's division of power thus reflects the "concern that a legislature should not be able unilaterally to impose a substantial deprivation on one person." INS v. Chadha, 462 U.S. 919, 962 (1983) (Powell, J., concurring in judgment). The Framers protected against that threat, both in "specific provisions, such as the Bill of Attainder Clause," and in the "general allocation" of the judicial power to the Judiciary alone. *Ibid.* As Chief Justice Marshall wrote, the Constitution created a straightforward distribution of authority: The Legislature wields the power "to prescribe general rules for the government of society," but "the application of those rules to individuals in society" is the "duty" of the Judiciary. Fletcher v. Peck, 6 Cranch 87, 136 (1810). Article III, in other words, sets out not only what the Judiciary can do, but also what Congress cannot.

Congress violates this arrangement when it arrogates the judicial power to itself and decides a particular case. We first enforced that rule in United States v. Klein, 13 Wall. 128 (1872)[.] * * *

* * * As we also explained in United States v. Sioux Nation, 448 U.S. 371, 398 (1980), because Congress has "no judicial powers" to render judgment "directly," it likewise cannot do so indirectly, by "direct[ing] . . . a court to find a judgment in a certain way." That sort of legislative intervention constitutes an exercise of the judicial power, leaving "the court no adjudicatory function to perform." *Id.*, at 392. * * *

II

Congress has previously approached the boundary between legislative and judicial power, but it has never gone so far as to target a single party for adverse treatment and direct the precise disposition of his pending case. Section 2(b)—remarkably—does just that.

The plurality cites a smattering of "narrow statutes" that this Court has previously upheld. Yet none is as brazen as § 2(b), either in terms of dictating a particular outcome or in singling out a particular party. Indeed, the bulk of those cases involved statutes that prospectively governed an open-ended class of disputes and left the courts to apply any new legal standard in the first instance. [Here, the dissent discussed Pennsylvania v. Wheeling & Belmont Bridge Co., 18 How. 421 (1856), and Robertson v. Seattle Audubon Soc., 503 U.S. 429 (1992), observing that in the latter case,] the statute at issue made reference to specific cases only as a shorthand for identifying preexisting environmental law requirements. *Id.*, at 440. The statute applied generally—"replac[ing] the legal standards" for timber harvesting across 13 national forests—and explicitly reserved for judicial determination whether pending and future timber sales complied with the new standards. *Id.*, at 437.

Even Bank Markazi, which disclaimed a number of limits on Congress's authority to intervene in ongoing litigation, did not suggest that Congress could dictate the result in a pending case. There, Congress inserted itself into a long-running dispute over whether terrorist victims could satisfy their judgments against Iran's central bank, enacting a statute that eliminated certain legal impediments to obtaining the bank's assets. We upheld the law because it "establish[ed] new substantive standards" and entrusted "application of those standards" to the court. 136 S.Ct., at 1326.

But the Court in Bank Markazi did not have before it anything like § 2(b), which prevents the court from applying any new legal standards and explicitly dictates the dismissal of a pending proceeding. The Court instead stressed that the judicial findings contemplated by the statute in Bank Markazi left "plenty" for the court "to adjudicate" before ruling that the bank was liable. *Id.*, at 1325, n.20. The law, for instance, did not define the terms "beneficial interest" and "equitable title." The District Court needed to resolve the scope of those phrases. Nor did it decide whether the assets were owned by the bank. That issue was also assigned to the court. And lastly, the statute did not settle whether the assets were held in New York or Luxembourg. The court had to sort that out too. See *ibid.* Section 2(b) goes much further * * * by disposing of the case outright, wresting any adjudicative responsibility from the courts. * * * [I]t is idle to suggest that § 2(b) preserves any role for the court beyond that of stenographer.

In addition, the Court in Bank Markazi repeatedly emphasized that the law was not a "one-case-only regime." 136 S.Ct., at 1317. The law instead governed a category of postjudgment execution claims filed by over a thousand plaintiffs who, in 16 different actions, had obtained judgments against Iran in excess of $1.75 billion—facts suggesting more generality than is true of many Acts of Congress.

By contrast, § 2(b) targets a single pending case. Although the formal language of the provision—reaching any action "relating to" the Bradley Property—could theoretically suggest a broader application, its practical operation unequivocally confirms that it concerns solely Patchak's suit. See Commodity Futures Trading Comm'n v. Schor, 478 U.S. 833, 851 (1986) (explaining that the Court "review[s] Article III challenges . . . with an eye to the practical effect that the congressional action will have on the constitutionally assigned role of the federal judiciary"). [Here, the dissent noted that no other cases were pending when Congress enacted § 2(b) and the Tribe conceded that no additional challenges could be brought "due to the expiration of the statute of limitations."] The plurality thus is simply incorrect when it asserts that the Act applies to a broad "class of cases." * * *

This is not a question of probing Congress's "unexpressed motives." The text and operation of the provision instead make clear that the range of potential applications is a class of one. Congress, in crafting a law tailored to Patchak's suit, has pronounced the equivalent of "Smith wins."

III

* * * In [the plurality's] view, § 2(b) falls comfortably within Congress's power to regulate the jurisdiction of the federal courts, and accordingly does not constitute an exercise of judicial power.

But nothing in § 2(b) specifies that the statute is jurisdictional. That has special significance: To rein in "profligate use of the term 'jurisdiction,'" this Court in recent cases has adopted a "bright line" rule treating statutory limitations as nonjurisdictional unless Congress "clearly states" otherwise. Sebelius v. Auburn Regional Medical Center, 568 U.S. 145, 153 (2013); Arbaugh v. Y & H Corp., 546 U.S. 500, 515–516 (2006). * * *

* * * [W]hile the greater power to create inferior federal courts generally includes the power to strip those courts of jurisdiction, at a certain point that lesser exercise of authority invades the judicial function. "Congress has the power (within limits) to tell the courts what *classes* of cases they may decide, but not to prescribe or superintend how they decide those cases." Arlington v. FCC, 569 U.S. 290, 297 (2013) (majority opinion of Scalia, J.) (emphasis added; citations omitted). In other words, Congress cannot, under the guise of altering federal jurisdiction, dictate the result of a pending proceeding.

Klein, after all, drew precisely the same distinction when it considered the provision stripping jurisdiction over any suit based on a pardon. Chief Justice Chase's opinion for the Court explained that if the statute had "simply" removed jurisdiction over "a particular class of cases," it would be regarded as "an exercise of the acknowledged power of Congress to make exceptions and prescribe regulations to the appellate power." 13 Wall., at 145, 146. But because the withdrawal of jurisdiction was a "means to an end," founded "solely on the application of a rule of decision," the Court held that the law violated the separation of powers. *Ibid.*; see R. Fallon, J. Manning, D. Meltzer, & D. Shapiro, Hart and Wechsler's The Federal Courts and the Federal System 324 (7th ed.2015) (recognizing that "not every congressional attempt to influence the outcome of cases, even if phrased in jurisdictional language, can be justified as a valid exercise of a power over jurisdiction").

Contrary to the plurality, I would hold that Congress exercises the judicial power when it manipulates jurisdictional rules to decide the outcome of a particular pending case. Because the Legislature has no authority to direct entry of judgment for a party, it cannot achieve the same result by stripping jurisdiction over a particular proceeding. Does the plurality really believe that there is a material difference between a law stating "The court lacks jurisdiction over Jones's pending suit against Smith" and one stating "In the case of Smith v. Jones, Smith wins"? In both instances, Congress has resolved the specific case in Smith's favor.

Over and over, the plurality intones that § 2(b) does not impinge on the judicial power because the provision "changes the law." But all that § 2(b) does is deprive the court of jurisdiction in a single proceeding. * * * In my view, the concept of "changing the law" must imply some measure of generality or preservation of an adjudicative role for the courts. * * *

The closest analogue is of course Ex parte McCardle, 7 Wall. 506 (1869)[.] * * *

The Court's decision in McCardle has been alternatively described as "caving to the political dominance" of the Radical Republicans or "acceding to Congress's effort to silence the Court." Meltzer, The Story of Ex parte McCardle, in Federal Courts Stories 73 (V. Jackson & J. Resnick eds. 2010). Read for all it is worth, the decision is also inconsistent with the approach the Court took just three years later in Klein, where Chief Justice Chase (a dominant character in this drama) stressed that "[i]t is of vital importance" that the legislative and judicial powers "be kept distinct." 13 Wall., at 147.

The facts of McCardle, however, can support a more limited understanding of Congress's power to divest the courts of jurisdiction. For starters, the repealer provision * * * applied to a class of cases, barring anyone from invoking the Supreme Court's appellate jurisdiction in habeas cases for the next two decades. In addition, the Court's decision did not foreclose all avenues for judicial review of McCardle's complaint. As Chase made clear in the penultimate paragraph of the opinion—and confirmed later that year in his opinion for the Court in Ex parte Yerger, 8 Wall. 85 (1869)—the statute did not deny "the whole appellate power of the Court." 7 Wall., at 515. McCardle, by taking a different procedural route and filing an original habeas action, could have had his case heard on the merits.[3]

Section 2(b), on the other hand, has neither saving grace. It ends Patchak's suit for good. * * * Because § 2(b) singles out Patchak's suit, specifies how it must be resolved, and deprives him of any judicial forum for his claim, the decision to uphold that provision surpasses even McCardle as the highwater mark of legislative encroachment on Article III.

---

[3] The plurality surmises that McCardle reserved an alternative avenue for relief in response to a perceived problem under the Suspension Clause. But regardless of the basis for that reservation, our point is simply that, in sustaining a jurisdictional repeal that leaves a claimant without any prospect for relief, the plurality goes beyond what the Court in McCardle upheld.

* * * In no uncertain terms, the plurality disavows any limitations on Congress's power to determine judicial results, conferring on the Legislature a colonial-era authority to pick winners and losers in pending litigation as it pleases. * * *

* * *

The Framers saw this case coming. They knew that if Congress exercised the judicial power, it would be impossible "to guard the Constitution and the rights of individuals from . . . serious oppressions." The Federalist No. 78, at 469 (A. Hamilton). Patchak thought his rights were violated, and went to court. He expected to have his case decided by judges whose independence from political pressure was ensured by the safeguards of Article III—life tenure and salary protection. It was instead decided by Congress, in favor of the litigant it preferred, under a law adopted just for the occasion. But it is our responsibility under the Constitution to decide cases and controversies according to law. It is our responsibility to, as the judicial oath provides, "administer justice without respect to persons." 28 U.S.C. § 453. And it is our responsibility to "firm[ly]" and "inflexibl[y]" resist any effort by the Legislature to seize the judicial power for itself. The Federalist No. 78, at 470.

I respectfully dissent.

NOTE ON JURISDICTION STRIPPING AS A MEANS TO AN END

(1) Klein and Article III. Though Delphic in its reasoning, Klein stands as an important Article III precedent because it was the first case, and remains one of the only cases, to invalidate a jurisdiction-stripping provision on Article III grounds. Klein stands for at least the proposition that Congress's attempt to regulate jurisdiction is not a talisman that renders any such legislative effort constitutional. The most straightforward reading of Klein is that Congress may not use its authority over jurisdiction to prescribe a rule of decision in a particular case.

The precise nature of the constitutional harm, however, is not fully evident from the Court's opinion. The Court reasons at a high level "that Congress has inadvertently passed the limit which separates the legislative from the judicial power," but it does not say precisely how. Could it be as simple as the idea that Congress cannot use its control over jurisdiction to usurp the law declaration authority implicit in "[t]he judicial Power"—to invade "the province and duty of the judicial department to say what the law is" when it decides a case or controversy? Marbury v. Madison, 5 U.S. (1 Cranch) 137, 177 (1803). If Congress told the Court how to interpret a presidential pardon, was it usurping the Marbury power plain and simple? More broadly, one could read Klein as supporting a conception of judicial integrity: Congress may not, in the guise of enacting jurisdictional legislation, direct a federal court to decide a case in a fashion that conflicts with the Constitution.

Broader still, Professor Young reads Klein as suggesting that Congress may not regulate a federal court's deliberative processes in a variety of ways. Young, *United States v. Klein, Then and Now*, 44 Loy.U.Chi.L.J. 265 (2012). Among the prohibited regulations would be some restrictions on fact-finding in constitutional cases (*e.g.*, conclusive or rebuttable presumptions that are probabilistically unreasonable) and some prescription of the interpretive methods followed when interpreting the Constitution and statutes.[1] Certainly, Congress has broad authority, presumably under the Necessary and Proper Clause,[2] to regulate judicial practice and procedure,[3] to prescribe rules of interpretation,[4] to establish standards of review for agency action,[5] and the like. What is the principle that distinguishes when Congress has moved from legitimately exercising authority over judicial procedure to impermissibly interfering with inherent Article III powers?

Perhaps the problem with the 1870 legislation was that it left the Court to hear the entire class of cases involving claims for the recovery of property confiscated during the Civil War—and lost jurisdiction only to decide cases in a particular way that Congress disfavored. In other words, it might be one thing for the Congress to say that the Supreme Court lacks jurisdiction to hear First Amendment cases, but another to say, "The Supreme Court shall have no jurisdiction to overrule Red Lion Broadcasting Co. v. FCC, 395 U.S. 367 (1969)." Even framed in that way, can it be that every congressional attempt to influence the outcome of cases, even if phrased in jurisdictional language, violates Article III? What criteria should inform the distinction between valid and invalid attempts to influence the outcome of cases?

(2) Limits on the Klein Principle. Read for all its worth, Klein might mean that Congress violates Article III whenever it uses jurisdiction to "prescribe rules of decision to the Judicial Department * * * in cases pending before it." It is doubtful, however, that this language can be taken at face

---

[1]   Professor Sager goes even farther, reading Klein to mean that "[t]he judiciary will not allow itself to be made to speak and act against its own best judgment on matters within its competence which have great consequence for our political community." Sager, *Klein's First Principle: A Proposed Solution*, 86 Geo.L.J. 2525, 2529 (1998). As an example, he mentions the Religious Freedom Restoration Act (RFRA), 107 Stat. 1488, codified at 42 U.S.C. § 2000bb *et seq.*, which enacted a rule of decision for religious freedom that the Court had rejected as a constitutional standard under the Free Exercise Clause. But isn't there a difference between statutes (arguably like that in Klein) that direct courts how to apply the Constitution, and statutes, like RFRA, that create statutory rules of decision whose content differs from that of the Constitution? See Meltzer, *Congress, Courts, and Constitutional Remedies*, 86 Geo.L.J. 2537, 2540–41 (1998) (suggesting Sager's reading of Klein is overly broad and would endanger other statutes—such as the Voting Rights Act Amendments of 1982 and the Pregnancy Discrimination Act of 1978—that created statutory bans on conduct the Supreme Court had ruled was not unconstitutional).

[2]   See generally Manning, *The Supreme Court, 2013 Term—Foreword: The Means of Constitutional Power*, 128 Harv.L.Rev. 1 (2014).

[3]   See, *e.g.*, Hanna v. Plumer, 380 U.S. 460, 463–64 (1965); Sibbach v. Wilson & Co., 312 U.S. 1, 9–10 (1941); Bank of the U.S. v. Halstead, 23 U.S. (10 Wheat.) 51, 53–54 (1825).

[4]   See 1 U.S.C. § 1 *et seq.* (the Dictionary Act). See also Rosenkranz, *Federal Rules of Statutory Interpretation*, 115 Harv.L.Rev. 2085 (2002).

[5]   See, *e.g.*, Allentown Mack Sales and Service, Inc. v. NLRB, 522 U.S. 359 (1998) (applying the "substantial evidence" test prescribed by the Administrative Procedure Act, 5 U.S.C. § 706); Universal Camera Corp. v. NLRB, 340 U.S. 474 (1951) (same).

value, given the Court's longstanding recognition that Congress has broad authority to make retroactive legislation applicable to pending cases.[6]

Consider Patchak. Justice Thomas's plurality opinion, joined by Justices Breyer, Alito, and Kagan, emphasized that a jurisdiction-stripping statute runs afoul of Article III if it "compel[s] . . . findings or results under old law," but not if it creates new law. The plurality ruled that the Gun Lake Act *changed* the law respecting federal jurisdiction, a permissible exercise of legislative power under Article I, § 8, and Article III, § 1. The plurality then distinguished Klein on the ground that the statute at issue there had sought to use jurisdiction to produce an outcome indirectly that Congress could not produce directly.

Is the plurality's reasoning persuasive? Chief Justice Roberts's dissenting opinion analogized the Gun Lake Act to a statute "directing that, in the hypothetical pending case of Smith v. Jones, 'Smith wins.' " For the dissent, it did not seem to matter that Congress could validly enact legislation retroactively confirming (or establishing) the trust status of the contested parcel of land. Instead, for Chief Justice Roberts, the form of the legislation was problematic because it resembled the founding-era state practice of legislative revision of judgments, something the Framers designed Article III to repudiate.

Patchak relied on two cases similarly rejecting Klein challenges. Bank Markazi v. Peterson, 578 U.S. 212 (2016) (6–2), arose out of an effort to enforce judgments entered against the Republic of Iran for terrorism-related harms under a "terrorism exception" to the Foreign Sovereign Immunities Act (FSIA). In consolidated litigation involving sixteen groups of respondents consisting of more than 1,000 plaintiffs, the enforcement proceedings in the U.S. District Court for the Southern District of New York focused on certain assets in a New York bank account that, according to the respondents, was owned by Bank Markazi, Iran's central bank. Petitioners contested the claim that the assets in question belonged to the Bank. In light of that dispute, a provision in the Iran Threat Reduction and Syria Human Rights Act of 2012, 22 U.S.C. § 8772, provided that, if the district court made several specified findings, it could enforce respondents' underlying judgments against the financial assets "that are identified in and the subject of * * * Case No. 10 Civ. 4518 (BSJ) (GWG)."

Petitioners argued that in enacting § 8772, Congress invaded the judicial function by imposing a rule of decision on the district court in a pending case. Justice Ginsburg's opinion for the Court rejected the

---

[6]   As Chief Justice Marshall wrote for the Court: "It is in the general true that the province of an appellate court is only to enquire whether a judgment when rendered was erroneous or not. But if subsequent to the judgment and before the decision of the appellate court, a law intervenes and positively changes the rule which governs, the law must be obeyed, or its obligation denied." United States v. Schooner Peggy, 5 U.S. (1 Cranch) 103, 110 (1801); see also, *e.g.*, Henderson v. United States, 568 U.S. 266, 271 (2013); Thorpe v. Housing Authority of Durham, 393 U.S. 268, 281 (1969); Ziffrin v. United States, 318 U.S. 73, 78 (1943). With ordinary economic legislation, the Court will uphold the retroactive adjustment of legal benefits and burdens provided that there is a rational basis for the retroactivity. See, *e.g.*, United States v. Carlton, 512 U.S. 26, 30–31 (1994); Pension Ben. Guar. Corp. v. R.A. Gray & Co., 467 U.S. 717, 728–29 (1984); Usery v. Turner Elkhorn Mining Co., 428 U.S. 1, 16–18 (1976).

contention, drawing a distinction between prescribing rules of decision and " 'amend[ing] applicable law.' " In this instance, the Court held, Congress had merely amended existing law, a conclusion that was unaffected by the fact that Congress specified the docket number of the proceedings to which its new policy applied. In a dissent joined by Justice Sotomayor, Chief Justice Roberts, as he would do again later in Patchak, argued that Congress rather than the judiciary had, in reality, decided the case. The dissent reasoned that if the legislature "targeted [the] specific case and eliminated [one party's] specific defenses so as to ensure [the other's] victory," then the judiciary "presided over [a] *fait accompli*," and the effect was no different from "a law saying 'respondents win.' " Such a statute, according to the Chief Justice, ignored the historical context and contradicted the purpose of the Founders' decision to establish an independent judiciary.

Patchak and Bank Markazi both relied, in turn, on Robertson v. Seattle Audubon Soc., 503 U.S. 429 (1992), which involved two lawsuits alleging that that the U.S. Forest Service's plan to permit timber harvesting in areas that were home to the Northern Spotted Owl violated the Endangered Species Act and other federal statutes. While those cases were pending, Congress, as part of an appropriations bill, enacted a provision, known as Section 318, that contained a management plan for timber harvesting only in such areas. Section 318 declared that management of the forests in accordance with the plan set forth in that section constituted "adequate consideration for the purpose of meeting the statutory requirements that are the basis for the consolidated cases captioned Seattle Audubon Society et al., v. F. Dale Robertson, Civil No. 89–160 and Washington Contract Loggers Assoc. et al., v. F. Dale Robertson, Civil No. 89–99 (order granting preliminary injunction) and the case Portland Audubon Society et al., v. Manuel Lujan, Jr., Civil No. 87–1160–FR." The Ninth Circuit, citing Klein, held Section 318 unconstitutional, concluding that Congress had not repealed or amended the environmental laws underlying the pending lawsuits, but had instead attempted to direct a result contrary to the law as judicially interpreted and thereby violated Article III. The Supreme Court, however, unanimously disagreed, contending that, even though it specified the relevant docket numbers of the pending cases affected, Section 318 did not instruct a court in how to apply pre-existing legal standards to pending cases, but rather amended those standards.

Is Congress really just "dot[ting] all the i's," as Justice Breyer said in Patchak, when it also strips jurisdiction in pending cases or when, as in Bank Markazi and Robertson, it also specifies the rule of decision in particular cases identified by docket number? Consider an Article II analogy: Congress at times has included in the appropriations for the U.S. Department of Justice a rider stating, "None of the funds appropriated * * * may be used for any activity, the purpose of which is to overturn * * * the per se prohibition on resale price maintenance in effect under Federal antitrust laws." Pub.L.No. 98–166, § 510, 97 Stat. 1071, 1102 (1983). The purpose of these riders was to prevent the Department from arguing that the Supreme Court should overrule its decision in Dr. Miles Medical Co. v. John D. Park & Sons Co., 220 U.S. 373 (1911). See H.R.Rep. No. 237, 102d Cong., 1st Sess. 3–7

(1991) (describing the aim of the Dr. Miles riders). Even though Congress could validly have codified Dr. Miles, did it infringe Article II for Congress instead to limit the executive's ability to argue, if that was its view, that Dr. Miles misread the antitrust laws and should be overruled? Is the problem in such a case, if any, one of transparency?[7]

(3) What Remains of Klein. After Patchak, Bank Markazi, and Robertson, does Klein now stand largely (or only) for the proposition that Congress cannot use jurisdiction to achieve indirectly a disposition that it could not achieve directly under the Constitution? The Court in Bank Markazi seems to suggest as much, reasoning that "the statute in Klein infringed the judicial power, not because it left too little for courts to do, but because it attempted to direct the result without altering the legal standards governing the effect of a pardon—standards Congress was powerless to prescribe." Perhaps this means that the problem in Klein was not that the Court used jurisdiction stripping as a means to an end or attempted to prescribe a rule of decision by specifying the evidentiary effect of a pardon. Is it possible to understand Klein instead as turning on Article II rather than Article III? Recall that the Court in Padelford had already held that a presidential pardon of someone who had given aid and comfort to the rebellion required return of property confiscated during the Civil War—or, at least, return of the net proceeds held in the U.S. Treasury from the sale of such confiscated property pursuant to the Act of March 12, 1863. Hence, the Court in Klein held that the practical effect of the jurisdiction stripping effected by the 1870 legislation was to impair the effect of a pardon and thus "infring[e] the constitutional power of the Executive." Perhaps Klein, then, despite its complicated reasoning stands for a straightforward proposition: Congress may not, in the guise of enacting jurisdictional legislation, direct a federal court to decide a case in a fashion that conflicts with the Constitution.

How far does this principle go? Does it support the position that legislation precluding Supreme Court jurisdiction, or jurisdiction of all federal courts, in cases challenging school prayer, for example, would be in service of a forbidden purpose and therefore beyond Congress's power to make exceptions to the Court's appellate jurisdiction?[8] If so, how strong is

---

[7] Another reading of Klein sees it as establishing that Congress may not deceive the electorate about the way in which legislation operates—a principle that Congress was said to have violated by enacting evidentiary rules the effect of which was to transform the meaning of the law that provided compensation to loyal owners of property. See Redish & Pudelski, *Legislative Deception, Separation of Powers, and the Democratic Process: Harnessing the Political Theory of United States v. Klein*, 100 Nw.U.L.Rev. 437 (2006); accord, Vladeck, *Why Klein (Still) Matters: Congressional Deception and the War on Terrorism*, 5 J.Nat'l Security L. & Pol'y 251 (2011). Professor Young, *supra*, casts doubt on this view of Klein and questions the appropriateness of judicial evaluation of purported legislative deceptiveness. (Moreover, how deceptive, really, was the statute at issue in Klein?) For a somewhat different take on Klein, see Zoldan, *The Klein Rule of Decision Puzzle and the Self-Dealing Solution*, 74 Wash. & Lee L.Rev. 2133 (2017), which argues that Klein is best understood as the instantiation of the background constitutional principle that Congress may not engage in self-dealing—in this case, by gerrymandering jurisdiction to favor the government and disfavor a claimant against the public fisc.

[8] Roughly contemporaneous cases decided on the authority of Klein include Armstrong v. United States, 80 U.S. (13 Wall.) 154 (1872), and Witkowski v. United States, 7 Ct.Cl. 393 (1872). In both, the courts refused to be bound by the provision of the statute involved in Klein ordering courts to dismiss suits for want of jurisdiction upon the introduction of a pardon.

that support given that the Klein judgment is adequately supported by narrower reasoning, including the entirely plausible understanding that the rule of decision whose application Congress directed would have required the courts to abridge the President's pardon power?

(4) Stripping Jurisdiction over Classes of Cases. The Court in Klein observed that if Congress "simply denied the right of appeal in a particular class of cases, there could be no doubt that it must be regarded as an exercise of the power of Congress to make 'such exceptions from the appellate jurisdiction' as should seem to it expedient." This, the Court said, stood in contrast with a jurisdiction-stripping statute "founded solely on the application of a rule of decision," which the Court associated with the idea that "[t]he court has jurisdiction of the cause to a given point; but when it ascertains that a certain state of things exists, its jurisdiction is to cease and it is required to dismiss the cause for want of jurisdiction."

Are the two types of situations readily distinguished in practice? What if Congress had succeeded in passing proposed legislation that eliminated federal jurisdiction over particular subject matter areas such as legislative reapportionment, school desegregation, abortion, or school prayer?[9] Should one distinguish laws stripping jurisdiction over particular subject areas from laws denying federal jurisdiction to hear constitutional challenges to certain kinds of laws?

There is little precedent that considers the constitutionality of congressional exclusion of a class of constitutional cases from lower federal court jurisdiction. But one decision possibly implicating such a situation involved the Norris-LaGuardia Act of 1932, 29 U.S.C. §§ 101–115, which sharply restricts the jurisdiction of "courts of the United States" to issue temporary or permanent injunctions in "a case involving or growing out of a labor dispute." The term "court of the United States" is defined to mean "any court of the United States whose jurisdiction has been or may be conferred or defined or limited by Act of Congress."

Before the Act's adoption, Truax v. Corrigan, 257 U.S. 312 (1921), had found *state* legislation similarly limiting employers' remedies to be

---

According to Professor Young, these decisions take an important step beyond Klein, which in his terms involved a "puppeteering" provision of the statute ordering the Supreme Court to reverse a decision rendered by a lower court. See Young, *A Critical Reassessment of the Case Law Bearing on Congress's Power to Restrict the Jurisdiction of the Lower Federal Courts*, 54 Md.L.Rev. 132, 158–59 (1995). By contrast, Young argues, Armstrong and Witkowski involved a "court-stripping" portion of the statute purporting to deprive *trial* courts of jurisdiction over a defined class of cases. He concludes that "[i]t seems impossible to distinguish * * * the plaintiff in Armstrong from plaintiffs today who might seek federal court enforcement of modern constitutional rights, such as busing or abortion rights, despite a statute which purports to close off the federal courts." *Id.* at 164.

Under a statute that authorizes lower courts to entertain claims, but orders them to dismiss those claims for want of jurisdiction upon proof of a presidential pardon, is the line between "puppeteering" and "court stripping" as clear as Young suggests?

[9] See Baucus & Kay, *The Court Stripping Bills: Their Impact on the Constitution, the Courts, and Congress*, 27 Vill.L.Rev. 998, 990–94 (1982) (collecting examples); Norton, *Reshaping Federal Jurisdiction: Congress's Latest Challenge to Judicial Review*, 41 Wake Forest L.Rev. 1003, 1008–10 (2006) (same). See also, *e.g.*, H.R. 326, 97th Cong., 1st Sess. (1981) (proposal to restrict federal jurisdiction over cases involving school prayer); H.R. 865, 97th Cong., 1st Sess. (1981) (school prayer); H.R. 867, 97th Cong., 1st Sess. (1981) (abortion).

unconstitutional. More specifically, Truax found that (a) the denial of *all* effective remedies for violation of common law rights would offend due process, and (b) state legislation depriving employers in labor disputes of injunctive remedies against the invasion of common law property rights, when injunctions were available to others who suffered similar invasions, denied equal protection.

Relying on those precedents, in Lauf v. E.G. Shinner & Co., 303 U.S. 323 (1938), an employer challenged the constitutionality of the Norris-LaGuardia Act insofar as it sharply restricted, but did not completely abolish, the authority of a federal court to enjoin allegedly unlawful picketing and related activities. As the Supreme Court noted, the substantive rights of the parties were governed by state law and federal jurisdiction rested on diversity. The district court (affirmed by the court of appeals) had issued an injunction, finding that there was no labor dispute regulated by the Act. The Supreme Court reversed, ruling that the Act did apply and that the district court, because it had not made the findings required by the Act in order to issue an injunction in a labor dispute, had exceeded its jurisdiction. "There can be no question," the Court said, "of the power of Congress thus to define and limit the jurisdiction of the inferior courts of the United States." But the Court did not discuss the Truax decision, even though both the employer's brief and the two dissenting Justices relied upon it, nor did the Court directly address the constitutionality of statutory limits on the provision of injunctive relief to employers.

With respect to internal restraints, given that the employer could have sued in state court, where the Norris-LaGuardia Act does not apply, does Lauf v. Shinner establish that the Constitution does not "give people any right to proceed or be proceeded against, in the first instance, in a federal rather than a state court"? Hart, *Dialogue*, 66 Harv.L.Rev. at 1363.[10] (Does that distinguish Lauf from Klein, given that the waiver of sovereign immunity to sue the United States would not have allowed Klein to pursue his claim in state court?) Or should Lauf be read more narrowly—for example, as resting on the ground that the limits imposed by the Act on issuance of a federal injunctive remedy were constitutionally unexceptionable? The latter view is supported by Young, note 8, *supra*. He argues, *inter alia*, that by 1938, when Lauf was decided, the Supreme Court no longer would have thought that the Due Process Clause required labor injunctions in any more than (at most) a narrow class of cases, to which Lauf did not belong. And he adds that the relevant holding of Truax v. Corrigan was that a *state* had denied the employer equal protection, a significant point given that the Court did not subject *federal* action to equal protection scrutiny until 1954, see Bolling v. Sharpe, 347 U.S. 497 (1954). On this view, the Norris-LaGuardia Act did not prevent the federal courts from awarding

---

[10]   The Senate and House Judiciary Committees that drafted the Norris-LaGuardia Act believed that the availability of state remedies satisfied the Constitution. See Frankfurter & Greene, The Labor Injunction 213–14 (1930). Is it fair to say that the theory of the legislation was that the Constitution may impose more stringent limitations on state power to restrict state court jurisdiction than on federal power to restrict federal jurisdiction? Does this make sense?

any relief that was constitutionally required by either the Due Process or Equal Protection Clauses.

What, then, does Lauf v. Shinner imply about external restraints? The Norris-LaGuardia Act was clearly motivated by objections to the substance of federal judicial decisions (including constitutional decisions like Truax) in labor disputes. See Cox, Law and National Labor Policy 4–8 (1960). Does the Act therefore unconstitutionally "burden" federal constitutional rights? Note that within a few years of the Norris-LaGuardia Act, Congress passed two other measures that also sharply limit federal court power in particular subject matter areas. The Tax Injunction Act, 28 U.S.C. § 1341, limits authority to issue injunctions in disputes about state taxes, and the Johnson Act, 28 U.S.C. § 1342, limits authority to enjoin state public utility rate orders.[11] See generally Chap. X, Sec. 1(B), *infra*.

Do these statutes, and the Supreme Court's acceptance of their constitutionality, establish that "the basic structure of article III affords" Congress the power to "redraw[ ] jurisdictional lines in part because it dislikes certain federal court decisions"? Gunther, *Congressional Power to Curtail Federal Court Jurisdiction: An Opinionated Guide to the Ongoing Debate*, 36 Stan.L.Rev. 895, 919–20 (1984). Would the analysis change if Congress's motive in withdrawing federal jurisdiction were to send cases to state courts that were viewed as less receptive to constitutional challenges?[12] If Congress sought to invite state court defiance of Supreme Court precedents interpreting the Constitution?[13] Consider in this regard a bill introduced in 2005 (but not enacted) that not only stripped the lower federal courts and the Supreme Court of jurisdiction to entertain challenges to governmental "acknowledgment of God as the sovereign source of law, liberty, or government," but also provided that any federal court or Supreme Court decision on such an issue (whether rendered before or after the effective date of the Act) "is not binding precedent on any State court."[14]

B. Stripping Federal and State Jurisdiction

The preceding discussion of congressional regulation of federal court jurisdiction has assumed in each case that, whatever the limits on federal court jurisdiction, the state courts remained open to litigate the merits of any claim. The next case raises the question of the constitutionality of

---

[11]   The Johnson Act, in particular, deprives the federal district courts of jurisdiction over rate orders where such jurisdiction "is based solely on diversity of citizenship or repugnance of the order to the Federal Constitution," where the order "does not interfere with interstate commerce," where it has been made "after reasonable notice and hearing," and where there is a "speedy and efficient" state court remedy. 28 U.S.C. § 1342. Does the Act operate like the problematic regime in Klein, preserving jurisdiction to give relief on some grounds but denying on others? Again, is the key difference that the state courts are open here?

[12]   There is limited evidence in the legislative record that some opponents of the Johnson Act feared that the state courts were less likely to vindicate the federal constitutional claims over which the Act eliminated federal jurisdiction. See 78 Cong.Rec. 2,029 (1934).

[13]   See Ely, *Legislative and Administrative Motivation in Constitutional Law*, 79 Yale L.J. 1205, 1306–08 (1970). See also Gressman & Gressman, *Necessary and Proper Roots of Exceptions to Federal Jurisdiction*, 51 Geo.Wash.L.Rev. 495 (1983).

[14]   Constitutional Restoration Act of 2005, S. 520, 109th Cong., 1st Sess.

congressional efforts to preclude the jurisdiction of both the federal courts and the state courts, leaving a litigant with no court in which to bring suit.[15]

Battaglia v. General Motors Corp.

169 F.2d 254 (2d Cir. 1948).
Appeals from the District Court of the United States for the
Western District of New York.

■ Before SWAN, AUGUSTUS N. HAND and CHASE, CIRCUIT JUDGES.

■ CHASE, CIRCUIT JUDGE:

[The Fair Labor Standards Act of 1938 (FLSA), 29 U.S.C. §§ 201–219, requires that covered employees be paid at least one and one-half times their regular wage rate for hours worked in excess of a 40-hour work week. The Act makes employers liable for unpaid overtime and for an additional, equal amount as liquidated damages.

[In three decisions in 1946, the Supreme Court unexpectedly interpreted the statutory term "work week" as including underground travel, and similar preliminary activities, of employees in iron ore mines. Under these decisions, many employees' work week now exceeded forty hours, resulting in monetary liability under the FLSA.

[Between July 1, 1946, and January 31, 1947, nearly two thousand lawsuits based on the Supreme Court's decisions were filed in federal district courts. Collectively, these actions sought more than $5 billion; the potential liability of the United States, on War Department cost-plus contracts, was estimated at $1.4 billion.

[Moved by these facts, on May 14, 1947, Congress enacted the Portal-to-Portal Act of 1947, 29 U.S.C. §§ 251–62. Finding that the recent decisions created immense and unexpected liabilities that would ruin many employers, bestow windfalls on employees, and seriously affect the United States Treasury, sections 2(a) and (b) of the Act eliminated the substantive liability that the Supreme Court had recognized. These subsections provided (with limited exceptions) that "[n]o employer shall be subject to any liability" under the FLSA for the failure to compensate employees for the preliminary work at issue.

[In addition, section 2(d) of the Act provided: "No court of the United States, of any State, Territory, or possession of the United States, or of the District of Columbia, shall have jurisdiction of any action or proceeding, whether instituted prior to or on or after May 14, 1947, to enforce liability or impose punishment for or on account of the failure of

---

[15]   The constitutional issues arising from the substitution of non-Article III federal tribunals for Article III courts are discussed in Section 2 of this Chapter. This Note addresses issues arising when Congress tries to withdraw jurisdiction from all "courts," with that term here understood to encompass so-called "Article I" or "legislative" courts—which are discussed extensively in Section 2—as well as Article III courts and state courts.

the employer to pay minimum wages or overtime compensation under the Fair Labor Standards Act of 1938 * * *, to the extent that such action or proceeding seeks to enforce any liability or impose any punishment with respect to an activity which was not compensable under subsections (a) and (b) of this section."

[The Battaglia decision involved four lawsuits filed against General Motors by employees alleging that the company had violated their right, under the Supreme Court's 1946 trio of decisions, to time and a half for hours over forty per week. While the actions were pending in the district court, the Portal-to-Portal Act was adopted. General Motors then moved to dismiss the complaints,] on the grounds that no cause of action was alleged and that the court was without jurisdiction by virtue of section 2 of the Portal-to-Portal Act. * * * [T]he appellants then questioned this statute upon constitutional grounds * * *. [Ultimately, the district court granted the motions to dismiss.]

* * * [T]he issue of the constitutionality of this section of the Portal-to-Portal Act has been presented by these appeals. * * * It was the duty of the court to ascertain whether it had jurisdiction before proceeding to hear and decide the case on the merits. * * * If subdivision (d) of section 2 of the Act is valid the lack of jurisdiction is clear and if subdivisions (a) and (b) of section 2 are valid it is equally apparent that no cause of action on the merits was alleged. We think the dismissal of each cause of action right, for the following reasons.

A few of the district court decisions sustaining section 2 of the Portal-to-Portal Act have done so on the ground that since jurisdiction of federal courts other than the Supreme Court is conferred by Congress, it may at the will of Congress be taken away in whole or in part. * * * [T]hese district court decisions would, in effect, sustain subdivision (d) of section 2 of the Act regardless of whether subdivisions (a) and (b) were valid. We think, however, that the exercise of Congress of its control over jurisdiction is subject to compliance with at least the requirements of the Fifth Amendment. That is to say, while Congress has the undoubted power to give, withhold, and restrict the jurisdiction of courts other than the Supreme Court,[4] it must not so exercise that power as to deprive any person of life, liberty, or property without due process of law or to take private property without just compensation. Thus, regardless of whether subdivision (d) of section 2 had an independent end in itself, if one of its effects would be to deprive the appellants of property without due process or just compensation, it would be invalid. Under this view, subdivision (d) on the one hand and subdivisions (a) and (b) on the other will stand or fall together. We turn then to a consideration of the question whether the appellants have been unconstitutionally deprived of any substantive rights.

---

    [4]   It also has the power, of course, to make "exceptions" to and "regulations" regarding the Supreme Court's appellate jurisdiction. U.S. Const. Art. III, § 2.

[After examining the statute and the employees' contracts, the court noted] three ways in which the employees' rights to compensation for these activities may be viewed: first, as wholly statutory up to the time the Portal-to-Portal Act was enacted; second, as purely statutory up to the time of the Supreme Court decisions and contractual thereafter; and finally, as wholly contractual from the beginning. * * * [W]e think that however appellants' rights are considered, the Portal-to-Portal Act is constitutional.

This seems plain enough, if we take the view that the claims rested purely on statute up to the time the Portal-to-Portal Act was enacted. Clearly, the general rule is that "powers derived wholly from a statute are extinguished by its repeal." Flanigan v. County of Sierra, 196 U.S. 553, 560. * * * This being true, so long as the claims, if they were purely statutory, had not ripened into final judgment, regardless of whether the activities on which they were based had been performed, they were subject to whatever action Congress might take with respect to them.

If however, the rights were statutory up to the time of the Supreme Court decisions and contractual thereafter, or if they were founded upon contract from the time of the enactment of the Fair Labor Standards Act, the problem is not so simple, for there are a number of cases holding that it is a violation of due process to deprive an individual of previously vested contractual rights.

But the solution to the problem seems quite as clear. * * * [If the FLSA previously made the employees' contracts include the right to compensation for portal-to-portal activities, the Portal-to-Portal Act did away with that aspect of the contracts.] Very closely in point is Louisville & Nashville R. Co. v. Mottley, 219 U.S. 467, where a contract to furnish transportation free of charge—valid when made * * *—was held unenforceable when Congress later * * * made it unlawful for railroads to provide such transportation. * * * The Supreme Court there said: "The agreement between the railroad company and the Mottleys must necessarily be regarded as having been made subject to the possibility that, as some future time, Congress might so exert its * * * power in regulating interstate commerce as to render that agreement unenforceable * * *. * * * If that principle be not sound, the result would be individuals and corporations could, by contracts between themselves, in anticipation of legislation, render of no avail the exercise of Congress, to the full extent authorized by the Constitution, of its power to regulate commerce. No power of Congress can be thus restricted." 219 U.S. at pages 482, 485, 486. * * *

Nor is the Portal-to-Portal Act a violation of Article III of the Constitution or an encroachment upon the separate power of the judiciary. True enough, decisions of the Supreme Court played their part in creating the conditions Congress undertook to remedy * * *. But those decisions were construing a previously enacted statute. The regulatory legislation did not attempt to change these decisions in any way, or to impose upon the courts any rule of decision not in conformity with basic legal concepts, as in United States v. Klein, 13 Wall. 128. On the contrary, it left express private contracts and those implied in fact, except to the extent that they may be said to have had reference to prior statutory law, untouched and enforceable in the courts as before under the applicable legal principles. It did not require repayment of any money paid in reliance upon the decisions of the Supreme Court. It left valid final judgments for portal-to-portal pay. Since Congress, for the reasons heretofore stated, otherwise had the power to enact the Portal-to-Portal Act, the fact that one of the Act's incidental effects is to prevent the courts from following the [Supreme Court's decisions interpreting the FLSA] is of no importance. * * *

Judgments affirmed.

NOTE ON PRECLUSION OF ALL JUDICIAL REVIEW AND ON THE RIGHT TO SEEK JUDICIAL REDRESS

(1) **The Reach of the Battaglia Principle.** Although the court of appeals found the plaintiffs' constitutional claim wanting on the merits, it did not treat Congress's preclusion of federal and state court jurisdiction as barring it from examining the merits. Rather, the court suggested that the validity of the jurisdiction-stripping provision and the substantive provisions of the Portal-to-Portal Act "stand or fall together." In other words, the court reasoned, if the substantive provisions of the Act deprived petitioners of property without due process or just compensation, then the jurisdiction-stripping provision would itself be invalid because it effectively denied petitioners redress for the deprivation of their property.

Importantly, despite a provision purporting to strip the lower federal courts (among others) of jurisdiction, the court of appeals took jurisdiction to determine whether that very provision was unconstitutional. Does Battaglia illustrate Professor Hart's contention that it is "a necessary postulate of constitutional government" that "a court must always be available to pass on claims of constitutional right to judicial process, and to provide such process if the claim is sustained"? Hart, *Dialogue*, 66 Harv.L.Rev. at 1372. If so, would that mean that a court always has jurisdiction to determine the validity of a provision denying it jurisdiction? What if the Portal-to-Portal Act had added a subsection (e) that explicitly said, "No court of the United States, of any State, Territory, or possession of the United States, or of the District of Columbia, shall have jurisdiction of any action or proceeding seeking to adjudicate the constitutionality of the jurisdictional provisions in subsection (d)"? Because the jurisdiction of the lower federal courts such as the court of appeals depends on a grant from Congress, should the presumption be that state courts, whose jurisdiction comes from the state itself, provide the more appropriate forum to review the validity of a thoroughgoing jurisdiction-stripping provision?

(2) Constitutional Avoidance by the Supreme Court. The Supreme
Court has ordinarily found ways to avoid squarely facing the question
whether Congress may strip all courts of jurisdiction to entertain
constitutional claims. Thus, in Webster v. Doe, 486 U.S. 592 (1988), an action
by a former CIA employee against the CIA Director alleging an unlawful
discharge, the Court interpreted a statutory review provision as barring
consideration of non-constitutional challenges but not constitutional
challenges. In finding that the provision did not satisfy the "heightened
showing" of intent required to construe it as barring judicial review of
constitutional challenges, the Court noted the " 'serious constitutional
question' that would arise if a federal statute were construed to deny any
judicial forum for a colorable constitutional claim."

Other cases have similarly strained to construe statutes to permit
judicial review of constitutional questions. See, *e.g.*, Bowen v. Michigan
Academy of Family Physicians, 476 U.S. 667, 681 n.12 (1986) (finding that a
statutory bar of judicial review of certain Medicare awards did not
encompass constitutional challenges—a ruling that avoided the "serious
constitutional question" that would otherwise be presented); Johnson v.
Robison, 415 U.S. 361, 366–67 (1974) (holding that a statute making benefits
decisions of the Veterans Administration "final" and nonreviewable did not
apply to constitutional challenges to the validity of legislative classifications,
since preclusion of such challenges would raise serious questions about the
provision's constitutionality). *Cf.* Cuozzo Speed Technologies, LLC v. Lee,
579 U.S. 261, 275 (2016) (reserving the question whether a statute barring
judicial review of certain decisions by the Director of the Patent Office
applies to constitutional questions).

(3) Preclusion of Review and Rights to Remedies. A litigant's claim to
possess a right to judicial redress for a constitutional violation necessarily
has two components. First, was there a constitutional violation: for example,
does a challenged government action abridge free speech or deny equal
protection? Second, even where there is a constitutional violation, to what
remedy, if any, is the litigant constitutionally entitled?

Any claim that the Constitution guarantees any particular remedy, or
indeed even that it guarantees some remedy, for a constitutional violation
can be in some tension with well-established doctrines. In Webster v. Doe,
Paragraph (2), *supra*, Justice Scalia's dissent noted that the Court has
"found some constitutional claims to be beyond judicial review because they
involve 'political questions.' " A second pertinent doctrine is that of sovereign
immunity, which loosely holds that neither the states nor the United States
can be sued in their own names without their consent—even for
constitutional violations.[1] Justice Scalia's dissent described sovereign
immunity as "a monument to the principle that some constitutional claims
can go unheard."

The constitutional text refers to only two remedies: (1) a right to just
compensation for takings and (2) the privilege of the writ of habeas corpus,

---

[1]   The political question doctrine is explored in Chap. II, Sec. 6, *supra*. Sovereign
immunity is extensively discussed in Chap. IX, Secs. 1 and 2A, *infra*.

a means of contesting the legality of executive detention. In Marbury v. Madison, 5 U.S. (1 Cranch) 137, 163 (1803), Chief Justice Marshall, quoting Blackstone, famously said that " 'it is a general and indisputable rule, that where there is a legal right, there is also a legal remedy by suit or action at law, whenever that right is invaded.' " William Marbury, of course, claimed a violation of a *non-constitutional* right to a judicial commission. And as a statement about remedies for constitutional violations, Marshall's dictum is more of an aspiration than a hard and fast rule. In numerous situations, there is no remedy for an acknowledged violation of constitutional rights— including in cases in which damages seem to be the only appropriate remedy, but all defendants are immune from damages liability (the government because of sovereign immunity, and individual officials because of official immunity). See generally Fallon, *Some Confusions About Due Process, Judicial Review, and Constitutional Remedies*, 93 Colum.L.Rev. 309, 329– 39, 366–72 (1993). By contrast, the right to seek a writ of habeas corpus, at least in circumstances falling within the core of the historical understanding of the writ, is more firmly grounded. Thus, the question whether one has a constitutional right to a remedy is neither a single nor a simple question.[2] Compare Fallon & Meltzer, *New Law, Non-Retroactivity, and Constitutional Remedies*, 104 Harv.L.Rev. 1731, 1778–79 (1991) (arguing that the U.S. constitutional tradition reflects two remedial principles: (1) a strong but not unyielding constitutional principle that there should be individually effective redress for all violations of constitutional rights—a principle that is sometimes outweighed by practical imperatives, such as those underlying the varied immunity doctrines; and (2) a structural principle that "demands a system of constitutional remedies adequate to keep government generally within the bounds of law"; it is "more unyielding in its own terms, but can tolerate the denial of particular remedies, and sometimes of [any] individual redress [to the victim of a constitutional violation]").

The availability of damages and injunctive relief for federal law violations, and Congress's role in regulating such relief, is explored more fully in Chap. VII, pp. 917–949, *infra*, and Chap. IX, pp. 1184–1190, 1200– 1210, *infra*. The distinctive questions relating to claims of a constitutional right to habeas corpus are explored in the immediately following Note and in Chapter XI, pp. 1506–1536, *infra*.

(4) Congress's Authority to Deprive State Courts of Jurisdiction over Constitutional Questions. As explored throughout this section, Congress's authority to regulate the jurisdiction of the federal courts springs from both Article I and Article III and, as is explored in the next section, Congress has broad authority to regulate statutory rights that it creates under Article I. As has also been explored in this section and is analyzed more fully in section 3 of this chapter, the Madisonian Compromise contemplates an important role for state courts in adjudicating federal rights along with a correlative role for Congress in regulating state court

---

[2]   For an analysis of congressional power to control jurisdiction, stressing its interconnection with the scope of Congress's power to preclude the award of a particular remedy, or in some cases to preclude any and all remedies, and suggesting that Congress may sometimes lack a valid source of legislative authority to strip all courts of jurisdiction, see Fallon, *Jurisdiction-Stripping Reconsidered*, 96 Va.L.Rev. 1043 (2010).

jurisdiction to some extent with respect to jurisdiction to adjudicate such rights. But where does Congress—if anywhere—draw constitutional authority to deprive willing state courts of jurisdiction to decide federal constitutional questions? Dorf, *Congressional Power to Strip State Courts of Jurisdiction*, 97 Tex.L.Rev. 1 (2018), suggests that the Necessary and Proper Clause may give Congress power to strip state and federal court jurisdiction over the constitutionality of *federal* statutes, but that Congress does not have the authority to strip state courts of their jurisdiction to determine the constitutionality of *state* statutes. What, if any, is the argument to the contrary?

FURTHER NOTE ON PRECLUSION OF ALL JUDICIAL REVIEW AND ON THE RIGHT TO SEEK JUDICIAL REDRESS: HABEAS CORPUS AND THE SUSPENSION CLAUSE

(1) The Writ and the Suspension Clause. A distinctive question about congressional power to preclude judicial review in both state and federal court concerns limitations on judicial authority to award the writ of habeas corpus. First developed in English common law courts, the writ is a means of testing the lawfulness of detention. Historically its central role was to permit a court to oversee the legality of detention imposed extra-judicially by executive officials. Traditionally, in such cases, if detention is deemed to be unlawful, a court exercising habeas corpus jurisdiction orders that the prisoner be discharged from confinement.

Any effort by Congress to preclude courts from providing the remedy of habeas corpus implicates not only Article III and the Due Process Clause but also the Suspension Clause of the Constitution, Article I, § 9, cl. 2, which states: "The Privilege of the Writ of Habeas Corpus shall not be suspended, unless when in Cases of Rebellion or Invasion the public Safety may require it." The provision testifies to the founding generation's understanding that the writ was an established and fundamental guarantee of liberty. Yet while the Clause plainly was designed to constrain power to suspend the writ, the text offers few clues as to the meaning of the "Privilege of the Writ" referenced therein. For greater discussion of what the constitutional privilege may entail, see pp. 1461–1465, *infra*. One uncertainty is whether the Suspension Clause, though not worded as an affirmative guarantee that habeas corpus will be available, should be so understood. Because Congress, beginning with the Judiciary Act of 1789, has always vested some form of habeas corpus jurisdiction in the federal courts, the question whether the Constitution requires the availability of such jurisdiction has rarely arisen. In recent decades, the Supreme Court has addressed that question when confronted by two different contexts in which Congress has moved to curtail the availability of habeas corpus—specifically, in legislating with respect to immigration and the attacks of September 11, 2001.

(2) Immigration Detention, the St. Cyr Case, and Thuraissigiam. In Immigration and Naturalization Serv. v. St. Cyr, 533 U.S. 289 (2001), the Court for the first time stated that the Suspension Clause restricts

Congress's power to preclude review of the legality of federal executive detentions. St. Cyr, a Haitian citizen lawfully resident in the United States, pled guilty to a criminal charge, triggering a provision of the immigration laws that in early 1996 presumptively required his deportation. At that time, however, the Attorney General had broad discretion to waive deportation. Because the INS commenced deportation proceedings against St. Cyr after the effective dates of two 1996 statutes, the Antiterrorism and Effective Death Penalty Act of 1996 (AEDPA), Pub. L. No. 104–132, 110 Stat. 1214, and the Illegal Immigration Reform and Immigrant Responsibility Act of 1996 (IIRIRA), Pub. L. No. 104–208, 110 Stat. 3009, the Attorney General took the position that those statutes withdrew her discretion to waive deportation.

St. Cyr brought a federal habeas corpus proceeding arguing that he had a statutory right to have the Attorney General consider (in her discretion) whether to waive deportation; that the Attorney General's contrary view was legally mistaken; and hence his deportation, a form of custody, was contrary to law. In response, the government argued that the court lacked jurisdiction to consider St. Cyr's legal arguments, because all judicial review was expressly precluded by a provision of AEDPA titled "Elimination of Custody Review by Habeas Corpus" and by three separate provisions of IIRIRA, including 8 U.S.C. § 1252(a)(2)(c), which reads: "Notwithstanding any other provision of law * * * no court shall have jurisdiction to review any final order of removal against an alien who is removable by reason of having committed [one or more enumerated] criminal offense[s]," including the offense of which St. Cyr had been convicted.

The statutes appeared to preclude judicial review of the deportation order in the federal court of appeals (as the Court held in a companion case, Calcano-Martinez v. INS, 533 U.S. 348 (2001)) and in the state courts. The question was whether there existed any court in which St. Cyr could make his legal argument. The Supreme Court concluded that the 1996 amendments had not foreclosed jurisdiction to reach St. Cyr's legal claim under the pre-existing general grant of habeas corpus jurisdiction in 28 U.S.C. § 2241. In reaching that conclusion, the Court relied heavily on a series of interpretive presumptions: "the strong presumption in favor of judicial review of administrative action" (citing, *e.g.*, Bowen v. Michigan Academy of Family Physicians, 476 U.S. 667 (1986), p. 462, *supra*);[1] "the longstanding rule requiring a clear statement of congressional intent to repeal habeas jurisdiction" (citing Ex parte Yerger, 75 U.S. (8 Wall.) 85 (1869), p. 419, *supra*, and Felker v. Turpin, 518 U.S. 651 (1996), p. 364, *supra*); and most important of all, the presumption that statutes should be construed, where possible, to avoid serious constitutional problems.

For present purposes, the key statement in Justice Stevens's majority opinion was that a finding of preclusion of review "of a pure question of law by any court would give rise to substantial constitutional questions" under the Suspension Clause: "[A]t the absolute minimum, the Suspension Clause protects the writ 'as it existed in 1789.' * * * At its historical core, the writ of

---

[1]   For a sustained critique of the presumption of reviewability, see Bagley, *The Puzzling Presumption of Reviewability*, 127 Harv.L.Rev. 1285 (2014).

habeas corpus has served as a means of reviewing the legality of executive detention * * *. [Historically,] the issuance of the writ was not limited to challenges to the jurisdiction of the custodian, but encompassed detentions based on errors of law, including the erroneous application or interpretation of statutes."

On the more specific question whether habeas corpus was available "to redress the improper exercise of official discretion," Justice Stevens viewed the historical evidence as equivocal, but noted the "substantial evidence to support the proposition that pure questions of law like the one raised by [St. Cyr] could have been answered in 1789 by a common-law judge with power to issue the writ of habeas corpus. It necessarily follows that a serious Suspension Clause issue would be presented if we were to accept the INS's submission that the 1996 statutes have withdrawn that power from federal judges and provided no adequate substitute for its exercise."

Justice Stevens next held that the language of IIRIRA precluding "judicial review" of and "jurisdiction to review" removal orders did not withdraw federal habeas corpus jurisdiction because "[i]n the immigration context, 'judicial review' and 'habeas corpus' have historically distinct meanings." He similarly concluded that the key provision of AEDPA should be read narrowly and, because it did not refer expressly to the general grant of habeas corpus jurisdiction under § 2241, it should not be construed to have eliminated it. The Court proceeded to reach the merits and hold that the elimination of the Attorney General's authority to grant discretionary relief did not apply retroactively to persons like St. Cyr who might have pled guilty in reliance on their eligibility at that time to seek waivers of deportation.

In dissent, Justice Scalia (joined by Chief Justice Rehnquist and Justice Thomas and in part by Justice O'Connor) protested that the majority found "ambiguity in the utterly clear" IIRIRA's language only by "fabricat[ing] a superclear statement, 'magic words' requirement * * * unjustified in law and unparalleled in any other area of our jurisprudence." He argued that constitutional avoidance was not implicated, as the Suspension Clause does not "guarantee[ ] any particular habeas right that enjoys immunity from suspension" but ensures only that whatever privileges of habeas corpus may exist at any particular time may not be suspended except in cases of rebellion or invasion. "In the present case, of course, Congress has not temporarily withheld operation of the writ, but has permanently altered its content. That is, to be sure, an act subject to majoritarian abuse * * *. But that is not the majoritarian abuse against which the Suspension Clause was directed." Justice Scalia also brusquely rejected arguments that preclusion of any review of St. Cyr's claim would violate the Due Process Clause or Article III.[2]

---

[2]   Justice O'Connor, who did not join Justice Scalia's discussion of the Suspension Clause, wrote her own dissent, arguing that even if the Suspension Clause guarantees some minimum habeas review, St. Cyr's claim falls outside the scope of that review. In response to the St. Cyr decision, Congress added a provision to the Immigration and Nationality Act restricting judicial review of removal orders in certain cases to "constitutional claims or questions of law." 8 U.S.C. § 1252(a)(2)(D). In Guerrero-Lasprilla v. Barr, 589 U.S. 221 (2020), the Court, per Justice Breyer, held that the phrase "questions of law" permits judicial review of "the application of a legal standard to undisputed or established facts." In dissent, Justice Thomas, joined in part by

Many commentators sympathetic to the majority's decision would not dispute Justice Scalia's claim that the Court's statutory interpretation bordered on a demand for "magic words."[3] Consider how that constitutional reasoning relates to the understanding that Congress need not create lower federal courts. Does St. Cyr presuppose that if Congress creates lower federal courts, it must vest them with the full scope of habeas corpus jurisdiction protected by the Suspension Clause? Or does the Suspension Clause apply only when Congress purports to restrict the jurisdiction of *both* federal and state courts? In pondering the last question, consider the significance of Tarble's Case, 80 U.S. (13 Wall.) 397 (1872), p. 575, *infra*, whose much-criticized reasoning appears to suggest that the Constitution precludes state courts from issuing writs of habeas corpus to federal officials.[4]

Over two decades after St. Cyr, in Department of Homeland Security v. Thuraissigiam, 591 U.S. 103 (2020), the Supreme Court rejected Suspension Clause and due process challenges to restrictions on the ability of an asylum seeker to obtain review of expedited administrative removal proceedings. Thuraissigiam crossed the border clandestinely, and a border patrol agent apprehended him within 25 yards of the border. Once in government custody, he sought asylum in the administrative proceedings that Congress prescribed, but failed to convince various immigration officials that he had a "credible fear of persecution" upon return to his native country. A different finding on the "credible fear" determination would have spared him "expedited removal" and afforded him additional procedural opportunities to seek asylum in the United States. After an Immigration Judge approved Thuraissigiam's removal from the country, Thuraissigiam sought a writ of habeas corpus in federal court, contending that he satisfied the credible fear test and that he had been denied a fair hearing. He further challenged the various provisions in IIRIRA purporting to restrict federal court review of his case[5] and requested a new opportunity to present his asylum claim before administrative officials.

Justice Alito, argued that "the majority effectively nullifies a jurisdiction-stripping statute, expanding the scope of judicial review well past the boundaries set by Congress."

[3] See also Demore v. Kim, 538 U.S. 510 (2003) (6–3) (quoting Justice Scalia's claim in St. Cyr as *supporting* the need for a "particularly clear statement" of congressional intent to bar habeas review and finding no such statement in a different provision of the immigration laws barring judicial review of decisions regarding the detention of aliens pending removal proceedings). For an expansive view of St. Cyr's implications, see Neuman, *The Habeas Corpus Suspension Clause After INS v. St. Cyr*, 33 Colum.Hum.Rts.L.Rev. 555 (2002).

[4] In assessing St. Cyr's arguments under the Due Process Clause and Article III, consider the case, suggested by Meltzer, *Congress, Courts, and Constitutional Remedies*, 86 Geo.L.J. 2537, 2573 (1998), of a resident alien with legal claims identical to those involved in St. Cyr, but who is physically removed from the country before filing a challenge to a removal order. Because the alien is no longer in federal detention, the Suspension Clause presumably no longer applies. Would preclusion of judicial review raise no serious constitutional issue? Compare the Court's dictum in Zadvydas v. Davis, 533 U.S. 678 (2001), which held as a matter of statutory construction, in light of the "avoidance" canon, that Congress had not authorized the indefinite detention of a removable alien whom no other country would accept: "This Court has suggested * * * that the Constitution may well preclude granting 'an administrative body the unreviewable authority to make determinations implicating fundamental rights.' "

[5] Section 1252(e)(2) provides for habeas review in limited circumstances: first, to ascertain "whether the petitioner is an alien"; second, "whether the petitioner was ordered removed"; and third, whether the petitioner has already been granted lawful entry to the United States. 8 U.S.C. §§ 1252(e)(2)(A)–(C). Section 1252(a)(2)(A)(iii) otherwise provides that

Justice Alito's opinion for the Court (joined by Chief Justice Roberts and Justices Thomas, Gorsuch, and Kavanaugh) analyzed the Suspension Clause claim against the backdrop of the understanding of the Clause that existed in 1789. The Court reasoned that habeas at the time of the founding was "a means to secure *release* from unlawful detention" and did not extend to an invocation of the writ, like petitioner's, "to achieve an entirely different end, namely, to obtain additional administrative review of his asylum claim and ultimately to obtain authorization to stay in this country."[6] The Court explained that the principle embraced by St. Cyr—applicable to "aliens already in the country * * * in custody pending deportation"—could not help Thuraissigiam, who was seeking *entry* into the United States. Speaking to the due process issues, the Court noted that "[w]hile aliens who have established connections in this country have due process rights in deportation proceedings, the Court long ago held that Congress is entitled to set the conditions for an alien's lawful entry into this country and that, as a result, an alien at the threshold of initial entry cannot claim any greater rights under the Due Process Clause" (citing Nishimura Ekiu v. United States, 142 U.S. 651, 660 (1892), and observing that Congress has "plenary authority to decide which aliens to admit" (citing *id.*, at 659)). Because Thuraissigiam had "attempted to enter the country illegally and was apprehended just 25 yards from the border," the Court held, he "has no entitlement to procedural rights other than those afforded by statute." Justice Alito also emphasized precedent supporting the proposition that "even those paroled elsewhere in the country for years pending removal * * * are 'treated' for due process purposes 'as if stopped at the border'" (quoting Shaughnessy v. United States ex rel. Mezei, 345 U.S. 206, 215 (1953)).

Justice Thomas's concurring opinion argued that the expedited removal procedures bore "little resemblance to a suspension as that term was understood at the founding," since they did "not allow the executive to detain based on mere suspicion of a crime or dangerousness."

Justice Breyer, joined by Justice Ginsburg, concurred in the judgment. Justice Breyer emphasized Thuraissigiam's "status" as akin to one stopped at the border and opined that "[t]o interpret the Suspension Clause as insisting upon habeas review of these claims would require, by constitutional command, that the habeas court make indeterminate and highly record-intensive judgments on matters of degree." Finding no precedent "suggesting that the Suspension Clause demands parsing procedural compliance at so

---

"[n]otwithstanding any other provision of law (statutory or nonstatutory), including section 2241 of title 28, or any other habeas corpus provision * * * no court shall have jurisdiction to review * * * [a] determination made [with respect to a credible fear claim]."

6   How does the Court's discussion of the relief sought by Thuraissigiam compare to the remedy awarded by the Court in Boumediene v. Bush, 553 U.S. 723 (2008), discussed below and at pp. 559, 581, 1473–1475, 1506–1536, *infra*? There, the Court remanded the habeas cases to the lower courts for expanded proceedings within which petitioners detained at Guantanamo Bay could challenge their classifications as enemy combatants in the war on terror. And how does the Court's methodology compare in the two cases? In Boumediene, the Court said that it "has been careful not to foreclose the possibility that the protections of the Suspension Clause have expanded along with post-1789 developments" (citing St. Cyr, 533 U.S. at 300–01). For further discussion, see p. 469, *infra*.

granular a level," he concluded that the expedited removal procedures were constitutional as applied here.

Justice Sotomayor, joined by Justice Kagan, dissented. The dissent maintained that the Court had long heard "claims indistinguishable from those" raised by the petitioner, which Justice Sotomayor characterized as raising both mixed questions of law and fact and legal challenges to "procedural defects" in the administrative procedures Congress prescribed. More generally, the dissent took issue with the majority's fixation upon 1789 to frame its analysis, pointing out that no analogous immigration restrictions were then in existence. Finally, in analyzing petitioner's claims under the Due Process Clause, Justice Sotomayor emphasized that he "was actually within the territorial limits of the United States" when captured, a fact that in her view raised a host of questions as to just how far the majority's holding would sweep in future cases.

For additional discussion of Thuraissigiam, see pp. 1544–1546, *infra*.

(3) Habeas Corpus, the Suspension Clause, and Detention Under the Laws of War. St. Cyr's constitutional reasoning became a constitutional holding seven years later in Boumediene v. Bush, 553 U.S. 723 (2008). Boumediene is the only Supreme Court decision clearly holding that a congressional enactment restricting jurisdiction—in that case, of both federal and state courts—is unconstitutional.[7]

The background to Boumediene began in Rasul v. Bush, 542 U.S. 466 (2004), p. 1505, *infra*, where the Court held, as a matter of statutory interpretation, that the general grant of habeas corpus jurisdiction, 28 U.S.C. § 2241, embraced petitions filed on behalf of aliens detained by the United States as enemy combatants at Guantanamo Bay, Cuba. Congress reacted by enacting the Detainee Treatment Act of 2005 (DTA)[8] and the Military Commissions Act of 2006 (MCA).[9] The MCA purported to eliminate habeas corpus jurisdiction for any alien, wherever held, who has "been determined by the United States to have been properly detained as an enemy combatant or is awaiting such a determination." *Id.* § 7(a) (codified at 28 U.S.C. § 2241(e)(1)). In place of habeas jurisdiction, the statutes authorized the D.C. Circuit to review, *inter alia*, decisions of military Combatant Status Review Tribunals (CSRTs) finding that a particular individual is in fact an enemy combatant, subject to non-punitive detention under the laws of war. But the statutes strictly limited judicial review to whether the CSRT's determination conforms to the applicable military standards and procedures.

In Boumediene, the Supreme Court confronted the question whether it had jurisdiction to decide habeas petitions filed on behalf of petitioners detained at Guantanamo Bay who had been determined by CSRTs to be enemy combatants and whether the MCA's jurisdiction-stripping provision

---

[7]   The decision in United States v. Klein, 80 U.S. (13 Wall.) 128 (1871), p. 434, *supra*, also invalidated a congressional statute framed in jurisdictional terms. But as discussed at p. 450, *supra*, the constitutional basis for Klein is murky, and the decision may be best understood as condemning Congress's attempt to enact *substantive* rules of decision that violated the Constitution.

[8]   Pub.L.No. 109–148, 119 Stat. 2739.

[9]   Pub.L.No. 109–366, 120 Stat. 2600.

violated the Suspension Clause. Writing for a 5–4 Court, Justice Kennedy held the provision unconstitutional on the ground that the Suspension Clause affirmatively guarantees, for those who fall within its scope, the right of habeas corpus or an adequate substitute.

The Court said that the Suspension Clause "ensures that, except during periods of formal suspension, the Judiciary will have a time-tested device, the writ, to maintain the 'delicate balance of governance' that is itself the surest safeguard of liberty. See Hamdi [v. Rumsfeld, 542 U.S. 507, 536 (2004)] (plurality opinion). The Clause protects the rights of the detained by affirming the duty and authority of the Judiciary to call the jailer to account." Continuing, Justice Kennedy wrote that "[t]he Court has been careful not to foreclose the possibility that the protections of the Suspension Clause have expanded" since the founding, though he observed that "the analysis may begin with precedents as of 1789, for the Court has said that 'at the absolute minimum' the Clause protects the writ as it existed when the Constitution was drafted and ratified" (quoting St. Cyr). He then went on to conclude that irrespective of the historical evidence, the petitioners were within the protection of the Suspension Clause on the basis of a functional understanding of the writ as part of the scheme of separation of powers.

Chief Justice Roberts and Justice Scalia both wrote dissents, joined by each other and by Justices Thomas and Alito. Unlike Justice Scalia's dissent in St. Cyr, neither dissent questioned that the Suspension Clause affirmatively guarantees habeas review. Instead, each advanced a reason why the Suspension Clause guarantee was not violated in the circumstances before the Court.

Justice Scalia's dissent contended that the Suspension Clause guarantee does not extend to aliens alleged to be enemy combatants and detained in a location like Guantanamo Bay that falls outside the formal territorial sovereignty of the United States.

Chief Justice Roberts's dissent started from the uncontroversial proposition that Congress may eliminate habeas corpus jurisdiction as long as it provides an adequate substitute. He then went on to challenge the majority's conclusion that the procedures Congress has provided for in the D.C. Circuit authorized by the DTA were constitutionally deficient.

The foregoing aspects of the Boumediene decision, and many of the questions that it leaves open, are explored at greater length in Chap. XI, Sec. 2. For present purposes, Boumediene's central importance relates to the scope of congressional power to regulate the jurisdiction of the federal courts. Although it rests on the distinctive protections of the Suspension Clause, does the decision support Professor Hart's general contention, in his celebrated *Dialogue*, that, notwithstanding congressional enactments purporting to withdraw jurisdiction, it is "a necessary postulate of constitutional government" that "a court must always be available to pass on claims of constitutional right to judicial process, and to provide such process if the claim is sustained"? Hart, *Dialogue*, 66 Harv.L.Rev. at 1372.

Professor Hart also argued that the *state* courts are the ultimate guardians of constitutional rights, a position with which the Boumediene opinion (like the St. Cyr opinion) does not even engage. See Fallon, *Jurisdiction-Stripping Reconsidered*, 96 Va.L.Rev. 1043, 1061 (2010). Does the Court's assumption in both cases, that any review should occur in federal court rather than state court, undercut Professor Hart's position and even suggest a right that any constitutionally-required review be provided by federal court? Or can the Court's assumption be explained on a narrower basis resting on statutory construction and severability analysis? In both cases, had Congress realized that it could bar judicial review of executive action in either federal court or state court but not both, surely it would have preferred that the ban on federal court review rather than on state court review be the one that was invalidated. The point is only reinforced in light of the suggestion (much criticized, but never repudiated) in Tarble's Case, 80 U.S. (13 Wall.) 397 (1872), p. 575, *infra*, that state courts lack authority to entertain habeas actions against federal custodians. And throughout, there remained in place the pre-existing general grant of habeas corpus jurisdiction in § 2241, under which the petitions could be entertained.

NOTE ON CONGRESSIONAL APPORTIONMENT OF JURISDICTION AMONG FEDERAL COURTS AND LIMITATIONS ON THE AUTHORITY OF ENFORCEMENT COURTS

(1) Introduction. The preceding material has focused on the scope of congressional power to restrict federal court jurisdiction, either to adjudicate at all or to provide particular remedies. This Note considers a distinct question: the scope of congressional power to confer jurisdiction on a court while limiting its authority to consider particular issues that are relevant to the controversy.[1]

That question has sometimes arisen in connection with legislation to establish specialized courts. Under its broad authority to apportion jurisdiction among federal courts, Congress can create specialized courts and vest them with exclusive jurisdiction over particular categories of cases. See Chap. I, pp. 47–49, *supra*, and Paragraph (2), *infra*. But hard issues can arise when Congress gives a federal court jurisdiction over a case while simultaneously providing that one or more issues in that case may be decided only by a different federal court.

(2) Specialized Courts.

(a) The Emergency Price Control Act. To combat wartime inflation, the Emergency Price Control Act of 1942, 56 Stat. 23, created the Office of Price Administration with the authority to issue regulations and orders fixing maximum prices and rents. The Act created an Article III court called the Emergency Court of Appeals (ECA), consisting of three or more federal district or circuit judges. The ECA was given "the powers of a district court with respect to the jurisdiction conferred on it," except that it had no

---

[1]   For a thoughtful discussion of Congress's power to divide aspects of the judicial function among Article III courts, see Caminker, *Allocating the Judicial Power in a "Unified Judiciary,"* 78 Tex.L.Rev. 1513 (2000).

power to issue any temporary restraining order or interlocutory decree staying the effectiveness of any order, regulation, or price schedule issued under the Act. The Act permitted a challenge to any order, regulation, or price schedule by filing a protest with the Administrator (§ 204(c));[2] if the protest was denied, the aggrieved party had thirty days to file a complaint with the ECA. Section 204(d) made the jurisdiction of the ECA to review the denial of a protest exclusive of all other federal and of state courts. ECA decisions were subject to Supreme Court review.

But the ECA lacked jurisdiction over other actions under the Act. In particular, federal district courts had jurisdiction over (i) actions by the Administrator to enjoin violations of the Act or secure an order directing compliance; (ii) treble damage actions by the Administrator or a buyer for over-ceiling sales; and (iii) criminal prosecutions for willful violations. The state courts had concurrent jurisdiction except in criminal prosecutions.[3]

(b) The Lockerty Decision. The Act's conferral of exclusive jurisdiction to the ECA over actions to enjoin regulations, orders, or price schedules was challenged in Lockerty v. Phillips, 319 U.S. 182 (1943), a suit brought by wholesale meat dealers in federal district court to restrain the United States Attorney from prosecuting them for violations of certain price regulations. The district court dismissed the suit on the ground that the ECA had exclusive jurisdiction over such an action. The Supreme Court affirmed, with Chief Justice Stone writing:

"The Congressional power to ordain and establish inferior courts includes the power 'of investing them with jurisdiction either limited, concurrent, or exclusive, and of withholding jurisdiction from them in the exact degrees and character which to Congress may seem proper for the public good.' Cary v. Curtis, 3 How. 236, 245 [(1845)]; Lauf v. E.G. Shinner & Co., 303 U.S. 323, 330 [(1938)]. * * * [I]t is plain that Congress has power to provide that the equity jurisdiction to restrain enforcement of the Act, or of regulations promulgated under it, be restricted to the Emergency Court, and, upon review of its decisions, to this Court. * * *

"Appellants also contend that the review in the Emergency Court is inadequate to protect their constitutional rights, and that § 204 is therefore unconstitutional, because § 204(c) prohibits all interlocutory relief by that court. We need not pass upon the constitutionality of this restriction. For, in any event, the separability clause of § 303 of the Act would require us to give effect to the other provisions of § 204, including that withholding from the district courts authority to enjoin enforcement of the Act—a provision which as we have seen is subject to no unconstitutional infirmity.

---

[2]   As originally enacted, the statute required such a protest to be filed within 60 days after the issuance of the regulation or after the grounds of protest had arisen, but this time limit was removed in the Stabilization Extension Act of June 30, 1944, 58 Stat. 632.

[3]   As originally enacted, the statute made no provision for a stay of enforcement proceedings by the government either to permit a regulatee to file a protest or to await the disposition of a protest previously filed. The Stabilization Extension Act of June 30, 1944, 58 Stat. 632, however, added a new § 204(e), which directed a stay of enforcement suits pending action on a protest already filed or review of its denial; it also gave a narrow scope for stays in some cases to permit suits to be filed in the ECA where no protest had been filed.

"Since appellants seek only an injunction which the district court is without authority to give, their bill of complaint was rightly dismissed."

Given that the jurisdiction of the ECA was explicitly defined to exclude the power to grant such relief, would the plaintiffs' position have been stronger there than in the district court? If not, does the foundation for the Court's separability ruling collapse?

(c) The Voting Rights Act of 1965. In South Carolina v. Katzenbach, 383 U.S. 301 (1966), the Court upheld a provision of the Voting Rights Act of 1965, 42 U.S.C. § 1973, requiring that actions to exempt states from the coverage of the Act and actions to permit certain "suspended" state voting regulations to go into effect be brought in the District Court for the District of Columbia. In declaring that "Congress might appropriately limit litigation under this provision to a single court in the District of Columbia, pursuant to its constitutional power under Art. III, § 1, to 'ordain and establish' inferior federal tribunals," the Court relied on the Lockerty decision and several others.

Assume that Congress's motivation for requiring litigation in the District of Columbia, rather than, for example, in federal court in South Carolina, was a belief that the former was less likely to uphold a state's constitutional objection to the Voting Rights Act. Does that motivation call the constitutionality of the jurisdictional provision into question? Does the answer to that question bear on the constitutionality of congressional limits on federal court jurisdiction over particular constitutional claims, leaving them to be adjudicated in state courts that Congress may believe are less likely to uphold those claims?

(3) Jurisdictional Limits on Enforcement Courts. When a federal court has jurisdiction to determine whether a defendant has violated federal law and, if so, to impose a sanction, may Congress limit the issues that may be raised by way of defense?

(a) The Yakus Decision. Yakus v. United States, 321 U.S. 414 (1944), presented the question whether a defendant prosecuted for a violation of the Price Control Act may defend the criminal case by challenging the validity of the Act or of a regulation. Section 204(d) was interpreted to bar attack upon a regulation (at least one not invalid on its face) but not upon the Act itself. Thus construed, the provision was sustained against contentions that it denied due process, violated the Sixth Amendment right to trial by a jury of the state and district where a crime was committed, and worked an unconstitutional legislative interference with judicial power.

On the due process issue, Chief Justice Stone's opinion for the Court treated as the central question whether the procedure for review in the ECA "affords to those affected a reasonable opportunity to be heard and present evidence." Concluding that it did, the opinion further held that in "the circumstances of this case" there was "no denial of due process in the statutory prohibition of a temporary stay or injunction. * * * If the alternatives, as Congress could have concluded, were war-time inflation or the imposition on individuals of the burden of complying with a price regulation while its validity is being determined, Congress could constitutionally make the choice in favor of the protection of the public interest from the dangers of inflation."

On the other issues, the opinion stated, *inter alia*: "[W]e are pointed to no principle of law or provision of the Constitution which precludes Congress from making criminal the violation of an administrative regulation, by one who has failed to avail himself of an adequate separate procedure for the adjudication of its validity, or which precludes the practice, in many ways desirable, of splitting the trial for violations of an administrative regulation by committing the determination of the issue of its validity to the agency which created it, and the issue of violation to a court which is given jurisdiction to punish violations. Such a requirement presents no novel constitutional issue. * * *

"* * * Nor has there been any denial * * * of the right, guaranteed by the Sixth Amendment, to a trial by a jury of the state and district where the crime was committed. * * * The indictment charged a violation of the regulation in the district of trial, and the question whether petitioners had committed the crime thus charged in the indictment and defined by Congress, namely, whether they had violated the statute by willful disobedience of a price regulation promulgated by the Administrator, was properly submitted to the jury."

Justice Rutledge's dissent, joined by Justice Murphy, found "the crux" of the case to lie in "the question whether Congress can confer jurisdiction upon federal and state courts in the enforcement proceedings, more particularly the criminal suit, and at the same time deny them 'jurisdiction or power to consider the validity' of the regulations for which enforcement is thus sought.

"It is one thing for Congress to withhold jurisdiction. It is entirely another to confer it and direct that it be exercised in a manner inconsistent with constitutional requirements or, what in some instances may be the same thing, without regard to them. * * * There are limits to the judicial power. Congress may impose others. And in some matters Congress or the President has final say under the Constitution. But whenever the judicial power is called into play, it is responsible directly to the fundamental law and no other authority can intervene to force or authorize the judicial body to disregard it. The problem therefore is not solely one of individual right or due process of law. It is equally one of the separation and independence of the powers of government and of the constitutional integrity of the judicial process, more especially in criminal trials."

(b) Subsequent Developments. Absent the exigency presented by the threat of wartime inflation, would a scheme like that involved in Yakus survive constitutional scrutiny? See United States v. Mendoza-Lopez, 481 U.S. 828, 839 n.15 (1987), p. 496, *infra*, which distinguished Yakus in part on the basis that it rested on the exigencies of wartime, and proceeded to hold that an enforcement court could not predicate a finding of criminal violation on a previous administrative determination where there had been no meaningful opportunity to seek judicial review of the administrative ruling.

Is there a division of responsibilities among courts whenever a claim of issue preclusion is upheld? Is it troubling to allow issue preclusion against a criminal defendant?[4] Especially troubling when the precluded issue was not fully and fairly litigated, even though there was an opportunity for full and fair litigation?

---

2. CONGRESSIONAL AUTHORITY TO ALLOCATE JUDICIAL POWER TO NON-ARTICLE III FEDERAL TRIBUNALS

INTRODUCTORY NOTE ON NON-ARTICLE III TRIBUNALS

This Section addresses the question of Congress's authority to assign federal adjudication to non-Article III tribunals. Familiar provisions of Article III again frame the issue. First, Article III, § 1, cl. 1, vests "[t]he judicial Power of the United States" in the federal courts and confers life tenure and salary protection upon the judges of those courts. Second, Article III, § 2, cl. 1, in turn, defines the subject areas to which such "judicial Power" shall extend.

Against the backdrop of the Madisonian Compromise, Article III has always been understood to be consistent with state court adjudication (at least in the first instance) of matters falling within the subject areas of federal judicial power. The understanding has gone unquestioned, moreover, despite the fact that most state judges lack the life tenure and salary protection of Article III judges.

Perhaps less intuitively, Article III has also long been understood to allow Congress to ordain *federal* tribunals that adjudicate various disputes without providing the adjudicators with life tenure or salary protection. The biggest category involves administrative adjudication, with federal agencies determining (at least in the first instance) federal rights and responsibilities in a host of areas, including government benefits, public lands, customs, immigration, and regulatory matters. These areas—largely but not exclusively consisting of matters known as "public rights"—harken back to a tradition of administrative adjudication dating from the early days of the Republic. The validity of this exercise of power depends, in part, on the

---

[4]   Bowles v. Willingham, 321 U.S. 503 (1944), decided the same day as Yakus, sustained preclusion of a challenge by the defendant to the validity of an Office of Price Administration regulation in a civil action brought by the Administrator to enjoin a landlord's state court suit to restrain the Administrator's issuance of an order reducing certain rentals. Concurring in the result, Justice Rutledge distinguished between such a civil enforcement proceeding and enforcement by criminal prosecution. He insisted, however, upon the following limitations, which he found to be satisfied: "(1) The order or regulation must not be invalid on its face; (2) the previous opportunity must be adequate for the purpose prescribed, in the constitutional sense; and (3) * * * the circumstances and nature of the substantive problem dealt with by the legislature must be such that they justify both the creation of the special remedy and the requirement that it be followed to the exclusion of others normally available."

nature of the matter adjudicated and, at least in some cases, on the scope and availability of review by Article III courts.

In addition to administrative agencies, history provides many examples of specialized federal courts the members of which are not appointed under Article III. These courts are often defined by their subject matter or their territorial status. For example, courts martial and military courts have long been thought to fall outside of Article III. So too have geographically specialized courts for U.S. territories and the District of Columbia. In addition, Congress has established a host of non-Article III specialty courts over particular subject matter areas, such as claims against the United States. As discussed below, what distinguishes these courts from agencies is typically the insulation of their judges from executive control and the issuance of judgments that are self-executing, subject to appeal.

This section considers the scope of congressional power to assign to non-Article III tribunals some role in adjudicating cases or controversies that fall within the scope of federal judicial power as defined by Article III, and, conversely, the extent to which the Constitution requires that an Article III court have authority to review the non-Article III tribunal's determinations.

A. THE CLASSIC FRAMEWORK: PUBLIC AND PRIVATE RIGHTS

The case that follows—Crowell v. Benson—defines the classic framework for assessing the validity of administrative adjudication in the United States. Note that, at the core of the opinion, the Court distinguishes private rights—cases, here, involving common law claims or statutory substitutes for such claims—and public rights relating to the regulatory and proprietary affairs of the U.S. government. In the Court's view, Congress has more latitude to provide for agency adjudication of public rights than it does for private rights. Does the Court explain where this distinction comes from? Consider whether it makes sense in light of the aims of Article III.

Crowell v. Benson

285 U.S. 22 (1932).
Certiorari to the Circuit Court of Appeals for the Fifth Circuit.

■ MR. CHIEF JUSTICE HUGHES delivered the opinion of the Court.

This suit was brought in the District Court to enjoin the enforcement of an award made by petitioner Crowell, as Deputy Commissioner of the United States Employees' Compensation Commission, in favor of the petitioner Knudsen and against the respondent Benson. The award was made under the Longshoremen's and Harbor Workers' Compensation Act [33 U.S.C. §§ 901–950 (LHWCA)], and rested upon the finding of the deputy commissioner that Knudsen was injured while in the employ of Benson and performing service upon the navigable waters of the United States. The complainant alleged that the award was contrary to law for the reason that Knudsen was not at the time of his injury an employee of the complainant and his claim was not "within the jurisdiction" of the Deputy Commissioner. An amended complaint charged that the act was unconstitutional upon the grounds that it violated the due process clause of the Fifth Amendment, the provision of the Seventh Amendment as to trial by jury, * * * and the provisions of Article III with respect to the judicial power of the United States. The District Judge denied motions to dismiss and granted a hearing de novo upon the facts and the law, expressing the opinion that the act would be invalid if not construed to permit such a hearing. [After the case was transferred to the admiralty docket,] the District Court decided that Knudsen was not in the employ of the petitioner and restrained the enforcement of the award. The decree was affirmed by the Circuit Court of Appeals and this Court granted writs of certiorari.

The question of the validity of the act may be considered in relation to (1) its provisions defining substantive rights and (2) its procedural requirements. * * *

[The first part of the opinion sustained the substantive provisions of the Act as a proper exercise of "the general authority of the Congress to alter or revise the maritime law which shall prevail throughout the country."

[The second part of the opinion began by describing the procedural provisions of the Act and the provisions for judicial review. Awards may be made by a deputy commissioner only after investigation, notice, and hearing. They may be enforced by a federal district court, on application of beneficiaries or of the deputy commissioner, if found to have been "made and served in accordance with law." Or they may be suspended or set aside, in whole or in part, on application of a respondent if "not in accordance with law."]

Second. The objections to the procedural requirements of the act relate to the extent of the administrative authority which it confers. * * *

1. The contention under the due process clause of the Fifth Amendment relates to the determination of questions of fact. Rulings of the deputy commissioner upon questions of law are without finality. * * *

Apart from cases involving constitutional rights to be appropriately enforced by proceedings in court, there can be no doubt that the act contemplates that as to questions of fact, arising with respect to injuries to employees within the purview of the act, the findings of the deputy commissioner, supported by evidence and within the scope of his authority, shall be final. To hold otherwise would be to defeat the obvious purpose of the legislation to furnish a prompt, continuous, expert, and inexpensive method for dealing with a class of questions of fact which are peculiarly suited to examination and determination by an administrative agency specially assigned to that task. The object is to secure within the prescribed limits of the employer's liability an immediate investigation and a sound practical judgment, and the efficacy of the plan depends upon the finality of the determinations of fact with respect to the circumstances, nature, extent, and consequences of the employee's injuries and the amount of compensation that should be awarded. And this finality may also be regarded as extending to the determination of the question of fact whether the injury "was occasioned solely by the intoxication of the employee or by the willful intention of the employee to injure or kill himself or another." While the exclusion of compensation in such cases is found in what are called "coverage" provisions of the act (section 3 [33 U.S.C. § 903]), the question of fact still belongs to the contemplated routine of administration, for the case is one of employment within the scope of the act, and the cause of the injury sustained by the employee as well as its character and effect must be ascertained in applying the provisions for compensation. The use of the administrative method for these purposes, assuming due notice, proper opportunity to be heard, and that findings are based upon evidence, falls easily within the principle of the decisions sustaining similar procedure against objections under the due process clauses of the Fifth and Fourteenth Amendments. * * *

2. The contention based upon the judicial power of the United States, as extended "to all cases of admiralty and maritime jurisdiction" (Const. Art. III), presents a distinct question. * * *

The question in the instant case, in this aspect, can be deemed to relate only to determinations of fact. The reservation of legal questions is to the same court that has jurisdiction in admiralty, and the mere fact that the court is not described as such is unimportant. * * * The Congress did not attempt to define questions of law, and the generality of the description leaves no doubt of the intention to reserve to the Federal court full authority to pass upon all matters which this Court had held to fall within that category. There is thus no attempt to interfere with, but rather provision is made to facilitate, the exercise by the court of its jurisdiction to deny effect to any administrative finding which is without evidence, or "contrary to the indisputable character of the evidence," or where the hearing is "inadequate," or "unfair," or arbitrary in any respect. Interstate Commerce Commission v. Louisville R. R. Co., [227 U. S. 88, 91, 92 (1913)]; Tagg Bros. & Moorhead v. United States, [280 U.S. 420 (1930)].

As to determinations of fact, the distinction is at once apparent between cases of private right and those which arise between the government and persons subject to its authority in connection with the performance of the constitutional functions of the executive or legislative departments. The Court referred to this distinction in Murray's Lessee v. Hoboken Land & improvement Company, 59 U.S. (18 How.) 272, 284

(1856), pointing out that "there are matters, involving public rights, which may be presented in such form that the judicial power is capable of acting on them, and which are susceptible of judicial determination, but which Congress may or may not bring within the cognizance of the courts of the United States, as it may deem proper." Thus the Congress, in exercising the powers confided to it, may establish "legislative" courts (as distinguished from "constitutional courts in which the judicial power conferred by the Constitution can be deposited") which are to form part of the government of territories or of the District of Columbia, or to serve as special tribunals "to examine and determine various matters, arising between the government and others, which from their nature do not require judicial determination and yet are susceptible of it." But "the mode of determining matters of this class is completely within congressional control. Congress may reserve to itself the power to decide, may delegate that power to executive officers, or may commit it to judicial tribunals." Ex parte Bakelite Corporation, 279 U.S. 438, 451 [(1929)]. Familiar illustrations of administrative agencies created for the determination of such matters are found in connection with the exercise of the congressional power as to interstate and foreign commerce, taxation, immigration, the public lands, public health, the facilities of the post office, pensions, and payments to veterans.

The present case does not fall within the categories just described, but is one of private right, that is, of the liability of one individual to another under the law as defined. But, in cases of that sort, there is no requirement that, in order to maintain the essential attributes of the judicial power, all determinations of fact in constitutional courts shall be made by judges. On the common-law side of the federal courts, the aid of juries is not only deemed appropriate but is required by the Constitution itself. In cases of equity and admiralty, it is historic practice to call to the assistance of the courts, without the consent of the parties, masters, and commissioners or assessors, to pass upon certain classes of questions, as, for example, to take and state an account or to find the amount of damages. * * *

The statute has a limited application, being confined to the relation of master and servant, and the method of determining the questions of fact, which arise in the routine of making compensation awards to employees under the act, is necessary to its effective enforcement. The act itself, where it applies, establishes the measure of the employer's liability, thus leaving open for determination the questions of fact as to the circumstances, nature, extent and consequences of the injuries sustained by the employee for which compensation is to be made in accordance with the prescribed standards. Findings of fact by the deputy commissioner upon such questions are closely analogous to the findings of the amount of damages that are made according to familiar practice by commissioners or assessors, and the reservation of full authority to the court to deal with matters of law provides for the appropriate exercise of the judicial function in this class of cases. For the purposes stated, we are unable to find any constitutional obstacle to the action of the Congress in availing itself of a method shown by experience to be essential in order to apply its standards to the thousands of cases involved, thus relieving the courts of a most serious burden while preserving their complete authority to insure the proper application of the law.

3. What has been said thus far relates to the determination of claims of employees within the purview of the act. A different question is presented where the determinations of fact are fundamental or "jurisdictional,"[17] in the sense that their existence is a condition precedent to the operation of the statutory scheme. These fundamental requirements are that the injury occur upon the navigable waters of the United States and that the relation of master and servant exist. These conditions are indispensable to the application of the statute, not only because the Congress has so provided explicitly (section 3), but also because the power of the Congress to enact the legislation turns upon the existence of these conditions. * * *

In relation to these basic facts, the question is not the ordinary one as to the propriety of provision for administrative determinations. Nor have we simply the question of due process in relation to notice and hearing. It is rather a question of the appropriate maintenance of the federal judicial power in requiring the observance of constitutional restrictions. It is the question whether the Congress may substitute for constitutional courts, in which the judicial power of the United States is vested, an administrative agency—in this instance a single deputy commissioner—for the final determination of the existence of the facts upon which the enforcement of the constitutional rights of the citizen depend. The recognition of the utility and convenience of administrative agencies for the investigation and finding of facts within their proper province, and the support of their authorized action, does not require the conclusion that there is no limitation of their use, and that the Congress could completely oust the courts of all determinations of fact by vesting the authority to make them with finality in its own instrumentalities or in the Executive Department. That would be to sap the judicial power as it exists under the Federal Constitution, and to establish a government of a bureaucratic character alien to our system, wherever fundamental rights depend, as not infrequently they do depend, upon the facts, and finality as to facts becomes in effect finality in law. * * *

In cases brought to enforce constitutional rights, the judicial power of the United States necessarily extends to the independent determination of all questions, both of fact and law, necessary to the

---

[17]   The term "jurisdictional," although frequently used, suggests analogies which are not complete when the reference is to administrative officials or bodies. In relation to administrative agencies, the question in a given case is whether it falls within the scope of the authority validly conferred.

performance of that supreme function. The case of confiscation is illustrative, the ultimate conclusion almost invariably depending upon the decisions of questions of fact. This court has held the owner to be entitled to "a fair opportunity for submitting that issue to a judicial tribunal for determination upon its own independent judgment as to both law and facts." Ohio Valley Water Company v. Ben Avon Borough, 253 U.S. 287 (1920). * * * Jurisdiction in the executive to order deportation exists only if the person arrested is an alien, and while, if there were jurisdiction, the findings of fact of the executive department would be conclusive, the claim of citizenship "is a denial of an essential jurisdictional fact" both in the statutory and the constitutional sense, and a writ of habeas corpus will issue "to determine the status." Persons claiming to be citizens of the United States "are entitled to a judicial determination of their claims," said this Court in Ng Fung Ho v. White, 259 U.S. 276, 285 (1922), and in that case the cause was remanded to the federal District Court "for trial in that court of the question of citizenship." * * *

[The Court then determined that, in order to avoid the serious constitutional question that would otherwise arise, the statute should be construed to permit the court "in determining whether a compensation order is in accordance with law" to "determine the fact of employment which underlies the operation of the statute."]

Assuming that the federal court may determine for itself the existence of these fundamental or jurisdictional facts, we come to the question,—Upon what record is the determination to be made? * * * We think that the essential independence of the exercise of the judicial power of the United States in the enforcement of constitutional rights requires that the federal court should determine such an issue upon its own record and the facts elicited before it. * * *

Decree affirmed.

■ MR. JUSTICE BRANDEIS, dissenting.

[The following excerpt from the long dissenting opinion indicates only one of the grounds of dissent.]

Sixth. Even if the constitutional power of Congress to provide compensation is limited to cases in which the employer-employee relation exists, I see no basis for a contention that the denial of the right to a trial de novo upon the issue of employment is in any manner subversive of the independence of the federal judicial power. Nothing in the Constitution, or in any prior decision of this Court to which attention has been called, lends support to the doctrine that a judicial finding of any fact involved in any civil proceeding to enforce a pecuniary liability may not be made upon evidence introduced before a properly constituted administrative tribunal, or that a determination so made may not be deemed an independent judicial determination. Congress has repeatedly exercised authority to confer upon the tribunals which it creates, be they administrative bodies or courts of limited jurisdiction, the power to receive evidence concerning the facts upon which the exercise of federal power must be predicated, and to determine whether those facts exist. The power of Congress to provide by legislation for liability under certain circumstances subsumes the power to provide for the determination of the existence of those circumstances. It does not depend upon the absolute existence in reality of any fact.

It is true that, so far as Knudsen is concerned, proof of the existence of the employer-employee relation is essential to recovery under the act. But under the definition laid down in Noble v. Union River Logging R. Co., 147 U.S. 165, 173, 174 [(1893)], that fact is not jurisdictional. It is quasi-jurisdictional. The existence of a relation of employment is a question going to the applicability of the substantive law, not to the jurisdiction of the tribunal. Jurisdiction is the power to adjudicate between the parties concerning the subject-matter. Obviously, the deputy commissioner had not only the power but the duty to determine whether the employer-employee relation existed. * * *

The "judicial power" of Article III of the Constitution is the power of the federal government, and not of any inferior tribunal. There is in that article nothing which requires any controversy to be determined as of first instance in the federal district courts. The jurisdiction of those courts is subject to the control of Congress. Matters which may be placed within their jurisdiction may instead be committed to the state courts. If there be any controversy to which the judicial power extends that may not be subjected to the conclusive determination of administrative bodies or federal legislative courts, it is not because of any prohibition against the diminution of the jurisdiction of the federal district courts as such, but because, under certain circumstances, the constitutional requirement of due process is a requirement of judicial process. An accumulation of precedents, already referred to, has established that in civil proceedings involving property rights determination of facts may constitutionally be made otherwise than judicially; and necessarily that evidence as to such facts may be taken outside of a court. I do not conceive that Article III has properly any bearing upon the question presented in this case. * * *

■ MR. JUSTICE STONE and MR. JUSTICE ROBERTS join in this opinion.

NOTE ON CROWELL V. BENSON AND ADMINISTRATIVE ADJUDICATION

(1) Historical Significance. Henry Hart claimed that "[m]ost people * * * reading Crowell concentrate on what it said Congress could *not* do," but criticized this emphasis as a "simple mistake." Hart, *The Power of Congress to Limit the Jurisdiction of Federal Courts: An Exercise in Dialectic*, 66 Harv.L.Rev. 1362, 1374–75 (1953) (hereinafter cited as "Hart, *Dialogue*").

What did the Court say in Crowell that Congress *could* do by way of investing federal administrative agencies with adjudicative authority?

In considering Professor Hart's statement, note that as of 2017, the federal government employed almost 2000 "administrative law judges" (ALJs)—executive branch officials assigned to various federal agencies. See Walker & Wasserman, *The New World of Agency Adjudication*, 107 Calif.L.Rev. 141, 154 (2019) ("the Office of Personnel Management (OPM) reports that there were 1,965 ALJs across the federal administrative state as of March 2017, 85 percent of whom work at the Social Security Administration"). ALJs perform exclusively adjudicative functions and enjoy some statutory safeguards of decisional independence—most importantly, they can be removed only "for good cause" and only by the Merit Systems Protection Board (MSPB), an independent agency. 5 U.S.C. § 7521.[1] Still, they lack life tenure and the Article III guarantee against reduction in salary. Indeed, a federal agency is frequently a party to proceedings before ALJs in whose selection the agency has participated and against whom the agency can initiate removal proceedings (although in practice removal is extraordinarily rare).[2] In addition, as of 2017, "there were 10,831 non-ALJ adjudicators" in surveyed agencies, approximately 73% of whom were Patent Examiners. Walker & Wasserman, *supra*, at 153–54. Although not designated as "administrative law judges" under the Administrative Procedure Act, these officials nonetheless conducted informal agency adjudications.

Because administrative adjudication is studied extensively in courses on Administrative Law, the discussion in this Note is brief and occasionally oversimplified. Nonetheless, any account of the contemporary role of the federal courts would be incomplete if it did not reckon with (i) the vast scope of administrative adjudication, (ii) the relationship between administrative adjudicators and Article III courts, and (iii) the strains that acceptance of administrative adjudication puts on efforts to develop a coherent theory of

---

[1]   In other words, the MSPB may remove an ALJ only "for good cause," and, pursuant to the terms of the Civil Service Reform Act, the President may remove members of the MSPB "only for inefficiency, neglect of duty, or malfeasance in office." 5 U.S.C. § 1202(d). Is that limitation constitutional in light of the Court's holding in Free Enter. Fund. v. Pub. Co. Accounting Oversight Bd., 561 U.S. 477, 484 (2010), that a multilayer tiered limitation on removal imposes an unconstitutional limitation on the President's Article II responsibility to "take Care that the Laws be faithfully executed" (U.S. Const., Art. II, § 3)? In Jarkesy v. Securities & Exchange Commission, 34 F.4th 446, 463–65 (5th Cir.2022), cert. granted, 143 S.Ct. 2688 (June 30, 2023), the Court of Appeals held the removal restriction on ALJs unconstitutional under Article II, but the Supreme Court ultimately affirmed on an alternate ground, 144 S.Ct. 2117 (2024). See also Lucia v. SEC, 585 U.S. 237 (2018) (declining to reach the removal question while holding that ALJs presiding over SEC enforcement actions are not merely employees, but "Officers of the United States" subject to the Appointments Clause and that appointment of SEC ALJs by SEC staff, rather than by the SEC's Commissioners themselves, therefore violated that Clause); United States v. Arthrex, Inc., 594 U.S. 1 (2021) (deeming Administrative Patent Judges to be inferior officers for purposes of the Appointments Clause and holding their decisions therefore must be subject to direct review by a principal officer).

For Article III purposes, does it matter if there is *some* limitation on removal if that limitation does not provide the full panoply of Article III guarantees?

[2]   See generally Barnett, *Resolving the ALJ Quandary*, 66 Vand.L.Rev. 797 (2013) (describing the selection and removal of ALJs and the debate about their independence).

the necessary role of courts under Article III, the separation of powers, and the Due Process Clause.

(2) Historical Foundations of Agency Adjudication. In assessing whether Congress's vesting of any form of adjudicative power in federal administrative agencies is justified under Article III, note that the first Congress assigned responsibilities to executive officials—including resolution of disputes involving veterans' benefits and customs duties—that might instead have been vested in constitutional courts. See Fallon, *Of Legislative Courts, Administrative Agencies, and Article III*, 101 Harv.L.Rev. 915, 919 (1988). Beyond the history lies a conceptual point, well-expressed in Bator, *The Constitution as Architecture: Legislative and Administrative Courts Under Article III*, 65 Ind.L.J. 233, 264–65 (1990): "Every time an official of the executive branch, in determining how faithfully to execute the laws, goes through the process of finding facts and determining the meaning and application of the relevant law, he is doing something which functionally is akin to the exercise of judicial power. Every time the Commissioner of Internal Revenue makes a determination that, on X facts, the Tax Code requires the collection of Y tax, and issues a tax assessment on that basis, or the Immigration Service determines that Z is a deportable alien and issues an order to deport, an implicit adjudicatory process is going on. Of course, many such executive determinations are informal. But it is only a step—and one quite consistent with the ideal of 'faithful' execution of the laws—from informal, implicit adjudication to the notion that in making these determinations the official should hear the parties, make a record of the evidence, and give explicit formulations to his interpretation of the law. Determinations by the executive to apply law and judicial adjudication have a symbiotic relationship and flow naturally from and into each other. There is no *a priori* wall between them. * * * It is history and custom and expediency, rather than logic, that determine what needs to be the participation of the judges in the adjudicatory enterprise. * * * The judicial power is neither a platonic essence nor a pre-existing empirical classification. It is a purposive institutional concept, whose content is a product of history and custom distilled in the light of experience and expediency."

Since not every application of law to fact to determine legal rights can be deemed inherently judicial, isn't the real question whether some exercises of adjudicative authority, though they may resemble the judicial process by applying law to fact, properly constitute an exercise of executive power? What criteria help sort between adjudications that are necessarily judicial and those which may be handled by the executive? Within the latter category, consider also whether, and to what extent, the Constitution requires judicial *remedies* for injuries resulting from erroneous or unlawful administrative actions or, instead, authorizes Congress to make administrative findings of fact and law *conclusive* on a court in subsequent litigation.

(3) Constitutional Values at Stake. Justice Brandeis, dissenting in Crowell, apparently viewed the Due Process Clause as the only constitutional limitation on Congress's power to vest in administrative agencies authority to adjudicate matters that could instead have been vested in Article III courts. And for the most part, he thought, the Constitution is satisfied if the administrative process is sufficiently fair to satisfy due process, though occasionally "the constitutional requirement of due process is a requirement of judicial process."

In contending that "Article III has properly [no] bearing upon the question presented," he noted that Congress could leave adjudication of cases like Crowell exclusively to the state courts, whose judges typically lack life tenure and salary protection (and none of whom enjoy such protection under the Constitution). If state court adjudication satisfies Article III, he reasoned, so too should adjudication before a federal administrative agency.

By contrast, the Court's opinion in Crowell reasoned that Article III was implicated when Congress assigned adjudication to an administrative agency but not when it relied on state courts. One possible distinction is that federal agencies may be more susceptible than state courts to influence by Congress or the President. A second possible distinction relates back to the thesis, discussed at pp. 410–413, 429–431, *supra*, that Congress must vest jurisdiction in "*all*" cases arising under federal law in some Article III court; if that premise were accepted, Supreme Court review of state court decisions might suffice, but federal agency decisions would require some federal *appellate* jurisdiction.

To what extent does Justice Brandeis's thesis about the Due Process Clause help to sort between matters that require Article III adjudication and those that do not? Perhaps one criterion for proper agency adjudication involves cases where administrative action does not threaten the deprivation of life, liberty, or property. Hence, Hayburn's Case, 2 U.S. (2 Dall.) 409 (1792), pp. 101–104, *supra*, offers a paradigmatic case of executive adjudication because it entailed the payment of pensions according to statutory criteria rather than the disposition of vested rights.

Others have taken a broader view of what Article III requires.[3] Consider the argument of Fallon, Paragraph (2), *supra*, that there are at least three Article III values at stake in cases such as Crowell: (i) ensuring fair adjudication to individual litigants, (ii) maintaining a system of judicial review and judicial remedies that suffices to keep government generally within the bounds of law, and (iii) preserving judicial integrity by not requiring a court to accept an agency's erroneous decision as conclusive of a legal issue and to make that decision a predicate for the judicial imposition of civil or criminal penalties.[4] How do these competing views map onto the distinction Crowell drew between public and private rights?

---

[3]   Meltzer, *Legislative Courts, Legislative Power, and the Constitution*, 65 Ind.L.J. 291 (1990), argues that review of federal administrative decisions is sometimes required by the Constitution, and, moreover, that if the constitutionally required review is by a federal tribunal, the judges must be Article III judges. Since due process does not generally require judges with life tenure (as, for example, in state court), Meltzer concludes that Article III must, at least in such cases, impose a requirement that the Due Process Clause does not impose.

[4]   Ordinarily, these values are promoted by review of agency decisions in Article III courts. But if Congress need not create lower federal courts, could it provide that state courts have exclusive jurisdiction, for example, to review federal administrative adjudications denying claims for disability benefits under the Social Security Act? To review Federal Trade Commission cease-and-desist orders (which impose enforceable duties whose violation can lead

(4) Public Rights. Crowell suggests broadly that public rights cases could be committed exclusively to administrative adjudication. Although as we will see, that suggestion may be somewhat overbroad, there is little doubt that the categorical distinction drawn in Crowell between public rights and private rights remains important in fixing the bounds of constitutionally permissible adjudication by federal administrative agencies.[5] Crowell relied on the foundational decision in Murray's Lessee v. Hoboken Land & Improvement Co., 59 U.S. (18 How.) 272 (1855), which upheld the power of an executive official to audit the accounts of a federal employee and, upon finding a deficit, to impose a summary attachment. In response to the argument that these were judicial acts that could be performed only by a court, the Court in Murray's Lessee said:

"[W]e do not consider congress can either withdraw from judicial cognizance any matter which, from its nature, is the subject of a suit at the common law, or in equity, or admiralty; nor, on the other hand, can it bring under the judicial power a matter which, from its nature, is not a subject for judicial determination. At the same time there are matters, involving public rights, which may be presented in such form that the judicial power is capable of acting on them, and which are susceptible of judicial determination, but which congress may or may not bring within the cognizance of the courts of the United States, as it may deem proper."

(a) Defining Public Rights. Despite its historical lineage, the public rights category has never received a canonical formulation. Notice that the Court in Crowell offered a fairly circular definition, followed by an enumeration of areas that historically implicated public rights. In particular, Crowell relied heavily on Ex parte Bakelite Corporation, 279 U.S. 438, 451 (1929), which referenced matters for which "Congress may reserve to itself the power to decide, may delegate that power to executive officers, or may commit it to judicial tribunals," and then cited administrative agencies handling matters arising from "congressional power as to interstate and foreign commerce, taxation, immigration, the public lands, public health, the facilities of the post office, pensions, and payments to veterans." What theory, if any, helps identify why the identified classes of cases fall on the public rights side of the ledger? Is the answer largely historical—a matter of accumulated constitutional practice—or is there some functional theory that connects those disparate but broad categories? Consider what common threads, if any, explain the following classes of cases often thought to be at the doctrine's core.

(i)   The first, and perhaps most familiar, category involves "claims against the United States." Ex parte Bakelite Corp., 279 U.S. 438, 452 (1929). This category follows from the doctrine of sovereign immunity (discussed in Chap. IX, Sec. 1, *infra*). As the Court said, with respect to

---

to contempt citations)? Though stressing how unusual such arrangements would be, Meltzer, note 3, *supra*, argues that they would satisfy Article III because the reviewing courts would be free from control by Congress and the federal executive.

    [5]   For a valuable history of the public rights doctrine, see Young, *Public Rights and the Federal Judicial Power: From Murray's Lessee Through Crowell to Schor*, 35 Buff.L.Rev. 765 (1986).

"claims for money against the United States," no claimants "have any right to sue * * * unless Congress consents; and Congress may attach to its consent such conditions as it deems proper," including adjudication before a non-Article III tribunal. *Id.* Referring to the deeply rooted congressional practice of enacting private bills to pay claims against the United States, the Court noted that resolution of such claims "is one which Congress has discretion either to exercise directly or to delegate to other agencies." *Id.* For further discussion, see, *e.g.*, Baude, *Adjudication Outside Article III*, 133 Harv.L.Rev. 1511, 1540–47 (2020); Harrison, *Public Rights and Private Privileges*, 54 Ga.L.Rev. 143 (2019); Harrison, *Legislative Power and Judicial Power*, 31 Const. Comm. 295, 304 (2016); Nelson, *Adjudication in the Political Branches*, 107 Colum.L.Rev. 559, 565–93 (2007). If, for example, a plaintiff has a claim for breach of contract or a claim that the government has wrongfully withheld benefits, sovereign immunity would bar suit against the United States absent its consent. Accordingly, if Congress may deny a remedy altogether, it may also condition the grant of a remedy on the adjudication's occurring in tribunals other than Article III courts. See, *e.g.*, Baude, *supra*, at 1543–44; Fallon, *supra*, at 919 (describing the public rights doctrine as being "mostly, although not invariably, associated with the doctrine of sovereign immunity").

(ii) A second, and related, category of public rights relates to the authority traditionally exercised by non-Article III tribunals, including administrative agencies, to allocate federal public lands or other federal benefits. See, *e.g.*, Smelting Co. v. Kemp, 104 U.S. 636, 640–41 (1881); Hayburn's Case, 2 U.S. (2 Dall.) 490 (1792). On one account, because the government held such assets on the public's behalf, and because private rights in public lands or benefits did not typically become vested property rights until the grant was completed, Congress could allocate such property or benefits itself or prescribe criteria by which the executive was to do so. See, *e.g.*, Baude, *supra*, at 1542–44; Harrison, *Public Rights*, *supra*, at 157–60, 167–71; Nelson, *supra*, at 566–69, 577–79.[6] On that account, Congress had wide discretion to determine the scope and availability of judicial review of the initial allocation of federal land or benefits. See, *e.g.*, Harrison, *Public Rights*, *supra*, at 174–75 (noting that it was up to Congress to prescribe judicial remedies in such cases); Young, *supra* note 5, at 800–01 (1986) (discussing the Court's deferential posture toward judicial review of federal land and benefits cases in cases such as Decatur v. Paulding, 39 U.S. (14 Pet.) 497, 516 (1840); Gaines v. Thompson, 74 U.S. (7 Wall.) 347, 350 (1868); and Johnson v. Towsley, 80 U.S. (13 Wall.) 72, 83 (1871)). At the same time, once the land office conveyed public land to a private party, such that property rights attached, any effort by the government to cancel or revoke the grant required resort to judicial rather than administrative process, as

---

[6]   In the land grant process, a property interest typically vested when the process came to its conclusion, but the property interest might vest earlier if a statute prescribed "preemption" rights—the option to purchase public land when individuals had made improvements or settled upon it. See Nelson, *supra*, at 579. There was some disagreement in the nineteenth century, however, about whether, even in such cases, Congress could confer on the executive the authority to determine whether an individual had acquired such preemption rights pursuant to the state. See *id.* 579–80.

did disputes among private parties about who in fact properly held a federal grant. See Nelson, *supra*, at 578.

Might Congress's power to rely on non-Article III tribunals in such cases reflect the fact that persons aggrieved by the government's failure to confer public lands or benefits would presumably also implicate sovereign immunity?

(iii) A third, and more conceptually complex, category involves disputes arising from coercive governmental conduct (outside of the criminal law). Customs disputes are illustrative: the government may coerce payment of duties at the border or seize disputed property and force the disputant to litigate later. See Nelson, *supra*, at 580. Here, too, settled Supreme Court decisions hold that Congress can provide for subsequent litigation in federal tribunals other than Article III courts. See, *e.g.*, Bakelite, 279 U.S. at 458; Buttfield v. Stranahan, 192 U.S. 470, 493–97 (1904). Some immigration cases were to similar effect, apparently reflecting an assumption about the scope of Congress's power over entry at the border. Fallon, *supra*, at 967.

This element of the public rights doctrine seems to reflect the principle that, in such cases, the legal system treated the underlying conduct—for instance, bringing goods into the country—as a privilege rather than a private or vested right. See, *e.g.*, Nelson, *supra*, at 580. Hence, Congress could prohibit importation of goods, subject to conditions whose existence could be ascertained by executive officers. See *id.*

(iv) A fourth category involves property deprivation but in a context in which, as a matter of historical practice, Congress could assign the adjudication to an administrative agency rather than the courts. This class of cases is exemplified by the decision in Murray's Lessee v. Hoboken Land & Improvement Co., 59 U.S. (18 How.) 272 (1855), see pp. 486–487, *supra*. To simplify a complex set of facts, at the time of Murray's Lessee, customs officials held customs revenues in their private bank accounts until they paid them to the U.S. Treasury. In the case of a deficiency, an 1820 statute authorized the Secretary of the Treasury to issue a "distress warrant" extrajudicially to recover the withheld funds. Though the summary administrative seizure of the collector's property does not fit neatly into any of the above categories, the Court noted that the distress warrant procedure had been used "in England from remote antiquity—and in many of the States * * * at the time the constitution was formed," and that summary procedures for tax collection had been widely accepted as a matter of "[i]mperative necessity." Murray's Lessee, 59 U.S. (18 How.) at 281–82. Though the collector had a right to a post-deprivation judicial hearing on the validity of the seizure of his bank accounts (that he did not invoke), the Court's reasoning did not depend on the existence of that procedure.

(v) What principles, if any, underlie these four categories? Building on Justice Brandeis's dissent in Crowell, if due process requires judicial process, perhaps the public benefits and private privileges categories are best explained by the fact that there was no vested liberty or property interest at stake requiring judicial process. See Baude, *supra*, at 1541–42. Or perhaps Congress's greater power to confer or withhold certain benefits—a waiver of sovereign immunity, a grant of federal public lands or monetary benefits, or the ability to enjoy privileges such as importing—also carries with it the lesser power of conditioning such benefits on adjudication occurring outside of Article III. See *id.* 1579. Would leveraging such legislative powers to require the waiver of constitutional rights implicate the doctrine of unconstitutional conditions? See *e.g.*, Sheetz v. Cnty. of El Dorado, California, 601 U.S. 267, 275–76 (2024); Agency for Int'l Dev. v. All. for Open Soc'y Int'l, Inc., 570 U.S. 205 (2013).

(b) Public Rights and Judicial Review. Although the Supreme Court has sometimes suggested that public rights disputes can be removed from the purview of the courts altogether, that broad pronouncement fits uneasily with other cases suggesting that there may be a right to judicial review of claims that administrative officials have violated constitutional rights. See pp. 476–481, *supra.* Similarly, a number of cases involving public rights make clear that, even in the absence of an express statutory grant of the right to judicial review of an agency decision, the Court may nonetheless review whether an agency adjudicating public rights has acted *ultra vires*— exercising authority clearly outside the scope of agency jurisdiction and thus beyond the administrator's power to act. See, *e.g.*, American School of Magnetic Healing v. McAnnulty, 187 U.S. 94, 109–10 (1902) (overturning a decision by the Postmaster General on the ground that "the case is not one which, by any construction of th[e] facts [of record], is covered or provided for by the statutes under which the Postmaster General has assumed to act"); Bartlett v. Kane, 57 U.S. (16 How.) 263, 272 (1853) (noting that challenges to customs appraisals allowed for examination of "power in the officer and fraud in the party").

Moreover, putting to one side suits against the United States itself or the agencies as such, the law has always included a range of common law and equitable remedies against government officers. See Chap. IX, *infra.* In a famous decision, for example, the Court held that even if an importer had no right of action against the Department of the Treasury itself for wrongfully detaining goods, the importer might still assert a common law action for replevin, detinue, or trover against the customs officer who had possession of the goods. See Cary v. Curtis, 44 U.S. (3 How.) 236, 250 (1845). Another striking example is the writ of habeas corpus, through which individuals whose liberty has been restrained may sue the government official who is responsible for the custody. Recall that in INS v. St. Cyr, 533 U.S. 289, 300 (2001), p. 464, *supra*, the majority reasoned that because of the Suspension Clause, Article I, § 9, cl. 2, "some 'judicial intervention in deportation cases' is unquestionably 'required by the Constitution' " (quoting Heikkila v. Barber, 345 U.S. 229, 235 (1953)). See also Chap. XI, *infra.* A decision like St. Cyr surely qualifies the broadest statements that public rights matters may always be decided with no judicial involvement. Nonetheless, there is little doubt that Congress generally has greater latitude to limit judicial involvement in the resolution of matters that involve public as compared to private rights.

(5) Private Rights. Crowell says it is a private rights case, which the Court defined as one involving the liability of one private party to another.

The dictum in Murray's Lessee suggests that in such a case Congress could not completely forgo judicial review. Nonetheless, Crowell held that Congress was under no obligation to ensure "all determinations of fact in constitutional courts shall be made by judges." Rather, as long as Congress assigned Article III courts sufficient authority over the decision, it could give the agency a role analogous to that of a judicial adjunct. In other words, the Court compared the deputy commissioner of the agency to juries in common law cases and to the masters, commissioners, or assessors who aided courts with factfinding in equity or admiralty cases. Key to determining whether Article III courts retained sufficient authority was the scope of judicial review over the agency's determinations of fact and of law.

(a) Questions of Fact. As summarized by Professor Hart, "the apparently solid thing about *Crowell* is the holding that administrative findings of non-constitutional and jurisdictional facts may be made conclusive upon the courts, if not infected with any error of law, as a basis for judicial enforcement of a money liability of one private person to another." Hart, *Dialogue*, 66 Harv.L.Rev. at 1375. Indeed, without this degree of agency conclusiveness, administrative adjudication would seem to be little more than a dry run for a later determination in court.

(i) Congress's reasons for vesting at least initial adjudicatory responsibility in administrative agencies have varied over time and across statutory regimes. Crowell stressed that the goal of the administrative factfinding process was "to furnish a prompt, continuous, expert, and inexpensive method for dealing with a class of questions of fact" and, in so doing, "to secure * * * a sound practical judgment" on the questions before the agency. The Court's observation aligns with recurrent themes of agency adjudication: taking advantage of specialized expertise, adapting law and administration swiftly to changing priorities, and avoiding an increase in the number of Article III judges that would diminish their prestige.

An additional motivation has been the sense that adjudication under a regulatory statute gives the agency an occasion to elaborate federal policies, combined with the sense that an agency fact-finder is more likely to reflect Congress's goals. This latter motivation may have seemed particularly important when Congress passed the Longshoreman's and Harbor Worker's Compensation Act, given the fact that Article III courts in the "Lochner era" were widely thought to have frustrated remedial schemes that departed from the common law. Where Article III business—a private right—is at stake, is the goal of making an adjudicator less independent and more aligned with Congress's preferences in tension with the aims of Article III? See Strauss, *Article III Courts and the Constitutional Structure*, 65 Ind.L.J. 307, 308–09 (1990).

(ii) Does the Court's suggestion in Crowell that the agency functioned as little more than a fact-finding "adjunct" seem naïve or disingenuous? How persuasive are the Court's analogies to the traditional judicial reliance on factfinding by juries, masters, and commissioners—all of whom operate more directly under judicial supervision and with far greater insulation from the influence of the political branches?[7] Notice how deferential the standard of review for ordinary facts was. The statute did not explicitly provide for any review of questions of fact, but rather authorized federal courts to set aside or refuse to enforce an order by the agency if it was not "in accordance with law." Building on its reading of that standard in past cases, the Court concluded that reviewing courts could hold that an agency's finding of ordinary fact was not in accordance with law if the agency acted "without evidence, or 'contrary to the indisputable character of the evidence.' " How often can we expect a court to determine that an agency has made an administrative finding "without evidence" or against the "indisputable character" of such evidence?

(b) **Questions of "Jurisdictional Fact."** The Court in Crowell insisted that constitutional values required de novo judicial review of questions of "jurisdictional fact"—that is, of those facts on which the jurisdiction of the agency depends. Earlier decisions had required de novo review of both "jurisdictional" facts, see Ng Fung Ho v. White, 259 U.S. 276 (1922) (involving the fact of citizenship in an immigration case), and also of "constitutional" facts—those facts on which the adjudication of constitutional rights depends, see Ohio Valley Water Co. v. Ben Avon Borough, 253 U.S. 287 (1920). In Crowell, the Court viewed the questions whether the injury occurred on navigable waters, and whether a master-servant relationship existed, as going to the jurisdiction of the agency. Justice Brandeis, by contrast, first called them quasi-jurisdictional, and then said, as to the master-servant issue, that it "go[es] to the applicability of the substantive law, not to the jurisdiction of the tribunal." Whenever an agency's action violates its governing statute, it seems possible to characterize the agency either as having exceeded its jurisdiction or as having erred substantively. As a result, any effort to distinguish those categories will be elusive. *Cf.* City of Arlington v. FCC, 569 U.S. 290, 297–98 (2013) ("Because the question— whether framed as an incorrect application of agency authority or an assertion of authority not conferred—is always whether the agency has gone beyond what Congress has permitted it to do, there is no principled basis for carving out some arbitrary subset of [legal] claims as 'jurisdictional.' ").

In Northern Pipeline Constr. Co. v. Marathon Pipe Line Co., 458 U.S. 50, 82 n.34 (1982), discussed in greater detail at pp. 501–505, *infra,* the plurality opinion summarized post-Crowell developments by stating: "Crowell's precise holding, with respect to the review of 'jurisdictional' and 'constitutional' facts that arise within ordinary administrative proceedings, has been undermined by later cases." Soon after Crowell, the decision in St. Joseph Stock Yards Co. v. United States, 298 U.S. 38, 53 (1936), rejected any requirement that the court must conduct its own evidentiary hearing;

---

[7]   Justice Thomas has suggested that, in cases of private right, administrative agencies may not make factual findings if subject only to deferential judicial review. See Axon Enter., Inc. v. FTC, 598 U.S. 175, 203 (2023) (Thomas, J., concurring) (arguing that factual finding lies "at the core of judicial power"). See also B & B Hardware, Inc. v. Hargis Industries, Inc., 575 U.S. 138, 171 (2015) (Thomas, J., dissenting) ("Because federal administrative agencies are part of the Executive Branch, it is not clear that they have power to adjudicate claims involving core private rights."). How significantly would acceptance of Justice Thomas's position alter the work of the administrative state? Do private rights constitute much of the agencies' business?

instead, the opinion suggested that all relevant evidence should ordinarily be submitted to the agency and that review on the agency's record would suffice in all but extraordinary cases. Other cases have refused to require courts to engage in de novo review of agency determinations of issues that are no less "jurisdictional" than the master-servant relationship in Crowell. See, *e.g.*, Myers v. Bethlehem Shipbuilding Corp., 303 U.S. 41, 49–50 (1938) (although the NLRB's jurisdiction over a labor dispute depends upon whether it affects interstate commerce, that question is for the Board to determine, with judicial review limited to whether the Board's finding lacks adequate evidence or is contrary to law). Thus, today any requirement of independent judicial judgment on questions of jurisdictional fact is at best infrequently applied, and independent judicial fact-finding—rather than redetermination of facts on the administrative record, ordinarily with considerable deference to the agency's determination—virtually never occurs. See generally Monaghan, *Constitutional Fact Review*, 85 Colum.L.Rev. 229 (1985).

(c) Questions of Law. The Court in Crowell appeared to assume that the Constitution required independent judicial decision of questions of law in private rights cases. But beginning as early as the 1940s, cases such as Gray v. Powell, 314 U.S. 402 (1941), and NLRB v. Hearst Publications., Inc., 322 U.S. 111 (1944), suggested that courts should defer to agency interpretations of their governing statutes, and in Chevron v. Natural Resources Defense Council, 467 U.S. 837, 842–43 (1984), the Court formally implemented a regime of deference to agency interpretations of ambiguous statutes.[8]

In 2024, however, a divided Court overturned Chevron in Loper Bright Enterprises v. Raimondo, 144 S.Ct. 2244 (2024), holding that the Administrative Procedure Act "codifies for agency cases the unremarkable, yet elemental proposition reflected by judicial practice dating back to *Marbury*: that courts decide legal questions by applying their own judgment." The Court specifically rejected earlier cases that deemed an agency interpretation "permissible" even if it was not the "best," holding that "[i]n the business of statutory interpretation, if it is not the best, it is not permissible." The Court bolstered its reasoning by asserting that "agencies have no special competence in resolving statutory ambiguities. Courts do."

Is the conclusion of Loper Bright required not just by the Administrative Procedure Act but by Article III? Justice Gorsuch and Justice Thomas wrote separately to argue that it is, suggesting that deference amounts to vesting part of the judicial power of the United States in administrative agencies. In evaluating this contention, consider the following colloquy from Hart, *Dialogue*, 66 Harv.L.Rev. at 1377–78:

"Q. The Crowell case * * * has a dictum that questions of law * * * must be open to judicial consideration. And * * * Brandeis * * * [said] *that* was necessary to the supremacy of law. Have those statements stood up? * * *

---

[8]   For an extensive discussion of Chevron and a valuable bibliography, see Manning & Stephenson, Legislation and Regulation 1108–37 (4th ed.2021).

"A. [Whether agencies are permitted 'to make final decisions of questions of law'] depends on how you define 'law'. * * *

"In recent years we've recognized increasingly a permissible range of administrative discretion in the shaping of judicially enforceable duties. How wide that discretion should be, and what are the appropriate ways to control it, are crucial questions in administrative law. But so long as the courts sit to answer the questions, the spirit of Brandeis' statement is maintained. And, since discretion by hypothesis is not law, the letter of it is not in question."

Compare Monaghan, *Marbury and the Administrative State*, 83 Colum.L.Rev. 1, 29, 33 (1983), arguing that "[t]he opposition of 'discretion' to 'law' cannot dissolve Hart's problem," since "the result of the exercise of discretion is * * * an administrative formulation of a rule of law." Professor Monaghan concludes, however, that "there has never been a pervasive notion that limited government mandated an all-encompassing judicial duty to supply all of the relevant meaning of statutes. Rather, the judicial duty is to ensure that the administrative agency stays within the zone of discretion committed to it by its organic act."

Along similar lines, the majority opinion in Loper Bright draws an important distinction between *ambiguous* statutes, which should be interpreted de novo by courts, and statutes that "expressly delegate to an agency the authority to give meaning to a particular statutory term[, or] * * * empower an agency to prescribe rules to fill up the details of a statutory scheme, or to regulate subject to the limits imposed by a term or phrase that leaves agencies with flexibility, such as 'appropriate' or 'reasonable.'"

In the latter cases, the Court holds: "When the best reading of a statute is that it delegates discretionary authority to an agency, the role of the reviewing court under the APA is, as always, to independently interpret the statute and effectuate the will of Congress subject to constitutional limits. The court fulfills that role by recognizing constitutional delegations, 'fix[ing] the boundaries of [the] delegated authority.'" (quoting Monaghan, *supra*, at 27). Did Loper Bright effectively return judicial review of the actions of the administrative state to the way it was originally conceived in Crowell?

(6) Agency Adjudication in Criminal Cases. Criminal cases have always been treated as "private rights" cases,[9] despite the involvement of the government as a party, and there seems to be no doubt that an administrative agency may not directly impose criminal punishments.[10] But may an Article III court, in imposing criminal punishment, rely in whole or in part on an agency's determination of fact or law? That question differs from the circumstances (a) in Yakus v. United States, 321 U.S. 414 (1944), p. 473, *supra*, where the Court held that Congress could require a criminal enforcement court to give conclusive effect to the decisions of a prior *judicial*

---

[9]   See, *e.g.*, Northern Pipeline Construction Co. v. Marathon Pipe Line Co., 458 U.S. 50, 70 n.24 (1982), p. 501, *infra*.

[10]   Under at least some circumstances, however, it has been held that *other* non-Article III federal tribunals—characteristically denominated as "legislative courts"—may do so. For discussion of the permissible use of "legislative courts" and the necessity, if any, of review of their judgments by Article III courts, see pp. 498–526, *infra*.

proceeding, and (b) in Crowell, where the Court held that in a *civil* action, a federal court could defer to agency determinations of the facts.

(a) Falbo, Estep, and the Views of Professor Hart. Consider the following excerpts from Professor Hart's *Dialogue*, 66 Harv.L.Rev. at 1380–83. Hart, who accepted Crowell without much difficulty but was troubled by Yakus, was even more troubled by the idea that federal criminal courts might accept the findings of federal agencies without searching independent inquiry:

"Q. Does Yakus mark the maximum inroad on the rights of a criminal defendant to judicial process?

"A. No, unfortunately it doesn't. We have to take account of two World War II selective service cases, Falbo v. United States[, 320 U.S. 549 (1944)], and Estep v. United States[, 327 U.S. 114 (1946)]. 'By the terms of' the selective service legislation, as Justice Douglas put it in Estep, 'Congress enlisted the aid of the federal courts only for enforcement purposes.' And so the question was sharply presented on what terms that could be done.

"The Court held in Falbo, with only Justice Murphy dissenting, that a registrant who was being prosecuted for failure to report for induction (or for work of national importance) could not defend on the ground that he had been wrongly classified and was entitled to a statutory exemption.

"Q. Doesn't that pretty well destroy your notion that there has to be some kind of reasonable means for getting a judicial determination of questions of law affecting liability for criminal punishment? All Congress has to do is to authorize an administrative agency to issue an individualized order, make the violation of the order a crime in itself, and at the same time immunize the order from judicial review. On the question of the violation of the order, all the defendant's rights are preserved in the criminal trial, except that they don't mean anything.

"A. Whoa! Falbo doesn't go that far. In Estep, after the fighting was over, the case was explained—and perhaps it had actually been decided—on the basis that the petitioner in failing to report for induction had failed to exhaust his administrative remedies. Considering the emergency, the requirement that claims be first presented at the induction center was pretty clearly a reasonable procedure.[11]

"Q. How about Estep?

"A. The petitioner there went to the end of the administrative road, and was indicted for refusing to submit to induction. The Court held that he was entitled to make the defense that the local board had 'acted beyond its jurisdiction'. Justice Douglas, speaking for himself and Justices Reed and Black, said:

" 'The provision making the decisions of the local boards "final" means to us that Congress chose not to give administrative action under this Act the customary scope of judicial review which obtains under other statutes. It

---

[11]   [Ed.] More recent cases indicate that even this "exhaustion" aspect of Falbo will be only selectively enforced, at least when the nation is not fully engaged in war. Compare McKart v. United States, 395 U.S. 185 (1969), with McGee v. United States, 402 U.S. 479 (1971).

means that the courts are not to weigh the evidence to determine whether the classification made by the local boards was justified. The decisions of the local boards made in conformity with the regulations are final even though they may be erroneous. The question of jurisdiction of the local board is reached only if there is no basis in fact for the classification which it gave the registrant.'

"Justices Murphy and Rutledge concurred specially on the ground that the Court's construction was required by the Constitution. Justice Frankfurter thought the construction wrong but concurred on the ground that there were other errors in the trial. Justice Burton and Chief Justice Stone dissented.

"Q. Well, the holding in the end wasn't such a departure after all, was it?

"A. Stop and think before you say that.

"Except for two Justices who are now dead, the whole Court dealt with the question as if it were merely one of statutory construction. Three Justices of the Supreme Court of the United States were willing to assume that Congress has power under Article I of the Constitution to direct courts created under Article III to employ the judicial power conferred by Article III to convict a man of a crime and send him to jail without his ever having had a chance to make his defenses. No decision in 164 years of constitutional history, so far as I know, had ever before sanctioned such a thing. Certainly no such decision was cited. For these three didn't even see it as a problem. There is ground to doubt whether the first three in the majority did either.

"Bear in mind that the three dissenters from the Court's construction expressly recognized that the order of induction might have been erroneous in law. They said that the remedy for that was habeas corpus after induction. They seemed to say that the existence of the remedy of habeas corpus saved the constitutionality of the prior procedure. That turns an ultimate safeguard of law into an excuse for its violation. And it strikes close to the heart of one of the main theses of this discussion—that so long at least as Congress feels impelled to invoke the assistance of courts, the supremacy of law in their decisions is assured."

Are Professor Hart's concerns obviously well grounded? Consider the following scenario: The Federal Aviation Administration has statutory authority under 49 U.S.C. § 44703, to issue a pilot's certificate to "an individual when the Administrator finds, after investigation, that the individual is qualified for, and physically able to perform the duties" of a pilot. Congress has made it a crime for someone to "knowingly and willfully serve[ ] or attempt[ ] to serve" as a pilot without a pilot's certificate. 49 U.S.C. § 46317. Assume for present purposes that the issuance of a pilot's certificate is a public right, and that Congress chose to vest the decision to issue a pilot's certificate in the FAA Administrator's discretion, making that decision unreviewable in court.[12] If an individual willfully and knowingly piloted a

---

[12]   In fact, the Federal Aviation Act provides for judicial review of the FAA Administrator's orders, making the Administrator's findings of fact "conclusive" if they are "supported by substantial evidence." 49 U.S.C. § 46110.

plane after having been denied a certificate, should the ability to impose criminal sanctions depend on whether the Administrator properly denied the certificate? Or should Congress have the power to attach criminal liability to the fact of someone's piloting a plane without a certificate? Or would it violate due process to deprive someone of liberty without an opportunity for such person to contest in court the legality of the order upon which criminal liability would rest? *Cf.* Walker v. City of Birmingham, 388 U.S. 307 (1967) (holding that a defendant in a contempt proceeding for violating a temporary injunction cannot raise constitutional challenges to that injunction, but relying on the fact the defendant had, but did not resort to, means of challenging the injunction in court beforehand). Consider the following decision.

(b) The Mendoza-Lopez Case. In United States v. Mendoza-Lopez, 481 U.S. 828 (1987), the Court held that a statutory provision that purported to prevent a federal court in a criminal case from reconsidering an administrative determination denied due process on the facts of the case. There, an alien was prosecuted for the crime of re-entering the United States after having previously been deported. The question was whether he was entitled, in the criminal proceeding, to challenge the validity of the administrative agency's prior deportation order, on the ground that the hearing conducted by the immigration judge failed to afford due process. Although he failed to seek judicial review of that order at the time of its issuance, he contended that he had not understood his rights, that the administrative judge did not adequately apprise him of his right to appeal, and that any waiver of that right was not knowing and intelligent.

The Court first ruled that the statute criminalizing re-entry purported to preclude this form of collateral attack on the earlier deportation orders. But resolution of that statutory question "does not end our inquiry." Turning to constitutional issues, the Court first cited Yakus (and other cases) for the proposition that "where a determination made in an administrative proceeding is to play a critical role in the subsequent imposition of a criminal sanction, there must be *some* meaningful review of the administrative proceeding." In a footnote, the Court added: "Even with this safeguard, the use of the result of an administrative proceeding to establish an element of a criminal offense is troubling. While the Court has permitted criminal conviction for violation of an administrative regulation where the validity of the regulation could not be challenged in the criminal proceeding, Yakus v. United States, the decision in that case was motivated by the exigencies of wartime, dealt with the propriety of regulations rather than the legitimacy of an adjudicative procedure, and, most significantly, turned on the fact that adequate judicial review of the validity of the regulation was available in another forum. Under different circumstances, the propriety of using an administrative ruling in such a way remains open to question. We do not reach this issue here, however, holding that, at a minimum, the result of an administrative proceeding may not be used as a conclusive element of a criminal offense where the judicial review that legitimated such a practice in the first instance has effectively been denied."

The Court proceeded to hold, 5–4, that when defects in a prior deportation proceeding "effectively eliminate[d] the right of [an] alien to obtain judicial review"—apparently because the immigration judge had failed to make clear the consequences of a deportation order and the availability of appeal—due process demanded that the alien could collaterally attack the use of that proceeding as an element of a later criminal offense.

In dissent, Chief Justice Rehnquist, joined by Justices White and O'Connor, agreed that "there may be exceptional circumstances where the Due Process Clause prohibits the Government from using an alien's prior deportation as a basis for imposing criminal liability," but argued that in this case the initial deportation proceedings did not violate due process and that there was no bar to relying on the prior deportation order.

In a separate dissent, Justice Scalia contended that no prior decision of the Court "squarely holds that the Due Process Clause invariably forbids reliance upon the outcome of unreviewable administrative determinations in subsequent criminal proceedings." He continued: "The Court's apparent adoption of that conclusion today seems to me wrong. To illustrate that point * * *, imagine that a State establishes an administrative agency that (after investigation and full judicial-type administrative hearings) periodically publishes a list of unethical businesses. Further imagine that the State, having discovered that a number of previously listed businesses are bribing the agency's investigators to avoid future listing, passes a law making it a felony for a business that has been listed to bribe agency investigators. It cannot be that the Due Process Clause forbids the State to punish violations of that law unless it either makes the agency's listing decisions judicially reviewable or permits those charged with violating the law to defend themselves on the ground that the original listing decisions were in some way unlawful."

(c) Questions About Mendoza-Lopez.

(i)   Does the Court's decision effectively vindicate Professor Hart's position, including his criticisms of the opinions in Falbo and Estep?

(ii) How broad is the Court's holding? In a prosecution for re-entry, could an alien collaterally attack a deportation order if the immigration judge did explain the right to seek judicial review of the deportation order, but because the alien could not afford a lawyer, no appeal was filed? If an alien, represented by counsel, had moved unsuccessfully to remove the immigration judge on the basis of alleged bias, but the lawyer failed to seek judicial review of the denied motion?

(iii) If agency findings can play a lesser role in criminal than in civil enforcement courts, why exactly is that? Because of Article III? The Due Process Clause? Presuppositions about the role of courts as guarantors of constitutional liberty that are reflected in Article III, the Due Process Clause, and the Suspension Clause? *Cf.* INS v. St. Cyr, p. 464, *supra*.

(7) Transitional Questions. In Mendoza-Lopez, as in Crowell, the statutory scheme gave ultimate responsibility for enforcing federal law to an Article III court, and the question therefore arose to what extent an "enforcement court" could rely on an agency's determination of fact or law. But may Congress bypass both Article III federal courts and state courts altogether, by authorizing a non-Article III federal tribunal to issue directly binding and enforceable rulings in private rights cases? In criminal prosecutions? Does the permissibility of using non-Article III tribunals depend upon the existence and extent of judicial review in an Article III court?

Although Congress has seldom purported to vest administrative "agencies" with powers that present this constitutional question, it has much more frequently done so through its use of so-called "legislative courts"— discussed in some of the materials that follow this Note.

B. FORMAL AND FUNCTIONAL APPROACHES TO AGENCY ADJUDICATION AND "LEGISLATIVE" COURTS

In the context of administrative agencies, Crowell v. Benson drew a sharp dichotomy between public rights and private rights, as discussed above. In addition to its analysis of agencies, the Court in Crowell also noted that, in certain contexts, Congress has relied on long-settled authority to establish "legislative" courts—federal tribunals denominated as "courts" but not organized under Article III, staffed by judges lacking life tenure and salary protection—in specialized contexts such as the territories and the District of Columbia, the military, and claims against the United States. Importantly, while some of these courts deal with public rights, some also handle business, including in some instances criminal cases, that meet the definition of private rights.

After elaborating on the main contexts in which Congress relies on legislative courts, the material that follows considers the Court's complex and often-shifting approach to justifying all non-Article III tribunals, including administrative agencies and legislative courts. Please keep the following questions in mind: To what extent has the Court, in its recent cases, continued to rely on the distinction between private and public rights? How much do formal or categorical factors such as history and tradition account for the Court's acceptance of non-Article III tribunals that handle what one would ordinarily think of as private rights? To what extent has the Court also embraced a "functional" approach to these questions, one that asks whether Congress's reliance on non-Article III tribunals, in particular contexts and subject to some form of Article III review, leaves intact the goals and policies that animate Article III? Finally, how important is the distinction between an administrative agency and a legislative court for purposes of constitutional analysis?

INTRODUCTORY NOTE ON LEGISLATIVE COURTS

(1) Historical Practice. Longstanding examples of legislative courts fall into three main categories.

(a) Territorial Courts. In American Ins. Co. v. Canter, 26 U.S. (1 Pet.) 511 (1828), Chief Justice Marshall upheld the use of non-Article III courts to adjudicate an admiralty dispute in the then-territory of Florida. Territorial courts, the Chief Justice said, were "not Constitutional Courts, in which the judicial power conferred by the Constitution on the general government, can be deposited." Instead, they were "legislative Courts, created in virtue of the general right of sovereignty, which exists in the government, or in virtue of [Article IV, Sec. 3's power in] Congress to make all needful rules and regulations respecting the territory belonging to the United States." While noting that the "admiralty jurisdiction can be exercised in the states [only in Article III courts], the same limitation does not extend to the territories. In legislating for them, Congress exercises the combined powers of the general, and of a state government."

As courts of general jurisdiction, territorial courts resemble state courts, which need not satisfy Article III's strictures. Moreover, had Congress established only Article III courts in the territory of Florida, hard questions might have arisen about whether all cases filed in those courts came within one of Article III's nine heads of jurisdiction. Do these considerations justify assigning a case like Canter, which clearly falls within one of those nine heads, to a non-Article III federal tribunal?

The Court relied on Canter, among other authorities, in Palmore v. United States, 411 U.S. 389 (1973), which upheld the constitutionality of a criminal prosecution before the local, non-Article III courts that Congress created in the District of Columbia, pursuant to Article I's conferral of legislative authority over the District.[1] For an article contending that Canter provides an inapt analogy for the historically and constitutionally unique status of the District of Columbia, see Durling, *The District of Columbia and Article III*, 107 Geo.L.J. 1205 (2019).

(b) Military Courts. From 1789 to the present, Congress has authorized military tribunals, whose judges are commissioned officers not protected by life tenure, to conduct courts martial to enforce military discipline and punish service members.[2] Their constitutionality was upheld in Dynes v. Hoover, 61 U.S. (20 How.) 65 (1858), and as a practical matter seems to be beyond question today,[3] although some issues have arisen at the margin about the reach of court-martial jurisdiction.[4] The justifications for

---

[1]   For descriptions of other territorial and related courts, see p. 499, *supra*.

[2]   See Schlueter, *The Court-Martial: An Historical Survey*, 87 Mil.L.Rev. 129, 150 (1980).

[3]   For a discussion of the relation of military justice to Article III, see Note, *Military Justice and Article III*, 103 Harv.L.Rev. 1909 (1990). For an article questioning the textual and historical basis for the Court's broad acceptance of military tribunals, see Vladeck, *Military Courts and Article III*, 103 Geo.L.J. 933 (2015) (proposing a limiting principle that authorizes military courts only in contexts in which "established norms of foreign and international practice" justify their use).

[4]   The holding of O'Callahan v. Parker, 395 U.S. 258 (1969), that a soldier may be tried by a court martial only for "service-connected" offenses, was overruled by Solorio v. United States, 483 U.S. 435 (1987). The Supreme Court has barred the use of military courts to try

establishing such a system outside of Article III have included (i) the physical separation of civilian society from the military, the latter of which requires a tribunal staffed with military officers to permit a quick determination of guilt; (ii) a concern that the military system differs from civilian society and that civilian officials unfamiliar with or even antagonistic to military life might misapply the legal standards of the military justice system; and (iii) the view that the goals of civilian and military justice differ, as the latter serves to preserve good order and discipline in the military as much as to punish, deter, incapacitate and rehabilitate offenders. See generally Vladeck, note 3, *supra*.

Other military tribunals have also been used from time to time to try enemy spies and other alleged unlawful combatants under the laws of war, to conduct trials under conditions of martial law, and to administer justice in foreign territories subject to military occupation. For discussion, see Note on Military Tribunals or Commissions, p. 551, *infra*.

(c) Courts to Adjudicate Public Rights Disputes. Numerous bodies fall within the elusive category (see pp. 486–489, *supra*) of federal tribunals that adjudicate public rights. Current examples include the Court of Federal Claims,[5] the Tax Court,[6] and the United States Court of Appeals for Veterans Claims.[7]

(2) Distinguishing Legislative Courts from Administrative Agencies. What is the difference between a legislative court and an administrative agency, and how does it bear on the appropriateness of adjudication outside of Article III? Consider the relevance of the following generalizations:

(a) Policymaking Functions. Administrative agencies typically engage in rulemaking, as well as adjudication, and are permitted to choose between and coordinate those processes to serve policy goals. See Shapiro, *The Choice of Rulemaking or Adjudication in the Development of Administrative Policy*, 78 Harv.L.Rev. 921 (1965). (Administrative law judges (ALJs), who characteristically make initial or recommended decisions, generally are not policymakers, but policymaking officials often review, and/or have some authority to establish standards and procedures governing, ALJ's decisions.) By contrast, legislative courts are less likely to have explicit and programmatic policymaking responsibilities, other than the exercise of discretion that comes through the resolution of indeterminacy in adjudication.

---

civilians, including the civilian dependents of service members, at least for non-military offenses in peacetime. See, *e.g.*, Kinsella v. United States ex rel. Singleton, 361 U.S. 234 (1960). In 2006, Congress extended court-martial jurisdiction to reach civilian contractors "serving with or accompanying an armed force in the field" during a "contingency operation." 10 U.S.C. § 802(a)(10); see United States v. Ali, 71 M.J. 256 (C.A.A.F.2012). See also Leider, *Retiring Military Jurisdiction over Military Retirees*, 68 Vill.L.Rev. 751 (2023) (questioning recent decisions upholding court-martial jurisdiction over retirees).

[5]   For discussions of the status and history of this court, see pp. 51, 109–112, *supra*.

[6]   See p. 51, *supra*.

[7]   See p. 51, *supra*. Earlier statutes also assigned adjudicative responsibilities to a Court of Private Land Claims and a Court of Customs Appeals. See Ex parte Bakelite Corp., 279 U.S. 438 (1929).

(b) Enforceability of Judgments. The decisions of administrative agencies often are not self-executing, but (as in Crowell v. Benson) instead require an enforcement action in a federal court. By contrast, the decisions of legislative courts (including the bankruptcy courts) are typically final and enforceable unless appealed. See Redish, *Legislative Courts, Administrative Agencies, and the Northern Pipeline Decision,* 1983 Duke L.J. 197, 216–17.

(c) Traditions of Justification. At least since Crowell v. Benson, agency adjudication is frequently justified *under* Article III on the theory that agencies are "adjuncts" or that judicial review of the agency's decisions retains "the essential elements" of the judicial power in an Article III court. See Fallon, *Of Legislative Courts, Administrative Agencies, and Article III,* 101 Harv.L.Rev. 915, 920–26, 946–47 (1988). By contrast, legislative courts have usually been justified as permissible "exceptions" to Article III's requirement of tenure and salary protection (although they are sometimes subject to Article III review as well). In the cases discussed below, consider how sharply that distinction holds up.

INTRODUCTORY NOTE ON COMPETING FRAMEWORKS FOR NON-ARTICLE III ADJUDICATION

The four cases discussed below frame the Court's modern approach to the constitutionality of non-Article III adjudication. Notice that the cases alternate between more formal and historically driven approaches (Northern Pipeline and Granfinanciera) and more functional and purpose-driven approaches (Thomas and Schor) to justifying non-Article III tribunals.

(1) The Northern Pipeline Case. The first Supreme Court decision to invalidate congressional employment of legislative courts was Northern Pipeline Constr. Co. v. Marathon Pipe Line Co., 458 U.S. 50 (1982), which held unconstitutional the jurisdiction given to non-Article III federal bankruptcy judges by the Bankruptcy Act of 1978. (Those judges were appointed by the President, with the consent of the Senate, to 14-year terms.) The case originated when Northern Pipeline filed a reorganization petition in the bankruptcy court. The Bankruptcy Act empowered that court to resolve not only what the plurality opinion characterized as "traditional matters of bankruptcy"—involving the adjudication of claims against the debtor and the adjustment of debtor-creditor relations—but also all civil claims "arising in or related to" bankruptcy proceedings. Decisions of the bankruptcy court were subject to appellate review by the court of appeals (and in some cases by the district court as well) and ultimately by the Supreme Court.

The precise question in Northern Pipeline was not the validity of the courts altogether, but the scope of the jurisdiction granted under the 1978 Act. Before 1978, bankruptcy proceedings had been heard by federal "referees" (also not Article III judges), who routinely adjudicated state-law issues in connection with the ordinary and traditional bankruptcy tasks of allowing and disallowing claims *against* the bankrupt's estate. The 1978 Act's innovation was to expand the bankruptcy courts' jurisdiction to actions brought *by* the bankrupt's estate against its debtors. The key issue in the case was the constitutionality of that expansion of jurisdiction (under which the bankrupt party, Northern Pipeline, had sued Marathon for breach of contract and misrepresentation).

(a) The Plurality Opinion. Justice Brennan's plurality opinion (joined by Justices Marshall, Blackmun, and Stevens) began by emphasizing that Article III was designed to ensure an independent and impartial judiciary and thereby maintain the separation of powers. The Court's precedents allowing the use of legislative courts, "properly understood, * * * represent no broad departure from the constitutional command that the judicial power of the United States must be vested in Art. III courts. Rather, they reduce to three narrow situations not subject to that command"— involving territorial courts, military tribunals, and the adjudication of public rights disputes. Each, Justice Brennan asserted, "recogniz[ed] a circumstance in which the grant of power to the Legislative and Executive Branches was historically and constitutionally so exceptional that the congressional assertion of a power to create legislative courts was consistent with, rather than threatening to, the constitutional mandate of separation of powers."

The jurisdiction conferred by the 1978 Bankruptcy Act, however, reached beyond these three categories. In particular, Justice Brennan rejected the argument that the claim at issue was a " 'public right,' similar to such congressionally created benefits as 'radio station licenses, pilot licenses, or certificates for common carriers' granted by administrative agencies." While "the restructuring of debtor-creditor relations, which is at the core of the federal bankruptcy power, * * * may well be a 'public right,' " "the adjudication of state-created private rights, such as the right to recover contract damages that is at issue in this case * * * obviously is not." Instead, the claim on behalf of the bankrupt corporation "to augment its estate is 'one of private right, that is, of the liability of one individual to another under the law as defined.' Crowell v. Benson, 285 U.S., at 51."

Justice Brennan then turned to a distinct argument for upholding the jurisdiction—that "the bankruptcy court is merely an 'adjunct' to the district court, and that the delegation of certain adjudicative functions to the bankruptcy court is accordingly consistent with the principle that the judicial power of the United States must be vested in Art. III courts." He wrote: "As support for their argument, appellants rely principally upon Crowell v. Benson, 285 U.S. 22 (1932), and United States v. Raddatz, 447 U.S. 667 (1980), cases in which we approved the use of administrative agencies and magistrates as adjuncts to Art. III courts. * * * The question to which we turn, therefore, is whether the Act has retained 'the essential attributes of the judicial power,' Crowell v. Benson, *supra*, at 51, in Art. III tribunals. * * *

"In United States v. Raddatz, *supra*, the Court upheld the 1978 Federal Magistrates Act, which permitted district court judges to refer certain pretrial motions, including suppression motions based on alleged violations of constitutional rights, to a magistrate for initial determination. The Court observed that the magistrate's proposed findings and recommendations were subject to *de novo* review by the district court, which was free to rehear the evidence or to call for additional evidence. Moreover, it was noted that the magistrate considered motions only upon reference from the district court, and that the magistrates were appointed, and subject to removal, by the district court.* * * *

"Together [Crowell and Raddatz] establish two principles that aid us in determining the extent to which Congress may constitutionally vest traditionally judicial functions in non-Art. III officers. First, it is clear that when Congress creates a substantive federal right, it possesses substantial discretion to prescribe the manner in which that right may be adjudicated— including the assignment to an adjunct of some functions historically performed by judges. * * * Second, the functions of the adjunct must be limited in such a way that 'the essential attributes' of judicial power are retained in the Art. III court."

Justice Brennan concluded that neither principle supported the constitutionality of the bankruptcy court's jurisdiction. On the first point, he noted simply that the claim of the bankrupt estate, for breach of contract and misrepresentation, was based on a right created by *state* law. As for whether the district courts retained the essential attributes of judicial power, Justice Brennan offered four reasons why the arrangement under the Bankruptcy Act compared unfavorably with the structure approved in Crowell. First, unlike the agency in Crowell, which "made only specialized, narrowly confined factual determinations regarding a particularized area of law," the bankruptcy courts adjudicated "not only traditional matters of bankruptcy, but also 'all civil proceedings arising under title 11 or arising in or *related to* cases under title 11.' 28 U.S.C. § 1471(b) (emphasis added)." "Second, while the agency in Crowell engaged in statutorily channeled factfinding functions, the bankruptcy courts exercise '*all* of the jurisdiction' conferred by the Act on the district courts, § 1471(c) (emphasis added)." Third, in Crowell the agency had only a limited power to issue compensation orders, which required enforcement by a district court; by contrast, "the bankruptcy courts exercise all ordinary powers of district courts * * *. Fourth, while orders issued by the agency in Crowell were to be set aside if 'not supported by the evidence,' the judgments of the bankruptcy courts are apparently subject to review only under the more deferential 'clearly erroneous' standard."

Justice Brennan stressed that the availability of conventional judicial review was not alone enough to constitute the bankruptcy courts as adjuncts: "Our precedents make it clear that the constitutional requirements for the exercise of the judicial power must be met at all stages of adjudication, and not only on appeal, where the court is restricted to considerations of law, as well as the nature of the case as it has been shaped at the trial level."

(b) Justice Rehnquist's Concurrence. Justice Rehnquist, joined by Justice O'Connor, concurred in the judgment only. He first noted that the claims filed by the bankrupt's estate "are the stuff of the traditional actions at common law tried by the courts at Westminster in 1789," arose exclusively under state law, and were to be tried "by the traditional common-law mode of judge and jury." He then acknowledged that "[t]he cases dealing with the authority of Congress to create courts other than by use of its power under

Art. III do not admit of easy synthesis. * * * I need not decide whether these cases in fact support a general proposition and three tidy exceptions, as the plurality believes, or whether instead they are but landmarks on a judicial 'darkling plain' where ignorant armies have clashed by night * * *. None of the cases has gone so far as to sanction the type of adjudication to which Marathon will be subjected against its will under the provisions of the 1978 Act." Nor could the bankruptcy courts be sustained under an "adjuncts" theory: "All matters of fact and law in whatever domains of the law to which the parties' dispute may lead are to be resolved by the bankruptcy court in the first instance, with only traditional appellate review by Art. III courts apparently contemplated. Acting in this manner the bankruptcy court is not an 'adjunct' of either the district court or the court of appeals."

(c)　The Dissent. Justice White, joined by Chief Justice Burger and Justice Powell, dissented. "The plurality concedes that in adjudications and discharges in bankruptcy, 'the restructuring of debtor-creditor relations, which is at the core of the federal bankruptcy power,' and 'the manner in which the rights of debtors and creditors are adjusted,' are matters of federal law. Under the plurality's own interpretation of the cases, therefore, these matters could be heard and decided by Art. I judges." But if this was so, said the dissent, it made no sense to hold that the bankruptcy court could not adjudicate state law claims: "[T]he distinction between claims based on state law and those based on federal law disregards the real character of bankruptcy proceedings. The routine in ordinary bankruptcy cases now, as it was before 1978, is to stay actions against the bankrupt, collect the bankrupt's assets, require creditors to file claims or be forever barred, allow or disallow claims that are filed, adjudicate preferences and fraudulent transfers, and make pro rata distributions to creditors, who will be barred by the discharge from taking further actions against the bankrupt. * * * [I]n the ordinary bankruptcy proceeding the great bulk of creditor claims are claims that have accrued under state law prior to bankruptcy—claims for goods sold, wages, rent, utilities, and the like. * * * Every such claim must be filed and its validity is subject to adjudication by the bankruptcy court. * * * Hence, the bankruptcy judge is constantly enmeshed in state-law issues."

Justice White then offered his own approach to the larger issues at stake in the case: "There is no difference in principle between the work that Congress may assign to an Art. I court and that which the Constitution assigns to Art. III courts. Unless we want to overrule a large number of our precedents upholding a variety of Art. I courts—not to speak of those Art. I courts that go by the contemporary name of 'administrative agencies'—this conclusion is inevitable." But that conclusion, he wrote, does not imply that "this Court must always defer to the legislative decision to create Art. I, rather than Art. III, courts. Article III is not to be read out of the Constitution; rather, it should be read as expressing one value that must be balanced against competing constitutional values and legislative responsibilities. This Court retains the final word on how that balance is to be struck." In Justice White's view, "[t]he burden on Art. III values should

* * * be measured against the values Congress hopes to serve through the use of Art. I courts."

Applying that approach, Justice White appeared to place dispositive weight on three considerations. First, "Crowell suggests that the presence of appellate review by an Art. III court will go a long way toward insuring a proper separation of powers." "Second, no one seriously argues that the Bankruptcy Act of 1978 represents an attempt by the political branches of government to aggrandize themselves at the expense of the third branch or an attempt to undermine the authority of constitutional courts in general." Third, Congress was justified both in wanting specialized bankruptcy judges and in not wanting to give them the protections of Article III: "Congress may have desired to maintain some flexibility in its possible future responses to the general problem of bankruptcy. There is no question that the existence of several hundred bankruptcy judges with life tenure would have severely limited Congress's future options. Furthermore, the number of bankruptcies may fluctuate, producing a substantially reduced need for bankruptcy judges. Congress may have thought that, in that event, a bankruptcy specialist should not as a general matter serve as a judge in the countless nonspecialized matters that come before the federal district courts."[1]

(2) The Thomas Decision. Soon after the decision in Northern Pipeline, the Supreme Court addressed the validity of another Article I tribunal in Thomas v. Union Carbide Agricultural Products Co., 473 U.S. 568 (1985). The case arose under the Federal Insecticide, Fungicide, and Rodenticide Act (FIFRA), 7 U.S.C. § 136 *et seq.*, which requires manufacturers of pesticides, as a precondition to obtaining the registration necessary to market a new product, to submit extensive data to EPA concerning the product's health and environmental effects. To streamline the registration process and make it less costly, the statute permits the EPA to use data previously submitted by another registrant in considering the registration application of a later ("follow-on") registrant—but only if the follow-on registrant agrees to compensate the original data submitter. If the original and follow-on registrants cannot agree on appropriate compensation, the issue must be submitted to binding arbitration before a private arbitrator, whose decision is subject to judicial review only for "fraud, misrepresentation, or other misconduct." 7 U.S.C. § 136a(c)(1)(D)(ii).

In upholding the statute's arbitration provision, Justice O'Connor's opinion for the Court stated that "an absolute construction of Article III is not possible," and that "the Court has long recognized that Congress is not

---

[1]   The Supreme Court stayed the effect of its decision in Northern Pipeline. After a short period during which an emergency rule, drafted by the Judicial Conference, was in effect in most districts, Congress in 1984 enacted a new Bankruptcy Act. Act of July 10, 1984, 98 Stat. 333. That Act makes the bankruptcy judges (who are appointed by the courts of appeals for 14-year terms) "units" of the district court; it directs that each district court "may provide" that "any or all" cases or proceedings arising under Title 11, or arising in or related to a case under Title 11, shall be referred to the bankruptcy judges of the district. If the matter is a "core" proceeding— corresponding, roughly, to the pre-1978 bankruptcy court's "summary" jurisdiction—the bankruptcy judge may "hear and determine" it. But if the matter is a non-core proceeding, the bankruptcy judge makes only proposed findings and conclusions, and the final order is entered by the district judge after "reviewing de novo" all matters as to which an objection was made. "Personal injury tort and wrongful death claims" must be adjudicated in the district court.

barred from acting pursuant to its powers under Article I to vest decisionmaking authority in tribunals that lack the attributes of Article III courts." The lead opinion in Northern Pipeline had spoken only for a plurality, Justice O'Connor emphasized. In addition, it adopted too categorical an approach in suggesting that the public rights/private rights dichotomy provides a bright-line test for determining the requirements of Article III and that for a case to come within the public rights category, the government must be a party. "Nor did a majority of the Court endorse the implication of the private right/public right dichotomy that Article III has no force simply because a dispute is between the Government and an individual." Instead, "[t]he enduring lesson of Crowell is that practical attention to substance rather than doctrinaire reliance on formal categories should inform application of Article III."

Turning to the dispute before it, the Court distinguished Northern Pipeline because here the claim rested on federal rather than state law, and distinguished Crowell because the federal claim did not replace a pre-existing state law right to compensation. Although the liability of one private party to another was at stake, the right to compensation under FIFRA "is not a purely 'private' right but bears many of the characteristics" of a public rights dispute because it arose under a complex regulatory scheme.

The administrative scheme, the Court stressed, gave effect to "a public purpose as an integral part of a program safeguarding the public health" pursuant to Congress's "power, under Article I, * * * to allocate costs and benefits among voluntary participants" in the regulatory program. In the context of creating a comprehensive regulatory scheme, the Court said, Congress "has the power to condition issuance of registrations or licenses on compliance with agency procedures"—in particular, FIFRA's arbitration scheme. Stressing the arbitration mechanism devised by Congress "incorporates its own system of internal sanctions and relies only tangentially, if at all, on the Judicial Branch for enforcement," Justice O'Connor concluded, "[t]he danger of Congress or the Executive encroaching on the Article III judicial powers is at a minimum when no unwilling defendant is subjected to judicial enforcement."

Finally, the Court found that FIFRA provided sufficient judicial review for a scheme involving the adjudication of "a seemingly 'private' right that is * * * so closely integrated into a public regulatory scheme." The statute provided judicial review of the arbitrator's determinations for "fraud, misconduct, or misrepresentation," which the Court construed to "protect[ ] against arbitrators who abuse or exceed their powers or willfully misconstrue their mandate under the governing law" and to preserve "review of constitutional error."

Justice Brennan, joined by Justices Blackmun and Marshall, concurred in the judgment. He first stated that the Northern Pipeline plurality had not sought to create "a generally applicable definition of 'public rights' but concluded that at a minimum public rights disputes must arise 'between the government and others.'" But then he seemed to switch gears, stating that (though the matter was not free from doubt) the FIFRA compensation scheme "should be viewed as involving a matter of public rights * * *. In one sense the question of proper compensation for a follow-on registrant's use of test data is * * * a dispute about 'the liability of one individual to another under the law as defined', Crowell v. Benson, at 51 (defining matters of private right). But the dispute arises in the context of a federal regulatory scheme that virtually occupies the field. Congress has decided that effectuation of the public policies of FIFRA demands not only a requirement of compensation from follow-on registrants in return for mandatory access to data but also an administrative process—mandatory negotiation followed by binding arbitration—to ensure that unresolved compensation disputes do not delay public distribution of needed products. This case, in other words, involves not only the congressional prescription of a federal rule of decision to govern a private dispute but also the active participation of a federal regulatory agency in resolving the dispute. Although a compensation dispute under FIFRA ultimately involves a determination of the duty owed one private party by another, at its heart the dispute involves the exercise of authority by a Federal Government arbitrator in the course of administration of FIFRA's comprehensive regulatory scheme."

In contrast with Northern Pipeline, Thomas conveyed the message that "practical attention to substance rather than doctrinaire reliance on formal categories should inform application of Article III." And the Court seemed to suggest that, in determining the permissibility of a non-Article III adjudicator, it should credit Congress's constitutionally valid public purpose in implementing a complex environmental scheme. But there were elements of formalism in Thomas's reasoning as well. Both the Court and the concurrence seemed to suggest that Congress, in the exercise of its Article I powers, may condition the parties' participation in the pesticide licensing scheme on agreeing to the arbitral mechanism prescribed by FIFRA. That could be seen to resemble an argument that the greater includes the lesser— the notion that if Congress can properly bar someone from selling pesticides altogether, it can condition a license to do so on factual determinations made by an agency, not a court. See Harrison, *Public Rights and Private Privileges*, 54 Ga.L.Rev. 143, 184–85, 198 (2019).

(3) CFTC v. Schor. CFTC v. Schor, 478 U.S. 833 (1986), arose under the Commodity Exchange Act (CEA), 7 U.S.C. § 1 *et seq.*, which a relevant committee report described as establishing a "comprehensive regulatory structure to oversee the volatile and esoteric futures trading complex." H.R.Rep. No. 93–975, at 1 (1974). The CEA, administered by the Commodity Futures Trading Commission, provided agency-administered remedies for fraudulent and manipulative practices in commodity futures trading.

Schor, a commodities trader, brought an action before the CFTC to seek statutory reparations from a commodity brokerage firm, ContiCommodity Services, Inc. (Conti), for alleged violations of the CEA and the CFTC's implementing regulations. Because Schor had a debit balance with Conti due to trading losses and unpaid commissions, Conti filed a state common law action for debt against Schor in federal district court. Schor moved to dismiss the court case, arguing that all the claims could be fully resolved in the reparations proceedings before the CFTC. Conti then voluntarily dismissed its judicial action and filed a counterclaim in Schor's CFTC reparations proceeding, which was permitted under CFTC regulations aimed at "promoting efficient dispute resolution."

After the CFTC ruled against Schor on both the reparations claim and Conti's counterclaim, he challenged the CFTC's authority to hear the counterclaim, arguing that its adjudication of that common-law private right violated Article III. In an opinion by Justice O'Connor, the Court noted that while its precedents "do not admit of easy synthesis," they establish that "the resolution of claims such as Schor's cannot turn on conclusory reference to the language of Article III," but rather that any congressional delegation of adjudicatory responsibility to a non-Article III entity "must be assessed by reference to the purposes underlying the requirements of Article III." The Court then articulated and applied the following framework for applying Article III's purposes:

"In determining the extent to which a given congressional decision to authorize the adjudication of Article III business in a non-Article III tribunal impermissibly threatens the institutional integrity of the Judicial Branch, the Court has declined to adopt formalistic and unbending rules. * * * Thus, in reviewing Article III challenges, we have weighed a number of factors, none of which has been deemed determinative, with an eye to the practical effect that the congressional action will have on the constitutionally assigned role of the federal judiciary. * * * Among the factors upon which we have focused are [1] the extent to which the 'essential attributes of judicial power' are reserved to Article III courts, and, conversely, the extent to which the non-Article III forum exercises the range of jurisdiction and powers normally vested only in Article III courts, [2] the origins and importance of the right to be adjudicated, and [3] the concerns that drove Congress to depart from the requirements of Article III."

The Court applied those three factors as follows:

"[1] The CFTC, like the agency in Crowell, deals only with a 'particularized area of law,' Northern Pipeline, *supra*, 458 U.S., at 85, whereas the jurisdiction of the bankruptcy courts found unconstitutional in Northern Pipeline extended to broadly 'all civil proceedings arising under title 11 or arising in *or related to* cases under title 11.' 28 U.S.C. § 1471(b) (emphasis added). CFTC orders, like those of the agency in Crowell, but unlike those of the bankruptcy courts under the 1978 Act, are enforceable only by order of the district court. CFTC orders are also reviewed under the same 'weight of the evidence' standard sustained in Crowell, rather than the more deferential standard found lacking in Northern Pipeline. See 7 U.S.C. § 9; Northern Pipeline, *supra*, at 85. The legal rulings of the CFTC, like the legal determinations of the agency in Crowell, are subject to de novo review. Finally, the CFTC, unlike the bankruptcy courts under the 1978 Act, does not exercise 'all ordinary powers of district courts,' and thus may not, for instance, preside over jury trials or issue writs of habeas corpus. * * *

"[2] Of course, the nature of the claim has significance in our Article III analysis quite apart from the method prescribed for its adjudication. The counterclaim asserted in this litigation is a 'private' right for which state law provides the rule of decision. It is therefore a claim of the kind assumed to be at the 'core' of matters normally reserved to Article III courts. * * * In this litigation, however, '[l]ooking beyond form to the substance of what' Congress has done, we are persuaded that the congressional authorization of limited CFTC jurisdiction over a narrow class of common law claims as an incident to the CFTC's primary, and unchallenged, adjudicative function does not create a substantial threat to the separation of powers. * * * Congress gave the CFTC the authority to adjudicate such matters, but the decision to invoke this forum is left entirely to the parties and the power of the federal judiciary to take jurisdiction of these matters is unaffected. In such circumstances, separation of powers concerns are diminished[.] * * *

"[3] When Congress authorized the CFTC to adjudicate counterclaims, its primary focus was on making effective a specific and limited federal regulatory scheme * * *. Congress intended to create an inexpensive and expeditious alternative forum through which customers could enforce the provisions of the CEA against professional brokers. Its decision to endow the CFTC with jurisdiction over such reparations claims is readily understandable * * * [and] is of unquestioned constitutional validity. * * * [And] the CFTC's assertion of counterclaim jurisdiction is limited to that which is necessary to make the reparations procedure workable."

In light of these factors, the Court concluded, "the magnitude of any intrusion on the Judicial Branch can only be termed *de minimis*," and a rejection of legislative power to "permit such limited cognizance of common law counterclaims at the election of the parties" would defeat Congress's purposes of creating "a prompt, continuous, expert and inexpensive" agency process for dealing with CEA claims.

Schor represents a decided shift toward the pragmatic approach in Justice White's Northern Pipeline dissent. Does that test leave the Court too much discretion, or does it represent a common-sense way of ensuring that there is enough judicial supervision to justify vesting jurisdiction over a contract claim, for good reason, in a non-Article III tribunal? How important is it to the Court that the parties have the power to decide whether to invoke that forum?

(4) Granfinanciera, S.A. v. Nordberg. Granfinanciera, S.A. v. Nordberg, 492 U.S. 33 (1989), is the final decision that frames the modern approach to non-Article III adjudication and highlights the dichotomy between the formal and pragmatic approaches. There, the Court took up the question of whether there was a right to a jury trial in a bankruptcy proceeding involving a fraudulent conveyance action, based on federal statutory law, filed on behalf of a bankruptcy estate against a noncreditor. The lower courts had rejected the defendants' claimed right to a jury trial on the ground that an action to recover a fraudulent conveyance is equitable, not legal. The Supreme Court reversed. Justice Brennan's opinion for the Court then declared that the question was the same under both Article III and the Seventh Amendment, with the crucial inquiry being whether the right to recover a fraudulent conveyance should be viewed as a "public" or "private" right. Reiterating his position in Thomas, Justice Brennan reasoned that a public right could be either a right "closely intertwined with a federal regulatory program Congress has power to enact" or one that "belongs to [or] exists against the Federal Government." Otherwise, he said, it was a private right that "must be adjudicated by an Article III court." From that starting point, he concluded that fraudulent conveyance claims "are quintessentially suits at common law that more nearly resemble state-law contract claims brought by a bankrupt corporation to augment the bankruptcy estate than they do creditors' hierarchically ordered claims to a pro rata share of the bankruptcy res." That is, they are legally similar to the common law claims that a majority of the Justices in Northern Pipeline deemed to be private rights. Having determined that the right was private, Justice Brennan concluded that the defendants were entitled to a jury trial.

Justice Scalia concurred in part and concurred in the judgment. Arguing that Thomas was wrongly decided, he contended that "public rights are rights *of the public*—that is, rights pertaining to claims brought by or against the United States." The permissibility of non-Article III adjudication in the public rights context, for him, turned on "the device of waiver of sovereign immunity," which "can only be implicated, of course, in suits where the Government is a party." Justice White's dissent (with which Justices Blackmun and O'Connor expressed general agreement) took a far broader view of public rights and criticized the Court for "call[ing] into question the longstanding assumption * * * that the equitable proceedings of [bankruptcy] courts, adjudicating creditor-debtor disputes," involve public rights. Justice White also argued that "[h]istory and our cases support the proposition that the right to a jury trial depends not solely on the nature of the issue to be resolved, but also on the forum in which it is to be resolved." He concluded that in a court of equity, where a jury trial would be anomalous, the Seventh Amendment does not apply.

The significance of Granfinanciera lies in (a) its assignment of greater importance to the public/private distinction than had Thomas or Schor; (b) its reliance on Justice Brennan's reformulation of the public rights doctrine, as offered in his earlier concurring opinion in Thomas; and (c) its invocation of the Seventh Amendment right to jury trial as an additional consideration.[2]

INTRODUCTORY NOTE ON THE SUPREME COURT'S MODERN APPROACH TO NON-ARTICLE III ADJUDICATION

The four cases that frame the Court's modern approach to non-Article III adjudication—Northern Pipeline, Thomas, Schor, and Granfinanciera—shift between categorical or formal analysis and pragmatic or functional analysis. In reading Stern v. Marshall and Oil States Energy Services v. Greene's Energy Group, the principal cases that follow, consider whether the Supreme Court now subscribes to one or the other of these approaches. Or is

---

[2]   In Securities and Exchange Commission v. Jarkesy, 144 S.Ct. 2117 (2024), the Court relied upon Granfinanciera in holding that the SEC's use of agency proceedings, rather than a federal court, to impose fines for securities fraud violated the Seventh Amendment right to a jury trial and was not shielded by the public rights doctrine. Jarkesy is discussed in more detail at p. 542, *infra*.

the Court still shifting back and forth to some degree? More generally, which approach is more persuasive? Why?

Stern v. Marshall

564 U.S. 462 (2011).
Certiorari to the U.S. Court of Appeals for the Ninth Circuit.

■ CHIEF JUSTICE ROBERTS delivered the opinion of the Court.

* * * This is the second time we have had occasion to weigh in on this long-running dispute between Vickie Lynn Marshall and E. Pierce Marshall over the fortune of J. Howard Marshall II * * *. [A] Texas state probate court and the Bankruptcy Court for the Central District of California * * * have reached contrary decisions on [the Marshalls' litigation.] * * *

* * * The Bankruptcy Court in this case exercised the judicial power of the United States by entering final judgment on a common law tort claim, even though the judges of such courts enjoy neither tenure during good behavior nor salary protection. We conclude that, although the Bankruptcy Court had the statutory authority to enter judgment on Vickie's counterclaim, it lacked the constitutional authority to do so.

I

* * * Known to the public as Anna Nicole Smith, Vickie was J. Howard's third wife and married him about a year before his death. Although J. Howard bestowed on Vickie many * * * gifts during their courtship and marriage, he did not include her in his will. Before J. Howard passed away, Vickie filed suit in Texas state probate court, asserting that Pierce—J. Howard's younger son—fraudulently induced J. Howard to sign a living trust that did not include her, even though J. Howard meant to give her half his property. * * *

After J. Howard's death, Vickie filed a petition for bankruptcy in the Central District of California. Pierce filed a complaint in that bankruptcy proceeding, contending that Vickie had defamed him by inducing her lawyers to tell members of the press that he had engaged in fraud to gain control of his father's assets. The complaint sought a declaration that Pierce's defamation claim was not dischargeable in the bankruptcy proceedings. Pierce subsequently filed a proof of claim for the defamation action, meaning that he sought to recover damages for it from Vickie's bankruptcy estate. Vickie responded to Pierce's initial complaint by * * * filing a counterclaim for tortious interference with the gift she expected from J. Howard. * * *

* * * [The Bankruptcy Court awarded Vickie $400 million in compensatory damages and $25 million in punitive damages.]

In post-trial proceedings, Pierce argued that [Vickie's counterclaim was not a "core proceeding" under 28 U.S.C. § 157(b)(2)(C) and hence was outside the Bankruptcy Court's statutory jurisdiction. Ultimately, the Court of Appeals for the Ninth Circuit agreed with Pierce's jurisdictional objection, in part because of doubts the Bankruptcy Court could constitutionally adjudicate Vickie's counterclaim.]

II

[In this part of the opinion, the Court ruled that Vickie's counterclaim was a "core proceeding" within the Bankruptcy Court's statutory jurisdiction, and that the statutory text was so clear on this point as to leave no room to construe the statute otherwise in order to avoid a constitutional question.]

III

Although we conclude that § 157(b)(2)(C) permits the Bankruptcy Court to enter final judgment on Vickie's counterclaim, Article III of the Constitution does not.

A

* * * Article III is "an inseparable element of the constitutional system of checks and balances" that "both defines the power and protects the independence of the Judicial Branch." Northern Pipeline [Constr. Co. v. Marathon Pipe Line Co,] 458 U.S. [50,] 58 [(1982)] (plurality opinion). * * *

In establishing the system of divided power in the Constitution, the Framers considered it essential that "the judiciary remain[ ] truly distinct from both the legislature and the executive." The Federalist No. 78, p. 466 (C. Rossiter ed. 1961) (A. Hamilton). * * *

We have recognized that the three branches are not hermetically sealed from one another, but it remains true that Article III imposes some basic limitations that the other branches may not transgress. Those limitations serve two related purposes. "Separation-of-powers principles are intended, in part, to protect each branch of government from incursion by the others. Yet the dynamic between and among the branches is not the only object of the Constitution's concern. The structural principles secured by the separation of powers protect the individual as well." Bond v. United States, 564 U.S. [211, 222] (2011). * * *

B

This is not the first time we have faced an Article III challenge to a bankruptcy court's resolution of a debtor's suit. In Northern Pipeline, we considered whether bankruptcy judges serving under the Bankruptcy Act of 1978—appointed by the President and confirmed by the Senate, but lacking the tenure and salary guarantees of Article III—could "constitutionally be vested with jurisdiction to decide [a] state-law contract claim" against an entity that was not otherwise part of the bankruptcy proceedings. 458 U.S., at 53, 87, n.40 (plurality opinion); see *id.,* at 89–92 (Rehnquist, J., concurring in judgment). The Court concluded that assignment of such state law claims for resolution by those judges "violates Art. III of the Constitution." *Id.*, at 52, 87 (plurality opinion); *id.*, at 91 (Rehnquist, J., concurring in judgment).

* * * A full majority of the Court, while not agreeing on the scope of the [public rights] exception, concluded that the doctrine did not encompass adjudication of the state law claim at issue in that case. *Id.*, at 69–72; see *id.*, at 90–91 (Rehnquist, J., concurring in judgment) * * *.[5] * * *

After our decision in Northern Pipeline, Congress revised the statutes governing bankruptcy jurisdiction and bankruptcy judges. In the 1984 Act, Congress provided that the judges of the new bankruptcy courts would be appointed by the courts of appeals for the circuits in which their districts are located. And * * * Congress permitted the newly constituted bankruptcy courts to enter final judgments only in "core" proceedings.

With respect to such "core" matters, however, the bankruptcy courts under the 1984 Act exercise the same powers they wielded under the Bankruptcy Act of 1978 (1978 Act). As in Northern Pipeline, for example, the newly constituted bankruptcy courts are charged * * * with resolving "[a]ll matters of fact and law in whatever domains of the law to which" a counterclaim may lead. 458 U.S., at 91 (Rehnquist, J., concurring in judgment). * * * And, as in Northern Pipeline, the district courts review the judgments of the bankruptcy courts in core proceedings only under the usual limited appellate standards. That requires marked deference to, among other things, the bankruptcy judges' findings of fact. See § 158(a); Fed. Rule Bkrtcy. Proc. 8013 (findings of fact "shall not be set aside unless clearly erroneous").

C

* * *

1

Vickie's counterclaim cannot be deemed a matter of "public right" that can be decided outside the Judicial Branch. * * * [I]n Northern Pipeline we rejected the argument that the public rights doctrine permitted a bankruptcy court to adjudicate a state law suit brought by a debtor against a company that had not filed a claim against the estate. Although our discussion of the public rights exception since that time has not been entirely consistent, and the exception has been the subject of some debate, this case does not fall within any of the various formulations of the concept that appear in this Court's opinions.

We first recognized the category of public rights in Murray's Lessee v. Hoboken Land & Improvement Co., 59 U.S. 272 (1856). That case involved the Treasury Department's sale of property belonging to a

---

[5]   The dissent is thus wrong in suggesting that less than a full Court agreed on the points pertinent to this case.

customs collector who had failed to transfer payments to the Federal Government that he had collected on its behalf. The plaintiff * * * objected that the Treasury Department's calculation of the deficiency and sale of the property was void, because it was a judicial act that could not be assigned to the Executive under Article III.

* * * [T]he Court * * * confirmed that Congress cannot "withdraw from judicial cognizance any matter which, from its nature, is the subject of a suit at the common law, or in equity, or admiralty." [*Id.*, at 284.] The Court also recognized that "[a]t the same time there are matters, involving public rights, which may be presented in such form that the judicial power is capable of acting on them, and which are susceptible of judicial determination, but which congress may or may not bring within the cognizance of the courts of the United States, as it may deem proper." *Ibid.*

As an example of such matters, the Court referred to "[e]quitable claims to land by the inhabitants of ceded territories" and cited cases in which land issues were conclusively resolved by Executive Branch officials. *Ibid.* In those cases "it depends upon the will of congress whether a remedy in the courts shall be allowed at all," so Congress could limit the extent to which a judicial forum was available. Murray's Lessee, 18 How., at 284. The challenge in Murray's Lessee to the Treasury Department's sale of the collector's land likewise fell within the "public rights" category of cases, because it could only be brought if the Federal Government chose to allow it by waiving sovereign immunity.

Subsequent decisions from this Court contrasted cases within the reach of the public rights exception—those arising "between the Government and persons subject to its authority in connection with the performance of the constitutional functions of the executive or legislative departments"—and those that were instead matters "of private right, that is, of the liability of one individual to another under the law as defined." Crowell v. Benson, 285 U.S. 22, 50, 51 (1932).[6] * * *

Shortly after Northern Pipeline, the Court rejected the limitation of the public rights exception to actions involving the Government as a party. The Court has continued, however, to limit the exception to cases in which the claim at issue derives from a federal regulatory scheme, or in which resolution of the claim by an expert government agency is

---

[6]   Although the Court in Crowell went on to decide that the facts of the private dispute before it could be determined by a non-Article III tribunal in the first instance, subject to judicial review, the Court did so only after observing that the administrative adjudicator had only limited authority to make specialized, narrowly confined factual determinations regarding a particularized area of law and to issue orders that could be enforced only by action of the District Court. In other words, the agency in Crowell functioned as a true "adjunct" of the District Court. That is not the case here.

Although the dissent suggests that we understate the import of Crowell in this regard, the dissent itself recognizes—repeatedly—that Crowell by its terms addresses the determination of facts outside Article III. Crowell may well have additional significance in the context of expert administrative agencies that oversee particular substantive federal regimes, but we have no occasion to and do not address those issues today. * * *

deemed essential to a limited regulatory objective within the agency's authority. In other words, it is still the case that what makes a right "public" rather than private is that the right is integrally related to particular federal government action.

Our decision in Thomas v. Union Carbide Agricultural Products Co., for example, involved a data-sharing arrangement between companies under a federal statute providing that disputes about compensation between the companies would be decided by binding arbitration. 473 U.S. 568, 571–575 (1985). This Court held that the scheme did not violate Article III, explaining that "[a]ny right to compensation . . . results from [the statute] and does not depend on or replace a right to such compensation under state law." *Id.,* at 584.

Commodity Futures Trading Commission v. Schor concerned a statutory scheme that created a procedure for customers injured by a broker's violation of the federal commodities law to seek reparations from the broker before the Commodity Futures Trading Commission (CFTC). 478 U.S. 833, 836 (1986). A customer filed such a claim to recover a debit balance in his account, while the broker filed a lawsuit in Federal District Court to recover the same amount as lawfully due from the customer. The broker later submitted its claim to the CFTC, but after that agency ruled against the customer, the customer argued that agency jurisdiction over the broker's counterclaim violated Article III. This Court disagreed, but only after observing that (1) the claim and the counterclaim concerned a "single dispute"—the same account balance; (2) the CFTC's assertion of authority involved only "a narrow class of common law claims" in a " 'particularized area of law' "; (3) the area of law in question was governed by "a specific and limited federal regulatory scheme" as to which the agency had "obvious expertise"; (4) the parties had freely elected to resolve their differences before the CFTC; and (5) CFTC orders were "enforceable only by order of the district court." *Id.,* at 844, 852–855 (quoting Northern Pipeline, 458 U.S., at 85). Most significantly, given that the customer's reparations claim before the agency and the broker's counterclaim were competing claims to the same amount, the Court repeatedly emphasized that it was "necessary" to allow the agency to exercise jurisdiction over the broker's claim, or else "the reparations procedure would have been confounded." *Id.,* at 856.

The most recent case in which we considered application of the public rights exception * * * is Granfinanciera, S.A. v. Nordberg, 492 U.S. 33 (1989). In Granfinanciera we rejected a bankruptcy trustee's argument that a fraudulent conveyance action filed on behalf of a bankruptcy estate against a noncreditor in a bankruptcy proceeding fell within the "public rights" exception. We explained that, "[i]f a statutory right is not closely intertwined with a federal regulatory program Congress has power to enact, and if that right neither belongs to nor exists against the Federal Government, then it must be adjudicated by an Article III court." *Id.,* at 54–55. We reasoned that fraudulent conveyance suits were "quintessentially suits at common law that more nearly resemble state law contract claims brought by a bankrupt corporation to augment the bankruptcy estate than they do creditors' hierarchically ordered claims to a pro rata share of the bankruptcy res." *Id.*, at 56. As a consequence, we concluded that fraudulent conveyance actions were "more accurately characterized as a private rather than a public right as we have used those terms in our Article III decisions." *Id.*, at 55.[7]

Vickie's counterclaim—like the fraudulent conveyance claim at issue in Granfinanciera—does not fall within any of the varied formulations of the public rights exception in this Court's cases. It is not a matter that can be pursued only by grace of the other branches, as in Murray's Lessee, or one that "historically could have been determined exclusively by" those branches, Northern Pipeline, *supra*, at 68 (citing Ex parte Bakelite Corp., 279 U.S. [438,] 458 [(1929)]. The claim is instead one under state common law between two private parties. * * *

In addition, Vickie's claimed right to relief does not flow from a federal statutory scheme, as in Thomas * * *. It is not "completely dependent upon" adjudication of a claim created by federal law, as in Schor. And in contrast to the objecting party in Schor, Pierce did not truly consent to resolution of Vickie's claim in the bankruptcy court proceedings. He had nowhere else to go if he wished to recover from Vickie's estate.[8]

Furthermore, the asserted authority to decide Vickie's claim is not limited to a "particularized area of the law," as in Crowell, Thomas, and Schor. Northern Pipeline, 458 U.S., at 85 (plurality opinion). We deal here not with an agency but with a court, with substantive jurisdiction reaching any area of the *corpus juris*. This is not a situation in which Congress devised an "expert and inexpensive method for dealing with a class of questions of fact which are particularly suited to examination and determination by an administrative agency specially assigned to that task." Crowell, 285 U.S., at 46. The "experts" in the federal system at resolving common law counterclaims such as Vickie's are the Article III courts * * *.

The dissent reads our cases differently, and in particular contends that more recent cases view Northern Pipeline as " 'establish[ing] only

---

7   We noted that we did not mean to "suggest that the restructuring of debtor-creditor relations is in fact a public right." 492 U.S., at 56, n.11. Our conclusion was that, "even if one accepts this thesis," Congress could not constitutionally assign resolution of the fraudulent conveyance action to a non-Article III court. *Ibid.* Because neither party asks us to reconsider the public rights framework for bankruptcy, we follow the same approach here.

8   Contrary to the claims of the dissent, Pierce did not have another forum in which to pursue his claim to recover from Vickie's prebankruptcy assets, rather than take his chances with whatever funds might remain after the Title 11 proceedings. Creditors who possess claims that do not satisfy the requirements for nondischargeability under 11 U.S.C. § 523 have no choice but to file their claims in bankruptcy proceedings if they want to pursue the claims at all. That is why * * * the notion of "consent" does not apply in bankruptcy proceedings as it might in other contexts.

that Congress may not vest in a non-Article III court the power to adjudicate, render final judgment, and issue binding orders in a traditional contract action arising under state law, without consent of the litigants, and subject only to ordinary appellate review.'" (quoting Thomas, *supra*, at 584). Just so: Substitute "tort" for "contract," and that statement directly covers this case.

We recognize that there may be instances in which the distinction between public and private rights—at least as framed by some of our recent cases—fails to provide concrete guidance as to whether, for example, a particular agency can adjudicate legal issues under a substantive regulatory scheme. Given the extent to which this case is so markedly distinct from the agency cases discussing the public rights exception in the context of such a regime, however, we do not in this opinion express any view on how the doctrine might apply in that different context.

What is plain here is that this case involves the most prototypical exercise of judicial power: the entry of a final, binding judgment *by a court* with broad substantive jurisdiction, on a common law cause of action, when the action neither derives from nor depends upon any agency regulatory regime. * * *

2

[The Court next rejected Vickie's contention that her counterclaim could be adjudicated under bankruptcy doctrine holding that a creditor who files a proof of claim in bankruptcy court (as Pierce did) must accept the further consequence of the bankruptcy court's adjudicating matters necessary to resolve the creditor's claim. See Katchen v. Landy, 382 U.S. 323 (1966); Langenkamp v. Culp, 498 U.S. 42 (1990) (per curiam). The Court instead concluded that there was never any reason to believe that the process of adjudicating Pierce's proof of claim would necessarily resolve Vickie's counterclaim.]

3

Vickie additionally argues that the Bankruptcy Court's final judgment was constitutional because bankruptcy courts under the 1984 Act are properly deemed "adjuncts" of the district courts. We rejected a similar argument in Northern Pipeline, and our reasoning there holds true today.

* * * The new bankruptcy courts, like the old, do not "ma[k]e only specialized, narrowly confined factual determinations regarding a particularized area of law" or engage in "statutorily channeled factfinding functions." Northern Pipeline, 458 U.S., at 85 (plurality opinion). Instead, bankruptcy courts under the 1984 Act resolve "[a]ll matters of fact and law in whatever domains of the law to which" the parties' counterclaims might lead. *Id.*, at 91 (Rehnquist, J., concurring in judgment).

In addition, whereas the adjunct agency in Crowell v. Benson "possessed only a limited power to issue compensation orders . . . [that] could be enforced only by order of the district court," Northern Pipeline, *supra*, at 85, a bankruptcy court resolving a counterclaim under 28 U.S.C. § 157(b)(2)(C) has the power to enter "appropriate orders and judgments"—including final judgments—subject to review only if a party chooses to appeal. * * * Given that authority, a bankruptcy court can no more be deemed a mere "adjunct" of the district court than a district court can be deemed such an "adjunct" of the court of appeals. * * *

It does not affect our analysis that * * * bankruptcy judges under the current Act are appointed by the Article III courts, rather than the President. If—as we have concluded—the bankruptcy court itself exercises "the essential attributes of judicial power [that] are reserved to Article III courts," Schor, 478 U.S., at 851 (internal quotation marks omitted), it does not matter who appointed the bankruptcy judge * * *.

D

Finally, Vickie and her amici predict as a practical matter that restrictions on a bankruptcy court's ability to hear and finally resolve compulsory counterclaims will create significant delays and impose additional costs on the bankruptcy process. It goes without saying that "the fact that a given law or procedure is efficient, convenient, and useful in facilitating functions of government, standing alone, will not save it if it is contrary to the Constitution." INS v. Chadha, 462 U.S. 919, 944 (1983). * * *

If our decision today does not change all that much, then why the fuss? Is there really a threat to the separation of powers where Congress has conferred the judicial power outside Article III only over certain counterclaims in bankruptcy? The short but emphatic answer is yes. A statute may no more lawfully chip away at the authority of the Judicial Branch than it may eliminate it entirely. * * * We cannot compromise the integrity of the system of separated powers and the role of the Judiciary in that system, even with respect to challenges that may seem innocuous at first blush.

* * *

* * * The Bankruptcy Court below lacked the constitutional authority to enter a final judgment on a state law counterclaim that is not resolved in the process of ruling on a creditor's proof of claim. Accordingly, the judgment of the Court of Appeals is affirmed.

It is so ordered.

■ JUSTICE SCALIA, concurring.

I agree with the Court's interpretation of our Article III precedents, and I accordingly join its opinion. I adhere to my view, however, that— our contrary precedents notwithstanding—"a matter of public rights . . . must at a minimum arise between the government and others,"

Granfinanciera, S.A. v. Nordberg, 492 U.S. 33, 65 (1989) (SCALIA, J., concurring in part and concurring in judgment) (internal quotation marks omitted).

The sheer surfeit of factors that the Court was required to consider in this case should arouse the suspicion that something is seriously amiss with our jurisprudence * * *. I count at least seven different reasons * * * for concluding that an Article III judge was required to adjudicate this lawsuit * * *.

Apart from their sheer numerosity, the more fundamental flaw in the many tests suggested by our jurisprudence is that they have nothing to do with the text or tradition of Article III. For example, Article III gives no indication that state-law claims have preferential entitlement to an Article III judge; nor does it make pertinent the extent to which the area of the law is "particularized." * * *

Leaving aside certain adjudications by federal administrative agencies, which are governed (for better or worse) by our landmark decision in Crowell v. Benson, 285 U.S. 22 (1932), in my view an Article III judge is required in all federal adjudications, unless there is a firmly established historical practice to the contrary. For that reason—and not because of some intuitive balancing of benefits and harms—I agree that Article III judges are not required in the context of territorial courts, courts-martial, or true "public rights" cases. Perhaps historical practice permits non-Article III judges to process claims against the bankruptcy estate; the subject has not been briefed, and so I state no position on the matter. But Vickie points to no historical practice that authorizes a non-Article III judge to adjudicate a counterclaim of the sort at issue here.

■ JUSTICE BREYER, with whom JUSTICE GINSBURG, JUSTICE SOTOMAYOR, and JUSTICE KAGAN join, dissenting.

* * *

I

My disagreement with the majority's conclusion stems in part from my disagreement about the way in which it interprets, or at least emphasizes, certain precedents. In my view, the majority overstates the current relevance of statements this Court made in * * * Murray's Lessee v. Hoboken Land & Improvement Co., 59 U.S. 272 (1856), and it overstates the importance of an analysis that did not command a Court majority in Northern Pipeline Constr. Co. v. Marathon Pipe Line Co., 458 U.S. 50 (1982), and that was subsequently disavowed. At the same time, I fear the Court understates the importance of a watershed opinion widely thought to demonstrate the constitutional basis for the current authority of administrative agencies to adjudicate private disputes, namely, Crowell v. Benson, 285 U.S. 22 (1932). And it fails to follow the analysis that this Court more recently has held applicable to the evaluation of claims of a kind before us here * * *. See Thomas v. Union

Carbide Agricultural Products Co., 473 U.S. 568 (1985); Commodity Futures Trading Comm'n v. Schor, 478 U.S. 833 (1986). * * *

A

In Murray's Lessee, the Court held that the Constitution permitted an executive official, through summary, nonjudicial proceedings, to attach the assets of a customs collector whose account was deficient. * * * In the course of its opinion, the Court wrote:

> "[W]e do not consider congress can either withdraw from judicial cognizance any matter which, from its nature, is the subject of a suit at the common law, or in equity, or admiralty; nor, on the other hand, can it bring under the judicial power a matter which, from its nature, is not a subject for judicial determination. At the same time there are matters, involving public rights, which may be presented in such form that the judicial power is capable of acting on them, and which are susceptible of judicial determination, but which congress may or may not bring within the cognizance of the courts of the United States, as it may deem proper." Id., at 284.

The majority reads the first part of the statement's first sentence as authoritatively defining the boundaries of Article III. I would read the statement in a less absolute way. For one thing, the statement is in effect dictum. For another, it is the remainder of the statement, announcing a distinction between "public rights" and "private rights," that has had the more lasting impact. Later Courts have seized on that distinction when upholding non-Article III adjudication, not when striking it down. [Citing cases.] The one exception is Northern Pipeline * * *. But in that case [it was] a plurality, not a majority, [that] read the statement roughly in the way the Court does today.

B

At the same time, I believe the majority places insufficient weight on Crowell * * *. The Court assumed that an Article III court would review the agency's decision de novo in respect to questions of law but it would conduct a less searching review (looking to see only if the agency's award was "supported by evidence in the record") in respect to questions of fact. The Court pointed out that the case involved a dispute between private persons (a matter of "private rights") and (with one exception not relevant here) it upheld Congress' delegation of primary factfinding authority to the agency. * * *

Crowell has been hailed as "the greatest of the cases validating administrative adjudication." Bator, The Constitution as Architecture: Legislative and Administrative Courts Under Article III, 65 Ind.L.J. 233, 251 (1990). Yet, in a footnote, the majority distinguishes Crowell as a case in which the Court upheld the delegation of adjudicatory authority to an administrative agency simply because the agency's power to make the "specialized, narrowly confined factual determinations" at issue arising in a "particularized area of law," made the agency a "true 'adjunct' of the District Court." Were Crowell's holding as narrow as the majority suggests, one could question the validity of Congress' delegation of authority to adjudicate disputes among private parties to other agencies such as the National Labor Relations Board, the Commodity Futures Trading Commission, the Surface Transportation Board, and the Department of Housing and Urban Development * * *.

C

The majority, in my view, overemphasizes the precedential effect of the plurality opinion in Northern Pipeline. * * *

Three years [after deciding that case], the Court held that Northern Pipeline

> "establishes only that Congress may not vest in a non-Article III court the power to adjudicate, render final judgment, and issue binding orders in a traditional contract action arising under state law, without consent of the litigants, and subject only to ordinary appellate review." Thomas, 473 U.S., at 584.

D

* * * I would look to this Court's more recent Article III cases Thomas and Schor—cases that commanded a clear majority. In both cases the Court took a more pragmatic approach to the constitutional question. It sought to determine whether, in the particular instance, the challenged delegation of adjudicatory authority posed a genuine and serious threat that one branch of Government sought to aggrandize its own constitutionally delegated authority by encroaching upon a field of authority that the Constitution assigns exclusively to another branch. * * *

II

A

This case law, as applied in Thomas and Schor, requires us to determine pragmatically whether a congressional delegation of adjudicatory authority to a non-Article III judge violates the separation-of-powers principles inherent in Article III. * * * [The relevant] factors include (1) the nature of the claim to be adjudicated; (2) the nature of the non-Article III tribunal; (3) the extent to which Article III courts exercise control over the proceeding; (4) the presence or absence of the parties' consent; and (5) the nature and importance of the legislative purpose served by the grant of adjudicatory authority to a tribunal with judges who lack Article III's tenure and compensation protections. The presence of "private rights" does not automatically determine the outcome of the question but requires a more "searching" examination of the relevant factors. Schor, *supra*, at 854.

Insofar as the majority would apply more formal standards, it simply disregards recent, controlling precedent.

B

Applying Schor's approach here, I conclude that * * * [a] grant of authority to a bankruptcy court to adjudicate compulsory counterclaims does not violate any constitutional separation-of-powers principle related to Article III.

First, I concede that *the nature of the claim to be adjudicated* argues against my conclusion. Vickie Marshall's counterclaim—a kind of tort suit—resembles "a suit at the common law." Murray's Lessee, 18 How., at 284. * * *

At the same time the significance of this factor is mitigated here by the fact that bankruptcy courts often decide claims that similarly resemble various common-law actions. * * *

Second, *the nature of the non-Article III tribunal* argues in favor of constitutionality. * * * [T]he tribunal is made up of judges who enjoy considerable protection from improper political influence. Unlike the 1978 Act which provided for the appointment of bankruptcy judges by the President with the advice and consent of the Senate, current law provides that the federal courts of appeals appoint federal bankruptcy judges. Bankruptcy judges are removable by the circuit judicial council (made up of federal court of appeals and district court judges) and only for cause. Their salaries are pegged to those of federal district court judges, and the cost of their courthouses and other work-related expenses are paid by the Judiciary. * * *

Third, *the control exercised by Article III judges over bankruptcy proceedings* argues in favor of constitutionality. * * * Any party may appeal * * * to the federal district court, where the federal judge will review all determinations of fact for clear error and will review all determinations of law de novo. But for the here-irrelevant matter of what Crowell considered to be special "constitutional" facts, the standard of review for factual findings here ("clearly erroneous") is more stringent than the standard at issue in Crowell (whether the agency's factfinding was "supported by evidence in the record"). 285 U.S., at 48; see Dickinson v. Zurko, 527 U.S. 150, 152, 153 (1999) ("unsupported by substantial evidence" more deferential than "clearly erroneous" (internal quotation marks omitted)). * * *

Moreover, in one important respect Article III judges maintain greater control over the bankruptcy court proceedings at issue here than they did over the relevant proceedings in any of the previous cases in which this Court has upheld a delegation of adjudicatory power. The District Court here may "withdraw, in whole or in part, any case or proceeding referred [to the Bankruptcy Court] . . . on its own motion or on timely motion of any party, for cause shown." 28 U.S.C. § 157(d).

Fourth, the fact that *the parties have consented* to Bankruptcy Court jurisdiction argues in favor of constitutionality, and strongly so. Pierce Marshall * * * appeared voluntarily in Bankruptcy Court as one of Vickie

Marshall's creditors * * *. He need not have filed a claim, * * * for he says his claim is "nondischargeable," in which case he could have litigated it in a state or federal court after distribution. * * *

Fifth, *the nature and importance of the legislative purpose served* by the grant of adjudicatory authority to bankruptcy tribunals argues strongly in favor of constitutionality.

* * * [T]o be effective, a single tribunal must have broad authority to restructure [debtor-creditor] relations, "having jurisdiction of the parties to controversies brought before them," "decid[ing] all matters in dispute," and "decree[ing] complete relief." Katchen v. Landy, 382 U.S. 323, 335 (1966) (internal quotation marks omitted).

The restructuring process requires a creditor to file a proof of claim in the bankruptcy court. In doing so, the creditor "triggers the process of 'allowance and disallowance of claims,' thereby subjecting himself to the bankruptcy court's equitable power." Langenkamp [v. Culp, 498 U.S. 42,44 (1990) (per curiam)] (quoting Granfinanciera, *supra,* at 58). By filing a proof of claim, the creditor agrees to the bankruptcy court's resolution of that claim, and if the creditor wins, the creditor will receive a share of the distribution of the bankruptcy estate. When the bankruptcy estate has a related claim against that creditor, that counterclaim may offset the creditor's claim, or even yield additional damages that augment the estate and may be distributed to the other creditors. * * *

Consequently a bankruptcy court's determination of [counterclaims] * * * plays a critical role in Congress' constitutionally based effort to create an efficient, effective federal bankruptcy system. At the least, that is what Congress concluded. We owe deference to that determination, which shows the absence of any legislative or executive motive * * * to encroach upon areas that Article III reserves to judges to whom it grants tenure and compensation protections.

Considering these factors together, I conclude that, as in Schor, "the magnitude of any intrusion on the Judicial Branch can only be termed *de minimis.*" 478 U.S., at 856. * * *

For these reasons, with respect, I dissent.

FURTHER NOTE ON LEGISLATIVE COURTS

(1) Formal Versus Functional Approaches and the Search for Constitutional Limits. How well does the Court in Stern reconcile the complex case law that preceded it? Justice Breyer's dissent unmistakably relies on the functional approach of Thomas and Schor. The opinion of the Court by Chief Justice Roberts, however, is harder to characterize. Certainly, he frames his opinion as a more formal approach, meant to protect against a series of pragmatic decisions, each seemingly "innocuous," that collectively lack a limiting principle and deprive the courts of their fundamental role in the constitutional scheme.

Yet is there as much of a difference between the majority and dissent as the differing tones and emphases suggest? The Court's opinion largely distinguishes prior cases on the basis of (some of) their facts. The Court's opinion does not set forth a generalized understanding about how to assess the constitutionality of a diverse array of existing institutional arrangements.

As Justice Scalia notes, the opinion of the Court instead adverts to a large number of considerations whose relative importance is unclear. How much easier is it to apply those factors than those invoked in Schor? Is the analysis in Stern all that different from the analysis in private rights cases such as Northern Pipeline and Crowell, which focused more tightly on whether the adjudicator could be understood as an Article III adjunct?

(2) The Significance of Consent. To what extent can a litigant's consent validate an adjudication that might otherwise be constitutionally questionable?

(a) Individual Versus Structural Interests. The Stern decision contends that Article III protects both the personal rights of litigants and the structural interest in the separation of powers.[1] The Schor decision, after drawing the same distinction, argued that litigants can waive their personal rights, but when the structural concern is implicated, consent cannot cure any constitutional difficulty. In his dissent in Schor, Justice Brennan contended that the distinction between personal and structural interests was artificial: individual interests are at risk only when federal adjudicators are subject to congressional or executive pressure. He then contended that consent should have no weight in assessing the validity of non-Article III adjudication.

Could one accept Justice Brennan's view that the two interests are inseparable without accepting his conclusion that consent is not relevant? Justice Brennan viewed the matter as similar to the inability of litigants to consent to Article III adjudication when the courts lack subject matter jurisdiction. But consider other analogies: (a) litigants who consent to private arbitration of a matter that otherwise would have fallen within the jurisdiction of the Article III courts; or (b) a litigant who might have a valid constitutional argument resting on the separation of powers but chooses not to assert that argument. (For example, even if the scheme in Crowell v. Benson was constitutional only if appellate review in an Article III tribunal is required, no litigant is obliged to seek such review.) Which analogy is more convincing?

(b) The Voluntariness of Consent. What constitutes *valid* consent? On the facts of Schor, the claim of consent was very strong, given Schor's motion to dismiss the parallel Article III court proceeding because of the

---

[1] Because the Court found that Pierce did not really consent to bankruptcy court adjudication, Stern does not clearly indicate what role consent should play when it does in fact exist. (That question is discussed at paragraph (2)(c), *infra*, and further in the Note on Magistrate Judges, pp. 546–550, *infra*).

pendency of the CFTC proceeding. But the Court said more broadly that merely proceeding before the CFTC constituted consent to a counterclaim. When federal programs provide for compulsory arbitration of disputes, has every participant consented to arbitration simply by participating in the program? See generally Bruff, *Public Programs, Private Deciders: The Constitutionality of Arbitration in Federal Programs*, 67 Tex.L.Rev. 441 (1989). If so, does that fact explain Thomas v. Union Carbide?

In Stern, the Court is far more skeptical about notions of constructive consent. On the facts there presented, doesn't the Chief Justice have the better of the argument? If Pierce's choice was either to file in bankruptcy court or to accept a non-trivial risk of forfeiting his claim if it was later deemed to have been discharged, how "voluntary" was his consent to counterclaim jurisdiction? More strikingly, if chemical companies had to agree to the arbitration scheme under FIFRA in order to get a license to sell their pesticides, how voluntary was the consent in Thomas?

(c) The Role of Consent Clarified. In Wellness International Network, Limited v. Sharif, 575 U.S. 665 (2015), Justice Sotomayor's opinion for the Court held that Article III permits bankruptcy judges to adjudicate Stern claims when both parties consent. The Court held that a litigant may waive his or her "personal" right to an Article III tribunal. Citing Schor, the Court explained that, with such a waiver, the proper question was what " 'practical effect' " non-Article III adjudication would have on the " 'constitutionally assigned role of the federal judiciary.' " In the bankruptcy context, the Court found such effects to be minimal because bankruptcy judges are appointed and removable by Article III judges and function as judicial officers within the district court. In addition, the bankruptcy courts' jurisdiction over Stern claims encompasses only a " 'narrow class' " of common law matters that are incidental to the primary jurisdiction over bankruptcy. Finally, the Court concluded that Congress had no evident purpose "to aggrandize itself or humble the Judiciary" by assigning Stern claims to bankruptcy judges. Rather, Congress merely sought to "supplement[ ] the capacity of district courts through the able assistance of bankruptcy judges."

In a dissent joined by Justice Scalia and, in part, by Justice Thomas, Chief Justice Roberts criticized the majority for reviving a functionalist approach that put efficiency, convenience, and utility ahead of the prophylactic protections that an independent judiciary assures. Casting the right to an Article III forum as central to liberty and accountability, the dissent argued that "an individual may not consent away the institutional interest protected by the separation of powers."[2] Justice Thomas also dissented separately.

Read together, do Thomas, Schor, Stern, and Wellness International suggest that the Court will apply (a) a strict, formalist approach to cases that

---

[2] For analysis questioning the relationship between party consent and the permissibility of non-Article III adjudication, see Dodge, *Reconceptualizing Non-Article III Tribunals*, 99 Minn.L.Rev. 905 (2015); Hessick, *Consenting to Adjudication Outside the Article III Courts*, 71 Vand.L.Rev. 715 (2018).

do not involve party consent and (b) a more forgiving, functionalist approach when consent is present?

(3) Why Not Article III Status? These complicated questions are of course necessitated by Congress's determination that non-Article III adjudicators, in some context, are to be preferred to those with life tenure and salary protection. And, at least in cases such as Schor and Thomas, the Court has relied heavily on legislative purpose in applying its balancing text. Why didn't Congress constitute bankruptcy courts as Article III courts? In connection with the Bankruptcy Reform Act of 1978 (the statute that was invalidated in Northern Pipeline), the organized federal judiciary lobbied against doing so, arguing that the Article III judiciary must remain relatively small to retain the elite status that has traditionally attracted first-rate lawyers to the federal bench. See Countryman, *Scrambling to Define Bankruptcy Jurisdiction: The Chief Justice, the Judicial Conference, and the Legislative Process*, 22 Harv.J. on Legis. 1, 7–12 (1985). How strong is this argument for making bankruptcy courts non-Article III courts?

(4) The (In)Significance of Crowell v. Benson. Northern Pipeline and Stern v. Marshall treat legislative courts and adjuncts as distinct categories, and view Crowell as involving the latter. That approach limits the generative force of Crowell as a precedent that can validate non-Article III tribunals that do not fit the agency model. By contrast, cases like Thomas and Schor tended to run the categories together and look at a wide range of factors in determining the constitutionality of a particular tribunal, and Justice Breyer's dissent takes that approach. But did his argument concerning Congress's power to substitute legislative courts for constitutional courts contain any limiting principle?

Was this also a problem with the government's "adjuncts" argument? Was the degree of oversight by Article III courts really that much less in Stern v. Marshall than in Crowell v. Benson? With respect to adjudicatory independence, how significant is it that judgments of the bankruptcy court were self-executing unless appealed, whereas the orders of the agency in Crowell required judicial enforcement? That bankruptcy courts' jurisdiction is not specialized but ranges broadly over diverse areas of law? That the tribunal in Stern, unlike the one in Crowell, resolved state rather than federal law claims?

On the last point, note that federal territorial courts (including the local courts of the District of Columbia) exercise jurisdiction over state law claims, and that the political branches might be more tempted to compromise adjudicatory independence with respect to federal law issues arising in congressionally created programs.

(5) The Continuing Relevance of the Public Rights Doctrine. Seven years after Stern, the Court again returned to the public rights doctrine, this time in the context of an agency adjudication.

Oil States Energy Servs., LLC v. Greene's Energy Group, LLC

584 U.S. 325 (2018).
Certiorari to the United States Court of Appeals for the District of Columbia Circuit.

■ JUSTICE THOMAS delivered the opinion of the Court.

The Leahy-Smith America Invents Act, 35 U.S.C. § 100 *et seq.*, establishes a process called "inter partes review." Under that process, the United States Patent and Trademark Office (PTO) is authorized to reconsider and to cancel an issued patent claim in limited circumstances. In this case, we address whether inter partes review violates Article III or the Seventh Amendment of the Constitution. We hold that it violates neither.

I

A

Under the Patent Act, the PTO is "responsible for the granting and issuing of patents." 35 U.S.C. § 2(a)(1). When an inventor applies for a patent, an examiner reviews the proposed claims and the prior art to determine if the claims meet the statutory requirements. See §§ 112, 131. Those requirements include utility, novelty, and nonobviousness based on the prior art. §§ 101, 102, 103. The Director of the PTO then approves or rejects the application. See §§ 131, 132(a). An applicant can seek judicial review of a final rejection. §§ 141(a), 145.

B

Over the last several decades, Congress has created administrative processes that authorize the PTO to reconsider and cancel patent claims that were wrongly issued. In 1980, Congress established "ex parte reexamination," which still exists today. See Act To Amend the Patent and Trademark Laws, 35 U.S.C. § 301 *et seq.* Ex parte reexamination permits "[a]ny person at any time" to "file a request for reexamination." § 302. If the Director determines that there is "a substantial new question of patentability" for "any claim of the patent," the PTO can reexamine the patent. §§ 303(a), 304. The reexamination process follows the same procedures as the initial examination. § 305.

In 1999, Congress added a procedure called "inter partes reexamination." See American Inventors Protection Act, §§ 4601–4608, 113 Stat. 1501A–567 to 1501A–572. Under this procedure, any person could file a request for reexamination. 35 U.S.C. § 311(a) (2006 ed.). * * * The reexamination [by the Director] would follow the general procedures for initial examination, but would allow the third-party requester and the patent owner to participate in a limited manner by filing responses and replies. §§ 314(a), (b) (2006 ed.). * * *

C

The America Invents Act replaced inter partes reexamination with inter partes review, the procedure at issue here. Any person other than the patent owner can file a petition for inter partes review. 35 U.S.C. § 311(a) (2012 ed.). The petition can request cancellation of "1 or more claims of a patent" on the grounds that the claim fails the novelty or nonobviousness standards for patentability. § 311(b). The challenges must be made "only on the basis of prior art consisting of patents or printed publications." *Ibid.* * * *

Before he can institute inter partes review, the [PTO] Director must determine "that there is a reasonable likelihood that the petitioner would prevail with respect to at least 1 of the claims challenged." § 314(a). * * *

Once inter partes review is instituted, the Patent Trial and Appeal Board—an adjudicatory body within the PTO created to conduct inter partes review—examines the patent's validity. See 35 U.S.C. §§ 6, 316(c). The Board sits in three-member panels of administrative patent judges. See § 6(c). During the inter partes review, the petitioner and the patent owner are entitled to certain discovery, § 316(a)(5); to file affidavits, declarations, and written memoranda, § 316(a)(8); and to receive an oral hearing before the Board, § 316(a)(10). The petitioner has the burden of proving unpatentability by a preponderance of the evidence. § 316(e). * * *

A party dissatisfied with the Board's decision can seek judicial review in the Court of Appeals for the Federal Circuit. § 319. * * * When reviewing the Board's decision, the Federal Circuit assesses "the Board's compliance with governing legal standards de novo and its underlying factual determinations for substantial evidence." Randall Mfg. v. Rea, 733 F.3d 1355, 1362 (C.A.Fed.2013).

II

* * * In 2001, Oil States obtained a patent relating to an apparatus and method for protecting wellhead equipment used in hydraulic fracturing. In 2012, Oil States sued Greene's Energy in Federal District Court for infringing that patent. Greene's Energy responded by challenging the patent's validity. Near the close of discovery, Greene's Energy also petitioned the Board to institute inter partes review. It argued that two of the patent's claims were unpatentable because they were anticipated by prior art not mentioned by Oil States in its original patent application. * * *

The proceedings before the District Court and the Board progressed in parallel. In June 2014, the District Court issued [an order rejecting] * * * Greene's Energy's arguments about the prior art. But a few months later, the Board issued a final written decision concluding that the claims were unpatentable. The Board acknowledged the District Court's contrary decision * * *.

Oil States sought review in the Federal Circuit [and] * * * argued that actions to revoke a patent must be tried in an Article III court before a jury. * * *

We granted certiorari to determine whether inter partes review violates Article III or the Seventh Amendment. * * *

III

Article III vests the judicial power of the United States "in one supreme Court, and in such inferior Courts as the Congress may from time to time ordain and establish." § 1. Consequently, Congress cannot "confer the Government's 'judicial Power' on entities outside Article III." Stern v. Marshall, 564 U.S. 462, 484 (2011). When determining whether a proceeding involves an exercise of Article III judicial power, this Court's precedents have distinguished between "public rights" and "private rights." Executive Benefits Ins. Agency v. Arkison, 573 U.S. [25, 32] (2014) (internal quotation marks omitted). Those precedents have given Congress significant latitude to assign adjudication of public rights to entities other than Article III courts. See *ibid.*; Stern, *supra*, at 488–492.

This Court has not "definitively explained" the distinction between public and private rights, Northern Pipeline Constr. Co. v. Marathon Pipe Line Co., 458 U.S. 50, 69 (1982), and its precedents applying the public-rights doctrine have "not been entirely consistent," Stern, 564 U.S., at 488. But this case does not require us to add to the "various formulations" of the public-rights doctrine. *Ibid.* Our precedents have recognized that the doctrine covers matters "which arise between the Government and persons subject to its authority in connection with the performance of the constitutional functions of the executive or legislative departments." Crowell v. Benson, 285 U.S. 22, 50 (1932). In other words, the public-rights doctrine applies to matters " 'arising between the government and others, which from their nature do not require judicial determination and yet are susceptible of it.' " *Ibid.* (quoting Ex parte Bakelite Corp., 279 U.S. 438, 451 (1929)). * * *

A

Inter partes review falls squarely within the public-rights doctrine. This Court has recognized, and the parties do not dispute, that the decision to grant a patent is a matter involving public rights— specifically, the grant of a public franchise. Inter partes review is simply a reconsideration of that grant, and Congress has permissibly reserved the PTO's authority to conduct that reconsideration. Thus, the PTO can do so without violating Article III.

1

This Court has long recognized that the grant of a patent is a " 'matte[r] involving public rights.' " United States v. Duell, 172 U.S. 576, 582–583 (1899) (quoting Murray's Lessee v. Hoboken Land & Improvement Co., 18 How. 272, 284 (1856)). It has the key features to fall within this Court's longstanding formulation of the public-rights doctrine.

Ab initio, the grant of a patent involves a matter "arising between the government and others." Ex parte Bakelite Corp., *supra*, at 451. As this Court has long recognized, the grant of a patent is a matter between " 'the public, who are the grantors, and . . . the patentee.' " Duell, *supra*, at 586 (quoting Butterworth v. United States ex rel. Hoe, 112 U.S. 50, 59 (1884)). By "issuing patents," the PTO "take[s] from the public rights of immense value, and bestow [s] them upon the patentee." United States v. American Bell Telephone Co., 128 U.S. 315, 370 (1888). Specifically, patents are "public franchises" that the Government grants "to the inventors of new and useful improvements." Seymour v. Osborne, 11 Wall. 516, 533 (1871)[.] * * * That right "did not exist at common law." Gayler v. Wilder, 10 How. 477, 494 (1851). Rather, it is a "creature of statute law." Crown Die & Tool Co. v. Nye Tool & Machine Works, 261 U.S. 24, 40 (1923).

Additionally, granting patents is one of "the constitutional functions" that can be carried out by "the executive or legislative departments" without " 'judicial determination.' " Crowell, *supra*, at 50–51 (quoting Ex parte Bakelite Corp., *supra*, at 452). Article I gives Congress the power "[t]o promote the Progress of Science and useful Arts, by securing for limited Times to Authors and Inventors the exclusive Right to their respective Writings and Discoveries." § 8, cl. 8. Congress can grant patents itself by statute. And, from the founding to today, Congress has authorized the Executive Branch to grant patents that meet the statutory requirements for patentability. When the PTO "adjudicate[s] the patentability of inventions," it is "exercising the executive power." Freytag v. Commissioner, 501 U.S. 868, 910 (1991) (Scalia, J., concurring in part and concurring in judgment) (emphasis deleted).

Accordingly, the determination to grant a patent is a "matte[r] involving public rights." Murray's Lessee, *supra*, at 284. It need not be adjudicated in Article III court.

2

Inter partes review involves the same basic matter as the grant of a patent. So it, too, falls on the public-rights side of the line.

Inter partes review is "a second look at an earlier administrative grant of a patent." [Cuozzo Speed Technologies, LLC v. Lee, 579 U.S. 261, 279 (2016)]. The Board considers the same statutory requirements that the PTO considered when granting the patent. See 35 U.S.C. § 311(b). * * *

The primary distinction between inter partes review and the initial grant of a patent is that inter partes review occurs after the patent has issued. But that distinction does not make a difference here. Patent claims are granted subject to the qualification that the PTO has "the authority to reexamine—and perhaps cancel—a patent claim" in an inter partes review. See Cuozzo, *supra*, at [267]. Patents thus remain "subject to [the Board's] authority" to cancel outside of an Article III court. Crowell, 285 U.S., at 50.

This Court has recognized that franchises can be qualified in this manner. For example, Congress can grant a franchise that permits a company to erect a toll bridge, but qualify the grant by reserving its authority to revoke or amend the franchise. See, *e.g.*, Louisville Bridge Co. v. United States, 242 U.S. 409, 421 (1917) (collecting cases). Even after the bridge is built, the Government can exercise its reserved authority through legislation or an administrative proceeding. See, *e.g.*, *id.*, at 420–421; Hannibal Bridge Co. v. United States, 221 U.S. 194, 205 (1911); Bridge Co. v. United States, 105 U.S. 470, 478–482 (1882). The same is true for franchises that permit companies to build railroads or telegraph lines. See, *e.g.*, United States v. Union Pacific R. Co., 160 U.S. 1, 24–25, 37–38 (1895).

Thus, the public-rights doctrine covers the matter resolved in inter partes review. The Constitution does not prohibit the Board from resolving it outside of an Article III court.

B

Oil States challenges this conclusion, citing three decisions that recognize patent rights as the "private property of the patentee." American Bell Telephone Co., 128 U.S., at 370; see also McCormick Harvesting Machine Co. v. Aultman, 169 U.S. 606, 609 (1898) ("[A granted patent] has become the property of the patentee"); Brown v. Duchesne, 19 How. 183, 197 (1857) ("[T]he rights of a party under a patent are his private property"). But those cases do not contradict our conclusion.

Patents convey only a specific form of property right—a public franchise. See Pfaff [v. Wells Electronics, Inc.], 525 U.S. [55,] 63–64 [(1998)]. * * * As a public franchise, a patent can confer only the rights that "the statute prescribes." Gayler, *supra*, at 494; Wheaton v. Peters, 8 Pet. 591, 663–664 (1834) (noting that Congress has "the power to prescribe the conditions on which such right shall be enjoyed"). It is noteworthy that one of the precedents cited by Oil States acknowledges that the patentee's rights are "derived altogether" from statutes, "are to be regulated and measured by these laws, and cannot go beyond them." Brown, *supra*, at 195.

One such regulation is inter partes review. * * * The Patent Act provides that, "[s]ubject to the provisions of this title, patents shall have the attributes of personal property." 35 U.S.C. § 261. This provision qualifies any property rights that a patent owner has in an issued patent, subjecting them to the express provisions of the Patent Act. See eBay Inc. v. MercExchange, L.L.C., 547 U.S. 388, 392 (2006). Those provisions include inter partes review. See §§ 311–319. * * *

C

Oil States and the dissent contend that inter partes review violates the "general" principle that "Congress may not 'withdraw from judicial cognizance any matter which, from its nature, is the subject of a suit at the common law, or in equity, or admiralty.'" Stern, 564 U.S., at 484 (quoting Murray's Lessee, 18 How., at 284). They argue that this is so because patent validity was often decided in English courts of law in the 18th century. * * *

But * * * there was another means of canceling a patent in 18th-century England, which more closely resembles inter partes review: a petition to the Privy Council to vacate a patent. See Lemley, [*Why Do Juries Decide If Patents Are Valid?*, 99 Va.L.Rev. 1673, 1681–1682 (2013)]; Hulme, *Privy Council Law and Practice of Letters Patent for Invention From the Restoration to 1794 (Pt. I)*, 33 L.Q.Rev. 63 (1917). The Privy Council was composed of the Crown's advisers. Lemley, *supra*, at 1681. From the 17th through the 20th centuries, English patents had a standard revocation clause that permitted six or more Privy Counsellors to declare a patent void if they determined the invention was contrary to law, "prejudicial" or "inconvenient," not new, or not invented by the patent owner. See 11 W. Holdsworth, A History of English Law 426–427, and n.6 (1938). * * *

[The Privy Council] had exclusive authority to revoke patents until 1753, and after that, it had concurrent jurisdiction with the courts. See Hulme (Pt. II), 33 L.Q.Rev., at 189–191, 193–194. The Privy Council continued to consider revocation claims and to revoke patents throughout the 18th century. * * *

* * * Based on the practice of the Privy Council, it was well understood at the founding that a patent system could include a practice of granting patents subject to potential cancellation in the executive proceeding of the Privy Council. * * *

For similar reasons, we disagree with the dissent's assumption that, because courts have traditionally adjudicated patent validity in this country, courts must forever continue to do so. Historical practice is not decisive here because matters governed by the public-rights doctrine "from their nature" can be resolved in multiple ways: Congress can "reserve to itself the power to decide," "delegate that power to executive officers," or "commit it to judicial tribunals." Ex parte Bakelite Corp., 279 U.S., at 451. That Congress chose the courts in the past does not foreclose its choice of the PTO today.

D

Finally, Oil States argues that inter partes review violates Article III because it shares "every salient characteristic associated with the exercise of the judicial power." Oil States highlights various procedures used in inter partes review: motion practice before the Board; discovery, depositions, and cross-examination of witnesses; introduction of evidence and objections based on the Federal Rules of Evidence; and an adversarial hearing before the Board. See 35 U.S.C. § 316(a); 77 Fed.Reg. 48758, 48761–48763 (2012). * * *

But this Court has never adopted a "looks like" test to determine if an adjudication has improperly occurred outside of an Article III court. The fact that an agency uses court-like procedures does not necessarily mean it is exercising the judicial power. * * * Nor does the fact that an administrative adjudication is final and binding on an individual who acquiesces in the result necessarily make it an exercise of the judicial power. See, *e.g.*, Murray's Lessee, 18 How., at 280–281 (permitting the Treasury Department to conduct "final and binding" audits outside of an Article III court). Although inter partes review includes some of the features of adversarial litigation, it does not make any binding determination regarding "the liability of [Greene's Energy] to [Oil States] under the law as defined." Crowell, 285 U.S., at 51. It remains a matter involving public rights, one "between the government and others, which from [its] nature do[es] not require judicial determination." Ex parte Bakelite Corp., 279 U.S., at 451. * * *

IV

In addition to Article III, Oil States challenges inter partes review under the Seventh Amendment. The Seventh Amendment preserves the "right of trial by jury" in "Suits at common law, where the value in controversy shall exceed twenty dollars." This Court's precedents establish that, when Congress properly assigns a matter to adjudication in a non-Article III tribunal, "the Seventh Amendment poses no independent bar to the adjudication of that action by a nonjury factfinder." Granfinanciera, S.A. v. Nordberg, 492 U.S. 33, 53–54 (1989)[.] * * * [O]ur rejection of Oil States' Article III challenge also resolves its Seventh Amendment challenge. Because inter partes review is a matter that Congress can properly assign to the PTO, a jury is not necessary in these proceedings. * * *

It is so ordered.

■ JUSTICE BREYER, with whom JUSTICE GINSBURG and JUSTICE SOTOMAYOR join, concurring.

I join the Court's opinion in full. The conclusion that inter partes review is a matter involving public rights is sufficient to show that it violates neither Article III nor the Seventh Amendment. But the Court's opinion should not be read to say that matters involving private rights may never be adjudicated other than by Article III courts, say, sometimes by agencies. Our precedent is to the contrary. Stern v. Marshall, 564 U.S. 462, 494 (2011); Commodity Futures Trading Comm'n v. Schor, 478 U.S. 833, 853–856 (1986); see also Stern, *supra*, at 513 (Breyer, J., dissenting) * * *.

■ JUSTICE GORSUCH, with whom THE CHIEF JUSTICE joins, dissenting.

After much hard work and no little investment you devise something you think truly novel. Then you endure the further cost and effort of applying for a patent, devoting maybe $30,000 and two years to that process alone. At the end of it all, the Patent Office agrees your invention is novel and issues a patent. The patent affords you exclusive rights to the fruits of your labor for two decades. But what happens if someone later emerges from the woodwork, arguing that it was all a mistake and your patent should be canceled? Can a political appointee and his administrative agents, instead of an independent judge, resolve the dispute? The Court says yes. Respectfully, I disagree.

We sometimes take it for granted today that independent judges will hear our cases and controversies. But it wasn't always so. Before the Revolution, colonial judges depended on the crown for their tenure and salary and often enough their decisions followed their interests. The problem was so serious that the founders cited it in their Declaration of Independence (see ¶ 11). Once free, the framers went to great lengths to guarantee a degree of judicial independence for future generations that they themselves had not experienced. * * *

Today, the government invites us to retreat from the promise of judicial independence. Until recently, most everyone considered an issued patent a personal right—no less than a home or farm—that the federal government could revoke only with the concurrence of independent judges. But in the statute before us Congress has tapped an executive agency, the Patent Trial and Appeal Board, for the job. Supporters say this is a good thing because the Patent Office issues too many low quality patents; allowing a subdivision of that office to clean up problems after the fact, they assure us, promises an efficient solution. And, no doubt, dispensing with constitutionally prescribed procedures is often expedient. Whether it is the guarantee of a warrant before a search, a jury trial before a conviction—or, yes, a judicial hearing before a property interest is stripped away—the Constitution's constraints can slow things down. But economy supplies no license for ignoring these— often vitally inefficient—protections. The Constitution "reflects a judgment by the American people that the benefits of its restrictions on the Government outweigh the costs," and it is not our place to replace that judgment with our own. United States v. Stevens, 559 U.S. 460, 470 (2010).

Consider just how efficient the statute before us is. The Director of the Patent Office is a political appointee who serves at the pleasure of the President. 35 U.S.C. §§ 3(a)(1), (a)(4). He supervises and pays the Board members responsible for deciding patent disputes. §§ 1(a), 3(b)(6), 6(a). The Director is allowed to select which of these members, and how many of them, will hear any particular patent challenge. See § 6(c). If they (somehow) reach a result he does not like, the Director can add more members to the panel—including himself—and order the case reheard. See §§ 6(a), (c) * * *. Nor has the Director proven bashful about asserting these statutory powers to secure the " 'policy judgments' " he seeks.

No doubt this efficient scheme is well intended. But can there be any doubt that it also represents a retreat from the promise of judicial independence? Or that when an independent Judiciary gives ground to bureaucrats in the adjudication of cases, the losers will often prove the unpopular and vulnerable? Powerful interests are capable of amassing armies of lobbyists and lawyers to influence (and even capture) politically accountable bureaucracies. But what about everyone else?

Of course, all this invites the question: how do we know which cases independent judges must hear? The Constitution's original public meaning supplies the key * * *. As originally understood, the judicial power extended to "suit[s] at the common law, or in equity, or admiralty." Murray's Lessee v. Hoboken Land & Improvement Co., 18 How. 272, 284 (1856). From this and as we've recently explained, it follows that, "[w]hen a suit is made of the stuff of the traditional actions at common law tried by the courts at Westminster in 1789 . . . and is brought within the bounds of federal jurisdiction, the responsibility for deciding that suit rests with" Article III judges endowed with the protections for their independence the framers thought so important. Stern v. Marshall, 564 U.S. 462, 484 (2011) (internal quotation marks omitted). * * *

As I read the historical record presented to us, only courts could hear patent challenges in England at the time of the founding. If facts were in dispute, the matter first had to proceed in the law courts. See, *e.g.*, Newsham v. Gray, 26 Eng. Rep. 575 (Ch. 1742). If successful there, a challenger then had to obtain a writ of scire facias in the law side of the Court of Chancery. See, *e.g.*, Pfander, *Jurisdiction-Stripping and the Supreme Court's Power To Supervise Inferior Tribunals*, 78 Tex.L.Rev. 1433, 1446 n.53 (2000); Lemley, *Why Do Juries Decide If Patents Are Valid?*, 99 Va.L.Rev. 1673, 1686–1687 (2013) (Lemley, Juries). The last time an executive body (the King's Privy Council) invalidated an invention patent on an ordinary application was in 1746, in Darby v. Betton, PC2/99, pp. 358–359; and the last time the Privy Council even considered doing so was in 1753, in Baker v. James, PC2/103, pp. 320– 321. After Baker v. James, the Privy Council "divest[ed] itself of its functions" in ordinary patent disputes, Hulme, *Privy Council Law and Practice of Letters Patent for Invention From the Restoration to 1794 (Pt. II)*, 33 L.Q.Rev. 180, 194 (1917), which "thereafter [were] adjudicated solely by the law courts, as opposed to the [crown's] prerogative courts," Mossoff, *Rethinking the Development of Patents: An Intellectual History, 1550–1800*, 52 Hastings L.J. 1255, 1286–1287 (2001) (Mossoff, Rethinking Patents).

This shift to courts paralleled a shift in thinking. Patents began as little more than feudal favors. *Id.*, at 1261. The crown both issued and revoked them. Lemley, Juries 1680–1681. And they often permitted the lucky recipient the exclusive right to do very ordinary things, like operate a toll bridge or run a tavern. *Ibid.* But by the 18th century, * * * invention patents * * * came to be viewed * * * as a procompetitive means to secure to individuals the fruits of their labor and ingenuity; encourage others to emulate them; and promote public access to new technologies that would not otherwise exist. Mossoff, Rethinking Patents 1288–1289. The

Constitution itself reflects this new thinking * * *. "In essence, there was a change in perception—from viewing a patent as a contract between the crown and the patentee to viewing it as a 'social contract' between the patentee and society." Walterscheid, *The Early Evolution of the United States Patent Law: Antecedents (Pt. 3)*, 77 J.Pat. & T.Off.Soc. 771, 793 (1995). And as invention patents came to be seen so differently, it is no surprise courts came to treat them more solicitously.

Unable to dispute that judges alone resolved virtually all patent challenges by the time of the founding, the Court points to three English cases that represent the Privy Council's dying gasp in this area * * *. Filed in 1779, 1782, and 1810, each involved an effort to override a patent on munitions during wartime, no doubt in an effort to increase their supply. But even then appealing to the Privy Council was seen as a last resort. * * * At most, [these cases] suggest that the Privy Council might have possessed some residual power to revoke patents to address wartime necessities. Equally, they might serve only as more unfortunate evidence of the maxim that in time of war, the laws fall silent. But whatever they do, these cases do not come close to proving that patent disputes were routinely permitted to proceed outside a court of law.

Any lingering doubt about English law is resolved for me by looking to our own. While the Court is correct that the Constitution's Patent Clause " 'was written against the backdrop' " of English practice, * * * it's also true that the Clause sought to reject some of early English practice. * * * In light of the Patent Clause's restrictions [to inventions that add to useful knowledge], courts took the view that when the federal government "grants a patent the grantee is entitled to it as a matter of right, and does not receive it, as was originally supposed to be the case in England, as a matter of grace and favor." James v. Campbell, 104 U.S. 356, 358 (1882). As Chief Justice Marshall explained, courts treated American invention patents as recognizing an "inchoate property" that exists "from the moment of invention." Evans v. Jordan, 8 F.Cas. 872, 873 (No. 4,564) (C.C.D.Va.1813). American patent holders thus were thought to "hol[d] a property in [their] invention[s] by as good a title as the farmer holds his farm and flock." Hovey v. Henry, 12 F.Cas. 603, 604 (No. 6,742) (C.C.D.Mass.1846) (Woodbury, J.). And just as with farm and flock, it was widely accepted that the government could divest patent owners of their rights only through proceedings before independent judges.

* * * [F]rom the time it established the American patent system in 1790 until about 1980, Congress left the job of invalidating patents at the federal level to courts alone. The only apparent exception to this rule cited to us was a 4-year period when foreign patentees had to "work" or commercialize their patents or risk having them revoked. Hovenkamp, *The Emergence of Classical American Patent Law*, 58 Ariz.L.Rev. 263, 283–284 (2016). And the fact that for almost 200 years "earlier Congresses avoided use of [a] highly attractive"—and surely more efficient—means for extinguishing patents should serve as good "reason

to believe that the power was thought not to exist" at the time of the founding. Printz v. United States, 521 U.S. 898, 905 (1997).

One more episode still underscores the point. When the Executive sought to claim the right to cancel a patent in the 1800s, this Court firmly rebuffed the effort. The Court explained:

> "It has been settled by repeated decisions of this court that when a patent has [been issued by] the Patent Office, it has passed beyond the control and jurisdiction of that office, and is not subject to be revoked or cancelled by the President, or any other officer of the Government. It has become the property of the patentee, and as such is entitled to the same legal protection as other property." McCormick Harvesting Machine Co. v. Aultman, 169 U.S. 606, 608–609 (1898) (citations omitted).

As a result, the Court held, "[t]he only authority competent to set a patent aside, or to annul it, or to correct it for any reason whatever, is vested in the courts of the United States, and not in the department which issued the patent." Id., at 609. * * *

With so much in the relevant history and precedent against it, the Court invites us to look elsewhere. Instead of focusing on the revocation of patents, it asks us to abstract the level of our inquiry and focus on their issuance. Because the job of issuing invention patents traditionally belonged to the Executive, the Court proceeds to argue, the job of revoking them can be left there too. But that doesn't follow. Just because you give a gift doesn't mean you forever enjoy the right to reclaim it. * * *

Still, the Court asks us to look away in yet another direction. At the founding, the Court notes, the Executive could sometimes both dispense and revoke public franchises. And because, it says, invention patents are a species of public franchises, the Court argues the Executive should be allowed to dispense and revoke them too. But labels aside, by the time of the founding the law treated patents protected by the Patent Clause quite differently from ordinary public franchises. Many public franchises amounted to little more than favors resembling the original royal patents the framers expressly refused to protect in the Patent Clause[, such as] the state-granted exclusive right to operate a toll bridge. By the founding, courts in this country (as in England) had come to view anticompetitive monopolies like that with disfavor, narrowly construing the rights they conferred. * * * As Justice Story explained, [however,] invention patents protected by the Patent Clause were "not to be treated as mere monopolies odious in the eyes of the law, and therefore not to be favored." Ames v. Howard, 1 F.Cas. 755, 756 (No. 326) (C.C.D.Mass.1833). For precisely these reasons and as we've seen, the law traditionally treated patents issued under the Patent Clause very differently than monopoly franchises when it came to governmental invasions. Patents alone required independent judges.* * *

Today's decision * * * signals a retreat from Article III's guarantees. Ceding to the political branches ground they wish to take in the name of efficient government may seem like an act of judicial restraint. But enforcing Article III isn't about protecting judicial authority for its own sake. It's about ensuring the people today and tomorrow enjoy no fewer rights against governmental intrusion than those who came before. And the loss of the right to an independent judge is never a small thing. It's for that reason Hamilton warned the judiciary to take "all possible care . . . to defend itself against" intrusions by the other branches. The Federalist No. 78, at 466. It's for that reason I respectfully dissent.

―――――――――――

FURTHER NOTE ON PUBLIC RIGHTS

(1) What Is a Public Right? If it is difficult to intuit what a public right is at this point, that may be because of the dizzying array of formulations that the Court has offered in recent decisions. Some decisions, like Crowell and Justice Scalia's opinion in Stern v. Marshall, suggest that it is a necessary condition that the United States be a party to the case. Thomas rejected that idea, instead emphasizing that the case arose under a complex federal regulatory scheme. In Stern, the Court noted the varied formulations of past cases and did not offer its own, simply arguing that the circumstances there are distinguishable from prior cases finding that a claim was a public right or that it bore many characteristics of one. If one were to return to first principles, is the public/private distinction intelligible, and useful, in considering the appropriateness of adjudication outside of Article III?[1]

(a) The United States as a Party. First consider Justice Scalia's suggestion that the presence of the United States as a party, is a necessary condition, if not a sufficient one, for a case to fall into the public rights category. On this suggestion, the law might sharply distinguish between (a) an agency like the NLRB, in which the United States commences agency proceedings (but does so after having received a complaint by a private party), and (b) an agency like those in Crowell, Thomas, Schor, and Oil States, in which one private party commences agency proceedings against another.

―――――――――――

[1]   For an argument that confusion will persist as long as the law is organized around this distinction, see Chemerinsky, *Ending the Marathon: It Is Time to Overrule Northern Pipeline*, 65 Am.Bankr.L.J. 311, 314–16 (1991). See also Redish & LaFave, *Seventh Amendment Right to Jury Trial in Non-Article III Proceedings: A Study in Dysfunctional Constitutional Theory*, 4 Wm. & Mary Bill Rts.J. 407 (1995), and Klein, *The Validity of the Public Rights Doctrine in Light of the Historical Rationale of the Seventh Amendment*, 21 Hastings Const.L.Q. 1013 (1994), both arguing, *inter alia*, that the public rights exception to the Seventh Amendment lacks sound foundations in history and doctrine. Baude, *Adjudication Outside Article III*, 133 Harv.L.Rev. 1511 (2020), argues that the public rights framework was inappropriate in Stern and Northern Pipeline for a different reason: "The public rights doctrine is a principle of executive power. But today's bankruptcy courts have not been vested with executive power. Their judges are appointed by Article III courts, supervised by Article III courts, and 'constitute[d]' as 'a unit of the district court.'" Baude concludes that bankruptcy courts must be sustained, if at all, as adjuncts to Article III courts.

But do Thomas and Oil States provide a plausible alternative? In Thomas, the Court noted that insisting upon the government being a party, at least in that instance, amounted to an artificial distinction. Recall that the question at issue was whether a compensation dispute between two parties who had registered their pesticides with the EPA involved a public right. Under the scheme at issue, when there was a dispute over whether a first-mover registrant was being adequately compensated by a follow-on registrant for the latter's reliance on proprietary information developed by the former, the matter went to mandatory arbitration, subject to limited judicial review. Noting that this dispute, though between private parties, did not necessarily involve a private right, the Court observed that "Congress, without implicating Article III, could have authorized EPA to charge follow-on registrants fees to cover the cost of data and could have directly subsidized [the first-mover] FIFRA data submitters for their contributions of needed data. * * * Instead, it selected a framework that collapses these two steps into one, and permits the parties to fix the amount of compensation, with binding arbitration to resolve intractable disputes." Does that analysis suggest that as long as the Court can envision a way of restructuring a complex regulatory scheme to make an agency as a party, the question at issue can potentially be understood as a public right, even if the actual structure involves adjudication of a dispute between private parties? Accord Securities and Exchange Commission v. Jarkesy, 144 S.Ct. 2117 (2024) ("[W]hat matters is the substance of the suit, not where it is brought, who brings it, or how it is labeled.").[2]

(b) The Power to Condition. Consider another possible explanation, one that also reflects a common theme in Thomas and Oil States. In Thomas, recall, the Court emphasized that "Congress has the power, under Article I, to authorize an agency administering a complex regulatory scheme to allocate costs and benefits among voluntary participants in the program without providing an Article III adjudication. It also has the power to condition issuance of registrations or licenses on compliance with agency procedures." In other words, because Congress can exercise its Article I power to prohibit the sale of pesticides, it can condition its permission to do so on the manufacturer's receiving a license from the EPA *and* complying with the specified "agency procedures" for obtaining such a license. Compare this with Oil States, in which the Court emphasized that a patent is a public franchise "granted subject to the qualification that the PTO has the authority to reexamine—and perhaps cancel—a patent claim in an inter partes review." This, the Court said, was akin to the doctrine holding that "Congress can grant a franchise that permits a company to erect a toll bridge, but qualify the grant by reserving its authority to revoke or amend the franchise." Taken to its logical extreme, does this mean that Congress can make a public right of anything that it has the power to subject to a public regulatory scheme and to condition regulatory permissions or exceptions on the regulated parties' compliance with (non-Article III) procedures? Does

---

[2]   Jarkesy (discussed further in this Note, *infra*) also makes clear that the presence of the United States as a party is not a *sufficient* condition for a public right. The Court held that a proceeding brought by the United States through the Securities and Exchange Commission seeking civil fines for common law fraud was the adjudication of a private right.

that seem more or less concerning, from an Article III perspective, than giving Bankruptcy Courts authority to handle common law counterclaims?

(c) The Role of History. Or does Oil States signal a different approach still to the public rights doctrine? Note that Justice Thomas relied heavily on the fact that, under the common law of England, the Privy Council—an executive body—had concurrent jurisdiction with the courts to revoke a patent, suggesting that patent challenges would have been seen as a permissible executive function at the time of the founding. Justice Gorsuch disagreed not with the Court's reliance on history, but rather with its reading of the historical record, which he took to establish that patent challenges had become an exclusive judicial function at common law prior to the founding and that they continued to be treated as such in subsequent U.S. practice. See also United States v. Arthrex, Inc., 594 U.S. 1, 27 (2021) (Gorsuch, J., concurring in part and dissenting in part) (reiterating the view that Oil States upset a "traditional understanding" that "an issued patent was considered a vested property right that could be taken from an individual only through a lawful process before a court").[3] Does that approach align with the Court's reasoning in Murray's Lessee, which seemed to rest on the proposition that extrajudicial distress warrants historically constituted an acceptable way of enforcing tax liability or arrearages in the accounts of public officials? Is the Court in Oil States signaling acceptance of this more granular historical approach? See also Securities and Exchange Commission v. Jarkesy, 144 S.Ct. 2117, 2134 (2024) ("The public rights exception is, after all, an *exception*. It has no textual basis in the Constitution and must therefore derive instead from background legal principles. Murray's Lessee itself, for example, took pains to justify the application of the exception in that particular instance by explaining that it flowed from centuries-old rules concerning revenue collection by a sovereign. Without such close attention to the basis for each asserted application of the doctrine, the exception would swallow the rule.").

(2) The Right to Jury Trial Before Non-Article III Tribunals. To what extent does the right to jury trial constrain Congress's ability to establish non-Article III tribunals? Until the Granfinanciera decision, emphatically reaffirmed in Jarkesy, the precedents had suggested that the Seventh

---

[3]   The explicitly historical approach used by both the Court and the dissent in Oil States has given rise to a new round of historical scholarship raising questions about the public rights/private rights framework used in that case. See, *e.g.*, Ablavsky, *Getting Public Rights Wrong: The Lost History of the Private Land Claims*, 74 Stan.L.Rev. 277 (2022) (arguing that the administrative adjudication of certain private land claims in newly acquired territory in the nineteenth century muddies the public rights inquiry and casts doubt on the Oil States test); Pfander & Borrasso, *Public Rights and Article III: Judicial Oversight of Agency Action*, 82 Ohio St.L.J. 493 (2021) (arguing that early doctrine distinguished between "constitutive authority" to establish new rights or obligations, which could be handled administratively, and retrospective adjudication of disputed matters, which could not); Nelson, *Vested Rights, "Franchises," and the Separation of Powers*, 169 U.Pa.L.Rev. 1429 (2021) (reconsidering an earlier article treating franchises as privileges and contending that, historically, patents had taken on a contractual character and, once granted, could be challenged only through judicial process). But see Golden & Lee, *Congressional Power, Public Rights, and Non-Article III Adjudication*, 98 Notre Dame L.Rev. 1113, 1167–68 (2023) (arguing that, while English practice was "in a state of flux" at the time of the founding, the majority properly relied on deeply rooted English practice permitting executive adjudication of patent rights, a reading that supports present congressional flexibility to rely on non-Article III adjudicators).

Amendment has little if any applicability to adjudication before administrative agencies.

(a) In NLRB v. Jones & Laughlin Steel Corp., 301 U.S. 1 (1937), in rejecting a Seventh Amendment challenge to an NLRB decision awarding back pay and reinstatement to union members whom the company had unlawfully dismissed, the Court said: "[The Seventh Amendment] has no application to cases where recovery of money damages is an incident to equitable relief even though damages might have been recovered in an action at law. It does not apply where the proceeding is not in the nature of a suit at common law.

"The instant case is not a suit at common law or in the nature of such a suit. The proceeding is one unknown to the common law. Reinstatement of the employee and payment for time lost are requirements imposed for violation of the statute and are remedies appropriate to its enforcement."

(b) Several decades later, the Court said that Jones & Laughlin "merely stands for the proposition that the Seventh Amendment is generally inapplicable in administrative proceedings, where jury trials would be incompatible with the whole concept of administrative adjudication and would substantially interfere with the NLRB's role in the statutory scheme." Curtis v. Loether, 415 U.S. 189, 194 (1974). But in Curtis, the Court held that Jones & Laughlin did not govern, as the action—one between private parties, under a federal civil rights law—was brought in a regular Article III court. The Supreme Court ruled that the Seventh Amendment conferred a right to jury trial.

(c) In Atlas Roofing Co. v. Occupational Safety & Health Review Comm'n, 430 U.S. 442 (1977), the Court upheld an agency's assessment of a civil money penalty for violation of workplace safety regulations. Relying on the distinction between public and private rights, the Court said: "At least in cases in which public rights are being litigated—e.g., cases in which the Government sues in its sovereign capacity to enforce public rights created by statutes within the power of Congress to enact—the Seventh Amendment does not prohibit Congress from assigning the factfinding function and initial adjudication to an administrative forum with which the jury would be incompatible."[4]

(d) Oil States reaffirmed the proposition that Seventh Amendment requirements follow the Article III analysis. Quoting Granfinanciera, 492 U.S. at 53–54, Justice Thomas emphasized "that when Congress properly assigns a matter to adjudication in a non-Article III tribunal, 'the Seventh Amendment poses no independent bar to the adjudication of that action by a

---

[4]   Sward, *Legislative Courts, Article III, and the Seventh Amendment*, 77 N.C.L.Rev. 1037 (1999), argues that the Seventh Amendment serves values distinct from those reflected in Article III—including citizen participation and securing deliberative, unanimous decisions. More generally, she finds "good reasons" for upholding a far broader right to jury trial than is currently recognized, "regardless of the nature of the [tribunal] in which the matter is pending." But acknowledging that a broader right would seriously disrupt administrative agencies and legislative courts, she concludes that "maintaining the status quo, however weak its constitutional base, may be more pragmatic and therefore more attractive."

nonjury factfinder.' " In other words, rejecting "Oil States' Article III challenge also resolve[d] [the] Seventh Amendment challenge."

(e) In Securities and Exchange Commission v. Jarkesy, 144 S.Ct. 2117 (2024), however, the Seventh Amendment played a central role. A 6–3 opinion for the Court by Chief Justice Roberts held it unconstitutional for the SEC to impose administrative fines for securities fraud without going through an Article III judge and jury. The Court began its analysis with the Seventh Amendment, relying on Granfinanciera and concluding that the Amendment was implicated because the statutory fines were "legal in nature." In so holding, the Court noted that the damages remedy had a punitive purpose, and also that the claim bore a kinship to common law fraud.

After concluding that the Seventh Amendment was implicated, the Court considered whether the public rights exception applied: "Under this exception, Congress may assign the matter for decision to an agency without a jury, consistent with the Seventh Amendment. But this case does not fall within the exception, so Congress may not avoid a jury trial by preventing the case from being heard before an Article III tribunal." Again the Court relied on Granfinanciera, which it said "effectively decides this case." It rejected the relevance of the statutory scheme that had regulated the securities fraud at issue and also rejected the relevance of the federal government as a plaintiff. See Paragraph (1), *supra*.

Finally, the Court rejected the relevance of Atlas Roofing, *supra* (which had described public rights broadly as "cases in which the Government sues in its sovereign capacity to enforce public rights created by statutes within the power of Congress to enact"). The Court distinguished Atlas Roofing on the ground that the OSHA claims in that case had been "unknown to the common law," rather than (like securities fraud) "akin to common law claims," and limited Atlas Roofing to that extent. The Court also described Atlas Roofing as "a departure from our legal tradition," denied that the case was of great importance or weight, and left open the possibility that Atlas Roofing had already been overruled by Granfinanciera, as Justice White's Granfinanciera dissent had suggested.

Dissenting in Jarkesy, Justice Sotomayor criticized the majority for "disregard[ing]" the "foundational principles" reflected in Atlas Roofing and other cases, and for "effect[ing] a seismic shift in this Court's jurisprudence." She argued that Congress had relied on precedent and past understandings in creating "more than two dozen agencies that can impose civil penalties in administrative proceedings," all of which now had their power threatened by the Court's decision.

(3) Surveying the Landscape. Few observers would view the Supreme Court's shifting decisions in this area as having provided a coherent approach to the general question of the constitutionality of non-Article III adjudication. Consider the plausibility of the following alternatives:

(a) Article III Exclusivity. A polar position would read Article III as mandating that all federal adjudicative tribunals must be Article III courts. As the early development of "exceptions" indicates, however, it is highly doubtful that this approach represented the original understanding of Congress's power, and as Professor Bator noted, p. 484, *supra*, there is a deep conceptual problem in seeking to distinguish adjudication from routine execution of the laws. In any event, by the time of the Northern Pipeline decision, wasn't it clearly too late to upset the myriad schemes of federal non-Article III adjudication—by both legislative courts and administrative agencies—already in existence?

(b) **Historical Exceptions.** The cases appear, for the moment, to accept a short list of exceptions to Article III (territorial courts, courts martial, and some combination of public rights cases and agency adjudication) as having been legitimated by a mixture of textual analysis and tradition. But the approach in Stern, like that in Northern Pipeline, strongly suggests that further exceptions will be hard if not impossible to justify. Isn't this categorical approach hard to apply and to justify without the identification of some guiding principles?

(c) **Text and Structure of Article III.** A related, but more textually grounded theory of non-Article III tribunals, suggests that the so-called "exceptions" may instead reflect a proper reading of the text of Article III. This theory—developed in detail in Baude, *Adjudication Outside Article III*, 133 Harv.L.Rev. 1511 (2020)—posits that not all federal adjudication properly constitutes an exercise of "[t]he judicial Power of the United States." Professor Baude starts from the basic fact that, pursuant to the Madisonian compromise, "state courts have always been able to adjudicate claims arising under federal law and other Article III business." When they do so, such courts are adjudicating federal rights and responsibilities but surely not exercising the judicial power of the United States. Similarly, he contends, when Congress establishes territorial courts pursuant to its powers under the Territory Clause, U.S. Const. art. IV, § 3, those courts have historically been understood to exercise the "judicial power of the territory," and not that of the United States. Public rights adjudication, according to Baude, reflects the proper exercise of executive rather than judicial power, which he identifies as historically permissible in contexts in which the adjudication does not threaten the deprivation of life, liberty, or property. Finally, Baude contends that military justice, properly understood, also constitutes a form of executive adjudication rather than an exercise of judicial power. Does it help clarify analysis to reconceptualize traditional classes of non-Article III adjudication as interpretations of the constitutional text rather than as exceptions to it?

(d) **Necessary and Proper Test.** At the opposite pole from Article III exclusivity would be an approach that views Article III as indifferent as to whether jurisdiction is vested in an Article III court, a legislative court, or an administrative agency. The only relevant questions would be whether use of a non-Article III federal tribunal was "necessary and proper" under Article I and whether it offended some other constitutional provision, such as the Due Process Clause or the Seventh Amendment.

(e) **Balancing.** Justice White, who dissented in Northern Pipeline, appeared there to endorse a case-by-case balancing approach, in which Article III values are weighed against the interests supporting adjudication by a non-Article III tribunal. All balancing tests raise the question whether courts can adequately specify which interests ought to count in the balance and how they ought to be weighed. Is that problem especially difficult in this context?

(f) Appellate Review. A final position, resting on the approach in Crowell v. Benson, would treat sufficiently searching appellate review by an Article III court as both necessary and sufficient to legitimate initial adjudication by a federal legislative court or administrative agency. See Fallon, *Of Legislative Courts, Administrative Agencies, and Article III*, 101 Harv.L.Rev. 915 (1988).[5] This approach claims the virtue of drawing only clear and enforceable lines.[6] As the price for doing so, it eschews efforts to inquire closely into the necessity or desirability of initial adjudication by a legislative court or administrative agency in a particular case. Compare Saphire & Solimine, *Shoring Up Article III: Legislative Court Doctrine in the Post CFTC v. Schor Era*, 68 B.U.L.Rev. 85, 135–51 (1988) (suggesting that review by an Article III court should be viewed as necessary, but not sufficient, to validate adjudication by a legislative court or administrative agency); Meltzer, *Legislative Courts, Legislative Power, and the Constitution*, 65 Ind.L.J. 291 (1990) (same). Moreover, as one of its advocates, Professor

---

[5]   Professor Merrill, in *Article III, Agency Adjudication, and the Origins of the Appellate Review Model of Administrative Law*, 111 Colum.L.Rev. 939 (2011), provides a careful historical study of the origins of the appellate review model of agency adjudication, which he views as hardly inevitable. The nineteenth century, he suggests, featured an all-or-nothing model in which courts either reviewed administrative action under one of the prerogative writs (like mandamus or habeas corpus), on a record produced in court, or afforded no review at all. He locates the origins of the modern appellate review model in the Supreme Court's retreat from its aggressive, and politically controversial, review of decisions of the Interstate Commerce Commission in the 1890s and 1900s, and contends that the approach then spread to other areas. Merrill suggests that while today scholars worry about whether the appellate review model permits the dilution of judicial power, the earlier concern was that Article III courts would be contaminated by being drawn into matters of administration, a concern that the appellate review model largely eliminated. Moving to the present, he doubts that the current allocation of authority—in which judges decide legal issues, while deferring to agencies on factual matters—is optimal, given the close ties of law to policy and the greater expertise and accountability of agencies as policymakers. But he acknowledges that the appellate review model is so deeply entrenched as to make unlikely any significant departure from it.

Pfander, *Article I Tribunals, Article III Courts, and the Judicial Power of the United States*, 118 Harv.L.Rev. 643 (2004), notes that Article I empowers Congress "[t]o constitute *Tribunals* inferior to the supreme Court," while Article III provides that the judicial power "shall be vested in one supreme Court, and in such inferior *Courts*" as Congress establishes (emphasis added). The "Tribunals" contemplated by Article I, he contends, are non-Article III tribunals. (Others dispute his linguistic claim that "tribunals" reaches farther than "courts." See Calabresi & Lawson, *The Unitary Executive, Jurisdiction Stripping, and the Hamdan Opinions: A Textualist Response to Justice Scalia*, 107 Colum.L.Rev. 1002, 1034 (2007).) Pfander acknowledges that the "inferior" status of non-Article III tribunals requires oversight by Article III courts, either through appeals or in some cases by writs such as habeas corpus or mandamus. But he contends that non-Article III tribunals may not adjudicate any disputes that would have lain "at the traditional core of the judicial power of the United States," even were appellate review provided. By contrast, he approves of adjudication by administrative agencies on the separate theory that they are "adjuncts" to Article III courts. Pfander's approach is thus less demanding than the appellate review theory in some respects but more demanding in others.

This brief summary does not capture all of Pfander's complex argument. But doesn't his approach, like that of the Northern Pipeline plurality, raise this question: if administrative adjudication can be justified by the fiction that agencies are "adjuncts" to Article III courts, why cannot adjudication by other non-Article III tribunals be justified on the same basis?

[6]   Note, however, that hard questions would remain about the necessary scope of review. See Fallon, *supra*, at 974–92.

Fallon, acknowledges, the requirement of Article III review, if it is at all robust, could call into question the validity of a number of extant and seemingly accepted regimes. See Fallon, *Jurisdiction-Stripping Reconsidered,* 96 Va.L.Rev. 1043 (2010).

(4) Supreme Court Review of Decisions by Non-Article III Tribunals. How court-like are legislative courts and other non-Article III tribunals? In Ortiz v. United States, 585 U.S. 427 (2018), the Court made clear that legislative courts operate as courts for purposes of Supreme Court review. At issue was whether the Supreme Court could exercise appellate jurisdiction over the final judgment of the Court of Appeals for the Armed Forces (CAAF)—a non-Article III tribunal that reviews the judgments of courts-martial in criminal cases. In Marbury v. Madison, 5 U.S. (1 Cranch) 137 (1803), p. 76, *supra*, Chief Justice Marshall established that "the essential criterion of appellate jurisdiction" is "that it revises and corrects the proceedings in a cause already instituted, and does not create that cause." In Ortiz, an amicus contended that, because the CAAF is in reality an adjudicative body within the Executive Branch—and not an Article III court—appellate jurisdiction did not lie under the criterion set forth in Marbury.

In an opinion for a divided (7–2) Court, Justice Kagan held that courts-martial and military courts possess a judicial "character" that gives them a certain "*court*-likeness," even if they are not Article III courts. She reasoned that military courts exercise a "vast swath" of jurisdiction over criminal offenses that overlaps with the jurisdiction of federal and state courts; military courts impose "terms of imprisonment and capital punishment" upon service members; render judgments that carry res judicata effect; and feature an appellate process that functions much like that of ordinary courts. Although military judges lack life tenure and salary protection, Justice Kagan emphasized that the tradition of non-Article III courts-martial goes back to the beginning of the Republic. She noted that in United States v. Coe, 155 U.S. 76 (1894), the Court upheld its appellate jurisdiction over the judgments of territorial courts, even though they are not Article III tribunals. In other cases, moreover, the Court had uncontroversially exercised appellate jurisdiction over judgments of the non-Article III D.C. local courts. In her view, the petition for a writ of certiorari to the CAAF was appellate because it asked the Court to revise the judgment in a case instituted "in a judicial system recognized since the founding as competent to render the most serious decisions."

In dissent, Justice Alito, joined by Justice Gorsuch, concluded that Article III authorized the Court to exercise appellate review only of an exercise of the judicial power. In the dissent's view, courts-martial "have always been understood to be Executive Branch entities that help the President, as Commander in Chief, to discipline the Armed Forces." According to Justice Alito, "Executive Branch adjudications * * * do not give rise to 'cases' that Article III grants us appellate jurisdiction to review, precisely because officers of the Executive Branch cannot lawfully be vested with judicial power." The dissent distinguished courts-martial from territorial and D.C. local courts on the ground that the latter reflect

Congress's "unique authority to create governments for the Territories and the District of Columbia and to confer on the various branches of those governments powers that are distinct from the legislative, executive, and judicial power of the United States."

Justice Alito's dissent finds support in Baude, *supra*, which, as noted, argues that certain categories of adjudication—even some involving the deprivation of liberty or property—are, by text and tradition, properly exercised by the executive rather than courts. These categories, according to Baude, include military justice. Note, however, that Baude also suggests that some forms of non-Article III adjudication, such as cases brought in territorial courts, properly constitute exercises of judicial power though not "[t]he judicial Power of the United States." How do these conclusions, if correct, sort between tribunals properly subject to Supreme Court review and those that are not? If Congress restyled the NLRB as the National Labor Relations Court, could Congress provide for direct Supreme Court review of the resulting adjudications? And if the Supreme Court could review directly a decision of the NLRB, could it also review directly a decision made by a single federal official, as when Secretary of State Madison "adjudicated" Marbury's claim that he was entitled to his commission?

NOTE ON MAGISTRATE JUDGES

(1) The Institution of Magistrates. Ever since 1789, the federal courts have employed officials other than Article III judges—sometimes called magistrates, sometimes commissioners—to handle certain adjudicative functions.[1] The current regime was established by the Federal Magistrates Act of 1968, codified at 28 U.S.C. § 631 *et seq.*[2] Magistrate judges are appointed for a term of eight years by the judges of the federal judicial district in which they are employed. 28 U.S.C. §§ 631(a), (e). During this term, a magistrate judge may be removed, by the judges of the judicial district, "only for incompetency, misconduct, neglect of duty, or physical or mental disability." *Id.* § 631(i).

(2) Statutory History and the Scope of Authority.

(a) The Federal Magistrates Act of 1968 authorized magistrates to serve as special masters, to provide "assistance to a district judge in the conduct of pretrial or discovery proceedings in civil or criminal actions" and to conduct "preliminary review of motions for posttrial relief." See Pub.L.No. 90–578, 82 Stat. 1107, 1113 (1968). The 1968 Act also contained an open-

---

[1]   The Judiciary Act of 1789 authorized magistrates to fix bail for those accused of federal crimes. In 1817, Congress redesignated magistrates as commissioners and modestly expanded their functions. Periodic revisions and expansions of commissioners' functions were enacted before passage of the 1968 Act. For historical background and analysis of the permissible role of federal magistrate judges, see Silberman, *Masters and Magistrates*, 50 N.Y.U.L.Rev. 1070 (*Part I: The English Model*), 1297 (*Part II: The American Analogue*) (1975).

[2]   A 1990 amendment renamed magistrates as "magistrate judges." Judicial Improvements Act of 1990, Pub.L.No. 101–650, § 321, 104 Stat. 5089 (1990).

ended grant of authority to district judges to charge magistrates with additional duties.

(b)   Amendments enacted in 1976 significantly expanded the range of functions that magistrate judges are expressly authorized to perform. Overruling the decision in Wingo v. Wedding, 418 U.S. 461 (1974), the 1976 amendments permit magistrate judges to conduct evidentiary hearings in habeas corpus cases and to "hear and determine" non-dispositive pre-trial motions, subject to review only to ensure that the decision is not "clearly erroneous or otherwise contrary to law," 28 U.S.C. § 636(b)(1)(A). The amendments further specify that dispositive motions may be referred to a magistrate judge, but only for "proposed findings of fact and recommendations for the disposition"; the presiding judge must make a "de novo" determination of those findings to which objection is raised. *Id.* § 636(b)(1)(B). A catch-all provision, still in effect, provides that magistrate judges "may be assigned such additional duties as are not inconsistent with the Constitution and laws of the United States." *Id.* § 636(b)(3).

(c)   The Federal Magistrates Act of 1979 took yet a further step by establishing that magistrate judges, with the consent of the parties, "may conduct any or all proceedings in a jury or nonjury civil matter and order the entry of judgment in the case, when specifically designated to exercise such jurisdiction by the district court." *Id.* § 636(c)(1).[3] Aggrieved parties then may appeal to the court of appeals. *Id.* § 636(c)(3).

(3)   The Significance of Magistrate Judges. As of 2023, there were 562 full-time and 25 part-time magistrate judges.[4] (By comparison, there were 677 authorized federal district judgeships.) The magistrate judges disposed of 1,192,782 judicial matters in 2022, including social security "appeals" and habeas petitions, and handled 246,886 references in criminal cases (involving motions, conferences, and other pretrial matters).[5] Magistrate judges conducted 283 civil trials with the consent of the parties.[6]

(4)   The Raddatz Case. United States v. Raddatz, 447 U.S. 667 (1980), presented questions about the statutory and constitutional authority of magistrates (as they were then called). There, after the defendant in a felony prosecution moved to suppress incriminating statements, the district judge referred the motion to a magistrate, who conducted an evidentiary hearing. The defendant's account of the encounters at which the statements were made differed sharply from that of federal agents. Crediting the latter, the magistrate proposed findings of fact and recommended that the motion be denied. Following a review of the magistrate's findings and recommendation,

---

[3]   "The court may, for good cause shown on its own motion, or under extraordinary circumstances shown by any party, vacate a reference of a civil matter to a magistrate." 28 U.S.C. § 636(c)(4).

[4]   U.S. Federal Courts, Judicial Facts and Figures (Sept. 30, 2023), at Table 1.1, https://www.uscourts.gov/sites/default/files/data_tables/jff_1.1_0930.2023.pdf.

[5]   See Judicial Business of the United States Courts: 2022 Annual Report of the Director of the Administrative Office of the United States Courts, at Table S-17, https://www.uscourts.gov/sites/default/files/data_tables/jb_s17_0930.2022.pdf.

[6]   See *id.* For further discussion, see p. 548, *supra.*

but not an independent review of the evidence, the district judge denied the motion.

In considering the defendant's challenge to this procedure, the Supreme Court first ruled that the Act does not require an Article III judge to hear the evidence of witnesses on a suppression motion, even when "determination" of the motion turned on issues of demeanor and credibility. The Act required a de novo decision by an Article III judge, but not a de novo hearing of the evidence. The Court then held that the Act, as so interpreted, did not deny due process. Writing for the majority, Chief Justice Burger noted that administrative agencies frequently follow an analogous procedure, with the agencies themselves making the ultimate findings based upon evidence presented to a hearing officer. Finally, the Court rejected the suggestion that Crowell v. Benson, 285 U.S. 22 (1932), p. 476, *supra*, requires an Article III trial de novo on the "constitutional facts" at stake in a suppression motion. The district court had "plenary discretion" whether to use a magistrate, to accept or reject the magistrate's recommendation, and to hear evidence de novo. It sufficed that "the entire process takes place under the district court's total control and jurisdiction."

In an elaborate dissent, Justice Marshall, joined by Justice Brennan, argued that the due process principle that the "one who decides must hear" is violated when a judge resolves a matter without hearing the witnesses in a case where "the factual issues turned on issues of credibility that cannot be fairly resolved on the basis of the record." He added that under Crowell and Ng Fung Ho v. White, 259 U.S. 276 (1922), p. 491, *supra*, an Article III court must make an independent determination of "case-dispositive facts," including credibility issues, in cases where individual liberty is at stake.[7]

(5) Jurisdiction with Consent.

(a) The courts of appeals have been unanimous in upholding the validity of 28 U.S.C. § 636(c), which permits magistrate judges to adjudicate any civil case brought in a federal district court if both parties consent, see, *e.g.*, Gairola v. Commonwealth of Virginia Department of General Services, 753 F.2d 1281 (4th Cir.1985) & cases cited, and the Supreme Court must

---

[7]   In a separate dissent, Justice Stewart, joined by Justices Brennan and Marshall, concluded that the statute required a de novo hearing where credibility issues are critical. In another opinion, Justice Powell dissented on the basis of the Due Process Clause.

The Raddatz Court assumed that it was unlikely that a district court, without conducting its own evidentiary hearing, would reject a magistrate's proposed finding of fact that is dispositive and that depends on a determination of credibility. But it turns out that district courts do just that with some regularity. In turn, six courts of appeals have held that such rejections of a magistrate's finding deny due process when they likely will lead to a defendant's criminal conviction. The cases are discussed in Pierce, *District Court Review of Findings of Fact Proposed by Magistrates: Reality Versus Fiction*, 81 Geo.Wash.L.Rev. 1236 (2013). Professor Pierce criticizes these appellate decisions as (i) inconsistent with the settled practice in administrative agencies of rejecting ALJs' credibility-based determinations, (ii) burdensome and at odds with the rationale for assigning factfinding to magistrates in the first instance, (iii) resting on a premise—that an observer can reliably determine from demeanor whether a person is telling the truth—that the empirical evidence belies, and (iv) inconsistent with Raddatz's argument that factfinding by magistrates comports with Article III because the entire process falls under the complete supervisory control of the district courts.

have implicitly agreed when it decided that consent could be inferred from a party's conduct in litigation. Roell v. Withrow, 538 U.S. 580 (2003).[8]

(b) In Peretz v. United States, 501 U.S. 923 (1991), the Court considered whether a magistrate judge may preside over jury selection in a felony trial when the parties consent.[9] Just two years earlier, in Gomez v. United States, 490 U.S. 858 (1989), a unanimous Court had ruled that presiding over jury selection in such a case, without the defendant's consent, is not among those "additional duties" that under 28 U.S.C. § 636 district courts may assign to magistrate judges. In so ruling the Court had adverted to the doctrine of constitutional avoidance as well as to its "serious doubts" about the feasibility of meaningfully reviewing determinations made by a magistrate judge in the course of jury selection.

But in the Peretz case, the Court held, 5–4, that consent rendered the assignment of jury selection constitutional. Any personal right of a defendant to an Article III judge may be waived, the Court found, and "[e]ven assuming that a litigant may not waive structural protections provided by Article III, we are convinced that no such structural protections are implicated by the procedure followed in this case. Magistrates are appointed and subject to removal by Article III judges. * * * Because 'the entire process takes place under the district court's total control and jurisdiction,' [quoting Raddatz, Paragraph (4), *supra*,] there is no danger that use of the magistrate involves" an attempt to transfer jurisdiction for purposes of crippling the Article III courts. As to review before an Article III judge, "nothing in the statute precludes a district court from providing the review that the Constitution requires." (The Court did not explain what the content of such a requirement might be in this setting.)

Justice Marshall, joined by Justices White and Blackmun, dissented. His opinion protested that the Court had not explained how the "serious doubts" about meaningful review expressed in Gomez were now resolved and concluded that, in the absence of such review, the district court could not be said to have "total control and jurisdiction."[10]

(6) The Underlying Issues. As courts and commentators have recognized, questions pertaining to the use of magistrate judges and other judicial

---

[8] At least four federal circuits have upheld § 636(c) consent jurisdiction in class actions, based on the consent of the class representative(s) and defendant(s), rejecting the view that unnamed class members are "parties" whose consent is required. See Koby v. ARS Nat'l Servs., Inc. 846 F.3d 1071, 1076 (9th Cir.2017); Day v. Persels & Associates, LLC, 729 F.3d 1309, 1324–25 (11th Cir.2013); Dewey v. Volkswagen Aktiengesellschaft, 681 F.3d 170, 180–81 (3d Cir.2012); Williams v. Gen. Elec. Capital Auto Lease, Inc. 159 F.3d 266, 268–70 (7th Cir.1998).

[9] Although the government had relied on a *waiver* theory, the Court rested on the conceptually distinct basis of *consent*. Should the distinction make a difference under Article III?

[10] For an argument that Peretz gives insufficient attention to the structural concerns embodied in Article III—concerns that might be analogized to the non-waivability of subject matter jurisdiction defects—see, *e.g.*, Note, 33 Wm. & Mary L.Rev. 253 (1991), and Note, 70 N.C.L.Rev. 1334 (1992). But see Meltzer, *Legislative Courts, Legislative Power, and the Constitution*, 65 Ind.L.J. 291, 304 (1990), concluding that "there is no inconsistency between an emphasis on Article III as the source of a right to judicial review * * * and a willingness to validate non-Article III adjudication to which litigants have consented."

auxiliaries within the Article III system are analytically distinct from the issue of the validity of legislative and administrative tribunals.

On the one hand, the congressional need to substitute magistrate judges for Article III judges might be thought to be weak. Because magistrate judges function just like Article III judges, the assignment of work to non-Article III officials cannot be justified on grounds that it requires specialized expertise, or the combination of adjudicatory and rulemaking functions, or different procedures (for example, arbitration) from those followed in Article III courts. Indeed, could one say Congress has *no* reason for providing for the assignment of adjudicative functions to magistrate judges, except that it prefers not to create more Article III judgeships? Is this a constitutionally adequate justification?

There have been strong dissents from the decisions of the courts of appeals upholding the consent jurisdiction under § 636(c). One theme of the dissents is that although there have always been judicial adjuncts like magistrates or special masters, their role should be to advise and assist, not to displace, the real judge. See, *e.g.*, Geras v. Lafayette Display Fixtures, Inc., 742 F.2d 1037 (7th Cir.1984) (Posner, J., dissenting); Pacemaker Diagnostic Clinic of America, Inc. v. Instromedix, Inc., 725 F.2d 537 (9th Cir.1984) (en banc) (Schroeder, J., dissenting).

On the other hand, the threat to judicial independence might be thought to be relatively minor. Magistrate judges are selected by Article III judges rather than by the political branches; they operate within the Article III judicial structure; and Article III judges not only review the decisions of magistrate judges but also have an unusually broad array of levers for supervising them.

But if those factors reduce any threat to independence from the political branches, do they create risks to independence from within the judicial branch? A provocative student Note, 88 Yale L.J. 1023, 1052–58 (1979), argues that caseload pressures will lead to appointment of more magistrate judges, with the matters referred to them disproportionately involving "simple cases and needy litigants." The upshot, the author fears, will be a form of discrimination both among classes of litigants and areas of the law. "In addition * * *, the magistrate is also subject to a qualitatively different form of bureaucratic control that may attend district court authority to determine his reappointment prospects and, more importantly, the day-to-day contents of his docket. * * * This ongoing, informal oversight [by district courts] creates the risk of impermissible intrusion on the magistrate's substantive decisions. The danger is not that magistrates will come to function as judicial alter egos, but rather that they may be encouraged to adopt a risk-averse strategy of adjudication by the pressure of judicial scrutiny, a strategy eschewing unconventional decisions that might otherwise be prompted by novel legal claims or pressing factual idiosyncracies [sic]."

NOTE ON MILITARY TRIBUNALS OR COMMISSIONS

(1) Introduction. Distinct from the courts-martial employed to try members of the U.S. military are military tribunals or "commissions" that have been constituted from time to time by the Executive Branch to deal with exigencies associated with war and whose jurisdiction embraces persons outside of the U.S. military. When authorized by Congress, they may be viewed as another form of legislative court. But the Executive Branch has established some commissions without clear legislative authorization.

The judges of such tribunals are typically military officers, and by their nature, military commissions involve adjudication outside the bounds of Article III. Moreover, the full safeguards of the Bill of Rights (for example, the jury trial right) do not apply. Although the Supreme Court has ruled that military commissions must afford due process, see Paragraph (2), *infra*, the Court has not resolved just how due process, and possibly other constitutional rights, apply before military tribunals.

Military commissions have most often been used abroad, in connection with military occupations of foreign territory, but they have sometimes been used domestically as well. They were employed during the Mexican-American War and more commonly during the Civil War "to enforce military discipline among civilian populations and to punish spies, saboteurs, provocateurs, and those that seriously disturbed the public order." Bederman, *Article II Courts*, 44 Mercer L.Rev. 825, 835 (1993). During and after World War II, the Supreme Court sustained the use of military tribunals to try both alleged war criminals[1] and civilians charged with ordinary criminal offenses in zones occupied by American forces.[2]

Following the attacks of September 11, 2001, military tribunals have been used to ascertain whether an individual is an enemy combatant who, under the laws of war, may be detained (without being subjected to criminal punishment) until the cessation of hostilities. After some delays, military commissions are now being used to prosecute alleged terrorists for violations of the laws of war.

(2) The Constitutionality of Military Tribunals. The most fundamental question raised by military commissions is whether adjudication before them, rather than before an Article III court, is ever constitutionally permissible. As is elaborated below, both history and Supreme Court precedent suggest that the answer to that question is yes. But that answer does not mean that every use of such commissions is constitutional. A range of variables may affect the constitutionality of their use, including:

(a) Whether the individual under its jurisdiction is a citizen or an alien;

(b) Whether the tribunal is located abroad or in the United States;

---

[1] See, *e.g.*, Application of Yamashita, 327 U.S. 1 (1946).

[2] See, *e.g.*, Madsen v. Kinsella, 343 U.S. 341 (1952) (upholding a murder trial of an American civilian before a military tribunal in occupied Germany following World War II).

(c) What procedural protections a particular commission affords;

(d) The existence and scope of review in an Article III court;

(e) Whether Congress has authorized the Executive Branch to use a particular kind of tribunal, or, conversely, has prohibited its use.

The present discussion is somewhat summary, seeking simply to provide an overview of the use of these non-Article III tribunals and to explore some of the questions they raise in connection with the themes of this Chapter—notably, the scope of congressional power to assign adjudication to particular tribunals. More detail on these matters is presented in Chapter XI, Sec. 2.

(3) 9/11, the War on Terror, and the Hamdi Decision. In Hamdi v. Rumsfeld, 542 U.S. 507 (2004), the Court addressed the constitutionality of the contemporary use of military tribunals—in that case, to detain an American citizen as an enemy combatant under the laws of war. Hamdi was captured in a field of combat in Afghanistan but then moved to the United States. Military officials determined that he was an "enemy combatant" and claimed the authority to detain him on that basis. When his challenge to his detention reached the Supreme Court, five Justices agreed that an enemy combatant, even if a citizen, could be lawfully detained. Justice O'Connor's plurality opinion (joined by Chief Justice Rehnquist and Justices Kennedy and Breyer) concluded that Congress, in enacting, one week after 9/11, an authorization for the use of military force, had validly authorized the seizure of enemy combatants (including citizens) in Afghanistan, in accordance with the laws and usages of war. But she also concluded that the Due Process Clause gave Hamdi the right to challenge, before an impartial adjudicator, his designation as an enemy combatant. Justice O'Connor referred without elaboration to "the possibility" that the process to which Hamdi was constitutionally entitled could be provided "by an appropriately authorized and properly constituted military tribunal." But because the hearing that Hamdi had previously been afforded was not adequate, she concluded that the decision below denying him any relief must be reversed and the case remanded for further proceedings. (Justices Souter and Ginsburg concluded that Hamdi's detention was not legislatively authorized, but in order to create a majority they joined the plurality's disposition.[3])

Justice Thomas agreed that Hamdi was not immune from detention at the hands of the Executive. He would have affirmed the denial of relief, however, because on his broad view of the scope of executive power, he found no constitutional shortcoming in the hearing that Hamdi had previously been afforded.

In dissent, Justice Scalia (joined by Justice Stevens) maintained that the traditions underlying the Constitution's guarantees of due process and of the privilege of the writ of habeas corpus barred Hamdi's non-punitive detention by the military. In his view, the government had to either try

---

[3] Justice Souter contended that because the government had not shown that its policy of incommunicado detention was consistent with the Geneva Conventions, it could not claim to be acting in accordance with the laws of war that Congress had authorized to be applied against citizens.

Hamdi for an ordinary crime in an Article III court or release him in the absence of a suspension. He explicitly stated, however, that his views applied only to citizens detained within the territorial jurisdiction of a federal court and that in wartime, aliens may lawfully be detained by the military outside of the ordinary criminal process.[4]

The Hamdi decision left open many questions, a number of which are addressed in Chapter XI, Sec. 2. But a majority of the Justices affirmed that there is a constitutionally valid role for military commissions to play, even with respect to American citizens.

(4) The Precedents at Issue in Hamdi. The various opinions in Hamdi discussed, and disagreed about the significance of, two important precedents on the use of military tribunals within the United States: Ex parte Milligan and Ex parte Quirin. Those two decisions are difficult to reconcile with each other.

(a) The Milligan Decision. In Ex parte Milligan, 71 U.S. (4 Wall.) 2 (1866), the Court held that a military tribunal lacked jurisdiction to try a U.S. citizen, living in Indiana, of conspiring to aid the Confederacy. Justice Davis's majority opinion began with the historical context: "During the late wicked Rebellion [when military tribunals were broadly employed], the temper of the times did not allow that calmness in deliberation and discussion so necessary to a correct conclusion of a purely judicial question." The Court emphasized the status of the rights to jury trial and of the Fourth, Fifth, and Sixth Amendments as "the birthright of every American citizen." Then, coming finally to the government's principal argument that the military tribunal could exercise jurisdiction whenever prosecutions were brought "under the 'laws and usages of war,'" the Court replied that those "laws and usages * * * can never be applied to citizens in states which have upheld the authority of the government, and where the courts are open and their process unobstructed. This court has judicial knowledge that, in Indiana, the Federal authority was always unopposed, and its courts always

---

[4]   Powerful support for Justice Scalia's position is provided by Tyler, *The Forgotten Core Meaning of the Suspension Clause*, 125 Harv.L.Rev. 901 (2012). Tyler reviews the history of the writ of habeas corpus, and its suspension, from the Stuart period in Britain through the American founding and up to the Civil War and Reconstruction. She concludes that persons owing allegiance to the government and thereby enjoying the protection of its law—most especially citizens—could not, absent suspension of the writ, be detained domestically except by the normal criminal process. That understanding extended, she argues, to persons suspected of aiding the enemy. Although most (though not all) of her evidence involves persons seized within a nation's sovereign territory, she contends that the extraterritorial seizure of Hamdi did not deprive him of protection and hence that he could not be detained outside of the criminal process absent suspension of the writ.

A quite different conclusion is offered by Professor Harrison, in *The Original Meaning of the Habeas Corpus Suspension Clause, the Right of Natural Liberty, and Executive Discretion*, 29 Wm. & Mary Bill Rts.J. 649 (2021). Harrison argues that neither the text of the Suspension Clause nor historical practice places citizens outside the scope of permissible detention, noting in particular that during the Revolutionary War, both the British and the Americans held captured citizens as prisoners of war. His review of English and early American history concludes that the Suspension Clause, despite its language, is not primarily about habeas corpus but rather about a substantive right to natural liberty. At the founding, he argues, the paradigmatic case of a suspension was a law that conferred on the executive extremely broad discretion to detain—whether or not the judicial remedy of habeas corpus remained intact, and whether or not the individual in custody was a citizen.

open to hear criminal accusations and redress grievances; and no usage of war could sanction a military trial there for any offence whatever of a citizen in civil life, in nowise connected with the military service."

Chief Justice Chase, joined by Justices Wayne, Swayne, and Miller, concurred in the judgment solely on the ground that Congress had not authorized trial by military commission on the facts of the case: "We think that Congress had power, though not exercised, to authorize the military commission which was held in Indiana."

(b) The Quirin Decision. The Court next addressed the use of military commissions in the midst of World War II. In Ex parte Quirin, 317 U.S. 1 (1942), it unanimously upheld the jurisdiction of a military tribunal to try eight German service members who, after landing on Long Island from a German submarine, buried their German military uniforms and set off on their sabotage mission in civilian garb. The Court determined that Congress, by statute, had "authorized trial of offenses against the law of war before [military] commissions," and then added: "the law of war draws a distinction between * * * lawful and unlawful combatants. Lawful combatants are subject to capture and detention as prisoners of war by opposing military forces. Unlawful combatants are likewise subject to capture and detention, but in addition they are subject to trial and punishment by military tribunals for acts which render their belligerency unlawful. The spy who secretly and without uniform passes the military lines of a belligerent in time of war * * * or an enemy combatant who without uniform comes secretly through the lines for the purpose of waging war by destruction of life or property, are familiar examples of belligerents who are generally deemed not to be entitled to the status of prisoners of war, but to be offenders against the law of war subject to trial and punishment by military tribunals."

The Court then held that the historical practice of trying such charges before military tribunals was conclusive of the question of constitutional validity: "§ 2 of Article III and the Fifth and Sixth Amendments cannot be taken to have extended the right to demand a jury to trials by military commission, or to have required that offenses against the law of war not triable by jury at common law be tried only in the civil courts." That conclusion applied equally, the Court said, to one of the saboteurs who claimed American citizenship.

The Court distinguished Ex parte Milligan in the following opaque passage: "Petitioners, and especially [the one claiming American citizenship], stress the pronouncement in the Milligan case that the law of war 'can never be applied to citizens in states which have upheld the authority of the government, and where the courts are open and their process unobstructed.' Elsewhere in its opinion the Court was at pains to point out that Milligan * * * was not an enemy belligerent either entitled to the status of a prisoner of war or subject to the penalties imposed upon unlawful belligerents. We construe the Court's statement as to the inapplicability of the law of war to Milligan's case as having particular reference to the facts before it. From them the Court concluded that Milligan, not being a part of or associated with the armed forces of the enemy, was a non-belligerent, not subject to the law of war save as—in circumstances found not there to be present, and not involved here—martial law might be constitutionally established."

(c) Hamdi's Discussion of Precedent. Unlike Quirin and Milligan, which involved *prosecutions for war crimes* before military tribunals, the Hamdi case involved the *non-criminal* detention of an enemy combatant during an armed conflict. Nonetheless, the Justices in Hamdi viewed Milligan and Quirin as the key precedents, although the various opinions differed sharply in their assessments of those decisions.

(i) Justice O'Connor's plurality opinion in Hamdi rested heavily on Quirin as establishing the constitutionality of military tribunals being used in accordance with the laws of war, even as to an American citizen. She emphasized that Quirin was a unanimous decision that "postdates and clarifies" Milligan. Justice Thomas's opinion went slightly further, asserting that "Quirin overruled Milligan to the extent that those cases are inconsistent."

(ii) By contrast, Justice Scalia's dissent contended that Quirin sought "to revise Milligan rather than describe it." He viewed Milligan as the more foundational precedent, one that resonated with the history of habeas corpus. Justice Scalia stressed Milligan's declaration that the "laws and usages [of war] * * * can never be applied to citizens in states which have upheld the authority of the government, and where the courts are open and their process unobstructed." Quirin, he said, was not the Court's "finest hour," noting that the denial of relief was announced the day after oral argument but the opinion justifying it was not issued for several months, after many of the defendants had been executed.[5] Justice Scalia added that Quirin was distinguishable in any event because it was uncontested that the defendants were members of enemy forces; but when, as in Hamdi, that question is in dispute, a citizen is entitled to a trial before an Article III court.

(d) Reconciling Milligan and Quirin. It is not certain that Milligan and Quirin can be reconciled. But consider these possible distinctions:

(i) One concerns the individual's relationship to the enemy. In the Milligan case, the "substance" of the charges included "holding communications with the enemy" and "conspiring to seize munitions of war stored in the arsenals" during the Civil War. But does a charge of providing support to or conspiring with the enemy fall short of a charge that an individual was a "part of or associated with" enemy forces? On some views, only a person charged with the latter may be detained under the laws of war. If that is a basis for distinction, the facts of Hamdi would seem to fall on the Quirin side of the line.

(ii) Justice Scalia suggests a distinction between cases of conceded and contested enemy status. (Quirin, of course, did not distinguish Milligan on

---

[5]   See also Katyal & Tribe, *Waging War, Deciding Guilt: Trying the Military Tribunals*, 111 Yale L.J. 1259, 1291 (2002) (suggesting that "some highly questionable ex parte arm-twisting by the executive may have spurred the Supreme Court's unanimous decision," and arguing that "Quirin plainly fits the criteria typically offered for judicial confinement or reconsideration").

this basis.) As he notes, on that view Hamdi falls on the Milligan side of the line.

(iii) Quirin found that Congress had authorized the use of military tribunals, whereas Milligan found the contrary. (But five of the nine Justices in Milligan expressed the view that any congressional authorization would have been invalid in any event.)

(5) Military Tribunals to Try Defendants Abroad. The use of military tribunals abroad to detain or punish individuals has provoked less controversy. During the occupations of Germany and Japan following World War II, the United States used military tribunals extensively, trying over 1600 persons in Germany and 1000 persons in the Far East.[6] The use of such tribunals seems to have rested on one of two bases: an occupying power may use military tribunals to try ordinary criminal offenses (including those committed by U.S. citizens) until domestic civil government is restored, see Madsen v. Kinsella, note 2, *supra*, or to try alleged violations of the laws of war (usually by aliens), even after hostilities have ended, see, *e.g.*, Application of Yamashita, note 1, *supra*.

In Johnson v. Eisentrager, 339 U.S. 763, 788–89 (1950), however, Justice Jackson's opinion for the Court can be read as going further; he suggested that challenges to the use of military tribunals to try aliens in foreign territories are challenges to the "conduct of diplomatic and foreign affairs, for which the President is exclusively responsible." He coupled this suggestion of constitutional authority with a further suggestion that enemy aliens detained on foreign soil have no constitutional right to be free from detention and trial by military commissions.

(6) The Relationship of Congress and the President in Determining the Appropriate Use of Military Tribunals. Insofar as the Constitution does not prohibit the use of military commissions, to what extent may the President constitute them without congressional authorization or in a fashion that conflicts with statutorily prescribed provisions?

(a) Quirin and Hamdi. That question did not arise in Quirin, in which the Court unanimously found congressional authorization. And five of the Justices in Hamdi concluded that at least in the circumstances there presented, Congress's authorization to the President to use "all necessary and appropriate force" against those responsible for the 9/11 attacks implicitly authorized the detention of enemy combatants, given that (as the plurality indicated) wartime detention was "fundamental and accepted [as] an incident to war." They declined to decide whether such authorization was necessary. But the other four Justices, who found no statutory authorization on varying bases,[7] appeared to assume that absent congressional authorization, the tribunals were not valid.

---

[6] American Bar Association Task Force on Terrorism and the Law, Report and Recommendations on Military Commissions (Jan. 4, 2002).

[7] Justice Souter's dissent (joined by Justice Ginsburg) argued that at most Congress authorized detention consistent with the laws of war, which, in his view, Hamdi's incommunicado detention violated. Justice Scalia's dissent focused on constitutional issues, but he also said that in view of the constitutional concerns, the congressional authorization of force was not sufficiently clear to warrant interpreting it to authorize the detention of a citizen.

(b) Conflict Between President and Congress: Hamdan v. Rumsfeld. When President Bush established military commissions after 9/11 to try enemy combatants for alleged violations of the laws of war, the Supreme Court found both that those tribunals violated statutorily rooted requirements that had taken effect after Quirin, and that as a result those tribunals lacked the power to proceed. In Hamdan v. Rumsfeld, 548 U.S. 557 (2006), a Yemeni national alleged to have been the bodyguard and driver for Osama bin Laden was captured during hostilities in Afghanistan, transported by the U.S. military to Guantanamo Bay, Cuba, and charged with conspiracy to commit war crimes. While those charges were pending, he filed suit in federal court challenging the jurisdiction of the military commission. On review, the Supreme Court upheld Hamdan's claim that the military commission lacked lawful authority to try him. Justice Stevens's opinion for the Court concluded that "[t]he [Uniform Code of Military Justice (UCMJ)] conditions the President's use of military commissions on compliance not only with the American common law of war, but also with * * * the 'rules and precepts of the law of nations,' Quirin, 317 U.S., at 28— including, *inter alia*, the four Geneva Conventions signed in 1949," seven years after the Quirin decision. The Court proceeded to find that the commission established to try Hamdan violated the UCMJ in two respects, both relating to the failure of the commission to conform to procedures that the UCMJ expressly prescribed for courts martial and that, the Court ruled, also applied to the proceedings in Hamdan's case.[8]

Dissents by Justices Scalia, Thomas, and Alito (each joined in full or in part by the others) disagreed with many aspects of the majority's reasoning. Justice Thomas contended that history and precedent supported the President's powers under the common law of war to prescribe the procedures for military commissions and questioned the majority's premise that Congress, in enacting the UCMJ, "intended to deprive [the President] of particular powers not specifically enumerated."

Some months after the Hamdan decision, Congress enacted the Military Commissions Act of 2006 (MCA), Pub.L.No. 109–366, 120 Stat. 2600, which expressly authorizes trials before military commissions of aliens alleged to be unlawful enemy combatants and which includes provisions that cured the legal defects identified in the Hamdan decision. For discussion, see pp. 1538–1539, *infra*.

(c) The Framework of the Steel Seizure Case. In Hamdan, all of the Justices appeared to agree that the validity of military commissions should be resolved within the framework of Justice Jackson's celebrated concurring opinion in Youngstown Sheet & Tube Co. v. Sawyer, 343 U.S. 579 (1952), which conceptualized presidential authority as (i) strongest when

---

[8]   First, the Court interpreted the UCMJ as requiring that the procedures used before military commissions be uniform with the procedures used before courts martial except to the extent that the President found them to be impracticable, a finding the Court concluded that the President had not made. Second, the Court interpreted the UCMJ as requiring compliance with Common Article 3 of the Geneva Conventions, which requires trial before a "regularly constituted court affording all the judicial guarantees which are recognized as indispensable by civilized peoples." The Court then determined that military commissions were not regularly constituted because they deviated from court-martial practice without an adequate justification.

asserted with the explicit or implicit authorization of Congress, (ii) uncertain when asserted in the absence of either a congressional grant or denial of authority, and (iii) at its lowest ebb when asserted contrary to the express or implied will of Congress. The Justices in Hamdan disagreed, however, about which of Justice Jackson's three categories the case occupied. The dissenters read the UCMJ and AUMF as broad authorizations of executive reliance on military tribunals, whereas the majority interpreted the UCMJ, in particular, as limiting presidential power.

When Congress and the Executive are in agreement, what limits are there on the scope of authority that can be vested in military tribunals rather than in Article III courts? Article I, § 8, cl. 10 gives Congress the power to "define and punish * * * Offences against the Law of Nations." Some have argued that Congress's power is limited to defining and specifying the punishment for offenses that are recognized as such by the international laws of war,[9] at least when there are no exigent circumstances arising, for example, from martial law or from the occupation of enemy territory. But the government has at times taken the view that the political branches may assign for trial before military tribunals a broader set of offenses, as recognized either by past U.S. practice or by legislation under Article I, § 8, cl. 10.[10]

---

[9]   See, *e.g.*, Vladeck, *The Laws of War as a Constitutional Limit on Military Jurisdiction*, 4 J.Nat'l Security L. & Pol'y 295 (2010); Hafetz, *Policing the Line: International Law, Article III, and the Constitutional Limits of Military Jurisdiction*, 2014 Wis.L.Rev. 681 (2014).

[10]   In Bahlul v. United States, 840 F.3d 757 (D.C.Cir.2016) (en banc), a badly splintered en banc decision of the D.C. Circuit affirmed a military tribunal's conviction of Bahlul for conspiracy to commit war crimes. Bahlul, who was a Pakistani national, argued that, under Articles I and III, the government could invoke non-Article III military commissions only to try offenses against "the *international* law of war" and that conspiracy was not such an offense.

In a brief per curiam opinion, the court affirmed Bahlul's conviction. The nine participating judges, however, produced five separate opinions (two of which concluded that Bahlul's conviction could be affirmed without reaching the constitutional question).

Then-Judge Kavanaugh, joined by two other judges, concurred on the ground that nothing in the Constitution or the Court's precedents requires Congress to restrict military tribunals only to offenses against the international laws of war. In addition, he concluded, "Congress's longstanding practice strongly supports the conclusion that international law is not a constitutional constraint on Congress's authority to [invoke a] . . . military commission." (A separate concurrence by Judge Henderson took a similar position). In a joint dissent, Judges Rogers, Tatel, and Pillard argued that Article III establishes a strong default rule of adjudication by judges with life-tenure and salary protection and that military commissions represent a limited historical exception for cases involving (a) courts in areas under martial law, (b) courts in areas of temporary military occupation, and (c) cases involving enemy combatants charged with violations of the international laws of war.

In a case such as Bahlul, how conclusive should historical practice be in determining the constitutionality of Congress's decision to assign adjudication of an offense such as conspiracy to a military commission? For the view that judges have done a poor job of capturing the historical complexities that surround the use of military commissions over the course of more than two centuries, see Lederman, *The Law(?) of the Lincoln Assassination*, 118 Colum.L.Rev. 323 (2018) (suggesting that divisions of opinion among Civil War-era officials and the Court's post-war decision in Ex parte Milligan, Paragraph (4)(a), *supra*, complicate modern reliance on Civil War-era practices relating to military commissions); and Lederman, *Of Spies, Saboteurs, and Enemy Accomplices: History's Lessons for the Constitutionality of Wartime Military Tribunals*, 105 Geo.L.J. 1529 (2017) (arguing that, without deep immersion in prior common law practice, it is easy for judges to overread Revolutionary War-era and early congressional practices relating to the use of military tribunals to try spies and those accused of giving aid and comfort to the enemy).

(d) The Question of Executive Authority. When Congress has neither authorized nor prohibited the use of military commissions, what is the scope of the President's power unilaterally to establish them?

(7) Judicial Review and Habeas Corpus. Article III courts have not typically had statutory jurisdiction to engage in appellate review of the decisions of military tribunals. But in some instances, the federal courts, in the exercise of their general habeas corpus jurisdiction, have reviewed whether "the Constitution or laws of the United States withhold [from the military] authority to proceed with the trial." Application of Yamashita, note 1, *supra*, 327 U.S. at 9. The decisions in Milligan, Quirin, Hamdi and Hamdan all arose under the habeas corpus jurisdiction.

Recall that in Boumediene v. Bush, 553 U.S. 723 (2008), p. 1507, *supra*, the Court, after first determining that an alien detained at Guantanamo Bay had a constitutional right to habeas corpus review, and that a procedure for appellate review in an Article III court of appeals was not an adequate substitute for habeas review, held that a congressional enactment purporting to bar all federal and state courts from exercising habeas corpus jurisdiction over those detained at Guantanamo like the petitioner violated the Suspension Clause. The Boumediene decision left open, however, a broad range of questions about the appropriate timing and scope of judicial inquiry. See generally pp. 1532–1536, *infra*.[11]

3. FEDERAL AUTHORITY AND STATE COURT JURISDICTION

INTRODUCTORY NOTE

So far, the material in this Chapter has focused on the power of Congress to vest, or deny, jurisdiction in federal tribunals. But there are closely related issues about congressional control of the jurisdiction of the state courts.

Four main questions are addressed in this section. The first, addressed in the next two principal cases, Tafflin v. Levitt and Tennessee v. Davis, concerns the scope of congressional power to preclude states from exercising jurisdiction, either by making federal court jurisdiction exclusive or by authorizing removal of cases from state to federal court. The second, raised by Tarble's Case, asks whether the Constitution itself precludes the exercise

---

[11] Based on a comprehensive historical analysis of the writ starting with its codification in England's Habeas Corpus Act of 1679, Professor Tyler argues that the privilege protects citizens and individuals in allegiance with the sovereign against being detained outside the formal criminal process, even in wartime, absent Congress's suspension of the writ for one of the reasons enumerated in the Suspension Clause. See Tyler, Habeas Corpus in Wartime: From the Tower of London to Guantanamo Bay (2017). To what extent should historical practice determine the present content of the habeas guarantee? Should it at least furnish a baseline below which the government may not go? For further discussion, see pp. 1526–1527, *infra*.

of state court jurisdiction in any way. The third concerns the extent to which state courts are obliged, by virtue of congressional action or the Supremacy Clause, to exercise jurisdiction over federal cases, even when state law does not authorize state court adjudication; the principal cases here are Testa v. Katt and Haywood v. Drown. And the last question, raised by a host of Supreme Court decisions, concerns the extent to which federal law governs the procedures and remedies followed by the state courts when litigating federal rights.

Tafflin v. Levitt

493 U.S. 455 (1990).
Certiorari to the United States Court of Appeals for the Fourth Circuit.

■ JUSTICE O'CONNOR delivered the opinion of the Court.

* * *

I

[Suit was brought in federal court against the officers and directors of a failed state-chartered savings and loan, and other defendants, by holders of unpaid certificates of deposit. The complaint included claims under the Racketeer Influenced and Corrupt Organizations Act (RICO), which prohibits various forms of participation in a criminal enterprise that is connected to a "pattern of racketeering activity." RICO is an unusual federal statute, as liability for a pattern of racketeering is based on the existence of at least two predicate acts, which are not defined by RICO itself. Instead, a predicate act can be any of a long list of federal or state crimes listed in the RICO statute. A person who violates RICO is subject not only to criminal prosecution, but also to private civil actions in which injured parties may collect treble damages and attorney's fees.

[The question before the Supreme Court in Tafflin was whether a state court may exercise jurisdiction over civil RICO actions. That question arose when, upon the defendants' motion, the lower federal courts held that they should "abstain" from resolving the RICO claims, effectively requiring them to be litigated in the state court. The lower courts reasoned that since (i) the underlying causes of action had been raised in pending litigation in Maryland state court, and (ii) Maryland had a "comprehensive scheme for the rehabilitation and liquidation of insolvent state-chartered savings and loan associations," abstention was appropriate under the doctrine of Burford v. Sun Oil Co., 319 U.S. 315 (1943), pp. 1398–1399, *infra*. The Supreme Court granted certiorari to determine whether the lower courts were correct in concluding, as a predicate for their abstention decision, that the state courts have concurrent jurisdiction over civil RICO actions.] We hold that they do * * *.

II

We begin with the axiom that, under our federal system, the States possess sovereignty concurrent with that of the Federal Government, subject only to limitations imposed by the Supremacy Clause. Under this system of dual sovereignty, we have consistently held that state courts have inherent authority, and are thus presumptively competent, to adjudicate claims arising under the laws of the United States. See, *e.g.*, Claflin v. Houseman, 93 U.S. 130, 136–137 (1876); Charles Dowd Box Co. v. Courtney, 368 U.S. 502, 507–508, 522–523 (1962); Gulf Offshore Co. v. Mobil Oil Corp., 453 U.S. 473, 477–478 (1981). As we noted in Claflin, "if exclusive jurisdiction be neither express nor implied, the State courts have concurrent jurisdiction whenever, by their own constitution, they are competent to take it." 93 U.S., at 136; see also Dowd Box, *supra*, 368 U.S. at 507–508 ("We start with the premise that nothing in the concept of our federal system prevents state courts from enforcing rights created by federal law. Concurrent jurisdiction has been a common phenomenon in our judicial history, and exclusive federal court jurisdiction over cases arising under federal law has been the exception rather than the rule"). See generally * * * The Federalist No. 82 (A. Hamilton) * * *.

This deeply rooted presumption in favor of concurrent state court jurisdiction is, of course, rebutted if Congress affirmatively ousts the state courts of jurisdiction over a particular federal claim. As we stated in Gulf Offshore:

> "In considering the propriety of state-court jurisdiction over any particular federal claim, the Court begins with the presumption that state courts enjoy concurrent jurisdiction. Congress, however, may confine jurisdiction to the federal courts either explicitly or implicitly. Thus, the presumption of concurrent jurisdiction can be rebutted by an explicit statutory directive, by unmistakable implication from legislative history, or by a clear incompatibility between state-court jurisdiction and federal interests." 453 U.S., at 478 (citations omitted).

* * * [T]hese principles, which have "remained unmodified through the years," Dowd Box, *supra*, 368 U.S. at 508, provide the analytical framework for resolving this case.

III

The precise question presented, therefore, is whether state courts have been divested of jurisdiction to hear civil RICO claims "by an explicit statutory directive, by unmistakable implication from legislative history, or by a clear incompatibility between state-court jurisdiction and federal interests." Gulf Offshore, *supra*, 453 U.S. at 478. * * *

At the outset, petitioners concede that there is nothing in the language of RICO—much less an "explicit statutory directive"—to suggest that Congress has, by affirmative enactment, divested the state courts of jurisdiction to hear civil RICO claims. The statutory provision authorizing civil RICO claims provides in full:

> "Any person injured in his business or property by reason of a violation of section 1962 of this chapter *may* sue therefor in any appropriate United States district court and shall recover threefold the damages he sustains and the cost of the suit, including a reasonable attorney's fee." 18 U.S.C. § 1964(c) (emphasis added).

This grant of federal jurisdiction is plainly permissive, not mandatory, for "[t]he statute does not state nor even suggest that such jurisdiction shall be exclusive. * * *" Dowd Box, *supra*, 368 U.S., at 506. Indeed, "[i]t is black letter law . . . that the mere grant of jurisdiction to a federal court does not operate to oust a state court from concurrent jurisdiction over the cause of action." Gulf Offshore, *supra*, 453 U.S., at 479 * * *.

Petitioners thus rely solely on the second and third factors suggested in Gulf Offshore, arguing that exclusive federal jurisdiction over civil RICO actions is established "by unmistakable implication from legislative history, or by a clear incompatibility between state-court jurisdiction and federal interests," 453 U.S., at 478.

Our review of the legislative history, however, reveals no evidence that Congress even considered the question of concurrent state court jurisdiction over RICO claims, much less any suggestion that Congress affirmatively intended to confer exclusive jurisdiction over such claims on the federal courts. * * * Petitioners nonetheless insist that if Congress had considered the issue, it would have granted federal courts exclusive jurisdiction over civil RICO claims. This argument, however, is misplaced, for even if we could reliably discern what Congress' intent might have been had it considered the question, we are not at liberty to so speculate; the fact that Congress did not even *consider* the issue readily disposes of any argument that Congress unmistakably intended to divest state courts of concurrent jurisdiction.

Sensing this void in the legislative history, petitioners rely, in the alternative, on our decisions in Sedima, S.P.R.L. v. Imrex Co., 473 U.S. 479 (1985), and Agency Holding Corp. v. Malley-Duff & Assocs., 483 U.S. 143 (1987), in which we noted that Congress modeled § 1964(c) after § 4 of the Clayton Act, 15 U.S.C. § 15(a). * * * Petitioners assert that, because we have interpreted § 4 of the Clayton Act to confer exclusive jurisdiction on the federal courts, see, *e.g.*, General Investment Co. v. Lake Shore & M.S.R. Co., 260 U.S. 261, 286–288 (1922), and because Congress may be presumed to have been aware of and incorporated those interpretations when it used similar language in RICO, Congress intended, by implication, to grant exclusive federal jurisdiction over claims arising under § 1964(c).

This argument is also flawed. To rebut the presumption of concurrent jurisdiction, the question is not whether any intent at all may be divined from legislative silence on the issue, but whether Congress in its deliberations may be said to have affirmatively or unmistakably intended jurisdiction to be exclusively federal. In the instant case, the lack of any indication in RICO's legislative history that Congress either considered or assumed that the importing of remedial language from the Clayton Act into RICO had any jurisdictional implications is dispositive. The "mere borrowing of statutory language does not imply that Congress also intended to incorporate all of the baggage that may be attached to the borrowed language." Lou [v. Belzberg, 834 F.2d 730, 737 (9th Cir.1987)]. * * *

Petitioners finally urge that state court jurisdiction over civil RICO claims would be clearly incompatible with federal interests. We noted in Gulf Offshore that factors indicating clear incompatibility "include the desirability of uniform interpretation, the expertise of federal judges in federal law, and the assumed greater hospitality of federal courts to peculiarly federal claims." 453 U.S., at 483–484 (citation and footnote omitted). Petitioners' primary contention is that concurrent jurisdiction is clearly incompatible with the federal interest in uniform interpretation of federal criminal laws, see 18 U.S.C. § 3231, because state courts would be required to construe the federal crimes that constitute predicate acts defined as "racketeering activity," see 18 U.S.C. §§ 1961(1)(B), (C), and (D) * * * [and the federal courts would] consequently lose control over the orderly and uniform development of federal criminal law.

We perceive no "clear incompatibility" between state court jurisdiction over civil RICO actions and federal interests. * * * [C]oncurrent jurisdiction over § 1964(c) suits is clearly not incompatible with § 3231 itself, for civil RICO claims are not "offenses against the laws of the United States," § 3231, and do not result in the imposition of criminal sanctions—uniform or otherwise. * * *

* * * Although petitioners' concern with the need for uniformity and consistency of federal criminal law is well-taken, see Ableman v. Booth, 62 U.S. (21 How.) 506, 517–518 (1859), federal courts, pursuant to § 3231, would retain full authority and responsibility for the interpretation and application of federal criminal law, for they would not be bound by state court interpretations of the federal offenses constituting RICO's predicate acts. State courts adjudicating civil RICO claims will, in addition, be guided by federal court interpretations of the relevant federal criminal statutes, just as federal courts sitting in diversity are guided by state court interpretations of state law * * *. State court judgments misinterpreting federal criminal law would, of course, also be subject to direct review by this Court. * * *

Moreover, contrary to petitioners' fears, we have full faith in the ability of state courts to handle the complexities of civil RICO actions, particularly since many RICO cases involve asserted violations of state law, such as state fraud claims, over which state courts presumably have greater expertise. See * * * BNA, Civil RICO Report, Vol. 2, No. 44, p. 7

(Apr. 14, 1987) (54.9% of all RICO cases after Sedima involved "common law fraud" and another 18% involved either "nonsecurities fraud" or "theft or conversion"). * * *

Finally, we note that, far from disabling or frustrating federal interests, "[p]ermitting state courts to entertain federal causes of action facilitates the enforcement of federal rights." Gulf Offshore, 453 U.S., at 478, n.4 * * *. Thus, to the extent that Congress intended RICO to serve broad remedial purposes, * * * concurrent state court jurisdiction over civil RICO claims will advance rather than jeopardize federal policies underlying the statute.

For all of the above reasons, we hold that state courts have concurrent jurisdiction to consider civil claims arising under RICO. * * * The judgment of the Court of Appeals is accordingly

Affirmed.

■ JUSTICE WHITE, concurring.

* * *

■ JUSTICE SCALIA, with whom JUSTICE KENNEDY joins, concurring.

I join the opinion of the Court, addressing the issues before us on the basis argued by the parties, which has included acceptance of the dictum in Gulf Offshore Co. v. Mobil Oil Corp., 453 U.S. 473, 478 (1981), that "the presumption of concurrent jurisdiction can be rebutted by an explicit statutory directive, by unmistakable implication from legislative history, or by a clear incompatibility between state-court jurisdiction and federal interests." * * * I write separately, before this * * * [dictum] has become too entrenched, to note my view that in one respect it is not a correct statement of the law, and in another respect it may not be.

State courts have jurisdiction over federal causes of action not because it is "conferred" upon them by the Congress; nor even because their inherent powers permit them to entertain transitory causes of action arising under the laws of foreign sovereigns, see, *e.g.*, McKenna v. Fisk, 1 How. 241, 247–249 (1843); but because "[t]he laws of the United States are laws in the several States, and just as much binding on the citizens and courts thereof as the State laws are. . . . The two together form one system of jurisprudence, which constitutes the law of the land for the State; and the courts of the two jurisdictions are not foreign to each other. . . ." Claflin v. Houseman, 93 U.S. 130, 136–137 (1876).

It therefore takes an affirmative act of power under the Supremacy Clause to oust the States of jurisdiction—an exercise of what one of our earliest cases referred to as "the power of congress to *withdraw*" federal claims from state-court jurisdiction. Houston v. Moore, 5 Wheat. 1, 26 (1820) (emphasis added).

As an original proposition, it would be eminently arguable that depriving state courts of their sovereign authority to adjudicate the law of the land must be done, if not with the utmost clarity, *cf.* Atascadero

State Hospital v. Scanlon, 473 U.S. 234, 243 (1985) (state sovereign immunity can be eliminated only by "clear statement"), at least *expressly*. That was the view of Alexander Hamilton:

> "When ... we consider the State governments and the national governments, as they truly are, in the light of kindred systems, and as parts of ONE WHOLE, the inference seems to be conclusive that the State courts would have a concurrent jurisdiction in all cases arising under the laws of the Union, where it was not expressly prohibited." The Federalist No. 82, p. 132 (E. Bourne ed. 1947).

* * * Although as early as Claflin, and as late as Gulf Offshore, we had *said* that the exclusion of concurrent state jurisdiction could be achieved by implication, the only cases in which to my knowledge we have acted upon such a principle are those relating to the Sherman Act and the Clayton Act—where the full extent of our analysis was the less than compelling statement that provisions giving the right to sue in United States District Court "show that [the right] is to be exercised *only* in a 'court of the United States.'" General Investment Co. v. Lake Shore & Michigan Southern R. Co., 260 U.S. 261, 287 (1922) (emphasis added). * * * In the standard fields of exclusive federal jurisdiction, the governing statutes specifically recite that suit may be brought "only" in federal court, Investment Company Act of 1940, as amended, 15 U.S.C. § 80a–35(b)(5); that the jurisdiction of the federal courts shall be "exclusive," Securities Exchange Act of 1934, as amended, 15 U.S.C. § 78aa; Natural Gas Act of 1938, 15 U.S.C. § 717u; Employee Retirement Income Security Act of 1974, 29 U.S.C. § 1132(e)(1); or indeed even that the jurisdiction of the federal courts shall be "exclusive of the courts of the States," 18 U.S.C. § 3231 (criminal cases); 28 U.S.C. §§ 1333 (admiralty, maritime, and prize cases), 1334 (bankruptcy cases), 1338 (patent, plant variety protection, and copyright cases), 1351 (actions against consuls or vice consuls of foreign states), 1355 (actions for recovery or enforcement of fine, penalty, or forfeiture incurred under Act of Congress), 1356 (seizures on land or water not within admiralty and maritime jurisdiction).

Assuming, however, that exclusion by implication is possible, surely what is required is implication in the text of the statute, and not merely, as the second part of the Gulf Offshore dictum would permit, through "unmistakable implication from legislative history." 453 U.S., at 478. * * * What is needed to oust the States of jurisdiction is congressional *action* (*i.e.*, a provision of law), not merely congressional discussion.

It is perhaps also true that implied preclusion can be established by the fact that a statute expressly mentions only federal courts, plus the fact that state-court jurisdiction would plainly disrupt the statutory scheme. That is conceivably what was meant by the third part of the Gulf Offshore dictum, "clear incompatibility between state-court jurisdiction and federal interests." 453 U.S., at 478. If the phrase is interpreted more broadly than that, however—if it is taken to assert some power on the part of this Court to exclude state-court jurisdiction when systemic federal interests make it undesirable—it has absolutely no foundation in our precedent. * * *

In sum: As the Court holds, the RICO cause of action meets none of the three tests for exclusion of state-court jurisdiction recited in Gulf Offshore. Since that is so, the proposition that meeting any one of the tests would have sufficed is dictum here, as it was there. In my view meeting the second test is assuredly not enough, and meeting the third may not be.

NOTE ON TAFFLIN V. LEVITT AND CONGRESSIONAL EXCLUSION OF STATE COURT JURISDICTION

(1) Federalist No. 82. Both the majority and the concurrence in Tafflin cite Federalist No. 82. In that paper, Alexander Hamilton started from the principles in Federalist No. 32, regarding legislative authority, writing that the states "will retain all *pre-existing* authorities" that are not exclusively delegated to the national government, either by (i) an express grant of exclusivity to the national government, (ii) a grant of authority to the union where "the exercise of a like authority is prohibited to the States," or (iii) an authority granted to the Union, with which the exercise of state authority would be "utterly incompatible." Being inclined to think these principles apply to the judiciary with similar force as to the legislature, he concluded that the "State courts will *retain* the jurisdiction they now have, unless it appears to be taken away in one of the enumerated modes."

He then said that Article III's language—in particular, that "[t]he JUDICIAL POWER of the United States *shall be vested* in one Supreme Court, and in *such* inferior courts as the Congress shall from time to time ordain and establish"—should not suggest that the federal judicial power is exclusive, as that would "amount to an alienation of State power by implication." Instead, he preferred interpreting the quoted language as merely identifying the courts that will exercise the judicial power.

Hamilton next seemed at first to state that "this doctrine of concurrent jurisdiction is only clearly applicable" to those causes of action "of which the State courts have previous cognizance" and that to deny state court jurisdiction over "cases which may grow out of, and be *peculiar* to, the Constitution * * * can hardly be considered as the abridgement of a pre-existing authority." But while proceeding to declare that the United States could, if it thought it expedient, make federal jurisdiction exclusive over "causes arising upon a particular regulation" (of which the RICO action in Tafflin would be an example), he then said that state courts would have concurrent jurisdiction not only of pre-existing causes but also of causes of action to which acts of Congress "may give birth." He noted that the judicial power of every government, in civil cases, "looks beyond its own * * * laws" and may apply the laws of foreign nations; when one considers that the state and federal governments are parts of "One Whole, the inference seems to be conclusive, that the State courts would have a concurrent jurisdiction in all cases arising under the laws of the Union, where it was not expressly prohibited."

(2) Constitutionally Mandated Exclusivity? The unqualified proposition that, absent congressional exclusion, state courts may adjudicate federal causes of action has not always appeared self-evident. Justice Story, for example, believed that Article III makes federal jurisdiction "unavoidably * * * exclusive" in at least some classes of cases. He clearly placed federal criminal cases and admiralty and maritime cases within with that category, and he suggested somewhat less clearly that the same might be true more generally of cases over which the state courts would not have had jurisdiction prior to adoption of the Constitution. See Martin v. Hunter's Lessee, 14 U.S. (1 Wheat.) 304, 337 (1816).[1] Tafflin v. Levitt and the cases on which it relies decisively reject the notion of constitutionally-based exclusivity. For additional discussion of whether the Constitution requires exclusive federal jurisdiction in particular classes of cases, see pp. 575–582, *infra*.

(3) Foundations of Congressional Authority. The Judiciary Act of 1789 provided for exclusive federal jurisdiction of cases involving "crimes and offences cognizable under the authority of the United States," "seizures" on land or water, "suits for penalties and forfeitures, incurred under the laws of the United States," "suits against consuls or vice-consuls," and "civil causes of admiralty and maritime jurisdiction * * * saving to suitors, in all cases, the right of a common law remedy, where the common law is competent to give it." Act of Sept. 24, 1789, §§ 9, 11, 1 Stat. 76–77, 79. The Act also conferred exclusive *original* Supreme Court jurisdiction in many civil actions to which states were parties. *Id.* § 13. Pockets of exclusive jurisdiction have existed ever since.[2] Justice Scalia's opinion in Tafflin lists most of the important statutes that make federal jurisdiction exclusive. (One important grant of exclusive jurisdiction that he does not list governs common law tort actions against the United States, brought under the Federal Tort Claims Act. See 28 U.S.C. § 1346(b).)

Because Congress's power to create exclusive federal jurisdiction has seldom been challenged, the Supreme Court did not discuss the question until The Moses Taylor, 71 U.S. (4 Wall.) 411 (1867). In reversing a state court judgment sustaining an *in rem* proceeding against a vessel, the Court

---

[1]   Justice Story's view appears to have rested in part on a distinction between jurisdiction that existed in state courts "previous to the adoption of the constitution," which they retained, and jurisdiction over cases that could not previously have arisen, which "could not afterwards be directly conferred on them." 14 U.S. (1 Wheat.) at 335. Whether intentionally or not, Justice Story's formulation echoes some of the language (though not the conclusion reached) in The Federalist No. 82. *Cf.* 3 Story, Commentaries on the Constitution § 1666, at 533 (1833) (noting the "peculiar wisdom in giving to the national government" admiralty jurisdiction, but stating that in many admiralty cases "the same reasons do not exist, as in cases of prize, for an exclusive jurisdiction; and, therefore, whenever the common law is competent to give a remedy in the state courts, they may retain their accustomed concurrent jurisdiction in the administration of it").

[2]   Section 256 of the former Judicial Code (28 U.S.C. § 371, 1940 ed.) purported to enumerate the areas from which state courts had been excluded, but the enumeration was incomplete and Congress repealed the section in the 1948 revision.

held that such relief fell within the exclusive grant of federal admiralty jurisdiction. With respect to the constitutional question, Justice Field said:

"The Judiciary Act of 1789 * * * is framed upon the theory that in all cases to which the judicial power of the United States extends, Congress may rightfully vest exclusive jurisdiction in the Federal courts. It declares that in some cases, from their commencement, such jurisdiction shall be exclusive; in other cases it determines at what stage of procedure such jurisdiction shall attach, and how long and how far concurrent jurisdiction of the State courts shall be permitted. * * *

"The constitutionality of these provisions cannot be seriously questioned, and is of frequent recognition by both State and Federal courts."[3]

Under which grant(s) of authority might Congress exclude state court jurisdiction of federal claims? For example, could Congress make diversity jurisdiction exclusive?

(4) The Scope of Implied Exclusion.

(a) The Claflin Presumption of Concurrency and Departures from It. The 1876 decision in Claflin v. Houseman established the presumption, generally followed ever since, that a grant of federal jurisdiction, unless explicitly exclusive, does not preclude the exercise of concurrent state court jurisdiction.[4] As noted in the Tafflin opinion, however, the Supreme Court has occasionally held that grants of federal jurisdiction *impliedly* exclude state jurisdiction. In the antitrust decision discussed by Justice Scalia, General Inv. Co. v. Lake Shore & M.S. Ry. Co., 260 U.S. 261 (1922), and the subsequent decision in Freeman v. Bee Machine Co., 319 U.S. 448 (1943), the Court did not refer to the Claflin presumption. Indeed, the Court's discussion of implied exclusivity was cursory.

Other statutes construed as impliedly excluding state court jurisdiction include 28 U.S.C. §§ 1346(a) (U.S. as defendant in suits for recovery in tax and certain non-tax cases), 1491(a)(1) (Court of Federal Claims jurisdiction over express or implied contract actions where U.S. is the defendant), and 2321–2322 (enforcement of Surface Transportation Board orders).

(b) The Current Law on Implied Exclusion. In Yellow Freight System, Inc. v. Donnelly, 494 U.S. 820 (1990), decided only a few months after Tafflin, a unanimous Court expressed stronger disfavor of implied exclusion. Holding that state courts have concurrent jurisdiction over private civil actions brought under Title VII of the 1964 Civil Rights Act, Justice Stevens's opinion said that the omission of any express provision making federal jurisdiction exclusive "is strong, and arguably sufficient, evidence that Congress had no such intent." The Court discussed only briefly the other two factors set forth in the Gulf Offshore decision—an "unmistakable implication from legislative history" or a "clear incompatibility between

---

[3]   The Moses Taylor, 71 U.S. (1 Wheat.) at 429–30. For similar affirmations, see Houston v. Moore, 18 U.S. (5 Wheat.) 1, 25–26 (1820); Lockerty v. Phillips, 319 U.S. 182, 187–88 (1943), p. 472, *supra*; Bowles v. Willingham, 321 U.S. 503, 511–12 (1944).

[4]   The Court has also held that an express statutory recognition of state court jurisdiction does not bar the exercise of federal court jurisdiction. See Mims v. Arrow Financial Services, LLC, 565 U.S. 368 (2012), p. 612, *infra*.

state-court jurisdiction and federal interests"—and attached little weight to statements in the legislative history indicating an expectation that all Title VII cases would be tried in federal courts or to the frequent statutory references to procedures applicable in federal courts.

Professor Solimine suggests that this decision implicitly abandons the three-part test employed in the Gulf Offshore and Tafflin cases and instead adopts Justice Scalia's view that only a clear statement by Congress suffices to oust state court jurisdiction. See Solimine, *Rethinking Exclusive Federal Jurisdiction*, 52 U.Pitt.L.Rev. 383, 385 (1991).[5]

(5) Implied Exclusion and the Judicial Function. What *should* be the courts' role in determining whether a grant of federal jurisdiction should be construed to exclude state jurisdiction? One approach insists that only Congress may oust state court jurisdiction. A textualist might add that Congress must make its intention evident in the statutory text rather than in a statute's legislative history. A second approach would have courts eschew any presumption of concurrent jurisdiction in determining statutory meaning, relying instead on an ordinary interpretation of the federal jurisdictional statute. (A final approach urges courts to exercise a "creative judicial lawmaking function" and determine whether federal jurisdiction is impliedly exclusive in light of "the potential impingement on important federal interests and programs that might result from [adjudication] by state judges who lack sufficient background, expertise or—on occasion—competence to deal with * * * uniquely federal concerns." Redish & Muench, *Adjudication of Federal Causes of Action in State Court*, 75 Mich.L.Rev. 311, 329 (1976).)

(6) Congressional Policy. The conjunction of congressional powers to define the scope of federal jurisdiction (discussed in Section 1 of this Chapter) and to make federal jurisdiction exclusive leaves Congress with an array of policy options. These include: (a) exclusive state original jurisdiction; (b) concurrent federal and state jurisdiction; (c) concurrent federal and state jurisdiction, but with a right of state court defendants to remove to federal court; and (d) exclusive federal jurisdiction.

Congress has employed each of these options for some kinds of federal claims. The considerations that Congress might weigh in choosing among them are complex. But one must bear in mind that cases frequently involve a mix of state and federal issues. In considering the appropriate forum for cases involving a mixture of state and federal issues, questions arise about how to weigh the competing state and federal interests in adjudicating the

---

[5]   The later decision in Nevada v. Hicks, 533 U.S. 353 (2001), can be viewed as raising the question whether the presumption of concurrent jurisdiction applies to tribal courts. There, the Court held that a tribal court lacked jurisdiction to adjudicate a federal civil rights claim under 42 U.S.C. § 1983 that was premised on the allegedly tortious conduct of a state warden executing, on tribal land, a search warrant for an off-reservation crime. Justice Scalia's majority opinion reasoned that the "historical and constitutional assumption of concurrent state-court jurisdiction over federal-law cases is completely missing with respect to tribal courts," which, unlike state courts, are not courts of general jurisdiction. Rather, "a tribe's inherent adjudicative jurisdiction over nonmembers is at most only as broad as its legislative jurisdiction." Finding that "tribal court jurisdiction would create serious anomalies * * * because the general federal-question removal statute refers only to removal from state court," the Court concluded that unlike state courts, "tribal courts cannot entertain § 1983 suits."

entire case, see generally Chap. VIII, *infra*, and about the benefits and drawbacks of carving a case into parts so that the state elements can be adjudicated in state court and federal issues resolved in federal court, see generally Chap. X, *infra*.

(a) Exclusive State Original Jurisdiction. State jurisdiction is necessarily exclusive in cases not within the jurisdictional headings of Article III (for example, state law claims between non-diverse parties), as it is in cases in which Congress has not seen fit to confer federal jurisdiction (for example, claims not satisfying a federal amount-in-controversy requirement).

(b) Concurrent Jurisdiction. Concurrent federal and state jurisdiction may promote convenience when it is easier for litigants to appear in a state court than in a federal court. Concurrent jurisdiction also "permits plaintiffs a relatively free choice of forum in the expectation that enlightened self-interest" will lead plaintiffs "into the forum most likely to enunciate an expansive vision of the rights of the individual." Neuborne, *Toward Procedural Parity in Constitutional Litigation*, 22 Wm. & Mary L.Rev. 725, 730 (1981).

(c) Concurrent Jurisdiction with Right of Removal. In civil cases arising under federal law, the most common jurisdictional arrangement is concurrent state and federal jurisdiction, subject to a right of the defendant to remove from state to federal court.[6] (Note that when there are multiple defendants, the general removal statute, 28 U.S.C. § 1441, requires the agreement of all of them to effect removal.) Ordinarily, the right to remove depends on the contents of the plaintiff's well-pleaded complaint; with a few exceptions, removal is not allowed based on a federal counterclaim, a federal defense, or a federal reply to a defense. For extensive consideration of the intricacies of this scheme and of policy arguments for and against it, see Chap. VIII, Sec. 3, *infra*.

The general diversity statute likewise couples original jurisdiction with a right of defendant(s) to remove, although in diversity actions the removal right is denied to in-state defendants. See 28 U.S.C. § 1441(b)(2).

(d) Exclusive Federal Jurisdiction. Arguments in favor of exclusive federal jurisdiction frequently invoke the desirability of uniform interpretation of federal law, the presumptive expertise of federal judges in dealing with federal issues, and the likelihood that federal courts will be more sympathetic to federal purposes than will state courts. To a considerable extent, these arguments assume lack of parity between state and federal courts. See Fallon, *The Ideologies of Federal Courts Law*, 74 Va.L.Rev. 1141, 1202–07 (1988); see generally pp. 403–406, *supra* (discussing the concept of "parity"). Insofar as that assumption is warranted, can the concern about the relative sympathy of state and federal tribunals to

---

[6]   See 28 U.S.C. § 1441. In some situations, statutes preclude removal of a federal question case that was initially filed in state court. See p. 1136, note 2, *infra*.

federal claims be adequately met by providing for concurrent state and federal jurisdiction and a right of removal?[7]

Tennessee v. Davis

100 U.S. (10 Otto) 257 (1880).
Certificate of division in opinion between the judges of the Circuit Court
of the United States for the Middle District of Tennessee.

[Davis, a federal revenue official, was indicted for murder in Tennessee state court. Before trial, he filed in the Circuit Court of the United States a petition to remove the case from the state court. The judges of the Circuit Court were divided in opinion, and certified to the Supreme Court, *inter alia*, the question, "Whether an indictment of a revenue officer (of the United States) for murder, found in a State court, under the facts alleged in the petition for removal in this case, is removable to the Circuit Court of the United States, under sect. 643 of the Revised Statutes."*]

■ MR. JUSTICE STRONG delivered the opinion of the court.

The first of the questions certified is one of great importance, bringing as it does into consideration the relation of the general government to the government of the States, and bringing also into view not merely the construction of an act of Congress, but its constitutionality. That * * * the defendant's petition for removal * * * was in the form prescribed by the act of Congress admits of no doubt. It represented that * * * he was acting by and under the authority of the internal-revenue laws of the United States; that what he did was done under and by right of his office, to wit, as deputy collector of internal revenue; that it was his duty to seize illicit distilleries and the apparatus that is used for the illicit and unlawful distillation of spirits; and that while so attempting to enforce the revenue laws of the United States, * * * he was assaulted and fired upon by a number of armed men, and that in defence of his life he returned the fire. * * * The language of the statute * * * is as follows: "When any civil suit or criminal prosecution is commenced in any court of a State against any officer appointed under, or acting by authority of, any revenue law of the United States * * *, or against any person acting by or under authority of any such officer, on account of any act done under color of his office or of any such law, or on account of any right, title, or authority claimed by such officer or other

---

[7]   See Redish, *Reassessing the Allocation of Federal Judicial Business Between State and Federal Courts: Federal Jurisdiction and "The Martian Chronicles,"* 78 Va.L.Rev. 1769, 1812 (1992) (urging the "virtual abandonment" of exclusive federal jurisdiction).

*   [Ed.] At the time of this decision, no statute gave the Supreme Court appellate jurisdiction over decisions of federal circuit courts in criminal cases. But the judges of a circuit court—which was a trial court composed of two judges—could certify to the Supreme Court for decision a question on which the circuit judges disagreed.

person under any such law," the case may be removed into the Federal court. * * *

We come, then, to the inquiry * * * whether sect. 643 is a constitutional exercise of the power vested in Congress. * * *

By the last clause of the eighth section of the first article of the Constitution, Congress is invested with power to make all laws necessary and proper for carrying into execution not only all the powers previously specified, but also all other powers vested by the Constitution in the government of the United States, or in any department or officer thereof. Among these is the judicial power of the government. That is declared by the second section of the third article to "extend to all cases in law and equity arising under the Constitution, the laws of the United States, and treaties made or which shall be made under their authority," &c. This provision embraces alike civil and criminal cases arising under the Constitution and laws. Cohens v. Virginia, 6 Wheat. 264 [(1821)]. Both are equally within the domain of the judicial powers of the United States, and there is nothing in the grant to justify an assertion that whatever power may be exerted over a civil case may not be exerted as fully over a criminal one. And a case arising under the Constitution and laws of the United States may as well arise in a criminal prosecution as in a civil suit. What constitutes a case thus arising was early defined in [Cohens v. Virginia]. It is not merely one where a party comes into court to demand something conferred upon him by the Constitution or by a law or treaty. A case consists of the right of one party as well as the other, and may truly be said to arise under the Constitution or a law or a treaty of the United States whenever its correct decision depends upon the construction of either. Cases arising under the laws of the United States are such as grow out of the legislation of Congress, whether they constitute the right or privilege, or claim or protection, or defence of the party, in whole or in part, by whom they are asserted. * * *

The constitutional right of Congress to authorize the removal before trial of civil cases arising under the laws of the United States has long since passed beyond doubt. It was exercised almost contemporaneously with the adoption of the Constitution, and the power has been in constant use ever since. The Judiciary Act of Sept. 24, 1789, was passed by the first Congress, many members of which had assisted in framing the Constitution; and though some doubts were soon after suggested whether cases could be removed from State courts before trial, those doubts soon disappeared. Whether removal from a State to a Federal court is an exercise of appellate jurisdiction, as laid down in Story's Commentaries on the Constitution, sect. 1745, or an indirect mode of exercising original jurisdiction, as intimated in Railway Company v. Whitton (13 Wall. 270 [(1871)]), we need not now inquire. Be it one or the other, it was ruled in the case last cited to be constitutional. But if there is power in Congress to direct a removal before trial of a civil case arising under the Constitution or laws of the United States, and direct its removal because such a case has arisen, it is impossible to see why the same power may not order the removal of a criminal prosecution, when a similar case has arisen in it. * * *

The argument so much pressed upon us, that it is an invasion of the sovereignty of a State to withdraw from its courts into the courts of the general government the trial of prosecutions for alleged offences against the criminal laws of a State, even though the defence presents a case arising out of an act of Congress, ignores entirely the dual character of our government. It assumes that the States are completely and in all respects sovereign. But when the national government was formed, some of the attributes of State sovereignty were partially, and others wholly, surrendered and vested in the United States. Over the subjects thus surrendered the sovereignty of the States ceased to extend. Before the adoption of the Constitution, each State had complete and exclusive authority to administer by its courts all the law, civil and criminal, which existed within its borders. Its judicial power extended over every legal question that could arise. But when the Constitution was adopted, a portion of that judicial power became vested in the new government created, and so far as thus vested it was withdrawn from the sovereignty of the State. Now the execution and enforcement of the laws of the United States, and the judicial determination of questions arising under them, are confided to another sovereign, and to that extent the sovereignty of the State is restricted. The removal of cases arising under those laws, from State into Federal courts, is, therefore, no invasion of State domain. On the contrary, a denial of the right of the general government to remove them, to take charge of and try any case arising under the Constitution or laws of the United States, is a denial of the conceded sovereignty of that government over a subject expressly committed to it. * * *

It follows that the first question certified to us from the Circuit Court of Tennessee must be answered in the affirmative. * * *

■ [The dissenting opinion of JUSTICE CLIFFORD, joined by JUSTICE FIELD, is omitted.]

NOTE ON THE POWER OF CONGRESS TO PROVIDE FOR REMOVAL FROM STATE TO FEDERAL COURTS

(1) Constitutional Background and Statutory Foundations. The constitutionality of removal before judgment has long been accepted,[1] as has broad congressional power in specifying how removal operates. See City of Greenwood v. Peacock, 384 U.S. 808, 833 (1966) ("We may assume that

---

[1]   Though declared to be beyond doubt in The Moses Taylor, 71 U.S. (4 Wall.) 411, 429–30 (1867), the power was not directly determined in a civil action until The Mayor v. Cooper, 73 U.S. (6 Wall.) 247, 251–52 (1868), a tort action challenging a seizure under claim of federal authority during the Civil War. Railway Co. v. Whitton, 80 U.S. (13 Wall.) 270, 288–90 (1872), reaffirmed this decision in a case in which removal rested on diversity of citizenship.

Congress has constitutional power to provide that all federal issues be tried in the federal courts, that all be tried in the courts of the States, or that jurisdiction of such issues be shared. And in the exercise of that power, we may assume that Congress is constitutionally fully free to establish the conditions under which civil or criminal proceedings involving federal issues may be removed from one court to another.").

(2) Current Statutes and Issues.[2]

(a) Civil Cases. The general removal statute applicable to civil cases, 28 U.S.C. § 1441, permits the defendant(s) to remove only when the action is one that could originally be filed in federal court.[3]

(b) Criminal Cases. No *general* provision, similar to § 1441, authorizes removal of state criminal cases. But where a more specialized provision authorizes removal of a criminal case, the notice of removal must be filed within thirty days of arraignment "or at any time before trial, whichever is earlier, except that for good cause shown the * * * [federal court] may enter an order granting the defendant or defendants leave to file the notice at a later time." 28 U.S.C. § 1455.

(c) Federal Officer Removal. The statute at issue in Davis authorized particular federal officials—those enforcing the revenue laws—to remove state court actions to federal court. Since 1948, 28 U.S.C. § 1442 has permitted removal of any civil or criminal action against any federal "officer" or "person acting under that officer" for "any act under color of such office." A later amendment extended the removal right to the United States or any agency thereof.

The scope of removal authorized by § 1442 is broader than that under § 1441, both because § 1442 applies to criminal as well as civil cases and because it permits removal not merely when the action could have been filed in federal court but also when the defendant asserts a federal defense. Tennessee v. Davis exemplifies both features of the broader coverage of the federal officer removal provision. Section 1442 has in general been broadly construed. See, *e.g.*, Willingham v. Morgan, 395 U.S. 402 (1969) (allowing the warden and chief medical officer of a federal penitentiary to remove to federal court on a showing that their only contact with a prisoner who alleged a range of abuses had occurred inside the penitentiary).

But in Mesa v. California, 489 U.S. 121 (1989), p. 1018, *infra*, the Court recognized an important limit on § 1442's reach, holding that it authorized removal only when the defendant federal officer raises a federal defense, rather than, as in Mesa, when the officer simply contests a state law criminal charge. In arguing for a broader interpretation, the United States contended that the defendant in Davis had not asserted a federal defense to the killing

---

[2]   For additional materials on removal, see pp. 1135–1146, *infra*.

[3]   Unlike most removal statutes, the Act of March 3, 1863, 12 Stat. 755, applied after as well as before judgment in the state court. In The Justices v. Murray, 76 U.S. (9 Wall.) 274 (1870), an action for assault and battery and false imprisonment that was removed after a jury trial and verdict for the plaintiff, the Court held that the Seventh Amendment governed and that "so much of the * * * act of Congress * * * as provides for the removal of a judgment in a State court, and in which the cause was tried by a jury, to the Circuit Court of the United States for a retrial on the facts and law, is not in pursuance of the Constitution, and is void."

but only a state law self-defense claim, which the Court held sufficient for removal. The Mesa Court rejected that interpretation of Davis, reasoning that whether Davis was acting in self-defense depended on whether he was lawfully trying to seize the still or was merely a thief; "[p]roof that Davis was not a thief depended on the federal revenue laws," and hence, adjudication of the self-defense claim required the application of federal law.

Clearly in the background in Mesa was a concern that, if § 1442 were construed to permit removal in the absence of a federal defense, the case might not "aris[e] under" federal law in the constitutional sense, and therefore would not come within any of the authorized categories of federal jurisdiction under Article III. But at least as long as there is some issue of federal law in a case, are there any "external" limits (arising from the Tenth Amendment or the Constitution's structure) on Congress's authority to provide for federal jurisdiction of civil and criminal actions rooted in state law?[4] *Cf.* Osborn v. Bank of the United States, 22 U.S. (9 Wheat.) 738 (1824), pp. 994–1002, *infra*. In this regard, consider whether any of the Supreme Court decisions in recent decades upholding state sovereign immunity suggest any limits upon the strong view of national supremacy articulated in the Davis decision.

INTRODUCTORY NOTE ON TARBLE'S CASE

The preceding cases concerned the scope of *congressional* power, in authorizing exclusive federal jurisdiction or removal jurisdiction, to divest the state courts of jurisdiction over federal cases. The next principal case raises the question whether the *Constitution* (rather than congressional legislation) sometimes precludes state courts from exercising jurisdiction.

Tarble's Case

80 U.S. (13 Wall.) 397 (1872).
Error to the Supreme Court of Wisconsin.

This was a proceeding on *habeas corpus* for the discharge of one Edward Tarble, held in the custody of a recruiting officer of the United States as an enlisted soldier, on the alleged ground that he was a minor, under the age of eighteen years at the time of his enlistment, and that he enlisted without the consent of his father.

[Acting under the authorization of state law, a Wisconsin state court commissioner issued a writ of habeas corpus.] It was issued in this case upon the petition of the father of Tarble, in which he alleged that his son, who had enlisted under the name of Frank Brown, was confined and

---

[4] But see Goldman, *The Neglected History of State Prosecutions for State Crimes in Federal Courts*, 52 Tex.Tech.L.Rev. 783, 786 (2020) (questioning Mesa's federal defense requirement on historical grounds).

restrained of his liberty by Lieutenant Stone, of the United States army, in the city of Madison, in that State and county * * *.

[The Supreme Court of Wisconsin affirmed] the order of the commissioner discharging the prisoner. This judgment was now before this court for examination on writ of error prosecuted by the United States. * * *

■ MR. JUSTICE FIELD, after stating the case, delivered the opinion of the court, as follows:

The important question is presented by this case, whether a State court commissioner has jurisdiction, upon *habeas corpus*, to inquire into the validity of the enlistment of soldiers into the military service of the United States, and to discharge them from such service when, in his judgment, their enlistment has not been made in conformity with the laws of the United States. The question presented may be more generally stated thus: Whether any judicial officer of a State has jurisdiction to issue a writ of *habeas corpus*, or to continue proceedings under the writ when issued, for the discharge of a person held under the authority, or claim and color of the authority, of the United States, by an officer of that government. * * *

The decision of this court in the two cases which grew out of the arrest of Booth, that of Ableman v. Booth, and that of The United States v. Booth,[3] disposes alike of the claim of jurisdiction by a State court, or by a State judge, to interfere with the authority of the United States, whether that authority be exercised by a Federal officer or be exercised by a Federal tribunal. * * * [The Supreme Court's 1859 decision in these consolidated cases involved one Booth, a federal prisoner charged with aiding in the escape of a fugitive enslaved person. Booth filed a habeas corpus petition in Wisconsin state court, challenging his arrest and detention by federal officials on the ground, *inter alia*, that the federal Fugitive Slave Act was unconstitutional. While federal criminal charges under that Act were pending against Booth, the Wisconsin courts held in his favor and ordered his release. Booth was thereafter tried and convicted in a federal court for violating the Fugitive Slave Act. He then filed a second habeas corpus petition in state court, attacking the Act on the same grounds, and the state court again ordered his discharge. Federal officials then filed writs of error in the U.S. Supreme Court, seeking review of both judgments of the Wisconsin Supreme Court.] * * * The cases were afterwards heard and considered together, and the decision of both was announced in the same opinion. In that opinion the Chief Justice [Taney] details the facts of the two cases at length, and comments upon the character of the jurisdiction asserted by the State judge and the State court * * *.

And in answer to this assumption of judicial power by the judges and by the Supreme Court of Wisconsin thus made, the Chief Justice said as

---

[3]   21 Howard, 506 [(1858)].

follows: If they "possess the jurisdiction they claim, they must derive it either from the United States or the State. It certainly has not been conferred on them by the United States; and it is equally clear it was not in the power of the State to confer it, even if it had attempted to do so; for no State can authorize one of its judges or courts to exercise judicial power, by *habeas corpus* or otherwise, within the jurisdiction of another and independent government. And although the State of Wisconsin is sovereign within its territorial limits to a certain extent, yet that sovereignty is limited and restricted by the Constitution of the United States. And the powers of the General government and of the State, although both exist and are exercised within the same territorial limits, are yet separate and distinct sovereignties, acting separately and independently of each other, within their respective spheres. And the sphere of action appropriated to the United States, is as far beyond the reach of the judicial process issued by a State judge or a State court, as if the line of division was traced by landmarks and monuments visible to the eye. And the State of Wisconsin had no more power to authorize these proceedings of its judges and courts, than it would have had if the prisoner had been confined in Michigan, or in any other State of the Union, for an offence against the laws of the State in which he was imprisoned."

It is in the consideration of this distinct and independent character of the government of the United States, from that of the government of the several States, that the solution of the question presented in this case, and in similar cases, must be found. There are within the territorial limits of each State two governments, restricted in their spheres of action, but independent of each other, and supreme within their respective spheres. * * *

Such being the distinct and independent character of the two governments, within their respective spheres of action, it follows that neither can intrude with its judicial process into the domain of the other, except so far as such intrusion may be necessary on the part of the National government to preserve its rightful supremacy in cases of conflict of authority. In their laws, and mode of enforcement, neither is responsible to the other. How their respective laws shall be enacted; how they shall be carried into execution; and in what tribunals, or by what officers; and how much discretion, or whether any at all shall be vested in their officers, are matters subject to their own control, and in the regulation of which neither can interfere with the other.

Now, among the powers assigned to the National government, is the power "to raise and support armies," and the power "to provide for the government and regulation of the land and naval forces." The execution of these powers falls within the line of its duties; and its control over the subject is plenary and exclusive. * * * Probably in every county and city in the several States there are one or more officers authorized by law to issue writs of *habeas corpus* on behalf of persons alleged to be illegally restrained of their liberty; and if soldiers could be taken from the army of the United States, and the validity of their enlistment inquired into by any one of these officers, such proceeding could be taken by all of them, and no movement could be made by the National troops without their commanders being subjected to constant annoyance and embarrassment from this source. The experience of the late rebellion has shown us that, in times of great popular excitement, there may be found in every State large numbers ready and anxious to embarrass the operations of the government, and easily persuaded to believe every step taken for the enforcement of its authority illegal and void. Power to issue writs of *habeas corpus* for the discharge of soldiers in the military service, in the hands of parties thus disposed, might be used, and often would be used, to the great detriment of the public service. In many exigencies the measures of the National government might in this way be entirely bereft of their efficacy and value. An appeal in such cases to this court, to correct the erroneous action of these officers, would afford no adequate remedy. Proceedings on *habeas corpus* are summary, and the delay incident to bringing the decision of a State officer, through the highest tribunal of the State, to this court for review, would necessarily occupy years, and in the meantime, where the soldier was discharged, the mischief would be accomplished. It is manifest that the powers of the National government could not be exercised with energy and efficiency at all times, if its acts could be interfered with and controlled for any period by officers or tribunals of another sovereignty.

It is true similar embarrassment might sometimes be occasioned, though in a less degree, by the exercise of the authority to issue the writ possessed by judicial officers of the United States, but the ability to provide a speedy remedy for any inconvenience following from this source would always exist with the National legislature. * * *

This limitation upon the power of State tribunals and State officers furnishes no just ground to apprehend that the liberty of the citizen will thereby be endangered. The United States are as much interested in protecting the citizen from illegal restraint under their authority, as the several States are to protect him from the like restraint under their authority * * *. Their courts and judicial officers are clothed with the power to issue the writ of *habeas corpus* in all cases, where a party is illegally restrained of his liberty by an officer of the United States, whether such illegality consists in the character of the process, the authority of the officer, or the invalidity of the law under which he is held. And there is no just reason to believe that they will exhibit any hesitation to exert their power, when it is properly invoked. Certainly there can be no ground for supposing that their action will be less prompt and efficient in such cases than would be that of State tribunals and State officers.

It follows, from the views we have expressed, that the court commissioner of Dane County was without jurisdiction to issue the writ of *habeas corpus* for the discharge of the prisoner in this case * * *. * * *

Judgment reversed.

■ THE CHIEF JUSTICE [CHASE], dissenting.

I cannot concur in the opinion just read. I have no doubt of the right of a State court to inquire into the jurisdiction of a Federal court upon *habeas corpus*, and to discharge when satisfied that the petitioner for the writ is restrained of liberty by the sentence of a court without jurisdiction. If it errs in deciding the question of jurisdiction, the error must be corrected in the mode prescribed by the 25th section of the Judiciary Act; not by denial of the right to make inquiry.

I have still less doubt, if possible, that a writ of *habeas corpus* may issue from a State court to inquire into the validity of imprisonment or detention, without the sentence of any court whatever, by an officer of the United States. The State court may err; and if it does, the error may be corrected here. The mode has been prescribed and should be followed.

To deny the right of State courts to issue the writ, or, what amounts to the same thing, to concede the right to issue and to deny the right to adjudicate, is to deny the right to protect the citizen by *habeas corpus* against arbitrary imprisonment in a large class of cases; and, I am thoroughly persuaded, was never within the contemplation of the Convention which framed, or the people who adopted, the Constitution. That instrument expressly declares that "the privilege of the writ of *habeas corpus* shall not be suspended, unless when, in case of rebellion or invasion, the public safety may require it."

NOTE ON TARBLE'S CASE AND STATE COURT PROCEEDINGS AGAINST FEDERAL OFFICIALS

(1) Historical Practice. The decisions in Ableman v. Booth and Tarble's Case departed from historic practice. Beginning in 1789, state courts, "for a period of eighty years, continued to assert a right, through the issue of writs of *habeas corpus*, to take persons out of the custody of federal officials." Warren, *Federal and State Court Interference*, 43 Harv.L.Rev. 345, 353 (1930). Many of these cases, like Tarble's Case, involved petitions seeking to free individuals from service in the military. See Oaks, *Habeas Corpus in the States: 1776–1865*, 32 U.Chi.L.Rev. 243 (1965); Pettys, *State Habeas Relief for Federal Extrajudicial Detainees*, 92 Minn.L.Rev. 265 (2007).[1]

(2) Ableman v. Booth and Tarble's Case Distinguished. The Wisconsin courts in Booth, in holding the Fugitive Slave Act unconstitutional, were acting in the teeth of Supreme Court and lower court decisions that that Act was valid. By contrast, Tarble's Case involved no such

---

[1]   There were also prominent instances of refusal to interfere with federal enforcement activities, notably with respect to the Fugitive Slave Law, even in areas where its validity was most contested. See, *e.g.*, Passmore Williamson's Case, 26 Pa. 9 (1855); Warren, *supra*, at 355–56.

frontal state court defiance, however nobly motivated, of governing precedent.

Perhaps a more significant distinction between the cases rests on the fact that in Booth, the state court's second writ of habeas corpus, issued after the federal court conviction, threatened the finality of federal judgments;[2] Tarble's Case posed no such threat, as there the state court challenged only the legality of extra-judicial detention—the historic core of the writ of habeas corpus. See Chap. XI, Sec. 1, *infra*. And in the thirteen years that separated the two decisions, although some state courts read the Booth decision broadly as denying them any power to issue habeas relief to individuals in federal custody, most read it more narrowly, as confined to cases in which detention was under the authority of a federal court judgment. See Pettys, Paragraph (1), *supra*, at 284–88. Thus, Professor Warren observes that "during the Civil War, New York, Ohio, Iowa and Maine judges granted *habeas corpus* for persons serving in the United States Army. And as late as 1871, the Massachusetts court said that this power was so well settled by judicial opinion and long practice that it was not 'to be now disavowed, unless in obedience to an express act of congress, or to a direct adjudication of the supreme court of the United States.' " Warren, Paragraph (1), *supra*, at 357, quoting Gray, J., in McConologue's Case, 107 Mass. 154, 160 (1871).[3]

(3) Constitutionally Mandated Exclusion? Much of the reasoning in Tarble's Case appears to rest on the proposition that the Constitution, of its own force, precludes the exercise of state habeas corpus jurisdiction against federal officials. Can such a proposition be squared with the Madisonian Compromise and the language of Article III making the establishment of "inferior" federal courts a matter of congressional discretion?

Imagine a case in which a petitioner seeking habeas corpus alleges that federal officials are detaining him unconstitutionally. The Suspension Clause, Article I, § 9, quoted at the end of Chief Justice Chase's dissent in Tarble's case, has been interpreted as conferring a constitutional right to habeas review of detention by federal officials (or to an adequate substitute) that would apply in many situations. See pp. 464–471, *supra*; Chap. XI, Sec. 2, *infra*. Tarble, of course, had the option of seeking a writ of habeas corpus from a federal court. But suppose Congress had not vested jurisdiction over his case, or some other case implicating the Suspension Clause, in the federal courts. If the state courts are not competent to entertain a petition, the detained individual would lack any court in which to seek to vindicate the

---

[2]   Following the Supreme Court's decision, the Wisconsin courts refused to issue a third writ of habeas corpus, after which an armed crowd freed Booth from federal custody. See Note, *Rethinking Ableman v. Booth and States' Rights in Wisconsin*, 93 Va.L.Rev. 1315, 1346 (2007).

[3]   The departure from historic practice in Ableman v. Booth might be ascribed to the political division that two years later ignited the Civil War. Professor Cover raises "the issue of whether the modern lawyer and scholar must forsake all the slavery cases as too infused with a substantive issue to be of any use in understanding our federal system" today. Cover, Justice Accused: Antislavery and the Judicial Process 166 n.* (1975). Tarble's Case was decided after the war's end and the Thirteenth Amendment's abolition of slavery. But might the Justices have had the recent rebellion in mind when considering the issues of state and national power in 1872?

constitutional habeas right.[4] That situation would conflict with Professor Hart's premise, that "a court must always be available to pass on claims of constitutional right to judicial process, and to provide such process if the claim is sustained." Hart, *The Power of Congress to Limit the Jurisdiction of Federal Courts: An Exercise in Dialectic*, 66 Harv.L.Rev. 1362, 1372 (1953); see p. 461, *supra*.

Professor Hart further thought that in cases of jurisdictional foreclosure the state courts were the ultimate guardians of constitutional rights—a position hard to square with Tarble's Case. Consider in this regard the decision in Boumediene v. Bush, 553 U.S. 723 (2008), p. 1507, *supra*, which involved a statutory provision purporting to bar all judicial review, in federal or state courts, of the detention of aliens as enemy combatants. The Court held the provision invalid, but proceeded to rule that the petitioners had a right to habeas corpus review in *federal* court. There was no discussion of Tarble's Case or of whether any constitutionally required review could be provided in state court. Thus, the Boumediene opinion is not clear whether the petitioners had (a) a constitutional right to federal court review (perhaps because Tarble's Case would preclude state court review), or, instead, (b) a constitutional right to judicial review that either federal or state courts could provide. If the latter, there were reasonably powerful statutory and historical arguments that any constitutionally required review should be undertaken by federal courts, see pp. 580–582, *infra*, but none of this is discussed in the Boumediene opinion, and therefore its implications for Tarble's Case, and for theories critical of Tarble's Case, remain uncertain.

(a) Historical Evidence. Professor Collins offers an *historical* argument that members of the founding generation and of its immediate successors widely understood that some categories of federal jurisdiction—including federal criminal cases and suits against federal officers for specific relief—were inherently exclusive of state court jurisdiction. See Collins, *Article III Cases, State Court Duties, and the Madisonian Compromise*, 1995 Wisc.L.Rev. 39, 46–135. Justice Story, Collins contends, was the most prominent but hardly the only example. According to Collins, as to cases in which the state courts lacked a "pre-existing" jurisdiction before the Constitution's ratification, the Constitution neither directly conferred jurisdiction nor empowered Congress to vest jurisdiction in state courts. He adds it appeared plausible to many eighteenth and nineteenth century lawyers that if Congress wished to see federal law enforced in cases in which the Constitution precluded state court jurisdiction, the solution could be to create lower federal courts—though such lawyers would not necessarily have endorsed the further conclusion that Congress was obliged to create lower federal courts. See Collins, *The Federal Courts, the First Congress, and the Non-Settlement of 1789*, 91 Va.L.Rev. 1515, 1560–61 (2005).

---

[4]   According to Duker, A Constitutional History of Habeas Corpus 126–80 (1980), a principal purpose of the Suspension Clause was to protect state habeas corpus jurisdiction from federal abrogation. That view would obviously create more serious tensions with Tarble's Case than alternative views that suggest, notwithstanding the Madisonian Compromise, that in some circumstances federal courts are constitutionally obliged to exercise habeas corpus jurisdiction. See generally *Note on the Suspension Clause of the Constitution*, pp. 1470–1477, *infra*.

The actual historical practice is contested but poses some challenges for Collins' thesis. Professor Warren has mustered evidence that early Congresses authorized state courts to entertain actions seeking fines and other penalties, including criminal penalties, under a variety of federal laws. See Warren, *Federal Criminal Laws and the State Courts*, 38 Harv.L.Rev. 545, 549–55, 570–73 (1925). Collins quarrels with Warren's characterization of the scope of state *criminal* jurisdiction contemplated by these federal statutes, see Collins, *supra*, 1995 Wisc.L.Rev. at 86–89, and in a subsequent article, Collins and co-author Nash argue that the evidence from the founding era—particularly the debate about the First Judiciary Act—is hard to square with state court authority to entertain federal criminal prosecutions. Collins & Nash, *Prosecuting Federal Crimes in State Courts*, 97 Va.L.Rev. 243 (2011).

Another historical practice that poses a challenge for Collins is the state courts' exercise, during the period before the Civil War, of habeas jurisdiction against federal officials, as described in Paragraph (1), *supra*.

(b) Constitutional Conundrums. Suppose, however, that it could be determined that Article III's public meaning at the time of the founding precluded state court jurisdiction of certain classes of claims. Would that *specific* determination necessarily dispose of the constitutional question? Would it be consistent with the structural logic of the constitutional plan for there to be no remedy available in any court for unconstitutional detentions or other unconstitutional actions by federal officials?

Redish & Woods, *Congressional Power to Control the Jurisdiction of Lower Federal Courts: A Critical Review and a New Synthesis*, 124 U.Pa.L.Rev. 45 (1975), give a negative answer to the latter question. They argue that Congress would violate the Constitution if it failed to create lower courts invested with jurisdiction to entertain suits that state courts may not entertain, unless Congress also expressly authorized the state courts to exercise jurisdiction in cases, like Tarble's Case, in which state court jurisdiction would otherwise be constitutionally forbidden. On this view, Tarble's Case does not establish an absolute constitutional bar to state court jurisdiction in the circumstances there presented, but only a constitutional default rule, subject to displacement by a clear congressional statement.

In assessing this argument, suppose that Congress neither created lower federal courts nor expressly authorized state courts to entertain suits seeking to compel action by federal officials. In that case, if the Suspension Clause gives individuals a right to habeas review in some court, as the Supreme Court has held, see pp. 469–470, *supra*, then wouldn't it follow either that the state courts must be able to hear such an action (in which case, even the "default rule" reading of Tarble's Case cannot be right) or that Congress must create lower federal courts and vest them with jurisdiction (a result at odds with the Madisonian Compromise)?[5]

---

[5] Hartnett, *The Constitutional Puzzle of Habeas Corpus*, 46 B.C.L.Rev. 251 (2005), argues that any demand for federal habeas jurisdiction under the Suspension Clause could be, and historically has been, reconciled with the Madisonian Compromise by a statute authorizing individual Justices of the Supreme Court to issue writs of habeas corpus. But that grant is not one of original jurisdiction (and under Marbury v. Madison, 5 U.S. (1 Cranch) 137 (1803), it

(4) Alternative Views of Tarble's Case. The foregoing discussion highlights the difficulties of any reading of Tarble's Case that suggests that the *Constitution* barred the exercise of state court jurisdiction in that case.

(a) Implied Exclusivity of Federal Jurisdiction? Could the narrow holding of Tarble's Case that the state court lacked jurisdiction be justified on the ground that federal *statutes* impliedly establish habeas corpus for persons in federal custody as a domain of exclusive federal jurisdiction? Might this attribution of congressional intent be warranted by the acts of Congress granting the federal courts habeas corpus jurisdiction? The acts of Congress governing the army? The conjunction of the two?

In the period after the Civil War, the authority of state courts (particularly in the states that had joined the Confederacy) to issue writs of habeas corpus or other orders to federal officials would seem to have posed a distinctive threat to national authority. And at that time, unlike today, the federal officials sued in Tarble's Case were unable to remove the matter to federal court. Perhaps the decision can be understood, and defended, as presuming that state courts are not sufficiently trustworthy to issue mandatory orders to federal officials, but as leaving open the prospect that the presumption could be overridden when Congress has either provided a sufficiently clear statement or has failed to confer federal jurisdiction.[6]

But such a rationale for the result in Tarble's Case would find federal jurisdiction to be exclusive without any clear statement to that effect in a statutory text. As such, it would be in tension with the approach to exclusivity taken in decisions like Tafflin v. Levitt, 493 U.S. 455 (1990), and Yellow Freight System, Inc. v. Donnelly, 494 U.S. 820 (1990), pp. 560, 568, *supra*. If those two approaches are in tension, which one is to be preferred?

(b) Was Tarble's Case Wrongly Decided? Alternatively, perhaps there is no justification, constitutional or sub-constitutional, for the result in Tarble's Case. Professor Pettys, Paragraph (1), *supra*, considers this question with particular attention to habeas corpus claims by those detained by the federal government in connection with the war on terror. He contends that state courts today should reject a constitutional basis for the result in Tarble's Case and should follow the modern approach (as set forth in a decision like Tafflin) in determining whether the grant of federal habeas jurisdiction excludes state court jurisdiction. Pettys notes that (1) Congress, in enacting the Judiciary Act of 1789, knew how to make federal court jurisdiction exclusive, as it did in some jurisdictional grants; (2) the legislative history of the Judiciary Act reflected a general concern to limit federal displacement of state court authority; and (3) state court habeas jurisdiction is not incompatible with federal purposes given that the state courts are presumptively competent to adjudicate federal rights and that,

---

could not be), nor is it an exercise of appellate jurisdiction, and so it must be viewed as the exercise of jurisdiction of an inferior court. (Recall that the Justices initially sat on the Circuit Courts as well as on the Supreme Court.) As such, Congress seemingly could repeal that grant as part of its authority to regulate the lower courts themselves. Thus, doesn't this suggestion fail to resolve the conundrum posed by Tarble's Case?

6   But *cf.* McClung v. Silliman, 19 U.S. (6 Wheat.) 598 (1821), Paragraph (5)(a), *infra*.

today at least, federal officials sued in state court may remove the action to federal court under § 1442.

On the last point, had a provision like today's § 1442 permitted the federal military officials to remove Tarble's habeas corpus action from state court to federal court, no decision on state court power would have been needed. Conversely, precisely because Congress had not provided for removal at that time, the legitimate concerns about potential state court interference with national policy may have made Tarble's a hard case that in turn made bad law.

(5) State Jurisdiction in Other Proceedings Against Federal Officials. How far does or should the rationale of Tarble's Case extend in barring state courts from issuing remedies other than a writ of habeas corpus in actions challenging the legality of federal official action? Any such action could have the potential, in the words of the Court in Tarble's Case, to place "the sphere of action appropriated to the United States" improperly within "the reach of the judicial process issued by a State judge or a State court." Yet one commentator, summarizing the decisions described in more detail below, suggested some years ago that various remedies line up along a spectrum, with mandamus joining habeas corpus jurisdiction as forbidden at one end, with jurisdiction to award damages and common law writs like replevin and ejectment that seek specific relief being just as clearly permitted at the other, and with injunctions from a court of equity in an uncertain middle. See Arnold, *The Power of State Courts to Enjoin Federal Officers*, 73 Yale L.J. 1385, 1397 (1964). Consider, in reading the materials below, whether any coherent policy supports such a pattern, or whether the pattern itself may be the product of historical accident.[7]

(a) Mandamus. In McClung v. Silliman, 19 U.S. (6 Wheat.) 598 (1821), the Court held that a state court lacked jurisdiction over a suit for mandamus to compel the register of a federal land office to make a conveyance. The Court's opinion seemed to rest on several intersecting lines of reason. The first was that because the federal courts lacked authority to issue mandamus to a federal executive official,[8] the states did also: "no one will seriously contend, it is presumed, that it is among the reserved powers of the states, because not communicated by law to the Courts of the United States." The second, which resonates with the opinion in Tarble's Case, was that the conduct of a federal official implementing a federal statute "can only be controlled by the power that created him." The third, building on the first, stressed that mandamus was an extraordinary remedy, and the absence of federal court power to issue it implied that those complaining that federal officials had violated their rights "should be referred to the ordinary mode of obtaining justice," such as damages or actions to recover specific property. The question left in the wake of McClung is how broadly to read the decision; specifically, should it be read to exclude state court mandamus against federal officials under any circumstances?[9]

---

[7]   See also Warren, *Federal and State Court Interference*, 43 Harv.L.Rev. 345 (1930).

[8]   See McIntire v. Wood, 11 U.S. (7 Cranch) 504 (1813).

[9]   In at least one case, the Supreme Court decided on the merits a state-court mandamus action against a federal officer. Northern Pac. Ry. Co. v. North Dakota ex rel. Langer, 250 U.S.

Note the tension between one interpretation of Tarble's Case noted above—that state court jurisdiction was excluded because the federal courts *possessed* habeas jurisdiction—and the holding in McClung that state court jurisdiction is excluded because the federal courts *lacked* mandamus jurisdiction.

In 1962, Congress authorized federal district courts to issue mandamus against federal officers. See 28 U.S.C. § 1361. What is left of McClung's rationale in light of the broad removal authority conferred by § 1442?

(b) Injunctions. The Supreme Court has not yet decided whether state courts have jurisdiction to entertain injunction actions against federal officers.[10] State and lower federal court decisions are divided, but "[t]he weight of reasoned opinion * * * supports the general denial of such state court power" to enjoin federal officers. Redish & Woods, Paragraph (3)(b), *supra*, at 89. See also General Atomic Co. v. Felter, 434 U.S. 12 (1977) (per curiam).

(c) Actions at Law for Specific Relief. Slocum v. Mayberry, 15 U.S. (2 Wheat.) 1 (1817), sustained a state court action for replevin of cargo illegally detained by federal customs officers. Chief Justice Marshall said that "the act of congress neither expressly, nor by implication, forbids the state courts to take cognizance of suits instituted for property in possession of an officer of the United States not detained under some law of the United States; consequently their jurisdiction remains." The Court has also assumed that state courts may try ejectment actions against federal officers. See, *e.g.*, Scranton v. Wheeler, 179 U.S. 141 (1900). See generally Arnold, *supra*, at 1397. But *cf.* Malone v. Bowdoin, 369 U.S. 643 (1962) (finding such actions barred by the doctrine of sovereign immunity).

How should modern courts consider the widely varying approaches to varying forms of specific relief? Insofar as, following the merger of law and equity, common law writs like replevin and ejectment have been displaced by injunctive relief, what sense is there to the distinctions in the cases just noted?

(d) Damages Actions. The Supreme Court has routinely sustained state court jurisdiction in damages actions averring tortious conduct by federal officials that was not authorized by federal law. See, *e.g.*, Teal v. Felton, 53 U.S. (12 How.) 284 (1852); Buck v. Colbath, 70 U.S. (3 Wall.) 334 (1866). But *cf.* Davis v. Passman, 442 U.S. 228, 245 n.23 (1979).[11]

---

135 (1919). See generally Arnold, *supra*, at 1391–92. And the Court held in Kendall v. United States ex rel. Stokes, 37 U.S. (12 Pet.) 524 (1838), that the territorial courts for the District of Columbia, apparently uniquely among the courts in the nation, possessed authority to issue writs of mandamus against federal officials.

[10]　Dictum in Keely v. Sanders, 99 U.S. 441, 443 (1878), stated that "no State court could, by injunction or otherwise, prevent Federal officers from collecting Federal taxes." The issue was raised in Brooks v. Dewar, 313 U.S. 354, 360 (1941), but the Court was unwilling to resolve an "asserted conflict touching issues of so grave consequence" where there was no case for injunction on the merits.

[11]　Whether sued in state or federal court, federal officials can ordinarily invoke qualified or absolute immunity as a shield from damages liability. See Chap. IX, Sec. 3.

INTRODUCTORY NOTE ON THE OBLIGATION OF STATE COURTS TO ENFORCE FEDERAL LAW

The preceding material discusses issues arising when federal law limits the *power* of *willing* state courts to exercise jurisdiction over federal rights of action. The material that follows concerns the opposite problem: issues that arise when federal law imposes an *obligation* on *unwilling* state courts to exercise jurisdiction over federal rights of action.

Testa v. Katt
330 U.S. 386 (1947).
Certiorari to the Superior Court for Providence and Bristol Counties, Rhode Island.

■ MR. JUSTICE BLACK delivered the opinion of the Court.

Section 205(e) of the Emergency Price Control Act provides that a buyer of goods above the prescribed ceiling price may sue the seller "in any court of competent jurisdiction" for not more than three times the amount of the overcharge plus costs and a reasonable attorney's fee. Section 205(c) provides that federal district courts shall have jurisdiction of such suits "concurrently with State and Territorial courts." Such a suit under § 205(e) must be brought "in the district or county in which the defendant resides or has a place of business * * *."

The respondent was in the automobile business in Providence, * * * Rhode Island. In 1944 he sold an automobile to petitioner Testa * * * for $1100, $210 above the ceiling price. The petitioner later filed this suit against respondent in the State District Court in Providence. Recovery was sought under § 205(e). The court awarded a judgment of treble damages and costs to petitioner. On appeal to the State Superior Court, where the trial was de novo, the petitioner was again awarded judgment, but only for the amount of the overcharge plus attorney's fees. * * * On appeal, the State Supreme Court reversed. It interpreted § 205(e) to be "a penal statute in the international sense." It held that an action for violation of § 205(e) could not be maintained in the courts of that State. The State Supreme Court rested its holding on its earlier decision in Robinson v. Norato, 1945, 71 R.I. 256, 43 A.2d 467, 468, in which it had reasoned that: A state need not enforce the penal laws of a government which is "foreign in the international sense"; § 205(e) is treated by Rhode Island as penal in that sense; the United States is "foreign" to the State in the "private international" as distinguished from the "public international" sense; hence Rhode Island courts, though their jurisdiction is adequate to enforce similar Rhode Island "penal" statutes, need not enforce § 205(e). Whether state courts may decline to enforce federal laws on these grounds is a question of great importance. For this reason, and because the Rhode Island Supreme Court's holding was alleged to conflict with this Court's previous holding in Mondou v. New York, N.H. & H.R. Co., 223 U.S. 1 [(1912)], we granted certiorari.

For the purposes of this case, we assume, without deciding, that § 205(e) is a penal statute in the "public international," "private international," or any other sense. * * * For we cannot accept the basic premise on which the Rhode Island Supreme Court held that it has no more obligation to enforce a valid penal law of the United States than it has to enforce a penal law of another state or a foreign country. Such a broad assumption flies in the face of the fact that the States of the Union constitute a nation. It disregards the purpose and effect of Article VI, § 2 of the Constitution which provides: "This Constitution, and the Laws of the United States which shall be made in Pursuance thereof; and all Treaties made, or which shall be made, under the Authority of the United States, shall be the supreme Law of the Land; and the Judges in every State shall be bound thereby, any Thing in the Constitution or Laws of any State to the Contrary notwithstanding."

It cannot be assumed, the supremacy clause considered, that the responsibilities of a state to enforce the laws of a sister state are identical with its responsibilities to enforce federal laws. Such an assumption represents an erroneous evaluation of the statutes of Congress and the prior decisions of this Court in their historic setting. Those decisions establish that state courts do not bear the same relation to the United States that they do to foreign countries. The first Congress that convened after the Constitution was adopted conferred jurisdiction upon the state courts to enforce important federal civil laws,[4] and succeeding Congresses conferred on the states jurisdiction over federal crimes and actions for penalties and forfeitures.[5]

Enforcement of federal laws by state courts did not go unchallenged. Violent public controversies existed throughout the first part of the Nineteenth Century until the 1860's concerning the extent of the constitutional supremacy of the Federal Government. During that period there were instances in which this Court and state courts broadly questioned the power and duty of state courts to exercise their jurisdiction to enforce United States civil and penal statutes or the power of the Federal Government to require them to do so. But after the fundamental issues over the extent of federal supremacy had been resolved by war, this Court took occasion in 1876 to review the phase of the controversy concerning the relationship of state courts to the Federal Government. Claflin v. Houseman, 93 U.S. 130 [(1876)]. The opinion of a unanimous court in that case was strongly buttressed by historic references and persuasive reasoning. It repudiated the assumption that federal laws can be considered by the states as though they were laws emanating from a foreign sovereign. Its teaching is that the Constitution

---

4   Judiciary Act of 1789, 1 Stat. 73, 77 (suits by aliens for torts committed in violation of federal laws and treaties; suits by the United States).

5   1 Stat. 376, 378 (1794) (fines, forfeitures and penalties for violation of the License Tax on Wines and Spirits); 1 Stat. 373, 375 (1794) (the Carriage Tax Act); 1 Stat. 452 (penalty for purchasing guns from Indians); 1 Stat. 733, 740 (1799) (criminal and civil actions for violation of the postal laws).

and the laws passed pursuant to it are the supreme laws of the land, binding alike upon states, courts, and the people, "anything in the Constitution or Laws of any State to the contrary notwithstanding." It asserted that the obligation of states to enforce these federal laws is not lessened by reason of the form in which they are cast or the remedy which they provide. And the Court stated that "If an act of Congress gives a penalty to a party aggrieved, without specifying a remedy for its enforcement, there is no reason why it should not be enforced, if not provided otherwise by some act of Congress, by a proper action in a state court." *Id.* 93 U.S. at page 137.

The Claflin opinion thus answered most of the arguments theretofore advanced against the power and duty of state courts to enforce federal penal laws. And since that decision, the remaining areas of doubt have been steadily narrowed. There have been statements in cases concerned with the obligation of states to give full faith and credit to the proceedings of sister states which suggested a theory contrary to that pronounced in the Claflin opinion. But when in Mondou v. New York, N.H. & H.R. Co., *supra*, this Court was presented with a case testing the power and duty of states to enforce federal laws, it found the solution in the broad principles announced in the Claflin opinion.

The precise question in the Mondou case was whether rights arising under the Federal Employers' Liability Act, 36 Stat. 291, could "be enforced, as of right, in the courts of the states when their jurisdiction, as prescribed by local laws, is adequate to the occasion. * * *" *Id.* 223 U.S. at page 46. The Supreme Court of Connecticut had decided that they could not. Except for the penalty feature, the factors it considered and its reasoning were strikingly similar to that on which the Rhode Island Supreme Court declined to enforce the federal law here involved. But this Court held that the Connecticut court could not decline to entertain the action. The contention that enforcement of the congressionally created right was contrary to Connecticut policy was answered as follows:

"The suggestion that the act of Congress is not in harmony with the policy of the State, and therefore that the courts of the state are free to decline jurisdiction, is quite inadmissible, because it presupposes what in legal contemplation does not exist. When Congress, in the exertion of the power confided to it by the Constitution, adopted that act, it spoke for all the people and all the states, and thereby established a policy for all. That policy is as much the policy of Connecticut as if the act had emanated from its own legislature, and should be respected accordingly in the courts of the state." Mondou v. New York, N.H. & H.R. Co., *supra*, 223 U.S. at page 57.

So here, the fact that Rhode Island has an established policy against enforcement by its courts of statutes of other states and the United States which it deems penal, cannot be accepted as a "valid excuse." Cf. Douglas v. New York, N.H. & H.R. Co., 279 U.S. 377, 388 [(1929)]. For the policy of the federal Act is the prevailing policy in every state. Thus, in a case which chiefly relied upon the Claflin and Mondou precedents, this Court stated that a state court cannot "refuse to enforce the right arising from the law of the United States because of conceptions of impolicy or want of wisdom on the part of Congress in having called into play its lawful powers." Minneapolis & St. L.R. Co. v. Bombolis, 241 U.S. 211, 222 [(1916)].

The Rhode Island court * * * cites cases of this Court which have held that states are not required by the full faith and credit clause of the Constitution to enforce judgments of the courts of other states based on claims arising out of penal statutes. But those holdings have no relevance here, for this case raises no full faith and credit question. Nor need we consider in this case prior decisions to the effect that federal courts are not required to enforce state penal laws.

* * * [T]hose decisions did not bring before us our instant problem of the effect of the supremacy clause on the relation of federal laws to state courts. Our question concerns only the right of a state to deny enforcement to claims growing out of a valid federal law.

It is conceded that this same type of claim arising under Rhode Island law would be enforced by that State's courts. Its courts have enforced claims for double damages growing out of the Fair Labor Standards Act, 29 U.S.C.A. § 201 *et seq.* Thus the Rhode Island courts have jurisdiction adequate and appropriate under established local law to adjudicate this action. Under these circumstances the State courts are not free to refuse enforcement of petitioners' claim. See McKnett v. St. Louis & S.F.R. Co., 292 U.S. 230 [(1934)]; and compare Herb v. Pitcairn, 324 U.S. 117 [(1945)]; 325 U.S. 77 [(1945)]. * * *

Reversed.

NOTE ON THE OBLIGATION OF STATE COURTS TO ENFORCE FEDERAL LAW

(1) From Power to Obligation. How long is the leap from Claflin v. Houseman, discussed in Testa, which upheld the *power* of a *willing* state court to exercise concurrent jurisdiction over a federal claim, to the holding of Testa that an *unwilling* state court was under an *obligation* to do so?[1]

---

[1]   The question of congressional power to obligate the states to exercise jurisdiction was apparently first discussed by the Supreme Court in Prigg v. Pennsylvania, 41 U.S. (16 Pet.) 539 (1842), where the precise issue involved Congress's authority to impose a mandatory, concurrent jurisdiction to enforce the Fugitive Slave Act. Writing for himself and Justices Catron and McKinley, Justice Story—echoing a position he had taken in Martin v. Hunter's Lessee, 14 U.S. (1 Wheat.) 304, 337 (1816)—suggested that Congress lacked power to force the states to exercise jurisdiction over federal criminal matters. Although Justice Story's opinion was styled as that of "the Court," "no five judges concurred in all of its reasoning." Cover, Justice Accused: Antislavery and the Judicial Process 166–68 (1975). The Court did not need to resolve this issue to reverse Prigg's conviction on the ground that the state kidnapping statute violated Article IV's Fugitive Slave Clause insofar as it forbade the forcible removal of an African-American from the state.

(2) State Obligations of Non-Discrimination.

(a) The Decisions. For more than a century, the Supreme Court has ruled that state courts may not discriminate against federal causes of action. Thus, Mondou v. New York, N.H. & H.R.R., 223 U.S. 1 (1912) (sometimes known as the Second Employers' Liability Cases), held unanimously that the state could not discriminate against a claim under the Federal Employers' Liability Act (FELA) by refusing to entertain it because of disagreement with the underlying federal policy.[2]

In line with Mondou is McKnett v. St. Louis & S.F. Ry., 292 U.S. 230 (1934), another FELA case, where an Alabama statute for the first time opened the state courts to suits against foreign corporations based on an out-of-state accident, but only for suits under the laws of sister states, not for those under federal law. The Court held that the state statute unlawfully discriminated against federal rights: "While Congress has not attempted to compel states to provide courts for the enforcement of the [FELA], the Federal Constitution prohibits state courts of general jurisdiction from refusing to do so solely because the suit is brought under a federal law. * * * A state may not discriminate against rights arising under federal laws."[3]

(b) The Source of the Non-Discrimination Principle. What federal law is the source of the non-discrimination obligation? One possibility is the Supremacy Clause. But that provision is often viewed merely as a rule of priority: when federal and state law conflict, federal law prevails. On that

---

For a collection of nineteenth century cases expressing doubts about Congress's power to impose jurisdiction on the state courts, see Collins, *Article III, State Court Duties, and the Madisonian Compromise*, 1995 Wisc.L.Rev. 39, 145–94.

For general discussion of state court obligations, see Jordan & Bader, *State Power to Define Jurisdiction*, 47 Ga.L.Rev. 1161 (2013); Katz, *State Judges, State Officers, and Federal Commands After Seminole Tribe and Printz*, 1998 Wisc.L.Rev. 1465; Neuborne, *Toward Procedural Parity in Constitutional Litigation*, 22 Wm. & Mary L.Rev. 725, 753–66 (1981); Redish & Muench, *Adjudication of Federal Causes of Action in State Court*, 75 Mich.L.Rev. 311, 340–61 (1976); Sandalow, *Henry v. Mississippi and the Adequate State Ground: Proposals for a Revised Doctrine*, 1965 Sup.Ct.Rev. 187, 203–09. See also Warren, *New Light on the History of the Federal Judiciary Act of 1789*, 37 Harv.L.Rev. 49 (1923); Warren, *Federal Criminal Laws and the State Courts*, 38 Harv.L.Rev. 545 (1925); Note, 73 Harv.L.Rev. 1551 (1960).

[2]   FELA, enacted in 1908, provides a federal right of action for railroad workers in interstate commerce who are injured on the job due to their employer's negligence. At the time it was enacted, the Act was designed to facilitate recovery by employees, by eliminating certain defenses that the employer might otherwise have had in a tort action.

In the years since Congress enacted FELA, virtually every American jurisdiction has moved to compensating victims of workplace injuries through workers' compensation schemes. FELA stands as an exception, providing that employees of railroads in interstate commerce will have their tort claims decided according to federal law standards in an ordinary jury trial, rather than by a state administrative agency administering a workers' compensation system.

Federal and state courts have concurrent jurisdiction over FELA actions. A special provision (28 U.S.C. § 1445(a)) denies to defendants in a state court FELA action the usual right to remove a federal cause of action to federal court.

[3]   Could Congress, if it relaxed the exclusivity of federal court jurisdiction over federal criminal cases, require state courts to entertain federal criminal cases? The Long Range Plan for the Federal Courts of the Judicial Conference of the United States, 166 F.R.D. 49, 86–87 (1996), proposed that some categories of federal criminal cases be heard in state court. See also Bellia, Jr., *Congressional Power and State Court Jurisdiction*, 94 Geo.L.J. 949 (2006); Carrington, *Federal Use of State Institutions in the Administration of Criminal Justice*, 49 S.M.U.L.Rev. 557, 560 (1996); Collins & Nash, *Prosecuting Federal Crimes in State Courts*, 97 Va.L.Rev. 243 (2011).

understanding, with what rule of federal law does a discriminatory state law conflict?

A second possibility is an implicit rule that every federal statutory right of action implicitly bars states from discriminating. Is that a plausible interpretive canon to apply across the board to all federal rights of action?

(c) Challenges to the Non-Discrimination Principle. Although some Justices have occasionally questioned application of the non-discrimination rule, few have doubted its validity. (Note that Testa was a unanimous decision.)[4] But in a dissent in Haywood v. Drown, 556 U.S. 729 (2009), the next principal case, Justice Thomas, speaking in this respect only for himself, broadly challenged the idea that federal law can *ever* oblige state courts to entertain an action over which they lack jurisdiction under state law. Distinguishing state court refusals to adjudicate based on disagreements with federal policy from those based on a lack of jurisdiction, he viewed Mondou and Testa as correctly decided: in both cases the state courts refused because of a policy disagreement to exercise jurisdiction they possessed. By contrast, he thought McKnett was wrongly decided because the Alabama statutes did not give the state courts jurisdiction over the FELA action there at issue.

(d) The Limits of the Non-Discrimination Rule: Cases Involving State Sovereign Immunity. One modern Supreme Court decision refused to invalidate what appeared to be state court discrimination against federal causes of action. Alden v. Maine, 527 U.S. 706 (1999), p. 1248, *infra*, upheld the authority of a state to waive its immunity in state court from state law actions but not from analogous federal law actions.[5] Rather than suggesting a general qualification of the rule against discrimination, however, Alden

---

[4]   For an argument that the Testa line of cases cannot be justified by the Supremacy Clause, and may actually undermine enforcement of federal law by diminishing the role of the states in fashioning different remedies, see Woolhandler & Collins, *State Jurisdictional Independence and Federal Supremacy*, 72 Fla.L.Rev. 73, 93–105, 119–125 (2020). In response, Vázquez & Vladeck, *Testa, Crain, and the Constitutional Right to Collateral Relief*, 72 Fla.L.Rev. 10, 13 (2021), argues that the Madisonian Compromise and the structures built around it reflect a default expectation of state court enforcement of federal rights. Consider, however, Justice Frankfurter's view, concurring, in Brown v. Gerdes, 321 U.S. 178, 188 (1944): "Since 1789, rights derived from federal law could be enforced in state courts unless Congress confined their enforcement to the federal courts. This has been so precisely for the same reason that rights created by the British Parliament or by the Legislature of Vermont could be enforced in New York courts. Neither Congress nor the British Parliament nor the Vermont Legislature has power to confer jurisdiction upon the New York courts. But the jurisdiction conferred upon them by * * * the State of New York * * * enables them to enforce rights no matter what the legislative source of the right may be." Is that view consistent with Testa (which Justice Frankfurter joined)?

Pfander, *Federal Supremacy, State Court Inferiority, and the Constitutionality of Jurisdiction-Stripping Legislation*, 101 Nw.U.L.Rev. 191, 227–28 (2007), contends that Article I, § 8, cl. 9's authorization "[t]o constitute Tribunals inferior to the supreme Court" does indeed permit Congress to "appoint" state courts to act as inferior federal tribunals and in that role to entertain federal claims.

[5]   In Alden, state employees contended that Maine had failed to pay overtime wages as required by the Fair Labor Standards Act. The Supreme Court ruled that under the Constitution, the state enjoys sovereign immunity from suit in its own courts under federal causes of action. It did not matter to the Court that Maine had waived its immunity to permit its state courts to entertain wage claims based on state law; the majority offered the cryptic observation that "there is no evidence that [the State] has manipulated its immunity in systematic fashion to discriminate against federal causes of action."

may be best understood as limited to cases involving claims of state sovereign immunity and as reflecting the Court's desire to address what it viewed as an effort to make an end run around that doctrine.

(3) Valid Excuses for State Courts to Not Adjudicate Federal Causes of Action. Several Supreme Court decisions have upheld, as a "valid excuse," non-discriminatory refusals by a state court to entertain a federal cause of action. The leading cases have involved rules relating in some way to the convenience of the state as a forum for resolving the case in question, and the refusal to adjudicate has typically left the courts of another, putatively more convenient state, as well as the federal courts, open to hear the dispute.

The leading example is Douglas v. New York, N.H. & H.R. Co., 279 U.S. 377 (1929), where the New York courts had dismissed a FELA action by a Connecticut resident against a Connecticut corporation based on an accident in Connecticut. A New York statute permitted actions by a nonresident against a foreign corporation only in certain cases, of which this was not one. On appeal, Justice Holmes said that FELA "does not purport to require State Courts to entertain suits arising under it but only to empower them to do so, so far as the authority of the United States is concerned. It may very well be that if the Supreme Court of New York were given no discretion, being otherwise competent, it would be subject to a duty. But there is nothing in the Act of Congress that purports to force a duty upon such Courts as against an otherwise valid excuse [citing Mondou]."

Consider also Herb v. Pitcairn, 324 U.S. 117 (1945), a FELA action in an Illinois city court that, under state law, lacked jurisdiction of causes of action, such as this one, arising outside the city. Before action on plaintiff's motion for a change of venue, FELA's two-year statute of limitations had run. The state court dismissed on the ground that there was no timely filed action to transfer, and the Supreme Court affirmed. Acknowledging the state's authority to allocate jurisdiction among its courts, the Court found no violation of the "qualification that the cause of action must not be discriminated against because it is a federal one."[6]

The next principal case further explores the "valid excuse" doctrine.

---

[6]   Pursuant to Missouri ex rel. Southern Ry. Co. v. Mayfield, 340 U.S. 1 (1950), it is understood that state courts may apply forum non conveniens doctrine to federal causes of action, but American Dredging Co. v. Miller, 510 U.S. 443 (1994), held, 7–2, that federal law does not require states to do so. Recognizing that a federal district court would apply a different forum non conveniens rule in the context of the federal cause of action, the Court ruled that forum non conveniens doctrine is procedural, not substantive, and that the policies of federal maritime law do not require complete procedural uniformity.

Haywood v. Drown

556 U.S. 729 (2009).
Certiorari to the New York Court of Appeals.

■ JUSTICE STEVENS delivered the opinion of the Court.

[New York Correction Law § 24 divests state courts of general jurisdiction over damages suits—including suits filed under 42 U.S.C. § 1983—against state corrections officers. Section 24 requires a plaintiff with a grievance against a state corrections officer to pursue a damages claim against the state in the Court of Claims, a court of limited jurisdiction, and denies the plaintiff attorney's fees, punitive damages, or injunctive relief. (The statute did not bar actions for declaratory or injunctive relief against corrections officials, or damages actions against police officers.) Haywood filed two § 1983 damages actions against correction employees in state court and sought punitive damages and attorney's fees. The trial court ruled that it lacked jurisdiction under § 24 and dismissed the actions. On appeal, the state's highest court rejected Haywood's argument that § 24 violated the Supremacy Clause. It reasoned that because § 24 denies damages suits against corrections officers in both state and federal courts, it was a neutral rule of judicial administration and thus a valid excuse for the trial court's refusal to entertain the federal cause of action.]

III

This Court has long made clear that federal law is as much the law of the several States as are the laws passed by their legislatures. * * * Although § 1983, a Reconstruction-era statute, was passed "to interpose the federal courts between the States and the people, as guardians of the people's federal rights," Mitchum v. Foster, 407 U.S. 225, 242 (1972), state courts as well as federal courts are entrusted with providing a forum for the vindication of federal rights violated by state or local officials acting under color of state law.

So strong is the presumption of concurrency that it is defeated only in two narrowly defined circumstances: first, when Congress expressly ousts state courts of jurisdiction, see [Minneapolis & St. Louis R. Co. v.] Bombolis, 241 U.S. [211,] at 221 [(1916)]; Claflin [v. Houseman], 93 U.S. [130], at 136 [1876]; and second, "[w]hen a state court refuses jurisdiction because of a neutral state rule regarding the administration of the courts," Howlett [v. Rose], 496 U.S. [356], at 372 [(1990)]. Focusing on the latter circumstance, we have emphasized that only a neutral jurisdictional rule will be deemed a "valid excuse" for departing from the default assumption that "state courts have inherent authority, and are thus presumptively competent, to adjudicate claims arising under the laws of the United States." Tafflin v. Levitt, 493 U.S. 455, 458 (1990).

In determining whether a state law qualifies as a neutral rule of judicial administration, our cases have established that a State cannot employ a jurisdictional rule "to dissociate [itself] from federal law because of disagreement with its content or a refusal to recognize the superior authority of its source." Howlett, 496 U.S., at 371. In other words, although States retain substantial leeway to establish the contours of their judicial systems, they lack authority to nullify a federal right or cause of action they believe is inconsistent with their local policies. * * *

It is principally on this basis that Correction Law § 24 violates the Supremacy Clause. In passing Correction Law § 24, New York made the judgment that correction officers should not be burdened with suits for damages arising out of conduct performed in the scope of their employment. Because it regards these suits as too numerous or too frivolous (or both), the State's longstanding policy has been to shield this narrow class of defendants from liability when sued for damages.[5] The State's policy, whatever its merits, is contrary to Congress' judgment that *all* persons who violate federal rights while acting under color of state law shall be held liable for damages. As we have unanimously recognized, "[a] State may not . . . relieve congestion in its courts by declaring a whole category of federal claims to be frivolous. Until it has been proved that the claim has no merit, that judgment is not up to the States to make." Howlett, 496 U.S., at 380. That New York strongly favors a rule shielding correction officers from personal damages liability and substituting the State as the party responsible for compensating individual victims is irrelevant. The State cannot condition its enforcement of federal law on the demand that those individuals whose conduct federal law seeks to regulate must nevertheless escape liability.

IV

While our cases have uniformly applied the principle that a State cannot simply refuse to entertain a federal claim based on a policy disagreement, we have yet to confront a statute like New York's that registers its dissent by divesting its courts of jurisdiction over a disfavored federal claim in addition to an identical state claim. * * *

Although the absence of discrimination is necessary to our finding a state law neutral, it is not sufficient. A jurisdictional rule cannot be used as a device to undermine federal law, no matter how evenhanded it may

---

[5]   In many respects, Correction Law § 24 operates more as an immunity-from-damages provision than as a jurisdictional rule. Indeed, the original version of the statute gave correction officers qualified immunity, providing that no officer would be "liable for damages if he shall have acted in good faith, with reasonable care and upon probable cause." And, more recently, a state legislative proposal seeking to extend Correction Law § 24's scheme to other state employees explained that its purpose was to grant "the same immunity from civil damage actions as all other State employees who work in the prisons." In Howlett v. Rose, we considered the question whether a Florida school board could assert a state-law immunity defense in a § 1983 action brought in state court when the defense would not have been available if the action had been brought in federal court. We unanimously held that the State's decision to extend immunity "over and above [that which is] already provided in § 1983 . . . directly violates federal law," and explained that the "elements of, and the defenses to, a federal cause of action are defined by federal law." Thus, if Correction Law § 24 were understood as offering an immunity defense, Howlett would compel the conclusion that it violates the Supremacy Clause.

appear. * * * Ensuring equality of treatment is thus the beginning, not the end, of the Supremacy Clause analysis.

In addition to giving too much weight to equality of treatment, respondents mistakenly treat this case as implicating the "great latitude [States enjoy] to establish the structure and jurisdiction of their own courts." [Howlett, 496 U.S.], at 372. Although Correction Law § 24 denies state courts authority to entertain damages actions against correction officers, this case does not require us to decide whether Congress may compel a State to offer a forum, otherwise unavailable under state law, to hear suits brought pursuant to § 1983. The State of New York has made this inquiry unnecessary by creating courts of general jurisdiction that routinely sit to hear analogous § 1983 actions. * * * For instance, if petitioner had attempted to sue a police officer for damages under § 1983, the suit would be properly adjudicated by a state supreme court. * * * It is only a particular species of suits—those seeking damages relief against correction officers—that the State deems inappropriate for its trial courts.[6]

We therefore hold that, having made the decision to create courts of general jurisdiction that regularly sit to entertain analogous suits, New York is not at liberty to shut the courthouse door to federal claims that it considers at odds with its local policy.[7] A State's authority to organize its courts while considerable, remains subject to the strictures of the Constitution. We have never treated a State's invocation of "jurisdiction" as a trump that ends the Supremacy Clause inquiry, see Howlett, 496 U.S., at 382–383, and we decline to do so in this case. * * *

Accordingly, the dissent's fear that "no state jurisdictional rule will be upheld as constitutional" is entirely unfounded. Our holding addresses only the unique scheme adopted by the State of New York—a law designed to shield a particular class of defendants (correction officers) from a particular type of liability (damages) brought by a particular class of plaintiffs (prisoners). Based on the belief that damages suits against correction officers are frivolous and vexatious, Correction Law § 24 is effectively an immunity statute cloaked in jurisdictional garb. Finding

---

[6]   While we have looked to a State's "common-law tort analogues" in deciding whether a state procedural rule is neutral, we have never equated "analogous claims" with "identical claims." Instead, we have searched for a similar claim under state law to determine whether a State has established courts of adequate and appropriate jurisdiction capable of hearing a § 1983 suit. Section 1983 damages claims against other state officials and equitable claims against correction officers are both sufficiently analogous to petitioner's § 1983 claims.

[7]   The dissent's contrary view is based on its belief that "States have unfettered authority to determine whether their local courts may entertain a federal cause of action." But this theory of the Supremacy Clause was raised and squarely rejected in Howlett. Respondents in that case "argued that a federal court has no power to compel a state court to entertain a claim over which the state court has no jurisdiction as a matter of state law." 496 U.S., at 381. We declared that this argument had "no merit" and explained that it ignored other provisions of the Constitution, including the Full Faith and Credit Clause and the Privileges and Immunities Clause, which compel States to open their courts to causes of action over which they would normally lack jurisdiction. 496 U. S., at 381–382. We saw no reason to treat the Supremacy Clause differently. Howlett, 496 U.S., at 382–383. Thus, to the extent the dissent resurrects this argument, we again reject it.

this scheme unconstitutional merely confirms that the Supremacy Clause cannot be evaded by formalism.[9] * * *

V

The judgment of the New York Court of Appeals is reversed, and the case is remanded to that court for further proceedings not inconsistent with this opinion.

It is so ordered.

■ JUSTICE THOMAS, with whom THE CHIEF JUSTICE, JUSTICE SCALIA, and JUSTICE ALITO join as to Part III, dissenting.

* * * Because neither the Constitution nor our precedent requires New York to open its courts to § 1983 federal actions, I respectfully dissent.

I

[Justice Thomas here detailed the drafting history at the Constitutional Convention.]

The assumption that state courts would * * * exercise concurrent jurisdiction over federal claims was essential to th[e Madisonian] compromise. * * *

The Constitution's implicit preservation of state authority to entertain federal claims, however, did not impose a duty on state courts to do so. * * * [T]here was at least one proposal [at the Federal Convention] to expressly require state courts to take original jurisdiction over federal claims (subject to appeal in federal court) that was introduced in an attempt to forestall the creation of lower federal courts. But in light of the failure of this proposal—which was offered before the adoption of the Madisonian Compromise—the assertions by its supporters that state courts would ordinarily entertain federal causes of action cannot reasonably be viewed as an assurance that the States would never alter the subject-matter jurisdiction of their courts. The Framers' decision to empower Congress to create federal courts that could either supplement or displace state-court review of federal claims, as well as the exclusion of any affirmative command requiring the States to consider federal claims in the text of Article III, confirms this understanding.

The earliest decisions addressing this question, written by then-serving and future Supreme Court Justices, confirm that state courts remain "tribunals over which the government of the Union has no adequate control, and which may be closed to any claim asserted under a law of the United States." Osborn v. Bank of United States, 9 Wheat. 738 (1824). "The states, in providing their own judicial tribunals, have a right

---

[9]   A contrary conclusion would permit a State to withhold a forum for the adjudication of any federal cause of action with which it disagreed as long as the policy took the form of a jurisdictional rule. That outcome, in turn, would provide a roadmap for States wishing to circumvent our prior decisions.

to limit, control, and restrict their judicial functions, and jurisdiction, according to their own mere pleasure." Mitchell v. Great Works Milling & Mfg. Co., 17 F.Cas. 496, 499 (No. 9,662) (C.C.D.Me.1843) (Story, J.). In short, there was "a very clear intimation given by the judges of the Supreme Court, that the state courts were not bound in consequence of any act of congress, to assume and exercise jurisdiction in such cases. It was merely permitted to them to do so as far, as was compatible with their state obligations." 1 J. Kent, Commentaries on American Law 375 (1826).

Under our federal system, therefore, the States have unfettered authority to determine whether their local courts may entertain a federal cause of action. Once a State exercises its sovereign prerogative to deprive its courts of subject-matter jurisdiction over a federal cause of action, it is the end of the matter as far as the Constitution is concerned.

The present case can be resolved under this principle alone. * * * The majority and petitioner agree that [NYCLA § 24] erects a jurisdictional bar that prevents the state courts from entertaining petitioner's claim for damages under § 1983. Because New York's decision to withdraw jurisdiction over § 1983 damages actions—or indeed, over any claims— does not offend the Constitution, the judgment below should be affirmed.

II

* * * There is no textual or historical support for the Court's incorporation of [an] antidiscrimination principle into the Supremacy Clause.

A

* * * Under [the Supremacy Clause], "[t]he laws of the United States are laws in the several States, and just as much binding on the citizens and courts thereof as the State laws are . . . The two together form one system of jurisprudence, which constitutes the law of the land for the State." Claflin, 93 U.S., at 136–137. Thus, a valid federal law is substantively superior to a state law; "if a state measure conflicts with a federal requirement, the state provision must give way." Swift & Co. v. Wickham, 382 U.S. 111, 120 (1965). As a textual matter, however, the Supremacy Clause does not address whether a state court must entertain a federal cause of action; it provides only a rule of decision that the state court must follow if it adjudicates the claim. * * *

The supremacy of federal law, therefore, is not impugned by a State's decision to strip its local courts of subject-matter jurisdiction to hear certain federal claims. Subject-matter jurisdiction determines only whether a court has the power to entertain a particular claim—a condition precedent to reaching the merits of a legal dispute. Although the line between subject-matter jurisdiction over a claim and the merits of that claim can at times prove difficult to draw, the distinction is crucial in the Supremacy Clause context. If the state court does not reach the merits of the dispute for lack of statutory or constitutional jurisdiction, the preeminence of federal law remains undiminished.

Accordingly, the superiority of federal law as a substantive matter does not trigger an obligation on States to keep their courts jurisdictionally neutral with respect to federal- and state-law claims. "The federal law in any field within which Congress is empowered to legislate is the supreme law of the land in the sense that it may supplant state legislation in that field, but not in the sense that it may supplant the existing rules of litigation in state courts. Congress has full power to provide its own courts for litigating federal rights. The state courts belong to the States." Brown v. Gerdes, 321 U.S. 178, 193 (1944) (Frankfurter, J., concurring). * * *

B

* * * [F]ederal law does not expressly require New York courts to accept jurisdiction over § 1983 suits. * * * The statute addresses who may sue and be sued for violations of federal law. But it includes no substantive command requiring New York to provide a state judicial forum to a § 1983 plaintiff. * * *

* * * NYCLA § 24 does not conflict with § 1983. * * * Congress did not grant § 1983 plaintiffs a "right" to bring their claims in state court or "guarantee" that the state forum would remain open to their suits. Moreover, Congress has created inferior federal courts that have the power to adjudicate all § 1983 actions. And this Court has expressly determined that § 1983 plaintiffs do not have to exhaust state-court remedies before proceeding in federal court. See Patsy [v. Board of Regents], 457 U.S. [496], at 516 [(1982)].

Therefore, even if every state court closed its doors to § 1983 plaintiffs, the plaintiffs could proceed with their claims in the federal forum. And because the dismissal of § 1983 claims from state court pursuant to NYCLA § 24 is for lack of subject-matter jurisdiction, it has no preclusive effect on claims refiled in federal court, and thus does not alter the substance of the federal claim. * * *

III

* * *

A

The majority mischaracterizes this Court's precedent when it asserts that jurisdictional neutrality is "the beginning, not the end, of the Supremacy Clause analysis." * * *

* * * A jurisdictional statute simply deprives the relevant court of the power to decide the case altogether. Such a statute necessarily operates without prejudice to the adjudication of the matter in a competent forum. Jurisdictional statutes therefore by definition are incapable of undermining federal law. NYCLA § 24 no more undermines § 1983 than the amount-in-controversy requirement for federal diversity

jurisdiction undermines state law. See 28 U.S.C. § 1332. The relevant law (state or federal) remains fully operative in both circumstances. The sole consequence of the jurisdictional barrier is that the law cannot be enforced in one particular judicial forum.[10] * * *

* * * [T]his Court has "never held that state courts must entertain § 1983 suits." Our decisions have held only that the States cannot use jurisdictional statutes to discriminate against federal claims. Because NYCLA § 24 does not violate this command, any policy-driven reasons for depriving jurisdiction over a "federal claim in addition to an identical state claim" are irrelevant for purposes of the Supremacy Clause.

This Court's decision in Howlett is not to the contrary. * * *

* * * Howlett * * * stands for the unremarkable proposition that States may not add immunity defenses to § 1983. A state law is not jurisdictional just because the legislature has "denominated" it as such. * * * The majority, therefore, is correct that a state court's decision "to nullify a federal right or cause of action [that it] believe[s] is inconsistent with [its] local policies" cannot evade the Supremacy Clause by hiding behind a jurisdictional label, because "the Supremacy Clause cannot be evaded by formalism." Rather, a state statute must in fact *operate* jurisdictionally: It must deprive the court of the power to hear the claim and it must not preclude relitigation of the action in a proper forum. * * *

* * * NYCLA § 24 is not merely "denominated" as jurisdictional—it actually is jurisdictional. The New York courts, therefore, have not declared a "category" of § 1983 claims to be " 'frivolous' " or to have " 'no merit' " in order to " 'relieve congestion' " in the state court system. [Howlett, 496 U.S., at 380]. These courts have simply recognized that they lack the power to adjudicate this category of claims regardless of their merit. * * *

B

* * * [A] statute's jurisdictional status turns on the grounds on which the state-law dismissal rests and the consequences that follow from such rulings. No matter how narrow the majority perceives NYCLA § 24 to be, it easily qualifies as jurisdictional under this established standard. Accordingly, it is immaterial that New York has chosen to allow its courts of general jurisdiction to entertain § 1983 actions against certain categories of defendants but not others (such as correction officers), or to entertain § 1983 actions against particular defendants for only certain types of relief. * * *

---

[10]   If by asserting that state law is not permitted to "undermine federal law," the majority instead is arguing that NYCLA § 24 is a procedural rule that too heavily "burdens the exercise of the federal right" in state court, see Felder [v. Casey], 487 U.S. [131], 141 [(1988)], its argument is equally misplaced. First, the majority concedes that NYCLA § 24 is not a state procedural rule. Second, applying the reasoning of Felder to a jurisdictional statute like NYCLA § 24 would overrule all of the Court's decisions upholding state laws that decline jurisdiction over federal claims, and would virtually ensure that in future cases, no state jurisdictional rule will be upheld as constitutional. * * *

* * * The majority is forcing States into an all-or-nothing choice that neither the Constitution nor this Court's decisions require.

Indeed, the majority's novel approach breaks the promise that the States still enjoy " 'great latitude ... to establish the structure and jurisdiction of their own courts.' " [Howlett, 496 U.S., at 372]. It cannot be that New York has forsaken the right to withdraw a particular class of claims from its courts' purview simply because it has created courts of general jurisdiction that would otherwise have the power to hear suits for damages against correction officers. The Supremacy Clause does not fossilize the jurisdiction of state courts in their original form. Under this Court's precedent, States remain free to alter the structure of their judicial system even if that means certain federal causes of action will no longer be heard in state court, so long as States do so on nondiscriminatory terms. * * *

NOTE ON HAYWOOD V. DROWN

(1) Questions About Haywood v. Drown. Haywood is the only decision in which the Court acknowledged that it was invalidating a nondiscriminatory jurisdictional rule. (One other decision, Felder v. Casey, 487 U.S. 131 (1988), also appears to have invalidated a nondiscriminatory rule, although the Court's opinion included an unconvincing contention that the state rule was discriminatory.[1])

Consider these questions raised by the Haywood decision:

(a) What Counts as Jurisdictional? Justice Stevens's opinion described the New York rule as jurisdictional, but he also said that in many respects it operates more as an immunity from damages than a jurisdictional rule; at another point he called it "an immunity statute cloaked in jurisdictional garb." In response, Justice Thomas essentially suggested that whatever substantive concerns might have motivated the rule, the key point was that a genuinely jurisdictional rule results in a dismissal without prejudice (thus permitting suit to go forward in another court), whereas a

---

[1] Felder involved a state law requiring that, before a state court action can be filed against a governmental body or its officials, the plaintiff must first have given the defendant notice of the claim within 120 days of the alleged injury. The plaintiff brought a federal civil rights action under 42 U.S.C. § 1983, naming a city and a police official as defendants. The state supreme court upheld dismissal of the action for failure to comply with the notice-of-claim statute. The Supreme Court reversed. Part of the Court's opinion argued, unpersuasively, that the statute, although it treated state law and federal law claims against governmental defendants identically, discriminated against the precise type of civil rights action that Congress had created in § 1983. But the Court also argued that the statute would burden civil rights plaintiffs in order to serve a purpose—minimizing governmental liability—that was impermissible under federal law. In particular, the Court reasoned that enforcement of the statute was inconsistent with the decision in Patsy v. Board of Regents, 457 U.S. 496 (1982), p. 1394, *infra*, that exhaustion of state administrative remedies is not required in § 1983 actions. For further discussion of Felder, see pp. 608–609, *infra*.

substantive immunity would result in dismissal with prejudice, which would preclude further pursuit of the claims.[2]

One possible reply to Justice Thomas is that, in view of the § 1983 suits that New York courts do entertain, the rule doesn't seem, in Justice Stevens's terms, to regulate judicial power over persons or competence over subject matter. But why can't a narrow rule depriving courts of a particular remedy be jurisdictional? A different reply to Justice Thomas might be that the policy underlying New York's law differs from the federal policy underlying § 1983. Compare the statement in the Mondou decision, quoted in Testa v. Katt: "When Congress, in the exertion of the power confided to it by the Constitution, adopted that act, it spoke for all the people and all the States, and thereby established a policy for all. That policy is as much the policy of Connecticut as if the act had emanated from its own legislature, and should be respected accordingly in the courts of the State."

(b) Why Displace Nondiscriminatory Rules? If application of the New York rule would merely have led to dismissal without prejudice of Haywood's action, what federal interest requires New York's courts to entertain it? Is it that a state court might be more convenient, speedier, or less costly than a federal court and that Congress wanted to give plaintiffs a forum choice? (The majority does not rely on that argument.) That state court resolution of the action helps reduce the federal courts' caseload, permitting their limited capacity to be directed elsewhere and avoiding burdens that might require an unwanted expansion of the federal judiciary? Does the latter rationale suggest that Congress is imposing an unfunded mandate upon the state courts? If so, is that problematic?

On the other hand, on Justice Thomas's view, are the state courts free to enforce any jurisdictional limitation that does not discriminate against federal rights so long as it requires a dismissal without prejudice? Consider a rule depriving state courts of jurisdiction over any employment discrimination case seeking more than $50,000 in damages, or over any actions challenging marriage rules under the state or federal constitution, or over any action challenging voting rules that relies on statistical evidence?[3]

(2) Justice Thomas's View of the Convention History. Justice Thomas placed considerable emphasis in his Haywood dissent on the debates surrounding the Madisonian Compromise and the adoption of the Supremacy Clause. How probative is the Convention history? Many motivations other than a rejection of state court obligation (including doubts that the Constitution itself should mandate state court jurisdiction over federal *crimes*, see p. 581, *supra*) might have underlain the rejection of the New Jersey Plan. (Recall the judiciary article of that plan would have

---

[2]   On this reasoning, both opinions in Haywood endorsed the decision in Howlett v. Rose, 496 U.S. 356 (1990), where the Court unanimously ruled that the Florida state courts were obliged to entertain a 42 U.S.C. § 1983 suit against a local school board. Since a state statute had waived sovereign immunity in comparable actions under state law, the Court found the state's excuse—that the waiver of immunity did not extend to § 1983 actions—discriminatory and therefore invalid. For Justice Thomas, key was the fact that the state rule there, though phrased in jurisdictional terms, led to dismissal of the claim with prejudice.

[3]   For further discussion of Haywood, see Seinfeld, *The Jurisprudence of Union*, 89 Notre Dame L.Rev. 1085 (2014).

expressly required state courts to entertain federal actions for punishments, fines, forfeitures, and penalties.) In other contexts, Justice Thomas has joined his colleagues in expressing skepticism about seeking to draw meaning from legislative inaction, see, *e.g.*, Brecht v. Abrahamson, 507 U.S. 619, 623–33 (1993), and that concern is especially potent with respect to inaction by the Convention, whose secret decisions were unknown to those in the state ratification conventions.

Suppose, however, that Justice Thomas is correct that neither the Supremacy Clause nor any other constitutional provision requires state courts to exercise jurisdiction over federal causes of action. How does that specific conclusion fit with foundational understandings of the constitutional structure? Consider, for example, the situation in which an individual has a constitutional right to judicial redress in some court, but Congress has not conferred jurisdiction on any federal court. Justice Thomas's approach would leave the state courts free to refuse jurisdiction, thereby foreclosing all relief for the individual. Is that a sensible understanding of the constitutional plan? Would his approach be more convincing if it were joined with the view that lower federal courts are constitutionally required in some cases?

(3) The Latest Chapter: Montgomery v. Louisiana. The Court's decision in Montgomery v. Louisiana, 577 U.S. 190 (2016), further suggests that state courts may have a duty to hear federal claims for reasons other than avoiding discrimination against such claims. At issue was whether a state court conducting collateral review of a state criminal conviction may preclude retroactive application of a new rule of substantive federal constitutional law. Specifically, more than four decades after being sentenced to life without parole as a juvenile, petitioner Montgomery sought to benefit from the Court's decision in Miller v. Alabama, 567 U.S. 460 (2012), holding that states may not, consistent with the Eighth Amendment, impose a life sentence without the possibility of parole for a crime committed by a juvenile. Montgomery brought a claim for relief under Miller under a state collateral review procedure that allows prisoners to challenge the legality of their sentences on Eighth Amendment grounds. As a matter of state practice, however, the state court declined to give Miller retroactive effect on state collateral review.

Writing for the Court, Justice Kennedy held that as a matter of federal constitutional law, state collateral proceedings must give retroactive effect to new substantive constitutional rules—those "that place certain criminal laws and punishments altogether beyond the State's power to impose."[4] Justice Kennedy reasoned that "when a State enforces a proscription or penalty barred by the Constitution, the resulting conviction or sentence is, by definition, unlawful." To buttress its conclusion, the Court cited "a long tradition" of federal courts giving retroactive effect to substantive constitutional rules on collateral review.

---

[4]   Here, Justice Kennedy read Teague v. Lane, 489 U.S. 288 (1989), discussed at pp. 1578–1587, *infra*, in which the Court held that the bar against retroactive application of new rules should not apply to new substantive constitutional rules, as "best understood as resting upon constitutional premises." This, in turn, he held, required that Montgomery be afforded the relief he sought.

In one of two dissents,[5] writing only for himself, Justice Thomas argued that nothing in the text of the Constitution or historical practice creates a right to collateral relief, either in state or federal court. According to Justice Thomas, the retroactivity requirement would not apply if the state eliminated state collateral review of all federal claims or perhaps even just Eighth Amendment claims. "Only when state courts have chosen to entertain a federal claim," he wrote, "can the Supremacy Clause conceivably command a state court to apply federal law." This conclusion, he added, reflects the idea that "the Constitution leaves the initial choice to entertain federal claims up to state courts, which are 'tribunals over which the government of the Union has no adequate control, and which may be closed to any claim asserted under a law of the United States' " (quoting Osborn v. Bank of the United States, 9 Wheat. 738, 821 (1824), see pp. 994–1002, *infra*).

Can Justice Thomas's position about state courts be squared with the majority's reasoning? The majority seems to say that the U.S. Constitution prohibits a state court from keeping a criminal defendant in confinement when the relevant conviction or sentence contravenes substantive constitutional rules limiting the state's power. Does that conclusion suggest that states have an affirmative constitutional duty to provide some form of collateral relief in such cases? Does your answer depend on whether federal habeas corpus relief is available in such cases? For further discussion of Montgomery v. Louisiana, see pp. 602–603, 1608, 1619–1625, *infra*.

(4) Statutory Interpretation Versus Constitutional Power to Displace State Jurisdictional Rules. When the Supreme Court decides that a state rule is a valid excuse (as in Douglas) or is not (as in Haywood), exactly what federal law is the Court applying? Is the Court determining whether a federal statute (like § 1983 in Haywood) and its associated policy are incompatible with the state's refusal to exercise jurisdiction?

Both Justice Stevens and Justice Thomas agreed that the Haywood case, in Justice Stevens's words, "does not require us to decide whether Congress may compel a State to offer a forum, otherwise unavailable under state law, to hear suits brought pursuant to § 1983." But suppose that New York eliminated all state court jurisdiction over civil rights actions, federal and state, and in turn Congress purported to compel the states to entertain § 1983 actions.

A series of Supreme Court decisions on constitutional federalism bear on the question of the ultimate scope of congressional power.

(a) Usery and Garcia. In National League of Cities v. Usery, 426 U.S. 833 (1976), the Court had ruled that substantive federal regulation of traditional state governmental functions involving matters "essential to [the] separate and independent existence" of the states lay beyond Congress's power under the Commerce Clause and the Tenth Amendment. Nine years later, the Court overruled Usery in Garcia v. San Antonio Metropolitan

---

[5]   Justice Scalia, joined by Justices Thomas and Alito, dissented on the ground that the Teague exception for new rules of substantive constitutional law was not constitutionally compelled.

Transit Auth., 469 U.S. 528 (1985). Both cases involved application of the Fair Labor Standards Act, and both resulted in 5–4 decisions.

(b) New York v. United States. In New York v. United States, 505 U.S. 144 (1992) (6–3), the Court made clear that, despite Garcia, it had not abandoned judicial enforcement of constitutional limits on Congress's power to regulate the states.[6] The Court invalidated, as outside the commerce power, a federal statute requiring states that failed to provide for disposal of internally generated radioactive waste by a certain date to take title to the waste and thereby to assume associated liabilities. In the Court's view, Congress lacked power either to "commandeer" the states into regulating waste disposal or to require states to take title to waste; accordingly, Congress lacked power to offer the states a choice between those two options. The Court distinguished Garcia because it involved a statute that, unlike the "take title" provision, "subjected a State to the same legislation applicable to private parties."

The Court also distinguished Testa on the following basis: "Federal statutes enforceable in state courts do, in a sense, direct state judges to enforce them, but this sort of federal 'direction' of state judges is mandated by the text of the Supremacy Clause. No comparable constitutional provision authorizes Congress to command state legislatures to legislate."

(c) The Printz Decision. The Court extended the "anti-commandeering" principle of New York v. United States in Printz v. United States, 521 U.S. 898 (1997) (5–4). Justice Scalia's opinion for the Court held that Congress overstepped constitutional bounds by directing local law enforcement officials to conduct background checks on would-be purchasers of handguns. The Court said that, just as the federal government may not order the states to legislate, it may not "command the States' officers, or those of their political subdivisions, to administer or enforce a federal regulatory program." The Printz Court distinguished Testa on the same basis that it had in New York v. United States.

(d) The Murphy Decision. In Murphy v. National Collegiate Athletic Ass'n, 584 U.S. 453 (2018), the Court (6–3) reaffirmed and extended its

---

[6]   Even before the Court overruled Usery, in Federal Energy Regulatory Comm'n [FERC] v. Mississippi, 456 U.S. 742 (1982), the Court rebuffed a Tenth Amendment challenge to the Public Utilities Regulatory Policies Act of 1978, 16 U.S.C. §§ 2601 *et seq.* That Act, *inter alia,* directed state utility regulatory authorities to implement certain federal rules, to "consider" the adoption of certain rate design and regulatory standards, and to follow specified procedures when considering these proposed standards. The Court distinguished Usery, and relied heavily on Testa v. Katt, in upholding the federal requirements. The Court stressed that Congress could choose to preempt state public utility regulation altogether and that the states could avoid the federal obligation by opting not to regulate.

In a partial dissent, the themes of which were later echoed by the majority in the New York decision and in Printz v. United States, Paragraph (4)(c), *infra,* Justice O'Connor, joined by Chief Justice Burger and Justice Rehnquist, argued that "[a]pplication of Testa to legislative power [such as that exercised by state utility regulatory commissions] * * * vastly expands the scope of that decision. Because trial courts of general jurisdiction do not choose the cases that they hear, the requirement that they evenhandedly adjudicate state and federal claims falling within their jurisdiction does not infringe any sovereign authority to set an agenda. * * * [But] the power to choose subjects for legislation is a fundamental attribute of legislative power, and interference with this power unavoidably undermines state sovereignty."

For further consideration of FERC, see p. 610, *infra.*

anticommandeering doctrine. The Professional and Amateur Sports Protection Act of 1992 (PASPA), 106 Stat. 4227, in relevant part made it unlawful for states to "authorize by law or compact" various forms of gambling on competitive sporting events. In the Court's view, this statute precluded a state from partially repealing any existing state legislation that barred such gambling. In effect, therefore, PASPA put state legislatures "under the direct control of Congress"—"as if federal officers were installed in state legislative chambers and were armed with the authority to stop legislators from voting on any offending proposals." This result, the Court said, constituted a "direct affront to state sovereignty" under the system of dual sovereignty affirmed by the Tenth Amendment.

(e) **The Brackeen Decision.** In Haaland v. Brackeen, 599 U.S. 255 (2023), the Court rejected an anticommandeering challenge to a provision of the Indian Child Welfare Act requiring state courts to apply a complex set of federal—rather than state—law preferences for child placement in state custody proceedings involving any child who is the member of a Native American tribe. See 25 U.S.C. §§ 1915(a), (b). Though acknowledging that "Congress can require state courts, unlike state executives and legislatures, to enforce federal law," petitioners drew "a distinction between requiring state courts to entertain federal causes of action and requiring them to apply federal law to state causes of action." In an opinion written by Justice Barrett, the Court held, 7–2, that petitioners' anticommandeering argument "runs headlong into . . . [t]he Supremacy Clause," reasoning that a federal law's preemptive effect is not limited due to the fact that it "modifies a state cause of action."

(f) **The Import of the Decisions.** Do concerns with state autonomy expressed in New York, Printz, and Murphy provide a basis for the Justices, in an appropriate case, to limit congressional power to require unwilling state courts to hear federal claims? For an affirmative answer, see Blackman, *State Judicial Sovereignty*, 2016 U.Ill.L.Rev. 2033. Does Brackeen help clarify the scope of federal power in state courts?

NOTE ON "SUBSTANCE" AND "PROCEDURE" IN THE ENFORCEMENT OF FEDERAL RIGHTS OF ACTION IN STATE COURTS

(1) State Court Procedures: The General Rule and the Dice v. Akron Exception. As a general rule, state courts apply existing state procedures when adjudicating federal rights. But the Supreme Court recognized a narrow exception to this rule in Dice v. Akron, Canton & Youngstown R.R., 342 U.S. 359 (1952).

In Dice, a railroad worker who sustained injuries on the job sued his employer for negligence under FELA in Ohio state court. The employer argued that it was not liable because the worker had signed a document releasing the employer from liability. The worker responded that the release was void, for he had signed it in reliance on the employer's "deliberately false statement that the document was nothing more than a mere receipt for back wages."

In an opinion by Justice Black, the Supreme Court held that federal law, not state law, governed whether such a release of claims under FELA was valid. The Court reasoned:

"Congress * * * granted petitioner a right to recover against his employer for damages negligently inflicted. State laws are not controlling in determining what the incidents of this federal right shall be. Manifestly the federal rights affording relief to injured railroad employees under a federally declared standard could be defeated if states were permitted to have the final say as to what defenses could and could not be properly interposed to suits under the Act. Moreover, only if federal law controls can the federal Act be given that uniform application throughout the country essential to effectuate its purposes. Releases and other devices designed to liquidate or defeat injured employees' claims play an important part in the federal Act's administration. Their validity is but one of the many interrelated questions that must constantly be determined in these cases according to a uniform federal law."

After emphasizing the need to protect the integrity of the federal right at issue and the uniformity of federal law, the Court further reasoned that allowing employers' misleading statements to defeat employees' rights under FELA would be "wholly incongruous" with the purposes of the Act: "to give railroad employees a right to recover just compensation for injuries negligently inflicted by their employers."

The Court also ruled that Ohio could not follow its ordinary practice of allowing judges—rather than juries—to decide certain elements of the question whether the release was fraudulently obtained. In Justice Black's view, the jury trial was a substantial portion of the remedy afforded by FELA,[1] and it followed that a state could not negate that federal remedy by way of a purported " 'local rule of procedure.' "

Writing for four Justices, Justice Frankfurter concurred only in the result. In his view, "simply because there is concurrent jurisdiction in Federal and State courts over actions under [FELA], a State is under no duty to treat actions arising under that Act differently from the way it adjudicates local actions for negligence, so far as the mechanics of litigation, the forms in which law is administered, are concerned." This principle, he argued, extends to "the distribution of functions as between judge and jury."

But, Justice Frankfurter continued, although "the method of trying" the relevant issue of fraud need not differ from how state courts try analogous state law issues, he agreed that "[i]n order to prevent diminution of railroad workers' nationally-uniform right to recover," the substantive "standard for the validity of a release of contested liability must be Federal."

(2) The Relationship of Dice to Testa v. Katt. The issue in Dice—whether states may follow their procedural rules in entertaining federal rights—echoes the issue in cases like Testa—whether states may follow their

---

[1]   Justice Black noted, for example, that the Court had "previously held that 'The right to trial by jury is "a basic and fundamental feature of our system of federal jurisprudence' " and that it is 'part and parcel of the remedy afforded railroad workers under [FELA]' " (quoting Bailey v. Central Vermont R. Co., 319 U.S. 350, 354 (1943)).

own jurisdictional or related rules in deciding whether to entertain federal causes of action. In both instances, there are questions of statutory interpretation or judicial policymaking, as well as questions of the ultimate scope of the constitutional authority of Congress.

(3) The Relationship of Dice to Minneapolis & St. Louis R. Co. v. Bombolis. Recall that the Court in Dice considered the jury trial right to be part of the federal remedy created by FELA, so states could not enforce procedural rules that would deprive litigants of that federal right. In reaching its conclusion, the Dice Court rejected an analogy to Minneapolis & St. Louis R. Co. v. Bombolis, 241 U.S. 211 (1916), where the Court had allowed state courts to try cases arising under FELA by nonunanimous verdicts. Justice Black wrote: "The Bombolis case might be more in point had Ohio abolished trial by jury in all negligence cases including those arising under the federal Act. But Ohio has not done this. It has provided jury trials for cases arising under the federal Act but seeks to single out one phase of the question of fraudulent releases for determination by a judge rather than by a jury. Compare Testa v. Katt, 330 U.S. 386."

In dissent, Justice Frankfurter relied on Bombolis to argue that FELA did not impose the jury trial right as a substantive remedy. After all, note that FELA's only textual reference to jury trials is in a provision stating that contributory negligence shall not bar a recovery "but the damages shall be diminished by the jury in proportion to the amount of negligence attributable to" the employee. 45 U.S.C. § 53. According to Justice Frankfurter, states are required only to conduct negligence suits under FELA in the same way as they "conduct[ ] the run of negligence litigation."

(4) Procedure Versus Substance. Notably, the Court has displaced nondiscriminatory procedural rules somewhat more freely than nondiscriminatory jurisdictional rules. Does a good reason exist for this difference in treatment? (Recall in this respect Justice Thomas's argument in his dissent in Haywood that applying state jurisdictional rules so as to dismiss a claim without prejudice does not harm federal rightholders. That argument plainly does not apply equally to the enforcement of state procedures.) In considering that question when reading the following exceptions (which have arisen principally in two specific contexts: FELA and § 1983 actions), keep in mind that these relatively few decisions depart from an otherwise consistent practice in which state courts, when adjudicating federal rights, apply the same procedures that apply when state law rights are adjudicated.

(a) Burden of Proof. Central Vermont Ry. Co. v. White, 238 U.S. 507 (1915), held that a state rule requiring the plaintiff to prove freedom from contributory negligence did not apply in FELA actions: the burden of proof on contributory negligence is not a "mere matter of state procedure," and Congress intended that FELA be interpreted in light of federal court decisions that uniformly required the defendant to prove contributory negligence.

(b) Non-Unanimous Juries. In Minneapolis & St. Louis R.R. v. Bombolis, 241 U.S. 211 (1916), another FELA action, the Court upheld a state provision for a civil verdict by five-sixths of the jury, after failure for twelve hours to achieve unanimity.[2] Why is that state rule valid but not a state rule on burden of proof? Can the difference be explained by whether each state rule was consistent with the (pro-plaintiff) policies of the FELA?[3]

(c) State Pleading Rules. In still another FELA case, Brown v. Western Ry., 338 U.S. 294 (1949), the plaintiff alleged certain injuries caused by "the negligence of the defendant" and provided various specifics of the circumstances of his injuries. The Georgia courts dismissed the complaint for failure to state a claim, apparently interpreting a rule that complaints must be construed "most strongly against the pleader" as requiring even more specific pleadings. The Supreme Court reversed. Justice Black's opinion acknowledged the "impossibility of laying down a precise rule to distinguish 'substance' from 'procedure,'" but found that the Court did not need to try to do so, as it was obliged to interpret the averments itself "to determine whether petitioner has been denied a right of trial granted him by Congress. This federal right cannot be defeated by the forms of local practice. * * * And we cannot accept as final a state court's interpretation of allegations in a complaint asserting it." He added: "Strict local rules of pleading cannot be used to impose unnecessary burdens upon rights of recovery authorized by federal laws."

Justice Frankfurter, joined by Justice Jackson, dissented, arguing that a litigant who chooses to enforce a federal right in state court cannot object to being treated no differently, with respect to the form in which the claim must be stated, from a litigant raising a state law claim, so long as the state requirement "does not add to, or diminish, the right as defined by Federal law, nor burden the realization of this right in the actualities of litigation." He stressed that "Congress has authorized State courts to enforce Federal rights, and Federal courts State-created rights. Neither system of courts can impair these respective rights, but both may have their own requirements for stating claims (pleading) and conducting litigation (practice)."

(d) Notice of Claim Requirements in § 1983 Actions. In Felder v. Casey, 487 U.S. 131 (1988), state law required that a plaintiff suing a governmental body or its officials must have first given the defendant notice of the claim within 120 days of the alleged injury. The state supreme court upheld dismissal of Felder's federal civil rights action under 42 U.S.C. § 1983 for failure to comply with the notice-of-claim statute. The Supreme Court reversed, concluding, *inter alia*, that the state statute burdened civil rights

---

[2]   Companion cases upheld verdicts by three-fourths, St. Louis & San Francisco R.R. v. Brown, 241 U.S. 223 (1916); Louisville & Nashville R.R. v. Stewart, 241 U.S. 261 (1916), and trial to a jury of seven, Chesapeake & Ohio Ry. v. Carnahan, 241 U.S. 241 (1916).

[3]   Despite the Bombolis decision, the Court has reversed state court judgments directing a verdict for the railroad, where the Court deemed the evidence sufficient to create an issue for the jury, although it would not overturn a jury verdict in defendant's favor. See, *e.g.*, Bailey v. Central Vermont Ry., 319 U.S. 350 (1943); Wilkerson v. McCarthy, 336 U.S. 53 (1949).

Suppose a state provided no jury in negligence actions. If the denial of a jury trial as to "one phase of fraud" diminishes a federal right in Dice, wouldn't the failure to provide any jury at all do so *a fortiori*? On the other hand, requiring state courts to convene juries when they otherwise would not is a greater burden than requiring submission of one additional issue to a jury that has already been convened. Does (should) the question whether a state procedure is displaced depend on a balancing of federal and state interests?

plaintiffs in order to serve a purpose—minimizing governmental liability—that was impermissible under federal law, and that enforcement of the statute was inconsistent with the decision in Patsy v. Board of Regents, 457 U.S. 496 (1982), p. 1394, *infra*, that exhaustion of state administrative remedies is not required in § 1983 actions. Justice Brennan's majority opinion, quoting Brown v. Western Ry., reasoned that "[f]ederal law takes state courts as it finds them only insofar as those courts employ rules that do not impose unnecessary burdens upon rights of recovery authorized by federal laws. * * * [T]he notice-of-claim statute in § 1983 actions brought in state court so interferes with and frustrates the substantive right Congress created that, under the Supremacy Clause, it must yield to the federal interest." The Court assumed that the notice-of-claim statute would not have applied in a federal court action. Comparing the question before it to the application of the Erie doctrine, the Court said that the state could not "demand[ ] compliance with outcome-determinative rules that are inapplicable when such claims are brought in federal courts." Justice O'Connor, joined by Chief Justice Rehnquist, dissented, finding that the state statute, unlike the rule in Brown, did not "diminish or alter any substantive right cognizable under § 1983."[4]

Is Felder's setting aside of a non-discriminatory state procedural rule reminiscent of Haywood's setting aside of a non-discriminatory state jurisdictional rule? Both seem concerned with states not unduly burdening federal rights. Are there grounds for defending one decision but not the other? Again, consider in this respect how Justice Thomas's argument in his dissent in Haywood—that federal rightholders are not harmed by dismissal of a claim without prejudice pursuant to state jurisdictional rules—does not apply equally to the enforcement of state procedures.

(5) Statutory Interpretation Versus Constitutional Power to Displace State Procedural Rules. In considering Dice and the power of federal courts to displace state procedural rules when adjudicating federal

---

[4]   Insofar as Felder could be read to suggest that state courts hearing § 1983 actions must follow (at least important) federal procedural rules, the Court unanimously rejected any such implication in Johnson v. Fankell, 520 U.S. 911 (1997). There, the Court ruled that, in a suit against a state official under § 1983, an Idaho court need not provide an interlocutory appeal from a trial judge's denial of a motion for summary judgment based on qualified immunity. Had the plaintiff filed her § 1983 action in federal court, such an appeal would have been permitted, on the theory that qualified immunity is " 'an entitlement not to stand trial or face the other burdens of litigation.' " Behrens v. Pelletier, 516 U.S. 299, 306 (1996). Nonetheless, the Court ruled in Johnson that Idaho rules precluding interlocutory appeals were not preempted in § 1983 actions. A key point was that the interlocutory appeal in federal court actions was provided to protect the state and its officials from overenforcement of federal rights. The state courts' failure to provide a similar protection "is thus less an interference with *federal* interests than a judgment about how best to balance the competing *state* interests of limiting interlocutory appeals and providing state officials with immediate review of the merits of their defense." The Court also concluded that Idaho's rules were "not 'outcome determinative' in the sense" used in Felder, since "postponement of the appeal until after final judgment will not affect the ultimate outcome of the case." Is that argument persuasive in view of the characterization of the purpose of immunity doctrine in the Behrens decision?

Would the Court's reasoning in Johnson apply to a federal civil rights action in state court filed against a *federal* officer (in an action under Bivens v. Six Unknown Named Agents, 403 U.S. 388 (1971), p. 918, *infra*) who had failed to remove the case to a federal court?

causes of action, consider the perspective of Hart, *The Relations Between State and Federal Law*, 54 Colum.L.Rev. 489, 508 (1954):

"The general rule, bottomed deeply in belief in the importance of state control of state judicial procedure, is that federal law takes the state courts as it finds them. * * * The Supreme Court in recent years has been disturbed by the recognition that differences between state and federal procedure may sometimes lead to different results in actions to enforce federally-created rights of which state and federal courts have concurrent jurisdiction. [Citing Dice and other FELA cases.] * * * Some differences in remedy and procedure are inescapable if the different governments are to retain a measure of independence in deciding how justice should be administered. If the differences become so conspicuous as to affect advance calculations of outcome, and so to induce an undesirable shopping between forums, the remedy does not lie in the sacrifice of the independence of either government. It lies rather in provision by the federal government, confident of the justice of its own procedure, of a federal forum equally accessible to both litigants."

Professor Hart's view has been clearly rejected by the Supreme Court in cases like Dice and Felder. But which position is more sound?

(a) Congressional Power to Prescribe Procedures in State Court. What is the scope of Congress's authority under Article I to require state courts to follow federally mandated procedures in adjudicating federal causes of action? In FELA cases, could Congress require state courts (a) to convene juries of 12, even though the state usually uses six-person juries; (b) to follow federal discovery rules; or (c) to use judges appointed by the governor (even though the state has long elected its judges)?

Consider in this regard the decision in Federal Energy Regulatory Comm'n v. Mississippi, 456 U.S. 742 (1982), also noted at p. 604, note 6, *supra*, where the Court upheld provisions of the Public Utility Regulatory Policies Act of 1978 that imposed important federal procedural requirements on state commissions regulating energy (as well as requiring the commissions to "consider" the adoption of federal substantive standards). The Court acknowledged that the Act's procedural provisions were "more intrusive" than its "hortatory" substantive provisions, but said: "If Congress can require a state administrative body to consider proposed regulations as a condition to its continued involvement in a pre-emptible field—and we hold today that it can—there is nothing unconstitutional about Congress' requiring certain procedural minima as that body goes about undertaking its tasks." Justice Powell's dissent stated that "I know of no other attempt by the Federal Government to supplant state-prescribed procedures that in part define the nature of their administrative agencies." Justice O'Connor's separate dissent objected that "[s]tate legislative and administrative bodies are not field offices of the national bureaucracy."

Neither the Court nor the dissenters alluded to Dice or the other FELA cases. Does the nature or scope of Congress's power to specify procedures that state adjudicators must follow differ for state agencies and state courts?

(b) Subconstitutional Questions: Statutory Interpretation and Judicial Policymaking. Would Professor Hart's argument be more tenable or attractive if understood to address not the *power* of Congress to impose obligations on state courts, but (i) the policies that Congress ought to follow in enacting substantive and jurisdictional legislation, (ii) the principles of statutory construction that courts should adopt in identifying the obligations that Congress has imposed, and/or (iii) the principles that should govern a judge-made federal common law of state-federal relations?

In this regard, recall that the Court in Dice was unanimous in holding that the standard governing the validity of the release is federal. If state law governing the validity of a release can be displaced as conflicting with federal purposes—even absent express statutory language so providing—why should the same not be true of state procedures? Perhaps Hart would have responded that state court procedures applied to the run of state and federal claims are unlikely to conflict with federal purposes. But even if that is true in general, what of cases where it is not? Clermont, *Reverse-Erie*, 82 Notre Dame L.Rev. 1 (2006), takes the view that these matters require interest balancing. If one agrees, does the state have a weightier interest in following its procedural rules than its rules on the validity of fraudulently obtained releases?[5]

(c) The Relevance of Plaintiff's Forum Choice. Professor Hart suggests that Dice, having chosen to file his FELA action in state rather than federal court, should be stuck with Ohio's allocation of responsibility between judge and jury. If the exercise of choice is the key, then should a state court *defendant* in a FELA action (who is barred from removing the case to federal court, see 28 U.S.C. § 1445(a)) be able to insist on a jury trial on the question of fraud in obtaining a release?

In assessing Hart's position, note that Congress may wish to give litigants the convenience of using state courts to enforce federal rights (a particularly salient point in FELA cases given the unusual statutory bar on removal) but may not be able to anticipate all of the procedural issues that might arise in the litigation of federal causes of action in state court. Further, isn't it doubtful to treat decisions about forum choice, which are motivated by many factors (for example, length of dockets; location of the court; geographical size of jury pool; identity and quality of judge), as if the parties and their lawyers had comprehensively analyzed every possible difference in state and federal procedure at the outset? Indeed, in Dice itself, when suit was filed in state court, neither the plaintiff nor his lawyer may have known that the plaintiff had signed a paper that the employee would then argue constituted a release.

(6) The Interpretation of Federal Statutes. Insofar as the question presented in cases like Testa, Douglas, and Haywood, as well as Dice and Felder, is one of statutory construction, consider the relevance of the decision in Gregory v. Ashcroft, 501 U.S. 452 (1991). There, the Court relied on some

---

[5] The decisions discussed in text involved state law rules thought to impair enforcement of federal rights in state courts. Does federal law ever preclude state courts from following procedural rules that make enforcement of those rights easier?

For two cases involving questions about the measure of damages in FELA cases, see Norfolk & Western Ry. Co. v. Liepelt, 444 U.S. 490 (1980); Monessen Southwestern Ry. Co. v. Morgan, 486 U.S. 330 (1988).

of the themes of the Usery decision and the anti-commandeering decisions in holding that the federal Age Discrimination in Employment Act, which forbids age-based mandatory retirement, does not apply to Missouri state judges, who are required by the state constitution to retire at age 70. Justice O'Connor's majority opinion reasoned that "[c]ongressional interference with this decision of the people of Missouri, defining their constitutional officers, would upset the usual constitutional balance of federal and state powers." Without questioning Congress's power to do so, Justice O'Connor held that " '[i]f Congress intends to alter "the usual constitutional balance between the States and the Federal Government," it must make its intention to do so "unmistakably clear in the language of the statute" ' " (quoting Will v. Michigan Dep't of State Police, 491 U.S. 58, 65 (1989)).

Given Gregory, does it upset the usual constitutional balance to override a discriminatory state jurisdictional rule? A non-discriminatory state rule? Should courts require that the statutory text include some language suggesting that state courts are *obliged* to hear a federal action? Recall that in deciding whether state courts are *precluded* from exercising jurisdiction, the Supreme Court has come close to holding that only statutory text can render a grant of federal jurisdiction exclusive.[6]

Is Justice Stevens's approach in Haywood, which assesses whether the state jurisdictional rule conflicts with federal policy, more appropriate, given the limited capacity of Congress both to anticipate how state jurisdictional rules might limit adjudication of federal actions and to decide up front whether those limitations should be overridden?[7]

What about state procedural rules? How clear must Congress be in order to upset the general rule that state courts adhere to their own state court procedures when adjudicating claims that arise under federal law?

(7) Reverse-Erie, the Constricted Scope of Modern Federal Common Law, & the Question of Dice's Vitality. As Justice Brennan suggested in his opinion for the Court in Felder, cases like Dice are often seen as raising "reverse-Erie" issues about the permissibility of state courts applying state procedural rules when enforcing federal rights.[8] Professor Clermont argues that cases such as Dice and Felder are properly viewed as exemplifying a broad doctrine central to understanding the relation of state and federal law in the federal system. Clermont, Paragraph (5)(a), *supra.* Criticizing Federal Courts casebooks (including earlier editions of this book)

---

[6]   In Mims v. Arrow Financial Services, LLC, 565 U.S. 368 (2012), the Court held that a statutory provision specifying that a person "may, if otherwise permitted by the laws or rules of court of a State, bring in an appropriate court of that State" an action for violation of a federal statute, did not bar the federal courts from exercising federal question jurisdiction. In response to the argument that the language authorizing state court suit would be superfluous, given the presumption of concurrent jurisdiction, unless it excluded federal jurisdiction, the Court said that "Congress arguably gave States leeway they would otherwise lack to decide whether to" exercise jurisdiction over such actions. Should that language be read to authorize states to invoke any non-discriminatory basis for declining to hear federal actions brought under this statute? To refuse to hear such actions even if their courts entertain analogous state law actions?

[7]   See generally Meltzer, *Preemption and Textualism*, 112 Mich.L.Rev. 1 (2013).

[8]   See Erie R.R. Co. v. Tompkins, 304 U.S. 64 (1938), pp. 760–764, *infra.* The term apparently originated in Baxter, *Choice of Law and the Federal System*, 16 Stan.L.Rev. 1, 34 (1963).

for treating the issue as solely one of preemption, he argues that there exists a zone of discretion in which judges must resolve "choice-of-law" issues, determining whether state or federal interests predominate, pursuant to a "balancing" test prescribed by the Supreme Court, apparently as a matter of federal common law.

Might the "reverse-Erie" label distract attention from a pertinent asymmetry, one that Clermont does acknowledge: Federal law can and frequently does preempt otherwise valid and applicable state law, whereas state law cannot preempt otherwise valid and applicable federal law? See generally Meltzer, *State Court Forfeitures of Federal Rights*, 99 Harv.L.Rev. 1128, 1176–85 (1986); Weinberg, *The Federal State Conflict of Laws: "Actual" Conflicts*, 70 Tex.L.Rev. 1743, 1773–96 (1992). However one answers that question, is Professor Clermont correct that the decisions such as Dice and Felder are better characterized as reflecting a judicial balancing of competing state and federal interests, conducted as a matter of federal common law, than as determining whether federal law preempts otherwise applicable state law?

If the decision to apply state or federal procedural law is a matter of federal common law, to what extent does the Supreme Court's recent narrowing of courts' federal common lawmaking powers call Dice and subsequent cases into question? See, *e.g.*, O'Melveny & Myers v. FDIC, 512 U.S. 79, 83–85 (1994); Hernandez v. Mesa, 589 U.S. 93, 99–102 (2020); Rodriguez v. FDIC, 589 U.S. 132, 136–38 (2020). That is, as the Court doubles down on Erie's teaching that "[t]here is no federal general common law" and grows more skeptical of expanding the scope of federal common law rules purportedly grounded in constitutional or statutory text, what is the basis for allowing Dice's exception to this rule to continue to stand?

(8) The Regulation of State Procedures When Adjudicating State Law Claims. What is the scope and appropriate use of congressional power to regulate state court procedures used in adjudicating *state law* claims? Only a few Supreme Court decisions bear directly on this question.[9]

(a) The Pierce County Decision. In Pierce County v. Guillen, 537 U.S. 129 (2003), the Court ruled unanimously that Congress possesses power under the Commerce Clause to enact a federal statute barring, in state as well as federal trials, the discovery or introduction into evidence of information "compiled or collected" in connection with certain federal highway safety programs. But the Court declined to decide (because the question had not been addressed below) whether the challenged statute "violates the principles of dual sovereignty embodied in the Tenth Amendment because it prohibits a State from exercising its sovereign powers to establish discovery and admissibility rules to be used in state court for a state cause of action."

---

[9]   For expressions of doubt about congressional power in this context, see Parmet, *Stealth Preemption: The Proposed Federalization of State Court Procedures*, 44 Vill.L.Rev. 1 (1999); Bellia, Jr., *Federal Regulation of State Court Procedures*, 110 Yale L.J. 947 (2001). For discussion of related issues, see Weinberg, *The Power of Congress Over Courts in Nonfederal Cases*, 1995 BYU L.Rev. 731; Steinman, *Reverse Removal*, 78 Iowa L.Rev. 1029 (1993).

(b) The Jinks Decision. In Jinks v. Richland County, 538 U.S. 456 (2003), the Court upheld a provision of the supplemental jurisdiction statute, 28 U.S.C. § 1367(d), that (under some circumstances) tolls the statute of limitations on state law claims while they are pending in federal court. The tolling provision requires state courts to hear claims, over which a federal court has declined to exercise supplemental jurisdiction, after the otherwise applicable state limitations period has expired. Justice Scalia's unanimous opinion first deemed the tolling provision "necessary and proper for carrying into execution Congress's power '[t]o constitute Tribunals inferior to the supreme Court,'" because it promotes the fair and efficient administration of justice by the federal courts. He then rejected a claim that, in light of principles of state sovereignty, it was not "proper" for Congress to prescribe procedural rules for the adjudication of state-law claims in state courts: assuming arguendo that federal laws regulating state court "procedure" could be distinguished from laws changing the "substance" of state-law rights of action, "we do not think that state-law limitations periods fall into the category of 'procedure' immune from congressional regulation." The Court cautioned, however, that "[t]o sustain § 1367(d) in this case, we need not (and do not) hold that Congress has unlimited power to regulate practice and procedure in state courts."

(c) Unresolved Questions. How should Congress understand the Court's reservation in both cases of the question of the ultimate scope of legislative power? As a suggestion that it is prepared to enforce as yet unstated limits on congressional action? An effort to forestall intrusive congressional action that might, however, ultimately be upheld? Or simply as a form of judicial minimalism, leaving undecided a broad question whose resolution was unnecessary to the cases at hand?

Suppose that Congress agreed with business interests that the procedures followed by certain state courts in adjudicating state law class actions are overly pro-plaintiff, have a harmful effect on interstate commerce, and are a much greater problem than the substantive law of tort or contract applied in such actions. Could Congress require state courts entertaining state law class actions to follow the procedures established in Fed.R.Civ.Proc. 23? (Note that on this score, rather than trying to regulate the state courts directly, Congress instead broadened the availability of removal of state court class actions to federal court, where federal procedures govern. See the Class Action Fairness Act of 2005 (CAFA), Pub.L.No. 109–2, 119 Stat. 4, discussed at p. 1081, *infra*.)

CHAPTER V

REVIEW OF STATE COURT DECISIONS BY THE SUPREME COURT

1. INTRODUCTION

From the beginning, proponents of the new Constitution understood it to provide for Supreme Court appellate jurisdiction over state court decisions with respect to federal matters. Thus, in Federalist No. 82, Hamilton took up the question "[w]hat relation would subsist between the national and State courts in * * * instances of concurrent jurisdiction?" To this, he answered:

"[A]n appeal would certainly lie from the latter, to the Supreme Court of the United States. The Constitution in direct terms gives an appellate jurisdiction to the Supreme Court in all the enumerated cases of federal cognizance in which it is not to have an original one, without a single expression to confine its operation to the inferior federal courts. The objects of appeal, not the tribunals from which it is to be made, are alone contemplated. From this circumstance, and from the reason of the thing, it ought to be construed to extend to the State tribunals. Either this must be the case, or the local courts must be excluded from a concurrent jurisdiction in matters of national concern, else the judiciary authority of the Union may be eluded at the pleasure of every plaintiff or prosecutor. Neither of these consequences ought, without evident necessity, to be involved; the latter would be entirely inadmissible, as it would defeat some of the most important and avowed purposes of the proposed government, and would essentially embarrass its measures. Nor do I perceive any foundation for such a supposition. Agreeably to the remark already made, the national and State systems are to be regarded as ONE WHOLE. The courts of the latter will of course be natural auxiliaries to the execution of the laws of the Union, and an appeal from them will as naturally lie to that tribunal which is destined to unite and assimilate the principles of national justice and the rules of national decisions. The evident aim of the plan of the convention is, that all the causes of the specified classes shall, for weighty public reasons, receive their original or final determination in the courts of the Union. To confine, therefore, the general expressions giving appellate jurisdiction to the Supreme Court, to appeals from the subordinate federal courts, instead of allowing their extension to the State courts, would be to abridge the latitude of the terms, in subversion of the intent, contrary to every sound rule of interpretation."[1]

This chapter sets out the framework of Article III appellate jurisdiction established by Congress, beginning with the Judiciary Act of 1789, before turning to explore the myriad questions that arise in the context of Supreme Court review of state court decisions.

---

2. THE ESTABLISHMENT OF THE JURISDICTION

NOTE ON THE DEVELOPMENT OF THE STATUTORY PROVISIONS

(1) The Judiciary Act of 1789 and the Amendments of 1867. Section 25 of the Judiciary Act of 1789[1] gave the Supreme Court mandatory jurisdiction to review specified state court judgments via a writ of error. (A writ of error was limited to matters in the record and, unlike a modern appeal, permitted review only of legal issues.[2]) The following text and accompanying footnotes show the original form of § 25 and the 1867 amendments to that provision:[3]

"Sec. 25. And be it further enacted, That a final judgment or decree in any suit, in the highest court [of law or equity][4] of a State in which a decision in the suit could be had, where is drawn in question the validity of a treaty or statute of, or an authority exercised under the United States, and the decision is against their validity; or where is drawn in question the validity of a statute of, or an authority exercised under any State, on the ground of their being repugnant to the constitution, treaties or laws of the United States, and the decision is in favour of such their validity, [or where is drawn in question the construction of any clause of the constitution, or of a treaty, or statute of, or commission held under the United States,][5] and the decision

---

[1]   Hamilton did not believe that the appellate jurisdiction was limited to the Supreme Court, continuing in No. 82 to answer in "the affirmative" the question whether an appeal could "be made to lie from the State courts to the subordinate federal judicatories." This followed, in his view, for several reasons, including the lack of specificity in the Constitution as to whether the inferior federal courts would enjoy authority "original or appellate, or both" in nature.

[1]   1 Stat. 73, 85.

[2]   See Cohens v. Virginia, 19 U.S. (6 Wheat.) 264, 409–10 (1821); Wiscart v. D'Auchy, 3 U.S. (3 Dall.) 321, 327–29 (1796) (Elsworth, C.J.).

[3]   Act of February 5, 1867 (14 Stat. 385, 386). The text is reproduced from Frankfurter & Shulman, Cases on Federal Jurisdiction and Procedure 627–28 (rev.ed.1937).

Congress re-enacted the 1867 version in substantially the same form as § 709 of the Revised Statutes (1874) and § 237 of the Judicial Code (1911); for the relevant texts, see Robertson & Kirkham, Jurisdiction of the Supreme Court of the United States, Appendix A, 931–41 (Wolfson & Kurland eds. 1951).

[4]   The 1867 Act deleted these words.

[5]   The 1867 Act substituted: "or where any title, right, privilege, or immunity is claimed under the constitution, or any treaty or statute of or commission held, or authority exercised under the United States."

is against the title, right, privilege or [exemption][6] specially set up or claimed by either party, under such [clause of the said][7] Constitution, treaty, statute [or] commission,[8] may be re-examined and reversed or affirmed in the Supreme Court of the United States upon a writ of error, the citation being signed by the chief justice, or judge or chancellor of the court rendering or passing the judgment or decree complained of, or by a justice of the Supreme Court of the United States, in the same manner and under the same regulations, and the writ shall have the same effect, as if the judgment or decree complained of had been rendered or passed in a [Circuit Court][9] and the proceeding upon the reversal shall also be the same, except that the Supreme Court, [instead of remanding the cause for a final decision as before provided,][10] may at their discretion, [if the cause shall have been once remanded before,][11] proceed to a final decision of the same, and award execution.[12] [But no other error shall be assigned or regarded as a ground of reversal in any such case as aforesaid, than such as appears on the face of the record, and immediately respects the before mentioned questions of validity or construction of the said constitution, treaties, statutes, commissions, or authorities in dispute.][13]"

(2) The Judiciary Act of 1914. As explored in Chapter III, Sec. 1, *supra*, the Judiciary Act of 1914 introduced two important features to the Supreme Court's jurisdiction. First, Congress for the first time authorized review of state court decisions *upholding* a claim of federal right;[14] previously, review extended only to judgments denying federal rights. This amendment was prompted largely by the decision in Ives v. South Buffalo Ry., 201 N.Y. 271, 94 N.E. 431 (1911), which held that the first American workers' compensation act violated both federal and state constitutional guarantees of due process. The state court's decision invalidating social legislation provoked widespread criticism and drew attention to the consequences of withholding Supreme Court review of state court decisions invalidating legislation on federal grounds. This limitation threatened disuniformity in the content of federal constitutional law among the states.[15]

---

[6] The 1867 Act substituted "immunity."

[7] The 1867 Act deleted these words.

[8] The 1867 Act added "or authority."

[9] The 1867 Act substituted "court of the United States."

[10] The 1867 Act deleted these words.

[11] The 1867 Act deleted these words.

[12] The 1867 Act added "or remand the same to an inferior court."

[13] The 1867 Act deleted these words.

[14] Act of December 23, 1914, c. 2, 38 Stat. 790. See Meltzer, *The History and Structure of Article III*, 138 U.Pa.L.Rev. 1569, 1585–92 (1990) (discussing decisions interpreting and often denying review under the pre-1914 jurisdictional statute); Hartnett, *Why Is the Supreme Court of the United States Protecting State Judges from Popular Democracy?*, 75 Tex.L.Rev. 907 (1997) (viewing the 1914 Act as a means of counteracting political pressure faced by state court judges rendering unpopular decisions, and taking the surprising view that under the Act, state officials should not have the same right as private litigants to seek Supreme Court review of unfavorable state court judgments).

[15] See Frankfurter & Landis, The Business of the Supreme Court 193–98 (1928).

Second, the 1914 Act introduced the discretionary writ of certiorari as a means of review of state court judgments.[16] Although the Act preserved mandatory review via a writ of error for cases within the pre-1914 jurisdiction, it made the newly conferred jurisdiction discretionary.

(3) Expansion of Certiorari Jurisdiction. Congress further extended the scope of discretionary review via certiorari in succeeding Acts in 1916[17] and 1925;[18] the latter preserved mandatory review only for state judgments invalidating a treaty or Act of Congress or upholding a state statute attacked on federal grounds. That distribution of mandatory and discretionary jurisdiction remained for more than a half century, with some minor changes in other provisions—most notably, the substitution, in 1928, of an appeal for a writ of error in all cases reviewable as of right.[19]

In 1988, Congress completed the gradual transition from mandatory to discretionary review of state court decisions by amending 28 U.S.C. § 1257

---

[16]   Thus, the Act made review discretionary where the state court decision was "in favor of the validity of the treaty or statute or authority exercised under the United States" or "against the validity of the State statute or authority claimed to be repugnant to the Constitution, treaties, or laws of the United States" or "in favor of the title, right, privilege, or immunity claimed under the Constitution, treaty, statute, commission, or authority of the United States."

The Evarts Act of 1891 had earlier provided for review via writ of certiorari of decisions of the federal circuit courts of appeals. See pp. 42–43, *supra.*

[17]   The Act of September 6, 1916, c. 448, § 2, 39 Stat. 726, substituted review on certiorari for the writ of error in cases where "any title, right, privilege or immunity is claimed under the Constitution, or any treaty or statute of, or commission held or authority exercised under the United States, and the decision is either in favor of or against the title, right, privilege, or immunity especially set up or claimed." The Act retained review on writ of error for decisions against the validity of "an authority exercised under the United States" and for decisions refusing to invalidate "an authority exercised under any State" as "repugnant to the Constitution, treaties, or laws of the United States." Review of the validity of claims asserted *under* an "authority," as distinguished from the validity of the authority itself, was only on certiorari. See, *e.g.,* Yazoo & Mississippi Valley R.R. v. Clarksdale, 257 U.S. 10, 15–16 & cases cited (1921). For discussion of the sometimes elusive distinction between review of the validity of legislation and review of the application of legislation, see Frankfurter & Landis, note 15, *supra,* at 211–16.

[18]   See Judges' Bill (Act of February 13, 1925, 43 Stat. 936). The Act abandoned the 1916 Act's subtle, and difficult, distinction between cases under an authority and those challenging the validity of an authority. See note 17, *supra.* A new § 237(c) authorized the Supreme Court to treat as a petition for a writ of certiorari papers improperly seeking a writ of error. Johnson, *The Origins of Supreme Court Question Selection,* 122 Colum.L.Rev. 793 (2022), observes that in the wake of the Judges' Bill, the Justices transformed certiorari review from a vehicle for deciding "the whole case" into a means of selecting specific questions for resolution (sometimes suggested by the Justices themselves) and contends the practice contravened the relevant jurisdictional statutes. For an elaborate discussion of the Judges' Bill and its aftermath, see Hartnett, *Questioning Certiorari: Some Reflections Seventy-Five Years After the Judges' Bill,* 100 Colum.L.Rev. 1643 (2000). Hartnett is critical of the certiorari jurisdiction and notes that although a denial of certiorari in a federal case merely allocates judicial power among federal courts, a denial in a state court case determines whether "the judicial power of the United States shall be called into play at all."

[19]   Act of January 31, 1928, c. 14, 45 Stat. 54, as amended, 45 Stat. 466. The 1948 revision of the Judicial Code reformulated, in 28 U.S.C. § 1257, the basic provisions conferring jurisdiction, without significant change in substance.

Under 28 U.S.C. § 2101(c), the time in which to seek Supreme Court review in civil cases is 90 days, and within this period, a Justice may extend the time to apply for not more than 60 days. Section 2101(d) defines the time in criminal cases as that "prescribed by rules of the Supreme Court," which state that a petition for a writ of certiorari is timely if filed within 90 days after the entry of the judgment of which review is sought (Rule 13.1) and that "[f]or good cause," an application to extend the time to file may be made but "is not favored" (Rule 13.5).

to eliminate appeals as of right and to make all state court judgments reviewable only by writ of certiorari.[20]

In the years since the 1988 change, the Supreme Court has reduced the number of cases that it hears annually, and the decline has been particularly sharp in cases coming from the state courts. The Court reviewed and decided with full opinions 41 cases from the state courts in 1989, 28 in 1990, and 25 in 1991. In the period spanning 1997–1999, the number ranged from 10 to 12, see Solimine, *Supreme Court Monitoring of State Courts in the Twenty-First Century*, 35 Ind.L.Rev. 335 (2002). During the 2020 Term, when the COVID-19 pandemic led the Court to decide fewer cases than it originally granted, the Court only deciding 3 cases from state courts with full opinions. That number rose to 5 in the 2022 Term. The net effect is clear: the Court is now reviewing only a handful of cases from the state courts each year.[21]

(4) Rules of the Supreme Court. Supreme Court Rules 10–16 set out the procedure on petitions for certiorari.[22] Among the considerations that the Court weighs in deciding whether to grant a petition are whether "a state court of last resort has decided an important federal question in a way that conflicts with the decision of another state court of last resort or of a United States court of appeals," and whether "a state court * * * has decided an important question of federal law that has not been, but should be, settled by this Court, or has decided an important federal question in a way that conflicts with relevant decisions of this Court." Rule 10.

INTRODUCTORY NOTE

The two principal cases that follow, Martin v. Hunter's Lessee and Murdock v. City of Memphis, are the twin pillars on which Supreme Court review of state court judgments rests. Martin is generally taken to affirm the Court's power to review *federal* issues decided in state court, while Murdock is taken to establish limits on the Court's power to review *non-federal* issues decided in state court. Both points are correct but require qualification: in the first round of Supreme Court review in Martin, the Court appears to have reviewed a non-federal issue, while in Murdock the Court discusses, at the end of its opinion, limitations on its power to review federal issues. Those complexities will be explored in more detail in Sec. 3(A), *infra*.

---

[20] Act of June 27, 1988, 102 Stat. 662. As part of this change, the 1988 Act repealed as superfluous § 2103, which permitted the Court to treat an improvidently taken appeal as a petition for certiorari. For further discussion, see Chap. III, Sec. 1, *supra*.

[21] See Statistics, J.S.Ct.U.S., Oct. Term 2020, at 487, 559, 713; Statistics, J.S.Ct.U.S., Oct. Term 2022, at 385, 613, 695.

[22] An authoritative work on Supreme Court practice is Shapiro et al., Supreme Court Practice (11th ed.2019). For further discussion, see Chap. III, Sec. 1, *supra*.

Martin v. Hunter's Lessee

14 U.S. (1 Wheat.) 304 (1816).
Error to the Court of Appeals of Virginia.

[At issue in this complex and long-running litigation was a portion of a partially unappropriated tract of Virginia land known as the Northern Neck. The land originally belonged to Lord Fairfax, a British subject but also a loyal citizen of Virginia. In 1781, Lord Fairfax bequeathed the Northern Neck to his nephew, Denny Martin Fairfax, who was a British subject. By virtue of a 1779 state statute providing for escheat of land held by a British subject, the vacant unappropriated lands of the Northern Neck became liable for escheat. Complicating Virginia's subsequent disposition of the land, however, was the fact that the commonwealth had never invoked the "inquest of office" procedure commonly required for escheat with which 1779 statute did not appear to do away, nor had it arguably effected escheat by any equivalent legislative act.* In 1785, the Virginia General Assembly passed legislation declaring that the commonwealth had the right to grant the unappropriated lands of the Northern Neck.** In 1789, Virginia then granted a portion of the Northern Neck to David Hunter.

[In 1791, Hunter initiated on behalf of his lessee an action for ejectment from a tract of land in Shenandoah County against Denny Martin Fairfax and later Philip Martin, who inherited Fairfax's interests. In the course of what turned out to be extensively drawn out litigation, Hunter's claim would rest at various points upon (a) the 1789 grant; (b) the assertion that Denny Martin Fairfax, as an alien, could not validly take ownership of the land and that his land had, in any case, escheated to the state pursuant to the 1779 Virginia statute; and (c) that any claims to the land had been resolved by a 1796 Virginia statute styled as an "Act of Compromise," which purported to settle the controversy, in part, by confirming Hunter's interest in the disputed lands. A potential conflict between state and federal law arose from Martin's counterarguments that the commonwealth had not taken the steps necessary for escheat under the 1779 Virginia statute (namely, there had been no inquest of office) and that the Treaty of Paris, adopted in 1783, and later the Jay Treaty of 1794 protected his interests.*** It followed, in

---

    *   [Ed.] The concept of escheatment is generally understood as the power of the state as sovereign to take ownership of property deemed abandoned. See Texas v. New Jersey, 379 U.S. 674, 675 (1965).

    The common law requirement of inquest of office involved extensive proceedings, including employment of jurors of the vicinage, to ensure that the Crown's claim to any lands had merit. For a more detailed description of the process. See 3 Blackstone Commentaries 258. The process was to protect "the liberties of England, and * * * the safety of the subject" from unlawful takings of property by the Crown. *Id.* 259.

    **   [Ed.] See Hobson, *John Marshall and the Fairfax Litigation: The Background of Martin v. Hunter's Lessee*, 1996 J.Sup.Ct.Hist. 36, 38 (vol. 2), from which some of the description is taken.

    ***   [Ed.] The 1783 Treaty of Paris provided that there should be no future confiscations of property against persons "for, or by reason of the part which he or they may have taken in the present war." Definitive Treaty of Peace Between the United States of America and his

Martin's view, that the federal treaties superseded any and all subsequent attempts by the commonwealth to transfer the Fairfax-Martin interests to Hunter.

[In 1794, a Virginia district court comprised of Judges St. George Tucker and William Nelson upheld title in the Fairfax line.**** After considerable delay, the Virginia Court of Appeals reversed that judgment in 1810. Writing for the appellate court, Judge Spencer Roane—John Marshall's political enemy—concluded that the commonwealth had validly obtained title under the terms of the 1779 Virginia statute prior to ratification of the Treaty of Paris. He also ruled that the Act of Compromise settled the matter in Hunter's favor. Hunter v. Fairfax's Devisee, 15 Va. (1 Munf.) 218, 231–32. Judge Fleming concurred solely on the basis of the Act of Compromise.

[On writ of error, the Supreme Court reversed. Fairfax's Devisee v. Hunter's Lessee, 11 U.S. (7 Cranch) 603 (1813). Justice Story's opinion held that none of the relevant Virginia acts altered the common law requirement of "inquest of office" to vest title in the Commonwealth; hence, the Fairfax-Martin title was undivested by the time of ratification of the 1794 Jay Treaty, which unquestionably protected the property interests of British subjects who owned American land. Justice Johnson dissented on the ground that the Virginia legislature was competent to dispense with an inquest of office. Justice Johnson agreed, however, that under § 25 of the Judiciary Act an inquiry into title was necessary and "must, in the nature of things, precede the consideration how far the law, treaty and so forth, is applicable to it, otherwise an appeal to this Court would be worse than nugatory." Neither Story nor Johnson mentioned the Act of Compromise. (Chief Justice Marshall, who had been a member of a syndicate that purchased part of the Fairfax estate, did not participate.)

[The Supreme Court mandate, which it directed to "the Honourable the Judges of the Court of Appeals in and for the Commonwealth of Virginia," "adjudged and ordered, that the judgment of the Court of Appeals * * * in this case be, and the same is hereby reversed and annulled, and that the judgment of the [Superior Court] be affirmed, with costs; and it is further ordered, that the said cause be remanded to the said Court of Appeals * * * with instructions to enter judgment for the appellant." It ended with the formal provision: "You therefore are hereby commanded that such proceedings be had in said cause, as according to right and justice, and the laws of the United States, and agreeably to said judgment and instructions of said Supreme Court ought to be had, the

---

Britannic Majesty, Gr. Brit.-U.S., art. VI, Sept. 3, 1783, 8 Stat. 80. The Jay Treaty provided that British subjects holding property in the United States would enjoy the same rights as U.S. citizens. Treaty of Amity, Commerce and Navigation, Between his Britannic Majesty and the United States of America, Gr. Brit.-U.S., Nov. 19, 1794, 8 Stat. 116.

**** [Ed.] The parties stipulated in the trial court that no inquest of office had occurred.

said writ of error notwithstanding." Hunter v. Martin, Devisee of Fairfax, 18 Va. (4 Munf. 1) 2–3.

["The question, whether this mandate should be obeyed, excited all that attention from the bench and bar, which its great importance truly merited"; and after oral argument, on December 16, 1815, the judges of that court (Cabell, Brooke, Roane and Fleming) expressed their separate opinions *seriatim* but unanimously joined in the following conclusion:

["[T]he appellate power of the Supreme Court of the United States, does not extend to this court, under a sound construction of the constitution of the United States;—that so much of the 25th section of the act of congress * * * as extends the appellate jurisdiction of the Supreme Court to this court, is not in pursuance of the constitution of the United States; that the writ of error in this case was improvidently allowed under the authority of that act; that proceedings thereon in the Supreme Court were *coram non judice* in relation to this court; and that obedience to its mandate be declined by this court."

[The common grounds for this conclusion of the Virginia judges are indicated by the following excerpts from Judge Cabell's opinion:

["The present government of the United States, grew out of the weakness and inefficacy of the confederation, and was intended to remedy its evils. Instead of a government of *requisition*, we have a government of power. But how does that power operate? On individuals in their individual capacities. No one presumes to contend, that the state governments can operate compulsively on the general government or any of its departments, even in cases of unquestionable encroachment on state authority. * * * I can perceive nothing in the constitution which gives to the Federal Courts any stronger claim to prevent or redress, *by any procedure acting on the state* Courts, an equally obvious encroachment on the Federal jurisdiction. The constitution of the United States contemplates the independence of both governments, and regards the *residuary* sovereignty of the states, as not less inviolable, than the *delegated* sovereignty of the United States. It must have been foreseen that controversies would sometimes arise as to the boundaries of the two jurisdictions. Yet the constitution has provided no umpire, has erected no tribunal by which they shall be settled. The omission proceeded, probably, from the belief, that such a tribunal would produce evils greater than those of the occasional collisions which it would be designed to remedy. * * *

["If this Court should now proceed to enter a judgment in this case, according to the instructions of the Supreme Court, the Judges of this Court, in doing so, must act either as Federal or as State Judges. But we cannot be made Federal Judges without our consent, and without commissions. * * * We must, then, in obeying this mandate, be considered still as State Judges. We are required, as State Judges to enter up a judgment, not our own, but dictated and prescribed to us by another Court. * * * But, before one Court can dictate to another, the judgment it shall pronounce, it must bear, to that other, the relation of an appellate Court. The term appellate, however, necessarily includes the idea of *superiority*. But one Court cannot be correctly said to be *superior* to another, unless both of them belong to the same sovereignty. It would be a misapplication of terms to say that a Court of Virginia is *superior* to a Court of Maryland, or *vice versa*. The Courts of the United States, therefore, belonging to one sovereignty, cannot be appellate Courts in relation to the State Courts, which belong to a different sovereignty * * *. * * *

["If, therefore, I am correct in this position, the appellate jurisdiction of the Supreme Court of the United States [under the constitution], must have reference to the inferior Courts of the United States, and not to the State Courts. * * * It has been contended that the constitution contemplated only the objects of appeal, and not the tribunals from which the appeal is to be taken * * *. But this argument proves too much * * *. It would give appellate jurisdiction, as well over the courts of England or France, as over the State courts; for, although I do not think the State Courts are *foreign* Courts in relation to the Federal Courts, yet I consider them not less *independent* than foreign Courts."

[To the argument that Supreme Court review of state decisions was necessary to ensure uniformity, Judge Cabell replied: "All the purposes of the constitution of the United States will be answered by the erection of Federal Courts, into which any party, plaintiff or defendant, concerned in a case of federal cognizance, *may* carry it for adjudication." Judges Brooke and Fleming apparently shared this opinion, on which Judge Roane expressed no view.

[Judges Roane and Fleming offered an additional ground for decision—that the case fell outside § 25 since the record did not show that the decision turned upon the federal treaty (see the last sentence of the text of section 25 on p. 617, *supra*) and that if the Supreme Court "had held itself at liberty, to go outside of the record," the report of the decision of the Virginia Court would have shown that it was based on the Act of Compromise.

[The case returned to the Supreme Court on a second writ of error brought by Philip Martin.*****]

■ STORY, J., delivered the opinion of the court.

     * * *

The constitution of the United States was ordained and established, not by the states in their sovereign capacities, but emphatically, as the preamble of the constitution declares, by "the People of the United

---

***** [Ed.] White, The Marshall Court and Cultural Change, 1815–1835, at 167–68 (1988), argues that John Marshall drafted the second petition for a writ of error. See also Hobson, note **, *supra*, at 48 (suggesting that Marshall helped prepare arguments for the use of counsel).

The third judge on the Court of Appeals was Judge St. George Tucker, who recused himself because by the time the case came up on appeal, his son had married Hunter's daughter.

States." There can be no doubt, that it was competent to the people to invest the general government with all the powers which they might deem proper and necessary * * * and to give them a paramount and supreme authority. As little doubt can there be, that the people had a right to prohibit to the states the exercise of any powers which were, in their judgment, incompatible with the objects of the general compact; to make the powers of the state governments, in given cases, subordinate to those of the nation, or to reserve to themselves those sovereign authorities which they might not choose to delegate to either. The constitution was not, therefore, necessarily carved out of existing state sovereignties, nor a surrender of powers already existing in state institutions * * *. On the other hand, it is perfectly clear that the sovereign powers vested in the state governments, by their respective constitutions, remained unaltered and unimpaired, except so far as they were granted to the government of the United States.

These deductions do not rest upon general reasoning, plain and obvious as they seem to be. They have been positively recognised by one of the articles in amendment of the constitution, which declares, that "the powers not delegated to the United States by the constitution, nor prohibited by it to the *states*, are reserved to the states respectively, or *to the people*." * * *

The third article of the constitution is that which must principally attract our attention. * * *

[Here, Justice Story developed the view that Article III's language is "designed to be mandatory" upon Congress. See pp. 410–413, *supra*.]

* * * [A]ppellate jurisdiction is given by the constitution to the supreme court in all cases where it has not original jurisdiction; subject, however, to such exceptions and regulations as congress may prescribe. It is, therefore, capable of embracing every case enumerated in the constitution, which is not exclusively to be decided by way of original jurisdiction. But the exercise of appellate jurisdiction is far from being limited by the terms of the constitution to the supreme court. There can be no doubt that congress may create a succession of inferior tribunals, in each of which it may vest appellate as well as original jurisdiction. * * *

As, then, by the terms of the constitution, the appellate jurisdiction is not limited as to the supreme court, and as to this court it may be exercised in all other cases than those of which it has original cognizance, what is there to restrain its exercise over state tribunals in the enumerated cases? The appellate power is not limited by the terms of the third article to any particular courts. The words are, "the judicial power (which includes appellate power) shall extend *to all cases*," & c., and "in all other cases before mentioned the supreme court shall have appellate jurisdiction." It is the *case*, then, and not *the court*, that gives the jurisdiction. * * *

If the constitution meant to limit the appellate jurisdiction to cases pending in the courts of the United States, it would necessarily follow that the jurisdiction of these courts would, in all the cases enumerated in the constitution, be exclusive of state tribunals. How otherwise could the jurisdiction extend to *all* cases arising under the constitution, laws, and treaties of the United States, or *to all cases* of admiralty and maritime jurisdiction? If some of these cases might be entertained by state tribunals, and no appellate jurisdiction as to them should exist, then the appellate power would not extend to *all*, but to *some*, cases. If state tribunals might exercise concurrent jurisdiction over all or some of the other classes of cases in the constitution without control, then the appellate jurisdiction of the United States might, as to such cases, have no real existence, contrary to the manifest intent of the constitution. Under such circumstances, to give effect to the judicial power, it must be construed to be exclusive; and this not only when the *casus foederis* should arise directly, but when it should arise, incidentally, in cases pending in state courts. This construction would abridge the jurisdiction of such court far more than has been ever contemplated in any act of congress.

On the other hand, if, as has been contended, a discretion be vested in congress to establish, or not to establish, inferior courts at their own pleasure, and congress should not establish such courts, the appellate jurisdiction of the supreme court would have nothing to act upon, unless it could act upon cases pending in the state courts. Under such circumstances it must be held that the appellate power would extend to state courts; for the constitution is peremptory that it shall extend to certain enumerated cases, which cases could exist in no other courts. Any other construction, upon this supposition, would involve this strange contradiction, that a discretionary power vested in congress, and which they might rightfully omit to exercise, would defeat the absolute injunctions of the constitution in relation to the whole appellate power. * * *

A moment's consideration will show us the necessity and propriety of this provision in cases where the jurisdiction of the state courts is unquestionable. * * * Suppose an indictment for a crime in a state court, and the defendant should allege in his defence that the crime was created by an *ex post facto* act of the state, must not the state court, in the exercise of a jurisdiction which has already rightfully attached, have a right to pronounce on the validity and sufficiency of the defence? It would be extremely difficult, upon any legal principles, to give a negative answer * * *. Innumerable instances of the same sort might be stated, in illustration of the position; and unless the state courts could sustain jurisdiction in such cases, this clause of the sixth article would be without meaning or effect, and public mischiefs, of a most enormous magnitude, would inevitably ensue.

It must, therefore, be conceded that the constitution not only contemplated, but meant to provide for cases within the scope of the judicial power of the United States, which might yet depend before state tribunals. It was foreseen that in the exercise of their ordinary jurisdiction, state courts would incidentally take cognizance of cases arising under the constitution, the laws, and treaties of the United States. Yet to all these cases the judicial power, by the very terms of the constitution, is to extend. It cannot extend by original jurisdiction if that was already rightfully and exclusively attached in the state courts * * *. It would seem to follow that the appellate power of the United States must, in such cases, extend to state tribunals * * *.

It is further argued, that no great public mischief can result from a construction which shall limit the appellate power of the United States to cases in their own courts: first, because state judges are bound by an oath to support the constitution of the United States, and must be presumed to be men of learning and integrity; and, secondly, because congress must have an unquestionable right to remove all cases within the scope of the judicial power from the state courts to the courts of the United States, at any time before final judgment, though not after final judgment. As to the first reason—admitting that the judges of the state courts are, and always will be, of as much learning, integrity, and wisdom, as those of the courts of the United States, (which we very cheerfully admit,) it does not aid the argument. It is manifest that the constitution has proceeded upon a theory of its own, and given or withheld powers according to the judgment of the American people, by whom it was adopted. We can only construe its powers, and cannot inquire into the policy or principles which induced the grant of them. The constitution has presumed (whether rightly or wrongly we do not inquire) that state attachments, state prejudices, state jealousies, and state interests, might sometimes obstruct, or control, or be supposed to obstruct or control, the regular administration of justice. Hence, in controversies between states; between citizens of different states; between citizens claiming grants under different states; between a state and its citizens, or foreigners, and between citizens and foreigners, it enables the parties, under the authority of congress, to have the controversies heard, tried, and determined before the national tribunals. No other reason than that which has been stated can be assigned, why some, at least, of those cases should not have been left to the cognizance of the state courts. In respect to the other enumerated cases—the cases arising under the constitution, laws, and treaties of the United States, cases affecting ambassadors and other public ministers, and cases of admiralty and maritime jurisdiction—reasons of a higher and more extensive nature, touching the safety, peace, and sovereignty of the nation, might well justify a grant of exclusive jurisdiction.

This is not all. A motive of another kind, perfectly compatible with the most sincere respect for state tribunals, might induce the grant of appellate power over their decisions. That motive is the importance, and even necessity of *uniformity* of decisions throughout the whole United States * * *. Judges of equal learning and integrity, in different states, might differently interpret a statute, or a treaty of the United States, or even the constitution itself: If there were no revising authority to control these jarring and discordant judgments, and harmonize them into uniformity, the laws, the treaties, and the constitution of the United States would be different in different states * * *. The public mischiefs that would attend such a state of things would be truly deplorable; * * * and the appellate jurisdiction must continue to be the only adequate remedy for such evils.

There is an additional consideration, which is entitled to great weight. * * * The judicial power was * * * not to be exercised exclusively for the benefit of parties who might be plaintiffs, and would elect the national forum, but also for the protection of defendants who might be entitled to try their rights, or assert their privileges, before the same forum. Yet, if the construction contended for be correct, it will follow, that as the plaintiff may always elect the state court, the defendant may be deprived of all the security which the constitution intended in aid of his rights. Such a state of things can, in no respect, be considered as giving equal rights. To obviate this difficulty, we are referred to the power which it is admitted congress possess to remove suits from state courts to the national courts; and this forms the second ground upon which the argument we are considering has been attempted to be sustained.

This power of removal is not to be found in express terms in any part of the constitution; if it be given, it is only given by implication * * *. [I]t presupposes an exercise of original jurisdiction to have attached elsewhere. * * * If, then, the right of removal be included in the appellate jurisdiction, it is only because it is one mode of exercising that power, and as congress is not limited by the constitution to any particular mode, or time of exercising it, it may authorize a removal either before or after judgment. * * * A writ of error is, indeed, but a process which removes the record of one court to the possession of another court, and enables the latter to inspect the proceedings, and give such judgment as its own opinion of the law and justice of the case may warrant. * * *

The remedy, too, of removal of suits would be utterly inadequate to the purposes of the constitution, if it could act only on the parties, and not upon the state courts. * * * If state courts should deny the constitutionality of the authority to remove suits from their cognizance, in what manner could they be compelled to relinquish the jurisdiction? In respect to criminal cases, there would at once be an end of all control, and the state decisions would be paramount to the constitution; and though in civil suits the courts of the United States might act upon the parties, yet the state courts might act in the same way; and this conflict of jurisdictions would not only jeopardise private rights, but bring into imminent peril the public interests.

On the whole, the court are of opinion, that the appellate power of the United States does extend to cases pending in the state courts; and that the 25th section of the judiciary act, which authorizes the exercise of this jurisdiction in the specified cases, by a writ of error, is supported by the letter and spirit of the constitution. * * *

Strong as this conclusion stands upon the general language of the constitution, it may still derive support from other sources. It is an historical fact, that this exposition of the constitution, extending its appellate power to state courts, was, previous to its adoption, uniformly and publicly avowed by its friends, and admitted by its enemies, as the basis of their respective reasonings, both in and out of the state conventions. It is an historical fact, that at the time when the judiciary act was submitted to the deliberations of the first congress, composed, as it was, not only of men of great learning and ability, but of men who had acted a principal part in framing, supporting, or opposing that constitution, the same exposition was explicitly declared and admitted by the friends and by the opponents of that system. It is an historical fact, that the supreme court of the United States have, from time to time, sustained this appellate jurisdiction in a great variety of cases, brought from the tribunals of many of the most important states in the union, and that no state tribunal has ever breathed a judicial doubt on the subject, or declined to obey the mandate of the supreme court, until the present occasion. * * *

The next question which has been argued, is, whether the case at bar be within the purview of the 25th section of the judiciary act, so that this court may rightfully sustain the present writ of error. * * *

That the present writ of error is founded upon a judgment of the court below, which drew in question and denied the validity of a statute of the United States, is incontrovertible, for it is apparent upon the face of the record. * * *

But it is contended, that the former judgment of this court was rendered upon a case not within the purview of this section of the judicial act, and that as it was pronounced by an incompetent jurisdiction, it was utterly void, and cannot be a sufficient foundation to sustain any subsequent proceedings. * * * [I]n ordinary cases a second writ of error has never been supposed to draw in question the propriety of the first judgment * * *. * * *

In this case, however, from motives of a public nature, we are entirely willing to wa[i]ve all objections, and to go back and re-examine the question of jurisdiction as it stood upon the record formerly in judgment. * * *

The objection urged at the bar is, that this court cannot inquire into the title, but simply into the correctness of the construction put upon the treaty by the court of appeals; and that their judgment is not re-examinable here, unless it appear on the face of the record that some construction was put upon the treaty. If, therefore, that court might have decided the case upon the invalidity of the title, (and, *non constat,* that they did not,) independent of the treaty, there is an end of the appellate jurisdiction of this court. In support of this objection much stress is laid upon the last clause of [§ 25, see p. 617, *supra*], which declares, that no other cause shall be regarded as a ground of reversal than such as appears *on the face* of the record and *immediately* respects the construction of the treaty, & c., in dispute.

If this be the true construction of the section, it will be wholly inadequate for the purposes which it professes to have in view, and may be evaded at pleasure. But we see no reason for adopting this narrow construction; and there are the strongest reasons against it, founded upon the words as well as the intent of the legislature. What is the case for which the body of the section provides a remedy by writ of error? The answer must be in the words of the section, a suit where is drawn in question the construction of a treaty, and the decision is against *the title set up by the party.* It is, therefore, the decision against the title set up with reference to the treaty, and not the mere abstract construction of the treaty itself, upon which the statute intends to found the appellate jurisdiction. How, indeed, can it be possible to decide whether a title be within the protection of a treaty, until it is ascertained what that title is, and whether it have a legal validity? From the very necessity of the case, there must be a preliminary inquiry into the existence and structure of the title, before the Court can construe the treaty in reference to that title. If the Court below should decide, that the title was bad, and, therefore, not protected by the treaty, must not this Court have a power to decide the title to be good, and, therefore, protected by the treaty? * * * One of the questions is as to the construction of a treaty upon a title specially set up by a party, and every error that immediately respects that question must, of course, be within the cognizance, of the court. The title set up in this case is apparent upon the face of the record, and immediately respects the decision of that question; any error, therefore, in respect to that title must be re-examinable, or the case could never be presented to the Court.

The restraining clause was manifestly intended for a very different purpose. It was foreseen that the parties might claim under various titles, and might assert various defences, altogether independent of each other. The court might admit or reject evidence applicable to one particular title, and not to all, and in such cases it was the intention of congress to limit what would otherwise have unquestionably attached to the court, the right of revising all the points involved in the cause. It therefore restrains this right to such errors as respect the questions specified in the section; and in this view, it has an appropriate sense, consistent with the preceding clauses. We are, therefore, satisfied, that, upon principle, the case was rightfully before us, and if the point were perfectly new, we should not hesitate to assert the jurisdiction. * * *

It has been asserted at the bar that, in point of fact, the court of appeals did not decide either upon the treaty or the title apparent upon the record, but upon a compromise made under an act of the legislature of Virginia. If it be true (as we are informed) that this was a private act, to take effect only upon a certain condition, viz. the execution of a deed of release of certain lands, which was matter *in pais*, it is somewhat difficult to understand how the court could take judicial cognizance of the act, or of the performance of the condition, unless spread upon the record. At all events, we are bound to consider that the court did decide upon the facts actually before them. The treaty of peace was not necessary to have been stated, for it was the supreme law of the land, of which all courts must take notice. And at the time of the decision in the court of appeals and in this court, another treaty had intervened, which attached itself to the title in controversy, and, of course, must have been the supreme law to govern the decision, if it should be found applicable to the case. It was in this view that this court did not deem it necessary to rest its former decision upon the treaty of peace, believing that the title of the defendant was, at all events, perfect under the treaty of 1794. * * *

We have not thought it incumbent on us to give any opinion upon the question, whether this court have authority to issue a writ of mandamus to the court of appeals to enforce the former judgments, as we do not think it necessarily involved in the decision of this cause.

It is the opinion of the whole court, that the judgment of the court of appeals of Virginia, rendered on the mandate in this cause, be reversed, and the judgment of the district court, held at Winchester, be, and the same is hereby affirmed.

■ JOHNSON, J., * * * In this act I can see nothing which amounts to an assertion of the inferiority or dependence of the state tribunals. The presiding judge of the state court is himself authorized to issue the writ of error, if he will, and thus give jurisdiction to the supreme court: and if he thinks proper to decline it, no compulsory process is provided by law to oblige him. The party who imagines himself aggrieved is then at liberty to apply to a judge of the United States, who issues the writ of error, which (whatever the form) is, in substance, no more than a mode of compelling the opposite party to appear before this court, and maintain the legality of his judgment obtained before the state tribunal. An exemplification of a record is the common property of every one who chooses to apply and pay for it, and thus the case and the parties are brought before us; and so far is the court itself from being brought under the revising power of this court, that nothing but the case, as presented by the record and pleadings of the parties, is considered, and the opinions of the court are never resorted to unless for the purpose of assisting this court in forming their own opinions.

The absolute necessity that there was for congress to exercise something of a revising power over cases and parties in the state courts, will appear from this consideration.

Suppose the whole extent of the judicial power of the United States vested in their own courts, yet such a provision would not answer all the ends of the constitution, for two reasons:

1st. Although the plaintiff may, in such case, have the full benefit of the constitution extended to him, yet the defendant would not; as the plaintiff might force him into the court of the state at his election.

2dly. Supposing it possible so to legislate as to give the courts of the United States original jurisdiction in all cases arising under the constitution, laws, & c., in the words of the 2d section of the 3d article, (a point on which I have some doubt, and which in time might, perhaps, under some *quo minus* fiction, or a willing construction, greatly accumulate the jurisdiction of those courts,) yet a very large class of cases would remain unprovided for. Incidental questions would often arise, and as a court of competent jurisdiction in the principal case must decide all such questions, whatever laws they arise under, endless might be the diversity of decisions throughout the union upon the constitution, treaties, and laws, of the United States * * *.

I should feel the more hesitation in adopting the opinions which I express in this case, were I not firmly convinced that they are practical, and may be acted upon without compromising the harmony of the union, or bringing humility upon the state tribunals. God forbid that the judicial power in these states should ever, for a moment, even in its humblest departments, feel a doubt of its own independence. Whilst adjudicating on a subject which the laws of the country assign finally to the revising power of another tribunal, it can feel no such doubt. An anxiety to do justice is ever relieved by the knowledge that what we do is not final between the parties. And no sense of dependence can be felt from the knowledge that the parties, not the court, may be summoned before another tribunal. With this view, by means of laws, avoiding judgments obtained in the state courts in cases over which congress has constitutionally assumed jurisdiction, and inflicting penalties on parties who shall contumaciously persist in infringing the constitutional rights of others—under a liberal extension of the writ of injunction and the *habeas corpus ad subjiciendum*, I flatter myself that the full extent of the constitutional revising power may be secured to the United States, and the benefits of it to the individual, without ever resorting to compulsory or restrictive process upon the state tribunals; a right which, I repeat again, congress has not asserted, nor has this court asserted, nor does there appear any necessity for asserting. * * *

NOTE ON THE ATTACKS UPON THE JURISDICTION

(1) **State Resistance to § 25.** Between 1789 and 1860 the courts of Virginia, Ohio, Georgia, Kentucky, South Carolina, California, and Wisconsin denied that the Supreme Court had the power to review state

court judgments on writs of error. The legislatures of all these states (except California), and of Pennsylvania and Maryland, adopted measures denying this power to the Supreme Court. Members of Congress introduced bills on at least ten occasions between 1821 and 1882 to deprive the Court of such jurisdiction.[1] The arguments advanced in these attacks ranged from the relatively narrow grounds adduced in the Martin case to the extreme position that each state had an equal right to adopt its own interpretation of the Constitution.[2] The Court's position, as defined by Justice Story, did not change throughout the period of controversy.[3]

---

[1]   Warren, *Legislative and Judicial Attacks on the Supreme Court of the United States— A History of the Twenty-Fifth Section of the Judiciary Act, Part I*, 47 Am.L.Rev. 1, 3–4 (1913); see also Part II of Warren's article, 47 *id.* 161. For an argument that the jurisdiction conferred upon the Supreme Court by § 25 may be constitutionally required by the political compromise that made the Supremacy Clause (rather than a congressional veto) the mechanism for enforcing federal supremacy, see LaCroix, *On Being "Bound Thereby"*, 27 Const.Comm. 507 (2011). Does that structural inference represent a plausible implied limitation on congressional power given Article III's Exceptions Clause? See pp. 422–428, *supra.*

[2]   See generally Haines, The Role of the Supreme Court in American Government and Politics 499–577 (1944); Reference Note, *Interposition vs. Judicial Power—A Study of Ultimate Authority in Constitutional Questions*, 1 Race Rel.L.Rep. 465 (1956); Goldstein, Constituting Federal Sovereignty: The European Union in Comparative Context 20, 22–33, 161–71 (2001).

Goldstein contends that the "American states, intermittently but in a steady, and not regionally concentrated stream, resisted federal authority when feelings in particular states on particular issues ran high. * * * Tax laws, debtor laws, controversies over land ownership, embargo laws, laws concerning Native Americans, laws concerning the banking system, laws concerning judicial procedures, laws regulating speech and press, fugitive slave laws—all at one time or another provoked state denial of federal judicial authority." She details more than fifty instances of resistance (defined to include formal public pronouncements by governors, majority decisions of state appellate courts, or majority votes or resolutions of legislative bodies) by 20 of the 33 states admitted to the Union prior to the Civil War.

[3]   Chief Justice Marshall authored multiple opinions defending the importance of state respect for federal decisions. Writing for the Court ten years before Martin in United States v. Peters, 5 Cranch. (9 U.S.) 115 (1809), for example, Marshall contended that it would undermine the basic structure of the new federal plan if state legislatures could disregard federal court decisions: "If the legislature of the several states may, at will, annul the judgments of the courts of the United States, and destroy the rights acquired under those judgments, the constitution itself becomes a solemn mockery, and the nation is deprived of the means of enforcing its laws by the instrumentality of its own tribunals." Peters involved the question whether the federal tribunal erected under the Articles of Confederation, the Committee of Appeals, see pp. 7–8, *supra*, "had full authority to revise and correct the sentences of the courts of admiralty of the several states, in prize causes." Having decided the question in the affirmative in earlier decisions, the Court responded in Peters to the Pennsylvania legislature's continuing recalcitrance to one such decision by declaring "[t]hat question" to be "at rest."

Later, in Cohens v. Virginia, 19 U.S. (6 Wheat.) 264 (1821), a writ of error to review a state court judgment affirming a criminal conviction, Chief Justice Marshall reiterated, for the Court, the position taken in Martin. He also rejected two additional contentions urged against the jurisdiction. The first was that the Eleventh Amendment (or general notions of state sovereign immunity) barred the writ of error as a prohibited suit against the state. (For a reaffirmation of this aspect of Cohens, see McKesson Corp. v. Division of ABT, 496 U.S. 18, 26–28 (1990).) The second was that Article III's grant of original jurisdiction to the Supreme Court in cases in which a state is a party precludes the Court's exercise of *appellate* jurisdiction in such a case. The Court did not respond to Virginia's third objection—that Article III's grant of federal question jurisdiction does not extend to criminal cases.

See generally Graber, *The Passive-Aggressive Virtues: Cohens v. Virginia and the Problematic Establishment of Judicial Power*, 12 Const.Comm. 67 (1995) (suggesting that the ruling on the merits in Cohens—that the state court conviction did not violate federal law—was implausible, but may have reflected the same strategy deployed in Marbury v. Madison: to make an assertion of judicial power politically palatable by refusing in the end to award relief); Newmyer, *John Marshall, McCulloch v. Maryland, and the Southern States' Rights Tradition*, 33 John Marshall L.Rev. 875 (2000) (discussing Cohens in the context of Marshall's response to

The remedies proposed by dissidents included repeal of § 25, *e.g.*, H.R.Rep. No. 43, 21st Cong., 2d Sess. (1831), and constitutional amendments depriving the courts of authority to annul legislation, vesting jurisdiction in the Senate, or establishing a new tribunal to mediate between the nation and the states.[4]

(2) Supreme Court Review Today. The constitutional validity of the Court's jurisdiction to review state court decisions has not been seriously challenged in recent years.[5] For example, although the Court's decision in Bush v. Gore, 531 U.S. 98 (2000), sparked great controversy, it did not generate attacks on the Court's jurisdiction.[6]

A half century before Bush v. Gore, however, Brown v. Board of Education, 347 U.S. 483 (1954), did provoke challenges to the authoritativeness of Court decisions, including "interposition" resolutions by state legislatures reminiscent of the pre-Civil War pattern.[7] There have also been more recent attempts—none successful—to restrict the Court's

---

anti-Court sentiment). For further discussion of Cohens, see LaCroix, *Federalists, Federalism, and Federal Jurisdiction*, 30 Law & Hist.Rev. 205, 237–40 (2012).

    [4]   See Ames, The Proposed Amendments to the Constitution of the United States During the First Century of its History 158–63 (1896).

    [5]   James v. City of Boise, 577 U.S. 306 (2016) (per curiam), summarily reversed a decision of the Idaho Supreme Court refusing to follow the Supreme Court's interpretation of a federal statute. In civil rights cases brought in state court pursuant to 42 U.S.C. § 1983, state court judges may "allow the prevailing party * * * a reasonable attorney's fee." *Id.* § 1988. Notwithstanding the fact that § 1988 refers to "the prevailing party" without qualification, the Court in Hughes v. Rowe, 449 U.S. 5 (1980) (per curiam), held that a prevailing *defendant* may recover fees only if the court finds that the plaintiff filed a frivolous lawsuit. In James, the Idaho Supreme Court held that the Supreme Court of the United States lacked " 'the authority to limit the discretion of state courts where such limitation is not contained in the statute.' " In a two-page per curiam opinion, the Supreme Court reversed. Quoting Justice Story's opinion for the Court in Martin, the Court wrote that "if state courts were permitted to disregard this Court's rulings on federal law, 'the laws, the treaties, and the constitution of the United States would be different in different states, and might, perhaps, never have precisely the same construction, obligation, or efficacy, in any two states. The public mischiefs that would attend such a state of things would be truly deplorable.' "

    Did the Idaho Supreme Court technically contradict Martin when it refused to follow a precedent rather than a judgment of the Supreme Court? Given the modern Court's sharply limited capacity to review cases, would the refusal of state courts to acquiesce in the Court's interpretation of federal law compromise federal uniformity almost as much?

    [6]   In fact, some commentators believe that the Court's exercise of "vertical" authority to review state court judgments helped it to establish and maintain "horizontal" authority to review the actions by the coordinate federal branches. For example, to the extent that national political leaders found it necessary to bolster the Court's final authority to enforce the supremacy of federal law against the states, those leaders often incidentally bolstered the Court's position as the final arbiter of legality more generally. In addition, particularly after the Court incorporated the Bill of Rights against the states, the exercise of federal judicial power to invalidate state statutes under provisions such as the First Amendment made it harder for Congress and the President to resist judicial enforcement of similar limitations against the federal government. See Friedman & Delaney, *Becoming Supreme: The Federal Foundation of Judicial Supremacy*, 111 Colum.L.Rev. 1137 (2011).

    [7]   See, *e.g.*, Driver, *Supremacies and the Southern Manifesto*, 92 Tex.L.Rev. 1053, 1089–93 (2014) (discussing the range of post-Brown positions taken toward the Court's authority by various southern states and by the congressional signatories of the so-called "Southern Manifesto"). For the Supreme Court's response to post-Brown challenges to its authority, see, for example, Cooper v. Aaron, 358 U.S. 1 (1958); Bush v. Orleans Parish Sch. Bd., 364 U.S. 803 (1960) (summarily rejecting the assertion that certain state statutes should be sustained on the ground that Louisiana "has interposed itself in the field of public education over which it has exclusive control").

jurisdiction over specific controversial subjects (*e.g.*, reapportionment, school prayer, abortion). See p. 432, *supra.*

(3) Review by Lower Federal Courts. Justice Story's opinion describes removal as an exercise of appellate jurisdiction. Does that suggest that Congress may authorize lower federal courts to review state court judgments? As set forth above, pp. 615–616, *supra*, Hamilton, in Federalist No. 82, perceived "no impediment" in Article III to such an arrangement. Under current law, a state court is not obliged to follow the decisions of any federal court of appeals on issues of federal law. Would it be constitutional for Congress to require a state court to treat as controlling precedent the decisions of the federal circuit court of appeals within whose boundaries the state sits?[8]

NOTE ON ENFORCEMENT OF THE MANDATE

(1) The Supreme Court's Mandate. Normally the Supreme Court, when reversing a state court judgment, remands the case for proceedings "not inconsistent" with the Court's opinion. The state court is therefore free to resolve any undecided questions or even to alter its determination of underlying state law. The reversal may not, therefore, be decisive of the final judgment.

Compare this form of decree with the firmness of the mandate issued in Fairfax's Devisee v. Hunter's Lessee, 11 U.S. (7 Cranch) 603 (1813), the Supreme Court's first decision in the Martin/Fairfax litigation. In what circumstances is each form preferable?

(2) Mandamus to Enforce Compliance. If a state court deviates from the Supreme Court's mandate, the proper remedy is to seek a new review of the judgment, as in Martin v. Hunter's Lessee. So long as such review is possible, issuance of a writ of mandamus as a means of obtaining compliance has been considered inappropriate. In re Blake, 175 U.S. 114 (1899).

When immediate review is precluded by the absence of a final judgment in the state court, the aggrieved party may seek leave from the Supreme Court to file a petition for mandamus. Even in such instances, the Court has generally denied leave without explanation. See, *e.g.*, Lavender v. Clark, 329 U.S. 674 (1946); Ex parte Kedroff, 346 U.S. 893 (1953); International Ass'n of Machinists v. Duckworth, 368 U.S. 982 (1962). On at least two occasions, however, the Court has taken a further step.

In Deen v. Hickman, 358 U.S. 57 (1958), the Supreme Court granted leave to file after determining that the Texas courts were treating as open an issue it considered foreclosed by its prior decision. The writ itself was not issued, however, since the Court assumed that the Texas court "will of course

---

[8]   For an argument that Congress could do so, see Frost, *Inferiority Complex: Should State Courts Follow Lower Federal Court Precedent on the Meaning of Federal Law?*, 68 Vand.L.Rev. 53 (2015). *Cf.* Pfander, One Supreme Court (2009) (positing that the Inferior Tribunals Clause permits Congress to "appoint" state courts as inferior tribunals in the federal judicial system).

conform to the disposition we now make * * *." The opinion did not discuss the Court's power to issue mandamus to a state court.

The Court again granted leave to file a petition for mandamus in General Atomic Co. v. Felter, 436 U.S. 493 (1978). There, the Court determined that a state trial court "has again done precisely what we held [in a prior decision] that it lacked the power to do * * *." The opinion invoked the principle that "a lower court" that fails to "give full effect" to the Court's mandate may be controlled by writ of mandamus (without discussing the assumption that state courts fall within this principle). As in Deen v. Hickman, the Court did not issue the formal writ, assuming that the state court "will now conform to our previous judgment * * *."

(3) Entry of Judgment. Another means by which the Supreme Court can deal with state recalcitrance is to enter judgment, as in Martin v. Hunter's Lessee, McCulloch v. Maryland, 17 U.S. (4 Wheat.) 316, 437 (1819), and Gibbons v. Ogden, 22 U.S. (9 Wheat.) 1, 239 (1824); to award execution, as in Tyler v. Magwire, 84 U.S. (17 Wall.) 253 (1873); or to remand with directions to enter a specific judgment, as in Stanley v. Schwalby, 162 U.S. 255 (1896), and Poindexter v. Greenhow, 114 U.S. 270 (1885).[1]

In NAACP v. Alabama ex rel. Flowers, 377 U.S. 288 (1964), after eight years of litigation (including four considerations by the Supreme Court) and obvious state court recalcitrance, the Court still refused the request to formulate its own decree for entry in the state courts. Accepting that it "undoubtedly" has the power to enter judgment, the Court "prefer[red] to follow our usual practice and remand the case to the Supreme Court of Alabama for further proceedings not inconsistent with this opinion." The opinion concluded: "Should we unhappily be mistaken in our belief that the Supreme Court of Alabama will promptly implement this disposition, leave is given the Association to apply to this Court for further appropriate relief"—which proved to be unnecessary, see 167 So.2d 171 (Ala.1964).

(4) Remedies for Violation of Mandates. If a state court were to defy a mandate to enter a specific judgment, which of the following procedures, if any, might be pursued: (a) recall of mandate and entry of judgment with award of execution or other process (28 U.S.C. §§ 561–566, 672, 1651, 2241); (b) mandamus to the state court to enter the proper judgment; or (c) punishment for contempt under 18 U.S.C. § 401 for disobedience to a "lawful * * * order * * * or command"?

In one instance, state *executive* officials have been punished for contempt of a Supreme Court order. In United States v. Shipp, 203 U.S. 563 (1906), 214 U.S. 386 (1909), 215 U.S. 580 (1909), the Court had ordered a stay of execution of a Black man who had been convicted of rape in Tennessee, pending an appeal, which the Court had allowed, from a federal circuit court's denial of his habeas corpus petition. A group of men (including a state sheriff with custody of the individual), with knowledge of the

---

[1]   The First Judiciary Act authorized the Supreme Court to enter judgment and award execution if the case had previously been remanded once; the requirement of one remand was eliminated in 1867, see pp. 616–617, *supra. Cf.* Judicial Code § 237(a), 28 U.S.C. § 344(a) (1940). In combination, 28 U.S.C. §§ 1651(a), 2104, and 2106 presumably confer no less authority than the Court had before the 1948 revision.

Supreme Court's order, lynched the man. After the Attorney General of the United States filed an information charging contempt of the Supreme Court, the Court appointed a commissioner to take testimony, rendered judgments of conviction, and sentenced the defendants to prison.

Should state judges, in a case of clear defiance, be any less subject to contempt sanctions than state executive officials?[2]

———————

Murdock v. City of Memphis

87 U.S. (20 Wall.) 590 (1875).
Error to the Supreme Court of Tennessee.

[Murdock filed a bill in Tennessee chancery court against the city of Memphis. He alleged that in July of 1844, after Congress had authorized establishment of a naval depot in Memphis and appropriated money for that purpose, Murdock's ancestors—"by ordinary deed of bargain and sale, without any covenants or declaration of trust on which the land was to be held by the city, but referring to the fact of 'the location of the naval depot lately established by the United States at said town'—conveyed to the city certain land 'for the location of the naval depot aforesaid.' By the same instrument * * * both the grantors and the city conveyed the same land to one Wheatley, in fee, in trust for the grantors and their heirs 'in case the same shall not be appropriated by the United States for that purpose.' "

[On September 14, 1844, the city sold the land to the United States. The conveyance included a covenant of general warranty; nothing in the deed to the United States designated "any purpose to which the land was to be applied, nor any conditions precedent or subsequent." "The United States took possession of the land for the purpose of the erection of a naval depot upon it" and made various improvements for that purpose. Ten years later, by an Act of Congress dated August 5, 1854, the United States transferred the land back to the city. The act stated: "All the grounds and appurtenances thereunto belonging, known as the Memphis Navy Yard, in Shelby County, Tennessee, be, and the same is hereby, ceded to the mayor and aldermen of the city of Memphis, *for the use and benefit of said city*."

[Murdock's bill alleged that when the United States abandoned any intention to establish a naval depot, "the land came within the clause of the deed of July, 1844, conveying it to Wheatley in trust; or if not, that it was held by the city in trust for the original grantors." Murdock therefore sought to subject the land to those trusts.

[The city's answer disputed Murdock's construction of the original 1844 deed and argued that the United States had appropriated the land

---

[2]   For additional discussion of the ability of federal courts to direct relief at state court judges, see pp. 1221–1224, *infra*.

as a naval depot within the terms of that deed, and contended that the perpetual occupation of it was not required by its terms. Thus, the city argued, the United States' abandonment of the land as a naval depot was not a breach of a condition of the deed that in turn divested the title that had been conveyed by the deed. The city also demurred to Murdock's bill "as seeking to enforce a forfeiture for breach of [a] condition subsequent" and argued the suit was untimely under the statute of limitations.

[The trial court sustained the city's demurrer, and also ruled that "the city had a perfect title to the property against the complainants both under the act of Congress and the statute of limitations." It therefore dismissed Murdock's suit. The Supreme Court of Tennessee affirmed that decree, stating that the act of Congress "cedes the property in controversy in this cause to the mayor and aldermen of the city of Memphis, for the use of the city only, and not in trust for the complainant; and that the complainant takes no benefit under the said act."

[Murdock sued out a writ of error to the Supreme Court.]

■ MR. JUSTICE MILLER * * * delivered the opinion of the court.

In the year 1867 Congress passed an act * * * entitled an act to amend "An act to establish the judicial courts of the United States, approved September the 24th, 1789." This act consisted of two sections, the first of which conferred upon the Federal courts * * * additional power in regard to writs of habeas corpus, and regulated appeals and other proceedings in that class of cases. The second section was a reproduction, with some changes, of the twenty-fifth section of the act of 1789, to which, by its title, the act of 1867 was an amendment, and it related to the appellate jurisdiction of this court over judgments and decrees of State courts. * * *

The proposition is that by a fair construction of the act of 1867 this court must, when it obtains jurisdiction of a case decided in a State court, by reason of one of the questions stated in the act, proceed to decide every other question which the case presents which may be found necessary to a final judgment on the whole merits. To this has been added the further suggestion that in determining whether the question on which the jurisdiction of this court depends has been raised in any given case, we are not limited to the record which comes to us from the State court * * * but we may resort to any such method of ascertaining what was really done in the State court as this court may think proper, even to *ex parte* affidavits. * * *

[After an initial argument, the Court propounded the following questions to counsel for reargument]:

1.   Does the second section of the act of February 5th, 1867, repeal all or any part of the twenty-fifth section of the act of 1789, commonly called the Judiciary Act?

2.   Is it the true intent and meaning of the act of 1867, above referred to, that when this court has jurisdiction of a case, by reason of

any of the questions therein mentioned, it shall proceed to decide all the questions presented by the record which are necessary to a final judgment or decree?

3.   If this question be answered affirmatively, does the Constitution of the United States authorize Congress to confer such a jurisdiction on this court? * * *

1.   [The Court answered the first question in the affirmative.]

2.   The affirmative of the second question propounded above is founded upon the effect of the omission or repeal of the last sentence of the twenty-fifth section of the act of 1789. That clause in express terms limited the power of the Supreme Court in reversing the judgment of a State court, to errors apparent on the face of the record and which respected questions, that for the sake of brevity, though not with strict verbal accuracy, we shall call Federal questions, namely, those in regard to the validity or construction of the Constitution, treaties, statutes, commissions, or authority of the Federal government.*

The argument may be thus stated: 1. That the Constitution declares that the judicial power of the United States shall extend to *cases* of a character which includes the questions described in the section, and that by the word *case*, is to be understood all of the case[s] in which such a question arises. 2. That by the fair construction of the act of 1789 in regard to removing those cases to this court, the power and the duty of re-examining the whole case would have been devolved on the court, but for the restriction of the clause omitted in the act of 1867; and that the same language is used in the latter act regulating the removal, but omitting the restrictive clause. And, 3. That by re-enacting the statute in the same terms as to the removal of cases from the State courts, without the restrictive clause, Congress is to be understood as conferring the power which that clause prohibited.

We will consider the last proposition first.

What were the precise motives which induced the omission of this clause it is impossible to ascertain with any degree of satisfaction. In a legislative body like Congress, it is reasonable to suppose that among those who considered this matter at all, there were varying reasons for consenting to the change. No doubt there were those who, believing that the Constitution gave no right to the Federal judiciary to go beyond the line marked by the omitted clause, thought its presence or absence immaterial; and in a revision of the statute it was wise to leave it out, because its presence implied that such a power was within the competency of Congress to bestow. There were also, no doubt, those who believed that the section standing without that clause did not confer the power which it prohibited, and that it was, therefore, better omitted. It may also have been within the thought of a few that all that is now claimed would follow the repeal of the clause. But if Congress, or the

---

*   [Ed.] For the text of this change, see pp. 616–617, *supra*.

Framers of the bill, had a clear purpose to enact affirmatively that the court *should consider* the class of errors which that clause forbids, nothing hindered that they should say so in positive terms; and in reversing the policy of the government from its foundation in one of the most important subjects on which that body could act, it is reasonably to be expected that Congress would use plain, unmistakable language in giving expression to such intention.

There is, therefore, no sufficient reason for holding that Congress, by repealing or omitting this restrictive clause, intended to enact affirmatively the thing which that clause had prohibited. * * *

There is * * * nothing in the language of the act, as far as we have criticized it, which in express terms defines the extent of the re-examination which this court shall give to such cases.

But we have not yet considered the most important part of the statute, namely, that which declares that it is only upon the existence of certain questions in the case that this court can entertain jurisdiction at all. Nor is the mere existence of such a question in the case sufficient to give jurisdiction—the question must have been *decided* in the State court. Nor is it sufficient that such a question was raised and was decided. It must have been decided in a certain way, that is, against the right set up under the Constitution, laws, treaties, or authority of the United States. The Federal question may have been erroneously decided. It may be quite apparent to this court that a wrong construction has been given to the Federal law, but if the right claimed under it by plaintiff in error has been conceded to him, this court cannot entertain jurisdiction of the case, so very careful is the statute, both of 1789 and of 1867, to narrow, to limit, and define the jurisdiction which this court exercises over the judgments of the State courts. Is it consistent with this extreme caution to suppose that Congress intended, when those cases came here, that this court should not only examine those questions, but all others found in the record?—questions of common law, of State statutes, of controverted facts, and conflicting evidence. Or is it the more reasonable inference that Congress intended that the case should be brought here that *those questions* might be decided and *finally* decided by the court established by the Constitution of the Union, and the court which has always been supposed to be not only the most appropriate but the only proper tribunal for their final decision? No such reason nor any necessity exists for the decision by this court of other questions in those cases. The jurisdiction has been exercised for nearly a century without serious inconvenience to the due administration of justice. The State courts are the appropriate tribunals, as this court has repeatedly held, for the decision of questions arising under their local law, whether statutory or otherwise. And it is not lightly to be presumed that Congress acted upon a principle which implies a distrust of their integrity or of their ability to construe those laws correctly.

Let us look for a moment into the effect of the proposition contended for upon the cases as they come up for consideration in the conference-room. If it is found that no such question is raised or decided in the court below, then all will concede that it must be dismissed for want of jurisdiction. But if it is found that the Federal question was raised and was decided against the plaintiff in error, then the first duty of the court obviously is to determine whether it was correctly decided by the State court. Let us suppose that we find that the court below was right in its decision on that question. What, then, are we to do? Was it the intention of Congress to say that while you can only bring the case here on account of this question, yet when it is here, though it may turn out that the plaintiff in error was wrong on that question, and the judgment of the court below was right, though he has wrongfully dragged the defendant into this court by the allegation of an error which did not exist, and without which the case could not rightfully be here, he can still insist on an inquiry into all the other matters which were litigated in the case? This is neither reasonable nor just.

In such case both the nature of the jurisdiction conferred and the nature and fitness of things demand that, no error being found in the matter which authorized the re-examination, the judgment of the State court should be affirmed, and the case remitted to that court for its further enforcement.

* * * We are of opinion that upon a fair construction of the whole language of the section the jurisdiction conferred is limited to the decision of the questions mentioned in the statute, and, as a necessary consequence of this, to the exercise of such powers as may be necessary to cause the judgment in that decision to be respected.

We will now advert to one or two considerations apart from the mere language of the statute, which seem to us to give additional force to this conclusion.

It has been many times decided by this court, on motions to dismiss this class of cases for want of jurisdiction, that if it appears from the record that the plaintiff in error raised and presented to the court * * * one of the questions specified in the statute, and the court ruled against him, the jurisdiction of this court attached, and we must hear the case on its merits. * * * But if when we once get jurisdiction, everything in the case is open to re-examination, it follows that every case tried in any State court, from that of a justice of the peace to the highest court of the State, may be brought to this court for final decision on all the points involved in it. * * *

It is impossible to believe that Congress intended this result, and equally impossible that they did not see that it would follow if they intended to open the cases that are brought here under this section to re-examination on all the points involved in them and necessary to a final judgment on the merits.

The twenty-fifth section of the act of 1789 has been the subject of innumerable decisions * * *. These form a system of appellate jurisprudence relating to the exercise of the appellate power of this court over the courts of the States. That system has been based upon the fundamental principle that this jurisdiction was limited to the correction of errors relating solely to Federal law. And though it may be argued with some plausibility that the reason of this is to be found in the restrictive clause of the act of 1789, which is omitted in the act of 1867, yet an examination of the cases will show that it rested quite as much on the conviction of this court that without that clause and on general principles the jurisdiction extended no further. It requires a very bold reach of thought, and a readiness to impute to Congress a radical and hazardous change of a policy vital in its essential nature to the independence of the State courts, to believe that that body contemplated, or intended, what is claimed, by the mere omission of a clause in the substituted statute, which may well be held to have been superfluous, or nearly so, in the old one.

Another consideration, not without weight in seeking after the intention of Congress, is found in the fact that where that body has clearly shown an intention to bring the whole of a case which arises under the constitutional provision as to its subject-matter under the jurisdiction of a Federal court, it has conferred its cognizance on Federal courts of original jurisdiction and not on the Supreme Court. * * *

There may be some plausibility in the argument that [rights under federal law] cannot be protected in all cases unless the Supreme Court has final control of the whole case. But the experience of eighty-five years of the administration of the law under the opposite theory would seem to be a satisfactory answer to the argument. It is not to be presumed that the State courts, where the rule is clearly laid down to them on the Federal question, and its influence on the case fully seen, will disregard or overlook it, and this is all that the rights of the party claiming under it require. Besides, by the very terms of this statute, when the Supreme Court is of opinion that the question of Federal law is of such relative importance to the whole case that it should control the final judgment, that court is authorized to render such judgment and enforce it by its own process. It cannot, therefore, be maintained that it is in any case necessary for the security of the rights claimed under the Constitution, laws, or treaties of the United States that the Supreme Court should examine and decide other questions not of a Federal character.

And we are of opinion that the act of 1867 does not confer such a jurisdiction.

This renders unnecessary a decision of the question whether, if Congress had conferred such authority, the act would have been constitutional. It will be time enough for this court to inquire into the existence of such a power when that body has attempted to exercise it in language which makes such an intention so clear as to require it. * * *

It is proper, in this first attempt to construe this important statute as amended, to say a few words on another point. What shall be done by this court when the question has been found to exist in the record, and to have been decided against the plaintiff in error, and *rightfully* decided, we have already seen, and it presents no difficulties.

But when it appears that the Federal question was decided erroneously against the plaintiff in error, we must then reverse the case undoubtedly, if there are no other issues decided in it than that. It often has occurred, however, and will occur again, that there are other points in the case than those of Federal cognizance, on which the judgment of the court below may stand; those points being of themselves sufficient to control the case.

Or it may be, that there are other issues in the case, but they are not of such controlling influence on the whole case that they are alone sufficient to support the judgment.

It may also be found that notwithstanding there are many other questions in the record of the case, the issue raised by the Federal question is such that its decision must dispose of the whole case.

In the two latter instances there can be no doubt that the judgment of the State court must be reversed, and under the new act this court can either render the final judgment or decree here, or remand the case to the State court for that purpose.

But in the other cases supposed, why should a judgment be reversed for an error in deciding the Federal question, if the same judgment must be rendered on the other points in the case? And why should this court reverse a judgment which is right on the whole record presented to us; or where the same judgment will be rendered by the court below, after they have corrected the error in the Federal question?

We have already laid down the rule that we are not authorized to examine these other questions for the purpose of deciding whether the State court ruled correctly on them or not. We are of opinion that on these subjects not embraced in the class of questions stated in the statute, we must receive the decision of the State courts as conclusive.

But when we find that the State court has decided the Federal question erroneously, then to prevent a useless and profitless reversal, which can do the plaintiff in error no good, and can only embarrass and delay the defendant, we must so far look into the remainder of the record as to see whether the decision of the Federal question alone is sufficient to dispose of the case, or to require its reversal; or on the other hand, whether there exist other matters in the record actually decided by the State court which are sufficient to maintain the judgment of that court, notwithstanding the error in deciding the Federal question. In the latter case the court would not be justified in reversing the judgment of the State court.

But this examination into the points in the record other than the Federal question is not for the purpose of determining whether they were correctly or erroneously decided, but to ascertain if any such have been decided, and their sufficiency to maintain the final judgment, as decided by the State court. * * *

Finally, we hold the following propositions on this subject as flowing from the statute as it now stands:

1.   That it is essential to the jurisdiction of this court over the judgment of a State court, that it shall appear that one of the questions mentioned in the act must have been raised, and presented to the State court.

2.   That it must have been decided by the State court, or that its decision was necessary to the judgment or decree, rendered in the case.

3.   That the decision must have been against the right claimed or asserted by plaintiff in error under the Constitution, treaties, laws, or authority of the United States.

4.   These things appearing, this court has jurisdiction and must examine the judgment so far as to enable it to decide whether this claim of right was correctly adjudicated by the State court.

5.   If it finds that it was rightly decided, the judgment must be affirmed.

6.   If it was erroneously decided against plaintiff in error, then this court must further inquire, whether there is any other matter or issue adjudged by the State court, which is sufficiently broad to maintain the judgment of that court, notwithstanding the error in deciding the issue raised by the Federal question. If this is found to be the case, the judgment must be affirmed without inquiring into the soundness of the decision on such other matter or issue.

7.   But if it be found that the issue raised by the question of Federal law is of such controlling character that its correct decision is necessary to any final judgment in the case, or that there has been no decision by the State court of any other matter or issue which is sufficient to maintain the judgment of that court without regard to the Federal question, then this court will reverse the judgment of the State court, and will either render such judgment here as the State court should have rendered, or remand the case to that court, as the circumstances of the case may require.

Applying the principles here laid down to the case now before the court, we are of opinion that this court has jurisdiction, and that the judgment of the Supreme Court of Tennessee must be affirmed. * * *

The complainants, in their bill, and throughout the case, insisted that the effect of the act of 1854 was to vest the title in the mayor or aldermen of the city in trust for them.

It may be very true that it is not easy to see anything in the deed by which the United States received the title from the city, or the act by which they ceded it back, which raises such a trust, but the complainants claimed a right under this act of the United States, which was decided against them by the Supreme Court of Tennessee, and this claim gives jurisdiction of that question to this court.

But we need not consume many words to prove that neither by the deed of the city to the United States, which is an ordinary deed of bargain and sale for a valuable consideration, nor from anything found in the Act of 1854, is there any such trust to be inferred. The act, so far from recognizing or implying any such trust, cedes the property to the mayor and aldermen *for the use of the city*. We are, therefore, of opinion that this, the only Federal question in the case, was rightly decided by the Supreme Court of Tennessee. * * *

[As for any claim based on the 1844 deed, it is] to be determined by the general principles of equity jurisprudence, and is unaffected by anything found in the Constitution, laws, or treaties of the United States. Whether decided well or otherwise by the State court, we have no authority to inquire. According to the principles we have laid down as applicable to this class of cases, the judgment of the Supreme Court of Tennessee must be

Affirmed.

■ MR. JUSTICE CLIFFORD, with whom concurred MR. JUSTICE SWAYNE, dissenting:

I dissent from so much of the opinion of the court as denies the jurisdiction of this court to determine the whole case, where it appears that the record presents a Federal question and that the Federal question was erroneously decided to the prejudice of the plaintiff in error; as in that state of the record it is, in my judgment, the duty of this court, under the recent act of Congress, to decide the whole merits of the controversy, and to affirm or reverse the judgment of the State court. * * *

Sufficient proof of the fact that the new law was not intended to be without meaning and effective operation is found in the fact that [the original restrictive clause] is wholly omitted in the new law.

■ MR. JUSTICE BRADLEY, dissenting:

* * * Proving that the government did not appropriate the land for a navy yard is a very different thing from setting up a claim to the land under an act of Congress.

I think, therefore, that in this case there was no title or right claimed by the appellants under any statute of, or authority exercised under, the United States; and consequently that there was no decision against any such title; and, therefore, that this court has no jurisdiction.

But supposing, as the majority of the court holds, that it has jurisdiction, I cannot concur in the conclusion that we can only decide the

Federal question raised by the record. If we have jurisdiction at all, * * * we have jurisdiction of the *case*, and not merely of a *question* in it. * * *

The [restrictive] clause by its presence in the original act meant something, and effected something. * * * The omission of the clause, according to a well-settled rule of construction, must necessarily have the effect of removing the restriction which it effected in the old law.

In my judgment, therefore, if the court had jurisdiction of the case, it was bound to consider not only the Federal question raised by the record, but the whole case. As the court, however, has decided otherwise, it is not proper that I should express any opinion on the merits.

■ [THE CHIEF JUSTICE, who was appointed only after reargument, took no part in the judgment.]

NOTE ON MURDOCK V. CITY OF MEMPHIS

(1) Murdock and Reconstruction. Is it possible that the Reconstruction Congress was so highly mistrustful of state courts that it did mean to authorize Supreme Court review of non-federal issues?[1] Although Murdock concerned only the second section of the Act of 1867, the first section of the Act gave the federal courts, for the first time, a general power to issue writs of habeas corpus to persons in state custody. See Chap. XI, Sec. 3, *infra*.[2] Further, no less a figure than Justice Story (author of not only of Martin, but also Swift v. Tyson, discussed at note 4, *infra*) at times appeared to criticize the final sentence of section 25 and its limitation of Supreme Court appellate review.[3] Was the Court justified in requiring a clearer statement than the Act's deletion of the restrictive language of section 25?

---

[1]   See generally Matasar & Bruch, *Procedural Common Law, Federal Jurisdictional Policy, and Abandonment of the Adequate and Independent State Grounds Doctrine*, 86 Colum.L.Rev. 1291, 1319 (1986) (so arguing). For a different perspective, see Collins, *Reconstructing Murdock v. Memphis*, 98 Va.L.Rev 1439 (2012).

[2]   Professor Wiecek argues that Congress, in deleting the proviso to § 25, may have approved a bill with far-reaching effects on American federalism without knowing what it was doing. He observes that many commentators believe that Congress did intend the expansion of jurisdiction implicit in deletion of § 25's proviso. Wiecek views Murdock as one of a group of decisions in the 1870s that narrowed federal jurisdiction and retreated from federal protection of persons newly freed from slavery. He asserts that the Court, already feeling overworked, was leery of taking on the added caseload that a contrary decision in Murdock would have generated. He concludes, however, that Murdock "was * * * a godsend for the American federal system." Wiecek, *Murdock v. Memphis: Section 25 of the 1789 Judiciary Act and Judicial Federalism*, in Origins of the Federal Judiciary 223, 243 (Marcus ed. 1992).

[3]   For example, in a prize case on appeal from the New York state courts in 1818 in which the parties disagreed as to the scope of the Supreme Court's authority to review the record below, including as relevant to the assessment of damages, Justice Story wrote:

"We have no right, on a writ of error from a state court, under the act of congress, to inquire into the legal correctness of the rule by which the damages were ascertained and assessed. There is no law of the United States, which interferes with, or touches, the question of damages. It is a question depending altogether upon the common law; and the act of congress has expressly precluded us from a consideration of such a question. Whether such a restriction can be defended upon public policy, or principle, may well admit of most serious doubts." Gelston v. Hoyt, 16 U.S. (3 Wheat.) 246, 325–26 (1818). For additional discussion, see Fletcher, *Congressional Power*

(2) Appellate Versus Original Federal Jurisdiction. Former Justice Benjamin R. Curtis, in an amicus curiae brief, argued in support of the extended jurisdiction that the Court ultimately rejected. On the question of the constitutionality of Supreme Court review of non-federal issues, Curtis asserted: "Unless, therefore, some distinction can be made between the power of Congress to confer original and appellate jurisdiction, and neither the Constitution nor the decisions of this court permit this distinction, it is clear that Congress may confer appellate power over all cases to which the judicial power of the United States extends, and is not restricted by the Constitution to particular questions, by reason of which the cases are brought within the judicial power * * *."4

Doesn't the Curtis syllogism ignore a fundamental structural difference between original and appellate adjudication? A federal trial court exercising original jurisdiction must decide the entire case, including non-federal law questions, in order to come to judgment. By contrast, when the Supreme Court exercises appellate jurisdiction, it need not resolve every issue presented in the case, which means that it need not necessarily decide non-federal law issues to ensure complete adjudication; those issues have been decided (or will be decided on remand) by the state courts.

Consider, for example, whether the undoubted power of a federal district court to entertain a diversity action based entirely on state law necessarily implies that the Supreme Court could exercise appellate jurisdiction over such an action that had been litigated in a state court.[5]

(3) The Dissent's Position. Suppose Murdock had been decided the other way, permitting the Supreme Court, in a case otherwise within its appellate jurisdiction, to review a state's highest court on "questions not of a Federal character." What would be the future precedential authority of such a Supreme Court determination, if the identical issues arose:

(a) in the state's courts, in a case that did not involve any issue of federal law and was not otherwise within the federal judicial power?

Over the Jurisdiction of Federal Courts: The Meaning of the Word "All" in Article III, 59 Duke L.J. 929, 948–49 (2010).

[4] The brief is summarized at 87 U.S. (20 Wall.) at 602–06 and printed in Curtis, Jurisdiction, Practice and Peculiar Jurisprudence of the Courts of the United States 54–58 (1880). *Cf.* 2 Crosskey, Politics and the Constitution in the History of the United States 711–817 (1953) (arguing on a much broader basis for the Court's power to decide state law). But see Hart, *The Relations Between State and Federal Law*, 54 Colum.L.Rev. 489, 499–506 (1954).

[5] Mitchell, *Reconsidering Murdock: State-Law Reversals as Constitutional Avoidance*, 77 U.Chi.L.Rev. 1335 (2010), argues that nothing in the language of Article III or 28 U.S.C. § 1257(a) forecloses Supreme Court review of state law issues, and that the Court already reviews questions of state law in many contexts. Starting from those premises, Professor Mitchell argues that the Supreme Court should review state law rulings of state courts when necessary to avoid a "novel and contentious" federal constitutional question. Such an approach, he contends, would serve the interests of the avoidance doctrine and allow the Court to forestall error costs sometimes incurred in difficult constitutional cases. Can Professor Mitchell's reading of Article III be squared with the constitutional considerations that influenced the decision in Murdock? *Cf.* Siler v. Louisville & Nashville R.R. Co., 213 U.S. 175 (1909) (it would be "much better" to resolve a case on a "question of a local nature * * * rather than to unnecessarily decide the various constitutional questions appearing in the record"); Sutton, 51 Imperfect Solutions: States and the Making of American Constitutional Law (2018) (urging federal courts to resolve state claims first in cases involving parallel state and federal claims).

(b)   in the state's courts, in a case that, because there was a federal question presented, would potentially be subject to the Supreme Court's appellate jurisdiction?

(c)   in the state's courts, in a case in which there was no federal question but there was diversity of citizenship?

(d)   in a federal district court of that state, in a diversity action in which there was not (or, alternatively, there was) also a federal question?

(e)   in a state court of a second state that, under applicable choice of law principles, would apply the law of the first state, and in which there was not (or, alternatively, there was) also a federal question?

Do these questions shed light on the correctness of Murdock as a matter of statutory interpretation? On whether the dissent's interpretation of the jurisdictional statute was constitutionally permissible?

(4)   Murdock and Erie. The Court's recognition in Murdock that it lacks authority to review state court resolutions of non-federal issues was echoed when the Court ruled over six decades later, in Erie R. Co. v. Tompkins, 304 U.S. 64 (1938), p. 760, *infra*, that the grant of diversity jurisdiction does not give federal courts a general lawmaking power to fashion common law. What accounts for the delay between Murdock and Erie? One response could be that the Murdock Court focused on the proper interpretation of § 25 rather than the potential lurking constitutional issues implicated by a broader reading of the section. This, of course, only raises the question whether, in light of Erie, the contrary result in Murdock would have been constitutional.[6]

As a separate matter, the Murdock Court may have viewed the non-federal trust law issue in the case as presenting a question of "local" law. Under the pre-Erie framework governed by Swift v. Tyson, 41 U.S. (16 Pet.) 1 (1842), p. 749, *infra*, such questions remained the domain of state courts for ultimate resolution. (Matters of "general" law, by contrast, were fair game for federal diversity courts under the Swift regime, even if state courts were not formally bound in subsequent cases to follow federal court pronouncements on such questions.) Supporting such a reading of Murdock is the Court's observation there that "[t]he State courts are the appropriate tribunals, as this court has repeatedly held, for the decision of questions arising under their local law, whether statutory or otherwise."

The Murdock Court also posited that "[i]t cannot * * * be maintained that it is in any case necessary for the security of the rights claimed under the Constitution, laws, or treaties of the United States that the Supreme Court should examine and decide other questions not of a Federal character." Does this latter observation lay at least some of the foundation for Erie? For greater discussion of Swift and Erie, see Chap. VI, Sec. 2, *infra*.

(5)   "Antecedent" Versus "Distinct" State Law Grounds. In Murdock, the non-federal issue of trust law was logically (and functionally) distinct from any issue of federal law; resolving that issue was not a necessary

---

[6]   Might the delay between the two decisions also have something to do with the differences between the exercise of appellate jurisdiction at issue in Murdock and original jurisdiction at issue in Erie?

antecedent to any question of federal law. Put differently, had the Supreme Court resolved the federal issue in favor of Murdock (the purported federal rightholder) and held that the 1854 Act of Congress conferred good title on him, he would have obtained all the relief he sought, regardless of the state court's resolution of the non-federal issues. There was no need to decide the non-federal issue of trust law in order to resolve the wholly independent federal question raised in the case.

In Martin v. Hunter's Lessee, by contrast, the state law question (did the Commonwealth of Virginia obtain title by escheat before any federal treaty took effect) was an essential antecedent to the application of the federal treaty provisions giving protection to then-existing land titles. If there was a proper escheat, there was no property interest for any federal treaty to protect in the Fairfax line. Thus, to obtain the relief he sought as a matter of federal law, Martin had to prevail on both the logically prior non-federal issue (that his chain of title had *not* been divested at the time of the Treaty of Peace) and then the federal law issue (that the Treaty protected that title against the Act of Compromise and other efforts to divest it). The two issues were, in effect, intertwined.

The distinction between these two types of cases is critical to understanding this area of the law. Where the state issue is wholly distinct, as in Murdock, is there any plausible argument that the Supreme Court, as a corollary to its authority over federal issues, needs power to review the correctness of the state court ruling? On the other hand, where a state law ruling serves as an antecedent for determining whether a federal right has been violated, some review of the basis for the state court's determination of the state law question is essential if the federal right is to be protected against evasion and discrimination—as Martin itself exemplifies. See Wechsler, *The Appellate Jurisdiction of the Supreme Court: Reflections on the Law and the Logistics of Direct Review*, 34 Wash. & Lee L.Rev. 1043, 1050–56 (1977).[7]

(6) The Disposition in Murdock. Justice Miller's seven propositions do not represent the Court's contemporary practice. Proposition (3) was the law prior to 1914, but that year Congress extended Supreme Court review to embrace state decisions that uphold as well as those that deny claims of federal right. Propositions (4)–(6) suggest an order of decision (first decide the federal issue, and if there was error, then determine whether the state judgment can nonetheless stand on the basis of a non-federal ground) that is the opposite of current practice. On this point, see the discussion of Fox Film Corp. v. Muller, 296 U.S. 207 (1935), p. 651, *infra*.

Further, given the statute of limitations issue in Murdock, which the Court appears to have viewed as one of non-federal law, there is an argument (at least under current practice) that the Court should not have reached the

---

[7]   For an argument (stimulated by Bush v. Gore, 531 U.S. 98 (2000) (per curiam)) that Article III permits the Supreme Court to review issues of state law in a case like Murdock, or in a state court case that involves diversity of citizenship, see Harrison, *Federal Appellate Jurisdiction Over Questions of State Law in State Courts*, 7 Green Bag 2d 353 (2004).

merits of even the federal issue. Return to this question after reading Section 3(A) of this Chapter.

(7) Federal Court Deference to State Courts. Notice the possible tension between Martin and Murdock with respect to how they discuss the conception of state courts contemplated by Article III and § 25. In Martin, Justice Story observes that "[t]he constitution has presumed (whether rightly or wrongly we do not inquire) that state attachments, state prejudices, state jealousies, and state interests, might sometimes obstruct, or control, or be supposed to obstruct or control, the regular administration of justice." This, he continues, explains Article III's grant of diversity jurisdiction to the federal courts. In Murdock, Justice Miller interprets § 25 in light of his observation that "it is not lightly to be presumed that Congress acted upon a principle which implies a distrust of [state courts'] integrity or of their ability to construe [non-federal law] correctly." Echoing the questions posed in Paragraph 1, *supra*, might the Reconstruction Congress have had reason to distrust the state courts? And what do these statements contribute to the larger debates over parity? See Chap. IV, Sec. 1, *supra*.

3. THE RELATION BETWEEN STATE AND FEDERAL LAW

A. SUBSTANTIVE LAW

INTRODUCTORY NOTE

(1) The Relationship of State and Federal Law. The material in this Section concerns the scope of Supreme Court review of state court decisions, but it also demands analysis of the diverse ways in which state and federal law interact. Only such analysis can illuminate why the Court sometimes lacks power to review issues of federal law decided by a state court,[1] and on other occasions may review (at least on a limited basis) determinations of state law.[2]

(2) The Interstitial Nature of Federal Law. A central aspect of the relationship of state and federal law was highlighted in the following discussion in the First Edition of this book, published in 1953:

"Federal law is generally interstitial in its nature. It rarely occupies a legal field completely, totally excluding all participation by the legal systems of the states. This was plainly true in the beginning when the federal legislative product (including the Constitution) was extremely small. It is significantly true today, despite the volume of Congressional enactments, and even within areas where Congress has been very active. Federal

---

[1]   See, *e.g.*, Fox Film Corp. v. Muller, 296 U.S. 207 (1935), p. 651, *infra*.
[2]   See, *e.g.*, Indiana ex rel. Anderson v. Brand, 303 U.S. 95 (1938), p. 674, *infra*.

legislation, on the whole, has been conceived and drafted on an *ad hoc* basis to accomplish limited objectives. It builds upon legal relationships established by the states, altering or supplanting them only so far as necessary for the special purpose. Congress acts, in short, against the background of the total *corpus juris* of the states in much the way that a state legislature acts against the background of the common law, assumed to govern unless changed by legislation.

"That this is so was partially affirmed in § 34 of the First Judiciary Act, now 28 U.S.C. § 1652, but an attentive canvass of the total product of the Congress would establish its surprising generality and force. Indeed, the strength of the conception of the central government as one of delegated, limited authority is most significantly manifested on this mundane plane of working, legislative practice.

"The point involved is vital to appreciation of the legal issues posed by the materials in this and later chapters (especially [Chapters VI and VII]), concerned with the relationship between the law of the United States and of the states. It explains why frequently in litigation federal law bears only partially upon the case: the basis of a right asserted by the plaintiff which is open to defenses grounded in state law, the basis of a defense when a state-created right has been advanced, the foundation of a replication to a state defense or only of the rejoinder to a replication that would otherwise be good. It explains why federal law often embodies concepts that derive their content, or some portion of their content, from the states. It makes it less anomalous, at least, that substantive rights may be defined by Congress but the remedies for their enforcement left undefined or relegated wholly to the states; or that *per contra* national law may do no more than formulate remedies for vindicating rights that have their source and definition in state law.

"The diversity of these relationships is shown most plainly in cases that reach the Supreme Court from the authorized expositors of state law, the state courts."

In the more than seventy years since Professors Hart and Wechsler published the First Edition, the expansion of federal legislation and administrative regulation noted in this discussion has accelerated; today one finds many more instances in which federal enactments supply both right and remedy in, or wholly occupy, a particular field. This same period has witnessed a broad extension of federal laws (constitutional and statutory) that protect individual rights and provide remedies for violations thereof. Thus, at present federal law appears to be more primary than interstitial in numerous areas. Nonetheless, consider, in reading the material in this Section, whether the First Edition's thesis does not remain accurate over an extremely broad range of applications.[3]

---

[3]   See generally Hart, *The Relations Between State and Federal Law*, 54 Colum.L.Rev. 489 (1954). For analysis of relevant institutional factors that help to preserve the primacy of state law in many areas, see, *e.g.*, Wechsler, *The Political Safeguards of Federalism: The Role of the States in the Composition and Selection of the National Government*, 54 Colum.L.Rev. 543 (1954); Choper, Judicial Review and the National Political Process (1980); Shapiro, Federalism: A Dialogue (1995); Baker, *Putting the Safeguards Back Into the Political Safeguards of*

Fox Film Corp. v. Muller

296 U.S. 207 (1935).
Certiorari to the Supreme Court of Minnesota.

■ MR. JUSTICE SUTHERLAND delivered the opinion of the Court.

[The case arose when Fox Film Corporation sued a licensee, Muller, for breach of two contracts governing Muller's right to exhibit certain motion pictures. In defense, Muller asserted that the contracts violated the Sherman Antitrust Act. All parties agreed that the contracts were essentially the same as the contract at issue in an earlier case in which the Supreme Court held the arbitration clause to be invalid under the Sherman Act, Paramount Famous Lasky Corp. v. United States, 282 U.S. 30 (1930).

[The Minnesota Supreme Court viewed the case as raising the question "whether the arbitration clause is severable from the contract, leaving the remainder of the contract enforceable, or not severable, permeating and tainting the whole contract with illegality and making it void." The state supreme court then] held the arbitration plan was inseparable from the other provisions of the contract. Whether this conclusion was right or wrong we need not determine. It is enough that it is, at least, not without fair support.

Respondent contends that the question of severability was alone decided and that no federal question was determined by the lower court. This contention petitioner challenges, and asserts that a federal question was involved and decided. We do not attempt to settle the dispute; but, assuming * * * that petitioner's view is the correct one, the case is controlled by the settled rule that where the judgment of a state court rests upon two grounds, one of which is federal and the other nonfederal in character, our jurisdiction fails if the nonfederal ground is independent of the federal ground and adequate to support the judgment. This rule had become firmly fixed at least as early as Klinger v. State of Missouri, 13 Wall. 257, 263 [(1871)], and has been reiterated in a long line of cases since that time. [Citing numerous decisions.]

Whether the provisions of a contract are non-severable, so that if one be held invalid the others must fall with it, is clearly a question of general and not of federal law.* The invalidity of the arbitration clause which the present contracts embody is conceded. It was held invalid * * * in the

Federalism, 46 Vill.L.Rev. 951 (2001); Kaden, *Politics, Money, and State Sovereignty: The Judicial Role*, 79 Colum.L.Rev. 847 (1979); Kramer, *Understanding Federalism*, 47 Vand.L.Rev. 1485 (1994); Kramer, *Putting the Politics Back into the Political Safeguards of Federalism*, 100 Colum.L.Rev. 215 (2000).

    *   [Ed.] Note the Court here refers to the severability question as "a question of general and not of federal law." The Court decided Fox Film three years before Erie R. Co. v. Tompkins, 304 U.S. 64 (1938), p. 760, *infra*, came to question the idea of "general law" as it had been recognized under the doctrine of Swift v. Tyson, 41 U.S. (16 Pet.) 1 (1842), p. 749, *infra*.

Paramount case, and its judgment was affirmed here. * * * [T]he primary question to be determined by the court below was whether the concededly invalid clause was separable from the other provisions of the contract. The ruling of the state Supreme Court that it was not, is sufficient to conclude the case without regard to the determination, if, in fact, any was made, in respect of the federal question. It follows that the non-federal ground is adequate to sustain the judgment.

The rule * * * to the effect that our jurisdiction attaches where the nonfederal ground is so interwoven with the other as not to be an independent matter, does not apply. The construction put upon the contracts did not constitute a preliminary step which simply had the effect of bringing forward for determination the federal question, but was a decision which automatically took the federal question out of the case if otherwise it would be there. The nonfederal question in respect of the construction of the contracts, and the federal question in respect of their validity under the Anti-trust Act, were clearly independent of one another. The case, in effect, was disposed of before the federal question said to be involved was reached. A decision of that question then became unnecessary; and whether it was decided or not, our want of jurisdiction is clear.

Writ dismissed for want of jurisdiction.

■ THE CHIEF JUSTICE took no part in the consideration or decision of this case.

PRELIMINARY NOTE ON THE INDEPENDENT AND ADEQUATE STATE GROUND

(1) Early Development and Present Administration of the Rule. In the early decisions after Murdock, the rule that the Court would not review a judgment resting on an adequate and independent state ground was apparently regarded merely as prudential on the ground that the Court need not decide an issue that could not affect the judgment. Later cases placed the rule squarely on lack of jurisdiction, see, *e.g.*, Enterprise Irrigation Dist. v. Farmers' Mut. Canal Co., 243 U.S. 157, 164 (1917), and in Herb v. Pitcairn, 324 U.S. 117, 126 (1945), the Court suggested that the jurisdictional barrier might be not merely statutory but constitutional: "[O]ur power is to correct wrong judgments, not to revise opinions. * * * [I]f the same judgment would be rendered by the state court after we corrected its view of federal laws, our review could amount to nothing more than an advisory opinion."[1]

---

[1]   See also *id.* at 125–26 ("Our only power over state judgments is to correct them to the extent that they incorrectly adjudge federal rights."). For endorsements of this suggestion, see, *e.g.*, Coleman v. Thompson, 501 U.S. 722, 729 (1991); Ake v. Oklahoma, 470 U.S. 68, 75 (1985); Fountaine, *Article III and the Adequate and Independent State Grounds Doctrine*, 48 Am.U.L.Rev. 1053 (1999) (arguing that the doctrine is demanded by the Article III standing requirement that the harm complained of be redressable). For greater discussion of the potential Article III jurisdictional barrier, review Chap. II, *supra*.

Because, as Fox Film indicates and Herb v. Pitcairn further explains, the Court regards the presence of an adequate and independent state ground as depriving it of jurisdiction to review the state court judgment, the proper disposition is to dismiss for lack of jurisdiction, rather than (as Murdock suggested) to affirm; and this has been the Court's practice since Eustis v. Bolles, 150 U.S. 361 (1893).[2] Today, the Court will simply deny a petition for certiorari that it lacks jurisdiction to entertain, without noting a reason, jurisdictional or otherwise.

(2) Application of the Rule. It is now an accepted principle that the Supreme Court will not review a federal question when the state court's decision of a state law issue precludes the Court from altering the outcome below, no matter how the Court might resolve the federal question.[3] But administration of that principle engenders impressive difficulties and requires careful analysis of the relationship between state and federal law in the case at hand.[4]

Fox Film is a good example. In that case, the Minnesota Supreme Court's decision relied on both state and federal precedents in concluding that the arbitration clause in the contracts at issue could not be severed. Further, as the Supreme Court described the state court's decision, it relied heavily on the federal proceedings in the earlier Paramount case to "reach[ ] the conclusion that the holding of the federal court was that the entire contract was illegal; and upon that view and upon what it conceived to be the weight of authority, held the arbitration plan was inseparable from the other provisions of the contract." Was the premise for finding no jurisdiction in Fox Film—that the question of separability was governed exclusively by non-federal law—as obvious as the Court seemed to think? Isn't there evidence to suggest that the line between federal antitrust law and the question of severability in the case was blurred?

---

[2]   The Eustis Court did not offer much in the way of explanation for the switch. After noting that the Court had been inconsistent in the past in disposing of cases that did not call upon the Court "to determine any federal question," the Eustis decision then observed: "This discrepancy may have originated in a difference of views as to the precise scope of the questions presented. However that may be, we think that when we find it unnecessary to decide any federal question, and when the state court had based its decision on a local or state question, our logical course is to dismiss the writ of error." 150 U.S. at 370. Isn't more than logic at play here? That is, if the Court views the problem with reviewing such cases as jurisdictional, from what source would the power to affirm derive?

[3]   Some decisions in the Court's qualified immunity caselaw, such as Camreta v. Greene, 563 U.S. 692 (2011), may be in tension with the Court's position on the adequate-and-independent-state-grounds doctrine insofar as they sometimes permit Supreme Court review sought by government officials who prevailed below on a qualified immunity defense but wish to challenge the breadth of a lower court's decision on the underlying merits, which has the potential to govern future conduct by the same officials. For greater discussion, see Chap. IX, Sec. 4(E), *infra*. How broadly should such a potential exception to Herb v. Pitcairn sweep? Are there situations analogous to the qualified immunity context in which it should apply? Do federalism concerns distinguish the adequate-and-independent-state-ground doctrine from the approach exemplified in Camreta?

[4]   See generally Hill, *The Inadequate State Ground*, 65 Colum.L.Rev. 943 (1965); Wechsler, *The Appellate Jurisdiction of the Supreme Court: Reflections on the Law and the Logistics of Direct Review*, 34 Wash. & Lee L.Rev. 1043 (1977); Note, *The Untenable Nonfederal Ground in the Supreme Court*, 74 Harv.L.Rev. 1375 (1961).

(3) State Law as Antecedent to Federal Law. In analyzing the relation of state and federal law, it is critical to keep in mind the key distinction (discussed at pp. 647–648, Paragraph (5), *supra*) between (i) state law as antecedent to federal law and (ii) state law as a distinct basis from federal law for relief.

In cases like Martin v. Hunter's Lessee, the federal rightholder must prevail on both state and federal grounds in order to obtain relief. This is what is meant by stating that state law is antecedent to the federal question. In such a case, if (i) the state court denies relief to the federal rightholder by deciding the issue of state law adversely, (ii) that ground is broad enough to support the judgment, and (iii) there is no basis for questioning or setting aside the state court's decision of the state law issue, then the Supreme Court lacks jurisdiction to review the federal question, because federal review could not change the judgment.[5] It is the third question here that is crucial to the analysis. As explored at pp. 674–690, *infra*, the question whether the state ground is "adequate" to support the judgment collapses with the question whether there is reason (as Justice Story thought there was in Martin) to set aside the state court's determination of the antecedent state law issue. Resolution of that question may require the Supreme Court to engage in some review of the correctness of the state court's decision of non-federal law issues (again, as in Martin) to ensure that federal rights are not undercut by serious misapplications of state law.

But if the state court resolves the state law issue *in favor* of the federal rightholder, it must then proceed to determine the federal issue. At that point, the Supreme Court has jurisdiction to review that determination respecting federal law, however the state court rules on it. Thus, federal reviewability ultimately depends on who prevailed on the antecedent non-federal issue in state court (and whether, if the determination of the non-federal issue supports the outcome below, there is any reason to question the integrity of that determination).

(4) State Law as a Distinct Basis for Relief. More complex possibilities are posed by cases like Fox Film and Murdock, in which state law provides a basis for relief that is entirely distinct from federal law—so that the federal rightholder (in Fox Film, the original defendant) can obtain the relief sought by prevailing on *either* state or federal grounds. Suppose, for example, that a taxpayer contends, in a state court refund action, that a state tax violates both the federal and state constitutions.

(a) If the state supreme court invalidates the tax under the state constitution, without reaching the federal question, the Supreme Court lacks jurisdiction to review. (This situation would have been presented in Murdock had the plaintiff prevailed in state court upon his claim under trust law;

---

[5]   This principle has been recognized in a variety of decisions refusing to review state court judgments resting on lack of remedial authority or similar quasi-procedural grounds. See, *e.g.*, Utley v. City of St. Petersburg, 292 U.S. 106 (1934) (laches is an adequate state ground); Enterprise Irrigation Dist. v. Farmers' Mutual Canal Co., 243 U.S. 157 (1917) (estoppel is an adequate state ground). The same principle operates when there is an antecedent state law *procedural* ground—ordinarily, that the party seeking Supreme Court review failed to raise the federal question in state court in accordance with state procedural rules. See Sec. 3(B), *infra*.

similarly, it parallels the defendant's interpretation of the state court's decision in Fox Film.)

(b)   If the state supreme court holds the tax invalid under the U.S. Constitution and independently invalid under the state constitution, there is no jurisdiction to review. Is it a problem that the state court's interpretation of federal law may be erroneous but unreviewable, thereby misleading other litigants or other courts? Is correcting such errors reason enough to justify Supreme Court review, even though the state court's judgment ordering a refund would not change, however the Supreme Court decided the federal issue? Compare Camreta v. Greene, note 3, *supra*.

(c)   If the state court holds the tax *valid* under both constitutions, the state ground cannot independently support the judgment, and the federal-law ruling is plainly subject to review.

(d)   If the state court invalidates the tax under the federal Constitution without reaching the state-law issue, the settled rule is that the judgment is reviewable: Supreme Court jurisdiction depends on the state court's actual grounds of decision rather than on possible grounds. See, *e.g.*, Grayson v. Harris, 267 U.S. 352, 358 (1925); Regents of the Univ. of California v. Bakke, 438 U.S. 265, 279–80 (1978); Orr v. Orr, 440 U.S. 268, 274–77 (1979). If it reverses the state court with respect to the federal question, the Supreme Court will remand to permit the state court to resolve the undetermined state law issue. See, *e.g.*, California v. Ramos, 463 U.S. 992, 997–98 n.7 (1983). The state court remains free to reinstate its prior judgment on that state-law ground. See, *e.g.*, Washington v. Chrisman, 455 U.S. 1 (1982), *reinstated on remand*, 676 P.2d 419 (Wash.1984); South Dakota v. Neville, 459 U.S. 553 (1983), *reinstated on remand*, 346 N.W.2d 425 (S.D.1984).

The Supreme Court's practice in cases like these has not been uniform, however. On occasion the Court, rather than deciding the federal constitutional question, has instead vacated the state court judgment and remanded for consideration of state grounds whose decision might obviate the need to reach the federal constitutional question. See Kirkpatrick v. Christian Homes of Abilene, Inc., 460 U.S. 1074 (1983); Musser v. Utah, 333 U.S. 95 (1948). What would justify use of this technique in some cases but not in others?[6]

(5)   The Responsibility of State Courts. In a case like the hypothetical challenge to a state tax, if a state court views the tax as invalid under both the federal and state constitutions, the state court may choose to rest its decision on state grounds alone, on federal grounds alone, or on both. In such cases, do state courts have an obligation to avoid decision of the federal

---

[6]   Consider Paschall v. Christie-Stewart Inc., 414 U.S. 100, 101–02 (1973), in which the Court declined to review a state court decision resting squarely on the Due Process Clause, deciding instead to remand because the suit might have been time-barred under state law and asserting that if so, "any decision by this Court would be advisory and beyond our jurisdiction." Though Paschall was a case in which state law (the statute of limitations) was antecedent to the federal right, rather than a case like the tax refund illustration, in which state law provides a distinct basis for relief, the Court's reason for remanding has more general applicability.

constitutional issue if possible?[7] Can the Supreme Court mandate such a canon of avoidance? Can Congress?[8]

(6) Further Problems in Application. Three further difficulties in the administration of the adequate and independent state ground rule are explored in the remaining materials in this Section:

(a) With the Court's jurisdiction turning on whether a given issue is one of federal or state law, surprisingly difficult questions of categorization sometimes arise.

(b) Once state and federal issues have been sorted out, the question may arise whether a state law ground is genuinely "independent" of the federal issue. Suppose, for example, that a state court rules that the state constitutional guarantee of free speech protects exactly what the federal First Amendment protects—no more and no less—and then strikes down a state statute as invalid under the state's constitutional guarantee. Is the state ground truly independent of federal law so as to bar Supreme Court review?

(c) Finally, a state court's opinion may be unclear about whether the judgment rested on an independent state-law ground, on federal law, or on both—a problem posed in the case that follows.

Michigan v. Long

463 U.S. 1032 (1983).
Certiorari to the Supreme Court of Michigan.

■ JUSTICE O'CONNOR delivered the opinion of the Court.

* * * In the present case, respondent David Long was convicted for possession of marihuana found by police in the passenger compartment and trunk of the automobile that he was driving. The police searched the passenger compartment because they had reason to believe that the vehicle contained weapons potentially dangerous to the officers. We hold that the protective search of the passenger compartment was reasonable under the principles articulated in Terry [v. Ohio, 392 U.S. 1 (1968),] and other decisions of this Court. We also examine Long's argument that the decision below rests upon an adequate and independent state ground, and we decide in favor of our jurisdiction.

---

[7] For a variety of views, see Kahn, *Interpretation and Authority in State Constitutionalism*, 106 Harv.L.Rev. 1147 (1993); Linde, *First Things First: Rediscovering the States' Bills of Rights*, 9 U.Balt.L.Rev. 379 (1980); Pollock, *State Constitutions as Separate Sources of Fundamental Rights*, 35 Rutgers L.Rev. 707 (1983); Utter, *Swimming in the Jaws of the Crocodile: State Court Comment on Federal Constitutional Issues When Disposing of Cases on State Constitutional Grounds*, 63 Tex.L.Rev. 1025 (1985). See also Kloppenberg, *Avoiding Constitutional Questions*, 35 B.C.L.Rev. 1003, 1061–65 (1994). *Cf.* Sutton, 51 Imperfect Solutions: States and the Making of American Constitutional Law (2018) (urging federal courts to resolve state claims before parallel federal claims and highlighting that Chief Justice Burger once suggested state courts should "first * * * resolv[e] issues arising under their constitutions and statutes [before] passing on matters concerning federal law").

[8] For additional discussion, see Wechsler, note 4, *supra*, at 1056.

I

[The trial court denied Long's motion to suppress the marihuana. Long's conviction for possession of marihuana was affirmed by the Michigan Court of Appeals. The Michigan Supreme Court reversed, however, holding that "the sole justification of the Terry search, protection of the police officers and others nearby, cannot justify the search in this case."]

We granted certiorari * * *.

II

Before reaching the merits, we must consider Long's argument that we are without jurisdiction to decide this case because the decision below rests on an adequate and independent state ground. The court below referred twice to the State Constitution in its opinion, but otherwise relied exclusively on federal law.[3] Long argues that the Michigan courts have provided greater protection from searches and seizures under the State Constitution than is afforded under the Fourth Amendment, and the references to the State Constitution therefore establish an adequate and independent ground for the decision below.

* * * Although we have announced a number of principles in order to help us determine whether various forms of references to state law constitute adequate and independent state grounds,[4] we openly admit that we have thus far not developed a satisfying and consistent approach for resolving this vexing issue. In some instances, we have taken the strict view that if the ground of decision was at all unclear, we would dismiss the case. See, *e.g.*, Lynch v. New York ex rel. Pierson, 293 U.S. 52 (1934). In other instances, we have vacated, see, *e.g.*, Minnesota v. National Tea Co., 309 U.S. 551 (1940), or continued a case, see, *e.g.*, Herb v. Pitcairn, 324 U.S. 117 (1945), in order to obtain clarification about the nature of a state court decision. See also California v. Krivda, 409 U.S. 33 (1972). In more recent cases, we have ourselves examined state law to determine whether state courts have used federal law to guide their

---

[3] On the first occasion, the court merely cited in a footnote both the State and Federal Constitutions. On the second occasion, at the conclusion of the opinion, the court stated: "We hold, therefore, that the deputies' search of the vehicle was proscribed by the Fourth Amendment to the United States Constitution and art. 1, § 11 of the Michigan Constitution."

[4] For example, we have long recognized that "where the judgment of a state court rests upon two grounds, one of which is federal and the other non-federal in character, our jurisdiction fails if the non-federal ground is independent of the federal ground and adequate to support the judgment." Fox Film Corp. v. Muller, 296 U.S. 207, 210 (1935). We may review a state case decided on a federal ground even if it is clear that there was an available state ground for decision on which the state court could properly have relied. Beecher v. Alabama, 389 U.S. 35, 37, n.3 (1967). Also, if, in our view, the state court " 'felt compelled by what it understood to be federal constitutional considerations to construe * * * its own law in the manner it did,' " then we will not treat a normally adequate state ground as independent, and there will be no question about our jurisdiction. Delaware v. Prouse, 440 U.S. 648, 653 (1979) (quoting Zacchini v. Scripps-Howard Broadcasting Co., 433 U.S. 562, 568 (1977)). Finally, "where the non-federal ground is so interwoven with the [federal ground] as not to be an independent matter, or is not of sufficient breadth to sustain the judgment without any decision of the other, our jurisdiction is plain." Enterprise Irrigation District v. Farmers Mutual Canal Co., 243 U.S. 157, 164 (1917).

application of state law or to provide the actual basis for the decision that was reached. See Texas v. Brown, 460 U.S. 730, 732–733, n.1 (1983) (plurality opinion). *Cf.* South Dakota v. Neville, 459 U.S. 553, 569 (1983) (Stevens, J., dissenting). In Oregon v. Kennedy, 456 U.S. 667, 670–671 (1982), we rejected an invitation to remand to the state court for clarification even when the decision rested in part on a case from the state court, because we determined that the state case itself rested upon federal grounds. We added that "[e]ven if the case admitted of more doubt as to whether federal and state grounds for decision were intermixed, the fact that the state court relied to the extent it did on federal grounds requires us to reach the merits." *Id.*, at 671.

This ad hoc method of dealing with cases that involve possible adequate and independent state grounds is antithetical to the doctrinal consistency that is required when sensitive issues of federal-state relations are involved. Moreover, none of the various methods of disposition that we have employed thus far recommends itself as the preferred method that we should apply to the exclusion of others, and we therefore determine that it is appropriate to reexamine our treatment of this jurisdictional issue in order to achieve the consistency that is necessary.

The process of examining state law is unsatisfactory because it requires us to interpret state laws with which we are generally unfamiliar, and which often, as in this case, have not been discussed at length by the parties. Vacation and continuance for clarification have also been unsatisfactory both because of the delay and decrease in efficiency of judicial administration, see Dixon v. Duffy, 344 U.S. 143 (1952), and, more important, because these methods of disposition place significant burdens on state courts to demonstrate the presence or absence of our jurisdiction. See Philadelphia Newspapers, Inc. v. Jerome, 434 U.S. 241, 244 (1978) (Rehnquist, J., dissenting); Department of Motor Vehicles v. Rios, 410 U.S. 425, 427 (1973) (Douglas, J., dissenting). Finally, outright dismissal of cases is clearly not a panacea because it cannot be doubted that there is an important need for uniformity in federal law, and that this need goes unsatisfied when we fail to review an opinion that rests primarily upon federal grounds and where the *independence* of an alleged state ground is not apparent from the four corners of the opinion. * * *

Respect for the independence of state courts, as well as avoidance of rendering advisory opinions, have been the cornerstones of this Court's refusal to decide cases where there is an adequate and independent state ground. It is precisely because of this respect for state courts, and this desire to avoid advisory opinions, that we do not wish to continue to decide issues of state law that go beyond the opinion that we review, or to require state courts to reconsider cases to clarify the grounds of their decisions. Accordingly, when, as in this case, a state court decision fairly appears to rest primarily on federal law, or to be interwoven with the federal law, and when the adequacy and independence of any possible state law ground is not clear from the face of the opinion, we will accept as the most reasonable explanation that the state court decided the case the way it did because it believed that federal law required it to do so. If a state court chooses merely to rely on federal precedents as it would on the precedents of all other jurisdictions, then it need only make clear by a plain statement in its judgment or opinion that the federal cases are being used only for the purpose of guidance, and do not themselves compel the result that the court has reached. * * * If the state court decision indicates clearly and expressly that it is alternatively based on bona fide separate, adequate, and independent grounds, we, of course, will not undertake to review the decision.

This approach obviates in most instances the need to examine state law in order to decide the nature of the state court decision, and will at the same time avoid the danger of our rendering advisory opinions.[6] It also avoids the unsatisfactory and intrusive practice of requiring state courts to clarify their decisions to the satisfaction of this Court. We believe that such an approach will provide state judges with a clearer opportunity to develop state jurisprudence unimpeded by federal interference, and yet will preserve the integrity of federal law. "It is fundamental that state courts be left free and unfettered by us in interpreting their state constitutions. But it is equally important that ambiguous or obscure adjudications by state courts do not stand as barriers to a determination by this Court of the validity under the federal constitution of state action." National Tea Co., *supra*, at 557.

The principle that we will not review judgments of state courts that rest on adequate and independent state grounds is based, in part, on "the limitations of our own jurisdiction." Herb v. Pitcairn, 324 U.S. 117, 125 (1945). The jurisdictional concern is that we not "render an advisory opinion, and if the same judgment would be rendered by the state court after we corrected its views of federal laws, our review could amount to nothing more than an advisory opinion." *Id.*, at 126. Our requirement of a "plain statement" that a decision rests upon adequate and independent state grounds does not in any way authorize the rendering of advisory opinions. Rather, in determining, as we must, whether we have jurisdiction to review a case that is alleged to rest on adequate and independent state grounds, we merely assume that there are no such grounds when it is not clear from the opinion itself that the state court relied upon an adequate and independent state ground and when it fairly appears that the state court rested its decision primarily on federal law.[8]

---

6   There may be certain circumstances in which clarification is necessary or desirable, and we will not be foreclosed from taking the appropriate action.

8   * * * In dissent, Justice Stevens proposes the novel view that this Court should never review a state court decision unless the Court wishes to vindicate a federal right that has been endangered. The rationale of the dissent is not restricted to cases where the decision is arguably supported by adequate and independent state grounds. Rather, Justice Stevens appears to

Our review of the decision below under this framework leaves us unconvinced that it rests upon an independent state ground. Apart from its two citations to the State Constitution, the court below relied *exclusively* on its understanding of Terry and other federal cases. Not a single state case was cited to support the state court's holding that the search of the passenger compartment was unconstitutional. Indeed, the court declared that the search in this case was unconstitutional because "[t]he Court of Appeals erroneously applied the principles of Terry v. Ohio * * * to the search of the interior of the vehicle in this case." The references to the state constitution in no way indicate that the decision below rested on grounds in any way *independent* from the state court's interpretation of federal law. Even if we accept that the Michigan Constitution has been interpreted to provide independent protection for certain rights also secured under the Fourth Amendment, it fairly appears in this case that the Michigan Supreme Court rested its decision primarily on federal law.

Rather than dismissing the case, or requiring that the state court reconsider its decision on our behalf solely because of a mere possibility that an adequate and independent ground supports the judgment, we find that we have jurisdiction in the absence of a plain statement that the decision below rested on an adequate and independent state ground. It appears to us that the state court "felt compelled by what it understood to be federal constitutional considerations to construe * * * its own law in the manner it did." Zacchini v. Scripps-Howard Broadcasting Co., 433 U.S. 562, 568 (1977).[10]

III

[The Court held that the search was valid under Terry v. Ohio.]

IV

[The Court concluded that a remand was necessary to permit the Michigan Supreme Court to address a different federal constitutional question that that court had not resolved in its earlier decision.]

---

believe that even if the decision below rests exclusively on federal grounds, this Court should not review the decision as long as there is no federal right that is endangered.

The state courts handle the vast bulk of all criminal litigation in this country. * * * The state courts are required to apply federal constitutional standards, and they necessarily create a considerable body of "federal law" in the process. It is not surprising that this Court has become more interested in the application and development of federal law by state courts in the light of the recent significant expansion of federally created standards that we have imposed on the States. * * *

[10]   There is nothing unfair about requiring a plain statement of an independent state ground in this case. Even if we were to rest our decision on an evaluation of the state law relevant to Long's claim, as we have sometimes done in the past, our understanding of Michigan law would also result in our finding that we have jurisdiction to decide this case. Under state search and seizure law, a "higher standard" is imposed under art. 1, § 11 of the 1963 Michigan Constitution. See People v. Secrest, 413 Mich. 521, 525, 321 N.W.2d 368, 369 (1982). If, however, the item seized is, *inter alia*, a "narcotic drug * * * seized by a peace officer outside the curtilage of any dwelling house in this state," art. 1, § 11 of the 1963 Michigan Constitution, then the seizure is governed by a standard identical to that imposed by the Fourth Amendment. See People v. Moore, 391 Mich. 426, 435, 216 N.W.2d 770, 775 (1974). * * *

V

The judgment of the Michigan Supreme Court is reversed, and the case is remanded for further proceedings not inconsistent with this opinion.

It is so ordered.

■ JUSTICE BLACKMUN, concurring in part and concurring in the judgment.

I join Parts I, III, IV, and V of the Court's opinion. While I am satisfied that the Court has jurisdiction in this particular case, I do not join the Court, in Part II of its opinion, in fashioning a new presumption of jurisdiction over cases coming here from state courts. Although I agree with the Court that uniformity in federal criminal law is desirable, I see little efficiency and an increased danger of advisory opinions in the Court's new approach.

■ [JUSTICE BRENNAN, with whom JUSTICE MARSHALL joined, dissented on the merits of the Fourth Amendment issue. On the jurisdictional question, he said only: "I agree that the Court has jurisdiction to decide this case. See [footnote 10 of the Court's opinion]."]

■ JUSTICE STEVENS, dissenting.

The jurisprudential questions presented in this case are far more important than the question whether the Michigan police officer's search of respondent's car violated the Fourth Amendment. The case raises profoundly significant questions concerning the relationship between two sovereigns—the State of Michigan and the United States of America.

The Supreme Court of the State of Michigan expressly held "that the deputies' search of the vehicle was proscribed by the Fourth Amendment to the United States Constitution and *art 1, § 11 of the Michigan Constitution.*" (emphasis added). The state law ground is clearly adequate to support the judgment, but the question whether it is independent of the Michigan Supreme Court's understanding of federal law is more difficult. Four possible ways of resolving that question present themselves: (1) asking the Michigan Supreme Court directly, (2) attempting to infer from all possible sources of state law what the Michigan Supreme Court meant, (3) presuming that adequate state grounds are independent unless it clearly appears otherwise, or (4) presuming that adequate state grounds are *not* independent unless it clearly appears otherwise. This Court has, on different occasions, employed each of the first three approaches; never until today has it even hinted at the fourth. In order to "achieve the consistency that is necessary," the Court today undertakes a reexamination of all the possibilities. It rejects the first approach as inefficient and unduly burdensome for state courts, and rejects the second approach as an inappropriate expenditure of our resources. Although I find both of those decisions defensible in themselves, I cannot accept the Court's decision to choose the fourth approach over the third * * *.

If we reject the intermediate approaches, we are left with a choice between two presumptions: one in favor of our taking jurisdiction, and one against it. Historically, the latter presumption has always prevailed. See, *e.g.*, Durley v. Mayo, 351 U.S. 277, 285 (1956); Lynch v. New York ex rel. Pierson, 293 U.S. 52 (1934). The rule, as succinctly stated in Lynch, was as follows:

> "Where the judgment of the state court rests on two grounds, one involving a federal question and the other not, or if it does not appear upon which of two grounds the judgment was based, and the ground independent of a federal question is sufficient in itself to sustain it, this Court will not take jurisdiction." *Id.*, at 54–55.

The Court today points out that in several cases we have weakened the traditional presumption by using the other two intermediate approaches identified above. Since those two approaches are now to be rejected, however, I would think that *stare decisis* would call for a return to historical principle. Instead, the Court seems to conclude that because some precedents are to be rejected, we must overrule them all. * * *

The nature of the case before us hardly compels a departure from tradition. These are not cases in which an American citizen has been deprived of a right secured by the United States Constitution or a federal statute. Rather, they are cases in which a state court has upheld a citizen's assertion of a right, finding the citizen to be protected under both federal and state law. The attorney for the complaining party is an officer of the state itself, who asks us to rule that the state court interpreted federal rights too broadly and "overprotected" the citizen.

Such cases should not be of inherent concern to this Court. The reason may be illuminated by assuming that the events underlying this case had arisen in another country, perhaps the Republic of Finland. If the Finnish police had arrested a Finnish citizen for possession of marihuana, and the Finnish courts had turned him loose, no American would have standing to object. If instead they had arrested an American citizen and acquitted him, we might have been concerned about the arrest but we surely could not have complained about the acquittal, even if the Finnish court had based its decision on its understanding of the United States Constitution. That would be true even if we had a treaty with Finland requiring it to respect the rights of American citizens under the United States Constitution. We would only be motivated to intervene if an American citizen were unfairly arrested, tried, and convicted by the foreign tribunal.

In this case the State of Michigan * * * simply provided greater protection to one of its citizens than some other State might provide or, indeed, than this Court might require throughout the country.

I believe that in reviewing the decisions of state courts, the primary role of this Court is to make sure that persons who seek to *vindicate* federal rights have been fairly heard. That belief resonates with statements in many of our prior cases. * * *

Until recently we had virtually no interest in cases [like the present one]. Thirty years ago, this Court reviewed only one. Nevada v. Stacher, 346 U.S. 906 (1953). Indeed, that appears to have been the only case during the entire 1953 Term in which a State even sought review of a decision by its own judiciary. Fifteen years ago, we did not review any such cases, although the total number of requests had mounted to three. Some time during the past decade, * * * our priorities shifted. The result is a docket swollen with requests by States to reverse judgments that their courts have rendered in favor of their citizens.[3] I am confident that a future Court will recognize the error of this allocation of resources. When that day comes, I think it likely that the Court will also reconsider the propriety of today's expansion of our jurisdiction.

The Court offers only one reason for asserting authority over cases such as the one presented today: "an important need for uniformity in federal law [that] goes unsatisfied when we fail to review an opinion that rests primarily upon federal grounds and where the independence of an alleged state ground is not apparent from the four corners of the opinion" (emphasis omitted). Of course, the supposed need to "review an opinion" clashes directly with our oft-repeated reminder that "our power is to correct wrong judgments, not to revise opinions." Herb v. Pitcairn, 324 U.S. 117, 126 (1945). The clash is not merely one of form: the "need for uniformity in federal law" is truly an ungovernable engine. That same need is no less present when it is perfectly clear that a state ground is both independent and adequate. In fact, it is equally present if a state prosecutor announces that he believes a certain policy of nonenforcement is commanded by federal law. Yet we have never claimed jurisdiction to correct such errors, no matter how egregious they may be, and no matter how much they may thwart the desires of the state electorate. We do not sit to expound our understanding of the Constitution to interested listeners in the legal community; we sit to resolve disputes. If it is not apparent that our views would affect the outcome of a particular case, we cannot presume to interfere.

Finally, I am thoroughly baffled by the Court's suggestion that it must stretch its jurisdiction and reverse the judgment of the Michigan Supreme Court in order to show "[r]espect for the independence of state courts." Would we show respect for the Republic of Finland by convening a special sitting for the sole purpose of declaring that its decision to release an American citizen was based upon a misunderstanding of American law?

I respectfully dissent.

---

[3]   This Term, we devoted argument time to [twelve such cases], as well as this case. And a cursory survey of the United States Law Week index reveals that so far this Term at least 80 petitions for certiorari to state courts were filed by the States themselves.

***

NOTE ON REVIEW OF STATE DECISIONS UPHOLDING CLAIMS OF FEDERAL RIGHT

(1) Justice Stevens's Argument. Justice Stevens's dissent in Long argues, quite apart from the problem of ambiguity (which is explored in the following Note), that the Court should not review state court judgments that *uphold* claims of federal right.[1] He returned to this theme in his dissent in Delaware v. Van Arsdall, 475 U.S. 673 (1986), where the Court reviewed a Delaware decision that had found a violation of the Confrontation Clause of the Sixth Amendment. Agreeing that the federal Constitution had been violated, the Supreme Court nonetheless vacated the state court's judgment reversing the conviction. The Court concluded that (a) as a matter of federal law, the violation was not grounds for automatic reversal if the error was "harmless"; (b) the state court's reversal did not clearly rest on a state-law "automatic reversal" rule; and (c) the case should therefore be remanded to allow the state court to determine whether the error was "harmless" under federal standards.

Justice Stevens objected that this disposition "operates to expand this Court's review of state remedies that over-compensate for violations of federal constitutional rights," adding that "the claim of these cases on our docket is secondary to the need to scrutinize judgments disparaging those rights." He also complained that reviewing such cases puts pressure on the state courts to confine *state* constitutional protections to the level required by the federal Constitution and noted that on remand the Delaware courts were free to apply an automatic reversal rule on the basis of state law. Despite these arguments, the Court has adhered to the position that it has both the power and responsibility to review state court decisions that uphold individual claims of federal right. See, *e.g.*, Arkansas v. Sullivan, 532 U.S. 769, 772 (2001) (per curiam). For an extended defense of Justice Stevens's position, see Mazzone, *When the Supreme Court is Not Supreme*, 104 Nw.U.L.Rev. 979 (2010).

(2) The 1914 Expansion of Supreme Court Jurisdiction. As Justice Stevens acknowledged in Van Arsdall (but not in Long), the Judiciary Act of 1914 gave the Supreme Court power for the first time to review state court determinations upholding claims of federal right. See p. 617, *supra*. Justice Stevens described that Act as designed to permit the Supreme Court to review "Lochner-style" overenforcement of supposed federal limits on the states' power to enact social legislation. Is there a principled distinction between review in "Lochner-style" cases and in Long or Van Arsdall? If so, what is it? And, to take one example, on which side of the divide would a hypothetical case of "overenforcement"—that is, an expansive interpretation—of a Second Amendment claim fall? *Cf.* District of Columbia v. Heller, 554 U.S. 570 (2008).

***

[1]   In Minnesota v. Clover Leaf Creamery, 449 U.S. 456 (1981), and City of Revere v. Massachusetts Gen. Hosp., 463 U.S. 239 (1983), Justice Stevens voiced the same objection.

Does the absence of review in cases of "overenforcement" before 1914 support the view (advanced by Justice Stevens in Van Arsdall) that the Court should adopt a systematic policy (as against the normal case-by-case operation of the certiorari practice) disfavoring review in such cases? If Justice Stevens's "low priority" approach is justified, should the Court, in its Rules, state that approach to be its policy—much as the Rules identify, for example, the priority assigned to reviewing cases involving conflicts among the lower courts?

(3) Uniformity Versus Federalism. The conventional wisdom is that a significant purpose of Article III (now implemented by § 1257) is to permit the Supreme Court to unify federal law by reviewing state court decisions of federal questions—a point stressed, for example, by Hamilton in Federalist No. 82 and by Justice Story in Martin v. Hunter's Lessee, see p. 620, *supra*. Assuming that to be the case,[2] how effectively can the Court play that role given that it rarely reviews state court decisions at all, much less those upholding claims of federal right? See p. 619, *supra*.

Beyond the uniformity problem lie other, deeper issues. Justice Stevens evidently assumes that the Constitution's guarantees of individual rights represent the only significant constitutional norms. Even were this true of the Bill of Rights and the other amendments when viewed in isolation, consider whether the Constitution as a whole "contains other sorts of values as well. It gives the federal government powers, but also enacts limitations on those powers. *The limitations, too, count as setting forth constitutional values.* * * * When a court upholds a state criminal statute against the claim that it violates the first amendment, it is rejecting one sort of constitutional claim, but it is also upholding principles of separation of powers and federalism which themselves have constitutional status." Bator, *The State Courts and Federal Constitutional Litigation*, 22 Wm. & Mary L.Rev. 605, 631–33 (1981). Does Justice Stevens's reference to Lochner illustrate these points?

Consider, also, the distinct point that states, when they complain of "overenforcement" of federal constitutional norms, often represent important individual or collective interests—as, for example, in Regents of the University of California v. Bakke, 438 U.S. 265, 279–80 (1978), where a state agency challenged a state court's invalidation under the federal Constitution of an affirmative action plan. See Shapiro, Federalism: A Dialogue 99–104 (1995). But see Sager, *Fair Measure: The Legal Status of Underenforced Constitutional Norms*, 91 Harv.L.Rev. 1212, 1242–63 (1978) (*inter alia*, urging the Stevens position while discussing a number of the objections to it).

(4) Supreme Court Review to "Unfreeze" State Political Processes. If a state's highest court provides broader protection of individual rights, under state statutory or constitutional provisions, than the federal Constitution demands, political actors in the state may express their

---

[2]   Compare Frost, *Overvaluing Uniformity*, 94 Va.L.Rev. 1567, 1619–20 (2008), which argues that, "[a]t best, Article III appears to be neutral with regard to uniformity, and several of its provisions can be read as antithetical to the idea that the federal judiciary was to devote significant resources to that project."

disagreement by amending the state statute or constitution to be narrower. But some have objected that a state court judgment that the federal Constitution bars the state government from action, if unreviewable by the Supreme Court, would effectively freeze the law in that state (subject only to an amendment of the United States Constitution): no change in state law could overcome the decision. (The possibility that the state court would, in a subsequent case, reconsider and reverse its own judgment on the federal issue may be remote, as may be the possibility that the United States Supreme Court would review the same issue in a case from another state court that *denied* the same federal claim.) Would this be a tolerable situation?

Consider the concerns expressed by then-California Attorney General Deukmejian, who criticized his state's highest court for improperly insulating its decisions from any review by relying on both state and federal grounds: the presence of a state ground bars Supreme Court review of the federal ground, while the presence of a federal ground makes futile, or at least discourages, popular review of the state law ground. See Deukmejian & Thompson, *All Sail and No Anchor—Judicial Review Under the California Constitution*, 6 Hast.Const.L.Q. 975, 996–97 (1979). Should the Court review such cases, even though reversal of the federal ground could not change the judgment below, in order to avoid "freezing" the state's political processes? Compare Bice, *Anderson and the Adequate State Ground*, 45 S.Calif.L.Rev. 750 (1972) (so arguing), with Falk, *The State Constitution: A More than "Adequate" Nonfederal Ground*, 61 Calif.L.Rev. 273 (1973) (criticizing the argument).[3]

(5) The Debate Renewed. In Kansas v. Carr, 577 U.S. 108 (2016), the Court revisited the debate over whether it should hear cases in which state courts "overprotect" federal rights. In its modern incarnation, the debate takes the form of asking whether the Court should exercise its discretion to deny certiorari in such cases, and not whether there is an adequate and independent state ground per se. Petitioner sought review of a Kansas Supreme Court decision vacating respondents' capital sentences on the ground that the trial court violated the Eighth Amendment by (a) giving the jury unclear instructions about mitigating circumstances and (b) declining to sever sentencing proceedings for respondents, who had been jointly tried. In his final opinion for the Court, Justice Scalia held that the state supreme court's opinion left "no room for doubt that it was relying on the Federal Constitution."

In a dissent that echoed some of the concerns voiced by Justice Stevens in his Michigan v. Long dissent, Justice Sotomayor argued that the Court

---

[3]   V. Amar & Brownstein, *When Avoiding Federal Questions Shouldn't Evade Federal Review*, 12 Green Bag 2d 381, 384 (2009), notes that without Long's presumption, "state courts * * * might fuzz up their opinions to foreclose U.S. Supreme Court reversal of results they favor, but at the same time invoke enough federal law to suggest—even when such federal law isn't really constraining—federal responsibility for the outcome of controversial disputes." Like Deukmejian & Thompson, the authors further observe that because an ambiguous state court decision *might* rest on federal grounds, "attempts by state electorates to amend their constitutions or to impose electoral sanctions on state court judges could be discouraged by the not-unrealistic possibility that the state law options were constrained by federal requirements."

should grant certiorari only when "the benefits of hearing a case outweigh the costs of so doing." In her view, reviewing state court cases that grant relief to criminal defendants imposes several systemic costs: First, the Supreme Court's review "may have little effect if a lower court is able to reinstate its holding as a matter of state law." Second, in cases involving "no suggestion" that the state court "violated any [individual's] federal constitutional right," federal review "intervene[s] in an intrastate dispute between the State's executive and its judiciary rather than entrusting the State's structure of government to sort it out." Third, granting review interferes with federalism interests in "state experimentation with how best to guarantee a fair trial." In this case, moreover, Justice Sotomayor saw few benefits to Supreme Court review because the key issues were hard to generalize beyond the particular state sentencing scheme or even the facts of the case. Finally, Justice Sotomayor stressed that the state court's rulings neither "indicate[d] a hostility to applying federal precedents" nor granted relief that was "particularly likely to destabilize or significantly interfere with federal policy." In that light, she concluded that "the Court should not have granted certiorari."

Justice Scalia's opinion for the Court responded that Supreme Court review was appropriate because the state court held that "the Federal Constitution *requires*" vacating the state sentences. The Court emphasized that "state courts may experiment all they want with their own constitutions, and often do in the wake of this Court's decisions." But, "what a state court cannot do is experiment with our federal Constitution and expect to elude this Court's review so long as victory goes to the criminal defendant." Such an approach, in Justice Scalia's view, undermines uniformity while "enabl[ing] state courts to blame the unpopular death-sentence reprieve of the most horrible criminals upon the Federal Constitution when it is in fact their own doing." Does shifting the debate to one about the appropriateness of granting certiorari alter the competing interests at stake? When, if ever, should the Court allow the posture of the parties to influence its decisions to grant or deny certiorari?

NOTE ON AMBIGUOUS STATE DECISIONS AND TECHNIQUES FOR CLARIFYING THEM

(1) Possible Approaches to Ambiguous State Court Judgments. When, as in Michigan v. Long, it is uncertain whether a state decision rested on a federal ground, a state ground, or both, the Court can (a) seek clarification from the state court (by vacating and remanding with a request for clarification);[1] (b) try to resolve the ambiguity itself by examining the

---

[1]   See, *e.g.*, Philadelphia Newspapers, Inc. v. Jerome, 434 U.S. 241, 242 (1978); Minnesota v. National Tea Co., 309 U.S. 551, 556–57 (1940). Although rarely done, the Court might also hold the case or defer consideration of the petition for a writ of certiorari so that counsel can apply to the state court for a certificate as to whether its judgment was intended to rest on an adequate and independent state ground. See, *e.g.*, Lynum v. Illinois, 368 U.S. 908 (1961), 372 U.S. 528, 535–36 (1963) (consideration of certiorari petition deferred for counsel to seek

relevant state-law materials;[2] (c) dismiss on the ground that, in view of the ambiguity, the obligation affirmatively to establish jurisdiction has not been satisfied;[3] or (d) presume that the decision rested on a federal ground (the opposite stance from alternative "(c)"). Over the years, the Court oscillated among the first three alternatives; Long was the first time it embraced the fourth.

(2) The Alternative of Vacation. In Long, none of the Justices favored vacation and remand. Yet might that approach best serve the two concerns that Justice O'Connor identified as underlying the adequate and independent state ground doctrine—the avoidance of unnecessary decisions of federal law (especially federal constitutional law) and respect for the independence of state courts? See Minnesota v. National Tea Co., 309 U.S. 551, 557 (1940) (so arguing). As Justice Jackson once contended (writing for the Court), where the state court opinion is unclear, "it seems consistent with the respect due the highest courts of states of the Union that they be asked rather than told what they have intended. If this imposes an unwelcome burden it should be mitigated by the knowledge that it is to protect their jurisdiction from unwitting interference as well as to protect our own from unwitting renunciation." Herb v. Pitcairn, 324 U.S. 117, 128 (1945). Indeed, even though the Court in Long declined to vacate and remand for clarification, its decision nevertheless required the Michigan Supreme Court, on remand, to clarify the basis for its original decision in order to dispose of the case. Hence, if the Court wishes to avoid "advisory opinions" or, at least, unnecessary decisions of federal law, isn't vacation and remand superior to the Court's current position?

The principal problem with vacation and remand is that it causes delay. Given that the Supreme Court is not a court of errors, and given the purposes for which it exercises its certiorari jurisdiction and its considerable discretion in doing so, how serious is that problem?

(3) Other Justifications for Long. If one looks beyond respect for state courts and the avoidance of possibly unnecessary decisions, do any of the following arguments offer convincing justifications for the approach adopted in Long?

(a) The certiorari jurisdiction assumes that Supreme Court review should be provided not because it is "necessary" to resolve a particular dispute but rather to decide important issues of federal law. By increasing the number of cases eligible for review, Long maximizes the Court's

---

certificate from state court; certificate treated as conclusive to establish jurisdiction); Herb v. Pitcairn, 324 U.S. 117, 128 (1945).

[2] See, *e.g.*, South Dakota v. Neville, 459 U.S. 553 (1983); Jankovich v. Indiana Toll Road Comm'n, 379 U.S. 487 (1965); compare footnote 10 of the Court's opinion in Long. As early as Johnson v. Risk, 137 U.S. 300 (1890), the Court examined prior state decisions before concluding that a state court judgment (rendered without opinion) could have rested on the state statute of limitations; it added that the party seeking review, if claiming that a federal question was in fact dispositive, should have obtained a certificate to that effect from the state supreme court.

[3] This was the approach of the earliest cases. See, *e.g.*, Klinger v. Missouri, 80 U.S. (13 Wall.) 257 (1871); Eustis v. Bolles, 150 U.S. 361 (1893). See also, *e.g.*, Lynch v. New York ex rel. Pierson, 293 U.S. 52, 54 (1934); Durley v. Mayo, 351 U.S. 277 (1956).

flexibility in managing its docket and in finding the right vehicle for resolving important federal issues.

(b)   Unlike most federal laws, the federal Constitution has not had a merely interstitial role; the federal Constitution is the primary protection of individual rights, and it remains so despite the recent invigoration of state constitutional guarantees. *Cf.* Brennan, *State Constitutions and the Protection of Individual Rights*, 90 Harv.L.Rev. 489 (1977) (promoting greater development of independent state constitutional law); Sutton, 51 Imperfect Solutions: States and the Making of American Constitutional Law (2018) (highlighting examples of where state constitutional law does not align perfectly with federal constitutional law). Thus, as a matter of probability, an ambiguous state court opinion is more likely to have rested on federal than on state constitutional law. (Note, however, that Long appears to apply to all ambiguous state court decisions, not merely to those involving federal constitutional questions.)

(c)   Long makes it more likely that, in order to avoid the possibility of reversal, state judges will clearly elaborate a state law ground when it exists. Since it is uniquely within the power of state courts to supply such clarity, does Long in effect operate as a penalty default rule—subjecting state court decisions to Supreme Court review unless they clearly articulate that the decision rests on an adequate and independent state ground?

(d)   If the Court reversed the Long presumption and instead held that ambiguity about the basis for a state court decision precludes Supreme Court review, then state courts might be better able to evade accountability for their decisions. See Paragraph (4), pp. 665–666, *supra*. Does that concern seem substantial enough to sustain the Long presumption?

(4)   The Meaning of Long. How significant a change in practice did Long introduce? Note that the application of Long's presumption depends on two "soft" requirements: the state decision must (a) "fairly appear" to rest "primarily" on federal law or be "interwoven" with federal law, *and* (b) the independence of the state ground must be "not clear" from the face of the state court opinion. These are not self-applying concepts. Subsequent decisions, however, have articulated the Long presumption more broadly than did the Long opinion.

(a)   In Ohio v. Johnson, 467 U.S. 493, 497 n.7 (1984), the Court stated Long's holding in the disjunctive: "we have jurisdiction * * * if the decision 'appears to rest primarily on federal law or to be interwoven with the federal law,' *or* if the 'adequacy and independence of any possible state law ground is not clear from the face of the opinion'" (emphasis added). Long said *and* rather than *or*. When might that difference in phrasing matter?

(b)   In Pennsylvania v. Labron, 518 U.S. 938 (1996) (per curiam), the Court ruled that a state court opinion that rested on the state constitution but cited federal constitutional precedents did not contain "a 'plain statement' sufficient to tell us 'the federal cases [were] being used only for the purpose of guidance, and d[id] not themselves compel the result that the court had reached'" (quoting Long). Justice Stevens's dissent (joined by Justice Ginsburg) objected that the state court had not rested "primarily" on federal law, nor was its holding "interwoven" with federal law; thus, the dissent argued, the Court's ruling "extends Michigan v. Long beyond its original scope."

(5) Long and Judicial Discretion. Since Long, the Court has often accepted jurisdiction in the face of ambiguities in the state court opinion. See, *e.g.*, Florida v. Powell, 559 U.S. 50 (2010). But does the Court's reservation in Long of the right to seek clarification from the state court where "necessary or desirable" (see footnote 6 of the Long opinion) suggest that the underlying policy tensions responsible for prior oscillations could still overcome the effort to work out a uniform approach?

In Capital Cities Media, Inc. v. Toole, 466 U.S. 378 (1984) (per curiam), the Court reverted to the practice of vacating and remanding. There, a state trial judge had restricted media access to a criminal trial. The Supreme Court of Pennsylvania, without opinion, denied a media petition (based on the First Amendment) for a writ of prohibition—a decision that might have rested on the ground that Pennsylvania law did not permit appellate review via writ of prohibition. The United States Supreme Court vacated and remanded to the state court for clarification.

Can this shift in technique be explained by the different relationship between state and federal law in Long and in Capital Cities? In Long, p. 656, *supra*, state and federal constitutional provisions provided distinct grounds of relief. In such cases, ambiguity about the presence of an adequate and independent state ground arises when the state court has upheld the position of the federal rightholder. In Capital Cities, by contrast, the possible state ground (lack of jurisdiction to issue a writ of prohibition) was antecedent to the federal right. In such cases, ambiguity about the presence of an adequate and independent state ground arises when the state court has denied the relief sought by the federal rightholder.[4]

The Court has also been inconsistent in three post-Long decisions concerning federal habeas applications by those in state custody. The district courts' habeas jurisdiction, for present purposes, should be thought of as, in substance, a form of federal review of a state court conviction. But habeas jurisdiction, unlike Supreme Court review, is (a) as of right rather than discretionary, and (b) one way—*i.e.*, an individual in custody may challenge a conviction as in violation of the federal Constitution, but the state may not use habeas to complain that a state court decision overprotected federal rights. See generally Chap. XI, Sec. 3, *infra*.

---

[4] The different approach followed in Capital Cities might seem to substantiate the many critics of Long who complained that the Burger Court, not generally known for its expansive view of federal jurisdiction, was extending Supreme Court jurisdiction in Long in order to permit review of a state court decision challenged as overprotecting federal rights. In Capital Cities, by contrast, the Court refused to apply Long's broad view of jurisdiction at the behest of a petitioner complaining that the state court failed to protect federal rights. On this score, consider the statistics noted in Sager, *Fair Measure: The Legal Status of Underenforced Constitutional Norms*, 91 Harv.L.Rev. 1212, 1244 (1978): from 1960–1969, the Supreme Court reviewed only eight cases in which state courts had upheld federal rights, affirming the state court in four of them; from 1970–1978, the Court granted review in 25 such cases, affirming the state court in only one. See also Hellman, *Case Selection in the Burger Court: A Preliminary Inquiry*, 60 Notre Dame L.Rev. 947, 1044–46 (1985); Hellman, *The Shrunken Docket of the Rehnquist Court*, 1996 Sup.Ct.Rev. 403.

Initially, the Court in Harris v. Reed, 489 U.S. 255 (1989), indicated that Long would apply in federal habeas proceedings to determine whether an ambiguous state court ruling had rested on the petitioner's procedural default or on a rejection of the federal constitutional merits in denying post-conviction relief. (If so, under established habeas rules, the petitioner ultimately would be barred from asserting any defaulted claims, subject only to extremely narrow exceptions.) In so holding, the Court in Harris rejected the contention that heightened interests in "finality, federalism, and comity" counseled against extending Long to this context. The Court noted that the Long presumption would impose only a minimal burden on state courts (articulating a clear basis for their decision), but that a different rule would impose significant costs on federal habeas courts (sifting through state court records to determine if a procedural default was asserted and/or researching state law to determine the potential existence of a procedural default). Justice Kennedy dissented, contending that it was not realistic to expect judges in lower state courts to internalize Long's plain statement rule and that the Court's approach would encourage those imprisoned "to burden state courts with a never-ending stream of petitions for postconviction relief."

Although Harris has never been overruled, the Court's subsequent habeas decisions appear to have significantly diluted its force by making it easier for the state to establish that an ambiguous state court decision rested on a finding of procedural default. See, *e.g.*, Coleman v. Thompson, 501 U.S. 722 (1991) (refusing to apply the Harris presumption in a capital case where the state court order dismissing a petition for post-conviction relief "fairly appear[ed]" to rest primarily on state law because it did not mention federal law and because the motion to dismiss had relied solely on the tardiness of a notice of appeal to the state trial court); Ylst v. Nunnemaker, 501 U.S. 797 (1991) (announcing, in an another capital case, the presumption that where the last reasoned state court opinion on a federal question rested on a finding of procedural default, subsequent state court summary orders denying relief also relied on the default rather than the merits, even if the orders and their surrounding circumstances gave no indication of such reliance). See also Wilson v. Sellers, 584 U.S. 122 (2018) (holding that for purposes of assessing whether an unexplained state court decision "unreasonabl[y]" applied federal law or determined questions of fact, a federal habeas court should presume that the decision rested on the same grounds as the last reasoned state court decision in the case); Foster v. Chatman, 578 U.S. 488, 498 n.3 (2016) (affirming the Court's practice of reviewing "a lower [state] court decision * * * in order to ascertain whether a federal question may be implicated in an unreasoned summary order from a higher court").

Does the pattern described in this Paragraph suggest that jurisdictional rules tend to move in the direction of allowing more intensive supervision of areas where the Supreme Court is in the process of changing the relevant substantive rules and wants to assure itself that the state courts are in compliance?

(6) The Importance of Long? Many commentators reacted to the Long decision with hostility.[5] But in the end, how important is Long, given that a state court that in fact relies on state law can, by simply so stating, avoid Supreme Court review? While many post-Long state court decisions fail to indicate clearly whether they rest on state or federal grounds (why do you think such ambiguity persists?), the New Hampshire Supreme Court routinely adds a declaration like the following: "when this court cites federal or other State court opinions in construing provisions of the New Hampshire Constitution or statutes, we rely on those precedents merely for guidance and do not consider our results bound by those decisions. See Michigan v. Long * * *." See, *e.g.*, State v. Ball, 471 A.2d 347, 352 (N.H.1983); see generally Gardner, *The Failed Discourse of State Constitutionalism*, 90 Mich.L.Rev. 761, 785–88, 801, 803–04 (1992).

Even when the Supreme Court does review an ambiguous decision and reverses on the federal issue, the state courts retain the power on remand to consider independent state-law grounds and, indeed, to rely on such grounds in reinstating their initial judgment. Of course, there is always the possibility that a Supreme Court decision on the merits of the federal issue might influence the state court's resolution, on remand, of an uncertain question of state constitutional law. For example, in See v. Commonwealth, 746 S.W.2d 401, 402 (Ky.1988), a criminal defendant claimed a violation of a constitutional right to confrontation that the Kentucky Supreme Court had recognized as a matter of federal law in a prior decision that in turn was reversed by the Supreme Court. On remand, the state court recognized that it remained free under the Kentucky Constitution to uphold the claimed right, but, in refusing to do so, stated that it was "not convinced that the [alleged error] is so violative of a basic right guaranteed by the Kentucky Constitution that we should place ourselves in direct opposition to an opinion of the United States Supreme Court * * *."

(7) The Choice for State Judges. Consider the options that judges on the states' highest courts face in many of the cases that come before their courts. If a judge believes a litigant has a valid claim of constitutional right which the judge could uphold, in good conscience, (i) on state constitutional grounds alone, (ii) on federal constitutional grounds alone, or (iii) on both state and federal grounds (making clear in the opinion that the state ground is separate and independent), which course should the judge take? Why? What legal, institutional, political, or personal motivations might lead other judges to take a different approach? See also Note (5), p. 655, *supra*.

---

[5] See, *e.g.*, Matasar & Bruch, *Procedural Common Law, Federal Jurisdictional Policy, and Abandonment of the Adequate and Independent State Grounds Doctrine*, 86 Colum.L.Rev. 1291, 1367–82 (1986); Seid, *Schizoid Federalism, Supreme Court Power and Inadequate Adequate State Ground Theory: Michigan v. Long*, 18 Creighton L.Rev. 1 (1984); Welsh, *Reconsidering the Constitutional Relationship Between State and Federal Courts: A Critique of Michigan v. Long*, 59 Notre Dame L.Rev. 1118 (1984). For more favorable treatments, see Althouse, *How to Build a Separate Sphere: Federal Courts and State Power*, 100 Harv.L.Rev. 1485 (1987); Baker, *The Ambiguous Independent and Adequate State Ground in Criminal Cases: Federalism Along a Möbius Strip*, 19 Ga.L.Rev. 799 (1985); Redish, *Supreme Court Review of State Court "Federal" Decisions: A Study in Interactive Federalism*, 19 Ga.L.Rev. 861 (1985); Solimine, *Supreme Court Monitoring of State Courts in the Twenty-First Century*, 35 Ind.L.Rev. 335 (2002).

(8) State Incorporation of Federal Law. The discussion so far has assumed that, however ambiguous a state court opinion may be, the content of state law does not depend on the content of federal law. But when a state court believes that its interpretation of a state constitutional or statutory provision is compelled by federal law, it would be difficult to regard that determination as an "independent" state ground. In Delaware v. Prouse, 440 U.S. 648 (1979), for example, the state supreme court affirmed the trial court's suppression of evidence after finding a violation of both the Fourth Amendment and the Delaware Constitution. On certiorari, the Supreme Court upheld its jurisdiction: "As we understand the opinion below, Art I, § 6, of the Delaware Constitution will automatically be interpreted at least as broadly as the Fourth Amendment; that is, every police practice authoritatively determined to be contrary to the Fourth and Fourteenth Amendments will, without further analysis, be held to be contrary to Art. I, § 6." In Prouse the state supreme court had done no more than give effect to what it perceived to be the compulsion of federal law.

In Prouse, the Fourth Amendment applied to the case of its own force, without regard to the content of state law. But sometimes federal law applies only because the state has gratuitously adopted federal criteria as the touchstone for the meaning of a state law. In such a case of gratuitous incorporation, what is the federal interest in reviewing the state court's (mis)interpretation? Consider some examples. If a state income tax statute piggybacked, as many do, on the federal definition of taxable income, does every question of taxable income in state tax returns present a reviewable federal question? Or if a state adopted as its rules of civil procedure the Federal Rules of Civil Procedure and indicated that they should be interpreted in the same fashion, would every interpretation of a state rule present a reviewable federal question? For the suggestion that in all such cases, the Court has an "implicit power to choose" whether the case is reviewable in light of "the strength of the federal interest," see Shapiro, *Jurisdiction and Discretion*, 60 N.Y.U.L.Rev. 543, 565 (1985). For a narrower conception of the authority of the Court to review state incorporation of federal law, see Greene, *Hybrid State Law in the Federal Courts*, 83 Harv.L.Rev. 289, 321 (1969) (suggesting that Supreme Court review of state law incorporating federal law is warranted "where harmonization of state and federal law serves federal objectives" or "where the state has determined to act to the full extent of its constitutional powers, thus transmuting every question of state law into a constitutional issue").[6]

To the extent that the Supreme Court can review the state court's determination of federal law when a question of state law turns on that

---

[6]   Sometimes a state court's interpretation of state law is influenced by a misconception about federal law, even if state law has not formally incorporated the federal provision—and in such cases, a correct Supreme Court resolution of the federal issue will permit the state court on remand to provide a sound interpretation of state law, free from any misconception. Consider, *e.g.*, Ohio v. Reiner, 532 U.S. 17 (2001) (per curiam); Three Affiliated Tribes v. Wold Engineering, P.C., 467 U.S. 138 (1984); St. Martin Evangelical Lutheran Church v. South Dakota, 451 U.S. 772 (1981).

Shapiro, *An Incomplete Discussion of "Arising Under" Jurisdiction*, 91 Notre Dame L.Rev. 1931 (2016), elaborates on the evolution of doctrinal and scholarly positions concerning the Supreme Court's authority to hear cases that turn on state incorporation of federal law.

interpretation, it does not necessarily follow that such claims fall within the arising-under jurisdiction of the district courts. See Chap. VIII, Sec. 3, considering issues of federal law embedded in state law claims.

(9) The Post-Script in Long. When the Long case returned to the Michigan Supreme Court, that court observed that its earlier decision pertaining to the police search of the passenger compartment "was based on our interpretation of Terry * * * and other federal cases." People v. Long, 359 N.W.2d 194 (Mich.1984). Further, the Michigan Supreme Court chastised Long for challenging on remand the passenger compartment search on state constitutional grounds, concluding that the challenge was "untimely" because "defendant did not raise any state constitutional claims until he was before the United States Supreme Court * * *." What, if anything, does this post-script suggest about the wisdom of the Long presumption that ambiguous state opinions should be understood to rest primarily on federal grounds?

INTRODUCTORY NOTE ON STATE LAW ANTECEDENTS TO FEDERAL RIGHTS

The next principal case, Indiana ex. rel. Anderson v. Brand, which arises under the Contract Clause, exemplifies the distinctive issues that can be presented when federal law protects interests created *primarily* by state law. Prominent examples include liberty and property interests, which the Fourteenth Amendment protects against deprivation without due process, and property interests, which the Takings Clause protects against taking without just compensation.

Indiana ex rel. Anderson v. Brand
303 U.S. 95 (1938).
Certiorari to the Supreme Court of Indiana.

■ MR. JUSTICE ROBERTS delivered the opinion of the Court.

The petitioner sought a writ of mandate to compel the respondent to continue her in employment as a public school teacher. [She alleged that she entered into contracts starting in 1924] to teach in the township schools and, pursuant to successive contracts, taught [through] the school year 1932–1933. [She also alleged] that her contracts for the school years 1931–1932 and 1932–1933 contained this clause: "It is further agreed by the contracting parties that all of the provisions of the Teachers' Tenure Law, approved March 8, 1927, shall be in full force and effect in this contract[.]" [Petitioner therefore argued] that by force of that act she had a contract, indefinite in duration, which could be canceled by the respondent only in the manner and for the causes specified in the act. She charged that in July, 1933, the respondent notified her he proposed to cancel her contract for cause * * *. [She further alleged that the respondent] then adhered to that decision after a hearing, after which the County Superintendent affirmed petitioner's termination. Petitioner alleged that she continued to teach during the 1933–1934 school year but remained under threat for termination by respondent.

[Respondent contended in state court that (1) he and the County Superintendent were authorized to adjudicate the matter and had ruled against petitioner; and (2) the Teachers' Tenure Law had been repealed with respect to teachers at township schools. The Indiana Supreme Court affirmed the judgment below for the respondent, resting its decision upon the conclusion that an act of 1933 had repealed the Teachers' Tenure Law with respect to teachers at township schools. That court went on to hold] that the repeal did not deprive the petitioner of a vested property right and did not impair her contract within the meaning of the Constitution. * * *

The court below holds that in Indiana teachers' contracts are made for but 1 year; that there is no contractual right to be continued as a teacher from year to year; that the law grants a privilege to one who has taught 5 years and signed a new contract to continue in employment under given conditions; that the statute is directed merely to the exercise of their powers by the school authorities and the policy therein expressed may be altered at the will of the legislature; that in enacting laws for the government of public schools, the legislature exercises a function of sovereignty and the power to control public policy in respect of their management and operation cannot be contracted away by one legislature so as to create a permanent public policy unchangeable by succeeding legislatures. In the alternative the court declares that if the relationship be considered as controlled by the rules of private contract the provision for re-employment from year to year is unenforceable for want of mutuality.

As in most cases brought to this court under the contract clause of the Constitution, the question is as to the existence and nature of the contract and not as to the construction of the law which is supposed to impair it. The principal function of a legislative body is not to make contracts but to make laws which declare the policy of the state and are subject to repeal when a subsequent legislature shall determine to alter that policy. Nevertheless, it is established that a legislative enactment may contain provisions which, when accepted as the basis of action by individuals, become contracts between them and the State or its subdivisions within the protection of Art. 1, § 10. If the people's representatives deem it in the public interest they may adopt a policy of contracting in respect of public business for a term longer than the life of the current session of the Legislature. This the petitioner claims has been done with respect to permanent teachers. The Supreme Court [of Indiana] has decided, however, that it is the state's policy not to bind school corporations by contract for more than 1 year.

On such a question, one primarily of state law, we accord respectful consideration and great weight to the views of the state's highest court but, in order that the constitutional mandate may not become a dead letter, we are bound to decide for ourselves whether a contract was made, what are its terms and conditions, and whether the State has, by later legislation, impaired its obligation. This involves an appraisal of the statutes of the State and the decisions of its courts.

The courts of Indiana have long recognized that the employment of school teachers was contractual and have afforded relief in actions upon teachers' contracts. * * *

In 1927, the State adopted the Teachers' Tenure Act under which the present controversy arises. * * * By this act it was provided that a teacher who has served under contract for 5 or more successive years, and thereafter enters into a contract for further service with the school corporation, shall become a permanent teacher and the contract, upon the expiration of its stated term, shall be deemed to continue in effect for an indefinite period * * * and shall remain in force unless succeeded by a new contract or canceled as provided in the Act. The corporation may cancel the contract, after notice and hearing, for incompetency, insubordination, neglect of duty, immorality, justifiable decrease in the number of teaching positions, or other good or just cause, but not for political or personal reasons. The teacher may not cancel the contract during the school term nor for a period of 30 days previous to the beginning of any term (unless by mutual agreement) and may cancel only upon 5 days' notice.

By an amendatory act of 1933 township school corporations were omitted from the provisions of the act of 1927. The court below construed this Act as repealing the act of 1927 so far as township schools and teachers are concerned and as leaving the respondent free to terminate the petitioner's employment. But we are of opinion that the petitioner had a valid contract with the respondent, the obligation of which would be impaired by the termination of her employment.

Where the claim is that the State's policy embodied in a statute is to bind its instrumentalities by contract, the cardinal inquiry is as to the terms of the statute supposed to create such a contract. The State long prior to the adoption of the act of 1927 required the execution of written contracts between teachers and school corporations * * *. These were annual contracts, covering a single school term. The act of 1927 announced a new policy that a teacher who had served for 5 years under successive contracts, upon the execution of another was to become a permanent teacher and the last contract was to be indefinite as to duration and terminable by either party only upon compliance with the conditions set out in the statute. The policy which induced the legislation evidently was that the teacher should have protection against the exercise of the right, which would otherwise inhere in the employer, of terminating the employment at the end of any school term without assigned reasons and solely at the employer's pleasure. The state courts in earlier cases so declared.

The title of the act is couched in terms of contract. It speaks of the making and cancelling of indefinite contracts. In the body the word "contract" appears ten times in section 1, defining the relationship; eleven times in section 2, relating to the termination of the employment by the employer, and four times in section 4, stating the conditions of termination by the teacher.

The tenor of the act indicates that the word "contract" was not used inadvertently or in other than its usual legal meaning. By section 6 it is expressly provided that the act is a supplement to that of March 7, 1921, requiring teachers' employment contracts to be in writing. By section 1 it is provided that the written contract of a permanent teacher "shall be deemed to continue in effect for an indefinite period and shall be known as an indefinite contract." Such an indefinite contract is to remain in force unless succeeded by a new contract signed by both parties or cancelled as provided in section 2. No more apt language could be employed to define a contractual relationship. By section 2 it is enacted that such indefinite contracts may be cancelled by the school corporation only in the manner specified. The admissible grounds of cancellation, and the method by which the existence of such grounds shall be ascertained and made a matter of record, are carefully set out. Section 4 permits cancellation by the teacher only at certain times consistent with the convenient administration of the school system and imposes a sanction for violation of its requirements. Examination of the entire act convinces us that the teacher was by it assured of the possession of a binding and enforceable contract against school districts.

Until its decision in the present case the Supreme Court of the State had uniformly held that the teacher's right to continued employment by virtue of the indefinite contract created pursuant to the act was contractual. [The opinion here reviews four decisions of the Indiana Supreme Court explicitly referring to teachers' contractual rights and indicating that mandamus to compel reinstatement was available.]

We think the decision in this case runs counter to the policy evinced by the act of 1927, to its explicit mandate and to earlier decisions construing its provisions. * * *

The respondent urges that every contract is subject to the police power and that in repealing the Teachers' Tenure Act the legislature validly exercised that reserved power of the state. The sufficient answer is found in the statute. By section 2 of the act of 1927 power is given to the school corporation to cancel a teacher's indefinite contract for incompetency, insubordination (which is to be deemed to mean willful refusal to obey the school laws of the State or reasonable rules prescribed by the employer), neglect of duty, immorality, justifiable decrease in the number of teaching positions or other good and just cause. The permissible reasons for cancellation cover every conceivable basis for such action growing out of a deficient performance of the obligations undertaken by the teacher, and diminution of the school requirements. Although the causes specified constitute in themselves just and reasonable grounds for the termination of any ordinary contract of employment, to preclude the assumption that any other valid ground was excluded by the enumeration, the legislature added that the relation might be terminated for any other good and just cause. Thus in the declaration of the state's policy, ample reservations in aid of the efficient administration of the school system were made. * * * It is significant that the act of 1933 left the system of permanent teachers and indefinite contracts untouched as respects school corporations in cities and towns of the state. * * *

Our decisions recognize that every contract is made subject to the implied condition that its fulfillment may be frustrated by a proper exercise of the police power but we have repeatedly said that, in order to have this effect, the exercise of the power must be for an end which is in fact public and the means adopted must be reasonably adapted to that end, and the Supreme Court of Indiana has taken the same view in respect of legislation impairing the obligation of the contract of a state instrumentality. The causes of cancellation provided in the act of 1927 and the retention of the system of indefinite contracts in all municipalities except townships by the act of 1933 are persuasive that the repeal of the earlier act by the latter was not an exercise of the police power for the attainment of ends to which its exercise may properly be directed.

As the court below has not passed upon one of the grounds of demurrer which appears to involve no federal question, and may present a defense still open to the respondent, we reverse the judgment and remand the cause for further proceedings not inconsistent with this opinion.

So ordered.

■ Mr. JUSTICE CARDOZO took no part in the consideration or decision of this case.

■ Mr. JUSTICE BLACK, dissenting. * * *

The Indiana Supreme Court has consistently held, even before its decision in this case, that the right of teachers, under the 1927 act, to serve until removed for cause, was *not given by contract, but by statute.* Such was the express holding in the two cases cited in the majority opinion * * *.

* * * In order to hold in this case that a contract was impaired, it is necessary to create a contract unauthorized by the Indiana Legislature and declared to be non-existent by the Indiana Supreme Court. * * *

The clear purport of Indiana law is that its legislature cannot surrender any part of its plenary constitutional right to repeal, alter or amend existing legislation relating to the school system whenever the conditions demand change for the public good. Under Indiana law the legislature can neither barter nor give away its constitutional investiture of power. * * * The construction of the constitution of Indiana by the Supreme Court of Indiana *must be accepted as correct.* That court * * * has here held that the legislature did not attempt or intend to surrender its constitutional power by authorizing *definite* contracts which would prevent the future exercise of this continuing, constitutional power. If the constitution and statutes of Indiana, as construed by its Supreme Court, prohibit the legislature from making a contract which is inconsistent with a continuing power to legislate, there could have been no *definite* contracts to be impaired. * * *

NOTE ON FEDERAL PROTECTION OF STATE-CREATED RIGHTS

How should the Supreme Court treat decisions involving federal interests established primarily or even exclusively by state law? At one extreme, one can imagine an approach under which the existence of a protected interest, for purposes of a particular federal provision, is defined by *federal* law; under that approach, the existence of a contract for purposes of the Contract Clause would be a matter of federal law. At the other extreme, the existence of a protected interest like a contractual right would depend only upon whether state law recognizes it. An intermediate approach, which Professor Merrill has called a "patterning definition" strategy, first establishes federal criteria that a protected interest must satisfy to merit federal protection, and then examines state law to determine if such an interest has been created. See generally Merrill, *The Landscape of Constitutional Property*, 86 Va.L.Rev. 885 (2000).

Which of these approaches (or which combination of them) is followed in a particular setting is a matter of interpretation of the federal provision that is the source of protection (in Brand, for example, the Contract Clause). But the choice of approach, once made, plainly affects the scope of review. For example, insofar as the federally protected interests are defined entirely by federal law, the Supreme Court would presumably engage in de novo review of a state court's determination whether a protected interest exists. Insofar as the existence of a protected interest depends only upon state law, a state court determination would presumably be reviewed more deferentially. The intermediate, patterning definition approach might involve de novo review of the content of the federal criteria and deferential review of a state court's determination whether those criteria have been satisfied.

Note that federal constitutional provisions may also protect liberty or property interests created by *federal* statutory law. For example, the Takings Clause or the Due Process Clause might provide protection against a statute or other government action that threatens a patent or other intellectual property rights that are created by federal statutes. Cases involving rights created by federal statute are considered here only insofar as they shed light on the primary focus of this material, which is Supreme Court review of state court judgments involving state-created entitlements.

With that background, consider the following examples.

A. The Contract Clause

(1) Choice of Law and Scope of Review. The question whether an acknowledged contractual obligation has been impaired, within the meaning of the Contract Clause, involves only interpretation of the Constitution. See, *e.g.*, El Paso v. Simmons, 379 U.S. 497, 506–08 (1965); Wright, The Contract Clause of the Constitution (1938); Hale, *The Supreme Court and the Contract Clause*, 57 Harv.L.Rev. 512, 621, 852 (1944).

But whose law governs the antecedent question whether there was a contract in the first place? The Brand opinion says that "the existence and nature of the contract" claimed to be impaired is a question "primarily of state law."[1]

Note that the key question under the Contract Clause is not what state law currently *is* but rather what it *was* in the past. And because the Clause prohibits impairment only by legislation, not by judicial decision, see Frankfurter & Landis, The Business of the Supreme Court 199–202 (1928), the critical time for judging whether an obligation existed would seem to be the time of enactment of the allegedly impairing legislation. The Court, however, appears to have emphasized the date of the agreement. See, *e.g.*, El Paso v. Simmons, *supra*. Does the backward-looking nature of the inquiry explain why in Brand the Supreme Court did not accept the Indiana court's determination on the matter of the existence of a contract? Is a state court less authoritative an expositor of what state law was than of what it now is?

Brand affirms an "independent judgment" rule, but as the opinion noted, the Supreme Court usually accords respectful weight to the state court's determination. The Court has not been entirely consistent as to the precise contours of such respect. In Hale v. Iowa State Bd., 302 U.S. 95, 101 (1937), for example, the Court said that it would accept the state court's judgment as to "the effect and meaning of the contract as well as its existence * * * unless manifestly wrong." Then, in General Motors Corp. v. Romein, 503 U.S. 181 (1992), the Court, in reviewing a state court determination that no contract existed, seemed to take a further step away from reliance on state law: "The question whether a contract was made is a federal question for purposes of Contract Clause analysis, * * * and 'whether it turns on issues of general or purely local law, we cannot surrender the duty to exercise our own judgment' " (quoting Appleby v. City of New York, 271 U.S. 364, 380 (1926)). At the same time, the Court in Romein acknowledged the "great weight" that it accords to—and in the end "saw no reason to disagree with"—the state court's views. Are the federal courts in a position to formulate a complete body of federal contract law for purposes of the Contract Clause? Doing so of course risks creating a system of rules under which the question whether a particular contract creates an obligation is governed by one set of rules (state law) in a suit for breach and by another (federal law) in litigation under the Contract Clause.

---

[1]   Accord, Ogden v. Saunders, 25 U.S. 213, 256–59, 326 (1827); Appleby v. City of New York, 271 U.S. 364, 380 (1926).

(2) Brand and Murdock. The Supreme Court's willingness in the Brand case to review a state court's determination of an issue of state law is at first blush hard to square with Murdock v. City of Memphis, p. 636, *supra*. But note that in Brand, as in Martin v. Hunter's Lessee, p. 620, *supra*, state law is antecedent to the claim for relief under federal law, whereas in Murdock v. City of Memphis, state and federal law provided distinct avenues for the relief sought. See Paragraph (5), pp. 647–648, *supra*.

B. The Due Process and Takings Clauses

More complex is the question of whose law governs the existence of property or liberty interests that are protected by the Fifth or Fourteenth Amendments against deprivation without due process or (in the case of property) against a taking without just compensation.

(1) "Old Property." The early cases involved traditional ("old") property interests. In Demorest v. City Bank Farmers Trust Co., 321 U.S. 36 (1944), the claimants argued that a New York statute retroactively deprived them of a property right (specifically, certain proceeds of a trust). In affirming the state court's determination that no such property right existed, the Supreme Court (per Jackson, J.) concluded that when the claim of constitutional deprivation turned on a determination of state law, the Court's role was merely "to inquire whether the decision of the state court rests upon a fair or substantial basis." The Court added that "if there is no evasion of the constitutional issue, * * * and the nonfederal ground of decision has fair support, * * * this Court will not inquire whether the rule applied by the state court is right or wrong."[2] Is that approach consistent with the approach in Brand to determining whether a contractual right existed?

In Stop the Beach Renourishment, Inc. v. Florida Department of Environmental Protection, 560 U.S. 702 (2010), a plurality opinion by Justice Scalia (joined by Chief Justice Roberts and Justices Thomas and Alito) struck what seems to be a middle position between Brand and Demorest. In reviewing the state court's decision concluding that no riparian property rights had been taken by state legislation, the plurality noted that "we make our own determination, without deference to state judges, whether the challenged decision deprives the claimant of an established property right" and that this was part and parcel of the Court's more general obligation to determine "state-court compliance with *all* constitutional imperatives." Still, the plurality added, in practice, such an approach will adopt "a considerable degree of deference to state courts," given that the test asks whether the state court decision resulted in the "deprivation of an *established* property right." As the plurality elaborated, no property right can be "established if there is doubt about its existence; and when there is doubt we do not make our own assessment but accept the determination of the state court."

Further, all eight participating Justices in Stop the Beach (Justice Stevens did not participate) joined the part of Justice Scalia's opinion holding that the Florida Supreme Court had not effected a taking of property because

---

[2]   See also Muhlker v. New York & Harlem R.R., 197 U.S. 544 (1905); Sauer v. New York, 206 U.S. 536 (1907); Fox River Paper Co. v. R.R. Comm'n of Wisconsin, 274 U.S. 651 (1927).

"[t]he Takings Clause only protects property rights as they are established under state law."

Does Stop the Beach's insistence upon identifying an "established" property interest under state law provide a way of reconciling Brand and Demorest? How does the Court's approach in Stop the Beach compare with its treatment of the Contract Clause question in General Motors Corp. v. Romein, 503 U.S. 181 (1992), Paragraph (1), p. 680, *supra*?

(2) "New" Property and Liberty. Many recent decisions involve alleged deprivations of so-called "new property" interests or of analogous liberty interests—when, for example, the government fires an employee, denies an individual social welfare benefits, or disadvantages an imprisoned person (for example, by denial of parole or transfer to less desirable conditions of confinement).[3] Where a protected "property" or "liberty" interest exists, federal law governs the questions (i) whether there has been a deprivation, and (ii) if so, whether due process was afforded. The more complicated issue is which law governs the determination whether, in the first instance, a protected interest exists.

(a) Property Interests. In Board of Regents v. Roth, 408 U.S. 564 (1972), a state university teacher alleged that the failure to re-appoint him at the end of his one-year term, without a statement of reasons or a hearing, deprived him of property without due process of law. In rejecting that claim, the Court stated: "Property interests, of course, are not created by the Constitution. Rather they are created and their dimensions are defined by existing rules or understandings that stem from an independent source such as state law * * *." Because nothing in the plaintiff's appointment, any state statute, or any university policy or rule created any legitimate claim to reemployment, the Court found that "he did not have a *property* interest sufficient to require the University authorities to give him a hearing * * *." Compare, *e.g.*, Memphis Light, Gas & Water Div. v. Craft, 436 U.S. 1, 9–12 (1978) (holding that a state law prohibiting the termination of utility service except "for cause" created a property interest in the non-termination of such service).[4]

---

[3] See generally Merrill, p. 679, *supra*; Farina, *Conceiving Due Process*, 3 Yale J.L. & Feminism 189 (1991); Monaghan, *Of Liberty and Property*, 62 Cornell L.Rev. 405 1977); Van Alstyne, *Cracks in "The New Property": Adjudicative Due Process in the Administrative State*, 62 Cornell L.Rev. 445 (1977); Herman, *The New Liberty*, 59 N.Y.U.L.Rev. 482 (1984).

[4] Even where state law itself creates a "new property" interest, the Court has made clear that the state cannot qualify the resultant interest by specifying in advance that it may impaired as long as certain procedures are followed. Compare Arnett v. Kennedy, 416 U.S. 134 (1974) (plurality opinion) (arguing that a new property holder must "take the bitter with the sweet"), with Cleveland Bd. of Educ. v. Loudermill, 470 U.S. 532 (1985) (8–1) (repudiating the bitter-with-the-sweet test and noting that state law defines the property interest but the Due Process Clause determines the procedural requirements for the deprivation). By the same token, because the procedures prescribed by state law do not define the *scope* of a liberty or property interest, a claimant cannot establish a due process violation merely by showing that the state has not complied with such procedures. See Swarthout v. Cooke, 562 U.S. 216 (2011) (per curiam) (observing in a federal habeas case that to treat state procedure as a judicially enforceable component of the resultant liberty interest "would subject to federal-court merits review the application of all state-prescribed procedures in cases involving liberty or property interests, including (of course) those in criminal prosecutions" in contradiction of the settled principle that violations of state law do not necessarily violate the Due Process Clause).

In Webb's Fabulous Pharmacies, Inc. v. Beckwith, 449 U.S. 155 (1980), however, the Court held that state law is not the sole determinant of property interests under the Takings Clause. The lawsuit alleged that a Florida statute, which authorized a county to take the interest accruing on an interpleader fund deposited in state court, constituted a taking of property from the claimants to the fund. The state court held that under the statute the interest was the property of the county, not of the claimants. The Supreme Court reversed. It acknowledged (citing Roth) that property rights are created not by the Constitution but by an independent source like state law. The Court, however, proceeded to cite numerous cases from jurisdictions other than Florida as supporting the proposition that, in the circumstances presented, the interest belonged to the claimants. Without examining Florida law further, the Court ruled that "a State, by *ipse dixit*, may not transform private property into public property without compensation."

Commentators have read Webb's Fabulous Pharmacies to suggest that, despite Roth, there is a core conception of "property" in the Due Process or Takings Clause that state law must respect. See Monaghan, note 3, *supra*, at 440; Fallon, *Some Confusions About Due Process, Judicial Review, and Constitutional Remedies*, 93 Colum.L.Rev. 309, 328–29 (1993). Does the same idea of constitutional constraint apply in the other direction—that is, are there federally derived constraints on what a state can recognize as a property right?[5] Professor Fallon argues that "no constitutional value typically precludes a state from choosing as expansive a conception [of property] as it may wish." If property is merely whatever "bundle of sticks" finds recognition in state law, doesn't Fallon's point have considerable force? On the other hand, could affording constitutional protection to whatever entitlement a state creates, no matter how unimportant, give rise to a flood of due process claims asserting the deprivation of quite trivial interests?

(b) Liberty Interests. The respective roles of state and federal law in defining entitlements are at least as complicated in cases involving "liberty" as in those involving "property." Significant authority recognizes a federal constitutional dimension to liberty, quite apart from entitlements based on positive law. Thus, without referring to state law, the Court has recognized a host of liberty interests, including that of a student in freedom from corporal punishment, see Ingraham v. Wright, 430 U.S. 651 (1977), of a parent in not having parental rights terminated, see Santosky v. Kramer, 455 U.S. 745, 754 (1982), of an intellectually disabled individual in the conditions of involuntary confinement, see Youngberg v. Romeo, 457 U.S. 307 (1982), and of individuals to marry someone of the same sex, see Obergefell v. Hodges, 576 U.S. 644 (2015).

At the same time, state law can create "liberty" interests, just as it can create property interests. See, *e.g.*, Board of Pardons v. Allen, 482 U.S. 369, 370–81 (1987) (state-law entitlement to parole). But the Court's cases have tended to be fairly parsimonious in recognizing a liberty interest on that

---

[5]   *Cf.* Town of Castle Rock v. Gonzales, 545 U.S. 748 (2005) (7–2) (given the public and traditionally discretionary character of law enforcement, a state court restraining order did not create a property interest in its enforcement, even though a state statute provided that a peace offer "*shall* use every reasonable means to enforce [such an] order").

basis.[6] In Sandin v. Conner, 515 U.S. 472 (1995), for example, the plaintiff filed suit in federal court, objecting to his placement in disciplinary segregation after having been found to have violated prison rules. Mandatory language in a state regulation set forth specific procedures by which discipline could be issued. With Chief Justice Rehnquist writing, however, the Court held that the plaintiff lacked a liberty interest in freedom from disciplinary segregation and therefore could not challenge the discipline as a denial of due process. Acknowledging that it was departing from its precedents, the Court refused to treat mandatory language alone as sufficient to generate a state-created liberty interest. Doing so, the Court contended, "creates disincentives for States to codify prison management procedures" and leads "to the involvement of federal courts in the day-to-day management of prisons." Instead, the Court held that a state-created liberty interest "will be generally limited to freedom from restraint which, while not exceeding the sentence in such an unexpected manner as to give rise to protection by the Due Process Clause of its own force, nonetheless imposes atypical and significant hardship on the inmate in relation to the ordinary incidents of prison life." But here, the Court concluded, the conditions of disciplinary segregation, when compared to ordinary prison life, did not "work a major disruption in [the individual's] environment."

Four Justices dissented. Justice Breyer (joined by Justice Souter) would have followed prior law, which he viewed as establishing three categories: deprivations so severe in kind or degree that as a matter of federal law they infringe liberty interests protected by the Due Process Clause directly; deprivations about minor matters (for example, the kind of lunch to be served) that are unprotected by the Due Process Clause, even if official conduct violated a clear-cut regulation; and an intermediate category of deprivations—like the one in the case at bar—in which the existence of a liberty interest depends upon state law. He argued forcefully that the disciplinary segregation here was not a mere "minor matter" that should be deemed unprotected despite the state regulation. Justice Ginsburg, joined by Justice Stevens, agreed with Justice Breyer that the deprivation was serious, but took the view that the plaintiff had a liberty interest rooted in the Due Process Clause itself—a result that avoided the concern (voiced by the majority) that states that formulate more rules subject themselves to stricter constitutional constraints.

Sandin is a prime example of what Professor Merrill terms a patterning approach—in which the Court first sets a constitutional floor of importance that interests created by the state must rise above to merit federal protection and then examines state law to determine if such an interest has been created. Merrill defends that approach as preferable to the alternatives; in

---

[6]   See, *e.g.*, Paul v. Davis, 424 U.S. 693 (1976) (state government official's defamation of private individual does not invade liberty interest); Connecticut Bd. of Pardons v. Dumschat, 452 U.S. 458, 465 (1981) (liberty interest in clemency does not arise out of institutional practice); Kentucky Dep't of Corrections v. Thompson, 490 U.S. 454, 462–63 (1989) (liberty interest is created only where official decisions are governed by "explicitly mandatory language" establishing "substantive predicates" whose satisfaction requires a particular outcome). *Cf.* Ohio Adult Parole Authority v. Woodard, 523 U.S. 272 (1998) (rejecting due process challenge to clemency procedures).

particular, he says that leaving the definition of entitlements entirely to state law risks generating increasing numbers of claims based on insubstantial or trivial state-created interests. See Merrill, p. 679, *supra*.

Under Sandin, what is the scope of review of a state court's decision that the state has not created "atypical and significant hardship"? Compare Wilkinson v. Austin, 545 U.S. 209 (2005), in which the Court, 9–0, recognized a state-created liberty interest in avoiding assignment to Ohio's "supermax" facility.[7]

C. Presidential Elections: The Role of State Legislatures and the Interpretation of State Statutes

(1) The Concurring Opinion in Bush v. Gore. Article II, § 1, cl. 2 provides: "Each State shall appoint, in such Manner as the Legislature thereof may direct," electors for the President and Vice President. In the litigation over the 2000 presidential election in Florida, parties advanced arguments that this constitutional provision (a) protects a state-created "right" of a different sort—the right to a have a presidential election conducted under the system established by the state legislature, unmodified by the state courts, and (b) demands Supreme Court review without the customary deference to state court determinations of state law.

After Florida officials had certified Governor George Bush as having won that state's electoral votes, Vice President Al Gore sued, invoking Florida statutes authorizing a "contest" of the certification of an election. The Florida Supreme Court ordered manual recounts in Florida counties in which ballots that voting machines had read as not casting a vote had not been manually tabulated. The state supreme court also ordered a change in vote totals previously certified by state officials to take account of votes that had been tallied in manual recounts in two counties as part of pre-certification "protests" but that had been excluded from the certified total because they had been submitted only after the deadline for the counties to file their election returns with Florida's Secretary of State.

In Bush v. Gore, 531 U.S. 98 (2000) (per curiam), the Supreme Court reversed on equal protection grounds and ordered an end to the recounts. Chief Justice Rehnquist, joined by Justices Scalia and Thomas, filed a concurring opinion in which he contended that the Florida Supreme Court's interpretation of Florida election law modified the scheme established by the Florida legislature and thereby violated Article II. The Chief Justice argued that Article II provides a basis for federal review of the correctness of a state

---

[7] Acknowledging the general difficulty of determining the appropriate baseline against which to measure whether a hardship is "atypical and significant," the Court in Wilkinson determined that "under any plausible baseline," assignment to the supermax prison qualified: "[A]lmost all human contact is prohibited, even to the point that conversation is not permitted from cell to cell; the light, though it may be dimmed, is on for 24 hours; exercise is for 1 hour per day, but only in a small indoor room. * * * [Further, u]nlike the 30-day placement in Sandin, placement * * * is indefinite and, after an initial 30-day review, is reviewed just annually. [And] placement disqualifies an otherwise eligible inmate for parole consideration. While any of these conditions standing alone might not be sufficient to create a liberty interest, taken together they impose an atypical and significant hardship within the correctional context." The Court proceeded to hold that the state's procedures for assigning individuals to the supermax prison satisfied due process requirements.

court's interpretation of state statutes regulating the selection of presidential electors.[8] But operating on that premise, the Chief Justice wrote that the state court's decision "empties certification of virtually all legal consequence during the contest," "virtually eliminat[es] both the [certification] deadline and the Secretary [of State]'s discretion to disregard recounts that violate it," and fails to defer to the Secretary's reasonable interpretation of what counts as a "legal vote," instead embracing the "peculiar reading of the statutes" that includes as a legal vote an improperly punched ballot.

He continued, "[t]hough we generally defer to state courts on the interpretation of state law, there are of course areas in which the Constitution requires this Court to undertake an independent, if still deferential, analysis of state law." Emphasizing that Article II, § 1, cl. 2 provides for the appointment of each state's presidential electors " 'in such Manner as the *Legislature* thereof may direct,' " the Chief Justice stressed that "the text of the election law itself, and not just its interpretation by the courts of the States, takes on independent significance." From that starting point, his concurring opinion concluded "that the Florida Supreme Court's interpretation of the Florida election laws impermissibly distorted them beyond what a fair reading required, in violation of Article II."

(2) The Response of the Dissenters. In separate dissents, Justices Stevens, Souter, and Breyer disputed that the Florida Supreme Court had changed, rather than merely interpreted, state law. All three of the dissents viewed differences between the Florida Supreme Court and the Secretary of State as routine disagreements about the interpretive merits. In still another dissent, Justice Ginsburg (joined in this respect by the other dissenters) argued less about the specifics of Florida law and more about the need to defer to state court interpretations of state law. Mere disagreement with a state court's interpretation of state law, she stressed, "does not warrant the conclusion that the justices of that court have legislated." She continued:

"Unavoidably, this Court must sometimes examine state law in order to protect federal rights. But we have dealt with such cases ever mindful of the full measure of respect we owe to interpretations of state law by a State's highest court. * * *

"The Chief Justice says that Article II * * * authorizes federal superintendence over the relationship between state courts and state legislatures, and licenses a departure from the usual deference we give to state-court interpretations of state law. * * * The Framers of our Constitution, however, understood that in a republican government, the judiciary would construe the legislature's enactments. * * * Yet * * * [b]y holding that Article II requires our revision of a state court's construction of state laws in order to protect one organ of the State from another, the Chief Justice contradicts the basic principle that a State may organize itself as it sees fit."

---

[8]   The concurrence did not explore whether a state's compliance with Article II presents a political question to be determined by Congress. See Chap. II, Sec. 6, *supra*.

(3) Moore v. Harper. Two decades after Bush v. Gore, a group of state legislators challenged the authority of the North Carolina Supreme Court to reject legislatively drawn voting districts as inconsistent with the state constitution. The legislators argued that the federal Elections Clause, which expressly assigns to "the Legislature" of each state the power to prescribe "[t]he Times, Places and Manner of" federal elections, Art. I, § 4, cl. 1, precludes state courts from rejecting legislative maps based on state constitutional principles because doing so interferes with the federal Constitution's delegation of exclusive power in this area to the legislature. In Moore v. Harper, 600 U.S. 1 (2023), the Supreme Court rejected the argument, concluding that "[t]he Elections Clause does not insulate state legislatures from the ordinary exercise of state judicial review." This result followed, Chief Justice Roberts wrote for the six-Justice majority, because "[w]hen a state legislature carries out its constitutional power to prescribe rules regulating federal elections, the 'commission under which' it exercises authority is twofold" (citing The Federalist No. 78, at 467). First, he observed, "[t]he legislature acts * * * as a lawmaking body created and bound by its state constitution." Second, it acts "as the entity assigned particular authority by the Federal Constitution." "Both constitutions," he concluded, "restrain the legislature's exercise of power."

The Court reiterated Murdock's principle that " 'State courts are the appropriate tribunals . . . for the decision of questions arising under their local law, whether statutory or otherwise" (citing Murdock v. City of Memphis, 87 U.S. (20 Wall.) 590, 626 (1875)). But, "[a]t the same time, the Elections Clause expressly vests power to carry out its provisions in 'the Legislature' of each State, a deliberate choice that this Court must respect." Thus, Chief Justice Roberts opined, "[a]s in other areas where the exercise of federal authority or the vindication of federal rights implicates questions of state law, we have an obligation to ensure that state court interpretations of that law do not evade federal law."[9] Referencing the debate in Bush v. Gore between Chief Justice Rehnquist and Justice Souter over how to carry out that obligation—that is, how to review state court interpretations of state law—the Court declined to adopt a specific test governing state court decisions respecting state law in Elections Clause disputes. Instead, the Court held "only that state courts may not transgress the ordinary bounds of judicial review such that they arrogate to themselves the power vested in state legislatures to regulate federal elections."

In dissent, Justice Thomas complained that the majority had improperly extended Bush v. Gore's review of state court determinations of state statutory law to state court determinations of state *constitutional* law. "When 'it is a *constitution* [courts] are expounding,' not a detailed statutory scheme, the standards to judge the fairness of a given interpretation are typically fewer and less definite" (quoting McCulloch v. Maryland, 17 U.S. (4

---

[9] *Cf.* Trump v. Anderson, 601 U.S. 100, 112 (2024) (holding with respect to "the Elections and Electors Clauses, which authorize States to conduct and regulate congressional and Presidential elections," see Art. I, § 4, cl. 1; Art. II, § 1, cl. 2, "there is little reason to think that these Clauses implicitly authorize the States to enforce Section 3 [of the Fourteenth Amendment] against federal officeholders and candidates. Granting the States that authority would invert the Fourteenth Amendment's rebalancing of federal and state power.").

Wheat.) 316, 407 (1819)). The result, he feared, would be to "invest[ ] potentially large swaths of state constitutional law with the character of a federal question not amenable to meaningful or principled adjudication by federal courts."

(4) Questions. Bush v. Gore was obviously an extraordinary case. The complexities of Florida election law, moreover, make it difficult to judge whether the Florida Supreme Court's interpretations were correct, were debatable but reasonable, or were, as the Chief Justice argued, "absurd" and "peculiar."[10] But was the basic problem facing the Supreme Court different from other cases involving federal protection of state-created rights? Was the Chief Justice correct that the Court should accord less deference to the Florida Supreme Court's interpretation of state election law than the Court would accord, for example, to a state court's interpretation of contract law underlying a Contract Clause claim?

It is true, of course, that Article II can be read as a directive to state *legislatures* to enact statutes establishing a method of appointing presidential electors; by contrast, the Contract Clause, although it presupposes that states will have a law of contracts, does not by its terms direct a particular branch of state government to create one. But does that difference bear on the appropriate degree of deference?[11]

Does Moore v. Harper add to this debate or just further prolong resolution whether federal court review of state court determinations of state law will depend on the context in which they arise? Chief Justice Roberts wrote in his opinion for the Court that "[t]he questions presented in this area are complex and context specific." Separately, is Justice Thomas right to fear that reviewing state court interpretations of state constitutional law (as opposed to statutory law) to ensure that they do "not transgress the ordinary bounds of judicial review" (the Court's phrase) will present special challenges?[12]

---

[10]   For differing perspectives on that issue, compare, *e.g.*, Tribe, *Erog v. Hsub and its Disguises: Freeing Bush v. Gore from Its Hall of Mirrors*, 115 Harv.L.Rev. 170, 184–217 (2001), and Klarman, *Bush v. Gore Through the Lens of Constitutional History*, 89 Calif.L.Rev. 1721, 1741–46 (2001) (both defending the Florida Supreme Court's interpretations of state law as correct or at least reasonable), with Posner, Breaking the Deadlock: The 2000 Election, the Constitution, and the Courts 92–128, 150–88 (2001), and Epstein, *Bush v. Gore: "In Such Manner as the Legislature Thereof May Direct": The Outcome in Bush v. Gore Defended*, 68 U.Chi.L.Rev. 613 (2001) (both sharply critical of those interpretations).

[11]   For articles arguing that the Florida Supreme Court's rulings on issues of state law were not entitled to deference, see, *e.g.*, Wells, *Were There Adequate State Grounds in Bush v. Gore?*, 18 Const.Comm. 403 (2001); Wells & Netter, *Article II and the Florida Election Case: A Public Choice Perspective*, 61 Md.L.Rev. 711 (2002). For those critical of the Supreme Court's scope of review of Florida law, see, *e.g.*, Krent, *Judging Judging: The Problem of Second-Guessing State Judges' Interpretation of State Law in Bush v. Gore*, 29 Fla.St.U.L.Rev. 493 (2001); Schapiro, *Conceptions and Misconceptions of State Constitutional Law in Bush v. Gore*, 29 Fla.St.U.L.Rev. 661, 662 (2001); Smith, *History of the Article II Independent State Legislature Doctrine*, 29 Fla.St.U.L.Rev. 731 (2001); Solimine, *Supreme Court Monitoring of State Courts in the Twenty-First Century*, 35 Ind.L.Rev. 335 (2002).

[12]   *Cf.* Litman & Shaw, *Textualism, Judicial Supremacy, and the Independent State Legislature Theory*, 2022 Wisc.L.Rev. 1235, 1263 (drawing upon several doctrines to posit that "states have, and should have, interpretive primacy over state laws, including the authority to decide how they should be interpreted").

D.   Other Federal Protections of State-Created Entitlements

The foregoing discussion of cases involving the Contract, Due Process, and Takings Clauses, and Articles I and II, merely exemplifies a broad set of situations in which federal constitutional or statutory law operates to protect an entitlement created primarily, if not exclusively, by state law. Another such situation was that involved in Martin v. Hunter's Lessee—where a federal treaty protected state-created rights in land against confiscation.

Other examples abound. The Full Faith and Credit Clause and implementing legislation (28 U.S.C. § 1738) protect entitlements under state-created judgments against non-recognition;[13] the Federal Arbitration Act protects state-created contractual rights to arbitrate against non-enforcement;[14] various federal constitutional provisions protect against criminal punishment except in accordance with previously enacted state laws.[15]

As the cases in this Note demonstrate, the Court has not embraced a consistent approach to reviewing state law issues embedded in questions of federal entitlement. Sometimes the Court has engaged in de novo review, sometimes settled for limited review, and sometimes deferred altogether to the state court determination. Is there any reason why the scope of review, on the question of the existence of an antecedent state-created entitlement, should not be the same in all cases?[16]

For a wide-ranging discussion of the problems raised in this Note, see Monaghan, *Supreme Court Review of State-Court Determinations of State*

---

[13]   See, *e.g.*, Clark v. Williard, 292 U.S. 112 (1934); Ford v. Ford, 371 U.S. 187 (1962). In Adam v. Saenger, 303 U.S. 59 (1938), the Texas courts denied enforcement to a California judgment on the ground that the California court that had rendered it lacked jurisdiction under California law. On review, Justice Stone said: "While this Court reexamines such an issue with deference after its determination by a state court, it cannot, if the laws and Constitution of the United States are to be observed, accept as final the decision of the state tribunal as to matters alleged to give rise to the asserted federal right. This is especially the case where the decision is rested * * * upon the law of another state, as readily determined here as in a state court."

[14]   Compare, *e.g.*, Volt Info. Sciences, Inc. v. Board of Trustees of Leland Stanford Jr. Univ., 489 U.S. 468 (1989) (deferring to a state court's decision, notwithstanding the Federal Arbitration Act, not to enforce a contractual arbitration clause and to enforce instead a distinct contractual clause under which arbitration was not compelled), with Green Tree Financial Corp. v. Bazzle, 539 U.S. 444 (2003) (plurality opinion) (declining to defer to a state court's determination that state law permits class arbitration when a contractual arbitration clause was silent on the question and concluding, instead, that ambiguities in such a clause were subject, in the first instance, to decision by the arbitrator).

[15]   See, *e.g.*, Splawn v. California, 431 U.S. 595, 600 (1977) (holding that in the Supreme Court's own assessment of an alleged retroactive expansion of a state law criminal prohibition, the state court's ruling on state law issues "is entitled to great weight in evaluating petitioner's constitutional contentions" under the Ex Post Facto and Due Process Clauses); Ricketts v. Adamson, 483 U.S. 1, 5 n.3 (1987) (holding that the Court would not "second-guess" the state courts' determination that new charges against the defendant were permissible because he had breached a plea agreement and asserting that "[w]hile we assess independently the plea agreement's effect on [the defendant's] double jeopardy rights, the construction of the plea agreement and the concomitant obligations flowing therefrom are, within broad bounds of reasonableness, matters of state law").

[16]   For an argument that the Court has too readily set aside state court rulings on issues of antecedent state law and should reverse state-law determinations only where it fairly suspects that the state court deliberately manipulated state law, see Fitzgerald, *Suspecting the States: Supreme Court Review of State-Court State-Law Judgments*, 101 Mich.L.Rev. 80 (2002).

Law in Constitutional Cases, 103 Colum.L.Rev. 1919 (2003). Professor Monaghan addresses cases that involve redetermination of state law—cases in which the Constitution assigns significance to a state's fidelity to state law as it stood at some point in the past.[17] Though he believes that ordinarily deferential review is the appropriate stance, more intrusive review may be necessary, he suggests, "particularly in times of change, or in certain controversial areas of the law." Uncertain whether criteria can be articulated to specify when de novo review should be exercised, he would leave it to the Court's sense of the situation, though he adds that de novo review would rarely be appropriate in cases involving federal statutory rather than constitutional provisions. Absent evidence that a state court's decision was unreasonable, motivated by hostility to federal rights, or lacking in fair support, is a "sense of the situation" an adequate basis for the Supreme Court to disregard a state court's view of state law?

B. PROCEDURAL REQUIREMENTS

Cardinale v. Louisiana
394 U.S. 437 (1969).
Certiorari to the Supreme Court of Louisiana.

■ MR. JUSTICE WHITE delivered the opinion of the Court.

Petitioner brutally murdered a woman near New Orleans. * * * His confession [to the police] was introduced in its entirety in the subsequent trial for murder in which petitioner was convicted and sentenced to death. Petitioner does not now contend that his confession was involuntary or that his admission of guilt * * * was inadmissible in evidence. He objects solely to the admission of those parts of his confession which he argues were both irrelevant and prejudicial in his trial for murder. A Louisiana statute requires that confessions must be admitted in their entirety, and petitioner contends that this is unconstitutional.

Although certiorari was granted to consider this question, the fact emerged in oral argument that the sole federal question argued here had never been raised, preserved, or passed upon in the state courts below. It was very early established that the Court will not decide federal constitutional issues raised here for the first time on review of state court decisions. In Crowell v. Randell, 10 Pet. 368 (1836), Justice Story reviewed the earlier cases commencing with Owings v. Norwood's Lessee, 5 Cranch 344 (1809), and came to the conclusion that the Judiciary Act

---

[17]   For example, referring to the state law questions raised by the Article II issue in Bush v. Gore, Monaghan argues that the Supreme Court had power to engage in de novo review to determine what state law was at the critical time. He finds support for that view in numerous cases, including Fairfax's Devisee (the prelude to Martin v. Hunter's Lessee) and Brand.

of 1789, § 25, vested this Court with no jurisdiction unless a federal question was raised and decided in the state court below. * * * The Court has consistently refused to decide federal constitutional issues raised here for the first time on review of state court decisions both before the Crowell opinion, Miller v. Nicholls, 4 Wheat. 311, 315 (1819), and since, *e.g.*, Safeway Stores, Inc. v. Oklahoma Retail Grocers Assn., Inc., 360 U.S. 334, 342, n.7 (1959); [citing additional cases].

In addition to the question of jurisdiction arising under the statute controlling our power to review final judgments of state courts, 28 U.S.C. § 1257, there are sound reasons for this. Questions not raised below are those on which the record is very likely to be inadequate, since it certainly was not compiled with those questions in mind. And in a federal system it is important that state courts be given the first opportunity to consider the applicability of state statutes in light of constitutional challenge, since the statutes may be construed in a way which saves their constitutionality. Or the issue may be blocked by an adequate state ground. Even though States are not free to avoid constitutional issues on inadequate state grounds, they should be given the first opportunity to consider them.

In view of the petitioner's admitted failure to raise the issue he presents here in any way below, the failure of the state court to pass on this issue, the desirability of giving the State the first opportunity to apply its statute on an adequate record, and the fact that a federal habeas remedy may remain if no state procedure for raising the issue is available to petitioner, the writ is dismissed for want of jurisdiction.

It is so ordered.

■ MR. JUSTICE BLACK, MR. JUSTICE DOUGLAS, and MR. JUSTICE FORTAS concur in the dismissal of the writ, believing it to have been improvidently granted.

NOTE ON THE PRESENTATION AND PRESERVATION OF FEDERAL QUESTIONS

(1) The Sources of the Rule. As sources for the requirement that a federal question have been presented to the state courts before brought to the Supreme Court on review, Cardinale invokes both 28 U.S.C. § 1257 (which requires that the federal question have been "drawn in question" or "specially set up or claimed") and a variety of policy concerns.[1] Despite such

---

[1]   See also Webb v. Webb, 451 U.S. 493, 499–501 (1981), elaborating on these sources. Supreme Court Rule 14.1(g)(i) provides that a petition for certiorari to a state court shall contain "specification of the stage in the proceedings, both in the court of first instance and in the appellate courts, when the federal questions sought to be reviewed were raised; the method or manner of raising them and the way in which they were passed on by those courts; and pertinent quotations of specific portions of the record or summary thereof, with specific reference to the places in the record where the matter appears (*e.g.*, court opinion, ruling on exception, portion of court's charge and exception thereto, assignment of error), so as to show that the federal

references to § 1257, the Court has repeatedly acknowledged that it is unsettled whether the rule is a jurisdictional requirement or is merely prudential.[2] The Court has also stressed, however, that whatever its precise nature, the rule is strictly enforced and exceptions to it are extraordinarily rare.[3]

(2) The Governing Standard. The requirement is often framed as one governed by federal-law standards: "There are various ways in which the validity of a state statute may be drawn in question on the ground that it is repugnant to the Constitution of the United States. No particular form of words or phrases is essential, but only that the claim of invalidity and the ground therefor be brought to the attention of the state court with fair precision and in due time." New York ex rel. Bryant v. Zimmerman, 278 U.S. 63, 67 (1928).[4]

(3) Problems in Application. The requirement of presentation to the state courts has been applied with varying strictness. A central difficulty in application is determining whether an issue raised before the Supreme Court is the same as one that was raised before and decided by the state courts.

(a) New Claims Versus New Arguments. One set of cases has addressed the question whether a party preserved a specific claim in state court versus a particular argument about that claim. For example, in Yee v. City of Escondido, 503 U.S. 519, 532 (1992), the Court reiterated the proposition that if a federal *claim* was properly raised in state court, a party can raise before the Supreme Court any *argument* in support of that claim, even if the *argument* was not raised in state court. The Court proceeded to hold that the argument that a rent control ordinance constituted a "regulatory taking" could be raised for the first time in the Supreme Court, since the litigant had raised in state court the claim that the ordinance was a "physical taking."[5] But, the Court held, the advancement of a substantive due process challenge to the ordinance, which was not advanced before the state courts, constituted a different claim not reviewable on appeal.

---

question was timely and properly raised and that this Court has jurisdiction to review the judgment on a writ of certiorari."

[2]   Compare the Court's treatment of the rule that it will not review a judgment resting on an adequate and independent state ground, discussed at pp. 651–656, *supra*.

[3]   See, *e.g.*, Adams v. Robertson, 520 U.S. 83, 86–88 (1997); Bankers Life & Cas. Co. v. Crenshaw, 486 U.S. 71, 79 (1988); Illinois v. Gates, 462 U.S. 213, 217–24 & cases cited (1983). For discussion of two decisions hard to square with the rule, see Paragraph (4), *infra*. That exceptions are hard to find in recent decades may be correlated with the fact that the Court's appellate jurisdiction over state court decisions is now entirely discretionary.

[4]   In Street v. New York, 394 U.S. 576, 582 (1969), the Court said that it is not bound by the state court's determination as to whether the federal question was sufficiently raised, but added: "[I]t is not entirely clear whether in such cases the scope of our review is limited to determining whether the state court has 'by-passed the federal right under forms of local procedure' or whether we should decide the matter 'de novo for ourselves.' Ellis v. Dixon, 349 U.S. 458, 463 (1955)." See also Herndon v. Georgia, 295 U.S. 441, 443 (1935), p. 702, *infra*, which appears to recite a federal standard in articulating "[t]he long-established general rule * * * that the attempt to raise a federal question after judgment [of the state's highest court], upon a petition for rehearing, comes too late * * *."

[5]   The Court nonetheless refused to decide the regulatory taking claim, on the distinct ground that it was not included within the question presented in the petition for certiorari (which was limited to the physical taking issue). See Paragraph (4)(a), *infra*.

The distinction between a new claim and a new argument is hardly clear-cut. For decisions in which the Justices divided on the question, see, *e.g.*, Eddings v. Oklahoma, 455 U.S. 104, 113–14 n.9 (1982) (defendant's claim that imposition of the death penalty in his particular circumstances violated the Eighth Amendment sufficed to put in issue the legality of the trial judge's refusal to consider mitigating evidence as required by Lockett v. Ohio, 438 U.S. 586 (1978)—despite the failure to mention Lockett in state court); Terminiello v. Chicago, 337 U.S. 1, 6 (1949) (defendant's objection that "his speech was protected by the constitution" sufficed to put in issue before the Supreme Court the question of the constitutionality of the ordinance under which he was prosecuted as it had been construed in the jury instructions).

(b) Federal Versus State Law Claims. A second set of cases has focused on whether a litigant adequately indicated in state court that a claim was based on federal rather than on state law. The Court has long required a litigant to show "that some provision of the Federal, as distinguished from the state, Constitution was relied upon," New York Central & H.R.Co. v. New York, 186 U.S. 269, 273 (1902), and claims that a state statute violates the Constitution or denies due process, without more, have been treated as referring to state and not federal provisions. See, *e.g.*, New York ex rel. Bryant v. Zimmerman, 278 U.S. 63, 67–68 (1928); Bowe v. Scott, 233 U.S. 658, 664–65 (1914). Is that treatment consistent with Michigan v. Long, p. 656, *supra*? Should the Court adopt the opposite inference?

The requirement that a litigant make clear that a claim rests on federal law is not limited to cases involving parallel federal and state constitutional provisions, and is sometimes applied with exorbitant rigor. For example, in Webb v. Webb, 451 U.S. 493 (1981), the Court, over Justice Marshall's lone dissent, held that a litigant who had complained in a state court custody suit about a failure to give "full faith and credit" to a prior judgment, but who had not mentioned the Full Faith and Credit Clause, had presented only a state law issue under the Uniform Child Custody Jurisdiction Act, and therefore could not raise the federal constitutional issue in the Supreme Court.

In Howell v. Mississippi, 543 U.S. 440 (2005), the petitioner argued that he had presented his federal claim in state court by implication, because the state-law rule on which he had relied was identical to the federal rule. The Court assumed without deciding that identical standards might overcome a failure to have identified as federal a claim pressed in state court, but ruled that state and federal law in fact differed and hence dismissed the petition.

(4) Exceptions to the Rule. Although exceptions to the rule that Cardinale reaffirms are extraordinarily rare, the Court has on at least two occasions decided federal questions in some tension with that rule.

(a) Vachon v. New Hampshire. In Vachon v. New Hampshire, 414 U.S. 478 (1974), the defendant had unsuccessfully challenged on appeal to the state supreme court the sufficiency of the evidence of willfulness as an element of the relevant charges. The Supreme Court, in a brief per curiam opinion, reversed, relying on the federal constitutional principle that due process is denied when there is "no evidence" to support one element of a crime (here, willfulness).

In dissent, Justice Rehnquist protested that the defendant on appeal had merely challenged " '[t]he State's failure to introduce any evidence of scienter * * *.' " That, Justice Rehnquist wrote, was simply "the customary appellate arguments of insufficiency of the evidence * * *." He added that the appellate brief did "not so much as mention either the United States Constitution or a single case decided by this Court" and that nothing in the Supreme Court of New Hampshire's "opinion remotely suggests that it was treating the claim as having a basis other than in state law."

In response, the Court relied on provisions in the Supreme Court's Rules stating that questions raised in the brief that were not presented in the jurisdictional papers "will be disregarded, save as the court, at its opinion, may notice a plain error not presented."[6] In Justice Rehnquist's view, however, that provision appeared only to authorize the Court, once it has previously noted probable jurisdiction or granted certiorari, to hear an issue properly raised in state court but not presented in the application for Supreme Court review, rather than an issue not raised at all in state court.

The Vachon decision takes an unusually flexible view of the requirement that the federal issue be raised in state court. Compare, *e.g.*, Bailey v. Anderson, 326 U.S. 203 (1945), ruling that a state court challenge to the denial of interest in a condemnation action could not be converted, in the Supreme Court, into a federal constitutional question under the Takings Clause. Note, however, that Vachon fell within the Court's then-existing mandatory appellate jurisdiction and by resolving the case as it did, the Court avoided having to decide more difficult constitutional claims that the appellant had properly raised. Today, the Court would have the option, in a case like Vachon, of simply denying certiorari. But do the circumstances in Vachon suggest that the Court's jurisdictional determinations are likely to be influenced by whether the Court is eager (or reluctant) to reach a particular issue? Is that appropriate? Inevitable?

(b) Wood v. Georgia. In Wood v. Georgia, 450 U.S. 261 (1981), the Court decided an issue that all the Justices acknowledged had not been raised in state court. The case involved three employees of a business who had been convicted of distributing obscene materials and sentenced to probation and ordered to pay substantial fines over time. When those payments were not made, the court revoked their probation. The Supreme Court granted review to decide whether imprisonment of a probationer who is unable to make such payments denies equal protection.

But the Court (per Powell, J.) vacated the convictions on due process grounds. Noting that the employees had been represented by a lawyer paid by their employer, and that the employer had promised to pay any fines imposed, the Court concluded that there was a potential conflict of interest.

---

6   For the current provisions, see Rule 14.1(a) (the Court will consider on the merits only those questions presented for its review in the petition) and Rule 24.1(a) (reserving to the Court the power to "consider a plain error not among the questions presented but evident from the record *and otherwise within its jurisdiction to decide*") (emphasis added).

It then remanded the case so that the state courts could determine the nature and implications of any such conflict.

In dissent, Justice White objected that the Court lacked jurisdiction to resolve the due process issue. The Court responded that the lack of any presentation of the issue "merely emphasize[s] * * * why it *is* appropriate for us to consider the issue. The party who argued the appeal and prepared the petition for certiorari was the lawyer on whom the conflict-of-interest charge focused." The Court added that the state could not claim lack of notice, as it had pointed out the conflict at the probation revocation hearing. The Court concluded: "In this context, it is appropriate to treat the due process issue as one 'raised' below, and proceed to consider it here. Even if one considers that the conflict-of-interest question was not technically raised below, there is ample support for a remand required in the interests of justice. See 28 U.S.C. § 2106 (authorizing the Court to 'require such further proceedings to be had as may be just under the circumstances')."

What is the holding of Wood? In Webb v. Webb, 451 U.S. 493 (1981), Justice Powell, in a concurring opinion joined by Justice Brennan, characterized Wood as having "reaffirmed * * * that the Court has jurisdiction to review plain error unchallenged in the state court when necessary to prevent fundamental unfairness." *Id.* 502. Should Wood be limited to circumstances in which some defect in the state process prevented the litigant from raising the issue in the first instance?[7]

National Association for the Advancement of Colored People v. Alabama ex rel. Patterson

357 U.S. 449 (1958).
Certiorari to the Supreme Court of Alabama.

■ MR. JUSTICE HARLAN delivered the opinion of the Court.

We review from the standpoint of its validity under the Federal Constitution a judgment of civil contempt entered against petitioner, the National Association for the Advancement of Colored People, in the courts of Alabama. The question presented is whether Alabama, consistently with the Due Process Clause of the Fourteenth Amendment, can compel petitioner to reveal to the State's Attorney General the names and addresses of all its Alabama members and agents, without regard to their positions or functions in the Association. The judgment of contempt was based upon petitioner's refusal to comply fully with a court order requiring in part the production of membership lists. Petitioner's claim is that the order, in the circumstances shown by this record, violated rights assured to petitioner and its members under the Constitution.

Alabama has a statute * * * which requires a foreign corporation, except as exempted, to * * * fil[e] its corporate charter with the Secretary

---

[7]   Compare the cases discussed at pp. 702–703, Paragraph (4), *infra.*

of State and designat[e] a place of business and an agent to receive service of process [before commencing activities within the state]. The statute imposes a fine on a corporation transacting intrastate business before qualifying and provides for criminal prosecution of officers of such a corporation. * * * [I]n 1951, the Association itself opened a regional office in Alabama * * *. The Association has never complied with the qualification statute, from which it considered itself exempt.

In 1956, the Attorney General of Alabama brought an equity suit in [state court] to enjoin the Association from conducting further activities within, and to oust it from, the State. Among other things, the bill in equity alleged that the Association had opened a regional office and had organized various affiliates in Alabama; had recruited members and solicited contributions within the State; had given financial support and furnished legal assistance to Negro students seeking admission to the state university, and had supported a Negro boycott of the bus lines in Montgomery to compel the seating of passengers without regard to race. [In the suit, the Attorney General argued that the NAACP] was "... causing irreparable injury to the property and civil rights of the residents and citizens of the State of Alabama for which criminal prosecution and civil actions at law afford no adequate relief ...." On the day the complaint was filed, the Circuit Court issued *ex parte* an order restraining the Association, *pendente lite,* from engaging in further activities within the State and forbidding it to take any steps to qualify itself to do business therein.

Petitioner demurred to the allegations of the bill and moved to dissolve the restraining order. It contended that its activities did not subject it to the qualification requirements of the statute and that, in any event, what the State sought to accomplish by its suit would violate rights to freedom of speech and assembly guaranteed under the Fourteenth Amendment to the Constitution of the United States. Before the date set for a hearing on this motion, the State moved for the production of a large number of the Association's records and papers, including bank statements, leases, deeds, and records containing the names and addresses of all Alabama "members" and "agents" of the Association. It alleged that all such documents were necessary for adequate preparation for the hearing, in view of petitioner's denial of the conduct of intrastate business within the meaning of the qualification statute. Over petitioner's objections, the court ordered the production of a substantial part of the requested records, including the membership lists * * *.

Thereafter petitioner filed its answer to the bill in equity. It admitted its Alabama activities substantially as alleged in the complaint and that it had not qualified to do business in the State. * * * [P]etitioner did not comply with the production order, and for this failure, was adjudged in civil contempt and fined $10,000. * * *

At the end of the five-day period, petitioner produced substantially all the data called for by the production order except its membership lists, as to which it contended that Alabama could not constitutionally compel disclosure, and moved to modify or vacate the contempt judgment, or stay its execution pending appellate review. This motion was denied. While a similar stay application, which was later denied, was pending before the Supreme Court of Alabama, the Circuit Court made a further order adjudging petitioner in continuing contempt and increasing the fine already imposed to $100,000. Under Alabama law, *see* Jacoby v. Goetter, Weil & Co., 74 Ala. 427 [(1883)], the effect of the contempt adjudication was to foreclose petitioner from obtaining a hearing on the merits of the underlying ouster action, or from taking any steps to dissolve the temporary restraining order which had been issued *ex parte,* until it purged itself of contempt.

The State Supreme Court thereafter twice dismissed petitions for certiorari to review this final contempt judgment, the first time, 265 Ala. 699, for insufficiency of the petition's allegations and the second time on procedural grounds. 265 Ala. 349. * * *

I

We address ourselves first to respondent's contention that we lack jurisdiction because the denial of certiorari by the Supreme Court of Alabama rests on an independent nonfederal ground, namely, that petitioner, in applying for certiorari, had pursued the wrong appellate remedy under state law. Respondent recognizes that our jurisdiction is not defeated if the nonfederal ground relied on by the state court is "without any fair or substantial support," Ward v. Board of County Commissioners, 253 U.S. 17, 22 [(1920)]. It thus becomes our duty to ascertain, ". . . in order that constitutional guaranties may appropriately be enforced, whether the asserted non-federal ground independently and adequately supports the judgment." Abie State Bank v. Bryan, 282 U.S. 765, 773 [(1931)].

The Alabama Supreme Court held that it could not consider the constitutional issues underlying the contempt judgment which related to the power of the State to order production of membership lists because review by certiorari was limited to instances ". . . where the court lacked jurisdiction of the proceeding, or where, on the face of it, the order disobeyed was void, or where procedural requirements with respect to citation for contempt and the like were not observed, or where the fact of contempt is not sustained. . . ." 265 Ala. at 353. The proper means for petitioner to obtain review of the judgment in light of its constitutional claims, said the court, was by way of mandamus to quash the discovery order prior to the contempt adjudication. Because of petitioner's failure to pursue this remedy, its challenge to the contempt order was restricted to the above grounds. Apparently not deeming the constitutional objections to draw into question whether, "on the face of it, the order disobeyed was void," the court found no infirmity in the contempt judgment under this limited scope of review. At the same time, it did go on to consider petitioner's constitutional challenge to the order to produce membership lists, but found it untenable, since membership lists were not privileged against disclosure pursuant to reasonable state demands and since the privilege against self-incrimination was not available to corporations.

We are unable to reconcile the procedural holding of the Alabama Supreme Court in the present case with its past unambiguous holdings as to the scope of review available upon a writ of certiorari addressed to a contempt judgment. As early as 1909, that court said in such a case, Ex parte Dickers, 162 Ala. 272, at 276, 279–280:

> "Originally, on certiorari, only the question of jurisdiction was inquired into; but this limit has been removed, and now the court 'examines the law questions involved in the case which may affect its merits.' . . . [T]he judgment of this court is that the proper way to review the action of the court in cases of this kind is by certiorari, and not by appeal."

> "We think that certiorari is a better remedy than mandamus, because the office of a 'mandamus' is to require the lower court or judge to act, and not 'to correct error or to reverse judicial action,' . . . whereas, in a proceeding by certiorari, errors of law in the judicial action of the lower court may be inquired into and corrected."

This statement was in full accord with the earlier case of Ex parte Boscowitz, 84 Ala. 463 [(1888)], and the practice in the later Alabama cases, until we reach the present one, appears to have been entirely consistent with this rule. [Citing three decisions of the Alabama Supreme Court.] For example, in Ex parte Morris, 252 Ala. 551, decided as late as 1949, the petitioner had been held in contempt for his refusal to obey a court order to produce names of members of the Ku Klux Klan. On writ of certiorari, constitutional grounds were urged in part for reversal of the contempt conviction. In denying the writ of certiorari, the Supreme Court concluded that petitioner had been accorded due process, and, in explaining its denial, the court considered and rejected various constitutional claims relating to the validity of the order. There was no intimation that the petitioner had selected an inappropriate form of appellate review to obtain consideration of all questions of law raised by a contempt judgment.

The Alabama cases do indicate, as was said in the opinion below, that an order requiring production of evidence ". . . *may* be reviewed on petition for mandamus." 265 Ala. at 353. (Italics added.) But we can discover nothing in the prior state cases which suggests that mandamus is the *exclusive* remedy for reviewing court orders after disobedience of them has led to contempt judgments. Nor, so far as we can find, do any of these prior decisions indicate that the validity of such orders can be drawn in question by way of certiorari only in instances where a defendant had no opportunity to apply for mandamus. Although the opinion below suggests no such distinction, the State now argues that this was, in fact, the situation in all of the earlier certiorari cases, because there, the contempt adjudications, unlike here, had followed almost immediately the disobedience to the court orders. Even if that is indeed the rationale of the Alabama Supreme Court's present decision, such a local procedural rule, although it may now appear in retrospect to form part of a consistent pattern of procedures to obtain appellate review, cannot avail the State here, because petitioner could not fairly be deemed to have been apprised of its existence. Novelty in procedural requirements cannot be permitted to thwart review in this Court applied for by those who, in justified reliance upon prior decisions, seek vindication in state courts of their federal constitutional rights. *Cf.* Brinkerhoff-Faris Co. v. Hill, 281 U.S. 673 [(1930)].

That there was justified reliance here is further indicated by what the Alabama Supreme Court said in disposing of petitioner's motion for a stay of the first contempt judgment in this case. * * * In denying the motion, 265 Ala. 356, 357, the Supreme Court stated:

> "It is the established rule of this Court that the proper method of reviewing a judgment for civil contempt of the kind here involved is by a petition for common law writ of certiorari. . . ."

> "But the petitioner here has not applied for writ of certiorari, and we do not feel that the petition [for a stay] presently before us warrants our interference with the judgment of the Circuit Court of Montgomery County here sought to be stayed."

We hold that this Court has jurisdiction to entertain petitioner's federal claims.

[The Supreme Court went on to hold that (1) the NAACP could assert its members' constitutional claims that the United States Constitution forbids the state to compel the disclosure of their affiliation with the Association; and (2) the judgment of civil contempt and the fine that resulted from the NAACP's refusal to produce its membership lists must be reversed because "the immunity from state scrutiny of membership lists which the Association claims on behalf of its members is here so related to the right of the members to pursue their lawful private interests privately and to associate freely with others in so doing as to come within the protection of the Fourteenth Amendment." Further, the Court added, the state "has fallen short of showing a controlling justification for the deterrent effect on the free enjoyment of the right to associate which disclosure of membership lists is likely to have."]

NOTE ON THE ADEQUACY OF STATE PROCEDURAL GROUNDS

(1) Cardinale and NAACP v. Alabama Compared. There is a subtle difference, not always appreciated in the decisions, between the jurisdictional questions in Cardinale and in NAACP v. Alabama. In Cardinale, the federal issue was never raised or considered in any fashion in state court. The Supreme Court's refusal to hear the issue was based on the litigant's failure to have complied with a *federal* rule requiring that some presentation be made in the state court.

In NAACP v. Alabama (and the other cases discussed in this Note), the federal issue was raised, but in a fashion that, the state court concluded, did not comply with state procedural law. With the state court having ruled that it could not reach the merits of the federal claim because of the procedural default, the question for the Supreme Court was whether that *state law ruling* constituted an adequate state procedural ground barring Supreme Court review.

(2) The Adequate State Procedural Ground and the Primacy of State Practice. Five months before NAACP v. Alabama, the Court decided Staub v. City of Baxley, 355 U.S. 313 (1958), a case raising similar issues. Staub involved a labor organizer whom a city sought to prosecute for conducting union-promoting efforts without obtaining a prior permit. Staub argued that the permitting requirement violated the First and Fourteenth Amendments, challenging the licensing statutory scheme in its entirety. After a state appellate court declined to reach Staub's constitutional claims on the basis that she had not challenged individual sections of the statutory scheme (something the court said state law required as a matter of procedure), the Supreme Court upheld its jurisdiction to review the conviction, ruled that state law as represented in a line of Georgia Supreme Court decisions did not require such detailed pleadings, and reversed Staub's conviction.

Justice Frankfurter dissented, joined by Justice Clark. He viewed the case as implicating "the distribution of power as between the Nation and the States, and more particularly the distribution of judicial power as between this Court and the judiciaries of the States." He continued:

"While the power to review the denial by a state court of a nonfrivolous claim under the United States Constitution has been centered in this Court, carrying with it the responsibility to see that the opportunity to assert such a claim be not thwarted by any local procedural device, equally important is observance by this Court of the wide discretion in the States to formulate their own procedures for bringing issues appropriately to the attention of their local courts * * *. Such methods and procedures may, when judged by the best standards of judicial administration, appear crude, awkward and even finicky or unnecessarily formal when judged in the light of modern emphasis on informality. But so long as the local procedure does not discriminate against the raising of federal claims and, in the particular case, has not been used to stifle a federal claim to prevent its eventual consideration here, this Court is powerless to deny to a State the right to have the kind of judicial system it chooses and to administer that system in its own way."[1]

Justice Frankfurter is surely correct that, in general, state rules of practice presumptively determine the time when, and the mode by which, federal claims must be asserted in the state courts. Thus, ordinarily when a state court litigant has committed a procedural default—that is, has failed to raise a federal question in accordance with state procedural rules—the state court will refuse to decide the federal question, and any effort to obtain Supreme Court review will be rejected on the basis that there is an adequate and independent state procedural ground precluding the exercise of jurisdiction. Decisions so holding are legion. See generally Shapiro et al., Supreme Court Practice 3-3-96 (11th ed.2019). And in many other such instances, the Court simply denies certiorari, without noting specifically that jurisdiction was wanting.

(3) The Inadequate State Ground. The decisions in NAACP v. Alabama and Staub are accordingly two of a small set of cases forming a limited exception to the general rule—cases in which the Supreme Court upholds its jurisdiction to review the federal issue in a case on the basis that the state procedural ground is "inadequate" to support the judgment below.[2] The remainder of this Note examines this set of cases.[3]

Many of the cases cited in this Note involved a refusal by courts in southern states to adjudicate the asserted federal rights of persons of color in civil rights and criminal cases, or, as in Staub, of members of locally unpopular social or political movements. Consider these questions: Did the Court bend its usual jurisdictional rules in order to give itself the capacity to deal with a pressing set of social, legal and political problems—and if so, was that appropriate?[4] Or did the Court fail to go far enough in protecting federal

---

[1]   Along similar lines, Justice Frankfurter contended that the Court risked imposing obligations upon the state courts that it did not follow itself:

"Th[is] Court has long insisted, certainly in precept, on rigorous requirements that must be fulfilled before it will pass on the constitutionality of legislation, on avoidance of such determinations even by strained statutory construction, and on keeping constitutional adjudication, when unavoidable, as narrow as circumstances will permit. * * * [T]his Court will consider only those very limited aspects of a statute that alone may affect the rights of a particular litigant before the Court. * * * Surely a state court is not to be denied the like right to protect itself from the necessity—sometimes even the temptation—of adjudicating overly broad claims of unconstitutionality. Surely it can insist that such claims be formulated under precise (even if, in our view, needlessly particularized) requirements and restricted to the limited issues that concrete and immediately pressing circumstances may raise."

[2]   Compare Walker v. City of Birmingham, 388 U.S. 307, 321 (1967), in which the Supreme Court upheld the criminal contempt convictions of petitioners, including Dr. Martin Luther King, Jr., when they did not pursue settled local procedures to have an injunction dissolved that the city had obtained to preclude petitioners' right to march: "This Court cannot hold that the petitioners were constitutionally free to ignore all the procedures of the law and carry their battle to the streets. One may sympathize with the petitioners' impatient commitment to their cause. But respect for judicial process is a small price to pay for the civilizing hand of law, which alone can give abiding meaning to constitutional freedom."

[3]   See generally Hill, *The Inadequate State Ground*, 65 Colum.L.Rev. 943 (1965); Meltzer, *State Court Forfeitures of Federal Rights*, 99 Harv.L.Rev. 1128 (1986); Sandalow, *Henry v. Mississippi and the Adequate State Ground: Proposals for a Revised Doctrine*, 1965 Sup.Ct.Rev. 187.

[4]   See Glennon, *The Jurisdictional Legacy of the Civil Rights Movement*, 61 Tenn.L.Rev. 869 (1994) (arguing that in the mid-1950s and the 1960s, the Supreme Court modified doctrines,

rights from being undermined in state court litigation? (Recall that, in criminal cases, an additional difficulty is the poor quality of representation afforded to many defendants, resulting in manifold failures by counsel properly to raise federal issues.[5]) In theory, Congress might have addressed defects in state court criminal proceedings by strengthening and/or expanding the collateral relief available in federal habeas actions. See Chap. XI, Sec. 3, *infra*. In the absence of such congressional action, how much discretion did the Supreme Court have to respond to the underlying problems? Compare Hart, *The Relations Between State and Federal Law*, 54 Colum.L.Rev. 489, 508 (1954), with Meltzer, note 3, *supra*, at 1176–78.

(4) Due Process Violations. Supreme Court review plainly cannot be foreclosed by a litigant's noncompliance with a state procedural rule that, on its face or as applied, violates the Due Process Clause. Rather, the validity of a state procedural rule under the Due Process Clause raises an independent federal question that the Court has jurisdiction to review, apart from any other federal issue in the case.

(a) Unforeseeable Appellate Court Rulings. In Brinkerhoff-Faris Trust & Savings Co. v. Hill, 281 U.S. 673 (1930), the state appellate court denied an equal protection challenge to a state tax because the taxpayer had failed first to seek administrative relief (which was no longer available)— even though earlier state decisions had held that the state administrative body lacked power to award relief. The Supreme Court viewed the state court's action as a denial of due process, and thus, brushing aside claims of procedural default, reversed and remanded for the state court to consider the equal protection issue on the merits.[6] But see Herndon v. Georgia, 295 U.S. 441 (1935) (treating First Amendment claim as defaulted where petitioner did not raise it until a motion for rehearing to the state supreme court).

(b) Strict Time Limits for Pre-Trial Motions. Reece v. Georgia, 350 U.S. 85 (1955), and Michel v. Louisiana, 350 U.S. 91 (1955), decided on the same day, both involved due process challenges by criminal defendants who failed to comply with state rules requiring prompt challenges to grand juries.

Reece was a capital case involving a Black man who "was convicted [in state court] of the rape of a white woman in Cobb County, Georgia." The Supreme Court reversed the state court's ruling that Reece's challenge to his conviction on the ground that Black jurors had been "systematically excluded" from grand jury service in Georgia was untimely. Specifically, the Court found fault in a state procedural rule requiring that such challenges

---

including that of the adequate state ground, that would otherwise have presented jurisdictional obstacles to the Court's support of the civil rights movement, and that subsequent changes in the southern states' legal and political systems have substantially diminished the need to do so).

[5]   Givelber, *Litigating State Capital Cases While Preserving Federal Questions: Can It Be Done Successfully?*, 29 St. Mary's L.J. 1009 (1998), explains the frequency with which federal issues are not successfully preserved in state criminal, and especially capital, cases on the bases, inter alia, that (i) trial counsel may overlook the need to raise and properly identify federal objections, and (ii) defense counsel may be wary of resting on federal law when the claim might also be based on state law that appears to be more favorable or clear-cut.

[6]   See also, *e.g.*, Saunders v. Shaw, 244 U.S. 317 (1917); *cf.* Missouri v. Gehner, 281 U.S. 313 (1930); Cole v. Arkansas, 333 U.S. 196 (1948).

be made prior to indictment when the trial court had not appointed Reece's lawyers until the day after his indictment, observing that "[t]he effective assistance of counsel in [a capital] case is a constitutional requirement of due process * * *."

But in Michel, the Court upheld application to several defendants of a state rule requiring that objections to the composition of the grand jury be raised before the expiration of the third judicial day following the end of the grand jury's term, or before trial, whichever was earlier. The relevant inquiry, the Court wrote, asks whether the state rule in question "raises an insuperable barrier to one making claim to federal rights. The test is whether the defendant has had 'a reasonable opportunity to have the issue as to the claimed right heard and determined by the state court.' Parker v. Illinois, 333 U.S. 571, 574 [(1948)]"—a test that the Court appeared to equate with the meaning of due process.

(5) Nonconstitutional Bases for Finding State Grounds Inadequate. Although the opinion in Michel v. Louisiana, 350 U.S. 91 (1955), Paragraph (4)(b), *supra*, appears to assume that a state procedural ground is inadequate only if it denies due process, in general, the Court's decisions do not equate the two doctrines.[7] For example, no language in NAACP v. Alabama suggests that Alabama's application of its new procedural rule to the Association denied due process. And if a state procedural rule denies due process, presumably it could not be enforced to prevent hearing a state law claim any more than it could prevent hearing a federal claim. There was, however, no suggestion in NAACP v. Alabama that Alabama was barred from applying its procedural rule to a challenge based on state constitutional grounds. And the Court has stated that an inadequate procedural ground may not block litigation of federal rights even when it might block litigation of state law claims. See Davis v. Wechsler, 263 U.S. 22 (1923), Paragraph (5)(b), *infra*.

The "nonconstitutional" bases for inadequacy can be broadly placed in two categories:

(a) The State Procedural Ground Is Novel or Has Been Inconsistently Applied. Part of the reasoning in the Court's unanimous decision in NAACP v. Alabama was that the procedural ruling was inadequate because the Alabama precedents did not support it.[8]

The Court's decision in Staub underscores the detailed examination of state law necessary to make such a determination. As noted *supra*, the majority there second-guessed the settled nature of the detailed pleading rule the state court cited as precluding review of Staub's underlying First Amendment arguments. In dissent, Justice Frankfurter listed five decisions of the Georgia Supreme Court that he read to support such a detailed pleading rule.

---

[7]   See generally Fay v. Noia, 372 U.S. 391, 448, 465–66 (1963) (Harlan, J., dissenting); Meltzer, note 3, *supra*, at 1159–60; Note, *The Untenable Nonfederal Ground in the Supreme Court*, 74 Harv.L.Rev. 1375 (1961). But *cf.* Hill, note 3, *supra*, at 971–80.

[8]   For additional decisions along similar lines, see, *e.g.*, Ford v. Georgia, 498 U.S. 411 (1991); James v. Kentucky, 466 U.S. 341, 345–48 (1984); Hathorn v. Lovorn, 457 U.S. 255 (1982).

When the Justices cannot agree as to the proper reading of state court precedent, should that counsel in favor of hesitation to second-guess the state court's application of a procedural bar in the case at bar? Like novelty, inadequacy is similarly established by a demonstration that the state courts had not previously applied their stated rule "with the pointless severity" shown in the present case. See, *e.g.*, Rogers v. Alabama, 192 U.S. 226 (1904) (two-page motion to quash indictment stricken as prolix); NAACP v. Alabama ex rel. Flowers, 377 U.S. 288, 294–302 (1964) (formal arrangement of points in brief); Barr v. City of Columbia, 378 U.S. 146, 149–50 (1964) (generality of stated exceptions; same form accepted in other cases, including an "identical" case a few weeks later).

Note that a state ruling that is novel or inconsistent could be characterized either as a misapplication of state law or as an implicit revision of state law. Under either view, the state procedural ground will be inadequate and therefore will not block Supreme Court review in the present case; but the latter characterization would presumably permit the new ruling to be applied to future cases "once notice of the new interpretation is provided." Meltzer, note 3, *supra*, at 1139 n.44.

Although, as in Staub, Court members may disagree as to what is settled state law, the Court has made clear that the "question whether a state procedural ruling is adequate is itself a question of federal law." Beard v. Kindler, 558 U.S. 53, 60 (2009). And despite saying it is only in "exceptional cases" that the Court will find a state ground inadequate, Lee v. Kemna, 534 U.S. 362, 376 (2002), the Court continues to do so on occasion. Cruz v. Arizona, 598 U.S. 17 (2023), is a good example. In Cruz, the Court held that a capital defendant's federal due process claim was subject to its appellate review despite a holding by the Arizona Supreme Court that the claim was procedurally barred from state post-conviction review for failing to rely upon a "significant change in the law" as required under Arizona Rule of Criminal Procedure 32.1(g). Writing for the Court, Justice Sotomayor emphasized that the state court had interpreted Rule 32.1(g) in Cruz's case in a manner that was "entirely new and in conflict with prior Arizona case law."[9] The Court concluded by reiterating the principle that "[i]n exceptional cases where a state-court judgment rests on a novel and unforeseeable state-court procedural decision lacking fair or substantial support in prior state law, that decision is not adequate to preclude review of a federal question." The Court then disposed of the case as follows: "[T]he judgment of the Supreme Court of Arizona is vacated, and the case is remanded for further proceedings not inconsistent with this opinion."

On remand, can the state court hold fast to its prior application of Rule 32.1(g) in the case? Given that the adequate and independent state ground doctrine is aimed at determining whether the Supreme Court has *jurisdiction* to review an underlying federal question on appeal, it is curious

---

[9]   Specifically, Justice Sotomayor held for the Court that settled state practice would have treated as a "significant change in the law" the Supreme Court's decision in Lynch v. Arizona, 578 U.S. 613 (2016) (per curiam), which rejected Arizona's application of the Court's earlier precedent in Simmons v. South Carolina, 512 U.S. 154 (1994) (requiring that capital juries be informed when a life sentence does not afford possibility of parole).

that the Court declined to review the petitioner's underlying due process claim on the merits and instead sent the case back to the state courts. On remand, are the Arizona courts obligated either to change their interpretation of state law or review the federal question? More generally, does Cruz suggest that the Court is blurring the distinction between constitutional and non-constitutional sources of inadequacy? Or does the case demonstrate a lack of attention or consistency to the difference between the two? *Cf.* Montgomery v. Louisiana, 577 U.S. 190 (2016), p. 1610, *infra* (requiring state post-conviction court to hear Eighth Amendment claim predicated on recent Supreme Court decision).

(b) The State Procedural Requirement Is Unacceptably Burdensome. On rare occasions, the Court finds state grounds inadequate not because state rules are applied in an inconsistent or novel fashion but rather because they are burdensome. In Davis v. Wechsler, 263 U.S. 22, 24 (1923), Justice Holmes said: "Whatever springes the State may set for those who are endeavoring to assert rights that the State confers, the assertion of federal rights, when plainly and reasonably made, is not to be defeated under the name of local practice." See *id.* (deeming inadequate state rule governing appearances and preservation of jurisdictional objections).

For examples of other decisions resting on undue burden, see Lee v. Kemna, 534 U.S. 362 (2002) (failing to comply with requirements that a motion for a continuance be in writing and make certain showings is not adequate in the particular circumstances of the case); Osborne v. Ohio, 495 U.S. 103, 123–25 (1990) (requiring a specific objection to jury instructions when the defendant had in substance previously raised the same objection in a motion to dismiss would " 'force resort to an arid ritual of meaningless form' " and would serve no perceivable state interest) (quoting Staub); Douglas v. Alabama, 380 U.S. 415, 422–23 (1965) (rejecting as inadequate a requirement that the defendant repeat, after every question to a witness, a constitutional objection that had been thrice made and whose repetition would have been futile and strategically harmful); Shuttlesworth v. City of Birmingham, 376 U.S. 339 (1964) (failing to use proper paper for petition to review criminal conviction; state forfeiture ruling held inadequate).[10]

(c) Relationship of the Varying Rubrics of Inadequacy. Individual cases may fit within more than one rubric of inadequacy. In Staub, some of the majority's language—"To require her, in these circumstances, to count off, one by one, the several sections of the ordinance would be to force resort to an arid ritual of meaningless form"—suggests that the state court's ruling would have been deemed inadequate (because unduly burdensome) even had the Court thought it was fairly supported by precedent.

Here, too, Justice Frankfurter disagreed and defended at length the state's prerogative to fashion its own procedural rules, observing: "There is

---

[10] Should the federal courts analyze the adequacy of state procedural grounds one by one, as in the previous cases, or focus more systematically on the fairness of the complex procedural mazes that criminal defendants must often clear before they can assert their federal claims in state court? See Primus, *Federal Review of State Criminal Convictions: A Structural Approach to Adequacy Doctrine*, 116 Mich.L.Rev. 75 (2017) (advancing the latter view).

nothing frivolous or futile (though it may appear 'formal') about a rule insisting that parties specify with arithmetic particularity those provisions in a legislative enactment they would ask a court to strike down. This is so, because such exactitude helps to make concrete the plaintiffs' relation to challenged provisions." Was the majority in Staub insufficiently respectful of the state's right to establish and apply its own procedures in its courts?

(6) State Court "Discretionary" Refusals to Excuse a Procedural Default. A handful of Supreme Court decisions raise the question whether a state court's failure to exercise "discretion" to excuse a litigant's failure to comply with state procedural rules calls into question the adequacy of a state procedural ground.

(a) In Williams v. Georgia, 349 U.S. 375 (1955) (6–3), after Williams, a Black man, had been convicted of an interracial murder, the U.S. Supreme Court held in a different case from the same county that the system used there to select juries was unconstitutional. Counsel for Williams first raised a jury discrimination claim six months later, in an extraordinary new trial motion filed after affirmance of the conviction. The state courts held the motion untimely on the ground that state practice required a challenge to the jury list, or array, before trial and that there had not been the due diligence necessary to justify an exception to that rule.

The Supreme Court, per Frankfurter, J., vacated and remanded. Although acknowledging the validity of the state rule, the Court said that "where a State allows questions of this sort to be raised at a later stage and be determined by its courts as a matter of discretion, we are not concluded from assuming jurisdiction and deciding whether the state court action in the particular circumstances is, in effect, an avoidance of the federal right." Noting numerous cases in which Georgia courts had exercised discretion to entertain extraordinary motions challenging individual jurors, and finding no basis for distinguishing challenges to the array, the Court stated that "the discretionary decision to deny the motion does not deprive this Court of jurisdiction to find that the substantive issue is properly before us."

All the same, Justice Frankfurter observed that "the fact that we have jurisdiction does not compel us to exercise it." Stressing that life was at stake and that the state had conceded the constitutional violation, the Court concluded that "orderly procedure requires a remand * * *. Fair regard for the principles which the Georgia courts have enforced in numerous cases and for the constitutional commands binding on all courts compels us to reject the assumption that the courts of Georgia would allow this man to go to his death as the result of a conviction secured from a jury which the State admits was unconstitutionally impaneled."[11]

---

[11]   To similar effect is Patterson v. Alabama, 294 U.S. 600 (1935), an appeal arising out of the infamous Scottsboro trials. In Patterson, Black defendants (including Patterson) had been convicted of interracial rape and sentenced to death for a third time after earlier convictions had been overturned. The Supreme Court of Alabama held that Patterson's challenge to the exclusion of Black jurors from the jury had not been made in timely fashion. Further, in a companion case, that court rejected the same claim of jury discrimination on the merits. Granting review in both cases, the U.S. Supreme Court held in the companion case that discrimination was established. Norris v. Alabama, 294 U.S. 587 (1935). In Patterson's case, the Court concluded that the state procedural ruling was supported by earlier Alabama decisions,

Was the Williams majority seeking "to cajole the Georgia court into reversing itself where the United States Supreme Court lacked grounds to do so"? Note, *Supreme Court, 1954 Term: Constitutional Law*, 69 Harv.L.Rev. 131, 160 (1955). Or was the Court concerned that the state courts were exercising their discretion in a discriminatory way? On remand, the Georgia Supreme Court, without briefing or argument, "[a]dhered to" its earlier judgment, while protesting that the Supreme Court had lacked jurisdiction. 88 S.E.2d 376 (Ga. 1954). When the case returned to the U.S. Supreme Court on a petition for certiorari, that Court denied review. 350 U.S. 950 (1956).[12] See also Sullivan v. Little Hunting Park, Inc., 396 U.S. 229 (1969) (deeming a state law notice requirement that was not consistently applied and "more properly deemed discretionary than jurisdictional" as "not bar[ring] review here by certiorari").

(b)   The Supreme Court's collateral review habeas case law seems to assign less significance to the existence of state court discretion in the adequacy analysis. (As explored in Chap. XI, Sec. 3, *infra*, federal habeas proceedings permit persons in state custody under certain circumstances to attack collaterally their state court convictions.) In Beard v. Kindler, 558 U.S. 53 (2009), for example, Kindler had been convicted of murder in Pennsylvania state court in 1985. While his post-verdict motions were pending, he escaped to Canada. After fighting extradition for several years, Kindler was extradited to the United States in 1991. The Pennsylvania trial court had dismissed Kindler's original post-verdict motions because of his escape. In 1991, the trial court rejected his motion to reinstate those earlier motions, reasoning that the original trial judge had not abused his discretion in dismissing them. The Pennsylvania Supreme Court affirmed, concluding that the trial court's dismissal of Kindler's postverdict motions constituted a "reasonable response" to his escape under Pennsylvania's fugitive forfeiture law. On state collateral review, the state courts again rejected Kindler's claims. Kindler then filed a petition for a writ of habeas corpus in federal court. The United States Court of Appeals for the Third Circuit held that because Pennsylvania's fugitive forfeiture law gave state courts "discretion" to hear an appeal by a fugitive who had been returned to custody, the fugitive forfeiture rule was not sufficiently "firmly established" to provide an adequate and independent state ground.

---

but nonetheless vacated the judgment: "We are not convinced that the [state] court, * * * confronting the anomalous and grave situation which would be created by a reversal of the judgment against Norris, and an affirmance of the judgment of death in the companion case of Patterson, * * * would have considered itself powerless to * * * provide appropriate relief. * * * At least the state court should have an opportunity to examine its powers in the light of the situation which has now developed." One commentator has argued that in Patterson, "the technical requirements of law were subordinated to the ends of justice." Hendel, Charles Evans Hughes and the Supreme Court 161 (1951). The state courts thereafter granted a new trial and sustained the resulting conviction in Patterson v. State, 175 So. 371 (Ala.), *cert. denied*, 302 U.S. 733 (1937).

[12]   For criticism, see Dickson, *State Court Defiance and the Limits of Supreme Court Authority: Williams v. Georgia Revisited*, 103 Yale L.J. 1423, 1478, 1481 (1994) (suggesting that the Court's failure to take up the Williams case anew stemmed from a desire "to secure Southern compliance with Brown [v. Board of Education]" and criticizing the Court's decision to "sacrific[e] individual justice for the sake of other institutional priorities," a decision that resulted in Williams' execution).

In reversing the court of appeals, Chief Justice Roberts, speaking for a unanimous Court, explained: "[A] discretionary state procedural rule can serve as an adequate ground to bar federal habeas review. Nothing inherent in such a rule renders it inadequate for purposes of the adequate state ground doctrine. To the contrary, a discretionary rule can be 'firmly established'—and 'regularly followed' even if the appropriate exercise of discretion may permit consideration of a federal claim in some cases but not others" (citing Meltzer, note 1, *supra*). The Court emphasized that a contrary principle would put states to a terrible choice. They "could preserve flexibility by granting courts discretion to excuse procedural errors, but only at the cost of undermining the finality of state court judgments." Alternatively, they could protect finality "by withholding such discretion, but only at the cost of precluding any flexibility in applying the rules." Noting that federal procedural norms frequently give the trial judge "broad discretion," the Court suggested that "the federalism and comity concerns that motivate the adequate state ground doctrine" would make it "particularly strange to disregard state procedural rules that are substantially similar to those to which we give full force in our own courts."

For decisions reaffirming Kindler's approach to discretion and procedural default in habeas, see Johnson v. Lee, 578 U.S. 605 (2016) (per curiam); Walker v. Martin, 562 U.S. 307, 320 (2011) (Ginsburg, J., for a unanimous Court) (holding that where a state court cannot be said to have "exercised its discretion in a surprising or unfair manner" to deem a state habeas petition untimely under its standard, such a conclusion is an adequate and independent state ground for denying a later federal habeas petition); see also *id.* ("A discretionary rule ought not be disregarded automatically upon a showing of seeming inconsistencies."). Is there any reason to think that the Court's reasoning in Kindler should have less force in the context of applying the adequate-state-ground doctrine on direct review? If not, what criteria should the Court apply in determining whether the exercise of such discretion negates an adequate and independent state ground?[13]

(7) The Source of Power to Find State Grounds Inadequate. What is the basis for the Supreme Court's assertion of the power to review a case where the state judgment rests on a procedural ruling that the Court finds "inadequate"? Could Supreme Court review of federal questions be adequately effectuated if state procedural rulings, once found constitutional, wholly insulated federal issues from review? See Wechsler, note 13, *supra*, at 1053–56. Consider whether the following justifications are persuasive.

(a) Traditional Explanations. First, one might ascribe to the Due Process Clause judicial power to find state grounds inadequate if (a) a state procedural bar denies a litigant a reasonable opportunity to raise the federal claim, or (b) if the novelty or inconsistency of a state procedural bar's

---

[13]   The Court's modern habeas jurisprudence allows for very few exceptions to procedural default. See Chap. XI, Sec. 3, *infra.* But for a time, it was more forgiving. See, *e.g.*, Fay v. Noia, 372 U.S. 391 (1963), pp. 1632–1634, *infra*; Henry v. Mississippi, 379 U.S. 443 (1965). For criticism of Henry, see Wechsler, *The Appellate Jurisdiction of the Supreme Court: Reflections on the Law and the Logistics of Direct Review*, 34 Wash. & Lee L.Rev. 1043, 1053–55 (1977).

application results in arbitrary decisionmaking. But the Due Process Clause, although occasionally invoked in the Court's decisions, see Paragraph (4), *supra*, provides at best a partial explanation for the doctrine. As Professor Meltzer writes, the Court has never held that mere inconsistency or lack of uniformity, standing alone, violates due process. In addition, he notes, if due process were the source of the inadequate state ground doctrine, it would provide a federal constitutional basis for challenging the application of state court procedural bars against *state* claims—something that the Court has not yet endeavored to do. See Meltzer, note 3, *supra*, at 1159–61.

Second, to the extent that the inadequate state ground doctrine suggests a purpose to prevent the use of state procedural rules to evade or deny federal claims of right, the source of judicial power to apply that doctrine might originate in the Supremacy Clause, U.S. Const. Art. VI. As Professor Hill writes, that theory would rest on the proposition "that there is jurisdiction to determine whether the state court has given federal law its due." Hill, note 3, *supra*, at 959. The anti-discrimination theory, however, does not necessarily account for cases that find inadequacy on the basis of an undue burden on the presentation of federal claims. See Paragraph 5(b), *supra*. Professor Meltzer is skeptical of this view, writing: "The supremacy clause is usually viewed * * * as creating not a substantive rule of federal law, but a rule of priority: if state and federal law conflict, federal law prevails. But this priority tells us little about what the federal law should be." Meltzer, note 3, *supra*, at 1162.[14]

Third, the source of the doctrine may be traced to the jurisdictional statute authorizing Supreme Court review—28 U.S.C. § 1257—which requires that "any title, right, privilege, or immunity [be] specially set up or claimed under the Constitution or the treaties or statutes of * * * the United States." Professor Roosevelt suggests that when the Supreme Court decides the adequacy of the ground for a state court procedural default, it is determining, as a matter of federal law, whether the federal right was "specially set up or claimed" in state court within the meaning of § 1257. Federal law, he adds, in general incorporates applicable state law, so as not to interfere with a state's ability to establish its own procedural rules. When, however, the federal statutory standard does not incorporate state rules (because the state ground is inadequate), that decision governs only the Supreme Court's jurisdiction; it does not preclude the state court from continuing to follow the rule in similar cases. See Roosevelt, *Light from Dead Stars: The Procedural Adequate and Independent State Ground Reconsidered*, 103 Colum.L.Rev. 1888 (2003).

One might plausibly attribute to § 1257 a purpose to maintain federal supremacy through the development of the inadequate state ground doctrine. But is there evidence that such an interpretation of § 1257 is rooted in its text or legislative background? Treating § 1257 as the source of the doctrine also would give rise to the odd situation in which a state court might

---

[14]　For additional discussion of the Supremacy Clause, see Armstrong v. Exceptional Child Center, 575 U.S. 320, 324 (2015) ("It is apparent that this Clause creates a rule of decision * * *. It is equally apparent that the Supremacy Clause is not the " 'source of any federal rights' " * * *.") (internal citations omitted), p. 1200, *infra*.

correctly apply a state procedural bar to a federal claim, only to have the Supreme Court, on review, correctly reverse the state court's decision on the merits on the basis that the state court's application of state procedural law cannot bar Supreme Court consideration of the federal claim. Changes in the applicable law as a case moves up the appellate ladder to the Supreme Court seem hard to reconcile with the broader implications of Murdock, p. 636, *supra*, as well as Erie R. Co. v. Tompkins, 304 U.S. 64 (1938), p. 760, *infra*.

(b) The Inadequate State Ground Doctrine as Federal Common Law. Could one explain the inadequate state ground doctrine as a form of "federal common law" that places limits, beyond those demanded by the Due Process Clause, on the freedom of states to refuse to entertain federal claims because not presented in compliance with state procedural rules? Meltzer, note 3, *supra*, adopts such a theory and then uses the reformulation to advocate somewhat more forgiveness in excusing state procedural defaults.[15]

According to Professor Meltzer, "special institutional factors" as relevant here mitigate the "inherent concerns about the legitimacy of federal common law"—concerns that center on the separation-of-powers and federalism implications of federal judicial lawmaking. See Chap. VII, Sec. 1, *infra*. First, because judges are experts in procedure, they have a comparative advantage in crafting rules in this space. Second, separation of powers concerns are minimized because "doctrines excusing procedural default" necessarily depend heavily on "factual nuance," which makes such doctrines "notoriously difficult to encapsulate in clear and specific codes." Third, federalism concerns about federal common lawmaking could be significantly mitigated if state courts participated in the formulation of a federal common law of state court forfeitures of federal rights. Assuming that Professor Meltzer's take on the institutional factors is correct, what is the source of authority for the formulation of such federal common law rules? Article III? Section 1257? Some other source?

Consider the implications of the federal common law approach if, just after the decision in Staub v. Baxley, a case raising an indistinguishable procedural issue were to arise in Georgia with respect to the forfeiture of a federal claim. Professor Meltzer argues that the Supreme Court's decision in Staub—finding inadequate the Georgia rule that a litigant must object to each separate section of the statute—should not be regarded simply as regulating Supreme Court jurisdiction to review, but rather as establishing a federal common law rule that must be honored in the state courts. Compare Dice v. Akron, Canton & Youngstown R.R., 342 U.S. 359 (1952), p. 605, *supra* (holding that in FELA actions, state courts must follow a federal procedural rule requiring jury trial on the issue whether a purported release of the claim was fraudulently obtained—even though the federal rule was not set forth in any federal constitutional or statutory enactment). *Cf.* Haywood v. Drown, 556 U.S. 729 (2009), p. 593, *supra*; Felder v. Casey, 487 U.S. 131 (1988), p.

---

[15]   Noting, however, that federal common law should be guided by federal legislative policy, Meltzer argues that the standards for excusing procedural defaults in the state courts should not be more forgiving than the standards applied in the federal courts, which themselves have numerous procedural rules whose violation results in the forfeiture of federal rights. Meltzer, note 3, *supra*, at 1202–08.

608, *supra*.[16] This conclusion would seem to follow under one of the most famous defenses of the so-called "new" federal common law. See Friendly, *In Praise of* Erie—*And of the New Federal Common Law*, 39 N.Y.U.L.Rev. 383, 405 (1964), discussed further at pp. 815–816, *infra* (positing that "Erie led to the emergence" of a new federal common law "that is truly uniform because, under the Supremacy Clause, it is binding in every forum.").

(8) State Court Excuse of Procedural Default. In the cases already discussed, the state courts enforced their procedural rules by refusing to reach federal claims that were not properly presented. But when a state court chooses instead to excuse a procedural violation and proceeds to reach the merits of the federal claim, the Supreme Court's jurisdiction to review the decision is secure.[17] This rule creates an obvious risk that the record may not be adequately developed, but the elimination of mandatory appeals in 1988 permits the Court to deny certiorari whenever that problem might exist.

(9) State Court Ambiguity. Sometimes it is unclear whether a state court's denial of relief rests on a state procedural ground (which would ordinarily foreclose Supreme Court review) or on the merits of the federal issue (which would permit such review). In such cases, the earlier decisions declined jurisdiction, presuming that the state judgment rested on the procedural default. See, *e.g.*, Mutual Life Ins. Co. v. McGrew, 188 U.S. 291, 309–10 (1903); Bailey v. Anderson, 326 U.S. 203, 206–07 (1945). The Court's later decision in Harris v. Reed, 489 U.S. 255 (1989), suggests that the presumption should be the reverse, so as to permit Supreme Court review.

Subsequent decisions have tried more nuanced approaches to deciphering unreasoned state court decisions. See Wilson v. Sellers, 584 U.S. 122 (2018) (applying the presumption, in the context of federal habeas corpus, that an unexplained state court decision rests on the same grounds as the last reasoned state court decision in the same case); Foster v. Chatman, 578 U.S. 488, 498 n.3 (2016) (employing a similar framework); Ylst v. Nunemaker, 501 U.S. 797 (1991), p. 671, *supra* (same); Coleman v. Thompson, 501 U.S. 722 (1991), p. 671, *supra* (relying in part on the content of the motion to dismiss as a means to decode an ambiguous state court decision). *Cf.* Capital Cities Media, Inc. v. Toole, 466 U.S. 378 (1984) (per curiam), p. 670, *supra* (instead of presuming one way or the other, vacating and remanding to the state court for clarification).

---

[16]   The question whether a finding of "inadequacy" should bind the state courts in future cases has divided the commentators. See Meltzer, note 3, *supra*, at 1150–52, 1202 n.70.

[17]   See, *e.g.*, Whitney v. California, 274 U.S. 357, 360–63 (1927); Orr v. Orr, 440 U.S. 268, 274–75 (1979); Payton v. New York, 445 U.S. 573, 582 n.19 (1980).

4. FINAL JUDGMENTS AND THE HIGHEST STATE COURT

Cox Broadcasting Corp. v. Cohn

420 U.S. 469 (1975).
Appeal from the Supreme Court of Georgia.

■ MR. JUSTICE WHITE delivered the opinion of the Court.

[During a criminal prosecution for rape and murder, a television reporter broadcasted a news story reporting the victim's name, which he had learned from records publicly available at the court. The victim's father sued the reporter and the television station for invasion of privacy, relying on Ga. Code Ann. § 26–9901, which made publication or broadcast of the identity of a rape victim a misdemeanor. Despite the defendants' claim that the imposition of civil liability would violate the First Amendment, the state trial court held that § 26–9901 implicitly created a civil remedy and granted summary judgment for the plaintiff on liability, with damages to be determined at a jury trial.

[On appeal, the Georgia Supreme Court initially ruled that the trial court's recognition of an implied right of action under § 26–9901 was in error (and therefore it did not further discuss the statute's constitutionality). The court added, though, that the complaint did state a cause of action for invasion of privacy or for the common law tort of public disclosure. The court also ruled that the award of summary judgment was improper because it was for a trier of fact to determine whether public disclosure of the victim's name actually invaded plaintiff's "zone of privacy," and if so, the extent to which it did. Further, the court wrote that "in formulating such an issue for determination by the fact-finder, it is reasonable to require the appellee to prove that the appellants invaded his privacy with willful or negligent disregard for the fact that reasonable men would find the invasion highly offensive." The Georgia Supreme Court nonetheless agreed with the trial court that defendants were not entitled to judgment as a matter of law based on the First and Fourteenth Amendments.]

Upon motion for rehearing the Georgia court countered the argument that the victim's name was a matter of public interest and could be published with impunity by relying on § 26–9901 as an authoritative declaration of state policy that the name of a rape victim was not a matter of public concern. This time the court felt compelled to determine the constitutionality of the statute and sustained it as a "legitimate limitation on the right of freedom of expression contained in the First Amendment." * * *

We postponed decision as to our jurisdiction over this appeal to the hearing on the merits. We conclude that the Court has jurisdiction, and reverse the judgment of the Georgia Supreme Court.

II

* * * Since 1789, Congress has granted this Court appellate jurisdiction with respect to state litigation only after the highest state court in which judgment could be had has rendered a "[f]inal judgment or decree." Title 28 U.S.C. § 1257 retains this limitation on our power to review cases coming from state courts. The Court has noted that "[c]onsiderations of English usage as well as those of judicial policy" would justify an interpretation of the final-judgment rule to preclude review "where anything further remains to be determined by a State court, no matter how dissociated from the only *federal* issue that has finally been adjudicated by the highest court of the State." Radio Station WOW, Inc. v. Johnson, 326 U.S. 120, 124 (1945). But the Court there observed that the rule had not been administered in such a mechanical fashion and that there were circumstances in which there has been "a departure from this requirement of finality for federal appellate jurisdiction." *Ibid.*

These circumstances were said to be "very few," *ibid.*; but as the cases have unfolded * * * [t]here are now at least four categories of * * * cases in which the Court has treated the decision on the federal issue as a final judgment for the purposes of 28 U.S.C. § 1257 and has taken jurisdiction without awaiting the completion of the additional proceedings anticipated in the lower state courts. * * *

In the first category are those cases in which there are further proceedings—even entire trials—yet to occur in the state courts but where for one reason or another the federal issue is conclusive or the outcome of further proceedings preordained. In these circumstances, because the case is for all practical purposes concluded, the judgment of the state court on the federal issue is deemed final. In Mills v. Alabama, 384 U.S. 214 (1966), for example, a demurrer to a criminal complaint was sustained on federal constitutional grounds by a state trial court. The State Supreme Court reversed, remanding for jury trial. This Court took jurisdiction on the reasoning that the appellant had no defense other than his federal claim and could not prevail at trial on the facts or any nonfederal ground. To dismiss the appeal "would not only be an inexcusable delay of the benefits Congress intended to grant by providing for appeal to this Court, but it would also result in a completely unnecessary waste of time and energy in judicial systems already troubled by delays due to congested dockets." (footnote omitted).

Second, there are cases such as Radio Station WOW, *supra*, and Brady v. Maryland, 373 U.S. 83 (1963), in which the federal issue, finally decided by the highest court in the State, will survive and require decision regardless of the outcome of future state court proceedings. In Radio Station WOW, the Nebraska Supreme Court directed the transfer of the properties of a federally licensed radio station and ordered an accounting, rejecting the claim that the transfer order would interfere with the federal license. The federal issue was held reviewable here despite the pending accounting on the "presupposition . . . that the federal questions that could come here have been adjudicated by the State court, and that the accounting which remains to be taken could not remotely give rise to a federal question . . . that may later come here . . . ." * * * Nothing that could happen in the course of the accounting, short of settlement of the case, would foreclose or make unnecessary decision on the federal question. Older cases in the Court had reached the same result on similar facts. * * *[9]

In the third category are those situations where the federal claim has been finally decided, with further proceedings on the merits in the state courts to come, but in which later review of the federal issue cannot be had, whatever the ultimate outcome of the case. Thus, in these cases, if the party seeking interim review ultimately prevails on the merits, the federal issue will be mooted; if he were to lose on the merits, however, the governing state law would not permit him again to present his federal claims for review. * * * California v. Stewart, 384 U.S. 436 (1966) (decided with Miranda v. Arizona), epitomizes this category. There the state court reversed a conviction on federal constitutional grounds and remanded for a new trial. Although the State might have prevailed at trial, we granted its petition for certiorari and affirmed, explaining that the state judgment was "final" since an acquittal of the defendant at trial would preclude, under state law, an appeal by the State.

A recent decision in this category is North Dakota State Board of Pharmacy v. Snyder's Drug Stores, Inc., 414 U.S. 156 (1973), in which the Pharmacy Board rejected an application for a pharmacy operating permit relying on a state statute specifying ownership requirements which the applicant did not meet. The State Supreme Court held the statute unconstitutional and remanded the matter to the Board for further consideration of the application, freed from the constraints of the ownership statute. * * * [When the Board sought review, we exercised jurisdiction.] The federal issue would not survive the remand, whatever the result of the state administrative proceedings. The Board might deny the license on state-law grounds, thus foreclosing the federal issue, and the Court also ascertained that under state law the Board could not bring the federal issue here in the event the applicant satisfied the requirements of state law except for the invalidated ownership statute. Under these circumstances, the issue was ripe for review.[10]

---

[9]   In Brady v. Maryland, 373 U.S. 83 (1963), the Maryland courts had ordered a new trial in a criminal case but on punishment only, and the petitioner asserted here that he was entitled to a new trial on guilt as well. We entertained the case, saying that the federal issue was separable and would not be mooted by the new trial on punishment ordered in the state courts.

[10]   Cohen v. Beneficial Industrial Loan Corp., 337 U.S. 541 (1949), was a diversity action in the federal courts in the course of which there arose the question of the validity of a state statute requiring plaintiffs in stockholder suits to post security for costs as a prerequisite to bringing the action. The District Court held the state law inapplicable, the Court of Appeals reversed, and this Court, after granting certiorari, held that the issue of security for costs was separable from and independent of the merits and that if review were to be postponed until the

Lastly, there are those situations where the federal issue has been finally decided in the state courts with further proceedings pending in which the party seeking review here might prevail on the merits on nonfederal grounds, thus rendering unnecessary review of the federal issue by this Court, and where reversal of the state court on the federal issue would be preclusive of any further litigation on the relevant cause of action rather than merely controlling the nature and character of, or determining the admissibility of evidence in, the state proceedings still to come. In these circumstances, if a refusal immediately to review the state court decision might seriously erode federal policy, the Court has entertained and decided the federal issue, which itself has been finally determined by the state courts for purposes of the state litigation.

In Construction Laborers v. Curry, 371 U.S. 542 (1963), the state courts temporarily enjoined labor union picketing over claims that the National Labor Relations Board had exclusive jurisdiction of the controversy. The Court took jurisdiction for two independent reasons. First, the power of the state court to proceed in the face of the preemption claim was deemed an issue separable from the merits and ripe for review in this Court, particularly "when postponing review would seriously erode the national labor policy requiring the subject matter of respondents' cause to be heard by the . . . Board, not by the state courts." Second, the Court was convinced that in any event the union had no defense to the entry of a permanent injunction other than the preemption claim that had already been ruled on in the state courts. Hence the case was for all practical purposes concluded in the state tribunals.

In Mercantile National Bank v. Langdeau, 371 U.S. 555 (1963), two national banks [that had been sued in a particular county asserted that, under a federal venue statute,] they could properly be sued only in another county. Although trial was still to be had and the banks might well prevail on the merits, the Court, relying on Curry, entertained the issue as a "separate and independent matter, anterior to the merits and not enmeshed in the factual and legal issues comprising the plaintiff's cause of action." Moreover, it would serve the policy of the federal statute "to determine now in which state court appellants may be tried rather than to subject them . . . to long and complex litigation which may all be for naught if consideration of the preliminary question of venue is postponed until the conclusion of the proceedings."

Miami Herald Publishing Co. v. Tornillo, 418 U.S. 241 (1974), is the latest case in this category. There a candidate for public office sued a newspaper for refusing, allegedly contrary to a state statute, to carry his reply to the paper's editorial critical of his qualifications. The trial court held the act unconstitutional, denying both injunctive relief and damages. The State Supreme Court reversed, sustaining the statute against the challenge based upon the First and Fourteenth Amendments

---

termination of the litigation, "it will be too late effectively to review the present order, and the rights conferred by the statute, if it is applicable, will have been lost, probably irreparably."

and remanding the case for a trial and appropriate relief, including damages. The newspaper brought the case here. We sustained our jurisdiction, relying on the principles elaborated in the North Dakota case and observing:

> "Whichever way we were to decide on the merits, it would be intolerable to leave unanswered, under these circumstances, an important question of freedom of the press under the First Amendment; an uneasy and unsettled constitutional posture of § 104.38 could only further harm the operation of a free press."

In light of the prior cases, we conclude that we have jurisdiction to review the judgment of the Georgia Supreme Court * * *, [which] is plainly final on the federal issue and is not subject to further review in the state courts. Appellants will be liable for damages if the elements of the state cause of action are proved. They may prevail at trial on nonfederal grounds, it is true, but if the Georgia court erroneously upheld the statute, there should be no trial at all. Moreover, even if appellants prevailed at trial and made unnecessary further consideration of the constitutional question, there would remain in effect the unreviewed decision of the State Supreme Court that a civil action for publishing the name of a rape victim disclosed in a public judicial proceeding may go forward despite the First and Fourteenth Amendments. Delaying final decision of the First Amendment claim until after trial will "leave unanswered . . . an important question of freedom of the press under the First Amendment," "an uneasy and unsettled constitutional posture [that] could only further harm the operation of a free press." Tornillo, *supra*, at 247 n.6. On the other hand, if we now hold that the First and Fourteenth Amendments bar civil liability for broadcasting the victim's name, this litigation ends. Given these factors—that the litigation could be terminated by our decision on the merits[13] and that a failure to decide the question now will leave the press in Georgia operating in the shadow of the civil and criminal sanctions of a rule of law and a statute the constitutionality of which is in serious doubt—we find that reaching the merits is consistent with the pragmatic approach that we have followed in the past in determining finality. * * *

[The Court proceeded to invalidate § 26–9901 and the common-law privacy action on the merits, holding that the First and Fourteenth Amendments preclude states from basing liability on the publication of

---

[13]   Mr. Justice Rehnquist is correct in saying that this factor involves consideration of the merits in determining jurisdiction. But it does so only to the extent of determining that the issue is substantial and only in the context that if the state court's final decision on the federal issue is incorrect, federal law forecloses further proceedings in the state court. That the petitioner who protests against the state court's decision on the federal question might prevail on the merits on nonfederal grounds in the course of further proceedings anticipated in the state court and hence obviate later review of the federal issue here is not preclusive of our jurisdiction. Curry, Langdeau, North Dakota State Board of Pharmacy, California v. Stewart, 384 U.S. 436 (1966) (decided with Miranda v. Arizona[, 384 U.S. 436 (1966)]), and Miami Herald Publishing Co. v. Tornillo, 418 U.S. 241 (1974), make this clear. In those cases, the federal issue having been decided, arguably wrongly, and being determinative of the litigation if decided the other way, the finality rule was satisfied. * * *

truthful information contained in official court records open to public inspection.]

Reversed.

■ [JUSTICE POWELL wrote a concurring opinion. CHIEF JUSTICE BURGER concurred in the judgment without opinion. JUSTICE DOUGLAS wrote an opinion concurring in the judgment.]

■ MR. JUSTICE REHNQUIST, dissenting.

* * * Over the years, * * * this Court has steadily discovered new exceptions to the finality requirement, such that they can hardly any longer be described as "very few." * * * Although the Court's opinion today does accord detailed consideration to this problem, I do not believe that the reasons it expresses can support its result.

I

The Court has taken what it terms a "pragmatic" approach to the finality problem presented in this case. In so doing, it has relied heavily on Gillespie v. United States Steel Corp., 379 U.S. 148 (1964). As the Court acknowledges, Gillespie involved 28 U.S.C. § 1291, which restricts the appellate jurisdiction of the federal courts of appeals to "final decisions of the district courts." Although acknowledging this distinction, the Court accords it no importance and adopts Gillespie's approach without any consideration of whether the finality requirement for this Court's jurisdiction over a "judgment or decree" of a state court is grounded on more serious concerns than is the limitation of court of appeals jurisdiction to final "decisions" of the district courts. * * *

Were judicial efficiency the only interest at stake there would be less inclination to challenge the Court's resolution in this case, although, as discussed below, I have serious reservations that the standards the Court has formulated are effective for achieving even this single goal. The case before us, however, is an appeal from a state court, and this fact introduces additional interests which must be accommodated in fashioning any exception to the literal application of the finality requirement. I consider § 1257 finality to be but one of a number of congressional provisions reflecting concern that uncontrolled federal judicial interference with state administrative and judicial functions would have untoward consequences for our federal system. This is by no means a novel view of the § 1257 finality requirement. In Radio Station WOW, Inc. v. Johnson, 326 U.S. [120, 124 (1945),] Mr. Justice Frankfurter's opinion for the Court explained the finality requirement as follows:

> "* * * *This prerequisite to review derives added force when the jurisdiction of this Court is invoked to upset the decision of a State court.* Here we are in the realm of potential conflict between the courts of two different governments. And so, ever since 1789, Congress has granted this Court the power to intervene in State litigation only after 'the highest court of a

State in which a decision in the suit could be had' has rendered a 'final judgment or decree.' § 237 of the Judicial Code, 28 U.S.C. § 344(a). *This requirement is not one of those technicalities to be easily scorned. It is an important factor in the smooth working of our federal system.*" (Emphasis added.) * * *

[W]e have in recent years emphasized and re-emphasized the importance of comity and federalism in dealing with a related problem, that of district court interference with ongoing state judicial proceedings. See Younger v. Harris, 401 U.S. 37 (1971). Because these concerns are important, and because they provide "added force" to § 1257's finality requirement, I believe that the Court has erred by simply importing the approach of cases in which the only concern is efficient judicial administration.

II

But quite apart from the considerations of federalism which counsel against an expansive reading of our jurisdiction under § 1257, the Court's holding today enunciates a virtually formless exception to the finality requirement, one which differs in kind from those previously carved out. * * *

While the totality of [the exceptions previously recognized by the Court] certainly indicates that the Court has been willing to impart to the language "final judgment or decree" a great deal of flexibility, each of them is arguably consistent with the intent of Congress in enacting § 1257, if not with the language it used, and each of them is relatively workable in practice.

To those established exceptions is now added one so formless that it cannot be paraphrased, but instead must be quoted:

> "Given these factors—that the litigation could be terminated by our decision on the merits and that a failure to decide the question now will leave the press in Georgia operating in the shadow of the civil and criminal sanctions of a rule of law and a statute the constitutionality of which is in serious doubt—we find that reaching the merits is consistent with the pragmatic approach that we have followed in the past in determining finality."

There are a number of difficulties with this test. One of them is the Court's willingness to look to the merits. It is not clear from the Court's opinion, however, exactly how great a look at the merits we are to take. On the one hand, the Court emphasizes that if we reverse the Supreme Court of Georgia the litigation will end, and it refers to cases in which the federal issue has been decided "arguably wrongly." On the other hand, it claims to look to the merits "only to the extent of determining that the issue is substantial." If the latter is all the Court means, then the inquiry is no more extensive than is involved when we determine whether a case is appropriate for plenary consideration; but if no more is meant, our decision is just as likely to be a costly intermediate step in the litigation as it is to be the concluding event. If, on the other hand, the Court really intends its doctrine to reach only so far as cases in which our decision in all probability will terminate the litigation, then * * * henceforth in determining our own jurisdiction we may be obliged to determine whether or not we agree with the merits of the decision of the highest court of a State.

Yet another difficulty with the Court's formulation is the problem of transposing to any other case the requirement that "failure to decide the question now will leave the press in Georgia operating in the shadow of the civil and criminal sanctions of a rule of law and a statute the constitutionality of which is in serious doubt." Assuming that we are to make this determination of "serious doubt" at the time we note probable jurisdiction of such an appeal, is it enough that the highest court of the State has ruled against any federal constitutional claim? If that is the case, then because § 1257 by other language imposes that requirement, we will have completely read out of the statute the limitation of our jurisdiction to a "final judgment or decree." Perhaps the Court's new standard for finality is limited to cases in which a First Amendment freedom is at issue. The language used by Congress, however, certainly provides no basis for preferring the First Amendment, as incorporated by the Fourteenth Amendment, to the various other Amendments which are likewise "incorporated," or indeed for preferring any of the "incorporated" Amendments over the due process and equal protection provisions which are embodied literally in the Fourteenth Amendment.

Another problem is that in applying the second prong of its test, the Court has not engaged in any independent inquiry as to the consequences of permitting the decision of the Supreme Court of Georgia to remain undisturbed pending final state-court resolution of the case. * * * In this case nothing more is at issue than the right to report the name of the victim of a rape. No hindrance of any sort has been imposed on reporting the fact of a rape or the circumstances surrounding it. Yet the Court unquestioningly places this issue on a par with the core First Amendment interest involved in Miami Herald Publishing Co. v. Tornillo, 418 U.S. 241 (1974), and Mills v. Alabama, [384 U.S. 214 (1966),] that of protecting the press in its role of providing uninhibited political discourse.

But the greatest difficulty with the test enunciated today is that it totally abandons the principle that constitutional issues are too important to be decided save when absolutely necessary, and are to be avoided if there are grounds for decision of lesser dimension * * *. [That principle is] primarily designed, not to benefit the lower courts, or state-federal relations, but rather to safeguard this Court's own process of constitutional adjudication. * * *

In this case there has yet to be an adjudication of liability against appellants, and unlike the appellant in Mills v. Alabama, they do not concede that they have no nonfederal defenses. Nonetheless, the Court rules on their constitutional defense. * * *

III

This Court is obliged to make preliminary determinations of its jurisdiction at the time it votes to note probable jurisdiction. * * * [S]uch determinations must of necessity be based on relatively cursory acquaintance with the record of the proceedings below. * * * It is thus especially disturbing that the rule of this case, unlike the more workable and straightforward exceptions which the Court has previously formulated, will seriously compound the already difficult task of accurately determining, at a preliminary stage, whether an appeal from a state-court judgment is a "final judgment or decree." * * *

I would dismiss for want of jurisdiction.

NOTE ON THE FINAL JUDGMENT RULE AND THE HIGHEST STATE COURT REQUIREMENT

(1) Evolution of the Finality Doctrine. As Cox indicates, out of the deceptively simple language "final judgment or decree," enacted in 1789 in § 25 of the first Judiciary Act and found today in 28 U.S.C. § 1257 ("final judgments or decrees"), the Court has developed a complicated body of doctrine.

For many years, the Court permitted review only when nothing was left to be done except entry or execution of judgment. See, *e.g.*, Houston v. Moore, 16 U.S. (3 Wheat.) 433 (1818). The first major inroad came with Carondelet Canal & Navigation Co. v. Louisiana, 233 U.S. 362 (1914), in which the state supreme court's judgment ordered the transfer of the company's property, despite its claim of federal protection, and remanded for an accounting. In reviewing that judgment, the Supreme Court noted that the remaining issue on remand was narrow and that the state supreme court's judgment disposed of the federal right asserted. Over time, a "penumbral area" developed within which state court judgments that left something to be adjudicated were nevertheless deemed final—often when they resolved a federal question in a manner threatening immediate and irreparable harm to a party. See, *e.g.*, Radio Station WOW, Inc. v. Johnson, 326 U.S. 120, 124 (1945).

The 1963 decisions in Curry and Langdeau (both discussed in Cox) substantially expanded the penumbra of finality. Curry's loose formulation, which treated as final cases where "postponing review would seriously erode" national policy, established the foundation for the fourth Cox category.

(2) The First Cox Category. The first Cox category—cases in which, despite a state court's remand to a lower state court, the federal question finally decided by the state court is likely to be decisive—has not been very controversial.[1] For example, in Duquesne Light Co. v. Barasch, 488 U.S. 299

---

[1]   See, *e.g.*, the Mills case discussed in Cox; Richfield Oil Corp. v. State Bd. of Equalization, 329 U.S. 69 (1946); Abood v. Detroit Bd. of Educ., 431 U.S. 209, 216 n.8 (1977),

(1989), the state public utilities commission authorized a rate increase to permit a utility to recoup costs incurred from canceled nuclear plants. The state supreme court reversed, remanding for the commission to set lower rates excluding those costs, and rejecting the utility's argument that the lower rates constituted an unconstitutional "taking." In hearing the utility's appeal, the Supreme Court (with only Justice Blackmun dissenting) ruled that the state court had finally adjudicated the constitutional challenge, leaving for remand only "straight-forward application of [the state supreme court's] clear directive to otherwise complete rate orders."

(3) The Second Cox Category. The second Cox category allows review of federal claims that will eventually require decision no matter what happens during further state court proceedings. Consider the suggestions (a) that each of the cases cited in Cox in support of this second category "arguably involved elements of hardship in addition to the simple burden of proceedings that might prove unnecessary" and that this category should be restricted to such situations, 16B Wright, Miller & Cooper, Federal Practice and Procedure § 4010, at 174, and (b) that in practice the prediction necessitated under this category is too difficult to make reliably, see Note, *The Finality Rule for Supreme Court Review of State Court Orders*, 91 Harv.L.Rev. 1004, 1017–20 (1978).[2]

(4) The Third Cox Category. The third Cox exception allows immediate review where further proceedings may render the federal question effectively unreviewable. Typical, and routinely reviewed, are criminal cases where the state court has decided a federal question in favor of the defendant—either in an interlocutory appeal or in reversing a conviction and remanding for retrial. See, *e.g.*, New York v. Quarles, 467 U.S. 649 (1984), California v. Trombetta, 467 U.S. 479 (1984), and Florida v. Meyers, 466 U.S. 380 (1984) (all reviewing decisions suppressing evidence on federal constitutional grounds).

(5) The Fourth Cox Category. The fourth Cox category requires that (i) reversal of the state court on the federal issue would end the litigation, and (ii) a refusal to review the federal issue would immediately threaten serious erosion of a significant federal policy. The range of federal policies encompassed has been broad. See, *e.g.*, Bullington v. Missouri, 451 U.S. 430 (1981), and Harris v. Washington, 404 U.S. 55 (1971) (constitutional policy against double jeopardy threatened if defendant tried a second time); Goodyear Atomic Corp. v. Miller, 486 U.S. 174 (1988) (federal preemption of state safety rules for nuclear facilities threatened by workers' compensation award based on violation of those rules); Southland Corp. v. Keating, 465

---

overruled on other grounds, Janus v. American Federation of State, County, and Municipal Employees, 585 U.S. 878 (2018).

    [2]   Recently, in Moore v. Harper, 600 U.S. 1 (2023), the Court held that despite the existence of ongoing state court proceedings, it enjoyed jurisdiction under the second Cox category to review the first round of a state supreme court's resolution of a federal Elections Clause challenge because that court had "finally decided" the relevant "federal issue" in a way that bound the parties. Also relevant to the Court's conclusion was the fact that the Court's decision had the potential to reverse the judgment of the state court and require implementation of legislative districting maps that the state supreme court had rejected. Accordingly, the Court ruled that it enjoyed "jurisdiction under both Article III and § 1257(a)." For further discussion, see p. 687, *supra*.

U.S. 1 (1984) (Federal Arbitration Act's policy of requiring arbitration eroded by decision refusing to compel arbitration and ordering state judicial proceedings); Belknap, Inc. v. Hale, 463 U.S. 491 (1983) (to permit state proceedings would erode federal policy giving the NLRB exclusive jurisdiction); Shaffer v. Heitner, 433 U.S. 186, 195–96 n.12 (1977), and Calder v. Jones, 465 U.S. 783 (1984) (due process limits on state court personal jurisdiction threatened if, after decision upholding jurisdiction, trial were to follow).

(6) First Amendment Cases. The Court has been especially willing to relax finality requirements in order to protect speech interests against the erosion that can attend delay. Such cases typically are accommodated by the fourth Cox category.

(a)   A notable example, which built on earlier decisions,[3] is National Socialist Party v. Skokie, 432 U.S. 43 (1977). There, Illinois appellate courts refused to stay a trial court order prohibiting petitioners from marching or parading. The U.S. Supreme Court, treating an application for a stay as a petition for certiorari from the order of the Illinois Supreme Court denying a stay, granted certiorari and reversed: "Th[e] order is a final judgment for purposes of our jurisdiction * * *. It finally determined the merits of petitioners' claim that the outstanding injunction will deprive them of rights protected by the First Amendment during the period of appellate review, which in the normal course may take a year or more to complete. If a State seeks to impose a restraint of this kind, it must provide strict procedural safeguards * * * including immediate appellate review * * *." Three Justices dissented, distinguishing Cox on the ground that there the state supreme court had finally decided the federal claim.[4]

(b)   In Fort Wayne Books, Inc. v. Indiana, 489 U.S. 46 (1989), the Court came close to holding reviewable any interlocutory order affecting the exercise of First Amendment rights. In a state RICO prosecution predicated on obscenity offenses, the trial court had dismissed the charges on the ground that the statute was unconstitutionally vague as applied to obscenity offenses. The Indiana Court of Appeals reversed, reinstating the charges. The Supreme Court (per White, J.) upheld its jurisdiction to review. Although acknowledging the general rule that in criminal cases finality is defined by judgment of conviction and imposition of sentence, the Court concluded that the case fell within Cox's fourth category. A decision for the defendants at trial would preclude review of their First Amendment challenges to the RICO statute, and, the Court argued, would intolerably

---

[3]   See Organization for a Better Austin v. Keefe, 402 U.S. 415 (1971); Nebraska Press Ass'n v. Stuart, 423 U.S. 1319 (1975) (Blackmun, J., in chambers).

[4]   For similar rulings, see, *e.g.*, M.I.C. Ltd. v. Bedford Township, 463 U.S. 1341 (1983) (Brennan, J., in chambers); Seattle Times Co. v. Rhinehart, 467 U.S. 20 (1984); Oklahoma Pub. Co. v. District Ct., 429 U.S. 967 (1976).

The cases in this line assume that the power of the Court (or of a Justice) to grant a stay is limited to cases where the state decision is "final." That assumption is plainly correct where the stay is sought pursuant to 28 U.S.C. § 2101(f), which authorizes a stay of a final judgment subject to Supreme Court review on writ of certiorari. But Sup.Ct.R. 23.1 says more generally that "[a] stay may be granted by a Justice as permitted by law." Does the All Writs Act, 28 U.S.C. § 1651, permit the Court to stay a concededly non-final state court judgment? See Shapiro et al., Supreme Court Practice 878–81 (10th ed.2013).

erode federal policy by leaving unresolved the question of First Amendment limits on government efforts to apply RICO laws in obscenity cases.

In dissent, Justice O'Connor (with whose views Justice Blackmun expressed agreement) relied heavily on Flynt v. Ohio, 451 U.S. 619 (1981) (per curiam) (5–4). There, after the state courts had denied defendants' motion to dismiss an obscenity prosecution on the ground that it constituted selective prosecution in violation of the First Amendment, the Supreme Court held the judgment not final. Although it arguably fell within the fourth Cox category, "there is no identifiable federal policy that will suffer if the state criminal proceeding goes forward. * * * The resolution of this [equal protection] question can await final judgment without any adverse effect upon important federal interests. A contrary conclusion would permit the fourth exception [of Cox] to swallow the rule."[5]

In the Fort Wayne case, the majority distinguished Flynt as involving a selective prosecution rather than a First Amendment claim—albeit in the context of a trial raising First Amendment issues. The majority added: "[N]o Member of the Court concluded in Flynt—as Justice O'Connor does today— that where an important First Amendment claim *is* before us, the Court should refuse to invoke Cox's fourth exception."[6]

(c)　Neither the criminal prosecution in the Fort Wayne case nor the tort action in Cox involved an injunction against speech. Was Supreme Court review urgently needed in either case? Does the Court's approach in these cases echo First Amendment overbreadth doctrine in trying to prevent the "chilling effect" from statutes that purport to prohibit protected activity? In this regard, recall Justice Rehnquist's invocation, in his Cox dissent, of the policy of constitutional avoidance. Does the Court's approach in First Amendment cases reflect a quite different conception of its role, in which articulation of constitutional values is to be encouraged rather than avoided? See generally pp. 241–244, *supra*.

(7)　Finality and Statutory Interpretation. Does the Court's assertion of a power to create desirable exceptions to a strict conception of finality (a) unjustifiably disregard a statutory limitation on its own jurisdiction, or (b) properly try to accommodate a necessarily general legislative directive to situations that Congress could not have anticipated?[7]

---

[5]　The four dissenters in Flynt found in the First Amendment an identifiable federal policy of preventing this sort of prosecution.

[6]　In Fort Wayne, a second proceeding was before the Court—a civil RICO action brought by the state, which had obtained an ex parte pretrial seizure order under which the defendants' stores were padlocked and their contents hauled away. On interlocutory appeal, the state supreme court upheld the constitutionality of the obscenity statute (the same constitutional issue presented in the criminal case) and of the pretrial seizure. Without dissent, the Supreme Court upheld its jurisdiction to review that judgment. Justice O'Connor's separate opinion expressed her agreement, noting that pretrial sanctions had already been imposed, and adding: "Where First Amendment interests are actually affected, we have held that such interlocutory orders are immediately reviewable by this Court." She asserted, however, that the availability of review in the civil case was another argument against the Court's decision that the criminal proceeding was reviewable.

[7]　For defense of the Court's departures from a strict view of finality, see Matasar & Bruch, *Procedural Common Law, Federal Jurisdictional Policy, and Abandonment of the*

The Court in Cox does not make clear whether the four categories it identifies exhaust the exceptions to the final judgment rule. Indeed, Justice White speaks of "at least" four categories of exceptions. In Florida v. Thomas, 532 U.S. 774 (2001), however, the Court said that Cox "divided cases [in which further state court proceedings were to occur] into four categories. None fits the judgment of the Florida Supreme Court, however, and we therefore conclude that its judgment is not final."[8]

Does the elimination in 1988 of mandatory appellate jurisdiction over state court judgments argue for a less strict interpretation of finality—because the Court can simply deny certiorari in any case?

(8) Finality and Federalism. In Cox, Justice Rehnquist's dissent argued that the finality rule of § 1257 should be more strictly construed than the analogous finality requirement in § 1291, governing review of district court decisions in the federal courts of appeals. The tradition has been to draw no distinction between the two statutes, and cases arising under them are apparently cited interchangeably.[9] Are there good reasons to distinguish between the finality rules of § 1257 and § 1291? If so, which way do they cut?

In Atlantic Richfield Co. v. Christian, 590 U.S. 1 (2020), the Supreme Court reviewed a state supreme court's determination that a federal environmental statute did not displace various common law claims notwithstanding the state's highest court having remanded the case to proceed to trial. The state supreme court had exercised review through a writ of supervisory control, which under state law presents "a self-contained case, not an interlocutory appeal" and "initiates a separate lawsuit." Under such circumstances, the Court held, "[i]t is the nature of the [state] proceeding, not the issues the state court reviewed, that establishes our jurisdiction."

(9) Reviewability of Issues Not Previously Reviewable. If a state court judgment is not final for purposes of Supreme Court review, the federal questions it determines will (if not mooted) be open in the Supreme Court on review of a later, final judgment—whether or not under state law the initial adjudication is the law of the case on the second state review. See, *e.g.*, Great Western Tel. Co. v. Burnham, 162 U.S. 339 (1896); Jefferson v. City of Tarrant, 522 U.S. 75 (1997). "[A] contrary rule would insulate interlocutory state court rulings on important federal questions from our consideration." Hathorn v. Lovorn, 457 U.S. 255, 262 (1982).

(10) The Highest State Court Requirement. The "highest court of a State in which a decision could be had" (28 U.S.C. § 1257) may be the lowest court in the state system, *e.g.*, the city's Police Court in Thompson v. City of Louisville, 362 U.S. 199 (1960), or the order of a judge in chambers, as in

---

Adequate and Independent State Grounds Doctrine, 86 Colum.L.Rev. 1291, 1355 (1986); Shapiro, *Jurisdiction and Discretion*, 60 N.Y.U.L.Rev. 543, 565–66 (1985).

8   For a particularly mysterious finding of finality that is hard to fit into any of the Cox categories, see American Export Lines, Inc. v. Alvez, 446 U.S. 274 (1980).

9   In Cox, Justice White cited Forgay v. Conrad, 47 U.S. (6 How.) 201 (1848), for the proposition that the final judgment rule is to be given a liberal, non-technical construction, and relied significantly on Gillespie v. United States Steel Corp., 379 U.S. 148 (1964). Both cases dealt with the question of finality of federal trial court decisions under what is now 28 U.S.C. § 1291.

Betts v. Brady, 316 U.S. 455 (1942). The sole criterion is whether further appellate review is possible within the state; if it is, even if such review is discretionary, it must have been sought to confer jurisdiction on the Supreme Court.[10]

In Pacific Gas & Elec. Co. v. PUC, 475 U.S. 1, 7 (1986), an order of the state utility commission was reviewable only in the discretion of the state supreme court, which had refused to accept the appeal. The Supreme Court noted probable jurisdiction and decided the appellant's First Amendment challenge. Was this an exercise of the Supreme Court's original jurisdiction? (If so, it would appear to lack authorization under 28 U.S.C. § 1251 and to run into problems under the Court's state sovereign immunity jurisprudence.) Before answering "yes," consider whether any federal criterion distinguishes state "courts" (review of whose decisions clearly falls within the Supreme Court's *appellate* jurisdiction) from other state tribunals that engage in adjudication. See Meltzer, *Legislative Courts, Legislative Power, and the Constitution*, 65 Ind.L.J. 291, 297–301 (1990). *Cf.* Baude, *Adjudication Outside Article III*, 133 Harv.L.Rev. 1511, 1523–25, 1561–63 (2020) (arguing that the key distinction is the exercise of state "judicial power").

---

[10]   See, *e.g.*, Costarelli v. Massachusetts, 421 U.S. 193 (1975); Gotthilf v. Sills, 375 U.S. 79 (1963) (leave to appeal on certified questions must be sought); Gorman v. Washington Univ., 316 U.S. 98 (1942) (review of judgment of division of state highest court by the court *en banc* is available and must be applied for).

CHAPTER VI

THE LAW APPLIED IN CIVIL ACTIONS IN THE DISTRICT COURTS

This is the first of two chapters that analyze the governing law in actions in the federal district courts, with an emphasis on civil actions. Section 1 overviews the history of and developments in procedural law since the founding. Section 2 covers federal courts' changing applications of the common law from the founding through the Supreme Court's revolutionary decision in Erie Railroad Co. v. Tompkins, 304 U.S. 64 (1938). Section 3 evaluates various strands of the "Erie doctrine" that emerged from that decision—an evaluation that continues in Chapter VII's analysis of the post-Erie "new" federal common law.

1. PROCEDURE

NOTE ON THE HISTORICAL DEVELOPMENT OF THE STATUTES AND RULES OF COURT

Today federal procedure in federal district courts is governed primarily by uniform federal rules prescribed by the Supreme Court pursuant to authorities and processes found in 28 U.S.C. §§ 2071–2077, as well as by statute or constitutional provision.[1] But for the first 150 years of the nation, not all federal procedure was uniform. In equity, admiralty, and bankruptcy, there was an early consensus that federal procedure should be uniform, rather than conforming to the varied practices among the states. In criminal actions and in civil actions at law, the move toward federal uniformity was considerably slower.[2] This history of procedure before 1938, though long superseded by the Federal Rules, provides essential context for many of the pre-1938 foundational decisions in this book.

---

[1] Section 2071 of the Judicial Code confers on the Supreme Court and on all courts established by act of Congress general authority to prescribe rules for the conduct of their own business. The proliferation of local rules issued by each district court and by the individual circuits has to some extent undermined the goal of uniformity across the entire federal court system.

[2] Even the Rules of Decision Act—the famous § 34 of the Judiciary Act of 1789—did not apply by its terms to equity. Not until the 1948 revision did Congress broaden the language to cover all "civil actions." 28 U.S.C. § 1652.

A.   Equity Before Merger

For nearly a century and a half, before law and equity were merged in 1938, equity had its own history as a distinctive branch of federal practice. From the outset, federal equity had to administer the substantive law of the states as well as of the United States. Particularly where rights under state law were at issue, state procedure governing equity, in principle, had a claim for acceptance in federal court. But in 1789, equity was either non-existent or undeveloped in the courts of many of the states. Federal procedure was thus able to establish itself without serious challenge.

When Congress first dealt directly with procedure in equity in the Process Act of September 29, 1789, 1 Stat. 93, 94, it provided that "the forms and modes of proceedings in causes of equity * * * shall be according to the course of the civil law." In the Process Act of 1792, the second Congress replaced this avowedly stopgap measure with a formulation that lasted until law and equity merged in 1938. The 1792 Act provided that the "forms and modes of proceeding" in cases "of equity" and "of admiralty and maritime jurisdiction" were to be "according to the principles, rules and usages which belong to courts of equity and to courts of admiralty respectively, as contradistinguished from courts of common law." Act of May 8, 1792, § 2, 1 Stat. 275, 276. The 1792 statute added an important qualification that provided needed flexibility: "* * * subject however to such alterations and additions as the said courts respectively shall in their discretion deem expedient, or to such regulations as the supreme court of the United States shall think proper from time to time by rule to prescribe to any circuit or district court concerning the same." The Supreme Court soon thereafter announced that "THE COURT considers the practice of the courts of King's Bench and Chancery in England, as affording outlines for the practice of this court; and that they will, from time to time, make such alterations therein, as circumstances may render necessary." 2 U.S. 411–12 (1792).

The Supreme Court first prescribed rules for lower federal courts in 1822, when it promulgated thirty-three Equity Rules. 20 U.S. (7 Wheat.) v–xiii. Twenty years later, the Court replaced these rules with ninety-two rules. 42 U.S. (1 How.) xli (1842).[3] These rules assumed the existence of traditional chancery practice and undertook only ad hoc modification or clarification of points of detail. The 1842 rules lasted for seventy years until the Equity Rules of 1912, 226 U.S. 649, worked a major reform. Three years later, Congress enacted the Law and Equity Act of 1915, 38 Stat. 956, making equitable defenses available in actions at law and providing for the transfer of cases brought on the wrong side of the court. These changes moved toward the merger of law and equity later accomplished more fully in 1938.

B.   Admiralty

In many respects, the story in admiralty parallels the one in equity. Admiralty was thought of in 1789 as a distinct body of law, quasi-international in character. This traditional law of admiralty comprised not

---

[3]   Congress affirmed the Supreme Court's rulemaking power, in language that swept beyond the confines of equity (and admiralty) and extended to "suits at common law," in § 6 of the Act of August 23, 1842, 5 Stat. 516, 518.

only distinctive principles of liability and distinctive remedies but also a distinctive set of procedures.

State law, to be sure, played a significant role in admiralty by virtue of the provision in § 9 of the Judiciary Act of 1789, 1 Stat. 73, 76, which conferred on the district courts "exclusive original cognizance of all civil causes of admiralty and maritime jurisdiction," while "saving to suitors, in all cases, the right of a common law remedy, where the common law is competent to give it." The saving clause preserved remedies in the state courts and on the law side of the federal courts. But it did not affect the federal character of proceedings on the admiralty side of the federal courts.

The first Congress in the Process Act of 1789 provided that in admiralty, as in equity, the forms and modes of proceedings "shall be according to the course of the civil law." And the second Congress in the Process Act of 1792 provided that they should be "according to the principles, rules and usages which belong * * * to courts of admiralty * * *, as contradistinguished from courts of common law," with the same important qualification as in equity concerning "alterations and additions" by lower federal courts and "regulations" by the Supreme Court.[4] For more than half a century after the 1792 Act, the Supreme Court left rulemaking in admiralty to the district courts, and divergent practices developed. Spurred apparently by the reaffirmation of its rulemaking authority in § 6 of the Act of August 23, 1842, see text accompanying note 3, *supra*, the Court in 1844 promulgated forty-seven "Rules of Practice of the Courts of the United States in Causes of Admiralty and Maritime Jurisdiction on the Instance Side of the Court." 44 U.S. (3 How.) iii. Like the first Equity Rules, the Admiralty Rules presupposed a traditional framework of procedure.

The 1844 rules remained in effect, with rather frequent amendments, until they were superseded in 1921. 254 U.S. 671. The 1921 rules, in turn, were frequently amended until in 1966 admiralty procedure was merged with civil procedure. 383 U.S. 1029. The Federal Rules of Civil Procedure now apply in admiralty, but a number of special provisions and supplemental rules now govern admiralty and maritime claims. Fed.R.Civ.Proc. A–G (Supplemental Rules for Admiralty or Maritime Claims and Asset Forfeiture Actions).

C. Bankruptcy

As in equity and admiralty, Congress before 1938 authorized the Supreme Court to promulgate general rules of bankruptcy. Within five months of the enactment of the Bankruptcy Act of July 1, 1898, 30 Stat. 544, the Court adopted the first "General Orders and Forms in Bankruptcy." 172 U.S. 653. Following enactment of the Bankruptcy Act (also known as the Chandler Act) on June 22, 1938, 52 Stat. 840, the Court revised these rules in 1939. 305 U.S. 677.

---

[4] This formulation survived until 1948, when it was swallowed entirely by the general rulemaking authorizations in 28 U.S.C. §§ 2071 and 2073. In 1966, Congress extended the general Enabling Act provision, § 2072, to admiralty, and repealed § 2073 in relevant part. (The present version of § 2073 deals with other matters.)

The authority to make bankruptcy rules is codified today at 28 U.S.C. § 2075. When Congress in 1978 enacted a comprehensive revision of the bankruptcy laws, 92 Stat. 2549, it provided that existing bankruptcy rules, to the extent not inconsistent with the new law, were to remain effective until "repealed or superseded" by new rules. 11 U.S.C. § 405(d). In Northern Pipeline Constr. Co. v. Marathon Pipe Line Co., 458 U.S. 50 (1982), p. 501, *supra*, the Supreme Court held that the 1978 Act's broad grant of jurisdiction to bankruptcy judges who lacked tenure and salary protection violated Article III. After a period of uncertainty, Congress made a number of changes in the bankruptcy laws as part of the Bankruptcy Amendments and Federal Judgeship Act of 1984. In 1985, an Advisory Committee proposed extensive amendments to the bankruptcy rules to conform to those statutory changes and for other purposes, 107 F.R.D. 403 (1985), and in March 1987, the Supreme Court approved amendments based on those proposals, 114 F.R.D. 193 (1987). Since then, a number of further changes in the rules have taken effect.

D. Criminal Prosecutions

Before adoption of the Rules of Criminal Procedure, federal criminal practice was a hodgepodge of judicial elaboration, common law rules, constitutional provisions, and ad hoc legislation. Though primarily uniform, the practice was interspersed with references to state law, called for by specific statutory direction or judicial interpretation.

Congress's first move addressed only proceedings after verdict, authorizing the Supreme Court to prescribe rules as to such proceedings by the Act of February 24, 1933, 47 Stat. 904, as amended by the Act of March 8, 1934, 48 Stat. 399. See 18 U.S.C. § 3772. The Court issued the first rules in 1934. 292 U.S. 661.

In the Act of June 29, 1940, 54 Stat. 688, Congress enlarged the Court's authority to include the promulgation of rules of procedure for criminal proceedings prior to and including verdict. See 18 U.S.C. § 3771. The Court exercised this authority in 1944. 323 U.S. 821.

The Rules of Criminal Procedure, which became effective on March 21, 1946, merged the 1934 post-verdict rules with the new rules. 327 U.S. 821 (1946). Since then, the rules have been amended on a number of occasions. As the pace of rulemaking increased and the subjects of rulemaking became more controversial, Congress became more deeply enmeshed in the process, especially in the 1970s, when it not infrequently modified, postponed, or disapproved particular rules. The Supreme Court has also promulgated (in addition to the criminal rules) rules governing habeas corpus and other collateral proceedings under 28 U.S.C. §§ 2254 and 2255—which became effective, with changes by Congress, in 1977—as well as rules for the trial of misdemeanors before United States magistrates. The latter are authorized by 18 U.S.C. § 3402. See 445 U.S. 975 (1980).

The Federal Rules of Evidence, discussed below, apply to criminal as well as civil cases.

E. Actions at Law Before Merger

(1) Origins. The Judiciary Act of 1789 addressed procedure in several sections. Section 14 gave federal courts the power to issue various writs "necessary for the exercise of their respective jurisdictions, and agreeable to the principles and usages of law." Section 17 proclaimed that federal courts had the authority (among other things) to grant new trials, administer oaths, punish contempt, and "make and establish all necessary rules for the orderly conducting business in the said courts, provided such rules are not repugnant to the laws of the United States." And the Rules of Decision Act, § 34 of the Judiciary Act of 1789, specified that state law "shall be regarded as rules of decision" in a wide area in actions at law in federal courts but left uncertain whether this area included procedure.

The Process Act of 1789, p. 728, *supra*, however, clearly called for application of state law to some elements of procedure. It provided: "That * * * except where by this act or other statutes of the United States is otherwise provided, the forms of writs and executions, except their style, and modes of process and rates of fees, except fees to judges, in the circuit and district courts, in suits at common law, shall be the same in each state respectively as are now used or allowed in the supreme courts of the same." The Process Act of 1792, p. 728, *supra*, reaffirmed this provision but made it subject to the same federal court rulemaking power, both in the Supreme Court and the lower courts, that applied in equity and admiralty.

(2) Wayman v. Southard. The Process Act of 1792 created a static conformity that required application of state law as it stood on the date of the Process Act of 1789. The requirement had no application to federal courts sitting in states that entered the union after 1789. In all states, including states already in the union in 1789, the act authorized federal courts to promulgate rules that would apply in federal court notwithstanding any state court procedure. See Clark & Moore, *A New Federal Civil Procedure*, 44 Yale L.J. 387, 399–401 (1935).

As time passed, state procedure changed—notably, in many states, in favor of debtors. Wayman v. Southard, 23 U.S. (10 Wheat.) 1 (1825), involved one such law—a Kentucky statute enacted after 1789 that required a judgment plaintiff either to accept Kentucky bank notes in payment of the judgment or else to take a replevin bond from the defendant for the debt. The Court's ruling on whether a federal court must apply this state law clarified the application of the Process Act. And more broadly, the Court's pioneering discussion of delegation of legislative power remains highly relevant today both to the inherent power of courts to make rules governing their own procedures for the resolution of controversies within their jurisdiction and to the broad congressional delegations to courts of rulemaking and lawmaking authority that were to follow in the next century.[5]

---

[5] On the contemporary significance of Wayman for federal courts, see Lemos, *The Other Delegate: Judicially Administered Statutes and the Nondelegation Doctrine*, 81 S.Calif.L.Rev. 405, 413–16 (2008); Volokh, *Judicial Non-Delegation, the Inherent-Powers Corollary, and Federal Common Law*, 66 Emory L.J. 1391, 1411 (2017); Barton, *An Article I Theory of the Inherent Powers of the Federal Courts*, 61 Cath.U.L.Rev. 1, 27–28 (2011); Iuliano, *The Judicial Nondelegation Doctrine*, 75 Ala.L.Rev. 51 (2024). Wayman has also become highly salient in

In an opinion by Chief Justice Marshall, the Court held that the procedure on executions in the federal courts, as well as the procedure before judgment, was governed by the Process Acts, which adopted the state law "as it existed in September, 1789 * * *, not as it might afterwards be made."[6]

The Court also rejected the argument that Congress lacked power to regulate executions on federal court judgments:

"The Court cannot accede to this novel construction. The constitution concludes its enumeration of granted powers, with a clause authorizing Congress to make all laws which shall be necessary and proper for carrying into execution the foregoing powers, and all other powers vested by this constitution in the government of the United States, or in any department or officer thereof. The judicial department is invested with jurisdiction in certain specified cases, in all which it has power to render judgment.

"That a power to make laws for carrying into execution all the judgments which the judicial department has power to pronounce, is expressly conferred by this clause, seems to be one of those plain propositions which reasoning cannot render plainer."

The Court later addressed the question whether the Process Acts' authorization to federal courts to make a federal court rule to govern the execution of a judgment "would be a delegation of legislative authority which Congress can never be supposed to intend, and has not the power to make." In a pioneering discussion on the delegation of legislative power, the Court stated:

"It will not be contended that Congress can delegate to the Courts, or to any other tribunals, powers which are strictly and exclusively legislative. But Congress may certainly delegate to others, powers which the legislature may rightfully exercise itself. * * * The Courts, for example, may make rules, directing the returning of writs and processes, the filing of declarations and other pleadings, and other things of the same description. It will not be contended, that these things might not be done by the legislature, without the intervention of the Courts; yet it is not alleged that the power may not be conferred on the judicial department.

"The line has not been exactly drawn which separates those important subjects, which must be entirely regulated by the legislature itself, from those of less interest, in which a general provision may be made, and power

---

debates over the non-delegation doctrine more generally. See Gundy v. United States, 588 U.S. 128, 157–58 (2019) (Gorsuch, J., dissenting); Mortenson & Bagley, *Delegation at the Founding*, 121 Colum.L.Rev. 277, 282–83 (2021); Posner & Vermeule, *Interring the Nondelegation Doctrine*, 69 U.Chi.L.Rev. 1721, 1738–39 (2002).

[6]   The Court recognized that the Rules of Decision Act, by contrast, called for a dynamic rather than a static conformity. But it rejected the claim that the section applied to executions: "This section has never, so far as is recollected, received a construction in this court; but it has, we believe, been generally considered by gentlemen of the profession, as furnishing a rule to guide the court in the formation of its judgment; not one for carrying that judgment into execution. It is 'a rule of decision,' and the proceedings after judgment are merely ministerial * * *[:] a phrase which presents clearly to the mind the idea of litigation in court, and could never occur to a person intending to describe an execution, or proceedings after judgment, or the effect of those proceedings. * * * The 34th section, then, has no application to the practice of the court, or to the conduct of its officer, in the service of an execution." 23 U.S. (10 Wheat.) at 24–26.

given to those who are to act under such general provisions to fill up the details. To determine the character of the power given to the Courts by the Process Act, we must inquire into its extent. [The Court describes what the Process Act authorizes federal courts to determine, including the "regulation of the conduct of the officer of the Court in giving effect to its judgments."] A general superintendence over this subject seems to be properly within the judicial province, and has been always so considered. It is, undoubtedly, proper for the legislature to prescribe the manner in which these ministerial offices shall be performed, and this duty will never be devolved on any other department without urgent reasons. But, in the mode of obeying the mandate of a writ issuing from a Court, so much of that which may be done by the judiciary, under the authority of the legislature, seems to be blended with that for which the legislature must expressly and directly provide, that there is some difficulty in discerning the exact limits within which the legislature may avail itself of the agency of its Courts.

"The difference between the departments undoubtedly is, that the legislature makes, the executive executes, and the judiciary construes the law; but the maker of the law may commit something to the discretion of the other departments, and the precise boundary of this power is a subject of delicate and difficult inquiry, into which a court will not enter unnecessarily."

Wayman's ruling was controversial because it allowed some out-of-state creditors to circumvent post-1789 debtor-favorable state procedural laws by suing in-state debtors in diversity in federal court. In the Process Act of May 19, 1828, 4 Stat. 278, Congress remedied this situation by "updating" the static conformity imposed by the Process Act of 1792. On writs of execution and other final process issued on judgments, the Process Act of 1828 required federal courts in all states to follow the procedure of the state courts in force on the day the act became effective, while providing that the lower courts should have the power to adopt future changes by the state legislature. As for proceedings before judgment, the Process Act of 1828 created two different dates for static conformity in federal courts: for courts sitting in states admitted after 1789, the Process Act of 1828 made the state procedure in force on the same date the rule; for the original states, the 1789 procedure remained the rule. In all states, rules regulating proceedings before judgment were subject to alterations and additions by the lower federal courts or the Supreme Court. Later legislation made parallel provisions for states admitted after 1828. See, *e.g.*, the Act of Aug. 1, 1842, 5 Stat. 499. Congress reaffirmed the Supreme Court's rulemaking power in the Act of Aug. 23, 1842, § 6, see text accompanying note 3, *supra*. But federal courts were reluctant to use the power.

(3) The Shift to Dynamic Conformity. The Conformity Act of June 1, 1872, 17 Stat. 196, withdrew the federal courts' unused rulemaking authority, and adopted, with qualifications, the principle of dynamic conformity. Section 5 of the Act provided: "That the practice, pleadings, and forms and modes of proceeding, in other than equity and admiralty causes in the circuit and district courts of the United States shall conform, as near as may be, to the practice, pleadings, and forms and modes of proceeding existing at the time in like causes in the courts of record of the State within which such circuit or district courts are held, any rule of court to the contrary notwithstanding: *Provided, however*, That nothing herein contained shall alter the rules of evidence under the laws of the United States, and as practiced in the courts thereof."

The Conformity Act eliminated the anachronism of federal adherence to no-longer-existent state practice. On more matters than not, a lawyer in a federal court in a particular state could now follow the procedure currently prevailing in the courts of that state—an advantage particularly appreciated in the code states. But this conformity was confined to actions at law, and even as to such actions, exceptions and qualifications soon appeared.

The earlier process acts did not affect "jurisdiction," and the Supreme Court similarly construed the 1872 Conformity Act. See, *e.g.*, Davenport v. County of Dodge, 105 U.S. 237 (1881). When the Act did apply, it required the federal courts to conform to state procedure only "as near as may be," a phrase that opened a wide door for adherence to distinctive federal practices. See generally Clark & Moore, *A New Federal Civil Procedure*, 44 Yale L.J. 387, 401–11 (1935).

Partly in reliance on this latter phrase and partly by a restrictive interpretation of the three categories of "practice, pleadings, and forms and modes of proceedings," the Court held that the Act did not reach a wide area of particularly important matters affecting the administration of federal justice. See, *e.g.*, Nudd v. Burrows, 91 U.S. 441, 442 (1875) (holding that a state statute regulating the manner in which a jury should be charged did not control in federal court because "the personal conduct and administration of a federal judge" is neither practice, pleading, nor a form nor mode of proceeding under the Conformity Act).

F.   The Enabling Act, Merger, and Beyond

(1)   The Rules Enabling Act. A desire to dispel the confusion created by the uneasy co-existence of several systems of procedure in the federal courts helped spur the next movement to reform federal procedure. Those who sought change believed that effective reform could be achieved only through the promulgation of nationwide court rules, drafted with the assistance of bench and bar. Federal-state conformity, they hoped, need not be sacrificed, if the federal rules served as a model for the states to follow. See generally Sunderland, *The Grant of Rule-Making Power to the Supreme Court of the United States*, 32 Mich.L.Rev. 1116 (1934).

The Act of June 19, 1934, known as the Rules Enabling Act (now principally contained as amended in 28 U.S.C. § 2072), followed several decades of debate and proposals for reform. Pub.L. 73–415, 48 Stat. 1064.[7] It provided:

"That the Supreme Court of the United States shall have the power to prescribe, by general rules, for the district courts of the United States and for the courts of the District of Columbia, the forms of process, writs,

---

[7]   For an exhaustive and informative study of the pre-1934 efforts at reform, see Burbank, *The Rules Enabling Act of 1934*, 130 U.Pa.L.Rev. 1015, 1035–98 (1982).

pleadings, and motions, and the practice and procedure in civil actions at law. Said rules shall neither abridge, enlarge, nor modify the substantive rights of any litigant. They shall take effect six months after their promulgation, and thereafter all laws in conflict therewith shall be of no further force or effect.

"The court may at any time unite the general rules prescribed by it for cases in equity with those in actions at law so as to secure one form of civil action and procedure for both: *Provided, however,* That in such union of rules the right of trial by jury as at common law and declared by the seventh amendment to the Constitution shall be preserved to the parties inviolate. Such united rules shall not take effect until they shall have been reported to Congress by the Attorney General at the beginning of a regular session thereof and until after the close of such session."

(2) The Exercise of Rulemaking Authority. On June 3, 1935, the Court appointed a distinguished Advisory Committee to draw up proposed rules. 295 U.S. 774. The Committee's proposals were subjected to considerable scrutiny and criticism, through the medium, among others, of special committees of the bench and bar established in the various circuits and districts. With minor changes, the Court approved the final proposals, and the rules became effective September 16, 1938. 308 U.S. 645–766.

Rule 2 of the new rules provided that "[t]here shall be one form of action to be known as 'civil action.' "[8] This provision rejected use of the common-law forms of action (then still operative in a number of states) and effectuated, with respect to the rules of procedure, the merger of law and equity.[9]

In 1958, in an amendment to 28 U.S.C. § 331, Congress instructed the Judicial Conference of the United States to "carry on a continuous study of the operation and effect of the general rules of practice and procedure now or hereafter in use as prescribed by the Supreme Court for the other courts of the United States pursuant to law. Such changes in and additions to those rules as the Conference may deem desirable * * * shall be recommended by the Conference from time to time to the Supreme Court for its consideration and adoption, modification or rejection, in accordance with law."

Pursuant to this provision, the Judicial Conference in 1960 established a Standing Committee on Rules of Practice and Procedure, together with five Advisory Committees (Civil, Criminal, Appellate, Bankruptcy, and Admiralty). The task of an Advisory Committee is to draft proposals, solicit public comment, and submit a report to the Standing Committee. The

---

[8]   Today Rule 2 provides: "There is one form of action—the civil action." Fed.R.Civ.P. 2.

[9]   Bray, *The System of Equitable Remedies,* 63 UCLA L.Rev. 530 (2016), argues that despite the merger of procedural rules nine decades ago, "there has been remarkably little merger of law and equity" for remedies. Challenging the "reigning view in the American legal academy" that the separation of legal and equitable remedies is irrational, Professor Bray argues that the "surviving equitable remedies and related doctrines work together as a system" to give courts the capacity to manage ongoing relief when damages at law are inadequate. The system, he maintains, has three components: (1) the equitable remedies themselves, which serve the need of compelling action or inaction; (2) equitable managerial devices, such as contempt, which enable courts to "manag[e] the parties and ensur[e] compliance"; and (3) equitable constraints, such as equitable ripeness requirements and equitable defenses, that serve as "frictions against the abuse of equitable remedies and managerial devices."

Standing Committee in turn reports to the Conference, which makes its recommendations to the Supreme Court.

(3) The Rules of Evidence. In 1965, the Conference appointed a sixth Advisory Committee, on Rules of Evidence, and after several drafts were submitted for public comment, see 46 F.R.D. 161 (1969); 51 F.R.D. 315 (1971), the Supreme Court transmitted the Federal Rules of Evidence to Congress in November 1972. 56 F.R.D. 183 (1972). Almost immediately, congressional opposition surfaced, centering both on the content of certain rules and on the question whether the Court was empowered by the Rules Enabling Act to promulgate rules of evidence at all. This opposition culminated in an enactment staying the effectiveness of the proposed rules until they should be affirmatively approved by Congress. 87 Stat. 9 (1973). Following this resolution, Congress redrafted the rules, leaving much of the original Court text substantially unchanged, but making significant modifications, *inter alia*, in the rules relating to privileges and presumptions. Finally, Congress enacted the Federal Rules of Evidence in statutory form. 88 Stat. 1926 (1975).[10]

The same statute contained a new "Enabling Act" (designated 28 U.S.C. § 2076) to govern amendments to the Rules of Evidence. This new Act extended the time allowed for congressional review of Supreme Court amendments to those rules from the ninety days of § 2072 (the general Enabling Act) to one hundred eighty days, and authorized *either* House of Congress to disapprove or defer a Supreme Court amendment.[11]

(4) The 1988 Revision of the Enabling Acts. Congress amended the Enabling Acts in 1988, repealing § 2076 and consolidating the rulemaking power with respect to civil procedure and evidence. Section 2074(a) now provides that no changes in the rules shall take effect until they have been reported to Congress and until the expiration of a specified period. In § 2074(b), however, Congress preserved the provision (formerly in § 2076) that any revision of the rules governing evidentiary privilege shall have no force unless approved by an Act of Congress. See generally Marcus, *Rulemaking's Second Founding*, 169 U.Pa.L.Rev. 2519 (2021) (reviewing background to and significance of 1988 revision).[12]

(5) Growing Controversy About Rulemaking. The pace of rulemaking in all areas has increased dramatically in recent years.[13] But at the same time, criticism of the process and the product has also increased, and

---

[10]   Several of the rules of evidence refer to state law in cases in which state law supplies the rule of decision. See, *e.g.*, Rule 302 (presumptions); Rule 501 (privileges); Rule 601 (competency of witnesses).

[11]   The "one-House veto" was successfully challenged, in another context, in INS v. Chadha, 462 U.S. 919 (1983), and eventually was eliminated in this context in the 1988 revision, Pub.L. 100–702 § 401, 102 Stat. 4642 (1988).

[12]   Congress in 1990 amended 28 U.S.C. § 2072 to add section (c), which provides: "Such rules may define when a ruling of a district court is final for the purposes of appeal under section 1291 of this title." Pub.L. 101–650 § 315, 104 Stat. 5089 (1990).

[13]   For a criticism of this pace, and a suggestion that the Advisory Committee should propose fewer rules, see Freer, *The Continuing Gloom about Federal Judicial Rulemaking*, 107 Nw.U.L.Rev. 447 (2013).

Congress's responses to these criticisms have in turn generated their own critiques.

From the beginning, a number of Supreme Court Justices have been skeptical or disapproving of their role in the process. In 1938, Justice Brandeis stated without explanation that he did not approve of the adoption of the original civil rules. See 308 U.S. at 649. And Justices Black and Douglas together on several occasions voiced objections, on grounds ranging from the undesirability of specific rules, to the inappropriateness of the Court's role in the rulemaking process, to the possible unconstitutionality of that role.[14]

The Court itself, in promulgating changes in the civil, criminal, appellate, and evidence rules in April 1993, expressed reservations about its role. (Some of these rules, especially as they related to disciplining lawyers for filing or pursuing matters thought to be frivolous and to radical changes in the rules governing discovery, were significant and controversial.) Each of the transmittal letters to Congress, signed by the Chief Justice "[b]y direction of the Supreme Court," stated: "While the Court is satisfied that the required procedures [pursuant to 28 U.S.C. § 2072] have been observed, this transmittal does not necessarily indicate that the Court itself would have proposed these amendments in the form submitted." See, *e.g.*, 146 F.R.D. 401, 403 (1993). A separate statement of Justice White noted that "[s]ome of us * * * have silently shared Justice Black's and Justice Douglas's suggestion that the enabling statutes be amended" to eliminate the Court's participation in rulemaking. Justice White added that if the rulemaking process were not changed, he believed the Court's role was "to transmit the Judicial Conference's recommendations without change and without careful study, as long as there is no suggestion that the committee system has not operated with integrity"—even though on several occasions he had "serious questions about the wisdom of particular proposals to amend certain rules." 146 F.R.D. 401, 503, 505 (1993). In an order issued on April 28, 2010, approving certain proposed changes in the Rules of Criminal Procedure, the Court took the rare action of recommitting to the Advisory Committee for further consideration a proposed amendment to Rule 15 (dealing with depositions). 559 U.S. 1152 (2010). There was no explanation.

Critics outside the Court contend that public notice and participation are inadequate and urge that the process be made more open.[15] Others have faulted the predominance of judges in the rulemaking process or have noted that those practitioners who are given a role tend to constitute a section of the bar more likely to represent the "haves" than the "have-nots."[16] Other

---

[14]   See, *e.g.*, 368 U.S. 1012 (1961); 374 U.S. 865 (1963); 383 U.S. 1032 (1966); 383 U.S. 1089 (1966); 398 U.S. 979 (1970); 401 U.S. 1019 (1971).

[15]   See, *e.g.*, Weinstein, Reform of Court Rule-Making Procedures (1977); Lesnick, *The Federal Rule-Making Process: A Time for Reexamination*, 61 A.B.A.J. 579 (1975); Hazard, *Undemocratic Legislation*, 87 Yale L.J. 1284 (1978) (reviewing Judge Weinstein's book). For a critical history of the rulemaking process for the Supreme Court Rules from the 1980s to 2022 that emphasizes the process's secrecy and insularity, see Dodson, *The Making of the Supreme Court Rules*, 90 Geo.Wash.L.Rev. 866 (2022).

[16]   See, *e.g.*, Meyn, *The Haves of Procedure*, 60 Wm. & Mary L.Rev. 1765 (2019) (arguing that the bifurcation of civil and criminal procedure with the Rules Enabling Act has allowed the "haves" to shape both procedures in self-serving ways); Macey, *Judicial Preferences, Public*

criticisms related to the federal rules include: (i) lack of adequate empirical investigation as a basis for proposed rule changes[17]; (ii) skepticism about "trans-substantive" rules[18]; (iii) the failure of the rulemakers to develop a "coherent normative theory of civil adjudication"[19]; (iv) a concern that the Enabling Act raises delegation concerns[20]; and (v) a concern that the Supreme Court has re-interpreted the rules in a fashion that circumvents the rulemaking process.[21]

(6) Changes in the Rulemaking Process. Some of these criticisms led to proposals for legislative change, and Congress has responded to these proposals on several occasions.

(a) The 1988 amendments to the Enabling Acts (see 28 U.S.C. §§ 2071–2077) specified procedures to be followed by the Judicial Conference and its committees (including the holding of open meetings by committees); provided mechanisms for the modification and abrogation of district and appellate court rules; and required notice and opportunity for comment as part of the rulemaking processes of the district and appellate courts. The new openness, while generally praised, led some to question whether the broadening of participation might increase the politicization of the process or affect the topics addressed.[22]

(b) In 1990, Congress enacted the Civil Justice Reform Act (CJRA), codified as amended at 28 U.S.C. §§ 471–482. This Act required every federal

---

Choice, and the Rules of Procedure, 23 J.Leg.Stud. 627 (1994) (arguing that judges engaged in rulemaking will try to serve their self-interest in a variety of ways); Yeazell, *Judging Rules, Ruling Judges*, 61 L. & Contemp.Probs. 229 (1998) (criticizing the increased involvement of judges in rulemaking and advocating adoption of a two-step rulemaking process in which lawyers draft and propose, while judges approve or disapprove).

[17] See, *e.g.*, Willging, *Past and Potential Uses of Empirical Research in Civil Rulemaking*, 77 Notre Dame L.Rev. 1121 (2002); Walker, *Perfecting Federal Civil Rules: A Proposal for Restricted Field Experiments*, 51 L. & Contemp.Probs. 67 (1988); Rosenberg, *The Impact of Procedure-Impact Studies in the Administration of Justice*, 51 L. & Contemp.Probs. 13 (1988).

[18] See Dobbins, *Legislative Transsubstantivity*, 12 Ne.U.L.Rev. 707, 723–29 (2020) (collecting criticisms); but see Marcus, *The Past, Present, and Future of Trans-Substantivity in Federal Civil Procedure*, 59 DePaul L.Rev. 371 (2010) (arguing that despite mounting legislation that has joined substantive change with substance-specific procedural change, trans-substantivity can and should continue to operate "as an institutional restraint on court-supervised rulemakers").

[19] Bone, *Making Effective Rules: The Need for Procedure Theory*, 61 Okla.L.Rev. 319 (2008).

[20] See Redish & Amuluru, *The Supreme Court, the Rules Enabling Act, and the Politicization of the Federal Rules: Constitutional and Statutory Implications*, 90 Minn.L.Rev. 1303 (2006); *see also* Volokh, note 5, *supra*, at 1427–28.

[21] Carrington, *Politics and Civil Procedure Rulemaking: Reflections and Experience*, 60 Duke L.J. 597 (2010). See also Burbank & Farhang, *Litigation Reform: An Institutional Approach*, 162 U.Pa.L.Rev. 1543 (2014) (arguing that conservative efforts to limit private enforcement actions have had more success in adjudication (by obtaining restrictive readings of the Federal Rules) than in efforts to change the Federal Rules).

[22] See, *e.g.*, Freer, *The Continuing Gloom About Federal Judicial Rulemaking*, 107 Nw.L.Rev. 447, 460 (2013); Mullenix, *Hope Over Experience: Mandatory Informal Discovery and the Politics of Rulemaking*, 69 N.C.L.Rev. 796 (1991); Bone, *The Process of Making Process: Court Rulemaking, Democratic Legitimacy, and Procedural Efficacy*, 87 Geo.L.J. 887 (1999) (rejecting as exaggerated the concerns about the substantive effects of the rules and arguing that political accountability and public participation are unnecessary to what he views as a deliberative process akin to common law adjudication). For a sympathetic account and defense of the 1988 Amendments, see Marcus, *Rulemaking's Second Founding*, 169 U.Pa.L.Rev. 2519 (2021).

district to create an advisory group (which was to include attorneys and representatives of major categories of litigants) to assess the causes of "cost and delay" in civil litigation and to formulate recommendations based at least in part on an assessment of certain specified factors. Each district was then required to adopt a plan addressed to these problems, which would be reviewed by the Judicial Conference and evaluated annually.

The CJRA resulted in the adoption and implementation of a variety of plans to reduce cost and delay, many of which focused on such matters as early control and scheduling by judges and/or magistrate judges, mandatory or optional use of alternative dispute resolution techniques (such as mediation or non-binding arbitration), and other devices for encouraging settlement or expedition. See *Reformers Tout ADR Programs*, A.B.A.J. 28 (Aug. 1994). When the CJRA expired, Congress made certain of its provisions permanent, including 28 U.S.C. § 476(a), which requires that the Director of the Administrative Office of the United States Courts prepare a semiannual report listing certain delayed matters on each judicial officer's docket. See 111 Stat. 1173 (1997).[23]

(7) The Scope of Rulemaking Authority. The Supreme Court decided Sibbach v. Wilson & Co., the principal case following this Note, shortly after promulgation of the Federal Rules under the Enabling Act. It remains one of the leading decisions interpreting the scope of the authority conferred by that Act.

Sibbach v. Wilson & Co., Inc.
312 U.S. 1 (1940).
Certiorari to the Circuit Court of Appeals for the Seventh Circuit.

■ MR. JUSTICE ROBERTS delivered the opinion of the Court.

This case calls for decision as to the validity of Rules 35 and 37 of the Rules of Civil Procedure for District Courts of the United States.

In an action brought by the petitioner in the District Court for Northern Illinois to recover damages for bodily injuries, inflicted in Indiana, respondent * * * moved for an order requiring the petitioner to submit to a physical examination by one or more physicians appointed by the court to determine the nature and extent of her injuries. The court ordered that the petitioner submit to such an examination by a physician so appointed.

Compliance having been refused, the respondent obtained an order to show cause why the petitioner should not be punished for contempt. In response the petitioner challenged the authority of the court to order her to submit to the examination, asserting that the order was void. It appeared that the courts of Indiana, the state where the cause of action

---

[23] For consideration of the impact of the six-month reporting rule, see de Figueiredo, Lahaw & Siegelman, *The Six-Month List and the Unintended Consequences of Judicial Accountability*, 105 Cornell L.Rev. 363 (2020).

arose, hold such an order proper, whereas the courts of Illinois, the state in which the trial court sat, hold that such an order cannot be made. Neither state has any statute governing the matter.

The court adjudged the petitioner guilty of contempt, and directed that she be committed until she should obey the order for examination or otherwise should be legally discharged from custody. The petitioner appealed.

The Circuit Court of Appeals decided that Rule 35, which authorizes an order for a physical examination in such a case, is valid, and affirmed the judgment. The writ of certiorari was granted * * *. * * *

The contention of the petitioner, in final analysis, is that Rules 35 and 37 are not within the mandate of Congress to this court. This is the limit of permissible debate, since argument touching the broader questions of Congressional power and of the obligation of federal courts to apply the substantive law of a state is foreclosed.

Congress has undoubted power to regulate the practice and procedure of federal courts,[6] and may exercise that power by delegating to this or other federal courts authority to make rules not inconsistent with the statutes or Constitution of the United States; but it has never essayed to declare the substantive state law, or to abolish or nullify a right recognized by the substantive law of the state where the cause of action arose, save where a right or duty is imposed in a field committed to Congress by the Constitution. On the contrary it has enacted that the state law shall be the rule of decision in the federal courts.

Hence we conclude that the Act of June 19, 1934, was purposely restricted in its operation to matters of pleading and court practice and procedure. Its two provisos or caveats emphasize this restriction. The first is that the court shall not "abridge, enlarge, nor modify the substantive rights", in the guise of regulating procedure. The second is that if the rules are to prescribe a single form of action for cases at law and suits in equity, the constitutional right to jury trial inherent in the former must be preserved. There are other limitations upon the authority to prescribe rules which might have been, but were not mentioned in the Act; for instance, the inability of a court, by rule, to extend or restrict the jurisdiction conferred by a statute.

Whatever may be said as to the effect of the Conformity Act while it remained in force, the rules, if they are within the authority granted by Congress, repeal that statute, and the District Court was not bound to follow the Illinois practice respecting an order for physical examination. On the other hand if the right to be exempt from such an order is one of substantive law, the Rules of Decision Act required the District Court, though sitting in Illinois, to apply the law of Indiana, the state where the cause of action arose, and to order the examination. To avoid this

---

6   Wayman v. Southard, 10 Wheat. 1, 21 [(1825)]; Bank of United States v. Halstead, 10 Wheat. 51, 53 [(1825)]; Beers v. Haughton, 9 Pet. 329, 359, 361 [(1835)].

dilemma the petitioner admits, and, we think, correctly, that Rules 35 and 37 are rules of procedure. She insists, nevertheless, that by the prohibition against abridging substantive rights, Congress has banned the rules here challenged. In order to reach this result she translates "substantive" into "important" or "substantial" rights. And she urges that if a rule affects such a right, albeit the rule is one of procedure merely, its prescription is not within the statutory grant of power embodied in the Act of June 19, 1934. * * *

[The Court here discussed and distinguished several cases, including Union Pac. Ry. v. Botsford, 141 U.S. 250 (1891), in which, the Court said, the refusal to order plaintiff to submit to a physical examination was based on a lack of authority for the issuance of such an order.]

We are thrown back, then, to the arguments drawn from the language of the Act of June 19, 1934. Is the phrase "substantive rights" confined to rights conferred by law to be protected and enforced in accordance with the adjective law of judicial procedure? It certainly embraces such rights. One of them is the right not to be injured in one's person by another's negligence, to redress infraction of which the present action was brought. The petitioner says the phrase connotes more; that by its use Congress intended that in regulating procedure this court should not deal with important and substantial rights theretofore recognized. Recognized where and by whom? The state courts are divided as to the power in the absence of statute to order a physical examination. In a number such an order is authorized by statute or rule. * * *

The asserted right, moreover, is no more important than many others enjoyed by litigants in District Courts sitting in the several states, before the Federal Rules of Civil Procedure altered and abolished old rights or privileges and created new ones in connection with the conduct of litigation. The suggestion that the rule offends the important right to freedom from invasion of the person ignores the fact that as we hold, no invasion of freedom from personal restraint attaches to refusal so to comply with its provisions. If we were to adopt the suggested criterion of the importance of the alleged right we should invite endless litigation and confusion worse confounded. The test must be whether a rule really regulates procedure,—the judicial process for enforcing rights and duties recognized by substantive law and for justly administering remedy and redress for disregard or infraction of them. That the rules in question are such is admitted.

Finally, it is urged that Rules 35 and 37 work a major change of policy and that this was not intended by Congress. Apart from the fact already stated, that the policy of the states in this respect has not been uniform, it is to be noted that the authorization of a comprehensive system of court rules was a departure in policy, and that the new policy envisaged in the enabling act of 1934 was that the whole field of court procedure be regulated in the interest of speedy, fair and exact determination of the truth. The challenged rules comport with this policy.

Moreover, in accordance with the Act, the rules were submitted to the Congress so that that body might examine them and veto their going into effect if contrary to the policy of the legislature.

The value of the reservation of the power to examine proposed rules, laws and regulations before they become effective is well understood by Congress. It is frequently, as here, employed to make sure that the action under the delegation squares with the Congressional purpose. * * * [T]his specific rule was attacked and defended before the committees of the two Houses. The Preliminary Draft of the rules called attention to the contrary practice indicated by the Botsford case,* as did the Report of the Advisory Committee and the Notes prepared by the Committee to accompany the final version of the rules. That no adverse action was taken by Congress indicates, at least, that no transgression of legislative policy was found. We conclude that the rules under attack are within the authority granted.

The District Court treated the refusal to comply with its order as a contempt and committed the petitioner therefor. Neither in the Circuit Court of Appeals nor here was this action assigned as error. We think, however, that in the light of the provisions of Rule 37 it was plain error of such a fundamental nature that we should notice it. * * * Rule 37 exempts from punishment as for contempt the refusal to obey an order that a party submit to a physical or mental examination. The District Court was in error in going counter to this express exemption. The remedies available under the rule in such a case are those enumerated in [the rule itself]. For this error we reverse the judgment and remand the cause to the District Court for further proceedings in conformity to this opinion.

Reversed and remanded.

■ MR. JUSTICE FRANKFURTER, dissenting.

* * * [I]t does not seem to me that the answer to our question is to be found by an analytic determination whether the power of examination here claimed is a matter of procedure or a matter of substance, even assuming that the two are mutually exclusive categories with easily ascertainable contents. The problem seems to me to be controlled by the policy underlying the Botsford decision. Its doctrine was not a survival of an outworn technicality. It rested on considerations akin to what is familiarly known in the English law as the liberties of the subject. To be sure, the immunity that was recognized in the Botsford case has no constitutional sanction. It is amenable to statutory change. But the "inviolability of a person" was deemed to have such historic roots in Anglo-American law that it was not to be curtailed "unless by clear and unquestionable authority of law." * * *

So far as national law is concerned, a drastic change in public policy in a matter deeply touching the sensibilities of people or even their

---

*   [Ed.] Union Pac. Ry. Co. v. Botsford, 141 U.S. 250 (1891).

prejudices as to privacy, ought not to be inferred from a general authorization to formulate rules for the more uniform and effective dispatch of business on the civil side of the federal courts. I deem a requirement as to the invasion of the person to stand on a very different footing from questions pertaining to the discovery of documents, pre-trial procedure and other devices for the expeditious, economic and fair conduct of litigation. That disobedience of an order under Rule 35 cannot be visited with punishment as for contempt does not mitigate its intrusion into an historic immunity of the privacy of the person. Of course the Rule is compulsive in that the doors of the federal courts otherwise open may be shut to litigants who do not submit to such a physical examination.

In this view little significance attaches to the fact that the Rules, in accordance with the statute, remained on the table of two Houses of Congress without evoking any objection to Rule 35 and thereby automatically came into force. * * * Having due regard to the mechanics of legislation and the practical conditions surrounding the business of Congress when the Rules were submitted, to draw any inference of tacit approval from non-action by Congress is to appeal to unreality. And so I conclude that to make the drastic change that Rule 35 sought to introduce would require explicit legislation.

Ordinarily, disagreement with the majority on so-called procedural matters is best held in silence. Even in the present situation I should be loath to register dissent did the issue pertain merely to diversity litigation. But Rule 35 applies to all civil litigation in the federal courts, and thus concerns the enforcement of federal rights and not merely of state law in the federal courts.

■ MR. JUSTICE BLACK, MR. JUSTICE DOUGLAS, and MR. JUSTICE MURPHY agree with these views.

NOTE ON CHALLENGES TO THE VALIDITY OF THE FEDERAL RULES

(1) Decisions Rejecting Challenges Under the Enabling Act. In Mississippi Pub. Corp. v. Murphree, 326 U.S. 438 (1946), the Supreme Court held that a provision of Rule 4, permitting service of process anywhere within the state in which the district court sits, rather than only within the district, did not "abridge, enlarge, nor modify the substantive rights of any litigant" within the meaning of the Enabling Act. It cited Sibbach for the proposition that the prohibition on altering substantive rights "was obviously not addressed to such incidental effects as necessarily attend the adoption of the prescribed new rules of procedure upon the rights of litigants who, agreeably to rules of practice and procedure, have been brought before a court authorized to determine their rights." But the Court noted that "[t]he fact that this Court promulgated the rules as formulated and recommended by the Advisory Committee does not foreclose consideration of their validity, meaning or consistency," and added that in ascertaining the meaning of the

Rules, "the construction given to them by the [Advisory] Committee is of weight."[1]

In several cases, the Court has given a rule a strained interpretation, apparently to avoid questions about its validity under the Enabling Act. See, *e.g.*, Palmer v. Hoffman, 318 U.S. 109 (1943) (Rule 8(c)); Anderson v. Yungkau, 329 U.S. 482 (1947) (Rules 6(b) and 25(a)); Walker v. Armco Steel Corp., 446 U.S. 740 (1980) (Rule 3); Semtek Int'l, Inc. v. Lockheed Martin Corp., 531 U.S. 497 (2001) (Rule 41(b)).[2] To date, the Court has never squarely invalidated a provision of the civil rules. In Business Guides, Inc. v. Chromatic Communications Enterprises, Inc., 498 U.S. 533 (1991), the Court took seriously, but ultimately rejected, an Enabling Act challenge to its interpretation of revised Rule 11 of the Federal Rules of Civil Procedure. See also Marek v. Chesny (and especially Justice Brennan's dissent), discussed in Paragraph (4), *infra*. In Ortiz v. Fibreboard Corp., 527 U.S. 815, 862 (1999), the Court cautioned against—but did not explicitly reject—an application of Rule 23 that would permit certification of a "mandatory" (non-opt-out) class action solely on the basis that the defendant might lack sufficient assets to satisfy all potential claims against it. The Court emphasized that the combination of the Enabling Act's limiting provisions and the effect on absent class members of certifying such a mandatory proceeding militated against so expansive an interpretation of the rule.

(2) Allocation of Authority Between the Legislative and Judicial Branches. The Enabling Act in § 2072(b) today specifies that "[a]ll laws in conflict [with rules promulgated under the Act] shall be of no further force or effect." Does this provision raise a constitutional issue? Does the Supreme Court's rulemaking power allow it to supersede acts of Congress passed *after* the rules became effective? If Congress overrides a particular rule, may the Court thereafter reinstate the rule? (Note that the opinion in Sibbach characterized the Enabling Act as giving the courts only the authority "to make rules not inconsistent with the statutes or Constitution of the United States.") For exploration of these issues, see Leib, *Are the Federal Rules of*

---

[1]   For criticism of the rationale in Murphree, and arguments that aspects of Rule 4 relating to amenability to jurisdiction exceed the Court's rulemaking authority, see Whitten, *Separation of Powers Restrictions on Rule Making: A Case Study of Federal Rule 4*, 40 Me.L.Rev. 41 (1988); Kelleher, *Amenability to Jurisdiction as a "Substantive Right": The Invalidity of Rule 4(k) Under the Rules Enabling Act*, 75 Ind.L.J. 1191 (2000). For additional reflection on the relationship between Rule 4 and the Enabling Act, see Spencer, *The Territorial Reach of Federal Courts*, 71 Fla.L.Rev. 979 (2019) (arguing that Rule 4(k) exceeds the rulemaking authority conferred by the Rules Enabling Act and should be revised to permit nationwide service of process); Woolley, *Rediscovering the Limited Role of the Federal Rules in Regulating Personal Jurisdiction*, 56 Hous.L.Rev. 565 (2019) (arguing that the Rules Enabling Act generally does not permit the Court to regulate amenability to suit and that Murphree is not to the contrary, but that Rule 4(k) is valid because it merely restates otherwise applicable law); Sachs, *The Unlimited Jurisdiction of the Federal Courts*, 106 Va.L.Rev. 1703 (2020) (defending Rule 4's validity, arguing that rules defining the scope of a federal court's service of process do not directly alter the court's jurisdiction and thus are authorized by the Rules Enabling Act, and further arguing that Congress has ratified Murphree's interpretation of the Rules Enabling Act).

[2]   For criticism of the Court's practice of interpreting the Rules narrowly to avoid conflict with the Rules Enabling Act, see Spencer, *Substance, Procedure, and the Rules Enabling Act*, 66 UCLA L.Rev. 654, 657–59 (2019); Steinman, *The End of an Era: The Federal Rules of Civil Procedure after the 2015 Amendments*, 66 Emory L.J. 1, 5–8 (2016).

Evidence Unconstitutional?, 71 Am.U.L.Rev. 911 (2022); Clinton, *Rule 9 of the Federal Habeas Corpus Rules: A Case Study on the Need for Reform of the Rules Enabling Acts*, 63 Iowa L.Rev. 15, 64–77 (1977).

The relationship between the Enabling Act and an Act of Congress arose in an unusual context in Henderson v. United States, 517 U.S. 654 (1996). In a provision unchanged since its enactment in 1920, the Suits in Admiralty Act (SAA), 46 U.S.C. App. § 742, permits certain actions in admiralty to be brought against the United States and further states that the plaintiff shall "forthwith" serve a copy of the complaint on the U.S. Attorney and shall mail a copy to the Attorney General. Rule 4 of the Federal Rules of Civil Procedure, however, as enacted by Congress in 1982, 96 Stat. 2527, authorizes an extendable 120-day period for service of process in all cases. In an action under the SAA, service of process was effected in accordance with Rule 4 but (the Court assumed) too late to meet the SAA requirement that service be made "forthwith." The Court held that the "procedural" provision of Rule 4 governing the time available for service superseded the shorter period specified in the SAA. Observing that the question did not arise squarely under the Enabling Act because Rule 4, as amended, had been enacted by Congress, the Court said: "As the United States acknowledges, * * * a Rule made law by Congress supersedes conflicting laws no less than a Rule this Court prescribes."[3]

(3) Sibbach and the Substance-Procedure Distinction. The substantive right asserted in the Sibbach case was state-created. What, if any, are the constitutional limits upon the power of Congress to regulate practice and procedure in actions for the enforcement of such rights? Does the Sibbach opinion yield a satisfactory test of what constitutes practice and procedure? Of when regulation of the former may transgress limits on the validity or appropriateness of federal regulation of the latter? Does the opinion cast any light on the difference, if any, between the constitutional power of Congress in this area and the power delegated by Congress to the Supreme Court? Is the Sibbach Court's statement correct that if the right asserted were one of "substantive law," the Rules of Decision Act would require the application of Indiana law?

(4) Marek v. Chesny and the Limits of Rulemaking Authority. The tension between the rulemaking authority and the legislative powers of Congress was highlighted by the controversy in Marek v. Chesny, 473 U.S. 1 (1985). In that case, the plaintiff, after prevailing in a civil rights action under 42 U.S.C. § 1983, moved for an award of attorney's fees as authorized by 42 U.S.C. § 1988. The district court denied the motion with respect to attorney's fees incurred after an offer of settlement by the defendant, since Rule 68 provided that when, as here, the amount recovered after trial was less than the amount of the offer, "the offeree must pay the costs incurred after the making of the offer." The Supreme Court agreed with the district court, holding that (a) the term "costs" in Rule 68 includes attorney's fees

---

[3]   Justice Thomas, joined by Chief Justice Rehnquist and Justice O'Connor, dissented, arguing that the SAA's requirement of service "forthwith" was a jurisdictional limitation on the waiver of sovereign immunity: (1) that could not be changed by a rule promulgated under the Enabling Act, and (2) that had not been impliedly repealed by Congress in 1982.

whenever the underlying statute (here, § 1988) defines costs to include those fees, and (b) as so construed Rule 68's policy of encouraging settlements is wholly consistent with § 1988's policy of encouraging meritorious civil rights suits.

Justice Brennan, joined by Justices Marshall and Blackmun, dissented on both grounds. He argued that the automatic provisions of Rule 68, if applied to attorney's fees, would put severe pressure on civil rights plaintiffs to settle even meritorious suits without adequate information and were thus wholly inconsistent with the broad discretion conferred by § 1988. He concluded that "[as] construed by the Court * * * Rule 68 surely will operate to 'abridge' and to 'modify' [the] statutory right to reasonable attorney's fees. * * * [Thus] the Rules Enabling Act requires that the Court's interpretation give way."[4]

2. THE COMMON LAW THROUGH 1938

INTRODUCTORY NOTE

A contested issue at the founding and for decades afterwards was the power of federal courts to identify and expound an unwritten "common law" in cases within federal jurisdiction. The term "common law" during this period was used in different contexts to mean one or a combination of the following: (i) the customs of the English people; (ii) the decisions and principles of law expounded by common law courts in England; (iii) basic tenets of liberty and justice emergent in those decisions; (iv) modes of reasoning common to courts (including Colonial courts) in the Anglo-American legal system; (v) certain transnational customs and practices; or (vi) non-written law. See Bridwell & Whitten, The Constitution and the Common Law 13–33 (1977); Jay, *Origins of Federal Common Law: Part Two*, 133 U.Pa.L.Rev. 1231, 1234–41 (1985).

In the early decades of the nation there was uncertainty about when federal courts could apply various elements of the common law; under what authority, if any, they could do so; the relationship of the common law that federal courts applied to state law; and the legal status of the law so applied. The closest that the Judiciary Act of 1789 came to speaking to these issues was in § 34, which provided: "That the laws of the several states, except where the constitution, treaties or statutes of the United States shall otherwise require or provide, shall be regarded as rules of decision in trials at common law in the courts of the United States in cases where they apply."

---

[4]   Justice Brennan's position finds support in Professor Burbank's study of the history of the Rules Enabling Act. See Burbank, *The Rules Enabling Act of 1934*, 130 U.Pa.L.Rev. 1015 (1982). In a later article, Burbank concludes that although the rules may *authorize* the award of fees and other costs in such circumstances, they may not *require* their imposition without running afoul of the Enabling Act. Burbank, *Sanctions in the Proposed Amendments to the Federal Rules of Civil Procedure: Some Questions About Power*, 11 Hofstra L.Rev. 997 (1983).

But § 34 was by its terms limited to rules of decision in trials at common law, failed to specify in which cases state law applies, and did not "indicate what law should be applied in cases, if any, in which state laws did not apply and in which federal law did not 'require or provide' anything." Fletcher, *The General Common Law and Section 34 of the Judiciary Act of 1789: The Example of Marine Insurance*, 97 Harv.L.Rev. 1513, 1516–17 (1984).

The two principal decisions that follow were important landmarks in the early debates about, and resolution of, these issues.

United States v. Hudson & Goodwin

11 U.S. (7 Cranch) 32 (1812).
On Certificate from the United States Circuit Court for the District of Connecticut.

[The defendants were indicted for criminal libel for having stated, in the *Connecticut Currant* of May 7, 1806, that the President and Congress of the United States had secretly voted $2,000,000 as a present to Bonaparte, for leave to make a treaty with Spain. The question whether the federal circuit court has a common law jurisdiction in cases of criminal libel divided that court's judges, who certified that question to the Supreme Court.]

■ * * * [T]he following opinion was delivered * * * by JOHNSON, J.

The only question which this case presents is, whether the Circuit Courts of the United States can exercise a common law jurisdiction in criminal cases. We state it thus broadly because a decision on a case of libel will apply to every case in which jurisdiction is not vested in those Courts by statute.

Although this question is brought up now for the first time to be decided by this Court, we consider it as having been long since settled in public opinion. In no other case for many years has this jurisdiction been asserted; and the general acquiescence of legal men shews the prevalence of opinion in favor of the negative of the proposition.

The course of reasoning which leads to this conclusion is simple, obvious, and admits of but little illustration. The powers of the general Government are made up of concessions from the several states—whatever is not expressly given to the former, the latter expressly reserve. The judicial power of the United States is a constituent part of those concessions * * *. * * * [Only the Supreme Court] possesses jurisdiction derived immediately from the constitution, and of which the legislative power cannot deprive it. All other Courts created by the general Government possess no jurisdiction but what is given them by the power that creates them, and can be vested with none but what the power ceded to the general Government will authorize them to confer.

It is not necessary to inquire whether the general Government * * * possesses the power of conferring on its Courts a jurisdiction in cases similar to the present; it is enough that such jurisdiction has not been conferred by any legislative act, if it does not result to those Courts as a consequence of their creation.

And such is the opinion of the majority of this Court: For, the power which congress possess to create Courts of inferior jurisdiction, necessarily implies the power to limit the jurisdiction of those Courts to particular objects; and when a Court is created, and its operations confined to certain specific objects, with what propriety can it assume to itself a jurisdiction—much more extended—in its nature very indefinite—applicable to a great variety of subjects—varying in every state in the Union—and with regard to which there exists no definite criterion of distribution between the district and Circuit Courts of the same district?

The only ground on which it has ever been contended that this jurisdiction could be maintained is, that, upon the formation of any political body, an implied power to preserve its own existence and promote the end and object of its creation, necessarily results to it. But, without examining how far this consideration is applicable to the peculiar character of our constitution, it may be remarked that it is a principle by no means peculiar to the common law. It is coeval, probably, with the first formation of a limited Government; belongs to a system of universal law, and may as well support the assumption of many other powers as those more peculiarly acknowledged by the common law of England.

But if admitted as applicable to the state of things in this country, the consequence would not result from it which is here contended for. If it may communicate certain implied powers to the general Government, it would not follow that the Courts of that Government are vested with jurisdiction over any particular act done by an individual in supposed violation of the peace and dignity of the sovereign power. The legislative authority of the Union must first make an act a crime, affix a punishment to it, and declare the Court that shall have jurisdiction of the offence.

Certain implied powers must necessarily result to our Courts of justice from the nature of their institution. But jurisdiction of crimes against the state is not among those powers. To fine for contempt— imprison for contumacy—inforce the observance of order, &c. are powers which cannot be dispensed with in a Court, because they are necessary to the exercise of all others: and so far our Courts no doubt possess powers not immediately derived from statute; but all exercise of criminal jurisdiction in common law cases we are of opinion is not within their implied powers.

Swift v. Tyson

41 U.S. (16 Pet.) 1 (1842).

Certificate of Division from the Circuit Court for the Southern District of New York.

■ MR. JUSTICE STORY delivered the opinion of the court.

This cause comes before us from the circuit court of the southern district of New York, upon a certificate of division of the judges of that court.

The action was brought by the plaintiff, Swift, as indorsee, against the defendant, Tyson, as acceptor, upon a bill of exchange dated at Portland, Maine, on [May 1,] 1836, for the sum of $1540.30, payable six months after date, and grace, drawn by one Nathaniel Norton and one Jairus S. Keith upon and accepted by Tyson, at the city of New York, in favor of the order of Nathaniel Norton, and by Norton indorsed to the plaintiff. The bill was dishonored at maturity.

At the trial, the acceptance and indorsement of the bill were admitted, and the plaintiff there rested his case. The defendant then introduced in evidence the answer of Swift to a bill of discovery, by which it appeared, that Swift took the bill, before it became due, in payment of a promissory note due to him by Norton & Keith; that he understood, that the bill was accepted in part payment of some lands sold by Norton to a company in New York; that Swift was a bona fide holder of the bill, not having any notice of anything in the sale or title to the lands, or otherwise impeaching the transaction, and with the full belief that the bill was justly due. * * * The defendant then offered to prove, that the bill was accepted by the defendant, as part consideration for the purchase of certain lands in the state of Maine, which Norton & Keith represented themselves to be the owners of, and also represented to be of great value, and contracted to convey a good title thereto; and that the representations were in every respect fraudulent and false, and Norton & Keith had no title to the lands, and that the same were of little or no value. The plaintiff objected to the admission of such testimony, or of any testimony, as against him, impeaching or showing a failure of the consideration, on which the bill was accepted, under the facts admitted by the defendant, and those proved by him, by reading the answer of plaintiff to the bill of discovery. The judges of the circuit court thereupon divided in opinion upon the following point or question of law—Whether, under the facts last mentioned, the defendant was entitled to the same defence to the action, as if the suit was between the original parties to the bill, that is to say, Norton, or Norton & Keith, and the defendant; and whether the evidence so offered was admissible as against the plaintiff in the action. And this is the question certified to us for our decision. * * *

In the present case, the plaintiff is a bona fide holder, without notice, for what the law deems a good and valid consideration, that is, for a preexisting debt; and the only real question in the cause is, whether, under the circumstances of the present case, such a pre-existing debt constitutes a valuable consideration, in the sense of the general rule applicable to negotiable instruments. * * * [T]he argument on behalf of the defendant is, that the contract is to be treated as a New York contract, and therefore, to be governed by the laws of New York, as expounded by its courts, as well upon general principles, as by the express provisions of the 34th section of the judiciary act of 1789, ch. 20. And then it is further contended, that by the law of New York, as thus expounded by its courts, a pre-existing debt does not constitute, in the sense of the general rule, a valuable consideration applicable to negotiable instruments.

[The Supreme Court first expressed doubt that the doctrine asserted can "be treated as finally established" by the New York cases.]

But, admitting the doctrine to be fully settled in New York, it remains to be considered, whether it is obligatory upon this court, if it differs from the principles established in the general commercial law. It is observable, that the courts of New York do not found their decisions upon this point, upon any local statute, or positive, fixed or ancient local usage; but they deduce the doctrine from the general principles of commercial law. It is, however, contended, that the 34th section of the judiciary act of 1789, ch. 20, furnishes a rule obligatory upon this court to follow the decisions of the state tribunals in all cases to which they apply. That section provides "that the laws of the several states, except where the constitution, treaties or statutes of the United States shall otherwise require or provide, shall be regarded as rules of decision, in trials at common law, in the courts of the United States, in cases where they apply." In order to maintain the argument, it is essential, therefore, to hold, that the word "laws," in this section, includes within the scope of its meaning, the decisions of the local tribunals. In the ordinary use of language, it will hardly be contended, that the decisions of courts constitute laws. They are, at most, only evidence of what the laws are, and are not, of themselves, laws. They are often re-examined, reversed and qualified by the courts themselves, whenever they are found to be either defective, or ill-founded, or otherwise incorrect. The laws of a state are more usually understood to mean the rules and enactments promulgated by the legislative authority thereof, or long-established local customs having the force of laws. In all the various cases, which have hitherto come before us for decision, this court have uniformly supposed, that the true interpretation of the 34th section limited its application to state laws, strictly local, that is to say, to the positive statutes of the state, and the construction thereof adopted by the local tribunals, and to rights and titles to things having a permanent locality, such as the rights and titles to real estate, and other matters immovable and intraterritorial in their nature and character. It never has been supposed by us, that the section did apply, or was designed to apply, to questions of a more general nature, not at all dependent upon local statutes or local usages of a fixed and permanent operation, as, for example, to the construction of ordinary contracts or other written instruments, and especially to questions of general commercial law, where the state tribunals are called upon to perform the like functions as ourselves, that is, to ascertain, upon general reasoning and legal analogies, what is the true exposition of the contract or instrument, or what is the just rule furnished by the principles of commercial law to govern the case. And we have not now the slightest difficulty in holding, that this section, upon its true intendment and construction, is strictly limited to local statutes and local usages of the character before stated, and does not extend to contracts and other instruments of a commercial nature, the true interpretation and effect whereof are to be sought, not in the decisions of the local tribunals, but in the general principles and doctrines of commercial jurisprudence. Undoubtedly, the decisions of the local tribunals upon such subjects are entitled to, and will receive, the most deliberate attention and respect of this court; but they cannot furnish positive rules, or conclusive authority, by which our own judgments are to be bound up and governed. The law respecting negotiable instruments may be truly declared in the language of Cicero, adopted by Lord Mansfield in Luke v. Lyde, 2 Burr. 883, 887, to be in a great measure, not the law of a single country only, but of the commercial world. * * *

It becomes necessary for us, therefore, upon the present occasion, to express our own opinion of the true result of the commercial law upon the question now before us. And we have no hesitation in saying, that a pre-existing debt does constitute a valuable consideration, in the sense of the general rule already stated, as applicable to negotiable instruments. * * * And why, upon principle, should not a pre-existing debt be deemed such a valuable consideration? It is for the benefit and convenience of the commercial world, to give as wide an extent as practicable to the credit and circulation of negotiable paper, that it may pass not only as security for new purchases and advances, made upon the transfer thereof, but also in payment of, and as security for, pre-existing debts. The creditor is thereby enabled to realize or to secure his debt, and thus may safely give a prolonged credit, or forbear from taking any legal steps to enforce his rights. The debtor also has the advantage of making his negotiable securities of equivalent value to cash. But establish the opposite conclusion, that negotiable paper cannot be applied in payment of, or as security for, pre-existing debts, without letting in all the equities between the original and antecedent parties, and the value and circulation of such securities must be essentially diminished, and the debtor driven to the embarrassment of making a sale thereof, often at a ruinous discount, to some third person, and then, by circuity, to apply the proceeds to the payment of his debts. What, indeed, upon such a doctrine, would become of that large class of cases, where new notes are given by the same or by other parties, by way of renewal or security to banks, in lieu of old securities discounted by them, which have arrived at maturity? Probably, more than one-half of all bank transactions in our country, as well as those of other countries, are of this nature. The doctrine would strike a fatal blow at all discounts of negotiable securities for pre-existing debts.

This question has been several times before this court, and it has been uniformly held, that it makes no difference whatsoever, as to the rights of the holder, whether the debt, for which the negotiable instrument is transferred to him, is a pre-existing debt, or is contracted at the time of the transfer. * * *

In England, the same doctrine has been uniformly acted upon. * * *

In the American courts, so far as we have been able to trace the decisions, the same doctrine seems generally, but not universally, to prevail. * * * We are all, therefore, of opinion, that the question on this point, propounded by the circuit court for our consideration, ought to be answered in the negative; and we shall, accordingly, direct it so to be certified to the circuit court.

■ [JUSTICE CATRON concurred in a separate statement, limiting his agreement to "the case made by the record."]

NOTE ON THE COMMON LAW IN FEDERAL COURTS BEFORE 1938

(1) The Early Debate over Common Law Crimes. Sections 9 and 11 of the Judiciary Act of 1789 granted federal courts exclusive "cognizance of all crimes and offences" that were "cognizable under the authority of the United States * * *."[1] But the Judiciary Act did not specify the sources of governing criminal law within this jurisdiction.[2] Congress in 1790 enacted the first federal criminal statute to punish certain specified crimes against the United States.[3]

In addition to applying statutory crimes, lower federal courts in the 1790s, often in opinions by Supreme Court Justices riding Circuit, upheld convictions for violations of unwritten common law crimes. See, *e.g.*, Williams' Case, 29 F.Cas. 1330, 1331 (C.C.D.Conn.1799) (No. 17,708) (upholding conviction of expatriate for hostilities against the United States) (Ellsworth, J.); United States v. Ravara, 27 F.Cas. 714, 715 (C.C.D.Pa.1794) (No. 16,122a) (upholding common law indictment of foreign consul for sending letters seeking to extort money) (Jay, C.J.); Henfield's Case, 11 F.Cas. 1099, 1120 (C.C.D.Pa.1793) (No. 6,360) (grand jury charge based on common law crime of violating neutrality) (Wilson, J., and Iredell, J.); see generally Goebel, History of the Supreme Court of the United States: Antecedents and Beginnings to 1801, at 623–33 (1971). Among the early

---

[1]   1 Stat. 73, 79. Section 9 granted jurisdiction to federal district courts but limited it to offenses for relatively minor crimes involving certain punishments, and § 11 provided jurisdiction to federal circuit courts, exclusive of the district court, for more serious crimes, and jurisdiction concurrent with the district court over the minor crimes cognizable in the district courts. Both grants of jurisdiction were exclusive of state court jurisdiction.

[2]   Section 34 of the 1789 Act was interpreted early on not to apply in criminal cases. See United States v. Burr, 25 F.Cas. 187, 188 (C.C.D.Va.1807) (No. 14,694) (Marshall, C.J.).

[3]   1 Stat. 112.

Federalist Justices, only Justice Chase denied the legitimacy of federal common law crimes. See United States v. Worrall, 28 F.Cas. 774, 779 (C.C.D.Pa.1798) (No. 16,766) (arguing that "the United States did not bring [the common law] with them from England; [that] the Constitution does not create it; and [that] no act of Congress has assumed it").

The federal judiciary's enforcement of common law crimes was a source of intense political controversy between the Jeffersonians and Federalists. See Jay, *Origins of Federal Common Law: Part One*, 133 U.Pa.L.Rev. 1003, 1019–24 (1985); Jay, *Origins of Federal Common Law: Part Two*, 133 U.Pa.L.Rev. 1231, 1233–35 (1985). The controversy peaked when the Federalist-dominated Congress passed the Alien Act, 1 Stat. 596 (1798), which codified seditious libel. In response to Jeffersonian opposition in Congress, Federalist supporters argued that federal courts could enforce seditious libel as a common law crime and that the Act provided safeguards (like an intent requirement and a truth defense) that the common law crime lacked. They argued more broadly that common law decision-making was familiar to those who adopted the Constitution and prevalent in every state. And they added that given the impossibility of codifying every wrong, a federal common law of crimes was needed to protect the lawful operations of the federal government. Jeffersonians denied the possibility of identifying a singular body of common law for the nation because each state had modified English common law to suit its circumstances. And they argued that a common law of the United States would circumvent the limitations on federal power embodied in Article I of the Constitution. See Currie, The Constitution in Congress: The Federalist Period, 1789–1801, at 260–74 & 273, n.299 (1999) (summarizing the congressional debates); Jay, *supra*, at 1077–83 (Part I) (same).

Federal common law became a major point of political contention outside Congress as part of a larger debate about the scope of national power versus the sovereignty of the states and the people. The Jeffersonian opposition was crystallized in a report prepared by Madison for the Virginia legislature in connection with (its half of) the Virginia and Kentucky Resolutions, both of which were passed to protest the asserted unconstitutionality of the Sedition Act and related Alien Acts. See Jay, *supra*, at 1089–91 (Part I). First, Madison contended that if the Constitution itself adopted the common law, "it follows that no part of the law can be altered by the legislature," thereby undermining the sovereignty of the people. Second, Madison argued that if Congress could alter or displace federal common law, it would destroy "the limitations marked out in the Constitution," because "some branch or other of the common law" extends to "every object of legislation * * *." Third, Madison added that "whether the common law be admitted as of legal or of constitutional obligation, it would confer on the judicial department a discretion little short of a legislative power," thus contravening the separation of powers. Madison's Report on the Virginia Resolutions, reprinted in 4 The Debates in the Several State Conventions on the Adoption of the Federal Constitution, 565–66 (Elliot ed. 1888).

Many commentators believe that a backlash against federal common law crimes helped to elect Jefferson in 1800. See, *e.g.*, 1 Warren, The Supreme Court in United States History 158–64 (1922); Presser, *A Tale of Two Judges: Richard Peters, Samuel Chase and the Broken Promise of Federalist Jurisprudence*, 73 Nw.U.L.Rev. 26, 47 (1978); Wilmarth, *Elusive Foundation: John Marshall, James Wilson, and the Problem of Reconciling Popular Sovereignty and Natural Law Jurisprudence in the New Federal Republic*, 72 Geo.Wash.L.Rev. 113, 187–88 (2003). Although the prosecution of federal common law crimes did not cease with Jefferson's election, prominent decisions by the Administration to discontinue such prosecutions confirmed its disapproval of such practice. See Preyer, *Jurisdiction to Punish: Federal Authority, Federalism and the Common Law of Crimes in the Early Republic*, 4 L. & Hist.Rev. 223, 238–41 (1986); Warren, *supra*, at 238, 435–36. Presumably, Justice Johnson's reference to "public opinion" and "the general acquiescence of legal men" referred to the Jeffersonian triumph and the apparent ratification of the Jeffersonian position on federal common law. See Jay, *supra*, at 1017–18 (Part I). See also Casto, The Supreme Court in the Early Republic: The Chief Justiceships of John Jay and Oliver Ellsworth 162 (1995).

(2) The Rationale of Hudson. Justice Johnson's opinion spoke in several places about the absence of a common law "jurisdiction" in criminal cases. But Section 11 gave Circuit courts "cognizance of all crimes and offences cognizable under the authority of the United States," so the Court must have believed—though it did not explain why—that the jurisdiction in the 1789 Act did not extend to common law crimes. From that premise, Johnson maintained that the enumerated power structure of the Constitution meant that the lower federal courts lacked any subject matter jurisdiction unless conferred in accordance with "the power ceded to the general Government," *i.e.* by Congress in a statute. According to the Court, no such jurisdiction had been conferred. But the Court went further and maintained that Congress must "make an act a crime, affix a punishment to it, and declare the Court that shall have jurisdiction of the offence," which seems to imply that Congress can only confer jurisdiction over statutory crimes, or that federal courts are incapable of receiving jurisdiction to develop common law crimes. If that is the right interpretation, why did Congress lack power to confer such jurisdiction on federal courts, especially in light of the nature of the crime at issue (a crime against the United States) and the Necessary and Proper Clause? Other values might argue in favor of statutory definitions of crimes, including fair notice and democratic accountability for punishment. Hessick, *The Myth of Common Law Crimes*, 105 Va.L.Rev. 965, 968, 975–78 (2019). But it is hard to locate these values in Article III. Note that common law prosecutions continued in state courts well into the twentieth century. *Id.* 980–81.[4]

---

[4]   Four years after Hudson, in United States v. Coolidge, 14 U.S. (1 Wheat.) 415 (1816), the Court followed Hudson, though not without some expression of doubt. Coolidge and a codefendant were indicted in the circuit court for having forcibly rescued a vessel captured as a prize, a crime on the high seas. In his opinion on circuit upholding the indictment, Justice Story argued for criminal common law powers in federal courts for "public offenses" and distinguished Coolidge from Hudson on the ground that it was an admiralty case where federal courts had

Hudson noted at the end of the opinion that although lower federal courts lack implied jurisdiction over common law crimes, federal courts possess an implied judicial power of contempt. For discussion of other such implied "procedural" powers, see Chap. VII, pp. 879–881, *infra*. For discussion of federal courts' residual lawmaking power to interpret and fill in gaps in federal criminal statutes, see Chap. VII, pp. 845–847, *infra*.

(3) Swift, Section 34, and General Law. Section 34 of the Judiciary Act required federal courts in cases not governed by federal enacted law to apply the "laws of the several states" as "rules of decision" in "trials at common law." Swift held that the term "laws" in § 34 refers to "local" state laws such as state statutes as interpreted by state courts, and long-established local customs, especially as they related to property in the state. (The Court during this period also treated state constitutions, as interpreted by state courts, as local law.) Swift further held that § 34 did not require federal courts to follow state court decisions on "general commercial law" topics like negotiable instruments. These aspects of the decision were not controversial at the time but rather formed the dominant view of § 34 since the founding. See generally Fletcher, *The General Common Law and Section 34 of the Judiciary Act of 1789: The Example of Marine Insurance*, 97 Harv.L.Rev 1513 (1984).[5]

The Court conceived of general common law—which it sometimes called "general principles," or "general jurisprudence," or "general law"—not as the law of a state, or even "the law of a single country," but rather law that governed "the commercial world." See also Sosa v. Alvarez-Machain, 542 U.S. 692, 725–26 (2004) (stating that in 1789, the common law was "outside of any particular State"); *id.* 739–40 (Scalia, J., concurring in part and concurring in the judgment) (viewing the general common law of Swift as neither federal nor state law). General law was thus trans-jurisdictional and "not attached to any particular sovereign," but rather "existed by common

---

long applied a non-statutory law in non-criminal cases. In the Supreme Court, the Attorney General declined to argue the case, treating Hudson as having settled the matter. Justice Johnson delivered the following opinion for the Court: "Upon the question now before the court a difference of opinion has existed, and still exists, among the members of the court. We should, therefore, have been willing to have heard the question discussed upon solemn argument. But the attorney-general has declined to argue the cause; and no counsel appears for the defendant. Under these circumstances the court would not choose to review their former decision in the case of the United States v. Hudson and Goodwin, or draw it into doubt." After Coolidge the prohibition on common law crimes was settled. See United States v. Eaton, 144 U.S. 677, 687 (1892); Clark, *Constitutional Structure, Judicial Discretion, and the Eighth Amendment*, 81 Notre Dame L.Rev. 1149, 1179–81 (2006).

[5]   This was not the uniform view early on, however. In Brown v. Van Bramm, 3 U.S. (3 Dall.) 344 (1797), for example, the plaintiff, in an action on bills of exchange in the United States Circuit Court for Rhode Island, obtained a default judgment for the principal, together with interest, protest charges, and (pursuant to a Rhode Island statute) damages of 10% of the principal. The Supreme Court affirmed the judgment with a brief statement that the result was warranted "under the laws, and the practical construction of the courts, of Rhode Island," and with the following footnote: "Chase, Justice, observed, that he concurred in the opinion of the court; but that it was on common law principles, and not in compliance with the laws and practice of the state." And as discussed in Collins, *Justice Iredell, Choice of Law, and the Constitution—A Neglected Encounter*, 23 Const.Comment. 163 (2006), the Circuit Court decision in United States v. Mundell, 27 F.Cas. 23 (C.C.D.Va.1795) (No. 15,834), concluded that "state law, *including its common law* as well as its statute law, should apply in cases governed by section 34 when federal law is silent" (emphasis added).

practice and consent among a number of sovereigns." Fletcher, *supra*, at 1517.

Commercial law was not the only general common law topic. At the time of Swift, it also included, at its substantive core, the law of nations and maritime law, as well as elements of procedure, evidence, conflict of laws, and equity. Since general law was not federal law, it did not preempt state law under the Supremacy clause. Both state and federal courts could independently apply general law, and their interpretations of that law were not binding on one another. Thus, one year after Swift, a New York state judge refused to follow Swift's commercial law ruling.[6] Nor was a state court's decision concerning the general common law considered "federal" law for purpose of the lower federal courts' original jurisdiction or the Supreme Court's appellate jurisdiction to review state court judgments.[7] Still, even if not binding, federal decisions were often influential and thus, in some domains (such as commercial law), may have led to greater uniformity among the state courts in practice than would have otherwise existed.[8]

Courts continued to apply state common law on local matters, which at the time included matters related to property and trusts. See, *e.g.,* Jackson v. Chew, 25 U.S. (12 Wheat.) 153 (1827). But in general, courts during this era before legal positivism took hold in the legal culture were often not attentive to the precise sources of law guiding decisions. What was clear for a long time after Hudson, however, was that federal courts denied that there was a common law *of the United States.* Consider Wheaton v. Peters, 33 U.S. (8 Pet.) 591 (1834), a federal court copyright action in which the plaintiff's claim for relief rested in part on the common law. The majority stated: "It is clear, there can be no common law of the United States. The federal government is composed of twenty-four sovereign and independent states; each of which may have its local usages, customs and common law. There is no principle which pervades the union, and has the authority of law, that is not embodied in the constitution or laws of the union. The common law could be made a part of our federal system by legislative adoption. When a common law right is asserted, we must look to the state in which the controversy originated."

In assessing the holding of Swift, consider: Would Congress have had power to enact the holding as a rule of decision in the federal courts? As a rule of decision in diverse citizenship cases in the state courts? As a rule of conduct between diverse citizens? As a general rule of conduct? Would a federal court in New York have been free to disregard a New York statute enacting a rule contrary to Swift v. Tyson?

(4) Reconciling Hudson and Swift? Swift was not a controversial decision at the time, and general common law was widely applied by federal

---

    6   See Stalker v. McDonald, 6 Hill 93, 95 (N.Y.1843). Some state courts chose to follow federal decisions as a matter of policy. See Nelson, *A Critical Guide to Erie Railroad Co. v. Tompkins,* 54 Wm. & Mary L.Rev. 921, 949 (2013).

    7   See, *e.g.,* San Francisco v. Itsell, 133 U.S. 65, 67 (1890); N.Y. Life Ins. v. Hendren, 92 U.S. 286 (1876); see also Collins, *Before Lochner—Diversity Jurisdiction and the Development of General Constitutional Law,* 74 Tul.L.Rev. 1263, 1304 & n.201 (2000).

    8   See Fletcher, *supra,* at 1562–63.

courts from the beginning of the nation. See Fletcher, Paragraph (3), *supra*, at 1514, 1518–21. Why did the Court so readily accept general common law long after it had rejected common law crimes in Hudson in 1812? Common law crimes were federal law, and their recognition implied to some that all of the English common law might apply as federal law—a controversial proposition that, as Madison argued in the Virginia and Kentucky Resolutions, had broad implications for the power of the federal government over the states. See Jay, Paragraph (1), *supra*, at 1090 (Part I). General common law, by contrast, was relatively limited in scope at the time of Swift and was not federal law, so it posed much less of a threat to state power. (This would change, as is explored below.) For other explanations for why the Court rejected common law crimes and embraced general common law in the nineteenth century, see Bellia & Clark, *General Law in Federal Court*, 54 Wm. & Mary L.Rev. 655, 705–06 (2013) (arguing that states received the common law—general law and local law—from England and the United States received no "municipal common law of its own," and so federal courts could apply general law, but not other forms of common law, when adopted by the state); Presser, *A Tale of Two Judges: Richard Peters, Samuel Chase and the Broken Promise of Federalist Jurisprudence*, 73 Nw.U.L.Rev. 26, 71–72 (1978) (the Court's treatment of the federal common law of crimes is explained less by legal doctrine than the politics of the time).

(5) Changes to General Common Law After Swift. Though Swift was not controversial when decided, the Supreme Court's application of general common law in the century after Swift grew very controversial due to a number of changes in how federal courts conceived of and applied it.

(a) The Growth of General Common Law. General common law after Swift grew in its substantive dimensions beyond its core early grounding in the law merchant, the law maritime, and the law of nations. Topics once seen as "local law" came to be viewed in some circumstances as general law, thus enhancing the federal courts' discretion to disregard state court common law decisions in federal court. The Court relied on general common law rather than state precedents in "the construction of ordinary contracts or other written instruments" like deeds and wills, *e.g.* Lane v. Vick, 44 U.S. (3 How.) 464 (1845), and commercial insurance contracts, *e.g.*, Carpenter v. Providence Washington Ins. Co., 41 U.S. (16 Pet.) 495 (1842). It came to view many aspects of tort law to be governed by general law as well, see Baltimore & Ohio R. Co. v. Baugh, 149 U.S. 368 (1893); Chicago v. Robbins, 67 U.S. (2 Black) 418 (1862). General law later came to include even a previously quintessential local law subject, real property law. See Kuhn v. Fairmont Coal Co., 215 U.S. 349 (1910).

(b) State Statutes and Constitutions. Soon after Swift, the Court began to assert authority in some cases to interpret state constitutions and statutes contrary to the constructions given to those enactments in state courts, especially when the cases involved state judicial decisions that altered commercial party expectations at the time of contracting. See, *e.g.*, Burgess v. Seligman, 107 U.S. (17 Otto) 20, 33–34 (1883) ("[W]hen contracts and transactions have been entered into, and rights have accrued thereon under a particular state of the decisions, or when there has been no decision of the state tribunals, the federal courts properly claim the right to adopt their own interpretation of the [statutory] law applicable to the case, although a different interpretation may be adopted by the state courts after such rights have accrued"); Watson v. Tarpley, 59 U.S. (18 How.) 517, 521 (1855) ("[A]ny state law or regulation, the effect of which would be to impair the rights [under and defined by the general commercial law] * * * or to devest the federal courts of cognizance thereof, * * * must be nugatory and unavailing.").

Among the most controversial of these decisions were ones governing federal court actions on defaulted municipal bonds. In Gelpcke v. City of Dubuque, 68 U.S. (1 Wall.) 175 (1863), the Court disregarded a state-court construction of the state constitution that would have rendered the state bonds invalid. The Court rested its decision on the fact that the state's construction overruled decisions outstanding at the time the bonds were issued. Justice Swayne wrote for the Court: "We are not unmindful of the importance of uniformity in the decisions of this court, and those of the highest local courts, giving constructions to the laws and constitutions of their own States. It is the settled rule of this court in such cases, to follow the decisions of the State courts. But there have been heretofore, in the judicial history of this court, as doubtless there will be hereafter, many exceptional cases. We shall never immolate truth, justice, and the law, because a State tribunal has erected the altar and decreed the sacrifice." Freyer, Harmony and Dissonance: The Swift and Erie Cases in American Federalism 58–61 (1981), notes that Gelpcke was the first of about 300 similar bond cases before the Supreme Court in the last third of the nineteenth century, and adds that, according to one report, "the total of defaulted bonds across the nation amounted to between $100,000,000 and $150,000,000."

(c) The Constitutional Dimension of General Law. Swift justified the application of general law without reliance on any statutory or constitutional authorization. But many later decisions rested on the view that Article III, and in particular diversity jurisdiction, guaranteed a federal forum for federal courts to protect the general law rights of parties in interstate transactions. See, *e.g.*, Seligman, 107 U.S. at 33; Tarpley, 59 U.S. at 521. This shift to positive constitutional law justification for the growing general law regime occurred in the same period that legal positivism was becoming entrenched in American judicial and legal culture.[9] Relying on this much different and broadened conception of general law, the Supreme Court disregarded state court interpretations of state constitutional and statutory provisions and developed a robust body of nonfederal law in federal courts on issues related to state takings of property, taxing and spending powers, state rate-making authority, and other elements of state government power. These nonfederal law precedents did not preempt state court interpretations, which (as nonfederal law) were not reviewable in the Supreme Court. But they were a powerful way to limit effective state legislative and constitutional power by circumventing the applicability of state law in

---

[9]   See, *e.g.*, Freyer, Paragraph (5)(b), *supra*, at 96–97; Goldsmith & Walt, *Erie and the Irrelevance of Legal Positivism*, 84 Va.L.Rev. 673, 683–84 & nn.38–43 (1998) (collecting sources).

federal court. And these precedents later provided a primary source of decisions for the later truly federal and preemptive substantive limits on state governmental action under the regime of Lochner v. New York, 198 U.S. 45 (1905).[10]

(d) The Controversy over General Law. The bulk of general law topics and precedents that the Court had developed by the turn of the twentieth century tended to be much more favorable to national corporations than the more progressive state written enactments and common law precedents.[11] The Court developed this nonfederal general law even in areas, such as commercial insurance, where Congress was thought to lack power to regulate under the Commerce Clause.[12] The many developments in general law sparked fierce criticism on the Court, see, *e.g.*, Southern Pac. Co. v. Jensen, 244 U.S. 205 (1917) (Holmes, J., dissenting); Kuhn v. Fairmont Coal Co., 215 U.S. 349 (1910) (Holmes, J., dissenting), and in Congress, where progressive and populist forces in the 1920s sought to curtail both general common law and the diversity jurisdiction in which it primarily arose.[13]

These criticisms reached a crescendo after the Court decided Black & White Taxicab & Transfer Co. v. Brown & Yellow Taxicab & Transfer Co., 276 U.S. 518 (1928). There a Kentucky taxicab company reincorporated in Tennessee in order to establish diversity of citizenship with a rival Kentucky taxicab company so that it could sue the rival in federal court, where general law permitted its monopoly contract at a Bowling Green railroad station even though Kentucky common law precedents barred such a monopoly. The Court upheld the application of general law. Justice Holmes filed a famous dissent in which he described general law as a "fallacy" and "illusion" that had resulted in "an unconstitutional assumption of powers by the Courts of the United States."

The Taxicab decision led to an outcry in Congress and a round of bills to overrule the Swift regime as it had come to be practiced.[14] Felix Frankfurter, an author of one of the bills, believed that legislative correction was necessary because Swift "is now too strongly imbedded in our law for judicial self-correction."[15]

---

[10]   On the claims in this paragraph, see Collins, *Before Lochner—Diversity Jurisdiction and the Development of General Constitutional Law*, 74 Tul.L.Rev. 1263 (2000). See also Post, *Federalism in the Taft Court Era: Can It Be "Revived"?*, 51 Duke L.J. 1513, 1599–1600 (2002); Woolhandler, *The Common Law Origins of Constitutionally Compelled Remedies*, 107 Yale L.J. 77 (1997).

[11]   See Purcell, Brandeis and the Progressive Constitution: Erie, the Judicial Power, and the Politics of the Federal Courts in Twentieth-Century America 12–69 (2000).

[12]   *Id.* 55.

[13]   *Id.* 64–94.

[14]   See Burbank, *The Rules Enabling Act of 1934*, 130 U.Pa.L.Rev. 1015, 1109–10 n.433 (1982).

[15]   Frankfurter, *Distribution of Judicial Power Between United States and State Courts*, 13 Cornell L.Q. 499, 530 (1928).

Erie Railroad Co. v. Tompkins

304 U.S. 64 (1938).
Certiorari to the Circuit Court of Appeals for the Second Circuit.

■ MR. JUSTICE BRANDEIS delivered the opinion of the Court.

The question for decision is whether the oft-challenged doctrine of Swift v. Tyson shall now be disapproved.

Tompkins, a citizen of Pennsylvania, was injured on a dark night by a passing freight train of the Erie Railroad Company while walking along its right of way at Hughestown in that state. He claimed that the accident occurred through negligence in the operation, or maintenance, of the train; that he was rightfully on the premises as licensee because on a commonly used beaten footpath which ran for a short distance alongside the tracks; and that he was struck by something which looked like a door projecting from one of the moving cars. To enforce that claim he brought an action in the federal court for Southern New York, which had jurisdiction because the company is a corporation of that state. * * *

The Erie insisted that its duty to Tompkins was no greater than that owed to a trespasser. It contended, among other things, that its duty to Tompkins, and hence its liability, should be determined in accordance with the Pennsylvania law; that under the law of Pennsylvania, as declared by its highest court, persons who use pathways along the railroad right of way—that is, a longitudinal pathway as distinguished from a crossing—are to be deemed trespassers; and that the railroad is not liable for injuries to undiscovered trespassers resulting from its negligence, unless it be wanton or willful. Tompkins denied that any such rule had been established by the decisions of the Pennsylvania courts; and contended that, since there was no statute of the state on the subject, the railroad's duty and liability is to be determined in federal courts as a matter of general law.

The trial judge refused to rule that the applicable law precluded recovery. The jury brought in a verdict of $30,000; and the judgment entered thereon was affirmed by the Circuit Court of Appeals, which held that it was unnecessary to consider whether the law of Pennsylvania was as contended, because the question was one not of local, but of general, law, and that "upon questions of general law the federal courts are free, in absence of a local statute, to exercise their independent judgment as to what the law is; and it is well settled that the question of the responsibility of a railroad for injuries caused by its servants is one of general law. * * * Where the public has made open and notorious use of a railroad right of way for a long period of time and without objection, the company owes to persons on such permissive pathway a duty of care in the operation of its trains. * * * It is likewise generally recognized law that a jury may find that negligence exists toward a pedestrian using a permissive path on the railroad right of way if he is hit by some object projecting from the side of the train."

The Erie had contended that application of the Pennsylvania rule was required, among other things, by section 34 of the Federal Judiciary Act of September 24, 1789 * * *.

Because of the importance of the question whether the federal court was free to disregard the alleged rule of the Pennsylvania common law, we granted certiorari.

First. Swift v. Tyson held that federal courts exercising jurisdiction on the ground of diversity of citizenship need not, in matters of general jurisprudence, apply the unwritten law of the state as declared by its highest court; that they are free to exercise an independent judgment as to what the common law of the state is—or should be * * *.

The Court in applying the rule of section 34 to equity cases, in Mason v. United States, 260 U.S. 545, 559 [(1923)], said: "The statute, however, is merely declarative of the rule which would exist in the absence of the statute." The federal courts assumed, in the broad field of "general law," the power to declare rules of decision which Congress was confessedly without power to enact as statutes. Doubt was repeatedly expressed as to the correctness of the construction given section 34, and as to the soundness of the rule which it introduced. But it was the more recent research of a competent scholar, who examined the original document, which established that the construction given to it by the Court was erroneous; and that the purpose of the section was merely to make certain that, in all matters except those in which some federal law is controlling, the federal courts exercising jurisdiction in diversity of citizenship cases would apply as their rules of decision the law of the state unwritten as well as written.[5]

Criticism of the doctrine became widespread after the decision of Black & White Taxicab & Transfer Co. v. Brown & Yellow Taxicab & Transfer Co., 276 U.S. 518 [(1928)] * * *.[*]

Second. Experience in applying the doctrine of Swift v. Tyson, had revealed its defects, political and social; and the benefits expected to flow from the rule did not accrue. Persistence of state courts in their own opinions on questions of common law prevented uniformity; and the impossibility of discovering a satisfactory line of demarcation between the province of general law and that of local law developed a new well of uncertainties.[8]

On the other hand, the mischievous results of the doctrine had become apparent. Diversity of citizenship jurisdiction was conferred in

---

[5]   Warren, *New Light on the History of the Federal Judiciary Act of 1789*, 37 Harv. L. Rev. 49, 51–52, 81–88, 108 (1923).

[*]   [Ed.] See p. 759, *supra.*

[8]   Compare 2 Warren, The Supreme Court in United States History 89 (rev.ed.1935): "Probably no decision of the Court has ever given rise to more uncertainty as to legal rights; and though doubtless intended to promote uniformity in the operation of business transactions, its chief effect has been to render it difficult for business men to know in advance to what particular topic the Court would apply the doctrine. * * *" * * *

order to prevent apprehended discrimination in state courts against those not citizens of the state. Swift v. Tyson introduced grave discrimination by noncitizens against citizens. It made rights enjoyed under the unwritten "general law" vary according to whether enforcement was sought in the state or in the federal court; and the privilege of selecting the court in which the right should be determined was conferred upon the noncitizen. Thus, the doctrine rendered impossible equal protection of the law. In attempting to promote uniformity of law throughout the United States, the doctrine had prevented uniformity in the administration of the law of the state.

The discrimination resulting became in practice far-reaching. This resulted in part from the broad province accorded to the so-called "general law" as to which federal courts exercised an independent judgment. In addition to questions of purely commercial law, "general law" was held to include the obligations under contracts entered into and to be performed within the state, the extent to which a carrier operating within a state may stipulate for exemption from liability for his own negligence or that of his employee; the liability for torts committed within the state upon persons resident or property located there, even where the question of liability depended upon the scope of a property right conferred by the state; and the right to exemplary or punitive damages. Furthermore, state decisions, construing local deeds, mineral conveyances, and even devises of real estate, were disregarded.

In part the discrimination resulted from the wide range of persons held entitled to avail themselves of the federal rule by resort to the diversity of citizenship jurisdiction. Through this jurisdiction individual citizens willing to remove from their own state and become citizens of another might avail themselves of the federal rule. And, without even change of residence, a corporate citizen of the state could avail itself of the federal rule by reincorporating under the laws of another state, as was done in the Taxicab Case.

The injustice and confusion incident to the doctrine of Swift v. Tyson have been repeatedly urged as reasons for abolishing or limiting diversity of citizenship jurisdiction. Other legislative relief has been proposed. If only a question of statutory construction were involved, we should not be prepared to abandon a doctrine so widely applied throughout nearly a century. But the unconstitutionality of the course pursued has now been made clear, and compels us to do so.

Third. Except in matters governed by the Federal Constitution or by acts of Congress, the law to be applied in any case is the law of the state. And whether the law of the state shall be declared by its Legislature in a statute or by its highest court in a decision is not a matter of federal concern. There is no federal general common law. Congress has no power to declare substantive rules of common law applicable in a state whether they be local in their nature or "general," be they commercial law or a part of the law of torts. And no clause in the Constitution purports to confer such a power upon the federal courts. As stated by Mr. Justice Field when protesting in Baltimore & Ohio R. Co. v. Baugh, 149 U.S. 368, 401 [(1893)], against ignoring the Ohio common law of fellow-servant liability: "I am aware that what has been termed the general law of the country—which is often little less than what the judge advancing the doctrine thinks at the time should be the general law on a particular subject—has been often advanced in judicial opinions of this court to control a conflicting law of a state. I admit that learned judges have fallen into the habit of repeating this doctrine as a convenient mode of brushing aside the law of a state in conflict with their views. And I confess that, moved and governed by the authority of the great names of those judges, I have, myself, in many instances, unhesitatingly and confidently, but I think now erroneously, repeated the same doctrine. But, notwithstanding the great names which may be cited in favor of the doctrine, and notwithstanding the frequency with which the doctrine has been reiterated, there stands, as a perpetual protest against its repetition, the constitution of the United States, which recognizes and preserves the autonomy and independence of the States—independence in their legislative and independence in their judicial departments. Supervision over either the legislative or the judicial action of the states is in no case permissible except as to matters by the constitution specifically authorized or delegated to the United States. Any interference with either, except as thus permitted, is an invasion of the authority of the state, and, to that extent, a denial of its independence."

The fallacy underlying the rule declared in Swift v. Tyson is made clear by Mr. Justice Holmes. The doctrine rests upon the assumption that there is "a transcendental body of law outside of any particular State but obligatory within it unless and until changed by statute," that federal courts have the power to use their judgment as to what the rules of common law are; and that in the federal courts "the parties are entitled to an independent judgment on matters of general law":

"But law in the sense in which courts speak of it today does not exist without some definite authority behind it. The common law so far as it is enforced in a State, whether called common law or not, is not the common law generally but the law of that State existing by the authority of that State without regard to what it may have been in England or anywhere else. * * *

"The authority and only authority is the State, and if that be so, the voice adopted by the State as its own [whether it be of its Legislature or of its Supreme Court] should utter the last word."

Thus the doctrine of Swift v. Tyson is, as Mr. Justice Holmes said, "an unconstitutional assumption of powers by the Courts of the United States which no lapse of time or respectable array of opinion should make us hesitate to correct." In disapproving that doctrine we do not hold unconstitutional section 34 of the Federal Judiciary Act of 1789 or any other act of Congress. We merely declare that in applying the doctrine this Court and the lower courts have invaded rights which in our opinion are reserved by the Constitution to the several states.

Fourth. The defendant contended that by the common law of Pennsylvania * * *, the only duty owed to the plaintiff was to refrain from willful or wanton injury. The plaintiff denied that such is the Pennsylvania law. * * * The Circuit Court of Appeals ruled that the question of liability is one of general law; and on that ground declined to decide the issue of state law. As we hold this was error, the judgment is reversed and the case remanded to it for further proceedings in conformity with our opinion.

Reversed.

■ [JUSTICE REED delivered a concurring opinion joining "in the conclusions reached in this case, in the disapproval of the doctrine of Swift v. Tyson, and in the reasoning of the majority opinion except in so far as it relies upon the unconstitutionality of the 'course pursued' by the federal courts." JUSTICE BUTLER dissented in an opinion in which JUSTICE MCREYNOLDS joined. JUSTICE CARDOZO did not participate.]

NOTE ON THE RATIONALE OF THE ERIE DECISION

(1) The "First" Ground of Decision. Under its *"First"* heading, the Court relies heavily on Warren, *New Light on the History of the Federal Judiciary Act of 1789*, 37 Harv.L.Rev. 49, 51–52, 81–88, 108 (1923). In that article Warren notes that § 34 was "not contained in the Draft Bill, as introduced in the Senate, but was proposed, probably by [Senator, later Chief Justice] Ellsworth, as an amendment * * *." Warren's examination of the records of the Senate revealed a slip of paper, believed to be in Ellsworth's handwriting, on which an earlier version of the amendment (including the italicized material in the following quotation) was written:

> "And be it further enacted, That the *Statute law of the several states in force for the time being and their unwritten or common law now in use, whether by adoption from the common law of England, the ancient statutes of the same or otherwise*, except where the Constitution, Treaties or Statutes of the United States shall otherwise require or provide, shall be regarded as rules of decision in the trials at common law in the courts of the United States in cases where they apply."

Warren's conclusion, endorsed by the Court in Erie, was that in light of the earlier draft, the phrase "laws of the several states" (which Ellsworth had written in as a substitute for the italicized phrase) was designed to cover unwritten law. That conclusion has been widely criticized on the ground that the change of language in the later draft might have been designed to alter rather than replicate the meaning of the earlier draft. See Nelson, *A Critical Guide to Erie Railroad Co. v. Tompkins*, 54 Wm. & Mary L.Rev. 921, 954–56 & n.104 (2013), and sources cited.

(2) The "Second" Ground. Under his "*Second*" heading, Justice Brandeis emphasized the "grave discrimination by noncitizens against citizens" introduced by the Swift decision. The point is oddly phrased, since every citizen of a state is a noncitizen of other states. Moreover, the Court seems to suggest that only noncitizens of a state may invoke diversity jurisdiction. This is true of removal but not of original jurisdiction, and the statutory ban on removal by in-state defendants, see 28 U.S.C. § 1441(b)(2), could be eliminated by Congress. The discrimination that Brandeis may have had in mind was that an out-of-state plaintiff could choose to file in federal court if the general law there was favorable, or in state court, where the in-state defendant could not remove, if general law there was more favorable.

The Court's related claim that the Swift approach "rendered impossible equal protection of the law" probably does not refer to the Equal Protection Clause, which is directed at the states, and did not apply to the federal government under the Fifth Amendment's Due Process Clause until 1954, see Bolling v. Sharpe, 347 U.S. 497 (1954). The Court thus may have had a different equal protection concern in mind—the idea that a diverse plaintiff could choose the most helpful governing law for an event after the event occurred on the basis of a strategic choice between federal or state court.[1] Compare Hart, *The Relations Between State and Federal Law*, 54 Colum.L.Rev. 489, 505 (1954) (observing that the Swift regime "subject[ed] citizens at the crucial level of everyday activity to dual and often inconsistent systems of substantive law, without means of foretelling which system, in the unforeseeable contingency of litigation, was going to apply").

A different "defect" of the Swift doctrine that Justice Brandeis discusses is the murkiness of the distinction between general and local unwritten law. Erie replaced this problem with a different murky distinction between substance and procedure.[2] See pp. 789–809, *infra*. See also Sherry, *Wrong, Out of Step, and Pernicious: Erie as the Worst Decision of All Time*, 39 Pepp.L.Rev. 129, 141–42 (2011).

Yet another "defect" of the Swift regime the Court identified was the disuniformity between state and federal courts in the content of general law and the resulting opportunities for forum shopping, as evinced in the Taxicab case. But as many have noted, Erie (combined with its important extension in Klaxon Co. v. Stentor Elec. Mfg. Co., Inc., 313 U.S. 487 (1941), see p. 768, *infra*) secured vertical uniformity on state law interpretations between federal and state courts in the same state at the expense of potential

---

[1] Note that the Erie holding and rationale are not limited to issues arising in litigation between citizens of different states. Consider, for example, a state law claim, joined to a federal law claim, that a federal court hears under its supplemental jurisdiction. The Supreme Court has suggested that Erie applies to the interpretation of the supplemental state law claim, see United Mine Workers of America v. Gibbs, 383 U.S. 715, 726 (1966), and that is the dominate approach in the lower courts, see Reinert, *Erie Step Zero*, 85 Fordham L.Rev. 2341, 2352–55 (2017) (collecting lower court cases). Professor Reinert challenges this conventional wisdom. See *id.* 2367–83.

[2] The Conformity Act, see pp. 733–734, *supra*, had required federal courts generally to follow state practice and procedure in actions at law, and thus to distinguish practice and procedure from substance (on which it might follow the general common law). Congress repealed the Act in 1948.

horizontal non-uniformity on governing law among federal courts. See Nelson, Paragraph (1), *supra*, at 964–70.

However valid the defects of the Swift regime cited by Erie may have been, the perceived existence of the defects, and their seeming reflection of the pro-business biases of federal courts, ignited a political storm in the decades prior to Erie that the Court alludes to when it talks about Swift's "injustice and confusion" leading to proposals in Congress to limit or eliminate diversity jurisdiction. See p. 762, *supra*.

(3) The "Third" Ground. Controversy has surrounded the scope and meaning of Erie's constitutional holding from the beginning.[3] The Court refers to the "unconstitutionality of the course pursued" but does "not hold unconstitutional section 34 of the Federal Judiciary Act of 1789 or any other act of Congress." Rather, it rules (with emphasis added) that in "applying the [Swift] doctrine" the "*Court and the lower courts* have invaded rights which in our opinion are reserved by the Constitution to the several states." Presumably this is a reference to the Tenth Amendment.

Despite the Court's reference to the judiciary invading the rights of states, some have argued that Erie holds that Congress or the federal government as a whole lacked the authority to draft a rule of decision to govern a case like Erie.[4] It is true that under the Swift regime, federal courts determined the substantive law to govern some matters that Congress, under the prevailing constitutional wisdom of the time, would have lacked the power to regulate. But even if in 1938 Congress would not have possessed authority to enact legislation purporting to govern the rights of a trespasser solely on the basis that the case was brought in a federal court (especially under the diversity jurisdiction), there was little doubt that Congress had power to prescribe a narrower rule of decision to govern the rights of trespassers on railroads whose activities affect interstate commerce.

The Court's statement that *federal courts* have invaded the rights of the states has drawn attention to the absence of power in the federal courts, in particular to declare rules of common law. On this view, which sounds more in separation of powers, the problem is that federal courts lack lawmaking power unless conferred by Congress or the Constitution, and neither source had authorized federal courts to develop common law in diversity cases.[5] Or as Erie put it in the first sentence under the third category, "Except in matters governed by the Federal Constitution or by acts of Congress, the law to be applied in any case is the law of the state."

Many other explanations of Erie's constitutional holding have been advanced.[6] Is it possible that both Swift and Erie were correctly decided, but

---

[3]   See generally Wright & Kane, Federal Courts § 56 and n.65 (8th ed.2017); Chemerinsky, Federal Jurisdiction § 5.3.5 and n.161 (8th ed.2021).

[4]   See, *e.g.*, Sherry, Paragraph (2), *supra*, at 143–44.

[5]   See Mishkin, *Some Further Last Words on Erie—The Thread*, 87 Harv.L.Rev. 1682, 1683–86 (1974); Young, *A General Defense of Erie Railroad Co. v. Tompkins*, 10 J.L.Econ. & Pol'y 17, 68–76 (2013).

[6]   Prominent scholarship on Erie's constitutional holding, beyond sources already mentioned in this Note, include Clark, *Erie's Constitutional Source*, 95 Calif.L.Rev. 1289 (2007); Ely, *The Irrepressible Myth of Erie*, 87 Harv.L.Rev. 693, 695 (1974); Green, *Erie and Problems of Constitutional Structure*, 96 Calif.L.Rev. 661 (2008); Roosevelt, *Valid Rule Due Process*

that changes occurring over the roughly 100 years between them—expansion of the reach of Swift, growing disuniformity, and decision-making by the federal judges that reflected their own views of policy rather than an effort to capture "the general law" as commonly understood, as well as the nature and sources of law[7]—called for different outcomes?[8]

---

3. THE "ERIE DOCTRINE"

INTRODUCTORY NOTE

Erie marked a revolution in federal courts law that had implications across numerous doctrines in this book. This section examines elements of what is sometimes called the "Erie doctrine": how federal courts should ascertain governing state law under Erie; how Erie applies in equity; how courts should determine whether a legal issue that is not obviously substantive should be governed by state law; and the relationship between the Federal Rules of Civil Procedure and Erie.

Challenges: Bond v. United States and Erie's Constitutional Source, 54 Wm. & Mary L.Rev. 987, 999–1000 (2013); Nielson, *Erie as Nondelegation*, 72 Ohio St.L.J. 239 (2011). For some of the better symposia on Erie, see 52 Akron L.Rev. 193–213 (2018); 10 J.L.Econ. & Pol'y. 1–299 (2013); see also Symposium, 83 Notre Dame L.Rev. No. 4 (2008).

[7]   See Casto, *The Erie Doctrine and the Structure of Constitutional Revolutions*, 62 Tul.L.Rev. 907 (1998) (relating the overruling of Swift to changes in the prevailing intellectual and jurisprudential climate); but see Goldsmith & Walt, *Erie and the Irrelevance of Legal Positivism*, 84 Va.L.Rev. 673 (1998) (arguing that Erie cannot be explained by changes of jurisprudence).

[8]   Despite Erie's declaration that there is "no federal general common law," many scholars have argued that something akin to general law persists even after Erie and can legitimately be applied by federal courts despite Erie. See Nelson, *The Legitimacy of (Some) Federal Common Law*, 101 Va.L.Rev. 1 (2015) (arguing that federal courts apply something akin to transjurisdictional customary practices that do not implicate separation of powers concerns because judges are not engaged in open-ended judicial lawmaking); Bellia & Clark, *General Law in Federal Court*, 54 Wm. & Mary L.Rev. 655, 706–23 (2013) (arguing that federal courts can, consistent with Erie, apply general law related especially to the law of nations in areas where states have no authority); see also Sachs, *Finding Law*, 107 Calif.L.Rev. 527 (2019) (seeking to revive the view "that unwritten law can be found, rather than made," and arguing that Erie was a "blunder" that "undermined the states' efforts" to adopt a general common law as their own law, and that unduly encouraged federal courts to recognize a category of "so-called" federal common law).

A. DIVINING STATE LAW

NOTE ON KLAXON AND PROBLEMS OF HORIZONTAL CHOICE OF LAW IN CASES INVOLVING STATE-CREATED RIGHTS

(1) The Klaxon Decision. The Erie decision assumed that, on remand, a New York federal court should apply Pennsylvania law in the case before it. This assumption must have been grounded on a further assumption: Either (i) a New York state court would apply Pennsylvania law on the facts of Erie, or (ii) the federal court gets to decide *which* state's law applied, even in a diversity case. The Court clarified this matter definitively in Klaxon Co. v. Stentor Elec. Mfg. Co., 313 U.S. 487 (1941), a diversity action brought in a Delaware federal court for breach of an agreement executed in New York and partially performed there. "The principal question in this case," said the Court, "is whether in diversity cases the federal courts must follow conflict of laws rules prevailing in the states in which they sit." The Court unanimously ruled that the federal court in Delaware must apply the rule that a Delaware state court would apply, and that the Full Faith and Credit Clause did not require Delaware to look to New York law on the issue of interest. On the first of these questions, the Court said:

"Any other ruling would do violence to the principle of uniformity within a state, upon which the Tompkins decision is based. Whatever lack of uniformity this may produce between federal courts in different states is attributable to our federal system, which leaves to a state, within the limits permitted by the Constitution, the right to pursue local policies diverging from those of its neighbors. It is not for the federal courts to thwart such local policies by enforcing an independent 'general law' of conflict of laws. Subject only to review by this Court on any federal question that may arise, Delaware is free to determine whether a given matter is to be governed by the law of the forum or some other law. * * * And the proper function of the Delaware federal court is to ascertain what the state law is, not what it ought to be."

(2) Klaxon and the Constitution. Assuming that the right to prejudgment interest at issue in Klaxon is governed by state law under Erie, the choice of *which* state's law applies in a federal court is surely a matter of federal concern that Congress could regulate under some combination of its powers to regulate interstate commerce, to make laws "necessary and proper" to the exercise of jurisdiction under Article III, and to "prescribe * * * the Effect" of the "public Acts, Records, and judicial Proceedings" of one state in another under Article IV. See Gottesman, *Draining the Dismal Swamp: The Case for Federal Choice of Law Statutes,* 80 Geo.L.J. 1, 16–28 (1991); Jackson, *Full Faith and Credit—The Lawyer's Clause of the Constitution,* 45 Colum.L.Rev. 1, 12 (1945). This conclusion is buttressed by the fact that at least in civil cases, the Constitution does not prohibit the territorial jurisdiction of the federal district courts from cutting across state boundaries. If Congress were to eliminate the district courts of New York and Delaware, and to create a single "Federal District Court for the Middle

Atlantic States," the Klaxon rule could not operate. See Hill, *The Erie Doctrine and the Constitution*, 53 Nw.U.L.Rev. 541, 558 (1958).

But it is a harder question whether federal courts have independent authority after Erie to develop federal choice-of-law rules in diversity cases. The implicit logic of Klaxon appears to be that choice-of-law rules for substantive state law matters are themselves deemed substantive law for Erie purposes, perhaps because the Court reads Erie to establish a "principle of uniformity within a state." The Court would qualify this "principle of uniformity" in later cases in the Erie line. See Hanna v. Plumer, 380 U.S. 460 (1965), p. 792, *infra*. Yet despite much criticism, the Court has never deviated from the basic rule in Klaxon.[1] See, *e.g.*, Atlantic Marine Constr. Co. v. U.S. Dist. Ct., 571 U.S. 49, 65 (2013); Day & Zimmermann, Inc. v. Challoner, 423 U.S. 3, 4 (1975).

Klaxon achieves vertical uniformity between state and federal courts at the expense of horizontal uniformity among federal courts on choice-of-law issues. While it might thus discourage forum shopping between federal and state courts within a state, it encourages forum shopping among federal courts sitting in different states. Is it more likely that forum shopping for a favorable choice-of-law rule would occur within a given state or among states? To what extent is horizontal disuniformity among state courts, and under Klaxon, among federal courts sitting in different states, not only inevitable but the very "*essence* of a federal system"? Young, *A General Defense of Erie Railroad Co. v. Tompkins*, 10 J.L.Econ. & Pol'y 17, 45 (2013).

(3) Existing Constitutional Limits on Horizontal Choice of Law. The Due Process and Full Faith and Credit Clauses place some limitations, but not strict ones, on the choice of law by state courts. Compare, *e.g.*, Phillips Petroleum Co. v. Shutts, 472 U.S. 797, 821–22 (1985) (since state lacks "significant contact or significant aggregation of contacts" with respect to claims of many members of plaintiff class, application of that state's law to those claims "is sufficiently arbitrary and unfair as to exceed constitutional limits"), with, *e.g.*, Allstate Ins. Co. v. Hague, 449 U.S. 302 (1981), and cases cited therein; Sun Oil Co. v. Wortman, 486 U.S. 717 (1988) (holding that the forum state could constitutionally apply its own, relatively long statute of limitations to claims as to which, under Shutts, it could not apply its own substantive law). Federal courts are controlled by the same limitations in

---

[1] For criticism, see, *e.g.*, Rosen, *Choice-of-Law as Non-Constitutional Federal Law*, 99 Minn.L. Rev. 1017, 1020–22 (2015); Wolff, *Choice of Law and Jurisdictional Policy in the Federal Courts*, 165 U.Pa.L.Rev. 1847, 1848–49, 1878–91 (2017); Roosevelt, *Choice of Law in Federal Courts: From Erie and Klaxon to CAFA and Shady Grove*, 106 Nw.U.L.Rev. 1, 17–23 (2012); Erbsen, *Erie's Four Functions: Reframing Choice of Law in Federal Courts*, 89 Notre Dame L.Rev. 579, 638–46 (2013); Laycock, *Equal Citizens of Equal and Territorial States: The Constitutional Foundations of Choice of Law*, 92 Colum.L.Rev. 249, 282 (1992); Childress, *When Erie Goes International*, 105 Nw.U.L.Rev. 1531 (2011). For defenders, see, *e.g.*, Clopton, *Horizontal Choice of Law In Federal Court*, 169 U.Pa.L.Rev. 2193 (2021); Parry, *Some Realism about Choice of Law Statutes and the Common Law: The Oregon Example*, 27 Lewis & Clark L.Rev. 197 (2023); Bradt, *Atlantic Marine and Choice-of-Law Federalism*, 66 Hastings L.J. 617 (2015); Slovin, *Stipulating to Overturn Klaxon*, 97 N.Y.U.L.Rev. 127 (2022); Cavers, *The Changing Choice-of-Law Process and the Federal Courts*, 28 L. & Contemp.Probs. 732 (1963); Ely, *The Irrepressible Myth of Erie*, 87 Harv.L.Rev. 693, 714–15 n.125 (1974).

administering the Klaxon doctrine—at least to the extent those limitations derive from the Due Process Clauses.

(4) Klaxon and Transfer of Venue. The Court has developed a qualification to Klaxon in actions that are transferred to another federal court under 28 U.S.C. § 1404(a), which provides that "[f]or the convenience of parties and witnesses, in the interest of justice, a district court may transfer any civil action to any other district or division where it might have been brought." In Van Dusen v. Barrack, 376 U.S. 612 (1964), the Court held in a case involving a § 1404 transfer that the transferee court must apply the choice-of-law rules followed by courts in the transferor state. The defendants in that case were seeking the transfer, and the law of the transferee state would have been more favorable to them. "The legislative history of § 1404(a)," the Court said, "certainly does not justify the rather startling conclusion that one might 'get a change of law as a bonus for a change of venue.' " See also Ferens v. John Deere Co., 494 U.S. 516 (1990) (holding that the transferor state's law governs in *all* cases transferred under § 1404, whether the transfer is initiated by the plaintiff, the defendant, or the court).

In Atlantic Marine Constr. Co. v. U.S. Dist. Ct., 571 U.S. 49 (2013), the Court recognized a significant exception to the Van Dusen choice-of-law principle. Atlantic Marine held that when a transfer of venue under § 1404 is made on the basis of a valid forum selection clause, the transferee court should apply the choice-of-law rules of the state in which it sits. The Court explained that the "policies motivating our exception [in Van Dusen] to the Klaxon rule for § 1404(a) transfers" did not apply because, in contrast with Van Dusen, a plaintiff who files suit in violation of a valid forum selection clause enjoys no "venue privilege" and thus is not entitled to "concomitant 'state-law advantages.' " Atlantic Marine assumed that the forum selection clause was valid and thus left open what law governs that question when the underlying claim is based on state law. For academic treatments of the issue, compare Steinman, *Atlantic Marine Through the Lens of Erie*, 66 Hastings L.J. 795, 804–19 (2015) (suggesting that Erie and Klaxon compel application of state law), with Sachs, *The Forum Selection Defense*, 10 Duke J.Const.L. & Pub.Pol'y 1, 14–26 (2014) (arguing that a range of federal interests justifies development of federal common law). For an argument that courts administering multidistrict litigation proceedings under 28 U.S.C. § 1407 should apply the choice-of-law rules of transferor courts notwithstanding the presence of a forum selection clause and the holding of Atlantic Marine, see Bock, *All Disputes Must Be Brought Here: Atlantic Marine and the Future of Multidistrict Litigation*, 106 Calif.L.Rev. 1657 (2018).

(5) The Applicability of Klaxon in Other Special Circumstances.

(a) In Griffin v. McCoach, 313 U.S. 498 (1941), decided the same day as Klaxon, the Court held that the forum state's choice-of-law rules must be applied in a statutory interpleader case.

(b) Scholars and some lower courts have questioned the applicability of the Klaxon rule to state-law issues that arise in bankruptcy, see, *e.g.,* Cross, *State Choice of Law Rules in Bankruptcy*, 42 Okla.L.Rev. 531 (1989), in cases under the Class Action Fairness Act of 2005 (CAFA), see, *e.g.,* Wolff, note 1, *supra*, and in cases subject to the multidistrict litigation statute, see, *e.g.*, Atwood, *The Choice-of-Law Dilemma in Mass Tort Litigation: Kicking Around Erie, Klaxon, and Van Dusen*, 19 Conn.L.Rev. 9 (1986). For a robust defense of the Klaxon rule in these and other special contexts, see Clopton, note 1, *supra*.

(c) In Cassirer v. Thyssen-Bornemisza Collection Foundation, 596 U.S. 107 (2022), a unanimous Supreme Court, in an opinion by Justice Kagan, followed the "long-settled precedent" in Klaxon and held that under § 1606 of the Foreign Sovereign Immunities Act, state choice-of-law rules determine which non-federal property law governs the dispute. The Court "express[ed] no view" on whether or when federal law might limit the application of state choice-of-law rules in an "unusual case" where their application "created foreign relations concerns." For contrasting views on the need for, and extent of, federal preemption of state choice-of-law rules when the choice-of-law question is international in scope, see Childress, note 1, *supra* (contending that, contrary to Day & Zimmerman, Inc. v. Challoner, 423 U.S. 3 (1975), federal courts should develop "specialized federal common law in international conflict-of-laws cases"), with Green, *Erie's International Effect*, 107 Nw.U.L.Rev. 1485 (2013) (arguing that the need for federal preemption in international choice-of-law cases should be based solely on the existence of a federal interest and that the existence of such an interest is likely to be rare).

NOTE ON THE WAYS OF ASCERTAINING STATE LAW

(1) Unresolved Questions of State Law. If a federal court confronts a question of state law not plainly resolved by the state's highest court, a range of issues can arise, including what weight should be given to state lower court decisions or to dicta in state decisions, even from the highest state court. There are also questions about whether the federal court should assume the same sense of responsibility for the creative development of law that a state court would have, and whether a federal court may disregard an applicable decision of the highest state court on the basis that the state court would not follow it today.

(2) Lower State Court Decisions. Two years after Erie, the Supreme Court held, in Fidelity Union Trust Co. v. Field, 311 U.S. 169 (1940), that a federal court in New Jersey was bound to follow a decision of the New Jersey Court of Chancery, a trial court of state-wide jurisdiction, "in the absence of more convincing evidence of what the state law is." But eight years after the Fidelity Union decision, in King v. Order of United Commercial Travelers, 333 U.S. 153 (1948), the Court unanimously upheld the refusal of a federal court of appeals to follow an unreported decision of a South Carolina court of common pleas (a trial court of limited territorial jurisdiction).

Eight years later, in Bernhardt v. Polygraphic Co., 350 U.S. 198 (1956), the Supreme Court had to determine whether a 1910 Vermont Supreme Court decision represented the state law on the question in 1956. The United States Supreme Court held that it did, stating: "Were the question in doubt

* * *, we would of course remand the case to the Court of Appeals to pass on this question of Vermont law. But * * * there appears to be no confusion in the Vermont decisions, no developing line of authorities that casts a shadow over the established ones, no dicta, doubts or ambiguities in the opinions of Vermont judges on the question, no legislative development that promises to undermine the judicial rule."

Wright and Kane, summarizing the state of the law since King and Bernhardt, say that a federal judge "no longer need be a ventriloquist's dummy. Instead he or she is free, just as state judges are, to consider all the data the highest court of the state would use in an effort to determine how the highest court of the state would decide." Wright & Kane, Federal Courts § 58, at 356 (8th ed.2017). A widely cited court of appeals decision states the test as follows: "a federal court attempting to forecast state law must consider relevant state precedents, analogous decisions, considered dicta, scholarly works, and any other reliable data tending convincingly to show how the highest court in the state would decide the issue at hand." McKenna v. Ortho Pharmaceutical Corp, 622 F.2d 657, 663 (3d Cir.1980).

But a welter of issues lies behind these general statements. Should a federal court (as some do) follow federal circuit precedent on the meaning of state law, even when one or more intervening state appellate court decisions have taken a different view? Should a federal trial court seek to predict how the state's highest court would rule in a state whose trial courts would not do so but instead would follow precedent of a state intermediate court? Insofar as different states articulate different approaches for their courts at various levels to address unsettled questions, should a federal court in a diversity case seek to mirror the practice and allocation of responsibility of the particular state in which it sits? See Erbsen, *Erie's Four Functions: Reframing Choice of Law in Federal Courts*, 89 Notre Dame L.Rev. 579, 646–59 (2013); Clark, *Ascertaining the Laws of the Several States: Positivism and Judicial Federalism After Erie*, 145 U.Pa.L.Rev. 1459 (1997).[1]

(3) Abstention and Other Refusals to Decide State Law Questions. In some cases, a federal court will abstain from determining a state law question because of the question's uncertainty and difficulty. Relatedly, nearly every state authorizes its highest court to answer questions that federal appellate courts, and often federal district courts, refer to it via certification procedures. For discussion of the use of abstention and certification by federal courts, see Chap. X, Sec. 2, *infra*.

---

[1]   There are also important questions, related to the questions in the text, concerning whether federal courts, in applying state statutory law, should follow the rules of statutory interpretation adopted by the courts of the relevant state. Gluck, *Intersystemic Statutory Interpretation: Methodology as "Law" and the Erie Doctrine*, 120 Yale L.J. 1898 (2011), criticizes the failure of most federal courts to recognize that the interpretive rules adopted by a state are integral to its substantive law. For her further exploration of the question of interpretive methodology, see Gluck, *The Federal Common Law of Statutory Interpretation: Erie for the Age of Statutes*, 54 Wm. & Mary L.Rev. 753 (2013). But see Bruhl, *Interpreting State Statutes in Federal Court*, 98 Notre Dame L.Rev. 61 (2022) (challenging some of Gluck's findings and arguing that federal courts do and should (with a few exceptions) employ state methods of interpretation when interpreting state statutes).

(4) Appellate Review of District Court Decisions. In Salve Regina College v. Russell, 499 U.S. 225 (1991), the Court held that a federal court of appeals should provide de novo review of the district court's determination of state law. The opinion relied not only on the traditional scope of review on questions of law and the "reflective dialogue and collective judgment" that attend appellate consideration, but also on the purposes of the Erie doctrine—to discourage forum shopping and to avoid inequitable administration of the laws. "[D]eferential appellate review," the Court said, "invites divergent development of state law among the federal trial courts even within a single State."

Is the rule of Salve Regina required by Erie? If not, is it preferable to a rule that in the absence of a conflict among district court decisions in a district, the circuit court will ordinarily defer to the district court's understanding of the content of local law—an interpretation usually rendered by a judge who hails from the state in question? See Nash, *Resuscitating Deference to Lower Federal Court Judges' Interpretations of State Law*, 77 S.Calif.L.Rev. 975 (2004).

B. STATE LAW AND FEDERAL EQUITY

Guaranty Trust Co. v. York
326 U.S. 99 (1945).
Certiorari to the Circuit Court of Appeals for the Second Circuit.

■ MR. JUSTICE FRANKFURTER delivered the opinion of the Court.

[Petitioner Guaranty Trust Co. was trustee for the holders of notes issued by a corporation. When it became apparent that the corporation could not meet its obligations on the notes, Guaranty negotiated an offer of exchange for less than the face value of the notes. After the offer had expired, respondent York, a noteholder, brought a diversity action against Guaranty in a New York federal court.]

The suit, instituted as a class action on behalf of non-accepting noteholders * * *, is based on an alleged breach of trust by Guaranty in that it failed to protect the interests of the noteholders in assenting to the exchange offer and failed to disclose its self-interest when sponsoring the offer. Petitioner moved for summary judgment, which was granted * * *. On appeal, the Circuit Court of Appeals, one Judge dissenting, * * * held that in a suit brought on the equity side of a federal district court that court is not required to apply the State statute of limitations that would govern like suits in the courts of a State where the federal court is sitting even though the exclusive basis of federal jurisdiction is diversity of citizenship. The importance of the question for the disposition of litigation in the federal courts led us to bring the case here. * * *

Our starting point must be the policy of federal jurisdiction which Erie R. Co. v. Tompkins, 304 U.S. 64 [(1938)], embodies. In overruling Swift v. Tyson, [41 U.S. (16 Pet.) 1 (1842)], Erie did not merely overrule a venerable case. It overruled a particular way of looking at law which dominated the judicial process long after its inadequacies had been laid bare. Law was conceived as a 'brooding omnipresence' of Reason, of which decisions were merely evidence and not themselves the controlling formulations. Accordingly, federal courts deemed themselves free to ascertain what Reason, and therefore Law, required wholly independent of authoritatively declared State law, even in cases where a legal right as the basis for relief was created by State authority and could not be created by federal authority and the case got into a federal court merely because it was 'between Citizens of different States' under Art. III, of the Constitution of the United States. * * *

In relation to the problem now here, the real significance of Swift v. Tyson lies in the fact that it did not enunciate novel doctrine. Nor was it restricted to its particular situation. It summed up prior attitudes and expressions in cases that had come before this Court and lower federal courts for at least thirty years, at law as well as in equity.[1] The short of it is that the doctrine was congenial to the jurisprudential climate of the time. Once established, judicial momentum kept it going. Since it was conceived that there was 'a transcendental body of law outside of any particular State but obligatory within it unless and until changed by statute', [Black & White Taxi. Co. v. B. & Y. Taxi. Co., 276 U.S. 518, 532 (1928) (Holmes, J., dissenting)], State court decisions were not 'the law' but merely someone's opinion—to be sure an opinion to be respected— concerning the content of this all-pervading law. Not unnaturally, the federal courts assumed power to find for themselves the content of such a body of law. The notion was stimulated by the attractive vision of a uniform body of federal law. To such sentiments for uniformity of decision and freedom from diversity in State law the federal courts gave currency, particularly in cases where equitable remedies were sought, because equitable doctrines are so often cast in terms of universal applicability when close analysis of the source of legal enforceability is not demanded.

In exercising their jurisdiction on the ground of diversity of citizenship, the federal courts, in the long course of their history, have not differentiated in their regard for State law between actions at law and suits in equity. Although § 34 of the Judiciary Act of 1789 directed that the "laws of the several States * * * shall be regarded as rules of decision in trials of common law * * *," this was deemed, consistently for

---

[1] In Russell v. Southard, 12 How. 139, 147 (1851), Mr. Justice Curtis, refusing to be bound by Kentucky law barring the reception of oral evidence to show that an absolute bill of sale was in reality a mortgage, declared that "upon the principles of general equity jurisprudence, this court must be governed by its own views of those principles." To support this statement, he cited, among others, Robinson v. Campbell, 3 Wheat. 212 (1818); Boyle v. Zacharie and Turner, 6 Pet. 648 (1832), and Swift v. Tyson, *supra. T*his commingling of law and equity cases indicates that the same views governed both and that Swift v. Tyson was merely another expression of the ideas put forth in the equity cases.

over a hundred years, to be merely declaratory of what would in any event have governed the federal courts and therefore was equally applicable to equity suits. Indeed, it may fairly be said that the federal courts gave greater respect to State-created "substantive rights," Pusey & Jones Co. v. Hanssen, 261 U.S. 491, 498 (1923), in equity than they gave them on the law side, because rights at law were usually declared by State courts and as such increasingly flouted by extension of the doctrine of Swift v. Tyson, while rights in equity were frequently defined by legislative enactment and as such known and respected by the federal courts.

Partly because the States in the early days varied greatly in the manner in which equitable relief was afforded and in the extent to which it was available, * * * Congress provided that "the forms and modes of proceeding in suits * * * of equity" would conform to the settled uses of courts of equity. Section 2, 1 Stat. 275, 276. But this enactment gave the federal courts no power that they would not have had in any event when courts were given "cognizance," by the first Judiciary Act, of suits "in equity." From the beginning there has been a good deal of talk in the cases that federal equity is a separate legal system. And so it is, properly understood. The suits in equity of which the federal courts have had "cognizance" ever since 1789 constituted the body of law which had been transplanted to this country from the English Court of Chancery. But this system of equity "derived its doctrines, as well as its powers, from its mode of giving relief." Langdell, Summary of Equity Pleading (1877) xxvii. * * * Congress never gave, nor did the federal courts ever claim, the power to deny substantive rights created by State law or to create substantive rights denied by State law.

This does not mean that whatever equitable remedy is available in a State court must be available in a diversity suit in a federal court, or conversely, that a federal court may not afford an equitable remedy not available in a State court. Equitable relief in a federal court is of course subject to restrictions: the suit must be within the traditional scope of equity as historically evolved in the English Court of Chancery, Payne v. Hook, 7 Wall. 425, 430 [(1868)]; a plain, adequate and complete remedy at law must be wanting, § 16, 1 Stat. 73, 82, 28 U.S.C. § 384; explicit Congressional curtailment of equity powers must be respected; the constitutional right to trial by jury cannot be evaded, Whitehead v. Shattuck, 138 U.S. 146 [(1891)]. That a State may authorize its courts to give equitable relief unhampered by any or all such restrictions cannot remove these fetters from the federal courts. State law cannot define the remedies which a federal court must give simply because a federal court in diversity jurisdiction is available as an alternative tribunal to the State's courts.[3] Contrariwise, a federal court may afford an equitable

---

[3]   In Pusey & Jones Co. v. Hanssen, 261 U.S. 491 (1923), the Court had to decide whether a Delaware statute had created a new right appropriate for enforcement in accordance with traditional equity practice or whether the statute had merely given the Delaware Chancery Court a new kind of remedy. * * * [T]he Court construed the Delaware statute merely to extend

remedy for a substantive right recognized by a State even though a State court cannot give it. Whatever contradiction or confusion may be produced by a medley of judicial phrases severed from their environment, the body of adjudications concerning equitable relief in diversity cases leaves no doubt that the federal courts enforced State-created substantive rights if the mode of proceeding and remedy were consonant with the traditional body of equitable remedies, practice and procedure, and in so doing they were enforcing rights created by the States and not arising under any inherent or statutory federal law.

Inevitably, therefore, the principle of Erie R. Co. v. Tompkins, an action at law, was promptly applied to a suit in equity. Ruhlin v. New York Life Ins. Co., 304 U.S. 202 [(1938)].

And so this case reduces itself to the narrow question whether, when no recovery could be had in a State court because the action is barred by the statute of limitations, a federal court in equity can take cognizance of the suit because there is diversity of citizenship between the parties. Is the outlawry, according to State law, of a claim created by the States a matter of "substantive rights" to be respected by a federal court of equity when that court's jurisdiction is dependent on the fact that there is a State-created right, or is such statute of "a mere remedial character," Henrietta Mills v. Rutherford Co., [281 U.S. 121, 128 (1930)], which a federal court may disregard?

Matters of "substance" and matters of "procedure" are much talked about in the books as though they defined a great divide cutting across the whole domain of law. But, of course, "substance" and "procedure" are the same key-words to very different problems. Neither "substance" nor "procedure" represents the same invariants. Each implies different variables depending upon the particular problem for which it is used. And the different problems are only distantly related at best, for the terms are in common use in connection with situations turning on such different considerations as those that are relevant to questions pertaining to ex post facto legislation, the impairment of the obligations of contract, the enforcement of federal rights in the State courts and the multitudinous phases of the conflict of laws. * * *

Here we are dealing with a right to recover derived not from the United States but from one of the States. When * * * such a right is enforceable in a federal as well as in a State court, the forms and mode of enforcing the right may at times, naturally enough, vary because the two judicial systems are not identic. But since a federal court adjudicating a state-created right solely because of the diversity of citizenship of the parties is for that purpose, in effect, only another court

---

the power to an equity court to appoint a receiver on the application of an ordinary contract creditor. By conferring new discretionary authority upon its equity court, Delaware could not modify the traditional equity rule in the federal courts that only someone with a defined interest in the estate of an insolvent person, *e.g.*, a judgment creditor, can protect that interest through receivership. * * *

of the State, it cannot afford recovery if the right to recover is made unavailable by the State nor can it substantially affect the enforcement of the right as given by the State.

And so the question is not whether a statute of limitations is deemed a matter of "procedure" in some sense. The question is whether such a statute concerns merely the manner and the means by which a right to recover, as recognized by the State, is enforced, or whether such statutory limitation is a matter of substance in the aspect that alone is relevant to our problem, namely does it significantly affect the result of a litigation for a federal court to disregard a law of a State that would be controlling in an action upon the same claim by the same parties in a State court?

It is therefore immaterial whether statutes of limitation are characterized either as "substantive" or "procedural" in State court opinions in any use of those terms unrelated to the specific issue before us. Erie R. Co. v. Tompkins was not an endeavor to formulate scientific legal terminology. It expressed a policy that touches vitally the proper distribution of judicial power between State and federal courts. In essence, the intent of that decision was to insure that, in all cases where a federal court is exercising jurisdiction solely because of the diversity of citizenship of the parties, the outcome of the litigation in the federal court should be substantially the same, so far as legal rules determine the outcome of a litigation, as it would be if tried in a State court. The nub of the policy that underlies Erie R. Co. v. Tompkins is that for the same transaction the accident of a suit by a non-resident litigant in a federal court instead of in a State court a block away, should not lead to a substantially different result. And so, putting to one side abstractions regarding "substance" and "procedure," we have held that in diversity cases the federal courts must follow the law of the State as to burden of proof, Cities Service Oil Co. v. Dunlap, 308 U.S. 208 [(1939)], as to conflict of laws, Klaxon Co. v. Stentor Co., 313 U.S. 487 [(1941)], as to contributory negligence, Palmer v. Hoffman, 318 U.S. 109, 117 [(1943)]. Erie R. Co. v. Tompkins has been applied with an eye alert to essentials in avoiding disregard of State law in diversity cases in the federal courts. A policy so important to our federalism must be kept free from entanglements with analytical or terminological niceties.

Plainly enough, a statute that would completely bar recovery in a suit if brought in a State court bears on a State-created right vitally and not merely formally or negligibly. As to consequences that so intimately affect recovery or nonrecovery a federal court in a diversity case should follow State law. * * *

To make an exception to Erie R. Co. v. Tompkins on the equity side of a federal court is to reject the considerations of policy which, after long travail, led to that decision. * * *

Diversity jurisdiction is founded on assurance to non-resident litigants of courts free from susceptibility to potential local bias. * * * The source of substantive rights enforced by a federal court under diversity jurisdiction, it cannot be said too often, is the law of the States. Whenever that law is authoritatively declared by a State, whether its voice be the legislature or its highest court, such law ought to govern in litigation founded on that law, whether the forum of application is a State or a federal court and whether the remedies be sought at law or may be had in equity.

Dicta may be cited characterizing equity as an independent body of law. To the extent that we have indicated, it is. But insofar as these general observations go beyond that, they merely reflect notions that have been replaced by a sharper analysis of what federal courts do when they enforce rights that have no federal origin. * * *

Reversed.

■ MR. JUSTICE ROBERTS and MR. JUSTICE DOUGLAS took no part in the consideration or decision of this case.

■ MR. JUSTICE RUTLEDGE.

I dissent. * * *

If any characteristic of equity jurisprudence has descended unbrokenly from and within "the traditional scope of equity as historically evolved in the English Court of Chancery," it is that statutes of limitations, often in terms applying only to actions at law, have never been deemed to be rigidly applicable as absolute barriers to suits in equity as they are to actions at law. That tradition, it would seem, should be regarded as having been incorporated in the various Acts of Congress which have conferred equity jurisdiction upon the federal courts. So incorporated, it has been reaffirmed repeatedly by the decisions of this and other courts. It is now excised from those Acts. If there is to be excision, Congress, not this Court, should make it. * * *

■ MR. JUSTICE MURPHY joins in this opinion.

Grupo Mexicano de Desarrollo, S.A.
v. Alliance Bond Fund, Inc.

527 U.S. 308 (1999).
Certiorari to the United States Court of Appeals for the Second Circuit.

■ JUSTICE SCALIA delivered the opinion of the Court.

[Respondent investment funds purchased unsecured notes from petitioner Grupo Mexicano de Desarrollo, S.A. (GMD), a Mexican holding company. Four GMD subsidiaries (also petitioners) guaranteed the Notes. After GMD fell into financial trouble and missed an interest payment on the Notes, respondents accelerated the Notes' principal amount and filed suit for the amount due in Federal District Court. Alleging that GMD was at risk of insolvency, or already insolvent, that it was preferring its Mexican creditors by its planned allocation to them of its most valuable assets, and that these actions would frustrate any judgment respondents could obtain, respondents requested a preliminary injunction restraining petitioners from transferring the assets. The district court issued the preliminary injunction and ordered respondents to post a $50,000 bond. The Second Circuit affirmed.]

III

We turn * * * to the merits question whether the District Court had authority to issue the preliminary injunction in this case pursuant to Federal Rule of Civil Procedure 65.[3] The Judiciary Act of 1789 conferred on the federal courts jurisdiction over "all suits . . . in equity." § 11, 1 Stat. 78. We have long held that "[t]he 'jurisdiction' thus conferred . . . is an authority to administer in equity suits the principles of the system of judicial remedies which had been devised and was being administered by the English Court of Chancery at the time of the separation of the two countries." Atlas Life Ins. Co. v. W.I. Southern, Inc., 306 U.S. 563, 568 (1939). See also, *e.g.*, Stainback v. Mo Hock Ke Lok Po, 336 U.S. 368, 382, n.26 (1949); Guaranty Trust Co. v. York, 326 U.S. 99, 105 (1945). "Substantially, then, the equity jurisdiction of the federal courts is the jurisdiction in equity exercised by the High Court of Chancery in England at the time of the adoption of the Constitution and the enactment of the original Judiciary Act, 1789 (1 Stat. 73)." A. Dobie, Handbook of Federal Jurisdiction and Procedure 660 (1928). "[T]he substantive prerequisites for obtaining an equitable remedy as well as the general availability of injunctive relief are not altered by [Rule 65] and depend on traditional principles of equity jurisdiction." 11A Charles Alan Wright, Arthur R. Miller, & Mary Kay Kane, Federal Practice and Procedure § 2941, 31 (2d ed.1995). We must ask, therefore, whether the relief respondents requested here was traditionally accorded by courts of equity.

A

Respondents do not even argue this point. The United States as *amicus curiae*, however, contends that the preliminary injunction issued in this case is analogous to the relief obtained in the equitable action known as a "creditor's bill." This remedy was used (among other purposes) to permit a judgment creditor to discover the debtor's assets, to reach equitable interests not subject to execution at law, and to set aside fraudulent conveyances. It was well established, however, that, as a general rule, a creditor's bill could be brought only by a creditor who had already obtained a judgment establishing the debt. See, *e.g.*, Pusey & Jones Co. v. Hanssen, 261 U.S. 491, 497 (1923); Hollins v. Brierfield Coal & Iron Co., 150 U.S. 371, 378–379 (1893); Cates v. Allen, 149 U.S. 451, 457 (1893); National Tube Works Co. v. Ballou, 146 U.S. 517, 523–

---

[3] Although this is a diversity case, respondents' complaint sought the injunction pursuant to Rule 65, and the Second Circuit's decision was based on that rule and on federal equity principles. Petitioners argue for the first time before this Court that under Erie R. Co. v. Tompkins, 304 U.S. 64 (1938), the availability of this injunction under Rule 65 should be determined by the law of the forum State (in this case New York). Because this argument was neither raised nor considered below, we decline to consider it.

524 (1892); Scott v. Neely, 140 U.S. 106, 113 (1891); Smith v. Railroad Co., 99 U.S. 398, 401 (1879); Adler v. Fenton, 24 How. 407, 411–413 (1861). The rule requiring a judgment was a product, not just of the procedural requirement that remedies at law had to be exhausted before equitable remedies could be pursued, but also of the substantive rule that a general creditor (one without a judgment) had no cognizable interest, either at law or in equity, in the property of his debtor, and therefore could not interfere with the debtor's use of that property. As stated by Chancellor Kent: "The reason of the rule seems to be, that until the creditor has established his title, he has no right to interfere, and it would lead to an unnecessary, and, perhaps, a fruitless and oppressive interruption of the exercise of the debtor's rights." Wiggins v. Armstrong, 2 Johns. Ch. 144, 145–146 (N.Y.1816). See also, *e.g.*, Guaranty Trust Co., *supra*, at 106–107, n.3; Pusey & Jones Co., *supra*, at 497. * * *

Justice Ginsburg concedes that federal equity courts have traditionally rejected the type of provisional relief granted in this case. She invokes, however, "the grand aims of equity," and asserts a general power to grant relief whenever legal remedies are not "practical and efficient," unless there is a statute to the contrary. This expansive view of equity must be rejected. * * * We do not question the proposition that equity is flexible; but in the federal system, at least, that flexibility is confined within the broad boundaries of traditional equitable relief. To accord a type of relief that has never been available before—and especially (as here) a type of relief that has been specifically disclaimed by longstanding judicial precedent—is to invoke a "default rule," not of flexibility but of omnipotence. When there are indeed new conditions that might call for a wrenching departure from past practice, Congress is in a much better position than we both to perceive them and to design the appropriate remedy. * * *

Respondents argue (supported by the United States) that the merger of law and equity changed the rule that a general creditor could not interfere with the debtor's use of his property. But the merger did not alter substantive rights. "Notwithstanding the fusion of law and equity by the Rules of Civil Procedure, the substantive principles of Courts of Chancery remain unaffected." Stainback, 336 U.S., at 382, n.26. Even in the absence of historical support, we would not be inclined to believe that it is merely a question of procedure whether a person's unencumbered assets can be frozen by general-creditor claimants before their claims have been vindicated by judgment. It seems to us that question goes to the substantive rights of all property owners. * * *

C

As further support for the proposition that the relief accorded here was unknown to traditional equity practice, it is instructive that the English Court of Chancery, from which the First Congress borrowed in conferring equitable powers on the federal courts, did not provide an injunctive remedy such as this until 1975. In that year, the Court of

Appeal decided Mareva Compania Naviera S.A. v. International Bulkcarriers S.A., 2 Lloyd's Rep. 509. Mareva * * * held (in the words of Lord Denning) that "[i]f it appears that the debt is due and owing—and there is a danger that the debtor may dispose of his assets so as to defeat it before judgment—the Court has jurisdiction in a proper case to grant an interlocutory judgment so as to prevent him [sic] disposing of those assets." 2 Lloyd's Rep., at 510. * * *

The parties debate whether Mareva was based on statutory authority or on inherent equitable power. Regardless of the answer to this question, it is indisputable that the English courts of equity did not actually exercise this power until 1975, and that federal courts in this country have traditionally applied the principle that courts of equity will not, as a general matter, interfere with the debtor's disposition of his property at the instance of a nonjudgment creditor. We think it incompatible with our traditionally cautious approach to equitable powers, which leaves any substantial expansion of past practice to Congress, to decree the elimination of this significant protection for debtors.

IV

The parties and *amici* discuss various arguments for and against creating the preliminary injunctive remedy at issue in this case. * * *

We do not decide which side has the better of these arguments. We set them forth only to demonstrate that resolving them in this forum is incompatible with the democratic and self-deprecating judgment we have long since made: that the equitable powers conferred by the Judiciary Act of 1789 did not include the power to create remedies previously unknown to equity jurisprudence. Even when sitting as a court in equity, we have no authority to craft a "nuclear weapon" of the law like the one advocated here. * * * The debate concerning this formidable power over debtors should be conducted and resolved where such issues belong in our democracy: in the Congress. * * *

It is so ordered.

■ JUSTICE GINSBURG, with whom JUSTICE STEVENS, JUSTICE SOUTER, and JUSTICE BREYER join, concurring in part and dissenting in part.

   * * *

II

The Judiciary Act of 1789 gave the lower federal courts jurisdiction over "all suits . . . in equity." § 11, 1 Stat. 78. We have consistently interpreted this jurisdictional grant to confer on the district courts "authority to administer . . . the principles of the system of judicial remedies which had been devised and was being administered" by the English High Court of Chancery at the time of the founding. Atlas Life Ins. Co. v. W.I. Southern, Inc., 306 U.S. 563, 568 (1939).

As I see it, the preliminary injunction ordered by the District Court was consistent with these principles. We long ago recognized that district courts properly exercise their equitable jurisdiction where "the remedy in equity could alone furnish relief, and . . . the ends of justice requir[e] the injunction to be issued." Watson v. Sutherland, 5 Wall. 74, 79 (1867). Particularly, district courts enjoy the "historic federal judicial discretion to preserve the situation [through provisional relief] pending the outcome of a case lodged in court." 11A Charles Alan Wright, Arthur R. Miller, & Mary Kay Kane, Federal Practice and Procedure § 2944, 79 (1995). The District Court acted in this case in careful accord with these prescriptions, issuing the preliminary injunction only upon well-supported findings that Alliance had "[no] adequate remedy at law," would be "frustrated" in its ability to recover a judgment absent interim injunctive relief, and was "almost certain" to prevail on the merits.

The Court holds the District Court's preliminary freeze order impermissible principally because injunctions of this kind were not "traditionally accorded by courts of equity" at the time the Constitution was adopted. In my view, the Court relies on an unjustifiably static conception of equity jurisdiction. From the beginning, we have defined the scope of federal equity in relation to the *principles* of equity existing at the separation of this country from England; we have never limited federal equity jurisdiction to the specific practices and remedies of the pre-Revolutionary Chancellor. * * *

III

* * *

B

Contrary to the Court's suggestion, this case involves no judicial usurpation of Congress' authority. Congress, of course, can instruct the federal courts to issue preliminary injunctions freezing assets pending final judgment, or instruct them not to, and the courts must heed Congress' command. Indeed, Congress has restricted the equity jurisdiction of federal courts in a variety of contexts.

The Legislature, however, has said nothing about preliminary freeze orders. The relevant question, therefore, is whether, absent congressional direction, the general equitable powers of the federal courts permit relief of the kind fashioned by the District Court. I would find the default rule in the grand aims of equity. Where, as here, legal remedies are not "practical and efficient," the federal courts must rely on their "flexible jurisdiction in equity . . . to protect all rights and do justice to all concerned." No countervailing precedent or principle holds the federal courts powerless to prevent a defendant from dissipating assets, to the destruction of a plaintiff's claim, during the course of judicial proceedings. Accordingly, I would affirm the judgment of the Court of Appeals and uphold the District Court's preliminary injunction.

NOTE ON STATE LAW AND FEDERAL EQUITY

(1) Federal Equity Before Merger and Erie. England had separate courts of common law and equity. Equity was the province of the English Court of Chancery, which had distinctive jurisdictional, procedural, remedial and substantive rules. As Justice Frankfurter suggests in Guaranty Trust, at the founding many states had no separate systems of equity and varied in only rudimentary equitable doctrines.

At the federal level, the Judiciary Act of 1789 did not create separate courts of law and equity, but instead established a unitary system in which every federal court had law and equity "sides." Section 11 of the 1789 Act gave the federal circuit courts diversity jurisdiction in suits "in equity" but provided in § 16 (repealed in 1948) that "suits in equity shall not be sustained in either of the courts of the United States, in any case where plain, adequate and complete remedy may be had at law."[1] The Rules of Decision Act (§ 34) applied only "in trials at common law," and thus by its terms did not apply in equity, see United States v. Burr, 25 F.Cas. 187, 188 (C.C.D.Va.1807) (No. 14,694) (Marshall, J.). The Process Act of 1792 provided that the "forms and modes of proceeding" in cases "of equity" were to be "according to the principles, rules and usages which belong to courts of equity * * *, as contradistinguished from courts of common law," subject to lower court regulations or to rules promulgated by the Supreme Court. See p. 728, *supra.*

The principles of equity that emerged from this system, and that were applied by federal courts before Erie, were extraordinarily complex.[2] Simplifying a good bit: Jurisdiction in federal courts over equity—including whether a claim sounded in equity, and the adequacy of a remedy at law— was determined by reference to the principles of the English Court of Chancery as they stood in 1789, as developed by federal courts, regardless of the jurisdictional rules (if any) in state courts. See, *e.g.,* Payne v. Hook, 74 U.S. (7 Wall.) 425, 430 (1868). Federal Court procedure was governed by Rules promulgated by the Supreme Court and by English Chancery procedures as a backstop, regardless of state law. See p. 728, *supra*; see also Russell v. Farley, 105 U.S. (15 Otto) 433, 437 (1881). By contrast, even though § 34 did not apply in suits in equity, federal courts would often apply state statutes that created new substantive equity rights on local law matters, such as rights to quiet title, see, *e.g.,* Clark v. Smith, 38 U.S. (13 Pet.) 195, 202–03 (1839).[3] The line between substance, on the one hand, and procedure and remedies, on the other, was often uncertain, see, *e.g.,* Pusey & Jones Co. v. Hanssen, 261 U.S. 491 (1923).

---

[1] Section 12 of the 1789 Act also excluded equity suits from the jury trial requirement, consistent with the Seventh Amendment. Judiciary Act of 1789, § 12, 1 Stat. at 80.

[2] See Morley, *The Federal Equity Power*, 59 B.C.L.Rev. 217, 230–44 (2018); Collins, *"A Considerable Surgical Operation": Article III, Equity, and Judge-Made Law in the Federal Courts*, 60 Duke L.J. 249, 257–90 (2010); Cross, *The Erie Doctrine in Equity*, 60 La.L.Rev. 173, 176–81 (1999).

[3] As Guaranty Trust notes, § 34 was deemed "to be merely declaratory of what would in any event have governed the federal courts and therefore was equally applicable to equity suits." See generally Fletcher, *The General Common Law and Section 34 of the Judiciary Act of 1789: The Example of Marine Insurance*, 97 Harv.L.Rev 1513, 1529–30 (1984).

The equitable remedies available in federal court were not constrained by state law. An equitable remedy—for example, an injunction, specific performance, rescission of a contract, a constructive trust—was traditionally available when nonmonetary relief did not suffice to redress an injury. As Guaranty Trust says, prior to Erie, federal courts felt free to apply their own body of equitable remedies, even in cases where the underlying action was governed by state law, as a form of general law akin to the law applied in Swift v. Tyson. For example, in Pusey (discussed in footnote 3 of the Guaranty Trust opinion), the Court refused to enforce a Delaware statute authorizing the appointment of a receiver upon the application of an unsecured simple contract creditor. In an opinion for the Court, Justice Brandeis said:

"That this suit could not be maintained in the absence of the [state] statute is clear. * * * That a remedial right to proceed in a federal court sitting in equity cannot be enlarged by a state statute is likewise clear. * * * The federal court may therefore be obliged to deny an equitable remedy which the plaintiff might have secured in a state court. * * * [I]t is not true that this statute confers upon the creditor a substantive right. * * * Insolvency is made a condition of the Chancellor's jurisdiction; but it does not give rise to any substantive right in the creditor. It makes possible a new remedy, because it confers upon the Chancellor a new power. * * * Whatever its exact nature, the power enables the Chancellor to afford a remedy which theretofore would not have been open to an unsecured simple contract creditor. But because that which the statute confers is merely a remedy, the statute cannot affect proceedings in the federal courts sitting in equity."

The 1938 Federal Rules of Civil Procedure, authorized by the 1934 Rules Enabling Act, made no change to "substantive rights" but merged law and equity into one form of action. See pp. 734–735, *supra*. And of course, the Court decided Erie that same year. As Guaranty Trust notes, a few weeks after Erie, the Court ruled, citing Erie, that a federal court must apply state court interpretations of insurance contract law even though "the question of construction arises not in an action at law, but in a suit in equity." Ruhlin v. New York Life Ins. Co., 304 U.S. 202, 205 (1938). Yet the meaning of Erie's application to equity remained complex.

(2) The Issues in Guaranty Trust. The narrow issue in Guaranty Trust was whether a federal court in a diversity suit for an alleged breach of trust—an equitable doctrine—can disregard the state statute of limitations that would bar the suit. The Court ruled that it cannot on the ground that a statute of limitation is a "matter of 'substantive rights' " for Erie purposes since its non-applicability would "significantly affect the result of a litigation" in federal court. This so-called "outcome-determination test" was widely criticized, and was later modified by the Court, as discussed pp. 790–792, *infra*.

A second important issue in Guaranty Trust was the status of equitable remedies in diversity cases after Erie. Guaranty Trust in dicta says that an independent body of equitable remedies remains available to some degree in federal court, even after Erie. Citing the pre-Erie decision in Pusey, it states that "State law cannot define the remedies which a federal court must give simply because a federal court in diversity jurisdiction is available as an alternative tribunal to the State's courts," and then adds that "a federal court may afford an equitable remedy for a substantive right recognized by a State even though a State court cannot give it."

But since equitable remedies operated akin to general common law prior to Erie, and since Erie repudiated general common law and applies in equity, why can federal courts after Erie continue to apply their own conception of remedies when state law remedies are different? Is it because remedies are akin to procedure, where Erie has less hold? See Chap. VII, pp. 879–881, *infra* (discussing the possibility that some judge-made procedural rules survive Erie). Because Article III authorizes federal courts to craft equitable remedies? See Gallogly, *Equity's Constitutional Source*, 132 Yale L.J. 1213, 1256–80 (2023); Cross, note 2, *supra*, at 206–14. Because the diversity statute should be viewed to authorize and limit equitable remedies? Olson, *Resolving Equity's Erie Problem*, 55 Ariz.St.L.J. 289, 337–40 (2024). Or should state law govern equitable remedies in diversity cases despite the dicta in Guaranty Trust? See Morley, note 2, *supra*; Burbank, *The Bitter with the Sweet: Tradition, History, and Limitations on Federal Judicial Power— A Case Study*, 75 Notre Dame L.Rev. 1291 (2000). Note that this issue has growing salience because states are increasingly by statute adopting "non-traditional equitable remedies for state law." Olson, *supra*, at 311 (providing examples).

(3) The Significance of Grupo Mexicano. Does Grupo Mexicano resolve these questions? It states that § 11 of the 1789 Judiciary Act—which granted lower federal courts diversity jurisdiction over "suits of a civil nature at common law or in equity"—"is an authority to administer in equity suits the principles of the system of judicial remedies which had been devised and was being administered by the English Court of Chancery at the time of the separation of the two countries." In 1948, ten years after the merger of law and equity and three years after Guaranty Trust, Congress, as part of a larger revision to the Judicial Code, changed "common law or in equity" in the diversity statute to "all civil actions." That is the current formulation in 28 U.S.C. § 1332, the statute invoked in Grupo Mexicano. Congress likely meant "all civil actions" to encompass equity jurisdiction, and in any event, the Court presumes that the 1948 Revision did not effect a change in the meaning of the statute unless such a change is specified in the Revisers' Notes or some other authoritative source. See, *e.g.*, John R. Sand & Gravel Co. v. U.S., 552 U.S. 130, 136 (2008); see generally Ch. III, p. 365, note 3.

Does Grupo Mexicano thus stand for the proposition that the diversity statute authorizes federal courts to apply equitable remedies traditionally available in federal court and disregard state equitable remedies in cases where the underlying dispute turns on state law? As in Guaranty Trust, the Court does not explain how or why the same diversity statute that Erie says cannot justify the development of general common law on an issue of negligence nonetheless authorizes federal courts to disregard state-law remedies and apply the same traditional equitable principles after Erie as before. See Chap. VII, pp. 850–852, *infra* (analyzing instances when jurisdictional statutes were deemed to authorize federal common lawmaking). Is it relevant that in the 1948 Amendments to the Judicial Code, Congress extended the Rules of Decision Act to apply not just to cases at common law but to all civil actions? For additional exploration of the different rules that govern damages versus injunctive relief in federal court, see Chapter IV, pp. 462–463, *supra*, and Chapter VII, pp. 911–917, *infra*.

Footnote 3 of Grupo Mexicano formally leaves the issue of governing law for equitable remedies in federal court open because the parties failed to raise the Erie issue. But does the Court's reliance on the diversity jurisdiction justification and on pre-Erie cases to give content to post-Erie equitable remedies, combined with the Guaranty Trust dicta, leave practical room for the application of state law?[4] Revisit this question after studying the modified outcome-determination test set forth in the next principal case, Hanna v. Plumer, 380 U.S. 460 (1965).[5]

(4) The New Equity and the Turn to History. Grupo Mexicano held that federal courts in diversity suits cannot issue an assets-freezing injunction before judgment because no such remedy, or any close analogue, was available in equity in 1789. Justice Ginsburg in dissent says this is an "unjustifiably static conception of equity," but how seriously does the Court take the 1789 baseline? Grupo Mexicano relies on nineteenth and twentieth century cases to ascertain the proper scope of assets-freezing injunctions. And it acknowledges that "equity is flexible" and says that only "*substantial* expansion of past practice" must be done in Congress. How does the Court draw the line between small evolutions in equity practice that it appears to countenance and the "expansive view of equity" of the dissent that it rejects?

Grupo Mexicano is the first decision in a line of cases that Professor Bray identifies as a "new equity jurisprudence." Bray, *The Supreme Court and the New Equity*, 68 Vand.L.Rev. 997 (2015).[6] The defining features of

---

[4] Morley, *Beyond the Elements:* Erie *and the Standards for Preliminary and Permanent Injunctions*, 52 Akron L.Rev. 457, 465–68, 474–75 (2018), examines competing lower federal court answers to the questions raised in this Note with regard to preliminary and permanent injunctions.

[5] One point that Hanna emphasizes is that federal courts should almost always apply the Federal Rules of Civil Procedure to control matters on which they purport to govern. See p. 792, *infra*. This raises the question of the relevance of Fed.R.Civ.Proc. 65, which governs certain procedural questions about injunctive relief, to the federal v. state choice-of-law issue for equitable remedies in federal court. The Supreme Court has articulated standards for equitable remedies in federal court in Grupo and in other important equitable remedies cases without reference to Rule 65, see, *e.g.*, Winter v. Natural Resources Defense Council, Inc., 555 U.S. 7 (2008); eBay Inc. v. MercExchange, L.L.C., 547 U.S. 388 (2006). For an argument that Rule 65 "may be read as a codification of the traditional federal equity practice," see Wright & Miller, 11A Fed. Prac. & Proc. Civ. § 2943 (3d ed.1995). For an argument that it has no relevance to the question of governing law for equitable remedies in federal court, see Morley, note 2, *supra*, at 252–55.

[6] In addition to Grupo Mexicano, the "new equity" cases identified by Professor Bray are Petrella v. Metro-Goldwyn-Mayer, Inc., 572 U.S. 663 (2014); US Airways, Inc. v. McCutchen, 569 U.S. 88 (2013); CIGNA Corp. v. Amara, 563 U.S. 421 (2011); Monsanto Co. v. Geertson Seed Farms, 561 U.S. 139 (2010); Nken v. Holder, 556 U.S. 418 (2009); Winter v. Natural Res. Def. Council, Inc., 555 U.S. 7 (2008); Munaf v. Geren, 553 U.S. 674 (2008); eBay Inc. v. MercExchange, L.L.C., 547 U.S. 388 (2006); Sereboff v. Mid Atl. Med. Servs., Inc., 547 U.S. 356 (2006); Great-West Life & Annuity Ins. Co. v. Knudson, 534 U.S. 204 (2002). Bray, *supra*, at 1000 n.5. Subsequent cases in this vein include Whole Woman's Health v. Jackson, 595 U.S. 30 (2021); Liu v. SEC, 591 U.S. 71 (2020); and Montanile v. Bd. of Trs. of Nat'l Elevator Indus. Health Benefit Plan, 577 U.S. 136 (2016).

this jurisprudence, Bray maintains, include a focus on history and tradition to define the scope of equitable relief, a reaffirmation of the "no adequate remedy at law" prerequisite for such relief, and an insistence that equitable remedies are exceptional and discretionary. Bray identifies some historical and doctrinal errors in many of the Court's "new equity" decisions (including Grupo Mexicano), and notes that the Court in cases after Grupo looked at nineteenth and twentieth century decisions and treatises to give content to the 1789 baseline. He nonetheless offers a qualified defense of the jurisprudence that emerges from the decisions on the grounds that it (a) is "well suited to judicial decisionmaking," and (b) constitutes a reasonable response to the challenge of making sense of equitable doctrines in a world without courts of equity. Is it right that the Court's historical analysis in the "new equity" decisions, though "not good as historians' history," can be "good as history for legal purposes because its very artificiality makes it more suited to the judicial resolution of cases," at least so long as this "artificial history" is a "sensible interpretation" of statutes that authorize "equitable relief" and is "largely consistent with traditional equitable principles"?

Pfander & Formo, *The Past and Future of Equitable Remedies: An Essay for Frank Johnson*, 71 Ala.L.Rev. 723 (2020), argues that, because equity adjusts in light of changes in the scope of common law remedies over time, Grupo Mexicano's emphasis on equity's past may render courts incapable of adjusting equitable remedies in light of intervening changes in the law. In any case, the authors contend that early decisions of the Supreme Court grant pre-judgment assets-freezing injunctive relief of the kind the Grupo Mexicano Court described as historically unprecedented.

(5) The Federal Arbitration Act and Federal Equity. In Bernhardt v. Polygraphic Co., 350 U.S. 198 (1956), a defendant, after removing a breach of contract action to a Vermont federal court on diversity grounds, moved to stay the proceedings pending arbitration, pursuant to an arbitration clause in the contract. (A stay is a form of injunction. See Chap. III, pp. 375–376, *supra.*). The district court denied the motion on the ground that under Vermont law an agreement to arbitrate was revocable at any time prior to an award and was therefore not enforceable. The Second Circuit reversed, but the Supreme Court agreed with the district court, saying: "If the federal court allows arbitration where the state court would disallow it, the outcome of litigation might depend on the courthouse where suit is brought. * * * The nature of the tribunal where suits are tried is an important part of the parcel of rights behind a cause of action."

The Court held, as a matter of statutory interpretation, that the provisions in the Federal Arbitration Act (FAA), 9 U.S.C. §§ 1–14, that authorize judicial enforcement of certain agreements to arbitrate did not apply to the case at hand. The Court noted that "[i]f respondent's contention [that the Act applied] is correct, a constitutional question might be presented. Erie R. Co. v. Tompkins indicated that Congress does not have the constitutional authority to make the law that is applicable to controversies in diversity of citizenship cases." For criticism of this holding, see Ely, *The Irrepressible Myth of Erie,* 87 Harv.L.Rev. 693, 705–06 (1974) (arguing that Erie did not fence off local law as immune from displacement by otherwise valid federal statutes, and that application of the FAA to diversity cases would be unconstitutional "only if it were so plainly nonprocedural as to fall outside Congress' undoubted power to formulate procedure for federal courts, which it quite clearly is not").

The constitutional concern raised in Bernhardt was dispelled, in part, in Prima Paint Corp. v. Flood & Conklin Mfg. Co., 388 U.S. 395 (1967). In this diversity action, Prima sought rescission of an agreement on the basis of fraudulent inducement. Flood & Conklin, relying on the FAA, moved to stay the action pending arbitration of the issue of fraud under an arbitration clause in the contract. The Supreme Court held, 6–3, that a stay was properly granted, even though it might not have been available in a state court action. The FAA applied because the contract here, unlike the one in Bernhardt, "evidenc[ed] a transaction involving commerce" within the meaning of § 2 of the Act. Application of the Act was constitutionally permissible because the question was "not whether Congress may fashion federal substantive rules to govern questions arising in simple diversity cases," but "whether Congress may prescribe how federal courts are to conduct themselves with respect to subject matter [interstate commerce] over which Congress plainly has power to legislate." The answer, the Court concluded, "can only be in the affirmative." But the Court carefully avoided any explicit endorsement of the view that the FAA embodied substantive policies that were to be applied to all contracts within its scope, whether sued on in state or federal courts.

The result in Prima Paint, which evidently contemplated different remedies in federal and state courts for breach of the same contract, was unstable and did not endure. In Southland Corp. v. Keating, 465 U.S. 1 (1984), the Court held that a state law rendering certain claims in franchise agreements not arbitrable directly conflicted with § 2 of the Act and therefore could not be applied by a state court to a contract within the scope of that Act. This reversal of the state court's judgment effectively required that court to compel arbitration.[7]

---

[7]   Southland has been reaffirmed, and extended, in several subsequent decisions. See, e.g., Allied-Bruce Terminix Companies, Inc. v. Dobson, 513 U.S. 265 (1995); Preston v. Ferrer, 552 U.S. 346 (2008). Justice Thomas, joined in dissent by Justice Scalia in Dobson, argued vigorously that Southland should be overruled, and that the FAA should be held inapplicable in state courts. Justice Thomas has continued to dissent on similar grounds in subsequent cases. See, e.g., Kindred Nursing Ctrs. Ltd. P'ship v. Clark, 581 U.S. 246 (2017); Viking River Cruises, Inc. v. Moriana, 596 U.S. 639 (2022).

Scholars have mainly been critical of these decisions. See, e.g., Leslie, The Arbitration Bootstrap, 94 Tex.L.Rev. 265, 315 (2015); Carrington & Haagen, Contract and Jurisdiction, 1996 Sup.Ct.Rev. 331; Moses, How the Supreme Court Created a Federal Arbitration Act Law Never Enacted by Congress, 34 Fla.St.U.L.Rev. 1 (2006) (sharply criticizing the decisions). But see Drahozal, In Defense of Southland: Reexamining the Legislative History of the Federal Arbitration Act, 78 Notre Dame L.Rev. 101, 169 (2002) (concluding, on the basis of a detailed examination of the legislative history of the Act, that "while the 'primary purpose' of the FAA was to make arbitration agreements enforceable in federal court, a secondary purpose was to make arbitration agreements enforceable in state court").

C. THE EVOLUTION OF THE "OUTCOME" TEST AND THE RELEVANCE OF THE FEDERAL RULES

INTRODUCTORY NOTE

Recall Justice Frankfurter's statement in Guaranty Trust that in diversity cases, "the outcome of the litigation in the federal court should be substantially the same, so far as legal rules determine the outcome of a litigation, as it would be if tried in a State court."

(1) "Same" Outcome. Consider these interpretations of the concept of the same outcome:

(i) Federal courts should not take a view of the parties' primary legal relations that differs from the view that the state court would take.

(ii) Federal courts should not give any form of relief that differs from the relief the state court would give.

(iii) Federal courts should (A) not act at all if the state court would refuse to act, even though the state court's refusal would be without prejudice, and (B) not refuse to act, even by dismissing without prejudice, if the state court would be willing to act.

In considering what the Guaranty Trust opinion meant by *"legal rules"* that "determine" the outcome of a lawsuit, note that any legal rule might determine the outcome if a litigant is sanctioned for violating it. But on that view, nearly any state rule could be outcome determinative in a particular case. Should *"legal rules"* be understood to exclude at least those rules whose application depends upon what the parties or counsel do after litigation begins and that might have been done differently under different rules of procedure?

(2) The 1949 Trilogy. Questions like those raised in Paragraph (1) have perplexed the federal courts at all levels ever since the Guaranty Trust decision. During the first thirteen years after the decision, the Court disposed of a number of important cases without suggesting a stopping place for the outcome test. Of particular interest are three cases decided on the same day: Ragan v. Merchants Transfer & Warehouse Co., 337 U.S. 530 (1949); Woods v. Interstate Realty Co., 337 U.S. 535 (1949); and Cohen v. Beneficial Indus. Loan Corp., 337 U.S. 541 (1949). Only four members of the Court joined in all three decisions (and only Justice Rutledge dissented in all three).

The Cohen and Woods decisions are summarized in the footnote.[1] In Ragan, a diversity action for injuries suffered in a highway accident had been

---

[1]   In Cohen, a stockholder filed a derivative action in a New Jersey federal court; jurisdiction rested on diversity of citizenship. The question arose whether the federal court should apply a New Jersey statute whose general effect was "to make a plaintiff having so small an interest liable for the reasonable expenses and attorney's fees of the defense if he fails to make good his complaint and to entitle the corporation to indemnity before the case can be prosecuted." The Court held, 6–3, that the statute should be applied. Rejecting the contention that the statute conflicted with Fed.R.Civ.Proc. 23 (now 23.1), the Court said: "We do not think

brought in a Kansas federal court. Kansas had a two-year statute of limitations; the action was filed within two years of the accident, but the summons and complaint were not served until after the two-year period had run. The Court held, 8–1, that summary judgment for the defendant should have been granted, on the basis of a state statute providing: "An action shall be deemed commenced * * *, as to each defendant, at the date of the summons which is served on him * * *." In a brief opinion that referred to but did not discuss the apparent conflict between the state statute and Fed.R.Civ.Proc. 3 (which provided that "[a] civil action is commenced by filing a complaint with the court"), the Court noted the holding of the court below that the Kansas statute was "an integral part" of its statute of limitations and said: "We can draw no distinction [from Guaranty Trust] in this case because local law brought the cause of action to an end after, rather than before, suit was started in the federal court. * * * We cannot give it longer life in the federal court than it would have had in the state court without adding something to the cause of action. We may not do that consistently with Erie R. Co. v. Tompkins."

(3) The Byrd v. Blue Ridge Decision: A New Approach.

(a) The first sign of a change of direction appeared in Byrd v. Blue Ridge Rural Elec. Coop., Inc., 356 U.S. 525 (1958). In a diversity action brought in a South Carolina federal court for injuries resulting from alleged negligence, the defendant asserted that because it was the plaintiff's employer, the plaintiff's exclusive remedy lay before South Carolina's Industrial Commission under the state's Workers' Compensation Law. Although the state supreme court had ruled that such a defense in this context should be passed on by the judge, alone, the United States Supreme Court held that issues of fact relevant to the defense should be tried to the jury in the federal action. After noting that the state supreme court had given no reasons for its decision, the Court continued:

"We find nothing to suggest that this rule was announced as an integral part of the special relationship created by the statute. Thus the requirement appears to be merely a form and mode of enforcing the immunity, Guaranty Trust Co. v. York, 326 U.S. 99, 108 [(1945)], and not a rule intended to be bound up with the definitions of the rights and obligations of the parties. * * *

"* * * [C]ases following Erie have evinced a broader policy to the effect that the federal courts should conform as near as may be—in the absence of

---

a statute which so conditions the stockholder's action can be disregarded by the federal court as a mere procedural device." The dissent argued that the statute "merely prescribes the method by which stockholders may enforce [a cause of action]."

In Woods, a Tennessee corporation had brought a diversity action in a Mississippi federal court against a Mississippi resident, seeking to recover a broker's commission allegedly due for the sale of real estate in Mississippi. The defense contended that since the plaintiff had not qualified to do business in the state, the action had to be dismissed under a state statute providing that any foreign corporation failing to qualify "shall not be permitted to bring or maintain any action or suit in any of the courts of this state." The Court held, 6–3, that the defense should be sustained, stating: "The York case was premised on the theory that a right which local law creates but which it does not supply with a remedy is no right at all for purposes of enforcement in a federal court in a diversity case; that where in such cases one is barred from recovery in the state court, he should likewise be barred in the federal court."

other considerations—to state rules even of form and mode where the state rules may bear substantially on the question whether the litigation would come out one way in the federal court and another way in the state court if the federal court failed to apply a particular local rule. [Citing Guaranty Trust and Bernhardt.] * * * It may well be that in the instant personal-injury case the outcome would be substantially affected by whether the issue [in question] * * * is decided by a judge or a jury. Therefore, were 'outcome' the only consideration, a strong case might appear for saying that the federal court should follow the state practice.

"But there are affirmative countervailing considerations at work here. The federal system is an independent system for administering justice to litigants who properly invoke its jurisdiction. An essential characteristic of that system is the manner in which, in civil common-law actions, it distributes trial functions between judge and jury and, under the influence— if not the command—of the Seventh Amendment, assigns the decisions of disputed questions of fact to the jury. The policy of uniform enforcement of state-created rights and obligations, see, *e.g.*, Guaranty Trust Co. v. York, *supra*, cannot in every case exact compliance with a state rule—not bound up with rights and obligations—which disrupts the federal system of allocating functions between judge and jury. Thus the inquiry here is whether the federal policy favoring jury decisions of disputed fact questions should yield to the state rule in the interest of furthering the objective that the litigation should not come out one way in the federal court and another way in the state court.

"We think that in the circumstances of this case the federal court should not follow the state rule."

(b) Note that in Byrd, perhaps for the first time since Erie, the Court sought to determine whether the policy behind a state rule would be frustrated if the federal court were not to follow it. At the same time, the Court said that even a state rule relating only to "form and mode"—if it might bear substantially on the outcome—should not be disregarded absent "affirmative countervailing considerations." Is that because there is no reason to adopt or follow a federal rule that encourages forum shopping but serves no other purpose?

The Court's analysis of the State's reason for assigning the issue in question to a judge rather than a jury was not particularly sympathetic. The South Carolina rule might be supported by arguments (a) that only a judge would be able to view the company's defense as an aspect of a comprehensive statutory scheme of liability without fault for industrial accidents, and (b) that a jury could not articulate the basis for its findings in a way that would help to assure predictability and consistency of decisions for litigants faced with many lawsuits raising the same issue. Wouldn't such bases for the state rule be undermined if the federal courts disregarded the rule?

As to the Court's reference to "affirmative countervailing considerations," it would have been simpler, and correct, to rest the result squarely on the Seventh Amendment. Instead, the Court said that even if the Seventh Amendment does not apply to the trial of a particular issue, there is nevertheless a federal policy favoring trial by jury on that issue. What is the source of the policy?

(4) From Byrd to Hanna. Byrd plainly approached the Erie question much differently than had Guaranty Trust.[2] Seven years after Byrd, the Court again engaged with the Erie question. In doing so, it helped to resolve some of the tension between Byrd and Guaranty Trust, while also giving new importance to the question whether federal practice was required by a Federal Rule of Civil Procedure.

Hanna v. Plumer

380 U.S. 460 (1965).
Certiorari to the United States Court of Appeals for the First Circuit.

■ MR. CHIEF JUSTICE WARREN delivered the opinion of the Court.

The question to be decided is whether, in a civil action where * * * jurisdiction * * * is based upon diversity of citizenship between the parties, service of process shall be made in the manner prescribed by state law or that set forth in Rule 4(d)(1) of the Federal Rules of Civil Procedure.

[On February 6, 1963, an Ohio citizen filed a diversity action in federal court in Massachusetts, seeking damages for personal injuries resulting from an automobile accident in South Carolina, allegedly caused by the negligence of a Massachusetts citizen who was deceased when the complaint was filed. The decedent's executor, also a Massachusetts citizen, was named as defendant. On February 8, service was made by leaving copies of the summons and the complaint with the defendant's wife at his residence, concededly in compliance with Rule 4(d)(1) (now embodied in substantial part in Rule 4(e)(2)), which then provided:]

> "The summons and complaint shall be served together. The plaintiff shall furnish the person making service with such copies as are necessary. Service shall be made as follows:

> "(1) Upon an individual other than an infant or an incompetent person, by delivering a copy of the summons and of the complaint to him personally or by leaving copies thereof at his dwelling house or usual place of abode with some person of suitable age and discretion then residing therein * * *."

[The defendant] filed his answer on February 26, alleging, *inter alia*, that the action could not be maintained because it had been brought "contrary to and in violation of the provisions of Massachusetts General Laws (Ter.Ed.) Chapter 197, Section 9." That section provides:

---

[2]   For discussions of the Erie doctrine during the period covered by this Note, see, *e.g.*, Smith, *Blue Ridge and Beyond: A Byrd's-Eye View of Federalism in Diversity Litigation*, 36 Tul.L.Rev. 443 (1962); Vestal, *Erie R.R. v. Tompkins: A Projection*, 48 Iowa L.Rev. 248 (1963).

"Except as provided in this chapter, an executor or administrator shall not be held to answer to an action by a creditor of the deceased which is not commenced within one year from the time of his giving bond for the performance of his trust, or to such an action which is commenced within said year unless before the expiration thereof the writ in such action has been served by delivery in hand upon such executor or administrator or service thereof accepted by him or a notice stating the name of the estate, the name and address of the creditor, the amount of the claim and the court in which the action has been brought has been filed in the proper registry of probate. * * *" Mass.Gen.Laws Ann., c. 197, § 9 (1958).

On October 17, 1963, the District Court granted [the defendant's] motion for summary judgment, citing Ragan v. Merchants Transfer & Warehouse Co., 337 U.S. 530 [(1949)], and Guaranty Trust Co. of New York v. York, 326 U.S. 99 [(1945)], in support of its conclusion that the adequacy of the service was to be measured by § 9, with which, the court held, [the plaintiff] had not complied. On appeal, [the plaintiff] admitted noncompliance with § 9, but argued that Rule 4(d)(1) defines the method by which service of process is to be effected in diversity actions. The Court of Appeals for the First Circuit, finding that "[r]elatively recent amendments [to § 9] evince a clear legislative purpose to require personal notification within the year,"[1] concluded that the conflict of state and federal rules was over "a substantive rather than a procedural matter," and unanimously affirmed. * * *

We conclude that the adoption of Rule 4(d)(1), designed to control service of process in diversity actions, neither exceeded the congressional mandate embodied in the Rules Enabling Act nor transgressed constitutional bounds, and that the Rule is therefore the standard against which the District Court should have measured the adequacy of the service. Accordingly, we reverse the decision of the Court of Appeals.

* * * Under the cases construing the scope of the Enabling Act, Rule 4(d)(1) clearly passes muster. Prescribing the manner in which a defendant is to be notified that a suit has been instituted against him, it relates to the "practice and procedure of the district courts."

"The test must be whether a rule really regulates procedure,— the judicial process for enforcing rights and duties recognized by substantive law and for justly administering remedy and redress for disregard or infraction of them." Sibbach v. Wilson & Co., 312 U.S. 1, 14 [(1941)].

---

[1] * * * The purpose of [the part of § 9 involved here] is, as the court below noted, to insure that executors will receive actual notice of claims. Actual notice is of course also the goal of Rule 4(d)(1); however, the Federal Rule reflects a determination that this goal can be achieved by a method less cumbersome than that prescribed in § 9. In this case the goal seems to have been achieved; although the affidavit filed by [defendant] in the District Court asserts that he had not been served in hand nor had he accepted service, it does not allege lack of actual notice.

In Mississippi Pub. Corp. v. Murphree, 326 U.S. 438 [(1945)], this Court upheld [then] Rule 4(f), which permits service of a summons anywhere within the State (and not merely the district) in which a district court sits * * *.

Thus were there no conflicting state procedure, Rule 4(d)(1) would clearly control. However, [the defendant], focusing on the contrary Massachusetts rule, calls to the Court's attention another line of cases, a line which—like the Federal Rules—had its birth in 1938. Erie R. Co. v. Tompkins, 304 U.S. 64 [(1938)], * * * held that federal courts sitting in diversity cases, when deciding questions of "substantive" law, are bound by state court decisions as well as state statutes. The broad command of Erie was therefore identical to that of the Enabling Act: federal courts are to apply state substantive law and federal procedural law. However, as subsequent cases sharpened the distinction between substance and procedure, the line of cases following Erie diverged markedly from the line construing the Enabling Act. Guaranty Trust Co. of New York v. York, 326 U.S. 99 [1945)], made it clear that Erie-type problems were not to be solved by reference to any traditional or common-sense substance-procedure distinction * * *.

[The defendant], by placing primary reliance on York and Ragan, suggests that the Erie doctrine acts as a check on the Federal Rules of Civil Procedure, that despite the clear command of Rule 4(d)(1), Erie and its progeny demand the application of the Massachusetts rule. Reduced to essentials, the argument is: (1) Erie, as refined in York, demands that federal courts apply state law whenever application of federal law in its stead will alter the outcome of the case. (2) In this case, a determination that the Massachusetts service requirements obtain will result in immediate victory for [the defendant]. If, on the other hand, it should be held that Rule 4(d)(1) is applicable, the litigation will continue, with possible victory for [the plaintiff]. (3) Therefore, Erie demands application of the Massachusetts rule. The syllogism possesses an appealing simplicity, but is for several reasons invalid.

In the first place, it is doubtful that, even if there were no Federal Rule making it clear that in-hand service is not required in diversity actions, the Erie rule would have obligated the District Court to follow the Massachusetts procedure. "Outcome-determination" analysis was never intended to serve as a talisman. Byrd v. Blue Ridge Rural Elec. Cooperative, 356 U.S. 525, 537 [(1945)]. Indeed, the message of York itself is that choices between state and federal law are to be made not by application of any automatic, "litmus paper" criterion, but rather by reference to the policies underlying the Erie rule.

The Erie rule is rooted in part in a realization that it would be unfair for the character or result of a litigation materially to differ because the suit had been brought in a federal court. * * * The decision was also in part a reaction to the practice of "forum-shopping" which had grown up in response to the rule of Swift v. Tyson. 304 U.S. [(16 Pet.) 1], 73–74

[(1842)]. That the York test was an attempt to effectuate these policies is demonstrated by the fact that the opinion framed the inquiry in terms of "substantial" variations between state and federal litigation. 326 U.S., at 109. Not only are nonsubstantial, or trivial, variations not likely to raise the sort of equal protection problems which troubled the Court in Erie; they are also unlikely to influence the choice of a forum. The "outcome-determination" test therefore cannot be read without reference to the twin aims of the Erie rule: discouragement of forum-shopping and avoidance of inequitable administration of the laws.[9]

The difference between the conclusion that the Massachusetts rule is applicable, and the conclusion that it is not, is of course at this point "outcome-determinative" in the sense that if we hold the state rule to apply, [the defendant] prevails, whereas if we hold that Rule 4(d)(1) governs, the litigation will continue. But in this sense *every* procedural variation is "outcome-determinative." For example, having brought suit in a federal court, a plaintiff cannot then insist on the right to file subsequent pleadings in accord with the time limits applicable in state courts, even though enforcement of the federal timetable will, if he continues to insist that he must meet only the state time limit, result in determination of the controversy against him. So it is here. Though choice of the federal or state rule will at this point have a marked effect upon the outcome of the litigation, the difference between the two rules would be of scant, if any, relevance to the choice of a forum. [The plaintiff] * * * was not presented with a situation where application of the state rule would wholly bar recovery; rather, adherence to the state rule would have resulted only in altering the way in which process was served. Moreover, it is difficult to argue that permitting service of defendant's wife to take the place of in-hand service of defendant himself alters the mode of enforcement of state-created rights in a fashion sufficiently "substantial" to raise the sort of equal protection problems to which the Erie opinion alluded.

There is, however, a more fundamental flaw in respondent's syllogism: the incorrect assumption that the rule of Erie R. Co. v. Tompkins constitutes the appropriate test of the validity and therefore the applicability of a Federal Rule of Civil Procedure. The Erie rule has never been invoked to void a Federal Rule. It is true that there have been cases where this Court has held applicable a state rule in the face of an argument that the situation was governed by one of the Federal Rules. But the holding of each such case was not that Erie commanded displacement of a Federal Rule by an inconsistent state rule, but rather

---

[9]   * * * Erie and its progeny make clear that when a federal court sitting in a diversity case is faced with a question of whether or not to apply state law, the importance of a state rule is indeed relevant, but only in the context of asking whether application of the rule would make so important a difference to the character or result of the litigation that failure to enforce it would unfairly discriminate against citizens of the forum State, or whether application of the rule would have so important an effect upon the fortunes of one or both of the litigants that failure to enforce it would be likely to cause a plaintiff to choose the federal court.

that the scope of the Federal Rule was not as broad as the losing party urged, and therefore, there being no Federal Rule which covered the point in dispute, Erie commanded the enforcement of state law. * * * [The Court here refers to Palmer v. Hoffman, p. 744, *supra*; Ragan v. Merchants Transfer & Whse Co., p. 789, *supra*; and Cohen v. Beneficial Indus. Loan Corp., p. 789, note 1, *supra*.] * * * At the same time, in cases adjudicating the validity of Federal Rules, we have not applied the York rule or other refinements of Erie, but have to this day continued to decide questions concerning the scope of the Enabling Act and the constitutionality of specific Federal Rules in light of the distinction set forth in Sibbach.

Nor has the development of two separate lines of cases been inadvertent. The line between "substance" and "procedure" shifts as the legal context changes. * * * When a situation is covered by one of the Federal Rules, the question facing the court is a far cry from the typical, relatively unguided Erie choice: the court has been instructed to apply the Federal Rule, and can refuse to do so only if the Advisory Committee, this Court, and Congress erred in their prima facie judgment that the Rule in question transgresses neither the terms of the Enabling Act nor constitutional restrictions.

We are reminded by the Erie opinion that neither Congress nor the federal courts can, under the guise of formulating rules of decision for federal courts, fashion rules which are not supported by a grant of federal authority contained in Article I or some other section of the Constitution; in such areas state law must govern because there can be no other law. But the opinion in Erie, which involved no Federal Rule and dealt with a question which was "substantive" in every traditional sense (whether the railroad owed a duty of care to Tompkins as a trespasser or a licensee), surely neither said nor implied that measures like Rule 4(d)(1) are unconstitutional. For the constitutional provision for a federal court system (augmented by the Necessary and Proper Clause) carries with it congressional power to make rules governing the practice and pleading in those courts, which in turn includes a power to regulate matters which, though falling within the uncertain area between substance and procedure, are rationally capable of classification as either. *Cf.* M'Culloch v. State of Maryland, 4 Wheat. 316, 421 [(1819)]. Neither York nor the cases following it ever suggested that the rule there laid down for coping with situations where no Federal Rule applies is coextensive with the limitation on Congress to which Erie had adverted. Although this Court has never before been confronted with a case where the applicable Federal Rule is in direct collision with the law of the relevant State, courts of appeals faced with such clashes have rightly discerned the implications of our decisions. * * *

Erie and its offspring cast no doubt on the long-recognized power of Congress to prescribe housekeeping rules for federal courts even though some of those rules will inevitably differ from comparable state rules.

* * * Thus, though a court, in measuring a Federal Rule against the standards contained in the Enabling Act and the Constitution, need not wholly blind itself to the degree to which the Rule makes the character and result of the federal litigation stray from the course it would follow in state courts, it cannot be forgotten that the Erie rule, and the guidelines suggested in York, were created to serve another purpose altogether. To hold that a Federal Rule of Civil Procedure must cease to function whenever it alters the mode of enforcing state-created rights would be to disembowel either the Constitution's grant of power over federal procedure or Congress' attempt to exercise that power in the Enabling Act. Rule 4(d)(1) is valid and controls the instant case.

Reversed.

■ MR. JUSTICE BLACK concurs in the result.

■ MR. JUSTICE HARLAN, concurring.

It is unquestionably true that up to now Erie and the cases following it have not succeeded in articulating a workable doctrine governing choice of law in diversity actions. I respect the Court's effort to clarify the situation in today's opinion. However, in doing so I think it has misconceived the constitutional premises of Erie and has failed to deal adequately with those past decisions upon which the courts below relied.

Erie was something more than an opinion which worried about "forum-shopping and avoidance of inequitable administration of the laws," although to be sure these were important elements of the decision. I have always regarded that decision as one of the modern cornerstones of our federalism, expressing policies that profoundly touch the allocation of judicial power between the state and federal systems. Erie recognized that there should not be two conflicting systems of law controlling the primary activity of citizens, for such alternative governing authority must necessarily give rise to a debilitating uncertainty in the planning of everyday affairs. And it recognized that the scheme of our Constitution envisions an allocation of law-making functions between state and federal legislative processes which is undercut if the federal judiciary can make substantive law affecting state affairs beyond the bounds of congressional legislative powers in this regard. Thus, in diversity cases Erie commands that it be the state law governing primary private activity which prevails.

The shorthand formulations which have appeared in some past decisions are prone to carry untoward results that frequently arise from oversimplification. The Court is quite right in stating that the "outcome-determinative" test of Guaranty Trust Co. of New York v. York, 326 U.S. 99, if taken literally, proves too much, for any rule, no matter how clearly "procedural," can affect the outcome of litigation if it is not obeyed. In turning from the "outcome" test of York back to the unadorned forum-shopping rationale of Erie, however, the Court falls prey to like oversimplification, for a simple forum-shopping rule also proves too much; litigants often choose a federal forum merely to obtain what they consider the advantages of the Federal Rules of Civil Procedure or to try their cases before a supposedly more favorable judge. To my mind the proper line of approach in determining whether to apply a state or a federal rule, whether "substantive" or "procedural," is to stay close to basic principles by inquiring if the choice of rule would substantially affect those primary decisions respecting human conduct which our constitutional system leaves to state regulation.[2] If so, Erie and the Constitution require that the state rule prevail, even in the face of a conflicting federal rule.

The Court weakens, if indeed it does not submerge, this basic principle by finding, in effect, a grant of substantive legislative power in the constitutional provision for a federal court system, and through it, setting up the Federal Rules as a body of law inviolate. * * * So long as a reasonable man could characterize any duly adopted federal rule as "procedural," the Court * * * would have it apply no matter how seriously it frustrated a State's substantive regulation of the primary conduct and affairs of its citizens. Since the members of the Advisory Committee, the Judicial Conference, and this Court who formulated the Federal Rules are presumably reasonable men, it follows that the integrity of the Federal Rules is absolute. Whereas the unadulterated outcome and forum-shopping tests may err too far toward honoring state rules, I submit that the Court's "arguably procedural, *ergo* constitutional" test moves too fast and far in the other direction.

The courts below relied upon this Court's decisions in [Ragan and Cohen]. Those cases deserve more attention than this Court has given them, particularly Ragan which, if still good law, would in my opinion call for affirmance of the result reached by the Court of Appeals. Further, a discussion of these two cases will serve to illuminate the "diversity" thesis I am advocating.

* * * I think that the [Ragan] decision was wrong. At most, application of the Federal Rule would have meant that potential Kansas tort defendants would have to defer for a few days the satisfaction of knowing that they had not been sued within the limitations period. The choice of the Federal Rule would have had no effect on the primary stages of private activity from which torts arise, and only the most minimal effect on behavior following the commission of the tort. In such circumstances the interest of the federal system in proceeding under its own rules should have prevailed.

* * * The proper view of Cohen is in my opinion, that the statute was meant to inhibit small stockholders from instituting "strike suits," and thus it was designed and could be expected to have a substantial impact

---

[2]   See Hart and Wechsler, The Federal Courts and the Federal System 678 [1st ed.1953]. Byrd v. Blue Ridge Rural Elec. Coop., Inc., 356 U.S. 525, 536–540, indicated that state procedures would apply if the State had manifested a particularly strong interest in their employment. However, this approach may not be of constitutional proportions.

on private primary activity. * * * [E]ven had the Federal Rules purported to [deal with this problem], and in so doing provided a substantially less effective deterrent to strike suits, I think the state rule should still have prevailed. That is where I believe the Court's view differs from mine; for the Court attributes such overriding force to the Federal Rules that it is hard to think of a case where a conflicting state rule would be allowed to operate, even though the state rule reflected policy considerations which, under Erie, would lie within the realm of state legislative authority.

It remains to apply what has been said to the present case. * * * If the Federal District Court in Massachusetts applies Rule 4(d)(1) of the Federal Rules of Civil Procedure instead of the Massachusetts service rule, what effect would that have on the speed and assurance with which estates are distributed? As I see it, the effect would not be substantial. It would mean simply that an executor would have to check at his own house or the federal courthouse as well as the registry of probate before he could distribute the estate with impunity. As this does not seem enough to give rise to any real impingement on the vitality of the state policy which the Massachusetts rule is intended to serve, I concur in the judgment of the Court.

NOTE ON HANNA AND ITS AFTERMATH

A. Introduction: Justice Harlan's Rationale in Hanna

Suppose the Court had adopted Justice Harlan's view that it should inquire whether "the choice of rule would substantially affect those primary decisions respecting human conduct which our constitutional system leaves to state regulation. If so, Erie and the Constitution require that the state rule prevail, even in the face of a conflicting federal rule." Consider rules of state law (a) allowing rescission or reformation of a contract for a mutual mistake of fact, (b) allocating the burden of proof with respect to comparative negligence, or (c) allowing the recovery of reliance damages for breach of a contract within the statute of frauds. Do any of these rules characteristically affect people's conduct at the stage of primary private activity? If not, should they be regarded as "quasi-procedural"—as rules that need not be followed in federal diversity actions? Isn't the more critical question whether the state rule embodies a significant state policy with respect to primary conduct and its effects?

B. The Significance of Whether a Federal
Rule of Civil Procedure Applies

To a significant extent, Hanna and later cases have distinguished between conflicts involving matters covered by a Federal Rule of Civil Procedure (or by another Federal Rule or statute) and conflicts to which no formal federal statute or rule applies. The following discussion is based on that distinction.

C. Matters Not Governed by a Federal Rule of Civil Procedure (or Other Federal Rule or Statute)

(1) The Analysis in Hanna. The Court in Hanna (in dictum) said that when the matter is *not* governed by a federal statute or Federal Rule of Civil Procedure, the question is whether failure to follow the state rule would make such an important difference as to "discriminate against citizens of the forum State" or as to lead the "plaintiff to choose the federal court." It is not clear why the courts should be unconcerned about discrimination against a *non-citizen* of the forum state, or whether the failure to follow the state rule leads the *defendant* to choose the federal court. But more fundamentally, the Court's emphasis on forum-shopping may make too short shrift of the Byrd analysis of the relationship between state and federal policies—an analysis that contemplates the presence of affirmative considerations justifying a uniform federal rule even in the absence of a statute or a Federal Rule of Civil Procedure.

Sharply contrasting views on these issues were expressed by Ely, p. 787, *supra,* at 714–17, and Redish & Phillips, *Erie and The Rules of Decision Act: In Search of the Appropriate Dilemma*, 91 Harv.L.Rev. 356, 394 (1977). Arguing that the Rules of Decision Act sought to mark out enclaves of exclusive state concern, Ely concludes that the Act requires state law to be followed whenever disregard of that law would be "likely to generate an outcome different from that which would result were the case litigated in the state court system and the state rules followed." "[I]n light of [the Act's] fairness rationale—or, for that matter in light of a desire either to minimize forum shopping or to avoid 'uncertainty in the planning of everyday affairs'— it becomes clear that there is no place in the analysis for the sort of balancing of federal and state interests contemplated by the Byrd opinion."

For Redish and Phillips, by contrast, Erie and the Rules of Decision Act warrant consideration not only of the interests of litigants in uniformity of outcome but also of the state's interest in enforcement of its substantive policies and of the federal interest in the fair and efficient administration of justice. Thus, they urge a "refined balancing test" that considers, *inter alia*, the federal interest in "doing justice" and in avoiding unnecessary cost or inconvenience.[1]

(2) The Gasperini Decision. Gasperini v. Center for Humanities, Inc., 518 U.S. 415 (1996), was an especially difficult case involving the relation between state and federal law governing review of a jury damages award.[2] A New York law (N.Y.Civ.Prac. Law & Rules § 5501(c)) empowered appellate courts to review the size of a jury verdict and to order a new trial when the award "deviates materially from what would be reasonable compensation"— a standard inviting more rigorous judicial review of awards than the "shock the conscience" test followed in federal courts in New York. In a diversity

---

[1]   See also Doernberg, *The Unseen Track of Erie Railroad: Why History and Jurisprudence Suggest a More Straightforward Form of Erie Analysis*, 109 W.Va.L.Rev. 611, 644–48 (2007) (advocating a Byrd-style balancing of interests in which a presumption that state law applies can be rebutted only by showing that it conflicts with a "dominant federal interest").

[2]   For an earlier case following federal law on the question of sanctions for improper conduct in the course of litigation, see Chambers v. NASCO, Inc., 501 U.S. 32 (1991).

action for the loss of certain slide transparencies, the jury in a New York federal court awarded the plaintiff $450,000. The district court denied the defendant's motion to set aside the verdict as excessive; the Second Circuit, after holding that § 5501(c) governed the controversy, reversed and remanded the case for a new trial unless the plaintiff agreed to a reduced award of $100,000.

(a) The Supreme Court concluded that New York law should apply under the Erie doctrine. Writing for the majority, Justice Ginsburg ruled that if New York had enacted a "statutory cap" on damage awards, that cap would clearly control in a diversity case. She then stated that § 5501 did not differ from such a cap in its substantive objective (of controlling jury awards) but only in its use of a procedural technique to be applied on a case-by-case basis. Given the aims of Erie, its doctrine "precludes a recovery in federal court significantly larger than the recovery that would have been tolerated in state court."

The Court then considered whether the federal interest in the allocation of authority between judge and jury, especially as reflected in the Seventh Amendment, in any way undercut or modified the obligation to follow state law. The Court noted that, under New York precedent, § 5501 governed the standard to be applied by trial judges as well as by appellate courts, and held that the application of that standard by a federal trial judge would not run afoul of the Seventh Amendment. In light of the "re-examination clause" of that Amendment, however, *appellate review*, while not entirely precluded, was limited to the question whether the district court's determination was an abuse of discretion. The Court concluded that this resolution accommodated both the interests served by the Erie doctrine and those reflected in the Seventh Amendment, and ordered the case returned to the district court for its review of the award under the New York standard.[3]

Justice Scalia's dissent, joined by Chief Justice Rehnquist and Justice Thomas, argued that, under the Seventh Amendment, appellate courts may not review (even for abuse of discretion) district court refusals to set aside civil jury awards as contrary to the weight of the evidence. He added that the majority departed significantly from precedent in holding that federal courts must follow a state's allocation of authority between judges and juries. Quoting Byrd, Justice Scalia contended that "changing the standard by which trial judges review jury verdicts does disrupt the federal system, and is plainly inconsistent with 'the strong federal policy against allowing state rules to disrupt the judge-jury relationship in federal court.' " The analogy to a statutory cap on damages was misleading, he said, because of the difference "between a rule of law * * * [that] would ordinarily be imposed upon the jury in the trial court's instructions, and a rule of review, which simply determines how closely the jury verdict will be scrutinized for compliance with the instructions."

(b) Assuming that the Seventh Amendment itself does not bar application of the New York standard in a federal *trial* court, the Supreme

---

3   The Court also rejected the argument that the result reached, with respect to the standard to be applied by the trial court, conflicted with Fed.R.Civ.Proc. 59. See p. 803, *infra*.

Court's decision with respect to the task of the trial judge seems to reject the approach in the Byrd case. Instead, the Court appears to favor the analysis in Hanna discussed above in Paragraph C(1) and/or the outcome-determinative analysis of Guaranty Trust.[4] The Byrd rationale does appear to play a larger role in the Court's holding as to the scope of *appellate* review, but that holding is also affected by the Court's understanding of the Seventh Amendment.[5]

D.   Matters Governed by the Federal Rules of Civil Procedure (or by Other Federal Rules or Statutes)

(1) The Analysis in Hanna. In Hanna, Justice Harlan criticizes the majority for clothing the Federal Rules of Civil Procedure with virtually absolute immunity by adopting an "arguably procedural, ergo constitutional" test. That test is surely appropriate for measuring the constitutionality of a rule of procedure laid down for the federal courts by Congress. And Sibbach v. Wilson & Co., 312 U.S. 1, 14 (1941), p. 739, *supra*, seems to endorse application of essentially the same test in determining the validity under the Enabling Act of a rule promulgated by the Supreme Court. Hanna is of a piece with Sibbach. But was the Sibbach opinion sufficiently sensitive to state interests and to the language and purpose of the Enabling Act?[6]

The majority in Hanna did recognize that courts applying federal rules and statutes must interpret them, and that the process of interpretation should reflect an awareness of legitimate state interests. Indeed, that awareness may account for the fact that the Court did not squarely confront the issue posed in Hanna until 27 years after Erie and 25 years after Sibbach.

---

[4]   See *The Supreme Court, 1995 Term—Leading Cases*, 110 Harv.L.Rev. 256, 265–66 (1996); Floyd, *Erie Awry: A Comment on Gasperini v. Center for Humanities, Inc.*, 1997 BYU L.Rev. 267, 303–04.

[5]   For an evaluation of Gasperini in the context of a comprehensive discussion of the Erie doctrine, see Rowe, *Not Bad for Government Work: Does Anyone Else Think the Supreme Court Is Doing a Halfway Decent Job in Its Erie-Hanna Jurisprudence?*, 73 Notre Dame L.Rev. 963, 1014–15 (1998). Rowe concludes that "in addition to being reasonably sensitive to federalist concerns and the nuances of a somewhat complex area," the Court's doctrine has been "fairly comprehensible and workable in its broad outlines" and "remarkably stable * * * over three decades." As for the Gasperini decision, it has left the "basic framework for analysis * * * very much intact," although it does suggest a greater willingness to construe potentially applicable Federal Rules to avoid "direct conflicts" with state policies and to preserve Byrd interest analysis "in a subset of cases involving judge-made federal procedural rules." Compare Freer, *Some Thoughts on the State of Erie After Gasperini*, 76 Tex.L.Rev. 1637, 1663 (1998) (arguing that the Court missed "perhaps its best [opportunity] in a generation—to make a meaningful contribution to [Rules of Decision Act] analysis * * *. Instead, the Court has left the field about as murky as it was before.").

[6]   Ely, *The Irrepressible Myth of Erie*, 87 Harv.L.Rev. 693 (1974), argues that the Court in Sibbach failed to give adequate scope to what was then the second sentence, and what is now subsection (b), of the Enabling Act. That provision, in his view, requires that a Federal Rule of Civil Procedure must yield in the face of a state rule that does not merely represent a procedural disagreement but embodies a substantive policy.

Professor Burbank, in *The Rules Enabling Act of 1934*, 130 U.Pa.L.Rev. 1015, 1025–26 (1982), also objects to the interpretation of the Enabling Act in Sibbach and Hanna, but on quite different grounds. Relying on his study of the pre-1934 history of the Act, he concludes (a) that the first two sentences of the original Act "were intended to allocate power between the Supreme Court as rulemaker and Congress and thus to circumscribe the delegation of legislative power, [(b) that those sentences] were thought to be equally relevant in all actions brought in a federal court, and [(c)] that the protection of state law was deemed a probable effect, rather than the primary purpose, of the allocation scheme established by the Act."

(2) Tension Between Hanna and Subsequent Decisions. After Hanna, the Supreme Court, in a number of cases, has interpreted the federal rules to avoid conflict with important state regulatory policies.[7]

(a) In Walker v. Armco Steel Corp., 446 U.S. 740 (1980), the Court unanimously decided that Ragan, p. 789, *supra*, was still good law, and that state law rather than Rule 3 ("A civil action is commenced by filing a complaint with the court.") determined when a diversity action was commenced for the purpose of tolling the statute of limitations. Beyond relying upon stare decisis, the Court reasoned that significant state policy interests would be frustrated if Rule 3 were to supersede the state rule requiring actual service on the defendant in order to stop the running of the statute. The Court did not reach the question of the validity of Rule 3 in this context because the lack of any reference in the rule to the tolling of state limitations statutes meant that there was no "direct conflict between the Federal Rule and the state law."[8]

Does the Walker decision cast some doubt on the Hanna result? If the state law at issue in Hanna was essentially a provision for determining when and how the statute of limitations was tolled, should it have prevailed even though its requirements for valid service went beyond those of Rule 4? Does Walker suggest an interpretive approach with respect to the Federal Rules that would have the federal courts read them narrowly as needed to account for federalism concerns?

(b) In Gasperini v. Center for Humanities, Inc., more fully discussed in Paragraph C(2), *supra*, Justice Scalia ended his dissent by contending that the decision to follow the state standard of review in ruling on a new trial motion in the district court was squarely in conflict with Fed.R.Civ.Proc. 59, which (as then worded) allowed a new trial "for any of the reasons for which new trials have heretofore been granted in actions at law in the courts of the United States." That provision, in his view, clearly imposed a federal standard. The majority (quoting the statement in the Fourth Edition of this book that the Court has "continued since Hanna to *interpret* the federal rules to avoid conflict with important state regulatory policies") responded that Rule 59 did not preclude reference to the only appropriate source of law for determining whether damages are excessive—the state law governing the cause of action.

(c) Finally, in Semtek Int'l, Inc. v. Lockheed Martin Corp., 531 U.S. 497 (2001) (more fully discussed at pp. 803–804, *infra*), a California federal court, applying a California statute of limitations, had dismissed a diversity

---

[7]   For an arguable exception, see Burlington N.R.R. v. Woods, 480 U.S. 1 (1987) (state rule requiring imposition of a fixed penalty on an appellant who obtains a stay of a money judgment and then loses the appeal is preempted by the federal appellate rule giving discretion to impose a penalty).

[8]   The Court also stated, in a footnote: "We do not here address the role of Rule 3 as a tolling provision for a statute of limitations, whether set by federal law or borrowed from state law, if the cause of action is based on federal law." That question was addressed in West v. Conrail, 481 U.S. 35 (1987), where the Court held that "when the underlying cause of action is based on federal law and the absence of an express federal statute of limitations makes it necessary to borrow a limitations period from another statute, the action is not barred if it has been 'commenced' in compliance with Rule 3 within the borrowed period."

suit "on the merits and with prejudice." The plaintiff then filed a new action on the same claim against the same defendant in a Maryland state court, because Maryland's statute of limitations had not yet run. The Maryland courts decided that the action was barred because under Rule 41(b) of the Federal Rules of Civil Procedure, the federal court dismissal "on the merits" had to be accorded claim preclusive effect. (Rule 41(b), as then worded, provided that "unless the dismissal order states otherwise," an involuntary dismissal (with certain exceptions not applicable in the Semtek case) "operates as an adjudication on the merits.")

A unanimous Supreme Court reversed. Justice Scalia's opinion stated first that a rule "governing the effect that must be accorded federal judgments * * * would arguably violate the jurisdictional limitation of the Rules Enabling Act" and in addition "would in many cases violate the federalism principle of [the Erie doctrine] by engendering 'substantial variations [in outcomes] between state and federal litigation' which would '[l]ikely influence the choice of a forum' " (quoting Hanna v. Plumer). He then concluded that the language of Rule 41(b) on which the Maryland court had relied simply meant "that, unlike a dismissal 'without prejudice,' the dismissal in the present case barred refiling of the same claim in the [same district court]." He added that the preclusive effect of the first judgment was governed by federal common law and that, in a diversity case, federal common law would usually refer to "the law that would be applied by state courts in the State in which the federal diversity court sits" (citing, *inter alia*, the decisions in Gasperini and Walker v. Armco).

Even in light of the decisions that sought, through interpretation, to avoid difficult questions under the Enabling Act and the principles underlying the Erie doctrine, was the interpretation of Rule 41(b) in Semtek nevertheless too much of a stretch? The Court might more plausibly have construed the rule as rendering a dismissal falling within its terms eligible for claim preclusive effect in *any* court, but only if that effect was required by the governing law of preclusion (which in Semtek would be federal common law). That interpretation would have avoided a novel and confusing distinction between the preclusive effect in the rendering court and in other courts.[9]

The Semtek decision could be read to cast doubt on the rationale of Hanna—that a valid and applicable Federal Rule of Civil Procedure trumps conflicting state law even in a diversity case. Justice Scalia's opinion in Semtek cited Hanna as supporting the proposition that even if the rejected interpretation of Rule 41(b) was consistent with the Enabling Act, it would "violate the federalism principle of Erie." Significantly, the portion of the Hanna opinion cited on this point dealt with the hypothetical case in which there was *no* conflicting Federal Rule of Civil Procedure. But note that

---

[9]   In a comment generally approving the Semtek result, Professor Burbank concludes that the Court's effort to cabin the rule was unpersuasive and that "[i]t might have been better, after all, to decide the Enabling Act question" (i.e., the question whether a federal rule of civil procedure that dictates the preclusive effect of a dismissal is valid under the Enabling Act). Burbank, Semtek, *Forum Shopping, and Federal Common Law*, 77 Notre Dame L.Rev. 1027, 1047 (2002). For a similar view, see Dudley & Rutherglen, *Deforming the Federal Rules: An Essay on What's Wrong with the Recent Erie Decisions*, 92 Va.L.Rev. 707, 708 (2006).

Semtek's discussion of this point was essentially dictum, given the Court's ultimate decision to adopt an interpretation of Rule 41(b) that rendered the Erie issue moot.[10]

(3) The Shady Grove Decision. The most important recent decision in this line, Shady Grove Orthopedic Associates, P.A. v. Allstate Ins. Co., 559 U.S. 393 (2010), suggests that the Court has yet to develop a consistent and predictable approach to determining when a Federal Rule is valid and should be read to govern the matter at hand. In striking contrast to the Walker, Gasperini, and Semtek decisions, a fractured Supreme Court decided that the provisions of Fed.R.Civ.Proc. 23 (on class actions) conflicted with, and trumped, state law.

The state law in question, N.Y.Civ.Prac. Law Ann. (CPLR) § 901(b), precludes the bringing of a class action to recover a "penalty," which the federal courts understood to include statutory interest. Notwithstanding this state law prohibition, Shady Grove filed a diversity class action in a New York federal district court to recover certain statutory interest on behalf of itself and a similarly situated class. The trial court decided, and the court of appeals agreed, that whether or not the action met the criteria for class certification under Rule 23, it could not be maintained as a class action in view of the prohibition in New York law, and since Shady Grove's individual claim was for less than the jurisdictional amount, dismissed the case.[11] The Supreme Court reversed.

(a) The Lead Opinion. In an opinion by Justice Scalia (joined by Chief Justice Roberts and Justices Stevens, Thomas, and Sotomayor), the Court held that Federal Rule 23 conflicted with the New York law. The Court stated that Rule 23—in providing that a class action "may be maintained" if certain conditions are met—confers "categorical permission" to maintain such an action. Justice Scalia rejected the Second Circuit's view that federal and state law do not conflict, because Rule 23 governs the "certifiability" of a class action with respect to a claim while the New York law governs the antecedent question of the eligibility of the claim for class treatment. And while agreeing that the federal courts should read ambiguous rules to avoid substantial variations in the outcome in federal and state litigation, Justice Scalia saw no ambiguity here: "there is only one reasonable reading of Rule 23."

Justice Scalia, now writing only for himself, Chief Justice Roberts and Justices Thomas and Sotomayor, went on to determine that because Rule 23 was a valid exercise of the authority granted by the Enabling Act, it trumped the conflicting state prohibition. Relying heavily on the holding of Sibbach v. Wilson & Co., p. 739, as well as its language (to the effect that the test of validity is whether the rule really regulates procedure—"the judicial process for enforcing rights and duties recognized by substantive law"), he concluded

---

[10]   For consideration of the relevance of state policy to a motion to transfer under § 1404, see Stewart Org., Inc. v. Ricoh Corp., 487 U.S. 22 (1988).

[11]   Under the Class Action Fairness Act, 28 U.S.C. § 1332(d), pp. 1081–1084, *infra*, it might have been possible to meet the jurisdictional amount threshold by aggregating the damages of class members. But an individual action could not meet § 1332's general threshold in diversity actions.

that "[a] class action * * * merely enables a federal court to adjudicate claims of multiple parties at once, instead of in separate suits." Whether or not New York's prohibition of class actions in this context had a "substantive nature" or "substantive purpose," he insisted, *makes no difference*." (Emphasis in original.) As long as the rule itself is procedural, it is "valid in all jurisdictions, regardless of its incidental effect upon state-created rights."

(b) The Concurrence. Justice Stevens, whose concurrence in part and concurrence in the judgment supplied the fifth vote for the outcome, contended that Rule 23 prevailed over New York law because the state law "is a procedural rule that is not part of New York's substantive law." Disagreeing with Justice Scalia's view that in the event of conflict, the sole question was the validity of the federal rule as a rule of procedure, Justice Stevens emphasized that the rule also had to satisfy the limitation of subsection (b) of the Enabling Act, *i.e.*, it could not "abridge, enlarge, or modify any substantive right."[12] Thus, a federal rule "cannot govern a particular case in which the rule would displace a state law that is procedural in the ordinary use of the term but is so intertwined with a state right or remedy that it functions to define the scope of the state-created right." He concluded, however, that the "high" bar for finding a violation of the Enabling Act had not been surmounted in this case. "The text of [New York's law] expressly and unambiguously applies not only to claims based on New York law but also to claims based on federal law or the law of any other State. * * * It is therefore hard to see how [the law] could be understood as a rule that, though procedural in form, serves the function of defining New York's rights or remedies." "In order to displace a federal rule, there must be more than just a possibility that a state rule is different than it appears."

(c) The Dissent. Justice Ginsburg (joined by Justices Kennedy, Breyer, and Alito) dissented. Her central theme was that Rule 23 need not, and should not, be read "to collide with New York's legitimate interest in keeping certain awards reasonably bounded." After discussing a number of earlier decisions in which the Court had avoided such conflicts by interpreting the federal rules "with awareness of, and sensitivity to, important state regulatory policies," she analyzed the history and purpose of the New York limitation and concluded that the state's decision "to block class-action proceedings for statutory damages * * * makes scant sense, except as a means to a manifestly substantive end: Limiting a defendant's liability in a single lawsuit in order to prevent the exorbitant inflation of penalties." Implementation of the state's substantive purpose, she contended, did not conflict with Rule 23 because that rule only "prescribes the considerations relevant to class certification and postcertification proceedings—but it does not command that a particular remedy be available when a party sues in a representative capacity." Justice Ginsburg also rejected as not in any way dispositive the placement of the New York limitation in the state's Civil Practice Law. And as to the fact that the

---

[12]   Justice Scalia, responding to Justice Stevens in a portion of his opinion joined by only Chief Justice Roberts and Justice Thomas, again relied heavily on the rationale of Sibbach. He conceded that "Sibbach's exclusive focus on the challenged federal rule—driven by the very real fear that Federal Rules which vary from State to State would be chaos—is hard to square with § 2072(b)'s terms."

provision was not expressly limited to claims under New York law, she said that "the most likely explanation for the absence of limiting language [was that] New York legislators make law with New York plaintiffs and defendants in mind." As in Gasperini, she said, the remedial provision could have been written, and should be understood, as a statutory cap.

(d) Questions and Comments About Shady Grove.

(i) The Nature of Class Actions. Justice Scalia asserts that a class action is only a procedural device for aggregating individual claims. Compare Shapiro, *Class Actions: The Class as Party and Client*, 73 Notre Dame L.Rev. 913 (1998), arguing that the availability of a class action has significant purposes and consequences that transcend the notion of joinder or aggregation. If Professor Shapiro is correct, how does that affect the appropriate scope of Rule 23 under the Enabling Act? If Justice Scalia is correct, is his reading of the rule the only "reasonable" one? Is the dissent's reading of Rule 23 any more of a stretch than the Court's reading of other rules in the cases discussed earlier in this Chapter (particularly its reading of Rule 41(b) in Semtek)?

(ii) The Tension Between Erie Concerns and the Uniform Application of the Federal Rules. Note that both Justice Stevens (in his understanding of the Rules Enabling Act) and Justice Ginsburg (in her reading of Rule 23) must inquire into the substantive purposes of state law. Is such an inquiry at odds with the notion that the Federal Rules of Civil Procedure are trans-substantive and should be uniformly applied (in both federal question and diversity cases)?[13] Could either of their approaches result in a Federal Rule being applicable in some cases (in states that lack New York's policy, and in federal question cases) but not in others (cases like Shady Grove)? Does that explain why the plurality (and the Sibbach decision itself) brushed aside arguments that the federal rule was invalid under the Enabling Act and did not delve extensively into what the state's substantive policy was? What weight should the Justices have given, in interpreting the Rule, to the obvious incentive that the Court's decision gives to class

---

[13] As a sign of the uncertain effect of the Shady Grove decision, several Justices disagreed on the appropriateness of the Court's subsequent per curiam decision granting certiorari, and summarily vacating and remanding for reconsideration in light of Shady Grove, the Second Circuit's refusal to permit a class action in another suit. See Holster v. Gatco, Inc., 559 U.S. 1060 (2010). In the view of Justice Ginsburg, whom Justice Breyer joined in dissent, the decision to vacate and remand was not warranted because the particular class action had been brought under a federal law (the Telephone Consumer Protection Act (TCPA)) that allowed a private action to be brought only if it was "otherwise permitted by the laws or rules of court of a State." But in the view of Justice Scalia, concurring in the per curiam, the remand was appropriate because the "independent ground" may have rested on an assumption (a) that Rule 23 did not "address whether class actions are available for specific claims" or (b) that the TCPA superseded Rule 23 because CPLR § 901(b) precludes an action under state law. In either event, he contended, the Shady Grove decision would affect the outcome in view of its holding that CPLR § 901(b) did not bar an action to recover a penalty but only the use of a procedural joinder device, and thus was trumped by Rule 23.

Recall, also, West v. Conrail, p. 803, note 8, *supra*, where the Court held that Rule 3 does govern the tolling of limitations periods in federal question cases, though not (under the Walker decision) in diversity cases resting on state law.

representatives to file actions seeking "penalties" under New York law in federal rather than state court?[14]

(iii) The Reach of the Decision. If New York were to replace CPLR § 901(b) with a provision, inserted into every law authorizing recovery of a statutory penalty, that "the remedy herein provided may not be sought on behalf of a class but only on behalf of an individual plaintiff," doesn't the majority accept that such a provision would have to be honored in a federal diversity action? If so, the long-term importance of the Shady Grove decision may be quite limited.

(iv) The State of the Law. In cases that implicate a federal rule, questions can arise both as to its meaning and its validity. On the question of meaning, Shady Grove takes an approach quite different from that in earlier cases. Indeed, the precedent closest in time was Gasperini, in which the Court narrowly interpreted a federal rule, and in that case, Justice Ginsburg wrote for the Court and Justice Scalia dissented.

On the question of validity, it remains true, more than 75 years after the adoption of the Federal Rules of Civil Procedure, that the Supreme Court has never held any rule invalid, on its face or as applied, under the Rules Enabling Act.

(v) Commentary. Shady Grove stimulated an outpouring of scholarly comment, which highlighted disagreement among scholars on such basic questions as the meaning and scope of the Erie decision, the proper approach to questions arising under the Rules of Decision Act and Rules Enabling Act, and the question whether the validity of a Federal Rule of Civil Procedure should ever be considered on an "as applied" basis.[15]

(4) Hanna and the Rulemaking Process. To a significant extent, the result of Hanna's permissive standards for measuring the validity of the Federal Rules has been to remit important issues of federalism from the Court as a decider of cases to the participants in the rulemaking process: the Rules Committees, the Court as a promulgator of rules, and Congress in its review of those rules. A case in point is the evolution of the rules relating to privilege in the Federal Rules of Evidence. As proposed by the Rules Committee and promulgated by the Supreme Court, the rules set out a federally-defined set of privileges for all civil and criminal litigation in the federal courts. Responding to the argument that at least in cases governed by state substantive law these rules might run afoul of Erie and the Enabling Act, the Advisory Committee Note argued that Hanna gave a large measure

---

[14]   For data confirming that the decision has led class representatives seeking a "penalty" to choose federal over state court, see Hubbard, *An Empirical Study of the Effect of Shady Grove v. Allstate on Forum Shopping in the New York Courts*, 10 J.L.Econ. & Pol'y 151 (2013).

[15]   Leading articles include Burbank & Wolff, *Redeeming the Missed Opportunities of Shady Grove*, 159 U.Pa.L.Rev. 17 (2010) (arguing that Shady Grove was erroneous because Rule 23 is a mechanism for implementing aggregate liability policy, and not itself the source of that policy; in Shady Grove, the source was the law of New York); and Tidmarsh, *Procedure, Substance, and Erie*, 64 Vand.L.Rev. 877 (2011) (defending the result in Shady Grove on the ground that the federal courts may properly apply their own rules to process a claim "as long as, in a world without transaction costs [including the costs of litigation], those rules do not affect the ex ante value of a claim"). For symposia on Shady Grove, see 44 Creighton L.Rev. 1–139 (2010); 86 Notre Dame L.Rev. 939–1239 (2011); 44 Akron L.Rev. 897–1209 (2011).

of choice to the rulemakers, that state privileges had at most a "tenuous" substantive aspect, that they would have to give way in federal question cases in any event, and that the practical dimensions of the problem were not great. See Revised Draft of Proposed Rules of Evidence, 51 F.R.D. 315, 358–60 (1971).

Congress refused to accept this approach. Moved by concern for privacy interests and by a desire to safeguard substantive state policies, Congress enacted a statute providing that in Federal Rule of Evidence 501, federal "common law" is controlling on matters of privilege *only* with respect to claims or defenses governed by federal substantive law. When the claim or defense is governed by state law, the state law of privilege applies.

CHAPTER VII

FEDERAL COMMON LAW

INTRODUCTION

On the same day that Erie R. Co. v. Tompkins, 304 U.S. 64 (1938), p. 760, *supra*, announced that "[t]here is no federal general common law" of the sort applied in Swift v. Tyson, 41 U.S. (16 Pet.) 1 (1842), p. 749, *supra*, the Supreme Court held that the apportionment of the water of an interstate stream between two states "is a question of 'federal common law' upon which neither the statutes nor the decisions of either State can be conclusive." Hinderlider v. La Plata Co., 304 U.S. 92, 110 (1938). As this chapter explains, the post-Erie federal common law, unlike pre-Erie general common law, is grounded, often dimly, in federal statutes or the Constitution. And because it is federal law, it is (again, in contrast to general law) binding on the states under the Supremacy Clause and can be the basis for federal question jurisdiction. See Illinois v. Milwaukee, 406 U.S. 91, 99–100 (1972); Banco Nacional de Cuba v. Sabbatino, 376 U.S. 398, 426 (1964).

Commentators have offered a range of definitions of federal common law. This book uses the term loosely to refer to federal rules of decision whose content cannot be traced directly by traditional methods of interpretation to federal statutory or constitutional commands. While that definition captures the conventional understanding of federal common law as judge-made law, the fact is that common lawmaking often cannot be sharply distinguished from statutory or constitutional interpretation. As specific evidence of statutory meaning with respect to the issue at hand diminishes, much interpretation shades into judicial lawmaking. Similarly, because constitutional interpretation routinely entails value judgments of sorts, some matters that are conventionally viewed as "federal common law" may also be treated, in the alternative, as implications from a constitutional provision or from the structure and relationship among clusters of such provisions. Hence, questions about the legitimacy of federal common lawmaking often overlaps with those concerning the legitimacy of particular interpretive techniques.

The broad topic of federal common law has a miscellaneous quality, in view of the wide variety of subject matters in which the power to formulate such law has been or might be recognized. Rather than attempting an exhaustive survey, this Chapter focuses on some of the major areas of judicial lawmaking in actions in the federal district courts.[1]

---

[1]   Federal common law is also formulated and applied in actions originating in the state courts. See, *e.g.*, Bellia, *State Courts and the Making of Federal Common Law*, 153 U.Pa.L.Rev. 825 (2005); Meltzer, *State Court Forfeitures of Federal Rights*, 99 Harv.L.Rev. 1128 (1986).

This Chapter draws a rough organizational distinction between common lawmaking that (i) defines primary legal obligations (Section 1) and (ii) shapes remedies to enforce primary obligations (Section 2). The boundary, however, can be blurry, as the nature of the remedy may have much to do with determining the significance and, at least as a practical matter, the very existence of the right.

1. DEFINING PRIMARY OBLIGATIONS

INTRODUCTORY NOTE

Erie's holding addressed the question of what law applies in diversity cases. It said nothing explicit about the law to be applied to fill in the gaps inevitably left in any complex federal statutory scheme. Not long after Erie, in a case involving the financial rights and responsibilities created by a federal statutory program, the Court had occasion to address whether such gap-filling calls for the application of state law or, instead, allows the federal judiciary to craft federal rules of decision to supply the omission.

Clearfield Trust Co. v. United States

318 U.S. 363 (1943).
Certiorari to the Circuit Court of Appeals for the Third Circuit.

■ MR. JUSTICE DOUGLAS delivered the opinion of the Court.

On April 28, 1936, a check was drawn on the Treasurer of the United States through the Federal Reserve Bank of Philadelphia to the order of Clair A. Barner in the amount of $24.20 * * *[,] for services rendered by Barner to the Works Progress Administration. The check was placed in the mail addressed to Barner * * *[, who] never received the check. Some unknown person obtained it in a mysterious manner and presented it to the J.C. Penney Co. store in Clearfield, Pa., representing that he was the payee and identifying himself to the satisfaction of the employees of J.C. Penney Co. He endorsed the check in the name of Barner and transferred it to J.C. Penney Co. in exchange for cash and merchandise. * * * J.C. Penney Co. endorsed the check over to the Clearfield Trust Co. which accepted it as agent for the purpose of collection and endorsed it as follows: "Pay to the order of Federal Reserve Bank of Philadelphia, Prior Endorsements Guaranteed."[1] Clearfield Trust Co. collected the check from the United States through the Federal Reserve Bank of Philadelphia and paid the full amount thereof to J.C. Penney Co. Neither

---

[1]   Guarantee of all prior endorsements on presentment for payment of such a check to Federal Reserve banks or member bank depositories is required by Treasury Regulations.

the Clearfield Trust Co. nor J.C. Penney Co. had any knowledge or suspicion of the forgery. Each acted in good faith. On or before May 10, 1936, Barner advised the timekeeper and the foreman of the W.P.A. project on which he was employed that he had not received the check in question. This information was duly communicated to other agents of the United States and on November 30, 1936, Barner executed an affidavit alleging that the endorsement of his name on the check was a forgery. No notice was given the Clearfield Trust Co. or J.C. Penney Co. of the forgery until January 12, 1937, at which time the Clearfield Trust Co. was notified. The first notice received by Clearfield Trust Co. that the United States was asking reimbursement was on August 31, 1937.

This suit was instituted in 1939 by the United States against the Clearfield Trust Co. * * *. The cause of action was based on the express guaranty of prior endorsements made by the Clearfield Trust Co. J.C. Penney Co. intervened as a defendant. * * * The District Court held that the rights of the parties were to be determined by the law of Pennsylvania and that since the United States unreasonably delayed in giving notice of the forgery to the Clearfield Trust Co., it was barred from recovery under the rule of Market Street Title & Trust Co. v. Chelten T. Co., 296 Pa. 230, 145 A. 848. It accordingly dismissed the complaint. * * * [T]he Circuit Court of Appeals reversed. * * *

We agree with the Circuit Court of Appeals that the rule of Erie R. Co. v. Tompkins, 304 U.S. 64, does not apply to this action. The rights and duties of the United States on commercial paper which it issues are governed by federal rather than local law. When the United States disburses its funds or pays its debts, it is exercising a constitutional function or power. This check was issued for services performed under the Federal Emergency Relief Act of 1935. The authority to issue the check had its origin in the Constitution and the statutes of the United States and was in no way dependent on the laws of Pennsylvania or of any other state. The duties imposed upon the United States and the rights acquired by it as a result of the issuance find their roots in the same federal sources.[2] In absence of an applicable Act of Congress it is for the federal courts to fashion the governing rule of law according to their own standards. * * *

In our choice of the applicable federal rule we have occasionally selected state law. But reasons which may make state law at times the appropriate federal rule are singularly inappropriate here. The issuance of commercial paper by the United States is on a vast scale and transactions in that paper from issuance to payment will commonly occur in several states. The application of state law, even without the conflict of laws rules of the forum, would subject the rights and duties of the

---

[2]   Various Treasury Regulations govern the payment and endorsement of government checks and warrants and the reimbursement of the Treasurer of the United States by Federal Reserve banks and member bank depositories on payment of checks or warrants bearing a forged endorsement. Forgery of the check was an offense against the United States. Criminal Code § 148, 18 U.S.C. § 262.

United States to exceptional uncertainty. It would lead to great diversity in results by making identical transactions subject to the vagaries of the laws of the several states. The desirability of a uniform rule is plain. And while the federal law merchant developed for about a century under the regime of Swift v. Tyson, 16 Pet. 1 [(1842)], represented general commercial law rather than a choice of a federal rule designed to protect a federal right, it nevertheless stands as a convenient source of reference for fashioning federal rules applicable to these federal questions.

United States v. National Exchange Bank, 214 U.S. 302 [(1909)], falls in that category. The Court held that the United States could recover as drawee from one who presented for payment a pension check on which the name of the payee had been forged, in spite of a protracted delay on the part of the United States in giving notice of the forgery. * * *

The National Exchange Bank case went no further than to hold that prompt notice of the discovery of the forgery was not a condition precedent to suit. It did not reach the question whether lack of prompt notice might be a defense. We think it may. If it is shown that the drawee on learning of the forgery did not give prompt notice of it and that damage resulted, recovery by the drawee is barred. [Citing lower federal court decisions.] The fact that the drawee is the United States and the laches those of its employees are not material. The United States as drawee of commercial paper stands in no different light than any other drawee. As stated in United States v. National Exchange Bank, 270 U.S. 527, 534 [(1926)], "The United States does business on business terms." It is not excepted from the general rules governing the rights and duties of drawees "by the largeness of its dealings and its having to employ agents to do what if done by a principal in person would leave no room for doubt." Id.[, at 535]. But the damage occasioned by the delay must be established and not left to conjecture. Cases such as Market St. Title & Trust Co. v. Chelten Trust Co., [145 A. 848 (Pa.1929)], place the burden on the drawee of giving prompt notice of the forgery—injury to the defendant being presumed by the mere fact of delay. But we do not think that he who accepts a forged signature of a payee deserves that preferred treatment. It is his neglect or error in accepting the forger's signature which occasions the loss. He should be allowed to shift that loss to the drawee only on a clear showing that the drawee's delay in notifying him of the forgery caused him damage. No such damage has been shown by Clearfield Trust Co. who so far as appears can still recover from J.C. Penney Co. The only showing on the part of the latter is contained in the stipulation to the effect that if a check cashed for a customer is returned unpaid or for reclamation a short time after the date on which it is cashed, the employees can often locate the person who cashed it. It is further stipulated that when J.C. Penney Co. was notified of the forgery in the present case none of its employees was able to remember anything about the transaction or check in question. The inference is that the more prompt the notice the more likely the detection of the forger. But that falls short of a showing that the delay caused a manifest loss. It is but another way of saying that mere delay is enough.

Affirmed.

■ [JUSTICES MURPHY and RUTLEDGE did not participate.]

NOTE ON THE EXISTENCE, SOURCES, AND SCOPE OF FEDERAL COMMON LAW

(1) The Logic of Clearfield Trust. The Brief for the United States in Clearfield explained why the choice between federal and state law in cases involving the proprietary interests of the government rarely presented itself before Erie: "Under the regime of Swift v. Tyson, since the law of commercial contracts and negotiable instruments was of course regarded as 'general law,' the courts found it unnecessary to consider separately the applicability of state decisional law to contracts or negotiable instruments involving the United States. The law merchant as interpreted by the federal courts was as a rule applied without discussion. Prior to Erie R. Co. v. Tompkins, an issue in regard to governing law insofar as the United States was concerned could have arisen only where the state law took the form of a state statute or state decisions interpreting such statutes. Such an issue seems to have been rarely presented and cannot be said to have been clearly considered or determined." Brief for Respondent at 11–12, Clearfield Trust Co. v. United States, 318 U.S. 363 (1943) (No. 490). Once Erie denied the existence of general law unattached to any sovereign, it became necessary to determine whether— and under what criteria—federal or state law would apply in such cases.

Why exactly did the Court conclude "that the rule of Erie * * * does not apply to this action" and that federal law instead governs? The Court said that the check paid for services performed under a federal statute. It added that the authority to issue the check, and the duties and rights that flowed from its issuance, were "rooted" in the Constitution and federal statutes, though it failed to identify the constitutional provision and cited only a federal statute that criminalized forgery. And it noted that Treasury regulations governed the operation of federal checks in various ways not at issue in the case. Was the Court claiming that these sources authorized the federal common law rule it made? That they preempted state law and required the Court to develop a federal rule? Did the federal common law rule result from an interpretation of these federal sources? In connection with this last question, note that the Court in crafting its federal common law rule relied on pre-Erie general law precedents that, when announced, lacked the status of federal law. Why did the Court look to these sources? Was it appropriate to do so?

(2) Erie and the "New" Federal Common Law. In a famous article, Judge Henry Friendly offered the following defense of the Court's choice to adopt federal common law in cases such as Clearfield: "[B]y banishing the spurious uniformity of Swift v. Tyson—what Mr. Justice Frankfurter was to call 'the attractive vision of a uniform body of federal law' but a vision only—

and by leaving to the states what ought to be left to them, Erie led to the emergence of a federal decisional law in areas of national concern that is truly uniform because, under the Supremacy Clause, it is binding in every forum, and therefore is predictable and useful as its predecessor, more general in subject matter but limited to the federal courts, was not. The clarion yet careful pronouncement of Erie, 'There is no federal general common law,' opened the way to what, for want of a better term, we may call specialized federal common law. * * *

"So, as it seems to me, the Supreme Court, in the years since Erie, has been forging a new centripetal tool incalculably useful to our federal system. It has employed a variety of techniques—spontaneous generation as in the cases of government contracts or interstate controversies, implication of a private federal cause of action from a statute providing other sanctions, construing a jurisdictional grant as a command to fashion federal law, and the normal judicial filling of statutory interstices. * * *

"The complementary concepts—that federal courts must follow state decisions on matters of substantive law appropriately cognizable by the states whereas state courts must follow federal decisions on subjects within national legislative power where Congress has so directed or the basic scheme of the Constitution demands—seem so beautifully simple, and so simply beautiful, that we must wonder why a century and a half was needed to discover them, and must wonder even more why anyone should want to shy away once the discovery was made." Friendly, *In Praise of Erie—And of the New Federal Common Law*, 39 N.Y.U.L.Rev. 383, 405, 421–22 (1964).

(3) The Need for Federal Common Law. Justice Jackson articulated an influential argument for federal common lawmaking in his concurrence in D'Oench, Duhme & Co. v. FDIC, 315 U.S. 447 (1942). There the FDIC sued D'Oench Duhme in federal court in Missouri to recover on a note that the defendant had executed and that was payable to an Illinois bank. The defendant initially had sold the bank some bonds that had become past due; the defendant then gave the bank the note in 1933, "with the understanding it will not be called for payment," to replace the bonds—so that they would not appear as assets of the bank. The FDIC insured the bank in 1934 and acquired the note in 1938 as collateral for a loan made in connection with the assumption of the bank's deposit liabilities by another bank. On review, the Supreme Court declared that "the liability of [D'Oench Duhme] on the note involves decision of a federal, not a state, question * * *." The Court found in various federal statutes "a federal policy to protect [the FDIC] and the public funds which it administers against misrepresentations as to the securities or other assets in the portfolios of the banks which [the FDIC] insures or to which it makes loans."

In concurrence, Justice Jackson noted that because "no federal statute purports to define the Corporation's rights," the Court had to determine whether to apply state law or to resolve the question as a matter of federal common law. Although acknowledging that there was no "general common law," Jackson added that "this is not to say that wherever we have occasion to decide a federal question which cannot be answered from federal statutes alone we may not resort to all the source materials of the common law, or that when we have fashioned an answer it does not become a part of the federal non-statutory or common law." He continued:

"Were we bereft of the common law, our federal system would be impotent. This follows from the recognized futility of attempting all-complete statutory codes, and is apparent from the terms of the Constitution itself. * * * In some cases [a federal court] may see fit for special reasons to give the law of a particular state highly persuasive or even controlling effect, but in the last analysis its decision turns upon the law of the United States, not that of any state. Federal law is no juridical chameleon, changing complexion to match that of each state wherein lawsuits happen to be commenced because of the accidents of service of process and of the application of the venue statutes. It is found in the federal Constitution, statutes, or common law. Federal common law implements the federal Constitution and statutes, and is conditioned by them. Within these limits, federal courts are free to apply the traditional common-law technique of decision and to draw upon all the sources of the common law in cases such as the present."

Assuming Justice Jackson is correct that Congress cannot anticipate and provide for all of the details necessary to complete a statute, why wouldn't state law have sufficed to provide the missing terms in D'Oench Duhme?

(4) The Sources of Federal Common Law. There is a consensus in the Supreme Court and among most scholars that post-Erie federal common law must be traceable, to some degree, to a constitutional or statutory source— even if a given common law rule does not flow from recognizably conventional approaches to constitutional or statutory interpretation.[1] Federal common law may be justifiable, for example, as an implication from the constitutional structure, as the product of an implicit delegation of power from Congress to supply an apparent omission in a statutory scheme, or as a tool for addressing a conflict between state law and federal statutory policy.

Four arguments might be marshaled in support of this general view.

(a) The first argument comes from Erie itself, p. 760, *supra,* which held (with emphasis added) that "*[e]xcept* in matters governed by the Federal Constitution or by Acts of Congress, the law to be applied in any case is the law of the State."

---

[1] Among scholars outside this consensus, Professor Weinberg argues that "there are no fundamental constraints on the fashioning of federal rules of decision" by federal courts. Weinberg, *Federal Common Law,* 83 Nw.U.L.Rev. 805, 805 (1989). For her, just as state courts have general lawmaking power in areas of state concern such as torts or contracts, federal courts have similar power in any area in which the Constitution authorizes federal legislative or executive action. As long as federal courts act "within their constitutional and statutory jurisdiction," she argues, the source of judicial lawmaking power "is the existence of a legitimate national governmental interest." *Id.* 813. Professor Weinberg says that hers is the "true position" of federal common law but acknowledges that it is not consonant with the "official position" of the Supreme Court. *Id.* 805–06.

At the other end of the spectrum, Professor Redish maintains that practically all federal common law is ruled out by the Rules Enabling Act, 28 U.S.C. § 1652. See Redish, *Federal Common Law, Political Legitimacy, and the Interpretive Process: An "Institutionalist" Perspective,* 83 Nw.U.L.Rev. 761 (1989).

(b) Second, the Rules of Decision Act, 28 U.S.C. § 1652, discussed in Erie, provides: "The laws of the several states, *except* where the Constitution or treaties of the United States or Acts of Congress otherwise require or provide, shall be regarded as rules of decision in civil actions in the courts of the United States, in cases where they apply."[2]

(c) The third argument is that lawmaking as a general matter should be made by politically accountable branches of government. See, *e.g.*, Redish, The Federal Courts in the Political Order 29–46 (1991); Merrill, *The Common Law Powers of Federal Courts*, 52 U.Chi.L.Rev. 1, 19–27 (1995). As the Court has said, "the federal lawmaking power is vested in the legislative, not the judicial, branch of government." Northwest Airlines v. Transport Workers Union, 451 U.S. 77, 95 (1981).

(d) A final argument sounds in federalism. The Tenth Amendment confirms the enumerated power structure of the Constitution, which entails that the federal government can exercise power only in accordance with the Constitution, which does not give federal courts naked lawmaking power. Relatedly, the cumbersome lawmaking procedures prescribed by the Constitution—for example, bicameral enactment and either presidential assent or a legislative supermajority—protect state interests. By constitutional design, congressional action is restrained by the "political safeguards of federalism"—the responsiveness of national legislators to the interests of the states. Lawmaking by federal courts, by contrast, lacks these important restraints. See Merrill, *supra*, at 13–19; Mishkin, *Some Further Last Words on Erie—The Thread*, 87 Harv.L.Rev. 1682, 1685 (1974); Field, *The Legitimacy of Federal Common Law*, 12 Pace L.Rev. 303, 305–06 (1992). See also Clark, *Separation of Powers as a Safeguard of Federalism*, 79 Tex.L.Rev. 1321 (2001) (The Supremacy Clause, U.S. Const. Art. VI, implicitly limits federal lawmaking to the three carefully chosen procedural methods for adopting or amending the "Constitution" (Articles VII and V), enacting "a Law" (Article I, § 7), and making "Treaties" (Article II, § 2, cl. 2)); but see Monaghan, *Supremacy Clause Textualism*, 110 Colum.L.Rev. 731, 750–51 (2010) (Supremacy Clause not framed to promote federalism).[3]

(5) The Scope of Federal Common Law. None of the arguments above speak to the degree or type of connection that a federal common law rule

---

[2]   A rare decision discussing the Rule of Decision Act's pertinence to federal common lawmaking is DelCostello v. International Bhd. of Teamsters, 462 U.S. 151, 158–59 n.13 (1983), p. 818, in which the Court rejected the view that the Act barred judicial creation of a statute of limitations for a federal right of action. Noting that the Act "authorizes application of state law only when federal law does not 'otherwise require or provide,'" the Court found no barrier to formulation of a federal rule of decision when called for by "the policies and requirements of the underlying cause of action * * *." One might also argue that the statutory phrase "in cases where [state rules] apply" means "in cases in which there is no federal common law preempting state rules of decision." See Meltzer, *State Court Forfeitures of Federal Rights*, 99 Harv.L.Rev. 1128, 1168 n.194 & sources cited (1986); Weinberg, *supra*. For the view that the Act places greater limits on federal common lawmaking than suggested by DelCostello, see Merrill, *supra*, at 27–32.

[3]   What about the legitimacy of state court common lawmaking? The Supreme Court has stated, "Federal courts, unlike state courts, are not general common-law courts and do not possess a general power to develop and apply their own rules of decision." City of Milwaukee v. Illinois, 451 U.S. 304, 312 (1981). For skepticism about this distinction, see Nelson, *The Legitimacy of (Some) Federal Common Law*, 101 Va.L.Rev. 1, 25–28 (2015).

must have to a federal enactment. The requisite connection is often elusive and tends to turn on one's conception of judicial power and theory of statutory or constitutional interpretation. Scholars have disagreed on these matters and the Supreme Court's view has fluctuated in the decades since Clearfield. Consider these scholarly viewpoints:

(a) Professor Hill would limit federal common lawmaking largely to areas where federal statutes or the Constitution preempts state lawmaking and implicitly leaves it to federal courts to fashion rules of decision in the absence of overt guidance from Congress. Hill, *The Law-Making Power of the Federal Courts: Constitutional Preemption*, 67 Colum.L.Rev. 1024, 1028–68 (1967). See also Clark, *Federal Common Law: A Structural Reinterpretation*, 144 U.Pa.L.Rev. 1245 (1996) (arguing that much of federal common law should only govern matters that the Constitution's structure places beyond state legislative competence).

(b) Professor Field would permit federal common lawmaking so long as the court can "point to a federal enactment, constitutional or statutory, that it interprets as authorizing the federal common law rule." Field, *Sources of Law: The Scope of Federal Common Law*, 99 Harv.L.Rev. 881, 887 (1986).

(c) Professor Kramer maintains that "federal courts can make common law * * * so long as whatever rules the courts fashion are consistent with and further an underlying federal enactment," or fall within areas (such as admiralty, foreign relations, and interstate disputes) in which the Constitution makes federal sovereignty exclusive. Kramer, *The Lawmaking Power of Federal Courts*, 12 Pace L.Rev. 263, 288 n.84, 289 (1992).

(d) Professor Merrill argues that "federal common law is legitimate insofar as it is the product of textual interpretation, understood to mean a search for the specific intentions of the draftsmen of the [statutory or constitutional] text," including a specific intention to establish a federal policy that preempts state law, or a specific intention to delegate lawmaking powers to federal courts. Merrill, Paragraph (4), *supra*, at 3; compare Merrill, *The Judicial Prerogative*, 12 Pace L.Rev. 327, 353–56 (1992) (acknowledging federal common law can be made in other ways).

(e) Professors Tidmarsh and Murray contend that federal common law should be limited to judicial lawmaking in six "enclaves" recognized in Supreme Court case law: cases affecting the rights and obligations of the United States, interstate controversies, cases affecting international relations, admiralty cases, "significant conflicts" between "uniquely federal interests" and the operation of state law, and cases involving preclusion. Tidmarsh & Murray, *A Theory of Federal Common Law*, 100 Nw.U.L.Rev. 585, 588, 594–609 (2006).

Consider which of these theories provides the best descriptive account of the cases in this Chapter, and which provides the best account of how federal common law should operate.

(6) Congressional Delegation of Federal Common Lawmaking. Congress sometimes expressly delegates lawmaking authority to the federal courts. For example, the first sentence of Rule 501 of the Federal Rules of Evidence, which Congress enacted (88 Stat. 1933 (1975)), provides: "Except as otherwise required * * * [by federal law], the privilege of a witness, person, government, State, or political subdivision thereof shall be governed by the principles of the common law as they may be interpreted by the courts of the United States in the light of reason and experience."

What about implied delegations of lawmaking power? The broad language of section 1 of the Sherman Act, 15 U.S.C. § 1, is often viewed as inviting the courts to fashion a common law of anti-competitive practices. See National Soc'y of Professional Eng'rs v. United States, 435 U.S. 679, 688 (1978) (noting that the "legislative history [of the Sherman Act] makes it perfectly clear that [Congress] expected the courts to give shape to the statute's broad mandate by drawing on common-law tradition"); but see Texas Indus., Inc. v. Radcliff Materials, Inc., 451 U.S. 630 (1981) (federal common lawmaking power recognized in National Soc'y of Professional Eng'rs does not extend to the fashioning of a right of contribution among antitrust co-conspirators); see generally Merrill, *supra*, 52 U.Chi.L.Rev. at 38, 40–46; Volokh, *Judicial Non-Delegation, the Inherent-Powers Corollary, and Federal Common Law*, 66 Emory L.J. 1391, 1438–43 (2017).

How far can the notion of implied delegation be taken? Might the Clearfield-D'Oench Duhme line of cases rest on the idea that a statute establishing a federal program can be understood to include an implied delegation to judges to supply omissions? See Young, *Preemption and Federal Common Law*, 83 Notre Dame L.Rev. 1639, 1642–43 (2008); compare Merrill, *supra*, 52 U.Chi.L.Rev. at 40–42 (arguing that delegated lawmaking can justify federal common law only if in accord with the specific intent of the enacting body). Would such a theory of "implied" delegation leave the judiciary without an intelligible principle to guide the resultant development of federal common law? See Nielson, *Erie as Nondelegation*, 72 Ohio St.L.J. 239, 296–301 (2011) (arguing that grants of federal common lawmaking authority are subject to the strictures of the nondelegation doctrine and maintaining that the Sherman Act as applied raises serious constitutional questions).

NOTE ON THE RELEVANCE OF THEORIES OF STATUTORY INTERPRETATION TO FEDERAL COMMON LAW

When the Supreme Court decided Clearfield and D'Oench Duhme, its dominant approach to statutory interpretation was the fulfillment of the overall statutory purpose rather than examination of the "plain meaning" of the statute.[1] Today that is no longer true. This Note sketches the evolving theoretical approaches to statutory interpretation most relevant to the

---

[1]   For examples of the earlier, "plain meaning" approach, see, *e.g.*, Caminetti v. United States, 242 U.S. 470, 490 (1917); White v. United States, 191 U.S. 545, 551 (1903); United States v. Hartwell, 73 U.S. (6 Wall.) 385, 396 (1867). Of course, the Court had long since recognized that federal courts may deviate from plain meaning when sources such as the legislative history offer clear evidence of contrary legislative intent or when a statute, literally construed, would produce an absurd result. See, *e.g.*, Church of the Holy Trinity v. United States, 143 U.S. 457 (1892). But the relative emphasis on purpose became considerably more pronounced in the era in which the Court decided Clearfield.

theory of federal common law and then considers the relevance of interpretive trends in the Supreme Court.[2]

(1) Statutory Purpose and the Legal Process School. In the leading case at the time of Clearfield and D'Oench Duhme, United States v. American Trucking Ass'ns, 310 U.S. 534, 543 (1940), the Court announced that when the literal or semantic meaning of a statute was " 'plainly at variance with the policy of the legislation as a whole,' " the Court's duty was to "follow[ ] that purpose, rather than the literal words." This statement reflected—and contributed to—a post-New Deal trend in statutory interpretation theory that posited (a) that legislatures enact all statutes for a purpose; and (b) that courts in our system of government act appropriately—indeed, advance the goal of legislative supremacy—when they interpret statutes to further the legislation's overall purpose, rather than hewing literally to texts often drafted in haste. See, *e.g.*, Cox, *Judge Learned Hand and the Interpretation of Statutes*, 60 Harv.L.Rev. 370, 370–71, 380 n.9 (1947); Frankfurter, *Some Reflections on the Reading of Statutes*, 47 Colum.L.Rev. 527, 536–37 (1947); Radin, A *Short Way with Statutes*, 56 Harv.L.Rev. 388 (1942); see also Parillo, *Leviathan and Interpretive Revolution: The Administrative State, the Judiciary, and the Rise of Legislative History, 1890–1950*, 123 Yale L.J. 266, 351 (2013) (explaining the rise in the judicial use of legislative history in the 1940s as a product of the new administrative state, and the connection of this trend to purposivism).

This "purposivist" approach was later captured in the canonical teaching materials prepared by Professors Hart and Sacks: The Legal Process: Basic Problems in the Making and Application of Law (tent.ed.1958) (Eskridge & Frickey eds. 1994). Hart and Sacks wrote that "[t]he idea of a statute without an intelligible purpose is foreign to the idea of law and inadmissible." *Id.* 1124. Accordingly, they believed that judges should use various tools of construction—including the overall policy evinced by the statutory text, the legislative history, and public knowledge of the mischief sought to be addressed—to determine what "purpose ought to be attributed to the statute" and to interpret the words "to carry out the purpose as best it can." *Id.* 1374. They emphasized that, in doing so, judges "should assume, unless the contrary unmistakably appears, that the legislature was made up of reasonable persons pursuing reasonable purposes reasonably." *Id.* 1378.

Courts applying the Legal Process approach could supply apparently omitted statutory terms by asking, in light of the available contextual evidence, how a "reasonable legislator" would have implemented the purposes underlying the statute. Such an approach, if accepted, would easily account for a federal court's authority to decide (a) whether an apparent omission should be addressed with a federal rather than a state rule of

---

[2] For discussion of the current debate, see generally Bressman, Rubin, & Stack, The Regulatory State (3d ed.2019); Eskridge, Brudney, Chafetz, Frickey, & Garrett, Cases and Materials on Legislation and Regulation: Statutes and the Creation of Public Policy (6th ed.2019); Eskridge, Gluck, & Nourse, Statutes, Regulation, and Interpretation: Legislation and Administration in the Republic of Statutes (2014); Manning & Stephenson, Legislation and Regulation (4th ed.2021); Nelson, Statutory Interpretation (2d ed.2023); Mikva, Lane, Gerhardt, & Hemel, Legislative Process (5th ed. 2022); Popkin, Materials on Legislation: Political Language and the Political Process (5th ed.2009).

decision because of the need for uniformity or the inconsistency of a state rule of decision with overall federal statutory policy; and (b) what federal rule of decision to prescribe when state law is deemed inappropriate.

(2) Textualism. Beginning in the late twentieth century, an approach that came to be known as the "new textualism" challenged the Legal Process school's purposive assumptions as inconsistent with the constitutional structure and the realities of the legislative process. See Eskridge, *The New Textualism*, 37 UCLA L.Rev. 621 (1990).

First, the leading judicial proponent of textualism, Justice Scalia, emphasized that Article I, § 7 of the Constitution prescribes the elaborate and cumbersome requirements of bicameralism and presentment and that judges must therefore pay close attention to the details of the enacted text, which is the only expression of policy that has made its way through that process.[3] Conroy v. Aniskoff, 507 U.S. 511, 519 (1993) (Scalia, J., concurring). Second, relying on the insights of public choice theory, other leading textualists maintained that the legislative process—which is marked by multiple veto gates (*e.g.*, committees), high procedural hurdles (*e.g.*, the Senate filibuster), and often hard-to-detect deals (*e.g.*, logrolling)—is simply too complex, opaque, and path dependent to allow judges to reconstruct what Congress would have intended to do about a matter that the text itself does not conclusively resolve. See, *e.g.*, Easterbrook, *Statutes' Domains*, 50 U.Chi.L.Rev. 533, 547 (1983); Shepsle, *Congress Is a "They," Not an "It": Legislative Intent as Oxymoron*, 12 Int'l.Rev.L. & Econ. 239, 244 (1992). Third, textualists stressed that the framing of statutory policy entails not merely the articulation of legislative purposes, but also the specification of the *means* for carrying out those purposes. Since the choice of means may be the product of hard-fought legislative compromise, textualists argued that abstracting from a statute's textual details to the broader purposes behind them "dishonors the legislative choice as effectively as expressly refusing to follow the law." Easterbrook, *Text, History, and Structure in Statutory Interpretation*, 17 Harv.J.L. & Pub.Pol'y 61, 68 (1994). But see Friedrich v. City of Chicago, 888 F.2d 511, 514 (7th Cir.1989) (Posner, J.) ("[J]udges * * * know that statutes are purposive utterances and that language is a slippery medium in which to encode a purpose. They know that legislatures, including the Congress of the United States, often legislate in haste, without considering fully the potential application of their words to novel settings.").

(3) Common Law Theories of Statutory Interpretation. Even if the new textualism accurately depicts the legislative process, does it necessarily follow that the role of the federal courts in our constitutional system is to enforce legislative compromise rather than to make statutory law more coherent and complete? An important strain of legal thought has long maintained that American judicial power should be understood to include common law powers in relation to statutes. See, *e.g.*, Landis, *Statutes and*

---

   3   Textualism presupposes that legislators can use words to communicate with judges, administrators, and the public—an assumption that rests on the idea that members of a social and linguistic community have shared conventions for decoding language in context. See, *e.g.*, Schauer, *Statutory Construction and the Coordinating Function of Plain Meaning*, 1990 Sup.Ct.Rev. 231, 251; Waldron, *Legislators' Intentions and Unintentional Legislation*, in Law and Interpretation 339 (Marmor ed. 1995).

the Sources of Law, 2 Harv.J. on Legis. 7, 7–12 (1965); Stone, *The Common Law in the United States*, 50 Harv.L.Rev. 4, 13, 15 (1936). Modern legal scholars have offered numerous arguments—some historical, some philosophical, and some pragmatic—to support the idea that courts should have robust inherent authority to make enacted law more coherent, adaptable, and/or just. See, *e.g.*, Dworkin, Law's Empire (1986); Eskridge, Dynamic Statutory Interpretation (1994); Aleinikoff, *Updating Statutory Interpretation*, 87 Mich.L.Rev. 20 (1988); Sunstein, *Interpreting Statutes in the Regulatory State*, 103 Harv.L.Rev. 405, 414–51 (1989); Strauss, *The Common Law and Statutes*, 70 U.Colo.L.Rev. 225 (1999).

Professor Eskridge argues that the original understanding of "the judicial Power of the United States" in Article III would have included the power to engage in equitable interpretation, a form of inherent authority that, as relevant here, empowered English judges to extend a statute to cover omitted cases that fell within the statute's reason or purpose. See Eskridge, *Textualism, the Unknown Ideal?*, 96 Mich.L.Rev. 1509 (1998); Eskridge, *All About Words: Early Understandings of the "Judicial Power" in Statutory Interpretation, 1776–1806*, 101 Colum.L.Rev. 990 (2001). According to Eskridge, it would have been natural for the founders—who had grown up within the English legal system—to assume that the judicial power included such authority. Professor Manning, by contrast, argues that English judicial practice—which involved considerable commingling of legislative and judicial functions (*e.g.*, the Upper House of Parliament was the court of last resort)—does not provide an appropriate model for understanding the interpretive powers of federal courts in the very different American system of separated powers. Manning, *Textualism and the Equity of the Statute*, 101 Colum.L.Rev. 1 (2001); Manning, *Deriving Rules of Statutory Interpretation from the Constitution*, 101 Colum.L.Rev. 1648 (2001).

(4) The Supreme Court and Textualism. The Supreme Court's statutory interpretation cases are today dominated by textualism. See Eskridge, Slocum, & Tobia, *Textualism's Defining Moment*, 123 Colum.L.Rev. 1611, 1615 (2023); Lee & Mouritsen, *Judging Ordinary Meaning*, 127 Yale L.J. 788, 792–93 (2018). One upshot is that the Court gives statutory text a more prominent and dominant role than in the era in which Clearfield and D'Oench Duhme were decided. In particular, it no longer elevates statutory purpose over text. See, *e.g.*, Luna Perez v. Sturgis Public Schools, 598 U.S. 142, 150 (2023) ("It is quite mistaken to assume * * * that any interpretation of a law that does more to advance a statute's putative goal must be the law") (internal quotation marks and citations omitted); Mohamad v. Palestinian Authority, 566 U.S. 449, 460 (2012) ("[N]o legislation pursues its purposes at all costs, and petitioners' purposive argument simply cannot overcome the force of the plain text") (internal quotation marks and citations omitted); Morrison v. National Australia Bank Ltd., 561 U.S. 247, 270 (2010) ("It is our function to give the statute the effect its language suggests, however modest that may be; not to extend it to admirable purposes it might be used to achieve.").

Yet textualism as practiced at the Court comes in many flavors. See Eskridge, Slocum, & Tobia, *supra*, at 1616 (showing that textualists on the

Supreme Court "frequently disagree" about "what the relevant rules [of textualism] are"); Grove, *Which Textualism?*, 134 Harv.L.Rev. 265, 267 (2020) (arguing that textualism in practice vacillates between a "formalistic textualism" that focuses on text and downplays policy concerns and practical consequences, and a "flexible textualism" that "make[s] sense of that text by considering policy and social context as well as practical consequences"). Of most significance to federal common law, the Court sometimes still considers "legislative scheme," or a statute's context or purpose, to discern the meaning of statutory text, albeit in a more restrained manner than during the Clearfield-D'Oench Duhme era. See, *e.g.*, West Virginia v. EPA, 597 U.S. 697, 721 (2022) (" 'It is a fundamental canon of statutory construction that the words of a statute must be read in their context and with a view to their place in the overall statutory scheme' ") (citation omitted); King v. Burwell, 576 U.S. 473, 486 (2015) (acknowledging that "[i]f the statutory language is plain, we must enforce it according to its terms," but noting that "oftentimes the 'meaning—or ambiguity—of certain words or phrases may only become evident when placed in context,' " and thus that in "deciding whether the language is plain, we must read the words 'in their context and with a view to their place in the overall statutory scheme' ") (citation omitted); Milner v. Dep't of the Navy, 562 U.S. 562, 571 n.5, 572 (2011) (noting, after textualist analysis of FOIA exemption, that the "statute's purpose reinforces this understanding of the exemption" because Congress's aim was to "confin[e] the provision's meaning to its words," and that the "judicial role is to enforce that congressionally determined balance").[4]

Is the rise of textualism in tension with the Clearfield-D'Oench Duhme approach to federal common law? To the extent that the Court has grown skeptical that legislative compromises pursue a statute's background purpose to its fullest, is it sound to presume that a statute has implicitly authorized the Court to supply apparent omissions in light of statutory purpose? How easy is it, without reference to statutory purpose or at least statutory context, to discern whether the relevant statutory text (i) marks out a point of legislative compromise, or (ii) contains an omission? If federal courts are not implicitly authorized to supply apparent statutory omissions, why shouldn't they rely on state law to supply the omission?

The Supreme Court has in recent decades taken a stricter approach to federal common law than is reflected in Clearfield Trust and D'Oench Duhme. The following two very different decisions can be seen as transition points to the modern approach.

---

[4]   For nuanced accounts of the Court's integration of statutory purpose into textualism, see Krishnakumar, *Backdoor Purposivism*, 69 Duke L.J. 1275, 1279 (2020) (arguing that modern textualist Justices "regularly employ pragmatic reasoning as well as supposedly neutral textualist tools to divine—or manufacture—congressional purpose and intent" that guides statutory interpretation); Re, *The New Holy Trinity*, 18 Green Bag 2d 407, 417 (2015) (explaining that the "key move is to view purposive and pragmatic considerations as relevant to the identification of textual clarity or ambiguity"); Manning, *The New Purposivism*, 2011 Sup.Ct.Rev. 113 (arguing that the Court's textualists are guided by the purposes of Congress as reflected in the specific choices Congress made to carry its purposes into effect).

United States v. Kimbell Foods, Inc.

440 U.S. 715 (1979).

This decision arose out of two cases. The facts of the first give the necessary context for the Court's decision. O.K. Super Markets ("O.K.") took out a $27,000 loan from Kimbell Foods that was secured by interests in O.K.'s equipment and merchandise. The security agreements were executed in compliance with the Texas Uniform Commercial Code. Subsequently, O.K. took out a $300,000 loan from Republic National Bank. That loan was secured by the same collateral as the Kimbell Foods loan. The Small Business Administration (SBA), a federal agency, guaranteed Republic's loan. When O.K. defaulted on its obligations, Kimbell Foods brought suit to recover its debt. Republic assigned its security interest to the SBA, which sued to recover from O.K. At issue was whether Kimbell Foods' or the SBA's security interest took priority and whether federal common law or state law governed the case. No provision of the Small Business Act—the statute under which the SBA guaranteed the loan—spoke to the question of priority.

In an opinion written by Justice Marshall, the Court began by noting, with a citation to Clearfield Trust, that it "has consistently held that federal law governs questions involving the rights of the United States arising under nationwide federal programs." It applied the principles of Clearfield to conclude that "the priority of liens stemming from federal lending programs must be determined with reference to federal law" because the SBA "unquestionably perform[s] federal functions within the meaning of Clearfield." It did not matter, the Court explained, that "the statutes authorizing these federal lending programs do not specify the appropriate rule of decision * * *. It is precisely when Congress has not spoken 'in an area comprising issues substantially related to an established program of government operation,' *id.*, at 593, quoting Mishkin [*The Variousness of 'Federal Law': Competence and Discretion in the Choice of National and State Rules for Decision*, 105 U.Pa.L.Rev. 797, 800 (1957)], that Clearfield directs federal courts to fill the interstices of federal legislation 'according to their own standards.' 318 U.S., at 367."

After determining that federal law "controls the Government's priority rights" because "federal interests are sufficiently implicated to warrant the protection of federal law," the Court turned to what it called the "more difficult task [of] giving content to this federal rule." It described the analysis as follows:

"Controversies directly affecting the operations of federal programs, although governed by federal law, do not inevitably require resort to uniform federal rules. See Clearfield Trust Co. v. United States, 318 U.S. 363, 367 (1943); United States v. Little Lake Misere Land Co., 412 U.S. 580, 594–595 (1973). Whether to adopt state law or to fashion a nationwide federal rule is a matter of judicial policy 'dependent upon a variety of considerations always relevant to the nature of the specific governmental interests and to the effects upon them of applying state law.' United States v. Standard Oil Co., 332 U.S. 301, 310 (1947)."

"Undoubtedly, federal programs that 'by their nature are and must be uniform in character throughout the Nation' necessitate formulation of controlling federal rules. United States v. Yazell, 382 U.S. 341, 354 (1966); [citing additional cases]. Conversely, when there is little need for a nationally uniform body of law, state law may be incorporated as the federal rule of decision. Apart from considerations of uniformity, we must also determine whether application of state law would frustrate specific objectives of the federal programs. If so, we must fashion special rules solicitous of those federal interests. Finally, our choice-of-law inquiry must consider the extent to which application of a federal rule would disrupt commercial relationships predicated on state law."

Applying this balancing test, the Court chose state law to govern. It rejected the government's argument that "nationwide standards favoring claims of the United States are necessary to ease program administration or to safeguard the Federal Treasury from defaulting debtors" and declined to "override intricate state laws of general applicability on which private creditors base their daily commercial transactions." The Court reached these conclusions through a fine-grained analysis of the impact of applying state law to determine the rights of the United States as against private creditors. It rebuffed the government's "generalized pleas for uniformity" and demanded "concrete evidence that adopting state law would adversely affect administration of the federal programs," which the Court concluded was lacking. The Court specifically rejected the arguments that the application of state law would "impede expeditious processing of loans" or would undermine the government's "ability to recover funds disbursed and therefore would conflict with program objectives."

The Court concluded by expressing concern that displacing state commercial law with a uniform judge-made rule in this context might undermine commercial stability: "Because the ultimate consequences of altering settled commercial practices are so difficult to foresee, we hesitate to create new uncertainties, in the absence of careful legislative deliberation. Of course, formulating special rules to govern the priority of the federal consensual liens in issue here would be justified if necessary to vindicate important national interests. But neither the Government nor the Court of Appeals advanced any concrete reasons for rejecting well-established commercial rules which have proven workable over time. Thus, the prudent course is to adopt the readymade body of state law as the federal rule of decision until Congress strikes a different accommodation."

Boyle v. United Technologies Corp.

487 U.S. 500 (1988).

Boyle, a United States Marine helicopter copilot, died when his military helicopter crashed and he drowned. His father filed a federal diversity action against the Sikorsky Division of United Technologies Corporation (Sikorsky), alleging under Virginia tort law that defective repairs had caused the crash and that a defective design of the emergency escape system had prevented Boyle from exiting the helicopter. The jury found Sikorsky liable and awarded petitioner $725,000. The court of appeals reversed, finding that petitioner had not met his burden of proof under state law on the defective repair claim and, as relevant here, that Sikorsky was not liable for the alleged design defect because it was entitled, on the facts, to invoke a newly recognized federal common law "military contractor defense." The Supreme Court affirmed in an opinion by Justice Scalia.

"[W]e have held that a few areas, involving 'uniquely federal interests,' Texas Industries, Inc. v. Radcliff Materials, Inc., 451 U.S. 630, 640 (1981), are so committed by the Constitution and laws of the United States to federal control that state law is pre-empted and replaced, where necessary, by federal law of a content prescribed (absent explicit statutory directive) by the courts—so-called 'federal common law.' See, *e.g.*, United States v. Kimbell Foods, Inc., 440 U.S. 715, 726–729 (1979); Banco Nacional v. Sabbatino, 376 U.S. 398, 426–427 (1964); Howard v. Lyons, 360 U.S. 593, 597 (1959); Clearfield Trust Co. v. United States, 318 U.S. 363, 366–367 (1943); D'Oench, Duhme & Co. v. FDIC, 315 U.S. 447, 457–458 (1942).

"The dispute in the present case borders upon two areas that we have found to involve such 'uniquely federal interests.' We have held that obligations to and rights of the United States under its contracts are governed exclusively by federal law. See, *e.g.*, Clearfield Trust, *supra*. The present case does not involve an obligation to the United States under its contract, but rather liability to third persons. That liability may be styled one in tort, but it arises out of performance of the contract * * *.

"Another area that we have found to be of peculiarly federal concern, warranting the displacement of state law, is the civil liability of federal officials for actions taken in the course of their duty. We have held in many contexts that the scope of that liability is controlled by federal law. See, *e.g.*, Howard v. Lyons, *supra*, 360 U.S., at 597. The present case involves an independent contractor performing its obligation under a procurement contract, rather than an official performing his duty as a federal employee, but there is obviously implicated the same interest in getting the Government's work done.

"We think the reasons for considering these closely related areas to be of 'uniquely federal' interest apply as well to the civil liabilities arising out of the performance of federal procurement contracts. * * *

"[It] is plain that the Federal Government's interest in the procurement of equipment is implicated by suits such as the present one—even though the dispute is one between private parties. It is true that where 'litigation is purely between private parties and does not touch the rights and duties of the United States,' Bank of America Nat. Trust & Sav. Assn. v. Parnell, 352 U.S. 29, 33 (1956), federal law does not govern. Thus, for example, in Miree v. DeKalb County, 433 U.S. 25, 30 (1977), which involved the question whether certain private parties could sue as third-party beneficiaries to an agreement between a municipality and the Federal Aviation Administration, we found that state law was not displaced because 'the operations of the United States in connection with FAA grants such as these . . . would [not] be burdened' by allowing state law to determine whether third-party beneficiaries could sue, *id.*, at 30, and because 'any federal interest in the outcome of the [dispute] before us "[was] far too speculative, far too remote a possibility to justify the application of federal law to transactions essentially of local concern.' " *Id.*, at 32–33, quoting Parnell, *supra*, at 352 U.S., at 33–34; see also Wallis v. Pan American Petroleum, 384 U.S. 63, 69 (1966). But the same is not true here. The imposition of liability on Government contractors will directly affect the terms of Government contracts: either the contractor will decline to manufacture the design specified by the Government, or it will raise its price. Either way, the interests of the United States will be directly affected.

"That the procurement of equipment by the United States is an area of uniquely federal interest does not, however, end the inquiry. That merely establishes a necessary, not a sufficient, condition for the displacement of state law.[3] Displacement will occur only where, as we have variously described, a 'significant conflict' exists between an identifiable 'federal policy or interest and the [operation] of state law,' [Wallis, *supra*, 384 U.S., at 68], or the application of state law would 'frustrate specific objectives' of federal legislation, Kimbell Foods, *supra*, 440 U.S., at 728. The conflict with federal policy need not be as sharp as that which must exist for ordinary pre-emption when Congress legislates 'in a field which the States have traditionally occupied.' Rice v. Santa Fe Elevator Corp., 331 U.S. [218, 230 (1947)]. Or to put the point differently, the fact that the area in question *is* one of unique federal concern changes what would otherwise be a conflict that cannot produce pre-emption into one that can. But conflict there must be. In some cases, for example where the federal interest requires a uniform rule, the entire body of state law applicable to the area conflicts and is replaced by federal rules. See, *e.g.*, Clearfield Trust, 318 U.S., at 366–367 * * *. In others, the conflict is more narrow, and only particular elements of state law are superseded. See, *e.g.*, Little Lake Misere Land Co., 412 U.S., at 595 (even assuming state law should generally govern federal land acquisitions, particular state law at issue may not). * * *

"Here the state-imposed duty of care that is the asserted basis of the contractor's liability (specifically, the duty to equip helicopters with the sort of escape-hatch mechanism petitioner claims was necessary) is precisely contrary to the duty imposed by the Government contract (the duty to manufacture and deliver helicopters with the sort of escape-hatch mechanism shown by the specifications). Even in this sort of situation, it would be unreasonable to say that there is always a 'significant conflict' between the state law and a federal policy or interest. If, for example, a federal procurement officer orders, by model number, a quantity of stock helicopters that happen to be equipped with escape hatches opening

---

[3]   We refer here to the displacement of state law, although it is possible to analyze it as the displacement of federal-law reference to state law for the rule of decision. Some of our cases appear to regard the area in which a uniquely federal interest exists as being entirely governed by federal law, with federal law deigning to "borro[w]," United States v. Little Lake Misere Land Co., 412 U.S. 580, 594 (1973), or "incorporat[e]" or "adopt[,]" United States v. Kimbell Foods, Inc., 440 U.S. 715, 728, 729, 730 (1979), state law except where a significant conflict with federal policy exists. We see nothing to be gained by expanding the theoretical scope of the federal pre-emption beyond its practical effect, and so adopt the more modest terminology. If the distinction between displacement of state law and displacement of federal law's incorporation of state law ever makes a practical difference, it at least does not do so in the present case.

outward, it is impossible to say that the Government has a significant interest in that particular feature. That would be scarcely more reasonable than saying that a private individual who orders such a craft by model number cannot sue for the manufacturer's negligence because he got precisely what he ordered."

The Court noted that the discretionary function exception to the Federal Tort Claims Act (FTCA) demonstrated the potential for a " 'significant conflict' between federal interests and state law in the context of government procurement" even though it technically did not apply in the case against a private contractor. In the FTCA, the federal government consents to damages lawsuits for harm "caused by the negligent or wrongful act or omission of any employee of the Government," 28 U.S.C. § 1346(b), but excepts from that consent any claims "based upon the exercise or performance or the failure to exercise or perform a discretionary function or duty on the part of a federal agency or an employee of the Government," 28 U.S.C. § 2680(a).

The Court stated that "the selection of the appropriate design for military equipment to be used by our Armed Forces" was a discretionary function since it involved judgments about, among other things, "the trade-off between greater safety and greater combat effectiveness." And it added that the second-guessing of these judgments through state-tort lawsuits would produce "the same effect sought to be avoided by the FTCA exemption," including the financial burden that would pass through to the United States. This was enough for the Court to conclude that "state law which holds Government contractors liable for design defects in military equipment does in some circumstances present a 'significant conflict' with federal policy, and must be displaced."

The Court then announced the content of its federal common law rule: "Liability for design defects in military equipment cannot be imposed, pursuant to state law, when (1) the United States approved reasonably precise specifications; (2) the equipment conformed to those specifications; and (3) the supplier warned the United States about the dangers in the use of the equipment that were known to the supplier but not to the United States." It explained that the first two conditions "assure that the suit is within the area where the policy of the 'discretionary function' would be frustrated," and that the third condition was needed to ensure that the defense contractor had no incentive to withhold knowledge of risks from the government.

In dissent, Justice Brennan argued that the Court "lacks both authority and expertise to fashion" its federal common law rule. He noted that "Erie was deeply rooted in notions of federalism, and is most seriously implicated when, as here, federal judges displace the state law that would ordinarily govern with their own rules of federal common law." He added that the Court's "power to create federal common law controlling the *Federal Government's* contractual rights and obligations does not translate into a power to prescribe rules that cover all transactions or contractual relationships collateral to Government contracts." He cited three decisions— Miree v. DeKalb County, 433 U.S. 25, 27 (1977), Bank of America Nat. Trust

& Sav. Assn. v. Parnell, 352 U.S. 29, 33 (1956), and Wallis v. Pan American Petroleum Corp., 384 U.S. 63, 68 (1966)—in support of the claim that the Court lacks the authority to make federal common law in litigation "between private parties" that does "not touch the rights and duties of the United States."

"Here, as in Miree, Parnell, and Wallis, a Government contract governed by federal common law looms in the background. But here, too, the United States is not a party to the suit and the suit neither 'touch[es] the rights and duties of the United States,' Parnell, *supra*, 352 U.S., at 33, nor has a 'direct effect upon the United States or its Treasury,' Miree, *supra*, 433 U.S., at 29."

Justice Brennan emphasized that the discretionary function exception to the FTCA did not apply here, and he rejected the possibility of the U.S. government's paying higher prices as a reason for the federal common law rule. "Even granting the Court's factual premise, which is by no means self-evident, the Court cites no authority for the proposition that burdens imposed on Government contractors, but passed on to the Government, burden the Government in a way that justifies extension of its immunity. * * *

"Perhaps tort liability is an inefficient means of ensuring the quality of design efforts, but '[w]hatever the merits of the policy' the Court wishes to implement, 'its conversion into law is a proper subject for congressional action, not for any creative power of ours.' [United States v.] Standard Oil, 332 U.S. [301,] 314–315 [(1947)]. It is, after all, 'Congress, not this Court or the other federal courts, [that] is the custodian of the national purse. By the same token [Congress] is the primary and most often the exclusive arbiter of federal fiscal affairs. And these comprehend, as we have said, securing the treasury or the Government against financial losses *however inflicted. . . .' Ibid.* (emphasis added)."

Justice STEVENS dissented as well. His central point was that "[w]hen the novel question of policy involves a balancing of the conflicting interests in the efficient operation of a massive governmental program and the protection of the rights of the individual—whether in the social welfare context, the civil service context, or the military procurement context—I feel very deeply that we should defer to the expertise of the Congress."

NOTE ON KIMBELL FOODS AND BOYLE

(1) Kimbell Foods and the Discretion to Adopt State Law. In his article on federal common law, Judge Friendly wrote that, properly understood, "Clearfield decided not one issue but two." The first issue, he wrote, was whether "the right of the United States to recover for conversion of a government check is a federal right, so that the courts of the United States may formulate a rule of decision." At the same time, the Court in Clearfield raised a second issue—specifically, whether "federal courts should adopt a uniform nation-wide rule or should follow state law." Friendly, *In*

Praise of Erie—And of the New Federal Common Law, 39 N.Y.U.L.Rev. 383, 410 (1964).

Kimbell Foods expressly disaggregates these issues. It makes clear that federal courts have authority to fashion a federal rule of decision to govern the proprietary interests of the United States. But it rules as a matter of discretion that uniform federal law need not be applied to the priority of liens in federal government litigation. The Court reached this conclusion based on a careful analysis of the asserted need for interstate uniformity, concern that a federal rule of decision would generate intrastate disuniformity, and a preference for incorporation of state law absent a demonstrated need for a uniform federal rule of decision.[1]

What is the point of the Court declaring that federal law "controls the Government's priority rights" but then giving content to this federal law by reference to non-uniform state law? Is the Supreme Court divining what it thinks Congress wants, or is it establishing its view of optimal federal policy until Congress acts? To the extent it is the latter, how good is the Court at assessing optimal policy? In the absence of congressional specification, is this task thrust on the Court, regardless of its competence, by its initial conclusion that federal law must control?

(2) Boyle and Private Litigation Involving Federally Created Interests. Kimbell foods reaffirmed that "federal law governs questions involving the rights of the United States arising under nationwide federal programs." 440 U.S. 715, 726 (1979). Before Boyle, however, the Court had suggested that purely private litigation involving federally created interests was governed directly by state law. Consider Miree v. DeKalb County, 433 U.S. 25 (1977), which involved a contractual dispute between a county-operated airport and a local garbage dump near the airport that allegedly attracted a horde of birds, causing the aircraft to crash. The Court held that despite the United States' regulation of and interest in aircraft travel and safety, state law governed the lawsuit because "the litigation is among private parties and no substantial rights or duties of the United States hinge on its outcome." *Id.* 31. See also Wallis v. Pan American Petroleum Corp., 384 U.S. 63, 68 (1966) (contractual dispute between private lessee of federal land and private assignee is governed by state law even though the Federal Mineral Leasing Act governed issuance of the lease and certain assignment rights, because the application of state law posed "no significant threat to any identifiable federal policy or interest"); Bank of America v. Parnell, 352 U.S. 29, 33 (1956) (state law governs dispute between bank and private party that allegedly converted bonds guaranteed by the United States because "litigation is purely between private parties and does not touch the rights and duties of the United States").

---

[1]   In United States v. Yazell, 382 U.S. 341 (1966), a decision relied upon in Kimbell Foods, the government sued on a Small Business Administration loan to a married couple. The question was whether the wife's separate property was exempt from recovery under a Texas law limiting the contractual powers of married women. The Court held (6–3) that state law governed, stressing that (1) the loan was individually negotiated, so that the government was chargeable with knowledge of Texas law; (2) there was no need for uniformity; (3) the financial consequences to the Treasury were small, as the Texas statute had been repealed; and (4) solicitude for state interests, particularly in the family-property area, was desirable.

Boyle distinguishes these cases on the ground that liability of government contractors will "directly affect" government contracts by leading the contractors to raise their prices or decline to manufacture a specified design. What evidence does the Court give for this claim, or for its implicit claim that these factors were absent in Miree, Wallis, or Parnell? Is speculation about the consequences of applying a state law rule to a private dispute in which the government has an interest a firm enough foundation, absent a clearer indication from Congress, that the United States has a unique federal interest that warrants preemption of state law? Is the presence of a unique federal interest that would justify federal judicial lawmaking clearer in Clearfield Trust and Kimbell Foods than in Boyle?

(3) Boyle and Textualism. Justice Scalia, the author of the majority opinion in Boyle, was the leading intellectual architect of textualism when he was on the Supreme Court. Is Boyle consistent with textualism? The Court's identification of the unique federal interest, and its crafting of a federal common law rule, both emerged from judicial policy analysis unmoored from statutory guidance from Congress. The majority opinion did point to a provision of the Federal Tort Claims Act (FTCA) that creates an exception, for "discretionary functions," to the Act's general recognition of governmental tort liability and concomitant waiver of the United States' sovereign immunity. See generally pp. 1345–1346, *infra*. But before extending the "policy" of the FTCA to a situation not covered by the statute, wouldn't textualism counsel consideration whether the exception in question was part of a legislative bargain that was tied to the waiver of sovereign immunity? Relatedly, Justice Brennan in dissent noted that Justice Scalia had two months earlier written in Puerto Rico Dept. of Consumer Affairs v. Isla Petroleum Corp., 485 U.S. 495, 500, 503 (1988) (additional internal quotation marks and citations omitted), that " 'we start with the assumption that the historic police powers of the States were not to be superseded . . . unless that was the clear and manifest purpose of Congress,' " and that " '[t]here is no federal pre-emption *in vacuo*, without a constitutional text or a federal statute to assert it.' " *Id.* 500, 503. For criticism of Boyle as a departure from textualism, see, *e.g.*, Doernberg, *Juridical Chameleons in the "New Erie" Canal*, 1990 Utah L.Rev. 759, 788–90; Zeppos, *Legislative History and the Interpretation of Statutes: Toward a Fact-Finding Model of Statutory Interpretation*, 76 Va.L.Rev. 1295, 1367 (1990).

(4) An Implied Structural Immunity? Instead of understanding Boyle as a federal common law decision, is it possible to read it as the implementation of a structural immunity against state interference with a federal constitutional function? Professor Clark argues that, properly understood, Boyle fits in a long line of precedents recognizing such implied immunity. See Clark, *Boyle as Constitutional Preemption*, 92 Notre Dame L.Rev. 2129, 2134–41 (2017); Clark, *Federal Common Law: A Structural Reinterpretation*, 144 U.Pa.L.Rev. 1245, 1368–75 (1996). In McCulloch v. Maryland, 17 U.S. 316, 436 (1819), the Court invalidated a state tax on the Bank of the United States on the ground that states may not, "by taxation or otherwise, * * * retard, impede, burden, or in any manner control, the operations of the constitutional laws enacted by Congress to carry into execution the powers vested in the general government." Similarly, in Osborn v. Bank of the United States, 22 U.S. 738, 867 (1824), p. 994, *infra*, Chief Justice Marshall wrote: "Can a contractor for supplying a military post with provisions, be restrained from making purchases within any State, or from transporting the provisions to the place at which the troops were stationed? or could he be fined or taxed for doing so? We have not yet heard these questions answered in the affirmative." According to Clark, allowing the state to impose liability for alleged design defects in Boyle would have intruded upon military functions that the Constitution assigns to the federal political branches. How convincing is that rationale for Boyle? What limiting principle distinguishes permissible from impermissible state regulations of private activity serving a federal purpose?

NOTE ON FEDERAL PREEMPTION AND FEDERAL COMMON LAW

This Note discusses the Supreme Court's federal preemption jurisprudence and considers its relationship to federal common law.

(1) The Forms of Preemption. The Supreme Court has identified several forms of federal preemption.

(a) A standard recitation of preemption doctrine is found in Crosby v. National Foreign Trade Council, 530 U.S. 363, 373 (2000):

"Even without an express provision for preemption, we have found that state law must yield to a congressional Act in at least two circumstances. When Congress intends federal law to 'occupy the field,' state law in that area is preempted. [California v. ARC America Corp., 490 U.S. 93, 100 (1989)]. And even if Congress has not occupied the field, state law is naturally preempted to the extent of any conflict with a federal statute. We will find preemption where it is impossible for a private party to comply with both state and federal law, and where 'under the circumstances of [a] particular case, [the challenged state law] stands as an obstacle to the accomplishment and execution of the full purposes and objectives of Congress.' Hines [v. Davidowitz, 312 U.S. 52,] 67 [(1941)]. What is a sufficient obstacle is a matter of judgment, to be informed by examining the federal statute as a whole and identifying its purpose and intended effects * * *."

(b) Field preemption is of notable importance in some areas, such as alien registration, see, *e.g.*, Arizona v. United States, 567 U.S. 387, 401 (2012), the regulation of locomotive equipment, see, *e.g.*, Kurns v. R.R. Friction Prods. Corp., 565 U.S. 625, 637 (2012), and nuclear safety, see, *e.g.*, English v. Gen. Elec. Co., 496 U.S. 72, 82–85 (1990). But it is not easily established, see, *e.g.*, Hillsborough County v. Automated Med. Labs., Inc., 471 U.S. 707, 717 (1985). And the Court often construes the recognized field narrowly. See, *e.g.*, Oneok, Inc. v. Learjet, Inc., 575 U.S. 373 (2015); PG & E Co. v. State Energy Res. Conservation & Dev. Comm'n, 461 U.S. 190 (1983). For the suggestion that the Court's standards for field preemption have become stricter in recent years, see Virginia Uranium, Inc. v. Warren, 587

U.S. 761, 773–76 (2019) (Gorsuch., J., joined by Thomas, J. and Kavanaugh, J.); Kurns v. Railroad Friction Products Corp., 565 U.S. 625, 638 (2012) (Kagan, J., concurring).

(c)   Conflict preemption, as the discussion in Crosby indicates, embraces two distinct situations. In the easier but far rarer case, compliance with both federal and state duties is simply impossible. See, *e.g.*, Southland Corp. v. Keating, 465 U.S. 1 (1984) (state law requiring judicial determination of certain claims preempted by federal law requiring arbitration of those claims). In the second and more common situation, sometimes called "obstacle preemption," compliance with both laws is possible, yet state law poses an obstacle to the achievement of federal purposes.

(d)   Crosby and other decisions (*e.g.*, English v. General Elec. Co., 496 U.S. 72, 79 n.5 (1990)) have recognized that field and conflict preemption are not "rigidly distinct." Field preemption, for example, can be recharacterized as conflict preemption (any state regulation of the field conflicts with a congressional decision to exclude state regulation). Relatedly, in any field preemption case, an important question is just how broadly the field should be defined; the narrower the definition, the more the case resembles conflict preemption.

(e)   The Court has said that "we start with the assumption that the historic police powers of the States were not to be superseded by the Federal Act unless that was the clear and manifest purpose of Congress." Rice v. Santa Fe Elevator Corp., 331 U.S. 218, 230 (1947). While this presumption against preemption applies in areas of traditional state regulatory authority, preemption is more easily inferred in areas in which "the federal interest is so dominant that the federal system will be assumed to preclude enforcement of state laws on the same subject." *Id.* See also, *e.g.*, United States v. Locke, 529 U.S. 89, 108, 114 (2000) (state regulation of the operation of oil tankers preempted by federal law; in national and international maritime commerce, "there is no beginning assumption that concurrent regulation by the State is a valid exercise of its police powers"); Ramah Navajo Sch. Bd., Inc. v. Bureau of Revenue, 458 U.S. 832, 838 (1982) (question of preemption of state regulation of Navajo Tribe members "is not controlled by standards * * * developed in other areas," but is informed by "traditional notions of tribal sovereignty, and the recognition and encouragement of this sovereignty in congressional Acts promoting tribal independence and economic development"); Hines, 312 U.S. at 68 (noting, in the course of assessing a Pennsylvania law that requires aliens to register annually and carry an identification card, that "[a]ny concurrent state power that may exist is restricted to the narrowest of limits" in this context because the state law "is in a field which affects international relations").

(2) Preemption and Textualism. Because the "obstacle" component of conflict preemption rests on judicial attribution of legislative purpose to Congress, it can be viewed as in tension with more text-focused theories of statutory interpretation. See generally pp. 822–824, *supra*. Indeed, Professor Nelson suggests it is inappropriate to interpret every congressional enactment (as implied preemption doctrine effectively does) as if it included a textual provision preempting any state law that is an obstacle to accomplishing the statutory purposes. See Nelson, *Preemption*, 86 Va.L.Rev. 225 (2000); see also Manning, *Foreword: The Means of Constitutional Power*, 128 Harv.L.Rev. 1, 72 (2014) ("obstacles and purposes" preemption hard to square with textualism). Yet the Court, despite its increasing emphasis on textual interpretation, continues to invoke implied preemption principles to invalidate state legislation that is contrary to federal purposes. See, *e.g.*, Lamps Plus, Inc. v. Varela, 587 U.S. 176 (2019); Hughes v. Talen Energy Mktg., LLC, 578 U.S. 150 (2016).

Several of the Court's most textually inclined Justices have sharply questioned "obstacle" preemption. Describing the Court's "entire body of 'purposes and objectives' pre-emption jurisprudence" as "inherently flawed," Justice Thomas's separate opinion in Wyeth v. Levine, 555 U.S. 555, 594 (2009) (Thomas, J., concurring in the judgment), argued that obstacle preemption cases "improperly rely on legislative history, broad atextual notions of congressional purpose, and even congressional inaction in order to pre-empt state law." Expressing similar concerns, a plurality opinion by Justice Gorsuch, joined by Justices Thomas and Kavanaugh, concluded that preemption based on asserted interference with the "purposes and objectives" of a federal statute "risk[s] displacing the legislative compromises actually reflected in the statutory text—compromises that sometimes may seem irrational to an outsider coming to the statute cold, but whose genius lies in having won the broad support our Constitution demands of any new law." Virginia Uranium, Inc. v. Warren, 587 U.S. 761, 778 (2019); see also Kansas v. Garcia, 589 U.S. 191, 213 (2020) (Thomas, J., joined by Gorsuch., J., concurring) (raising similar concerns about "purposes and objectives" preemption); AT&T Mobility LLC v. Concepcion, 563 U.S. 333, 353 (2011) (Thomas, J., concurring) (same); Williamson v. Mazda Motor of America, Inc., 562 U.S. 323, 341–43 (2011) (Thomas, J., concurring in the judgment) (same).

These arguments align with views about legislative compromise and bicameralism that the Court has embraced in some of its recent statutory interpretation opinions. See p. 822, *supra*. Yet a majority of the Court has continued to accept the validity of obstacle preemption even while applying it strictly. See, *e.g.*, Kansas v. Garcia, 589 U.S. 191 (2020). In view of the challenges Congress would face if it were to try to anticipate, specify, and accurately express the proper resolution to all of the preemption questions that would arise in the lifetime of even a moderately complex regulatory statute, can textualism plausibly supply a workable approach to preemption questions? See Meltzer, *Textualism and Preemption*, 112 Mich.L.Rev. 1 (2013) (arguing that the answer is no); see also Fallon, *On Viewing the Courts as Junior Partners of Congress in Statutory Interpretation Cases: An Essay Celebrating the Scholarship of Daniel J. Meltzer*, 91 Notre Dame L.Rev. 1743, 1762–69 (2016) (situating Meltzer's critique in a broader theory of purposive interpretation).

(3) Preemption and Federal Common Law. Citing Kimbell, Clearfield, and D'Oench Duhme, Boyle described federal common law as follows: "We have held that a few areas, involving uniquely federal interests, are so committed by the Constitution and laws of the United States to federal control that state law is *pre-empted* and replaced, where necessary, by federal law of a content prescribed (absent explicit statutory directive) by the courts—so-called federal common law." Boyle v. United Technologies Corp., 487 U.S. 500, 504 (1988) (internal quotation marks and citations omitted) (emphasis added). Neither Kimbell, nor Clearfield, nor D'Oench Duhme, invoked preemption doctrine or purported to do a preemption analysis. But they all concluded in the first step of the federal common law analysis that federal law rather than state law governed the issue before moving on to fashion the federal rule. Federal preemption of state competence is also an initial step in many of the federal common law decisions related to jurisdictional grants or structural constitutional inference, discussed in the next Section. For scholarly treatment on the relationship between preemption and federal common law, see Hill, *The Law-Making Power of the Federal Courts: Constitutional Preemption*, 67 Colum.L.Rev. 1024, 1028–68 (1967); Clark, *Federal Common Law: A Structural Reinterpretation,* 144 U.Pa.L.Rev. 1245, 1368–75 (1996); Merrill, *The Common Law Powers of Federal Courts*, 52 U.Chi.L.Rev. 1, 36–39 (1985).

In recent decades the Supreme Court has taken a stricter approach to its federal common lawmaking powers drawn from federal statutory schemes. The next decision is representative.

O'Melveny & Myers v. Federal Deposit Insurance Corp.

512 U.S. 79 (1994).

Certiorari to the United States Court of Appeals for the Ninth Circuit.

■ JUSTICE SCALIA delivered the opinion of the Court.

The issue in this case is whether, in a suit by the Federal Deposit Insurance Corporation (FDIC) as receiver of a federally insured bank, it is a federal-law or rather a state-law rule of decision that governs the tort liability of attorneys who provided services to the bank.

I

[Ranbir Sahni and Lester Day engaged in fraudulent acts through their ownership of American Diversified Savings Bank (ADSB), a California-chartered and federally insured savings and loan. On February 14, 1986, federal regulators concluded that ADSB was insolvent and that it had incurred substantial losses because of legal violations and unsound business practices. The respondent, the Federal Deposit Insurance Corporation (FDIC), became receiver for ADSB and sued Sahni and Day in federal court for breach of fiduciary duty and (as to Sahni) violations of the Racketeer Influenced and Corrupt Organizations Act. It later sued petitioner O'Melveny & Myers

(O'Melveny), a law firm that represented ADSB in connection with two real estate syndications, for professional negligence and breach of fiduciary duty. O'Melveny moved for summary judgment and argued, among other things, that knowledge of the conduct of Sahini and Day must be imputed to ADSB and hence to the FDIC, which, as receiver, stood in its shoes; and that this imputed knowledge estopped the FDIC from pursuing its tort claims against O'Melveny. The district court granted summary judgment, but the court of appeals reversed on grounds discussed below.]

II

It is common ground that the FDIC was asserting in this case causes of action created by California law. Respondent contends that in the adjudication of those causes of action (1) a federal common-law rule and not California law determines whether the knowledge of corporate officers acting against the corporation's interest will be imputed to the corporation; and (2) even if California law determines the former question, federal common law determines the more narrow question whether knowledge by officers so acting will be imputed to the FDIC when it sues as receiver of the corporation.

The first of these contentions need not detain us long, as it is so plainly wrong. "There is no federal general common law," Erie R. Co. v. Tompkins, 304 U.S. 64, 78, 58 (1938), and (to anticipate somewhat a point we will elaborate more fully in connection with respondent's second contention) the remote possibility that corporations may go into federal receivership is no conceivable basis for adopting a special federal common-law rule divesting States of authority over the entire law of imputation. [The Court explains that the Ninth's Circuit's holding that judge-made federal law rather than state law governs the application of defenses against FDIC, including the imputation question, was contrary to the federal court case law on which it relied.]

In seeking to defend the Ninth Circuit's holding, respondent contends (to quote the caption of its argument) that "The Wrongdoing Of ADSB's Insiders Would Not Be Imputed To ADSB Under Generally Accepted Common Law Principles"—in support of which it attempts to show that nonattribution to the corporation of dishonest officers' knowledge is the rule applied in the vast bulk of decisions from 43 jurisdictions, ranging from Rhode Island to Wyoming. The supposed relevance of this is set forth in a footnote: "It is our position that federal common law does govern this issue, but that the content of the federal common law rule corresponds to the rule that would independently be adopted by most jurisdictions." If there were a federal common law on such a generalized issue (which there is not), we see no reason why it would necessarily conform to that "independently . . . adopted by most jurisdictions." But the short of the matter is that California law, not federal law, governs the imputation of knowledge to corporate victims of alleged negligence, and that is so whether or not California chooses to follow "the majority rule."

We turn, then, to the more substantial basis for the decision below, which asserts federal pre-emption not over the law of imputation generally, but only over its application to the FDIC suing as receiver. Respondent begins its defense of this principle by quoting United States v. Kimbell Foods, Inc., 440 U.S. 715, 726 (1979), to the effect that "federal law governs questions involving the rights of the United States arising under nationwide federal programs." But the FDIC is not the United States, and even if it were we would be begging the question to assume that it was asserting its *own* rights rather than, as receiver, the rights of ADSB. In any event, knowing whether "federal law governs" in the Kimbell Foods sense—a sense which includes federal adoption of state-law rules—does not much advance the ball. The issue in the present case is whether the California rule of decision is to be applied to the issue of imputation or displaced, and if it *is* applied it is of only theoretical interest whether the basis for that application is California's own sovereign power or federal adoption of California's disposition. See Boyle v. United Technologies Corp., 487 U.S. 500, 507, n.3 (1988).

In answering the central question of displacement of California law, we of course would not contradict an explicit federal statutory provision. Nor would we adopt a court-made rule to supplement federal statutory regulation that is comprehensive and detailed; matters left unaddressed in such a scheme are presumably left subject to the disposition provided by state law. See Northwest Airlines, Inc. v. Transport Workers, 451 U.S. 77, 97 (1981); Milwaukee v. Illinois, 451 U.S. 304, 319 (1981). Petitioner asserts that both these principles apply in the present case, by reason of 12 U.S.C. § 1821(d)(2)(A)(i), and the comprehensive legislation of which it is a part, the Financial Institutions Reform, Recovery, and Enforcement Act of 1989 (FIRREA), Pub.L. 101–73, 103 Stat. 183.

[The Court interprets 12 U.S.C. § 1821(d)(2)(A)(i) to mean that "the FDIC as receiver 'steps into the shoes' of the failed S & L," which means that in litigation by the FDIC asserting the claims of ADSB, any defense good against ADSB is good against the receiver. It rejects the FDIC's argument that the statute "should be read as a *nonexclusive* grant of rights to the FDIC receiver, which can be supplemented or modified by federal common law; and that FIRREA as a whole, by demonstrating the high federal interest in this area, confirms the courts' authority to promulgate such common law. This argument is demolished by those provisions of FIRREA which specifically create special federal rules of decision regarding claims by, and defenses against, the FDIC as receiver. *Inclusio unius, exclusio alterius*. It is hard to avoid the conclusion that § 1821(d)(2)(A)(i) places the FDIC in the shoes of the insolvent S & L, to work out its claims under state law, except where some provision in the extensive framework of FIRREA provides otherwise. To create additional 'federal common-law' exceptions is not to 'supplement' this scheme, but to alter it." But the Court did not rest its decision on this interpretation of FIRREA alone, since it was enacted three years after the FDIC became receiver for ADSB, and its retroactive effect was unclear and unbriefed. The Court stated that "even assuming the inapplicability of FIRREA this is not one of those cases in which judicial creation of a special federal rule would be justified."]

Such cases are, as we have said in the past, "few and restricted," Wheeldin v. Wheeler, 373 U.S. 647, 651 (1963), limited to situations where there is a "significant conflict between some federal policy or interest and the use of state law." Wallis v. Pan American Petroleum Corp., 384 U.S. 63, 68 (1966). Our cases uniformly require the existence of such a conflict as a precondition for recognition of a federal rule of decision. See, *e.g.,* Kamen v. Kemper Financial Services, Inc., 500 U.S. 90, 98 (1991); Boyle, *supra,* 487 U.S., at 508; Kimbell Foods, 440 U.S., at 728. Not only the permissibility but also the scope of judicial displacement of state rules turns upon such a conflict. See, *e.g.,* Kamen, *supra,* at 98; Boyle, *supra,* 487 U.S., at 508. What is fatal to respondent's position in the present case is that it has identified *no* significant conflict with an identifiable federal policy or interest. There is not even at stake that most generic (and lightly invoked) of alleged federal interests, the interest in uniformity. The rules of decision at issue here do not govern the primary conduct of the United States or any of its agents or contractors, but affect only the FDIC's rights and liabilities, as receiver, with respect to primary conduct on the part of private actors that has already occurred. Uniformity of law might facilitate the FDIC's nationwide litigation of these suits, eliminating state-by-state research and reducing uncertainty—but if the avoidance of those ordinary consequences qualified as an identifiable federal interest, we would be awash in "federal common-law" rules.

The closest respondent comes to identifying a specific, concrete federal policy or interest that is compromised by California law is its contention that state rules regarding the imputation of knowledge might "deplet[e] the deposit insurance fund." But neither FIRREA nor the prior law sets forth any anticipated level for the fund, so what respondent must mean by "depletion" is simply the forgoing of *any* money which, under any *conceivable* legal rules, might accrue to the fund. That is a broad principle indeed, which would support not just elimination of the defense at issue here, but judicial creation of new, "federal-common-law" causes of action to enrich the fund. Of course we have no authority to do that, because there is no federal policy that the fund should always win. Our cases have previously rejected "more money" arguments remarkably similar to the one made here. See Kimbell Foods, *supra,* 440 U.S., at 737–738.

Even less persuasive—indeed, positively probative of the dangers of respondent's facile approach to federal-common-law-making—is respondent's contention that it would "disserve the federal program" to permit California to insulate "the attorney's or accountant's malpractice," thereby imposing costs "on the nation's taxpayers, rather than on the negligent wrongdoer." By presuming to judge what constitutes malpractice, this argument demonstrates the runaway tendencies of "federal common law" untethered to a genuinely identifiable (as opposed to judicially constructed) federal policy. What sort of tort liability to impose on lawyers and accountants in general, and on lawyers and accountants who provide services to federally insured financial institutions in particular, 'involves a host of considerations that must be weighed and appraised,' " Northwest Airlines, Inc. v. Transport Workers Union], 451 U.S. [77,] 98, n.41 (1981) (quoting United States v. Gilman, 347 U.S. 507, 512–513 (1954))—including, for example, the creation of incentives for careful work, provision of fair treatment to third parties, assurance of adequate recovery by the federal deposit insurance fund, and enablement of reasonably priced services. Within the federal system, at least, we have decided that that function of weighing and appraising " 'is more appropriately for those who write the laws, rather than for those who interpret them.' " Northwest Airlines, 451 U.S., at 98, n.41 (quoting Gilman, 347 U.S., at 513).

We conclude that this is not one of those extraordinary cases in which the judicial creation of a federal rule of decision is warranted. As noted earlier, the parties are in agreement that if state law governs it is the law of California; but they vigorously disagree as to what that law provides. * * * The judgment is reversed and the case remanded for proceedings consistent with this opinion.

So ordered.

■ JUSTICE STEVENS, with whom JUSTICE BLACKMUN, JUSTICE O'CONNOR, and JUSTICE SOUTER join, concurring.

While I join the Court's opinion, I add this comment to emphasize an important difference between federal courts and state courts. It would be entirely proper for a state court of general jurisdiction to fashion a rule of agency law that would protect creditors of an insolvent corporation from the consequences of wrongdoing by corporate officers even if the corporation itself, or its shareholders, would be bound by the acts of its agents. Indeed, a state court might well attach special significance to the fact that the interests of taxpayers as well as ordinary creditors will be affected by the rule at issue in this case. Federal courts, however, "unlike their state counterparts, are courts of limited jurisdiction that have not been vested with open-ended lawmaking powers." Northwest Airlines, Inc. v. Transport Workers, 451 U.S. 77, 95 (1981). Because state law provides the basis for respondent FDIC's claim, that law also governs both the elements of the cause of action and its defenses. Unless Congress has otherwise directed, the federal court's task is merely to interpret and apply the relevant rules of state law.

Cases like this one, however, present a special problem. They raise issues, such as the imputation question here, that may not have been definitively settled in the state jurisdiction in which the case is brought, but that nevertheless must be resolved by federal courts. The task of the federal judges who confront such issues would surely be simplified if Congress had provided them with a uniform federal rule to apply. As matters stand, however, federal judges must do their best to estimate how the relevant state courts would perform their lawmaking task, and then emulate that sometimes purely hypothetical model. The Court correctly avoids any suggestion about how the merits of the imputation issue should be resolved on remand or in similar cases that may arise elsewhere. * * *

NOTE ON CONTEMPORARY APPROACHES TO FEDERAL COMMON LAW RELATED TO STATUTORY REGULATION

(1) O'Melveny's Higher Bar to Federal Common Law. O'Melveny is factually and legally similar to D'Oench Duhme, see Lund, *The Decline of Federal Common Law*, 76 B.U.L.R. 895, 920–35 (1996), yet in several ways takes a noticeably stricter approach to federal common law related to a federal statutory program than that of D'Oench Duhme and other cases studied thus far in this Chapter. See Monaghan, *Supremacy Clause Textualism*, 110 Colum.L.Rev. 731, 758 (2010) ("The relatively freewheeling era of federal judicial lawmaking (akin to that of a state common law court) to 'fill in the gaps' in a federal statutory regime, sanctioned by such eminent figures as Justice Jackson and Judge Friendly, is long gone.") Compare how the tests and showings needed for federal common lawmaking in Clearfield Trust, D'Oench Duhme, Kimbell Foods, and Boyle, differ from those in O'Melveny:

(a) O'Melveny seems to raise the bar to the type of conflicts with a federal statutory regime that will warrant preemption and thus displacement of state law. There must as a "precondition" be " 'significant conflict between some federal policy or interest and the use of state law,' " and that policy must be "genuinely identifiable (as opposed to judicially constructed) federal policy." See also Empire HealthChoice Assurance, Inc. v. McVeigh, 547 U.S. 677, 692 (2006) (quoting Boyle for the proposition that involvement of "an area of uniquely federal interest * * * establishes a necessary, not a sufficient, condition for the displacement of state law" because in some cases, an " 'entire body of state law' may conflict with the federal interest and therefore require replacement," while "in others, the conflict is confined, and 'only particular elements of state law are superseded' ").

(b) Relatedly, O'Melveny draws different inferences from the existence of a comprehensive federal scheme: "Nor would we adopt a court-made rule to supplement federal statutory regulation that is comprehensive and detailed; matters left unaddressed in such a scheme are presumably left subject to the disposition provided by state law." To similar effect more recently is Rodriguez v. FDIC, 589 U.S. 132 (2020), where a unanimous Court declined to adopt a federal common law rule to resolve disputes over the distribution of joint tax refunds among affiliated banks (one of which was in a FDIC receivership) because federal law was silent on that question even though it specified how the government should receive taxes from corporate groups and how it should deliver a tax refund to such groups. The Court concluded that there was no need to protect "uniquely federal interests" and that state law was "well equipped to handle disputes involving corporate property rights" even "in the context of a federal bankruptcy and a tax dispute." *Id.* 136, 137 (internal quotation marks and citations omitted). Compare Atherton v. FDIC, 519 U.S. 213 (1997) ("Nor does the existence of related federal statutes automatically show that Congress intended courts to create federal common-law rules, for 'Congress acts * * * against the background of the total corpus juris of the states' ") (quoting Wallis v. Pan American Petroleum Corp., 384 U.S. 63, 68 (1966) (quoting H. Hart & H. Wechsler, The Federal Courts and the Federal System 435 (1953)) (internal quotation marks omitted).

(c)   O'Melveny also expresses a different attitude toward the competence of the Justices to engage in policy analysis to determine the right federal rule, and, relatedly, toward the relevance of federalism and separation of powers. After noting that the best tort regime to serve the federal program "involves a host of considerations that must be weighed and appraised," the decision concludes by saying that "[w]ithin the federal system, at least, we have decided that that function of weighing and appraising is more appropriately for those who write the laws, rather than for those who interpret them." 512 U.S. at 89 (internal quotation marks and citations omitted).

(d)   For a critical assessment of O'Melveny, see Lund, *supra*, at 935–37. For a sympathetic take, see Clark, *Federal Common Law: A Structural Reinterpretation*, 144 U.Pa.L.Rev. 1245, 1363–64 (1996).

(e)   Not every contemporary federal common law case takes the stricter approach outlined in this Note. See Sosa v. Alvarez-Machain, 542 U.S. 692 (2004); Semtek Int'l, Inc. v. Lockheed Martin Corp., 531 U.S. 497 (2001).

(2) Two Steps or One? O'Melveny seems to collapse the Kimbell Foods two-step analysis into a single test of whether a judge-made federal rule of decision should govern: "knowing whether 'federal law governs' in the Kimbell Foods sense—a sense which includes federal adoption of state-law rules—does not much advance the ball," said the Court, adding that the "issue in the present case is whether the California rule of decision is to be applied to the issue of imputation or displaced * * *." O'Melveny at this point cited footnote 3 of Boyle, which stated: "Some of our cases appear to regard the area in which a uniquely federal interest exists as being entirely governed by federal law, with federal law deigning to * * * 'incorporat[e]' or 'adopt,' Kimbell Foods, state law except where a significant conflict with federal policy exists. We see nothing to be gained by expanding the theoretical scope of the federal preemption beyond its practical effect, and so adopt the more modest terminology." These decisions together seem to say that the Court will apply state law to a matter unless it is preempted by the federal scheme. But see Semtek Int'l, Inc. v. Lockheed Martin Corp., 531 U.S. 497, 508 (2001) (applying the Kimbell Foods two-step framework).

Professor Young suggests that collapsing the inquiry into a single step—one that predicates federal common lawmaking power on a finding of incompatibility between state and federal law—puts federal common law on firmer ground. Starting from the premise that any genuine link between federal common lawmaking and implied congressional authorization is "tenuous indeed," he argues that "competence" to make federal common law must come, if anywhere, "from the existence of a conflict between state law and some preexisting federal policy"—a circumstance that gives rise to preemption under the Supremacy Clause. Citing familiar federalism concerns, he contends that federal courts may craft a federal common law rule only "to fill in the gap created by a finding that state law is preempted in a particular case." On this view, in cases such as Kimbell Foods, state law would "apply of its own force," not because federal courts choose to adopt it as a federal rule of decision. Young, *Preemption and Federal Common Law*, 83 Notre Dame L.Rev. 1639, 1653, 1660, 1664–65 (2008).

(3) The Persistence of General Law? Professor Nelson maintains that when federal courts formulate binding federal rules of decision that are not clearly specified by statute, they typically do not make them up from scratch, but rather seek guidance in the background doctrines and practices of multiple jurisdictions. Nelson, *The Persistence of General Law*, 106 Colum.L.Rev. 503 (2006); see also Nelson, *The Legitimacy of (Some) Federal Common Law*, 101 Va.L.Rev. 1 (2015). He describes the law so applied as "general law" to emphasize its multi-jurisdictional quality and argues that the application of such law attenuates separation of powers concerns because it is not invented "out of whole cloth" but rather is "firmly grounded in sources outside the federal judiciary * * *." Nelson, *Legitimacy, supra*, at 9, 18, 25. If federal courts reject judicial creativity and resort to off-the-rack legal doctrines and assumptions to fill in the gaps in federal law, do they mitigate separation-of-powers concerns with federal common law? Or should federal common law related to statutory programs make some effort to shape itself to the contours of those programs? Compare O'Melveny, 512 U.S. at 84 ("[W]e see no reason why [federal common law] would necessarily conform to [the rule] independently . . . adopted by most jurisdictions") (internal quotation marks omitted).

Nelson further suggests that federal courts may need "no special justification" beyond a grant of jurisdiction to identify and apply this conception of general law. *Id.* 18–19. See also Sachs, *Finding Law*, 107 Calif.L.Rev. 527, 578 (2019) (arguing that "[w]henever the Constitution vests judicial power in the federal courts but leaves them without a rule of decision," federal courts can and perhaps must " 'apply preexisting sources of law that the Constitution left intact," including 'known and settled principles of national and municipal jurisprudence' "). Are these arguments consistent with Erie's claims that there "is no federal general common law" and that "[e]xcept in matters governed by the Federal Constitution or by Acts of Congress, the law to be applied in any case is the law of the State," or with its holding that the diversity jurisdiction statute did not authorize federal courts to apply general common law? 304 U.S. 64, 78 (1938), p. 762, *supra*.

Compare Sachs, *supra*, at 571–79 (arguing that Erie was theoretically flawed in its rejection of general law, among other things).

(4) The Various Ways in Which State Law Applies. Consider several possible meanings of the proposition that state law "applies" as the rule of decision for an issue in federal court:

(a) The federal government (Congress as well as the federal courts) lacks lawmaking authority.

(b) Congress has lawmaking authority, but in the absence of legislative action, state law governs. This was true, for example, in Erie and O'Melveny.

(c) Federal legislation calls for the application of state law as part of a federal scheme. The Federal Tort Claims Act is an example. See 28 U.S.C. § 1346(b)(1).

(d) The Supreme Court interprets a federal statutory term to embody a state law definition. See, *e.g.*, De Sylva v. Ballentine, 351 U.S. 570, 582 (1956) (holding that the federal copyright renewal rights of deceased authors' "children" depended on state law rules defining whether a child would qualify as an heir of the author).

(e) Although federal common law governs a given question, state law furnishes an appropriate and convenient measure of the content of this federal law. See, *e.g.*, Kimbell Foods, p. 825, *supra*.

O'Melveny suggests that "it is of only theoretical interest" whether state law applies of its own force or by incorporation into federal common law. See p. 836, *supra*. But this suggestion is wrong. Whether a federal court applies state law of its own force or by direction of federal law can matter in at least two ways:

(a) If state law applies at the direction of federal law, a cause arising under that state law might establish federal jurisdiction under 28 U.S.C. § 1331. If state law applies of its own force, a cause with no other federal ingredients arising under it cannot establish federal jurisdiction.

(b) If state law applies of its own force absent any conflict with federal law, then presumably the rules for "finding" state law developed under Erie, see p. 767, *supra*, should apply. But if state law applies at the direction of federal law, then the content of "state law" arguably becomes a federal question that can be subject to review by the Supreme Court.

On these points see Young, Paragraph (2), *supra*, at 1651–55; Mishkin, *The Variousness of "Federal Law": Competence and Discretion in the Choice of National and State Rules for Decision*, 105 U.Pa.L.Rev. 797, 802–10 (1957).

NOTE ON FEDERAL COMMON LAW RELATED TO CRIMINAL MATTERS

Although nonstatutory federal prosecutions ended with United States v. Hudson & Goodwin, 11 U.S. (7 Cranch) 32 (1812), p. 747, *supra*, federal courts still make law in criminal cases.

(1) Common Law Enforcement. Federal courts have continued to enforce law by use of the contempt power—a role the Court approved in the last paragraph of the Hudson opinion, see p. 748, *supra*—and to use a variety of common law techniques, forms, and writs in the enforcement of congressionally defined crimes.

(2) Common Law Crimes? Although the Supreme Court adheres to the principle that "[i]t is the legislature, not the Court, which is to define a crime, and ordain its punishment," United States v. Wiltberger, 18 U.S. (5 Wheat.) 76, 95 (1820) (Marshall, C.J.), it has sometimes appeared to premise criminal liability more on judge-made policy analysis than conventional methods of statutory interpretation.

In Pinkerton v. United States, 328 U.S. 640 (1946), for example, the Court ruled that a conspirator can be liable for substantive crimes that he did not commit but that were committed by another conspirator, even though no federal statute attached liability in such circumstances. The Court reasoned that since an overt act was an essential ingredient of the crime of conspiracy under what was then 18 U.S.C. § 88, "we fail to see why the same or other acts in furtherance of the conspiracy are likewise not attributable to the others for the purpose of holding them responsible for the substantive offense." *Id.* 647. See generally Hessick, *The Myth of Common Law Crimes*, 105 Va.L.Rev. 965, 985–86 (2019) (concluding that Pinkerton "found criminal liability despite the absence of any supporting statutory language or legislative history").

The Court has also recognized the crime of insider trading without identifying a clear textual basis for it in federal enactments that prohibit deceptive practices or fraudulent schemes. See Securities Exchange Act of 1934, 15 U.S.C. § 78j(b); 17 C.F.R. § 240.10b–5. It has done so based on the insiders' violation of a fiduciary obligation to shareholders, see Chiarella v. United States, 445 U.S. 222, 228–29 (1980), or on the theory that the insider "misappropriates confidential information for securities trading purposes," United States v. O'Hagan, 521 U.S. 642, 652 (1997), combined with policy reasons why a prohibition on insider trading furthers the purposes of securities laws and helps markets, see *id.* 658–59. See generally Bainbridge, *Incorporating State Law Fiduciary Duties into the Federal Insider Trading Prohibition*, 52 Wash. & Lee L.Rev. 1189, 1192 (1995) (describing "the insider trading prohibition [as] a species of federal common law"); Hessick, supra, at 983–86 (noting the difficulty of conceptualizing insider trading as anything other than "judicial crime creation").

(3) The Supervisory Power. The Supreme Court has recognized that federal courts may exercise a "supervisory power to formulate and apply proper standards for enforcement of the criminal law in the federal courts * * *." That statement is from Marshall v. United States, 360 U.S. 310, 313

(1959), in which the Court, invoking this "supervisory power," set aside a jury verdict when the jurors had been exposed to potentially prejudicial publicity. Is judicial lawmaking with respect to methods of enforcement and remediation, as distinguished from the definition of legal rights and duties, easier to defend against a charge that it usurps the legislative prerogative?

Later Supreme Court decisions narrowed the scope of the supervisory power. For example, in United States v. Williams, 504 U.S. 36, 45–47 (1992), the Court ruled that the supervisory power did not extend to prescribing standards of prosecutorial conduct before a federal grand jury; the opinion distinguished, however: (i) the power of federal courts to fashion doctrines that enforce rules of conduct prescribed by the Constitution, statutes, or court rules, and (ii) their power with respect to rules governing the conduct of litigants before the courts themselves. And in United States v. Tsarnaev, 595 U.S. 302, 315–16 (2022), the Court held that a court of appeals could not invoke its supervisory powers to displace a district court's broad discretion to manage voir dire by prescribing specific lines of questioning. Along the way, the Court emphasized the "clear limits" on such authority, including that "supervisory rules cannot conflict with or circumvent a constitutional provision or federal statute," or "conflict with or circumvent a Federal Rule," or "circumvent or supplement legal standards set out in decisions of this Court."[1]

(4) Common Law Defenses. In the face of Congress's failure, in general, to prescribe the scope or even the existence of defenses (*e.g.*, self-defense or duress) to federal crimes, federal courts have freely crafted such defenses. See, *e.g.*, Brown v. United States, 256 U.S. 335 (1921) (self-defense); but *cf.* United States v. Oakland Cannabis Buyers' Cooperative, 532 U.S. 483, 490 (2001) (stating in dictum that it "is an open question whether federal courts ever have *authority* to recognize a necessity defense not provided by statute") (emphasis added). Why are federal courts competent to recognize defenses but not new offenses? One justification is that Congress passes criminal statutes against the backdrop of well-established common law norms of defense. Smith v. United States, 568 U.S. 106, 112 (2013); Dixon v. United States, 548 U.S. 1, 17 (2006); United States v. Bailey, 444 U.S. 394, 415 n.11

---

[1] Because the government did not "challenge the general existence of the Court of Appeals' supervisory power," the Court did not address the question. 595 U.S. at 315 n.1. In a concurrence joined by Justice Gorsuch, Justice Barrett expressed "skepticism" about a courts of appeals' supervisory power that extends beyond adopting "a rule regulating its own proceedings" to include "a blanket rule that all district courts in its jurisdiction must follow on pain of reversal." *Id.* 325 (Barrett, J., concurring). Justice Barrett acknowledged that the Supreme Court had "suggested that the courts of appeals possess authority to dictate procedural rules for district courts," citing as example Cuyler v. Sullivan, 446 U.S. 335, 346 n.10 (1980), but urged the Court to reconsider the issue and limit the practice. 595 U.S. at 325–26. She explained that while the Supreme Court's arguable basis for supervisory power to regulate procedure in lower federal courts lay in "the Constitution's establishment of this Court as 'supreme,' as distinct from the 'inferior Courts' that Congress has discretion to create," it is "difficult, if not impossible, to find" a "comparable constitutional hook" or statutory authority "for such power in the courts of appeals." *Id.* 326–27. She also suggested that supervisory power was not entailed by a general power of appellate review. *Id.* In dissent, Justice Breyer noted that the Court's precedents "clearly recognize" the existence of a supervisory authority in the courts of appeals, arguing that "[a] degree of [supervisory] authority for the courts of appeals, closer to the fray, to issue at least some supervisory rules facilitates the flexibility needed in our geographically dispersed multicircuit system." *Id.* 343 (Breyer, J., dissenting).

(1980). According to Easterbrook, *The Case of the Speluncean Explorers: Revisited*, 112 Harv.L.Rev. 1913, 1913–14 (1999), because familiar norms of "justification" have been applied to criminal statutes for "thousands of years," they simply form part of the legislators' background social and linguistic assumptions, in much the same way that rules of "grammar and diction" do. Given the varied formulations—and, frequently, also the vagueness—of "established" defenses, does Easterbrook's theory adequately answer the question of judicial authority?

(5) Delegation. Finally, consider the thesis of Professor Kahan in *Lenity and Federal Common Law Crimes*, 1994 Sup.Ct.Rev. 345, 347–48, 371, 373–75, "that Congress may *delegate* criminal lawmaking power to courts"; "that federal criminal law, no less than other statutory domains, is dominated by judge-made law crafted to fill the interstices of open-textured statutory provisions"; and that "a regime of delegated criminal lawmaking is much more * * * effective than one in which Congress is obliged to make criminal law without judicial assistance." One illustration Kahan offers is the Crimes Act of 1790, 1 Stat. 112, the text of which "merely identified" without defining various offenses on the high seas and in federal enclaves. He also mentions a number of modern statutes; for example, the offense of mail fraud, 18 U.S.C. § 1341, has been interpreted to encompass many forms of misconduct not generally recognized as fraud at common law—including public corruption and misappropriation of confidential information. Is a statute like § 1341 fairly viewed as an implicit delegation? Consider whether, notwithstanding Kahan's argument, Hudson's limits on the judicial definition of primary duties in criminal cases are stricter than the parallel limits in civil cases—and if so, whether the difference in approach is justified. Compare Hessick, Paragraph (2), *supra*, at 973–78 (noting special reasons for concern about federal common lawmaking in the criminal context, including the principle of legality and the special importance of notice and generality in criminal law).

INTRODUCTORY NOTE ON FEDERAL COMMON LAW IMPLIED BY JURISDICTIONAL GRANTS AND STRUCTURAL INFERENCE

In previous cases in this Chapter, federal common law is generally fashioned in support of statutory regulation enacted by Congress, and the judge-made law is interstitial, addressing matters allied to a legislative program that are not specifically addressed by any statutory provision. By contrast, the next principal case concerns federal common lawmaking in an area (admiralty matters) in which federal courts, exercising the admiralty jurisdiction granted by Article III and congressional legislation, initially provided an entire corpus juris without prior congressional regulation. Thus, common lawmaking cannot be justified as filling the gaps in a legislative program, nor can it be characterized merely as interstitial; and if it is viewed as field preemption, the only enactments on which it is based are constitutional and statutory grants of federal jurisdiction.

Chelentis v. Luckenbach S. S. Co.

247 U.S. 372 (1918).
Certiorari to the Circuit Court of Appeals for the Second Circuit.

■ MR. JUSTICE MCREYNOLDS delivered the opinion of the Court.

* * * [P]etitioner was employed by respondent * * * on board the steamship "J. L. Luckenbach" * * *. While at sea, * * * petitioner undertook to perform certain duties on deck during a heavy wind; a wave came aboard, knocked him down and broke his leg. * * * [W]hen the vessel arrived [in New York] he was taken to the marine hospital, where he remained for three months; during that time it became necessary to amputate his leg. After discharge from the hospital claiming that his injuries resulted from the negligence and an improvident order of a superior officer, he instituted a common law action in Supreme Court, New York County, demanding full indemnity for damage sustained. The cause was removed to the United States District Court because of diverse citizenship. Counsel did not question [the] seaworthiness of [the] ship or her appliances and announced that no claim was made for maintenance, cure, or wages.* At [the] conclusion of plaintiff's evidence the court directed verdict for respondent, and judgment thereon was affirmed by the Circuit Court of Appeals. [The court of appeals noted that "[t]he contract of a seaman is maritime and has written into it those peculiar features of the maritime law that were considered in the case of The Osceola[, 189 U.S. 158] (1903)."] * * *

In The Osceola, a libel *in rem* to recover damages for personal injuries to a seaman while on board and alleged to have resulted from the master's negligence, * * * we held:

"1.   That the vessel and her owners are liable, in case a seaman falls sick, or is wounded, in the service of the ship, to the extent of his maintenance and cure, and to his wages, at least so long as the voyage is continued.

"2.   That the vessel and her owner are * * * liable to an indemnity for injuries received by seamen in consequence of the unseaworthiness of the ship * * *.

"3.   That all the members of the crew, except perhaps the master, are, as between themselves, fellow servants, and hence seamen cannot recover for injuries sustained through the negligence of another member of the crew beyond the expense of their maintenance and cure.

"4.   That the seaman is not allowed to recover an indemnity for the negligence of the master, or any member of the crew, but is entitled to maintenance and cure, whether the injuries were received by negligence or accident."

---

*   [Ed.] "'Maintenance' is the right of a seaman to food and lodging if he falls ill or becomes injured while in the service of the ship. 'Cure' is the right to necessary medical services." Schoenbaum, Admiralty and Maritime Law, § 4–28, at 334 (5th ed.2012).

After reference to article 1, § 8, and article 3, § 2, of the Constitution, we declared in Southern Pacific Co. v. Jensen, 244 U.S. 205, 215, 216 [(1917)]: "Considering our former opinions, it must now be accepted as settled doctrine that in consequence of these provisions Congress has paramount power to fix and determine the maritime law which shall prevail throughout the country. * * * And further, that in the absence of some controlling statute the general maritime law as accepted by the federal courts constitutes part of our national law applicable to matters within the admiralty and maritime jurisdiction." Concerning [the] extent to which the general maritime law may be changed, modified or affected by state legislation this was said: "No such legislation is valid if it contravenes the essential purpose expressed by an act of Congress or works material prejudice to the characteristic features of the general maritime law or interferes with the proper harmony and uniformity of that law in its international and interstate relations. This limitation, at the least, is essential to the effective operation of the fundamental purposes for which such law was incorporated into our national laws by the Constitution itself. These purposes are forcefully indicated in the foregoing quotations from The Lottawanna, 21 Wall. 558, 575 [(1874)]." Among such quotations is the following: "One thing, however, is unquestionable; the Constitution must have referred to a system of law coextensive with, and operating uniformly in, the whole country. It certainly could not have been the intention to place the rules and limits of maritime law under the disposal and regulation of the several States, as that would have defeated the uniformity and consistency at which the Constitution aimed on all subjects of a commercial character affecting the intercourse of the states with each other or with foreign states."

* * * [T]he parties' rights and liabilities were matters clearly within the admiralty jurisdiction. * * * Under the doctrine approved in Southern Pacific Co. v. Jensen, no state has power to abolish the well recognized maritime rule concerning measure of recovery and substitute therefor the full indemnity rule of the common law. Such a substitution would distinctly and definitely change or add to the settled maritime law; and it would be destructive of the "uniformity and consistency at which the Constitution aimed on all subjects of a commercial character affecting the intercourse of the States with each other or with foreign states."

* * * [Petitioner argues that he has the right to recover full indemnity according to the common law under section 9 of the Judiciary Act of 1789], whereby District Courts of the United States were given exclusive original cognizance of all civil causes of admiralty and maritime jurisdiction, "saving to suitors, in all cases, the right of a common law remedy, where the common law is competent to give it" * * *.

The precise effect of the quoted clause of the original Judiciary Act has not been delimited by this court and different views have been entertained concerning it. In Southern Pacific Co. v. Jensen we definitely ruled that it gave no authority to the several states to enact legislation which would work "material prejudice to the characteristic features of the general maritime law or interfere with the proper harmony and uniformity of that law in its international and interstate relations." In The Moses Taylor, 4 Wall. 411, 431 [(1866)], we said: "That clause only saves to suitors 'the right of a common-law remedy, where the common law is competent to give it.' It is not a remedy in the common-law courts which is saved, but a common-law remedy. A proceeding *in rem*, as used in the admiralty courts, is not a remedy afforded by the common law; it is a proceeding under the civil law." And in Knapp, Stout & Co. v. McCaffrey, 177 U.S. 638, 644, 648 [(1900)]: "Some of the cases already cited recognize the distinction between a common law action and a common law remedy. * * * If the suit be *in personam* against an individual defendant, with an auxiliary attachment against a particular thing, or against the property of the defendant in general, it is essentially a proceeding according to the course of the common law, and within the saving clause of the statute * * * of a common law remedy. The suit in this case being one in equity to enforce a common law remedy, the state courts were correct in assuming jurisdiction."

The distinction between rights and remedies is fundamental. A right is a well founded or acknowledged claim; a remedy is the means employed to enforce a right or redress an injury. Plainly, we think, under the saving clause a right sanctioned by the maritime law may be enforced through any appropriate remedy recognized at common law; but we find nothing therein which reveals an intention to give the complaining party an election to determine whether the defendant's liability shall be measured by common-law standards rather than those of the maritime law. Under the circumstances here presented, without regard to the court where he might ask relief, petitioner's rights were those recognized by the law of the sea. * * *

The judgment of the court below is

Affirmed.

■ [MR. JUSTICE HOLMES concurred in the result. MR. JUSTICE PITNEY, MR. JUSTICE BRANDEIS, and MR. JUSTICE CLARKE dissented without opinion.]

NOTE ON FEDERAL COMMON LAW IMPLIED BY JURISDICTIONAL GRANTS

A. Introduction

Erie R. Co. v. Tompkins, 304 U.S. 64 (1938), p. 760, *supra*, made clear that, as the Court later said, "[t]he vesting of jurisdiction in the federal courts does not in and of itself give rise to authority to formulate federal common law * * *." Texas Indus., Inc. v. Radcliff Materials, Inc., 451 U.S. 630, 640–41 (1981). Chelentis exemplifies one area—admiralty—in which the federal courts' lawmaking power is often viewed as based, at least substantially, on the grant of jurisdiction in Article III and federal statutes. Indeed, this exercise of lawmaking power is particularly dramatic not only because it arose in the absence of statutory regulation but also because the recognition of judicial lawmaking power was in turn deemed to be a source of Congress's power to legislate on admiralty matters.[1] A second area in which federal court lawmaking power is often viewed as grounded, at least in part, on a grant of jurisdiction is that involving controversies between two states. A third but more contested example—Textile Workers Union of Am. v. Lincoln Mills of Ala., 353 U.S. 448 (1957)—involves what some see as the implication of substantive lawmaking power from a labor statute granting federal jurisdiction over collective bargaining disputes between unions and management.

Given Erie's holding that the grant of federal jurisdiction over diversity actions does not authorize formulation of federal common law, should such grants of jurisdiction be treated as sources of lawmaking authority? As you read this Note, consider whether lawmaking authority in these areas rests on factors other than a jurisdictional grant—and, indeed, whether it is a mistake to think of lawmaking in admiralty and in interstate disputes as resting (exclusively? primarily?) on jurisdictional grants rather than on a structural constitutional inference that the area is inherently federal.[2]

Finally, consider how the Court should treat the fact that founding-era assumptions about the nature of law have changed over time. Although it is sometimes difficult for modern lawyers to appreciate the concept, late-eighteenth and early-nineteenth century lawyers subscribed to the idea of "general law" embodied in the "law of nations"—a set of rules and norms that did not emanate from the will of a particular sovereign, but rather emerged over a long period of time from "common practice and consent among a number of sovereigns." Fletcher, *The General Common Law and Section 34 of the Judiciary Act of 1789: The Example of Marine Insurance*, 97 Harv.L.Rev. 1513, 1517 (1984). To the extent that certain jurisdictional grants (such as those governing admiralty and maritime matters and state-state disputes) presupposed that certain branches of the law of nations (the law maritime and law of inter-sovereign relations) would supply uniform rules of decision, how should a modern Court maintain fidelity to the original purposes of those jurisdictional grants after Erie rejected the concept of general law on which they were premised?[3]

B. Admiralty[4]

(1) The Origins of Admiralty Jurisdiction and Admiralty Law.
Article III's conferral of admiralty and maritime jurisdiction was among the

---

[1] For an account of the historical development, see Note, *From Judicial Grant to Legislative Power: The Admiralty Clause in the Nineteenth Century*, 67 Harv.L.Rev. 1214 (1954).

[2] See Meltzer, *Customary International Law, Foreign Affairs, and Federal Common Law*, 42 Va.J.Int'l.L. 513, 540–41 (2002). *Cf.* Hill, *The Law-Making Power of the Federal Courts: Constitutional Preemption*, 67 Colum.L.Rev. 1024 (1967) (viewing these areas as ones in which the Constitution preempts state lawmaking, leaving federal common law to govern).

[3] For discussion of the idea of translation, see generally Lessig, *Understanding Changed Readings: Fidelity and Theory*, 47 Stan.L.Rev. 395 (1995).

[4] For extensive accounts of the development of the law, see Robertson, Admiralty and Federalism (1970); Currie, *Federalism and the Admiralty: "The Devil's Own Mess,"* 1960

least controversial of those in Article III. See, *e.g.*, The Federalist, No. 80 (Hamilton) ("The most bigoted idolizers of State authority have not thus far shown a disposition to deny the national judiciary the cognizance of maritime causes."). A central concern involved the relationship of admiralty matters to international affairs; consider, for example, the possible implications of prize cases, which adjudicated the legality under the law of nations of captures of one nation's ships and cargo by the nationals of another. These cases involved determination of the rights and status of foreign claimants and nations, neutral and belligerent. Accordingly, the proper disposition of such cases was a matter of obvious national concern. In addition, the emerging American states lacked a well-developed body of maritime law on which courts could rely.

But admiralty and maritime law has come to govern not only the high seas and tidal waters, but also navigable waters generally, and thus embraces matters—such as a collision between two pleasure boats on Lake Michigan—far removed from foreign affairs or international commerce. Policy support for the broader understanding has been found in the perceived value of uniformity in admiralty and maritime law—a notion reflecting the traditional view of the law of the sea as an independent and international body of rules transcending the power of territorial jurisdictions—and in the contemporary federal interest in furthering maritime commerce. For all of these reasons, admiralty and maritime law developed as a freestanding body of judge-made law.

(2) From General Law to Preemptive Federal Law. As noted, early Americans understood admiralty and maritime law to be of the same genus of "general law" as the "law merchant" applied in diversity in Swift v. Tyson, 41 U.S. 1, 19 (1842), originating not in the will of a particular sovereign but in the commonly shared customs and practices that made up the law of nations. See Fletcher, p. 747, *supra*, at 1517. See also, *e.g.*, Clark, *Federal Common Law: A Structural Reinterpretation*, 144 U.Pa.L.Rev. 1245, 1280–81 (1996); Gilmore & Black, note 4, *supra*, § 1–3, at 6; Jay, *Origins of Federal Common Law: Part Two*, 133 U.Pa.L.Rev. 1231, 1309–11 (1985); Young, *Preemption at Sea*, 67 Geo.Wash.L.Rev. 273, 318–22 (1999). Given the character of the law of nations, neither federal nor state courts had the authority to bind the other to its view of its content in cases within their respective jurisdictions. See, *e.g.*, Clark, *supra*, at 1283–86. Nonetheless, reliance on such law supplied (albeit imperfectly) a degree of needed uniformity. See Fletcher, p. 747, *supra*, at 1518–21, 1532, 1538.

The modern doctrine that admiralty and maritime law is a uniform body of substantive *federal* law, applicable not only in federal admiralty courts but also binding upon the state courts, is conventionally thought to have originated in Chelentis and in the decision one year earlier in Southern Pac. Co. v. Jensen, 244 U.S. 205 (1917). Although predating by more than two decades the post-Erie emergence of modern federal common law, the Jensen

---

Sup.Ct.Rev. 158. Other valuable sources include Gilmore & Black, The Law of Admiralty (2d ed.1975); Lucas & Schmidt, Admiralty: Cases and Materials (6th ed.2012); Robertson, Friedell & Sturley, Admiralty and Maritime Law in the United States (4th ed.2020); Schoenbaum, Admiralty and Maritime Law (6th ed.2018).

Court viewed admiralty law, in a similar vein, as the product of an implicit grant of constitutional authority, derived from the Admiralty Clause of Article III, to adopt a body of preemptive federal law that could serve the evident purpose of ensuring " 'the uniformity and consistency at which the Constitution aimed on all subjects of a commercial character affecting the intercourse of the States with each other or with foreign states' " (quoting The Lottawanna, 88 U.S. (21 Wall.) 558, 575 (1874)). Jensen involved a longshoreman killed while loading a vessel in the port of New York. His next of kin obtained a workers' compensation award under the New York Compensation Law, which the state courts sustained. The Supreme Court reversed. Justice McReynolds declared that "no [state] legislation is valid if it * * * works material prejudice to the characteristic features of the general maritime law or interferes with the proper harmony and uniformity of that law in its international and interstate relations." Without explaining why a workers' compensation law would be more destructive of "harmony and uniformity" than state wrongful death statutes (which could be relied on to remedy maritime deaths, see The Hamilton, 207 U.S. 398, 403–06 (1907)), he concluded that "freedom of navigation between the States and with foreign countries would be seriously hampered" if the compensation law applied. Justice Holmes dissented and famously asserted that "[t]he common law is not a brooding omnipresence in the sky but the articulate voice of some sovereign or quasi-sovereign that can be identified * * *."[5]

Note that the Jensen case came to the Supreme Court on review of a state court decision. As the Chelentis opinion notes, ever since 1789, Congress has conferred on the federal courts exclusive jurisdiction over all civil cases in admiralty and maritime jurisdiction, "saving to suitors, in all cases, the right of a common law remedy, where the common law is competent to give it."[6] The saving clause limits not federal jurisdiction but rather the scope of federal exclusivity, which is restricted to admiralty and maritime actions brought *in rem*, see The Moses Taylor, 71 U.S. (4 Wall.) 411 (1867). However, the "uniformity" doctrine of Jensen and Chelentis, insofar as it applies, governs a case whether litigated in a federal admiralty court, a state court, or on the "law" side of a federal court; if uniform federal law must be applied, any conflicting state law is preempted.

(3) The Remaining Scope of State Law. Ever since Jensen and Chelentis, courts have faced vexing questions in trying to define what matters are governed by uniform federal admiralty law and in what areas state law remains free to operate. See Currie, note 4, *supra*, at 164–65. Jensen's formulation—whether application of state law "works material prejudice to" or "interferes with the proper harmony and uniformity of"

---

[5]   After Jensen, Congress twice explicitly authorized states to provide workers' compensation schemes for maritime workers, but the Court held that both statutes had unconstitutionally delegated authority to the states to impair maritime uniformity. See Knickerbocker Ice Co. v. Stewart, 253 U.S. 149 (1920); Washington v. W.C. Dawson & Co., 264 U.S. 219 (1924). Subsequent decisions cast doubt on that view of congressional incapacity. See Wilburn Boat Co. v. Fireman's Fund Ins. Co., 348 U.S. 310, 321 n.29 (1955); Askew v. American Waterways Operators Inc., 411 U.S. 325, 344 (1973). For a defense of the earlier position, see Bederman, *Uniformity, Delegation and the Dormant Admiralty Clause*, 28 J.Mar.L. & Com. 1 (1997).

[6]   For the present wording and further discussion, see p. 1107, *infra*.

federal maritime law—is not easy to apply. Nor are the other formulations the Court has supplied over time: that state law may (a) provide remedies but not rights (Chelentis); (b) fill gaps in federal maritime law (Western Fuel Co. v. Garcia, 257 U.S. 233, 242 (1921)); (c) regulate matters maritime but local (see *id.*); (d) govern when state interests outweigh federal interests (Kossick v. United Fruit Co., 365 U.S. 731, 738–42 (1961)); or (e) govern procedure but not substance (American Dredging Co. v. Miller, 510 U.S. 443, 453–54 (1994)).[7] In American Dredging, the Court conceded that the "line separating permissible from impermissible state regulation" is neither "readily discernible" nor "entirely consistent" in the Court's decisions, and Justice Stevens's separate opinion argued that Jensen's assertion of judicial authority to preempt state law was unwarranted—and, in view of the Commerce Clause's broad grant of legislative authority and its dormant effect, unnecessary.

(4) The Relevance of Federal Legislation. Though originally governed by judicially defined common law rules, maritime matters are increasingly regulated by federal enactments, making for a complex mixture of statutory and common law. Federal statutes, of course, prevail over contrary federal common law,[8] but the appropriate relationship between judge-made and statutory law has presented challenging questions. A notable example is found in the area of wrongful death.

Although maritime law long recognized a right of action for harm suffered as the result of negligence or unseaworthiness, The Harrisburg, 119 U.S. 199 (1886), adopted for maritime law the longstanding rule at common law that, absent a wrongful death statute, no remedy exists for wrongful death. A later decision in The Tungus v. Skovgaard, 358 U.S. 588 (1959), held that when neither general maritime law nor any federal statute provides a remedy, a wrongful death remedy may be provided under an applicable state statute.

The Court revisited the question whether federal admiralty law should recognize a wrongful death remedy in Moragne v. States Marine Lines, Inc., 398 U.S. 375 (1970), an action by the widow of a longshoreman killed while working on a vessel on navigable waters. After removing the case to federal court on the basis of diversity, the defendants successfully moved to dismiss the wrongful death claim based on unseaworthiness, on the ground that state law did not encompass unseaworthiness as a basis for liability. The Supreme Court unanimously reversed. Justice Harlan's opinion noted that whatever the correctness of The Harrisburg at the time of its decision, legislative developments had changed the legal background against which the Court must assess the common law of admiralty. In particular, Justice Harlan observed:

---

[7]   See generally Robertson, *Displacement of State Law by Federal Maritime Law*, 26 J.Mar.L. & Com. 325, 338–46 (1995) (finding all the approaches unsuccessful); Force, *Choice of Law in Admiralty Cases: "National Interests" and the Admiralty Clause*, 75 Tul.L.Rev. 1421 (2001). See also Robertson & Sturley, *The Admiralty Extension Act Solution*, 34 J.Mar.L. & Com. 209 (2003).

[8]   But *cf.* note 5, *supra*.

"In the United States, every State today has enacted a wrongful-death statute. The Congress has created actions for wrongful deaths of railroad employees, Federal Employers' Liability Act, 45 U.S.C. §§ 51–59; of merchant seamen, Jones Act, 46 U.S.C. § 688; and of persons on the high seas, Death on the High Seas Act, 46 U.S.C. §§ 761, 762. Congress has also, in the Federal Tort Claims Act, 28 U.S.C. § 1346(b), made the United States subject to liability in certain circumstances for negligently caused wrongful death to the same extent as a private person.

"These numerous and broadly applicable statutes, taken as a whole, make it clear that there is no present public policy against allowing recovery for wrongful death. The statutes evidence a wide rejection by the legislatures of whatever justifications may once have existed for a general refusal to allow such recovery. This legislative establishment of policy carries significance beyond the particular scope of each of the statutes involved. The policy thus established has become itself a part of our law, to be given its appropriate weight not only in matters of statutory construction but also in those of decisional law."

The action in Moragne fell within a gap in what had become an extensive system of state and federal remedies for wrongful death. The Jones Act provided no remedy because the decedent was not a merchant seaman. The Death on the High Seas Act did not apply because the death did not occur outside the Act's three-mile limit. And, as noted, the accident happened within the territorial limits of a state whose wrongful death cause of action happened not to extend to seaworthiness. The resultant gap highlighted discrepancies in coverage under existing maritime law. For example, although federal admiralty law required "the furnishing of a seaworthy vessel," identical violations of that duty "within territorial waters" would give rise to liability "if the victim is merely injured, but frequently not if he is killed." In light of the statutory developments since The Harrisburg and the discrepancies in coverage that now resulted from that precedent, the Court found The Harrisburg rule to be "such an unjustifiable anomaly in the present maritime law that it should no longer be followed." See also The Dutra Grp. v. Batterton, 588 U.S. 358, 369–74 (2019) (following Jones Act's policy, which was consistent with overwhelming historical evidence, to hold that a seaman could not recover punitive damages on a claim of unseaworthiness); Norfolk Shipbuilding & Drydock Corp. v. Garris, 532 U.S. 811, 815 (2001) (extending Moragne to wrongful death actions based on negligence and finding that negligence "is no less a distinctively maritime duty than seaworthiness"); Miles v. Apex Marine Corp., 498 U.S. 19, 30 (1990) (recognizing a general maritime cause of action, based on unseaworthiness, for the wrongful death of a sailor, rather than a longshore worker like Moragne, killed in territorial waters); but see Atlantic Sounding Co. v. Townsend, 557 U.S. 404, 422–25 (2009) (holding that the common law of admiralty authorizes the recovery of punitive damages when a shipowner willfully denies a crew member maintenance and cure after an injury despite the fact that such damages would not be recoverable in an action brought pursuant to the Jones Act, 46 U.S.C. § 30104, which allows someone in the plaintiff's position to elect between a common law and statutory remedy).[9]

Central to Justice Harlan's opinion in Moragne was the conviction that it is "the duty of the common-law court to perceive the impact of major legislative innovations and to interweave the new legislative policies with the inherited body of common-law principles * * *." Was Justice Harlan's discussion of congressional purpose persuasive? Compare Posner, *Legal Formalism, Legal Realism, and the Interpretation of Statutes and the Constitution*, 37 Case W.Res.L.Rev. 179, 203 (1986) ("Essentially the Court deleted the word 'High' from the Death on the High Seas Act. Congress thought it was legislating for the high seas. It thought wrong."). Does his approach fully account for the limits that statutes such as the Death on the High Seas Act place upon the reach of the legislative policies they embody? Is it consistent with the stricter approach to judicial creativity in federal common lawmaking in such cases as O'Melveny?

(5) Contemporary Debate About the Sources of Law in Admiralty. A number of scholars have questioned the justification for federal judicial lawmaking in admiralty. See, *e.g.*, Redish, Federal Jurisdiction: Tensions in the Allocation of Judicial Power 138–47 (2d ed.1990); Clark, Paragraph (2), *supra*; Young, Paragraph (2), *supra*. Critics of the Court's approach argue that post-Jensen federal common law attributes to the Admiralty Clause an unjustifiably broad purpose. Historically, they say, such jurisdiction was designed principally to deal with concerns arising out of certain classes of cases—crimes on the high seas, prize cases, and revenue cases. See generally Casto, *The Origins of Federal Admiralty Jurisdiction in an Age of Privateers, Smugglers, and Pirates*, 37 Am.J. Legal Hist. 117 (1993). And because those categories touched on questions involving foreign relations and the war power, they lay outside the competence of the states and posed few federalism concerns. Acknowledging that the Admiralty Clause historically also covered private maritime claims, the modern critics add that, insofar as uniformity was desired for such cases, this goal was to be implemented through the judicial application of "general maritime law"—the analogue to the law merchant applied in Swift v. Tyson. See Paragraph (2), *supra*. Given the resulting similarity of the pre-Jensen regime to the Swift regime in diversity, critics of admiralty preemption maintain that the Jensen-Chelentis doctrine should not survive Erie, whose federalism and separation-of-powers concerns apply no less to most admiralty and maritime claims than

---

[9]   The Court in Dutra Group reaffirmed the view that " 'an admiralty court should look primarily to * * * legislative enactments for policy guidance,' " (quoting Miles v. Apex Marine Corp., 498 U.S. 19, 27 (1990)), and distinguished Atlantic Sounding based on established maritime law tradition: "We may depart from the policies found in the statutory scheme in discrete instances based on long-established history, see, *e.g.*, Atlantic Sounding Co. v. Townsend, 557 U.S. 404, 424–25 (2009), but we do so cautiously in light of Congress's persistent pursuit of 'uniformity in the exercise of admiralty jurisdiction.' " (quoting Miles, *supra*, at 26 (quoting Moragne v. States Marine Lines, Inc., 398 U.S. 375, 401 (1970))). Compare Exxon Shipping Co. v. Baker, 554 U.S. 471, 508 n.21 (2008) (noting, in the course of limiting the permissible ratio of punitive to compensatory damages in an admiralty action, that although an admiralty court should look primarily to pertinent legislation in formulating common law rules, "we may not slough off our responsibilities for common law remedies because Congress has not made a first move, and the absence of federal legislation constraining punitive damages does not imply a congressional decision that there should be no quantified rule").

to diversity cases. See Clark, Paragraph (2), *supra*, at 1332–60; Young, Paragraph (2), *supra*, at 312–28.

Is the foregoing argument a convincing translation of the original understanding of admiralty and maritime jurisdiction to the post-Erie context in which general law is no longer recognized? Insofar as the purpose of the Diversity Clause was to ensure a neutral forum while that of the Admiralty Clause was to assure uniformity in maritime commerce, does Erie's insistence upon the application of state law in diversity cases necessarily extend to the admiralty and maritime context? See Currie, The Constitution in the Supreme Court: The Second Century, 1888–1986, at 243 (1990) (suggesting such a distinction).

Professor Young further contends that today maritime commerce no more requires uniform rules than do other forms of commerce. He adds (along with Professor Clark) that even if the Court abandoned the Jensen-Chelentis doctrine, judge-made federal maritime law would be appropriate for cases that fall outside state competence (*e.g.*, those arising beyond territorial waters) or that implicate a compelling federal interest (*e.g.*, the conduct of foreign affairs). And while taking seriously the concern that overruling Jensen and Chelentis would subject maritime commerce to "a crazy-quilt" of state laws, Young finds it sufficient to rely on "Congress's power to impose uniformity by statute" and on the dormant Commerce Clause "prohibition on measures that discriminate against or unduly burden commerce." Young, Paragraph (2), *supra*, at 349. See also American Dredging Co. v. Miller, 510 U.S. 443, 461–62 (1994) (Stevens, J., concurring in part and concurring the judgment) (outlining similar grounds for overruling Jensen).

Consider the following responses to the modern critique of the Jensen-Chelentis doctrine: (1) the original understanding of admiralty and maritime jurisdiction treated private law cases (whether brought in state or federal court) as governed by a single body of judge-made law; (2) admiralty law often involves relations with other nations, in which uniformity is an international objective; (3) any effort today to de-federalize admiralty law would generate chaos, for often there exists no corresponding state law that could be substituted; (4) creation of a body of federal admiralty law is consistent with the original wording of the Rules of Decision Act, whose directive to apply state law extended only to "trials at common law" and not to admiralty; and (5) admiralty jurisprudence already leaves considerable room for the application of state law. See Force, *An Essay on Federal Common Law and Admiralty*, 43 St. Louis U.L.J. 1367 (1999); Gutoff, *Original Understandings and the Private Law Origins of the Federal Admiralty Jurisdiction: A Reply to Professor Casto*, 30 J.Mar.L. & Com. 361 (1999). Compare Gutoff, *Federal Common Law and Congressional Delegation: A Reconceptualization of Admiralty*, 61 U.Pitt.L.Rev. 367, 405 (2000) (arguing, *inter alia*, that admiralty is properly viewed as an instance of congressional delegation of authority, and that congressional extensions of admiralty jurisdiction in various statutes enacted between 1845 and 1994 were "premised on the existence of a body of supreme federal maritime law that the federal courts had articulated"), with Young, *It's Just Water: Toward the Normalization of Admiralty*, 35 J.Mar.L. & Com. 469, 485–507 (2004) (disagreeing).

(6) Choice of Forum and Choice of Law Clauses in Admiralty. The Supreme Court in a series of federal common law decisions in admiralty has shown receptivity to enforcement of a private agreement that precludes suit from being brought in a federal court originally or on removal, and to enforcement of parties' choice of governing law.[10]

(a) Private Agreements Limiting Choice of Forum. The Court took a first step in the forum selection clause context in The M/S Bremen v. Zapata Off-Shore Co., 407 U.S. 1 (1972). Zapata, an American corporation, had contracted with Unterweser, a German corporation, for towage of Zapata's ocean-going drilling rig from Louisiana to the Adriatic Sea. The contract specified that "[a]ny dispute arising must be treated before the London Court of Justice." After the rig sustained damage, Zapata brought an admiralty action in a Florida federal court seeking damages against Unterweser *in personam* and against Unterweser's deep sea tug, The Bremen, *in rem*. Unterweser moved to dismiss on the basis of the contract's forum selection clause or on forum non conveniens grounds, or, in the alternative, to stay the action pending submission of the dispute to the London Court of Justice.

Reversing the lower courts, the Supreme Court upheld enforcement of the forum selection clause, stating that for federal courts sitting in admiralty, "such clauses are prima facie valid and should be enforced unless enforcement is shown by the resisting party to be 'unreasonable' under the circumstances * * *." The Court noted that much undesirable uncertainty in international transactions can be eliminated by an advance agreement as to forum and that the party seeking to avoid its impact on such grounds as fraud, undue influence, "overweening bargaining power," or, perhaps, serious inconvenience should have a heavy burden of proof.

Zapata also argued that enforcement of the forum selection clause would violate public policy because the contract also contained a clause, exculpating Unterweser from liability, that an English court would honor but a federal admiralty court presumably would not. See Bisso v. Inland Waterways Corp., 349 U.S. 85 (1955). The Supreme Court rejected this argument on the ground that the policy invoked did not reach "a freely negotiated international commercial transaction between a German and an American corporation for towage of a vessel from the Gulf of Mexico to the Adriatic Sea." Finally, the Court distinguished Insurance Co. v. Morse, Paragraph (1), *supra*, on the basis that in that case "a state statutory requirement was viewed as imposing an unconstitutional condition on the exercise of the federal right of removal."

The Supreme Court extended the rationale of The Bremen beyond international transactions in Carnival Cruise Lines, Inc. v. Shute, 499 U.S.

---

[10]   The focus of the discussion in text is on an agreement that suit may be brought only in the court of another forum (*i.e.*, a court of a state or of another country). Agreements to submit disputes to arbitration, though once disfavored, are now generally enforced under a variety of state and federal statutes.

585 (1991). At issue in this admiralty action was a forum-selection clause contained in a standard form passenger ticket. That the clause was undoubtedly not negotiated between the parties did not make it "unreasonable," the Court argued, stressing the advantages of such clauses. The Court did state, however, that such clauses "are subject to judicial scrutiny for fundamental fairness."

(b) Private Agreements on Governing Law. The Supreme Court relied on the "analogous" forum selection clause context in The Bremen and Carnival Cruise in upholding the validity of a choice-of-law clause in admiralty in Great Lakes Ins. SE v. Raiders Retreat Reality Co., LLC, 601 U.S. 65 (2024). The case involved a marine insurance contract between Raiders, a Pennsylvania firm, and Great Lakes, a German firm headquartered in the United Kingdom, that chose New York law to govern disputes. The Court rejected Great Lakes' argument that the parties' choice of New York law must give way to the strong public policy of Pennsylvania in applying its insurance law. As a matter of uniform federal admiralty law, the Court ruled, choice-of-law provisions in maritime contracts are presumptively enforceable for the same efficiency and uncertainty-reducing reasons that forum selection clauses are. This presumption can be overcome, the Court stated, "when the chosen law would contravene a controlling federal statute" or "an established federal maritime policy," or if there is "no reasonable basis" for the chosen law. But the Court rejected the argument that a state's contrary "public policy" could overcome the presumption.

C. Interstate Disputes

(1) The Law Governing Interstate Disputes. A second area in which lawmaking power is recognized despite the absence of federal substantive legislation is that involving interstate disputes. Article III gives the Supreme Court original jurisdiction of suits between states, and the implementing legislation, 28 U.S.C. § 1251, makes such jurisdiction exclusive. The Court has fashioned a body of federal common law in interstate disputes as an implication of the jurisdictional grant and the obvious difficulty with applying the law of either disputant. See generally Hill, note 2, *supra*, at 1031–32.

For example, in Connecticut v. Massachusetts, 282 U.S. 660 (1931), a suit to enjoin Massachusetts "from diverting waters from the watershed of the Connecticut River," Connecticut asked the Court to follow the common law of both states, which, it argued, gave riparian owners "a vested right in the use of the flowing waters" unimpaired by such a diversion. The Court replied:

"For the decision of suits between States, federal, state and international law are considered and applied by this Court as the exigencies of the particular case may require. The determination of the relative rights of contending States in respect of the use of streams flowing through them does not depend upon the same considerations and is not governed by the same rules of law that are applied in such States for the solution of similar questions of private right. And, while the municipal law relating to like questions between individuals is to be taken into account, it is not to be deemed to have controlling weight. * * * [T]he principles of right and equity shall be applied having regard to the 'equal level or plane on which all the States stand * * * under our constitutional system' and * * *, upon a consideration of the pertinent laws of the contending States and all other relevant facts, this Court will determine what is an equitable apportionment of the use of such waters."

(2) The Hinderlider Decision and the Problem of Translation. Hinderlider v. La Plata River & Cherry Creek Ditch Co., 304 U.S. 92 (1938), handed down on the same day as Erie R. Co. v. Tompkins, p. 760, *supra*, and, like Erie, authored by Justice Brandeis, made clear that the law applicable to interstate disputes was *federal* common law. The action was brought by a private company against Colorado officials whose actions, the company alleged, deprived it of water rights under an 1898 Colorado decree. The state supreme court had ruled for the plaintiff, finding that an interstate compact pursuant to which the defendants had acted was invalid because it deprived the company of its rights in violation of the Fourteenth Amendment. The Supreme Court reversed, finding that private parties are bound by a decree or compact to which their state is a party, and that "whether the water of an interstate stream must be apportioned between the two States is a question of 'federal common law' upon which neither the statutes nor the decisions of either State can be conclusive."

Previously, the Court had not been so self-conscious in identifying the basis for its choice of law in interstate disputes. See Kansas v. Colorado, 206 U.S. 46, 97 (1907) ("Sitting, as it were, as an international, as well as a domestic tribunal, we apply Federal law, state law, and international law, as the exigencies of the particular case may demand."). The Court could often draw upon general law principles because many disputes between the (formerly independent and still partly sovereign) states—such as border or water-rights disputes—had pertinent analogues in the law of nations that governs relations among sovereigns. See, *e.g.*, Weisburd, *State Courts, Federal Courts, and International Cases*, 20 Yale J.Int'l.L. 1, 51 (1995); Nelson, *The Persistence of General Law*, 106 Colum.L.Rev. 503, 508–09 (2006).

But once Erie rejected the notion of general common law, wasn't it obvious that the law to be applied in suits between states would have to be treated as federal rather than state law? Several commentators have suggested that the Hinderlider doctrine represents a necessary implication of the constitutional structure. As Professor Monaghan has put it: "Some tribunal must exist for settling interstate controversies; but it is a basic presumption of the Constitution that the state courts may be too parochial to administer fairly disputes in which important state interests are at issue. Nor does it seem appropriate to restrict the choice of controlling substantive law to that of one of the contending states. * * * Thus the authority to create federal common law springs of necessity from the structure of the Constitution, from its basic division of authority between the national government and the states." Monaghan, *Foreword: Constitutional Common Law*, 89 Harv.L.Rev. 1, 14 (1975); see also Hill, note 2, *supra*, at 1076

(Hinderlider's lawmaking authority is "established not by Congress but by the Constitution").

The Supreme Court now seems to have accepted, at least in dicta, the structural reading of Hinderlider, concluding that "implicit alterations to the States' relationships with each other" at the time of the founding opened the door for application of a federal rule of decision to interstate disputes. Franchise Tax Bd. v. Hyatt, 587 U.S. 230, 246 (2019). Does it matter if the Hinderlider doctrine is treated as an implication from the jurisdictional grant or from some deeper understanding of the federal structure?[11]

(3) Interstate Compacts. Federal common law governs questions about the obligations created by compacts between states. While not all interstate compacts require congressional approval, where such approval is provided, interpretation of the compact in effect requires interpretation of an act of Congress. See generally Kansas v. Nebraska, 574 U.S. 445, 455–56 (2015); Carchman v. Nash, 473 U.S. 716, 719 (1985). In such a case, is there any role for state law? Compare Petty v. Tennessee-Missouri Bridge Comm'n, 359 U.S. 275, 285 (1959) (Frankfurter, J., dissenting) (contending that, at least where the states do not disagree, the language of a compact, which Congress had not modified, should be given the legal significance that the member states placed upon it, just as the interpretation of an ordinary contract depends on the meaning that the parties attribute to its words).

(4) Interstate Pollution. Does federal common law have a special role in disputes that pit interests from two different states against each other, even if the states themselves are not parties? The problem has arisen in the context of interstate water pollution, in which the Court has traveled up and down the hill on the role of federal common law—though in this area, unlike most interstate disputes, congressional legislation exists and has been taken as a source of guidance.

(a) A dictum in Ohio v. Wyandotte Chems. Corp., 401 U.S. 493, 498–99 n.3 (1971), suggested that state law would govern in an action by Ohio to abate, as a nuisance, the pollution of Lake Erie by private corporations in Michigan and Ontario. But a year later, in an action in the Court's original jurisdiction by Illinois against four Wisconsin cities and two sewer commissions to enjoin pollution of Lake Michigan, the Court held that federal common law governed (and then proceeded to dismiss on the ground that the suit should be filed in federal district court). Illinois v. Milwaukee,

---

[11] Compare Clark, *Federal Common Law: A Structural Reinterpretation,* 144 U.Pa.L.Rev. 1245, 1322–31 (1996), which argues that the federal common law of interstate disputes, properly understood, rests on a structural constitutional inference from the admission of states on an "equal footing," which permitted the Court to draw on extant law-of-nations principles that implemented the corresponding principle of "perfect equality" of sovereigns; see also Sachs, *Constitutional Backdrops,* 80 Geo.Wash.L.Rev. 1813 (2012) (arguing that a considerable body of common law predating the Constitution, including the law of nations, survived its adoption without having been formally incorporated into the document and became the relevant source of law for cases brought pursuant to the grant of jurisdiction for controversies between states, and adding that because U.S. Const. Art. IV, § 3, preserves the territorial integrity of the states, except insofar as the legislatures of the affected states and Congress agree, the Court may not retroactively alter the preexisting common law rules for determining state boundaries).

406 U.S. 91 (1972) (Milwaukee I). After noting a variety of federal statutes asserting an interest in the problem, Justice Douglas said:

"The Federal Water Pollution Control Act in § 1(b) declares that it is federal policy 'to recognize, preserve, and protect the primary responsibilities and rights of the States in preventing and controlling water pollution.' But the Act makes clear that it is federal, not state, law that in the end controls the pollution of interstate or navigable waters. * * *

"The remedy sought by Illinois is not within the precise scope of remedies prescribed by Congress. Yet the remedies which Congress provides are not necessarily the only federal remedies available. * * * When we deal with air and water in their ambient or interstate aspects, there is a federal common law * * *.

"The application of federal common law to abate a public nuisance in interstate or navigable waters is not inconsistent with the Water Pollution Control Act. Congress provided in § 10(b) of that Act that, save as a court may decree otherwise in an enforcement action, '[s]tate and interstate action to abate pollution of interstate or navigable waters shall be encouraged and shall not * * * be displaced by Federal enforcement action.' "

(b)   After this decision, Congress enacted the extensive Water Pollution Control Act Amendments of 1972, 33 U.S.C. § 1311 *et seq.*, which, among other things, made it illegal to discharge pollutants into the nation's waters without a permit. Illinois, meanwhile, re-filed its action in a federal district court in Illinois and served the defendants, who had obtained such permits. The district court held that a nuisance had been established under federal common law and issued an elaborate decree. The court of appeals affirmed in part. But the Supreme Court, in an early decision marking retrenchment of federal common law, reversed, 6–3. Milwaukee v. Illinois, 451 U.S. 304 (1981) (Milwaukee II).

The Court, citing the separation of powers implications of Erie, p. 760, *supra*, and Hudson, p. 747, *supra*, noted: "Federal courts, unlike state courts, are not general common-law courts and do not possess a general power to develop and apply their own rules of decision. The enactment of a federal rule in an area of national concern, and the decision whether to displace state law in doing so, is generally made not by the federal judiciary, purposefully insulated from democratic pressures, but by the people through their elected representatives in Congress." After noting that the Court can develop federal common law when there is "a significant conflict between some federal policy or interest and the use of state law," the Court added: "Nothing in this process suggests that courts are better suited to develop national policy in areas governed by federal common law than they are in other areas, or that the usual and important concerns of an appropriate division of functions between the Congress and the federal judiciary are inapplicable. * * * [W]hen Congress addresses a question previously governed by a decision rested on federal common law the need for such an unusual exercise of lawmaking by federal courts disappears."

Then the Court turned to the relevance of the Water Pollution Control Act Amendments of 1972: "Congress has not left the formulation of appropriate federal standards to the courts through application of often vague and indeterminate nuisance concepts and maxims of equity jurisprudence, but rather has occupied the field through the establishment of a comprehensive regulatory program supervised by an expert administrative agency. The 1972 Amendments to the Federal Water Pollution Control Act were not merely another law 'touching interstate waters' of the sort surveyed in Illinois v. Milwaukee, and found inadequate to supplant federal common law. Rather, the Amendments were viewed by Congress as a 'total restructuring' and 'complete rewriting' of the existing water pollution legislation considered in that case."

The 1972 amendments had explicitly preserved more stringent remedies under state law. For the majority, however, a less clear showing sufficed to establish that Congress had displaced federal common law—a matter that did not implicate the concerns underlying the reluctance to displace state authority. "Indeed, * * * 'we start with the assumption' that it is for Congress, not federal courts, to articulate the appropriate standards to be applied as a matter of federal law."

Justice Blackmun, for the dissenters, thought that the 1972 Act meant to preserve the federal common law of nuisance. The Court, he complained, "in effect is encouraging recourse to state law wherever the federal statutory scheme is perceived to offer inadequate protection against pollution from outside the State," a prospect that would lead states to turn to their own courts and would disserve the objective of uniformity.[12] See also Epstein, *Federal Preemption, and Federal Common Law, in Nuisance Cases*, 102 Nw.U.L.Rev. 551, 573 (2008) ("[T]he entire thrust of the [1972 Amendments] is to toughen the laws, so it seems gratuitous to knock out the extra protections that the federal common law offered.").

D. Lincoln Mills and § 301 of the Taft-Hartley Act

(1) The Lincoln Mills Decision. Can lawmaking authority be implied from a statutory grant of jurisdiction? The decision in Textile Workers Union v. Lincoln Mills, 353 U.S. 448 (1957), is sometimes viewed as an example of such a phenomenon.[13]

There, the union sued an employer to compel arbitration of grievances, as called for by the collective bargaining agreement. Section 301(a) of the Labor Management Relations Act of 1947 (the Taft-Hartley Act), 29 U.S.C. § 185, confers federal court jurisdiction on suits for violation of a collective bargaining agreement between union and employer. Section 301(b) provides a few slivers of substantive federal law: a union and employer shall be bound by the acts of their agents; a union may sue or be sued as an entity in a federal court; and any money judgment against a union in a federal district court is enforceable only against the organization, not against individual

---

[12] For a comprehensive history of the role of federal common law in interstate pollution disputes, see Percival, *The Clean Water Act and the Demise of the Federal Common Law of Interstate Nuisance*, 55 Ala.L.Rev. 717 (2004).

[13] For discussion of other areas sometimes viewed in this way, see pp. 949–970, *infra* (Alien Tort Statute); pp. 778–781, 785, *supra* (federal equity jurisdiction); Brilmayer, *State Forfeiture Rules and Federal Review of State Criminal Convictions*, 49 U.Chi.L.Rev. 741, 765–70 (1982) (federal habeas corpus jurisdiction).

members. The Act does not indicate whose law governs the enforceability of collective bargaining agreements.

Justice Douglas' opinion for the Court noted the holdings of a majority of lower courts that § 301(a) was more than jurisdictional—that it authorized federal courts to fashion federal common law to enforce collective bargaining agreements, including the promise to arbitrate. Analyzing the legislative history, he reasoned that under the Act, the enforceability of the agreement to arbitrate grievances was the quid pro quo for an agreement not to strike and that the purpose of § 301 was to promote labor peace. Thus, in suits under § 301(a), federal courts should apply federal law, fashioned from national labor policy: "The range of judicial inventiveness will be determined by the nature of the problem. Federal interpretation of the federal law will govern, not state law. But state law, if compatible with the purpose of § 301, may be resorted to in order to find the rule that will best effectuate the federal policy. See Board of Commissioners v. United States, [308 U.S. 343], 351–52 [(1939)]. Any state law applied, however, will be absorbed as federal law and will not be an independent source of private rights." He proceeded to rule that federal law permitted suit to enforce the agreement to arbitrate.[14]

A lengthy dissent by Justice Frankfurter took issue with the Court's reading of the legislative history, interpreted § 301(a) as a mere jurisdictional grant, and argued that it was unconstitutional because it purported to confer jurisdiction beyond the scope of Article III. For criticism of that claim, see Pfander, *Judicial Purpose and the Scholarly Process: The Lincoln Mills Case*, 69 Wash.U.L.Q. 243 (1991). For further analysis of the claim, see pp. 1016–1017, *infra*.

NOTE ON FEDERAL STATUTORY DISPLACEMENT OF FEDERAL COMMON LAW

In the federal common law decisions in this chapter, the Court faces a vertical federalism question about whether federal or state authority controls, and then a horizontal separation of powers question about how the judge-made rule relates to congressional legislation. One trajectory that federal common law cases have traveled has been from a relatively undemanding test for the identification of unique federal interests to a relatively demanding one. A related trajectory, outlined in this Note, has been from an expansive view of the Court's power to supplement a

---

[14]   In Local 174 v. Lucas Flour Co., 369 U.S. 95 (1962), the Court held that federal common law governs in suits within the scope of § 301 that are brought in state court. How can state court application of federal common law in labor-management disputes be justified by reference to § 301, a grant of jurisdiction to the federal courts? Does that question reinforce concerns about grounding federal common lawmaking power in a jurisdictional grant alone? The problem also exists in admiralty and interstate matters: federal admiralty law governs in state court actions under the saving clause; and while disputes between two states are subject to the exclusive original jurisdiction of the Supreme Court, federal common law also governs in state court disputes between a private company and state officials concerning interstate matters, as in Hinderlider, p. 860, *supra*.

congressional statutory scheme to a view that more readily reads congressional statutes to supplant, or "displace," federal common law. One can see this move, for example, in the interstate pollution cases discussed in Paragraph (C)(4), pp. 861–863, *supra*, and in the general solicitude for statutory enactments in recent admiralty cases. One can also see it, perhaps, in the move from D'Oench, Duhme, where the Court identified a federal policy in several statutes and then extended it by federal common law, to O'Melveny, where the Court declined "to supplement federal statutory regulation that is comprehensive and detailed" because "matters left unaddressed in such a scheme are presumably left subject to the disposition provided by state law."

Federal legislation will not displace federal common law when Congress's language explicitly preserves it. See Milwaukee v. Illinois, 451 U.S. at 327–29. When Congress is silent on the relationship between a federal statutory scheme and federal common law, however, the test for displacement is set forth in American Elec. Power Co. v. Connecticut, 564 U.S. 410 (2011), a case involving interstate air pollution. There the plaintiffs—a number of states, the city of New York, and several private land trusts—filed public nuisance actions against several large power companies, alleging that the companies' carbon dioxide emissions contributed to global warming. The Second Circuit held that the plaintiffs had stated a claim under the federal common law of nuisance and that the Clean Air Act did not displace that federal common law right of action. In an opinion by Justice Ginsburg, joined in full by Chief Justice Roberts and Justices Scalia, Kennedy, Breyer, and Kagan, the Court reversed. Given its previous holding in Massachusetts v. EPA, 549 U.S. 497 (2007), that the Clean Air Act authorized the EPA to regulate greenhouse gases, the Court concluded that the Act displaced any federal common law right of action that the plaintiffs might otherwise have had.[1]

After emphasizing that "[l]egislative displacement of federal common law does not require the 'same sort of evidence of a clear and manifest [congressional] purpose' demanded for preemption of state law" (quoting Milwaukee v. Illinois, 451 U.S. 304, 316–319 (1981) (Milwaukee II), Paragraph (C)(4), p. 862, *supra*), the Court stated that "[t]he test for whether congressional legislation excludes the declaration of federal common law is simply whether the statute 'speak[s] directly to [the] question' at issue" (quoting Mobil Oil Corp. v. Higginbotham, 436 U.S. 618, 625 (1978)). Since Massachusetts v. EPA "made plain that emissions of carbon dioxide qualify as air pollution subject to regulation under the [Clean Air] Act," the Court held that the Act "speaks directly" to the claims brought by the plaintiffs. It made no difference that the EPA had not yet fully implemented its previously recognized regulatory authority. If the EPA declined to set emissions standards for a particular pollutant or pollution source, the remedy would lie in the judicial review prescribed by the Act itself. The important point, for the Court, was that Congress entrusted the "complex balancing" of environmental, energy, and economic considerations, in the first instance, to

---

[1]   The Court declined to reach the question whether the plaintiffs would have had a federal common law right of action if the Clean Air Act had not addressed the issue.

an expert agency. For that reason, the Court found it inappropriate to attribute parallel authority to inexpert, unelected federal judges.

In Milwaukee II, *supra*, the Court emphasized that the Clean Water Act "occupied the field through the establishment of a comprehensive regulatory program supervised by an expert administrate agency"; that the EPA had issued regulations and permits authorizing the exact conduct for which the plaintiffs sought to hold the defendants liable; and that the Water Act's legislative history indicated that Congress had sought to create an "all-encompassing program of water pollution regulation." In contrast, the American Electric Power Court found displacement simply because the Clean Air Act authorized the EPA to address the subject matter of the lawsuit and allowed private parties to petition the EPA to act. Does this more relaxed displacement standard signal a broader reticence on the part of the Court about the federal common law of interstate pollution? About federal common law?

More broadly, why is the test for displacement easier to satisfy than the test for preemption? Because federal courts after Erie presumptively lack lawmaking powers? How should the Court decide when a federal statute "speaks directly" to the question at stake? For an exhaustive and elucidating analysis of these and related questions, see Raab, *Displacement of Federal Common Law*, 58 Wake Forest L.Rev. 709 (2023). Based on a close reading of Supreme Court and lower court decisions, Raab argues that, unless Congress otherwise specifies, "federal legislation displaces a federal common law cause of action when it (1) bears on the same or similar conduct as the common-law action and (2) creates a remedial scheme in which private parties can (to some extent) enforce the legislatively created rule as a matter of right." For an analysis of displacement in the admiralty law context, see Pojanowski, *Private Law in the Gaps*, 82 Fordham L.Rev. 1689, 1716–22 (2014).

INTRODUCTORY NOTE ON FEDERAL COMMON LAW AND FOREIGN RELATIONS

Article III creates several heads of jurisdiction that touch directly upon the foreign relations of the United States. Article III, § 2, clause 1, for example, extends federal jurisdiction "to all Cases * * * arising under * * * Treaties"; "to all Cases affecting Ambassadors, other public Ministers and Consuls"; and "to Controversies * * * between a State, or the Citizens thereof, and foreign States, Citizens or Subjects." In cases arising under treaties or under federal statutes related to foreign relations, the federal source of law—and of federal jurisdiction—is straightforward. But the history of the federal courts has generated many cases involving foreign relations that do not arise under a specific treaty or federal statute. In these cases, is the source of law state law, federal common law, or something else? The next principal case, Banco Nacional De Cuba v. Sabbatino, frames these issues.

Banco Nacional de Cuba v. Sabbatino

376 U.S. 398 (1964).

Certiorari to the United States Court of Appeals for the Second Circuit.

■ MR. JUSTICE HARLAN delivered the opinion of the Court.

The question which brought this case here * * * is whether the so-called act of state doctrine serves to sustain petitioner's claims in this litigation. * * * The act of state doctrine in its traditional formulation precludes the courts of this country from inquiring into the validity of the public acts a recognized foreign sovereign power committed within its own territory.

I

[A New York corporation contracted to buy sugar from a subsidiary of a Cuban corporation, whose stock was owned primarily by Americans.* After President Eisenhower reduced the sugar quota for Cuba, the Cuban government expropriated the sugar under a decree that passed title to petitioner, a state-owned Cuban bank. Although the decree purported to provide a system of compensation, the prospect of adequate recovery was dim. The New York corporation secured a Cuban export license for the sugar by promising to pay the proceeds to the petitioner, but after export, it refused to honor this promise and transferred the funds to Sabbatino, a receiver for the Cuban corporation that had sold the sugar. Petitioner then brought a diversity action in federal district court against the purchaser and Sabbatino for conversion of the proceeds. In defense they argued that the expropriation violated international law and that title to the sugar therefore had not validly passed to Cuba. Petitioner responded that the court could not consider this argument because the act of state doctrine required it to accept the validity of a foreign act of state committed on foreign soil. The district court disagreed, ruled the taking to be invalid under principles of international law, and held that the Cuban decree had not conveyed good title to the petitioner. The court of appeals affirmed, relying in part "on two letters * * * written by State Department officers which it took as evidence that the Executive Branch had no objection to a judicial testing of the Cuban decree's validity."]

II

[The Court first considered whether the Banco Nacional, an instrumentality of an unfriendly power that does not permit American nationals to obtain relief in its courts, should be permitted to sue in American courts. The Court refused to hold that America's severance of diplomatic relations with and commercial embargo on Cuba, along with the freezing of Cuban assets in this country, manifested such hostility that American courts should be closed to the Cuban government. The Court concluded that it lacked competence to assess the state of relations with a recognized sovereign power and that any relationship short of war

---

*   [Ed.] The summary of the case has been simplified in minor respects.

permitted resort to American courts. It added that "[p]olitical recognition is exclusively a function of the Executive."] * * *

IV

The classic American statement of the act of state doctrine * * * is found in Underhill v. Hernandez, 168 U.S. 250, [252 (1897)] * * *:

> "Every sovereign State is bound to respect the independence of every other sovereign State, and the courts of one country will not sit in judgment on the acts of the government of another done within its own territory. Redress of grievances by reason of such acts must be obtained through the means open to be availed of by sovereign powers as between themselves."

Following this precept the Court in that case refused to inquire into acts of Hernandez, a revolutionary Venezuelan military commander whose government had been later recognized by the United States, which were made the basis of a damage action in this country by Underhill, an American citizen, who claimed that he had been unlawfully assaulted, coerced, and detained in Venezuela by Hernandez.

* * * [T]he doctrine as announced in Underhill was [later] reaffirmed in unequivocal terms. [The Court here discussed Oetjen v. Central Leather Co., 246 U.S. 297 (1918), and Ricaud v. American Metal Co., 246 U.S. 304 (1918).]

In deciding the present case the Court of Appeals relied in part upon an exception to the unqualified teachings of Underhill, Oetjen, and Ricaud which that court had earlier indicated. In Bernstein v. Van Heyghen Freres Societe Anonyme, 163 F.2d 246 [(2d Cir.1947)], suit was brought to recover from an assignee property allegedly taken, in effect, by the Nazi Government because plaintiff was Jewish. Recognizing the odious nature of this act of state, the court, through Judge Learned Hand, nonetheless refused to consider it invalid on that ground. Rather, it looked to see if the Executive had acted in any manner that would indicate that United States Courts should refuse to give effect to such a foreign decree. Finding no such evidence, the court sustained dismissal of the complaint. In a later case involving similar facts the same court again assumed examination of the German acts improper, Bernstein v. N.V. Nederlandsche-Amerikaansche Stoomvaart-Maatschappij, 173 F.2d 71 [(2d Cir.1949)], but, quite evidently following the implications of Judge Hand's opinion in the earlier case, amended its mandate to permit evidence of alleged invalidity, 210 F.2d 375 [(2d Cir.1954)], subsequent to receipt by plaintiff's attorney of a letter from the Acting Legal Adviser to the State Department written for the purpose of relieving the court from any constraint upon the exercise of its jurisdiction to pass on that question.[18]

---

[18]   The letter stated:

This Court has never had occasion to pass upon the so-called Bernstein exception, nor need it do so now. For whatever ambiguity may be thought to exist in the two letters from State Department officials on which the Court of Appeals relied, is now removed by the position which the Executive has taken in this Court on the act of state claim; respondents do not indeed contest the view that these letters were intended to reflect no more than the Department's then wish not to make any statement bearing on this litigation.

The outcome of this case, therefore, turns upon whether any of the contentions urged by respondents against the application of the act of state doctrine in the premises is acceptable: (1) that the doctrine does not apply to acts of state which violate international law, as is claimed to be the case here; (2) that the doctrine is inapplicable unless the Executive specifically interposes it in a particular case; and (3) that, in any event, the doctrine may not be invoked by a foreign government plaintiff in our courts.

V

Preliminarily, we discuss the foundations on which we deem the act of state doctrine to rest, and more particularly the question of whether state or federal law governs its application in a federal diversity case.[20]

We do not believe that [the act of state] doctrine is compelled either by the inherent nature of sovereign authority * * * or by some principle of international law. * * * While historic notions of sovereign authority do bear upon the wisdom of employing the act of state doctrine, they do not dictate its existence.

* * * The traditional view of international law is that it establishes substantive principles for determining whether one country has wronged another. Because of its peculiar nation-to-nation character the usual method for an individual to seek relief is to exhaust local remedies and then repair to the executive authorities of his own state to persuade them to champion his claim in diplomacy or before an international tribunal. Although it is, of course, true that United States courts apply international law as a part of our own in appropriate circumstances, The Paquete Habana, 175 U.S. 677, 700 [(1900)], the public law of nations can hardly dictate to a country which is in theory wronged how to treat that wrong within its domestic borders.

"1. This government has consistently opposed the forcible acts of dispossession of a discriminatory and confiscatory nature practiced by the Germans on the countries or peoples subject to their controls.

"3. The policy of the Executive, with respect to claims asserted in the United States for the restitution of identifiable property (or compensation in lieu thereof) lost through force, coercion, or duress as a result of Nazi persecution in Germany, is to relieve American courts from any restraint upon the exercise of their jurisdiction to pass upon the validity of the acts of Nazi officials."

[20] Although the complaint in this case alleged both diversity and federal question jurisdiction, the Court of Appeals reached jurisdiction only on the former ground. We need not decide, for reasons appearing hereafter, whether federal question jurisdiction also existed.

Despite the broad statement in Oetjen that "The conduct of the foreign relations of our Government is committed by the Constitution to the Executive and Legislative * * * Departments," 246 U.S., at 302, it cannot of course be thought that "every case or controversy which touches foreign relations lies beyond judicial cognizance." Baker v. Carr, 369 U.S. 186, 211. The text of the Constitution does not require the act of state doctrine; it does not irrevocably remove from the judiciary the capacity to review the validity of foreign acts of state.

The act of state doctrine does, however, have "constitutional" underpinnings. It arises out of the basic relationships between branches of government in a system of separation of powers. It concerns the competency of dissimilar institutions to make and implement particular kinds of decisions in the area of international relations. The doctrine as formulated in past decisions expresses the strong sense of the Judicial Branch that its engagement in the task of passing on the validity of foreign acts of state may hinder rather than further this country's pursuit of goals both for itself and for the community of nations as a whole in the international sphere. Many commentators disagree with this view; they have striven * * * to stimulate a narrowing of the apparent scope of the rule. Whatever considerations are thought to predominate, it is plain that the problems involved are uniquely federal in nature. If federal authority, in this instance this Court, orders the field of judicial competence in this area for the federal courts, and the state courts are left free to formulate their own rules, the purposes behind the doctrine could be as effectively undermined as if there had been no federal pronouncement on the subject.

We could perhaps in this diversity action avoid the question of deciding whether federal or state law is applicable to this aspect of the litigation. New York has enunciated the act of state doctrine in terms that echo those of federal decisions decided during the reign of Swift v. Tyson, 16 Pet. 1 [(1842)]. * * * Thus, our conclusions might well be the same whether we dealt with this problem as one of state law, see Erie R. Co. v. Tompkins, 304 U.S. 64 [(1938)]; Klaxon Co. v. Stentor Elec. Mfg. Co., 313 U.S. 487 [(1941)], or federal law.

However, we are constrained to make it clear that an issue concerned with a basic choice regarding the competence and function of the Judiciary and the National Executive in ordering our relationships with other members of the international community must be treated exclusively as an aspect of federal law.[23] It seems fair to assume that the Court did not have rules like the act of state doctrine in mind when it decided Erie R. Co. v. Tompkins. Soon thereafter, Professor Philip C. Jessup, now a judge of the International Court of Justice, recognized the potential dangers were Erie extended to legal problems affecting

---

[23]   At least this is true when the Court limits the scope of judicial inquiry. We need not now consider whether a state court might, in certain circumstances, adhere to a more restrictive view concerning the scope of examination of foreign acts than that required by this Court.

international relations.[24] He cautioned that rules of international law should not be left to divergent and perhaps parochial state interpretations. His basic rationale is equally applicable to the act of state doctrine.

The Court in the pre-Erie act of state cases, although not burdened by the problem of the source of applicable law, used language sufficiently strong and broad-sweeping to suggest that state courts were not left free to develop their own doctrines (as they would have been had this Court merely been interpreting common law under Swift v. Tyson, *supra*). The Court of Appeals in the first Bernstein case, *supra*, a diversity suit, plainly considered the decisions of this Court, despite the intervention of Erie, to be controlling in regard to the act of state question, at the same time indicating that New York law governed other aspects of the case. We are not without other precedent for a determination that federal law governs; there are enclaves of federal judge-made law which bind the States. A national body of federal-court-built law has been held to have been contemplated by § 301 of the Labor Management Relations Act, Textile Workers v. Lincoln Mills, 353 U.S. 448 [(1957)]. Principles formulated by federal judicial law have been thought by this Court to be necessary to protect uniquely federal interests, D'Oench, Duhme & Co. v. Federal Deposit Ins. Corp., 315 U.S. 447 [(1942)]; Clearfield Trust Co. v. United States, 318 U.S. 363 [(1943)]. Of course the federal interest guarded in all these cases is one the ultimate statement of which is derived from a federal statute. Perhaps more directly in point are the bodies of law applied between States over boundaries and in regard to the apportionment of interstate waters.

In Hinderlider v. La Plata River Co., 304 U.S. 92, 110 [(1938)], in an opinion handed down the same day as Erie and by the same author, Mr. Justice Brandeis, the Court declared, "For whether the water of an interstate stream must be apportioned between the two States is a question of 'federal common law' upon which neither the statutes nor the decisions of either State can be conclusive." Although the suit was between two private litigants and the relevant States could not be made parties, the Court considered itself free to determine the effect of an interstate compact regulating water apportionment. The decision implies that no State can undermine the federal interest in equitably apportioned interstate waters even if it deals with private parties. * * * The problems surrounding the act of state doctrine are, albeit for different reasons, as intrinsically federal as are those involved in water apportionment or boundary disputes. The considerations supporting exclusion of state authority here are much like those which led the Court in United States v. California, 332 U.S. 19 [(1947)], to hold that the Federal Government possessed paramount rights in submerged lands though within the three-mile limit of coastal States. We conclude that

---

[24] *The Doctrine of Erie Railroad v. Tompkins Applied to International Law*, 33 Am.J.Int'l.L. 740 (1939).

the scope of the act of state doctrine must be determined according to federal law.[25]

VI

If the act of state doctrine is a principle of decision binding on federal and state courts alike but compelled by neither international law nor the Constitution, its continuing vitality depends on its capacity to reflect the proper distribution of functions between the judicial and political branches of the Government on matters bearing upon foreign affairs. It should be apparent that the greater the degree of codification or consensus concerning a particular area of international law, the more appropriate it is for the judiciary to render decisions regarding it, since the courts can then focus on the application of an agreed principle to circumstances of fact rather than on the sensitive task of establishing a principle not inconsistent with the national interest or with international justice. It is also evident that some aspects of international law touch much more sharply on national nerves than do others; the less important the implications of an issue are for our foreign relations, the weaker the justification for exclusivity in the political branches. The balance of relevant considerations may also be shifted if the government which perpetrated the challenged act of state is no longer in existence * * * for the political interest of this country may, as a result, be measurably altered. Therefore, rather than laying down or reaffirming an inflexible and all-encompassing rule in this case, we decide only that the Judicial Branch will not examine the validity of a taking of property within its own territory by a foreign sovereign government, extant and recognized by this country at the time of suit, in the absence of a treaty or other unambiguous agreement regarding controlling legal principles, even if the complaint alleges that the taking violates customary international law. * * *

The possible adverse consequences of a conclusion to the contrary * * * is highlighted by contrasting the practices of the political branch with the limitations of the judicial process in matters of this kind. Following an expropriation of any significance, the Executive engages in diplomacy aimed to assure that United States citizens who are harmed are compensated fairly. Representing all claimants of this country, it will often be able, either by bilateral or multilateral talks, by submission to the United Nations, or by the employment of economic and political sanctions, to achieve some degree of general redress. Judicial determinations of invalidity of title can, on the other hand, have only an occasional impact, since they depend on the fortuitous circumstance of the property in question being brought into this country. Such decisions would, if the acts involved were declared invalid, often be likely to give

---

[25] Various constitutional and statutory provisions indirectly support this determination, see U.S. Const., Art, I, § 8, cls. 3, 10; Art. II, §§ 2, 3; Art. III, § 2; 28 U.S.C. §§ 1251(a)(2), (b)(1), (b)(3), 1332(a)(2), 1333, 1350–1351, by reflecting a concern for uniformity in this country's dealings with foreign nations and indicating a desire to give matters of international significance to the jurisdiction of federal institutions.

offense to the expropriating country; since the concept of territorial sovereignty is so deep seated, any state may resent the refusal of the courts of another sovereign to accord validity to acts within its territorial borders. Piecemeal dispositions of this sort involving the probability of affront to another state could seriously interfere with negotiations being carried on by the Executive Branch and might prevent or render less favorable the terms of an agreement that could otherwise be reached. Relations with third countries which have engaged in similar expropriations would not be immune from effect.

The dangers of such adjudication are present regardless of whether the State Department has, as it did in this case, asserted that the relevant act violated international law. If the Executive Branch has undertaken negotiations with an expropriating country, but has refrained from claims of violation of the law of nations, a determination to that effect by a court might be regarded as a serious insult, while a finding of compliance with international law would greatly strengthen the bargaining hand of the other state with consequent detriment to American interests.

Even if the State Department has proclaimed the impropriety of the expropriation, the stamp of approval of its view by a judicial tribunal, however impartial, might increase any affront and the judicial decision might occur at a time, almost always well after the taking, when such an impact would be contrary to our national interest. Considerably more serious and far-reaching consequences would flow from a judicial finding that international law standards had been met if that determination flew in the face of a State Department proclamation to the contrary. When articulating principles of international law in its relations with other states, the Executive Branch speaks not only as an interpreter of generally accepted and traditional rules, as would the courts, but also as an advocate of standards it believes desirable for the community of nations and protective of national concerns. In short, whatever way the matter is cut, the possibility of conflict between the Judicial and Executive Branches could hardly be avoided. * * *

It is suggested that if the act of state doctrine is applicable to violations of international law, it should only be so when the Executive Branch expressly stipulates that it does not wish the courts to pass on the question of validity. We should be slow to reject the representations of the Government that such a reversal of the Bernstein principle would work serious inroads on the maximum effectiveness of United States diplomacy. Often the State Department will wish to refrain from taking an official position, particularly at a moment that would be dictated by the development of private litigation but might be inopportune diplomatically. * * * We do not now pass on the Bernstein exception, but even if it were deemed valid, its suggested extension is unwarranted. * * *

VII

* * * The judgment of the Court of Appeals is reversed and the case is remanded to the District Court for proceedings consistent with this opinion. It is so ordered.

■ MR. JUSTICE WHITE, dissenting.

[Justice White's lengthy dissent did not question the view that federal law governed. He argued, however, that the act of state doctrine does not require American courts to disregard customary international law in deciding cases. "As stated in The Paquete Habana, 175 U.S. 677, 700 [(1900)], '[i]nternational law is part of our law, and must be ascertained and administered by the courts of justice of appropriate jurisdiction, as often as questions of right depending upon it are duly presented for their determination.' Principles of international law have been applied in our courts to resolve controversies not merely because they provide a convenient rule for decision but because they represent a consensus among civilized nations on the proper ordering of relations between nations and the citizens thereof. Fundamental fairness to litigants as well as the interest in stability of relationships and preservation of reasonable expectations call for their application whenever international law is controlling in a case or controversy."

[As for the Court's concern about embarrassing the Executive Branch, he responded: "Without doubt political matters in the realm of foreign affairs are within the exclusive domain of the Executive Branch * * *.[20] But this is far from saying that the Constitution vests in the executive exclusive absolute control of foreign affairs or that the validity of a foreign act of state is necessarily a political question. * * * And it cannot be contended that the Constitution allocates this area to the exclusive jurisdiction of the executive, for the judicial power is expressly extended by that document to controversies between aliens and citizens or States, aliens and aliens, and foreign states and American citizens or States."]

NOTE ON SABBATINO AND THE FEDERAL COMMON LAW OF FOREIGN RELATIONS

(1) The Basis for Federal Common Law. What is the basis for judicial lawmaking in Sabbatino? Should the decision be read narrowly as addressing the allocation of powers between the judiciary and the political branches on matters implicating foreign relations—that is, as a decision calling for judicial self-restraint and deference to the Executive Branch? Or does it suggest a broader role for federal common law (which would preempt

---

[20]   These issues include whether a foreign state exists or is recognized by the United States; the status that a foreign state or its representatives shall have in this country (sovereign immunity); the territorial boundaries of a foreign state; and the authorization of its representatives for state-to-state negotiation.

conflicting state law) in at least some "uniquely federal" areas relating to foreign affairs? What is the relevance of the federal enactments cited in footnote 25? For various perspectives, see Clark, *Federal Common Law: A Structural Reinterpretation*, 144 U.Pa.L.Rev. 1245 (1996); Hill, *The Law-Making Power of the Federal Courts: Constitutional Preemption*, 67 Colum.L.Rev. 1024, 1028–68 (1967); Moore, *Federalism and Foreign Relations*, 1965 Duke L.J. 248 (1965); Henkin, *The Foreign Affairs Power of the Federal Courts: Sabbatino*, 64 Colum.L.Rev. 805 (1964).

Note that Sabbatino said that although "the Constitution does not require the act of state doctrine," the doctrine has " 'constitutional' underpinnings." One consequence of this view is that Congress could override the Court's decision. And it promptly did so to bar judicial invocation of the act of state doctrine except under specified circumstances. See 22 U.S.C. § 2370(e).

(2)　The Implications of Sabbatino for Federal Common Lawmaking. Many commentators viewed Sabbatino to establish an enclave of federal common lawmaking power in areas that touched on the foreign relations of the United States. See Goldsmith, *Federal Courts, Foreign Affairs, and Federalism*, 83 Va.L.Rev. 1617, 1632–33 (1997) (collecting sources). And the Court has often suggested the same, albeit in dicta. See, *e.g.*, Texas Indus., Inc. v. Radcliff Materials, Inc., 451 U.S. 630, 641 (1981) ("[F]ederal common law exists only in such narrow areas as those concerned with * * * interstate and international disputes implicating the conflicting rights of States or our relations with foreign nations * * *."). But the actual scope of federal common lawmaking in this area since Sabbatino has been narrow.

(a)　The high water mark for the preemption component of federal common lawmaking related to foreign affairs came four years after Sabbatino in Zschernig v. Miller, 389 U.S. 429, 432 (1968). There, the Court invalidated—as "an intrusion by the State into the field of foreign affairs which the Constitution entrusts to the President and the Congress"—an Oregon statute that, as interpreted and administered, barred foreigners from inheriting if their country did not (a) grant U.S. citizens reciprocal rights to inherit and (b) permit foreign legatees or heirs to enjoy the inherited property without confiscation. "The statute as construed seems to make unavoidable judicial criticism of nations established on a more authoritarian basis than our own" and could "impair the effective exercise of the Nation's foreign policy," reasoned the Court. Justice Harlan concurred on the basis that the Oregon statute conflicted with a federal treaty, but disagreed with the Court's rationale, noting, *inter alia*, that state courts often inquire into the administration of foreign law. As examples, he pointed to doctrines refusing to enforce foreign judgments rendered without an impartial tribunal or procedures compatible with due process, or refusing to apply the law of a country shown to be "uncivilized." Justice White's dissent agreed with Justice Harlan's criticism of the Court's rationale.

(b)　In subsequent cases, the Court has shown greater reluctance to supplant state law based on the raw judicial assessment that enforcement of such law would interfere with the foreign relations of the United States. See Wuerth, *The Future of the Federal Common Law of Foreign Relations*, 106

Geo.L.J. 1825, 1825 (2018) (arguing that the "overall scope and effect [of the federal common law of foreign relations] have been declining for decades" as part of "broader trends in foreign relations and constitutional law, including an increase in formalism, a growth in the difficulties in distinguishing foreign from domestic cases, and an overall normalization of the foreign relations field").

In Barclays Bank, PLC v. Franchise Tax Bd., 512 U.S. 298 (1994), the Court deemed unmeritorious a federal constitutional challenge to California's method of apportioning taxes on multinational corporations. In rejecting arguments that the challenged method impaired national uniformity in international trade and was likely to provoke international retaliation, the Court stressed that the nuances of foreign policy " 'are much more the province of the Executive Branch and Congress than of this Court' " and that "[t]he judiciary is not vested with power to decide 'how to balance a particular risk of retaliation against the sovereign right of the United States as a whole to let the States tax as they please' " (quoting Container Corp. of America v. Franchise Tax Bd., 463 U.S. 159, 194, 196 (1983)). The Court did not mention Zschernig. See also W.S. Kirkpatrick & Co. v. Environmental Tectonics Corp., Int'l, 493 U.S. 400, 409–10 (1990) (declining to extend the act of state doctrine to a case that would not require invalidating the act of a foreign sovereign within its own territory, even though the lawsuit in question might otherwise "embarrass [a] foreign government[ ]").

(c) Despite the Court's increased reluctance to supplant state laws based on perceived interference with foreign relations, it has shown continued willingness to do so in order to enforce the nation's foreign relations interests as determined by the President or Congress. Compare Sosa v. Alvarez-Machain, 542 U.S. 692, 726 (2004) ("[A]lthough we have even assumed competence to make judicial rules of decision of particular importance to foreign relations, such as the act of state doctrine, see Sabbatino, the general practice has been to look for legislative guidance before exercising innovative authority over substantive law.").

In American Ins. Ass'n v. Garamendi, 539 U.S. 396 (2003), the Court, 5–4, held that certain executive agreements with Germany and other European nations preempted a California law that, in response to the confiscation of and refusal to honor life insurance policies held by Jewish persons before and during World War II, required insurance companies doing business in California to "disclose information about all policies sold in Europe" from 1920–45. The Court ruled that the California law had been preempted by an executive agreement in 2000 between President Clinton and German Chancellor Schröder, in which Germany agreed to compensate victims of Nazi persecution by "establishing a foundation funded with 10 billion deutsche marks contributed equally by the German Government and German companies." In exchange for this pledge, the U.S. Government agreed to submit to "any American court" in which "a German company was sued on a Holocaust-era claim," a statement that "it would be in the foreign policy interests of the United States for the Foundation to be the exclusive forum and remedy for the resolution of all asserted claims against German companies" arising from the Nazi regime and World War II and "that U.S.

policy interests favor dismissal on any valid legal ground." Although the relevant executive agreements contained no explicit preemption provision, Justice Souter's opinion for the Court found preemption based on a "clear conflict" between the President's policies and those of California. The dissent argued that the agreement did not preempt state law. Both the majority opinion and the dissent questioned Zschernig's reasoning.

Similarly, even though Crosby v. Nat'l Foreign Trade Council, 530 U.S. 363 (2000), ruled that a Massachusetts law restricting the power of state entities to buy goods or services from companies doing business with Myanmar was preempted by a federal law imposing similar sanctions, the Court's opinion eschewed reliance on freestanding foreign affairs preemption doctrine. Compare First Nat'l City Bank v. Banco Para El Comercio Exterior De Cuba, 462 U.S. 611 (1983) (federal common law informed both by "international law principles and by articulated congressional policies" governs when to pierce the corporate veil of separate juridical entities in suits under the Foreign Sovereign Immunities Act).

(d) Why might the Court hesitate to preempt state law based on its own assessment of U.S. foreign relations interests but readily do so when it can identify a political branch directive that plausibly preempts state law?

Goldsmith, *supra*, maintains that constitutional structure supports the distinction. Article I, § 10 carefully specifies which external matters lie beyond the states' authority (*e.g.*, no treaties, no alliances, no granting letters of marque and reprisal), and Articles I and II adopt explicit mechanisms for the political branches to preempt state laws that interfere with national foreign affairs interests in other ways. Goldsmith further contends that the Constitution's procedural obstacles to the exercise of the political branches' authority to abrogate state law (for example, the hurdles set by the Treaty Clause, or the hurdles to enacting federal legislation) were designed to protect state prerogatives. In functional terms, moreover, he adds that any distinction between foreign and domestic matters is problematic in the face of growing global integration and the involvement of states in transnational activities such as trade, investment, tourism, border issues, and environmental cooperation. Finally, Goldsmith argues that Congress and the President have appropriate resources to monitor and, when necessary, to override state practices affecting foreign relations, while the federal courts lack the capacity to determine when international interests call for preempting state law.[1]

Few would disagree with Professor Henkin's observation that "[j]udge-made law * * * can serve foreign policy only interstitially, grossly, and spasmodically; [judges'] attempts to draw lines and make exceptions must be bound in doctrine and justified in reasoned opinions, and they cannot provide flexibility, completeness, and comprehensive coherence." Henkin, Foreign Affairs and the United States Constitution 140 (2d ed.1996). But how does

---

[1] See also Weisburd, *State Courts, Federal Courts, and International Cases*, 20 Yale J.Int'l.L. 1, 59 (1995) (criticizing broad claims that federal law governs all matters of foreign relations, and arguing that federal common law preempts state law only in cases that (i) require a decision about what counts as a foreign state, (ii) require formal judicial evaluation of a foreign state's public policy, or (iii) involve immigration).

the limited capacity of federal courts compare with the capacity of state courts (or of state legislatures, as in Crosby)? Should state courts be free, for example, to deny foreign diplomats or heads of state immunity from suit except to the extent that a federal enactment confers such immunity? See Koh, *Is International Law Really State Law?*, 111 Harv.L.Rev. 1824, 1855 (1998) (raising concerns about such a scenario).

(3) Judicial Deference to the Political Branches. Sabbatino is paradoxical in premising its federal common law rule on the need to accommodate executive branch primacy over certain foreign relations matters while at the same time crafting the federal common act of state doctrine based on "the strong sense *of the Judicial Branch*" that "passing on the validity of foreign acts of state may hinder rather than further this country's pursuit of goals both for itself and for the community of nations * * *." The Court in Sabbatino refused to pass on the validity of the "Bernstein exception," which counseled that courts will not apply the act of state doctrine when the Executive branch affirmatively indicates that it has no objection to adjudication of the act of state. In First Nat'l City Bank v. Banco Nacional de Cuba, 406 U.S. 759 (1972), the Court splintered on the validity of this exception in a case holding that the act of state doctrine did not preclude adjudication of a counterclaim filed by a foreign state-owned bank. An opinion by Justice Rehnquist in support of the judgment, joined by two other Justices, supported the exception on the ground that "[i]t would be wholly illogical to insist that [the act of state doctrine], fashioned because of fear that adjudication would interfere with the conduct of foreign relations, be applied in the face of an assurance from that branch of the Federal Government that conducts foreign relations that such a result would not obtain." But in separate concurring opinions, Justices Douglas and Powell rejected the Bernstein exception. Justice Brennan for four Justices in dissent agreed and stated: "As six members of this Court recognize today, the reasoning of that case is clear that the representations of the Department of State are entitled to weight for the light they shed on the permutation and combination of factors underlying the act of state doctrine [but] cannot be determinative."

The issue of judicial deference to the political branches in foreign relations in drafting judge-made rules in foreign relations contexts has also arisen in determining foreign immunities from suit. Prior to 1976, the federal courts enforced common law immunities from suit for both foreign sovereigns and foreign officials. Foreign sovereign immunity cases were the more common of the two. Traditionally, if the State Department granted a "suggestion of immunity" requested by a foreign sovereign, district courts would dismiss for lack of jurisdiction. Ex parte Peru, 318 U.S. 578, 581 (1943), Ch. II, *supra*, at p. 358. If the State Department did not recognize immunity, the district court remained free to decide the question itself under the common law. Although rare, cases involving suits against foreign *officials* employed a similar set of procedures. See Samantar v. Yousuf, 560 U.S. 305, 312 (2010).

For foreign sovereigns, the Foreign Sovereign Immunities Act of 1976 (FSIA), 28 U.S.C. §§ 1330, 1602 *et seq.*, "replac[ed] the old executive-driven, factor-intensive, loosely common-law-based immunity regime with [a] * * * 'comprehensive set of legal standards governing claims of immunity in every civil action against a foreign state.'" Republic of Argentina v. NML Capital, Ltd., 573 U.S. 134, 141 (2014) (quoting Verlinden B.V. v. Central Bank of Nigeria, 461 U.S. 480, 488 (1983)). As the Court in Samantar explained, the availability of immunity for foreign sovereigns now depends upon the district court's determination of whether the claimed immunity satisfies the criteria set forth in the FSIA itself.

Samantar also held, however, that the enactment of comprehensive statutory criteria for foreign *sovereign* immunity did not displace the preexisting common law of foreign *official* immunity. Yet, in so holding, Samantar left unresolved key questions about the present scope and implementation of foreign official immunity doctrine. See also Turkiye Halk Bankasi A.S. v. United States, 598 U.S. 264 (2023) (holding that the FSIA does not apply in criminal cases, but declining to consider whether foreign sovereign bank might be immune under "common-law-immunity principles" outside the FSIA). To what extent should federal courts, in enforcing that doctrine, defer to executive determinations about the appropriateness of immunity in particular cases? Even though the FSIA does not directly apply to official immunity, should the approach taken by the FSIA to foreign sovereign immunity also inform the approach federal courts take in shaping the common law of official immunity? *Cf.* Moragne v. States Marine Lines, Inc., 398 U.S. 375, 390–91 (1970) ("[L]egislative establishment of policy carries significance beyond the particular scope of each of the statutes involved. The policy thus established has become itself a part of our law, to be given its appropriate weight not only in matters of statutory construction but also in those of decisional law.").

NOTE ON PROCEDURAL COMMON LAW

Federal procedural law consists primarily of rules promulgated by the Supreme Court pursuant to the Rules of Decision Act, 28 U.S.C. § 2072, and local rules promulgated by courts pursuant to 28 U.S.C. § 2071. See Chap. VI, Sec. 1, *supra*. Federal courts also have authority to craft a wide range of judge-made doctrines and rules related to procedure and the litigation process that do not have an obvious source in a Federal Rule or congressional enactment. The Court outlined this authority in Chambers v. Nasco, Inc., 501 U.S. 32 (1991), a case where the federal district court, sitting in diversity, exercised its "inherent power" to sanction a party almost $1 million in attorney's fees and expenses for acts of fraud aimed to deprive the court of jurisdiction, false and frivolous pleadings, and delay and harassment tactics:

"It has long been understood that '[c]ertain implied powers must necessarily result to our Courts of justice from the nature of their institution,' powers 'which cannot be dispensed with in a Court, because they are necessary to the exercise of all others.' United States v. Hudson, 7 Cranch 32, 11 U.S. 34 (1812). For this reason, 'Courts of justice are universally acknowledged to be vested, by their very creation, with power to impose silence, respect, and decorum, in their presence, and submission to their lawful mandates.' Anderson v. Dunn, 6 Wheat. 204, 19 U.S. 227 (1821). These powers are 'governed not by rule or statute, but by the control necessarily vested in courts to manage their own affairs so as to achieve the orderly and expeditious disposition of cases.' Link v. Wabash R. Co., 370 U.S. 626, 370 U.S. 630–631 (1962)."

Chambers stated that "the inherent power of the federal courts" includes the power "to control admission to its bar and to discipline attorneys who appear before it"; "to punish for contempts"; to "vacate [a] judgment upon proof that a fraud has been perpetrated upon the court"; to "bar from the courtroom a criminal defendant who disrupts a trial"; and to "act sua sponte to dismiss a suit for failure to prosecute." The Court noted that "[b]ecause of their very potency, inherent powers must be exercised with restraint and discretion." It then ruled that inherent power extends to the sanctions for bad faith imposed by the district court and is not displaced by the related sanctioning schemes in Fed.R.Civ.P. 11 and 28 U.S.C. § 1927 because the federal courts' inherent power was "both broader and narrower than other means of imposing sanctions." Finally, the Court rejected the argument that Erie required application of state law to govern these issues in diversity, agreeing with the court of appeals that the sanctions were "not a matter of substantive remedy, but of vindicating judicial authority." Justices Scalia and Kennedy filed separate dissents to disagree primarily on the Erie point.

Barrett, *Procedural Common Law*, 94 Va.L.Rev. 813, 816, 882–83 & n.203 (2008), says that Chambers is an example of a federal court's power to "sanction misbehavior and regulate those who serve it," which she says the Court has long recognized to fall within a federal court's inherent power, the basis of which, she argues, is Article III. Compare Chambers, *supra*, at 58 (Scalia, J., dissenting) ("I agree with the Court that Article III courts, as an independent and coequal Branch of Government, derive from the Constitution itself, once they have been created and their jurisdiction established, the authority to do what courts have traditionally done in order to accomplish their assigned tasks.") She distinguishes a separate component of procedural common law—the judicial power "to prescribe procedural regulations" which include the multitude of rules within a federal court's "supervisory power," such as ones related to voir dire questioning, see Rosales-Lopez v. United States, 451 U.S. 182 (1981), discovery in criminal cases, see United States v. Nobles, 422 U.S. 225 (1975), and the time period in which criminal cases must be brought, see Barker v. Wingo, 407 U.S. 514, 523 n.18, 530 n.29 (1972).[1] Barrett argues that Article III "empowers federal courts to adopt procedural rules in the course of adjudication" beyond those authorized in the Rules Enabling Act, a proposition for which she finds modest support in sources of law between 1789–1820. 94 Va.L.Rev. at 846–78. She further maintains, contrary to Supreme Court precedent, see, *e.g.*, Cuyler v. Sullivan, 446 U.S. 335, 346, n.10 (1980), that "Article III empowers

---

[1]   Barrett argues that procedural common law also includes other litigation-related doctrines like abstention, forum non conveniens, stare decisis, remittitur, and preclusion. Barrett, *supra*, at 815.

a court to regulate its own proceedings, but it does not empower a reviewing court to supervise the proceedings of a lower court by prescribing procedures that the lower court must follow." 94 Va.L.Rev. at 817. For further exploration of this claim, see United States v. Tsarnaev, 595 U.S. 302, 325–27 (2022) (Barrett, J., concurring); Barrett, *The Supervisory Power of the Supreme Court*, 106 Colum.L.Rev. 324 (2006); p. 845, *supra*.

Barrett rightly maintains that procedural common law, in contrast to the "substantive" federal common law rules analyzed thus far in this Chapter, generally applies only in federal court and does not purport to be preemptive or to bind state courts. 94 Va.L.Rev. at 814–15. It also, she argues, may in some instances be an exclusive judicial power that is immune from congressional revision, see *id*. 814, 823 n.22, though the case law support on this point is scant.

---

2. ENFORCING PRIMARY OBLIGATIONS

A. CIVIL ACTIONS

INTRODUCTORY NOTE ON IMPLIED STATUTORY PRIVATE RIGHTS OF ACTION

Federal statutes do not always fully specify the means by which the rights or duties they create are to be effectuated. Some such statutes, for example, do not articulate the burden of persuasion upon plaintiffs or the order of proof. Others might not state whether a cause of action survives a plaintiff's death. Sometimes, moreover, federal statutes lack any statute of limitations, raising the question whether Congress could really have meant for the legal peril created by the statute to continue indefinitely. Some federal statutes create rights without specifying whether or how private litigants may bring federal lawsuits to vindicate those rights. The presence of these gaps poses the inevitable question of the proper judicial role in filling them. In some of these contexts—for example, the order of proof and burden of persuasion—the courts must inevitably supply what Congress has omitted; a case cannot proceed without the courts articulating standards of proof. In other areas, the role of the federal courts is less obvious. To what extent should the federal judiciary supply a missing statute of limitations or even the right of action itself?

The question of implied private rights of action—or of private rights to sue to enforce statutes that do not expressly authorize private suits—offers the best and most thoroughly debated example of this phenomenon. Federal statutes sometimes state explicitly that private parties may sue to redress harm suffered as the result of another's violation of statutory duties. For example, the patent laws expressly authorize patentholders to sue infringers for damages and injunctive relief. But many federal statutes do not expressly authorize suit by persons injured as the result of statutory violations. Some statutes say nothing about remedies; others provide criminal sanctions but are silent about the availability of civil remedies; still others establish certain civil remedies (for example, by authorizing a federal administrative agency to take specified measures to enforce the statute) but say nothing about private actions. In each of these instances, if a private person seeks legal redress against another who has violated the statute, the courts may have to determine whether to recognize remedies not expressly authorized by the governing statute. The next two principal cases and the Note that follows address the appropriate role of the federal courts in implying private remedies for violations of federal statutes.

Cannon v. University of Chicago

441 U.S. 677 (1979).

Certiorari to the United States Court of Appeals for the Seventh Circuit.

■ MR. JUSTICE STEVENS delivered the opinion of the Court.

[Cannon alleged that the University of Chicago's medical school, which receives federal funds, denied her admission on account of her sex. She sued the university under § 901(a) of Title IX of the Education Amendments of 1972, as amended, 20 U.S.C. § 1681, which provides in relevant part: "No person * * * shall, on the basis of sex, be excluded from participation in, be denied the benefits of, or be subjected to discrimination under any education program or activity receiving Federal financial assistance * * *." Cannon sought declaratory, injunctive, and monetary relief. Section 901, however, does not expressly authorize a private right of action by an injured person. The district court refused to infer such a right of action and dismissed the action. The court of appeals affirmed.]

* * * As our recent cases—particularly Cort v. Ash, 422 U.S. 66 [(1975)]—demonstrate, the fact that a federal statute has been violated and some person harmed does not automatically give rise to a private cause of action in favor of that person. Instead, before concluding that Congress intended to make a remedy available to a special class of litigants, a court must carefully analyze the four factors that Cort identifies as indicative of such an intent.[9] Our review of those factors

---

[9]   "In determining whether a private remedy is implicit in a statute not expressly providing one, several factors are relevant. First, is the plaintiff 'one of the class for whose *especial* benefit the statute was enacted,' Texas & Pacific R. Co. v. Rigsby, 241 U.S. 33, 39 (1916) (emphasis supplied)—that is, does the statute create a federal right in favor of the plaintiff? Second, is there any indication of legislative intent, explicit or implicit, either to create such a remedy or to deny one? Third, is it consistent with the underlying purposes of the legislative scheme to imply such a remedy for the plaintiff? See, *e.g.*, [National R.R. Passenger Corp. v. National Ass'n of R.R. Passengers, 414 U.S. 453 (1974)]. And finally, is the cause of action one traditionally relegated to state law, in an area basically the concern of the States, so that it would be inappropriate to infer a cause of action based solely on federal law?" 422 U.S., at 78.

persuades us, however, that * * * petitioner does have a statutory right to pursue her claim that respondents rejected her application on the basis of her sex. * * *

I

First, the threshold question under Cort is whether the statute was enacted for the benefit of a special class of which the plaintiff is a member. That question is answered by looking to the language of the statute itself. Thus, the statutory reference to "any employee of any such common carrier" in the 1893 legislation requiring railroads to equip their cars with secure "grab irons or handholds," made "irresistible" the Court's earliest "inference of a private right of action"—in that case in favor of a railway employee who was injured when a grab iron gave way. Texas & Pacific R. Co. v. Rigsby, 241 U.S. 33, 40 [(1916)].

Similarly, it was statutory language describing the special class to be benefited by § 5 of the Voting Rights Act of 1965 that persuaded the Court that private parties within that class were implicitly authorized to seek a declaratory judgment against a covered State. Allen v. State Board of Elections, 393 U.S. 544, 554–555 [(1969)]. The dispositive language in that statute—"no person shall be denied the right to vote for failure to comply with [a new state enactment covered by, but not approved under, § 5]"—is remarkably similar to the language used by Congress in Title IX.

The language in these statutes—which expressly identifies the class Congress intended to benefit—contrasts sharply with statutory language customarily found in criminal statutes, such as that construed in Cort, *supra*, and other laws enacted for the protection of the general public. There would be far less reason to infer a private remedy in favor of individual persons if Congress, instead of drafting Title IX with an unmistakable focus on the benefited class, had written it simply as a ban on discriminatory conduct by recipients of federal funds or as a prohibition against the disbursement of public funds to educational institutions engaged in discriminatory practices.

Unquestionably, therefore, the first of the four factors identified in Cort favors the implication of a private cause of action. * * *

Second, the Cort analysis requires consideration of legislative history. We must recognize, however, that the legislative history of a statute that does not expressly create or deny a private remedy will typically be equally silent or ambiguous on the question. Therefore, in situations such as the present one "in which it is clear that federal law has granted a class of persons certain rights, it is not necessary to show an intention to *create* a private cause of action, although an explicit purpose to *deny* such cause of action would be controlling." Cort, 422 U.S., at 82 (emphasis in original). But this is not the typical case. Far from evidencing any purpose to *deny* a private cause of action, the history of

Title IX rather plainly indicates that Congress intended to create such a remedy.

Title IX was patterned after Title VI of the Civil Rights Act of 1964. Except for the substitution of the word "sex" in Title IX to replace the words "race, color, or national origin" in Title VI, the two statutes use identical language to describe the benefited class.* Both statutes provide the same administrative mechanism for terminating federal financial support for institutions engaged in prohibited discrimination. * * * The drafters of Title IX explicitly assumed that it would be interpreted and applied as Title VI had been during the preceding eight years.

In 1972 when Title IX was enacted, the critical language in Title VI had already been construed as creating a private remedy. Most particularly, in 1967, a distinguished panel of the Court of Appeals for the Fifth Circuit squarely decided this issue in an opinion that was repeatedly cited with approval and never questioned during the ensuing five years. In addition, at least a dozen other federal courts reached similar conclusions in the same or related contexts during those years. It is always appropriate to assume that our elected representatives, like other citizens, know the law; in this case, because of their repeated references to Title VI and its modes of enforcement, we are especially justified in presuming both that those representatives were aware of the prior interpretation of Title VI and that that interpretation reflects their intent with respect to Title IX.

Moreover, * * * during the period between the enactment of Title VI in 1964 and the enactment of Title IX in 1972, this Court had consistently found implied remedies [under other statutory schemes]—often in cases much less clear than this. It was after 1972 that this Court decided Cort v. Ash * * *. We, of course, adhere to the strict approach followed in our recent cases, but our evaluation of congressional action in 1972 must take into account its contemporary legal context. In sum, it is not only appropriate but also realistic to presume that Congress was thoroughly familiar with these unusually important precedents from this and other federal courts and that it expected its enactment to be interpreted in conformity with them.

It is not, however, necessary to rely on these presumptions. The package of statutes of which Title IX is one part also contains a provision * * * that authorizes federal courts to award attorney's fees to the prevailing parties, other than the United States, in private actions brought against public educational agencies to enforce Title VI in the context of elementary and secondary education. The language of this provision explicitly presumes the availability of private suits to enforce Title VI in the education context. For many such suits, no express cause

---

* [Ed.] Section 601 of Title VI of the Civil Rights Act of 1964, 78 Stat. 252, 42 U.S.C. § 2000d, provides: "No person in the United States shall, on the ground of race, color, or national origin, be excluded from participation in, be denied the benefits of, or be subjected to discrimination under any program or activity receiving Federal financial assistance."

of action was then available; hence Congress must have assumed that one could be implied under Title VI itself. * * *

Finally, the very persistence—before 1972 and since, among judges and executive officials, as well as among litigants and their counsel, and even implicit in decisions of this Court[33]—of the assumption that both Title VI and Title IX created a private right of action for the victims of illegal discrimination and the absence of legislative action to change that assumption provide further evidence that Congress at least acquiesces in, and apparently affirms, that assumption. * * *

Third, under Cort, a private remedy should not be implied if it would frustrate the underlying purpose of the legislative scheme. On the other hand, when that remedy is necessary or at least helpful to the accomplishment of the statutory purpose, the Court is decidedly receptive to its implication under the statute.

Title IX, like its model Title VI, sought to accomplish two related, but nevertheless somewhat different, objectives. First, Congress wanted to avoid the use of federal resources to support discriminatory practices; second, it wanted to provide individual citizens effective protection against those practices. * * *

The first purpose is generally served by the statutory procedure for the termination of federal financial support for institutions engaged in discriminatory practices. That remedy is, however, severe and often may not provide an appropriate means of accomplishing the second purpose if merely an isolated violation has occurred. In that situation, the violation might be remedied more efficiently by an order requiring an institution to accept an applicant who had been improperly excluded. Moreover, in that kind of situation it makes little sense to impose on an individual, whose only interest is in obtaining a benefit for herself, or on [the Department of Health, Education, and Welfare], the burden of demonstrating that an institution's practices are so pervasively discriminatory that a complete cutoff of federal funding is appropriate. * * *

The Department of Health, Education, and Welfare, which is charged with the responsibility for administering Title IX, * * * takes the unequivocal position that the individual remedy will provide effective assistance to achieving the statutory purposes. The agency's position is unquestionably correct.[42]

Fourth, the final inquiry suggested by Cort is whether implying a federal remedy is inappropriate because the subject matter involves an area basically of concern to the States. No such problem is raised by a

---

[33]   [The Court here cited Lau v. Nichols, 414 U.S. 563, 566–69 (1974), and Hills v. Gautreaux, 425 U.S. 284, 286 (1976), both private actions to enforce Title VI in which the Court, without discussing whether the statute confers a private right of action, reached the merits and granted relief.] * * *

[42]   * * * HEW has candidly admitted that it does not have the resources necessary to enforce Title IX in a substantial number of circumstances * * *. * * *

prohibition against invidious discrimination of any sort, including that on the basis of sex. * * * Moreover, it is the expenditure of federal funds that provides the justification for this particular statutory prohibition. * * *

In sum, there is no need in this case to weigh the four Cort factors; all of them support the same result. * * *

II

Respondents' principal argument against implying a cause of action under Title IX is that it is unwise to subject admissions decisions of universities to judicial scrutiny at the behest of disappointed applicants on a case-by-case basis. * * *

This argument * * * addresses a policy issue that Congress has already resolved.

History has borne out the judgment of Congress. Although victims of discrimination on the basis of race, religion, or national origin have had private Title VI remedies available at least since 1965, respondents have not come forward with any demonstration that Title VI litigation has been so costly or voluminous that either the academic community or the courts have been unduly burdened. * * *

III

[The Court here discussed, *inter alia*, the university's argument "that a comparison of Title VI with other Titles of the Civil Rights Act of 1964 demonstrated that Congress created express private remedies whenever it found them desirable." The Court responded that "[e]ven if these arguments were persuasive with respect to Congress' understanding in 1964 when it passed Title VI, they would not overcome the fact that in 1972 when it passed Title IX, Congress was under the impression that Title VI could be enforced by a private action and that Title IX would be similarly enforceable." It added that "[t]he fact that other provisions of a complex statutory scheme create express remedies has not been accepted as a sufficient reason for refusing to imply an otherwise appropriate remedy under a separate section. See, *e.g.*, J.I. Case Co. v. Borak, 377 U.S. 426 [(1964)]."]

IV

When Congress intends private litigants to have a cause of action to support their statutory rights, the far better course is for it to specify as much when it creates those rights. But * * * under certain limited circumstances the failure of Congress to do so is not inconsistent with an intent on its part to have such a remedy available to the persons benefited by its legislation. Title IX presents the atypical situation in which *all* of the circumstances that the Court has previously identified as supportive of an implied remedy are present. We therefore conclude that petitioner may maintain her lawsuit * * *.

The judgment of the Court of Appeals is reversed, and the case is remanded for further proceedings consistent with this opinion.

■ MR. CHIEF JUSTICE BURGER concurs in the judgment.

■ MR. JUSTICE REHNQUIST, with whom MR. JUSTICE STEWART joins, concurring.

* * * The question of the existence of a private right of action is basically one of statutory construction. And while state courts of general jurisdiction still enforcing the common law as well as statutory law may be less constrained than are federal courts enforcing laws enacted by Congress, the latter must surely look to those laws to determine whether there was an intent to create a private right of action under them.

We do not write on an entirely clean slate, however, and the Court's opinion demonstrates that Congress, at least during the period of the enactment of the several Titles of the Civil Rights Act, tended to rely to a large extent on the courts to *decide* whether there should be a private right of action, rather than determining this question for itself. * * *

I fully agree with the Court's statement that "[when] Congress intends private litigants to have a cause of action to support their statutory rights, the far better course is for it to specify as much when it creates those rights." It seems to me that the factors to which I have here briefly adverted apprise the lawmaking branch of the Federal Government that the ball, so to speak, may well now be in its court. Not only is it "far better" for Congress to so specify when it intends private litigants to have a cause of action, but for this very reason this Court in the future should be extremely reluctant to imply a cause of action absent such specificity on the part of the Legislative Branch.

■ [The dissent of JUSTICE WHITE, joined by JUSTICE BLACKMUN, is omitted.]

■ MR. JUSTICE POWELL, dissenting.

I agree with Mr. Justice White that even under the standards articulated in our prior decisions, it is clear that no private action should be implied here. * * * But as mounting evidence from the courts below suggests, and the decision of the Court today demonstrates, the mode of analysis we have applied in the recent past cannot be squared with the doctrine of the separation of powers. The time has come to reappraise our standards for the judicial implication of private causes of action.

* * * Congress * * * should determine when private parties are to be given causes of action under legislation it adopts. As countless statutes demonstrate, including Titles of the Civil Rights Act of 1964, Congress recognizes that the creation of private actions is a legislative function and frequently exercises it. When Congress chooses not to provide a private civil remedy, federal courts should not assume the legislative role of creating such a remedy and thereby enlarge their jurisdiction.

* * * The "four factor" analysis of [Cort] is an open invitation to federal courts to legislate causes of action not authorized by Congress. It is an analysis not faithful to constitutional principles and should be rejected. Absent the most compelling evidence of affirmative congressional intent, a federal court should not infer a private cause of action.

I

The implying of a private action from a federal regulatory statute has been an exceptional occurrence in the past history of this Court. * * *

A

The origin of implied private causes of actions in the federal courts is said to date back to Texas & Pacific R. Co. v. Rigsby, 241 U.S. 33 (1916). * * * The narrow question presented for decision was whether the standards of care defined by the Federal Safety Appliance Act's penal provisions applied to a tort action brought against an interstate railroad by an employee not engaged in interstate commerce at the time of his injury. The jurisdiction of the federal courts was not in dispute, the action having been removed from state court on the ground that the defendant was a federal corporation. Under the regime of Swift v. Tyson, 16 Pet. 1 (1842), then in force, the Court was free to create the substantive standards of liability applicable to a common-law negligence claim brought in federal court. The practice of judicial reference to legislatively determined standards of care was a common expedient to establish the existence of negligence. Rigsby did nothing more than follow this practice * * *.

For almost 50 years after Rigsby, this Court recognized an implied private cause of action in only one other statutory context.[3] * * *

During this same period, the Court frequently turned back private plaintiffs seeking to imply causes of action from federal statutes. Throughout these cases, the focus of the Court's inquiry generally was on the availability of means other than a private action to enforce the statutory duty at issue. * * *

---

[3]   During this period, the Court did uphold the implication of civil remedies in favor of the Government, see Wyandotte Transportation Co. v. United States, 389 U.S. 191 (1967); United States v. Republic Steel Corp., 362 U.S. 482 (1960), and strongly suggested that private actions could be implied directly from particular provisions of the Constitution, Bell v. Hood, 327 U.S. 678, 684 (1946). Both of these issues are significantly different from the implication of a private remedy from a federal statute. In Wyandotte and Republic Steel, the Government already had a "cause of action" in the form of its power to bring criminal proceedings under the pertinent statutes. Thus, the Court was confronted only with the question whether the Government could exact less drastic civil penalties as an alternative means of enforcing the same obligations. And this Court's traditional responsibility to safeguard constitutionally protected rights, as well as the freer hand we necessarily have in the interpretation of the Constitution, permits greater judicial creativity with respect to implied constitutional causes of action. Moreover, the implication of remedies to enforce constitutional provisions does not interfere with the legislative process in the way that the implication of remedies from statutes can.

A break in this pattern occurred in J.I. Case Co. v. Borak, 377 U.S. 426 (1964). There the Court held that a private party could maintain a cause of action under § 14(a) of the Securities Exchange Act of 1934, in spite of Congress' express creation of an administrative mechanism for enforcing that statute. I find this decision both unprecedented and incomprehensible as a matter of public policy. The decision's rationale, which lies ultimately in the judgment that "[p]rivate enforcement of the proxy rules provides a necessary supplement to Commission action," 377 U.S., at 432, ignores the fact that Congress, in determining the degree of regulation to be imposed on companies covered by the Securities Exchange Act, already had decided that private enforcement was unnecessary. More significant for present purposes, however, is the fact that Borak, rather than signaling the start of a trend in this Court, constitutes a singular and, I believe, aberrant interpretation of a federal regulatory statute.

Since Borak, this Court has upheld the implication of private causes of actions derived from federal statutes in only three extremely limited sets of circumstances. First, the Court in Jones v. Alfred H. Mayer Co., 392 U.S. 409 (1968); Sullivan v. Little Hunting Park, Inc., 396 U.S. 229 (1969); and Johnson v. Railway Express Agency, Inc., 421 U.S. 454 (1975), recognized the right of private parties to seek relief for violations of 42 U.S.C. §§ 1981 and 1982. But to say these cases "implied" rights of action is somewhat misleading, as Congress at the time these statutes were enacted expressly referred to private enforcement actions. Furthermore, as in the Railway Labor Act cases, Congress had provided no alternative means of asserting these rights. Thus, the Court was presented with the choice between regarding these statutes as precatory or recognizing some kind of judicial proceeding.

Second, the Court in Allen v. State Board of Elections, 393 U.S. 544 (1969), permitted private litigants to sue to enforce the preclearance provisions of § 5 of the Voting Rights Act of 1965. As the Court seems to concede, this decision was reached without substantial analysis, and in my view can be explained only in terms of this Court's special and traditional concern for safeguarding the electoral process. In addition * * * the remedy implied was very limited, thereby reducing the chances that States would be exposed to frivolous or harassing suits.

Finally, the Court in Superintendent of Insurance v. Bankers Life & Cas. Co., 404 U.S. 6 (1971), ratified 25 years of lower-court precedent that had held a private cause of action available under the Securities and Exchange Commission's Rule 10b–5. As the Court concedes, this decision reflects the unique history of Rule 10b–5, and did not articulate any standards of general applicability.

These few cases applying Borak must be contrasted with the subsequent decisions where the Court refused to imply private actions. * * *

B

It was against this background of almost invariable refusal to imply private actions, absent a complete failure of alternative enforcement mechanisms and a clear expression of legislative intent to create such a remedy, that Cort v. Ash, 422 U.S. 66 (1975), was decided. In holding that no private action could be brought to enforce 18 U.S.C. § 610 (1970 ed. and Supp. III), a criminal statute, the Court referred to four factors said to be relevant to determining generally whether private actions could be implied. * * * But, as the opinion of the Court today demonstrates, the Cort analysis too easily may be used to deflect inquiry away from the intent of Congress, and to permit a court instead to substitute its own views as to the desirability of private enforcement.

Of the four factors mentioned in Cort, only one refers expressly to legislative intent. The other three invite independent judicial lawmaking. Asking whether a statute creates a right in favor of a private party, for example, begs the question at issue. What is involved is not the mere existence of a legal right, but a particular person's right to invoke the power of the courts to enforce that right. Determining whether a private action would be consistent with the "underlying purposes" of a legislative scheme permits a court to decide for itself what the goals of a scheme should be, and how those goals should be advanced. Finally, looking to state law for parallels to the federal right simply focuses inquiry on a particular policy consideration that Congress already may have weighed in deciding not to create a private action. * * *

II

In my view, the implication doctrine articulated in Cort and applied by the Court today engenders incomparably greater problems than the possibility of occasionally failing to divine an unexpressed congressional intent. If only a matter of statutory construction were involved, our obligation might be to develop more refined criteria which more accurately reflect congressional intent. "But the unconstitutionality of the course pursued has now been made clear" and compels us to abandon the implication doctrine of Cort. Erie R. Co. v. Tompkins, 304 U.S. 64, 77–78 (1938).

* * * Cort allows the Judicial Branch to assume policymaking authority vested by the Constitution in the Legislative Branch. It also invites Congress to avoid resolution of the often controversial question whether a new regulatory statute should be enforced through private litigation. * * * Because the courts are free to reach a result different from that which the normal play of political forces would have produced, the intended beneficiaries of the legislation are unable to ensure the full measure of protection their needs may warrant. For the same reason, those subject to the legislative constraints are denied the opportunity to forestall through the political process potentially unnecessary and disruptive litigation. * * *

The Court's implication doctrine encourages, as a corollary to the political default by Congress, an increase in the governmental power exercised by the federal judiciary. * * *

It is true that the federal judiciary necessarily exercises substantial powers to construe legislation, including, when appropriate, the power to prescribe substantive standards of conduct that supplement federal legislation. But this power normally is exercised with respect to disputes over which a court already has jurisdiction, and in which the existence of the asserted cause of action is established. Implication of a private cause of action, in contrast, involves a significant additional step. By creating a private action, a court of limited jurisdiction necessarily extends its authority to embrace a dispute Congress has not assigned it to resolve.[17] This runs contrary to the established principle that "[t]he jurisdiction of the federal courts is carefully guarded against expansion by judicial interpretation . . . [.]" American Fire & Cas. Co. v. Finn, 341 U.S. 6, 17 (1951) * * *.

The facts of this case illustrate how the implication of a right of action not authorized by Congress denigrates the democratic process. * * * Arming frustrated applicants with the power to challenge in court his or her rejection inevitably will have a constraining effect on admissions programs. The burden of expensive, vexatious litigation upon institutions whose resources often are severely limited may well compel an emphasis on objectively measured academic qualifications at the expense of more flexible admissions criteria that bring richness and diversity to academic life. If such a significant incursion into the arena of academic polity is to be made, it is the constitutional function of the Legislative Branch, subject as it is to the checks of the political process, to make this judgment.

Congress already has created a mechanism for enforcing the mandate found in Title IX against gender-based discrimination. * * * The current position of the Government notwithstanding, overlapping judicial and administrative enforcement of these policies inevitably will lead to conflicts and confusion * * *. * * *

---

[17]   * * * [A] private action implied from a federal statute * * * universally has been considered to present a federal question over which a federal court has jurisdiction under 28 U.S.C. § 1331. Thus, when a federal court implies a private action from a statute, it necessarily expands the scope of its federal-question jurisdiction.

It is instructive to compare decisions implying private causes of action to those cases that have found nonfederal causes of action cognizable by a federal court under § 1331. E.g., Smith v. Kansas City Title & Trust Co., 255 U.S. 180 (1921). Where a court decides * * * that federal-law elements * * * present in a state-law cause of action * * * predominate to the point that the action can be said to present a "federal question" cognizable in federal court, the net effect is the same as implication of a private action directly from the constitutional or statutory source of the federal-law elements. To the extent an expansive interpretation of § 1331 permits federal courts to assume control over disputes which Congress did not consign to the federal judicial process, it is subject to the same criticisms of judicial implication of private actions discussed in the text.

III

* * * I would start afresh. Henceforth, we should not condone the implication of any private action from a federal statute absent the most compelling evidence that Congress in fact intended such an action to exist. Where a statutory scheme expressly provides for an alternative mechanism for enforcing the rights and duties created, I would be especially reluctant ever to permit a federal court to volunteer its services for enforcement purposes. Because the Court today is enlisting the federal judiciary in just such an enterprise, I dissent.

Alexander v. Sandoval

532 U.S. 275 (2001).

Certiorari to the United States Court of Appeals for the Eleventh Circuit.

■ JUSTICE SCALIA delivered the opinion of the Court.

This case presents the question whether private individuals may sue to enforce disparate-impact regulations promulgated under Title VI of the Civil Rights Act of 1964.

I

[The Alabama Department of Public Safety (Department) receives federal funds from the Department of Justice (DOJ) and the Department of Transportation (DOT), and thus is subject to the restrictions of Title VI of the Civil Rights Act of 1964. Section 601 of that Title provides that no person shall, "on the ground of race, color, or national origin, be excluded from participation in, be denied the benefits of, or be subjected to discrimination under any program or activity" covered by Title VI. Section 602 authorizes federal agencies "to effectuate the provisions of [§ 601] . . . by issuing rules, regulations, or orders of general applicability," and DOJ promulgated a regulation forbidding funding recipients to "utilize criteria or methods of administration which have the effect of subjecting individuals to discrimination because of their race, color, or national origin. . . ." 28 CFR § 42.104(b)(2) (1999).

[Sandoval brought a class action to enjoin the Department's policy—adopted after an amendment to the Alabama Constitution declared English "the official language of the state"—of administering driver's license examinations only in English. The federal district court and court of appeals agreed with Sandoval's position that the English-only policy violated the DOJ regulation because it "had the effect of discriminating on the basis of national origin."] Both courts rejected petitioners' argument that Title VI did not provide respondents a cause of action to enforce the regulation.

We do not inquire here whether the DOJ regulation was authorized by § 602 * * *. The petition for writ of certiorari raised, and we agreed to review, only the question * * * whether there is a private cause of action to enforce the regulation.

II

* * * [T]hree aspects of Title VI must be taken as given. First, private individuals may sue to enforce § 601 of Title VI and obtain both injunctive relief and damages. [Cannon upheld a private right of action under Title IX, and its reasoning embraced Title VI.] Congress has since ratified Cannon's holding. * * * We recognized in Franklin v. Gwinnett County Public Schools, 503 U.S. 60[, 72] (1992), that [Section 1003 of the Rehabilitation Act Amendments of 1986, 42 U.S.C. § 2000d–7] "cannot be read except as a validation of Cannon's holding." It is thus beyond dispute that private individuals may sue to enforce § 601.

Second, it is similarly beyond dispute—and no party disagrees—that § 601 prohibits only intentional discrimination. * * *

Third, we must assume for purposes of deciding this case that regulations promulgated under § 602 of Title VI may validly proscribe activities that have a disparate impact on racial groups, even though such activities are permissible under § 601. [Though no prior opinion of the Court has so held, and although the stated assumption is in considerable tension with other decisions,] petitioners have not challenged the regulations here. We therefore assume for the purposes of deciding this case that the * * * regulations proscribing activities that have a disparate impact on the basis of race are valid.

* * * [Cannon] *held* that Title IX created a private right of action to enforce its ban on intentional discrimination, but had no occasion to consider whether the right reached regulations barring disparate-impact discrimination.[2] * * *

Nor does it follow straightaway from the three points we have taken as given that Congress must have intended a private right of action to enforce disparate-impact regulations. We do not doubt that regulations applying § 601's ban on intentional discrimination are covered by the cause of action to enforce that section. Such regulations, if valid and reasonable, authoritatively construe the statute itself, see Chevron U.S.A. Inc. v. Natural Resources Defense Council, Inc., 467 U.S. 837, 843–844 (1984), and it is therefore meaningless to talk about a separate cause of action to enforce the regulations apart from the statute. A Congress that intends the statute to be enforced through a private cause of action intends the authoritative interpretation of the statute to be so enforced as well. The many cases that respondents say have "assumed" that a cause of action to enforce a statute includes one to enforce its regulations illustrate * * * only this point; each involved regulations of

---

[2]   Although the dissent acknowledges that "the breadth of [Cannon's] precedent is a matter upon which reasonable jurists may differ," it disagrees with our reading of Cannon's holding because it thinks the distinction we draw between disparate-impact and intentional discrimination was "wholly foreign" to that opinion * * *.

the type we have just described * * *. See National Collegiate Athletic Ass'n v. Smith, 525 U.S. 459, 468 (1999) (regulation defining who is a "recipient" under Title IX); School Bd. of Nassau Cty. v. Arline, 480 U.S. 273, 279–281 (1987) (regulations defining the terms "physical impairment" and "major life activities" in § 504 of the Rehabilitation Act of 1973) * * *. Our decision in Lau v. Nichols, 414 U.S. 563 (1974), falls within the same category. The Title VI regulations at issue in Lau, similar to the ones at issue here, forbade funding recipients to take actions which had the effect of discriminating on the basis of race, color, or national origin. Unlike our later cases, however, the Court in Lau interpreted § 601 itself to proscribe disparate-impact discrimination * * *.

* * * [W]e have since rejected Lau's interpretation of § 601 as reaching beyond intentional discrimination. It is clear now that the disparate-impact regulations do not simply apply § 601—since they indeed forbid conduct that § 601 permits—and therefore clear that the private right of action to enforce § 601 does not include a private right to enforce these regulations. That right must come, if at all, from the independent force of § 602. As stated earlier, we assume for purposes of this decision that § 602 confers the authority to promulgate disparate-impact regulations;[6] the question remains whether it confers a private right of action to enforce them. If not, we must conclude that a failure to comply with regulations promulgated under § 602 that is not also a failure to comply with § 601 is not actionable.

Implicit in our discussion thus far has been a particular understanding of the genesis of private causes of action. Like substantive federal law itself, private rights of action to enforce federal law must be created by Congress. Touche Ross & Co. v. Redington, 442 U.S. 560, 578 (1979) (remedies available are those "that Congress enacted into law"). The judicial task is to interpret the statute Congress has passed to determine whether it displays an intent to create not just a private right but also a private remedy. Transamerica Mortgage Advisors, Inc. v. Lewis, 444 U.S. 11, 15 (1979). Statutory intent on this latter point is determinative. Without it, a cause of action does not exist and courts may not create one, no matter how desirable that might be as a policy matter, or how compatible with the statute. "Raising up causes of action where a statute has not created them may be a proper function for common-law courts, but not for federal tribunals." Lampf, Pleva, Lipkind, Prupis & Petigrow v. Gilbertson, 501 U.S. 350, 365 (1991) (Scalia, J., concurring in part and concurring in judgment).

Respondents would have us revert in this case to the understanding of private causes of action that held sway 40 years ago when Title VI was

---

[6]   For this reason, the dissent's extended discussion of the scope of agencies' regulatory authority under § 602 is beside the point. We cannot help observing, however, how strange it is to say that disparate-impact regulations are "inspired by, at the service of, and inseparably intertwined with" § 601, when § 601 permits the very behavior that the regulations forbid. * * *

enacted. That understanding is captured by the Court's statement in J.I. Case Co. v. Borak, 377 U.S. 426, 433 (1964), that "it is the duty of the courts to be alert to provide such remedies as are necessary to make effective the congressional purpose" expressed by a statute. We abandoned that understanding in Cort v. Ash, 422 U.S. 66, 78 (1975)— which itself interpreted a statute enacted under the *ancien regime*—and have not returned to it since. * * * Having sworn off the habit of venturing beyond Congress's intent, we will not accept respondents' invitation to have one last drink.

Nor do we agree with the Government that our cases interpreting statutes enacted prior to Cort v. Ash have given "dispositive weight" to the "expectations" that the enacting Congress had formed "in light of the 'contemporary legal context.'" Brief for United States 14. Only three of our legion implied-right-of-action cases have found this sort of "contemporary legal context" relevant,* and two of those involved Congress's enactment (or reenactment) of the verbatim statutory text that courts had previously interpreted to create a private right of action. See Merrill Lynch, Pierce, Fenner & Smith, Inc. v. Curran, 456 U.S. 353, 378–379 (1982); Cannon v. University of Chicago, 441 U.S., at 698–699. In the third case, this sort of "contemporary legal context" simply buttressed a conclusion independently supported by the text of the statute. See Thompson v. Thompson, 484 U.S. 174 (1988). We have never accorded dispositive weight to context shorn of text. In determining whether statutes create private rights of action, as in interpreting statutes generally, legal context matters only to the extent it clarifies text.

We therefore begin (and find that we can end) our search for Congress's intent with the text and structure of Title VI. Section 602 authorizes federal agencies "to effectuate the provisions of [§ 601] . . . by issuing rules, regulations, or orders of general applicability." It is immediately clear that the "rights-creating" language so critical to the Court's analysis in Cannon of § 601 is completely absent from § 602. Whereas § 601 decrees that "[n]o person . . . shall . . . be subjected to discrimination," the text of § 602 provides that "[e]ach Federal department and agency . . . is authorized and directed to effectuate the provisions of [§ 601]." Far from displaying congressional intent to create new rights, § 602 limits agencies to "effectuat[ing]" rights already created by § 601. And the focus of § 602 is twice removed from the individuals who will ultimately benefit from Title VI's protection. Statutes that focus on the person regulated rather than the individuals protected create "no

---

*   [Ed.] Neither the majority nor dissent cited Morse v. Republican Party of Virginia, 517 U.S. 186 (1996), a suit alleging that the Republican Party of Virginia's imposition of a registration fee for delegates to a nominating convention for the party's candidate for the U.S. Senate constituted a poll tax prohibited by § 10 of the Voting Rights Act of 1965. Although there was no opinion for the Court, five Justices recognized a private right of action to enforce § 10, and two of those Justices noted that the Voting Rights Act was passed the year after the Borak decision, in a legal context in which generous standards were applied.

implication of an intent to confer rights on a particular class of persons." *California v. Sierra Club*, 451 U.S. 287, 294 (1981). Section 602 is yet a step further removed: it focuses neither on the individuals protected nor even on the funding recipients being regulated, but on the agencies that will do the regulating. Like the statute found not to create a right of action in *Universities Research Assn., Inc. v. Coutu*, 450 U.S. 754 (1981), § 602 is "phrased as a directive to federal agencies engaged in the distribution of public funds," id., at 772. When this is true, "[t]here [is] far less reason to infer a private remedy in favor of individual persons," *Cannon v. University of Chicago*, *supra*, at 690–691. * * *

Nor do the methods that § 602 goes on to provide for enforcing its authorized regulations manifest an intent to create a private remedy; if anything, they suggest the opposite. Section 602 empowers agencies to enforce their regulations either by terminating funding to the "particular program, or part thereof," that has violated the regulation or "by any other means authorized by law." No enforcement action may be taken, however, "until the department or agency concerned has advised the appropriate person or persons of the failure to comply with the requirement and has determined that compliance cannot be secured by voluntary means." And every agency enforcement action is subject to judicial review. If an agency attempts to terminate program funding, still more restrictions apply. The agency head must "file with the committees of the House and Senate having legislative jurisdiction over the program or activity involved a full written report of the circumstances and the grounds for such action." And the termination of funding does not "become effective until thirty days have elapsed after the filing of such report." Whatever these elaborate restrictions on agency enforcement may imply for the private enforcement of rights created *outside* of § 602, compare Cannon, they tend to contradict a congressional intent to create privately enforceable rights through § 602 itself. The express provision of one method of enforcing a substantive rule suggests that Congress intended to preclude others. * * *

Both the Government and respondents argue that the *regulations* contain rights-creating language and so must be privately enforceable, but that argument skips an analytical step. Language in a regulation may invoke a private right of action that Congress through statutory text created, but it may not create a right that Congress has not. * * *

[Finally the Court rejected the argument that the Rehabilitation Act Amendments of 1986, § 1003, 42 U.S.C. § 2000d–7, and the Civil Rights Restoration Act of 1987, § 6, 42 U.S.C. § 2000d–4a, ratified Supreme Court decisions finding an implied private right of action to enforce the disparate-impact regulations. First, the Court said, no such decisions existed; second, at best the statutes speak to suits for violation of a *statute*, like § 601, rather than one, like this one, for violation of a *regulation*.] Respondents point to Merrill Lynch, Pierce, Fenner & Smith, Inc. v. Curran, 456 U.S., at 381–382, which inferred congressional intent to ratify lower court decisions regarding a particular statutory provision when Congress comprehensively revised the statutory scheme but did not amend that provision. But we recently criticized Curran's reliance on congressional inaction, saying that "[a]s a general matter . . . [the] argumen[t] deserve[s] little weight in the interpretive process." Central Bank of Denver, N.A. v. First Interstate Bank of Denver, N. A., 511 U.S., at 187. * * *

Neither as originally enacted nor as later amended does Title VI display an intent to create a freestanding private right of action to enforce regulations promulgated under § 602. We therefore hold that no such right of action exists. Since we reach this conclusion applying our standard test for discerning private causes of action, we do not address petitioners' additional argument that implied causes of action against States (and perhaps nonfederal state actors generally) are inconsistent with the clear statement rule of Pennhurst State School and Hospital v. Halderman, 451 U.S. 1 (1981).

The judgment of the Court of Appeals is reversed.

■ JUSTICE STEVENS, with whom JUSTICE SOUTER, JUSTICE GINSBURG, and JUSTICE BREYER join, dissenting.

[Justice Stevens's lengthy dissent is only summarized here. He first asserted, contrary to the majority, that prior Supreme Court decisions had already recognized a private right of action to enforce the disparate impact regulation, as had every court of appeals to address the question.

[Beyond relying on precedent, he criticized the majority's treatment of § 601 and § 602 as entirely separate provisions; instead, he argued that the two sections are part of an integrated scheme and that § 602 has the "sole purpose of forwarding the antidiscrimination ideals laid out in § 601." He added: "On its own terms, the statute supports an action challenging policies of federal grantees that explicitly or unambiguously violate antidiscrimination norms (such as policies that on their face limit benefits or services to certain races). With regard to more subtle forms of discrimination (such as schemes that limit benefits or services on ostensibly race-neutral grounds but have the predictable and perhaps intended consequence of materially benefiting some races at the expense of others), the statute does not establish a static approach but instead empowers the relevant agencies to evaluate social circumstances to determine whether there is a need for stronger measures.[13]"

---

[13]   "It is important, in this context, to note that regulations prohibiting policies that have a disparate impact are not necessarily aimed only—or even primarily—at unintentional discrimination. Many policies whose very intent is to discriminate are framed in a race-neutral manner. It is often difficult to obtain direct evidence of this motivating animus. Therefore, an agency decision to adopt disparate-impact regulations may very well reflect a determination by that agency that substantial intentional discrimination pervades the industry it is charged with regulating but that such discrimination is difficult to prove directly. As I have stated before: 'Frequently the most probative evidence of intent will be objective evidence of what actually happened rather than evidence describing the subjective state of mind of the actor.' Washington

[Justice Stevens also disputed the Court's textual analysis, contending that there was no reason to repeat in § 602 the rights-creating language of § 601, as the two sections were obviously designed to protect the same people. Whether the disparate impact regulation was viewed as an interpretation of discrimination in § 601 or a prophylactic measure broader than § 601, it made no sense to differentiate private actions under § 601 from those under § 602.

[More generally, Justice Stevens criticized the majority's approach to implied rights of action: "The majority couples its flawed analysis of the structure of Title VI with an uncharitable understanding of the substance of the divide between those on this Court who are reluctant to interpret statutes to allow for private rights of action and those who are willing to do so if the claim of right survives a rigorous application of the criteria set forth in Cort v. Ash, 422 U.S. 66 (1975). As the majority narrates our implied right of action jurisprudence, the Court's shift to a more skeptical approach represents the rejection of a common-law judicial activism in favor of a principled recognition of the limited role of a contemporary 'federal tribunal.' According to its analysis, the recognition of an implied right of action when the text and structure of the statute do not absolutely compel such a conclusion is an act of judicial self-indulgence.

["* * * [I]t is the majority's approach that blinds itself to congressional intent. While it remains true that, if Congress intends a private right of action to support statutory rights, 'the far better course is for it to specify as much when it creates those rights,' Cannon, 441 U.S., at 717, its failure to do so does not absolve us of the responsibility to endeavor to discern its intent. In a series of cases since Cort v. Ash, we have laid out rules and developed strategies for this task." Justice Stevens proceeded to explain how in Cannon, the Court applied those factors to find an "implicit intent" to create a private right of action.

[Finally, he contended that the Court's argument that provision of an express statutory remedy suggests that Congress intends to preclude other remedies was squarely inconsistent with Cannon's reasoning.]

NOTE ON IMPLIED RIGHTS OF ACTION[1]

(1) The Evolution of the Court's Approach. As Justice Powell notes in his dissent in Cannon, prior to Erie, it appears that plaintiffs who believed

---

v. Davis, 426 U.S. 229, 253 (1976) (concurring opinion). On this reading, Title VI simply accords the agencies the power to decide whether or not to credit such evidence."

[1]   In addition to sources cited elsewhere in this Note, see, *e.g.*, Bellia, *Justice Scalia, Implied Rights of Action, and Historical Practice*, 92 Notre Dame L.Rev. 2077 (2017); Beske, *The Court and the Private Plaintiff*, 58 Wake Forest L.Rev. 1 (2023); Brown, *Of Activism and Erie—Implication Doctrine's Implications for the Nature and Role of the Federal Courts*, 69 Iowa L.Rev. 617, 627–49 (1984); Marcantel, *Abolishing Implied Private Rights of Action Pursuant to*

they suffered a federal statutory violation could sue for relief if they could find a cause of action under general law for the type of injury suffered, and courts then looked (in Justice Powell's words) to "legislatively determined standards of care" to determine negligence under general law. See generally Thayer, *Public Wrong and Private Action*, 27 Harv.L.Rev. 317, 320 (1914). As the Court stated in 1933, "the right to recover damages sustained by the injured employee through the breach of [a federal duty under the Safety Appliance Act] sprang from the principle of the common law" in the absence of a state or federal statutory cause of action. Moore v. Chesapeake & Ohio Ry. Co, 291 U.S. 205, 215–16 (1933). After Erie, the Supreme Court needed to find a basis for the right to sue either in state law or in federal law. But perhaps since states likely lacked authority to determine the scope of federal rights, federal courts began to locate the cause of action in a federal law source. See Nelson, *State and Federal Models of the Interaction between Statutes and Unwritten Law*, 80 U.Chi.L.Rev. 657, 734 (2013).

This in turn led to the implication of causes of action under the statute in cases like J.I. Case Co. v. Borak, 377 U.S. 426 (1964), which was the high-water mark of judicially inferred remedies. Borak was a case in which a unanimous Court upheld a private party's right to sue under § 14(a) of the Securities Exchange Act of 1934, which prohibits fraud in the solicitation of proxy material. The Court adopted a broad, purposive rationale for embracing an implied right of action. Noting that "it is the duty of the courts to be alert to provide such remedies as are necessary to make effective the congressional purpose," the Court concluded that "[w]hile [§ 14(a)] makes no specific reference to a private right of action, among its chief purposes is 'the protection of investors,' which certainly implies the availability of judicial relief where necessary to achieve that result." The 1934 Act provided for SEC enforcement, but Borak emphasized the value of private enforcement as a "necessary supplement" to SEC action. Reflecting what was then the dominant Legal Process approach to statutes (see p. 821, *supra*), Borak's framework was followed, in cases in other statutory settings, by the Supreme Court and by lower federal courts.

(a) **Retrenchment and Cort v. Ash.** Beginning in 1974, the Court started to narrow the Borak approach. Particularly significant was its decision in Cort v. Ash, 422 U.S. 66 (1975). In Cort, the Court refused to infer—from a provision of the Federal Election Campaign Act making it a crime for a corporation to make certain campaign contributions—a shareholder's right to bring a derivative action against corporate directors alleged to have violated the criminal prohibition. The decision was especially noteworthy for its effort, through its four-part test (quoted in footnote 9 of Cannon), to harmonize and rationalize the law.[2] Though stricter than Borak, Cort stated (in language on which Cannon relied) that when "federal law has granted a class of persons certain rights, it is not necessary to show an

---

Federal Statutes, 39 J.Legis. 251 (2013); Preis, *How the Federal Cause of Action Relates to Rights, Remedies, and Jurisdiction*, 67 Fla.L.Rev. 849 (2016).

[2] Several post-1975 decisions, applying that test, refused to infer a private right of action. See, *e.g.*, Piper v. Chris-Craft Indus., Inc., 430 U.S. 1 (1977) (§ 14(e) of the Securities Exchange Act); Santa Clara Pueblo v. Martinez, 436 U.S. 49 (1978) (Indian Civil Rights Act of 1968).

intention to *create* a private cause of action, although an explicit purpose to *deny* such cause of action would be controlling."

(b) The Post-Cannon Shift. Justice Powell lost the battle in Cannon, but he won the war. His dissent in Cannon maintained that separation of powers demanded that Congress and not the Court make the policy-laden decision whether to authorize private parties to sue for relief under a statute. He rejected the idea that implying causes of action was a component of the traditional judicial function of crafting remedies or of filling in gaps in a statutory scheme, and associated the practice instead with groundless judge-made lawmaking of the sort that he believed Erie ruled out. He concluded that "[a]bsent the most compelling evidence of affirmative congressional intent, a federal court should not infer a private cause of action."

The same year that Cannon was decided, the Court began to embrace Justice Powell's approach. In Touche Ross & Co. v. Redington, 442 U.S. 560, 578 (1979), the Court refused to imply a right of action under § 17(a) of the Securities Act of 1934. While nominally purporting to apply Cannon, including its guidance to look to legislative purpose and history, the Court emphasized that its "task is limited solely to determining whether Congress intended to create the private right of action" and it focused on the absence of textual evidence that Congress intended a private cause of action. Because it was "not at liberty to legislate," the Court concluded that "[i]f there is to be a federal damages remedy under these circumstances, Congress must provide it."

(2) The Test for Implying Statutory Causes of Action. The Sandoval opinion treats Cannon as good law but advances three propositions that are difficult to square with Cannon: (i) a private right of action must be based on legislative intent as reflected in "text and structure"; (ii) "legal context matters only to the extent it clarifies text"; and (iii) "the express provision of one method of enforcing a substantive rule [the fund cutoff mechanism under Titles VI and IX] suggests that Congress intended to preclude others."

Sandoval's focus on text and structure to ascertain congressional intent is the Court's current test. See, *e.g.*, Ziglar v. Abbasi, 582 U.S. 120, 131–35 (2017); Stoneridge Investment Partners, LLC v. Scientific-Atlanta, 552 U.S. 148, 164 (2008). But Sandoval's focus on text does not entail a clear statement rule. In Maine Community Health Options v. United States, 590 U.S. 296 (2020), the Court held that because a statute that stated that the government "shall pay" insurers for losses exceeding a statutory threshold could "fairly be interpreted as mandating compensation by the Federal Government," the insurers could bring a Tucker Act claim against the government for damages in the Court of Federal Claims. Justice Alito in lone dissent objected that this conclusion was hard to square with Sandoval's requirement that congressional intent had to be apparent in statutory text. See *id*. 335 n.5. The Court responded: "Relying on Alexander v. Sandoval, 532 U.S. 275 (2001), the dissent's logic suggests that a federal statute could never provide a cause of action for damages absent magic words explicitly inviting suit. We have repeatedly rejected that notion—including in opinions written by Sandoval's author. See, *e.g.*, United States v. Bormes, 568 U.S. 6, 15–16 (2012); United States v. Navajo Nation, 556 U.S. 287, 290 (2009)."[3]

(3) The Role of Contemporaneous Legal Context. Cannon maintained courts should more easily recognize rights of action under statutes enacted during a period when Congress's expectations may have been influenced by the Borak line of decisions. See also Merrill Lynch, Pierce, Fenner & Smith, Inc. v. Curran, 456 U.S. 353, 381 (1982) (implying a private cause of action under the Commodity Exchange Act, primarily on the theory that such a remedy was part of the "contemporary legal context" that was preserved when Congress undertook a comprehensive revision of the Act in 1974). The Court began to move away from this approach in Central Bank of Denver v. First Interstate Bank of Denver, 511 U.S. 164 (1994), in which the Court (5–4) refused to imply a right of action for aiding and abetting a violation of § 10(b) of the Securities Exchange Act. The Court rejected the contention that Congress had acquiesced in the widespread recognition of aiding and abetting liability under § 10(b) of the Securities Exchange Act in the courts of appeals, even though Congress had left those interpretations untouched while otherwise amending the Act on several occasions. The Court explained that even in the face of serial amendments, "Congress' failure to overturn a statutory precedent" cannot be equated with " 'affirmative congressional approval of the [courts'] statutory interpretation,' " which can be effected only through bicameral passage and presentment to the President (quoting Patterson v. McLean Credit Union, 491 U.S. 164, 175, n.1 (1989)).[4]

Sandoval more generally held that courts should interpret a statute of any vintage according to *current* principles governing the implication of private rights of action, rather than reverting to those that prevailed when the statute was enacted. The Court's post-Sandoval decisions, however, have not uniformly rejected reliance on contemporaneous legal context to resolve questions about private rights of action. In Jackson v. Birmingham Bd. of

---

[3] What about the implication of private causes of action under *treaties*? A treaty, like a statute, is "the supreme Law of the Land" under Article VI and can operate as domestic law both by preempting state law and by superseding prior inconsistent statutes. See Cook v. United States, 288 U.S. 102 (1933). But there are two hurdles to the implication of private causes of action under treaties. First, as a general matter, only a subset of treaties—"self-executing" ones—operate as domestic law. See Medellín v. Texas, 552 U.S. 491 (2008) (treaty is " 'equivalent to an act of the legislature,' and hence self-executing, when it 'operates of itself without the aid of any legislative provision' ") (quoting Foster & Elam v. Neilson, 27 U.S. (2 Pet.) 253, 254 (1829)). The test for a self-executing treaty is elusive, but appears to depend primarily on the text of the treaty. See Medellín, 552 U.S. at 514–15. Second, "[e]ven when treaties are self-executing in the sense that they create federal law, the background presumption is that '[i]nternational agreements, even those directly benefiting private persons, generally do not create private rights or provide for a private cause of action in domestic courts.' " *Id.* 506 n.3 (quoting 2 Restatement (Third) of Foreign Relations Law of the United States § 907, Comment a (1986)). The Court in Medellín further noted without endorsement that "a number of the Courts of Appeals have presumed that treaties do not create privately enforceable rights in the absence of express language to the contrary." *Id.* Compare Restatement (Fourth) of the Foreign Relations Law of the United States § 311(1) (2018) ("A treaty provision, even if it is self-executing, does not by virtue of that fact alone establish a private right of action or confer a right to seek particular remedies such as damages.").

[4] The following year, Congress partially restored enforcement authority against aiders and abettors, by giving the SEC (but not private parties) the right to sue those who knowingly provide substantial assistance to principal violators. See Private Securities Litigation Reform Act of 1995, § 104, codified as amended at 15 U.S.C. § 78t(e) (2006).

Educ., 544 U.S. 167 (2005), the Court held (5–4) that Title IX's implied right of action embraced a suit by a male teacher who alleged discrimination "on the basis of sex" stemming from the school board's retaliation for his protest of sex discrimination in school athletics. Writing for the majority, Justice O'Connor relied in part on the fact that three years before the enactment of Title IX, the Court had construed 42 U.S.C. § 1982's basic prohibition against race discrimination to cover an analogous retaliation claim. Justice O'Connor described that earlier decision as "valuable context for understanding" how Congress would have understood Title IX. Does this reasoning signal, as Justice Thomas's dissent suggested, some retrenchment from Sandoval's strict approach? Or does it merely recognize the continuing effects of a decision from an earlier era, with the majority simply delineating the scope of the right of action recognized in Cannon—a right of action that might not have been recognized at all had the question first arisen in 2005 rather than in 1979?

(4) Sandoval and Alternate Bases for Injunctive Relief to Enjoin Illegal State Action. Sandoval held that § 602 does not authorize a cause of action for injunctive relief to redress an alleged state official violation of a federal statute, but the plaintiffs might have been able to invoke another ground as authorization to sue for such relief. For example, 42 U.S.C. § 1983 authorizes "any person" whose federal law rights are violated by a state official to sue the official "in an action at law [or] suit in equity." The plaintiffs in Sandoval apparently failed to mention § 1983 in their lawsuit, but Justice Stevens in dissent argued that they could have (and indeed might have been able to on remand). 532 U.S. at 299–300. The operation of the § 1983 cause of action is discussed at length in Chapter IX.

The plaintiffs also might have been able to invoke Ex parte Young, 209 U.S. 123 (1908), p. 1184, *infra*, a case that recognized the authority of federal courts to issue injunctive relief against officials who violate federal law. See also Armstrong v. Exceptional Child Ctr., Inc., 575 U.S. 320, 326 (2015), p. 1205, *infra* (noting without reference to statutory cause of action that the Court has "long held that federal courts may in some circumstances grant injunctive relief against state officers who are violating, or planning to violate, federal law"); Shaw v. Delta Air Lines, Inc., 463 U.S. 85 (1983) (assuming without consideration of statutory cause of action that federal courts can "enjoin state officials from interfering with federal rights"). This latter line of cases is also analyzed in Chapter IX.

For discussions of the seemingly disparate evolution of these lines of decisions, see Monaghan, *A Cause of Action, Anyone?: Federal Equity and the Preemption of State Law*, 91 Notre Dame L.Rev. 1807 (2016). Sloss, *Constitutional Remedies for Statutory Violations*, 89 Iowa L.Rev. 355 (2004).

(5) Arguments of Principle and Policy. Consider this argument: Allowing a private plaintiff to sue for a violation of a federal statute always adds force to the deterrent effect of a statutory prohibition. Because Congress must have meant the prohibition to be taken seriously, why shouldn't courts always imply private remedies to promote the statutory purpose?

Note the following five objections to this argument—and possible responses to each, focusing on the context of the Cannon case.

First, the argument assumes that a statutory prohibition is motivated by a one-dimensional purpose to deter or require certain kinds of conduct. In fact, a statute is often the product of a pitched battle between competing interest groups, one outcome of which may be a compromise that the available remedies would be limited—that full compliance was neither desired nor desirable.[5] And modern federal statutes tend to be attentive to remedial detail, making it more likely that when no express remedy exists, an implied remedy will be in tension with congressional objectives.[6]

Were Titles VI and IX parts of such a compromise, and if so what were the terms? Can a court reliably answer such questions?

Second, even when full compliance with the prohibition is the statutory goal, private enforcement in the courts leads to serious problems of overinclusion or excessive deterrence that discourage socially productive conduct outside the scope of the prohibition.

Did the right of action recognized in Cannon pose such a threat? Does the force of the objection depend on how meritorious most such actions are? The likely response of universities to the threat of lawsuits? The costs of litigation?

Third, Congress may have wished to give an administrative agency authority to flesh out statutory meaning and to determine appropriate levels of enforcement. Indeed, regulatory statutes frequently issue commands to administrative officials rather than directly to regulated parties, and judicial recognition of a private remedy may thwart congressional efforts to centralize enforcement in an administrative body.[7]

Did Congress wish to give federal agencies a monopoly over enforcement of Titles VI and IX? If so, does it follow that a state law remedy for violation of federal regulatory statutes like those provisions should be held to be preempted—even if, in Cannon, the majority was correct that the government's only remedy, a fund cutoff, is too draconian to be regularly enforced?

Fourth, whether and to what extent to provide a private remedy is an important question that the legislature should decide. Treating it as left to

---

[5] See Easterbrook, *Foreword: The Court and the Economic System*, 98 Harv.L.Rev. 4, 45–51 (1984).

[6] Mashaw, *Textualism, Constitutionalism, and the Interpretation of Federal Statutes*, 32 Wm. & Mary L.Rev. 827, 842 (1991).

[7] See generally Stewart & Sunstein, *Public Programs and Private Rights*, 95 Harv.L.Rev. 1193 (1982). The authors consider private rights of action as one of several available forms of private initiative in the operation of regulatory programs. They suggest that such a private remedy is of greatest worth in programs emphasizing "entitlement values"—for example, the value of being treated with respect and without invidious discrimination—and is considerably more problematic in programs designed primarily to increase productive efficiency. In the latter cases, however, they argue that a remedy limited to damages for injuries suffered is far less likely than broader remedies (sweeping injunctions or damages not tied to harm suffered) to generate overdeterrence.

judicial implication makes it too easy for Congress to dodge the question and unduly taxes the ingenuity and capacity of the federal courts.

If this objection is valid, is it equally valid as to a congressional failure to provide, for example, a statute of limitations for federal causes of action? Or is there a categorical difference, as Justice Powell contends in his Cannon dissent, between the federal common law power to "supplement federal legislation" in a dispute over which jurisdiction and a cause of action are established, and the power to create the cause of action in the first place, which would involve "a court of limited jurisdiction necessarily extend[ing] its authority to embrace a dispute Congress has not assigned it to resolve"?

Fifth, the current regime of refusing to imply a statutory cause of action provides a clear and predictable baseline against which Congress can legislate.

But wasn't the regime of broad implication of a cause of action also a clear and predictable baseline? Which default rule—broad implication or no implication—is more likely to induce Congress to clarify its intent and overcome the attributes of the legislative process (inertia, lack of time, lack of foresight, sloppiness, incapacity or unwillingness to reach agreement on various matters) that might give rise to uncertainties in the first place? See generally Elhauge, Statutory Default Rules 149–223 (2008) (discussing the conditions under which courts should craft "preference-eliciting default rules").

(6) The Range of Remedies. Should the appropriateness of recognizing an implied right of action depend on just what remedy is sought? Note that Justice Powell, in Cannon, distinguished Allen v. State Board of Elections, 393 U.S. 544 (1969)—in which the Court had permitted private litigants to seek a declaratory judgment that certain legislation had to be submitted for preclearance under § 5 of the Voting Rights Act of 1965—on the ground that "the remedy implied was very limited, thereby reducing the chances that States would be exposed to frivolous or harassing suits."

Are those chances greater when actions for compensatory (or punitive) damages are recognized? More generally, might the Court's increased restrictiveness reflect, in part, changes in the Justices' view, for example, of the extent to which discrimination lawsuits or securities class actions constitute (i) an important enforcement tool or (ii) meritless strike suits instituted by unscrupulous plaintiffs' lawyers?

(a)   The post-Cannon decision in Transamerica Mortgage Advisors, Inc. (TAMA) v. Lewis, 444 U.S. 11 (1979), involved § 206 of the Investment Advisers Act of 1940, which makes it unlawful for an investment adviser to "employ any device, scheme, or artifice to defraud," as well as § 215, which renders "void" any contract made in violation of the Act. Treating the remedial issue as one of legislative intent, the Court construed § 215 as implying a private remedy for rescission of the void contract and restitution of money paid, but refused (over four dissents) to recognize a right of action for damages under § 206.

(b)   The TAMA decision appears, however, to be limited to the specifics of the Investment Advisers Act. In Franklin v. Gwinnett County Pub.

Schools, 503 U.S. 60 (1992), all nine Justices agreed that when a private right of action exists, "[t]he general rule * * * is that absent clear direction to the contrary by Congress, the federal courts have the power to award any appropriate relief." Thus, the Court held that in a private action under the same statute involved in Cannon—Title IX of the Education Amendments of 1972—a damages remedy was available.

(c)   Franklin's holding that "any appropriate relief" may be afforded in actions under Title IX and similar statutes imposing conditions on recipients of federal funds was narrowly construed in Barnes v. Gorman, 536 U.S. 181 (2002). In that case, an action alleging that the municipal defendant had discriminated on the basis of disability, the Court held, without dissent, that punitive damages were unavailable under the Americans with Disabilities Act and the Rehabilitation Act, which incorporate by reference the remedies available under Title VI. Noting that Title VI's remedial scheme originates in Congress's Spending Power, the Court's opinion (per Scalia, J.) stressed that spending programs are similar in nature to a contract; that " 'if Congress intends to impose a condition on the grant of federal moneys, it must do so unambiguously' " (quoting Pennhurst State Sch. & Hosp. v. Halderman, 451 U.S. 1, 17 (1981)); and that because punitive damages are generally unavailable for contractual breach, funding recipients are not on notice that they might be subject to such damages. Justice Stevens, joined by Justices Ginsburg and Breyer, concurred in the judgment on the narrower basis that a municipality is not ordinarily subject to punitive damages. See City of Newport v. Fact Concerts, Inc., 453 U.S. 247 (1981), p. 1296, *infra*. He objected, *inter alia*, to the Court's extension of the Pennhurst decision from the question of the scope of conduct for which recipients are liable to the question of the scope of remedies.

(d)   More recently, the Court held in Cummings v. Premier Rehab Keller, 596 U.S. 212 (2022), that emotional distress damages are not available for implied causes of action under two Spending Clause statutes, the Rehabilitation Act of 1973 and the Patient Protection and Affordable Care Act of 2010. The Court emphasized that Barnes requires damages to be "traditionally available in suits for breach of contract" so that the funding recipient receives "clear notice" of the possibility of damages. It determined that such notice did not exist for emotional distress damages, which are "highly unusual" for breach of contract, and which do not reflect "the consensus rule among American jurisdictions." In a concurring opinion, Justice Kavanaugh, joined by Justice Gorsuch, argued that the contract-law analogy deployed by the majority and dissent, and in the prior Spending Clause cases, should be replaced by a separation-of-powers approach which counsels that, "with respect to existing implied causes of action, Congress, not this Court, should extend those implied causes of action and expand available remedies."

(7) Implied Rights of Contribution. The Court has held that an express statutory right of action does not authorize judges to recognize an implied right of contribution, but that an implied primary right of action does carry with it that further authority. In Texas Industries, Inc. v. Radcliff Materials, Inc., 451 U.S. 630 (1981), the Court held that a company sued for conspiring to fix prices under the Sherman Act cannot seek contribution against other alleged participants in the scheme in the absence of express statutory recognition of such a right. First, applying the Cort v. Ash test, the Court found that Congress had neither expressly nor implicitly intended to create such a right, stressing that alleged conspirators were not "beneficiaries" of the antitrust laws. Second, turning to what it saw as the distinct question of whether it was appropriate to fashion a right of contribution as a matter of federal common law, the Court found that the claim for contribution did not implicate the narrow class of "uniquely federal interests" that justify federal common lawmaking. (Some of the language is quoted in Justice Brennan's dissent in the Boyle case, pp. 829–830, *supra*.) Finally, the Court ruled that although Congress had delegated broad authority to the courts to develop substantive rules specifying what conduct violates the antitrust laws, that delegation did not extend to the development of remedial rules like contribution.[8]

In contrast, the Court was willing to fashion a right of contribution in Musick, Peeler & Garrett v. Employers Ins. of Wausau, 508 U.S. 286 (1993). That suit was based on the implied private right of action, previously recognized by the Court, under § 10(b) of the Securities Exchange Act of 1934 and SEC Rule 10b–5. See Superintendent of Insurance v. Bankers Life & Cas. Co., 404 U.S. 6 (1971). The Court found Texas Industries to be distinguishable, because its central inquiries—whether Congress " 'expressly or by clear implication' envisioned" a right to contribution, or "whether Congress 'intended courts to have the power to alter or supplement the remedies enacted' "—are not helpful in the context of a *judicially* created private right of action like the one under Rule 10b–5. Rather, in that context, the Court must ask "how the 1934 Congress would have addressed the issue had the 10b–5 action been included as an express provision in the 1934 Act." Because analogous provisions in the Act that do create express private rights of action also provide a right to contribution, the Court concluded that Congress would have wanted a similar contribution right in 10b–5 actions.

Viewed from the standpoint of protecting Congress's policymaking prerogatives, does its specification of *express* rights and remedies carry negative implications concerning the right of contribution that are absent when the right of contribution would supplement an *implied* right of action? Or does Musick, Peeler just reflect the old adage, "in for a penny, in for a pound"?[9]

(8) Implied Rights of Action on Behalf of the United States. It has been long settled law that the United States needs no specific statutory

---

[8] See also Northwest Airlines, Inc. v. Transport Workers Union, 451 U.S. 77 (1981) (refusing to recognize a right of contribution in an employment discrimination case and noting that, in the face of a comprehensive statutory scheme of remedies, the "judiciary may not * * * fashion new remedies that might upset carefully considered legislative programs").

[9] Compare Lampf, Pleva, Lipkind, Prupis & Petigrow v. Gilbertson, 501 U.S. 350, 365–66 (1991) (Scalia, J., concurring) (arguing that while the Court should ordinarily address an omitted federal statute of limitations by applying the analogous state limitations period, it appropriately borrows an analogous federal limitations period for an implied right of action, since Congress never had "the opportunity * * * to consider whether it is content with the state limitations or would prefer to craft its own rule").

authorization to bring common law actions of a kind that private citizens could also bring—for example, for trespass or breach of contract. See, *e.g.*, United States v. San Jacinto Tin Co., 125 U.S. 273, 285 (1888) (noting that "the right of the government of the United States to institute such a suit depends upon the same general principles which would authorize a private citizen to apply to a court of justice for relief"). But the Court has, at times, recognized a much broader governmental authority to sue, without statutory authorization, to vindicate the public interest against federal law infractions or, on rarer occasion, against intrusion upon federal interests. See, *e.g.*, United States v. American Bell Tel. Co., 128 U.S. 315, 367 (1888) (concluding that the government need not have a "direct pecuniary interest" in a case, but may sue "to protect the public from the monopoly of the patent which was procured by fraud"); In re Debs, 158 U.S. 564 (1895) (holding that the United States could sue for a labor injunction against a railroad strike and observing that the government has "all the attributes of sovereignty," which include the power to go to court to seek injunctive relief "to remove all obstructions upon highways, natural or artificial, to the passage of interstate commerce or the carrying of the mail"); Sanitary Dist. of Chicago v. United States, 266 U.S. 405 (1925) (relying on a similar theory to uphold an injunction against an Illinois corporation from diverting more water from Lake Michigan than the Secretary of War had authorized).

Note that these are *not* recent cases.[10] To the extent that they fail to insist upon prior congressional creation of an actionable right, do they suggest that a different rule obtains with respect to the government's ability to invoke common law principles to impose civil—as opposed to criminal— liability? Even if the defendant has violated a preexisting federal statutory duty, is it consistent with the private-right-of-action cases discussed above to recognize a non-statutory right, on behalf of the federal government, to sue to enforce that duty?[11]

---

[10] In 2021, the United States invoked these cases, most prominently Debs, in a lawsuit to enjoin the Texas Heartbeat Act, 87th Leg., Reg. Sess., also known as S.B. 8. See Brief for the United States at 14–15, United States v. Texas (No. 21–588). The Act prohibits physicians from performing an abortion on a pregnant woman after approximately six weeks of pregnancy, in violation of the then-governing precedents of Roe v. Wade, 410 U.S. 113 (1973), and Planned Parenthood of Southeastern Pa. v. Casey, 505 U.S. 833 (1992). After the United States Court of Appeals for the Fifth Circuit in a private-party challenge to S.B. 8 rejected a request for an injunction pending appeal, largely on sovereign immunity grounds, the United States sued Texas on the theory that Texas has no immunity in a suit brought by the federal government. The United States relied primarily on Debs to argue that it could seek equitable relief against S.B. 8's threats to its sovereign interests in protecting the supremacy of the Constitution, even absent an express statutory cause of action. The Supreme Court granted certiorari to determine the propriety of the United States's suit but later dismissed the writ as improvidently granted. United States v. Texas, 595 U.S. 74 (2021). For a comprehensive analysis of Debs and its continuing significance that reads the decision narrowly to authorize the federal government to seek an injunction to protect rights of U.S. citizens connected to some kind of proprietary interest, see Bamzai & Bray, *Debs and the Federal Equity Jurisdiction*, 98 Notre Dame L.Rev. 699 (2022).

[11] For a range of views, see Bamzai & Bray, note 10, *supra*, at 703–04 (2022); Monaghan, *The Protective Power of the Presidency*, 93 Colum.L.Rev. 1 (1993); Yackle, *A Worthy Champion for Fourteenth Amendment Rights: The United States in Parens Patriae*, 92 Nw.U.L.Rev. 111 (1997); Hartnett, *The Standing of the United States: How Criminal Prosecutions Show That Standing Doctrine Is Looking for Answers in All the Wrong Places*, 97 Mich.L.Rev. 2239 (1999).

B. REMEDIES FOR CONSTITUTIONAL VIOLATIONS

This Section begins exploration of whether the Constitution should be construed to provide particular remedies for violations of federal constitutional rights. It focuses on the availability of monetary relief for constitutional violations.

Ward v. Love County

253 U.S. 17 (1920).
Certiorari to the Supreme Court of Oklahoma.

■ MR. JUSTICE VAN DEVANTER delivered the opinion of the Court.

[Ward and sixty-six other members of the Choctaw Tribe sought to recover taxes that, they alleged, had been coercively collected from them in violation of federal law. After the "county commissioners disallowed the claim," the claimants appealed to the state district court, which entered judgment for the claimants. That Oklahoma Supreme Court, however, reversed the judgment.]

The claimants, who were members of the Choctaw Tribe and wards of the United States, received their allotments out of the tribal domain under a congressional enactment of 1898, which subjected the right of alienation to certain restrictions and provided that "the lands allotted shall be nontaxable while the title remains in the original allottee, but not to exceed twenty-one years from date of patent." In the act of 1906, enabling Oklahoma to become a state, Congress made it plain that no impairment of the rights of property pertaining to the Indians was intended; and the state included in its Constitution a provision exempting from taxation "such property as may be exempt by reason of treaty stipulations, existing between the Indians and the United States government, or by federal laws, during the force and effect of such treaties or federal laws." Afterwards Congress, by an act of 1908, removed the restrictions on alienation as to certain classes of allottees, including the present claimants, and declared that all land from which the restrictions were removed "shall be subject to taxation, * * * as though it were the property of other persons than allottees."

Following the last enactment the officers of Love and other counties began to tax the allotted lands from which restrictions on alienation were removed. [In previous litigation, allottees brought suit in state court to enjoin the threatened taxation, arguing "that the tax exemption was a vested property right which could not be abrogated or destroyed" without

---

For an in-depth analysis of federal and state public authorities' standing to bring both private and public actions, see Davis, *Implied Public Rights of Action*, 114 Colum.L.Rev. 1 (2014).

violating the Constitution. "[O]ne of the suits [was] prosecuted by some 8,000 allottees against the officers of Love and other counties. When the case was reviewed by the United States Supreme Court, it held that the exemption was a vested property right that Congress could not repeal consistently with the Fifth Amendment, the exemption was binding on the taxing authorities in Oklahoma, and that the state courts had erred in refusing to enjoin them from taxing the lands."]

While those suits were pending the officers of Love county, with full knowledge of the suits, and being defendants in one, proceeded with the taxation of the allotments, demanded of these claimants that the taxes on their lands be paid to the county, threatened to advertise and sell the lands unless the taxes were paid, did advertise and sell other lands similarly situated, and caused these claimants to believe that their lands would be sold if the taxes were not paid. So, to prevent such a sale and to avoid the imposition of a penalty of eighteen per cent, for which the local statute provided, these claimants paid the taxes. They protested and objected at the time that the taxes were invalid, and the county officers knew that all the allottees were pressing the objection in the pending suits.

* * * In reversing the judgment which the district court had given for the claimants the [Oklahoma] Supreme Court held, first, that the taxes were not collected by coercive means, but were paid voluntarily, and could not be recovered back as there was no statutory authority therefor; and, secondly, that there was no statute making the county liable for taxes collected and then paid over to the state and municipal bodies other than the county—which it was assumed was true of a portion of these taxes—and that the petition did not show how much of the taxes was retained by the county, or how much paid over to the state and other municipal bodies, and therefore it could not be the basis of any judgment against the county.

The county challenges our jurisdiction * * * [and] insists that the [Oklahoma] Supreme Court put its judgment entirely on independent nonfederal grounds which were broad enough to sustain the judgment.

* * * [I]t is certain that the lands were nontaxable. This was settled in [this Court's earlier decisions]; and it also was settled in those cases that the exemption was a vested property right arising out of a law of Congress and protected by the Constitution of the United States. This being so, the state and all its agencies and political subdivisions were bound to give effect to the exemption. It operated as a direct restraint on Love County, no matter what was said in local statutes. The county did not respect it, but, on the contrary, assessed the lands allotted to these claimants, placed them on the county roll, and there charged them with taxes like other property. * * *

We accept so much of the [Oklahoma] Supreme Court's decision as held that, if the payment was voluntary, the moneys could not be recovered back in the absence of a permissive statute, and that there was no such statute. But we are unable to accept its decision in other respects.

The right to the exemption was a federal right * * *. Whether the right was denied, or not given due recognition, by the [Oklahoma] Supreme Court is a question as to which the claimants were entitled to invoke our judgment. It therefore is within our province to inquire not only whether the right was denied in express terms, but also whether it was denied in substance and effect, as by putting forward nonfederal grounds of decision that were without any fair or substantial support. [Citing numerous Supreme Court decisions.] * * *

The facts set forth in the petition * * * make it plain, as we think, that the finding or decision that the taxes were paid voluntarily was without any fair or substantial support. The claimants were Indians just emerging from a state of dependency and wardship. Through the pending suits and otherwise they were objecting and protesting that the taxation of their lands was forbidden by a law of Congress. But, notwithstanding this, the county demanded that the taxes be paid, and by threatening to sell the lands of these claimants and actually selling other lands similarly situated made it appear to the claimants that they must choose between paying the taxes and losing their lands. To prevent a sale and to avoid the imposition of a penalty of eighteen per cent, they yielded to the county's demand and paid the taxes, protesting and objecting at the same time that the same were illegal. The moneys thus collected were obtained by coercive means—by compulsion. The county and its officers reasonably could not have regarded it otherwise; much less the Indian claimants. Atchison, Topeka & Santa Fe Ry. Co. v. O'Connor, 223 U.S. 280 [(1912)]; Gaar, Scott & Co. v. Shannon, 223 U.S. 471 [(1912)].

As the payment was not voluntary, but made under compulsion, no statutory authority was essential to enable or require the county to refund the money. It is a well-settled rule that "money got through imposition" may be recovered back; and, as this court has said on several occasions, "the obligation to do justice rests upon all persons, natural and artificial, and if a county obtains the money or property of others without authority, the law, independent of any statute, will compel restitution or compensation." Marsh v. Fulton County, 10 Wall. 676, 684 [(1870)]. To say that the county could collect these unlawful taxes by coercive means and not incur any obligation to pay them back is nothing short of saying that it could take or appropriate the property of these Indian allottees arbitrarily and without due process of law. Of course this would be in contravention of the Fourteenth Amendment, which binds the county as an agency of the state.

If it be true, as the Supreme Court assumed, that a portion of the taxes was paid over, after collection, to the state and other municipal bodies, we regard it as certain that this did not alter the county's liability to the claimants. The county had no right to collect the money, and it took the same with notice that the rights of all who were to share in the taxes were disputed by these claimants and were being contested in the pending suits. In these circumstances it could not lessen its liability by paying over a portion of the money to others whose rights it knew were disputed and were no better than its own. In legal contemplation it received the money for the use and benefit of the claimants and should respond to them accordingly.

The county calls attention to the fact that * * * the [state] statute of limitation * * * was relied on [by Love County below]. This point was not discussed by the [Oklahoma] Supreme Court and * * * when the case is remanded it will be open to that court to deal with the point as to the whole claim or any item in it as any valid local law in force when the claim was filed may require.

Judgment reversed.

NOTE ON REMEDIES FOR FEDERAL CONSTITUTIONAL RIGHTS

(1) The Sources of Constitutional Remedies. "Constitutional rights do not typically come with a built-in cause of action to allow for private enforcement in courts." DeVillier v. Texas, 601 U.S. 285, 286 (2024). The need for constitutional remedies likely appeared unnecessary to the Framers "because the Constitution presupposed a going legal system, with ample remedial mechanisms, in which constitutional guarantees would be implemented." Fallon & Meltzer, *New Law, Non-Retroactivity, and Constitutional Remedies*, 104 Harv.L.Rev. 1731, 1779 (1991). As discussed in more detail in Chapter IX, pp. 1150–1151, *infra*, those mechanisms at the founding were the recognized forms of action at common law and in equity.[1] And since the founding Congress has additionally supplied statutory authority for defined plaintiffs to bring claims for constitutional violations against defined official defendants. See, *e.g.*, 42 U.S.C. § 1983 (providing a right to sue state officials for, among other things, federal constitutional violations).

Historically, in an action to enforce a legal duty *other* than one imposed by the Constitution itself, a litigant could invoke the Constitution to nullify that duty. See DeVillier, *supra*, at 291 (noting that "constitutional rights are generally invoked defensively in cases arising under other sources of law"); see generally Dellinger, *Of Rights and Remedies: The Constitution as a Sword*, 85 Harv.L.Rev. 1532, 1532 (1972) ("The sanction most frequently imposed in response to a constitutional violation is the sanction of nullification: the courts decline to convict on a criminal charge, or decline to

---

[1]   For the argument that the only constitutionally mandated remedy for constitutional violations is nullification of a void enactment—and that Congress accordingly may eliminate all affirmative federal remedies now provided, leaving persons harmed by constitutional violations to state law remedies for violation of "private rights"—see Harrison, *Jurisdiction, Congressional Power and Constitutional Remedies*, 86 Geo.L.J. 2513 (1998). For a critical reply, which both questions the textual and historical premises underlying Harrison's claims and disputes the appropriateness of his originalist framework, see Meltzer, *Congress, Courts, and Constitutional Remedies*, 86 Geo.L.J. 2537, 2549–65 (1998).

admit evidence, or decline to allow the imposition of civil liability."). Thus, if state or county officials had sued Ward and his fellow tribe members to enforce tax obligations imposed by state or local law, Ward and those similarly situated could have defended on the ground that assessment of the tax was unconstitutional.

It is often said that the text of the Constitution refers to remedies for constitutional violations in two instances. First, the privilege of the writ of habeas corpus is safeguarded against "suspension" by Congress. U.S. Const., Art. I, § 9. Recall, however, that Ex parte Bollman, 8 U.S. 75 (1807), suggested that the Suspension Clause was not operative in federal court absent an affirmative conferral of federal jurisdiction. See p. 355, *supra*. The Suspension Clause was not clearly recognized as an affirmative constitutionally compelled remedy until Boumediene v. Bush, 553 U.S. 723 (2008).

Second, the Just Compensation Clause of the Fifth Amendment states: "nor shall private property be taken for public use, without just compensation." The Court has said that this provision "dictates the remedy for interference with property rights amounting to a taking." First English Evangelical Lutheran Church v. County of Los Angeles, 482 U.S. 304, 316 n.9 (1987).[2] But as the Court clarified in DeVillier in a unanimous opinion, while the Takings Clause provides "an irrevocable right to just compensation immediately upon a taking," the Court's precedents "do not cleanly answer the question whether a plaintiff has a cause of action arising directly under the Takings Clause." 601 U.S. at 292. DeVillier was a suit by property owners against Texas for a taking of their property brought under both the Texas Constitution and the federal Takings Clause. The Court declined to address whether the federal Takings Clause provided a cause of action because it concluded that plaintiffs could sue on their federal just compensation claim through a state law cause of action.[3] In assessing constitutional remedies, DeVillier therefore seems to distinguish between (i) a right to certain forms of relief, and (ii) a "cause of action," or right to sue, to seek certain forms of relief.

(2) The Sources of Constitutional Remedy in Ward. What was the source of the affirmative refund remedy in Ward? State law apparently provided a refund for taxes paid involuntarily. Perhaps the Supreme Court, in finding no fair or substantial support for the state court's conclusion that

---

[2]   Brauneis, *The First Constitutional Tort: The Remedial Revolution in Nineteenth-Century State Just Compensation Law*, 52 Vand.L.Rev. 55 (1999), suggests that in the nineteenth century, the remedy for a violation of just compensation clauses in state constitutions was not an award of compensation but rather a declaration that the offending act was a nullity. That approach left property owners free to seek common law remedies (like trespass) against individual officers, who could be held liable once any purported legislative justification had been nullified as unconstitutional. Brauneis contends that state courts began, in the post-bellum period, to view just compensation provisions as the source of a right to bring an action for damages, and that beginning in the 1920s, some state courts also viewed those provisions as abrogating state sovereign immunity.

[3]   The lawsuit in DeVillier began in state court but was removed to federal court, which was the posture in which the Supreme Court reviewed the case. In ruling that the plaintiffs on remand "should be permitted to pursue their claim under the Takings Clause through the cause of action available under Texas law," the Supreme Court did not specify whether plaintiffs could seek such relief in federal court or had to pursue the remedy in state court. 601 U.S. at 293.

the taxes had been paid voluntarily, was seeking to ensure that the state courts were applying *state* remedial rules on a nondiscriminatory basis to claims based on federal law. See generally Chap. V, Sec. 2(B), *supra*. But how does that reading square with the Supreme Court's statement: "As the payment was not voluntary * * *, no statutory authority was essential to enable or require the county to refund the money"?

In any event, the Supreme Court did not assert that fair or substantial support was lacking for the state court's alternative holding that state law afforded no remedy against the county with respect to monies already paid over to the state. The Act of Congress did not explicitly create a right of action to recover taxes paid under compulsion. Did it create such a right by implication? Did such a right exist as a matter of the general common law, as then understood? Of federal common law? Or did it arise from the Constitution itself? Consider the Court's observation that "[t]o say that the county could collect these unlawful taxes by coercive means and not incur any obligation to pay them back is nothing short of saying that it could take * * * property * * * arbitrarily and without due process of law."

(3) The Virginia Coupon Cases. A precursor of sorts to Ward that appeared to hold that federal law confers a right to recover and informs the availability of a remedy in state court was the set of 1885 Virginia Coupon Cases. In 1871, Virginia's legislature refinanced the state's debt with new bonds and coupons that could be used to pay state taxes. In 1882, the legislature prohibited the use of the coupons to pay taxes, requiring the taxpayer to pay in hard money under protest and then, as the sole remedy, initiate a suit to recover the taxes paid. If the taxpayer tendered coupons, the law directed the collector to consider the taxes unpaid and seize the taxpayer's property for sale in satisfaction of the tax debt.

In Poindexter v. Greenhow, 114 U.S. 270 (1885), the lead of several consolidated Virginia Coupon Cases growing out of the 1882 law, Poindexter tendered coupons in partial payment of the taxes, but the collector for the City of Richmond, Greenhow, rejected the tender and seized his property. Poindexter sued in state court, seeking through the writ of detinue to secure the return of the property, and arguing that the Virginia law foreclosing acceptance of tax-payment coupons violated the federal Constitution by impairing the obligation of its contract. The state court maintained that the refund action was the exclusive remedy. The Supreme Court disagreed. It held that the Virginia statute impaired the obligation of contract and, by restricting taxpayers to a suit to recover back taxes initially paid in specie, violated the taxpayers' due process rights. "No one would contend that a law of a State, forbidding all redress by actions at law for injuries to property, would be upheld in the courts of the United States, for that would be to deprive one of his property without due process of law." 114 U.S. at 303. Does this mean, as argued in Woolhandler, *The Common Law Origins of Constitutionally Compelled Remedies*, 107 Yale L.J. 77, 121 (1997), that the Due Process Clause compelled the state law common law remedy "quite apart from the Contracts Clause issues implicated by the repeal of such remedies"? Or was the state common law remedy simply available under general law once the exclusive statutory remedy in the 1882 law was struck down as a violation of the Contracts Clause? In any event, as a result of this ruling, Poindexter could sue Greenhow in an action in detinue and Greenhow lacked a defense because the 1882 law violated the Contracts Clause.

Note that the Supreme Court had upheld remedial substitution in allowing Congress to limit the individual's right to sue an officer for unlawful tax collection. See Cary v. Curtis, 44 U.S. (3 How.) 236 (1845). See generally Hill, *Constitutional Remedies*, 69 Colum.L.Rev. 1109, 1115–16 & n.29 (1969) (when the Supreme Court requires a state to furnish a remedy unavailable as a matter of state law, the Court does so to effectuate federal constitutional rights).[4]

(4) Remedies for Equal Protection Violations. Should an equal protection violation be redressed by granting better treatment to the previously disfavored class or by imposing harsher burdens on the previously favored class? In Iowa-Des Moines Nat'l Bank v. Bennett, 284 U.S. 239 (1931), taxpayers, alleging a denial of equal protection, sought a refund of taxes levied on the plaintiffs' stock at a higher rate than was applied to the shares of competing domestic corporations. Without denying that systematic discrimination existed, the Supreme Court of Iowa affirmed a judgment denying relief, holding that the auditor had violated state law in reducing taxes on the competitors, and that the plaintiffs' remedy was to await (or to initiate proceedings to compel) collection of the higher tax from their competitors. The Supreme Court (per Brandeis, J.) reversed, holding that the taxpayers were entitled to a refund of the excess of taxes exacted from them: "It may be assumed that all ground for a claim for refund would have fallen if the State, promptly upon discovery of the discrimination, had removed it by collecting the additional taxes from the favored competitors. * * * The right invoked is that to equal treatment; and such treatment will be attained if either their competitors' taxes are increased or their own reduced. But it is well settled that a taxpayer who has been subjected to discriminatory taxation * * * cannot be required himself to assume the burden of seeking an increase of the taxes which the others should have paid. Nor may he be remitted to the necessity of awaiting such action by the state officials upon their own initiative."[5]

(5) The McKesson and Reich Decisions.

(a) The source of the remedial obligation in Ward and Bennett was clarified in McKesson Corp. v. Division of ABT, 496 U.S. 18 (1990), a state court action seeking a refund of state taxes paid under a discriminatory tax that was held to violate the dormant Commerce Clause. The state court had

---

[4]   Nineteenth century tax collectors, sheriffs, marshals, and other officials handled government money subject to strict rules of accounting that required them to pay funds collected to the treasury less any allowable offsets (including their fees). For an overview of the sheriff's accounting obligations, see Pfander & Borrasso, *Public Rights and Article III: Judicial Oversight of Agency Action,* 82 Ohio St.L.J. 493, 508–10 (2021). Relying on Osborn v. Bank of the United States, Poindexter indicates that state officials have available a "perfect defence" in judgments for the claimants if forced by a federal court to return money or property to them. 114 U.S. at 293–94.

[5]   Compare Heckler v. Mathews, 465 U.S. 728 (1984) (upholding plaintiff's standing to challenge sex discrimination in the award of social security benefits—even though a congressional mandate limited relief to reducing benefits received by others rather than increasing plaintiff's benefits).

enjoined future enforcement of the tax but had refused, on the basis of "equitable considerations," to award a refund of taxes previously paid. A unanimous Supreme Court held that if (as in this case) a state requires taxpayers to pay first and obtain review of the tax's validity later, the Due Process Clause requires the state to afford a meaningful opportunity to secure postpayment relief. The Court held that the state must either refund to the complaining taxpayer the constitutionally excessive portion of the taxes paid, or (to the extent consistent with other constitutional restrictions[6]) assess and collect back taxes from the taxpayer's competitors to eliminate the discrimination. The opinion considered and rejected several arguments made by the state that such a requirement would cause serious economic dislocation and heavy administrative burdens. Concluding that the state's interest in financial stability did not justify a refusal to provide relief, the Court observed that there are procedural measures that states could take in the future to "protect [their] fiscal security when weighed against their obligation to provide meaningful relief for their unconstitutional taxation."

(b)   Was it significant that the Court treated the remedial obligation as arising not from the constitutional provision that was violated (the dormant Commerce Clause) but from the Due Process Clause?

(c)   In McKesson, the Court placed some emphasis on the fact that Florida had opened its courts to refund actions and did not contend that they were barred by sovereign immunity. But in Reich v. Collins, 513 U.S. 106 (1994), also a state court action for a state tax refund, the Supreme Court unanimously stated the constitutional obligation more unqualifiedly. It cited, *inter alia*, McKesson, Bennett, and Ward, as support for the proposition that due process requires that a state provide a "clear and certain" remedy for taxes collected in violation of federal law, and that while the state may choose between predeprivation and postdeprivation remedies, it must provide one or the other. Thus, exaction of taxes in violation of a federal statute or the Constitution, by compulsion, violated the Fourteenth Amendment. The Court added that the obligation exists notwithstanding "the sovereign immunity States traditionally enjoy in their own courts." (That statement was dictum, as the state court's denial of a refund did not rest on immunity grounds.)[7]

---

[6]   On the permissible scope of retroactive taxation of the favored class as a remedy for discrimination, see Rakowski, *Harper and Its Aftermath*, 1 Fla.Tax.Rev. 445, 489–99 & authorities cited (1993); cf. United States v. Carlton, 512 U.S. 26 (1994) (applying doctrine that retroactive tax legislation is constitutional so long as there is a rational basis for retroactive application).

[7]   In an opinion by Justice Jackson for six Justices, the Supreme Court distinguished McKesson and Reich in Office of the United States Trustee v. John Q. Hammons Fall 2006, 144 S.Ct. 1588 (2024), holding that prospective fee parity rather than a refund was the appropriate remedy for the federal government's high differential fees imposed on certain Chapter II debtors, which the Court had previously held in Siegel v. Fitzgerald, 596 U.S. 464 (2022), violated the Bankruptcy Clause's uniformity requirement. Citing cases involving requests for non-monetary prospective injunctive relief, the Court stated broadly that "the touchstone for any decision about remedy is legislative intent" (quoting Ayotte v. Planned Parenthood of Northern New England, 546 U.S. 320, 330 (2006)), and thus that "the key question in determining how to remedy a constitutional violation wrought by the legislative process is always 'what the legislature would have willed had it been apprised of the constitutional infirmity.'" (quoting Sessions v. Morales-Santana, 582 U.S. 47, 73–74 (2017) (further internal quotations omitted)). After concluding that "Congress would have wanted prospective parity,

(d)   The Court has more recently recast the required refund remedy in light of its sovereign immunity jurisprudence. In Alden v. Maine, 527 U.S. 706 (1999), p. 1248, *infra*, the Supreme Court held that state sovereign immunity does not derive simply from the Eleventh Amendment (the text of which addresses only federal judicial power) but rather is embedded in the Constitution and is generally co-extensive in state and federal courts. In so holding, the Alden Court reaffirmed Reich v. Collins on narrow grounds: "We held [in Reich] that, despite its immunity from suit in federal court, a State which holds out what plainly appears to be 'a clear and certain' postdeprivation remedy for taxes collected in violation of federal law may not declare, after disputed taxes have been paid in reliance on this remedy, that the remedy does not in fact exist. This case arose in the context of tax-refund litigation, where a State may deprive a taxpayer of all other means of challenging the validity of its tax laws by holding out what appears to be a 'clear and certain' postdeprivation remedy. In this context, due process requires the State to provide the remedy it has promised. The obligation arises from the Constitution itself; Reich does not speak to the power of Congress to subject States to suits in their own courts."

Does Alden suggest that a state is merely prohibited from using bait-and-switch tactics and that no remedy would be required if the state clearly provides that no remedy for the exaction of unconstitutional taxes exists?

(6) Retroactivity and Remedies. A series of cases has addressed the question whether the remedial obligation recognized in McKesson and Reich extends to claims for tax refunds based upon "new" principles of federal law not clearly established at the time the tax was collected.

In Harper v. Virginia Dept. of Taxation, 509 U.S. 86, 113 (1993) (5–4), the Court determined that its decision in Davis v. Michigan Dept. of Treasury, 489 U.S. 803 (1989)—which held unconstitutional a state tax on federal pension income—should be applied retroactively. The Court relied, in part, on the narrow ground that in Davis itself, the new rule was applied retroactively, leaving no basis for denying retroactive relief to similarly situated taxpayers in Virginia. But some language in Justice Thomas's majority opinion indicated that retroactive relief must be afforded even in situations in which the new constitutional rule had not already been applied retroactively in a prior case, reasoning that the Court lacks the constitutional authority, in effect, to disregard substantive law when deciding a case or controversy or to treat similarly situated litigants differently by denying a new rule retroactive effect.

Justice O'Connor tried in her Harper dissent to recast the question of retroactivity as one of remedial discretion, allowing courts in appropriate circumstances to deny a full refund even where no predeprivation process was provided. Courts often consider factors like surprise, arguable injustice

---

not a refund or retrospective raising of fees," the Court distinguished the due process analysis in McKesson and Reich (among other cases) on the ground that they were tax cases that might not apply to cases involving other forms of monetary injury, and that due process was satisfied in any event because respondents "had the opportunity to challenge their fees before they paid them," which was all that McKesson and subsequent cases required. Justice Gorsuch, joined by Justices Thomas and Barrett, dissented.

from retroactive application of unforeseeable rulings, and relative hardship to litigants, in framing remedies. May they consider such factors in framing remedies for *constitutional* violations?

A subsequent decision outside the tax context, Reynoldsville Casket Co. v. Hyde, 514 U.S. 749 (1995), cast doubt on the permissibility of invoking remedial discretion to deny relief for the violation of a "novel" constitutional rule. In retroactively applying an earlier precedent that had invalidated Ohio's statute of limitations, the Court emphasized that Harper's nonretroactivity principle should not be avoidable simply by asserting that the denial of relief was "based on 'remedy' rather than 'non-retroactivity.' "

The plaintiff had drawn an analogy to the law of qualified immunity in constitutional tort actions, under which courts will deny damages if an official's conduct, though illegal, did not violate "clearly established" law. Conceding that that doctrine "does reflect certain remedial considerations," the Court attempted to distinguish it on the ground that "a set of special federal policy considerations have led to the creation of a well-established, independent rule of law," whereas Ohio had tried to create "what amounts to an ad hoc exemption from retroactivity." (Is that an adequate distinction?) The Court also found wanting a second analogy offered by the plaintiff—the general unavailability of habeas corpus relief when sought on the basis of "new" rulings of constitutional law. That doctrine, the Court said, was not a "remedial" limitation on retroactivity but rather a limitation inherent in retroactivity itself, and one based on special concerns about the finality of criminal convictions. (But because the Court's decisions had authorized habeas relief based on new law in exceptional circumstances, see generally Teague v. Lane, 489 U.S. 288 (1989), p. 1580, *infra*, isn't there in fact a remedial calculus at work in such cases?)

The Hyde opinion recognized, however, that sometimes a new rule of law will not require a retroactive remedy, pointing to the "well-established general legal rule" of official immunity, which, the Court said, "reflects *both* reliance interests and other significant policy justifications," and which "trumps the new rule of [constitutional] law."

INTRODUCTORY NOTE ON BIVENS AND IMPLIED CAUSES OF ACTION AGAINST FEDERAL OFFICIALS

As already noted, Congress has created an express statutory cause of action for constitutional violations by *state* officials in 42 U.S.C. § 1983. See pp. 1279–1297, *infra*. The following decisions and Notes deal with the question whether federal courts will imply a cause of action for damages against *federal* officials for constitutional violations.

Bivens v. Six Unknown Named Agents
of Federal Bureau of Narcotics

403 U.S. 388 (1971).
Certiorari to the United States Court of Appeals for the Second Circuit.

■ MR. JUSTICE BRENNAN delivered the opinion of the Court.

* * * In Bell v. Hood, 327 U.S. 678 (1946), we reserved the question whether violation of that command by a federal agent acting under color of his authority gives rise to a cause of action for damages consequent upon his unconstitutional conduct. Today we hold that it does.

* * * Petitioner's complaint alleged that * * * respondents, agents of the Federal Bureau of Narcotics acting under claim of federal authority, entered his apartment and arrested him for alleged narcotics violations. The agents manacled petitioner in front of his wife and children, and threatened to arrest the entire family. They searched the apartment from stem to stern. Thereafter, petitioner was taken to the federal courthouse in Brooklyn, where he was interrogated, booked, and subjected to a visual strip search.

* * * [P]etitioner brought suit in Federal District Court [pro se]. In addition to the allegations above, his complaint asserted that the arrest and search were effected without a warrant, and that unreasonable force was employed in making the arrest; fairly read, it alleges as well that the arrest was made without probable cause. Petitioner claimed to have suffered great humiliation, embarrassment, and mental suffering as a result of the agents' unlawful conduct, and sought $15,000 damages from each of them. The District Court * * * dismissed the complaint on the ground, *inter alia*, that it failed to state a cause of action. The Court of Appeals * * * affirmed on that basis. We granted certiorari. We reverse.

I

Respondents do not argue that petitioner should be entirely without remedy for an unconstitutional invasion of his rights by federal agents. In respondents' view, however, the rights that petitioner asserts—primarily rights of privacy—are creations of state and not of federal law. Accordingly, they argue, petitioner may obtain money damages to redress invasion of these rights only by an action in tort, under state law, in the state courts. In this scheme the Fourth Amendment would serve merely to limit the extent to which the agents could defend the state law tort suit by asserting that their actions were a valid exercise of federal power: if the agents were shown to have violated the Fourth Amendment, such a defense would be lost to them and they would stand before the state law merely as private individuals. Candidly admitting that it is the policy of the Department of Justice to remove all such suits from the state to the federal courts for decision, respondents nevertheless urge that we uphold dismissal of petitioner's complaint in federal court, and remit him to filing an action in the state courts in order that the case may properly be removed to the federal court for decision on the basis of state law.

We think that respondents' thesis rests upon an unduly restrictive view of the Fourth Amendment's protection against unreasonable searches and seizures by federal agents, a view that has consistently been rejected by this Court. Respondents seek to treat the relationship between a citizen and a federal agent unconstitutionally exercising his authority as no different from the relationship between two private citizens. In so doing, they ignore the fact that power, once granted, does not disappear like a magic gift when it is wrongfully used. An agent acting—albeit unconstitutionally—in the name of the United States possesses a far greater capacity for harm than an individual trespasser exercising no authority other than his own. Accordingly, as our cases make clear, the Fourth Amendment operates as a limitation upon the exercise of federal power regardless of whether the State in whose jurisdiction that power is exercised would prohibit or penalize the identical act if engaged in by a private citizen. It guarantees to citizens of the United States the absolute right to be free from unreasonable searches and seizures carried out by virtue of federal authority. And "where federally protected rights have been invaded, it has been the rule from the beginning that courts will be alert to adjust their remedies so as to grant the necessary relief." Bell v. Hood, 327 U.S., at 684. * * *

First. Our cases have long since rejected the notion that the Fourth Amendment proscribes only such conduct as would, if engaged in by private persons, be condemned by state law. * * * In light of these cases, respondents' argument that the Fourth Amendment serves only as a limitation on federal defenses to a state law claim, and not as an independent limitation upon the exercise of federal power, must be rejected.

Second. The interests protected by state laws regulating trespass and the invasion of privacy, and those protected by the Fourth Amendment's guarantee against unreasonable searches and seizures, may be inconsistent or even hostile. Thus, we may bar the door against an unwelcome private intruder, or call the police if he persists in seeking entrance. The availability of such alternative means for the protection of privacy may lead the State to restrict imposition of liability for any consequent trespass. A private citizen, asserting no authority other than his own, will not normally be liable in trespass if he demands, and is granted, admission to another's house. But one who demands admission under a claim of federal authority stands in a far different position. The mere invocation of federal power by a federal law enforcement official will normally render futile any attempt to resist an unlawful entry or arrest by resort to the local police; and a claim of authority to enter is likely to unlock the door as well. * * *

Nor is it adequate to answer that state law may take into account the different status of one clothed with the authority of the Federal Government. For just as state law may not authorize federal agents to violate the Fourth Amendment, * * * neither may state law undertake to limit the extent to which federal authority can be exercised. The inevitable consequence of this dual limitation on state power is that the federal question becomes not merely a possible defense to the state law action, but an independent claim both necessary and sufficient to make out the plaintiff's cause of action. * * *

Third. That damages may be obtained for injuries consequent upon a violation of the Fourth Amendment by federal officials should hardly seem a surprising proposition. * * * See Nixon v. Condon, 286 U.S. 73 (1932); Nixon v. Herndon, 273 U.S. 536, 540 (1927); Swafford v. Templeton, 185 U.S. 487 (1902); Wiley v. Sinkler, 179 U.S. 58 (1900). Of course, the Fourth Amendment does not in so many words provide for its enforcement by an award of money damages for the consequences of its violation. But "it is * * * well settled that where legal rights have been invaded, and a federal statute provides for a general right to sue for such invasion, federal courts may use any available remedy to make good the wrong done." Bell v. Hood, 327 U.S., at 684 (footnote omitted). The present case involves no special factors counseling hesitation in the absence of affirmative action by Congress. We are not dealing with a question of "federal fiscal policy," as in United States v. Standard Oil Co., 332 U.S. 301, 311 (1947). * * * Nor are we asked in this case to impose liability upon a congressional employee for actions contrary to no constitutional prohibition, but merely said to be in excess of the authority delegated to him by the Congress. Wheeldin v. Wheeler, 373 U.S. 647 (1963). Finally, we cannot accept respondents' formulation of the question as whether the availability of money damages is necessary to enforce the Fourth Amendment. For we have here no explicit congressional declaration that persons injured by a federal officer's violation of the Fourth Amendment may not recover money damages from the agents, but must instead be remitted to another remedy, equally effective in the view of Congress. The question is merely whether petitioner, if he can demonstrate an injury consequent upon the violation by federal agents of his Fourth Amendment rights, is entitled to redress his injury through a particular remedial mechanism normally available in the federal courts. *Cf.* J.I. Case Co. v. Borak, 377 U.S. 426, 433 (1964); Jacobs v. United States, 290 U.S. 13, 16 (1933). "The very essence of civil liberty certainly consists in the right of every individual to claim the protection of the laws, whenever he receives an injury." Marbury v. Madison, 1 Cranch 137, 163 (1803). Having concluded that petitioner's complaint states a cause of action under the Fourth Amendment, we hold that petitioner is entitled to recover money damages for any injuries he has suffered as a result of the agents' violation of the Amendment.

II

In addition to holding that petitioner's complaint had failed to state facts making out a cause of action, the District Court ruled that in any event respondents were immune from liability by virtue of their official position. This question was not passed upon by the Court of Appeals, and accordingly we do not consider it here. The judgment of the Court of Appeals is reversed and the case is remanded for further proceedings consistent with this opinion.

■ MR. JUSTICE HARLAN, concurring in the judgment.

My initial view of this case was that the Court of Appeals was correct in dismissing the complaint, but for reasons stated in this opinion I am now persuaded to the contrary. * * *

I am of the opinion that federal courts do have the power to award damages for violation of "constitutionally protected interests" and I agree with the Court that a traditional judicial remedy such as damages is appropriate to the vindication of the personal interests protected by the Fourth Amendment.

I

I turn first to the contention that the constitutional power of federal courts to accord Bivens damages for his claim depends on the passage of a statute creating a "federal cause of action." Although the point is not entirely free of ambiguity, I do not understand either the Government or my dissenting Brothers to maintain that Bivens' contention that he is entitled to be free from the type of official conduct prohibited by the Fourth Amendment depends on a decision by the State in which he resides to accord him a remedy. Such a position would be incompatible with the presumed availability of federal equitable relief, if a proper showing can be made in terms of the ordinary principles governing equitable remedies. See Bell v. Hood, 327 U.S. 678, 684 (1946). However broad a federal court's discretion concerning equitable remedies, it is absolutely clear—at least after Erie R. Co. v. Tompkins, 304 U.S. 64 (1938)—that in a nondiversity suit a federal court's power to grant even equitable relief depends on the presence of a substantive right derived from federal law. Compare Guaranty Trust Co. v. York, 326 U.S. 99, 105–107 (1945), with Holmberg v. Armbrecht, 327 U.S. 392, 395 (1946). See also H. Hart & H. Wechsler, The Federal Courts and the Federal System 818–819 (1953).

Thus the interest which Bivens claims—to be free from official conduct in contravention of the Fourth Amendment—is a federally protected interest.[3] Therefore, the question of judicial power to grant

---

[3] The Government appears not quite ready to concede this point. Certain points in the Government's argument seem to suggest that the "state-created right—federal defense" model reaches not only the question of the power to accord a federal damages remedy, but also the claim to any judicial remedy in any court. * * *

In truth, the legislative record as a whole behind the Bill of Rights is silent on the rather refined doctrinal question whether the framers considered the rights therein enumerated as dependent in the first instance on the decision of a State to accord legal status to the personal interests at stake. That is understandable since the Government itself points out that general federal-question jurisdiction was not extended to the federal district courts until 1875. The most that can be drawn from this historical fact is that the authors of the Bill of Rights assumed the adequacy of common-law remedies to vindicate the federally protected interest. One must first combine this assumption with contemporary modes of jurisprudential thought which appeared to link "rights" and "remedies" in a 1:1 correlation, cf. Marbury v. Madison, 1 Cranch 137, 163

Bivens damages is not a problem of the "source" of the "right"; instead, the question is whether the power to authorize damages as a judicial remedy for the vindication of a federal constitutional right is placed by the Constitution itself exclusively in Congress' hands.

II

The contention that the federal courts are powerless to accord a litigant damage for a claimed invasion of his federal constitutional rights until Congress explicitly authorizes the remedy cannot rest on the notion that the decision to grant compensatory relief involves a resolution of policy considerations not susceptible of judicial discernment. Thus, in suits for damages based on violations of federal statutes lacking any express authorization of a damage remedy, this Court has authorized such relief where, in its view, damages are necessary to effectuate the congressional policy underpinning the substantive provisions of the statute. J.I. Case Co. v. Borak, 377 U.S. 426 (1964); [citing two other decisions].[4]

If it is not the nature of the remedy which is thought to render a judgment as to the appropriateness of damages inherently "legislative," then it must be the nature of the legal interest offered as an occasion for invoking otherwise appropriate judicial relief. But I do not think that the fact that the interest is protected by the Constitution rather than statute or common law justifies the assertion that federal courts are powerless to grant damages in the absence of explicit congressional action authorizing the remedy. * * *

More importantly, the presumed availability of federal equitable relief against threatened invasions of constitutional interests appears entirely to negate the contention that the status of an interest as constitutionally protected divests federal courts of the power to grant damages absent express congressional authorization. * * *

If explicit congressional authorization is an absolute prerequisite to the power of a federal court to accord compensatory relief regardless of the necessity or appropriateness of damages as a remedy simply because of the status of a legal interest as constitutionally protected, then it

---

(1803), before reaching the conclusion that the framers are to be understood today as having created no federally protected interests. And, of course, that would simply require the conclusion that federal equitable relief would not lie to protect those interests guarded by the Fourth Amendment. * * *

   [4]   The Borak case is an especially clear example of the exercise of federal judicial power to accord damages as an appropriate remedy in the absence of any express statutory authorization of a federal cause of action. There we "implied"—from what can only be characterized as an "exclusively procedural provision" affording access to a federal forum—a private cause of action for damages for violation of § 14(a) of the Securities Exchange Act of 1934, 48 Stat. 895, 15 U.S.C. § 78n(a). We did so in an area where federal regulation has been singularly comprehensive and elaborate administrative enforcement machinery had been provided. The exercise of judicial power involved in Borak simply cannot be justified in terms of statutory construction; nor did the Borak Court purport to do so. The notion of "implying" a remedy, therefore, as applied to cases like Borak, can only refer to a process whereby the federal judiciary exercises a choice among traditionally available judicial remedies according to reasons related to the substantive social policy embodied in an act of positive law.

seems to me that explicit congressional authorization is similarly prerequisite to the exercise of equitable remedial discretion in favor of constitutionally protected interests. Conversely, if a general grant of jurisdiction to the federal courts by Congress is thought adequate to empower a federal court to grant equitable relief for all areas of subject-matter jurisdiction enumerated therein, see 28 U.S.C. § 1331(a), then it seems to me that the same statute is sufficient to empower a federal court to grant a traditional remedy at law. Of course, the special historical traditions governing the federal equity system, might still bear on the comparative appropriateness of granting equitable relief as opposed to money damages. That possibility, however, relates, not to whether the federal courts have the power to afford one type of remedy as opposed to the other, but rather to the criteria which should govern the exercise of our power. To that question, I now pass.

III

The major thrust of the Government's position is that, where Congress has not expressly authorized a particular remedy, a federal court should exercise its power to accord a traditional form of judicial relief at the behest of a litigant, who claims a constitutionally protected interest has been invaded, only where the remedy is "essential," or "indispensable for vindicating constitutional rights." Govt. Brief, 19, 24. * * *

These arguments for a more stringent test to govern the grant of damages in constitutional cases seem to be adequately answered by the point that the judiciary has a particular responsibility to assure the vindication of constitutional interests such as those embraced by the Fourth Amendment. To be sure, "it must be remembered that legislatures are ultimate guardians of the liberties and welfare of the people in quite as great a degree as the courts." But it must also be recognized that the Bill of Rights is particularly intended to vindicate the interests of the individual in the face of the popular will as expressed in legislative majorities; at the very least, it strikes me as no more appropriate to await express congressional authorization of traditional judicial relief with regard to these legal interests than with respect to interests protected by federal statutes.

The question then, is, as I see it, whether compensatory relief is "necessary" or "appropriate" to the vindication of the interest asserted. * * * In resolving that question, it seems to me that the range of policy considerations we may take into account is at least as broad as the range of a legislature would consider with respect to an express statutory authorization of a traditional remedy. In this regard I agree with the Court that the appropriateness of according Bivens compensatory relief does not turn simply on the deterrent effect liability will have on federal official conduct.[8] * * *

I think it is clear that Bivens advances a claim of the sort that, if proved, would be properly compensable in damages. The personal interests protected by the Fourth Amendment are those we attempt to capture by the notion of "privacy"; while the Court today properly points out that the type of harm which officials can inflict when they invade protected zones of an individual's life are different from the types of harm private citizens inflict on one another, the experience of judges in dealing with private trespass and false imprisonment claims supports the conclusion that courts of law are capable of making the types of judgment concerning causation and magnitude of injury necessary to accord meaningful compensation for invasion of Fourth Amendment rights.

On the other hand, the limitations on state remedies for violation of common-law rights by private citizens argue in favor of a federal damages remedy. The injuries inflicted by officials acting under color of law, while no less compensable in damages than those inflicted by private parties, are substantially different in kind, as the Court's opinion today discusses in detail. See Monroe v. Pape, 365 U.S. 167 (1961) (Harlan, J., concurring). It seems to me entirely proper that these injuries be compensable according to uniform rules of federal law, especially in light of the very large element of federal law which must in any event control the scope of official defenses to liability. Certainly, there is very little to be gained from the standpoint of federalism by preserving different rules of liability for federal officers dependent on the State where the injury occurs.

Putting aside the desirability of leaving the problem of federal official liability to the vagaries of common-law actions, it is apparent that some form of damages is the only possible remedy for someone in Bivens' alleged position. It will be a rare case indeed in which an individual in Bivens' position will be able to obviate the harm by securing injunctive relief from any court. However desirable a direct remedy against the Government might be as a substitute for individual official liability, the sovereign still remains immune to suit. Finally, assuming Bivens' innocence of the crime charged, the "exclusionary rule" is simply irrelevant. For people in Bivens' shoes, it is damages or nothing.

---

[8]   And I think it follows from this point that today's decision has little, if indeed any, bearing on the question whether a federal court may properly devise remedies—other than traditionally available forms of judicial relief—for the purpose of enforcing substantive social policies embodied in constitutional or statutory policies. Compare today's decision with Mapp v. Ohio, 367 U.S. 643 (1961), and Weeks v. United States, 232 U.S. 383 (1914). The Court today simply recognizes what has long been implicit in our decisions concerning equitable relief and remedies implied from statutory schemes; i.e., that a court of law vested with jurisdiction over the subject matter of a suit has the power—and therefore the duty—to make principled choices among traditional judicial remedies. Whether special prophylactic measures—which at least arguably the exclusionary rule exemplifies—are supportable on grounds other than a court's competence to select among traditional judicial remedies to make good the wrong done is a separate question.

Of course, for a variety of reasons, the remedy may not often be sought. And the countervailing interests in efficient law enforcement of course argue for a protective zone with respect to many types of Fourth Amendment violations. But, while I express no view on the immunity defense offered in the instant case, I deem it proper to venture the thought that at the very least such a remedy would be available for the most flagrant and patently unjustified sorts of police conduct. Although litigants may not often choose to seek relief, it is important, in a civilized society, that the judicial branch of the Nation's government stand ready to afford a remedy in these circumstances. * * *

For these reasons, I concur in the judgment of the Court.

■ MR. JUSTICE BLACK, dissenting.

* * * There can be no doubt that Congress could create a federal cause of action for damages for an unreasonable search in violation of the Fourth Amendment. Although Congress has created such a federal cause of action against state officials acting under color of state law, it has never created such a cause of action against federal officials. If it wanted to do so, Congress could, of course, create a remedy against federal officials who violate the Fourth Amendment in the performance of their duties. But the point of this case and the fatal weakness in the Court's judgment is that neither Congress nor the State of New York has enacted legislation creating such a right of action. For us to do so is, in my judgment, an exercise of power that the Constitution does not give us.

[CHIEF JUSTICE BURGER also dissented, arguing that the Court's creation of a damages remedy usurped a legislative function in violation of the separation of powers. JUSTICE BLACKMUN's separate dissent sounded a similar theme. He contended that the Court's "judicial legislation" would provide an "avalanche of new federal cases." He added: "The Fourth Amendment was adopted in 1791, and, in all the intervening years, neither the Congress nor the Court has seen fit to take this step. I had thought that, for the truly aggrieved person, other quite adequate remedies have always been available. If not, it is the Congress, and not this Court, that should act."]

―――――――――

NOTE ON BIVENS

(1) Background. In evaluating Bivens' implication of an implied right of action for constitutional violations by federal officers, consider six points about the state of the law at the time of Bivens.

(a) A plaintiff could pursue a claim for money damages against a federal officer in state court or in federal court in diversity, alleging such common law torts as trespass and invasion of privacy. In such a proceeding, the officer would claim immunity under federal authority as a defense unless the officer's conduct exceeded the scope of designated authority or violated the Fourth Amendment. (This was the standard model of officer suit litigation underlying nineteenth century decisions such as Little v. Barreme, 6 U.S. (2 Cranch) 170, 179 (1804), p. 1148, *infra*.) If brought in state court, the officers could tender a federal authority defense and remove the action to federal court for litigation there under 28 U.S.C. § 1442. Thus, while state law would provide the right of action, liability, including damages, would turn on the court's interpretation of the Fourth Amendment and the scope of official authority, both questions of federal law. In this manner state-law causes of action (and general law causes of action before Erie) were central to federal officer liability for damages. The availability and scope of recovery for Bivens under New York tort law at the time of the decision was unclear. See Dellinger, *Of Rights and Remedies: The Constitution as a Sword*, 85 Harv.L.Rev. 1532, 1535–36 (1972); Brief of Respondent United States in Bivens, at 34–38.

(b)   As noted in the introduction, 42 U.S.C. § 1983 provides a statutory right to sue officials acting under color of *state law* for constitutional violations but does not apply to action under color of *federal* law, such as the search and seizure at issue in Bivens.

(c)   At the time of Bivens, *equitable* remedies were, as Justice Harlan maintained, presumptively available in federal court to vindicate "a substantive right derived from federal law" even in the absence of an overt congressional authorization. This proposition is analyzed thoroughly in Chapter IX.

(d)   As Justice Harlan also noted, at the time of Bivens, the Court was readily implying causes of action under federal statutes in order to effectuate the policies and purposes of the statutes. The controlling case at the time was J.I. Case Co. v. Borak, 377 U.S. 426 (1964). See pp. 898–899, *supra*.

(e)   In Bell v. Hood, 327 U.S. 678 (1946), the Court noted that it had not decided "whether federal courts can grant money recovery for damages" in this context, but also noted that "where federally protected rights have been invaded, it has been the rule from the beginning that courts will be alert to adjust their remedies so as to grant the necessary relief." Against that background, the Court held that a federal district court had subject matter jurisdiction under 28 U.S.C. § 1330 over a claim that sought money damages against a federal officer for violating the Fourth Amendment because the claim was not "insubstantial or frivolous," and because it "raise[d] serious questions, both of law and fact, which the district court can decide only after it has assumed jurisdiction over the controversy."

(f)   In the same year that the Court decided Bell v. Hood, Congress provided a vehicle for recovering damages for certain torts committed by federal officials. In the Federal Tort Claims Act, it waived the federal government's sovereign immunity and allowed suits against the United States to recover damages for the negligent acts of its employees. Pub.L.No. 79–601, ch. 753, § 410, 60 Stat. 842, 843–844 (1946). But the Act did not apply to intentional torts like assault, false arrest, false imprisonment, or abuse of process, see 28 U.S.C. § 2680(h), and it is thus unlikely that Bivens could have recovered under the FTCA. See Dellinger, *supra*, at 1535 & n.20.

(2) The Debate over Implied Constitutional Rights of Action. Consider the following questions about the holding and analysis in Bivens.

(a)   The Fourth Amendment provides in part: "The right of the people to be secure in their persons, houses, papers, and effects, against unreasonable searches and seizures, shall not be violated * * *." The majority and concurrence in Bivens maintain that this language confers an affirmative right in need of federal law protection, and not merely a tool for negating official authority defenses to claims predicated on common law rights. Is that right? The two camps further maintain that a judge-made remedy for damages is necessary because—despite the long history of enforcing constitutional rights through the adjudication of defenses to common law claims—common law rights circa 1971 were not adequately broad to ensure the vindication of constitutional rights circa 1971. Is this gap a justification for federal courts to develop constitutional causes of action?

(b)   The dissenting Justices argue on separation of powers grounds that it is the job of Congress, not the Court, to confer a right to sue for damages for federal officer violations of the Constitution.[1] Is this argument consistent with the presumptive availability of injunctive relief as a remedy for constitutional violations by federal officers? Is there a special justification for a damages remedy for Fourth Amendment violations when injunctive relief and the exclusionary rule are unavailable? What reasons might there be for judicial caution in recognizing a right to sue for damages?

(c)   What are the separation of powers implications of Congress having (i) conferred an express cause of action for damages for state officer violations of the Constitution but not for federal officer violations, and (ii) waived immunity from suit against the United States for some federal official torts but not the ones at issue in Bivens? Should officer suits for monetary relief be seen as different from suits against the government itself—because the relief does not come from the treasury—or instead as a functionally necessary surrogate for governmental immunity, without which such immunity would not be tolerable?

(d)   The practice at the time of Bivens of easily recognizing implied rights of action to enforce statutory rights has ended; the Court will no longer supplement the legislative scheme by recognizing non-statutory private rights to sue. See Alexander v. Sandoval, 532 U.S. 275 (2001), p. 892, *supra*. Should the change in thinking about the implication of private causes of action to vindicate statutory rights require a rethinking of the Court's authority and competence to recognize non-statutory rights of action to enforce constitutional rights?

---

[1]   In calling for deference to Congress, the Bivens dissenters appear to assume that Congress has power to furnish a right to sue, albeit not one rooted in the Fourteenth Amendment. The enforcement power in § 5 of the Fourteenth Amendment operates on the states. For the argument that congressional power may be inferred from Article I's provision for Congress to carry into execution the power vested in Article III courts to adjudicate cases arising under the Constitution, see Dellinger, *Of Rights and Remedies: The Constitution as a Sword*, 85 Harv.L.Rev. 1532, 1546–49 (1972). For doubts about the use of Article III to justify the judicial role, see Monaghan, *Constitutional Common Law*, 89 Harv.L.Rev. 1, 24 (1975).

(3) Initial Extension of the Bivens Approach. The Bivens opinion suggested that recognition of a damages remedy might not be inappropriate in a case presenting (i) "special factors counselling hesitation in the absence of affirmative action by Congress" or (ii) "an explicit congressional declaration that * * * [plaintiff should be] remitted to another remedy, equally effective in the view of Congress." But the Court's next two decisions in the Bivens line suggested a narrow compass for those limitations.

(a)   In Davis v. Passman, 442 U.S. 228 (1979), the Court held, 5–4, that Davis could bring a Bivens action alleging that she had been fired from her job as administrative assistant to Congressman Passman because of her gender, in violation of the equal protection component of the Due Process Clause of the Fifth Amendment. Starting from the premise that "the judiciary is clearly discernible as the primary means through which [constitutional] rights may be enforced," Justice Brennan's opinion for the Court emphasized that "unless such rights are to become merely precatory," litigants with "no [other] effective means [to] * * * enforce these rights[ ] must be able to invoke the existing jurisdiction of the courts for the protection of their justiciable constitutional rights." Because Passman was no longer in Congress, the Court concluded that "for Davis, as for Bivens, it is damages or nothing."

(b)   The next year, in Carlson v. Green, 446 U.S. 14 (1980), the Court upheld the availability of a damages remedy in an action alleging that the failure of federal prison officials to provide medical attention to plaintiff's deceased son constituted cruel and unusual punishment in violation of the Eighth Amendment. The Court, again per Justice Brennan, stated flatly that "the victims of a constitutional violation by a federal agent have a right to recover damages against the official in federal court despite the absence of any statute conferring such a right," unless (1) the defendant demonstrates "special factors counselling hesitation," or (2) "Congress has provided an alternative remedy which it explicitly declared to be a *substitute* for recovery directly under the Constitution and viewed as equally effective" (emphasis in original).

The Court ruled that 1974 changes to the FTCA did not constitute such a substitute. Three years after Bivens, Congress amended the FTCA to impose vicarious liability on the government for certain intentional torts— "assault, battery, false imprisonment, false arrest, abuse of process, or malicious prosecution"—committed by its "investigative or law enforcement officers." 88 Stat. 50 (1974), codified at 28 U.S.C. § 2680(h). The Court in Carlson acknowledged that plaintiffs had an action under FTCA against the United States but concluded that Congress did not intend the amendment to be a substitute rather than an alternative remedy. And the Court suggested four ways in which the Bivens remedy might be more effective than the FTCA remedy: (a) an action against the individual wrongdoer is a more effective deterrent than an action against the government; (b) unlike the FTCA, the Bivens remedy permits punitive damages; (c) a Bivens plaintiff can opt for jury trial, unavailable under the FTCA; and (d) the FTCA applies only to conduct that would be actionable under state law if committed by a private person, whereas uniform federal rules govern the extent of Bivens liability.

(4) Retrenchment in the Face of Alternative Congressional Remedies. Carlson represents the high-water mark of Bivens, from which the Court has retreated ever since. Ever since Carlson, the Court has refused to recognize a constitutional damages remedy primarily because of the existence of alternative remedies provided by Congress.

In Bush v. Lucas, 462 U.S. 367 (1983), Bush, an aerospace engineer employed by the federal government, sued his superior for damages, alleging, *inter alia*, that he had been demoted in retaliation for exercising his First Amendment rights. The Civil Service Commission's Appeals Review Board had previously restored him to his former position and awarded him back pay. Although assuming that the civil service remedy was "less than complete," the Court held (per Stevens, J.) that in this matter of "federal personnel policy" the "elaborate remedial system" constructed by Congress should not be "augmented by the creation of a new judicial remedy." The Court also stated that the remedy afforded by Congress was "constitutionally adequate," even though it was not an "equally effective substitute" for the judicial remedy sought. Justice Marshall, joined by Justice Blackmun, wrote a separate concurrence.

In Schweiker v. Chilicky, 487 U.S. 412 (1988), plaintiffs sued federal and state policymaking officials, alleging that defendants had denied them due process by adopting policies that resulted in the improper denials of disability benefits under the Social Security Act. The complaint sought equitable relief and damages for "emotional distress and for loss of food, shelter and other necessities proximately caused by [defendants'] denial of benefits." The Supreme Court declined to recognize a Bivens action, stressing that the Social Security Act provided an elaborate administrative and judicial remedy. While acknowledging that the statutory remedy permitted only the restoration of improperly denied benefits and that a Bivens remedy would offer the prospect of recovering damages for emotional distress or other hardships caused by the delay in awarding benefits, the Act nonetheless "provide[d] meaningful safeguards or remedies for the rights of persons situated as [plaintiffs] were." Justice Brennan (joined by Justices Marshall and Blackmun) dissented.

For analogous reasons, Hui v. Castaneda, 559 U.S. 799 (2010), rejected a Bivens claim alleging that Public Health Service (PHS) officials had shown "deliberate indifference" to Casteneda's "serious medical needs," in violation of the Fifth, Eighth, and Fourteenth Amendments, while he was in the custody of U.S. Immigration and Customs Enforcement (ICE). Justice Sotomayor for a unanimous Court explained that the Bivens action was precluded by 42 U.S.C. § 233(a), which provides: "The Federal Tort Claims [FTCA] remedy against the United States * * * for damage for personal injury, including death, resulting from the performance of medical * * * or related functions * * * by any [PHS] commissioned officer or employee * * * while acting within the scope of his office or employment, shall be exclusive of any other civil action or proceeding by reason of the same subject-matter against the officer or employee." Although Carlson v. Green, Paragraph 3(b), *supra*, had extended Bivens to Eighth Amendment claims and held that the remedies supplied by the FTCA did *not* provide an equally effective alternative to a Bivens action, the Court in Castaneda nonetheless held it dispositive that § 233(a) "grants absolute immunity to PHS officers and employees" in the circumstances of the case. (No defendant in Carlson had invoked that immunity.)

(5) Special Factors Counseling Hesitation. The Court has also declined to recognize Bivens actions when "special factors [might] counsel[ ] hesitation [even] in the absence of affirmative action by Congress."

(a) The most prominent cases implicating "special factors" have involved claims against military officers. In Chappell v. Wallace, 462 U.S. 296 (1983), the Court unanimously held that a constitutional claim for race discrimination by Navy enlisted men against their superior officers could not be maintained, stating that "the unique disciplinary structure of the Military Establishment and Congress' activity in the field constitute 'special factors' which dictate that it would be inappropriate to provide enlisted military personnel a Bivens-type remedy against their superior officers." The activity of Congress to which the Court referred embraced "a comprehensive internal system of justice to regulate military life" that included procedures "for the review and remedy of complaints and grievances such as those presented by respondents." The Court said nothing about that system's effectiveness.

In United States v. Stanley, 483 U.S. 669 (1987), a former servicemember sued military officers and civilians for injuries resulting from the administration to him of the drug LSD without his consent, as part of an army experiment. The Court held, 5–4, that the special factors found in Chappell "extend beyond the situation in which an officer-subordinate relationship exists, and require abstention in the inferring of Bivens actions * * * for injuries that 'arise out of or are in the course of activity incident to [military] service'" (quoting Feres v. United States, 340 U.S. 135 (1950)). Dissenting in part, Justice O'Connor contended that "conduct of the type alleged in this case is so far beyond the bounds of human decency that as a matter of law it simply cannot be considered a part of the military mission." Justice Brennan's partial dissent, joined by Justice Marshall and in part by Justice Stevens, distinguished Chappell and argued that unlike in that case, no intramilitary system "'provides for the * * * remedy' of Stanley's complaint" (quoting Chappell).

(b) In Correctional Services Corp. v. Malesko, 534 U.S. 61 (2001), a closely divided Court declined to extend Bivens to an Eighth Amendment claim brought by a plaintiff serving a sentence in federal prison who challenged his treatment by a private contractor that operated the prison for the federal Bureau of Prisons. Chief Justice Rehnquist's opinion for the majority emphasized, among other things, the Court's consistent refusal to extend Bivens since Carlson and the fact that Malesko could pursue administrative remedies with the Bureau of Prisons or sue the officials for negligence under state tort law, which (unlike in Bivens) was not inconsistent with or hostile to a constitutional remedy. Concurring and joined by Justice Thomas, Justice Scalia argued in favor of "abandon[ing]" implying causes of action in the Bivens line, "since an 'implication' imagined in the Constitution can presumably not even be repudiated by Congress." Writing for four dissenters, Justice Stevens emphasized that, contrary to the majority's position, "Bivens and its progeny [were not] cases in which plaintiffs lacked '*any alternative remedy*.'"

(c) The Court in Wilkie v. Robbins, 551 U.S. 557 (2007), applied the "special factors" analysis to reject claims brought by a rancher (Robbins) against federal Bureau of Land Management (BLM) officials for alleged retaliation against his property rights after he refused to re-grant an easement that the BLM had forfeited by failing to record it. The Court noted the existence of "administrative" and "ultimately judicial" remedies for the government's alleged wrongs and stressed the "difficulty in defining a workable cause of action" to describe Robbins' claim. Because the BLM could legitimately make some efforts to induce Robbins to grant an easement, the Court concluded that Robbins's claim boiled down to the proposition "that defendants simply demanded too much and went too far." The relative unworkability of that standard, the Court said, "counts against recognizing freestanding liability in a case like this." Finally, the Court emphasized that "a Bivens action to redress retaliation against those who resist Government impositions on their property rights would invite claims in every sphere of legitimate governmental action affecting property interests, from negotiating tax claim settlements to enforcing Occupational Safety and Health Administration regulations." Justice Ginsburg, joined by Justice Stevens, dissented.[2]

INTRODUCTION TO THE MODERN BIVENS DOCTRINE

In more recent cases, the Court has expressed increasing doubt about the legitimacy of the Bivens enterprise and has called for yet greater deference to the role of Congress in deciding when individuals may sue in this context.

Ziglar v. Abbasi

582 U.S. 120 (2017).

This case arose from the detention of the respondents in the wake of the terrorist attacks of September 11, 2001, and led the Court to place renewed emphasis on the "special factors" analysis developed in prior cases. Government officials arrested respondents on immigration charges and then detained them without bail in a maximum-security facility under a "hold-until-cleared policy" that applied to individuals whom the FBI deemed of potential interest to the investigation of terrorism. Respondents—all of whom were of Arab or South Asian descent and five of whom were Muslim—filed a Bivens action against three officials of the U.S. Department of Justice

---

[2] For other cases declining to recognize a non-statutory right to sue, see Minneci v. Pollard, 565 U.S. 118 (2012) (Bivens action was not available against employees of a privately operated federal prison alleged to have violated the Eighth Amendment); Ashcroft v. Iqbal, 556 U.S. 662 (2009) (rejecting respondeat superior liability under Bivens); Federal Deposit Insurance Corp. v. Meyer, 510 U.S. 471 (1994) (rejecting a Bivens action against the FDIC for due process property right arising from allegedly wrongful discharge).

and two wardens of the federal facility at which respondents had been held. Respondents sought damages on that grounds that the petitioners had (1) held them in "harsh pretrial conditions for a punitive purpose," in violation of substantive due process; (2) singled them out because of their "race, religion, or national origin," contrary to the equal protection component of the Fifth Amendment; (3) subjected them to strip searches "without any legitimate penological interest," in contravention of the Fourth and Fifth Amendments; and (4) knowingly permitted the guards to abuse them, again in violation of due process.

In an opinion for the Court (joined by Chief Justice Roberts and Justices Thomas and Alito), Justice Kennedy concluded that a Bivens action did not lie for respondents' claims. Noting that Bivens was the product of a time in which the Court more freely recognized statutory implied rights of action, Justice Kennedy explained that the Court today thinks "separation-of-powers principles are or should be central to the analysis" in both contexts. "The question is 'who should decide' whether to provide for a damages remedy, Congress or the courts? The answer most often will be Congress." While not overruling Bivens, the Court made clear that "expanding the Bivens remedy is now a 'disfavored' judicial activity." It held that when asked to extend Bivens to a new context, it would ask "whether the Judiciary is well suited, absent congressional action or instruction, to consider and weigh the costs and benefits of allowing a damages action to proceed." In this case, even though the claims were at some level related to those recognized under Bivens and its progeny, the Court reasoned that the challenged actions—undertaken "pursuant to a high-level executive policy created in the wake of a major terrorist attack on American soil"—in fact bore "little resemblance" to previously recognized Bivens claims. More generally, the Court concluded that "special factors" counseled hesitation against extending Bivens to respondents' claims against large-scale executive policy concerning "sensitive issues of national security." The Court found it "telling" that Congress has not prescribed liability for post-9/11 detention policy even though the USA PATRIOT Act required the Department of Justice to provide Congress with periodic reports on civil rights and civil liberties abuses in the fight against terrorism.

In dissent, Justice Breyer (joined by Justice Ginsburg) reasoned that the Court had previously recognized implied rights of action for unlawful searches and seizures, invidious discrimination, and unconstitutional conditions of confinement. Justice Breyer further argued that, although the Constitution vests "primary power" over national security in the political branches, it "also delegates to the Judiciary the duty to protect an individual's fundamental constitutional rights." It followed, in his view, that the judiciary had a proper "role to play" in crafting remedies when national security interests and individual rights conflict. The Court, he added, could rely on doctrines of qualified immunity, heightened pleading, and tailored discovery to mitigate potential intrusions upon national security interests. (Justices Sotomayor, Kagan, and Gorsuch did not participate in the case.)

Notably, the Court did not face a situation in which its refusal to recognize a non-statutory right to sue top officials in the Department of

Justice would deprive the individuals of all redress. To the contrary, the Court acknowledged that claims might well proceed against the warden and line officers at the detention facility, either under the Bivens doctrine or the FTCA. In Hernández v. Mesa, the next principal case, however, the Court clarified that it understood the denial of Bivens relief to foreclose all redress.

Hernández v. Mesa

589 U.S. 93 (2020).
Certiorari to the United States Court of Appeals for the Fifth Circuit.

■ JUSTICE ALITO delivered the opinion of the Court.

We are asked in this case to extend Bivens v. Six Unknown Fed. Narcotics Agents, 403 U.S. 388 (1971), and create a damages remedy for a cross-border shooting. As we have made clear in many prior cases, however, the Constitution's separation of powers requires us to exercise caution before extending Bivens to a new "context," and a claim based on a cross-border shooting arises in a context that is markedly new. Unlike any previously recognized Bivens claim, a cross-border shooting claim has foreign relations and national security implications. In addition, Congress has been notably hesitant to create claims based on allegedly tortious conduct abroad. Because of the distinctive characteristics of cross-border shooting claims, we refuse to extend *Bivens* into this new field.

I

* * * Sergio Adrián Hernández Güereca, a 15-year-old Mexican national, was with a group of friends in a concrete culvert that separates El Paso, Texas, from Ciudad Juarez, Mexico. The border runs through the center of the culvert, which was designed to hold the waters of the Rio Grande River but is now largely dry. Border Patrol Agent Jesus Mesa, Jr., detained one of Hernández's friends who had run onto the United States' side of the culvert. After Hernández, who was also on the United States' side, ran back across the culvert onto Mexican soil, Agent Mesa fired two shots at Hernández; one struck and killed him on the other side of the border. * * *

The shooting quickly became an international incident, with the United States and Mexico disagreeing about how the matter should be handled. On the United States' side, the Department of Justice conducted an investigation. When it finished, the Department, while expressing regret over Hernández's death, concluded that Agent Mesa had not violated Customs and Border Patrol policy or training, and it declined to bring charges or take other action against him. Mexico was not and is not satisfied with the U.S. investigation. It requested that Agent Mesa be extradited to face criminal charges in a Mexican court, a request that the United States has denied.

Petitioners, Hernández's parents, were also dissatisfied and therefore brought suit for damages in the United States District Court for the Western District of Texas. Among other claims, they sought recovery of damages under Bivens, alleging that Mesa violated Hernández's Fourth and Fifth Amendment rights. [The District Court granted Mesa's motion to dismiss, and the Court of Appeals for the Fifth Circuit sitting en banc ruled that "the action presented a 'new context' for Bivens" and that "special factors counseled its hesitation."] * * *

We granted certiorari and now affirm.

II

* * * Bivens, Davis [v. Passman, 442 U.S. 228 (1979)], and Carlson [v. Green, 446 U.S. 14 (1980),] were the products of an era when the Court routinely inferred "causes of action" that were "not explicit" in the text of the provision that was allegedly violated. As [Ziglar v.] Abbasi[, 582 U.S. 120 (2017),] recounted:

> "During this '*ancien regime*,' . . . the Court assumed it to be a proper judicial function to 'provide such remedies as are necessary to make effective' a statute's purpose . . . . Thus, as a routine matter with respect to statutes, the Court would imply causes of action not explicit in the statutory text itself." *Ibid.* (quoting Alexander v. Sandoval, 532 U.S. 275, 287 (2001)).

Bivens extended this practice to claims based on the Constitution itself. Bivens, 403 U.S., at 402 (Harlan, J., concurring in judgment) (Court can infer availability of damages when, "in its view, damages are necessary to effectuate" the "policy underpinning the substantive provisio[n]").

In later years, we came to appreciate more fully the tension between this practice and the Constitution's separation of legislative and judicial power. The Constitution grants legislative power to Congress; this Court and the lower federal courts, by contrast, have only "judicial Power." Art. III, § 1. But when a court recognizes an implied claim for damages on the ground that doing so furthers the "purpose" of the law, the court risks arrogating legislative power. No law " 'pursues its purposes at all costs.' " * * * Thus, a lawmaking body that enacts a provision that creates a right or prohibits specified conduct may not wish to pursue the provision's purpose to the extent of authorizing private suits for damages. For this reason, finding that a damages remedy is implied by a provision that makes no reference to that remedy may upset the careful balance of interests struck by the lawmakers.

This problem does not exist when a common-law court, which exercises a degree of lawmaking authority, fleshes out the remedies available for a common-law tort. Analogizing Bivens to the work of a common-law court, petitioners and some of their *amici* make much of the fact that common-law claims against federal officers for intentional torts were once available. But Erie R. Co. v. Tompkins, 304 U.S. 64, 78 (1938), held that "[t]here is no federal general common law," and therefore federal courts today cannot fashion new claims in the way that they could before 1938. See Alexander, 532 U.S., at 287 (" 'Raising up causes of action where a statute has not created them may be a proper function for common law courts, but not for federal tribunals' ").

With the demise of federal general common law, a federal court's authority to recognize a damages remedy must rest at bottom on a statute enacted by Congress, see *id.*, at 286 ("private rights of action to enforce federal law must be created by Congress"), and no statute expressly creates a Bivens remedy. Justice Harlan's Bivens concurrence argued that this power is inherent in the grant of federal question jurisdiction, but our later cases have demanded a clearer manifestation of congressional intent.

In both statutory and constitutional cases, our watchword is caution. For example, in Jesner v. Arab Bank, PLC, 584 U.S. 241 (2018), we expressed doubt about our authority to recognize any causes of action not expressly created by Congress. See also Abbasi, 582 U.S., at 133–134 * * *.

In constitutional cases, we have been at least equally reluctant to create new causes of action. We have recognized that Congress is best positioned to evaluate "whether, and the extent to which, monetary and other liabilities should be imposed upon individual officers and employees of the Federal Government" based on constitutional torts. Abbasi, 582 U.S., at 134. We have stated that expansion of Bivens is "a 'disfavored' judicial activity," *id.*, at 135, and have gone so far as to observe that if "the Court's three Bivens cases [had] been . . . decided today," it is doubtful that we would have reached the same result. And for almost 40 years, we have consistently rebuffed requests to add to the claims allowed under Bivens [citing cases].

When asked to extend Bivens, we engage in a two-step inquiry. We first inquire whether the request involves a claim that arises in a "new context" or involves a "new category of defendants." Correctional Svcs. Corp. v. Malesko, 534 U.S. 61, 68 (2001). And our understanding of a "new context" is broad. We regard a context as "new" if it is "different in a meaningful way from previous Bivens cases decided by this Court." Abbasi, 582 U.S., at 139.

When we find that a claim arises in a new context, we proceed to the second step and ask whether there are any " ' "special factors [that] counse[l] hesitation" ' " about granting the extension. If there are—that is, if we have reason to pause before applying Bivens in a new context or to a new class of defendants—we reject the request.

We have not attempted to "create an exhaustive list" of factors that may provide a reason not to extend Bivens, but we have explained that "central to [this] analysis" are "separation-of-powers principles." Abbasi, 582 U.S., at 135. We thus consider the risk of interfering with the authority of the other branches, and we ask whether "there are sound reasons to think Congress might doubt the efficacy or necessity of a damages remedy," *id.*, at 137, and "whether the Judiciary is well suited, absent congressional action or instruction, to consider and weigh the costs and benefits of allowing a damages action to proceed," *id.* at 136.

III

A

The Bivens claims in this case assuredly arise in a new context. Petitioners contend that their Fourth and Fifth Amendment claims do not involve a new context because Bivens and Davis involved claims under those same two amendments, but that argument rests on a basic misunderstanding of what our cases mean by a new context. A claim may arise in a new context even if it is based on the same constitutional provision as a claim in a case in which a damages remedy was previously recognized. And once we look beyond the constitutional provisions invoked in Bivens, Davis, and the present case, it is glaringly obvious that petitioners' claims involve a new context, *i.e.*, one that is meaningfully different. Bivens concerned an allegedly unconstitutional arrest and search carried out in New York City; Davis concerned alleged sex discrimination on Capitol Hill. There is a world of difference between those claims and petitioners' cross-border shooting claims, where "the risk of disruptive intrusion by the Judiciary into the functioning of other branches" is significant.

Because petitioners assert claims that arise in a new context, we must proceed to the next step and ask whether there are factors that counsel hesitation. As we will explain, there are multiple, related factors that raise warning flags.

B

The first is the potential effect on foreign relations. "The political branches, not the Judiciary, have the responsibility and institutional capacity to weigh foreign-policy concerns." Jesner, 584 U.S., at 265. Indeed, we have said that "matters relating 'to the conduct of foreign relations ... are so exclusively entrusted to the political branches of government as to be largely immune from judicial inquiry or interference.'" Haig v. Agee, 453 U.S. 280, 292 (1981). "Thus, unless Congress specifically has provided otherwise, courts traditionally have been reluctant to intrude upon the authority of the Executive in [these matters]." Department of Navy v. Egan, 484 U.S. 518, 530 (1988). We must therefore be especially wary before allowing a Bivens remedy that impinges on this arena.

A cross-border shooting is by definition an international incident; it involves an event that occurs simultaneously in two countries and affects both countries' interests. Such an incident may lead to a disagreement between those countries, as happened in this case.

The United States, through the Executive Branch, which has " 'the lead role in foreign policy,' " Medellín v. Texas, 552 U.S. 491, 524 (2008) (alteration omitted), has taken the position that this incident should be handled in a particular way—namely, that Agent Mesa should not face charges in the United States nor be extradited to stand trial in Mexico. * * *

The Government of Mexico has taken a different view of what should be done. It has requested that Agent Mesa be extradited for criminal prosecution in a Mexican court under Mexican law, and it has supported petitioners' Bivens suit. * * *

Both the United States and Mexico have legitimate and important interests that may be affected by the way in which this matter is handled. The United States has an interest in ensuring that agents assigned the difficult and important task of policing the border are held to standards and judged by procedures that satisfy United States law and do not undermine the agents' effectiveness and morale. Mexico has an interest in exercising sovereignty over its territory and in protecting and obtaining justice for its nationals. It is not our task to arbitrate between them.

In the absence of judicial intervention, the United States and Mexico would attempt to reconcile their interests through diplomacy—and that has occurred. The broad issue of violence along the border, the occurrence of crossborder shootings, and this particular matter have been addressed through diplomatic channels. In 2014, Mexico and the United States established a joint Border Violence Prevention Council, and the two countries have addressed cross-border shootings through the United States-Mexico bilateral Human Rights Dialogue. Following the Justice Department investigation in the present case, the United States reaffirmed its commitment to "work with the Mexican government within existing mechanisms and agreements to prevent future incidents." DOJ Press Release.

For these reasons, petitioners' assertion that their claims have "nothing to do with the substance or conduct of U.S. foreign . . . policy" is plainly wrong.

C

Petitioners are similarly incorrect in deprecating the Fifth Circuit's conclusion that the issue here implicates an element of national security.

One of the ways in which the Executive protects this country is by attempting to control the movement of people and goods across the border, and that is a daunting task. * * *

Unfortunately, there is also a large volume of illegal cross-border traffic. During the last fiscal year, approximately 850,000 persons were apprehended attempting to enter the United States illegally from Mexico, and large quantities of drugs were smuggled across the border.

In addition, powerful criminal organizations operating on both sides of the border present a serious law enforcement problem for both countries.

On the United States' side, the responsibility for attempting to prevent the illegal entry of dangerous persons and goods rests primarily with the U.S. Customs and Border Protection Agency, and one of its main responsibilities is to "detect, respond to, and interdict terrorists, drug smugglers and traffickers, human smugglers and traffickers, and other persons who may undermine the security of the United States." 6 U.S.C. § 211(c)(5). While Border Patrol agents often work miles from the border, some, like Agent Mesa, are stationed right at the border and have the responsibility of attempting to prevent illegal entry. For these reasons, the conduct of agents positioned at the border has a clear and strong connection to national security, as the Fifth Circuit understood.

Petitioners protest that " 'shooting people who are just walking down a street in Mexico' " does not involve national security, but that misses the point. The question is not whether national security requires such conduct—of course, it does not—but whether the Judiciary should alter the framework established by the political branches for addressing cases in which it is alleged that lethal force was unlawfully employed by an agent at the border.

We have declined to extend Bivens where doing so would interfere with the system of military discipline created by statute and regulation, and a similar consideration is applicable here. Since regulating the conduct of agents at the border unquestionably has national security implications, the risk of undermining border security provides reason to hesitate before extending Bivens into this field.

D

Our reluctance to take that step is reinforced by our survey of what Congress has done in statutes addressing related matters. We frequently "look to analogous statutes for guidance on the appropriate boundaries of judge-made causes of action." * * * Accordingly, it is "telling" that Congress has repeatedly declined to authorize the award of damages for injury inflicted outside our borders.

A leading example is 42 U.S.C. § 1983, which permits the recovery of damages for constitutional violations by officers acting under color of *state* law. We have described Bivens as a "more limited" "federal analog" to § 1983. Hartman v. Moore, 547 U.S. 250, 254, n.2 (2006). It is therefore instructive that Congress chose to make § 1983 available only to "citizen[s] of the United States or other person[s] within the jurisdiction thereof." It would be "anomalous to impute . . . a judicially implied cause of action beyond the bounds [Congress has] delineated for [a] comparable express caus[e] of action." Thus, the limited scope of § 1983 weighs against recognition of the Bivens claim at issue here

Section 1983's express limitation to the claims brought by citizens and persons subject to United States jurisdiction is especially significant, but even if this explicit limitation were lacking, we would presume that § 1983 did not apply abroad. We presume that statutes do not apply extraterritorially to "ensure that the Judiciary does not erroneously adopt an interpretation of U.S. law that carries foreign policy consequences not clearly intended by the political branches." Kiobel v. Royal Dutch Petroleum Co., 569 U.S. 108, 116 (2013).

If this danger provides a reason for caution when Congress has enacted a statute but has not provided expressly whether it applies abroad, we have even greater reason for hesitation in deciding whether to extend a judge-made cause of action beyond our borders. "[T]he danger of unwarranted judicial interference in the conduct of foreign policy is magnified" where "the question is not what Congress has done but instead what courts may do." Kiobel, 569 U.S., at 116. Where Congress has not spoken at all, the likelihood of impinging on its foreign affairs authority is especially acute.

Congress's treatment of ordinary tort claims against federal officers is also revealing. As petitioners and their *amici* stress, the traditional way in which civil litigation addressed abusive conduct by federal officers was by subjecting them to liability for common-law torts. For many years, such claims could be raised in state or federal court, and this Court occasionally considered tort suits against federal officers for extraterritorial injuries. See, *e.g.*, Mitchell v. Harmony, 13 How. 115 (1852) (affirming award in trespass suit brought by U.S. citizen against U.S. Army officer who seized personal property in Mexico during the Mexican-American war). After Erie, federal common-law claims were out, but we recognized the continuing viability of state-law tort suits against federal officials as recently as Westfall v. Erwin, 484 U.S. 292 (1988).

In response to that decision, Congress passed the so-called Westfall Act, formally the Federal Employees Liability Reform and Tort Compensation Act of 1988, 28 U.S.C. § 2679. That Act makes the Federal Tort Claims Act (FTCA) "the exclusive remedy for most claims against Government employees arising out of their official conduct." Hui v. Castaneda, 559 U.S. 799, 806 (2010).[9] Thus, a person injured by a federal employee may seek recovery directly from the United States under the FTCA, but the FTCA bars "[a]ny claim arising in a foreign country." The upshot is that claims that would otherwise permit the recovery of damages are barred if the injury occurred abroad.

Yet another example is provided by the Torture Victim Protection Act of 1991, note following 28 U.S.C. § 1350, which created a cause of

---

[9]   The Act also permits claims "brought for a violation of the Constitution." 28 U.S.C. § 2679(b)(2)(A). By enacting this provision, Congress made clear that it was not attempting to abrogate Bivens, but the provision certainly does not suggest, as one of petitioners' amici contends, that Congress "intended for a robust enforcement of Bivens remedies." Instead, the provision simply left Bivens where it found it. It is not a license to create a new Bivens remedy in a context we have never before addressed, see Correctional Services Corp. v. Malesko, 534 U.S. 61, 68 (2001).

action that may be brought by an alien in a U.S. court under the Alien Tort Statute, § 1350. Under the Torture Victim Protection Act, a damages action may be brought by or on behalf of a victim of torture or an extrajudicial killing carried out by a person who acted under the authority of a foreign state. Consequently, this provision, which is often employed to seek redress for acts committed abroad, cannot be used to sue a United States officer.

These statutes form a pattern that is important for present purposes. When Congress has enacted statutes creating a damages remedy for persons injured by United States Government officers, it has taken care to preclude claims for injuries that occurred abroad.

Instead, when Congress has provided compensation for injuries suffered by aliens outside the United States, it has done so by empowering Executive Branch officials to make payments under circumstances found to be appropriate. Thus, the Foreign Claims Act, 10 U.S.C. § 2734, first enacted during World War II, ch. 645, 55 Stat. 880, allows the Secretary of Defense to appoint claims commissions to settle and pay claims for personal injury and property damage resulting from the noncombat activities of the Armed Forces outside this country. § 2734(a). Similarly, § 2734a allows the Secretary of Defense and the Secretary of Homeland Security to make payments pursuant to "an international agreement which provides for the settlement or adjudication and cost sharing of claims against the United States" that arise out of "acts or omissions" of the Armed Forces.

This pattern of congressional action—refraining from authorizing damages actions for injury inflicted abroad by Government officers, while providing alternative avenues for compensation in some situations— gives us further reason to hesitate about extending Bivens in this case.

E

In sum, this case features multiple factors that counsel hesitation about extending Bivens, but they can all be condensed to one concern— respect for the separation of powers. * * * To avoid upsetting the delicate web of international relations, we typically presume that even congressionally crafted causes of action do not apply outside our borders. These concerns are only heightened when judges are asked to fashion constitutional remedies. Congress, which has authority in the field of foreign affairs, has chosen not to create liability in similar statutes, leaving the resolution of extraterritorial claims brought by foreign nationals to executive officials and the diplomatic process.

Congress's decision not to provide a judicial remedy does not compel us to step into its shoes. "The absence of statutory relief for a constitutional violation . . . does not by any means necessarily imply that courts should award money damages against the officers responsible for the violation." Schweiker v. Chilicky, 487 U.S. 412, 421–422 (1988).

When evaluating whether to extend Bivens, the most important question "is 'who should decide' whether to provide for a damages remedy, Congress or the courts?" Abbassi, 582 U.S. at 135. The correct "answer most often will be Congress." *Ibid.* That is undoubtedly the answer here.

* * *

The judgment of the United States Court of Appeals for the Fifth Circuit is affirmed.

It is so ordered.

■ JUSTICE THOMAS, with whom JUSTICE GORSUCH joins, concurring.

* * * I [join the Court's opinion but] write separately because, in my view, the time has come to consider discarding the Bivens doctrine altogether. The foundation for Bivens—the practice of creating implied causes of action in the statutory context—has already been abandoned. And the Court has consistently refused to extend the Bivens doctrine for nearly 40 years, even going so far as to suggest that Bivens and its progeny were wrongly decided. *Stare decisis* provides no "veneer of respectability to our continued application of [these] demonstrably incorrect precedents." To ensure that we are not "perpetuat[ing] a usurpation of the legislative power," we should reevaluate our continued recognition of even a limited form of the Bivens doctrine. * * *

■ JUSTICE GINSBURG, with whom JUSTICE BREYER, JUSTICE SOTOMAYOR, and JUSTICE KAGAN join, dissenting.

* * * Rogue U.S. officer conduct falls within a familiar, not a "new," Bivens setting. Even if the setting could be characterized as "new," plaintiffs lack recourse to alternative remedies, and no "special factors" counsel against a Bivens remedy. Neither U.S. foreign policy nor national security is in fact endangered by the litigation. Moreover, concerns attending the application of our law to conduct occurring abroad are not involved, for plaintiffs seek the application of U.S. law to conduct occurring inside our borders. I would therefore hold that the plaintiffs' complaint crosses the Bivens threshold. * * *

III

Plaintiffs' Bivens action arises in a setting akin to Bivens itself. * * *

The only salient difference here: the fortuity that the bullet happened to strike Hernández on the Mexican side of the embankment. But Hernández's location at the precise moment the bullet landed should not matter one whit. After all, "[t]he purpose of Bivens is to deter the *officer*." Ziglar v. Abbasi, 582 U.S. 120, 140 (2017). And primary conduct constrained by the Fourth Amendment is an *officer*'s unjustified resort to excessive force. Mesa's allegedly unwarranted deployment of deadly force occurred on United States soil. It scarcely makes sense for a remedy trained on deterring rogue officer conduct to turn upon a happenstance subsequent to the conduct—a bullet landing in one half of a culvert, not the other. * * *

IV

Even accepting, *arguendo*, that the setting in this case could be characterized as "new," there is still no good reason why Hernández's parents should face a closed courtroom door. As in Bivens, plaintiffs lack recourse to alternative remedies. And not one of the "special factors" the Court identifies weigh any differently based on where a bullet happens to land. * * *

B

The special factors featured by the Court relate, in the main, to foreign policy and national security. But, as suggested earlier, no policies or policymakers are challenged in this case. Plaintiffs target the rogue actions of a rank-and-file law enforcement officer acting in violation of rules controlling his office. See 8 CFR § 287.8(a)(2)(ii) (2019) (limiting use of deadly force). The situation here presented resembles cases Abbasi distinguished—cases involving "individual instances of . . . law enforcement overreach." 582 U.S., at 144.

The Court nevertheless asserts that the instant suit has a "potential effect on foreign relations" because it invites courts "to arbitrate between" the United States and Mexico. Plaintiffs, however, have brought a civil damages action, no different from one a federal court would entertain had the fatal shot hit Hernández before he reached the Mexican side of the border. True, cross-border shootings spark bilateral discussion, but so too does a range of smuggling and other border-related issues that courts routinely address "concurrently with whatever diplomacy may also be addressing them." The Government has identified no deleterious effect on diplomatic negotiations in any case after the Ninth Circuit held that the mother of a boy killed in a cross-border shooting could institute a Bivens action.

Moreover, the Court, in this case, cannot escape a "potential effect on foreign relations," by declining to recognize a Bivens action. As the Mexican Government alerted the Court: "[R]efus[al] to consider [Hernández's] parents' claim on the merits . . . is what has the potential to negatively affect international relations." * * *

The Court also asserts, as cause for hesitation, "the risk of undermining border security." But the Court speaks with generality of the national-security involvement of Border Patrol officers. It does not home in on how a Bivens suit for an unjustified killing would in fact undermine security at the border. Abbasi cautioned against invocations of national security of this very order: "[N]ational-security concerns must not become a talisman used to ward off inconvenient claims—a 'label' used to cover a multitude of sins." 582 U.S., at 143. Instructions regulating Border Patrol agents tell them to guard against deploying unjustified deadly force. Given that instruction, I do not grasp how allowing a Bivens action here would intrude upon the political branches' national-security prerogatives.

Congress, although well aware of the Court's opinion in Bivens, has not endeavored to dislodge the decision. The Court cites several statutes in support of the argument that affording a Bivens action to Hernández's parents would be inconsistent with measures Congress has taken. None of the cited statutes should stand in plaintiffs' way.

Section 1983 actions, the Court points out, are available only to "person[s] within the jurisdiction" of the United States. 42 U.S.C. § 1983. That statute has, as its provenance, Reconstruction-era policies aiming to secure to former slaves federal rights and to ward off state and local incursion on those rights. "It is inconceivable that . . . Congress [then] thought about (and deliberately excluded liability for) cross-border incidents involving federal officials."

The FTCA is also inapposite. Its exclusion of "claim[s] arising in a foreign country," 28 U.S.C. § 2680(k), reflects "Congress's unwilling[ness] to subject the United States to liabilities depending upon the laws of a foreign power." Sosa v. Alvarez-Machain, 542 U.S. 692, 707 (2004). Here, however, the suit arises under U.S. law. Even as the Westfall Act amended the FTCA to make it the "exclusive" remedy for scope-of-employment claims against Government officers, § 2679(b)(1), Congress carved out an exception for Bivens suits, § 2679(b)(2)(A) (excepting civil claims "brought for a violation of the Constitution of the United States"). The Torture Victim Protection Act of 1991 applies exclusively to wrongdoers acting under color of *foreign* law. 28 U.S.C. § 1350 Note. The conduct of federal and state officers is outside that Act's purview. * * *

V

Regrettably, the death of Hernández is not an isolated incident. One report reviewed over 800 complaints of alleged physical, verbal, or sexual abuse lodged against Border Patrol agents between 2009 and 2012; in 97% of the complaints resulting in formal decisions, no action was taken. According to *amici* former Customs and Border Protection officials, "the United States has not extradited a Border Patrol agent to stand trial in Mexico, and to [*amici's*] knowledge has itself prosecuted only one agent in a cross-border shooting." These *amici* warn that, "[w]ithout the possibility of civil liability, the unlikely prospect of discipline or criminal prosecution will not provide a meaningful deterrent to abuse at the border." In short, it is all too apparent that to redress injuries like the one suffered here, it is Bivens or nothing.

* * *

I resist the conclusion that "nothing" is the answer required in this case. I would reverse the Fifth Circuit's judgment and hold that plaintiffs can sue Mesa in federal court for violating their son's Fourth and Fifth Amendment rights.

Egbert v. Boule

596 U.S. 482 (2022).

Boule, a federal informant, alleged that a U.S. Border Patrol Agent unlawfully entered his property (an inn abutting the U.S.-Canada border often used by smugglers). After an exchange of words, the agent allegedly threw Boule against a vehicle in the midst of an enforcement action, and later retaliated by, among other things, prompting the Internal Revenue Service to audit him. Boule brought Bivens claims against the agent under the Fourth Amendment for excessive force and the First Amendment for unlawful retaliation.

In an opinion by Justice Thomas (joined by Chief Justice Roberts and Justices Alito, Kavanaugh, and Barrett), the Court rejected the Fourth Amendment claim for two independent reasons. First, after reducing the two-step test from Hernández to the question "whether there is any rational reason (even one) to think that Congress is better suited" to decide whether a damages action is appropriate, the Court concluded that Congress was better suited here because the case involved border security and, by extension, national security. Second, the Court explained that courts may not fashion a Bivens remedy "if Congress has already provided, or authorized the Executive to provide," an alternate remedial scheme. Here the executive branch's investigation of Egbert's actions and its provision of a grievance procedure sufficed to preclude a cause of action even though respondent claimed the grievance procedure lacked adequate process. The Court also ruled that a Bivens action can never lie for First Amendment retaliation because Congress is better suited than courts to weigh the social costs of such an action.[1]

Justice Sotomayor, joined by Justices Breyer and Kagan, dissented on the Fourth Amendment excessive force claim but concurred in the judgment on the First Amendment retaliation claim. Relying on the two-step inquiry from Hernández, she concluded that the Fourth Amendment claim should be recognized because the context was materially indistinguishable from Bivens, and in any event, there was no special factor because the case's mere proximity to the border raised no national security issue. But she agreed with the First Amendment ruling, albeit on the different ground that a First Amendment retaliation claim presents a special factor because it "raises line-drawing concerns similar to those identified in Wilkie." More broadly, Justice Sotomayor criticized as contrary to Ziglar and Hernández—decisions that themselves had circumscribed the Bivens inquiry in new ways—the Court's holding that only Congress, not the courts, may weigh the costs and benefits of a new cause action. She further argued that the Court's "alternative remedies" analysis was flawed because the internal executive branch grievance procedure provided "no remedy at all." While criticizing the Court's relentless narrowing of the Bivens doctrine, Justice Sotomayor stated that

---

[1] Justice Gorsuch concurred in the judgment. He agreed with the majority's new formulation of the Bivens test but argued that because Congress is always better situated than courts "to weigh the value of a new cause of action," the Court should "return the power to create new causes of action" to Congress.

"lower courts should not read [the majority opinion] to render Bivens a dead letter."

NOTE ON THE DECLINE OF THE BIVENS DOCTRINE

In rejecting any Bivens remedy, the Court in Ziglar, Hernández, and Egbert makes clear that the doctrine has little prospect for growth. Indeed, the Egbert Court's unanimous rejection of the retaliation claim suggests that a similar disposition awaits any claim that arises in a new context or invokes a constitutional provision other than the Fourth, Fifth, and Eighth Amendments. See Egbert v. Boule, 596 U.S. 482, 502 (2022) ("[I]f we were called to decide Bivens today, we would decline to discover any implied causes of action in the Constitution.").

(1) Implied Causes of Action for Statutory and Constitutional Violations. The Supreme Court's trend away from implying causes of action for constitutional violations mirrors, and indeed purports to be justified by, the trend away from implying statutory causes of action. Is the analogy apt? Justice Kennedy for the majority in Ziglar acknowledged that the two contexts "involve[ ] somewhat different considerations": When "Congress enacts a statute, there are specific procedures and times for considering its terms and the proper means for its enforcement," and it is thus "logical * * * to assume that Congress will be explicit if it intends to create a private cause of action"; but with respect to the Constitution, "there is no single, specific congressional action to consider and interpret." He nonetheless justified the Court's "caution as to implied causes of actions" in the constitutional context as follows:

"[I]t is a significant step under separation-of-powers principles for a court to determine that it has the authority, under the judicial power, to create and enforce a cause of action for damages against federal officials in order to remedy a constitutional violation. When determining whether traditional equitable powers suffice to give necessary constitutional protection—or whether, in addition, a damages remedy is necessary—there are a number of economic and governmental concerns to consider. Claims against federal officials often create substantial costs, in the form of defense and indemnification. Congress, then, has a substantial responsibility to determine whether, and the extent to which, monetary and other liabilities should be imposed upon individual officers and employees of the Federal Government. In addition, the time and administrative costs attendant upon intrusions resulting from the discovery and trial process are significant factors to be considered."

Are these policy arguments persuasive? Injunctive suits can be expensive to litigate and prospective injunctive relief can often impose significant costs on the government. See Chap. IX, *infra*. Independent of this concern, why do federal courts need additional authority to vindicate constitutional rights by damages actions since they unquestionably have authority to issue injunctive relief for these purposes, and since Article III and federal jurisdictional statutes do not, as a general matter, distinguish these remedies?

(2) The Erosion of Common Law Alternatives. As noted, see pp. 925–926, *supra*, at the time Bivens came down, a plaintiff could pursue a common law tort action against federal officials to redress constitutional violations. Congress eliminated this possibility in an amendment to the FTCA known as the Westfall Act, 28 U.S.C. § 2679. That statute was a response to Westfall v. Erwin, 484 U.S. 292, 300 (1988), where the Court held that "absolute immunity does not shield official functions from state-law tort liability unless the challenged conduct is within the outer perimeter of an official's duties and is discretionary in nature," and that "absolute immunity does not attach simply because the precise conduct of the federal official is not prescribed by law." This holding exposed federal employees to personal liability for run-of-the-mill torts. But the Court stated that it would be "useful" for Congress to clarify the "standards governing the immunity of federal employees involved in state-law tort actions," and Congress obliged. The Westfall Act made the FTCA the "excusive" remedy for conduct that it covered except for "a civil action against an employee of the Government * * * which is brought for a violation of the Constitution of the United States." 28 U.S.C. § 2679(b). And the Court later read this provision to displace state tort claims against federal employees acting within the scope of their employment, even where the FTCA does not impose correlative liability on the federal government. See Gutierrez de Martinez v. Lamagno, 515 U.S. 417 (1995); United States v. Smith, 499 U.S. 160 (1991).

Counsel for the Hernández family argued that the FTCA's displacement of traditional common law remedies against federal officers made it vital for the Court to recognize the existence of a Bivens remedy for the cross-border shooting. The Court rejected this view. Instead of using the common law baseline of the nineteenth century to give content to the non-statutory Bivens doctrine, it reasoned that Erie had put an end to the old remedial system, and that the FTCA, limited as it was to torts in the United States, furnished an additional reason to refrain from affording victims a non-statutory remedy for constitutional violations in other countries.

Professor Vázquez argues these developments result in "a remedial regime far narrower than that which had prevailed for most of our history." He maintains that since the framers expected that common law damages remedies would be available to redress constitutional violations, the Court should preserve this expectation in the post-Erie era by crafting a federal common law right to damages for constitutional violations. Such federal common law is justified, he maintains, because, as with other federal common law doctrines, it implicates a unique federal interest that justifies federal courts to develop appropriate law unless and until Congress acts. The "pre-Erie regime of common-law remedies for constitutional violations by federal officials was much closer to a post-Erie regime that regards such remedies as having a federal-law status than a post-Erie regime that regards them as having a state-law status," he concludes. Vázquez, *Bivens and the Ancien Régime*, 96 Notre Dame L.Rev. 1923 (2021). See also Fallon, *Bidding Farewell to Constitutional Torts*, 107 Calif.L.Rev. 933, 989 (2019) ("With the

Westfall Act creating a substantially broadened category of victims of constitutional lawbreaking for whom it is Bivens actions or nothing, the historically well-grounded principle that damages remedies should normally be available to victims of constitutional misconduct ought to control."); Vladeck, *Constitutional Remedies in Federalism's Forgotten Shadow*, 107 Calif.L.Rev. 1043 (2019) (similar).

(3) Changing Conceptions of Remedial Adequacy. One indication of how dramatically the recent wave of Bivens cases departs from the cases closer to Bivens is the Court's differing attitude toward alternate forms of relief. In earlier cases such as Bush v. Lucas, p. 929, *supra*, and Schweicker v. Chilicky, p. 929, *supra*, the Court presumed the viability of a Bivens action and asked whether some alternative form of relief served as an effective substitute. In both instances, the petitioner had secured redress through alternative channels and was seeking more substantial compensation via a Bivens action. The rejection of non-statutory remedies there effectively deferred to a more tailored remedial scheme. Something similar occurs in connection with an evaluation of the implied displacement of remedies under § 1983. See Fitzgerald v. Barnstable School Comm., 555 U.S. 246 (2009). By contrast, in Hernández and Egbert v. Boule, the Court did not identify any such remedial substitute. Instead, it relied on administrative grievance processes and the uncertain prospect of gratuitous executive payments to justify, in part, a refusal to recognize a Bivens remedy. Hernández was expressly decided on the assumption that the family had no alternative judicially cognizable right to secure redress for the shooting. Compare Egbert, 596 U.S. at 498 ("[T]he question whether a given remedy is adequate is a legislative determination that must be left to Congress, not the federal courts. So long as Congress or the Executive has created a remedial process that it finds sufficient to secure an adequate level of deterrence [against unconstitutional conduct], the courts cannot second-guess that calibration by superimposing a Bivens remedy.").

(4) Critiques of the Decline of Bivens. For critiques of the state of Bivens jurisprudence after Hernández, see Kent, *Lessons for Bivens and Qualified Immunity Debates from Nineteenth-Century Damages Litigation Against Federal Officers*, 96 Notre Dame L.Rev. 1755 (2021); Sisk, *Recovering the Tort Remedy for Federal Official Wrongdoing*, 96 Notre Dame L.Rev. 1789 (2021); Schwartz, Reinert & Pfander, *Going Rogue: The Supreme Court's Newfound Hostility to Policy-Based Bivens Claims*, 96 Notre Dame L.Rev. 1835 (2021); Vladeck, *The Inconsistent Originalism of Judge-Made Remedies Against Federal Officials*, 96 Notre Dame L.Rev. 1869 (2021); Woolhandler & Collins, *Was Bivens Necessary?*, 96 Notre Dame L.Rev. 1893 (2021).

(5) Constitutional Common Law. Recall that the Court appears to have recognized a constitutional obligation on the part of the government (rather than government officials) to provide a monetary remedy in at least two settings: (a) actions under the Just Compensation Clause, see First English Evangelical Lutheran Church v. County of Los Angeles, 482 U.S. 304 (1987), p. 912, *supra*, and (b) actions seeking a refund of unconstitutionally exacted taxes, see McKesson Corp. v. Division of ABT, 496 U.S. 18 (1990), and Reich

v. Collins, 513 U.S. 106 (1994), p. 915, *supra*—at least when no adequate predeprivation remedy exists.[1] Although neither obligation is quite as clear-cut as it might be, see pp. 916–917, *supra*, insofar as those two lines of decision establish a constitutional right to compensatory relief, on what basis can the Court justify a refusal to provide a monetary remedy for violations of other constitutional provisions, especially as in Bivens and Hernández, when no other relief is available? Do the Due Process and Takings Clauses contemplate judicial remedies for monetary relief in ways that other constitutional provisions do not?

The Court's modern Bivens jurisprudence—which denies a judge-made right of action for constitutional violations even in cases where there are very thin alternative remedies (as in Egbert), or no remedies at all (as in Hernández)—assumes that the cause of action is not constitutionally compelled and that Congress rather than federal courts should take the lead in providing one. But if that is so, then by what authority do the federal courts recognize Bivens remedies in the absence of legislative authorization? Professor Monaghan, in *Foreword: Constitutional Common Law*, 89 Harv.L.Rev. 1 (1975), views Bivens as one example of what he terms "constitutional common law"—a body of judge-made law that implements constitutional guarantees rather than statutory provisions. Other examples noted by Monaghan include the Fourth Amendment's exclusionary rule and the invalidation of state statutes under the dormant Commerce Clause.

Unlike simple interpretations of the Constitution, which Congress cannot overturn, constitutional common law is subject to legislative modification or repeal precisely because it is not constitutionally required. Thus, for example, Congress responded to Banco Nacional de Cuba v. Sabbatino, 376 U.S. 398 (1964), p. 867, *supra*—a decision that was at least partially influenced by structural constitutional considerations—by narrowing the Court's federal common law rule. See p. 875, *supra*. What source of lawmaking power authorizes judicial development of a penumbra of supplemental, quasi-constitutional protection? If there is a valid source for constitutional common law, can that body of law adequately be distinguished from "real" constitutional law? For a critical response to Monaghan, see Schrock & Welsh, *Reconsidering the Constitutional Common Law*, 91 Harv.L.Rev. 1117 (1978). If Monaghan is correct that Bivens actions are at least constitutionally inspired, should the Court require a clear statement from Congress before finding legislative preclusion of a Bivens action? See Grey, *Preemption of Bivens Claims: How Clearly Must Congress Speak?*, 70 Wash.U.L.Q. 1087 (1992) (so arguing). See also Brown, *Letting Statutory Tails Wag Constitutional Dogs—Have the Bivens Dissenters Prevailed?*, 64 Ind.L.J. 263, 265 (1989).

(6) Should the Court Overrule Bivens? Can It? The Court has not extended Bivens to new fact situations since Carlsen v. Green in 1980, and the successively stricter tests announced in Ziglar, Hernández, and Boule give rise to serious doubt whether it ever will. Should the Court go further

---

[1]   And with the further possible qualification, not greatly significant in practice, that in cases of unconstitutional discrimination, retroactive tax increases on the favored class might substitute for refunds to the disfavored class.

and overrule Bivens and the two subsequent decisions recognizing implied constitutional causes of action, as Justices Thomas and Gorsuch have argued? The Bivens remedy is still technically available in cases factually close to Bivens, Davis, and Carlson, and is most robust in lower courts for Fourth amendment claims. See Pfander, Reinert, & Schwartz, *The Myth of Personal Liability: Who Pays When Bivens Claims Succeed*, 72 Stan.L.Rev. 561, 566 (2020) (noting that $18.9 million was paid to plaintiffs resulting from Bivens claims against Federal Bureau of Prisons officials from 2007–2017); but see Schwartz, Reinert, & Pfander, *Going Rogue*, Paragraph (4), *supra*, at 1839 ("[A]t least in some circuits, Ziglar appears to threaten the viability of even well-settled forms of Bivens liability.") As recently as Ziglar, the Court noted that it did "not inten[d] to cast doubt on the continued force, or even necessity, of Bivens in the search-and-seizure context in which it arose," and added that the "settled law of Bivens in this common and recurrent sphere of law enforcement, and the undoubted reliance upon it as a fixed principle in the law, are powerful reasons to retain it in that sphere."

Further, as Justice Sotomayor noted in dissent in Boule, Congress "has recognized and relied on the Bivens cause of action in creating and amending other remedies, including the FTCA." Recall that the Westfall Act reserved civil action remedies against a federal governmental employee "brought for a violation of the Constitution of the United States." See 28 U.S.C. § 2679(b)(2)(A). The Court in Hernández noted that "[b]y enacting this provision, Congress made clear that it was not attempting to abrogate Bivens," but rather "simply left Bivens where it found it." 589 U.S. at 111 n.9. Pfander & Baltmanis, *Rethinking Bivens: Legitimacy and Constitutional Adjudication*, 98 Geo.L.J. 117 (2009), have gone further and claimed that the Westfall Act "ratified" Bivens. See also Vázquez & Vladeck, *State Law, the Westfall Act, and the Nature of the Bivens Question*, 161 U.Pa.L.Rev. 509 (2013) (drawing similar inferences from the Westfall Act). How do these varying interpretations of the Westfall Act's impact on Bivens affect the Court's discretion to overrule Bivens? If the Westfall Act affirmatively "ratified" the Bivens framework, should the Court assume that the Act ratified the framework as of 1971, when Bivens was decided, or as of 1988 when the Court had already begun its retrenchment in cases such as Bush v. Lucas, Chappell v. Wallace, and United States v. Stanley, see pp. 929–930, *supra*?

INTRODUCTORY NOTE ON CAUSES OF ACTION UNDER THE ALIEN TORT STATUTE

The Alien Tort Statute (ATS), 28 U.S.C. § 1350, a law enacted by the First Congress in the Judiciary Act of 1789, today gives district courts "original jurisdiction of any civil action by an alien for a tort only, committed in violation of the law of nations or a treaty of the United States," 28 U.S.C. § 1350. Judge Friendly called the ATS "a kind of legal Lohengrin; although it has been with us since the first Judiciary Act, no one seems to know whence it came." IIT v. Vencap, Ltd., 519 F.2d 1001, 1015 (2d Cir.1975). Prior to 1980 federal courts had found jurisdiction under the statute in only a handful of cases.

The statute became a prominent source of international human rights litigation in Filartiga v. Pena-Irala, 630 F.2d 876 (2d Cir.1980), which held that § 1350 provided jurisdiction over a claim by Paraguayan citizens against a former Paraguayan official (served while in the United States) for acts of torture allegedly committed in Paraguay. The court rejected the argument that premising subject matter jurisdiction on § 1350 violated Article III because there was neither a federal question nor the requisites for party-based jurisdiction: "The constitutional basis for the Alien Tort Statute is the law of nations, which has always been part of the federal common law." Filartiga did not decide what law governed the lawsuit, however, and suggested that under the proper choice-of-law analysis, Paraguayan tort law might apply.

Filartiga sparked a wave of human rights lawsuits that were initially brought primarily, as in Filartiga, by alien plaintiffs against alien defendants for human rights abuses committed outside the United States.[1] The decision and its progeny provoked a wide-ranging debate over the proper interpretation of the ATS and the proper Article III basis for federal jurisdiction in ATS cases that did not present distinctive grounds for federal question jurisdiction.[2] This debate unfolded for almost a quarter century until the Court resolved many questions about the ATS's meaning in the next principal case, Sosa v. Alvarez-Machain, a decision that implicates many of the themes of Chapters VI and VII.

———————

Sosa v. Alvarez-Machain

542 U.S. 692 (2004).
Certiorari to the United States Court of Appeals for the Ninth Circuit.

[Petitioner Sosa and other Mexican nationals kidnapped respondent Alvarez, also a Mexican national, in Mexico pursuant to a plan developed by the U.S. Drug Enforcement Administration (DEA). They then brought

---

[1]   Two developments have limited the generative capacity of ATS litigation. The first is the relatively cautious approach the Court took toward the recognition of new federal common law rights of action under the ATS in the next principal case, Sosa v. Alvarez-Machain, 542 U.S. 692 (2004), and in Jesner v. Arab Bank PLC, 584 U.S. 241 (2018). The second development is the Court's determination in Kiobel v. Royal Dutch Petroleum Co., 569 U.S. 108 (2013), Paragraph (4), *infra*, that the ATS does not reach "violations of the law of nations occurring within the territory of a sovereign other than the United States." See Ewell, Hathaway & Nohle, *Has the Alien Tort Statute Made a Difference? A Historical, Empirical, and Normative Assessment*, 107 Cornell L.Rev. 1205 (2022).

[2]   See, for example, Bradley, *The Alien Tort Statute and Article III*, 42 Va.J.Int'l.L. 587 (2002); Bradley & Goldsmith, *The Current Illegitimacy of International Human Rights Litigation*, 66 Fordham L.Rev. 319, 357–63 (1997); Casto, *The Federal Courts' Protective Jurisdiction over Torts Committed in Violation of the Law of Nations*, 18 Conn.L.Rev. 467 (1986); Dodge, *The Constitutionality of the Alien Tort Statute: Some Observations on Text and Context*, 42 Va.J.Int'l.L. 687 (2002); Randall, *Federal Jurisdiction over International Law Claims: Inquiries into the Alien Tort Statute*, 18 N.Y.U.J.Int'l.L. & Pol. 1, 15–21 (1985); Sweeney, *A Tort Only in Violation of the Law of Nations*, 18 Hastings Int'l & Comp.L.Rev. 445 (1995).

him to stand trial in the United States for a DEA agent's torture and murder. After his acquittal, Alvarez claimed that Sosa violated customary international law prohibitions on arbitrary arrest and detention and sued him to recover damages under the Alien Tort Statute (ATS), 28 U.S.C. § 1350, which gives district courts "original jurisdiction of any civil action by an alien for a tort only, committed in violation of the law of nations or a treaty of the United States." Alvarez also sued the Government under the Federal Tort Claims Act (FTCA), 28 U.S.C. § 1346(b)(1), §§ 2671–2680. "The District Court granted the Government's motion to dismiss the FTCA claim, but awarded summary judgment and $25,000 in damages to Alvarez on the ATS claim. [The] Ninth Circuit then affirmed the ATS judgment, but reversed the dismissal of the FTCA claim." The Supreme Court granted certiorari on both issues. It dismissed the FTCA claim based on the statute's exception to waiver of sovereign immunity for claims "arising in a foreign country," 28 U.S.C. § 2680(k). What follows is the Court's analysis of the ATS claim.]

■ JUSTICE SOUTER delivered the opinion of the Court.

III

       * * *

A

* * * The parties and *amici* here advance radically different historical interpretations of [the ATS]. Alvarez says that the ATS was intended not simply as a jurisdictional grant, but as authority for the creation of a new cause of action for torts in violation of international law. We think that reading is implausible. As enacted in 1789, the ATS gave the district courts "cognizance" of certain causes of action, and the term bespoke a grant of jurisdiction, not power to mold substantive law. The fact that the ATS was placed in § 9 of the Judiciary Act, a statute otherwise exclusively concerned with federal-court jurisdiction, is itself support for its strictly jurisdictional nature. Nor would the distinction between jurisdiction and cause of action have been elided by the drafters of the Act or those who voted on it. * * * In sum, we think the statute was intended as jurisdictional in the sense of addressing the power of the courts to entertain cases concerned with a certain subject.

But holding the ATS jurisdictional raises a new question, this one about the interaction between the ATS at the time of its enactment and the ambient law of the era. Sosa would have it that the ATS was stillborn because there could be no claim for relief without a further statute expressly authorizing adoption of causes of action. *Amici* professors of federal jurisdiction and legal history take a different tack, that federal courts could entertain claims once the jurisdictional grant was on the books, because torts in violation of the law of nations would have been recognized within the common law of the time. We think history and practice give the edge to this latter position.

1

"When the United States declared their independence, they were bound to receive the law of nations, in its modern state of purity and refinement." Ware v. Hylton, 3 Dall. 199, 281 (1796) (Wilson, J.). In the years of the early Republic, this law of nations comprised two principal elements, the first covering the general norms governing the behavior of national states with each other * * *. This aspect of the law of nations thus occupied the executive and legislative domains, not the judicial.

The law of nations included a second, more pedestrian element, however, that did fall within the judicial sphere, as a body of judge-made law regulating the conduct of individuals situated outside domestic boundaries and consequently carrying an international savor. To Blackstone, the law of nations in this sense was implicated "in mercantile questions, such as bills of exchange and the like; in all marine causes, relating to freight, average, demurrage, insurances, bottomry . . .; [and] in all disputes relating to prizes, to shipwrecks, to hostages, and ransom bills." W. Blackstone, Commentaries on the Laws of England 67 (1769). The law merchant emerged from the customary practices of international traders and admiralty required its own transnational regulation. * * *

There was, finally, a sphere in which these rules binding individuals for the benefit of other individuals overlapped with the norms of state relationships. Blackstone referred to it when he mentioned three specific offenses against the law of nations addressed by the criminal law of England: violation of safe conducts, infringement of the rights of ambassadors, and piracy. 4 Commentaries 68. An assault against an ambassador, for example, impinged upon the sovereignty of the foreign nation and if not adequately redressed could rise to an issue of war. It was this narrow set of violations of the law of nations, admitting of a judicial remedy and at the same time threatening serious consequences in international affairs, that was probably on minds of the men who drafted the ATS with its reference to tort. * * *

3

* * * There is no record of congressional discussion about private actions that might be subject to the jurisdictional provision, or about any need for further legislation to create private remedies; there is no record even of debate on the section. * * * [D]espite considerable scholarly attention, it is fair to say that a consensus understanding of what Congress intended has proven elusive.

Still, the history does tend to support two propositions. First, there is every reason to suppose that the First Congress did not pass the ATS as a jurisdictional convenience to be placed on the shelf for use by a future Congress or state legislature that might, some day, authorize the creation of causes of action or itself decide to make some element of the law of nations actionable for the benefit of foreigners. The anxieties of the preconstitutional period cannot be ignored easily enough to think that the statute was not meant to have a practical effect. * * *

The second inference to be drawn from the history is that Congress intended the ATS to furnish jurisdiction for a relatively modest set of actions alleging violations of the law of nations. Uppermost in the legislative mind appears to have been offenses against ambassadors; violations of safe conduct were probably understood to be actionable; and individual actions arising out of prize captures and piracy may well have also been contemplated. But the common law appears to have understood only those three of the hybrid variety as definite and actionable, or at any rate, to have assumed only a very limited set of claims. * * *

IV

We think it is correct, then, to assume that the First Congress understood that the district courts would recognize private causes of action for certain torts in violation of the law of nations, though we have found no basis to suspect Congress had any examples in mind beyond those torts corresponding to Blackstone's three primary offenses: violation of safe conducts, infringement of the rights of ambassadors, and piracy. We assume, too, that no development in the two centuries from the enactment of § 1350 to the birth of the modern line of cases beginning with Filartiga v. Pena-Irala, 630 F.2d 876 (2d Cir.1980), has categorically precluded federal courts from recognizing a claim under the law of nations as an element of common law; Congress has not in any relevant way amended § 1350 or limited civil common law power by another statute. Still, there are good reasons for a restrained conception of the discretion a federal court should exercise in considering a new cause of action of this kind. Accordingly, we think courts should require any claim based on the present-day law of nations to rest on a norm of international character accepted by the civilized world and defined with a specificity comparable to the features of the 18th-century paradigms we have recognized. This requirement is fatal to Alvarez's claim.

A

A series of reasons argue for judicial caution when considering the kinds of individual claims that might implement the jurisdiction conferred by the early statute. First, the prevailing conception of the common law has changed since 1789 in a way that counsels restraint in judicially applying internationally generated norms. When § 1350 was enacted, the accepted conception was of the common law as "a transcendental body of law outside of any particular State but obligatory within it unless and until changed by statute." Black and White Taxicab & Transfer Co. v. Brown and Yellow Taxicab & Transfer Co., 276 U.S. 518, 533 (1928) (Holmes, J., dissenting). Now, however, in most cases where a court is asked to state or formulate a common law principle in a new context, there is a general understanding that the law is not so much found or discovered as it is either made or created. * * *

Second, along with, and in part driven by, that conceptual development in understanding common law has come an equally significant rethinking of the role of the federal courts in making it. Erie R. Co. v. Tompkins, 304 U.S. 64 (1938), was the watershed in which we denied the existence of any federal "general" common law, which largely withdrew to havens of specialty, some of them defined by express congressional authorization to devise a body of law directly. Elsewhere, this Court has thought it was in order to create federal common law rules in interstitial areas of particular federal interest. And although we have even assumed competence to make judicial rules of decision of particular importance to foreign relations, such as the act of state doctrine, see Banco Nacional de Cuba v. Sabbatino, 376 U.S. 398, 427 (1964), the general practice has been to look for legislative guidance before exercising innovative authority over substantive law. It would be remarkable to take a more aggressive role in exercising a jurisdiction that remained largely in shadow for much of the prior two centuries.

Third, this Court has recently and repeatedly said that a decision to create a private right of action is one better left to legislative judgment in the great majority of cases. Correctional Services Corp. v. Malesko, 534 U.S. 61, 68 (2001); Alexander v. Sandoval, 532 U.S. 275, 286–287 (2001). The creation of a private right of action raises issues beyond the mere consideration whether underlying primary conduct should be allowed or not, entailing, for example, a decision to permit enforcement without the check imposed by prosecutorial discretion. Accordingly, even when Congress has made it clear by statute that a rule applies to purely domestic conduct, we are reluctant to infer intent to provide a private cause of action where the statute does not supply one expressly. While the absence of congressional action addressing private rights of action under an international norm is more equivocal than its failure to provide such a right when it creates a statute, the possible collateral consequences of making international rules privately actionable argue for judicial caution.

Fourth, the subject of those collateral consequences is itself a reason for a high bar to new private causes of action for violating international law, for the potential implications for the foreign relations of the United States of recognizing such causes should make courts particularly wary of impinging on the discretion of the Legislative and Executive Branches in managing foreign affairs. It is one thing for American courts to enforce constitutional limits on our own State and Federal Governments' power, but quite another to consider suits under rules that would go so far as to claim a limit on the power of foreign governments over their own citizens, and to hold that a foreign government or its agent has transgressed those limits. Yet modern international law is very much concerned with just such questions, and apt to stimulate calls for vindicating private interests in § 1350 cases. Since many attempts by federal courts to craft remedies for the violation of new norms of international law would raise risks of adverse foreign policy consequences, they should be undertaken, if at all, with great caution. * * *

The fifth reason is particularly important in light of the first four. We have no congressional mandate to seek out and define new and debatable violations of the law of nations, and modern indications of congressional understanding of the judicial role in the field have not affirmatively encouraged greater judicial creativity. It is true that a clear mandate appears in the Torture Victim Protection Act of 1991, providing authority that "establishes an unambiguous and modern basis for" federal claims of torture and extrajudicial killing, H.R.Rep. No. 102–367, pt. 1, p. 3 (1991).* But that affirmative authority is confined to specific subject matter, and although the legislative history includes the remark that § 1350 should "remain intact to permit suits based on other norms that already exist or may ripen in the future into rules of customary international law," Congress as a body has done nothing to promote such suits. Several times, indeed, the Senate has expressly declined to give the federal courts the task of interpreting and applying international human rights law, as when its ratification of the International Covenant on Civil and Political Rights declared that the substantive provisions of the document were not self-executing.

B

These reasons argue for great caution in adapting the law of nations to private rights. * * *

Whereas Justice Scalia sees these developments as sufficient to close the door to further independent judicial recognition of actionable international norms, other considerations persuade us that the judicial power should be exercised on the understanding that the door is still ajar subject to vigilant doorkeeping, and thus open to a narrow class of international norms today. Erie did not in terms bar any judicial recognition of new substantive rules, no matter what the circumstances, and post-Erie understanding has identified limited enclaves in which federal courts may derive some substantive law in a common law way. For two centuries we have affirmed that the domestic law of the United States recognizes the law of nations. See, *e.g.*, Sabbatino, 376 U.S., at 423 ("[I]t is, of course, true that United States courts apply international law as a part of our own in appropriate circumstances"); The Paquete Habana, 175 U.S., at 700 ("International law is part of our law, and must be ascertained and administered by the courts of justice of appropriate jurisdiction, as often as questions of right depending upon it are duly

---

    *   [Ed.] The Torture Victim Protection Act of 1991 (TVPA), 106 Stat. 73 (1992) (codified at 28 U.S.C. § 1350 note), provides for a damages action against "an individual who, under actual or apparent authority, or color of law, of any foreign nation, subjects an individual to torture" or "extrajudicial killing." The TVPA is a substantive, not a jurisdictional, provision; suits under it may ordinarily be brought in federal court under 28 U.S.C. § 1331 or § 1350. The TVPA is broader than § 1350 in some respects (*e.g.*, it permits suit by American citizens as well as by aliens), but narrower in others (*e.g.*, it limits actionable violations to torture or extrajudicial killing under color of law).

presented for their determination"); The Nereide, 9 Cranch 388, 423 (1815) (Marshall, C. J.) ("[T]he Court is bound by the law of nations which is a part of the law of the land"). It would take some explaining to say now that federal courts must avert their gaze entirely from any international norm intended to protect individuals.

We think an attempt to justify such a position would be particularly unconvincing in light of what we know about congressional understanding bearing on this issue lying at the intersection of the judicial and legislative powers. The First Congress, which reflected the understanding of the framing generation and included some of the Framers, assumed that federal courts could properly identify some international norms as enforceable in the exercise of § 1350 jurisdiction. We think it would be unreasonable to assume that the First Congress would have expected federal courts to lose all capacity to recognize enforceable international norms simply because the common law might lose some metaphysical cachet on the road to modern realism. Later Congresses seem to have shared our view. The position we take today has been assumed by some federal courts for 24 years, ever since the Second Circuit decided Filartiga v. Pena-Irala, 630 F.2d 876 (2d Cir.1980) * * *. Congress, however, has not only expressed no disagreement with our view of the proper exercise of the judicial power, but has responded to its most notable instance by enacting legislation supplementing the judicial determination in some detail. *See supra* (discussing the Torture Victim Protection Act).

While we agree with Justice Scalia to the point that we would welcome any congressional guidance in exercising jurisdiction with such obvious potential to affect foreign relations, nothing Congress has done is a reason for us to shut the door to the law of nations entirely. It is enough to say that Congress may do that at any time (explicitly, or implicitly by treaties or statutes that occupy the field) just as it may modify or cancel any judicial decision so far as it rests on recognizing an international norm as such.[19]

C

We must still, however, derive a standard or set of standards for assessing the particular claim Alvarez raises, and for this case it suffices to look to the historical antecedents. Whatever the ultimate criteria for accepting a cause of action subject to jurisdiction under § 1350, we are persuaded that federal courts should not recognize private claims under

---

[19]   Our position does not, as Justice Scalia suggests, imply that every grant of jurisdiction to a federal court carries with it an opportunity to develop common law (so that the grant of federal-question jurisdiction would be equally as good for our purposes as § 1350). Section 1350 was enacted on the congressional understanding that courts would exercise jurisdiction by entertaining some common law claims derived from the law of nations; and we know of no reason to think that federal-question jurisdiction was extended subject to any comparable congressional assumption. Further, our holding today is consistent with the division of responsibilities between federal and state courts after Erie, as a more expansive common law power related to 28 U.S.C. § 1331 might not be.

federal common law for violations of any international law norm with less definite content and acceptance among civilized nations than the historical paradigms familiar when § 1350 was enacted. * * *

[Looking at a number of international and domestic law sources, the Court concludes that Alvarez's allegations against Sosa "violate[ ] no norm of customary international law so well defined as to support the creation of a federal remedy."]

The judgment of the Court of Appeals is

Reversed.

■ JUSTICE SCALIA, with whom THE CHIEF JUSTICE and JUSTICE THOMAS join, concurring in part and concurring in the judgment.

There is not much that I would add to the Court's detailed opinion, and only one thing that I would subtract: its reservation of a discretionary power in the Federal Judiciary to create causes of action for the enforcement of international-law-based norms. * * *

I

* * * At the time of its enactment, the ATS provided a federal forum in which aliens could bring suit to recover for torts committed in "violation of the law of nations." The law of nations that would have been applied in this federal forum was at the time part of the so-called general common law.

General common law was not federal law under the Supremacy Clause, which gave that effect only to the Constitution, the laws of the United States, and treaties. U.S. Const., Art VI, cl. 2. Federal and state courts adjudicating questions of general common law were not adjudicating questions of federal or state law, respectively—the general common law was neither. The nonfederal nature of the law of nations explains this Court's holding that it lacked jurisdiction in New York Life Ins. Co. v. Hendren, 92 U.S. 286 (1876), where it was asked to review a state-court decision regarding "the effect, under the general public law, of a state of sectional civil war upon [a] contract of life insurance." *Ibid.* Although the case involved "the general laws of war, as recognized by the law of nations applicable to this case," *ibid.*, it involved no federal question. The Court concluded: "The case, . . . having been presented to the court below for decision upon principles of general law alone, and it nowhere appearing that the constitution, laws, treaties, or executive proclamations, of the United States were necessarily involved in the decision, we have no jurisdiction." *Id.*, at 287.

This Court's decision in Erie R. Co. v. Tompkins, 304 U.S. 64 (1938), signaled the end of federal-court elaboration and application of the general common law. Erie repudiated the holding of Swift v. Tyson, 16 Pet. 1 (1842), that federal courts were free to "express our own opinion" upon "the principles established in the general commercial law." *Id.*, at 19, 18. After canvassing the many problems resulting from "the broad province accorded to the so-called 'general law' as to which federal courts exercised an independent judgment," 304 U.S., at 75, the Erie Court extirpated that law with its famous declaration that "[t]here is no federal general common law." Erie affected the status of the law of nations in federal courts not merely by the implication of its holding but quite directly, since the question decided in Swift turned on the "law merchant," then a subset of the law of nations.

After the death of the old general common law in Erie came the birth of a new and different common law pronounced by federal courts. There developed a specifically federal common law (in the sense of judicially pronounced law) for a "few and restricted" areas in which "a federal rule of decision is necessary to protect uniquely federal interests, and those in which Congress has given the courts the power to develop substantive law." Texas Industries, Inc. v. Radcliff Materials, Inc., 451 U.S. 630, 640 (1981) (internal quotation marks and citation omitted). Unlike the general common law that preceded it, however, federal common law was self-consciously "made" rather than "discovered," by judges who sought to avoid falling under the sway of (in Holmes's hyperbolic language) "[t]he fallacy and illusion" that there exists "a transcendental body of law outside of any particular State but obligatory within it unless and until changed by statute." Black and White Taxicab & Transfer Co. v. Brown and Yellow Taxicab & Transfer Co., 276 U.S. 518, 533 (1928) (dissenting opinion).

Because post-Erie federal common law is made, not discovered, federal courts must possess some federal-common-law-making authority before undertaking to craft it. "Federal courts, unlike state courts, are not general common-law courts and do not possess a general power to develop and apply their own rules of decision." Milwaukee v. Illinois, 451 U.S. 304, 312 (1981).

The general rule as formulated in Texas Industries, 451 U.S., at 640–641, is that "[t]he vesting of jurisdiction in the federal courts does not in and of itself give rise to authority to formulate federal common law." This rule applies not only to applications of federal common law that would displace a state rule, but also to applications that simply create a private cause of action under a federal statute. * * *

The rule against finding a delegation of substantive lawmaking power in a grant of jurisdiction is subject to exceptions, some better established than others. The most firmly entrenched is admiralty law, derived from the grant of admiralty jurisdiction in Article III, § 2, cl. 3, of the Constitution. In the exercise of that jurisdiction federal courts develop and apply a body of general maritime law, "the well-known and well-developed venerable law of the sea which arose from the custom among seafaring men." R.M.S. Titanic, Inc. v. Haver, 171 F.3d 943, 960 (4th Cir.1999) (Niemeyer, J.) (internal quotation marks omitted). At the other extreme is Bivens v. Six Unknown Fed. Narcotics Agents, 403 U.S. 388 (1971), which created a private damages cause of action against federal officials for violation of the Fourth Amendment. We have said that the authority to create this cause of action was derived from "our general jurisdiction to decide all cases 'arising under the Constitution, laws, or treaties of the United States.'" Correctional Services Corp. v. Malesko, 534 U.S. 61, 66 (2001) (quoting 28 U.S.C. § 1331). While Bivens stands, the ground supporting it has eroded. For the past 25 years, "we have consistently refused to extend Bivens liability to any new context." Correctional Services Corp., *supra*, at 68. Bivens is "a relic of the heady days in which this Court assumed common-law powers to create causes of action." 534 U.S., at 75 (Scalia, J., concurring). * * *

III

The analysis in the Court's opinion departs from my own in this respect: After concluding * * * that "the ATS is a jurisdictional statute creating no new causes of action," the Court addresses at length * * * the "good reasons for a restrained conception of the *discretion* a federal court should exercise in considering a new cause of action" under the ATS. (Emphasis added.) By framing the issue as one of "discretion," the Court skips over the antecedent question of authority. This neglects the "lesson of Erie," that "grants of jurisdiction alone" (which the Court has acknowledged the ATS to be) "are not themselves grants of law-making authority." Meltzer, *Customary International Law, Foreign Affairs, and Federal Common Law*, 42 Va.J.Int'l.L. 513, 541 (2002). On this point, the Court observes only that no development between the enactment of the ATS (in 1789) and the birth of modern international human rights litigation under that statute (in 1980) "has categorically *precluded* federal courts from recognizing a claim under the law of nations as an element of common law." (Emphasis added). This turns our jurisprudence regarding federal common law on its head. The question is not what case or congressional action *prevents* federal courts from applying the law of nations as part of the general common law; it is what *authorizes* that peculiar exception from Erie's fundamental holding that a general common law *does not exist*.

The Court would apparently find authorization in the understanding of the Congress that enacted the ATS, that "district courts would recognize private causes of action for certain torts in violation of the law of nations." But as discussed above, that understanding rested upon a notion of general common law that has been repudiated by Erie.

The Court recognizes that Erie was a "watershed" decision heralding an avulsive change, wrought by "conceptual development in understanding common law ... [and accompanied by an] equally significant rethinking of the role of the federal courts in making it." The Court's analysis, however, does not follow through on this insight, interchangeably using the unadorned phrase "common law" * * * to refer to pre-Erie general common law and post-Erie federal common law. This lapse is crucial, because the creation of post-Erie federal common law is rooted in a positivist mindset utterly foreign to the American common-law tradition of the late 18th century. Post-Erie federal common lawmaking (all that is left to the federal courts) is so far removed from that general-common-law adjudication which applied the "law of nations" that it would be anachronistic to find authorization to do the former in a statutory grant of jurisdiction that was thought to enable the latter.[*] Yet that is precisely what the discretion-only analysis * * * suggests.

Because today's federal common law is not our Framers' general common law, the question presented by the suggestion of discretionary authority to enforce the law of nations is not whether to extend old-school general-common-law adjudication. Rather, it is whether to create new federal common law. The Court masks the novelty of its approach when it suggests that the difference between us is that we would "close the door to further independent judicial recognition of actionable international norms," whereas the Court would permit the exercise of judicial power "on the understanding that the door is still ajar subject to vigilant doorkeeping." The general common law was the old door. We do not close that door today, for the deed was done in Erie. Federal common law is a *new* door. The question is not whether that door will be left ajar, but whether this Court will open it. * * *

Jesner v. Arab Bank PLC

584 U.S. 241 (2018).

Petitioners were foreign nationals who alleged that Hamas and other terrorist groups injured them or their families in the Middle East. Petitioners brought several ATS suits arising out of their alleged injuries against Arab Bank, PLC, a Jordanian financial institution with a New York branch. They alleged that Arab Bank financed attacks by, among other things, "maintain[ing] bank accounts for terrorists and their front groups and allow[ing] the accounts to be used to pay the families of suicide bombers." The district court and Court of Appeals for the Second Circuit dismissed the case on the ground that suits against corporations cannot be maintained under the ATS.

---

[*] The Court conjures the illusion of common-law-making continuity between 1789 and the present by ignoring fundamental differences. The Court's approach places the law of nations on a federal-law footing unknown to the First Congress. At the time of the ATS's enactment, the law of nations, being part of general common law, was not supreme federal law that could displace state law. By contrast, a judicially created federal rule based on international norms would be supreme federal law. Moreover, a federal-common-law cause of action of the sort the Court reserves discretion to create would "arise under" the laws of the United States, not only for purposes of Article III but also for purposes of statutory federal-question jurisdiction. The lack of genuine continuity is thus demonstrated by the fact that today's opinion renders the ATS unnecessary for federal jurisdiction over (so-called) law-of-nations claims. If the law of nations can be transformed into federal law on the basis of (1) a provision that merely grants jurisdiction, combined with (2) some residual judicial power (from whence nobody knows) to create federal causes of action in cases implicating foreign relations, then a grant of federal-question jurisdiction would give rise to a power to create international-law-based federal common law just as effectively as would the ATS. This would mean that the ATS became largely superfluous as of 1875, when Congress granted general federal-question jurisdiction subject to a $500 amount-in-controversy requirement, and entirely superfluous as of 1980, when Congress eliminated the amount-in-controversy requirement.

The Supreme Court affirmed in an opinion by Justice Kennedy that garnered a majority on some grounds but only a plurality on others. Of relevance here, Justice Kennedy wrote for a majority:

"Sosa is consistent with this Court's general reluctance to extend judicially created private rights of action. The Court's recent precedents cast doubt on the authority of courts to extend or create private causes of action even in the realm of domestic law, where this Court has 'recently and repeatedly said that a decision to create a private right of action is one better left to legislative judgment in the great majority of cases.' Sosa, 542 U. S., at 727 (citing Correctional Services Corp. v. Malesko, 534 U.S. 61, 68 (2001); Alexander v. Sandoval, 532 U.S. 275, 286–287 (2001)). That is because 'the Legislature is in the better position to consider if the public interest would be served by imposing a new substantive legal liability.' Ziglar v. Abbasi, 582 U.S. 120, 136 (2017). Thus, 'if there are sound reasons to think Congress might doubt the efficacy or necessity of a damages remedy, . . . courts must refrain from creating the remedy in order to respect the role of Congress.' *Id.,* at 137.

"This caution extends to the question whether the courts should exercise the judicial authority to mandate a rule that imposes liability upon artificial entities like corporations. Thus, in Correctional Services Corp. v. Malesko, 534 U.S. 61, 68 (2001), the Court held that corporate defendants may not be held liable in Bivens actions. See Bivens v. Six Unknown Fed. Narcotics Agents, 403 U.S. 388 (1971). Allowing corporate liability would have been a 'marked extension' of Bivens that was unnecessary to advance its purpose of holding individual officers responsible for 'engaging in unconstitutional wrongdoing.' Malesko, 534 U.S., at 74. Whether corporate defendants should be subject to suit was 'a question for Congress, not us, to decide.' *Id.,* at 72.

"Neither the language of the ATS nor the precedents interpreting it support an exception to these general principles in this context. In fact, the separation-of-powers concerns that counsel against courts creating private rights of action apply with particular force in the context of the ATS. The political branches, not the Judiciary, have the responsibility and institutional capacity to weigh foreign-policy concerns. See Kiobel, 569 U.S., at 116–117. That the ATS implicates foreign relations 'is itself a reason for a high bar to new private causes of action for violating international law.' Sosa, *supra,* at 727.

"In *Sosa,* the Court emphasized that federal courts must exercise 'great caution' before recognizing new forms of liability under the ATS. 542 U.S., at 728. * * * Either way, absent further action from Congress it would be inappropriate for courts to extend ATS liability to foreign corporations.* * *"

NOTE ON INTERNATIONAL LAW-BASED CAUSES OF ACTION UNDER THE ATS

(1) Sosa and the Problem of Translation. The Court in Sosa acknowledged that the ATS was a "strictly jurisdictional statute" and that the international law-based causes of action that would have been applied under that jurisdiction in 1789 was non-federal general common law. The Court thus faced a situation not unlike the one faced in Erie, Hinderlider, and Clearfield Trust: an area of law governed in the 18th and 19th centuries by general common law had to be rethought in view of the profound shift reflected in Erie. Sosa's approach was to begin with the ATS framers' expectation that federal courts in ATS cases would "recognize private causes of action for certain torts in violation of the law of nations," and then translate that expectation in a post-Erie context to mean that federal courts could exercise "discretion" to "recognize" a narrow band of international law-based federal common law causes of action akin to the eighteenth century ones.

Is this approach akin to what the Court did in an interstate apportionment case, which before Erie was governed by general common law grounded in part in international law, and after Erie was deemed to be federal law? See Hinderlider, p. 860, *supra*. Is it akin in its approach to admiralty jurisdiction, which as Justice Scalia notes is an exception to the "rule against finding a delegation of substantive lawmaking power in a grant of jurisdiction"? Compare Lincoln Mills, p. 863, *supra*, which is cited favorably in Sosa. Is it akin to the structural analysis in Sabbatino, which Sosa also relies on? In light of these analogies, is Justice Scalia right that the "avulsive change" of Erie, combined with the other reasons for "judicial caution" noted by the majority opinion, rule out any federal common lawmaking in this context?

In a concurring opinion in Jesner, Justice Gorsuch notes that since the law of nations was general common law and not federal law at the founding, an ATS suit between aliens (as in both Sosa and Jesner) would not have arisen under federal law for purposes of Article III, and thus could not have been brought. See 584 U.S. at 285–91. Sosa avoided this problem in its suit between aliens because of the Court's holding that ATS causes of action are federal common law causes of action. But is it a problem that Sosa translates the ATS framers' expectations for the post-Erie world to justify a lawsuit that could not have been brought in 1789?

(2) Sosa and Implied Causes of Action. Sosa overcame the Court's "reluctan[ce] to infer intent to provide a private cause of action where the statute does not supply one expressly," and yet at the same time invoked this reluctance as justification for "a restrained conception of the discretion a federal court should exercise in considering a new cause of action of this kind." Is this approach consistent with Sandoval? And can one square Sosa's extensive focus on vindicating the aims and expectations of the ATS framers on the Court's attenuated consideration of statutory purpose in recent decades in other federal common law contexts? Is there something about the international law basis for federal common law that leads the Court to reason differently here?

The Court seemed to revert to a more restrictive approach to ATS causes of action in Jesner, which relies on the analysis in Sandoval and other cases that have refused in recent decades to imply a cause of action for damages for constitutional violations. Note that in declining to extend ATS liability to foreign corporations, Jesner left open the question whether "a proper application of Sosa would preclude courts from *ever* recognizing any new causes of action under the ATS."[1]

(3) Sosa and Statutory Federal Question Jurisdiction. Justice Souter and Justice Scalia disagree on whether the analysis in Sosa implies that international law-based causes of action recognized under the decision can form a basis for statutory jurisdiction, and perhaps for the further development of federal common law, under 28 U.S.C. § 1331, presumably because the causes of actions recognized in Sosa are federal law. Who has the better of the argument? It is typically true that a case arising under federal common law can form the basis for jurisdiction under § 1331. See Illinois v. Milwaukee, 406 U.S. 91, 99–100 (1972). Yet the logic of Sosa's holding is closely tied to the original purposes of the ATS. And as Justice Souter suggests in footnote 19, there would have been no expectation by the drafters of the 1875 federal question jurisdiction statute that the law of nations would implicate a federal question or would justify application of the law of nations. See Ker v. Illinois, 119 U.S. 436, 444 (1886) (question whether forcible seizure abroad is basis to invalidate trial in state court is "a question of common law, or of the law of nations" that the Supreme Court has "no right to review"); N.Y. Life Ins. Co. v. Hendren, 92 U.S. 286, 286–87 (1876) (Supreme Court lacks jurisdiction to review "general laws of war, as recognized by the law of nations applicable to this case," which do not involve "the constitution, laws, treaties, or executive proclamations, of the United States").

(4) The Extraterritorial Application of the ATS. In Kiobel v. Royal Dutch Petroleum Co., 569 U.S. 108 (2012), the Supreme Court unanimously affirmed the dismissal of an ATS suit by a foreign national against foreign corporations for conduct that occurred in a foreign country. In an opinion by Chief Justice Roberts (joined by Justices Scalia, Kennedy, Thomas, and Alito), the Court held that the presumption against extraterritorial application of U.S. law governs claims brought pursuant to the ATS. The Court acknowledged that the presumption, which serves to prevent the U.S. from becoming embroiled in international disputes that might arise from conflicts between U.S. and foreign law, ordinarily reaches only the extraterritorial application of statutes that "regulat[e] conduct." The ATS, in

---

[1]   In Nestle USA, Inc. v. Doe, 593 U.S. 628 (2021), a case about the extraterritorial application of the ATS, see Paragraph (4), *infra,* the Justices in numerous opinions, none of which garnered a majority, commented again on when causes of action were available under the ATS. Justice Thomas, in an opinion joined by Justices Gorsuch and Kavanaugh, maintained that "federal courts should not recognize private rights of action for violations of international law beyond the three historical torts identified in Sosa." Justice Gorsuch's concurrence, joined on this point by Justice Kavanaugh, emphasized that while corporations enjoy no immunity from ATS actions, the Court should "jettison the misguided notion that courts have discretion to create new causes of action under the ATS." Justice Sotomayor, in a concurrence joined by Justices Breyer and Kagan, argued that corporations were not immune from ATS liability and took issue with Justice Thomas's argument for limiting the ATS to the three historical causes of action identified in Sosa. Finally, Justice Alito in a lone dissent argued that domestic corporations were not immune under the ATS. In sum, five Justices across three opinions, one in dissent, agreed that the domestic corporations could be sued in ATS cases. But none explained how this conclusion was consistent with the holding in Jesner that separation of powers concerns preclude extension of ATS liability to foreign corporations. Can Nestle and Jesner be reconciled on this point?

contrast, is strictly jurisdictional and thus "does not directly regulate conduct or afford relief." Still, the Court found that "the principles underlying the canon of interpretation similarly constrain courts considering causes of action that may be brought under the ATS." In particular, because Sosa concluded that the ATS authorizes federal courts "to recognize certain causes of action based on * * * international law," the Court in Kiobel asserted that the risk of "unwarranted judicial interference" in U.S. foreign policy is, if anything, "magnified."

Justice Breyer, joined by Justices Ginsburg, Sotomayor, and Kagan, concurred only in the judgment and disputed the majority's reliance on the presumption against extraterritoriality. Justice Breyer emphasized that the presumption was inapt as applied to a statute that "was enacted with 'foreign matters' in mind." Indeed, noting that Congress passed the ATS "to permit recovery of damages from pirates and others who violated basic international law norms as understood in 1789," Justice Breyer emphasized that piracy was extraterritorial and often required the application of U.S. law to ships that flew the flag of foreign nations and thus lay within their jurisdiction.[2]

The Court relied heavily on Kiobel in Nestlé USA, Inc. v. Doe, 593 U.S. 628 (2021), a case in which plaintiffs alleged in an ATS suit that two U.S. corporations aided and abetted child slavery when they provided resources to, and bought cocoa from, farms in Ivory Coast to which plaintiffs were trafficked as children. In an opinion by Justice Thomas, the Court ruled, 8–1, that plaintiffs' claims were impermissibly extraterritorial. The Court reasoned that "[n]early all the conduct that they say aided and abetted forced labor * * * occurred in Ivory Coast," and plaintiffs' allegation that "every major operational decision by both companies is made in or approved in the U.S." did not render the claims domestic for ATS purposes. On the latter point, the Court explained that "[b]ecause making 'operational decisions' is an activity common to most corporations, generic allegations of this sort do not draw a sufficient connection between the cause of action respondents seek—aiding and abetting forced labor overseas—and domestic conduct."

Two centuries after the fact, it is obviously difficult to reconstruct the purposes of a statute with very little legislative history, especially when one can find but few interpretations of the statute before modern times. Is the majority's reliance on a presumption against extraterritoriality itself a form of federal common law? Does the Court convincingly explain why it makes

---

[2]   Legal scholars have expressed a range of views on Kiobel. See, *e.g.*, Vázquez, *Things We Do With Presumptions: Reflections on Kiobel v. Royal Dutch Petroleum*, 89 Notre Dame L.Rev. 1719 (2014) (arguing, *inter alia*, that the presumption against extraterritoriality does not apply to a jurisdictional statute purporting to give courts power to adjudicate universal norms); Weinberg, *What We Don't Talk About When We Talk About Extraterritoriality: Kiobel and the Conflict of Laws*, 99 Cornell L.Rev. 1471 (2014) (contending that Kiobel's facts fall within the literal terms of the ATS's jurisdictional grant and that the national interest in having U.S. courts hear a case like Kiobel lies in the "mutual, reciprocal interest" of all nations in "protecting human rights"); Young, *Universal Jurisdiction, the Alien Tort Statute, and Transnational Public-Law Litigation After Kiobel*, 64 Duke L.J. 1023, 1100 (2015) (arguing that Kiobel "was a particularly appropriate case for judicial caution about the extraterritorial reach of American law" because of the foreign relations implications of recognizing an implied right of action in wholly extraterritorial cases).

sense to apply that presumption to a statute enacted, in part, to deal with piracy?

NOTE ON FEDERAL COMMON LAW AND INTERNATIONAL LAW BEYOND THE ATS

Sosa holds that federal courts can recognize a limited range of international law-based causes of action in ATS cases. The form of international law that Sosa focused on was customary international law (CIL), which emerges from the consistent practice of nations followed from a sense of legal obligation. A fiercely debated question, before and after Sosa, is whether federal courts should view CIL as a kind of federal common law, which preempts conflicting state law and provides the basis for federal question jurisdiction. That question is difficult in part because the matters regulated by CIL vary widely: they include the immunity of governmental officials, human rights, limits on legislative and adjudicative jurisdiction, the enforcement of foreign judgments, the law of the sea, and the law of the environment.[1] This Note reviews the debate and considers Sosa's and Jesner's impact on it.

(1) Customary International Law and Federal Common Law. Older federal decisions are full of statements like that from The Paquete Habana, 175 U.S. 677, 700 (1900), quoted by Justice White in Sabbatino, p. 874, *supra*: "International Law is part of our law, and must be ascertained and administered by the courts of justice of appropriate jurisdiction, as often as questions of right depending upon it are duly presented for their determination." Some legal scholars read such statements, as well as similar utterances by prominent members of the founding generation, to indicate that from the early days of the Republic, CIL was understood to be federal common law.[2] But nearly all recent scholarship starts from the proposition that CIL was applied, in the years before Erie, as part of the *general* common law, rather than as either state or federal law.[3] And the Supreme Court in Sosa has now endorsed that position. Accordingly, at the heart of the current

---

[1] See, *e.g.*, 1 Restatement (Third) of Foreign Relations 456–57 (1987) (discussing CIL regarding the immunity of government officials); 2 *id.* 144–47, § 701 cmt. b, at 152–53, § 701 reporters' note 2, at 153–55 (discussing CIL and human rights law); 1 *id.* 235–37 (discussing jurisdiction to prescribe); 1 *id.* 304–05 (discussing jurisdiction to adjudicate); 2 *id.* 5–7 (discussing CIL sources of law of the sea); 2 *id.* 99–102 (discussing CIL sources of environmental law).

[2] See, *e.g.*, Paust, International Law as the Law of the United States 7–8 (2d ed.2003); Glennon, *Raising The Paquete Habana: Is Violation of Customary International Law by the Executive Unconstitutional?*, 80 Nw.U.L.Rev. 321, 343–47 (1985).

[3] That pre-Erie CIL was "general law" is a central tenet of the "revisionist position," discussed below. See Paragraph (3), *infra*. For leading proponents of the "modern position," discussed at Paragraph (2), *infra*, who acknowledge the general law status of pre-Erie law, see, *e.g.*, Koh, *Is International Law Really State Law?*, 111 Harv.L.Rev. 1824, 1830–31 (1998); Henkin, *International Law as Law in the United States*, 82 Mich.L.Rev. 1555, 1557–58 (1984); Neuman, *Sense and Nonsense About Customary International Law: A Response to Professors Bradley and Goldsmith*, 66 Fordham L.Rev. 371, 373–74 (1997). For an excellent account of the relevant history, see Jay, *The Status of the Law of Nations in Early American Law*, 42 Vand.L.Rev. 819 (1989).

debate lies the familiar question of translation that has arisen in various contexts after Erie: Once Erie rejected the idea of general law and insisted that, in our system, law must emanate from the authority of a (state or federal) sovereign, how should one understand the status of CIL? Commentators have extensively debated this question.[4] Although the relevant literature is too copious to capture fairly in its entirety, it is possible to describe some of the high points of the competing positions.

(2) The Modern Position. Many international law scholars argue that CIL is presumptively incorporated into the American legal system and given effect as federal law—a view reflected in the Restatement (Third) of Foreign Relations § 111, editors' note 3 (1987). Support for the so-called "modern position" rests on several closely related historical, structural, and functional propositions:[5] First, the founders, chastened by the inadequacies of the Articles of Confederation, sought to ensure uniform and effective federal implementation of the law of nations, in part, by giving the federal courts jurisdiction over those cases most likely to implicate foreign relations (those concerning foreign envoys, admiralty cases, and alienage-based diversity jurisdiction). And even though Erie itself rejected the concept of "general law" that underlay the law of nations, nothing in that decision "require[d] that federal courts stop citing cases decided before 1938 and reinvent federal common law from scratch. * * * [Rather,] [f]ormer doctrines of 'general common law' have been reconceptualized as doctrines of federal common law that continue to govern in areas of dominant federal concern," Neuman, note 7, *supra*, at 380. Second, state-by-state variation in the content of CIL would undermine the goals underlying the constitutional structure and contradict embedded understandings about the national character of foreign relations. Third, treating customary international law as federal common law does not pose the federalism concerns highlighted by Erie because the Constitution does not reserve power to the states over foreign relations, but rather vests it exclusively in the federal government. Fourth, separation-of-powers concerns about the judiciary's exercising legislative discretion are addressed by the fact that judges *find* CIL based on an existing body of law derived from the common consent and practice of sovereigns. And fifth, certain anomalies that would occur if post-Erie CIL were regarded as state, rather than federal, law. As Professor Koh writes, "how would the President's lawyers advise a visiting head of state about her chances of civil immunity while traveling on a classic State visit from Hawaii, to Williamsburg, Virginia, to Washington, D.C., and to New York (and the U.N. headquarters district)?" Koh, note 3, *supra*, at 1851.

Under the modern position, could a state law permitting the imposition of capital punishment in certain contexts be invalidated by a court if it were shown to violate a CIL norm? What if the United States, in assenting to

---

[4]   For a superb review of the debate, see Young, *Sorting Out the Debate Over Customary International Law*, 42 Va.J.Int'l.L. 365 (2002), which also cites the voluminous commentary on this matter.

[5]   The summary in this paragraph derives primarily from Henkin, note 7, *supra*, at 1651–52; Koh, note 7, *supra*, at 1831–32, 1853–58; Neuman, note 7, *supra*, at 382–83; and Stephens, *The Law of Our Land: Customary International Law as Federal Law After Erie*, 66 Fordham L.Rev. 393, 402–08 (1997).

various international agreements relating to human rights, expressed reservations or understandings that the agreements would not preempt state law?

(3) The Revisionist Position. The prevailing or "modern" position is challenged in Bradley & Goldsmith, *Customary International Law as Federal Common Law: A Critique of the Modern Position*, 110 Harv.L.Rev. 815 (1997).[6] First, they emphasize that prior to Erie the Court had never suggested that CIL was federal common law, and that Sabbatino did not alter that result, having invoked the act of state doctrine as an off-the-rack rule to implement the separation-of-powers principle of limited "judicial involvement in foreign affairs." Second, they say that treating CIL as federal common law is inconsistent with Erie, noting Erie's positivist insistence that law be associated with a particular sovereign and its realist recognition that judicial decisionmaking is a form of lawmaking. Third, in the absence of any textual source of constitutional or statutory authorization for courts to adopt CIL as federal common law,[7] they suggest that the modern position departs from constitutional norms of democratic self-governance. CIL is not "generated by U.S. lawmaking processes," but rather "is derived from the views and practices of the international community," which is not representative of the American polity. Finally, these difficulties, they say, have become more acute as CIL has evolved beyond its traditional concern with relations among nations to embrace a nation's relations with its citizens (as in human rights law), thus increasing the likelihood that CIL will conflict with domestic law.

Consider a *federal* cause of action that presents an issue relating to international relations—*e.g.*, the immunity of a foreign head of state, or the extraterritorial application of a statute—that is not addressed by a federal statute. Should that issue be governed by federal common law?

(4) Intermediate Positions. Professors Weisburd and Young contend that CIL should be viewed as neither state nor federal law: Weisburd, note 11, *supra*, suggests an analogy to the law of a foreign nation, while Young, note 8, *supra*, views CIL as a contemporary and valid analogue of the general common law of the pre-Erie variety. That approach has some attractions, including a greater capacity for achieving uniformity, and a greater role for federal courts in formulating CIL, than would be true if CIL were merely state law. But it raises some tricky questions about choice of law, the implications of Erie, and about how to distinguish CIL from state law. For critical examinations, see Meltzer, *Customary International Law, Foreign Affairs, and Federal Common Law*, 42 Va.J.Int'l.L. 513 (2002); Ramsey,

---

[6]   Some elements of the following critique of the modern position are foreshadowed in Trimble, *A Revisionist View of Customary International Law*, 33 UCLA L.Rev. 665 (1986), and Weisburd, *State Courts, Federal Courts, and International Cases*, 20 Yale J.Int'l.L. 1, 51 (1995), *supra*.

[7]   Bradley and Goldsmith note that in contrast with the Admiralty Clause and interstate dispute clause, "Article III of the Constitution does not even list CIL as a basis for the exercise of federal judicial power, much less authorize federal courts to incorporate CIL wholesale into federal law. Nor does [the Supremacy Clause of] Article VI list CIL as a source of supreme federal law." Bradley & Goldsmith, *supra*, at 856.

International Law as Non-preemptive Federal Law, 42 Va.J.Int'l.L. 555 (2002).

Professors Bellia and Clark, in turn, have argued that neither the modern position nor the revisionist critique adequately explains the role of CIL in the federal system. See Bellia & Clark, *The Federal Common Law of Nations*, 109 Colum.L.Rev. 1 (2009); see also Bellia & Clark, *The Law of Nations as Constitutional Law*, 98 Va.L.Rev. 729 (2012). They maintain that early statements characterizing the law of nations (the precursor to modern customary international law) as part of the law of the land were carried over from England (where the common law incorporated the law of nations) and thus were not addressed to the distinctly American question whether the law of nations qualified as the *supreme* law of the land in the technical sense of the Supremacy Clause. They argue that, beginning in early prize cases and continuing through Sabbatino, the Supreme Court applied a subset of the law of nations—the so-called "perfect rights" of sovereigns—as a means of preserving the constitutional prerogatives of the Congress and the President to recognize foreign nations, conduct foreign relations, and decide momentous questions of war and peace. Under the law of nations, a violation of perfect rights gave a nation just cause for waging war. Bellia and Clark argue that courts used perfect rights as a baseline (even in the absence of federal incorporation by statute or treaty) that served to preserve the Constitution's allocation of powers. This approach ties the application of such rules to Articles I and II, but stops short of endorsing broad Article III power to create federal common law.[8]

Even assuming that one or more of the foregoing accounts finds support in the historical record, has too much water passed over the dam to return to an eighteenth-century understanding of general law? Or would treating CIL as general law or incorporating certain aspects of it selectively into our understanding of separated powers resolve some of the anomalies produced by both the modern and revisionist positions?

(5) Supreme Court Cases. The Sabbatino decision does not provide a definitive answer in this debate. On the one hand, footnote 24 of the opinion cited with approval an article by Professor Jessup, *The Doctrine of Erie Railroad v. Tompkins Applied to International Law*, 33 Am.J.Int'l.L. 740 (1939), which argued that Erie did not compel federal courts to apply state views of international law. On the other hand, the Sabbatino ruling *precluded* the application of CIL to the matter at hand, and Justice Harlan's opinion is reasonably clear that the rule of decision there announced implements "the basic relationships between branches of government in a system of separation of powers," rather than international law.

---

[8]   Professor Vázquez argues that Bellia and Clark's position is "thoroughly convincing," but that it "actually provides substantial support for most of the modern position." Vázquez, *Customary International Law as U.S. Law: A Critique of the Intermediate Positions and a Defense of the Modern Position*, 86 Notre Dame L.Rev. 1495 (2011). To the extent that Bellia and Clark's analysis simply seeks to put existing CIL cases on firmer conceptual footing, what practical implications attach to treating CIL as implied constitutional law rather than federal common law?

The impact of Sosa on these questions is contested. The Court's statement that § 1350 is entirely jurisdictional may suggest that the substantive law applied in actions properly brought under that statute is a preexisting federal common law of CIL. See, *e.g.*, Koh, *The Ninth Annual John W. Hager Lecture, The 2004 Term: The Supreme Court Meets International Law*, 12 Tulsa J.Comp. & Int'l.L. 1 (2005) (reading Sosa to endorse the modern position); Flaherty, *The Future and Past of U.S. Foreign Relations Law*, 67 Law & Contemp.Probs. 169, 174 (2004) (same). But isn't it unlikely that, had the ATS never been enacted, the Court would have ruled that those violations of CIL that Sosa does recognize state good claims under the federal common law? Insofar as the Court relies on the fact that "the ATS was meant to underwrite litigation of a narrow set of common law actions derived from the law of nations," doesn't it give the ATS more than jurisdictional significance? Bradley, Goldsmith, and Moore view Sosa as reading the ATS also to be a source of authority under which the federal courts may recognize at least some federal common law rights of action (whose recognition would be inappropriate absent that statutory authorization). Bradley, Goldsmith, & Moore, Sosa, *Customary International Law, and the Continuing Relevance of* Erie, 120 Harv.L.Rev. 869 (2007). If that is correct, then the Court would seem to be rejecting the view that some urged, prior to Sosa, that § 1350 neither establishes a federal cause of action for violations of CIL nor authorizes the federal courts to do so. See, *e.g.*, Bradley & Goldsmith, *The Current Illegitimacy of International Human Rights Litigation*, 66 Fordham L.Rev. 319, 357–63 (1997).

On the other hand, the Court's caution in setting forth the kinds of CIL claims that can be brought under the ATS, and its linking the validity of those CIL claims to the action of Congress in 1789, appears to reject the modern view that all CIL is, by its nature, federal common law. In that regard, should the ATS be viewed, notwithstanding the language in Sosa that it is only jurisdictional, as authorizing the federal courts within a limited domain to fashion federal common law whose creation would be inappropriate without that statutory authorization—much like the jurisdictional grant in Textile Workers Union v. Lincoln Mills, 353 U.S. 448 (1957)?[9] Is there an intelligible way to understand the ATS without

---

[9] Compare Sosa v. Alvarez-Machain, 542 U.S. 692, 731 n.19 (2004): "Our position does not * * * imply that every grant of jurisdiction to a federal court carries with it an opportunity to develop common law (so that the grant of federal-question jurisdiction would be equally as good for our purposes as § 1350). Section 1350 was enacted on the congressional understanding that courts would exercise jurisdiction by entertaining some common law claims derived from the law of nations; and we know of no reason to think that federal-question jurisdiction was extended subject to any comparable congressional assumption."

assuming that Congress meant to authorize the federal courts to develop a specialized federal common law of international torts?[10]

---

[10]   Professors Bellia and Clark argue that the original meaning of the ATS did not authorize the development of a CIL of torts; rather, in their view, the First Congress understood the statute to permit an alien to sue a U.S. citizen for any intentional tort to person or personal property because any such tort would have violated the law of nations in 1789. See Bellia & Clark, *The Alien Tort Statute and the Law of Nations*, 78 U.Chi.L.Rev. 445 (2011). Under law of nations principles, a nation became responsible for its citizens' intentional torts against an alien unless it extradited the offender, imposed criminal punishment, or gave the alien a civil remedy. Bellia and Clark maintain that by granting federal courts jurisdiction to hear alien tort claims against U.S. citizens, the ATS merely sought to establish a self-executing means of satisfying the United States' obligations under the law of nations. Bellia and Clark add that the tort law causes of action under the ATS would have come from the Process Act of 1789, which required federal courts to apply the forms of action and modes of process then used or allowed in the supreme courts of the states in which they sat. Act of Sept. 29, 1789, ch. 21, 1 Stat. 93. See Bellia & Clark, *The Original Source of the Cause of Action in Federal Courts: The Example of the Alien Tort Statute*, 101 Va.L.Rev. 609 (2015). According to Bellia and Clark, the Process Act of 1789—and its successor, the Process Act of 1792, Act of May 8, 1792, ch. 36, 1 Stat. 275—would have made the relevant state forms of action applicable in federal court. If correct, how (if at all) should this conclusion affect the understanding of the ATS today?

CHAPTER VIII

THE CIVIL JURISDICTION OF THE DISTRICT COURTS: FEDERAL QUESTION, ADMIRALTY, AND DIVERSITY

INTRODUCTION

This chapter examines the subject matter jurisdiction of the federal district courts, focusing on cases that present a question of federal law (federal question jurisdiction); controversies between identified parties, including citizens and subjects of different states or nations (diversity or party-alignment jurisdiction); and cases that touch or concern the navigable waters of the United States (admiralty and maritime jurisdiction). Much of this litigation begins in federal court; the parties can also remove civil actions from state to federal court. In both original and removed actions, district courts frequently exercise supplemental jurisdiction over state-law claims that lack any jurisdictional predicate aside from their relationship to claims that do qualify for federal subject matter jurisdiction. After treating the various heads of subject matter jurisdiction, this chapter concludes with a discussion of supplemental and removal jurisdiction.

The chapter begins with the special rules that govern the identification and judicial enforcement of jurisdictional limits as a general matter. The section on jurisdictional limits considers such questions as when and how parties and courts raise these issues; in what order courts decide them; and when courts assign jurisdictional status to some element of a claim or defense.

---

1. IDENTIFYING AND ENFORCING JURISDICTIONAL LIMITS

A. THE "FIRST PRINCIPLE" OF FEDERAL JURISDICTION

The Supreme Court has long ascribed special importance to issues of subject matter jurisdiction. The first edition of this book described the duty of a federal court to ensure that it has subject matter jurisdiction as the "first principle" of federal jurisdiction.[1] This obligation applies both at the district court level, see Fed.R.Civ.P. 12(h)(3) (declaring that the district court must dismiss a civil action if at any time it discovers that it lacks subject matter jurisdiction), and on appeal. When appellate jurisdiction depends on a showing that the lower court or courts had jurisdiction to enter the judgment or decree (as it often does), the appellate court must consider both its own and the lower courts' subject matter jurisdiction.

Mansfield, Coldwater, & Lake Michigan Ry. Co. v. Swan

111 U.S. 379 (1884).
Error to the Circuit Court of the United States for the Northern District of Ohio.

■ MR. JUSTICE MATTHEWS delivered the opinion of the Court.

[The plaintiffs sued in Ohio state court, seeking damages from the railway company for breach of contract. Invoking diversity, the defendant removed the action to the federal circuit court, which at the time exercised original and removal jurisdiction in such matters. After a trial, the federal circuit court entered judgment for the plaintiffs for extensive damages. The defendant sought appellate review of that judgment in the Supreme Court.]

* * * An examination of the record * * * discloses that the circuit court had no jurisdiction to try the action, and as, for this reason, we are constrained to reverse the judgment, we have not deemed it within our province to consider any other questions involved in it. It appears from the petition for removal, and not otherwise by the record elsewhere, that, at the time the action was first brought in the state court, one of the plaintiffs, and a necessary party, McMann, was a citizen of Ohio, the same state of which the defendants were citizens. It does not affirmatively appear that at the time of the removal he was a citizen of any other state. * * * [T]he difference of citizenship on which the right of removal depends must have existed at the time when the suit was begun, as well as at the time of the removal; and, according to the uniform decisions of this court, the jurisdiction of the circuit court fails, unless the necessary citizenship affirmatively appears in the pleadings or elsewhere in the record. It was error, therefore, in the circuit court to assume jurisdiction in the case, and not to remand it, on the motion of the plaintiffs below.

It is true that the plaintiffs below, against whose objection the error was committed, do not complain of being prejudiced by it, and it seems to be an anomaly and a hardship that the party at whose instance it was

---

[1] Hart & Wechsler, The Federal Courts and the Federal System 719 (1953). See Collins, *Jurisdictional Exceptionalism*, 93 Va.L.Rev. 1829, 1831 n.2 (2007).

committed should be permitted to derive an advantage from it; but the rule, springing from the nature and limits of the judicial power of the United States, is inflexible and without exception which requires this court, of its own motion, to deny its own jurisdiction, and, in the exercise of its appellate power, that of all other courts of the United States, in all cases where such jurisdiction does not affirmatively appear in the record on which, in the exercise of that power, it is called to act. On every writ of error or appeal the first and fundamental question is that of jurisdiction, first, of this court, and then of the court from which the record comes. This question the court is bound to ask and answer for itself, even when not otherwise suggested, and without respect to the relation of the parties to it. This rule was adopted in Capron v. Van Noorden, [6 U.S. (2 Cranch) 126 (1804)], where a judgment was reversed on the application of the party against whom it had been rendered in the circuit court, for want of the allegation of his own citizenship, which he ought to have made to establish the jurisdiction which he had invoked. * * *

It remains, however, to dispose of the question of costs. It is clear that the plaintiffs in error, having wrongfully caused the removal of the cause from the state court, ought to pay the costs incurred in the circuit court, and there is no want of power in the court to award a judgment against them to that effect. [Citing "section 5 of the act of March 3, 1875."]

As to costs in this court, the question is not covered by any statutory provision, and must be settled on other grounds. Ordinarily, by the long established practice and universally recognized rule of the common law, in actions at law, the prevailing party is entitled to recover a judgment for costs, the exception being that where there is no jurisdiction in the court to determine the litigation, the cause must be dismissed for that reason, and, as the court can render no judgment for or against either party, it cannot render a judgment even for costs. Nevertheless there is a judgment or final order in the cause dismissing it for want of jurisdiction. Accordingly, in Winchester v. Jackson, [7 U.S. (3 Cranch) 514 (1806)], costs were allowed where a writ of error was dismissed for want of jurisdiction, the parties not appearing upon the record to be citizens of different states, the plaintiff in error being plaintiff below. * * *

* * * In the present case the writ of error is not dismissed for want of jurisdiction in this court; on the contrary, the jurisdiction of the court is exercised in reversing the judgment for want of jurisdiction in the circuit court; and although, in a formal and nominal sense, the plaintiffs in error prevail in obtaining a reversal of a judgment against them, the cause of that reversal is their own fault in invoking a jurisdiction to which they had no right to resort, and its effect is to defeat the entire proceeding which they originated and have prosecuted. In a true and proper sense the plaintiffs in error are the losing and not the prevailing party, and, this court having jurisdiction, upon their writ of error, so to determine,

and in that determination being compelled to reverse the judgment, of which, on other grounds, they complain, although denying their right to be heard for that purpose, has jurisdiction, also, in order to give effect to its judgment upon the whole case against them, to do what justice and right seem to require, by awarding judgment against them for the costs that have accrued in this court.

The judgment of the circuit court is accordingly reversed, with costs against the plaintiffs in error, and the cause is remanded to the circuit court, with directions to render a judgment against them for costs in that court, and to remand the cause to the court of common pleas of Fulton County, Ohio; and it is so ordered.

NOTE ON JURISDICTIONAL CHALLENGES

(1) The First Principle and Subject Matter Jurisdiction. In describing the "first principle" of limited subject matter jurisdiction, Professors Hart and Wechsler identified an essential federal judicial obligation: to notice and address jurisdictional issues even when the parties do not raise them. Mansfield explains that the rule, "inflexibl[y] and without exception," "requires this court, of its own motion, to deny its own jurisdiction, and, in the exercise of its appellate power, that of all other courts of the United States, in all cases where such jurisdiction does not affirmatively appear in the record." On the centrality of jurisdictional limits in the development of American law, see Baude, *The Judgment Power*, 96 Geo.L.J. 1807 (2008).

Rooted in Article III and the idea of the federal government as one of limited and enumerated powers, subject matter restrictions have been judicially raised and enforced in a variety of familiar cases. In Marbury v. Madison, 5 U.S. (1 Cranch) 137 (1803), p. 76, *supra,* for example, the Court raised the question itself and found that it lacked original jurisdiction under Article III. See also Capron v. Van Norden, 6 U.S. (2 Cranch) 126 (1804) (dismissing for want of jurisdiction on suggestion of the plaintiff who had invoked the jurisdiction of the lower court). Lower federal courts, too, must abide by the first principle. Congress has authority under the Madisonian Compromise to create such courts (or not) and to confer jurisdiction on them by statute, acting within the limits of Article III. See pp. 9–10, *supra.* In general, both the Supreme Court and lower federal courts routinely consider both statutory and constitutional limits on their authority before entertaining a case.[1]

---

[1] The Supreme Court sometimes describes its jurisdiction as conferred directly by the Constitution. By pressing that view to its logical extreme, the Court might exercise original and appellate jurisdiction without enabling legislation or in defiance of legislation that curtailed its authority. But in the context of its appellate jurisdiction, the Court has treated statutory grants of appellate jurisdiction as creating implicit exceptions, valid under Article III's exceptions and regulations clause. See Durousseau v. United States, 10 U.S. 307 (1810); p. 362, *supra.* Consequently, the Court typically considers itself bound by statutory and constitutional limits on its appellate jurisdiction, although it may refuse to give effect to statutes that unconstitutionally restrict its jurisdiction. See generally Chap. IV, Sec. 1. Note that the

(2) Jurisdiction to Determine Jurisdiction. As explored in Chapter II, Sec. 1, there was a debate over the validity of the Marbury Court's long discussion of mandamus, all offered as a prelude to a jurisdictional dismissal. Some critics, including President Jefferson, think the Court should have announced the absence of subject matter jurisdiction and said no more. More generally, a question that arises not infrequently is whether a court that lacks jurisdiction (literally, the power to "speak" the law) can say anything at all. "Jurisdiction is power to declare the law, and when it ceases to exist, the only function remaining to the court is that of announcing the fact and dismissing the cause." Ex parte McCardle, 74 U.S. 506, 514 (1868).

Notwithstanding these formal limits, Mansfield confirms a longstanding view that federal courts have jurisdiction to determine their own jurisdiction. Such jurisdiction may appear at first blush to be little more than a bootstrap but has seemed essential to enable federal courts to issue binding jurisdictional decisions; parties might otherwise ignore all jurisdictional denials on the basis that they were issued by a court that lacks jurisdiction. As Mansfield indicates, moreover, jurisdiction to determine jurisdiction enables the federal court to award costs and sanctions, where appropriate, to moderate the inconvenience and expense imposed by one party's mistaken jurisdictional invocation.

(3) Is the First Principle Constitutionally Required? The Mansfield Court mildly observed that jurisdiction's first principle produces anomalous results and hardship to the litigants. More recent decisions speak more vividly. See Newman-Green, Inc. v. Alfonzo-Larrain, 490 U.S. 826, 836 (1989) ("requiring dismissal after years of litigation would impose unnecessary and wasteful burdens on the parties, judges, and other litigants waiting for judicial attention"). Such draconian results help to enforce jurisdictional limits by aligning the incentives of judges and parties to address and correctly answer jurisdictional questions. Aside from the instrumental value of harsh results, the first principle might appear to have constitutional underpinnings rooted in the separation of powers. In considering that proposition, note that the first principle operates more stringently on direct review in cases like Mansfield. On collateral review, the Court has not insisted on similarly rigid enforcement of jurisdictional limits.[2] See Paragraph (6), *infra.*

Durousseau rule does not extend to matters assigned by Article III to the Court's original jurisdiction; Congress has no explicit power to qualify or regulate that jurisdiction, except under the Necessary and Proper Clause. See Chap. III, Sec. 2.

Other institutional structures, including salaries that do not automatically adjust as the judicial workload increases, may help to encourage federal judges to respect the separation of powers. See Pfander, *Judicial Compensation and the Definition of Judicial Power in the Early Republic*, 107 Mich.L.Rev. 1 (2008).

[2]   Scholars debate the degree to which jurisdiction should retain its first-principle qualities on direct and collateral review. Compare Lee, *The Dubious Concept of Jurisdiction*, 54 Hastings L.J. 1613 (2003) (questioning the power conception of jurisdiction), and Dodson, *Jurisdiction and Its Effects*, 105 Geo.L.J. 619, 634 (2017) (proposing to redefine jurisdiction less as power than as a rule of forum determination), with Williams, *Jurisdiction as Power*, 89 U.Chi.L.Rev. 1719 (2022) (defending the jurisdiction as power metaphor as historically grounded and doctrinally useful even as moderated in the context of collateral review).

In perhaps the clearest challenge to the first principle's constitutional status, the American Law Institute's *Study of the Division of Jurisdiction Between State and Federal* Courts § 1386 (1969), proposed to preclude jurisdictional objections after the beginning of trial. Although the proposal made exceptions for previously unknown and unavailable facts or collusion between the parties, critics challenged the ALI proposal as unconstitutional, at least insofar as it would enable federal courts to adjudicate claims that exceed the limits of Article III. Defenders of the ALI's model statute understood Congress to have power to adopt procedures for timely resolution of jurisdictional issues.[3]

(4) Moderating Jurisdictional Defects. Under the Mansfield rule, federal courts must identify jurisdictional problems at both the trial and appellate stages of the process, even where the parties fail to do so. Once the jurisdictional defect has been identified, courts may consider how to moderate the impact of the dismissal.

(a) Costs. One possible moderating strategy was deployed in Mansfield, the award of costs. Having found that the defendant railway had erroneously invoked diversity jurisdiction in removing the action to federal court, the Court ordered the defendant to pay the plaintiffs' costs at the trial and appellate court levels. Given the narrow definition of costs applicable both in the nineteenth century and today, such awards fall well short of repaying plaintiffs the value of their lost judgments.[4]

(b) Sanctions. The Supreme Court has held that a district court may impose Rule 11 sanctions for misconduct in a proceeding over which it lacks subject matter jurisdiction. See Willy v. Coastal Corp., 503 U.S. 131 (1992). Unlike civil contempt, which seeks to induce compliance with a court order and necessarily implicates the merits of the order in question, Rule 11 sanctions were said to be punitive and separate from the merits.[5]

(c) Restitution. Suppose that the plaintiffs in Mansfield collected their judgment from the defendant railway before the judgment was set aside on appeal for want of subject matter jurisdiction. On remand, the plaintiffs might contend that the lower court, lacking jurisdiction, had no power to order restitution of the amount in question. In Northwestern Fuel Co. v. Brock, 139 U.S. 216, 219 (1891), the Court confirmed lower court power to order restitution: "Jurisdiction to correct what had been wrongfully done must remain with the court so long as the parties and the case are properly before it, either in the first instance or when remanded to it by an appellate tribunal."

(d) Subsequent Litigation. Assume that the plaintiffs in Mansfield later pursued their claims against the railway in Ohio state court. The state

---

[3]   For a qualified defense of some relaxation of the first principle based on an early practice of according prima facie weight to jurisdictional allegations in the record, see Collins, *Jurisdictional Exceptionalism*, 93 Va.L.Rev. 1829 (2007).

[4]   See Act of Feb. 26, 1853, Ch. 80, 10 Stat. 161, 168 (limiting costs to such matters as docket fees, judgment fees, fees for issuance of certain writs, and fees for removal).

[5]   *Cf.* Belleville Catering Co. v. Champaign Marketplace LLC, 350 F.3d 691, 694 (7th Cir.2003) (finding opposing attorneys responsible for jurisdictional dismissal and ordering them to relitigate the matter in state court without charging their clients additional fees).

court might attempt to moderate the jurisdictional dismissal's wasteful consequences by according some legal effect to the federal proceedings. Documents and depositions obtained through the discovery process and trial testimony might (absent a prior protective order) be used as grist for the subsequent litigation. In one case, the Supreme Court assumed that the prior adjudication (via summary judgment in federal court) might prefigure the result in a subsequent proceeding. See Newman-Green, 490 U.S. at 837 (observing that dismissal of the first proceeding on jurisdictional grounds would trigger a new federal lawsuit against the diverse defendants, which would "proceed to a preordained [summary] judgment"). But one should distinguish a preordained summary judgment from preclusive effect: had the first proceeding been resolved on disputed facts by a jury, before its vacatur on jurisdictional grounds, the earlier judgment would lack preclusive effect in a second proceeding.

(5) Curing Jurisdictional Defects. Congress has adopted some cures to avoid the disruptive effects of a jurisdictional dismissal. Thus, in 28 U.S.C. § 1653, Congress authorized the amendment of defective allegations of jurisdiction "in the trial or appellate courts." So long as the facts support an amendment to defective pleadings, the statute can prevent some jurisdictional disruption that might flow from mistaken allegations. But allegations alone do not establish the citizenship of the parties. If doubts arise, district courts will sometimes hold an evidentiary hearing to establish jurisdictional facts.[6]

District courts can address jurisdictional spoilers by dismissing a (not indispensable) non-diverse party under Fed.R.Civ.P. 21.[7] Significantly, the Supreme Court has held that a district court that lacked jurisdiction due to the presence of a non-diverse party may enter a binding judgment so long as the jurisdictional spoiler dropped out of the case before judgment was entered. See Caterpillar Inc. v. Lewis, 519 U.S. 61, 75 (1996). In addition, the Court has held that the appellate court can invoke Rule 21 to dismiss a jurisdictional spoiler on appeal, at least where the non-diverse party was not indispensable. See Newman-Green, 490 U.S. at 836. Non-diverse members of partnerships, associations, and LLCs do not qualify as parties subject to dismissal to cure jurisdictional defects. See Grupo Data v. Atlas Global L.P., 541 U.S. 567 (2004) (post-filing exclusion of non-diverse members of partnership did not cure jurisdictional defect; citizenship of an association depends on the members' citizenship at the time of filing).

(6) Relief from Judgments and Collateral Attack. The Mansfield Court dismissed for want of jurisdiction on direct appeal, but parties may attack the validity of a judgment in collateral proceedings. It is possible that the same unyielding attitude toward jurisdictional limits would control in all

---

[6]   The Court ruled in State Farm Fire & Cas. Co. v. Tashire, 386 U.S. 523 (1967), that Article III of the Constitution does not require complete diversity. Congress might adopt curative legislation relaxing the complete diversity requirement as a general matter and thereby lessening the likelihood of first-principle dismissals. Consider whether Congress might authorize incomplete diversity to validate otherwise problematic judgments in which incompletely diverse parties were mistakenly included in the litigation.

[7]   See Fed.R.Civ.P. 21 ("On motion or on its own, the court may at any time, on just terms, add or drop a party.").

contexts, requiring a federal court to grant relief from judgment on motion
and to reconsider jurisdictional issues when raised in collateral proceedings.
But in practice, the federal courts have tended to moderate the rigor of their
jurisdictional inquiry on collateral review.

Consider a motion under Federal Rule of Civil Procedure 60(b)(4)
seeking relief from a void judgment. In Gonzalez v. Crosby, 545 U.S. 524, 534
(2005), the Court stated in dicta that Rule 60(b)(4) "preserves parties'
opportunity to obtain vacatur of a judgment that is void for lack of subject-
matter jurisdiction . . . since absence of jurisdiction altogether deprives a
federal court of the power to adjudicate the rights of the parties." In practice,
though, as the Court has explained, federal courts have been less exacting.
See United Student Aid Funds, Inc. v. Espinosa, 559 U.S. 260, 270–71 (2010)
("Federal courts considering Rule 60(b)(4) motions that assert a judgment is
void because of a jurisdictional defect generally have reserved relief only for
the exceptional case in which the court that rendered judgment lacked even
an 'arguable basis' for jurisdiction").

In collateral proceedings, the Court has taken much the same approach
in treating many, but not all, jurisdictional errors as foreclosed from further
review. See Durfee v. Duke, 375 U.S. 106 (1963) (treating the adjudication of
a jurisdictional issue in a Nebraska proceeding as foreclosing the relitigation
of that issue in a subsequent suit brought in Missouri). See also Stoll v.
Gollieb, 305 U.S. 165 (1938). In Chicot County Drainage District v. Baxter
State Bank, 308 U.S. 371 (1940), the Court went further, refusing to allow a
collateral attack on an earlier judgment that resulted from proceedings in
which the parties did not actually contest jurisdiction. The Court explained
that, on the general principles governing the defense of res judicata, the
challengers had "the opportunity to raise the question of invalidity [and]
were not the less bound by the decree because they failed to raise it."

Together, Durfee and Chicot suggest that the first principle of
jurisdiction rigorously applies only on direct review. But the Court has not
been quite so consistent. In United States v. United States Fidelity &
Guaranty Co., 309 U.S. 506 (1940), the Court held that the United States
government and certain Native American tribes under its protection were
immune from suit; that the immunity could not be waived by failure to assert
it; and that an earlier judgment against them was open to collateral attack
in a later proceeding. See also Kalb v. Fuerstein, 308 U.S. 433 (1940) (holding
that, because a preemptive federal insolvency statute had rendered void a
state court judgment ordering a foreclosure sale of certain real property,
owners could reclaim the property in a subsequent proceeding).

Attempts to reconcile the two lines of decision recognize both the
interest in finality and the interest in jurisdictional limitation. See
Restatement (Second) Judgments § 12 (1980) (stating a general rule
precluding collateral attack on judgments for lack of jurisdiction except in
cases of "manifest abuse of authority"; substantial infringement of other
government authority; or an inability in the court rendering the judgment to
make an informed decision). The Restatement's general rule appears to track
Chicot County in recognizing preclusion in contested matters without regard
to whether the issue of subject matter jurisdiction was actually litigated as

it was in Durfee v. Duke. In addition, the exceptions seemingly accommodate both Fidelity & Guaranty and Kalb v. Fuerstein, without necessarily clarifying what qualifies as a substantial infringement of other government authority.

B. JURISDICTIONAL SEQUENCING

Steel Co. v. Citizens for a Better Environment
523 U.S. 83 (1998).
Certiorari to the United States Court of Appeals for the Seventh Circuit.

■ JUSTICE SCALIA delivered the opinion of the Court.

This is a private enforcement action under the citizen-suit provision of the Emergency Planning and Community Right-To-Know Act of 1986 (EPCRA), 42 U.S.C. § 11046(a)(1). The case presents the merits question, answered in the affirmative by the United States Court of Appeals for the Seventh Circuit, whether EPCRA authorizes suits for purely past violations. It also presents the jurisdictional question whether respondent, plaintiff below, has standing to bring this action.

I

Respondent, an association of individuals interested in environmental protection, sued petitioner, a small manufacturing company in Chicago, for past violations of EPCRA. EPCRA establishes a framework of state, regional, and local agencies designed to inform the public about the presence of hazardous and toxic chemicals, and to provide for emergency response in the event of health-threatening release. Central to its operation are reporting requirements compelling users of specified toxic and hazardous chemicals to file annual [reports providing details regarding chemical use].

Enforcement of EPCRA can take place on many fronts [including actions brought by the EPA and by state and local governments. In addition,] "any person may commence a civil action on his own behalf against . . . [a]n owner or operator of a facility for failure" [to file a required report]. [42 U.S.C.] § 11046(a)(1). As a prerequisite to bringing such a suit, the plaintiff must, 60 days prior to filing his complaint, give notice to [the EPA, the state], and the alleged violator. § 11046(d). * * *

In 1995 respondent sent a notice [that petitioner had failed to file the required reports. Petitioner promptly cured that failure during the 60-day waiting period. When the statutory period expired, Respondent sued for penalties.] Petitioner promptly filed a motion to dismiss under Federal Rules of Civil Procedure 12(b)(1) and (6), contending that, because its filings were up to date when the complaint was filed, the court had no jurisdiction to entertain a suit for a present violation; and that, because EPCRA does not allow suit for a purely historical violation, respondent's allegation of untimeliness in filing was not a claim upon which relief could be granted.

The district court agreed with petitioner on both points. The Court of Appeals reversed, concluding that citizens may seek penalties against EPCRA violators who file after the statutory deadline and after receiving notice.

II

We granted certiorari in this case to resolve a [circuit] conflict. * * * Petitioner, however, both in its petition for certiorari and in its briefs on the merits, has raised the issue of respondent's standing to maintain the suit, and hence this Court's jurisdiction to entertain it. Though there is some dispute on this point, see Part III, *infra*, this would normally be considered a threshold question that must be resolved in respondent's favor before proceeding to the merits. Justice Stevens' opinion concurring in the judgment, however, claims that the question whether § 11046(a) permits this cause of action is *also* "jurisdictional," and so has equivalent claim to being resolved first. Whether that is so has significant implications for this case and for many others, and so the point warrants extended discussion.

It is firmly established in our cases that the absence of a valid (as opposed to arguable) cause of action does not implicate subject-matter jurisdiction, *i.e.*, the courts' statutory or constitutional *power* to adjudicate the case. As we stated in Bell v. Hood, 327 U.S. 678, 682 (1946), "[j]urisdiction . . . is not defeated . . . by the possibility that the averments might fail to state a cause of action on which petitioners could actually recover." Rather, the district court has jurisdiction if "the right of the petitioners to recover under their complaint will be sustained if the Constitution and laws of the United States are given one construction and will be defeated if they are given another," *id.*, at 685, unless the claim "clearly appears to be immaterial and made solely for the purpose of obtaining jurisdiction or where such a claim is wholly insubstantial and frivolous." *Id.*, at 682–683. Dismissal for lack of subject-matter jurisdiction because of the inadequacy of the federal claim is proper only when the claim is "so insubstantial, implausible, foreclosed by prior decisions of this Court, or otherwise completely devoid of merit as not to involve a federal controversy." Oneida Indian Nation of N.Y. v. County of Oneida, 414 U.S. 661, 666 (1974). * * *

Justice Stevens relies on our treatment of a similar issue as jurisdictional in Gwaltney of Smithfield, Ltd. v. Chesapeake Bay Foundation, Inc., 484 U.S. 49 (1987). The statute at issue in that case, however, after creating the cause of action, went on to say that "[t]he district courts shall have jurisdiction, *without regard to the amount in controversy or the citizenship of the parties*," to provide various forms of relief. 33 U.S.C. § 1365(a) (emphasis added). The italicized phrase strongly suggested (perhaps misleadingly) that the provision was addressing genuine subject-matter jurisdiction. The corresponding provision in the present case, however, reads as follows:

> "The district court shall have jurisdiction in actions brought under subsection (a) of this section against an owner or operator of a facility to enforce the requirement concerned and to impose any civil penalty provided for violation of that requirement." 42 U.S.C. § 11046(c).

It is unreasonable to read this as making all the elements of the cause of action under subsection (a) jurisdictional, rather than as merely specifying the remedial *powers* of the court, viz., to enforce the violated requirement and to impose civil penalties. "Jurisdiction," it has been observed, "is a word of many, too many, meanings" * * *. * * *

It is also the case that the Gwaltney opinion does not display the slightest awareness that anything *turned upon* whether the existence of a cause of action for past violations was technically jurisdictional—as indeed nothing of substance did. The District Court had statutory jurisdiction over the suit in any event, since continuing violations were also alleged. It is true, as Justice Stevens points out, that the issue of Article III standing which is addressed at the end of the opinion should technically have been addressed at the outset if the statutory question was not jurisdictional. But that also did not really matter, since Article III standing was in any event found. The short of the matter is that the jurisdictional character of the elements of the cause of action in Gwaltney made no substantive difference (nor even any procedural difference that the Court seemed aware of), had been assumed by the parties, and was assumed without discussion by the Court. We have often said that drive-by jurisdictional rulings of this sort (if Gwaltney can even be called a ruling on the point rather than a dictum) have no precedential effect. [Citing cases.] * * *

Justice Stevens' concurrence devotes a large portion of its discussion to cases in which a statutory standing question was decided before a question of constitutional standing. They also are irrelevant here, because it is not a statutory *standing* question that Justice Stevens would have us decide first. He wishes to resolve, not whether EPCRA authorizes this plaintiff to sue (it assuredly does), but whether the scope of the EPCRA right of action includes past violations. Such a question, we have held, goes to the merits and not to statutory standing. See Northwest Airlines, Inc. v. County of Kent, 510 U.S. 355, 365 (1994) ("The question whether a federal statute creates a claim for relief is not jurisdictional").

Though it is replete with extensive case discussions, case citations, rationalizations, and syllogoids, Justice Stevens' opinion conspicuously lacks one central feature: a single case in which this Court has done what he proposes, to wit, call the existence of a cause of action "jurisdictional," and decide that question before resolving a dispute concerning the existence of an Article III case or controversy. Of course, even if there were not solid precedent contradicting Justice Stevens' position, the consequences are alone enough to condemn it. It would turn every statutory question in an EPCRA citizen suit into a question of jurisdiction. * * * If Justice Stevens is correct that all cause-of-action questions may be regarded as jurisdictional questions, and thus capable of being decided where there is no genuine case or controversy, it is hard to see what is left of that limitation in Article III.

III

In addition to its attempt to convert the merits issue in this case into a jurisdictional one, Justice Stevens' concurrence proceeds to argue the bolder point that jurisdiction need not be addressed first anyway. Even if the statutory question is not "fram[ed] . . . in terms of 'jurisdiction,'" but is simply "characterize[d] . . . as whether respondent's complaint states a 'cause of action,'" "it is also clear that we have the power to decide the statutory question first." This is essentially the position embraced by several Courts of Appeals, which find it proper to proceed immediately to the merits question, despite jurisdictional objections, at least where (1) the merits question is more readily resolved, and (2) the prevailing party on the merits would be the same as the prevailing party were jurisdiction denied. [Citing cases.] The Ninth Circuit has denominated this practice—which it characterizes as "assuming" jurisdiction for the purpose of deciding the merits—the "doctrine of hypothetical jurisdiction." See, e.g., United States v. Troescher, 99 F.3d 933, 934, n.1 ([9th Cir.]1996).

We decline to endorse such an approach because it carries the courts beyond the bounds of authorized judicial action and thus offends fundamental principles of separation of powers. This conclusion should come as no surprise, since it is reflected in a long and venerable line of our cases. "Without jurisdiction the court cannot proceed at all in any cause. Jurisdiction is power to declare the law, and when it ceases to exist, the only function remaining to the court is that of announcing the fact and dismissing the cause." Ex parte McCardle, [74 U.S.] 7 Wall. 506, 514 (1868). * * * The requirement that jurisdiction be established as a threshold matter "spring[s] from the nature and limits of the judicial power of the United States" and is "inflexible and without exception." Mansfield, C. & L.M.R. Co. v. Swan, 111 U.S. 379, 382 (1884).

This Court's insistence that proper jurisdiction appear begins at least as early as 1804, when we set aside a judgment for the defendant at the instance of the losing plaintiff *who had himself* failed to allege the basis for federal jurisdiction. Capron v. Van Noorden, [6 U.S.] 2 Cranch 126 (1804). * * *

Justice Stevens' arguments contradicting all this jurisprudence—and asserting that a court may decide the cause of action before resolving Article III jurisdiction—are readily refuted. * * *

Much more extensive defenses of the practice of deciding the cause of action before resolving Article III jurisdiction have been offered by the Courts of Appeals. * * *

While some of the * * * cases must be acknowledged to have diluted the absolute purity of the rule that Article III jurisdiction is always an antecedent question, none of them even approaches approval of a doctrine of "hypothetical jurisdiction" that enables a court to resolve contested questions of law when its jurisdiction is in doubt. Hypothetical jurisdiction produces nothing more than a hypothetical judgment—which comes to the same thing as an advisory opinion, disapproved by this Court from the beginning. Muskrat v. United States, 219 U.S. 346, 362 (1911); Hayburn's Case, 2 [U.S.] Dall. 409 (1792). Much more than legal niceties are at stake here. The statutory and (especially) constitutional elements of jurisdiction are an essential ingredient of separation and equilibration of powers, restraining the courts from acting at certain times, and even restraining them from acting permanently regarding certain subjects. For a court to pronounce upon the meaning or the constitutionality of a state or federal law when it has no jurisdiction to do so is, by very definition, for a court to act ultra vires.

IV

Having reached the end of what seems like a long front walk, we finally arrive at the threshold jurisdictional question: whether respondent, the plaintiff below, has standing to sue. [The Court held no, emphasizing the inability of declaratory and injunctive relief to redress any injury from past reporting failures.]

* * *

Having found that none of the relief sought by respondent would likely remedy its alleged injury in fact, we must conclude that respondent lacks standing to maintain this suit, and that we and the lower courts lack jurisdiction to entertain it. However desirable prompt resolution of the merits EPCRA question may be, it is not as important as observing the constitutional limits set upon courts in our system of separated powers. EPCRA will have to await another day.

The judgment is vacated, and the case is remanded with instructions to direct that the complaint be dismissed.

It is so ordered.

■ JUSTICE O'CONNOR, with whom JUSTICE KENNEDY joins, concurring.

[Justice O'Connor agreed with the Court's conclusion that federal courts should be certain of their jurisdiction before reaching the merits of a case.] I write separately to note that, in my view, the Court's opinion should not be read as cataloging an exhaustive list of circumstances under which federal courts may exercise judgment in "reserv[ing] difficult questions of . . . jurisdiction when the case alternatively could be resolved on the merits in favor of the same party."

■ JUSTICE BREYER, concurring in part and concurring in the judgment.

[Justice Breyer agreed as to Article III standing.] I further agree that federal courts often, and typically should, decide standing questions at the outset of a case. That order of decision (first jurisdiction then the merits) helps better to restrict the use of the federal courts to those adversarial disputes that Article III defines as the federal judiciary's business. * * *

* * * I would not make the ordinary sequence an absolute requirement. Nor, even though the case before us is ordinary, not exceptional, would I simply reserve judgment about the matter. I therefore join only Parts I and IV of the Court's opinion.

■ JUSTICE STEVENS, with whom JUSTICE SOUTER joins as to Parts I, III, and IV, and with whom JUSTICE GINSBURG joins as to Part III, concurring in the judgment.

This case presents two questions: (1) whether [EPCRA] confers federal jurisdiction over citizen suits for wholly past violations; and (2) if so, whether respondent has standing under Article III of the Constitution. The Court has elected to decide the constitutional question first and, in doing so, has created new constitutional law. Because it is always prudent to avoid passing unnecessarily on an undecided constitutional question, the Court should answer the statutory question first. Moreover, because EPCRA, properly construed, does not confer jurisdiction over citizen suits for wholly past violations, the Court should leave the constitutional question for another day.

I

The statutory issue in this case can be viewed in one of two ways: whether EPCRA confers "jurisdiction" over citizen suits for wholly past violations, or whether the statute creates such a "cause of action." Under either analysis, the Court has the power to answer the statutory question first.

EPCRA frames the question in terms of "jurisdiction." Section 326(c) states:

> "The district court shall have jurisdiction in actions brought under [§ 326(a)] against an owner or operator of a facility to enforce the requirement concerned and to impose any civil penalty provided for violation of that requirement." 42 U.S.C. § 11046(c).

Thus, if § 326(a) authorizes citizen suits for wholly past violations, the district court has jurisdiction over these actions; if it does not, the court lacks jurisdiction.

Given the text of the statute, it is not surprising that the parties and the District Court framed the question in jurisdictional terms. * * *

The threshold issue concerning the meaning of § 326 is virtually identical to the question that we decided in Gwaltney of Smithfield, Ltd.

v. Chesapeake Bay Foundation, Inc., 484 U.S. 49 (1987). In that case, we considered whether § 505(a) of the Clean Water Act allows suits for wholly past violations. We unanimously characterized that question as a matter of "jurisdiction." * * * If we resolve the comparable statutory issue in the same way in this case, federal courts will have no jurisdiction to address the merits in future similar cases. Thus, this is not a case in which the choice between resolving the statutory question or the standing question first is a choice between a merits issue and a jurisdictional issue; rather, it is a choice between two jurisdictional issues.

We have routinely held that when presented with two jurisdictional questions, the Court may choose which one to answer first. [Here, Justice Stevens relied upon, among other decisions, Sierra Club v. Morton, 405 U.S. 727 (1972).]

* * * See also and Bennett v. Spear, 520 U.S. 154, 164 (1997) (opinion of Scalia, J.) (stating that "[t]he first question in the present case is whether the [Endangered Species Act's] citizen-suit provision . . . negates the zone-of-interests test," and turning to the constitutional standing question only after determining that standing existed under the statute). Thus, our precedents clearly support the proposition that, given a choice between two jurisdictional questions—one statutory and the other constitutional—the Court has the power to answer the statutory question first. * * *

Thus, regardless of whether we characterize this issue in terms of "jurisdiction" or "causes of action," the Court clearly has the power to address the statutory question first. Gwaltney itself powerfully demonstrates this point. As noted, that case involved a statutory question virtually identical to the one presented here—whether the statute permitted citizens to sue for wholly past violations. While the Court framed the question as one of "jurisdiction," it could also be said that the case presented the question whether the plaintiffs had a "cause of action." Regardless of the label, the Court resolved the statutory question without pausing to consider whether the plaintiffs had standing to sue for wholly past violations. Of course, the fact that we did not discuss standing in Gwaltney does not establish that the plaintiffs had standing there. Nonetheless, it supports the proposition that—regardless of how the issue is characterized—the Court has the power to address the virtually identical statutory question in this case as well.

The Court disagrees, arguing that the standing question must be addressed first. Ironically, however, before "first" addressing standing, the Court takes a long excursion that entirely loses sight of the basic reason why standing is a matter of such importance to the proper functioning of the judicial process. The "gist of the question of standing" is whether plaintiffs have "alleged such a personal stake in the outcome of the controversy as to assure that concrete adverseness which sharpens the presentation of issues upon which the court so largely depends for illumination of difficult constitutional questions." The Court completely disregards this core purpose of standing in its discussion of "hypothetical jurisdiction." Not only is that portion of the Court's opinion pure dictum because it is entirely unnecessary to an explanation of the Court's decision; it is also not informed by any adversary submission by either party. Neither the topic of "hypothetical jurisdiction," nor any of the cases analyzed, distinguished, and criticized in Part III, was the subject of any comment in any of the briefs submitted by the parties or their amici. It therefore did not benefit from the "concrete adverseness" that the standing doctrine is meant to ensure. * * *

The doctrine of "hypothetical jurisdiction" is irrelevant because this case presents us with a choice between two threshold questions that are intricately interrelated—as there is only a standing problem if the statute confers jurisdiction over suits for wholly past violations. The Court's opinion reflects this fact, as its analysis of the standing issue is predicated on the hypothesis that § 326 may be read to confer jurisdiction over citizen suits for wholly past violations. If, as I think it should, the Court were to reject that hypothesis and construe § 326, the standing discussion would be entirely unnecessary. Thus, ironically, the Court is engaged in a version of the "hypothetical jurisdiction" that it has taken pains to condemn at some length.

II

There is an important reason for addressing the statutory question first: to avoid unnecessarily passing on an undecided constitutional question. Whether correct or incorrect, the Court's constitutional holding [denying standing to the plaintiff citizens group] represents a significant extension of prior case law.

[Justice Stevens next questioned the Court's analysis of the standing issue, viewing it as based on a contestable application of a "redressability" requirement that was judicially created in the past twenty-five years.]

It is thus quite clear that the Court's holding today represents a significant new development in our constitutional jurisprudence. Moreover, it is equally clear that the Court has the power to answer the statutory question first. It is, therefore, not necessary to reject the Court's resolution of the standing issue in order to conclude that it would be prudent to answer the question of statutory construction before announcing new constitutional doctrine.

III

[Justice Stevens evaluated the text and history of EPCRA's citizen-suit provision, found it ambiguous, but reasoned that other sections of EPCRA demonstrate that Congress did not intend to allow suit for wholly past violations.]

[He concluded,] our settled policy of adopting acceptable constructions of statutory provisions in order to avoid the unnecessary adjudication of constitutional questions—here, the unresolved standing question—strongly supports a construction of the statute that does not authorize suits for wholly past violations.

IV

For these reasons, I concur in the Court's judgment, but do not join its opinion.

■ JUSTICE GINSBURG, concurring in the judgment.

[Expressing agreement with Justice Stevens that EPCRA did not authorize suits for wholly past violations, Justice Ginsburg proposed to] resist expounding or offering advice on the constitutionality of what Congress might have done, but did not do.

NOTE ON JURISDICTIONAL SEQUENCING

Decisional sequencing occurs in a variety of settings, perhaps most famously in Marbury v. Madison, 5 U.S. (1 Cranch) 137 (1803), p. 76, *supra*, a case the Steel Co. Court failed to cite. Before reaching the jurisdictional question in Marbury, Chief Justice Marshall considered whether mandamus was proper to compel delivery of Marbury's commission; whether the suit was cognizable, notwithstanding Madison's government office; and whether the statute conferred the jurisdiction in question. Only then did Marshall conclude that the statute violated Article III's limitation on the scope of the Court's original jurisdiction. Something similar occurred in Ex parte Christy, 44 U.S. 292, 323 (1845), where the Court, per Justice Story, delivered a lengthy disquisition on the district court's equity jurisdiction in bankruptcy before concluding that it lacked jurisdiction to review that court's work on a writ of prohibition. Justice Catron wrote separately to argue that the Court should not "hazard an opinion where no case was before the court, and when that opinion might be justly arraigned as extra-judicial." *Id.* 322 (Catron, J.).

In Steel Co., the Court viewed sequencing as an obligatory implication of the jurisdictional character of the Article III inquiry. By according jurisdictional status to the standing doctrine and demanding its threshold consideration, the Court increased the output of standing and other subject matter jurisdiction decisions by the federal appellate courts and encouraged first-principle jurisdictional dismissals. Yet the Court apparently left open the issue of sequencing when the defendant's threshold objections do not entail an adjudication of the merits.

(1) Non-Merits Jurisdictional Sequencing. In Ruhrgas AG v. Marathon Oil Co., 526 U.S. 574 (1999), the Marathon group and its affiliates had sued Ruhrgas in Texas state court, alleging fraud and breach of fiduciary duty in connection with a contract calling for Marathon to extract oil and gas from the Norwegian North Sea and sell it to Ruhrgas for distribution to the European market. Ruhrgas removed the matter to federal court, invoking that court's diversity and federal question jurisdiction. In so doing, Ruhrgas also argued that Texas courts (and by implication, the federal court[1]) lacked personal jurisdiction over it and the case should be dismissed. The district court conducted jurisdictional discovery and concluded that none of the allegedly fraudulent acts had occurred in Texas. Applying circuit precedent, the district court found that it had sequencing discretion to grant the motion to dismiss on what it viewed as a relatively straightforward personal jurisdiction defense without first resolving the more complicated subject matter jurisdiction issue raised by the plaintiffs in support of remand, which was rooted in the proper interpretation of the complete diversity rule. Relying on Steel Co., the Fifth Circuit reversed the dismissal on personal jurisdiction grounds, concluded there was no subject matter jurisdiction over the suit in federal court, and remanded the proceeding to state court.

A unanimous Court reversed and remanded, upholding the sequencing discretion of the district court. Writing for the Court, Justice Ginsburg first rejected the argument that subject matter jurisdiction was "ever and always the more 'fundamental.' " The subject matter issue in the case, she wrote, did not implicate any constitutional limitation, whereas the personal jurisdiction question turned on an assessment of the Due Process Clause. Justice Ginsburg acknowledged that Steel Co. viewed subject matter jurisdiction as necessarily preceding a ruling on the merits. But "the same principle does not dictate a sequencing of jurisdictional issues." Justice Ginsburg pointed to instances in which the federal courts might permissibly choose among threshold grounds for declining to address the merits, including discretionary decisions about the exercise of supplemental jurisdiction and whether to abstain in deference to a pending state proceeding.

In reaching its holding, the Court also rejected additional arguments advanced by the Marathon group. To begin, the Marathon group urged that removal presents especially sensitive questions of federal-state relations, given the likely application of issue preclusion to block any litigation in state court after dismissal of the federal proceeding. Marathon also argued that allowing the district courts to dismiss on other grounds would encourage defendants to "abuse the federal system with opportunistic removals" based on "convoluted" theories of federal subject matter jurisdiction. The Court did not deny that issue preclusion might block further state court litigation, only that such issue preclusive effect could also attach to subject-matter jurisdictional dismissals. As for the concern with opportunistic removals, the Court expressed confidence that district courts would fairly apply removal limits and thereby discourage defendant gamesmanship.

(2) Ruhrgas Extended. In Sinochem International Co. Ltd. v. Malaysia International Shipping Corp., 549 U.S. 422 (2007), the Court extended Ruhrgas sequencing to dismissals based on forum non conveniens. The dispute arose when a Chinese firm, Sinochem, alleged fraud by the Malaysian shipping firm in triggering payment under a letter of credit. Sinochem invoked the jurisdiction of a Chinese admiralty court, securing the arrest of the Malaysian firm's vessel to secure payment of any amounts owed.

---

[1]   See Fed.R.Civ.P. 4(k)(1)(A) (establishing default rule that federal courts analyze matters of personal jurisdiction the same as the state courts in the state in which the federal court is located).

When the Malaysian firm brought suit in federal district court in Pennsylvania, that court dismissed for forum non conveniens. The Court, citing Ruhrgas, affirmed the dismissal, despite the federal court's failure to first resolve issues of subject matter and personal jurisdiction. Justice Ginsburg wrote again for a unanimous Court, concluding that "where subject-matter or personal jurisdiction is difficult to determine, and forum non conveniens considerations weigh heavily in favor of dismissal, the court properly takes the less burdensome course." *Id.* 436.[2]

(3) Ruhrgas Questioned. Scholars have questioned both the Court's approach to jurisdictional sequencing and its tendency, in cases like Ruhrgas, to enable defendants to defeat claims through removal and the presentation of a non-merits but nonetheless fatal defense. On sequencing generally, see Trammell, *Jurisdictional Sequencing*, 47 Ga.L.Rev. 1099 (2013); Clermont, *Sequencing the Issues for Judicial Decisionmaking: Limitations from Jurisdictional Primacy and Intrasuit Preclusion*, 63 Fla.L.Rev. 301 (2011). On the use of procedural grounds to dismiss claims after removal, see Clopton, *Catch and Kill Jurisdiction*, 121 Mich.L.Rev. 171 (2022). Contrast the Ruhrgas Court's decision to downplay the significance of the issue preclusive effects of a personal jurisdiction dismissal with the approach taken in Mansfield, which returned the matter to state court for de novo litigation, free from any issue preclusive effects.

NOTE ON JURISDICTIONAL CHARACTERIZATION

The Steel Co. Court's distinction between jurisdictional questions and merits-based issues has informed both jurisdictional sequencing and jurisdictional characterization. A growing body of law has elaborated on Steel Co. while often insisting on a narrower definition of the issues to be treated as jurisdictional within the meaning of Mansfield's first principle.[1]

(1) Statutory Elements of a Claim. In Arbaugh v. Y & H Corporation, 546 U.S. 500 (2006), the Court rejected an employer's argument that Title VII's employee-numerosity requirement operated as a jurisdictional limitation on the district court's power to adjudicate a claim of sexual harassment in the workplace. After the jury returned a verdict in favor of the plaintiff, finding harassment and awarding $40,000 in compensatory and punitive damages, Y & H questioned the district court's jurisdiction. Upon conducting a hearing, the district court found that Y & H employed fewer than the 15 persons needed to meet the statute's definition of a covered employer and dismissed for lack of subject matter jurisdiction. Reversing and

---

[2]   Would the federal forum non conveniens decision bind the parties if the action were re-filed in a Pennsylvania state court? See Chick Kam Choo v. Exxon Corp., 486 U.S. 140 (1988) (proceeding on the assumption that the Texas state courts could apply a different body of forum non conveniens law in subsequent state court litigation).

[1]   See Dodson, *In Search of Removal Jurisdiction*, 102 Nw.U.L.Rev. 55, 88–89 (2008); Wasserman, *Jurisdiction and Merits*, 80 Wash.L.Rev. 643 (2005); Wasserman, *Jurisdiction, Merits, and Procedure: Thoughts on a Trichotomy*, 102 Nw.U.L.Rev. 1547 (2008); Wasserman, *The Demise of "Drive-By Jurisdictional Rulings,"* 105 Nw.U.L.Rev. 947 (2011).

remanding in an opinion written by Justice Ginsburg, the Court reasoned as follows:

"Of course, Congress could make the employee-numerosity requirement 'jurisdictional,' just as it has made an amount-in-controversy threshold an ingredient of subject-matter jurisdiction in delineating diversity-of-citizenship jurisdiction under 28 U.S.C. § 1332. But neither § 1331, nor Title VII's jurisdictional provision, 42 U.S.C. § 2000e–5(f)(3) (authorizing jurisdiction over actions 'brought under' Title VII), specifies any threshold ingredient akin to 28 U.S.C. § 1332's monetary floor. Instead, the 15-employee threshold appears in a separate provision that 'does not speak in jurisdictional terms or refer in any way to the jurisdiction of the district courts.' Zipes v. Trans World Airlines, Inc., 455 U.S. 385, 394 (1982). Given the 'unfair[ness]' and 'waste of judicial resources,' entailed in tying the employee-numerosity requirement to subject-matter jurisdiction, we think it the sounder course to refrain from constricting § 1331 or Title VII's jurisdictional provision, 42 U.S.C. § 2000e–5(f)(3), and to leave the ball in Congress's court. If the Legislature clearly states that a threshold limitation on a statute's scope shall count as jurisdictional, then courts and litigants will be duly instructed and will not be left to wrestle with the issue. But when Congress does not rank a statutory limitation on coverage as jurisdictional, courts should treat the restriction as non-jurisdictional in character. Applying that readily administrable bright line to this case, we hold that the threshold number of employees for application of Title VII is an element of a plaintiff's claim for relief, not a jurisdictional issue." 546 U.S. at 514–16.

(2) Distinguishing Jurisdiction and Claim-Processing Rules. Some courts have treated time limitations as jurisdictional, thereby ascribing first-principle status to objections based on the timeliness of claims and defenses. In Kontrick v. Ryan, 540 U.S. 443 (2004), a unanimous Court held, per Justice Ginsburg, that the rules governing the assertion of claims and defenses in bankruptcy should be regarded as mandatory claim-processing rules, rather than jurisdictional rules.

"Characteristically, a court's subject-matter jurisdiction cannot be expanded to account for the parties' litigation conduct; a claim-processing rule, on the other hand, even if unalterable on a party's application, can nonetheless be forfeited if the party asserting the rule waits too long to raise the point." Id. 456. The Court viewed the timeliness rule as mandatory, but non-jurisdictional, and found that it was forfeited by the debtor's failure to raise the issue before the court below ruled on the merits.

In contrast to unanimity on display in Arbaugh and Kontrick, a closely divided Court in Bowles v. Russell, 551 U.S. 205 (2007), held that statutory timeliness rules for filing a notice of appeal were jurisdictional.[2] Subsequent

---

[2]   Relying on the federal appellate rules and 28 U.S.C. § 2107(c), the district court had enlarged the time for petitioner Bowles to file a notice of appeal from denial of his application for habeas corpus. But the district court gave more time than the statute allowed. In concluding that the time limit was jurisdictional, the Court relied on earlier decisions that characterized the time for appeal as a jurisdictional restriction and on the fact that the limitation appeared in a federal statute rather than (as in Kontrick) in a bankruptcy rule. The dissent found no clear statement in the applicable statute. For criticism, see Dodson, *The Failure of Bowles v. Russell*, 43 Tulsa L.Rev. 631 (2008).

cases have returned to the clear-statement rule of Arbaugh in assessing the jurisdictional significance of statutory time limits. See Harrow v. Department of Defense, 601 U.S. 480 (2024) (holding unanimously while applying clear statement rule that sixty-day limit for filing petition for review in the Federal Circuit of any agency decision was non-jurisdictional and therefore subject to equitable tolling); Boechler, P.C. v. Comm'r of Internal Review, 596 U.S. 199 (2022) (holding unanimously that thirty-day limit for filing of petition seeking review of assessment in Tax Court was non-jurisdictional and subject to equitable tolling); United States v. Wong, 575 U.S. 402 (2015) (5–4) (concluding that Congress did not clearly state its intention that time limits for the submission of claims under the Federal Tort Claims Act were jurisdictional restrictions); Henderson v. Shinseki, 562 U.S. 428 (2011) (rejecting government's argument that statutory 120-day deadline for the submission of a veteran's disability appeal should be treated as jurisdictional; unlike the statute in Bowles, time limit applied to proceedings in the non-Article III U.S. Court of Veterans Appeals). But where its earlier decisions had adopted a jurisdictional characterization of statutory time limits, the Court has reaffirmed that treatment. See John R. Sand & Gravel Co. v. United States, 552 U.S. 130 (2008) (history compels treatment of six-year time limit for initiating suit in Court of Claims as jurisdictional) (citing Finn v. United States, 123 U.S. 227 (1887) (holding that a time limit on suit against the government should be treated as jurisdictional, and that the ordinary legal principle that "limitation . . . is a defence [that a defendant] must plead . . . *has no application to suits in the Court of Claims against the United States*")).[3]

(3) State Sovereign Immunity. The Court has sometimes suggested that the state's immunity from suit in federal court serves as a jurisdictional limitation. See Edelman v. Jordan, 415 U.S. 651, 678 (1974) (declaring that a state's immunity "sufficiently partakes of the nature of a jurisdictional bar so that it need not be raised in the trial court"); *cf.* Sosna v. Iowa, 419 U.S. 393, 396 n.2 (1975) (noting that states may waive their quasi-jurisdictional immunity through consent or waiver by the conduct of their attorneys). If state consent to suit overrides sovereign immunity, can the issue be sensibly characterized as jurisdictional? Might the characterization depend on the source of the state's immunity defense? Jurisdictional restrictions imposed by the text of the Eleventh Amendment might deserve more inflexible

---

[3]   The Court has frequently rejected arguments that time limits and other defenses available in suits against the United States should be characterized as conditions on the waiver of sovereign immunity and accorded jurisdictional treatment. See Wilkins v. United States, 598 U.S. 152 (2023) (holding twelve-year time limit on suits to challenge the United States' rights in real property, in the absence of any clear statement, non-jurisdictional). Compare Case v. Terrell, 78 (11 Wall.) U.S. 199 (1871) (reversing on its own motion a circuit court decree awarding the plaintiff some $200,000 against the United States; reasoning that the officials named as defendants lacked the power to waive the government's immunity from suit). The contrast between Wilkins and Terrell suggests that a congressional decision to authorize a certain category of litigation against the United States may waive sovereign immunity as a general matter and call for the treatment of defenses to litigation within the category as non-jurisdictional. See United States v. Wong, 575 U.S. 402, 419 (2015) (rejecting government's sovereign-immunity-based argument that time limits in the Federal Tort Claims Act were jurisdictional; describing the FTCA as treating the government "more like a commoner than like the Crown").

treatment than the broader unwritten state immunity identified in such cases as Seminole Tribe v. Florida, 517 U.S. 44 (1996), and Alden v. Maine, 527 U.S. 706 (1999). For greater discussion, see Chap. IX, Sec. 3.

(4) Appellate Review of Remand Orders. Jurisdictional issues arise in appellate review of remand orders issued by district courts in removal cases. The governing statute forecloses routine appellate review of district court decisions remanding a case to state court for want of subject matter jurisdiction. See 28 U.S.C. § 1447(d).

The Court has attempted to offer some guidance on the question of how closely appellate courts should scrutinize the purported jurisdictional basis of remand orders. In Kirchner v. Putnam Funds Trust, 547 U.S. 643 (2006), the Court ruled that the district court had correctly characterized its remand decision as jurisdictional and had thus reached a conclusion that foreclosed appellate review. In engaging in any review of the matter, the Court's approach suggests that appellate courts may at least consider the plausibility of a district court order remanding on jurisdictional grounds and potentially may reverse the remand order if it concludes that the district court wrongly characterized its disposition as jurisdictional. Such a regime could invite appellate litigation over the proper characterization of district court remand orders. *Cf.* Powerex Corp. v. Reliant Energy Services, Inc., 551 U.S. 224 (2007) (barring appellate review when the district court's remand order rested on a colorable assertion of lack of subject matter jurisdiction and noting a division within the Court on the proper handling of such jurisdictional issues). See Pfander, *Collateral Review of Remand Orders: Reasserting the Supervisory Role of the Supreme Court*, 159 U.Pa.L.Rev. 493 (2011).

(5) Exhaustion. In Santos-Zacaria v. Garland, 598 U.S. 141 (2023), the Court held that 8 U.S.C. § 1252(d)(1)'s exhaustion requirement for appealing an immigration removal order from an Immigration Judge is not jurisdictional. Viewing exhaustion as a quintessential claim-processing rule, the Court reasoned that allowing the issue to be raised at any point in litigation would defeat its purpose of promoting efficiency. The Court rejected an argument that Congress's placement of the exhaustion requirement in a broader section concerning judicial review warranted interpreting the requirement as jurisdictional.

(6) Clarity of the Statement. Building on the assumption that that Congress can define specified elements of a statutory claim as jurisdictional, the Court in MOAC Mall Holdings v. Transform Holdco LLC, 598 U.S. 288, 298 (2023), addressed the necessary clarity of the required congressional statement. The Court said that Congress need not use "magic words" to convey its intent that a matter be treated as jurisdictional and approved the use of traditional tools of statutory construction in assessing the clarity of Congress's statement. At the same time, the Court said that the statement must actually be clear; a jurisdictional reading must be more than merely "plausible" or the "better" reading.

2. THE SCOPE OF THE CONSTITUTIONAL GRANT OF FEDERAL QUESTION JURISDICTION

INTRODUCTORY NOTE

Article III, § 2 empowers the federal courts to hear "cases," essentially defined by the subject matter of the litigation, and "controversies" between specified categories of parties. This section focuses on the lower federal courts' original jurisdiction over federal question cases; a later section takes up jurisdiction based on party alignment.

As the cases that follow underscore, lower federal courts may exercise subject matter jurisdiction only if Congress has so provided and if doing so respects the limits set forth in Article III. In the next principal case, Osborn v. Bank of the United States, the Court located the relevant statutory authority in the legislation that created the Bank. (The general federal question statute, now 28 U.S.C. § 1331, was not available as an enduring source of federal jurisdiction until 1875). That finding set the stage for the Osborn Court's now classic discussion of the scope of Congress's authority under Article III to confer federal question jurisdiction on the lower federal courts.

Today, most plaintiffs pursuing federal question claims in the lower federal courts rely on § 1331. As explored in a principal case below, Louisville & Nashville R.R. Co. v. Mottley, 211 U.S. 149 (1908), p. 1024, *infra*, the Court has interpreted the statute to apply only where a relatively substantial question of federal law appears on the face of the well-pleaded complaint. As a practical matter, then, most claims that "arise under" federal law for purposes of § 1331 will so arise for purposes of the constitutional grant. But occasionally, Congress enacts particular jurisdictional statutes that authorize the federal courts to hear cases that implicate federal law but do not fall under § 1331 and in which federal law figures less centrally than it does in cases that would fall under § 1331. Some of these jurisdictional grants embrace cases in which a question of federal law is uncontested or subsidiary, and on rare occasions a statute may appear to confer jurisdiction in cases in which federal law is absent altogether. Statutes such as these test the outer limits of Article III's "arising under" jurisdiction.

The materials that follow present a range of understandings about the scope of Article III. The decision in Osborn and the accompanying Note discuss just what kind of federal issue must be present for a case to arise under federal law within the meaning of Article III. As explored further below, similar questions arise today in litigation under modern statutes, such as claims in bankruptcy, suits to enforce labor contracts, and claims for compensation for losses sustained in the September 11, 2001, attacks. And complicated questions of jurisdiction arise as well when Congress assigns the adjudication of claims to federal court in which state law provides the rule of decision. As the materials that follow demonstrate, the Court has been suspicious of arguments that would premise jurisdiction not on the need to adjudicate an issue of federal law but on the need to protect federal interests in a case governed by state law.

A. THE BROAD SWEEP OF OSBORN

Osborn v. Bank of the United States

22 U.S. (9 Wheat.) 738 (1824).
Appeal from the Circuit Court of Ohio.

[The Bank of the United States sued to enjoin Ralph Osborn, auditor of the State of Ohio, from enforcing an Ohio statute that, after reciting that the Bank's operations violated an Ohio law, provided that the Bank, if it continued to transact business in Ohio after September 1, 1819, would be liable for an annual tax of $50,000 on each office of discount and deposit. In September of 1819—six months after the Bank's immunity from state taxation had been recognized in M'Culloch v. Maryland, 17 U.S. (4 Wheat.) 316 (1819)—the federal circuit court issued the requested injunction, which was served upon Osborn and also upon Harper, whom Osborn had allegedly employed to collect the tax.

[An amended bill charged that Harper, after service of the injunction, took $100,000 in specie and bank notes from a Bank office in Ohio. Sullivan, the State treasurer, was apparently holding $98,000 of this money separately, with notice of the circumstances; the location of the remaining $2,000 was unclear. The circuit court ordered Osborn and Harper to restore $100,000 to the bank, with interest on $19,830 (the amount of specie held by Sullivan).]* * *

■ MR. CHIEF JUSTICE MARSHALL delivered the opinion of the Court, and, after stating the case, proceeded as follows:

At the close of the argument, a point was suggested, of such vital importance, as to induce the Court to request that it might be particularly spoken to. That point is, the right of the Bank to sue in the Courts of the United States. It has been argued, and ought to be disposed of, before we proceed to the actual exercise of jurisdiction, by deciding on the rights of the parties.

The appellants contest the jurisdiction of the Court on two grounds:

1st. That the act of Congress has not given it.

2d. That, under the constitution, Congress cannot give it.

1.   The first part of the objection depends entirely on the language of the act. The words are, that the Bank shall be "made able and capable in law," "to sue and be used, plead and be impleaded, answer and be answered, defend and be defended, in all State Courts having competent jurisdiction, and in any Circuit Court of the United States."

These words seem to the Court to admit of but one interpretation. They cannot be made plainer by explanation. They give, expressly, the right 'to sue and be sued,' 'in every Circuit Court of the United States,' and it would be difficult to substitute other terms which would be more direct and appropriate for the purpose. The argument of the appellants is founded on the opinion of this Court, in The Bank of the United States v. Deveaux, [9 U.S.] 5 Cranch 85 [(1809)]. In that case it was decided, that the former Bank of the United States was not enabled, by the act which incorporated it, to sue in the federal courts. The words of the 3d section of that act are, that the Bank may "sue and be sued," &c. "in Courts of record, or any other place whatsoever." The Court was of opinion, that these general words, which are usual in all acts of incorporation, gave only a general capacity to sue, not a particular privilege to sue in the Courts of the United States * * *. Whether this decision be right or wrong, it amounts only to a declaration, that a general capacity in the Bank to sue, without mentioning the Courts of the Union, may not give a right to sue in those Courts. To infer from this, that words expressly conferring a right to sue in those Courts, do not give the right, is surely a conclusion which the premises do not warrant.

The act of incorporation, then, confers jurisdiction on the Circuit Courts of the United States, if Congress can confer it.

2.   We will now consider the constitutionality of the clause in the act of incorporation, which authorizes the Bank to sue in the federal Courts.

In support of this clause, it is said, that the legislative, executive, and judicial powers, of every well constructed government, are co-extensive with each other; that is, they are potentially co-extensive. The executive department may constitutionally execute every law which the Legislature may constitutionally make, and the judicial department may receive from the Legislature the power of construing every such law. All governments which are not extremely defective in their organization, must possess, within themselves, the means of expounding, as well as enforcing, their own laws. If we examine the constitution of the United States, we find that its framers kept this great political principle in view. The 2d article vests the whole executive power in the President; and the 3d article declares, "that the judicial power shall extend to all cases in law and equity arising under this constitution, the laws of the United States, and treaties made, or which shall be made, under their authority."

This clause enables the judicial department to receive jurisdiction to the full extent of the constitution, laws, and treaties of the United States, when any question respecting them shall assume such a form that the judicial power is capable of acting on it. That power is capable of acting only when the subject is submitted to it by a party who asserts his rights in the form prescribed by law. It then becomes a case, and the constitution declares, that the judicial power shall extend to all cases arising under the constitution, laws, and treaties of the United States.

The suit of The Bank of the United States v. Osborn and others, is a case, and the question is, whether it arises under a law of the United States?

The appellants contend, that it does not, because several questions may arise in it, which depend on the general principles of the law, not on any act of Congress.

If this were sufficient to withdraw a case from the jurisdiction of the federal Courts, almost every case, although involving the construction of a law, would be withdrawn; and a clause in the constitution, relating to a subject of vital importance to the government, and expressed in the most comprehensive terms, would be construed to mean almost nothing. There is scarcely any case, every part of which depends on the constitution, laws, or treaties of the United States. The questions, whether the fact alleged as the foundation of the action, be real or fictitious; whether the conduct of the plaintiff has been such as to entitle him to maintain his action; whether his right is barred; whether he has received satisfaction, or has in any manner released his claims, are questions, some or all of which may occur in almost every case; and if their existence be sufficient to arrest the jurisdiction of the Court, words which seem intended to be as extensive as the constitution, laws, and treaties of the Union, which seem designed to give the Courts of the government the construction of all its acts, so far as they affect the rights of individuals, would be reduced to almost nothing.

In those cases in which original jurisdiction is given to the Supreme Court, the judicial power of the United States cannot be exercised in its appellate form. In every other case, the power is to be exercised in its original or appellate form, or both, as the wisdom of Congress may direct. With the exception of these cases, in which original jurisdiction is given to this Court, there is none to which the judicial power extends, from which the original jurisdiction of the inferior Courts is excluded by the constitution. Original jurisdiction, so far as the constitution gives a rule, is co-extensive with the judicial power. We find, in the constitution, no prohibition to its exercise, in every case in which the judicial power can be exercised. It would be a very bold construction to say, that this power could be applied in its appellate form only, to the most important class of cases to which it is applicable.

The constitution establishes the Supreme Court, and defines its jurisdiction. It enumerates cases in which its jurisdiction is original and exclusive; and then defines that which is appellate, but does not insinuate, that in any such case, the power cannot be exercised in its original form by Courts of original jurisdiction. It is not insinuated, that the judicial power, in cases depending on the character of the cause, cannot be exercised in the first instance, in the Courts of the Union, but must first be exercised in the tribunals of the State; tribunals over which the government of the Union has no adequate control, and which may be closed to any claim asserted under a law of the United States.

We perceive, then, no ground on which the proposition can be maintained, that Congress is incapable of giving the Circuit Courts original jurisdiction, in any case to which the appellate jurisdiction extends.

We ask, then, if it can be sufficient to exclude this jurisdiction, that the case involves questions depending on general principles? A cause may depend on several questions of fact and law. Some of these may depend on the construction of a law of the United States; others on principles unconnected with that law. If it be a sufficient foundation for jurisdiction, that the title or right set up by the party, may be defeated by one construction of the constitution or law of the United States, and sustained by the opposite construction, provided the facts necessary to support the action be made out, then all the other questions must be decided as incidental to this, which gives that jurisdiction. Those other questions cannot arrest the proceedings. Under this construction, the judicial power of the Union extends effectively and beneficially to that most important class of cases, which depend on the character of the cause. On the opposite construction, the judicial power never can be extended to a whole case, as expressed by the constitution, but to those parts of cases only which present the particular question involving the construction of the constitution or the law. We say it never can be extended to the whole case, because, if the circumstance that other points are involved in it, shall disable Congress from authorizing the Courts of the Union to take jurisdiction of the original cause, it equally disables Congress from authorizing those Courts to take jurisdiction of the whole cause, on an appeal, and thus will be restricted to a single question in that cause; and words obviously intended to secure to those who claim rights under the constitution, laws, or treaties of the United States, a trial in the federal Courts, will be restricted to the insecure remedy of an appeal upon an insulated point, after it has received that shape which may be given to it by another tribunal, into which he is forced against his will.

We think, then, that when a question to which the judicial power of the Union is extended by the constitution, forms an ingredient of the original cause, it is in the power of Congress to give the Circuit Courts jurisdiction of that cause, although other questions of fact or of law may be involved in it.

The case of the Bank is, we think, a very strong case of this description. The charter of incorporation not only creates it, but gives it every faculty which it possesses. The power to acquire rights of any description, to transact business of any description, to make contracts of any description, to sue on those contracts, is given and measured by its charter, and that charter is a law of the United States. This being can acquire no right, make no contract, bring no suit, which is not authorized

by a law of the United States. It is not only itself the mere creature of a
law, but all its actions and all its rights are dependent on the same law.
Can a being, thus constituted, have a case which does not arise literally,
as well as substantially, under the law?

Take the case of a contract, which is put as the strongest against the
Bank.

When a Bank sues, the first question which presents itself, and
which lies at the foundation of the cause, is, has this legal entity a right
to sue? Has it a right to come, not into this Court particularly, but into
any Court? This depends on a law of the United States. The next question
is, has this being a right to make this particular contract? If this question
be decided in the negative, the cause is determined against the plaintiff;
and this question, too, depends entirely on a law of the United States.
These are important questions, and they exist in every possible case. The
right to sue, if decided once, is decided for ever; but the power of Congress
was exercised antecedently to the first decision on that right, and if it
was constitutional then, it cannot cease to be so, because the particular
question is decided. It may be revived at the will of the party, and most
probably would be renewed, were the tribunal to be changed. But the
question respecting the right to make a particular contract, or to acquire
a particular property, or to sue on account of a particular injury, belongs
to every particular case, and may be renewed in every case. The question
forms an original ingredient in every cause. Whether it be in fact relied
on or not, in the defence, it is still a part of the cause, and may be relied.
on. The right of the plaintiff to sue, cannot depend on the defence which
the defendant may choose to set up. His right to sue is anterior to that
defence, and must depend on the state of things when the action is
brought. The questions which the case involves, then, must determine its
character, whether those questions be made in the cause or not.

The appellants say, that the case arises on the contract; but the
validity of the contract depends on a law of the United States, and the
plaintiff is compelled, in every case, to show its validity. The case arises
emphatically under the law. The act of Congress is its foundation. The
contract could never have been made, but under the authority of that act.
The act itself is the first ingredient in the case, is its origin, is that from
which every other part arises. That other questions may also arise, as the
execution of the contract, or its performance, cannot change the case, or
give it any other origin than the charter of incorporation. The action still
originates in, and is sustained by, that charter.

The clause giving the Bank a right to sue in the Circuit Courts of the
United States, stands on the same principle with the acts authorizing
officers of the United States who sue in their own names, to sue in the
Courts of the United States. The Postmaster General, for example,
cannot sue under that part of the constitution which gives jurisdiction to
the federal Courts, in consequence of the character of the party, nor is he
authorized to sue by the Judiciary Act. He comes into the Courts of the

Union under the authority of an act of Congress, the constitutionality of which can only be sustained by the admission that his suit is a case arising under a law of the United States. If it be said, that it is such a case, because a law of the United States authorizes the contract, and authorizes the suit, the same reasons exist with respect to a suit brought by the Bank. That, too, is such a case; because that suit, too, is itself authorized, and is brought on a contract authorized by a law of the United States. It depends absolutely on that law, and cannot exist a moment without its authority.

If it be said, that a suit brought by the Bank may depend in fact altogether on questions unconnected with any law of the United States, it is equally true, with respect to suits brought by the Postmaster General. The plea in bar may be payment, if the suit be brought on a bond, or non assumpsit, if it be brought on an open account, and no other question may arise than what respects the complete discharge of the demand. Yet the constitutionality of the act authorizing the Postmaster General to sue in the Courts of the United States, has never been drawn into question. It is sustained singly by an act of Congress, standing on that construction of the constitution which asserts the right of the Legislature to give original jurisdiction to the Circuit Courts, in cases arising under a law of the United States.

The clause in the patent law, authorizing suits in the Circuit Courts, stands, we think, on the same principle. Such a suit is a case arising under a law of the United States. Yet the defendant may not, at the trial, question the validity of the patent, or make any point which requires the construction of an act of Congress. He may rest his defense exclusively on the fact, that he has not violated the right of the plaintiff. That this fact becomes the sole question made in the cause, cannot oust the jurisdiction of the Court, or establish the position, that the case does not arise under a law of the United States.

It is said, that a clear distinction exists between the party and the cause; that the party may originate under a law with which the cause has no connexion; and that Congress may, with the same propriety, give a naturalized citizen, who is the mere creature of a law, a right to sue in the Courts of the United States, as give that right to the Bank.

This distinction is not denied; and, if the act of Congress was a simple act of incorporation, and contained nothing more, it might be entitled to great consideration. But the act does not stop with incorporating the Bank. It proceeds to bestow upon the being it has made, all the faculties and capacities which that being possesses. Every act of the Bank grows out of this law, and is tested by it. To use the language of the constitution, every act of the Bank arises out of this law.

A naturalized citizen is indeed made a citizen under an act of Congress, but the act does not proceed to give, to regulate, or to prescribe his capacities. He becomes a member of the society, possessing all the rights of a native citizen, and standing, in the view of the constitution, on the footing of a native. The constitution does not authorize Congress to enlarge or abridge those rights. The simple power of the national Legislature, is to prescribe a uniform rule of naturalization, and the exercise of this power exhausts it, so far as respects the individual. The constitution then takes him up, and, among other rights, extends to him the capacity of suing in the Courts of the United States, precisely under the same circumstances under which a native might sue. He is distinguishable in nothing from a native citizen, except so far as the constitution makes the distinction. The law makes none.

There is, then, no resemblance between the act incorporating the Bank, and the general naturalization law.

Upon the best consideration we have been able to bestow on this subject, we are of opinion, that the clause in the act of incorporation, enabling the Bank to sue in the Courts of the United States, is consistent with the constitution, and to be obeyed in all Courts.

[On considering the merits, the Court affirmed the circuit court's order that Sullivan return $98,000, and that Osborn and Harper pay the remaining $2,000, to the Bank, but the Court reversed the award of interest on the specie.]

■ MR. JUSTICE JOHNSON [dissenting].

* * * I have very little doubt that the public mind will be easily reconciled to the decision of the Court here rendered; for, whether necessary or unnecessary originally, a state of things has now grown up, in some of the States, which renders all the protection necessary, that the general government can give to this Bank. The policy of the decision is obvious, that is, if the Bank is to be sustained; and few will bestow upon its legal correctness, the reflection, that it is necessary to test it by the constitution and laws, under which it is rendered.

* * * [The Bank of the United States imposed monetary discipline on state banks, adopting an approach that restricted state power and met great resistance. Nonetheless, in] the present instance, I cannot persuade myself, that the constitution sanctions the vesting of the right of action in this Bank, in cases in which the privilege is exclusively personal, or in any case, merely on the ground that a question might *possibly* be raised in it, involving the constitution, or constitutionality of a law, of the United States.

When laws were heretofore passed for raising a revenue by a duty on stamped paper, the tax was quietly acquiesced in, notwithstanding it entrenched so closely on the unquestionable power of the States over the law of contracts. [On the majority's view, Congress could transfer jurisdiction over disputes concerning contracts, property, and decedents' estates from the state to the federal courts by declaring such federal stamps essential to the legal validity of formal legal instruments.] But still farther, as was justly insisted in argument, there is not a tract of land of the United States, acquired under laws of the United States, whatever be the number of mesne transfers that it may have undergone, over which the jurisdiction of the Courts of the United States might not be extended by Congress, upon the very principle [ ] here maintained. Nor is the case of the alien, put in argument, at all inapplicable. The [Bank] acquires its character of individual property, as the [naturalized citizen] does his political existence, under a law of the United States; and there is not a suit which may be instituted to recover the one, nor an action of ejectment to be brought by the other, in which a right acquired under a law of the United States, does not lie as essentially at the basis of the right of action.

[Having established that Congress did not intend] to vest in the Bank of the United States, the right of suit to the extent here claimed, I next proceed to consider] the constitutional question. * * *

[Here, Justice Johnson denied that counsel for Ohio had suggested that the occurrence of issues of general law should arrest a jurisdiction otherwise vested.] No one can question, that the Court which has jurisdiction of the principal question, must exercise jurisdiction over every question. Neither did I understand them as denying, that [the matters within the potential scope of a federal court's appellate jurisdiction could provide a basis for original jurisdiction as well.] The argument went to deny the right to assume jurisdiction on a mere hypothesis. [In short, until] a question involving the construction or administration of the laws of the United States did actually arise, the *casus federis* was not presented, on which the constitution authorized the government to take to itself the jurisdiction of the cause. * * *

[In defining the constitutional scope of jurisdiction in cases arising under the laws of the United States, Justice Johnson distinguished federal rights of action that were cognizable in the lower federal courts as an original matter and those based on general principles of law that were, instead, proper objects of appellate jurisdiction if and when a federal question appeared in the litigation. In the original category, Johnson placed cases in which a law of the United States confers a right to sue, such as that given for the violation of a patent-right. In the appellate category, Johnson described suits in which the plaintiff relies on a general law form of action, such as trespass,] but in which the pleadings or evidence raised the question on the law or constitution of the United States. In this class of cases, the occurrence of a question makes the case, and transfers it, as provided for under the [grant of appellate jurisdiction in the] twenty-fifth section of the Judiciary Act, to the jurisdiction of the United States.

[Explaining that jurisdiction depended on a live dispute over a question of federal law, Justice Johnson evidently viewed any federal questions in Osborn as entirely speculative until the officers of Ohio actually put into issue the constitutionality of the Bank of the United States.] But until the plaintiff can control the defendant in his pleadings, I see no practical mode of determining when the case does occur, otherwise than by permitting the cause to advance [in state court] until the case for which the constitution provides shall actually arise. [Admittedly, the] cause might be transferred to the [federal circuit court] before an adjudication takes place [in state court]; but I can perceive no earlier stage at which [jurisdiction can attach.] It is not, therefore, because Congress may not vest an *original* jurisdiction, where they can constitutionally vest in the Circuit Courts *appellate* jurisdiction, that I object to this general grant of the right to sue. [Rather, Justice Johnson objected to the principle that the possible occurrence of a federal question can ground federal jurisdiction. Such a principle transcends] the bounds of the constitution, [ ] placing it on a ground which will admit of an *enormous accession*, if not an *unlimited assumption*, of jurisdiction. * * *

Bank of the United States v. Planters' Bank

22 U.S. 904 (1824).

In this case, later consolidated with Osborn for review in the Supreme Court, the Bank of the United States sued in Georgia federal circuit court to collect the value in specie of bank notes issued by the Planters' Bank, a bank chartered by the state of Georgia. Such redemption suits pressured state banks to maintain adequate gold and silver reserves to support their circulating bank notes (promissory notes payable to bearer) and limited the amount of paper money in circulation—elements of monetary discipline that state banks did not welcome.[1] Today, in a post-Erie world, one would describe the Bank's suit to enforce the state bank's promissory notes as posing issues of state contract law. As a general matter, suits based entirely on state (or general) law do not arise under federal law for jurisdictional purposes.

Divided as to the existence of subject matter jurisdiction, the judges of the Georgia circuit court certified the question to the Supreme Court. When the Court announced its decision in Osborn, the majority opinion referred to the Georgia litigation as the "case of the contract" and explained why Article III allowed the federal circuit court to hear such claims. One day after deciding Osborn, the Supreme Court, in an opinion by Chief Justice Marshall, formally upheld the jurisdiction of the Georgia federal circuit court.

Notably, as in Osborn, the Planters' Bank litigation presented issues of federal law, apart from those posed by the Bank's right to sue under its federal charter. In defense, the state bank argued that it was entitled to invoke the state's Eleventh Amendment immunity and that suits based on the assignment of promissory notes were exempted from federal subject matter jurisdiction. The Court rejected these federal-law defenses on the

---

[1]   On the states' hostile reaction to the Bank's use of redemption suits to enforce monetary discipline, see Catterall, The Second Bank of the United States 36, 88–89 (1903). The author reports that Georgia adopted a state statute, empowering state banks to refuse to pay specie to the Bank of United States when it tendered state bank notes for redemption. The Planters Bank litigation may have sought to test that statute; the author reports that the Georgia legislature repealed the law in 1824 after the Supreme Court's ruling. If so, the constitutionality of state discrimination against the Bank may have lurked in the background of the litigation in Georgia. *Id.* 89. On President Jackson's decision to kill the Bank of the United States in 1833, see *id.* 238–42, 285–313.

merits and said nothing to indicate that they bore on the decision to uphold subject matter jurisdiction. Justice Johnson wrote separately, acknowledging the controlling authority of the Osborn decision as to jurisdiction but raising questions about the Court's application of the Eleventh Amendment.

NOTE ON THE SCOPE OF THE CONSTITUTIONAL GRANT

(1) The Bank of the United States as a Party. As an instrumentality of the federal government's monetary policy, the Bank of the United States was re-chartered in bipartisan legislation signed into law by President Madison after the War of 1812. Yet the controversy sparked by the Bank's role in enforcing monetary restraint (as reflected in the Planters' Bank litigation) spurred state hostility and retaliation, often in the form of punitive taxation. In McCulloch v. Maryland, 17 U.S. (4 Wheat.) 316 (1819), the Court held that Congress had power to charter a Bank and that such a federal instrumentality was immune from state taxes. The Ohio tax at issue in Osborn, seeking to destroy the economic viability of the Bank's Ohio branches, was apparently invalid under McCulloch.

One might assume that the Bank, like today's Federal Reserve, operated as an arm or agency of the federal government. On that view, it might appear that claims by the Bank would qualify for Article III subject matter jurisdiction over controversies to which the United States is a party. But neither the Bank's federal charter nor the national government's partial ownership of the Bank's shares made the United States a "party" to suits by or against the Bank for this purpose. See Planters' Bank, 22 U.S. at 908 ("The government of the Union held shares in the old Bank of the United States; but the privileges of the government were not imparted by that circumstance to the Bank. The United States was not a party to suits brought by or against the Bank in the sense of the constitution. So with respect to the present Bank."). See also Lebron v. National R.R. Passenger Corp., 513 U.S. 374, 398–99 (1995) (analyzing whether federally-created entity should be treated as government actor for purposes of the First Amendment). This remains true today; federally chartered corporations cannot invoke the party-based jurisdiction of the United States under 28 U.S.C. § 1345 unless authorized to do so as agencies of the federal government. See *id.* § 1349; Lund, *Federally Chartered Corporations and Federal Jurisdiction*, 36 Fla.St.U.L.Rev. 317 (2009).

(2) Identifying the Federal Question in the Osborn and Planters' Bank Cases. In the absence of a right to invoke federal judicial power under a grant of party-based jurisdiction, the Bank of the United States relied in both Osborn and Planters' Bank on federal question jurisdiction. The Court upheld jurisdiction in a two-step analysis. First, the Court held that Congress had by statute authorized subject matter jurisdiction over the Bank's claims. Explored below is the role of federal charters as grants of statutory (and constitutional) subject matter jurisdiction. Second, the Court held that the Bank's claim was one arising under federal law for purposes of Article III's grant of subject matter jurisdiction.

In doing so, the Court proceeded on two premises that remain widely accepted today. First, the claims in both Osborn and Planters' Bank were based on common law theories of liability. Whether seen as matters of general law (as they were by both the majority and dissent in Osborn) or as state common law (as they would be today), such non-federal claims do not arise under federal law for jurisdictional purposes. Second, and a corollary to the first point, a *statutory* grant of jurisdiction does not in itself supply the needed federal question to justify the exercise of jurisdiction under the *Constitution.*

Working within these premises, Chief Justice Marshall's decision upholding jurisdiction has been the subject of at least three different interpretations, summarized here.

(a) Jurisdiction over the Whole Case. The Bank anticipated that its suit in Ohio would lead to litigation over the constitutionality of the state tax (raising the issue in McCulloch v. Maryland). By the time the case reached the Supreme Court, it was littered with federal questions, including those concerning the constitutionality of the state tax and the defendant officials' entitlement to the state's Eleventh Amendment immunity from suit. Some argue that Marshall's opinion relies on these evidently federal questions, even though they might enter the litigation after the Bank filed its bill of complaint for an injunction against trespass in circuit court. Justice Johnson's dissent argues that while federal issues that arise during litigation can support adjudication in the Supreme Court on appeal from a state court decision or removal of the action to a lower federal court, they cannot support original federal jurisdiction in the circuit court. See also Textile Workers Union v. Lincoln Mills, 353 U.S. 448, 471 (1957) (Frankfurter, J., dissenting).

(b) Protective Jurisdiction. Some understand Chief Justice Marshall's opinion as designed to extend a protective jurisdiction to claims by and against the Bank as a federal instrumentality. On that view, the need to ensure the Bank's ability to perform federal functions free from the controlling power of presumptively hostile state courts necessitates jurisdiction over non-federal claims. Justice Johnson's dissent offered that explanation of the majority opinion even as he expressed disagreement with such an approach. The idea that Congress can confer protective jurisdiction, explored in more detail below, has been the subject of a cogent criticism by those who argue that the party-based heads of jurisdiction in Article III fully exhaust the potential scope of protective jurisdiction to address state court hostility to identified claimants as to matters of non-federal law. See Textile Workers Union v. Lincoln Mills, 353 U.S. 448, 475 (1957) (Frankfurter, J., dissenting).

(c) Jurisdiction over Claims of Right Under Federal Law. Consider finally the possibility that Chief Justice Marshall viewed the Bank's complaint as stating a claim of right under federal law. The decision in McCulloch establishes the Bank's constitutional immunity from state taxes and the suit in Osborn was brought to vindicate that right by enjoining a trespassory taking of the Bank's property to satisfy the tax. Viewing the Bank's tax challenge as based on federal constitutional right, many believe that the Ohio trespass suit presented a stronger case for federal question jurisdiction than the Georgia contract suit to redeem the bank notes of Planters' Bank.

Yet the Marshall Court did not view the Ohio litigation as a direct claim to enforce a federal right conferred by the Constitution and did not regard the Ohio and Georgia suits as presenting different jurisdictional problems. In the formal world of nineteenth-century litigation, the Bank's tax immunity was not directly enforceable in a suit on the Constitution but only indirectly as an incident of litigation based on private law. Thus, the Bank relied on trespass and equity in asserting the claim, the states' officials invoked state power to collect what they viewed as a lawful tax, and the Bank contested the tax's legality on constitutional grounds in reply to the state's defense. On this view, the Constitution negated state-law defenses set up by Ohio officials; it did not confer an affirmative right to relief (as it might today if invoked in a suit under § 1983). The prospect that constitutional questions might arise (in Ohio or Georgia) did not ground original jurisdiction.

Indeed, Chief Justice Marshall did not rest his jurisdictional analysis on the possibility that the parties would (as they ultimately did) present claims and defenses under the Constitution. Instead, Marshall described the federal question as an "original ingredient" in the plaintiff's cause. The right of the plaintiff to sue in federal court, Marshall explained in Osborn, "cannot depend" on any "defense that the defendant may choose to set up." The "right" was said to be anterior to any defenses and must depend on the state of things when the action is brought. Such comments appear to reject the "whole" case characterization proposed in Justice Johnson's dissent. They also appear to anticipate the Court's later articulation of the well-pleaded complaint rule, which as will be seen reflects an understanding that the party invoking federal question jurisdiction must set up a federal right, title, or interest. See p. 1025, *infra*.

The Chief Justice regarded the Bank's charter as creating a new jural person with rights to own property, to contract, and to sue that it would lack as a matter of state or general law. Marshall analogized the Bank's charter rights to federal patent law, which (then as now) authorized those holding federal patents to enforce them in a suit brought in federal court. Marshall explained that those suing to enforce patent rights may do so, even when the defendant accepts the law as settled and contests only the patent's validity on the facts. The Bank's right "to make a particular contract, or to acquire a particular property, or to sue on account of a particular injury" "belongs to every particular case" and "may be renewed in every case." It thus appears that the Osborn Court viewed the Bank's federal right to enforce its contract and vindicate injuries to its property as an "original ingredient" in any claim the Bank might pursue. Professor Bellia has argued that, under the pleading conventions of the day, corporations were expected to allege affirmatively that they had been duly incorporated under governing law, see Bellia, *Article III and the Cause of Action*, 89 Iowa L.Rev. 777 (2004), thereby suggesting that the fact of incorporation and the rights thereby conferred were proper elements of the initial complaint.

The Osborn dissent rejected the argument that the Bank's charter conferred federal rights to pursue otherwise non-federal claims in tort and contract.[1] The dissent observed that the Bank's act of incorporation authorized "four or five" specific forms of litigation, including those brought against the Bank's officers. Anticipating the modern debate over express and implied rights of action, Justice Johnson would have limited the Bank's federal rights to sue to those specified in federal law. The right to sue, according to Justice Johnson, must "live, move and have its being" in a law of the United States.

(3) Original and Appellate Federal Question Jurisdiction. Chief Justice Marshall defended a broad view of original jurisdiction in the lower federal courts by analogy to federal question jurisdiction on appeal. He proposed that original jurisdiction "is coextensive with judicial power" and that Congress is capable of "giving the Circuit Courts original jurisdiction, in any case to which the appellate jurisdiction extends." Marshall also suggested that appellate jurisdiction may be exercised in any case over which there would have been original jurisdiction. Both these statements appear to be overbroad. A federal question first injected into litigation in a state appellate court proceeding would warrant further appellate review in the Supreme Court but would not justify original jurisdiction. Similarly, questions of federal law that might establish original federal jurisdiction would not—if undisputed and irrelevant to the outcome in a state court proceeding—justify Supreme Court review.

As these examples illustrate, appellate jurisdiction can be tailored to the case as it develops: the presence (or absence) of a dispositive federal "ingredient" is known by the time Supreme Court review is sought. Original jurisdiction, on the other hand, must often be based on the state of affairs at the time of filing: it cannot be known with certainty which issues will turn out to be decisive. As a result, the constitutional scope of the appellate jurisdiction may not be wholly congruent with that of the original jurisdiction. See Note on Murdock v. Memphis, p. 645, *supra*.

Marshall's discussion makes more sense if viewed as defending the general proposition that federal question cases, though mostly assigned by statute at the time of Osborn to the Court's appellate docket, could properly be assigned instead to lower federal courts. True, circuit court jurisdiction under the Judiciary Act of 1789 was dominated by party-alignment proceedings; Congress did not enduringly confer general federal question jurisdiction on the lower federal courts until 1875. But specific grants of federal question jurisdiction did appear before then, some catalogued in the Court's opinion (jurisdiction over patent claims, naturalization proceedings, and suits by officers of the postal service). Congress also assigned admiralty

---

[1]   Chief Justice Marshall made much of the Bank's charter. The same provision that authorizes the Bank to sue and be sued gives the Bank a right to acquire and sell property, presumably by contract. But it does not expressly confer a right to sue on account of tortious injury. See Act to Incorporate the Bank of the United States, 14th Cong., 1st Sess., ch. 44, § 7, 3 Stat. 266, 269 (1816).

and maritime jurisdiction to the federal district courts. The Court's decision in Osborn indicates (without dissent on this point) that Congress can assign matters within the Court's Article III grant of appellate jurisdiction (including cases arising under federal law) to the lower federal courts for initial adjudication.

In linking original and appellate jurisdiction in a defense of judicial power over issues of general law. Marshall may have had in mind cases like Martin v. Hunter's Lessee, 14 U.S. (1 Wheat.) 304 (1816), p. 411, *supra*, in which a federal treaty right might provide a foundation either for original federal question jurisdiction (at least in a quiet title action) or for appellate federal question jurisdiction on review of a state court decision. The antecedent question of state law that the Court agreed to consider in Martin could complicate the effective enforcement of the federal treaty right whether pursued in an original complaint in a lower federal court or on appeal from a state court.

(4) Other Notable Features of Osborn. As befits a foundational case, much that appears in Osborn has continued to shape modern conceptions of judicial power. Among other canonical features, Osborn addresses the purpose of federal courts, the distinction between cases and controversies, the principle of co-extensivity, and the definition of a case within the meaning of Article III.

(a) The Purpose of Federal Courts. The majority explains that every government must have the power of "expounding and enforcing" its laws and understands the Constitution to have assigned these powers to the judiciary. True, the Court expounds federal law on review of state court decisions. But exposition might furnish only "the insecure remedy of an appeal upon an insulated point, after it has received that shape which may be given to it by another tribunal, into which [the party] is forced against his will." Appeal might come too late in cases like Planters' Bank, given popular hostility to the Bank and its use of redemption suit to compel payment in specie.[2] Or suppose the Bank had sued in Ohio state courts and those courts denied preliminary relief to the Bank. By the time of any appeal, deposit of the Bank's assets into the state treasury could complicate any subsequent recovery on review a final state court decision denying relief.

(b) Co-Extensivity. Marshall views the co-extensivity of the judicial power with that of the legislative and executive powers as a key feature in any constitution not "extremely defective." By extending to cases arising under the Constitution, laws, and treaties, the Article III judicial power necessarily expands and contracts as the substantive content of federal law changes over time. Congress authorized jurisdiction over claims to enforce the Reconstruction Amendments with a series of statutes; no amendment to Article III was needed to secure a federal forum for their adjudication. On the axiomatic quality of coextensivity, see Amar, *A Neo-Federalist View of*

---

[2] See Catterall, The Second Bank of the United States 63 (1903) (reporting that the people in the affected states came to attribute the failure of state banks to the pressure of redemption suits).

Article III: Separating the Two Tiers of Federal Jurisdiction, 65 B.U.L.Rev. 205, 250–52 (1985).

(c) The Case-Controversy Distinction. Marshall distinguishes, as he did in Cohens v. Virginia, 19 U.S. (6 Wheat.) 264 (1821), and as Justice Story did in Martin v. Hunter's Lessee, between jurisdiction by virtue of the character of the cause (cases) and jurisdiction by virtue of the alignment of the parties (controversies). Marshall describes jurisdiction over cases arising under federal law as the most important grant of power in Article III. See Amar, Two Tiers, *supra*; Pushaw, *Article III's Case/Controversy Distinction and the Dual Functions of Federal Courts*, 69 Notre Dame L.Rev. 447 (1994). Today's Court often speaks of an Article III case-or-controversy requirement but it can often be important to keep the two forms of jurisdiction conceptually distinct.

(d) Definition of a Case. In a section of the opinion often overlooked, Marshall defines federal question jurisdiction as "capable of acting" only when the federal subject is submitted to court "by a party who asserts his rights in the form prescribed by law." Marshall found that the Bank had presented a case or claim of right in the form prescribed, leaving only the determination as to its federal character. But the definition may have more general significance. Marshall says nothing that would limit the definition of a "case" to a claim seeking redress for an injury inflicted by an opposing party. Many federal claims of right, including those for naturalized citizenship (a form of federal adjudication that figured in Osborn's majority and dissenting opinions), began with an ex parte petition and did not trigger an adversary proceeding. See Pfander & Birk, *Article III Judicial Power, the Adverse-Party Requirement, and Non-Contentious Jurisdiction*, 124 Yale L.J. 1346 (2015) (identifying naturalization petitions, pension claims, warrant applications, and *in rem* proceedings in admiralty as examples of uncontested inquisitorial-style adjudication).[3]

(e) Federal Ingredient Jurisdiction. By concluding that the presence of a right-conferring element of federal law, or federal ingredient, was enough to warrant jurisdiction over matters otherwise controlled by state or general law, Osborn wrestled with an enduring source of jurisdictional ambiguity. Absent jurisdiction based on party alignment, Congress cannot assign disputes wholly governed by state law to federal courts. But nor must Congress create an express federal right to sue (as Justice Johnson would have required). The Court's subsequent decisions, applying Osborn, typically insist that Congress confer some new federal right or title, apart from a mere grant of jurisdiction, as the basis for litigation in federal court.

(5) Applying Osborn.

(a) Other Federally Chartered Entities. Osborn may go far to establish that federal corporations, as such, were entitled to litigate in

---

[3] On the assertion of no-injury claims to enforce public law under qui tam and other informer statutes, see Pfander, *Public Law Litigation in Eighteenth Century America: Diffuse Law Enforcement for a Partisan World*, 92 Fordham L.Rev. 469 (2023); Beck, *The False Claims Act and the English Eradication of Qui Tam Legislation*, 78 N.C.L.Rev. 539 (2000).

federal court. But in accepting the distinction between the party and the cause, Marshall seemingly viewed federal incorporation without more as jurisdictionally insufficient. The Bank had more: its "right to make a particular contract, or to acquire a particular property, [and] to sue on account of a particular injury" were conferred by federal law. Does anything more than the thinnest formal line separate a corporate charter that confers juridical status and capacity to sue and be sued from one that confers federal rights to make and enforce contracts and to sue on account of injuries? Perhaps unsurprisingly, subsequent decisions tend to collapse the distinction and focus on the fact of federal incorporation alone.

(i) **Pacific Railroad Removal Cases.** Relying on Osborn, the Court upheld the removal from state to federal court of tort actions against federally chartered railroad corporations. Pacific Railroad Removal Cases, 115 U.S. 1 (1885) (7–2). Unlike the Bank of the United States, these railroads were not primarily carrying out government policy, a difference that Justice Frankfurter later viewed as significant. See Textile Workers Union v. Lincoln Mills, 353 U.S. 448, 471 n.4 (1957) (Frankfurter, J., dissenting). In identifying a statutory source of federal question jurisdiction, the Pacific Railroad Court relied on the 1875 precursor to today's general grant of jurisdiction over cases arising under federal law. In identifying federal substantive rights, the Court said that "the corporations now before us not only derive their existence, but their powers, their functions, their duties, and a large portion of their resources, from [Acts of Congress], and by virtue thereof sustain important relations to the government of the United States."[4]

(ii) **American Red Cross.** In American Nat'l Red Cross v. S.G., 505 U.S. 247 (1992), plaintiffs filed a tort suit claiming injuries when one contracted AIDS allegedly from a blood transfusion. In upholding the Red Cross' removal of the action from state court, the Court ruled that the congressional charter authorizing the Red Cross "to sue and be sued in courts of law and equity, State or Federal, within the jurisdiction of the United States" conferred federal question jurisdiction. The Court viewed Deveaux, Osborn, and other precedents as supporting "the rule that a congressional charter's 'sue and be sued' provision may be read to confer federal court jurisdiction if, but only if, it specifically mentions the federal courts." The Court distinguished the Deveaux decision, discussed in the Osborn Court's opinion, principally on the ground that there, the act of incorporation did not mention the federal courts but simply referred to all "courts of record."

Turning to the constitutional question, the Court invoked Osborn's holding that Article III's "arising under" jurisdiction is "broad enough to

---

4   Congress narrowed jurisdiction over federal corporations on two occasions. It declared in 1915, 38 Stat. 83, 84, that "no court of the United States shall have jurisdiction of any action or suit by or against any railroad company upon the ground that said railroad company was incorporated under an act of Congress." See Banker's Trust Co. v. Texas & P. R. Co., 241 U.S. 295 (1916) (broadly construing the jurisdiction restriction). In 1925, Congress declared as later amended that district courts "shall not have jurisdiction of any civil action by or against any corporation upon the ground that it was incorporated by or under an Act of Congress, unless the United States is the owner of more than one-half of its capital stock." 28 U.S.C. § 1349. While it forecloses use of federal incorporation as the ingredient essential to jurisdiction under 28 U.S.C. § 1331, § 1349 does not block jurisdiction where the charter itself confers Osborn-like statutory jurisdiction.

authorize Congress to confer federal-court jurisdiction over actions involving federally chartered corporations." In a brief paragraph, the Court assumed that all rights at issue in the tort litigation were governed by state law. It nonetheless concluded that the charter's grant of corporate capacity sufficed to establish the existence of a federal question. Four dissenting Justices contended that the Red Cross' charter established the Red Cross as a juridical entity but did not confer statutory jurisdiction; the dissenters did not address the constitutional issue.

No doubt, political exigencies help to account in part for the broad interpretation of corporate charter rights and jurisdiction in Osborn. But no such exigency would necessitate a similar approach to charters like that in Red Cross, enabling federal court litigation of state-law actions. If inclined to narrow the scope of Osborn-inflected charter jurisdiction, the Court might proceed by more narrowly interpreting Article III, by more narrowly defining the substantive rights said to derive from sue and be sued clauses, or by more narrowly reading the statutory jurisdiction conferred by such clauses.

(iii) Lightfoot v. Cendant Mortgage. In Lightfoot v. Cendant Mortgage Corp., 580 U.S. 82 (2017), the Court chose the third option, clarifying and narrowing the Red Cross approach to "sue and be sued" clauses. The federal corporate charter of the (privately owned) Federal National Mortgage Association (Fannie Mae) grants Fannie Mae the power "to sue and to be sued, and to complain and to defend, in any court of competent jurisdiction, State or Federal." 12 U.S.C. § 1723(a). The Court held that this provision established Fannie Mae's capacity to sue and be sued but did not grant federal jurisdiction over cases involving Fannie Mae. The Court acknowledged that the specific reference to federal court, taken alone, pointed toward federal jurisdiction. But the Court further reasoned that the phrase "any court of competent jurisdiction" required an extant, independent source of subject-matter jurisdiction. The Court concluded that Fannie Mae's corporate charter permits suit by or against Fannie Mae only in a "state or federal court already endowed with subject-matter jurisdiction over the suit."

The Court has now interpreted a "sue and be sued" clause in six federal corporate charters stretching back to the charter of the first Bank of the United States at issue in Deveaux. One might read Lightfoot as a significant restriction on the Osborn/Red Cross "rule" of statutory interpretation. Alternatively, one might read Lightfoot as holding only that a specific reference in the "sue and be sued" clause to federal court will confer federal jurisdiction unless some other provision in the clause indicates a need for an independent basis of jurisdiction.[5]

(b) Federal Statutes that Confer Federal Jurisdiction over Claims Based on State Law. Congress often confers federal jurisdiction over claims based largely on state law that nonetheless include a controlling

---

[5]   Federally chartered corporations also invoke the diversity jurisdiction of the federal courts. The Court has refused to view them as citizens of any state for diversity purposes. See Banker's Trust Co. v. Texas & P. R. Co., 241 U.S. 295 (1916). But Congress has sometimes conferred state-citizen status on federal corporations by statute. See Wachovia Bank v. Schmidt, 546 U.S. 303 (2006) (interpreting 28 U.S.C. § 1348). See generally Lund, *Federally Chartered Corporations and Federal Jurisdiction*, 36 Fla.St.U.L.Rev. 317 (2009).

element of federal law. The Court upholds such statutes when it can conclude that the claims in question implicate a federal title or right, in Osborn's terms, and satisfy Article III's arising under standard.

(i) Jurisdiction Under the Foreign Sovereign Immunities Act. In Verlinden B.V. v. Central Bank of Nigeria, 461 U.S. 480 (1983), a Dutch corporation sued an instrumentality of the Government of Nigeria for breach of contract in federal court. Statutory jurisdiction over the action was provided by the Foreign Sovereign Immunities Act (FSIA), which confers on federal district courts original jurisdiction over "any nonjury civil action against a foreign state * * * as to any claim * * * with respect to which the foreign state is not entitled to immunity" under either the FSIA or any applicable international agreement. 28 U.S.C. § 1330(a). Implementing the so-called "restrictive" theory, the FSIA limits immunity to the sovereign's public acts, and thus deprives the foreign government of immunity in cases arising out of its strictly commercial acts. Once the plaintiff shows that federal law allows the suit to go forward against a foreign government, state law supplies the substantive measure of liability, as the Court later confirmed in Cassirer v. Thyssen-Bornemisza Collection Foundation, 596 U.S. 107 (2022).

The defendant in Verlinden B.V. moved to dismiss the complaint for want of subject matter jurisdiction. The court of appeals held that the Act was unconstitutional insofar as it purported to authorize the federal courts to entertain an action when the substantive claim is not based on federal law and when diversity jurisdiction was absent (because neither party was a citizen of the United States).

In a unanimous opinion by Chief Justice Burger, the Supreme Court reversed, upholding the FSIA's jurisdictional grant. The Court described Osborn as the "controlling decision," one that "reflects a broad conception of 'arising under' jurisdiction, according to which Congress may confer on the federal courts jurisdiction over any case or controversy that might call for the application of federal law." The Court continued:

"The breadth of that conclusion has been questioned. * * * We need not now resolve that issue or decide the precise boundaries of Art. III jurisdiction, however, since the present case does not involve a mere speculative possibility that a federal question may arise at some point in the proceeding. Rather, a suit against a foreign state under this Act necessarily raises questions of substantive federal law at the very outset, and hence clearly 'arises under' federal law, as that term is used in Art. III.

"By reason of its authority over foreign commerce and foreign relations, Congress has the undisputed power to decide, as a matter of federal law, whether and under what circumstances foreign nations should be amenable to suit in the United States. Actions against foreign sovereigns in our courts raise sensitive issues concerning the foreign relations of the United States, and the primacy of federal concerns is evident.

"To promote these federal interests, Congress exercised its Art. I powers by enacting a statute comprehensively regulating the amenability of foreign nations to suit in the United States. The statute must be applied by the district courts in every action against a foreign sovereign, since subject-matter jurisdiction in any such action depends on the existence of one of the specified exceptions to foreign sovereign immunity, 28 U.S.C. § 1330(a). At the threshold of every action in a district court against a foreign state, therefore, the court must satisfy itself that one of the exceptions applies—and in doing so it must apply the detailed federal-law standards set forth in the Act. Accordingly, an action against a foreign sovereign arises under federal law, for purposes of Art. III jurisdiction.

"* * * Congress deliberately sought to channel cases against foreign sovereigns away from the state courts and into federal courts, thereby reducing the potential for a multiplicity of conflicting results among the courts of the 50 States. The resulting jurisdictional grant is within the bounds of Art. III, since every action against a foreign sovereign necessarily involves application of a body of substantive federal law, and accordingly 'arises under' federal law, within the meaning of Art. III."

The lower courts regarded the issue of foreign sovereign immunity as a defense to a claim otherwise based on state law. But the Court read the statute as refining foreign sovereign immunity law in a way that reshaped the ability of plaintiffs to pursue claims against foreign governments. See Vázquez, *The Federal "Claim" in the District Courts: Osborn, Verlinden, and Protective Jurisdiction*, 95 Calif.L.Rev. 1731 (2007). All claims under the FSIA must satisfy a threshold inquiry into the suability of the defendant. After Verlinden, consider whether Congress can treat its statutory abrogation of existing defenses as the substantive federal ingredient that justifies federal jurisdiction over claims otherwise based on state law. Even if such a strategy might work in some circumstances, one might question jurisdiction under a statute that countermands an extremely rare defense as the basis for federalizing state-law claims.

(ii) Jurisdiction Under the Federal Tort Claims Act. The Federal Tort Claims Act imposes vicarious tort liability on the federal government for the acts and omissions of its officers and employees within the scope of their employment. Thus, the government bears liability where "a private person would be liable to the claimant in accordance with the law of the place where the act or omission occurred." 28 U.S.C. § 1346(b)(1). Prior to the FTCA's adoption, the government owed no vicarious liability for the torts of its officers. The FTCA thus resembles the FSIA in overriding an immunity and subjecting the government to civil liability as defined by state law. Suits under the FTCA presumably arise under federal law within the meaning of Osborn and Verlinden.

Under the Westfall Act, a 1988 amendment to the FTCA, codified at 28 U.S.C. § 2679(b)(1), Congress conferred statutory immunity on federal employees for tort claims arising under the FTCA and provided for the substitution of the government as the defendant. But the statute preserved the personal liability of federal employees if they committed torts while acting outside the scope of their employment. In Osborn v. Haley, 549 U.S. 225 (2007), a state-law claim brought in state court against a federal official was removed to federal court after the Attorney General certified that the official was acting within the scope of employment. The district court concluded that the certification was invalid. On review, the Supreme Court held that the certification was valid and remanded for further proceedings. In doing so, the Court clarified that Article III would permit the district court to retain the case even if the claim were to proceed against the employee under state law for conduct outside the scope of federal employment. In accounting for why a garden variety state-law claim would stay in federal court, Justice Ginsburg's opinion for the Court explained: "Because a significant federal question (whether [the defendant] has Westfall Act immunity) would have been raised at the outset, the case would 'aris[e] under' federal law, as that term is used in Article III" (citing Verlinden B.V. v. Central Bank of Nigeria, 461 U.S. 480 (1983)).

B. DEFINING THE OUTER LIMITS OF ARTICLE III

Classical theories of enumeration and limited power would suggest that Congress cannot authorize federal courts to adjudicate matters that do not fit within the heads of subject matter jurisdiction listed in Article III. But that understanding has been tested on occasion, both in the decisions of the Supreme Court and in commentary on the power of Congress to confer a protective jurisdiction on federal courts.

National Mutual Tidewater Co. v. Tidewater Transfer Co.

337 U.S. 582 (1949).

A corporate citizen of the District of Columbia brought suit in a Maryland federal district court against a Virginia corporation on an insurance contract; the dispute involved only issues of state law. A 1940 statute gave the district courts jurisdiction in actions between citizens of the states and citizens of the District, even though the Court had previously ruled that a citizen of the District was not a citizen of a "State" within the meaning of the Diversity Clause. See Hepburn & Dundas v. Ellzey, 6 U.S. (2 Cranch) 445 (1805) (Marshall, C.J.).

The Tidewater Court upheld the constitutionality of the 1940 statute but the five Justices who voted for that result offered radically different explanations.[1] Justices Rutledge and Murphy thought that Hepburn should be overruled, concluding that the matter fell within Article III's grant of diversity jurisdiction. The other seven Justices would have followed Hepburn and found no diversity. Justice Jackson's plurality opinion, joined by Justices Black and Burton, supplied the other three votes to uphold the statute.

---

[1]   Justice Frankfurter called attention to a paradox: "conflicting minorities in combination bring to pass a result—paradoxical as it may appear—which differing majorities find insupportable." Justice Frankfurter's paradox has been the subject of a large and growing literature on the legal import of voting protocols on multimember courts. See Nash, *A Context-Sensitive Voting Paradigm Protocol for Multimember Courts*, 56 Stan.L.Rev. 75 (2003); Stearns, *Constitutional Process: A Social Choice Analysis of Supreme Court Decision Making* 111–24 (2000); Hartnett, *A Matter of Judgment, Not a Matter of Opinion*, 74 N.Y.U.L.Rev. 123 (1999); Sherry, *Justice O'Connor's Dilemma: The Baseline Question*, 39 Wm. & Mary L.Rev. 865 (1998). Perhaps Tidewater stands for the proposition that Congress may not give an Article III court jurisdiction over a non-Article III case or function—with the case itself being a counterexample to the proposition for which it stands.

Accepting that Hepburn was still good law and that the dispute did not present any federal questions, Justice Jackson contended that Congress, acting pursuant to its Article I powers, may authorize Article III courts to adjudicate cases beyond Article III's nine heads of jurisdiction. He relied in particular on Congress's Article I power over the District of Columbia, which Congress had used to authorize citizens of the District to sue and be sued in the courts of the District. Allowing such suits to proceed in federal district courts outside the District was said to occasion only a small extension of congressional power.

Justice Jackson also urged that the Court had previously upheld federal adjudication of matters assigned under Article I that went beyond the limits of Article III. First, it had approved Article III adjudication of money claims against the United States, despite earlier decisions suggesting (perhaps on dubious grounds) that these matters were not properly characterized as implicating the judicial power under Article III.[2] Second, Justice Jackson pointed to bankruptcy decisions, in which the Court had approved federal court adjudication of state-law claims brought by the bankruptcy trustee against debtors of the estate. Reasoning that such claims did not arise under federal law within the meaning of Osborn, Justice Jackson concluded that the bankruptcy power in Article I "can supply a source of judicial power for their adjudication." Although he concluded that Congress may give the federal courts judicial business that lies outside the enumeration in Article III, Justice Jackson contended that it must be judicial business. He asserted that Congress lacks any similar power to authorize federal courts to decide matters that are not cases or controversies within the meaning of Article III.

The other six Justices objected strongly to Justice Jackson's opinion, calling it among other things a "dangerous doctrine." Justice Frankfurter, joined by Justice Reed, wrote a passionate dissent reaffirming the classical proposition that the federal courts are courts of limited jurisdiction with no authority to adjudicate except in the instances enumerated in Article III. He asked: "what justification is there for interpreting Article III as imposing one restriction in the exercise of those other powers of the Congress—the restriction to the exercise of 'judicial power'—yet not interpreting it as imposing the restrictions that are most explicit, namely, the particularization of the 'cases' to which 'the judicial power shall extend'?" He continued: "To find a source for the 'judicial power,' therefore, which may be exercised by courts established under Article III of the Constitution outside that Article would be to disregard the distribution of powers made by the Constitution."

Textile Workers Union v. Lincoln Mills

353 U.S. 448 (1957).

Congress amended the nation's labor laws in 1947, adopting the Taft-Hartley Act and authorizing federal courts to hear claims by and against labor organizations. See § 301 of the Labor Management Relations Act of 1947, 61 Stat. 156. Among other things, the statute conferred entity status

---

[2]   National Mutual v. Tidewater, 337 U.S. at 592 (citing Williams v. United States, 289 U.S. 553 (1933)).

on unions, enabled them to sue and be sued in federal court, and subjected them to liability for secondary boycotts. Doubts arose about a provision authorizing federal courts to exercise jurisdiction over "suits for violation" of collective bargaining agreements between unions and employers in an industry affecting commerce. See 29 U.S.C. § 185. Some interpreted the provision to confer substantive law-making power on the federal courts; others viewed it as merely incorporating such rules of state contract law as were applicable to the matter at hand.

In this case, the Textile Workers Union sued to enforce an arbitration clause in its collective bargaining agreement with Lincoln Mills.[1] The district court upheld its jurisdiction and ordered the employer to arbitrate; the court of appeals reversed. In an opinion by Justice Douglas, the Court reversed in turn. Instead of addressing Article III issues, the majority opinion interpreted the statute as authorizing the federal courts to create federal common law to govern such contract breach claims. That interpretive move solved the jurisdictional problem: instead of state contract law, all claims for breach of collective agreements were to be governed by and arise under a body of (judge-made but congressionally authorized) federal contract law. Disagreeing with the majority's attribution of federal substance to the statute, three Justices addressed the protective jurisdiction alternative. Justice Burton, joined by Justice Harlan, voted to uphold the statutory grant of jurisdiction, noting "that some federal rights may necessarily be involved in a § 301 case, and hence that the constitutionality of § 301 can be upheld as a congressional grant to Federal District Courts of what has been called 'protective jurisdiction.'"

Justice Frankfurter, in a lone dissent, read the statute as leaving state contract law intact. That interpretation of the statute, in turn, raised serious constitutional questions that the majority had elided. Frankfurter began by questioning the wisdom of any federal judicial role in fashioning a common law of labor relations, a policy perspective that shaped his help with drafting the Norris-LaGuardia Act's twenty-five years earlier. Frankfurter then considered a variety of arguments that might justify federal adjudication. He found that Osborn failed to justify the jurisdictional provision. At its broadest, Frankfurter worried that Osborn might be read as permitting "assertion of original federal jurisdiction on the remote possibility of presentation of a federal question."

Justice Frankfurter also rejected the doctrine of protective jurisdiction, developed by scholars to defend the judicial role under § 301. One view, developed by Professor Wechsler, held that the power of Congress to confer federal question jurisdiction "should extend * * * to all cases in which Congress has authority to make the rule to govern disposition of the controversy but is content instead to let the states provide the rule so long as jurisdiction to enforce it has been vested in a federal court."[2] Wechsler

---

[1]   For accounts of the litigation, see Shapiro, *The Story of Lincoln Mills: Jurisdiction and Choice of Law in Federal Courts* Stories 389 (Resnik & Jackson eds. 2009); Pfander, *Judicial Purpose and the Scholarly Process: The Lincoln Mills Case*, 69 Wash.U.L.Q. 243 (1991).

[2]   Wechsler, *Federal Jurisdiction and the Revision of the Judicial Code*, 13 Law & Contemp.Probs. 216, 224–25 (1948).

added, "A grant of jurisdiction is in short, one mode by which the Congress may assert its regulatory powers. A case is one 'arising under' federal law within the sense of Article III whenever it is comprehended in a valid grant of jurisdiction * * *." A second view, put forward by Professor Mishkin, proposed to limit protective jurisdiction to situations, like labor relations and bankruptcy, "where there is an articulated and active federal policy regulating a field."[3] As to such fields of active regulation, Article III would authorize "the conferring of jurisdiction on the national courts of all cases in the area—including those substantively governed by state law."

Justice Frankfurter's evaluation of protective jurisdiction remains the most complete judicial assessment of that theory. In his view, "Surely the truly technical restrictions of Article III are not met or respected by a beguiling phrase that the greater power [Congress's power to regulate] must necessarily include the lesser [its power to confer jurisdiction]. In the compromise of federal and state interests leading to distribution of jealously guarded judicial power in a federal system, it is obvious that very different considerations apply to cases involving questions of federal law and those turning solely on state law." He objected to the breadth of congressional power under Wechsler's theory, noting that it would permit conferral of federal court jurisdiction over every state-law contract or tort affecting commerce. Frankfurter also suggested that insofar as protective jurisdiction rested on mistrust of state tribunals, Article III confined the grant of jurisdiction on this basis to cases falling within its party-based clauses, notably the diversity clause. He added that Chief Justice Marshall's failure to rely on a theory of protective jurisdiction "at a time when conditions might have presented more substantial justification strongly suggests its lack of constitutional merit." Finally, as to Mishkin's theory, he said dismissively that it "has the dubious advantage of limiting incursions on state judicial power to situations in which the State's feelings may have been tempered by early substantive federal invasions."

NOTE ON TIDEWATER, LINCOLN MILLS, AND PROTECTIVE JURISDICTION

(1) Understanding the Enumerated Powers Question. Both Tidewater and the separate opinions in Lincoln Mills wrestle with the power of federal courts to entertain state-law claims for relief where the parties lack citizenship diversity, and the case fails obviously to present a controlling question of federal law. In Tidewater, most of the Justices thought that diversity was lacking, but nonetheless agreed on a result that effectively treats citizens of the District as state citizens for that purpose. In Lincoln Mills, most of the Justices viewed labor contract enforcement as presenting controlling questions of federal law sufficient to satisfy the Osborn test.

---

[3]   Mishkin, *The Federal "Question" in the District Courts*, 53 Colum.L.Rev. 157, 184–96 (1953).

Under Justice Douglas's majority opinion in Lincoln Mills, the Osborn problem disappears entirely.

Assessing Justice Jackson's Tidewater opinion rejecting enumerated limits on the judicial power invites a return to the principle of co-extensivity in Osborn. Chief Justice Marshall apparently expected Article III federal question jurisdiction to operationalize the principle, authorizing grants of jurisdiction to address claims specified in all statutes that Congress enacted under Article I. Justice Jackson appears to view federal question jurisdiction as inadequate for the purpose of assuring co-extensivity. In assessing that claim, consider one proposed characterization of the statute upheld in Tidewater as permissible legislation, adopted under § 5 of the Fourteenth Amendment to protect the privileges and immunities of national citizens, including citizens of the District of Columbia, from biased adjudication in state courts.[1]

Contrast Justice Jackson's expansive view with Justice Frankfurter's classic view of enumeration in Lincoln Mills, which was premised on the conclusion that state law furnished the rule of decision under § 301 for claims to enforce the labor agreement. Even assuming that was correct, one might find analogies to the Bank's charter in the Taft-Hartley Act. The Act confers entity status on labor unions, with a right to sue and be sued, and establishes a form of limited liability, making the union as such financially accountable for violations of federal law rather than the union's members. On the majority's view of the statute, these potential federal ingredients were not essential to the presence of a federal question. But they may have deserved closer attention in Frankfurter's dissent. See Bellia, *Article III and the Cause of Action*, 89 Iowa L.Rev. 777 (2004) (arguing that Frankfurter misread Osborn insofar as he suggested that it construes Article III as permitting Congress to confer jurisdiction over any case in which a federal issue might possibly arise). A more charitable view might read Osborn as upholding jurisdiction when the plaintiff must affirm the federal ingredient (even if the defendant does not contest it) to obtain relief.

(2) The Theory of Protective Jurisdiction. The opinions in Osborn assume that federal question jurisdiction requires the presence in the case of a federal right or a question of federal law that must be applied to resolve the dispute. Yet the opinions also express concern that state court hostility to the Bank might manifest itself in discriminatory application of state law or unfavorable treatment of evidence. Building on that possibility, especially as applied to the labor contract enforcement problem in Lincoln Mills, many scholars have defended Congress's power to extend federal jurisdiction to protect defined federal interests. See, *e.g.*, Wechsler, *supra*, and Mishkin, *supra*. Proponents of these varied forms of "protective" jurisdiction contend that Congress can permit litigation in federal court of state-law matters without making federal substantive law an ingredient in the lawsuit. Justice Frankfurter, by contrast, viewed the heads of party-alignment jurisdiction

---

[1]   See Pfander, *The Tidewater Problem: Article III and Constitutional Change*, 79 Notre Dame L.Rev. 1925 (2004) (making the argument).

(including diversity) as an exhaustive specification of the available forms of protective jurisdiction.

(a) The Greater Includes the Lesser. Professor Wechsler took the position that Congress has power to regulate a field within its Article I competence by adopting a grant of jurisdiction that enables the federal courts to adjudicate matters entirely governed by state law. In other words, power to fashion federal rules of decision under Article I entailed the lesser power simply to confer federal jurisdiction over the subject matter. On Wechsler's view, p. 1015 n.2, *supra*, a "grant of jurisdiction is in short, one mode by which the Congress may assert its regulatory powers."

(b) To Protect Active Federal Policy. Professor Mishkin offered a different conception of protective jurisdiction. Viewing Wechsler's account as too broad, Mishkin linked protective jurisdiction to fields of law where Congress had "an articulated and active federal policy." See p. 1016 n.3, *supra*. The exercise of a permissible protective jurisdiction, on this account, was driven not by the identity of the party (a national bank or labor union) but by the nature of the legislative program and the risks posed by state court adjudication.

(c) Building on Mishkin's Theory. In a symposium devoted to Mishkin's scholarship, Professor Vázquez defended protective jurisdiction so long as Congress "formally" adopts state law as federal law, thereby supplying at least as a formal matter the substantive federal law supposedly missing from other models. See Vázquez, *The Federal "Claim" in the District Courts: Osborn, Verlinden, and Protective Jurisdiction*, 95 Calif.L.Rev. 1731 (2007). Compare Young, *Stalking the Yeti: Protective Jurisdiction, Foreign Affairs Removal, and Complete Preemption*, 95 Calif.L.Rev. 1775 (2007) (expressing a federalism-based concern with the use by Congress of protective jurisdiction and asking whether, if the adopted state law is treated as real federal law under the Vázquez model, federal courts would no longer be required to follow state court interpretations of the law's content).[2]

(3) The Practice of Protective Jurisdiction. The Court has so far refrained from relying on protective jurisdiction theories to uphold an exercise of federal jurisdiction (aside from the modest reliance in the Lincoln Mills concurring opinion). When the parties invoke the theory, the Court has applied the Osborn test instead. See Verlinden B.V. v. Central Bank of Nigeria, 461 U.S. 480 (1983), p. 1011, *supra* (ruling that Article III jurisdiction encompasses claims arising under the Foreign Sovereign Immunities Act and declining to "consider petitioner's alternative argument that the Act is constitutional as an aspect of so-called 'protective jurisdiction'").

Later, in Mesa v. California, 489 U.S. 121 (1989), the Court again avoided the question, this time by narrowly construing a jurisdictional statute. There, two Postal Service employees faced state criminal

---

[2] For other important contributions, see Goldberg-Ambrose, *The Protective Jurisdiction of the Federal Courts*, 30 UCLA L.Rev. 542, 549 (1983); Seinfeld, *Article I, Article III, and the Limits of Enumeration*, 108 Mich.L.Rev. 1389 (2010); Segall, *Article III as a Grant of Power: Protective Jurisdiction, Federalism and the Federal Courts*, 54 Fla.L.Rev. 361 (2002).

prosecutions arising out of traffic violations committed in connection with their jobs. The prosecutions were removed to federal court under 28 U.S.C. § 1442(a)(1), which authorizes removal of any civil or criminal action against an officer of the United States for any act "under color of such office." The government argued that removal was proper even though the defendants asserted no colorable federal defense to the state charges. Congress's desire to protect federal officials from interference by hostile state courts was said to suffice for jurisdictional purposes. The Supreme Court rejected that view out of hand: "Adopting the Government's view, which would eliminate the federal defense requirement, would in turn eliminate the substantive Art. III foundation of § 1442(a)(1) and unnecessarily present grave constitutional problems." Instead, the Court read § 1442(a) to permit federal officer removal only when the defendant-officer avers a federal defense, explaining as follows: "There is no need to adopt a theory of 'protective jurisdiction' to support Art. III 'arising under' jurisdiction, as the Government urges, because in this case there are no federal interests that are not protected by limiting removal to situations in which a federal defense is alleged." Compare Mesa with the federal officer removal regime in the Federal Tort Claims Act as interpreted in Osborn v. Haley, 549 U.S. 225 (2007), p. 1012, *supra*. Note that under the FTCA, the immunity issue on which subject matter jurisdiction was predicated was thought to attach to actions within the scope of employment whereas the defendants in Mesa did not identify any similar colorable claim to immunity.

(4) Some Testing Cases. The reach of Osborn and the validity of protective jurisdiction implicate many questions. The following jurisdictional statutes test the limits of Article III.

(a) The Problem of Bankruptcy Jurisdiction. Bankruptcy offers indebted firms and individuals an orderly way to manage excessive debt. A simple bankruptcy proceeding does three things: establishes a new jural entity (called the bankruptcy estate), collects or marshals the debtor's assets and deposits them in the estate, and distributes the assets to those creditors who have legitimate claims on the estate. The bankruptcy code facilitates asset collection and distribution by conferring power on the estate's "representative" (a federal trustee or debtor in possession) to sue and be sued. In addition, the bankruptcy petition triggers an automatic stay of other litigation against the debtor, enforcing the creditors' duty to pursue the debtor's assets through the bankruptcy proceeding. Whether it leads to reorganization or liquidation, bankruptcy (like interpleader) allocates rights in a limited fund.

Today, applicable law confers jurisdiction on district courts over two kinds of claims: those "arising under" the bankruptcy laws and those "arising in" or "related to" cases in bankruptcy. 28 U.S.C. § 1334(b). District courts, in turn, typically refer such matters to bankruptcy judges. "Core" proceedings arise under the bankruptcy laws; bankruptcy judges can hear and determine them. 11 U.S.C. § 157(a). "Non-core" proceedings arise in or relate to bankruptcy; bankruptcy judges can "hear" them, 11 U.S.C. § 157(b), and recommend a disposition for ultimate "determination" by the district court.

For jurisdictional purposes, it helps to distinguish those who want money from the bankruptcy estate (creditors) from those who owe the estate money (estate debtors).[3] The filing of a bankruptcy petition changes the legal position of estate creditors; bankruptcy rules force them to file proofs of claim and often to accept less than full satisfaction. Even though many of these claims depend on state law, no one questions the power of federal courts to adjudicate them as part of the bankruptcy. By convention, such claims arise under bankruptcy law and fall within the "core" purview of the bankruptcy judge.

By contrast, the bankruptcy filing does not fundamentally alter the legal obligations of the estate's debtors; they still owe money, but the estate "owns" and brings the claim. Many of the claims against these third-party debtors rest on state law, raising jurisdictional questions. Without fully explaining why, the Court has long treated such claims as arising under federal law for purposes of Article III. See Schumacher v. Beeler, 293 U.S. 367 (1934) ("Congress, by virtue of its constitutional authority over bankruptcies, could confer or withhold jurisdiction to entertain such [estate] suits and could prescribe the conditions upon which the federal courts should have jurisdiction"); Lathrop v. Drake, 91 U.S. 516, 517–18 (1875) (emphasizing without directly addressing constitutionality that "a uniform system of bankruptcy, national in its character, ought to be capable of execution in the national tribunals, without dependence upon those of the States in which it is possible that embarrassments might arise").

Much of the controversy centers on the breadth of jurisdiction over matters of state law that arise in or relate to bankruptcy. In many cases, litigation targets assets held by third parties who may owe money to the bankruptcy estate. For example, in Celotex Corp. v. Edwards, 514 U.S. 300 (1995), personal injury claimants had won substantial state-law judgments against Celotex based on exposure to its asbestos products. To recover from Celotex after its initiation of bankruptcy, those judgment creditors were obliged to pursue core proceedings. But the creditors also sued third-party sureties, seeking to recover on bonds posted as part of an ongoing coverage dispute between Celotex and its insurance carriers. Even though Celotex was not a party, and the suits were based on state law, the Court upheld the bankruptcy court's jurisdiction to enjoin their separate litigation. Surety payments directly to creditors could deplete the funds available for reorganization.

Bankruptcy scholars tend to agree that Article III authorizes jurisdiction over matters that arise in or relate to bankruptcy but disagree as to how to defend such jurisdiction under Article III. Consider claims brought by the estate against third-party debtors. While the Schumacher Court did not invoke Osborn, one scholar argues that federal law makes the bankruptcy estate a new federal entity with new powers and duties to sue and be sued, arguably supplying a federal ingredient for all such claims. See Brubaker, *On the Nature of Federal Bankruptcy Jurisdiction: A General*

---

[3]   The distinction between suits by and against the bankruptcy estate shows up in the debate, explored in Chapter IV, see pp. 633–647, over the power of Congress to shift the litigation of certain state-law claims from Article III courts to non-Article III bankruptcy courts.

Statutory and Constitutional Theory, 41 Wm. & Mary L.Rev. 743 (2000). Osborn-style ingredient jurisdiction, coupled with supplemental jurisdiction, might cover most instances of related-to jurisdiction.[4]

Not everyone has embraced the Osborn theory, however. Justice Jackson viewed jurisdiction over state-law claims in bankruptcy as proof of his argument in Tidewater that federal jurisdiction was not limited to federal question cases but extended to state-law matters assigned to federal court in the exercise of Article I powers (such as the bankruptcy power). Justice Frankfurter rejected these arguments in Tidewater and Lincoln Mills, taking a narrow view of Osborn and bankruptcy jurisdiction. Following Frankfurter, Pathak, *Breaking the "Unbreakable Rule": Federal Courts, Article I, and the Problem of 'Related To' Bankruptcy Jurisdiction*, 85 Or.L.Rev. 59 (2006), finds that none of the theories provides an acceptable basis for the jurisdiction.

(b) Other Statutes Protecting Federal Interests.

(i) The Diplomatic Relations Act of 1978. Pub.L.No. 95–393, as amended in 1987 by Pub.L.No. 100–204, 28 U.S.C. § 1364, was designed to facilitate recovery of damages, particularly from automobile accidents, caused by foreign diplomats who are themselves immune from suit, by permitting suit, in some circumstances, against an insurer of members of diplomatic missions or their families. In such direct actions, the insurer may not defend on the ground that the insured is immune from suit or is an indispensable party, nor (absent fraud or collusion) on the ground that the insured has breached the insurance contract. The Senate Report accompanying the bill (S.Rep. No. 1108, 95th Cong., 2d Sess. 5 (1978)) indicated that state law would govern such suits.

Some of the contemplated litigation would proceed in connection with injuries inflicted by members of diplomatic missions who would not themselves qualify as "ambassadors, other public ministers, or consuls" within the terms of Article III. Direct actions against insurance policies held by the mission's employees might nonetheless be regarded as "affecting" higher level foreign diplomats within the meaning of Article III. One might also defend the statute as effectively conferring new rights on the victims of a diplomatic mission's tortious wrongdoing, much the way Congress authorized tort claims against foreign sovereigns by countermanding immunity in the statute upheld in Verlinden.

(ii) The Clean Air Act. Under 42 U.S.C. § 7604, the district courts have jurisdiction over private civil actions against any person alleged to be

---

[4]   For a skeptical assessment of broad bankruptcy jurisdiction, see Block-Lieb, *The Case Against Supplemental Bankruptcy Jurisdiction: A Constitutional, Statutory, and Policy Analysis*, 62 Fordham L.Rev. 721 (1994) (expressing doubts about Osborn's application and the breadth of supplemental jurisdiction). Cross, *Congressional Power to Extend Federal Jurisdiction to Disputes Outside Article III: A Critical Analysis from the Perspective of Bankruptcy*, 87 Nw.U.L.Rev. 1188, 1238 (1993), contends that such jurisdiction is best explained as a species of "ancillary jurisdiction," because bankruptcy creates a fund comprised of many assets and subject to many claims. But *cf.* Galligan, *Article III and the "Related To" Bankruptcy Jurisdiction: A Case Study in Protective Jurisdiction*, 11 U. Puget Sound L.Rev. 1 (1987) (criticizing the "essential ingredient" and "ancillary jurisdiction" approaches and arguing that bankruptcy is a valid form of protective jurisdiction).

in violation of any "emission standard or limitation" issued under the Act. "Emission standards" appear to include standards contained in state-promulgated "Implementation Plans"; these plans must meet federal requirements and be approved by EPA, but otherwise constitute detailed programs of implementation, maintenance, and enforcement of air quality standards as a matter of state law. The lower courts have heard cases based on violations of state plans without raising any question about jurisdiction. *E.g.*, Save Our Health Org. v. Recomp of Minnesota, Inc., 37 F.3d 1334, 1336 (8th Cir.1994). Although it may not qualify as "express," the statute may illustrate the law-incorporation model of protective jurisdiction advanced by Vázquez, Paragraph (2)(c), *supra*.

(iii) The Air Transportation Safety and System Stabilization Act. A statute passed shortly after September 11, 2001, creates a "Federal cause of action for damages" arising from the four terrorist-related airline crashes on that date. Pub.L.No. 107–42, 49 U.S.C. § 408(b)(1), 115 Stat. 230, 240–41 (2001). The Act provides that the new federal cause of action is the exclusive remedy and declares that the substantive law to be applied "shall be derived from the law, including choice of law principles, of the State in which the crash occurred unless such law is inconsistent with or preempted by Federal law." 49 U.S.C. § 408(b)(2). The only substantive rule of decision that the statute prescribes is that an air carrier's liability for all claims arising out of the four crashes shall not exceed the limits of the carrier's liability insurance coverage. *Id.* § 408(a).

The Act confers on the Southern District of New York "original and exclusive jurisdiction over all actions brought for any claim [including property and personal injury claims] resulting from or relating to the terrorist-related aircraft crashes of September 11, 2001." *Id.* § 408(b)(3). Consider whether the provision limiting the liability of air carriers might help to sustain federal question jurisdiction in a damage action against an air carrier. If so, consider a damage action against some other defendant (for example, a security firm alleged to have been lax in operating airport metal detectors). Congress did not limit the liability of such defendants, but they may have claims for contribution or indemnity against the air carriers. Such claims might be said to implicate the federal limits on air carrier liability, somewhat in the way state-law claims were thought in Celotex to "relate to" a bankruptcy proceeding. The Second Circuit rejected an argument that the Act's limit on liability necessarily required coordinated administration of claims to a limited fund.[5] Does that decision cast doubt on the exercise of federal question jurisdiction?

(5) Protective Jurisdiction and the Problem of Regulation by Jurisdiction. For a skeptical view of protective jurisdiction, see Young, Paragraph (2)(c), *supra*. Professor Young argues that recognition of protective jurisdiction undermines valuable diversification in the political control of the judiciary, by permitting Congress more broadly to assign cases to federal rather than state courts, which are subject to different methods of

---

[5] See In re September 11 Property Damage Litigation, 650 F.3d 145 (2d Cir.2011). On the implications of a limited fund for the coordination of concurrent state and federal court jurisdiction, see Chap. X, Sec. 3.

selection and political control. He suggests, additionally, that the supposedly "lesser" power of Congress to confer protective jurisdiction may be more worrisome than the supposedly "greater" power to enact substantive federal rules and confer jurisdiction, for it may be easier in the national political process to reach agreement on jurisdiction than on substance. Young adds that protective jurisdiction threatens to reduce state control over the content of state law for entire categories of cases.

Similar concerns may arise from federal statutes that authorize federal litigation of matters of perceived federal concern by using minimal diversity as a basis for jurisdictional expansion. The Class Action Fairness Act of 2005, Pub.L.No. 109–2, 119 Stat. 4, transfers sizable state-law class actions to federal court based on any minimal diversity between the defendants and any member of the plaintiff class. See 28 U.S.C. § 1332(d)(2). Rather than regulate the substantive rights of consumers and firms (which would have facilitated federal question class action jurisdiction under § 1331 within the areas regulated), Congress left state substantive law intact, as Professor Young's critique highlights. But the shift to federal court ensured coordinated pre-trial management of overlapping class actions, 28 U.S.C. § 1407, and uniform application of the federal procedural rules governing class certification. See Shady Grove Orthopedic Associates, P.A. v. Allstate Ins. Co., 559 U.S. 393 (2010). Young's concerns may apply with less force if one views the federal "interests" protected by minimal diversity statutes as fundamentally procedural.

Also consider the Multi-Party, Multi-Forum Trial Jurisdiction Act of 2002, Pub.L.No. 107–273, 116 Stat. 1826, enacted shortly after 9/11. Congress authorized federal district courts to exercise original jurisdiction based on minimal diversity between adverse parties where at least seventy-five people died in a single accident at a discrete location. 28 U.S.C. § 1369(a). Such legislation does not impose a federal cap on defendant liability, but it would have presumably authorized consolidated adjudication of much of the 9/11 litigation without Osborn or a theory of protective jurisdiction. On the overlap of protective jurisdiction and minimal diversity, see Pfander, *Protective Jurisdiction, Aggregate Litigation, and the Limits of Article III*, 95 Calif.L.Rev. 1423 (2007).

---

3. THE SCOPE OF THE STATUTORY GRANT OF FEDERAL QUESTION JURISDICTION

The general grant of federal question jurisdiction, adopted in 1875 and now codified at 28 U.S.C. § 1331, has long been interpreted to require the appearance of a federal question on the face of the well-pleaded complaint. This section explores the origins of this longstanding rule and a host of related topics.

A. THE WELL-PLEADED COMPLAINT RULE AND FEDERAL QUESTION JURISDICTION

Louisville & Nashville R.R. Co. v. Mottley

211 U.S. 149 (1908).
Appeal from the Circuit Court of the United States
for the Western District of Kentucky.

■ MR. JUSTICE MOODY * * * delivered the opinion of the court.

[Mr. and Mrs. Mottley sued the Louisville & Nashville Railroad for specific performance of a contract under which the railroad agreed to issue free passes to the Mottleys for life, in exchange for their release of damage claims arising from a collision. The complaint alleged that, beginning in 1907, the railroad refused to renew the passes, relying on a 1906 Act of Congress forbidding free passes, and further alleged that (i) the 1906 Act did not prohibit free passes pursuant to contracts made before its enactment, but (ii) if construed retroactively to invalidate the Mottleys' contract, the Act deprived them of property without due process. After the federal circuit court entered a decree of specific performance, the railroad appealed to the Supreme Court.]

* * * We do not deem it necessary, however, to consider either of [the questions raised by the bill of complaint,] because, in our opinion, the court below was without jurisdiction of the cause. Neither party has questioned that jurisdiction, but it is the duty of this court to see to it that the jurisdiction of the Circuit Court, which is defined and limited by statute, is not exceeded. This duty we have frequently performed of our own motion. [See, *e.g.,*] Mansfield, C & L.M. Railway Company v. Swan, 111 U.S. 379, 382 [(1884)].

There was no diversity of citizenship and it is not and cannot be suggested that there was any ground of jurisdiction, except that the case was a "suit . . . arising under the Constitution and laws of the United States." It is the settled interpretation of these words, as used in this statute, conferring jurisdiction, that a suit arises under the Constitution and laws of the United States only when the plaintiff's statement of his own cause of action shows that it is based upon those laws or that Constitution. It is not enough that the plaintiff alleges some anticipated defense to his cause of action and asserts that the defense is invalidated by some provision of the Constitution of the United States. Although such allegations show that very likely, in the course of the litigation, a question under the Constitution would arise, they do not show that the suit, that is, the plaintiff's original cause of action, arises under the Constitution. In Tennessee v. Union & Planters' Bank, 152 U.S. 454 [(1894)], the plaintiff, the State of Tennessee, brought suit * * * to recover from the defendant certain taxes alleged to be due under the laws of the

State. The plaintiff alleged that the defendant claimed an immunity from the taxation by virtue of its charter, and that therefore the tax was void, because in violation of the provision of the Constitution of the United States, which forbids any State from passing a law impairing the obligation of contracts. The cause was held to be beyond the jurisdiction of the Circuit Court, the court saying, by Mr. Justice Gray [152 U.S. at 464], "a suggestion of one party, that the other will or may set up a claim under the Constitution or laws of the United States, does not make the suit one arising under that Constitution or those laws." * * *

The interpretation of the act which we have stated was first announced in Metcalf v. Watertown, 128 U.S. 586 [(1888)], and has since been repeated and applied in * * * [citing numerous cases]. The application of this rule to the case at bar is decisive against the jurisdiction of the Circuit Court.

It is ordered that the judgment be reversed and the case remitted to the circuit court with instructions to dismiss the suit for want of jurisdiction.

NOTE ON MOTTLEY AND THE WELL-PLEADED COMPLAINT RULE

(1) A Brief History of the Rule. Congress expanded federal jurisdiction considerably in 1875, doing so in part to address state court hostility to the newly free citizens of the United States and in part for other reasons. See Wiecek, *The Reconstruction of the Federal Judicial Power, 1863–1875*, 13 Am.J.Leg.Hist. 333 (1969). The bill took shape in the Senate where Senator Carpenter, a leading proponent and former railroad attorney, explained the need to update jurisdictional provisions designed for the water-borne commerce of 1789 to accommodate a rail-borne commerce that "crosses the continent." *Id*. 342.[1] Among other provisions, the 1875 Act conferred broad original and removal jurisdiction on the lower federal courts in matters arising under the Constitution and laws of the United States. Taking cues from Osborn v. Bank of the United States, 22 U.S. (9 Wheat.) 738 (1824), early interpretations of the Act were often quite expansive. Thus, in Pacific Railroad Removal Cases, 115 U.S. 1 (1885), p. 1026, *infra*, the Court upheld federal jurisdiction on removal of non-federal claims brought in state court against a railroad chartered by the federal government. Claims against the Pacific Railroad, like those brought by the Bank in Osborn, were said to arise under federal law.[2]

The Court articulated the well-pleaded complaint rule in Metcalf v. City of Watertown, 128 U.S. 586 (1888). Like the Mottleys, Metcalf sued in federal

---

[1]   On Senator Carpenter's role in the adoption of the Act of 1875, see Frankfurter & Landis, *The Business of the Supreme Court* 65–69 (1928); Chadbourn & Levin, *Original Jurisdiction of Federal Questions*, 90 U.Pa.L.Rev. 639, 642–45 (1942); Forrester, *The Nature of a "Federal Question,"* 16 Tul.L.Rev. 362, 374–77 (1942).

[2]   Congress has overruled the more specific holding of the Pacific Railroad Removal Cases that the general federal question statute embraces suits by or against federally incorporated bodies. See 28 U.S.C. § 1349.

court to enforce a non-federal contract right and anticipated certain federal issues. Interpreting a statutory provision that extended jurisdiction to "suits" arising under federal law, the Court held that Metcalf's suit did not so arise: "it must appear, in that class of cases, that the suit was one of which the circuit court, at the time its jurisdiction is invoked, could properly take cognizance." Metcalf, 128 U.S. at 589. That conclusion was thought to follow both from statute's reference to the plaintiff's suit, and from jurisdictional first principles: "If the city had not answered in the present suit, and judgment by default had been rendered against it, this court, upon writ of error, would have been compelled to reverse the judgment, upon the ground that the record did not show jurisdiction in the circuit court." *Id.* The Court acknowledged that earlier decisions, like Pacific Railroad, upheld jurisdiction over federal issues that entered the proceeding by "the answer or plea of the defendant."[3] But those were removal cases, "in each of which the grounds of federal jurisdiction were disclosed either in the pleadings, or in the petition or affidavit for removal." *Id.*

The Metcalf Court thus offered an "invocation" account of federal jurisdiction under the Act of 1875: the party invoking the federal forum must identify a claim grounded in federal law. Such an account treats the presence of a federal question as less a matter of good policy or convenience and more as a basic necessity for the exercise of judicial power. For plaintiffs, invoking federal jurisdiction as an original matter, the complaint must present a federal question. On removal, defendants might point either to the plaintiff's own complaint or to federal defenses they assert by plea or answer. Congress reworked this framework in the Act of 1887, adopting the modern rule that general removal jurisdiction was to be defined by reference to the existence of original jurisdiction over the plaintiff's "suit." See generally 28 U.S.C. § 1441. That made the presence of federal grounds in the plaintiff's "suit" conclusive as to both original and removal jurisdiction, thereby setting the rule against removal on the basis of federal law defenses that remains largely in place today.[4] For greater discussion of removal jurisdiction, see Sec. 8, *infra.*

(2) The Merits of the "Well-Pleaded Complaint" Rule. Although its holding was based on settled law, the Mottley decision has lent its name to the well-pleaded complaint rule. However effective as a rule for identifying federal questions that can ground the invocation of federal jurisdiction at the

---

[3]   Apart from claims by and against federal corporations, the Court upheld federal question jurisdiction over claims sounding in trespass when the plaintiff alleged that the state was attempting to justify its seizure of property under an unconstitutional state law. See White v. Greenhow, 114 U.S. 307 (1885). Rather than looking as in Metcalf and Mottley to the well-pleaded complaint, the Court based jurisdiction on "the face of the declaration," a narrative statement of the plaintiff's claim that anticipated and responded to the state's defense.

[4]   Compare 28 U.S.C. § 1442 (authorizing removal by federal officers and agencies sued in state court). Note that the Act of 1875 Act tracked the arising-under language of Article III, except as to Congress's choice of the word "suits" instead of "cases." Justice Miller, dissenting in New Orleans, M. & T. Railroad Co. v. Mississippi, 102 U.S. 135, 143 (1880), seized upon this difference in arguing that under the statute, jurisdiction depended on the law under which the plaintiff claimed and could not rest on a federal defense. That view was apparently adopted in Metcalf and later decisions. The Court continued to apply the well-pleaded complaint rule, despite the substitution, in the Act of Mar 3, 1911, ch. 231, § 24, 36 Stat. 1087, 1091, of the phrase "matter in controversy" for "suits." Today, § 1331 confers jurisdiction over "civil actions."

outset of litigation, its application does not invariably identify disputes that "really" turn on federal law.[5] In evaluating the Mottley rule, one must consider what claims deserve an original federal docket and what matters should be left to the state courts, subject to the possibility of an appeal to the Supreme Court as to any ultimately controlling issues of federal law.

(a) **The Value of a Systemic Perspective.** Mottley itself illustrates the importance of assessing the well-pleaded complaint rule from a systemic perspective. If federal jurisdiction seeks to ensure the uniform and effective enforcement of federal law, the Mottley rule seems obviously imperfect, as Mottley itself illustrates. While the Mottleys' claim was said to fail the statutory well-pleaded complaint test, their dispute with the railroad clearly turned on the resolution of federal questions. Indeed, after the Supreme Court's decision, the case was adjudicated in Kentucky state court, where the federal questions proved decisive, and were ultimately reviewed by the Supreme Court on appeal. See Louisiana & N. R. Co. v. Mottley, 219 U.S. 467 (1911) (Mottley II) (reversing state court judgment in favor of the Mottleys). It is also true that in some cases squarely within the statutory grant of federal jurisdiction, the only decisive questions may involve state law—for example, when the dispute centers on whether there was a valid settlement and release pertaining to a federal claim, or in a suit for patent or copyright infringement where the only dispute concerns the validity or meaning of a licensing contract.

Notably, the exercise of removal jurisdiction does little to improve the ability of the Mottley test to select cases for lower federal court adjudication that genuinely turn on federal law. As noted, ever since 1887, the general removal statute (now 28 U.S.C. § 1441) reaches only cases that fall within the original jurisdiction of the district courts. Except when permitted by a more specialized removal statute (for example, 28 U.S.C. § 1442, governing suits against federal officers and agencies), Congress does not permit removal based on a federal defense. Thus, a case like Mottley, if brought as required in a state court, could not have been removed to federal court under the governing statute (then or now) even after federal issues were raised by the railroad's answer and in turn by the Mottleys' reply.[6]

(b) **The Role of Appellate Review in the Mottley System.** The rule tying removal to original jurisdiction has a profound effect on the jurisdictional structure and even on our ways of thinking about that structure. Debates about the "need for a federal forum" frequently focus on

---

[5]   For criticism of the well-pleaded complaint rule, see Doernberg, *There's No Reason for It; It's Just Our Policy: Why the Well-Pleaded Complaint Rule Sabotages the Purposes of Federal Question Jurisdiction*, 38 Hastings L.J. 597 (1987).

[6]   Until 1986, subject matter jurisdiction in cases removed under § 1441 turned not only on the existence of original federal court jurisdiction in the removed case but also on the existence of state subject matter jurisdiction. Thus, if the state court lacked jurisdiction because the case was one within exclusive federal jurisdiction, it could not be removed to federal court. See, *e.g.*, Lambert Run Coal Co. v. Baltimore & Ohio R.R. Co., 258 U.S. 377 (1922). This rule, much-criticized, was repealed in 1986 in a new subsection [now subsection (f) to § 1441 (100 Stat. 637 (1986)): "The court to which a civil action is removed * * * is not precluded from hearing and determining any claim in such civil action because the State court from which such civil action is removed did not have jurisdiction over that claim." But the rule was apparently restored in part through a later amendment. See pp. 1142–1143, *infra*.

whether plaintiffs with a claim of federal right should have access to a federal court. But that argument overlooks defendants with a federal defense. See Bator, *The State Courts and Federal Constitutional Litigation*, 22 Wm. & Mary L.Rev. 605, 608–11 (1981). One might justify a narrow view of original and removal jurisdiction, as Justice Johnson did dissenting in Osborn v. Bank of the United States, by pointing to the parties' right to seek appellate review in the Supreme Court. Such review, at the time of both Osborn and Mottley, was available as of right for any dispositive state court errors in the interpretation of federal law. Parties were thus assured of a federal forum for controlling federal questions, even those that were first injected into state court proceedings by the defendant.

Two things about this earlier structure deserve attention. First, the ability of the parties to raise controlling federal issues on appeal from state court judgments lessens to some extent the importance of securing initial access to a lower federal court. Instead of allowing initial lower federal court adjudication of *all* federal defenses to state-law claims, the nineteenth-century jurisdictional rules relied on as-of-right review in the Supreme Court to address controlling federal issues that did not appear in the complaint. Second, and apart from its possible merit as a filtration system, the appellate review structure operated (like the well-pleaded complaint rule) on an invocation theory: the party seeking federal review (like the railroad in Mottley II) was entitled to a federal forum by making a claim of federal right on appeal from the state court.

Since 1988, when Congress switched to a fully discretionary model of Supreme Court review of final state court decisions, defendants no longer enjoy assured access to a federal forum for the adjudication of controlling federal defenses to state-law claims. Much of the pressure for relaxation of the well-pleaded complaint rule now stems from the fact that, absent original or removal jurisdiction, state courts finally decide virtually all questions that arise in state court litigation, including those governed by federal law. The Court takes only a handful of state court cases each year and no longer routinely corrects errors in the state court application of federal law. See Chap. V, Sec. 4.

(c) **Recasting Federal Defenses.** In evaluating Mottley from a post-1988 perspective, note that federal statutory or constitutional defenses can frequently be recast as affirmative claims of federal right. For example, suppose that a telephone and internet company sued by state regulators defends on the grounds that federal communication law preempts the state regulation. Such a case would fail the Mottley test and would not be removable. But the company, before being sued, might first bring a federal court action to enjoin enforcement of the state regulation as preempted. And if, as is generally true, the relevant federal remedial law (express or implied) gives the company a federal cause of action for injunctive relief against preempted state law, the company's action for an injunction would fall within the federal question jurisdiction. See pp. 1276–1279, *infra*. The example illustrates the important point that litigants' contingent status as "plaintiffs" and "defendants" varies depending on applicable remedial and substantive rules. The Mottley scheme does not, therefore, uniquely burden defendants.

One striking example further confirms the contingent relationship between claims and defenses. Consider the jurisdictional consequences of a case in which the telecom struck first and sued, in *state court*, to enjoin the state law as preempted by federal law. In that (perhaps unlikely) case, the defendant officials could remove the case to federal court. Such a result implicates the debate in Chapter V over appellate review of state court decisions (as in Michigan v. Long, 463 U.S. 1032 (1983), p. 656, *supra*), in which the state court has arguably overprotected federal rights. Removal by state regulators of a state court proceeding poses some of the same concerns and explains in part why some observers argue that Congress should extend a federal forum to the party that puts forth (or in Metcalf's terms, invokes) federal law. See Wechsler, *Federal Jurisdiction and the Revision of the Judicial Code*, 13 Law & Contemp.Probs. 216, 233–34 (1948). Such an approach would allow the railroad to remove the Mottley case by asserting a substantial federal defense but would not permit the state regulators to remove the telecom's state court preemption action. More generally, the approach would deny removal rights to defendants in cases where the plaintiff invoked federal law in the complaint but chose the state forum.

(d) Frivolity of the Federal Defense. Some propose to address concerns with the Supreme Court's inability to correct state court errors on appeal by expanding removal jurisdiction under § 1441 to encompass federal-law defenses to state court claims. Consider Judge Posner's defense of existing law: "In many [cases] the federal defense would have little merit—would, indeed, have been concocted purely to confer federal jurisdiction—yet this fact might be impossible to determine with any confidence without having a trial before the trial. I grant that frivolous federal claims are also a problem when only plaintiffs can use them to get into court, but a less serious problem. If the plaintiff gets thrown out of federal court because his claim is frivolous, and he must therefore start over in state court, he has lost time, and the loss may be fatal if meanwhile the statute of limitations has run. But the defendant may be delighted to see the plaintiff's case thrown out of federal court when the court discovers that the federal defense is frivolous. Thus, it would not be a complete solution to the problem of the frivolous federal defense to allow removal on the basis of a federal question first raised by way of defense but to give the district court discretion to remand the case back to the state court." Posner, The Federal Courts: Challenge and Reform 302–03 (1996).

(3) Counterclaims and the Well-Pleaded Complaint Rule. In Holmes Group, Inc. v. Vornado Air Circulation Systems, Inc., 535 U.S. 826 (2002), the Court held without dissent that a federal counterclaim, even when compulsory, does not establish "arising under" jurisdiction. Justice Scalia's opinion for the Court reasoned that a contrary rule would (i) permit the defendant to defeat the plaintiff's forum choice by raising a federal counterclaim, (ii) "radically expand the class of removable cases" and thereby fail to respect "the rightful independence of state governments," and (iii) undermine   administrative   simplicity   by   making   jurisdictional determinations depend on the content not only of the complaint but also of responsive pleadings.[7]

B. ASSESSING THE SUFFICIENCY OF THE FEDERAL QUESTION

The Mottley decision instructs that under § 1331, jurisdiction depends on the appearance of a federal question in the well-pleaded complaint. But neither § 1331 nor Mottley defines what federal questions qualify as sufficient to ground jurisdiction. On appeal to the Supreme Court from a state court decision, as Chapter V explains, the parties must identify a controlling question of federal law. But litigants do not always know when they file an original action in state or federal court what legal questions will ultimately prove decisive. This section explores the Court's rules for assessing the sufficiency of a federal question under § 1331.

1. THE CAUSE OF ACTION TEST

American Well Works Co. v. Layne & Bowler Co.

241 U.S. 257 (1916).
Error to the District Court of the United States for the Eastern District of Arkansas.

■ MR. JUSTICE HOLMES delivered the opinion of the court.

[The question presented is whether the district court properly concluded that the cause of action arises under the federal patent laws.]
* * *

---

[7]   The case actually involved the interpretation of 28 U.S.C. § 1295(a)(1), which, with certain exceptions not pertinent here, gives the Court of Appeals for the Federal Circuit exclusive appellate jurisdiction over the decision of a district court whose jurisdiction "was based, in whole or in part, on [28 U.S.C.] § 1338." Section 1338 confers exclusive district court jurisdiction over, *inter alia*, cases "arising under" any Act of Congress relating to patents. In Holmes Group, the plaintiff's complaint raised a federal claim but not one relating to patents; the defendant counterclaimed for patent infringement. The Supreme Court ruled that the case did not "arise under" the patent laws by virtue of the patent counterclaim, and hence held that the Federal Circuit lacked appellate jurisdiction under § 1295(a)(1).

In reaching that decision, the Court's opinion rested more broadly on the premises that (i) the meaning of "arising under" in § 1331 and § 1338 is the same, and (ii) a counterclaim, because it appears in the answer, cannot provide the basis for "arising under" jurisdiction consistently with the well-pleaded complaint rule. The Court specifically noted that its approach also governs whether a case is removable from state court under § 1441(a). But *cf.* Horton v. Liberty Mut. Ins. Co., 367 U.S. 348 (1961).

With respect to patent and other cases embraced by § 1338, Congress has overturned the specific holding of the Holmes Group decision. See Paragraph (4)(b), *infra*. But the decision's rationale remains the law with respect to the interpretation of § 1331 and of other statutes using the "arising under" language.

Of course the question depends upon the plaintiff's declaration. That may be summed up in a few words. The plaintiff alleges that it owns, manufactures and sells a certain pump, has or has applied for a patent for it, and that the pump is known as the best in the market. It then alleges that the defendants have falsely and maliciously libeled and slandered the plaintiff's title to the pump by stating that the pump and certain parts thereof are infringements upon the defendants' pump and certain parts thereof and that without probable cause they have brought suits against some parties who are using the plaintiff's pump, and that they are threatening suits against all who use it. * * *

It is evident that the claim for damages is based upon conduct, or, more specifically, language, tending to persuade the public to withdraw its custom from the plaintiff and having that effect to its damage. Such conduct having such effect is equally actionable whether it produces the result by persuasion, by threats or by falsehood, and it is enough to allege and prove the conduct and effect, leaving the defendant to justify if he can. If the conduct complained of is persuasion, it may be justified by the fact that the defendant is a competitor, or by good faith and reasonable grounds. If it is a statement of fact, it may be justified, absolutely or with qualifications, by proof that the statement is true. But all such justifications are defences and raise issues that are no part of the plaintiff's case. In the present instance it is part of the plaintiff's case that it had a business to be damaged; whether built up by patents or without them does not matter. It is no part of it to prove anything concerning the defendants' patent or that the plaintiff did not infringe the same—still less to prove anything concerning any patent of its own. The material statement complained of is that the plaintiff infringes— which may be true notwithstanding the plaintiff's patent. That is merely a piece of evidence. Furthermore, the damage alleged presumably is rather the consequence of the threat to sue than of the statement that the plaintiff's pump infringed the defendants' rights.

A suit for damages to business caused by a threat to sue under the patent law is not itself a suit under the patent law. And the same is true when the damage is caused by a statement of fact—that the defendant has a patent which is infringed. What makes the defendants' act a wrong is its manifest tendency to injure the plaintiff's business, and the wrong is the same whatever the means by which it is accomplished. But whether it is a wrong or not depends upon the law of the State where the act is done, not upon the patent law, and therefore the suit arises under the law of the State. A suit arises under the law that creates the cause of action. The fact that the justification may involve the validity and infringement of a patent is no more material to the question under what law the suit is brought than it would be in an action of contract. If the State adopted for civil proceedings the saying of the old criminal law: the greater the truth, the greater the libel, the validity of the patent would not come in question at all. In Massachusetts the truth would not be a defence if the statement was made from disinterested malevolence. The State is master of the whole matter, and if it saw fit to do away with actions of this type altogether, no one, we imagine, would suppose that they still could be maintained under the patent laws of the United States.

Judgment reversed.

■ MR. JUSTICE MCKENNA dissents, being of the opinion that the case involves a direct and substantial controversy under the patent laws.

NOTE ON "ARISING UNDER" JURISDICTION AND THE CAUSE OF ACTION TEST

(1) The Cause of Action Test. The "cause of action" test that Justice Holmes announced should not be viewed as a canonical statement of the reach of § 1331. As Judge Friendly famously remarked, "Justice Holmes' formula is more useful for inclusion than for the exclusion for which it was intended." T.B. Harms Co. v. Eliscu, 339 F.2d 823, 827 (2d Cir.1964). Justice Holmes's formula does, however, remain helpful as a rule of inclusion. With only the most uncertain and limited exceptions (see Paragraph (4), *infra*), § 1331 confers federal question jurisdiction when the plaintiff's complaint pleads a non-frivolous federal cause of action. That is so even when the only dispute between the parties is about the facts (or indeed when there is no dispute about facts or law, as may be true, for example, when a default judgment is entered).

But Justice Holmes's test fails as a rule of exclusion. As is explored more fully in the next principal case, Grable & Sons Metal Prods., Inc. v. Darue Eng'g & Mfg., 545 U.S. 308 (2005), and in the Notes that precede and follow that opinion, jurisdiction under § 1331 has been upheld in some cases not involving a federal cause of action, on the basis that a state-law cause of action incorporates a question of federal law in a fashion that merits the exercise of federal question jurisdiction.[1]

(2) The Substantiality of the Asserted Federal Cause of Action. Complaints alleging doubtful or frivolous federal causes of action pose distinctive problems. In Bell v. Hood, 327 U.S. 678 (1946), the plaintiff sued FBI agents, seeking damages for arrests, searches, and seizures in violation of the Fourth and Fifth Amendments. The complaint's theory, that those constitutional provisions gave victims of the violations an implied federal right of action for damages, was novel twenty-five years before the Bivens doctrine was recognized in 1971. See Bivens v. Six Unknown Named Agents of Federal Bureau of Narcotics, 403 U.S. 388 (1971), p. 918, *supra*. With

---

[1]   Professors Woolhandler & Collins, in *Federal Question Jurisdiction and Justice Holmes*, 84 Notre Dame L.Rev. 2151 (2009), contend that cases in which federal law was a substantial ingredient but not the source of the cause of action may well have constituted the "paradigm" of "arising under" cases both before and after passage of the general federal question jurisdiction statute in 1875. They conclude, however, that allowing all such cases into federal court today might prove unworkable and suggest that "federal ingredient" cases might appropriately be limited to those in which the ingredient was a constitutional (and not merely a statutory) one.

Justice Black writing, the Bell v. Hood Court upheld the district court's jurisdiction, reasoning that "[j]urisdiction * * * is not defeated * * * by the possibility that the averments might fail to state a cause of action on which petitioners could actually recover"; that question "must be decided after and not before the court has assumed jurisdiction." True, Justice Black acknowledged that "a suit may sometimes be dismissed for want of jurisdiction"—where the claim "appears to be immaterial and made solely for the purpose of obtaining jurisdiction or where such a claim is wholly insubstantial and frivolous." But those exceptions did not apply, as the Court had never decided whether the federal courts can award compensation for violations of the Fourth and Fifth Amendments by federal officers. Justice Black's opinion, confirming jurisdiction before reaching the merits, thus bears some resemblance to the jurisdictional sequencing decision in Steel Co. v. Citizens for a Better Environment, 523 U.S. 83 (1998), which similarly called upon courts to decide jurisdictional issues before reaching the merits question of a statutory right to sue. See p. 979, *supra*.

In evaluating the import of Justice Black's approach, consider the range of issues that might be affected by a jurisdictional characterization of wholly insubstantial complaints. Such a jurisdictional characterization imposes a "first-principle" obligation on federal judges to raise the issue sua sponte, even on appeal. Such a characterization may also trigger the rule that jurisdictional dismissals do not enjoy claim preclusive effect. But a jurisdictional dismissal of a "wholly insubstantial" claim would presumably enjoy issue preclusive effect on the question of jurisdiction, thereby barring further litigation in federal court. Issue preclusive effect might extend, a fortiori, to the validity of the claim on the merits. In any case, a claim dismissed as "wholly insubstantial" seems like a poor candidate for further litigation. Finally, consider the role Bell v. Hood played in Shapiro v. McManus, 577 U.S. 39 (2015). There, a unanimous Court in an opinion by Justice Scalia ruled that a district court lacked discretion to refrain from calling for a three-judge court to resolve a constitutional challenge to a legislative apportionment map. The complaint was not so wholly insubstantial or frivolous as to warrant dismissal for want of jurisdiction; hence, the district court was obliged to refer the merits to the three-judge court rather than deciding them.

(3) Causes of Action Created by Federal Common Law. Although most federal causes of action are created expressly by statute, it is now settled that causes of action that are properly "implied" from federal statutes or from the federal Constitution, or that are otherwise recognized by federal common law, do "arise under" federal law within the meaning of § 1331.[2] No plausible reason was ever advanced why—once a claim was determined to rest on federal rather than state law—the appropriateness of and need for a federal forum should turn on whether the claim arose under a federal statute or under federal common law. The proposition that § 1331 embraces actions based on federal common law was implicit in Bell v. Hood, and it was made explicit in Illinois v. City of Milwaukee, 406 U.S. 91 (1972). There, the Court

---

[2] For a partial exception to that rule in the distinctive area of admiralty jurisdiction, see Sec. 6, *infra*.

denied a motion for leave to file an original action in the Supreme Court, seeking to enjoin pollution of Lake Michigan, on the ground that a district court would be a more appropriate forum. As a predicate for its decision, the Court determined that pollution of navigable interstate waters is governed by federal common law (as well as by statutes) and that the district courts had jurisdiction because actions asserting such common law rights arise under the "laws" of the United States. See generally Chap. VII, *supra*.

(4) Do All Federal Causes of Action Arise Under Federal Law? For an unusual exception to the general rule that a case alleging a non-frivolous federal cause of action arises under federal law within the meaning of § 1331, see Shoshone Mining Co. v. Rutter, 177 U.S. 505 (1900). A federal law established conditions for issuance of federal patents (exclusive grants) for mining claims. The law provided that if, after notice of an application, an adverse claim were filed, "it shall be the duty of the adverse claimant, within thirty days after filing his claim, to commence proceedings in a court of competent jurisdiction, to determine the question of the right of possession"; in turn, the patent should issue in accordance with the judgment in those proceedings. Congress provided that this right of possession could be determined by "local customs or rules of miners in the several mining districts, so far as the same are applicable and not inconsistent with the laws of the United States, or "by the statute of limitations for mining claims of the state or territory where the same may be situated." 177 U.S. at 508.

In Shoshone, the Court held that such an adverse suit to determine the right to possession fell outside the general grant of federal question jurisdiction, as it "may not involve any question as to the construction or effect of the Constitution or laws of the United States, but may present simply a question of fact as to the time of the discovery of mineral, the location of the claim on the ground, or a determination of the meaning and effect of certain local rules and customs prescribed by the miners of the district, or the effect of state statutes, it would seem to follow that it is not one which necessarily arises under the Constitution and laws of the United States." *Id.* 509. Earlier in its opinion the Court had said: "[It is] well settled that a suit to enforce a right which takes its origin in the laws of the United States is not necessarily one arising under the Constitution or laws of the United States, within the meaning of the jurisdiction clauses; for if it did, every action to establish title to real estate (at least in the newer states) would be such a one, as all titles in those states come from the United States or by virtue of its laws." *Id.* 507.

Note the ambiguity of the phrase "a suit to enforce a right which takes its origin in the laws of the United States." The "for if it did" clause in the rest of that sentence shows that the Court was thinking of a vast range of cases in which the chain of title includes a federal grant but there is no federal question in the forefront of the case and the right of action is entirely state-created. But many have understood the statutory scheme in Shoshone as one in which Congress created the right to sue. If that understanding is correct, why wasn't that decisive? As a general matter, there is federal jurisdiction when a federal statute creates a federal right of action, even if the statute incorporates state-law standards of liability in substantial part;

a leading example is the Federal Tort Claims Act, 28 U.S.C. §§ 1346(b), 2671–2680, which creates a right of action in tort against the United States for actions of its employees, but borrows state tort law as the measure of liability.

Several Supreme Court decisions have described the Shoshone decision as an extremely rare exception to the rule that the presence of a federal right of action suffices to establish subject matter jurisdiction under the statutory grant of arising under jurisdiction.[3] For an argument that this exception is justified as a matter of statutory interpretation, see Shapiro, *Jurisdiction and Discretion*, 60 N.Y.U.L.Rev. 543, 569–70 (1985).[4]

(5) The Cause of Action Test in Arbitration. The Federal Arbitration Act, 9 U.S.C. §§ 1–16 (FAA), provides for the enforcement of arbitration agreements and the recognition and enforcement of arbitral awards. But while the Act directs the federal courts on petition in an appropriate case to compel, vacate, and confirm arbitral proceedings in specified circumstances, these proceedings do not apparently qualify as federal rights of action within the general grant of federal question jurisdiction. Rather, the federal court must have an "independent jurisdictional basis" to resolve the matter. Hall Street Associates, L.L.C. v. Mattel, Inc., 552 U.S. 576, 582 (2008).[5] The analysis varies depending on the nature of the relief sought. But the Act illustrates a situation in which federal law apparently confers a right of action without necessarily triggering federal question jurisdiction under § 1331. The approach may represent less an exception to the cause-of-action test than a decision by Congress to modify the presumptive jurisdictional scheme.

(a) Jurisdiction over Actions to Compel Arbitration. In Vaden v. Discover Bank, 556 U.S. 49 (2009), the Court divided, 5–4, on a difficult issue involving a federal court action seeking to compel arbitration. The litigation

---

[3] See, *e.g.*, footnote 5 of the next principal case, Grable & Sons Metal Prods., Inc. v. Darue Eng'g & Mfg., p. 1044, *infra*; see also Gunn v. Minton, 568 U.S. 251 (2013); Mims v. Arrow Fin. Services, LLC, 565 U.S. 368, 377 n.8 (2012); Merrell Dow Pharmaceuticals v. Thompson, 478 U.S. 804, 814 n.12 (1986), p. 1039, *infra*.

Professor Oakley, by contrast, contends that the Shoshone case did not in fact present a federal cause of action; he suggests that the statute did not confer a federal right (and thus a basis for federal question jurisdiction) until after the invocation of non-federal judicial processes or the expiration of time for initiating such processes. See American Law Institute, Judicial Code Revision Project644–45 (2004) (reporter's memorandum). On this view, no federal right of action would exist at the time of filing, and thus Shoshone would not stand as an exception to the general rule that there is "arising under" jurisdiction over federal causes of action.

[4] With Shoshone, compare Oneida Indian Nation v. County of Oneida, 414 U.S. 661, 677 (1974), upholding jurisdiction under § 1331 over the Indian Nation's action for ejectment. The Court found that "the assertion of a federal controversy does not rest solely on the claim of a right to possession derived from a federal grant of title whose scope will be governed by state law. Rather, it rests on the not insubstantial claim that federal law now protects, and has continuously protected from the time of the formation of the United States, possessory rights to tribal lands, wholly apart from the application of state-law principles which normally and separately protect a valid right of possession." Thus, the Court upheld jurisdiction on the theory that in the unique area of Indian affairs, the matter of competing claims to land, which would ordinarily be thought to arise under state law (even where some of the claims are based on a grant of federal title), is governed entirely by federal law.

[5] *Cf.* Southland Corp. v. Keating, 465 U.S. 1, 15, n.9 (1984) ("While the Federal Arbitration Act creates federal substantive law requiring the parties to honor arbitration agreements, it does not create any independent federal-question jurisdiction under 28 U.S.C. § 1331 or otherwise.").

began when Discover Bank (through an affiliate) sued Vaden under state law in state court to recover past-due charges on a credit card. Vaden counterclaimed that the charges and fees in question violated state law, though both parties later agreed, and the dissent assumed, that the counterclaims were entirely based on federal law, because a provision of the Federal Deposit Insurance Act (FDIA) "completely preempted" any applicable state law and supplied the only possible basis for relief. At this point in the litigation, Discover filed a federal court action against Vaden under § 4 of the FAA, seeking to compel arbitration, which it contended was prescribed by the credit card agreement. Section 4 authorizes a party to seek federal district court enforcement of a written agreement to arbitrate if "save for such agreement, [the district court] would have jurisdiction under title 28 * * * of the subject matter of a suit arising out of the controversy between the parties."

On review, the Supreme Court held that the federal district court lacked jurisdiction over Discover's petition to compel arbitration. First, the Court unanimously agreed that the quoted language in § 4 did not refer to a "controversy" concerning an arbitration agreement (even though such a controversy might be governed in part by federal law under the FAA), but rather directed the federal court to "look through" the dispute over arbitrability to see whether the court would have had subject matter jurisdiction over the underlying controversy between the parties. In other words, the Court refused to treat the suit to compel arbitration as a federal right of action entitled to jurisdiction under American Well Works, but instead looked to the nature of the parties' underlying dispute. Then the majority, per Justice Ginsburg, went on to hold that the "whole" controversy between the parties was one arising under state law (based as it was on Discover's claim for unpaid charges and fees), and that under the well-pleaded complaint rule as interpreted in Holmes Group, Inc. v. Vornado Air Circulation Systems, Inc., 535 U.S. 826 (2002), Vaden's counterclaim did not give rise to federal question jurisdiction under § 1331.

Dissenting in part, Chief Justice Roberts (joined by Justices Stevens, Breyer, and Alito) did not disagree with the majority's look-through approach as a general matter. Instead, the dissent contended that the underlying "controversy" for purposes of § 4 was Vaden's federal-law counterclaim (the only matter on which Discover sought arbitration). Federal question jurisdiction would have clearly existed had the only litigation been an original action by Vaden for violation of the FDIA (or, perhaps, by Discover for a declaratory judgment that the FDIA had not been violated); thus, the sequence of the actual litigation in the case should not control. That Discover could have sought to compel arbitration of the counterclaim in state court (a point made by the majority) should not, the Chief Justice argued, deprive it of access to a federal forum.[6]

---

[6] The Court's approach bears some resemblance to that followed in the context of declaratory judgment actions, as in both settings the determination of jurisdiction over the pending federal court action requires the court to "look through" that action to assess whether there would be jurisdiction over the dispute between the parties as framed in some other way. See pp. 1051–1059, *infra*. However, under the majority's opinion in Vaden, in "looking through," the court considers only whether there would be jurisdiction over the actual litigation already

(b) Jurisdiction over Actions to Confirm or Vacate Arbitral Awards. In Badgerow v. Walters, 596 U.S. 1 (2022), the Court refused to extend the look-through method of jurisdictional assessment to actions brought to confirm or vacate arbitral awards. In a decision by Justice Kagan, for eight Justices, the Badgerow Court held that the look-through approach was necessitated by and limited to the specific language of § 4. Because Congress had not included the same language in §§ 9 and 10 of the FAA, dealing with confirmation and vacatur of arbitral awards, Justice Kagan held that it did not intend courts to follow a similar look-through approach to the jurisdictional analysis of those proceedings. Justice Breyer dissented for himself alone, arguing that the look-through model for assessing jurisdiction worked equally well for actions to compel and for those to vacate or confirm.

The employment dispute arose from Badgerow's termination—after which she invoked a contractual right to arbitration and sought compensation for a discharge that was said to violate state and federal law. (Had there been an action to compel arbitration under Vaden, the federal questions would have presumably conferred look-through federal question jurisdiction.) After losing the arbitration, Badgerow sued in state court to vacate the award, contending it was tainted by fraud. The employer removed the action to federal court, arguing that the federal-law nature of the original dispute over Badgerow's discharge meant that a claim to vacate or confirm the resulting award would also arise under federal law.

In rejecting use of the look-through method, the Court based its decision on the contrasting language of the applicable sections of the FAA. Section 4 provides for jurisdiction in a federal district court that, "save for [the arbitration] agreement, would have jurisdiction" over "the controversy between the parties." By contrast, the sections that govern petitions to confirm or vacate an award do not contain the "save for" language and do not confer jurisdiction on the district courts. The Court regarded the textual difference as decisive; the district courts were to apply standard jurisdictional analysis, looking either for diversity or for a federal question on the face of the well-pleaded complaint to confirm or vacate an award. Rejecting policy arguments, the Court found that extending the look-through method would not materially simplify the jurisdictional analysis. Nor did the Court see signs of a congressional desire to broaden federal judicial engagement with arbitral matters, many of which Congress left to state courts.

As for how to evaluate a petition to vacate or confirm an award, Justice Kagan called for use of the usual well-pleaded-complaint rule. Conducting that evaluation directed attention not to the employee's invocation of federal law in challenging her termination as an initial matter but to the law that would govern the enforcement of the arbitral award. The Court explained

---

pending, whereas under the Declaratory Judgment Act, the court looks through the declaratory action to assess whether there is *any* hypothetical non-declaratory action (whether or not yet filed) between the parties that raises the same federal issue as the declaratory action. And in the declaratory judgment context, the plaintiff in the hypothetical action could be either the plaintiff or the defendant in the pending declaratory action.

that the award is "no more than a contractual resolution of the parties' dispute—a way of settling legal claims." Legal settlements—even settlements of federal claims—were said to typically involve only state law, like disagreements about other contracts. *Cf.* Metcalf v. City of Watertown, 128 U.S. 586 (1888) (suit to enforce a federal money judgment did not arise under federal law).

In concluding that Badgerow's claim arose under state law, Justice Kagan acknowledged that FAA § 9 authorizes courts of the United States to vacate awards "procured by corruption, fraud, or undue means." But she explained in a footnote that the Court has yet to decide whether the "FAA's more procedural provisions," including § 9, also apply in state courts. Badgerow, 596 U.S. at n.2. The Court thus had no reason to consider whether, assuming federal law specified the rule of decision governing vacatur due to fraud, Badgerow's state-law claim to vacate might incorporate a federal ingredient sufficient to confer federal jurisdiction. The next section addresses the ingredient theory of federal question jurisdiction.

---

2. THE SUFFICIENCY OF A FEDERAL ELEMENT OR INGREDIENT

Federal causes of action, with rare exceptions, present questions of federal law sufficient to support federal question jurisdiction. But some state-created causes of action also qualify for federal question jurisdiction, considerably complicating the analysis. They do so, as the Court has explained, when the state-created cause of action incorporates a federal element or ingredient deemed significant enough to warrant an exercise of original federal question jurisdiction. The balancing of state and federal interests entailed in assessments of the significance of the federal element or ingredient has led to inconsistent outcomes in tension with the goal of a rule-based approach to jurisdictional definition.

Smith v. Kansas City Title & Trust Co.

255 U.S. 180 (1921).

Smith, the vice president of the defendant trust company, brought a friendly shareholder's suit to enjoin the company from investing in federal bonds issued by Federal Land Banks or Joint-Stock Land Banks under authority of an Act of Congress. That Act explicitly provided that these federal bonds constituted lawful investments for all fiduciary and trust funds. The shareholder claimed a right to relief on the ground that state law prohibited the trust company from investing in bonds not issued pursuant to a valid law, and that the federal statute under which the bonds were issued was invalid under the federal Constitution.

Despite the fact that state law supplied both the claimed right and the claimed remedy, the Supreme Court upheld the district court's jurisdiction, on the ground that "the controversy concerns the constitutional validity of an act of Congress, which is directly drawn in question. The decision depends upon the determination of this issue." More broadly, the Court said: "The general rule is that, where it appears from the bill or statement of the plaintiff that the right to relief depends upon the construction or application of the Constitution or laws of the United States, and that such federal claim is not merely colorable, and rests upon a reasonable foundation, the District Court has jurisdiction under [§ 1331]."

Decided just five years after American Well Works, Smith v. Kansas City Title remains a leading decision upholding federal question jurisdiction over a case alleging a state-law cause of action that incorporates an element of federal law. Not surprisingly, Justice Holmes dissented, relying in significant part on his own opinion for the Court in American Well Works. He argued that "a suit cannot be said to arise under any other law than that which creates the cause of action." He then discussed Osborn, which he could have distinguished as arising under a special jurisdictional statute rather than under the predecessor to § 1331. Instead, he viewed Osborn as suggesting that "[i]t may be enough that the law relied upon creates a part of the cause of action," but he insisted that even that minimal standard had not been met in the case at hand.[1]

Merrell Dow Pharmaceuticals Inc. v. Thompson

478 U.S. 804 (1986).

In two state-law tort actions, the plaintiffs alleged that the defendants had misbranded a drug in violation of the Federal Food, Drug, and Cosmetic Act (FDCA). Under Ohio law, such a violation created a rebuttable presumption of negligence. Thus, embedded within a state-law claim was a federal issue about the meaning and application of the FDCA to consumers who ingested such drugs in other countries. The defendant removed the actions from state to federal court, but on review, the Supreme Court, 5–4, held the removal improper because the case did not arise under federal law within the meaning of § 1331.

Justice Stevens's majority opinion acknowledged that "a case may arise under federal law where the vindication of a right under state law necessarily turned on some construction of federal law." But in rejecting federal question jurisdiction over the state tort claim, Justice Stevens emphasized the negative implications that were said to flow from the parties'

---

[1]   For a fascinating study of the Smith case, see Yackle, *Federal Banks and Federal Jurisdiction in the Progressive Era: A Case Study of Smith v. K.C. Title & Trust Co.*, 62 U.Kan.L.Rev. 255 (2013). Among other things, Professor Yackle finds that (1) the mere institution of the suit in Smith "wrecked the rural financial system established by the Act" of Congress; (2) the lawsuit was a "friendly matter," as Smith was not a disgruntled shareholder but a vice president of the Trust Company, and, moreover, he was a "shill for the mortgage banks sponsoring the suit"; (3) the jurisdictional holding in Smith was unexceptional, as "jurisdiction was commonly sustained when plaintiffs raised federal questions in actions that were almost certainly conceived to be warranted by nonfederal law."

Yackle distinguishes two readings of the Smith decision and Justice Holmes's dissent. One reading of the dissent is that Holmes found jurisdiction wanting "because federal law supplied no 'remedies' for shareholders in Smith's position." But a different reading is that both the majority and dissent "treated the substantive legal claim and the shareholder's ability to take it to court as one and the same." On this account, the majority and the dissent disagreed about whether the shareholder's claim was genuinely federal but did not view the source of the plaintiff's authority to sue as the key issue. Under the second account, the idea "that a private litigant's entitlement to pursue judicial relief constitutes a separate, threshold issue distinct from a legal claim is an artifact of the administrative state," in which a legal claim might be enforced not by private litigants but by an administrative agency.

assumption that Congress had failed to recognize a private federal right of action to vindicate the interest at stake. "For the ultimate import of such a conclusion * * * is that it would flout congressional intent to provide a private federal remedy for the violation of the federal statute. We think it would similarly flout, or at least undermine, congressional intent to conclude that the federal courts might nevertheless exercise federal-question jurisdiction and provide remedies for violations of that federal statute" under state law.

In an important footnote, the Court identified two additional factors: the nature of the federal interest and the potential impact on the federal docket. As the docket impact grows and the federal issue becomes less significant, the exercise of federal question jurisdiction becomes harder to justify. The Court "conclude[d] that a complaint alleging a violation of a federal statute as an element of a state cause of action, when Congress has determined that there should be no private, federal cause of action for the violation, does not state a claim" arising under federal law for purposes of § 1331.

In a spirited dissent, Justice Brennan described the majority as endorsing an "infinitely malleable" case-by-case appraisal of the importance of the federal issue. Smith v. Kansas City Title, by contrast, had endorsed a rule-based approach, upholding jurisdiction whenever the right of the plaintiff turned on a non-frivolous question of federal law. Justice Brennan also objected to the Court's reliance on Congress's presumed failure to create a private right of action, explaining that the Court's appellate review of state court decisions could not ensure the uniform and effective enforcement of the federal rights at issue.

While the majority in Merrel Dow refrained from overruling Smith,[1] its reliance on the absence of a federal right of action threatened to end much federal ingredient jurisdiction. The next principal case addresses the conflict between Smith and Merrell Dow.

Grable & Sons Metal Products, Inc. v. Darue Engineering and Manufacturing

545 U.S. 308 (2005).
Certiorari to the United States Court of Appeals for the Sixth Circuit.

■ JUSTICE SOUTER delivered the opinion of the Court.

The question is whether want of a federal cause of action to try claims of title to land obtained at a federal tax sale precludes removal to federal court of a state action with non-diverse parties raising a disputed issue of federal title law. We answer no, and hold that the national interest in providing a federal forum for federal tax litigation is sufficiently substantial to support the exercise of federal question

---

[1]   Two years after Merrell Dow, in Christianson v. Colt Industries Operating Corp., 486 U.S. 800, 808 (1988), the Court, per Justice Brennan, said that a case arises under federal law if "the plaintiff's right to relief necessarily depends on resolution of a substantial question of federal law."

jurisdiction over the disputed issue on removal, which would not distort any division of labor between the state and federal courts, provided or assumed by Congress.

I

[The Internal Revenue Service seized real property belonging to Grable to satisfy a federal tax delinquency. Grable received notice, by certified mail, of the seizure before the IRS sold the property to Darue. Grable also received notice of the sale but did not exercise its statutory right to redeem the property within 180 days of the sale, and after that period had passed, the Government gave Darue a quitclaim deed.]

Five years later, Grable brought a quiet title action in state court, claiming that Darue's record title was invalid because the IRS had failed to notify Grable of its seizure of the property in the exact manner required by [26 U.S.C.] § 6335(a), which provides that written notice must be "given * * * to the owner of the property [or] left at his usual place of abode or business." Grable said that the statute required personal service, not service by certified mail.

Darue removed the case to Federal District Court as presenting a federal question, because the claim of title depended on the interpretation of the notice statute in the federal tax law. The District Court declined to remand the case * * *. On the merits, the court granted summary judgment to Darue, holding that although § 6335 by its terms required personal service, substantial compliance with the statute was enough.

The Court of Appeals for the Sixth Circuit affirmed. * * * We granted certiorari on the jurisdictional question alone to resolve a split within the Courts of Appeals on whether Merrell Dow Pharmaceuticals Inc. v. Thompson, 478 U.S. 804 (1986), always requires a federal cause of action as a condition for exercising federal-question jurisdiction. We now affirm.

II

Darue was entitled to remove the quiet title action if Grable could have brought it in federal district court originally, 28 U.S.C. § 1441(a), as a civil action "arising under the Constitution, laws, or treaties of the United States," § 1331. This provision for federal-question jurisdiction is invoked by and large by plaintiffs pleading a cause of action created by federal law * * *. There is, however, another longstanding, if less frequently encountered, variety of federal "arising under" jurisdiction, this Court having recognized for nearly 100 years that in certain cases federal question jurisdiction will lie over state-law claims that implicate significant federal issues. E.g., Hopkins v. Walker, 244 U.S. 486, 490–491 (1917). The doctrine captures the commonsense notion that a federal court ought to be able to hear claims recognized under state law that nonetheless turn on substantial questions of federal law, and thus justify resort to the experience, solicitude, and hope of uniformity that a federal forum offers on federal issues.

The classic example is Smith v. Kansas City Title & Trust Co., 255 U.S. 180 (1921), a suit by a shareholder claiming that the defendant corporation could not lawfully buy certain bonds of the National Government because their issuance was unconstitutional. Although Missouri law provided the right to sue the trust company, the Court recognized federal-question jurisdiction because the principal issue in the case was the federal constitutionality of the bond issue. Smith thus held, in a somewhat generous statement of the scope of the doctrine, that a state-law claim could give rise to federal-question jurisdiction so long as it "appears from the [complaint] that the right to relief depends upon the construction or application of [federal law]." *Id.*, at 199.

The Smith statement has been subject to some trimming to fit earlier and later cases recognizing the vitality of the basic doctrine, but shying away from the expansive view that mere need to apply federal law in a state-law claim will suffice to open the "arising under" door. As early as 1912, this Court had confined federal-question jurisdiction over state-law claims to those that "really and substantially involv[e] a dispute or controversy respecting the validity, construction or effect of [federal] law." Shulthis v. McDougal, 225 U.S. 561, 569 (1912). This limitation was the ancestor of Justice Cardozo's later explanation that a request to exercise federal-question jurisdiction over a state action calls for a "common-sense accommodation of judgment to [the] kaleidoscopic situations" that present a federal issue, in "a selective process which picks the substantial causes out of the web and lays the other ones aside." Gully v. First Nat. Bank in Meridian, 299 U.S. 109, 117–118 (1936). It has in fact become a constant refrain in such cases that federal jurisdiction demands not only a contested federal issue, but a substantial one, indicating a serious federal interest in claiming the advantages thought to be inherent in a federal forum. *E.g.*, Chicago v. International College of Surgeons, 522 U.S. 156, 164 (1997); Merrell Dow, *supra*, at 814, and n.12; Franchise Tax Bd. of Cal. v. Construction Laborers Vacation Trust for Southern Cal., 463 U.S. 1, 28 (1983).

But even when the state action discloses a contested and substantial federal question, the exercise of federal jurisdiction is subject to a possible veto. For the federal issue will ultimately qualify for a federal forum only if federal jurisdiction is consistent with congressional judgment about the sound division of labor between state and federal courts governing the application of § 1331. Thus, Franchise Tax Bd. explained that the appropriateness of a federal forum to hear an embedded issue could be evaluated only after considering the "welter of issues regarding the interrelation of federal and state authority and the proper management of the federal judicial system." *Id.*, at 8. Because arising-under jurisdiction to hear a state-law claim always raises the possibility of upsetting the state-federal line drawn (or at least assumed) by Congress, the presence of a disputed federal issue and the ostensible importance of a federal forum are never necessarily dispositive; there must always be an assessment of any disruptive portent in exercising federal jurisdiction.

These considerations have kept us from stating a "single, precise, all-embracing" test for jurisdiction over federal issues embedded in state-law claims between nondiverse parties. Christianson v. Colt Industries Operating Corp., 486 U.S. 800, 821 (1988) (Stevens, J., concurring). We have not kept them out simply because they appeared in state raiment, as Justice Holmes would have done, see Smith, *supra*, at 214 (dissenting opinion), but neither have we treated "federal issue" as a password opening federal courts to any state action embracing a point of federal law. Instead, the question is, does a state-law claim necessarily raise a stated federal issue, actually disputed and substantial, which a federal forum may entertain without disturbing any congressionally approved balance of federal and state judicial responsibilities.

III

A

This case warrants federal jurisdiction. Grable's state complaint must specify "the facts establishing the superiority of [its] claim," Mich. Ct. Rule 3.411(B)(2)(c) (West 2005), and Grable has premised its superior title claim on a failure by the IRS to give it adequate notice, as defined by federal law. Whether Grable was given notice within the meaning of the federal statute is thus an essential element of its quiet title claim, and the meaning of the federal statute is actually in dispute; it appears to be the only legal or factual issue contested in the case. The meaning of the federal tax provision is an important issue of federal law that sensibly belongs in a federal court. The Government has a strong interest in the "prompt and certain collection of delinquent taxes," United States v. Rodgers, 461 U.S. 677, 709 (1983), and the ability of the IRS to satisfy its claims from the property of delinquents requires clear terms of notice to allow buyers like Darue to satisfy themselves that the Service has touched the bases necessary for good title. The Government thus has a direct interest in the availability of a federal forum to vindicate its own administrative action, and buyers (as well as tax delinquents) may find it valuable to come before judges used to federal tax matters. Finally, because it will be the rare state title case that raises a contested matter of federal law, federal jurisdiction to resolve genuine disagreement over federal tax title provisions will portend only a microscopic effect on the federal-state division of labor. See n.3, *infra*.

This conclusion puts us in venerable company, quiet title actions having been the subject of some of the earliest exercises of federal-question jurisdiction over state-law claims. In Hopkins, 244 U.S., at 490–491, the question was federal jurisdiction over a quiet title action based on the plaintiffs' allegation that federal mining law gave them the superior claim. Just as in this case, "the facts showing the plaintiffs' title and the existence and invalidity of the instrument or record sought to be eliminated as a cloud upon the title are essential parts of the plaintiffs' cause of action."[3] *Id.*, at 490. As in this case again, "it is plain that a controversy respecting the construction and effect of the [federal] laws is involved and is sufficiently real and substantial." *Id.*, at 489. This Court therefore upheld federal jurisdiction in Hopkins, as well as in * * * similar quiet title matters * * *. Consistent with those cases, the recognition of federal jurisdiction is in order here.

B

Merrell Dow Pharmaceuticals Inc. v. Thompson, 478 U.S. 804 (1986), on which Grable rests its position, is not to the contrary. Merrell Dow considered a state tort claim resting in part on the allegation that the defendant drug company had violated a federal misbranding prohibition, and was thus presumptively negligent under Ohio law. *Id.*, at 806. The Court assumed that federal law would have to be applied to resolve the claim, but after closely examining the strength of the federal interest at stake and the implications of opening the federal forum, held federal jurisdiction unavailable. Congress had not provided a private federal cause of action for violation of the federal branding requirement, and the Court found "it would ... flout, or at least undermine, congressional intent to conclude that federal courts might nevertheless exercise federal-question jurisdiction and provide remedies for violations of that federal statute solely because the violation ... is said to be a ... 'proximate cause' under state law." *Id.*, at 812.

Because federal law provides for no quiet title action that could be brought against Darue, Grable argues that there can be no federal jurisdiction here, stressing some broad language in Merrell Dow (including the passage just quoted) that on its face supports Grable's position. But an opinion is to be read as a whole, and Merrell Dow cannot be read whole as overturning decades of precedent, as it would have done by effectively adopting the Holmes dissent in Smith, and converting a federal cause of action from a sufficient condition for federal-question jurisdiction[5] into a necessary one.

In the first place, Merrell Dow disclaimed the adoption of any bright-line rule, as when the Court reiterated that "in exploring the outer reaches of § 1331, determinations about federal jurisdiction require sensitive judgments about congressional intent, judicial power, and the federal system." 478 U.S., at 810. The opinion included a lengthy footnote

---

[3]   The quiet title cases also show the limiting effect of the requirement that the federal issue in a state-law claim must actually be in dispute to justify federal-question jurisdiction. In Shulthis v. McDougal, 225 U.S. 561 (1912), this Court found that there was no federal question jurisdiction to hear a plaintiff's quiet title claim in part because the federal statutes on which title depended were not subject to "any controversy respecting their validity, construction, or effect." *Id.*, at 570. As the Court put it, the requirement of an actual dispute about federal law was "especially" important in "suit[s] involving rights to land acquired under a law of the United States," because otherwise "every suit to establish title to land in the central and western states would so arise [under federal law], as all titles in those States are traceable back to those laws." *Id.*, at 569–570.

[5]   For an extremely rare exception to the sufficiency of a federal right of action, see Shoshone Mining Co. v. Rutter, 177 U.S. 505, 507 (1900).

explaining that questions of jurisdiction over state-law claims require "careful judgments," *id.*, at 814, about the "nature of the federal interest at stake," *id.*, at 814, n.12 (emphasis deleted). And as a final indication that it did not mean to make a federal right of action mandatory, it expressly approved the exercise of jurisdiction sustained in Smith, despite the want of any federal cause of action available to Smith's shareholder plaintiff. Merrell Dow then, did not toss out, but specifically retained the contextual enquiry that had been Smith's hallmark for over 60 years. At the end of Merrell Dow, Justice Holmes was still dissenting.

Accordingly, Merrell Dow should be read in its entirety as treating the absence of a federal private right of action as evidence relevant to, but not dispositive of, the "sensitive judgments about congressional intent" that § 1331 requires. The absence of any federal cause of action affected Merrell Dow's result two ways. The Court saw the fact as worth some consideration in the assessment of substantiality. But its primary importance emerged when the Court treated the combination of no federal cause of action and no preemption of state remedies for misbranding as an important clue to Congress's conception of the scope of jurisdiction to be exercised under § 1331. The Court saw the missing cause of action not as a missing federal door key, always required, but as a missing welcome mat, required in the circumstances, when exercising federal jurisdiction over a state misbranding action would have attracted a horde of original filings and removal cases raising other state claims with embedded federal issues. For if the federal labeling standard without a federal cause of action could get a state claim into federal court, so could any other federal standard without a federal cause of action. And that would have meant a tremendous number of cases.

One only needed to consider the treatment of federal violations generally in garden variety state tort law. "The violation of federal statutes and regulations is commonly given negligence per se effect in state tort proceedings."[6] Restatement (Third) of Torts § 14, Reporters' Note, Comment *a*, p.195 (Tent. Draft No.1, Mar. 28, 2001). A general rule of exercising federal jurisdiction over state claims resting on federal mislabeling and other statutory violations would thus have heralded a potentially enormous shift of traditionally state cases into federal courts. Expressing concern over the "increased volume of federal litigation," and noting the importance of adhering to "legislative intent," Merrell Dow thought it improbable that the Congress, having made no provision for a federal cause of action, would have meant to welcome any state-law tort case implicating federal law "solely because the violation of the federal statute is said to [create] a rebuttable presumption [of negligence] . . . under state law." 478 U.S., at 811–812 (internal quotation marks omitted). In this situation, no welcome mat meant keep out. Merrell

---

[6]   Other jurisdictions treat a violation of a federal statute as evidence of negligence or, like Ohio itself in Merrell Dow * * *, as creating a rebuttable presumption of negligence. Restatement [(Third) of Torts (proposed final draft)], § 14, Reporters' Note, Comment c at 196. Either approach could still implicate issues of federal law.

Dow's analysis thus fits within the framework of examining the importance of having a federal forum for the issue, and the consistency of such a forum with Congress's intended division of labor between state and federal courts.

As already indicated, however, a comparable analysis yields a different jurisdictional conclusion in this case. Although Congress also indicated ambivalence in this case by providing no private right of action to Grable, it is the rare state quiet title action that involves contested issues of federal law, see n.3, *supra*. Consequently, jurisdiction over actions like Grable's would not materially affect, or threaten to affect, the normal currents of litigation. Given the absence of threatening structural consequences and the clear interest the Government, its buyers, and its delinquents have in the availability of a federal forum, there is no good reason to shirk from federal jurisdiction over the dispositive and contested federal issue at the heart of the state-law title claim.[7]

IV

The judgment of the Court of Appeals, upholding federal jurisdiction over Grable's quiet title action, is affirmed.

It is so ordered.

■ JUSTICE THOMAS, concurring.

The Court faithfully applies our precedents interpreting 28 U.S.C. § 1331 * * *. In this case, no one has asked us to overrule those precedents and adopt the rule Justice Holmes set forth in American Well Works Co. v. Layne & Bowler Co., 241 U.S. 257 (1916), limiting § 1331 jurisdiction to cases in which federal law creates the cause of action pleaded on the face of the plaintiff's complaint. *Id.*, at 260. In an appropriate case, and perhaps with the benefit of better evidence as to the original meaning of § 1331's text, I would be willing to consider that course.

Jurisdictional rules should be clear. Whatever the virtues of the Smith standard, it is anything but clear. *Ante*, at 313 (the standard "calls for a 'common-sense accommodation of judgment to [the] kaleidoscopic situations' that present a federal issue, in 'a selective process which picks the substantial causes out of the web and lays the other ones aside'" (quoting Gully v. First Nat. Bank in Meridian, 299 U.S. 109, 117–118 (1936))); *ante*, at 314 ("[T]he question is, does a state-law claim necessarily raise a stated federal issue, actually disputed and substantial, which a federal forum may entertain without disturbing any congressionally approved balance of federal and state judicial responsibilities"); *ante*, at 317, 318 ("'[D]eterminations about federal

---

[7] At oral argument Grable's counsel espoused the position that after Merrell Dow, federal-question jurisdiction over state-law claims absent a federal right of action could be recognized only where a constitutional issue was at stake. There is, however, no reason in text or otherwise to draw such a rough line. As Merrell Dow itself suggested, constitutional questions may be the more likely ones to reach the level of substantiality that can justify federal jurisdiction. 478 U.S., at 814, n.12. But a flat ban on statutory questions would mechanically exclude significant questions of federal law like the one this case presents.

jurisdiction require sensitive judgments about congressional intent, judicial power, and the federal system' "; "the absence of a federal private right of action [is] evidence relevant to, but not dispositive of, the 'sensitive judgments about congressional intent' that § 1331 requires" (quoting Merrell Dow, *supra*, at 810)).

Whatever the vices of the American Well Works rule, it is clear. Moreover, it accounts for the " 'vast majority' " of cases that come within § 1331 under our current case law, Merrell Dow, *supra*, at 808 (quoting Franchise Tax Bd. of Cal. v. Construction Laborers Vacation Trust for Southern Cal., 463 U.S. 1, 9 (1983))—further indication that trying to sort out which cases fall within the smaller Smith category may not be worth the effort it entails. See R. Fallon, D. Meltzer, & D. Shapiro, Hart and Wechsler's The Federal Courts and the Federal System 885–886 (5th ed.2003). Accordingly, I would be willing in appropriate circumstances to reconsider our interpretation of § 1331.

NOTE ON THE SUFFICIENCY OF FEDERAL INGREDIENTS UNDER 28 U.S.C. § 1331

(1) Assessing the Grable Factors. Consider the various Grable factors that inform the assessment of jurisdiction over state-created claims with federal ingredients.

(a) Claims That Necessarily Raise a Stated Federal Question. Grable's incorporation of a requirement that the complaint necessarily raise a stated federal question replicates the Mottley rule. That means the jurisdictional determination depends on pleading conventions, often drawn from state law.[1] In Grable, the rules governing the assertion of a quiet title action called for the plaintiff to tell the whole story, a pleading convention that nicely identified the parties' dispute over the adequacy of notice under federal law. By contrast, jurisdiction was denied in Joy v. City of St. Louis, 201 U.S. 332 (1906), an action in ejectment, where pleading conventions do not demand that the plaintiff allege chain of title or identify a dispute about the validity of that title. Compare Hopkins v. Walker, 244 U.S. 486 (1917), where the Court upheld jurisdiction over an action to remove a cloud on title.[2] The Hopkins Court's assessment of both "general" and state law revealed that the plaintiff's title under a federal grant and the existence and invalidity of the cloud upon the title were "essential parts of the plaintiff's cause of action."

(b) Actually Disputed. Grable's requirement that the federal element be actually disputed seeks to identify federal questions that most obviously deserve a federal forum. The Court may have drawn this

---

[1]   Federal statutes or rules that prescribe pleading requirements on particular issues arising in a state-law cause of action (*e.g.*, Fed.R.Civ.P. 8(c)) may override state pleading rules. *Cf.* Palmer v. Hoffman, 318 U.S. 109 (1943).

[2]   Although the Grable Court describes Hopkins as a quiet title action, the case was actually one to remove a cloud on title.

requirement from Hopkins, which was decided in a context that left no doubt that the validity of competing federal land grants was in dispute. By contrast, five years before Hopkins, jurisdiction was denied in Shulthis v. McDougal, 225 U.S. 561 (1912), an action to quiet title in which, as Grable explained, the litigation may have had nothing to do with a dispute over the validity of the title as a matter of federal law.

Two features of the actually disputed requirement deserve mention. First, the requirement serves to distinguish the statutory jurisdictional test from that the Court announced in Osborn, where the appearance of the federal issue (contested or not) was thought sufficient to satisfy Article III. Second, the requirement apparently seeks to privilege the federal adjudication of unsettled questions of federal law. Consider whether the embedded federal question in a case like Grable itself would continue to deserve (or qualify for) federal adjudication after the Court resolved any question about the sufficiency of certified-mail notice of tax delinquency sales. Or suppose Merrell Dow went the other way, accepting the importance of resolving doubts as to the overseas application of the FDCA to residents of Scotland and Canada. In both cases, Grable & Sons at least suggests the possibility that resolution of the federal question would remit future plaintiffs to state court and reduce the threat to the federal docket.

This line of inquiry highlights a significant puzzle about the breadth of any approval of jurisdiction in a case like Grable & Sons. One might argue that Grable & Sons approves all litigation contesting the validity of federal tax delinquency sales on federal grounds, rather than only those addressed to the sufficiency of notice. On such a view, the model of litigation would remain available to any tax delinquent challenge. It appears that the Court decided Merrell Dow on the assumption that a suit for tort-based damages would be available under the FDCA for any injured plaintiff. Note in thinking about the impact of a decision upholding jurisdiction that the Court's decision in Smith v. Kansas City Title, approving a friendly shareholder challenge to contemplated corporate activity, had substantial staying power as a vehicle for contesting the constitutionality of other federal programs. See Ashwander v. Tennessee Valley Authority, 297 U.S. 288 (1936) (reaffirming the Smith model of friendly, shareholder-initiated constitutional litigation). Congress later moderated the Smith litigation model by statute. See 28 U.S.C. § 2403 (entitling United States to notice of and intervention in such litigation). Resolution of the disputed federal issue may not eliminate the docket threat posed by the approval of federal ingredient jurisdiction.

(c) **Substantial.** Grable includes a substantiality prong but does not appear to assign much independent weight to that question in its analysis. One might understand the Grable Court's passing reference to the requirement as incorporating the substantiality rule from elsewhere in the law of federal jurisdiction, where the term means colorable, non-frivolous, or not wholly insubstantial. See Bell v. Hood, 327 U.S. 678 (1946), p. 926, *supra*.

(d) **Avoiding Disturbance of the Congressional Balance.** Perhaps the most amorphous of the Grable factors—the inquiry into the jurisdictional balance approved by Congress—sets up a consideration of the key issue in

Merrell Dow: how to reckon with the absence of a congressionally created private right of action. In Merrell Dow, recall, the Court relied in part on the absence of a private right of action under the FDCA in rejecting federal jurisdiction over a state tort claim with a federal ingredient. There was no private right of action to enforce in Grable & Sons either; instead, suits to contest title to property in the wake of a tax delinquency sale were left to state law. The Grable Court observes that one would not expect Congress to have legislated such a private right of action into place when it could leave such matters to state law. Hence, the negative implication said to influence the result in Merrell Dow had little resolving power in Grable.

Apart from negative inferences from statutory silences, the Grable Court considered both the docket impact and the significance or importance of the federal question. Its point of departure for this analysis was its perception that Congress would generally prefer to narrow federal dockets and focus federal court attention on the most important questions. Grable thus contrasted the "microscopic" docket impact threatened by jurisdiction over a tax delinquency claim with the "horde of original filings and removal cases" that the embedded federal issue in Merrell Dow would have shifted to federal court. The microscopic docket impact, coupled with its perception of the importance of tax delinquency sales to the administration of the federal tax laws, informed the Grable Court's approval of jurisdiction.

Reconsider Smith v. Kansas City Title from Grable's perspective. Grable classified the constitutional claim at issue in Smith as among those thought significant enough to justify federal jurisdiction. One might also view the exercise of jurisdiction in Smith as posing little threat of disturbing the congressional balance: there was no private federal remedy for shareholders but nor would one expect Congress to enact a statute authorizing shareholders to sue a state-created corporation for breach of duty in proposing to purchase bonds issued under an invalid federal statute. From the Grable Court's perspective, congressional silence might appear to have little significance in this context. That conclusion points to a concern with the ability of federal courts to rightly assess the jurisdictional implications of a congressional failure to act.

Note also that in both Grable & Sons and Smith, the suits sought equitable relief and thus invited the federal court to exercise discretion in assessing the need for intervention and the adequacy of alternative remedies. The private suit for damages in Merrell Dow, by contrast, would not have occasioned any such discretionary assessment.

(2) Post-Grable Decisions. In decisions applying Grable's framework, the Court has found little room for the recognition of jurisdiction absent a federal cause of action. In Empire HealthChoice Assurance, Inc. v. McVeigh, 547 U.S. 677 (2006), the Court considered and rejected the argument that a health plan reimbursement claim governed by state law incorporated a federal ingredient weighty enough to satisfy § 1331. The Court stressed that the federal issue in Grable was triggered by the action of a federal agency (the IRS) and was "a nearly 'pure issue of law,' one 'that could be settled once and for all and thereafter would govern numerous tax sale cases.'" The instant claim, by contrast, is "fact-bound and situation specific." Moreover, the state court was competent to apply federal law "to the extent it is relevant." In sum, the case could not "be squeezed into the slim category" Grable exemplifies. Similarly, in Gunn v. Minton, 568 U.S. 251 (2013), p. 1069, *infra*, the Court found that a state-law legal malpractice claim arising from litigation over the validity of a federal patent did not present a substantial federal issue for jurisdictional purposes.

(3) Simple Versus Refined Jurisdictional Rules. Since reaffirming the well-pleaded complaint rule in Mottley, the Supreme Court has upheld § 1331 jurisdiction over claims lacking a federal cause of action in only four contexts—Hopkins and similar cases, Smith, Grable, and College of Surgeons. See p. 1133, *supra*.[3] Even in the lower courts, rather few decisions uphold jurisdiction in such cases.

Powerful arguments have been made that rules of subject matter jurisdiction should strive to identify "bright lines." See Chafee, Some Problems of Equity 1–102 (1950). Consider Justice Thomas's concurrence in Grable, asking if the systemic value of getting a few cases right justifies the cost in terms of uncertainty and inconsistency. Professor Meltzer made a similar point, in Meltzer, *Jurisdiction and Discretion Revisited*, 79 Notre Dame L.Rev. 1891, 1913 (2004), suggesting that the lower court decisions after Merrell Dow and before Grable raise the question "whether federal judges, as intelligent and dedicated as most of them are, can in fact establish a coherent framework for the boundaries of subject matter jurisdiction predicated not upon a federal claim for relief but instead upon a federal ingredient in a state-law claim for relief"). Scholarship cited by the majority in Grable found that since 1994, the courts of appeals had discussed Smith jurisdiction in 69 reported cases and in 45 of them had reversed the district court. See Note, *Mr. Smith Goes to Federal Court: Federal Question Jurisdiction Over State Law Claims Post-Merrell Dow*, 115 Harv.L.Rev. 2272, 2280 (2002).

To be sure, reported appeals are often an unrepresentative sample of cases generally. Moreover, Professor Meltzer's assessment, and a reversal rate of 65%, may have been the product of the uncertainty generated by Merrell Dow, which the Grable and Gunn decisions may have reduced. But the doctrinal uncertainty reflected in reversal rates may understate the costs associated with federal ingredient jurisdiction. Uncertainty may encourage defendants to remove doubtful cases from state to federal court, gaining the benefit of litigation delay even in circumstances where the district court orders a remand to state court. Yet in the Court's most recent decision, Gunn v. Minton, 568 U.S. 251 (2013), no Justice advocated for a return to Justice Holmes's "cause of action" test as the exclusive measure of arising under jurisdiction.[4]

---

[3] See also De Sylva v. Ballentine, 351 U.S. 570 (1956) (deciding on the merits—without discussing any jurisdictional question—a federal court action involving a state-law claim to partial ownership of copyright renewal terms).

[4] For the view that the Holmes test lacks the "nuance and balancing" needed for sound jurisdictional determinations and is too grudging given the Court's limited capacity to review state court judgments, see Freer, *Of Rules and Standards: Reconciling Statutory Limitations on 'Arising Under' Jurisdiction*, 82 Ind.L.J. 309, 320 (2007).

C. JURISDICTION OVER SUITS FOR DECLARATORY AND INJUNCTIVE RELIEF

Plaintiffs seeking relief from threatened or continuing violations of their federal rights, whether statutory or constitutional, often bring suits for injunctive and declaratory relief. Such suits, though well-established forms of adjudication, can pose tricky questions of federal subject matter jurisdiction. To see why, consider for starters that 42 U.S.C. § 1983 authorizes suits for relief in law and equity and thus squarely confers a right of action for injunctive relief under the American Well Works cause-of-action rule for federal question jurisdiction. But with its focus on defendants who act under color of state law, § 1983 does not specifically authorize suits for injunctive relief against private parties or federal officials. Plaintiffs seeking such relief may invoke other federal statutes or rely on the equitable right of action underlying the decision in Ex parte Young, 209 U.S. 123 (1908), p. 1184, *infra*. There, the Supreme Court recognized that a suit to enjoin state actors from violating constitutional rights presented a case arising under federal law for jurisdictional purposes, even though it was based on general principles of federal equity rather than a more explicit statutory right to sue. One possible implication of the Young framework is that suits based on general equitable principles, at least when brought to secure enforcement of a federal right, qualify for jurisdiction as federal equitable rights of action within the meaning of the cause-of-action test of American Well Works. See p. 1030, *supra*.

Declaratory judgment claims present conceptual and practical challenges as well. Although the Declaratory Judgment Act of 1934 seemingly confers an express right of action to secure a declaration of rights in a "case of actual controversy," 28 U.S.C. § 2201, the Court's decision in the next principal case, Skelly Oil v. Phillips Petroleum, does not evaluate jurisdiction over claims under the statute by reference to a well-pleaded declaratory judgment complaint. Rather than the content of the complaint itself, Skelly Oil requires consideration of the hypothetical coercive complaint a plaintiff might have brought had Congress never enacted the Declaratory Judgment Act. This section considers both jurisdictional puzzles, beginning with declaratory judgments.

1. JURISDICTION OVER DECLARATORY JUDGMENT CLAIMS

In what was once described as the "the greatest one-man job of legal reform to occur in this country," Professor Edwin Borchard led a multi-year effort to persuade state and federal legislators to authorize suits for a declaratory judgment.[1] Such proceedings had long been part of civil law and had been approved by the British parliament in the nineteenth century. They seek to provide parties with a clarification of their legal relations in cases where the traditional forms of relief (suits for damages or equitable relief) might require them to act at their peril. Consider a building contractor whose client raises a legal question as to the quality of materials being used on a project. Whether the contractor decides to build anyway, incorporating arguably substandard materials, or suspends construction, the client may sue for breach. Or consider a protester who wishes to demonstrate within the bounds of the law, believing the First Amendment overrides threatened criminal sanctions. In both cases, declaratory relief at the outset would allow the parties conduct their affairs with knowledge of their legal rights.[2]

Congress drafted the Act against the background of arguments that a declaratory remedy was tantamount to a prohibited advisory opinion.[3] The key provision of the Act, codified at 28 U.S.C. § 2201, authorizes a federal court to issue a declaratory judgment "[i]n a case of actual controversy *within its jurisdiction*" (emphasis added). Suppose that on the facts of the Mottley case, the plaintiffs sought a declaration that (1) the Act of Congress did not retroactively invalidate railroad passes previously issued by contract, or (2) if it did, the Act was unconstitutional. Both questions of federal law appear as part of a well-pleaded claim for declaratory relief and an "actual controversy" exists between the parties. Yet in the next principal case, the Court refused to allow federal question jurisdiction over such a hypothetical claim.

Skelly Oil Co. v. Phillips Petroleum Co.

339 U.S. 667 (1950).

Certiorari to the United States Court of Appeals for the Tenth Circuit.

■ MR. JUSTICE FRANKFURTER delivered the opinion of the Court.

In 1945, Michigan-Wisconsin Pipe Line Company sought from the Federal Power Commission a certificate of public convenience and necessity, required by § 7(c) of the Natural Gas Act, 52 Stat. 825, as amended, 15 U.S.C. § 717f, for the construction and operation of a pipe line to carry natural gas from Texas to Michigan and Wisconsin. A prerequisite for such a certificate is adequate reserves of gas. To obtain these reserves Michigan-Wisconsin entered into an agreement with

---

[1]   Clark, *Edwin Borchard,* 60 Yale L.J. 1071–72 (1951).

[2]   Doernberg & Mushlin, *The Trojan Horse: How the Declaratory Judgment Act Created a Cause of Action and Expanded Federal Jurisdiction While the Supreme Court Wasn't Looking,* 36 UCLA L.Rev. 529, 552–53 (1989).

[3]   The Supreme Court put those concerns to rest in Nashville, C. & St. Louis Ry. v. Wallace, 288 U.S. 249 (1933), in which it reviewed a state court decision in a suit under a state declaratory judgment provision, and in Aetna Life Insurance Co. v. Haworth, 300 U.S. 227 (1937), which upheld the federal Act.

Phillips Petroleum Company * * * whereby the latter undertook to make available gas * * * which it produced or purchased from others. Phillips had contracted with petitioners, Skelly Oil Company, Stanolind Oil and Gas Company, and Magnolia Petroleum Company, to purchase gas produced by them * * * for resale to Michigan-Wisconsin. Each contract provided that "in the event Michigan-Wisconsin Pipe Line Company shall fail to secure from the Federal Power Commission on or before (October 1, 1946) a certificate of public convenience and necessity for the construction and operation of its pipe line, Seller (a petitioner) shall have the right to terminate this contract by written notice to Buyer (Phillips) delivered to Buyer at any time after December 1, 1946, but before the issuance of such certificate." The legal significance of this provision is at the core of this litigation.

The Federal Power Commission * * * on November 30, 1946, ordered that "A certificate of public convenience and necessity be and it is hereby issued to applicant [Michigan-Wisconsin], upon the terms and conditions of this order," listing among the conditions [that gas not be transported to Detroit and Ann Arbor] except with due regard for the rights and duties of Panhandle Eastern Pipe Line Company * * * in its established service for resale in these areas, such rights and duties to be set forth in a supplemental order. It was also provided that Michigan-Wisconsin should have fifteen days from the issue of the supplemental order to notify the Commission whether the certificate "as herein issued is acceptable to it." Finally, the Commission's order provided that for purposes of computing the time within which applications for rehearing could be filed, "the date of issuance of this order shall be deemed to be the date of issuance of the opinions, or of the supplemental order referred to herein, whichever may be the later."

News of the Commission's action was released on November 30, 1946, but the actual content of the order was not made public until December 2, 1946. Petitioners * * *, on December 2, 1946, gave notice to Phillips of termination of their contracts on the ground that Michigan-Wisconsin had not received a certificate of public convenience and necessity. Thereupon Michigan-Wisconsin and Phillips brought suit against petitioners in the District Court for the Northern District of Oklahoma. Alleging that a certificate of public convenience and necessity, "within the meaning of said Natural Gas Act and said contracts" had been issued prior to petitioners' attempt at termination of the contracts, they invoked the Federal Declaratory Judgment Act for a declaration that the contracts were still "in effect and binding upon the parties thereto." * * * [T]he District Court decreed that the contracts between Phillips and petitioners have not been "effectively terminated and that each of such contracts remain (sic) in full force and effect." The Court of Appeals for the Tenth Circuit affirmed, and we brought the case here because it raises in sharp form the question whether a suit like this "arises under the Constitution, laws or treaties of the United States," 28 U.S.C. § 1331, so as to enable District Courts to give declaratory relief under the Declaratory Judgment Act, * * * 28 U.S.C. § 2201.

"[T]he operation of the Declaratory Judgment Act is procedural only." Aetna Life Ins. Co. v. Haworth, 300 U.S. 227, 240 [(1937)]. Congress enlarged the range of remedies available in the federal courts but did not extend their jurisdiction. * * * Prior to [the Declaratory Judgment] Act, a federal court would entertain a suit on a contract only if the plaintiff asked for an immediately enforceable remedy like money damages or an injunction, but such relief could only be given if the requisites of jurisdiction, in the sense of a federal right or diversity, provided foundation for resort to the federal courts. The Declaratory Judgment Act allowed relief to be given by way of recognizing the plaintiff's right even though no immediate enforcement of it was asked. But the requirements of jurisdiction—the limited subject matters which alone Congress had authorized the District Courts to adjudicate—were not impliedly repealed or modified.

If Phillips sought damages from petitioners or specific performance of their contracts, it could not bring suit in a United States District Court on the theory that it was asserting a federal right. * * * Whatever federal claim Phillips may be able to urge would in any event be injected into the case only in anticipation of a defense to be asserted by petitioners. * * * [But it has long been settled that t]he plaintiff's claim itself must present a federal question "unaided by anything alleged in anticipation of avoidance of defenses which it is thought the defendant may interpose." Taylor v. Anderson, 234 U.S. 74, 75–76 [(1914)].

These decisions reflect the current of jurisdictional legislation since the Act of March 3, 1875, 18 Stat. 470, first entrusted to the lower federal courts wide jurisdiction in cases "arising under this Constitution, the Laws of the United States, and Treaties." U.S. Const. Art. III, § 2. * * * With exceptions not now relevant Congress has narrowed the opportunities for entrance into the federal courts, and this Court has been more careful than in earlier days in enforcing these jurisdictional limitations. See Gully v. First National Bank in Meridian, 299 U.S. [109,] 113 [(1936)].

To be observant of these restrictions is not to indulge in formalism or sterile technicality. It would turn into the federal courts a vast current of litigation indubitably arising under State law, in the sense that the right to be vindicated was State-created, if a suit for a declaration of rights could be brought into the federal courts merely because an anticipated defense derived from federal law. Not only would this unduly swell the volume of litigation in the District Courts but it would also embarrass those courts—and this Court on potential review—in that matters of local law may often be involved, and the District Courts may either have to decide doubtful questions of State law or hold cases pending disposition of such State issues by State courts. To sanction suits for declaratory relief as within the jurisdiction of the District Courts merely because, as in this case, artful pleading anticipates a defense based on federal law would contravene the whole trend of jurisdictional legislation by Congress, disregard the effective functioning of the federal judicial system and distort the limited procedural purpose of the Declaratory Judgment Act. Since the matter in controversy as to which Phillips asked for a declaratory judgment is not one that "arises under the . . . laws . . . of the United States" and since as to Skelly and Stanolind jurisdiction cannot be sustained on the score of diversity of citizenship, the proceedings against them should have been dismissed.

[The Court proceeded to reach the merits as to Magnolia because, based on its citizenship and that of Phillips, diversity jurisdiction existed.]

■ MR. JUSTICE BLACK agrees with the Court of Appeals and would affirm its judgment.

■ MR. JUSTICE DOUGLAS took no part in the consideration or disposition of this case.

■ MR. CHIEF JUSTICE VINSON, with whom MR. JUSTICE BURTON joins, dissenting in part.

I concur in that part of the Court's judgment that directs dismissal of the cause as to Skelly and Stanolind. I have real doubts as to whether there is a federal question here at all, even though interpretation of the contract between private parties requires an interpretation of a federal statute and the action of a federal regulatory body. But the Court finds it unnecessary to reach that question because it holds that the federal question, if any, is not a part of the plaintiff's claim and that jurisdiction does not, therefore, attach. While this result is not a necessary one, I am not prepared to dissent from it at this time. * * *

NOTE ON JURISDICTION OVER DECLARATORY CLAIMS

(1) The Progressive Concern with Declaratory Claims. Although the Court upheld the Declaratory Judgment Act in Aetna Life v. Haworth, 300 U.S. 227 (1937), progressive-era hostility toward declaratory-style relief may have informed Justice Frankfurter's approach to the statute in Skelly Oil.[1] Consider the separate opinion in Ashwander v. Tennessee Valley Authority, 297 U.S. 288 (1936) (Brandeis J., concurring), expressing concern with a range of cases, including Smith v. Kansas City Title, p. 1038, *supra*, in which

---

[1]   Two commentators argue that then-Professor Frankfurter opposed enactment of the Declaratory Judgment Act, primarily because he thought it would facilitate adjudication of constitutional issues without an adequate factual record and thereby aggravate the judicial tendency of the era to declare social and economic legislation to be unconstitutional. See Doernberg & Mushlin, *History Comes Calling: Dean Griswold Offers New Evidence About the Jurisdictional Debate Surrounding the Enactment of the Declaratory Judgment Act*, 37 UCLA L.Rev. 139 (1989). The authors suggest that Professor Frankfurter's concerns about justiciability evolved into Justice Frankfurter's concerns in Skelly Oil about subject matter jurisdiction.

private shareholders contrived to procure an adjudication of constitutional issues in a friendly proceeding. To ward off contrived, declaratory-style constitutional adjudication, Justice Brandeis's Ashwander opinion encouraged the avoidance of constitutional issues and the use of prudential doctrines, like standing, to limit contrived litigation. *Id.* 346–48.

(2) Assessing the Legal Basis for the Skelly Decision. The statute authorizes suit in a case of actual controversy "within" the jurisdiction of the federal court. Scholars have argued that this language was meant to preclude advisory opinions by limiting jurisdiction to cases that present a genuine dispute. Such a dispute was clearly present in Skelly Oil, but the Court read the statute to limit declaratory judgment claims to those coercive suits that already came "within" federal jurisdiction *before* the Act's adoption. Instead of evaluating the actual complaint in Skelly Oil, which incorporated a federal question, the Court called for an assessment of the hypothetical well-pleaded complaint that a plaintiff would have filed had it sought coercive (rather than declaratory) relief. Evaluating Phillips's claim for damages or specific performance, the Court found that the federal issue would arise (like the Fifth Amendment issue in the Mottley case) as a response to an anticipated defense.

Note the problems with the Court's approach. Granting that the Declaratory Judgment Act extends only to claims "within" federal question and diversity jurisdiction, the well-pleaded complaint rule in place when the Act took effect required an examination of the complaint within the pleading conventions applicable to claims of the relevant character. Mottley applied contract pleading rules to a contract dispute, just as Grable & Sons (and some earlier cases it cited) applied quiet title pleading rules to determine if the federal question appeared in a well-pleaded complaint. Quiet title actions closely resemble suits for declaratory relief in that they call for a recitation of the nature of the dispute and seek a decree quieting title by an essentially declaratory statement of the rights of the plaintiff. Such pleading conventions potentially expand the range of claims that will present federal questions yet the Grable & Sons Court accepted the conventions as given and proceeded to conduct its jurisdictional analysis within their framework. See p. 1040, *supra.* Skelly Oil applies hypothetical pleading conventions drawn from a different form of action to govern jurisdictional assessments of the complaint. How much does that approach differ from the Mottley Court's refusal to consider anticipated federal law defenses?

(3) Applying the Skelly Oil Test. Under the Skelly Oil interpretation, the existence of jurisdiction over a declaratory action depends on the answer to a hypothetical question: had the Declaratory Judgment Act not been enacted, would there have been a non-declaratory (or coercive) action (i) concerning the same issue, (ii) between the same parties, (iii) that itself would have been within the federal courts' subject matter jurisdiction? In Skelly Oil, there was no such hypothetical non-declaratory action (at least as to the non-diverse parties) and, as a result, there was no jurisdiction over the declaratory action. Similarly, in the hypothetical Mottley claim for declaratory relief, no § 1331 jurisdiction would exist under the approach of Skelly Oil.

Skelly Oil's test for federal jurisdiction over declaratory actions has been much criticized.[2] After all, the drafters and advocates of the Declaratory Judgment Act clearly saw it as an innovation that permitted suit by parties who previously would not have had effective access to coercive relief. Chief among those whom the Act sought to authorize to sue were persons who would be defendants in traditional coercive actions if and when their adversaries brought suit. But Skelly Oil's interpretation bars some prospective defendants from seeking declaratory relief in federal court on matters of federal law that they would raise as defenses to a coercive proceeding.

On the other hand, one can understand the Court's reluctance to treat the Declaratory Judgment Act as creating a federal cause of action that triggers application of the American Well Works cause-of-action test for jurisdiction. The Act did not create rights so much as formulate a new remedy for existing rights. Skelly Oil complicated the assessment of the jurisdictional significance of those existing rights by abstracting away from a well-pleaded complaint for declaratory relief.

(4) An Alternative to the Skelly Oil Test. Consider the road not taken in Skelly Oil. The plaintiffs were seeking to enforce rights grounded in state law; the Court ultimately concluded that the federal question did not appear on the face of the hypothesized coercive complaint for breach of contract. Had the Court instead treated the usual pleading conventions for declaratory claims as controlling, the federal question would have so appeared. But a case otherwise governed by state law qualifies for federal adjudication only where such a federal ingredient satisfies the Grable & Sons test.

Application of that test would cast doubt on the existence of federal question jurisdiction in Skelly Oil. Chief Justice Vinson doubted that any substantial federal question appeared in the litigation; the federal law in question did not confer rights on the parties but was incorporated by them in defining their contract rights under state law. Consider the absence of a significant or substantial federal question in connection with Justice Frankfurter's worry that artful pleading could shift many state-law claims into federal court, thereby upsetting an approved congressional jurisdictional balance. Together, those factors suggest that the claims in Skelly Oil would fail the Grable & Sons test even though the federal question might qualify as necessarily stated and actually disputed.

Consider how this alternative approach, using a Grable & Sons analysis, would apply to a hypothetical complaint for declaratory relief filed by the Mottleys in federal court that duly recited the contract and the dispute over the interpretation of the federal statute and its constitutional implications. (Of course, at the time the Mottleys filed, declaratory relief was unavailable in federal court.) In Mottley, unlike Skelly Oil, the federal issues were disputed, substantial, and decisive; everyone appears to have agreed that the Mottleys' contract rights were enforceable against the railroad unless superseded by federal law. Amending the Skelly Oil test to focus on the

---

[2]   See, *e.g.*, Doernberg & Mushlin, note 1, *supra*; see also Mishkin, *The Federal "Question" in the District Courts*, 53 Colum.L.Rev. 157, 178 n.99 (1953).

jurisdictional significance of the federal ingredients in a well-pleaded declaratory complaint might better serve the purposes of "arising under" jurisdiction[3] and avoid some extreme complexity. Instead of analyzing all the *hypothetical* non-declaratory claims for relief that might relate to the same dispute, courts and litigants could attend to the terms of the declaratory complaint as filed.

The road not taken in Skelly Oil might help address problems critics have identified with the Mottley well-pleaded complaint rule. Recall suggestions that Congress authorize removal jurisdiction when the defendant invokes a federal-law defense; recall too Judge Posner's rejoinder that parties can often assert barely plausible federal-law defenses to many state claims for relief and would likely do so to gain a federal docket. See p. 1029, *supra*. Instead of opening federal courts to all federal defenses, the suggested alternative to Skelly Oil's analysis of the hypothetical coercive claim would allow the district court to consider the significance of the federal defense as an ingredient in a declaratory judgment complaint. Federal courts exercise discretion both in applying the Grable & Sons factors and deciding whether to issue declaratory relief. Today, in a replay under the hypothesized Grable framework, both the Mottleys and the railroad might pursue a declaration of their rights in federal court.

(5) Further Complexities of Skelly Oil: Which Coercive Claim? Skelly Oil clearly rejected the view that jurisdiction exists merely because a federal question is properly set forth in the complaint for a declaratory judgment, when that question would have arisen only by way of defense or reply in a non-declaratory action between the same parties. But the Court failed to clarify the nature of the hypothetical coercive claims it meant to consider. Narrowly interpreted, Skelly Oil would permit the exercise of jurisdiction over a declaratory action only if jurisdiction would also exist in a hypothetical non-declaratory action brought by the declaratory judgment *plaintiff*. Broadly read, Skelly Oil would uphold jurisdiction over a declaratory action if jurisdiction would exist in a hypothetical non-declaratory action brought *by either party* against the other. See Note, *Developments in the Law—Declaratory Judgments—1941–1949*, 62 Harv.L.Rev. 787, 802–03 (1949) (discussing, before the Skelly Oil decision, various approaches and favoring the broader view). Notably, the Court later adopted the broader view. See Franchise Tax Board v. Construction Laborers Vacation Trust, 463 U.S. 1 (1983) (stating that federal courts have "regularly" assumed jurisdiction over declaratory judgment actions in which the declaratory *defendant* could have brought a coercive federal action against the declaratory plaintiff).

An important example of suits falling within this broader view are those in which an alleged patent infringer (who would, of course, be the defendant in any coercive action for patent infringement) asks a federal court for a declaration of noninfringement or of the invalidity of the patent. Apart from seeking declaratory relief, the alleged infringer would have no way to bring the dispute before a federal court; only the patent holder could have done so.

---

[3]   For discussion of the Court's similar approach to the question of arising under jurisdiction over actions to compel arbitration, see pp. 1035–1036, *supra*.

But the leading and widely followed decision in E. Edelmann Co. v. Triple-A Specialty Co., 88 F.2d 852 (7th Cir.1937), held that an alleged infringer's claim for declaratory relief "arises under" the patent laws. In the Franchise Tax Board case, the Court approved of the Edelmann holding, and in other decisions the Court has reached the merits of such actions for a declaratory judgment without raising any question of jurisdiction.

A different question about the reach of Skelly Oil arises from the fact that sometimes more than one possible coercive action can be imagined. For example, suppose that a patent licensor and licensee disagree about whether a product made by the licensee infringes the licensor's patent; the licensee refuses to pay royalties with respect to that product; and then one of the disputants seeks a declaration about the scope of the patent. The licensor could have brought either of two coercive actions, one for breach of contract and one for patent infringement. In such a case, the Supreme Court has held that it suffices to establish arising under jurisdiction over the declaratory action that one hypothetical coercive action—that for patent infringement—would arise under federal law. See Medtronic, Inc. v. Mirowski Family Ventures, LLC, 571 U.S. 191 (2014).

---

2. FEDERAL QUESTION JURISDICTION OVER SUITS FOR INJUNCTIVE RELIEF

Litigants often sue state or local officials, claiming that a state statute, regulation, or other action is preempted by a federal statute or by the federal Constitution and seeking injunctive relief. If federal law gives a right of action (express or implied) to a plaintiff to bring such an action, there is no doubt that the lawsuit "arises under" federal law within the meaning of § 1331 under the rule of American Well Works. The harder questions concern the source and scope of any federal right of action, matters explored in depth in both Chapters VII and IX.

(1) **Express Rights of Action.** Sometimes a federal statute confers an express right to sue a state official for injunction against a state law that the plaintiff contends is preempted. Consider, for example, the Employee Retirement Income Security Act (ERISA), which provides protection for employee benefit plans; § 502(a) of the Act, 29 U.S.C. § 1132(a), expressly authorizes suit by participants, beneficiaries, and fiduciaries of benefit plans to enjoin conduct that violates the Act. Section 502(a) has been construed as including the right to sue state officials for an injunction against enforcing state laws that are inconsistent with ERISA.

(2) **The Shaw Decision and Implied Rights of Action.** The Supreme Court has suggested more broadly that an action seeking to enjoin preempted state regulation may be brought even if the federal statute alleged to have preemptive effect does not expressly authorize such a suit. In the leading decision, Shaw v. Delta Air Lines, Inc., 463 U.S. 85 (1983), the Court in effect upheld federal question jurisdiction over an implied right of action to bring such an action. In the Shaw case, private

plaintiffs sued state officials for declaratory and injunctive relief, alleging that ERISA preempted provisions of New York's Human Rights Law and Disability Benefits Law. In upholding federal question jurisdiction, the Court did not rest on the narrow ground that § 502(a) of ERISA specifically authorized the action. Instead, the Court relied on general principles seemingly applicable to any claim that a federal statute preempts state law:

"It is beyond dispute that federal courts have jurisdiction over suits to enjoin state officials from interfering with federal rights. See Ex parte Young, 209 U.S. 123, 160–62 (1908). A plaintiff who seeks injunctive relief from state regulation, on the ground that such regulation is preempted by a federal statute which, by virtue of the Supremacy Clause of the Constitution, must prevail, thus presents a federal question which the federal courts have jurisdiction under 28 U.S.C. § 1331 to resolve. This Court, of course, frequently has resolved pre-emption disputes in a similar jurisdictional posture."

The decision in Ex parte Young, 209 U.S. 123 (1908), p. 1184, *infra*, cited by the Shaw opinion, upheld an injunction against a state statute regulating railroad rates on the ground that the statute was confiscatory and denied due process. The Court did not treat the right to sue as having been conferred by statute, although the statute that became 42 U.S.C. § 1983 was on the books at the time. Instead, the Court invoked general equitable principles in holding that parties can enforce the Due Process Clause in an affirmative suit to enjoin unconstitutional state laws, rather than using the Clause only as a defense to a state court enforcement proceeding. The Court has also approved the use of Ex parte Young suits to enforce federal statutes. See, *e.g.*, Edelman v. Jordan, 415 U.S. 651 (1974) (suit to compel state official compliance with federal standards). See p. 1196, *infra*.

The Court continues to assert federal jurisdiction over suits for injunctive relief against preempted state law. In Verizon Md. Inc. v. Public Serv. Comm'n, 535 U.S. 635, 642 (2002), the Court quoted Shaw in explaining: "Verizon seeks relief from the Commission's order on the ground that such regulation is pre-empted by a federal statute which, by virtue of the Supremacy Clause of the Constitution, must prevail, and its claim thus presents a federal question which the federal courts have jurisdiction under 28 U.S.C. § 1331 to resolve."[1] See also Sprint Communications, Inc. v. Jacobs, 571 U.S. 69, 76 (2013) (treating the jurisdictional question as settled law).

(3) Implied Rights of Action in a Post-Erie World. Under the Court's holdings that an implied right of action exists to enjoin state regulation as preempted, the American Well Works rule suggests that

---

[1] Although the majority treated the Verizon case as one, like Shaw, involving a claim that state law was preempted, in fact the claim was (in the words of Justice Souter's concurring opinion) that "the Maryland Public Service Commission has wrongly decided a question of federal law under a decisional power conferred by" a federal statute. Verizon, 535 U.S. at 650.

jurisdiction under § 1331 extends to such claims. But conceptual questions arise from the tension between the recognition of implied rights of action in cases like Shaw and Ex parte Young and more recent Supreme Court decisions holding that Congress, rather than the federal courts, should take the lead in conferring rights to sue on a regulatory beneficiary. For greater discussion, see Chap. VII, Sec. 2, *supra*. Consider, for example, a hypothetical federal drug law that authorizes judicial review of agency action but makes no provision for other private litigation by interested parties. Under the current state of the Court's implied-right-of-action jurisprudence, a drug company can bring an implied right of action claiming preemption of state law. But an individual cannot bring an implied right of action to recover compensation for injuries inflicted by the drug company's violation of federal standards.[2] A similar distinction in the approach to implied suits for injunctive relief (presumptively valid) and implied suits for damages (presumptively invalid) shows up elsewhere in the law of government accountability. See Chap. VII, Sec. 1, *supra*, Chap. IX, Sec. 2, *infra*.

The express right to sue conferred in by 42 U.S.C. § 1983 does not entirely resolve the conceptual problem. In Golden State Transit Corp. v. City of Los Angeles, 493 U.S. 103 (1989), the Court held that § 1983 extends to suits seeking relief from preempted state law. But note that even after the Golden State decision, federal courts (including the Supreme Court) have continued to uphold their jurisdiction over actions to enjoin preempted state or local regulations without relying on § 1983. For example, the Verizon decision, noted above, makes no reference to § 1983. Chapter IX more fully considers the interaction between suits based on federal equity and those based on § 1983. See pp. 1300–1302, *infra*.

(4) Declaratory Judgments of Preemption. The Skelly Oil approach to assessing federal question jurisdiction over claims for declaratory relief poses conceptual challenges in connection with suits for relief from preempted state law. To begin with, the analytical approach of Skelly Oil might appear to cast doubt on the viability of federal jurisdiction over suits for injunctive relief in cases such as Shaw and Verizon. In both those cases, the plaintiff sought relief from a threatened state court enforcement proceeding on grounds of federal preemption. The federal issue would ordinarily arise as a defense to such an enforcement proceeding and fail to satisfy Mottley's well-pleaded complaint rule for jurisdictional purposes. Note that the suits approved in Shaw and Verizon ignore this defensive characterization of the federal preemption issue and instead treat the implied right to injunctive relief from preemption as part of the plaintiff's affirmative claim under federal law, thereby satisfying Mottley. The Skelly Oil rule, requiring consideration

---

[2]   For an argument that historically the federal courts possessed equitable power to issue injunctive relief in constitutional cases, which has not been withdrawn by congressional enactments, see Preis, *In Defense of Implied Injunctive Relief in Constitutional Cases*, 22 Wm. & Mary Bill of Rts.L.J. 1 (2013).

of a hypothetical coercive action, thus applies only to declaratory judgment claims.

The Court's approval of federal jurisdiction over suits for injunctive relief may have two implications for suits for declaratory relief in the preemption context. For starters, if federal question jurisdiction extends to the suit for injunctive relief, supplemental jurisdiction (as discussed more fully below) would surely extend to a related claim for a declaration of rights. Even if the plaintiff were to bring a stand-alone suit for declaratory relief, one can argue that the proper application of the Skelly Oil test should take account of the availability of federal jurisdiction over the hypothetical Shaw/Verizon suits for injunctive relief. In either posture, then, the district courts would seem to have federal question jurisdiction over the declaratory judgment action.

A federal plaintiff might seek declaratory relief, however, in circumstances that do not support injunctive relief. (One purpose of the Declaratory Judgment Act was to authorize relief in circumstances in which the requirements for issuance of an injunction have not been met.) The absence of a plausible claim for injunctive relief might appear, under Skelly Oil, to cast doubt on the existence of federal question jurisdiction. Nonetheless, the Supreme Court suggested in a dictum in Lawrence County v. Lead-Deadwood School Dist., 469 U.S. 256, 259 n.6 (1985), that § 1331 jurisdiction extends to an action seeking a declaration of state law's preemption. Relying on Shaw, the Court did not specifically analyze the availability of a coercive action for an injunction. One might interpret the dictum either as recognizing an implied right of action to secure declaratory relief in such cases or as relying on Shaw/Verizon as the operative hypothetical claim within the Skelly Oil framework. See also Schneidewind v. ANR Pipeline Co., 485 U.S. 293 (1988). In Franchise Tax Board, discussed immediately below, the Court further complicated the analytical framework by unanimously refusing to allow federal jurisdiction over a claim seeking a declaratory judgment that federal law did *not* preempt state law.

Franchise Tax Board v. Construction Laborers Vacation Trust

463 U.S. 1 (1983).

The litigation arose from efforts of the Franchise Tax Board, the agency charged with enforcement of California income tax, to reach the assets of delinquent taxpayers by pursuing their accumulated vacation benefits in an ERISA Trust fund. The Franchise Tax Board filed a complaint in state court against the Trust. The first claim sought to enforce three levies, which would require the Trust to pay to the Board amounts equal to the tax delinquencies of employee beneficiaries of the trust. The second claim sought a declaration that the Board's regulatory authority was not preempted by ERISA.

After the Trust removed the case to federal court under 28 U.S.C. § 1441, the Board moved to remand. The first claim in the complaint invoked California tax law, and hence could not, under the well-pleaded complaint rule, support jurisdiction. The second claim, invoking the state declaratory judgment act, posed as a central question whether ERISA shielded the Trust's assets from seizure in payment of delinquent state taxes, an issue of federal preemption.

In deciding whether the second claim arose under federal law, Justice Brennan's opinion for a unanimous Court first considered whether to extend Skelly Oil to suits brought under state declaratory judgment regimes. He reasoned that "while Skelly Oil itself is limited to the federal Declaratory Judgment Act, fidelity to its spirit leads us to extend it to state declaratory judgment actions as well." To hold otherwise would make the rule of Skelly Oil a "dead letter," for "litigants could get into federal court for a declaratory judgment despite our interpretation of § 2201, simply by pleading an adequate state claim for a declaration of federal law." Therefore, the Court held that complaints for a state declaratory judgment were to be analyzed for jurisdictional purposes under Skelly Oil.

In applying Skelly Oil, the Court first acknowledged that the Board's request for a declaratory judgment presented an issue—and only an issue—of federal law. Moreover, in considering hypothetical non-declaratory actions between the same parties that raised the same issue of federal law, the Court assumed that the Trust "could have sought an injunction under ERISA against application to it of state regulations that require acts inconsistent with ERISA." On that assumption, Skelly Oil would seemingly authorize the assertion of jurisdiction.

Nonetheless, the Court refused to allow jurisdiction, creating a new wrinkle in the Skelly Oil analysis. "There are good reasons why the federal courts should not entertain suits by the States to declare the validity of their regulations despite possibly conflicting federal law. States are not significantly prejudiced by an inability to come to federal court for a declaratory judgment in advance of a possible injunctive suit by a person subject to federal regulation. They have a variety of means by which they can enforce their own laws in their own courts, and they do not suffer if the preemption questions such enforcement may raise are tested there." In an associated footnote, the Court found little prospect that States will "flood the federal courts with declaratory judgment actions." Instead the cases would come to federal court if at all on removal. "[C]onsiderations of comity make us reluctant to snatch cases which a State has brought from the courts of that State, unless some clear rule demands it." The Court concluded, "The express grant of federal jurisdiction in ERISA is limited to suits brought by certain parties, as to whom Congress presumably determined that a right to enter federal court was necessary to further the statute's purposes. It did not go so far as to provide that any suit *against* such parties must also be brought in federal court when they themselves did not choose to sue."

NOTE ON THE REJECTION OF JURISDICTION IN FRANCHISE TAX BOARD

(1) The Majority's Reasoning. The Court's reasoning in Franchise Tax Board is difficult to accept at face value. It should not matter that the state would not be prejudiced by a remand to state court, when the notice of removal was filed by the Trust, which sought a federal court adjudication of the preemption question and may have feared that the state court would give an unduly narrow scope to federal preemption. Further, given that Congress has made federal jurisdiction over nearly all ERISA actions exclusive, see 29 U.S.C. § 1132(e)(1), the Court offered little support for its ad hoc decision to leave an important question concerning ERISA preemption to the state courts. It is equally hard to justify the odd state of the law after Franchise Tax Board and Shaw—that a federal court may entertain a private litigant's action, against a government agency or official, seeking a determination that state regulation *is preempted* by federal law (Shaw), but may not entertain an action by the government agency or official against the private litigant, seeking a determination that the state regulation *is not preempted* (Franchise Tax Board).

(2) An Alternative Rationale. Consider, however, a different rationale for the Court's outcome. Suppose that the state had filed only Count I of its complaint—a simple state court enforcement action against the Trust for a tax lien, without including Count II (the request for a declaration of non-preemption). Had the Trust then filed a separate federal court action seeking declaratory or injunctive relief against enforcement of state tax law on the ground that it was preempted by ERISA, the federal court would have had subject matter jurisdiction under § 1331. Under established principles, however, the abstention doctrine of Younger v. Harris, 401 U.S. 37 (1971), would have required the federal district court to abstain from exercising that jurisdiction, in order to prevent federal interference with important state interests implicated in the enforcement action. See Chap. X, Sec. 4, *infra*.

In the actual Franchise Tax Board case, the Trust proposed to remove both the state court declaratory action and the state-law claim to impress a tax lien. Removal, if successful, would have brought into federal court not only the federal preemption issues in the dispute but also the tax lien claim, which was governed entirely by state law. Thus, if the abstention doctrine would have precluded the Trust from litigating a separate federal court action to enjoin the state court proceeding as preempted, it would seem to follow a fortiori that the Trust was precluded from removing the entire state court action and thereby obstructing state court enforcement of the tax lien provision. Justice Brennan's reference in the opinion to "comity" hints at such considerations but does not put them forward clearly. Consider whether such an unspoken abstention-based rationale for Franchise Tax Board adequately justifies the Court's conclusion. After all, a straightforward application of Skelly Oil, upholding removal, would have presumably informed state tax authorities who wish to litigate in state court that they should refrain from seeking a non-preemption declaration in any similar suits brought in the future.

4. EXCLUSIVE GRANTS OF FEDERAL QUESTION JURISDICTION

Apart from the general grant of federal question jurisdiction in § 1331, Congress has sometimes provided specialized grants of subject matter jurisdiction tailored to specific statutory schemes. Several of these specialized jurisdictional provisions confer exclusive jurisdiction on the federal courts, thereby foreclosing the exercise of state court concurrent jurisdiction. See, *e.g.*, 28 U.S.C. § 1337 (antitrust cases); *id.* § 1338 (patent and copyright cases); 15 U.S.C. § 78aa (certain securities cases). Typically, these provisions use the same statutory phrase ("arising under") as does § 1331. See, *e.g.*, 28 U.S.C. § 1338 (providing in part for exclusive federal jurisdiction "of any civil action arising under any Act of Congress relating to patents"). Many such claims would qualify for federal adjudication as cases "arising under" federal law for purposes of § 1331, inviting the question of what (aside from a declaration of exclusivity) such specialized statutes add to the jurisdictional aspects of the federal courts. This section briefly examines that question.

(1) Extension of the Well-Pleaded Complaint Rule. Grants of exclusive jurisdiction have generally been interpreted as embodying the well-pleaded complaint rule. See, *e.g.*, Holmes Group, Inc. v. Vornado Air Circulation Systems, Inc., 535 U.S. 826, 829–30 (2002). As a result, when important questions of federal antitrust, patent, or copyright law arise as defenses to state law claims, the case lies outside of original federal question jurisdiction. Suppose, for example, that a plaintiff sues a non-diverse party for breach of the defendant's promise to pay royalties in exchange for a patent license; the defendant concedes the failure to pay but defends on the ground that the patent is invalid and as a result the promise is unenforceable. Although the case will turn exclusively on the federal issue of patent validity, that issue will be litigated entirely in state court.[1]

In one important area of exclusive jurisdiction, cases arising under federal intellectual property laws, Congress altered the regime to restrict the role of state courts. The Leahy-Smith America Invents Act, Pub.L.No. 112–29, § 19, 125 Stat. 284, 331 (2011), a major patent reform measure,

---

[1]   Sometimes plaintiffs have a choice of theories on which to bring suit for what is essentially the same complaint, and that choice determines where the litigation can occur. Consider disputes about whether the licensee of a patent or copyright has exploited the intellectual property right in a fashion unauthorized by the license. If the licensor alleges infringement, the federal courts plainly have jurisdiction, even if the only dispute is whether the licensee's action exceeded the scope of the license contract. See, *e.g.*, The Fair v. Kohler Die & Specialty Co., 228 U.S. 22 (1913). See also Medtronic, Inc. v. Mirowski Family Ventures, LLC, 571 U.S. 191 (2014) (if a licensee and a licensor dispute whether the licensee's product infringes the licensor's patent, and the licensee fails to pay royalties under license agreement, the licensor may sue for patent infringement). Indeed, 28 U.S.C. § 1338(a) makes federal jurisdiction over such an infringement action *exclusive*. On the other hand, if the licensor frames its claim as one for breach of contract—because the defendant violated an agreement to use the licensed property in only a specified way—the case would not arise under federal law. See, *e.g.*, Luckett v. Delpark, Inc., 270 U.S. 496, 510–11 (1926).

amended 28 U.S.C. § 1338, the statute conferring exclusive federal court jurisdiction over patent, plant variety protection, and copyright cases, to read as follows:

"(a) The district courts shall have original jurisdiction of any civil action arising under any Act of Congress relating to patents, plant variety protection, copyrights and trademarks. No State court shall have jurisdiction over any claim for relief arising under any Act of Congress relating to patents, plant variety protection, or copyrights. For purposes of this subsection, the term 'State' includes any State of the United States, the District of Columbia, the Commonwealth of Puerto Rico, the United States Virgin Islands, American Samoa, Guam, and the Northern Mariana Islands."

The first sentence is unchanged; the second and third sentences substitute for the second sentence of the previous provision.[2]

Note that while the first sentence of section § 1338(a), like § 1331 and many other jurisdictional provisions, speaks of federal court jurisdiction over *a civil action*, the second sentence of § 1338(a) excludes state court jurisdiction over *a claim for relief*. Federal Rule of Civil Procedure 8(a) makes clear that a claim for relief is not limited to claims in a plaintiff's complaint; it includes, for example, counterclaims. As amended, § 1338(a) thus appears to preclude a state court from hearing a patent, plant variety, or copyright counterclaim. The jurisdictional provisions of the Leahy-Smith Act appear to contemplate that a state court defendant may file a patent, plant variety, or copyright counterclaim in state court (and perhaps must if the counterclaim is compulsory under state law)—even though under § 1338(a) the state courts lack jurisdiction to decide that counterclaim—and then the defendant or the plaintiff may, under § 1454, remove the action to federal court.[3]

---

[2] Before 2011, the second sentence read: "Such jurisdiction shall be exclusive of the courts of the states in patent, plant variety protection and copyright cases."

[3] The 2011 Act also contains a new provision, codified as 28 U.S.C. § 1454, that authorizes *any party* to remove a civil action in state court in which any party asserts a claim for relief under the patent, plant variety, or copyright laws; by contrast, the general removal statute, 28 U.S.C. § 1441, which previously governed removal of civil actions filed under § 1338(a), authorizes only the defendant to remove. New § 1454 also specifies that removal is not precluded because the state court lacked jurisdiction over the claim.

The 2011 Act also changes the jurisdiction of the Court of Appeals for the Federal Circuit. Under 28 U.S.C. § 1295(a)(1), that court was initially given exclusive appellate jurisdiction over patent and plant variety cases arising under § 1338, in order to centralize appellate resolution of such matters in a specialized court. Holmes Group, Inc. v. Vornado Air Circulation Systems, Inc., 535 U.S. 826 (2002), held that a civil action in which a defendant asserted a patent counterclaim did not arise under the patent laws within the meaning of § 1338, and hence, appellate jurisdiction lay in the regional court of appeals, not in the Court of Appeals for the Federal Circuit. As amended in 2011, 28 U.S.C. § 1295(a)(1) now gives the Federal Circuit exclusive jurisdiction "in any civil action arising under, *or in any civil action in which a party has asserted a compulsory counterclaim arising under,* any Act of Congress relating to patents or plant variety protection." The pre-2011 grant of appellate jurisdiction to the Federal Circuit was too narrow to ensure centralized review of patent cases, see note 8, *supra*, and the grant in 2011 of appellate jurisdiction over counterclaims makes enormous sense. (Indeed, what is the

Note, however, that the Leahy-Smith Act did not completely strip state courts of authority to decide patent issues: a patent law defense (as distinguished from a counterclaim or other claim for relief) still does not provide a basis for removal. Does this power of state courts to decide issues of federal law embraced by a scheme of exclusive jurisdiction undermine the justification for such exclusivity?[4] Should the Leahy-Smith Act have authorized removal of cases in which a federal patent law defense has been raised?

More broadly, consider whether the jurisdictional policy expressed in the Leahy-Smith Act should extend to claims for relief under other federal regimes that confer exclusive jurisdiction (for example, the antitrust laws or ERISA). Indeed, Congress could surely expand federal question jurisdiction to encompass removal of any compulsory counterclaim under federal law, without requiring a direct link to a statute conferring exclusive federal jurisdiction. Should it do so?

(2) Extension of the Federal Ingredient Rule. Apart from its general use of the well-pleaded complaint rule as the test of federal jurisdiction, the Court has extended the Grable & Sons federal ingredient rule to claims arising under exclusive jurisdictional statutes.

Merrill Lynch, Pierce, Fenner & Smith, Inc. v. Manning

578 U.S. 374 (2016).

Section 27 of the Securities Exchange Act of 1934 grants federal district courts exclusive jurisdiction "of all suits in equity and actions at law brought to enforce any liability or duty created by [the Exchange Act] or the rules or regulations thereunder." Manning sued several financial institutions in New Jersey state court under New Jersey law for allegedly illegal "naked short sales" of stock that, according to the complaint, also violated a Securities and Exchange Commission regulation. The defendants removed the case to federal court, but the court of appeals remanded. It ruled that the district court lacked subject matter jurisdiction under § 1331 because Manning's claims were "brought under state law" and none "necessarily raised" a federal issue. This ruling decided the question of subject matter jurisdiction under § 27, which, the court held, was co-extensive with § 1331. On review of only the § 27 issue, the Supreme Court affirmed.

In explaining why it was appropriate for § 27 to include the "federal element" component of § 1331's jurisdictional test, the Court noted that a

---

reason, under current law, to exclude from the Federal Circuit's appellate jurisdiction review of patent counterclaims that are not *compulsory*?).

But the jurisdiction that remains after the 2011 Act is also too broad. Imagine a case in which a plaintiff files a patent infringement action in federal court, the defendant counterclaims for a state-law business tort, and the only issue raised on appeal concerns the trial court's decision of the business tort counterclaim. Under § 1295(a)(1), both before and after 2011, the Federal Circuit would have exclusive jurisdiction over the appeal, because the civil action arose under the patent laws. But it makes little sense to direct that appeal, which includes no patent law issue, to the Federal Circuit rather than to the regional court of appeals.

[4]   *Cf.* pp. 1388–1389, *infra* (discussing whether state court determinations of issues arising under schemes of exclusive federal jurisdiction should have issue-preclusive effect in federal court).

state-law action could be brought in federal court to enforce an Exchange Act duty under § 27 if it "necessarily depends on a showing that the defendant breached the Exchange Act." The Court offered this hypothetical:

"Suppose, for example, that a state statute simply makes illegal 'any violation of the Exchange Act involving naked short selling.' A plaintiff seeking relief under that state law must undertake to prove, as the cornerstone of his suit, that the defendant infringed a requirement of the federal statute. (Indeed, in this hypothetical, that is the plaintiff's *only* project.) Accordingly, his suit, even though asserting a state-created claim, is also 'brought to enforce' a duty created by the Exchange Act."

The Court then noted that such a claim, whose "very success depends on giving effect to a federal requirement," is like a claim for federal jurisdiction under § 1331 when the state-law claim " 'necessarily raise[s] a stated federal issue, actually disputed and substantial, which a federal forum may entertain without disturbing any congressionally approved balance' of federal and state power" (quoting Grable & Sons Metal Prods., Inc. v. Darue Eng'g & Mfg., 545 U.S. 308, 314 (2005)).

Justice Thomas, in a concurrence in the judgment joined by Justice Sotomayor, rejected the assimilation of the "federal element" prong of the § 1331 test to § 27. He argued that the better reading of § 27 would be to allow federal jurisdiction over all state-law claims that necessarily raise an Exchange Act issue without importing the "arising under" test's additional inquiries about substantiality, disputedness, and the federal-state balance. The Court responded:

"[T]his Court has not construed any jurisdictional statute, whether using the words 'brought to enforce' or 'arising under' (or for that matter, any other), to draw the concurrence's line. For as long as we have contemplated exercising federal jurisdiction over state-law claims necessarily raising federal issues, we have inquired as well into whether those issues are 'really and substantially' disputed. See, *e.g.*, Hopkins v. Walker, 244 U.S. 486, 489 (1917); Shulthis v. McDougal, 225 U.S. 561, 569 (1912). And similarly, we have long emphasized the need in such circumstances to make 'sensitive judgments about congressional intent, judicial power, and the federal system.' Merrell Dow Pharmaceuticals Inc. v. Thompson, 478 U.S. 804, 810 (1986). At this late juncture, we see no virtue in trying to pull apart these interconnected strands of necessity and substantiality-plus. Indeed, doing so here—and thus creating a gap between our 'brought to enforce' and 'arising under' standards—would conflict with this Court's precedent and undermine important goals of interpreting jurisdictional statutes."

The Court acknowledged the oddity of construing the very different language in § 1331 and § 27 to mean the same thing. But it said that the test for "arising under" jurisdiction has never been based on the statute's "particular phrasing," and noted that that § 1331 was given a narrower construction than the identical words in Article III due to the statute's "history[,] the demands of reason and coherence, and the dictates of sound judicial policy" (quoting Romero v. Int'l Terminal Operating Co., 358 U.S. 354, 379 (1959)). Because the "arising under" test does not turn on § 1331's text, "there is nothing remarkable in its fitting as, or even more, neatly a differently worded statutory provision."[1]

Gunn v. Minton

568 U.S. 251 (2013).

The case began when, in Minton's action for patent infringement, the federal district court found Minton's patent invalid, on the basis that the invention had been on sale more than a year prior to the patent application. In a motion for reconsideration, Gunn, the lawyer for Minton, raised for the first time an argument that the prior uses of the invention were "experimental" and thus, under the patent laws, did not render the patent invalid. The district court denied the motion, and the U.S. Court of Appeals for the Federal Circuit affirmed, ruling that the district court had properly found Minton's experimental-use argument to have been waived by its belated assertion.

Minton then sued Gunn for malpractice in Texas state court, complaining of Gunn's tardiness in raising the experimental-use argument. After losing on the merits in the trial court, Minton argued on appeal that the state courts lacked subject matter jurisdiction, contending that his malpractice claim, because it was founded on a question of patent law, arose under federal patent law and hence was within the exclusive jurisdiction of the federal courts. On review, the Supreme Court held that the case did not arise under federal law and that the state courts had therefore properly entertained the malpractice action. (In so holding, the Court reaffirmed that the same analysis governs federal question jurisdiction under § 1331 and § 1338(a).)

Chief Justice Roberts's opinion for a unanimous Court observed that the Court has identified a "slim category" in which claims originating under state law nonetheless arise under federal law. The Grable decision sought "to bring some order to" a doctrine that had previously been "unruly" by providing that federal jurisdiction lies over a state claim "if a federal issue is: (1) necessarily raised, (2) actually disputed, (3) substantial, and (4) capable of resolution in federal court without disrupting the federal-state balance approved by Congress." Applying those requirements, the Court acknowledged that the federal patent issue was necessarily raised and actually disputed, but it concluded that the last two requirements were not satisfied.

---

[1] Does the Manning Court in downplaying the text take adequate account of the role of Congress? Consider Mulligan, *28 U.S.C. § 1331 Jurisdiction in the Roberts Court: A Rights-Inclusive Approach*, 51 Stetson L.Rev. 201 (2022). Mulligan identifies in recent cases a more rights-inclusive approach to federal question jurisdiction—one that departs from the Holmes cause-of-action test and aligns more closely with Mulligan's own understanding of what Congress meant to accomplish when the statute became law in the nineteenth century. For a similar approach, rejecting the Holmes test and more generally defending a faithful agent role for the federal courts in interpreting jurisdictional statutes, see Redish, et al., *Federal Jurisdiction As Statutory Interpretation: A Majordomo Purposivist Perspective*, 74 SMU L.Rev. 303 (2021). Whatever one might say about the proper judicial role in interpreting § 1331, should the Court evaluate the jurisdictional implications of subsequent statutes, such as the 1934 federal securities law implicated in Manning, by reference to the congressional intent surrounding the 1875 enactment of the precursor to § 1331?

As to the third criterion, the Court said that an issue was not "substantial" just because it was important to the plaintiff's case; rather, the relevant question was "the importance of the issue to the federal system as a whole." In both Grable and Smith v. Kansas City Title & Trust, the issue of federal law embedded in the state-law claim for relief was of general importance to the federal government. Here, the federal question—whether timely presentation of the experimental-use argument would have changed the outcome of the patent infringement lawsuit—would not change the outcome of the patent action, nor would it threaten the uniformity of federal law. The Chief Justice also noted that a state court determination of the patent issue would not bind the federal courts and that state courts addressing patent issues could be expected to "hew closely to the pertinent federal precedents." And he expressed some doubt that a possibly erroneous state court decision would have broad precedential or preclusive effect; at most, he said, it could bind the parties with regard to the patents at issue.

Finally, as to Grable's fourth requirement, the Court noted that it was the states' responsibility to maintain standards of practice for members of their bars. Accordingly, "state legal malpractice claims based on underlying patent matters will rarely, if ever, arise under federal patent law for purposes of § 1338(a)."

NOTE ON THE EXTENSION OF THE FEDERAL INGREDIENT TEST

In Manning, the Court insisted that the extension of the scope of § 1331's "arising under" jurisprudence to § 27 promoted administrative simplicity because "judges and litigants are familiar with the 'arising under' standard and how it works," the test "[f]or the most part * * * provides ready answers to jurisdictional questions," and "an existing body of precedent gives guidance whenever borderline cases crop up." Do the decisions studied in this Section support this happy assessment? Or is it more accurate to say, with Justice Thomas, that the "arising under" standard "is anything but clear" and "involves numerous judgments about matters of degree that are not readily susceptible to bright lines"?

Consider whether the extension of the general principles for arising under jurisdiction give adequate weight to the special interests that moved Congress to confer exclusive jurisdiction over the proceedings in question. As a result of the Gunn decision, the standards of practice before a federal administrative agency (the Patent and Trademark Office) and the federal courts, for lawyers whose practice may be almost exclusively before those bodies, will be regulated by state law, and enforced by state courts whose jurisdiction to consider issues of patent law is unusually restricted. Is that a cause for concern?

------

5. THE DIVERSITY JURISDICTION OF THE FEDERAL DISTRICT COURTS

A. INTRODUCTION

STATUTORY DEVELOPMENT

Federal diversity jurisdiction has existed ever since the Judiciary Act of 1789. Section 11 of that Act, 1 Stat. 79, conferred jurisdiction when the "matter in dispute" exceeded the sum or value of $500 and (1) an alien was a party, or (2) the suit was between a citizen of the state where the action was brought and a citizen of another state. The requirement in the second category that one of the parties be a citizen of the forum state was eliminated in 1875, 18 Stat. 470. The 1875 Act also modified the first category by conferring jurisdiction in controversies between "citizens of a State and foreign states, citizens, or subjects."

The statute has been amended many times in the past hundred years as well. For example, a 1940 amendment extended diversity jurisdiction to suits "between * * * citizens of the District of Columbia, the Territory of Hawaii, or Alaska, and any State or Territory." 54 Stat. 143. (The constitutionality of this amendment is discussed at pp. 1013–1017, *infra.*) And in 1958, Congress explicitly addressed corporate citizenship, providing that for diversity purposes "a corporation shall be deemed a citizen of any State by which it has been incorporated and of the State where it has its principal place of business." (This provision is discussed at pp. 1085–1087, *infra.*) In 2005, Congress enacted the Class Action Fairness Act, 119 Stat. 4 (2005), significantly expanding federal court jurisdiction over certain class actions, as well as certain "mass action[s]" in which "monetary relief claims of 100 or more persons are proposed to be tried jointly." (The Act is discussed in detail at pp. 1081–1084, *infra*). In 2011, Congress enacted the Federal Courts Jurisdiction and Venue Clarification Act of 2011, Pub.L.No. 112–63, 125 Stat. 758, making a number of clarifications and changes to the wording of the statute.

Finally, several other statutes contain provisions allowing diversity jurisdiction in circumstances not covered by § 1332. These include the Interpleader Act, 28 U.S.C. §§ 1335 (discussed at pp. 1077–1079, *infra*) and 1369, dealing with certain actions involving a large number of casualties and arising out of a single accident (discussed at p. 1080, *infra*).

NOTE ON THE HISTORICAL BACKGROUND AND CONTEMPORARY UTILITY OF THE DIVERSITY JURISDICTION

A. Historical Background

The conventional account of the diversity jurisdiction has found its roots in fear of prejudice against out-of-state litigants in the state courts. The most quoted statement is Chief Justice Marshall's in Bank of the United States v. Deveaux, 9 U.S. (5 Cranch) 61, 87 (1809): "However true the fact may be that the tribunals of the states will administer justice as impartially as those of the nation to parties of every description, it is not less true that the constitution itself either entertains apprehensions on this subject or views with such indulgence the possible fears and apprehensions of suitors that it has established national tribunals for the decision of controversies between aliens and a citizen, or between citizens of different states."

Perhaps the best-known study of the origins of the diversity jurisdiction is Friendly, *The Historic Basis of Diversity Jurisdiction*, 41 Harv.L.Rev. 483 (1928). As he noted, the principal discussion took place in the debates on ratification, in which the proposed jurisdiction was bitterly denounced. What Judge Friendly found "astounding," however, was "not the vigor of the attack but the apathy of the defense." He questioned the "sincerity" of the argument about apprehension of local prejudice because of the failure of Madison and other proponents to adduce specific examples. Reviewing the scanty reports of contemporary decisions, Judge Friendly concluded that the evidence "entirely fails to show the existence of prejudice on the part of the state judges."

What Judge Friendly did find was that "the real fear was not of state courts so much as of state legislatures. * * * In summary, we may say that the desire to protect creditors against legislation favorable to debtors was a principal reason for the grant of diversity jurisdiction, and that as a reason it was by no means without validity." To this he added a general lack of confidence in state judges and fear of the practice of legislative review of judicial decisions that prevailed in some states. (Note also state legislative control of judicial salaries and, in many states, the removability of judges at the behest of governors or on address of the legislatures.) "Not unnaturally the commercial interests of the country were reluctant to expose themselves to the hazards of litigation before such courts as these. They might be good enough for the inhabitants of their respective states, but merchants from abroad felt themselves entitled to something better. There was a vague feeling that the new courts would be strong courts, creditors' courts, business men's courts."

Friendly's research and conclusions have not gone unchallenged. Yntema & Jaffin, *Preliminary Analysis of Concurrent Jurisdiction*, 79 U.Pa.L.Rev. 869, 873–76 & n.13 (1931), argue that the available evidence "precludes extensive inference" and that "the theory of no local prejudice is presumptively improbable." Frank, *Historical Bases of the Federal Judicial System*, 13 Law & Contemp.Probs. 3, 22–28 (1948), reviews the question and concludes that the relevant considerations in creating the jurisdiction were "1. The desire to avoid regional prejudice against commercial litigants, based in small part on experience and in large part on common-sense anticipation. 2. The desire to permit commercial, manufacturing, and speculative interests to litigate their controversies, and particularly their controversies with other classes, before judges who would be firmly tied to their own interests. 3. The desire to achieve more efficient administration of justice for the classes thus benefitted."

And more recently, Jones, *Finishing a Friendly Argument: The Jury and the Historical Origins of Diversity Jurisdiction*, 82 N.Y.U.L.Rev. 997 (2007), argues that (a) the Federalists' goal in creating the diversity jurisdiction transcended purely commercial matters and (b) the Federalists did not fear state legislatures but instead state court *juries*, whose primarily rural agrarian composition and power to decide issues of both law and fact had transformed them into powerful pro-debtor, quasi-legislative bodies. Jones posits that diversity jurisdiction was devised by the Federalists to present commercial (and other) cases instead to federal juries, which were designed to be composed primarily of urban merchants more sympathetic to commercial interests.[1]

B.   Contemporary Utility

(1) The Relevance of Erie. Diversity jurisdiction has always been controversial. During the era before the decision in Erie R.R. Co. v. Tompkins, 304 U.S. 64 (1938), see Chap. VI, Sec. 2, *supra*, opposition to the jurisdiction was buttressed by the belief that federal courts were using the diversity power to favor business interests and to exercise law-making authority that exceeded both federal and judicial bounds.[2]

The effect of the Erie decision has been to make diversity jurisdiction less consequential in one respect, by diminishing the differences between the substantive law that will be applied to litigants in federal courts and state courts in a particular case. Writing a decade after Erie, Professor Wechsler argued that diversity jurisdiction could not be justified solely on the basis of the "original fear of prejudice against the litigant from out of state." Wechsler, *Federal Jurisdiction and the Revision of the Judicial Code*, 13 Law

---

[1]   For the view that alienage jurisdiction was "historically the single most important grant of national court jurisdiction embodied in the [First Judiciary] Act," and that the "poor record" of the state courts in enforcing the treaty obligations of the union was the main impetus behind the creation of national courts, see Holt, *The Origins of Alienage Jurisdiction*, 14 Okla. City U.L.Rev. 547, 548–49 (1989). For discussions of the origins of the diversity jurisdiction that emphasize the nationalizing functions it served, see Marbury, *Why Should We Limit Federal Diversity Jurisdiction?*, 46 A.B.A.J. 379 (1960); Moore & Weckstein, *Diversity Jurisdiction: Past, Present, and Future*, 43 Tex.L.Rev. 1 (1964). For an argument that emphasizes the founding generation's experience judging prize case appeals during the Revolutionary War, see Mask & MacMahon, *The Revolutionary War Prize Cases and the Origins of Diversity Jurisdiction*, 63 Buff.L.Rev. 477 (2015).

[2]   For conflicting views in the decade prior to Erie, see Frankfurter, *Distribution of Judicial Power Between United States and State Courts*, 13 Cornell L.Q. 499, 520–30 (1928); Yntema & Jaffin, *Limiting Jurisdiction of Federal Courts—Pending Bills—Comments by Members of Chicago University Law Faculty*, 31 Mich.L.Rev. 59 (1932); Clark, *Diversity of Citizenship Jurisdiction of the Federal Courts*, 19 A.B.A.J. 499 (1933). For a summary of earlier views, see Frankfurter & Landis, The Business of the Supreme Court 86–102, 136–41 (1928). And for a contemporary review of the pre-Erie period that focuses on the concerns of Justice Brandeis, see Purcell, Brandeis and the Progressive Constitution: Erie, the Judicial Power, and the Politics of the Federal Courts in Twentieth-Century America (2000), cited at p. 759, note 11, *supra*.

& Contemp.Probs. 216, 235–39 (1948). But he went on to say: "There is, I think, a solid case for preservation of the jurisdiction in any instance where a concrete showing of state prejudice can be established. There may be cases, too, where there is need for process that outruns state borders, as in the interpleader under present law." The challenge, he argued, is to limit federal intervention to the situations in which it in fact responds to such needs.

Conversely, one might view the constitutional and statutory determinations to vest federal courts with significant diversity jurisdiction as a reason to question aspects of the Erie decision, or at least some applications or extensions of it. Several possibilities are discussed in the following paragraph.

(2) The Possible Uses of the Diversity Jurisdiction. Consider the contemporary persuasiveness of the following possible justifications for the diversity jurisdiction.

(a) *As a vehicle for building up and administering a uniform body of common law in areas in which Congress either has not legislated or could not.*

This was the goal of Swift v. Tyson, 41 U.S. (16 Pet.) 1 (1842), p. 749, *supra*, on which, presumably, the books are now closed—absent a basis for the formulation of "new" federal common law. See Chaps. VI, VII, *supra*.

(b) *As a means of encouraging out-of-state individuals and enterprises to engage in local investment and other activities, by providing an assurance of impartial decision of disputes growing out of those activities.*

Notice the varying kinds of injustice against which a safeguard may be desired: *e.g.*, invocation of unjust or discriminatory rules of law; unjust factfinding or application of law to the facts; delays and inefficiencies in judicial administration. Should an in-state plaintiff be able to invoke the jurisdiction, especially given that an in-state defendant may not remove a state court action brought by an out-of-state plaintiff? See 28 U.S.C. § 1441(b)(2).

There are other federal protections against these evils: *e.g.*, the Privileges and Immunities Clause of Article IV, § 2; the Privileges or Immunities Clause of the Fourteenth Amendment; the Commerce Clause; the Due Process Clause of the Fourteenth Amendment; and the Equal Protection Clause. Do these constitutional provisions sufficiently protect against the potential injustices described above? Is the need for diversity jurisdiction decreased or eliminated by the lessening of provincialism and the improvement of state judicial systems?[3]

(c) *As a means of providing for the just resolution of conflicts of laws in controversies between citizens of different states.*

In Klaxon Co. v. Stentor Elec. Mfg. Co., 313 U.S. 487 (1941), p. 768, *supra*, the Supreme Court held that federal courts sitting in diversity should use the choice of law rules of the state in which the federal district court is

---

[3]   Some justification for the diversity jurisdiction may be based on "rational prejudice"— situations in which a state's residents (including the judges they have chosen) have an *economic* incentive to discriminate against nonresidents. See Posner, The Federal Courts: Challenge and Reform 215–16 (1996).

located. This justification for diversity implicates the question whether Klaxon was correctly decided, or whether federal courts ought to enforce a neutral set of choice of law principles to decide what state law applies in a particular case. For scholarship arguing that the Klaxon decision is difficult to reconcile with the purposes of diversity jurisdiction, see Laycock, *Equal Citizens of Equal and Territorial States: The Constitutional Foundations of Choice of Law*, 92 Colum.L.Rev. 249, 282–83 (1992); Nelson, *A Critical Guide to Erie Railroad Co. v. Tompkins*, 54 Wm. & Mary L.Rev. 921, 963 (2013).

Even as Klaxon remains good law, should legislative action be taken under the Full Faith and Credit Clause to alter its holding, in all or some specific area(s) of diversity jurisdiction? See Gottesman, *Draining the Dismal Swamp: The Case for Federal Choice of Law Statutes*, 80 Geo.L.J. 1 (1991).[4] See also Ch. VI, Sec. 3, *supra*.

(d) *As a means of assuring out-of-state litigants and their lawyers that a familiar procedural system will be available for the resolution of disputes.*

The adoption of the Federal Rules of Civil Procedure in 1938 made it possible to think about this objective as a justification for the diversity jurisdiction. Has its value been undercut by the extent to which those very rules have influenced the development of procedural systems in virtually every state? How does this value relate to the application of Erie to questions of federal procedure explored in Guaranty Trust v. York, 326 U.S. 99 (1945), Hanna v. Plumer, 380 U.S. 460 (1965), and other such cases, set forth in Chap. VI, Sec. 3?

(e) *As a means of facilitating the settlement of controversies that, because of the multiplicity of parties and their diversity of citizenship, cannot be effectually settled in the courts of any one state.*

The notion that diversity jurisdiction should be available to resolve controversies that involve similar claims of many parties in a number of states (or class claims involving class members residing in many states) has gained increasing traction in recent decades. The first special enactment providing for such use was the Federal Interpleader Act of 1936, now codified in 28 U.S.C. §§ 1335, 1397, 2361. Many years later, proposals for broader uses of diversity in multiparty litigation appeared. See, *e.g.*, American Law Institute, Study of the Division of Jurisdiction Between State and Federal Courts, proposed §§ 2371–2376 (1969); Rowe & Sibley, *Beyond Diversity: Federal Multiparty, Multiforum Jurisdiction*, 135 U.Pa.L.Rev. 7 (1986). Legislation ensued, first in 2002 with the enactment of § 1369, providing for jurisdiction based on "minimal diversity" in certain mass tort cases, see p. 1079, *infra*, and most important, in the Class Action Fairness Act of 2005, see pp. 1081–1084, *infra*.[5]

---

[4] In cases involving complex litigation, especially litigation likely to take the form of lawsuits brought in a number of courts (state and/or federal), are the arguments for such action especially strong? For proposed federal legislation governing choice of law in such cases, see American Law Institute, Complex Litigation: Statutory Recommendations and Analysis (1994). See also the extensive discussion of this and other aspects of the proposals made by the ALI Project in the Symposium appearing in 54 La.L.Rev. No. 4 (1994).

[5] For an analysis of these developments, and their implications for the federal courts, see Underwood, *The Late, Great Diversity Jurisdiction*, 57 Case W.Res.L.Rev. 179 (2006).

Are there other justifications for the diversity jurisdiction to which consideration should be given? Should it matter if the federal courts of first instance are in fact, or are perceived to be, of higher quality than their state counterparts? (See Chap. IV, Sec. 1, *supra*.) For an argument that it should not, see Friendly, Federal Jurisdiction: A General View 145–47 (1973).[6]

Recent decades have seen much discussion of the desirability and proper scope of the diversity jurisdiction. Those favoring abolition suggest not only that local prejudice is no longer a serious concern,[7] but that diversity cases burden the federal courts, whose resources could better be devoted to cases turning on federal law, and that these cases pose complexities. Those include: the need to ascertain jurisdiction, difficult questions of whether federal or state law applies, and, where state law does apply, to determine its content. Such complexities would be avoided were such cases litigated in state court.[8] In response, proponents of retention not only cite some of the foregoing possible justifications for the jurisdiction, but also argue that lightening federal court burdens will increase the burdens on state courts and that experience with the jurisdiction suggests that "[t]here is no widespread, obvious abuse to be corrected." Frank, *The Case for Diversity Jurisdiction*, 16 Harv.J. on Legis. 403, 409 (1979).[9]

(3) Diversity Filings in the District Courts. According to the annual reports of the Administrative Office of the United States Courts, the number of diversity cases filed in the district courts continued to rise prior to the 1988 increase in the jurisdictional amount, but the ratio of such cases to all civil actions filed in those courts declined—from approximately one-third in 1960 to one-quarter in 1988. After some fluctuation in the intervening years, the ratio of diversity filings to all civil filings had returned to slightly less than

---

[6] Compare Professor Seinfeld's argument, *The Federal Courts as a Franchise: Rethinking the Justifications for Federal Question Jurisdiction*, 97 Calif.L.Rev. 95 (2009), that the primary purpose of *federal question jurisdiction* is to provide litigants and their lawyers with a high quality "franchise" provided by federal courts.

[7] See, *e.g.*, Testimony of Professor Charles Allen Wright, Hearings on Federal Diversity of Citizenship Jurisdiction Before the Subcommittee on Improvements in Judicial Machinery of the Senate Committee on the Judiciary, 95th Cong. 45–49 (1978).

[8] See especially Rowe, *Abolishing Diversity Jurisdiction: Positive Side Effects and Potential for Further Reforms*, 92 Harv.L.Rev. 963 (1979).

[9] Among those favoring abolition of general diversity jurisdiction have been Judge Friendly, in Federal Jurisdiction: A General View 3–4, 139–52 (1973), and then-Chief Justice Burger in *Annual Report on the State of the Judiciary*, 62 A.B.A.J. 443, 444 (1976). See also Rowe, note 8, *supra*; Kramer, *Diversity Jurisdiction*, 1990 B.Y.U.L.Rev. 97 (concluding that, with the exception of cases involving aliens, interpleader actions, and complex multistate litigation, the jurisdiction should be abolished, a conclusion that paralleled the contemporaneous recommendation of the Federal Courts Study Committee, on which he served as a reporter).

With the foregoing, compare, *e.g.*, Arnold, *The Future of the Federal Courts*, 60 Mo.L.Rev. 533, 538–39 (1995) (noting that Congress "created the lower [federal] court[s] primarily to hear diversity cases"); Frank, *supra*; Shapiro, *Federal Diversity Jurisdiction: A Survey and a Proposal*, 91 Harv.L.Rev. 317, 319 (1977) (suggesting a " 'local option plan,' under which each federal district would have limited freedom to retain, curtail, or virtually eliminate diversity jurisdiction within its borders"); Freer, *The Political Reality of Diversity Jurisdiction*, 94 S.Calif.L.Rev. 1083 (2021) (arguing that diversity jurisdiction is now justified both by concerns about region-based bias and by the need for efficient resolution of complex litigation). See also Dodson, *Beyond Bias in Diversity Jurisdiction*, 69 Duke L.J. 267 (2019) (arguing that bias against out-of-state litigants no longer justifies diversity jurisdiction but "[p]romoting aggregation [of litigation] across state lines" may do so).

25% in 1994. Following the 1996 increase in the jurisdictional amount threshold, diversity filings declined by approximately 15% during the next three years. Bak, Golmant & O'Conor, *Reducing Federal Diversity Jurisdiction Filings: A Qualified Success*, 39 Judges' J., Summer 2000, at 20, 24 tbl 1. But that trend did not continue, and in the fiscal year ending March 31, 2023, diversity filings totaled 109,095, representing 38.4% of all civil cases filed.

B. ELEMENTS OF DIVERSITY JURISDICTION

Strawbridge v. Curtiss
7 U.S. (3 Cranch) 267 (1806).
Appeal from the Circuit Court for the District of Massachusetts.

[In this case, the question before the Court was whether a federal court could exercise diversity jurisdiction in a multi-party case in which one of the plaintiffs was a citizen of the same state as several of the defendants. The lower court had dismissed the action.]

■ MARSHALL, CH.J., delivered the opinion of the court.

The court has considered this case, and is of opinion that the jurisdiction cannot be supported.

The words of the act of congress are, "where an alien is a party; or the suit is between a citizen of a state where the suit is brought, and a citizen of another state."

The court understands these expressions to mean that each distinct interest should be represented by persons, all of whom are entitled to sue, or may be sued, in the federal courts. That is, that where the interest is joint, each of the persons concerned in that interest must be competent to sue, or liable to be sued, in those courts.

But the court does not mean to give an opinion in the case where several parties represent several distinct interests, and some of those parties are, and others are not, competent to sue, or liable to be sued, in the courts of the United States.

Decree affirmed.

State Farm Fire & Casualty Co. v. Tashire
386 U.S. 523 (1967).
Certiorari to the United States Court of Appeals for the Ninth Circuit.

[Following a collision between a bus and a pick-up truck in California, four injured passengers on the bus filed a suit for damages in excess of $1,000,000 in California state court against the bus company, the owner of the truck, and the drivers of the bus and the truck. Soon after, State Farm, which had insured the truck driver with a policy limit of $10,000 per person and $20,000 per accident, filed a federal interpleader action against the four state plaintiffs and all other potential claimants alleging that interpleader was appropriate because the aggregate damages in actions already pending and others it anticipated far exceeded the policy limits. It asked, *inter alia*, that (a) all claimants be required to establish their claims against the insured and State Farm in the interpleader proceeding and (b) State Farm be discharged from all further obligations under the policy. Several but not all of the claimants named as defendants were co-citizens, but there was diversity between some of the claimants and between all claimants and State Farm. State Farm based federal jurisdiction on the Interpleader Act of 1935, codified in part in 28 U.S.C. § 1335, which confers jurisdiction on the district courts over "any civil action of interpleader * * * filed by any * * * [corporation having issued an insurance policy in the amount] of $500 or more * * * if * * * [t]wo or more adverse claimants, of diverse citizenship * * * are claiming or may claim to be entitled to [the benefits of that policy]."*

[On appeal from a preliminary injunction restraining all defendants from prosecuting any other action against State Farm and its insured relating to the accident, the Ninth Circuit reversed, holding that interpleader was not available in the circumstances of the case. The Supreme Court granted certiorari.]

■ MR. JUSTICE FORTAS delivered the opinion of the Court.

* * * Before considering the issues presented by the petition for certiorari, we find it necessary to dispose of a question neither raised by the parties nor passed upon by the courts below. Since the matter concerns our jurisdiction, we raise it on our own motion. The interpleader statute, 28 U.S.C. § 1335, applies where there are "Two or more adverse claimants, of diverse citizenship * * *." This provision has been uniformly construed to require only "minimal diversity," that is, diversity of citizenship between two or more claimants, without regard to the circumstance that other rival claimants may be cocitizens. The language of the statute, the legislative purpose broadly to remedy the problems posed by multiple claimants to a single fund, and the consistent judicial interpretation tacitly accepted by Congress, persuade us that the statute requires no more. There remains, however, the question whether such a statutory construction is consistent with Article III of our Constitution, which extends the federal judicial power to "Controversies * * * between Citizens of different States * * * and between a State, or the Citizens

---

* [Ed.] Because there was complete diversity between State Farm and all the defendants, State Farm also alleged jurisdiction on the basis of the general diversity statute, 28 U.S.C. § 1332, but as the Court noted, jurisdiction had to be upheld under § 1335 in order for State Farm to take advantage of the other provisions of the Interpleader Act governing venue (§ 1397) and service of process (§ 2361).

thereof, and foreign States, Citizens or Subjects." In Strawbridge v. Curtiss, 3 Cranch 267 (1806), this Court held that the diversity of citizenship statute required "complete diversity": where co-citizens appeared on both sides of a dispute, jurisdiction was lost. But Chief Justice Marshall there purported to construe only "The words of the act of congress," not the Constitution itself. And in a variety of contexts this Court and the lower courts have concluded that Article III poses no obstacle to the legislative extension of federal jurisdiction, founded on diversity, so long as any two adverse parties are not co-citizens.[7] Accordingly, we conclude that the present case is properly in the federal courts.

[The Court went on to hold that State Farm had properly invoked federal interpleader jurisdiction, but that it was not entitled to the injunctive relief granted by the district court. Justice Douglas, dissenting, expressed his agreement "with the Court's view as to 'minimal diversity,'" but disagreed with the holding that, in the particular circumstances, federal interpleader was available.]

NOTE ON COMPLETE VERSUS MINIMAL DIVERSITY

(1) The Strawbridge Holding. The Strawbridge opinion is one of Chief Justice Marshall's more cryptic efforts. The case involved a suit brought by co-executors, neither of whom could bring suit without the other joining as a plaintiff. Strawbridge's requirement of complete diversity could have been read narrowly, as applying only to cases in which the interests of the several plaintiffs and/or defendants were "joint." But the decision has consistently been interpreted more broadly, under all the varying formulations of the general grant of diversity jurisdiction in successive judiciary acts, as requiring "complete" diversity—that is, diversity of citizenship as between each plaintiff and each defendant. Does the co-citizenship of two adverse parties always assure that the state court will be impartial in the disposition of every aspect of the litigation?[1]

---

[7]   See, *e.g.*, American Fire & Cas. Co. v. Finn, 341 U.S. 6, 10, n.3 (1951), and Barney v. Latham, 103 U.S. 205, 213 (1881), construing the removal statute, now 28 U.S.C. § 1441 (c); Supreme Tribe of Ben-Hur v. Cauble, 255 U.S. 356 (1921), concerning class actions; Wichita R. R. & Light Co. v. Public Util. Comm., 260 U.S. 48 (1922), dealing with intervention by co-citizens. Full-dress arguments for the constitutionality of "minimal diversity" in situations like interpleader, which arguments need not be rehearsed here, are set out in Judge Tuttle's opinion in Haynes v. Felder, 239 F.2d 868, 875–876 (5th Cir.1957); in Judge Weinfeld's opinion in Twentieth Century-Fox Film Corp. v. Taylor, 239 F.Supp. 913, 918–921 (S.D.N.Y. 1965); and in ALI, Study of the Division of Jurisdiction Between State and Federal Courts 180–190 (Official Draft, Pt. 1, 1965); 3 Moore, Federal Practice para. 22.09, at 3033–3037; Chafee, *Federal Interpleader Since the Act of 1936*, 49 Yale L.J. 377, 393–406 (1940); Chafee, *Interpleader in the United States Courts*, 41 Yale L.J. 1134, 1165–1169 (1932). * * *

[1]   For an argument that the complete diversity requirement contravenes the history and purposes of Article III's diversity clause and "rests on a construction of the diversity statute that the Supreme Court has acknowledged was erroneous," see Cooper & Nielson, Jr.,*Complete Diversity and the Closing of the Federal Courts*, 37 Harv.J.L. & Pub.Pol'y. 295 (2014).

(2) Realignment. In applying the doctrine of Strawbridge v. Curtiss, a court is not controlled by the plaintiff's alignment of the parties. The Court "will look beyond the pleadings and arrange the parties according to their sides in the dispute," whether the result is to establish or to defeat jurisdiction. City of Dawson v. Columbia Ave. Saving Fund, Safe Deposit, Title & Trust Co., 197 U.S. 178, 180 (1905) (realigning to defeat jurisdiction); see also City of Indianapolis v. Chase Nat'l Bank, 314 U.S. 63 (1941) (same). Realignment is particularly important in stockholders' derivative suits, since the defendants are often directors or officers of the corporation and thus co-citizens of the corporation. See generally Smith v. Sperling, 354 U.S. 91 (1957).[2]

(3) Statutory Jurisdiction in Cases of Less than Complete Diversity.

(a) Interpleader. The Tashire case appeared to put to rest a debate over the constitutionality of diversity jurisdiction based on less than complete diversity between adversaries. Does that decision stand for the proposition that minimal diversity is always enough to satisfy Article III? The question is especially relevant to the constitutionality of the Class Action Fairness Act, discussed in subparagraph (d), below.

(b) 28 U.S.C. § 1369: "Multiparty, Multiforum Jurisdiction." In response to calls from several quarters for the use of "minimal diversity" as a basis of federal jurisdiction in cases involving claims of substantial harm to many people, Congress took a step in that direction in 2002 by adding a new provision to the Judicial Code (§ 1369), along with related provisions governing venue (new § 1391(g)), removal (new § 1441(e)), nationwide service of process (new § 1697), and subpoenas (new § 1785). See Pub.L.No. 107–273, § 11020. Section 1369 itself provides for original jurisdiction "of any civil action involving minimal diversity between adverse parties that arises from a single accident" if any one of three additional conditions is met (for example, if any two defendants reside in different states), and also requires that prompt notice of the action be given to the Judicial Panel on Multidistrict Litigation, which supervises transfers under § 1407. "Minimal diversity" between "adverse parties" exists if any party is a citizen of a state and any adverse party is a citizen of another state, a citizen or subject of a foreign state, or a foreign state. An "accident" is defined as a "sudden accident, or a natural event culminating in an accident that results in death incurred in a discrete location by at least 75 natural persons." There is no jurisdictional amount requirement, but the district court is required to "abstain" if (a) both the primary defendants and the substantial majority of all plaintiffs are citizens of a single state and (b) the claims will be governed primarily by the law of that state.

This section, together with its related provisions, addresses only one of a range of instances in which harm may occur to a large number of people.

---

[2]   For critiques of the doctrine, see Sherkow, *A Call for the End of the Doctrine of Realignment*, 107 Mich.L.Rev. 525 (2008); Bassett & Perschacher, *Realigning Parties*, 2014 Utah L.Rev. 109 (2014).

It does not deal, for example, with claims of harm caused in many locations as a result of an allegedly defective product.

(c) The Class Action Fairness Act of 2005.

(i) Background and Summary. For a number of years, there had been intense debate, and lobbying, on the question whether federal court jurisdiction should be expanded with respect to class actions involving significant sums of money and class members and/or defendants from several states. Arguments favoring such expansion focused on claims that many state courts were too willing to certify inappropriate, even frivolous, class actions, and then to approve settlements that defendants felt compelled to accept in order to avoid litigation, or that benefited the lawyers for the plaintiff class far more than the class members themselves, or both. Congress responded to these arguments by enacting the Class Action Fairness Act of 2005 (CAFA), Pub.L.No. 109–2, 119 Stat. 4. The Act considerably expanded the original and removal jurisdiction of the federal courts over certain class actions (and related actions) and adopted a number of special provisions regarding the settlement of such actions and the award of attorney's fees. Following is a brief summary of the Act's principal provisions as they relate to the diversity jurisdiction.[3]

— Section 2 of the Act contains findings about the importance of class actions and abuses of the device that have adversely affected interstate commerce, plaintiff class members, and defendants, and includes among the purposes of the Act the assurance of prompt and fair recovery for class members and of "Federal court consideration of interstate cases of national importance under diversity jurisdiction."

— Section 4 inserted into the original jurisdiction provision of 28 U.S.C. § 1332 a new subsection (d), which is the heart of the expansion of federal diversity jurisdiction. It confers original federal court jurisdiction over class actions (as defined) in which the matter in controversy (after *aggregating* the claims of all class members) exceeds $5,000,000,[4] and in which any member of a class of plaintiffs is (i) a citizen of a state different

---

[3]   Beyond its expansion of diversity jurisdiction, the Act added new §§ 1711–1715 to Title 28. These provisions deal with the settlement of class actions in the federal courts. Section 1712 imposes substantive and procedural limitations on settlements that involve the recovery of "coupons" (to be used, for example, in purchasing the defendant's product(s)) and on the calculation of attorney's fees in such cases. Sections 1713 and 1714 provide protection against a net loss by class members as a result of a settlement and against discrimination in settlements based on the geographic locations of class members. Section 1715 provides that particular state and federal officials, and certain institutions, must be given notice of and opportunity for comment on certain proposed settlements.

In addition, the Act required the Judicial Conference to submit a report containing recommendations for ensuring fair settlements and fair attorney's fee awards and specifying the actions taken to achieve those goals; explicitly approved the 2003 Supreme Court amendments to Federal Rule 23 (on class actions); reaffirmed the role of the Judicial Conference and the authority of the Supreme Court in promulgating rules of practice and procedure; and provided that the Act shall apply to any civil action commenced on or after the date of enactment.

[4]   In Standard Fire Ins. Co. v. Knowles, 568 U.S. 588 (2013), the Court held that a state court stipulation by the class representative that he and absent class members would seek less than $5 million in damages does not prevent removal under CAFA, because the stipulation could not bind absent members.

from any defendant, *or* (ii) a foreign state or citizen of a foreign state if any defendant is a citizen of a state, *or* (iii) a citizen of a state if any defendant is a foreign state or citizen of a foreign state. The provision then goes on (a) to *authorize* the district court, after consideration of six enumerated factors, to decline to exercise jurisdiction in any case in which more than 1/3 but less than 2/3 of the plaintiff class members, as well as the "primary defendants," are citizens of the forum state; and (b) to *mandate* the decline of jurisdiction if more than 2/3 of the plaintiff class members are citizens of the forum state, if at least one defendant from whom significant relief is sought is also a citizen of the forum state, and if certain other conditions are met. Remaining provisions of new § 1332(d) serve, among other things, (a) to exempt certain class actions from the section's coverage (including classes consisting of fewer than 100 members), (b) to define, for purposes of CAFA only, an unincorporated association as a citizen of the state where it is organized and of the state where it has its principal place of business, and (c) to include in the definition of "class action" certain "mass action[s]" involving the joinder of 100 or more plaintiffs even if not formally certified as a class under Rule 23.[5]

— Section 5 added a new § 1453 to Title 28, authorizing removal of class actions (as defined in the Act) "by any defendant without the consent of all defendants" and "without regard to whether any defendant is a citizen of the State in which the action is brought." Section 1453 further provides that the one-year limitation on removal (in § 1446(c)) does not apply, and creates a specific exception to the general prohibition (in § 1447(d)) of appellate review of a remand order; instead, under new § 1453, "a court of appeals may accept an appeal from an order of a district court granting or denying a motion to remand * * * if application is made to the court of appeals not more than 10 days after entry of the order."[6]

---

[5]   See Mullenix, *Class Actions Shrugged: Mass Actions and the Future of Aggregate Litigation*, 32 Rev.Litig. 591 (2013) (arguing that scholars' focus on CAFA's implications for state law class actions has obscured the law's significant changes to mass action litigation, which can be a more powerful tool for plaintiffs than the class action model).

In Mississippi ex rel. Hood v. AU Optronics Corp. 571 U.S. 161 (2014), the state had brought an action in state court to recover (under state law) restitution for purchases made by itself and by (more than 100 unnamed) citizens of the state. Resolving a circuit conflict, the Supreme Court held unanimously that the case was not removable under CAFA as a "mass action" because Mississippi was the only named plaintiff and the statutory definition of a mass action required 100 or more "actual named parties." In answer to the argument that the Court should consider whether the form of the action constituted an improper effort to defeat removal jurisdiction, the Court held that Congress did not intend that judge-made principle to apply to the mass action provision.

[6]   The Supreme Court clarified the scope of § 1453(b) in Home Depot U.S.A., Inc. v. Jackson, 587 U.S. 435 (2019). The issue in Home Depot was whether a third-party counterclaim defendant—that is, a new party brought into the suit by the original defendant's counterclaim against the original plaintiff—can remove a suit that otherwise qualifies for original federal jurisdiction. In an opinion by Justice Thomas, the Court ruled that a third-party counterclaim defendant cannot remove because it is not a "defendant" under the relevant removal statutes. The Court first addressed removal under 28 U.S.C. § 1441(a), which permits a "defendant" to remove a "civil action * * * of which the district courts" have "original jurisdiction." It reasoned that since the original complaint alone determines whether a federal court has original jurisdiction over a civil action, the defendant who can remove is the one named in the original complaint, not a party named in a counterclaim. The Court then turned to § 1453(b), which presented "a closer question" primarily because its broader language permits removal by "any defendant" to a "class action." It concluded that removal was not available under the section

The definition of "class action" in § 1332(d)(1), which is incorporated by reference in § 1453, is very broad: "any civil action filed under rule 23 of the Federal Rules of Civil Procedure or similar State statute or rule of judicial procedure authorizing an action to be brought by 1 or more representative persons as a class action." This definition contains none of CAFA's limitations on original jurisdiction, found in other provisions of § 1332(d)— although the legislative history leaves no doubt that the scope of the removal provision was intended to be co-extensive with that original jurisdiction.[7]

(ii) Comments and Questions. CAFA expands the diversity jurisdiction not only by requiring only minimal diversity, but also by departing from existing rules generally barring plaintiffs from aggregating their claims for purposes of satisfying a jurisdictional amount requirement, see Snyder v. Harris, 394 U.S. 331 (1969), and by departing significantly from existing statutory limitations on removal (such as the bar on removal when a properly joined defendant is a citizen of the forum state, 28 U.S.C. § 1441(b)(2)).

Among the broad policy questions raised by this Act are: whether, and to what extent, the Act is warranted by state court abuses and overreaching in class action cases; whether the Act may overburden federal courts with the adjudication of matters not involving federal law; and whether Congress should have considered addressing not only procedural and remedial issues in class action cases significantly affecting commerce but also issues of substantive tort liability (particularly in the area of responsibility for defective products).

In addition, no consensus yet exists with respect to a number of more specific problems raised by these provisions. For example: Who is a "primary" defendant? How does a court determine—particularly in cases involving large classes, at least some of whose members are not known or may not even

---

either. The Court explained that the clauses in § 1453(b) that use the term "any defendant" concern CAFA's relaxed removal requirements—namely, its elimination of both the requirement that all defendants in a diversity case must consent to removal, see 28 U.S.C. § 1446(b)(2)(A), and the bar on removal if any defendant is a citizen of the state where the action is brought, see 28 U.S.C. § 1441(b)(2). But nothing in § 1453(b) alters § 1441(a)'s limitation on what type of party can remove. Section 1453(b) thus does not expand who is a "defendant" under the removal statutes, but rather clarifies what restrictions apply to eligible parties seeking removal for certain class actions. The Court noted that this conclusion was reinforced by the fact that §§ 1453(b) and 1441(a) both rely on the procedures for removal in 28 U.S.C. § 1446, which employs the term "defendant" and thus suggests that that term should have the same meaning in both Sections. In dissent, Justice Alito disagreed sharply with the Court's statutory analysis of both removal provisions and argued that the Court created an unjustified "loophole" in § 1453(b) to Congress's clear aim of making class action removal easier. For a useful discussion of the issues in Home Depot, see Tidmarsh, *Finding Room For State Class Actions in a Post-CAFA World: The Case of the Counterclaim Class Action,* 35 W.St.U.L.Rev. 193 (2007).

[7] Steinman, *Sausage-Making, Pigs' Ears, and Congressional Expansions of Federal Jurisdiction: Exxon Mobil v. Allapattah and Its Lessons for the Class Action Fairness Act,* 81 Wash.L.Rev. 279 (2006), proposes a resolution of the resulting tension based in part on the rationale and result of Exxon Mobil v. Allapattah, 545 U.S. 546 (2005), p. 1122, *infra.* Section 1453, Steinman suggests, should be read not as conferring removal jurisdiction but only as providing more "defendant-friendly" removal provisions "for class actions that have an independent basis for removal elsewhere under federal law." He concedes that this approach does not square easily with either the text or the legislative history of the provision but sees it as the best solution to a problem made especially difficult by the combination of poor legislative drafting and a growing judicial insistence on adherence to the statutory text.

have been born—what percentage of class members are citizens of the forum state? To what extent, if any, should the Act be interpreted to modify the Erie doctrine (and especially the determination of which state's laws shall apply) in cases arising under it? Does the Act affect the authority of federal courts to enjoin state court proceedings, or the preclusive effects of judgments granting or denying certification, approving settlements, or entered after trial?

Moreover, since the Act applies "to any class action before or after the entry of a class certification order by the court," what happens if, for example, in a removed action, the federal court refuses to certify under Rule 23? Must the entire action be remanded to state court, or are there situations in which any remaining individual action(s) by the named plaintiff(s) may remain in federal court? In the event of remand, is it still open to the state court to certify the action as a class action under state rules? If so, would the result undermine one of the goals of CAFA? If not, would the result unconstitutionally interfere with state administration of a case not governed by federal law?[8]

NOTE ON THE DEFINITION OF CITIZENSHIP FOR PURPOSES OF DIVERSITY JURISDICTION

(1) Individuals. State citizenship of an individual, for the purposes of diversity jurisdiction, has traditionally depended upon two elements: first, United States citizenship; and second, domicile in the state, in the accepted conflict-of-laws sense of the term "domicile." See, *e.g.*, Brown v. Keene, 33 U.S. (8 Pet.) 112 (1834). "Domicile" in this sense is usually a person's home, *i.e.*, the place "where a person dwells and which is the center of his domestic,

---

[8]   A large body of literature deals with CAFA. Studies of particular interest include Vairo, The Class Action Fairness Act of 2005: A Review and Preliminary Analysis (2005); Issacharoff, *Settled Expectations in a World of Unsettled Law: Choice of Law After the Class Action Fairness Act*, 106 Colum.L.Rev. 1839 (2006); Marcus, *Erie, the Class Action Fairness Act, and Some Federalism Implications of Diversity Jurisdiction*, 48 Wm. & Mary L.Rev. 1247 (2007); Nagareda, *Aggregation and Its Discontents: Class Settlement Pressure, Class-Wide Arbitration, and CAFA*, 106 Colum.L.Rev. 1872 (2006); Scribner, *Protecting Federalism Interests After the Class Action Fairness Act of 2005: A Reply to Professor Vairo*, 51 Wayne L.Rev. 1417 (2005); Burbank, *Aggregation on the Couch: The Strategic Uses of Ambiguity and Hypocrisy*, 106 Colum.L.Rev. 1924 (2006); Floyd, *The Inadequacy of the Interstate Commerce Justification for the Class Action Fairness Act of 2005*, 55 Emory L.J. 487 (2006); Cabraser, *Just Choose: The Jurisprudential Necessity To Select a Single Governing Law for Mass Claims Arising from Nationally Marketed Consumer Goods and Services*, 14 Roger Williams U.L.Rev. 29 (2009); Richardson, *Class Dismissed, Now What? Exploring the Exercise of CAFA Jurisdiction After the Denial of Class Certification*, 39 N.M.L.Rev. 121 (2009); Silberman, *Choice of Law in National Class Actions: Should CAFA Make a Difference?*, 14 Roger Williams U.L.Rev. 54, 67 (2009); Wood, *The Changing Face of Diversity Jurisdiction*, 82 Temp.L.Rev. 593, 605 (2009); Note, *Class Certification as a Prerequisite for CAFA Jurisdiction*, 96 Minn.L.Rev. 1151 (2012); Roosevelt, *Choice of Law in Federal Courts: From Erie and Klaxon to CAFA and Shady Grove*, 106 Nw.U.L.Rev. 1, 40–50 (2012); Steinman, *Kryptonite for CAFA?*, 32 Rev.Litig. 649 (2013); Wolff, *Choice of Law and Jurisdictional Policy in the Federal Courts*, 165 U.Pa.L.Rev. 1847 (2017). For broad-ranging discussions of these and other issues raised by CAFA, see Symposium, *Fairness to Whom?: Perspectives on the Class Action Fairness Act of 2005*, 156 U.Pa.L.Rev. 1439 (2008); Symposium, *Developments in the Law—The Class Action Fairness Act of 2005*, 39 Loy.L.A.L.Rev. 979 (2006).

social and civil life." Also, "no person has more than one domicil at a time." Restatement (Second) of Conflict of Laws §§ 11, 12 (1971).

Innumerable cases hold that a mere allegation of residence in a state is insufficient to found diversity jurisdiction, since such an allegation may not connote domicile and hence state citizenship. See, *e.g.*, Wolfe v. Hartford Life & Annuity Ins. Co., 148 U.S. 389 (1893). This doctrine survived the Fourteenth Amendment, despite its statement that all persons born or naturalized in the United States are citizens of the United States and "the State wherein they reside." See Robertson v. Cease, 97 U.S. 646, 648–50 (1878).

(2) Corporations.

(a) In 1958, Congress addressed for the first time the question of the status of corporations in determining diversity of citizenship. It provided, in 28 U.S.C. § 1332(c), that "a corporation shall be deemed a citizen of any State by which it has been incorporated and of the State where it has its principal place of business." A 2011 amendment changed the words "any state" to "every State and foreign state."

Additionally, in 2010, the Supreme Court unanimously resolved a disagreement about the meaning of "principal place of business." Hertz Corp. v. Friend, 559 U.S. 77 (2010). Placing "primary weight upon the need for judicial administration of a jurisdictional statute to remain as simple as possible," the Court held that the principal place of business is what some lower courts had called the "nerve center," which is "the place where a corporation's officers direct, control and coordinate the corporation's activities," usually the same as its "headquarters."

(b) Before Congress acted in 1958, the question was controlled entirely by judicial decision. In the Supreme Court's first major pronouncement on the subject, Chief Justice Marshall said: "That invisible, intangible, and artificial being, that mere legal entity, a corporation aggregate, is certainly not a citizen." Bank of the United States v. Deveaux, 9 U.S. (5 Cranch) 61, 86 (1809).

From this premise the Court might have moved to any of three conclusions: first, that despite its capacity to sue and be sued, a corporation was barred altogether from the diversity jurisdiction; second, that actions by and against corporations should be regarded as conducted, on behalf of the members, by the president and directors, and that the citizenship of these managers controlled; or third, that because such actions should be treated as, in substance, actions by or against all the members, the citizenship of all the members controlled. In the Deveaux case, the Court reached the third conclusion. Together with the rule of Strawbridge v. Curtiss, this approach effectively barred the use of diversity jurisdiction in much corporate litigation.

Thirty-five years later, the Court yielded to the pressure of the bar for a different result. In Louisville, C. & C.R.R. v. Letson, 43 U.S. (2 How.) 497, 555 (1844), the Court said: "A corporation created by a state to perform its functions under the authority of that state and only suable there, though it may have members out of the state, seems to us to be a person, though an artificial one, inhabiting and belonging to that state, and therefore entitled, for the purpose of suing and being sued, to be deemed a citizen of that state."

While the Letson opinion said that a corporation was "entitled to be deemed" a citizen, and elsewhere that it was "substantially" a citizen, the Court carefully avoided saying that a corporation *was* a citizen. Under the hammering of a minority of the Justices, the Court later rephrased its position so as to bring it into closer accord with the Deveaux decision. Marshall v. Baltimore & O.R.R., 57 U.S. (16 How.) 314, 329 (1853). As Chief Justice Taney later explained, the Court decided "that where a corporation is created by the laws of a State, the legal presumption is, that its members are citizens of the State * * * and that a suit by or against a corporation, in its corporate name, must be presumed to be a suit by or against citizens of the State which created the corporate body * * *." Ohio & M.R.R. v. Wheeler, 66 U.S. (1 Black) 286, 296 (1861). See also Steamship Co. v. Tugman, 106 U.S. 118 (1882), applying a similar presumption to corporations created by foreign states.[1]

(c)   Is § 1332(c) constitutional? Professors Moller and Solum argue that as a matter of the original public meaning of Article III, corporations could not be "citizens" of any state and that Congress lacks the power to change the constitutional meaning of "citizen" through legislation. Moller & Solum, *Corporations and the Original Meaning of "Citizens" in Article III*, 72 Hastings L.J. 169, 225–26 (2020). That conclusion standing alone could still be consistent with Chief Justice Marshall's approach in Deveaux, looking to the citizenship of all of a corporation's stockholders when considering diversity jurisdiction over a corporation. And combined with the principal of minimal diversity for Article III, it could still allow § 1332(c) to be upheld as applied in many cases.

In a second article, though, Professors Moller and Solum further argue that Deveaux is wrong as a matter of original public meaning, because the phrase "Controversies * * * between Citizens of different States" turned on technicalities of the law of parties, and that the members of a corporation were not parties to a suit involving the corporation and thus they could not be considered for diversity purposes. Moller & Solum, *The Article III "Party" and the Originalist Case Against Corporate Diversity Jurisdiction*, 64 Wm. & Mary L.Rev. 1345 (2023). Will there be an originalist defense of Deveaux?

(d)   Finally, what is the status for diversity purposes of a corporation incorporated under the laws of the United States but not of any state? Section 1348 of Title 28 provides that national banking associations shall "be deemed citizens of the States in which they are respectively located."[2] This

---

[1]   For details about these developments, from sharply conflicting points of view, see McGovney, *A Supreme Court Fiction*, 56 Harv.L.Rev. 853, 1090, 1225 (1943), and Green, *Corporations as Persons, Citizens, and Possessors of Liberty*, 94 U.Pa.L.Rev. 202 (1946). See also Henderson, The Position of Foreign Corporations in American Constitutional Law (1918); Moore & Weckstein, *Corporations and Diversity of Citizenship Jurisdiction: A Supreme Court Fiction Revisited*, 77 Harv.L.Rev. 1426 (1964).

[2]   In Wachovia Bank, Nat'l Ass'n v. Schmidt, 546 U.S. 303 (2006), a unanimous Supreme Court held that for purposes of determining the state citizenship of a national bank, the word "located" in § 1348 refers to the state in which the bank has its main branch, and does not include any other states in which the bank has branch offices.

provision codified a result that had previously been reached without the aid of statute and has also been reached with respect to federal corporations other than national banks. Perhaps a similar result should be reached with respect to other nationally chartered corporations, at least if "localized" within one state. The only effect of such a decision would be to expand the reach of the diversity jurisdiction. But would a decision sustaining jurisdiction in such a case be consistent with the provisions of 28 U.S.C. § 1349, which provides that "The district courts shall not have jurisdiction of any civil action by or against any corporation upon the ground that it was incorporated by or under an Act of Congress, unless the United States is the owner of more than one-half of its capital stock." Consider also, after you have read about the Bouligny decision discussed below, whether such a decision could be squared with the Court's approach in that case.[3]

(3) Unincorporated Entities.

(a)   The leading decision on the citizenship of *unincorporated* entities is United Steelworkers v. R.H. Bouligny, Inc., 382 U.S. 145 (1965). There, a union was sued in a state court and sought to remove the case, on diversity grounds, to a federal court. The union argued that, like a corporation, it should be treated as a citizen for diversity purposes despite the absence of any statutory provision relating to unincorporated entities and despite the holding in Chapman v. Barney, 129 U.S. 677 (1889), that a joint stock company could not be treated as if it were a corporation. (As a result, jurisdiction for diversity purposes was determined in the Chapman case on the basis of the citizenship of all of the company's members.)

The Court rejected these arguments, concluding that "however appealing, [they] are addressed to an inappropriate forum, and that pleas for extension of the diversity jurisdiction to hitherto uncovered broad categories of litigants ought to be made to the Congress and not to the courts."[4] Moreover, the Court reasoned, acceptance of the union's invitation to "amend diversity jurisdiction" would create considerable difficulty for the Court in fashioning "a test for ascertaining of which State the labor union is a citizen."

(b)   In Carden v. Arkoma Associates, 494 U.S. 185 (1990), the Court reaffirmed the distinction between incorporated and unincorporated entities, in the context of limited partnerships, in which there are both "general" and "limited" partners. Citing Bouligny and Chapman v. Barney, the Court concluded that diversity jurisdiction in a suit by or against an artificial entity other than a corporation "depends on the citizenship of 'all the members' " (quoting Chapman), including the limited as well as the general partners.

(c)   In Americold Realty Trust v. ConAgra Foods, Inc., 577 U.S. 378 (2016), the Court again reaffirmed Bouligny and Chapman, in deciding

---

[3]   See Lund, *Federally Chartered Corporations and Federal Jurisdiction*, 36 Fla.St.U.L.Rev. 317 (2009) (questioning the judicial recognition of a "localization" rule for federally chartered corporations and urging Congress to enact a statute defining the citizenship (for diversity purposes) of all such corporations).

[4]   Note that in the Class Action Fairness Act, as discussed at p. 1081, *supra*, Congress provided that for purposes of the Act, "an unincorporated association shall be deemed to be a citizen of the State where it has its principal place of business and the State under whose laws it is organized." 28 U.S.C. § 1332(d)(10).

whether the citizenship for diversity purposes of a Maryland "real estate investment trust" should be determined by the citizenship of the trust or of its members. The Court stated broadly that "[w]hile humans and corporations can assert their own citizenship, other entities take the citizenship of their members." The Court further explained that the appropriate "membership" of unincorporated entities is determined by state law, and that under the law of Maryland, which created the investment trust, the relevant members were its shareholders.

(d) For a discussion of the complex question of the citizenship, for diversity purposes, of Native American tribes or tribal entities, see Nicolas, *American-Style Justice in No Man's Land*, 36 Ga.L.Rev. 895, 942–47, 942–47, 1061–73 (2002). Professor Nicolas sees this question as an aspect of a broad range of issues relevant to the solution of what he describes as the "no forum" and "biased forum" problems in Indian law. The former arises when "no court has jurisdiction over disputes involving Indian tribes, tribal entities, or tribal members," and the latter when a substantial risk exists that a state or tribal court with jurisdiction over a dispute will not treat the litigants fairly.

C. JURISDICTIONAL AMOUNT

INTRODUCTORY NOTE

The Judiciary Act of 1789, 1 Stat. 73, 78, fixed the jurisdictional amount, in those cases in which some amount was requisite, at $500. Ninety-eight years later, 24 Stat. 552 (1887), Congress raised the amount to $2,000. In 1911, 36 Stat. 1087, 1091, it was set at $3,000; in 1958, 72 Stat. 415, at $10,000; in 1988, 102 Stat. 4646, at $50,000; and in 1996, 110 Stat. 3847, at $75,000, where it remains today for diversity cases brought under 28 U.S.C. § 1332.

From 1875, when Congress enacted general federal question, to 1976, there was a jurisdictional amount requirement in such cases identical to that in diversity cases. In 1976, Congress excepted actions against federal officers and agencies from the jurisdictional amount requirement of § 1331, and in 1980 Congress deleted the requirement from § 1331 altogether.

Burns v. Anderson

502 F.2d 970 (1974).
United States Court of Appeals for the Fifth Circuit.

■ JOHN R. BROWN, CHIEF JUDGE:

The question on this appeal is whether a district court may dismiss a personal injury diversity suit where it appears "to a legal certainty" that the claim was "really for less than the jurisdictional amount."[1]

The suit grew out of an auto accident in which plaintiff Burns' automobile was struck amidships by that of defendant Anderson. Burns' principal injury was a broken thumb. He brought the action in the Eastern District of Louisiana, claiming $1,026.00 in lost wages and medical expenses and another $60,000.00 for pain and suffering. After a pre-trial conference and considerable discovery, the District Court dismissed for want of jurisdiction. Plaintiff appeals.

The test for jurisdictional amount was established by the Supreme Court in St. Paul Mercury Indemnity Co. v. Red Cab Co.[2] There, the Court held that the determinant is plaintiff's good faith claim and that to justify dismissal it must appear to a legal certainty that the claim is really for less than the jurisdictional amount. There is no question but that this is a test of liberality, and it has been treated as such by this Court. This does not mean, however, that Federal Courts must function as small claims courts. The test is an objective one and, once it is clear that as a matter of law the claim is for less than $10,000.00 [the statutory figure at that time], the Trial Judge is required to dismiss.

In the instant case, the District Judge dismissed only after examination of an extensive record. * * * The accident occurred on May 26. The evidence is without contradiction that by the middle of August only very minimal disability remained. By December, even this minor condition had disappeared. Burns' actions speak even more strongly than the medical testimony. In his deposition he testified that he took a job as a carpenter's assistant on June 21 or 22—less than a month after the accident. He did heavy manual labor for the remainder of the summer with absolutely no indication of any difficulty with his thumb. It is equally clear that any pain he suffered was not of very great magnitude or lasting duration. Burns admitted that by the end of July there was no pain whatsoever. * * * [T]he evidence reveals that the only medication he ever received was a single prescription on the day of the accident for Empirin, a mild aspirin compound. Nor did his special damages take him a significant way down the road to the $10,000.00 minimum. His total medical bills were less than $250.00. Although he claims $800.00 in lost wages, it is difficult to see how this could have amounted to even $300.00 at Burns' rate of pay that summer.

---

[1]   St. Paul Mercury Indemnity Co. v. Red Cab Co., 303 U.S. 283, 289 (1938).

[2]   *Id.*

The point of this fact recitation is that it really does appear to a legal certainty that the amount in controversy is less than $10,000. * * * Here the Trial Court examined an extensive record and determined as a matter of law that the requisite amount in controversy was not present. Indeed, had the case gone to trial and had the jury returned an award of $10,000, a Gorsalitz-girded Judge [see footnote 7] would have been compelled as a matter of law to order a remittitur. He would have inescapably found that the verdict was "so inordinately large as obviously to exceed the maximum of the reasonable range within which the jury may properly operate.[7]" * * *

Neither are we affected by plaintiff's plaintive plea that he is being deprived of a jury trial. The question in this case is not whether Burns is entitled to a trial by jury but rather where that trial is to be. We hold only that the case cannot be tried in the Federal Court because competence over it has not been granted to that Court by Congress.

Affirmed.

NOTE ON THE AMOUNT IN CONTROVERSY

(1) Questions About the Burns Decision. After the decision in Burns, was a state court jury still free to award plaintiff more than $10,000? Was plaintiff's jury trial argument in Burns properly disposed of?

(2) Removal. Additional considerations apply to the amount in controversy when a case is removed by the defendant to federal court, rather than initially filed by the plaintiff. In St. Paul Mercury Indem. Co. v. Red Cab Co., 303 U.S. 283 (1938), cited in the Burns opinion, the Court held, in a case removed by the defendant to federal court, that federal jurisdiction, once it had attached by virtue of the plaintiff's good faith claim in excess of the jurisdictional threshold, was not defeated by the plaintiff's later amendment reducing the ad damnum below that amount.

Additionally, The Federal Courts Jurisdiction and Venue Clarification Act of 2011, Pub.L.No. 112–63, 125 Stat. 758, provides rules for the amount in controversy in removed cases, including allowing the defendant's notice of removal to assert the amount in controversy if the plaintiff's state court complaint seeks non-monetary relief is sought or if state law does not permit demand for a specific sum or allows recovery of a larger amount than that demanded.[1]

(3) Unliquidated Damages. A "short and plain statement" that a case satisfies the jurisdictional amount requirement suffices; the pleading need not include evidence backing up the allegation. See Dart Cherokee Basin Operating Co. v. Owens, 574 U.S. 81 (2014).

----

[7]   Gorsalitz v. Olin Mathieson Chemical Corp., 429 F.2d 1033, 1046 (5th Cir.1970).

[1]   For discussion of some ambiguities in the Act, see Baude, *Clarification Needed: Fixing the Jurisdiction and Venue Clarification Act*, 110 Mich.L.Rev. First Impressions 33 (2012).

(4)   The Effect of a Recovery of Less than the Jurisdictional Amount.
Suppose it is established at trial that any recovery to which plaintiff is
entitled falls short of the jurisdictional amount, or that plaintiff is not
entitled to recover at all. Should the action be dismissed for lack of
jurisdiction? In Mt. Healthy City Sch. Dist. Bd. of Educ. v. Doyle, 429 U.S.
274, 277 (1977), at a time when the jurisdictional threshold was $10,000, the
plaintiff had sought $50,000 damages and reinstatement but was awarded
only $5,158 damages, together with reinstatement. In upholding jurisdiction,
the Court said: "Even if the District Court had chosen to award only
compensatory damages [of $5,158] and not reinstatement, it was far from a
'legal certainty' at the time of suit that Doyle would not have been entitled
to more than $10,000." See also Rosado v. Wyman, 397 U.S. 397, 405 n.6
(1970).[2]

D. DEVICES FOR CREATING OR AVOIDING DIVERSITY JURISDICTION

Kramer v. Caribbean Mills, Inc.

394 U.S. 823 (1969).
Certiorari to the United States Court of Appeals for the Fifth Circuit.

■ MR. JUSTICE HARLAN delivered the opinion of the Court.

The sole question presented by this case is whether the Federal
District Court in which it was brought had jurisdiction over the cause, or
whether that court was deprived of jurisdiction by 28 U.S.C. § 1359. * * *

The facts were these. Respondent Caribbean Mills, Inc. (Caribbean)
is a Haitian corporation. In May 1959 it entered into a contract with an
individual named Kelly and the Panama and Venezuela Finance
Company (Panama), a Panamanian corporation. The agreement provided
that Caribbean would purchase from Panama 125 shares of corporate
stock, in return for payment of $85,000 down and an additional $165,000
in 12 annual installments.

No installment payments ever were made, despite requests for
payment by Panama. In 1964, Panama assigned its entire interest in the
1959 contract to petitioner Kramer, an attorney in Wichita Falls, Texas.
The stated consideration was $1. By a separate agreement dated the
same day, Kramer promised to pay back to Panama 95% of any net
recovery on the assigned cause of action, "solely as a Bonus."

Kramer soon thereafter brought suit against Caribbean for $165,000
in the United States District Court for the Northern District of Texas,

---

[2]   Section 1332(b), enacted in 1958, provides that a plaintiff who recovers less than the
jurisdictional amount may be saddled with the opponent's court costs. The provision does not
seem to have had much impact.

alleging diversity of citizenship between himself and Caribbean. The District Court denied Caribbean's motion to dismiss for want of jurisdiction. The case proceeded to trial, and a jury returned a $165,000 verdict in favor of Kramer.

On appeal, the Court of Appeals for the Fifth Circuit reversed, holding that the assignment was "improperly or collusively made" within the meaning of 28 U.S.C. § 1359, and that in consequence the District Court lacked jurisdiction. * * * For reasons which follow, we affirm the judgment of the Court of Appeals.

I

The issue before us is whether Kramer was "improperly or collusively made" a party "to invoke the jurisdiction" of the District Court, within the meaning of 28 U.S.C. § 1359. We look first to the legislative background.

Section 1359 has existed in its present form only since the 1948 revision of the Judicial Code. Prior to that time, the use of devices to create diversity was regulated by two federal statutes. The first, known as the "assignee clause," provided that, with certain exceptions not here relevant:

> "No district court shall have cognizance of any suit . . . to recover upon any promissory note or other chose in action in favor of any assignee . . . unless such suit might have been prosecuted in such court . . . if no assignment had been made."[3]

The second pre-1948 statute, 28 U.S.C. § 80 (1940 ed.), stated that a district court should dismiss an action whenever:

> "it shall appear to the satisfaction of the . . . court . . . that such suit does not really and substantially involve a dispute or controversy properly within the jurisdiction of [the] court, or that the parties to said suit have been improperly or collusively made or joined . . . for the purpose of creating [federal jurisdiction]."

As part of the 1948 revision, § 80 was amended to produce the present § 1359. The assignee clause was simultaneously repealed. The Reviser's Note describes the amended assignee clause as a "jumble of legislative jargon," and states that "[t]he revised section changes this clause by confining its application to cases wherein the assignment is improperly or collusively made . . . . Furthermore, . . . the original purpose of [the assignee] clause is better served by substantially following section 80." That purpose was said to be "to prevent the manufacture of Federal jurisdiction by the device of assignment." *Ibid.*

---

[3]   28 U.S.C. § 41(1) (1940 ed.). The clause first appeared as § 11 of the Judiciary Act of 1789, 1 Stat. 79.

II

* * * Because the approach of the former assignee clause was to forbid the grounding of jurisdiction upon *any* assignment, regardless of its circumstances or purpose, decisions under that clause are of little assistance. However, decisions of this Court under the other predecessor statute, 28 U.S.C. § 80 (1940 ed.), seem squarely in point. These decisions, together with the evident purpose of § 1359, lead us to conclude that the Court of Appeals was correct in finding that the assignment in question was "improperly or collusively made."

The most compelling precedent is Farmington v. Pillsbury, 114 U.S. 138 (1885). There Maine holders of bonds issued by a Maine village desired to test the bonds' validity in the federal courts. In an effort to accomplish this, they cut the coupons from their bonds and transferred them to a citizen of Massachusetts, who gave in return a non-negotiable two-year note for $500 and a promise to pay back 50% of the net amount recovered above $500. The jurisdictional question was certified to this Court, which held that there was no federal jurisdiction because the plaintiff had been "improperly or collusively" made a party within the meaning of the predecessor statute to 28 U.S.C. § 80 (1940 ed.). The Court pointed out that the plaintiff could easily have been released from his non-negotiable note, and found that apart from the hoped-for creation of federal jurisdiction the only real consequence of the transfer was to enable the Massachusetts plaintiff to "retain one-half of what he collects for the use of his name and his trouble in collecting." 114 U.S., at 146. The Court concluded that "the transfer of the coupons was 'a mere contrivance, a pretence, the result of a collusive arrangement to create' " federal jurisdiction. *Ibid.*

We find the case before us indistinguishable from Farmington and other decisions of like tenor. When the assignment to Kramer is considered together with his total lack of previous connection with the matter and his simultaneous reassignment of a 95% interest back to Panama, there can be little doubt that the assignment was for purposes of collection, with Kramer to retain 5% of the net proceeds "for the use of his name and his trouble in collecting."[9] If the suit had been unsuccessful, Kramer would have been out only $1, plus costs. Moreover, Kramer candidly admits that the "assignment was in substantial part motivated by a desire by [Panama's] counsel to make diversity jurisdiction available . . . ."

---

[9]   Hence, we have no occasion to re-examine the cases in which this Court has held that where the transfer of a claim is absolute, with the transferor retaining no interest in the subject matter, then the transfer is not "improperly or collusively made," regardless of the transferor's motive.

Nor is it necessary to consider whether, in cases in which suit is required to be brought by an administrator or guardian, a motive to create diversity jurisdiction renders the appointment of an out-of-state representative "improper" or "collusive." See, *e.g.,* McSparran v. Weist, 402 F.2d 867 (3d Cir.1968); *cf.* Mecom v. Fitzsimmons Drilling Co., 284 U.S. 183 (1931). * * *

The conclusion that this assignment was "improperly or collusively made" within the meaning of § 1359 is supported not only by precedent but also by consideration of the statute's purpose. If federal jurisdiction could be created by assignments of this kind, which are easy to arrange and involve few disadvantages for the assignor, then a vast quantity of ordinary contract and tort litigation could be channeled into the federal courts at the will of one of the parties. Such "manufacture of Federal jurisdiction" was the very thing which Congress intended to prevent when it enacted § 1359 and its predecessors.

III

Kramer nevertheless argues that the assignment to him was not "improperly or collusively made" within the meaning of § 1359, for two main reasons. First, he suggests that the undisputed legality of the assignment under Texas law necessarily rendered it valid for purposes of federal jurisdiction. We cannot accept this contention. * * * [To do so] would render § 1359 largely incapable of accomplishing its purpose; this very case demonstrates the ease with which a party may "manufacture" federal jurisdiction by an assignment which meets the requirements of state law.

Second, Kramer urges that this case is significantly distinguishable from earlier decisions because it involves diversity jurisdiction under 28 U.S.C. § 1332(a)(2), arising from the alienage of one of the parties, rather than the more common diversity jurisdiction based upon the parties' residence in different States. We can perceive no substance in this argument: by its terms, § 1359 applies equally to both types of diversity jurisdiction, and there is no indication that Congress intended them to be treated differently.

IV

In short, we find that this assignment falls not only within the scope of § 1359 but within its very core. It follows that the District Court lacked jurisdiction to hear this action, and that petitioner must seek his remedy in the state courts. The judgment of the Court of Appeals is affirmed.

Affirmed.

■ MR. JUSTICE FORTAS took no part in the consideration or decision of this case.

NOTE ON DEVICES FOR CREATING OR AVOIDING FEDERAL JURISDICTION

(1) Appointment of Legal Representatives.

(a) Footnote 9 of the Kramer opinion refers to the appointment of an administrator or guardian for the purpose of creating diversity jurisdiction. The problem presented by this practice had become particularly acute in the Eastern District of Pennsylvania, where it was common for lawyers to arrange for the appointment—as guardians, administrators, or executors— of secretaries or other office staff who commuted to work from New Jersey, thus laying the basis for a diversity action against a Pennsylvania defendant. In McSparran v. Weist, 402 F.2d 867 (3d Cir.1968), decided a few months before Kramer, the plaintiff conceded that the fiduciary (a guardian for a minor) was "a straw party, chosen solely to create diversity jurisdiction." The Third Circuit, overruling its own precedent, sustained a challenge to the jurisdiction, saying: "[A] nominal party designated simply for the purpose of creating diversity of citizenship, who has no real or substantial interest in the dispute or controversy, is improperly or collusively named."

(b)   In 1988, Congress addressed the McSparran problem by adopting a "bright line" test for determining jurisdiction: 28 U.S.C. § 1332(c)(2) specifies that the representative of an estate shall be deemed to be a citizen only of the state of citizenship of the decedent, and the representative of an infant or incompetent shall be deemed to be a citizen only of the state of citizenship of the person represented.

(2) Variations on the Theme: Matters Not Covered by Kramer or by § 1332(c)(2). The Kramer Court deliberately left open the status under § 1359 of a variety of events, thus casting doubt on a number of its own precedents. As stated in the Court's footnote 9, an absolute transfer not subject to the former assignee clause had been held not improper or collusive, regardless of the transferor's motive. See, *e.g.*, Cross v. Allen, 141 U.S. 528 (1891). And if a plaintiff effectively changes domicile prior to the bringing of suit, it did not matter that the sole motive was to create jurisdiction. Williamson v. Osenton, 232 U.S. 619 (1914). Finally, although reincorporation would fail to create diversity jurisdiction if the old corporation continued in existence with power to control the new, *e.g.*, Lehigh Mining & Mfg. Co. v. Kelly, 160 U.S. 327 (1895), the device would succeed if the new corporation was a genuine one not subject to control by any predecessor, Black & White Taxicab & Transfer Co. v. Brown & Yellow Taxicab & Transfer Co., 276 U.S. 518 (1928), p. 759, *supra*.

Should any or all of these holdings be overruled? What is the effect, if any, of Congress's decision, in § 1332(c)(2), to deal specifically with the case of the legal representative?

(3) Avoidance Devices. No statutory provision aids a district court in disregarding devices to *avoid* federal jurisdiction, and such devices have often been successful. In Provident Savings Life Assurance Society v. Ford, 114 U.S. 635 (1885), the Court held that an assignment to the plaintiff made to prevent removal, even if only "merely colorable," raised at most a defense to the action in the state court, and thus the case could not be removed. See also Oakley v. Goodnow, 118 U.S. 43 (1886) (assignment to defeat jurisdiction precludes removal); Mecom v. Fitzsimmons Drilling Co., 284 U.S. 183 (1931) (appointment of co-citizen administrator to defeat jurisdiction precludes removal).[1]

---

[1]   But in Gentle v. Lamb-Weston, Inc., 302 F.Supp. 161 (D.Me.1969), each of the plaintiffs, who were citizens of Maine, transferred 1% of his claim to an Oregon citizen (a law school classmate of their Maine attorney), and the Oregon citizen then joined as a plaintiff in an action against an Oregon defendant in a Maine state court. The admitted purpose of the

---

6. THE ADMIRALTY JURISDICTION OF THE FEDERAL DISTRICT COURTS

INTRODUCTORY NOTE

The need for federal tribunals exercising admiralty jurisdiction was a key reason for establishing a system of lower federal courts. The Founders were particularly concerned with the relationship of maritime matters to international affairs—for example, prize cases required adjudication of the rights and status of foreign claimants and nations, both neutral and belligerent. See The Federalist, No. 80 (Hamilton). Indeed, Professor Casto, in *The Origins of Federal Admiralty Jurisdiction in an Age of Privateers, Smugglers, and Pirates*, 37 Am.J. Legal Hist. 117 (1993), contends that the original vision of the jurisdiction focused not on private claims but on such "public" matters as prize cases, revenue cases, and criminal prosecutions. But the Admiralty Clause in Article III has given rise to a broader jurisdiction that includes a large area of private law. Policy support for the broader scope has been found in the perceived value of uniformity in maritime law—a notion reflecting the traditional view of the law of the sea as an independent and international body of rules, transcending the reach of territorial jurisdictions—and in the contemporary federal interest in furthering maritime commerce. See Gutoff, *Original Understandings and the Private Law Origins of the Federal Admiralty Jurisdiction: A Reply to Professor Casto*, 30 J.Mar.L. & Com. 361 (1999) (contending that this broader view squares with the original understanding). Although some academics have criticized its soundness, this broader understanding is deeply rooted in the case law, as the following two cases exemplify. In reading these cases, consider both the proper scope of admiralty jurisdiction and the possible parallels or lack thereof between the development of admiralty jurisdiction and other heads of subject matter jurisdiction.

The Propeller Genesee Chief v. Fitzhugh
53 U.S. (12 How.) 443 (1851).
On appeal from the Circuit Court of the United States
for the Northern District of New York.

■ MR. CHIEF JUSTICE TANEY delivered the opinion of the court.

This is a case of collision on Lake Ontario. The libellants were the owners of the schooner Cuba, and the respondents and present

---

transfer, to prevent removal, failed when Judge Gignoux denied a motion to remand the case to the state court. He relied on the Kramer rationale, *inter alia*, and concluded that "the essential diversity of citizenship of the parties at bar has not been vitiated by plaintiffs' sham transaction."

appellants the master and owners of the propeller Genesee Chief. The libellants state that on the 6th of May, 1847, as the Cuba was on her voyage from Sandusky, in the state of Ohio, to Oswego, in the state of New York, the Genesee Chief, which was proceeding on a voyage up the lake, ran foul of her and damaged her so seriously that she shortly afterwards sunk, with her cargo on board; and they also allege that the collision was occasioned by the carelessness and mismanagement of the officers and crew of the propeller, without any fault of the officers or crew of the Cuba. The respondents deny that it was occasioned by the fault of the steamboat, and impute it to the carelessness with which the schooner was managed.

[The suit was filed under the Act of Fed. 26, 1845, 5 Stat. 726, Ch. 20, which extended admiralty jurisdiction that previously existed "upon the high seas, or tidewaters" to "matters * * * concerning steamboats and other vessels of twenty tons burden and upwards" that occurred "upon the lakes and navigable waters connecting said lakes," such as the Great Lakes.]

Before, however, we can look into the merits of the dispute there is question of jurisdiction which meets us at the threshold. When the act of Congress was passed, under which these proceedings were had, serious doubts were entertained of its constitutionality. The language and decision of this court, whenever a question of admiralty jurisdiction had come before it, seemed to imply that under the Constitution of the United States, the jurisdiction was confined to tide-waters. Yet the conviction that this definition of admiralty powers was narrower than the Constitution contemplated, has been growing stronger every day with the growing commerce on the lakes and navigable rivers of the western States. * * *

If this law * * * is constitutional, it must be supported on the ground that the lakes and navigable waters connecting them are within the scope of admiralty and maritime jurisdiction, as known and understood in the United States when the Constitution was adopted.

If the meaning of these terms was now for the first time brought before this court for consideration, there could, we think, be no hesitation in saying that the lakes and their connecting waters were embraced in them. These lakes are in truth inland seas. Different States border on them on one side, and a foreign nation on the other. A great and growing commerce is carried on upon them between different States and a foreign nation, which is subject to all the incidents and hazards that attend commerce on the ocean. Hostile fleets have encountered on them, and prizes been made; and every reason which existed for the grant of admiralty jurisdiction to the general government on the Atlantic seas, applies with equal force to the lakes. There is an equal necessity for the instance and for the prize power of the admiralty court to administer international law, and if the one cannot be established neither can the other.

* * * The union is formed upon the basis of equal rights among all the States. * * * That equality does not exist, if the commerce on the lakes and on the navigable waters of the West are denied the benefits of the same courts and the same jurisdiction for its protection which the Constitution secures to the States bordering on the Atlantic. * * *

In England, undoubtedly the writers upon the subject, and the decisions in its courts of admiralty, always speak of the jurisdiction as confined to tide-water. And this definition in England was a sound and reasonable one, because there was no navigable stream in the country beyond the ebb and flow of the tide; nor any place where a port could be established to carry on trade with a foreign nation, and where vessels could enter or depart with cargoes. In England, therefore, tide-water and navigable water are synonymous terms, and tide-water, with a few small and unimportant exceptions, meant nothing more than public rivers, as contradistinguished from private ones; and they took the ebb and flow of the tide as the test, because it was a convenient one, and more easily determined the character of the river. Hence the established doctrine in England, that the admiralty jurisdiction is confined to the ebb and flow of the tide. In other words, it is confined to public navigable waters.

At the time the Constitution of the United States was adopted, and our courts of admiralty went into operation, the definition which had been adopted in England was equally proper here. * * * [U]ntil the discovery of steamboats, there could be nothing like foreign commerce upon waters with an unchanging current resisting the upward passage. The courts of the United States, therefore, naturally adopted the English mode of defining a public river, and consequently the boundary of admiralty jurisdiction. * * * It was under the influence of these precedents and this usage, that the case of the Thomas Jefferson, 23 U.S. (10 Wheat.) 428 (1825), was decided in this court; and the jurisdiction of the courts of admiralty of the United States declared to be limited to the ebb and flow of the tide. * * *

It is the decision in the case of the Thomas Jefferson which mainly embarrasses the court in the present inquiry. We are sensible of the great weight to which it is entitled. But at the same time we are convinced that, if we follow it, we follow an erroneous decision into which the court fell, when the great importance of the question as it now presents itself could not be foreseen; and the subject did not therefore receive that deliberate consideration which at this time would have been given to it by the eminent men who presided here when that case was decided. For the decision was made in 1825, when the commerce on the rivers of the west and on the lakes was in its infancy, and of little importance, and but little regarded compared with that of the present day. * * *

■ MR. JUSTICE DANIEL.

From so much of the opinion just announced as claims jurisdiction in this case * * * I find myself constrained to declare my dissent. * * *

* * * [T]he doctrine at present promulged by this Court, is based upon assumptions [that are] irregular [and] dangerous * * * because it claims for this court, wholly irrespective either of the Constitution or the legislation of Congress, powers to be assumed and carried into execution by some rule which in the judgment of this court is to be applied according to its own opinions of convenience or necessity. * * * [A]lthough it is admitted that the power was once clearly understood as being limited to the ebb and flow of the tide, yet now, without there having been engrafted any new provision on the Constitution, without the alteration of one letter of that instrument, designed to be the charter of all federal power, the jurisdiction of the admiralty is to be measured by miles, and by the extent of territory which may have been subsequently acquired * * *. My opinions may be deemed to be contracted and antiquated, unsuited to the day in which we live; but they are founded upon deliberate conviction as to the nature and objects of limited government, and by myself at least cannot be disregarded * * *. * * *

Jerome B. Grubart, Inc. v. Great Lakes Dredge & Dock Co.

513 U.S. 527 (1995).
Certiorari to the United States Court of Appeals for the Seventh Circuit.

■ JUSTICE SOUTER delivered the Opinion of the Court.

On April 13, 1992, water from the Chicago River poured into a freight tunnel running under the river and thence into the basements of buildings in the downtown Chicago Loop. Allegedly, the flooding resulted from events several months earlier, when respondent Great Lakes Dredge and Dock Company had used a crane, sitting on a barge in the river next to a bridge, to drive piles into the riverbed above the tunnel. The issue before us is whether a court of the United States has admiralty jurisdiction to determine and limit the extent of Great Lakes's tort liability. We hold this suit to be within federal admiralty jurisdiction. * * *

II

* * *

A

A federal court's authority to hear cases in admiralty flows initially from the Constitution, which "extend[s]" federal judicial power "to all Cases of admiralty and maritime Jurisdiction." U.S. Const., Art. III, § 2. Congress has embodied that power in a statute giving federal district courts "original jurisdiction . . . of . . . [a]ny civil case of admiralty or maritime jurisdiction. . . ." 28 U.S.C. § 1333(1).

The traditional test for admiralty tort jurisdiction asked only whether the tort occurred on navigable waters. If it did, admiralty jurisdiction followed; if it did not, admiralty jurisdiction did not exist. See, *e.g.*, Thomas v. Lane, 23 F.Cas. 957, 960 (No. 13902) (CC Me.1813) (Story, J., on Circuit). This ostensibly simple locality test was complicated by the rule that the injury had to be "wholly" sustained on navigable waters for the tort to be within admiralty. The Plymouth, [70 U.S.] 3 Wall. 20, 34 (1866) (no jurisdiction over tort action brought by the owner of warehouse destroyed in a fire that started on board a ship docked nearby). Thus, admiralty courts lacked jurisdiction over, say, a claim following a ship's collision with a pier insofar as it injured the pier, for admiralty law treated the pier as an extension of the land. Martin v. West, 222 U.S. 191, 197 (1911).

This latter rule was changed in 1948, however, when Congress enacted the Extension of Admiralty Jurisdiction Act, 62 Stat. 496. The Act provided that

> "[t]he admiralty and maritime jurisdiction of the United States shall extend to and include all cases of damage or injury, to person or property, caused by a vessel on navigable water, notwithstanding that such damage or injury be done or consummated on land." 46 U.S.C.App. § 740.

The purpose of the Act was to end concern over the sometimes confusing line between land and water, by investing admiralty with jurisdiction over "all cases" where the injury was caused by a ship or other vessel on navigable water, even if such injury occurred on land. See, *e.g.*, Gutierrez v. Waterman S.S. Corp., 373 U.S. 206, 209–210 (1963); Executive Jet Aviation, Inc. v. Cleveland, 409 U.S. 249, 260 (1972).

After this congressional modification to gather the odd case into admiralty, the jurisdictional rule was qualified again in three decisions of this Court aimed at keeping a different class of odd cases out. In the first case, Executive Jet, *supra*, tort claims arose out of the wreck of an airplane that collided with a flock of birds just after takeoff on a domestic flight and fell into the navigable waters of Lake Erie. We held that admiralty lacked jurisdiction to consider the claims. * * * We held that "claims arising from airplane accidents are not cognizable in admiralty" despite the location of the harm, unless "the wrong bear[s] a significant relationship to traditional maritime activity." *Id.*, at 268.

The second decision, Foremost Ins. Co. v. Richardson, 457 U.S. 668 (1982), dealt with tort claims arising out of the collision of two pleasure boats in a navigable river estuary. We held that admiralty courts had jurisdiction * * *. * * *

In the most recent of the trilogy, Sisson v. Ruby, 497 U.S. 358 (1990), we held that a federal admiralty court had jurisdiction over tort claims arising when a fire, caused by a defective washer/dryer aboard a pleasure boat docked at a marina, burned the boat, other boats docked nearby, and the marina itself. *Id.*, at 367. We elaborated on the enquiry exemplified in Executive Jet and Foremost by focusing on two points to determine the relationship of a claim to the objectives of admiralty jurisdiction. We noted, first, that the incident causing the harm, the burning of docked boats at a marina on navigable waters, was of a sort "likely to disrupt [maritime] commercial activity." 497 U.S., at 363. Second, we found a "substantial relationship" with "traditional maritime activity" in the kind of activity from which the incident arose, "the storage and maintenance of a vessel . . . on navigable waters." *Id.*, at 365–367.

After Sisson, then, a party seeking to invoke federal admiralty jurisdiction pursuant to 28 U.S.C. § 1333(1) over a tort claim must satisfy conditions both of location and of connection with maritime activity. A court applying the location test must determine whether the tort occurred on navigable water or whether injury suffered on land was caused by a vessel on navigable water. 46 U.S.C.App. § 740. The connection test raises two issues. A court, first, must "assess the general features of the type of incident involved," 497 U.S., at 363, to determine whether the incident has "a potentially disruptive impact on maritime commerce," *id.*, at 364, n.2. Second, a court must determine whether "the general character" of the "activity giving rise to the incident" shows a "substantial relationship to traditional maritime activity." *Id.*, at 365, 364, and n.2. We now apply the tests to the facts of this suit.

B

The location test is, of course, readily satisfied. If Great Lakes caused the flood, it must have done so by weakening the structure of the tunnel while it drove in new pilings or removed old ones around the bridge piers. The weakening presumably took place as Great Lakes's workers lifted and replaced the pilings with a crane that sat on a barge stationed in the Chicago River. The place in the river where the barge sat, and from which workers directed the crane, is in the "navigable waters of the United States." Escanaba Co., 107 U.S., at 683. Thus, if Great Lakes committed a tort, it must have done it while on navigable waters.

It must also have done it "by a vessel." Even though the barge was fastened to the river bottom and was in use as a work platform at the times in question, at other times it was used for transportation. Petitioners do not here seriously dispute the conclusion of each court below that the Great Lakes barge is, for admiralty tort purposes, a "vessel." The fact that the pile driving was done with a crane makes no difference under the location test, given the maritime law that ordinarily treats an "appurtenance" attached to a vessel in navigable waters as part of the vessel itself. See, *e.g.*, Victory Carriers, Inc. v. Law, 404 U.S. 202, 210–211 (1971). * * *

C

We now turn to the maritime connection enquiries, the first being whether the incident involved was of a sort with the potential to disrupt maritime commerce. * * *

The first Sisson test turns * * * on a description of the incident at an intermediate level of possible generality. To speak of the incident as "fire" would have been too general to differentiate cases; at the other extreme, to have described the fire as damaging nothing but pleasure boats and their tie-up facilities would have ignored, among other things, the capacity of pleasure boats to endanger commercial shipping that happened to be nearby. We rejected both extremes and instead asked whether the incident could be seen within a class of incidents that posed more than a fanciful risk to commercial shipping.

[T]he "general features" of the incident at issue here may be described as damage by a vessel in navigable water to an underwater structure. So characterized, there is little question that this is the kind of incident that has a "potentially disruptive impact on maritime commerce." As it actually turned out in this suit, damaging a structure beneath the riverbed could lead to a disruption in the water course itself, App. 33 (eddy formed above the leak); and, again as it actually happened, damaging a structure so situated could lead to restrictions on the navigational use of the waterway during required repairs. See Pet. for Cert. in No. 93–1094, p. 22a (District Court found that after the flood "[t]he river remained closed for over a month," "[r]iver traffic ceased, several commuter ferries were stranded, and many barges could not enter the river system . . . because the river level was lowered to aid repair efforts").

In the second Sisson enquiry, we look to whether the general character of the activity giving rise to the incident shows a substantial relationship to traditional maritime activity. * * * Navigation of boats in navigable waters clearly falls within the substantial relationship; storing them at a marina on navigable waters is close enough, Sisson, *supra,* 497 U.S., at 367; whereas in flying an airplane over the water, Executive Jet, 409 U.S., at 270–271, as in swimming, *id.,* at 255–256, the relationship is too attenuated.

On like reasoning, the "activity giving rise to the incident" in this suit, Sisson, *supra,* 497 U.S., at 364, should be characterized as repair or maintenance work on a navigable waterway performed from a vessel. Described in this way, there is no question that the activity is substantially related to traditional maritime activity, for barges and similar vessels have traditionally been engaged in repair work similar to what Great Lakes contracted to perform here. * * *

III

Perhaps recognizing the difficulty of escaping the case law, petitioners ask us to change it. In cases "involving land based parties and injuries," the city would have us adopt a condition of jurisdiction that

"the totality of the circumstances reflects a federal interest in protecting maritime commerce sufficiently weighty to justify shifting what would otherwise be state-court litigation into

federal court under the federal law of admiralty." City Brief 32.
* * *

Although the arguments [for this test] are not frivolous, they do not persuade. It is worth recalling that the Sisson tests are aimed at the same objectives invoked to support a new multifactor test, the elimination of admiralty jurisdiction where the rationale for the jurisdiction does not support it. If the tort produces no potential threat to maritime commerce or occurs during activity lacking a substantial relationship to traditional maritime activity, Sisson assumes that the objectives of admiralty jurisdiction probably do not require its exercise, even if the location test is satisfied. If, however, the Sisson tests are also satisfied, it is not apparent why the need for admiralty jurisdiction in aid of maritime commerce somehow becomes less acute merely because land-based parties happen to be involved. Certainly Congress did not think a land-based party necessarily diluted the need for admiralty jurisdiction or it would have kept its hands off the primitive location test. * * *

Finally, on top of these objections * * * there is added a most powerful one based on the practical consequences of adopting a multifactor test. Although the existing case law tempers the locality test with the added requirements looking to potential harm and traditional activity, it reflects customary practice in seeing jurisdiction as the norm when the tort originates with a vessel in navigable waters, and in treating departure from the locality principle as the exception. For better or worse, the case law has thus carved out the approximate shape of admiralty jurisdiction in a way that admiralty lawyers understand reasonably well. As against this approach, so familiar and relatively easy, the proposed four- or seven-factor test would be hard to apply, jettisoning relative predictability for the open-ended rough-and-tumble of factors, inviting complex argument in a trial court and a virtually inevitable appeal. * * *

Reasons of practice, then, are as weighty as reasons of theory for rejecting the city's call to adopt a multifactor test for admiralty jurisdiction for the benefit of land-based parties to a tort action.

Accordingly, we conclude that the Court of Appeals correctly held that the District Court had admiralty jurisdiction over the respondent Great Lakes's Limitation Act suit. The judgment of the Court of Appeals is

Affirmed.

■ JUSTICE STEVENS and JUSTICE BREYER took no part in the decision of these cases.

■ [The concurring opinion of JUSTICE O'CONNOR is omitted.]

■ JUSTICE THOMAS, with whom JUSTICE SCALIA joins, concurring in the judgment.

I agree with the majority's conclusion that 28 U.S.C. § 1333(1) grants the District Court jurisdiction over the great Chicago flood of 1992. But I write separately because I cannot agree with the test the Court applies to determine the boundaries of admiralty and maritime jurisdiction. Instead of continuing our unquestioning allegiance to the multi-factor approach of Sisson v. Ruby, 497 U.S. 358 (1990), I would restore the jurisdictional inquiry to the simple question whether the tort occurred on a vessel on the navigable waters of the United States. If so, then admiralty jurisdiction exists. This clear, bright-line rule, which the Court applied until recently, ensures that judges and litigants will not waste their resources in determining the extent of federal subject-matter jurisdiction.

I

This action requires the Court to redefine once again the line between federal admiralty jurisdiction and state power due to an ambiguous balancing test. The fact that we have had to revisit this question for the third time in a little over 10 years indicates the defects of the Court's current approach. The faults of balancing tests are clearest, and perhaps most destructive, in the area of jurisdiction. Vague and obscure rules may permit judicial power to reach beyond its constitutional and statutory limits, or they may discourage judges from hearing disputes properly before them. Such rules waste judges' and litigants' resources better spent on the merits, as this action itself demonstrates. It is especially unfortunate that this has occurred in admiralty, an area that once provided a jurisdictional rule almost as clear as the 9th and 10th verses of Genesis: "And God said, Let the waters under the heaven be gathered together unto one place, and let the dry land appear: and it was so. And God called the dry land Earth; and the gathering together of the waters called he Seas: and God saw that it was good." The Holy Bible, Genesis 1:9–10 (King James Version). * * *

II

* * * In place of Sisson I would follow the test described at the outset. When determining whether maritime jurisdiction exists under § 1333(1), a federal district court should ask if the tort occurred on a vessel on the navigable waters. * * * Although this approach "might leave within admiralty jurisdiction a few unusual actions," 497 U.S., at 374, such freakish cases will occur rarely. In any event, the resources needed to resolve them "will be saved many times over by a clear jurisdictional rule that makes it unnecessary to decide" what is a traditional maritime activity and what poses a threat to maritime commerce. *Id.*, at 374–375.

In this action, a straightforward application of the proposed test easily produces a finding of admiralty jurisdiction. As the majority quite ably demonstrates, the situs requirement is satisfied because the tort was caused by a "spud barge" on the Chicago River. Although the accident's effects were felt on land, the Extension of Admiralty Jurisdiction Act brings the event within § 1333(1). While I agree with the majority's analysis of this question, I disagree with its decision to continue on to other issues. A simple application of the situs test would yield the same result the Court reaches at the end of its analysis.

This Court pursues clarity and efficiency in other areas of federal subject-matter jurisdiction, and it should demand no less in admiralty and maritime law. * * *

NOTE ON ADMIRALTY JURISDICTION

(1) Further Doctrinal Context. While the details of admiralty jurisdiction and its substantive law could of course encompass an entire course, this paragraph offers a few pieces of additional context.

(a) The Genesee Chief was followed by Jackson v. The Steamboat Magnolia, 61 U.S. (20 How.) 296 (1857), which applied the principle of Genesee Chief to an accident that took place on a river above tide-water and located entirely within a single state and county. The majority opinion by Justice Grier treated the matter as largely resolved by Genesee Chief. Several other justices filed extended separate opinions. Justice McLean wrote a concurring opinion that argued against placing much weight on historical understandings of admiralty jurisdiction: "Antiquity has its charms, as it is rarely found in the common walks of professional life; but it may be doubted whether wisdom is not more frequently found in experience and the gradual progress of human affairs; and this is especially the case in all systems of jurisprudence which are matured by the progress of human knowledge. Whether it be common, chancery, or admiralty law, we should be more instructed by studying its present adaptations to human concerns, than to trace it back to its beginnings. Every one is more interested and delighted to look upon the majestic and flowing river, than by following its current upwards until it becomes lost in its mountain rivulets."

Justice Daniel, as he had in Genesee Chief, filed a dissent on originalist grounds. He argued that the courts should "interpret[ ] the Constitution and laws as they should have been fairly expounded at the times of their enactment," and criticized the majority for judicial activism. He attributed the following sentiment to the majority: "The Constitution, which at its adoption suited perfectly well the situation of the country * * * we now adjudge to have become unequal to the exigencies of the times; it must therefore be substituted by something more efficient; and as the people, and the States, and the Federal Legislature, are tardy or delinquent in making this substitution, the duty or the credit of this beneficent work must be devolved upon the judiciary."

Justice Campbell filed a separate dissent as well, joined by Justice Catron, stressing the impact of admiralty jurisdiction on state sovereignty. He expressed his opinion "that the present case carries the jurisdiction to an incalculable extent beyond any other, and all others, that have heretofore been pronounced, and that it must create a revolution in the admiralty administration of the courts of the United States; that the change will produce heart-burning and discontent, and involve collisions with State Legislatures and State jurisdictions. And, finally, it is a violation of the rights reserved in the Constitution of the United States to the States and the people."

(b) Most of the Grubart decision focuses on the connection to maritime activity. The two other elements of its test for jurisdiction—"navigable waters" and "vessels"—were easily satisfied in that case, but they can produce harder cases as well.

(i) For navigable waters, the leading case is The Daniel Ball, 77 U.S. (10 Wall.) 557 (1870), which states: "Those rivers must be regarded as public navigable rivers in law which are navigable in fact when they are used or are susceptible of being used, in their ordinary condition, as highways for commerce, over which trade or travel are or may be conducted in the customary modes of travel and trade on water. And they constitute navigable waters of the United States when they form in their ordinary condition themselves, or by uniting with other waters, a continued highway over which commerce is or may be carried on with other states or foreign countries in the customary modes in which such commerce is conducted by water." *Id.* 563.

(ii) For vessels, which are defined in the Dictionary Act as including "every description of watercraft or other artificial contrivance used, or capable of being used, as a means of transportation on water," the Supreme Court has issued two somewhat recent constructions. In Stewart v. Dutra Constr. Co., 543 U.S. 481 (2005), which held that a gigantic dredge used in Boston's "Big Dig" was a vessel, the Court interpreted this definition to extend to watercraft that were "practically capable" of transportation on water—not extending to those that were only "theoretical[ly]" capable of transportation, but not limited to those that were actively or primarily capable of transportation. In Lozman v. City of Rivera Beach, Fla, 568 U.S. 115 (2012), which held that a floating home moored in a Florida marina was not a vessel, the Court further clarified that this test should be approached from the standpoint of a "reasonable observer," and did not include "anything that floats."

(c) Both Genesee Chief and Grubart were maritime tort cases. The Supreme Court has also upheld very broad admiralty jurisdiction over maritime contracts. In Norfolk Southern Railway Co. v. James N. Kirby, Pty Ltd., 543 U.S. 14 (2004), the Court stressed that in contract cases, admiralty jurisdiction is "conceptual" rather than "spatial." A contract falls within admiralty jurisdiction if it substantially deals with maritime commerce or transactions, even if it also includes substantial non-maritime aspects. Given the growth of containerized shipping, this can extend admiralty jurisdiction to many inland transactions, thus explaining Kirby's first sentence: "This is a maritime case about a train wreck."

(2) The Constitutional Limits of Admiralty Jurisdiction. As Genesee Chief, Grubart, and Paragraph (1) all demonstrate, the scope of admiralty jurisdiction has evolved greatly over the years. The legislative extension upheld by the Genesee Chief allowed admiralty jurisdiction to expand from the traditional high seas and tidewaters to include all navigable waters, because of the development of maritime commerce on the Great Lakes and the invention of the steamship. The Admiralty Extension Act of 1948 discussed in Grubart extended admiralty jurisdiction to many cases of injuries on land. There are other examples as well.[1]

Is there some constitutional ceiling to the jurisdiction that Congress may vest in the name of "admiralty and maritime jurisdiction"? To what extent could Congress permissibly expand admiralty jurisdiction to smaller bodies of water, or to less-traditional maritime concerns, or to more remote consequences of things that did occur in the water? Finally, is it relevant to the constitutional scope of jurisdiction that the substantive law of admiralty has been treated, for the last century or so, as a special enclave of judge-made federal common law? See Chap. VI, pp. 852–854, *supra*.[2]

(3) Methodology for Understanding the Scope of the Grant. Two noticeable themes in the admiralty cases are a certain amount of openly practical reasoning (for instance about the role of maritime commerce and the effects on it) and a certain preference for relatively predictable rules over relatively open-ended ones (especially evidenced in Grubart). Are these themes justified by the particular purpose and province of admiralty jurisdiction, or do they signal considerations that should be used more broadly in jurisdictional inquiries under the other heads of subject matter jurisdiction discussed in this chapter?

For instance, in Grubart Justice Souter defends the "familiar and relatively easy" approach in which the Court relies on "the approximate shape of admiralty jurisdiction in a way that admiralty lawyers understand reasonably well." Would one or could one make similar claims about the scope of federal jurisdiction under the test in Grable & Sons v. Darue, 545 U.S. 308 (2005), discussed p. 1040, *supra*?

(4) The Scope of Exclusivity, the Saving Clause and the Role of State Law. As with its predecessors dating back to the Judiciary Act of 1789, § 1333(1) contains an *exclusive* grant of admiralty jurisdiction as well as a "saving" clause that preserves the option of common law courts in some

---

[1]   See, *e.g.*, The Thomas Barlum, 293 U.S. 21, 42–52 (1934) (upholding the Ship Mortgage Act of 1920 and collecting other examples of expansions). See also United States v. Matson Navigation Co., 201 F.2d 610, 614–16 (9th Cir.1953) (discussing and upholding the constitutionality of the Admiralty Extension Act); Robertson & Sturley, *The Admiralty Extension Act Solution*, 34 J.Mar.L. & Com. 209, 243–63 (2003) (discussing and defending the constitutionality of the Admiralty Extension Act); Young, *It's Just Water: Toward the Normalization of Admiralty*, 35 J.Mar.L. & Com. 469, 493–96 (2004) (questioning Robertson & Sturley's understanding of the force of and constitutional basis for the Admiralty Extension Act).

[2]   Robertson & Sturley, *supra* note 5, note the "large question that has nagged U.S. maritime law for almost two centuries: To what extent does Congress have the power to enlarge the federal courts' admiralty and maritime jurisdiction?" The authors suggest that many past cases and commentary rest on an important "distinction between simply expanding the admiralty jurisdiction (which was thought to be prohibited to Congress) and redefining the substantive maritime law in a manner that effectively expands the admiralty jurisdiction (which was thought to be permitted)," and that both The Thomas Barlum and the constitutionality of the Admiralty Extension Act rest on the latter account. Is this a satisfactory account of admiralty jurisdiction, and one consistent with the treatment of "protective" jurisdiction, discussed at p. 1017, *supra*?

cases. It reads: "The district courts shall have original jurisdiction, exclusive of the courts of the States, of * * * [a]ny civil case of admiralty or maritime jurisdiction, saving to suitors in all cases all other remedies to which they are otherwise entitled."

In general, what this means is that the exclusivity of federal admiralty jurisdiction under § 1333 is limited to maritime actions brought *in rem* against a vessel or its cargo. See The Moses Taylor, 71 U.S. (4 Wall.) 411 (1866). An *in personam* action may be brought in federal admiralty court, or, where state law provides a remedy, in state court by virtue of the Saving Clause. And under the traditional division among cases in equity, at law, or in admiralty, state law actions permitted by the Saving Clause may be brought on the "law" side of the federal court if otherwise within the court's jurisdiction—*e.g.*, if diversity or supplemental jurisdiction exists.

(5) The Romero Decision.

(a) Actions in Admiralty Versus Actions at Law. Historically, admiralty was considered to be a distinct body of jurisprudence separate from law or equity, just as law and equity were historically thought to be distinct from each other. But may a claim in admiralty also be brought on the "law" side of the federal courts, under the "arising under" jurisdiction? That question seems highly conceptual, but its resolution could have important consequences; for example, in admiralty actions, unlike actions at law brought under 28 U.S.C. § 1331, jury trials are generally unavailable.

This issue was presented in Romero v. International Terminal Operating Co., 358 U.S. 354 (1959). There, an injured seaman sued for damages, asserting a statutory claim under the Jones Act, 46 U.S.C. App. § 688, and claims under general judge-made maritime law for unseaworthiness and maintenance and cure. His complaint attempted to invoke federal jurisdiction under § 1331 as well as under the Jones Act, which explicitly confers jurisdiction on the district courts over actions under the Act for a seaman's injury. The plaintiff's complaint did not invoke § 1333.

Justice Frankfurter, writing for a five-Justice majority, concluded that § 1331 did not confer federal question jurisdiction over claims arising out of judge-made maritime law. Stressing the distinctness of Article III's grants of admiralty jurisdiction and of federal question jurisdiction, he saw no reason for assuming that Congress, when it conferred general federal question jurisdiction in 1875, meant to change the historic operation of admiralty jurisdiction. If § 1331 were to embrace admiralty claims, "the sole remaining justification for the federal admiralty courts which have played such a vital role in our federal judicial system for 169 years will be to provide a federal forum for the small number of maritime claims which derive from state law, and to afford the ancient remedy of a libel *in rem* in those limited instances when an *in personam* judgment would not suffice to satisfy a claim." He objected that the expanded view of § 1331 would remove "the historic option of a maritime suitor pursuing a common-law remedy to select his forum, state or federal," since saving-clause actions would then be freely removable under 28 U.S.C. § 1441. And he added that "[i]f jurisdiction of maritime claims were allowed to be invoked under § 1331, it would become necessary for courts to decide whether the action 'arises under federal law,' and this jurisdictional decision would largely depend on whether the governing law is state or federal. Determinations of this nature are among the most difficult and subtle that federal courts are called upon to make."

But the Court did uphold § 1331 jurisdiction over the Jones Act claim, which was based on the negligence of the employer.[3] The Court then proceeded to hold that Romero's unseaworthiness and maintenance and cure claims, although they did not arise under federal law, could be heard under the district court's pendent jurisdiction, given its jurisdiction over the Jones Act claim.

Justice Brennan's dissent argued that because the causes of action for unseaworthiness and for maintenance and cure were created by federal law, Romero's case arose under federal law within the meaning of § 1331. The issue before the Court, he stressed, was narrow: it did not involve a remedy that the common law could not provide and in which suit under § 1333 was exclusive, but only actions at law under the Saving Clause, and only actions based on federal substantive law. "The issue before us is only whether the fact that an action is a Saving Clause action excludes it from § 1331 where it would otherwise be maintainable thereunder." Noting that § 1333 does not exclude the exercise of diversity jurisdiction over actions under the Saving Clause, he saw no reason why § 1333 should exclude the exercise of § 1331 jurisdiction over Romero's general maritime law claims that were based on federal law.

(b) Romero and Jury Trial. In Romero, the Court ruled on the merits that the Jones Act and unseaworthiness and maintenance and cure doctrines were inapplicable, on the facts presented, to a foreign seaman like Romero. That ruling avoided any need to reach the question whether the "pendent" claims under the general maritime law could be submitted to the jury. Four years later, the Court held that when (as is the usual case) a seaman's claims for unseaworthiness and for maintenance and cure are joined in an action under the Jones Act on the "law side" of the district court, the general maritime claims must be submitted to the jury with the Jones Act claim as a matter of trial convenience. Fitzgerald v. United States Lines, 374 U.S. 16 (1963).

Given that holding, what is the ultimate significance of the Romero decision? Is the elaborateness of treatment explained by the suggestion that its question "wakes echoes in the deepest metaphysics of admiralty"? Gilmore & Black, The Law of Admiralty 33 n.118 (1st ed.1957).[4] See also Bederman, *Romero's Enduring Legacy*, 39 J.Mar.L. & Com. 27 (2008).

---

[3] Notwithstanding Romero's holdings that actions under the Jones Act against employers for personal injuries can be brought under § 1331, some have argued that Romero does not apply to statutory claims generally. See Wetherington, *Jurisdictional Bases of Maritime Claims Founded on Acts of Congress*, 18 U.Miami L.Rev. 163 (1963).

[4] For thorough analyses, see Currie, *The Silver Oar and All That: A Study of the Romero Case*, 27 U.Chi.L.Rev. 1 (1959); Kurland, *The Romero Case and Some Problems of Federal Jurisdiction*, 73 Harv.L.Rev. 817 (1960).

7. THE SUPPLEMENTAL JURISDICTION OF THE DISTRICT COURTS

INTRODUCTORY NOTE

Litigants in federal courts often join a wide range of claims and parties in a civil action. Such bundled litigation poses questions about the scope and purpose of federal jurisdiction. On the one hand, as Chief Justice Marshall in Osborn v. Bank of the United States, p. 994, *supra*, explained, a substantial claim under federal law can confer subject matter jurisdiction over an entire case within the meaning of Article III, including non-federal claims that would not independently qualify for federal adjudication. But in Strawbridge v. Curtiss, p. 1077, *supra*, Marshall rejected proffered expansion of the scope of jurisdiction when the joinder of additional parties would destroy complete diversity of citizenship. Some two centuries later, federal courts continue to struggle with when to give effect to Osborn's whole case impulse and when to adhere to Strawbridge's narrow view of diverse-citizenship jurisdiction.

With the adoption in 1990 of the federal supplemental jurisdiction statute, 28 U.S.C. § 1367, Congress provided a statutory framework for defining the proper scope of federal jurisdiction. One can best understand the impetus for and operation of the statute by examining it against the background of leading judicial decisions. Those decisions embraced doctrines of pendent and ancillary jurisdiction that allowed federal district courts to hear some "non-federal" claims that did not independently satisfy jurisdictional requirements but bore a close relationship to "federal" claims that did. United Mine Workers of America v. Gibbs, detailed below, helped redefine the scope of federal jurisdiction following the expansion of joinder under the Federal Rules of Civil Procedure, and remains a touchstone for analysis of the scope of supplemental jurisdiction under the statute.

United Mine Workers of America v. Gibbs

383 U.S. 715 (1966).

Paul Gibbs recovered damages at trial against United Mine Workers of America (UMW) for violations of § 303 of the Labor Management Relations Act, 1947 and of the common law of Tennessee. The case grew out of the rivalry between the United Mine Workers and the Southern Labor Union over representation of workers in the southern Appalachian coal fields. Gibbs had contracts to haul coal from a mine employing SLU workers. But the UMW struck the mine. As a result, Gibbs lost his job as superintendent, never entered into performance of his haulage contract, and testified that he began to lose other trucking contracts and mine leases he held.

Before evaluating the jury's award of damages under § 303 and state law, the Court considered whether the district court properly entertained jurisdiction of the claim based on Tennessee law. In a deliberate decision to broaden the scope of pendent claim jurisdiction to take account of the expansive rules of joinder under the Federal Rules of Civil Procedure, the Court switched from the restrictive same cause of action test, as specified in Hurn v. Oursler, 289 U.S. 238 (1933), to a more expansive consideration of whether the federal and state claims arise from a common nucleus of operative fact. The Court explained:

"Hurn was decided in 1933, before the unification of law and equity by the Federal Rules of Civil Procedure. At the time, the meaning of "cause of action" was a subject of serious dispute * * *. * * *

"With the adoption of the Federal Rules of Civil Procedure and the unified form of action, much of the controversy over "cause of action" abated. The phrase remained as the keystone of the Hurn test, however, and, as commentators have noted, has been the source of considerable confusion. Under the Rules, the impulse is toward entertaining the broadest possible scope of action consistent with fairness to the parties; joinder of claims, parties and remedies is strongly encouraged. Yet because the Hurn question involves issues of jurisdiction as well as convenience, there has been some tendency to limit its application to cases in which the state and federal claims are, as in Hurn, 'little more than the equivalent of different epithets to characterize the same group of circumstances.' 289 U.S., at 246.

"This limited approach is unnecessarily grudging. Pendent jurisdiction, in the sense of judicial *power*, exists whenever there is a claim 'arising under [the] Constitution, the Laws of the United States, and Treaties made, or which shall be made, under their Authority . . .,' U.S. Const., Art. III, § 2, and the relationship between that claim and the state claim permits the conclusion that the entire action before the court comprises but one constitutional 'case.' The federal claim must have substance sufficient to confer subject matter jurisdiction on the court. The state and federal claims must derive from a common nucleus of operative fact. But if, considered without regard to their federal or state character, a plaintiff's claims are such that he would ordinarily be expected to try them all in one judicial proceeding, then, assuming substantiality of the federal issues, there is *power* in federal courts to hear the whole.[13]

"That power need not be exercised in every case in which it is found to exist. It has consistently been recognized that pendent jurisdiction is a doctrine of discretion, not of plaintiff's right. Its justification lies in considerations of judicial economy, convenience and fairness to litigants; if these are not present a federal court should hesitate to exercise jurisdiction over state claims, even though bound to apply state law to them, Erie R. Co. v. Tompkins, 304 U.S. 64 (1938). Needless decisions of state law should be avoided both as a matter of comity and to promote justice between the parties, by procuring for them a surer-footed reading of applicable law. Certainly, if the federal claims are dismissed before trial, even though not insubstantial in a jurisdictional sense, the state claims should be dismissed as well. Similarly, if it appears that the state issues substantially

---

[13] * * * While it is commonplace that the Federal Rules of Civil Procedure do not expand the jurisdiction of federal courts, they do embody "the whole tendency of our decisions . . . to require a plaintiff to try his . . . whole case at one time," Baltimore S.S. Co. v. Phillips, 274 U.S. 316 (1927), and to that extent emphasize the basis of pendent jurisdiction.

predominate, whether in terms of proof, of the scope of the issues raised, or of the comprehensiveness of the remedy sought, the state claims may be dismissed without prejudice and left for resolution to state tribunals. There may, on the other hand, be situations in which the state claim is so closely tied to questions of federal policy that the argument for exercise of pendent jurisdiction is particularly strong. In the present case, for example, the allowable scope of the state claim implicates the federal doctrine of pre-emption; while this interrelationship does not create statutory federal question jurisdiction, Louisville & N. R. Co. v. Mottley, 211 U.S. 149 (1908), its existence is relevant to the exercise of discretion. Finally, there may be reasons independent of jurisdictional considerations, such as the likelihood of jury confusion in treating divergent legal theories of relief, that would justify separating state and federal claims for trial. If so, jurisdiction should ordinarily be refused.

"The question of power will ordinarily be resolved on the pleadings. But the issue whether pendent jurisdiction has been properly assumed is one which remains open throughout the litigation. Pretrial procedures or even the trial itself may reveal a substantial hegemony of state-law claims, or likelihood of jury confusion, which could not have been anticipated at the pleading stage. Although it will of course be appropriate to take account in this circumstance of the already completed course of the litigation, dismissal of the state claim might even then be merited. For example, it may appear that the plaintiff was well aware of the nature of his proofs and the relative importance of his claims; recognition of a federal court's wide latitude to decide ancillary questions of state law does not imply that it must tolerate a litigant's effort to impose upon it what is in effect only a state law case. Once it appears that a state claim constitutes the real body of a case, to which the federal claim is only an appendage, the state claim may fairly be dismissed."

Having formulated a regime of discretion, the Court concluded that the district court had not erred in proceeding to judgment on the state claim. "It is true that the § 303 claims ultimately failed and that the only recovery allowed respondent was on the state claim. We cannot confidently say, however, that the federal issues were so remote or played such a minor role at the trial that in effect the state claim only was tried. * * * Moreover, the question whether the permissible scope of the state claim was limited by the doctrine of pre-emption afforded a special reason for the exercise of pendent jurisdiction; the federal courts are particularly appropriate bodies for the application of pre-emption principles. We thus conclude that although it may be that the district court might, in its sound discretion, have dismissed the state claim, the circumstances show no error in refusing to do so."

NOTE ON SUPPLEMENTAL JURISDICTION IN FEDERAL QUESTION AND OTHER NONDIVERSITY CASES

(1) The Rationale and Consequences of the Gibbs Rule. In assessing the justifications for supplemental jurisdiction, note first that Chief Justice Marshall's opinion in Osborn does not necessarily lead to the result in Gibbs.

Marshall upheld federal court power to adjudicate non-federal questions that were intermingled with questions federal law in a single claim for relief. No such justification is available, however, for the pendent jurisdiction at issue in Gibbs; decision of the federal claim under § 303 did not necessitate decision of the separate state-law claims for tortious interference with business relations. Nor can Gibbs be justified solely by the policy of avoiding piecemeal litigation; when Congress (as it usually does) allows state courts to exercise concurrent jurisdiction over federal claims, state courts offer a forum for consolidated litigation of federal and state claims.

Consider, however, whether the denial of supplemental jurisdiction in a case like Gibbs might burden the federal plaintiff's congressionally conferred right to a federal forum for the adjudication of his federal claims. Without supplemental jurisdiction, a litigant like Gibbs could bring separate state court and federal court actions, but doing so would be costly and could create claim preclusion problems if the state case comes to judgment first. Alternatively, Gibbs could consolidate his claims in a single action in state court—thereby surrendering his right to a federal forum on the federal claim. And when a federal plaintiff's claim falls within exclusive federal jurisdiction, then, absent supplemental jurisdiction, pursuit of both claims would require separate federal and state court actions. Many, but perhaps not quite all, observers regard these concerns of litigation efficiency and convenience as establishing a persuasive argument for the result in Gibbs.[1]

(2) The Statutory and Constitutional Bases of the Gibbs Holding. The Gibbs opinion focuses on whether Article III permits the exercise of what it describes as pendent jurisdiction. If so, the Court assumes that the federal courts have power to hear the whole case and "discretion" in deciding whether to do so. But the Court's analysis does not focus directly on the text of the statute granting subject matter jurisdiction. The opinion does not mention either § 303(b) (conferring a federal right to recover damages for secondary boycotts) or § 1331 (conferring jurisdiction over "civil actions" that arise under federal law).[2]

Consider how the Court might have understood the statutory grant of jurisdiction over "civil actions" to apply. In Gibbs, the civil action consisted of at least two different claims for relief: one federal claim under § 303 for secondary boycott damages and one non-federal claim under state law for a business tort. The Court may have viewed the two separate but closely related claims as comprising a single civil action for statutory purposes, just as they were part of a single case for Article III purposes. See McLaughlin, *The Federal Supplemental Jurisdiction Statute: A Constitutional and Statutory Analysis*, 24 Ariz.St.L.J. 849 (1992).

---

[1]   Professor Bone thinks not. He notes that most cases settle; contends that absent two trials, the cost of litigating in different courts is not so great (*e.g.*, discovery in one action may be usable in the other); and suggests that claim preclusion difficulties could be addressed directly by eliminating interjurisdictional preclusion. See Bone, *Revisiting the Policy Case for Supplemental Jurisdiction*, 74 Ind.L.J. 139 (1998).

[2]   Is it at all significant that § 1331 speaks of "civil actions" while Article III speaks of "cases"?

Understanding the distinction between a civil action, as a unit of jurisdictional analysis, and the specific claims that make up the civil action helps to clarify both the development and application of supplemental jurisdiction. It will often simplify analysis to follow the analytical framework proposed by the American Law Institute's Federal Judicial Code Revision Project 5–7 (2004). In analyzing supplemental jurisdiction anchored by claims arising under federal law, as in Gibbs, the ALI suggests that a court should ask not whether it has jurisdiction over an entire action. Instead, the analysis should consider (i) whether it has jurisdiction over a "freestanding" federal question claim and (ii) if so, whether another claim not within federal question jurisdiction may be adjudicated based on its relationship to the freestanding claim. The ALI refers to this as a "claim-specific" approach to supplemental jurisdiction.[3] As will be seen in the next case and more generally, a claim-specific approach presents challenges when the "freestanding" claim qualifies for federal adjudication on the basis of citizenship diversity.

Owen Equipment & Erection Co. v. Kroger

437 U.S. 365 (1978).

In this case, Kroger (a citizen of Iowa) first sued Omaha Public Power District (a citizen of Nebraska) in federal court on the basis of diversity, seeking redress for the death of her husband. The complaint alleged that Kroger was electrocuted while walking past a crane near an electrical line owned and operated by OPPD. In due course, OPPD filed a third-party complaint under Fed.R.Civ.P. 14 against the owner of the allegedly defective or mishandled crane, Owen Equipment. Sometime later, Kroger added a direct claim against the third-party defendant, Owen. Complicating these assertions of jurisdiction, Owen was both a citizen of Nebraska and a citizen of Iowa, meaning that there was no diversity of citizenship to support either OPPD's third-party claim or the plaintiff's direct claim against Owen. After OPPD's dismissal from the action, the jury returned a verdict for Kroger against Owen, deeming Owen responsible for the accident. Owen unsuccessfully challenged the jurisdiction of the district court to enter a judgment, pointing to the absence of diversity between plaintiff and defendant. On appeal, the Eighth Circuit upheld the judgment, reasoning that Kroger's claim against Owen arose from the same common nucleus of operative fact and thereby met the requirements for supplemental jurisdiction announced in Gibbs.

Reversing in a 7–2 decision, the Court, per Justice Stewart, held that there was no jurisdiction over Kroger's claim against Owen. While conceding that Article III was not a bar to the federal court's exercise of jurisdiction over the claim, the Court emphasized instead the statutory requirement of complete diversity. The Court acknowledged that the doctrine of ancillary jurisdiction, traceable to Freeman v. Howe, 65 U.S. (24 How.) 450 (1860), had created exceptions to the complete diversity rule; indeed, the Court indicated that ancillary jurisdiction had been properly extended to the third-party

---

[3] *Cf.* 28 U.S.C. §§ 1338(a), 1454, p. 1066, *supra* (provisions enacted in 2011 that move in the direction of asking whether a claim for relief arises under federal law).

claim of OPPD as well as to many other defensive claims such as counterclaims, crossclaims, and interventions of right. See 437 U.S. at 375 n.18. But the Court found no justification for the doctrine's application in the circumstances of the case. Rather than an ancillary or defensive claim, Kroger's was a "new and independent one." Allowance of ancillary jurisdiction would encourage future plaintiffs to circumvent the complete diversity rule by naming only the completely diverse defendant (OPPD), awaiting the predictable impleader of a non-diverse defendant (Owen), and then pursuing claims against the newly joined non-diverse defendant. Justice White, dissenting for himself and Justice Brennan, argued that the result was not required by any rule of constitutional or statutory jurisdiction, that it too casually brushed aside considerations of "convenience, judicial economy, and fairness."

NOTE ON THE ORIGINS OF ANCILLARY JURISDICTION IN DIVERSITY

The exercise of supplemental jurisdiction in diversity runs up against the complete diversity requirement, which forecloses jurisdiction over related claims against non-diverse parties. Had the plaintiff Kroger joined claims against OPPD and Owen at the outset, the civil action would fail the complete diversity test even though the claims satisfied Gibbs' common nucleus test. Traditionally, in assessing diversity, courts have evaluated the civil action as a whole. And, a strict application of Strawbridge rules out, in its interpretation of the diversity statute, the notion that one might anchor diversity jurisdiction with a "freestanding" claim against a diverse defendant and then join an additional claim against a non-diverse defendant.

(1) Origins of Ancillary Jurisdiction in Diversity. As Kroger suggests, however, a doctrine of ancillary jurisdiction arose in diversity litigation that side-stepped the complete diversity rule. Convention, as reflected in Kroger, traces ancillary jurisdiction to Freeman v. Howe, 65 U.S. 450 (1860), but the doctrine has deep roots in the practice of courts of equity in the nineteenth century. Briefly, when a court seized control of property and brought it within the "custody of the court," other courts were barred from interfering with its administrative priority. Chapter X explores in greater detail the implications of such priority for the development of rules to coordinate overlapping state and federal jurisdiction. But exclusive federal control could pose problems if the complete diversity rules would block the federal court from adjudicating competing claims to the property. The Freeman Court solved that problem by allowing the non-diverse claimant to file an ancillary bill in equity. As the Court explained: "The principle is, that a bill filed on the equity side of the [federal] court to restrain or regulate judgments or suits at law in the same court, and thereby prevent injustice, or an inequitable advantage under mesne or final process, is not an original suit, but ancillary and dependent, supplementary merely to the original suit, out of which it had arisen, and is maintained without reference to the citizenship or residence of the parties."

(2) The Growth of Ancillary Jurisdiction. In time, the rule of Freeman v. Howe led to the use of ancillary jurisdiction to support nineteenth-century equitable receiverships, which came to operate something like bankruptcy administration. In such proceedings, judgment creditors who satisfied the diversity requirement would file a bill to initiate a receivership, naming the debtor (often a railroad company) as defendant and inviting the court to appoint a receiver to administer the railroad's property for the protection of creditors. Such an appointment would establish administrative priority and force all parties with competing claims to the railroad's property to satisfy them in the context of the receivership; on the logic of Freeman, it would necessitate ancillary jurisdiction to encompass all such claims without regard to diversity. See Reihle v. Margolies, 279 U.S. 218, 223 (1929) ("The appointment of a receiver of a debtor's property by a federal court confers upon it, regardless of citizenship and of the amount in controversy, federal jurisdiction to decide all questions incident to the preservation, collection, and distribution of the assets.").

The Court developed rules to govern the use of intervention that were layered atop the distinction between complete diversity (required at the outset) and ancillary jurisdiction (available after initial filing). The Court thus sometimes allowed parties to intervene in litigation without insisting on maintaining complete diversity. See, *e.g.*, Phelps v. Oaks, 117 U.S. 236 (1886); Wichita R.R. & Light Co. v. Public Util. Comm'n, 260 U.S. 48 (1922) (jurisdiction once acquired is not "defeated by the intervention, by leave of the court, of a party whose presence is not essential to a decision of the controversy between the original parties"). But when the party was thought to have been essential to the proper resolution of the claims from the outset, the Court regarded that party as part of the complete diversity calculus and refused to expand the litigation unit. See, *e.g.*, Kentucky Natural Gas Corp. v. Duggins, 165 F.2d 1011 (6th Cir.1948); Chance v. County Bd., 332 F.2d 971 (7th Cir.1964). In such cases, there was no preexisting jurisdiction to which the intervention could be regarded as ancillary.

Ancillary jurisdiction also shaped the development of class action litigation, and in time the rule emerged that the citizenship of a class action must be determined by reference to the named plaintiffs, rather than all class members. The issue arose in Supreme Tribe of Ben-Hur v. Cauble, 255 U.S. 356 (1921), a class action suit contesting the devaluation of beneficial membership in an Indiana-based fraternal organization. The first action, brought by plaintiffs from outside Indiana in federal court, resulted in a judgment favorable to the association. The second action, brought by Indiana citizens in state court, sought to litigate the same questions. The Supreme Court ruled that the federal court should grant a requested injunction against further prosecution of the Indiana state court proceeding; the state court plaintiffs were bound by the earlier decision on behalf of all members. Acknowledging that the Indiana plaintiffs would have destroyed complete diversity had they joined the federal suit at the outset, the Court explained that intervention after the suit began "would not have defeated the jurisdiction already acquired." In effect, the citizenship of the representatives rather than that of the entire class came to define class citizenship for diversity, at least in cases where the interrelationship of the class interests would trigger what today would be viewed as a class action under Fed.R.Civ.P. 23(b)(1).

Eventually, ancillary jurisdiction lost its connection to the administration of property brought within the custody of a court of equity and came to support forms of jurisdiction based on litigation convenience. In Kroger, the Court refers to a variety of such accepted forms of relatedness jurisdiction: that over cross claims, counterclaims, and impleader actions in contexts (like Kroger itself) where the initial suit itself does not present issues of equitable administration. But the acceptance of ancillary jurisdiction to expand litigation after a suit begins did not alter the Court's insistence on the relatively strict application of complete diversity rules at the outset. Thus, for example, the Court consistently refused to permit multiple plaintiffs to aggregate *in personam* claims to satisfy the amount in controversy. See Zahn v. Int'l Paper Co., 414 U.S. 291, 301 (1973) (federal court, in a class action, lacks jurisdiction over any plaintiff whose claim falls short of the jurisdictional amount); Snyder v. Harris, 394 U.S. 332 (1969) (no aggregation of plaintiffs' claims to satisfy amount in controversy requirement).

Finley v. United States

490 U.S. 545 (1989).

Pendent claim jurisdiction as applied in Gibbs allowed only the addition of related non-federal claims against a party already properly before a federal court on a claim within federal question jurisdiction. Some lower courts also authorized "pendent party" jurisdiction over related non-federal claims against a defendant who could not be otherwise sued in federal court. In one example of such a configuration of parties, Finley sued the United States under the Federal Tort Claims Act (FTCA), alleging that the FAA's negligence caused a plane crash in which her husband and two of her children died. The FTCA confers exclusive federal court jurisdiction over such claims. The question presented was whether the federal district court could exercise jurisdiction over a state-law tort claim against the (non-diverse) city of San Diego and the local electric company (whose transmission lines the plane had struck) arising out of the same events.

Justice Scalia's majority opinion for a closely divided (5–4) Court broadly rejected pendent party jurisdiction. The Court rested on the principle that federal court jurisdiction must be within the bounds of Article III and also conferred by act of Congress. On the Article III question, the Court "assume[d], without deciding, that the constitutional criterion for pendent-party jurisdiction is analogous to Gibbs' constitutional criterion for pendent-claim jurisdiction, and that [plaintiff's] state-law claims pass that test." But in the Court's view, Gibbs' assertion of jurisdiction over pendent claims, "without specific examination of jurisdictional statutes," was in tension with the principle that jurisdiction must be conferred by Congress. The Court continued: "Our cases show * * * that with respect to the addition of parties, as opposed to the addition of only claims, we will not assume that the full constitutional power has been congressionally authorized, and will not read jurisdictional statutes broadly." Here, the Court cited both the diversity precedents, Zahn and Kroger, as well as Aldinger v. Howard, 427 U.S. 1 (1976), which rejected pendent party in a case arising under 42 U.S.C. § 1983 on less sweeping terms. Justice Scalia recognized that because of the exclusivity of federal jurisdiction over FTCA actions against the federal government, the Court's decision would require plaintiff to file two suits, one in state court and one in federal court, but he viewed that result as an inevitability under the limitations of existing jurisdictional grants to the federal courts.

NOTE ON THE LEGISLATIVE RESPONSE: 28 U.S.C. § 1367

Following considerable criticism of Finley, the Federal Courts Study Committee recommended that the decision be legislatively overruled, and Congress responded by adding § 1367 to Title 28 as part of the Judicial Improvements Act of 1990, 104 Stat. 5089. See Mengler, Burbank & Rowe, *Congress Accepts Supreme Court's Invitation to Codify Supplemental Jurisdiction*, 74 Judicature 213 (1991). Section 1367 substitutes the term "supplemental" jurisdiction for the prevailing (and often confusing) references to pendent and ancillary jurisdiction. Section 1367 broadly confers supplemental jurisdiction, including pendent party jurisdiction, while otherwise seeking to codify existing decisional law.[1]

Subsection (a) provides in sweeping terms that (except as stated in subsections (b) and (c) or in another federal law) a district court with original jurisdiction over a "civil action" "shall have supplemental jurisdiction over all other claims" that "form part of the same case or controversy under Article III"—including claims involving additional parties (thus overruling Finley). Subsection (b), which applies to diversity cases, excepts from the scope of subsection (a) a variety of claims by plaintiffs against additional parties, or by persons proposed to be joined or seeking to intervene, "when exercising supplement jurisdiction over such claims would be inconsistent with the jurisdictional requirements of [28 U.S.C. §] 1332."

(1) The Scope of Supplemental Jurisdiction in Nondiversity Cases. Section § 1367(a) speaks in broad terms, and thus governs admiralty as well as cases generally "arising under" federal law. Section 1367 also contemplates the availability of supplemental jurisdiction with respect to such devices as counterclaims, crossclaims, intervention, and permissive and necessary joinder, so long as the specified criteria are met. See generally McLaughlin, *The Federal Supplemental Jurisdiction Statute—A Constitutional and Statutory Analysis*, 24 Ariz.St.L.J. 849, 925–34 (1992).

---

[1]   Prior to enactment of § 1367, 28 U.S.C. § 1338(b), as set forth by the 1948 Revision of the Judicial Code, had conferred jurisdiction over "a claim of unfair competition when joined with a substantial and related claim under the copyright, patent or trade-mark laws." That provision was designed to codify the decision in Hurn v. Oursler, 289 U.S. 238 (1933), discussed in the Gibbs opinion. See generally 13B Wright, Miller & Cooper, Federal Practice and Procedure § 3582.

There remain, however, a number of questions concerning the application of § 1367 in federal question and other nondiversity litigation, only some of which have been resolved by decisions to date. These include at the outset questions concerning the constitutional reach of § 1367.

Specifically, what is the permissible reach of jurisdiction over "all other claims that are so related to claims in the action within * * * original jurisdiction that they form part of the same case or controversy under Article III"? Must there be a "common nucleus of operative fact," as required by Gibbs, or are the constitutional bounds broad enough to reach other kinds of relationships?

Permissive counterclaims, for example, by definition do not arise "out of the transaction or occurrence that is the subject matter of the opposing party's claim," Fed.R.Civ.P. 13(a), and thus generally will not share a common nucleus of operative fact with the plaintiff's claim. But Professor McLaughlin argues that a "logical relationship" to the claim over which arising under jurisdiction does exist is constitutionally sufficient, and thus he argues that in some instances permissive counterclaims, as well as some permissive joinder, may qualify. See McLaughlin, *supra*. Three circuits have held that at least some permissive counterclaims, which once were thought to require an independent basis of jurisdiction, fall within the scope of § 1367.[2]

Professor Matasar takes a still broader view of the permissible scope of § 1367. Arguing that Gibbs' conflation of statutory and constitutional tests unduly restricted the latter, he contends that the only limit to supplemental jurisdiction under Article III is the existence of a case or controversy as defined under lawfully adopted procedural rules for the joinder of claims and parties, and that no common nucleus of operative fact is constitutionally required. Matasar, *Rediscovering "One Constitutional Case": Procedural Rules and the Rejection of the Gibbs Test for Supplemental Jurisdiction*, 71 Calif.L.Rev. 1399 (1983).

Professor Floyd responds that Matasar's approach would give Congress essentially unlimited power. Supplemental jurisdiction, he argues, should extend only as far as is necessary to permit the federal courts to perform the tasks assigned to them by Article III. Applying that standard, he approves of supplemental jurisdiction over permissive counterclaims, without which, he contends, defendants would be unfairly deprived of security for the payment of their own claims. But he disapproves of supplemental jurisdiction over claims filed under Fed.R.Civ.P. 18, which permits a party asserting one claim against another party to join with that claim any other claim, no matter how unrelated, against the same party. See Floyd, *Three Faces of Supplemental Jurisdiction After the Demise of United Mine Workers v. Gibbs*, 60 Fla.L.Rev. 277 (2008).

(2) Other Issues in the Application of § 1367. In addition to complicated questions raised by § 1367(b)'s interaction with diversity jurisdiction grant

---

[2]   See Jones v. Ford Motor Credit Co., 358 F.3d 205, 213 (2d Cir.2004); Channell v. Citicorp Nat'l Servs., Inc., 89 F.3d 379, 384–87 (7th Cir.1996); Global Naps, Inc. v. Verizon New Eng. Inc., 603 F.3d 71, 76 (1st Cir.2010).

in § 1332, explored below, several other matters arise in the application of § 1367.

(a) Discretion to Decline. Section 1367(c) rejects the language in Gibbs appearing to *require* dismissal of the supplemental claim if the federal claim is disposed of before trial. But does the statute alter the criteria that a district court should consider in deciding whether to exercise supplemental jurisdiction? The legislative history can be read to suggest that Congress meant to codify the judge-made principles set forth in Gibbs and other decisions.[3] However, some courts have read the specific list of four factors in § 1367(c) as narrowing the scope of district court discretion by excluding consideration of the "fairness" or "efficiency" concerns articulated in Gibbs or of any other concern not set forth in the statute. See Sherry, *Logic Without Experience: The Problem of Federal Appellate Courts*, 82 Notre Dame L.Rev. 97, 125–26 (2006).

(b) Tolling the Statute of Limitations. Section 1367(d) specifies the time period in which an asserted supplemental claim that is later dismissed may be refiled in state court. It provides that the state law period of limitations for any such claim "shall be tolled while the claim is pending [in federal court] and for a period of 30 days after it is dismissed unless State law provides for a longer tolling period." In Artis v. District of Columbia, 583 U.S. 71 (2018), the Court, in an opinion by Justice Ginsburg for five Justices, rejected the view that § 1367(d) permits the state limitation period to run during the pendency of the supplemental claim but imposes a 30-day grace period to refile. It instead held that § 1367(d) "stops the clock" on the state limitations period during the claim's pendency in federal court, thereby giving the plaintiff whatever time remained under state law on the stopped clock, plus 30 days, to refile. The Court reasoned that this conclusion best comported with the language of subsection (d) and the dominant usage of the term "tolled."[4]

The Court rejected the argument that § 1367(d), so interpreted, exceeds Congress's enumerated powers. Relying on Jinks v. Richland County, 538 U.S. 456 (2003) (rejecting constitutional objections to § 1367(d)'s 30-day grace period for claim refiled in state court and otherwise time-barred there), the Artis Court ruled that the subsection was "necessary and proper" for carrying out Congress's power to establish inferior federal courts in a fair and efficient manner because it provides an alternative to the unsatisfactory options that federal courts otherwise faced when deciding whether to retain jurisdiction over supplemental claims that might be time-barred in state court. The Court further ruled that the provision does not unduly infringe state sovereignty. It acknowledged that a different interpretation of the

---

[3] Possibly supporting this view is language in the Supreme Court's decision in City of Chicago v. International College of Surgeons, Paragraph (1)(b), *supra*: " '[D]istrict courts [should] deal with cases involving pendent claims in the manner that best serves the principles of economy, convenience, fairness, and comity which underlie the pendent jurisdiction doctrine' " [and] "[t]he supplemental jurisdiction statute codifies these principles." 522 U.S. at 172–73 (citation omitted; alterations in original).

[4] *Cf.* Harrow v. Department of Defense, 144 S.Ct 1178 (2024) (holding that 5 U.S.C. § 7703(b)(1)'s 60-day filing deadline for a federal employee to petition the Federal Circuit to review a final decision of the Merit Systems Protection Board is not jurisdictional).

"grace period" in § 1367(d) might be less intrusive on state authority, but ruled that the Constitution did not limit Congress's discretion to that degree. Justice Gorsuch, joined by Justices Kennedy, Thomas, and Alito, dissented. He disagreed with the Court's interpretation of § 1367(d) and expressed particular concern about its impact on state authority to define time limitations on state law claims.

(c) **Remand: Total or Partial?** Section 1367(c) states that a federal court may refuse to exercise supplemental jurisdiction, but leaves open the question whether the court may remand to state court the entire case or only the state-law claims. Most decisions have held that a federal court must retain jurisdiction over properly removed federal claims. See Steinman, *Crosscurrents: Supplemental Jurisdiction, Removal, and the ALI Revision Project*, 74 Ind.L.J. 76, 107–09 (1998).

(3) **The Role of the Courts and of Congress.** One might characterize the Finley decision and the legislature's response as an example of successful dialogue between the Court and Congress. On the contrary, one might understand the statute as a specific remonstrance to a Court that had taken too crabbed a view of the scope of federal jurisdiction. On this view, Justice Scalia's approach in the Finley case reduced judicial flexibility to shape the contours of supplemental jurisdiction, requiring Congress to take on that responsibility. Granted that Congress sets the broad parameters of judicial power, many of the rules collected in this chapter represent judicial elaborations of general statutory directives. (Consider, in this regard, the well-pleaded complaint rule, see p. 1025, *supra*.)

Note that the legislative response, though it authorizes pendent party jurisdiction, does not overturn the Finley Court's interpretive emphasis on congressional specificity in jurisdictional statutes. Indeed, § 1367 provides a relatively detailed specification of jurisdictional rules tends to instantiate the Finley Court's jurisprudential commitment to legislative primacy and interpretive textualism. In thinking about the various interpretive approaches represented in the supplement jurisdiction caselaw (*e.g.*, in comparing Gibbs to Finley), consider the institutional competence of Congress to address unforeseen consequences in detailed efforts to codify. In Professor Shapiro's view, the better approach would have been for Congress to adopt a general grant, with details to be worked out by the courts. See Shapiro, *Supplemental Jurisdiction: A Confession, an Avoidance, and a Proposal*, 74 Ind.L.J. 211, 218 (1998); see also Meltzer, *The Supreme Court's Judicial Passivity*, 2002 Sup.Ct.Rev. 343, 396–403 (2003) (suggesting the same). True, courts might struggle to work out some elements, such as the 30-day tolling provision in § 1367(d). But other problems might yield more readily to judicial elaboration, as the next principal case might be read to illustrate.

Exxon Mobil Corporation v. Allapattah Services, Inc.

545 U.S. 546 (2005).
Certiorari to the United States Court of Appeals for the Eleventh Circuit.

■ JUSTICE KENNEDY delivered the opinion of the Court.

These consolidated cases present the question whether a federal court in a diversity action may exercise supplemental jurisdiction over additional plaintiffs whose claims do not satisfy the minimum amount-in-controversy requirement, provided the claims are part of the same case or controversy as the claims of plaintiffs who do allege a sufficient amount in controversy. Our decision turns on the correct interpretation of 28 U.S.C. § 1367. * * *

We hold that, where the other elements of jurisdiction are present and at least one named plaintiff in the action satisfies the amount-in-controversy requirement, § 1367 does authorize supplemental jurisdiction over the claims of other plaintiffs in the same Article III case or controversy, even if those claims are for less than the jurisdictional amount specified in the statute setting forth the requirements for diversity jurisdiction. * * *

I

[In both of the two cases consolidated for decision, at least one of the named plaintiffs asserted a claim in excess of the statutory amount-in-controversy threshold ($75,000). But other plaintiffs asserted below-threshold claims, arguing that § 1367 overrode the traditional rule that all claimants must satisfy the amount-in-controversy requirement on their own. In one case, a class action against Exxon Mobil, the Eleventh Circuit had upheld supplemental jurisdiction over the claims of all members of a plaintiff class, joined under Fed.R.Civ.P. 23, to recoup certain fuel price overcharges. In the second case, a child and certain family members asserted personal injury and related claims against Star Kist after the child suffered a serious injury from a tuna can; family members joined the child's claim under Fed.R.Civ.P. 20. The First Circuit held that § 1367 did not permit the exercise of jurisdiction over the individuals claims that did not independently satisfy § 1332's amount-in-controversy requirement.]

II

A

* * * Although the district courts may not exercise jurisdiction absent a statutory basis, it is well established—in certain classes of cases—that, once a court has original jurisdiction over some claims in the action, it may exercise supplemental jurisdiction over additional claims that are part of the same case or controversy. The leading modern case for this principle is Mine Workers v. Gibbs, 383 U.S. 715 (1966). * * *

We have not, however, applied Gibbs' expansive interpretive approach to other aspects of the jurisdictional statutes. For instance, we have consistently interpreted § 1332 as requiring complete diversity * * *. The complete diversity requirement is not mandated by the Constitution, State Farm Fire & Casualty Co. v. Tashire, 386 U.S. 523, 530–531 (1967), or by the plain text of § 1332(a). The Court, nonetheless, has adhered to the complete diversity rule in light of the purpose of the diversity requirement, which is to provide a federal forum for important disputes where state courts might favor, or be perceived as favoring, home-state litigants. * * *

In contrast to the diversity requirement, most of the other statutory prerequisites for federal jurisdiction, including the federal-question and amount-in-controversy requirements, can be analyzed claim by claim. True, it does not follow by necessity from this that a district court has authority to exercise supplemental jurisdiction over all claims provided there is original jurisdiction over just one. Before the enactment of § 1367, the Court declined in contexts other than the pendent-claim instance to follow Gibbs' expansive approach to interpretation of the jurisdictional statutes. The Court took a more restrictive view of the proper interpretation of these statutes in so-called pendent-party cases involving supplemental jurisdiction over claims involving additional parties—plaintiffs or defendants—where the district courts would lack original jurisdiction over claims by each of the parties standing alone.

Thus, with respect to plaintiff-specific jurisdictional requirements, the Court held in Clark v. Paul Gray, Inc., 306 U.S. 583 (1939), that every plaintiff must separately satisfy the amount-in-controversy requirement [in a federal question case]. * * * The Court reaffirmed this rule, in the context of a class action brought invoking § 1332(a) diversity jurisdiction, in Zahn v. International Paper Co., 414 U.S. 291 (1973). It follows "inescapably" from Clark, the Court held in Zahn, that "any plaintiff without the jurisdictional amount must be dismissed from the case, even though others allege jurisdictionally sufficient claims." 414 U.S., at 300.

The Court took a similar approach with respect to supplemental jurisdiction over claims against additional defendants that fall outside the district courts' original jurisdiction. [Here the Court discussed Aldinger v. Howard and Finley v. United States, 490 U.S. 545 (1989), p. 1117, supra.]

As the jurisdictional statutes existed in 1989, then, here is how matters stood: First, the diversity requirement in § 1332(a) required complete diversity * * *. Second, if the district court had original jurisdiction over at least one claim, the jurisdictional statutes implicitly authorized supplemental jurisdiction over all other claims between the same parties arising out of the same Article III case or controversy. Third, even when the district court had original jurisdiction over one or more claims between particular parties, the jurisdictional statutes did not authorize supplemental jurisdiction over additional claims involving other parties.

B

In Finley we emphasized that "[w]hatever we say regarding the scope of jurisdiction conferred by a particular statute can of course be changed by Congress." 490 U.S., at 556. In 1990, Congress accepted the invitation. * * *

Section 1367 provides, in relevant part:

"(a) Except as provided in subsections (b) and (c) or as expressly provided otherwise by Federal statute, in any civil action of which the district courts have original jurisdiction, the district courts shall have supplemental jurisdiction over all other claims that are so related to claims in the action within such original jurisdiction that they form part of the same case or controversy under Article III of the United States Constitution. Such supplemental jurisdiction shall include claims that involve the joinder or intervention of additional parties.

"(b) In any civil action of which the district courts have original jurisdiction founded solely on section 1332 of this title, the district courts shall not have supplemental jurisdiction under subsection (a) over claims by plaintiffs against persons made parties under Rule 14, 19, 20, or 24 of the Federal Rules of Civil Procedure, or over claims by persons proposed to be joined as plaintiffs under Rule 19 of such rules, or seeking to intervene as plaintiffs under Rule 24 of such rules, when exercising supplemental jurisdiction over such claims would be inconsistent with the jurisdictional requirements of section 1332."

All parties to this litigation and all courts to consider the question agree that § 1367 overturned the result in Finley. There is no warrant, however, for assuming that § 1367 did no more than to overrule Finley and otherwise to codify the existing state of the law of supplemental jurisdiction. We must not give jurisdictional statutes a more expansive interpretation than their text warrants, but it is just as important not to adopt an artificial construction that is narrower than what the text provides. * * *

Section 1367(a) is a broad grant of supplemental jurisdiction over other claims within the same case or controversy, as long as the action is one in which the district courts would have original jurisdiction. The last sentence of § 1367(a) makes it clear that the grant of supplemental jurisdiction extends to claims involving joinder or intervention of additional parties. The single question before us, therefore, is whether a diversity case in which the claims of some plaintiffs satisfy the amount-in-controversy requirement, but the claims of other plaintiffs do not, presents a "civil action of which the district courts have original jurisdiction." * * *

We now conclude the answer must be yes. When the well-pleaded complaint contains at least one claim that satisfies the amount-in-controversy requirement, and there are no other relevant jurisdictional defects, the district court, beyond all question, has original jurisdiction over that claim. The presence of other claims in the complaint, over which the district court may lack original jurisdiction, is of no moment. If the court has original jurisdiction over a single claim in the complaint, it has original jurisdiction over a "civil action" within the meaning of § 1367(a), even if the civil action over which it has jurisdiction comprises fewer claims than were included in the complaint. Once the court determines it has original jurisdiction over the civil action, it can turn to the question whether it has a constitutional and statutory basis for exercising supplemental jurisdiction over the other claims in the action. * * *

If § 1367(a) were the sum total of the relevant statutory language, our holding would rest on that language alone. The statute, of course, instructs us to examine § 1367(b) to determine if any of its exceptions apply, so we proceed to that section. While § 1367(b) qualifies the broad rule of § 1367(a), it does not withdraw supplemental jurisdiction over the claims of the additional parties at issue here. The specific exceptions to § 1367(a) contained in § 1367(b), moreover, provide additional support for our conclusion that § 1367(a) confers supplemental jurisdiction over these claims. Section 1367(b), which applies only to diversity cases, withholds supplemental jurisdiction over the claims of plaintiffs proposed to be joined as indispensable parties under Federal Rule of Civil Procedure 19, or who seek to intervene pursuant to Rule 24. Nothing in the text of § 1367(b), however, withholds supplemental jurisdiction over the claims of plaintiffs permissively joined under Rule 20 * * * or certified as class-action members pursuant to Rule 23 * * *. The natural, indeed the necessary, inference is that § 1367 confers supplemental jurisdiction over claims by Rule 20 and Rule 23 plaintiffs. This inference, at least with respect to Rule 20 plaintiffs, is strengthened by the fact that § 1367(b) explicitly excludes supplemental jurisdiction over claims against defendants joined under Rule 20.

We cannot accept the view * * * that a district court lacks original jurisdiction over a civil action unless the court has original jurisdiction over every claim in the complaint. As we understand this position, it requires assuming either that all claims in the complaint must stand or fall as a single, indivisible "civil action" as a matter of definitional necessity—what we will refer to as the "indivisibility theory"—or else that the inclusion of a claim or party falling outside the district court's original jurisdiction somehow contaminates every other claim in the complaint, depriving the court of original jurisdiction over any of these claims—what we will refer to as the "contamination theory."

The indivisibility theory is easily dismissed, as it is inconsistent with the whole notion of supplemental jurisdiction. If a district court must have original jurisdiction over every claim in the complaint in order to have "original jurisdiction" over a "civil action," then in Gibbs there was no civil action of which the district court could assume original jurisdiction under § 1331, and so no basis for exercising supplemental jurisdiction over any of the claims. The indivisibility theory is further belied by our practice—in both federal-question and diversity cases—of allowing federal courts to cure jurisdictional defects by dismissing the offending parties rather than dismissing the entire action. * * *

We also find it unconvincing to say that the definitional indivisibility theory applies in the context of diversity cases but not in the context of federal-question cases. The broad and general language of the statute does not permit this result. The contention is premised on the notion that the phrase "original jurisdiction of all civil actions" means different things in §§ 1331 and 1332. It is implausible, however, to say that the identical phrase means one thing (original jurisdiction in all actions where at least one claim in the complaint meets the following requirements) in § 1331 and something else (original jurisdiction in all actions where every claim in the complaint meets the following requirements) in § 1332.

The contamination theory, as we have noted, can make some sense in the special context of the complete diversity requirement because the presence of nondiverse parties on both sides of a lawsuit eliminates the justification for providing a federal forum. The theory, however, makes little sense with respect to the amount-in-controversy requirement, which is meant to ensure that a dispute is sufficiently important to warrant federal-court attention. The presence of a single nondiverse party may eliminate the fear of bias with respect to all claims, but the presence of a claim that falls short of the minimum amount in controversy does nothing to reduce the importance of the claims that do meet this requirement.

It is fallacious to suppose, simply from the proposition that § 1332 imposes both the diversity requirement and the amount-in-controversy requirement, that the contamination theory germane to the former is also relevant to the latter. * * * After all, federal-question jurisdiction once had an amount-in-controversy requirement as well. If such a requirement were revived under § 1331, it is clear beyond peradventure that § 1367(a) provides supplemental jurisdiction over federal-question cases where some, but not all, of the federal-law claims involve a sufficient amount in controversy. In other words, § 1367(a) unambiguously overrules the holding and the result in Clark. If that is so, however, it would be quite extraordinary to say that § 1367 did not also overrule Zahn, a case that was premised in substantial part on the holding in Clark. * * *

We also reject the argument * * * that while the presence of additional claims over which the district court lacks jurisdiction does not mean the civil action is outside the purview of § 1367(a), the presence of additional parties does. The basis for this distinction is not altogether clear, and it is in considerable tension with statutory text. * * * The argument that the presence of additional parties removes the civil action from the scope of § 1367(a) also would mean that § 1367 left the Finley result undisturbed. Finley, after all, involved a Federal Tort Claims Act suit against a federal defendant and state-law claims against additional defendants not otherwise subject to federal jurisdiction. Yet all concede that one purpose of § 1367 was to change the result reached in Finley. * * *

C

The proponents of the alternative view of § 1367 insist that the statute is at least ambiguous and that we should look to other interpretive tools, including the legislative history of § 1367, which supposedly demonstrate Congress did not intend § 1367 to overrule Zahn. We can reject this argument at the very outset simply because § 1367 is not ambiguous. * * * Even if we were to stipulate, however, that the reading these proponents urge upon us is textually plausible, the legislative history cited to support it would not alter our view as to the best interpretation of § 1367. * * *

First of all, the legislative history of § 1367 is far murkier than selective quotation from the House Report [reflecting an understanding that the text of § 1367 did not overrule the Zahn case] would suggest. * * *

Second, the worst fears of critics who argue legislative history will be used to circumvent the Article I process were realized in this case. The telltale evidence is the statement, by three law professors who participated in drafting § 1367, see House Report, at 27, n.13, that § 1367 "on its face" permits "supplemental jurisdiction over claims of class members that do not satisfy section 1332's jurisdictional amount requirement, which would overrule [Zahn]. * * * So there exists an acknowledgment, by parties who have detailed, specific knowledge of the statute and the drafting process, both that the plain text of § 1367 overruled Zahn and that language to the contrary in the House Report was a *post hoc* attempt to alter that result. One need not subscribe to the wholesale condemnation of legislative history to refuse to give any effect to such a deliberate effort to amend a statute through a committee report. * * *

D

Finally, we note that the Class Action Fairness Act (CAFA), Pub.L. 109–2, 119 Stat. 4, enacted this year, has no bearing on our analysis of these cases. Subject to certain limitations, the CAFA confers federal diversity jurisdiction over class actions where the aggregate amount in controversy exceeds $5 million. It abrogates the rule against aggregating claims, a rule this Court recognized in [Supreme Tribe of] Ben-Hur [v. Cauble, 255 U.S. 356 (1921),] and reaffirmed in Zahn. The CAFA, however, is not retroactive * * *. The CAFA, moreover, does not moot the significance of our interpretation of § 1367, as many proposed exercises of supplemental jurisdiction, even in the class-action context, might not fall within the CAFA's ambit. * * *

* * *

The judgment of the Court of Appeals for the Eleventh Circuit is affirmed. The judgment of the Court of Appeals for the First Circuit is reversed, and the case is remanded for proceedings consistent with this opinion.

It is so ordered.

■ JUSTICE STEVENS, with whom JUSTICE BREYER joins, dissenting.

Justice Ginsburg's carefully reasoned opinion demonstrates the error in the Court's rather ambitious reading of this opaque jurisdictional statute. She also has demonstrated that "ambiguity" is a term that may have different meanings for different judges, for the Court has made the remarkable declaration that its reading of the statute is so obviously correct—and Justice Ginsburg's so obviously wrong—that the text does not even qualify as "ambiguous." * * * I remain convinced that it is unwise to treat the ambiguity *vel non* of a statute as determinative of whether legislative history is consulted. Indeed, I believe that we as judges are more, rather than less, constrained when we make ourselves accountable to *all* reliable evidence of legislative intent.

The legislative history of 28 U.S.C. § 1367 provides powerful confirmation of Justice Ginsburg's interpretation of that statute. [Justice Stevens's discussion of that history is omitted.] * * *

The Court's reasons for ignoring this virtual billboard of congressional intent are unpersuasive. That a subcommittee of the Federal Courts Study Committee believed that an earlier, substantially similar version of the statute overruled Zahn only highlights the fact that the statute is ambiguous. What is determinative is that the House Report explicitly rejected that broad reading of the statutory text. Such a report has special significance as an indicator of legislative intent. In Congress, committee reports are normally considered the authoritative explication of a statute's text and purposes, and busy legislators and their assistants rely on that explication in casting their votes.

The Court's second reason—its comment on the three law professors who participated in drafting § 1367—is similarly off the mark. In the law review article that the Court refers to, the professors were merely saying that the text of the statute was susceptible to an overly broad (and simplistic) reading, and that clarification in the House Report was therefore appropriate. * * *

* * * Given Justice Ginsburg's persuasive account of the statutory text and its jurisprudential backdrop, and given the uncommonly clear legislative history, I am confident that the majority's interpretation of § 1367 is mistaken. I respectfully dissent.

■ JUSTICE GINSBURG, with whom JUSTICE STEVENS, JUSTICE O'CONNOR, and JUSTICE BREYER join, dissenting.

[In the initial portions of her dissent, Justice Ginsburg traced the history of the concepts of pendent and ancillary jurisdiction, and of the proposals leading up to the enactment of § 1367. Before turning to her reading of that section, she addressed some aspects of the Court's interpretation of the general diversity statute, § 1332.]

The statute today governing federal-court exercise of diversity jurisdiction in the generality of cases, § 1332, like all its predecessors, incorporates both a diverse-citizenship requirement and an amount-in-controversy specification.[5] * * * This Court has long held that, in determining whether the amount-in-controversy requirement has been satisfied, a single plaintiff may aggregate two or more claims against a single defendant, even if the claims are unrelated. But in multiparty cases, including class actions, we have unyieldingly adhered to the nonaggregation rule * * *. * * *

The Court's reading [of § 1367(a)] is surely plausible, especially if one detaches § 1367(a) from its context and attempts no reconciliation with prior interpretations of § 1332's amount-in-controversy requirement. But § 1367(a)'s text * * * can be read another way, one that would involve no rejection of Clark and Zahn. * * *

* * * [Section] 1367(a) addresses "civil action[s] of which the district courts have original jurisdiction," a formulation that, in diversity cases, is sensibly read to incorporate the rules on joinder and aggregation tightly tied to § 1332 at the time of § 1367's enactment. On this reading, a complaint must first meet that "original jurisdiction" measurement. If it does not, no supplemental jurisdiction is authorized. If it does, § 1367(a) authorizes "supplemental jurisdiction" over related claims. In other words, § 1367(a) would preserve undiminished, as part and parcel of § 1332 "original jurisdiction" determinations, both the "complete diversity" rule and the decisions restricting aggregation to arrive at the amount in controversy.[9] Section 1367(b)'s office, then, would be "to

---

[5]   Endeavoring to preserve the "complete diversity" rule first stated in Strawbridge v. Curtiss, the Court's opinion drives a wedge between the two components of 28 U.S.C. § 1332, treating the diversity-of-citizenship requirement as essential, the amount-in-controversy requirement as more readily disposable. Section 1332 itself, however, does not rank order the two requirements. * * * [T]he Court asserts that amount in controversy can be analyzed claim-by-claim, but the diversity requirement cannot. It is not altogether clear why that should be so. The cure for improper joinder of a nondiverse party is the same as the cure for improper joinder of a plaintiff who does not satisfy the jurisdictional amount. In both cases, original jurisdiction can be preserved by dismissing the nonqualifying party.

[9]   On this reading of § 1367(a), it is immaterial that § 1367(b) "does not withdraw supplemental jurisdiction over the claims of the additional parties at issue here." Because those

prevent the erosion of the complete diversity [and amount-in-controversy] requirement[s] that might otherwise result from an expansive application of what was once termed the doctrine of ancillary jurisdiction." See Pfander, *Supplemental Jurisdiction and Section 1367: The Case for a Sympathetic Textualism*, 148 U.Pa.L.Rev. 109, 114 (1999). In contrast to the Court's construction of § 1367, which draws a sharp line between the diversity and amount-in-controversy components of § 1332, the interpretation presented here does not sever the two jurisdictional requirements. * * *

The less disruptive view I take of § 1367 also accounts for the omission of Rule 20 plaintiffs and Rule 23 class actions in § 1367(b)'s text. If one reads § 1367(a) as a plenary grant of supplemental jurisdiction to federal courts sitting in diversity, one would indeed look for exceptions in § 1367(b). Finding none for permissive joinder of parties or class actions, one would conclude that Congress effectively, even if unintentionally, overruled Clark and Zahn. But if one recognizes that the nonaggregation rule delineated in Clark and Zahn forms part of the determination whether "original jurisdiction" exists in a diversity case, then plaintiffs who do not meet the amount-in-controversy requirement would fail at the § 1367(a) threshold. Congress would have no reason to resort to a § 1367(b) exception to turn such plaintiffs away from federal court, given that their claims, from the start, would fall outside the court's § 1332 jurisdiction. See Pfander, *supra*, at 148.

Nor does the more moderate reading assign different meanings to "original jurisdiction" in diversity and federal-question cases. As the First Circuit stated:

" '[O]riginal jurisdiction' in § 1367(a) has the same meaning in every case: [An] underlying statutory grant of original jurisdiction must be satisfied. What differs between federal question and diversity cases is not the meaning of 'original jurisdiction' but rather the [discrete] requirements of sections 1331 and 1332. Under § 1331, the sole issue is whether a federal question appears on the face of the plaintiff's well-pleaded complaint; the [citizenship] of the parties and the amounts they stand to recover [do not bear on that determination]. Section 1332, by contrast, predicates original jurisdiction on the identity of the parties (*i.e.*, [their] complete diversity) and their [satisfaction of the amount-in-controversy specification]. [In short,] the 'original jurisdiction' language in § 1367 operates differently in federal-question and diversity cases not because the meaning of that term varies, but because the [jurisdiction-granting] statutes are different." 370 F.3d [124,] 139–140 [(1st Cir.2004)].

---

claims would not come within § 1367(a) in the first place, Congress would have had no reason to list them in § 1367(b).

What is the utility of § 1367(b) under my reading of § 1367(a)? Section 1367(a) allows parties other than the plaintiff to assert *reactive* claims once entertained under the heading ancillary jurisdiction. * * * [Section] 1367(b) stops plaintiffs from circumventing § 1332's jurisdictional requirements by using another's claim as a hook to add a claim that the plaintiff could not have brought in the first instance. [Owen Equipment & Erection Co. v.] Kroger[, 437 U.S. 365 (1978),] is the paradigm case. * * * Section 1367(b), then, is corroborative of § 1367(a)'s coverage of claims formerly called ancillary, but provides exceptions to ensure that accommodation of added claims would not fundamentally alter "the jurisdictional requirements of section 1332." See Pfander, 148 U.Pa.L.Rev., at 135–37.

While § 1367's enigmatic text defies flawless interpretation,[13] the precedent-preservative reading, I am persuaded, better accords with the historical and legal context of Congress's enactment of the supplemental jurisdiction statute, and the established limits on pendent and ancillary jurisdiction. It does not attribute to Congress a jurisdictional enlargement broader than the one to which the legislators adverted, and it follows the sound counsel that "close questions of [statutory] construction should be resolved in favor of continuity and against change." Shapiro, *Continuity and Change in Statutory Interpretation*, 67 N.Y.U.L.Rev. 921, 925 (1992).

* * *

For the reasons stated, I would hold that § 1367 does not overrule Clark and Zahn. * * *

NOTE ON SUPPLEMENTAL JURISDICTION IN DIVERSITY CASES UNDER § 1367

(1) Engaging with the Statutory Text. The text of § 1367(a) identifies a "civil action" within the district court's original jurisdiction as the foundation for exercising supplemental jurisdiction. It then authorizes supplemental jurisdiction over "claims" that bear an appropriate relationship to the "claims" in the "action" such that together they comprise a single constitutional case or controversy. As applied to Finley v. United States, 490 U.S. 545 (1989), p. 1117, *supra*, the statute apparently assumes that the "civil action" comprises the federal question "claim" against the United

---

[13] If § 1367(a) itself renders unnecessary the listing of Rule 20 plaintiffs and Rule 23 class actions in § 1367(b), then it is similarly unnecessary to refer, as § 1367(b) does, to "persons proposed to be joined as plaintiffs under Rule 19." On one account, Congress bracketed such persons with persons "seeking to intervene as plaintiffs under Rule 24" to modify pre-§ 1367 practice. Before enactment of § 1367, courts entertained, under the heading ancillary jurisdiction, claims of Rule 24(a) intervenors "of right," but denied ancillary jurisdiction over claims of "necessary" Rule 19 plaintiffs. Congress may have sought simply to underscore that those seeking to join as plaintiffs, whether under Rule 19 or Rule 24, should be treated alike, *i.e.*, denied joinder when "inconsistent with the jurisdictional requirements of section 1332." See 370 F.3d at 140, and n.15 (internal quotation marks omitted).

States and treats the additional "claims" against the non-diverse state-law defendants as implicating supplemental (pendent party) jurisdiction. On that view, supplemental jurisdiction would have a claim-specific focus and would govern the joinder of claims and parties in the initial complaint.

Extension of such a claim-specific approach to diversity presents the problem the Court was forced to address in Exxon Mobil and its companion case, Rosario-Ortega v. Star Kist. In both cases, the "claim" of at least one plaintiff satisfied the citizenship and amount-in-controversy requirements for diversity jurisdiction; other plaintiffs, joined under Rules 20 and 23, wished to assert related claims. Understood as applying a claim-specific approach, the statute conferred supplemental jurisdiction over such pendent party claims and § 1367(b) failed to include any exception. This was the so-called "literal" interpretation of § 1367 that critics of the statute advanced in arguing that Congress had unwittingly overruled the venerable complete diversity rule. The Exxon Mobil majority adopted a modified version of the literal account, viewing the statute as allowing the joinder of additional diverse parties even where they were asserting claims below the amount-in-controversy threshold.

Justice Ginsburg, by contrast, argued that the supplemental jurisdiction statute worked differently in diversity. Instead of evaluating a specific claim, Justice Ginsburg called for consideration of the whole civil action as presented in the plaintiffs' complaint to determine if the action qualified as one within the district court's original jurisdiction. Applying then-applicable precedents governing diversity jurisdiction (Clark v. Paul Gray, Inc., 306 U.S. 583 (1939), and Zahn v. International Paper Co., 414 U.S. 291 (1973)), Justice Ginsburg concluded that the civil action failed at the threshold to satisfy the requirements of "original jurisdiction." Such a view preserves the rules governing diversity-based jurisdiction; supplemental jurisdiction in diversity would operate solely on an ancillary basis under the logic of Owen Equipment & Erection Co. v. Kroger, 437 U.S. 365 (1978), p. 1114, *supra*. Justice Ginsburg's view therefore treats § 1367(b) as operating to limit claims that plaintiffs might want to assert, as in Kroger itself, after new parties were added to the litigation on a permissible ancillary basis. The close division in the Exxon Mobil case reflects the difficulty of interpreting a statute that tried perhaps too hard to deal in elaborate detail with an area that did not easily yield to codification.

(2) Questions About Exxon Mobil. Both sides had to confront difficulties in reaching their conclusions.[1] For the majority, perhaps the major problem lay in explaining why its "contamination theory" was consistent with the textualism it otherwise sought to defend. The contamination theory was meant to prevent the erosion of the complete diversity rule, but the majority does not explain why as a textual matter the theory does not also preserve the amount-in-controversy requirement: both jurisdictional elements appear in § 1332. In any case, the rules scarcely achieve the majority's goal of limiting diversity jurisdiction to situations of threatened, citizenship-based

---

[1]　Although the Court held that the Class Action Fairness Act was not relevant to the outcome, and did not moot the case, that Act, in authorizing aggregation in many diversity class actions, clearly reduced the significance of the decision.

bias. The statutory availability of diversity jurisdiction in the plaintiff's home state is difficult to square with this view, as is the strained definition of complete diversity in class actions under the rule of Supreme Tribe of Ben-Hur v. Cauble, 255 U.S. 356 (1921), p. 1116, *supra*.

Moreover, the majority's conception of incomplete diversity as jurisdictionally contaminating from the start seems hard to square with decisions in cases that allow dismissal of a non-diverse party on appeal and affirmance of the relief awarded against the remaining defendants. See Newman-Green, Inc. v. Alfonzo-Larrain, 490 U.S. 826 (1989). Finally, the Court fails to grapple with the implications of its account for cases in which more than one defendant has been joined under Rule 20, a circumstance that renders supplemental jurisdiction unavailable in diversity under the text of § 1367(b).

For the dissent, the principal problem was to explain why section 1367(a) applies to federal question proceedings on a claim-specific basis and diversity proceedings on a broader basis that considers the civil action as a whole. After all, Justice Ginsburg's whole-case approach in Exxon Mobil, if applied to Finley, would lead to the conclusion that original jurisdiction was lacking over Finley's civil action and perhaps imply that § 1367(a) failed in its central mission to overrule that decision. Justice Ginsburg grapples with this problem, highlighting the difference in the meaning of "original jurisdiction" in the different contexts of federal question and diversity jurisdiction. Moreover, her account of § 1367(b), as she recognizes, does not explain some of its provisions. The Rule 20 exception for claims by plaintiffs *against* persons made parties under that rule would appear to restrict jurisdiction over claims in the original complaint.[2] Which interpretation is most faithful to the statutory language? Congressional intent? (And is the statute as "unambiguous" as the majority concludes?)

(3) The Applicability of § 1367 to Removed Cases. Despite some uncertainty in the language of § 1367, the Supreme Court held, in City of Chicago v. International College of Surgeons, 522 U.S. 156 (1997), that the provision applies to removed cases. But the question remains whether the limitations in § 1367(b) apply to claims asserted in state court before removal. For a forceful argument that they do not, see Steinman, *Supplemental Jurisdiction in § 1441 Removed Cases: An Unsurveyed Frontier of Congress's Handiwork*, 35 Ariz.L.Rev. 305 (1993). Professor Steinman's argument is supported by the phrasing of § 1367(b) in terms of the relationship of the *Federal* Rules of Civil Procedure to the assertion of claims and the joinder of parties. Indeed, given this terminology, rejection of her argument might raise difficult questions about the application of

---

[2]   In a critique of the rationale of Exxon Mobil, Steinman, *Claims, Civil Actions, Congress & the Court: Limiting the Reasoning of Cases Construing Poorly Drawn Statutes*, 65 Wash. & Lee L.Rev. 1593 (2008), contends that the Court has redefined the terms "claim" and "civil action" by sometimes conflating them. Noting that the lower courts have not extended this redefinition to other statutory contexts though they may have a duty to do so under accepted notions of the effects of a binding Supreme Court precedent, Steinman argues that such an extension would have undesirable consequences, particularly in cases removed from state courts. She concludes by urging congressional action to clarify the law and to prevent such consequences.

subsection (b) to removed cases in which claims have been asserted and/or parties joined under state rules that differ significantly from the relevant federal rules.[3]

(4) Preservation of the Kroger Rule. Both the wording of § 1367(b) and the legislative history indicate that the drafters did not intend to change the result in Owen Equipment and Erection Co. v. Kroger. However sound that legislative choice, its application may generate interpretive difficulties. Consider a plaintiff who wishes to assert a direct claim against a third-party nondiverse defendant in a suit initially brought in state court and removed to federal court. One might argue that the last sentence of § 1367(b), foreclosing claims brought under Fed.R.Civ.P. 14 only when "inconsistent with the jurisdictional requirements" of diversity would allow the district court to hear such a claim. When suit begins in state court, it does not threaten the same erosion of complete diversity that concerned the Court in Kroger. Suppose, by contrast, the plaintiff asserts a claim against a nondiverse third party defendant as a *counterclaim* under Fed.R.Civ.P. 13 to a claim set up by the third party. The statute might be interpreted to treat the plaintiff as a defendant for purposes of assessing the jurisdictional implications.

(5) Additional Problems of Interpreting § 1367(b). Difficult questions also arise under subsection (b) with respect to the addition of necessary parties under Fed.R.Civ.P. 19 and intervention under Rule 24. For example, are *all* claims excluded if they are asserted by plaintiffs against persons made parties under these rules, or only those that "would be inconsistent" with the requirements of § 1332? (And what are those?) An aspect of this question is grammatical: does the final clause of subsection (b) relate to the entire subsection, or only to claims by persons joined as, or seeking to intervene as, plaintiffs? As another example, since subsection (b) does not purport to affect claims made by persons seeking to intervene as *defendants*, the problem of alignment, and possible realignment, becomes critical.

(6) Other Sources of Ancillary Jurisdiction. Section 1367 does not fully authorize the exercise of what was once characterized as "ancillary jurisdiction." Thus, in Kokkonen v. Guardian Life Ins. Co., 511 U.S. 375 (1994), the Court first held that the doctrine did *not* confer authority on a federal court to enforce the terms of a settlement agreement in a diversity case, but then suggested (without reference to § 1367) that such authority would exist had the district court "embod[ied] the settlement contract in its dismissal order (or, what has the same effect, retain[ed] jurisdiction over the settlement contract) if the parties [had] agree[d]." The distinction drawn in Kokkonen between an independent action and an ancillary proceeding was buttressed by the decision two years later in Peacock v. Thomas, 516 U.S. 349 (1996). In that case the Court held, 8–1, that federal courts do not possess ancillary jurisdiction over a new action in which a federal judgment

---

[3] 28 U.S.C. § 1441(c) now permits removal of a state court action containing both a removable claim falling within the district court's original federal question jurisdiction (within the meaning of § 1331) and a claim not within the original or supplemental jurisdiction (for example, a state-law claim that is entirely unrelated to the federal question claim)—but then requires severance, and remand to the state court, of any claim falling outside the federal court's original or supplemental jurisdiction.

creditor sues to impose liability on a person who has not previously been held liable for a monetary judgment against another defendant. The Court noted, in passing, that "Congress codified much of the common-law doctrine of ancillary jurisdiction" in § 1367, and then went on to reject any common-law basis of ancillary jurisdiction on the facts presented.[4]

---

8. THE REMOVAL JURISDICTION OF THE FEDERAL DISTRICT COURTS

INTRODUCTION TO THE REMOVAL STATUTES

Beginning with the Judiciary Act of 1789, Congress has allowed parties (usually but not always defendants) to remove civil actions from state to federal court. Congress may have drawn on the common law writ of certiorari as a model for its initial removal provisions; that common law writ authorized the removal of the record from an inferior to a superior court, often for a trial on the merits. But unlike certiorari, which was directed to an inferior court and its judges, early removal procedure was designed to allow the defendant to invoke the jurisdiction of the federal court by filing a removal petition with the state court and then lodging the papers with the federal court for litigation "in the same manner as if it had been brought there by original process." Act of September 24, 1789, ch. 23, § 12. Removal authority extended only where the matter in controversy exceeded $500 and the suit was brought in state court against a foreign national or against a citizen of another state, sued by a "citizen of the state in which the suit is brought." *Id*.

On occasion through the nineteenth century, Congress expanded removal rights to include some state court suits brought against federal officials. See pp. 573–585, *supra*. Congress considerably expanded removal rights in the Act of 1875, 18 Stat. 470, alongside its first enduring general grant of original federal question jurisdiction. As initially structured, the statute allowed removal of virtually every civil case within the scope of Article III on the petition of either plaintiff or defendant. Congress changed

---

[4]   Ancillary jurisdiction once extended to the adjudication of an attorney's lien, impressed on the proceeds of successful litigation to secure payment of fees. See Wilkinson v. Tilden, 14 F. 778, 780–81 (C.C.S.D.N.Y.1883) (in a suit at equity, and on the attorney's motion, placing a lien on any recovered funds—by decree or settlement—to cover a dismissed attorney's contingency fee prior to allowing substitution of counsel); Isaacs v. Abraham, 13 F.Cas. 151, 151 (C.C.D.Mass.1878) (noting that "substitution of solicitors in equity is made on motion, . . . granted as a matter of course, [but] subject to the lien of the former solicitors"). Some circuit courts have evaluated the continued viability of such litigation by aligning the parties and evaluating the amount in controversy as if the claim for fees were a freestanding civil action. Others have characterized such claims as invoking jurisdiction ancillary to the merits proceeding. Compare Griffin v. Lee, 621 F.3d 380 (5th Cir.2010) (considering the attorney's citizenship in relation not to his client but to opposing parties for purposes of determining the existence of jurisdiction) with Exact Software North America, Inc. v. DeMoisey, 718 F.3d 535, 542–44 (6th Cir.2013) (drawing on the history of ancillary jurisdiction in upholding district court's power over an attorney's fee petition).

course twelve years later, limiting removal rights to defendants and allowing removal only in cases that could have been originally filed in federal court, thereby ruling out removal on the basis of a federal defense.[1] The current statute, 28 U.S.C. § 1441(a), preserves those features and the requirement that, in cases in which multiple defendants are sued on a claim, all the defendants must join in or consent to the notice of removal. 28 U.S.C. § 1446(b)(2)(A). Finally, some statutory provisions qualify § 1441(a)'s general right of removal by making actions under particular federal statutes non-removable.[2]

A. Federal Question Removal and Complete Preemption

Beneficial National Bank v. Anderson

539 U.S. 1 (2003).

Plaintiffs sued in state court, alleging that Beneficial National, a bank chartered under the National Bank Act, had violated state usury law. The Bank responded by removing the action from state to federal court, arguing that the National Bank Act set forth exclusive and preemptive usury regulations for national banks and thereby displaced state law. But rather than asserting preemption as a defense in state court, the Bank argued that the National Bank Act was like a small group of other federal statutes with such completely preemptive force as to transform nominally state-law claims into federal-law claims for removal purposes. Thus, although the plaintiffs pleaded usury claims under state law, the Bank argued that a well-pleaded complaint for usury was viable only as a matter of federal law and removal was therefore proper.

The Court, with Justice Stevens writing, upheld removal, agreeing with the Bank that the federal statute had completely preempted the plaintiffs' state-law claims. Justice Stevens relied on two decisions, Avco Corp. v. Aero Lodge No. 735, 390 U.S. 557 (1968), and Metropolitan Life Ins. Co. v. Taylor, 481 U.S. 58 (1987), both of which had embraced a version of preemption removal theory. In Avco, the state court suit was brought to enforce a collective bargain agreement under state law. But as the Court held in Textile Workers v. Lincoln Mills, 353 U.S. 448 (1957), p. 1014, *supra*, Congress had authorized suits to enforce collective agreements under the federal common law formulated under the aegis of § 301 of the Taft-Hartley Act. Similarly, in Metropolitan Life, plaintiffs sued in state court to recover benefits from a trust fund, despite governing provisions in ERISA that authorized such claims to brought under federal law. Justice Stevens summarized the two decisions as permitting removal "when a federal statute wholly displaces the state-law cause of action through complete pre-

---

[1] For detailed discussion of the background of federal question removal, see Collins, *The Unhappy History of Federal Question Removal*, 71 Iowa L.Rev. 717 (1986).

[2] These include (i) damage actions under the Federal Employers' Liability Act, see Act of Apr. 22, 1908, 35 Stat. 65, amended by Act of Apr. 5, 1910, 36 Stat. 291, now codified as 28 U.S.C. § 1445(a); (ii) actions under the Jones Act, which made the FELA applicable to seamen by generic reference, see 46 U.S.C. App. § 688; (iii) actions against railroads sued under federal law for damages to goods shipped of less than $3,000, Act of Jan. 20, 1914, 38 Stat. 278 (a threshold since raised to $10,000, see 28 U.S.C. § 1445(b)); and (iv) actions under the 1933 Securities Act, Act of May 27, 1933, § 22(a), 48 Stat. 74. 87, now codified as amended at 15 U.S.C. § 77v.

emption," and noted that in both instances "the federal statutes at issue provided the exclusive cause of action for the claim asserted and also set forth procedures and remedies governing that cause of action."

Turning to the case at hand, the Court found that the National Bank Act "unquestionably pre-empts any [state-law] rule that would treat * * * as usurious" rates that were lawful under the Act. But a federal preemption defense would not alone justify removal; "[o]nly if Congress intended [the pertinent provision of the federal Act] to provide the exclusive cause of action for usury claims against national banks would the statute be comparable to the provisions" in Avco and Metropolitan Life. Analyzing the federal scheme, the Court found that provisions of the National Bank Act "supersede both the substantive and the remedial provisions of state usury laws and create a federal remedy for overcharges that is exclusive." The Court accordingly found that the usury claim could arise only under federal law. A footnote added that "the proper inquiry focuses on whether Congress intended the federal cause of action to be exclusive rather than on whether Congress intended that the cause of action be removable."

Insofar as Avco and Metropolitan Life included language referring to the extraordinary preemptive effect of a particular statute or to an intent in the legislative history to permit removal, Beneficial National Bank seems to make clear that complete preemption does not require either such element. Instead, the Court suggests that any federal statute that both preempts state law and creates an "exclusive cause of action" may trigger the complete preemption doctrine. The federal remedy need not be as complete as that provided by the preempted state-law cause of action. Thus, the National Bank Act provides a remedy for usury—compensation in twice the amount of any unlawful interest charge—far less generous than the remedy under some state laws (which may provide compensatory and punitive damages). Nonetheless, the Court viewed federal banking law as having supplied a preemptive substitute remedy.

Dissenting in Beneficial National Bank, Justice Scalia (joined by Justice Thomas) attacked the foundations of the complete preemption doctrine. He characterized Avco as a radical departure from the well-pleaded complaint rule and Metropolitan Life simply as following suit because ERISA was modeled on § 301 of the Taft-Hartley Act. To observe that federal preemption may render a state cause of action non-viable did not, he contended, "magically transform[ ]" or "transmogrify[y]" it into a claim arising under federal law. Criticizing the entire doctrine as illogical, he urged that it be confined to cases under the Taft Hartley Act or statutes modeled on it.

NOTE ON REMOVAL JURISDICTION AND THE COMPLETE PREEMPTION EXCEPTION

(1) The Standard Removal Model. 28 U.S.C. § 1441(a) authorizes removal of any civil action brought in state court "of which the district courts . . . have original jurisdiction." The Court has long interpreted the statute's reference to original jurisdiction as incorporating by reference the many rules that govern federal question and diversity-based jurisdiction in the federal courts under 28 U.S.C. §§ 1331 and 1332. As to federal question claims, the rules of Louisville & Nashville R.R. Co. v. Mottley, 211 U.S. 149 (1908), p. 1024, *supra*, Grable & Sons Metal Products, Inc. v. Darue Engineering & Mfg., 545 U.S. 308 (2005), p. 1040, *supra*, and Skelly Oil Co. v. Phillips Petroleum Co., 338 U.S. 667 (1950), p. 1052, *supra*, apply to the jurisdictional assessment of the removability of the state court complaint (thereby ruling out § 1441(a) removal based on the assertion of a federal defense). As to diversity-based removal, the complete diversity and amount-in-controversy rules apply as well as some more particular limitations. See 28 U.S.C. § 1441(b)(2) (prohibiting removal where one or more defendants is a citizen of the forum state). Generally, defendants must initiate removal by notice to the federal court for the geographic district in which the state court action was filed within 30 days of the filing of the action. *Id.* § 1446(b)(1). Following removal, the state court must refrain from further proceedings unless and until the case has been returned to it by a remand order. Plaintiffs may contest compliance with removal procedure and jurisdiction by moving to remand within 30 days of the notice's filing. *Id.* § 1447(c). Remands for lack of subject matter jurisdiction may occur at any time. Remand orders do not ordinarily occasion federal appellate review; litigation will presumptively continue in state court. See 28 U.S.C. § 1447(d); Carlsbad Tech., Inc. v. HIF Bio, Inc., 556 U.S. 635 (2009) (recognizing the rule and exceptions).

(2) Uncertain Foundations of Complete Preemption Removal. Judged by the standard model, complete preemption removal deserves some explanation. In Beneficial National Bank, the state court complaint asserted only state-law claims for usury and thus failed the well-pleaded complaint test; federal preemption ordinarily operates as a defense to such claims. Given that, Justice Scalia rightly observes that the complete preemption doctrine seemingly lacks a settled legal foundation. Justice Douglas's unanimous opinion in Avco offered little by way of justification; he briefly noted that, under § 301, substantive federal law governs a claim for breach of a collective bargaining agreement between union and employer, whether the case is filed in federal or state court. As later elaborated in Franchise Tax Bd. v. Construction Laborers Vacation Trust, 463 U.S. 1, 23–24 (1983), Avco was said to stand "for the proposition that if a federal cause of action completely preempts a state cause of action, any complaint that comes within the scope of the federal cause of action necessarily 'arises under' federal law." In Metropolitan Life Ins. Co. v. Taylor, 481 U.S. 58 (1987), the Court extended the approach of the Avco decision to federal regulation of employee benefit plans under ERISA but did not justify the doctrine as a matter of first principles. It based its jurisdictional decision on legislative intent, concluding that Congress wished "to make [ERISA] suits brought by participants or beneficiaries federal questions for the purposes of federal court jurisdiction in like manner as § 301 of the [Taft-Hartley Act]."

For a time, complete preemption was thought to have something in common with the equally confusing but apparently short-lived "artful pleading" doctrine of Federated Dep't Stores, Inc. v. Moitie, 452 U.S. 394, 397 n.27 (1981). There, the Court allowed removal on the basis of a "factual finding" by a lower federal court that state court plaintiffs had attempted by "artful pleading" to disguise the federal nature of their complaint. The Court proceeded to find the removed action barred by claim preclusion, an issue that would normally have arisen as a defense to the state court proceeding. Moitie caused some confusion in the lower courts until it was retired in Rivet v. Regions Bank of La., 522 U.S. 470 (1998). Stating that the "enigmatic footnote" in Moitie "did not create a preclusion exception to the rule * * * that a defendant could not remove on the basis of a federal defense," the Court unanimously ruled that a state court action removed on the basis that the state-law claim was precluded by a prior federal judgment should be remanded to the state court.[1]

In Beneficial National Bank, the Court declined to cabin or retire the complete preemption doctrine but instead restated the doctrine on less confusing grounds that may lead to its expansion.[2] Consider Justice Scalia's criticism and his intermediate position—to confine the doctrine to cases under the Taft-Hartley Act and statutes (like ERISA) that were modeled on it. Given the procedural character of the issue and the absence of any significant reliance interests, stare decisis does not militate strongly against scrapping the doctrine altogether.

(3) Justifying Complete Preemption. One can assess complete preemption's possible policy justifications by asking "compared to what?" If the doctrine did not exist, the Beneficial National Bank would presumably assert a preemption defense in state court. If the state court agreed and dismissed the state-law usury claim as preempted, the plaintiff could presumably file an amended complaint setting out the usury claim under federal law. The assertion of a federal claim would trigger the defendant's right to remove. In the end, then, the litigation might well proceed if at all in federal court.

Viewed from this perspective, the complete preemption removal doctrine contributes two features to the law of federal subject matter jurisdiction. First, it shifts responsibility for determining the preemptive force of federal law from the state to the federal court. Second, it triggers an early evaluation of the preemption question as part of the removal decision. If successful, the defendant's removal, somewhat curiously, transforms a defective state-law claim into a nominally viable federal-law claim. Defendants invoking the doctrine either prefer the federal liability scheme or have an effective defense to the transformed federal claim. In the end, the doctrine confers a right to federal judicial determination of the claimed exclusivity of a federal right of action.

---

[1]   See generally Miller, *Artful Pleading: A Doctrine in Search of a Definition*, 76 Tex.L.Rev. 1781, 1824–25 (1998) (praising the Rivet decision and concluding that the Court's language "[c]onfining Moitie to its context" is simply a courteous way of saying that the "footnote has gone gently into the night").

[2]   One year after the Beneficial decision, in Aetna Health Inc. v. Davila, 542 U.S. 200 (2004), a case involving ERISA, the Court unanimously upheld removal under the complete preemption doctrine, which it described as "an exception" to the well-pleaded complaint rule.

Supreme Court decisions addressing complete preemption have come in suits between private parties, rather than in litigation between a regulated firm and the state. Note that under Shaw v. Delta Air Lines, Inc., 463 U.S. 85 (1983), and Verizon, Md., Inc. v. Public Serv. Comm'n of Md., 535 U.S. 635 2002), a regulated party can often pursue a federal suit for injunctive and declaratory relief from the threatened enforcement of preempted state law. See pp. 1140–1141, *infra*. Prospective state court defendants cannot always anticipate the initiation of private litigation and may have greater difficulty securing similar anticipatory relief in such cases as Avco, Metropolitan Life, and Beneficial National. Once named in state court, they might try to invoke the Skelly Oil rule, in a suit brought to secure declaratory and injunctive relief from the continued prosecution of a preempted state-law claim. But the Anti-Injunction Act, 28 U.S.C. § 2283, as more fully explored in Chapter 10, will bar many such suits seeking relief from a pending state court proceeding. See p. 1370, *infra*.

Complete preemption thus provides a federal forum for determination of the preemptive force of some private federal rights of action. Instead of protecting defendants from overly broad state agency regulation, as in Shaw/Verizon, complete preemption ensures a federal judicial role in preventing state-law supplementation of the exclusively federal regulation of private conduct.[3]

(4) Complete Preemption and Statutory Text. If complete preemption rests on some form of intent imputed to Congress, one might ask if the Court should await clearer legislative signals. For starters, as more fully discussed in Chapter VII, the Court has emphasized textualism in recent years as it has cut back on other preemption doctrines, narrowing field preemption and the recognition of federal common law to fill gaps in federal regulatory schemes. See pp. 833–836, *infra*. The turn to textualism poses a significant threat to complete preemption, as Justice Scalia observed in dissent from Beneficial National.

The argument for insisting on clearer textual guidance could also rely on Congress's decision to fashion forms of text-based complete preemption in some familiar settings. In the Federal Employees Liability Reform and Tort Compensation Act of 1988, § 5, 102 Stat. 4563–64 (sometimes known as the Westfall Act), for example, Congress authorized federal officials sued in state court for certain common law torts committed within the scope of their employment to seek the removal of those actions to federal court and the transformation of the claims into suits against the federal government under the Federal Tort Claims Act. See 28 U.S.C. § 2679(d). Similarly, the Securities Litigation Uniform Standards Act of 1998, Pub.L.No. 105–353, 112 Stat. 3227, authorizes removal by those asserting a federal defense of preemption to certain state-law class actions alleging fraud in the purchase

---

[3] The distinctive function of complete preemption removal may inform assessments of its wisdom in relation to other preemption doctrines. Compare Seinfeld, *The Puzzle of Complete Preemption*, 155 U.Pa.L.Rev. 537, 566–77 (2007) (defending a role for complete preemption that may be served adequately through Shaw/Verizon litigation) with McGreal, *In Defense of Complete Preemption*, 156 U.Pa.L.Rev. PENNumbra 147 (2007) (defending complete preemption in light of worries about lawyerly manipulation and the potential for state court error in application of preemption standards).

or sale of securities. Assuming Congress has the legislative capacity to create a statutory regime of complete preemption or federal defense removal, consider what role the courts should play in fashioning similar regimes without more explicit guidance.[4]

B. Specialized Removal Statutes

Apart from the general removal statute, 28 U.S.C. § 1441, federal law confers a variety of specialized rights to removal. This section briefly examines two such provisions. The first, in § 1442, broadly authorizes removal by federal officers and agencies. The second, in § 1443, authorizes removal to address a threatened denial of civil rights in state court litigation.

NOTE ON REMOVAL OF ACTIONS AGAINST FEDERAL DEFENDANTS

(1) The 1948 Revision. Building on a string of statutes dating from 1815, Congress in 1948 authorized the removal of state court actions brought against federal officers. The Revision of the Judicial Code enacted that year included a provision, 28 U.S.C. § 1442(a)(1), that in sweeping terms authorized removal of any civil action or criminal prosecution against "[a]ny officer of the United States or any agency thereof, or person acting under him, for any act under color of such office."[1] This grant of federal officer removal authority differs from the general removal model in two respects: it allows the removal of criminal as well as civil cases and it allows removal on the basis of federal questions set up as defenses by the removing defendant. In Mesa v. California, 489 U.S. 121 (1989), p. 1018, *supra*, the Court clarified that § 1442(a)(1) permits an officer to remove a state-law action only when the officer sets up a colorable federal defense.

(2) Subsequent Amendments. Responding to the Court's decision in International Primate Protection League v. Administrators of Tulane Educational Fund, 500 U.S. 72 (1991), Congress amended § 1442(a)(1) to expressly authorize removal by the United States and federal agencies.[2] After subsequent amendment in 2011,[3] the provision now authorizes removal by "[t]he United States or any agency thereof" as well as by "any officer (or any person acting under that officer) of the United States or of any agency thereof, in an official or individual capacity, for or relating to any act under color of such office."

(3) Persons Acting "Under That Officer." Although framed in terms that would appear to embrace deputies and assistants working at the direction of federal officers, the provision for removal by persons acting "under" a federal officer has been widely invoked by corporate defendants with less evidently subordinate relationships to federal officials. Consider

---

[4]   See Morrison, *Complete Preemption and the Separation of Powers*, 155 U.Pa.L.Rev. 186 (2007).

[1]   Act of June 25, 1948, Pub.L.No. 80–773, ch. 646, § 1442, 62 Stat. 869, 938.

[2]   See Federal Courts Improvement Act of 1996, Pub.L.No. 104–317, § 206, 110 Stat. 3847, 3480.

[3]   Removal Clarification Act of 2011, Pub.L.No. 112–51, § 2, 125 Stat. 545.

the strategy adopted in Watson v. Philip Morris Companies, Inc., 551 U.S. 142 (2007), a state court action alleging false advertising by the defendant tobacco company in violation of state law. The defendant removed the action, arguing that the plaintiffs were attacking a testing process that was mandated and supervised by the Federal Trade Commission. After consulting the language, history, and purpose of the statute, the Court found that it applied only to persons engaged in "an effort to *assist*, or to help *carry out*, the duties or tasks of the federal superior." Applying that test, the Court unanimously concluded that the tobacco company did not qualify as a person acting under a federal officer for purposes of removal.[4]

The Watson Court's narrow definition has not ended corporate reliance on the federal officer removal statute, as the saga of Boulder County climate change litigation confirms. In one of a cluster of similar state court actions, Boulder County brought state-law claims against major extractive energy producers alleging nuisance, trespass, unjust enrichment, and civil conspiracy. Like other localities, Boulder claimed that it was facing massive costs due to climate change, including wild-fire prevention and control, loss of agricultural productivity, and infrastructure destruction. Energy companies removed these claims on various theories, including complete preemption, federal ingredient jurisdiction under Grable & Sons, and federal officer removal under § 1442 on the theory that they were acting under federal officials in conducting their business and extractive activities. See Boulder County, Colorado v. Suncor, Energy USA Inc., 405 F.Supp.3d 947 (D.Colo.2019) (rejecting these grounds for removal). After considerable litigation, the United States Court of Appeals for the Tenth Circuit rejected all asserted grounds for removal. See BCCBC v. Suncor Energy Inc., 25 F.4th 1238 (10th Cir.2022).

(4) Appellate Review of Remand Orders. When the district court concludes on a timely motion that a case was mistakenly removed from state to federal court, federal law directs a remand of the action to state court. In general, Congress has foreclosed routine appellate review of such remand orders. See 28 U.S.C. § 1447(d). In the case of federal officers and agencies, however, Congress has created an exception. See *id.* § 1447(d) (authorizing appeal from remand orders in cases removed under § 1442(a)).

As noted above, in Boulder County v. Suncor, *supra*, and similar cases, oil and gas defendants invoked a variety of theories in support of removal, including the claim that they were acting under a federal officer. In BP P.L.C. v. Mayor & City Council of Baltimore, 593 U.S. 230 (2021), the Supreme Court held that appellate jurisdiction in such cases extended not only to the federal officer removal theory but to all theories invoked in support of removal. Broad appellate jurisdiction over remand orders explains in part why Boulder County's state-law claims spent five years in the federal courts before being returned to state courts for consideration of the merits.

---

[4] See Isaacson v. Dow Chem. Co., 517 F.3d 129 (2d Cir.2008) (upholding removal of a state court suit against a private contractor asserting the "government contractor" defense recognized in Boyle v. United Technologies Corp., 487 U.S. 500 (1988), p. 826, *supra*).

(5) Derivative Removal Jurisdiction. Under an earlier version of the removal statute, federal courts took the position that removal jurisdiction was derivative of jurisdiction that first attached in the state court from which the action was removed. See General Inv. Co. v. Lake Shore & M.S. Ry. Co., 260 U.S. 261, 288 (1922); Lambert Run Coal Co. v. Baltimore & O.R. Co., 258 U.S. 377, 382 (1922). That meant a federal court could not exercise removal jurisdiction over a matter removed to federal court if the state court lacked subject matter jurisdiction of the matter. Derivative jurisdiction problems arise when federal courts enjoy exclusive jurisdiction of claims under federal law, such as suits to enforce the antitrust laws or suits under ERISA. If the defendant removes such cases from state to federal court, federal courts were expected to dismiss for want of subject matter jurisdiction on the theory that the state court could not have acquired jurisdiction of the proceeding. See Minnesota v. United States, 305 U.S. 382, 389 (1939) (explaining that federal jurisdiction on removal depends on the state court's first having acquired jurisdiction of the subject matter and the parties). Following a derivative jurisdiction dismissal, the plaintiff could attempt to cure by re-filing the claims in federal court as an original matter. But the passage of the applicable limitation period might foreclose such a renewed filing. What sense any of this made eluded most observers. Removal would seem to vindicate the federal interest in federal subject matter exclusivity.

In all events, Congress overruled derivative jurisdiction in 1986, providing: "The court to which such civil action is removed is not precluded from hearing and determining any claim in such civil action because the State court from which such civil action is removed did not have jurisdiction over that claim."[5] After some judicial debate as to the import of the change, Congress repositioned the language slightly and added the terms "under this section," apparently limiting its operation to removals effected under § 1441 and thereby restoring the doctrine as to removals under § 1442. Efforts to understand the rationale for the amendment have fallen short. See, *e.g.*, High Lonesome Ranch, LLC v. Garfield County, 61 F.4th 1225, 1239 (10th Cir.2023) ("For no clear reason, the 2002 amendment limited abolition of derivative jurisdiction to cases removed under § 1441.")

While most circuits agree that derivative jurisdiction has been restored for federal officer removals, some have chosen to treat the issue as one the parties can waive. See, *e.g.*, Rodas v. Seidlin, 656 F.3d 610 (7th Cir.2011). For criticism of derivate jurisdiction, see 14C Wright & Miller, Federal Practice and Procedure § 3722 (Rev.4th ed.2023).

NOTE ON CIVIL RIGHTS REMOVAL UNDER 28 U.S.C. § 1443

Dating from Reconstruction, the civil rights removal statute authorizes defendants to remove a case if they can show both that the right upon which they rely is a "right under any law providing for * * * equal civil rights" and that they are "denied or cannot enforce" that right in the state courts. 28

---

[5]   Judicial Improvements Act of 1985, Pub. L. No. 99–336, § 3, 100 Stat. 633, 637 (1986).

U.S.C. § 1443. Yet the statute was sharply limited in early interpretations and does not play a robust role in the protection of civil rights today.

(1) Early Decisions. Two cases decided on the same day significantly narrowed the potential scope of civil rights removal. In Strauder v. West Virginia, 100 U.S. 303 (1880), the Court upheld removal of a murder prosecution, brought against a Black man who argued that his equal civil rights were violated by a state law limiting jury service to white males. But in Virginia v. Rives, 100 U.S. 313 (1880), the Court refused to allow removal of murder proceedings against Black defendants who alleged that the county had never allowed Black people to serve on juries. Limiting removal to situations in which the state's constitution or laws required differential treatment (as in Strauder), the Rives Court viewed pre-trial misconduct by state officials (however ingrained in local custom) as something the state court was left to address in the first instance, subject to correction on appeal to the Court. If a state official discriminated in selecting the jury, it "can hardly be said that [a defendant] is denied, or cannot enforce, 'in the judicial tribunals of the State' the rights which belong to him." The Court did not explain why the removal statute operated only on written rather than customary forms of legal discrimination. Presumably, the Supremacy Clause would have also obligated the state court in Strauder to invalidate the state law and that court's failure to do so would have been open to review on appeal.

(2) The Second Reconstruction: Rachel and Peacock. There matters rested for over 80 years, at least in the Supreme Court. In the Civil Rights Act of 1964, Congress amended 28 U.S.C. § 1447(d) to create an exception to its general ban on appellate review of remand orders for cases removed under § 1443. That brought new cases to the Court, applying the Strauder-Rives framework to the civil rights protests of the 1960s. In Georgia v. Rachel, 384 U.S. 780 (1966), the Court upheld the removal of criminal trespass proceedings against 20 protesters who were arrested after being told to leave a restaurant that was said to qualify as a place of public accommodation under the Civil Rights Act. But in a companion decision, City of Greenwood v. Peacock, 384 U.S. 808 (1966), the Court refused to allow removal of proceedings against 29 state criminal defendants who alleged that their arrests were motivated by racial animus and a desire to punish them for exercising their constitutional rights to register voters, protest racial discrimination, and freely associate. They further alleged that they could not enforce their rights in a state judicial system in which they would be tried in segregated courtrooms in which Blacks would be excluded from the juries; that the judges and prosecutors had gained office in elections from which Black voters had been excluded; and that the statutes and ordinances under which they were charged were unconstitutional and unconstitutionally vague as applied to their conduct.[1]

---

[1] On the history of the civil rights removal statute, see Amsterdam, *Criminal Prosecutions Affecting Federally Guaranteed Civil Rights: Federal Removal and Habeas Corpus Jurisdiction to Abort State Court Trial*, 113 U.Pa.L.Rev. 793 (1965); Bator, *The State Courts and Federal Constitutional Litigation*, 22 Wm. & Mary L.Rev. 605, 611–21 (1981). See also Goldstein, *Blyew: Variations on a Jurisdictional Theme*, 41 Stan.L.Rev. 469 (1989) (discussing the origins and development of § 1443 in the context of the original 1866 Act).

The Court approached both cases with the Strauder-Rives limits in mind, explaining that the requirement of formal discrimination on the face of state law served to ease the task of deciding when a state court would deny civil rights. The Court worried that predicating removal on a prediction as to likely state court behavior would impose a difficult analytical burden on federal judges by involving them in "the unseemly process of prejudging their brethren of the state courts." Removal rights were extended "primarily, if not exclusively," to a denial resulting from "the Constitution or laws of the State." In the absence of a discriminatory state enactment, removal was available only if "an equivalent basis could be shown for an equally firm prediction that the defendant would be 'denied or cannot enforce' the specified federal rights in the state court."

Applying this standard, the Court distinguished the arrests in Rachel from those in Peacock. In Rachel, a unanimous Court found that any proceedings in state court would violate the defendants' right to enter places of public accommodation; they enjoyed a federal immunity from racially motivated demands that they leave the premises. In Peacock, by contrast, a narrow 5–4 majority explained that the conduct charged in the indictments (to "obstruct a public street, to contribute to the delinquency of a minor, to drive an automobile without a license, or to bite a policeman") did not enjoy any federal immunity. The Peacock Court acknowledged that police officers may act from corrupt motives "but that does not show that the state trial court will find the defendant guilty if he is innocent." The removal statute did not "permit the judges of the federal courts to put their brethren of the state judiciary on trial."

The Peacock Court also noted that remedies other than removal— including, in appropriate cases, injunctions, actions for damages under 42 U.S.C. § 1983, and habeas corpus—were available to vindicate defendants' constitutional rights. A broad construction of § 1443 would cause an explosion of state criminal litigation in the federal courts, a change that, the Court said, raised fundamental issues of policy for Congress to consider: "Has the historic practice of holding state criminal trials in state courts * * * been such a failure that the relationship of the state and federal courts should now be revolutionized? Will increased responsibility of the state courts in the area of federal civil rights be promoted and encouraged by denying those courts any power at all to exercise that responsibility?" Compare Johnson v. Mississippi, 421 U.S. 213 (1975) (narrowly construing the "murky" language of § 1443(1) as inapplicable to a state criminal prosecution for conspiracy and unlawful boycott brought against individuals protesting racial discrimination in the hiring practices of certain Vicksburg, Mississippi merchants).

Rachel and Peacock both display great reluctance to open federal courts to the removal of state criminal proceedings, partly due to an unwillingness to make jurisdiction depend on an assessment of the competence and fairness of state judges and partly due to the perceived adequacy of other remedies, including appellate review in the Supreme Court. The Court noted in Peacock that the protests in Rachel were peaceful and that they occurred under the protection of a federal immunity conferred by statute. But that does not explain why the defendants in Rachel could not enforce their rights in state court as effectively as those in Peacock and Johnson. Consider the possibility that Rachel allows removal only when federal law protects the conduct *charged as violating state law* (entry into a restaurant) rather than merely the conduct (registering voters) that was said to have occasioned prosecution for other offenses. That understanding would leave little if any room in which § 1443(1) can operate—a conclusion supported by the small number of cases successfully removed under the provision.

CHAPTER IX

SUITS CHALLENGING OFFICIAL ACTION

INTRODUCTION

This chapter examines suits to hold the governments of the United States—federal, state, local, and tribal—accountable for legal wrongs. After introducing the coordinate role of nineteenth century courts and legislative assemblies in ensuring government accountability, this chapter considers the early debate over state sovereign immunity and the adoption of the Eleventh Amendment. With the ratification of the Fourteenth Amendment during Reconstruction, state compliance with federal law took on renewed urgency. During Reconstruction, Congress adopted the statute later codified as 42 U.S.C. § 1983 and the Supreme Court later decided Ex parte Young, 209 U.S. 123 (1908), upholding anticipatory relief from threatened constitutional violations. After examining use of officer suits under Ex parte Young and § 1983 and the qualified power of Congress to abrogate state governmental immunity, the chapter turns to issues of federal governmental accountability, including the scope of federal judicial power to grant universal injunctive relief.

1. OFFICER SUITS AND SOVEREIGN IMMUNITY IN THE NINETEENTH CENTURY

Where applicable, the doctrine of sovereign immunity bars unconsented suits against the United States, the states, and Native American tribes. Without an assured remedy through direct suits against these government bodies, however, plaintiffs have long sought alternative redress in "officer suits" against the officials who act for governments. See generally Jaffe, *Suits Against Governments and Officers: Sovereign Immunity*, 77 Harv.L.Rev. 1 (1963). In reading the next two cases, both of which involve the federal government, consider how sovereign immunity shaped the choice of a proper defendant and allocated institutional responsibility between Congress and the federal courts.

Little v. Barreme

6 U.S. (2 Cranch) 170 (1804).
Appeal from the Circuit Court of Massachusetts.

■ MARSHALL, CHIEF JUSTICE, now delivered the opinion of the Court.

The *Flying-Fish* a *Danish* vessel having on board *Danish* and neutral property, was captured on the 2d of *December* 1799, on a voyage from *Jeremie* to *St. Thomas's*, by the *United States* frigate *Boston*, commanded by Captain *Little*, and brought into the port of *Boston*, where she was libelled as an *American* vessel that had violated the non-intercourse law.

The judge before whom the cause was tried, directed a restoration of the vessel and cargo as neutral [*i.e.*, Danish] property, but refused to award damages for the capture and detention, because in his opinion, there was probable cause to suspect the vessel to be *American*.

On an appeal to the circuit court this sentence was reversed, because the *Flying-Fish* was on a voyage *from*, not *to*, a *French* port, and was therefore, had she even been an *American* vessel, not liable to capture on the high seas.

[The first section of the non-intercourse law authorized the forfeiture and sale of American vessels engaged in any "traffic or commerce" with persons resident in French territory. The fifth section narrowed the law's operation on the high seas to authorize forfeiture only in cases in which the American ship or vessel "is bound or sailing to any port or place within the territory of the French Republic."]

It is by no means clear that the president of the *United States* whose high duty it is to "take care that the laws be faithfully executed," and who is commander in chief of the armies and navies of the *United States*, might not, without any special authority for that purpose, in the then existing state of things, have empowered the officers commanding the armed vessels of the *United States*, to seize and send into port for adjudication, *American* vessels which were forfeited by being engaged in this illicit commerce. But when it is observed that the general clause of the first section * * * obviously contemplates a seizure within the *United States*; and that the 5th section gives a special authority to seize on the high seas, and limits that authority to the seizure of vessels bound or sailing *to* a *French* port, the legislature seem to have prescribed that the manner in which this law shall be carried into execution, was to exclude a seizure of any vessel not bound *to* a *French* port. Of consequence, however strong the circumstances might be, which induced captain *Little* to suspect the *Flying-Fish* to be an *American* vessel, they could not excuse the detention of her, since he would not have been authorized to detain her had she been really *American*.

It was so obvious, that if only vessels sailing to a *French* port could be seized on the high seas, that the law would be very often evaded, that this act of congress appears to have received a different construction from the executive of the *United States*; a construction much better calculated to give it effect.

A copy of this act was transmitted by the secretary of the navy, to the captains of the armed vessels, who were ordered to consider the 5th section as a part of their instructions. The same letter contained the following clause. "A proper discharge of the important duties enjoined on you, arising out of this act, will require the exercise of a sound and an impartial judgment. You are not only to do all that in you lies, to prevent all intercourse, whether direct or circuitous, between the ports of the *United States*, and those of *France* or her dependencies, where the vessels *are apparently as well as really American*, and protected by *American* papers only, but you are to be vigilant that vessels or cargoes really *American*, but covered by *Danish* or other foreign papers, and bound *to* or *from French* ports, do not escape you."

These orders given by the executive under the construction of the act of congress made by the department to which its execution was assigned, enjoin the seizure of *American* vessels sailing from a *French* port. Is the officer who obeys them liable for damages sustained by this misconstruction of the act, or will his orders excuse him? If his instructions afford him no protection, then the law must take its course, and he must pay such damages as are legally awarded against him; if they excuse an act not otherwise excusable, it would then be necessary to inquire whether this is a case in which the probable cause which existed to induce a suspicion that the vessel was *American*, would excuse the captor from damages when the vessel appeared in fact to be neutral.

I confess the first bias of my mind was very strong in favour of the opinion that though the instructions of the executive could not give a right, they might yet excuse from damages. I was much inclined to think that a distinction ought to be taken between acts of civil and those of military officers; and between proceedings within the body of the country and those on the high seas. That implicit obedience which military men usually pay to the orders of their superiors, which indeed is indispensably necessary to every military system, appeared to me strongly to imply the principle that those orders, if not to perform a prohibited act, ought to justify the person whose general duty it is to obey them, and who is placed by the laws of his country in a situation which in general requires that he should obey them. I was strongly inclined to think that where, in consequence of orders from the legitimate authority, a vessel is seized with pure intention, the claim of the injured party for damages would be against that government from which the orders proceeded, and would be a proper subject for negotiation. But I have been convinced that I was mistaken, and I have receded from this first opinion. I acquiesce in that of my brethren, which is, that the instructions cannot change the nature of the transaction, or legalize an act which without those instructions would have been a plain trespass.

It becomes therefore unnecessary to inquire whether the probable cause afforded by the conduct of the *Flying-Fish* to suspect her of being an *American*, would excuse Captain *Little* from damages for having seized and sent her into port, since had she actually been an *American*, the seizure would have been unlawful?

Captain *Little* then must be answerable in damages to the owner of this neutral vessel, and as the account taken by order of the circuit court is not objectionable on its face, and has not been excepted to by coun[sel] before the proper tribunal, this court can receive no objection to it.

There appears then to be no error in the judgment of the circuit court, and it must be affirmed with costs.

NOTE ON COMMON LAW ACTIONS AGAINST FEDERAL OFFICERS

(1) The Right of Action. The plaintiff, Barreme, recovered damages from Captain Little for a maritime tort—the unlawful taking of private property on the high seas. Notably, common law imposed the duty on the individual officer, rather than the government itself. In this respect, the law of the United States followed that of England, where individual government officials were accountable in trespass suits. See Entick v. Carrington, 19 Howell's State Trials 1029, 95 Eng.Rep. 807 (1765) (government officers liable for trespass after court found that the warrant for search of plaintiff's home was issued without legal authority).[1] Officers, like Captain Little, often defended by pointing to statutory authority. But that defense did not work if the officer's actions exceeded the bounds of statutory authority or violated the Constitution. In the circumstances presented, the statute interdicting commerce during the Quasi-War did not authorize seizure of American, let alone Danish, vessels. Having exceeded his official authority, Little was held personally liable for damages.

Although the writ of trespass did much of the work in suits seeking redress for positive government wrongs, other common law forms were available to contest government action. Compare Crowell v. McFadon, 12 U.S. (8 Cranch) 94, 98 (1814) (rejecting suit for conversion of the cargo of a vessel detained under Jefferson's embargo), with Slocum v. Mayberry, 15 U.S. (2 Wheat.) 1, 9–12 (1817) (allowing owner to sue in replevin to recover cargo from an embargoed vessel). Suits to challenge the collection of taxes, including on constitutional grounds, typically named the tax collector as a defendant. See, *e.g.*, Poindexter v. Greenhow, 114 U.S. 270 (1885) (suit brought in detinue to recover property seized by the collector in payment of

------

[1]   On the significance of Entick to founding-era conceptions of government accountability, see Stuntz, *The Substantive Origins of Criminal Procedure*, 105 Yale L.J. 393, 396–404 (1995). For an accessible version of the decision, see Burset & Arvind, *A New Report of Entick v. Carrington (1765)*, 110 Ky.L.J. 265, 298–332 (2022). Jaffe & Henderson, *Judicial Review and the Rule of Law: Historical Origins*, 72 L.Q.Rev. 345, 348 (1956), explain that the "structure of judicial review derives from two sources: the prerogative writs (particularly certiorari and mandamus) and actions for damages" based on such theories as trespass and assumpsit. On the law governing maritime torts today, see Chap. VII, Sec. 1 and Chap. VIII, Sec. 6, *supra*.

taxes); Elliott v. Swartwout, 35 U.S. 137 (1836) (suit in assumpsit to recover back taxes paid under protest); see generally Woolhandler, *The Common Law Origins of Constitutionally Compelled Remedies*, 107 Yale L.J. 77, 135–37 (1997). None of these common law forms was understood, as such, to present a federal question or confer subject matter jurisdiction on the federal courts, see p. 1004, *supra*. Where diversity or maritime jurisdiction was unavailable, plaintiffs sued in state court. See Merriam v. Mitchell, 13 Me. 439 (1836) (upholding award of damages against federal postal official for false imprisonment).

(2) The Relevance of Good Faith and Superior Orders. Chief Justice Marshall addressed the possibility (and may have firmly believed) that Captain Little deserved some protection from damages based on the nature of his military office, the mitigating consequences of his duty to obey superior orders, and the entire good faith in which he proceeded. But the Court found it unnecessary to decide on the good faith defense and instead affirmed a judicial decree awarding over $8000, a substantial sum at the time. The Little decision has come to stand for the proposition that presidential directives do not immunize a federal officer from liability and cannot alter the rule of executive conduct specified in an act of Congress. See Barron & Lederman, *The Commander in Chief at Lowest Ebb—A Constitutional History*, 121 Harv.L.Rev. 941, 967–970 (2008).

In assessing the Court's choice to impose substantial personal liability on Captain Little, consider the alternative: to affirm the restoration of the vessel and remit the owner's compensation claim to the political branches. Such an approach (at least in a dispute between the United States and a foreign nation) would have required an assessment of the seizure's legality and a determination of the proper compensatory sum. Is it clear why political actors might prefer a federal adjudication of legality and damages in the first instance? Although Congress could have appropriated the necessary funds before any such adjudication, Secretary of State James Madison encouraged foreign nationals and their government representatives to pursue their Quasi-War loss-of-property claims in court before seeking compensation from the government. See Pfander & Hunt, *Public Wrongs and Private Bills: Indemnification and Government Accountability in the Early Republic*, 85 N.Y.U.L.Rev. 1862, 1895–1903 (2010).

(3) The "Right" to Indemnity. Little did not pay the judgment from his personal resources. Responding to Little's petition for indemnity, Congress appropriated funds to pay both the judgment and the cost of legal representation. See Pfander & Hunt, Paragraph (2), *supra*, at 1933 (reporting appropriation in excess of $10,000). Similar measures were enacted throughout the nineteenth century to indemnify other federal officers as to personal tort-based liability incurred for good faith actions in the line of duty. While indemnity was not guaranteed, legislative practice during the early republic resulted in payment to most officers who petitioned for relief. See *id.* 1905. Indemnity denials tended to occur when officers acted in bad faith or erred in discharging their duties. Reflecting on indemnity practice, the Court would explain that personal liability imposed no personal hardship because the government was "bound" to indemnify its officers. See, *e.g.*, Tracy v. Swartwout, 35 U.S. 80, 98–99 (1836).[2]

The coordinate role of the courts in adjudicating tort claims and the legislature in passing on official indemnity petitions achieved four goals. First, victims of government wrongdoing were ensured an adjudication of their claim in court and, if successful, an award of damages against the responsible officer. Second, the grant of indemnity secured a fund from which the victim could satisfy the judgment. Third, the grant of indemnity protected the officer from any personal liability for actions taken on behalf of the government, perhaps explaining why the Court rejected judge-made immunity in Little's case. Fourth, enactment of indemnifying legislation shifted responsibility to the United States for the payment of judgments resulting from the government's activities. Liability for the wrongful interdiction of commercial shipping thus fell on the U.S. Treasury as part of the cost of conducting the Quasi-War, despite the government's nominal immunity from tort-based claims for damages.

Sovereign immunity was a form of institutional settlement; it was less a matter of immunizing governments from liability than assigning functions to the proper department. Executive officers carried out government activities; courts assessed legality; and legislatures appropriated funds to pay government obligations. How well did this system work in practice? One would hesitate to speak today of a right to indemnity when compensation depends on congressional willingness to enact an appropriations bill. Yet during the nineteenth century, Congress devoted considerable time to assessing individual petitions for redress of grievances.[3] The challenges of keeping up with this work helped persuade Congress to transfer contract claims to the Court of Claims in 1855 and to accept Treasury liability for the torts of government officials in 1946. Both statutes shifted the task of assessing claims from the legislature to the courts.[4]

(4) The Transitory Tort Doctrine. As Little v. Barreme confirms, the system of government accountability applied to tort-based claims wherever

---

[2]   Officers who collected or handled government money, such as tax collectors, sheriffs, and marshals, maintained a running account in which they paid over to the treasury the sums they collected, less allowable fees and other appropriate deductions. For an overview of accounting obligations, see Pfander & Borrasso, *Public Rights and Article III: Judicial Oversight of Agency Action*, 82 Ohio St.L.J. 493, 508–10 (2021). When federal courts ordered the officer to repay a tax wrongly collected or compensate an individual for property wrongly seized, governments owed a federal duty to indemnify the officer by crediting the officer's account. See Poindexter v. Greenhow, 114 U.S. 270, 294 (1885) (citing Osborn v. Bank of the United States, 22 U.S. (9 Wheat.) 738, 853–54 (1824)).

[3]   Both the House and Senate set up committees to investigate and recommend payment of meritorious claims. See Pfander & Hunt, Paragraph (2), *supra*, at 1937. On the nature of legislative petitioning, see Pfander, *Sovereign Immunity and the Right to Petition*, 91 Nw.U.L.Rev. 899 (1997); Blackhawk, *Legislative Constitutionalism and Federal Indian Law*, 132 Yale L.J. 2205 (2023); Desan, *The Constitutional Commitment to Legislative Adjudication in the Early American Tradition*, 111 Harv.L.Rev. 1381 (1998); Bailey, Popular Influence Upon Public Policy: Petitioning in Eighteenth-Century Virginia (1979).

[4]   See Shimomura, *The History of Claims Against the United States: The Evolution from a Legislative Toward a Judicial Model of Payment*, 45 La.L.Rev. 625 (1985); United States v. Yellow Cab Co., 340 U.S. 543, 548–49 (1951) (noting that prior to the FTCA, "each Congress for many years ha[d] recognized the Government's obligation to pay claims on account" of officer torts through "hundreds of private relief acts").

they might arise. Invoking the transitory tort doctrine, victims could sue federal officers for torts committed within the United States, as well as those that arose outside the country. For example, the victim of a taking of personal property that occurred in Mexico during the Mexican-American War brought suit in New York federal court and recovered a judgment in excess of $100,000 against the responsible federal officer. See Mitchell v. Harmony, 54 U.S. 115 (1851). (Congress indemnified Colonel Mitchell.) On the incorporation of the transitory tort doctrine from English law, see McKenna v. Fisk, 42 U.S. 241, 249 (1843) (citing Mostyn v. Fabrigas, 1 Cowp. 161, 98 Eng.Rep. 1021, 1025–26 (1775)) (explaining that courts of the United States have jurisdiction that extends, like that in England, to claims by citizens and foreign nationals alike for "trespasses committed within the realm and out of the realm, or within or without the king's foreign dominions").[5]

(5) Specific Relief Against Government Officers. Apart from suits for damages by way of trespass and assumpsit, the common law tradition recognized a variety of writs for specific relief against government officials. These writs included replevin and detinue (to recover back property), ejectment (to secure possession of landed property rightfully owned), and a series of extraordinary (or, in England, "prerogative") writs that directed officials to take certain specified action on pain of contempt. The extraordinary writs in question—mandamus, prohibition, quo warranto, habeas corpus, certiorari, and scire facias—were typically administered at the discretion of a superior court.[6] See generally Jaffe, Judicial Control of Administrative Action 165–93 (1965); de Smith, *The Prerogative Writs*, 11 Cambridge L.J. 40 (1951). Of the six writs often characterized as extraordinary, Congress conferred judicial power to issue all but two (quo warranto and certiorari) in §§ 13 and 14 of the Judiciary Act of 1789 (now

---

[5] On the connection between the transitory tort doctrine and the assertion of personal jurisdiction based on the defendant's presence in the forum state, see Mallory v. Norfolk Southern Railway Co., 600 U.S. 122 (2023) (Gorsuch, J.) (suit for an injury " 'that might have happened any where' was generally considered a *'transitory'* action that followed the individual" and could be "maintained * * * in any place the defendant could be found") (quoting Story, Commentaries on the Conflict of Laws § 538, at 450 (1834)).

[6] For an introduction to mandamus, see the discussion of Marbury v. Madison, 5 U.S. (1 Cranch) 137 (1803), p. 76, *supra.* The writ of quo warranto ("by what authority") would inquire into the authority by which a public office is held or power to act is claimed. Historically, it was used to discover whether an official or state-chartered corporation was acting without authorization. If so, the remedy was to oust the relevant party from power. See Black's Law Dictionary 1371 (9th ed.2011). The writ of habeas corpus ("to hold the body") serves to test the legality of official detention or custody. For detailed discussion, see Chap. XI, *infra.* Courts issued the writ of prohibition at the threshold of litigation to block an inferior judicial or quasi-judicial body from exceeding its jurisdiction. The writ would issue, among other reasons, to inquire into the constitutionality of state tax statutes. See Weston v. City Council of Charleston, 27 U.S. 449 (1829). The writ of certiorari ("to be more fully informed") would direct a lower tribunal to certify its record for review in a superior court. Unlike prohibition, certiorari generally operated after a trial below to secure review of judicial or quasi-judicial action, but later fell into disuse as a means of reviewing administrative action. See Degge v. Hitchcock, 229 U.S. 162 (1913). The writ of scire facias ("you are to show cause") was useful in a great many settings; its role in offering extraordinary relief was to vacate a matter of record, such as a land or invention patent, an official's commission, or a corporation's charter, where the official record was tainted by illegality. Modern procedural rules abolished the form, but not the substance, of certain of these writs. See Fed.R.Civ.P. 81(b) (abolishing the writs of scire facias and mandamus but preserving the relief previously available through them).

codified in the All Writs Act, 28 U.S.C. § 1651). As officer suits, none of these extraordinary writ proceedings was thought to implicate the government's sovereign immunity even though, like injunctions, they effectively compelled government officers to act or refrain from acting in specific ways. See Houston v. Ormes, 252 U.S. 469, 472–74 (1920); Minnesota v. Hitchcock, 185 U.S. 373, 386 (1902).[7]

United States v. Lee

106 U.S. 196 (1882).
Appeal from the Circuit Court for the Eastern District of Virginia.

[The United States purchased the Arlington, Virginia plantation of General Robert E. Lee's wife, after an alleged failure to pay a $92 assessment under a tax to support the Civil War. The tax commissioners had refused a proffer of payment on behalf of the property's owner, under a rule (later held invalid) that only the owner in person could pay overdue taxes. The United States proceeded to use the property, known today as Arlington National Cemetery, as a burial ground and a fort.

[The Lees' son (who claimed title under his grandfather's will) filed an ejectment action in state court against the two federal officers who, under authority of the Secretary of War, had charge of the property. The defendants removed the action to the Circuit Court of the United States for the Eastern District of Virginia. Though the United States was not a party, the Attorney General filed a pleading in the Circuit Court seeking dismissal of the suit, stating that the United States possessed the property in the exercise of its sovereign and constitutional powers, and that "the court has no jurisdiction of the subject in controversy." Plaintiff's demurrer to this pleading was sustained, and after a jury trial, judgment for the plaintiff was entered.

[Both the individual defendants and the United States filed a writ of error in the Supreme Court. The Solicitor General argued the case for the individual defendants and for the United States.]

■ MR. JUSTICE MILLER delivered the opinion of the Court.

[The Court expressed doubt that the United States, a non-party, could file a writ of error, but noted that the defendants' writ raised all the issues pressed by the United States. After upholding the jury's determination that the United States did not acquire valid title under the tax sale proceeding because of the illegal refusal to accept payment

---

[7]   In England, mandamus, certiorari, and prohibition were issued by King's Bench, over which the sovereign once presided. Royal presence eventually became a fiction. Because the writs issued in the Crown's name, demanding that officers account for the legality of their actions, sovereign immunity played no role in these proceedings. The High Court of Chancery mostly stayed out of public law matters, instead handling private disputes over property rights. Scire facias in its extraordinary form originated on the "law side" of the Court of Chancery, where the records were kept. See Pfander & Wentzel, *The Common Law Origins of Ex parte Young*, 72 Stan.L.Rev. 1269 (2020).

on behalf of the owner, the Court turned to the question of sovereign immunity.]

The counsel for plaintiffs in error and in behalf of the United States assert the proposition, that though it has been ascertained by the verdict of the jury, in which no error is found, that the plaintiff has the title to the land in controversy, and that what is set up in behalf of the United States is no title at all, the court can render no judgment in favor of the plaintiff against the defendants in the action, because the latter hold the property as officers and agents of the United States, and it is appropriated to lawful public uses.

This proposition rests on the principle that the United States cannot be lawfully sued without its consent in any case, and that no action can be maintained against any individual without such consent, where the judgment must depend on the right of the United States to property held by such persons as officers or agents for the government.

The first branch of this proposition is conceded to be the established law of this country and of this court at the present day; the second, as a necessary or proper deduction from the first, is denied.

In order to decide whether the inference is justified from what is conceded, it is necessary to ascertain, if we can, on what principle the exemption of the United States from a suit by one of its citizens is founded, and what limitations surround this exemption. In this, as in most other cases of like character, it will be found that the doctrine is derived from the laws and practices of our English ancestors; and * * * it is beyond question that from the time of Edward the First until now the King of England was not suable in the courts of that country, except where his consent had been given on petition of right * * *.

There is in this country, however, no such thing as the petition of right, as there is no such thing as a kingly head to the nation, or to any of the States which compose it. There is vested in no officer or body the authority to consent that the State shall be sued except in the law-making power, which may give such consent on the terms it may choose to impose. Congress has created a court [the Court of Claims] in which it has authorized suits to be brought against the United States, but has limited such suits to those arising on contract, with a few unimportant exceptions.

What were the reasons which forbid that the King should be sued in his own court, and how do they apply to the political body corporate which we call the United States of America? As regards the King, one reason given by the old judges was the absurdity of the King's sending a writ to himself to command the King to appear in the King's court. No such reason exists in our government, as process runs in the name of the President, and may be served on the Attorney-General, as was done in Chisholm v. Georgia, 2 Dall. 419 [(1793)]. Nor can it be said that the government is degraded by appearing as a defendant in the courts of its own creation, because it is constantly appearing as a party in such courts, and submitting its rights as against the citizen to their judgment. * * *

That the doctrine [of sovereign immunity] met with a doubtful reception in the early history of this court may be seen from the opinions of two of its justices in the case of Chisholm v. Georgia, where Mr. Justice Wilson, a member of the convention which framed the Constitution, after a learned examination of the laws of England and other states and kingdoms, sums up the result by saying: "We see nothing against, but much in favor of, the jurisdiction of this court over the State of Georgia, a party to this cause." Mr. Chief Justice Jay also considered the question as affected by the difference between a republican State like ours and a personal sovereign, and held that there is no reason why a state should not be sued, though doubting whether the United States would be subject to the same rule.

The first recognition of the general doctrine by this court is to be found in the case of Cohens v. Virginia, 6 Wheat. 264 [(1821)].

The terms in which Mr. Chief Justice Marshall there gives assent to the principle does not add much to its force. "The counsel for the defendant," he says, "has laid down the general proposition that a sovereign independent State is not suable except by its own consent." This general proposition, he adds, will not be controverted.

* * * [W]hile acceding to the general proposition that in no court can the United States be sued directly by original process as a defendant, there is abundant evidence in the decisions of this court that the doctrine, if not absolutely limited to cases in which the United States are made defendants by name, is not permitted to interfere with the judicial enforcement of the established rights of plaintiffs when the United States is not a defendant or a necessary party to the suit.

But little weight can be given to the decisions of the English courts on this branch of the subject, for two reasons:—

1. In all cases where the title to property came into controversy between the crown and a subject, whether held in right of the person who was king or as representative of the nation, the petition of right presented a judicial remedy,—a remedy which this court, on full examination in a case which required it, held to be practical and efficient. There has been, therefore, no necessity for suing the officers or servants of the King who held possession of such property, when the issue could be made with the King himself as defendant.

2. Another reason of much greater weight is found in the vast difference in the essential character of the two governments as regards the source and the depositaries of power. * * *

Under our system the *people*, who are there called *subjects*, are the sovereign. Their rights, whether collective or individual, are not bound to give way to a sentiment of loyalty to the person of a monarch. The citizen here knows no person, however near to those in power, or however powerful himself, to whom he need yield the rights which the law secures to him when it is well administered. When he, in one of the courts of competent jurisdiction, has established his right to property, there is no reason why deference to any person, natural or artificial, not even the United States, should prevent him from using the means which the law gives him for the protection and enforcement of that right. * * *

The earliest case in this court in which the true rule is laid down, and which, bearing a close analogy to the one before us, seems decisive of it, is United States v. Peters, 5 Cranch 115 [(1809)]. In an admiralty proceeding, * * * the District Court of the United States for Pennsylvania * * * had decided that the libellants were entitled to the proceeds of the sale of a vessel condemned as prize of war, which had come to the possession of David Rittenhouse as treasurer of Pennsylvania. * * * [O]n an application therefor, a writ of *mandamus* to compel the judge of the District Court to proceed in the execution of his decree was granted. In delivering the opinion, Mr. Chief Justice Marshall says: "The State cannot be made a defendant to a suit brought by an individual, but it remains the duty of the courts of the United States to decide all cases brought before them by citizens of one State against citizens of a different State, when a State is not necessarily a defendant. In this case, the suit was not instituted against the State or its treasurer, but against the executrixes of David Rittenhouse, for the proceeds of a vessel condemned in the Court of Admiralty, which were admitted to be in their possession. If these proceeds had been the actual property of Pennsylvania, however wrongfully acquired, the disclosure of that fact would have presented a case on which it was unnecessary to give an opinion; *but it certainly can never be alleged that a mere suggestion of title in a State to property in possession of an individual must arrest the proceedings of the court, and prevent their looking into the suggestion and examining the validity of the title.*" * * *

It may be said—in fact it is said—that the present case differs from the one in 5 Cranch, because the officers who are sued assert no personal possession, but are holding as the mere agents of the United States, while the executors of Rittenhouse held the money until a better right was established. But the very next case in this court of a similar character, Meigs v. McClung's Lessee, 9 Cranch 11 [(1815)], shows that this distinction was not recognized as sound. [In Meigs, the plaintiff brought an action against military officers in possession of property and prevailed over the objection that the action could not be maintained against the officers because they were acting for the benefit of the United States and under their direction. The lower court held that since title was in the plaintiff, he was entitled to recover possession, and the Supreme Court upheld the judgment.]

* * * Osborn v. Bank of United States, 9 Wheat. 738 [(1824)], is a leading case, remarkable in many respects, and in none more than in those resembling the one before us. * * *

One of the objections pressed with pertinacity all through the case to the jurisdiction of the court was the conceded fact that the State of Ohio, though not made a defendant to the bill, was the real party in interest. That all the parties sued were her officers,—her auditor, her treasurer, and their agents,—concerning acts done in their official character, and in obedience to her laws. It was conceded that the State could not be sued, and it was earnestly argued there, as here, that what could not be done directly could not be done by suing her officers. And it was insisted that while the State could not be brought before the court, it was a necessary party to the relief sought, namely, the return of the money and obedience to the injunction, and that the bill must be dismissed.

A few citations from the opinion of Mr. Chief Justice Marshall will show the views entertained by the court on the question thus raised. * * *

[Chief Justice Marshall stated]: "* * * In cases where a State is a party on the record, the question of jurisdiction is decided by inspection. If jurisdiction depend not on this plain fact, but on the interest of the State, what rule has the Constitution given by which this interest is to be measured? If no rule is given, is it to be settled by the court? If so, the curious anomaly is presented of a court examining the whole testimony of a cause, inquiring into and deciding on the extent of a State's interest, without having a right to exercise any jurisdiction in the case. Can this inquiry be made without the exercise of jurisdiction?" * * *

The objection [of sovereign immunity] is also inconsistent with the principle involved in the last two clauses of article 5 of the amendments to the Constitution of the United States, whose language is: "That no person * * * shall be deprived of life, liberty, or property without due process of law, nor shall private property be taken for public use without just compensation."

Conceding that the property in controversy in this case is devoted to a proper public use, and that this has been done by those having authority to establish a cemetery and a fort, the verdict of the jury finds that it is and was the private property of the plaintiff, and was taken without any process of law and without any compensation. Undoubtedly those provisions of the Constitution are of that character which it is intended the courts shall enforce, when cases involving their operation and effect are brought before them. The instances in which the life and liberty of the citizen have been protected by the judicial writ of *habeas corpus* are too familiar to need citation, and many of these cases, indeed almost all of them, are those in which life or liberty was invaded by persons assuming to act under the authority of the government. Ex parte Milligan, 4 Wall. 2 [(1866)].

If this constitutional provision is a sufficient authority for the court to interfere to rescue a prisoner from the hands of those holding him under the asserted authority of the government, what reason is there that the same courts shall not give remedy to the citizen whose property has been seized without due process of law, and devoted to public use without just compensation? * * *

No man in this country is so high that he is above the law. No officer of the law may set that law at defiance with impunity. All the officers of the government, from the highest to the lowest, are creatures of the law, and are bound to obey it. * * *

Courts of justice are established, not only to decide upon the controverted rights of the citizens as against each other, but also upon rights in controversy between them and the government; and the docket of this court is crowded with controversies of the latter class.

Shall it be said, in the face of all this, and of the acknowledged right of the judiciary to decide in proper cases, statutes which have been passed by both branches of Congress and approved by the President to be unconstitutional, that the courts cannot give a remedy when the citizen has been deprived of his property by force, his estate seized and converted to the use of the government without lawful authority, without process of law, and without compensation, because the President has ordered it and his officers are in possession?

If such be the law of this country, it sanctions a tyranny which has no existence in the monarchies of Europe, nor in any other government which has a just claim to well-regulated liberty and the protection of personal rights. * * *

The evils supposed to grow out of the possible interference of judicial action with the exercise of powers of the government essential to some of its most important operations, will be seen to be small indeed compared to this evil, and much diminished, if they do not wholly disappear, upon a recurrence to a few considerations.

* * * [One such] consideration is, that since the United States cannot be made a defendant to a suit concerning its property, and no judgment in any suit against an individual who has possession or control of such property can bind or conclude the government, * * * the government is always at liberty, notwithstanding any such judgment, to avail itself of all the remedies which the law allows to every person, natural or artificial, for the vindication and assertion of its rights. Hence, taking the present case as an illustration, the United States may proceed by a bill in chancery to quiet its title, in aid of which, if a proper case is made, a writ of injunction may be obtained. Or it may bring an action of ejectment, in which, on a direct issue between the United States as plaintiff, and the present plaintiff as defendant, the title of the United States could be judicially determined. Or, if satisfied that its title has been shown to be invalid, and it still desires to use the property, or any part of it, for the purposes to which it is now devoted, it may purchase such property by fair negotiation, or condemn it by a judicial proceeding, in which a just compensation shall be ascertained and paid according to the Constitution.

If it be said that the proposition here established may subject the property, the officers of the United States, and the performance of their indispensable functions to hostile proceedings in the State courts, the answer is, that no case can arise in a State court, where the interests, the property, the rights, or the authority of the Federal government may come in question, which cannot be removed into a court of the United States under existing laws. * * *

The Circuit Court was competent to decide the issues in this case between the parties that were before it; in the principles on which these issues were decided no error has been found; and its judgment is

Affirmed.

■ MR. JUSTICE GRAY, with whom concurred MR. CHIEF JUSTICE WAITE, MR. JUSTICE BRADLEY, and MR. JUSTICE WOODS, dissenting.

* * * The case so deeply affects the sovereignty of the United States, and its relations to the citizen, that it is fit to announce the grounds of our dissent. * * *

This [action] * * * is brought to recover possession of land which the United States have for years held, and still hold, for military and other public purposes, claiming title under a certificate of sale for direct taxes, which is declared by the act of Congress of June 7, 1862, to be *prima facie* evidence of the regularity and validity of the sale and of the title of the purchaser * * *.

The principles upon which we are of opinion that the court below had no authority to try the question of the validity of the title of the United States in this action, and that this court has therefore no authority to pass upon that question, may be briefly stated.

The sovereign is not liable to be sued in any judicial tribunal without its consent. The sovereign cannot hold property except by agents. To maintain an action for the recovery of possession of property held by the sovereign through its agents, not claiming any title or right in themselves, but only as the representatives of the sovereign and in its behalf, is to maintain an action to recover possession of the property against the sovereign; and to invade such possession of the agents, by execution or other judicial process, is to invade the possession of the sovereign, and to disregard the fundamental maxim that the sovereign cannot be sued.

That maxim is not limited to a monarchy, but is of equal force in a republic. In the one, as in the other, it is essential to the common defence and general welfare that the sovereign should not, without its consent, be dispossessed by judicial process of forts, arsenals, military posts, and ships of war, necessary to guard the national existence against insurrection and invasion; of custom-houses and revenue cutters, employed in the collection of the revenue; or of light-houses and light-ships, established for the security of commerce with foreign nations and among the different parts of the country.

These principles appear to us to be axioms of public law, which would need no reference to authorities in their support, were it not for the exceeding importance and interest of the case, the great ability with which it has been argued, and the difference of opinion that has been manifested as to the extent and application of the precedents.

The exemption of the United States from being impleaded without their consent is, as has often been affirmed by this court, as absolute as that of the Crown of England or any other sovereign. * * *

To maintain this action, independently of any legislation by Congress, is to declare that the exemption of the United States from being impleaded without their consent does not embrace lands held by a disputed title; to defeat the exemption from judicial process in the very cases in which it is of the utmost importance to the public that it should be upheld; and to compel the United States to submit to the determination of courts and juries the validity of their title to any land held and used for military, naval, commercial, revenue, or police purposes.

[Justice Gray then argued that several precedents relied upon by the plaintiff, including Chisholm, Osborn, and Meigs, were distinguishable— Chisholm because the case did not hold that the United States could be sued without its consent, Osborn because the money in issue was in the personal possession of the defendants and the suit was one to enjoin federal constitutional violations, and Meigs because "[n]o objection to the exercise of jurisdiction was made by the defendants or by the United States, or noticed by the Court."] * * *

NOTE ON SOVEREIGN IMMUNITY AS A DEFENSE TO OFFICER SUITS

(1) The Origin of Sovereign Immunity. Justice Miller, writing for the Court in Lee, attributed the doctrine of sovereign immunity partly to the English monarchy and partly to the common law's failure to provide authority for asserting claims against the government. But Justice Miller distinguished governments in the republican United States, which lacked a "kingly head" or any person or body (aside from the law-making power) with power to consent to suit. Acknowledging that the petition of right arose in England to facilitate certain claims against the Crown, primarily those to property, Justice Miller explained that the procedure had not taken hold in the United States. Hence, the Court's emphasis on officer suits, which were said to extend to all officers however "high" and assure remedies to prevent "tyranny."[1]

Sovereign immunity today protects federal and state governments from unauthorized suits in federal court. The doctrine owes much to the idea that the payment of government money requires legislative adoption of an

---

[1] On the petition of right and its role in property disputes in England, see Jaffe, *Suits Against Governments and Officers: Sovereign Immunity*, 77 Harv.L.Rev. 1 (1963).

appropriations bill. Article I, § 9, cl. 7, provides that "No Money shall be drawn from the Treasury, but in Consequence of Appropriations made by Law." See Reeside v. Walker, 52 U.S. 272, 291 (1850); Figley & Tidmarsh, *The Appropriations Power and Sovereign Immunity*, 107 Mich.L.Rev. 1207 (2009). Yet judicial deference to legislative disposition of government money and property does not fully explain the doctrine.[2] The Lee Court effectively ousted the federal government from the property in question after rejecting its claim of good title, much the way the Osborn Court ordered a return of the Bank's assets after rejecting the validity of the Ohio tax. See Osborn v. Bank of the United States, 22 U.S. (9 Wheat.) 738 (1824), p. 994, *supra*. It did so by exercising control over government officers under the party-of-record rule.

(2) Officer Suits and the Party of Record Rule. However well-grounded in the theory of republican government, sovereign immunity means as a practical matter that plaintiffs are expected to pursue many of their claims against responsible officers instead of the government. Suits against the government were permissible only when Congress adopted a statutory waiver of immunity, as it did (Justice Miller notes) by creating the Court of Claims in 1855 to hear suits for breach of government contracts. See Shimomura, *The History of Claims Against the United States: The Evolution from a Legislative Toward a Judicial Model of Payment*, 45 La.L.Rev. 625 (1985). For more details on the statutory provisions that now more broadly authorize suits against the federal government, see Sec. 5.A, *infra*.

The Lees' claim to eject federal officials from their land sounded in tort and fell outside the jurisdiction of the Court of Claims. After the Supreme Court upheld the jury's verdict, rejecting the government's ownership claim, Congress appropriated $150,000 to purchase the Lee estate. See Poole, On Hallowed Ground: The Story of Arlington National Cemetery 282 (2009) (recounting the property's acquisition and its use to the present day as Arlington National Cemetery). As in Little v. Barreme, the Court in Lee addressed legality and left Congress to reckon with the financial implications of wrongful possession.[3]

The Court limited sovereign immunity to those cases in which the government was a formal party of record, joined as such by the plaintiff, or was "a necessary party to the suit." Applying its earlier decisions in United States v. Peters, 9 U.S. (5 Cranch) 115 (1809), and Osborn, the Lee Court

---

[2]   For other suggested justifications of sovereign immunity, consider Federal Maritime Comm'n v. South Carolina State Ports Auth., 535 U.S. 743 (2002) (advancing a "dignity"-based rationale for state sovereign immunity); Chisholm v. Georgia, 2 U.S. (2 Dall.) 419, 478 (1793) (Jay, C.J.) (identifying difficulty with the enforcement of a judgment against the government rather than its officers); Kawananakoa v. Polyblank, 205 U.S. 349, 353 (1907) (Holmes, J.) (citing the "logical and practical ground that there can be no legal right as against the authority that makes the law on which the right depends"); United States v. Shearer, 473 U.S. 52, 58–59 (1985) (avoiding judicial interference with government control over its instrumentalities, funds, and property).

[3]   After the Civil War ended, General Robert E. Lee was indicted for treason by a federal grand jury sitting in Virginia. For a variety of reasons, the indictment fizzled and Lee served as a university president until his death in 1870. See Guelzo, Robert E. Lee: A Life (2021). The government's claim to ownership of the Lee plantation, rejected by the Court, was based on Lee's failure to pay taxes during the Civil War.

took a very narrow view of the government's "necessary" party status. The government's obvious and acknowledged interest in the question of title to the Lee estate did not suffice; a focus on government interests would presumably arrest any proceeding against government officials for action taken in the line of duty. Instead, the Court emphasized the importance of providing a test of legality through suit against the official.

The "necessary party" calculus changed in suits for relief on government contracts. In contrast to their personal responsibility in tort, officers entering into and administering contracts on behalf of the government were not, at common law, personally liable if the government committed a breach. Lacking a responsible individual defendant, those seeking compensation for breach of government contracts were expected to petition the legislative branch for payment; breach of contract suits were cognizable in court only as Congress or the state assembly provided. If the legislature made no such provision, suits for breach of government contracts were barred by immunity. See, *e.g.*, Louisiana ex rel. Elliott v. Jumel, 107 U.S. 711, 721, 727 (1883) (immunizing state of Louisiana). That was true even where the plaintiff attempted to name the officer as the party of record and secure relief without naming the government. Thus, In re Ayers, 123 U.S. 443, 487 (1887), held that the doctrine of state sovereign immunity and the Eleventh Amendment precluded a federal court from entering an injunction against state officials "the object of which is * * * indirectly, to compel the specific performance of [a] contract." The Lee Court seemingly anticipated these results, acknowledging that immunity may not be "absolutely limited to cases in which the United States are made defendants by name."

The Lee Court's application of the party-of-record rule, as qualified by a narrow necessary party exception, left in place a broad scope for suits against officers, if it could be shown that the officer had personally committed an actionable wrong. Subsequent decisions confirm that government officials can be not only enjoined from causing harm, *e.g.*, Philadelphia Co. v. Stimson, 223 U.S. 605 (1912), but also compelled to perform affirmative acts if they are required by law to discharge some duty, see, *e.g.*, Wilbur v. United States ex rel. Krushnic, 280 U.S. 306 (1930). Summarizing the general pattern of judicial responses to officer suits, Professor Jaffe found that the "sensitive areas—the areas where consent to suit [was] likely to be required—[were] those involving the enforcement of contracts, treasury liability for tort, and the adjudication of interests in property which [had] come unsullied by tort" into the treasury of the government. Jaffe, *Suits Against Governments and Officers: Sovereign Immunity*, 77 Harv.L.Rev. 1, 29 (1963). If the legislature did not provide for the litigation of such claims, individuals sought relief by petition to the assembly.

(3) Retrenchment: Larson and Its Progeny. In several twentieth century decisions, the Supreme Court retreated to a significant extent from the broad implications of United States v. Lee respecting the availability of specific relief against federal officers.

(a) In the first and perhaps the most controversial of these cases, Larson v. Domestic & Foreign Commerce Corp., 337 U.S. 682 (1949), a sharply divided Court upheld the defense of sovereign immunity in a suit by a plaintiff who claimed to have purchased some coal from the United States and sought to enjoin federal officers from transferring it to any other person. Writing for the Court, Chief Justice Vinson reasoned that the suit was "in substance, a suit against the Government over which the court, in the absence of consent, has no jurisdiction." In a suit against a government officer, "the question is * * * whether, by obtaining relief against the officer, relief will not, in effect, be obtained against the sovereign. For the sovereign can act only through agents and, when an agent's actions are restrained, the sovereign itself may, through him, be restrained."

Officer suits seeking to compel official action should be treated as *not* barred by sovereign immunity, the Chief Justice said, only when the actions are *ultra vires*, either because they exceed statutory bounds on official authority such that the officer is "not doing the business which the sovereign has empowered him to do or he is doing it in a way which the sovereign has forbidden." Deeming action in violation of the Constitution to be necessarily *ultra vires*, the Court distinguished Lee as a case involving official action in violation of the Takings Clause.

Applying these principles to the case at hand, Chief Justice Vinson concluded that although the defendant official might have violated the substantive law by failing to deliver coal to which the plaintiff had a legal right, the decision whether to deliver the coal lay within the bounds of his statutory authority, and he had not violated the Constitution by failing to deliver it.

Justice Frankfurter dissented, writing: "[T]he policy behind the immunity of the sovereign from suit without its consent does not call for disregard of a citizen's right to pursue an agent of the government for a wrongful invasion of a recognized legal right unless the legislature deems it appropriate to displace the right of suing the individual defendant with the right to sue the Government."

How useful is it to ask whether a particular action against government officials is "really" against the government? Government interests were fully implicated in Lee as they are in other actions not barred by sovereign immunity. Is it a fiction that such suits against officers are not against the state even when they implicate important government interests? Or is the fiction that there ever existed a broad doctrine of sovereign immunity that, outside of a few specific areas, barred relief at the behest of individuals complaining of government illegality?

(b) Subsequent decisions upholding a sovereign immunity defense in suits nominally against officials include Malone v. Bowdoin, 369 U.S. 643 (1962), in which the plaintiffs sought to eject a federal forest service officer from certain land to which both plaintiffs and the federal government claimed title, and Dugan v. Rank, 372 U.S. 609 (1963), a suit to enjoin federal officers from impounding waters behind a federally financed dam, on the ground that the impoundment interfered with the plaintiffs' downstream uses of the water. Although Malone was otherwise similar on its facts to United States v. Lee, the cases were distinguishable, the Court reasoned, because Lee involved an alleged violation of the Takings Clause and

Malone—in which subsequent changes in the statutory law would have authorized a suit against the government for just compensation—did not.

For now, issues involving the availability of an immunity defense in cases such as these have been essentially mooted, or at least transformed, by the enactment of statutes waiving the government's sovereign immunity, especially including the 1976 amendment to the Administrative Procedure Act, discussed at p. 1341, *infra*, which waived immunity in all federal court actions seeking relief other than money damages. Nevertheless, Larson and its progeny appear to state the currently controlling law on the conditions under which a suit against a government officer that has not been authorized by statute may be barred on the ground that it is really one against the sovereign and thus falls under the doctrine of federal sovereign immunity. Sisk, *A Primer on the Doctrine of Federal Sovereign Immunity*, 58 Okla.L.Rev. 439, 457 (2006), offers this summary:

"[U]nder the Larson-Malone sovereign immunity doctrine, a suit may be maintained directly against a governmental officer under two circumstances. First, if the officer allegedly acted outside of the authority conferred on his or her office by Congress, that is, beyond delegated statutory authority, then his or her conduct will be treated as individual in nature and will be neither attributed to the sovereign nor barred by sovereign immunity. Second, if the officer acted within the conferred statutory limits of the office, but his or her conduct allegedly offended a provision of the Constitution, then sovereign immunity again is lifted."

Note that the law of federal sovereign immunity, as thus summarized, assumes that Congress not only can, but does, authorize federal officials to violate otherwise applicable law establishing statutory or common law rights in private citizens. When if ever should the Court assume that Congress has decided to deny a remedy for lawbreaking by federal officials? Did the Larson Court so assume or were other remedies available?[4]

---

2. THE ELEVENTH AMENDMENT AND STATE SOVEREIGN IMMUNITY

Modern law retains some recognizable features of the nineteenth-century framework, with its reliance on officer suits to challenge state official action. Today, states enjoy a presumptive sovereign immunity from suit that requires plaintiffs to identify alternative modes of securing redress for legal wrongs. Those alternatives include officer suits under 42 U.S.C. § 1983 and Ex parte Young, 209 U.S. 123 (1908), which pose questions of their own, and suits under federal statutes in which

---

[4]   In the Tucker Act, discussed at p. 1343, *infra*, Congress authorized the Court of Claims to adjudicate claims seeking compensation for the federal government's takings of property and breaches of contract. The Court's perception that such remedies were adequate may go far to explain its decision to foreclose equitable relief in the Larson-Malone line of cases. Compare Knick v. Township of Scott, 588 U.S. 180 (2019), p. 1305, *infra*, where the Court reaffirmed the validity of an officer suit for injunctive relief against a taking of property but acknowledged its possible displacement through the provision of an adequate just compensation remedy.

Congress has properly exercised its power to subject the states to liability. Complicating this framework, the Court's expansive view of state immunity blocks suits that the Eleventh Amendment's text does not in terms foreclose.

No single principle or mode of interpretation explains the resulting body of law. The Court's analysis often emphasizes the Constitution's purpose and structure and discounts the text in assessing the meaning of the constitutional plan. See Manning, *The Eleventh Amendment and the Reading of Precise Constitutional Texts*, 113 Yale L.J. 1663 (2004). Moreover, the avowed purposes vary from case to case, from the assurance of adequate remedies in one decision to the protection of government interests in the next. See Jeffries, *In Praise of the Eleventh Amendment and Section 1983*, 84 Va.L.Rev. 47 (1998) (noting the doctrine's arbitrary stops in reasoning).

Additionally, the theory of "remedial equilibration" suggests that the Court adjusts the availability of legal remedies as part of a much broader picture considering what rights and remedies are available in the system as a whole. See Levinson, *Rights Essentialism and Remedial Equilibration*, 99 Colum.L.Rev. 857 (1999); see also Fallon, *The Linkage Between Justiciability and Remedies—And Their Connection to Substantive Rights*, 92 Va.L.Rev. 633 (2006). On this account, the wisdom of any particular grant of immunity must be considered in the context of what other remedies are available, as well as in the context of the Court's interpretations of the substantive law.

NOTE ON CHISHOLM V. GEORGIA AND THE ELEVENTH AMENDMENT

(1) The Ratification-Era Immunity Debate. Article III of the Constitution confers jurisdiction over state-party litigation, including "controversies" between the states; between a state and a foreign nation; between a state and diverse citizens or foreign nationals. In addition, Article III's grant of federal question jurisdiction has been thought to extend to federal law claims by and against the states. Finally, Article III confers original jurisdiction on the Supreme Court in "those" cases in which a state shall be party. In referring to states as parties the Constitution posed but did not specifically answer the question of state sovereign immunity. It says nothing in terms that would preserve such immunity, promote it to constitutional status, set it aside, or authorize Congress to set it aside.

Opponents of ratification argued that, by conferring jurisdiction, the Constitution's provision for state-party litigation stripped the states of their sovereign immunity from suit and could lead to federal enforcement of state debts. In Virginia, responding to such arguments from George Mason and Patrick Henry, James Madison said: "jurisdiction in controversies between a State and citizens of another State is much objected to, and perhaps without reason. It is not in the power of individuals to call any State into court. The only operation it can have is that, if a State should wish to bring a suit against a citizen, it must be brought before the federal court." Henry called Madison's argument "perfectly incomprehensible." Apparently a textualist, Henry asked: "What says the paper? That it shall have cognizance of all controversies between a State, and citizens of another State, without discriminating between plaintiff or defendant." John Marshall replied: "I hope that no gentleman will think that a State will be called at the bar of the federal court. . . . It is not rational to suppose that the sovereign power should be dragged before a court. . . . I see a difficulty in making a State defendant which does not prevent its being plaintiff."[1]

Writing in Federalist No. 81, Alexander Hamilton also offered a qualified denial of state amenability to suit: "It is inherent in the nature of sovereignty not to be amenable to the suit of an individual *without its consent*. This is the general sense, and the general practice of mankind; and the exemption, as one of the attributes of sovereignty, is now enjoyed by the government of every State in the Union. Unless, therefore, there is a surrender of this immunity in the plan of the convention, it will remain with the States, and the danger intimated must be merely ideal." In denying that the grant of diversity jurisdiction worked a surrender of immunity, Hamilton explained that the debts had been incurred under the Articles of Confederation when the states were "free from every constraint but that which flows from the obligations of good faith." To use diversity jurisdiction to render those obligations federally enforceable "would be altogether forced and unwarrantable."[2]

Hamilton acknowledged that states could accept limits on their sovereignty by ratifying the Constitution or "plan of the convention" but did not directly discuss what role the federal courts would play in enforcing the federal restrictions on state action that would take effect on the "plan's" adoption. Hamilton did not address the Constitution's declarations, in Article I, § 10, that "[n]o state shall" emit bills of credit, authorize payment of debts except in gold and silver, or impair the obligation of contract. Hamilton's discussion of immunity and waiver in the "plan of the convention" has been revived in recent Supreme Court decisions as one source of congressional power to subject states to suit in federal court. See pp. 1252–1262, *infra*.

Following ratification, Congress enacted § 13 of the Judiciary Act of 1789, conferring original jurisdiction on the Court to hear "all controversies of a civil nature" in which "a state is a party." Individual suitors hastened to the Court to institute claims against the states of Georgia, Maryland, Massachusetts, New York, South Carolina, and Virginia, thereby posing the issue of sovereign immunity that Hamilton, the Virginians, and others had

---

[1]   10 The Documentary History of the Ratification of the Constitution 1406, 1414, 1422–23, 1433 (Kaminski ed. 1993). Nelson, *Sovereign Immunity as a Doctrine of Personal Jurisdiction*, 115 Harv.L.Rev. 1559 (2002), defends the Madison-Marshall distinction between party-based litigation by and against the states on the theory that Article III requires a case or controversy, a dispute between parties amenable to judicial power. To the extent existing law failed to recognize state amenability, Nelson argues that Article III courts lacked power to join states as defendants due to limits better understood as matters of personal than subject matter jurisdiction.

[2]   The Federalist No. 81 (Hamilton).

debated. See 5 Documentary History of the Supreme Court: Suits Against the States, 1789–1800 (Marcus ed. 1994). Among those suits was Chisholm's claim against Georgia.

(2) Chisholm v. Georgia. In Chisholm v. Georgia, 2 U.S. (2 Dall.) 419 (1793), a South Carolina citizen, Chisholm, filed an assumpsit claim against the State of Georgia as an original action in the Supreme Court, seeking to enforce contractual obligations dating from 1777. When Georgia refused to enter an appearance, Chisholm moved for the entry of a default judgment.

Each of the five Justices wrote separately. Justices Blair and Cushing both relied on what they said was the clear language of Article III, noting that its grant of jurisdiction over controversies between two states contemplated that an unconsenting state could be a defendant. Generalizing, Justice Blair thought it followed that jurisdiction in diversity also contemplated suits against state defendants. To the argument that, by listing the states first in the diversity grant of judicial power, Article III meant to allow jurisdiction over states as plaintiffs only, Blair responded: "A dispute between A. and B. [is] surely a dispute between B. and A. Both cases, I have no doubt, were intended." Blair also pointed to the grant of original jurisdiction in Article III; he thought its reference to states as parties contemplated their appearance as both plaintiffs and defendants. Justice Cushing agreed with Blair's analysis of Article III. In addition, he observed that the Constitution had made serious inroads on state sovereignty: the powers of "declaring war, making peace, raising and supporting armies for public defence, levying duties, excises and taxes" were all "lodged in Congress." Finally, he described the no-state-shall provisions in Article I, section 10 as "important restrictions of the power of States" thought necessary "to maintain the Union; and to establish some fundamental uniform principles of public justice, throughout the whole Union."

Chief Justice Jay likewise relied on Article III's language but argued in addition that the "feudal" doctrine of sovereign immunity was incompatible with popular sovereignty. Troubled, though, that this argument implied that the United States itself could be sued, notwithstanding the difficulty of enforcing a judgment against it, he left that question open. Justice Wilson argued most fully that the doctrine of sovereign immunity was incompatible with principles of public law, popular sovereignty, and a republican form of government, reasoning that a state was no more sovereign, and no less subject to the law, than an individual.

Justice Iredell's lengthy and lone dissent focused on "the particular question * * * will an action of assumpsit lie against a State? * * * If it will, it must be in virtue of the Constitution of the United States, and of some law of Congress conformable thereto." The attorney general of the United States, serving in a private capacity as Chisholm's lawyer, argued that the Court had ample power under § 14 of the 1789 Judiciary Act to fashion any writs "necessary for the exercise" of its jurisdiction and agreeable to the "principles and usages of law." Counsel also argued that the Supreme Court had inherent power to fashion incidental remedies to make its jurisdiction effective. Justice Iredell rejected both views. Federal courts "must receive, not merely their organization as to the number of Judges of which they are to consist; but all their authority, as to the manner of their proceeding, from the Legislature only." Turning to the fashioning of writs under § 14, Justice Iredell explained that the limiting reference to the "principles and usages" of law must refer either to the pre-constitutional practice of the state courts or that in England, neither one of which would have allowed "a compulsory suit for the recovery of money against a State." After grounding his opinion in the absence of statutory authority, Justice Iredell also added that "it may not be improper to intimate that my present opinion is strongly against any construction of [the Constitution] which will admit, under any circumstances, a compulsive suit against a State." He noted that "[t]his opinion I hold, however, with all the reserve proper for one, which, according to my sentiments in this case, may be deemed in some measure extrajudicial."[1]

(3) The Adoption of the Eleventh Amendment. Chisholm provoked a strong reaction that more recent opinions of the Supreme Court have characterized as "a shock of surprise." *E.g.* Seminole Tribe v. Florida, 517 U.S. 44, 69 (1996). Constitutional amendments to overrule Chisholm were introduced in February 1793, shortly after the decision, and one version was formally adopted by the House and Senate nearly a year later.[2] With state ratification complete in 1795, the Eleventh Amendment became law, providing that:

"The Judicial power of the United States shall not be construed to extend to any suit in law or equity, commenced or prosecuted against one of the United States by Citizens of another State, or by Citizens or Subjects of any Foreign State."

As history has revealed, these words have meant different things to different readers. All agree that the Eleventh Amendment was adopted to overrule the Supreme Court's decision in Chisholm, which had "construed" Article III to "extend to [a] * * * suit in law * * * against one of the United States by Citizens of another State." But what else the Amendment does— or does not do—and what immunity principles apply in the absence of the Eleventh Amendment have puzzled generations of lawyers and jurists. Some read the Amendment's failure to block all state suits as a gap to be filled through judicial recognition of some form of sovereign immunity that extends beyond the text's jurisdictional restrictions. Others regard the Amendment as a compromise, foreclosing diversity-based suits to collect old state debts but preserving state suability to enforce obligations imposed by federal and maritime law. For greater discussion, see pp. 1181–1183, 1244, *infra.*

---

[1]   On founding-era controversies over advisory opinions and other extrajudicial statements, see Chap. II., Sec. 1, *supra.*

[2]   Another early proposed amendment read as follows: "That no state shall be liable to be made a party defendant in any of the judicial courts, established, or which shall be established under the authority of the United States, at the suit of any person or persons whether a citizen or citizens, or a foreigner or foreigners, of any body politic or corporate, whether within or without the United States." See Fletcher, *The Diversity Explanation of the Eleventh Amendment: A Reply to Critics,* 56 U.Chi.L.Rev. 1261, 1269 & n.45 (1989) (attributing the draft to Theodore Sedgwick, a member of Congress from Massachusetts). Later, a rejected amendment, proffered by then Senator and later Treasury Secretary Albert Gallatin, would have added a savings clause for suits to enforce treaties. See *id.* 1285.

(4) The Eleventh Amendment: Early Applications. In its first encounter with the Eleventh Amendment, the Court dismissed the many pending state-party suits on its original docket after concluding that the Amendment deprived it of subject matter jurisdiction. See Hollingsworth v. Virginia, 3 U.S. 378 (1798). Such a jurisdictional characterization of the Amendment both vindicated the states' claimed immunity from suit and deprived the Court of power to use its jurisdiction to recognize rights to sue in assumpsit or otherwise.

In other early cases, the Court limited the Amendment to its specific text and allowed suits to proceed under the unamended language of Article III. Thus, in Rhode Island v. Massachusetts, 37 U.S. 657 (1838), the Court upheld its jurisdiction over controversies between two states and rejected the defendant's argument that sovereign immunity blocked the claim of its sibling state. Similarly in Cohens v. Virginia, 19 U.S. (6 Wheat.) 264 (1821), the Court rejected the state's contention that it was being sued without its consent. Because the petition for the writ of error, filed by the Cohens after they were convicted in state court criminal proceedings, was entirely defensive and sought no affirmative relief, Chief Justice Marshall concluded that it was not a "suit" within the meaning of the Amendment.

The Court also generally applied a rule focused on the "party on the record" in assessing the viability of litigation against state officials. See Osborn v. Bank of the United States, 22 U.S. (9 Wheat.) 738 (1824), p. 994, *supra* (ordering Ohio state officials to return assets taken from the bank and limiting the Eleventh Amendment's operation "to those suits in which a State is a party on the record"). The Osborn Court further explained, in an oft-quoted passage, that the "amendment has its full effect, if the constitution be construed as it would have been construed, had the jurisdiction of the Court never been extended to suits brought against a State, by the citizens of another State, or by aliens." At the same time, earlier in the opinion, the Court observed that it "was not in the power of the Bank" to "make [the State] a party" even though the case was grounded in federal question jurisdiction, because of the Eleventh Amendment. Other cases also wrestled with the party-of-record rule. Compare Governor of Georgia v. Madrazo, 26 U.S. (1 Pet.) 110 (1828) (concluding that the proper party defendant was the state of Georgia; suit against the governor for an authorized taking did not give rise to personal liability), with Ex parte Madrazzo [sic], 32 U.S. (7 Pet.) 627, 632 (1833) (dismissing an original suit against Georgia where jurisdiction was based on party-alignment within the express terms of the Eleventh Amendment and the dispute's subject matter did not implicate admiralty or federal question jurisdiction).

In reading the next principal case, consider whether the Court's refusal to allow the suit to proceed rests on Article III, the Eleventh Amendment, a federal statute, a reluctance to recognize a judge-made right to sue, or something else.

Hans v. Louisiana

134 U.S. 1 (1890).

Error to the Circuit Court of the United States for the Eastern District of Louisiana.

This was an action brought in the Circuit Court of the United States * * * against the State of Louisiana by Hans, a citizen of that State, to recover the amount of certain coupons annexed to bonds of the State, issued under the provisions of an act of the legislature approved January 24, 1874. [The coupons sued on were for interest accrued as of January 1, 1880. Hans alleged that an amendment to the state constitution barring the state from paying the interest owing was an impairment of the obligation of contract in violation of the U.S. Constitution. The lower court dismissed the action for lack of jurisdiction, and Hans appealed to the Supreme Court.]

■ MR. JUSTICE BRADLEY delivered the opinion of the court.

The question is presented, whether a State can be sued in a Circuit Court of the United States by one of its own citizens upon a suggestion that the case is one that arises under the Constitution or laws of the United States.

The ground taken is, that under the Constitution, as well as under the act of Congress passed to carry it into effect, a case is within the jurisdiction of the federal courts, without regard to the character of the parties, if it arises under the Constitution or laws of the United States * * *. It is conceded that where the jurisdiction depends alone upon the character of the parties, a controversy between a State and its own citizens is not embraced within it; but it is contended that though jurisdiction does not exist on that ground, it nevertheless does exist if the case itself is one which necessarily involves a federal question; and with regard to ordinary parties this is undoubtedly true. The question now to be decided is, whether it is true where one of the parties is a State, and is sued as a defendant by one of its own citizens.

That a State cannot be sued by a citizen of another State, or of a foreign state, on the mere ground that the case is one arising under the Constitution or laws of the United States, is clearly established by the decisions of this court in several recent cases. Louisiana v. Jumel, 107 U.S. 711 [(1883)]; Hagood v. Southern, 117 U.S. 52 [(1886)]; In re Ayers, 123 U.S. 443 [(1887)]. Those were cases arising under the Constitution of the United States, upon laws complained of as impairing the obligation of contracts, one of which was the constitutional amendment of Louisiana complained of in the present case. Relief was sought against state officers who professed to act in obedience to those laws. This court held that the suits were virtually against the States themselves and were consequently violative of the Eleventh Amendment of the Constitution, and could not be maintained. It was not denied that they presented cases arising under the Constitution; but, notwithstanding that, they were held to be prohibited by the amendment referred to.

In the present case the plaintiff in error contends that he, being a citizen of Louisiana, is not embarrassed by the obstacle of the Eleventh Amendment, inasmuch as that amendment only prohibits suits against a State which are brought by the citizens of another State, or by citizens or subjects of a foreign State. It is true, the amendment does so read: and if there were no other reason or ground for abating his suit, it might be maintainable; and then we should have this anomalous result, that in cases arising under the Constitution or laws of the United States, a State may be sued in the federal courts by its own citizens, though it cannot be sued for a like cause of action by the citizens of other States, or of a foreign state; and may be thus sued in the federal courts, although not allowing itself to be sued in its own courts. If this is the necessary consequence of the language of the Constitution and the law, the result is no less startling and unexpected than was the original decision of this court, that under the language of the Constitution and of the judiciary act of 1789, a State was liable to be sued by a citizen of another State, or of a foreign country. That decision was made in the case of Chisholm v. Georgia, 2 Dall. 419 [(1793)], and created such a shock of surprise throughout the country that, at the first meeting of Congress thereafter, the Eleventh Amendment to the Constitution was almost unanimously proposed, and was in due course adopted by the legislatures of the States. This amendment, expressing the will of the ultimate sovereignty of the whole country, superior to all legislatures and all courts, actually reversed the decision of the Supreme Court. It did not in terms prohibit suits by individuals against the States, but declared that the Constitution should not be construed to import any power to authorize the bringing of such suits. The language of the amendment is that "the judicial power of the United States shall *not be construed to extend* to any suit in law or equity, commenced or prosecuted against one of the United States by citizens of another State or by citizens or subjects of any foreign state." The Supreme Court had construed the judicial power as extending to such a suit, and its decision was thus overruled. The court itself so understood the effect of the amendment * * * [as shown by its later decisions].

This view of the force and meaning of the amendment is important. It shows that, on this question of the suability of the States by individuals, the highest authority of this country was in accord rather with the minority than with the majority of the court in the decision of the case of Chisholm v. Georgia; and this fact lends additional interest to the able opinion of Mr. Justice Iredell on that occasion. The other justices were more swayed by a close observance of the letter of the Constitution, without regard to former experience and usage; and because the letter said that the judicial power shall extend to controversies "between a State and citizens of another State;" and "between a State and foreign states, citizens or subjects," they felt constrained to see in this language a power to enable the individual citizens of one State, or of a foreign state, to sue another State of the Union in the federal courts. Justice Iredell, on the contrary, contended that it was not the intention to create new and unheard of remedies, by subjecting sovereign States to actions at the suit of individuals, (which he conclusively showed was never done before,) but only, by proper legislation, to invest the federal courts with jurisdiction to hear and determine controversies and cases, between the parties designated, that were properly susceptible of litigation in courts.

Looking back from our present standpoint at the decision in Chisholm v. Georgia, we do not greatly wonder at the effect which it had upon the country. Any such power as that of authorizing the federal judiciary to entertain suits by individuals against the States, had been expressly disclaimed, and even resented, by the great defenders of the Constitution whilst it was on its trial before the American people. As some of their utterances are directly pertinent to the question now under consideration, we deem it proper to quote them. [The Court then quoted passages from Hamilton, Madison, and Marshall, discussed at pp. 1166–1167, *supra*.] * * *

It seems to us that these views of those great advocates and defenders of the Constitution were most sensible and just, and they apply equally to the present case as to that then under discussion. The letter is appealed to now, as it was then, as a ground for sustaining a suit brought by an individual against a State. The reason against it is as strong in this case as it was in that. It is an attempt to strain the Constitution and the law to a construction never imagined or dreamed of. Can we suppose that, when the Eleventh Amendment was adopted, it was understood to be left open for citizens of a State to sue their own state in the federal courts, whilst the idea of suits by citizens of other states, or of foreign states, was indignantly repelled? Suppose that Congress, when proposing the Eleventh Amendment, had appended to it a proviso that nothing therein contained should prevent a State from being sued by its own citizens in cases arising under the Constitution or laws of the United States[:] can we imagine that it would have been adopted by the States? The supposition that it would is almost an absurdity on its face. * * *

The suability of a State without its consent was a thing unknown to the law. This has been so often laid down and acknowledged by courts and jurists that it is hardly necessary to be formally asserted. It was fully shown by an exhaustive examination of the old law by Mr. Justice Iredell in his opinion in Chisholm v. Georgia; and it has been conceded in every case since, where the question has, in any way, been presented, even in the cases which have gone farthest in sustaining suits against the officers or agents of States. Osborn v. Bank of United States, 9 Wheat. 738 [(1824)]; Davis v. Gray, 16 Wall. 203 [(1872)]; Board of Liquidation v. McComb, 92 U.S. 531 [(1875)]; United States v. Lee, 106 U.S. 196 [(1882)]; Poindexter v. Greenhow, 109 U.S. 63 [(1883)]; Virginia Coupon Cases, 114 U.S. 269 [(1884)]. In all these cases the effort was to show, and the court held, that the suits were not against the State or the United States, but against the individuals; conceding that if they had been against either the State or the United States, they could not be maintained. * * *

Undoubtedly a State may be sued by its own consent, as was the case in Curran v. Arkansas et al., 15 How. 304, 309 [(1853)], and in Clark v. Barnard, 108 U.S. 436, 447 [(1883)]. * * *

[B]esides the presumption that no anomalous and unheard-of proceedings or suits were intended to be raised up by the Constitution—anomalous and unheard of when the Constitution was adopted—an additional reason why the jurisdiction claimed for the Circuit Court does not exist, is the language of the act of Congress by which its jurisdiction is conferred. The words are these: "The circuit courts of the United States shall have original cognizance, concurrent with the courts of the several States, of all suits of a civil nature at common law or in equity, . . . arising under the Constitution or laws of the United States, or treaties," etc.—"Concurrent with the courts of the several States." Does not this qualification show that Congress, in legislating to carry the Constitution into effect, did not intend to invest its courts with any new and strange jurisdictions? The state courts have no power to entertain suits by individuals against a State without its consent. Then how does the Circuit Court, having only concurrent jurisdiction, acquire any such power? It is true that the same qualification existed in the judiciary act of 1789, which was before the court in Chisholm v. Georgia, and the majority of the court did not think that it was sufficient to limit the jurisdiction of the Circuit Court. Justice Iredell thought differently. In view of the manner in which that decision was received by the country, the adoption of the Eleventh Amendment, the light of history and the reason of the thing, we think we are at liberty to prefer Justice Iredell's views in this regard.

Some reliance is placed by the plaintiff upon the observations of Chief Justice Marshall, in Cohens v. Virginia, 6 Wheat. 264, 410 [(1821)]. The Chief Justice was there considering the power of review exercisable by this court over the judgments of a state court, wherein it might be necessary to make the State itself a defendant in error. He showed that this power was absolutely necessary in order to enable the judiciary of the United States to take cognizance of all cases arising under the Constitution and laws of the United States. He also showed that making a State a defendant in error was entirely different from suing a State in an original action in prosecution of a demand against it, and was not within the meaning of the Eleventh Amendment; that the prosecution of a writ of error against a State was not the prosecution of a suit in the sense of that amendment, which had reference to the prosecution, by suit, of claims against a State. * * *

After * * * showing by incontestable argument that a writ of error to a judgment recovered by a State, in which the State is necessarily the defendant in error, is not a suit commenced or prosecuted against a State in the sense of the amendment, he added, that if the court were mistaken in this, its error did not affect that case, because the writ of error therein was not prosecuted by "a citizen of another State" or "of any foreign state," and so was not affected by the amendment; but was governed by the general grant of judicial power, as extending "to all cases arising under the Constitution or laws of the United States, without respect to parties".

It must be conceded that the last observation of the Chief Justice does favor the argument of the plaintiff. But the observation was unnecessary to the decision, and in that sense *extra judicial*, and though made by one who seldom used words without due reflection, ought not to outweigh the important considerations referred to which lead to a different conclusion. With regard to the question then before the court, it may be observed, that writs of error to judgments in favor of the crown, or of the State, had been known to the law from time immemorial; and had never been considered as exceptions to the rule, that an action does not lie against the sovereign. * * *

It is not necessary that we should enter upon an examination of the reason or expediency of the rule which exempts a sovereign State from prosecution in a court of justice at the suit of individuals. This is fully discussed by writers on public law. It is enough for us to declare its existence. The legislative department of a State represents its polity and its will, and is called upon by the highest demands of natural and political law to preserve justice and judgment, and to hold inviolate the public obligations. Any departure from this rule, except for reasons most cogent, (of which the legislature, and not the courts, is the judge,) never fails in the end to incur the odium of the world, and to bring lasting injury upon the State itself. But to deprive the legislature of the power of judging what the honor and safety of the State may require, even at the expense of a temporary failure to discharge the public debts, would be attended with greater evils than such failure can cause. The judgment of the Circuit Court is

Affirmed.

■ MR. JUSTICE HARLAN, concurring.

I concur with the court in holding that a suit directly against a State by one of its own citizens is not one to which the judicial power of the United States extends, unless the State itself consents to be sued. Upon this ground alone I assent to the judgment. But I cannot give my assent to many things said in the opinion. The comments made upon the decision in Chisholm v. Georgia do not meet my approval. They are not necessary to the determination of the present case. Besides, I am of opinion that the decision in that case was based upon a sound interpretation of the Constitution as that instrument then was.

NOTE ON THE SCOPE OF THE ELEVENTH AMENDMENT

(1) Eleventh Amendment Immunity and Constitutional Enforcement. Note the effect of Hans v. Louisiana: The Court does not doubt that the state is to some extent legally bound by the Contract Clause and other provisions of the Constitution. But it holds that the Eleventh Amendment bars the federal adjudication of the plaintiff's suit against the state and leaves the state legislature in charge of deciding when and whom to pay. The Court reached its result in a federal question case involving an in-state citizen to whom the terms of the Eleventh Amendment do not apply. The Court suggested that a state would retain a similar immunity from such suits in its own courts, remitting individuals to whatever compensation the legislature might choose to award. It therefore might seem to make the Constitution effectively unenforceable against the state.

In evaluating the Hans immunity, consider when suits against officers will still provide an adequate means of enforcing the Constitution. Five years earlier the Court had decided Poindexter v. Greenhow, 114 U.S. 270 (1885), p. 1176, *infra*—a suit brought against Virginia officials to contest coercive tax collection as violative of the Constitution. In that case, and others known together as the Virginia Coupon Cases, plaintiffs sued to challenge a state law overriding earlier statutes that allowed use of coupons attached to state bonds in payment of taxes. The Court, 5–4, upheld suits against state officials, invoking the party of record rule and invalidating the new law as an unconstitutional impairment of the state's obligation of contract. The Court did so not by authorizing a suit against the state but by imposing trespass liability on the officers who, after refusing to accept coupons tendered in payment of taxes, seized taxpayer property for sale to satisfy the disputed tax obligation. The unanimous decision in Hans, rejecting direct enforcement of the Contract Clause by suit against the state, thus came after the officer suit option had been reaffirmed. Well into the twentieth century, the Court continued to force state courts to entertain suits against agents of the state where necessary to ensure constitutional remedies. See General Oil Co. v. Crain, 209 U.S. 211 (1908) (concluding that Tennessee courts must make injunctive relief available if necessary to prevent state interference with the federal commerce power); Ettor v. City of Tacoma, 228 U.S. 148 (1913) (invalidating remedial restriction as unconstitutional and thereby compelling Washington courts to entertain suits against the city for destruction of plaintiff's property). See generally Woolhandler, *The Common Law Origins of Constitutionally Compelled Remedies*, 107 Yale L.J. 77 (1997); Chap. VII, Sec. 2.B, *supra*. These issues are further considered in the context of the subsequent decision of Ex parte Young, 209 U.S. 123 (1908), p. 1184, *infra*.

(2) The Legal Basis of the Hans Decision. Because Hans was a citizen of Louisiana, the case fell outside of the terms of the Eleventh Amendment, as the Court acknowledged. Given the inapplicability of the text of the Eleventh Amendment, Hans appears to rest on as many as five possible rationales:

(a) The Purpose of the Eleventh Amendment. The Court suggests that the purpose of the Eleventh Amendment was to overrule Chisholm and to reinstate a regime of state immunity from suit, especially suits brought to enforce state contracts. Even though the Eleventh Amendment does not foreclose all individual suits against the states by its terms, the Court indicates that it should be interpreted to achieve its broadly immunizing purpose. For a critique, see Manning, *The Eleventh Amendment and the Reading of Precise Constitutional Texts*, 113 Yale L.J. 1663, 1669–70 (2004), arguing that "at least where the Constitution speaks in precise, rule-like terms, as the Eleventh Amendment does," the Court should apply it as written, rather than adopting a "strongly purposive" approach.

In analyzing the merits of purposive arguments about the Eleventh Amendment, consider also the view expressed by Justice Bradley (and joined by three other Justices) in his Poindexter dissent, that the Eleventh Amendment, though addressed in terms to the judicial power, effected an implied repeal of the Contract Clause. According to Justice Bradley: "If the contract clause and the eleventh amendment come into conflict, the latter has paramount force. It was adopted as an amendment to the constitution, and operates as an amendment of every part of the constitution to which it is at any time found to be repugnant. * * * The language of the constitution was not changed, but it became subject and subordinate to the paramount declaration of the amendment." He emphasized that the Eleventh Amendment should not be limited to its text: "Moreover, the eleventh amendment is not intended as a mere formula of words, to be slurred over by subtle methods of interpretation, so as to give it a literal compliance, without regarding its substantial meaning and purpose. It is a grave and solemn condition, exacted by sovereign states, for the purpose of preserving and vindicating their sovereign right to deal with their creditors and others propounding claims against them, according to their own views of what may be required by public faith and the necessities of the body politic." Poindexter v. Greenhow, 114 U.S. 269, 331–32 (1885) (Bradley J., dissenting).

(b) The Meaning of Article III. The Hans Court treats Chisholm as having mistakenly interpreted Article III. (The concurring Justice Harlan did not agree.) If Hans altered the controlling interpretation of Article III, then federal courts could be said to lack jurisdiction over suits by individuals, even when the jurisdictional basis for the suit (federal question or admiralty) was not addressed in terms by the Eleventh Amendment. For a critique, see Manning, *supra*, at pp. 1743–1747 (arguing that the Eleventh Amendment should be taken to confirm those aspects of the Chisholm interpretation that were left intact).[1]

---

[1]   Clark, *The Eleventh Amendment and the Nature of the Union*, 123 Harv.L.Rev. 1817 (2010), argues that the Constitution's structural assumptions foreclose suit against states based on federal law. With the power to issue commands directly to individuals, Professor Clark argues that Congress cannot act on the states either by imposing statutory duties or by authorizing collective remedies for constitutional violations. With the possibility of suits against the states based on federal law being ruled out by a shared original understanding, Hans properly restores an across-the-board immunity. *Cf.* Vázquez, *The Unsettled Nature of the Union,* 123 Harv.L.Rev. Forum 79 (2011) (maintaining that most of the evidence that Professor Clark cites to support his claim that the federal government lacked the power to regulate the

(c) **The Limits of the Applicable Statute.** Hans also offers a statutory basis for decision. The Act of 1875 conferred concurrent jurisdiction on the lower federal courts in federal question cases. The Court read concurrency to mean that Congress expected federal courts to apply state law limits on the suability of states, much the way Justice Iredell read the Judiciary Act of 1789 in Chisholm. Such a reading would seem to confirm the Court's general view, as expressed at the end of its opinion, that remedial options should be roughly equivalent in state and federal court.

(d) **The Absence of a Right of Action.** Following Justice Iredell, the Hans Court noted that the common law did not furnish a right of action to enforce contracts against a state debtor. Nor had Congress supplied a right to sue. The Court viewed the common law history, coupled with the Eleventh Amendment, as reason to refrain from "rais[ing] up" a judge-made right to sue. On this view, the court needs a case, brought by a plaintiff with a recognized right to sue the defendant, to ground its jurisdiction.

(e) **The Defense of State Sovereign Immunity.** If regarded as a restriction on federal jurisdiction, the state's traditional immunity from suit might foreclose federal adjudication of all individual suits against the states (as contemplated in the rejected early draft of the Eleventh Amendment). The Hans Court expressed some sympathy for this view. Does it provide an independent basis for decision, or is it fully encompassed by the four other rationales above?

(3) Legacy of Non-Literalism. The Supreme Court has continued to accord the states an immunity from suit in contexts that do not implicate the text of the Eleventh Amendment. Contrary to earlier dicta to the contrary, *e.g.*, Cherokee Nation v. Georgia, 30 U.S. (5 Pet.) 1, 15–16 (1831), the Court held in Monaco v. Mississippi, 292 U.S. 313, 322 (1934), that the Hans principle bars suit against a state by a foreign country, despite the Amendment's textual limitation to suits by individual plaintiffs. In Ex parte New York, 256 U.S. 490 (1921), the Court applied the principle of immunity to bar a suit in admiralty, notwithstanding the Amendment's limiting reference to suits "in law or equity." More recently, and despite the Eleventh Amendment's application only to the "judicial power of the United States," the Court has held the states immune from suit on certain federal law claims in state court, Alden v. Maine, 527 U.S. 706 (1999) p. 1248, *infra*, and before a federal administrative agency, Federal Maritime Comm'n v. S.C. State Ports Auth., 535 U.S. 743 (2002). In such decisions, the Court appears to acknowledge that the Amendment's text does not compel the result. *E.g.*, Monaco v. Mississippi, *supra* (behind the text are "postulates" that "limit and control"); Alden v. Maine, *supra* (despite the Amendment's inapplicability to state court litigation, constitutional structure forecloses Congress from subjecting states to suit in state court under disfavored federal statutes).

(4) Hans and the Enforcement of Contracts. Other factors may inform the Hans decision. First, as explained in Shapiro, *Wrong Turns: The Eleventh Amendment and the Pennhurst Case*, 98 Harv.L.Rev. 61, 69–70 (1984), Hans

---

states unequivocally supports only the narrower conclusion that Congress could not subject the states (rather than their officers) to coercive suits).

involved a suit to enforce a contract, something that had long been viewed as a matter for legislative adjustment. As noted above, Poindexter v. Greenhow, Paragraph (1), *supra*, involving a tort-based claim against an officer, came out the other way.[2] Second, as explained in Orth, The Judicial Power of the United States: The Eleventh Amendment in American History 47–120 (1987), the end of Reconstruction meant that the Court may have had difficulty enforcing any judgment compelling Southern states (Virginia, Louisiana) to honor their debts.[3]

(5) State Waivers of Sovereign Immunity. Hans did not purport to question the rule that a state, like any sovereign entity, may waive its immunity and consent to suit. See Clark v. Barnard, 108 U.S. 436, 447 (1883); Petty v. Tenn.-Mo. Bridge Comm'n, 359 U.S. 275 (1959).[4]

(a) Consent to Suit Confined to State Tribunals. Smith v. Reeves, 178 U.S. 436, 441 (1900), held that a state may waive sovereign immunity as to suits for tax refunds in its own courts, while retaining its Eleventh Amendment immunity from such lawsuits in federal court. Earlier cases looked the other way, *e.g.*, Reagan v. Farmers' Loan & Trust Co., 154 U.S. 362, 391 (1894), but Smith reasoned that a limitation upon tax refund actions could not be seen as "hostile to the General Government, or as trenching upon any right granted or secured by the Constitution of the United States." Subsequent cases have permitted selective waiver by the state without regard to Smith's qualifications. See, *e.g.*, Edelman v. Jordan, 415 U.S. 651 (1974); Alden v. Maine, 527 U.S. 706 (1999) (consent to suit on state law claims does not selectively discriminate against federal law claims).

(b) Consent Based on the State's Conduct in Litigation. When a state files suit in federal court, it necessarily waives its sovereign immunity from the court's jurisdiction to determine the validity of its claims and of any defenses that might be asserted against those claims. See, *e.g.*, Gardner v.

---

[2]   Officers owed duties in tort to refrain from trespassory property takings but no duty to provide redress for a state's breach of its contracts; the duty ran to the state itself. As a result, the officer suit did not guarantee a remedy when the claim sounded in contract, rather than tort. Moreover, the state's status as a necessary party to contract enforcement proceedings triggered the immunity later articulated in Hans. See In re Ayers, 123 U.S. 443 (1887) (suit to enjoin state officers from suing to collect taxes was a prohibited suit against the state to compel recognition of contract rights); Hagood v. Southern, 117 U.S. 52 (1886) (suits nominally against officers were barred as seeking specific performance of state contract); Louisiana v. Jumel, 107 U.S. 711 (1883) (rejecting mandamus and injunctive relief that would have compelled state performance of its contract duties).

[3]   Note that officer suits simplify judgment-enforcement by imposing liability on individuals, rather than on the state as an entity. Nonetheless, the Court's decision in the Virginia Coupon Cases, 114 U.S. 269 (1884), though nominally addressed to state officials, would oblige the state legislature to take measures to honor such coupons, despite the impact on the state treasury. *Cf.* United States v. Lee, 106 U.S. 196 (1882), p. 1154, *supra* (declaring legal rights in an officer suit that led to substantial payments from the U.S. treasury).

[4]   Under the first principle of jurisdiction, see Chap. VIII, Sec. 1, *supra*, parties lack power to confer subject matter jurisdiction on the federal courts by consent. But the Court has yet to resolve the apparent tension between the subject matter roots of the Eleventh Amendment immunity and the idea of jurisdiction by consent. Compare Edelman v. Jordan, 415 U.S. 651 (1974) (treating the immunity as jurisdictional), with Patsy v. Board of Regents, 457 U.S. 496, 515–16 n.19 (1982) (stating that an Eleventh Amendment question is not jurisdictional "in the sense that it must be raised and decided by this Court on its own motion"). and Wisconsin Department of Corrections v. Schacht, 524 U.S. 381, 391 (1998) (explaining that the issue has yet to be resolved).

New Jersey, 329 U.S. 565 (1947). A similar consent results from a state's decision to remove a state court action to federal court under 28 U.S.C. § 1441. See Lapides v. Board of Regents, 535 U.S. 613 (2002) (holding that removal operated as consent to suit in federal court on state-law claim from which the state had no immunity in state court).

(6) "Exceptions" to Hans. Although Hans continues to establish the states' immunity from a range of unconsented actions, it has never been understood to bar all actions through which the Constitution and laws of the United States might be enforced against states, their subdivisions, and their officers. In addition to the example of officer suits, discussed in the next principal case, consider three "exceptions" to Hans:

(a) Appeals of Actions Initiated by the States in State Court. Hans accepted the ruling of Cohens v. Virginia, 19 U.S. (6 Wheat.) 264 (1821), that appeals to the Supreme Court of state criminal convictions are not suits against the state within the meaning of the Eleventh Amendment. Neither are appeals of civil actions instituted by the states.

(b) Suits by Other States and the United States. The Supreme Court has declined to bar either suits against a state by another state, see, *e.g.*, Kansas v. Colorado, 206 U.S. 46, 83 (1907), or suits against a state by the United States, see, *e.g.*, United States v. Mississippi, 380 U.S. 128, 140–41 (1965); Idaho v. United States, 533 U.S. 262, 271 n.4 (2001). In Monaco v. Mississippi, the Court explained that the former holding "was essential to the peace of the Union" and "a necessary feature of the formation of a more perfect Union," while the latter was "inherent in the constitutional plan."

(c) Suits Against Local Governments. Lincoln County v. Luning, 133 U.S. 529 (1890), decided the same day as Hans, held that the Eleventh Amendment does not bar an individual's suit in federal court against a county for nonpayment of a debt. (By contrast, a suit against a statewide agency is considered a suit against the state under the Eleventh Amendment. See, *e.g.*, Edelman v. Jordan, 415 U.S. 651 (1974); Ford Motor Co. v. Department of Treasury, 323 U.S. 459 (1945)). In allowing suits against counties and municipalities, the Court was unanimous, relying in part on its "general acquiescence" in such suits over the prior thirty years. The Court has adhered to this position as to local government bodies ever since. See, *e.g.*, Mount Healthy City School Dist. Bd. of Educ. v. Doyle, 429 U.S. 274, 280–81 (1977); Northern Ins. Co. v. Chatham County, 547 U.S. 189 (2006).

Does it make sense for local governments to be treated differently from state agencies for Eleventh Amendment purposes when both are creatures of the state? Then-Professor Fletcher explained the different treatment on the ground that in the nineteenth century, a municipal corporation was viewed as more closely analogous to a private corporation than to a state government. Fletcher, *A Historical Interpretation of the Eleventh Amendment: A Narrow Construction of an Affirmative Grant of Jurisdiction Rather than a Prohibition Against Jurisdiction*, 35 Stan.L.Rev 1033, 1099–1107 (1983). By contrast, Professor Orth, Paragraph (4), *supra*, traces the opposing outcomes in Hans and Lincoln County to the comparative ease with which courts can enforce their judgments against counties.

(7) The Eleventh Amendment After Hans: Textual Core and Unwritten Immunity? For many observers, the law of state suability in the aftermath of Hans can be best understood as including two elements: a text-based jurisdictional core set forth in the Eleventh Amendment and a judge-made body of state sovereign immunity law that extends beyond the text. This account distinguishes the subject matter "judicial power" limits imposed by the text of the Eleventh Amendment from the broader unwritten sovereign immunity that derives from other sources. Advocates of this view believe that the unwritten immunity doctrine can yield to such factors as state consent and congressional override but that the textual core of the Eleventh Amendment imposes more unyielding subject matter jurisdiction restrictions.

(a) **The Textual Core: Diversity and Literal Interpretations.** The Eleventh Amendment's text forbids the exercise of federal judicial power over suits against states only by two disfavored plaintiffs (diverse citizens and foreign nationals) and only in suits at law or in equity. It does not foreclose suits by in-state plaintiffs (as in Hans itself), suits in admiralty (as in Ex parte New York), or suits by foreign states (as in Monaco). Attempting to make sense of the words, Justice Brennan's dissenting opinion in Atascadero State Hosp. v. Scanlon, 473 U.S. 234 (1985), drew on the work of several commentators[5] in proposing a diversity theory of the Eleventh Amendment that would have permitted federal jurisdiction in cases such as Hans in which plaintiffs assert federal causes of action. Justice Brennan's "diversity" account rested on two central distinctions. First, he sharply differentiated "sovereign immunity"—a traditional concept barring uncontested suit against the sovereign in any court—from the jurisdictional bar to suit in *federal* court erected by the Eleventh Amendment. The Eleventh Amendment, he argued, had nothing to do with sovereign immunity (in suits in state court, for example); it was designed exclusively to regulate the scope of federal judicial power.[6]

Second, Justice Brennan distinguished between two grounds of federal jurisdiction under Article III: jurisdiction based on subject matter (such as suits arising under federal law) and that dependent on party status (such as citizen-state diversity). The Eleventh Amendment, he contended, barred federal jurisdiction in suits based on party status, but not those based on subject matter. More specifically, it barred jurisdiction in suits against a state brought under the state-citizen diversity clause, in which state rather

---

[5] *E.g.*, Fletcher, Paragraph (6)(c), *supra*, at 1058–59; Gibbons, *The Eleventh Amendment and State Sovereign Immunity: A Reinterpretation*, 83 Colum.L.Rev. 1889 (1983); Orth, *The Interpretation of the Eleventh Amendment, 1798–1908: A Case Study of Judicial Power*, 1983 U.Ill.L.Rev. 423. For a later account on this score, see also Lee, *Making Sense of the Eleventh Amendment: International Law and State Sovereignty*, 96 Nw.U.L.Rev. 1027 (2002).

[6] Other Justices have embraced this understanding. See Seminole Tribe of Fla. v. Florida, 517 U.S. 44, 76–100 (1996) (Stevens, J., dissenting) (describing the two sources of state immunity). See also PennEast Pipeline Co. v. New Jersey, 594 U.S. 482, 509–11 (2021) (Gorsuch and Thomas, JJ., dissenting) (describing "two distinct federal-law immunities" from suit: "an ironclad rule for a particular category of diversity suits" and a personal privilege that states may waive).

than federal law would ordinarily supply the plaintiff's cause of action but did not restrict suits against an unconsenting state brought under admiralty or federal question jurisdiction.

In support of his "diversity" account, Justice Brennan reviewed the ratification debates over Article III:

"The various references to state sovereign immunity all appear in discussions of the state-citizen diversity clause. Virtually all of the comments were addressed to the problem created by state debts that predated the Constitution, when the State's creditors may often have had meager judicial remedies in the case of default. Yet, even in this sensitive context, a number of participants in the debates welcomed the abrogation of sovereign immunity that they thought followed from the state-citizen and state-alien clauses."[7]

Justice Brennan concluded that the language of the Eleventh Amendment "would represent a particularly cryptic way to embody" in the Constitution a consensus that the doctrine of state sovereign immunity would bar cases brought to enforce the Constitution and laws of the United States. Rather, the language chosen—"The Judicial power of the United States shall not be construed to extend * * *"—parallels the phrasing of Article III, and was meant merely to abandon the construction of Article III in Chisholm, which permitted federal court suit against a state based simply upon party status. The Amendment, accordingly, bars only suits against a state brought by aliens or citizens of another state, in order to track (and restrict) the party-based jurisdiction in Article III.[8]

An alternative text-based account would read the Amendment "literally" to block all claims against states brought by the two identified plaintiffs, including those based on non-federal law and those that seek to enforce federal law and thus do not depend jurisdictionally on the alignment of parties.[9] Defenders of the "literal" account observe that the Amendment bars "any suit" by the disfavored plaintiffs rather than tracking the language of Article III in curtailing jurisdiction over "controversies." The literal

---

[7]   [Ed.] The view that the Constitution abrogated immunity was advanced as an argument against ratification by some opponents (such as George Mason and Patrick Henry in Virginia) and various anti-Federalist publicists, but the view was also held by proponents of ratification (like Edmund Pendleton and Edmund Randolph of Virginia and Timothy Pickering and James Wilson of Pennsylvania). See generally Gibbons, note 5, *supra*, at 1902–08.

[8]   See Manning, Paragraph (2)(a), *supra*; Nelson, *Sovereign Immunity as a Doctrine of Personal Jurisdiction*, 115 Harv.L.Rev. 1559 (2002) (arguing that the Eleventh Amendment itself created a core, non-waivable, subject matter immunity in cases falling within its specific terms and likening the unwritten Hans immunity to a waivable personal jurisdiction defense); Baude & Sachs, *The Misunderstood Eleventh Amendment*, 169 U.Pa.L.Rev. 609, 616 (2021) (following Nelson); Pfander, *Rethinking the Supreme Court's Original Jurisdiction in State-Party Cases*, 82 Calif.L.Rev. 555 (1994) (distinguishing the constitutional limits imposed by the Eleventh Amendment from the sovereign immunity embedded in the common law and law of nations).

[9]   See, *e.g.*, Baude & Sachs, *supra* note 8; Marshall, *Fighting the Words of the Eleventh Amendment*, 102 Harv.L.Rev. 1342 (1989); Massey, *State Sovereignty and the Tenth and Eleventh Amendments*, 56 U.Chi.L.Rev. 61 (1989). For responses by defenders of a "diversity" theory similar to Justice Brennan's, see Amar, *Marbury, Section 13, and the Original Jurisdiction of the Supreme Court*, 56 U.Chi.L.Rev. 443, 496 (1989); Fletcher, *The Diversity Explanation of the Eleventh Amendment: A Reply to Critics*, 56 U.Chi.L.Rev. 1261 (1989).

reading would leave federal question jurisdiction intact for suits (like that in Hans) brought by in-state citizens but would block federal question and admiralty litigation by non-citizen plaintiffs. Literal theorists support their account with historical arguments, explaining that the drafters may have worried that non-citizen plaintiffs would recast their general law debt claims against the states as suits to enforce the Contract Clause or rights conferred by federal treaties and thereby evade the force of an Amendment that curtailed only party-alignment claims.[10]

In reading the Amendment to foreclose all claims by disfavored plaintiffs, the literal account creates a party-alignment gap in federal question jurisdiction. Such a gap would introduce a form of disparate treatment that the Constitution otherwise deprecates, allowing in-state citizens access to federal court to enforce federal law against their own state but denying that same privilege to out-of-staters. In a departure from current law, that reading would block out-of-staters who have been authorized to sue in state court from seeking appellate review of errors of federal law in the Supreme Court. Compare Baude & Sachs, note 8, *supra*, with Jackson, *The Supreme Court, the Eleventh Amendment, and State Sovereign Immunity*, 98 Yale L.J. 1, 72–104 (1988).

Despite disagreement about how to define the core, diversity and literal theorists agree that the text-based limits of the Eleventh Amendment operate as true jurisdictional restrictions. As such, jurisdiction over claims within the Amendment's core cannot be conferred by legislation "abrogating" state immunity or by consent of the parties.[11] Diversity and literal theorists also agree that a substantial amount of federal question jurisdiction remains intact for suits brought by in-state citizens and agree that Hans and some of its non-literal progeny were wrongly decided if said to rest on the Amendment's text alone.

(b) The Unwritten Immunity Doctrine. Justice Brennan distinguished between the jurisdictional core of the Eleventh Amendment and the unwritten rules of state sovereign immunity. Hans, Ex parte New York, and Monaco—all of which lack textual support in the Eleventh Amendment—may rest on an unwritten body of federal law. As in Hans, that body of law might have many ingredients: the absence of any common law right to sue the government; the judicial reluctance to raise up new rights of action against the states; the failure of the common law and law of nations to sanction the joinder of a state as a party to a suit brought by a private individual. Professor Nelson, note 8, *supra*, weaves these elements together in arguing that state sovereign immunity operates much like a doctrine of personal jurisdiction in being understood to deprive federal courts of a

---

[10] For doubts that suits such as those brought by Chisholm could have been readily repackaged as brought directly under the Contracts Clause, see Atascadero State Hosp. v. Scanlon, 473 U.S. 234 (1985) (Brennan, J., dissenting) (questioning the Clause's application to state contracts and the existence of a right of action to sue the state for damages). In any case, the Contracts Clause did not take effect until the Constitution was ratified in 1788, long after the debt in Chisholm was contracted. See Pfander & Dwinell, *A Declaratory Theory of State Accountability*, 102 Va.L.Rev. 153, 174 (2016).

[11] On the unyielding quality of subject matter restrictions on federal judicial power, see Chap. VIII, Sec. 1.

dispute between properly joined adverse parties. On the view taken by Nelson and others, note 8 *supra*, state sovereign immunity would operate as a presumptive (but not a subject-matter jurisdictional) limit on state suability.

There would remain the question about the power of Congress to alter or override this immunity. Professor Jackson maintains that as a sub-constitutional, common law doctrine rooted in federal law, the unwritten doctrine of state immunity would remain subject to waiver by the state and to congressional override. Jackson, *supra*, at 72–104. For Professors Baude and Sachs, however, the unwritten doctrine of state sovereign immunity can better be understood as a constitutional backdrop, which could not generally be overridden by Congress under Article I. See Baude & Sachs, *supra*.[12] Professor Nelson appears to view the question of abrogation as a close one. Nelson, note 8, *supra*, at 1626–51. For more on the abrogation of state sovereign immunity under Article I, see p. 1226, *infra*.

(8) Officer Suits. As the suit named the state as a party of record, the Hans Court had no occasion to revisit the use of "officer suits" to ensure state compliance with the Constitution and laws of the United States. But the officer suit continued to play a vital role in government accountability litigation throughout the nineteenth century, as the 1885 decision in Poindexter v. Greenhow, Paragraph (1), *supra*, confirms. The changing nature of officer suits was among the issues before the Court in the next principal case.

Ex parte Young

209 U.S. 123 (1908).
Petition for Writs of Habeas Corpus and Certiorari.

[Shareholders of various railroads brought derivative actions in federal circuit court in Minnesota, alleging that state legislation regulating railroad rates was confiscatory and violated the Fourteenth Amendment. The companies' managements, plaintiffs alleged, had refused their demands that the companies not comply with the legislation.

[The trial court entered a temporary restraining order prohibiting Edward Young, the state's Attorney General, from enforcing the legislation, and after denying Young's motion under the Eleventh Amendment to dismiss, entered a preliminary injunction to the same effect. Young then defied the injunction by filing a state court action seeking to enforce the legislation against the railroads.

[The circuit court held Young in contempt, again rejecting his Eleventh Amendment defense. He then filed an application in the

---

[12]   See also Baude, *Sovereign Immunity and the Constitutional Text*, 103 Va.L.Rev. 1 (2017); Sachs, *Constitutional Backdrops*, 80 Geo.Wash.L.Rev. 1813 (2012).

Supreme Court for leave to file a petition for writs of habeas corpus and certiorari.]

■ MR. JUSTICE PECKHAM * * * delivered the opinion of the court.

[The Court first concluded that the circuit court had "arising under" jurisdiction, as the suit raised several federal questions: (i) whether enforcement of the rates would take property without due process of law, (ii) whether the penalties for violation were so enormous as to deny equal protection and due process, and (iii) whether the legislation interfered with interstate commerce.]

Coming to the inquiry regarding the alleged invalidity of these acts, we take up the contention that they are invalid on their face on account of the penalties. For disobedience to the freight act the officers, directors, agents and employés of the company are made guilty of a misdemeanor, and upon conviction each may be punished by imprisonment in the county jail for a period not exceeding ninety days. Each violation would be a separate offense, and, therefore, might result in imprisonment of the various agents of the company who would dare disobey for a term of ninety days each for each offense. Disobedience to the passenger rate act renders the party guilty of a felony and subject to a fine not exceeding five thousand dollars or imprisonment in the state prison for a period not exceeding five years, or both fine and imprisonment. The sale of each ticket above the price permitted by the act would be a violation thereof. * * * The company, in order to test the validity of the acts, must find some agent or employé to disobey them at the risk stated. The necessary effect and result of such legislation must be to preclude a resort to the courts (either state or Federal) for the purpose of testing its validity. * * * It may therefore be said that when the penalties for disobedience are by fines so enormous and imprisonment so severe as to intimidate the company and its officers from resorting to the courts to test the validity of the legislation, the result is the same as if the law in terms prohibited the company from seeking judicial construction of laws which deeply affect its rights.

* * * Ordinarily a law creating offenses in the nature of misdemeanors or felonies relates to a subject over which the jurisdiction of the legislature is complete in any event. In the case, however, of the establishment of certain rates without any hearing, the validity of such rates necessarily depends upon whether they are high enough to permit at least some return upon the investment (how much it is not now necessary to state), and an inquiry as to that fact is a proper subject of judicial investigation. If it turns out that the rates are too low for that purpose, then they are illegal. Now, to impose upon a party interested the burden of obtaining a judicial decision of such a question (no prior hearing having ever been given) only upon the condition that if unsuccessful he must suffer imprisonment and pay fines as provided in these acts, is, in effect, to close up all approaches to the courts, and thus

prevent any hearing upon the question whether the rates as provided by the acts are not too low, and therefore invalid. * * *

We hold, therefore, that the provisions of the acts relating to the enforcement of the rates, either for freight or passengers, by imposing such enormous fines and possible imprisonment as a result of an unsuccessful effort to test the validity of the laws themselves, are unconstitutional on their face, without regard to the question of the insufficiency of those rates. * * *

* * * The question that arises is whether there is a remedy that the parties interested may resort to, by going into a Federal court of equity, in a case involving a violation of the Federal Constitution, and obtaining a judicial investigation of the problem, and pending its solution obtain freedom from suits, civil or criminal, by a temporary injunction, and if the question be finally decided favorably to the contention of the company, a permanent injunction restraining all such actions or proceedings.

This inquiry necessitates an examination of the most material and important objection made to the jurisdiction of the Circuit Court, the objection being that the suit is, in effect, one against the State of Minnesota * * *. This objection is to be considered with reference to the Eleventh and Fourteenth Amendments to the Federal Constitution. * * *

We may assume that each [Amendment] exists in full force, and that we must give to the Eleventh Amendment all the effect it naturally would have, without cutting it down or rendering its meaning any more narrow than the language, fairly interpreted, would warrant. It applies to a suit brought against a State by one of its own citizens as well as to a suit brought by a citizen of another State. Hans v. Louisiana, 134 U.S. 1 [(1890)]. * * *

The cases * * * [following adoption of the Eleventh Amendment] were reviewed, and it was held, In re Ayers, 123 U.S. 443 [(1887)], that a bill in equity brought against officers of a State, who, as individuals, have no personal interest in the subject-matter of the suit, and defend only as representing the State, where the relief prayed for, if done, would constitute a performance by the State of the alleged contract of the State, was a suit against the State (page 504), following in this respect Hagood v. Southern, [117 U.S. 52, 67 (1886)].

A suit of such a nature was simply an attempt to make the State itself, through its officers, perform its alleged contract, by directing those officers to do acts which constituted such performance. The State alone had any interest in the question, and a decree in favor of plaintiff would affect the treasury of the State.

[The Court then discussed a number of its recent decisions that it viewed as "ample justification" for determining that a state official who is about to commence civil or criminal proceedings to enforce unconstitutional state legislation may be enjoined from such action by a federal court of equity. Those cases included Reagan v. Farmers' Loan & Trust Co., 154 U.S. 362 (1894), and Smyth v. Ames, 169 U.S. 466, 518 (1898). The Court continued:]

* * * In those cases the only wrong or injury or trespass involved was the threatened commencement of suits to enforce the statute as to rates, and the threat of such commencement was in each case regarded as sufficient to authorize the issuing of an injunction to prevent the same. The threat to commence those suits under such circumstances was therefore necessarily held to be equivalent to any other threatened wrong or injury to the property of a plaintiff which had theretofore been held sufficient to authorize the suit against the officer.

* * * It is contended that the complainants do not complain and they care nothing about any action which Mr. Young might take or bring as an ordinary individual, but that he was complained of as an officer, to whose discretion is confided the use of the name of the State of Minnesota so far as litigation is concerned, and that when or how he shall use it is a matter resting in his discretion and cannot be controlled by any court.

The answer to all this is the same as made in every case where an official claims to be acting under the authority of the State. The act to be enforced is alleged to be unconstitutional, and if it be so, the use of the name of the State to enforce an unconstitutional act to the injury of complainants is a proceeding without the authority of and one which does not affect the State in its sovereign or governmental capacity. It is simply an illegal act upon the part of a state official in attempting by the use of the name of the State to enforce a legislative enactment which is void because unconstitutional. If the act which the state Attorney General seeks to enforce be a violation of the Federal Constitution, the officer in proceeding under such enactment comes into conflict with the superior authority of that Constitution, and he is in that case stripped of his official or representative character and is subjected in his person to the consequences of his individual conduct. The State has no power to impart to him any immunity from responsibility to the supreme authority of the United States. * * *

It is further objected (and the objection really forms part of the contention that the State cannot be sued) that a court of equity has no jurisdiction to enjoin criminal proceedings, by indictment or otherwise, under the state law. This, as a general rule, is true. But there are exceptions. When such indictment or proceeding is brought to enforce an alleged unconstitutional statute, which is the subject matter of inquiry in a suit already pending in a Federal court, the latter court having first obtained jurisdiction over the subject matter, has the right, in both civil and criminal cases, to hold and maintain such jurisdiction, to the exclusion of all other courts, until its duty is fully performed. But the Federal court cannot, of course, interfere in a case where the proceedings were already pending in a state court. * * *

It is proper to add that the right to enjoin an individual, even though a state official, from commencing suits under circumstances already stated, does not include the power to restrain a court from acting in any case brought before it, either of a civil or criminal nature, nor does it include power to prevent any investigation or action by a grand jury. The latter body is part of the machinery of a criminal court, and an injunction against a state court would be a violation of the whole scheme of our Government. * * *

It is further objected that there is a plain and adequate remedy at law open to the complainants and that a court of equity, therefore, has no jurisdiction in such case. It has been suggested that the proper way to test the constitutionality of the act is to disobey it, at least once, after which the company might obey the act pending subsequent proceedings to test its validity. But in the event of a single violation the prosecutor might not avail himself of the opportunity to make the test, as obedience to the law was thereafter continued, and he might think it unnecessary to start an inquiry. If, however, he should do so while the company was thereafter obeying the law, several years might elapse before there was a final determination of the question, and if it should be determined that the law was invalid the property of the company would have been taken during that time without due process of law, and there would be no possibility of its recovery.

Another obstacle to making the test on the part of the company might be to find an agent or employé who would disobey the law, with a possible fine and imprisonment staring him in the face if the act should be held valid. Take the passenger rate act, for instance: A sale of a single ticket above the price mentioned in that act might subject the ticket agent to a charge of felony, and upon conviction to a fine of five thousand dollars and imprisonment for five years. It is true the company might pay the fine, but the imprisonment the agent would have to suffer personally. It would not be wonderful if, under such circumstances, there would not be a crowd of agents offering to disobey the law. The wonder would be that a single agent should be found ready to take the risk.

* * * [I]t must be remembered that jurisdiction of this general character has, in fact, been exercised by Federal courts from the time of Osborn v. United States Bank up to the present; the only difference in regard to the case of Osborn and the case in hand being that in this case the injury complained of is the threatened commencement of suits, civil or criminal, to enforce the act, instead of, as in the Osborn case, an actual and direct trespass upon or interference with tangible property. A bill filed to prevent the commencement of suits to enforce an unconstitutional act, under the circumstances already mentioned, is no new invention, as we have already seen. The difference between an actual and direct interference with tangible property and the enjoining of state officers from enforcing an unconstitutional act, is not of a radical nature, and does not extend, in truth, the jurisdiction of the courts over the subject

matter. * * * The sovereignty of the State is, in reality, no more involved in one case than in the other. The State cannot in either case impart to the official immunity from responsibility to the supreme authority of the United States.

This supreme authority, which arises from the specific provisions of the Constitution itself, is nowhere more fully illustrated than in the series of decisions under the Federal *habeas corpus* statute, in some of which cases persons in the custody of state officers for alleged crimes against the State have been taken from that custody and discharged by a Federal court or judge, because the imprisonment was adjudged to be in violation of the Federal Constitution. The right to so discharge has not been doubted by this court, and it has never been supposed there was any suit against the State by reason of serving the writ upon one of the officers of the State in whose custody the person was found. * * *

The rule to show cause is discharged and the petition for writs of *habeas corpus* and certiorari is dismissed. * * *

■ MR. JUSTICE HARLAN, dissenting.

* * * Let it be observed that the suit * * * in the Circuit Court of the United States was, as to the defendant Young, one against him *as, and only because he was*, Attorney General of Minnesota. No relief was sought against him individually but only in his capacity *as* Attorney General. And the manifest, indeed the avowed and admitted, object of seeking such relief was *to tie the hands* of the *State* so that it could not in any manner or by any mode of proceeding, *in its own courts*, test the validity of the statutes and orders in question. It would therefore seem clear that within the true meaning of the Eleventh Amendment the suit brought in the Federal court was one, in legal effect, against the State—as much so as if the State had been formally named on the record as a party—and therefore it was a suit to which, under the Amendment, so far as the State or its Attorney General was concerned, the judicial power of the United States did not and could not extend.

* * * [T]he intangible thing, called a State, however extensive its powers, can never appear or be represented or known in any court in a litigated case, except by and through its officers. When, therefore, the Federal court forbade the defendant Young, as Attorney General of Minnesota, from taking any action, suit, step or proceeding whatever looking to the enforcement of the statutes in question, it said in effect to the State of Minnesota: " * * * the Federal court adjudges that you, the State, although a sovereign for many important governmental purposes, shall not appear in your own courts, by your law officer, with the view of enforcing, or even for determining the validity of the state enactments which the Federal court has, upon a preliminary hearing, declared to be in violation of the Constitution of the United States."

This principle, if firmly established, would work a radical change in our governmental system. It would inaugurate a new era in the American judicial system and in the relations of the National and state governments. It would enable the subordinate Federal courts to supervise and control the official action of the States as if they were "dependencies" or provinces. It would place the States of the Union in a condition of inferiority never dreamed of when the Constitution was adopted or when the Eleventh Amendment was made a part of the Supreme Law of the Land. * * * Too little consequence has been attached to the fact that the courts of the States are under an obligation equally strong with that resting upon the courts of the Union to respect and enforce the provisions of the Federal Constitution as the Supreme Law of the Land, and to guard rights secured or guaranteed by that instrument. We must assume—a decent respect for the States requires us to assume—that the state courts will enforce every right secured by the Constitution. If they fail to do so, the party complaining has a clear remedy for the protection of his rights; for, he can come by writ of error, in an orderly, judicial way, from the highest court of the State to this tribunal for redress in respect of every right granted or secured by that instrument and denied by the state court. * * *

NOTE ON EX PARTE YOUNG AND SUITS AGAINST STATE OFFICERS

(1) The Significance of Ex parte Young. One can hardly overstate the importance of Ex parte Young's decision to authorize individual suits for injunctive relief from unconstitutional state official action. (Similar suits may be brought against federal officers, as discussed pp. 1347–1349, *infra*.) Of course, the tradition of "officer suits" as a means of redress for official misconduct was already well established. But Ex parte Young does more than reaffirm that the officer suit survived the broad interpretation of the Eleventh Amendment announced eighteen years earlier in Hans. It recognizes that officers owe duties under *federal law* to refrain from enforcing unconstitutional state laws, rather than centering litigation on officers' private duties at common law to refrain from trespassory and other tortious activity. Indeed, Attorney General Young's announced readiness to prosecute for conduct in violation of state law may not have been tortious at common law. Ex parte Young enforces constitutional rights directly, moving perceptibly away from a nineteenth-century litigation model in which constitutional issues arose incidentally (if predictably) in litigation to enforce private duties imposed by general or common law.[1]

The Ex parte Young action now provides what some have called a "bedrock" foundation for suits to enjoin enforcement of unconstitutional state (and federal) law. See Friedman, *The Story of Ex parte Young: Once Controversial, Now Canon*, in Federal Courts Stories 247 (Jackson & Resnik eds. 2010). Over time, the Ex parte Young action became the "normal

---

[1]   For illustrations of the common law model, see the Osborn v. Bank of the United States, 22 U.S. (9 Wheat.) 738 (1824), p. 994, *supra*; Poindexter v. Greenhow, 114 U.S. 270 (1885), p. 1176, *supra*.

mechanism" for such litigation, Fallon, *Constitutional Remedies: In One Era and Out the Other*, 136 Harv.L.Rev. 1300, 1317 (2023). In its wake, Judge Henry Friendly described the decision as the "fountainhead" of civil rights enforcement; Professor Charles Alan Wright called it "indispensable"; even Professor Currie who saw the case's reasoning as "outlandish," accepted the plausibility of the Court's use of injunctive relief to protect constitutional rights.[2]

Over the course of the twentieth century, the Court extended the Ex parte Young model of direct constitutional enforcement to claims for damages as well. Thus, in Monroe v. Pape, 365 U.S. 167 (1961), p. 1280, *infra*, the Court interpreted 42 U.S.C. § 1983 to authorize direct enforcement of constitutional rights in suits against state and local officials. As noted in Chapter VII, see pp. 918–931, *supra*, in a similar conceptual move, the Court based the right to sue federal officials under the Bivens doctrine on the Constitution instead of private tort law. Private law duties no longer play a central role in constitutional litigation, although as noted at pp. 1302–1311, *infra*, the Court draws on traditional tort law in elaborating the elements of certain § 1983 claims.

Despite its widespread use, the Ex parte Young suit remains a topic of controversy. Progressives in and out of Congress initially viewed the decision with some suspicion as a jurisdictional predicate for expanded Lochner-style due process litigation, and responded in turn. See Chap. X, Sec. 4.A, *infra* (reviewing federal statutes enacted to limit access to injunctive relief in response to Ex parte Young). During the Warren and Burger Court eras, use of the injunction as the foundation for public law and structural reform litigation provoked scholarly criticism, judicial retrenchment, and congressional reform. For a summary, see Jeffries & Rutherglen, *Structural Reform Revisited*, 95 S.Calif.L.Rev. 1387 (2007) (tracing the origins of and defending a limited role for structural reform litigation), see also p. 281, *supra*.

Beneath the surface of the debate over constitutional remedies and the role of injunctive and structural relief, commentators identify three key holdings in the Ex parte Young decision: its conclusion that the Eleventh Amendment does not block the suit; that the suit presents federal questions in a posture that confers federal question jurisdiction; and that federal equitable remedies are generally available to authorize federal courts to grant relief. Because all three holdings depend importantly on the nature of the duty of state officials to refrain from enforcing an unconstitutional law, this Note first discusses the question of duty.

(2) The Source of Official Duty. As noted, much nineteenth century constitutional litigation was set in motion by a suit to enforce an official's duty under private law. Tortious conduct could lead to individual liability if the officers exceeded their official authority under applicable statutes or if the statutory authority conferred violated the Constitution. Thus, Osborn

---

[2]   See also Friedman, *The Story of Ex parte Young, supra*, at 272 (collecting sources); Monaghan, *The Sovereign Immunity "Exception"*, 110 Harv.L.Rev. 102 (1996) (describing the decision as more important than Hans v. Louisiana).

(an Ohio state official) was held subject to injunctive relief to prevent a tortious taking of the Bank's property under color of an unconstitutional state tax; the duty was based on the law of trespass. See Osborn v. Bank of the United States, 22 U.S. (9 Wheat.) 738 (1824), p. 994, *supra*. So long as the officer's duty was based on private law and operated on the officer as an individual rather than on the state as such, the Court's view was that the state's sovereign immunity was not implicated.

On one conventional understanding, Ex parte Young's central innovation was to recognize an actionable duty imposed on the official by *public* law (the Fourteenth Amendment) rather than *private* tort law. There are passages in the opinion that can be read to support this understanding. The Court explained that a threatened suit to enforce an unconstitutional law was "equivalent to any other threatened wrong or injury to the property of a plaintiff which had theretofore been held sufficient to authorize the suit against the officer." Justice Peckham's majority opinion explained that: "jurisdiction of this general character has, in fact, been exercised by Federal courts from the time of Osborn * * * up to the present; the only difference in regard to the case of Osborn and the case in hand being that in this case the injury complained of is the threatened commencement of suits, civil or criminal, to enforce the act, instead of, as in the Osborn case, an actual and direct trespass upon or interference with tangible property." The majority pointed to post-Osborn decisions that had similarly upheld injunctive relief against state officials for threatened enforcement of unconstitutional state laws. (Specifically, the majority cited Pennoyer v. McConnaughy, 140 U.S. 1 (1891), and Reagan v. Farmers' Loan & Trust Co., 154 U.S. 362 (1894)).[3]

Dissenting, Justice Harlan did not reject the idea of a federal duty so much as the imposition of that duty on the state attorney general, in his official capacity, notwithstanding his attenuated enforcement obligations. In an earlier opinion for the Court, Justice Harlan had approved injunctive relief to prevent constitutional violations, explaining that the "suits are not against the state, but against certain individuals charged with the administration of a state enactment." Smyth v. Ames, 169 U.S. 466, 518 (1898). Without disavowing that decision, Justice Harlan cited his own later opinion for the Court in Fitts v. McGhee, 172 U.S. 516 (1899), which barred suit against officers with no direct enforcement obligations; Justice Harlan argued that Young too lacked any direct role in law enforcement. Injunctions against officers without specific enforcement duties, he believed, were tantamount to injunctions against the state, with the state official serving as only a nominal defendant. (A similar argument was central to the Court's rejection of broad Ex parte Young relief in Whole Woman's Health v. Jackson, 595 U.S. 30 (2021), p. 1211, *infra*.)

(3) The Eleventh Amendment and the Ex parte Young Paradox. Consider whether Ex parte Young, if interpreted as upholding the

---

[3]   See A.C.L.U. of Mississippi, Inc. v. Finch, 638 F.2d 1336, 1340 n.6 (5th Cir.1981) (Wisdom, J.) (suggesting that the "true contribution of Ex parte Young to our constitutional jurisprudence was to confirm and generalize a development first enunciated in Reagan . . . : it implied a new form of action directly from the Constitution, to restrain [as] a newly-recognized constitutional tort threatened prosecution under an unconstitutional state statute") (citing Bator, et al., Hart and Wechsler's The Federal Courts and the Federal System 935 (2d ed.1973)).

enforcement of a duty imposed by the Fourteenth Amendment, rests on a paradox. On the one hand, Attorney General Young acted to enforce the Minnesota state statute in his role as an officer of the state and was a state actor for purposes of the Fourteenth Amendment. On the other hand, the Court held that the violation of supreme federal law "stripped" Young of his official character and "subjected" him to remedial consequences as an individual.[4] Because only state actors owe the sort of public law duty that the Court seemingly recognized in Ex parte Young, many see a paradox in the Court's treatment of the same officials as non-state actors for Eleventh Amendment purposes.[5]

Although no single explanation dispels the paradox, an earlier account in a similar case may shed some light on the Court's Eleventh Amendment thinking. In Reagan v. Farmers' Loan & Trust Co., 154 U.S. 362 (1894), the Court confronted a suit for injunctive relief against allegedly unconstitutional state railroad regulation and an invocation of the Eleventh Amendment. As the Reagan Court explained in response to the state's immunity claim,

"So far from the state being the only real party in interest, and upon whom alone the judgment effectively operates, it has, in a pecuniary sense, no interest at all. Going back of all matters of form, the only parties pecuniarily affected are the shippers and the carriers * * *. There is a sense, doubtless, in which it may be said that the state is interested in the question, but only a governmental sense. It is interested in the well-being of its citizens, in the just and equal enforcement of all its laws; but such governmental interest is not the pecuniary interest which causes it to bear the burden of an adverse judgment. Not a dollar will be taken from the treasury of the state, no pecuniary obligation of it will be enforced, none of its property affected by any decree which may be rendered. It is not nearly so much affected by the decree in this case as it would be by an injunction against officers, staying the collection of taxes; and yet a frequent and unquestioned exercise of jurisdiction of courts, state and federal, is in restraining the collection of taxes, illegal in whole or in part." Id. 390. Applying the Reagan distinction, the Ex parte Young Court may have viewed the suit to enjoin rate enforcement as implicating Minnesota's "governmental interest" in the autonomous enforcement of its laws rather than its "pecuniary interest" in avoiding monetary liability imposed by an adverse judgment.[6]

---

[4]   See In re Ayers, 123 U.S. 443 (1883) (stating in the context of a dispute over a state's breach of contract that a suit to restrain state officials from enforcing state law would be, in effect, a suit against the state). Compare Smyth v. Ames, 169 U.S. 466, 518–19 (1898) (declaring "settled doctrine" that a "suit against individuals for the purpose of preventing them as officers of a state from enforcing an unconstitutional enactment to the injury of the rights of the plaintiff, is not a suit against the state within the meaning of that amendment").

[5]   See Currie, *The Three-Judge District Court in Constitutional Litigation*, 32 U.Chi.L.Rev. 1, 4 (1964) (describing the authority-stripping rationale on which the Court relied as "outlandish"). Compare Monaghan, note 2, *supra*.

[6]   A tort-contract distinction in gauging the permissible scope of officer suits has been defended by some as consistent with the historically prevailing idea that an official could be enjoined only from the commission (or threatened commission) of a wrong for which the official would be personally liable at common law. *E.g.*, Engdahl, *Immunity and Accountability for*

Today, the Ex parte Young action rests on a hybrid conception of constitutional duty, understood to bind officers in both their individual and official capacities. Thus, if the state replaces one official with a new individual, the constitutional duties attach to the new officer, and the federal courts will routinely substitute the new officer as the defendant in any pending Ex parte Young action.[7] At the same time, any injunctive relief will at least in theory bind official defendants in their individual capacity with the threat of contempt sanctions to ensure compliance.[8] Federal law imposes the same hybrid duty on official custodians named as defendants in habeas proceedings. See generally Chap. XI, *infra.*

Although state officers appear in some cases as somewhat nominal defendants, those seeking Ex parte Young relief must respect the formal distinction between the state and the officer as they craft their complaints. The Eleventh Amendment bars unconsented suits against the states themselves, including those in which the plaintiffs seek injunctive relief only. See, *e.g.*, Alabama v. Pugh, 438 U.S. 781 (1978) (per curiam). In other words, the doctrine and rationale of Ex parte Young require that plaintiffs, seeking to avoid the Eleventh Amendment, sue state officials, not the state in its own name. Sometimes, as the Court concluded in Whole Woman's Health v. Jackson, 595 U.S. 30 (2021), p. 1211, *infra*, the plaintiff's inability to name the state may severely limit access to constitutional remedies.

(4) Direct Constitutional Enforcement and Jurisdictional Expansion. The idea that Ex parte Young recognizes a federal duty to refrain from threatening to enforce an unconstitutional law is also important to analyzing the federal courts' subject-matter jurisdiction over such suits. Viewed as a suit brought to enforce a federal law duty, the railroad's equitable claim in Ex parte Young presents a well-pleaded question of federal law properly brought in a lower federal court under the general grant of federal question jurisdiction.[9] That conclusion contrasts with the earlier

---

Positive Governmental Wrongs, 44 U.Colo.L.Rev. 1, 15–16, 37–38 (1972). But the distinction has been attacked by Woolhandler, *Patterns of Official Immunity and Accountability*, 37 Case W.Res.L.Rev. 396, 436–45 (1986–87), on the basis that the historical pattern of decisions was mixed and that given "the flexibility of the common law, the legal duty strand easily merges with the tort strand." See also Vázquez, *Night and Day: Coeur D'Alene, Breard, and the Unraveling of the Prospective-Retrospective Distinction in Eleventh Amendment Doctrine*, 87 Geo.L.J. 1 (1998) (urging an approach in which a suit against an officer for a violation of federal law does not run afoul of the Eleventh Amendment if it seeks only nonmonetary relief).

[7]   Rule 25(d) of the Federal Rules of Civil Procedure calls for the free substitution of government officials sued in their official capacity. According to the Advisory Committee note accompanying the 1961 amendment to Rule 25(d), "the amended rule will apply to actions against officers to compel performance of official duties [and] to prevent officers from acting in excess of their authority or under authority not validly conferred or from enforcing unconstitutional enactments, *cf.* Ex parte Young, 209 U.S. 123 (1908)."

[8]   See Seminole Tribe v. Florida, 517 U.S. 44, 75 (1996) (noting the availability of individual contempt sanctions). In practice, such remedies appear unusual at least against federal officers and agencies. See Parrillo, *The Endgame of Administrative Law: Governmental Disobedience and the Judicial Contempt Power*, 131 Harv.L.Rev. 685 (2018).

[9]   See Ex parte Young, 209 U.S. at 143 (noting the absence of diversity jurisdiction and explaining that jurisdiction was predicated on the claim that the state's regulatory scheme violated due process); see also Smyth v. Ames, 169 U.S. 466, 518 (1898) (in suit to restrain acts of state officials on the ground of their "being repugnant to rights secured to the plaintiffs by the constitution of the United States, the cases may be regarded as arising under that

private right litigation model in which the actionable wrong was non-federal and constitutional issues arising within the litigation after the complaint was filed would be deemed not to satisfy the well-pleaded complaint rule.[10]

(5) The Crain Decision, Remedial Parity, and Remedy Forcing. In General Oil Co. v. Crain, 209 U.S. 211 (1908), the Court imposed on state courts an obligation to furnish injunctive remedies similar to those available in federal court under Ex parte Young. General Oil sued in Tennessee state court to enjoin a state official from enforcing a tax alleged, inter alia, to burden interstate commerce. The plaintiff based its claim for anticipatory injunctive relief on the heavy penalties for any violation, doubts that payments under protest could be recovered, and concern that a multiplicity of refund actions would be necessary to obtain complete relief.

The Supreme Court of Tennessee held that the state courts lacked jurisdiction to grant the injunction sought, applying a Tennessee statute treating such officer suits as suits against the state, barred by state sovereign immunity. On review in the Supreme Court, the state urged that the judgment "involved no Federal question, but only the powers and jurisdiction of the courts of the State of Tennessee, in respect to which the Supreme Court of Tennessee is the final arbiter." The Court assumed jurisdiction (although it sustained the tax on the merits). Justice McKenna said:

"It seems to be an obvious consequence that as a State can only perform its functions through its officers, a restraint upon them is a restraint upon its sovereignty from which it is exempt without its consent in the state tribunals, and exempt by the Eleventh Amendment of the Constitution of the United States, in the national tribunals. The error is in the universality of the conclusion, as we have seen. Necessarily to give adequate protection to constitutional rights a distinction must be made between valid and invalid state laws, as determining the character of the suit against state officers. And the suit at bar illustrates the necessity. If a suit against state officers is precluded in the national courts by the Eleventh Amendment to the Constitution, and may be forbidden by a state to its courts, * * * without power of review by this court, * * * an easy way is open to prevent the enforcement of many provisions of the Constitution, and the Fourteenth Amendment, which is directed at state action, could be nullified as to much of its operation * * *."[11]

---

instrument"). For a summary of congressional responses to this expansion of federal jurisdiction, including the institution of three-judge courts, see Chap. X, Sec. 4.A, *infra.*

[10]   See Chap. VIII, Sec. 3.A, *supra.* For one exception, announced before the Court adopted the well-pleaded complaint rule, see White v. Greenhow, 114 U.S. 307 (1885), (authorizing federal question jurisdiction over a suit predicated on a common law trespass claim where the plaintiff's common law declaration made clear that the claim was one to enforce a state official's federal duty to accept tax coupons).

[11]   Consider Crain's relevance to the later decision in Haywood v. Drown, 556 U.S. 729 (2009), p. 593, *supra,* which forced the state of New York to entertain § 1983 claims against state officers, despite a state statute depriving the state courts of jurisdiction for that purpose. *Cf.* Kenney v. Supreme Lodge, 252 U.S. 411, 415 (1920) (Crain foreshadows the rule "that a State cannot escape its constitutional obligations by the simple device of denying jurisdiction in such cases to Courts otherwise competent").

Given Ex parte Young's assurance of a federal forum for injunctive relief, in a decision announced the same day, why did the Court in Crain worry that states might nullify the Fourteenth Amendment by shutting off access to injunctive relief in both the national and state courts? Consider the possibility that acceptance of Tennessee's narrow view of officer suits and its correspondingly broad view of state sovereign immunity could undermine both state and federal court enforcement of federal rights. More generally, the Court often forced remedies on state courts, one consequence of which was to ensure that plaintiffs could secure similar relief in suits in state and federal court. Compare Poindexter v. Greenhow, 114 U.S. 270 (1885), p. 1176, *supra* (Constitution required state courts to furnish remedies, unavailable as a matter of Virginia state law, for trespassory seizure of taxpayer's property), and Chafin v. Taylor, 114 U.S. 309 (1885) (same), with White v. Greenhow, 114 U.S. 307 (1885) (suit for redress of trespassory taking of property to satisfy a disputed tax obligation was viable in federal court despite Virginia statute foreclosing such relief). See also Ward v. Love County, 253 U.S. 17 (1920) (forcing an assumpsit remedy on state court to allow challenge to taxes paid under protest).

Some commentators reason that, lacking any other federal law justification for forcing remedies on state courts that were otherwise unavailable under state law, decisions such as Poindexter, Crain, and Ward rest on the Court's perception that the Constitution obliges the states to afford remedies in the circumstances presented. See Hill, *Constitutional Remedies*, 69 Colum.L.Rev. 1109, 1128–29, 1132–35 (1969); Woolhandler, *The Common Law Origins of Constitutionally Compelled Remedies*, 107 Yale L.J. 77, 121 (1997); Vázquez, *What Is Eleventh Amendment Immunity?*, 106 Yale L.J. 1683, 1778–79 (1997). That perspective has been thought to support the conclusion that Ex parte Young's provision for injunctive relief in federal court has a similar constitutional core. See Hill, *supra*, at 1138–39.

(6) Prospective Enforcement of Federal Statutes. The Court has extended Ex parte Young to encompass orders directing state compliance with federal rights conferred by statute. Thus, in Edelman v. Jordan, 415 U.S. 651 (1974), the Court approved the issuance of "declaratory and injunctive relief" ordering state officials to administer the federal-state program for Aid to the Aged, Blind, or Disabled in accordance "with various federal regulations and with the Fourteenth Amendment."

At the same time, the Edelman Court made clear that the equitable relief available was limited to an order compelling future compliance with law and did not extend to an award of retroactive monetary relief. It thus invalidated on Eleventh Amendment grounds the lower court's "equitable restitution" order, which would have compelled the state to pay wrongfully withheld past benefits to the members of the plaintiff class. The Court acknowledged that compliance with a purely prospective decree permitted under Ex parte Young could substantially burden the state's treasury, making the line between permissible prospective relief and prohibited retrospective relief less obvious than that between "night" and "day." But the Court upheld "such an ancillary effect on the state treasury" as "a permissible and often an inevitable consequence" of giving effect to federal law.

Consider whether the following forms of relief should be characterized as permissibly prospective within the meaning of the Edelman rule:

(a)   Georgia Railroad & Banking Co. v. Redwine, 342 U.S. 299 (1952), allowed suit to enjoin the state revenue commissioner from imposing taxes on property exempted from taxation under a state charter. Yet, an order preventing taxation may burden the state treasury as significantly as one ordering equitable restitution of benefits.

(b)   Milliken v. Bradley, 433 U.S. 267 (1977) (Milliken II), upheld a decree ordering the state to pay half of the cost of providing remedial education for pupils and in-service training for teachers and administrators as part of the Detroit school desegregation remedy. Although it resembles the equitable restitution forbidden in Edelman, the Milliken decree required the state to purchase services for (rather than to pay cash to) the plaintiffs and to make the payments over a long period, giving more time for budgetary planning.

(c)   Hutto v. Finney, 437 U.S. 678 (1978), upheld an award of attorney's fees, payable by the state to the prevailing plaintiffs following a successful class action challenge to the constitutionality of the conditions of confinement in the Arkansas penal system. Although the Court upheld the fees in part on the theory that Congress, in authorizing fee awards, was enforcing the Fourteenth Amendment, the Court also invoked prospectivity: "[w]hen a State defends a suit for prospective relief, it is not exempt from the ordinary discipline of the courtroom."

(7)   Pennhurst and the Balancing of State and Federal Interests. In Pennhurst State School & Hospital v. Halderman, 465 U.S. 89 (1984), the Court held that a state's Eleventh Amendment immunity from suit blocked federal courts from ordering state officials to comply with state law. As Justice Powell explained for a narrowly divided Court, the application of the party-of-record rule in Ex parte Young was a "fiction[al]" exception to the Eleventh Amendment meant to accommodate the interest in ensuring the supremacy of federal law. But there was no need to reconcile competing interests in state immunity and the supremacy of federal law "when a plaintiff alleges that a state official has violated *state* law." Viewing such litigation as a serious intrusion on state sovereignty and a violation of principles of federalism, the Court held that "[Ex parte] Young and Edelman are inapplicable in a suit against state officials on the basis of state law."

Justice Stevens's dissent, joined by Justices Brennan, Marshall, and Blackmun rejected the Ex parte Young doctrine's characterization as "merely an unprincipled accommodation between federal and state interests." Instead, the doctrine of official accountability was said to have "deep roots" in broader claims of illegality rather than in claims of unconstitutionality alone.

(a)   Interest Balancing in Pennhurst. Pennhurst presents both conceptual and practical puzzles. From a conceptual perspective, the authority-stripping rationale of Ex parte Young might seem to apply at least as strongly to an officer's violation of state law. Indeed, as a matter of tradition, suits in state or federal court to enforce an officer's state law duties did not implicate state sovereign immunity. Instead of framing Pennhurst as the product of state sovereign immunity, the Court might have reasoned instead that federal courts exercising equity powers should defer to the role of state courts in enforcing state law duties. Had Pennhurst been framed this way, it might be more akin to doctrines of abstention and judicial federalism explored more fully in Chapter X, *infra*.[12]

From a practical perspective, Pennhurst complicates the litigation choices of plaintiffs with plausible claims under state and federal law. When a plaintiff brings federal law claims in federal district court, that court's supplemental jurisdiction ordinarily extends to related state law claims. See 28 U.S.C. § 1367, discussed at pp. 1118–1135, *supra*. But Pennhurst forecloses the assertion of such jurisdiction. If plaintiffs wish to file the federal claim in federal court, they must either forgo their state law claim altogether, or assert the state law claim in a second lawsuit in state court, with the attendant risk of claim and issue preclusion.

(b) Post-Pennhurst Interest Balancing. In Idaho v. Coeur D'Alene Tribe, 521 U.S. 261 (1997), the Court refused to allow a Native American tribe to test the legality of state ownership of submerged land through a federal declaratory and injunctive claim against a variety of state officials and agencies. In what the Justices referred to as the principal opinion, Justice Kennedy urged a discretionary case-by-case view of the Ex parte Young doctrine. Following the approach in Pennhurst, Justice Kennedy proposed to characterize Ex parte Young as an exception to state immunity the correct application of which requires "a proper understanding of its role in our federal system and respect for state courts instead of a reflexive reliance on an obvious fiction." *Id.* 270. Justices O'Connor wrote separately, concurring in part and concurring in the judgment and joined by Justices Scalia and Thomas, and rejected Justice Kennedy's case-by-case analysis in favor of a more "straightforward" approach to Ex parte Young but nonetheless joined Justice Kennedy in holding "the Young exception inapplicable" under the "particular circumstances" that the case presented.

(c) The "Straightforward" Alternative. Seemingly rejecting ad hoc balancing, the Court in Verizon Md., Inc. v. Public Service Commission, 535 U.S. 635 (2002) embraced the views set forth in Justice O'Connor's separate opinion in Coeur d'Alene Tribe. Verizon had filed a federal court action against a state agency, its members (in their official capacity), and others, seeking declaratory and injunctive relief from an agency decision that allegedly violated both a federal statute and a federal agency ruling. A unanimous Supreme Court, in an opinion by Justice Scalia, held that the Ex parte Young doctrine allowed Verizon to proceed against the individual commissioners. Justice Scalia explained that, under Ex parte Young, a court need only conduct a "straightforward inquiry into whether [the] complaint

---

[12]   See Shapiro, *Wrong Turns: The Eleventh Amendment and the Pennhurst Case*, 98 Harv.L.Rev. 61, 79 (1984) (describing the Eleventh Amendment and sovereign immunity as "inappropriately blunt instruments for dealing with" collisions of state and individual interests, given the availability of more precise doctrine of restraint").

alleges an ongoing violation of federal law and seeks relief properly characterized as prospective."

The Court followed the same approach in Virginia Office for Protection and Advocacy (VOPA) v. Stewart, 563 U.S. 247 (2011). Writing for a 6–2 majority, Justice Scalia acknowledged that the suit—brought by one Virginia state agency to compel another agency to comply with federal disability law—presented an unusual alignment of state parties. But the Court refused to treat the identity of the plaintiffs or the supposed affront to state dignity as a controlling consideration. Content to give effect to the premise of the doctrine, sometimes "less delicately called a 'fiction,' " the Court ruled that a prospective suit against officials does not implicate the state's immunity. Chief Justice Roberts, joined by Justice Alito, dissented. In his view, the "fiction" of Ex parte Young constituted " 'a narrow exception' to a State's sovereign immunity" and was inapplicable to an intra-state litigation setting.

Can Coeur D'Alene Tribe, Verizon, and VOPA be reconciled by invoking the distinction made in Reagan v. Farmers' Loan & Trust Co., 154 U.S. 362 (1894), Paragraph (3), *supra*, between the state's "governmental" and "pecuniary" interests? The straightforward view of Ex parte Young in Verizon and VOPA rejects immunity arguments based on concerns with state dignity and regulatory autonomy that appear "governmental" within the Reagan framework. By contrast, the claims rejected in the earlier decision in Coeur D'Alene Tribe may have more directly implicated state property interests that should be deemed pecuniary within the Reagan framework.

(8) The Source of the Right to Sue in Ex parte Young. Despite agreement that suits seeking Ex parte Young relief arise under federal law for jurisdictional purposes, debate continues over the source of the Court's authority to issue injunctive relief. One account holds that Ex parte Young viewed the Constitution itself as implying a federal right of action to secure relief from threatened enforcement of an unconstitutional law. Such a conception of the right to sue as springing directly from the Fourteenth Amendment was once widely shared. See Fallon, *Constitutional Remedies: In One Era and Out the Other*, 136 Harv.L.Rev. 1300, 1316 n.102 (2023) (citing Hart, *The Relations Between State and Federal Law*, 54 Colum.L.Rev. 489, 523–24, 524 n.124 (1954); Purcell, *Ex parte Young and the Transformation of the Federal Courts, 1890–1917*, 40 U.Tol.L.Rev. 931, 962–63 (2009); Woolhandler, *Common Law Origins*, Paragraph (5), *supra*, at 99–111). Claims based on such implied federal rights of action would (as recognized in the Bivens line of cases) plainly arise for jurisdictional purposes under federal law.

In an important challenge to that view, Harrison, *Ex parte Young*, 60 Stan.L.Rev. 989 (2008), argues that Ex parte Young did not "rest on a novel cause of action derived from the Fourteenth Amendment." Rather, he writes, the plaintiff asserted a traditional, equitable cause of action to enjoin a prosecution on the basis of what would have been a valid defense at law; that equitable cause of action would today be classified as arising under state law; and federal jurisdiction was proper, despite the absence of diversity, only because equity pleading rules required the plaintiff to recite his Fourteenth

Amendment defense to enforcement on the face of his well-pleaded complaint in equity.[13] For a similar account of the impact of pleading rules on remedial development, see Hill, Paragraph (5), *supra*, at 1128–29. The next principal case considers these questions about the source of federal injunctive relief in the context of a suit to enjoin allegedly preempted state law.

Armstrong v. Exceptional Child Center, Inc.

575 U.S. 320 (2015).
Certiorari to the United States Court of Appeals for the Ninth Circuit.

■ JUSTICE SCALIA delivered the opinion of the Court, except as to Part IV.

We consider whether Medicaid providers can sue to enforce § (30)(A) of the Medicaid Act. 81 Stat. 911 (codified as amended at 42 U.S.C. § 1396a(a)(30)(A)).

I

* * * Like other Spending Clause legislation, Medicaid offers the States a bargain: Congress provides federal funds in exchange for the States' agreement to spend them in accordance with congressionally imposed conditions.

In order to qualify for Medicaid funding, the State of Idaho adopted, and the Federal Government approved, a Medicaid "plan," which Idaho administers through its Department of Health and Welfare. Idaho's plan includes "habilitation services"—in-home care for certain individuals * * *. Providers of these services are reimbursed by the Department of Health and Welfare.

Section 30(A) of the Medicaid Act requires Idaho's plan to:

"provide such methods and procedures relating to the utilization of, and the payment for, care and services available under the plan . . . as may be necessary to safeguard against unnecessary utilization of such care and services and to assure that payments are consistent with efficiency, economy, and quality of care and are sufficient to enlist enough providers so that care and services are available under the plan at least to the extent that such care and services are available to the general population in the geographic area . . . ." 42 U.S.C. § 1396a(a)(30)(A).

---

[13]   Professor Harrison's argument that Young recognized no cause of action directly under the Fourteenth Amendment depends heavily on his claim that federal question jurisdiction over the case could be supported based on the presence of a federal element in Young's well-pleaded complaint asserting a common law cause of action. The idea that federal question jurisdiction could exist in the absence of a federal cause of action is seemingly incompatible with what Justice Holmes stated to be the controlling standard eight years later in American Well Works Co. v. Layne & Bowler Co., 241 U.S. 257 (1916), p. 1030, *supra*, but consistent with the Court's position five years after that in Smith v. Kansas City Title & Trust Co., 255 U.S. 180 (1921), p. 1038, *supra*. See also Paragraph (4), *supra*.

Respondents are providers of habilitation services to persons covered by Idaho's Medicaid plan. They sued petitioners—two officials in Idaho's Department of Health and Welfare—in the United States District Court for the District of Idaho, claiming that Idaho violates § 30(A) by reimbursing providers of habilitation services at rates lower than § 30(A) permits. They asked the court to enjoin petitioners to increase these rates.

The District Court entered summary judgment for the providers, holding that Idaho had not set rates in a manner consistent with § 30(A). The Ninth Circuit affirmed. It said that the providers had "an implied right of action under the Supremacy Clause to seek injunctive relief against the enforcement or implementation of state legislation." We granted certiorari.

II

The Supremacy Clause, Art. VI, cl. 2, reads:

> "This Constitution, and the Laws of the United States which shall be made in Pursuance thereof; and all Treaties made, or which shall be made, under the Authority of the United States, shall be the supreme Law of the Land; and the Judges in every State shall be bound thereby, any Thing in the Constitution or Laws of any State to the Contrary notwithstanding."

It is apparent that this Clause creates a rule of decision: Courts "shall" regard the "Constitution," and all laws "made in Pursuance thereof," as "the supreme Law of the Land." They must not give effect to state laws that conflict with federal laws. Gibbons v. Ogden, 9 Wheat. 1, 210 (1824). It is equally apparent that the Supremacy Clause is not the " 'source of any federal rights,' " Golden State Transit Corp. v. Los Angeles, 493 U.S. 103, 107 (1989) (quoting Chapman v. Houston Welfare Rights Organization, 441 U.S. 600, 613 (1979)), and certainly does not create a cause of action. It instructs courts what to do when state and federal law clash, but is silent regarding who may enforce federal laws in court, and in what circumstances they may do so.

Hamilton wrote that the Supremacy Clause "only declares a truth, which flows immediately and necessarily from the institution of a Federal Government." The Federalist No. 33, p. 207 (J. Cooke ed. 1961). And Story described the Clause as "a positive affirmance of that, which is necessarily implied." 3 Commentaries on the Constitution of the United States § 1831, p. 693 (1833). These descriptions would have been grossly inapt if the Clause were understood to give affected parties a constitutional (and hence congressionally unalterable) right to enforce federal laws against the States. And had it been understood to provide such significant private rights against the States, one would expect to find that mentioned in the preratification historical record, which contained ample discussion of the Supremacy Clause by both supporters and opponents of ratification. We are aware of no such mention, and respondents have not provided any. Its conspicuous absence militates strongly against their position.

Additionally, it is important to read the Supremacy Clause in the context of the Constitution as a whole. Article I vests Congress with broad discretion over the manner of implementing its enumerated powers, giving it authority to "make all Laws which shall be necessary and proper for carrying [them] into Execution." Art. I, § 8. We have said that this confers upon the Legislature "that discretion, with respect to the means by which the powers [the Constitution] confers are to be carried into execution, which will enable that body to perform the high duties assigned to it," McCulloch v. Maryland, 4 Wheat. 316, 421 (1819). It is unlikely that the Constitution gave Congress such broad discretion with regard to the enactment of laws, while simultaneously limiting Congress's power over the manner of their implementation, making it impossible to leave the enforcement of federal law to federal actors. If the Supremacy Clause includes a private right of action, then the Constitution *requires* Congress to permit the enforcement of its laws by private actors, significantly curtailing its ability to guide the implementation of federal law. It would be strange indeed to give a clause that makes federal law supreme a reading that *limits* Congress's power to enforce that law, by imposing mandatory private enforcement—a limitation unheard-of with regard to state legislatures.

To say that the Supremacy Clause does not confer a right of action is not to diminish the significant role that courts play in assuring the supremacy of federal law. For once a case or controversy properly comes before a court, judges are bound by federal law. Thus, a court may not convict a criminal defendant of violating a state law that federal law prohibits. See, *e.g.*, Pennsylvania v. Nelson, 350 U.S. 497, 499, 509 (1956). Similarly, a court may not hold a civil defendant liable under state law for conduct federal law requires. See, *e.g.*, Mutual Pharmaceutical Co. v. Bartlett, 570 U.S. 472, 486–487 (2013). And, as we have long recognized, if an individual claims federal law immunizes him from state regulation, the court may issue an injunction upon finding the state regulatory actions preempted. Ex parte Young, 209 U.S. 123, 155–156 (1908).

Respondents contend that our preemption jurisprudence—specifically, the fact that we have regularly considered whether to enjoin the enforcement of state laws that are alleged to violate federal law—demonstrates that the Supremacy Clause creates a cause of action for its violation. They are incorrect. It is true enough that we have long held that federal courts may in some circumstances grant injunctive relief against state officers who are violating, or planning to violate, federal law. See, *e.g.*, Osborn v. Bank of United States, 9 Wheat. 738, 838–839, 844 (1824); Ex parte Young, *supra*, at 150–151 (citing Davis v. Gray, 16 Wall. 203, 220 (1873)). But that has been true not only with respect to violations of federal law by state officials, but also with respect to violations of federal law by federal officials. Thus, the Supremacy Clause need not be (and in light of our textual analysis above, cannot be) the explanation. What our cases demonstrate is that, "in a proper case, relief may be given in a court of equity . . . to prevent an injurious act by a public officer." Carroll v. Safford, 3 How. 441, 463 (1845).

The ability to sue to enjoin unconstitutional actions by state and federal officers is the creation of courts of equity, and reflects a long history of judicial review of illegal executive action, tracing back to England. See Jaffe & Henderson, *Judicial Review and the Rule of Law: Historical Origins*, 72 L.Q.Rev. 345 (1956). It is a judge-made remedy, and we have never held or even suggested that, in its application to state officers, it rests upon an implied right of action contained in the Supremacy Clause. That is because, as even the dissent implicitly acknowledges, it does not. The Ninth Circuit erred in holding otherwise.

III

A

We turn next to respondents' contention that, quite apart from any cause of action conferred by the Supremacy Clause, this suit can proceed against Idaho in equity.

The power of federal courts of equity to enjoin unlawful executive action is subject to express and implied statutory limitations. See, *e.g.*, Seminole Tribe of Fla. v. Florida, 517 U.S. 44, 74 (1996). " 'Courts of equity can no more disregard statutory and constitutional requirements and provisions than can courts of law.' " INS v. Pangilinan, 486 U.S. 875, 883 (1988) (quoting Hedges v. Dixon County, 150 U.S. 182, 192 (1893); brackets omitted). In our view the Medicaid Act implicitly precludes private enforcement of § 30(A), and respondents cannot, by invoking our equitable powers, circumvent Congress's exclusion of private enforcement.

Two aspects of § 30(A) establish Congress's "intent to foreclose" equitable relief. Verizon Md., Inc. v. Public Serv. Comm'n of Md., 535 U.S. 635, 647 (2002). First, the sole remedy Congress provided for a State's failure to comply with Medicaid's requirements—for the State's "breach" of the Spending Clause contract—is the withholding of Medicaid funds by the Secretary of Health and Human Services. 42 U.S.C. § 1396c. As we have elsewhere explained, the "express provision of one method of enforcing a substantive rule suggests that Congress intended to preclude others." Alexander v. Sandoval, 532 U.S. 275, 290 (2001).

The provision for the Secretary's enforcement by withholding funds might not, *by itself*, preclude the availability of equitable relief. But it does so when combined with the judicially unadministrable nature of § 30(A)'s text. It is difficult to imagine a requirement broader and less specific than § 30(A)'s mandate that state plans provide for payments that are "consistent with efficiency, economy, and quality of care," all the while "safeguard[ing] against unnecessary utilization of . . . care and services." Explicitly conferring enforcement of this judgment-laden standard upon the Secretary alone establishes, we think, that Congress "wanted to make the agency remedy that it provided exclusive," thereby achieving "the expertise, uniformity, widespread consultation, and resulting administrative guidance that can accompany agency decisionmaking," and avoiding "the comparative risk of inconsistent interpretations and misincentives that can arise out of an occasional inappropriate application of the statute in a private action." Gonzaga Univ. v. Doe, 536 U.S. 273, 292 (2002) (Breyer, J., concurring in the judgment). The sheer complexity associated with enforcing § 30(A), coupled with the express provision of an administrative remedy, § 1396c, shows that the Medicaid Act precludes private enforcement of § 30(A) in the courts. * * *

IV

[Here, writing for a plurality, Justice Scalia considered and rejected an argument the respondents had not raised: that the Medicaid Act itself contained "the sort of rights-creating language needed to imply a private right of action."] * * * The judgment of the Ninth Circuit Court of Appeals is reversed.

It is so ordered.

■ [JUSTICE BREYER joined Parts I–III, but not IV, of the Court's opinion. His concurrence is omitted.]

■ JUSTICE SOTOMAYOR, with whom JUSTICE KENNEDY, JUSTICE GINSBURG, and JUSTICE KAGAN join, dissenting.

* * *

I

A

That parties may call upon the federal courts to enjoin unconstitutional government action is not subject to serious dispute. Perhaps the most famous exposition of this principle is our decision in Ex parte Young, 209 U.S. 123 (1908), from which the doctrine derives its usual name. * * * This Court had earlier recognized similar equitable authority in Osborn v. Bank of United States, 9 Wheat. 738 (1824), in which a federal court issued an injunction prohibiting an Ohio official from executing a state law taxing the Bank of the United States. *Id.*, at 838–839. We affirmed in relevant part, concluding that the case was "cognizable in a Court of equity," and holding it to be "proper" to grant equitable relief insofar as the state tax was "repugnant" to the federal law creating the national bank. *Id.*, at 839, 859. More recently, we confirmed the vitality of this doctrine in Free Enterprise Fund v. Public Company Accounting Oversight Bd., 561 U.S. 477 (2010). There, we found no support for the argument that a challenge to " 'governmental action under the Appointments Clause or separation-of-powers principles' " should be treated "differently than every other constitutional claim" for which "equitable relief 'has long been recognized as the proper means for preventing entities from acting unconstitutionally.' " *Id.*, at 491, n.2.

A suit, like this one, that seeks relief against state officials acting pursuant to a state law allegedly preempted by a federal statute falls comfortably within this doctrine. A claim that a state law contravenes a federal statute is "basically constitutional in nature, deriving its force from the operation of the Supremacy Clause," Douglas v. Seacoast Products, Inc., 431 U.S. 265, 271–272 (1977), and the application of preempted state law is therefore "unconstitutional," Crosby v. National Foreign Trade Council, 530 U.S. 363, 388 (2000). We have thus long entertained suits in which a party seeks prospective equitable protection from an injurious and preempted state law without regard to whether the federal statute at issue itself provided a right to bring an action. See, *e.g.*, Shaw v. Delta Air Lines, Inc., 463 U.S. 85 (1983) (state law preempted in part by the federal Employee Retirement Income Security Act of 1974). Indeed, for this reason, we have characterized "the availability of prospective relief of the sort awarded in Ex parte Young" as giving "life to the Supremacy Clause." Green v. Mansour, 474 U.S. 64, 68 (1985).

Thus, even though the Court is correct that it is somewhat misleading to speak of "an implied right of action contained in the Supremacy Clause," that does not mean that parties may not enforce the Supremacy Clause by bringing suit to enjoin preempted state action. As the Court also recognizes, we "have long held that federal courts may in some circumstances grant injunctive relief against state officers who are violating, or planning to violate, federal law."

B

Most important for purposes of this case is not the mere existence of this equitable authority, but the fact that it is exceedingly well established—supported, as the Court puts it, by a "long history." Congress may, if it so chooses, either expressly or implicitly preclude Ex parte Young enforcement actions with respect to a particular statute or category of lawsuit. See, *e.g.*, 28 U.S.C. § 1341 (prohibiting federal judicial restraints on the collection of state taxes); Seminole Tribe of Fla. v. Florida, 517 U.S. 44, 75–76 (1996) (comprehensive alternative remedial scheme can establish Congress' intent to foreclose Ex parte Young actions). But because Congress is undoubtedly aware of the federal courts' long-established practice of enjoining preempted state action, it should generally be presumed to contemplate such enforcement unless it affirmatively manifests a contrary intent. "Unless a statute in so many words, or by a necessary and inescapable inference, restricts the court's jurisdiction in equity, the full scope of that jurisdiction is to be recognized and applied." Porter v. Warner Holding Co., 328 U.S. 395, 398 (1946).

In this respect, equitable preemption actions differ from suits brought by plaintiffs invoking 42 U.S.C. § 1983 or an implied right of action to enforce a federal statute. Suits for "redress designed to halt or prevent the constitutional violation rather than the award of money damages" seek "traditional forms of relief." United States v. Stanley, 483 U.S. 669, 683 (1987). By contrast, a plaintiff invoking § 1983 or an implied statutory cause of action may seek a variety of remedies—including damages—from a potentially broad range of parties. Rather than simply pointing to background equitable principles authorizing the action that Congress presumably has not overridden, such a plaintiff must demonstrate specific congressional intent to *create* a statutory right to these remedies. See Gonzaga Univ. v. Doe, 536 U.S. 273, 290 (2002); Alexander v. Sandoval, 532 U.S. 275, 286 (2001). For these reasons, the principles that we have developed to determine whether a statute creates an implied right of action, or is enforceable through § 1983, are not transferable to the Ex parte Young context.

II

In concluding that Congress has "implicitly preclude[d] private enforcement of § 30(A)," the Court ignores this critical distinction and threatens the vitality of our Ex parte Young jurisprudence. The Court identifies only a single prior decision—Seminole Tribe—in which we have ever discerned such congressional intent to foreclose equitable enforcement of a statutory mandate. Even the most cursory review of that decision reveals how far afield it is from this case.

[The dissent went on to argue that Seminole Tribe inferred congressional foreclosure of Ex parte Young due the statute's "carefully crafted and intricate remedial scheme," while contending that the statute in the case at bar did not meet that standard. The dissent concluded by decrying the fact that "[t]he Court's error today has very real consequences" and positing that "a faithful application of our precedents would have led to a contrary result" in the case.]

———————

NOTE ON THE SOURCE OF FEDERAL INJUNCTIVE RELIEF

(1) The Uncertain Basis for Equitable Relief Prior to Armstrong. As explained in Chapter VI, Sec. 6.2, *supra*, courts prior to Erie R.Co. v. Tompkins, 304 U.S. 64 (1938), p. 760, *supra*, applied the equitable remedy of injunctive relief as a form of general common law. Federal courts also issued injunctive relief in cases involving violations of federal law in pre-Erie cases such as Ex parte Young, 209 U.S. 123 (1908), though views differ, as noted above, about whether the relief was grounded in federal law or general law. See pp. 1194–1196, *supra*. The Court continued after Erie to approve injunctive relief for federal constitutional violations without insisting on overt authorization. See, *e.g.,* Brown v. Board of Education of Topeka, 347

U.S. 483 (1954); Youngstown Sheet & Tube Co. v. Sawyer, 343 U.S. 579 (1952).

Eight years after Erie, Guaranty Trust Co. v. York, 326 U.S. 99 (1945), p. 773, *supra*, stated in dicta that equitable remedies like injunctions continued to be available in federal courts in diversity cases but failed to explain the basis for this conclusion. In Bivens v. Six Unknown Fed. Narcotics Agents, 403 U.S. 388, 404 (1971), p. 918, *supra*, Justice Harlan's concurrence referred to "the presumed availability of federal equitable relief against threatened invasions of constitutional interests," and federal courts' "inherent equitable powers" (citation omitted), both in the absence of express congressional authorization, as a justification for federal court power to craft a damages remedy for constitutional violations. Even as the Court narrowed implied damages remedies in this context, it continued to presume, again without explanation, that equitable remedies would be available. See Ziglar v. Abbasi, 582 U.S. 120, 133, 136, 142, 148 (2017), p. 931, *supra*. And in Grupo Mexicano de Desarrollo, S.A. v. Alliance Bond Fund, Inc., 527 U.S. 308, 318 (1999), p. 778, *supra*, a diversity case, the Court stated:

"The Judiciary Act of 1789 conferred on the federal courts jurisdiction over 'all suits . . . in equity.' § 11, 1 Stat. 78. We have long held that '[t]he "jurisdiction" thus conferred . . . is an authority to administer in equity suits the principles of the system of judicial remedies which had been devised and was being administered by the English Court of Chancery at the time of the separation of the two countries.' Atlas Life Ins. Co. v. W. I. Southern, Inc., 306 U.S. 563, 568 (1939). See also, *e.g.*, Stainback v. Mo Hock Ke Lok Po, 336 U.S. 368, 382, n.26 (1949); Guaranty Trust Co. v. York, 326 U.S. 99, 105 (1945); Gordon v. Washington, 295 U.S. 30, 36 (1935). 'Substantially, then, the equity jurisdiction of the federal courts is the jurisdiction in equity exercised by the High Court of Chancery in England at the time of the adoption of the Constitution and the enactment of the original Judiciary Act, 1789 (1 Stat. 73).' A. Dobie, Handbook of Federal Jurisdiction and Procedure 660 (1928)."

(2) The Three Holdings of Armstrong.

(a) The Supremacy Clause. The Court rejected the Ninth Circuit's ruling that the providers had "an implied right of action under the Supremacy Clause to seek injunctive relief against the enforcement or implementation of state legislation." Earlier editions of this book and commentators had read Shaw v. Delta Air Lines, Inc., 463 U.S. 85 (1983), to support the Ninth Circuit view. See, *e.g.*, Fallon, Manning, Meltzer & Shapiro, Hart & Wechsler's The Federal Courts and the Federal System 844–45 (7th ed. 2015); Sloss, *Constitutional Remedies for Statutory Violations*, 89 Iowa L.Rev. 355 (2004). In Shaw, private plaintiffs, alleging that ERISA preempted provisions of New York's Human Rights Law and Disability Benefits Law, sued state officials for declaratory and injunctive relief. Without examining ERISA on this point, the Court stated:

"It is beyond dispute that federal courts have jurisdiction over suits to enjoin state officials from interfering with federal rights. See Ex parte Young, 209 U.S. 123, 160–162 (1908). A plaintiff who seeks injunctive relief from state regulation, on the ground that such regulation is pre-empted by a federal statute which, by virtue of the Supremacy Clause of the Constitution, must prevail, thus presents a federal question which the federal courts have jurisdiction under 28 U.S.C. § 1331 to resolve. This Court, of course, frequently has resolved pre-emption disputes in a similar jurisdictional posture."

While the Court in Shaw presumed that federal courts could enjoin preempted state action, it spoke in the language of jurisdiction and not about implying a right of action. Compare Green v. Mansour, 474 U.S. 64, 68 (1985) ("the availability of prospective relief of the sort awarded in Ex parte Young gives life to the Supremacy Clause").

Armstrong squarely rejected the view that the Supremacy Clause gives rise to an implied cause of action as the source of injunctive relief in this context. Compare Bray & Miller, *Getting Into Equity*, 97 Notre Dame L.Rev. 1763 (2022) (suggesting that equitable remedies do not rest on a cause of action). Viewing the Supremacy Clause as a "rule of decision" but not a "source of any federal rights," the Court explained that it "does not create a cause of action" or say anything "regarding who may enforce federal laws in court, and in what circumstances they may do so." This conclusion rested in part on the presumed availability of the Ex parte Young remedy in suits against both state and federal officers to enjoin violations of federal law. The Court also made plain the significance of its holding: "If the Supremacy Clause includes a private right of action, then the Constitution requires Congress to permit the enforcement of its laws by private actors, significantly curtailing its ability to guide the implementation of federal law."

(b) The Source of Authority for Equitable Relief. Armstrong also holds that the "ability to sue to enjoin unconstitutional actions by state and federal officers is the creation of courts of equity, and reflects a long history of judicial review of illegal executive action, tracing back to England," and is a "judge-made remedy." Does this mean that equitable remedies are a form of federal common law, and if so, on what basis can federal courts make it? Is the judge-made remedy in equity attached to the substantive federal right that is being enforced, akin to the view once embraced in cases like Bivens v. Six Unknown Fed. Narcotics Agents, 403 U.S. 388 (1971), and Cort v. Ash, 422 U.S. 66 (1975)? See Chap. VII, Sec. 2, *supra*. Does it flow from a jurisdictional statute, as Grupo suggested in the diversity context, perhaps by analogy to the judicial lawmaking power in admiralty? Is the source "the judicial Power" in Article III? Or did the Court just continue the pre-Erie general law, which was consonant with "long history of judicial review of illegal executive action, tracing back to England," yet without an obvious source of authorization? Can this view be squared with Erie?[1]

---

[1]   For post-Erie defenses of the legitimacy of judge-made federal equity in the context of non-statutory review of federal administrative action, see Duffy, *Administrative Common Law in Judicial Review*, 77 Tex.L.Rev. 113 (1998) (tracing "non-statutory" review to statutory provisions, dating from 1789, and general federal question jurisdiction, dating from 1875, assigning federal courts power over cases in law and equity).

Armstrong did not address Erie or cite Grupo, Paragraph (1), *supra*, which was also written by Justice Scalia. Grupo stated that in the diversity context equitable remedies were governed by "the principles of the system of judicial remedies which had been devised and was being administered by the English Court of Chancery at the time of the separation of the two countries." Are these principles different from the ones derived from the "long history of judicial review of illegal executive action" that the Court in Armstrong says is the touchstone for equitable remedies in federal question cases reviewing the legality of action under federal law?[2]

Whatever else Armstrong's conception of federal equity may entail, it affirms presumptive enforcement of federal rights through injunctive relief in federal court, though the proper scope of that relief remains uncertain. Why does the Court persist in recognizing the presumptive availability of injunctive relief even as it has in recent decades cut back on judge-made remedies for damages in the Bivens line of cases, cut back on implied statutory rights of action, and narrowed its conception of federal common law? Do the questions raised here pose doubts about judge-made federal equity or about the more restrictive approach to judge-made remedies in these other areas?

(c) Implied Displacement of Injunctive Relief.

(i) The Test for Displacement. Equity's status as "judge-made law" means that Congress can revise it, at least to some degree. Note that the Court had previously held that Congress in the Indian Gaming Regulatory Act had displaced the presumptive Ex parte Young remedy on the grounds that "where Congress has prescribed a detailed remedial scheme for the enforcement against a State of a statutorily created right, a court should hesitate before casting aside those limitations and permitting an action against a state officer based upon Ex parte Young." Seminole Tribe of Fla. v. Florida, 517 U.S. 44, 74 (1996), p. 1226, *infra*. The Court in Verizon Md., Inc. v. Public Serv. Comm'n of Md., 535 U.S. 635 (2002), described the Seminole Tribe test as whether the relevant congressional statute evinces an "intent to foreclose jurisdiction under Ex parte Young." It ruled that the relevant provisions of the Telecommunications Act of 1996 did not evince that intent because it lacked a detailed remedial scheme and rather simply authorized federal court review of state utility commission decisions. See also Virginia Office for Protection and Advocacy v. Stewart, 563 U.S. 247, 256 n.3 (2011) (rejecting displacement argument raised for first time in Supreme Court because the fact that "the Federal Government can exercise oversight of a federal spending program and even withhold or withdraw funds * * * does not demonstrate that Congress has 'displayed an intent not to provide the

---

[2]   The article on which Armstrong relies, Jaffe & Henderson, *Judicial Review and the Rule of Law: Historical Origins*, 72 L.Q. Rev. 345, 348 (1956), explains that the "structure of judicial review derives from two sources: the prerogative writs (particularly certiorari and mandamus) and actions for damages." All such writs were administered by the common law courts, primarily King's Bench. The High Court of Chancery did not figure in such matters. Is Armstrong thus suggesting that the practices of the English chancellor in 1789 are not reliable guidance as to the contours of federal equitable enforcement of federal law?

"more complete and more immediate relief" that would otherwise be available under Ex parte Young' ").

Applying these principles, Armstrong held that the Medicaid Act § 30(A) impliedly foreclosed or displaced the conventional federal equity remedy. The statute's authorization of a federal agency to withhold Medicaid funds for state non-compliance with the statute's requirements did not by itself establish Congress's "intent to foreclose" equitable relief, but it did so in combination "with the judicially unadministrable nature of § 30(A)'s text," which, the Court concluded, signaled a congressional desire for an exclusive agency remedy that could draw on "agency expertise."[3] Is the search for congressional intent to foreclose an Ex parte Young remedy a meaningful inquiry or judicial speculation?

The Court may have taken pains to indicate that a funds cut-off remedy does not alone suffice to displace the Ex parte Young action because many spending power statutes include such remedies. The deference given the Idaho state agency in Armstrong, though the product of a different analysis, bears some resemblance to that accorded federal agencies on issues that have been "committed to agency discretion" by law. See Citizens to Preserve Overton Park v. Volpe, 401 U.S. 402 (1971) (describing a "very narrow exception" to the presumptive reviewability of agency action under the APA).

(ii) Comparison to Other Displacement Doctrines. The Court has developed a statutory displacement doctrine for other remedies—notably for § 1983 claims, and for Bivens actions. See p. 1299, *infra*; pp. 945–947, *supra*. While earlier decisions pegged displacement to the availability of "comprehensive" remedies, see Bush v. Lucas, 462 U.S. 367, 388 (1983), more recent decisions recognize that any other political-branch remedy, including a regulatory grievance procedure, cuts against recognition of the judicial remedy for damages. See Egbert v. Boule, 596 U.S. 482 (2022). What accounts for the differential approach to displacement of the "judge-made remedy" of injunctive relief under cases like Ex parte Young and in the Bivens context? Is it because of the much longer and deeper tradition of federal injunctive relief? Or is it because the Court's narrowing of the Bivens doctrine has been based in part on the presumed availability of injunctive relief?

By contrast to Bivens, an injunctive remedy against state officials for federal law violations is available by statute under 42 U.S.C. § 1983. The relevant test, akin on the surface to the test for displacing the Ex parte Young remedy, is whether "Congress intended a statute's remedial scheme to 'be the exclusive avenue through which a plaintiff may assert [the] claim[ ],' " Fitzgerald v. Barnstable School Comm., 555 U.S. 246, 252 (2009) (citing Smith v. Robinson, 468 U.S. 992, 1009 (1984)). While the Court has not always applied the test evenly, see p. 1299, *infra*, the test is much harder to satisfy than in the Bivens line of cases, in part because the "burden to demonstrate that Congress has expressly withdrawn the remedy is on the

---

[3]   Justice Breyer's concurring opinion highlighted "the complexity and nonjudicial nature" of setting rates for the reimbursement of patient care services. Armstrong, 575 U.S. at 334 (Breyer, J., concurring in part).

defendant." Golden State Transit Corp. v. Los Angeles, 493 U.S. 103, 107 (1989).[4]

(iii) Broader Implications for Constitutional Remedies. Recall that in earlier cases beyond Ex parte Young, including General Oil Co. v. Crain, 209 U.S. 211 (1908), p. 1195, *supra*, and Ward v. Love County, 253 U.S. 17 (1920), p. 908, *supra*, the Court has been read to hold or to imply that the Constitution ultimately requires some remedies to ensure the supremacy of constitutional law. And Free Enterprise Fund v. Public Company Accounting Oversight Bd., 561 U.S. 477 (2010), says that injunctions are presumptively available to enforce federal rights, although it does not identify the source of that rule. In viewing the Supremacy Clause as a "rule of decision" but not a "source of any federal rights," Armstrong rejects the idea that the Supremacy Clause serves as the source of authority for injunctive remedies against state law that conflicts with a federal statute and reaffirms more generally that Congress controls the preemptive consequences of rights conferred by federal statute. What implications does this holding under the Supremacy Clause have for cases like Crain and Ward in which the federal right derives from the Fourteenth Amendment, rather than from a federal statute?

(3) Relevant Scholarship. For analysis of the issues discussed in this Note, see Bray & Miller, Paragraph (2)(a), *supra*; Gallogly, *Equity's Constitutional Source*, 132 Yale L.J. 1213 (2023); Fallon, *Constitutional Remedies: In One Era and Out the Other*, 136 Harv.L.Rev. 1300 (2023); Fallon, *Bidding Farewell to Constitutional Torts*, 107 Calif.L.Rev. 933 (2019); Hill, *Constitutional Remedies*, 69 Colum.L.Rev. 1109 (1969); Monaghan, *A Cause of Action, Anyone?: Federal Equity and the Preemption of State Law*, 91 Notre Dame L.Rev. 1807 (2016); Vázquez, *The Constitution as a Source of Remedial Law*, 132 Yale L.J. Forum 1062 (2023).

Whole Woman's Health v. Jackson

595 U.S. 30 (2021).
On Writ of Certiorari to the United States Court
of Appeals for the Fifth Circuit.

■ JUSTICE GORSUCH announced the judgment of the Court, and delivered the opinion of the Court except as to Part II-C.

The Court granted certiorari before judgment in this case to determine whether, under our precedents, certain abortion providers can pursue a pre-enforcement challenge to a recently enacted Texas statute. We conclude that such an action is permissible against some of the named defendants but not others.

---

[4]   See Note, *Interpreting Congress's Creation of Alternative Remedial Schemes*, 134 Harv.L.Rev. 1499 (2021) ("the Court's Young foreclosure jurisprudence * * * functionally fall[s] somewhere between § 1983 and Bivens").

I

* * * In their complaint, petitioners alleged that S. B. 8 violates the Federal Constitution and sought an injunction barring the following defendants from taking any action to enforce the statute: [a state-court judge (Jackson); a state-court clerk (Clarkston); the Texas Attorney General (Paxton); the executive directors of Texas medical, nursing, and pharmacy licensing boards (Carlton, Thomas, and Benz); the executive commissioner of the Texas Health and Human Services Commission (Young); and a single private party (Dickson). Shortly after the complaint was filed, the State-employed individuals moved to dismiss, mainly on sovereign immunity grounds.] The sole private defendant * * * also moved to dismiss, claiming that the petitioners lacked standing to sue him. The District Court denied the motions.

[On interlocutory review, the Fifth Circuit Court of Appeals stayed proceedings in the district court pending its resolution of the defendants' appeals and rejected the petitioners' request for an injunction suspending S. B. 8's enforcement. On an emergency petition to stay enforcement of S. B. 8 before it took effect two days later, the Court denied relief. See Whole Woman's Health v. Jackson, 595 U.S. 30 (2021) (Whole Woman's Health I). The Court then granted certiorari before judgment and set the case for expedited briefing and argument.]

II

* * * In this preliminary posture, the ultimate merits question—whether S. B. 8 is consistent with the Federal Constitution—is not before the Court. Nor is the wisdom of S. B. 8 as a matter of public policy.

A

* * * [W]e begin with the sovereign immunity appeal involving the state-court judge, Austin Jackson, and the state-court clerk, Penny Clarkston. While this lawsuit names only one state-court judge and one state-court clerk as defendants, the petitioners explain that they hope eventually to win certification of a class including all Texas state-court judges and clerks as defendants. In the end, the petitioners say, they intend to seek an order enjoining all state-court clerks from docketing S. B. 8 cases and all state-court judges from hearing them.

Almost immediately, however, the petitioners' theory confronts a difficulty. Generally, States are immune from suit under the terms of the Eleventh Amendment and the doctrine of sovereign immunity. See, *e.g.,* Alden v. Maine, 527 U.S. 706, 713 (1999). To be sure, in Ex parte Young, this Court recognized a narrow exception grounded in traditional equity practice—one that allows certain private parties to seek judicial orders in federal court preventing state executive officials from enforcing state laws that are contrary to federal law. 209 U.S. 123, 159–60 (1908). But as Ex parte Young explained, this traditional exception does not normally permit federal courts to issue injunctions against state-court judges or clerks. Usually, those individuals do not enforce state laws as executive officials might; instead, they work to resolve disputes between parties. If a state court errs in its rulings, too, the traditional remedy has been some form of appeal, including to this Court, not the entry of an *ex ante* injunction preventing the state court from hearing cases. As Ex parte Young put it, "an injunction against a state court" or its "machinery" "would be a violation of the whole scheme of our Government." *Id.*, at 163.

Nor is that the only problem confronting the petitioners' court-and-clerk theory. Article III of the Constitution affords federal courts the power to resolve only "actual controversies arising between adverse litigants." Muskrat v. United States, 219 U.S. 346, 361 (1911). Private parties who seek to bring S. B. 8 suits in state court may be litigants adverse to the petitioners. But the state-court clerks who docket those disputes and the state-court judges who decide them generally are not. Clerks serve to file cases as they arrive, not to participate as adversaries in those disputes. Judges exist to resolve controversies about a law's meaning or its conformance to the Federal and State Constitutions, not to wage battle as contestants in the parties' litigation. As this Court has explained, "no case or controversy" exists "between a judge who adjudicates claims under a statute and a litigant who attacks the constitutionality of the statute." Pulliam v. Allen, 466 U.S. 522, 538 n.18 (1984).

Then there is the question of remedy. Texas Rule of Civil Procedure 24 directs state-court clerks to accept complaints and record case numbers. The petitioners have pointed to nothing in Texas law that permits clerks to pass on the substance of the filings they docket—let alone refuse a party's complaint based on an assessment of its merits. Nor does Article III confer on federal judges some "amorphous" power to supervise "the operations of government" and reimagine from the ground up the job description of Texas state-court clerks. Raines v. Byrd, 521 U.S. 811, 829 (1997) (internal quotation marks omitted).

Troubling, too, the petitioners have not offered any meaningful limiting principles for their theory. If it caught on and federal judges could enjoin state courts and clerks from entertaining disputes between private parties under *this* state law, what would stop federal judges from prohibiting state courts and clerks from hearing and docketing disputes between private parties under *other* state laws? And if the state courts and clerks somehow qualify as "adverse litigants" for Article III purposes in the present case, when would they not? * * *

* * * Under the petitioners' theory, would clerks have to assemble a blacklist of banned claims subject to immediate dismissal? What kind of inquiry would a state court have to apply to satisfy due process before dismissing those suits? How notorious would the alleged constitutional defects of a claim have to be before a state-court clerk would risk legal jeopardy merely for filing it? Would States have to hire independent legal counsel for their clerks—and would those advisers be the next target of suits seeking injunctive relief? When a party hales a state-court clerk

into federal court for filing a complaint containing a purportedly unconstitutional claim, how would the clerk defend himself consistent with his ethical obligation of neutrality? See Tex. Code of Judicial Conduct Canon 3(B)(10) (2021) (instructing judges and court staff to abstain from taking public positions on pending or impending proceedings). Could federal courts enjoin those who perform other ministerial tasks potentially related to litigation, like the postal carrier who delivers complaints to the courthouse? Many more questions than answers would present themselves if the Court journeyed this way.

Our colleagues writing separately today * * * point to Pulliam. But that case had nothing to do with state-court clerks, injunctions against them, or the doctrine of sovereign immunity. Instead, the Court faced only the question whether the suit before it could proceed against a judge consistent with the distinct doctrine of judicial immunity. 466 U.S., at 541–543. * * *

If anything, the remainder of our colleagues' cases are even further afield. Mitchum v. Foster did not involve state-court clerks, but a judge, prosecutor, and sheriff. When it came to these individuals, the Court held only that the Anti-Injunction Act did not bar suit against them. 407 U.S. 225, 242–243 (1972). Once more, the Court did not purport to pass judgment on any sovereign immunity defense, let alone suggest any disagreement with Ex parte Young. * * * Simply put, nothing in any of our colleagues' cases supports their novel suggestion that we should allow a pre-enforcement action for injunctive relief against state-court clerks, all while simultaneously holding the judges they serve immune.

B

Perhaps recognizing the problems with their court-and-clerk theory, the petitioners briefly advance an alternative. They say they seek to enjoin the Texas attorney general from enforcing S. B. 8. Such an injunction, the petitioners submit, would also automatically bind any private party who might try to bring an S. B. 8 suit against them. But the petitioners barely develop this back-up theory in their briefing, and it too suffers from some obvious problems.

Start with perhaps the most straightforward. While Ex parte Young authorizes federal courts to enjoin certain state officials from enforcing state laws, the petitioners do not direct this Court to any enforcement authority the attorney general possesses in connection with S. B. 8 that a federal court might enjoin him from exercising. * * *

Even if we could overcome this problem, doing so would only expose another. Supposing the attorney general did have some enforcement authority under S. B. 8, the petitioners have identified nothing that might allow a federal court to parlay that authority, or any defendant's enforcement authority, into an injunction against any and all unnamed private persons who might seek to bring their own S. B. 8 suits. The equitable powers of federal courts are limited by historical practice. "A court of equity is as much so limited as a court of law." Alemite Mfg. Corp. v. Staff, 42 F.2d 832 ([2d Cir.]1930) (L. Hand, J.). Consistent with historical practice, a federal court exercising its equitable authority may enjoin named defendants from taking specified unlawful actions. But under traditional equitable principles, no court may "lawfully enjoin the world at large," *ibid.*, or purport to enjoin challenged "laws themselves." Whole Woman's Health, 595 U.S., at ___ (citing California v. Texas, 593 U.S.659, 672–73 (2021)). * * *

C

While this Court's precedents foreclose some of the petitioners' claims for relief, others survive. The petitioners also name as defendants Stephen Carlton, Katherine Thomas, Allison Benz, and Cecile Young. On the briefing and argument before us, it appears that these particular defendants fall within the scope of Ex parte Young's historic exception to state sovereign immunity. Each of these individuals is an executive licensing official who may or must take enforcement actions against the petitioners if they violate the terms of Texas's Health and Safety Code, including S. B. 8. Accordingly, we hold that sovereign immunity does not bar the petitioners' suit against these named defendants at the motion to dismiss stage.

* * * Justice Thomas suggests that the licensing-official defendants lack authority to enforce S. B. 8 because that statute says it is to be "exclusively" enforced through private civil actions "[n]otwithstanding . . . any other law." * * * Of course, Texas courts and not this one are the final arbiters of the meaning of state statutory directions. See Railroad Comm'n of Texas v. Pullman Co., 312 U.S. 496, 500 (1941). But at least based on the limited arguments put to us at this stage of the litigation, it appears that the licensing defendants do have authority to enforce S. B. 8. * * *

D

[Without objection from any Justice, the Court dismissed the claims against the private defendant for want of standing, accepting Mr. Dickson's sworn statement that he did not plan to sue the petitioners to enforce S. B. 8.]

III

While this should be enough to resolve the petitioners' appeal, a detour is required before we close. Justice Sotomayor charges this Court with "shrink[ing]" from the task of defending the supremacy of the Federal Constitution over state law. That rhetoric bears no relation to reality.

The truth is, many paths exist to vindicate the supremacy of federal law in this area. Even aside from the fact that eight Members of the Court agree sovereign immunity does not bar the petitioners from bringing this pre-enforcement challenge in federal court, everyone acknowledges that other pre-enforcement challenges may be possible in state court as well.

In fact, 14 such state-court cases already seek to vindicate both federal and state constitutional claims against S. B. 8—and they have met with some success at the summary judgment stage. Separately, any individual sued under S. B. 8 may pursue state and federal constitutional arguments in his or her defense. Still further viable avenues to contest the law's compliance with the Federal Constitution also may be possible; we do not prejudge the possibility. * * *

The truth is, too, that unlike the petitioners before us, those seeking to challenge the constitutionality of state laws are not always able to pick and choose the timing and preferred forum for their arguments. This Court has never recognized an unqualified right to pre-enforcement review of constitutional claims in federal court. In fact, general federal question jurisdiction did not even exist for much of this Nation's history. And pre-enforcement review under the statutory regime the petitioners invoke, 42 U.S.C. § 1983, was not prominent until the mid-20th century. See Monroe v. Pape, 365 U.S. 167 (1961); see also R. Fallon, J. Manning, D. Meltzer, & D. Shapiro, Hart and Wechsler's The Federal Courts and the Federal System 994 (7th ed.2015). To this day, many federal constitutional rights are as a practical matter asserted typically as defenses to state-law claims, not in federal pre-enforcement cases like this one.

Finally, Justice Sotomayor contends that S. B. 8 "chills" the exercise of federal constitutional rights. If nothing else, she says, this fact warrants allowing further relief in this case. Here again, however, it turns out that the Court has already and often confronted—and rejected—this very line of thinking. As our cases explain, the "chilling effect" associated with a potentially unconstitutional law being " 'on the books' " is insufficient to "justify federal intervention" in a pre-enforcement suit. Younger v. Harris, 401 U.S. 37, 42, 50–51 (1971). Instead, this Court has always required proof of a more concrete injury and compliance with traditional rules of equitable practice. See Muskrat, 219 U.S., at 361; Ex parte Young, 209 U.S., at 159–160. The Court has consistently applied these requirements whether the challenged law in question is said to chill the free exercise of religion, the freedom of speech, the right to bear arms, or any other right. The petitioners are not entitled to a special exemption. * * *

IV

* * * The order of the District Court is affirmed in part and reversed in part, and the case is remanded for further proceedings consistent with this opinion.

So ordered.

■ JUSTICE THOMAS, concurring in part and dissenting in part.

[Justice Thomas interpreted Texas law to foreclose enforcement of S. B. 8 by state licensing officials. He also viewed the likely enforcement of S. B. 8 as too remote to satisfy the standard of imminently threatened enforcement that he saw as essential to bringing traditional equity powers into play.]

■ CHIEF JUSTICE ROBERTS, with whom JUSTICE BREYER, JUSTICE SOTOMAYOR, and JUSTICE KAGAN join, concurring in the judgment in part and dissenting in part.

* * * [S. B. 8.] is contrary to this Court's decisions in Roe v. Wade, 410 U.S. 113 (1973), and Planned Parenthood of Southeastern Pa. v. Casey, 505 U.S. 833 (1992). It has had the effect of denying the exercise of what we have held is a right protected under the Federal Constitution.

Texas has employed an array of stratagems designed to shield its unconstitutional law from judicial review. * * *

These provisions, among others, effectively chill the provision of abortions in Texas. Texas says that the law also blocks any pre-enforcement judicial review in federal court. On that latter contention, Texas is wrong. As eight Members of the Court agree, petitioners may bring a pre-enforcement suit challenging the Texas law in federal court under Ex parte Young, 209 U.S. 123 (1908), because there exist state executive officials who retain authority to enforce it. Given the ongoing chilling effect of the state law, the District Court should resolve this litigation and enter appropriate relief without delay.

In my view, several other respondents are also proper defendants. First, under Texas law, the Attorney General maintains authority coextensive with the Texas Medical Board to address violations of S. B. 8. * * * Under Texas law, then, the Attorney General maintains authority to "take enforcement actions" based on violations of S. B. 8. He accordingly also falls within the scope of Ex parte Young's exception to sovereign immunity.

The same goes for Penny Clarkston, a court clerk. Court clerks, of course, do not "usually" enforce a State's laws. But by design, the mere threat of even unsuccessful suits brought under S. B. 8 chills constitutionally protected conduct, given the peculiar rules that the State has imposed. Under these circumstances, the court clerks who issue citations and docket S. B. 8 cases are unavoidably enlisted in the scheme to enforce S. B. 8's unconstitutional provisions, and thus are sufficiently "connect[ed]" to such enforcement to be proper defendants. Young, 209 U.S., at 157. The role that clerks play with respect to S. B. 8 is distinct from that of the judges. Judges are in no sense adverse to the parties subject to the burdens of S. B. 8. But as a practical matter clerks are—to the extent they "set[ ] in motion the machinery" that imposes these burdens on those sued under S. B. 8. Sniadach v. Family Finance Corp. of Bay View, 395 U.S. 337, 338 (1969).

The majority contends that this conclusion cannot be reconciled with Young, pointing to language in Young that suggests it would be improper to enjoin courts from exercising jurisdiction over cases. Decisions after Young, however, recognize that suits to enjoin state court proceedings may be proper. See Mitchum v. Foster, 407 U.S. 225, 243 (1972); see also Pulliam v. Allen, 466 U.S. 522, 525 (1984). And this conclusion is consistent with the entire thrust of Young itself. Just as in Young, those sued under S. B. 8 will be "harass[ed] . . . with a multiplicity of suits or litigation generally in an endeavor to enforce penalties under an unconstitutional enactment." 209 U.S., at 160. Under these circumstances, where the mere "commencement of a suit," and in fact just the threat of it, is the "actionable injury to another," the principles underlying Young authorize relief against the court officials who play an essential role in that scheme. *Id.*, at 153. Any novelty in this remedy is a direct result of the novelty of Texas's scheme.

* * *

The clear purpose and actual effect of S. B. 8 has been to nullify this Court's rulings. It is, however, a basic principle that the Constitution is the "fundamental and paramount law of the nation," and "[i]t is emphatically the province and duty of the judicial department to say what the law is." Marbury v. Madison, 1 Cranch 137, 177 (1803). Indeed, "[i]f the legislatures of the several states may, at will, annul the judgments of the courts of the United States, and destroy the rights acquired under those judgments, the constitution itself becomes a solemn mockery." United States v. Peters, 5 Cranch 115, 136 (1809). The nature of the federal right infringed does not matter; it is the role of the Supreme Court in our constitutional system that is at stake.

■ JUSTICE SOTOMAYOR, with whom JUSTICE BREYER and JUSTICE KAGAN join, concurring in the judgment in part and dissenting in part.

For nearly three months, the Texas Legislature has substantially suspended a constitutional guarantee: a pregnant woman's right to control her own body. * * * The chilling effect has been near total, depriving pregnant women in Texas of virtually all opportunity to seek abortion care within their home State after their sixth week of pregnancy. Some women have vindicated their rights by traveling out of State. For the many women who are unable to do so, their only alternatives are to carry unwanted pregnancies to term or attempt self-induced abortions outside of the medical system.

The Court should have put an end to this madness months ago, before S. B. 8 first went into effect. It failed to do so then, and it fails again today. * * * By foreclosing suit against state-court officials and the state attorney general, the Court effectively invites other States to refine S. B. 8's model for nullifying federal rights. The Court thus betrays not only the citizens of Texas, but also our constitutional system of government.

I

I have previously described the havoc S. B. 8's unconstitutional scheme has wrought for Texas women seeking abortion care and their medical providers. [Citing, inter alia, Whole Woman's Health I, 595 U.S. ___, ___–___ (Sotomayor, J., dissenting).] * * *

As a whole, these provisions go beyond imposing liability on the exercise of a constitutional right. If enforced, they prevent providers from seeking effective pre-enforcement relief (in both state and federal court) while simultaneously depriving them of effective post-enforcement adjudication, potentially violating procedural due process. To be sure, state courts cannot restrict constitutional rights or defenses that our precedents recognize, nor impose retroactive liability for constitutionally protected conduct. * * * Unenforceable though S. B. 8 may be, however, the threat of its punitive measures creates a chilling effect that advances the State's unconstitutional goals.

II

This Court has confronted State attempts to evade federal constitutional commands before, including schemes that forced parties to expose themselves to catastrophic liability as state-court defendants in order to assert their rights. Until today, the Court had proven equal to those challenges.

In 1908, this Court decided Ex parte Young, 209 U.S. 123. In Young, the Court considered a Minnesota law fixing new rates for railroads and adopting high fines and penalties for failure to comply with the rates. The law purported to provide no option to challenge the new rates other than disobeying the law and taking "the risk . . . of being subjected to such enormous penalties." Id., at 145. Because the railroad officers and employees "could not be expected to disobey any of the provisions . . . at the risk of such fines and penalties," the law effectively resulted in "a denial of any hearing to the company." Id., at 146.

The Court unequivocally rejected this design. Concluding that the legislature could not "preclude a resort to the courts . . . for the purpose of testing [the law's] validity," the Court decided the companies could obtain pre-enforcement relief by suing the Minnesota attorney general based on his "connection with the enforcement" of the challenged act. Id., at 146, 157. The Court so held despite the fact that the attorney general's only such connection was the "general duty imposed upon him, which includes the right and the power to enforce the statutes of the State, including, of course, the act in question." Id., at 161. * * *

Like the stockholders in Young, abortion providers face calamitous liability from a facially unconstitutional law. To be clear, the threat is not just the possibility of money judgments; it is also that, win or lose, providers may be forced to defend themselves against countless suits, all across the State, without any prospect of recovery for their losses or expenses. * * *

Under normal circumstances, providers might be able to assert their rights defensively in state court. These are not normal circumstances.

S. B. 8 is structured to thwart review and result in "a denial of any hearing." Young, 209 U.S., at 146. * * *

[Justice Sotomayor next argued that state court clerks are proper defendants under Shelley v. Kraemer, 334 U.S. 1, 14 (1948).] In Shelley, private litigants sought to enforce restrictive racial covenants designed to preclude Black Americans from home ownership and to preserve residential segregation. The Court explained that these ostensibly private covenants involved state action because "but for the active intervention of the state courts, supported by the full panoply of state power," the covenants would be unenforceable. *Id.*, at 19. * * *

* * * Modern cases, however, have recognized that suit may be proper even against state court judges, including to enjoin state-court proceedings. See Mitchum v. Foster, 407 U.S. 225, 243 (1972); see also Pulliam v. Allen, 466 U.S. 522, 525 (1984). The Court responds that these cases did not expressly address sovereign immunity or involve court clerks. If language in Young posed an absolute bar to injunctive relief against state-court proceedings and officials, however, these decisions would have been purely advisory.

Moreover, the Court has emphasized that "the principles undergirding the Ex parte Young doctrine" may "support its application" to new circumstances, "novelty notwithstanding." [Virginia Office for Protection and Advocacy v.] Stewart, 563 U.S. [247,] 261 [(2011)]. No party has identified any prior circumstance in which a State has delegated an enforcement function to the populace, disclaimed official enforcement authority, and skewed state-court procedures to chill the exercise of constitutional rights. Because S. B. 8's architects designed this scheme to evade Young as historically applied, it is especially perverse for the Court to shield it from scrutiny based on its novelty. * * *

Finally, the Court raises "the question of remedy." For the Court, that question cascades into many others about the precise contours of an injunction against Texas court clerks in light of state procedural rules. Vexing though the Court may find these fact-intensive questions, they are exactly the sort of tailoring work that District Courts perform every day. * * *

III

My disagreement with the Court runs far deeper than a quibble over how many defendants these petitioners may sue. The dispute is over whether States may nullify federal constitutional rights by employing schemes like the one at hand. The Court indicates that they can, so long as they write their laws to more thoroughly disclaim all enforcement by state officials, including licensing officials. This choice to shrink from Texas' challenge to federal supremacy will have far-reaching repercussions. I doubt the Court, let alone the country, is prepared for them. * * *

* * * [B]y foreclosing suit against state-court officials and the state attorney general, the Court clears the way for States to reprise and perfect Texas' scheme in the future to target the exercise of any right recognized by this Court with which they disagree.

This is no hypothetical. New permutations of S. B. 8 are coming. In the months since this Court failed to enjoin the law, legislators in several States have discussed or introduced legislation that replicates its scheme to target locally disfavored rights. * * *

* * *

* * * While the Court properly holds that this suit may proceed against the licensing officials, it errs gravely in foreclosing relief against state-court officials and the state attorney general. By so doing, the Court leaves all manner of constitutional rights more vulnerable than ever before, to the great detriment of our Constitution and our Republic.

NOTE ON EX PARTE YOUNG RELIEF AFTER WHOLE WOMAN'S HEALTH

(1) The Elements of S. B. 8. Texas enacted the Texas Heartbeat Act, also known as S. B. 8, prohibiting physicians (with exceptions for medical emergencies) from "knowingly perform[ing] or induc[ing] an abortion on a pregnant woman if the physician detected a fetal heartbeat for the unborn child." Tex. Health & Safety Code, §§ 171.204–205 (West Cum. Supp. 2021). In pegging its prohibition to a fetal heartbeat that physicians can detect six weeks into the pregnancy, the Texas statute departed from the 23-week viability standard of Planned Parenthood v. Casey, 505 U.S. 833 (1992). Rather than authorize or direct state officials to bring criminal prosecutions or civil enforcement actions, S. B. 8 authorizes "any person" to enforce the law by bringing a private civil action to collect a penalty of $10,000 or more from anyone who performs or assists in a prohibited abortion, unless doing so would place an "undue burden" on women seeking abortions. Tex. Health & Safety Code, §§ 171.207, 208. In addition, S. B. 8 confers a state-wide venue privilege on plaintiffs, protects plaintiffs from any award of costs or fees if they pursue frivolous enforcement claims, and invites plaintiffs to pursue duplicative litigation by foreclosing non-mutual claim and issue preclusion. *Id.* §§ 171.208(a), 208(i), 208(e)(5).

(2) Subsequent Proceedings. Following the Court's decision, the Fifth Circuit did not immediately return the case to the district court. Instead, over plaintiffs' objections,[1] that court certified to the Texas Supreme Court questions specific to the authority of state licensing officials to enforce S. B. 8. See Whole Woman's Health v. Jackson, 23 F.4th 380 (5th Cir.2022). The Texas Supreme Court ruled that the relevant statutes conferred no such authority. See Whole Woman's Health v. Jackson, 642 S.W.3d 569 (Tex.

---

[1]   See In re Whole Woman's Health, 142 S.Ct. 701 (2022) (denying plaintiffs' application for mandamus to compel Fifth Circuit to return case to district court).

2022). With one judge dissenting, the Fifth Circuit then remanded the case to the district court with instructions to dismiss all claims. Whole Woman's Health v. Jackson, 31 F.4th 1004 (5th Cir.2022).

(3) Applying Ex parte Young. Consider the way the Whole Woman's Health decision applied Ex parte Young, which had reasoned as follows:

"If, because they were law officers of the state, a case could be made for the purpose of testing the constitutionality of the statute, by an injunction suit brought against them, then the constitutionality of every act passed by the legislature could be tested by a suit against the governor and the attorney general, based upon the theory that the former, as the executive of the state, was, in a general sense, charged with the execution of all its laws, and the latter, as attorney general, might represent the state in litigation involving the enforcement of its statutes." A state official "must have some connection with the enforcement of the act," otherwise, the suit is making the official "a party as a representative of the state, and thereby attempting to make the state a party." 209 U.S. at 157.

Embracing this desire to ward off purely declaratory anticipatory litigation, the Whole Woman's Health Court explained that limiting relief to officers with enforcement authority protects Eleventh Amendment values and ensures a concrete case or controversy under Article III. Both these Eleventh Amendment and Article III concerns were thought to overlap with the obligation of a federal court, when evaluating the merits of an application for preliminary injunctive relief, to assess the threat of concrete harm alongside other considerations such as the clarity of the constitutional violation.

Whole Woman's Health viewed state judges and clerks as applying rather than enforcing the law, and thus entitled to claim the state's immunity from suit under the Eleventh Amendment. In doing so, it could also draw direct support from passages in Ex parte Young denying the suability of judicial officers.

The Court did not consider, however, the common law writ of prohibition. Prohibition issued from superior courts, directing lower court judges to refrain from exceeding the bounds of their jurisdiction on pain of contempt. Nineteenth century state supreme court decisions treated the federal Constitution as setting boundaries to state authority enforceable through writs of prohibition the disposition of which was in turn reviewable on appeal to the Supreme Court. See Weston v. City of Charleston, 27 U.S. 449 (1829). Drawing on the prohibition tradition, cases cited by Justice Sotomayor in Whole Woman's Health had recognized the suability of state judicial officials in Ex parte Young suits brought to enforce the Constitution. See, *e.g.*, Pulliam v. Allen, 466 U.S. 522, 525 (1984) (allowing injunctive relief against state magistrate to compel prompt arraignment and admission to bail over objection based on judicial immunity rather than the Eleventh Amendment).[2] Unlike the writ of prohibition, the anti-suit tradition in equity

---

[2]   For the history, see Nickerson & Funk, *When Judges Were Enjoined: Text and Tradition in the Federal Review of State Judicial Action*, 111 Calif.L.Rev. 1763 (2023); Pfander, *Judicial Review of Unconventional Enforcement Regimes*, 102 Tex.L.Rev. 769 (2024). Given the writ's historic role as a check on inferior courts, arguments from tradition that justify the

emphasized injunctive relief against private parties, rather than relief against the court or judge in which the action was pending. Which tradition was more relevant to a state statute that authorizes private enforcement of public law?

(4) Assessing the Impact on Anticipatory Relief. Critics of the Whole Women's Health decision have characterized its holding, refusing to stay the Texas abortion law, as a retreat from a model of presumptively available remedies for threatened constitutional violations. See Fallon, *Constitutional Remedies: In One Era and Out the Other*, 136 Harv.L.Rev. 1300 (2023); Strauss, *Rights, Remedies, and Texas's S.B. 8*, 2022 Sup.Ct.Rev. 81. Such critics highlight the majority's failure to block the statute's operation and its suggestion that defendants can vindicate their constitutional rights by asserting them defensively in response to state court S. B. 8 enforcement proceedings.[3]

As the critics observe, S. B. 8's provisions make it difficult to secure effective pre-enforcement review. Even assuming the viability of suits to restrain licensing officials, as the Court tentatively ruled, such suits would do little to forestall private enforcement until such time as the Court finally settled the validity of S. B. 8. See Strauss, *supra*, at 87. In addition, the statute poses challenges for the defensive assertion of constitutional rights. By foreclosing any award of costs or attorney's fees for frivolous litigation, Texas law subjects defendants to the prospect of repeat litigation. Further, S. B. 8 allows suit in any court in Texas, a venue generosity that threatens defendants with the prospect of litigation throughout the state. Finally, by apparently limiting the claim preclusive effect of litigation to those who have paid a judgment, the statute would deny defendants repose even if they secured a favorable judgment in an initial proceeding. Ex parte Young viewed arguably analogous burdens on the defensive assertion of constitutional rights as the basis for equitable intervention, noting that few individuals would have the temerity to violate Minnesota state law to procure a test of its constitutionality. Compare General Oil Co. v. Crain, 209 U.S. 211 (1908) (viewing the threat of multiple proceedings as a justification for equitable relief).

Supreme Court's use of the writ of prohibition to block state court proceedings might not readily extend to lower federal courts.

[3]   Apart from the burdens of multifarious litigation to defend against private civil enforcement, S. B. 8 threatened abortion providers with retroactive criminal liability for actions that became subject to sanctions under Texas law only after the Supreme Court's decision in Dobbs v. Jackson Women's Health Organization, 597 U.S. 215 (2022), broadened state regulatory authority with respect to abortion. Following the overruling of Roe v. Wade, 410 U.S. 113 (1973), in Dobbs, a Texas "trigger ban" statute went into effect, criminalizing abortions under Texas law and confronting abortion providers with that possibility. See Act of May 25, 2021, 87th Leg., R.S., ch. 800, § 3, 2021 Tex.Gen. Laws 1886, 1887 (H.B. 1280) (codified at Tex. Health & Safety Code § 170A). Yet the reinstatement of criminal enforcement did not displace private enforcement under S. B. 8. Litigation continued in Texas state courts to challenge aspects of the private enforcement regime. For a summary, see Texas Equal Access Fund v. Maxwell, 2024 WL 853320 (Tex. Ct. App. Feb. 29, 2024) (party threatened with private enforcement may not seek review of statute's constitutionality in state court declaratory judgment proceeding). Do these developments confirm the wisdom of the Court's approach to S. B. 8 in Whole Woman's Health v. Jackson?

(5) Static and Dynamic Approaches to Equity. In light of the foregoing two paragraphs, can one view Whole Woman's Health as taking a "static" rather than a "dynamic" approach to equity? The Court asked whether the specific kind of equitable relief sought by the plaintiffs was consistent with the specific kinds of equitable relief that were described as available in Ex parte Young. But the Court did *not* consider the possibility that just as Ex parte Young had arguably broadened or reconceptualized the availability of equitable relief in response to a new statutory scheme designed to frustrate the assertion of federal rights, so too the Court might be justified in broadening or reconceptualizing the availability of equitable relief again. Is that the correct approach for a federal court to take to equitable relief in the twenty-first century? How does this question compare to the debates about history and equity in Grupo Mexicano de Desarrollo, S.A. v. Alliance Bond Fund, Inc., 527 U.S. 308 (1999), p. 778, *supra*?

(6) The Relevance of Dobbs. Barely six months after the Court's decision in Whole Woman's Health, the Court issued its opinion in Dobbs v. Jackson Women's Health Organization, 597 U.S. 215 (2022), overruling Roe v. Wade, 410 U.S. 113 (1973), and Planned Parenthood of Southeastern Pa. v. Casey, 505 U.S. 833 (1992), and largely eliminating federal constitutional recognition of a right to an abortion. The Dobbs case was argued on December 1, 2021, nine days before the decision in Whole Woman's Health was announced. How much does the pendency of Dobbs explain the Court's diffidence in Whole Woman's Health? Can one see the decision, in hindsight, as an effort to temporize, smoothing the transition to a post-Dobbs world?

(7) Expanding Popular Enforcement? Other states have adopted laws like S. B. 8, some that authorize popular enforcement of abortion restrictions, some that target other issues.[4] State legislatures may more broadly rely on private enforcement mechanisms to avoid pre-enforcement review but can apparently do so only by forswearing traditional forms of public enforcement. Lower federal courts may consider expanding state sovereign immunity into new contexts, such as voting rights litigation, where state laws may not clearly define official enforcement authority.[5] That said, a post-S. B. 8 decision may signal a return to what the Court earlier described as a "straightforward" approach to Ex parte Young. In Reed v. Goertz, 598 U.S. 230 (2023), the Court rejected a claim by Texas that the Eleventh Amendment blocked a suit against a prosecutor to challenge on due process grounds the state's refusal to authorize DNA testing in connection with litigation to invalidate a criminal conviction and death sentence. Justice Thomas, dissenting alone, argued that the state official was named as a nominal defendant and lacked the enforcement role necessary to trigger the Ex parte Young exception. See 598 U.S. at 253–54 & n.7 (Thomas, J., dissenting).

---

[4]   See Michaels & Noll, *Vigilante Federalism*, 108 Cornell L.Rev. 1187 (2023); Norris, *The Promise and Perils of Private Enforcement*, 108 Va.L.Rev. 1483, 1497 (2022) (reporting that Oklahoma and Idaho adopted laws based on S. B. 8).

[5]   See Texas Alliance for Retired Americans v. Scott, 28 F.4th 669 (5th Cir.2022) (holding that a suit to contest the constitutionality of state voting laws was barred by the Eleventh Amendment when brought against a state official with ambiguous enforcement authority).

3. CONGRESSIONAL CONTROL OF SOVEREIGN IMMUNITY

Although Hans v. Louisiana held that the states' sovereign or Eleventh Amendment immunity constitutes a barrier to unconsented suits in federal court seeking to enforce federal law, the Court had no occasion to consider whether Congress has power to lift any jurisdictional restriction or confer a right to sue by statute. As the twentieth century progressed, Congress brought states and other governmental entities within the scope of federal regulatory programs. States challenged congressional power to authorize enforcement of such regulations through individual suits brought against the states as such. The Supreme Court has taken up such challenges in a number of cases.

In Parden v. Terminal Ry., 377 U.S. 184 (1964), the Court held, 5–4, that the states had impliedly consented to an employee's federal court negligence action under the Federal Employers' Liability Act (FELA) by operating a state-owned railway. (The Court subsequently overruled Parden in College Savings Bank v. Florida Prepaid Postsecondary Education Expense Board, 527 U.S. 666 (1999), p. 1248, *infra*.)

Next, Fitzpatrick v. Bitzer, 427 U.S. 445 (1976), more directly concluded that Congress had power to subject states to suit to enforce Title VII of the 1964 Civil Rights Act. (In 1972, Congress had amended Title VII to prohibit discrimination by state and local governments, agencies and political subdivisions.) The case involved a federal court action alleging that Connecticut's retirement plan discriminated against male employees in violation of Title VII. In an opinion by then-Justice Rehnquist, the Supreme Court held that the Eleventh Amendment did not bar an award of retroactive retirement benefits and attorney's fees under Title VII, to be paid from the state treasury, as long as "the 'threshold fact of congressional authorization' * * * is clearly present," as it was in the case.

In explaining the Court's ruling, Justice Rehnquist emphasized that Congress enacted the 1972 amendment pursuant to § 5 of the Fourteenth Amendment. That amendment as a whole represented a "shift in the federal-state balance," with § 5 serving as a potent source of legislative power. He added, "we think that the Eleventh Amendment, and the principle of state sovereignty which it embodies, are necessarily limited by the enforcement provisions of § 5 of the Fourteenth Amendment. * * * We think that Congress may, in determining what is 'appropriate legislation' for the purpose of enforcing the provisions of the Fourteenth Amendment, provide for private suits against State or state officials which are constitutionally impermissible in other contexts."

Finally, a fractured Supreme Court majority upheld Congress's power to subject states to suit in legislation adopted pursuant to the Commerce Clause in Pennsylvania v. Union Gas, 491 U.S. 1 (1989) (5–

4). Writing for the plurality, Justice Brennan argued that the states had ceded their sovereignty to Congress insofar as the Constitution vests Congress with power to regulate the states, and he concluded that the Eleventh Amendment posed no bar to suits to enforce federal law when Congress has abrogated the states' immunity. (The necessary fifth vote for the Court's judgment came from Justice White, who, in a cryptic and brief opinion, stated only that he concurred in the plurality's conclusion but did not agree "with much of [its] reasoning.")

Seven years later, in the next principal case, the Court revisited the question of Congress's power to abrogate the states' immunity when legislating pursuant to Article I.

A. CONGRESSIONAL POWER TO ABROGATE STATE IMMUNITY

Seminole Tribe of Florida v. Florida
517 U.S. 44 (1996).
Certiorari to the United States Court of Appeals for the Eleventh Circuit.

■ CHIEF JUSTICE REHNQUIST delivered the opinion of the Court.

The Indian Gaming Regulatory Act provides that an Indian tribe may conduct certain gaming activities only in conformance with a valid compact between the tribe and the State in which the gaming activities are located. 25 U.S.C. § 2710(d)(1)(C). The Act, passed by Congress under the Indian Commerce Clause, U.S. Const., Art. I, § 8, cl. 3, imposes upon the States a duty to negotiate in good faith with an Indian tribe toward the formation of a compact, § 2710(d)(3)(A), and authorizes a tribe to bring suit in federal court against a State in order to compel performance of that duty, § 2710(d)(7). We hold that notwithstanding Congress' clear intent to abrogate the States' sovereign immunity, the Indian Commerce Clause does not grant Congress that power, and therefore § 2710(d)(7) cannot grant jurisdiction over a State that does not consent to be sued. We further hold that the doctrine of Ex parte Young, 209 U.S. 123 (1908), may not be used to enforce § 2710(d)(3) against a state official.

I

Congress passed the Indian Gaming Regulatory Act in 1988 in order to provide a statutory basis for the operation and regulation of gaming by Indian tribes. [The Act provides that certain types of Indian gaming are lawful where they are:] "conducted in conformance with a Tribal-State compact entered into by the Indian tribe and the State under paragraph (3) that is in effect." § 2710(d)(1).* * *

[The statute authorizes a tribe to sue in federal district court if, after 180 days, the state has failed to negotiate in good faith.] * * *

In September 1991, the Seminole Tribe of Indians, petitioner, sued the State of Florida and its Governor, Lawton Chiles, respondents, [alleging a violation of the good faith negotiation requirement. The district court denied the state's motion to dismiss, but the Eleventh Circuit reversed, sustaining the state's sovereign immunity defense.] * * *

* * * Although the text of the Amendment would appear to restrict only the Article III diversity jurisdiction of the federal courts, "we have understood the Eleventh Amendment to stand not so much for what it says, but for the presupposition . . . which it confirms." Blatchford v. Native Village of Noatak, 501 U.S. 775, 779 (1991). That presupposition, first observed over a century ago in Hans v. Louisiana, 134 U.S. 1 (1890), has two parts: first, that each State is a sovereign entity in our federal system; and second, that " '[i]t is inherent in the nature of sovereignty not to be amenable to the suit of an individual without its consent.' " *Id.*, at 13 (emphasis deleted) (quoting The Federalist No. 81) * * *. For over a century we have reaffirmed that federal jurisdiction over suits against unconsenting States "was not contemplated by the Constitution when establishing the judicial power of the United States." Hans, *supra*, at 15.

Here, petitioner has sued the State of Florida and it is undisputed that Florida has not consented to the suit. See Blatchford, *supra*, at 782 (States by entering into the Constitution did not consent to suit by Indian tribes). Petitioner nevertheless contends that its suit is not barred by state sovereign immunity. First, it argues that Congress through the Act abrogated the States' sovereign immunity. Alternatively, petitioner maintains that its suit against the Governor may go forward under Ex parte Young, *supra*. We consider each of those arguments in turn.

II

Petitioner argues that Congress through the Act abrogated the States' immunity from suit. In order to determine whether Congress has abrogated the States' sovereign immunity, we ask two questions: first, whether Congress has "unequivocally expresse[d] its intent to abrogate the immunity," Green v. Mansour, 474 U.S. 64, 68 (1985); and second, whether Congress has acted "pursuant to a valid exercise of power." *Ibid.*

A

Congress' intent to abrogate the States' immunity from suit must be obvious from "a clear legislative statement." Blatchford, *supra*, at 786. * * *

Here, we agree with the parties, with the Eleventh Circuit in the decision below, and with virtually every other court that has confronted the question that Congress has in § 2710(d)(7) provided an "unmistakably clear" statement of its intent to abrogate. * * *

B

* * *

* * * [O]ur inquiry into whether Congress has the power to abrogate unilaterally the States' immunity from suit is narrowly focused on one question: Was the Act in question passed pursuant to a constitutional provision granting Congress the power to abrogate? See, *e.g.*, Fitzpatrick v. Bitzer, 427 U.S. 445, 452–456 (1976). Previously, in conducting that inquiry, we have found authority to abrogate under only two provisions of the Constitution. In Fitzpatrick, we recognized that the Fourteenth Amendment, by expanding federal power at the expense of state autonomy, had fundamentally altered the balance of state and federal power struck by the Constitution. *Id.*, at 455. We noted that § 1 of the Fourteenth Amendment contained prohibitions expressly directed at the States and that § 5 of the Amendment expressly provided that "The Congress shall have the power to enforce, by appropriate legislation, the provisions of this article." See *id.*, at 453 (internal quotation marks omitted). We held that through the Fourteenth Amendment, federal power extended to intrude upon the province of the Eleventh Amendment and therefore that § 5 of the Fourteenth Amendment allowed Congress to abrogate the immunity from suit guaranteed by that Amendment.

In only one other case has congressional abrogation of the States' Eleventh Amendment immunity been upheld. In Pennsylvania v. Union Gas Co., 491 U.S. 1 (1989), a plurality of the Court found that the Interstate Commerce Clause, Art. I, § 8, cl. 3, granted Congress the power to abrogate state sovereign immunity, stating that the power to regulate interstate commerce would be "incomplete without the authority to render States liable in damages." Union Gas, 491 U.S., at 19–20. Justice White added the fifth vote necessary to the result in that case, but wrote separately in order to express that he "[did] not agree with much of [the plurality's] reasoning." *Id.*, at 57 (opinion concurring in judgment in part and dissenting in part). * * *

Both parties make their arguments from the plurality decision in Union Gas, and we, too, begin there. We think it clear that Justice Brennan's opinion finds Congress' power to abrogate under the Interstate Commerce Clause from the States' cession of their sovereignty when they gave Congress plenary power to regulate interstate commerce. See Union Gas, 491 U.S., at 17 ("The important point . . . is that the provision both expands federal power and contracts state power"). * * *

[The Court viewed the Indian Commerce Clause as effecting, "[i]f anything, * * * a greater transfer of power from the States to the Federal Government than does the Interstate Commerce Clause." But the Court agreed to reconsider Union Gas after explaining that the principle of stare decisis, a policy rather than an "inexorable command," has been accorded less weight in constitutional cases, where correction through legislative action is "practically impossible."]

The Court in Union Gas reached a result without an expressed rationale agreed upon by a majority of the Court. We have already seen that Justice Brennan's opinion received the support of only three other Justices. Of the other five, Justice White, who provided the fifth vote for the result, wrote separately in order to indicate his disagreement with the majority's rationale, and four Justices joined together in a dissent that rejected the plurality's rationale. * * *

The plurality's rationale also deviated sharply from our established federalism jurisprudence and essentially eviscerated our decision in Hans. It was well established in 1989 when Union Gas was decided that the Eleventh Amendment stood for the constitutional principle that state sovereign immunity limited the federal courts' jurisdiction under Article III. * * * As the dissent in Union Gas recognized, the plurality's conclusion—that Congress could under Article I expand the scope of the federal courts' jurisdiction under Article III—"contradict[ed] our unvarying approach to Article III as setting forth the *exclusive* catalog of permissible federal court jurisdiction." Union Gas, *supra*, 491 U.S., at 39.

Never before the decision in Union Gas had we suggested that the bounds of Article III could be expanded by Congress operating pursuant to any constitutional provision other than the Fourteenth Amendment. Indeed, it had seemed fundamental that Congress could not expand the jurisdiction of the federal courts beyond the bounds of Article III. Marbury v. Madison, 1 Cranch 137 (1803). The plurality's citation of prior decisions for support was based upon what we believe to be a misreading of precedent. * * *

The plurality's extended reliance upon our decision in Fitzpatrick v. Bitzer, 427 U.S. 445 (1976), that Congress could under the Fourteenth Amendment abrogate the States' sovereign immunity was also, we believe, misplaced. Fitzpatrick was based upon a rationale wholly inapplicable to the Interstate Commerce Clause, viz., that the Fourteenth Amendment, adopted well after the adoption of the Eleventh Amendment and the ratification of the Constitution, operated to alter the pre-existing balance between state and federal power achieved by Article III and the Eleventh Amendment. As the dissent in Union Gas made clear, Fitzpatrick cannot be read to justify "limitation of the principle embodied in the Eleventh Amendment through appeal to antecedent provisions of the Constitution." Union Gas, *supra*, at 42 (Scalia, J., dissenting).

In the five years since it was decided, Union Gas has proven to be a solitary departure from established law. * * * Reconsidering the decision in Union Gas, we conclude that none of the policies underlying *stare decisis* require our continuing adherence to its holding. The decision has, since its issuance, been of questionable precedential value, largely because a majority of the Court expressly disagreed with the rationale of the plurality. The case involved the interpretation of the Constitution and therefore may be altered only by constitutional amendment or revision by this Court. Finally, both the result in Union Gas and the plurality's rationale depart from our established understanding of the Eleventh Amendment and undermine the accepted function of Article III. We feel bound to conclude that Union Gas was wrongly decided and that it should be, and now is, overruled.

The dissent makes no effort to defend the decision in Union Gas, but nonetheless would find congressional power to abrogate in this case.[11] Contending that our decision is a novel extension of the Eleventh Amendment, the dissent chides us for "attend[ing]" to dicta. We adhere in this case, however, not to mere *obiter dicta*, but rather to the well-established rationale upon which the Court based the results of its earlier decisions. When an opinion issues for the Court, it is not only the result but also those portions of the opinion necessary to that result by which we are bound. For over a century, we have grounded our decisions in the oft-repeated understanding of state sovereign immunity as an essential part of the Eleventh Amendment. In Principality of Monaco v. Mississippi, 292 U.S. 313 (1934), the Court held that the Eleventh Amendment barred a suit brought against a State by a foreign state. Chief Justice Hughes wrote for a unanimous Court:

> "[N]either the literal sweep of the words of Clause one of § 2 of Article III, nor the absence of restriction in the letter of the Eleventh Amendment, permits the conclusion that in all controversies of the sort described in Clause one, and omitted from the words of the Eleventh Amendment, a State may be sued without her consent. Thus Clause one specifically provides that the judicial power shall extend 'to all Cases, in Law and Equity, arising under this Constitution, the Laws of the United States, and Treaties made, or which shall be made, under their Authority.' But, although a case may arise under the Constitution and laws of the United States, the judicial power does not extend to it if the suit is sought to be prosecuted against a State, without her consent, by one of her own citizens. . . .

> "Manifestly, we cannot rest with a mere literal application of the words of § 2 of Article III, or assume that the letter of the Eleventh Amendment exhausts the restrictions upon suits against non-consenting States. Behind the words of the constitutional provisions are postulates which limit and control. There is the essential postulate that the controversies, as contemplated, shall be found to be of a justiciable character. There is also the postulate that States of the Union, still possessing attributes of sovereignty, shall be immune from suits, without their consent, save where there has been a

---

[11]   Unless otherwise indicated, all references to the dissent are to the dissenting opinion authored by Justice Souter.

'surrender of this immunity in the plan of the convention.' " *Id.*, at 321–323 (citations and footnote omitted).

* * * It is true that we have not had occasion previously to apply established Eleventh Amendment principles to the question whether Congress has the power to abrogate state sovereign immunity (save in Union Gas). But consideration of that question must proceed with fidelity to this century-old doctrine.

The dissent, to the contrary, disregards our case law in favor of a theory cobbled together from law review articles and its own version of historical events. The dissent cites not a single decision since Hans (other than Union Gas) that supports its view of state sovereign immunity, instead relying upon the now-discredited decision in Chisholm v. Georgia, 2 Dall. 419 (1793). Its undocumented and highly speculative extralegal explanation of the decision in Hans is a disservice to the Court's traditional method of adjudication. * * *

Hans—with a much closer vantage point than the dissent—recognized that the decision in Chisholm was contrary to the well-understood meaning of the Constitution. The dissent's conclusion that the decision in Chisholm was "reasonable," certainly would have struck the Framers of the Eleventh Amendment as quite odd: that decision created "such a shock of surprise that the Eleventh Amendment was at once proposed and adopted." Monaco, *supra*, at 325. The dissent's lengthy analysis of the text of the Eleventh Amendment is directed at a straw man—we long have recognized that blind reliance upon the text of the Eleventh Amendment is " 'to strain the Constitution and the law to a construction never imagined or dreamed of.' " Monaco, *supra*, at 326, quoting Hans, *supra*, 134 U.S., at 15. The text dealt in terms only with the problem presented by the decision in Chisholm; in light of the fact that the federal courts did not have federal-question jurisdiction at the time the Amendment was passed (and would not have it until 1875), it seems unlikely that much thought was given to the prospect of federal-question jurisdiction over the States.

That same consideration causes the dissent's criticism of the views of Marshall, Madison, and Hamilton to ring hollow. The dissent cites statements made by those three influential Framers, the most natural reading of which would preclude all federal jurisdiction over an unconsenting State.[12] Struggling against this reading, however, the dissent finds significant the absence of any contention that sovereign

---

[12] We note here also that the dissent quotes selectively from the Framers' statements that it references. The dissent cites the following, for instance, as a statement made by Madison: "[T]he Constitution 'give[s] a citizen a right to be heard in the federal courts; and if a state should condescend to be a party, this court may take cognizance of it.' " * * * But that statement, perhaps ambiguous when read in isolation, was preceded by the following: "[J]urisdiction in controversies between a state and citizens of another state is much objected to, and perhaps without reason. It is not in the power of individuals to call any state into court. The only operation it can have, is that, if a state should wish to bring a suit against a citizen, it must be brought before the federal courts. It appears to me that this can have no operation but this[.]" See 3 J. Elliot, Debates on the Federal Constitution 533 (2d ed.1836).

immunity would affect the new federal-question jurisdiction. But the lack of any statute vesting general federal-question jurisdiction in the federal courts until much later makes the dissent's demand for greater specificity about a then-dormant jurisdiction overly exacting.[13]

In putting forward a new theory of state sovereign immunity, the dissent develops its own vision of the political system created by the Framers, concluding with the statement that "[t]he Framer's principal objectives in rejecting English theories of unitary sovereignty . . . would have been impeded if a new concept of sovereign immunity had taken its place in federal-question cases, and would have been substantially thwarted if that new immunity had been held untouchable by any congressional effort to abrogate it."[14] This sweeping statement ignores the fact that the Nation survived for nearly two centuries without the question of the existence of such power ever being presented to this Court. And Congress itself waited nearly a century before even conferring federal-question jurisdiction on the lower federal courts.[15]

In overruling Union Gas today, we reconfirm that the background principle of state sovereign immunity embodied in the Eleventh Amendment is not so ephemeral as to dissipate when the subject of the suit is an area, like the regulation of Indian commerce, that is under the exclusive control of the Federal Government. Even when the Constitution vests in Congress complete law-making authority over a particular area, the Eleventh Amendment prevents congressional

---

[13] Although the absence of any discussion dealing with federal-question jurisdiction is therefore unremarkable, what is notably lacking in the Framers' statements is any mention of Congress' power to abrogate the States' immunity. The absence of any discussion of that power is particularly striking in light of the fact that the Framers virtually always were very specific about the exception to state sovereign immunity arising from a State's consent to suit. See, *e.g.*, The Federalist No. 81, pp. 487–488 (C. Rossiter ed. 1961) (A. Hamilton) ("It is inherent in the nature of sovereignty not to be amenable to the suit of an individual *without its consent*. . . . Unless, therefore, there is a surrender of this immunity in the plan of the convention, it will remain with the States and the danger intimated must be merely ideal") (emphasis in the original); 3 Elliot, *supra*, at 533 (J. Madison) ("It is not in the power of individuals to call any state into court. . . . [The Constitution] can have no operation but this: . . . if a state should condescend to be a party, this court may take cognizance of it").

[14] This argument wholly disregards other methods of ensuring the States' compliance with federal law: The Federal Government can bring suit in federal court against a State, see, *e.g.*, United States v. Texas, 143 U.S. 621, 644–645 (1892) (finding such power necessary to the "permanence of the Union"); an individual can bring suit against a state officer in order to ensure that the officer's conduct is in compliance with federal law, see, *e.g.*, Ex parte Young, 209 U.S. 123 (1908); and this Court is empowered to review a question of federal law arising from a state-court decision where a State has consented to suit, see, *e.g.*, Cohens v. Virginia, 6 Wheat. 264 (1821).

[15] Justice Stevens, in his dissenting opinion, makes two points that merit separate response. First, he contends that no distinction may be drawn between state sovereign immunity and the immunity enjoyed by state and federal officials. But even assuming that the latter has no constitutional foundation, the distinction is clear: The Constitution specifically recognizes the States as sovereign entities, while government officials enjoy no such constitutional recognition. Second, Justice Stevens criticizes our prior decisions applying the "clear statement rule," suggesting that they were based upon an understanding that Article I allowed Congress to abrogate state sovereign immunity. His criticism, however, ignores the fact that many of those cases arose in the context of a statute passed under the Fourteenth Amendment, where Congress's authority to abrogate is undisputed. * * *

authorization of suits by private parties against unconsenting States.[16] The Eleventh Amendment restricts the judicial power under Article III, and Article I cannot be used to circumvent the constitutional limitations placed upon federal jurisdiction. Petitioner's suit against the State of Florida must be dismissed for a lack of jurisdiction.

III

Petitioner argues that we may exercise jurisdiction over its suit to enforce § 2710(d)(3) against the Governor notwithstanding the jurisdictional bar of the Eleventh Amendment. Petitioner notes that since our decision in Ex parte Young, 209 U.S. 123 (1908), we often have found federal jurisdiction over a suit against a state official when that suit seeks only prospective injunctive relief in order to "end a continuing violation of federal law." Green v. Mansour, 474 U.S., at 68. The situation presented here, however, is sufficiently different from that giving rise to the traditional Ex parte Young action so as to preclude the availability of that doctrine. * * *

Where [as here] Congress has created a remedial scheme for the enforcement of a particular federal right, we have, in suits against federal officers, refused to supplement that scheme with one created by the judiciary. Schweiker v. Chilicky, 487 U.S. 412, 423 (1988) * * *. Here, of course, the question is not whether a remedy should be created, but instead is whether the Eleventh Amendment bar should be lifted, as it was in Ex parte Young, in order to allow a suit against a state officer. Nevertheless, we think that the same general principle applies * * *.

[After summarizing the statutory scheme described above, the Court continued:] By contrast with this quite modest set of sanctions, an action brought against a state official under Ex parte Young would expose that official to the full remedial powers of a federal court, including, presumably, contempt sanctions. If § 2710(d)(3) could be enforced in a suit under Ex parte Young, § 2710(d)(7) would have been superfluous; it is difficult to see why an Indian tribe would suffer through the intricate scheme of § 2710(d)(7) when more complete and more immediate relief would be available under Ex parte Young.

---

[16]   Justice Stevens understands our opinion to prohibit federal jurisdiction over suits to enforce the bankruptcy, copyright, and antitrust laws against the States. He notes that federal jurisdiction over those statutory schemes is exclusive, and therefore concludes that there is "no remedy" for state violations of those federal statutes.

That conclusion is exaggerated both in its substance and in its significance. First, Justice Stevens' statement is misleadingly overbroad. We have already seen that several avenues remain open for ensuring state compliance with federal law. Most notably, an individual may obtain injunctive relief under Ex parte Young in order to remedy a state officer's ongoing violation of federal law. See n.14, *supra*. Second, contrary to the implication of Justice Stevens' conclusion, it has not been widely thought that the federal antitrust, bankruptcy, or copyright statutes abrogated the States' sovereign immunity. * * * Although the copyright and bankruptcy laws have existed practically since our nation's inception, and the antitrust laws have been in force for over a century, there is no established tradition in the lower federal courts of allowing enforcement of those federal statutes against the States. * * *

Here, of course, we have found that Congress does not have authority under the Constitution to make the State suable in federal court under § 2710(d)(7). Nevertheless, the fact that Congress chose to impose upon the State a liability which is significantly more limited than would be the liability imposed upon the state officer under Ex parte Young strongly indicates that Congress had no wish to create the latter under § 2710(d)(3). Nor are we free to rewrite the statutory scheme in order to approximate what we think Congress might have wanted had it known that § 2710(d)(7) was beyond its authority. If that effort is to be made, it should be made by Congress, and not by the federal courts. We hold that Ex parte Young is inapplicable to petitioner's suit against the Governor of Florida, and therefore that suit is barred by the Eleventh Amendment and must be dismissed for a lack of jurisdiction. * * *

IV

* * * The Eleventh Circuit's dismissal of petitioner's suit is hereby affirmed.

It is so ordered.

■ JUSTICE STEVENS, dissenting.

This case is about power—the power of the Congress of the United States to create a private federal cause of action against a State, or its Governor, for the violation of a federal right. In Chisholm v. Georgia, 2 Dall. 419 (1793), the entire Court—including Justice Iredell whose dissent provided the blueprint for the Eleventh Amendment—assumed that Congress had such power. In Hans v. Louisiana, 134 U.S. 1 (1890)—a case the Court purports to follow today—the Court again assumed that Congress had such power. In Fitzpatrick v. Bitzer, 427 U.S. 445 (1976), and Pennsylvania v. Union Gas Co., 491 U.S. 1, 24 (1989) (Stevens, J., concurring), the Court squarely held that Congress has such power. In a series of cases beginning with Atascadero State Hospital v. Scanlon, 473 U.S. 234, 238–239 (1985), the Court formulated a special "clear statement rule" to determine whether specific Acts of Congress contained an effective exercise of that power. Nevertheless, in a sharp break with the past, today the Court holds that with the narrow and illogical exception of statutes enacted pursuant to the Enforcement Clause of the Fourteenth Amendment, Congress has no such power.

The importance of the majority's decision to overrule the Court's holding in Pennsylvania v. Union Gas Co. cannot be overstated. The majority's opinion does not simply preclude Congress from establishing the rather curious statutory scheme under which Indian tribes may seek the aid of a federal court to secure a State's good faith negotiations over gaming regulations. Rather, it prevents Congress from providing a federal forum for a broad range of actions against States, from those sounding in copyright and patent law, to those concerning bankruptcy, environmental law, and the regulation of our vast national economy.

There may be room for debate over whether, in light of the Eleventh Amendment, Congress has the power to ensure that such a cause of action may be enforced in federal court by a citizen of another State or a foreign citizen. There can be no serious debate, however, over whether Congress has the power to ensure that such a cause of action may be brought by a citizen of the State being sued. Congress' authority in that regard is clear. * * *

I

* * * Justice Brennan has persuasively explained that the Eleventh Amendment's jurisdictional restriction is best understood to apply only to suits premised on diversity jurisdiction, see Atascadero State Hospital v. Scanlon, 473 U.S., at 247 (dissenting opinion), and Justice Scalia has agreed that the plain text of the Amendment cannot be read to apply to federal-question cases. See Pennsylvania v. Union Gas, 491 U.S., at 31 (dissenting opinion).[8] Whatever the precise dimensions of the Amendment, its express terms plainly do *not* apply to all suits brought against unconsenting States. The question thus becomes whether the relatively modest jurisdictional bar that the Eleventh Amendment imposes should be understood to reveal that a more general jurisdictional bar implicitly inheres in Article III. * * *

II

The majority appears to acknowledge that one cannot deduce from either the text of Article III or the plain terms of the Eleventh Amendment that the judicial power does not extend to a congressionally created cause of action against a State brought by one of that State's citizens. Nevertheless, the majority asserts that precedent compels that same conclusion. I disagree. The majority relies first on our decision in Hans v. Louisiana, 134 U.S. 1 (1890), which involved a suit by a citizen of Louisiana against that State for a claimed violation of the Contracts Clause. The majority suggests that by dismissing the suit, Hans effectively held that federal courts have no power to hear federal-question suits brought by same-state plaintiffs.

Hans does not hold, however, that the Eleventh Amendment, or any other constitutional provision, precludes federal courts from entertaining actions brought by citizens against their own States in the face of contrary congressional direction. * * * Hans instead reflects, at the most, this Court's conclusion that, as a matter of federal common law, federal courts should decline to entertain suits against unconsenting States. Because Hans did not announce a constitutionally mandated jurisdictional bar, one need not overrule Hans, or even question its

---

[8]   Of course, even if the Eleventh Amendment applies to federal-question cases brought by a citizen of another State, its express terms pose no bar to a federal court assuming jurisdiction in a federal-question case brought by an in-state plaintiff pursuant to Congress's express authorization. As that is precisely the posture of the suit before us, and as it was also precisely the posture of the suit at issue in Pennsylvania v. Union Gas, there is no need to decide here whether Congress would be barred from authorizing out-of-state plaintiffs to enforce federal rights against States in federal court. * * *

reasoning, in order to conclude that Congress may direct the federal courts to reject sovereign immunity in those suits not mentioned by the Eleventh Amendment. Instead, one need only follow it. * * *

* * * Hans deduced its rebuttable presumption in favor of sovereign immunity largely on the basis of its extensive analysis of cases holding that the sovereign could not be forced to make good on its debts via a private suit. * * *

In Hans, the plaintiff asserted a Contracts Clause claim against his State and thus asserted a federal right. To show that Louisiana had impaired its federal obligation, however, Hans first had to demonstrate that the State had entered into an enforceable contract as a matter of state law. That Hans chose to bring his claim in federal court as a Contract Clause action could not change the fact that he was, at bottom, seeking to enforce a contract with the State. * * *

The view that the rule of Hans is more substantive than jurisdictional comports with Hamilton's famous discussion of sovereign immunity in The Federalist Papers. Hamilton offered his view that the federal judicial power would not extend to suits against unconsenting States only in the context of his contention that no contract with a State could be enforceable against the State's desire. He did not argue that a State's immunity from suit in federal court would be absolute. * * *

III

* * * The fundamental error that continues to lead the Court astray is its failure to acknowledge that its modern embodiment of the ancient doctrine of sovereign immunity "has absolutely nothing to do with the limit on judicial power contained in the Eleventh Amendment." [Pennsylvania v. Union Gas Co, 491 U.S.,] at 25 (Stevens, J., concurring). It rests rather on concerns of federalism and comity that merit respect but are nevertheless, in cases such as the one before us, subordinate to the plenary power of Congress. * * *

* * * For these reasons, as well as those set forth in Justice Souter's opinion, I respectfully dissent.

■ JUSTICE SOUTER, with whom JUSTICE GINSBURG and JUSTICE BREYER join, dissenting.

[Justice Souter began by characterizing the Court as holding for the "first time since the founding of the Republic that Congress has no authority to subject a State to the jurisdiction of a federal court at the behest of an individual asserting a federal right." Then, Justice Souter conducted a lengthy review of the history of sovereign immunity, the decision in Chisholm, and the ratification of the Eleventh Amendment. As did Justice Brennan in Atascadero State Hospital v. Scanlon, 473 U.S. 234, 247 (1985) (Brennan, J., dissenting), see pp. 1181–1183, *supra*, Justice Souter concluded that the Amendment applied only to claims brought to federal court based on diversity of citizenship. As for claims based on federal law, he argued, the Eleventh Amendment did not apply;

any background norm of state sovereign immunity was a matter of common law that Congress could override in the exercise of its delegated powers.]

I

A

Whatever the scope of sovereign immunity might have been in the Colonies * * * or during the period of Confederation, the proposal to establish a National Government under the Constitution drafted in 1787 presented a prospect unknown to the common law prior to the American experience: the States would become parts of a system in which sovereignty over even domestic matters would be divided or parceled out between the States and the Nation, the latter to be invested with its own judicial power and the right to prevail against the States whenever their respective substantive laws might be in conflict. With this prospect in mind, the 1787 Constitution might have addressed state sovereign immunity by eliminating whatever sovereign immunity the States previously had, as to any matter subject to federal law or jurisdiction; by recognizing an analogue to the old immunity in the new context of federal jurisdiction, but subject to abrogation as to any matter within that jurisdiction; or by enshrining a doctrine of inviolable state sovereign immunity in the text, thereby giving it constitutional protection in the new federal jurisdiction.

The 1787 draft in fact said nothing on the subject, and it was this very silence that occasioned some, though apparently not widespread, dispute among the Framers and others over whether ratification of the Constitution would preclude a State sued in federal court from asserting sovereign immunity as it could have done on any matter of nonfederal law litigated in its own courts. As it has come down to us, the discussion gave no attention to congressional power under the proposed Article I but focused entirely on the limits of the judicial power provided in Article III. * * *

B

[Justice Souter here recounted the decision in Chisholm v. Georgia.]

C

The Eleventh Amendment, of course, repudiated Chisholm * * *. * * * There are two plausible readings of this provision's text. Under the first, it simply repeals the Citizen-State Diversity Clauses of Article III for all cases in which the State appears as a defendant. Under the second, it strips the federal courts of jurisdiction in any case in which a state defendant is sued by a citizen not its own, even if jurisdiction might otherwise rest on the existence of a federal question in the suit. Neither reading of the Amendment, of course, furnishes authority for the Court's view in today's case * * *.

The history and structure of the Eleventh Amendment convincingly show that it reaches only to suits subject to federal jurisdiction exclusively under the Citizen-State Diversity Clauses. In precisely tracking the language in Article III providing for citizen-state diversity jurisdiction, the text of the Amendment does, after all, suggest to common sense that only the Diversity Clauses are being addressed. If the Framers had meant the Amendment to bar federal question suits as well, they could not only have made their intentions clearer very easily, but could simply have adopted the first post-Chisholm proposal, introduced in the House of Representatives by Theodore Sedgwick of Massachusetts on instructions from the Legislature of that Commonwealth. Its provisions would have had exactly that expansive effect:

> "[N]o state shall be liable to be made a party defendant, in any of the judicial courts, established, or which shall be established under the authority of the United States, at the suit of any person or persons, whether a citizen or citizens, or a foreigner or foreigners, or of any body politic or corporate, whether within or without the United States." Gazette of the United States 303 (Feb. 20, 1793). * * *

Congress took no action on Sedgwick's proposal, however, and the Amendment as ultimately adopted two years later could hardly have been meant to limit federal-question jurisdiction, or it would never have left the States open to federal-question suits by their own citizens. * * *

It should accordingly come as no surprise that the weightiest commentary following the Amendment's adoption described it simply as constricting the scope of the Citizen-State Diversity Clauses. [Discussion of Cohens v. Virginia, 6 Wheat. 264 (1821), and Osborn v. Bank of the United States, 9 Wheat. 738 (1824), omitted.]

The good sense of this early construction of the Amendment as affecting the diversity jurisdiction and no more has the further virtue of making sense of this Court's repeated exercise of appellate jurisdiction in federal-question suits brought against states in their own courts by out-of-staters. Exercising appellate jurisdiction in these cases would have been patent error if the Eleventh Amendment limited federal-question jurisdiction, for the Amendment's unconditional language ("shall not be construed") makes no distinction between trial and appellate jurisdiction. And yet, again and again we have entertained such appellate cases, even when brought against the State in its own name by a private plaintiff for money damages. * * *

II

* * * Hans v. Louisiana * * * was indeed a leap in the direction of today's holding, even though it does not take the Court all the way. * * * Although the Court invoked a principle of sovereign immunity to cure what it took to be the Eleventh Amendment's anomaly of barring only those state suits brought by noncitizen plaintiffs, the Hans Court had no

occasion to consider whether Congress could abrogate that background immunity by statute. * * * [But since Hans was wrongly decided,] [i]t follows that the Court's further step today of constitutionalizing Hans's rule against abrogation by Congress compounds and immensely magnifies the century-old mistake of Hans itself and takes its place with other historic examples of textually untethered elevations of judicially derived rules to the status of inviolable constitutional law. * * *

III

Three critical errors in Hans weigh against constitutionalizing its holding as the majority does today. The first we have already seen: the Hans Court misread the Eleventh Amendment. It also misunderstood the conditions under which common-law doctrines were received or rejected at the time of the Founding, and it fundamentally mistook the very nature of sovereignty in the young Republic that was supposed to entail a State's immunity to federal question jurisdiction in a federal court. While I would not, as a matter of *stare decisis*, overrule Hans today, an understanding of its failings on these points will show how the Court today simply compounds already serious error in taking Hans the further step of investing its rule with constitutional inviolability against the considered judgment of Congress to abrogate it.

[Justice Souter argued that the sovereign immunity known to the founding generation was a common law immunity. He argued that such common law doctrines were not generally received into the new constitutional order but remained subject to congressional override; it was not reasonable to argue that "the old immunity doctrine somehow slipped in as a tacit but enforceable background principle." Justice Souter contended that the majority's decision, "constitutionalizing common-law rules at the expense of legislative authority," could not be squared with the Framers' "abhorrence" of the notion that any common law rules "received into the new legal systems would be beyond legislative power to alter or repeal." He then expressed doubt that the Constitution left individuals without any way to enforce "their federal rights directly against an intransigent state." Finally, he likened the majority's decision to the "practice in the century's early decades that brought this Court to the nadir of competence that we identify with Lochner v. New York, 198 U.S. 45 (1905)."]

IV

The Court's holding that the States' Hans immunity may not be abrogated by Congress leads to the final question in this case, whether federal-question jurisdiction exists to order prospective relief enforcing IGRA against a state officer, [the Governor], who is said to be authorized to take the action required by the federal law. * * *. The answer to this question is an easy yes, the officer is subject to suit under the rule in Ex parte Young, 209 U.S. 123 (1908), and the case could, and should, readily be decided on this point alone.

* * * I do not in theory reject the Court's assumption that Congress may bar enforcement by suit even against a state official. But because in practice, in the real world of congressional legislation, such an intent would be exceedingly odd, it would be equally odd for this Court to recognize an intent to block the customary application of Ex parte Young without applying the rule recognized in our previous cases, which have insisted on a clear statement before assuming a congressional purpose to "affec[t] the federal balance," United States v. Bass, 404 U.S. 336, 349 (1971). * * *

IGRA's jurisdictional provision reads as though it had been drafted with the specific intent to apply to officer liability under Young. * * * The door is so obviously just as open to jurisdiction over an officer under Young as to jurisdiction over a State directly that it is difficult to see why the statute would have been drafted as it was unless it was done in anticipation that Young might well be the jurisdictional basis for enforcement action. * * *

It may be that even the Court agrees, for it falls back to the position that only a State, not a state officer, can enter into a compact. This is true but wholly beside the point. The issue is whether negotiation should take place as required by IGRA and an officer (indeed, only an officer) can negotiate. * * *

Finally, one must judge the Court's purported inference by stepping back to ask why Congress could possibly have intended to jeopardize the enforcement of the statute by excluding application of Young's traditional jurisdictional rule, when that rule would make the difference between success or failure in the federal court if state sovereign immunity was recognized. Why would Congress have wanted to go for broke on the issue of state immunity in the event the State pleaded immunity as a jurisdictional bar? Why would Congress not have wanted IGRA to be enforced by means of a traditional doctrine giving federal courts jurisdiction over state officers, in an effort to harmonize state sovereign immunity with federal law that is paramount under the Supremacy Clause? There are no plausible answers to these questions. * * *

V

[Justice Souter concluded that the Eleventh Amendment's limited application to diverse-citizen claims left Congress free to authorize federal jurisdiction over suits against the states in the exercise of its Article I powers. Although the Tenth Amendment's requirement that Congress clearly state its intent to subject states to suit would control, no further restriction was required.]

* * * In the past, we have assumed that a plain-statement requirement is sufficient to protect the States from undue federal encroachments upon their traditional immunity from suit. It is hard to contend that this rule has set the bar too low, for (except in Union Gas) we have never found the requirement to be met outside the context of

laws passed under § 5 of the Fourteenth Amendment. The exception I would recognize today proves the rule, moreover, because the federal abrogation of state immunity comes as part of a regulatory scheme which is itself designed to invest the States with regulatory powers that Congress need not extend to them. This fact suggests to me that the political safeguards of federalism are working, that a plain statement rule is an adequate check on congressional overreaching, and that today's abandonment of that approach is wholly unwarranted. * * *

NOTE ON CONGRESSIONAL POWER TO ABROGATE STATE IMMUNITY

(1) The Stakes. In holding that Congress lacks power to abrogate the states' Eleventh Amendment immunity under the Indian Commerce Clause of Article I, the Seminole Tribe Court did not question that Congress, when legislating under that clause, can impose valid legal obligations on the states. In theory then, Seminole Tribe did not free the states from congressionally imposed restraints, but only exempted them from statutes authorizing individuals to sue in federal court to enforce the states' federal statutory obligations. When Seminole Tribe came down, available alternative enforcement mechanisms included suits for prospective injunctive relief under Ex parte Young (as qualified in Seminole Tribe itself), suits brought by the federal government on behalf of individuals under certain statutes, and suits brought pursuant to a state's consent to litigation in federal court. One potential alternative, individual suit against the state in state court, was apparently left open by Seminole Tribe's reliance on the Eleventh Amendment, but later foreclosed in Alden v. Maine, 527 U.S. 706 (1999), p. 1248, *infra.*

(2) Seminole Tribe and the New Federalism "Revolution." In evaluating the impetus for and impact of Seminole Tribe, consider its relationship to other new federalism initiatives introduced by the Burger and Rehnquist Courts. See generally Young, *State Sovereign Immunity After the Revolution*, 102 Tex.L.Rev. 697 (2024). In National League of Cities v. Usery, 426 U.S. 833 (1976), the Court blocked Congress from regulating the states as states pursuant to the Commerce Clause (thereby invalidating the federal Fair Labor Standards Act as to state employers). Had Usery remained good law, it may have blocked state regulation altogether and obviated any issue of state immunity from suit. But the Court overruled Usery in Garcia v. San Antonio Metropolitan Transit Authority, 469 U.S. 528 (1985), restoring congressional power under the Commerce Clause to regulate the states and posing the question of state immunity that the Court addressed in Seminole Tribe. Garcia based its decision in part on the perception that the political safeguards of federalism would protect the states from congressional overreach. Do such safeguards provide a similar basis for entrusting the issue of state sovereign immunity to congressional control?

In its anti-commandeering cases, the Court invalidated federal laws that directed states to enact certain laws and required state officers to administer federal programs. See New York v. United States, 505 U.S. 144 (1992); Printz v. United States, 521 U.S. 898 (1997). Aimed at preserving a measure of state government autonomy, these doctrines leave Congress free to use reasonable conditional spending inducements to encourage states to implement federal law initiatives. Compare NFIB v. Sebelius, 567 U.S. 519 (2012) (invalidating an inducement deemed coercive). Congress might use similar inducements to secure a state's consent to suit as a condition of its acceptance of federal funds.[1]

The Court's anti-commandeering doctrine was predicated in part on the notion that the Constitution contemplates the regulation of individuals rather than states. That principle has been thought to support a structural argument for a general rule of state sovereign immunity. See Clark, *The Eleventh Amendment and the Nature of the Union*, 123 Harv.L.Rev. 1817 (2010) (arguing that the Constitution's anti-commandeering principle prohibits Congress from imposing regulations and monetary liability on the states as such). In assessing Professor Clark's contention, consider the difference between federal statutes that commandeer the states' legislative or administrative apparatus and those that authorize suit to vindicate federal rights that apply across the board to state and private actors.[2]

(3) The Restriction on Ex parte Young Relief. The relief sought by the Seminole Tribe, an order directing Florida state officials to bargain in good faith over the siting of a casino as contemplated in IGRA, would appear to fall squarely within the doctrine of Ex parte Young, as extended in Edelman v. Jordan. In an amicus submission, the United States argued that the Court could avoid the abrogation issue, given the clarity of the Tribe's right to seek Ex parte Young relief against the Florida governor (who was also named as a defendant). Consider the Court's explanation for its rejection of Ex parte Young relief: The federal statute was said to create a limited set of remedies against the state itself that displaced the more sweeping relief available through an officer suit under Ex parte Young. Commentators reacted, some with alarm and others with placidity, to the implied displacement ruling.[3] That ruling might also be criticized on severability grounds: it treats a constitutionally invalid portion of the statute (its provision for suit against the state) as displacing a remedy for legally binding rules governing state behavior that the invalidation of state suability presumptively left intact.[4]

---

[1]   Mere acceptance of funds to which Congress did not attach explicit conditions does not serve as an implied consent to suit. See Edelman v. Jordan, 415 U.S. 651 (1974).

[2]   See Murphy v. Nat'l Colleg. Athletic Ass'n, 584 U.S. 453, 475–76 (2018) (declaring the anticommandeering doctrine inapplicable when Congress "evenhandedly regulates an activity in which both States and private actors engage").

[3]   Compare Jackson, *Seminole Tribe, The Eleventh Amendment, and the Potential Evisceration of Ex parte Young*, 72 N.Y.U.L.Rev. 495 (1997) (viewing implied displacement as inconsistent with presumed availability of Ex parte Young relief under § 1983) with Currie, *Response: Ex parte Young after Seminole Tribe*, 72 N.Y.U.L.Rev. 547 (1997) (viewing Ex parte Young as "alive and well" but criticizing the doctrine as resting on the premise that the Eleventh Amendment was ratified only to change "the caption on the complaint").

[4]   Current law establishes a presumption of severability under which the Court treats the invalidation of an unconstitutional portion of a statute (such as the statutory provision at issue in Seminole Tribe authorizing suit against the state) as leaving the remainder of the statute intact (such as the provisions lawfully obligating the state to negotiate over the siting of casinos). See Alaska Airlines, Inc. v. Brock, 480 U.S. 678, 684 (1987). With those provisions

Building on this aspect of Seminole Tribe, the Court also found implied displacement in Armstrong v. Exceptional Child Center, 575 U.S. 320 (2015), p. 1200, *supra*, ruling that Ex parte Young relief was unavailable to supplement the remedial scheme under the Medicaid Act.

(4) Congress's Limited Abrogation Authority. At the heart of the Seminole Tribe decision, the Court distinguished between the (reaffirmed) power of Congress to abrogate state immunity pursuant to the Fourteenth Amendment, Fitzpatrick v. Bitzer, 427 U.S. 445 (1976), and its inability to do so pursuant to its Article I powers. The Seminole Tribe Court framed its analysis in jurisdictional terms and seemingly based its decision on the Eleventh Amendment. But rather than a decision that allows Congress limited power to modify the Eleventh Amendment's textual core, Seminole Tribe makes more sense as a decision about Congress's power to manage the unwritten body of state sovereign immunity law that overlaps with and extends beyond the narrow terms of the Eleventh Amendment. One finds hints to that effect in the Seminole Tribe opinion, which acknowledges that the text of the Amendment would appear to curtail only diversity-based suits against the states and later speaks of the "background principle of state sovereign immunity embodied in the Eleventh Amendment" as interpreted in Hans. Much the same formulation appeared in Fitzpatrick v. Bitzer's reference to "the Eleventh Amendment, and the principle of state sovereignty which it embodies."

Identifying the "background principle" of state sovereign immunity, rather than the Amendment's text, as the source of the presumptive Hans immunity helps explain as a formal matter how Congress can regulate state suability. But it does not explain why Congress may exercise its authority only when acting pursuant to legislative authority conferred in later-in-time constitutional amendments. The Seminole Tribe Court rationalized differential treatment by emphasizing the distinctive character of the Fourteenth Amendment, which came after the Eleventh Amendment and altered the "pre-existing balance between state and federal power achieved by Article III and the Eleventh Amendment." But the Eleventh Amendment speaks to judicial, rather than legislative power, and the Fourteenth Amendment does not address judicial power at all.[5] Moreover, the source of unwritten state sovereign immunity lies in the pre-constitutional past, before Article III was adopted, implemented, interpreted, and amended. It

---

preserved as law, relief under Ex parte Young would have presumptively taken them into account. See generally Baude, *Severability First Principles*, 109 Va.L.Rev. 1 (2023). On the Seminole Tribe theory of implied displacement after Armstrong v. Exceptional Child Center, Inc., see p. 1349, *infra*.

[5]   Meltzer, *The Seminole Decision and State Sovereign Immunity*, 1996 S.Ct.Rev. 1, 20–24, criticizes the Court's distinction between abrogation under § 5 and abrogation pursuant to Article I on several grounds. With respect to the "temporal argument," he notes the long-established practice of viewing an amended enactment as a whole and observes that the argument rests in significant part on the purely stylistic convention of reproducing constitutional amendments after the text of the original document. He then points out that the Civil War and its aftermath had a profound impact on all aspects of constitutional theory and practice—an impact not limited to the post-Civil War amendments—and that the distinction drawn by the Court between § 5 and other constitutional provision is especially ironic, coming as it did in a case involving federal Indian law, where the limitation on state sovereignty is particularly stringent.

was interpreted in Hans to establish a constitutional basis for blocking federal question claims, well after the Fourteenth Amendment's ratification.

(5) The "Diversity" Interpretation and Its Implications for Abrogation. The dissenting opinions in Seminole Tribe view the Eleventh Amendment as inapplicable to suits based on federal law, extending the "diversity" account of the Eleventh Amendment as formulated by scholars and restated in Justice Brennan's dissenting opinion in Atascadero State Hospital v. Scanlon, 473 U.S. 234, 247 (1985), p. 1181, *supra*. Having narrowed the Eleventh Amendment to its textual core, the dissenters viewed unwritten law of state sovereign immunity as subject to congressional override pursuant to any grant of legislative power. A broad range of scholars share this view, subscribing both to the diversity account and to Congress's power to override the states' unwritten immunity. See Nelson, *Sovereign Immunity as a Doctrine of Personal Jurisdiction*, 115 Harv.L.Rev. 1559 (2002) (tracing sovereign immunity to the traditional view that states were not amenable to suit at common law). For Professor Nelson and others, immunity from suit (unlike the subject matter limits in the Eleventh Amendment) may be overridden by state consent and appropriate federal legislation.[6]

Professors Baude & Sachs, in contrast, embrace the "literal" view of the textual core of the Eleventh Amendment as proposed by earlier scholars.[7] In addition, they ascribe an entrenched status to unwritten state sovereign immunity that makes it impervious to some forms of congressional control. They do so by characterizing the personal jurisdictional form of immunity identified by Nelson as an unwritten but sticky constitutional backdrop that Congress cannot override except through especially potent forms of legislative power, such as that conferred by the Fourteenth Amendment. See Baude & Sachs, *The Misunderstood Eleventh Amendment*, 169 U.Pa.L.Rev. 609 (2021); see also Baude, *Sovereign Immunity and the Constitutional Text*, 103 Va.L.Rev. 1 (2017); Sachs, *Constitutional Backdrops*, 80 Geo.Wash.L.Rev. 1813 (2012). The Baude-Sachs account broadly aligns with the abrogation limits specified in Seminole Tribe. Compare Young, *Our Prescriptive Judicial Power: Constitutive and Entrenchment Effects of Historical Practice in Federal Courts Law*, 58 Wm. & Mary L.Rev. 535, 593

---

[6]   See Fletcher, *A Historical Interpretation of the Eleventh Amendment: A Narrow Construction of an Affirmative Grant of Jurisdiction Rather than a Prohibition Against Jurisdiction,* 35 Stan.L.Rev. 1033, 1036 (1983); Gibbons, *The Eleventh Amendment and State Sovereign Immunity: A Reinterpretation,* 83 Colum.L.Rev. 1889 (1983); Amar, *Of Sovereignty and Federalism,* 96 Yale L.J. 1425 (1987); Jackson, *The Supreme Court, the Eleventh Amendment, and State Sovereign Immunity,* 98 Yale L.J. 1 (1988); Pfander, *History and State Suability: An "Explanatory" Account of the Eleventh Amendment,* 83 Cornell L.Rev. 1269 (1998).

[7]   For literal accounts of the Eleventh Amendment, see W. Marshall, *The Diversity Theory of the Eleventh Amendment: A Critical Evaluation,* 102 Harv.L.Rev. 1372 (1989); L. Marshall, *Fighting the Words of the Eleventh Amendment,* 102 Harv.L.Rev. 1342 (1989); Massey, *State Sovereignty and the Tenth and Eleventh Amendments,* 56 U.Chi.L.Rev. 61 (1989). For doubts that the Framers shared the literalists' concern with federal question suits by non-citizens, see Pfander, note 6, *supra* (state debts contracted prior to constitution's ratification did not implicate federal constitutional limits on state action). Justice Souter's dissent expressed the further concern that a literal view of the Eleventh Amendment would depart from practice in depriving the Court of federal question jurisdiction on appeal from state court decisions rejecting claims set up under state statutes consenting to suit in state court. See also Jackson, note 6, *supra.*

(2016) (noting that selective constitutional entrenchment of unwritten historical practice as reflected in Seminole Tribe poses line-drawing problems and threatens the Court's legitimacy).

Much of the debate over state sovereign immunity sounds in the register of originalism, as the Justices offer competing accounts of the history of Article III and the Eleventh Amendment. Leaving aside questions about originalism as an interpretive modality, consider the likelihood that the votes of the Justices turn on the answer to sharply contested historical questions.

NOTE ON ABROGATION UNDER THE FOURTEENTH AMENDMENT

(1) The Practice of Abrogation as Applied to Particular Statutes. Although it did not address abrogation of state sovereign immunity, the Court's decision in City of Boerne v. Flores, 521 U.S. 507 (1997), now frames judicial assessment of the exercise of Congress's Fourteenth Amendment § 5 enforcement powers. There, the lower court found that the City's zoning rules burdened the exercise of religion in violation of the Religious Freedom Restoration Act. The Court reversed, reasoning that Congress had unconstitutionally attempted to overrule an earlier Supreme Court decision interpreting the First Amendment as applied to the states through the Fourteenth Amendment. Acknowledging that Congress's power under § 5 extends to the creation of remedies, the Court found that it does not include the power to alter substantive rights. Under City of Boerne, for § 5 legislation to be valid, it must exhibit "congruence and proportionality between the [constitutional violations] to be prevented or remedied and the means"— including abrogation of the states' immunity—"adopted to that end." The congruence and proportionality test defines Congress's authority to create remedial schemes either to prevent future violations or to protect statutory rights that lack a firm basis in the Fourteenth Amendment (as explicated by the Supreme Court).

　　(a) Race and Sex-Based Employment Discrimination. In Title VII, Congress conferred statutory rights to freedom from race- and sex-based workplace discrimination and extended those rights to individuals working for both private sector and state government employers. Given that the equal protection clause of the Fourteenth Amendment prohibits states from intentionally discriminating on the basis of race and sex, Title VII's abrogation of immunity enables the exercise of jurisdiction to remedy constitutional violations. Although it did not apply the Boerne analysis, the Court's decision in Fitzpatrick v. Bitzer, 427 U.S. 445 (1976), p. 1225, *supra*, upholding abrogation under Title VII, illustrates a situation in which a federal statute would seem to meet the congruence and proportionality test. In light of the Court's interpretation of the Fourteenth Amendment to reach intent-based but not effect-based discrimination claims, how far can Congress go in authorizing effect-based claims against state employers? *Cf.* Alexander v. Sandoval, 532 U.S. 275 (2001), p. 892, *supra*.

(b) Age and Disability-Based Employment Discrimination. The Age Discrimination in Employment Act (ADEA) and the Americans with Disabilities Act (ADA) protect both private sector and state government workers from age and disability discrimination on the job. Because the Supreme Court does not recognize age or disability as a suspect classification for purposes of Fourteenth Amendment equal protection analysis, discrimination by a state actor does not violate the Fourteenth Amendment unless it lacks any rational basis. The Court has held that Congress's abrogation of state sovereign immunity in both the ADEA and ADA were invalid under Boerne's congruence and proportionality test. See Kimel v. Fla. Bd. of Regents, 528 U.S. 62 (2000) (ruling that ADEA's substantive provisions were "disproportionate to any unconstitutional conduct that conceivably could be targeted by the Act"); Univ. of Ala. v. Garrett, 531 U.S. 356 (2001) (invalidating provision for state suits to enforce ADA after finding no pattern of constitutional violations).

(c) Intellectual Property Rights and Due Process. Congress has power under Article I of the Constitution to recognize and regulate a host of intellectual property rights, including patents, trademarks, and copyrights. While Congress can create statutory remedies against private parties for infringement of these property rights, abrogation of state immunity from monetary remedies has so far failed the Boerne test of congruence and proportionality. See Florida Prepaid Postsecondary Education Expense Board v. College Savings Bank, 527 U.S. 627 (1999) (Congress identified no pattern of unremedied state patent infringements warranting enforcement of due process); Allen v. Cooper, 589 U.S. 248 (2020) (as with patent infringement, Congress lacked authority to subject states to suit for copyright infringement).

(d) Prophylactic Measures: Family and Medical Leave Act. Decisions upholding some but not all abrogations of state sovereign immunity under the Family and Medical Leave Act of 1993 (FMLA) highlight the importance of identifying a Fourteenth Amendment violation and assessing the abrogation of immunity in relation to that violation. The FMLA confers on employees the right to twelve weeks of unpaid leave annually for any of several reasons, including the onset of a "serious health condition" in the employee's spouse, child, or parent. In addition to these family-care provisions, the FMLA provides leave for purposes of self-care. The Fourteenth Amendment prohibits state employers from discriminating on the basis of sex; the statutory right to unpaid leave sought in part to prevent such discrimination.

Nevada Dep't of Human Resources v. Hibbs, 538 U.S. 721 (2003), upheld, by a vote of 6–3, the abrogation of state sovereign immunity in the FMLA to enforce the unpaid leave entitlement. The Court, per Chief Justice Rehnquist, held that Congress had met its burden under § 5: it had sufficient evidence of a "pattern of constitutional violations on the part of the States in this area" to warrant the provision of the FMLA's private rights and remedies as "appropriate prophylactic legislation." The Court noted that it had subjected gender-based discrimination to heightened judicial scrutiny and pointed to evidence that women had been disadvantaged in both private and public employment because of mutually enforcing, prevailing stereotypes that women are responsible for family caregiving and that men lack domestic responsibilities.

By contrast, in Coleman v. Court of Appeals of Maryland, 566 U.S. 30 (2012), the Court held, without a majority opinion, that Congress had no abrogation authority in respect of the FMLA's self-care provisions. Assuming that denial of self-care options as such did not implicate the Fourteenth Amendment, Justice's Kennedy's opinion for a four-Justice plurality found that Congress had not adequately linked the provision to a pattern of constitutional violations and, in particular, had not shown it to be a response to sex discrimination in sick leave policies. Justice Scalia concurred in the judgment only, reiterating his view that, aside from racial discrimination, "Congress's § 5 power [should be limited] to the regulation of conduct that itself violates the Fourteenth Amendment."

In a dissenting opinion, Justice Ginsburg, joined in pertinent part by three Justices, relied heavily on the FMLA's legislative history in arguing that the contested provision was directed at the exclusion of women from the workplace based on pregnancy-related health issues, even though it was deliberately framed in gender-neutral terms. In light of the record before Congress, Justice Ginsburg concluded that the statute was congruent and proportional to an identified pattern of sex discrimination.[1]

(2) As-Applied Abrogation. As Hibbs and Coleman suggest, statutes abrogating immunity may be valid in some applications and invalid in others. The Court has upheld as-applied abrogation under the public accommodation provisions of the Americans with Disabilities Act (despite its refusal to uphold abrogation under the ADA's workplace protections). See Tennessee v. Lane, 541 U.S. 509 (2004) (upholding suit for damages under the public accommodation provisions of the Americans with Disabilities Act (ADA) as applied to disabled claimants denied their Fourteenth Amendment due process right of access to the courts); United States v. Georgia, 546 U.S. 151 (2006) (upholding right of disabled plaintiff to seek damages under the ADA for an alleged violation of his right to be free from cruel and unusual punishment).

Consider this possible summary of the Court's abrogation doctrine. First, when plaintiffs seek compensation under a statute that authorizes suit against the states for violations of the Fourteenth Amendment, the Court has upheld abrogation as a matter of course. Thus, the federal statutes in the ADA cases involving Tennessee and Georgia and the employment discrimination claim in Fitzpatrick v. Bitzer, were applied to state conduct that was unconstitutional. Second, when the statute confers rights that diverge from or go beyond those specified in the Fourteenth Amendment, the Court has been more circumspect. The Court viewed intellectual property rights and employment rights under the ADA and ADEA as the product of Article I regulatory power and found that the congressional record did not

---

[1] Justice Ginsburg also argued at length that the Court should revisit and overrule the holding of Geduldig v. Aiello, 417 U.S. 484 (1974), that discrimination on the basis of pregnancy does not constitute discrimination on the basis of sex.

support their treatment as Due Process rights under the Fourteenth Amendment. In the FMLA cases, the statutory rights were designed to prevent rather than remedy Fourteenth Amendment violations; the conduct alleged as a statutory violation did not violate the Constitution. Here, Boerne's congruence and proportionality factors take center stage in the analysis.

(3) Congressional Power Under Article I to Induce, Identify, or Compel State "Consent" to Suit. Congress may use its Spending Clause power to condition financial grants on a state's agreement to do something that Congress could not compel the state to do under other provisions of Article I, so long as it stops short of coercion. See National Federation of Independent Business v. Sebelius, 567 U.S. 519 (2012). Congress can also induce state legislation through a conditional proposal to preempt state law.[2] Does Congress's power to condition the "gift" of funds on a state's waiver of immunity necessarily entail a power to condition the "gift" of entry into an activity that Congress has extensively regulated? In College Savings Bank v. Florida Prepaid Postsecondary Education Expense Board, 527 U.S. 666 (1999), the Supreme Court said no. In a 5–4 decision, rejecting the so-called "constructive waiver" theory of Parden v. Terminal Ry., 377 U.S. 184 (1964), the Court held that Congress lacks power under Article I to deem a state to have waived its sovereign immunity simply because the state engaged in otherwise lawful conduct. To impose a constructive waiver was tantamount to exercising a regulatory power foreclosed by Seminole Tribe.

Justice Breyer's dissent, joined by Justices Stevens, Souter, and Ginsburg, expressed continuing disagreement with the Seminole decision. He also argued that in order to avoid giving the states a strong competitive advantage over regulated private entities, Congress must have "the power to condition entry into the market upon a waiver of sovereign immunity * * * for to deny Congress that power would deny Congress the power effectively to regulate private conduct." Accordingly, the authority to impose such a condition was "necessary and proper" to the effective exercise of the commerce power.

———————————

NOTE ON ALDEN V. MAINE AND IMMUNITY FROM SUIT IN STATE COURT

(1) Alden v. Maine. In Alden v. Maine, 527 U.S. 706 (1999). a group of state probation officers filed suit against the state in a Maine court, seeking money damages for the state's alleged violation of the overtime provisions of

———————————

[2] Congress can also induce state compliance by threatening to preempt state regulatory power unless the state agrees to regulate in accordance with federal standards. See Murphy v. National Collegiate Athletic Ass'n, 584 U.S. 453 (2018). Under Murphy, Congress's power to induce state compliance must be based on federal laws that would lawfully regulate individuals rather than the states themselves. See *id.* 478–80. Yet imposing federal regulations on the states and private actors alike avoids any anti-commandeering challenge. See *id.* 475–76; Hartnett, *Distinguishing Permissible Preemption from Unconstitutional Commandeering*, 96 Notre Dame L.Rev. 351 (2020). Consider whether Congress could condition preemption based on the states' willingness to allow suits against itself in state or federal court.

the Fair Labor Standards Act of 1938 (FLSA), 29 U.S.C. § 201 *et seq*. The plaintiffs had initially filed their action in federal district court and had secured injunctive relief; they turned to the state court only after the federal court, following the Supreme Court's decision in Seminole Tribe, dismissed their claims for backpay.

The state responded to the state court action by invoking its sovereign immunity from suit. Maine law allowed suits by state employees for wage claims based on state law even though it denied those same employees the ability to enforce wage claims based on federal law. State law did not require overtime pay, while the FLSA does. The Supreme Court affirmed the state court's dismissal of the action on sovereign immunity grounds.

Writing for a 5–4 majority, Justice Kennedy began by addressing the point that the Eleventh Amendment limits the federal judicial power and says nothing about suit in state court. He explained that the phrase "Eleventh Amendment immunity" was "something of a misnomer, for the sovereign immunity of the States neither derives from, nor is limited by, the terms of the Eleventh Amendment." Instead, the state's immunity derived from "the Constitution's structure, its history, and the authoritative interpretations by this Court," which have made the States' immunity from suit a fundamental aspect of their sovereignty, and "which they retain today (either literally or by virtue of their admission into the Union upon an equal footing with the other States) except as altered by the plan of the Convention or certain constitutional Amendments."

Justice Kennedy distinguished statements in earlier cases that the Eleventh Amendment does not apply in state court,[1] explaining that the Amendment does not exhaustively describe "the States' constitutional immunity from suit." Having cleared away prior decisions, Justice Kennedy viewed Congress's power under Article I to abrogate a State's immunity from suit in its own courts as "a question of first impression" appropriately answered in the negative. Both the silence of the founding generation and early congressional practice supported this conclusion. The first statute that "even arguably purported" to subject the States to private actions was adopted in 1908. Moreover, several decisions, including Ex parte Young, were said to be premised on the absence of suit against the states as such.

Drawing on policy considerations, Justice Kennedy explained that the states had a dignitary and financial interest in avoiding suit for money damages. True, the doctrine of Testa v. Katt, 330 U.S. 386 (1947), p. 586, *supra*, requires state courts of competent jurisdiction to enforce valid federal laws and to refrain from discriminating against federal rights of action, but the Court dismissed the doctrine as inapplicable to Maine's exercise of sovereign choice as to what forms of suability to allow. Justice Kennedy expressed confidence that states would honor their federal obligations within

---

[1]   Among others, the Court distinguished Hilton v. South Carolina Public Railway Comm'n, 502 U.S. 197 (1991) (holding that an injured employee of a state-owned railroad could sue his employer (an arm of the State) in state court); Nevada v. Hall, 440 U.S. 410 (1979) (holding that the Constitution did not bar California from subjecting Nevada to suit in a California state court), overruled, Franchise Tax Board v. Hyatt, 587 U.S. 230 (2019); and Reich v. Collins, 513 U.S. 106 (1994).

the remedial framework that remained in place, which included suits brought under Ex parte Young, those brought against states under statutes adopted pursuant to the Fourteenth Amendment, and those brought by the federal government against the state to enforce federal law. "Suits brought by the United States itself require the exercise of political responsibility for each suit prosecuted against a State, a control which is absent from a broad delegation to private persons to sue nonconsenting States."

Justice Souter, joined by Justices Stevens, Ginsburg, and Breyer, filed a long and passionate dissenting opinion. "[T]he Court * * * confronts the fact that the state forum renders the Eleventh Amendment beside the point, and it has responded by discerning a simpler and more straightforward theory of state sovereign immunity than it found in Seminole Tribe: a State's sovereign immunity from all individual suits is a 'fundamental aspect' of state sovereignty 'confirm[ed]' by the Tenth Amendment. As a consequence, Seminole Tribe's contorted reliance on the Eleventh Amendment and its background was presumably unnecessary; the Tenth would have done the work with an economy that the majority in Seminole Tribe would have welcomed." But the Court's analysis, he said, was mistaken.

Justice Souter emphasized the distinction between rights based on state or common law, as were at issue in Chisholm v. Georgia, and those based on federal law. Under the Constitution, the states are sovereign with respect to the matters committed to them, but not with respect to matters committed to the national government. Accordingly, "[t]he State of Maine is not sovereign with respect to the national objective of the FLSA." And it was "sheer circularity for the Court to talk of the 'anomaly' that would arise if the State could be sued on federal law in its own courts, when it may not be sued under federal law in federal court" under Seminole Tribe: "The short and sufficient answer is that the anomaly is the Court's own creation: the Eleventh Amendment was never intended to bar federal-question suits against the States in federal court."

Justice Souter also found the majority's arguments based on policy and history unconvincing. Citizens of Maine with federal rights should be entitled to pursue their claims in a republican government based on respect for the rule of law. That such commerce-clause based litigation had no precursors in the practice of the early Republic did not trouble Justice Souter; times had changed and innovation in response to such changes does not raise a "presumption of unconstitutionality." Justice Souter urged consideration of the matter "in the light of our whole experience and not merely in that of what was said a hundred years ago." Missouri v. Holland, 252 U.S. 416, 433 (1920) (Holmes, J.).

(2) The Constitutional Source of State Immunity. Unlike Seminole Tribe, which framed its denial of federal power in terms of federal jurisdiction, the Alden Court applied structural limits on Congress's power to authorize individual suits against the states under Article I of the Constitution. Congress after Alden has power to impose federal standards on the states under the Commerce Clause (and other Article I powers), but cannot provide for the individual enforcement of those standards in suits brought against the states in either federal court or state court. Is the immunity recognized in Alden best understood as an implied limit on congressional power imposed by the Tenth Amendment, the Eleventh Amendment, or some combination of the two? Compare Vázquez, *What is Eleventh Amendment Immunity?*, 106 Yale L.J. 1683 (1997).

In evaluating the Alden decision, consider the range of available alternative remedies and their adequacy in securing state compliance with federal law. The Court highlighted a variety of such remedies, including suits against consenting states, suits pursuant to legislation abrogating immunity under the Fourteenth Amendment, and suits against state officers. (Of course, none of those would secure monetary remedies in Alden itself.) In addition, Congress can presumably adopt provisions, like that in the FLSA itself, authorizing the federal government to pursue money claims on behalf of affected employees. See 29 U.S.C. § 216(c). Finally, the plaintiffs can pursue compensation through petition to the state legislature, a strategy that apparently led to the adoption of Maine legislation compensating the affected employees. See Pfander & Dwinell, *A Declaratory Theory of State Accountability*, 102 Va.L.Rev. 153, 209 (2016) (reporting the passage of a bill to compensate the employees involved in the Alden litigation).

(3) The Implications of Alden. Among the cases Alden distinguished, Nevada v. Hall, 440 U.S. 410 (1979), refused to extend a federal law sovereign immunity defense to states sued on state law claims in the courts of another state. In Franchise Tax Board v. Hyatt, 587 U.S. 230 (2019), the Court overruled Nevada v. Hall, holding that the decision had misread the constitutional structure. At the time of the founding, the Franchise Tax majority noted, states were entitled to common law immunity from suit in their own courts and to law-of-nations immunity from suit in other state courts. Rather than a defeasible entailment of comity, as expounded in Nevada v. Hall, the Court viewed the rule of interstate sovereign immunity as embedded in the constitutional design. For a critique, see Baude & Sachs, *The Misunderstood Eleventh Amendment*, 169 U.Pa.L.Rev. 609, 622 (2021) (arguing that states have broader power to override the immunity of sibling states than does Congress).

Whatever the source of state immunity, Seminole Tribe and Alden establish a rough sort of remedial parity in state and federal courts. States enjoy immunity in both state and federal court from unconsented suits to enforce federal statutes enacted pursuant to Article I. But as Alden itself confirms, suits may proceed in state and federal court under abrogating legislation adopted pursuant to § 5 of the Fourteenth Amendment, provided the statute meets the congruence and proportionality test. Similar state-federal parity obtains in suits brought against state officials under § 1983; state courts cannot, under Testa v. Katt, p. 586, *supra*, refuse to hear such claims without a valid excuse. But the Seminole-Alden settlement was thrown into doubt by the Court's subsequent expansive view of state waiver of immunity in the "plan of the convention."

B. WAIVER OF STATE IMMUNITY IN THE "PLAN OF THE CONVENTION"

Torres v. Texas Department of Public Safety
597 U.S. 580 (2022).
Certiorari to the Supreme Court of Texas.

■ JUSTICE BREYER delivered the opinion of the Court.

The Constitution vests in Congress the power "[t]o raise and support Armies" and "[t]o provide and maintain a Navy." Art. I, § 8, cls. 1, 12–13. Pursuant to that authority, Congress enacted a federal law that gives returning veterans the right to reclaim their prior jobs with state employers and authorizes suit if those employers refuse to accommodate them. See Uniformed Services Employment and Reemployment Rights Act of 1994 (USERRA), 38 U.S.C. § 4301 *et seq.* This case asks whether States may invoke sovereign immunity as a legal defense to block such suits.

In our view, they cannot. Upon entering the Union, the States implicitly agreed that their sovereignty would yield to federal policy to build and keep a national military. States thus gave up their immunity from congressionally authorized suits pursuant to the "'plan of the Convention,'" as part of "'the structure of the original Constitution itself.'" PennEast Pipeline Co. v. New Jersey, 594 U.S. 482 (2021) (quoting Alden v. Maine, 527 U.S. 706 (1999)).

I

A

* * * Since before the United States' entry into World War II, Congress has sought, in particular, to smooth volunteers' reentry into civilian life by recognizing veterans' "right to return to civilian employment without adverse effect on . . . career progress" in the federal work force and private employment. H.R. Rep. No. 105–448, p. 2 (1998). * * *

The Vietnam War prompted Congress to extend these protections to employment by States. Amidst political opposition to the war, "some State and local jurisdictions ha[d] demonstrated a reluctance, and even an unwillingness, to reemploy" returning servicemembers. S. Rep. No. 93–907, p. 110 (1974). So Congress authorized private damages suits against States to ensure that "veterans who [had] previously held jobs as school teachers, policemen, firemen, and other State, county, and city employees" would not be denied their old jobs as reprisal for their service. *Ibid.* The statute at issue, USERRA, embodies these protections today.

B

[Upon his return from active-duty deployment to Iraq in 2007, reservist Le Roy Torres sought to return to his job with his former employer, Texas Department of Public Safety (Texas). Although he applied for an alternative position that would accommodate disabling injuries to his lungs sustained during his deployment, Texas refused to re-employ him. Torres sued Texas in state court.]

II

* * * The question before us is whether the Constitution allows Congress to enforce these federal reemployment protections by authorizing private litigation against noncompliant state employers that do not wish to consent to suit.

A

* * * Basic tenets of sovereign immunity teach that courts may not ordinarily hear a suit brought by any person against a nonconsenting State.

But States still remain subject to suit in certain circumstances. States may, of course, consent to suit. See Sossamon v. Texas, 563 U.S. 277, 284 (2011). Congress may also enact laws abrogating their immunity under the Fourteenth Amendment. See Fitzpatrick v. Bitzer, 427 U.S. 445 (1976). And, as relevant here, States may be sued if they agreed their sovereignty would yield as part of the "plan of the Convention," PennEast, 594 U.S., at ___—that is, if "the structure of the original Constitution itself" reflects a waiver of States' sovereign immunity. Alden, 527 U.S., at 728. * * *

Alexander Hamilton described three circumstances where the "plan of the Convention" implied that the States waived their sovereign immunity: "where the Constitution in express terms granted an exclusive authority to the Union; where it granted in one instance an authority to the Union and in another prohibited the States from exercising the like authority; and where it granted an authority to the Union, to which a similar authority in the States would be absolutely and totally contradictory and repugnant." The Federalist No. 32, p. 200 (J. Cooke ed. 1961) (emphasis in original); see id., No. 81, at 548–549 (A. Hamilton).

Consistent with these principles, this Court has found structural waiver as to suits between States, in South Dakota v. North Carolina, 192 U.S. 286 (1904), and suits by the United States against a State, in United States v. Texas, 143 U.S. 621 (1892). The States, we said, must have recognized that these waivers of immunity from suit were "a necessary feature of the formation of a more perfect Union" and thus "inherent in the constitutional plan." Principality of Monaco v. Mississippi, 292 U.S. 313, 329 (1934). The alternative to consenting to litigation between sovereigns, after all, could be civil war.

A century later, in Central Va. Community College v. Katz, 546 U.S. 356 [(2006)], the Court recognized another structural waiver. We held that States could not assert sovereign immunity to block suits by private parties pursuant to federal bankruptcy laws. Id., at 359. There, too, we based our holding on the constitutional structure. We noted the text's insistence on "uniform Laws on the subject of Bankruptcies," U.S. Const., Art. I, § 8, cl. 4, the Framers' concerns about States' passing patchwork legislation and refusing to discharge the debts of noncitizens (as had happened under the Articles of Confederation), and the history of habeas laws related to bankruptcy. See 546 U.S. at 368–377. All that evidence led us to conclude that, by ratifying the Constitution, the States had agreed that their sovereignty would yield to ensure the effectiveness of national bankruptcy policy. See *id.*, at 379. * * *

Last Term, in PennEast Pipeline Co. v. New Jersey, 594 U.S. 482 (2021), we considered whether Congress could, pursuant to its eminent domain power, authorize private parties to sue States to enforce federally approved condemnations necessary to build interstate pipelines. We held that "when the States entered the federal system, they renounced their right to the 'highest dominion in the[ir] lands,'" meaning they agreed their "eminent domain power would yield to that of the Federal Government." *Id.*, at 502. Congress could therefore authorize private actions against States.

PennEast defined the test for structural waiver as whether the federal power at issue is "complete in itself, and the States consented to the exercise of that power—in its entirety—in the plan of the Convention." 594 U.S., at 508 (internal quotation marks and citation omitted). Where that is so, the States implicitly agreed that their sovereignty "would yield to that of the Federal Government 'so far as is necessary to the enjoyment of the powers conferred upon it by the Constitution.'" *Id.*, at 502 (quoting Kohl v. United States, 91 U.S. 367, 372 (1876)). By committing not to "thwart" or frustrate federal policy, the States accepted upon ratification that their "consent," including to suit, could "never be a condition precedent to" Congress' chosen exercise of its authority. 594 U.S., at 495 (internal quotation marks omitted). * * *

B

Congress' power to build and maintain the Armed Forces fits PennEast's test. The Constitution's text, its history, and this Court's precedents show that "when the States entered the federal system, they renounced their right" to interfere with national policy in this area. *Id.* at 502.

For one thing, the Constitution's text, across several Articles, strongly suggests a complete delegation of authority to the Federal Government to provide for the common defense. Unlike most of the powers given to the National Government, the Constitution spells out the war powers not in a single, simple phrase, but in many broad, interrelated provisions. The Preamble makes the "common defence" one of the document's central projects. Article I gives Congress authority to "provide for th[at] common Defence" in six numbered paragraphs: to "declare War"; "raise and support Armies"; "provide and maintain a Navy"; "make Rules" for the Armed Forces; "provide for calling forth the Militia"; and "provide for [their] organizing, arming, and disciplining."

§ 8, cls. 1, 11–16. Article II makes the President the "Commander in Chief of the Army and Navy of the United States, and of the Militia of the several States." § 2, cl. 1. And the Federal Government is charged with "protect[ing] each" State "against Invasion." Art. IV, § 4.

The Constitution also divests the States of like power. States may not "engage in War, unless actually invaded," "enter into any Treaty," or "keep Troops, or Ships of War in time of Peace." Art. I, § 10, cls. 1, 3. States retain a role in "the Appointment of the Officers" to and the "training [of] the Militia," but that delegation is strictly cabined. Art. I, § 8, cl. 16. States must do so "according to the discipline prescribed by Congress." *Ibid.* These substantial limitations on state authority, together with the assignment of sweeping power to the Federal Government, provide strong evidence that the structure of the Constitution prevents States from frustrating national objectives in this field. * * *

The Constitution, by design, worked "an entire change in the first principles of the system." The Federalist No. 23, at 148 (A. Hamilton). * * * Some state conventions pitched proposals to limit the reach of Congress' war powers, but those amendments "die[d] away." [3 Story] § 1186, at 74. The States ultimately ratified the Constitution knowing that their sovereignty would give way to national military policy. * * *

It follows that Congress' power to build and maintain a national military is "complete in itself." PennEast, 594 U.S., at 503 (internal quotation marks omitted). Text, history, and precedent show the States agreed that their sovereignty would "yield . . . so far as is necessary" to national policy to raise and maintain the military. *Id.* at 502. And because States committed themselves not to "thwart" the exercise of this federal power, "[t]he consent of a State," including to suit, "can never be a condition precedent to [Congress'] enjoyment" of it. *Id.* at 495 (internal quotation marks omitted). We consequently hold that, as part of the plan of the Convention, the States waived their immunity under Congress' Article I power "[t]o raise and support Armies" and "provide and maintain a Navy." § 8, cls. 12–13.

III

* * * Texas asserts that "Congress cannot abrogate state sovereign immunity through the exercise of Article I powers." But, as explained, "congressional abrogation is not the only means of subjecting States to suit. . . . States can also be sued if they have consented to suit in the plan of the Convention." PennEast, 594 U.S., at 501. * * *

Texas and the dissent go on to suggest that the fact that an area of law "is under the exclusive control of the Federal Government" is not alone sufficient to do away with sovereign immunity. Seminole Tribe [Tribe of Fla. v. Florida,], 517 U.S. [44,] 72 [(1996)]. We agree. In Seminole Tribe, we held that Congress could not rely on its Article I commerce powers to abrogate state sovereign immunity simply because that power was exclusive. But later, in PennEast, we found that the federal eminent domain power was "complete in itself," and held that *was* enough to find a waiver of sovereign immunity in the constitutional structure. 594 U.S., at 503. It thus matters to the analysis that federal regulation of commerce (at issue in Seminole Tribe) involves goods that, before they travel between States or outside a tribe, are subject to regulation by a sovereign other than the Federal Government (a State or tribe). That feature of commerce arguably makes the federal regulatory power less than "complete." * * *

In any event, the text, history, and precedent we have described indicate that an assertion of state sovereignty to frustrate federal prerogatives to raise and maintain military forces would be strongly "*contradictory* and *repugnant*" to the constitutional order. The Federalist No. 32, at 200 (A. Hamilton) (emphasis in original). * * * None of those powers (*e.g.*, Indian commerce, interstate commerce, or intellectual property) is expressly denied to the States, or operates for the benefit of the entire Nation, or proves comparably essential to the survival of the Union—itself a foundational purpose for drafting the Constitution. These factors, taken together, lead us to conclude that the results in PennEast and Katz, not dicta in Seminole Tribe, control this case.

[The dissent argues that PennEast and Katz create special rules regarding waivers of sovereign immunity in federal courts that do not apply in state courts. But a waiver pursuant to the plan of the Convention displaces the background principles of state sovereign immunity in whichever court those suits proceed.]

[Texas argues that PennEast (eminent domain) and Katz (bankruptcy) both involved *in rem* proceedings. But while PennEast discussed the close connection between the exercise of eminent domain and condemnation actions, the Court read PennEast] as resting on a broader point: The Federal Government's eminent domain power is complete, such that no State may frustrate its exercise by claiming immunity to forestall the transfer of property. And that conclusion applies equally to Congress' powers to raise and maintain the military. * * *

* * * Text, history, and precedent show that the States, in coming together to form a Union, agreed to sacrifice their sovereign immunity for the good of the common defense.

* * *

We consequently reverse the judgment of the Texas Court of Appeals and remand the case for further proceedings not inconsistent with this opinion.

It is so ordered.

■ [The concurring opinion of JUSTICE KAGAN is omitted.]

■ JUSTICE THOMAS, with whom JUSTICE ALITO, JUSTICE GORSUCH, and JUSTICE BARRETT join, dissenting.

* * * Today, by adopting contrived interpretations of Alden and the recent decision in PennEast Pipeline Co. v. New Jersey, 594 U.S. 482 (2021), the Court holds that at least two (and perhaps more) Article I "war powers" do, in fact, include "the power to subject nonconsenting States to private suits for damages in state courts," Alden [v. Maine], 527 U.S. [706,] 712 [(1999)] * * *. Alden should have squarely foreclosed that holding. As the Court there already explained, constitutional text, history, and precedent all show that when the States ratified the Constitution, they did not implicitly consent to private damages actions filed in their own courts—whether authorized by Congress' war powers or any other Article I power. Because the Court today holds otherwise, I respectfully dissent.

I

[Despite its general reluctance to countenance suits against the states, "in the last two decades, the Court has recognized two [plan-of-convention] surrenders of sovereign immunity," in Central Va. Community College v. Katz, 546 U.S. 356 (2006), and PennEast, 594 U.S. 482.]

These cases contrast with those that involve congressional "abrogation" of state sovereign immunity. Abrogation rests on some "statement Congress ha[s] made on the subject of state sovereign immunity." Katz, 546 U.S. at 378–379. Specifically, we have held that Congress must enact "unequivocal statutory language" abrogating States' immunity. Seminole Tribe of Fla. v. Florida, 517 U.S. 44, 56 (1996) (internal quotation marks omitted). That said, the line between "plan-of-the-Convention waiver" and "congressional abrogation" is a murky one. Both inquiries ask the same basic question: whether Congress has authorized suit against a nonconsenting State pursuant to "a valid exercise of constitutional authority." Kimel v. Florida Bd. of Regents, 528 U.S. 62, 78 (2000). * * *

II

In answering that question, the Court discounts two important points. First, it creates a constitutional problem by adopting a questionable interpretation of USERRA that assumes Congress intended to legislate with indifference to States' state-law immunity. Second, the Court cannot escape the fact that Alden already answered the question presented and held that the States did not surrender their state-court immunity when ratifying Article I of the Constitution.

A

[Justice Thomas examined the text of USERRA, finding no evidence that Congress intended to require nonconsenting States to defend themselves in their own courts. He argued that the majority should have avoided the constitutional question by narrowly construing the statute.]

B

[Justice Thomas next argued that Alden directly controls this case.]

* * *

* * * Both Katz and PennEast considered plan-of-the-Convention waivers applicable to federal, not state, court. Nothing in those decisions, therefore, undermined Alden's categorical holding. * * *

III

Even if Alden's holding were not alone dispositive, thus requiring us to consider our "plan of the Convention" precedents applicable to private actions *in federal court*, I would still conclude that the States have not waived their immunity to private damages actions authorized by the war powers. * * *

A

* * * First, Seminole Tribe long ago explained that the breadth and exclusivity of a federal power does not authorize Congress to subject nonconsenting States to private damages actions. * * *

Nor is the answer different when the exclusive federal exercise of a particular power is reinforced by an explicit divestment of state authority under Article I, § 10. * * *

Second, even if express textual divestment of state power were relevant, Torres and the Court incorrectly conclude that the specific divestments listed in Article I, § 10, "provide strong evidence" supporting "a complete delegation of authority to the Federal Government to provide for the common defense." * * *

* * * [E]ven though the Army and Navy Clauses grant Congress "exclusive" authority over raising and supporting armies and navies, that exclusivity is no different from that which attends any other Article I power.

To nonetheless find plan-of-the-Convention waiver, as Torres proposes and the Court accepts, * * * proves too much. The upshot is that the States would have consented in the plan of the Convention to surrender their immunity against the exercise of any Article I power. * * *

B

Constitutional history and practice do Torres and the Court no better. To begin, we must view the historical evidence in light of the "presumption that no anomalous and unheard-of proceedings or suits were intended to be raised up by the Constitution." Hans [v. Louisiana], 134 U.S. [1,] 18 [(1890)]. Applying that presumption, the Court in the past has "attribute[d] great significance" to the absence of analogous suits "at the time of the founding or for many years thereafter." Federal Maritime Comm'n [v. South Carolina Ports Authority], 535 U.S. [743,] 755 [(2002)]. Moreover, the presumption is arguably at its strongest here, for private damages actions were precisely "the type of proceedings from which the Framers would have thought the States possessed immunity." *Id.*, at 756. * * *

To overcome that presumption, Torres and the Court invoke some historical sources that generally discuss the scope and importance of Congress' war-related powers. But virtually none of them addresses directly the central question here: whether the States understood that they had surrendered their sovereign immunity from suit in their own courts when delegating those powers to Congress. * * *

C

Constitutional structure also cuts decisively against inferring a surrender of state sovereign immunity in this context.

First and most fundamentally, all private suits against nonconsenting States present " 'the indignity of subjecting a State to the coercive process of judicial tribunals at the instance of private parties.' " [Alden, 527 U.S.], at 749. * * *

Second, congressional authorization of private damages actions "threaten[s] the financial integrity of the States." *Id.*, at 750. It can "create staggering burdens" and give "Congress a power and a leverage over the States that is not contemplated by our constitutional design." *Ibid.*

Third, representative government itself is jeopardized when "deliberation by the political process established by the citizens of the State" is replaced with "judicial decree mandated by the Federal Government and invoked by the private citizen." *Id.*, at 751. Political accountability—"essential to our liberty and republican form of government"—breaks down when "the Federal Government asserts authority over a State's most fundamental political processes." *Ibid.* * * *

IV

The Court nevertheless holds that States surrendered their sovereign immunity for any congressional causes of action passed pursuant to Article I's Army and Navy Clauses. * * *

In my view, the Court is asking the wrong question. It unjustifiably asserts that the entire plan-of-the-Convention inquiry rests on whether a power is "complete in itself." * * * By saddling "completeness" with more analytical weight than it can bear, the Court has devised a method that has the certainty and objectivity of a Rorschach test. Beyond its inconsistency with PennEast, this contrivance also threatens to rework or erase the Court's prevailing sovereign immunity jurisprudence.

A

* * * Worse still, today's decision removes the one important guardrail on the "completeness" inquiry that PennEast described. Absent that limit, the Court's indefinite test will provide future courts cover to further erode the States' sovereign immunity.

B

To the extent that the Court's new "complete in itself" standard has any definable contours, it is inconsistent with our modern sovereign immunity doctrine and, in particular, Seminole Tribe. * * *

* * *

* * * To * * * deem USERRA constitutional, the Court brushes aside a 23-year-old, pathbreaking precedent, while elevating a single phrase, made in passing in a one-year-old, highly circumscribed precedent. It then uses that phrase to fashion a test for plan-of-the-Convention waiver that mimics earlier attempts by this Court to deny States the dignity owed to them in our system of dual federalism.

Our sovereign States deserved better. I respectfully dissent.

NOTE ON WAIVER OF STATE IMMUNITY IN THE PLAN OF THE CONVENTION

In Torres v. Texas Department of Public Safety, a closely divided Court held in the last majority opinion announced by a retiring Justice Breyer that the states had waived their immunity from suit as to certain forms of federal legislation by agreeing to ratify the Constitution. The majority opinion builds on earlier decisions in Katz and PennEast, authorizing Congress to subject states to suit pursuant to Article I powers that would not support abrogation of immunity under the Seminole-Alden framework.

(1) Katz and Its Critics. In Central Virginia Community College v. Katz, 546 U.S. 356 (2006), the Court upheld the power of federal courts to hear suits to recover preferential transfers made by a debtor in bankruptcy to several state agencies. Writing for a majority of five, Justice Stevens relied on the breadth of the bankruptcy power vested in Congress under Article I and the idea that states ratifying the Constitution necessarily consented to suit to enforce so broad a power. The question was not whether Congress could "abrogate" state sovereign immunity, something that earlier decisions in the Seminole Tribe line had seemingly rejected. Rather, the Court focused on the nature of the Bankruptcy Clause, which granted legislative authority to Congress and authorized "limited subordination of state sovereign immunity in the bankruptcy arena." Justice Thomas, in an opinion joined by three other members of the Court, dissented vigorously, sounding themes he would reiterate in the Torres dissent. He concluded: "Nothing in the text, structure, or history of the Constitution indicates that the Bankruptcy Clause, in contrast to all of the other provisions of Article I, manifests the States' consent to be sued by private citizens."

Commentators looked unkindly on the rationale if not the result in Katz.[1] In Allen v. Cooper, 589 U.S. 248 (2020), the Court rebuffed an

---

[1]   Compare Redish & Greenfield, *Bankruptcy, Sovereign Immunity and the Dilemma of Principled Decision Making*, 15 Am.Bankr.Inst.L.Rev. 13 (2007) (describing Katz as curious, surprising, and "unambiguously indefensible"), with Brubaker, *Explaining Katz's New*

invitation to extend Katz beyond the bankruptcy power to a suit brought against a state for copyright infringement. Writing for a unanimous Court, Justice Kagan explained that the question was one of abrogation, controlled by Seminole Tribe and its progeny. The Court described Katz's "plan of the Convention" analysis as "good for one clause only"—a reference to the Bankruptcy Clause. See *id.* 258–59. The Allen consensus was short-lived, however. PennEast, below, stands at odds with Allen's "one-clause only" dictum and Justice Kagan shifted her position from a dissent in PennEast to a concurrence in Torres.

(2) The PennEast Revival of Katz. In PennEast Pipeline Co. v. New Jersey, 594 U.S. 482 (2021), the Court rejected the state's claim of immunity from suit under a federal statute allowing pipeline companies to employ the federal government's right of eminent domain in the construction of an approved pipeline project. PennEast invoked that eminent domain authority in a suit against the state of New Jersey. In an opinion by Chief Justice Roberts, the Court rejected the state's claim of immunity.

The majority emphasized that Congress has always enjoyed the power of eminent domain, and that Congress has long delegated that power to private parties to advance public purposes. Given this historical background, the Chief Justice concluded that the states had surrendered their sovereign immunity from eminent domain actions by the United States when they ratified the Constitution, and he further inferred that the surrender extended to "condemnation proceedings brought by private delegatees" such as PennEast.

Justice Barrett dissented in an opinion joined by Justices Thomas, Kagan, and Gorsuch. In her view, the Chief Justice's opinion mischaracterized the issue before the Court. Acting pursuant to its Article I power to regulate commerce, Congress had sought to authorize a private company to take property for a public purpose through the exercise of a delegated power of eminent domain. But it was well settled, Justice Barrett argued, that Congress, acting pursuant to Article I, could not authorize private suits against nonconsenting states.

Justice Gorsuch also dissented separately in an opinion joined by Justice Thomas to point out that the suit by PennEast, a Delaware citizen, against New Jersey was barred by the literal language of the Eleventh Amendment, which he thought controlling (citing Baude & Sachs, *The Misunderstood Eleventh Amendment*, 169 U.Pa.L.Rev. 609 (2021)). The Court responded that no party had asked the Court to reconsider precedents holding that the Eleventh Amendment immunity was waivable, and held that consent to actions such as the one before it was implicit in the constitutional plan.

The central dispute in the PennEast case, as framed by the majority opinion and Justice Barrett's dissent, hinged on whether "the eminent domain power," as the Chief Justice characterized it, uniquely entails a

---

Bankruptcy Exception to State Sovereign Immunity, 15 Am.Bankr.Inst.L.Rev. 95, 97 (2007) (acknowledging that some would view Katz as a "silver bullet" exempting bankruptcy from the Seminole Tribe regime).

surrender of state sovereign immunity that extends to cases in which the federal government has delegated a power to sue to private parties. As the Chief Justice noted, if Congress can delegate to private parties the power to take private property for public use, the most efficient mechanism for effecting a taking of property may be a suit against the property owner, even when the property owner is a state. Consider Justice Barrett's rejoinder in dissent that "[s]tate sovereign immunity indisputably makes it harder for Congress to accomplish its goals, as we have recognized many times before."

(3) Convention-Plan Waivers Before Katz. Until Katz, the Court had based plan of convention waiver on the language of Article III, such as that extending the judicial power and the Court's original jurisdiction to controversies between states. See Rhode Island v. Massachusetts, 37 U.S. 657, 720 (1838) (explaining in response to Massachusetts' invocation of sovereign immunity that the "states waived their exemption from judicial power, as sovereigns by original and inherent right by their own grant of its exercise over themselves in such cases"). Katz, PennEast, and Torres focus instead on Article I's grants of legislative authority. That change appears to confirm that current doctrine focuses less on the scope of jurisdiction than on the power of Congress to manage the sovereign immunity recognized by Hans and reaffirmed in Seminole Tribe and Alden. For a critique of PennEast and Torres, see Clark & Bellia, *State Sovereign Immunity and the New Purposivism*, 65 Wm. & Mary L.Rev. 485, 542–45 (2024) (arguing that the Court's decisions misunderstand the plan-of-convention waiver analysis put forward by Alexander Hamilton in the Federalist Papers).

(4) Other Congressional Powers. Consider what other powers conferred on Congress in Article I qualify as "complete" enough to trigger a convention-plan waiver of state sovereign immunity. Some powers (commerce, intellectual property) have been previously addressed within Seminole Tribe's abrogation framework. Article I also confers arguably exclusive powers on Congress to ratify and implement treaties, coin money, and establish post offices and post roads. The treaty provision has a counterpart in the Article I, § 10 prohibition against state entry into treaties or alliances. In addition, the "no-state-shall" provisions of Article I, § 10 (enact tender laws or impair the obligation of contract) bear some resemblance to the due process and equal protection provisions of the Fourteenth Amendment but do not include enforcement provisions. Hans v. Louisiana refused to allow suit to enforce the Contract Clause, but a right to sue had not been legislatively conferred.

Consider also, as do the PennEast and Torres dissenters, whether the "plan of convention" waiver doctrine provides a legitimate analytical alternative to the otherwise controlling Seminole-Alden framework. Should a Court committed to principled decision-making restore Seminole-Alden or establish a new framework based on deference to the political safeguards of federalism that inform congressional choices about state suability under Article I? *Cf.* Garcia v. San Antonio Transit Authority, 469 U.S. 528 (1985) (overruling the Court's earlier decision prohibiting congressional regulation of the states as states in part due to concerns with unprincipled decision-making).

C. FEDERAL INDIAN LAW AND TRIBAL SOVEREIGN IMMUNITY

Suits by and against Native American tribes pose some of the same challenges of immunity and accountability that arise in connection with state-party litigation. In general, as reflected in the next principal case, tribal governments can invoke sovereign immunity from unconsented suit in state and federal court and control their own exposure to litigation in tribal courts. Yet Congress has "plenary and exclusive" authority over commerce with Native American tribes and tribal citizens, derived from its Article I power to regulate commerce with "the Indian tribes," Article II's Treaty Clause, and principles inherent in the Constitution's structure. Haaland v. Brackeen, 599 U.S. 255, 272 (2023). Congress can thus abrogate tribal sovereign immunity in statutes that speak with appropriate clarity.

Michigan v. Bay Mills Indian Community
572 U.S. 782 (2014).
Supreme Court of the United States.

■ JUSTICE KAGAN delivered the opinion of the Court.

The question in this case is whether tribal sovereign immunity bars Michigan's suit against the Bay Mills Indian Community for opening a casino outside Indian lands. We hold that immunity protects Bay Mills from this legal action. Congress has not abrogated tribal sovereign immunity from a State's suit to enjoin gaming off a reservation or other Indian lands. And we decline to revisit our prior decisions holding that, absent such an abrogation (or a waiver), Indian tribes have immunity even when a suit arises from off-reservation commercial activity. Michigan must therefore resort to other mechanisms, including legal actions against the responsible individuals, to resolve this dispute.

I

The Indian Gaming Regulatory Act (IGRA or Act), 102 Stat. 2467, 25 U.S.C. § 2701 et seq., creates a framework for regulating gaming activity on Indian lands. See § 2702(3) (describing the statute's purpose as establishing "regulatory authority . . . [and] standards for gaming on Indian lands"). * * *

Pursuant to the Act, Michigan and Bay Mills, a federally recognized Indian Tribe, entered into a compact in 1993. The compact empowers Bay Mills to conduct class III gaming on "Indian lands"; conversely, it prohibits the Tribe from doing so outside that territory. The compact also contains a dispute resolution mechanism, which sends to arbitration any contractual differences the parties cannot settle on their own. A provision within that arbitration section states that "[n]othing in this Compact shall be deemed a waiver" of either the Tribe's or the State's sovereign immunity. Since entering into the compact, Bay Mills has operated class III gaming, as authorized, on its reservation in Michigan's Upper Peninsula.

In 2010, Bay Mills opened another class III gaming facility in Vanderbilt, a small village in Michigan's Lower Peninsula about 125 miles from the Tribe's reservation. Bay Mills had bought the Vanderbilt property with accrued interest from a federal appropriation, which Congress had made to compensate the Tribe for 19th century takings of its ancestral lands. * * * According to the legislation, any land so acquired "shall be held as Indian lands are held." [111 Stat.] at 2658. Citing that provision, Bay Mills contended that the Vanderbilt property was "Indian land" under IGRA and the compact; and the Tribe thus claimed authority to operate a casino there.

Michigan disagreed: The State sued Bay Mills in federal court to enjoin operation of the new casino, alleging that the facility violated IGRA and the compact because it was located outside Indian lands. [The Sixth Circuit vacated an injunction against continued operation of the casino, concluding that the tribe enjoyed sovereign immunity from suit unless Congress had provided otherwise and interpreting IGRA to authorize suit only as to gaming activity located on Indian lands, while agreeing the new casino was not on Indian land.]

We granted certiorari to consider whether tribal sovereign immunity bars Michigan's suit against Bay Mills, and we now affirm the Court of Appeals' judgment.

II

Indian tribes are " 'domestic dependent nations' " that exercise "inherent sovereign authority." Oklahoma Tax Comm'n v. Citizen Band Potawatomi Tribe of Okla., 498 U.S. 505, 509 (1991) (Potawatomi) (quoting Cherokee Nation v. Georgia, 5 Pet. 1, 17 (1831)). As dependents, the tribes are subject to plenary control by Congress. And yet they remain "separate sovereigns pre-existing the Constitution." Santa Clara Pueblo v. Martinez, 436 U.S. 49, 45 (1978). Thus, unless and "until Congress acts, the tribes retain" their historic sovereign authority. United States v. Wheeler, 435 U.S. 313, 323 (1978).

Among the core aspects of sovereignty that tribes possess—subject, again, to congressional action—is the "common-law immunity from suit traditionally enjoyed by sovereign powers." Santa Clara Pueblo, 436 U.S., at 58. * * * And the qualified nature of Indian sovereignty modifies that principle only by placing a tribe's immunity, like its other governmental powers and attributes, in Congress's hands. * * *

Our decisions establish as well that such a congressional decision must be clear. The baseline position, we have often held, is tribal immunity; and "[t]o abrogate [such] immunity, Congress must 'unequivocally' express that purpose." C & L Enterprises, Inc. v. Citizen Bank of Potawatomi Tribe of Okla., 532 U.S. 411, 418 (2001) (quoting Santa Clara Pueblo, 436 U.S., at 58). That rule of construction reflects an enduring principle of Indian law: Although Congress has plenary authority over tribes, courts will not lightly assume that Congress in fact intends to undermine Indian self-government.

The upshot is this: Unless Congress has authorized Michigan's suit, our precedents demand that it be dismissed. And so Michigan, naturally enough, makes two arguments: first, that IGRA indeed abrogates the Tribe's immunity from the State's suit; and second, that if it does not, we should revisit—and reverse—our decision in Kiowa [Tribe of Okla. v. Manufacturing Technologies, Inc., 523 U.S. 751 (1998)], so that tribal immunity no longer applies to claims arising from commercial activity outside Indian lands. We consider—and reject—each contention in turn.

III

IGRA partially abrogates tribal sovereign immunity in § 2710(d)(7)(A)(ii)—but this case, viewed most naturally, falls outside that term's ambit. The provision, as noted above, authorizes a State to sue a tribe to "enjoin a class III gaming activity located on Indian lands and conducted in violation of any Tribal-State compact." A key phrase in that abrogation is "on Indian lands"—three words reflecting IGRA's overall scope. A State's suit to enjoin gaming activity *on* Indian lands * * * falls within § 2710(d)(7)(A)(ii); a similar suit to stop gaming activity off Indian lands does not. * * *

Michigan first attempts to fit this suit within § 2710(d)(7)(A)(ii) by relocating the "class III gaming activity" to which it is objecting. True enough, Michigan states, the Vanderbilt casino lies outside Indian lands. But Bay Mills "authorized, licensed, and operated" that casino from within its own reservation. According to the State, that necessary administrative action—no less than, say, dealing craps—is "class III gaming activity," and because it occurred on Indian land, this suit to enjoin it can go forward.

But that argument comes up snake eyes, because numerous provisions of IGRA show that "class III gaming activity" means just what it sounds like—the stuff involved in playing class III games. [Detailed statutory analysis omitted]. * * *

Stymied under § 2710(d)(7)(A)(ii), Michigan next urges us to adopt a "holistic method" of interpreting IGRA that would allow a State to sue a tribe for illegal gaming off, no less than on, Indian lands. * * * Michigan argues: Whatever words Congress may have used in IGRA, it could not have intended that senseless outcome.

But this Court does not revise legislation, as Michigan proposes, just because the text as written creates an apparent anomaly as to some subject it does not address. * * * This Court [cannot] disregard clear language simply on the view that (in Michigan's words) Congress "must have intended" something broader. And still less do we have that warrant when the consequence would be to expand an abrogation of immunity, because (as explained earlier) "Congress must 'unequivocally' express [its] purpose" to subject a tribe to litigation. C & L Enterprises, 532 U.S., at 418.

In any event, IGRA's history and design provide a more than intelligible answer to the question Michigan poses about why Congress would have confined a State's authority to sue a tribe as § 2710(d)(7)(A)(ii) does. * * * Everything—literally everything—in IGRA affords tools (for either state or federal officials) to regulate gaming on Indian lands, and nowhere else. Small surprise that IGRA's abrogation of tribal immunity does that as well.

And the resulting world, when considered functionally, is not nearly so "enigma[tic]" as Michigan suggests. * * * So, for example, Michigan could, in the first instance, deny a license to Bay Mills for an off-reservation casino. And if Bay Mills went ahead anyway, Michigan could bring suit against tribal officials or employees (rather than the Tribe itself) seeking an injunction for, say, gambling without a license. As this Court has stated before, analogizing to Ex parte Young, 209 U.S. 123 (1908), tribal immunity does not bar such a suit for injunctive relief against *individuals*, including tribal officers, responsible for unlawful conduct. See Santa Clara Pueblo, 436 U.S., at 59. And to the extent civil remedies proved inadequate, Michigan could resort to its criminal law, prosecuting anyone who maintains—or even frequents—an unlawful gambling establishment. In short * * *, the panoply of tools Michigan can use to enforce its law on its own lands—no less than the suit it could bring on Indian lands under § 2710(d)(7)(A)(ii)—can shutter, quickly and permanently, an illegal casino.

Finally, if a State really wants to sue a tribe for gaming outside Indian lands, the State need only bargain for a waiver of immunity. Under IGRA, a State and tribe negotiating a compact "may include remedies for breach of contract," 25 U.S.C. § 2710(d)(3)(C)(v) * * *. * * * Many states have taken that path. * * * Michigan did not * * *. * * *

IV

Because IGRA's plain terms do not abrogate Bay Mills' immunity from this suit, Michigan (and the dissent) must make a more dramatic argument: that this Court should "revisit[ ] Kiowa's holding" and rule that tribes "have no immunity for illegal commercial activity outside their sovereign territory." Michigan argues that tribes increasingly participate in off-reservation gaming and other commercial activity, and operate in that capacity less as governments than as private businesses. Further, Michigan contends, tribes have broader immunity from suits arising from such conduct than other sovereigns—most notably, because Congress enacted legislation limiting foreign nations' immunity for commercial activity in the United States. It is time, Michigan concludes, to "level[ ] the playing field."

But this Court does not overturn its precedents lightly. *Stare decisis*, we have stated, "is the preferred course because it promotes the evenhanded, predictable, and consistent development of legal principles, fosters reliance on judicial decisions, and contributes to the actual and perceived integrity of the judicial process." Payne v. Tennessee, 501 U.S. 808, 827 (1991). * * * For that reason, this Court has always held that "any departure" from the doctrine "demands special justification." Arizona v. Rumsey, 467 U.S. 203, 212 (1984).

And that is more than usually so in the circumstances here. First, Kiowa itself was no one-off: Rather, in rejecting the identical argument Michigan makes, our decision reaffirmed a long line of precedents, concluding that "the doctrine of tribal immunity"—without any exceptions for commercial or off-reservation conduct—"is settled law and controls this case." 523 U.S., at 756. Second, we have relied on Kiowa subsequently: In another case involving a tribe's off-reservation commercial conduct, we began our analysis with Kiowa's holding that tribal immunity applies to such activity (and then found that the Tribe had waived its protection). See C & L Enterprises, 532 U.S., at 418. Third, tribes across the country, as well as entities and individuals doing business with them, have for many years relied on Kiowa (along with its forebears and progeny), negotiating their contracts and structuring their transactions against a backdrop of tribal immunity. * * * And fourth * * *, Congress exercises primary authority in this area and "remains free to alter what we have done"—another factor that gives "special force" to *stare decisis*. Patterson v. McLean Credit Union, 491 U.S. 164, 172–173 (1989). To overcome all these reasons for this Court to stand pat, Michigan would need an ace up its sleeve.

But instead, all the State musters are retreads of assertions we have rejected before. [Here the Court cited the arguments, rejected in Kiowa, as to the growing tribal engagement in commercial activities and the recognition that foreign sovereigns enjoy no immunity in the courts of the United States from suits based on commercial activities. Although Kiowa expressed some sympathy with these arguments, the Court still refused to] "confine [immunity] to reservations or to noncommercial activities." [523 U.S., at 758.]

We ruled that way for a single, simple reason: because it is fundamentally Congress's job, not ours, to determine whether or how to limit tribal immunity. The special brand of sovereignty the tribes retain—both its nature and its extent—rests in the hands of Congress. Kiowa chose to respect that congressional responsibility (as Potawatomi had a decade earlier) when it rejected the precursor to Michigan's argument: Whatever our view of the merits, we explained, "we defer to the role Congress may wish to exercise in this important judgment." 523 U.S., at 758. * * *

All that we said in Kiowa applies today, with yet one more thing: Congress has now reflected on Kiowa and made an initial (though of course not irrevocable) decision to retain that form of tribal immunity. Following Kiowa, * * * Congress has continued to exercise its plenary authority over tribal immunity, specifically preserving immunity in some contexts and abrogating it in others, but never adopting the change Michigan wants. So rather than confronting, as we did in Kiowa, a legislative vacuum as to the precise issue presented, we act today against the backdrop of a congressional choice: to retain tribal immunity (at least for now) in a case like this one.

* * * [I[t is for Congress, now more than ever, to say whether to create an exception to tribal immunity for off-reservation commercial activity. As in Kiowa—except still more so—"we decline to revisit our case law[,] and choose" instead "to defer to Congress." *Id.*, at 760.

V

* * * We affirm the Sixth Circuit's judgment and remand the case for further proceedings consistent with this opinion.

It is so ordered.

■ JUSTICE SOTOMAYOR, concurring.

The doctrine of tribal immunity has been a part of American jurisprudence for well over a century. * * *

The majority compellingly explains why *stare decisis* and deference to Congress' careful regulatory scheme require affirming the decision below. I write separately to further detail why both history and comity counsel against limiting Tribes' sovereign immunity in the manner the principal dissent advances.

I

Long before the formation of the United States, Tribes "were self-governing sovereign political communities." United States v. Wheeler, 435 U.S. 313, 322–323 (1978). * * * In this case then, the question is what type of immunity federal courts should accord to Tribes, commensurate with their retained sovereignty.

In answering this question, the principal dissent analogizes tribal sovereign immunity to foreign sovereign immunity. Foreign sovereigns (unlike States) are generally not immune from suits arising from their commercial activities. * * * This analogy, however, lacks force. Indian Tribes have never historically been classified as "foreign" governments in federal courts even when they asked to be.

The case of Cherokee Nation v. Georgia, 5 Pet. 1 (1831), is instructive. In 1828 and 1829, the Georgia Legislature enacted a series of laws that purported to nullify acts of the Cherokee government and seize Cherokee land, among other things. The Cherokee Nation sued Georgia in this Court, alleging that Georgia's laws violated federal law and treaties. As the constitutional basis for jurisdiction, the Tribe relied on Article III, § 2, cl. 1, which extends the federal judicial power to cases "between a state, or the citizens thereof, and foreign states, citizens, or subjects." But this Court concluded that it lacked jurisdiction because Tribes were not "foreign state[s]." *Id.*, at 20. The Court reasoned that "[t]he condition of the Indians in relation to the United States is perhaps unlike that of any other two people in existence." *Id.*, at 16. Tribes were more akin to "domestic dependent nations," the Court explained, than to foreign nations. *Id.*, at 17. * * * Two centuries of jurisprudence therefore weigh against treating Tribes like foreign visitors in American courts.

II

* * * Principles of comity strongly counsel in favor of continued recognition of tribal sovereign immunity, including for off-reservation commercial conduct.

Comity—"that is, 'a proper respect for [a sovereign's] functions,'" Sprint Communications, Inc. v. Jacobs, 571 U.S. 69, 77 (2013), fosters "respectful, harmonious relations" between governments. Wood v. Milyard, 566 U.S. 463, 471 (2012). For two reasons, these goals are best served by recognizing sovereign immunity for Indian Tribes, including immunity for off-reservation conduct, except where Congress has expressly abrogated it. First, a legal rule that permitted States to sue Tribes, absent their consent, for commercial conduct would be anomalous in light of the existing prohibitions against Tribes' suing States in like circumstances. Such disparate treatment of these two classes of domestic sovereigns would hardly signal the Federal Government's respect for tribal sovereignty. Second, Tribes face a number of barriers to raising revenue in traditional ways. If Tribes are ever to become more self-sufficient, and fund a more substantial portion of their own governmental functions, commercial enterprises will likely be a central means of achieving that goal.

A

We have held that Tribes may not sue States in federal court, Blatchford v. Native Village of Noatak, 501 U.S. 775 (1991), including for commercial conduct that chiefly impacts Indian reservations, Seminole Tribe of Fla. v. Florida, 517 U.S. 44 (1996). * * *

Importantly, [in Seminole Tribe,] the Court barred the Tribe's suit against Florida even though the case involved the State's conduct in the course of commercial negotiations. As this Court later observed, relying in part on Seminole Tribe, the doctrine of state sovereign immunity is not "any less robust" when the case involves conduct "that is undertaken for profit, that is traditionally performed by private citizens and corporations, and that otherwise resembles the behavior of 'market participants.'" College Savings Bank v. Florida Prepaid Postsecondary Ed. Expense Bd., 527 U.S. 666, 684 (1999). Nor did Seminole Tribe adopt a state corollary to the "off-reservation" exception to tribal sovereign immunity that the principal dissent urges today. To the contrary, the negotiations in Seminole Tribe concerned gaming on Indian lands, not state lands.

* * * This Court would hardly foster respect for the dignity of Tribes by allowing States to sue Tribes for commercial activity on State lands, while prohibiting Tribes from suing States for commercial activity on Indian lands. Both States and Tribes are domestic governments who come to this Court with sovereignty that they have not entirely ceded to the Federal Government.

Similar asymmetry would result if States could sue Tribes in state courts. In Nevada v. Hicks, 533 U.S. 353, 355 (2001), this Court considered whether a tribal court had "jurisdiction over civil claims against state officials who entered tribal land to execute a search warrant against a tribe member suspected of having violated state law outside the reservation." It held that the tribal court did not. In reaching that conclusion, the Court observed that "[s]tate sovereignty does not end at a reservation's border." *Id.*, at 361. And relying on similar principles, some federal courts have more explicitly held that tribal courts may not entertain suits against States. To the extent Tribes are barred from suing in tribal courts, it would be anomalous to permit suits against Tribes in state courts.

Two of the dissenting opinions implicitly address this asymmetry. The principal dissent reasons that States and Tribes should be treated differently for purposes of sovereign immunity because—unlike tribal sovereign immunity—state sovereign immunity has constitutional origins. Justice Ginsburg * * * expresses concerns about cases like Seminole Tribe, pointing to dissents that have catalogued the many problems associated with the Court's sprawling state sovereign immunity jurisprudence.

As things stand, however, Seminole Tribe and its progeny remain the law. And so long as that is so, comity would be ill-served by unequal treatment of States and Tribes. If Tribes cannot sue States for commercial activities on tribal lands, the converse should also be true. Any other result would fail to respect the dignity of Indian Tribes.

B

The principal dissent contends that Tribes have emerged as particularly "substantial and successful" commercial actors. The dissent expresses concern that, although tribal leaders can be sued for prospective relief, Tribes' purportedly growing coffers remain unexposed to broad damages liability. These observations suffer from two flaws.

First, not all Tribes are engaged in highly lucrative commercial activity. Nearly half of federally recognized Tribes in the United States do not operate gaming facilities at all. And even among the Tribes that do, gaming revenue is far from uniform. As of 2009, fewer than 20% of Indian gaming facilities accounted for roughly 70% of the revenues from such facilities. One must therefore temper any impression that Tribes across the country have suddenly and uniformly found their treasuries filled with gaming revenue.

Second, even if all Tribes were equally successful in generating commercial revenues, that would not justify the commercial-activity exception urged by the principal dissent. For tribal gaming operations cannot be understood as mere profit-making ventures that are wholly separate from the Tribes' core governmental functions. [Justice Sotomayor cataloged the difficulties tribes face in raising revenue through taxes, both because much reservation land has been transferred to non-Indians under the Dawes Act, 24 Stat. 388 (1887), and because poverty and unemployment deprive many tribal governments of a stable tax base.]

* * *

Both history and proper respect for tribal sovereignty—or comity— counsel against creating a special "commercial activity" exception to tribal sovereign immunity. For these reasons, and for the important reasons of *stare decisis* and deference to Congress outlined in the majority opinion, I concur.

■ [The dissenting opinion of JUSTICE SCALIA is omitted.]

■ JUSTICE THOMAS, with whom JUSTICE SCALIA, JUSTICE GINSBURG, and JUSTICE ALITO join, dissenting.

In Kiowa Tribe of Okla. v. Manufacturing Technologies, Inc., 523 U.S. 751 (1998), this Court extended the judge-made doctrine of tribal sovereign immunity to bar suits arising out of an Indian tribe's commercial activities conducted outside its territory. That was error. Such an expansion of tribal immunity is unsupported by any rationale for that doctrine, inconsistent with the limits on tribal sovereignty, and an affront to state sovereignty.

* * * Still lacking a substantive justification for Kiowa's rule, the majority relies on notions of deference to Congress and *stare decisis*. Because those considerations do not support (and cannot sustain) Kiowa's unjustifiable rule and its mounting consequences, I respectfully dissent.

I

A

1

[The majority justifies immunity as a retained attribute of the tribes' historic sovereignty.] * * * But this notion cannot support a tribe's claim of immunity in the courts of another sovereign—either a State (as in Kiowa) or the United States (as here). * * * Outside of tribal courts, the majority's inherent-immunity argument is hardly persuasive.

2

Immunity for independent foreign nations in federal courts is grounded in international "comity" * * *. But whatever its relevance to tribal immunity, comity is an ill-fitting justification for extending immunity to tribes' off-reservation commercial activities. Even with respect to fully sovereign foreign nations, comity has long been discarded as a sufficient reason to grant immunity for commercial acts. In 1976, Congress provided that foreign states are not immune from suits based on their "commercial activity" in the United States or abroad.

There is a further reason that comity cannot support tribal immunity for off-reservation commercial activities. At bottom, comity is about one sovereign respecting the dignity of another. But permitting immunity for a tribe's off-reservation acts represents a substantial affront to a different set of sovereigns—the States, whose sovereignty is guaranteed by the Constitution. * * *

Nor does granting tribes immunity with respect to their commercial conduct in state territory serve the practical aim of comity: allaying friction between sovereigns. We need look no further than this case (and many others cited by petitioner and *amici* States) to see that such broad immunity has only aggravated relationships between States and tribes throughout the country.

3

This Court has previously suggested that recognizing tribal immunity furthers a perceived congressional goal of promoting tribal self-sufficiency and self-governance. Whatever the force of this assertion as a general matter, it is easy to reject as a basis for extending tribal immunity to off-reservation commercial activities. * * *

B

Despite acknowledging that there is scant substantive justification for extending tribal immunity to off-reservation commercial acts, this Court did just that in Kiowa. The Kiowa majority admitted that the Court—rather than Congress—"has taken the lead in drawing the bounds of tribal immunity." [523 U.S.], at 759. Nevertheless, the Court adopted a rule of expansive immunity purportedly to "defer to the role Congress may wish to exercise in this important judgment." *Id.*, at 758. * * *

II

* * * The Court's failure to justify Kiowa's rule and the decision's untoward consequences outweigh the majority's arguments for perpetuating the error.

A

[Justice Thomas argued that stare decisis does not justify retention of the Kiowa rule. The rule has created a substantial impediment to Michigan's efforts to halt the casino's operation permanently and has also been exploited in new areas that are often heavily regulated by States, such as payday lending.]

B

In support of its adherence to *stare decisis*, the majority asserts that "Congress has now reflected on Kiowa" and has decided to "retain" the decision. * * *

This argument from legislative inaction is unavailing. * * *

Even assuming the general validity of arguments from legislative inaction, they are a poor fit in this common-law context. * * * Allowing legislative inaction to guide common-law decisionmaking is not deference, but abdication. * * *

* * *

In Kiowa, this Court adopted a rule without a reason: a sweeping immunity from suit untethered from commercial realities and the usual justifications for immunity, premised on the misguided notion that only Congress can place sensible limits on a doctrine we created. The decision was mistaken then, and the Court's decision to reaffirm it in the face of the unfairness and conflict it has engendered is doubly so. I respectfully dissent.

■ JUSTICE GINSBURG, dissenting.

I join Justice Thomas' dissenting opinion with one reservation. * * * I also believe that the Court has carried beyond the pale the immunity possessed by States of the United States. [Citing, among other decisions, Seminole Tribe and Alden.] Neither brand of immoderate, judicially confirmed immunity, I anticipate, will have staying power.

NOTE ON TRIBAL SOVEREIGN IMMUNITY

(1) Federal Indian Law: A Brief Overview. Federal Indian law has long posed questions of sovereignty and federalism, as the Court defines spheres of regulatory authority against the backdrop of constitutional structure and federal statutes. In general, the Court has long viewed Native American tribes as enjoying an inherent but now limited sovereignty that pre-dates the Constitution.[1] Broadly speaking, "tribal law" describes the tribe's regulation of its own members and "federal Indian law" regulates inter-governmental relations between the tribes, states, and federal government, such as that implicated in Bay Mills. See Reese, *The Other American Law*, 73 Stan.L.Rev. 555 (2021) (identifying the categories of tribal and Federal Indian law).

---

[1] Three cases make up the Marshall Court trilogy on federal Indian law. See Johnson v. McIntosh, 21 U.S. (8 Wheat.) 543 (1823); Cherokee Nation v. Georgia, 30 U.S. (5 Pet.) 1 (1831); and Worcester v. Georgia, 31 U.S. (6 Pet.) 515 (1832). See Blackhawk, *Federal Indian Law as Paradigm Within Public Law*, 132 Harv.L.Rev. 1787 (2019); Ablavsky, *Beyond the Indian Commerce Clause*, 124 Yale L.J. 1012 (2015).

Although the Bill of Rights and other constitutional limits on federal and state governmental action do not themselves apply to tribal governments, Congress imposed many such limits by statute in the Indian Civil Rights Act of 1968 (ICRA), 25 U.S.C. §§ 1301–1304. Tribal citizens can enforce such rights against tribal governments in habeas proceedings brought in federal court or through suits for monetary and injunctive relief in tribal courts. See Santa Clara Pueblo v. Martinez, 436 U.S. 49, 65–66 (1978).

The Court applied general principles of immunity to tribal litigation as early as Parks v. Ross, 52 U.S. (11 How.) 362, 374 (1850), holding that tribal official diplomatic immunity blocked federal courts from exercising "power * * * to arrest the public representatives or agents of Indians nations * * * and compel them to pay the debts of their nation." See Struve, *Tribal Immunity and Tribal Courts*, 36 Ariz.St.L.J. 137, 149–50 (2004) (connecting the rationale of Parks v. Ross to the Court's contemporaneous refusal to permit officer suits to enforce government contracts or reach the public treasury).[2]

(2) State and Tribal Sovereign Immunity Compared. In Bay Mills, all the Justices agreed that, although some measure of tribal sovereign immunity from suit inheres in tribal governance, such immunity does not enjoy constitutional protection from congressional override. In this and other ways, Native tribes do not stand on an equal footing with the states for immunity purposes.

(a) Constitutional Status. For starters, Native tribes do not enjoy sovereign status conferred by or recognized in the Constitution. Early in the nineteenth century, the Court refused to exercise original jurisdiction over a tribe's claim against a state; the tribes were not "foreign nations" within the meaning of the original jurisdiction clause but were "domestic dependent nations." See Cherokee Nation v. Georgia, 30 U.S. (5 Pet.) 1, 17 (1831). Similarly in Blatchford v. Native Village of Noatak, 501 U.S. 775 (1991), a Native tribe sought to bring an unconsented suit against the state of Alaska, invoking the state's waiver of its immunity in the plan of the convention. Rejecting that argument, the Court explained:

"What makes the States' surrender of immunity from suit by sister States plausible is the mutuality of that concession. There is no such mutuality with either foreign sovereigns or Indian tribes. We have repeatedly held that Indian tribes enjoy immunity against suits by States, as it would be absurd to suggest that the tribes surrendered immunity in a convention to which they were not even parties. But if the convention could not surrender *the tribes'* immunity for the benefit of the *States*, we do not believe that it surrendered the States' immunity for the benefit of the tribes." *Id.* 782.

---

[2]   Tribal governments operate on and off reservation land, within a framework specified by federal law. Tribal courts have power to hear criminal and civil proceedings that stem from conduct in "Indian country," a term of art that recognizes the continuing importance of reservation boundaries. See 18 U.S.C. § 1151 (defining "Indian country"). At the same time, the state and federal governments regulate much Native American activity outside the reservation.

(b) The Governmental-Commercial Distinction. In proposing to distinguish the tribe's governmental from its commercial activities, Justice Thomas's dissent analogizes to foreign nations under the Foreign Sovereign Immunity Act (FSIA), 28 U.S.C. §§ 1601 *et seq.* Adopting a limiting or restrictive theory of foreign sovereign immunity, Congress adopted the FSIA in response to growing governmental participation in the marketplace, often in competition with private sector producers of goods and services. Is Justice Thomas right that tribal governments' market participation warrants judge-made restrictions on tribal sovereign immunity? For a similar argument that states should be subject to suit when they participate in the marketplace, see Fletcher, *Eleventh Amendment: Unfinished Business*, 75 Notre Dame L.Rev. 843, 855–58 (2000).

(c) Arms of the Tribe. Tribes exercising inherent governmental authority can create corporate entities, much the way states do. Such entities may claim tribal sovereign immunity, invoking their status as an "arm of the tribe" in much the way state agencies claim sovereign immunity as an "arm of the state."[3]

(d) A Clear Statement Doctrine? In Bay Mills, the Court asked if the "plain terms" of IGRA overrode tribal sovereign immunity. Compare Lac du Flambeau Band of Lake Superior Chippewa Indians v. Coughlin, 599 U.S. 382 (2023) (concluding that the Bankruptcy Code unambiguously abrogated tribal sovereign immunity despite the Code's failure to mention Native tribes in plain terms).

---

4. FEDERAL PROTECTION AGAINST STATE OFFICIAL ACTION

Given the limits on suits against the states as such, much constitutional litigation proceeds against state and local officials under the party-of-record rule. This section explores such litigation, beginning with the use of 42 U.S.C. § 1983 to enforce federal constitutional rights. The section then evaluates the application of that statute to suits against state and local officials, including those to enforce federal statutes. After assessing the interaction between § 1983 and the Ex parte Young doctrine, the section assesses the origins and growth of official immunity doctrines, including a brief summary of the Court's decision in Trump v. United States, 144 S.Ct. 2312 (2024).

---

[3]   For arm-of-the-tribe analysis, see Breakthrough Mgmt. Grp., Inc. v. Chukchansi Gold Casino & Resort, 629 F.3d 1173, 1181 (10th Cir.2010) (setting forth a multi-factor test). A similar multi-factor test governs arm-of-the-state analysis, albeit over the objections of one judge who would define the state for sovereign immunity purposes in historical terms. See Springboards to Education, Inc. v. McAllen Indep. School Dist., 62 F.4th 174, 178–79 (5th Cir.2023); *id.* 187 (Oldham, J., concurring).

A. The Home Telephone Puzzle

Suits brought against state officers for violating the federal Constitution, though now familiar, pose a conceptual issue if the officials' alleged acts also violate state law. The next principal case explains that conduct in violation of state law counts as "state action" in violation of the Constitution. Yet available state law remedies continue to inform and complicate the Court's task in fashioning constitutional remedies under 42 U.S.C. § 1983.

Home Telephone & Telegraph Co. v. City of Los Angeles

227 U.S. 278 (1913).

Appeal from the United States District Court for the Southern District of California.

■ Mr. Chief Justice White delivered the opinion of the Court.

The appellant, a California corporation furnishing telephone service in the city of Los Angeles, sued the city and certain of its officials to prevent the putting into effect of a city ordinance establishing telephone rates for the year commencing July 1, 1911.

[The company alleged that the city fixed telephone rates "so unreasonably low" that their enforcement would confiscate property in violation of the due process clause of the 14th Amendment.] * * *

Being of the opinion that no jurisdiction was disclosed by the bill, the court refused to grant a restraining order or allow a preliminary injunction, and thereafter, on the filing of a formal plea to the jurisdiction the bill was dismissed for want of power as a Federal court to consider it. This direct appeal was then taken. * * *

The ground of challenge to the jurisdiction advanced by the plea may be thus stated: As the acts of the state officials (the city government) complained of were alleged to be wanting in due process of law, and therefore repugnant to the 14th Amendment,—a ground which, on the face of the bill, if well founded, also presumptively caused the action complained of to be repugnant to the due-process clause of the state Constitution,—there being no diversity of citizenship, there was no Federal jurisdiction. In other words, the plea asserted that where, in a given case, taking the facts averred to be true, the acts of state officials violated the Constitution of the United States, and likewise, because of the coincidence of a state constitutional prohibition, were presumptively repugnant to the state Constitution, such acts could not be treated as acts of the state within the 14th Amendment, and hence no power existed in a Federal court to consider the subject until, by final action of an appropriate state court, it was decided that such acts were authorized by the state, and were therefore not repugnant to the state Constitution. * * *

In the first place, the proposition addresses itself not to the mere distribution of the judicial power granted by the Constitution, but substantially denies the existence of power under the Constitution over the subject with which the proposition is concerned. It follows that the limitation which it imposes would be beyond possible correction by legislation. Its restriction would, moreover, attach to the exercise of Federal judicial power under all circumstances, whether the issue concerned original jurisdiction or arose in the course of a controversy to which otherwise jurisdiction would extend. Thus, being applicable equally to all Federal courts, under all circumstances, in every stage of a proceeding, the enforcement of the doctrine would hence render impossible the performance of the duty with which the Federal courts are charged under the Constitution. Such paralysis would inevitably ensue, since the consequence would be that, at least in every case where there was a coincidence between a national safeguard or prohibition and a state one, the power of the Federal court to afford protection to a claim of right under the Constitution of the United States, as against the action of a state or its officers, would depend on the ultimate determination of the state courts, and would therefore require a stay of all action to await such determination. * * * [Moreover,] it would come to pass that in every case where action of a state officer was complained of as violating the Constitution of the United States, the Federal courts, in any form of procedure, or in any stage of the controversy, would have to await the determination of a state court as to the operation of the Constitution of the United States. It is manifest that, in necessary operation, the doctrine which was sustained would, in substance, cause the state courts to become the primary source for applying and enforcing the constitution of the United States in all cases covered by the 14th Amendment.

* * * [I]f there be no right to exert [Federal judicial] power until, by the final action of a state court of last resort, the act of a state officer has been declared rightful and to be the lawful act of the state as a governmental entity, the inquiry naturally comes whether, under such circumstances, a suit against the officer would not be a suit against the state, within the purview of the 11th Amendment. The possibility of such a result, moreover, at once engenders a further inquiry; that is, whether the effect of the proposition would not be to cause the 14th Amendment to narrow Federal judicial power instead of enlarging it and making it more efficacious. It must be borne in mind, also, that the limitations which the proposition, if adopted, would impose upon Federal judicial power, would not be in reason solely applicable to an exertion of such power as to the persons and subjects covered by the 14th Amendment, but would equally govern controversies concerning the contract and possibly other clauses of the Constitution.

The vice which not only underlies but permeates the proposition is not far to seek. It consists, first, in causing by an artificial construction the provisions of the 14th Amendment not to reach those to whom they are addressed when reasonably construed; and, second, in wholly misconceiving the scope and operation of the 14th Amendment, thereby removing from the control of that Amendment the great body of rights which it was intended it should safeguard, and in taking out of reach of its prohibitions the wrongs which it was the purpose of the Amendment to condemn. * * *

* * * By the proposition the prohibitions and guaranties of the Amendment are addressed to and control the states only in their complete governmental capacity, and as a result give no authority to exert Federal judicial power until, by the decision of a court of last resort of a state, acts complained of under the 14th Amendment have been held valid, and therefore state acts in the fullest sense. To the contrary, the provisions of the Amendment as conclusively fixed by previous decisions are generic in their terms, are addressed, of course, to the states, but also to every person, whether natural or juridical, who is the repository of state power. By this construction the reach of the Amendment is shown to be coextensive with any exercise by a state of power, in whatever form exerted. * * *

To speak broadly, the difference between the proposition insisted upon and the true meaning of the Amendment is this: that the one assumes that the Amendment virtually contemplates alone wrongs authorized by a state, and gives only power accordingly, while in truth the Amendment contemplates the possibility of state officers abusing the powers lawfully conferred upon them by doing wrongs prohibited by the Amendment. In other words, the Amendment, * * * [conceiving] that state powers might be abused by those who possessed them, and as a result might be used as the instrument for doing wrongs, provided against all and every such possible contingency. * * * [A] state officer cannot, on the one hand, as a means of doing a wrong forbidden by the Amendment, proceed upon the assumption of the possession of state power, and at the same time, for the purpose of avoiding the application of the Amendment, deny the power, and thus accomplish the wrong. * * *

Reversed.

———————

NOTE ON THE SCOPE OF FEDERAL CONSTITUTIONAL PROTECTION AGAINST UNAUTHORIZED STATE ACTION

In holding that the Fourteenth Amendment reaches all state official action, including action that also violates state law, the Home Telephone Court portrays the rejected "proposition" as a threat to the federal judicial role in constitutional litigation. One can see that threat in Home Telephone itself, where the lower federal court dismissed a Fourteenth Amendment challenge on the ground that the state constitution might also be interpreted to invalidate the city's rate structure. Anytime state action was thought to violate both state and federal law, the proposition would seemingly defer any federal law remedy until the state law question was settled. It would complicate the litigation of state and federal challenges to state action if the federal issue would not ripen for adjudication until the state law matter was resolved.

Consider the complexity of a litigation model in which plaintiffs must first challenge allegedly wrongful conduct through the state court system and then initiate a federal constitutional claim only after the state court rules definitively that the conduct in question was lawful under state law. Such a two-stage model of litigation would threaten fairness and judicial efficiency; indeed, the state's disposition of a state law challenge might preclude a later claim based on parallel federal law. See San Remo Hotel, L.P. v. City & County of San Francisco, 545 U.S. 323 (2005) (viewing the state court's rejection of a state law just-compensation claim as preclusive of a pending federal court takings challenge). A variant of this two-stage model was introduced by the Pullman abstention doctrine, a topic explored in Chapter X, Sec. 4, *infra*.

Note that the Home Telephone plaintiff's suit challenging the city's rate structure did not raise an Eleventh Amendment issue. The Court focused instead on the "proposition" that unlawful state official conduct does not qualify as state action for Fourteenth Amendment purposes. Despite its rejection in Home Telephone, the argument that federal law reaches only duly authorized acts of the state has proven to be a persistent one. The question resurfaced in Monroe v. Pape, the next principal case, involving the interpretation of 42 U.S.C. § 1983. In another set of cases addressed to the random and unauthorized torts of state officials, pp. 1288–1291, *infra*, the Court has viewed adequate post-deprivation state remedies as providing "due process of law," thereby forestalling any procedural due process claim under the Constitution.

B. FEDERAL STATUTORY PROTECTION AGAINST STATE OFFICIAL ACTION: 42 U.S.C. § 1983

In 1871, in response to an ongoing pattern of violence and intimidation against the nation's newly freed citizens and those in sympathy with them, especially in the former Confederacy, Congress enacted the Ku Klux Klan Act, 17 Stat. 13. But while the Act's most immediate target was the Klan, its first section created a federal cause of action, now codified at 42 U.S.C. § 1983, that was not so limited:

"Every person who, under color of any statute, ordinance, regulation, custom, or usage, of any State or Territory or the District of Columbia, subjects, or causes to be subjected, any citizen of the United States or other person within the jurisdiction thereof to the deprivation of any rights, privileges, or immunities secured by the Constitution and laws, shall be liable to the party injured in an action at law, suit in equity, or other proper proceeding for redress."

This provision spawned relatively few cases for many decades, apparently because its language partly tracks the wording of the Fourteenth Amendment's Privileges or Immunities Clause, which the Supreme Court rendered a near constitutional dead letter in The Slaughter-House Cases, 83 U.S. (16 Wall.) 36 (1873). (One commentator reports that there were only 19 case annotations under § 1983 in its first 65 years. See Note, *Limiting the Section 1983 Action in the Wake of Monroe v. Pape,* 82 Harv.L.Rev. 1486, 1486 n.4 (1969).) During this period, many suits that might have been brought under § 1983 as it has more recently been interpreted were brought as non-statutory actions predicated on general law and governing traditions of equity.[1]

Since the 1960s, § 1983 has emerged as easily the most important statute authorizing suits against state officials for violations of the Constitution and laws of the United States. What follows examines the scope of the § 1983 cause of action, the interpretive issues to which the statute has given rise, and the evolving course of the Supreme Court's implementing decisions.

Monroe v. Pape

365 U.S. 167 (1961).

Certiorari to the United States Court of Appeals for the Seventh Circuit.

■ MR. JUSTICE DOUGLAS delivered the opinion of the Court.

This case presents important questions concerning the construction of 42 U.S.C. § 1983 * * *. * * *

The complaint alleges that 13 Chicago police officers broke into petitioners' home in the early morning, routed them from bed, made them stand naked in the living room, and ransacked every room, emptying drawers and ripping mattress covers. It further alleges that Mr. Monroe was then taken to the police station and detained on "open" charges for 10 hours, while he was interrogated about a two-day-old murder, that he was not taken before a magistrate, though one was accessible, that he was not permitted to call his family or attorney, that he was subsequently released without criminal charges being preferred against him. It is alleged that the officers had no search warrant and no arrest warrant and that they acted "under color of the statutes, ordinances, regulations, customs and usages" of Illinois and of the City of Chicago. Federal jurisdiction was asserted under [§ 1983], which we have set out above, and 28 U.S.C. § 1343 and 28 U.S.C. § 1331.

---

[1] Compare Carter v. Greenhow, 114 U.S. 317 (1885) (rejecting suit under Rev.Stat. 1979, now 42 U.S.C. § 1983, seeking damages for seizure of property in payment of disputed taxes), with Allen v. Baltimore & Ohio R.R. Co., 114 U.S. 311 (1885) (allowing suit for injunctive relief under general equitable principles to block anticipated seizure of property).

The City of Chicago moved to dismiss the complaint on the ground that it is not liable under the Civil Rights Acts nor for acts committed in performance of its governmental functions. All defendants moved to dismiss, alleging that the complaint alleged no cause of action under those Acts or under the Federal Constitution. The District Court dismissed the complaint. The Court of Appeals affirmed. * * *

I.

Petitioners claim that the invasion of their home and the subsequent search without a warrant and the arrest and detention of Mr. Monroe without a warrant and without arraignment constituted a deprivation of their "rights, privileges, or immunities secured by the Constitution" within the meaning of [§ 1983]. * * *

Section [1983] came onto the books as § 1 of the Ku Klux Act of April 20, 1871. 17 Stat. 13. * * *

Its purpose is plain from the title of the legislation, "An Act to enforce the Provisions of the Fourteenth Amendment to the Constitution of the United States, and for other Purposes." 17 Stat. 13. Allegation of facts constituting a deprivation under color of state authority of a right guaranteed by the Fourteenth Amendment satisfies to that extent the requirement of [§ 1983]. So far petitioners are on solid ground. For the guarantee against unreasonable searches and seizures contained in the Fourth Amendment has been made applicable to the States by reason of the Due Process Clause of the Fourteenth Amendment. Wolf v. Colorado, 338 U.S. 25 [(1949)].

II.

There can be no doubt at least since Ex parte Virginia, 100 U.S. 339, 346–347 [(1879)], that Congress has the power to enforce provisions of the Fourteenth Amendment against those who carry a badge of authority of a State and represent it in some capacity, whether they act in accordance with their authority or misuse it. See Home Tel. & Tel. Co. v. Los Angeles, 227 U.S. 278, 287–296 [(1913)]. The question with which we now deal is the narrower one of whether Congress, in enacting § [1983], meant to give a remedy to parties deprived of constitutional rights, privileges and immunities by an official's abuse of his position. We conclude that it did so intend.

It is argued that "under color of" enumerated state authority excludes acts of an official or policeman who can show no authority under state law, state custom, or state usage to do what he did. In this case it is said that these policemen, in breaking into petitioners' apartment, violated the Constitution and laws of Illinois. It is pointed out that under Illinois law a simple remedy is offered for that violation and that, so far as it appears, the courts of Illinois are available to give petitioners that full redress which the common law affords for violence done to a person; and it is earnestly argued that no "statute, ordinance, regulation, custom or usage" of Illinois bars that redress. * * *

The legislation—in particular the section with which we are now concerned—had several purposes. * * * One who reads [the debates] in their entirety sees that the present section had three main aims.

First, it might, of course, override certain kinds of state laws. * * *

Second, it provided a remedy where state law was inadequate. * * *

But the purposes were much broader. The *third* aim was to provide a federal remedy where the state remedy, though adequate in theory, was not available in practice. * * *

This Act of April 20, 1871, sometimes called "the third 'force bill,'" was passed by a Congress that had the Klan "particularly in mind." The debates are replete with references to the lawless conditions existing in the South in 1871. * * * It was not the unavailability of state remedies but the failure of certain States to enforce the laws with an equal hand that furnished the powerful momentum behind this "force bill." Mr. Lowe of Kansas said:

> "While murder is stalking abroad in disguise, while whippings and lynchings and banishment have been visited upon unoffending American citizens, the local administrations have been found inadequate or unwilling to apply the proper corrective. * * * Immunity is given to crime, and the records of the public tribunals are searched in vain for any evidence of effective redress." * * *

There was, it was said, no quarrel with the state laws on the books. It was their lack of enforcement that was the nub of the difficulty. [Further excerpts from the legislative history are omitted.]

The debates were long and extensive. It is abundantly clear that one reason the legislation was passed was to afford a federal right in federal courts because, by reason of prejudice, passion, neglect, intolerance or otherwise, state laws might not be enforced and the claims of citizens to the enjoyment of rights, privileges, and immunities guaranteed by the Fourteenth Amendment might be denied by the state agencies. * * *

Although the legislation was enacted because of the conditions that existed in the South at that time, it is cast in general language and is as applicable to Illinois as it is to the States whose names were mentioned over and again in the debates. It is no answer that the State has a law which if enforced would give relief. The federal remedy is supplementary to the state remedy, and the latter need not be first sought and refused before the federal one is invoked. Hence the fact that Illinois by its constitution and laws outlaws unreasonable searches and seizures is no barrier to the present suit in the federal court.

We had before us in United States v. Classic, [313 U.S. 299 (1941)], § 20 of the Criminal Code, 18 U.S.C. § 242, which provides a criminal punishment for anyone who "under color of any law, statute, ordinance, regulation, or custom" subjects any inhabitant of a State to the deprivation of "any rights, privileges, or immunities secured or protected by the Constitution or laws of the United States." Section 242 first came into the law as § 2 of the Civil Rights Act, Act of April 9, 1866, 14 Stat. 27. After passage of the Fourteenth Amendment, this provision was re-enacted and amended by §§ 17, 18, Act of May 31, 1870, 16 Stat. 140, 144. The right involved in the Classic case was the right of voters in a primary to have their votes counted. The laws of Louisiana required the defendants "to count the ballots, to record the result of the count, and to certify the result of the election." United States v. Classic, *supra*, 325–326. But according to the indictment they did not perform their duty. In an opinion written by Mr. Justice (later Chief Justice) Stone, in which Mr. Justice Roberts, Mr. Justice Reed, and Mr. Justice Frankfurter joined, the Court ruled, "Misuse of power, possessed by virtue of state law and made possible only because the wrongdoer is clothed with the authority of state law, is action taken 'under color of' state law." *Id.*, 326. There was a dissenting opinion; but the ruling as to the meaning of "under color of" state law was not questioned.

That view of the meaning of the words "under color of" state law, 18 U.S.C. § 242, was reaffirmed in Screws v. United States, [325 U.S. 91, 108–113 (1945)], * * * [and] in Williams v. United States, [341 U.S. 97, 99 (1951)].

Mr. Shellabarger, reporting out the bill which became the Ku Klux Act, said of the provision with which we now deal:

> "The model for it will be found in the second section of the act of April 9, 1866, known as the 'civil rights act.' . . . This section of this bill, on the same state of facts, not only provides a civil remedy for persons whose former condition may have been that of slaves, but also to all people where, under color of State law, they or any of them may be deprived of rights. . . ."

Thus, it is beyond doubt that this phrase should be accorded the same construction in both statutes—in § [1983] and in 18 U.S.C. § 242. * * *

So far, then, the complaint states a cause of action. There remains to consider only a defense peculiar to the City of Chicago.

III.

The City of Chicago asserts that it is not liable under § [1983]. We do not stop to explore the whole range of questions tendered us on this issue at oral argument and in the briefs. For we are of the opinion that Congress did not undertake to bring municipal corporations within the ambit of § [1983]. [The Court concluded that the complaint was properly dismissed against the city, but reversed dismissal of the complaint against the officials.]

■ MR. JUSTICE HARLAN, whom MR. JUSTICE STEWART joins, concurring.

Were this case here as one of first impression, I would find the "under color of any statute" issue very close indeed. However, in Classic and Screws this Court considered a substantially identical statutory phrase to have a meaning which, unless we now retreat from it, requires that issue to go for the petitioners here. * * *

Those aspects of Congress' purpose which are quite clear in the earlier congressional debates, as quoted by my Brothers Douglas and Frankfurter in turn, seem to me to be inherently ambiguous when applied to the case of an isolated abuse of state authority by an official. * * * If attention is directed at the rare specific references to isolated abuses of state authority, one finds them neither so clear nor so disproportionately divided between favoring the positions of the majority or the dissent as to make either position seem plainly correct. * * *

The dissent considers that the "under color of" provision of § 1983 distinguishes between unconstitutional actions taken without state authority, which only the State should remedy, and unconstitutional actions authorized by the State, which the Federal Act was to reach. If so, then the controlling difference for the enacting legislature must have been either that the state remedy was more adequate for unauthorized actions than for authorized ones or that there was, in some sense, greater harm from unconstitutional actions authorized by the full panoply of state power and approval than from unconstitutional actions not so authorized or acquiesced in by the State. I find less than compelling the evidence that either distinction was important to that Congress.

I.

If the state remedy was considered adequate when the official's unconstitutional act was unauthorized, why should it not be thought equally adequate when the unconstitutional act was authorized? * * *

Since the suggested narrow construction of § 1983 presupposes that state measures were adequate to remedy unauthorized deprivations of constitutional rights and since the identical state relief could be obtained for state-authorized acts with the aid of Supreme Court review, this narrow construction would reduce the statute to having merely a jurisdictional function, shifting the load of federal supervision from the Supreme Court to the lower courts and providing a federal tribunal for fact findings in cases involving authorized action. Such a function could be justified on various grounds. It could, for example, be argued that the state courts would be less willing to find a constitutional violation in cases involving "authorized action" and that therefore the victim of such action would bear a greater burden in that he would more likely have to carry his case to this Court, and once here, might be bound by unfavorable state court findings. But the legislative debates do not disclose congressional concern about the burdens of litigation placed upon the victims of "authorized" constitutional violations contrasted to the victims of unauthorized violations. Neither did Congress indicate an interest in relieving the burden placed on this Court in reviewing such cases.

The statute becomes more than a jurisdictional provision only if one attributes to the enacting legislature the view that a deprivation of a constitutional right is significantly different from and more serious than a violation of a state right and therefore deserves a different remedy even though the same act may constitute both a state tort and the deprivation of a constitutional right. This view, by no means unrealistic as a common-sense matter,[5] is, I believe, more consistent with the flavor of the legislative history than is a view that the primary purpose of the statute was to grant a lower court forum for fact findings. * * *

II.

I think [the] limited interpretation of § 1983 fares no better when viewed from the other possible premise for it, namely that state-approved constitutional deprivations were considered more offensive than those not so approved. For one thing, the enacting Congress was not unaware of the fact that there was a substantial overlap between the protections granted by state constitutional provisions and those granted by the Fourteenth Amendment. * * * I hesitate to assume that the proponents of the present statute, who regarded it as necessary even though they knew that the provisions of the Fourteenth Amendment were self-executing, would have thought the remedies unnecessary whenever there were self-executing provisions of state constitutions also forbidding what the Fourteenth Amendment forbids. * * *

These difficulties in explaining the basis of a distinction between authorized and unauthorized deprivations of constitutional rights fortify my view that the legislative history does not bear the burden which *stare decisis* casts upon it. For this reason and for those stated in the opinion of the Court, I agree that we should not now depart from the holdings of the Classic and Screws cases.

■ MR. JUSTICE FRANKFURTER, dissenting except insofar as the Court holds that this action cannot be maintained against the City of Chicago.

* * *

III.

* * * [A]lthough this Court has three times found that conduct of state officials which is forbidden by state law may be "under color" of state law for purposes of the Civil Rights Acts, it is accurate to say that

---

[5] There will be many cases in which the relief provided by the state to the victim of a use of state power which the state either did not or could not constitutionally authorize will be far less than what Congress may have thought would be fair reimbursement for deprivation of a constitutional right. * * * Even the remedy for such an unauthorized search and seizure as Monroe was allegedly subjected to may be only the nominal amount of damages to physical property allowable in an action for trespass to land. It would indeed be the purest coincidence if the state remedies for violations of common-law rights by private citizens were fully appropriate to redress those injuries which only a state official can cause and against which the Constitution provides protection.

that question has never received here the consideration which its importance merits. * * *

The issue in the present case concerns directly a basic problem of American federalism: the relation of the Nation to the States in the critically important sphere of municipal law administration. In this aspect, it has significance approximating constitutional dimension. * * * This imposes on this Court a corresponding obligation to exercise its power within the fair limits of its judicial discretion. * * *

IV.

* * * [Plaintiffs] assert that they have been deprived of due process of law and of equal protection of the laws under color of state law, although from all that appears the courts of Illinois are available to give them the fullest redress which the common law affords for the violence done them, nor does any "statute, ordinance, regulation, custom, or usage" of the State of Illinois bar that redress. Did the enactment by Congress of § 1 of the Ku Klux Act of 1871 encompass such a situation? * * *

The original text of the present § [1983] contained words, left out in the Revised Statutes, which clarified the objective to which the provision was addressed:

> "That any person who, under color of any law, statute, ordinance, regulation, custom, or usage of any State, shall subject, or cause to be subjected, any person within the jurisdiction of the United States to the deprivation of any rights, privileges, or immunities secured by the Constitution of the United States, shall, *any such law, statute, ordinance, regulation, custom, or usage of the State to the contrary notwithstanding*, be liable to the party injured. . . ." * * *

The Court now says, however, that "It was not the unavailability of state remedies but the failure of certain States to enforce the laws with an equal hand that furnished the powerful momentum behind this 'force bill.'" Of course, if the notion of "unavailability" of remedy is limited to mean an absence of statutory, paper right, this is in large part true. Insofar as the Court undertakes to demonstrate—as the bulk of its opinion seems to do—that § [1983] was meant to reach some instances of action not specifically authorized by the avowed, apparent, written law inscribed in the statute books of the States, the argument knocks at an open door. No one would or could deny this, for by its express terms the statute comprehends deprivations of federal rights under color of any "statute, ordinance, regulation, *custom, or usage*" of a State. (Emphasis added.) The question is, *what* class of cases other than those involving state statute law were meant to be reached. And, with respect to this question, the Court's conclusion is undermined by the very portions of the legislative debates which it cites. For surely the misconduct of individual municipal police officers, subject to the effective oversight of appropriate state administrative and judicial authorities, presents a situation which differs *toto coelo* from one in which "Immunity is given to crime, and the records of the public tribunals are searched in vain for any evidence of effective redress," or in which murder rages while a State makes "no successful effort to bring the guilty to punishment or afford protection or redress," or in which the "State courts . . . [are] unable to enforce the criminal laws . . . or to suppress the disorders existing," or in which, in a State's "judicial tribunals one class is unable to secure that enforcement of their rights and punishment for their infraction which is accorded to another" * * *. These statements indicate that Congress— made keenly aware by the post-bellum conditions in the South that States through their authorities could sanction offenses against the individual by settled practice which established state law as truly as written codes—designed § [1983] to reach, as well, official conduct which, because engaged in "permanently and as a rule," or "systematically," came through acceptance by law-administering officers to constitute "custom, or usage" having the cast of law. They do not indicate an attempt to reach, nor does the statute by its terms include, instances of acts in defiance of state law and which no settled state practice, no systematic pattern of official action or inaction, no "custom, or usage, of any State," insulates from effective and adequate reparation by the State's authorities.

* * * [A]ll the evidence converges to the conclusion that Congress by § [1983] created a civil liability enforceable in the federal courts only in instances of injury for which redress was barred in the state courts because some "statute, ordinance, regulation, custom, or usage" sanctioned the grievance complained of. This purpose, manifested even by the so-called "Radical" Reconstruction Congress in 1871, accords with the presuppositions of our federal system. The jurisdiction which Article III of the Constitution conferred on the national judiciary reflected the assumption that the state courts, not the federal courts, would remain the primary guardians of that fundamental security of person and property which the long evolution of the common law had secured to one individual as against other individuals. The Fourteenth Amendment did not alter this basic aspect of our federalism.

Its commands were addressed to the States. Only when the States, through their responsible organs for the formulation and administration of local policy, sought to deny or impede access by the individual to the central government in connection with those enumerated functions assigned to it, or to deprive the individual of a certain minimal fairness in the exercise of the coercive forces of the State, or without reasonable justification to treat him differently than other persons subject to their jurisdiction, was an overriding federal sanction imposed. * * *

* * * Suppose that a state legislature or the highest court of a State should determine that within its territorial limits no damages should be recovered in tort for pain and suffering, or for mental anguish, or that no

punitive damages should be recoverable. * * * Should an unlawful intrusion by a policeman in Chicago entail different consequences than an unlawful intrusion by a hoodlum? These are matters of policy in its strictly legislative sense, not for determination by this Court. And if it be, as it is, a matter for congressional choice, the legislative evidence is overwhelming that § [1983] is not expressive of that choice. * * *

[Justice Frankfurter concluded that the general allegation that the police intrusion was under color of Illinois law failed to state a claim under § 1983 in the face of Illinois decisions holding such intrusions unlawful. However, the averment that it was the "custom or usage" of the Chicago police department to detain individuals for long periods on "open charges" did state a valid claim of unlawful detention.]

NOTE ON 42 U.S.C. § 1983: AN OVERVIEW[1]

(1) **An Introduction to § 1983.** In the decades since Monroe v. Pape, litigation under § 1983 has been both controversial and important. All agree that that § 1983 litigation has grown rapidly since Monroe,[2] though the statistics kept by the Administrative Office of the United States Courts make it hard to disaggregate § 1983 actions from suits filed under other civil rights statutes. But the overall number of civil rights actions has risen markedly, with § 1983 cases accounting for a large if uncertain percentage of the increase. In 1961 there were 296 civil rights cases filed in federal courts (the 1961 records do not indicate whether the plaintiffs were imprisoned[3]); in 1986 there were over 40,000, half of which were filed by imprisoned plaintiffs.[4] The most recent available figures show a total of 64,805 civil

---

[1]   For further discussion of § 1983, see Chap. X, Sec. 4, *infra.* For extensive treatment of § 1983 as well as additional references to secondary materials, see Schwartz on Section 1983 (2021).

[2]   Professor Weinberg contends that the large increase in civil rights cases after Monroe was caused not so much by Monroe's holding as by the Warren Court's expansion of protections afforded by the Bill of Rights—especially those relating to the criminal process. See Weinberg, *The Monroe Mystery Solved: Beyond the "Unhappy History" Theory of Civil Rights Litigation,* 1991 BYU L.Rev. 737. Section 1983 suits tend to include one central issue; however, many cases raise multiple types of issues (*e.g.,* inadequate medical treatment concerns as well as excessive force by correctional officers). See Hanson & Daley, *Challenging the Conditions of Prisons and Jails: A Report on Section 1983 Litigation,* Department of Justice, 12 (Dec. 1994) (noting the relative frequency of single-issue Section 1983 lawsuits at 62%).

[3]   References to imprisoned people include those in prisons and jails.

[4]   More refined analysis of data available during this period suggests that § 1983 actions account for less of the increase than some have assumed. Eisenberg & Schwab, *The Reality of Constitutional Tort Litigation,* 72 Cornell L.Rev. 641 (1987), conducted a detailed review of one federal judicial district, and concluded that (i) only fewer than 50% of the Administrative Office's "civil rights cases" were constitutional tort actions brought under § 1983 or the Bivens line of cases, see Chap. VII, Sec. 2, *supra* (exploring Bivens litigation); (ii) much of the increase reflected in the Administrative Office's data was attributable to the burgeoning of other kinds of actions, such as employment discrimination actions under Title VII of the 1964 Civil Rights Act; (iii) though civil rights suits by imprisoned plaintiffs rose by nearly 200% between 1975 and 1984, from less than 7,000 to more than 18,000, when one adjusts for increases in prison population, the rate of increase was only 101%, compared with a 119% increase in all other civil rights actions. See also Kreimer, *Exploring the Dark Matter of Judicial Review: A Constitutional Census of the 1990s,* 5 Wm. & Mary Bill Rts.J. 427, 485–90 (1997) (reporting that the growth in

rights actions filed in federal court in 2022 (of which roughly 25,000 were filed by imprisoned plaintiffs[5]).

Some regard the growth in § 1983 claims as validating Justice Frankfurter's preference for continued reliance on state law. Others see federal docket growth as confirming doubts about state court quality, reflecting the once widely held view among civil rights lawyers that federal courts offered a more hospitable forum for the vindication of the rights in question. In a world of concurrent jurisdiction, where plaintiffs can choose a state or federal court, changes in forum selection may reveal something about the comparative capacity of the two systems to secure the rights in question. Much of the so-called parity debate centers on these questions of comparative institutional capacity. See Chap. IV, Sec. 1, *supra*.

Recently, growing doubts about the effectiveness of federal remedies under § 1983 have led some civil rights lawyers to assert their claims in state court. In the aftermath of George Floyd's murder in 2020, reform efforts at the national level stalled, but some states moved to make state law remedies more effective for both state and federal constitutional violations. For a description, see Reinert, Schwartz & Pfander, *New Federalism and Civil Rights Enforcement*, 116 Nw.U.L.Rev. 737 (2021) (highlighting new police reform statutes in Colorado and New Mexico).

(2) Proper Defendants and Forms of Relief. The Court in Monroe interpreted § 1983's reference to "persons" to authorize suit against Officer Pape but not the City of Chicago. Several years later, the Court reversed course and included municipalities within the definition of suable persons under § 1983. See Monell v. Department of Social Services, 436 U.S. 658 (1978), discussed pp. 1293–1294, *infra*. Later still, the Court found that states were not suable under § 1983. See Will v. Michigan Dep't of State Police, 491 U.S. 58 (1989). Section 1983 therefore authorizes suit against local officials, local governments, and state officials. Federal government and tribal officials do not ordinarily act under color of state law within the meaning of § 1983.

Section 1983 authorizes both damages and injunctive relief to redress federal law violations. But the liability rule varies depending on the nature of the relief sought and the identity of the defendant. Suitors can secure injunctive relief from violations of federal law in suits naming state and local officers and local governments. Such injunctive suits typically name officers in their *official* capacity and the rules of qualified immunity do not apply. In suits for damages, by contrast, suitors typically name officers in their

---

filings by imprisoned people was "largely attributable to the growth in the American prison population").

[5]   Suits by imprisoned plaintiffs peaked in 1995, see Schlanger, *Inmate Litigation*, 116 Harv.L.Rev. 1555 (2003), just before the enactment of the Prison Litigation Reform Act (PLRA), 110 Stat. 1321 (1996), discussed at p. 1310, *infra*. Since the passage of that Act, there has been a dramatic decline in such filings (which consist primarily but not exclusively of actions based on § 1983). The decline appears to be due to several aspects of the PLRA, including a nonwaivable filing fee requirement and provisions limiting the amount of lawyer's fees that may be awarded to prevailing plaintiffs. (The requirement of the exhaustion of administrative remedies, while undoubtedly affecting outcomes, may not have significantly affected the number of filings.)

personal or *unofficial* capacity and seek, if successful, a judgment payable by the officer personally. Studies show that the government entity almost invariably indemnifies its officers by paying judgments that in form bind only the officer. See Schwartz, *Shielded: How the Police Became Untouchable* 184–85 (2023) (reporting indemnity rate in excess of 99%). In addition, a complex and controversial body of qualified and absolute immunity doctrine, discussed below, shields officials from some personal liability.

If the suit seeks damages from officials in their *official* capacity, the law presumes that payments will come from the treasury of the employing government. The Eleventh Amendment, where applicable, will therefore bar official-capacity suits against state officials and the rules of municipal liability will govern such suits against local officials. As explored in the Note that follows, see p. 1293, *infra*, Monell limits the liability of municipal governments to action taken pursuant to official custom or policy.

Liability for attorney's fees, as described in Paragraph (4) below, tracks the capacity of the defendant. Personal capacity suits against government officials thus threaten the officer with personal liability for compensatory damages, punitive damages, and attorney's fees. See Kentucky v. Graham, 473 U.S. 159, 168 (1985) ("[F]ee liability runs with merits liability."). But official capacity suits for injunctive relief, if successful, threaten the government (including the state in a proper case) with liability for such fees. See, *e.g.*, Hutto v. Finney, 437 U.S. 678, 693 (1978). Although indemnity has become routine, even a guaranteed right to indemnity does not convert a personal capacity officer suit into a suit against the employing government. See Lewis v. Clarke, 581 U.S. 155 (2017). The party-of-record rule remains intact.

Note that the § 1983 liability of officers sued in their personal capacity extends only to action under "color of state law." State action, as defined in the Court's decisions, necessarily meets the "color of law" requirement. See Lugar v. Edmondson Oil Co., 457 U.S. 922, 928, 930 (1982); Home Telephone & Telegraph Co. v. City of Los Angeles, 227 U.S. 278 (1913), p. 1276, *supra*.

(3) Exhaustion and the Meaning of "Under Color of" Law. In equating action "under color of" state law with the state action requirement, Monroe establishes that § 1983 remedies are available even in cases in which a state official *violates* state law.[6] Now well accepted, this aspect of the Monroe decision underlies the common-place notion that § 1983 claimants have no obligation to exhaust state judicial remedies before initiating suit in federal court. See also Patsy v. Board of Regents, 457 U.S. 496 (1982) (no duty to exhaust state administrative remedies). Monroe thus bears some resemblance to Home Telephone & Telegraph Co., in refusing to limit federal constitutional litigation to claims challenging state action that has been authorized or upheld as lawful under state law.

---

[6]　See Achtenberg, *A 'Milder Measure of Villainy': The Unknown History of 42 U.S.C. § 1983 and the Meaning of 'Under Color of' Law*, 1999 Utah L.Rev. 1 (tracing in great detail previously unexplored aspects of the legislative history of § 1983, and concluding that "this history should dispel the remarkably persistent myth that the Forty-second Congress never intended the provision to cover constitutional wrongs unless those wrongs were actually authorized by state law").

By adopting a broad view of actions taken under color of state law, Monroe extended the evolving model of direct constitutional remediation confirmed in Ex parte Young. Before Monroe was decided, as noted at pp. 1190–1192, *supra*, and confirmed in the separate opinions of both Justice Harlan and Justice Frankfurter, claimants often brought private tort law claims to remedy state official violations of the federal Constitution. Justice Harlan's characterization of the Fourteenth Amendment as self-executing seemingly had in mind its role in negating official-authority defenses to private trespass claims; Justice Frankfurter's analogy would place trespass claims against the hoodlum and the police officer on an equal footing, both governed by private law of trespass and both largely consigned to state court in keeping with Justice Frankfurter's vision of federalism.

Justice Harlan captures the essence of the change wrought by Monroe, explaining that the deprivation of a constitutional right is "significantly different from and more serious than a violation of a state right and therefore deserves a different remedy even though the same act may constitute both a state tort and the deprivation of a constitutional right." Monroe thus distinguishes between the private law that governs the hoodlum's trespass and the public law applicable to the police officer. Justice Harlan defended the switch as one apparently contemplated by the drafters of § 1983. He also questioned the wisdom of a litigation model that would treat state court remedies as presumptively adequate for unauthorized official conduct but would allow suit in federal district court for challenges to authorized official activities. In both cases, state courts would owe the same obligation to effectuate supreme federal law and in both their failures would be subject to review in the Supreme Court. (Today, of course, after the Supreme Court's 1988 switch to a discretionary docket, see p. 345, *supra*, plaintiffs can no longer rely on review in that court.)

Note, finally, the complex inquiry that Justice Frankfurter's test would force on the federal courts in determining whether state "statute, ordinance, regulation, custom, or usage" sanctions an individual defendant's unconstitutional acts. The reading of § 1983 given in Monroe elides such difficulties by making the custom or usage inquiry unnecessary in actions against individual officials. But the Court in Monell v. Department of Social Services, 436 U.S. 658 (1978), p. 1293, *infra*, later introduced much the same complex standard as the measure of municipal liability.

(4) Jurisdiction, Fees, and Procedure in § 1983 Litigation.

(a) Jurisdiction. Federal courts have subject matter jurisdiction of § 1983 claims under the general federal question statute, 28 U.S.C. § 1331, without regard to any amount in controversy. (Federal courts also have subject matter jurisdiction over § 1983 claims pursuant to 28 U.S.C. § 1343, an outgrowth of the original jurisdictional grant in the 1871 Act.) State courts have concurrent jurisdiction of such actions. See Martinez v. California, 444 U.S. 277, 283–84 n.7 (1980); Maine v. Thiboutot, 448 U.S. 1, 3 n.1 (1980).

(b) Attorney's Fees. The Civil Rights Attorney's Fees Awards Act of 1976, codified in 42 U.S.C. § 1988, provides that a court "in its discretion, may allow the prevailing party, other than the United States, a reasonable attorney's fee as part of the costs." This provision applies to § 1983 actions in state as well as federal courts. Maine v. Thiboutot, 448 U.S. 1, 8–11 (1980). As a result, while the prospect of a fee award may encourage the assertion of § 1983 claims, it will not necessarily make the state or federal forum more attractive.

Although prevailing plaintiffs can generally recover fees, the same rule of automatic fee-shifting does not apply when the defendant prevails; defendants recover fees only when the plaintiff's action was frivolous or vexatious. See Hughes v. Rowe, 449 U.S. 5 (1980) (per curiam). The essentially one-way shifting of fees may encourage § 1983 litigation and may also increase the total number of civil rights actions filed. See Rowe, *Predicting the Effects of Attorney Fee Shifting*, 47 Law & Contemp.Prob. 139, 147 (1984). But see Schwab & Eisenberg, *Explaining Constitutional Tort Litigation: The Influence of the Attorney Fees Statute and the Government as Defendant*, 73 Cornell L.Rev. 719, 780 (1988) ("attorney fees statutes may have less of an effect on filing rates than is commonly believed").

To decide when a plaintiff can be said to have prevailed in the litigation for fee-award purposes, the Court has established the following rules: (i) absent special circumstances, the "prevailing party" language applies to plaintiffs whose litigation terminates in judicially approved consent decrees, Maher v. Gagne, 448 U.S. 122 (1980); (ii) a plaintiff does not qualify as a "prevailing party" when the defendant changes its conduct under the terms of a private settlement or makes a unilateral change in policy to ward off further litigation, even where the plaintiff's suit was the "catalyst" for the change in adopted, Buckhannon Bd. & Care Home, Inc. v. W. Virginia Dep't of Health & Hum. Res., 532 U.S. 598, 604–05 (2001); and (iii) the usual "lodestar" model that governs calculation of attorney's fees (multiplying an appropriate hourly rate by the number of hours devoted to the representation) does not apply when the plaintiff secures something less than full relief, such as an award of only nominal damages, see Farrar v. Hobby, 506 U.S. 103, 114 (1992) (calling for a downward adjustment in the fee to reflect the degree of success obtained). Clear rules may help the parties anticipate the fee payment consequences of the various settlement options. In addition, attorneys' contingency fee contracts with their clients may assure some payment in the absence of any explicit provision in the settlement agreement. See generally Carroll, *Fee-Shifting Statutes and Compensation for Risk*, 95 Ind.L.J. 1021 (2020).

(c) Adjective Law. Section 1983 provides a barebones cause of action, without specifying such important matters as the measure of damages, the statute of limitations, and any official immunities from liability. In filling out the contours of the claim, the Court has sometimes fashioned rules of federal common law and has sometimes chosen to borrow rules of law from state sources. See, *e.g.*, Wilson v. Garcia, 471 U.S. 261 (1985) (treating constitutional torts as personal injury claims for purposes of selecting an applicable state statute of limitations period). A third possible approach, which the Court has not taken, would be to borrow analogous doctrines from other federal civil rights statutes.

NOTE ON LOCAL GOVERNMENTS AS DEFENDANTS IN § 1983 LITIGATION

(1) Monell v. Department of Social Services. In Monell v. Department of Social Services, 436 U.S. 658 (1978), the Court revisited and overruled Monroe v. Pape's rejection of municipal liability. In Monell, a class of female employees sued municipal agencies for back pay and injunctive relief, challenging defendants' policy of requiring pregnant employees to take unpaid leaves of absence. Reversing the lower courts, the Supreme Court, per Justice Brennan, ruled that cities and counties may be sued directly under § 1983 for damages or for declaratory and injunctive relief "where * * * the action that is alleged to be unconstitutional implements or executes a policy statement, ordinance, regulation or decision officially adopted and promulgated by that body's officers. Moreover * * * local governments * * * may be sued for constitutional deprivations visited pursuant to governmental 'custom' even though such a custom has not received formal approval through the body's official decision-making channels."

The opinion determined that Monroe v. Pape had misinterpreted the import of the 42nd Congress's rejection of the so-called Sherman Amendment. That amendment would have made municipalities liable not simply for violations of federal rights by municipal officials, but also for certain wrongful acts of private citizens within the municipality. In the view of the Monell Court, rejection of the Sherman Amendment could not justify an inference that Congress sought to exclude municipal liability for the conduct of officials. The Court found support for municipal liability in the legislative debates, and in the general understanding in 1871 that the term "person" included municipal corporations.

But the Court clearly stated, albeit in dictum, that "a municipality cannot be held liable solely because it employs a tortfeasor—or, in other words, a municipality cannot be held liable under § 1983 on a respondeat superior theory." 436 U.S. at 691. The language of the statute (in particular, "[a]ny person who * * * shall subject, or causes to be subjected," a person to the deprivation of federal rights) "cannot be easily read to impose liability vicariously on governing bodies solely on the basis of the existence of an employer-employee relationship." *Id.* 692. The Court viewed the primary rationales for respondeat superior liability—loss-spreading and reduction of harm—as too close to the justifications for the Sherman Amendment to be the predicate for municipal liability. Thus, "it is [only] when execution of a government's policy or custom, whether made by its lawmakers or by those whose edicts or acts may fairly be said to represent official policy, inflicts the injury that the government as an entity is responsible under § 1983." *Id.* 694.

(2) The Meaning of "Policy" or "Custom." In Monell, the city's policy of discrimination in employment was quite clearly specified in binding rules. Yet the Court also recognized that informal practices or customs might establish official policy. The Supreme Court has dealt with the meaning of Monell's "policy or custom" standard in at least two important contexts:

(a) Policymakers. In Pembaur v. City of Cincinnati, 475 U.S. 469 (1986), the Court ruled that a single decision of a high official like the county prosecutor, who had authority under state law to decide whether police officers should enter a premises and whose decision "may fairly be said to represent official policy," was an adequate basis for imposing governmental liability under § 1983 (quoting Monell). In City of St. Louis v. Praprotnik, 485 U.S. 112 (1988), Justice O'Connor's plurality opinion—later endorsed by a majority in Jett v. Dallas Independent School District, 491 U.S. 701 (1989)—affirmed that state law determines who is a policymaking official and found state and local regulations limited policymaking authority over personnel decisions to the mayor and aldermen of St. Louis and the Civil Service Commission.

(b) Deliberate Indifference/Failure to Train. The Court has recognized the potential viability of claims based on the municipality's deliberate indifference to the threat that its officers will commit constitutional violations and its failure to train officers to avoid such violations.[1] Assuming the plaintiff can demonstrate a pattern of activity that triggers the duty to train, City of Canton v. Harris, 489 U.S. 378 (1989), suggests that the evaluation of training should focus on the "adequacy of the training program in relation to the tasks the particular officers must perform." The Court's emphasis on the need for and adequacy of the training program wards off undue consideration of the lapses of a particular officer. See Board of County Commissioners of Bryan Cty. v. Brown, 520 U.S. 397 (1997) (rejecting claim based on sheriff's failure to conduct a background check on a deputy who used excessive force in arresting the plaintiff). Notwithstanding the programmatic focus of the analysis, Canton did recognize potential liability in single incident scenarios, where certain obvious risks, such as that posed by authorizing armed police officers to use lethal force, give rise to a duty to train without any required showing of a pattern of activity. See Canton, 489 U.S. at 390.[2]

(3) Failure to Train in Connick v. Thompson. In Connick v. Thompson, 563 U.S. 51 (2011), the Court narrowed the right of individuals to pursue failure to train claims against municipalities. Invoking 42 U.S.C. § 1983, John Thompson sued for wrongful conviction, naming Harry Connick in his official capacity as head of the district attorney's office of Orleans Parish in Louisiana. Connick conceded that, in prosecuting Thompson for attempted armed robbery, prosecutors failed to disclose evidence that should have been turned over to the defense under Brady v. Maryland, 373 U.S. 83 (1963). That violation occurred when a swatch of fabric stained with blood revealed that the perpetrator had blood type B. Thompson had blood type O. Rather than test Thompson's blood type or reveal the swatch evidence to defense

---

[1]   Although the Court in Ashcroft v. Iqbal, 566 U.S. 662 (2009), refused to recognize supervisor liability on a deliberate indifference theory, see p. 931, *supra*, that decision has not been thought to foreclose proof of deliberate indifference to support municipal liability. See Connick v. Thompson, 563 U.S. 51 (2011).

[2]   For a survey of cases that address Monell liability in the context of employment decisions, see Leong, Civil *Liability for Bad Hiring*, 108 Minn.L.Rev. 1 (2023). For a suggested emphasis on failure to supervise as a theory of Monell liability, see Leong, *Municipal Failures*, 108 Cornell L.Rev. 345 (2022).

counsel, prosecutors removed the swatch from the courthouse property room. No one disclosed the swatch or blood type evidence to the defense.

Thompson spent 18 years in prison, including 14 years on death row. One month before Thompson's scheduled execution, his investigator discovered a reference to the undisclosed blood-type evidence in a crime lab report. Both of Thompson's convictions were vacated and he was acquitted on retrial. In his subsequent civil action, the jury awarded Thompson $14 million, concluding that Connick had failed to train his prosecutors as to their duty to produce exculpatory evidence, thereby causing the nondisclosure in Thompson's robbery case.

Writing for a 5–4 majority, Justice Thomas explained the narrow scope of failure-to-train liability:

"In limited circumstances, a local government's decision not to train certain employees about their legal duty to avoid violating citizens' rights may rise to the level of an official government policy for purposes of § 1983. A municipality's culpability for a deprivation of rights is at its most tenuous where a claim turns on a failure to train. To satisfy the statute, a municipality's failure to train its employees in a relevant respect must amount to 'deliberate indifference to the rights of persons with whom the [untrained employees] come into contact.' Canton, 489 U.S. at 388. Only then can such a shortcoming be properly thought of as a city 'policy or custom' that is actionable under § 1983.

" '[D]eliberate indifference' is a stringent standard of fault, requiring proof that a municipal actor disregarded a known or obvious consequence of his action. Thus, when city policymakers are on actual or constructive notice that a particular omission in their training program causes city employees to violate citizens' constitutional rights, the city may be deemed deliberately indifferent if the policymakers choose to retain that program. * * * A less stringent standard of fault for a failure-to-train claim "would result in de facto respondeat superior liability on municipalities."

Finding little evidence of pattern of sufficiently similar misconduct and distinguishing the Canton single-incident scenario, the Court explained that attorneys are trained in the law and equipped with the tools to interpret and apply legal principles, understand constitutional limits, and exercise legal judgment. Education and admission to the bar were said to ensure that all new attorneys have learned how to find, understand, and apply legal rules.

Dissenting for herself and Justices Breyer, Sotomayor, and Kagan, Justice Ginsburg found ample evidence of Connick's deliberate indifference through failure to train attorneys working in the office. The jury learned of several Brady oversights in Thompson's trials and heard testimony that Connick's office had one of the worst Brady records in the country. Nor did the dissent view legal education as adequately training lawyers on a prosecutor's unique obligations under Brady.

(4) Municipal Liability After Monell and Connick. The important consequence of Monell was to render city, county, and school board treasuries liable in § 1983 damages actions for violations of federal constitutional and statutory rights by their officials—but only when the violation occurred pursuant to government policy or custom. Monell thus adopts a liability rule like that Justice Frankfurter's Monroe dissent proposed for officer suits under § 1983.

One might fairly ask what municipal liability adds to the framework of § 1983 litigation. As noted above, nearly all state and local governments routinely pay judgments and settlements in suits in which their police officers are sued in their individual capacities for constitutional violations. Schwartz, *Police Indemnification,* 89 N.Y.U.L.Rev. 885 (2014), Given this practice—which neither the Constitution nor § 1983 mandates—cities, counties, and their taxpayers almost invariably pick the tab for the constitutional torts of the workforce. For skeptical assessments of modern practice under the Monell rule, see Schwartz, *Municipal Immunity,* 109 Va.L.Rev. 1181 (2023); Smith, *Local Sovereign Immunity,* 116 Colum.L.Rev. 409 (2016).

With indemnity in place, municipal liability may play its most important role as a supplement to the regime of official liability under § 1983. In Monell, for example, the officers of the New York agency were subject to injunctive relief foreclosing discrimination in employment. But members of the plaintiff class were likely unable to secure back pay from the officers in charge of administering employee compensation; such liability sounds in contract and runs against the government rather than its employees. Municipal liability thus provided compensation for past violations that officer suits could not guarantee. In actions like that in Connick, prosecutors often claim absolute immunity from suit for misconduct in their prosecutorial capacity (unless their actions be deemed investigative and entitled only to qualified immunity). See p. 1313, *infra.* That immunity makes municipal liability the only pathway to recovery for claims seeking redress for a wrongful conviction linked to prosecutorial misconduct.

Other aspects of municipal liability come into sharper focus when viewed against the backdrop of routine officer-suit indemnification. Consider Owen v. City of Independence, 445 U.S. 622, 638 (1980), a suit to recover damages for the wrongful discharge of a city employee without due process of law. The Court proceeded on the assumption that any official defendants could claim qualified immunity from suit because the entitlement to due process had not been clearly established at the time of the discharge. (Such immunity freed the officers from liability and the city from any corresponding duty to indemnify.) But the Court refused to allow the city to assert its own qualified immunity defense to liability based on city policies. Justice Brennan's opinion for a 5–4 majority relied in part on the common law's refusal to allow municipalities to assert such defenses and in part on the compensatory and deterrent purposes of § 1983. The Court deemed the public's interest adequately protected by the policy or custom liability standard, citing Monell which imposed retrospective money liability in the context of evolving constitutional law.

Consider also City of Newport v. Fact Concerts, Inc., 453 U.S. 247, 258–71 (1981), which held that municipalities cannot be sued under § 1983 for punitive damages. The Court in Newport stressed that the common law did not subject municipalities to punitive awards and expressed the view that such an award would be a windfall to the plaintiff, while unfairly punishing "blameless or unknowing taxpayers." In contrast, the Court has upheld punitive damage awards in suits against individual officers who engage in willful or wanton misconduct. What's more, the empirical evidence suggests that the practice of indemnity almost invariably extends to payment of such punitive awards (effectively saddling the taxpayer with such costs). See Schwartz, *Police Indemnification, supra*, at 947. The upshot of the two decisions: § 1983 allows punitive awards but directs the jury to calculate the proper deterrent amount by reference to the assets of an individual officer rather than those of a deeper-pocketed municipality.[3]

(5) Rethinking Vicarious Liability. Just as Justice Ginsburg did dissenting in Connick, Justice Souter's dissent in Board of County Commissioners, Paragraph (2) *supra*, argued that the Court had raised the requirements for establishing deliberate indifference far too high. In a separate dissent in Board of County Commissioners, Justice Breyer called for a reexamination of Monell's rejection of the principle of municipal respondeat superior liability. In evaluating Justice Breyer's call for reexamination, note that criticisms of the Monell regime come both from those who believe that it should be easier for plaintiffs to recover damages and from those who believe that any local governmental liability was a mistake in the first place.

C. REMEDIES FOR STATE VIOLATIONS OF FEDERAL STATUTES

(1) Background: Maine v. Thiboutot. In Maine v. Thiboutot, 448 U.S. 1 (1980), the Court confronted the meaning of § 1983's provision for suit against state officials who violate rights "secured by the Constitution *and laws*" of the United States. As originally enacted in 1871 (17 Stat. 13), the provision that is now § 1983 authorized suit only for the deprivation of *constitutional* rights. The phrase "and laws" was added, without helpful explanation, and some argue by mistake, as part of a revision of the statutes in 1874, at the same time the jurisdictional provisions of the 1871 Act were severed from its remedial provisions. In Maine v. Thiboutot, the petitioner state of Maine argued that the term "and laws" should be narrowly construed to encompass only federal statutes that address equal or civil rights. The respondents, a class of welfare beneficiaries seeking to enforce standards in the federal program, Aid to Families with Dependent Children (AFDC), argued that § 1983's

---

[3]   One might ask whether liability induces government entities to supervise their employees to reduce the incidence of official misconduct. Compare Schwartz, *How Governments Pay: Lawsuits, Budgets, and Police Reform*, 63 UCLA L.Rev. 1144 (2016) (reporting survey evidence that many agencies feel no direct budget impact from constitutional tort liability, due to budgeting and insurance practices), with Rappaport, *How Private Insurers Regulate Public Police*, 130 Harv.L.Rev. 1539 (2017) (reporting that "insurance companies can and do shape police behavior" in jurisdictions that purchase liability insurance).

reference to laws encompassed legislation enacted pursuant to Congress's Spending Clause power.

The Court agreed with the respondents, ruling, 6–3, in an opinion by Justice Brennan that the plaintiff class could sue to compel compliance with AFDC standards in a suit against the state's officials. The Court also concluded that the plaintiff class could qualify as prevailing parties entitled to payment of attorney's fees under § 1988. The Court based its decision both on the text of the statute and on its practice of allowing suits like that in Edelman v. Jordan, 415 U.S. 651, 675 (1974), to secure injunctive relief to enforce federal spending clause statutes. Justice Powell's dissent emphasized the absence of any legislative history to support the Court's interpretation. The dissent also expressed concern that the majority's interpretation would threaten states with costly compliance litigation to enforce spending statutes that made no specific provision for individual remedies against the states.

(2) Defining the "Rights" Enforceable Through § 1983: Gonzaga Univ. v. Doe. In later decisions, the Court continued to read "laws" broadly but narrowed federal enforcement by requiring that the laws in question clearly establish the existence of a private right, enforceable through § 1983. In Gonzaga University v. Doe, 536 U.S. 273 (2002), the plaintiff sued the university for damages, alleging a violation of privacy norms set forth in the Family Educational Rights and Privacy Act of 1974 (FERPA). The relevant provision of FERPA, enacted as spending clause legislation, declared that federal funds were to be denied to any institution "permitting the release of education records (or personally identifiable information contained therein") without the permission of the student or the student's parents. 20 U.S.C. § 1232g(b)(1). The state court upheld a jury verdict in excess of $1 million against the university after concluding that the privacy guarantees were actionable under § 1983.

The Court reversed, 7–2, in an opinion by Chief Justice Rehnquist. Drawing on its reluctance to recognize implied rights of action, see Chap. VII, Sec. 2, *supra*, the Court explained that a similar reluctance should govern the recognition of spending-clause rights for enforcement through § 1983. As the Court explained: "[I]f Congress wishes to create new rights enforceable under § 1983, it must do so in clear and unambiguous terms—no less and no more than what is required for Congress to create new rights enforceable under an implied private right of action." 536 U.S. at 290. Finding no such clarity in the text of FERPA's expression of a general policy of privacy enforceable through agency oversight, the Court rejected private enforcement through § 1983. Justice Stevens, in a dissent joined by Justice Ginsburg, objected among other things to the majority's reliance on the implied right of action cases, which, he argued, were predicated on separation of powers concerns not present when § 1983 provides an express right of action.

(3) Implied Displacement of § 1983 Remedies. Even where the language of a federal statute confers rights enforceable through § 1983, the Court has sometimes found that the relative completeness of the statute's remedial scheme impliedly displaces any supplemental remedy under § 1983. Such implied displacement has been found when the statute in question creates a self-contained right of action, see Middlesex County Sewerage Authority v. National Sea Clammers Assn., 453 U.S. 1 (1981) (applicable statute permitted private enforcement suits), or a detailed administrative enforcement scheme, see Smith v. Robinson, 468 U.S. 992 (1984) (statute provided for administrative process and judicial review). Compare Fitzgerald v. Barnstable School Comm., 555 U.S. 246, 252–255 (2009) (considering and unanimously rejecting the argument that remedies under Title IX for sex discrimination by public schools that receive federal funds impliedly displaced a suit under § 1983 to enforce rights to equal protection under the Fourteenth Amendment).

(4) Health & Hospital Corp. v. Talevski. In Health & Hospital Corp. v. Talevski, 599 U.S. 166 (2023), the Court reaffirmed much of the settled law governing the use of § 1983 to enforce federal Spending Clause statutes. The plaintiff sued a nursing home acting for the state of Indiana to enforce rights under the Federal Nursing Home Reform Act (FNHRA), including restrictions on chemical restraints and rules governing discharge or transfer. In an opinion by Justice Jackson, the Court ruled, 7–2, that the rights in question were enforceable under § 1983.

In addition to a set of "residents' rights," some of which plaintiff sued to enforce, FNHRA establishes a detailed administrative scheme for government inspections of nursing facilities. "Surveys" (in the statute's parlance) must be conducted to detect nursing homes that are falling short of the FNHRA's minimum standards, and state and federal officials must periodically file certifications, based on these surveys, regarding nursing-home compliance, see § 1396r(g)(1)(A). In addition, the statute authorizes government actors to sanction and correct noncompliant facilities, or, if appropriate, exclude them from the Medicaid program entirely.

In challenging enforcement of Spending Clause legislation, the petitioner depicted FNHRA as a contract between the federal government and any states that opted into the program. On the petitioner's contract theory, the plaintiff was said to lack authority as a third-party beneficiary to bring an enforcement action. The majority rejected the contract analogy and resolved the case by applying the "and laws" provision of § 1983, as interpreted in previous decisions to encompass Spending Clause legislation.

The Court assessed FNHRA's rights-conferring language within the framework of Gonzaga Univ. v. Doe, 536 U.S. at 273. The unnecessary-restraint and predischarge-notice provisions were said to meet the Gonzaga test. Both were included in the "residents' rights" provision, and both included mandatory, rights-conferring language. Thus, residents were given a right to be free of unnecessary restraints and to family notification before being discharged or transferred.

Noting the absence of statutory language foreclosing enforcement under § 1983, the Court considered and rejected petitioner's implied displacement argument that FNHRA created a "comprehensive enforcement scheme that is incompatible with individual enforcement under § 1983." Unlike previous cases of implied displacement, the Court found nothing in FNHRA's provision for inspections and oversight that was incompatible with private enforcement. In addition, FNHRA itself stated that "[t]he remedies provided under" its enforcement-process subsection are "in addition to those otherwise available under State or Federal law and shall not be construed as limiting such other remedies." § 1396r(h)(8).

The dissenting opinion of Justice Alito, joined by Justice Thomas, agreed with the majority that FNHRA created individual rights but concluded that allowing remedies under § 1983 would upset the Act's careful balance of federal and state remedies. Also dissenting for himself alone on originalist grounds, Justice Thomas reasoned that federal spending legislation can impose only contractual duties on those who accept federal largesse and cannot "secure rights" within the meaning of § 1983. Relying on the scholarship of Engdahl, *The Spending Power*, 44 Duke L.J. 1 (1994), and others, Justice Thomas distinguished between Congress's broad but enumerated powers to regulate and its power to spend federal money.

(5) The Special Problem of the Application of § 1983 to Preemption Claims. In Golden State Transit Corp. v. City of Los Angeles, 493 U.S. 103 (1989), the question involved the application of § 1983 to a claim of federal statutory preemption of state law. The plaintiff, Golden State, had challenged Los Angeles' effort to condition renewal of its taxicab franchise on settlement of a labor dispute. The Court upheld Golden State's ability to sue under § 1983 for both injunctive and compensatory relief for interference with a federally protected bargaining relationship. The Court reasoned that (a) the National Labor Relations Act (NLRA) did not benefit private parties merely "as an incident" of federal regulation; rather the Act "creates rights in labor and management both against one another and against the State"; and (b) those rights are secured against state interference by the Supremacy Clause.

Measured by the standard of Gonzaga Univ. v. Doe, 536 U.S. 273 (2002), the NLRA would seem to lack the specific rights-conferring language now thought essential to support enforcement through § 1983. For a perceptive analysis, see Monaghan, *Federal Statutory Review Under Section 1983 and the APA*, 91 Colum.L.Rev. 233 (1991). As the next note explores more fully, preemption follows from a conflict between state and federal law that courts often resolve in suits for declaratory and injunctive relief that, if successful, invalidate state regulation.

(6) Preemption Issues in Suits Brought Under the Authority of Ex parte Young. As noted earlier, p. 902, *supra*, the Court has long authorized Ex parte Young-style suits to enjoin the application of preempted state law. See Shaw v. Delta Air Lines, Inc., 463 U.S. 85 (1983). Yet despite its pedigree, such litigation poses important questions of judicial authority, congressional control, and remedial coordination that the Court in Armstrong v. Exceptional Child Center, Inc., 575 U.S. 320 (2015), p. 1200, *supra*, addressed in part but did not definitively resolve. After concluding that the Supremacy Clause did not confer judicial authority to entertain a suit for injunctive relief from preempted state law, Part II of the Armstrong decision located the authority instead in historical practice as the "creation of courts of equity." But that authority was said in Part III of the Armstrong opinion to have been displaced by the Medicaid Act, a federal statute adopted pursuant to the Spending Clause (as in Talevski, *supra*), with a funds cut-off remedy for state non-compliance. For a partial defense of Armstrong, see Fallon, *Constitutional Remedies: In One Era and Out the Other*, 136 Harv.L.Rev. 1300, 1328 (2023) ("Congress should be able to authorize whatever enforcement mechanisms it chooses in cases not involving alleged deprivations of constitutional rights").

Part IV of Justice Scalia's lead opinion in Armstrong, speaking for a plurality of only four Justices, reached and rejected a claim that the parties had not raised. Justice Scalia found that the right conferred under the Medicaid Act was not enforceable in an implied right of action under the standard specified in Alexander v. Sandoval, 532 U.S. 275 (2001), p. 892, *supra*. That finding raises but does not resolve important questions about the interplay between the Ex parte Young action upheld in Armstrong Part II and the implied right of action rejected in Armstrong Part IV. The puzzle is deepened by the fact that Sandoval itself, also written by Justice Scalia, was a case about injunctive relief. There, in overturning a grant of equitable relief, the Court endorsed "a particular understanding of the genesis of private causes of action," namely that "private rights of action to enforce federal law must be created by Congress." In doing so, the Sandoval Court rejected the kind of relief that Part II of Armstrong makes presumptively available unless foreclosed by Congress. Why did the plaintiffs need a cause of action in Sandoval? Why not use Ex parte Young? Put another way, how can Sandoval be squared with Armstrong's presumption favoring the availability of injunctive relief to enforce preemption claims?

Consider the possibility that an anti-suit injunction theory of Ex parte Young might help to make sense of the puzzle. Although the theory has yet to secure a firm foothold at the Court, it has appeared in dissenting and concurring opinions that propose to read the decision in Ex parte Young as authorizing only the preemptive assertion of defenses to state enforcement suits. See Douglas v. Independent Living Center of Southern California, 565 U.S. 606 (2012) (Roberts, C.J., dissenting);

Virginia Office for Protection and Advocacy v. Stewart, 563 U.S. 247, 262 (2011) (Kennedy, J., concurring) (citing Harrison, *Ex parte Young*, 60 Stan.L.Rev. 989 (2008)). No state enforcement proceeding was threatened in Armstrong; instead, the plaintiffs sought to compel the state to comply with federal Medicaid law by setting higher patient care reimbursement rates. If as Professor Harrison argues, Ex parte Young does not extend to such claims for affirmative relief, then the distinction between Ex parte Young and Sandoval could matter. Ex parte Young would provide presumptive access to anticipatory suits asserting defenses to state enforcement proceedings, but a plaintiff would need an implied right of action under Sandoval to secure relief of the kind at issue in Sandoval itself and in Armstrong. Compare Whole Woman's Health v. Jackson, 595 U.S. 30, 39 (2021), p. 1211, *supra* (characterizing Ex parte Young as a "narrow exception" to state sovereign immunity "grounded in traditional equity practice" and "allowing an action to prevent state officials from enforcing state laws that are contrary to federal law").

There is a final complexity. Suit under 42 U.S.C. § 1983 has been broadly available as an alternative to Ex parte Young, authorizing federal courts to issue injunctive relief against state violations of federal law. The primary context in which plaintiffs need recourse to Ex parte Young over § 1983 is when the latter is not available due to the absence of an "unambiguously conferred right" for the § 1983 action to enforce. Compare Talevski, *supra* (concluding that the statutory rights at issue met the Gonzaga standard for enforcement through § 1983). As the Armstrong majority speculated, in a footnote, the plaintiffs may have believed in declining to assert a § 1983 claim in that case that they lacked such a right under the Medicaid Act. See 575 U.S. at 330 n.*. The possible availability of § 1983 as a substitute for an Ex parte Young injunction narrows the scope in which the uncertainty about the anti-suit injunction theory of Ex parte Young has practical relevance mainly to those cases in which a right is not available under Gonzaga. It also narrows the impact of the Court's displacement holding more broadly, at least to the extent that the Court's test for displacement of injunctive relief under § 1983 is harder to satisfy than its test for displacement of relief under Ex parte Young. See Note, *Interpreting Congress's Creation of Alternative Remedial Schemes*, 134 Harv.L.Rev. 1499, 1508–12 (2021).

―――――――――――

D. CONSTITUTIONAL TORT LITIGATION UNDER § 1983: DEFINING THE ELEMENTS OF CLAIMS

Just as state courts define the elements of common law claims, the Supreme Court determines whether and in what circumstances plaintiffs can mount constitutional tort claims under § 1983. The process of defining actionable wrongs takes account of a range of factors, including whether the right in question can be enforced at all under § 1983, whether the elements of a particular constitutional tort claim derive from the Constitution alone or from other sources, including common law rules in place at the time § 1983 was enacted, and what role post-deprivation remedies in state court may play in shaping the availability of suit. The decisions summarized below, far from an exhaustive collection, illustrate the Court's approach. Note the interaction between the definition of rights and remedies. In keeping with the idea of remedial equilibration, see p. 1166, *supra*, the Court sometimes redefines the scope of the constitutional right and sometimes moderates the force of remedies under § 1983. State law and state remedial options figure prominently in these adjustments.

(1) Constitutional Torts and State Law Remedial Alternatives. Although Monroe v. Pape, 365 U.S. 167 (1961), p. 1280, *supra*, rejected a requirement that constitutional tort plaintiffs pursue available state remedies, such remedies have remained critical considerations as the Court defines the elements of claims that include a due process component. Two examples are explored below: procedural due process claims for random and unauthorized state action under the regime of Parratt v. Taylor, 451 U.S. 527 (1981), and Fifth Amendment takings claims under Knick v. Township of Scott, 588 U.S. 180 (2019).

(a) Parratt v. Taylor. During the mid-twentieth century, the Supreme Court considerably broadened the Fourteenth Amendment's guarantee of procedural due process to protect interests in "new" forms of liberty and property, including the right of individuals to a hearing before their government benefits were terminated. See Goldberg v. Kelly, 397 U.S. 254 (1970); *cf.* Mathews v. Eldridge, 424 U.S. 319 (1976) (recognizing a property interest in social security benefits but rejecting the argument for a pre-deprivation hearing). Building on such due process cases, plaintiffs argued that common law torts committed under color of state law were actionable under § 1983 as a deprivation of liberty or property without due process. The Supreme Court has recoiled from the notion that either § 1983 or the Due Process Clause should function as a "font of tort law." See, *e.g.*, Castle Rock v. Gonzales, 545 U.S. 748, 768 (2005).

In Parratt v. Taylor, 451 U.S. 527 (1981), the Court relied on available remedies under state tort law to reject a § 1983 claim for the value of hobby materials lost through the negligence of prison officials. Taylor claimed that he had been deprived of property without due process of law but did not seek compensation under a Nebraska statute that allowed individuals in Taylor's position to recover damages for the torts committed by state employees within the scope of their office. The Court concluded that Taylor had failed to allege a viable constitutional tort claim under § 1983; claimants seeking compensation for random and unauthorized property deprivations by state actors must establish that the state's post-deprivation remedy was inadequate. Writing for the majority, then-Justice Rehnquist explained that past cases require some kind of hearing before the state finally deprives an individual of a property interest. But due process had not been inflexibly read to require a pre-deprivation hearing in every instance.

"The justifications which we have found sufficient to uphold takings of property without any pre-deprivation process are applicable to a situation such as the present one involving a tortious loss of a prisoner's property as a result of a random and unauthorized act by a state employee. In such a case, the loss is not a result of some established state procedure and the State cannot predict precisely when the loss will occur. It is difficult to conceive of how the State could provide a meaningful hearing before the deprivation takes place. The loss of property, although attributable to the State as action under 'color of law,' is in almost all cases beyond the control of the State. Indeed, in most cases it is not only impracticable, but impossible, to provide a meaningful hearing before the deprivation. That does not mean, of course, that the State can take property without providing a meaningful post-deprivation hearing. The prior cases which have excused the prior-hearing requirement have rested in part on the availability of some meaningful opportunity subsequent to the initial taking for a determination of rights and liabilities." *Id.* 541.

Justices Blackmun and White concurred, calling for limits on the Parratt doctrine that anticipated the approach later taken in Zinermon v. Burch, 494 U.S. 113 (1990), discussed below. Justices Powell and Stewart concurred, arguing that mere negligence on the part of state officials leading to property loss should not be regarded as a "deprivation" within the meaning of the due process clause.[1] Justice Marshall alone dissented in part, arguing that the state's tort-claims statute was irrelevant to claims brought by imprisoned plaintiffs absent an affirmative showing that prison officials had informed the claimant of its availability.

(b) Parratt Refined. In a series of cases, all brought under § 1983, the Court further narrowed the range of procedural due process tort litigation. Thus, in Hudson v. Palmer, 468 U.S. 517 (1984), the Court affirmed a judgment for a prison official who intentionally and unjustifiably destroyed the plaintiff's personal property during a prison shakedown. Even though the official's actions were intentional, the Parratt principle applied. Whenever the deprivation occurs "through random and unauthorized conduct of a state employee, pre-deprivation procedures are simply 'impracticable' since the state cannot know when such deprivations will occur." But Parratt does not apply, the Court held, "where a deprivation of property is caused by conduct pursuant to established state procedure, rather than random and unauthorized action."

---

[1]　　The Court later adopted the Powell view. See Daniels v. Williams, 474 U.S. 327 (1986) (holding that allegations of injury due to negligence of a prison official do not state a Fourteenth Amendment claim for deprivation and overruling Parratt on the point).

The importance of the distinction between established procedures and random official misconduct became clear in Zinermon v. Burch, 494 U.S. 113 (1990), where the Court restated the impact of available state remedies on the legal sufficiency of three kinds of Due Process claims under the Fourteenth Amendment:

"[The general rule of Monroe v. Pape—that] overlapping state remedies are generally irrelevant to the question of the existence of a cause of action under § 1983— * * * applies in a straightforward way to two of the three kinds of § 1983 claims that may be brought against the State under the Due Process Clause of the Fourteenth Amendment. First, the Clause incorporates many of the specific protections defined in the Bill of Rights. A plaintiff may bring suit under § 1983 for state officials' violation of his rights to, e.g., freedom of speech or freedom from unreasonable searches and seizures. Second, the Due Process Clause contains a substantive component that bars certain arbitrary, wrongful government actions 'regardless of the fairness of the procedures used to implement them.' "

For these two categories of claims, the constitutional violation occurs when the wrongful action is taken. Thus, a plaintiff, under Monroe v. Pape, may invoke § 1983 regardless of any state-tort remedy that might redress the wrong suffered.[2]

Turning to the third type of claim, one for violation of procedural due process, the Court reaffirmed that plaintiffs must meet the Parratt standard (demonstrating state post-deprivation remedial inadequacy) in cases of random and authorized state action. But where the plaintiff can show that the deprivation occurred as a predictable consequence of inadequate procedures, as on the facts of Zinermon itself, post-deprivation remedies (and the Parratt limits) drop out of the case. For an assessment of the Parratt regime, see Fallon, *Some Confusions about Due Process, Judicial Review, and Constitutional Remedies*, 93 Colum.L.Rev. 309 (1993).

(c) Takings Claims. The adequacy of post-deprivation state remedies also shapes the availability of Fifth Amendment suits to block uncompensated takings of private property. In Knick v. Township of Scott, 588 U.S. 180 (2019), the Court redefined the elements of a claim for the unconstitutional taking of private property to exclude any requirement that the plaintiff first show a denial of compensation under

---

[2]   Parratt looks superficially analogous to the position championed by Justice Frankfurter in his dissenting opinion in Monroe v. Pape, p. 1280, *supra*. But whereas Justice Frankfurter rested his case on an interpretation of § 1983, Parratt reflects an interpretation of the Fourteenth Amendment. In requiring the plaintiff to establish the inadequacy of state procedural remedies as an element of the due process claim, Parratt also appears to differ from the position, rejected by a unanimous Court in Home Telephone v. City of Los Angeles, p. 1276, *supra*, that state court litigation of an available state law claim was an essential precursor to a finding of state action. Compare Monaghan, *State Law Wrongs, State Law Remedies, and the Fourteenth Amendment*, 86 Colum.L.Rev. 979, 990–91 (1986). Rather than requiring the plaintiff to exhaust remedies as the prelude to federal litigation, the Parratt line of cases consigns the plaintiff to adequate state remedies alone.

state law. Knick sued the Township of Scott, Pennsylvania to challenge an ordinance requiring property owners to provide public access to cemeteries during daylight hours; Township officials interpreted the ordinance as applying to the small family plot on Knick's otherwise private land. In defending against the claim in federal court, the Township invoked Williamson Cty. Regional Planning Comm'n v. Hamilton Bank of Johnson City, 473 U.S. 172 (1985), which held that claimants like Knick could not bring a Takings Clause claim for injunctive relief until the state or county had denied them just compensation. Overruling Williamson County, 5–4, in a decision by Chief Justice Roberts, the Court held that the violation of the Taking Clause was complete and therefore actionable when the invasion of the plaintiff's property rights occurred without payment of just compensation. No pre-suit invocation of state inverse condemnation or other compensation procedures was required.

The Court reconsidered prior opinions that had treated viable post-deprivation compensation remedies as precluding a takings claim. The cases in question did not require payment in advance of occupancy but only an assurance that the owner would be given "reasonable, certain, and adequate provision for obtaining compensation" after a taking. Cherokee Nation v. Southern Kansas R. Co., 135 U.S. 641, 659 (1890). Noting that the cases in question began as suits for injunctive relief, the Court treated them as establishing only that compensatory remedies made equitable relief inappropriate.[3] Reframing the denial of injunctive relief as a matter of remedial discretion, the Court treated the earlier cases as assuming that the state had committed a fully complete violation of the Takings Clause at the time of suit. The Court concluded by reassuring governments that provisions for adequate post-deprivation compensation would continue to forestall federal injunctive relief.

In dissent, Justice Kagan viewed the state's failure to pay just compensation as an essential element of a takings claim:

"The right that Clause confers is not to be free from government takings of property for public purposes. Instead, the right is to be free from those takings when the government fails to provide 'just compensation.' In other words, the government can take private property for public purposes, so long as it fairly pays the property owner. That precept, which the majority does not contest, comes straight out of the constitutional text which prohibits the taking of private property 'for public use, without just compensation.' "

In considering the impact of the changing definition of when a taking occurs, note that prior law encouraged litigants to contest the adequacy

---

[3]   See Regional Rail Reorganization Act Cases, 419 U.S. 102, 107, 149 (1974) (reversing a decision "enjoin[ing]" the enforcement of a federal statute because "the availability of the Tucker Act guarantees an adequate remedy at law for any taking which might occur"); Hurley v. Kincaid, 285 U.S. 95, 99, 105 (1932) (rejecting a request to "enjoin the carrying out of any work" on a flood control project because the Tucker Act provided the plaintiff with "a plain, adequate, and complete remedy at law").

of state remedies in state court, rather than doing so as a factor bearing on the availability of equitable relief in federal court.

(2) Borrowing Elements from State Law. The Supreme Court sometimes borrows state law in defining the elements of constitutional tort claims. Note that, in the cases described below, the Court's decision to borrow state law represents an elaboration of an avowedly federal law claim, rather than an entailment of the Erie doctrine as discussed in Chapter VI, Section 3.

(a) Retaliatory-Arrest Claims Under the First Amendment. In Nieves v. Bartlett, 587 U.S. 391 (2019), the Court found that a First Amendment retaliatory arrest claim must ordinarily establish absence of probable cause. Bartlett was arrested during the "Arctic Man" celebration in a remote corner of Alaska. The arrest came after two confrontations between Bartlett and the police officers working the event during which Bartlett advised other celebrants that they should avoid talking to the police. Officer Nieves arrested Bartlett as he addressed individuals in discussion with another officer. After he was handcuffed, Bartlett claimed that Nieves said "bet you wish you would have talked to me now."

After charges were dismissed, Bartlett sued under 42 U.S.C. § 1983, claiming that the officers violated his First Amendment rights by arresting him in retaliation for his speech—*i.e.*, his initial refusal to speak with Nieves and his intervention in a separate discussion with other individuals. Finding that the officers had probable cause to arrest, the district court dismissed the claim on summary judgment. Upholding that decision in an opinion by Chief Justice Roberts, the Court relied in part on Hartman v. Moore, 547 U.S. 250 (2006), which read a probable cause element into First Amendment retaliatory prosecution claims. To prevail on such claims, the Court explained, a plaintiff must show that retaliation for speech was the but-for cause of the retaliatory response, ordinarily by proving absence of probable cause. But the Chief Justice also drew on § 1983: "When defining the contours of a claim under § 1983, we look to 'common-law principles that were well settled at the time of its enactment.'" At common law, the Chief Justice found, the most analogous precedents—involving false imprisonment and malicious prosecution—either required proof of the absence of probable cause or made probable cause a complete defense. The Court recognized an exception allowing the claim to proceed even where there was probable cause to arrest if the plaintiff can provide "objective evidence that [the plaintiff] was arrested when otherwise similarly situated individuals not engaged in . . . protected speech had not been." Nieves, 587 U.S. at 407.

Justice Gorsuch, concurring in part and dissenting in part, and Justice Sotomayor, dissenting, both argued that the decisive question should be whether the plaintiff had adequately alleged a violation of his First Amendment rights. If so, neither Justice thought that the common-law background to the enactment of § 1983 could justify denying the plaintiff a remedy. In evaluating the majority's view, recall that the Court in Monroe v. Pape portrayed § 1983 actions as claims brought directly to vindicate constitutional values rather than as common law claims structured to trigger incidental constitutional adjudication. Neither § 1983 nor the First Amendment makes any specific reference to probable cause.

Five years later, in Gonzalez v. Trevino, 144 S.Ct. 1663 (2024), the Court considered the contours of the Nieves exception to the probable cause requirement. Admitting that there was probable cause to arrest, Gonzalez invoked the Nieves exception for claims supported by "objective evidence." Gonzalez had surveyed arrest records in the county and found that no one had been arrested under applicable state law for conduct comparable to hers. She argued that the absence of comparable arrests bolstered her claim that her arrest was politically motivated. The district court allowed the claim to proceed, but the Fifth Circuit reversed in a divided opinion that required plaintiffs invoking the Nieves exception to show that other similarly situated individuals had engaged in the same conduct but had not been arrested. Gonzalez did not provide evidence of non-arrests, nor does it appear immediately apparent how a plaintiff could make such a showing.

In a short per curiam opinion, the Court reversed. It held that Gonzalez had offered evidence sufficiently objective to satisfy the Nieves exception. The fact that no one had ever been arrested for engaging in a certain kind of conduct made "it more likely that an officer has declined to arrest someone for engaging in such conduct in the past." Justice Alito's lengthy concurring opinion expressed skepticism of the claim, viewed in context, and argued more broadly that common-law principles relating to a question the majority did not reach were best understood as "helpful guides" rather than "prefabricated components of a § 1983 claim." Justice Thomas dissented for himself alone, objecting to the exception "created in Nieves and expanded upon today."

(b) Malicious Prosecution Claims. In McDonough v. Smith, 588 U.S. 109 (2019), the plaintiff brought suit, seeking damages under § 1983 for the fabrication of evidence. The Court defined the elements of the claim in deciding when the statute of limitations began to run. In an opinion joined by five other Justices, Justice Sotomayor began by stating the generally governing rule: "Although courts look to state law for the length of the limitations period, the time at which a § 1983 claim accrues 'is a question of federal law,' 'conforming in general to common-law tort principles'" (quoting Wallace v. Kato, 549 U.S. 384, 388 (2007)). Pursuant to that rule, Justice Sotomayor concluded that "the most natural common-law analogy" was the tort of malicious prosecution. In addition, the Court emphasized "practical considerations that have previously led this Court to defer accrual of claims that would otherwise constitute an untenable collateral attack on a criminal judgment," a reference to the doctrine under Heck v. Humphrey, 512 U.S. 477 (1994), explored at pp. 1681–1693, *infra*. The Court concluded that the statute of limitations for fabricated evidence claims did not "begin to run until the criminal proceedings against the defendant (the § 1983 plaintiff) have terminated in his favor."

Justice Thomas, joined by Justices Kagan and Gorsuch, dissented. The petitioner McDonough had "declined to take a definitive position on" the particular constitutional provision on which his fabricated-evidence claim was based. Believing this to be a necessary antecedent question to the statute-of-limitations issue, the dissenters would have dismissed the petition as improvidently granted. For further discussion of McDonough, see p. 1690, *infra*.

The Court again drew on common law precursors in Thompson v. Clark, 596 U.S. 36 (2022), holding that a § 1983 plaintiff in a malicious prosecution claim for an unreasonable seizure under the Fourth Amendment need only show, for purposes of satisfying the favorable termination element of the claim, that his prosecution ended without a conviction. In an opinion by Justice Kavanaugh for six Justices, the Court relied heavily on the common law elements of the tort at the time § 1983 was enacted, rejecting the argument that the plaintiff must show some affirmative evidence of innocence. Justice Alito, in a dissent joined by Justices Thomas and Gorsuch, objected that the Court had wrongly conjoined the tort of malicious prosecution with a Fourth Amendment unreasonable seizure claim—two claims that were said to have "almost nothing in common."

(3) Finding No Enforceable Constitutional Right. The Court has also rejected claims under § 1983 on the theory that the plaintiff has failed to allege the violation of a constitutional right. In one example, the Court found that negligent conduct on the part of state officials did not constitute a "deprivation" of liberty or property for procedural due process purposes. See Daniels v. Williams, 474 U.S. 327 (1986). In a second example, Justice Alito wrote an opinion for a six-Justice majority in Vega v. Tekoh, 597 U.S. 134 (2022), holding that the failure of a sheriff's deputy to provide the warnings required under Miranda v. Arizona, 384 U.S. 436 (1966), is not actionable in a suit for damages under § 1983. Tekoh was acquitted at trial, despite the admission of what he challenged as an un-Mirandized statement taken by the defendant during a criminal investigation. Having no reason to appeal from his acquittal, Tekoh sued for damages, arguing that the statement's wrongful admission violated the Fifth Amendment. Characterizing Miranda as a prophylactic rule rather than a constitutional right, the Court applied a cost-benefit analysis in refusing to allow the suit to proceed. What little would be gained in terms of preventing self-incrimination was outweighed in the majority's view by the costs of allowing duplicative federal litigation of issues the state court had addressed in denying a suppression motion.

Justice Kagan dissented for three Justices, rejecting the majority's characterization of Miranda as merely prophylactic. Viewing the question as whether Miranda's protections are a "right[ ]" that is "secured by the Constitution" within the meaning of § 1983, the dissent thought the answer was plainly yes, as stated in earlier decisions that view Miranda as a "constitutional rule." Dickerson v. United States, 530 U.S. 428, 444 (2000). Consider the implications of the Court's approach for the continued vitality of Withrow v. Williams, 507 U.S. 680 (1993), p. 1571, *infra*, treating Miranda issues as cognizable in habeas for those who, unlike Tekoh, were convicted at trial. To what extent does specification of the elements of a claim for damages govern other forms of constitutional litigation?

(4) Special Rules for Prisoners. In 1996, Congress enacted the Prison Litigation Reform Act (PLRA), 110 Stat. 1321–66 to 1321–77. The PLRA imposes restrictions on suits by prisoners that do not apply to other § 1983 actions. Among the innovations are:

(a) A requirement that plaintiffs, for whom filing fees had previously been waived, pay the customary filing fee (if necessary, in installments from the small prison financial account that they would otherwise use to pay for sundries).

(b) A requirement that before filing suits challenging prison conditions, plaintiffs must first exhaust administrative remedies.

(c) A provision addressed to "frequent filers" that prohibits a plaintiff who has brought three or more previous actions that were dismissed as frivolous or malicious or for failure to state a claim from filing additional actions unless in imminent danger of serious physical injury.

(d) A prohibition on the award of damages for mental and emotional distress unaccompanied by physical injury.

(e) Limits on the permissible scope of consent decrees and injunctive orders, designed to keep judicial intrusion into prison management to the minimum required by the Constitution.

(f) Special limits on attorney's fees.

Schlanger, *Inmate Litigation*, 116 Harv.L.Rev. 1555, 1559–60 (2003), describes the PLRA as having had "an impact on inmate litigation that is hard to exaggerate; to set out the most obvious effect, 2001 filings by inmates were down forty-three percent since their peak in 1995 [from 39,008 to 22,206], notwithstanding a simultaneous twenty-three percent increase in the number of people incarcerated nationwide." Without contesting the Act's success in reducing strain on federal dockets, critics express concern that it poses traps for legally unsophisticated plaintiffs (notably through its "exhaustion" requirement) and precludes the filing of meritorious as well as frivolous claims. Apart from the Act's effectiveness, consider whether the Court should treat Congress's decision to impose a series of specific limits on claims by incarcerated individuals as foreclosing new judge-made restrictions on such claims.

E. CONSTITUTIONAL TORT LITIGATION UNDER § 1983 AND THE BIVENS DOCTRINE: QUALIFIED IMMUNITY

This section examines the various official immunity doctrines that now operate as defenses to constitutional tort liability under 42 U.S.C. § 1983 and the Bivens doctrine, see Bivens v. Six Unknown Fed. Narcotics Agents, 403 U.S. 388, 400 (1971), p. 918, *supra* (recognizing an implied cause of action against federal officers under the Fourth Amendment).[1] The section begins with an overview of the evolution of qualified immunity doctrine, from a nineteenth-century world in which officers acting in good faith were protected through the payment of indemnity to the modern world of judge-made immunity. It then examines the absolute immunity doctrines that govern suits against legislators, judges, prosecutors, and the President of the United States.

(1) The Nineteenth Century's Rule of Official Liability and Indemnity. In overseeing government action in the nineteenth century, the Supreme Court often applied a relatively strict form of official liability that was meant to ensure a remedy for victims of government misconduct and presumed that the legislature would protect officials through indemnity. See generally Pfander & Hunt, *Public Wrongs and Private Bills*, 85 N.Y.U.L.Rev. 1862 (2010). Modern observers might criticize such an approach as wrongheaded in two respects: personal liability could threaten well-meaning officials with financial ruin and could deter effective responses to emergent national security concerns. Speaking to such criticisms for a unanimous Court in The Appollon, 22 U.S. (9 Wheat.) 362 (1824), a decision upholding the award of damages against government revenue officers for seizing a vessel in international waters, Justice Story explained:

"It may be fit and proper for the government, in the exercise of the high discretion confided to the executive, for great public purposes, to act on a sudden emergency, or to prevent an irreparable mischief, by summary measures, which are not found in the text of the laws. Such measures are properly matters of state, and if the responsibility is taken, under justifiable circumstances, the Legislature will doubtless apply a proper indemnity. But this Court can only look to the questions, whether the laws have been violated; and if they were, justice demands, that the injured party should receive a suitable redress." *Id*. 366–67. On this view, rooted in the separation of powers, courts were responsible for

---

[1]   On the application of a single immunity doctrine to state and federal officials alike, see Butz v. Economou, 438 U.S. 478, 504 (1978) (deeming "it untenable to draw a distinction for purposes of immunity law between suits brought against state officials under § 1983 and suits brought directly under the Constitution against federal officials"). In one exception, the President enjoys a broader immunity from civil liability than do governors, see p. 1333, *infra*.

adjudication of the claim for redress and left the protection of executive branch officials to the legislature.

Still, nineteenth century courts did recognize limits on official liability, applying something like the ministerial-discretionary distinction adverted to in Marbury v. Madison, 5 U.S. (1 Cranch) 137 (1803). These doctrines treated the legislature as competent to invest officials with delegated power to make discretionary decisions that, once announced, were immune from judicial review. So long as the official acted within the bounds of the discretion conferred, the official's action was deemed lawful, unless it willfully injured another or exceeded constitutional limits. Accounting for some ebbs and flows in the Court's conception of what was meant by discretionary, see Woolhandler, *Patterns of Official Immunity and Accountability*, 37 Case W.Res.L.Rev. 396 (1987), the officer's discretionary judgment would control within the bounds of a lawful delegation, see Spalding v. Vilas, 161 U.S. 483 (1896).

Such quasi-judicial immunity did not attach to ministerial actions or to positive government wrongs by law enforcement officials. In broad terms and allowing for some changes in the definition of the categories over time, ministerial actions were those that the courts deemed lacking in any discretionary component; they were compelled by clear law (much the way Marbury's right to an office was said to be complete and thus enforceable through mandamus). Positive government wrongs were those that invaded rights of liberty and property; tortious invasions of bodily integrity or property typified the category. See Engdahl, *Immunity and Accountability for Positive Governmental Wrongs,* 44 U.Colo.L.Rev. 1 (1972); Woolhandler, *supra*, at 437; see generally Jaffe, Judicial Control of Administrative Action 235 (1965) (distinguishing between summary government action, such as that to seize property for a tax sale, and adjudicatory action, such as judicial proceedings brought to establish a taxpayer's liability). For suits brought to compel ministerial action or to redress positive government wrongs, no discretionary function defense was available, even where the officer exercised broad discretion. See Buck v. Colbath, 70 U.S. 334 (1865) (federal marshal held strictly liable for wrongful seizure of property in execution of a court judgment notwithstanding the Court's recognition of the breadth of discretion marshals must exercise in carrying out their duties). Good faith was also largely beside the point. See, *e.g.*, Shanley v. Wells, 71 Ill. 78, 81 (1873) (affirming jury verdict for wrongful arrest by Chicago police officer and explaining that if "the plaintiff was assaulted and beaten, or imprisoned, by the defendant, without authority of law, it cannot be doubted that he is entitled to recover, whatever may have been the defendant's motives").

Precursors to official immunity appear in the nineteenth-century system of remedies. Thus, Professors Fallon and Meltzer point to doctrines of absolute immunity (discussed below) that were thought to immunize judges and legislators from all tort-based individual liability. Fallon & Meltzer, *New Law, Non-Retroactivity, and Constitutional*

Remedies, 104 Harv.L.Rev. 1731 (1991). Professor Kent identifies pockets of law protecting good faith official acts from liability in the context of maritime torts. Kent, *Lessons for Bivens and Qualified Immunity Debates from Nineteenth-Century Damages Litigation Against Federal Officers*, 96 Notre Dame L.Rev. 1755 (2021). Pointing to treatises on officer litigation that appeared in the late nineteenth century, Keller argues that forms of immunity took root in common law. Keller, *Qualified and Absolute Immunity at Common Law*, 73 Stan.L.Rev. 1337 (2021). For the suggestion that Keller's authorities recognize the legality of official action taken within the boundaries of discretion lawfully conferred, rather than an immunity for officers who violate the law, see Baude, *Is Quasi-Judicial Immunity Qualified Immunity?*, 74 Stan.L.Rev. Online 115 (2022); Pfander, *Zones of Discretion at Common Law*, 116 Nw.U.L.Rev. Online 148 (2021).

(2) The Rise of Policy-Based Immunity in the Twentieth Century. Courts began to recognize forms of official immunity in the twentieth century as the product of a broader balance of policy considerations. In one oft-cited example, Gregoire v. Biddle, 177 F.2d 579 (2d Cir.1949) (L. Hand, J.) upheld the absolute prosecutorial immunity of the Attorney General, and mid-level Justice Department officials, in a suit claiming that the defendants had, with malice and without justification, falsely imprisoned the plaintiff. As Judge Hand explained:

"There must indeed be means of punishing public officers who have been truant to their duties; but that is quite another matter from exposing such as have been honestly mistaken to suit by anyone who has suffered from their errors. As is so often the case, the answer must be found in a balance between the evils inevitable in either alternative. In this instance it has been thought in the end better to leave unredressed the wrongs done by dishonest officers than to subject those who try to do their duty to the constant dread of retaliation."

The Court first considered the extension of policy-based immunity to constitutional tort claims under § 1983 in Tenney v. Brandhove, 341 U.S. 367 (1951). There, the Court immunized state legislators from suit for actions taken in a legislative capacity after concluding that the enacting Congress in 1871 must have meant to incorporate existing immunity doctrines. See also Pierson v. Ray, 386 U.S. 547, 554–55 (1967) (stating that the legislative history of the Civil Rights Act did not support the notion that Congress meant to abrogate the common law doctrine of judicial immunity). The Court subsequently characterized Tenney as "establish[ing] that § 1983 is to be read in harmony with general principles of tort immunities and defenses rather than in derogation of them." Imbler v. Pachtman, 424 U.S. 409, 418 (1976).

The legislative and judicial immunities at issue in Tenney and Pierson were accepted features of the nineteenth century dispensation. Extension of immunity to executive branch officials posed a different question. Yet Pierson v. Ray also held that police officers sued for false arrest had a defense of "good faith and probable cause," by analogy to defenses at common law. The Court first used the term "qualified immunity" in Scheuer v. Rhodes, 416 U.S. 232, 243 (1974), indicating that the doctrine's contours would depend on "the scope of discretion and responsibilities of the office and all the circumstances as they reasonably appeared at the time of the action on which liability is sought to be based." For doubts that common law justifies the recognition of qualified immunity defenses to liability imposed by a statute that says nothing on the subject, see Reinert, *Qualified Immunity's Flawed Foundation*, 111 Calif.L.Rev. 201 (2023) (questioning the Court's presumptive allowance of qualified immunity both as a matter of statutory text and of then-governing canons of statutory interpretation); Baude, *Is Qualified Immunity Unlawful?*, 106 Calif.L.Rev. 45 (2018).

Harlow v. Fitzgerald

457 U.S. 800 (1982).

Noted whistleblower Arthur (Ernie) Fitzgerald was discharged from his position in the Air Force after testifying before Congress about cost overruns. He sued President Richard Nixon and two presidential aides, Harlow and Butterfield, seeking damages under the Bivens doctrine for retaliatory discharge in violation of his First Amendment rights. The Supreme Court dismissed Fitzgerald's claim against Nixon, applying the doctrine of absolute presidential immunity. See Nixon v. Fitzgerald, 457 U.S. 731 (1982), p. 1335, *infra*. But the Court refused to extend such absolute immunity to Harlow and Butterfield, taking the position that for most executive branch officials, "qualified immunity represents the norm." Then the Court articulated a new qualified immunity standard that switched from a subjective assessment of official good faith to an objective inquiry into the clarity of established law.

In justifying continued application of a qualified immunity doctrine, the Court recognized competing interests. On the one hand, "in situations of abuse of office, an action for damages may offer the only realistic avenue for vindication of constitutional guarantees." On the other hand, "claims frequently run against the innocent as well as the guilty—at a cost not only to the defendant officials, but to society as a whole." Social costs include "the expenses of litigation, the diversion of official energy from pressing public issues, and the deterrence of able citizens from acceptance of public office." Finally, the Court expressed concern lest the fear of being sued will "dampen the ardor of all but the most resolute, or the most irresponsible" public officials.

In attempting to strike the proper balance, the Court observed that its prior cases had defined qualified immunity by reference to the official's state of mind. Thus, its prior cases asked if the official "should have known" that the conduct in question would violate constitutional rights or took the action "with the malicious intention" to cause a deprivation of rights or injury. But because these subjective inquiries could complicate an official's motion for summary judgment, given the fact-based quality of state-of-mind issues, the Court deemed them inconsistent with the goal of ensuring that "insubstantial claims should not proceed to trial." Apart from complicating summary adjudication, broad-ranging discovery into subjective motivation could be "disruptive of effective government." The Court accordingly pronounced a new standard: "we conclude today that bare allegations of malice should not suffice to subject government officials either to the costs of trial or to the burdens of broad-reaching discovery. We therefore hold that government officials performing discretionary functions, generally are shielded from liability for civil damages insofar as their conduct does not violate clearly established statutory or constitutional rights of which a reasonable person would have known."

The Court explained that it did not intend to license "lawless conduct." The interest in deterring unlawful conduct and in compensating victims was "protected by a test that focuses on the objective legal reasonableness of an official's acts." Thus, official conduct that evidently violates constitutional or statutory rights will support a claim for relief. "But where an official's duties legitimately require action in which clearly established rights are not implicated, the public interest may be better served by action taken "with independence and without fear of consequences." Three Justices concurred separately, expressing agreement with the substantive standard articulated. Only Chief Justice Burger dissented, arguing that presidential aides should receive absolute immunity, comparable to the absolute immunity accorded legislative aides in Gravel v. United States, 408 U.S. 606 (1972), p. 1332, *infra*.

Kisela v. Hughes

584 U.S. 100 (2018).
On writ of certiorari to the United States Court of Appeals for the Ninth Circuit.

[In a per curiam opinion, the Court reversed a Ninth Circuit decision that would have allowed Amy Hughes to pursue a Fourth Amendment excessive force suit under § 1983 against Andrew Kisela, a Tucson, Arizona police officer.]

* * * In May 2010, someone in Hughes' neighborhood called 911 to report that a woman was hacking a tree with a kitchen knife. Kisela and another police officer, Alex Garcia, heard about the report over the radio in their patrol car and responded. A few minutes later the person who had called 911 flagged down the officers; gave them a description of the woman with the knife; and told them the woman had been acting erratically. About the same time, a third police officer, Lindsay Kunz, arrived on her bicycle.

Garcia spotted a woman, later identified as Sharon Chadwick, standing next to a car in the driveway of a nearby house. A chain-link fence with a locked gate separated Chadwick from the officers. The officers then saw another woman, Hughes, emerge from the house carrying a large knife at her side. Hughes matched the description of the woman who had been seen hacking a tree. Hughes walked toward Chadwick and stopped no more than six feet from her.

All three officers drew their guns. At least twice they told Hughes to drop the knife. Viewing the record in the light most favorable to Hughes, Chadwick said "take it easy" to both Hughes and the officers. Hughes appeared calm, but she did not acknowledge the officers' presence or drop the knife. The top bar of the chain-link fence blocked Kisela's line of fire, so he dropped to the ground and shot Hughes four times through the fence. Then the officers jumped the fence, handcuffed Hughes, and called paramedics, who transported her to a hospital. There she was treated for non-life-threatening injuries. Less than a minute had transpired from the moment the officers saw Chadwick to the moment Kisela fired shots.

* * * After the shooting, the officers discovered that Chadwick and Hughes were roommates, that Hughes had a history of mental illness, and that Hughes had been upset with Chadwick over a $20 debt. In an affidavit produced during discovery, Chadwick said that a few minutes before the shooting her boyfriend had told her Hughes was threatening to kill Chadwick's dog, named Bunny. Chadwick "came home to find" Hughes "somewhat distressed," and Hughes was in the house holding Bunny "in one hand and a kitchen knife in the other." Hughes asked Chadwick if she "wanted [her] to use the knife on the dog." The officers knew none of this, though. Chadwick went outside to get $20 from her car, which is when the officers first saw her. In her affidavit Chadwick said that she did not feel endangered at any time. Based on her experience as Hughes' roommate, Chadwick stated that Hughes "occasionally has episodes in which she acts inappropriately," but "she is only seeking attention." * * *

In Graham v. Connor, 490 U.S. 386, 396 (1989), the Court held that the question whether an officer has used excessive force "requires careful attention to the facts and circumstances of each particular case, including the severity of the crime at issue, whether the suspect poses an immediate threat to the safety of the officers or others, and whether he is actively resisting arrest or attempting to evade arrest by flight." "The 'reasonableness' of a particular use of force must be judged from the perspective of a reasonable officer on the scene, rather than with the 20/20 vision of hindsight." *Ibid.* And "[t]he calculus of reasonableness must embody allowance for the fact that police officers are often forced to make split-second judgments—in circumstances that are tense, uncertain, and rapidly evolving—about the amount of force that is necessary in a particular situation." *Id.*, at 396–397.

Here, the Court need not, and does not, decide whether Kisela violated the Fourth Amendment when he used deadly force against Hughes. For even assuming a Fourth Amendment violation occurred—a proposition that is not at all evident—on these facts Kisela was at least entitled to qualified immunity.

"Qualified immunity attaches when an official's conduct does not violate clearly established statutory or constitutional rights of which a reasonable person would have known." White v. Pauly, 580 U.S. 73, 78–

79 (2017) (per curiam) (alterations and internal quotation marks omitted). "Because the focus is on whether the officer had fair notice that her conduct was unlawful, reasonableness is judged against the backdrop of the law at the time of the conduct." Brosseau v. Haugen, 543 U.S. 194, 198 (2004) (per curiam).

Although "this Court's caselaw does not require a case directly on point for a right to be clearly established, existing precedent must have placed the statutory or constitutional question beyond debate." White, 580 U.S., at 79. "In other words, immunity protects all but the plainly incompetent or those who knowingly violate the law." *Ibid.* (internal quotation marks omitted). This Court has " 'repeatedly told courts—and the Ninth Circuit in particular—not to define clearly established law at a high level of generality.' " City and County of San Francisco v. Sheehan, 575 U.S. 600, 613 (2015) (quoting Ashcroft v. al-Kidd, 563 U.S. 731, 742 (2011)).

"[S]pecificity is especially important in the Fourth Amendment context, where the Court has recognized that it is sometimes difficult for an officer to determine how the relevant legal doctrine, here excessive force, will apply to the factual situation the officer confronts." Mullenix v. Luna, 577 U.S. 7, 12 (2015) (per curiam) (internal quotation marks omitted). Use of excessive force is an area of the law "in which the result depends very much on the facts of each case," and thus police officers are entitled to qualified immunity unless existing precedent "squarely governs" the specific facts at issue. *Id.*, at 13 (internal quotation marks omitted and emphasis deleted). Precedent involving similar facts can help move a case beyond the otherwise "hazy border between excessive and acceptable force" and thereby provide an officer notice that a specific use of force is unlawful. *Id.*, at 18 (internal quotation marks omitted).

"Of course, general statements of the law are not inherently incapable of giving fair and clear warning to officers." White, 580 U.S., at 79. But the general rules set forth in "Garner and Graham do not by themselves create clearly established law outside an 'obvious case.' " *Ibid.* Where constitutional guidelines seem inapplicable or too remote, it does not suffice for a court simply to state that an officer may not use unreasonable and excessive force, deny qualified immunity, and then remit the case for a trial on the question of reasonableness. An officer "cannot be said to have violated a clearly established right unless the right's contours were sufficiently definite that any reasonable official in the defendant's shoes would have understood that he was violating it." Plumhoff v. Rickard, 572 U.S. 765, 778–779 (2014). * * *

Kisela says he shot Hughes because, although the officers themselves were in no apparent danger, he believed she was a threat to Chadwick. Kisela had mere seconds to assess the potential danger to Chadwick. He was confronted with a woman who had just been seen hacking a tree with a large kitchen knife and whose behavior was erratic enough to cause a concerned bystander to call 911 and then flag down

Kisela and Garcia. Kisela was separated from Hughes and Chadwick by a chain-link fence; Hughes had moved to within a few feet of Chadwick; and she failed to acknowledge at least two commands to drop the knife. Those commands were loud enough that Chadwick, who was standing next to Hughes, heard them. This is far from an obvious case in which any competent officer would have known that shooting Hughes to protect Chadwick would violate the Fourth Amendment.

[The Court next parsed a series of Ninth Circuit decisions and found that none of them provided Kisela with notice that the specific use of force was unlawful.]

For these reasons, the petition for certiorari is granted; the judgment of the Court of Appeals is reversed; and the case is remanded for further proceedings consistent with this opinion.

It is so ordered.

■ JUSTICE SOTOMAYOR, with whom JUSTICE GINSBURG joins, dissenting.

[After restating the Court's excessive force precedents, Justice Sotomayor applied them to the use of force by Kisela.]

First, Hughes committed no crime and was not suspected of committing a crime. The officers were responding to a "check welfare" call, which reported no criminal activity, and the officers did not observe any illegal activity while at the scene. The mere fact that Hughes held a kitchen knife down at her side with the blade pointed away from Chadwick hardly elevates the situation to one that justifies deadly force.

Second, a jury could reasonably conclude that Hughes presented no immediate or objective threat to Chadwick or the other officers. It is true that Kisela had received a report that a woman matching Hughes' description had been acting erratically. But the police officers themselves never witnessed any erratic conduct. Instead, when viewed in the light most favorable to Hughes, the record evidence of what the police encountered paints a calmer picture. It shows that Hughes was several feet from Chadwick and even farther from the officers, she never made any aggressive or threatening movements, and she appeared "composed and content" during the brief encounter.

Third, Hughes did not resist or evade arrest. Based on this record, there is significant doubt as to whether she was aware of the officers' presence at all, and evidence suggests that Hughes did not hear the officers' swift commands to drop the knife.

Finally, the record suggests that Kisela could have, but failed to, use less intrusive means before deploying deadly force. For instance, Hughes submitted expert testimony concluding that Kisela should have used his Taser and that shooting his gun through the fence was dangerous because a bullet could have fragmented against the fence and hit Chadwick or his fellow officers. Consistent with that assessment, the other two officers on the scene declined to fire at Hughes, and one of them explained that he was inclined to use "some of the lesser means" than shooting, including verbal commands, because he believed there was time "[t]o try to talk [Hughes] down." * * *

Taken together, the foregoing facts would permit a jury to conclude that Kisela acted outside the bounds of the Fourth Amendment by shooting Hughes four times. * * *

[Justice Sotomayor went on to criticize the majority for intervening in a case in which the Ninth Circuit had not erred at all, let along erred at a level that would justify a summary reversal.] * * *

The majority today exacerbates [a] troubling asymmetry. Its decision is not just wrong on the law; it also sends an alarming signal to law enforcement officers and the public. It tells officers that they can shoot first and think later, and it tells the public that palpably unreasonable conduct will go unpunished. Because there is nothing right or just under the law about this, I respectfully dissent.

NOTE ON JUSTIFICATIONS FOR QUALIFIED IMMUNITY

Qualified immunity, especially as applied to suits seeking redress for use of excessive force by law enforcement officers, has attracted broad criticism but retains substantial support in the Court's decisional law. Consider whether the following legal and policy-based arguments offer a persuasive defense for the doctrine.

(1) Defining the Elements of a Constitutional Tort Claim. Note the contrast between nineteenth century's reliance on common law tort claims and the twentieth century's turn to constitutional torts under § 1983. Monroe v. Pape hastened the transition from a private tort-based law of government accountability to one focused on direct enforcement of constitutional rights. In defining the elements of constitutional tort, the Court has exercised some freedom of choice, often incorporating common law rules as it calibrates the remedial potency of the constitutional rights at issue. Some defend the Court's largely judge-made body of qualified immunity law as an appropriate response to a largely judge-made body of remedial rights. See, *e.g.*, Crawford-El v. Britton, 523 U.S. 574, 611 (1998) (Scalia, J., dissenting) (defending judge-made qualified immunity doctrine as necessary to temper Monroe's extension of constitutional tort liability well beyond § 1983's terms). As the source of the remedial rights invoked in Harlow, the Bivens doctrine also rests on what some portray as "judicial legislation" and might, on the same theory, warrant judicial trimming. Consider Baude, *Is Qualified Immunity Unlawful?*, 106 Calif.L.Rev. 45 (2018) (contesting the view that qualified immunity represents a legitimate compensating adjustment); Mims-Crocker, *Qualified Immunity and Constitutional Structure,* 117 Mich.L.Rev. 1405 (2019) (same).

Some have argued that the Court should transform the clear-law requirement from a defense to an element of the plaintiff's constitutional tort claim. See Wyatt v. Cole, 504 U.S. 158, 172 (1992) (Kennedy, J., concurring) (explaining it was "something of a misnomer to describe the common law as creating a good-faith defense; we are in fact concerned with the essence of the wrong itself, with the essential elements of the tort"). Compare Wood v. Moss, 572 U.S. 744 (2014) (explaining that "the doctrine of qualified immunity protects government officials from liability for civil damages 'unless a plaintiff pleads facts showing (1) that the official violated a statutory or constitutional right, and (2) that the right was "clearly established" at the time of the challenged conduct' "). Would such a change in the allocation of the burden of pleading make qualified immunity easier to understand or defend?

(2) Legal Change and Prospectivity. Others defend qualified immunity as a tool to facilitate changes in constitutional doctrine. See Fallon & Meltzer, *New Law, Non-Retroactivity, and Constitutional Remedies*, 104 Harv.L.Rev. 1731 (1991); Jeffries, *The Right-Remedy Gap in Constitutional Law*, 109 Yale L.J. 87 (1999). On this view, the Harlow v. Fitzgerald clear law requirement immunizes officers (and their indemnifying employers) from the cost of failing to anticipate changes in the law and avoids unfairly imposing damages liability for that failure of foresight. In addition, the doctrine "fosters the development of constitutional law" by lowering the cost of adjusting rules of constitutional law. Jeffries, *supra*. Landmark decisions, such as Miranda v. Arizona, 384 U.S. 436 (1966), and Brown v. Board of Education, 347 U.S. 483 (1954), might have failed to gain the support of a majority of Justices had the Court been forced, as the price of implementing them, to order the release all those convicted on the basis of un-Mirandized statements or the payment of compensation for the manifold injuries incident to government-sponsored segregation.

In reflecting on qualified immunity and legal change, consider the remedial moderation reflected in the Brown II formula, "all deliberate speed," the rise of massive resistance, and the challenges of implementing the Brown decision. Klarman, From Jim Crow to Civil Rights: The Supreme Court and the Struggle for Racial Equality (2004). At the time Brown came down, some argued that an award of damages to students and their parents against principals and school boards, perhaps modeled on those allowed for denial of the right to vote, might be more effective than alternative remedies in securing compliance. Leflar & Davis, *Segregation in the Public Schools— 1953*, 67 Harv.L.Rev. 377, 425–26 (1954).

(3) Remedial Equilibration. Related to the arguments for prospectivity and constitutional development, scholars have identified qualified immunity as one of several legal doctrines by which the Court adjusts the remedial potency of the constitutional rights it chooses to recognize. See Levinson, *Rights Essentialism and Remedial Equilibration*, 99 Colum.L.Rev. 857 (1999). Fallon, *Asking the Right Questions About Officer Immunity*, 80 Fordham L.Rev. 479, 480 (2011) observes: "[O]fficial immunity is not a variable among constants but * * * one potential variable among others. * * * In the absence of official immunity, even some currently well-established constitutional rights and authorizations to sue to enforce them would likely *shrink*, and sometimes appropriately so." To adjust or eliminate qualified immunity might invite a narrower definition of the elements of a constitutional tort claim or a scaling back of the remedies available on proof of an invasion. Recall the discussion of the Court's control over the elements of a constitutional tort claim, pp. 1303–1307, *supra*.

One can accept the inevitability of some equilibration without necessarily embracing its legitimacy in all contexts or its wisdom as applied. One broad, equilibrating move—the across-the-board application of qualified immunity to all constitutional tort claims, without regard to office or context—reflects the Court's preference for declaratory style adjudication and distrust of damage awards. Kent, *Are Damages Different?: Bivens and National Security*, 87 S.Calif.L.Rev. 1123 (2014) (noting the Court's preference for law declaration). Yet such a move may foreclose the only available remedy for positive government wrongs and hamper the development of law. See Jeffries, *Reversing the Order of Battle in Constitutional Torts*, 2009 Sup.Ct.Rev. 115, 120 ("[R]epeated invocation of qualified immunity will reduce the meaning of the Constitution to the lowest plausible conception of its content.").

(4) Fault and Fair Warning. The Court has defended Harlow's clear-law requirement as ensuring that officers will have fair notice or warning that their conduct violates the law. See Brosseau v. Haugen, 543 U.S. 194, 198 (2004) (per curiam) ("Because the focus is on whether the officer had fair notice that her conduct was unlawful, reasonableness is judged against the backdrop of the law at the time of the conduct"). For a development of the fair warning justification, see Chapman, *Fair Warning, the Rule of Law, and Reforming Qualified Immunity*, 75 Fla.L.Rev. 1 (2023). But see Baude, Paragraph (1), *supra*, Calif.L.Rev.at 73 (concluding that the doctrine of lenity as connected to the interest in fair warning does not translate well to civil proceedings under § 1983). Jeffries, *The Liability Rule for Constitutional Torts*, 99 Va.L.Rev. 207 (2013), argues for shifting the immunity inquiry "from whether the defendant violated a 'clearly established' right to whether the defendant's actions were 'clearly unconstitutional.'" According to Professor Jeffries, the latter standard would "signal a less technical requirement, less tied to specific precedent, and more accommodating of notice through 'common social duty'" in cases involving egregious official misconduct but no closely on-point judicial precedents clearly establishing constitutional rights.

(5) Preventing Ruinous Personal Liability and Overdeterrence. In expanding qualified immunity, in cases such as Pierson v. Ray and Harlow v. Fitzgerald, the Court has assumed, following Judge Hand in Gregoire v. Biddle, 177 F.2d 579 (2d Cir.1949) (L. Hand, J.), p. 1313, *supra*, that personal capacity suits threaten potentially ruinous personal liability. Immunity has been said to moderate that threat, encouraging individuals to accept government jobs and carry out their assignments with suitable ardor and zeal. But the Court has announced these justifications for immunity without any apparent consideration of the practice of indemnification.

An important empirical study, Schwartz, *Police Indemnification*, 89 N.Y.U.L.Rev. 885 (2014), reveals a widespread governmental practice of indemnifying officers sued for tortious misconduct. Based on a survey involving forty-four of the nation's seventy largest law enforcement agencies and thirty-seven of seventy randomly selected smaller jurisdictions, Professor Schwartz found that between 2006 and 2011, in the over 9200 suits against officers in the larger jurisdictions that ended in either damages awards or settlements (which collectively totaled over $730 million), "officers paid just .02% of the dollars awarded to plaintiffs in police misconduct suits. In thirty-seven small and mid-sized law enforcement agencies, officers never contributed to settlements or judgments [that totaled over $9 million]. No officer in any of the eighty-one jurisdictions satisfied a punitive damages judgment entered against him. * * * And officers were indemnified even when they were disciplined, terminated, or prosecuted for their misconduct."

Based on her findings, Professor Schwartz argues that qualified immunity is unnecessary to protect officials from unfair liability or to avoid overdeterrence and concludes that it should be "eliminated or restricted." According to her, "[w]hen officers are indemnified * * * there is less injustice in 'subjecting to liability an officer who is required, by the legal obligations of his position, to exercise discretion'" (quoting Owen v. City of Independence, 445 U.S. 622, 654 (1980)). A study of practice in connection with Bivens suits brought against officers of the federal Bureau of Prisons reveals a similar pattern of government payment. See Pfander, Schwartz & Reinert, *The Myth of Personal Liability: Who Pays When Bivens Claims Succeed?*, 72 Stan.L.Rev. 561 (2020) (reporting that in over 95% of successful claims "the officials named as defendants made no contribution to the payment of settlements and judgments").

NOTE ON POLICE MISCONDUCT AND CLEARLY ESTABLISHED LAW

(1) Qualified Immunity and Police Misconduct. For an illustration of how the judicial assessment of law enforcement practices has changed over the decades, compare the decision in Kisela v. Hughes with that in Buck v. Colbath, 70 U.S. 334 (1865). In Buck, the Court recognized that federal marshals must exercise discretion in performing their official duties but nonetheless held the marshal liable for mistaken seizure of property in satisfaction of a judgment. The Kisela Court ruled, by contrast, that the law in the Ninth Circuit did not establish with the necessary clarity that Officer Kisela was wrong to shoot in the circumstances of that case. In the Court's telling, liability should extend only to the "plainly incompetent or those who knowingly violate the law." See generally Baude, *Is Qualified Immunity Unlawful?*, 106 Calif.L.Rev. 45, 82 (2018) (reporting, as of that writing, that the Supreme Court found a violation of clearly established law in just two of thirty qualified immunity cases since 1982).[1]

In evaluating the clearly established law standard in police misconduct cases, consider what role legal precedents play in shaping the conduct of

----

[1] For the conclusion that the "discretionary function" element of Harlow's qualified immunity standard was met when an officer terminated a subordinate in the state highway patrol, see Davis v. Scherer, 468 U.S. 183, 196 n.14 (1984) ("A law that fails to specify the precise action that the official must take in each instance creates only discretionary authority; and that authority remains discretionary [and entitled to qualified immunity protections] however egregiously it is abused.").

police officers. The officer in Buck v. Colbath was expected to know the law governing attachment of property and to apply it correctly at his peril. Nuanced understanding of the law does not necessarily shape official use of force today. Schwartz, *Qualified Immunity's Boldest Lie*, 88 U.Chi.L.Rev. 605 (2021), reports on an empirical study of the training and educational materials provided to California law enforcement officials. While police departments regularly inform their officers about watershed decisions, they do not update officers about the application of those decisions "in different factual scenarios." Even assuming better information, officers may not consult legal precedents when making decisions about the use of force and other aspects of policing.

(2) Qualified Immunity and the Meaning of Clearly Established Law. As Kisela confirms, Harlow makes the availability of qualified immunity turn on whether the plaintiff has alleged a violation of "clearly established" federal law. According to the Court in Ashcroft v. Al-Kidd, 563 U.S. 731, 741 (2011), a "government official's conduct violates clearly established law when, at the time of the challenged conduct, '[t]he contours of [a] right [are] sufficiently clear' that every 'reasonable official would [have understood] that what he is doing violates that right.' We do not require a case directly on point, but existing precedent must have placed the statutory or constitutional question beyond debate." A variety of factors inform the analysis, including Supreme Court and circuit court authority, the context in which the officer acted, and the specificity with which relevant courts have spoken to the legality of official conduct.

(a) Supreme Court Decisions and the Level of Generality Problem. Supreme Court decisions clearly establish controlling principles of law. But the Court has repeatedly admonished lower courts that, as in Kisela, qualified immunity will attach unless the controlling precedents provide notice "sufficiently definite that any reasonable official in the defendant's shoes would have understood that he was violating it." One leading case, Anderson v. Creighton, 483 U.S. 635 (1987), arose in the context of an unquestioned Fourth Amendment rule barring a warrantless search of a home absent probable cause or exigent circumstances. Reversing a ruling by the court of appeals, the Supreme Court held, 6–3, that the availability of qualified immunity should turn not on the general right, but on its application to particular facts.

(b) Lower Court Disagreement and "Clearly Established" Law. Lower federal courts may adopt varying interpretations of Supreme Court's decisions, creating uncertainty as to the content of the law. The Court cited disagreement among lower court judges as its principal ground for upholding a qualified immunity defense in Safford Unified School District #1 v. Redding, 557 U.S. 364 (2009). In an opinion by Justice Souter, the Court first held that the defendant school officials had violated the Fourth Amendment when they strip-searched a thirteen-year-old middle school student without adequate reason to suspect her of hiding dangerous contraband in her underwear. But the defendants possessed qualified immunity, the Court said, largely because lower courts had "reached divergent conclusions regarding how" the controlling precedent allowing school searches under a reasonableness standard, New Jersey v. T.L.O., 469 U.S. 325 (1985), applied to strip searches: "We would not suggest that entitlement to qualified immunity is the guaranteed product of disuniform views of the law in the other federal, or state, courts, and the fact that a single judge, or even a group of judges, disagrees about the contours of a right does not automatically render the law unclear. That said, however, the cases viewing strip searches differently from the way we see them are numerous enough, with well-reasoned majority and dissenting opinions, to counsel doubt that we were sufficiently clear in the prior statement of the law." Justice Stevens, joined by Justice Ginsburg, filed an opinion concurring in part and dissenting in part, asserting that "the clarity of a well-established right should not depend on whether jurists have misread our precedents." (Justice Ginsburg also filed an opinion concurring in part and dissenting in part; Justice Thomas filed an opinion concurring in the judgment and dissenting in part.)

When, if ever, would "disuniform views" among lower courts fail to demonstrate that the law was not "clearly established?" In thinking about this question, note that in Groh v. Ramirez, 540 U.S. 551 (2004), a five-Justice majority held that the defendant had violated clearly established rights, even though Justices Scalia and Thomas concluded that the defendants had not violated the Constitution at all.

(c) **Law of the Circuit and Clearly Established Law.** Consider the possibility that a circuit court precedent might conflict with the decisions of one or more other circuits and still clearly establish the law *within that circuit* for qualified immunity purposes. One might argue that, just as federal district courts within the circuit would be bound to follow circuit law, so too would state and federal officials within the circuit have notice of the law's content. At least some decisions point in that direction. For example, in Camreta v. Greene, 563 U.S. 692 (2011), the Court agreed to hear an appeal from a Ninth Circuit decision holding that Oregon child protective services workers must obtain a warrant before interviewing a school child about domestic sexual abuse. In a twist, however, the appellant school officials had won below, persuading the Ninth Circuit that they were entitled to qualified immunity because the law was not clear when they conducted the interview.

In concluding that the officers had standing to appeal despite the judgment of non-liability, the Court emphasized that the Ninth Circuit's decision would establish the law throughout the state and limit the investigative freedom of the officers going forward. That adverse impact was thought to confer standing to appeal. In so ruling, the Court appears to have assumed that a Ninth Circuit decision would establish clear law for the state, whatever else might have been said on the subject in other circuits and state courts. In Kisela v. Hughes, the Court analyzed Ninth Circuit precedent to determine the content of applicable law, apparently on the assumption that circuit precedent could clarify the law sufficiently to overcome the officer's qualified immunity defense.

Circuit court authority may have less clarifying power as to officers with a national portfolio, in contrast to the local officials in Camreta and Kisela whose official conduct occurred within the boundaries of a single state. See

Ashcroft v. al-Kidd, 563 U.S. 731, 746 (2011) (Kennedy, J., concurring) (opining that the Attorney General of the United States, as "[a] national officeholder" "need not abide by the most stringent standard adopted anywhere in the United States"). Imagine that the Attorney General and a county sheriff are both sued in the Ninth Circuit for ordering seizures that would be unreasonable under Ninth Circuit precedent. With the rise of joint state-federal criminal task forces, such a geographic approach to clear law could produce liability for a local official that the national official would not face. More generally, consider whether assigning authority to circuit court interpretations of federal law gives adequate weight to state court decisions (which may diverge from circuit law). Consider as well the fact that lower federal courts have no local lawmaking authority as to matters of federal law but apply, at least in theory, a body of federal law that aspires to national uniformity. See Bennett, *There Is No Such Thing as Circuit Law*, 107 Minn.L.Rev. 1681 (2023).

District court decisions have less clarifying power altogether. See Ashcroft v. al-Kidd, 563 U.S. 731, 741 (2011) (stating in dictum that a single district court decision could not "clearly establish" that a course of action by the Attorney General violates the Constitution).

(d) Clear Law in Cases of Deliberate Misconduct. Outside the context of use-of-force cases that call for an assessment of split-second decisions, the Court has found that the law sufficiently clear to overcome claims of qualified immunity as to some deliberate official misconduct. In Taylor v. Riojas, 592 U.S. 7 (2020), the Court issued a per curiam opinion reversing a grant of qualified immunity to prison officials who allegedly confined an incarcerated person "in a pair of shockingly unsanitary cells" teeming with human waste. Despite the absence of specifically on-point authority, "no reasonable correctional officer" could have thought the defendants' alleged conduct constitutionally permissible "under the extreme circumstances of this case").[2] Compare McCoy v. Alamu, 141 S.Ct. 1364 (2021) (treating Taylor as relevant in prison excessive force case). See also Hope v. Pelzer, 536 U.S. 730 (2002) (holding in the absence of controlling circuit authority that an Alabama prison guard violated clearly established Eighth Amendment law by tying the plaintiff to a hitching post without a shirt for seven hours in the hot sun, with only one or two water breaks and no bathroom break).

(e) Reliance on a Judicial Warrant. In Malley v. Briggs, 475 U.S. 335 (1986), a police officer presented arrest warrants to a state judge, who approved and signed them. The officer was later sued under § 1983 for having caused the arrest of individuals without probable cause. The Supreme Court refused to hold that the officer was absolutely immune because he had relied "on the judgment of a judicial officer in finding that probable cause exist[ed] and hence issuing the warrant." Though in an ideal system no judge would approve a defective application, it was not unreasonable to minimize the risk of error by holding an officer liable if "the warrant application is so lacking in indicia of probable cause as to render

---

[2]   On the implications of Taylor, see Laurin, *Reading Taylor's Tea Leaves: The Future of Qualified Immunity*, 17 Duke J.Const'n.L. & Pub.Pol'y. 241 (2022).

official belief in its existence unreasonable." The Court remanded for application of the Harlow standard.[3] Contrast Malley with Messerschmidt v. Millender, 565 U.S. 535 (2012), where the Court viewed the magistrate's decision to issue a search warrant as normally establishing the objective legal reasonableness of its execution. The Court treated Malley as establishing an "exception" applicable only when "the magistrate so obviously erred that any reasonable officer would have recognized the error." In evaluating the Court's rule, consider how well the ex ante assessment by a neutral magistrate substitutes for the ex post judicial review of the warrant's legality that a suit under § 1983 would occasion.

(3) Order of Decision in Qualified Immunity Cases. Constitutional tort claims for damages present two questions: did the official violate the Constitution and was the relevant right established with the clarity necessary to overcome qualified immunity. After following a different approach, the Court ruled unanimously in Pearson v. Callahan, 555 U.S. 223, 236 (2009), that lower court judges "should be permitted to exercise their sound discretion in deciding which of the two prongs of the qualified immunity analysis should be addressed first in light of the particular circumstances in the particular case at hand." Lower court judges had rebelled against the prior rule, announced in Saucier v. Katz, 533 U.S. 194 (2001), which had inflexibly required them to decide the constitutional issue first and only then consider if the matter was clearly established. See Leval, *Judging Under the Constitution: Dicta About Dicta*, 81 N.Y.U.L.Rev. 1249 (2006) (explaining that a mandatory merits-first rule frequently required courts to address difficult issues of constitutional law that would have been easily avoided by a ruling on the absence of clear law). The Pearson Court recognized the value of avoidance and discretion but continued to regard the merits-first protocol as "often beneficial," especially in promoting the development of constitutional law as to "questions that do not frequently arise." For an assessment, see Jeffries, *The Order of Battle in Constitutional Torts*, 2009 S.Ct.Rev. 115.[4]

---

[3]   A closely divided Court has refused to recognize immunity for private parties acting under color of law. See Wyatt v. Cole, 504 U.S. 158 (1992); Richardson v. McKnight, 521 U.S. 399 (1997). In Filarsky v. Delia, 566 U.S. 377 (2012), however, a unanimous Court held that a person hired directly by the government to work on its behalf need not be a permanent or full-time employee in order to claim official immunity.

[4]   For defense of the Saucier approach, see Wells, *The "Order-of-Battle" in Constitutional Litigation*, 60 SMU L.Rev. 1539 (2007). Empirical studies disagree sharply about whether Saucier's order-of-decision rule had a significant impact in promoting the identification of new constitutional rights. Compare Leong, *The Saucier Qualified Immunity Experiment: An Empirical Analysis*, 36 Pepperdine L.Rev. 667, 670 (2009) (finding the "the decline in avoidance" mandated by Saucier "was accompanied only by a sharp increase in the percentage of cases in which courts explicitly held that no constitutional violation had occurred"), and Healy, *The Rise of Unnecessary Constitutional Rulings*, 83 N.C.L.Rev. 847, 930 (2005) (reporting similar findings), with Note, *An Empirical Analysis of Section 1983 Qualified Immunity Actions and Implications of Pearson v. Callahan*, 62 Stan.L.Rev. 523 (2010) (concluding that the frequency of rights-affirming outcomes—in which courts found that the plaintiffs had alleged the violation of a constitutional right—"jumped from 34.2% of all pre-Saucier dispositions to 50.4% of all post-Saucier dispositions").

Examining circuit court practice in the wake of Pearson v. Callahan, Sampsell-Jones & Yauch, *Measuring Pearson in the Circuits*, 80 Fordham L.Rev. 623 (2011), conclude that circuit courts that had the option of ruling only on the immunity question followed the Saucier approach of deciding the merits question anyway in over 68% of all cases that cited Pearson in

The order of decision introduces complexity on review of lower court decisions that accept Pearson's invitation to resolve the merits first. In Camreta v. Greene, *supra*, the Ninth Circuit ruled that the Fourth Amendment barred Camreta, a child services officer, from conducting a warrantless interview of a nine-year-old school child as part of a sexual abuse investigation. But the lower court went on to hold that qualified immunity blocked the suit; the law was not clear. The officer sought review in the Supreme Court, despite the fact that he had prevailed below. He argued that the court of appeals' ruling on the Fourth Amendment issue interfered with his capacity as a child services worker to protect his clients against abuse. The Court upheld its appellate jurisdiction, concluding that the officer had standing to contest the Ninth Circuit's decision even though he prevailed below.

Although the Court ultimately dismissed the proceeding as moot, it put in place structures by which it can exercise appellate oversight over lower courts that declare the content of constitutional law (as Pearson allows) as a prelude to dismissing for lack of clearly established law. But doing so came at some cost: a decision allowing prevailing parties to seek review on appeal. In assessing that choice, consider what would have happened if the Court had dismissed Camreta's appeal as one brought by a prevailing party. That decision would have left the Ninth Circuit decision intact as a source of clearly established law and would have subjected state officials to tort liability for failure to comply with the warrant requirement. True, an official like Camreta could appeal from the imposition of such liability and contest the constitutional rule in the Supreme Court. But other child services officers might choose instead to comply with the Ninth Circuit's rule. Should state officials have to violate clearly established circuit law to procure Supreme Court review?

(4) Official Immunity from Statutory Claims. In the last section of its opinion in Ziglar v. Abbasi, 582 U.S. 120 (2017), the Court rejected civil conspiracy claims under 42 U.S.C. § 1985(3), after concluding that qualified immunity applied to such claims and that the requisite clarity of law was not sufficiently established. Justice Thomas concurred, expressing doubt about qualified immunity without questioning its extension to federal statutory rights. *Id.* 158 (Thomas J., concurring). Congress can often impose money liability on the government for breach of a federal statute; normally, no doctrine of qualified immunity applies to such claims. What default rule should apply when Congress chooses to create a money remedy running against the government's officials instead? Consider Tanzin v. Tanvir, 592 U.S. 43 (2020) (interpreting the Religious Freedom Restoration Act to impose personal liability on officers but declining to address the qualified immunity issue). For an argument against qualified immunity in that setting, see Godfrey, *The Religious Freedom Restoration Act, Federal Prison Officials,*

the calendar years 2009 and 2010. See also Beermann, *Qualified Immunity and Constitutional Avoidance,* 2009 S.Ct.Rev. 139 (criticizing Pearson for giving lower courts "standardless, unreviewable discretion" about the order of decision in qualified immunity cases and urging a presumption in favor of ruling on the merits first); Jeffries, *supra* (arguing for a merits-first approach in cases involving constitutional rights that are difficult to enforce except through suits for money damages).

and the Doctrinal Dinosaur of Qualified Immunity, 98 N.Y.U.L.Rev. 1045 (2023).

(5) Official Immunity in State Law Actions. The immunity of *state* officials in actions based on state law is itself governed by state law; absent wholly arbitrary action by the state, there is no distinctive federal interest. See Martinez v. California, 444 U.S. 277 (1980). This rule applies in actions that fall within the federal courts' jurisdiction. See, *e.g.*, Oyler v. National Guard Ass'n, 743 F.2d 545 (7th Cir.1984).

F. Absolute Immunity: Judges, Prosecutors, Legislators, Presidents

Unlike many executive branch officers, who enjoy qualified immunity, the law confers absolute immunity on judges, prosecutors, legislators, and the President of the United States. Absolute immunity means that such officials cannot be held liable for damages for conduct within the scope of their official duties under any circumstances, even if they intentionally or maliciously violate clearly established federal rights. Because an official with absolute immunity has no obligation to justify action taken, a suit barred by the doctrine can ordinarily be dismissed at the threshold. Absolute immunity thus eliminates the threat and burden of litigation and, in the unusual case in which a constitutional violation was caused by the actions of a single official, bars all civil recourse. (Aside from the President, as explored below, most officials remain subject to criminal sanctions, even if they enjoy absolute immunity from damages.)

(1) General Principles.

(a) Alternative Remedies. In many cases in which officials have been accorded absolute immunity, other forms of redress may be available. For example, in a decision upholding the absolute immunity of legislators, the Court clarified that the sergeant-at-arms—the official charged with executing legislative orders—was subject to liability in tort for compelling an individual to appear and testify before a committee of Congress. See Kilbourn v. Thompson, 103 U.S. 168, 196–97, 200 (1880) (recognizing legislative immunity but confirming that the assembly's sergeant-at-arms bore responsibility in tort for trespass or false arrest). Similarly, accounts of the development of absolute judicial immunity point to the fact that individuals injured by a judicial decision ordinarily have a firm right to seek appellate review. See Jeffries, *The Liability Rule for Constitutional Torts*, 99 Va.L.Rev. 207, 212 (2013) (absolute judicial immunity, like absolute legislative immunity, is justified by the existence of alternative remedies). Presidents enjoy an absolute immunity that the Court has declined to extend to presidential advisors and to state governors. See Harlow v. Fitzgerald, 457 U.S. 800 (1982) (according presidential advisors only a qualified immunity); Sheuer v. Rhodes, 416 U.S. 232 (1974) (rejecting absolute immunity for governors).

(b) Functions v. Offices. Although judicial and prosecutorial immunity are absolute, and officials engaging in executive functions are protected only by qualified immunity, the Court's decisions make clear that immunity attaches to functions, not offices. Accordingly, executive officials enjoy absolute judicial immunity from suit for actions taken in a judicial capacity. See, *e.g.*, Butz v. Economou, 438 U.S. 478 (1978). By contrast, judges have only qualified immunity when sued for non-judicial actions such as firing a probation officer. See Forrester v. White, 484 U.S. 219 (1988).

(c) Individual Capacity v. Official Capacity. Official immunities apply only in suits in which officials are sued in their "individual" capacities, meaning that damages are at least nominally sought from the officials themselves, rather than from government treasuries. (Damages actions against state and federal officials in their "official" capacities will often be barred by sovereign immunity.) When officials act outside the scope of office for their personal account, no governmental immunities attach to their conduct. Judges and legislators can be held liable for breach of a contract to purchase a private home and for negligent operation of a private automobile.

(2) Absolute Immunities Associated with the Judicial Process.

(a) Judicial Immunity. The considerations offered by the Court as justifications for absolute judicial immunity have been summarized as follows: "(1) the need for a judge to 'be free to act upon his own conviction, without apprehension of personal consequences to himself'; (2) the controversiality and importance of the competing interests adjudicated by judges and the likelihood that the loser, feeling aggrieved, would wish to retaliate; (3) the record-keeping to which self-protective judges would be driven in the absence of immunity; (4) the availability of alternative remedies, such as appeal and impeachment, for judicial wrongdoing; and (5) the ease with which bad faith can be alleged and made the basis for vexatious litigation." Schuck, Suing Government: Citizen Remedies for Official Wrongs 90 (1983) (citations omitted).

The only way to circumvent judicial immunity is to show that a judge was acting "in the clear absence of all jurisdiction" or was not performing a "judicial act." These tests, dating back at least to Bradley v. Fisher, 80 U.S. (13 Wall.) 335, 351 (1871), were applied in Stump v. Sparkman, 435 U.S. 349 (1978), in which an Indiana judge had approved *ex parte* a petition filed by parents of a fifteen-year-old girl to have her sterilized without her knowledge. When she later sued the judge for damages under § 1983, the Supreme Court ruled that he was absolutely immune: since he presided over a court of general jurisdiction, he had not acted wholly outside his jurisdiction, and he did not lose his immunity simply because no state statute specifically authorized his conduct.

The Court also rejected the argument that because the petition was never docketed or filed with the clerk, no hearing was held, and no guardian *ad litem* was appointed, the judge's approval of the petition was not a "judicial act." In the Court's view, whether a judge's action is a "judicial act" depends on whether (i) "it is a function normally performed by a judge," and (ii) "the expectations of the parties, *i.e.*, whether they dealt with the judge in his judicial capacity." The Court found both criteria to be met, noting as to the former that Indiana judges are often called upon to approve petitions about minors' affairs.

Justice Stewart, joined by Justices Marshall and Powell, wrote an angry dissent, arguing that *ex parte* approval of a parent's petition was not an act normally performed by Indiana judges. He continued by insisting that "false illusions as to a judge's power can hardly convert a judge's response to those illusions into a judicial act," and that "[a] judge is not free, like a loose cannon, to inflict indiscriminate damage whenever he announces that he is acting in his judicial capacity." Justice Powell's separate dissent emphasized that "[t]he complete absence of normal judicial process" made inoperative the assumption underlying judicial immunity that "there exist alternative forums and methods for vindicating [private] rights."

Since Stump, most of the cases finding judges not to have acted in a judicial capacity have involved off-beat situations. Compare Mireles v. Waco, 502 U.S. 9 (1991) (per curiam) (extending absolute immunity to a state judge who allegedly ordered police officers to seize "with excessive force," and bring to the judge's chambers, a public defender who had missed a calendar call, since it was a properly judicial function to direct officers to bring a person in the courthouse before a judge), with Zarcone v. Perry, 572 F.2d 52 (2d Cir.1978) (judge who ordered court officials to bring "in front of me in cuffs" the vendor of coffee that the judge thought tasted "putrid," and who then interrogated the vendor and threatened his "livelihood," acted outside his judicial capacity). But in Forrester v. White, Paragraph (1), *supra*, the Supreme Court unanimously ruled that a judge was acting in an administrative rather than a judicial capacity, and hence was not entitled to absolute immunity, when he fired a probation officer, allegedly on account of her sex and thus in violation of the Fourteenth Amendment.

(b) Absolute Prosecutorial Immunity. The purposes and scope of prosecutorial immunity are similar to those of judicial immunity. In Imbler v. Pachtman, 424 U.S. 409 (1976), a § 1983 action alleging that a state prosecutor had knowingly introduced perjured testimony, the Court found that prosecutorial immunity was well-established at common law and that absolute rather than qualified immunity was appropriate. Otherwise, a criminal defendant could "transform his resentment * * * into the ascription of improper and malicious actions to the State's advocate," and suits "could be expected with some frequency." These suits would require a retrial of the criminal case, could discourage the prosecutor from presenting relevant evidence, and might skew postconviction procedures because of a judge's subconscious knowledge that a decision favorable to the accused could lead to a prosecutor's civil liability. There was "no occasion," the Court added, "to consider whether like or similar reasons require immunity for those aspects of the prosecutor's responsibility that cast him in the role of an administrator or investigative officer rather than that of advocate."[1]

In subsequent cases the Court has made clear that prosecutorial immunity extends only to prosecutorial functions related to courtroom advocacy and not to administrative tasks. In Mitchell v. Forsyth, 472 U.S. 511 (1985), the Court thus held with little discussion that former Attorney General John N. Mitchell, in authorizing a warrantless wiretap for reasons of national security, was not acting in a prosecutorial capacity and hence was not shielded by absolute immunity. Burns v. Reed, 500 U.S. 478 (1991), then further limited the reach of a prosecutor's absolute immunity. In Burns, the plaintiff alleged, *inter alia*, that the defendant had violated her constitutional rights (i) by improperly advising the police that they could question her under hypnosis and that they "probably had probable cause" to arrest her and (ii) by presenting false and misleading evidence at a court appearance in support of an application for a search warrant. The Supreme Court held that the defendant's court appearance and his presentation of evidence at the hearing on the search warrant were protected by absolute immunity, but that his acts of providing advice to the police were subject only to a qualified immunity defense. The Court noted the lack of any historical or common law support for extending absolute immunity to the provision of advice and stressed the rationale behind absolute prosecutorial immunity—"to free the *judicial process* from the harassment and intimidation associated with litigation." Moreover, one significant check on constitutional violations in the course of the judicial process—the availability of appellate review—"will not necessarily restrain out-of-court activities by a prosecutor that occur prior to the initiation of a prosecution," particularly "if a suspect is not eventually prosecuted."[2]

---

[1]   Jurors and witnesses in judicial proceedings also enjoy absolute immunity. See Briscoe v. LaHue, 460 U.S. 325 (1983). Rehberg v. Paulk, 566 U.S. 356 (2012), held unanimously that a witness in a grand jury proceeding enjoys the same absolute immunity from suit as a witness at trial. Public defenders, who do not ordinarily act under color of state law, see Polk County v. Dodson, 454 U.S. 312 (1981), are likely to be liable under § 1983 only if they conspire with state officials, and Tower v. Glover, 467 U.S. 914 (1984), held that in such a § 1983 action a defender has *no* immunity.

[2]   In Buckley v. Fitzsimmons, 509 U.S. 259 (1993), the plaintiff alleged that prosecutors had fabricated evidence during the preliminary investigation of a crime by obtaining testimony about a boot print from an expert known to be unreliable. The suit also alleged that prosecutors had made false statements at a press conference announcing the return of an indictment. The Court ruled that the prosecutors were entitled only to qualified immunity with respect to both the press conference (on this point, the Court was unanimous) and the alleged fabrication (here, the Court divided, 5–4). See also Kalina v. Fletcher, 522 U.S. 118 (1997) (holding that a prosecutor who allegedly filed a false "Certification of Determination of Probable Cause" in support of an application for an arrest warrant was not entitled to absolute immunity from suit

Compare Van de Kamp v. Goldstein, 555 U.S. 335 (2009), which held that absolute prosecutorial immunity barred claims based on the prosecution's non-disclosure of impeachment material, which was allegedly due to the defendants' failure to (1) train and supervise prosecutors and (2) establish an information system containing potential impeachment material concerning informants. Although the alleged constitutional violations involved "administrative activities," absolute prosecutorial immunity applied, Justice Breyer reasoned for a unanimous Court, because "[t]he management tasks at issue * * * concern how and when to make impeachment information available at trial" and "are thereby directly connected with the prosecutor's basic trial advocacy duties." It would "prove difficult," the Court said, "to draw a line between *general* office supervision or office training * * * and *specific* supervision or training related to a particular case."

Consider whether the Court's approach can be best understood as defining the proper reach of prosecutorial immunity, the limits of the § 1983 cause of action, or the scope of the underlying constitutional right. Compare the Court's approach to municipal liability for similar failures to train in Connick v. Thompson, 563 U.S. 51 (2011), p. 1294, *supra*.

(3) The Absolute Immunity of Legislators. The only explicit source in the Constitution for official immunity of any kind appears in Article I, § 6, which states that Senators and Representatives "shall in all Cases, except Treason, Felony, and Breach of Peace, be privileged from Arrest during their Attendance at the Session of their respective Houses, and in going to and returning from the same; and for any Speech or Debate in either House, they shall not be questioned in any other Place."

The Supreme Court first considered the Speech or Debate Clause in Kilbourn v. Thompson, 103 U.S. 168, 200–05 (1880). Relying on the English tradition of parliamentary privilege, the Court held that federal legislators who had voted for a resolution ordering the plaintiff to be imprisoned for contempt of Congress were immune from damages liability in a suit for false imprisonment. Subsequent cases have interpreted the Speech or Debate Clause to shield all "legislative acts"— matters that are "an integral part of the deliberative and communicative processes by which Members participate in committee and House proceedings with respect to the consideration and passage or rejection of proposed legislation or with respect to other matters which the Constitution places within the jurisdiction of either House." Gravel v.

---

because, in filing the certification, the prosecutor was acting as a complaining witness, not as a lawyer).

For a forceful argument that neither history nor considerations of policy lend support to absolute prosecutorial immunity, see Johns, *Reconsidering Absolute Prosecutorial Immunity*, 2005 BYU L.Rev. 53. For further attacks on absolute prosecutorial immunity, largely predicated on the claim that current law includes too few deterrents to prosecutorial misconduct, see Johns, *Unsupportable and Unjustified: A Critique of Absolute Prosecutorial Immunity*, 80 Fordham L.Rev. 509 (2011); Rudin, *The Supreme Court Assumes Errant Prosecutors Will Be Disciplined by Their Offices or the Bar: Three Case Studies that Prove that Assumption Wrong*, 80 Fordham L.Rev. 537 (2011).

United States, 408 U.S. 606, 625 (1972).[3] The Gravel case held, contrary to prior authority, that the immunity extends not only to members of Congress but also to their aides.

Although the Speech or Debate Clause extends only to members of Congress, Tenney v. Brandhove, 341 U.S. 367 (1951), p. 1313, *supra*, held a state legislator absolutely immune from damages liability in a § 1983 action that alleged that the defendant had called a hearing not for a legitimate legislative purpose but instead to deprive plaintiff of his constitutional rights.[4]

(4) Absolute Immunity of the President: Civil Actions. In Nixon v. Fitzgerald, 457 U.S. 731 (1982), Fitzgerald (the plaintiff in the Harlow case) sought damages from President Nixon, who allegedly shared responsibility for the decision to fire Fitzgerald. Justice Powell's opinion for the Court ruled that the President enjoyed an absolute immunity from damages liability for all acts within the "outer perimeter" of his official responsibilities. This immunity, he argued, was a "functionally mandated incident of the President's unique office, rooted in the constitutional tradition of the separation of powers."[5] The Court stressed that the President's prominence made the Chief Executive an easy target for damages actions, and that if Presidents had only a qualified immunity, the resulting diversion of their energies in defending themselves would jeopardize the effective functioning of government. Justice White wrote a vigorous dissent, in which Justices Brennan, Marshall, and Blackmun joined, accusing the Court of mistakenly conferring immunity on an office rather than a function, and finding nothing in the nature of executive personnel decisions to warrant absolute rather than qualified immunity.[6]

---

[3] Compare Doe v. McMillan, 412 U.S. 306 (1973) (House Members responsible for preparing a committee report were absolutely immune in a suit for invasion of privacy filed by schoolchildren identified in the report, though the Superintendent of Documents and the Public Printer, who publicly disseminated the report, were not immune), with Hutchinson v. Proxmire, 443 U.S. 111 (1979) (Senator was not immune from a defamation action arising out of his publicizing his "Golden Fleece" award—for wasteful federal spending—in a press release, newsletter, and television program).

[4] In Bogan v. Scott-Harris, 523 U.S. 44 (1998), the Court held that local legislators are entitled to the same absolute immunity from § 1983 civil liability as are state and federal legislators. The Court then determined that a mayor's preparation of a budget eliminating the plaintiff's position and his signing of the ordinance so providing, as well as the city council vice president's vote on the measure, were legislative actions entitled to absolute immunity. In its opinion, the Court stated that the determination whether a particular activity should be classified as legislative hinges on the nature of the activity, not the subjective intent of the actor.

[5] The Court left open the question whether the President could be subjected to damages liability by explicit and affirmative congressional action.

[6] A different question is that of the ability of a litigant to bring a civil suit against a sitting President for conduct occurring prior to the President's taking office. In Clinton v. Jones, 520 U.S. 681 (1997), a case involving sexual harassment claims against President Clinton that arose out of alleged conduct prior to his Presidency (when he was governor of Arkansas), the Supreme Court denied a claim of broad Presidential "temporary immunity" from civil damages actions relating to events outside the scope of his Presidential duties. The Court did not decide whether a *state* court could entertain a private action in such a case, or whether the trial court in the case at hand could compel the President's appearance at any specific time or place. The Court held that the trial court had broad discretion to control its own docket and that the respect

Trump v. Vance, 591 U.S. 786 (2020), held that a sitting President has no absolute immunity from state court subpoenas issued in conjunction with a criminal investigation. Chief Justice Roberts's majority opinion emphasized, however, that the President, "like any other citizen," can "raise subpoena-specific constitutional challenges," including objections "that compliance with a particular subpoena would impede his constitutional duties," "in either a state or federal forum." See also Trump v. Mazars USA, LLP, 591 U.S. 848 (2020) (holding that courts must weigh separation-of-powers principles in assessing whether a congressional subpoena "directed at the President's personal information" is valid and enforceable).

Although Harlow held that absolute immunity might be appropriate for presidential aides with discretionary authority in national security matters or foreign affairs, the Court rejected a claim of absolute immunity in Mitchell v. Forsyth, 472 U.S. 511 (1985), Paragraph (2)(b), *supra*, a Bivens action against former Attorney General John N. Mitchell for having authorized a warrantless wiretap for the purpose of protecting national security. The Court reasoned that the secrecy of national security matters reduced both the likelihood of unfounded and burdensome lawsuits and the effectiveness of other possible mechanisms of restraining misconduct. See also Butz v. Economou, 438 U.S. 478 (1978) (rejecting absolute immunity for cabinet officials). Consider what remains of such potential liability after the rejection of a Bivens claim against high-level government officials in Ziglar v. Abbasi, 582 U.S. 120 (2017), p. 931, *supra*.

(5) Absolute Immunity of the President: Criminal Actions. In Trump v. United States, 144 S.Ct. 2312 (2024), the Supreme Court considered for the first time a former president's immunity from criminal prosecution. A Special Counsel appointed by Attorney General Merrick Garland indicted former President Donald Trump for conspiring to overturn the results of the 2020 election "by spreading knowingly false claims of election fraud to obstruct the collecting, counting, and certifying of the election results," in violation of several federal criminal statutes. Trump sought to dismiss the indictment on the ground that a former President enjoys "absolute immunity" from criminal prosecution for official acts. The Court, in an opinion by Chief Justice Roberts, recognized that a former president enjoys significant immunity from criminal prosecution for official acts. The Court's immunity analysis had three primary holdings with subsidiary moving parts.

First, the Court held that a president enjoys no immunity for "unofficial acts" committed in office. The Court built on Harlow's statement that official action includes presidential acts pursuant to

---

owed the Presidency should inform the exercise of that discretion, but that staying the action was premature. Justice Breyer, concurring in the judgment, argued at length that "ordinary case-management principles" must be "supplemented with a constitutionally based requirement that district courts schedule proceedings so as to avoid significant interference with the President's ongoing discharge of his official responsibilities."

"constitutional and statutory authority," including "discretionary responsibilities" under these authorities "in a broad variety of areas, many of them highly sensitive." (quoting Nixon v. Fitzgerald, 457 U.S. 731, 757 (1982)). It noted that "some Presidential conduct—for example, speaking to and on behalf of the American people, see Trump v. Hawaii, 585 U.S. 667, 701 (2018)—certainly can qualify as official even when not obviously connected to a particular constitutional or statutory provision." The Court reiterated Nixon v. Fitzgerald's "outer perimeter" protection for presidential acts to mean that immunity covers "actions so long as they are not manifestly or palpably beyond his authority." (internal quotation marks and citation omitted). And the Court said that "[i]n dividing official from unofficial conduct, courts may not inquire into the President's motives," which, the Court stated, "would risk exposing even the most obvious instances of official conduct to judicial examination on the mere allegation of improper purpose, thereby intruding on the Article II interests that immunity seeks to protect."

Second, the Court held that "the President is absolutely immune from criminal prosecution for conduct within his exclusive sphere of constitutional authority." This principle is unremarkable in the abstract, since the Court understood exclusive Article II authority to be one that "disabl[es] the Congress from acting upon the subject" (quoting Youngstown Sheet & Tube Co. v. Sawyer, 343 U.S. 579, 637–38 (1952) (Jackson, J., concurring)). In addition to stating that the president's removal power was exclusive, the Court in a significant ruling of uncertain scope held that investigative and prosecutorial decisionmaking falls within the president's exclusive sphere as well. On this basis, the Court concluded that elements of the indictment that alleged that Trump and his co-conspirators "attempted to leverage the Justice Department's power and authority to convince certain States to replace their legitimate electors with Trump's fraudulent slates of electors" via meetings with senior Justice Department officials and threats to replace the Acting Attorney General impinged on the president's exclusive power and thus that Trump was "absolutely immune from prosecution for the alleged conduct involving his discussions with Justice Department officials."

Third, for presidential acts that are official but do not implicate exclusive powers, the Court drew heavily on the functional analysis in Nixon v. Fitzgerald. It concluded that "separation of powers principles * * * necessitate at least a *presumptive* immunity from criminal prosecution," and possibly absolute immunity (the Court did not decide), "for a President's acts within the outer perimeter of his official responsibility." This immunity was needed in order to "safeguard the independence and effective functioning of the Executive Branch, and to enable the President to carry out his constitutional duties without undue caution." Although Nixon v. Fitzgerald had suggested that the balance of functional considerations might cut differently for criminal immunity as opposed to immunity for civil damages, see 457 U.S. at 755 & n.37, the

Court in Trump v. United States maintained that the danger to presidential prerogatives from criminal prosecution was "akin to, indeed greater than" the factors that led it to recognize absolute presidential immunity from civil damages. While the Court at this stage did not specify if this category of immunity was presumptive or absolute, it stated that "[a]t a minimum, the President must * * * be immune from prosecution for an official act unless the Government can show that applying a criminal prohibition to that act would pose no 'dangers of intrusion on the authority and functions of the Executive Branch.' "

One consequence of presidential immunity from criminal prosecution, the Court made clear, was that evidence of official acts for which the president receives immunity cannot be introduced at trial to support charges for unofficial acts, since to do so "would permit a prosecutor to do indirectly what he cannot do directly—invite the jury to examine acts for which a President is immune from prosecution to nonetheless prove his liability on any charge." The Court remanded the case without definitively resolving how these principles applied to the indictment (other than the charges involving presidential discussions with the Justice Department).

Justice Barrett concurred in all except Part III-C, which contained the Court's analysis on the introduction of official acts evidence to prove crimes for unofficial acts. "The Constitution does not require blinding juries to the circumstances surrounding conduct for which Presidents can be held liable," she explained. She added that the Court's concern "that allowing into evidence official acts for which the President cannot be held criminally liable may prejudice the jury" could be handled on a case-by-case basis through evidentiary rules about prejudice in the trial court. Justice Thomas also concurred. He argued that the Attorney General's appointment of the Special Counsel, a private citizen, violated the requirement in the Appointments Clause (Art. II, § 2, cl. 2.) that all federal offices be "established by Law."

Justice Sotomayor, joined by Justices Kagan and Jackson, dissented. She argued that the Court's exclusive presidential power analysis was "unnecessary on the facts of the indictment" and yet, as applied to the president's interactions with the Justice Department, "expands the concept of core powers beyond any recognizable bounds." She further maintained that the Court's official acts immunity ruling lacked a constitutional textual basis; was unsupported by history, including Justice Department understandings about the president's criminal liability; was contrary to Nixon v. Fitzgerald's functional analysis in overstating the chilling effect on presidencies from criminal prosecution and understated the public interest in such a prosecution and in presidential accountability; and would make "a President's use of any official power for any purpose, even the most corrupt, * * * immune from prosecution." Justice Jackson also filed a dissenting opinion to emphasize the deleterious consequences of the Court's ruling on presidential accountability.

NOTE ON JUDICIAL CONTROL OF LEGISLATIVE AND EXECUTIVE FUNCTIONS

Adjacent to doctrines of absolute judicial, legislative, and presidential immunity from suit for damages, the Court has formulated a set of rules that govern judicial issuance of specific forms of relief. Such relief includes mandamus and habeas decrees, both of which direct official action on pain of contempt. It also includes suits for injunctive relief, aimed at directing official action, and subpoenas to compel production of information. Marbury v. Madison, 5 U.S. (1 Cranch) 137 (1803), p. 76, *supra*, calls on federal courts to enforce individual rights and to refrain from interfering with the discretionary exercise of executive authority. The same principle shields legislative action from judicial control. This note briefly discusses cases that have examined the line between rights enforcement and improper interference in the exercise of branch-specific discretion.

The Court has addressed the problem in part by allowing litigation to proceed against subordinates, rather than against high-ranking officials and legislators. The Court issued the writ of habeas corpus to invalidate President Jefferson's detention of the Burr conspirators, in Ex parte Bollman, 8 U.S. (4 Cranch) 75 (1807), p. 355, *supra*, p. 1471, *infra*, just as it invalidated President Truman's seizure of the steel mills in Youngstown Sheet & Tube Co. v. Sawyer, 343 U.S. 579 (1952). In both cases, the Court did so in litigation that proceeded against a subordinate official.

On occasion, however, the Court issues or affirms decrees that directly bind high government officials or legislators. In Powell v. McCormack, 395 U.S. 486 (1969), the Court ordered reinstatement of a member of Congress in a decree directed at the speaker of the House of Representatives. In United States v. Nixon, 418 U.S. 683 (1974), the Supreme Court unanimously affirmed an order requiring President Nixon to respond to a grand jury subpoena seeking, *inter alia*, tape recordings of presidential conversations. The Court stressed the special importance of the government's demonstrated need for evidence in a criminal trial. Other sitting Presidents, including Jefferson, Reagan, Clinton, and Trump, have produced evidence pursuant to subpoena.

(1) Limiting Specific Relief in the Case of the President.

(a)   In Mississippi v. Johnson, 71 U.S. (4 Wall.) 475 (1867), the state, in an original action in the Supreme Court, sought to restrain the President from executing allegedly unconstitutional provisions of the Reconstruction Acts. Without ruling on the constitutionality of the challenged acts, the Court dismissed the action. After referring to cases on mandamus against executive officers, and expressly reserving the question whether the President may be ordered to perform a purely ministerial act, Chief Justice Chase said:

"Very different is the duty of the President in the exercise of the power to see that the laws are faithfully executed, and among these laws the acts named in the bill. By the first of these acts he is required to assign generals to command in the several military districts, and to detail sufficient military force to enable such officers to discharge their duties under the law. By the supplementary act, other duties are imposed on the several commanding generals, and these duties must necessarily be performed under the supervision of the President as commander-in-chief. The duty thus imposed on the President is in no just sense ministerial. It is purely executive and political. * * *

"It is true that in the instance before us the interposition of the court is not sought to enforce action by the Executive under constitutional legislation, but to restrain such action under legislation alleged to be unconstitutional. But we are unable to perceive that this circumstance takes the case out of the general principles which forbid judicial interference with the exercise of Executive discretion. * * *

"The impropriety of such interference will be clearly seen upon consideration of its possible consequences.

"Suppose the bill filed and the injunction prayed for allowed. If the President refuse obedience, it is needless to observe that the court is without power to enforce its process. If, on the other hand, the President complies with the order of the court and refuses to execute the acts of Congress, is it not clear that a collision may occur between the executive and legislative departments of the government?"

As is evident from the quoted language, the Court's analysis in Johnson subsumed the question of presidential immunity under concerns involving the scope of unreviewable executive discretion and the hazards of creating a direct conflict between Congress and the President—hazards that may have achieved an historical zenith in the face-off between President Johnson and a Republican-dominated Reconstruction Congress.

(b) In Franklin v. Massachusetts, 505 U.S. 788 (1992), plaintiffs challenging the reapportionment of congressional seats following the 1990 census named President Bush as well as various other federal officials as defendants. In an opinion for a plurality of four Justices, Justice O'Connor stated: "We have left open the question whether the President might be subject to a judicial injunction requiring the performance of a purely 'ministerial' duty, Mississippi v. Johnson, and we have held that the President may be subject to a subpoena to provide information relevant to an ongoing criminal prosecution, United States v. Nixon, *supra*, but in general 'this court has no jurisdiction of a bill to enjoin the President in the performance of his official duties'" (quoting Mississippi v. Johnson, 71 U.S. (4 Wall.) at 501).

Justice Scalia concurred in the judgment. He noted that Mississippi v. Johnson "left open the question whether the President might be subject to a judicial injunction requiring the performance of a purely 'ministerial' duty," but argued that "no court has authority to direct the President to take an official act" or to enter a declaratory judgment with respect to the concededly nonministerial function presented in the case at bar.

(c)   Several habeas corpus cases litigated in the Supreme Court have included the President as a named respondent, apparently without triggering any immunity-based objection. See Rasul v. Bush, 542 U.S. 466 (2004); Boumediene v. Bush, 553 U.S. 723 (2008), discussed at pp. 1526–1530, *infra.* Consider why the Court might grant habeas relief in a suit that names the President but refrain from enjoining the President from implementing the program that led to the imprisonment contested by the habeas petition. Contempt sanctions for non-compliance with a habeas judgment would presumably run against the official with custody of the petitioner.

(2) Limiting Specific Relief in the Case of Legislators. In general, courts do not tell legislative bodies how to conduct their investigations, how to vote, or how to regulate their internal affairs. When legislative action has been completed, and individuals seek to challenge the result, they do so by initiating suit against those who execute the legislative will. Consider the application of that principle in Supreme Court of Virginia v. Consumers Union of the U.S., Inc., 446 U.S. 719 (1980). There a consumer group sued the Virginia state supreme court and its chief justice under § 1983, seeking to enjoin (as inconsistent with the First Amendment) state bar rules restricting plaintiffs' ability to gather information about lawyers' fees. A three-judge federal court ultimately awarded the injunctive relief sought, as well as attorney's fees under 42 U.S.C. § 1988. On appeal, the Supreme Court ruled that officials acting in a legislative capacity could not be enjoined. But observing that the state supreme court also had enforcement authority over bar discipline proceedings, the Court upheld the injunction on that basis. "We need not decide whether judicial immunity would bar prospective relief, for we believe that the Virginia court and its chief justice properly were held liable in their enforcement capacities," much as prosecutors—who enjoy absolute immunity from damages liability—may be enjoined from enforcing laws that violate the Constitution.

Compare Eastland v. United States Servicemen's Fund, 421 U.S. 491 (1975), a suit brought by an organization critical of the Vietnam War to contest a Senate subpoena of its bank records as a violation of its rights under the First Amendment. The Court found that the named defendants, the chair, members, and chief counsel of the Senate subcommittee that issued the subpoena, were acting in their legislative capacity and thus enjoyed a Speech and Debate Clause immunity from suit. Three Justices concurred, agreeing that the Senators and their lawyer were immune from suit but noting that such immunity did not foreclose other forms of litigation by parties who wish to challenge a subpoena. The subpoenas themselves indicated that they were to be served by the U.S. Marshals service, an executive branch agency that was presumably subject to injunctive relief.

Consider also the Court's approach to litigation brought to compel the city of Yonkers, New York to end its practice of segregated public housing. Four members of the city council voted against an ordinance that would have authorized court-ordered changes to the city's public housing policy and the ordinance failed. The district court imposed contempt sanctions on the city and the individual members. Without addressing the members' argument that legislative immunity barred contempt sanctions for the way they cast their votes, the Court ruled in Spallone v. United States, 493 U.S. 265 (1990), that sanctions should have been granted, at least initially, against the city alone.

(3) Limiting Specific Relief in the Case of Judges. Judicial immunity does not extend to suits for prospective relief, according to the Court's 5–4 decision in Pulliam v. Allen, 466 U.S. 522 (1984). Pulliam, a state magistrate, had a practice in criminal cases involving nonjailable offenses of setting bail and incarcerating persons who could not post it. Two arrestees subjected to this policy brought suit against the magistrate under § 1983, seeking injunctive and declaratory relief. The district court ruled that the practice was unconstitutional and enjoined Pulliam from continuing it. The court also awarded the plaintiffs $7,691 in costs, of which $7,038 was attorney's fees awarded under 42 U.S.C. § 1988. The Supreme Court upheld the injunction and the fee award, noting that the writ of prohibition traditionally authorized specific relief against inferior courts and judges.

Subsequently, Congress took up the question in The Federal Courts Improvement Act of 1996, Pub.L.No. 104–317, § 309(b)–(c), 110 Stat. 3847. That act amended § 1988 to bar the collection of any costs, including attorney's fees, from judicial officers in suits against them arising from actions taken in their judicial capacity, and also amended § 1983 to bar suits against judicial officers for injunctive relief, except when declaratory relief was unavailable or the officer was acting contrary to a prior declaratory decree. See Nickerson & Funk, *When Judges Were Enjoined: Text and Tradition in the Federal Review of State Judicial Action*, 111 Calif.L.Rev. 1763 (2023) (explaining that Congress effectively ratified judicial power to enjoin state court judges while shielding them from attorney's fees).

---

5. REMEDIES FOR WRONGFUL FEDERAL OFFICIAL ACTION

As explored above, nineteenth century courts presumed the immunity of state and federal governments from suit and relied instead the suability of government officials. Today, Congress has authorized suits against the federal government for a broad range of claims sounding in tort, property, contract, and seeking review of agency action. But Congress has never seen fit to adopt an all-purpose provision for the assertion of constitutional claims against either the federal government itself or its officials acting under color of federal law. (Section 1983 applies only to action under color of state law.) As a result, most constitutional litigation (aside from takings claims in the Court of Federal Claims) proceeds against federal officials as the parties of record. Such officer suit litigation takes various forms, including habeas petitions to contest the legality of custody (covered in Chapter XI), Bivens claims for a short list of constitutional torts (covered in Chapter VII), and Ex parte Young claims to secure injunctive and declaratory relief against threatened or continuing constitutional violations. This part first sketches the statutory waivers of federal sovereign immunity and then considers questions of authority, coordination, and judicial administration that arise from the practice of allowing individuals to pursue Ex parte Young style suits against federal officials.

A. STATUTES AUTHORIZING SUIT AGAINST THE UNITED STATES

The federal statutes summarized here fall into two groups, those that authorize judicial review of federal agency action and those that waive the federal government's immunity as to money claims.

1. REVIEW OF FEDERAL AGENCY ACTION

Statutory review, largely a development of the twentieth century, has become the predominant method of reviewing federal official action, though it has not wholly displaced the nonstatutory "officer suits" traditionally available at common law and in equity.

(a) Specific Statutory Provisions Authorizing Judicial Review. Regulatory statutes often authorize judicial review at the instance of a private person who wishes to challenge official action. Though these statutory review provisions vary widely, probably the most common authorize a petition in a federal court of appeals to set aside an administrative order. Thus, the National Labor Relations Act specifies that final orders of the National Labor Relations Board may be reviewed in an appropriate court of appeals, see 29 U.S.C. § 160(f), and similar provisions govern other agencies. Other statutes authorize review in a federal district court. An important example is § 205(g) of the Social Security Act, 42 U.S.C. § 405(g), which provides for district court review of final and adverse administrative decisions on claims for social security benefits.

(b) The Administrative Procedure Act. In addition to specific statutory review provisions, Congress in 1946 enacted the Administrative Procedure Act (APA), which in § 10, 5 U.S.C. §§ 701–06, generally authorizes judicial review at the behest of a person who suffers legal wrong because of final agency action or who is adversely affected by such action. Though review under the APA may be denied, *inter alia*, when (1) the action is committed to agency discretion, (2) the governing regulatory statute expressly or impliedly precludes judicial review, (3) the challenge is not ripe, or (4) the petitioner has failed to meet specific requirements for the exhaustion of administrative remedies, decisions have established a strong presumption that federal agency action is reviewable.

(c) Suits for Relief Other than Money Damages. In a statute enacted in 1976, now codified as the last three sentences of § 10(b) of the Administrative Procedure Act, 5 U.S.C. § 702, Congress eliminated three barriers to federal court actions seeking specific relief against federal official action. First, the statute amended 28 U.S.C. § 1331 to abolish any jurisdictional minimum in suits thereunder "brought against the United States, any agency thereof, or any officer or employee thereof in his official capacity." Second, the statute waived sovereign immunity in federal court suits seeking relief other than money damages against federal agencies or officials. Third, the statute relaxed the party-of-record rule, allowing the United States to be named as a defendant and to have judgment entered against it, provided that any mandatory or injunctive order specify the officer(s) responsible for compliance. Provisos declare that: "Nothing herein (1) affects other limitations on judicial review or the power or duty of the court to dismiss any action or deny relief on any other appropriate legal or equitable ground; or (2) confers authority to grant relief if any other statute that grants consent to suit expressly or impliedly forbids the relief which is sought." The House Report explained that the statute does not change existing limitations on specific relief, if any, derived from statutes dealing with such matters as government contracts, patent infringement, tort claims, and tax claims.[1]

---

2.   FEDERAL STATUTES ALLOWING MONEY CLAIMS AGAINST THE UNITED STATES

Important statutes authorizing money claims against the United States include the Tucker Act, governing non-tort monetary claims against the United States and the Federal Tort Claims Act (FTCA), governing tort suits against the United States. A separate statute, often referred to as the Judgment Fund, authorizes treasury payments to judgment creditors of the United States, and obviates the necessity for special appropriations to pay contract, tort, and other claims. See 31 U.S.C. § 1304 (providing for payment of judgments rendered against the United States under specified statutes). Prevailing parties in litigation with the government may also recover attorneys' fees in many cases.

In cases presenting the question whether a particular statute waives sovereign immunity, the Court has failed to settle on a consistent interpretive approach. The traditional view held that such waivers must be clearly expressed. See, *e.g.*, Borchard, *Government Liability in Tort*, 34 Yale L.J. 1, 28–41 (1924). But more recent decisions treat sovereign

---

[1]   For the suggestion that the statute "rendered fictional officer suits far less important than they previously were," see Siegel, *Suing the President: Nonstatutory Review Revisited*, 97 Colum.L.Rev. 1612, 1665 (1997).

immunity as disfavored. See FDIC v. Meyer, 510 U.S. 471 (1994). According to Sisk, *Twilight for the Strict Construction of Waivers of Federal Sovereign Immunity*, 92 N.C.L.Rev. 1245 (2014), modern cases treat most issues as matters of ordinary statutory interpretation, once satisfied as a threshold matter that Congress consented to suit on claims seeking relief of the kind presented. See United States v. Wong, 575 U.S. 402 (2015) (refusing, in suit based on the FTCA, to read statutory provisions narrowly in favor federal government immunity; the statute treats the government "more like a commoner than like the Crown").

(a) The Tucker Act. During the early republic, Congress chose to address money claims against the government of the United States by special legislative process instead of judicial process. Concluding that its reliance on legislative adjudication and appropriation was burdensome and inequitable, Congress created the Court of Claims in 1855 and authorized it to determine all claims against the government founded upon any statute, executive regulation, or express or implied contract with the United States. Such authority included suits to recover for authorized takings of private property on the theory that the government impliedly promised to make the property owner whole. See Pfander, *Dicey's Nightmare: An Essay on the Rule of Law*, 107 Calif.L.Rev. 737, 764–66 (2019).

In 1887, the Tucker Act broadened the Court of Claims' jurisdiction to include all "claims founded upon the Constitution of the United States or any law of Congress * * * or upon any regulation of an Executive Department, or upon any contract, expressed or implied, with the Government of the United States, or for damages, liquidated or unliquidated, in cases not sounding in tort." 28 U.S.C. § 1491(a)(1). In 1982 Congress established what it later renamed as the United States Court of Federal Claims, an Article I court, to assume the trial jurisdiction formerly possessed by the Court of Claims. This tribunal has jurisdiction over all claims governed by the Tucker Act. Its jurisdiction over claims (other than for a tax refund) in excess of $10,000 is exclusive, while the district courts have concurrent jurisdiction of claims not exceeding $10,000. There is no right in either forum to jury trial. 28 U.S.C. § 2402.

As a grant of jurisdiction, the Tucker Act proceeds on the assumption that the government owes a duty to compensate for taken property and breach of contract; the statute does not itself create any substantive rights. A suit under the Tucker Act must therefore demonstrate that the source of substantive law relied upon "can fairly be interpreted as mandating compensation by the Federal Government." United States v. Navajo Nation, 556 U.S. 287, 290 (2009) (involving suit under the Indian Tucker Act, 28 U.S.C. § 1505). Constitutional claims founded on the Takings Clause satisfy this standard. See, *e.g.*, United States v. Causby, 328 U.S. 256 (1946). But a consistent line of lower court authority rejects Tucker Act suits based on violations of other constitutional provisions.

Appeals from decisions involving Tucker Act claims go to the U.S. Court of Appeals for the Federal Circuit, a specialized Article III tribunal established in 1982. See 28 U.S.C. § 1295(a); United States v. Hohri, 482 U.S. 64 (1987).

The Tucker Act is strictly limited to claims for money. It gives no jurisdiction to hear claims for specific performance, delivery of property in kind, or injunctive relief, although other provisions give the Court of Federal Claims a limited power to award equitable remedies. These restrictions give rise to the Tucker Act shuffle, where litigants seeking complete relief must pursue injunctive relief in district courts and monetary relief in the Court of Federal Claims. See Sisk, *The Tapestry Unravels: Statutory Waivers of Sovereign Immunity and Money Claims Against the United States*, 71 Geo.Wash.L.Rev. 602, 611–15 (2003).

A second kind of jurisdictional overlap poses challenges for litigants. The APA provision sketched above, 5 U.S.C. § 702, waives the government's immunity for relief other than money damages. In Bowen v. Massachusetts, 487 U.S. 879, 910 (1988), the Court held that the provision enabled federal district courts to order some monetary relief, so long as it results as a "mere by-product of [the district court's] primary function of reviewing the [agency's] interpretation of federal law." The Court thus upheld prospective declaratory and injunctive relief compelling reimbursement under Medicaid for certain state-provided services. By contrast, in Maine Community Health Options v. United States, 590 U.S. 296 (2020), the Court ruled that a federal statute mandated compensation in the circumstance of that case and therefore triggered exclusive Tucker Act jurisdiction.

Congress could eliminate many problems of conflicting jurisdiction by abolishing the Court of Federal Claims and empowering the district courts to entertain all claims against the United States under the Tucker Act, the FTCA, and every other statute consenting to suit. History and path dependence explain but do not necessarily justify continued reliance on a non-Article III tribunal for the determination of money claims against the United States. For an argument that the district courts could easily absorb the docket of a disbanded Court of Federal Claims, see Schooner, *The Future: Scrutinizing the Empirical Case for the Court of Federal Claims*, 71 Geo.Wash.L.Rev. 714 (2002).

(b) The Federal Tort Claims Act. At common law, tort liability runs against the officers themselves, rather than against their employing government. But Congress nonetheless spent a good deal of legislative time considering petitions for indemnity by officers held liable for torts committed in the scope of their employment. After decades of consideration, Congress in 1946 adopted the FTCA. The FTCA establishes federal district court jurisdiction and imposes substantive liability on the United States "for injury or loss of property, or personal injury or death caused by the negligent or wrongful act or omission of any employee of the Government while acting within the scope of his office or employment, under circumstances where the United States, if a private person, would be liable to the claimant in accordance with the law of the place [which is typically a state] where the act or omission occurred." 28 U.S.C. § 1346(b). Though it contains significant exceptions and limitations, the FTCA established governmental liability in tort and effectively transferred the responsibility for making the scope of employment determinations from Congress (in passing on indemnity petitions) to the federal courts.

(i)   Procedures and Remedies. Procedure under the FTCA differs from that in ordinary tort suits in important respects. No suit may be filed unless (1) the claimant has made a timely application to the involved agency for administrative settlement, and (2) the claim has been denied or not acted upon for six months. 28 U.S.C. § 2675. Trial is de novo, however, and is without jury. Relief is limited to money damages, and punitive damages are barred.

(ii)   The "Discretionary Function" Exception. There are a number of express exceptions to the FTCA. The most important, which has caused difficulty from the outset, excludes any claim "based upon the exercise or performance or the failure to exercise or perform a discretionary function or duty on the part of a federal agency or an employee of the Government, whether or not the discretion involved be abused." 28 U.S.C. § 2680(a).

(a)   The Dalehite Case. The Supreme Court first considered the scope of this exception in Dalehite v. United States, 346 U.S. 15 (1953). Pursuant to a high-level government decision, agents of the federal government manufactured large quantities of an ammonium nitrate fertilizer for shipment to occupied Germany, Japan, and Korea. The material was being loaded on ships at Texas City when spontaneous combustion led to an explosion that killed 560 people, injured some 3,000, and leveled a portion of the city. Over a strong dissent, the Court rejected money claims against the government, reasoning that the program in question had been planned "at a high level under a direct delegation of plan-making authority from the apex of the Executive Department."

(b)   The Berkovitz Decision. A later decision, Berkovitz v. United States, 486 U.S. 531 (1988), clarified the application of the discretionary function exception in the context of federal regulatory programs. Berkovitz held unanimously that the exception does not preclude liability for all acts arising out of such programs, calling instead for an analysis of the degree to which federal law confers discretion on federal officials to act as they had in releasing untested vaccine that later caused injury.

(c)   Limits on Discretion. At common law, officers who acted within a zone of discretion conferred by statute were shielded from tort-based liability. But the Constitution was thought to set an independent limit on the scope of their discretionary-function immunity subjecting them to liability for actions in violation of the Constitution. Lower courts view the Constitution as imposing similar limits on the breadth of the FTCA's statutory discretionary function exception. See Loumiet v. United States, 828 F.3d 935 (D.C. Cir.2016) (collecting cases).

(iii) The Feres Doctrine. Numerous cases have considered the FTCA's application to injuries suffered by military personnel. In 1950, the Court unanimously held the Act inapplicable to injuries to service members that "arise out of or are in the course of activity incident to service," notwithstanding the absence of any statutory language supporting that result. Feres v. United States, 340 U.S. 135, 146 (1950). The Court later explained this doctrine as based primarily upon three considerations: the distinctively federal character of military relationships, the existence of alternative compensation systems, and the deleterious effect that tort suits could have upon military discipline. Stencel Aero Eng'g Corp. v. United States, 431 U.S. 666, 673 (1977). Some years later, the Court stressed that the last of these considerations is the most important, and that "[t]he Feres doctrine cannot be reduced to a few bright-line rules." United States v. Shearer, 473 U.S. 52 (1985).

With Congress having created numerous specific exceptions to FTCA liability, a textualist Court may struggle to approve judicial creation of additional exceptions. See United States v. Johnson, 481 U.S. 681, 693–701 (1987) (Scalia, J., dissenting) (arguing that there are none). For an account that explains the doctrine as transforming tort-based liability into a form of worker's compensation, see Taber v. Maine, 67 F.3d 1029 (2d Cir.1995) (Calabresi, J.).

(iv) The Relation Between the FTCA and the Bivens Doctrine. Carlson v. Green, 446 U.S. 14 (1980), held that the government's liability under the FTCA does not preclude a Bivens action against individual officers for the same tortious conduct. Some lower courts have held that the FTCA's judgment bar, 28 U.S.C. § 2676, precludes Bivens litigation anytime a suit based on the FTCA suffers dismissal. For a summary and criticism, see Pfander & Aggarwal, *Bivens, the Judgment Bar, and the Perils of Dynamic Textualism*, 8 U.St. Thomas L.J. 417 (2011). *Cf.* Simmons v. Himmelreich, 578 U.S. 621 (2016) (dismissal of FTCA claim under discretionary function exception does not trigger judgment bar); Brownback v. King, 592 U.S. 209 (2021) (dismissal on grounds that implicate the merits triggers the judgment bar).

In the 1988 Westfall Act, Congress protected federal officials from certain tort-based liability as to claims made actionable under the FTCA, 28 U.S.C. § 2678(b)(1), but specifically preserved suits against federal officials for violation of the Constitution and federal statutes. See 28 U.S.C. § 2678(b)(2). For the Act's impact on Bivens litigation, see Chap. VII, Sec. 2, *supra*. On the displacement of private tort remedies against federal officers acting within the scope of their employment, a mainstay of nineteenth century government accountability litigation, see United States v. Smith, 499 U.S. 160 (1991) (certain defenses available to the government under the FTCA also bar suits against individual federal officers).[1]

---

3. ATTORNEY'S FEES

The Equal Access to Justice Act of 1980, codified at 28 U.S.C. § 2412(b), authorizes the award of attorney's fees to a party who prevails against the United States in the same circumstances in which courts would award fees against private parties. In addition, § 2412(d) provides that courts shall award attorney's fees to certain persons who prevail against the United States in non-tort civil actions, unless the United States' position was "substantially justified" or "special circumstances make an award unjust." There are, moreover, many statutory provisions authorizing the award of attorney's fees in particular kinds of actions. See generally Bennett, Winning Attorneys' Fees from the U.S. Government (rev.ed.2015).

B. INJUNCTIVE RELIEF FROM FEDERAL OFFICIAL ACTION

The Supreme Court has long relied on the use of Ex parte Young-style litigation to test the legality of both state and federal official action. See Free Enterprise Fund v. Public Company Accounting Oversight Board, 561 U.S. 477 (2010) (allowing constitutional challenge under Ex parte Young, 209 U.S. 123 (1908), p. 1211, *supra*, to structure of federal agency). In addition to individual litigants, states today often bring such suits, challenging federal programs on constitutional and statutory grounds. See United States v. Texas, 579 U.S. 547 (2016) (upholding Fifth Circuit decision blocking President Obama's deferred action immigration program); Trump v. Hawaii, 585 U.S. 667 (2018) (addressing challenge to President Trump's travel ban); Biden v. Nebraska, 600 U.S. 477 (2023) (invalidating President Biden's loan forgiveness program).[1] Such litigation invokes jurisdiction conferred by 28 U.S.C. § 1331 and poses questions about the nature and source of the right to proceed in equity that arise from the Court's reliance on traditional equity in Armstrong v. Exceptional Child Center, 575 U.S. 320 (2015) (explaining that suits "to enjoin unconstitutional actions by state and federal officers" were "the creation of courts of equity"), p. 1303, *supra*.

---

[1] The Court undermined the interpretive foundation of Smith in Simmons v. Himmelreich, 578 U.S. 621, 627–29 (2016), holding over the government's objection that certain FTCA exceptions render the statute inapplicable to claims against officials. *Cf.* Brownback v. King, 592 U.S. 209, 223 (2021) (Sotomayor, J., concurring) (calling for careful reconsideration of the FTCA's text).

[1] On state standing to pursue such litigation, see Chap. II, Sec. 3, *supra*.

This part first summarizes the post-Erie R.R. Co. v. Tompkins, 304 U.S. 64 (1938), p. 760, *supra*, concern with the authority to grant injunctive relief in the context of suits to challenge federal official action, drawing on the earlier discussion of Armstrong. Second, it considers the issues of coordination and displacement that arise from the availability of suits in equity to contest federal official action. Third, it considers one of the more contested exercises of contemporary equitable remedies: universal injunctions.

1. THE SOURCE OF JUDICIAL POWER OVER EQUITABLE CHALLENGES TO FEDERAL OFFICIAL ACTION

Both before and after Erie, the Supreme Court recognized the availability of Ex parte Young-style litigation to challenge the legality of federal official action. Compare American School of Magnetic Healing v. McAnnulty, 187 U.S. 94 (1902) (pre-Erie injunctive relief upholding right of access to the US mails); Ashwander v. Tennessee Valley Authority, 297 U.S. 288 (1936) (pre-Erie suit against federal agency) with Shields v. Utah Idaho Central R. Co., 305 U.S. 177, 183–84 (1938) (post-Erie suit against law enforcement official); Joint Anti-Fascist Refugee Committee v. McGrath, 341 U.S. 123 (1951) (post-Erie suit against attorney general); Stark v. Wickard, 321 U.S. 288, 290 (1944) (post-Erie suit against agency head).

As with suits to challenge state action in Armstrong, the Court has continued to uphold the power of federal courts to enjoin unlawful federal official action without suggesting a need for overt authorization. In Free Enterprise Fund v. Public Company Accounting Oversight Bd., 561 U.S. 477 (2010), p. 1211, *supra*, an accounting firm under investigation by the defendant Board sued the Board and its members, alleged that the members were unconstitutionally insulated from presidential removal, and sought to enjoin the Board from exercising its powers. The U.S. government argued that "petitioners have not pointed to any case in which this Court has recognized an implied private right of action directly under the Constitution to challenge governmental action under the Appointments Clause or separation-of-powers principles." The Court responded:

"The Government does not appear to dispute such a right to relief as a general matter, without regard to the particular constitutional provisions at issue here. See, *e.g.*, Correctional Services Corp. v. Malesko, 534 U.S. 61, 74 (2001) (equitable relief "has long been recognized as the proper means for preventing entities from acting unconstitutionally"); Bell v. Hood, 327 U.S. 678, 684 (1946) ("[I]t is established practice for this Court to sustain the jurisdiction of federal courts to issue injunctions to protect rights safeguarded by the Constitution"); see also Ex parte Young, 209 U.S. 123, 149, 165, 167 (1908). If the Government's point is that an Appointments Clause or separation-of-powers claim should be treated differently than every other constitutional claim, it offers no reason and cites no authority why that might be so." *Id.* 491 n.2.

As noted earlier, the Free Enterprise Court's willingness to presume the availability of injunctive relief (even in what the Court appears to have recognized as a new context) contrasts with its refusal to broaden judge-made implied rights of action against federal officers into new contexts under the Bivens doctrine and with its generally restrictive approach to implied statutory rights of action. See Chap. VII, Sec. 2, *supra.* As the next section explains, the presumptive availability of federal equity also gives rise to coordination challenges and arguments for implied displacement not unlike those the Court addressed in Armstrong.

---

2. IMPLIED DISPLACEMENT OR PRECLUSION OF FEDERAL EQUITY

As noted above, p. 1341, *supra,* Congress created a presumption favoring judicial review of federal agency action in the Administrative Procedure Act. Litigants seeking such review typically proceed by first exhausting their remedies before the agency and then seeking judicial review as provided in the agency's organic statute, often through appellate-style proceedings in a federal circuit court of appeals. The availability of two avenues of judicial review, one based on the agency's organic statute and one based on Ex parte Young and 28 U.S.C. § 1331, raises questions of coordination and implied displacement.

In Axon Enterprise, Inc. v. Federal Trade Commission, 598 U.S. 175 (2023), the Court clarified the circumstances in which plaintiffs can pursue Ex parte Young-style constitutional challenges in a federal district court, notwithstanding the availability of statutory appellate-style review in a federal circuit court. The plaintiffs in suits consolidated on appeal asserted that the agencies' administrative law judges (ALJs) were insufficiently accountable to the President, in violation of separation-of-powers principles. The government argued that jurisdiction under 28 U.S.C. § 1331 had been displaced by the statutes governing review of agency action, which require parties to litigate first before the agency and then seek review in a federal circuit court of appeals.

Applying Thunder Basin Coal Co. v. Reich, 510 U.S. 200 (1994), the Axon Enterprise Court, speaking through Justice Kagan, held that the plaintiffs were free to pursue Ex parte Young relief in federal district court. All three Thunder Basin factors were said to point to the preservation of district court jurisdiction. First, the Court ruled that precluding district court jurisdiction could "foreclose all meaningful judicial review" of the claim by denying the plaintiffs an opportunity to contest the structure of agency adjudication before submitting to its operation. Review on appeal would come too late to remedy the harm. Second, and for much the same reason, the Court viewed the claims as "wholly collateral to [the] statute's [agency-specific] review provisions." In the Court's view, "[t]he parties' separation-of-powers claims do not relate to the subject of the enforcement actions—in the one case auditing practices, in the other a business merger. * * * Nor do the parties' claims address the sorts of procedural or evidentiary matters an agency often resolves on its way to a merits decision." Finally, the Court concluded that the claims in question fell "outside the agency's expertise." Claims that ALJ tenure protections violate Article II were said to raise " 'standard questions of administrative' and constitutional law, detached from 'considerations of agency policy.' " See also Free Enterprise Fund v. Public Company Accounting Oversight Board, 561 U.S. 477 (2010) (authorizing suit in a federal district court to challenge the structure of a federal agency).

Compare the coordination of overlapping remedies in Axon Enterprise with that in Armstrong v. Exceptional Child Center, 575 U.S. 320 (2015), p. 1200, *supra*. Axon Enterprise followed Thunder Basin in conducting its analysis in terms of jurisdiction. Armstrong, by contrast, eschewed jurisdictional language and framed the question in terms of whether Congress impliedly displaced equitable relief traditionally available under Ex parte Young. Consider whether the jurisdictional framework deployed in Axon Enterprise coheres with the Court's preference for a more thoughtful use of jurisdictional doctrines following Steel Co. v. Citizens for a Better Environment, 523 U.S. 83 (1998), p. 979, *supra*. The Axon Enterprise Court may have adopted a jurisdictional calculus in reliance on Thunder Basin, which came down before Steel Co., or in the belief that a jurisdictional framework would place firm limits on the invocation of collateral review in district courts and better preserve the primacy of appellate-style review. Justice Gorsuch concurred separately in Axon Enterprise, arguing that the Thunder Basin factors were an inappropriate judicial gloss on a straightforward jurisdictional statute. Adopting Justice Gorsuch's approach to jurisdiction would presumably leave the Court free to apply something comparable to the Thunder Basin factors within a framework of equitable or remedial preclusion.

------

3. THE SCOPE OF INJUNCTIVE RELIEF: UNIVERSAL INJUNCTIONS

In litigating with the federal government, plaintiffs have increasingly sought and often obtained a form of relief known as a "nationwide" or "universal" injunction.[1] Similar injunctions sometimes

------

[1]   In an ongoing debate over terminology, some scholars label problematic injunctions as "nationwide," others as "universal." Universal perhaps best describes the way these injunctions extend protection to non-parties; federal courts have ample power to provide relief throughout the nation on behalf of parties to the litigation. See Steele v. Bulova Watch Co., Inc., 344 U.S.

issue against state governments on a statewide basis. Such injunctions bind the governments as a general matter, prohibiting the enforcement of a challenged statute, rule, or order against anyone, anywhere. In their broadest form, universal injunctions operate statewide or nationwide and universally bar the government from enforcing the challenged rule against parties and non-parties alike.

Although it has approved the issuance of universal relief on occasion, the Court has not defined its parameters. After introducing the issue with a sketch of the 2017 litigation over the legality of President Trump's travel ban regulations, this part evaluates the constitutional, statutory, and remedial policy issues that such relief poses for the federal courts.

(a) The 2017 Travel Ban. In January 2017, President Trump issued an executive order altering refugee policy and suspending entry of foreign nationals from seven countries identified as presenting heightened terrorism risks—Iran, Iraq, Libya, Somalia, Sudan, Syria, and Yemen. The President's order was the immediate target of litigation brought in Washington state and elsewhere in which plaintiffs argued that the ban unlawfully singled out countries with predominantly Muslim populations. The Washington federal district court entered a universal temporary restraining order, upheld on appeal, that enjoined enforcement of several key provisions. Rather than seek further review, President Trump issued a more tailored travel ban in an executive order in March 2017. When further litigation led district and appellate courts (for Maryland and Hawaii) to grant and affirm universal injunctions against that order as well, the government sought an emergency stay from the Court.

In Trump v. International Refugee Assistance Project (IRAP), 582 U.S. 571 (2017) (per curiam), the Court affirmed in part and left intact universal aspects of the injunctions that operated for the benefit of non-parties. The Court first summarized the task of the district court in crafting a preliminary injunction as "an exercise of discretion and judgment" that takes account of the equities, the interests of the parties, and the "overall public interest." Its own task in considering a proposed stay was to reach "an equitable judgment of our own" through a balance of equities that explores "the relative harms to applicant and respondent, as well as the interests of the public at large." (For developments in the Court's approach to stays, see Chap. III, Sec. 4, *supra*.) Applying that standard, the Court stayed the injunctions, to the extent they operated with respect to "foreign nationals who lack any bona fide relationship with a person or entity in the United States." Where such a bona fide relationship existed, by contrast, the Court left the injunctions in place

---

280, 289 (1952) (explaining that "the District Court in exercising its equity powers may command persons properly before it to cease or perform acts outside its territorial jurisdiction") Compare Wasserman, *"Nationwide" Injunctions Are Really "Universal" Injunctions and They Are Never Appropriate*, 22 Lewis & Clark L.Rev. 335 (2018).

both as to the plaintiffs themselves and as to any non-party individuals and institutions "similarly situated" to the plaintiffs.

The travel ban litigation illustrates the factors that encourage greater reliance on universal injunctions. First, Presidents of both parties increasingly use executive orders to implement policy preferences that Congress will not support. Consider President Obama's Deferred Action for Parents of Americans (DAPA), which accorded benefits to undocumented immigrants if they were parents of American citizens. Like President Trump's travel ban, the Obama administration initiated the program by administrative action, without first securing legislative support. For an account, see Ahdout, *Enforcement Lawmaking and Judicial Review*, 135 Harv.L.Rev. 937 (2022) (linking the rise of universal injunctions to increased presidential reliance on orders that use structured enforcement discretion to establish policies that lack bi-partisan support in Congress).

Second, the acceptance of broad state standing, as more fully described in Chap. II, pp. 210–221, *supra*, facilitates challenges to such programs by state attorneys general opposed to the President's policy initiatives. See Davis, *The New Public Standing*, 71 Stan.L.Rev. 1229 (2019); Lemos & Young, *State Public-Law Litigation in an Age of Polarization*, 97 Tex.L.Rev. 43 (2018). The Texas state attorney general initiated the challenge to DAPA in a federal court located in Texas, yielding a universal injunction against the 2014 program that was upheld on appeal. See United States v. Texas, 579 U.S. 547 (2016) (per curiam) (affirming Texas v. United States, 809 F.3d 134 (5th Cir.2015), by equally divided vote). Challenges to President Trump's travel ban were brought by the attorneys general of the states of Hawaii and Washington. The combination of presidential initiatives and broad state standing has fueled a rise in universal injunctions in recent years. See Ahdout, *supra* (listing dozens of universal injunctions against Obama, Trump, and Biden administration initiatives and describing them as a "fixture" of modern remedial practice).[2]

(b) Developments at the Court. In contrast to its decision to let stand in part a universal preliminary injunction in Trump v. IRAP, *supra*, the Court stayed statewide universal relief granted by the district court of Idaho in a challenge to that state's Vulnerable Child Protection Act of 2023. See Labrador v. Poe, 144 S.Ct. 921 (2024). The plaintiffs in Labrador—two children and their parents proceeding anonymously—challenged the statute's restriction on the children's access to gender-affirming puberty blockers and estrogen as a severe threat to the children's mental health. The district court granted an injunction blocking the enforcement of any provision of the law in any circumstances so long as the litigation remained ongoing. Following an affirmance on appeal, the Court stayed the injunction "except as to the provision to the

---

[2]   An updated count appears in *Developments: District Court Reform: Nationwide Injunctions*, 137 Harv.L.Rev. 1701 (2024).

plaintiffs of the treatments they sought below." The stay thus barred the enforcement of the non-party specific elements of the injunction.

Although the Court did not explain its decision, a plurality opinion by Justice Gorsuch, joined by Justices Thomas and Alito, applauded the restriction on universal injunctions as a "welcome development" and invited lower courts to "take heed." Reiterating themes that Justices Thomas and Gorsuch had sounded in earlier concurrences,[3] the plurality opinion explained that injunctions should not be " 'more burdensome to the defendant than necessary to [redress]' the plaintiff's injuries." Ordinarily, that will require the district court to tailor its remedy to "the inadequacy that produced the injury in fact that the plaintiff has established" (quoting Gill v. Whitford, 585 U.S. 48, 68 (2018). The plurality also observed that such injunctions were apparently a relatively recent phenomenon, raising doubts as to their legitimacy under a conception of equitable power as limited by the rules in place at the time of the founding, in keeping with Grupo Mexicano de Desarrollo, S.A. v. Alliance Bond Fund, Inc., 527 U.S. 308 (1999), p. 778, *supra*.

Justice Kavanaugh, joined by Justice Barrett, also concurred, primarily to discuss criticisms of the Court's handling of its emergency docket. But Justice Kavanaugh's concurrence also explained that limits on universal injunctions, if adopted by the Court, would not forestall all high-stakes emergency litigation, such as suits challenging federal laws by a state or a national plaintiffs' class. Justice Jackson's dissent from the stay order, joined by Justice Sotomayor, argued in relevant part that the Court had erred in using its emergency docket to decide a factbound question about the proper scope of an injunction that might have defensibly benefited nonparties.

On the scope of injunctive relief against states, also consider Horne v. Flores, 557 U.S. 433 (2009). Parents of the children in one school district in Arizona secured a consent decree ordering statewide compliance with federal educational standards. On review of denial of the state's motion for relief from the decree, the Court questioned the district court's "jurisdiction to issue a statewide injunction when it is not apparent that plaintiffs—a class of [students and parents from only one

---

[3]   See Trump v. Hawaii, 585 U.S. 667 (2018) (Thomas, J., concurring) (characterizing universal injunctions as "a recent development, emerging for the first time in the 1960s and expressing doubt that federal courts have either statutory or constitutional jurisdiction to issue them); see also Dep't of Homeland Security v. New York, 140 S.Ct. 599 (2020) (Gorsuch, J., concurring) (urging the Court to "take up some of the underlying equitable and constitutional questions raised by the rise of universal injunctions," and noting that such remedies can preclude the percolation of issues through multiple circuits). Other Justices have spoken separately in defense of universal injunctions. In Little Sisters of the Poor v. Pennsylvania, 591 U.S. 657 (2020), Justices Ginsburg and Sotomayor dissented from the Court's decision upholding government exemptions of religious institutions from the employer contraception mandate of the Affordable Care Act. They also defended the district court's injunction, explaining that the Administrative Procedure Act "contemplates nationwide relief from invalid agency action." Nationwide relief was thought "necessary to provide complete relief to the plaintiffs" on the basis that loss of employer contraception benefits would force women in the plaintiff states, Pennsylvania and New Jersey, to seek healthcare elsewhere, including across state lines. See Little Sisters, 140 S.Ct. at 2412 n.28.

of the state's many school districts]—had standing to seek such relief."
Id. 470–71. See also Griffin v. HM Florida-ORL, LLC, 144 S.Ct. 1 (2023)
(Kavanaugh, J.) (questioning grant of non-party protective relief in a
state-wide injunction as something no federal statute expressly
authorizes). Contrast Horne with Pierce v. Society of Sisters, 268 U.S.
510 (1925) (upholding universal statewide injunctive relief against state
compulsory education requirement in a suit brought by two school
districts, suing for themselves alone); West Virginia State Board of Educ.
v. Barnette, 319 U.S. 624 (1943) (affirming injunctive relief that
protected children of the plaintiff religious group and any other children
having religious scruples against saluting the flag). See generally Sohoni,
The Lost History of the "Universal" Injunction, 133 Harv.L.Rev. 920
(2020).

(c) Questions of Judicial Power. Critics argue that universal
injunctions exceed the judicial power conferred by Article III. See
generally Bray, *Multiple Chancellors: Reforming the National Injunction*,
131 Harv.L.Rev. 417 (2017) (arguing that the Article III "judicial Power"
is solely "a power to decide a case for parties").[4] Contending that federal
courts can protect only parties with standing to pursue claims, critics
portray universal injunctive relief for non-parties as a violation of the
case-or-controversy requirement. Critics also argue that history and
tradition define and limit federal equity courts to those powers exercised
by the High Court of Chancery at the time of the framing. Professor Bray
dates the origins of universal injunctions to the 1960s.

Responding to the argument that universal injunctions are a recent
innovation, Sohoni, *The Lost History*, *supra*, offers historical evidence
that "Article III courts have issued injunctions that extend beyond just
the plaintiff for well over a century." Sohoni's article complements an
earlier argument by Frost, *In Defense of Nationwide Injunctions*, 93
N.Y.U.L.Rev. 1065 (2018), that universal injunctions lie within the
Article III judicial power. Both Professors Sohoni and Frost argue that
federal practice allows class action relief on behalf of those similarly
situated and allows representative parties to seek relief that extends
beyond defined injuries. Non-party protective relief also inheres in the
acceptance of states and associations as representative litigants.

(d) Questions of Statutory Interpretation. While Congress has
not authorized or forbidden universal injunctions in terms, the
Administrative Procedure Act's provision for the vacatur of federal
agency action may confer similar power by statute. While the Court has

---

4   See also Morley, *De Facto Class Actions? Plaintiff- and Defendant-Oriented Injunctions
in Voting Rights, Election Law, and Other Constitutional Cases*, 39 Harv.J.L. & Pub.Pol'y 487
(2016) (mounting a multifaceted attack on the casual issuance of universal injunctions against
the enforcement of federal statutes, orders, and regulations); Siddique, *Nationwide Injunctions*,
117 Colum.L.Rev. 2095 (2017) (arguing that federal courts should, and normally do, adhere to
the principle that an injunction should extend no further than necessary to provide "complete
relief to the plaintiffs" and proposing an amendment to Rule 65 of the Federal Rules of Civil
Procedure to codify this requirement).

yet to address the question, Justice Kavanaugh has suggested in a separate statement that statutory authorization distinguishes vacatur under the APA from universal injunctive relief:

"The APA expressly authorizes a court to 'hold unlawful and set aside agency action' that violates the Act. 5 U.S.C. § 706(2); see Sohoni, *The Power to Vacate a Rule*, 88 Geo.Wash.L.Rev. 1121, 1173 (2020) ("The term 'set aside' means invalidation—and an invalid rule may not be applied to anyone"). As a leading article explained: "Judicial review of agency action presents a different situation because the Administrative Procedure Act instructs a reviewing court to 'hold unlawful and set aside' agency rules and orders that it deems unlawful or unconstitutional." Mitchell, *The Writ-of-Erasure Fallacy*, 104 Va.L.Rev. 933, 1012 (2018). Therefore, "[u]nlike judicial review of statutes, in which courts enter judgments and decrees only against litigants, the APA . . . go[es] further by empowering the judiciary to act directly against the challenged agency action. This statutory power to 'set aside' agency action is more than a mere non-enforcement remedy. . . . In these situations, the courts do hold the power to 'strike down' an agency's work, and the disapproved agency action is treated as though it had never happened." *Id.* 1012–13. Of course, if a lower court sets aside an agency rule under the APA, the Federal Government may promptly seek a stay in the relevant court of appeals or in this Court if the Government wants the rule to remain in effect while the appellate litigation over the rule's legality is ongoing." Griffin v. HM Florida-ORL, LLC, 144 S.Ct. 1, 2 n.1 (2023) (statement of Kavanaugh, J.).[5]

In contrast to the APA's approval of vacatur, Congress has, on rare occasions, imposed limits on the availability of broad, class-wide relief. One such statute, 8 U.S.C. § 1252(f)(1), reads as follows:

"Regardless of the nature of the action or claim or of the identity of the party or parties bringing the action, no court (other than the Supreme Court) shall have jurisdiction or authority to enjoin or restrain the operation of [Immigration and Nationality Act programs], other than with respect to the application of such provisions to an individual alien against whom proceedings under [those provisions] have been initiated."

In 2022, the statute was the subject of two successive Supreme Court decisions. First, in Garland v. Aleman Gonzalez, 596 U.S. 543 (2022), the Court interpreted § 1252(f)(1) to bar class-wide injunctive relief. The plaintiffs sought certification of a class action brought on behalf of undocumented foreign nationals who had been detained and were awaiting removal. After certification, the district courts "enjoined [the government] from detaining [respondents] and the class members * * * for more than 180 days without providing each a bond hearing." On

---

[5]   For an example of vacatur, see Nat'l Mining Ass'n v. U.S. Army Corps of Eng'rs, 145 F.3d 1399, 1409 (D.C. Cir.1988). Some evidence suggests that district courts addressing unlawful federal government action have increasingly chosen vacatur as a less controversial remedy than a universal injunction. See *Developments*, note 2, *supra*.

review, the Court found that the class-wide injunction was barred by § 1252(f)(1) because it would control the operation of government programs other than in respect to the " 'application of such provisions to an individual alien.' " *Id.* 548 (quoting statute).

Two weeks later, the Court applied the statute again, this time to vacate universal injunctive relief. In Biden v. Texas, 597 U.S. 785 (2022), the state of Texas sued to block the Biden administration from terminating a Trump-era immigration program that required certain foreign nationals to remain in Mexico as they awaited the result of their applications for asylum in the United States. Concluding that the Biden administration had failed to ensure proper detention of the migrants in question, pending their asylum determination, the district court granted a universal injunction against the Biden program. But that form of relief, the Court ruled, operated across-the-board rather than on an alien-specific basis and was barred by the statute.

Like the vacatur provision, the statute construed in Garland and Biden v. Texas represents an unusual instance in which Congress has directly addressed the propriety of issuing forms of universal and class-wide injunctive relief. Does congressional engagement with the problem of broad relief in these two instances have any implications for the Court's role in shaping the availability of such relief?

(e) Questions of Remedial Policy. Assuming its Article III and statutory bona fides, the universal injunction still poses a host of questions of remedial policy, including concerns with forum shopping, loss of percolation, and asymmetric preclusion.

(i) Forum Shopping. As leading players in suits against the federal government, state attorneys general (AGs) can often choose from among several venue options. Conservative AGs may choose to contest Democratic presidential programs in Texas; liberal AGs may prefer to challenge Republican programs in California or Hawaii. Forum shopping may occur within specific states, as state AGs steer litigation to single-judge district courts with congenial judicial incumbents. Commentators have supported legislation that would combat forum shopping by transferring such litigation to three-judge courts or elsewhere. See Mank & Solimine, *State Standing and National Injunctions*, 94 Notre Dame L.Rev. 1955 (2019) (noting and criticizing the use of three-judge courts to combat forum shopping and proposing instead the D.C. courts). For criticism of another venue option, consolidated treatment through multidistrict litigation, see Bradt & Clopton, *MDL v. Trump: The Puzzle of Public Law in Multidistrict Litigation*, 112 Nw.U.L.Rev. 905 (2018) (universal injunction litigation could politicize the MDL process). The Justices have noticed, observing that with "a little bit of forum shopping for a willing judge," a plaintiff can win a broad decree. Labrador v. Poe, 144 S.Ct. 921, 927 (2024) (Gorsuch, J., concurring), Paragraph (b), *supra*.

(ii) Percolation. Universal injunctions raise the stakes, pressuring the government to seek an immediate stay in the appellate court. Often, the issue arrives at the Supreme Court a short time later as it did in the mifepristone litigation, described in Chapter III, see p. 383, *supra*. Such hurried litigation deprives the Court of the benefits of percolation—the process of lower court adjudication and perhaps disagreement that frequently sets the stage for the Court's intervention to clarify a question of federal law. In a world without universal injunctions, percolation might more naturally occur as the government defended its policy initiatives in litigation across the country.[6]

(iii) Asymmetric Preclusion. As Justice Gorsuch noted, concurring in Dep't of Homeland Security v. New York, 140 S.Ct. 599 (2020), universal injunctions introduce claim and issue preclusion asymmetries into federal practice. Preclusion typically operates on the parties to litigation, foreclosing a second round of litigation after a decision on the merits. In a class action, for example, the judgment binds both the members of a certified class and the defendants. But in litigation aimed at securing a universal injunction, the plaintiffs may not seek class certification (as with suits brought by the states). Hence the asymmetry: non-parties may benefit from a favorable universal decree, but they cannot be precluded by an unfavorable decision. Without preclusion, various non-parties might pursue a second, third, or fourth claim against the Government, litigating until they win an injunction that will benefit all. See Morley, *De Facto Class Actions? Plaintiff- and Defendant-Oriented Injunctions in Voting Rights, Election Law, and Other Constitutional Cases*, 39 Harv.J.L. & Pub.Pol'y 487 (2016) (criticizing universal injunctions as inconsistent with the rules governing class actions).

The concern with asymmetry builds on United States v. Mendoza, 464 U.S. 154 (1984), which declined to apply the doctrine of offensive non-mutual collateral estoppel to litigation with the federal government. In general, non-parties can invoke non-mutual collateral estoppel to take advantage of a prior judgment against the defendant in a closely related case (such as one that establishes the defendant's liability in tort for a plane crash). The doctrine does not guarantee access to estoppel; rather, it invites the court to consider the equities including fairness to defendants and gamesmanship by plaintiffs. Citing the special concerns posed by government litigation and the desire to assure percolation, the Court in Mendoza rejected non-mutual estoppel, thereby enabling the government to press a previously rejected defense in later proceedings against another party. Universal injunctions confer protections on non-parties that resemble those rejected in Mendoza. For doubts about Mendoza in general and about its resolving power in the debate over universal injunctions, see Clopton, *National Injunctions and Preclusion*,

---

[6]   Views differ about the value of percolation. Compare Bray, Paragraph (3)(c), *supra*, at 461–62 (emphasizing its importance) with Coenen & Davis, *Percolation's Value*, 73 Stan.L.Rev. 363, 388 (2021) (collecting criticisms of percolation). See generally Estreicher & Revesz, *Nonacquiescence by Federal Administrative Agencies*, 98 Yale L.J. 679 (1989).

118 Mich.L.Rev. 1 (2019); Trammell, *Demystifying Nationwide Injunctions*, 98 Tex.L.Rev. 67 (2019).

(f)   The Practice of Non-Party Protection. As they consider the proposed issuance of universal injunctions, district courts seem to consider at least three factors, in addition to likely success on the merits, in deciding if the balance of equities tips in favor of such broad-gauged relief:

(i)   The Need for National Settlement. As the travel ban cases illustrate, many universal injunction cases involve temporary restraining orders and preliminary injunctions issued to resolve the legality of challenged government action on a nationwide basis. But the national scope of the federal policy or program does not alone justify a universal injunction to secure uniformity. See Frost, Paragraph (c), *supra*, at 1103 (given the dispersed structure of lower court adjudication, district judges cannot justify universal injunctions as "essential to achieve immediate uniformity in the interpretation of federal law"). Indeed, such injunctions may force the Court's hand, allowing district courts that lack the Court's national perspective to determine which matters deserve nationwide resolution.[7]

(ii)   Complete Relief. Equity directs that "injunctive relief should be no more burdensome to the defendant than necessary to provide complete relief to the plaintiffs." Califano v. Yamasaki, 442 U.S. 682, 702 (1979). Striking that balance poses challenges. Unlike a party-specific judgment for damages, an injunctive decree redressing harm to a single party may have consequences for other members of the community. Consider a nuisance decree: shutting down a polluting plant will assure cleaner air for all members of the community (not just the plaintiff) and will burden workers who lose their jobs. Or consider a desegregation decree: a single child cannot obtain an integrated public-school education except through enrollment policies that affect all children. In both instances, complete relief for parties may confer protections (or burdens) on non-parties, including those similarly situated to the plaintiffs. In balancing the equities, the Court has insisted on due regard for these spillover effects and "public consequences." Weinberger v. Romero-Barcelo, 456 U.S. 305, 312 (1982). Taking account of these effects, the issuing court must find "that an injunction is in the public interest." Winter v. Natural Resources Defense Council, Inc., 555 U.S. 7 (2008).

(iii) Administrative Complexity. Sometimes the lower courts will grant non-party relief because of the breadth and complexity of the administrative scheme. In one early example, the D.C. Circuit universally enjoined the operation of a government regulation that

---

[7]   See Labrador v. Poe, 144 S.Ct. 921, 928 (2024) (Gorsuch, J, concurring) ("A rising number of universal injunctions virtually guarantees that a rising number of 'high-profile' cases will find their way to this Court."); Dep't of Homeland Security v. New York, 140 S.Ct. 599 (2020) (Gorsuch, J., concurring) (lamenting that "universal injunctions tend to force judges into making rushed, high-stakes, low-information decisions"); see also Bray, Paragraph 3(c), *supra*, at 422, 461–62.

defined "locality" very broadly in setting the "prevailing wage" payable by firms bidding in a national market to supply steel to government procurement projects. See Perkins v. Lukens Steel Co., 310 U.S. 113 (1940) (vacating and remanding on other grounds). Administrative complexity was also said to support universal injunctions against the travel ban and DAPA. The states of Hawaii (travel ban) and Texas (DAPA) argued that free travel between states would undermine any remedy tailored to protect one state alone. For an account, including the difficulties that ensued when one district court granted travel ban relief limited to a single state, see Frost, Paragraph (c), *supra*, at 1092–94, 1099.

CHAPTER X

COORDINATING CONCURRENT JURISDICTION IN A FEDERAL SYSTEM

INTRODUCTORY NOTE

Much of the law in this book deals with the allocation of adjudicative authority between state and federal courts. These allocational decisions have produced a judicial federalism in which the jurisdiction of state and federal courts overlaps pervasively. Federal district courts hear state law matters in their diversity and supplemental jurisdiction, see Chap. VIII, Secs. 5, 7, and state courts presumptively enjoy concurrent jurisdiction over claims arising under federal law, see Chap. IV, Sec. 3. The overlap extends to matters nominally within exclusive federal jurisdiction, such as patent and antitrust issues that sometimes arise as defenses in state court to claims based on state law.

Given pervasive jurisdictional overlap, parties to disputes often invoke the concurrent jurisdiction of both a state and a federal court. This chapter examines the rules of coordination that govern when the parties pursue such overlapping claims. First, the chapter introduces the problem by examining the choice between a first-to-file and first-to-judgment rule of coordination. As will be seen, the Supreme Court has generally followed a first-to-judgment rule in cases of concurrent *in personam* litigation but has recognized a first-to-file exception for *in rem* claims. The first section explores these *in personam* and *in rem* coordination rules.

The remainder of the chapter explores the injunction's role as a tool of coordination and the exceptions to presumed concurrency that the Supreme Court has recognized in the name of judicial federalism. The Anti-Injunction Act, 28 U.S.C. § 2283, limits the power of federal courts to enjoin pending state court proceedings, subject to important exceptions. But the decision in Ex parte Young, 209 U.S. 123 (1908), p. 1184, *supra*, holds that federal courts may enjoin state enforcement if they act *before* the commencement of any state proceeding. This chapter examines rules that restrict anticipatory federal injunctive relief, focusing particular attention on judge-made abstention doctrines that require federal judicial deference to pending or contemplated state court proceedings.

1. COORDINATION RULES: FIRST TO FILE OR FIRST TO JUDGMENT

Kline v. Burke Construction Company

260 U.S. 226 (1922).

Certiorari to the Circuit Court of Appeals for the Eighth Circuit.

■ MR. JUSTICE SUTHERLAND delivered the opinion of the Court.

[On February 16, 1920, Burke Construction Company, a Missouri corporation, brought an action for damages in Arkansas federal district court against petitioners (citizens of Arkansas), invoking diversity jurisdiction. The suit alleged breach of a contract under which Burke was to pave certain streets in the town of Texarkana.

[On March 19, 1920, petitioners brought a suit in equity in an Arkansas Chancery Court against Burke and the sureties on the bond given for the faithful performance of the contract. The bill alleged that Burke had abandoned the contract; it sought an accounting for all the work, completed and yet unfinished, and prayed for judgment in the sum of $88,000. Burke removed the equity suit to federal district court, which remanded the case to the Arkansas Chancery Court.

[Both actions were *in personam* and sought monetary compensation; they presented substantially the same issues; and the defendants' answer and cross-complaint in each alleged, in substance, the matters set forth as plaintiffs in the other. The principal difference between the suits was the addition of the sureties as defendants in the equitable action.

[In the federal action, following a mistrial, Burke sought to enjoin petitioners from further prosecuting the state court action. The federal district court denied the injunction, but the court of appeals reversed and remanded with instructions to issue the injunction.] From that decree the case comes here upon writ of certiorari.

Section 265 of the Judicial Code [the Anti-Injunction Act, now codified, as amended, as 28 U.S.C. § 2283] provides:

> "The writ of injunction shall not be granted by any court of the United States to stay proceedings in any court of a State, except in cases where such injunction may be authorized by any law relating to proceedings in bankruptcy."

But this section is to be construed in connection with section 262 [the All Writs Act, now codified, as amended, as 28 U.S.C. § 1651], which authorizes the United States courts "to issue all writs not specifically provided for by statute, which may be necessary for the exercise of their respective jurisdictions and agreeable to the usages and principles of law." It is settled that where a federal court has first acquired jurisdiction of the subject-matter of a cause, it may enjoin the parties from proceeding in a state court of concurrent jurisdiction where the effect of the action would be to defeat or impair the jurisdiction of the federal court. Where the action is *in rem* the effect is to draw to the federal court the possession or control, actual or potential, of the *res*, and the exercise by the state court of jurisdiction over the same *res* necessarily impairs, and may defeat, the jurisdiction of the federal court already attached. The converse of the rule is equally true, that where the jurisdiction of the state court has first attached, the federal court is precluded from exercising its jurisdiction over the same *res* to defeat or impair the state court's jurisdiction. * * *

But a controversy * * * over a mere question of personal liability does not involve the possession or control of a thing, and an action brought to enforce such a liability does not tend to impair or defeat the jurisdiction of the court in which a prior action for the same cause is pending. Each court is free to proceed in its own way and in its own time, without reference to the proceedings in the other court. Whenever a judgment is rendered in one of the courts and pleaded in the other, the effect of that judgment is to be determined by the application of the principles of *res adjudicata* by the court in which the action is still pending * * *. The rule, therefore, has become generally established that where the action first brought is *in personam* and seeks only a personal judgment, another action for the same cause in another jurisdiction is not precluded. [Citing numerous cases.]

* * * In the case now under consideration, however, the court below held otherwise, upon the ground that:

> "By the Constitution of the United States, article III, section 2, and the acts of Congress, the constitutional right was granted to the Burke Company to ask and to have a trial and adjudication by the federal court." * * *

The force of the cases above cited is sought to be broken by the suggestion that in none of them was this question of constitutional right presented or considered.

The right of a litigant to maintain an action in a federal court on the ground that there is a controversy between citizens of different States is not one derived from the Constitution of the United States, unless in a very indirect sense. * * *

* * * Only the jurisdiction of the Supreme Court is derived directly from the Constitution. Every other court created by the general government derives its jurisdiction wholly from the authority of Congress. * * * A right which thus comes into existence only by virtue of an act of Congress * * * cannot well be described as a constitutional right. The Construction Company, however, had the undoubted right under the

statute to invoke the jurisdiction of the federal court and that court was bound to take the case and proceed to judgment. It could not abdicate its authority or duty in favor of the state jurisdiction. But, while this is true, it is likewise true that the state court had jurisdiction of the suit instituted by petitioners. Indeed, since the case presented by that suit was such as to preclude its removal to the federal jurisdiction, the state jurisdiction in that particular suit was exclusive. It was, therefore, equally the duty of the state court to take the case and proceed to judgment. There can be no question of judicial supremacy, or of superiority of individual right. * * * The rank and authority of the courts are equal but both courts cannot possess or control the same thing at the same time, and any attempt to do so would result in unseemly conflict. The rule, therefore, that the court first acquiring jurisdiction shall proceed without interference from a court of the other jurisdiction is a rule of right and of law based upon necessity, and where the necessity, actual or potential, does not exist, the rule does not apply. Since that necessity does exist in actions *in rem* and does not exist in actions *in personam*, involving a question of personal liability only, the rule applies in the former but does not apply in the latter.

The decree of the Circuit Court of Appeals is therefore reversed and the case remanded to the District Court for further proceedings in conformity with this opinion.

Princess Lida of Thurn and Taxis v. Thompson

305 U.S. 456 (1939).

Lida Purcell married Gerald Fitzgerald in 1899. When the marriage ended, Fitzgerald settled a trust to provide support for his former wife and children. Sometime later, she married Prince Victor of Thurn and Taxis, a minor German noble. All was (more or less) well until the stock market crashed in 1929 and the trustees filed their accounts in 1930 with the Pennsylvania court of common pleas. A day later, Princess Lida and her son sued in Pennsylvania federal district court, alleging trust fund mismanagement and demanding removal of trustees and an accounting. The state court of common pleas, meanwhile, found that the filing of the trustees' accounts brought the trust and its property before that court for administration. Concluding that it had exclusive jurisdiction of the *res*, the state court enjoined prosecution of the later-filed federal proceeding. On appeal, Pennsylvania's supreme court upheld the injunction.

The Supreme Court affirmed. Under state law, the submission of trustee accounts triggered a proceeding seeking judicial approval of asset management. That meant, the Court explained, that the state court's administrative powers were fully engaged, including oversight of the trustee's compensation, expenses, asset management decisions, and investment performance. Interested parties were authorized to object to the account, raising all pertinent questions respecting the management of the trust, and invoking the powers of the court. If an audit were to show grounds for the trustee's removal, the court could compel the removed trustee to transfer the trust assets to his successor.

Evaluating the potential for conflict, the Court found that only two of the trust's five beneficiaries had appeared in federal court. Another had appeared in state court, objecting to the trustees' accounts. That meant, the Court explained,

"that if both courts were to proceed they would be required to cover the same ground. This of itself is not conclusive of the question of the [federal court's] jurisdiction, for it is settled that where the judgment sought is strictly *in personam*, both the state court and the federal court, having concurrent jurisdiction, may proceed with the litigation at least until judgment is obtained in one of them which may be set up as *res judicata* in the other. On the other hand, if the two suits are *in rem*, or *quasi in rem*, so that the court, or its officer, has possession or must have control of the property which is the subject of the litigation in order to proceed with the cause and grant the relief sought the jurisdiction of the one court must yield to that of the other. [T]he principle applicable to both federal and state courts that the court first assuming jurisdiction over property may maintain and exercise that jurisdiction to the exclusion of the other, is not restricted to cases where property has been actually seized under judicial process before a second suit is instituted, but applies as well where suits are brought to marshal assets, administer trusts, or liquidate estates, and in suits of a similar nature where, to give effect to its jurisdiction, the court must control the property. The doctrine is necessary to the harmonious cooperation of federal and state tribunals. While it has no application to a case in a federal court based upon diversity of citizenship, wherein the plaintiff seeks merely an adjudication of his right of his interest as a basis of a claim against a fund in the possession of a state court, this is not such a case. No question is presented in the federal court as to the right of any person to participate in the *res* or as to the quantum of his interest in it. The contentions are solely as to administration and restoration of corpus."

NOTE ON COORDINATION: FIRST TO FILE OR FIRST TO JUDGMENT?

In a leading decision on coordination of overlapping state and federal jurisdiction, the Kline Court ruled that the federal court in Arkansas lacked power to enjoin an overlapping and subsequently filed state court proceeding. In emphasizing the concurrent jurisdiction of state and federal courts and the *in personam* nature of the proceedings, the Court held that the federal court did not obtain priority by virtue of being the first court to secure jurisdiction over the disputing parties. Priority on this view begins not on the date of filing but on the date one court (state or federal) enters a final judgment, resolving the dispute. At that point, the doctrines of claim and issue preclusion will require the second court to give effect to the prior adjudication. Critics of Kline's first-to-judgment rule worry that it invites wasteful and duplicative litigation.

The Kline Court viewed the Anti-Injunction Act (AIA), now 28 U.S.C. § 2283, as consistent with its approach; as then codified, the AIA barred federal courts from issuing the "writ of injunction" to stay proceedings in state court. The Court has imposed the same regime of presumptive concurrency on state courts (albeit without explicit statutory guidance), denying them power to enjoin overlapping and arguably claim-precluded federal court suits to impose a personal liability. See Donovan v. City of Dallas, 377 U.S. 408 (1964); M'Kim v. Voorhies, 11 U.S. (7 Cranch) 279 (1812).

As an alternative to Kline's first-to-judgment rule, some commentators propose, and some complex federated judicial systems have chosen, to give priority (absolute or presumptive) to the suit first filed. Under the doctrine of *lis pendens*, as codified in European Union regulations, the courts of the member states in Europe must defer to the primacy of the first member state court seized with jurisdiction of a dispute between the parties.[1] Europe thus features a race to a single courthouse, while litigants in the United States may find themselves racing through multiple courthouses on their way to a judgment.[2]

The presumptive concurrency contemplated by the first-to-judgment rule means that, in general, parties and courts owe no deference to earlier-filed litigation. But in addition to the *in rem* exception to presumptive concurrency mentioned in Kline, the Court has recognized a range of abstention doctrines, which later sections of this chapter explore in some detail. Such doctrines owe much to the traditional rule that courts of equity will refuse to interpose when the plaintiff has adequate remedies at law. Something of the sort occurs under abstention doctrines that require federal courts to abstain in deference to state court litigation when doing so might avoid constitutional issues and preserve the state court's role in hearing federal law issues that arise in certain state proceedings.

Posing questions of their own, these abstention doctrines seriously complicate the apparent clarity and simplicity of Kline's presumptive-concurrency/first-to-judgment rule. See, *e.g.*, Rehnquist, *Taking Comity Seriously: How to Neutralize the Abstention Doctrine*, 46 Stan.L.Rev. 1049, 1068 (1994) (advocating replacement of all of the various abstention doctrines—under which a federal court may dismiss or stay proceedings within its statutory jurisdiction—with the rule that "[a] federal court should abstain if, and only if, the federal plaintiff has an adequate opportunity to litigate his federal claim in a duplicative suit already pending in state court").[3] In reading more about the abstention doctrines, consider whether

---

[1] State property law often require litigants contesting title to file a caveat or *lis pendens* with the recording office to provide notice of a pending claim to the property in question. But such rules of notice differ from Europe's general rule of deference to the first-filed proceeding.

[2] See Article 29, Regulation (EU) No 1215/2012 of the European Parliament and of the Council of 12 December 2012 on Jurisdiction and the Recognition and Enforcement of Judgments in Civil and Commercial Matters (providing "any court other than the court first seised shall of its own motion stay its proceedings until such time as the jurisdiction of the court first seised is established").

[3] See also Currie, *The Federal Courts and the American Law Institute (II)*, 36 U.Chi.L.Rev. 268, 335 (1969).

Rehnquist's proposed approach would give adequate weight to the decision of Congress to confer jurisdiction on the federal courts. If it seems essential to furnish a federal forum for certain claims, Congress might achieve that goal through expanded access to removal jurisdiction for any important federal questions that current jurisdictional rules otherwise consign to state court. Removal may pose fewer threats to harmonious federal-state judicial relations than Rehnquist's proposed reliance on routine stay orders.

NOTE ON THE FIRST-TO-FILE RULE IN THE EQUITABLE ADMINISTRATION OF PROPERTY

As Kline acknowledges and Princess Lida illustrates, the Supreme Court has long recognized an exception to the first-to-judgment rule for *in rem* proceedings. As to such proceedings, the Court's articulated rule of coordination gives primacy to the first court (state or federal) to assert jurisdiction over a specified fund, trust, estate, asset, or property.[1] This Note describes the origins and current application of this first-to-file rule in property cases, explaining the distinction between the "liquidation" of a claim to a fund or asset and the "administration" of those assets to ensure the orderly payment of competing claims. The chapter sometimes uses the term equitable priority to describe the Court's decision to assign decisional primacy to the first court to secure jurisdiction in property cases.

(1) The Origins of Equitable Priority. Equitable administration arose in England, where the High Court of Chancery would enter a decree for the administration of assets when it became clear that the available fund or property was insufficient to fully satisfy all legitimate claims. Langdell, *A Brief Survey of Equity Jurisdiction*, 5 Harv.L.Rev. 101, 104–05 (1891), described the process as follows:

"The administration of an estate consists in dividing it among the several persons who have interests in it or claims upon it, according to their respective rights; and, to enable a court so to divide an estate, it must ascertain, not only who such persons are, but what are their respective rights; and, in order to enable it to do the latter, it must have all such persons before it * * *; and this latter object can be accomplished only by means of one suit or proceeding. In short, when a court undertakes to administer an estate, it must consider the claim of every particular person in connection with the claims of all other persons, and it cannot dispose of any one person's claim separately and by itself."

Such forms of equitable administration could arise in a variety of now-familiar proceedings, including bankruptcy, the equitable oversight of trusts and decedent's estates, equitable receiverships, and interpleader claims to a

---

[1]   On the origins of property-based primacy, see Buck v. Colbath, 70 U.S. 334 (1865). There, the Court explained that a state court could not proceed directly against property that a federal marshal seized to satisfy a federal judgment. But state courts could hear a trespass claim, seeking damages from the marshal for wrongly seizing the property in question. Unlike specific relief, the *in personam* trespass claim would not interfere with marshal's prior possession.

limited fund. In these situations, it was understood that all claimants were obliged to seek satisfaction in the context of a single equitable proceeding. See Hazard & Moskovitz, *An Historical and Critical Analysis of Interpleader*, 52 Calif.L.Rev. 706 (1964) (explaining the process in interpleader actions).

In England, the primary challenge to effective equitable coordination of claims was posed when one creditor secured or sought a separate judgment in a common law court. But the High Court of Chancery would grant an injunction against proceedings at law, insisting that the creditor seek satisfaction of any such claim as part of the pending equity action. See Robert Henley Eden, A Treatise on the Law of Injunctions 31–33 (1821) (explaining Chancery's power to enjoin the pursuit of conflicting claims as deriving from its "having taken the fund into its hands"). As Kline explains, federal courts could coordinate claims to property within their control by staying overlapping state court actions (notwithstanding the limits on equitable relief in the Anti-Injunction Act, a topic explored below). As Princess Lida makes clear, a state court enjoyed corresponding authority to enjoin a competing federal proceeding (notwithstanding structural limits on the power of state courts to control federal adjudication).

Adapting this conception of unified equitable administration for litigation in the United States posed distinctive problems of federalism and territoriality that the English unitary state did not confront. The Supreme Court managed these problems in the nineteenth century through broad conceptions of *in rem* jurisdiction (thereby overcoming territorial limits on judicial jurisdiction) and ancillary jurisdiction, which arose as an exception to the subject matter jurisdictional limits imposed by the complete diversity rule. See Chap. VIII, Sec. 5.

(2) Distinguishing Equitable Administration from Claim Liquidation. Despite a preference for coordinated treatment, the Court has distinguished between the administrative distribution of assets among creditors and the liquidation of claims of indebtedness brought by creditors of the estate. In Riehle v. Margolies, 279 U.S. 218, 224 (1929), the Court explained that the court with equitable priority had exclusive control over matters of distribution: "no one can obtain any part of the assets, or enforce a right to specific property in the possession of a receiver, except upon application to the court which appointed him." But no such exclusivity extended to a suit brought by a creditor to "liquidate" a claim to the property of the defendant or estate. As the product of a proceeding *in personam*, such a liquidating judgment "does not purport to deal with the property." The Riehle Court thus upheld the validity of a state court judgment as proof of the claim in question. Once the claim has been liquidated, then any distribution in satisfaction of the claim must be handled by the court with equitable priority.

In Princess Lida, the Court acknowledged the distinction between claim administration and claim liquidation but concluded that the federal court proceeding went beyond mere liquidation. As the Court viewed matters, the federal plaintiffs did not seek to establish their right to assets in the trust but to challenge the performance of the trustees. That issue of trustee performance had been drawn into issue when the trustees sought state court approval of their accounts. The Court thus recognized the state court's constructive control of the trust and related questions about its proper management. The trustees' suit therefore qualified as one for the equitable administration of trust assets that triggered state court equitable priority.[2]

(3) Evaluating the Kline/Princess Lida Distinction. Unlike the Kline Court, which allowed duplicative litigation of *in personam* claims, the Princess Lida Court upheld the state court's exclusive control over the issues of fiduciary performance after finding that the trustees' petition for approval of accounts initiated an *in rem* or quasi *in rem* proceeding. Consider whether the formal distinction between *in personam* and *in rem* claims can bear the weight of justifying the Court's differential approach to Kline and Princess Lida. In other contexts, the Court has downplayed the distinction's significance, describing "(t)he phrase, 'judicial jurisdiction over a thing', [as] a customary elliptical way of referring to jurisdiction over the interests of persons in a thing." Shaffer v. Heitner, 433 U.S. 186, 207 (1977) (quoting Restatement (Second) of Conflict of Laws § 56, Introductory Note (1971)). Note too that the argument from wasteful duplication might appear stronger in Kline, where the parties and claims were essentially identical. The federal plaintiffs in Princess Lida, by contrast, did not formally appear in state court (but would likely have been bound by its disposition nonetheless).

Consider the possibility that differential treatment has less to do with the formal distinction between personal and property-based judgments than with a functional difference in the systemic interest in consolidated proceedings. When personal claims overlap as in Kline, coordination through a first-to-file rule coupled with an anti-suit injunction would advance systemic interests in the avoidance of duplicative litigation. But existing law compels both state and federal courts to give claim preclusive effect to the judgments of coordinate courts, thereby vindicating that interest to some degree. See Donovan v. City of Dallas, 377 U.S. 408 (1964) (rejecting state court power to enjoin a federal proceeding and emphasizing the obligation of the federal court to accord the Texas judgment claim preclusive effect). One can of course argue that our system should, like that in Europe, accord greater weight to the interest in avoiding duplicative proceedings.

In Princess Lida, by contrast, coordination through a first-to-file rule coupled with an anti-suit injunction advances a systemic interest in securing unitary administration of claims to a specified fund, trust, or estate. Fairness to all parties, especially in cases of insolvency, was thought to require consolidation to ensure that no one gets too much or too little. The argument

---

[2]   One can better understand that conclusion with a sense of the close working relationship that arises between a court of equity and the parties who bear a fiduciary responsibility for the day-to-day management of property that belongs to others. These fiduciaries go by various names—receiver, executor, administrator, trustee—and they may be either court-appointed (receivers) or chosen in a legal instrument, such as a will (executor) or a trust (trustee). Fiduciaries bear primary responsibility for hands-on management of the assets in question, and may seek judicial approval of their fees and their managerial and investment decisions. When courts of equity approve a fiduciary's accounts and fee application, they distribute assets and effectively adjudicate and uphold the legality of the transactions reflected in them. Preclusive effect may attach even in the absence of party contestation, a fact that helps to explain the Court's insistence that trustees notify interested parties of the pendency of such proceedings. See Mullane v. Central Hanover Bank & Trust Co., 339 U.S. 306 (1950).

for unitary administration of property now finds its most obvious analogs in state court trust and probate proceedings and federal court bankruptcy proceedings and may also inform the Burford and Colorado River abstention doctrines explored later in this chapter, see pp. 1398, 1400, *infra*.

---

2. STATUTORY PROVISIONS FOR COORDINATION

A. THE ANTI-INJUNCTION ACT

From its adoption in 1793, the Anti-Injunction Act (AIA) has imposed a statutory restriction on the power of federal courts to stay proceedings in state court. As first adopted, the Act provided that no "writ of injunction [shall] be granted to stay proceedings in any court of a state." Act of Mar. 2, 1793, ch. 22, § 5, 1 Stat. 333. Congress amended the Act in 1874, creating an exception where authorized by "any law relating to proceedings in bankruptcy." See Rev. Stat. § 720, 18 Stat. 136 (1874). But as suggested in Kline v. Burke Construction Co., 260 U.S. 226 (1922), the statutory bar to anti-suit injunctions was long understood as less than absolute. The AIA's history, purpose, and early application have shaped its codification in 1948 and its operation today.

(1) History and Purpose. Conventional accounts portray the original AIA as having the purpose of preventing tension between state and federal courts. Disputing that assumption, Professor Mayton argues that the original Act of 1793 was designed merely to prohibit a *single Justice* of the Supreme Court from enjoining such proceedings while riding circuit. Mayton, *Ersatz Federalism under the Anti-Injunction Statute*, 78 Colum.L.Rev. 330 (1978). The original meaning was lost, Mayton argues, when, in Peck v. Jenness, 48 U.S. (7 How.) 612 (1849), the Supreme Court asserted without discussion that the Act barred federal injunctions against state court proceedings.

Pfander & Nazemi, *The Anti-Injunction Act and the Problem of Federal-State Jurisdictional Overlap*, 92 Tex.L.Rev. 1 (2013), offer an alternative account of the statute's text and history. According to the authors, in limiting use of the "writ of injunction" to stay proceedings in state court, the original AIA sought to prevent a federal court, sitting in equity, from enforcing equitable defenses to a pending state court proceeding. At the time of enactment, common law courts did not recognize equitable defenses (fraud, accident, mistake); parties seeking to assert such defenses initiated a new proceeding in a court of equity and, if successful, secured an anti-suit injunction staying any continued prosecution of the common law proceeding. By preventing federal courts from interposing equitable defenses to pending state court actions, the AIA forced state court defendants to pursue their equitable defenses in a competent state court.

When by contrast a federal court of equity first asserted power over a dispute within its jurisdiction, it had ancillary or auxiliary authority to stay conflicting proceedings in other tribunals. See *id.* 20–31. Such ancillary relief operated in the nature of an injunction; but because the parties were already before the court on a bill of complaint, it was not necessary to sue out a new "writ of injunction." Thus, the prohibition in the AIA applied to original, after-filed suits in equity to stay a state court proceeding but did not apply when the federal court first obtained jurisdiction. Pfander and Nazemi argue that, where the federal equity court had secured jurisdiction over property or entered a binding decree, its authority to enforce its equitable control over the property or to compel compliance with its decrees was ancillary to a pending action and did not implicate the ban on original proceedings for a "writ of injunction."[1]

(2) Pre-1948 Applications. Several pre-1948 decisions treated the AIA as less than an absolute prohibition on federal stays of state court proceedings. Many of these injunctions lacked explicit statutory support but were defensible on the view that ancillary relief was proper to defend a federal court's jurisdiction and decrees.

(a) The *In Rem*/Property Exception. A line of cases beginning with Hagan v. Lucas, 35 U.S. (10 Pet.) 400 (1836), and reaffirmed in Freeman v. Howe, 65 U.S. 450 (1860), declared that the court (state or federal) that first assumes jurisdiction over property may exercise that jurisdiction to the exclusion of any other court—if necessary by enjoining another court's proceedings. The *in rem*/property exception was recognized in Kline v. Burke Construction and applied in Princess Lida (although obviously not in a context that implicated the AIA).[2] In Providence & N.Y.S.S. Co. v. Hill Mfg. Co., 109 U.S. 578, 600–01 (1883), the Court extended the property exception to encompass after-initiated federal proceedings under a federal statute limiting the maritime tort liability of a shipowner to the value of the vessel. The statute in question declared that, when the owner pays the vessel's value into the registry of an admiralty court, "all claims and proceedings * * * shall cease." 46 U.S.C. § 185. On review of a Massachusetts state court judgment that refused to give effect to the statute and awarded damages in a separate proceeding against the shipowner, the Court reversed. Explaining the need for coordination, the Court found it "obvious on the face of the thing that proceedings for limited liability cannot be participated in by two jurisdictions without interference and conflict between them." *Id.* 595. As

---

[1] In a separate article, *Morris v. Allen and the Lost History of the Anti-Injunction Act of 1793*, 108 Nw.U.L.Rev. 187 (2014), Pfander and Nazemi argue that the impetus for adopting the AIA stemmed in part from a high-profile federal suit by financier and Senator Robert Morris that largely duplicated a pending state court equitable action and from a report by Attorney General Edmund Randolph (which the AIA follows only in part) recommending congressional action to avoid bifurcated proceedings.

[2] Compare Mandeville v. Canterbury, 318 U.S. 47 (1943) (holding that because federal court action concerning a trust was *in personam*, related state court action could not be enjoined).

for the federal district court's injunction against continued prosecution of the Massachusetts state proceeding, the Court explained that although the issue was not directly presented on appeal "we have little doubt of its legality." *Id.* 600.

(b) Fraudulent State Court Judgments. Several Supreme Court decisions sustained the power of federal courts to enjoin litigants from enforcing judgments fraudulently obtained in state courts. See, *e.g.*, Wells Fargo & Co. v. Taylor, 254 U.S. 175, 184–86 (1920); Simon v. S. Ry. Co., 236 U.S. 115, 128 (1915); Marshall v. Holmes, 141 U.S. 589, 601 (1891). Apart from ignoring the AIA, these decisions effectively denied preclusive effect to prior state court judgments and allowed collateral attack on judgments that were subject to appellate review in the Supreme Court. (The interaction of preclusion and appellate jurisdiction now shapes the Rooker-Feldman doctrine, as discussed at p. 1387, *infra*.)

(c) The Relitigation Exception. When the AIA was drafted, it was understood that courts of law did not give claim or issue preclusive effect to some equitable decrees. See Eden, A Treatise on the Law of Injunctions 31 (1821) (observing that courts of law did "not tak[e] notice of a decree in equity, which therefore compel[led] them, in support of their jurisdiction, to establish their decrees by injunction"). In Root v. Woolworth, 150 U.S. 401 (1893), the Court viewed as "well settled" the principle that "a court of equity has jurisdiction to carry into effect it[s] own orders, decrees, and judgments, which remain unreversed, when the subject-matter and the parties are the same in both proceedings." *Id.* 410–11. Affirming a decision below that enjoined a duplicative state proceeding, the Court characterized the relief in question as "ancillary" to the "original" bill and "supplementary" to an earlier decree. *Id.* 413. This ancillary quality was apparently thought to render the AIA inapplicable.

(d) The Toucey Decision. In Toucey v. New York Life Ins. Co., 314 U.S. 118 (1941), the Court (per Justice Frankfurter) broke with historical practice, holding that the federal courts lacked authority to enjoin state relitigation of issues settled in a prior federal action. The opinion found the precedents upholding such injunctions to be at most "a tenuous basis for the exception which we are now asked explicitly to sanction;" "[w]e must be scrupulous in our regard for the limits within which Congress has confined the authority of the courts of its own creation." *Id.* 140–41. Although acknowledging the existence of the "*res*" exception, the Court argued that "[t]he fact that one exception has found its way into [the statute] is no justification for making another."[3]

---

[3]   Compare Pfander & Nazemi, Paragraph (1), supra, at 8: "[C]ontrary to Justice Frankfurter's view, the AIA exceptions were often well grounded in the Act's qualified language. In the main, federal courts granted injunctive relief against state proceedings when the former had first obtained authority over the dispute, when the relief sought was ancillary to the federal action, and when the relief sought to defend the federal court's equitable priority. Indeed, in many of the leading cases, the Supreme Court expressly invoked the distinction between original and ancillary injunctive relief in support of federal authority."

(e) The 1948 Revision. Section 2283, the current embodiment of the Anti-Injunction Act, dates from the 1948 revision of the Judicial Code: "A court of the United States may not grant an injunction to stay proceedings in a State court except as expressly authorized by Act of Congress, or where necessary in aid of its jurisdiction, or to protect or effectuate its judgments." 28 U.S.C. § 2283. The Revisers' Notes offered this explanation:

"An exception as to acts of Congress relating to bankruptcy was omitted and the general exception substituted to cover all exceptions.

"The phrase 'in aid of its jurisdiction' was added to conform to section 1651 of this title and to make clear the recognized power of the Federal courts to stay proceedings in State cases removed to the district courts.

"The exceptions specifically include the words 'to protect or effectuate its judgments,' for lack of which the Supreme Court held that the Federal courts are without power to enjoin relitigation of cases and controversies fully adjudicated by such courts. (See Toucey v. New York Life Ins. Co. * * *. A vigorous dissenting opinion * * * notes that at the time of the 1911 revision of the Judicial Code, the power of the courts of the United States to protect their judgments was unquestioned and that the revisers of that code noted no change and Congress intended no change).

"Therefore the revised section restores the basic law as generally understood and interpreted prior to the Toucey decision.

"Changes were made in phraseology."

Smith v. Bayer Corp.

564 U.S. 299 (2011).
Certiorari to the United States Court of Appeals for the Eighth Circuit.

■ JUSTICE KAGAN delivered the opinion of the Court.*

In this case, a Federal District Court enjoined a state court from considering a plaintiff's request to approve a class action. The District Court did so because it had earlier denied a motion to certify a class in a related case, brought by a different plaintiff against the same defendant alleging similar claims. The federal court thought its injunction appropriate to prevent relitigation of the issue it had decided.

We hold to the contrary. In issuing this order to a state court, the federal court exceeded its authority under the "relitigation exception" to the Anti-Injunction Act. That statutory provision permits a federal court to enjoin a state proceeding only in rare cases, when necessary to "protect or effectuate [the federal court's] judgments." 28 U.S.C. § 2283. Here, that standard was not met for two reasons. First, the issue presented in

---

*   JUSTICE THOMAS joins Parts I and II-A of this opinion.

the state court was not identical to the one decided in the federal tribunal. And second, the plaintiff in the state court did not have the requisite connection to the federal suit to be bound by the District Court's judgment.

I

[Two class actions, initiated in West Virginia state court, sought to recover damages allegedly caused by Bayer's sale of a prescription drug called Baycol. One class action, brought in the name of Smith as class representative, stayed in state court. The other, brought in the name of McCollins, was removed to federal court and transferred to the District of Minnesota for consolidated proceedings by the Judicial Panel on Multi-District Litigation. Lengthy pre-trial proceedings ensued in both West Virginia and Minnesota.]

Applying Federal Rule of Civil Procedure 23, the District Court declined to certify McCollins' proposed class of West Virginia Baycol purchasers. The District Court's reasoning proceeded in two steps. The court first ruled that, under West Virginia law, each plaintiff would have to prove "actual injury" from his use of Baycol to recover. The court then held that because the necessary showing of harm would vary from plaintiff to plaintiff, "individual issues of fact predominate[d]" over issues common to all members of the proposed class, and so the case was not suitable for class treatment. * * *

Although McCollins' suit was now concluded, Bayer asked the District Court for another order based upon it, this one affecting Smith's case in West Virginia. In a motion—receipt of which first apprised Smith of McCollins' suit—Bayer explained that the proposed class in Smith's case was identical to the one the federal court had just rejected. Bayer therefore requested that the federal court enjoin the West Virginia state court from hearing Smith's motion to certify a class. According to Bayer, that order was appropriate to protect the District Court's judgment in McCollins' suit denying class certification. The District Court agreed and granted the injunction. * * *

We granted certiorari * * * and we now reverse.

II

* * * This case involves the last of the Act's three exceptions, known as the relitigation exception. That exception is designed to implement "well-recognized concepts" of claim and issue preclusion. Chick Kam Choo [v. Exxon Corp.], 486 U.S. [140,] 147 [(1988)]. The provision authorizes an injunction to prevent state litigation of a claim or issue "that previously was presented to and decided by the federal court." *Ibid.* But in applying this exception, we have taken special care to keep it "strict and narrow." *Id.*, at 148. After all, a court does not usually "get to dictate to other courts the preclusion consequences of its own judgment." 18 C. Wright, A. Miller, & E. Cooper, Federal Practice and Procedure § 4405, p. 82 (2d ed.2002) (hereinafter Wright & Miller). Deciding

whether and how prior litigation has preclusive effect is usually the bailiwick of the *second* court (here, the one in West Virginia). So issuing an injunction under the relitigation exception is resorting to heavy artillery.[5] For that reason, every benefit of the doubt goes toward the state court; an injunction can issue only if preclusion is clear beyond peradventure.

The question here is whether the federal court's rejection of McCollins' proposed class precluded a later adjudication in state court of Smith's certification motion. For the federal court's determination of the class issue to have this preclusive effect, at least two conditions must be met.[6] First, the issue the federal court decided must be the same as the one presented in the state tribunal. And second, Smith must have been a party to the federal suit, or else must fall within one of a few discrete exceptions to the general rule against binding nonparties. In fact, as we will explain, the issues before the two courts were not the same, and Smith was neither a party nor the exceptional kind of nonparty who can be bound. So the courts below erred in finding the certification issue precluded, and erred all the more in thinking an injunction appropriate.

A

In our most recent case on the relitigation exception, Chick Kam Choo v. Exxon, we applied the "same issue" requirement of preclusion law to invalidate a federal court's injunction. 486 U.S., at 151. [In that case, after ordering dismissal of a federal suit on grounds of *forum non conveniens*, the federal district court enjoined a similar Texas state court proceeding. But this Court reversed after concluding that Texas courts would apply "a significantly different *forum non conveniens* analysis," *id.*, at 149, and reject the strictness of the federal doctrine.] Because the legal standards in the two courts differed, the issues before the courts differed, and an injunction was unwarranted.

The question here closely resembles the one in Chick Kam Choo. The class Smith proposed in state court mirrored the class McCollins sought to certify in federal court: Both included all Baycol purchasers resident in West Virginia. Moreover, the substantive claims in the two suits broadly overlapped: Both complaints alleged that Bayer had sold a defective product in violation of the state's consumer protection law and the company's warranties. So far, so good for preclusion. But not so fast:

---

[5]   That is especially so because an injunction is not the only way to correct a state trial court's erroneous refusal to give preclusive effect to a federal judgment. As we have noted before, "the state appellate courts and ultimately this Court" can review and reverse such a ruling. Atlantic Coast Line R. Co. v. Locomotive Engineers, 398 U.S. 281, 287 (1970).

[6]   We have held that federal common law governs the preclusive effect of a decision of a federal court sitting in diversity. See Semtek Int'l, Inc. v. Lockheed Martin Corp., 531 U.S. 497, 508 (2001). Smith assumes that federal common law should here incorporate West Virginia's preclusion law, whereas Bayer favors looking only to federal rules of preclusion because of the federal interests at stake in this case. We do not think the question matters here. Neither party identifies any way in which federal and state principles of preclusion law differ in any relevant respect. Nor have we found any such divergence. We therefore need not decide whether, in general, federal common law ought to incorporate state law in situations such as this.

a critical question—the question of the applicable legal standard—remains. The District Court ruled that the proposed class did not meet the requirements of Federal Rule 23 (because individualized issues would predominate over common ones). But the state court was poised to consider whether the proposed class satisfied *West Virginia* Rule 23. If those two legal standards differ (as federal and state *forum non conveniens* law differed in Chick Kam Choo)—then the federal court resolved an issue not before the state court. * * *

The Court of Appeals and Smith offer us two competing ways of deciding whether the West Virginia and Federal Rules differ, but we think the right path lies somewhere in the middle. The Eighth Circuit relied almost exclusively on the near-identity of the two Rules' texts. That was the right place to start, but not to end. Federal and state courts, after all, can and do apply identically worded procedural provisions in widely varying ways. If a state's procedural provision tracks the language of a Federal Rule, but a state court interprets that provision in a manner federal courts have not, then the state court is using a different standard and thus deciding a different issue. At the other extreme, Smith contends that the source of law is all that matters: a different sovereign must in each and every case "have the opportunity, if it chooses, to construe its procedural rule differently." But if state courts have made crystal clear that they follow the same approach as the federal court applied, we see no need to ignore that determination; in that event, the issues in the two cases would indeed be the same. So a federal court considering whether the relitigation exception applies should examine whether state law parallels its federal counterpart. But as suggested earlier, the federal court must resolve any uncertainty on that score by leaving the question of preclusion to the state courts.

Under this approach, the West Virginia Supreme Court has gone some way toward resolving the matter before us by declaring its independence from federal courts' interpretation of the Federal Rules—and particularly of Rule 23. * * *

But here the case against an injunction is even stronger, because the West Virginia Supreme Court has *disapproved* the approach to Rule 23(b)(3)'s predominance requirement that the Federal District Court embraced. Recall that the federal court held that the presence of a single individualized issue—injury from the use of Baycol—prevented class certification. The court did not identify the common issues in the case; nor did it balance these common issues against the need to prove individual injury to determine which predominated. The court instead applied a strict test barring class treatment when proof of each plaintiff's injury is necessary. By contrast, the West Virginia Supreme Court in In re [W. Va.] Rezulin [Litigation, 214 W.Va. 52, 585 S.E.2d 52 (2003),] adopted an all-things-considered, balancing inquiry in interpreting its Rule 23. Rejecting any "rigid test," the state court opined that the predominance requirement "contemplates a review of many factors."

[*Id.*], at 72, 585 S.E.2d, at 72. * * * A state court using the In re Rezulin standard would decide a different question than the one the federal court had earlier resolved.[9] * * *

B

The injunction issued here runs into another basic premise of preclusion law: A court's judgment binds only the parties to a suit, subject to a handful of discrete and limited exceptions. 18A Wright & Miller s 4449, at 300. * * * Against this backdrop, Bayer defends the decision below by arguing that Smith—an unnamed member of a proposed but uncertified class—qualifies as a party to the McCollins litigation. Alternatively, Bayer claims that the District Court's judgment binds Smith under the recognized exception to the rule against nonparty preclusion for members of class actions. We think neither contention has merit. * * *

Bayer's strongest argument comes not from established principles of preclusion, but instead from policy concerns relating to use of the class action device. Bayer warns that under our approach class counsel can repeatedly try to certify the same class "by the simple expedient of changing the named plaintiff in the caption of the complaint." And in this world of "serial relitigation of class certification," Bayer contends, defendants "would be forced in effect to buy litigation peace by settling."

But this form of argument flies in the face of the rule against nonparty preclusion. That rule perforce leads to relitigation of many issues, as plaintiff after plaintiff after plaintiff (none precluded by the last judgment because none a party to the last suit) tries his hand at establishing some legal principle or obtaining some grant of relief. * * *

And to the extent class actions raise special problems of relitigation, Congress has provided a remedy that does not involve departing from the usual rules of preclusion. In the Class Action Fairness Act of 2005 (CAFA), 28 U.S.C. §§ 1332(d), 1453 (2006 ed. and Supp. III), Congress enabled defendants to remove to federal court any sizable class action involving minimal diversity of citizenship. Once removal takes place, Federal Rule 23 governs certification. * * * CAFA may be cold comfort to Bayer with respect to suits like this one beginning before its enactment. But Congress's decision to address the relitigation concerns associated with class actions through the mechanism of removal provides yet another reason for federal courts to adhere in this context to longstanding

---

[9] Bayer argues that In re Rezulin does not preclude an injunction in this case because the West Virginia court there decided that common issues predominated over individual issues of damages, not over individual issues of liability (as exist here). We think Bayer is right about this distinction, but wrong about its consequence. Our point is not that In re Rezulin dictates the answer to the class certification question here; the two cases are indeed too dissimilar for that to be true. The point instead is that In re Rezulin articulated a general approach to the predominance requirement that differs markedly from the one the federal court used. Minor variations in the application of what is in essence the same legal standard do not defeat preclusion; but where, as here, the state's courts "would apply a significantly different . . . analysis," Chick Kam Choo v. Exxon Corp., 486 U.S. 140, 149 (1988), the federal and state courts decide different issues.

principles of preclusion. And once again, that is especially so when the federal court is deciding whether to go so far as to enjoin a state proceeding.

* * *

* * * For these reasons, the judgment of the Court of Appeals is

Reversed.

NOTE ON EXCEPTIONS TO THE ANTI-INJUNCTION ACT (28 U.S.C. § 2283)

In addressing the relitigation exception, the Bayer Court emphasized the importance of giving the AIA's exceptions a "strict and narrow" reading. But the Court has not always been quite as strict and narrow as that statement would suggest. In Leiter Minerals, Inc. v. United States, 352 U.S. 220 (1957), the Court recognized an unwritten exception for injunctions sought by the United States.[1] This Note surveys the Court's interpretation of the three written exceptions to the AIA's prohibition of injunctive relief in light of the principle of strict and narrow interpretation.

(1) Expressly Authorized by Congress. Interpreting the exception for injunctions "expressly authorized" by Congress in Mitchum v. Foster, 407 U.S. 225 (1972), discussed more fully at p. 1440, *infra*, the Court held that § 1983's reference to suits in law and equity authorized federal courts to stay state court proceedings when necessary to vindicate federal rights. Section 1983 was thus said to qualify as a statute that "expressly" authorizes anti-suit injunctions, even though it says nothing in terms about the issuance of such stays. In support of its conclusion, Mitchum listed a series of federal statutes that it characterized as having authorized injunctive relief against pending state court proceedings:

(a)   Removal under 28 U.S.C. §§ 1446(d) (declaring that after removal the state court shall proceed no further until the case is remanded). See French v. Hay, 89 U.S. 250 (1874).

(b)   Shipowner's limitation of liability under 46 U.S.C. § 185 (following deposit of the value of the ship in registry of federal admiralty court, "all claims and proceedings against the owner * * * shall cease"). See Providence & N.Y.S.S. Co. v. Hill Mfg. Co., 109 U.S. 578 (1883).

(c)   Interpleader litigation under 28 U.S.C. § 2361 (authorizing a federal court in civil interpleader actions to restrain all claimants "from instituting or prosecuting any proceeding" affecting property involved in the interpleader action). See Treinies v. Sunshine Mining Co., 308 U.S. 66 (1939).

---

[1]   In NLRB v. Nash-Finch Co., 404 U.S. 138 (1971), the Court extended the Leiter rationale to an application for an injunction by the National Labor Relations Board, an "independent" federal agency.

(d)   Federal habeas corpus under 28 U.S.C. § 2251 (authorizing stay of any proceeding against "the person detained" in state court as to any matter involved in the habeas proceeding). See Ex parte Royall, 117 U.S. 241, 248–49 (1886).

(e)   Stays under the Emergency Price Control Act of 1942, 56 Stat. 33 (providing that the Price Administrator could request a federal district court to enjoin acts that violated or threatened to violate the Act). See Porter v. Dicken, 328 U.S. 252 (1946) (construing the statute as authority to restrain state court proceedings).

Two of these statutes (interpleader and habeas) expressly authorize stays; the others appear to operate as what one might view as implied "express authorizations." Recognition of such exceptions might appear to support the Mitchum Court's decision to authorize anti-suit injunctions under § 1983 as yet another implied exception. But some of those implied exceptions can be attributed to other factors: the price control act contemplated enforcement by an agency of the United States, thereby triggering the Leiter exception, and the shipowner's liability act brought property into the custody of a federal maritime court for equitable administration. With control of property, an injunction to stay competing state court proceedings might be better understood as operating in aid of equitable administration than as an implied exception. The pattern on which Mitchum relied, in short, may not support its apparent departure from the AIA's requirement of express authority.

Subsequent decisions (like that in Smith v. Bayer Corp.) signal a more literal approach to the statute's interpretation. In Vendo Co. v. Lektro-Vend Corp., 433 U.S. 623 (1977), a splintered Supreme Court refused to allow a federal court to enjoin the enforcement of a state court judgment that was said to have violated the federal antitrust laws. While § 16 of the Clayton Act, 15 U.S.C. § 26, authorizes private suits for injunctive relief against antitrust violations, it says nothing about the stay of state court proceedings. The plurality found no indication that Congress "was concerned with the possibility that state-court proceedings would be used to violate the Sherman or Clayton Acts." *Id.* 634. Justice Blackmun, joined by Chief Justice Burger, concurred, but on the very different theory that § 16 was an "expressly authorized" exception only in the "narrowly limited circumstances," not found in the present case, where state court proceedings "are themselves part of a 'pattern of baseless, repetitive claims' that are being used as an anticompetitive device." *Id.* 643–44. Justice Stevens, for the four dissenters, contended that prosecution of even a single state-court proceeding could (and in this case did) violate the antitrust laws; that to deny an injunction would deprive § 16 of its intended scope; and thus that § 16 was an "expressly authorized" exception.

(2) "In Aid of Its Jurisdiction." The exception for injunctions "in aid of [the federal court's] jurisdiction" has two primary objectives. First, it confirms the twin rules in Kline v. Burke Construction Company, 260 U.S. 226 (1922), p. 1362, *supra*, upholding the issuance of injunctions to stay state proceedings that would interfere with a federal court's *in rem* jurisdiction over a fund or property and foreclosing such injunctions as to *in personam* actions.[2] See Atlantic Coast Line R. Co. v. Brotherhood of Locomotive Engineers, 398 U.S. 281, 295–96 (1970) (the exercise of concurrent state court jurisdiction does not "hinder the federal court's jurisdiction so as to make an injunction necessary to aid that jurisdiction"). Second, it authorizes federal courts, after removal of an action to federal court, to stay further proceedings if the state court fails to heed the requirement, in 28 U.S.C. § 1446(b), that after removal that the state court "shall proceed no further" until the case has been remanded. In keeping with these limits, the Court has refused to allow injunctions on the theory that state court jurisdiction has been preempted by federal law. See Amalgamated Clothing Workers v. Richman Brothers, 348 U.S. 511 (1955).

(3) The Relitigation Exception. The relitigation exception permits but does not require a federal court to enjoin a state court proceeding that threatens or disregards the preclusive effect of a federal judgment. But as Kline v. Burke Construction, Company, 260 U.S. 226 (1922), and Donovan v. City of Dallas, 377 U.S. 408 (1964), reveal, state and federal courts alike owe a federal obligation to accord preclusive effect to the prior judgments of coordinate courts. This assured preclusive effect represents a change from practice in the early nineteenth century, when the relitigation exception arose to enable courts of equity to enforce decrees that separate common law courts would sometimes ignore. Today, rules of inter-systemic claim and issue preclusion require both state and federal courts to respect one another's judgments and decrees. See Semtek Int'l, Inc. v. Lockheed Martin Corp., 531 U.S. 497 (2001) (recognizing state court obligation, rooted in federal common law, to effectuate federal judgment). Inter-systemic preclusion coupled with the joinder of law and equity in a single civil action make it more difficult to justify equitable intervention to prevent relitigation today.

Without addressing the equities, Smith v. Bayer narrows the relitigation exception to situations in which continued prosecution of the state proceeding would disregard the preclusive effect of a prior federal judgment. Yet even if the federal movant can show a clear entitlement to relief from relitigation, the state court's obligation to effectuate claim preclusion defenses will provide an adequate remedy in many instances. On this view, the relitigation exception confers no right to an anti-suit injunction but only a right to apply for an injunction where state court remedies seem inadequate.

Consider what would establish state court remedial inadequacy for such purposes. Notably, if the state court declines to accord preclusive effect to the federal judgment, the state defendant can appeal through the state system and then to the Supreme Court. But if the state court finally rejects the preclusion defense, the state court defendant cannot return to federal court to seek an anti-suit injunction. In Parsons Steel, Inc. v. First Alabama Bank, 474 U.S. 518 (1986), the Supreme Court unanimously overturned such a federal injunction against completed state court proceedings, concluding that the federal court was bound by 28 U.S.C. § 1738 (the full faith and credit statute) to give the state court judgment the same effect that it would have

---

[2]   For a collection of cases, see 17A Wright, Miller & Cooper, Federal Practice & Procedure § 4225.

under state law. By precluding injunctive relief after a failed effort to secure state court recognition of a federal decree, Parsons Steel encourages a litigant who has obtained a favorable federal judgment to seek an immediate federal injunction against state court relitigation. Consider whether a federal movant who seeks but fails to secure such a federal anti-suit injunction should be issue precluded from raising the preclusion defense in state court.[3] The answer may depend on why the federal court denied injunctive relief.

(4) The Meaning of "Proceedings." When do the state court "proceedings" referred to in § 2283 begin? Ex parte Young, 209 U.S. 123 (1908), held the Act inapplicable to an injunction against criminal proceedings not yet instituted.[4] Consider how critical that holding has been to the vindication of federal rights. In Lynch v. Household Finance Corp., 405 U.S. 538 (1972), the Court held (6–3) that a prejudgment garnishment was not a "proceeding" in state court within the scope of § 2283, and hence could be enjoined by a federal court, even though the garnishment might be necessary to obtain satisfaction of any subsequent judgment obtained by the creditor. The opinion emphasized that the garnishment could be instituted by the creditor's attorney, without judicial order, before filing suit.

The language of the Act suggests that when proceedings end in state court, the statute no longer curtails federal court authority to grant injunctive relief. But the Court has viewed the results of completed state court proceedings as within the Act's continuing protection. In Atlantic Coast Line R. Co. v. Brotherhood of Locomotive Engineers, 398 U.S. 281, 287 (1970), the Court overturned a federal injunction against the enforcement of a state court injunction that was said to interfere with an earlier federal decision that was said to have authorized the picketing in question. While the state court proceeding had ended, its injunction remained in effect. The Court explained that the federal movant must bring its request for injunctive relief within the terms of the statute; "the prohibition of § 2283 cannot be evaded by . . . prohibiting utilization of the results of a completed state proceeding." See also Hill v. Martin, 296 U.S. 393, 402 (1935) (finding that the Act barred federal suit to enjoin further enforcement of state tax levy; although they had yet to begin, further state proceedings "to compel satisfaction of the [state] decree . . . do not differ in essence from those

---

[3]   For a generally critical discussion of federal injunctions against state court judicial proceedings asserted to be in violation of contractual arbitration provisions—injunctions that a number of courts have entered, sometimes without careful attention to § 2283—see Sternlight, *Forum Shopping for Arbitration Decisions: Federal Courts' Use of Antisuit Injunctions Against State Courts*, 147 U.Pa.L.Rev. 91 (1998).

[4]   Note that the question can arise even when a federal action is filed first. Dombrowski v. Pfister, 380 U.S. 479, 484 n.2 (1965), appears to hold (in the alternative) that when state grand jury indictments are returned after the filing of a federal complaint but before injunctive relief is issued, "no state 'proceedings' [are] pending within the intendment of § 2283." Nevertheless, the circuits appear to be split on the question whether the Anti-Injunction Act bars injunctions against state court litigation commenced subsequent to the filing of a federal action. See, *e.g.*, Denny's, Inc. v. Cake, 364 F.3d 521, 529 (4th Cir.2004). *Cf.* Hicks v. Miranda, 422 U.S. 332, 349 (1975), p. 1453, *infra*, holding that the equitable restraint doctrine of Younger v. Harris, 401 U.S. 37 (1971), p. 1430, *infra*, applies "in full force" when a state prosecution is filed after the federal action but "before any proceedings of substance on the merits" in federal court.

required to satisfy any judgment for a debt recovered at law or any decree in chancery for the payment of money"); *cf.* County of Imperial v. Munoz, 449 U.S. 54 (1980) (suggesting that strangers to an initial proceeding in state court may institute a separate action in federal court to enjoin illegal state action).[5]

(5) Declaratory Judgments. How should a federal court respond if one party to an ongoing state proceeding brings an overlapping application for a federal declaration of rights under 28 U.S.C. § 2201? Under the rule of Kline v. Burke Construction, the presumption of concurrency would seem to allow the maintenance of such an action as part of the race to judgment. What's more, while § 2283 bars federal injunctions, it says nothing in terms to prohibit a federal suit for declaratory relief.[6] Some courts refuse to allow declaratory judgment actions in such cases of overlap, reasoning that they would have the same effect as an injunction and should also be barred. See, *e.g.,* American Airlines, Inc. v. Department of Transp., 202 F.3d 788 (5th Cir.2000); *cf.* California v. Grace Brethren Church, 457 U.S. 393, 407–11 (1982) (reading Tax Injunction Act's denial of federal jurisdiction to "suspend or restrain" state tax proceedings as barring declaratory judgment). See also 17A Wright, Miller & Cooper § 4222. But instead of seeking an injunction to enforce the declaratory judgment, as 28 U.S.C. § 2202 contemplates, the federal plaintiff might seek recognition of the declaratory judgment in state court, thereby inviting the state court to evaluate its preclusive effect on further state court proceedings. Such an approach would enforce a federal declaration without use of an injunction to stay proceedings in state court.

B. STATUTORY AGGREGATION AND COORDINATION MECHANISMS

Congress now takes the lead in identifying, through jurisdictional statutes, situations that demand consolidated proceedings and equitable administration. But consolidation alone does not typically justify equitable administration and coordination. On the one hand, federal statutes, such as the interpleader statute, 28 U.S.C. § 1335, and the bankruptcy laws, confer jurisdiction and call for equitable administration of competing claims to a potentially limited fund. On the other hand, provisions for consolidated pre-trial management of multi-district litigation (MDL), 28 U.S.C. § 107, the Class Action Fairness Act of 2005 (CAFA), *id.* §§ 1332(d), 1453, and the Multiparty, Multiforum Trial Jurisdiction Act of 2002, *id.* §§ 1369(a), 1441(e), do not call for equitable administration of an estate or a limited fund.

---

[5]   Justice Blackmun, concurring in Munoz, expressed the view that § 2283 may apply even when the state litigation involves different parties. The Supreme Court later disapproved of "virtual representation" in a different context. See Taylor v. Sturgell, 553 U.S. 880 (2008).

[6]   Justice Brennan (joined by Justices White and Marshall) opined that § 2283 does not extend to declarations. See Perez v. Ledesma, 401 U.S. 82, 128–29 n.18 (1971) (separate opinion). But in a companion case, Samuels v. Mackell, 401 U.S. 66 (1971), the Court viewed declarations and injunctions as subject to the same equitable and policy-based limitations.

(1) Statutory Provisions for Consolidated Adjudication.

(a) Multi-District Litigation. Among important consolidation provisions, 28 U.S.C. § 1407 provides for the transfer of multi-district litigation to a single district court, appointed by the Judicial Panel on Multi-District Litigation (MDL), for consolidated pre-trial proceedings. Adopted in 1968 to deal with what was perceived as a flood of electrical equipment antitrust suits, MDL today routinely provides a forum for consolidated treatment of a variety of mass tort and other claims, including claims based on exposure to hazardous drugs and other mass disasters.[1]

The MDL statute does not confer subject matter jurisdiction on the federal courts and thus does not ensure consolidated litigation of disputes governed by state law, except as properly brought to federal court through diversity jurisdiction. Plaintiffs pursuing such state law claims may avoid MDL consolidation by structuring their claims to defeat diversity-based removal. Many states like California have their own state procedures for consolidated treatment of mass tort claims and many state courts cooperate with the federal MDL court in regulating the pretrial process.[2]

(b) The Class Action Fairness Act of 2005. In the years preceding the adoption of the Class Action Fairness Act of 2005 (CAFA), critics identified a series of problems with class action practice in state courts. Apart from concerns with unjustified class certification decisions, and the settlement pressure such decisions place on defendants, critics pointed to the "reverse auctions" that can result when the plaintiffs' lawyers in dueling lawsuits compete with one another to offer the lowest settlement price to the defendants.[3]

CAFA addressed some of these problems, allowing certain class actions to be brought in, or removed to, federal court based on minimal, rather than complete, diversity of citizenship and an amount in controversy keyed to the aggregate value of the class members' claims. See 28 U.S.C. § 1332(d); Chap. VIII, Sec. 4. Under CAFA, defendants can alleviate the threat of inappropriate state court class certification by removing to federal court and securing application of more restrictive federal procedures. *Id.* § 1453. Parties in federal court, concerned with lack of coordination, may move for consolidated pre-trial proceedings in the MDL. Such coordinated pre-trial proceedings encompass the

---

[1]   Mullenix, *Aggregate Litigation and the Death of Democratic Dispute Resolution,* 107 Nw.U.L.Rev. 511, 521–23 (2013) (describing MDL proceedings that led to the resolution of mass tort litigation regarding asbestos, Agent Orange, and the Dalkon Shield). For a detailed history of the adoption of the Multidistrict Litigation Act of 1968, see Bradt, *"A Radical Proposal": The Multidistrict Litigation Act of 1968,* 165 U.Pa.L.Rev. 831 (2017).

[2]   See Clopton & Rave, *MDL in the States,* 115 Nw.U.L.Rev. 1649 (2021) (roughly half the states have MDL procedures in place, many of which differ markedly from federal practice).

[3]   See Coffee, *Class Wars: The Dilemma of the Mass Tort Class Action,* 95 Colum.L.Rev. 1343, 1370–72 (1995) (describing the incentives that produce "reverse auctions").

discovery process, summary judgment motions, and class certification decisions.[4]

CAFA does not address all potential sources of unfairness. For example, the Act did not include a provision aimed at protecting "absent class members"—those who are not named plaintiffs in class actions in state court. Such absentees have no removal option comparable to that of defendants and, accordingly, face some risk of reverse auctions. (If class counsel behave self-interestedly and offer bargain-rate settlements, then defendants cannot be counted on to remove a state court action against them to federal court.) Absentees can, of course, opt out and pursue their own claims separately. But many of the claims cannot be cost-effectively pursued in individual litigation. (Although an earlier version of CAFA would have permitted absent class members to remove state court class actions to federal court, the relevant provision was deleted in the final Senate bill. See Klonoff & Herrmann, *The Class Action Fairness Act: An Ill-Conceived Approach to Class Settlements*, 80 Tul.L.Rev. 1695, 1710 (2006) (citing S.Rep. No. 108–123, at 94–95 (2003)).

(c) Multiparty, Multiforum Trial Jurisdiction Act. Enacted in the aftermath of the September 11, 2001 attacks, the Multiparty, Multiforum Trial Jurisdiction of 2002 provides for consolidated federal jurisdiction over disputes arising from a single accident in which "at least 75 natural persons" have died at a discrete location. While the statute leaves state law in place as the measure of liability, it bases jurisdiction on the presence of any minimal diversity between adverse parties. See 28 U.S.C. § 1369.[5]

(2) Consolidation and Coordination Tools for Mass Litigation. Problems that have arisen in the administration of consolidated proceedings, whether through the MDL or through CAFA, bear some resemblance to those with which nineteenth century courts wrestled. When nineteenth century courts of equity were charged with administering the assets of a company in receivership, for example, they were relatively single-minded in working to consolidate all related claims (by expanding the receivership court's subject matter jurisdiction to include ancillary claimants) and to foreclose opt-out litigation in the state courts by granting injunctive relief against conflicting claims on the "property" or estate before the court. In Ex parte Tyler, 149 U.S. 164 (1893), the Supreme Court upheld contempt sanctions imposed on a local

---

[4]   A 2008 study concluded that the federal courts "have embraced CAFA with coolness." Clermont & Eisenberg, *CAFA Judicata: A Tale of Waste and Politics*, 156 U.Pa.L.Rev. 1553, 1592 (2008); see also Lee & Willging, *The Impact of the Class Action Fairness Act on the Federal Courts: An Empirical Analysis of Filings and Removals*, 156 U.Pa.L.Rev. 1723, 1724–25 (2008) (finding "an increase in diversity class action filings and removals in the federal courts * * * [though] a less dramatic increase than some anticipated").

[5]   See Wallace v. Louisiana Citizens Property Ins. Co., 444 F.3d 697 (5th Cir.2006) (approving removal and consolidation of claims arising from Hurricane Katrina); Pettitt v. Boeing Co., 606 F.3d 340 (7th Cir.2010) (approving removal of a handful of cases arising from Cameroon plane crash in which 114 people died).

sheriff who seized property in the custody of a receivership court to satisfy the railroad's local tax obligations. The Court held that the sheriff had notice of the receivership and was bound to pursue the tax claim in that proceeding, rather than in separate litigation. The receivership court's subject matter jurisdiction was flexible enough to encompass the tax claims, even though they would not have met jurisdictional requirements on their own.

Much the same instinct underlay early efforts to secure consolidated treatment of related claims through class action proceedings. Judge Weinstein worked to bring all conceivable Agent Orange claims to the Eastern District of New York where he was presiding over class action proceedings brought by injured Vietnam veterans.[6] Apart from aggressive consolidation efforts, Judge Weinstein worked intensely to shape the settlement, helping to broker a deal that reflected his own perception of claim validity and defendant capacity to pay.[7] Years later, many veterans mounted a successful collateral attack on the settlement, after showing that they were not fairly represented by class counsel. See Stephenson v. Dow Chemical Co., 273 F.3d 249 (2d Cir.2001), aff'd, 539 U.S. 111 (2003). *Cf.* Ortiz v. Fibreboard Corp., 527 U.S. 815 (1999).

Parties made similar attempts to consolidate tobacco and asbestos litigation. But the Court found that such class actions could not be certified without taking account of state-to-state variation in controlling law. See Castano v. American Tobacco Co., 84 F.3d 734 (5th Cir.1996). Parties have tried to work around consolidation problems with the creative construction of settlement class actions, but the Supreme Court has rejected such efforts as well, unless structured in ways that otherwise largely met the certification requirements and satisfied due process concerns. See, *e.g.*, Amchem Products, Inc. v. Windsor, 521 U.S. 591 (1997) (rejecting certification of settlement class for lack of predominance and adequate representation). To be sure, scholars contended that class actions had effectively become at least for some purposes the kind of entity that was entitled to unitary administration.[8] But underlying the Court's rejection of consolidated litigation models has been its perception that individual claimants were pursuing personal claims that did not comprise together the inter-connected estate or property interests that justify the consolidation tools used in equity receiverships and bankruptcy proceedings.

---

[6] Available tools then included use of the All Writs Act, which some lower courts interpreted as authorizing the removal, transfer, and consolidation of state court claims that did not otherwise qualify for federal jurisdiction. The Supreme Court eventually rejected this form of removal and the consolidation it facilitated, reaffirming that the All Writs Act did not confer jurisdiction. See Syngenta Crop Protection, Inc. v. Henson, 537 U.S. 28 (2002).

[7] For an account and questions, see Marcus, *Apocalypse Now?*, 85 Mich.L.Rev. 1267 (1987); see also Schuck, Agent Orange on Trial: Mass Toxic Disasters in the Courts (1986).

[8] See Shapiro, *Class Actions: The Class as Party and Client*, 73 Notre Dame L.Rev. 913 (1998).

Notably, mass tort class action consolidations pose challenges because they seek to join individual claims for damages under Rule 23(b)(3). When parties propose class actions that touch upon inter-connected property interests, such as those implicated in Rule 23(b)(1) class actions, consolidated treatment was traditionally more readily available. Thus, in Supreme Tribe of Ben-Hur v. Cauble, 255 U.S. 356 (1921), a pre-cursor to the (b)(1) class action, the Court treated the judgment as disposing of all challenges to the financial restructuring of a beneficial association, even when some individual members of the class had claims that did not meet subject matter jurisdiction requirements. So long as the named plaintiff met the diversity requirements, and the litigation brought claims to a fund before the court, jurisdictional requirements were met.

Some courts and scholars continue to press for further expansion and the consolidation it would enable. In F5 Capital v. Pappas, 856 F.3d 61 (2d Cir.2017), for example, the court held that jurisdiction over a class action under CAFA conferred supplemental jurisdiction over related state law claims that did not meet the requirements of complete diversity. In doing so, the court treated a CAFA class action as an anchor for expanded litigation. With expansion have come calls for coordination. Wolff, *Federal Jurisdiction and Due Process in the Era of the Nationwide Class Action*, 156 U.Pa.L.Rev. 2035, 2069–73 (2008), argues that federal courts with jurisdiction over a class action should be able to enjoin parallel state court actions "in aid of" their jurisdiction under CAFA. In a subtle and thorough treatment, Professor Wolff likens CAFA to other "targeted" grants of jurisdiction to protect discretely identified federal interests that deserve protection from overlapping state litigation. Such arguments may prove challenging after Smith v. Bayer Corp.

In personam consolidation through MDL, now the primary site for coordinated management of mass tort litigation, poses similar challenges. Under current jurisdictional statutes, MDL cannot ensure a federal forum for consolidation of all claims from any particular mass tort. Nor does the existence of consolidated mass tort claims justify an anti-suit injunction against the pursuit of similar claims by other parties in state courts. Yet modes of administration, comparable to those used in the judicial oversight of trusts and estates, have arisen. MDL judges oversee the selection and approval of lead plaintiffs' counsel and oversee the payment of attorney's fees. Similar oversight of counsel occurs in class action litigation as district courts consider the adequacy of representation and approve any ultimate settlement and attorney fee request. Even the doctrine of *cy pres*, which arose to allow a redirection of the trust's assets in cases where the settlor's purpose had been frustrated by intervening events, has been adapted for use in distributing unclaimed funds in a class action settlement pool.[9] While the model of

---

[9]   *See* Redish, Julian & Zyontz, *Cy Pres Relief and the Pathologies of the Modern Class Action: A Normative and Empirical Analysis,* 62 Fla.L.Rev. 617 (2010); Tidmarsh, *Cy Pres and*

individual representation remains intact, MDL settlements place pressure on the model and give, critics argue, too little attention to the individual claimant.[10]

Further coordination of complex litigation remains possible if Congress chooses to create a limited fund. In the Air Transportation Safety and System Stabilization Act of 2001 ("ATSSSA"), Pub.L.No. 107–42, 115 Stat. 230 (2001) (codified as amended at 49 U.S.C. § 40101, note), Congress authorized adjudication of all claims arising from the 9/11 attacks to proceed in the Southern District of New York and capped recovery at the total value of the defendants' insurance coverage. Litigants argued that the statutory cap required consolidated resolution and equitable administration, but the Second Circuit disagreed. See In re September 11 Property Damage Litigation, 650 F.3d 145 (2d Cir.2011) (finding no evidence that "Congress intended to create a 'limited fund' from which plaintiffs * * * are entitled to an equitable share"). Notably, neither MDL nor Rule 23(b)(3) class actions typically entail claims to a limited fund. Parties confronting such litigation may secure equitable administration by initiating proceedings in bankruptcy.

(3) Coordination Through Appellate Review: 28 U.S.C. § 1257 and Rooker-Feldman. During the nineteenth century, separate courts of equity granted relief when common law judgments were infected with fraud or mistake. Under the so-called "fraud" exception to the Anti-Injunction Act, federal courts, exercising equity power, sometimes played this role as to state court judgments. Notably difficult to defend under the AIA as then phrased, injunctions directed at pending or completed state court proceedings would seem clearly to violate the current version of the AIA, which as amended in 1948 no longer includes a "fraud" exception. Rather than rely on the AIA or rules of claim preclusion, however, the Court chose in Rooker v. Fidelity Trust Co., 263 U.S. 413 (1923), to foreclose such fraud-based federal equitable relitigation by invoking the statutory provision for Supreme Court appellate review of state court decisions, now codified at 28 U.S.C. § 1257. Viewing the statute as conferring exclusive appellate jurisdiction, the Court held that lower federal courts had no jurisdiction to conduct the functional equivalent of appellate review through relitigation of state court judgments. The Court reiterated that view 60 years later, in District of Columbia Court of Appeals v. Feldman, 460 U.S. 462 (1983), giving voice to what would come to be known as the Rooker-Feldman doctrine.

After several years of unruly decisions in the lower federal courts,[11] the Supreme Court narrowed and clarified the doctrine in Exxon Mobil

---

the Optimal Class Action, 82 Geo.Wash.L.Rev. 767 (2014); Wasserman, Cy Pres in Class Action Settlements, 88 S.Calif.L.Rev. 97 (2014).

[10] Redish & Karaba, One Size Doesn't Fit All: Multidistrict Litigation, Due Process, and the Dangers of Procedural Collectivism, 95 B.U.L.Rev. 109 (2015).

[11] During this period, the doctrine attracted a good deal of scholarly attention. Of particular interest was a 1999 symposium in the Notre Dame Law Review, in which most (but not all) of the commentators were critical of the doctrine, in whole or in substantial part. See

Corp. v. Saudi Basic Industries Corp., 544 U.S. 280 (2005). In that case, the parties brought concurrent suits in Delaware state and New Jersey federal court, contesting aspects of their business relationship. Saudi Basic invoked foreign sovereign immunity as a defense to the federal litigation and sought interlocutory review of the denial of its motion to dismiss. On appeal, the Third Circuit raised the Rooker-Feldman doctrine on its own motion. During the pendency of the federal proceeding, the Delaware state court had entered judgment on a substantial jury verdict in favor of Exxon Mobil. Although Exxon Mobil argued that its federal suit was not appellate when initiated, the Third Circuit held that it became effectively appellate when the Delaware proceeding went to judgment. That judgment deprived the federal court of subject matter jurisdiction under Rooker-Feldman.

The Supreme Court reversed in a unanimous opinion by Justice Ginsburg. The Court began by reaffirming the continued vitality of the principle of concurrent state and federal court litigation articulated in Kline v. Burke. Then, the Court gave voice to a very narrow view of Rooker-Feldman, limiting the doctrine to "cases brought by state-court losers complaining of injuries caused by state-court judgments rendered before the district court proceedings commenced and inviting district court review and rejection of those judgments." *Id.* 284. In the case at hand, Exxon Mobil initiated the federal proceeding only a few weeks after Saudi Basic sued in Delaware state court, well before the state court judgment, thereby rendering the Rooker-Feldman doctrine inapplicable. Rather than coordinate such overlapping litigation with a jurisdictional doctrine, the Court explained the matter was governed by preclusion law. "In parallel litigation, a federal court may be bound to recognize the claim- and issue-preclusive effects of a state-court judgment, but federal jurisdiction over an action does not terminate automatically on the entry of judgment in the state court." *Id.* 293.

The Court's decision, in both its holding and its general tone, tempered the enthusiasm of many lower courts for applying the Rooker-Feldman doctrine. Subsequent decisions point in the same direction. In Lance v. Dennis, 546 U.S. 459 (2006), the Court reversed the dismissal of a federal action brought by plaintiffs who were said to be in privity

---

Rowe, *Rooker-Feldman: Worth Only the Powder To Blow it Up?*, 74 Notre Dame L.Rev. 1081 (1999) (quoting David Shapiro and setting the stage for the debate). See also Sherry, *Judicial Federalism in the Trenches: The Rooker-Feldman Doctrine in Action*, 74 Notre Dame L.Rev. 1085, 1100, 1128 (1999) (defending the doctrine as a "valuable tool" for plugging gaps in the rules governing res judicata and Younger abstention "that would otherwise wreak havoc on our system of dual courts"); Friedman & Gaylord, *Rooker-Feldman from the Ground Up*, 74 Notre Dame L.Rev. 1129 (1999) (analyzing the overlap of various doctrines and concluding that Rooker-Feldman performs a unique function only in situations in which the lower courts have extended the doctrine well beyond its precedential roots); Bandes, *The Rooker-Feldman Doctrine: Evaluating Its Jurisdictional Status*, 74 Notre Dame L.Rev. 1175 (1999) (tracing the jurisdictional lineage of the doctrine and arguing that it can properly be applied only in certain narrowly defined instances); Beermann, *Comments on Rooker-Feldman or Let State Law Be Our Guide*, 74 Notre Dame L.Rev. 1209 (1999) (joining with those who question both the value and significance of the doctrine).

with state court losers: Rooker-Feldman "does not bar actions by nonparties to the earlier state-court judgment simply because, for purposes of preclusion law, they could be considered in privity with a party to the judgment." *Id.* 466. The question of preclusion under state law, which the Court insisted should not be conflated with Rooker-Feldman, was left open on remand. Similarly, in Skinner v. Switzer, 562 U.S. 521 (2011), the Court again refused to find that Rooker-Feldman defeated jurisdiction, unanimously ruling that Skinner's § 1983 action "[did] not challenge the adverse [state court] decisions themselves; instead, he target[ed] as unconstitutional the Texas statute they authoritatively construed." See also Reed v. Goertz, 598 U.S. 230 (2023).

Unresolved questions persist. Just as federal courts recognized a fraud exception to the early AIA, fraud sometimes operates as an exception to state court finality and claim preclusion. Pointing to such an exception, some federal plaintiffs (losers in state court) have challenged earlier state court judgments as having been obtained by fraud. See Baker, *The Fraud Exception to the Rooker-Feldman Doctrine: How It Almost Wasn't (and Probably Shouldn't Be)*, 5 Fed.Cts.L.Rev. 139 (2011) (describing a division in authority concerning federal challenges to allegedly fraudulent state court mortgage foreclosure judgments). Should the federal courts use Rooker-Feldman to bar such suits? Or should the federal courts coordinate remedies by allowing state law to dictate the extent of any federal court relitigation under 28 U.S.C. § 1738? On that view, federal courts might ordinarily stay their hand and require would-be federal plaintiffs to seek relief in state court, by moving to reopen the judgment there or set it aside on appeal. A federal collateral attack could proceed only when the state affords litigants that option in state court.

———————

3. COORDINATING STATE AND FEDERAL COURT REVIEW OF STATE ADMINISTRATIVE ACTION

———————

New Orleans Public Service, Inc. v. Council of New Orleans
491 U.S. 350 (1989).
Certiorari to the Circuit Court of Appeals for the Fifth Circuit.

■ JUSTICE SCALIA delivered the opinion of the Court.

[The dispute arose from efforts to allocate cost overruns in the construction of the Grand Gulf nuclear reactor located in Mississippi. On one side was the New Orleans Public Service Inc. (NOPSI), a public utility supplying electricity to customers in Louisiana. NOPSI and other subsidiaries of Middle South Utilities had agreed to finance the construction of the reactor in exchange for a share of the energy it supplied. On the other side was the Council of New Orleans, a state regulatory body with the power to set rates for the city's electricity customers within a federal framework overseen by the Federal Energy Regulatory Commission (FERC). Both NOPSI and the Council appeared in a ratemaking proceeding in which FERC decided to allocate construction costs to the various Middle South subsidiaries roughly in proportion to their energy usage. FERC therefore assigned 17% of Grand Gulf's costs to NOPSI as "just, reasonable, and non-discriminatory" within the meaning of federal law. Instead of granting an immediate rate increase to NOPSI to implement the federal determination, the Council undertook further deliberations. Ultimately, the Council decided that, having failed to act prudently to hold down costs, NOPSI could not recapture some $135 million in construction costs through its rates. NOPSI took the position that the Council was obliged by federal law and the FERC decision to set rates that would authorize full recapture.

[Simplifying somewhat, NOPSI filed two proceedings, one in state court to challenge the rate decision as a violation of state law and the Takings Clause of the federal Constitution and a second in federal court seeking injunctive and declaratory relief from the Council's failure to accord preemptive effect to FERC's rate-making determination as to cost allocation. The Council asked the federal court to abstain from deciding the preemption issue and allow that issue to be resolved in NOPSI's pending state court proceeding. Ultimately, the Fifth Circuit agreed with the Council, concluding that two decisions—Burford v. Sun Oil Co., 319 U.S. 315 (1943), and Younger v. Harris, 401 U.S. 37 (1971), p. 1430, *infra*—required the federal court to abstain. On review, the Supreme Court reversed as to both doctrines.]

II

* * * With [the federal courts' "virtually unflagging" obligation to adjudicate claims within their jurisdiction] in mind, we address the question whether the District Court, relying on Burford * * * and Younger * * *, properly declined to exercise its jurisdiction in the present case. While we acknowledge that "[t]he various types of abstention are not rigid pigeonholes into which federal courts must try to fit cases," Pennzoil Co. v. Texaco, Inc., 481 U.S. 1, 11, n.9 (1987), the policy considerations supporting Burford are sufficiently distinct to justify independent analyses.

A

In Burford v. Sun Oil, a Federal District Court sitting in equity was confronted with a Fourteenth Amendment challenge to the reasonableness of the Texas Railroad Commission's grant of an oil drilling permit. The constitutional challenge was of minimal federal importance, involving solely the question whether the commission had properly applied Texas' complex oil and gas conservation regulations. [319 U.S.], at 331, and n.28. Because of the intricacy and importance of the regulatory scheme, Texas had created a centralized system of judicial review of commission orders, which "permit[ted] the state courts, like the Railroad Commission itself, to acquire a specialized knowledge" of the regulations and industry, *id.*, at 327. We found the state courts' review of commission decisions "expeditious and adequate," *id.*, at 334, and, because the exercise of equitable jurisdiction by comparatively unsophisticated Federal District Courts alongside state-court review had repeatedly led to "[d]elay, misunderstanding of local law, and needless federal conflict with the state policy," *id.*, at 327, we concluded that "a sound respect for the independence of state action requir[ed] the federal equity court to stay its hand," *id.*, at 334.

    * * * [W]e have [since] distilled the principle now commonly referred to as the "Burford doctrine." Where timely and adequate state-court review is available, a federal court sitting in equity must decline to interfere with the proceedings or orders of state administrative agencies: (1) when there are "difficult questions of state law bearing on policy problems of substantial public import whose importance transcends the result in the case then at bar"; or (2) where the "exercise of federal review of the question in a case and in similar cases would be disruptive of state efforts to establish a coherent policy with respect to a matter of substantial public concern." Colorado River Water Conservation Dist. v. United States, 424 U.S.[800,] 814 [(1976)].

    The present case does not involve a state-law claim, nor even an assertion that the federal claims are "in any way entangled in a skein of state-law that must be untangled before the federal case can proceed," The Fifth Circuit acknowledged as much in NOPSI I, but found "the absence of a state law claim ... not fatal" because, it thought, "[t]he motivating force behind Burford abstention is ... a reluctance to intrude into state proceedings where there exists a complex state regulatory system." Finding that this case involved a complex regulatory scheme of "paramount local concern and a matter which demands local administrative expertise," it held that the District Court appropriately applied Burford.

    While Burford is concerned with protecting complex state administrative processes from undue federal interference, it does not require abstention whenever there exists such a process, or even in all cases where there is a "potential for conflict" with state regulatory law or policy. Colorado River Water Conservation Dist., 424 U.S., at 815–816. Here, NOPSI's primary claim is that the Council is prohibited by federal law from refusing to provide reimbursement for FERC-allocated wholesale costs. Unlike a claim that a state agency has misapplied its lawful authority or has failed to take into consideration or properly weigh relevant state-law factors, federal adjudication of this sort of pre-emption claim would not disrupt the State's attempt to ensure uniformity in the treatment of an "essentially local problem."

    [The Court here invoked Public Util. Comm'n of Ohio v. United Fuel Gas Co., 317 U.S. 456, 468–469 (1943), in which it approved the issuance of injunctive relief to block a "plainly invalid" state order regulating interstate natural gas rates.] Similarly in the case at bar, no inquiry beyond the four corners of the Council's retail rate order is needed to determine whether it is facially pre-empted by FERC's allocative decree and relevant provisions of the Federal Power Act. Such an inquiry would not unduly intrude into the processes of state government or undermine the State's ability to maintain desired uniformity. It may, of course, result in an injunction against enforcement of the rate order, but "there is . . . no doctrine requiring abstention merely because resolution of a federal question may result in the overturning of a state policy."

It is true that in its initial complaint, NOPSI asserted, as an alternative to its facial pre-emption challenge, that the rate order's nominal emphasis on NOPSI's failure in 1979–1980 to diversify its power supply by selling off a portion of its Grand Gulf allocation was merely a cover for the determination that the original Grand Gulf investment was itself unwise. Unlike the facial challenge, this claim cannot be resolved on the face of the rate order, because it hinges largely on the plausibility of the Council's finding that NOPSI should have, and could have, diversified its supply portfolio and thereby lowered its average wholesale costs. Analysis of this pretext claim requires an inquiry into industry practice, wholesale rates, and power availability during the relevant time period, an endeavor that demands some level of industry-specific expertise. But since, as the facts of this case amply demonstrate, wholesale electricity is not bought and sold within a predominantly local market, it does *not* demand significant familiarity with, and will not disrupt state resolution of, distinctively local regulatory facts or policies. The principles underlying Burford are therefore not implicated.

B

[In a portion of the opinion discussed later in this chapter, see p. 1455, *infra*, the Court concluded that the doctrine of equitable restraint enunciated in Younger v. Harris, did not require federal judicial abstention in view of NOPSI's pending state court challenge to the Council's order. (In Younger, the Court observed, "we held that absent extraordinary circumstances federal courts should not enjoin pending state criminal prosecutions.") In resolving that question, the Court also considered whether the Louisiana state court proceedings might implicate the Prentis doctrine, which holds that federal courts should await the completion of "legislative" state court processes—those that occur as part of an integrated agency-court partnership in the setting of rates. The Court reviewed Prentis and its distinction between "judicial" and "legislative" proceedings.]

In Prentis v. Atlantic Coast Line Co., 211 U.S. 210 (1908), several railroads requested a [federal court] "to enjoin . . . the Virginia State Corporation Commission from publishing or taking any steps to enforce a certain order fixing passenger rates," on the ground that the proposed rates were confiscatory. *Id.*, at 223. To decide whether the federal court was at liberty to issue the requested injunction, we examined first the nature of the challenged agency action. Under Virginia law the commission was invested with both legislative and judicial powers, and we assumed, without deciding, that "if it were proceeding against [a railroad] to enforce [the rate] order or to punish [the railroad] for a breach, "it then would be sitting as a court and would be protected from interference on the part of courts of the United States," *id.*, at 226. But, upon analysis, we found the proceedings in the case at hand to be legislative. Justice Holmes, writing for the Court, explained as follows:

> "A judicial inquiry investigates, declares and enforces liabilities as they stand on present or past facts and under laws supposed already to exist. That is its purpose and end. Legislation on the other hand looks to the future and changes existing conditions by making a new rule to be applied thereafter to all or some part of those subject to its power. The establishment of a rate is the making of a rule for the future, and therefore is an act legislative and not judicial in kind. . . ." *Ibid.*

He then considered and rejected the notion that the nature of the agency's proceedings might depend on their form:

> "[The proper characterization of an agency's actions] depends not upon the character of the body but upon the character of the proceedings. . . . And it does not matter what inquiries may have been made as a preliminary to the legislative act. Most legislation is preceded by hearings and investigations. But the effect of the inquiry, and of the decision upon it, is determined by the nature of the act to which the inquiry and decision lead up. . . . The nature of the final act determines the nature of the previous inquiry. As the judge is bound to declare the law he must know or discover the facts that establish the law. So when the final act is legislative the decision which induces it cannot be judicial in the practical sense, although the questions considered might be the same that would arise in the trial of a case." *Id.*, at 226–227 (citations omitted).

We have since reaffirmed both the general mode of analysis of Prentis, see District of Columbia Court of Appeals v. Feldman, 460 U.S. 462, 476–479 (1983), and its specific holding that ratemaking is an essentially legislative act, Colorado Interstate Gas Co. v. FPC, 324 U.S. 581, 589 (1945). Thus, the Council's proceedings here were plainly legislative.

That characterization does not, however, end the inquiry. In Prentis, while we found the challenged agency proceeding legislative in character, we nonetheless held equitable intervention inappropriate because, we determined, the attack on the rate order was premature. Although we made clear that those challenging the rates "were not bound to wait for proceedings brought to enforce the rate and to punish them for departing from it," 211 U.S., at 228, because Virginia provided for legislative review of commission rates by appeal to the state courts, we concluded that the challengers "should make sure that the State in its final legislative action would not respect what they think their rights to be, before resorting to the courts of the United States." *Id.*, at 230. We were as concerned, in other words, to preserve the integrity of a unitary and still-to-be-completed legislative process as we were [in another case] to preserve the integrity of judicial proceedings. Similarly in the present case, if the Louisiana courts' review of Council ratemaking was legislative in nature, NOPSI's challenge to the Council's order should have been dismissed as unripe.

There is no contention here that the Louisiana courts' review involves anything other than a judicial act—that is, not "the making of a rule for the future," but the declaration of NOPSI's rights vis-a-vis the Council "on present or past facts and under laws supposed already to exist," Prentis, 211 U.S., at 226. Nor does there seem to be room for such a contention. Since the state-court review is not an extension of the legislative process, NOPSI's pre-emption claim was ripe for federal review when the Council's order was entered.

As a challenge to completed legislative action, NOPSI's suit represents neither the interference with ongoing judicial proceedings against which Younger was directed, nor the interference with an ongoing legislative process against which our ripeness holding in Prentis was directed. It is, insofar as our policies of federal comity are concerned, no different in substance from a facial challenge to an allegedly unconstitutional statute or zoning ordinance—which we would assuredly not require to be brought in state courts. See Wooley v. Maynard, 430 U.S. 705, 711 (1977). It is true, of course, that the federal court's disposition of such a case may well affect, or for practical purposes pre-empt, a future—or, as in the present circumstances, even a pending—state-court action. But there is no doctrine that the availability or even the pendency of state judicial proceedings excludes the federal courts. Viewed, as it should be, as no more than a state-court challenge to completed legislative action, the Louisiana suit comes within none of the exceptions that Younger and later cases have established.

For the reasons stated, the judgment of the Court of Appeals is reversed, and the cases remanded for further proceedings consistent with this opinion.

So ordered.

■ [JUSTICE BRENNAN, with JUSTICE MARSHALL joining, concurred in a separate opinion. CHIEF JUSTICE REHNQUIST concurred in Parts I and II-B, and concurred in the judgment in a separate opinion. JUSTICE BLACKMUN concurred in the judgment in a separate opinion.]

Patsy v. Board of Regents of the State of Florida

457 U.S. 496 (1982).

Alleging that her employer, a state university in Florida, had discriminated against her on the basis of race and gender, Patsy filed a civil rights action in federal district court. The district court dismissed, based on Patsy's failure to exhaust administrative remedies provided by the university itself. The en banc court of appeals reversed, ruling that a § 1983 plaintiff was required to exhaust administrative remedies when (but only when): (i) an orderly system of review is provided by statute or agency rule; (ii) the agency can grant relief more or less commensurate with the claim; (iii) relief is available without undue delay; (iv) the procedures are fair, not burdensome, and are not used to harass those with legitimate claims; and (v) interim relief is available in appropriate cases. It remanded to allow the district court to determine whether exhaustion was appropriate under those standards.

The Supreme Court, per Justice Marshall, reversed. The Court noted its ruling in McNeese v. Board of Education, 373 U.S. 668 (1963), that exhaustion should not be required in § 1983 actions and its adherence to that view in seven subsequent cases. That position was also supported by the legislative history of § 1 of the Civil Rights of 1871, the precursor to § 1983, the "very purpose" of which "was to interpose the federal courts between the States and the people, as guardians of the people's federal rights" (quoting Mitchum v. Foster, 407 U.S. 225, 242 (1972)). Though Congress in 1871 did not consider the question of exhaustion, the Court believed that the "tenor of the debates" did not support an exhaustion requirement. The Court based this conclusion on three recurring themes in the legislative history: Congress's assignment "to the federal courts [of] a paramount role in protecting constitutional rights;" Congress's belief "that the state authorities had been unable or unwilling to protect the constitutional rights of individuals or to punish those who violated [those] rights;" and "the fact that many legislators interpreted the bill to provide dual or concurrent forums in the state and federal system, enabling the plaintiff to choose the forum in which to seek relief."

Justice Marshall also found support for the Court's holding in a 1980 amendment to the Civil Rights of Institutionalized Persons Act, 42 U.S.C. § 1997 *et seq.* That amendment requires adult incarcerated people, before seeking relief under § 1983, to exhaust administrative remedies that satisfy statutorily specified conditions. In the Court's view, "[t]his detailed scheme is inconsistent with discretion to impose, on an ad hoc basis, a judicially developed exhaustion rule in other cases."

Justice Powell, joined by Chief Justice Burger, dissented. The court of appeals' exhaustion requirement was based, he said, on "sound considerations. It does not defeat federal-court jurisdiction, it merely defers it. It permits the States to correct violations through their own procedures, and it encourages the establishment of such procedures. It is consistent with the principles of comity that apply whenever federal courts are asked to review state action or supersede state proceedings." A rule requiring exhaustion also conserves federal court resources, Justice Powell argued, a matter particularly important given the rapid growth of § 1983 litigation.

In Justice Powell's view, many of the Court's past decisions suggesting that exhaustion was not required in a § 1983 action "can be explained as applications of traditional exceptions to the exhaustion requirement. Other decisions speak to the question in an offhand and conclusory fashion without full briefing and argument." Nor did § 1997e support the Court's decision: that provision focused on the particular question of incarcerated people's suits, and simply did not bear on the general question of exhaustion in § 1983 actions.[1]

NOTE ON EXHAUSTION OF REMEDIES FOR UNLAWFUL STATE ADMINISTRATIVE ACTION

(1) The No-Exhaustion Rule. Patsy builds on the rule of Monroe v. Pape, 365 U.S. 167 (1961), p. 1280, *supra*, under which § 1983 claimants may pursue their federal court challenges as soon as an invasion of their rights occurs, without first availing themselves of state remedies. Recall that Monroe considered an argument for deference to available state *judicial* remedies, p. 1282, *supra*, whereas the university argued in Patsy for deference to an *administrative* process the university made available to aggrieved employees. In NOPSI, by contrast, the Court indicated that the challenge to the Council's decision had become ripe for judicial review upon the completion of the administrative process and the final decision fixing rates. The two decisions may seem superficially inconsistent, in that Patsy rejects any required exhaustion of administrative remedies whereas NOPSI seems to embrace a form of exhaustion in suggesting that litigation must await completion of the rate-making process.

The Prentis doctrine helps to resolve some of the apparent tension between NOPSI and Patsy. See Prentis v. Atlantic Coast Line Co., 211 U.S. 210 (1908). As Prentis explained, ratemaking decisions are legislative in nature, creating a new rule for future application. Judicial process, by contrast, typically entails the resolution of a dispute over past events. Prentis and NOPSI defer judicial review in federal court until the state's legislative ratemaking process ends and a final decision has been reached, setting new rates for future application. Then, judicial review may commence. Sometimes, as NOPSI and Prentis suggest, state courts play a continuing legislative role in setting rates. But where no such legislative role has been assigned to the state courts, a regulated party (like NOPSI) may proceed to the federal court as soon as the judicial stage of the dispute has been reached. See Bacon v. Rutland R.R., 232 U.S. 134 (1914). Note that in Patsy, the majority apparently concluded that the "judicial" stage of the process had arrived when the plaintiff was terminated from employment. Both the majority and dissent in Patsy assumed that the university's administrative proceedings were "judicial" or remedial in character.

(2) Federal Review of State Court "Legislative" Action. The prospect that state courts may act legislatively, rather than judicially, complicates the

---

[1]   Justice O'Connor wrote a concurring opinion, in which Justice Rehnquist joined, endorsing an exhaustion requirement as sound policy, but noting that, "for the reasons set forth in the Court's opinion," that view had already been rejected by prior decisions. Justice White concurred in part, expressing his disagreement with the Court's view that Congress's enactment of § 1997e supported the Court's decision.

task of determining the timing and locus of federal judicial review. In general, if legislative, then the final decision of the state's supreme court may be subject to an initial federal judicial challenge in district court. As Prentis explained: "If the rate should be affirmed by the supreme court of appeals and the railroads still should regard it as confiscatory, * * * they will be at liberty then to renew their application to the [federal trial court], without fear of being met by a plea of res judicata."[1] If, by contrast, the state's supreme court has conducted "judicial" review of a federal claim, a party must typically pursue an appeal to the Supreme Court. See District of Columbia Court of Appeals v. Feldman, 460 U.S. 462 (1983) (federal district court lacks jurisdiction to hear challenge when appeals from the "judicial" decisions of the D.C. Court of Appeals have been assigned by statute to the Supreme Court). In characterizing state proceedings as legislative or judicial, the Court apparently looks to state law. See Oklahoma Packing Co. v. Oklahoma Gas & Elec. Co., 309 U.S. 4 (1940).

Other forms of court-related work may be said to have a legislative quality. Consider, as noted in the discussion of the domestic relations and probate exceptions, pp. 1405–1413, *infra*, that state (and federal) courts often preside over forms of non-contentious adjudication, in which one party may seek the recognition of a claim of right or the creation of a new status or relationship, often in uncontested proceedings brought before a court of record. Such proceedings may result in the entry of a constitutive decree, one that establishes new rights going forward, rather than in an adjudication of rights based on past events. As further discussed below, federal courts may refrain from handling such uncontested matters in the first instance when they present questions of state law. But once a new right or status has been established, a dispute over the enforcement of that right or status or a challenge to its legality may be adjudicated in state or (assuming jurisdiction) federal court. See Barber v. Barber, 62 U.S. 582 (1860) (authorizing federal judicial enforcement of alimony obligation); Spindel v. Spindel, 283 F.Supp. 797 (E.D.N.Y.1968) (upholding federal court power to adjudicate disputes over legality of divorce challenged as fraudulent).

(3) Exhaustion Imposed by Statute. The Prison Litigation Reform Act of 1995 ("PLRA"), 110 Stat. 1321 (1996), requires the exhaustion of "such administrative remedies as are available" prior to the filing of federal suits by plaintiffs challenging prison conditions under § 1983 "or any other Federal law." 42 U.S.C. § 1997e(a). The court may, however, dismiss the underlying claim without requiring exhaustion "[i]n the event that a claim, on its face, is frivolous or malicious, fails to state a claim on which relief can be granted, or seeks monetary relief from a defendant who is immune from such relief." § 1997e(c)(2).

---

[1]   Accord, Porter v. Investors' Syndicate, 286 U.S. 461 (1932), 287 U.S. 346 (1932), holding that a legislative remedy in a state district court against an administrative order under a state blue sky law must be exhausted before resort to a federal court. But *cf.* Pacific Tel. & Tel. Co. v. Kuykendall, 265 U.S. 196 (1924), where the utility alleged that existing rates were confiscatory and that no stay was available: "Under such circumstances comity yields to constitutional right, and the fact that the procedure on appeal in the legislative fixing of rates has not been concluded will not prevent a federal court of equity from suspending the daily confiscation, if it finds the case to justify it." *Id.* 204–05.

When a plaintiff fails to comply with state administrative requirements—including time limits for filing grievances or administrative appeals—a number of circuits have held that suit in federal court is foreclosed, unless stringent conditions are satisfied, on the theory that no sanction for noncompliance with state procedures would otherwise exist. The net result can be not only to defer federal court jurisdiction, but to defeat it altogether.[2]

Booth v. Churner, 532 U.S. 731 (2001), applied the exhaustion requirement to a plaintiff seeking only money damages, despite the unavailability of monetary relief in the administrative forum. The Court unanimously concluded that "one 'exhausts' processes, not forms of relief." It also attached significance to the PLRA's failure to require the exhaustion only of "effective" remedies, as had a prior version of § 1997(e).[3]

In Jones v. Bock, 549 U.S. 199 (2007), however, the Court held that a court of appeals had overstepped its authority by erecting procedural barriers to individual suits that went beyond the requirements of the PLRA. More specifically, the Court rejected rulings that had required individual plaintiffs to plead exhaustion in their complaints (rather than treating non-exhaustion as an affirmative defense), barred suits against a defendant who had not been specifically named in an administrative grievance, and mandated total dismissal of complaints in which petitioners had failed to exhaust some, but not all, of their claims.

In Ross v. Blake, 578 U.S. 632 (2016), the Court rejected the rule adopted by some circuits that the exhaustion requirement of the Prison Litigation Reform Act (PLRA) is not absolute and need not be satisfied in cases involving "special circumstances." The Court emphasized, however, that the PLRA's exhaustion requirement "hinges" on administrative remedies being " 'available,' " 42 U.S.C. § 1997e(a), a term that should not be understood to encompass administrative procedures that are a mere "dead end"; a scheme that is "so opaque that it becomes, practically speaking, incapable of use"; or a situation in which "prison administrators thwart inmates from taking advantage of a grievance process through machination, misrepresentation, or intimidation." *Id.* 643–44.

Burford v. Sun Oil Co.

319 U.S. 315 (1943).

The case arose as an action to enjoin the execution of an order of the Railroad Commission of Texas granting a neighboring leaseholder a permit to drill new wells. The plaintiffs, oil companies with existing leases, attacked the order on state-law grounds, but also alleged an unlawful deprivation of property under the federal Due Process Clause. Jurisdiction rested on both diversity of citizenship and the presence in the case of a federal question. The Court held, 5–4, that the federal district court "as a matter of sound

---

[2]   See generally Schlanger, *Inmate Litigation*, 116 Harv.L.Rev. 1555 (2003).

[3]   The Court construed the PLRA broadly in Porter v. Nussle, 534 U.S. 516 (2002), which unanimously held the exhaustion requirement applicable to all suits brought by incarcerated individuals based on conditions of prison life, including actions alleging use of excessive force and those involving discrete acts rather than general conditions.

equitable discretion" should have declined to exercise jurisdiction and dismissed the case.

Justice Black's opinion emphasized the complexity of the problems of oil and gas regulation and the role of state courts as collaborators with a state agency in administering the state's regulatory scheme: "Since * * * oil moves through the entire field, one operator can not only draw oil from under his own surface area, but can also, if he is advantageously located, drain oil from the most distant parts of the reservoir. * * * For these, and many other reasons based on geologic realities, each oil and gas field must be regulated as a unit for conservation purposes. * * *

"Texas['] interests in this matter are more than that very large one of conserving gas and oil, two of our most important natural resources. It must also weigh the impact of the industry on the whole economy of the state and must consider its revenue, much of which is drawn from taxes on industry and from mineral lands preserved for the benefit of its educational and eleemosynary institutions. * * * The primary task of attempting adjustment of these diverse interests is delegated to the Railroad Commission which Texas has vested with 'broad discretion' in administering the law."

Justice Black condemned the results of previous federal court injunctions, particularly those that had proved to be based on "misunderstanding of local law." He continued: "In describing the relation of the Texas court to the Commission[,] no useful purpose will be served by attempting to label the court's position as legislative, [citing Prentis], or judicial, [citing Bacon v. Rutland Railroad Co., 232 U.S. 134 (1914)]—suffice it to say that the Texas courts are working partners with the Railroad Commission in the business of creating a regulatory system for the oil industry. * * *

"The State provides a unified method for the formation of policy and determination of cases by the Commission and by the state courts. The judicial review of the Commission's decisions in the state courts is expeditious and adequate. Conflicts in the interpretation of state law, dangerous to the success of state policies, are almost certain to result from the intervention of the lower federal courts. On the other hand, if the state procedure is followed from the Commission to the State Supreme Court, ultimate review of the federal questions is fully preserved here. * * * Under such circumstances, a sound respect for the independence of state action requires the federal equity court to stay its hand."

Justice Frankfurter, joined by three other Justices, dissented vigorously. He argued that the Court's refusal to allow the federal district court to adjudicate issues of state law was inconsistent with the congressional grant of diversity-based subject matter jurisdiction.

NOTE ON BURFORD ABSTENTION

Note that the doctrines at issue in Patsy and Prentis addressed the timing of federal judicial engagement, whereas Burford forecloses all lower federal court adjudication of matters of state law in deference to state administrative and judicial primacy. Despite Justice Frankfurter's criticism of the decision as inconsistent with judicial duty under the diversity grant of subject matter jurisdiction, the Court has continued to consider and reject arguments for Burford abstention that appear to imply the continuing vitality of the doctrine. Apart from NOPSI, see Quackenbush v. Allstate Ins. Co., 517 U.S. 706 (1996). It appears that the Court itself has ordered Burford-based abstention in only one subsequent case. See Alabama Pub. Serv. Comm'n v. Southern Ry., 341 U.S. 341 (1951) (ordering abstention in a case involving intrastate railroad regulation that the Court described as "primarily the concern of the state").

NOPSI's two-part formulation would appear to suggest that Burford abstention applies most sensibly to cases in which a particular state court, through its exclusive appellate jurisdiction, works as a de facto partner with a state administrative agency in developing state regulatory policy, and review of the agency's decision by a federal district court would disrupt the partnership relationship.[1] In clearing a pathway to federal court for federal law challenges to state regulation, the NOPSI Court had little occasion to define what sort of state administrative-judicial partnership would qualify for abstention.

Justice Black's account in Burford may help. He suggested that the regulation of oil and gas fields was different in various ways from the typical state regulatory scheme. First, the owners of competing leases may tap into a single reservoir and drain the field. More for one may mean less for another, creating the sort of regulatory interdependence that has long been thought to justify unitary administration. Burford also treats the inter-connected role of the Texas courts and the commission as a factor; Texas had assigned judicial review to a single state court in Travis county, rather than allowing dispersed review. True, Burford stops short of characterizing the state courts' role as "legislative" within the Prentis framework. But one might view the Texas oil field as one (sizable) property under the regulatory control of the Texas court-agency partnership. Such a characterization might support the result in Burford as an elaboration of a state's property-based equitable primacy, such as that recognized in cases like Princess Lida, see p. 1364, *supra*. Yet such an account of Burford would leave room for federal adjudication of disputes that posed no threat to unitary administration, perhaps explaining in part the tenor of Justice Frankfurter's dissent.

Colorado River Water Conservation Dist. v. United States

424 U.S. 800 (1976).

The McCarran Amendment, 43 U.S.C. § 666, authorized suit against the United States in state court "(1) for the adjudication of rights to the use of water of a river system or other source, or (2) for the administration of such rights, where it appears that the United States is the owner of or is in the

---

[1]   See Rehnquist, *Taking Comity Seriously: How to Neutralize the Abstention Doctrine*, 46 Stan.L.Rev. 1049, 1077–78 (1994). See also Young, *Federal Court Abstention and State Administrative Law From Burford to Ankenbrandt: Fifty Years of Judicial Federalism Under Burford v. Sun Oil Co. and Kindred Doctrines*, 42 DePaul L.Rev. 859, 886–99 (1993) (arguing that the decision in Burford reflected concerns such as these).

process of acquiring water rights by appropriation under State law." Instead of claiming water rights in pending state court proceedings in one of the state's seven water districts, the United States sued over 1,000 water users in Colorado federal district court in Denver seeking establishment of rights through declaratory judgments. Colorado applies the doctrine of prior appropriation, assigning priority according to the date of the initial diversion of water for beneficial use. The federal district court in Denver was located some 300 miles from the state court where parallel litigation over rights in the river system was underway.

In response, parties to litigation in both state and federal court moved to join the United States as a claimant in state court and then asked the federal court to abstain. On review of a Tenth Circuit decision allowing the federal action to proceed, the Supreme Court reversed. Acknowledging that the state and federal courts had concurrent jurisdiction over the water claims of the United States, the Court observed that the rule of Kline v. Burke Construction would ordinarily counsel in favor of allowing parallel litigation to proceed. But the Court ordered dismissal of the federal action nonetheless, identifying a range of factors that together were said to create "exceptional circumstances" warranting abstention.

"It has been held, for example, that the court first assuming jurisdiction over property may exercise that jurisdiction to the exclusion of other courts. Donovan v. City of Dallas, [377 U.S. 408, 412 (1964)]; Princess Lida v. Thompson, 305 U.S. 456, 466 (1939). This has been true even where the Government was a claimant in existing state proceedings and then sought to invoke district-court jurisdiction * * *. In assessing the appropriateness of dismissal in the event of an exercise of concurrent jurisdiction, a federal court may also consider such factors as the inconvenience of the federal forum, the desirability of avoiding piecemeal litigation, and the order in which jurisdiction was obtained by the concurrent forums. No one factor is necessarily determinative; a carefully considered judgment taking into account both the obligation to exercise jurisdiction and the combination of factors counselling against that exercise is required. Only the clearest of justifications will warrant dismissal.

"Turning to the present case, a number of factors clearly counsel against concurrent federal proceedings. The most important of these is the McCarran Amendment itself. The clear federal policy evinced by that legislation is the avoidance of piecemeal adjudication of water rights in a river system. This policy is akin to that underlying the rule requiring that jurisdiction be yielded to the court first acquiring control of property, for the concern in such instances is with avoiding the generation of additional litigation through permitting inconsistent dispositions of property. This concern is heightened with respect to water rights, the relationships among which are highly interdependent. Indeed, we have recognized that actions seeking the allocation of water essentially involve the disposition of property and are best conducted in unified proceedings. The consent to jurisdiction given by the McCarran Amendment bespeaks a policy that recognizes the availability of comprehensive state systems for adjudication of water rights as the means for achieving these goals."

Beyond the congressional policy, the Court emphasized that federal proceedings had not progressed past the motion to dismiss stage; that 1,000 defendants were named; that 300 miles separated Denver from the state court managing the other litigation, and that the federal government had apparently submitted its claims to state court adjudication in other Colorado water districts. The Court was at pains to portray its decision as a narrow one, explaining that changes in any of these factors might call for a different result.

In a dissenting opinion for three Justices, Justice Stewart distinguished the property cases (Princess Lida) at the center of the majority's abstention decision. The dissent argued that the federal court did not need *in rem* jurisdiction to declare the rights of the parties as to whether the United States had reserved water rights. The district court could make such a determination "without having control of the river." In Princess Lida, the dissent observed, state court primacy did not apply to plaintiffs who seek merely an adjudication of a right or interest as the basis for a claim on a fund in the possession of the state court. Here, the United States asked the federal court to determine only its specific rights in the flow of water in the river. Once such decisions were made on the government's claims, the state court would "integrate" any new awards of water rights with past decisions into what the dissent described as "one all-inclusive tabulation for each water source."

NOTE ON ABSTENTION IN DEFERENCE TO "PARALLEL" STATE COURT PROCEEDINGS

(1) Parallel Proceedings. Note that the same form of abstention ordered in Burford—dismissal of the federal proceeding—was approved in Colorado River. But unlike in Burford, there were in Colorado River parallel proceedings pending in state court and federal court involving the same parties and claims. To what extent does the presence or absence of parallel proceedings inform the abstention decision? After an abstention-based dismissal of federal suits like that in Burford, the federal plaintiffs could pursue any timely relief in state court much the way the United States would presumably pursue its water claims to the Colorado River in state court. Abstention-based stays and dismissals do not adjudicate the merits; they contemplate further litigation.

Consider the duplication of proceedings in NOPSI, where the utility sued in both state and federal court to challenge the Council's denial of a full cost-recovery rate increase. NOPSI explained that it filed duplicative proceedings as a hedge in case the federal court chose to abstain from adjudicating its preemption claim. See also Sprint Communications, Inc. v. Jacobs, 571 U.S. 69 (2013).

(2) Equitable Administration. In both Burford (oil and gas) and Colorado River (water), disputes over competing claims to a natural resource had been assigned to a unitary state administrative process. In both cases federal litigation would establish (or "liquidate") legal rights rather than integrate and adjust competing claims to a limited resource. The dissent in Colorado River emphasized the absence of any federal interference in the state administrative process, comparing the federal litigation to that approved in such cases as Princess Lida and Riehle v. Margolies, 279 U.S. 218 (1929), p. 1368, *supra*. In response, the majority said it was recognizing only a limited exception to the normal Kline v. Burke Construction rule allowing litigation of parallel proceedings.

In evaluating the scope of the Colorado River exception, consider how to value or weigh the fact that the state court was conducting administrative proceedings aimed at the allocation of a scarce resource between competing claimants. The argument for abstention seems stronger when federal litigation could disrupt such an administrative process. The Burford Court cited a series of injunctive decrees that were said to have disrupted the ability of the Texas state court-agency partnership to achieve administrative coherence in the Texas oil patch. Similarly, in Colorado River, the Court emphasized the inconvenience of the federal forum and the number of litigants (over 1000) named there. The sheer number of parties suggests that the government's *in personam* litigation strategy in Colorado bore some resemblance to proceedings *in rem* to establish rights in the flow of the river.

(3) Beyond Equitable Administration. Later cases apply the Burford and Colorado River abstention doctrines to a broader range of parallel proceedings. The decisions have an ad hoc quality and do not seemingly rest on a policy of protecting unitary state administration.

(a) Moses H. Cone Memorial Hosp. v. Mercury Constr. Corp., 460 U.S. 1 (1983). In state court, the hospital sued for breach of contract and a stay of any proposed arbitration. In federal court, the construction firm sued to compel arbitration, as agreed to in the contract and as authorized by the Federal Arbitration Act. The federal district court tentatively stayed its proceedings in deference to the parallel state court proceeding. The Fourth Circuit reversed, directing the district court to grant an order compelling arbitration. The Supreme Court upheld that decision, concluding that the various Colorado River factors did not support abstention and that the federal plaintiff was invoking a federal right to compel arbitration. The principle of Kline v. Burke Construction, had it been applied by the Court, would seemingly support non-abstention.

(b) Quackenbush v. Allstate Ins. Co., 517 U.S. 706 (1996). A California state insurance commissioner sued Allstate for breach of reinsurance contracts, asserting as trustee the rights of an insolvent insurance company that had been placed into receivership. Allstate removed to federal court, invoking diversity jurisdiction, and moved to compel arbitration. Quackenbush sought a remand, arguing on Burford grounds that federal adjudication or arbitration would interfere with litigation pending in the receivership. The district court remanded on Burford grounds but the Ninth Circuit reversed, viewing abstention doctrines as a creature of equity inapplicable to suits for money damages. The Supreme Court affirmed, finding that abstention doctrines were largely if not strictly confined to suits seeking equitable relief.

Note the important difference between a suit for equitable relief, like that in NOPSI, and an argument for the equitable adjustment of money claims. The set-off claim in Quackenbush nicely illustrates the distinction. If Allstate were permitted to set-off its entire claim and thereby reduce its financial obligations to the insolvent company, Allstate might recover more than its fair share of the limited assets available in the receivership proceeding. In other words, set-off might interfere with the equitable distribution of receivership assets in violation of the principle of unitary administration. The Court's refusal to order abstention should not be read to foreclose equitable administration of the set-off claim, once it has been liquidated.

(c) Expansive Application of Colorado River in Lower Courts. Lower federal courts have extended Colorado River abstention well beyond its banks. Consider the Seventh Circuit's approach in Driftless Area Land Conservancy v. Valcq, 16 F.4th 508 (7th Cir.2021), a case that presented parallel state and federal court challenges to a Wisconsin state agency's decision to authorize construction of an electricity transmission line. Raising Colorado River abstention on its own motion, the appellate court found that the state and federal court proceedings were "parallel" in the sense that they involved the same parties, roughly speaking, and the same due process challenge to conflicts of interest that allegedly infected the state agency's authorization decision. Identifying a ten-factor checklist that had emerged in earlier decisions, the court deemed two factors controlling: the availability of relief in state court and the state's "sovereign" interest in "the proper functioning of its administrative law and procedure." Notably, the Driftless court did not confront a state court's administration of a scarce natural resource, as in Burford and Colorado River, but only a question of legality as in NOPSI, where the Supreme Court rejected any abstention requirement.[1]

(4) Parallel Claims and the Declaratory Judgment Act. In Wilton v. Seven Falls Co., 515 U.S. 277 (1995), the Court acknowledged that, under Colorado River, federal courts should not in general abstain in deference to parallel state proceedings unless they find the requisite "exceptional circumstances." But the Court ruled that the Colorado River test does not govern parallel federal proceedings under the Declaratory Judgment Act. The case began when an insurance company sued in federal court for a declaration of non-coverage. The policyholder responded with a suit in state court seeking to recover for breach of the insurance contract. The policyholder asked the federal court for a stay to allow resolution of the coverage dispute in the pending state proceeding. When the federal court granted the stay, the insurance company argued on appeal that the controlling exceptional circumstances test of Colorado River had not been met.

---

[1]   See also Baek v. Clausen, 886 F.3d 652 (7th Cir.2018) (upholding district court order staying parallel federal proceeding to allow state court action to proceed to a final, claim preclusive judgment). Other courts have applied related doctrines, such as the prohibition against claim splitting and "other action pending," in staying or dismissing a federal action that overlaps with a pending state proceeding. For a persuasive rejection of such authority, treating Colorado River as the controlling framework, see Maldonado-Cabrera v. Anglero-Alfaro, 26 F.4th 523, 527–28 (1st Cir.2022).

In concluding that the Colorado River test did not apply, the Court in a unanimous opinion by Justice O'Connor emphasized instead the controlling language of the Declaratory Judgment Act, 28 U.S.C. § 2201, which provides that a district court "*may* declare the rights and other legal relations of any interested party." Justice O'Connor noted that the Act's "textual commitment to discretion, and the breadth of leeway we have always understood it to suggest, distinguish the declaratory judgment context from other areas of the law in which concepts of discretion surface." *Id.* 286–87. Here, "the normal principle that federal courts should adjudicate claims within their jurisdiction yields to considerations of practicality and wise judicial administration." *Id.* 288. Without trying "to delineate the outer boundaries of [the district court's] discretion in other cases, for example, cases raising issues of federal law or cases in which there are no parallel state proceedings," the Court found that the district court had not abused its discretion in granting the stay. *Id.* 290.

(5) The Implications of Pennhurst. In Pennhurst State School & Hosp. v. Halderman, 465 U.S. 89 (1984), p. 1197, *supra,* the Supreme Court held that the Eleventh Amendment denies federal courts jurisdiction to award injunctive relief aimed at compelling state officials to comply with state law. Pennhurst does not bar federal court suits challenging state action under either state or federal law if the relief is not of the kind barred by the Eleventh Amendment—as with injunctive relief against a local government or its officials and damages payable out of a state or local official's own pocket. See Chap. IX, Sec. 2. Nor is Pennhurst relevant to cases in which a plaintiff attempts to attack a state statute and the validity of the attack depends on how the statute would be construed by the state's courts. But if the Burford case were filed today in federal court, that court would lack power under Pennhurst to entertain a suit to enjoin Texas officials from violating Texas law in the issuance of drilling permits.[2]

NOTE ON JURISDICTIONAL RESTRICTION AS COORDINATION: THE PROBATE AND DOMESTIC RELATIONS EXCEPTIONS

As the material surveyed thus far makes clear, the Supreme Court has sometimes chosen in the face of a clear grant of jurisdiction to require abstention in deference to state proceedings. On other occasions, the Court has chosen to achieve much the same result by recognizing a judge-made exception to an existing grant of jurisdiction that preserves an area of state court primacy. This section briefly surveys two instances of deference through jurisdictional restriction. What is now commonly known as the "domestic relations" exception narrows the federal judicial role in certain family law matters. In the probate exception, the Court has excluded federal courts from hearing certain claims that implicate the administration of decedents' estates. While these exceptions operate as formal limits on federal

---

[2]   For a persuasive argument that federal courts in the nineteenth century did not shy away from overseeing state and local agency compliance with state law, see Woolhandler & Collins, *Judicial Federalism and the Administrative States,* 87 Calif.L.Rev. 613 (1999).

jurisdiction, they overlap with the abstention doctrines and implement a form of coordination comparable to that articulated in Kline v. Burke Construction and Princess Lida.

Ankenbrandt v. Richards

504 U.S. 689 (1992).

Carol Ankenbrandt sued her former spouse and his partner in tort, seeking damages for the alleged sexual abuse of her children. After the court of appeals upheld the dismissal of Ankenbrandt's claims as falling within the domestic relations exception, the Court granted review to clarify the doctrine's legal basis and scope. After tracing the exception's origins to Barber v. Barber, 62 U.S. 582 (1859), the Ankenbrandt Court ultimately concluded that the doctrine was not constitutionally compelled but operated as a gloss on the statutory grant of diversity jurisdiction. Confining the exception to suits that seek entry of divorce, alimony, and child custody decrees, the Ankenbrandt Court reversed and remanded to allow the plaintiff to pursue her tort claims in district court.

On the origin of the doctrine, the Ankenbrandt Court quoted language in Barber: "Our first remark is—and we wish it to be remembered—that this is not a suit asking the court for the allowance of alimony. That has been done by a court of competent jurisdiction. The court in Wisconsin was asked to interfere to prevent that decree from being defeated by fraud.

"We disclaim altogether any jurisdiction in the courts of the United States upon the subject of divorce, or for the allowance of alimony, either as an original proceeding in chancery or as an incident to divorce."

Ankenbrandt, 504 U.S. at 694 (quoting Barber, 62 U.S. at 584). Though dicta, the Barber Court's statements were said to have given rise to an exclusion of "domestic relations" cases from the jurisdiction of the lower federal courts. Unwilling to cast aside a doctrine with so lengthy a pedigree, the Court found that Congress implicitly ratified the doctrine by re-enacting the statutory grant of diversity jurisdiction without disclaiming its application.

The Court supported its conclusions by what it described as "sound policy considerations." "Issuance of decrees of this type not infrequently involves retention of jurisdiction by the court and deployment of social workers to monitor compliance. As a matter of judicial economy, state courts are more eminently suited to work of this type than are federal courts, which lack the close association with state and local government organizations dedicated to handling issues that arise out of conflicts over divorce, alimony, and child custody decrees. Moreover, * * * [the state courts have developed special proficiency] * * * over the past century and a half in handling issues that arise in the granting of such decrees." In framing the doctrine as an exception to statutory grants of diversity jurisdiction, the Court rejected the argument that the exception was better understood as an application of one or more federal abstention doctrines.

Justice Blackmun concurred, rejecting the majority's interpretation of the diversity statute but concluding that the district court might properly abstain from adjudicating claims that fall within the core state court competence over domestic relations matters. On the jurisdictional issue, Justice Blackmun concluded that "Congress likely had no idea until the Court's decision today that the diversity statute contained an exception for domestic relations matters." Nevertheless, Justice Blackmun discerned in the cases a concern best described as "abstentional—and not jurisdictional—in nature." He viewed the cases as premised upon virtually exclusive state court primacy "in the regulation of domestic relations." Noting like the majority that the states have "developed specialized courts and institutions in family matters," he thought abstention proper in actions "seeking divorce, alimony, and child custody."

Justice Blackmun viewed the Court's approach—"invent[ing] statutory exceptions that are simply not there"—as the greater affront to Congress than using "principles of abstention." As for what kind of abstention, he agreed with the majority that Younger abstention was inappropriate in view of the absence of any pending state court proceeding. See Sec. 3(c). But he declined to identify a doctrine or "affix a label" on the principles he would apply. Instead, Justice Blackmun explained that the plaintiff "does not seek a determination of status or obligations arising from status," apparently a reference to divorce, alimony, and custody. Nor would a federal adjudication "upset a prior state court determination of status or obligations appurtenant to status nor pre-empt a pending state court determination of this nature."

NOTE ON FEDERAL JURISDICTION IN MATTERS OF DOMESTIC RELATIONS

(1) History. The view, repudiated in Ankenbrandt, that Article III excludes jurisdiction in domestic relations cases, was bound up with the assertion that certain matters were beyond the historical scope of law and equity. See, *e.g.*, Fontain v. Ravenel, 58 U.S. (17 How.) 369, 393 (1854) (Taney, C.J., dissenting) (arguing that the federal courts lacked power to enforce a charitable bequest, as the "chancery jurisdiction" of the federal courts conferred by Article III extended only to matters of which chancery had jurisdiction "in its judicial character as a court of equity," and not to the "prerogative powers, which the king, as *parens patriae*, in England, exercised through the courts," and which remained with the states as sovereigns).

(2) The Spindel Decision. In Spindel v. Spindel, 283 F.Supp. 797 (E.D.N.Y.1968), Judge Weinstein offered a searching analysis and criticism of the whole development of the federal domestic relations exception. On the historical point, he challenged the premise that matrimonial matters were handled exclusively in the ecclesiastical courts and not in chancery acting in its judicial capacity. He also noted that Article III requires only a "controversy" (not a "case in law or equity") between citizens of different states for federal jurisdiction to exist and that Congress could therefore confer on the federal courts authority to grant divorces in such cases. *Id.* 801.

(3) The Legal Basis for the Ankenbrandt Exception. Ankenbrandt treats the domestic relations exception as a limit on the statutory grant of diversity jurisdiction, rather than Article III. That interpretive move accomplishes two things: (1) it clears the way for Supreme Court review of federal questions that arise in the course of state domestic relations proceedings and allows district courts to entertain federal law claims that implicate domestic relations;[1] and (2) it opens up the possibility, however unlikely, that Congress might enact a new law, broadening diversity jurisdiction to reach some matters within the scope of the narrow exception specified in Ankenbrandt.

Consider Justice Blackmun's concurring view that abstention doctrines would provide a more legally justified, effective, and sensitive tool to avoid federal interference with state court primacy. Some abstention doctrines, including Burford and Colorado River, reflect a concern with the preservation of the state court's role in the unitary administration of a limited resource and might provide the "principles" to which Justice Blackmun pointed in urging abstention. Whatever the wisdom of the Ankenbrandt Court's choice of the alternative "jurisdictional" view, the majority opinion leaves open the possibility that federal courts may more broadly abstain from deciding certain domestic matters within their jurisdiction.

The Ankenbrandt Court unanimously agreed that federal deference was owed to state court control of some domestic relations decisions but that the deference did not extend to the plaintiff's tort claims. Consider the factors that should inform its choice as to how best to implement its dual concern with access to federal court and preservation of some state court primacy. As Chapter VIII explains, p. 971, *supra*, jurisdictional limits enjoy first-principle status in that they remain open throughout the litigation process. Choosing a jurisdictional foundation for the Court's doctrine thus threatens to disrupt efficient dispute resolution. At the same time, the Court has come to share the concern that abstention doctrines sometimes operate as unprincipled refusals to exercise jurisdiction Congress has conferred. See, *e.g.*, Sprint Communications, Inc. v. Jacobs, 571 U.S. 69 (2013).

(4) A Critique of the Domestic Relations Exception. Responding to those who defend federal court deference to traditional state court competence in matters of domestic relations, Professor Resnik argues that the exception marginalizes the domestic sphere, based on an assumption that it is dominated by women: "Women and the families they sometimes inhabit are not only assumed to be outside the federal courts, they also are assumed not to be related to the 'national issues' to which the federal

---

[1]   Confirming the importance of preserving access to a federal forum for federal question claims, the Court has repeatedly enforced constitutional rights in the domestic relations sphere. See, *e.g.*, Obergefell v. Hodges, 576 U.S. 644 (2015) (holding that the Fourteenth Amendment requires states to recognize same-sex marriages); V.L. v. E.L., 577 U.S. 404 (2016) (per curiam) (summarily reversing one state's refusal to give full faith and credit to an adoption decree awarded in another state); Pavan v. Smith, 582 U.S. 563 (2017) (holding that state law must recognize same-sex spouse of biological mother as second parent on birth certificate where it would otherwise by default recognize opposite-sex spouse on birth certificate); Troxel v. Granville, 530 U.S. 57 (2000) (holding that state court order granting visitation rights to paternal grandparents impermissibly infringed upon mother's due process rights to make decisions concerning the raising of her children). Compare Abbott v. Abbott, 560 U.S. 1 (2010) (federal law entitled parent to enforce Chilean custody decree by suit brought in federal court under the federal International Child Abduction Remedies Act (ICARA)).

judiciary is to devote its interests. Jurisdictional lines have not been drawn according to the laws of nature but by men, who today are seeking to confirm their prestige as members of the most important judiciary in the country * * *. Dealing with women * * * is not how they want to frame their job." Resnik, *"Naturally" Without Gender: Women, Jurisdiction, and the Federal Courts*, 66 N.Y.U.L.Rev. 1682, 1749 (1991).[2]

Marshall v. Marshall

547 U.S. 293 (2006).

The Court granted review in this long-running dispute over the assets of a wealthy decedent (Howard Marshall) to clarify the scope of the so-called "probate" exception to federal jurisdiction. The dispute pitted the decedent's son (Pierce Marshall) against the decedent's widow (Vickie Marshall). Vickie claimed that, before he died, Howard had promised her a "catchall" trust fund, but Howard failed to provide for her in his will or otherwise. Vickie charged son Pierce with meddling, asserting in the Texas state probate proceeding that Pierce had tortiously interfered with her expected legacy. Pierce regarded that claim as defamatory. When Vickie filed for bankruptcy in California, Pierce brought a defamation claim there and Vickie counterclaimed by reasserting her tortious interference claim. Pierce argued that the counterclaim fell within the exclusive jurisdiction of the pending Texas state court proceeding. After rejecting Pierce's argument that the probate exception barred the federal court from hearing Vickie's counterclaim, the California federal district court awarded her some $90 million in compensatory and punitive damages.

The Ninth Circuit reversed. It recognized that Vickie's tortious interference claim did not involve the administration of an estate, the probate of a will, or any other purely probate matter, but it broadly applied the "probate" exception to bar federal jurisdiction. It also relied in part on Texas state law, which assigns exclusive jurisdiction over such matters to a special probate court.

With Justice Ginsburg writing, a unanimous Court reversed in turn. The Court acknowledged the debate over the origins of the probate exception and noted its connection to a related exception for matters of domestic relations, as more fully explored in Ankenbrandt v. Richards, 504 U.S. 689 (1992), p. 1406, *supra*. The exceptions, the Court explained, are not "compelled by the text of the Constitution or federal statute. Both are judicially created doctrines stemming in large measure from misty understandings of English legal history." Justice Ginsburg recalled that the Ankenbrandt Court had narrowed the domestic relations exception considerably by confining it to claims in federal courts based on diversity of citizenship and clarifying that only "divorce, alimony, and child custody decrees" remain outside federal jurisdictional bounds.

---

[2]   See also Cahn, *Family Law, Federalism, and the Federal Courts*, 79 Iowa L.Rev. 1073 (1994); Stein, *The Domestic Relations Exception to Federal Jurisdiction: Rethinking an Unsettled Federal Courts Doctrine*, 36 B.C.L.Rev. 669 (1995); Jackson, *Empiricism, Gender, and Legal Pedagogy: An Experiment in a Federal Courts Seminar at Georgetown University Law Center*, 83 Geo.L.J. 461, 494–95 & n.113 (1994).

Having recounted the downsizing of the domestic relations exception, the Marshall Court considered the proper scope of the probate exception. Acknowledging "enigmatic" language in an earlier decision, Markham v. Allen, 326 U.S. 490 (1946), the Court explained that case as standing for "the general principle that, when one court is exercising *in rem* jurisdiction over a *res*, a second court will not assume *in rem* jurisdiction over the same *res*. Thus, the probate exception reserves to state probate courts the probate or annulment of a will and the administration of a decedent's estate; it also precludes federal courts from endeavoring to dispose of property that is in the custody of a state probate court. But it does not bar federal courts from adjudicating matters outside those confines and otherwise within federal jurisdiction."

Applying this narrow view of the probate exception, the Court readily concluded that Vickie's claim could proceed in federal court. Vickie's claim does not "involve the administration of an estate, the probate of a will, or any other purely probate matter." Alleging a widely recognized tort, "Vickie seeks an *in personam* judgment against Pierce. [She does not] seek to reach a *res* in the custody of a state court."

The Court also rejected the argument that the claims in question fell within the exclusive jurisdiction of the Texas state probate court. Federal jurisdiction was not subject to the control of state law. Indeed, earlier cases had held that the jurisdiction of the federal courts cannot be "impaired by subsequent state legislation creating courts of probate." McClellan v. Carland, 217 U.S. 268, 281 (1910). Nor do the federal courts owe full faith and credit to the exclusive jurisdiction Texas had conferred on its probate courts. "Under our federal system, Texas cannot render its probate courts exclusively competent to entertain a claim of that genre." Having concluded that the district court properly exercised jurisdiction, the Court remanded for consideration of whether Vickie's federal judgment was claim precluded by her unsuccessful submission of a similar claim to the Texas probate court.

Justice Steven concurred, arguing that the Court should go further in restricting the scope of the probate exception.

NOTE ON JURISDICTIONAL ALLOCATION IN PROBATE MATTERS

(1) Development of the Exception. Perhaps reflecting a heritage in which the probate of wills was vested in special courts in England—first the ecclesiastical courts and then chancery courts—nineteenth century decisions of the Supreme Court recognized a "probate exception" to federal jurisdiction that the Court in Marshall v. Marshall viewed as analogous to the so-called domestic relations exception. At its core, the decisions barred efforts by lower federal courts to take over, generally, the administration of a decedent's estate. *E.g.*, Hook v. Payne, 81 U.S. (14 Wall.) 252 (1871); Byers v. McAuley, 149 U.S. 608 (1893). *Cf.* Waterman v. Canal-Louisiana Bank & Trust Co., 215 U.S. 33 (1909) (denying jurisdiction, in an otherwise proper case, over a prayer for an accounting of an estate). Like the domestic relations exception, the probate exception has generated uncertainties in application and triggered controversy.[1]

(2) Fixing the Legal Basis of the Exception. The Marshall v. Marshall Court did not explicitly disavow earlier decisions that viewed the probate exception as a limit on federal jurisdiction. But it did narrow the exception to the specific claims identified: probate or annulment of a will; the administration of a decedent's estate; and the disposition of property in the custody of a state probate court. The Court had no occasion to say whether the exception applied only to federal diversity proceedings, or more broadly to claims that present federal questions as well.

Note the distinction between the *allocation* of federal jurisdiction and the *coordination* of overlapping state and federal jurisdiction. Pierce argued for a first-to-file rule of coordination; once the Texas state probate court had asserted jurisdiction over all claims relating to Howard's estate, the federal courts should stay their hand in deference to state court priority. But the Court rejected this rule of coordination, applying instead the presumption of concurrency and the first-to-judgment rule of Kline v. Burke Construction. That explains the Court's conclusion that the state courts cannot assert exclusive jurisdiction over matters within federal judicial power and its decision to remand for an assessment of the preclusive effect of any Texas judgment.

Despite its rejection of a first-to-file rule, the Court's approach in Marshall v. Marshall to allocating or defining the scope of federal jurisdiction owes much to the conception of equitable priority and *in personam* concurrency that underlies the decisions in Princess Lida, 305 U.S. 456 (1939), p. 1364, *supra*, and Riehle v. Margolies, 279 U.S. 218 (1929), p. 1368, *supra*. In effect, the Marshall Court acknowledged state court equitable priority in matters of *in rem* administration, or what it calls "pure" probate, but upheld concurrent federal jurisdiction over an action that seeks to "liquidate" an *in personam* claim to the assets in question. Given its consistency with an established framework of equitable priority, consider what the probate exception adds to the analysis. Recall that in Princess Lida, the state court proceeding was first filed, thereby triggering equitable priority, and foreclosing federal court interference. By contrast, a jurisdictional restriction on federal diversity or bankruptcy authority, as in Marshall v. Marshall, limits federal judicial power even where a federal proceeding was first initiated.

(3) An Alternative Account of the Exceptions. In evaluating the origins of the two doctrines, consider that nineteenth century divorce proceedings typically triggered a form of estate administration not unlike that involved in the probate of a decedent's estate. For recognition of the estate-like quality of domestic relations, see Jones v. Brennan, 465 F.3d 304, 307 (7th Cir.2006) (likening disputes over the marital estate to an *in rem* proceeding). Proceedings ancillary to a divorce might include marshaling of the marital

---

[1]   See generally Nicolas, *Fighting the Probate Mafia: A Dissection of the Probate Exception to Federal Court Jurisdiction*, 74 S.Calif.L.Rev. 1479 (2001) (discussing and critically analyzing a variety of proffered justifications for the exception); Pfander & Downey, *In Search of the Probate Exception*, 67 Vand.L.Rev. 1533 (2014).

estate's assets and ordering a fair division of those assets through alimony awards or property settlements. The initiation of divorce proceedings could thus lead to a form of state court property administration not unlike that undertaken in connection with the oversight of trustee performance in Princess Lida and probate in Marshall v. Marshall. A suit for tort damages, like that brought by Ankenbrandt, poses little threat to the state court's administrative function. See generally Pfander & Damrau, *A Non-Contentious Account of Article III's Domestic Relations Exception*, 92 Notre Dame L.Rev. 117 (2016).

As part of a broader project on the meaning of "cases" and "controversies" in Article III, Pfander, Cases Without Controversies: Uncontested Adjudication in Article III Courts (2021), argues on historical and conceptual grounds that the domestic relations and probate exceptions derive from diversity-based limits on the nature of federal judicial power. Pfander draws on civil law in suggesting a distinction between the resolution of disputes between adverse parties (contentious adjudication) and the judicial recognition or registration of a new right or status (non-contentious adjudication). While Article III power over "cases" encompasses both contentious and non-contentious forms of adjudication, power over "controversies" may extend only to contested matters. As a consequence, federal courts were authorized to use non-contentious forms of adjudication to establish new rights or status based on federal law; they were foreclosed from doing so as to matters of state law by the absence of a controversy.[2]

For much of the nineteenth century, Pfander argues, the federal courts applied these distinctions. They routinely heard uncontested applications to claim federal rights, such as petitions for naturalized citizenship, but they consistently disclaimed authority over similar matters of state law. The probate exception may reflect in part the fact that the proceeding often began with an uncontested or ex parte application for admission of a will to probate "in the common form." The court's admission of the will to probate triggered the creation of a decedent's estate and appointment of an executor, bringing into play the principle of equitable priority that forecloses any federal judicial role in estate administration. But under the theory of Princess Lida and Riehle v. Margolies, the liquidation of claims to the estate could proceed in an alternative forum (much the way Vickie Marshall was allowed to pursue her defamation claim in bankruptcy).

In contrast to probate proceedings in the common form, nineteenth century divorce proceedings often presented contested disputes for the courts to resolve. But as recognized in Spindel v. Spindel, 283 F.Supp. 797 (E.D.N.Y.1968) and reiterated in Justice Blackmun's Ankenbrandt concurrence, many family law proceedings, including those for divorce, alimony, and child custody, propose to establish a new status or jural relationship. The Spindel court explained that federal courts might well resolve disputes over the legality of past transactions but should refrain from the creation of a new status or jural relationship as a matter of state law. The creation of new constitutive rights under state law may lie beyond the

---

[2]   See also Pfander & Birk, *Article III Judicial Power, the Adverse-Party Requirement, and Non-Contentious Jurisdiction*, 124 Yale L.J. 1346 (2015).

adjudicatory power of a federal court limited to the resolution of "controversies" over state law.

Like Ankenbrandt, Pfander's account would leave federal question jurisdiction intact but qualify the exercise of diversity jurisdiction by limiting it to the resolution of disputes. Both the tort claim for domestic abuse in Ankenbrandt and the tortious interference claim in Marshall fit comfortably within federal diversity jurisdiction, so conceived.

NOTE ON STAYS TO ALLOW CLARIFICATION OF UNSETTLED STATE LAW

Lehman Brothers v. Schein

416 U.S. 386 (1974)

This shareholder's derivative action was brought in New York federal district court based on diversity. The suit sought damages from corporate insiders on the theory that they had misappropriated an asset of the firm in trading on insider information. While Florida law controlled, the Florida Supreme Court had yet to rule on whether such a theory of misappropriation applied to Florida corporate insiders. The Court vacated and remanded to allow the lower court to consider certifying the question to the Florida state supreme court through available procedures, offering the following guidance:

"[W]hen state law does not make the certification procedure available, a federal court not infrequently will stay its hand, remitting the parties to the state court to resolve the controlling state law on which the federal rule may turn. Numerous applications of that practice are reviewed in Meredith v. Winter Haven, 320 U.S. 228 (1943), which teaches that the mere difficulty in ascertaining local law is no excuse for remitting the parties to a state tribunal for the start of another lawsuit. We do not suggest that where there is doubt as to local law and where the certification procedure is available, resort to it is obligatory. It does, of course, in the long run save time, energy, and resources and helps build a cooperative judicial federalism. Its use in a given case rests in the sound discretion of the federal court."

NOTE ON CERTIFICATION TO STATE SUPREME COURTS

(1) Doctrinal History. An early statute empowered the Supreme Court to answer questions of federal law certified by a divided federal circuit court.[1] It was not until 1960 that the Supreme Court first ordered a lower federal court to avail itself of state certification procedures in Clay v. Sun Ins. Office Ltd., 363 U.S. 207 (1960). (The Clay case arose in Florida, which from 1945–1965 was the only state with a statute authorizing its courts to answer certified questions.) Before certification took hold, federal courts would

---

[1]   See Act of Apr. 29, 1802, ch. 31, § 6, 2 Stat. 156, 159. For greater discussion, see Chap. III, Sec. 1.

sometimes direct the parties to institute state court proceedings (perhaps through a declaratory judgment action) to clarify the content of state law.

Today, at least 49 states have some form of certification, although some state supreme courts have narrowed access to the process by demanding genuine uncertainty as to the meaning of state law and a strong showing that legal clarification will control the outcome of the federal case. By contrast, some state supreme courts welcome certified questions from a much broader set of institutions. In Delaware, for example, the state supreme court may answer certified questions from federal courts, from other state courts, from federal bankruptcy courts, from the Securities Exchange Commission, and from courts in the European Union. See Del.R.Sup.Ct. 41(a)(ii).

(2) Mechanics. Virtually every state with certification procedures authorizes the submission of certified questions by the Supreme Court and from a federal court of appeals.[2] Most, but not all, also authorize the certification of questions by federal district courts.[3] Some states also authorize certification from lower state courts to the court of last resort. If a state supreme court will answer certified questions only from a federal court of appeals, should a district court feel encouraged to attempt to resolve a difficult state law issue, knowing that certification will be possible on appeal? Or is classic Pullman abstention, as described p. 1419, *infra*, a better option?

Certification sometimes occurs at the request of one of the parties, but federal courts can also decide to certify on their own motion. As noted, most states require that the certified question be potentially determinative of the case. Thus, in Abrams v. West Virginia Racing Comm'n, 263 S.E.2d 103 (W.Va.1980), the state court refused to decide a certified question because it believed that federal law would control regardless of the answer. Some states, moreover, impose the stricter requirement that the answer will certainly determine the case.[4] How often will an answer *either way* determine the outcome? Apart from the requirement that a certified question be actually or potentially dispositive of the case, most if not all state supreme courts retain discretion to refuse to answer certified questions that they adjudge inappropriate for their decision.

(3) Certification in Practice. Formal and informal studies confirm widespread use of certification,[5] a trend that seems almost certain to

---

[2]   New Jersey only authorizes certified questions from the Third Circuit. See N.J.Ct.R. 2:12A-1.

[3]   As of 2003, 36 states permitted district courts to certify questions directly to their supreme courts. See Cochran, *Federal Court Certification of Questions of State Law to State Courts: A Theoretical and Empirical Study*, 29 J.Legis. 157, 223 (2003). See also Ripple & Gallagher, *Certification Comes of Age: Reflections on the Past, Present and Future of Cooperative Judicial Federalism*, 95 Notre Dame L.Rev. 1927, 1955 (2020) ("Of the forty-nine states that now have certification procedures, thirty-nine allow certification by federal district courts.").

[4]   See Newman, *Certification of State Law Questions: Pennsylvania's Experience in the First Five Years*, 75 Penn. Bar Assoc.Q. 47, 53 (2004) (reporting 13 states in this category).

[5]   See, *e.g.*, Prefatory Note, Uniform Certification of Questions of Law [Act]. An informal search of an electronic database revealed 78 federal cases handed down in 2007 in which federal courts considered certifying a state law question. Within that sample, federal courts ordered certification in 31 cases and declined to do so in 47. A comparable search in 2001 found 62 reported cases in which federal courts considered certifying questions to a state supreme court and 24 in which they actually did so.

continue. In response to a survey conducted by the American Judicature Society, "[a]lmost all of the [responding] circuit judges (93%), district judges (86%), and state justices (87%) *agree[d]* that certification improves federal-state comity." Goldschmidt, Certification of Questions of Law 66 (1995). The literature, which includes numerous articles by both state and federal judges, is also generally supportive of certification as a model of cooperative federal-state judicial interaction.[6] The perceived benefits of a state certification procedure include increased cooperation and respect between state and federal courts and uniform judgments on unsettled issues of state law.[7] Some observers argue that certification may discourage forum shopping, and yet concerns have been raised about the use of certification in diversity cases.

But the literature is by no means monolithic. In addition to tributes, it includes a number of negative assessments of certification's operation in practice, including some by both federal judges and state supreme court justices.[8] There are well-documented instances in which state courts have declined to respond to certified questions, either because they were badly drafted or for other reasons.[9]

NOTE ON ABSTENTION TO SECURE CLARIFICATION OF STATE LAW

The wide availability of certification may reduce the significance of a curious pair of abstention decisions, handed down on the same day in 1959. In one, Louisiana Power & Light Co. v. Thibodaux, 360 U.S. 25 (1959), the Court affirmed an appellate court decision calling for abstention to allow the parties to pursue remedies in state court that might clarify state law as applied to eminent domain proceedings. By contrast, in County of Allegheny v. Frank Mashuda Co., 360 U.S. 185 (1959), the Court refused to uphold an abstention order in a somewhat comparable diversity action. In later accounting for the distinction, the Court explained in Quackenbush v. Allstate Ins. Co., 517 U.S. 706 (1996), that Thibodaux involved a permissible "stay" of the federal suit pending state court action, whereas Mashuda involved an outright dismissal of the federal suit. That distinction maps nicely onto the perception, expressed in Lehman Brothers v. Schein, that a

---

[6]   See Nash, *Examining the Power of Federal Courts to Certify Questions of State Law,* 88 Cornell L.Rev. 1672, 1699–1700 (2003) (collecting sources).

[7]   See Cantone & Griffin, *Certified Questions of State Law: An Empirical Examination of Use in Three U.S. Courts of Appeals,* 53 Univ. Toledo L.Rev. 1 (2021).

[8]   See, *e.g.*, Schneider, *"But Answer Came There None": The Michigan Supreme Court and the Certified Question of State Law,* 41 Wayne L.Rev. 273, 316–22 (1995). Judge Selya of the United States Court of Appeals for the First Circuit complains that certification "frequently adds time and expense to litigation that is already overlong and overly expensive" without achieving its intended purposes. Selya, *Certified Madness: Ask a Silly Question . . .,* 29 Suffolk U.L.Rev. 677, 691 (1995). The Chief Justice of Indiana's supreme court has also sounded notes of caution. See Shepard, *Is Making State Constitutional Law Through Certified Questions a Good Idea or a Bad Idea?,* 38 Val.U.L.Rev. 327, 346 (2004).

[9]   See, *e.g.*, Eley v. Pizza Hut of America, 500 N.W.2d 61 (Iowa 1993), in which the Supreme Court of Iowa declined to answer a certified question on the ground that, because the question was poorly drafted and did not include sufficient facts, the court could respond in a variety of ways and had no basis to choose the right answer.

district court may stay proceedings in diversity while awaiting the answer to an unsettled question of state law that it has certified to the state supreme court. For a discussion, see Challener, *Distinguishing Certification From Abstention in Diversity Cases: Postponement Versus Abdication of the Duty to Exercise Jurisdiction*, 38 Rutgers L.J. 847, 874 (2007). Professor Challener reports some disagreement as to the standard governing certification stays in diversity; some courts apply an "exceptional circumstances" test while others exercise the broader discretion Lehman Brothers recognizes.

4. COORDINATING CONSTITUTIONAL LITIGATION AFTER EX PARTE YOUNG

A. STATUTORY LIMITS ON SUITS FOR FEDERAL RELIEF

Much of the controversy following Ex parte Young, 209 U.S. 123 (1908), explored in Chapter IX, pp. 1184–1199, *supra*, centered on the power of a single federal judge to stop the implementation of state legislation in its tracks.[1] Congress responded quickly, adopting a three-judge court requirement that has waxed and waned over time. Later responses include the Johnson Act of 1934, now 28 U.S.C. § 1342, and the Tax Injunction Act of 1937, now 28 U.S.C. § 1341. A brief summary of each statutory scheme follows.

(1) The Rise and Decline of Three-Judge Courts. Responding to the particular abuses of *ex parte* restraining orders and interlocutory injunctions, Congress in 1910 required that applications for interlocutory injunctions against enforcement of state statutes on constitutional grounds be heard by a district court of three judges (at least one of whom had to be a judge of the court of appeals). Decisions of a three-judge court were appealable as of right directly to the Supreme Court.[2] The statute was extended in 1913 to cover interlocutory injunctions against state administrative orders, and in 1925 and 1948 to encompass permanent injunctions. From 1948–1976, this three-judge court requirement was codified as 28 U.S.C. § 2281. A parallel provision, enacted in 1937 and codified from 1948–1976 as 28 U.S.C. § 2282, required a three-judge court in suits seeking to enjoin federal statutes as unconstitutional.

As time passed, Congress grew concerned with the burdens imposed by three-judge hearings and mandatory appeals, which could account for

---

[1]   See generally Frankfurter, *Distribution of Judicial Power Between United States and State Courts*, 13 Cornell L.Q. 499, 519 (1928); Lilienthal, *The Federal Courts and State Regulation of Public Utilities*, 43 Harv.L.Rev. 379 (1930); Lockwood, Maw, & Rosenberry, *The Use of the Federal Injunction in Constitutional Litigation*, 43 Harv.L.Rev. 426 (1930); Hutcheson, *A Case for Three Judges*, 47 Harv.L.Rev. 795 (1934).

[2]   36 Stat. 557. Three-judge courts had previously been used in certain antitrust cases, see 32 Stat. 823 (1903), and in suits challenging ICC orders, see 34 Stat. 584, 592 (1906).

upwards of 20% of the argued cases on the Court's docket in a given year.[3] In 1976, Congress abolished nearly all three-judge courts, repealing the general requirement and substituting a new provision that calls for three-judge courts only in suits "challenging the constitutionality of the apportionment of congressional districts or the apportionment of any statewide legislative body,"[4] or "when otherwise required by Act of Congress." 28 U.S.C. § 2284.[5]

(2) The Johnson Act of 1934. Responding to concerns over federal judicial interference in the operation of state regulatory schemes, the Johnson Act of 1934, now 28 U.S.C. § 1342, deprives the district courts of jurisdiction to enjoin the operation of, or compliance with, any order of a state administrative agency or local body fixing rates for a public utility. At the time, most utilities were government-regulated monopolies. Commissions fixed rates to ensure payment of production costs and a reasonable return for investors. During and after the 1990s, many states deregulated their utility services and allowed competition in lieu of a regulated monopoly. Today, roughly half the states rely on competition.[6] As a result, direct price regulation through government ratemaking has become less common and the Johnson Act has correspondingly less work to do. Where ratemaking continues, however, the federal courts lack power to enjoin the resulting rates whenever four conditions are met:

> "(1) Jurisdiction is based solely on diversity of citizenship or repugnance of the order to the Federal Constitution; and,
>
> "(2) The order does not interfere with interstate commerce; and,
>
> "(3) The order has been made after reasonable notice and hearing; and,
>
> "(4) A plain, speedy and efficient remedy may be had in the courts of such State."

The Johnson Act limits federal injunctive relief to situations of inadequate state remediation. All state remedies count in the adequacy

---

[3] S.Rep. No. 201, 94th Cong., 2d Sess. 4 (1976).

[4] This language eliminates the distinction between suits for declaratory judgments, which the Supreme Court had held could be heard by a single judge under the former § 2282 (in Kennedy v. Mendoza-Martinez, 372 U.S. 144 (1963)), and suits for injunctions subject to the three-judge requirement.

The requirement of three-judge courts in certain antitrust actions, see note 2, *supra*, was abolished in 1974, 88 Stat. 1706, and the following year, the requirement in suits to enjoin ICC orders was also repealed, 88 Stat. 1918.

[5] The latter phrase refers primarily to provisions of the Civil Rights Act of 1964, 42 U.S.C. §§ 1971(g), 2000a–5(b), 2000e–6(b), and the Voting Rights Act of 1965, as amended, *id.* §§ 1973b(a), 1973c, 1973h(c), 1973aa–2, 1973bb(a)(2)—although other statutes occasionally employ the device. See generally Williams, *The New Three-Judge Courts of Reapportionment and Continuing Problems of Three-Judge-Court Procedure*, 65 Geo.L.J. 971 (1977); Solimine, *Congress, Ex parte Young, and the Fate of the Three-Judge District Court*, 70 U.Pitt.L.Rev. 101 (2008) (tracing the history of political support for three-judge district courts and attributing their near abolition in 1976 to considerations involving judicial workload).

[6] See Elec. Energy Mkt. Competition Task Force, Report to Congress on Competition in Wholesale and Retail Markets for Electric Energy 27 (2007).

calculus, including suits in law, in equity, and statutory forms of judicial review.[7]

(3) The Tax Injunction Act of 1937. The Tax Injunction Act of 1937, now 28 U.S.C. § 1341, states: "The district courts shall not enjoin, suspend or restrain the assessment, levy or collection of any tax under State law where a plain, speedy and efficient remedy may be had in the courts of such State." Previous language restricting the district courts' "jurisdiction" was removed in the 1948 statutory revision. For purposes of the Act, local taxes have uniformly been held to be collected "under State law." See 17A Wright, Miller & Cooper, Federal Practice & Procedure § 4237.

The Supreme Court has broadly construed "suspend or restrain" to encompass federal remedies that stop short of enjoining the state tax. In California v. Grace Brethren Church, 457 U.S. 393 (1982), the Court squarely ruled that § 1341 bars the issuance of declaratory judgments. In so holding, the Court relied on language from an earlier decision, in Great Lakes Dredge & Dock Co. v. Huffman, 319 U.S. 293 (1943), that equated the practical effect of a declaration with that of an injunction and on the Act's prohibition of actions that not only "enjoin" but also "suspend or restrain" collection of state taxes.

The Court has also concluded that the principle of deference to state tax remedies applies to suits for damages brought under 42 U.S.C. § 1983. In Fair Assessment in Real Estate Ass'n, Inc. v. McNary, 454 U.S. 100 (1981), plaintiffs alleged constitutional violations in tax assessment and enforcement and sought compensatory and punitive damages from the officials in charge. The Court (per Justice Rehnquist) deemed it unnecessary to decide whether § 1341 barred plaintiffs' action, as "the principle of comity" that had been held to bar declaratory relief in Great Lakes applied in the instant case as well. That principle, the Court said, barred any federal intervention the practical effect of which was to suspend collection of state taxes, regardless of the form of relief sought.[8] In an opinion for four concurring Justices, Justice Brennan viewed the comity ground as inapplicable outside suits for equitable relief but found it reasonable to require suitors to exhaust their administrative remedies before mounting a claim under § 1983.

In a subsequent case, nonresident plaintiffs brought suit in Oklahoma state court, seeking a refund of taxes that were imposed in violation of the dormant commerce clause. The plaintiffs also sought declaratory and injunctive relief under § 1983. Despite the Tax Injunction Act's inapplicability (given its application only to suits in the

---

[7]   Consider the possibility that the claim of FERC preemption in NOPSI v. Council of New Orleans, 491 U.S. 350 (1989), p. 1389, *supra*, rendered the Johnson Act inapplicable.

[8]   The McNary Court reserved the question "whether * * * comity * * * would also bar a claim under § 1983 which requires no scrutiny whatever of state tax assessment practices, such as a facial attack on tax laws colorably claimed to be discriminatory as to race." 454 U.S. at 107 n.4.

"district courts"), the Supreme Court affirmed a state court judgment refusing § 1983 relief (including attorney's fees). In an opinion by Justice Thomas, the Court ruled that "Congress never authorized federal [or state] courts to entertain damages actions under § 1983 against state taxes when state law furnishes an adequate remedy." National Private Truck Council, Inc. v. Oklahoma Tax Comm'n, 515 U.S. 582, 587 (1995). Is this reading, which relies on an implicit limit in § 1983 that would have made the Tax Injunction Act unnecessary in 1937, more persuasive than the claim in McNary that a suit for damages operates in effect to suspend the operation of government activities?

In contrast, the Court has narrowly defined the forms of state (and federal) action that qualify as an "assessment, levy, or collection" of a tax within the meaning of the Act. (The Tax Injunction Act's operative language was modeled on an analogous provision in the federal tax code, 26 U.S.C. § 7421(a), and has been read to mean much the same thing in both contexts.) Seeking to draw a clear definitional line, the Court unanimously concluded in Direct Marketing Association v. Brohl, 575 U.S. 1 (2015), that a federal court could enjoin reporting requirements that Colorado imposed on out-of-state retailers without running afoul of the Act. The Court reasoned that while an injunction against such reporting requirements may complicate the administrative process, it would not prevent the "assessment, levy or collection" of a state tax. In a later case under the federal tax code's analogous limit on injunctive relief, the Court arguably extended the Direct Marketing rule. The plaintiff in CIC Servs., LLC v. IRS, 593 U.S. 209 (2021), challenged an IRS rule that imposed reporting obligations enforceable through a tax penalty and criminal sanctions. In concluding that an injunction against the rule did not run afoul of the Act, a unanimous Court characterized the Act as imposing a "familiar pay-now-sue-later procedure." But that procedure was inapplicable to the notice in question, which did not levy a tax. Without an injunction, the plaintiff would have been forced to violate the regulation, and risk criminal penalties, to secure a test of legality.

B. PULLMAN AND THE AVOIDANCE OF FEDERAL QUESTIONS

Railroad Commission of Texas v. Pullman Co.

312 U.S. 496 (1941).

Appeal from the United States District Court for the Western District of Texas.

■ MR. JUSTICE FRANKFURTER delivered the opinion of the Court.

In those sections of Texas where the local passenger traffic is slight, trains carry but one sleeping car. These trains, unlike trains having two or more sleepers, are without a Pullman conductor; the sleeper is in charge of a porter who is subject to the train conductor's control. As is well known, porters on Pullmans are colored and conductors are white. Addressing itself to this situation, the Texas Railroad Commission after due hearing ordered that "no sleeping car shall be operated on any line of railroad in the State of Texas * * * unless such cars are continuously in the charge of an employee * * * having the rank and position of Pullman conductor". Thereupon, the Pullman Company and the railroads affected brought this action in a federal district court to enjoin the Commission's order. Pullman porters were permitted to intervene as complainants, and Pullman conductors entered the litigation in support of the order. Three judges having been convened, the court enjoined enforcement of the order. From this decree, the case came here directly.

The Pullman Company and the railroads assailed the order as unauthorized by Texas law as well as violative of the Equal Protection, the Due Process and the Commerce Clauses of the Constitution. The intervening porters adopted these objections but mainly objected to the order as a discrimination against Negroes in violation of the Fourteenth Amendment.

The complaint of the Pullman porters undoubtedly tendered a substantial constitutional issue. It is more than substantial. It touches a sensitive area of social policy upon which the federal courts ought not to enter unless no alternative to its adjudication is open. Such constitutional adjudication plainly can be avoided if a definitive ruling on the state issue would terminate the controversy. It is therefore our duty to turn to a consideration of questions under Texas law.

The Commission found justification for its order in a Texas statute * * *.[1] It is common ground that if the order is within the Commission's authority its subject matter must be included in the Commission's power to prevent "unjust discrimination * * * and to prevent any and all other abuses" in the conduct of railroads. Whether arrangements pertaining to the staffs of Pullman cars are covered by the Texas concept of "discrimination" is far from clear. What practices of the railroads may be deemed to be "abuses" subject to the Commission's correction is equally doubtful. Reading the Texas statutes and the Texas decisions as

---

[1]   Vernon's Anno. Texas Civil Statutes, Article 6445:

"Power and authority are hereby conferred upon the Railroad Commission of Texas over all railroads, and suburban, belt and terminal railroads, and over all public wharves, docks, piers, elevators, warehouses, sheds, tracks and other property used in connection therewith in this State, and over all persons, associations and corporations, private or municipal, owning or operating such railroad, wharf, dock, pier, elevator, warehouse, shed, track or other property to fix, and it is hereby made the duty of the said Commission to adopt all necessary rates, charges and regulations, to govern and regulate such railroads, persons, associations and corporations, and to correct abuses and prevent unjust discrimination in the rates, charges and tolls of such railroads, persons, associations and corporations, and to fix division of rates, charges and regulations between railroads and other utilities and common carriers where a division is proper and correct, and to prevent any and all other abuses in the conduct of their business and to do and perform such other duties and details in connection therewith as may be provided by law."

outsiders without special competence in Texas law, we would have little confidence in our independent judgment regarding the application of that law to the present situation. The lower court did deny that the Texas statutes sustained the Commission's assertion of power. And this represents the view of an able and experienced circuit judge of the circuit which includes Texas and of two capable district judges trained in Texas law. Had we or they no choice in the matter but to decide what is the law of the state, we should hesitate long before rejecting their forecast of Texas law. But no matter how seasoned the judgment of the district court may be, it cannot escape being a forecast rather than a determination. The last word on the meaning of Article 6445 of the Texas Civil Statutes, and therefore the last word on the statutory authority of the Railroad Commission in this case, belongs neither to us nor to the district court but to the supreme court of Texas. In this situation a federal court of equity is asked to decide an issue by making a tentative answer which may be displaced tomorrow by a state adjudication. The reign of law is hardly promoted if an unnecessary ruling of a federal court is thus supplanted by a controlling decision of a state court. The resources of equity are equal to an adjustment that will avoid the waste of a tentative decision as well as the friction of a premature constitutional adjudication.

An appeal to the chancellor, as we had occasion to recall only the other day, is an appeal to the "exercise of the sound discretion, which guides the determination of courts of equity". Beal v. Missouri Pacific R.R., 312 U.S. 45, decided January 20, 1941. The history of equity jurisdiction is the history of regard for public consequences in employing the extraordinary remedy of the injunction. There have been as many and as variegated applications of this simple principle as the situations that have brought it into play. Few public interests have a higher claim upon the discretion of a federal chancellor than the avoidance of needless friction with state policies, whether the policy relates to the enforcement of the criminal law, Fenner v. Boykin, 271 U.S. 240 [(1926)]; Spielman Motor Co. v. Dodge, 295 U.S. 89 [(1935)]; or the administration of a specialized scheme for liquidating embarrassed business enterprises, Pennsylvania v. Williams, 294 U.S. 176 [(1935)]; or the final authority of a state court to interpret doubtful regulatory laws of the state, Gilchrist v. Interborough Co., 279 U.S. 159 [(1929)]; cf. Hawks v. Hamill, 288 U.S. 52, 61 [(1933)]. These cases reflect a doctrine of abstention appropriate to our federal system whereby the federal courts, "exercising a wise discretion", restrain their authority because of "scrupulous regard for the rightful independence of the state governments" and for the smooth working of the federal judiciary. See Cavanaugh v. Looney, 248 U.S. 453, 457 [(1919)]; Di Giovanni v. Camden Ins. Ass'n, 296 U.S. 64, 73 [(1935)]. This use of equitable powers is a contribution of the courts in furthering the harmonious relation between state and federal authority without the need of rigorous congressional restriction of those powers.

Regard for these important considerations of policy in the administration of federal equity jurisdiction is decisive here. If there was no warrant in state law for the Commission's assumption of authority there is an end of the litigation; the constitutional issue does not arise. The law of Texas appears to furnish easy and ample means for determining the Commission's authority. Article 6453 of the Texas Civil Statutes gives a review of such an order in the state courts. Or, if there are difficulties in the way of this procedure of which we have not been apprised, the issue of state law may be settled by appropriate action on the part of the State to enforce obedience to the order. Article 6476, Texas Civil Statutes. In the absence of any showing that these obvious methods for securing a definitive ruling in the state courts cannot be pursued with full protection of the constitutional claim, the district court should exercise its wise discretion by staying its hands. Compare Thompson v. Magnolia Co., 309 U.S. 478 [(1940)].

We therefore remand the cause to the district court, with directions to retain the bill pending a determination of proceedings, to be brought with reasonable promptness, in the state court in conformity with this opinion.

Reversed and remanded.

■ MR. JUSTICE ROBERTS took no part in the consideration or decision of this case.

Arizonans for Official English v. Arizona

520 U.S. 43 (1997).

An Arizona ballot initiative established English as the official language of the state. Passed on November 8, 1988, by a margin of one percentage point, the measure became effective on December 5 as Arizona State Constitution Article XXVIII. Among key provisions, the Article declares that, with specified exceptions, the state "shall act in English and in no other language." It also declared that "English [shall be] the language of the ballot, the public schools and all government functions and actions."

The provision was challenged in federal court by Maria-Kelly Yniguez, an Arizona state employee, as a violation of her free speech rights under the First Amendment. She worried that the provision threatened her with employment-related sanctions for using Spanish on the job. In defending the measure, Arizona's Attorney General asked both the federal district court and the Ninth Circuit on appeal to seek, through the state's statutory certified-question process, an authoritative construction of the new measure from the state supreme court. Both federal courts refused to certify and ultimately entered and upheld a judgment invalidating the measure.

The Supreme Court unanimously vacated and remanded, concluding that the dispute had become moot when Yniguez left her job as an Arizona state employee and should now be dismissed in its entirety. In reaching that conclusion, the Court viewed the lower courts' erroneous failure to certify the constitutional issues to the state supreme court as reason to broadly vacate the constitutional ruling:

"Certification today covers territory once dominated by a deferral device called 'Pullman abstention,' after the generative case, Railroad Comm'n of Tex. v. Pullman Co., 312 U.S. 496 (1941). Designed to avoid federal-court error in deciding state-law questions antecedent to federal constitutional issues, the Pullman mechanism remitted parties to the state courts for adjudication of the unsettled state-law issues. If settlement of the state-law question did not prove dispositive of the case, the parties could return to the federal court for decision of the federal issues. Attractive in theory because it placed state-law questions in courts equipped to rule authoritatively on them, Pullman abstention proved protracted and expensive in practice, for it entailed a full round of litigation in the state court system before any resumption of proceedings in federal court.

"Certification procedure, in contrast, allows a federal court faced with a novel state-law question to put the question directly to the State's highest court, reducing the delay, cutting the cost, and increasing the assurance of gaining an authoritative response. Most States have adopted certification procedures. Arizona's statute * * * permits the State's highest court to consider questions certified to it by federal district courts, as well as courts of appeals and this Court."

NOTE ON ABSTENTION TO AVOID RESOLUTION OF A FEDERAL QUESTION

(1) The Basis of the Pullman Doctrine. In explaining its decision to order abstention in the Pullman case, the Supreme Court cited a number of considerations, including the following: resolution of a state law question in a particular way would avoid the necessity to decide a federal constitutional question; the relevant state law was unclear; the three-judge district court, after Erie, lacked power to determine the meaning of state law except as to the parties before the court; resolution of the federal constitutional question adversely to the defendants might generate "needless friction" with state policies; and the federal constitutional question "touche[d] a sensitive area of social policy." Do these factors, individually or jointly, justify the decision to abstain?[1]

(a) How significant is the worry that a federal court's decision of a difficult state law issue, in a case such as Pullman, might be "supplanted by a controlling decision of a state court"? If a state court decision in a suit between other parties was contrary to that of the federal court, the federal

---

[1]   Even before Pullman, the Supreme Court had endorsed federal court abstention on difficult, unsettled questions of state law. See, *e.g.*, Gilchrist v. Interborough Rapid Transit Co., 279 U.S. 159 (1929) (federal court action to prevent state commission from interfering with fare increase; action was filed only a few hours before commission sued in state court to compel compliance with existing fare); Railroad Comm'n v. Rowan & Nichols Oil Co., 310 U.S. 573 (1940), *reh'g denied*, 311 U.S. 614 (1940) (rejecting on the merits a federal due process challenge to a regulatory order, and refusing to decide whether under state law there was a "reasonable basis" for the commission's order, so as to avoid supplanting the commission's expert judgment). See also Thompson v. Magnolia Petroleum Co., 309 U.S. 478 (1940) (although federal bankruptcy court had jurisdiction to determine the title to property in trustee's possession, trustee should be directed to bring state court proceeding to settle the issue).

court could withdraw or modify any injunction that it had issued previously. Although this result might be embarrassing, federal courts are frequently called upon to resolve hard questions of state law that they could potentially decide erroneously.[2]

(b) In suggesting that the friction generated by a federal remedy for unconstitutional state action might be "needless," Justice Frankfurter appeared to assume that it is preferable for a state court, rather than a federal court, to invalidate a state law or state policy. Recall Justice Frankfurter's position, dissenting from Monroe v. Pape, 365 U.S. 167 (1961), p. 1280, *supra*, and proposing to remit the plaintiff to state law remedies for an unlawful search and seizure. Consider how well Pullman's use of state law as an avoidance strategy fits with the policy of making constitutional rights directly enforceable that Monroe subsequently held to have been reflected in § 1983.

(c) What did Justice Frankfurter mean in suggesting that the constitutional question "touche[d] a sensitive area of social policy"? According to Resnik, *Rereading "The Federal Courts": Revising the Domain of Federal Courts Jurisprudence at the End of the Twentieth Century*, 47 Vand.L.Rev. 1021, 1039 (1994) (footnotes omitted):

"The testimony [in the record] in Pullman is filled with discussion of how white women feel 'a little bit safer . . . with a white man conductor in charge of that car.' * * * Further, in an effort to prop up the porters' claims, the record also includes testimony aimed at distinguishing 'the Pullman porter[s],' as 'pretty high-classed colored men,' from those other kinds of 'colored men.'

"* * * In 1941 it was, I take it, not obvious how federal constitutional law would decide [the equal protection] question [that Pullman presented]. It was not easy because national norms did not readily trump local customs and prejudices, indeed because national norms may well have shared such prejudices. [As Professor Resnik observes in a footnote, the United States Army remained segregated in 1941.] Thus, the case was 'sensitive,' the engagement between federal and state law fraught with anxiety, and if some other point of law could determine the outcome without having to consider

---

[2] See generally Shapiro, *State Courts and Federal Declaratory Judgments*, 74 Nw.U.L.Rev. 759 (1979) (suggesting that after a federal court has resolved a dispute in an action for equitable relief, its decision should have claim and issue preclusive effect in subsequent litigation between the same parties, but that issue preclusion ought not apply against the state with regard to other parties). For specific discussion of the effect of federal judgments that state statutes are overbroad and therefore unenforceable—judgments that necessarily rest on a possibly erroneous determination of the meaning of those statutes as a matter of state law—see Fallon, *Making Sense of Overbreadth*, 100 Yale L.J. 853, 877–83, 898–903 (1991).

One of the situations in which federal courts may be asked to resolve difficult state law questions is specifically addressed by the supplemental jurisdiction statute, 28 U.S.C. § 1367, under which a federal court may refuse jurisdiction over a pendent state law claim in a federal question case if it "raises a novel or complex issue of State law." On the relationship between § 1367(c) and abstention, see Schapiro, *Polyphonic Federalism: State Constitutions in the Federal Courts*, 87 Calif.L.Rev. 1409, 1421–22 (1999).

announcing federal constitutional rules about discrimination based on race, more the better."[3]

The Supreme Court decided Pullman in 1941, thirteen years before Brown v. Board of Education, 347 U.S. 483 (1954). Consider whether avoidance tactics like those deployed in Pullman could be defended as making Brown later possible, or criticized for frustrating equal protection under law without a principled basis.

(2) Abstention and the Separation of Powers. The federal district court possessed undoubted statutory jurisdiction over the Pullman case. In his much-quoted opinion in Cohens v. Virginia, 19 U.S. (6 Wheat.) 264 (1821), Chief Justice Marshall wrote: "We have no more right to decline the exercise of a jurisdiction which is given, than to usurp that which is not given. The one or the other would be treason to the constitution." Did the Court in Pullman commit "treason to the constitution"?

In approaching this question, recall Justice Frankfurter's invocation of the tradition of judicial discretion in the award of equitable remedies. But the traditions of equity developed in England, and considerations of federalism therefore had no role in early equitable practice. Under these circumstances, Professor Redish argues that reference to equity simply begs the question whether the federal courts possess authority under the separation of powers to decline to exercise a congressionally authorized jurisdiction based on their own federalism-based notions of sound policy. Redish, The Federal Courts in the Political Order: Judicial Jurisdiction and American Political Theory 59–60 (1991). In his view, there is no demonstrated justification for assuming that Congress would have intended courts to retain discretionary authority to decline jurisdiction based on federalism-related concerns. He sees a judicial claim of power to abstain as a power grab—a usurpation of congressional power to define the jurisdiction of the federal courts—that is incompatible with basic premises of constitutional democracy.

Compare Shapiro, *Jurisdiction and Discretion*, 60 N.Y.U.L.Rev. 543, 543–45, 574–75 (1985) (some paragraphing omitted): "Judges and lawyers have often said that the federal courts are obligated to exercise the jurisdiction conferred on them by the Constitution and by Congress. * * * [S]uggestions of an overriding obligation, subject only and at most to a few narrowly drawn exceptions, are far too grudging in their recognition of judicial discretion in matters of jurisdiction. * * * [T]he existence of this discretion is much more pervasive than is generally realized, and * * * it has ancient and honorable roots at common law as well as in equity. * * *

---

[3] See also Robel, *Riding the Color Line: The Story of Railroad Commission of Texas v. Pullman Co.*, in Federal Courts Stories (Jackson & Resnik eds. 2009) (detailing the proceedings in the case and noting that Pullman abstention frustrated efforts by the NAACP to enforce the mandate of Brown v. Board of Education, 347 U.S. 483 (1954). Professor Robel notes that only one month after handing down the decision in Pullman, the Supreme Court resisted calls to abstain from determining whether the Interstate Commerce Act mandated equal accommodations for passengers regardless of race and held that the Act required equal accommodations. See Mitchell v. United States, 313 U.S. 80 (1941).

"My point is not that the Constitution expressly 'provides' that a grant of jurisdiction carries with it certain discretion not to proceed, or that Congress necessarily 'intends' to confer such discretion when it authorizes the exercise of jurisdiction. Rather, I submit that, as experience and tradition teach, the question whether a court must exercise jurisdiction and resolve a controversy on its merits is difficult, if not impossible, to answer in gross. And the courts are functionally better adapted to engage in the necessary fine tuning than is the legislature. * * *

"A grant of jurisdiction obligates the court to receive and consider the plaintiff's complaint and, on appropriate occasions, to determine whether the ends of justice will be served best by declining to proceed. At the same time, nothing in our history or traditions permits a court to interpret a normal grant of jurisdiction as conferring unbridled authority to hear cases simply at its pleasure. * * * [W]hen jurisdiction is conferred, I believe that there is at least a 'principle of preference' that a court should entertain and resolve on its merits an action within the scope of the jurisdictional grant. For this preference to yield in a particular case, the court must provide an explanation based on the language of the grant, the historical context in which the grant was made, or the common law tradition behind it."[4]

(3) What Issues of State Law Qualify as Unsettled? As Pullman itself suggests, the newness of a state statute and the total absence of judicial precedent are clearly significant considerations in evaluating the necessity for clarification through abstention. On the other hand, the mere presence of judicially unconstrued state law does not automatically require abstention. See, *e.g.*, Brockett v. Spokane Arcades, Inc., 472 U.S. 491 (1985); Wisconsin

---

[4]   The question whether judicially crafted abstention doctrines are permissible under the jurisdictional statutes and the separation of powers is a general one, by no means limited to Pullman abstention, and it has stimulated a broad debate. Professor Redish remains the leading proponent of the view that, in the absence of clear statutory authorization, abstention violates separation-of-powers principles. See, *e.g.*, Redish, *supra*, at 47–74; Redish, *Abstention, Separation of Powers, and the Limits of the Judicial Function*, 94 Yale L.J. 71 (1984). See also Doernberg, *"You Can Lead a Horse to Water . . .": The Supreme Court's Refusal to Allow the Exercise of Original Jurisdiction Conferred by Congress*, 40 Case W.Res.L.Rev. 999 (1989–1990). For critical analyses of this view, in addition to Shapiro, *supra*, see Wells, *Why Professor Redish is Wrong About Abstention*, 19 Ga.L.Rev. 1097 (1985); Althouse, *The Humble and the Treasonous: Judge-Made Jurisdiction Law*, 40 Case W.Res.L.Rev. 1035 (1989–1990); Beerman, *"Bad" Judicial Activism and Liberal Federal-Courts Doctrine: A Comment on Professor Doernberg and Professor Redish*, 40 Case W.Res.L.Rev. 1053 (1989–1990); Brown, *When Federalism and Separation of Powers Collide—Rethinking Younger Abstention*, 59 Geo.Wash.L.Rev. 114 (1990); and Marshall, *Abstention, Separation of Powers, and Recasting the Meaning of Judicial Restraint*, 107 Nw.U.L.Rev. 881 (2013). For an argument that abstention doctrines do not merely involve questions of policy, but are rooted in the Constitution, see Massey, *Abstention and the Constitutional Limits of the Judicial Power of the United States*, 1991 B.Y.U.L.Rev. 811.

Fallon, *Why Abstention Is Not Illegitimate: An Essay on the Distinction Between "Legitimate" and "Illegitimate" Statutory Interpretation and Judicial Lawmaking*, 107 Nw.U.L.Rev. 847 (2013), argues that if abstention involves an illegitimate judicial usurpation of congressional prerogatives (as Professor Redish maintains), then so do a number of other federal courts doctrines discussed by Professors Shapiro and Friedman, with whom he agrees in rejecting Redish's characterization. But Professor Fallon also rejects the view, which he ascribes to Professors Shapiro and Friedman, that past latitudinarian interpretations of jurisdictional statutes would necessarily legitimate future judicial claims of comparably broad interpretive and lawmaking prerogative.

v. Constantineau, 400 U.S. 433, 439 (1971); Toomer v. Witsell, 334 U.S. 385 (1948).

Most important, the uncertainty in state law must be such that construction by the state court might obviate the need for decision (or at least help to limit the scope) of the federal constitutional question. See, *e.g.*, Baggett v. Bullitt, 377 U.S. 360 (1964) (rejecting an argument for abstention in a case challenging a statute as unconstitutionally vague where it was "fictional to believe that anything less than extensive adjudications, under the impact of a variety of factual situations," would cure the vagueness). First Amendment claims frequently lead to Pullman abstention issues, as the defendant urges limiting interpretations that might obviate issues of vagueness or overbreadth. See Hawaii Housing Auth. v. Midkiff, 467 U.S. 229 (1984) (although in the abstract the possibility of a limiting construction always exists, " '[w]e have frequently emphasized that abstention is not to be ordered unless the statute is of an uncertain nature, and is obviously susceptible of a limiting construction' ") (citation omitted; alteration in original).

The Court in Arizonans for Official English warmly embraced the need for clarification of state constitutional provisions to inform and perhaps obviate a federal constitutional challenge. Compare Wisconsin v. Constantineau, 400 U.S. 433 (1971) (declining to order abstention, despite the possibility that the state court might have invalidated the challenged practice of publicly shaming those with drinking problems on state constitutional grounds) with Harris County Comm'rs Court v. Moore, 420 U.S. 77 (1975) (ordering abstention to obtain a state court construction of state constitutional rules governing office-holder rights as a prelude to assessing the federal constitutionality of a redistricting plan). The Harris Court treated Constantineau as a case in which abstention could yield an alternative remedy for the asserted violation. Abstention in that setting would seemingly violate the no-exhaustion principle of Home Telephone & Telegraph Co. v. Los Angeles, 227 U.S. 278 (1913), p. 1276, *supra*, and Monroe v. Pape, 365 U.S. 167 (1961), p. 1280, *supra*, both of which held (Monroe in the context of interpreting § 1983) that the adjudication of federal constitutional claims under the Fourteenth Amendment need not await a state court's determination regarding whether the state or local official alleged to have violated the Amendment did so with the official sanction of state law. See Zwickler v. Koota, 389 U.S. 241, 251 (1967) (rejecting abstention aimed at giving "state courts the first opportunity to vindicate the federal claim"). In Arizonans, the Court sought clarification of the nature of the free speech implications of the state constitutional provision.

(4) What Constitutional Issues Qualify for Pullman Abstention? One might suppose, given the burden it imposes on the vindication of federal rights, that Pullman abstention would apply only to cases of considerable "sensitivity," where the need to avoid resolution strikes the Court as unusually pressing. One might also suppose that the doctrine, at least at the Supreme Court, would decline in significance now that the Court can avoid issues through the denial of certiorari, an option unavailable in connection with mandatory review of the three-judge court's decision in Pullman.

Pullman abstention has nonetheless expanded to encompass a much broader range of issues than the constitutionality of Jim Crow laws.[5]

(5) The Procedural Complexity of Pullman Abstention. During the early years of the Pullman doctrine, pursuit of the prescribed procedure sometimes occasioned delays of six or eight years before the final resolution of litigation. Such delays do not seem surprising, given the procedural burdens that Pullman imposes on the parties.[6] They must initiate a new proceeding in state court, or re-focus a pending proceeding, and present the unsettled question of state law to the court for resolution. To the extent state courts hear them, declaratory judgment-style proceedings may simplify the task of law clarification. But the trial court's decision may be subject to further review within the state court system before a clear answer emerges.

The process by which the litigants secure a clarification of state law presents further procedural wrinkles. For starters, the parties cannot discharge their clarification duty by inviting the state court to answer an abstract legal question; state courts must be asked to interpret state law "in light of the constitutional objections" presented to the federal court. Government & Civic Employees Organizing Committee, CIO v. Windsor, 353 U.S. 364 (1957). Without such exposure of the constitutional issues, the state court cannot effectively perform the constitutional avoidance function contemplated by the Pullman abstention doctrine. But having exposed the federal constitutional issue, the federal plaintiff has a choice: either to submit that claim to preclusive state court adjudication or to reserve it for ultimate federal court resolution.

(6) The England Reservation. Federal plaintiffs eager to retain the opportunity to secure federal court adjudication of their federal constitutional claim make an England reservation, the name of which derives from England v. Louisiana State Bd. of Medical Examiners, 375 U.S. 411 (1964). Specifically, so long as the federal plaintiff expresses an intent to reserve the issue for federal court, preclusive effect will not attach to the state court's evaluation of the merits of the constitutional claim. See *id.* More severe preclusive consequences may result, however, if the federal plaintiff asserts in state court a state constitutional challenge to state practice that broadly resembles the federal constitutional claim. See San Remo Hotel, L.P. v. City and County of San Francisco, 545 U.S. 323 (2005).

---

[5] For cases assessing abstention arguments in areas deemed sensitive and vital, see, *e.g.*, C-Y Development Co. v. City of Redlands, 703 F.2d 375 (9th Cir.1983) (land-use planning); Planned Parenthood of Greater Texas Surgical Health Services v. City of Lubbock, 542 F.Supp.3d 465 (N.D.Tx.2021) (threatened private enforcement of abortion restrictions); Brown v. Vail, 623 F.Supp.2d 1241 (W.D.Wash.2009) (death penalty protocols); Pennsylvania Medical Soc. v. Marconis, 679 F.Supp. 452 (M.D.Pa.1987) (drug abuse and medical care).

[6] See, *e.g.*, Spector Motor Serv., Inc. v. O'Connor, 340 U.S. 602 (1951) (eight years); United States v. Leiter Minerals, Inc., 381 U.S. 413 (1965) (dismissed as moot eight years after abstention was ordered). For concerns with the problem of delay, see Kurland, *Toward a Cooperative Judicial Federalism: The Federal Court Abstention Doctrine*, 24 F.R.D. 481 (1960); Field, *The Abstention Doctrine Today*, 125 U.Pa.L.Rev. 590, 605–07 (1977); Currie, *The Federal Courts and the American Law Institute, Part II*, 36 U.Chi.L.Rev. 268, 317 (1969). See also England v. Louisiana State Bd. of Medical Exam'rs, 375 U.S. 411, 423 (1964) (Douglas, J., concurring) (urging that the doctrine be reconsidered).

(7) The Impact of Pennhurst. In Pennhurst State School & Hosp. v. Halderman, 465 U.S. 89 (1984), the Supreme Court held that the Eleventh Amendment denies federal courts jurisdiction to award injunctive relief against state officials based upon state law. Pennhurst does not prevent Pullman abstention if unsettled questions of state law turn up in the course of litigation; as Pullman itself illustrates, a federal court may decide to abstain on its own motion.[7] But Pennhurst may mean that federal plaintiffs challenging the constitutionality of state action will present fewer issues of state law in their complaints that might serve as candidates for Pullman abstention.[8]

(8) Considerations Governing the Use of Certification. Despite the Supreme Court's suggestion in Arizonans for Official English, *supra*, that the standards for certification are somehow more relaxed than those necessary for Pullman abstention,[9] the Court has not laid down a clear test for when federal courts should avail themselves of the certification option, and patterns appear to vary among the circuits. See generally 17A Wright, Miller & Cooper, Federal Practice & Procedure § 4248. There is an obvious threshold question of how uncertain a state law issue should be in order for a federal court to hesitate to decide it. Further questions involve how important and difficult the potentially avoidable federal question ought to be in order for the parties to be asked to bear the expense and delay of certification.[10] Clark, *Ascertaining the Laws of the Several States: Positivism and Judicial Federalism After Erie*, 145 U.Pa.L.Rev. 1459 (1997), argues that the federal courts should employ a presumption in favor of certifying unsettled questions of state law to state courts in order to avoid inequitable administration of state law and encroachment on states' lawmaking powers, on the one hand, and separation-of-powers objections to abstention, on the

---

[7]   See also Ohio Bureau of Emp't Servs. v. Hodory, 431 U.S. 471, 480 n.11 (1977); Bellotti v. Baird, 428 U.S. 132, 143 n.10 (1976).

[8]   Sutton, 51 Imperfect Solutions: States and the Making of American Constitutional Law (2018), urges federal courts to eschew "intruding on sensitive and complicated issues of state law without giving the state courts a chance to review, and perhaps resolve, the matter first." Further, he suggests that where a federal court maintains jurisdiction over a case involving arguably parallel state and federal claims, it should resolve the state claim first and even consider pointing out "the relevance of state constitutional guarantees to certain disputes" to foster greater development of state constitutional law. Do you agree? Why should a federal court resolve a (possibly more difficult) state claim before addressing a federal claim that it may be more qualified to decide and that may moot the state claim?

[9]   See also Bellotti, 428 U.S. at 151 ("Although we do not mean to intimate that abstention would be improper in this case were certification not possible, the availability of certification greatly simplifies the analysis."). But *cf.* Houston v. Hill, 482 U.S. 451, 470–71 (1987) (the availability of certification, though important in deciding whether to abstain, "is not in itself sufficient to render abstention appropriate").

[10]   Researchers for the Federal Judicial Center compiled a dataset of over 200 certification events in the Third, Sixth, Ninth Circuits from 2010 to 2018, finding a fair amount of variation across circuits in the rate and timing of certification. Cantone & Giffin, *Certified Questions of State Law: An Empirical Examination of Use in Three U.S. Courts of Appeal*, 53 U.Tol.L.Rev. 1 (2021). The data suggest that it often takes some time, roughly two years on appeal, before a federal circuit court certifies a question of state law. Once the certification occurs, however, circuit courts typically terminate a case within roughly one year. The authors conclude that the circuit courts do an effective job in identifying, often on their own motion, what matters would benefit from certification.

other hand.[11] *Cf.* Glassman, *Making State Law in Federal Court*, 41 Gonz.L.Rev. 237, 254–55 (2005–2006), maintaining that while state supreme courts are likely to welcome the opportunity to resolve "political hot-button issue[s]," they may appropriately prefer to postpone decision of more mundane state law issues until they have the benefit of being able to review lower court opinions. Should it matter whether a state court is likely to welcome the certified question?

C. EQUITABLE RESTRAINT

INTRODUCTORY NOTE

At the dawn of the twentieth century, Ex parte Young, 209 U.S. 123 (1908), p. 1184, *supra*, upheld federal court power to enjoin threatened enforcement of a state law that violates the federal Constitution. At the same time, the Court reiterated that equity rarely interferes with pending criminal prosecutions. In allowing anticipatory relief, the Court refused to insist that those facing prosecution first violate the statute as a condition of securing judicial review of their challenges to its constitutionality. Defining the interplay between the anticipatory relief authorized in Ex parte Young and the perceived need to preserve state authority to enforce criminal law became more challenging as the Court expanded the range of constitutional protections under the Due Process and Equal Protection components of the Fourteenth Amendment and the (incorporated) Bill of Rights. Facing the need to establish coordination rules for the litigation of federal court challenges to the constitutionality of contemplated or pending state criminal proceedings, the Court in 1971 reviewed a set of cases, many brought in federal court under § 1983, that sought to restrain state criminal proceedings. The resulting doctrine, set out in the next principal case, largely preserves the suit for anticipatory relief but ordinarily requires federal abstention (or equitable restraint) if the constitutional right can be vindicated in pending state court proceedings.

Younger v. Harris

401 U.S. 37 (1971).

Appeal from the United States District Court for the Central District of California.

■ MR. JUSTICE BLACK delivered the opinion of the Court.

Appellee, John Harris, Jr., was indicted in a California state court, charged with violation of the California Penal Code §§ 11400 and 11401,

---

[11]   See also Calabresi, *Federal and State Courts: Restoring a Workable Balance*, 78 N.Y.U.L.Rev. 1293 (2003) (arguing, *inter alia*, for increased use of certification and suggesting congressional authorization of state court appellate review of federal appellate decisions on issues of state law).

known as the California Criminal Syndicalism Act * * *. He then filed a complaint in the Federal District Court, asking that court to enjoin the appellant, Younger, the District Attorney of Los Angeles County, from prosecuting him, and alleging that the prosecution and even the presence of the Act inhibited him in the exercise of his rights of free speech and press, rights guaranteed him by the First and Fourteenth Amendments. [Appellees Jim Dan, Diane Hirsch, and Farrell Broslawsky intervened as plaintiffs, arguing that Harris's prosecution inhibited them in their advocacy on behalf of the Progressive Labor Party and in teaching the doctrines of Karl Marx. A three-judge court found that the state's statute violated the First Amendment and enjoined Younger] from "further prosecution of the currently pending action against plaintiff Harris for alleged violation of the Act."

[Without reaching the constitutional issue,] we have concluded that the judgment of the District Court, enjoining appellant Younger from prosecuting under these California statutes, must be reversed as a violation of the national policy forbidding federal courts to stay or enjoin pending state court proceedings except under special circumstances.[2] We express no view about the circumstances under which federal courts may act when there is no prosecution pending in state courts at the time the federal proceeding is begun.

I

Appellee Harris has been indicted, and was actually being prosecuted by California for a violation of its Criminal Syndicalism Act at the time this suit was filed. He thus has an acute, live controversy with the State and its prosecutor. But none of the other parties plaintiff in the District Court, Dan, Hirsch, or Broslawsky, has such a controversy. None has been indicted, arrested, or even threatened by the prosecutor. * * * Whatever right Harris, who is being prosecuted under the state syndicalism law may have, Dan, Hirsch, and Broslawsky cannot share it with him. If these three had alleged that they would be prosecuted for the conduct they planned to engage in, and if the District Court had found this allegation to be true—either on the admission of the State's district attorney or on any other evidence—then a genuine controversy might be said to exist. But here appellees, Dan, Hirsch, and Broslawsky do not claim that they have ever been threatened with prosecution, that a prosecution is likely, or even that a prosecution is remotely possible. They claim the right to bring this suit solely because, in the language of their complaint, they "feel inhibited." We do not think this allegation even if true, is sufficient to bring the equitable jurisdiction of the federal courts into play to enjoin a pending state prosecution. A federal lawsuit to stop

---

2   Appellees did not explicitly ask for a declaratory judgment in their complaint. They did, however, ask the District Court to grant "such other and further relief as to the Court may seem just and proper," and the District Court in fact granted a declaratory judgment. For the reasons stated in our opinion today in Samuels v. Mackell, 401 U.S. 66 [(1971)], we hold that declaratory relief is also improper when a prosecution involving the challenged statute is pending in state court at the time the federal suit is initiated.

a prosecution in a state court is a serious matter. And persons having no fears of state prosecution except those that are imaginary or speculative, are not to be accepted as appropriate plaintiffs in such cases. Since Harris is actually being prosecuted under the challenged laws, however, we proceed with him as a proper party.

II

Since the beginning of this country's history Congress has, subject to few exceptions, manifested a desire to permit state courts to try state cases free from interference by federal courts. In 1793 an Act unconditionally provided: "[N]or shall a writ of injunction be granted to stay proceedings in any court of a state * * *." A comparison of the 1793 Act with 28 U.S.C. § 2283, its present-day successor, graphically illustrates how few and minor have been the exceptions granted from the flat, prohibitory language of the old Act. During all this lapse of years from 1793 to 1970 the statutory exceptions to the 1793 congressional enactment have been only three: (1) "except as expressly authorized by Act of Congress"; (2) "where necessary in aid of its jurisdiction"; and (3) "to protect or effectuate its judgments." In addition, a judicial exception to the longstanding policy evidenced by the statute has been made where a person about to be prosecuted in a state court can show that he will, if the proceeding in the state court is not enjoined, suffer irreparable damages. See Ex parte Young, 209 U.S. 123 (1908).

The precise reasons for this longstanding public policy against federal court interference with state court proceedings have never been specifically identified but the primary sources of the policy are plain. One is the basic doctrine of equity jurisprudence that courts of equity should not act, and particularly should not act to restrain a criminal prosecution, when the moving party has an adequate remedy at law and will not suffer irreparable injury if denied equitable relief. The doctrine may originally have grown out of circumstances peculiar to the English judicial system and not applicable in this country, but its fundamental purpose of restraining equity jurisdiction within narrow limits is equally important under our Constitution, in order to prevent erosion of the role of the jury and avoid a duplication of legal proceedings and legal sanctions where a single suit would be adequate to protect the rights asserted. This underlying reason for restraining courts of equity from interfering with criminal prosecutions is reinforced by an even more vital consideration, the notion of "comity," that is, a proper respect for state functions, a recognition of the fact that the entire country is made up of a Union of separate state governments, and a continuance of the belief that the National Government will fare best if the States and their institutions are left free to perform their separate functions in their separate ways. This, perhaps for lack of a better and clearer way to describe it, is referred to by many as "Our Federalism," and one familiar with the profound debates that ushered our Federal Constitution into existence is bound to respect those who remain loyal to the ideals and dreams of "Our

Federalism." The concept does not mean blind deference to "States' Rights" any more than it means centralization of control over every important issue in our National Government and its courts. The Framers rejected both these courses. What the concept does represent is a system in which there is sensitivity to the legitimate interests of both State and National Governments, and in which the National Government, anxious though it may be to vindicate and protect federal rights and federal interests, always endeavors to do so in ways that will not unduly interfere with the legitimate activities of the States. It should never be forgotten that this slogan, "Our Federalism," born in the early struggling days of our Union of States, occupies a highly important place in our Nation's history and its future.

This brief discussion should be enough to suggest some of the reasons why it has been perfectly natural for our cases to repeat time and time again that the normal thing to do when federal courts are asked to enjoin pending proceedings in state courts is not to issue such injunctions. * * *

In all of these cases the Court stressed the importance of showing irreparable injury, the traditional prerequisite to obtaining an injunction. In addition, however, the Court also made clear that in view of the fundamental policy against federal interference with state criminal prosecutions, even irreparable injury is insufficient unless it is "both great and immediate." Certain types of injury, in particular, the cost, anxiety, and inconvenience of having to defend against a single criminal prosecution, could not by themselves be considered "irreparable" in the special legal sense of that term. Instead, the threat to the plaintiff's federally protected rights must be one that cannot be eliminated by his defense against a single criminal prosecution. * * *

This is where the law stood when the Court decided Dombrowski v. Pfister, 380 U.S. 479 (1965), and held that an injunction against the enforcement of certain state criminal statutes could properly issue under the circumstances presented in that case.[4] In Dombrowski, unlike many

---

[4]   Neither the cases dealing with standing to raise claims of vagueness or overbreadth, e.g., Thornhill v. Alabama, 310 U.S. 88 (1940), nor the loyalty oath cases, e.g., Baggett v. Bullitt, 377 U.S. 360 (1964), changed the basic principles governing the propriety of injunctions against state criminal prosecutions. In the standing cases we allowed attacks on overly broad or vague statutes in the absence of any showing that the defendant's conduct could not be regulated by some properly drawn statute. But in each of these cases the statute was not merely vague or overly broad "on its face"; the statute was held to be vague or overly broad as construed and applied to a particular defendant in a particular case. If the statute had been too vague as written but sufficiently narrow as applied, prosecutions and convictions under it would ordinarily have been permissible. See Dombrowski, supra, 380 U.S., at 491 n.7.

In Baggett and similar cases we enjoined state officials from discharging employees who failed to take certain loyalty oaths. We held that the States were without power to exact the promises involved, with their vague and uncertain content concerning advocacy and political association, as a condition of employment. Apart from the fact that any plaintiff discharged for exercising his constitutional right to refuse to take the oath would have had no adequate remedy at law, the relief sought was of course the kind that raises no special problem—an injunction against allegedly unconstitutional state action (discharging the employees) that is not part of a criminal prosecution.

of the earlier cases denying injunctions, the complaint made substantial allegations that:

> "the threats to enforce the statutes against appellants are not made with any expectation of securing valid convictions, but rather are part of a plan to employ arrests, seizures, and threats of prosecution under color of the statutes to harass appellants and discourage them and their supporters from asserting and attempting to vindicate the constitutional rights of Negro citizens of Louisiana." 380 U.S., at 482.

The appellants in Dombrowski had offered to prove that their offices had been raided and all their files and records seized pursuant to search and arrest warrants that were later summarily vacated by a state judge for lack of probable cause. They also offered to prove that despite the state court order quashing the warrants and suppressing the evidence seized, the prosecutor was continuing to threaten to initiate new prosecutions of appellants under the same statutes, was holding public hearings at which photostatic copies of the illegally seized documents were being used, and was threatening to use other copies of the illegally seized documents to obtain grand jury indictments against the appellants on charges of violating the same statutes. These circumstances, as viewed by the Court sufficiently establish the kind of irreparable injury, above and beyond that associated with the defense of a single prosecution brought in good faith, that had always been considered sufficient to justify federal intervention. * * *

It is against the background of these principles that we must judge the propriety of an injunction under the circumstances of the present case. Here a proceeding was already pending in the state court, affording Harris an opportunity to raise his constitutional claims. There is no suggestion that this single prosecution against Harris is brought in bad faith or is only one of a series of repeated prosecutions to which he will be subjected. In other words, the injury that Harris faces is solely "that incidental to every criminal proceeding brought lawfully and in good faith," and therefore under the settled doctrine we have already described he is not entitled to equitable relief "even if such statutes are unconstitutional".

The District Court, however, thought that the Dombrowski decision substantially broadened the availability of injunctions against state criminal prosecutions and that under that decision the federal courts may give equitable relief, without regard to any showing of bad faith or harassment, whenever a state statute is found "on its face" to be vague or overly broad, in violation of the First Amendment. We recognize that there are some statements in the Dombrowski opinion that would seem to support this argument. But, as we have already seen, such statements were unnecessary to the decision of that case, because the Court found that the plaintiffs had alleged a basis for equitable relief under the long-established standards. In addition, we do not regard the reasons adduced to support this position as sufficient to justify such a substantial departure from the established doctrines regarding the availability of injunctive relief. It is undoubtedly true, as the Court stated in Dombrowski, that "[a] criminal prosecution under a statute regulating expression usually involves imponderables and contingencies that themselves may inhibit the full exercise of First Amendment freedoms." 380 U.S., at 486. But this sort of "chilling effect," as the Court called it, should not by itself justify federal intervention. In the first place, the chilling effect cannot be satisfactorily eliminated by federal injunctive relief. In Dombrowski itself the Court stated that the injunction to be issued there could be lifted if the State obtained an "acceptable limiting construction" from the state courts. The Court then made clear that once this was done, prosecutions could then be brought for conduct occurring before the narrowing construction was made, and proper convictions could stand so long as the defendants were not deprived of fair warning. 380 U.S., at 491 n.7. The kind of relief granted in Dombrowski thus does not effectively eliminate uncertainty as to the coverage of the state statute and leaves most citizens with virtually the same doubts as before regarding the danger that their conduct might eventually be subjected to criminal sanctions. The chilling effect can, of course, be eliminated by an injunction that would prohibit any prosecution whatever for conduct occurring prior to a satisfactory rewriting of the statute. But the States would then be stripped of all power to prosecute even the socially dangerous and constitutionally unprotected conduct that had been covered by the statute, until a new statute could be passed by the state legislature and approved by the federal courts in potentially lengthy trial and appellate proceedings. Thus, in Dombrowski itself the Court carefully reaffirmed the principle that even in the direct prosecution in the State's own courts, a valid narrowing construction can be applied to conduct occurring prior to the date when the narrowing construction was made, in the absence of fair warning problems. * * *

Beyond all this is another, more basic consideration. Procedures for testing the constitutionality of a statute "on its face" in the manner apparently contemplated by Dombrowski, and for then enjoining all action to enforce the statute until the State can obtain court approval for a modified version, are fundamentally at odds with the function of the federal courts in our constitutional plan. The power and duty of the judiciary to declare laws unconstitutional is in the final analysis derived from its responsibility for resolving concrete disputes brought before the courts for decision; a statute apparently governing a dispute cannot be applied by judges, consistently with their obligations under the Supremacy Clause, when such an application of the statute would conflict with the Constitution. Marbury v. Madison, 5 U.S. (1 Cranch) 137 (1803). But this vital responsibility, broad as it is, does not amount to an unlimited power to survey the statute books and pass judgment on laws before the courts are called upon to enforce them. Ever since the Constitutional Convention rejected a proposal for having members of the

Supreme Court render advice concerning pending legislation it has been clear that, even when suits of this kind involve a "case or controversy" sufficient to satisfy the requirements of Article III of the Constitution, the task of analyzing a proposed statute, pinpointing its deficiencies, and requiring correction of these deficiencies before the statute is put into effect, is rarely if ever an appropriate task for the judiciary. The combination of the relative remoteness of the controversy, the impact on the legislative process of the relief sought, and above all the speculative and amorphous nature of the required line-by-line analysis of detailed statutes ordinarily results in a kind of case that is wholly unsatisfactory for deciding constitutional questions, whichever way they might be decided. In light of this fundamental conception of the Framers as to the proper place of the federal courts in the governmental processes of passing and enforcing laws, it can seldom be appropriate for these courts to exercise any such power of prior approval or veto over the legislative process.

For these reasons, fundamental not only to our federal system but also to the basic functions of the Judicial Branch of the National Government under our Constitution, we hold that the Dombrowski decision should not be regarded as having upset the settled doctrines that have always confined very narrowly the availability of injunctive relief against state criminal prosecutions. We do not think that opinion stands for the proposition that a federal court can properly enjoin enforcement of a statute solely on the basis of a showing that the statute "on its face" abridges First Amendment rights. There may, of course, be extraordinary circumstances in which the necessary irreparable injury can be shown even in the absence of the usual prerequisites of bad faith and harassment. For example, as long ago as the Buck case, [Watson v. Buck, 313 U.S. 387 (1941)], we indicated:

> "It is of course conceivable that a statute might be flagrantly and patently violative of express constitutional prohibitions in every clause, sentence and paragraph, and in whatever manner and against whomever an effort might be made to apply it." 313 U.S., at 402.

Other unusual situations calling for federal intervention might also arise, but there is no point in our attempting now to specify what they might be. It is sufficient for purposes of the present case to hold, as we do, that the possible unconstitutionality of a statute "on its face" does not in itself justify an injunction against good-faith attempts to enforce it, and that appellee Harris has failed to make any showing of bad faith, harassment, or any other unusual circumstance that would call for equitable relief. Because our holding rests on the absence of the factors necessary under equitable principles to justify federal intervention, we have no occasion to consider whether 28 U.S.C. § 2283, which prohibits an injunction against state court proceedings "except as expressly authorized by Act of Congress" would in and of itself be controlling under the circumstances of this case.

The judgment of the District Court is reversed, and the case is remanded for further proceedings not inconsistent with this opinion.

Reversed.

■ MR. JUSTICE BRENNAN with whom MR. JUSTICE WHITE and MR. JUSTICE MARSHALL join, concurring in the result.

I agree that the judgment of the District Court should be reversed. Appellee Harris had been indicted for violations of the California Criminal Syndicalism Act before he sued in federal court. He has not alleged that the prosecution was brought in bad faith to harass him. His constitutional contentions may be adequately adjudicated in the state criminal proceeding, and federal intervention at his instance was therefore improper. * * *

■ MR. JUSTICE STEWART, with whom MR. JUSTICE HARLAN joins, concurring.

The questions the Court decides today are important ones. Perhaps as important, however, is a recognition of the areas into which today's holdings do not necessarily extend. In all of these cases, the Court deals only with the proper policy to be followed by a federal court when asked to intervene by injunction or declaratory judgment in a criminal prosecution which is contemporaneously pending in a state court.

In basing its decisions on policy grounds, the Court does not reach any questions concerning the independent force of the federal anti-injunction statute, 28 U.S.C. § 2283. Thus we do not decide whether the word "injunction" in § 2283 should be interpreted to include a declaratory judgment, or whether an injunction to stay proceedings in a state court is "expressly authorized" by § 1 of the Civil Rights Act of 1871, now 42 U.S.C. § 1983. And since all these cases involve state criminal prosecutions, we do not deal with the considerations that should govern a federal court when it is asked to intervene in state civil proceedings, where, for various reasons, the balance might be struck differently.[2] Finally, the Court today does not resolve the problems involved when a federal court is asked to give injunctive or declaratory relief from *future* state criminal prosecutions.

The Court confines itself to deciding the policy considerations that in our federal system must prevail when federal courts are asked to

---

[2]   Courts of equity have traditionally shown greater reluctance to intervene in criminal prosecutions than in civil cases. See [the majority holding]; Douglas v. City of Jeannette, 319 U.S. 157, 163–164 [(1943)]. The offense to state interests is likely to be less in a civil proceeding. A State's decision to classify conduct as criminal provides some indication of the importance it has ascribed to prompt and unencumbered enforcement of its law. By contrast, the State might not even be a party in a proceeding under a civil statute.

These considerations would not, to be sure, support any distinction between civil and criminal proceedings should the ban of 28 U.S.C. § 2283, which makes no such distinction, be held unaffected by 42 U.S.C. § 1983.

interfere with pending state prosecutions. Within this area, we hold that a federal court must not, save in exceptional and extremely limited circumstances, intervene by way of either injunction or declaration in an existing state criminal prosecution.[3] Such circumstances exist only when there is a threat of irreparable injury "both great and immediate." A threat of this nature might be shown if the state criminal statute in question were patently and flagrantly unconstitutional on its face * * * or if there has been bad faith and harassment—official lawlessness—in a statute's enforcement * * *. * * *

■ MR. JUSTICE DOUGLAS, dissenting.

* * * Dombrowski represents an exception to the general rule that federal courts should not interfere with state criminal prosecutions. The exception does not arise merely because prosecutions are threatened to which the First Amendment will be the proffered defense. Dombrowski governs statutes which are a blunderbuss by themselves or when used *en masse*—those that have an "overbroad" sweep. * * *

* * * Harris is charged only with distributing leaflets advocating political action toward his objective. He tried unsuccessfully to have the state court dismiss the indictment on constitutional grounds. He resorted to the state appellate court for writs of prohibition to prevent the trial, but to no avail. He went to the federal court as a matter of last resort in an effort to keep this unconstitutional trial from being saddled on him. * * *

NOTE ON YOUNGER V. HARRIS AND THE DOCTRINE OF EQUITABLE RESTRAINT

Younger establishes a rule for the coordination of overlapping state and federal court remedies. Individuals in Harris's position as defendants in a pending state court prosecution must ordinarily assert their constitutional rights defensively and then appeal to the Supreme Court. Federal district courts may not grant equitable relief against such pending state court proceedings except in extraordinary circumstances. Younger does not address the problem of suits to block threatened (but non-pending) state criminal proceedings. But under the law in place at the time, prospective defendants could often seek Ex parte Young relief from a threatened prosecution if they could show harm from the threat of imminent enforcement more substantial than the "inhibition" alleged by Dan, Hirsh, and Broslawski.

As described in Justice Black's opinion, the doctrine of equitable restraint rests on the principles of equity jurisdiction and Our Federalism, a judicial policy informed but not fully defined by the state-federal balance

---

[3]   The negative pregnant in this sentence—that a federal court may, as a matter of policy, intervene when such "exceptional and extremely limited circumstances" are found—is subject to any further limitations that may be placed on such intervention by 28 U.S.C. § 2283.

identified in the Anti-Injunction Act (AIA). This Note first examines the legal basis for equitable restraint and then explores the doctrine's impact on those who wish to exercise their constitutional rights within the bounds of the law. True, rights-holders like Harris can always engage in conduct (passing out leaflets) and then assert their rights defensively in any subsequent prosecution. But uncertainty about the contours of the right coupled with a threat of severe punishment for violations may make the violate-and-defend strategy constitutionally problematic. *Cf.* Whole Woman's Health v. Jackson, 595 U.S. 30 (2021), p. 1211, *supra*.

(1) The Right to Equitable Relief: Ex parte Young and § 1983. In Ex parte Young, 209 U.S. 123 (1908), p. 1184, *supra*, a case well known for its Eleventh Amendment holding, the Supreme Court addressed concerns with the adequacy of the violate-and-defend model of constitutional litigation. The Court sustained a federal injunction forbidding the Minnesota Attorney General from enforcing railroad rate regulations alleged to deny due process. The Court noted that the "general rule" that "equity has no jurisdiction to enjoin [state] criminal proceedings * * * [was subject to] exceptions. When such * * * [a] proceeding is brought to enforce an alleged unconstitutional statute, which is the subject-matter of inquiry in a suit already pending in a Federal court, the latter court, having first obtained jurisdiction over the subject-matter, has the right, in both civil and criminal cases, to hold and maintain such jurisdiction, to the exclusion of all other courts, until its duty is fully performed. But the Federal court cannot, of course, interfere in a case where the proceedings were already pending in a state court." *Id.* 161–62.

The Court in Young also rejected the Attorney General's argument that the railroads had an adequate remedy at law—namely, to disobey the statute and then challenge its constitutionality in a subsequent prosecution. In part, this conclusion was based on the difficulty for the railroad of setting up a test case. But the Court also advanced a broader argument: To force the railroad "[t]o await proceedings against the company in a state court, grounded upon a disobedience of the act, [and then if necessary seek Supreme Court review,] would place the company in peril of large loss and its agents in great risk of fines and imprisonment if it should be finally determined that the act was valid. This risk the company ought not to be required to take."[1] *Id.* 165.

Together, Ex parte Young and the right to sue conferred in § 1983 as interpreted in Monroe v. Pape, 365 U.S. 167 (1961), authorize federal claims to enjoin unconstitutional state action. But in keeping with Ex parte Young's distinction between threatened and pending proceedings, federal courts in the run-up to the Warren Court era seldom if ever enjoined pending criminal prosecutions. During the same period, as one scholar reports, injunctions against *future* prosecutions "in practice * * * became routine."[2]

---

[1]   For discussion of the precedents prior to Young, see Isseks, *Jurisdiction of the Lower Federal Courts to Enjoin Unauthorized Action of State Officials*, 40 Harv.L.Rev. 969 (1927); Taylor & Willis, *The Power of Federal Courts to Enjoin Proceedings in State Courts*, 42 Yale L.J. 1169, 1190–92 (1942); Warren, *Federal and State Court Interference*, 43 Harv.L.Rev. 345, 372–74 (1930); B. Wechsler, *Federal Courts, State Criminal Law and the First Amendment*, 49 N.Y.U.L.Rev. 740, 753–62 (1974).

[2]   Laycock, *The Death of the Irreparable Injury Rule*, 103 Harv.L.Rev. 687 (1990); Laycock, *Federal Interference with State Prosecutions: The Need for Prospective Relief*, 1977

(2) Policy-Based Answers and Statutory Questions. At the time of Younger, then, decisional law and the AIA barred most suits for injunctive relief against pending state court proceedings. But the Court in Younger nonetheless felt pressed to clarify and restate that general rule in terms of Our Federalism. To see why, consider that cases had arrived on the Court's appellate docket, mostly from three-judge courts empaneled to address applications for injunctive relief against enforcement of state laws criminalizing political speech and obscenity. Relying on § 1983 and applying Dombrowski v. Pfister, 380 U.S. 479 (1965), discussed at length in Younger, many of these decisions granted relief after concluding that pending state prosecutions were based on unconstitutionally overbroad state laws. Apart from the six cases that were consolidated and decided with Younger in February 1971, the Court dealt summarily later that Term with some twenty pending appeals posing questions controlled by Younger v. Harris.

The cases presented both the question whether, under controlling statutes, the federal courts had the power to issue injunctive and declaratory relief against pending prosecutions and, assuming they do, what policies should govern the federal courts' equitable discretion. The Court chose to address only the policy questions but clarified in one of Younger's companion cases that the same policies applied to suits for declaratory relief. See Samuels v. Mackell, 401 U.S. 66 (1971) (citing Great Lakes Dredge & Dock Co. v. Huffman, 319 U.S. 293 (1943)). The Court's decision to resolve the pending cases on "policy" grounds, Justice Stewart explained in his concurrence, meant that "we do not decide whether the word 'injunction' in § 2283 [the Anti-Injunction Act] should be interpreted to include a declaratory judgment, or whether an injunction to stay proceedings in a state court is 'expressly authorized' by § 1 of the Civil Rights Act of 1871, now 42 U.S.C. § 1983." The Court took up that unresolved question one year later in Mitchum v. Foster.

Mitchum v. Foster

407 U.S. 225 (1972).

The case arose from a proceeding in a Florida state court to close the appellant's bookstore as a public nuisance under the claimed authority of Florida law. After the state court entered a preliminary order prohibiting continued operation of the bookstore, the appellant filed a complaint in federal court, invoking § 1983 and alleging that state judicial and law enforcement officials were depriving him of rights protected by the First and Fourteenth Amendments. The district court ruled that § 1983 did not come within the "expressly authorized" exception of the AIA. Before tackling that statutory question, Justice Stewart, writing for a unanimous Court, set the stage: "Last Term, in Younger v. Harris, 401 U.S. 37 [(1971)], and its companion cases, the Court dealt at length with the subject of federal judicial

---

Sup.Ct.Rev. 193, 197; see Soifer & MacGill, *The Younger Doctrine: Reconstructing Reconstruction*, 55 Tex.L.Rev. 1141, 1158 (1977). Without questioning Professor Laycock's showing that injunctions have become routinely available against future prosecution, Bray, *The System of Equitable Remedies*, 63 UCLA L.Rev. 530, 581 (2016), argues that the judicial inquiry into adequacy of alternative relief remains important in marking out the conceptual distinction between legal and equitable remedies.

intervention in pending state criminal prosecutions. In Younger a three-judge federal district court in a § 1983 action had enjoined a criminal prosecution pending in a California court. In asking us to reverse that judgment, the appellant argued that the injunction was in violation of the federal anti-injunction statute. But the Court carefully eschewed any reliance on the statute in reversing the judgment, basing its decision instead upon what the Court called 'Our Federalism'—upon 'the national policy forbidding federal courts to stay or enjoin pending state court proceedings except under special circumstances.'

"* * * At the same time, however, the Court clearly left room for federal injunctive intervention in a pending state court prosecution in certain exceptional circumstances—where irreparable injury is 'both great and immediate,' where the state law is 'flagrantly and patently violative of express constitutional prohibitions,' or where there is a showing of 'bad faith, harassment, or * * * other unusual circumstances that would call for equitable relief.'

"* * * While the Court in Younger and its companion cases expressly disavowed deciding the question now before us—whether § 1983 comes within the 'expressly authorized' exception of the anti-injunction statute—it is evident that our decisions in those cases cannot be disregarded in deciding this question. In the first place, if § 1983 is not within the statutory exception, then the anti-injunction statute would have absolutely barred the injunction issued in Younger, as the appellant in that case argued, and there would have been no occasion whatever for the Court to decide that case upon the 'policy' ground of 'Our Federalism.' Secondly, if § 1983 is not within the 'expressly authorized' exception of the anti-injunction statute, then we must overrule Younger and its companion cases insofar as they recognized the permissibility of injunctive relief against pending criminal prosecutions in certain limited and exceptional circumstances."

With the stakes thus specified, the Court ruled that § 1983 conferred the requisite express statutory authority. The Court first concluded, on reviewing the history of the AIA, that express authority was not strictly required: "In the first place, it is evident that, in order to qualify under the 'expressly authorized' exception of the anti-injunction statute, a federal law need not contain an express reference to that statute. * * * Indeed, none of the previously recognized statutory exceptions contains any such reference. Secondly, a federal law need not expressly authorize an injunction of a state court proceeding in order to qualify as an exception. Three of the six previously recognized statutory exceptions contain no such authorization.[1] Thirdly, it is clear that, in order to qualify as an 'expressly authorized' exception to the anti-injunction statute, an Act of Congress must have created a specific and uniquely federal right or remedy, enforceable in a federal court of equity, that could be frustrated if the federal court were not empowered to enjoin a state court proceeding."

---

[1] For a criticism of this aspect of the opinion, see p. 1379, *supra* (noting that some of the statutes identified as implied exceptions called for the equitable administration of property, thereby triggering a separate AIA exception for injunctions in aid of the federal court's jurisdiction).

Turning to the legislative history of § 1983, the Court found ample evidence that Congress meant to empower federal courts to address state court frustration of federal purposes. Section 1983 was "a product of a vast transformation from the concepts of federalism that had prevailed in the late 18th century when the anti-injunction statute was enacted. The very purpose of § 1983 was to interpose the federal courts between the States and the people, as guardians of the people's federal rights—to protect the people from unconstitutional action under color of state law, 'whether that action be executive, legislative, or judicial.' In carrying out that purpose, Congress plainly authorized the federal courts to issue injunctions in § 1983 actions, by expressly authorizing a 'suit in equity' as one of the means of redress. And this Court long ago recognized that federal injunctive relief against a state court proceeding can in some circumstances be essential to prevent great, immediate, and irreparable loss of a person's constitutional rights. Ex parte Young, 209 U.S. 123 [(1908)]."

NOTE ON EQUITABLE RELIEF FROM PENDING STATE PROCEEDINGS

(1) Younger's Exceptions. Mitchum holds that federal courts have power, in exceptional circumstances, to grant equitable relief against pending state criminal prosecutions. Consider the factors identified in Younger and repeated in Mitchum that were said to warrant equitable intervention.

(a) Bad Faith Prosecution or Harassment. Although the Supreme Court has never upheld an injunction on this basis, the exception may derive from the circumstances recounted in Dombrowski v. Pfister, 380 U.S. 479 (1965). (Note that in Dombrowski, no state prosecution was pending in which the federal plaintiffs could challenge the prosecution's motives.) Among the cases in which the Court has refused to find bad faith are Cameron v. Johnson, 390 U.S. 611 (1968) (rejecting the notion that bad faith could be inferred from the innocence of the accused and framing the question as whether enforcement was undertaken "with no expectation of convictions but only to discourage exercise of protected rights"), and Hicks v. Miranda, 422 U.S. 332 (1975) (refusing to credit the districts court's characterization of the prosecutor's "pattern" of bad faith in part because the actions were authorized by state judicial orders).

If Younger itself is sound, why should there be such an exception? Consider alternative remedies for prosecutorial bad faith. A state court defendant might move to abate a state criminal proceeding. *Cf.* Bank of Nova Scotia v. United States, 487 U.S. 250 (1988) (district court may dismiss indictment where prosecutorial misconduct prejudiced defendant). Alternatively, a state defendant might initiate a claim for malicious prosecution after an acquittal in state court. Or is the real problem one of harassment—of repeated, unfounded prosecutions that are dismissed before the defendant can obtain a favorable ruling?

(b) Patent and Flagrant Unconstitutionality. Younger also suggested that federal courts might be justified in restraining prosecutions under statutes that are "flagrantly and patently violative of express constitutional prohibitions in every clause, sentence, and paragraph, and in whatever manner and against whomever an effort might be made to apply it." The language is from Watson v. Buck, 313 U.S. 387 (1941), which refused to enjoin an entire statute when parts could be severed or the legislation could be given a narrowing construction. Why might an exception for patently and flagrantly unconstitutional statutes be warranted at all? Isn't it a particular insult to the state courts to suggest that they will be unable to detect patent unconstitutionality in state statutes? Indeed, what sense does this exception make in Younger itself? Two years earlier, Brandenburg v. Ohio, 395 U.S. 444 (1969), had invalidated a statute almost identical to the one under which Harris was being prosecuted.

Whatever the rationale, little remains of this "exception" after Trainor v. Hernandez, 431 U.S. 434, 446–47 (1977). There, the defendants in a state court action filed a federal suit challenging the constitutionality of a state court attachment against their property that had been obtained without any prior hearing, as authorized by state law. The lower court, in enjoining the attachment, held that the state's attachment procedure was "on its face patently violative of the due process clause." 405 F.Supp. 757 (N.D.Ill. 1975). Dividing 5–4, the Supreme Court reversed. Without expressly reaffirming a Younger exception for flagrantly unconstitutional statutes, the majority simply said the cases did not warrant the lower court's patent-violation conclusion.[1] See also New Orleans Public Serv., Inc. v. Council of New Orleans, 491 U.S. 350 (1989), p. 1389, *supra* (concluding that an allegation that "requires further factual inquiry can hardly be deemed" to have satisfied the test for flagrant unlawfulness "for purposes of a threshold abstention determination").

(c) Other Extraordinary Circumstances. What else might constitute "extraordinary circumstances" meriting an exception to Younger's policy of non-interference? In Gibson v. Berryhill, 411 U.S. 564 (1973), the Court refused to require Younger deference to administrative proceedings before a state agency that the lower court had found to be "incompetent by reason of bias to adjudicate the issues pending before it. If the District Court's conclusion was correct in this regard, it was also correct that it need not defer to the Board. Nor, in these circumstances, would a different result be required simply because judicial review, de novo or otherwise, would be forthcoming at the conclusion of the administrative proceedings."[2]

---

[1]   Justices Brennan, Stewart, Marshall, and Stevens dissented. Justice Brennan's dissent argued that "a requirement that the * * * formulation [defining this exception] must be literally satisfied renders the exception meaningless." Analyzing the statute in some detail, Justice Brennan found it clearly unconstitutional under existing precedent. Justice Stevens's dissent objected that the majority's view made the exception inapplicable whenever the statute had a separability clause, and argued that there was no reason "why all sections of any statute must be considered invalid in order to justify an injunction against a portion that is itself flagrantly unconstitutional."

[2]   In Kugler v. Helfant, 421 U.S. 117 (1975), the Court described Gibson as an example of an "extraordinary circumstance," other than bad faith/harassment or patent unconstitutionality, but concluded that the case was distinguishable because the plaintiff's claim (in Kugler) that he could not obtain a fair hearing in the state courts was without merit.

The Younger "exceptions" bear some resemblance to the factors—likely success on the merits, adequacy of alternative remedies, and irreparable harm—that ordinarily inform decisions to grant preliminary injunctive relief. See Winter v. Natural Resources Defense Council, Inc., 555 U.S. 7 (2008). Consider the possibility that Younger can be better understood as calling for a multi-factored evaluation of the equities rather than a set of discrete exceptions.

(2) Criticisms of Younger. Three criticisms of Younger are especially common.

(a) First, numerous commentators have objected that Younger fails to respect congressional policy by requiring abstention in suits under 42 U.S.C. § 1983—a statute the purpose of which (according to Mitchum v. Foster) "was to interpose the federal courts between the States and the people, as guardians of the people's federal rights."[3] Consider, however, whether the alternative outcome in Younger might have been in tension with Congress's having given the state courts exclusive jurisdiction over state criminal prosecutions that involve federal defenses (apart from prosecutions of federal officers covered by the removal statute in 28 U.S.C. § 1442).

(b) A second, related complaint is that Younger relegates plaintiffs claiming constitutional rights violations to state forums that they, at least, expect to be less sympathetic to their claims than the federal court in which they would prefer to litigate. For discussion of the "parity" or "disparity" of state and federal courts, see Chap. IV, Sec. 3.

(c) A third objection is that Younger erects a frequently insuperable barrier to prospective and class relief—remedies typically unavailable from a criminal court. See Laycock, Federal Interference with *State Prosecutions: The Need for Prospective Relief*, 1977 Sup.Ct.Rev. 193.

(3) The Relationship of Younger to Pullman Abstention. Note the differences between the Pullman "abstention" doctrine and the equitable restraint doctrine of Younger. In conventional Pullman-type cases, the issue is whether federal plaintiffs—as a necessary condition of having the federal court adjudicate their federal claims—should be forced to obtain a state court resolution of state law issues. In the normal Younger-type case, on the other hand, the whole point is that a state proceeding either has been or is about to be commenced by the state authorities, and that the entire case (of which key aspects will be federal in nature) should be litigated in that proceeding.

The two doctrines thus have sharply different impacts on federal plaintiffs' ability to obtain federal court resolution of their federal claims. The Pullman doctrine ordinarily entails postponement, not relinquishment, of federal jurisdiction to pass on claims of federal right. In Younger cases, by contrast, the federal court dismisses the suit, and the underlying federal claims must typically be adjudicated in the context of a state criminal case, subject only to Supreme Court review. The state court adjudication will have res judicata effect in subsequent federal court proceedings, see Allen v.

---

[3]   See also Redish, *Abstention, Separation of Powers, and the Limits of the Judicial Function*, 94 Yale L.J. 71 (1984).

McCurry, 449 U.S. 90 (1980), but would not typically bar a subsequent claim under 42 U.S.C. § 1983 if the state defendant is acquitted.

The policies of the two doctrines sometimes overlap, as when the Court deploys Younger abstention as a means of allowing state courts to provide narrowing constructions that might avoid constitutional questions. See, *e.g.*, Pennzoil Co. v. Texaco, Inc., 481 U.S. 1, 11–12 (1987); Moore v. Sims, 442 U.S. 415, 429–30 (1979). But Younger abstention does not depend on the existence of unsettled state law questions in need of state court clarification.

(4) Equitable Restraint—Mandatory or Permissive? In Ohio Bureau of Employment Servs. v. Hodory, 431 U.S. 471 (1977), the state, in appealing a three-judge court's injunction against the enforcement of a state statute, argued for reversal on the merits but not for dismissal under Younger. The Supreme Court reached the merits and reversed, over the suggestion of an amicus that Younger called for dismissal. On this point, the Court said: "If the State voluntarily chooses to submit to a federal forum, principles of comity do not demand that the federal court force the case back into the State's own system." Accord, Brown v. Hotel & Rest. Employees & Bartenders Local 54, 468 U.S. 491, 500 n.9 (1984).

Steffel v. Thompson

415 U.S. 452 (1974).

Certiorari to the United States Court of Appeals for the Fifth Circuit.

■ MR. JUSTICE BRENNAN delivered the opinion of the Court.

[In October 1970, Steffel and a companion faced arrest for handing out leaflets opposing the Vietnam War at a shopping center in Decatur, Georgia. Steffel left the mall to avoid arrest, but his companion stayed, continued to handbill, and was arrested for criminal trespass. Steffel filed suit in federal court, seeking relief from threatened arrest for constitutionally protected speech. The lower courts dismissed the action, finding no evidence of bad faith on the part of police officials and the absence of any real controversy.

I

[In an opinion by Justice Brennan, a unanimous Court reversed. The Court first held that Steffel presented an actual controversy within the meaning of the declaratory judgment act and Article III. Steffel faced a more concrete threat of arrest than did the three intervening plaintiffs in Younger v. Harris, 401 U.S. 37 (1971), p. 1430, *supra*: Dan, Hirsh, and Broslawski. (In the Court's view, the threat in Steffel's case "cannot be characterized as 'imaginary or speculative' " (quoting Younger, 401 U.S., at 42). "In these circumstances, it is not necessary that petitioner first expose himself to actual arrest or prosecution to be entitled to challenge a statute that he claims deters the exercise of his constitutional rights." Next, the Court concluded that in the absence of any pending state prosecution, the policy of Our Federalism applied in Younger and

Samuels v. Mackell, 401 U.S. 66 (1971), did not govern federal declaratory relief from enforcement of a disputed state criminal statute.

II

[In reserving the question of relief in the absence of a pending state prosecution, Younger and Samuels recognized] that the relevant principles of equity, comity, and federalism "have little force in the absence of a pending state proceeding." Lake Carriers' Assn. v. MacMullan, 406 U.S. 498, 509 (1972). When no state criminal proceeding is pending at the time the federal complaint is filed, federal intervention does not result in duplicative legal proceedings or disruption of the state criminal justice system; nor can federal intervention, in that circumstance, be interpreted as reflecting negatively upon the state court's ability to enforce constitutional principles. In addition, while a pending state prosecution provides the federal plaintiff with a concrete opportunity to vindicate his constitutional rights, a refusal on the part of the federal courts to intervene when no state proceeding is pending may place the hapless plaintiff between the Scylla of intentionally flouting state law and the Charybdis of forgoing what he believes to be constitutionally protected activity in order to avoid becoming enmeshed in a criminal proceeding. Cf. Dombrowski v. Pfister, 380 U.S. 479, 490 (1965).

When no state proceeding is pending and thus considerations of equity, comity, and federalism have little vitality, the propriety of granting federal declaratory relief may properly be considered independently of a request for injunctive relief. Here, the Court of Appeals held that, because injunctive relief would not be appropriate since petitioner failed to demonstrate irreparable injury—a traditional prerequisite to injunctive relief—it followed that declaratory relief was also inappropriate. * * * [T]he court erred in treating the requests for injunctive and declaratory relief as a single issue. "[W]hen no state prosecution is pending and the only question is whether declaratory relief is appropriate[,] . . . the congressional scheme that makes the federal courts the primary guardians of constitutional rights, and the express congressional authorization of declaratory relief, afforded because it is a less harsh and abrasive remedy than the injunction, become the factors of primary significance." Perez v. Ledesma, 401 U.S. 82, 104 (1971) (separate opinion of Brennan, J.).

The subject matter jurisdiction of the lower federal courts was greatly expanded in the wake of the Civil War. A pervasive sense of nationalism led to enactment of the Civil Rights Act of 1871, empowering the lower federal courts to determine the constitutionality of actions, taken by persons under color of state law, allegedly depriving other individuals of rights guaranteed by the Constitution and federal law, see 42 U.S.C. § 1983, 28 U.S.C. § 1343(3). Four years later, in the Judiciary Act of March 3, 1875, Congress conferred upon the lower federal courts, for but the second time in their nearly century-old history, general federal-question jurisdiction subject only to a jurisdictional-amount requirement, see 28 U.S.C. § 1331. With this latter enactment, the lower federal courts "ceased to be restricted tribunals of fair dealing between citizens of different states and became the *primary* and powerful reliances for vindicating every right given by the Constitution, the laws, and treaties of the United States." F. Frankfurter & J. Landis, The Business of the Supreme Court 65 (1928) (emphasis added). These two statutes, together with the Court's decision in Ex parte Young, 209 U.S. 123 (1908)—holding that state officials who threaten to enforce an unconstitutional state statute may be enjoined by a federal court of equity and that a federal court may, in appropriate circumstances, enjoin future state criminal prosecutions under the unconstitutional Act—have "established the modern framework for federal protection of constitutional rights from state interference." Perez v. Ledesma, *supra*, 401 U.S., at 107 (separate opinion of Brennan, J.).

* * * The highlights of th[e] history [of the Declaratory Judgment Act], particularly pertinent to our inquiry today, emphasize that:

> "The express purpose of the Federal Declaratory Judgment Act was to provide a milder alternative to the injunction remedy. . . . Of particular significance on the question before us, the Senate report makes it even clearer that the declaratory judgment was designed to be available to test state criminal statutes in circumstances where an injunction would not be appropriate. . . . * * *

> * * * Moreover, the Senate report's clear implication that declaratory relief would have been appropriate in Pierce v. Society of Sisters, 268 U.S. 510 (1925), and Village of Euclid v. Ambler Realty Co., 272 U.S. 365 (1926), both cases involving federal adjudication of the constitutionality of a state statute carrying criminal penalties, and the report[ ] * * * make[s] it plain that Congress anticipated that the declaratory judgment procedure would be used by the federal courts to test the constitutionality of state criminal statutes." * * *

III

[The Court next considered the propriety of declaratory relief in the as-applied context in which Steffel's claim arose. The Court described the state officials as arguing that] the State's interest in unencumbered enforcement of its laws outweighs the minimal federal interest in protecting the constitutional rights of only a single individual. We reject the argument. * * *

Indeed, the State's concern with potential interference in the administration of its criminal laws is of lesser dimension when an attack is made upon the constitutionality of a state statute as applied. A declaratory judgment of a lower federal court that a state statute is invalid *in toto*—and therefore incapable of any valid application—or is overbroad or vague—and therefore no person can properly be convicted under the statute until it is given a narrowing or clarifying construction—will likely have a more significant potential for disruption of state enforcement policies than a declaration specifying a limited number of impermissible applications of the statute. While the federal interest may be greater when a state statute is attacked on its face, since there exists the potential for eliminating any broad-ranging deterrent effect on would-be actors, see Dombrowski v. Pfister, 380 U.S. 479 (1965), we do not find this consideration controlling. The solitary individual who suffers a deprivation of his constitutional rights is no less deserving of redress than one who suffers together with others. * * *

We therefore hold that, regardless of whether injunctive relief may be appropriate, federal declaratory relief is not precluded when no state prosecution is pending and a federal plaintiff demonstrates a genuine threat of enforcement of a disputed state criminal statute, whether an attack is made on the constitutionality of the statute on its face or as applied. The judgment of the Court of Appeals is reversed, and the case is remanded for further proceedings consistent with this opinion.

It is so ordered.

■ Mr. Justice Stewart, with whom The Chief Justice joins, concurring.

[Justice Stewart emphasized the limits of the Court's opinion to rare cases in which genuine threats of enforcement create a concrete controversy for resolution by the federal courts.]

* * * Our decision today must not be understood as authorizing the invocation of federal declaratory judgment jurisdiction by a person who thinks a state criminal law is unconstitutional, even if he genuinely feels "chilled" in his freedom of action by the law's existence, and even if he honestly entertains the subjective belief that he may now or in the future be prosecuted under it. * * *

The petitioner in this case has succeeded in objectively showing that the threat of imminent arrest, corroborated by the actual arrest of his companion, has created an actual concrete controversy between himself and the agents of the State. He has, therefore, demonstrated "a genuine threat of enforcement of a disputed state criminal statute * * *." Cases where such a "genuine threat" can be demonstrated will, I think be exceedingly rare.

■ Mr. Justice White, concurring.

[In response to Justice Rehnquist's concurrence], I would anticipate that a final declaratory judgment entered by a federal court holding particular conduct of the federal plaintiff to be immune on federal constitutional grounds from prosecution under state law should be accorded res judicata effect in any later prosecution of that very conduct. There would also, I think, be additional circumstances in which the federal judgment should be considered as more than a mere precedent bearing on the issue before the state court.

Neither can I at this stage agree that the federal court, having rendered a declaratory judgment in favor of the plaintiff, could not enjoin a later state prosecution for conduct that the federal court has declared immune. The Declaratory Judgment Act itself provides that a "declaration shall have the force and effect of a final judgment or decree," 28 U.S.C. § 2201; eminent authority anticipated that declaratory judgments would be res judicata, E. Borchard, Declaratory Judgments 10–11 (2d ed. 1941); and there is every reason for not reducing declaratory judgments to mere advisory opinions. * * * The statute provides for "[f]urther necessary or proper relief * * * against any adverse party whose rights have been determined by such judgment," 28 U.S.C. § 2202, and it would not seem improper to enjoin local prosecutors who refuse to observe adverse federal judgments.

Finally, I would think that a federal suit challenging a state criminal statute on federal constitutional grounds could be sufficiently far along so that ordinary consideration of economy would warrant refusal to dismiss the federal case solely because a state prosecution has subsequently been filed and the federal question may be litigated there.

■ MR. JUSTICE REHNQUIST, with whom THE CHIEF JUSTICE joins, concurring.

I concur in the opinion of the Court. * * * Congress apparently was aware at the time it passed the Act that persons threatened with state criminal prosecutions might choose to forego the offending conduct and instead seek a federal declaration of their rights. Use of the declaratory judgment procedure in the circumstances presented by this case seems consistent with that congressional expectation.

[Justice Rehnquist offered a "few remarks" on whether a declaratory judgment by a federal court will have any subsequent res judicata effect or will perhaps support the issuance of a later federal injunction.]

First, the legislative history of the Declaratory Judgment Act and the Court's opinion in this case both recognize that the declaratory judgment procedure is an alternative to pursuit of the arguably illegal activity. * * * The plaintiff who continues to violate a state statute after the filing of his federal complaint does so both at the risk of state prosecution and at the risk of dismissal of his federal lawsuit. For any arrest prior to resolution of the federal action would constitute a pending prosecution and bar declaratory relief under the principles of Samuels.

Second, I do not believe that today's decision can properly be raised to support the issuance of a federal injunction based upon a favorable declaratory judgment. The Court's description of declaratory relief as "a milder alternative to the injunction remedy," having a "less intrusive effect on the administration of state criminal laws" than an injunction, indicates to me critical distinctions which make declaratory relief appropriate where injunctive relief would not be. * * *

A declaratory judgment is simply a statement of rights, not a binding order supplemented by continuing sanctions. State authorities may choose to be guided by the judgment of a lower federal court, but they are not compelled to follow the decision by threat of contempt or other penalties. If the federal plaintiff pursues the conduct for which he was previously threatened with arrest and is in fact arrested, he may not return the controversy to federal court, although he may, of course, raise the federal declaratory judgment in the state court for whatever value it may prove to have.[3] In any event, the defendant at that point is able to present his case for full consideration by a state court charged, as are the federal courts, to preserve the defendant's constitutional rights. Federal interference with this process would involve precisely the same concerns discussed in Younger and recited in the Court's opinion in this case.

* * * If the federal court finds that the threatened prosecution would depend upon a statute it judges unconstitutional, the State may decide to forgo prosecution of similar conduct in the future, believing the judgment persuasive. Should the state prosecutors not find the decision persuasive enough to justify forbearance, the successful federal plaintiff will at least be able to bolster his allegations of unconstitutionality in the state trial with a decision of the federal district court in the immediate locality. The state courts may find the reasoning convincing even though the prosecutors did not. Finally, of course, the state legislature may decide, on the basis of the federal decision, that the statute would be better amended or repealed. All these possible avenues of relief would be reached voluntarily by the States and would be completely consistent with the concepts of federalism discussed above. Other more intrusive forms of relief should not be routinely available. * * *

NOTE ON DECLARATORY RELIEF IN THE ABSENCE OF PENDING STATE PROCEEDINGS

In authorizing declaratory judgments, Steffel emphasized the absence of any pending state prosecution and the difference between declaratory and injunctive relief. This Note explores those distinctions.

(1) The Declaratory/Injunctive Relief Distinction. Steffel places some weight on the relatively "mild" character of the remedy contemplated in the federal Declaratory Judgment Act, viewing it as less abrasive to federal-state relations than an injunction barring future prosecution. In Samuels v. Mackell, 401 U.S. 66 (1971), decided the same day as Younger, the Court took a different position, explaining that in cases where the criminal

---

[3]   The Court's opinion notes that the possible res judicata effect of a federal declaratory judgment in a subsequent state court prosecution is a question " 'not free from difficulty.' " I express no opinion on that issue here. * * *

proceeding was begun prior to the federal civil suit: "the propriety of declaratory and injunctive relief should be judged by essentially the same standards. In both situations deeply rooted and long-settled principles of equity have narrowly restricted the scope for federal intervention, and ordinarily a declaratory judgment will result in precisely the same interference with and disruption of state proceedings that the longstanding policy limiting injunctions was designed to avoid. This is true for at least two reasons. In the first place, the Declaratory Judgment Act provides that after a declaratory judgment is issued the district court may enforce it by granting '(f)urther necessary or proper relief,' 28 U.S.C. § 2202, and therefore a declaratory judgment issued while state proceedings are pending might serve as the basis for a subsequent injunction against those proceedings to 'protect or effectuate' the declaratory judgment, 28 U.S.C. § 2283, and thus result in a clearly improper interference with the state proceedings. Secondly, even if the declaratory judgment is not used as a basis for actually issuing an injunction, the declaratory relief alone has virtually the same practical impact as a formal injunction would."[1]

Samuels thus depicts the declaratory judgment in terms far closer to the position articulated in Steffel by Justice White's concurring opinion than by Justice Brennan's majority opinion or Justice Rehnquist's concurrence. Scholars agree that the portrait of declaratory judgments as mild alternatives to injunctive relief misses the fact that such judgments represent binding resolutions of disputed legal issues that can only serve their function if accorded claim and issue preclusive effect.[2] Justice Rehnquist's account appears to treat the declaratory judgment as something akin to an advisory opinion that state courts and prosecutors may regard as entitled only to persuasive rather than binding effect.

Subsequent cases recognize the power of federal courts to grant preliminary and permanent injunctive relief in circumstances where no pending state prosecution brings the doctrine of Younger abstention into play. See Doran v. Salem Inn, Inc., 422 U.S. 922 (1975); Wooley v. Maynard, 430 U.S. 705 (1977). Federal plaintiffs today may pursue both forms of relief in federal court.

(2) Anticipatory Relief and the Pending/Non-Pending Distinction. In evaluating the Court's conclusion in Steffel that the "principles of equity, comity, and federalism" underlying Younger v. Harris "have little force in the absence of a pending state proceeding," consider Redish, Federal Jurisdiction: Tensions in the Allocation of Judicial Power 356 (2d ed.1990): "[Steffel] appears to contradict two * * * recognized bases of Younger deference—the desire to avoid interference with state substantive legislative policies and with state prosecutorial discretion. For whether or not a prosecution has been filed, federal relief tells the prosecutor 'when and how'—and indeed if—he or she is to bring a prosecution." Given Steffel's

---

[1]   The Kline model of presumptively overlapping state and federal litigation, discussed at pp. 1362–1370, *supra*, rests on the premise that the first final judgment should be given claim and issue preclusive effect in the other proceeding, A final declaratory judgment may enjoy such effect in state court even in the absence of an injunction.

[2]   See Bray, *The Myth of the Mild Declaratory Judgment*, 63 Duke L.J. 1091 (2014).

similar impact on prosecutorial discretion, the Supreme Court's nearly total unanimity in *both* Younger and Steffel may require an alternative explanation.[3]

One leading alternative explanation points to the powerful interests that plaintiffs such as Steffel have in obtaining *anticipatory* relief from what they believe to be unconstitutional applications of state laws. Both Steffel and Ex parte Young rejected the violate-and-defend model of constitutional litigation. To clarify the interests at stake, and to evaluate the extent to which they are in tension with the values underlying Younger v. Harris, it is useful to distinguish claims to federal relief against state prosecution for future, past, and continuing conduct.

(a) Future Conduct. Suppose that Steffel had never violated the Georgia anti-trespassing statute, but that he had definite plans to do so, and was deterred from carrying out those plans only by the threat of a criminal prosecution. As Justice Brennan points out in Steffel, to allow plaintiffs to obtain a declaration of their rights in such cases would appear to be a central purpose of the Declaratory Judgment Act. Exposing oneself to criminal prosecution is a perilous business; anticipatory federal relief is important to relieve parties acting in good faith from having to choose between forgoing conduct they believe to be constitutionally protected and risking criminal liability.

For a declaratory judgment to be available under these circumstances, the standing and ripeness barriers must of course be surmounted, as they were in Steffel. Although the Supreme Court's standing and ripeness decisions have taken a sometimes perplexing path, on the whole Justice Stewart's forecast in Steffel—that cases where a genuine threat of prosecution can be demonstrated will be "exceedingly rare"—has not been borne out.[4] For further discussion, see Chap. II.

(b) Past Conduct. Consider the case of someone who has engaged in conduct in the past but has no plan to continue that conduct in the future, and who seeks a federal declaration that the past conduct was constitutionally protected. Declaratory relief designed to immunize past, noncontinuing conduct from state prosecution cannot spare a litigant the choice between violating the statute and forgoing possibly lawful activity; that choice has already been made. And if the state prevails in the federal action, a subsequent prosecution is likely to be highly duplicative, since the federal litigation will have at best very limited res judicata effect against the state criminal defendant.[5]

---

[3]   The decision in Steffel was unanimous, while eight of the nine Justices concurred in the result in Younger.

[4]   See, *e.g.,* Laycock, Modern American Remedies 596 (4th ed.2010) (observing that "[m]ost of the Court's cases hold or assume that a suit to enjoin enforcement is ripe when the statute is on the books and plaintiff wants to violate it").

[5]   Although preclusion might apply to a pure issue of law—such as the facial validity of a statute—differences in the burden of proof in civil and criminal cases would ordinarily require relitigation of the application of law to fact. See generally Restatement (Second) of Judgments §§ 27, 28 (1982). Does this suggest that there may be a stronger argument for federal intervention in cases involving past conduct if the federal plaintiff is challenging the state statute on its face rather than as applied?

(c) Continuing Conduct. Consider now the case of a plaintiff, like Steffel, engaged in a continuing course of conduct—someone who has already violated a criminal statute, but who seeks federal equitable relief from prosecution for similar actions not yet undertaken. In such a case, anticipatory federal intervention offers the federal plaintiff distinctive advantages over defending against a state prosecution. First, in appropriate cases interlocutory relief may be available, thereby largely eliminating the need for the federal plaintiff to choose, *pendente lite*, between desisting from conduct that the plaintiff believes to be constitutionally protected and risking additional criminal penalties. Second, if the federal court awards equitable relief based upon the protected nature of the plaintiff's conduct, the plaintiff has protection against prosecution for similar conduct undertaken in the future. By contrast, a defendant's victory in the pending state criminal case will not necessarily preclude prosecution for engaging thereafter in the same conduct: an acquittal, or even a trial judge's dismissal of the charges, may not have preclusive effect, especially where the state could not appeal.[6] Such considerations make the arguments for allowing federal equitable intervention much stronger in a case involving continuing conduct than in a case involving past conduct only.

(3) Blurring the Pending/Non-Pending Distinction: Hicks v. Miranda. Suppose that the prosecutor responded to Steffel's federal suit for declaratory relief by initiating a criminal trespass prosecution against Steffel for his admitted prior handbilling activity. Such an after-filed prosecution would afford Steffel an opportunity to litigate the constitutional issue as a defense in state court. Justices White and Rehnquist, concurring in Steffel, both thought federal deference might be appropriate in such a setting. One year later, a divided Court ruled in an opinion by Justice Rehnquist that federal courts should exercise Younger-style equitable restraint in respect of such after-filed prosecutions unless the federal court has conducted "proceedings of substance on the merits." Hicks v. Miranda, 422 U.S. 332, 349 (1975). That means that a federal suit viable under Steffel when filed, must be dismissed in deference to a later-filed state court prosecution, so long as no substantive proceedings have occurred in federal court. Any other result, the Court explained, would trivialize Younger. In a vigorous dissent for four Justices, Justice Stewart argued that Hicks instead trivialized Steffel and departed from the usual rule that a court of equity retains jurisdiction even where an adequate legal remedy has become available after the equitable action was filed. See, *e.g.*, American Life Ins. Co. v. Stewart, 300 U.S. 203, 215 (1937) (Cardozo, J.); Dawson v. Kentucky Distilleries & Whse. Co., 255 U.S. 288, 296 (1921) (Brandeis, J.).

In Hicks, the federal court had conducted a hearing in connection with its consideration of the federal plaintiff's motion for a temporary restraining order before the prosecution began. But the Court found that the TRO hearing did not meet the "proceedings of substance" test it had formulated. On the other hand, had the federal court granted the TRO or a preliminary injunction, the state would have been barred from instituting a state court

---

[6] See generally Laycock, *Federal Interference with State Prosecutions: The Need for Prospective Relief*, 1977 Sup.Ct.Rev. 193.

prosecution to which Younger abstention would apply. In Hawaii Housing Auth. v. Midkiff, 467 U.S. 229 (1984), the Supreme Court found that Younger/Hicks did not bar consideration of a federal action seeking injunctive relief against a state land reform scheme, stating: "Whether issuance of the February temporary restraining order was a substantial federal court action or not, issuance of the June preliminary injunction certainly was;" the court had by then "proceeded well beyond the 'embryonic stage,'" and no state judicial proceedings had yet been filed.

(4) Multiple Parties, Preliminary Relief, and Preclusive Effect. In Doran v. Salem Inn, Inc., 422 U.S. 922 (1975), the Court clarified the interplay of Younger and Steffel in multi-party litigation. A municipal ordinance prohibited exotic dancing in bars; three local bars initially complied with the ordinance. But the corporate owners (M & L, Salem, and Tim-Robb) sued in federal court seeking a declaration that the ordinance was unconstitutional as well as a temporary restraining order and a preliminary injunction against its enforcement. The day after the complaint was filed, M & L (but not the other two plaintiffs) resumed exotic dancing; a criminal prosecution against M & L was commenced immediately. The district court granted plaintiffs' prayer for a preliminary injunction, and the court of appeals affirmed.

The Supreme Court first concluded that the three plaintiffs should not "be thrown into the same hopper for Younger purposes"; although there "may be some circumstances in which legally distinct parties are so closely related that they should all be subjected to the Younger considerations which govern any one of them, this is not such a case." M & L was barred from securing an injunction by Younger and a declaratory judgment by Samuels v. Mackell. "When the criminal summonses issued against M & L on the days immediately following the filing of the federal complaint, the federal litigation was in an embryonic stage." With regard to Salem and Tim-Robb, the Court held their prayers for declaratory relief squarely governed by Steffel, since they were not subject to state criminal prosecution at any time. Further, the Court held that under the circumstances the issuance of a preliminary injunction barring enforcement of the ordinance was not subject to the restrictions of Younger. The Court reasoned that, at the end of trial on the merits, the plaintiffs' interests can generally be protected by a declaratory judgment; but "prior to final judgment there is no established declaratory remedy comparable to a preliminary injunction."

Yet the grant of declaratory and preliminary injunctive relief at the district court level by no means settles the issue if the prosecutor insists on enforcing the ordinance. For one thing, the prosecutor might continue to prosecute M & L, urging the state court to conclude that the federal court's constitutional ruling lacks persuasive force. For another thing, the prosecutor could certainly appeal from the federal decree protecting Salem and Tim-Robb from prosecution. If successful, the prosecutor might later indict Salem and Tim-Robb for any exotic dancing those bars offered while the injunction was in place.

Prosecution for conduct shielded by a preliminary injunction that was later vacated poses a difficult question of immunity. While the Court did not reach the question in Edgar v. MITE Corp., 457 U.S. 624 (1982), Justices Stevens and Marshall staked out different views in separate opinions. Neither opinion cited Oklahoma Operating Co. v. Love, 252 U.S. 331 (1920) (Brandeis, J.), where, in unanimously affirming the award of a preliminary injunction against allegedly confiscatory rate regulation, the Court said: "If upon final hearing the maximum rates fixed should be found not to be confiscatory, a permanent injunction should, nevertheless, issue to restrain enforcement of penalties accrued pendente lite, provided that it also be found that the plaintiff had reasonable ground to contest them as being confiscatory." See generally Morley, *Erroneous Injunctions*, 71 Emory L.J. 1137 (2022).

Both Steffel and Doran view federal plaintiffs as entitled to pursue federal relief without regard to the existence of pending state proceedings against related non-parties that present the same constitutional issue. Preclusion doctrine points in the same direction, rejecting concepts of virtual representation. In Taylor v. Sturgell, 553 U.S. 880 (2008), the Court rejected non-party preclusion except "at a minimum" where "[t]he interests of the nonparty and her representative are aligned" and "either the party understood herself to be acting in a representative capacity or the original court took care to protect the interests of the nonparty." *Id.* 900. The various bar owners in Doran engaged one lawyer but were said to exercise separate ownership and control. Compare County of Imperial v. Munoz, 449 U.S. 54 (1980), holding that the plaintiffs' federal action challenging on federal grounds a state court injunction against a different person was barred under the Anti-Injunction Act, 28 U.S.C. § 2283, unless the federal plaintiffs were "strangers to the state court proceeding." The Munoz Court used "stranger" as a term of art to refer to doctrines of privity that determine when the federal plaintiffs would be bound "as though [they were parties] to the litigation in the state court." The logic of Kline v. Burke Construction Company, 260 U.S. 226 (1922), p. 1362, *supra*, suggests that such issues should be resolved through application of claim preclusion rather than abstention doctrine.

(5) The Adequacy of State Court Defensive Vindication. The Court has refused to extend Younger abstention to claims in federal court that challenge aspects of the state criminal justice system that do not function as defenses to criminal liability. Thus, in Gerstein v. Pugh, 420 U.S. 103 (1975), the Court explained that a class action brought to contest the absence of a probable cause hearing did not implicate Younger: "The injunction was not directed at the state prosecutions as such, but only at the legality of pretrial detention without a judicial hearing, an issue that could not be raised in defense of the criminal prosecution." *Id.* 108 n.9. The same rule presumably applies to federal litigation that challenges the administration of bail and the conditions of confinement. See, *e.g.*, Pulliam v. Allen, 466 U.S. 522 (1984) (approving fee award in litigation challenging bond requirements that resulted in detention of impecunious defendants for non-jailable offenses).[7]

---

[7]   For a thorough consideration of the limits of Younger, see Smith, *Abstention in the Time of Ferguson*, 131 Harv.L.Rev. 2283 (2018). See also Traum, *Distributed Federalism: The Transformation of Younger*, 106 Cornell L.Rev. 1759 (2021).

Sprint Communications, Inc. v. Jacobs

571 U.S. 69 (2013).

Sprint Communications, Inc. (Sprint), a nationwide telecom, initiated two proceedings in Iowa, one before the Iowa Utilities Board (IUB) and one in federal court naming the IUB's officials as defendants. In both, Sprint argued that federal law preempted any requirement that it pay intrastate access charges for telephone calls transported to Iowa customers via the internet. The IUB ultimately rejected Sprint's claim of preemption and moved to dismiss the federal court proceeding as barred by the Younger doctrine. On review of an Eighth Circuit decision requiring Younger abstention, the Court reversed in a unanimous opinion by Justice Ginsburg.

The Court began by reaffirming the general rule that the pendency of overlapping state and federal proceedings does not ordinarily justify abstention. Acknowledging that it had applied Younger outside the criminal context to certain pending civil actions, the Court deliberately limited Younger to what it described as three "exceptional" categories identified in New Orleans Public Service, Inc. v. Council of City of New Orleans, 491 U.S. 350, 367–68 (1989) (NOPSI), p. 1389, *supra*: criminal proceedings, like those in Younger itself; certain "civil enforcement proceedings," such as those in Huffman v. Pursue, Ltd., 420 U.S. 592 (1975); and "civil proceedings involving certain orders . . . uniquely in furtherance of the state courts' ability to perform their judicial functions." Juidice v. Vail, 430 U.S. 327, 336, n.12 (1977); Pennzoil Co. v. Texaco, Inc., 481 U.S. 1, 13 (1987)). Apparently intent on warding off further expansion, the Court held that the three categories "define Younger's scope."

Dismissing categories one and three as plainly inapplicable, the Court considered whether the IUB proceeding would rank as an act of civil enforcement "akin to a criminal prosecution." The Court explained that such "enforcement actions are characteristically initiated to sanction the federal plaintiff, *i.e.*, the party challenging the state action, for some wrongful act. *E.g.*, Middlesex [County Ethics Comm'n v. Garden State Bar Ass'n], 457 U.S. [423,] 433–434 [(1982) (disciplinary proceedings against lawyer)]. In cases of this genre, a state actor is routinely a party to the state proceeding and often initiates the action. See, *e.g.*, Ohio Civil Rights Comm'n v. Dayton Christian Schools, Inc., 477 U.S. 619 (1986) (state-initiated administrative proceedings to enforce state civil rights laws); Moore v. Sims, 442 U.S. 415, 419–420 (1979) (state-initiated proceeding to gain custody of children allegedly abused by their parents); Trainor v. Hernandez, 431 U.S. 434, 444 (1977) (civil proceeding 'brought by the State in its sovereign capacity' to recover welfare payments defendants had allegedly obtained by fraud); Huffman, 420 U.S., at 598 (state-initiated proceeding to enforce obscenity laws). Investigations are commonly involved, often culminating in the filing of a formal complaint or charges.

"The IUB proceeding does not resemble the state enforcement actions this Court has found appropriate for Younger abstention. It is not 'akin to a criminal prosecution.' Nor was it initiated by 'the State in its sovereign capacity.' A private corporation, Sprint, initiated the action. No state authority conducted an investigation into Sprint's activities, and no state actor lodged a formal complaint against Sprint."

Relying on the Court's decision in Middlesex, the Eighth Circuit had viewed Younger abstention as warranted whenever three conditions are met: (1) "an ongoing state judicial proceeding, which (2) implicates important state interests, and (3) . . . provide[s] an adequate opportunity to raise [federal] challenges." But the Court explained that Middlesex, barring a federal court from entertaining a lawyer's challenge to a pending state ethics investigation, did not go so far. "Unlike the IUB proceeding here, the state ethics committee's hearing in Middlesex was indeed 'akin to a criminal proceeding.' As we noted, an investigation and formal complaint preceded the hearing, an agency of the State's Supreme Court initiated the hearing, and the purpose of the hearing was to determine whether the lawyer should be disciplined for his failure to meet the State's standards of professional conduct. 457 U.S., at 433–435. The three Middlesex conditions recited above were not dispositive; they were, instead, additional factors appropriately considered by the federal court before invoking Younger.

"Divorced from their quasi-criminal context, the three Middlesex conditions would extend Younger to virtually all parallel state and federal proceedings, at least where a party could identify a plausibly important state interest. That result is irreconcilable with our dominant instruction that, even in the presence of parallel state proceedings, abstention from the exercise of federal jurisdiction is the 'exception, not the rule.' Hawaii Housing Authority v. Midkiff, 467 U.S. 229, 236 (1984). In short, to guide other federal courts, we today clarify and affirm that Younger extends to the three 'exceptional circumstances' identified in NOPSI but no further."

NOTE ON YOUNGER'S EXTENSION TO CIVIL PROCEEDINGS

(1) **State Civil Enforcement Proceedings.** As Sprint suggests, the Court initially extended Younger abstention to state court civil proceedings of a quasi-criminal character. See Huffman v. Pursue, Ltd., 420 U.S. 592 (1975) (state court action to close adult bookstore as a nuisance); *cf.* Mitchum v. Foster, 407 U.S. 225 (1972) (same). The Court further extended the doctrine to state administrative proceedings of a coercive nature. See Middlesex County Ethics Comm'n v. Garden State Bar Ass'n, 457 U.S. 423 (1982) (state-initiated disciplinary proceedings against lawyer for violation of state ethics rules); Ohio Civil Rights Comm'n v. Dayton Christian Schools, Inc., 477 U.S. 619 (1986) (state-initiated administrative proceedings to enforce state civil rights laws).

Both Middlesex and Ohio Civil Rights found that § 1983 claims were foreclosed by the pendency of state administrative proceedings, raising questions about the Younger doctrine's interaction with the no-exhaustion rule of Patsy v. Board of Regents of the State of Florida, 457 U.S. 496 (1982), p. 1394, *supra*. In Ohio Civil Rights, the Court explained that, unlike Patsy, "the administrative proceedings here are coercive rather than remedial, began before any substantial advancement in the federal action took place, and involve an important state interest." The Court has thus articulated three different kinds of administrative proceedings: those of a remedial nature in Patsy (which § 1983 claimants need not exhaust); those of a legislative character in NOPSI (which must run their course before a judicial challenge may commence); and those of a coercive nature in Ohio Civil Rights (which may give rise to Younger abstention).

The line between the remedial proceedings in Patsy and the coercive proceedings in Ohio may prove hard to draw. Sprint's initial proceeding before the IUB sought to ward off a threat (by the Iowa Baby Bell, Windstream) to block all calls to Sprint's Iowa customers. When that threat was retracted, the IUB kept the proceeding alive to address the preemption issue, a decision to which it pointed in describing that proceeding as state-initiated. Yet the Sprint Court characterized the IUB proceeding as a civil dispute, rather than an enforcement proceeding. But many such disputes, carried to judgment, threaten enforcement of the resulting decree. In NOPSI, for example, the completion of the rate-making process would threaten the utility with coercive disallowance of any rate increases in excess of those allowed by state processes. Perhaps the punitive or quasi-criminal characterization of the proceeding in cases such as Huffman v. Pursue offers a more useful distinguishing construct than does coercive.

(2) State Executive Proceedings. In Rizzo v. Goode, 423 U.S. 362 (1976), a lawsuit under § 1983 charging the mayor and other high officials of the City of Philadelphia with responsibility for a wide variety of discriminatory and arbitrary police practices, the Supreme Court held that there was no justification for equitable relief against the named defendants, since there was no showing that they had themselves invaded or authorized any invasions of the plaintiffs' constitutional rights. The opinion then went on, quite unnecessarily, to suggest that "principles of federalism" would independently bar relief. After citing Doran v. Salem Inn, Inc., 422 U.S. 922 (1975), and Huffman v. Pursue, Ltd., 420 U.S. 592 (1975), the Court said: "[T]he principles of federalism which play such an important part in governing the relationship between federal courts and state governments, though initially expounded and perhaps entitled to their greatest weight in cases where it was sought to enjoin a criminal prosecution in progress * * * likewise have applicability where injunctive relief is sought, not against the judicial branch of the state government, but against those in charge of an executive branch of an agency of state or local governments such as petitioners here."[1] The Younger-based aspect of Rizzo conflicts with a long line of federal cases including Ex parte Young, 209 U.S. 123 (1908), and was apparently repudiated in Sprint's restriction of Younger-based abstention to three categories that did not encompass Rizzo.

(3) Orders Central to State Judicial Functions. As Sprint suggests, the Court has mandated abstention when confronting federal court challenges to "civil proceedings involving certain orders . . . uniquely in furtherance of the

---

[1] For criticisms of Rizzo, see Weinberg, *The New Judicial Federalism*, 29 Stan.L.Rev. 1191, 1219–27 (1977); Eisenberg & Yeazell, *The Ordinary and the Extraordinary in Institutional Litigation*, 93 Harv.L.Rev. 465, 503–06 (1980); Fiss, *Dombrowski*, 86 Yale L.J. 1103, 1159 (1977).

state courts' ability to perform their judicial functions." Thus, in Juidice v. Vail, 430 U.S. 327, 336 n.12 (1977), the Court refused to allow a federal court to adjudicate a challenge to the constitutionality of state contempt proceedings. Similarly, in Pennzoil Co. v. Texaco Inc., 481 U.S. 1, 13 (1987), the Court rejected a federal court challenge to the state's requirement that appellants post an appeal bond as a condition of securing review of a challenged judgment. Consider if the Sprint Court's decision to foreclose further expansion of the civil-Younger doctrine limits the growing power of this abstention category.

CHAPTER XI

FEDERAL HABEAS CORPUS

1. INTRODUCTION

INTRODUCTORY NOTE ON THE FUNCTION OF THE WRIT

The writ of *habeas corpus ad subjiciendum*—what Blackstone described as a "bulwark of our liberties" and many have called the Great Writ[1]—has enjoyed celebrated status in the common law tradition for centuries. It played an historic part in the English struggle with royal prerogative,[2] and in the lead up to the American Revolutionary War, the Continental Congress declared that the habeas privilege and trial by jury were rights "without which a people cannot be free and happy * * *."[3] The writ's underlying premise is that only legal authority can justify detention. Thus, an individual whose liberty is restrained may file a petition seeking issuance of the writ, and thereby require a custodian to respond in court and justify the restraint as lawful. If that justification cannot be made, the court will order the discharge of the petitioner.[4]

---

[1] 1 Blackstone Commentaries 133. Translated loosely, the writ of *habeas corpus ad subjiciendum* means "to undergo and receive" the corpus, or body, of the person detained. Other forms of the writ of habeas corpus at common law were: (1) *ad respondendum* (to remove a person confined by process of an inferior court to answer to an action in a higher court); (2) *ad satisfaciendum* (to remove one imprisoned to a higher court to be charged with process of execution); (3) *ad prosequendum, testificandum, deliberandum* (to remove one imprisoned to enable prosecution, testimony, or trial in the proper jurisdiction); and (4) *ad faciendum et recipiendum* (to remove a cause at the behest of one imprisoned from an inferior court to Westminster). 3 Blackstone, *supra*, at 129–132.

[2] The most elaborate explication of this struggle is found in Halliday, Habeas Corpus: From England to Empire (2010). See also Tyler, Habeas Corpus in Wartime: From the Tower of London to Guantanamo Bay (2017); Duker, A Constitutional History of Habeas Corpus (1980); Walker, The Constitutional and Legal Development of Habeas Corpus as the Writ of Liberty (1960); Farbey, Sharpe & Atrill, The Law of Habeas Corpus (3d ed.2011). For other sources, see 1 Hertz & Liebman, Federal Habeas Corpus Practice & Procedure § 2.3, at 22 n.1 (6th ed.2011).

[3] [1774] 1 Journals of the Continental Congress 1774–1789, at 108 (Ford ed. 1904).

[4] Professor Halliday, note 2, *supra,* provides a rich account of the writ from 1500–1800. He notes that by 1605, the writ had become "fundamentally an instrument of judicial power derived from the king's prerogative, a power more concerned with the wrongs of jailers than with the rights of prisoners." Thus, the Court of King's Bench could act on behalf of the king in "demand[ing] an account for his subject who is restrained of his liberty." Halliday's other themes with particular relevance to this Chapter include: (1) the King's Bench used procedural innovations in "transform[ing] habeas corpus * * * into an instrument for controlling other jurisdictions"; (2) the writ was not limited to citizens but was available to individuals who came under the King's protection; (3) courts administering the writ had power over people, not places, and the common law writ could follow those subject to the King's protection wherever they traveled, limited only by the practicalities created by distance; (4) though not strictly an equitable writ, habeas was administered equitably to do justice; and (5) although a petitioner could not challenge the factual accuracy of the return (the custodian's response to a petition),

Legend ties the origins of the writ of habeas corpus to Chapter 39 of Magna Carta.[5] Important events then occurred in the evolution of the writ in England during the seventeenth century. Under the reign of Charles I, the writ had failed to check summary executive detention, including in the "Case of the Five Knights," which involved five nobles who had refused to loan Charles I funds to enable him to continue fighting the Thirty Years' War. The king ordered the nobles arrested and imprisoned. The Court of King's Bench declined to act on the nobles' habeas petitions, leaving the crown's justification for the detention—that the nobles were being held by the special command of the king—unquestioned. Instead, the court told the petitioners that to win their freedom, their only option was to ask the King for "mercy." Darnel's Case (1627) 3 Cobbett's St. Tr. 1 (Eng.).[6] In the decades that followed, those in power increasingly employed the practice of sending persons taken into custody to "legal islands"—whether true islands or the Tower of London—to escape the writ's reach.

In response, Parliament enacted a series of habeas statutes, culminating in the English Habeas Corpus Act of 1679, all to the end of wrestling greater legislative control of the law governing executive detention and judicial deployment of the writ. Parliament declared the Act was "[f]or the prevention whereof and the more speedy Releife of all persons imprisoned for any such criminall or supposed criminall Matters." 31 Car. II, c. 2. Among its many provisions responding to the abuses of the preceding decades, the Act's seventh section provided that where the crown did not indict "any person or persons * * * committed for High Treason or Fellony" within two courts terms (a period typically spanning three to six months), the justices of King's Bench and other criminal courts were "required * * * to sett at Liberty the Prisoner upon Baile." To bolster its application, the Act's

---

judges nonetheless found ways to ascertain additional information not found in the return. Over time, he argues, the writ came to be viewed as a protection of individual liberty. See also Freedman, *Habeas Corpus in Three Dimensions, Dimension I: Habeas Corpus as a Common Law Writ*, 46 Harv.C.R.-C.L.L.Rev. 591 (2011) (arguing that in the colonial and early national period, demands for release from unlawful custody were made through habeas corpus and through a variety of other common law writs).

Litman, *The Myth of the Great Writ*, 100 Tex.L.Rev. 219 (2021), ties aspects of the writ's function during the nineteenth century to Halliday's account of it as "an instrument for seizing and building power and control, not solely for constraining it." Professor Litman argues that when studying the writ's historical role in the American legal system, one must avoid oversimplifying it as a "great writ of liberty" and confront the ways that courts and other actors wielded the writ "to discriminate on the bases of race and citizenship and to legitimate government power" over historically subordinated groups. See *id.* (exploring case studies in immigration, Native American affairs, and the law of slavery and freedom).

[5]   Chapter 39 declared, "No free man shall be taken or imprisoned or dispossessed, or outlawed, or banished, or in any way destroyed * * * except by the legal judgment of his peers or by the law of the land." Great Charter of Liberties, ch. 39 (1215), reprinted in Select Documents of English Constitutional History 42, 47 (Adams & Stephens eds. 1904). In the seventeenth century, Sir Edward Coke connected Chapter 39 with the writ, writing, "Now it may be demanded, if a man be taken, or committed to prison *contra legem terrae*, against the law of the land, what remedy hath the party grieved?" To this he answered, "He may have an *habeas corpus.*" Coke, The Second Part of the Institutes of the Laws of England (1628).

[6]   For more details, see Halliday, note 2, *supra*; Kishlansky, *Tyranny Denied: Charles I, Attorney General Heath, and the Five Knights' Case*, 42 Hist.J. 53 (1999); Guy, *The Origins of the Petition of Right Reconsidered*, 25 Hist.J. 289 (1982).

tenth section threatened judges with financial penalties for violating the Act's terms.[7]

Just ten years later during the Glorious Revolution, however, Parliament temporarily displaced the Act in the first of what would be many acts of suspension over the course of the next century. Parliament entitled the first such legislation "An Act for Impowering His Majestie to Apprehend and Detaine such Persons as He shall finde just Cause to Suspect are Conspireing against the Government." 1688, 1 W. & M., c. 2. By its terms, the suspension set aside "the Benefitt and Advantage" of the Habeas Corpus Act of 1679. As Professor Halliday's work documents, waves of arrests followed under the suspensions enacted during this period.[8]

The founding generation was well aware of the writ's English history. Among other things, Parliament had suspended application of the English Habeas Corpus Act to American "Rebels" detained on English soil during the American Revolutionary War. 17 Geo. 3, c. 9 (1777). Many states, meanwhile, moved during the founding period to adopt the English Habeas Corpus Act's terms as their own, and many in turn suspended its application in response to British threats during the Revolutionary War.[9] Informed by this backdrop, the founding generation adopted the Constitution's Suspension Clause, Article I, sec. 9, cl. 2, which provides: "The Privilege of the Writ of Habeas Corpus shall not be suspended, unless when in Cases of Rebellion or Invasion the public Safety may require it."

The Supreme Court has often declared that "[t]o ascertain its meaning and the appropriate use of the writ in the federal courts, recourse must be had to the common law, from which the term was drawn, and to the decisions of this Court interpretating and applying th[ose] common law principles." McNally v. Hill, 293 U.S. 131, 136 (1934). The Court also has pointed specifically to the writ's "use" as "defined and regulated by the Habeas Corpus Act of 1679, 31 Car. II, c. 2. This legislation and the decisions of the English courts interpreting it have been accepted by this Court as authoritative guides in defining the principles which control the use of the writ in the federal courts." *Id.* See also Ex parte Watkins, 28 U.S. (3 Pet.) 193, 202 (1830)[10]; Ex parte Yerger, 75 U.S. (8 Wall.) 85, 95 (1868), p. 419, *supra* (observing that the writ "guaranteed" by the 1679 Act "was brought to America by the colonists, and claimed as among the immemorial rights descended to them from their ancestors").

---

[7]   For details on the Habeas Corpus Act of 1679, see Halliday, note 2, *supra*; Nutting, *The Most Wholesome Law—The Habeas Corpus Act of 1679*, 65 Am.Hist.Rev. 527 (1960); Tyler, *A "Second Magna Carta": The English Habeas Corpus Act and the Statutory Origins of the Habeas Privilege*, 91 Notre Dame L.Rev. 1949 (2016).

[8]   See Halliday, note 2, *supra*; see also Tyler, note 2, *supra*, at 35–61.

[9]   For more details, see Tyler, note 2, *supra*, at 63–121.

[10]   Chief Justice Marshall explained the importance of the Act in Watkins: "The English judges, being originally under the influence of the crown, neglected to issue th[e] writ where the government entertained suspicions which could not be sustained by evidence; and the writ when issued was sometimes disregarded or evaded, and great individual oppression was suffered in consequence of delays in bringing prisoners to trial. To remedy this evil the celebrated *habeas corpus* act of the 31st of Charles II. was enacted, for the purpose of securing the benefits for which the writ was given." 28 U.S. (3 Pet.) 193, 202 (1830).

Today, the most common use of federal habeas corpus is as a post-conviction remedy for incarcerated persons claiming that an error of federal law—almost always of constitutional law—infected the criminal judicial proceedings that resulted in detention. But post-conviction relief was not the original office of habeas corpus, which focused instead on whether extrajudicial detention—most often by the executive—was authorized by law. In recent decades, the original office of the writ has regained prominence in connection with the government's detention of so-called "enemy combatants" following the terrorist attacks of September 11, 2001.

Other uses of the writ include challenges to (i) the legality of detention (including confinement, exclusion, and deportation) in immigration matters, see Paragraph (2), p. 464, *supra*; (ii) the holding of individuals for military service, the conduct of trials before military commissions,[11] and the relocation and detention of Japanese Americans during World War II;[12] (iii) the determination of preliminary matters in criminal cases, involving, for example, the sufficiency of cause for detention on the basis of a criminal complaint[13] or for removal to another federal district,[14] the legality of interstate rendition[15] or of extradition to a foreign country,[16] the denial of bail,[17] the failure to provide a prompt post-arrest hearing[18] or a speedy trial,[19] or a claim under the Double Jeopardy Clause;[20] and (iv) according to some authorities, the legality of conditions of confinement.[21] Historically, the writ also served as a vehicle by which enslaved persons could win their freedom[22] and as a tool of abolitionists to protect fugitive enslaved persons from federal authority, at least until Ableman v. Booth, 62 (21 How.) U.S. 506 (1859).[23] In cases potentially falling within the scope of the writ, habeas

---

[11]   See, *e.g.*, Ex parte Quirin, 317 U.S. 1 (1942), p. 554, *infra*; Ex parte Milligan, 71 U.S. (4 Wall.) 2 (1866), p. 553, *infra*.

[12]   See Ex parte Endo, 323 U.S. 283 (1944), p. 1500, *infra*.

[13]   See, *e.g.*, Ex parte Bollman, 8 U.S. (4 Cranch) 75 (1807), p. 1465, *infra*. See also Jurney v. MacCracken, 294 U.S. 125 (1935) (power of Senate to order arrest for contempt of a committee).

[14]   See, *e.g.*, Tinsley v. Treat, 205 U.S. 20 (1907); United States ex rel. Kassin v. Mulligan, 295 U.S. 396 (1935).

[15]   See, *e.g.*, Roberts v. Reilly, 116 U.S. 80 (1885); Biddinger v. Commissioner of Police, 245 U.S. 128 (1917). But *cf.* Sweeney v. Woodall, 344 U.S. 86 (1952) (person escaped from prison).

[16]   See, *e.g.*, Fernandez v. Phillips, 268 U.S. 311 (1925); Factor v. Laubenheimer, 290 U.S. 276 (1933).

[17]   This historical use of habeas has been displaced, in the federal courts, by the statutory right to apply for bail, see 18 U.S.C. §§ 3142, 3144; Fed.R.Crim.Proc. 46, and the right to move in court for a reduction of excessive bail, see Stack v. Boyle, 342 U.S. 1 (1951).

[18]   See, *e.g.*, Gerstein v. Pugh, 420 U.S. 103 (1975).

[19]   See, *e.g.*, Braden v. 30th Judicial Cir. Ct., 410 U.S. 484 (1973), pp. 1503, 1665, *infra*.

[20]   See Justices of Boston Municipal Ct. v. Lydon, 466 U.S. 294 (1984), p. 1664, *infra*.

[21]   The Supreme Court has not resolved whether a person in custody can challenge conditions of confinement in a habeas petition or exclusively via a claim brought under 42 U.S.C. § 1983. See Ziglar v. Abbasi, 582 U.S. 120, 144–45 (2017). For discussion, see p. 1694, *infra*.

[22]   Somerset v. Stewart, (1772) 98 Engl.Rep. 499 (K.B.), 1 Lofft.1.

[23]   See, *e.g.*, Morris, Free Men All: The Personal Liberty Laws of the North, 1780–1861 (1974). This being said, the writ was also employed to the end of keeping enslaved persons in bondage, see Neeley, The Fate of Liberty: Abraham Lincoln and Civil Liberties (1991), and the Fugitive Slave Act of 1850, which provided for expedited proceedings for returning fugitive enslaved persons to the states from which they had fled, undermined the writ's use as a tool of

review may not be available where a distinct and adequate form of judicial review has been provided.[24]

This chapter first offers an overview of the historical development of the statutory governance of habeas corpus in the federal courts. Section 2 explores many questions surrounding the scope and use of habeas corpus in the context of extrajudicial detention by the executive. Finally, Section 3 explores analogous questions as they arise in the context of federal and state court post-conviction review of federal and state criminal convictions.

NOTE ON THE JURISDICTIONAL STATUTES

(1) The First Judiciary Act. Section 14 of the First Judiciary Act (1 Stat. 81–82) provided:

"That all the before-mentioned courts of the United States, shall have power to issue writs of *scire facias*, *habeas corpus*, and all other writs not specially provided for by statute, which may be necessary for the exercise of their respective jurisdictions, and agreeable to the principles and usages of law. And that either of the justices of the supreme court, as well as judges of the district courts, shall have power to grant writs of *habeas corpus* for the purpose of an inquiry into the cause of commitment.—*Provided*, That writs of *habeas corpus* shall in no case extend to prisoners in gaol, unless where they are in custody, under or by colour of the authority of the United States, or are committed for trial before some court of the same, or are necessary to be brought into court to testify."

(2) Ex parte Bollman. Section 14 came before the Court in Ex parte Bollman, 8 U.S. (4 Cranch) 75 (1807), also discussed at pp. 355–358, 362–364, *supra*. Military officials arrested Bollman and Swartwout, two individuals linked to Aaron Burr's expedition in the Louisiana Territory in 1805–1806, in New Orleans and then transported them to military detention in Washington, D.C. After the two filed habeas petitions and one day after suspension legislation failed in the House, the U.S. Attorney obtained an arrest warrant from the U.S. Circuit Court for the District of Columbia to have the two committed to stand trial for treason. Bollman and Swartwout then petitioned the Supreme Court, which issued the writ, finding the existing evidence of treason insufficient to support the charges.[1] Chief Justice Marshall's opinion included several important rulings concerning the habeas jurisdiction.

---

abolitionists. See also Litman, note 4, *supra*; Arkin, *The Ghost at the Banquet: Slavery, Federalism, and Habeas Corpus for State Prisoners*, 70 Tulane L.Rev. 1 (1995).

[24] See note 17, *supra*.

[1] The Court declined to rule out that "fresh proceedings" could be initiated upon stronger evidence. For more background, see Tyler, Habeas Corpus in Wartime: From the Tower of London to Guantanamo Bay 145–55 (2017). Ex parte Bollman came on the heels of Ex parte Burford, 7 U.S. (3 Cranch) 448, 450–53 (1806). Burford had been detained as "an evil doer and disturber of the peace" in the absence of formal criminal charges. The Court explained that to determine "what authority * * * the jailor [has] to detain him * * * we must look to the warrant of commitment only." Because Burford's warrant "state[d] no offence," the Court concluded it "was illegal" and Burford should be discharged from custody.

First, he rejected the view that § 14 authorized issuance of the writ only as an auxiliary to jurisdiction otherwise conferred. Instead, he read § 14 as authorizing an independent action in habeas corpus. (The opinion held the power expressly conferred on the *justices* and *judges* to be vested in the courts by implication.)

Second, he declared that when (as in Bollman) a petitioner applies for the writ directly in the Supreme Court, the Court may use the writ as a means of reviewing the legality of a commitment ordered by a lower federal court. This was held to be an exercise of *appellate* jurisdiction, thus avoiding any difficulty under Marbury v. Madison's holding that Congress may not expand the scope of the Supreme Court's *original* jurisdiction.[2]

Finally, Chief Justice Marshall stated that the jurisdiction of the federal courts to issue the writ is not an "inherent" power but must be conferred by statute. At the same time, the opinion in Bollman stated: "Acting under the immediate influence of [the Suspension Clause, the members of the First Congress] must have felt, with peculiar force, the obligation of providing efficient means by which this great constitutional privilege should receive life and activity; for if the means be not in existence, the privilege itself would be lost, although no law for its suspension should be enacted. Under the impression of this obligation, they give, to all the courts, the power of awarding writs of *habeas corpus*."

Commentators have offered a range of criticisms of Bollman's conclusion that the federal courts lack inherent power to issue the writ.[3] And tension exists between Bollman's insistence that jurisdiction be granted by statute

---

[2]   The view that the Supreme Court had a duty to inquire into the cause of commitment, Ex parte Yarbrough, 110 U.S. 651, 653 (1884), gave way, by the time of Ex parte Abernathy, 320 U.S. 219, 220 (1943), to the view that "this Court does not, save in exceptional circumstances, exercise [jurisdiction] in cases where an adequate remedy may be had in" a different court. The current Sup.Ct.R. 20.4(a) states: "To justify the granting of a writ of habeas corpus, the petitioner must show that exceptional circumstances warrant the exercise of the Court's discretionary powers, and that adequate relief cannot be obtained in any other form or from any other court. This writ is rarely granted."

Since 1900, the Court appears to have granted relief in only three cases involving direct recourse to its habeas jurisdiction. See Ex parte Grossman, 267 U.S. 87 (1925); Ex parte Hudgings, 249 U.S. 378 (1919); In re Heff, 197 U.S. 488 (1905). See also In re Davis, 557 U.S. 952 (2009) (transferring a petition for an original writ of habeas jurisdiction, filed in the Supreme Court, to a district court). See generally Felker v. Turpin, 518 U.S. 651 (1996), p. 1577, *infra*; Oaks, *The "Original" Writ of Habeas Corpus in the Supreme Court*, 1962 Sup.Ct.Rev. 153.

[3]   See, *e.g.*, Freedman, *Just Because John Marshall Said It Doesn't Make It So: Ex parte Bollman and the Illusory Prohibition on the Federal Writ of Habeas Corpus for State Prisoners in the Judiciary Act of 1789*, 51 Ala.L.Rev. 531 (2000) (reading the ratification debates as assuming that all courts had power to issue the writ); Paschal, *The Constitution and Habeas Corpus*, 1970 Duke L.J. 605 (arguing that § 14 merely ratified a court's power to employ habeas corpus in aid of jurisdiction otherwise conferred and that the Suspension Clause directs the courts to make habeas available); Neuman, *The Habeas Corpus Suspension Clause After INS v. St. Cyr*, 33 Colum.Hum.Rts.L.Rev. 555, 580–81 (2002) (contending the Constitution obliges Congress to provide some means through which the writ can be made available); Halliday & White, *The Suspension Clause: English Text, Imperial Contexts, and American Implications*, 94 Va.L.Rev. 575, 683–98 (2008) (questioning Bollman's denial that federal courts possess common law habeas jurisdiction). If Professors Fallon and Meltzer are correct that the Constitution "presupposed a going legal system, with ample remedial mechanisms," Fallon & Meltzer, *New Law, Non-Retroactivity, and Constitutional Remedies*, 104 Harv.L.Rev. 1731, 1779 (1991), wouldn't it be odd to read the Suspension Clause as not promising a habeas privilege be available in some court? See also pp. 1471–1474, *infra*.

and the apparent presupposition of the Suspension Clause that (absent a congressional act of suspension) habeas corpus review would be available. Some two hundred years later, in Boumediene v. Bush, 553 U.S. 723 (2008), the Supreme Court embraced the view that the Suspension Clause itself affirmatively confers a right to habeas corpus review in some circumstances, even when Congress has not conferred statutory jurisdiction. See pp. 464–471, *supra,* 1471–1474, *infra.*

(3) Legislation Before the Civil War. Section 14 reached only persons held in *federal* custody. Subsequent enactments extended the federal courts' power to small categories of individuals held in *state* custody.[4]

(a) The Force Act of 1833, countering South Carolina's resistance to the "Tariff of Abominations," conferred power to grant writs when persons were confined "for any act done, or omitted to be done, in pursuance of a law of the United States, or any order, process, or decree, of any judge or court thereof, any thing in any act of Congress to the contrary notwithstanding." Section 7, 4 Stat. 634–35.

(b) Nine years later, following British protests that the New York murder trial of a Canadian soldier violated the law of nations (the homicide was claimed to be an act of state),[5] Congress vested the federal courts with power to grant writs in certain cases involving "subjects or citizens of a foreign State, and domiciled therein" in the custody "of the United States, or of any one of them." Act of Aug. 29, 1842, 5 Stat. 539–40.

(4) The Act of 1867. The most significant expansion of the writ—to encompass generally persons in *state* custody—came during Reconstruction with the Act of February 5, 1867, 14 Stat. 385. It conferred power on all federal courts, and the judges and Justices thereof, "within their respective jurisdictions, * * * to grant writs of habeas corpus in all cases where any person may be restrained of his or her liberty in violation of the constitution, or of any treaty or law of the United States," whether held in federal or in state custody.[6]

(5) The 1948 Revision. The foregoing provisions survived without important change until 1948, when they were codified in 28 U.S.C. §§ 2241–2255. The revision placed the general grant of habeas corpus jurisdiction to the federal courts in § 2241, without significantly altering the bases for challenging the lawfulness of custody. But the revision did effect some procedural changes;[7] established a new provision (§ 2254) addressing

---

[4] In addition, the Bankruptcy Act of 1800 authorized federal courts exercising bankruptcy jurisdiction to issue writs of habeas corpus to state officials ordering the release of debtors arrested after having received a discharge in bankruptcy. See Act of Apr. 4, 1800, ch. 19, § 38, 2 Stat. 19, 31.

[5] See People v. McLeod, 25 Wend. 483 (N.Y. 1841); 2 Warren, The Supreme Court in United States History 98 (rev.ed.1947).

[6] Decisions under each of the foregoing statutory formulations are collected in 18 Fed. 68 (1884). For further discussion of the 1867 Act, see p. 1555, *infra.*

[7] Unlike prior law, the 1948 revision, without explanation, did not authorize district judges (as distinguished from courts) to issue the writ. Compare 28 U.S.C. § 452 (1940). The courts of appeals (as distinguished from their judges) have never had such authority, see Whitney v. Dick, 202 U.S. 132 (1906), except under the "all writs" provision, 28 U.S.C. § 1651, in aid of appellate jurisdiction in a pending case, see, *e.g.*, Price v. Johnston, 334 U.S. 266 (1948).

specifically challenges to custody resulting from conviction in state court; and gave statutory recognition to the judge-made rule requiring exhaustion of state remedies prior to seeking the writ, see § 2254(b–c), p. 1662, *infra*. In addition, the revision created, in § 2255, a new statutory motion for those incarcerated by the federal government for collaterally attacking their convictions, which is similar in substance but different in form from a habeas petition. See generally Sec. 3(B), *infra*.

(6) The Antiterrorism and Effective Death Penalty Act of 1996. The structure established in 1948 remained in effect, with only minor changes,[8] until, in the wake of the 1995 bombing of the Oklahoma City Federal Building, Congress passed the Antiterrorism and Effective Death Penalty Act of 1996 (AEDPA), 110 Stat. 1214. AEDPA contains numerous provisions restricting the availability of the writ in post-conviction cases.[9] One of its most important provisions, codified in § 2254(d)(1), states that habeas relief cannot be awarded to a person in state custody solely because a federal court disagrees with the state court's application of established constitutional principles to the particular case; rather, relief may be issued only when the state court determination was "contrary to, or involved an unreasonable application of, clearly established Federal law, as determined by the Supreme Court of the United States." In addition, AEDPA sharply narrows the power of federal habeas courts to conduct evidentiary hearings, to disregard factfindings made in state court, and to entertain multiple petitions from a single petitioner. The Act also established, for the first time, a statute of limitations (of one year) governing collateral attacks by those in both state and federal custody. §§ 2244(d), 2255(f).[10] The provisions added by AEDPA are discussed throughout Section 3, *infra*.

(7) The Detainee Treatment Act of 2005 and the Military Commissions Act of 2006. Following the 9/11 attacks, Congress modified the habeas corpus jurisdiction as it applies to suspected terrorists. The first legislation, the Detainee Treatment Act of 2005 (DTA), 119 Stat. 2739, codified at 10 U.S.C. § 801 note, precluded, subject to limited exceptions, federal court review of habeas petitions brought on behalf of an alien detained at Guantanamo Bay as an enemy combatant. See *id*. § 1005(e)(1).

The following year, § 7(a) of the Military Commissions Act of 2006 (MCA of 2006), Pub.L.No. 109–366, 120 Stat. 2600, significantly broadened the DTA such that § 2241(e) now reads:

> "(e)(1)   No court, justice, or judge shall have jurisdiction to hear or consider an application for a writ of habeas corpus filed by or on behalf of an alien detained by the United States who has been

---

[8]   In 1966, Congress added §§ 2244(b–c) (further specifying the effect of previous federal adjudications on a federal habeas petition) and § 2254(d) (providing that state court factfindings made in a procedurally fair manner must be treated as presumptively correct).

[9]   See generally Yackle, *A Primer on the New Habeas Corpus Statute*, 44 Buff.L.Rev. 381 (1996); Tushnet & Yackle, *Symbolic Statutes and Real Laws: The Pathologies of the Antiterrorism and Effective Death Penalty Act and the Prison Litigation Reform Act*, 47 Duke L.J. 1 (1997).

[10]   AEDPA also includes provisions designed to speed adjudication of capital cases, see 28 U.S.C. §§ 2261–2266; pp. 1553–1555, *infra*, along with provisions relating to immigration removal proceedings, see pp. 1542–1546, *infra*.

determined by the United States to have been properly detained as an enemy combatant or is awaiting such determination.

"(2) Except as provided in paragraphs (2) and (3) of section 1005(e) of the [DTA], no court, justice, or judge shall have jurisdiction to hear or consider any other action against the United States or its agents relating to any aspect of the detention, transfer, treatment, trial, or conditions of confinement of an alien who is or was detained by the United States and has been determined by the United States to have been properly detained as an enemy combatant or is awaiting such determination."

The DTA provisions incorporated into § 2241(e) granted the D.C. Circuit jurisdiction (exclusive of all other courts) to entertain actions by aliens detained at Guantanamo Bay in two circumstances.

(a) Review of Enemy Combatant Status. First, the D.C. Circuit had "jurisdiction to determine the validity of any final decision of a Combatant Status Review Tribunal that an alien is properly detained as an enemy combatant," so long as the alien was still detained when review was sought. DTA § 1005(e)(2)(A–B). (A Combatant Status Review Tribunal (CSRT) is a panel of three military officers. See p. 1506, *infra*.) The provision in turn authorized the court of appeals to review (i) whether a CSRT's status determination complies with standards and procedures adopted by the Secretary of Defense for CSRTs and (ii) if the Constitution applies, whether such standards and procedures are constitutional. DTA § 1005(e)(2)(C).

In Boumediene v. Bush, p. 1507, *infra*, the Supreme Court ruled that the combined effect of the DTA and MCA violated the Suspension Clause and hence aliens detained at Guantanamo Bay as enemy combatants were constitutionally entitled to file a petition for a writ of habeas corpus.[11]

(b) Review of Military Commission Proceedings. The DTA also gave the D.C. Circuit jurisdiction to review a "final" decision of a military commission convened to try a war crime prosecution, with a scope of review similar to that for review of CSRT determinations.[12] DTA § 1005(e)(3). Congress replaced this provision in the Military Commissions Act of 2009, discussed in the next paragraph.

(8) The Military Commissions Act of 2009. The Military Commissions Act of 2009 (MCA of 2009) amended the 2006 Act in a variety of ways, one of which was to establish a new system of post-conviction review of military commission proceedings that replaced the system established under the

---

[11] In Kiyemba v. Obama, 561 F.3d 509 (D.C.Cir.2009), the D.C. Circuit ruled that Boumediene had invalidated § 2241(e)(1)'s effort to limit habeas petitions with respect to all claims by persons detained at Guantanamo. The D.C. Circuit also held, however, that § 2241(e)(2)'s jurisdictional limits remain in effect in non-habeas actions. See Al-Zahrani v. Rodriguez, 669 F.3d 315 (D.C.Cir.2012) (statute precludes jurisdiction over claims brought by survivors of persons detained at Guantanamo under Alien Tort Claims Act, Federal Tort Claims Act, and Fifth and Eighth Amendments); see also Ameur v. Gates, 759 F.3d 317 (4th Cir.2014) (statute precludes claims brought by plaintiff formerly detained at Guantanamo predicated upon allegations of abuse and torture).

[12] Initially, the DTA granted review as of right only in cases of capital punishment or imprisonment of at least 10 years; otherwise, review was within the discretion of the D.C. Circuit. A 2006 amendment made all review as of right. See MCA of 2006, § 9(2).

DTA. See 10 U.S.C. §§ 950a–950j. A defendant convicted by a military commission may first seek review before the Defense Department's Convening Authority, after which defendants have a right to appellate review—unusually, of fact as well as of law—by the United States Court of Military Commission Review, an Article I court.[13] Thereafter, review by an Article III court is available in the D.C. Circuit, which has jurisdiction "only with respect to matters of law, including the sufficiency of the evidence to support the verdict." Finally, the Act permits certiorari review in the Supreme Court.[14]

Certain aspects of the 2006 MCA's amendments to the habeas statute have continuing relevance. Section 5(a) of the 2006 MCA expressly precludes litigants from relying on the Geneva Conventions and their protocols as a source of rights in any civil action (specifically including a habeas corpus action) against the United States or its officials.[15] And because the 2009 MCA did not purport to amend 28 U.S.C. § 2241(e), discussed at p. 1468, *supra*, its preclusion of specified actions remains, to the extent allowed by the Constitution. For example, after Boumediene, it remains unclear whether some habeas petitions filed on behalf of aliens detained abroad may be precluded by § 2241(e)(1), see Paragraph (3), p. 1528, *infra*; likewise, actions complaining, *e.g.*, about conditions of confinement may be barred by § 2241(e)(2).

---

2. HABEAS CORPUS AND EXECUTIVE DETENTION

NOTE ON THE SUSPENSION CLAUSE OF THE CONSTITUTION

A. Introduction

The Suspension Clause (Art. I, § 9, cl. 2) provides: "The Privilege of the Writ of Habeas Corpus shall not be suspended, unless when in Cases of Rebellion or Invasion the public Safety may require it."[1] That the original Constitution included this Clause testifies that the founding generation viewed the writ as an established and fundamental guarantee of liberty.

Records from the Convention and ratification debates reveal a few clues as to the Clause's meaning but also leave many questions unresolved. The Convention delegates originally placed the draft habeas clause in the

---

[13] The appellate panels of that court have at least three military judges, but can have additional military or civilian judges; the latter are appointed by the President with the advice and consent of the Senate.

[14] The 2009 Act repealed a provision of the 2006 Act—former 10 U.S.C. § 950j(b)—which had restricted the availability of habeas jurisdiction for persons prosecuted under the Military Commissions Act.

[15] Compare the general provision in § 2241(c), providing that habeas jurisdiction does not exist unless the petitioner alleges "custody in violation of the Constitution or laws or treaties of the United States."

[1] On the significance of the reference to the "Privilege of the Writ" rather than simply the Writ itself, see Ex parte Milligan, 71 U.S. (4 Wall.) 2, 130–31 (1866) (dictum).

Judiciary Article alongside the guarantee of a jury trial in criminal proceedings.[2] Also, during the debates, some states objected to recognition of any power to suspend habeas; they were, in the end, outnumbered. Subsequently, some participants in the ratification debates feared the suspension power could be wielded to illegitimate ends, such as to entrench political power. At the same time, both critics and supporters of the draft Constitution lauded the role of the Suspension Clause as a font of liberty. The Anti-Federalist publication the Federal Farmer, for example, pointed to the Clause and its neighboring provisions as a "partial bill of rights."[3] Hamilton, meanwhile, asserted that there was no need for further enumeration of individual rights, in part because the Constitution provided for "trial by jury in criminal cases, aided by the *habeas corpus act*."[4]

The wording of the Clause presents a puzzle, since it appears to presuppose the existence of habeas corpus jurisdiction without affirmatively guaranteeing a right to habeas corpus—a failing to which four of the state ratifying conventions objected. See Collings, *Habeas Corpus for Convicts— Constitutional Right or Legislative Grace?*, 40 Calif.L.Rev. 335, 340–41 (1952).[5] And Ex parte Bollman, p. 1465, *supra*, held that the federal courts' habeas jurisdiction must be given by statute. Since enactment of the Judiciary Act of 1789, however, Congress has affirmatively vested habeas corpus jurisdiction in the federal courts, and in 1867 Congress broadened the jurisdiction to embrace individuals in state as well as federal custody. Consequently, for two centuries, the Supreme Court was not required to address what power, if any, the federal courts could exercise by virtue of the Suspension Clause in the absence of statutory habeas jurisdiction.

Matters changed as a result of legislation enacted in 1996, 2005–2006, and 2009, which either withdrew habeas corpus jurisdiction over a particular set of cases or could be interpreted as having done so.

B. The Suspension Clause as an Affirmative Guarantee of Judicial Review

(1) Immigration and the St. Cyr Decision. In INS v. St. Cyr, 533 U.S. 289 (2001), Paragraph (2), p. 464, *supra*, the Immigration and Naturalization Service ordered St. Cyr to be removed from the United States. Provisions of 1996 amendments to the immigration laws broadly precluded recourse to state or federal court to challenge the legality of the INS's actions, and the

---

[2]   The Committee on Style later moved the Clause to its present location in Article I as part of the stylistic reworking of the entire draft.

[3]   The pamphlet argued that the draft should go further in enumerating rights. Letter IV from the Federal Farmer to the Republican, Oct. 12, 1787.

[4]   The Federalist, No. 83 (Hamilton). Citing Hamilton and others, Tyler, Habeas Corpus in Wartime: From the Tower of London to Guantanamo Bay (2017), surveys the Convention and ratification debates to conclude that "a wealth of evidence from this period demonstrates that in the Suspension Clause, the founding generation sought to constitutionalize the protections associated with the seventh section of the English Habeas Corpus Act and import the English suspension model, while also severely limiting the circumstances when the suspension power could be invoked." For additional discussion, see Paragraph (4), p. 1495, *infra*.

[5]   Paschal, *The Constitution and Habeas Corpus*, 1970 Duke L.J. 605, reads the negative phraseology as "only a circumlocution to propose a suspending power in the least offensive way" and asserts that the Clause "is a direction to all superior courts of record, state as well as federal, to make the habeas privilege routinely available."

government contended that the preclusion of judicial review was total and barred the exercise of habeas corpus jurisdiction. The Supreme Court disagreed, construing the amendments as not precluding the exercise of federal habeas jurisdiction under the general grant in § 2241, and stating that "a serious Suspension Clause issue would be presented if we were to accept the INS' submission that the 1996 statutes have withdrawn [the power to issue the writ] from federal judges and provided no adequate substitute for its exercise." Justice Stevens's majority opinion did not read Ex parte Bollman, p. 1465, *supra*, as having interpreted the Suspension Clause to "proscribe a temporary abrogation of the writ, while permitting its permanent suspension. Indeed, Marshall's comment expresses the far more sensible view that the Clause was intended to preclude any possibility that 'the privilege itself would be lost' by either the inaction or the action of Congress." Justice Stevens next posited that "at the absolute minimum, the Suspension Clause protects the writ 'as it existed in 1789,' " adding that "[a]t its historical core, the writ of habeas corpus has served as a means of reviewing the legality of Executive detention * * *" (quoting Felker v. Turpin, 518 U.S. 651 (1996)).

Turning to the scope of the right protected by the Suspension Clause, Justice Stevens first concluded that aliens had always been protected by the writ.[6] He then declared that historically, habeas review extended not only to constitutional claims but also to "errors of law, including the erroneous application or interpretation of statutes." In the Court's view, the writ therefore embraced St. Cyr's legal claim that the INS had erred in interpreting amendments to the immigration laws as having withdrawn, in this case, the Attorney General's discretionary power to waive deportation.

In dissent, Justice Scalia (joined on this issue by Chief Justice Rehnquist and Justice Thomas) disputed the majority's reading of the Suspension Clause. Relying in part on the statement in Ex parte Bollman that the power to issue the writ must be given by written law, he argued that the Clause was designed only to limit temporary suspension of the writ as it existed under the statutory law in effect at the time—an abuse he said was well known to the founding generation. Thus, the Clause did not "guarantee[ ] any particular habeas right that enjoys immunity from suspension." And even if one assumed that the Suspension Clause protected some right to review, he added, it surely would not extend to "the right to judicial compulsion of the exercise of Executive *discretion*."[7]

In the end, St. Cyr rested on statutory interpretation. But the textual argument that Congress had indeed withdrawn federal habeas corpus jurisdiction was powerful, see p. 465, *supra,* and the statutory ruling was plainly driven by the Court's desire to avoid the constitutional question that

---

[6]   On this point, see Neuman, *Habeas Corpus, Executive Detention, and the Removal of Aliens*, 98 Colum.L.Rev. 961 (1998).

[7]   In a separate dissent, Justice O'Connor said: "assuming, *arguendo*, that the Suspension Clause guarantees some minimum extent of habeas review, the right asserted by the alien in this case falls outside the scope of that review * * *."

For discussion of St. Cyr, see Neuman, *The Habeas Corpus Suspension Clause After INS v. St. Cyr*, 33 Colum.Hum.Rts.L.Rev. 555 (2002).

would have been presented had the Court determined that Congress had withdrawn habeas corpus jurisdiction in the circumstances presented.

(2) "Enemy Combatants" Detained at Guantanamo Bay and the Boumediene Decision. The Court next confronted the question whether the Suspension Clause guarantees an affirmative right to habeas corpus review in Boumediene v. Bush, 553 U.S. 723 (2008). This time, none of the Justices doubted that Congress had indeed purported to abolish habeas corpus review. The Court, 5–4, held for the first time that the Suspension Clause confers an affirmative right to habeas review and struck down as unconstitutional a federal statutory provision purporting to preclude any federal or state court from exercising habeas corpus jurisdiction.[8]

Boumediene involved provisions of the Detainee Treatment Act of 2005 and the Military Commissions Act of 2006, which purported to limit judicial review of challenges by aliens held at Guantanamo Bay to the legality of their detention as suspected enemy combatants. The four dissenters argued that the petitioners fell outside the scope of the Suspension Clause's protection (because they were aliens detained as enemy combatants beyond the territorial sovereignty of the United States) and that, in any event, the alternative procedure that Congress had provided was a constitutionally adequate substitute for habeas review. Unlike in St. Cyr, however, none of the dissenters (who included Justices Scalia and Thomas) questioned the premise that for persons who do fall within its ambit, the Suspension Clause confers an affirmative right to habeas corpus review or to an adequate substitute. See pp. 1519–1526, *infra.*

(3) Federal Versus State Court. Is the affirmative right to habeas review guaranteed by the Suspension Clause a right to *federal* habeas corpus review? In both St. Cyr and Boumediene, the government argued that the jurisdictional statutes precluded all review in federal or state court; holding such a total preclusion constitutionally suspect or invalid, the Court, without real discussion, assumed that any constitutionally required review should be provided in federal court.

Does that assumption cast doubt on Professor Hart's position that the state courts are the ultimate guardians of constitutional rights? Or can the Court's assumption that review should occur in federal court be explained on a narrower basis? In both cases, that assumption seems entirely justified as a matter of statutory construction and severability analysis. Had Congress realized that judicial review of executive action was required in either federal or state court, surely it would have preferred that review of immigration matters and of federal military detention occur in federal court. The point is

---

[8] See also Meltzer, *Habeas Corpus, Suspension, and Guantánamo: The Boumediene Decision,* 2008 Sup.Ct.Rev. 1, 1. Subsequently, in Department of Homeland Security v. Thuraissigiam, 591 U.S. 103 (2020), the Court could be read to cast some doubt on this holding. See *id.* 116 n.12 (stating that "[t]he original meaning of the Suspension Clause is the subject of controversy" and that it would not "revisit the question" "whether the Clause independently guarantees the availability of the writ or simply restricts the temporary withholding of its operation"). For criticism of this inconsistency, see Tyler, *Thuraissigiam and the Future of the Suspension Clause,* Lawfare (July 2, 2020), https://www.lawfaremedia.org/article/thuraissigiam-and-future-suspension-clause; Kovarsky, *Habeas Privilege Origination and INS v. Thuraissigiam,* 121 Colum.L.Rev. Forum 23 (2021).

only reinforced by the language (much criticized, but never repudiated) in Tarble's Case, 80 U.S. (13 Wall.) 397 (1872), p. 575, *supra*, stating that state courts lack authority to entertain habeas actions against federal custodians. And in both cases, once the Court had dealt with the jurisdiction-stripping provisions (invalidating them in Boumediene, narrowly construing them in St. Cyr), there remained in place the pre-existing general grant of habeas corpus jurisdiction in § 2241, under which the relevant petitions could be entertained.

But in light of the Madisonian Compromise and the possibility that Congress might never have established federal courts at all (or might never have conferred on them any habeas corpus jurisdiction), what might be the relationship between the Clause and state courts? It has been argued that the Clause, at its core, precludes Congress, where it has not established the requisite habeas jurisdiction in federal court, from interfering with the power of the state courts to issue habeas relief. See Duker, A Constitutional History of Habeas Corpus (1980); see generally pp. 579–585, *supra*. On this view, Congress could presumably eliminate federal review for a particular class of detained persons while leaving them free to seek habeas corpus relief in state court. In such a circumstance, would a state court be obliged to entertain a habeas action—even one against a federal custodian? See Chap. IV, Sec. 3.

C.   The Power to Suspend the Writ

Whether federal court power rests on a statutory grant of jurisdiction, inherent common law authority, or the Suspension Clause, the Constitution by its terms contemplates that the writ may be suspended—the Constitution's only "express provision for exercise of extraordinary authority because of a crisis." Youngstown Sheet & Tube Co. v. Sawyer, 343 U.S. 579, 650 (1952) (Jackson, J., concurring). But this in turn raises many questions.

(1) Which Branch of Government Has the Power to Suspend the Writ? Given the Clause's placement in Article I, there seems little question that Congress has the power to suspend the writ. Congress has authorized suspension of the writ four times in the nation's history—twice within the United States (during the Civil War and Reconstruction), once in the Philippines in 1905, and once, during World War II, in what was then the territory of Hawaii. See Tyler, *Suspension as an Emergency Power*, 118 Yale L.J. 600 (2009) (providing details). On each occasion, rather than declaring a suspension itself, Congress delegated to executive officials the authority to suspend the writ under specified circumstances. See Barrett, *Suspension and Delegation*, 99 Cornell L.Rev. 251, 270–92 (2014). Is there a limit on Congress's authority to delegate the power to suspend the writ? See *id.* 325 (acknowledging some power to delegate but arguing that Congress must itself decide that an invasion or rebellion has occurred and that protecting the public safety may require suspension—a standard not satisfied by three of the four historical acts of suspension in her view).[9]

---

[9]   See *id.* 280 (noting General Lee surrendered at Appomattox on April 9, 1865, but President Johnson did not revoke in full President Lincoln's nationwide suspension until August 20, 1866); 287–92 (observing the territorial suspensions in the Philippines and Hawaii followed under standing delegations in the territorial organic acts made to the territorial governors). See also Tyler, note 4, *supra*, at 194–95, 205–06.

May the President suspend the writ without any delegation of authority by Congress? Two years before Congress enacted suspension legislation, President Lincoln purported to suspend the writ at the outset of the Civil War. Chief Justice Taney rejected Lincoln's claim that he could do so without congressional authorization in Ex parte Merryman, 17 F.Cas. 144, 151–52 (C.C.D.Md.1861) (No. 9487), which involved a habeas petition addressed to Taney in both his capacity as Chief Justice and as circuit justice. Drawing on English legal tradition and pointing to the English Habeas Corpus Act of 1679 and Parliament's subsequent suspensions of the same, Taney wrote, "[i]f the president of the United States may suspend the writ, then the constitution of the United States has conferred upon him more regal and absolute power over the liberty of the citizen, than the people of England have thought it safe to entrust to the crown." See also Hamdi v. Rumsfeld, 542 U.S. 507, 562 (2004) (Scalia, J., dissenting) (highlighting both English practice and the Suspension Clause's placement in Article I).[10]

(2) What Constitutes a Suspension of the Writ? The Supreme Court has repeatedly recognized that Congress may replace habeas corpus with a different form of judicial review, so long as the substitute is adequate. See, *e.g.*, Boumediene v. Bush, p. 1507, *infra*; Swain v. Pressley, 430 U.S. 372 (1977); United States v. Hayman, 342 U.S. 205 (1952). But whether a limitation on habeas jurisdiction, or on a substitute remedy, constitutes a suspension is bound up with the question of what scope of habeas corpus review is required by the Suspension Clause.

(3) Interpretation of Congressional Statutes. In Boumediene, there was no doubt that Congress had eliminated habeas corpus jurisdiction in § 2241(e)(1). The government did not argue, and the Supreme Court did not conclude, however, that the congressional action purported to suspend the writ; instead, the Court treated the absence of habeas jurisdiction as a violation of the affirmative right guaranteed by the Suspension Clause (a right the government argued the petitioners did not have).

Congress clearly did not want cases like Boumediene heard in federal court (or indeed in any court). Was the Supreme Court correct in refusing to treat the relevant legislation as an effort to suspend the writ? One could argue that given the fundamental role of habeas in protecting individual liberty, a clear statement rule requiring Congress to be explicit when purporting to suspend the privilege of the writ is appropriate. See INS v. St. Cyr, 533 U.S. 289, 298 (2001) (recognizing a "longstanding rule requiring a clear statement of congressional intent to repeal habeas jurisdiction"). In each of the four instances in which Congress historically authorized suspension of the writ, the statutory authorization was clear in its delegation of a power to suspend.

(4) Is the Act of Suspension Subject to Judicial Review? Some opinions have broadly asserted (all in dictum) that the courts may not review a congressional decision to suspend. See, *e.g.*, Hamdi v. Rumsfeld, 542 U.S.

---

[10]   See generally Jackson, *The Power to Suspend Habeas Corpus: An Answer from the Arguments Surrounding Ex parte Merryman*, 34 U.Balt.L.Rev. 11 (2004); see also McGinty, The Body of John Merryman: Abraham Lincoln and the Suspension of Habeas Corpus 28 (2011); Tyler, note 4, *supra*, at 160–67.

507, 577–78 (2004) (Scalia, J., dissenting); *id.* 594 n.4 (Thomas, J., dissenting); Ex parte Merryman, 17 F.Cas. 144, 148 (C.C.D.Md.1861) (No. 9487) (Taney, C.J.) ("[C]ongress is, of necessity, the judge of whether the public safety does or does not require [suspension]; and their judgment is *conclusive.*"); Ex parte Bollman, 8 U.S. (4 Cranch) 75, 101 (1807) (Marshall, C.J.) (legislation may suspend "[i]f at any time the public safety shall require [it] * * *. That question depends on political considerations, on which the legislature is to decide.").[11] Note that a petitioner confronting an act allegedly suspending the writ might object that (i) there was no rebellion or invasion, (ii) the public safety did not require suspension, (iii) the measure in question was not in fact an exercise of the power to suspend, (iv) the branch that purported to suspend the writ lacked the constitutional authority to do so, or (v) the terms of the suspension were limited by time, geography, or in some other respect and did not encompass the detention.

Is there any reason why the last three of these issues should not be subject to judicial review? Ex parte Milligan, 71 U.S. (4 Wall.) 2 (1866), p. 553, *supra,* determined that Milligan's custody was illegal only after concluding that it fell outside the scope of the suspension that Congress had authorized during the Civil War. Ex parte Merryman, Paragraph (1), *supra,* reviewed (and found wanting) the President's power, acting without congressional authorization, to suspend the writ. And in Hamdi v. Rumsfeld, the next principal case, Justice Scalia's dissenting opinion addressed the question of whether the resolution passed by Congress shortly after 9/11 constituted a suspension of the writ (concluding that it did not).

What about judicial review of the existence of a rebellion or invasion? In suggesting that the issue is not immune from all review, Professor Shapiro offers the example of a suspension based on a legislative determination that the flow of undocumented immigrants crossing from Mexico into the United States constitutes an "invasion." Shapiro, *Habeas Corpus, Suspension, and Detention: Another View,* 82 Notre Dame L.Rev. 59 (2006). As for reviewability of a determination that "the public Safety may require" suspension, Professor Shapiro suggests that the text of the Suspension Clause indicates that Congress has, at a minimum, very broad discretion on that question. For a forceful argument that the validity of a suspension does not present a political question, see Tyler, *Is Suspension a Political Question?,* 59 Stan.L.Rev. 333 (2006).[12]

(5) What Is the Effect of a Suspension? Justice Souter once suggested that "a suspension of the writ * * * is just about the most stupendously significant act that the Congress of the United States can take."[13] But what

---

[11]   See also Story, Commentaries on the Constitution of the United States § 1336 ("It would seem, as the power is given to congress to suspend the writ of habeas corpus, in cases of rebellion or invasion, that the right to judge, whether the exigency had arisen, must exclusively belong to that body.").

[12]   *Cf.* Sterling v. Constantin, 287 U.S. 378, 393, 400 (1932) (rejecting the argument that "courts may not review the sufficiency of facts upon which martial law is declared," concluding instead that "[w]hat are the allowable limits of military discretion, and whether or not they have been overstepped in a particular case, are judicial questions").

[13]   Transcript of Oral Argument at 57–58, Hamdan v. Rumsfeld, 548 U.S. 557 (2007) (No. 05–184).

does a suspension accomplish? Does a valid suspension merely withdraw the privilege of the writ (thereby requiring dismissal of habeas petitions falling within its scope)? Or does it go further, so that a petitioner may not assert the right to be free from unlawful detention through other procedural vehicles or obtain other remedies for alleged unlawful detention? (The issue might arise, for example, were one held in custody subject to a suspension of the writ later to seek damages for an illegal detention.) Relatedly, does a valid suspension legalize detentions that come within its scope? For an argument that other remedies remain available, see Morrison, *Hamdi's Habeas Puzzle: Suspension as Authorization?*, 91 Cornell L.Rev. 411 (2006), and Morrison, *Suspension and the Extrajudicial Constitution*, 107 Colum.L.Rev. 1533 (2007); for criticism of that view, see Shapiro, Paragraph (4), *supra*, and Tyler, Paragraph (1), *supra*.[14] In debating these questions, what might historical episodes of suspension teach?[15]

INTRODUCTORY NOTE ON HAMDI V. RUMSFELD

In 2004, the Supreme Court decided three habeas cases involving alleged enemy combatants. Two of them reached only the question whether habeas jurisdiction existed. But in the third, Hamdi v. Rumsfeld, the Court considered a case in which habeas jurisdiction was not in doubt. Hamdi presented the question whether the military could lawfully detain a United States citizen on American soil without trial and in the absence of a suspension. Before reading Hamdi, it is helpful to review the earlier discussion of Ex parte Milligan and Ex parte Quirin, both of which figure prominently in the Hamdi opinions, at pp. 553–555, *supra*.

Hamdi v. Rumsfeld

542 U.S. 507 (2004).
Certiorari to the United States Court of Appeals for the Fourth Circuit.

■ JUSTICE O'CONNOR announced the judgment of the Court and delivered an opinion, in which THE CHIEF JUSTICE, JUSTICE KENNEDY, and JUSTICE BREYER join.

At this difficult time in our Nation's history, we are called upon to consider the legality of the Government's detention of a United States citizen on United States soil as an "enemy combatant" and to address the process that is constitutionally owed to one who seeks to challenge his classification as such. * * * We hold that although Congress authorized

---

[14] Consider in this connection the argument of Professor Harrison, in *The Original Meaning of the Habeas Corpus Suspension Clause, the Right of Natural Liberty, and Executive Detention*, 29 Wlm. & Mary Bill of Rts.J. 649 (2021), that the Suspension Clause is primarily a protection not of the remedy of habeas corpus but rather of a substantive right to natural liberty.

[15] For additional details on English and British suspensions pre-dating American independence and during the American Revolutionary War, as well as suspensions over the course of American history, see Tyler, note 4, *supra*.

the detention of combatants in the narrow circumstances alleged here, due process demands that a citizen held in the United States as an enemy combatant be given a meaningful opportunity to contest the factual basis for that detention before a neutral decisionmaker.

I

* * * [One week after the 9/11 attacks,] Congress passed a resolution authorizing the President to "use all necessary and appropriate force against those nations, organizations, or persons he determines planned, authorized, committed, or aided the terrorist attacks" or "harbored such organizations or persons, in order to prevent any future acts of international terrorism against the United States by such nations, organizations or persons." Authorization for Use of Military Force (AUMF), 115 Stat. 224. Soon thereafter, the President ordered United States Armed Forces to Afghanistan, with a mission to subdue al Qaeda and quell the Taliban regime that was known to support it.

[In 2001, members of the Northern Alliance (a coalition of military groups opposed to the Taliban government) seized Yaser Hamdi, a United States American citizen, in Afghanistan and turned him over to the United States military. After authorities learned that he had been born in the United States, the government transferred him to military detention at a naval brig in South Carolina. The government designated him as an "enemy combatant" and took the position that he could be detained indefinitely on that basis.

[Hamdi's father filed a habeas corpus petition, alleging that his son's detention was unlawful and that as an American citizen, Hamdi was entitled to an impartial tribunal, the assistance of counsel, and the full protections of the Constitution. The petition alleged that Hamdi went to Afghanistan to do relief work and had received no military training, and requested an evidentiary hearing.

[The government did not contest the district court's jurisdiction, but eventually filed a motion to dismiss the petition, supported by a declaration from a Defense Department official, Michael Mobbs. Mobbs stated that he was generally familiar with the war against al Qaeda and the Taliban, and that "based upon my review of the relevant records and reports, I am also familiar with the facts and circumstances related to the capture of * * * Hamdi and his detention by U.S. military forces." In the only evidentiary support for Hamdi's detention that the government submitted, Mobbs stated that after Hamdi traveled to Afghanistan in July or August of 2001, he "affiliated with a Taliban military unit and received weapons training," he stayed on with his Taliban unit following the attacks of September 11, his unit surrendered in battle to the Northern Alliance, and Hamdi himself surrendered his assault rifle. Mobbs also stated that a series of "U.S. military screening team[s]" determined that Hamdi met the "criteria for enemy combatants" and that "a subsequent interview of Hamdi has confirmed that he surrendered and gave his firearm to Northern Alliance forces."

[The district court ruled that Mobbs's declaration, given its "generic and hearsay nature," fell "far short" of supporting Hamdi's detention. The court ordered the government to turn over, for *in camera* review, numerous materials, including copies of Hamdi's statements and notes from his interviews as well as further details regarding Hamdi's interrogators; the role of the Northern Alliance in Hamdi's capture; and the American officials who classified Hamdi as an enemy combatant. The Fourth Circuit reversed, concluding "that because it was 'undisputed that Hamdi was captured in a zone of active combat in a foreign theater of conflict,' no factual inquiry or evidentiary hearing allowing Hamdi to be heard or to rebut the Government's assertions was necessary or proper. Concluding that the factual averments in the Mobbs Declaration, 'if accurate,' provided a sufficient basis upon which to conclude that the President had constitutionally detained Hamdi pursuant to the President's war powers, it ordered the habeas petition dismissed."]

II

The threshold question before us is whether the Executive has the authority to detain citizens who qualify as "enemy combatants." * * * [T]he government has never provided any court with the full criteria that it uses in classifying individuals as such. It has made clear, however, that, for purposes of this case, the "enemy combatant" that it is seeking to detain is an individual who, it alleges, was " 'part of or supporting forces hostile to the United States or coalition partners' " in Afghanistan and who " 'engaged in an armed conflict against the United States' " there. We therefore answer only the narrow question before us: whether the detention of citizens falling within that definition is authorized.

The Government maintains that no explicit congressional authorization is required, because the Executive possesses plenary authority to detain pursuant to Article II of the Constitution. We do not reach the question whether Article II provides such authority, however, because we agree with the Government's alternative position, that Congress has in fact authorized Hamdi's detention, through the AUMF.

* * * [Hamdi] * * * posits that his detention is forbidden by 18 U.S.C. § 4001(a). Section 4001(a) states that "[n]o citizen shall be imprisoned or otherwise detained by the United States except pursuant to an Act of Congress." Congress passed § 4001(a) in 1971 as part of a bill to repeal the Emergency Detention Act of 1950, 50 U.S.C. § 811 *et seq.*, which [permitted the President to declare a national emergency and order the detention, without trial, of persons suspected of espionage and sabotage]. Congress was particularly concerned about the possibility that the [Emergency Detention] Act could be used to reprise the Japanese-American internment camps of World War II. * * * [W]e conclude that the AUMF is explicit congressional authorization for the detention of individuals in the narrow category we describe * * * and that the AUMF satisfied § 4001(a)'s requirement that a detention be "pursuant to an Act

of Congress" (assuming, without deciding, that § 4001(a) applies to military detentions).

* * * There can be no doubt that individuals who fought against the United States in Afghanistan as part of the Taliban, an organization known to have supported the al Qaeda terrorist network responsible for those attacks, are individuals Congress sought to target in passing the AUMF. We conclude that detention of individuals falling into the limited category we are considering, for the duration of the particular conflict in which they were captured, is so fundamental and accepted an incident to war as to be an exercise of the "necessary and appropriate force" Congress has authorized the President to use.

The capture and detention of lawful combatants and the capture, detention, and trial of unlawful combatants, by "universal agreement and practice," are "important incident[s] of war." Ex parte Quirin, [317 U.S. 1, 28, 30 (1942)]. The purpose of detention is to prevent captured individuals from returning to the field of battle and taking up arms once again. * * *

There is no bar to this Nation's holding one of its own citizens as an enemy combatant. In Quirin, one of the detainees, Haupt, alleged that he was a naturalized United States citizen. 317 U.S., at 20. We held that "[c]itizens who associate themselves with the military arm of the enemy government, and with its aid, guidance and direction enter this country bent on hostile acts, are enemy belligerents within the meaning of . . . the law of war." Id., at 37–38. While Haupt was tried for violations of the law of war, nothing in Quirin suggests that his citizenship would have precluded his mere detention for the duration of the relevant hostilities. Id., at 30–31. * * * A citizen, no less than an alien, can be "part of or supporting forces hostile to the United States or coalition partners" and "engaged in an armed conflict against the United States"; such a citizen, if released, would pose the same threat of returning to the front during the ongoing conflict.

In light of these principles, it is of no moment that the AUMF does not use specific language of detention. Because detention to prevent a combatant's return to the battlefield is a fundamental incident of waging war, in permitting the use of "necessary and appropriate force," Congress has clearly and unmistakably authorized detention in the narrow circumstances considered here.

Hamdi objects, nevertheless, that Congress has not authorized the *indefinite* detention to which he is now subject. * * * As the Government concedes, "given its unconventional nature, the current conflict is unlikely to end with a formal cease-fire agreement." * * * Hamdi's detention could last for the rest of his life.

It is a clearly established principle of the law of war that detention may last no longer than active hostilities. * * *

Hamdi contends that the AUMF does not authorize indefinite or perpetual detention. Certainly, we agree that indefinite detention for the purpose of interrogation is not authorized. Further, we understand Congress' grant of authority for the use of "necessary and appropriate force" to include the authority to detain for the duration of the relevant conflict * * *. If the practical circumstances of a given conflict are entirely unlike those of the conflicts that informed the development of the law of war, that understanding may unravel. But that is not the situation we face as of this date. Active combat operations against Taliban fighters apparently are ongoing in Afghanistan. The United States may detain, for the duration of these hostilities, individuals legitimately determined to be Taliban combatants who "engaged in an armed conflict against the United States." * * *

Ex parte Milligan, 4 Wall. 2, 125 (1866), does not undermine our holding about the Government's authority to seize enemy combatants, as we define that term today. In that case, the Court made repeated reference to the fact that its inquiry into whether the military tribunal had jurisdiction to try and punish Milligan turned in large part on the fact that Milligan was not a prisoner of war, but a resident of Indiana arrested while at home there. That fact was central to its conclusion. Had Milligan been captured while he was assisting Confederate soldiers by carrying a rifle against Union troops on a Confederate battlefield, the holding of the Court might well have been different. The Court's repeated explanations that Milligan was not a prisoner of war suggest that had these different circumstances been present he could have been detained under military authority for the duration of the conflict, whether or not he was a citizen.

Moreover, as Justice Scalia acknowledges, the Court in Ex parte Quirin dismissed the language of Milligan that the petitioners had suggested prevented them from being subject to military process. * * * Haupt * * * was accused of being a spy. The Court in Quirin found him "subject to trial and punishment by [a] military tribuna[l]" for those acts, and held that his citizenship did not change this result. 317 U.S., at 31, 37–38.

Quirin was a unanimous opinion. It both postdates and clarifies Milligan, providing us with the most apposite precedent that we have on the question of whether citizens may be detained in such circumstances. Brushing aside such precedent—particularly when doing so gives rise to a host of new questions never dealt with by this Court—is unjustified and unwise.

To the extent that Justice Scalia accepts the precedential value of Quirin, he argues that it cannot guide our inquiry here because "[i]n Quirin it was uncontested that the petitioners were members of enemy forces," while Hamdi challenges his classification as an enemy combatant. But it is unclear why, in the paradigm outlined by Justice Scalia, such a concession should have any relevance. Justice Scalia envisions a system in which the only options are congressional suspension of the writ of habeas corpus or prosecution for treason or some other crime. He does not explain how his historical analysis supports the addition of a third option—detention under some other process after concession of enemy-combatant status—or why a concession should carry any different effect than proof of enemy-combatant status in a proceeding that comports with due process. * * *

Further, Justice Scalia largely ignores the context of this case: a United States citizen captured in a *foreign* combat zone. Justice Scalia refers to only one case involving this factual scenario—a case in which a United States citizen-prisoner of war (a member of the Italian army) from World War II was seized on the battlefield in Sicily and then held in the United States. The court in that case held that the military detention * * * was lawful. See In re Territo [156 F.2d 142, 148 (9th Cir.1946)]. * * *

Moreover, Justice Scalia presumably would come to a different result if Hamdi had been kept in Afghanistan or even Guantanamo Bay. This creates a perverse incentive. Military authorities faced with the stark choice of submitting to the full-blown criminal process or releasing a suspected enemy combatant captured on the battlefield will simply keep citizen-detainees abroad. * * *

III

Even in cases in which the detention of enemy combatants is legally authorized, there remains the question of what process is constitutionally due to a citizen who disputes his enemy-combatant status. Hamdi argues that he is owed a meaningful and timely hearing and that "extra-judicial detention [that] begins and ends with the submission of an affidavit based on third-hand hearsay" does not comport with the Fifth and Fourteenth Amendments. The Government counters that any more process than was provided below would be both unworkable and "constitutionally intolerable." Our resolution of this dispute requires a careful examination both of the writ of habeas corpus * * * and of the Due Process Clause, which informs the procedural contours of that mechanism in this instance.

A

* * * All agree that, absent suspension, the writ of habeas corpus remains available to every individual detained within the United States. * * * All agree suspension of the writ has not occurred here. Thus, * * * Hamdi was properly before an Article III court to challenge his detention under 28 U.S.C. § 2241. Further, all agree that § 2241 and its companion provisions provide at least a skeletal outline of the procedures to be afforded a petitioner in federal habeas review. Most notably, § 2243 provides that "the person detained may, under oath, deny any of the facts set forth in the return or allege any other material facts," and § 2246 allows the taking of evidence in habeas proceedings by deposition, affidavit, or interrogatories.

The simple outline of § 2241 makes clear both that Congress envisioned that habeas petitioners would have some opportunity to present and rebut facts and that courts in cases like this retain some ability to vary the ways in which they do so as mandated by due process. The Government recognizes the basic procedural protections required by the habeas statute, but asks us to hold that, given both the flexibility of the habeas mechanism and the circumstances presented in this case, the presentation of the Mobbs Declaration * * * completed the required factual development. * * *

B

First, the Government urges the adoption of the Fourth Circuit's holding below—that because it is "undisputed" that Hamdi's seizure took place in a combat zone, the habeas determination can be made purely as a matter of law, with no further hearing or factfinding necessary. This argument is easily rejected. * * * [Justice O'Connor here stressed that Hamdi had not been permitted to respond to the government's allegations and that he disputed whether he was " 'part of or supporting forces hostile to the United States or coalition partners' and 'engaged in an armed conflict against the United States.' "]

C

The Government's second argument requires closer consideration. * * * Under the Government's most extreme rendition of this argument, "[r]espect for separation of powers and the limited institutional capabilities of courts in matters of military decision-making in connection with an ongoing conflict" ought to eliminate entirely any individual process, restricting the courts to investigating only whether legal authorization exists for the broader detention scheme. At most, the Government argues, courts should review its determination that a citizen is an enemy combatant under a very deferential "some evidence" standard. Under this review, a court would assume the accuracy of the Government's articulated basis for Hamdi's detention, as set forth in the Mobbs Declaration, and assess only whether that articulated basis was a legitimate one.

In response, Hamdi emphasizes that this Court consistently has recognized that an individual challenging his detention may not be held at the will of the Executive without recourse to some proceeding before a neutral tribunal to determine whether the Executive's asserted justifications for that detention have basis in fact and warrant in law. * * *

Both of these positions highlight legitimate concerns. * * * The ordinary mechanism that we use for balancing such serious competing interests, and for determining the procedures that are necessary to ensure that a citizen is not "deprived of life, liberty, or property, without due process of law," U.S. Const., Amdt. 5, is the test that we articulated in Mathews v. Eldridge, 424 U.S. 319 (1976). Mathews dictates that the process due in any given instance is determined by weighing "the private interest that will be affected by the official action" against the Government's asserted interest, "including the function involved" and the burdens the Government would face in providing greater process. 424 U.S., at 335. The Mathews calculus then contemplates a judicious balancing of these concerns, through an analysis of "the risk of an erroneous deprivation" of the private interest if the process were reduced and the "probable value, if any, of additional or substitute procedural safeguards." *Ibid.* We take each of these steps in turn.

1

* * * Hamdi's "private interest . . . affected by the official action," *ibid.,* is the most elemental of liberty interests—the interest in being free from physical detention by one's own government. "In our society liberty is the norm," and detention without trial "is the carefully limited exception." * * *

Nor is the weight on this side of the Mathews scale offset by the circumstances of war or the accusation of treasonous behavior, for "[i]t is clear that commitment for *any* purpose constitutes a significant deprivation of liberty that requires due process protection," Jones v. United States, 463 U.S. 354, 361 (1983) (emphasis added; internal quotation marks omitted), and at this stage in the Mathews calculus, we consider the interest of the erroneously detained individual. Indeed, * * * the risk of erroneous deprivation of a citizen's liberty in the absence of sufficient process here is very real. Moreover, as critical as the Government's interest may be in detaining those who actually pose an immediate threat to the national security of the United States during ongoing international conflict, history and common sense teach us that an unchecked system of detention carries the potential to become a means for oppression and abuse of others who do not present that sort of threat. * * *

2

On the other side of the scale are the weighty and sensitive governmental interests in ensuring that those who have in fact fought with the enemy during a war do not return to battle against the United States. * * * Without doubt, our Constitution recognizes that core strategic matters of warmaking belong in the hands of those who are best positioned and most politically accountable for making them.

The Government also argues at some length that its interests in reducing the process available to alleged enemy combatants are heightened by the practical difficulties that would accompany a system of trial-like process. In its view, military officers who are engaged in the serious work of waging battle would be unnecessarily and dangerously distracted by litigation half a world away, and discovery into military operations would both intrude on the sensitive secrets of national defense and result in a futile search for evidence buried under the rubble of war.

To the extent that these burdens are triggered by heightened procedures, they are properly taken into account in our due process analysis.

3

Striking the proper constitutional balance here is of great importance to the Nation during this period of ongoing combat. But it is equally vital that our calculus not give short shrift to the values that this country holds dear or to the privilege that is American citizenship. * * *

With due recognition of these competing concerns, we * * * hold that a citizen-detainee seeking to challenge his classification as an enemy combatant must receive notice of the factual basis for his classification, and a fair opportunity to rebut the Government's factual assertions before a neutral decisionmaker. * * *

At the same time, the exigencies of the circumstances may demand that, aside from these core elements, enemy-combatant proceedings may be tailored to alleviate their uncommon potential to burden the Executive at a time of ongoing military conflict. Hearsay, for example, may need to be accepted as the most reliable available evidence from the Government in such a proceeding. Likewise, the Constitution would not be offended by a presumption in favor of the Government's evidence, so long as that presumption remained a rebuttable one and fair opportunity for rebuttal were provided. Thus, once the Government puts forth credible evidence that the habeas petitioner meets the enemy-combatant criteria, the onus could shift to the petitioner to rebut that evidence with more persuasive evidence that he falls outside the criteria. [This] will ensur[e] that the errant tourist, embedded journalist, or local aid worker has a chance to [secure their freedom]. * * *

We think it unlikely that this basic process will have the dire impact on the central functions of warmaking that the Government forecasts. The parties agree that initial captures on the battlefield need not receive the process we have discussed here; that process is due only when the determination is made to *continue* to hold those who have been seized. The Government has made clear in its briefing that documentation regarding battlefield detainees already is kept in the ordinary course of military affairs. Any factfinding imposition created by requiring a knowledgeable affiant to summarize these records to an independent tribunal is a minimal one. Likewise, arguments that military officers ought not have to wage war under the threat of litigation lose much of their steam when factual disputes at enemy-combatant hearings are limited to the alleged combatant's acts. This focus meddles little, if at all, in the strategy or conduct of war, inquiring only into the appropriateness of continuing to detain an individual claimed to have taken up arms against the United States. * * *

D

In so holding, we necessarily reject the Government's assertion that separation of powers principles mandate a heavily circumscribed role for the courts in such circumstances. * * * We have long since made clear that a state of war is not a blank check for the President when it comes to the rights of the Nation's citizens. Youngstown Sheet & Tube, 343 U.S. [579,] 587 [(1952)]. * * * Likewise, we have made clear that, unless Congress acts to suspend it, the Great Writ of habeas corpus allows the Judicial Branch to play a necessary role in maintaining [the] delicate balance of governance, serving as an important judicial check on the Executive's discretion in the realm of detentions. * * * Absent suspension of the writ by Congress, a citizen detained as an enemy combatant is entitled to this process.

Because we conclude that due process demands some system for a citizen-detainee to refute his classification, the proposed "some evidence" standard is inadequate. Any process in which the Executive's factual assertions go wholly unchallenged or are simply presumed correct without any opportunity for the alleged combatant to demonstrate otherwise falls constitutionally short. * * * This [is especially true where] a habeas petitioner has received no prior proceedings before any tribunal and had no prior opportunity to rebut the Executive's factual assertions before a neutral decisionmaker. * * *

There remains the possibility that the standards we have articulated could be met by an appropriately authorized and properly constituted military tribunal. Indeed, it is notable that military regulations already provide for such process in related instances, dictating that tribunals be made available to determine the status of enemy detainees who assert prisoner-of-war status under the Geneva Convention. In the absence of such process, however, a court that receives a petition for a writ of habeas corpus from an alleged enemy combatant must itself ensure that the minimum requirements of due process are achieved. * * *

IV

* * * Since our grant of certiorari in this case, Hamdi has been appointed counsel * * *. He unquestionably has the right to access to counsel in connection with the proceedings on remand. * * *

The judgment of the United States Court of Appeals for the Fourth Circuit is vacated, and the case is remanded for further proceedings.

It is so ordered.

■ JUSTICE SOUTER, with whom JUSTICE GINSBURG joins, concurring in part, dissenting in part, and concurring in the judgment.

[Unlike the plurality, Justice Souter concluded that the AUMF was not the kind of clearly expressed congressional authorization to detain a citizen that he believed was required by the Non-Detention Act. He began by stressing the origins of § 4001(a) and "the fact that Congress intended to guard against a repetition of the World War II internments" of Japanese Americans when it passed the law. Section 4001(a), he argued, "intended to preclude reliance on vague congressional authority * * * as authority for detention or imprisonment at the discretion of the

Executive." Justice Souter next emphasized that while the AUMF "is fairly read to authorize the use of armies and weapons * * * it never so much as uses the word detention, and there is no reason to think Congress might have perceived any need to augment Executive power to deal with dangerous citizens within the United States, given the well-stocked statutory arsenal of defined criminal offenses covering the gamut of actions that a citizen sympathetic to terrorists might commit."

[Concluding that Hamdi's detention violated the Non-Detention Act, Justice Souter thought the Court should simply vacate and remand on the basis that his detention was unauthorized. But, he wrote, "the need to give practical effect to the conclusions of eight members of the Court rejecting the Government's position calls for me to join with the plurality in ordering remand on terms closest to those I would impose." Justice Souter added, however, "I do not adopt the plurality's resolution of constitutional issues that I would not reach."]

■ JUSTICE SCALIA, with whom JUSTICE STEVENS joins, dissenting.

* * * Where the Government accuses a citizen of waging war against it, our constitutional tradition has been to prosecute him in federal court for treason or some other crime. Where the exigencies of war prevent that, the Constitution's Suspension Clause, Art. I, § 9, cl. 2, allows Congress to relax the usual protections temporarily. Absent suspension, however, the Executive's assertion of military exigency has not been thought sufficient to permit detention without charge. No one contends that the congressional Authorization for Use of Military Force * * * is an implementation of the Suspension Clause. Accordingly, I would reverse the judgment below.

I

The very core of liberty secured by our Anglo-Saxon system of separated powers has been freedom from indefinite imprisonment at the will of the Executive. * * *

> "To make imprisonment lawful, it must either be, by process from the courts of judicature, or by warrant from some legal officer, having authority to commit to prison; which warrant must be in writing, under the hand and seal of the magistrate, and express the causes of the commitment, in order to be examined into (if necessary) upon a *habeas corpus*. If there be no cause expressed, the gaoler is not bound to detain the prisoner. For the law judges in this respect, . . . that it is unreasonable to send a prisoner, and not to signify withal the crimes alleged against him." 1 W. Blackstone, Commentaries on the Laws of England 131–133 (1765) (hereinafter Blackstone).

These words were well known to the Founders. Hamilton quoted from this very passage in The Federal No. 84. * * * The two ideas central to Blackstone's understanding—due process as the right secured, and habeas corpus as the instrument by which due process could be insisted upon by a citizen illegally imprisoned—found expression in the Constitution's Due Process and Suspension Clauses.

The gist of the Due Process Clause, as understood at the founding and since, was to force the Government to follow those common-law procedures traditionally deemed necessary before depriving a person of life, liberty, or property. When a citizen was deprived of liberty because of alleged criminal conduct, those procedures typically required committal by a magistrate followed by indictment and trial. * * *

To be sure, certain types of permissible *non* criminal detention * * * did not require the protections of criminal procedure. However, these fell into a limited number of well-recognized exceptions—civil commitment of the mentally ill, for example, and temporary detention in quarantine of the infectious. * * *

[Justice Scalia next recounted the story leading up to Parliament's adoption of] the Petition of Right, accepted by the King in 1628, which expressly prohibited imprisonment without formal charges, see 3 Car. 1, ch. 1, §§ 5, 10.

The struggle between subject and Crown continued, and culminated in the Habeas Corpus Act of 1679, 31 Car. 2, ch. 2, described by Blackstone as a "second *magna carta,* and stable bulwark of our liberties." 1 Blackstone 133. The Act governed all persons "committed or detained . . . for any crime." [The act provided, *inter alia*, that for felony or treason, "the Crown" was "required * * * to commence criminal proceedings within a specified time": in practice not more than three to six months.] [I]f the prisoner was not brought to trial [within that time period], the Act provided that "he shall be discharged from his Imprisonment." * * *

* * * Hamilton lauded "the establishment of the writ of *habeas corpus*" in his Federalist defense as a means to protect against "the practice of arbitrary imprisonments . . . in all ages, [one of] the favourite and most formidable instruments of tyranny." The Federalist No. 84, at 444. Indeed, availability of the writ under the new Constitution (along with the requirement of trial by jury in criminal cases, see Art. III, § 2, cl. 3) was his basis for arguing that additional, explicit procedural protections were unnecessary. See The Federalist No. 83, at 433.

II

The allegations here, of course, are no ordinary accusations of criminal activity. * * * [T]he Government believes [Hamdi] participated in the waging of war against the United States. The relevant question, then, is whether there is a different, special procedure for imprisonment of a citizen accused of wrongdoing *by aiding the enemy in wartime.*

A

Justice O'Connor, writing for a plurality of this Court, asserts that captured enemy combatants (other than those suspected of war crimes) have traditionally been detained until the cessation of hostilities and then released. That is probably an accurate description of wartime practice with respect to enemy *aliens*. The tradition with respect to American citizens, however, has been quite different. Citizens aiding the enemy have been treated as traitors subject to the criminal process.

[Justice Scalia next discussed English sources setting out a distinction between foreign enemies and English subjects adhering to the crown's enemies, who were treated as traitors. He then observed, "[t]he Founders inherited the understanding that a citizen's levying war against the Government was to be punished criminally." Justice Scalia also highlighted numerous examples of American citizens being charged in Article III courts for acts of war against the United States during World Wars I and II (other than Haupt in the Quirin case) and in connection with military hostilities against the United States.]

B

There are times when military exigency renders resort to the traditional criminal process impracticable. English law accommodated such exigencies by allowing legislative suspension of the writ of habeas corpus for brief periods. * * * Where the Executive has not pursued the usual course of charge, committal, and conviction, it has historically secured the Legislature's explicit approval of a suspension. * * *

III

* * * Even if suspension of the writ on the one hand, and committal for criminal charges on the other hand, have been the only *traditional* means of dealing with citizens who levied war against their own country, it is theoretically possible that the Constitution does not *require* a choice between these alternatives.

I believe, however, that substantial evidence does refute that possibility. First, the text of the 1679 Habeas Corpus Act makes clear that indefinite imprisonment on reasonable suspicion is not an available option of treatment for those accused of aiding the enemy, absent a suspension of the writ. In the United States, this Act was read as "enforc[ing] the common law," Ex parte Watkins, 3 Pet. 193, 202, and shaped the early understanding of the scope of the writ. * * * The Act does not contain any exception for wartime. That omission is conspicuous, since § 7 [of the Act] explicitly addresses the offense of "High Treason," which often involved offenses of a military nature.

[Justice Scalia next discussed a host of historical materials supporting his position, including President Lincoln's view "that suspension was required if the prisoner was to be held without criminal trial."]

Further evidence comes from this Court's decision in Ex parte Milligan, *supra*. There, the Court issued the writ to an American citizen who had been tried by military commission for offenses that included conspiring to overthrow the Government, seize munitions, and liberate prisoners of war. The Court rejected in no uncertain terms the Government's assertion that military jurisdiction was proper "under the 'laws and usages of war,'" *id.*, at 121:

> "It can serve no useful purpose to inquire what those laws and usages are, whence they originated, where found, and on whom they operate; they can never be applied to citizens in states which have upheld the authority of the government, and where the courts are open and their process unobstructed," *ibid.*[1]

* * * The Government justifies imprisonment of Hamdi on principles of the law of war and admits that, absent the war, it would have no such authority. But if the law of war cannot be applied to citizens where courts are open, then Hamdi's imprisonment without criminal trial is no less unlawful than Milligan's trial by military tribunal. * * *

* * * Thus, criminal process was viewed as the primary means—and the only means absent congressional action suspending the writ—not only to punish traitors, but to incapacitate them.

The proposition that the Executive lacks indefinite wartime detention authority over citizens is consistent with the Founders' general mistrust of military power permanently at the Executive's disposal. * * *

IV

The Government * * * places primary reliance upon Ex parte Quirin, 317 U.S. 1 (1942), a World War II case upholding the trial by military commission of eight German saboteurs, one of whom, Herbert Haupt, was a U.S. citizen. The case was not this Court's finest hour. The Court * * * denied relief in a brief *per curiam* issued the day after oral argument concluded; a week later the Government carried out the commission's death sentence upon six saboteurs, including Haupt. The Court eventually explained its reasoning in a written opinion issued several months later.

Only three paragraphs of the Court's lengthy opinion dealt with the particular circumstances of Haupt's case. * * * Quirin purported to interpret the language of Milligan quoted above (the law of war "can never be applied to citizens in states which have upheld the authority of the government, and where the courts are open and their process unobstructed") in the following manner:

> "Elsewhere in its opinion . . . the Court was at pains to point out that Milligan, a citizen twenty years resident in Indiana, who had never been a resident of any of the states in rebellion, was not an enemy belligerent either entitled to the status of a prisoner of war or subject to the penalties imposed upon

---

[1]   As I shall discuss presently, the Court purported to limit this language in Ex parte Quirin, 317 U.S. 1, 45. Whatever Quirin's effect on Milligan's precedential value, however, it cannot undermine its value as an indicator of original meaning.

unlawful belligerents. We construe the Court's statement as to the inapplicability of the law of war to Milligan's case as having particular reference to the facts before it. From them the Court concluded that Milligan, not being a part of or associated with the armed forces of the enemy, was a non-belligerent, not subject to the law of war . . . ." 317 U.S., at 45.

In my view this seeks to revise Milligan rather than describe it. Milligan had involved (among other issues) two separate questions: (1) whether the military trial of Milligan was justified by the laws of war, and if not (2) whether the President's suspension of the writ, pursuant to congressional authorization, prevented the issuance of habeas corpus. The Court's categorical language about the law of war's inapplicability to citizens where the courts are open * * * was contained in its discussion of the first point. The factors pertaining to whether Milligan could reasonably be considered a belligerent and prisoner of war * * * were made relevant and brought to bear in the Court's later discussion of whether Milligan came within the statutory provision that effectively made an exception to Congress's authorized suspension of the writ for (as the Court described it) "all parties, not prisoners of war, resident in their respective jurisdictions, . . . who were citizens of states in which the administration of the laws in the Federal tribunals was unimpaired," *id.*, at 116. Milligan thus understood was in accord with the traditional law of habeas corpus I have described: Though treason often occurred in wartime, there was, absent provision for special treatment in a congressional suspension of the writ, no exception to the right to trial by jury for citizens who could be called "belligerents" or "prisoners of war."[2]

But even if Quirin gave a correct description of Milligan, or made an irrevocable revision of it, Quirin would still not justify denial of the writ here. In Quirin it was uncontested that the petitioners were members of enemy forces. * * * The specific holding of the Court was only that, "upon the *conceded* facts," the petitioners were "plainly within [the] boundaries" of military jurisdiction, *id.*, at 46 (emphasis added).[3] But where those jurisdictional facts are *not* conceded—where the petitioner insists that he is *not* a belligerent—Quirin left the pre-existing law in place * * *.

---

[2]   Without bothering to respond to this analysis, the plurality states that Milligan "turned in large part" upon the defendant's lack of prisoner-of-war status, and that the Milligan Court explicitly and repeatedly *said* so. Neither is true. To the extent, however, that prisoner-of-war status was relevant in Milligan, it was only because prisoners of war *received different statutory treatment* under the conditional suspension then in effect.

[3]   The only two Court of Appeals cases from World War II cited by the Government in which citizens were detained without trial likewise involved petitioners who were conceded to have been members of enemy forces. See In re Territo, 156 F.2d 142, 143–45 (9th Cir.1946); Colepaugh v. Looney, 235 F.2d 429, 432 (10th Cir.1956). The plurality complains that Territo is the only case I have identified in which "a United States citizen [was] captured in a *foreign* combat zone." Indeed it is; such cases must surely be rare. But given the constitutional tradition I have described, the burden is not upon me to find cases in which the writ was *granted* to citizens in this country *who had been captured on foreign battlefields;* it is upon those who would carve out an exception for such citizens (as the plurality's complaint suggests it would) to find a single case (other than one where enemy status was admitted) in which habeas was *denied*.

V

It follows from what I have said that Hamdi is entitled to a habeas decree requiring his release unless (1) criminal proceedings are promptly brought, or (2) Congress has suspended the writ of habeas corpus. * * *

[Justice Scalia next argued that the AUMF did not overcome the statutory prescription in § 4001(a). He next criticized the Court's "judicial balancing" in reliance on Mathews v. Eldridge, which he described as "a case involving . . . *the withdrawal of disability benefits!*" He continued: "Whatever the merits of this technique when newly recognized property rights are at issue * * *, it has no place where the Constitution and the common law already supply an answer."]

* * * [T]he plurality finishes up by transmogrifying the Great Writ— * * * by remanding for the District Court to "engag[e] in a factfinding process that is both prudent and incremental." * * * This judicial remediation of executive default is unheard of. The role of habeas corpus is to determine the legality of executive detention, not to supply the omitted process necessary to make it legal. * * *

VI

Several limitations give my views * * * a relatively narrow compass. They apply only to citizens, accused of being enemy combatants, who are detained within the territorial jurisdiction of a federal court. * * * Where the citizen is captured outside and held outside the United States, the constitutional requirements may be different. Moreover, even within the United States, the accused citizen-enemy combatant may lawfully be detained once prosecution is in progress or in contemplation. * * *

I frankly do not know whether these tools are sufficient to meet the Government's security needs, including the need to obtain intelligence through interrogation. * * * If the situation demands it, the Executive can ask Congress to authorize suspension of the writ—which can be made subject to whatever conditions Congress deems appropriate, including even the procedural novelties invented by the plurality today. To be sure, suspension is limited by the Constitution to cases of rebellion or invasion. But whether the attacks of September 11, 2001, constitute an "invasion," and whether those attacks still justify suspension several years later, are questions for Congress rather than this Court.[6] If civil rights are to be curtailed during wartime, it must be done openly and democratically, as the Constitution requires, rather than by silent erosion through an opinion of this Court. * * *

■ JUSTICE THOMAS, dissenting.

---

6   Justice Thomas worries that the constitutional conditions for suspension of the writ will not exist "during many . . . emergencies during which . . . detention authority might be necessary." It is difficult to imagine situations in which security is so seriously threatened as to justify indefinite imprisonment without trial, and yet the constitutional conditions of rebellion or invasion are not met.

[Justice Thomas was the only member of the Court voting to uphold the government's authority to detain Hamdi without further process. Agreeing with the plurality that the AUMF authorized the detention of enemy combatants generally, he thought that the determination by the Executive Branch, within the scope of its war powers, that Hamdi was an enemy combatant sufficed to establish the legality of detention. Stressing the breadth of the President's power to protect national security and conduct foreign affairs, he reasoned that while Congress has a substantial role to play here, "*judicial* interference in these domains destroys the purpose of vesting primary responsibility in a unitary Executive." Because much intelligence is appropriately secret, courts lack the information needed to make judgments in these domains, and even if they could require some form of disclosure, " 'the very nature of executive decisions as to foreign policy is political, not judicial' " (quoting Chicago & Southern Air Lines, Inc. v. Waterman S.S. Corp., 333 U.S. 103, 111 (1948)). Thus, resolution of the question whether Hamdi is an enemy combatant "is committed to other branches."

[Justice Thomas therefore disagreed with Justice Scalia's position and concluded:] [T]he fact that the writ may not be suspended "unless when in Cases of Rebellion or Invasion the public Safety may require it," Art. I, § 9, cl. 2, poses two related problems. First, this condition might not obtain here or during many other emergencies during which this detention authority might be necessary. Congress would then have to choose between acting unconstitutionally[4] and depriving the President of the tools he needs to protect the Nation. Second, I do not see how suspension would make constitutional otherwise unconstitutional detentions ordered by the President. It simply removes a remedy. Justice Scalia's position might therefore require one or both of the political branches to act unconstitutionally in order to protect the Nation. * * *

NOTE ON HAMDI V. RUMSFELD AND THE SCOPE OF HABEAS INQUIRY IN CASES OF EXECUTIVE DETENTION

(1) The Function of Habeas Corpus Jurisdiction. All nine Justices in Hamdi agreed that the federal courts' role was to examine the legality of Hamdi's detention; their considerable disagreements rested on divergent substantive views about the interpretation of relevant statutes (particularly the AUMF and the Non-Detention Act), the scope of executive war power, and the requirements of the Suspension Clause and due process. Further, in Hamdi and subsequent cases, the Justices have diverged in their views as to what the appropriate remedy is for a Suspension Clause violation—namely, discharge and/or additional process.

---

[4]   I agree with Justice Scalia that this Court could not review Congress' decision to suspend the writ.

(2) A New Kind of Armed Conflict. The kind of armed conflict authorized by the AUMF differs in important respects from traditional wars. In the words of Professors Bradley and Goldsmith, "[t]he enemy intermingles with civilians and attacks civilian and military targets alike. The traditional concept of 'enemy alien' is inapplicable in this conflict; instead of being affiliated with particular states that are at war with the United States, terrorist enemies are predominantly citizens and residents of friendly states or even the United States. The battlefield lacks a precise geographic location and arguably includes the United States. It is unclear how to conceptualize the defeat of terrorist organizations, and thus unclear how to conceptualize the end of the conflict." Bradley & Goldsmith, *Congressional Authorization and the War on Terrorism*, 118 Harv.L.Rev. 2047, 2048–49 (2005).[1]

The new kind of conflict presented by the war on terrorism presents enormous challenges in "translation"—that is, how to draw upon the legal frameworks of past wars to shed light on what rules should govern the scope of government authority in modern armed conflicts. It bears paying close attention to these complications in reading the materials that follow while asking how much historical models of war can and should inform the legal calculus today.

(3) A Common Law Model of Habeas. In Hamdi, the plurality adopted what might be viewed as a common law model of habeas corpus, viewing Hamdi's detention as raising distinctive issues calling for a flexible adaptation of due process requirements to the circumstances presented by the armed conflict with al Qaeda and the Taliban. Under this view, the judiciary is best-suited to craft the contours of the habeas privilege, with habeas proceedings themselves providing the relevant process due. In support of her position, Justice O'Connor also noted other contexts in which the Constitution authorizes detention outside of the criminal process.

Defending the plurality's approach in Hamdi, Professors Fallon and Meltzer argue that "[m]uch of the most important jurisdictional and substantive doctrine [in the habeas context] has been and remains judge-made." Fallon & Meltzer, *Habeas Corpus Jurisdiction, Substantive Rights, and the War on Terror*, 120 Harv.L.Rev. 2029, 2044 (2007). Tracing the common law origins of the writ in English legal history, Professor Halliday in turn identifies "the writ's core principle" as this: "*that* the judge judges." Halliday, Habeas Corpus: From England to Empire 7 (2010). Surveying how English and British courts employed the common law writ in the lead up to United States independence, he concludes "the writ had always been at its most effective when judges used it to address new problems." *Id.* 308.[2]

---

[1]   In subsequent work, the authors detail the expansion of the reach of the AUMF to encompass military operations against the Islamic State. See Bradley & Goldsmith, *Obama's AUMF Legacy*, 110 Am.J.Int'l.L. 628 (2016). *Cf.* Al-Alwi v. Trump, 901 F.3d 294 (D.C.Cir.2018) (rejecting claim brought by petitioner detained at Guantanamo Bay that the end of operations in Afghanistan, during which he was taken into custody, terminated the government's power to detain him under the terms of the AUMF).

[2]   For elaboration of the arguments favoring a common law model in this context, see Fallon, *On Viewing the Courts as Junior Partners of Congress in Statutory Interpretation Cases: An Essay Celebrating the Scholarship of Daniel J. Meltzer*, 91 Notre Dame L.Rev. 1743 (2016).

(4) The Hamdi Dissent, the English Habeas Corpus Act, and the Post-Ratification Evolution of the Suspension Model. Justice Scalia's dissent, joined by Justice Stevens, embraced an entirely different approach. It was not, in his view, the role of habeas to provide necessary process; habeas, he argued, instead asked whether appropriate process had *already* been afforded the petitioner. Because, on this account, due process in this context equated historically with the protections afforded in criminal proceedings, the question for a habeas court in the absence of a valid suspension was whether such process had been provided—*i.e.*, whether the petitioner had been charged and timely tried. Under the historical model, moreover, Justice Scalia argued that there was nothing for the judiciary to adapt or balance—in the absence of timely criminal trial or a valid suspension, the Constitution demanded Hamdi's release.[3]

In reaching this conclusion, Justice Scalia relied heavily on the English Habeas Corpus Act of 1679 and its importance to early Supreme Court habeas jurisprudence in cases like Ex parte Watkins, 28 U.S. (3 Pet.) 193 (1830), see note 10, p. 1463, *supra*. Tyler, *A "Second Magna Carta": The English Habeas Corpus Act and the Statutory Origins of the Habeas Privilege*, 91 Notre Dame L.Rev. 1949 (2016), elaborates on the importance of the English Habeas Corpus Act of 1679 and observes that "extensive evidence of the Act's influence across the Atlantic dating from well before, during, and after the Revolutionary War demonstrates that much of early American habeas law was premised upon efforts to incorporate the Act's key protections rather than developed through judicial innovation."

In separate work, Tyler details the role that the English Habeas Corpus Act played in the Revolutionary War legal framework, noting that "determinations regarding the reach and application of the English Habeas Corpus Act of 1679 were of tremendous consequence" during this important period in American history. Tyler, *Habeas Corpus and the American Revolution*, 103 Calif.L.Rev. 635 (2015). She writes that when asked for guidance as to the legal status of American "Rebels" brought to English soil for detention during the war, Lord Mansfield advised the North Administration that "in England, where the Habeas Corpus Act was unquestionably in force, it promised a timely criminal trial to those who

---

See also Vladeck, *Constitutional Remedies in Federalism's Forgotten Shadow*, 107 Calif.L.Rev. 1043 (2019); Freedman, Making Habeas Work: A Legal History (2018).

[3]   Although Justice Thomas saw no Suspension Clause problem in Hamdi, subsequently, in Department of Homeland Security v. Thuraissigiam, 491 U.S. 103 (2020), his concurring opinion observed that "[t]he Founders * * * enshrined" the English suspension model "in the Suspension Clause, which they understood to protect a substantive right"—specifically, "freedom from discretionary detention" at the hands of the executive. *Id.* 143 (Thomas, J., concurring). Suspension, Justice Thomas added, "likely meant a statute granting the executive the power to detain without bail or trial based on mere suspicion of a crime or dangerousness." Do these statements suggest that Justice Thomas's position has evolved since Hamdi, possibly moving closer to Justice Scalia's? For more on Thuraissigiam, see pp. 467–469, *supra*; 1544–1546, *infra*.

For criticism of the Hamdi dissent's all-or-nothing approach, see Farber & Sherry, Judgment Calls: Principle and Politics in Constitutional Law 137 (2009) (arguing that Justice Scalia's view puts the government in a "straightjacket," unable to account for "changing conditions," and observing that "if invoked [a suspension] might be far more destructive of civil liberties than a judicially defined solution").

could and did claim the protection of domestic law—a category of persons long understood to encompass traitors."[4] Accordingly, in the absence of a suspension, Mansfield counseled that a petitioner under such circumstances could win their freedom via habeas. It was against this backdrop that the Administration requested a suspension from Parliament, with Lord North asserting that the law was "necessary for the crown to have a power of confining them like other prisoners of war." By its terms, the Revolutionary War suspension (and its extensions) applied to American colonists captured outside the geographic reach of the Habeas Corpus Act who were then brought within the realm, where the Act was otherwise in full force and theirs to claim as British subjects. As Tyler also explains, it was not until independence became a foregone conclusion that Parliament allowed the suspension legislation to lapse and declared Americans remaining in custody to be prisoners of war subject to exchange under the laws of war.

Tyler, Habeas Corpus in Wartime: From the Tower of London to Guantanamo Bay (2017), then surveys the Convention and ratification debates and concludes that the founding generation sought to constitutionalize the English suspension model and with it the protections long associated with the English Habeas Corpus Act.[5] She posits that this understanding of the constraints that the Clause imposed on executive detention largely controlled through Reconstruction, but contends that the model broke down during World War II with the mass incarceration of Japanese Americans under President Roosevelt's Executive Order 9066 and resulting military regulations. See id. 222–43.[6]

Assessing this same history, White, *Looking Backward and Forward at the Suspension Clause*, 117 Mich.L.Rev. 1313 (2019), focuses on the Civil War as a turning point in the story of the writ, observing that by acting unilaterally ahead of Congress, President Lincoln effectively defended "the outbreak of war [as] justifying suspension of the privilege, and as a result the privilege really did not exist in wartime." This, White suggests, established a new model of "limited executive 'suspensions'" like that which occurred during World War II under Executive Order 9066. He concludes by asserting that each of these "strategic decisions of the Executive, and their legitimation by the Court, suggest that, at least since World War II, the

---

[4]　19 The Parliamentary History of England, From the Earliest Period to the Year 1803, at 4 (T.C. Hansard 1814) (remarks of Lord Frederick North given Feb. 6, 1777).

[5]　As one example, Tyler highlights that Georgia included in its Constitution of 1777 an express provision stating, "[t]he principles of the *habeas-corpus* act, shall be a part of this constitution," and annexed verbatim copies of the English Habeas Corpus Act to the constitution's original distribution. GA. CONST. of 1777, art. LX.

[6]　For a different view contending that the habeas privilege should be understood as "'only' a procedural remedy and * * * not the source of distinct substantive anti-detention rules," see Kovarsky, *Citizenship, National Security Detention, and the Habeas Remedy*, 107 Calif.L.Rev. 867 (2019). Professor Harrison, in *The Original Meaning of the Habeas Corpus Suspension Clause, the Right of Natural Liberty, and Executive Detention*, 29 Wlm. & Mary Bill of Rts.J. 649 (2021), contends that neither the text of the Suspension Clause nor historical practice places citizens outside the scope of permissible detention. Harrison also contends, based on his review of English and early American history, that the Suspension Clause, despite its language, is not primarily about habeas corpus but rather about a substantive right to natural liberty. At the founding, he argues, the central concept of a suspension was a law that conferred on the executive extremely broad discretion to detain—whether or not the judicial remedy of habeas corpus remained intact, and whether or not the person in custody was a citizen.

Suspension Clause has not so much been 'forgotten' as deliberately bypassed," including in cases like Hamdi.

Assuming that the English model provided the foundation of the Suspension Clause in the United States Constitution, what bearing, if any, should this history have on questions such as those raised in Hamdi?[7] And if Professor White is right that whatever the original understanding of the privilege, in practice it has come to mean something less over time, what bearing, if any, should that conclusion have on the interpretation of the Suspension Clause today?[8]

(5) The "One Way Ratchet" Expansion of Habeas. Another question left in the wake of Hamdi is what, if any, constitutional significance should be assigned to expansions of the writ along various dimensions that have occurred under the statutory grant of jurisdiction that has existed since 1789. Professor Shapiro says that "[s]urely, the guarantee is not a one-way ratchet, in which every advance in the availability of the writ becomes part of the [Suspension Clause] guarantee itself," but that "the guarantee would be stripped of virtually all meaning if it did not include what might fairly be viewed as the essence of the writ at the time of ratification." Shapiro, *Habeas Corpus, Suspension, and Detention: Another View*, 82 Notre Dame L.Rev. 59, 74 (2006). Shapiro suggests, *inter alia*, that the heart of the writ involves a determination of the adequacy of the custodian's return—that is, the custodian's response to the allegations in the petition—but not necessarily of the accuracy of factual statements in the return. He suggests that the essence of the writ did not necessarily permit the court to probe behind the competency of the committing authority to order the commitment. Shapiro notes that the review for lawfulness was especially rigorous when the committing authority was the executive or an inferior court and when the commitment was not pursuant to conviction by a competent superior court. If Professor Shapiro is right, then a great deal turns on what was "the essence of the writ at the time of ratification."

(6) Variations on a Theme: Aliens Versus Citizens, the Circumstances of Seizure, and the Location of Detention. The Hamdi case involved only one of a range of situations in which persons alleged to be enemy combatants might contest the legality of their custody. The existence of habeas jurisdiction or the appropriate scope of habeas review may depend on (a) the location of detention, see pp. 1503–1506, *infra*; (b) whether the

---

[7] See also Meyler, *Originalism and a Forgotten Conflict over Martial Law*, 113 Nw.U.L.Rev. 1335 (2019) (exploring the intersection of habeas corpus with martial law in the century leading up to ratification).

[8] Pfander, *Constructive Constitutional History and Habeas Corpus Today*, 107 Calif.L.Rev. 1005 (2019), poses a similar question this way: "With habeas sidelined, how should we restore the rule of law in light of Lincoln's action?" He responds by proposing that the law recognize damages suits by persons detained against responsible officers. Doing so, Pfander argues, "would preserve the Constitution and the rule of law, while signaling to future presidents that actions taken in the name of military necessity must ultimately face a test of legality."

person detained is a citizen or an alien;[9] and (c) the location of seizure—for example, on or off a battlefield, or within or outside of the United States.[10]

(a) The Padilla Case. The government arrested José Padilla, a United States citizen detained in connection with the war on terror, upon arrival at Chicago's O'Hare Airport traveling from Pakistan. The government alleged that he had been armed in a combat zone in Afghanistan during fighting between the American military and Taliban and al Qaeda forces, and that, upon his escape to Pakistan, he was involved with al Qaeda operatives. Designating him an "enemy combatant," President George W. Bush declared that Padilla "represent[ed] a continuing, present and grave danger to the national security of the United States." In ruling on Padilla's habeas petition on appeal, the Second Circuit held Padilla's detention unlawful on several grounds: the President lacked inherent constitutional authority to detain Padilla, the Non-Detention Act prohibited detention of a citizen captured on American soil absent a separate specific statutory authorization, and the AUMF did not provide such authorization. The Supreme Court then vacated that decision for want of jurisdiction. See Rumsfeld v. Padilla, 542 U.S. 426 (2004) (assigning significance to the government's transfer of Padilla before the filing of Padilla's petition to a different jurisdiction), p. 1539, *infra*. Justice Stevens's dissent (joined by Justices Souter, Ginsburg, and Breyer) argued that jurisdiction existed, and declared, "[a]t stake in this case is nothing less than the essence of a free society. * * * Unconstrained executive detention for the purpose of investigating and preventing subversive activity is the hallmark of the Star Chamber."

When Padilla refiled his habeas petition and the matter eventually reached the Fourth Circuit, that court ruled that there was no difference in principle between Hamdi and Padilla, both of whom allegedly fought against the United States in Afghanistan and posed the same threat of returning to battle if not detained. Padilla v. Hanft, 423 F.3d 386, 391–92 (4th Cir.2005). After Padilla sought review in the Supreme Court anew, the government indicted him on various criminal charges and transferred him to the control of civilian authorities. The Court thereafter declined review. Padilla v. Hanft, 547 U.S. 1062 (2006).

(b) The Al-Marri Case. In Al-Marri v. Pucciarelli, 534 F.3d 213 (4th Cir.2008) (en banc) (per curiam), a lawful resident alien seized in the United States and held by the military challenged the legality of his custody. Al-

---

[9]   Support for the relevance of the distinction between a citizen and alien to the application of the Suspension Clause may be found in Department of Homeland Security v. Thuraissigiam, 591 U.S. 103 (2020). There, after holding that the Suspension Clause does not apply to an asylum seeker, the Court distinguished the situation of a citizen who is detained for deportation, emphasizing that its decision "would not prevent the citizen from petitioning for release." For additional discussion of Thuraissigiam, see pp. 467–469, *supra*; 1544–1546, *infra*.

[10]   For an effort to outline how these kinds of factors influence the exercise of habeas jurisdiction, see Fallon & Meltzer, Paragraph (3), *supra*.

Goldstein, *Habeas Without Rights*, 2007 Wis.L.Rev. 1165, argues that recent decisions considering military detention have focused unduly on whether a petitioner has legally cognizable rights, rather than on whether the custodian had lawful authority to detain and offers evidence that historically the latter question was the focus of courts exercising habeas jurisdiction in both England and the United States.

Marri disputed a government affidavit asserting that he was closely associated with al Qaeda and had come to this country as a sleeper agent. (Unlike Padilla and Hamdi, al-Marri was not alleged to have directly engaged in hostilities.) The Fourth Circuit held en banc, 5–4, that the government's allegations, if true, established an adequate basis for detention.

The five judges in the majority expressed overlapping but differing points of view in four separate opinions. The themes voiced included: neither the language nor the purpose of the AUMF is limited to persons who took hostile action on a battlefield; the scope of detention authorized by the AUMF, even if broader than that traditionally recognized by the laws of war, was justified in view of the dangers posed by stateless actors who target innocent civilians; and the opposing view would have prevented the government, had it apprehended the 9/11 hijackers in the United States before they could carry out their plans, from detaining them militarily. The four dissenters argued that detention was not authorized by the AUMF (or by principles of the laws of war); al-Marri, they stressed, was neither a citizen of, nor affiliated with the armed forces of, any nation at war with the United States and never directly participated in hostilities against the United States; thus, al-Marri was a civilian analogous to Milligan.

(c) **Questions Left in the Balance.** When Hamdi's petition came before the United States Court of Appeals for the Fourth Circuit, Judge Wilkinson argued that "[t]o compare [Hamdi's] battlefield capture to the domestic arrest in Padilla * * * is to compare apples and oranges." Hamdi v. Rumsfeld, 337 F.3d 335, 344 (4th Cir.2003) (en banc) (Wilkinson, J., concurring in the denial of rehearing en banc). To him, Hamdi's capture on a foreign battlefield made all the difference. Should it? Does domestic capture and/or detention change the constitutional analysis? Consider this question in light of the cases that follow, as well as the discussion of the mass incarceration of Japanese Americans during World War II, discussed in Paragraph (7), *infra*. Consider as well that when authorities took a citizen-suspect into custody for the 2013 bombing at the Boston Marathon in nearby Watertown, Massachusetts, Senators McCain and Graham, among others, declared that "[t]he accused perpetrators of these acts were not common criminals attempting to profit from a criminal enterprise, but terrorists trying to injure, maim, and kill innocent Americans * * *. Under the Law of War we can hold this suspect as a potential enemy combatant."[11] Could Hamdi be read to permit this approach? Or did the domestic capture and detention of the marathon suspect require his prosecution in due course?[12]

---

[11] *GOP Lawmakers want Boston bombing suspect treated as "enemy combatant,"* Wash. Post, Apr. 20, 2013. See Press Release, Offs. of Sens. Graham and McCain, Statement from Sens. Graham and McCain (Apr. 19, 2013), https://www.lgraham.senate.gov/public/index.cfm/press-releases?ID=28509AF5-D294-994C-13DB-AEB71345ACE5.

[12] Doe v. Mattis, 928 F.3d 1 (D.C.Cir.2019), involved an American citizen captured in Syrian territory controlled by the Islamic State of Iraq and the Levant (ISIL) and subsequently detained by the United States government as an enemy combatant at a military facility in Iraq. The United States Court of Appeals for the D.C. Circuit held that under Hamdi, Doe had a right to challenge his classification as an enemy combatant, even though he had never been detained on American soil. The court went to hold that the government could not, in the absence of such a hearing upholding Doe's classification, transfer him to the custody of another country

(7) The Mass Incarceration of Japanese Americans During World War II and the Non-Detention Act. In the immediate wake of the bombing of Pearl Harbor on December 7, 1941, the United States declared war on Japan and Germany. Meanwhile, the Hawaiian territorial governor declared martial law and suspended habeas corpus on the Islands. Then, on February 19, 1942, President Roosevelt signed Executive Order 9066, authorizing the Secretary of War, *inter alia*, to designate military zones "from which any or all persons may be excluded" and "to provide for residents of any such area who are excluded therefrom, such transportation, food, shelter, and other accommodations as may be necessary." 3 C.F.R. 1092 (1942) (repealed 1976). In a matter of months, the military proclaimed a host of regulations targeting "all persons of Japanese ancestry" living in the western United States mainland. The escalating regulations ordered curfews, exclusion, registration, evacuation (with only what individuals could carry), and eventually detention in "Assembly Centers" and "Relocation Centers" scattered around the western states.[13] By war's end, the government detained for an average period of three years approximately 120,000 persons of Japanese ancestry, over 70,000 of whom were natural-born United States citizens.

During the period between Pearl Harbor and Roosevelt's issuance of 9066, Attorney General Francis Biddle told members of Congress that "[u]nless the Writ of Habeas Corpus is suspended, I do not know of any way in which Japanese born in this country and therefore American citizens could be interned."[14] But when the matter came before the Supreme Court in a set of companion cases, it sidestepped the relevant constitutional issues. First, in Korematsu v. United States, 323 U.S. 214 (1944), a divided Court upheld Fred Korematsu's conviction for violating an exclusion order and remaining in a designated military zone in Northern California, eschewing discussion of the fact that compliance with such orders inevitably led (as it did in his case) to detention in the camps. In Ex parte Endo, 323 U.S. 283 (1944), decided the same day as Korematsu, the Court faced its only habeas petition directly challenging the constitutionality of the mass incarceration of Japanese Americans. Mitsuye Endo, ordered to leave her home in Sacramento, California, and then detained in a series of camps, cited Bollman, Merryman, and Milligan as dictating that her detention was unconstitutional in the absence of a suspension. In her view, if, as Milligan holds, the military could not try a civilian for an alleged offense outside the courts when they are open, it followed that the military had even less power to detain an individual not charged or even suspected of criminal activity.

---

partnering with the United States in the campaign against ISIL. The decision suggests that Hamdi's prescriptions apply forcefully in situations involving citizens, even where both capture and detention lie outside the United States. Are there functional reasons to suggest that imposing such a burden on the government in such circumstances is unwise? At the other end of the spectrum, are there reasons to be concerned about a rule that permits the transfer of an American citizen to foreign custody after the limited requirements of a Hamdi-style hearing are satisfied?

[13]   Legislation enacted by Congress criminalized violations of the military orders. See Act of Mar. 21, 1942, Pub.L.No. 77–503, 56 Stat. 173 (repealed 1976).

[14]   For details on the lead up to 9066, see Tyler, Habeas Corpus in Wartime, Paragraph (4), *supra*, at 222–43.

Declining to reach the constitutional issues in the case, the Court first emphasized that Endo "is detained by a *civilian* agency," and "not by the military," and therefore "no questions of military law are involved." (distinguishing Milligan and Quirin as inapposite). The Court then held that the relevant military regulations required the release of concededly loyal citizens, like Endo, because "[a] citizen who is concededly loyal presents no problem of espionage or sabotage."[15] Justice Douglas's opinion for the Court "mention[ed]" a list of constitutional provisions—including the Suspension Clause—"not to stir the constitutional issues which have been argued at the bar," but instead to explain why the Court would "give[ ] a narrower scope" to the relevant military orders.[16] ("We must assume, when asked to find implied powers in a grant of legislative or executive authority, that the law makers intended to place no greater restraint on the citizen than was clearly and unmistakably indicated by the language they used.") Likely tipped off that the Court would order Endo's release, the White House preempted the decision by announcing that it would begin closing the camps forthwith.[17]

For purposes of Suspension Clause jurisprudence, Ex parte Endo proved the case that wasn't. But had the Court reached her Suspension Clause arguments, how should it have ruled?[18] Does the Court's reluctance to reach the issues undercut or support the position of Justices Scalia and Stevens in Hamdi, if either? Or does Hamdi's foreign capture materially distinguish his case? What about the fact that Hamdi was alleged to be fighting with the enemy? On this last point, is the better analogy to Hamdi that of Americans (sometimes dual citizens) held as prisoners of war on American soil during World War II?[19] With the exception of the case of In re Territo, 156 F.2d 142 (9th Cir.1946), such persons did not challenge their detentions in habeas. Should they have? Or does the reasoning of Quirin and Hamdi suggest that such challenges would have been without basis? In answering that question,

---

[15]   Justice Douglas continued: "Loyalty is a matter of the heart and mind, not of race, creed, or color * * *. When the power to detain is derived from the power to protect the war effort against espionage and sabotage, detention which has no relationship to that objective is unauthorized." In the lead up to the decision, the War Relocation Authority, which ran the camps, had instituted loyalty screenings as part of its release program. What, if anything, does the Constitution have to say about how loyalty is assessed?

[16]   In separate opinions, Justice Roberts argued that the Court should reach the constitutional issues in the case, arguing that "[a]n admittedly loyal citizen * * * should be free to come and go as she pleases." Justice Murphy labeled the detention policy a product of "the unconstitutional resort to racism." A Commission charged by Congress to study the episode later concluded that the push for mass detention of Japanese Americans stemmed from "race prejudice, war hysteria, and a failure of political leadership." Commission on Wartime Relocation and Internment of Civilians, Personal Justice Denied: Part 2: Recommendation 5 (1983); *id.* 3 (concluding that "no documented acts of espionage, sabotage or fifth column activity were shown to have been committed by any identifiable American citizen of Japanese ancestry or resident Japanese alien on the West Coast" in the period leading up to the orders).

[17]   Public Proclamation No. 21, 10 Fed. Reg. 53 (Dec. 17, 1944) (effective Jan. 2, 1945).

[18]   In analyzing the constitutionality of executive detention, should it matter whether a person is detained by civilian or military authorities?

[19]   The United States military detained hundreds of thousands of prisoners of war on American soil during the war. See Bradley & Goldsmith, *Congressional Authorization and the War on Terrorism*, 118 Harv.L.Rev. 2047, 2108 n.271 (2005) (citing Krammer, Nazi Prisoners of War in America 3 (1979), and U.S. Army Prisoner of War Info. Bureau, American Nationals Detained in the Custody of the United States Armed Forces During World War II (1956) (listing more than twenty American nationals so detained)).

is it relevant that the Supreme Court held dual citizenship not to preclude criminal liability for treason for a Japanese American prosecuted after the war for acts taken in Japan during World War II? See Kawakita v. United States, 343 U.S. 717, 734 (1952) (emphasizing that "American citizenship, until lost, carries obligations of allegiance as well as privileges and benefits").

More generally, what, if anything, does the mass incarceration of Japanese Americans during World War II teach about the normative stakes at issue in Suspension Clause debates? What about the role of the various branches in protecting civil liberties?[20] Writing in their immediate wake, Professor Rostow was deeply critical of Endo and Korematsu. In his view, "[i]t is hard to imagine what courts are for if not to protect people against unconstitutional arrest." Rostow, *The Japanese American Cases—A Disaster*, 54 Yale L.J. 489, 511 (1945). Compare Justice Frankfurter's opinion joining the majority in Korematsu, stating that the Court's holding should not be read as "approval of that which Congress and the Executive did. That is their business, not ours." 323 U.S. at 225 (Frankfurter, J., concurring).

(8) Jurisdiction over "The Body" and Mootness. Sensing the threat that Endo's case posed to the policy of mass incarceration of Japanese Americans, government lawyers offered Endo early release after she filed her habeas petition (conditioned upon her not returning to restricted areas on the west coast). The government likely believed that had she accepted release, her habeas case would have been mooted, since jurisdiction of habeas courts traditionally has been conceived of as over the "corpus," or body, of the petitioner. Moving or releasing individuals in custody has long served as a vehicle for evading habeas jurisdiction. See, *e.g.*, Zimmerman v. Walker, 319 U.S. 744 (1943) (in a case that challenged the lawfulness of the World War II suspension in the Hawaiian Territory: "Petition * * * denied on the ground that the cause is moot, it appearing that Hans Zimmerman, on whose behalf the petition is filed, has been released from the respondent's custody."); see also Padilla, Paragraph (6), *supra* (declining to revisit constitutionality of petitioner's military detention following his transfer to civilian custody in conjunction with filing of criminal charges against him).[21]

(9) The AUMF and the 2012 National Defense Authorization Act. In Hamdi, the Justices disagreed over whether the AUMF displaced the Non-Detention Act. Subsequently, Congress stepped in and "affirm[ed] that the

---

[20]   Tyler, *Courts and the Executive in Wartime: A Comparative Study of the American and British Approaches to the Internment of Citizens during World War II and Their Lessons for Today*, 107 Calif.L.Rev. 789 (2019), compares the actions of Prime Minister Churchill and President Roosevelt with respect to the British and American policies governing domestic detention of citizens outside the criminal process during the war, noting that Churchill pointed to the role of habeas corpus in English legal tradition in ending the British program.

For more on the Non-Detention Act's origins, see Chafee, *The Most Important Human Right in the Constitution*, 32 B.U.L.Rev. 143 (1952).

[21]   Tyler, Habeas Corpus in Wartime, Paragraph (4), *supra*, notes that one of the objects of the English Habeas Corpus Act of 1679 was to address the proclivity of the Earl of Clarendon regularly to dispatch persons in custody in the seventeenth century to "remote islands' garrisons and other places, thereby to prevent them from the benefit of the law." She also notes that during the Civil War, the Johnson Administration moved several conspirators in the Lincoln assassination to the Florida Keys in an attempt to put them, along with their constitutional challenges to the military tribunals that convicted them, beyond the reach of habeas courts.

authority of the President to use all necessary and appropriate force pursuant to" the AUMF "includes the authority" to "detain" persons who "w[ere] a part of or substantially supported al-Qaeda, the Taliban, or associated forces that are engaged in hostilities against the United States." National Defense Authorization Act for Fiscal Year 2012, Pub.L.No. 112–81, §§ 1021(a), (b)(2), 125 Stat. 1298, 1562 (2011). Congress granted authority to detain such persons "under the law of war without trial until the end of the hostilities authorized by the" AUMF. *Id.* § 1021(c)(1).

NOTE ON THE TERRITORIAL REACH OF THE WRIT

(1) Territorial Jurisdiction: Location of the Petitioner. Section 2241(a) vests authority to grant the writ in the Supreme Court and the district courts, any Justice of the Supreme Court and any circuit judge, but only "within their respective jurisdictions." In Ahrens v. Clark, 335 U.S. 188 (1948), the Court held that the District Court for the District of Columbia could not issue the writ because the petitioners, who were held at Ellis Island, New York, by order of the Attorney General, were not within the district court's territorial jurisdiction. It did not suffice, the Court held, that a custodian was within the district court's jurisdiction; instead, it was fatal to jurisdiction that the petitioners were not. Over time, amendments to the habeas statute and judicial decisions have eroded Ahrens' restriction.

(2) Statutory and Judicial Expansion of Territorial Jurisdiction.

(a) Legislative Revisions. In 1948, Congress added a provision (§ 2255) that, for persons "in custody under sentence of a court established by Act of Congress"—ordinarily those convicted of federal crimes—requires filing a motion in the sentencing court rather than a habeas petition in the district of incarceration. See Section 3(B), *infra*. Then, in 1966, Congress added a provision, codified in § 2241(d), that permits individuals in state custody attacking convictions in states containing more than one federal district to file in the district either of conviction or of confinement.

(b) The Braden Decision. Caselaw has also retreated from Ahrens' interpretation of § 2241(a). In Braden v. 30th Judicial Cir. Ct., 410 U.S. 484 (1973) (6–3), the Court recognized the jurisdiction of a district court to entertain a petition from one physically confined in another state. In the case, a detainer had been filed against an individual imprisoned by Alabama on behalf of the state of Kentucky, to assure that he would be turned over to Kentucky for trial when his Alabama sentence expired. He filed a petition in federal court in Kentucky against his future Kentucky custodians, alleging denial of his constitutional right to a speedy trial in Kentucky and seeking an order compelling his immediate trial there. The Supreme Court upheld the district court's jurisdiction, concluding that § 2241(a) requires only that the court "have jurisdiction over the custodian." The Court pointed to §§ 2255 and 2241(d) (neither of which applied here) as exemplifying Congress's recognition of the desirability of resolving habeas cases in a court closely connected to the underlying controversy. It also argued in favor of "a more expansive definition of the 'custody' requirement," see pp. 1665–1667, *infra*, permitting new forms of challenge, such as Braden's. The Court concluded that Ahrens should be confined to its facts, emphasizing that there both the petitioners and their custodians were in New York and no showing had been made that the District of Columbia was a more convenient forum.

(3) Persons Detained Outside of the United States. The foregoing discussion concerns detentions within American territory. What is the reach of habeas jurisdiction when detention lies outside of the United States?

(a) Aliens Detained in Foreign Nations: Johnson v. Eisentrager. In Johnson v. Eisentrager, 339 U.S. 763 (1950), the Court held that the federal district court in the District of Columbia (and, by implication, all other district courts) could not issue a writ sought by German citizens detained abroad. The petitioners had been captured in China and convicted by a U.S. military tribunal there of violating the laws of war by continuing hostilities against the United States after the surrender of Germany in 1945. After conviction, they were sent to an American military prison in occupied Germany, where they were being held when they filed their petitions. The precise basis for the Supreme Court's decision—how far it rested on a lack of statutory jurisdiction, and how far it was based on a determination on the merits that the petitioners had suffered no violation of their constitutional rights—became the subject of elaborate debate in Rasul v. Bush, Paragraph (4), *infra*, and the next principal case, Boumediene v. Bush, p. 1507, *infra*.

(b) Citizens Detained Abroad. In Burns v. Wilson, 346 U.S. 137 (1953), two American servicemembers detained overseas, after having been convicted by court martial of crimes committed in Guam, filed habeas petitions in federal court in the District of Columbia, naming the Secretary of Defense as respondent. Although in the end it refused to grant the writ, the Supreme Court did not question the district court's jurisdiction, even though both the petitioners and their immediate custodian were abroad and therefore outside the territorial jurisdiction of any district court. Justice Frankfurter only raised the jurisdictional issue several months later in an opinion dissenting from the denial of rehearing, 346 U.S. 844 (1953).

In United States ex rel. Toth v. Quarles, 350 U.S. 11 (1955), the Court granted habeas relief against the Secretary of the Air Force to an ex-servicemember arrested in the United States and taken to Korea for military trial. The jurisdictional issue, though again not discussed, could hardly have been overlooked in view of Justice Frankfurter's opinion two years earlier.[1] Note that in both cases a strict territorial limitation on jurisdiction could have left the petitioners with no chance to reach an Article III court in which to assert their constitutional challenges to the legality of custody—a circumstance that might itself have raised a serious constitutional question.

Is it justifiable for extraterritorial jurisdiction to turn on a distinction between citizens and aliens not found in the text of § 2241? In answering that question, is it relevant that the extent to which particular constitutional

---

[1]   The Court decided Burns and Toth nearly contemporaneous with a recognition that citizens detained abroad could assert constitutional rights in challenging court martial convictions. See Reid v. Covert, 354 U.S. 1 (1957). For discussion of the cases, see Fallon & Meltzer, *Habeas Corpus Jurisdiction, Substantive Rights, and the War on Terror*, 120 Harv.L.Rev. 2029, 2053–55 (2007).

provisions have extraterritorial application—and therefore whether a habeas petitioner has substantive constitutional rights to invoke—may depend on citizenship?

(4) Detention at Guantanamo Bay: The Rasul Decision. Insofar as Eisentrager could be interpreted as barring habeas jurisdiction over aliens held outside of territory over which the United States exercises de jure sovereignty, the Court limited its holding in Rasul v. Bush, 542 U.S. 466 (2004). Rasul involved two Australians and twelve Kuwaitis captured during hostilities between the United States and the Taliban regime in Afghanistan and held at the United States Naval Base at Guantanamo Bay in Cuba. The United States' agreements with Cuba, dating from 1903 and 1934, recognize the ultimate sovereignty of Cuba over the leased areas but grant the United States, as long as it retains a naval base there, "complete jurisdiction and control." Treating actions on petitioners' behalf filed in federal court in the District of Columbia as habeas petitions, the lower courts ruled that under Eisentrager, they lacked jurisdiction.[2] The Supreme Court reversed.

(a) Justice Stevens's opinion for the Court began by describing the Eisentrager decision, which had reversed a lower court's decision upholding habeas jurisdiction. As Justice Stevens described it, the Eisentrager Court viewed itself as " 'confronted with a decision whose basic premise is that these prisoners are entitled, as a constitutional right, to sue in some court of the United States for a writ of *habeas corpus*,' " even in the face of a host of factors distancing the petitioners from ties to the United States (quoting Eisentrager, 339 U.S. at 777).

The Guantanamo petitioners, Justice Stevens reasoned, differed from the Eisentrager petitioners in important respects: "They are not nationals of countries at war with the United States, and they deny that they have engaged in or plotted acts of aggression against the United States; they have never been afforded access to any tribunal, much less charged with and convicted of wrongdoing; and for more than two years they have been imprisoned in territory over which the United States exercises exclusive jurisdiction and control."

The Rasul Court then stated a critical premise of its opinion: that the six factors mentioned in Eisentrager "were relevant only to the question of the prisoners' *constitutional* entitlement to habeas corpus." Given that Braden overruled Ahrens and held that "the prisoner's presence within the territorial jurisdiction of the district court is not 'an invariable prerequisite' " to jurisdiction under § 2241, the Court held that for purposes of statutory jurisdiction, what now matters is that the custodian can be reached by service of process (quoting Braden), a point no party questioned.

The principle that federal statutes are presumed to lack extraterritorial application, Justice Stevens reasoned, was inapposite because given the

---

[2] The government chose Guantanamo Bay to detain individuals taken into custody in the wake of 9/11 in part because government lawyers at the time believed precedent supported the conclusion that the location was beyond the jurisdiction of the courts. See Memorandum from Patrick F. Philbin, Deputy Assistant Attorney Gen., and John C. Yoo, Deputy Assistant Attorney Gen., on Possible Habeas Jurisdiction over Aliens Held in Guantanamo Bay, Cuba, to William J. Haynes II, Gen. Counsel, Dep't of Defense (Dec. 28, 2001).

terms of the lease agreements, the Guantanamo petitioners were within the territorial jurisdiction of the United States. Going further and noting the government's concession that habeas jurisdiction would lie over a petition by an American citizen held at Guantanamo, he highlighted that § 2241 does not distinguish citizens from aliens.

(b)   Justice Scalia, joined by Chief Justice Rehnquist and Justice Thomas, filed a lengthy dissent. He argued that the court of appeals in Eisentrager, motivated by the policy of constitutional avoidance, had upheld statutory jurisdiction, and the Supreme Court, in reversing the court of appeals, necessarily held that § 2241 conferred no jurisdiction.

For Justice Scalia, the text of § 2241 "could not be clearer that a necessary requirement for issuing the writ is that *some* federal district court have territorial jurisdiction over the detainee."[3] He acknowledged that enforcing that limitation so as to deny any habeas review to a *citizen* detained abroad might raise constitutional doubts, thereby "justifying a strained construction of the habeas statute, or (more honestly) a determination of [the] constitutional right to habeas." But a case like this one, he argued, "raises no constitutional doubt."

(c)   Concurring in the judgment, Justice Kennedy distinguished Eisentrager on two grounds: "First, Guantanamo Bay is in every practical respect a United States territory, and it is one far removed from any hostilities." Second, the government was detaining the petitioners indefinitely without trial or other proceedings, which suggests a weaker case of military necessity and "much greater alignment with the traditional function of habeas corpus."

INTRODUCTORY NOTE ON BOUMEDIENE V. BUSH

At the end of its opinion in Hamdi, the plurality stated: "There remains the possibility that the standards we have articulated could be met by an appropriately authorized and properly constituted military tribunal." In response, the Department of Defense established Combatant Status Review Tribunals (CSRTs)—panels of three "neutral" military officers charged with reviewing, in the case of each alien detained at Guantanamo Bay, the government's initial determination that the individual could lawfully be detained as an enemy combatant.

Meanwhile, the Court held that the statutory grant of habeas jurisdiction in 28 U.S.C. § 2241 extended to aliens detained as enemy combatants at Guantanamo Bay in Rasul v. Bush, 542 U.S. 466 (2004), p. 1505, *supra*. In 2005 and 2006, Congress enacted legislation designed to override the Rasul decision and to strip federal (and state) courts of habeas or other jurisdiction to entertain challenges by aliens to the legality of their

---

[3]   Justice Scalia also relied on § 2242, which states that an application "addressed to the Supreme Court, a justice thereof or a circuit judge . . . shall state the reasons for not making application to *the district court of the district in which the applicant is held.*" (Emphasis added by Justice Scalia.)

detention as enemy combatants, and permit only limited review, in the D.C. Circuit, of decisions of the CSRTs. See pp. 1468–1470, *supra*.

After enactment of the jurisdiction-stripping provisions, the government moved to dismiss pending habeas petitions that had been filed by individuals detained at Guantanamo Bay. In the next principal case, Boumediene v. Bush, the Supreme Court faced two principal issues. The first was whether the Suspension Clause's guarantee of habeas review (or of an adequate substitute) extended to aliens detained as enemy combatants at the U.S. Naval Base in Guantanamo Bay, Cuba. The second was whether the legal structure Congress provided for those detained at Guantanamo constituted an adequate substitute for the review guaranteed by the Suspension Clause, assuming the Clause applied.

Boumediene v. Bush

553 U.S. 723 (2008).
Certiorari to the United States Court of Appeals for the District of Columbia Circuit.

■ JUSTICE KENNEDY delivered the opinion of the Court.

Petitioners are aliens designated as enemy combatants and detained at the United States Naval Station at Guantanamo Bay, Cuba. * * *

Petitioners present a question not resolved by our earlier cases * * *: whether they have the constitutional privilege of habeas corpus, a privilege not to be withdrawn except in conformance with the Suspension Clause, Art. I, § 9, cl. 2. We hold these petitioners do have the habeas corpus privilege. Congress has enacted a statute, the Detainee Treatment Act of 2005 (DTA), 119 Stat. 2739, that provides certain procedures for review of the detainees' status. We hold that those procedures are not an adequate and effective substitute for habeas corpus. Therefore § 7 of the Military Commissions Act of 2006 (MCA), 28 U.S.C. § 2241(e)[, which purports to strip the federal and state courts of habeas corpus jurisdiction,] operates as an unconstitutional suspension of the writ. * * *

I

* * * All [of the petitioners] are foreign nationals, but none is a citizen of a nation now at war with the United States. Each denies he is a member of the al Qaeda terrorist network that carried out the September 11 attacks or of the Taliban regime that provided sanctuary for al Qaeda. Each petitioner appeared before a separate CSRT; was determined to be an enemy combatant; and has sought a writ of habeas corpus in the United States District Court for the District of Columbia. * * *

[In 2005, Congress passed the DTA, subsection 1005(e) of which amended § 2241] to provide that "no court, justice, or judge shall have jurisdiction to hear or consider . . . an application for a writ of habeas corpus filed by or on behalf of an alien detained by the Department of Defense at Guantanamo Bay, Cuba." Section 1005 further provides that the Court of Appeals for the District of Columbia Circuit shall have "exclusive" jurisdiction to review decisions of the CSRTs.

[In 2006, Congress enacted the MCA, 10 U.S.C.A. § 948a *et seq.* (Supp. 2007), which again amended § 2241 so as to eliminate habeas corpus jurisdiction for cases like those of petitioners.] The Court of Appeals concluded that MCA § 7 must be read to strip from it, and all federal courts, jurisdiction to consider petitioners' habeas corpus applications * * *. * * *

II

[In this Part, the Court concluded that the jurisdiction-stripping provisions of MCA § 7 applied to pending cases, "so that, if the statute is valid, petitioners' cases must be dismissed."]

III

In deciding the constitutional questions now presented we must determine whether petitioners are barred from seeking the writ or invoking the protections of the Suspension Clause either because of their status, *i.e.*, petitioners' designation by the Executive Branch as enemy combatants, or their physical location, *i.e.*, their presence at Guantanamo Bay. The Government contends that noncitizens designated as enemy combatants and detained in territory located outside our Nation's borders have no constitutional rights and no privilege of habeas corpus. [Petitioners dispute both of those contentions.]

We begin with a brief account of the history and origins of the writ. Our account proceeds from two propositions. First, * * * [i]n the system conceived by the Framers the writ had a centrality that must inform proper interpretation of the Suspension Clause. Second, to the extent there were settled precedents or legal commentaries in 1789 regarding the extraterritorial scope of the writ or its application to enemy aliens, those authorities can be instructive for the present cases.

A

The Framers viewed freedom from unlawful restraint as a fundamental precept of liberty, and they understood the writ of habeas corpus as a vital instrument to secure that freedom. Experience taught, however, that the common-law writ all too often had been insufficient to guard against the abuse of monarchial power. That history counseled the necessity for specific language in the Constitution to secure the writ * * *.

* * * [The Court observed that historically, "the writ proved to be an imperfect check. Even when the importance of the writ was well understood in England, habeas relief often was denied by the courts or suspended by Parliament." The Court then traced important parliamentary developments in the evolution of the writ, including, *inter alia*, adoption of the Petition of Right, 3 Car. 1, ch. 1 (1627), 5 Statutes of

the Realm 23, 24 (condemning executive "imprison[ment] without any cause" shown), and the English Habeas Corpus Act of 1679, 31 Car. 2, ch. 2, which the Court noted "was the model upon which the habeas statutes of the 13 American Colonies were based." The Court also noted that Parliament's suspensions along with the resulting protests were known to the Framers and confirmed their "inherent distrust of government power" and "was the driving force behind the constitutional plan that allocated powers among three independent branches."]

That the Framers considered the writ a vital instrument for the protection of individual liberty is evident from the care taken to specify the limited grounds for its suspension: "The Privilege of the Writ of Habeas Corpus shall not be suspended, unless when in Cases of Rebellion or Invasion the public Safety may require it." Art. I, § 9, cl. 2. * * *

* * * [T]he Suspension Clause * * * ensures that, except during periods of formal suspension, the Judiciary will have a time-tested device, the writ, to maintain the "delicate balance of governance" that is itself the surest safeguard of liberty. See Hamdi [v. Rumsfeld, 542 U.S. 507, 536 (2004)] (plurality opinion). The Clause protects the rights of the detained by affirming the duty and authority of the Judiciary to call the jailer to account. The separation-of-powers doctrine, and the history that influenced its design, therefore must inform the reach and purpose of the Suspension Clause.

B

* * * The Court has been careful not to foreclose the possibility that the protections of the Suspension Clause have expanded along with post-1789 developments that define the present scope of the writ. See INS v. St. Cyr, 533 U.S. 289, 300–301 (2001). But the analysis may begin with precedents as of 1789, for the Court has said that "at the absolute minimum" the Clause protects the writ as it existed when the Constitution was drafted and ratified. Id., at 301.

* * * The Government argues the common-law writ ran only to those territories over which the Crown was sovereign. Petitioners argue that jurisdiction followed the King's officers. * * * In none of the cases cited [by the parties] do we find that a common-law court would or would not have granted, or refused to hear for lack of jurisdiction, a petition for a writ of habeas corpus brought by a prisoner deemed an enemy combatant, under a standard like the one the Department of Defense has used in these cases, and when held in a territory, like Guantanamo, over which the Government has total military and civil control.

We know that at common law a petitioner's status as an alien was not a categorical bar to habeas corpus relief. See, e.g., Sommersett's Case, 20 How. St. Tr. 1, 80–82 (1772). We know as well that common-law courts entertained habeas petitions brought by enemy aliens detained in England—"entertained" at least in the sense that the courts held hearings to determine the threshold question of entitlement to the writ.

See Case of Three Spanish Sailors, 2 Black. W. 1324, 96 Eng. Rep. 775 (C.P. 1779); King v. Schiever, 2 Burr. 765, 97 Eng. Rep. 551 (K.B. 1759); Du Castro's Case, Fort. 195, 92 Eng. Rep. 816 (K.B. 1697).

In the Schiever and the Spanish Sailors' case, [it is unclear whether the denial of relief was for lack of jurisdiction or because the detention was lawful. In Du Castro's Case, although relief was granted, the petitioner was detained in England.] To the extent these authorities suggest the common-law courts abstained altogether from matters involving prisoners of war, there was greater justification for doing so in the context of declared wars with other nation states. Judicial intervention might have complicated the military's ability to negotiate exchange of prisoners with the enemy, a wartime practice well known to the Framers.

[As to the geographic scope of the writ at common law, Petitioners cite cases offering relief to persons detained outside the realm of England though under the Crown's control, but those areas, unlike Guantanamo, may have been considered sovereign territory.

[The Government points to cases denying the power to issue writs to Scotland and Hanover, territories controlled by the English Monarch in his capacity as King of Scotland and Elector of Hanover. But in view of England's "delicate and complicated relationships" with those territories and the fact that they maintained their own laws, the refusal to issue the writ may have rested on "prudential concerns."]

[Those prudential concerns] are not relevant here. We have no reason to believe an order from a federal court would be disobeyed at Guantanamo. No Cuban court has jurisdiction to hear these petitioners' claims, and no law other than the laws of the United States applies at the naval station. * * *

Each side in the present matter argues that the very lack of a precedent on point supports its position. The Government points out there is no evidence that a court sitting in England granted habeas relief to an enemy alien detained abroad; petitioners respond there is no evidence that a court refused to do so for lack of jurisdiction.

Both arguments are premised, however, upon the assumption that the historical record is complete and that the common law, if properly understood, yields a definite answer to the questions before us. There are reasons to doubt both assumptions. * * * [G]iven the unique status of Guantanamo Bay and the particular dangers of terrorism in the modern age, the common-law courts simply may not have confronted cases with close parallels to this one. We decline, therefore, to infer too much, one way or the other, from the lack of historical evidence on point.

IV

* * * [T]he Government says the Suspension Clause affords petitioners no rights because the United States does not claim sovereignty over the place of detention.

Guantanamo Bay is not formally part of the United States. And under the terms of the lease between the United States and Cuba, Cuba retains "ultimate sovereignty" over the territory while the United States exercises "complete jurisdiction and control." [Citing Lease Agreement.] Under the terms of the 1934 Treaty, however, Cuba effectively has no rights as a sovereign until the parties agree to modification of the 1903 Lease Agreement or the United States abandons the base. * * *

[It is not improper "to inquire into the objective degree of control the Nation asserts over foreign territory." Although Cuba "retains *de jure* sovereignty over Guantanamo Bay," we note the] uncontested fact that the United States, by virtue of its complete jurisdiction and control over the base, maintains *de facto* sovereignty over this territory.

* * * [T]he history of common-law habeas corpus provides scant support for [the proposition that *de jure* sovereignty is the touchstone of habeas corpus jurisdiction, and] that position would be inconsistent with our precedents and contrary to fundamental separation-of-powers principles.

A

* * * Fundamental questions regarding the Constitution's geographic scope first arose at the dawn of the 20th century when the Nation acquired * * * Puerto Rico, Guam, and the Philippines * * * at the conclusion of the Spanish-American War [and then annexed Hawaii in 1898.] * * *

In a series of opinions later known as the Insular Cases, the Court addressed whether the Constitution, by its own force, applies in any territory that is not a State. [Citing six decisions from the early twentieth century.] The Court held that the Constitution has independent force in these territories, a force not contingent upon acts of legislative grace. [Yet the Court was wary of applying the Anglo-American legal tradition (for example, the use of grand and petit juries) to territories that followed the civil law system, especially when, as with the Philippines, the United States intended to grant independence to the territory.]

These considerations resulted in the doctrine of territorial incorporation, under which the Constitution applies in full in incorporated Territories surely destined for statehood but only in part in unincorporated Territories. * * * [T]he Court took for granted that even in unincorporated Territories the * * * United States was bound to provide to noncitizen inhabitants "guaranties of certain fundamental personal rights declared in the Constitution" [Balzac v. Porto Rico, 258 U.S. 298, 312 (1922), while recognizing] the inherent practical difficulties of enforcing all constitutional provisions "always and everywhere" * * *. * * *

Practical considerations likewise influenced the Court's analysis a half century later in Reid [v. Covert, 354 U.S. 1 (1957). There, spouses of American servicemen living on military bases overseas were tried by military courts for crimes committed abroad. In upholding their claim of a right to jury trial, the Court placed great weight on their status as citizens. But] practical considerations, related not to the petitioners' citizenship but to the place of their confinement and trial, were relevant to each Member of the Reid majority. * * *

Practical considerations weighed heavily as well in Johnson v. Eisentrager, 339 U.S. 763 (1950) * * *. The prisoners were detained at Landsberg Prison in Germany during the Allied Powers' post-War occupation. The Court stressed the difficulties of ordering the Government to produce the prisoners in a habeas corpus proceeding. It "would require allocation of shipping space, guarding personnel, billeting and rations" and would damage the prestige of military commanders at a sensitive time. *Id.*, at 779. * * *

True, the Court in Eisentrager denied access to the writ, and it noted the prisoners "at no relevant time were within any territory over which the United States is sovereign, and [that] the scenes of their offense, their capture, their trial and their punishment were all beyond the territorial jurisdiction of any court of the United States." 339 U.S., at 778. The Government seizes upon this language as proof positive that the Eisentrager Court adopted a formalistic, sovereignty-based test for determining the reach of the Suspension Clause. We reject this reading for three reasons.

First, we do not accept the idea that the above-quoted passage from Eisentrager is the only authoritative language in the opinion and that all the rest is dicta. * * *

Second, because the United States lacked both *de jure* sovereignty and plenary control over Landsberg Prison, it is far from clear that the Eisentrager Court used the term sovereignty only in the narrow technical sense * * *. * * * That the Court devoted [significant discussion to practical matters] suggests that the Court was not concerned exclusively with the formal legal status of Landsberg Prison but also with the objective degree of control the United States asserted over it. * * *

Third, * * * [the Government's reading] of Eisentrager overlooks what we see as a common thread uniting the Insular Cases, Eisentrager, and Reid: the idea that questions of extraterritoriality turn on objective factors and practical concerns, not formalism.

B

The Government's formal sovereignty-based test [would mean] that by surrendering formal sovereignty over any unincorporated territory to a third party, while at the same time entering into a lease that grants total control over the territory back to the United States, it would be possible for the political branches to govern without legal constraint.

Our basic charter cannot be contracted away like this. * * * [To hold otherwise] would permit a striking anomaly in our tripartite system of government, leading to a regime in which Congress and the President, not this Court, say "what the law is." Marbury v. Madison, 1 Cranch 137, 177 (1803).

These concerns have particular bearing upon the Suspension Clause * * *. The test for determining the scope of this provision must not be subject to manipulation by those whose power it is designed to restrain.

C

As we recognized in Rasul, the outlines of a framework for determining the reach of the Suspension Clause are suggested by the factors the Court relied upon in Eisentrager. * * * [T]he Court [there] found relevant that each petitioner:

> "(a) is an enemy alien; (b) has never been or resided in the United States; (c) was captured outside of our territory and there held in military custody as a prisoner of war; (d) was tried and convicted by a Military Commission sitting outside the United States; (e) for offenses against laws of war committed outside the United States; (f) and is at all times imprisoned outside the United States." 339 U.S., at 777.

Based on this language * * * and the reasoning in our other extraterritoriality opinions, we conclude that at least three factors are relevant in determining the reach of the Suspension Clause: (1) the citizenship and status of the detainee and the adequacy of the process through which that status determination was made; (2) the nature of the sites where apprehension and then detention took place; and (3) the practical obstacles inherent in resolving the prisoner's entitlement to the writ.

Applying this framework, we note at the onset that the status of these detainees is a matter of dispute[, for they, unlike the detainees in Eisentrager, deny they are enemy combatants.] They have been afforded some process in CSRT proceedings to determine their status; but, unlike in Eisentrager, there has been no trial by military commission for violations of the laws of war. The difference is not trivial. [The Eisentrager petitioners were afforded a rigorous adversarial process to test the legality of their detention, in which they were represented by counsel and could introduce evidence and cross-examine the prosecution's witnesses.]

In comparison the procedural protections afforded to the detainees in the CSRT hearings are far more limited, and * * * fall well short of the procedures and adversarial mechanisms that would eliminate the need for habeas corpus review. Although the detainee is assigned a "Personal Representative" to assist him during CSRT proceedings, * * * that person is not the detainee's lawyer or even his "advocate." The Government's evidence is accorded a presumption of validity. The detainee is allowed to present "reasonably available" evidence, but his ability to rebut the Government's evidence against him is limited by the circumstances of his confinement and his lack of counsel at this stage. And although the detainee can seek review of his status determination in the Court of Appeals, that review process cannot cure all defects in the earlier proceedings. See Part V, *infra.*

As to the second factor relevant to this analysis, [the sites of apprehension and detention], * * * there are critical differences between Landsberg Prison, circa 1950, and the United States Naval Station at Guantanamo Bay in 2008. * * * [T]he United States' control over the prison in Germany was neither absolute nor indefinite. [The United States was answerable to the combined Allied Forces, which did not intend to occupy Germany indefinitely or even to displace all German institutions during the occupation.] Guantanamo Bay, on the other hand, is no transient possession. In every practical sense Guantanamo is not abroad; it is within the constant jurisdiction of the United States.

As to the third factor, we recognize, as the Court did in Eisentrager, that there are costs to holding the Suspension Clause applicable in a case of military detention abroad. * * * While we are sensitive to these concerns, we do not find them dispositive. * * * The Government presents no credible arguments that the military mission at Guantanamo would be compromised if habeas corpus courts had jurisdiction to hear the detainees' claims. * * *

The situation in Eisentrager was far different * * *. [The United States was responsible for an occupation zone in Germany exceeding 57,000 square miles, with a population of 18 million. American forces faced potential security threats from a defeated enemy. By contrast, Guantanamo is a secure prison facility located on an isolated and heavily fortified military base consisting of 45 square miles of land and water, where the only long-term residents are American military personnel, their families, and a small number of workers.]

* * * Under the facts presented here * * * there are few practical barriers to the running of the writ. To the extent barriers arise, habeas corpus procedures likely can be modified to address them. See Part VI-B, *infra.*

It is true that before today the Court has never held that noncitizens detained by our Government in territory over which another country maintains *de jure* sovereignty have any rights under our Constitution. But the cases before us lack any precise historical parallel. They involve individuals detained by executive order for the duration of a conflict that, if measured from September 11, 2001, to the present, is already among the longest wars in American history. The detainees, moreover, are held in a territory that * * * is under the complete and total control of our Government. * * *

We hold that Art. I, § 9, cl. 2, of the Constitution has full effect at Guantanamo Bay. * * * The MCA does not purport to be a formal suspension of the writ; and the Government * * * has not argued that it is. Petitioners, therefore, are entitled to the privilege of habeas corpus to challenge the legality of their detention.*

V

In light of this holding the question becomes whether * * * Congress has provided adequate substitute procedures for habeas corpus [in the review process in the D.C. Circuit authorized by the Detainee Treatment Act to satisfy the Suspension Clause.] Congress has granted that court jurisdiction to consider

> "(i) whether the status determination of the [Combatant Status Review Tribunal] . . . was consistent with the standards and procedures specified by the Secretary of Defense . . . and (ii) to the extent the Constitution and laws of the United States are applicable, whether the use of such standards and procedures to make the determination is consistent with the Constitution and laws of the United States." § 1005(e)(2)(c), 119 Stat. 2742.

The Court of Appeals * * * found it unnecessary to consider whether an adequate substitute has been provided. [Although our normal practice would be to remand, in exceptional circumstances such as here where "these detainees have been denied meaningful access to a judicial forum for a period of years" we may appropriately depart from that practice.]

A

Our case law does not contain extensive discussion of standards defining suspension of the writ or of circumstances under which suspension has occurred. * * *

The two leading cases addressing habeas substitutes, Swain v. Pressley, 430 U.S. 372 (1977), and United States v. Hayman, 342 U.S. 205 (1952) * * * provide little guidance here. [Those cases considered statutory procedures designed as a substitute for *post-conviction* habeas review.]

[The Court here contrasted DTA review with review under § 2241, observing that the latter "accommodates the necessity for factfinding that will arise in some cases" and that a petition initially filed with a Justice or a circuit judge can be transferred to a district court for factfinding.] By granting the Court of Appeals "exclusive" jurisdiction over petitioners' cases, Congress has foreclosed that option. * * * The DTA should be interpreted to accord some latitude to the Court of Appeals to fashion procedures necessary to make its review function a meaningful one, but, if congressional intent is to be respected, the procedures adopted cannot be as extensive or as protective of the rights

---

*   [Ed.] In a concurring opinion joined by Justices Ginsburg and Breyer, Justice Souter stated that "no one who reads the Court's opinion in Rasul could seriously doubt that the jurisdictional question must be answered the same way in purely constitutional cases, given the Court's reliance on the historical background of habeas generally in answering the statutory question."

of the detainees as they would be in a § 2241 proceeding. Otherwise there would have been no, or very little, purpose for enacting the DTA. * * *

B

We do not endeavor to offer a comprehensive summary of the requisites for an adequate substitute for habeas corpus. We do consider it uncontroversial, however, that the privilege of habeas corpus entitles the prisoner to a meaningful opportunity to demonstrate that he is being held pursuant to "the erroneous application or interpretation" of relevant law. St. Cyr, 533 U.S., at 302. And the habeas court must have the power to order the conditional release of an individual unlawfully detained * * *. * * * [D]epending on the circumstances, more may be required.

Indeed, common-law habeas corpus was, above all, an adaptable remedy. Its precise application and scope changed depending upon the circumstances. It appears the common-law habeas court's role was most extensive in cases of pretrial and noncriminal detention, where there had been little or no previous judicial review of the cause for detention. Notably, the black-letter rule that prisoners could not controvert facts in the jailer's return was not followed (or at least not with consistency) in such cases. [Citing authorities.]

[Evidence from 19th-century American sources indicates that habeas courts] routinely allowed prisoners to introduce exculpatory evidence that was either unknown or previously unavailable to the prisoner. [Citing authorities.] * * *

The idea that the necessary scope of habeas review in part depends upon the rigor of any earlier proceedings accords with our test for procedural adequacy in the due process context. See Mathews v. Eldridge, 424 U.S. 319, 335 (1976). * * *

Where a person is detained by executive order, rather than, say, after being tried and convicted in a court, the need for collateral review is most pressing. A criminal conviction in the usual course occurs after a judicial hearing before a tribunal disinterested in the outcome and committed to procedures designed to ensure its own independence. These dynamics are not inherent in executive detention orders or executive review procedures. * * * Habeas corpus proceedings need not resemble a criminal trial, even when the detention is by executive order. But * * * [t]he habeas court must have sufficient authority to conduct a meaningful review of both the cause for detention and the Executive's power to detain.

[The Court next turned to the CSRT process.]

Petitioners identify what they see as myriad deficiencies in the CSRTs. The most relevant for our purposes are the constraints upon the detainee's ability to rebut the factual basis for the Government's assertion that he is an enemy combatant. [In addition to limitations already mentioned, the detained party] may not be aware of the most critical allegations that the Government relied upon to order his detention. The detainee can confront witnesses that testify during the CSRT proceedings. But given that there are in effect no limits on the admission of hearsay evidence—the only requirement is that the tribunal deem the evidence "relevant and helpful"—the detainee's opportunity to question witnesses is likely to be more theoretical than real.

The Government [argues that the CSRT] was designed to conform to the procedures suggested by the plurality in Hamdi. Setting aside the fact that the relevant language in Hamdi did not garner a majority of the Court * * *, [there, t]he § 2241 habeas corpus process remained in place. * * * [T]he Court had no occasion to define the necessary scope of habeas review, for Suspension Clause purposes, in the context of enemy combatant detentions. * * *

Although we make no judgment as to whether the CSRTs, as currently constituted, satisfy due process standards, we agree with petitioners that * * * there is considerable risk of error in the tribunal's findings of fact. * * * And given that the consequence of error may be detention of persons for the duration of hostilities that may last a generation or more, this is a risk too significant to ignore.

For the writ of habeas corpus, or its substitute, to function as an effective and proper remedy in this context, the court that conducts the habeas proceeding must have the means to correct errors that occurred during the CSRT proceedings. This includes some authority to assess the sufficiency of the Government's evidence against the detainee. It also must have the authority to admit and consider relevant exculpatory evidence that was not introduced during the earlier proceeding. Federal habeas petitioners long have had the means to supplement the record on review, even in the postconviction habeas setting. Here that opportunity is constitutionally required.

Consistent with the historic function and province of the writ, habeas corpus review may be more circumscribed if the underlying detention proceedings are more thorough than they were here. [Here the Court contrasted two habeas cases involving enemy aliens tried for war crimes, In re Yamashita, 327 U.S. 1 (1946), and Ex parte Quirin, 317 U.S. 1 (1942), where the proceedings, "like those in Eisentrager, had an adversarial structure that is lacking here." Thus, it was appropriate for the Court to limit review in those cases to whether "the Executive had legal authority to try the petitioners by military commission."] * * *

C

[The Court next considered the DTA procedures. The Court first read the DTA to permit the court to order release, "a constitutionally required remedy." Next, the Court held that the DTA "might be read * * * to allow the petitioners to assert most, if not all, of the legal claims they seek to advance, including their most basic claim: that the President has no authority under the AUMF to detain them indefinitely." The court then turned to whether the DTA permits the lower court to find facts.]

Assuming the DTA can be construed to allow the Court of Appeals to review or correct the CSRT's factual determinations, as opposed to merely certifying that the tribunal applied the correct standard of proof, we see no way to construe the statute to allow what is also constitutionally required in this context: an opportunity for the detainee to present relevant exculpatory evidence that was not made part of the record in the earlier proceedings.

On its face the statute allows the Court of Appeals to consider no evidence outside the CSRT record. [But, the Court noted, the D.C. Circuit had decided in parallel litigation] that the DTA allows it to order the production of all " 'reasonably available information in the possession of the U.S. Government bearing on the issue whether the detainee meets the criteria to be designated as an enemy combatant,' " regardless of whether this evidence was put before the CSRT. See Bismullah v. Gates (I), 501 F.3d 178, 180 (D.C.Cir.2007). * * * [Even assuming the correctness of that interpretation of the DTA, constitutional problems remain because] the detainee still would have no opportunity to present evidence discovered after the CSRT proceedings concluded.

* * * [N]ewly discovered evidence * * * may be critical to the detainee's argument that he is not an enemy combatant and there is no cause to detain him. * * *

The Government * * * [points out] that if a detainee obtains such evidence, he can request that the Deputy Secretary of Defense convene a new CSRT. [This] is an insufficient replacement for the factual review these detainees are entitled to receive through habeas corpus. [The decision whether to initiate new proceedings is wholly discretionary.] And we see no way to construe the DTA to allow a detainee to challenge the Deputy Secretary's decision not to open a new CSRT * * *. * * *

[We cannot interpret the DTA to satisfy the Suspension Clause especially when] read in light of Congress' reasons for enacting it. * * *

Although we do not hold that an adequate substitute must duplicate § 2241 in all respects, * * * MCA § 7 * * * effects an unconstitutional suspension of the writ. * * *

VI

A

* * * The only law we identify as unconstitutional is MCA § 7. Accordingly, both the DTA and the CSRT process remain intact. Our holding * * * should not be read to imply that a habeas court should intervene the moment an enemy combatant steps foot in a territory where the writ runs. The Executive is entitled to a reasonable period of time to determine a detainee's status before a court entertains that detainee's habeas corpus petition. The CSRT process is the mechanism Congress and the President set up to deal with these issues. Except in cases of undue delay, federal courts should refrain from entertaining an

enemy combatant's habeas corpus petition at least until after the Department, acting via the CSRT, has had a chance to review his status.

B

* * * We make no attempt to anticipate all of the evidentiary and access-to-counsel issues that will arise during the course of the detainees' habeas corpus proceedings. We recognize, however, that the Government has a legitimate interest in protecting sources and methods of intelligence gathering * * *. * * *

["In considering both the procedural and substantive standards used to impose detention to prevent acts of terrorism," the Executive, which, unlike the judiciary, has access to intelligence, should be accorded substantial deference. But security depends not only on the actions of intelligence and military officials, but also on "freedom from arbitrary and unlawful restraint and the personal liberty that is secured by adherence to the separation of powers."]

* * * The judgment of the Court of Appeals is reversed. The cases are remanded to the Court of Appeals with instructions that it remand the cases to the District Court for proceedings consistent with this opinion.

It is so ordered.

■ CHIEF JUSTICE ROBERTS, with whom JUSTICE SCALIA, JUSTICE THOMAS, and JUSTICE ALITO join, dissenting.

Today the Court strikes down as inadequate the most generous set of procedural protections ever afforded aliens detained by this country as enemy combatants, * * * without bothering to say what due process rights the detainees possess, without explaining how the statute fails to vindicate those rights, and before a single petitioner has exhausted the procedures under the law. And to what effect? The majority merely replaces a review system designed by the people's representatives with a set of shapeless procedures to be defined by federal courts at some future date. * * * [T]his decision is not really about the detainees at all, but about control of federal policy regarding enemy combatants.

* * * I regard the issue [whether the detainees are entitled to the protections of habeas corpus] as a difficult one, primarily because of the unique and unusual jurisdictional status of Guantanamo Bay. I nonetheless agree with Justice Scalia's analysis of our precedents and the pertinent history of the writ, and accordingly join his dissent. The important point for me, however, is that the Court should have resolved these cases on other grounds. Habeas is most fundamentally a procedural right * * *. The critical threshold question in these cases * * * is whether the system the political branches designed protects whatever rights the detainees may possess. If so, there is no need for any additional process, whether called "habeas" or something else.

* * * [T]he habeas process the Court mandates will most likely end up looking a lot like the DTA system it replaces, as the district court

judges shaping it will have to reconcile review of the prisoners' detention with the undoubted need to protect the American people from the terrorist threat—precisely the challenge Congress undertook in drafting the DTA. All that today's opinion has done is shift responsibility for those sensitive foreign policy and national security decisions from the elected branches to the Federal Judiciary.

I believe the system the political branches constructed adequately protects any constitutional rights aliens captured abroad and detained as enemy combatants may enjoy. I therefore would dismiss these cases on that ground. * * *

I

* * * The plurality in Hamdi v. Rumsfeld, 542 U. S. 507, 533 (2004), explained that the Constitution guaranteed an American *citizen* challenging his detention as an enemy combatant the right to "notice of the factual basis for his classification, and a fair opportunity to rebut the Government's factual assertions before a neutral decisionmaker." The plurality specifically stated that constitutionally adequate collateral process could be provided "by an appropriately authorized and properly constituted military tribunal," given the "uncommon potential to burden the Executive at a time of ongoing military conflict." *Id.*, at 533, 538. This point is directly pertinent here, for surely the Due Process Clause does not afford *non*-citizens in such circumstances greater protection than citizens are due.

If the CSRT procedures meet the minimal due process requirements outlined in Hamdi, and if an Article III court is available to ensure that these procedures are followed in future cases, there is no need to reach the Suspension Clause question. * * *

II

* * * [The existing system] is adequate to vindicate whatever due process rights petitioners may have.

A

[The CSRTs are a means for challenging the Government's initial determination of enemy combatant status, based on the very Army Regulation that] the plurality in Hamdi said provided the type of process an enemy combatant could expect from a habeas court. The CSRTs operate much as habeas courts would if hearing the detainee's collateral challenge for the first time * * *. * * *

* * * Congress went further in the DTA [than Hamdi requires]. * * * The majority attempts to dismiss Hamdi's relevance[, but] Hamdi was all about the scope of habeas review in the context of enemy combatant detentions. * * *

B

* * * The scope of federal habeas review is traditionally more limited in some contexts than in others, depending on the status of the detainee

and the rights he may assert. See St. Cyr, 533 U.S., at 306 ("In [immigration cases], other than the question whether there was some evidence to support the [deportation] order, the courts generally did not review factual determinations made by the Executive" (footnote omitted)); Burns v. Wilson, 346 U.S. 137, 139 (1953) (plurality opinion) ("[I]n military habeas corpus the inquiry, the scope of matters open for review, has always been more narrow than in civil cases"); In re Yamashita, 327 U.S. 1, 8 (1946) ("* * * If the military tribunals have lawful authority to hear, decide and condemn, their action is not subject to judicial review"); Ex parte Quirin, 317 U.S. 1, 25 (1942) (federal habeas review of military commission verdict limited to determining commission's jurisdiction).* * *

* * * The majority admits that a number of historical authorities suggest that at the time of the Constitution's ratification, "common-law courts abstained altogether from matters involving prisoners of war." If this is accurate, the process provided prisoners under the DTA is plainly more than sufficient * * *.

Assuming the constitutional baseline is more robust, the DTA still provides adequate process * * *. * * *

C

* * * None of [the Court's] complaints [about the DTA] is persuasive.

[Detainees may call any witness who is "reasonably available," a standard drawn from Army Regulations that permits the government to avoid a futile search for evidence that might burden the military. And Hamdi expressly approved the use of hearsay evidence.

[The access to classified information afforded to the detainee's Personal Representative, and to counsel on appeal, is broader than that ever before provided to alleged alien enemy combatants. Prisoners of war who challenge status determinations under the Geneva Convention enjoy no such access and have no right to assistance from counsel or from a personal representative.]

Keep in mind that all this is just at the CSRT stage. [Before the D.C. Circuit, detainees have counsel and the right to challenge the factual and legal bases of their detentions.] * * *

D

Despite these guarantees, the Court finds the DTA system an inadequate habeas substitute, for one central reason: Detainees are unable to introduce at the appeal stage exculpatory evidence discovered after the conclusion of their CSRT proceedings. The Court hints darkly that the DTA may suffer from other infirmities, but it does not bother to name them, making a response a bit difficult. * * *

[If new evidence materializes after CSRT proceedings but before review in the Court of Appeals, the DTA permits the D.C. Circuit to remand for a new CSRT determination.]

* * * The DTA [also] expressly directs the Secretary of Defense to "provide for periodic review of any new evidence that may become available relating to the enemy combatant status of a detainee." DTA § 1005(a)(3). Regulations issued by the Department of Defense provide that when a detainee puts forward new, material evidence "not previously presented to the detainee's CSRT," the Deputy Secretary of Defense " 'will direct that a CSRT convene to reconsider the basis of the detainee's . . . status in light of the new information.' " * * *2 * * *

E

[Under the DTA framework, the D.C. Circuit, the CSRTs, and the head of the Administrative Review Boards can order release. The Court's conclusion that the DTA system is not an adequate substitute for habeas relies on a simple premise: "Congress could not possibly have intended to enact an adequate substitute for habeas."]

III

* * * [The Court] simply ignores the many difficult questions its holding presents. What, for example, will become of the CSRT process? * * * [T]o what deference, if any, is that CSRT determination entitled?

There are other problems. Take witness availability. What makes the majority think witnesses will become magically available when the review procedure is labeled "habeas"? Will the location of most of these witnesses change—will they suddenly become easily susceptible to service of process? Or will subpoenas issued by American habeas courts run to Basra? * * * [W]ill detainees be able to call active-duty military officers as witnesses? If not, why not?

The majority has no answers for these difficulties. What it does say leaves open the distinct possibility that its "habeas" remedy will, when all is said and done, end up looking a great deal like the DTA review it rejects. * * *

So who has won? Not the detainees. The Court's analysis leaves them with only the prospect of further litigation to determine the content of their new habeas right, followed by further litigation to resolve their particular cases, followed by further litigation before the D.C. Circuit— where they could have started had they invoked the DTA procedure. Not Congress, whose attempt to "determine—through democratic means— how best" to balance the security of the American people with the detainees' liberty interests, has been unceremoniously brushed aside. Not the Great Writ, whose majesty is hardly enhanced by its extension to a jurisdictionally quirky outpost, with no tangible benefit to anyone. Not the rule of law, unless by that is meant the rule of lawyers, who will

---

2   The Court wonders what might happen if the detainee puts forward new material evidence but the Deputy Secretary refuses to convene a new CSRT. The answer is that the detainee can petition the D.C. Circuit for review. The DTA directs that the procedures for review of new evidence be included among "[t]he procedures submitted under paragraph (1)(A)" governing CSRT review of enemy combatant status[.] § 1405(a)(3), 119 Stat. 3476. It is undisputed that the D.C. Circuit has statutory authority to review and enforce these procedures.

now arguably have a greater role than military and intelligence officials in shaping policy for alien enemy combatants. And certainly not the American people, who today lose a bit more control over the conduct of this Nation's foreign policy to unelected, politically unaccountable judges.

I respectfully dissent.

■ JUSTICE SCALIA, with whom THE CHIEF JUSTICE, JUSTICE THOMAS, and JUSTICE ALITO join, dissenting.

Today, for the first time in our Nation's history, the Court confers a constitutional right to habeas corpus on alien enemies detained abroad by our military forces in the course of an ongoing war. * * * The writ of habeas corpus does not, and never has, run in favor of aliens abroad; the Suspension Clause thus has no application, and the Court's intervention in this military matter is entirely ultra vires. * * *

I

America is at war with radical Islamists. * * *

* * * [T]oday's opinion * * * will almost certainly cause more Americans to be killed. * * *

[At least 30 of the prisoners that the military had chosen to release from Guantanamo Bay have returned to the battlefield. "These, mind you, were detainees whom *the military* had concluded were not enemy combatants." Despite the "incredible difficulty" of assessing who is and is not an enemy combatant, "[a]stoundingly, the Court today raises the bar" by requiring the military to defend its decisions in civilian courts under rules beyond those specified by Congress.] * * *

* * * The Court today decrees that no good reason to accept the judgment of the other two branches is "apparent." * * * What competence does the Court have to second-guess the judgment of Congress and the President on such a point? None whatever. But the Court blunders in nonetheless. Henceforth, as today's opinion makes unnervingly clear, how to handle enemy prisoners in this war will ultimately lie with the branch that knows least about the national security concerns that the subject entails.

II

A

* * * The Court admits that it cannot determine whether the writ historically extended to aliens held abroad, and it concedes (necessarily) that Guantanamo Bay lies outside the sovereign territory of the United States. Together, these two concessions establish that it is (in the Court's view) perfectly ambiguous whether the common-law writ would have provided a remedy for these petitioners. If that is so, the Court has no basis to strike down the Military Commissions Act * * *.[2] * * *

2　The opinion seeks to avoid this straightforward conclusion by saying that the Court has been "careful not to foreclose the possibility that the protections of the Suspension Clause

B

* * * [T]he most pertinent * * * precedent[ ] [is] Johnson v. Eisentrager, 339 U.S. 763. * * * Writing for the Court, Justice Jackson held that American courts lacked habeas jurisdiction:

> "We are cited to [*sic*] no instance where a court, in this or any other country where the writ is known, has issued it on behalf of an alien enemy who, at no relevant time and in no stage of his captivity, has been within its territorial jurisdiction. Nothing in the text of the Constitution extends such a right, nor does anything in our statutes." *Id.*, at 768.

Justice Jackson then elaborated on the historical scope of the writ:

> * * * "[I]n extending constitutional protections beyond the citizenry, the Court has been at pains to point out that it was the alien's presence within its territorial jurisdiction that gave the Judiciary power to act." *Id.*, at 770–771.

[Justice Jackson also] distinguished [Quirin and Yamashita] in which aliens had been permitted to seek habeas relief, on the ground that the prisoners in those cases were in custody within the sovereign territory of the United States. * * *

The Court would have us believe that Eisentrager rested on "[p]ractical considerations," such as the "difficulties of ordering the Government to produce the prisoners in a habeas corpus proceeding." * * * This is a sheer rewriting of the case. Eisentrager mentioned practical concerns, to be sure—* * * to support *its holding* that the Constitution does not empower courts to issue writs of habeas corpus to aliens abroad *in any circumstances.* * * *

[Nor, Justice Scalia argued, can a "functional" reading of Eisentrager be supported by the Insular Cases, which concerned sovereign territories of the United States, or by the decision in Reid v. Covert, which concerned only the rights of citizens abroad.]

The category of prisoner comparable to these detainees are not the Eisentrager criminal defendants, but the more than 400,000 prisoners of war detained in the United States alone during World War II. Not a single one was accorded the right to have his detention validated by a habeas corpus action in federal court—and that despite the fact that they were present on U.S. soil. The Court's analysis produces a crazy result: Whereas those convicted and sentenced to death for war crimes are without judicial remedy, all enemy combatants detained during a war, at least insofar as they are confined in an area away from the battlefield

---

have expanded along with post-1789 developments that define the present scope of the writ" (citing INS v. St. Cyr, 533 U.S. 289, 300–01 (2001)). But not foreclosing the possibility that they have expanded is not the same as demonstrating * * * that they have expanded. The Court must either hold that the Suspension Clause has "expanded" * * * to aliens abroad, or acknowledge that it has no basis to set aside the actions of Congress and the President. It does neither.

over which the United States exercises "absolute and indefinite" control, may seek a writ of habeas corpus in federal court. * * *

C

What drives today's decision is * * * an inflated notion of judicial supremacy. * * * Our power "to say what the law is" is circumscribed by the limits of our statutorily and constitutionally conferred jurisdiction. And that is precisely the question in these cases: whether the Constitution confers habeas jurisdiction on federal courts to decide petitioners' claims. It is both irrational and arrogant to say that the answer must be yes, because otherwise we would not be supreme. * * *

III

Putting aside the conclusive precedent of Eisentrager, it is clear that the original understanding of the Suspension Clause was that habeas corpus was not available to aliens abroad * * *.

The Suspension Clause * * * [should be given] the meaning it was understood to have at the time of its adoption by the people. That course is especially demanded when (as here) the Constitution limits the power of Congress to infringe upon a pre-existing common-law right. * * *

[At English common law, the writ did not extend beyond the Crown's sovereign territory, and the Habeas Corpus Act of 1679 was limited in its territorial application to the sovereign territory of the Crown.]

* * * The possibility of evading judicial review through * * * spiriting-away [of prisoners beyond the Act's reach] was eliminated, not by expanding the writ abroad, but by forbidding (in Section XII of the Act) the shipment of prisoners to places where the writ did not run or where its execution would be difficult." * * *

In sum, *all* available historical evidence points to the conclusion that the writ would not have been available at common law for aliens captured and held outside the sovereign territory of the Crown. * * *

What history teaches is confirmed by the nature of the limitations that the Constitution places upon suspension of the common-law writ. It can be suspended only "in Cases of Rebellion or Invasion." Art. I, § 9, cl. 2. The latter case (invasion) is plainly limited to the territory of the United States; and while it is conceivable that a rebellion could be mounted by American citizens abroad, surely the overwhelming majority of its occurrences would be domestic. If the extraterritorial scope of habeas turned on flexible, "functional" considerations, as the Court holds, why would the Constitution limit its suspension almost entirely to instances of domestic crisis? Surely there is an even greater justification for suspension in foreign lands where the United States might hold prisoners of war during an ongoing conflict. And correspondingly, there is less threat to liberty when the Government suspends the writ's (supposed) application in foreign lands, where even on the most extreme view prisoners are entitled to fewer constitutional rights. * * *

[The limited reach of the writ is not disproved by its availability for citizens held abroad, for the common law writ, when absorbed into] the new constitutional Republic, took on such changes as were demanded by a system in which rule is derived from the consent of the governed, and in which citizens (not "subjects") are afforded defined protections against the Government. * * *

The Nation will live to regret what the Court has done today. I dissent.

NOTE ON BOUMEDIENE AND THE TERRITORIAL REACH OF HABEAS CORPUS

(1) Interpretive Methodology in Boumediene. Justice Scalia's dissent argues that fidelity to original intent is especially important "when (as here) the Constitution limits the power of Congress to infringe upon a pre-existing common-law right." Is that argument convincing, given that other constitutional guarantees have similar effect? (Consider, for example, the rights to a jury trial and to be free from unreasonable searches and seizures.)

Is the majority's view of the relevance of original understanding clear? Justice Kennedy says both that "[t]he Court has been careful not to foreclose the possibility that the protections of the Suspension Clause have expanded" since the founding and that "the analysis may begin with precedents as of 1789, for the Court has said that 'at the absolute minimum' the Clause protects the writ as it existed when the Constitution was drafted and ratified" (quoting St. Cyr). In turn, Justice Scalia's dissent (see footnote 2) takes the Court to task for not being explicit about whether the Suspension Clause's protection is broader today than it was two centuries ago.

One might view the majority's extensive historical discussion (of which only a summary is provided) as having accepted, at least to some extent, an originalist approach, only to determine that history yields no definitive answer. But the majority's emphasis on functional assessments, the particularities of the detention site, and prudential and practical considerations together seems to depart from originalism, for that cluster of factors will have quite different significance today than it did two centuries ago. (Could a federal court in the nation's capital have effectively exercised jurisdiction over a location like Guantanamo Bay in the eighteenth century?) Or should the Court's opinion be read as holding that the original understanding of the Suspension Clause was a functional one? Does the Suspension Clause's reference to a common law writ implicitly contemplate a continued common law-like development of constitutional meaning? And is the Court's opinion consistent with a "common law" approach to interpretation of the scope of the writ, under which courts have "a creative, discretionary function in adapting constitutional and statutory language—which is frequently vague, and even more frequently reflects imperfect foresight—to novel circumstances"? Fallon & Meltzer, *Habeas Corpus*

Jurisdiction, Substantive Rights, and the War on Terror, 120 Harv.L.Rev. 2029, 2033 (2007).[1]

In Department of Homeland Security v. Thuraissigiam, 591 U.S. 103 (2020), the Court held that the Suspension Clause did not apply to a petitioner seeking asylum in the United States captured 25 yards inside the border and then ordered removed via expedited administrative proceedings. Writing for the Court, Justice Alito asked whether petitioner's claims would have come within the reach of the Suspension Clause as it was understood in 1789. Finding no support for the idea that "the writ of habeas corpus was understood at the time of the adoption of the Constitution to permit a petitioner to claim the right to enter or remain in a country or to obtain administrative review potentially leading to that result," the Court held that the Suspension Clause inapplicable. (At the founding, he observed, "[t]he writ simply provided a means of contesting the lawfulness of restraint and securing release.") For the majority, that was the end of the matter.[2] Compare the Court's approach in Boumediene, which moved beyond an historical record that it viewed as providing no clear analogy to explore functional considerations in determining the application of the Suspension Clause in the case. For more discussion, see pp. 467–469, *supra*; 1544–1546, *infra*.

(2) Hamdi and Boumediene; Suspension and Due Process. The Court's decisions in Hamdi and Boumediene came down four years apart. How might the added temporal distance from 9/11 have impacted the Court's approach in Boumediene?

Consider the various positions of the Justices in the two cases. Justices Kennedy and Breyer both voted with the plurality in Hamdi and majority in Boumediene (with Justices Souter and Ginsburg concurring in Hamdi and joining Boumediene), all toward the end of upholding procedural protections to any person detained as an enemy combatant. At the other extreme, Justice Thomas viewed both cases as not warranting any judicial intervention or additional process beyond that afforded by the executive and/or Congress. Justices Scalia and Stevens, by contrast, joined together in Hamdi and divided in Boumediene. For Justice Scalia, an avowed originalist, the fact that historically the writ had never reached aliens abroad was dispositive. (Note he also argued in both cases that the appropriate remedy for violations of the Suspension Clause is discharge as opposed to more process.) For Justice Stevens, by contrast, the founding period established a constitutional floor but not a ceiling. Going further, Justice Stevens's position in the two cases suggests a belief that the Suspension Clause can function both as a

---

[1]   Compare Al-Waheed v. Ministry of Defence & Ministry of Defence v. Mohammed [2017] UKSC 2, ¶¶ 100–102 (opinion of Lord Sumption) (citing Boumediene while holding that an Iraqi citizen detained by British forces in Afghanistan as an alleged enemy combatant may challenge that detention in the British courts via habeas).

[2]   It was also irrelevant to the majority that during the founding period and for decades thereafter, federal policy provided an " 'open door to the immigrant' " (citation omitted), rendering it such that a challenge to a limitation on review of immigration determinations would never have arisen. Concurring in the judgment in Thuraissigiam, Justices Breyer and Ginsburg relied upon Boumediene for the proposition that habeas corpus "is an 'adaptable remedy,' and the 'precise application and scope' of the review it guarantees may change 'depending upon the circumstances' " (quoting 553 U.S. at 779).

restraint on certain kinds of executive detention (like that at issue in Hamdi) and as a right of access to the courts (with certain procedures then promised) for a broader category of persons than the Clause may have protected at the time of its ratification (as in Boumediene).

Justice Stevens's position in the two cases draws attention to the question what protections, exactly, the Suspension Clause encapsulates: release from detention outside the criminal process, additional process in habeas, or both? Note that in Hamdi, at least two Justices believed the detention unlawful regardless of whether additional process would be provided in habeas proceedings. In Boumediene, by contrast, no Justice questioned the government's authority to detain enemy combatants outside the criminal process as part of the war on terrorism. Agreeing with Justices Scalia and Stevens in Hamdi that the Suspension Clause, drawing influence from the English Habeas Corpus Act of 1679, imposes substantive limitations on executive detention, Professor Tyler argues Boumediene, by contrast, solely implicated the question "what procedural rights attach in habeas proceedings." Tyler, Habeas Corpus in Wartime: From the Tower of London to Guantanamo Bay (2017). Tyler then questions "whether there is room for both cases under the umbrella of Suspension Clause jurisprudence"—something Justice Stevens clearly thought possible—or whether "the Suspension Clause and due process elements of the war on terrorism decisions should be rendered conceptually distinct." Tyler suggests that drawing such a distinction would have the benefit of "guard[ing] against the tendency to allow the process-oriented inquiry posed in cases like *Boumediene* to weaken the substantive limitations historically at the core of the Suspension Clause, as occurred in *Hamdi*."[3] *Id.* 275–76. Should the Court adopt such a distinction?

(3)   The Suspension Clause and Aliens Abroad.

(a)   The reasoning of the Rasul decision on the reach of § 2241 (before that statute's amendment by the DTA and the MCA of 2006) was ambiguous about whether the writ extended generally to detentions throughout the world. Some language in Boumediene could be viewed as opening up arguments that habeas jurisdiction can reach aliens detained by the U.S. government in foreign countries—for example, the statement that questions of extraterritoriality turn on objective factors and practical concerns, not formalism, and the concern about efforts by the government to avoid habeas jurisdiction. But the majority sharply distinguished the circumstances in Eisentrager from those in Boumediene, and the Court emphasized American "de facto sovereignty" at Guantanamo Bay. Those features of the opinion strongly suggest (as did Justice Kennedy in his concurrence in Rasul) that Boumediene's reach is limited to the "unique status" of Guantanamo Bay.

(b)   Whether aliens detained abroad enjoy any rights under the Suspension Clause (or the Constitution more generally) is a much-debated question. Among arguments supporting constitutional protection are these:

---

[3]   See also Tyler, Habeas Corpus: A Very Short Introduction 120–21 (2021) (observing that "one possible approach * * * would associate the common law writ of habeas corpus within modern due process jurisprudence * * *, while leaving the Suspension Clause to enforce the core protections of the English Habeas Corpus Act").

(1) historically, habeas corpus was concerned with the actions of the officials, wherever located, and with their fidelity to the King's prerogative (in England) or to the law (in the United States), see Halliday & White, *The Suspension Clause: English Text, Imperial Contexts, and American Implications*, 94 Va.L.Rev. 575 (2008); (2) the Suspension Clause protects aliens when detained in the United States and persons detained overseas when they are citizens and should therefore protect aliens detained overseas; (3) modern transportation and communication permit the extraterritorial exercise of habeas jurisdiction; and (4) a variety of normative arguments supporting such constitutional protection.[4] Some scholars are far more skeptical about extraterritorial application of constitutional protections.[5]

(c)   One might argue that the functional approach of Boumediene at least introduces the possibility that aliens abroad might sometimes be protected under the Suspension Clause. But a critic of Boumediene like Justice Scalia could offer a functional argument that, as a general matter, habeas jurisdiction is more awkward for detentions outside sovereign territory than those inside such territory—without distinguishing Guantanamo from other areas beyond American sovereignty.

Alternatively, one could establish three categories: sovereign American territory, areas with the distinctive attributes of Guantanamo, and "truly" foreign areas, where in general the functional arguments against the exercise of habeas corpus jurisdiction are stronger than is true at Guantanamo. See Fallon & Meltzer, Paragraph (1), *supra*, at 2057 (discussing concerns over the application of habeas to noncitizens abroad in the context of conventional wars and with respect to "such sensitive activities as foreign espionage," as well as the many "practical problems" that would be posed in such cases).

Or one could subdivide still further, asking in each individual case whether the exercise of habeas jurisdiction is practicable in the circumstances presented—which might depend, for example, on whether the detention was on a battlefield or in an area over which American de facto control was secure, or on whether habeas inquiry would reveal sensitive intelligence.[6]

(d)   In Al Maqaleh v. Gates, 605 F.3d 84 (D.C.Cir.2010), the D.C. Circuit considered whether, in light of the Boumediene decision, the Suspension Clause grants a right to habeas review to persons seized outside Afghanistan and then moved for detention by the United States as suspected

---

[4]   For discussion of these normative arguments, see generally Neuman, Strangers to the Constitution 5–8 (1996).

[5]   See, *e.g.*, Kent, *A Textual and Historical Case Against a Global Constitution*, 95 Geo.L.J. 463 (2007); Hamburger, *Beyond Protection*, 109 Colum.L.Rev. 1823 (2009). See also Kent, *Piracy and Due Process*, 39 Mich.J.Int'l.L. 385 (2018) (exploring the political and legal treatment of piracy in the period leading up to and following ratification and concluding that the history cuts against any historically inflected arguments supporting the concept of global due process).

[6]   Even if in general the Suspension Clause does not reach aliens detained abroad, might some cases call for an exception? See Fallon & Meltzer, Paragraph (1), *supra*, at 2058 (imagining "a resident alien who ventured abroad to serve the United States as a military translator and was detained [overseas] on allegations of complicity with terrorists").

enemy combatants at the American-operated Bagram Theater Internment Facility outside Kabul. Relying on Boumediene, the district court denied the government's motion to dismiss for want of jurisdiction.

On an interlocutory appeal, the D.C. Circuit reversed, applying the three factors that the Boumediene Court had found relevant: "(1) the citizenship and status of the detainee and the adequacy of the process through which that status determination was made; (2) the nature of the sites where apprehension and then detention took place; and (3) the practical obstacles inherent in resolving the prisoner's entitlement to the writ." As to the first factor, citizenship and status were the same as in Boumediene and the administrative hearing afforded at Bagram was more rudimentary than the CSRT hearings afforded individuals detained at Guantanamo. Thus, the first factor weighed in the petitioners' favor. The second factor weighed in the government's favor, as the U.S. had no intention to occupy Bagram permanently and did not exercise the kind of de facto sovereignty present at Guantanamo. Most important, however, and also favoring the government, was the third factor, in view of Afghanistan's status as an active war zone. The court acknowledged that a government transfer of detained persons to an active theater of war for the purpose of evading habeas jurisdiction might in some cases be a factor relevant to jurisdiction, but deemed it unnecessary to assess the significance of that factor given the lack of evidence that the government had been so motivated in this case.[7]

(e) In applying the Suspension Clause, how should a court determine whether a petitioner is inside the United States? In Department of Homeland Security v. Thuraissigiam, 591 U.S. 103 (2020), the Court concluded that an alien seeking asylum in the United States should be treated differently than one who is "already in the country [and] held in custody pending deportation" for purposes of both the Suspension Clause and due process. This conclusion followed from Congress's "plenary authority to decide which aliens to admit."[8] It was therefore of no relevance to the inquiry that petitioner had actually crossed the border and been apprehended some 25 yards inside the United States.

Thuraissigiam reveals that the border remains an important factor in constitutional analysis and that the Court defers extensively to Congress in the immigration context. See also pp. 467–469, *supra*; 1544–1546, *infra*.

(4) The Application of the Due Process Clause to Aliens Detained Abroad. In Al-Hela v. Trump, 972 F.3d 120 (D.C.Cir.2020), a D.C. Circuit panel rejected claims brought by an individual held at Guantanamo Bay that his detention violated both substantive and procedural due process. In the panel's view, "the Due Process Clause may not be invoked by aliens without property or presence in the sovereign territory of the United States." The D.C. Circuit then vacated the panel opinion and reviewed the case en banc. The en banc majority declined to "decide whether due process protections apply to Guantanamo detainees, because," it held, "even assuming the Due

---

[7]   See also Al Maqaleh v. Hagel, 738 F.3d 312 (D.C.Cir.2013) (reaffirming the lack of jurisdiction).

[8]   The Thuraissigiam Court distinguished Boumediene as involving individuals who had "sought only to be released from Guantanamo, not to enter this country."

Process Clause applie[d]" to al-Hela, his hearing in the district court afforded him procedural due process and satisfied the Suspension Clause. Al-Hela v. Biden, 66 F.4th 217, 222 (D.C.Cir.2023) (en banc). The court also concluded that even if the Due Process Clause applies as a substantive matter to persons detained at Guantanamo Bay (a matter that it did not decide), al-Hela's claims that his detention violated substantive due process also failed.

The decision in al-Hela underscores the continuing lack of clarity over the relationship between the Suspension Clause and due process. Further unsettled is whether there remain any claims under the Due Process Clause that those detained at Guantanamo Bay may advance challenging the fact or length of their detention and/or how they came to be classified as enemy combatants.[9] Also unresolved is the question whether those in custody may bring due process claims challenging the procedures or rulings of the military commissions operating at Guantanamo.

(5) Agency for International Development v. Alliance for Open Society International, Inc. The Supreme Court's most recent intervention in the debate over the application of constitutional protections overseas to non-citizens came in Agency for International Development v. Alliance for Open Society International, Inc., 591 U.S. 430 (2020). There, the Court rejected the proposition that foreign affiliates of American organizations could bring a First Amendment challenge to conditions that Congress attached to funding grants to combat HIV/AIDS abroad. Writing for the Court, Justice Kavanaugh (joined by Chief Justice Roberts and Justices Thomas, Alito, and Gorsuch), posited that "it is long settled as a matter of American constitutional law that foreign citizens outside U. S. territory do not possess rights under the U.S. Constitution." Justice Kavanaugh emphasized that "[i]f the rule were otherwise, actions by American military, intelligence, and law enforcement personnel against foreign organizations or foreign citizens in foreign countries would be constrained by the foreign citizens' purported rights under the U.S. Constitution. That has never been the law" (citing United States v. Verdugo-Urquidez, 494 U.S. 259, 273–74 (1990); Eisentrager, 339 U.S. at 784). He distinguished the situation of foreign citizens inside the United States, who "may enjoy certain constitutional rights," such as "the right to due process in a criminal trial." Finally, Justice Kavanaugh set apart those cases in which "under some circumstances, foreign citizens in the U.S. Territories—or in 'a territory' under the 'indefinite' and 'complete and total control' and 'within the constant jurisdiction' of the United States—may possess certain constitutional rights" (quoting Boumediene, 553 U.S. at 755–71).

In dissent, Justice Breyer, joined by Justices Ginsburg and Sotomayor, rejected the Court's assessment of prior caselaw on matters of extraterritoriality, writing that it "does not reflect the current state of the law." "At most, one might say that [foreign citizens abroad] are unlikely to

---

[9] For example, one could imagine claims challenging continuing detention being predicated upon arguments that the hostilities justifying detention are no longer ongoing, a contention al-Hela did not advance in his case, or claims that continuing detention once an individual has been cleared for transfer runs afoul of constitutional concerns similar to those flagged by the Court in the immigration context in Zadvydas v. Davis, 533 U.S. 678 (2001), p. 467, note 4, *supra*.

enjoy very often extraterritorial protection under the Constitution. Or one might say that the matter is undecided. But this Court has studiously avoided establishing an absolute rule that forecloses that protection in all circumstances." The dissent further relied upon Boumediene's rejection of a "formalistic" approach and its holding that " 'questions of extraterritoriality turn on objective factors and practical concerns' present in a given case." Ultimately, the dissent would have left unresolved such questions in light of the many complications that may arise in future cases presenting different circumstances. (Justice Kagan did not participate in the case.)

After this decision and Thuraissigiam, what is left of Boumediene's functional approach?

NOTE ON BOUMEDIENE V. BUSH AND THE CONSTITUTIONALLY REQUIRED SCOPE OF HABEAS REVIEW

(1) The Adequacy of DTA Review. In Boumediene, Chief Justice Roberts complains that while the majority "hints darkly" that the DTA may have other infirmities, the only one plainly found was the inability of the D.C. Circuit to consider exculpatory evidence that materializes after conclusion of the CSRT process. Was that a sufficient basis for a broad holding that the DTA is not an adequate substitute for habeas corpus—even for petitioners who do not wish to present such evidence? The Court could have interpreted § 1005(a)(3) of the DTA, which requires that CSRT procedures "shall provide for periodic review of any new evidence that may become available relating to the enemy combatant status of a detainee," as *requiring* reconsideration by a CSRT—thereby overriding the Defense Department's regulation that made the decision to reconsider discretionary.[1]

(2) The Quality of CSRT Proceedings. Although the Court focused on the petitioner's inability to introduce exculpatory evidence in CSRT proceedings, it may have had broader concerns about the process by which enemy combatant status was determined.

(a) Two critical descriptions of that process, both publicly available, raised numerous objections to the CSRT proceedings, including:

(1) The information used to prepare files for CSRT proceedings was often generic, outdated intelligence not specific to the individuals in question and lacking in detail, and failed to identify sources;

(2) In almost every case, the government's evidence was exclusively documentary and was not presented to the detained individual before the hearing; the government also furnished only conclusory summaries of classified evidence; and it was doubtful whether the government turned over all exculpatory information for use in the CSRT proceedings;

---

[1] Alternatively, the majority might have held that exculpatory evidence could be presented to a special master in accordance with Fed.R.App.Proc. 48, which specifically authorizes a court of appeals to appoint a special master to recommend factual findings in matters ancillary to proceedings in the appellate court, and expressly contemplates that the master can be a judge.

(3)   Personal representatives did not participate in any meaningful way in the CSRT proceedings; and

(4)   The government often re-opened or convened a new CSRT when a panel found an individual was not an enemy combatant.[2]

There is reason to believe that knowledge of these issues may have influenced the Court.[3]

(b)   Chief Justice Roberts says that federal appellate courts reviewing factual determinations routinely remand cases to permit the tribunal that initially decided the case to consider new evidence in the first instance. The examples that he provides, however, involve remands to district courts. Doesn't the attractiveness of the remand option depend upon the faith one has that the tribunal to which the case is being returned will respond appropriately to any court order?

In this regard, Chief Justice Roberts mentions more than once that the procedures followed by CSRTs are rooted in the Hamdi plurality's opinion, which suggested that due process might be provided by an appropriately constituted military panel. Might Justices Kennedy and Breyer, who both joined the plurality opinion in Hamdi and were in the majority in Boumediene, have lost faith over the course of four years in the approach that Hamdi described and, more particularly, in the reliability of the CSRT determinations? Would concerns like these adequately answer the dissenters' accusations that the majority was essentially engaged in a power grab? For greater discussion, see Meltzer, *Habeas Corpus, Suspension, and Guantánamo: The Boumediene Decision*, 2008 Sup.Ct.Rev. 1.

(3)   Unanswered Questions About the Scope of Habeas Review. The Court's opinion leaves unanswered many questions concerning the scope of the constitutional entitlement to habeas corpus.

(a)   At various times the Court refers to practice under § 2241 in assessing the adequacy of review under the DTA. Note, however, that Congress may vest broader jurisdiction by statute than is required by the Suspension Clause—a point the Court seemed to acknowledge when stating: "we do not hold that an adequate substitute must duplicate § 2241 in all respects." Is the constitutional entitlement to be measured by practice at the time of the founding (to the extent that can be determined)? By evolving practice over time in dealing with captives during wartime? By a judicial calculus that might view the struggle against terrorism as not necessarily fitting neatly within the paradigms of either war or crime?

---

[2]   See Declaration of Lt. Col. Stephen Abraham, an intelligence officer assigned to the Office for the Administrative Review of the Detention of Enemy Combatants, found in Reply to Opposition to Petition for Rehearing at i–viii, Al Odah v. United States, 551 U.S. 1161 (2007); Denbeaux et al., *No-Hearing Hearings: An Analysis of the Proceedings of the Combatant Status Review Tribunals at Guantánamo*, 41 Seton Hall L.Rev. 1231 (2011).

[3]   On April 2, 2007, the Supreme Court denied the original petition for certiorari in the case—over the dissent of Justice Breyer, joined by Justice Souter and in part by Justice Ginsburg. 549 U.S. 1328. In an extraordinary reversal, on June 29, 2007, the Court granted rehearing, vacated the April 2 order, and granted certiorari. The petitioners' Reply Brief in support of the Petition for Rehearing prominently featured the Abraham declaration, note 2, *supra*.

(b)   Although the historical materials concerning the scope of habeas review are anything but clear, several themes emerge from the history. First, early American precedents often state that habeas review is limited to questions of jurisdiction. Over time, however, decisional law stretched the notion of jurisdiction, thereby making it difficult at times to distinguish jurisdiction from the legal merits. See pp. 1555–1558, *infra*. Second, as the majority notes, the scope of review has often turned on the quality of any prior determination concerning the legality of custody: the more trustworthy the prior determination, the more limited subsequent habeas review might be. Third, review of questions of law, where courts generally are thought to have comparative expertise, has generally been broader than review of questions of fact. In the context of collateral review of criminal convictions, however, some cases have suggested that not all legal errors are cognizable on habeas. See, *e.g.*, Hill v. United States, 368 U.S. 424, 428 (1962) (claim predicated upon trial judge's failure to comply with formal requirements of Federal Rule of Criminal Procedure 32(a) is not cognizable in collateral proceedings under 28 U.S.C. § 2255); Stone v. Powell, 428 U.S. 465 (1976) (Fourth Amendment claims not cognizable in collateral proceedings), discussed p. 1570, *infra*. The Court expressed a broader view in INS v. St. Cyr, pp. 464, 1471, *supra*, an immigration case, where it said that historically, habeas review extended to "errors of law, including the erroneous application or interpretation of statutes." Fourth, as to review of fact, while some English and early American decisions barred petitioners from introducing evidence to contest the facts presented by a custodian in a return to the writ, the practice was not consistent, the limitation was sometimes evaded,[4] and it eventually eroded in the nineteenth century. Finally, the scope of review has varied in different circumstances, and as Chief Justice Roberts noted, has often been considerably narrower when reviewing military decisions and matters arising out of war.[5]

(4)   Unanswered Questions About the Conduct of Future Habeas Proceedings. Apart from questions about scope of review, an enormous number of procedural issues have arisen in the numerous habeas cases filed by individuals detained at Guantanamo.[6] In addressing those questions, are

---

[4]   See pp. 1461–1462, note 4, *supra*.

[5]   In considering the appropriate scope of review by a habeas court, does the DTA have any relevance? Following Boumediene, the D.C. Circuit held that DTA review is no longer available, reasoning that the DTA's provision for review in the D.C. Circuit could not be severed from the provision purporting to preclude habeas jurisdiction, which Boumediene had invalidated. See Bismullah v. Gates, 551 F.3d 1068 (D.C.Cir.2009).

But note that the Boumediene Court drew on the DTA's framework in stating that it would be appropriate for all Guantanamo habeas petitions to be heard in (or transferred to) the District Court for the District of Columbia. Note as well that the DTA appears to preclude the D.C. Circuit from entertaining a challenge based on an alleged violation of a treaty, and § 5(a) of the MCA precludes a habeas petitioner from invoking the Geneva Conventions as a source of rights. If, apart from those provisions, petitioners could have relied upon the Geneva Conventions in habeas proceedings, what is the statutes' effect in habeas proceedings under Boumediene? For discussion, see Vázquez, *The Military Commissions Act, the Geneva Conventions, and the Courts: A Critical Guide*, 101 Am.J.Int'l.L. 73 (2007). Is it an adequate answer that Congress has simply determined, as it may, that the Geneva Conventions do not confer privately enforceable rights?

[6]   Following Boumediene, the district court judges in the D.C. Circuit consolidated most pending habeas cases for administrative purposes and entered a case management order setting

the courts implicitly determining what the Suspension Clause does, and does not, require when habeas courts review the detention of aliens, asserted to be subject to detention under the laws of war? Or does the invalidation of the jurisdiction-stripping provisions in Boumediene leave the courts with their normal jurisdiction under § 2241, which might provide more procedural protection than the Constitution requires?

Examples of the procedural questions include:

(a) **Admissibility of Hearsay Evidence.** In Al-Bihani v. Obama, 590 F.3d 866, 879 (D.C.Cir.2010), the court held that hearsay is always admissible in these cases and that the only question is "what probative weight to ascribe to whatever indicia of reliability it exhibits."

(b) **Burden of Proof.** The Al-Bihani decision also ruled that the district court had permissibly adopted a preponderance of the evidence standard in reviewing the factual determinations of a CSRT. Thereafter, in Al-Adahi v. Obama, 613 F.3d 1102 (D.C.Cir.2010), the court of appeals went further to doubt that the Suspension Clause requires the government to meet the preponderance of the evidence standard, citing cases from other contexts in which habeas courts applied a lesser standard—sometimes, only a requirement that there be "some evidence" to support the decision.

(c) **Presumption of Regularity of the Government's Evidence.** In Latif v. Obama, 666 F.3d 746 (D.C.Cir.2011), the D.C. Circuit held that Government intelligence reports merit a presumption of regularity, permitting courts to presume, absent clear contrary evidence, that officials have properly discharged their official duties. The court justified the presumption by arguing that "courts have no special expertise in evaluating the nature and reliability of * * * wartime records" and therefore should defer to the Executive Branch.[7] Judge Tatel's dissent argued that the presumption of regularity applies only when government documents are the product of reliable processes, an assumption that his opinion went on to question in the specific circumstances of the case. Judge Tatel concluded by suggesting that a presumption of authenticity with respect to a report should still permit the factfinder a role in deciding how much probative weight to accord the evidence.

(5) The Net Effect of Boumediene in the Lower Courts. To date, the D.C. Circuit has failed to order release of an individual detained at Guantanamo,[8] and only a single release has followed directly pursuant to a

---

forth the procedures for discovery and merits determinations for the relevant petitions. See In re Guantanamo Bay Detainee Litig., Misc. No. 08–0442, 2008 WL 4858241 (D.D.C. Nov. 6, 2008), as amended 2008 WL 5245890 (D.D.C. Dec. 16, 2008). For surveys of early developments in the D.C. federal courts following Boumediene, see Wittes, Chesney, & Reynolds, The Emerging Law of Detention 2.0: The Guantánamo Habeas Cases as Lawmaking (2012), https://www.brookings.edu/wp-content/uploads/2016/06/05_guantanamo_wittes.pdf; Hafetz, *Calling the Government to Account: Habeas Corpus in the Aftermath of Boumediene*, 57 Wayne L.Rev. 99 (2011); Vladeck, *The D.C. Circuit After Boumediene,* 41 Seton Hall L.Rev. 1451 (2011).

[7] The court stressed, however, that "[t]he presumption of regularity * * * presumes the government official accurately identified the source and accurately summarized his statement, but it implies nothing about the truth of the underlying non-government source's statement."

[8] Alexander, *The Law-Free Zone and Back Again*, 2013 U.Ill.L.Rev. 551, argues that the D.C. Circuit has "effectively reversed" Boumediene.

district court order that was not reversed on appeal.[9] That said, Dycus, Banks, Raven-Hansen, & Vladeck, National Security Law 926 (7th ed.2020), report that "of the 64 detainees who have had their habeas claims adjudicated on the merits as of December 1, 2019, 39 (60.9%) prevailed in the district court. Three of those rulings were subsequently dismissed or held in abeyance pending the detainees' transfer, and another six were reversed by the D.C. Circuit. But that still left 30 out of 61 detainees (not counting the dismissed or stayed cases) who prevailed even under the D.C. Circuit's decisional law." *Id.* (For example, some cases include petitions in which the district court held the government lacked authority to detain, but then did not order outright release.) Still other petitioners obtained release before fully litigating their claims in habeas proceedings. Thus, the impact of Boumediene in the lower courts is not altogether easy to measure, but the number of releases connected in various ways to then-pending litigation suggests that the decision and proceedings in its wake have not been without effect.

What, if anything, do these statistics reveal about the merits of Boumediene and the disagreement among the Justices? The fidelity of the D.C. Circuit to that decision? The competence and appropriateness of Article III courts to evaluate challenges to enemy combatant designations?

NOTE ON EXHAUSTION OF NON-HABEAS REMEDIES

(1) Timing of Habeas Review. A court possessing habeas jurisdiction may nonetheless sometimes abstain from exercising it until other legal processes have concluded. For example, the rule that individuals in state custody seeking post-conviction federal habeas corpus review must first exhaust state court remedies was developed as judge-made law before it was codified. See generally pp. 1662–1665, *infra.* The question of exhaustion of non-habeas remedies has arisen in other contexts, notably when habeas courts are asked to intervene in federal military proceedings. Because the tension between any decision to abstain and the role of the habeas court in redressing unlawful detention, the Court has struggled to identify clear guideposts identifying when abstention is appropriate.

(2) Exhaustion and Courts Martial. In Schlesinger v. Councilman, 420 U.S. 738 (1975) (6–3), an army captain facing court martial proceedings for sale and possession of marijuana sought immediate federal court review, alleging that the offense was not service-connected and that therefore, under the decisional law then governing, the military courts could not

---

[9]   In 2021, a district judge ordered the release of a petitioner detained at Guantanamo over government opposition on the basis that the petitioner "was not a part of or substantial supporter of al Qaeda," Gul v. Biden, 2021 WL 5206199 (D.D.C. Nov. 9, 2021), after which the government repatriated the petitioner to Afghanistan. See Rosenberg, *U.S. Repatriates Afghan Whose Guantánamo Detention Was Unlawful*, N.Y. Times (June 24, 2022), https://www.nytimes.com/2022/06/24/us/politics/guantanamo-afghan-prisoner-released.html. *Cf.* Kiyemba v. Obama, 605 F.3d 1046 (D.C.Cir.2010) (reversing district court order compelling release of Uighur petitioners into United States).

constitutionally exercise jurisdiction.[1] The Supreme Court, relying on decisions calling on federal courts to abstain from exercising jurisdiction to enjoin state court proceedings, held that the lower federal courts should have abstained: "While the peculiar demands of federalism are not implicated, the deficiency is supplied by factors equally compelling"—the need for deference to the military and the federal courts' respect for Congress's judgment that "the military court system will vindicate servicemen's constitutional rights."

The Court distinguished habeas decisions that had permitted anticipatory relief against courts-martial acting in excess of their constitutionally permissible jurisdiction on the basis that (a) those decisions involved civilian petitioners and (b) the jurisdictional question "turned on the status of the persons as to whom the military asserted its power." By contrast, here the petitioner was unquestionably subject to military authority, and the question whether the charges were service-related depended on judgments about which "the expertise of military courts is singularly relevant."

(3) Abstention and Military Commission Trials. In Hamdan v. Rumsfeld, 548 U.S. 557 (2006), p. 557, *supra*, the government, alleging that Hamdan, a Yemeni national, had, in violation of the laws of war, conspired with members of al Qaeda to attack civilians and commit acts of terrorism, brought criminal charges against him in a military commission. Before trial, Hamdan sought writs of habeas corpus and mandamus, challenging the authority of the military commission to try him. In upholding Hamdan's challenge, the Supreme Court rejected, 5–3, the contention that the federal courts should have abstained until completion of the military proceedings. For the majority, Justice Stevens reasoned that "neither of the comity considerations identified in Councilman weighs in favor of abstention * * *. First, Hamdan is not a member of our Nation's Armed Forces, so concerns about military discipline do not apply. Second, the tribunal convened to try Hamdan is not part of the integrated system of military courts, complete with independent review panels, that Congress has established." Further, Justice Stevens noted, the Court had exercised pre-conviction review of war crimes trials before military commission proceedings in Ex parte Quirin, 317 U.S. 1, 19 (1942), justifying intervention by the importance of the questions and the judicial duty in war as in peacetime to preserve constitutional liberties. Without foreclosing the possibility that some military commission proceedings (such as those convened on the battlefield) might call for abstention, Justice Stevens found none applicable in this case, and he observed that both the government and Hamdan had "a compelling interest in knowing in advance whether Hamdan may be tried by a military commission that arguably is without any basis in law."[2]

---

[1]   See O'Callahan v. Parker, 395 U.S. 258 (1969), *overruled*, Solorio v. United States, 483 U.S. 435 (1987). Captain Councilman sought to enjoin further proceedings, but the Court made clear it was applying principles equally applicable to, and indeed drawn from, habeas corpus practice.

[2]   The government also objected, more specifically, to the Court's consideration of any challenges to the commission's procedures, contending that Hamdan could obtain review of any procedural issue after final decision and that there was no reason to presume that a violation

In dissent, Justice Scalia (joined by Justices Thomas and Alito) offered three reasons supporting abstention. First, if "military necessities" required abstention in Councilman, surely the necessities recognized by the political branches "relating to the * * * terrorists of September 11 require abstention all the more here." Second, the absence of an integrated scheme and independent review stressed by the Court was more than compensated for by the provision in the Detainee Treatment Act (DTA) for review of any final decision by the D.C. Circuit—a form of review not available in Quirin. Third, "considerations of *interbranch* comity * * * weigh heavily against" judicial intervention, which would create a "direct conflict with the Executive in an area where the Executive's competence is maximal and ours is virtually nonexistent."[3]

(4) Exhaustion and Boumediene. In Boumediene, the Court said that ordinarily a habeas court should not entertain a petition from a party detained at Guantanamo until a CSRT had completed its status determination but held that the petitioners need not exhaust DTA review in the D.C. Circuit. The Court stressed that some of the petitioners had been detained for six years without judicial oversight and doubted that DTA review could be performed expeditiously. But if those conditions do not hold, might exhaustion be warranted?

(5) Reconciling the Decisions. The Hamdan decision found abstention inappropriate when there is a substantial question about a military tribunal's personal jurisdiction over a defendant. Does the "jurisdictional" label provide a clear benchmark for the appropriate scope of abstention? (Compare the argument in Councilman.) If not, note the multiplicity of factors on which the Court's judgments about whether to abstain have rested. And in the end, isn't there an inherent tension between any kind of abstention, on the one hand, and the language in Boumediene about the importance of habeas in preserving a role for the judiciary in the separation of powers?[4]

(6) Exhaustion and Military Trials Today: Congressional Power and Constitutional Limits. Four months after the Hamdan decision, Congress enacted the Military Commissions Act of 2006 (MCA of 2006), and three years later, the Military Commissions Act of 2009. Together these acts were designed to alter the procedures followed in military commission proceedings against aliens charged criminally for law of war violations to address the defects that the Supreme Court had found in the Hamdan decision. As noted on p. 1469–1470, *supra,* under current law, a conviction by military commission is subject to review within the Department of Defense, then to review of law and fact before the United States Court of Military Commission Review, an Article I court staffed by military and civilian judges, and then to further review in the U.S. Court of Appeals for

---

would occur. In response, Justice Stevens said, *inter alia,* that procedural harm was not conjectural as Hamdan had already been excluded from proceedings in his own case.

[3]   For subsequent proceedings in Hamdan, see Hamdan v. Gates, 565 F.Supp.2d 130 (D.D.C.2008); see also Al Odah v. Bush, 593 F.Supp.2d 53 (D.D.C.2009).

[4]   Compare the material on pre-trial intervention by habeas courts into state criminal proceedings, p. 1664–1665, *infra.*

the D.C. Circuit, see 10 U.S.C. § 950f, whose decisions can be reviewed on certiorari by the Supreme Court.

Does that structure effectively undercut a key basis for Hamdan's holding on exhaustion—namely, that Congress had not created an integrated system of review? Even if so, does the Suspension Clause permit withholding habeas review until all remedies under that elaborate review procedure have been exhausted? Consider this language in the Boumediene opinion: "This Court may not impose a *de facto* suspension by abstaining from these controversies. See Hamdan, 548 U.S. at 585, n.16 ('[A]bstention is not appropriate in cases . . . in which the legal challenge "turn[s] on the status of the persons as to whom the military asserted its power" ' (quoting Schlesinger v. Councilman, 420 U.S. 738, 759 (1975)))."[5]

NOTE ON PROPER RESPONDENTS

When a habeas petitioner challenges the lawfulness of custody, who is the proper respondent? The official who operates the detention facility? That official's supervisor? How far up the chain of authority may a petitioner go in naming a respondent? These questions matter because a misstep by the habeas petitioner can result in dismissal for want of jurisdiction.

(1) The Padilla Decision. After the government took Padilla, an American citizen, into custody at Chicago's O'Hare airport, it then detained Padilla in New York City as a material witness in connection with a federal grand jury investigation of the 9/11 attacks. While his motion to vacate the material witness warrant was pending in federal court in New York, the government designated him as an "enemy combatant" and transferred him to military custody at the Naval Brig in Charleston, South Carolina. Two days later and unaware that Padilla had been moved, his counsel filed a federal habeas corpus petition in New York, naming as respondents President Bush, Secretary of Defense Rumsfeld, and Melanie Marr, Commander of the Naval Brig. When the case reached the Supreme Court, it held in Rumsfeld v. Padilla, 542 U.S. 426 (2004), 5–4, that (a) only Commander Marr, the immediate custodian, was a proper respondent, and (b) the district court in New York lacked jurisdiction over her.

(a) On the former point, Chief Justice Rehnquist's opinion emphasized that the habeas statute consistently refers to "the" custodian; he likewise cited longstanding authority and practice confirming "that in habeas challenges to present physical confinement—'core challenges'—the default rule is that the proper respondent is the warden of the facility where the prisoner is being held, not the Attorney General or some other remote supervisory official." Cases departing from that rule involved challenges to something other than present physical confinement—as, for example, in

---

[5] See also In Obaydullah v. Obama, 609 F.3d 444 (D.C.Cir.2010) (declining to abstain in a habeas action filed by Guantanamo petitioner who did not yet face a prosecution); In re al-Nashiri, 791 F.3d 71 (D.C.Cir.2015) (declining to review preemptive separation of powers challenge to the composition of the Court of Military Commission Review while proceedings before military commission were ongoing); In re Khadr, 823 F.3d 92 (D.C.Cir.2016) (same).

Braden v. 30th Judicial Cir. Ct., 410 U.S. 484 (1973), p. 1503, *supra*, where the petitioner challenged future confinement.

(b) In finding no jurisdiction, the Court invoked the "traditional rule" grounded in precedent and various statutory provisions that the writ may issue only in the district in which the immediate custodian is located.[1]

(c) Justice Stevens, joined by Justices Souter, Ginsburg, and Breyer, dissented. Although agreeing that "the immediate custodian rule should control in the ordinary case," he noted that when Padilla's lawyer filed a habeas petition, she apparently had not received official notice of Padilla's location following the Attorney General's announcement the day before that Padilla would be transferred to the Defense Department. Justice Stevens objected that if the government had notified her of its intention to transfer Padilla to military custody, she would presumably have filed immediately, when both Padilla and his immediate custodian were in New York.

Justice Stevens stressed that the Court's "bright-line rule" admits many exceptions—including when physical custody is not at issue (as in Braden),[2] when citizens are confined overseas, see Paragraph (2), *infra*, and when the petitioner is transferred from a judicial district *after* having filed a petition.[3] He likewise argued that Padilla's detention followed from exceptional circumstances. Justice Stevens therefore would have upheld jurisdiction in New York over Secretary Rumsfeld on the basis of his order to military personnel to seize Padilla and remove him to South Carolina.

(2) Custodians of Persons Held Overseas.

(a) Citizens Held by U.S. Officials. In Padilla, the Court acknowledged that "[w]e have long implicitly recognized an exception to the immediate custodian rule in the military context where an American citizen is detained outside the territorial jurisdiction of any district court." The Court cited Burns v. Wilson, 346 U.S. 137 (1953), and United States ex rel. Toth v. Quarles, 350 U.S. 11 (1955), both discussed at pp. 1504, *supra*, in

---

[1] Those provisions include §§ 2241(d) and 2255, which in some circumstances permit persons convicted in state or federal proceedings to file in districts other than the district of confinement; both would have been unnecessary, the Court said, if § 2241 generally permitted one imprisoned to do so.

Padilla relied on Strait v. Laird, 406 U.S. 341 (1972), where an inactive Army reservist petitioned for habeas in California, where he was domiciled to review a failure to grant discharge on conscientious objector grounds. The Court ruled that the petitioner's superior officers, though located in Indiana, were "present" in California because Strait's discharge application was processed through Army personnel there. The majority in Padilla distinguished Strait as involving no challenge to present physical confinement and involving a case in which the petitioner "had always resided in California and had his only meaningful contacts with the Army there * * *."

[2] Justice Stevens also relied on Strait v. Laird, note 1, *supra*.

[3] Justice Stevens referred here to Ex parte Endo, 323 U.S. 283 (1944), p. 1500, *supra*, a case in which the petitioner sought the writ in the Northern District of California while being detained in that jurisdiction in a Japanese American detention camp during World War II. The Endo Court held that the district court retained jurisdiction, despite petitioner's subsequent movement by the government to another camp in Utah, because a custodian—the assistant director of the War Relocation Authority—remained within the district. In Padilla, the majority responded by stating that "Endo stands for the important but limited proposition that when the Government moves a habeas petitioner after she properly files a petition naming her immediate custodian, the District Court retains jurisdiction and may direct the writ to any respondent within its jurisdiction who has legal authority to effectuate the prisoner's release."

which the Court did not question the district court's jurisdiction to consider petitions on behalf of servicemembers, detained abroad, who challenged the constitutionality of their convictions in courts martial proceedings. Both cases appear to hold, albeit implicitly, that at least when the immediate custodian is outside the jurisdiction of any federal district court, a petitioner may name as the respondent a high official located within the United States—in Burns, the Secretary of Defense, and in Toth, the Secretary of the Air Force.

(b) Citizens Detained Under Multinational Auspices. Munaf v. Geren, 553 U.S. 674 (2008), involved petitions filed on behalf of American citizens who, after allegedly committing crimes in Iraq, were detained by American forces there. The government relied on Hirota v. MacArthur, 338 U.S. 197 (1948), p. 368, *supra*, for the proposition that American courts lack habeas jurisdiction when, as in Iraq, American military forces are part of a multinational force. In rejecting that view, a unanimous Court, per Roberts, C.J., said that in Hirota, it was not clear that the multinational tribunal whose decision was at issue was subject to plenary United States authority; here, by contrast, the government conceded that American forces were subject to plenary control by the American chain of command. The Court also emphasized that the petitioners, unlike those in Hirota, were American citizens.[4]

(c) Aliens Detained Abroad by U.S. Officials. Does the recognized exception to the immediate custodian rule when *citizens* are held abroad apply equally to *aliens*? In Rasul v. Bush, 542 U.S. 466 (2004), p. 1505, *supra*, the Guantanamo petitioners named as respondents the President, the Secretary of Defense, the Chairman of the Joint Chiefs of Staff, the Commandant of Camp X-Ray/Camp Delta at Guantanamo, and other military officials. The Supreme Court did not address who was a proper respondent in light of the government's failure to challenge the district court's jurisdiction over the petitioner's custodians. In Boumediene v. Bush, 553 U.S. 723 (2008), p. 1507, *supra*, the Court, in upholding habeas jurisdiction, did not even discuss the identity of the respondents.

---

[4]   In Munaf, the Court proceeded, again unanimously, to deny relief on the merits. The petitioners sought an order barring their transfer for criminal prosecution to the Iraqi government, which the petitioners alleged would likely torture them. The Court said that the Executive's policy is not to transfer individuals when torture likely will result, the State Department had found that the Iraqi Justice Ministry "generally met internationally accepted standards for basic prisoner needs," and the judiciary was not well suited to second-guess such determinations. More broadly, the Court rejected the notion that the judiciary should shelter petitioners from a sovereign government seeking to hold them accountable for alleged crimes committed within the sovereign's borders. *Cf.* Doe v. Mattis, 928 F.3d 1 (D.C.Cir.2019), discussed at p. 1499, note 12, *supra*.

For discussion of the Hirota decision, see generally Huq, *The Hirota Gambit*, 63 N.Y.U. Ann.Surv.Am.L. 63 (2007); Vladeck, *Deconstructing Hirota: Habeas Corpus, Citizenship, and Article III*, 95 Geo.L.J. 1497 (2007).

NOTE ON THE SCOPE OF REVIEW IN IMMIGRATION CASES

(1) The Pre-1996 Practice. The United States did not formally begin to restrict immigration under federal law until 1875. Until then, the country maintained an "open door" policy to immigrants. Between 1875 and 1961, federal courts assumed jurisdiction to review immigration cases of those held in government custody under the 1867 Reconstruction-era habeas statute, which provided for habeas review of those held in federal or state custody in violation of federal law. Through such review, courts inquired whether a person was being detained in violation of the immigration laws.

One early habeas case in this context was United States v. Jung Ah Lung, 124 U.S. 621 (1888). The petitioner, a Chinese immigrant, had lived in the United States but left to visit China. When he returned to the United States having lost the papers he needed for re-entry, immigration authorities refused to admit him and detained him. Concluding he had a lawful right to enter the country, the district court ordered his release into the United States, a decision affirmed by the Supreme Court. Congress responded by passing immigration legislation in 1891 that purported to restrict judicial review of immigration proceedings and render them "final." See Act of March 3, 1891, §§ 7, 8, 26 Stat. 828. In Nishimura Ekiu v. United States, 142 U.S. 651 (1892), the Supreme Court interpreted the new statute to allow habeas review over a range of legal and constitutional questions arising in immigration cases and only to limit judicial review of basic facts. Citing Nishimura Ekiu, the Supreme Court proceeded to uphold habeas review in a host of cases, including those of persons seeking to enter the country as well as other would-be immigrants who had been seized by authorities after entering the United States. See, *e.g.*, Brownell v. We Shung, 352 U.S. 180, 182 n.1 (1956); Shaughnessy v. United States ex rel. Mezei, 345 U.S. 206, 213 (1953). *Cf.* Heikkila v. Barber, 345 U.S. 229, 235 (1953).

In INS v. St. Cyr, 533 U.S. 289, 306–09 (2001), the Supreme Court described the pre-1996 practice this way (most citations are omitted):

"Until the enactment of the 1952 Immigration and Nationality Act, the sole means by which an alien could test the legality of his or her deportation order was by bringing a habeas corpus action in district court. In such cases, other than the question whether there was some evidence to support the order, the courts generally did not review factual determinations made by the Executive. However, * * * [i]n case after case, courts answered questions of law in habeas corpus proceedings brought by aliens challenging Executive interpretations of the immigration laws.

"Habeas courts also regularly answered questions of law that arose in the context of discretionary relief. Traditionally, courts recognized a distinction between eligibility for discretionary relief * * * and the favorable exercise of discretion * * *. Eligibility that was 'governed by specific statutory standards' provided 'a right to a ruling on an applicant's eligibility,' even though the actual granting of relief was 'not a matter of right under any circumstances, but rather is in all cases a matter of grace.' * * *

"[Beginning in 1952, Congress established procedures other than habeas corpus for federal court review of immigration matters. Under the

1952 Immigration and Nationality Act, Pub.L.No. 82–414, 66 Stat. 163,] district courts had broad authority to grant declaratory and injunctive relief in immigration cases, including orders adjudicating deportability and those denying suspensions of deportability. [Then, by the Act of Sept. 26, 1961, Pub.L.No. 87–301, 75 Stat. 650, Congress] withdrew that jurisdiction from the district courts and provided that the procedures set forth in the Hobbs Act [governing direct review in the federal courts of appeals of agency actions] would be the 'sole and exclusive procedure' for judicial review of final orders of deportation, subject to a series of exceptions. See 75 Stat. 651. The last of those exceptions stated that 'any alien held in custody pursuant to an order of deportation may obtain review thereof by habeas corpus proceedings.' See *id.*, at 652, codified at 8 U.S.C. § 1105a(10) (repealed Sept. 30, 1996)."

(2) The Effect of Statutory Changes in 1996 and 2005. In 1996, Congress enacted a set of statutory provisions that merged deportation and exclusion cases into "removal" proceedings and purported to limit, or in some cases preclude altogether, judicial review of decisions made by immigration officers in such proceedings. Specifically, in the government's view, the new legislation precluded all judicial review (including habeas review) in federal and state courts of the Attorney General's decision that the 1996 amendments had eliminated her discretion to waive deportation in specified circumstances. In the St. Cyr decision, pp. 464, 1471, *supra*, and the companion decision in Calcano-Martinez v. INS, 533 U.S. 348 (2001), the Court agreed that the 1996 amendments did strip the courts of appeals of the reviewing jurisdiction they had been given in 1961, but held that that Congress had not precluded the exercise of habeas corpus jurisdiction to review the legality of removal decisions. In the aftermath of St. Cyr, Congress enacted the REAL ID Act of 2005, Pub.L.No. 109–13, 119 Stat. 302 (2005), which eliminated habeas corpus jurisdiction in removal cases, substituting review in the federal courts of appeals. A provision of the Act, codified at 8 U.S.C. § 1252(a)(2)(D), authorizes review of "constitutional claims or questions of law." The legislative history indicates that this section was designed to "permit judicial review over those issues that were historically reviewable on habeas." H.R.Rep. No. 109–72, 175 (2005). In immigration matters, however, the relevant history is particularly tortured. See, *e.g.*, Neuman, *Habeas Corpus, Executive Detention, and the Removal of Aliens*, 98 Colum.L.Rev. 961 (1998); Neuman, *Jurisdiction and the Rule of Law After the 1996 Immigration Act*, 113 Harv.L.Rev. 1963 (2000).

Days on the heels of St. Cyr, the court decided Zadvydas v. Davis, 533 U.S. 678 (2001), p. 467, note 4, *infra*, again by a 5–4 margin. In an opinion by Justice Breyer, the majority reaffirmed that the 1996 amendments did not displace § 2241 habeas jurisdiction, this time in a case challenging the indefinite detention by the attorney general of an alien who had been ordered deported. Going further, the court held that the relevant post-removal detention statute, "read in light of the Constitution's demands * * * does not permit indefinite detention." Instead, the majority read the statute to "contain an implicit 'reasonable time' limitation, the application of which is subject to federal-court review." Like St. Cyr, Zadvydas did not purport to be a constitutional decision; all the same, both were heavily influenced by the idea that the Suspension Clause may have compelled their outcomes.

Neither decision, however, spoke to what the Constitution might require with respect to those seeking entry to the United States, including persons seeking asylum. The Court addressed this question in Department of Homeland Security v. Thuraissigiam, 591 U.S. 103 (2020). Thuraissigiam, a Sri Lankan national, entered the United States clandestinely and was apprehended by a Border Patrol agent some 25 yards inside the border. He then sought asylum in administrative proceedings, but he failed to convince immigration officials that he had a "credible fear of persecution" upon return to his native country. Had he succeeded on that score, Thuraissigiam would have been spared expedited removal as provided for under the 1996 legislation and afforded additional procedural opportunities to seek asylum in the United States. Notwithstanding a provision restricting judicial review of "the determination" by immigration officials that an applicant lacks a credible fear of persecution, 8 U.S.C. § 1252(a)(2)(A)(iii), Thuraissigiam sought a writ of habeas corpus in federal court, contending that he satisfied the credible fear test while also challenging the fairness of the proceedings and arguing that under both the Suspension Clause and the Due Process Clause, he was entitled to a new, more extensive hearing and, ultimately, entry to the United States.

The Supreme Court rejected his claims, 5–4. Writing for the majority, Justice Alito posited that the relevant inquiry should ask how the founding generation understood the Suspension Clause in 1789. Thuraissigiam's claim failed because, in his view, habeas during that period was "a means to secure *release* from unlawful detention" and did not extend to an invocation of the writ "to achieve an entirely different end, namely, to obtain additional administrative review of his asylum claim and ultimately to obtain authorization to stay in this country." Nothing in St. Cyr counseled otherwise. That case was distinguishable, Justice Alito wrote, because it applied to "aliens already in the country who were held in custody pending deportation," as opposed to those seeking entry. Nor did Boumediene help Thuraissigiam, because it involved petitioners who "sought only to be released from Guantanamo, not to enter th[e] country."

As for Thuraissigiam's due process argument, Justice Alito noted that "[w]hile aliens who have established connections in this country have due process rights in deportation proceedings, the Court long ago held that Congress is entitled to set the conditions for an alien's lawful entry into this country and that, as a result, an alien at the threshold of initial entry cannot claim any greater rights under the Due Process Clause." It did not matter that Thuraissigiam was taken into custody on United States soil because Congress possesses "plenary authority to decide which aliens to admit" to the country. Further, the Court emphasized that its precedents provide that even aliens paroled in the country while pending removal are treated for due process purposes as if they had been stopped at the border. It followed, in Justice Alito's view, that an asylum seeker like Thuraissigiam had "no entitlement to procedural rights other than those afforded by statute."

Justices Breyer, joined by Justice Ginsburg, concurred in the judgment, agreeing that the statutory scheme was constitutional as applied to Thuraissigiam. Justice Breyer characterized Thuraissigiam's primary claims as "at their core, challenges to factual findings." He similarly characterized Thuraissigiam's challenge to the asylum officer's application of the relevant legal standard, observing that "[a]t the heart of [what are] purportedly legal contentions * * * lies a disagreement with immigration officials' findings" relating to the underlying facts. He concluded that the Suspension Clause does not require that a "habeas court make indeterminate and highly record-intensive judgments on matters of degree." He added that there existed no precedent "suggesting that the Suspension Clause demands parsing procedural compliance at so granular a level."

Justice Sotomayor, joined by Justice Kagan, dissented. She contended that in countless habeas cases following Nishimura Ekiu, the court had heard "claims indistinguishable from those" raised by Thuraissigiam, which encompassed both mixed questions of law and fact and legal challenges to "procedural defects" in the removal procedures that Congress had prescribed. Justice Sotomayor further argued that Nishimura Ekiu should be read as a Suspension Clause decision. Finally, Justice Sotomayor worried that "taken to its extreme, a rule conditioning due process rights on lawful entry would permit Congress to constitutionally eliminate all procedural protections for any noncitizen the Government deems unlawfully admitted and summarily deport them no matter how many decades they have lived here."

In response, the majority disagree with the dissent's reading of Nishimura Ekiu and stated that it had no occasion to address whatever distinctions existed between petitioner's claims, which raised "at best a mixed question of law," and those advanced in St. Cyr. The Court instead relied upon the distinction that St. Cyr was already within the United States when he sought review of his claims.

In most cases, won't the application of law to fact be as or more critical to the individual than broad questions of statutory meaning? On the other hand, would upholding jurisdiction to review the application of law to fact risk bringing in routine questions of administration, rather than the kind of fundamental questions to which habeas jurisdiction is sometimes thought to be limited? In all events, can pure questions of law easily be distinguished from the applications of law to fact, or do the categories blend into each other?

Separately, note Justice Alito's emphasis on the fact that the remedy associated with the English Habeas Corpus Act of 1679 was discharge. Both Hamdi and Boumediene, the latter expressly a decision grounded in the Suspension Clause, held that the petitioner in question should be afforded additional *process*—precisely what Thuraissigiam sought in his petition. Recall as well that Boumediene cited the writ's common law origins as a basis for interpreting the writ as capable of confronting new circumstances. Does Thuraissigiam walk back these aspects of Boumediene, or do so only in connection with unlawful entry? Relatedly, when paired with another 2020 Supreme Court decision, Agency for International Development v. Alliance for Open Society International, Inc., 591 U.S. 430 (2020), p. 1531, *supra*,

Thuraissigiam may be read to emphasize geographical boundaries as highly significant to the application of the Constitution. For additional discussion of Thuraissigiam, see pp. 467–469, 1527, 1530, *supra*.

---

3. COLLATERAL ATTACK ON CRIMINAL CONVICTIONS

INTRODUCTION

This Section explores the scope and use of habeas corpus in the context of post-conviction, or collateral, review of federal and state criminal convictions. Similar issues arise in collateral habeas review as in the context of habeas review of executive detention. But distinct issues also arise in this context because the habeas court is here confronted with cases previously adjudicated in state and federal courts.

A. COLLATERAL ATTACK ON STATE CONVICTIONS

INTRODUCTORY NOTE ON THE OPERATION OF FEDERAL HABEAS CORPUS JURISDICTION FOR PETITIONERS IN STATE CUSTODY

In 1867, during Reconstruction, Congress extended federal court habeas corpus jurisdiction so that it generally reached cases challenging the lawfulness of *state* custody. From 1867 to 1996, Congress made few significant changes to the jurisdiction; instead, decisional law wove an intricate web of rules that changed significantly over time. In 1867, it was hardly clear what the role of federal habeas corpus courts should be with respect to those held in state custody. Over time, Supreme Court decisions interpreted the statutory grant of jurisdiction as conferring federal courts with the power to review federal issues decided adversely to persons held in state custody by a state criminal court of competent jurisdiction.

Perhaps unsurprisingly, the Warren Court generally defined the habeas jurisdiction broadly. In turn, the Burger and Rehnquist Courts narrowed the jurisdiction and tightened procedural requirements. Then Congress, in the Antiterrorism and Effective Death Penalty Act of 1996 (AEDPA), p. 1468, *supra*, enacted provisions significantly restricting the writ's availability, while leaving intact many judge-made doctrines that pre-date that Act. Both those doctrines and the provisions of AEDPA are immensely complex, erecting a maze of requirements through which only a handful of petitions successfully emerge. The following offers an overview of the operation of the habeas jurisdiction in actions commenced by persons convicted in state court before studying key issues in greater depth.

A. Cognizable Issues

(1) The Statutory Grant. In practice, habeas relitigation for those held in state custody involves almost exclusively questions of federal *constitutional* law, as few state prosecutions implicate federal statutes or treaties.[1] In Estelle v. McGuire, 502 U.S. 62 (1991), the Supreme Court held that federal habeas corpus does not reach errors of *state* law.

Under the Warren Court, a habeas court could review all constitutional issues that the Supreme Court could have considered on direct review of a state criminal conviction. The Burger and Rehnquist Courts created two major exceptions to that general rule: (i) one precluded claims that the state court erred in refusing to suppress evidence under the Fourth Amendment, so long as the state court provided a full and fair opportunity to litigate that question, see pp. 1570–1571, *infra*; (ii) the second, subject only to extraordinarily narrow exceptions, excluded claims founded on "new law"—*i.e.*, a constitutional rule that was not dictated by precedent at the time that the petitioner's conviction became final on direct review, see pp. 1580–1585, *infra*.

B. Prerequisites to Review

A petitioner seeking federal habeas relief must satisfy two pre-conditions.

(1) Custody. Because habeas corpus is a remedy for unlawful custody, the petitioner must be in custody when the petition is filed. See 28 U.S.C. § 2241(c)(3); pp. 1665–1667, *infra*. "Custody" includes not only physical detention but also being subject to parole or probation conditions. But an individual who has served their entire sentence (including parole or probation terms) before filing a habeas petition, or whose only penalty was a fine, is considered not in custody.

(2) Exhaustion of State Remedies. Before seeking habeas relief, a petitioner must exhaust state remedies, including direct appellate review in the state courts (but not direct Supreme Court review of the state court conviction). See 28 U.S.C. § 2254(b–c); pp. 1662–1665, *infra*. Ordinarily, state post-conviction remedies must be exhausted only as to issues not previously presented to the state courts during a defendant's trial and direct appeals (as might be true of claims of ineffective assistance of counsel or of failure to disclose exculpatory evidence). One study following AEDPA's enactment concluded that courts dismissed 11% of habeas petitions for failure to exhaust.[2]

Note that in cases involving short sentences, a petitioner may no longer be in custody by the time state remedies have been exhausted.

---

[1] In Reed v. Farley, 512 U.S. 339 (1994), five Justices indicated that a non-constitutional violation must constitute a "fundamental defect" to be cognizable, and that a violation of an interstate compact requiring commencement of trial within 120 days of an incarcerated person's transfer from one state to another did not qualify, at least when the person had not made a timely objection and had suffered no prejudice.

[2] See King, Cheesman & Ostrom, *Final Technical Report: Habeas Litigation in U.S. District Courts*, National Center for State Courts, Aug. 21, 2007, at 48, 57.

C.   Initiation and Nature of the Proceedings

(1) Filing a Petition. A habeas petition (sometimes called an "application") names as the respondent a state officer having custody of the petitioner—ordinarily the prison warden or the director of the state correctional system. A habeas petition is not an appeal from, but rather a collateral attack upon, the state criminal conviction. Although most defendants in state criminal proceedings are convicted by guilty plea, one study published in 2007 found that 97% of habeas petitioners under sentence of death, and 65% of non-capital habeas petitioners, were convicted at trial.[3]

(2) Civil Nature of Proceedings and Applicable Rules. Habeas corpus actions are civil proceedings. Since 1977, they have been subject to the "Rules Governing Section 2254 Cases in the United States District Courts" ("§ 2254 Rules"), Rule 12 of which states: "The Federal Rules of Civil Procedure, to the extent that they are not inconsistent with any statutory provisions or these rules, may be applied to a proceeding under these rules." The Supreme Court has recognized the ability of habeas petitioners to invoke Rules 59(e) and 60(b) of the Federal Rules of Civil Procedure to reopen judgments. See, *e.g.*, Banister v. Davis, 590 U.S. 504 (2020), p. 1660, *infra* (Rule 59(e)), Buck v. Davis, 580 U.S. 100 (2017), p. 1625, *infra* (Rule 60(b)). At the same time, the Court has declined to permit amendments under Rule 15 where doing so would conflict with the statute of limitations for collateral habeas petitions. See Mayle v. Felix, 545 U.S. 644 (2005).

(3) Time Limits. No statute of limitations existed until 1996, when AEDPA added a one-year limitations period running from the latest of four specified dates. Ordinarily, the operative date is that "on which the judgment became final by the conclusion of direct review or the expiration of the time for seeking such review." 28 U.S.C. § 2244(d)(1)(A). The other three are the dates on which (a) an impediment to filing, created by state action in violation of the Constitution or federal law, was removed; (b) the Supreme Court initially recognized a new constitutional right, retroactively applicable to cases on collateral review, see Paragraph (4), p. 1608, *infra*; and (c) the factual predicate of the claim could have been discovered with due diligence. § 2244(d). In addition, the Supreme Court has indicated that petitions filed more than one year after the dates specified in § 2244(d) are nonetheless not time-barred if the claim falls within the doctrine of equitable tolling or if the petitioner can satisfy an exacting standard of actual innocence.[4] The

---

[3]   See *id.* 20. For earlier studies, see Flango, Habeas Corpus in State and Federal Courts 36 (1994); Robinson, An Empirical Study of Federal Habeas Corpus Review of State Court Judgments 7 (1979); Faust, Rubenstein & Yackle, *The Great Writ in Action: Empirical Light on the Federal Habeas Corpus Debate*, 18 N.Y.U.Rev.L. & Soc. Change 637, 678 (1991). Petitions from defendants convicted by guilty plea could become even rarer in light of the rise of the practice of requiring defendants, as a condition of plea agreements, to waive the right to seek habeas relief. See Malani, *Habeas Settlements*, 92 Va.L.Rev. 1, 7–10 (2006).

[4]   On equitable tolling, see Holland v. Florida, 560 U.S. 631 (2010) (deeming equitable tolling available in appropriate cases because § 2244(d) is properly considered "nonjurisdictional" and observing that equitable principles have traditionally governed habeas corpus and equitable tolling would not undermine statutory purposes). On actual innocence, see McQuiggin v. Perkins, 569 U.S. 383 (2013) (5–4) (holding that a petition that can demonstrate that in light of new evidence, no juror, acting reasonably, would have found the petitioner guilty beyond a reasonable doubt is not time-barred). In both cases, Justice Scalia dissented,

limitations period is tolled during the pendency of properly filed state post-conviction proceedings, but not during the pendency of a prior federal habeas proceeding. See Duncan v. Walker, 533 U.S. 167 (2001).

Many other complexities have arisen in the application of the limitations period.[5] Roughly one-fifth of non-capital cases (but a smaller percentage of capital cases) are dismissed as time-barred.[6]

(4) Availability of Counsel. Incarcerated persons, the great majority of whom are indigent, generally have no constitutional right to appointed counsel in state or federal collateral attacks on their convictions.[7] Any federal right to counsel derives from statutes or court rules.

(a) Capital Cases. In 1988, Congress conferred a right to appointed counsel upon indigent federal habeas petitioners attacking a capital sentence or conviction.[8] About 7% of capital petitioners proceed pro se.[9] (Nearly every state provides counsel to indigent capital defendants in state post-conviction proceedings, although there is little monitoring of their performance.)

(b) Non-Capital Cases. In non-capital cases, the § 2254 Rules require appointment of counsel for an indigent petitioner if an evidentiary hearing is warranted (Rule 8(c)) or when necessary to utilize effectively discovery authorized by the court (Rule 6(a)); both circumstances are extraordinarily rare. Otherwise, the court may appoint counsel if "the interests of justice so require." 18 U.S.C. § 3006A(a)(2). More than 90% of non-capital petitioners proceed pro se.[10]

D. Processing of Cases

(1) Petition and Response. Many petitions are frivolous, and the same 2007 study found that more than 40% of non-capital petitions are dismissed

---

contending that the Court lacked authority to create additional qualifications or exceptions to the limitations period spelled out in § 2244(d).

⁵ See, *e.g.*, Day v. McDonough, 547 U.S. 198 (2006) (5–4) (district court may raise a limitations defense sua sponte); Wood v. Milyard, 566 U.S. 463 (2012) (when state expressly disclaimed reliance on a limitations defense of which it was aware, the court of appeals abused its discretion by resurrecting the defense); Lawrence v. Florida, 549 U.S. 327 (2007) (5–4) (limitations period is not tolled by filing a petition for certiorari seeking review of an otherwise final state post-conviction proceeding); Mayle v. Felix, 545 U.S. 644 (2005) (amended petition, filed outside limitation period, that seeks to add a claim to a pending timely petition does not relate back when claims lack common core of operative facts); Pace v. DiGuglielmo, 544 U.S. 408 (2005) (5–4) (state post-conviction petition dismissed as untimely by the state court is not "properly filed" under § 2244(d) and hence does not toll federal limitations period). See also Dodd v. United States, 545 U.S. 353 (2005) (5–4), p. 1609, note 5, *infra* (in a § 2255 action the one-year period from initial recognition by the Supreme Court of a new constitutional right, retroactively applicable to cases on collateral review, runs from the date on which the Supreme Court recognizes the new right, rather than the date on which the right is made retroactive).

⁶ King, Cheesman & Ostrom, note 2, *supra*, at 46.

⁷ See, *e.g.*, Pennsylvania v. Finley, 481 U.S. 551, 554–55 (1987); Johnson v. Avery, 393 U.S. 483, 488 (1969).

⁸ See Anti-Drug Abuse Act of 1988, Pub.L.No. 100–690, § 7001(b), 102 Stat. 4393–4394, codified at 21 U.S.C. § 848(q)(4)(B), repealed and recodified without change at 18 U.S.C. § 3599 by the Terrorist Death Penalty Enhancement Act of 2005, Pub.L.No. 109–177, Tit. II, § 222, 120 Stat. 231–232 (2006). This statutory right to counsel applies both before a habeas petition is filed, to provide assistance in preparing the petition, see McFarland v. Scott, 512 U.S. 849 (1994), and also during state clemency proceedings, see Harbison v. Bell, 556 U.S. 180 (2009).

⁹ King, Cheesman & Ostrom, note 2, *supra*, at 23.

¹⁰ *Id.*

without the state even filing a response.[11] A state's response, when filed, often establishes a basis for dismissal without further proceedings. Discovery proceeds only as authorized by the judge for good cause shown, § 2254 Rules, Rule 6(a), and in practice is extremely limited. Evidentiary hearings to develop the facts are also rare[12]: in the twelve months ending September 30, 2022, of 9,881 petitions on which courts took action, 9,811 were terminated "Before Trial," 67 "During or After Pretrial," and only three "During or After Trial."[13]

(2) The Role of Magistrate Judges. In many districts, federal magistrate judges have primary responsibility for handling habeas petitions. If a party objects to the magistrate judge's proposed findings and recommendations, the district judge must make a "de novo determination" with respect to any contested matter. 28 U.S.C. § 636(b)(1).

(3) Deference to State Court Determinations. Although res judicata does not apply in habeas proceedings,[14] Congress sharply limited the federal courts' role in reviewing underlying facts in 1996's AEDPA and its new provision in § 2254(d)(2), which precludes relief unless the court finds that the state court made an unreasonable determination of the facts based on the evidence in the state court record. See pp. 1627–1628, *infra*.

Traditionally, a habeas court was not bound to defer to a state court's decision on a question of law or the application of law to the facts. See Brown v. Allen, 344 U.S. 443, 497–513 (1953) (opinion of Frankfurter, J.), pp. 1560–1563, *infra*. But § 2254(d)(1)—the most significant restriction that Congress added in 1996—now requires deference by precluding habeas relief unless the state court's determination was "contrary to, or involved an unreasonable application of, clearly established Federal law, as determined by the Supreme Court of the United States." See generally pp. 1588–1609, *infra*.

E.   Procedural Default

When a claim raised in a federal habeas petition was not presented to the state courts or was not presented in accordance with state procedural rules (*e.g.*, was not raised on a timely basis), ordinarily the state courts will not have reached the merits of the claim. When that is so, subject to only the narrowest exceptions, the federal habeas court will not consider the defaulted claim. See pp. 1631–1657, *infra*. (A procedural default involves a failure to pursue opportunities to litigate in state court that once were but no longer are available; a failure to exhaust state remedies, by contrast, involves a failure to pursue opportunities to litigate in state court that *remain* available.) A 2007 study found that approximately 13% of non-capital petitions are dismissed because of procedural default, and in nearly half of capital habeas proceedings, at least one claim is dismissed on this basis.[15]

---

[11]   *Id.* 34.

[12]   See Weisselberg, *Evidentiary Hearings in Federal Habeas Corpus Cases*, 1990 B.Y.U.L.Rev. 131, 165–68.

[13]   Annual Report of the Director of the Administrative Office of the United States Courts, Table C-4 (2022).

[14]   See Darr v. Burford, 339 U.S. 200 (1950); Salinger v. Loisel, 265 U.S. 224 (1924).

[15]   King, Cheesman & Ostrom, note 2, *supra*, at 48.

F.   Harmless Error

In Brecht v. Abrahamson, 507 U.S. 619 (1993) (5–4), the Court held that habeas courts should *not* apply the rule—followed by state and federal courts on direct review—that upon finding a constitutional violation, a court should grant relief unless the government can prove that the error was harmless beyond a reasonable doubt. See Chapman v. California, 386 U.S. 18 (1967). Instead, Brecht held that application of the Chapman standard on collateral review was unnecessary to incentivize state courts to apply that standard faithfully on direct review, and hence habeas courts should apply a less stringent standard under which an error is harmless unless it "had substantial and injurious effect or influence in determining the jury's verdict" (quoting Kotteakos v. United States, 328 U.S. 750, 776 (1946)).

G.   Relief, Appeals, and Successive Petitions

(1)   Relief. Ordinarily the only remedy awarded is release from custody, but the remedy is tailored to the nature of the constitutional violation. Thus, a petitioner convicted for conduct that is constitutionally protected (for example, burning the American flag) would obtain unconditional release from custody; a petitioner who established a procedural error (for example, admission of a confession in violation of the Miranda rules) would in practice obtain a retrial (through award of a conditional remedy, requiring release only if a retrial is not commenced within a specified period); and a petitioner who established a sentencing error would in practice be granted a new sentencing hearing.

(2)   Appeals. The custodian may appeal a district court's grant of relief. Before appealing a denial of relief, a petitioner must obtain, from either the district court or the court of appeals,[16] a "certificate of appealability," which issues upon "a substantial showing of the denial of a constitutional right" and which must indicate the specific issue(s) satisfying that standard. 28 U.S.C. § 2253(c).[17]

(3)   Successive Petitions. A petitioner may file more than one habeas petition only in exceedingly narrow circumstances. See pp. 1657–1662, *infra.*

---

[16]   See, *e.g.*, Tiedeman v. Benson, 122 F.3d 518, 522 & cases cited (8th Cir.1997).

[17]   In Slack v. McDaniel, 529 U.S. 473, 483 (2000), the Court ruled that § 2253(c)(2), also added in 1996, codified precedent calling for issuance of a certificate if the appeal presented a federal question of substance that was "debatable among jurists of reason" or not "squarely foreclosed by statute, rule or authoritative court decision," Barefoot v. Estelle, 463 U.S. 880, 893 n.4, 894 (1983) (internal quotations omitted), except that § 2253(c)(2) substitutes "constitutional" for "federal." For discussion of the application of that standard in light of § 2254(d)(1)'s deferential standard, see Medellín v. Dretke, 544 U.S. 660 (2005) (O'Connor, J., dissenting); Miller-El v. Cockrell, 537 U.S. 322 (2003).

H. Filing and Success Rates

(1) Number of Petitions Filed. The trend in filings is as follows:

	Number of Habeas Corpus Petitions Filed by Petitioners in State Custody[18]	Number of Persons Incarcerated by the States[19]	Habeas Petitions Filed by Petitioners in State Custody as % of Persons Incarcerated by the States	Number of Private Civil Cases Filed in the Federal Courts[20]	Habeas Petitions Filed by Petitioners in State Custody as % of Private Civil Cases
1950	560	149,031	0.38%	32,193	1.74%
1955	660	165,692	0.40%	39,225	1.68%
1960	871	189,735	0.46%	38,444	2.27%
1965	4,845	189,855	2.55%	46,027	10.53%
1970	9,063	176,403	5.14%	62,356	14.53%
1975	7,843	216,462	3.62%	85,541	9.17%
1980	7,031	305,458	2.30%	105,161	6.69%
1985	8,534	462,284	1.85%	156,182	5.46%
1990	10,823	708,393	1.53%	161,579	6.70%

---

[18] See Annual Report of the Director of the Administrative Office of the United States Courts, Table C-3, for the years indicated. Where numbers have been revised, the most recent figure is used. Through 1990, statistics are for a June 30 fiscal year and thereafter for a September 30 fiscal year. The figures include the very small number of petitions listed (a) under "local jurisdiction" and (b) in 2000, 2005, 2010, 2015, 2020, and 2022, in a separate category of death penalty cases.

Studies have found that roughly 80% of habeas petitions attacked convictions or sentences; the rest related to pretrial matters, conditions of confinement, or revocation of probation or parole. See Allen, Schachtman & Wilson, *Federal Habeas Corpus and Its Reform: An Empirical Analysis*, 13 Rutgers L.J. 675, 755 n.367 (1982); King, Cheesman & Ostrom, note 2, *supra*, at 26–27.

[19] See Bureau of Justice Statistics (BJS), Historical Statistics on Prisoners in State and Federal Institutions, Yearend 1925–1986 (May 1988) (1950–1975 figures); BJS, Prisoners in State and Federal Institutions on December 31, 1981, Table 1 (1980 figure); BJS, Correctional Populations in the United States, 1986, 1991, and 1996, respectively, Table 5 (1985–1995 figures); BJS, Bulletin: Prisoners in 2011 (December 2012), at 1 (2000–2010 figure); BJS, Prisoners in 2021—Statistical Tables (December 2022), at 6 (2015–2021 figures); BJS, Prisons Report Series—Preliminary Data Release, Table 2: Prisoners under the jurisdiction of state or federal correctional authorities, by sex and jurisdiction, 2021 and 2022 (Sep. 20, 2023). Where numbers have been revised, the most recent figure is used. Statistics are as of December 31 for the indicated year.

The figures through 1975 are of persons "in custody," which refers to those under direct physical control by the state. Beginning in 1978, BJS published statistics of persons "under jurisdiction," which refers to the legal power to incarcerate the person and includes persons in custody but not in the state's own prisons—for example, parties housed in local jails, other states, federal prisons, or hospitals outside the correctional system, and individuals on work release, furlough, or bail. The above table uses the "under jurisdiction" statistic starting in 1980.

[20] See Annual Report, note 13, *supra*, Tables C-2, C-3, for the years indicated. Statistics through 1990 are based on a fiscal year ending June 30, and thereafter for a fiscal year ending September 30.

1995	13,632	1,025,624	1.33%	205,177	6.64%
2000	21,349	1,248,815	1.71%	188,408	11.33%
2005	19,190	1,338,292	1.43%	200,887	9.55%
2010	17,042	1,404,032	1.21%	239,858	7.11%
2015	16,217	1,330,148	1.22%	237,453	6.83%
2020	13,371	1,069,008	1.25%	423,059	3.16%
2022	11,079	1,070,834	1.03%	236,343	4.69%

(2) Success Rates. Studies conducted during the 1970s and early 1980s found that only 3–4% of persons incarcerated by the states who filed a petition obtained any kind of relief in the district courts[21]—and relief may result only in a further hearing or retrial that sustains the conviction. As judge-made and statutory restrictions on the exercise of habeas jurisdiction tightened, success rates in the district courts declined: to 1% in a study of petitions filed in 1990 and 1992,[22] and then, in a study of petitions filed in 2003–2004 (when the 1996 amendments were fully operative), to less than 0.6% for non-capital petitioners.[23] (As noted below in Section I of this Note, relief is more common in capital cases.)

(3) The Impact of the System. Do these statistics suggest that habeas review is a waste of time? That the jurisdiction exacts few costs while providing the valuable promise of federal review of federal questions arising in state criminal cases? (Consider the assessment by Professor Shapiro, note 21, *supra*, at 340–42, that in a significant number of cases in which no relief is awarded, habeas review nonetheless serves useful functions—including helping get state processes that have been derailed back on track.) That uncounseled petitioners cannot navigate the procedural complexities or surmount the strict limits on the scope of federal review? That it is doubtful that any purpose that one might posit for habeas review is substantially fulfilled in practice?

I. Procedures in Capital Cases

Capital cases, although they constituted only 113 of the 9,881 habeas cases on which the district courts took action in the twelve-month period ending on September 30, 2022,[24] pose special difficulties. On the one hand, the finality of execution calls for special solicitude, and the complexity of capital cases provides fertile ground for constitutional errors. One study found that petitioners obtained some relief in roughly 40% of the cases in which a death sentence was imposed between 1973 and 1995. Liebman,

---

[21]   See Faust, Rubenstein & Yackle, note 3, *supra*, at 681; Robinson, note 3, *supra*, at 23; Shapiro, *Federal Habeas Corpus: A Study in Massachusetts*, 87 Harv.L.Rev. 321, 333 (1973). Capital cases aside, very few petitioners who lose in the district court obtain relief on appeal. See, *e.g.*, King, *Non-Capital Habeas Cases After Appellate Review: An Empirical Analysis*, 24 Fed. Sent'g Rep. 308, 310 (2012) (in a study in which 2,188 cases terminated in the district courts, only 18 petitioners received favorable rulings on appeal).

[22]   Flango, note 3, *supra*, at 62–63.

[23]   King, Cheesman & Ostrom, note 2, *supra*, at 52, as modified by King, note 21, *supra*. King's article found that after appeals were resolved, another 0.3% of petitioners obtained relief.

[24]   See Annual Report, note 13, *supra*, Table C-4.

Fagan, & West, A Broken System: Error Rates in Capital Cases, 1973–1995 (https://scholarship.law.columbia.edu/faculty_scholarship/1219/).   A more recent study of capital petitions in 2000–2002 found that 33 of 368 petitioners in the sample, or roughly 9%, obtained some form of relief, which two-thirds of the time was from the sentence rather than from conviction.[25] That rate, though dramatically lower than 40%, was nearly 30 times higher than the rate for non-capital cases.[26] (Recall that only capital petitioners are entitled by statute to counsel in federal habeas proceedings.)

On the other hand, critics of capital habeas litigation have expressed concern about perceived abuses and unnecessary delays (such as filing multiple petitions and/or petitions at the eleventh hour and then seeking a stay of execution). AEDPA, enacted in 1996 and amended in 2006, provides that various additional procedural restrictions take effect if a state has established a mechanism for providing "competent counsel" and "payment of reasonable litigation expenses" in state post-conviction proceedings brought by indigent petitioners under sentence of death. 28 U.S.C. §§ 2261(b), 2265(a)(1).[27] To date, only one state, Arizona, has qualified for the procedural benefits available to states in federal capital habeas corpus cases. It did so under new procedures that empower the Attorney General to certify qualifying states.[28] No other state has qualified, perhaps because although most do provide for appointment of counsel in capital state post-conviction

---

[25]   See King, Cheesman & Ostrom, note 2, *supra*, at 51–52.

[26]   Another recent study found that between 2013 and 2017, federal habeas courts granted relief for claims relating to the guilt phase at a significantly higher rate in capital murder cases than non-capital murder cases. See Note, *Is Death Different to Federal Judges?*, 72 Stan.L.Rev. 1655 (2020).

[27]   Section 507 of the USA PATRIOT Improvement and Reauthorization Act of 2005, Pub.L.No. 109–177, 120 Stat. 192, 250 (2006), amended AEDPA by shifting from the federal courts to the Attorney General the authority initially to certify states and specified no additional certification requirements shall be imposed beyond those set forth in the statute, § 2265(a)(1)).

One restriction triggered by a state's qualification is a limitations period for filing a petition of 180 days rather than one year. 28 U.S.C. § 2263. A second is the specification of deadlines within which courts must render decisions: for the district courts, the earlier of (i) 450 days after filing or (ii) 60 days after the case was submitted for decision; for the courts of appeals, the deadline is 120 days after the reply brief is filed. *Id.* § 2266. A third restriction limits the issuance of stays of execution. Pre-AEDPA decisions had come close to laying down a rule that a capital petitioner is entitled to a stay of execution in connection with a first habeas petition, see Lonchar v. Thomas, 517 U.S. 314, 324 (1996), while suggesting that a stay in connection with a successive petition will be far more difficult to obtain, see Bowersox v. Williams, 517 U.S. 345 (1996) (per curiam). AEDPA does not disturb this approach but provides that any stay of execution shall expire if the petitioner (a) fails to file a timely petition, (b) "fails to make a substantial showing of the denial of a Federal right," or (c) "is denied relief in the district court or at any subsequent stage of review." *Id.* § 2262(b). Upon expiration, "no Federal court thereafter shall have the authority to enter a stay of execution in the case, unless the court of appeals approves the filing of a second or successive application under section 2244(b)." *Id.* § 2262(c). For a detailed analysis of the relevant provisions, see Yackle, *The New Habeas Corpus in Death Penalty Cases*, 63 Am.U.L.Rev. 1791 (2014).

[28]   In 2013, in keeping with § 507, the Attorney General issued a final rule implementing the certification procedure. See 78 Fed. Reg. 58,160 (Sept. 23, 2013) (to be codified at 28 C.F.R. pt. 26). The Attorney General thereafter certified Arizona in 2020, see 85 Fed. Reg. 20,705. The certification was under review in the D.C. Circuit, see Office of the Federal Public Defender et al. v. Barr, No. 20–1144 (D.C.Cir.), but in response to a motion by the Department of Justice, that court remanded the matter back to the Department for further consideration, see Order dated Mar. 26, 2021.

cases, most find the benefits not worth the cost of supporting counsel at a level sufficient to meet the Attorney General's standards.

INTRODUCTORY NOTE ON THE HISTORICAL DEVELOPMENT AND ROLE OF FEDERAL RELITIGATION IN CRIMINAL CASES

Many scholars have discussed the historic scope of the writ of habeas corpus as a post-conviction remedy and the implications of the history for contemporary interpretation of the jurisdictional grant. Drawing lessons from the history is difficult, as the precedents involve a broad range of variables—federal vs. state custody; pre-trial vs. post-trial detention; ordinary criminal cases vs. contempt proceedings; unfamiliar and shifting conceptions of jurisdiction; evolving conceptions of due process; and changes in the Supreme Court's appellate jurisdiction—whose significance is not always discussed. Further, many decisions do not articulate a clear understanding of habeas corpus—particularly one that corresponds to modern categories and perceptions.[1] Nonetheless, it is worth noting several key points about the historical development and debate.

(1) The Historical Limits of Post-Conviction Review. Numerous authorities suggest that both before and after the founding, one held pursuant to a criminal conviction could challenge, in a habeas corpus petition, only the jurisdiction of the court that rendered the judgment of conviction. See, *e.g.*, Ex parte Watkins, 28 U.S. (3 Pet.) 193 (1830).[2]

(2) The Habeas Corpus Act of 1867. The Act of February 5, 1867, 14 Stat. 385, extended the federal writ to a new class of petitioners—all of those in state custody, empowering federal courts to grant the writ "in all cases where any person may be restrained of his or her liberty in violation of the constitution, or of any treaty or law of the United States." Wiecek, *The Great Writ and Reconstruction: The Habeas Corpus Act of 1867*, 36 J.So.Hist. 530 (1970), notes the original bill from which the Act emerged was intended to extend the writ to citizens newly freed from slavery and observes that

---

[1] For example, Arkin, *The Ghost at the Banquet: Slavery, Federalism, and Habeas Corpus for State Prisoners*, 70 Tulane L.Rev. 1 (1995), notes that in the period before the Civil War, (i) post-conviction habeas petitions were rare because imprisonment was not a common sanction, and (ii) the most prominent use of federal habeas jurisdiction to promote federal supremacy was in enforcing the Fugitive Slave Act—hardly a comfortable foundation for modern understandings.

[2] See Bator, *Finality in Criminal Law and Federal Habeas Corpus for State Prisoners*, 76 Harv.L.Rev. 441 (1963); Oaks, *Habeas Corpus in the States: 1776–1865*, 32 U.Chi.L.Rev. 243, 258–61 (1965). For discussion of the British foundations of habeas, see the authorities cited at p. 1461, note 2, *supra*.

Professor Peller explains decisions like Watkins differently. He contends that it would have been anomalous for the Supreme Court, which until 1891 lacked jurisdiction to review federal criminal convictions directly, to review convictions indirectly on habeas; but, he argues, lower federal courts exercised plenary power to relitigate constitutional claims. Peller, *In Defense of Federal Habeas Corpus Relitigation*, 16 Harv.C.R.-C.L.L.Rev. 579 (1982). For doubts about this explanation, see Woolhandler, *Demodeling Habeas*, 45 Stan.L.Rev. 575, 585–96 & n.67 (1993); Liebman, *Apocalypse Next Time?: The Anachronistic Attack on Habeas Corpus/Direct Review Parity*, 92 Colum.L.Rev. 1997, 2046 (1992). Against the tide of the literature, Kovarsky, *A Constitutional Theory of Habeas Power*, 99 Va.L.Rev. 753, 768–69 (2013), asserts that King's Bench in England reviewed criminal convictions in habeas proceedings.

subsequent debates leading up to adoption of the 1867 Act "are remarkable for their scantiness and opacity." Scholars dispute whether the Reconstruction Congress, mistrustful as it was of state courts, intended the Act to broaden the scope of the writ to reach not merely jurisdictional defects but violations of federal law more broadly.[3]

(3) Evolution in the Nineteenth Century. After 1867, the Court held that the writ embraced claims by those held in federal custody alleging that the statute under which a criminal conviction had been obtained was unconstitutional, see, *e.g.*, Ex parte Siebold, 100 U.S. 371, 376–77 (1879), or that the sentence imposed exceeded what the statute authorized, see, *e.g.*, Ex parte Lange, 85 U.S. (18 Wall.) 163, 176 (1873). Some view these decisions as merely "softening," but not departing from, the jurisdictional concept.[4] Others view them as part of a trend in which habeas courts reached beyond jurisdictional defects to consider most constitutional claims. On one interpretation, for much of the nineteenth century, constitutional claims were generally limited to challenges to statutes. But as the understanding of constitutional wrongs expanded to encompass ad hoc or unauthorized actions of state officials, the effective scope of habeas relitigation expanded.[5]

(4) Early Twentieth Century Precedents. Two decisions from the early twentieth century involved due process claims arising from alleged mob domination of state trial proceedings. In Frank v. Mangum, 237 U.S. 309 (1915), the Court refused to grant the writ; eight years later, in Moore v. Dempsey, 261 U.S. 86 (1923), it changed course. Justice Holmes, who had dissented in Frank, wrote for the Court in Moore and held due process is denied where "the whole proceeding is a mask [and] counsel, jury and judge were swept to the fatal end by an irresistible wave of public passion, and * * * the State Courts failed to correct the wrong." One explanation for the differing results is that in Frank, the state appellate court, in reviewing the trial proceedings, had already provided fair corrective process, whereas in Moore, the Court may have viewed the state appellate review of the alleged mob domination as so perfunctory as not to constitute an adequate state corrective process, therefore permitting federal habeas review.[6] Others view

---

[3]   Compare Bator, note 2, *supra*, at 465–66 (arguing there was no expansion of the writ); Forsythe, *The Historical Origins of Broad Federal Habeas Review Reconsidered*, 70 Notre Dame L.Rev. 1079, 1101–24 (1995) (same); and Mayers, *The Habeas Corpus Act of 1867: The Supreme Court as Legal Historian*, 33 U.Chi.L.Rev. 31 (1965) (same), with Peller, note 2, *supra*, at 618–20 (contending Congress meant to expand the writ). Wiecek, *supra*, suggests that "[p]erhaps all that can be concluded about the intent of Congress * * * is that * * * [it] enacted a statute of comprehensive terminology, being vaguely aware of the possibilities inherent in the act and willing to see how it would be nurtured and matured in the courts."

[4]   See Bator, note 2, *supra*.

[5]   See Woolhandler, note 2, *supra*, at 596–630. Should this expansion be viewed as an evolution of the not uncommon practice in the early nineteenth century of federal courts granting pre-trial habeas review over challenges to the adequacy of evidence relied upon to commit one under criminal charges, as in Ex parte Bollman, 8 U.S. (4 Cranch) 75 (1807), discussed at pp. 1465–1467, *supra*?

[6]   See Bator, note 2, *supra*, at 483–93.

Moore as overruling Frank on either the scope of the writ[7] or on the meaning of due process.[8]

Either way, over the course of the next three decades, the Court's decisions expanded the scope of collateral habeas proceedings, as exemplified in cases like Johnson v. Zerbst, 304 U.S. 458 (1938). There, the Court held that habeas relief would be warranted if, on remand, the district court concludes that the petitioner did not "competently and intelligently waive his right to counsel" at trial, because in such circumstances "the trial court did not have jurisdiction to proceed to judgment and conviction." A few years later, in Waley v. Johnston, 316 U.S. 101 (1942), the Court remanded for a hearing on a claim that the federal criminal defendant's guilty plea had been coerced while holding that "the use of the writ in the federal courts to test the constitutional validity of a conviction for crime is not restricted to those cases where the judgment of conviction is void for want of jurisdiction of the trial court to render it. It extends also to those exceptional cases where the conviction has been in disregard of the constitutional rights of the accused, and where the writ is the only effective means of preserving his rights."

Professor Vázquez notes that during the nineteenth century, those convicted in state courts enjoyed direct appeal as of right to the Supreme Court of any federal question decided against them. Surveying the cases between the 1916 expansion of discretionary review of state court criminal cases by the Supreme Court and the next principal case, Brown v. Allen, decided in 1953, Vázquez concludes that during this period the Justices debated whether review of such questions appropriately remained the exclusive province of the Supreme Court on direct appeal or whether lower federal courts could examine them in habeas proceedings. Thus, Vázquez argues, disagreement centered not on *whether* a federal court would review such questions generally, but instead over *which* federal forum should do so. See Vázquez, *Habeas as Forum Allocation: A New Synthesis*, 71 U. Miami L.Rev. 645 (2017).[9]

(5) The 1953 Decision in Brown v. Allen. The next principal case, Brown v. Allen, is one landmark decision the holding of which is not in dispute.[10]

---

[7]   See Wechsler, *Habeas Corpus and the Supreme Court: Reconsidering the Reach of the Great Writ*, 59 U.Colo.L.Rev. 167, 173 (1988).

[8]   See Peller, note 2, *supra*, at 646. A distinct explanation of the more expansive role for habeas exemplified by Moore rests on the premise that "[s]ince 1789, Congress has entitled federal and state prisoners incarcerated in violation of any fundamental legal (typically, any constitutional) principle to one meaningful federal court review as of right." When, in 1914, however, the Supreme Court's jurisdiction to review state court judgments became discretionary rather than mandatory, federal habeas corpus jurisdiction expanded to fill the gap. Liebman, note 2, *supra*, at 2081, 2096. See also Freedman, *Leo Frank Lives: Untangling the Historical Roots of Meaningful Federal Habeas Corpus Review of State Convictions*, 51 Ala.L.Rev. 1467 (2000).

[9]   Vázquez's conclusion therefore contrasts with that reached by Professor Bator in his survey of the same period, see Bator, note 2, *supra*, at 483–99, and builds on Professor Liebman's analysis of the expansion of the writ during the period, see Liebman, note 2, *supra*, at 2072–78.

[10]   The Brown Court applied the then-governing statutory habeas provisions stemming from the 1948 revisions to the Judicial Code. As Justice Reed's opinion in Brown noted, federal court relief was "only authorized when a state prisoner is in custody in violation of the Constitution of the United States" (citing § 2241) and where " 'it appears that the applicant has exhausted the remedies available in the courts of the State, or that there is either an absence of

Brown clearly ruled that a federal habeas court should routinely relitigate the merits of federal constitutional issues that the state court had decided adversely to a petitioner in state custody. Some commentators viewed Brown as a dramatic expansion of the historic role of habeas,[11] while others saw Brown as merely confirming a trend by which violations of fundamental law—a term that encompassed evolving notions of due process—could be reviewed by a habeas court.[12] Whatever its consistency with the history, Brown ushered in a regime of broad federal relitigation during the Warren Court years and in the early years of the Burger Court. That same era witnessed the incorporation of almost all of the provisions of the Bill of Rights through the Fourteenth Amendment so as to make them applicable to the states as well as a dramatic expansion of the reach of constitutional rights concerning criminal procedure. Many observers believe that without the broad scope of habeas review authorized by Brown, the federal judiciary could not have effectively supervised the compliance by state courts (particularly in Southern states) with Supreme Court decisions recognizing new and controversial federal constitutional rights governing state criminal processes.

Judicial decisions from the 1970s on, coupled with AEDPA's 1996 amendments to the habeas jurisdiction, sharply limited the scope of relitigation that Brown had recognized. Although Brown no longer states the governing law, the current scope of review and the issues it raises cannot be understood without studying the backdrop it provides.

Brown v. Allen

344 U.S. 443 (1953).

Certiorari to the United States Court of Appeals for the Fourth Circuit.

[Brown involved three consolidated cases (those of Brown, Speller, and Daniels), all involving Black defendants sentenced to death in North Carolina for interracial rape or murder. All three habeas petitions alleged unconstitutional racial discrimination in the selection of the petit

---

available State corrective process or the existence of circumstances rendering such process ineffective to protect the rights of the prisoner' " (quoting § 2254).

[11]   The leading proponent of that view was Bator, note 2, *supra*. Accord, *e.g.*, Duker, A Constitutional History of Habeas Corpus (1980); Mayers, note 3, *supra*; Oaks, *Legal History in the High Court—Habeas Corpus*, 64 Mich.L.Rev. 451 (1966). See also, *e.g.*, Felker v. Turpin, 518 U.S. 651, 663 (1996); Wright v. West, 505 U.S. 277, 285–86 (1992) (opinion of Thomas, J., joined by Rehnquist, C.J., and Scalia, J.); McCleskey v. Zant, 499 U.S. 467, 477–79 (1991); Stone v. Powell, 428 U.S. 465, 475–76 (1976).

[12]   That view was taken by Justice Brennan, for the Court, in Fay v. Noia, 372 U.S. 391 (1963). See also Vázquez, Paragraph (4), *supra*; Yackle, *Form and Function in the Administration of Justice: The Bill of Rights and Federal Habeas Corpus*, 23 U.Mich.J.L. Reform 685, 695–702 (1990). Freedman, *Brown v. Allen: The Habeas Corpus Revolution That Wasn't*, 51 Ala.L.Rev. 1541 (2000), concludes, after examining internal Court documents, that the Justices did not perceive Brown to be revolutionary. (The documents do reveal the Court's recognition of considerable uncertainty about the scope of habeas jurisdiction.)

As explored below, this debate is revived by Justices Kagan and Gorsuch in Brown v. Davenport, 596 U.S. 118 (2022), p. 1568, *infra*.

jury; Brown and Daniels also complained of discrimination in the selection of the grand jury and of the admission at trial of a coerced confession.*

[In the Daniels case, the Supreme Court of North Carolina, on direct appeal from the conviction, refused to consider the merits of the constitutional claims because the appeal had been filed one day late. The U.S. Supreme Court held that this state court procedural default precluded federal habeas review.

[Brown's and Speller's petitions raised constitutional issues that had been fully litigated with the aid of counsel at trial, rejected on the merits in their direct appeal, and set forth in an unsuccessful petition for certiorari. In considering their habeas petitions, the federal district court examined the state court record, and, in Speller's case, took additional evidence. It then denied relief, essentially on the basis that the state court's determinations were supported by the evidence and should not be relitigated. In Speller's case, the district judge stated that a "habeas corpus proceeding is not available * * * for the purpose of raising the identical question passed upon in [the state] Courts," but added, as an alternative ground, that Speller had failed to substantiate his constitutional claims. The Fourth Circuit affirmed in both cases.

[In the Supreme Court, eight opinions resulted. The Justices divided both on the central question presented by the Brown and Speller petitions—whether a federal court exercising habeas jurisdiction may re-examine the merits of federal constitutional claims that were denied by the state courts—and on the merits of those claims.

[The Court's handling of the case was unusual. Justice Reed delivered the "opinion of the Court"—even though on one issue, he spoke for a minority.** His opinion, joined by Chief Justice Vinson and Justices Burton, Clark, and Minton, sends conflicting signals on whether federal courts should defer to the state court's substantive determinations. In the end, Justice Reed reached the merits of Brown's and Speller's constitutional claims and found them wanting. Justice Frankfurter filed an elaborate opinion that no other Justice formally joined, but with which four other Justices (Black, Douglas, Burton, and Clark) indicated their agreement in separate opinions. Justice Frankfurter described his opinion as "designed to make explicit and detailed matters that are also the concern of Mr. Justice Reed's opinion," and he stated that "[t]he views of the Court * * * may thus be drawn from the two opinions jointly." Because Justice Frankfurter's opinion reflects the way that Brown v. Allen has been understood and was followed by federal habeas courts in its immediate wake, substantial portions of it are presented here.]

---

*　　[Ed.] Note that the Court decided Brown v. Allen while Brown v. Board of Education, 347 U.S. 483 (1954), was pending before the Court.

**　　[Ed.] That issue was whether the Supreme Court's earlier denial of certiorari should be treated as a determination that there was no constitutional violation. The majority held no.

■ Opinion of FRANKFURTER, J.

* * *

II

* * * I deem it appropriate to begin by making explicit some basic considerations underlying the federal habeas corpus jurisdiction. Experience may be summoned to support the belief that most claims in these attempts to obtain review of State convictions are without merit. Presumably they are adequately dealt with in the State courts. Again, no one can feel more strongly than I do that a casual, unrestricted opening of the doors of the federal courts to these claims not only would cast an undue burden upon those courts, but would also disregard our duty to support and not weaken the sturdy enforcement of their criminal laws by the States. That wholesale opening of State prison doors by federal courts is, however, not at all the real issue before us is best indicated by a survey recently prepared in the Administrative Office of the United States Courts for the Conference of Chief Justices: of all federal question applications for habeas corpus, some not even relating to State convictions, only 67 out of 3,702 applications were granted in the last seven years. And "only a small number" of these 67 applications resulted in release from prison: "a more detailed study over the last four years shows that out of 29 petitions granted, there were only 5 petitioners who were released from state penitentiaries."[11] The meritorious claims are few, but our procedures must ensure that those few claims are not stifled by undiscriminating generalities. * * *

For surely it is an abuse to deal too casually and too lightly with rights guaranteed by the Federal Constitution, even though they involve limitations upon State power and may be invoked by those morally unworthy. Under the guise of fashioning a procedural rule, we are not justified in wiping out the practical efficacy of a jurisdiction conferred by Congress on the District Courts. Rules which in effect treat all these cases indiscriminately as frivolous do not fall far short of abolishing this head of jurisdiction.

Congress could have left the enforcement of federal constitutional rights governing the administration of criminal justice in the States exclusively to the State courts. These tribunals are under the same duty as the federal courts to respect rights under the United States Constitution. Indeed, * * * [i]t was not until the Act of 1867 that the power to issue the writ was extended to an applicant under sentence of a State court. It is not for us to determine whether this power should have been vested in the federal courts. As Mr. Justice Bradley * * * commented not long after the passage of that Act, "although it may appear unseemly that a prisoner, after conviction in a state court, should be set at liberty by a single judge on *habeas corpus*, there seems to be no escape from the

---

[11] Habeas Corpus Cases in the Federal Courts Brought by State Prisoners, Administrative Office of the United States Courts 4 (Dec. 16, 1952). * * *

law." Ex parte Bridges, 2 Woods (5th Cir.) 428, 432 [(1875)]. * * * It is for this Court to give fair effect to the habeas corpus jurisdiction as enacted by Congress. By giving the federal courts [habeas] jurisdiction, Congress has embedded into federal legislation the historic function of habeas corpus adapted to reaching an enlarged area of claims.

In exercising the power thus bestowed, the District Judge must take due account of the proceedings that are challenged by the application for a writ. All that has gone before is not to be ignored as irrelevant. But the prior State determination of a claim under the United States Constitution cannot foreclose consideration of such a claim, else the State court would have the final say which the Congress, by the Act of 1867, provided it should not have. * * * That most claims are frivolous has an important bearing upon the procedure to be followed by a district judge. The prior State determination may guide his discretion in deciding upon the appropriate course to be followed in disposing of the application before him. The State record may serve to indicate the necessity of further pleadings or of a quick hearing to clear up an ambiguity, or the State record may show the claim to be frivolous or not within the competence of a federal court because solely dependent on State law.

It may be a matter of phrasing whether we say that the District Judge summarily denies an application for a writ by accepting the ruling of the State court or by making an independent judgment, though he does so on the basis of what the State record reveals. But since phrasing mirrors thought, it is important that the phrasing not obscure the true issue before a federal court. * * * If we are to give effect to the statute and at the same time avoid improper intrusion into the State criminal process by federal judges * * *[,] we must direct them to probe the federal question while drawing on available records of prior proceedings to guide them in doing so.

Of course, experience cautions that the very nature and function of the writ of habeas corpus precludes the formulation of fool-proof standards which the 225 District Judges can automatically apply. * * * But it is important, in order to preclude individualized enforcement of the Constitution in different parts of the Nation, to lay down as specifically as the nature of the problem permits the standards or directions that should govern the District Judges in the disposition of applications for habeas corpus by prisoners under sentence of State courts.

First. Just as in all other litigation, a prima facie case must be made out by the petitioner. The application should be dismissed when it fails to state a federal question, or fails to set forth facts which, if accepted at face value, would entitle the applicant to relief.

Care will naturally be taken that the frequent lack of technical competence of prisoners should not strangle consideration of a valid constitutional claim that is bunglingly presented. * * *

Second. Failure to exhaust an available State remedy is an obvious ground for denying the application. * * *

Third. If the record of the State proceedings is not filed, the judge is required to decide * * * whether it is more desirable to call for the record or to hold a hearing. * * *

Fourth. When the record of the State court proceedings is before the court, it may appear that the issue turns on basic facts and that the facts (in the sense of a recital of external events and the credibility of their narrators) have been tried and adjudicated against the applicant. Unless a vital flaw be found in the process of ascertaining such facts in the State court, the District Judge may accept their determination in the State proceeding * * *. On the other hand, State adjudication of questions of law cannot, under the habeas corpus statute, be accepted as binding. It is precisely these questions that the federal judge is commanded to decide. * * *

Fifth. Where the ascertainment of the historical facts does not dispose of the claim but calls for interpretation of the legal significance of such facts, the District Judge must exercise his own judgment on this blend of facts and their legal values. Thus, so-called mixed questions or the application of constitutional principles to the facts as found leave the duty of adjudication with the federal judge.

For instance, the question whether established primary facts underlying a confession prove that the confession was coerced or voluntary cannot rest on the State decision. * * * Although there is no need for the federal judge, if he could, to shut his eyes to the State consideration of such issues, no binding weight is to be attached to the State determination. * * * The State court cannot have the last say when it, though on fair consideration and what procedurally may be deemed fairness, may have misconceived a federal constitutional right. * * *

These standards, addressed as they are to the practical situation facing the District Judge, recognize the discretion of judges to give weight to whatever may be relevant in the State proceedings, and yet preserve the full implication of the requirement of Congress that the District Judge decide constitutional questions presented by a State prisoner even after his claims have been carefully considered by the State courts. Congress has the power to distribute among the courts of the States and of the United States jurisdiction to determine federal claims. It has seen fit to give this Court power to review errors of federal law in State determinations, and in addition to give to the lower federal courts power to inquire into federal claims, by way of habeas corpus. Such power is in the spirit of our inherited law. It accords with, and is thoroughly regardful of, "the liberty of the subject" * * *.

The reliable figures of the Administrative Office of the United States Courts, showing that during the last four years five State prisoners, all told, were discharged by federal district courts, prove beyond peradventure that it is a baseless fear, a bogey man, to worry lest State convictions be upset by allowing district courts to entertain applications for habeas corpus on behalf of prisoners under State sentence. Insofar as this jurisdiction enables federal district courts to entertain claims that State Supreme Courts have denied rights guaranteed by the United States Constitution, it is not a case of a lower court sitting in judgment on a higher court. It is merely one aspect of respecting the Supremacy Clause of the Constitution whereby federal law is higher than State law. It is for the Congress to designate the member in the hierarchy of the federal judiciary to express the higher law. * * *

The uniqueness of habeas corpus in the procedural armory of our law cannot be too often emphasized. It differs from all other remedies in that it is available to bring into question the legality of a person's restraint and to require justification for such detention. Of course this does not mean that prison doors may readily be opened. It does mean that explanation may be exacted why they should remain closed. * * *

■ MR. JUSTICE JACKSON, concurring in the result.

Controversy as to the undiscriminating use of the writ of habeas corpus by federal judges to set aside state court convictions is traceable to three principal causes: (1) this Court's use of the generality of the Fourteenth Amendment to subject state courts to increasing federal control, especially in the criminal law field; (2) *ad hoc* determination of due process of law issues by personal notions of justice instead of by known rules of law; and (3) the breakdown of procedural safeguards against abuse of the writ. * * *

In 1867, Congress authorized federal courts to issue writs of habeas corpus to prisoners "in custody in violation of the Constitution or laws or treaties of the United States." At that time, the writ was not available here nor in England to challenge any sentence imposed by a court of competent jurisdiction. The historic purpose of the writ has been to relieve detention by executive authorities without judicial trial. It might have been expected that if Congress intended a reversal of this traditional concept of habeas corpus it would have said so. * * *

The fact that the substantive law of due process is and probably must remain so vague and unsettled as to invite farfetched or border-line petitions makes it important to adhere to procedures which enable courts readily to distinguish a probable constitutional grievance from a convict's mere gamble on persuading some indulgent judge to let him out of jail. Instead, this Court has sanctioned progressive trivialization of the writ until floods of stale, frivolous and repetitious petitions inundate the docket of the lower courts and swell our own. Judged by our own disposition of habeas corpus matters, they have, as a class, become peculiarly undeserving. It must prejudice the occasional meritorious application to be buried in a flood of worthless ones. He who must search a haystack for a needle is likely to end up with the attitude that the needle is not worth the search. Nor is it any answer to say that few of these petitions in any court really result in the discharge of the petitioner. That is the condemnation of the procedure which has encouraged frivolous cases. In this multiplicity of worthless cases, states are compelled to default or to defend the integrity of their judges and their official records, sometimes concerning trials or pleas that were closed many years ago. * * *

It cannot be denied that the trend of our decisions is to abandon rules of pleading or procedure which would protect the writ against abuse. Once upon a time the writ could not be substituted for appeal * * * but challenged only the legal competence or jurisdiction of the committing court. We have so departed from this principle that the profession now believes that the issues we *actually consider* on a federal prisoner's habeas corpus are substantially the same as would be considered on appeal.

Conflict with state courts is the inevitable result of giving the convict a virtual new trial before a federal court sitting without a jury. Whenever decisions of one court are reviewed by another, a percentage of them are reversed. That reflects a difference in outlook normally found between personnel comprising different courts. However, reversal by a higher court is not proof that justice is thereby better done. There is no doubt that if there were a super-Supreme Court, a substantial proportion of our reversals of state courts would also be reversed. We are not final because we are infallible, but we are infallible only because we are final. * * *

It is sometimes said that *res judicata* has no application whatever in habeas corpus cases and surely it does not apply with all of its conventional severity. Habeas corpus differs from the ordinary judgment in that, although an adjudication has become final, the application is renewable, at least if new evidence and material is discovered or if, perhaps as the result of a new decision, a new law becomes applicable to the case. This is quite proper so long as its issues relate to jurisdiction. But call it *res judicata* or what one will, courts ought not to be obliged to allow a convict to litigate again and again exactly the same question on the same evidence. * * *

My conclusion is that * * * no lower federal court should entertain a petition except on the following conditions: (1) that the petition raises a jurisdictional question involving federal law on which the state law allowed no access to its courts, either by habeas corpus or appeal from the conviction and that he therefore has no state remedy; or (2) that the petition shows that although the law allows a remedy, he was actually improperly obstructed from making a record upon which the question could be presented, so that his remedy by way of ultimate application to this Court for certiorari has been frustrated. There may be circumstances so extraordinary that I do not now think of them which would justify a departure from this rule, but the run-of-the-mill case certainly does not. * * *

NOTE ON BROWN V. ALLEN AND HABEAS CORPUS POLICY

A. The Scope of Federal Prelitigation

The basic principle of Brown v. Allen—that federal habeas courts should relitigate questions of federal constitutional law that were fully and fairly litigated in state court—was controversial from its inception. But as Justice Frankfurter noted, the scope of relitigation did not routinely extend to the basic, or historical, facts. Thus, for example, if in Brown the admissibility of the confession turned on the length of the interrogation, or on whether certain threats had been made, Brown permitted (though it did not require) a federal court to accept the state court's factfindings about what happened.[1] The federal obligation was limited to determining the appropriate standard for deciding whether a confession was admissible (a question of legal principle), and applying that standard to the facts as found (an application of law to fact, or a "mixed" question). As a result, the vast majority of cases were resolved on the state court record without evidentiary proceedings in federal court.

A distinct set of cases addresses efforts to litigate in federal court claims that, unlike those in Brown, were not resolved on the merits in state court, usually because of a procedural default by the petitioner. A companion case to Brown, Daniels v. Allen, 344 U.S. 443 (1953), announced a general rule that federal habeas courts may not hear defaulted claims. For discussion of Daniels and subsequent developments, see pp. 1631–1657, *infra*.

B. Justifications for Federal Relitigation and a Federal Forum Model of Collateral Habeas Corpus

(1) A Surrogate for Appellate Review. One justification for Brown v. Allen rests on the inability of the Supreme Court adequately to protect constitutional rights through its direct review of state court judgments. On this view, habeas jurisdiction, though not technically appellate review by district courts, serves as a substitute for Supreme Court review to ensure federal constitutional claims are heard by a federal court.[2] Consider these questions:

(a) If state courts can be trusted to find the facts, why can't they be trusted to apply the law? Compare Townsend v. Sain, 372 U.S. 293, 312

---

[1] Statutory amendments in 1966 and 1996 narrowed the district courts' discretion by making state court factfindings presumptively binding. See pp. 1627–1628, *infra*.

[2] See, *e.g.*, Justice Brennan's dissent in Stone v. Powell, 428 U.S. 465 (1976), p. 1570, *infra*; Hart, *The Supreme Court, 1958 Term—Foreword: The Time Chart of the Justices*, 73 Harv.L.Rev. 84, 105–07 (1959); Friedman, *A Tale of Two Habeas*, 73 Minn.L.Rev. 247 (1988); Liebman, *Apocalypse Next Time?: The Anachronistic Attack on Habeas Corpus/Direct Review Parity*, 92 Colum.L.Rev. 1997 (1992). See also Vázquez, *Habeas as Forum Allocation: A New Synthesis*, 71 U. Miami L.Rev. 645 (2017) (arguing that Supreme Court Justices favored shifting review of state criminal cases from direct appeals to federal habeas proceedings during the period leading up to Brown).

Judge Friendly, in *Is Innocence Irrelevant? Collateral Attack on Criminal Judgments*, 38 U.Chi.L.Rev. 142, 166–67 (1970), raised the possibility of substituting for habeas a system of appeals in state criminal cases to an intermediate federal court of appeals. See also Meador, *Straightening Out Federal Review of State Criminal Cases*, 44 Ohio St.L.J. 273 (1983).

(1963) ("It is the typical, not the rare, case in which constitutional claims turn upon the resolution of contested factual issues.").

(b)   If habeas courts are a surrogate for Supreme Court review, why should they (unlike the Supreme Court) be limited to reviewing only state court decisions that deny, rather than that uphold, claims of federal constitutional right?

(c)   Why should federal relitigation of constitutional issues be limited only to criminal cases leading to custody—thereby excluding issues arising in state court civil cases or in the many state criminal cases in which the defendant is never in custody (because the punishment was only by a fine) or is no longer in custody by the time state remedies have been exhausted?[3]

(2)   Independent Inquiry into Detention. A different justification for federal relitigation was offered by Justice Brennan for the Court in Fay v. Noia, 372 U.S. 391, 430–31 (1963), p. 1632, *infra*: "The jurisdictional prerequisite [in habeas] is not the judgment of a state court but detention *simpliciter.* * * * And the broad power of the federal courts under [the habeas statute,] 28 U.S.C. § 2243 * * * to 'determine the facts, and dispose of the matter as law and justice require,' is hardly characteristic of an appellate jurisdiction. Habeas lies to enforce the right of personal liberty * * *. * * * [I]t cannot revise the state court judgment; it can act only on the body of the petitioner."[4]

(a)   Is the premise that a party should always be able to litigate a federal question in federal court convincing? If accepted, shouldn't it require abolition of the custody requirement—which blocks many persons convicted of crimes by the states from federal court—as well as full relitigation of the facts? Compare Meltzer, *Habeas Corpus Jurisdiction: The Limits of Models*, 66 S.Calif.L.Rev. 2507, 2507–13 (1993), with Yackle, Reclaiming the Federal Courts 287–88 n.157 (1994).[5]

(b)   If state courts do not adequately protect federal rights, can habeas relief—which comes only after conviction and incarceration—undo the damage? *Cf.* Amsterdam, *Criminal Prosecutions Affecting Federally*

---

[3]   For a response to this question, see Friedman, *Pas de Deux: The Supreme Court and the Habeas Courts*, 66 S.Calif.L.Rev. 2467, 2485–90 (1993).

[4]   See also Townsend v. Sain, 372 U.S. 293 (1963), p. 1628, *infra*; Reitz, *Federal Habeas Corpus: Postconviction Remedy for State Prisoners*, 108 U.Pa.L.Rev. 461 (1960); Wright & Sofaer, *Federal Habeas Corpus for State Prisoners: The Allocation of Fact-Finding Responsibility*, 75 Yale L.J. 895 (1966).

In support of this understanding, Professor Yackle argues: (a) in principle, federal courts should have original or removal jurisdiction over all cases in which federal issues are raised (whether as part of the complaint or by defense); (b) that principle is not observed in state criminal cases, where there is no general removal provision; (c) the absence of removal jurisdiction is justifiable because, among other things, federal issues often arise only late in the game; but (d) habeas review must be available after conviction to provide the needed federal forum for federal constitutional issues. See Yackle, *Explaining Habeas Corpus*, 60 N.Y.U.L.Rev. 991 (1985); Yackle, *The Habeas Hagioscope*, 66 S.Calif.L.Rev. 2331 (1993).

[5]   According to Cover & Aleinikoff, *Dialectical Federalism: Habeas Corpus and the Court*, 86 Yale L.J. 1035 (1977), habeas jurisdiction generates a healthy dialogue between state and federal courts about the scope of federal constitutional rights and accounts for the different perspectives of each set of courts in this context. See also Meltzer, *State Court Forfeitures of Federal Rights*, 99 Harv.L.Rev. 1128, 1233–34 n.505 (1986).

Guaranteed Civil Rights: Federal Removal and Habeas Corpus Jurisdiction to Abort State Court Trial, 113 U.Pa.L.Rev. 793, 801 (1965).

(c) Does Justice Brennan's notion of an independent inquiry justify habeas courts in disregarding limits on the scope of review that would apply on direct review by the Supreme Court? Justice Harlan's dissent in Fay v. Noia said that the answer was no, reasoning that "[i]n habeas as on direct review, ordering the prisoner's release invalidates the judgment of conviction" on which the detention was based.

(3) Finality in the Criminal Process. In Sanders v. United States, 373 U.S. 1, 8 (1963), Justice Brennan declared: "Conventional notions of finality of litigation have no place where life or liberty is at stake and infringement of constitutional rights is alleged." Judge Friendly responded: "Why do they have *no* place? One will readily agree that * * * different rules should govern the determination of guilt than when only property is at issue * * *. * * * But this shows only that 'conventional notions of finality' should not have *as much* place in criminal as in civil litigation, not that they should have *none*." Friendly, note 2, *supra*, at 149–50.

C. Objections to Federal Relitigation: Process and Jurisdictional Models for Collateral Habeas Corpus

(1) Professor Bator's Argument. Bator, *Finality in Criminal Law and Federal Habeas Corpus for State Prisoners*, 76 Harv.L.Rev. 441 (1963), built on Justice Jackson's opinion in Brown v. Allen and articulated a narrow conception, often called the "process" view, of the appropriate scope of habeas review. Among Professor Bator's objections to routine federal relitigation were these: (a) "[I]f a job can be well done once, it should not be done twice"; (b) "I could imagine nothing more subversive of a [state] judge's sense of responsibility * * * than an indiscriminate acceptance of the notion that all the shots will always be called by someone else"; and (c) Broad habeas review undermines the swiftness and certainty of punishment, and thus the educative, deterrent, and rehabilitative functions of the criminal law.

Echoing Justice Jackson, Bator's argument was skeptical that any legal process can assure the ultimate correctness of the results reached. Thus, he doubted that when state and federal court decisions differed, the latter were necessarily correct, and he resisted "the notion that sound remedial institutions can be built on the premise that state judges are not in sympathy with federal law." Professor Bator therefore concluded that habeas jurisdiction should be limited to determining whether the state provided a fair process for resolving constitutional claims. Under this view, habeas review would be appropriate, for example, to consider an alleged deprivation of the effective assistance of counsel or a claim that evidence discovered only after a conviction was affirmed shows that the trial judge had been bribed, but not in many other circumstances.[6]

(2) Recent Criticism of the Federal Forum Model: A Jurisdictional Model for Collateral Habeas Corpus. In Edwards v. Vannoy, 593 U.S. 255 (2021), Justice Gorsuch, joined by Justice Thomas, criticized Brown v.

---

[6]   In Bator's view, for example, if an allegation of bribery at the trial level had been rejected by a state appellate court after a fair hearing, no habeas relief should follow.

Allen in a concurring opinion. In his view, "Brown not only upended centuries of settled precedent and invited practical problems; it produced anomalies as well." In his view, Brown also denigrated the role of state courts, which are obligated to follow federal law under the Supremacy Clause.[7]

Justice Gorsuch returned to these themes while writing for the Court in Brown v. Davenport, 596 U.S. 118 (2022). Invoking Justice Jackson's dissent in Brown v. Allen, Justice Gorsuch criticized that decision for disregarding "[t]he traditional distinction between jurisdictional defects and mere errors in adjudication." As in Vannoy, Justice Gorsuch asserted that in the period leading up to Brown v. Allen, federal habeas courts granted relief only to petitioners in state custody whose convictions arose out of proceedings in which state courts did not have proper jurisdiction.

Writing for three dissenters in Davenport, Justice Kagan challenged Justice Gorsuch's assertion that Brown v. Allen broke new ground. She emphasized the breadth of the grant of habeas jurisdiction in the 1789 Judiciary Act and its expansion in 1867. As to the 1867 Act, she noted that its terms broadly permitted federal courts " 'to grant writs of habeas corpus in all cases where any person may be restrained of his or her liberty' in violation of the Federal Constitution." She then catalogued a number of the Court's decisions and contemporary treatises pre-dating Brown, all of which, in her view, demonstrate that Brown "built on decades and decades of history." (citing, among others, Ex parte Lange, 85 U.S. (18 Wall.) 163 (1874) (granting habeas relief to a petitioner under the Double Jeopardy Clause); Ex parte Wilson, 114 U.S. 417 (1885) (granting habeas relief where petitioner had not been indicted by a grand jury); Callan v. Wilson, 127 U.S. 540 (1888) (granting habeas relief where petitioner had been denied jury trial); Moore v. Dempsey, 261 U.S. 86 (1923) (granting relief in habeas proceedings where petitioners were denied due process in their state court trial); Johnson v. Zerbst, 304 U.S. 458 (1938) (holding that habeas may provide relief for denial of effective assistance of counsel at trial)).

One of the habeas cases relied upon by Justice Kagan, Moore v. Dempsey, 261 U.S. 86 (1923), discussed at p. 1556, *supra*, involved the prosecution of several Black men for an alleged interracial murder in Arkansas. In response to mob domination of the trial, the Court set aside the state convictions for denying the defendants due process of law. Moore v. Dempsey, which predated Brown v. Allen by decades, seems to sweep well beyond the narrow jurisdictional model of habeas that Justice Gorsuch describes in Vannoy and Davenport. Should the context in which Congress adopted the 1867 Act along with its expansive terms also matter to this debate? For additional discussion of Davenport, see p. 1603, note 6, *infra*. Recent scholarship exploring habeas jurisprudence in the decades preceding Brown v. Allen describes Brown as the culmination of a decades-long expansion of federal habeas review of state convictions, see, *e.g.*, Vázquez,

---

[7]   Justice Gorsuch also contrasted Brown with the Court's decision in Burns v. Wilson, 346 U.S. 137 (1953) (plurality opinion), which, on his description, rejected Brown's "fix-any-error approach for final judgments issued by military courts," resulting in the oddity that "federal courts wound up with more power to reopen the judgments of a different sovereign's courts than the administrative proceedings of the federal government itself."

Habeas as Forum Allocation: A New Synthesis, 71 U. Miami L.Rev. 645 (2017), p. 1557, *supra*, with some scholars noting that terminology employed by habeas courts in the past may not equate with modern understandings, see, *e.g.*, Siegel, *Habeas, History, and Hermeneutics*, 64 Ariz.L.Rev. 505 (2022) (exploring use of the term "jurisdiction" in habeas cases); see also *id.* 510 (observing that "[a]s amended by AEDPA, the federal habeas statute plainly assumes and confirms the availability of habeas relief in cases beyond" those Justice Gorsuch outlines in his Vannoy opinion).

D. The Relevance of Guilt or Innocence to the Scope of the Writ

(1) An Innocence Model for Collateral Habeas Corpus. In his article, *Is Innocence Irrelevant? Collateral Attack on Criminal Judgments*, 38 U.Chi.L.Rev. 142 (1970), Judge Friendly contended that, subject to limited exceptions, a petitioner who received a fair hearing in state court should not be able to attack a criminal conviction collaterally without making "a colorable showing that an error, whether 'constitutional' or not, may be producing the continued punishment of an innocent" person. He defined the necessary showing as "a fair probability that, in light of all the evidence, including that alleged to have been illegally admitted (but with due regard to any unreliability of it) and evidence tenably claimed to have been wrongly excluded or to have become available only after the trial, the trier of the facts would have entertained a reasonable doubt of [the defendant's] guilt."[8]

(2) Justice Powell's Approach. In Schneckloth v. Bustamonte, 412 U.S. 218 (1973), Justice Powell's concurrence (joined by Chief Justice Burger and Justice Rehnquist)[9] echoed many of Judge Friendly's concerns, and would have held that a Fourth Amendment claim was cognizable on habeas only where the petitioner did not have a fair opportunity to litigate in state court: "I am aware that history reveals no exact tie of the writ of habeas corpus to a constitutional claim relating to innocence or guilt. * * * We are now faced, however, with the task of accommodating the historic respect for the finality of the judgment of a committing court with recent Court expansions of the role of the writ. This accommodation can best be achieved * * * by recourse to the central reason for habeas corpus: the affording of means, through an extraordinary writ, of redressing an unjust incarceration."

Justice Powell's approach differed subtly from Judge Friendly's. Justice Powell favored limiting habeas based on the general nature of the claim; coerced confession claims would be permitted, Fourth Amendment exclusionary rule claims would not. Judge Friendly favored a focus on the specific facts of the case: upon a proper showing of innocence, the petitioner could raise any constitutional claim (even a Fourth Amendment claim); absent the requisite showing, habeas would be unavailable (even on a coerced confession claim).

---

[8] Judge Friendly advocated exceptions to his proposed requirement where (i) the original tribunal lacked jurisdiction or the criminal process had broken down; (ii) the constitutional claim was based on facts outside the record and only collateral attack could vindicate the claim; (iii) the state failed to provide a proper procedure for making a defense; or (iv) the governing constitutional law had changed.

[9] Justice Blackmun agreed with "nearly all" of, but did not join, Justice Powell's opinion.

(3) Questions About Guilt and Innocence. Would petitioners simply plead around any innocence-based limitation, by alleging innocence and/or including innocence-related claims in their petitions? And would acceptance of Judge Friendly's position burden habeas courts by requiring threshold, fact-specific inquiries into questions of innocence? More generally, insofar as state court underenforcement of federal constitutional norms may be greatest when conviction of the innocent is not at issue, would any innocence limitation eliminate federal oversight in exactly the cases in which it is most important?

(4) Stone v. Powell. In Stone v. Powell, 428 U.S. 465 (1976) (6–3), the Court, overturning prior authority, held that a petitioner in state custody generally cannot obtain relief in federal habeas proceedings on the ground that evidence obtained in an unconstitutional search or seizure was introduced at trial. Relying on the premise that the exclusionary rule is not a personal constitutional right of the defendant but rather a judicially created remedy designed to safeguard Fourth Amendment rights by deterring police misconduct, see Mapp v. Ohio, 367 U.S. 643 (1961), Justice Powell argued for the majority that enforcing the rule on habeas imposed serious costs while providing little incremental deterrence of Fourth Amendment violations. Thus, the Court ruled "that where the State has provided an opportunity for full and fair litigation of a Fourth Amendment claim, a state prisoner may not be granted federal habeas corpus relief on the ground that evidence obtained in an unconstitutional search or seizure was introduced at his trial."

Although the Court's holding rested on distinctive features of the exclusionary remedy and stated that "[o]ur decision today is *not* concerned with the scope of the habeas corpus statute as authority for litigating constitutional claims generally," some the opinion's reasoning appeared to reach more broadly and apply to all claims unrelated to guilt or innocence. For example, the Court dismissed the argument that state courts cannot be trusted to enforce Fourth Amendment rights: whatever was true of those courts in the past, "we are unwilling to assume" that they now lack "appropriate sensitivity to constitutional rights." And the opinion stressed that habeas relitigation imposes resource costs, erodes finality, generates friction between federal and state courts, and threatens the constitutional balance on which federalism rests. "We nevertheless afford broad habeas corpus relief, recognizing the need in a free society for an additional safeguard against compelling an innocent man to suffer an unconstitutional loss of liberty." But relitigation on habeas of a typical Fourth Amendment claim, the Court said, "has no bearing on the basic justice" of incarceration.

Justice Brennan, joined by Justice Marshall, dissented. Declaring that a state court that admits evidence obtained in violation of the Fourth Amendment "has committed a *constitutional* error," he argued that in such a case, the petitioner is " 'in custody in violation of the Constitution' within the comprehension of 28 U.S.C. § 2254." He also observed that in the habeas statute, "Congress, which has the power to do so under Art. III of the Constitution, has effectively cast the district courts sitting in habeas in the role of surrogate Supreme Courts." Calling the Court's decision a "novel reinterpretation of the habeas statutes," Justice Brennan argued "the groundwork is being laid today for a drastic withdrawal of federal habeas jurisdiction * * * at least for claims * * * that this Court later decides are not 'guilt-related.' "[10]

(5) The Limitation of Stone. Despite Justice Brennan's fears, decisions since Stone v. Powell have not adopted a general rule limiting habeas corpus to matters relating to guilt or innocence.[11]

(a) Rose v. Mitchell, 443 U.S. 545 (1979), involved an allegation of racial discrimination in selection of the grand jury. When, as in that case, an untainted trial jury finds the defendant guilty beyond a reasonable doubt, discrimination in selection of the grand jury—which typically has to find only a prima facie case of guilt—is highly unlikely to have led to conviction of an innocent person. But Justice Blackmun, writing for the Court, reached the merits of the discrimination claim and confined Stone to its context.[12]

(b) The Court also declined to extend Stone in Withrow v. Williams, 507 U.S. 680 (1993), where the petitioner claimed a violation of the Miranda rules. Justice Souter's majority opinion argued that unlike the Fourth Amendment's exclusionary rule, the Miranda decision "safeguards 'a fundamental *trial* right' " that is not "necessarily divorced from the correct ascertainment of guilt." Most importantly, eliminating habeas review of Miranda claims would not significantly unburden the courts: petitioners would simply allege instead that their confessions were involuntary and therefore inadmissible under the Due Process Clause, which would require difficult determinations under a totality of the circumstances test rather than under Miranda's "brighter-line" rules. Dissenting from this portion of the decision, Justice O'Connor (joined by Chief Justice Rehnquist) argued, *inter alia*, that (1) confessions obtained in violation of Miranda, but that are not involuntary under the Due Process Clause, are reliable, and (2) any impact of habeas review in improving police compliance with Miranda is slight and, under the approach of Stone v. Powell, is outweighed by considerations of finality, equity, and federalism.[13]

---

[10] Justice White dissented separately "[f]or many of the reasons stated by Mr. Justice Brennan."

Articles critical of Stone v. Powell include Seidman, *Factual Guilt and the Burger Court: An Examination of Continuity and Change in Criminal Procedure*, 80 Colum.L.Rev. 436, 449–59 (1980), and Tushnet, *Constitutional and Statutory Analyses in the Law of Federal Jurisdiction*, 25 UCLA L.Rev. 1301, 1316–18 (1978). More supportive is Halpern, *Federal Habeas Corpus and the Mapp Exclusionary Rule After Stone v. Powell*, 82 Colum.L.Rev. 1 (1982).

[11] The Court did rely on Stone in reshaping the harmless error doctrine applied in habeas proceedings in Brecht v. Abrahamson, 507 U.S. 619 (1993) (5–4), discussed at p. 1551, *supra*.

[12] Nonetheless, the Court held petitioners' prima facie case of discrimination wanting.

[13] Justice O'Connor also argued, consistently with language in various Supreme Court decisions, that Miranda announced a set of prophylactic rules, not a core constitutional right. The Court later rejected that position in Dickerson v. United States, 530 U.S. 428 (2000), 7–2. The Court in turn arguably revived this view in Vega v. Tekoh, 597 U.S. 134 (2022), where, 6–3, the Court again labeled the Miranda warnings as "prophylactic" and concluded that "a violation of Miranda does not necessarily constitute a violation of the Constitution" for purposes of 42 U.S.C. § 1983.

In Withrow, Justice Scalia (joined by Justice Thomas) would have denied relief on the ground that the equitable discretion possessed by habeas courts is abused by granting relief to a petitioner who had a full and fair opportunity to litigate in state court, unless the claim "goes

Even though it has not been extended in cases like Withrow, the exception to habeas review set forth in Stone v. Powell remains good law today.[14]

E.   The Cognizability of Claims of Innocence in Habeas Corpus Proceedings

(1) Claims Relating to Innocence. How far does the habeas jurisdiction extend to a claim that alleges no specific constitutional violation (like introduction of a coerced confession) but simply asserts that the petitioner is in fact innocent?

(2) Jackson v. Virginia. In Jackson v. Virginia, 443 U.S. 307 (1979), the Court held that the due process requirement of proof beyond a reasonable doubt means not only that a jury must be so instructed, but also that the question whether a properly instructed jury could reasonably have found the evidence in the record to establish guilt beyond a reasonable doubt is itself a federal constitutional question cognizable on habeas. The Court largely treated the case as a routine exercise of habeas jurisdiction, in which the habeas court reviews applications of a federal constitutional standard (proof beyond a reasonable doubt) to the historical facts (the evidence in the state court record). But the Court did note that unlike the Fourth Amendment issue in Stone, "[t]he question whether a defendant has been convicted upon inadequate evidence is central to the basic question of guilt or innocence."

(3) Freestanding Claims of Innocence. A different question arises when the record at trial suffices to uphold the finding of guilt, but a petitioner claims that evidence obtained after conviction establishes innocence.

(a)   In Herrera v. Collins, 506 U.S. 390 (1993), the evidence at Herrera's murder trial included two eyewitness identifications and a handwritten letter in which Herrera appeared to admit his guilt. Ten years after his conviction and death sentence, his habeas petition contended that newly discovered evidence (affidavits declaring that Herrera's now-dead brother had confessed to the murder) showed that Herrera was actually innocent and argued that his execution would violate the Eighth and Fourteenth Amendments. Holding that his petition should be denied, the Court ruled that "[c]laims of actual innocence based on newly discovered evidence have never been held to state a ground for federal habeas relief absent an independent constitutional violation occurring in the underlying state criminal proceeding." The function of habeas review, the Court submitted, was to redress constitutional violations, not to correct factual errors, and review of freestanding innocence claims would severely disrupt the strong state interest in finality. The Court resisted petitioner's formulation of the question—whether it is constitutional to execute the innocent—stressing

---

to the fairness of the trial process or to the accuracy of the ultimate result." He viewed the Court's broader position as inconsistent with the history of federal habeas corpus in the nineteenth century and with the presumption, drawn from Article III's failure to mandate creation of lower federal courts, that state courts will faithfully apply federal law.

[14]   See, *e.g.*, Hampton v. Wyant, 296 F.3d 560 (7th Cir.2002) (AEDPA "does not affect *Stone*" because "a person imprisoned following a trial that relies, in part, on unlawfully seized evidence is not 'in custody in violation of the Constitution or laws or treaties of the United States'" under § 2254(a)).

that Herrera, having been convicted after a fair trial, was to be treated as guilty. The Court distinguished the claim in Jackson v. Virginia because it (i) established an independent constitutional violation; (ii) could be adjudicated by reviewing the adequacy of the record evidence, without new factfinding; and (iii) asked only if the verdict of guilt was rational, not whether it was correct.

The Court added: "We may assume, for the sake of argument * * *, that in a capital case a truly persuasive demonstration of 'actual innocence' " would warrant habeas relief "if there were no state avenue open to process such a claim." But Herrera's showing fell far short of the "extraordinarily high" threshold for such an "assumed right." Four Justices (White, Blackmun, Stevens, and Souter), in separate concurring or dissenting opinions, assumed, in Justice White's words, "that a persuasive showing of 'actual innocence' * * * would render unconstitutional the execution of petitioner"; Justices O'Connor and Kennedy said they would not reach that "sensitive" and "troubling" issue given the strong evidence of Herrera's guilt; and Justices Scalia and Thomas criticized the Court for failing to declare firmly that there is no constitutional right to consideration of evidence of innocence discovered after conviction.

(b)   The Court has yet to resolve the uncertainty generated by the array of views expressed in Herrera about the circumstances (if any) in which freestanding claims of innocence are cognizable—either in capital cases or more generally. In House v. Bell, 547 U.S. 518 (2006), discussed at p. 1654, *infra*, a unanimous Court said that *if* a freestanding innocence claim may be brought on habeas, relief was not warranted by the evidence presented there, even though five Justices concluded that it was more likely than not that no reasonable juror would have found the petitioner guilty beyond a reasonable doubt. The Court instead held the circumstances warranted excusing the procedural default of two claims, permitting House to advance them on remand. Then, in In re Davis, 557 U.S. 952 (2009), p. 1466, note 2, *supra*, the Court transferred an original petition for habeas corpus to a district court with instructions that it should hold an evidentiary hearing on a freestanding innocence claim raised in the petition. Dissenting from the order, Justice Scalia, joined by Justice Thomas, emphasized that the Court had never held, and indeed had expressed considerable doubt, that a freestanding innocence claim is constitutionally cognizable.

Few habeas petitions in fact advance freestanding claims of innocence.[15]

(4) Questions About Freestanding Claims of Innocence. Is any purpose of post-conviction review more central than overturning the conviction of an innocent person? Even if federal habeas jurisdiction exists only when custody violates the federal Constitution or some other

---

[15]   See King, Cheesman & Ostrom, *Final Technical Report: Habeas Litigation in U.S. District Courts*, National Center for State Courts, Aug. 21, 2007, at 29–30 (finding such claims asserted in 11% of capital cases and 4% of non-capital cases). One review of 173 reported decisions involving such claims found no outright grants of relief and only seven instances in which some relief (*e.g.*, an evidentiary hearing or required DNA testing) was provided. See Note, *Turning a Blind Eye to Innocence: The Legacy of Herrera v. Collins,* 42 Am.Crim.L.Rev. 121 (2005).

fundamental federal law, can one persuasively argue that Congress and the Court have always reshaped the writ based on an evaluation of competing concerns? Is this view illustrated, for example, by the evolution of the writ over the centuries into a regime of federal relitigation, and by the qualification to that regime established in Stone v. Powell? See Steiker, *Innocence and Federal Habeas*, 41 UCLA L.Rev. 303, 309 (1993).

Consider, however, these countervailing arguments: (i) the burdens of entertaining "actual innocence" claims would be high, for such claims can be raised in every case and their adjudication can be labor-intensive; and (ii) federal review of such claims may be relatively less appropriate because their resolution often requires interpretation of the elements of the offense, a question of state law.

(5) The Availability of State Court Post-Conviction Remedies. As the Herrera opinion noted, every state permits motions for a new trial based on new evidence, but such motions are subject to many limitations. When the Court decided Herrera in 1993, 17 states (including Texas, where Herrera was convicted) required such a motion to be made within 60 days after judgment, while another 18 had time limits of one to three years. In addition, many states require the evidence to have come to light after trial, not to have been obtainable earlier in the exercise of due diligence, and to be likely to lead to a different result upon retrial.[16] Succeeding on such motions is rare.

Instead of simply claiming that he was innocent, could Herrera have argued that Texas' short time period for filing a new trial motion based on new evidence denied due process? Framed that way, the petition does assert a federal constitutional claim.[17] But were such a claim upheld, should the remedy be an inquiry by the habeas court itself into petitioner's innocence, or instead an order requiring the state court to conduct such an inquiry?

F.   Assessing Possible Models for Collateral Habeas Corpus Review

(a) What are the advantages and disadvantages of each model for collateral habeas corpus review? Is any approach to the scope of habeas review necessarily appropriate for all eras? Some have argued that post-conviction habeas served an important role through the 1970s to force state

---

[16] See Berger, *Herrera v. Collins: The Gateway of Innocence for Death-Sentenced Prisoners Leads Nowhere*, 35 Wm. & Mary L.Rev. 943, 958 (1994).

[17] See Thomas et al., *Is It Ever Too Late for Innocence? Finality, Efficiency, and Claims of Innocence*, 64 U.Pitt.L.Rev. 263 (2003) (arguing that due process "require[s] courts to be open to powerful claims of innocence without regard to whether procedural deadlines for challenging a conviction have expired"); Berger, *supra* note 16 (arguing for a right to state post-conviction relief in some circumstances).

All fifty states have enacted statutes giving convicted defendants the right (which can be more or less broadly defined) to obtain post-conviction DNA testing. Such tests are now quite inexpensive, and the evidence of innocence can be (though often is not) conclusive. Note, however, that even when favorable DNA results are obtained, it is a separate question whether relief from criminal conviction is available, and the limitations in state post-conviction proceedings, noted above, may create hurdles hard to overcome.

Insofar as Herrera rested on the importance of finality, on the premise that post-hoc determinations are less reliable than those at trial, and on the resource costs of relitigating innocence after conviction, does the availability of DNA testing substantially change the calculus? For discussion, see Garrett, *Claiming Innocence*, 92 Minn.L.Rev. 1629 (2008).

court judges who defied expansive Warren Court criminal procedure rulings to obey the federal Constitution, but it is no longer needed in view of the improvement of state courts processes. See, *e.g.*, Hoffman & King, *Rethinking the Federal Role in State Criminal Justice*, 84 N.Y.U.L.Rev. 791 (2009).[18] For a critical response, see Blume, Johnson & Weyble, *In Defense of Noncapital Habeas: A Response to Hoffman and King*, 96 Cornell L.Rev. 435 (2011) (contending, *inter alia*, that in many state court systems there are impediments to meaningful appellate and post-conviction review; that racial discrimination in state criminal justice systems persists; and that the prospect of habeas review affects state court behavior).

(b)   The reasonably broad habeas review recognized in Brown has been sharply narrowed by subsequent judicial and legislative developments. But how realistic is it to view habeas review, whatever its scope, as significantly affecting state court behavior, given that: most criminal defendants plead guilty (thereby waiving most rights), most do not receive sufficiently long sentences to file a proper habeas petition, the success rate for those who do file is minuscule, and post-hoc litigation has inherent limitations, particularly in addressing claims of ineffective assistance of counsel? Should federal efforts be redirected to address the greatest barrier to the enforcement of constitutional rights for state criminal defendants—the lack of adequate defense representation?[19]

(c)   In assessing the different approaches to collateral habeas review, is it relevant that the Supreme Court today takes exceedingly few direct appeals of state criminal convictions? For example, in three successive recent Terms, the Supreme Court only reviewed two criminal cases on direct review from state courts each Term.[20]

(d)   When considering the landscape of the statutory and judicially announced rules surveyed in this chapter that govern habeas today, what (if any) model of habeas review does it embody?

NOTE ON THE SUSPENSION CLAUSE AND POST-CONVICTION REVIEW

(1) Executive Detention Versus Post-Conviction Cases. The Constitution's Suspension Clause guarantees access to habeas corpus (or an adequate substitute) in some cases involving executive detention. See p. 1470–1474, *supra*. But it is uncertain whether the Clause confers a right to habeas corpus as a means of post-conviction review. Such review was not the

---

[18]   Accordingly, Hoffman and King argue that habeas review should be limited to capital cases and cases involving claims of innocence.

[19]   See King & Hoffman, Habeas for the Twenty-First Century (2011) (so arguing). Compare Huq, *Habeas and the Roberts Court*, 81 U.Chi.L.Rev. 519 (2014) (criticizing King and Hoffman's proposal to scale back collateral federal habeas review and questioning the plausibility of the fiscal tradeoffs they propose), and Wiseman, *What is Federal Habeas Worth?*, 67 Fla.L.Rev. 1157 (2015) (estimating expenditures associated with non-capital habeas review in the federal courts to constitute "a tiny fraction" of criminal justice spending).

[20]   See Statistics, J.S.Ct.U.S., Oct. Term 2022, at 385, 695; Statistics, J.S.Ct.U.S., Oct. Term 2021, at 349, 707; Statistics, J.S.Ct.U.S., Oct. Term 2020, at 559, 713.

original office of the writ, and numerous decisions state that "at common law a judgment of conviction rendered by a court of general criminal jurisdiction was conclusive proof that confinement was legal. Such a judgment prevented issuance of the writ without more." United States v. Hayman, 342 U.S. 205, 211 (1952).[1] Indeed, absent some limiting conception, no decision denying relief could be immune from a further claim that the decision was in error and the detention therefore illegal.[2]

Over time, *statutory* authority to issue the writ reached well beyond the common law limit on post-conviction review. See pp. 1555–1558, *supra*. Might the scope of the Suspension Clause similarly evolve over time to afford a constitutional right to post-conviction review? *Cf.* Boumediene v. Bush, 553 U.S. 723, 746 (2008), p. 1507, *supra* ("The Court has been careful not to foreclose the possibility that the protections of the Suspension Clause have expanded along with post-1789 developments that define the present scope of the writ.").

(2) The Right of Those Imprisoned by the *State* to Federal Post-Conviction Review. Any argument that the Suspension Clause gives petitioners complaining of *state* custody pursuant to a criminal conviction a right to *federal* habeas review faces two hurdles beyond the general question about whether or when the Suspension Clause guarantees post-conviction review. First, at its origins, the Suspension Clause appears to have been directed only to detention under *federal* authority, as was the grant of habeas jurisdiction in the Judiciary Act of 1789. See pp. 1465–1466, *supra*. Second, a claimed right to habeas review in *federal* court must take account of the Madisonian Compromise—the constitutional understanding, reflected in the text of Article III, that it was for Congress to decide whether to create lower federal courts at all. See pp. 9–10, *supra*.[3]

---

[1] See Collings, *Habeas Corpus for Convicts—Constitutional Right or Legislative Grace?*, 40 Calif.L.Rev. 335, 340–41 (1952) (concluding that suspension of the writ historically was not aimed at those convicted, but rather at suspects deprived of their right to a speedy trial). For a survey of the historical materials on the Suspension Clause, see the authorities cited at p. 1461, note 2, *supra*, and p. 1466, note 3, *supra*. See also Freedman, *The Suspension Clause in the Ratification Debates*, 44 Buff.L.Rev. 451 (1996); Neuman, *Habeas Corpus, Executive Detention, and the Removal of Aliens*, 98 Colum.L.Rev. 961 (1998); Oaks, *The "Original" Writ of Habeas Corpus in the Supreme Court*, 1962 Sup.Ct.Rev. 153. See also Kovarsky, *A Constitutional Theory of Habeas Power*, 99 Va.L.Rev. 753 (2013).

[2] See generally Bator, *Finality in Criminal Law and Federal Habeas Corpus for State Prisoners*, 76 Harv.L.Rev. 441, 447 (1963).

[3] Additional questions abound. If the Suspension Clause does protect post-conviction review, can such review be suspended during war? Separately, at what point does limitation of post-conviction review become a suspension? When the scope of relief available for a first petition is contracted? What about successive petitions?

Professor Jordan Steiker, while acknowledging the difficulties discussed in the text above, argues that persons in state custody enjoy a constitutional right to habeas review in federal court of constitutional challenges to their criminal convictions. See Steiker, *Incorporating the Suspension Clause: Is There a Constitutional Right to Federal Habeas Corpus for State Prisoners?*, 92 Mich.L.Rev. 862, 874–78 (1994). He contends that by the time the Fourteenth Amendment's ratification, the writ had evolved far beyond its common law origins and the Amendment's Due Process Clause incorporated the "privilege" of that broadened writ against state authority. But even accepting those conclusions, the hardest part of his argument is the further claim that the Fourteenth Amendment, a provision directed to the *states*, implicitly obliges the *federal* government to vest federal courts with habeas corpus jurisdiction.

(3) Supreme Court Interpretation. Supreme Court decisions in the post-conviction setting have only rarely and in limited fashion discussed the Suspension Clause.[4]

(a) In Swain v. Pressley, 430 U.S. 372 (1977), the Court upheld a provision of the District of Columbia Code that replaced federal habeas corpus with a statutory motion in the local D.C. courts for persons convicted of local crimes in the District. The majority noted that the statutory motion was "commensurate" with habeas corpus and was not inadequate merely because the local judges who administer it are not Article III judges. Chief Justice Burger, joined by Justices Blackmun and Rehnquist, concurred on the broader ground that the Suspension Clause protects only the writ as known to the founding generation and does not require collateral review after conviction by a court of competent jurisdiction.

(b) Felker v. Turpin, 518 U.S. 651 (1996), involved a statutory provision added in 1996 that sharply restricts the ability of those in state custody to file more than one habeas petition in federal court. Chief Justice Rehnquist's opinion for a unanimous Court began by stating that before 1867, habeas jurisdiction was not generally available for persons in state custody and that collateral attacks on judgments of conviction rendered by courts of competent jurisdiction were not permitted until well into the twentieth century. Nonetheless, he said that "we assume, for purposes of decision here, that the Suspension Clause * * * refers to the writ as it exists today, rather than as it existed in 1789." Even still, the Court held the restriction was not a suspension of the writ. Further, relying on Chief Justice Marshall's language in Ex parte Bollman stating that a federal court's power to award the writ must be given by positive law, the Court declared that judgments about the proper scope of the writ are normally left to Congress and concluded that the restrictions on filing multiple petitions "are well within the compass of this evolutionary process * * *."[5]

(c) In Jones v. Hendrix, 599 U.S. 465 (2023), the Supreme Court rejected a Suspension Clause challenge to statutory limits on the filing of successive motions under 28 U.S.C. § 2255 by those in federal custody. The case involved a claim of legal innocence predicated upon intervening Supreme Court authority narrowing the scope of the federal criminal statute under which Jones had been convicted. Writing for the Court, Justice

---

For an effort to surmount that and other difficulties while arguing that the Fourteenth Amendment's Privileges and Immunities Clause guarantees petitioners in state custody a right to habeas review in federal court, see Kovarsky, *Prisoners and Habeas Privileges under the Fourteenth Amendment*, 67 Vand.L.Rev. 609 (2014).

[4]   Besides the decisions discussed in text, see Sanders v. United States, 373 U.S. 1, 11–12 (1963), and Fay v. Noia, 372 U.S. 391, 406 (1963). Both provide liberal interpretations of the scope of statutory federal court habeas jurisdiction while suggesting in dictum that narrower interpretations might raise constitutional questions. Both decisions have been overruled. See pp. 1567, 1632, *infra*. For other judicial statements about the Suspension Clause, see Yackle, *Form and Function in the Administration of Justice: The Bill of Rights and Federal Habeas Corpus*, 23 U.Mich.J.L.Ref. 685, 694 nn.39–40 (1990); see also Lindh v. Murphy, 96 F.3d 856 (7th Cir.1996) (en banc) (rejecting Suspension Clause challenge to AEDPA's revisions to collateral habeas corpus review of petitions brought by those in state custody).

[5]   Five years after Felker, in INS v. St. Cyr, 533 U.S. 289 (2001), pp. 464, 1471, *supra*, the Court observed: "At its historical core, the writ * * * served as a means of reviewing the legality of Executive detention." *Id.* 301.

Thomas held the Suspension Clause inapplicable because "[a]t the Founding, a sentence after conviction 'by a court of competent jurisdiction' was " 'in *itself* sufficient cause' " for continued detention. 599 U.S. at 483 (quoting Brown v. Davenport, 596 U.S. 118, 129 (2022) (quoting in turn Ex parte Watkins, 38 U.S. (3 Pet.) 193, 202 (1830))). For this proposition, the Jones Court relied heavily on Chief Justice Marshall's opinion in Ex parte Watkins, which observed that a habeas court has no power to "look beyond the judgment" of a criminal proceeding to "re-examine the charges on which it was rendered"—even where the "court ha[d] misconstrued the law, and ha[d] pronounced an offence to be punishable criminally, which [was] not so." 38 U.S. (3 Pet.) at 202, 209. Going further, the Jones Court observed that "[t]he principles of Watkins guided this Court's understanding of the habeas writ throughout the 19th century and well into the 20th." 599 U.S. at 485.

NOTE ON RETROACTIVITY AND NEW LAW IN HABEAS CORPUS

A.   The Warren Court and the Background to Teague v. Lane

(1) The Problem. Traditionally, judicial decisions, no matter how novel, apply retroactively to the parties in the litigation and to other litigants in all pending cases that have not yet become "final" on direct review. (For these purposes, "final" means that certiorari has been denied or that the time for seeking further direct appellate review has expired.) The key question of retroactivity that arises in the habeas context is whether that tradition of full retroactivity should also apply to cases that have concluded direct review—that is, all pending or future cases of *collateral attack* on a final conviction. Note that until 1996, no federal statute of limitations applied in habeas corpus. Accordingly, following the decision in Miranda v. Arizona, 384 U.S. 436 (1966), a broad retroactivity rule would have permitted every person incarcerated by the states whose trial had not been conducted in accordance with the Miranda rules to file a habeas petition and, unless the error was harmless, to obtain relief.[1]

The retroactivity question grew in significance during the 1960s due to the sharp increase in the number of habeas petitions filed, the expansive scope of habeas review recognized by the Warren Court, and that Court's numerous broad and novel criminal procedure decisions expanding the rights of defendants, of which Miranda is an example. In the decades that followed, the rise in the population of those incarcerated by the states—a nearly eight-fold increase between 1970 and 2010—also gave the question great significance.[2]

Ever since 1965, the Supreme Court has been unwilling to treat all constitutional criminal procedure decisions as fully retroactive in post-conviction habeas corpus cases, adopting different approaches

---

[1]   Note further that although today a petitioner who had not raised a claim in state court would ordinarily be barred from pursuing it on habeas corpus, that was not the law when Miranda was decided. See generally pp. 1631–1657, *infra*.

[2]   See p. 1552–1553, *supra*.

commensurate with the Court's contemporary approach to criminal procedure more generally. Then in 1996, Congress enacted a provision, codified as 28 U.S.C. § 2254(d)(1), that bars federal habeas courts from granting relief on a claim that was adjudicated on the merits by a state court, unless the state court's decision "was contrary to, or involved an unreasonable application of, clearly established Federal law, as determined by the Supreme Court of the United States" as of the time of the state court decision. As a result of § 2254(d)(1), today habeas claims seeking retroactive application of new federal constitutional norms are excluded from habeas jurisdiction if those claims were decided on the merits by state courts. In such cases, the federal courts have no reason to reach issues of retroactivity when the petitioner is relying on new law.

Nonetheless, the non-retroactivity doctrines that governed between 1965 and 1996 still govern in certain circumstances[3] and form an important backdrop to the enactment and understanding of § 2254(d)(1). Further, recent Supreme Court jurisprudence has held that a longstanding exception to the Court's non-retroactivity doctrines is constitutional in nature, therefore superseding state law restrictions on habeas relief where it applies. See Montgomery v. Louisiana, 577 U.S. 190 (2016), p. 1610, *infra*.

(2) The Warren Court's Approach: Non-Retroactivity.[4] In Linkletter v. Walker, 381 U.S. 618 (1965), the Court for the first time asserted the power to render a constitutional decision not fully retroactive. There, it ruled that its decision in Mapp v. Ohio, 367 U.S. 643 (1961), which applied the Fourth Amendment's exclusionary remedy to the states, would not be retroactively applied to state court convictions that had become final before Mapp was decided. A year later, in Johnson v. New Jersey, 384 U.S. 719, 733–35 (1966), the Court held that the Miranda rules did not apply to trials that commenced before the date of the Miranda decision. In adopting this approach of non-retroactivity, the Warren Court was able to hand down sweeping decisions reforming criminal procedure while minimizing the disruption they caused.

Eventually, the Court held that the retroactivity of new constitutional rulings depended on three factors: the purpose of the new rule, the extent of reliance on the old rule, and the effect on the administration of justice of retroactive application of the new rule. See Stovall v. Denno, 388 U.S. 293, 297 (1967).[5]

---

[3]   For example, the non-retroactivity doctrine still applies in the rare habeas case in which a federal claim, not decided by the state courts on the merits and not barred procedurally, rests on a new rule of constitutional law.

[4]   See generally Fallon & Meltzer, *New Law, Non-Retroactivity, and Constitutional Remedies*, 104 Harv.L.Rev. 1731, 1738–44 (1991), which cites much bibliographic material.

[5]   Under this approach, a new rule like Miranda always applied to the case in which it was announced, whether that case reached the Supreme Court on direct or collateral review. When a subsequent case implicating the new rule reached the Court, the Court applied the three-factor test to determine whether the new decision applied retroactively to cases both on direct and collateral review. Thus, by way of example, unlike the decisions in Mapp and Miranda, the Sixth Amendment right to the assistance of counsel recognized in Gideon v. Wainwright, 372 U.S. 335 (1963)), was enforced in all proceedings, whether on direct review or on habeas review.

(3) Justice Harlan's Critique. Justice Harlan's separate opinions in Desist v. United States, 394 U.S. 244, 256–69 (1969), and Mackey v. United States, 401 U.S. 667, 675–702 (1971), strongly criticized the Warren Court's approach to retroactivity. In his view, cases still subject to adjudication or on appeal differed importantly from cases on habeas review. On direct review, he argued, courts must apply all decisions retroactively; to do otherwise would suggest that their function was not one of adjudication but of legislation. But because habeas corpus is an extraordinary remedy, no such judicial obligation exists, and the state's interest in finality called for a narrower judicial inquiry. In Desist, he argued that habeas review must be adequate to "serve[ ] as a necessary additional incentive for trial and appellate courts throughout the land to conduct their proceedings in a manner consistent with established constitutional standards." That purpose did not require the retroactive application of *new* rules, which, he said in Mackey, should apply retroactively only when they (i) held previously punishable conduct to be constitutionally protected, or (ii) recognized constitutional rights of procedure so fundamental as to be " 'implicit in the concept of ordered liberty.' "

(4) Griffith v. Kentucky. In Griffith v. Kentucky, 479 U.S. 314 (1987), a divided Supreme Court endorsed Justice Harlan's view that new rules should be fully retroactive on direct review. Justice Blackmun wrote for the Court that the "failure to apply a newly declared constitutional rule to criminal cases pending on direct review violates basic norms of constitutional adjudication." He stressed that "the integrity of judicial review" requires the application of the new rule to "all similar cases pending on direct review" and that "selective application of new rules violates the principle of treating similarly situated defendants the same." Justice White, joined by Chief Justice Rehnquist and Justice O'Connor, dissented, contending that the majority's concerns about judicial legislation "go more to the substance of the Court's decisions than to whether or not they are retroactive." He deemed the concern about inequality to be "hollow," because the Court will tolerate comparable inequalities between defendants based on whether their cases come up on direct or collateral review—inequalities that depend on how long ago the unconstitutional conduct occurred and how quickly cases move through the judicial system.

Since 1987, the Court has generally adhered to the approach of Griffith in deciding cases on direct review.[6]

B. The Approach of Teague v. Lane

(1) The Teague Decision. In Teague v. Lane, 489 U.S. 288 (1989), the Court completed its rejection of the Warren Court's approach, holding that, with only the most limited exceptions, new constitutional rules do not apply retroactively on collateral review. Although Justice O'Connor's opinion announcing the Court's judgment spoke only for a plurality of four, in

---

[6]   But see Davis v. United States, 564 U.S. 229 (2011) (Breyer, J., dissenting) (contending that the majority departed from Griffith's approach in a Fourth Amendment case involving a search the circumstances of which the Court held unconstitutional in another case while Davis's direct appeal was pending).

numerous subsequent decisions, the Court endorsed and followed Justice O'Connor's approach.

Justice O'Connor began by stating that "[r]etroactivity is properly treated as a threshold question, for, once a new rule is applied to the defendant in the case announcing the rule, evenhanded justice requires that it be applied retroactively to all who are similarly situated." Endorsing Justice Harlan's views, she stated that, subject to two exceptions, new constitutional rules of criminal procedure will not apply to cases that "have become final before the new rules are announced." To provide state judges with the incentive to comply with established constitutional principles requires only that habeas courts apply constitutional standards prevailing when the state proceedings took place; to apply new rules in habeas undermines finality and unfairly burdens states that provided trials that were entirely fair under then-governing standards.

Noting the difficulty of determining whether a case announces a new rule, Justice O'Connor stated the relevant question is whether "it breaks new ground or imposes a new obligation on the States or the Federal Government. * * * To put it differently, a case announces a new rule if the result was not *dictated* by precedent existing at the time the defendant's conviction became final."[7]

Justice O'Connor next endorsed two exceptions to the nonretroactivity rule identified by Justice Harlan. First, she observed that a new rule should apply retroactively if it provides that the conduct for which the defendant was prosecuted is constitutionally protected. She then proposed a second, procedural, exception for a new rule (a) that implicates the fundamental fairness of the trial and (b) without which the likelihood of an accurate conviction is seriously diminished. Yet Justice O'Connor also doubted that any new rules falling within the latter category had yet to emerge.

Justice O'Connor next turned to the claims presented in Teague. Teague first sought the benefit of Batson v. Kentucky, 476 U.S. 79 (1986), which the Court had decided after his conviction became final. See *id.* (holding that prosecution's use of racially motivated peremptory challenges violates the Fourteenth Amendment's Equal Protection Clause). Teague separately argued that his prosecution violated the Sixth Amendment's fair cross section requirement, a claim that the Court had not previously recognized and had declined to reach in Batson. Justice O'Connor concluded that because both claims sought by Teague relied upon new rules and fell within neither exception, they were not cognizable on collateral review.[8]

In dissent, Justice Brennan, joined by Justice Marshall, objected that the plurality "would erect a formidable new barrier to relief. * * * Few decisions on appeal or collateral review are '*dictated*' by what came before. Most such cases involve a question of law that is at least debatable * * *.

---

[7]   Are these statements saying the same thing?

[8]   Justice Stevens, joined by Justice Blackmun, generally endorsed Justice Harlan's approach, but differed with the plurality in some respects. In particular, he disputed that retroactivity should be treated as a threshold issue. Instead, he suggested following the approach of harmless error decisions, which frequently decide the constitutional merits and only thereafter assess whether relief should nonetheless be denied because the error was harmless.

Virtually no case that prompts a dissent on the relevant legal point, for example, could be said to be '*dictated*' by prior decisions. This meant, in his view, that habeas would now be contracted dramatically, a problem exacerbated, he believed, by the limited exceptions embraced by the plurality. Justice Brennan concluded by arguing that the better model would decide Teague's claim and grant relief if the claim were meritorious, while waiting for a subsequent case in which to determine whether the right applied retroactively.

(2)   The Meaning of "New" Law. After Teague, subsequent decisions gave a wide definition to the concept of "new" law, thereby sharply contracting the scope of federal post-conviction review.

A notable example is Butler v. McKellar, 494 U.S. 407 (1990). The background to Butler lay in two decisions elaborating the Miranda rules: Edwards v. Arizona, 451 U.S. 477 (1981), which held that after a suspect has requested counsel, the police may not initiate further interrogation until counsel has been made available, and Arizona v. Roberson, 486 U.S. 675 (1988), which held that Edwards applies equally when the second interrogation concerns a different crime from the one that was the subject of the initial questioning.

Butler's claim was similar to that in Roberson, but Butler's conviction had become final in 1982, before Roberson was decided. The Supreme Court ruled, 5–4, that Butler could not obtain habeas relief because the Roberson decision, on which Butler's claim depended, had established a new rule. Chief Justice Rehnquist wrote that "[t]he 'new rule' principle * * * validates reasonable, good-faith interpretations of existing precedents made by state courts even though they are shown to be contrary to later decisions." The fact that the Court, in Roberson, had viewed the case as within the scope of its Edwards decision "is not conclusive * * *. Courts frequently view their decisions as being 'controlled' or 'governed' by prior opinions even when aware of reasonable contrary conclusions reached by other courts." He continued by observing that differing positions taken by judges in the courts of appeals indicate that "the outcome in Roberson was susceptible to debate among reasonable minds * * *." The four dissenters in Butler objected that under the Court's approach, "a state prisoner can secure habeas relief only by showing that the state court's rejection of the constitutional challenge was *so* clearly invalid under then-prevailing legal standards that the decision could not be defended by any reasonable jurist."[9]

---

[9]   In Chaidez v. United States, 568 U.S. 342 (2013), the Court, in concluding that its decision in Padilla v. Kentucky, 559 U.S. 356 (2010), had announced a new rule, articulated a distinction between "threshold" issues about whether a constitutional right applies and "garden-variety" applications of established law to new facts.

In Padilla, the Court held that an attorney's failure to provide competent advice about the risk of deportation resulting from a guilty plea constitutes ineffective assistance of counsel in violation of the Sixth Amendment. Relying on Padilla, Chaidez filed a collateral attack on her federal conviction. Applying the principles of Teague v. Lane, the Supreme Court ruled that the Padilla decision did not apply retroactively. Justice Kagan's opinion for the Court acknowledged that a decision does not announce a new rule when it merely applies a governing principle to a new set of facts. But the Court found that "Padilla did something more." It "considered a threshold question: Was advice about deportation 'categorically removed' from the scope of the Sixth Amendment right to counsel because it involved only a 'collateral consequence' of a

(3) The Teague Exceptions.

(a) Constitutionally Protected Primary Conduct. Teague's first exception would permit retroactive application of cases like Loving v. Virginia, 388 U.S. 1 (1967), and Lawrence v. Texas, 539 U.S. 558 (2003). In this respect, Teague's first exception echoes the historic notion that habeas lies when the sentencing court lacked jurisdiction—and that jurisdiction is lacking when the statute under which the defendant was convicted is unconstitutional. See p. 1555, *supra*. In such a case, is relief less prejudicial to state interests because no trial should have been held and no retrial can be commenced?

(b) Constitutional Limitations on Sentences. The question how Teague's first exception applies to constitutional challenges to sentences arose in Penry v. Lynaugh, 492 U.S. 302 (1989), where the Court addressed the claim that execution of a person with the mental capacity of a seven-year old violated the Eighth Amendment. A unanimous Court ruled that although the claim was "new," the first exception extends to new rules "prohibiting a certain category of punishment for a class of defendants because of their status or offense." But the Court proceeded to reject Penry's claim, 5–4.[10]

(c) Teague's Second Exception. The Supreme Court never held a claim to fit within Teague's second exception.[11] A divided Supreme Court then eliminated the second exception altogether in Edwards v. Vannoy, 593 U.S. 255 (2021). The case presented the question whether Teague's second exception encompasses a habeas claim seeking the benefit of the Court's holding in Ramos v. Louisiana, 590 U.S. 83 (2020) (overruling Apodaca v. Oregon, 406 U.S. 404 (1972)), that the Sixth Amendment's requirement of a unanimous jury applies to the states under the Fourteenth Amendment. Writing for six Justices, Justice Kavanaugh began by observing that "applying Ramos retroactively would potentially overturn decades of convictions. . . ." Turning to the Teague inquiry, he observed that "[t]he starkest example of a decision announcing a new rule is a decision that overrules an earlier case." Thus, it was clear that Ramos established a new rule. The Ramos rule was procedural, moreover, because it "affects 'only the

---

conviction, rather than a component of the criminal sentence?" Before the Padilla decision, the Supreme Court had explicitly left that question open, and nearly all state and federal appellate courts to consider the question had found no Sixth Amendment violation. Padilla held otherwise, but, Justice Kagan said, "[i]f that does not count as 'break[ing] new ground' or 'impos[ing] a new obligation,' we are hard pressed to know what would." (Justice Thomas concurred in the judgment separately, and Justice Sotomayor, joined by Justice Ginsburg, dissented.)

[10]   The Court overruled the merits of Penry in Atkins v. Virginia, 536 U.S. 304 (2002) (holding that the Eighth Amendment precluded imposition of a death sentence on a developmentally disabled defendant).

[11]   Cases finding the exception inapplicable include Whorton v. Bockting, 549 U.S. 406 (2007) (rule of Crawford v. Washington, 541 U.S. 36 (2004), that the Confrontation Clause prohibits the admission of hearsay that is "testimonial," whether or not it would be deemed reliable, unless the declarant is unavailable and the defendant had a prior opportunity to cross-examine); Sawyer v. Smith, 497 U.S. 227, 244 (1990) (rule of Caldwell v. Mississippi, 472 U.S. 320 (1985), that the Eighth Amendment bars imposition of death sentence by a sentencer that has been led to the false belief that responsibility for determining the appropriateness of such a sentence lies elsewhere); and Gilmore v. Taylor, 508 U.S. 333 (1993) (claim that homicide instructions denied due process because they permitted a jury to convict for murder rather than voluntary manslaughter without considering whether killing was in the heat of passion).

manner of determining the defendant's culpability'" (quoting Schriro v. Summerlin, 542 U.S. 348, 353 (2004)).

But, Justice Kavanaugh stressed, Teague's second exception has "[i]n practice * * * been theoretical, not real."[12] After identifying a number of important decisions that the Court has declined to bring within the watershed exception, Justice Kavanaugh saw no reason to hold differently with respect to the rule of Ramos. This conclusion, he explained, also begged a larger question: "If landmark and historic criminal procedure decisions— including Mapp, Miranda, Duncan, Crawford, Batson, and now Ramos—do not apply retroactively on federal collateral review, how can any additional new rules of criminal procedure apply retroactively on federal collateral review? At this point, some 32 years after Teague, we think the only candid answer is that none can." Justice Kavanaugh observed that "[c]ontinuing to articulate a theoretical exception that never actually applies in practice offers false hope to defendants, distorts the law, misleads judges, and wastes the resources of defense counsel, prosecutors, and courts."

Justice Thomas, joined by Justice Gorsuch, concurred, opining that the Court need go no further than apply 28 U.S.C. § 2254(d) to resolve the case and deny relief because in his view, AEDPA superseded Teague, including its exceptions. For additional discussion, see p. 1622, note 7, *infra*. Justice Gorsuch, joined by Justice Thomas, also concurred. In his view, "Teague did much to return the writ to its original station" by "insisting that final judgments cannot be reopened as a 'general rule,'" but, he observed, its prohibition on retroactive application of "new" rules does not make sense with respect to Supreme Court holdings, like Ramos, that purport to "realign th[e] Court's decisions with the original meaning" of the Constitution. He then argued that Teague's default proposition should govern in all cases: habeas corpus should "not authorize federal courts to reopen a judgment issued by a court of competent jurisdiction once it has become final."[13]

Dissenting and joined by Justices Breyer and Sotomayor, Justice Kagan labeled the Ramos decision "historic." She observed that "[i]f you were scanning a thesaurus for a single word to describe the decision, you would stop when you came to 'watershed.'" Justice Kagan also believed that the precedents on which the majority relied in rejecting classifying the Ramos rule as "watershed" were not comparable. Ramos, she noted, emphasized the importance of jury unanimity, declaring it "an 'essential element[ ]' of the jury trial right," and therefore "'fundamental to the American scheme of justice'" (quoting Ramos, 590 U.S. at 92–93). Going further, the dissent reiterated that Ramos did away with nonunanimous juries because the practice was adopted "'to dilute the influence [on juries] of racial, ethnic, and religious minorities,'—and particularly, 'to ensure that African-American juror service would be meaningless'" (quoting Ramos, 590 U.S. at 88).

---

[12] Notwithstanding the Court's failure to recognize any watershed procedural rules within Teague's second exception, several state courts have done so. See Fox & Stein, *Constitutional Retroactivity in Criminal Procedure*, 91 Wash.L.Rev. 463 (2016) (listing examples).

[13] Although Justice Gorsuch was writing about Teague's second exception in his Edwards v. Vannoy opinion, could his views be read to suggest that he questions the legitimacy of Teague's first exception as well?

Justice Kagan concluded, "[i]f the right to a unanimous jury is so fundamental—if a verdict rendered by a divided jury is 'no verdict at all'—then Thedrick Edwards should not spend his life behind bars over two jurors' opposition."

In the wake of Teague, the Court had never found a single one of its decisions to establish a watershed rule of criminal procedure.[14] In some respects, therefore, the decision in Edwards is not remarkable. One might argue, however, that this conclusion begs the question whether the Court should have identified more watershed rules. Then there is the separate question whether Teague should apply a "new" rule retroactively when declared to be better aligned with the Constitution's original meaning? Couldn't one argue that such a rule is not "new"?

To be sure, the majority's approach respects state reliance interests by avoiding the need for retrials, sometimes years after the fact when witnesses' memories have faded, and evidence may be lost. See Bator, *Finality in Criminal Law and Federal Habeas Corpus for State Prisoners*, 76 Harv.L.Rev. 441 (1963); Friendly, *Is Innocence Irrelevant? Collateral Attack on Criminal Judgments*, 38 U.Chi.L.Rev. 142, 149–50 (1970). And it is also possible, at least in theory, that the majority's position could encourage the Court to recognize more procedural rights on behalf of criminal defendants if doing so will prove less disruptive.[15]

(d) Substantive Rights Versus Procedural Rights. In Schriro v. Summerlin, 542 U.S. 348 (2004), the Court recharacterized the first Teague exception as follows: "New *substantive* rules generally apply retroactively. This includes decisions that narrow the scope of a [federal] criminal statute by interpreting its terms, see Bousley v. United States, [523 U.S. 614 (1998), p. 1669, *infra*], as well as constitutional determinations that place particular conduct or persons covered by the statute beyond the State's power to punish." A footnote added: "We have sometimes referred to rules of this latter type as falling under an exception to Teague's bar on retroactive application of procedural rules; they are more accurately characterized as substantive rules not subject to the bar."[16]

---

[14] Note that in Vannoy Justice Kagan disputed the majority's assertion that the Court had never applied a procedural rule retroactively *before* Teague, citing Brown v. Louisiana, 447 U.S. 323 (1980), which, she explained, retroactively applied the rule of Burch v. Louisiana, 441 U.S. 130 (1979) (holding that a six-person jury verdict must be unanimous). The majority challenged her reading of Brown's application of Burch to collateral cases.

[15] Consider Jeffries, *The Right-Remedy Gap in Constitutional Law*, 109 Yale L.J. 87 (1999) (doctrines like Teague and official immunity, which withhold remedies for violations of new constitutional rules, enable courts more easily to develop rights-protective doctrines—an approach that redistributes constitutional benefits from past to future claimants).

[16] The Court extended this reasoning in Montgomery v. Louisiana, 577 U.S. 190 (2016), holding that its decision in Miller v. Alabama, 567 U.S. 460 (2012), was substantive for Teague purposes. See p. 1610, *infra*. In Welch v. United States, 578 U.S. 120 (2016), the Court also held retroactive its decision in Johnson v. United States, 576 U.S. 591 (2015). See p. 1670, *infra*. Given these extensions of Teague's first exception, and with Teague's second exception now eliminated, it would be accurate to restate Teague and its exceptions this way: new substantive rules apply retroactively; new procedural rules do not.

C. Questions About Teague

(1) Criticisms. A common criticism of Teague is that the Court's conception of "new law" is too broad: by including rules that reflect ordinary legal evolution, it reduces the incentives for state courts, and state law enforcement officials, to take account of the direction of legal developments. See, *e.g.*, Fallon & Meltzer, note 4, *supra*, at 1816–17.[17]

(2) Equal Treatment of Litigants. Justice O'Connor's opinion in Teague objected that the Warren Court's approach to retroactivity treated similarly situated litigants differently. But, as Justice White's dissent in Griffith noted, an approach turning on when a conviction became final on direct review merely redirects any inequality. Consider a defendant whose conviction became final one day before Ramos and a defendant whose conviction became final one day after Ramos. Why should one receive a new trial and the other not receive a new trial? Any approach that is neither fully retroactive nor fully prospective necessarily treats some litigants differently from others. Which dividing line is the most principled?

(3) A Threshold Issue? Does deciding whether a habeas petition rests on "new law" at the threshold, as Justice O'Connor said a court should do, make sense, given how intertwined that question often is with the merits? A different approach might sometimes establish more promptly the contours of new constitutional protections, thereby providing useful guidance for state officials and state courts. See generally Fallon & Meltzer, note 4, *supra*, at 1797–1807. As Justice Stevens noted in his Teague concurrence, courts often discuss the merits even if relief is ultimately denied on harmless error grounds. Compare as well the Court's shifting approach to officer immunity. See pp. 1311–1328, *supra*.

(4) Teague's Foundations. What is the basis for Teague's mandate? The Constitution or the federal habeas statute? The Court explored this important question in Danforth v. Minnesota, 552 U.S. 264 (2008), discussed below in Paragraph (5), and more recently in Montgomery v. Louisiana, 577 U.S. 190 (2016), included below as a principal case, p. 1610, *infra*.

(5) The Application of Teague in State Court. Does Teague govern state post-conviction proceedings? That issue arose in Danforth v. Minnesota, 552 U.S. 264 (2008). After Danforth's conviction became final, the Supreme Court decided Crawford v. Washington, 541 U.S. 36 (2004), which reshaped a defendant's rights under the Confrontation Clause. The Court then held that Crawford announced a "new" rule not retroactively applicable in federal habeas corpus proceedings. Whorton v. Bockting, 549 U.S. 406 (2007). When Danforth filed a state post-conviction petition relying on Crawford, the state supreme court ruled that it was precluded from giving

---

[17]   See also, *e.g.*, Feldman, *Diagnosing Power: Postmodernism in Legal Scholarship and Judicial Practice (with an Emphasis on the Teague Rule Against New Rules in Habeas Corpus Cases)*, 88 Nw.U.L.Rev. 1046, 1065 (1994); Meyer, *"Nothing We Say Matters": Teague and New Rules*, 61 U.Chi.L.Rev. 423 (1994); Liebman, *More Than "Slightly Retro": The Rehnquist Court's Rout of Habeas Corpus Jurisdiction in Teague v. Lane*, 18 N.Y.U.Rev.L. & Soc. Change 537 (1990–1991); Hoffman, *Retroactivity and the Great Writ: How Congress Should Respond to Teague v. Lane*, 1990 B.Y.U.L.Rev. 183.

retroactive effect to a federal constitutional ruling that, under Teague, does not apply retroactively in federal habeas proceedings.

The Supreme Court reversed. Justice Stevens's majority opinion reasoned that Teague rested on an interpretation of the federal habeas statute in light of equitable and prudential considerations and it was for the state courts to evaluate whether the state's interest in finality calls for precluding reliance on new law in state post-conviction proceedings.[18]

The Court next held in Montgomery v. Louisiana, 577 U.S. 190 (2016), a principal case below, p. 1610, *infra*, that Teague's first exception establishes a constitutional rule that state courts must apply in collateral proceedings.[19]

INTRODUCTORY NOTE ON 28 U.S.C. § 2254(d)(1)

The Antiterrorism and Effective Death Penalty Act of 1996 (AEDPA) includes a provision, codified at 28 U.S.C. § 2254(d)(1), that, like the Teague decision, limits the retroactive application of new decisions to cases in collateral review. Unlike Teague, § 2254(d)(1) applies only when a state court has decided the constitutional issue. But when it does apply, § 2254(d)(1) curtails the scope of federal habeas review even more sharply than Teague.

The next principal case, Terry Williams v. Taylor, provides the Supreme Court's first and fullest discussion of § 2254(d)(1).[1] Although Justice Stevens delivers the majority opinion in the case that follows, note that on the key issue in the case—the interpretation of § 2254(d)(1)—he is in the minority, while Justice O'Connor speaks for the majority.

---

[18]   Justice Stevens added that any other rule would be anomalous given that the state political branches may waive a Teague defense.

[19]   In applying Griffith and Teague, the threshold question whether a state court proceeding is direct or collateral is significant. In McKinney v. Arizona, 589 U.S. 139 (2020), a divided Court concluded that where a federal habeas court orders a state court to reweigh aggravating and mitigating factors in determining the appropriateness of a death sentence, the subsequent proceeding should be treated as collateral for Teague purposes. Accordingly, Griffith did not apply, and the state court was not required to apply intervening Supreme Court decisions that postdated the conclusion of the petitioner's original direct appeal.

Dissenting for four Justices, Justice Ginsburg understood the majority opinion to "look[ ] first to the State's classification of a proceeding, and then ask[ ] whether the character of the proceeding warrants the classification." Applying that test, Justice Ginsburg viewed the reweighing proceeding in McKinney's as a reinstatement of his direct appeal: the state supreme court conducted a de novo review of McKinney's sentence, used the docket number from his original direct appeal, and labeled the original appeal as " 'reinstated.' " In her view, that meant Griffith applied and McKinney should benefit from subsequent decisions.

After McKinney, will any new proceedings ordered by a federal habeas court short of a full retrial alter the date of finality for Teague purposes? Separately, what is the distinction between McKinney and Magwood v. Patterson, 561 U.S. 320 (2010)? In Magwood, the Court held that where a federal habeas court orders a state court to resentence the petitioner, the ensuing proceeding results in a "new" judgment for purposes of AEDPA and a subsequent federal habeas petition is therefore not "second or successive" to any prior petition; instead, the petition should be treated as "challeng[ing] a new judgment for the first time." See also p. 1661, note 6, *infra*.

[1]   During its 2000 Term, the Court decided two habeas cases against Virginia's Warden, Taylor, in which the petitioner's surname was Williams; hence, in discussing each, the petitioner's first name is included as well.

Terry Williams v. Taylor

529 U.S. 362 (2000).

Certiorari to the United States Court of Appeals for the Fourth Circuit.

■ JUSTICE STEVENS announced the judgment of the Court and delivered the opinion of the Court with respect to Parts I, III, and IV, and an opinion with respect to Parts II and V.*

The questions presented are whether Terry Williams' constitutional right to the effective assistance of counsel as defined in Strickland v. Washington, 466 U.S. 668 (1984), was violated, and whether the judgment of the Virginia Supreme Court refusing to set aside his death sentence "was contrary to, or involved an unreasonable application of, clearly established Federal law, as determined by the Supreme Court of the United States," within the meaning of 28 U.S.C. § 2254(d)(1) (1994 ed., Supp. III). We answer both questions affirmatively.

I

[Having been sentenced to death, Williams alleged, in a state postconviction proceeding, that his lawyers denied him the effective assistance of counsel at the sentencing hearing by failing to introduce mitigating evidence of Williams' childhood neglect and abuse, significant intellectual disabilities, repeated head injuries, and possible mental impairment that was organic in origin. Williams also complained that after the government's experts testified to a "high probability" that he would pose a continuing threat to society, his counsel failed on cross-examination to elicit the experts' view that Williams would not pose such a threat if kept in a structured environment.

[Applying the Strickland standard, the state trial judge ruled that Williams had been denied his right to counsel, holding that (a) his lawyer's performance fell below the range of competent assistance, and (b) that deficiency was prejudicial, as there was a reasonable probability that the sentencing outcome would have differed had counsel been effective. The Virginia Supreme Court disagreed, reasoning that even assuming that counsel's performance was deficient, there was no prejudice. In so doing, that court read Lockhart v. Fretwell, 506 U.S. 364 (1993), as having modified the Strickland standard of prejudice.

[Lockhart was an unusual case in which the petitioner's lawyer failed to raise a constitutional objection based on an established lower court precedent that the Supreme Court later rejected. Ruling against the petitioner, the Supreme Court held that no prejudice results from a lawyer's failure to have made an objection that is no longer meritorious.

---

*   JUSTICE SOUTER, JUSTICE GINSBURG, and JUSTICE BREYER join this opinion in its entirety. JUSTICE O'CONNOR and JUSTICE KENNEDY join Parts I, III, and IV of this opinion.

[In Williams' case, the Virginia Supreme Court ruled that, in light of Lockhart, the trial judge erred in relying on "mere outcome determination" when assessing prejudice under the Sixth Amendment. The state supreme court also found no reasonable possibility that the omitted mitigating evidence would have changed the jury's recommendation.

[Williams then sought federal habeas corpus relief. The district judge upheld the claim of ineffective assistance of counsel. The Fourth Circuit reversed, construing § 2254(d)(1) as barring relief unless the state court "decided the question by interpreting or applying the relevant precedent in a manner that reasonable jurists would all agree is unreasonable." In so doing, the Court of Appeals] explained that the evidence that Williams presented a future danger to society was "simply overwhelming," it endorsed the Virginia Supreme Court's interpretation of Lockhart, and it characterized the state court's understanding of the facts in this case as "reasonable."

We granted certiorari, and now reverse.

II

* * * The warden here contends that federal habeas corpus relief is prohibited by the amendment to 28 U.S.C. § 2254, enacted as a part of the Antiterrorism and Effective Death Penalty Act of 1996 (AEDPA). The relevant portion of that amendment provides:

> "(d) An application for a writ of habeas corpus on behalf of a person in custody pursuant to the judgment of a State court shall not be granted with respect to any claim that was adjudicated on the merits in State court proceedings unless the adjudication of the claim—

> "(1) resulted in a decision that was contrary to, or involved an unreasonable application of, clearly established Federal law, as determined by the Supreme Court of the United States. . . ."

* * * The inquiry mandated by the amendment relates to the way in which a federal habeas court exercises its duty to decide constitutional questions; the amendment does not alter the underlying grant of jurisdiction in § 2254(a). When federal judges exercise their federal-question jurisdiction under the "judicial Power" of Article III of the Constitution, it is "emphatically the province and duty" of those judges to "say what the law is." Marbury v. Madison, 1 Cranch 137, 177 (1803). At the core of this power is the federal courts' independent responsibility * * * to interpret federal law. A construction of AEDPA that would require the federal courts to cede this authority to the courts of the States would be inconsistent with the practice that federal judges have traditionally followed in discharging their duties under Article III of the Constitution. If Congress had intended to require such an important change in the exercise of our jurisdiction, we believe it would have spoken with much greater clarity than is found in the text of AEDPA.

This basic premise informs our interpretation of both parts of § 2254(d)(1): first, the requirement that the determinations of state courts be tested only against "clearly established Federal law, as determined by the Supreme Court of the United States," and second, the prohibition on the issuance of the writ unless the state court's decision is "contrary to, or involved an unreasonable application of," that clearly established law. We address each part in turn.

The "clearly established law" requirement

In Teague v. Lane, 489 U.S. 288 (1989), we held that the petitioner was not entitled to federal habeas relief because he was relying on a rule of federal law that had not been announced until after his state conviction became final. The antiretroactivity rule recognized in Teague, which prohibits reliance on "new rules," is the functional equivalent of a statutory provision commanding exclusive reliance on "clearly established law." Because there is no reason to believe that Congress intended to require federal courts to ask both whether a rule sought on habeas is "new" under Teague—which remains the law—and also whether it is "clearly established" under AEDPA, it seems safe to assume that Congress had congruent concepts in mind.[11] It is perfectly clear that AEDPA codifies Teague to the extent that Teague requires federal habeas courts to deny relief that is contingent upon a rule of law not clearly established at the time the state conviction became final.[12]

* * * [Under Teague,] a federal habeas court operates within the bounds of comity and finality if it applies a rule "dictated by precedent existing at the time the defendant's conviction became final." 489 U.S., at 301 (emphasis deleted). A rule that "breaks new ground or imposes a new obligation on the States or the Federal Government," *ibid.*, falls outside this universe of federal law.

To this, AEDPA has added, immediately following the "clearly established law" requirement, a clause limiting the area of relevant law to that "determined by the Supreme Court of the United States." * * * [T]he lower federal courts cannot themselves establish such a principle with clarity sufficient to satisfy the AEDPA bar. * * *

In the context of this case, we also note that * * * rules of law may be sufficiently clear for habeas purposes even when they are expressed

---

[11]   It is not unusual for Congress to codify earlier precedent in the habeas context. [citing examples].

[12]   We are not persuaded by the argument that because Congress used the words "clearly established law" and not "new rule," it meant * * * to codify an aspect of the doctrine of executive qualified immunity rather than Teague's antiretroactivity bar. The warden refers us specifically to § 2244(b)(2)(A) and 28 U.S.C. § 2254(e)(2), in which the statute does in so many words employ the "new rule" language familiar to Teague and its progeny. * * * [But] the verbatim adoption of the Teague language in these other sections bolsters our impression that Congress had Teague—and not any unrelated area of our jurisprudence—specifically in mind in amending the habeas statute. * * * We will not assume that in a single subsection of an amendment entirely devoted to the law of habeas corpus, Congress made the anomalous choice of reaching into the doctrinally distinct law of qualified immunity for a single phrase that just so happens to be the conceptual twin of a dominant principle in habeas law of which Congress was fully aware.

in terms of a generalized standard rather than as a bright-line rule. As Justice Kennedy has explained:

> "If the rule * * * requires a case-by-case examination of the evidence, then we can tolerate a number of specific applications without saying that those applications themselves create a new rule. . . . [When a general rule is] * * * designed for the specific purpose of evaluating a myriad of factual contexts, it will be the infrequent case that yields a result so novel that it forges a new rule, one not dictated by precedent." Wright v. West, 505 U.S. 277 (1992) (opinion concurring in judgment). * * *

It has been urged, in contrast, that we should read Teague and its progeny to encompass a broader principle of deference requiring federal courts to "validat[e] 'reasonable, good-faith interpretations' of the law" by state courts. * * * This presumption of deference was in essence the position taken by three Members of this Court in Wright, 505 U.S., at 290–291 (opinion of Thomas, J.) ("[A] federal habeas court 'must defer to the state court's decision rejecting the claim unless that decision is patently unreasonable' ") (quoting Butler [v. McKellar], 494 U.S. [407], 422 [(1990)] (Brennan, J., dissenting)).

Teague, however, does not extend this far. The often repeated language that Teague endorses "reasonable, good-faith interpretations" by state courts is an explanation of policy, not a statement of law. * * * [W]e have long insisted that federal habeas courts attend closely to [considered decisions of state courts], and give them full effect when their findings and judgments are consistent with federal law. See Thompson v. Keohane, 516 U.S. 99, 107–116 (1995). But as Justice O'Connor explained in Wright:

> "[T]he duty of the federal court in evaluating whether a rule is 'new' is not the same as deference * * *. * * *
>
> * * * "We have always held that federal courts, even on habeas, have an independent obligation to say what the law is." 505 U.S., at 305 (opinion concurring in judgment).

We are convinced that in the phrase, "clearly established law," Congress did not intend to modify that independent obligation.

The "contrary to, or an unreasonable application of," requirement

The message that Congress intended to convey by using the phrases "contrary to" and "unreasonable application of" is not entirely clear. The prevailing view in the Circuits is that the former phrase requires *de novo* review of "pure" questions of law and the latter requires some sort of "reasonability" review of so-called mixed questions of law and fact.

We are not persuaded that the phrases define two mutually exclusive categories of questions. Most constitutional questions that arise in habeas corpus proceedings * * * require the federal judge to apply a rule of law to a set of facts * * *. For example, an erroneous conclusion that particular circumstances established the voluntariness of a confession, or that there exists a conflict of interest when one attorney represents multiple defendants, may well be described either as "contrary to" or as an "unreasonable application of" the governing rule of law. In constitutional adjudication, as in the common law, rules of law often develop incrementally as earlier decisions are applied to new factual situations. But rules that depend upon such elaboration are hardly less lawlike than those that establish a bright-line test.

Indeed, our pre-AEDPA efforts to distinguish questions of fact, questions of law, and "mixed questions," and to create an appropriate standard of habeas review for each, generated some not insubstantial differences of opinion as to which issues of law fell into which category of question, and as to which standard of review applied to each. * * *

The statutory text likewise does not obviously prescribe a specific, recognizable standard of review for dealing with either phrase. * * * Rather, the text is fairly read simply as a command that a federal court not issue the habeas writ unless the state court was wrong as a matter of law or unreasonable in its application of law in a given case. The suggestion that a wrong state-court "decision" * * * may no longer be redressed through habeas (because it is unreachable under the "unreasonable application" phrase) is based on a mistaken insistence that the § 2254(d)(1) phrases have not only independent, but mutually exclusive, meanings. Whether or not a federal court can issue the writ "under [the] 'unreasonable application' clause," the statute is clear that habeas may issue under § 2254(d)(1) if a state-court "decision" is "contrary to . . . clearly established Federal law." We thus anticipate that there will be a variety of cases, like this one, in which both phrases may be implicated.

Even though we cannot conclude that the phrases establish "a body of rigid rules," they do express a "mood" that the Federal Judiciary must respect. Universal Camera Corp. v. NLRB, 340 U.S. 474, 487 (1951). * * * [I]t seems clear that Congress intended federal judges to attend with the utmost care to state-court decisions, including all of the reasons supporting their decisions, before concluding that those proceedings were infected by constitutional error * * *. * * *

On the other hand, it is significant that the word "deference" does not appear in the text of the statute itself. Neither the legislative history nor the statutory text suggests any difference in the so-called "deference" depending on which of the two phrases is implicated. Whatever "deference" Congress had in mind with respect to both phrases, it surely is not a requirement that federal courts actually defer to a state-court application of the federal law that is, in the independent judgment of the federal court, in error. * * *[14]

---

14   [Justice Stevens deemed unpersuasive the three reasons advanced by Justice O'Connor in support of the majority's interpretation of the phrase "unreasonable application of."

Our disagreement with the Court about the precise meaning of the phrase "contrary to," and the word "unreasonable," is, of course, important, but should affect only a narrow category of cases. The simplest and first definition of "contrary to" as a phrase is "in conflict with." Webster's Ninth New Collegiate Dictionary 285 (1983). * * * [W]e think the phrase surely capacious enough to include a finding that the state-court "decision" is simply "erroneous" or wrong. * * * And there is nothing in the phrase "contrary to"—as the Court appears to agree—that implies anything less than independent review by the federal courts. * * * Our difference is as to the cases in which, at first blush, a state-court judgment seems entirely reasonable, but thorough analysis by a federal court produces a firm conviction that that judgment is infected by constitutional error. In our view, such an erroneous judgment is "unreasonable" within the meaning of the Act * * *.

In sum, the statute directs federal courts to attend to every state-court judgment with utmost care, but it does not require them to defer to the opinion of every reasonable state-court judge on the content of federal law. If, after carefully weighing all the reasons for accepting a state court's judgment, a federal court is convinced that a prisoner's custody—or, as in this case, his sentence of death—violates the Constitution, that independent judgment should prevail. Otherwise the federal "law as determined by the Supreme Court of the United States" might be applied by the federal courts one way in Virginia and another way in California. In light of the well-recognized interest in ensuring that federal courts interpret federal law in a uniform way, we are convinced that Congress did not intend the statute to produce such a result.

III

[The Court here observed that to prevail on his claim of ineffective assistance of counsel at his sentencing hearing, Williams must show, under Strickland v. Washington, (a) that "counsel's representation fell below an objective standard of reasonableness," and (b) "that there is a

---

[As to the suggestion that Congress, in using the word "unreasonable," was directly influenced by the "patently unreasonable" standard advocated by Justice Thomas's opinion in Wright v. West, 505 U.S. 277, 287 (1992), Justice Stevens responded that the debate in Wright was "not about the *standard of review* habeas courts should use for law-application questions, but about whether a rule is 'new' or 'old' " for purposes of Teague. * * * "Teague, of course, as Justice O'Connor correctly pointed out, 'did not establish a standard of review at all,' 505 U.S., at 303–304 * * *."

[As to the suggestion that the legislative history supports the Court's interpretation, Justice Stevens said that the only two passages on which the Court relies "do no more than beg the question. One merely quotes the language of the statute without elaboration, and the other goes to slightly greater length in stating that state-court judgments must be upheld unless 'unreasonable.' "

[Finally, as to the claim that Congress must have intended to change the law more substantially than his reading of 28 U.S.C. § 2254(d)(1) permits, he responded that although AEDPA "wrought substantial changes in habeas law [citing various provisions], there is an obvious fallacy in the assumption that because the statute changed pre-existing law in some respects, it must have rendered this specific change here."]

reasonable probability that, but for counsel's unprofessional errors, the result of the proceeding would have been different."] * * *

It is past question that the rule set forth in Strickland qualifies as "clearly established Federal law, as determined by the Supreme Court of the United States." * * * Williams is therefore entitled to relief if the Virginia Supreme Court's decision rejecting his ineffective-assistance claim was either "contrary to, or involved an unreasonable application of," that established law. It was both.

IV

[Writing for the Court, Justice Stevens concluded that the Virginia Supreme Court's understanding of Lockhart v. Fretwell was contrary to clearly established law. Lockhart dealt with the unusual case in which a lawyer failed to make a then-meritorious objection but that subsequent decisions have held to be without merit. Lockhart did not change the law in a case, like Williams', in which counsel's ineffectiveness "*does* deprive the defendant of a substantive or procedural right to which the law entitles him." * * *

[Justice Stevens proceeded to determine that Williams' counsel was ineffective at the sentencing phase. The opinion pointed to numerous investigatory failures that could have uncovered "extensive records graphically describing Williams' nightmarish childhood," which would have permitted the jury to learn] that Williams' parents had been imprisoned for the criminal neglect of Williams and his siblings, that Williams had been severely and repeatedly beaten by his father, and that he had been committed to the custody of the social services bureau for two years during his parents' incarceration (including one stint in an abusive foster home). [Justice Stevens also highlighted how counsel failed to introduce evidence of Williams' significant intellectual disabilities, limited education, and the aid he had provided officials in cracking a prison drug ring. Finally, Justice Stevens noted that counsel failed to seek testimony of prison officials who described Williams as among the least likely to be violent in the prison population.] * * *

We are also persuaded * * * that counsel's unprofessional service prejudiced Williams within the meaning of Strickland. * * *

The Virginia Supreme Court's own analysis of prejudice reaching the contrary conclusion was * * * unreasonable in at least two respects. First, * * * the court's decision turned on its erroneous view that a "mere" difference in outcome is not sufficient to establish constitutionally ineffective assistance of counsel. Its analysis in this respect was thus not only "contrary to," but also, inasmuch as the Virginia Supreme Court relied on the inapplicable exception recognized in Lockhart, an "unreasonable application of" the clear law as established by this Court.

Second, the State Supreme Court's prejudice determination was unreasonable insofar as it failed to evaluate the totality of the available mitigation evidence—both that adduced at trial, and the evidence adduced in the habeas proceeding in reweighing it against the evidence in aggravation. * * *

[T]he state court failed even to mention the sole argument in mitigation that trial counsel did advance—Williams turned himself in, alerting police to a crime they otherwise would never have discovered, expressing remorse for his actions, and cooperating with the police after that. While this, coupled with the prison records and guard testimony, may not have overcome a finding of future dangerousness, the graphic description of Williams' childhood, filled with abuse and privation, or the reality that he was "borderline mentally retarded," might well have influenced the jury's appraisal of his moral culpability. * * * Mitigating evidence unrelated to dangerousness may alter the jury's selection of penalty, even if it does not undermine or rebut the prosecution's death-eligibility case. The Virginia Supreme Court did not entertain that possibility. It thus failed to accord appropriate weight to the body of mitigation evidence available to trial counsel.

V

* * * [T]he Virginia Supreme Court rendered a "decision that was contrary to, or involved an unreasonable application of, clearly established Federal law." * * *

Accordingly, the judgment of the Court of Appeals is reversed, and the case is remanded for further proceedings.

It is so ordered.

■ JUSTICE O'CONNOR delivered the opinion of the Court with respect to Part II (except as to the footnote), concurred in part, and concurred in the judgment.*

[I agree with the Court's determination that the Virginia Supreme Court's decision was contrary to, or involved an unreasonable application of, clearly established federal law, as determined by the Supreme Court of the United States,] and join Parts I, III, and IV of the Court's opinion. Because I disagree, however, with the interpretation of § 2254(d)(1) set forth in Part II of Justice Stevens' opinion, I write separately to explain my views.

I

Before 1996, this Court held that a federal court entertaining a state prisoner's application for habeas relief must exercise its independent judgment when deciding both questions of constitutional law and mixed constitutional questions (*i.e.*, application of constitutional law to fact). See, *e.g.*, Miller v. Fenton, 474 U.S. 104, 112 (1985). * * * In 1991, in the case of Wright v. West, 502 U.S. 1021, we revisited our prior holdings by asking the parties to address the following question in their briefs:

---

    *   JUSTICE KENNEDY joins this opinion in its entirety. The CHIEF JUSTICE and JUSTICE THOMAS join this opinion with respect to Part II. JUSTICE SCALIA joins this opinion with respect to Part II, except as to the footnote.

"In determining whether to grant a petition for writ of habeas corpus by a person in custody pursuant to the judgment of a state court, should a federal court give deference to the state court's application of law to the specific facts of the petitioner's case or should it review the state court's determination *de novo?" Ibid.*

Although our ultimate decision did not turn on the answer to that question, our several opinions did join issue on it.

Justice Thomas * * * acknowledged that our precedents had "treat[ed] as settled the rule that mixed constitutional questions are 'subject to plenary federal review' on habeas." *Id.,* at 289 (quoting Miller, *supra,* at 112). * * * Justice Thomas suggested that the time to revisit our decisions may have been at hand, given that our more recent habeas jurisprudence in the nonretroactivity context, see, *e.g.,* Teague v. Lane, 489 U.S. 288 (1989), had called into question the then-settled rule of independent review of mixed constitutional questions.

I wrote separately in Wright because I believed Justice Thomas had "understate[d] the certainty with which Brown v. Allen rejected a deferential standard of review of issues of law." *Id.,* at 300. * * * I noted that "Teague did not establish a 'deferential' standard of review" because "[i]t did not establish a standard of review at all." 505 U.S., at 303–304. * * *

Finally, * * * I stated my disagreement with Justice Thomas' suggestion that *de novo* review is incompatible with the maxim that federal habeas courts should "give great weight to the considered conclusions of a coequal state judiciary," Miller, *supra,* at 112. Our statement in Miller signified only that a state-court decision is due the same respect as any other "persuasive, well-reasoned authority." Wright, 505 U.S., at 305. "But this does not mean that * * * federal courts must presume the correctness of a state court's legal conclusions on habeas, or that a state court's incorrect legal determination has ever been allowed to stand because it was reasonable. * * *" *Ibid.* * * *

II

A

* * * Justice Stevens' opinion in Part II essentially contends that § 2254(d)(1) does not alter the previously settled rule of independent review. Indeed, the opinion concludes its statutory inquiry with the somewhat empty finding that § 2254(d)(1) does no more than express a " 'mood' that the Federal Judiciary must respect." For Justice Stevens, the congressionally enacted "mood" has two important qualities. First, "federal courts [must] attend to every state-court judgment with utmost care" by "carefully weighing all the reasons for accepting a state court's judgment." Second, if a federal court undertakes that careful review and yet remains convinced that a prisoner's custody violates the Constitution, "that independent judgment should prevail."

One need look no further than our decision in Miller to see that Justice Stevens' interpretation of § 2254(d)(1) gives the 1996 amendment no effect whatsoever. The command that federal courts should now use the "utmost care" by "carefully weighing" the reasons supporting a state court's judgment echoes our pre-AEDPA statement in Miller that federal habeas courts "should, of course, give great weight to the considered conclusions of a coequal state judiciary." 474 U.S., at 112. Similarly, the requirement that the independent judgment of a federal court must in the end prevail essentially repeats the conclusion we reached in the very next sentence in Miller with respect to the specific issue presented there: "But, as we now reaffirm, the ultimate question whether, under the totality of the circumstances, the challenged confession was obtained in a manner compatible with the requirements of the Constitution *is a matter for independent federal determination*." *Ibid.* (emphasis added).

That Justice Stevens would find the new § 2254(d)(1) to have no effect on the prior law of habeas corpus is remarkable given his apparent acknowledgement that Congress wished to bring change to the field. * * *

Justice Stevens arrives at his erroneous interpretation by means of one critical misstep. He fails to give independent meaning to both the "contrary to" and "unreasonable application" clauses of the statute. * * *

The word "contrary" is commonly understood to mean "diametrically different," "opposite in character or nature," or "mutually opposed." Webster's Third New International Dictionary 495 (1976). The text of § 2254(d)(1) therefore suggests that the state court's decision must be substantially different from the relevant precedent of this Court. * * * A state-court decision will certainly be contrary to our clearly established precedent if the state court applies a rule that contradicts the governing law set forth in our cases. Take, for example, our decision in Strickland v. Washington, 466 U.S. 668 (1984). If a state court were to reject a prisoner's claim of ineffective assistance of counsel on the grounds that the prisoner had not established by a preponderance of the evidence that the result of his criminal proceeding would have been different, that decision would be "diametrically different," "opposite in character or nature," and "mutually opposed" to our clearly established precedent because we held in Strickland that the prisoner need only demonstrate a "reasonable probability that . . . the result of the proceeding would have been different." *Id.*, at 694. A state-court decision will also be contrary to this Court's clearly established precedent if the state court confronts a set of facts that are materially indistinguishable from a decision of this Court and nevertheless arrives at a result different from our precedent. * * *

On the other hand, a run-of-the-mill state-court decision applying the correct legal rule from our cases to the facts of a prisoner's case would not fit comfortably within § 2254(d)(1)'s "contrary to" clause. Assume, for example, that a state-court decision on a prisoner's ineffective-assistance claim correctly identifies Strickland as the controlling legal authority and, applying that framework, rejects the prisoner's claim. * * * [E]ven assuming the federal court considering the prisoner's habeas application might reach a different result applying the Strickland framework itself[, i]t is difficult * * * to describe such a run-of-the-mill state-court decision as "diametrically different" from, "opposite in character or nature" from, or "mutually opposed" to Strickland, our clearly established precedent. * * *

Justice Stevens would instead construe § 2254(d)(1)'s "contrary to" clause to encompass such a routine state-court decision. That construction, however, saps the "unreasonable application" clause of any meaning. If a federal habeas court can, under the "contrary to" clause, issue the writ whenever it concludes that the state court's *application* of clearly established federal law was incorrect, the "unreasonable application" clause becomes a nullity. We must, however, if possible, give meaning to every clause of the statute. * * *

The Fourth Circuit's interpretation of the "unreasonable application" clause of § 2254(d)(1) is generally correct. * * * [The Fourth Circuit correctly reasoned that] a state-court decision can involve an "unreasonable application" of this Court's clearly established precedent * * * if the state court identifies the correct governing legal rule from this Court's cases but unreasonably applies it to the facts of the particular state prisoner's case. * * **

The Fourth Circuit also held * * * that state-court decisions that unreasonably extend a legal principle from our precedent to a new context where it should not apply (or unreasonably refuse to extend a legal principle to a new context where it should apply) should be analyzed under § 2254(d)(1)'s "unreasonable application" clause. Although that holding may perhaps be correct, the classification does have some problems of precision. Just as it is sometimes difficult to distinguish a mixed question of law and fact from a question of fact, it will often be difficult to identify separately those state-court decisions that involve an unreasonable application of a legal principle (or an unreasonable failure to apply a legal principle) to a new context. Indeed, on the one hand, in some cases it will be hard to distinguish a decision involving an unreasonable extension of a legal principle from a decision involving an unreasonable application of law to facts. On the other hand, in many of the same cases it will also be difficult to distinguish a decision involving an unreasonable extension of a legal principle from a decision that "arrives at a conclusion opposite to that reached by this Court on a question of law." Today's case does not require us to decide how such "extension of legal principle" cases should be treated under § 2254(d)(1). For now it is sufficient to hold that when a state-court decision

---

＊   The legislative history of § 2254(d)(1) also supports this interpretation. See, *e.g.*, 142 Cong. Rec. 7799 (1996) (remarks of Sen. Specter) ("[U]nder the bill deference will be owed to State courts' decisions on the application of Federal law to the facts. Unless it is unreasonable, a State court's decision applying the law to the facts will be upheld") * * *.

unreasonably applies the law of this Court to the facts of a prisoner's case, a federal court applying § 2254(d)(1) may conclude that the state-court decision falls within that provision's "unreasonable application" clause.

B

There remains the task of defining what exactly qualifies as an "unreasonable application" of law under § 2254(d)(1). The Fourth Circuit held * * * that a state-court decision involves an "unreasonable application of . . . clearly established Federal law" only if the state court has applied federal law "in a manner that reasonable jurists would all agree is unreasonable." The placement of this additional overlay on the "unreasonable application" clause was erroneous. * * *

* * * Stated simply, a federal habeas court making the "unreasonable application" inquiry should ask whether the state court's application of clearly established federal law was objectively unreasonable. The federal habeas court should not transform the inquiry into a subjective one by resting its determination instead on the simple fact that at least one of the Nation's jurists has applied the relevant federal law in the same manner the state court did in the habeas petitioner's case. * * *

The term "unreasonable" is no doubt difficult to define. * * * For purposes of today's opinion, the most important point is that an *unreasonable* application of federal law is different from an *incorrect* application of federal law. Our opinions in Wright, for example, make that difference clear. [Justice O'Connor noted that Justice Thomas's opinion in Wright argued that Brown v. Allen did not indicate whether a habeas court must grant relief unless the state court's decision was deemed to be *correct*, as opposed to merely *reasonable*. Her own opinion in Wright maintained that "a state court's *incorrect* legal determination has [never] been allowed to stand because it was *reasonable*. * * *"] In § 2254(d)(1), Congress specifically used the word "unreasonable," and not a term like "erroneous" or "incorrect." * * *

Justice Stevens turns a blind eye to the debate in Wright because he finds no indication in § 2254(d)(1) itself that Congress was "directly influenced" by Justice Thomas' opinion in Wright. As Justice Stevens himself apparently recognizes, however, Congress need not mention a prior decision of this Court by name in a statute's text in order to adopt either a rule or a meaning given a certain term in that decision. In any event, * * * Wright is important for the light it sheds on § 2254(d)(1)'s requirement that a federal habeas court inquire into the reasonableness of a state court's application of clearly established federal law. * * * The Wright opinions confirm what § 2254(d)(1)'s language already makes clear—that an *unreasonable* application of federal law is different from an *incorrect* or *erroneous* application of federal law.

Throughout this discussion the meaning of the phrase "clearly established Federal law, as determined by the Supreme Court of the United States" has been put to the side. That statutory phrase refers to the holdings, as opposed to the dicta, of this Court's decisions as of the time of the relevant state-court decision. In this respect, the "clearly established Federal law" phrase bears only a slight connection to our Teague jurisprudence. With one caveat, whatever would qualify as an old rule under our Teague jurisprudence will constitute "clearly established Federal law, as determined by the Supreme Court of the United States" under § 2254(d)(1). The one caveat, as the statutory language makes clear, is that § 2254(d)(1) restricts the source of clearly established law to this Court's jurisprudence.

In sum, § 2254(d)(1) places a new constraint on the power of a federal habeas court * * * with respect to claims adjudicated on the merits in state court. Under § 2254(d)(1), the writ may issue only if * * * [(1)] the state court arrives at a conclusion opposite to that reached by this Court on a question of law or if the state court decides a case differently than this Court has on a set of materially indistinguishable facts[,] or (2) * * * the state court identifies the correct governing legal principle from this Court's decisions but unreasonably applies that principle to the facts of the prisoner's case.

III

Although I disagree with Justice Stevens concerning the standard we must apply under § 2254(d)(1) * * *, [the Court's discussion] in Parts III and IV is correct and * * * demonstrates the reasons that the Virginia Supreme Court's decision in Williams' case, even under the interpretation of § 2254(d)(1) I have set forth above, was both contrary to and involved an unreasonable application of our precedent. * * *

Accordingly, * * * I join Parts I, III, and IV of the Court's opinion and concur in the judgment of reversal.

■ CHIEF JUSTICE REHNQUIST, with whom JUSTICE SCALIA and JUSTICE THOMAS join, concurring in part and dissenting in part.

I agree with the Court's interpretation of 28 U.S.C. § 2254(d)(1) but disagree with its decision to grant habeas relief in this case.

[The Chief Justice argued that the Virginia Supreme Court had properly applied the prejudice standard of Strickland v. Washington; hence, the state court's decision was not contrary to clearly established precedent. Nor, he argued, was the decision an unreasonable application of Strickland, for given the strong evidence of the petitioner's dangerousness, the state court could reasonably have determined that evidence related to his childhood and intellectual disabilities would not have swayed the jury.]

Accordingly, I would hold that habeas relief is barred by 28 U.S.C. § 2254(d).

NOTE ON TERRY WILLIAMS V. TAYLOR AND 28 U.S.C. § 2254(d)(1)

(1) The Significance of the Terry Williams Decision and the Role of Standards Versus Rules in the Analysis. The situation in the Terry Williams case—in which a state court is found to have misunderstood the meaning of a Supreme Court precedent—is unusual. More often, a state court decision will properly recite the applicable doctrine and the petitioner's complaint will be about the doctrine's application to the facts. Accordingly, the "unreasonable application" clause will typically be the critical one in determining whether § 2254(d)(1) bars relief.

Consider in this regard Lockyer v. Andrade, 538 U.S. 63 (2003) (5–4), where the petitioner claimed that the imposition, under California's "three strikes" law, of two consecutive sentences of 25 years to life for each of two thefts of a handful of videotapes violated the Eighth Amendment's Cruel and Unusual Punishment Clause. Justice O'Connor's opinion stressed that the Court's decisions "in this area have not been a model of clarity" and "have not established a clear or consistent path for courts to follow." The only "clearly established" doctrine is a "gross disproportionality principle, the precise contours of which are unclear, applicable only in the 'exceedingly rare' and 'extreme' case." Concluding that the sentence at issue fell between two Supreme Court precedents, one invalidating a life sentence without parole and the other upholding a life sentence with the possibility of parole, the Court held that the state court's application of the gross disproportionality principle was not unreasonable.

If the "precise contours" of an established principle must be clear, § 2254(d)(1) is especially likely to preclude habeas relief when the petitioner invokes constitutional doctrine framed as a standard rather than as a rule. The Court suggested as much in Yarborough v. Alvarado, 541 U.S. 652 (2004), where the state courts had ruled there was no error in the admission of a confession because the suspect had not been "in custody" for purposes of the Miranda rules when he made his statement. Writing for the majority, Justice Kennedy held that § 2254(d)(1) barred relief, observing that "[a]pplying a general standard to a specific case can demand a substantial element of judgment. As a result, evaluating whether a rule application was unreasonable requires considering the rule's specificity. The more general the rule, the more leeway courts have in reaching outcomes in case-by-case determinations." He continued to emphasize that where "fair-minded jurists could disagree" over the application of a legal rule to the facts at bar, that is enough to conclude that the state court's decision was reasonable.[1]

(2) How "Clear" Is the Text of § 2254(d)(1)? Justice Souter once described AEDPA this way: "[I]n a world of silk purses and pigs' ears, the Act is not a silk purse of the art of statutory drafting." Lindh v. Murphy, 521 U.S. 320, 336 (1997). Is Justice O'Connor nonetheless correct that Congress intended to scale back dramatically the role of federal courts reviewing state

---

[1] Compare Justice Kennedy's pre-AEDPA approach in Wright v. West, 505 U.S. 277 (1992), quoted by Justice Stevens in his Terry Williams opinion, p. 1591, *supra.*

court convictions under § 2254(d)(1)? Is Justice O'Connor's criticism that Justice Stevens fails to assign independent significance to the phrases "contrary to" and "unreasonable application of" persuasive? Or is Justice Stevens's interpretation a better approximation of what Congress may have intended? *Cf.* Shapiro, *Continuity and Change in Statutory Interpretation*, 67 N.Y.U.L.Rev. 921, 925 (1992) (posting that "close questions of [statutory] construction should be resolved in favor of continuity and against change").[2]

(3) Section 2254(d)(1) in Operation. The hurdle interposed by § 2254(d)(1) has proved to be extremely difficult for petitioners to overcome. In Harrington v. Richter, 562 U.S. 86 (2011), the Court, after describing the § 2254(d) standard, stated: "If this standard is difficult to meet, that is because it was meant to be," as § 2254(d) was designed to be a " 'guard against extreme malfunctions in the state criminal justice systems,' not a substitute for ordinary error correction through appeal" (quoting Jackson v. Virginia, 443 U.S. 307, 332 n.5 (1979) (Stevens, J., concurring in judgment)). The Court added that to obtain relief, a petitioner must show that the state court ruling "was so lacking in justification that there was an error well understood and comprehended in existing law beyond any possibility for fairminded disagreement."[3]

In the wake of Terry Williams, the Court's decisions underscore the limited opportunity for relief afforded under § 2254(d)(1). For example, for the period spanning from the 2005 Term (the first for Chief Justice Roberts and Justice Alito) through the end of the 2015 Term, the Court decided 43 habeas cases in which section § 2254(d)(1) figured. In 37 of those cases, the Court ruled that § 2254(d)(1) barred relief.[4] Over time, the few cases in which the Court has held that § 2254(d)(1) did not bar relief have tended to involve death sentences.[5] Meanwhile, some Supreme Court opinions have expressed frustration with what the Justices view as disobedience of § 2254(d)(1) by the lower courts. See, *e.g.,* White v. Woodall, 572 U.S. 415, 417 (2014) (the Sixth Circuit "disregarded the limitations of 28 U.S.C. § 2254(d)—a provision of law that some federal judges find too confining, but that all federal judges must obey"); White v. Wheeler, 577 U.S. 73, 81 (2015) (per curiam) ("again

---

[2]   In support of Justice Stevens's minority position, Professor Vázquez contends that the weight of the legislative history and President Clinton's signing statement both strongly support the conclusion that AEDPA was not intended to alter prior de novo review applied to questions of federal law in collateral habeas corpus cases. Vázquez, *AEDPA as Forum Allocation: The Textual and Structural Case for Overruling Williams v. Taylor*, 56 Am.Crim.L.Rev. 1 (2019).

[3]   More recently in Brown v. Davenport, 596 U.S. 118 (2022), the Court declined relief under § 2254(d)(1) stating that "[e]ven if some fairminded jurist applying [the relevant clearly established law] could reach a different conclusion, we cannot say that every fairminded jurist must." How different in this standard from the Fourth Circuit's standard rejected by the Court in Terry Williams v. Taylor? (Recall the Fourth Circuit had interpreted § 2254(d)(1) as barring relief unless the state court "decided the question by interpreting or applying the relevant precedent in a manner that reasonable jurists would all agree is unreasonable.")

[4]   Overwhelmingly, these cases came to the Court from the Sixth and Ninth Circuits.

[5]   One of the very few examples in which the Court deemed § 2254(d)(1) satisfied is McWilliams v. Dunn, 582 U.S. 183 (2017). Reversing the Court of Appeals, the Court held, 5–4, that Alabama's provision of mental health assistance to a capital defendant "fell so dramatically short" of the requirements set forth in Ake v. Oklahoma, 470 U.S. 68 (1985) (holding that where certain threshold criteria are met, states must provide indigent defendants with access to a mental health expert to "assist in evaluation, preparation, and presentation of the defense"), that no deference was owed to a state court decision refusing relief to petitioner.

advis[ing] the Court of Appeals that the provisions of AEDPA apply with full force even when reviewing a conviction and sentence imposing the death penalty"); Mays v. Hines, 592 U.S. 385, 391 (2021) (per curiam) ("If [§ 2254(d)] means anything, it is that a federal court must carefully consider all the reasons and evidence supporting the state court's decision").

Several of the Court's opinions also posit that state court decisions involving claims generally reviewed deferentially are entitled to "double" deference under AEDPA. See, *e.g.,* Woods v. Etherton, 578 U.S. 113 (2016) (per curiam) (applying deference under § 2254(d)(1) in addition to Strickland's "strong" presumption that counsel provided adequate representation); Wheeler, *supra* (applying "doubly deferential" review under AEDPA to claim challenging trial judge's decision to excuse a juror for cause). *Cf.* Shinn v. Kayer, 592 U.S. 111 (2020) (per curiam) (because " 'the Strickland standard is a general standard, a state court has even more latitude to reasonably determine that a defendant has not satisfied that standard' ") (quoting Knowles v. Mirzayance, 556 U.S. 111, 123 (2009)).[6]

Recall the criticism of Teague v. Lane for having defined new law so broadly that it reduced the incentive for state courts faithfully to enforce federal constitutional standards. How strong is the incentive provided by habeas review in light of the Court's interpretation of § 2254(d)(1)?[7]

(4) The Constitutionality of the Court's Interpretation. Justice Stevens's opinion in the Terry Williams case states that a deferential standard of review would be so extraordinary that Congress would surely have spoken with greater clarity than it did in § 2254(d)(1) had it intended such a standard. That statement, together with his citation to Marbury v. Madison, carries a suggestion that the statute, as interpreted by the majority, raises constitutional concerns. An article predating the Terry Williams decision, Liebman & Ryan, *"Some Effectual Power": The Quantity and Quality of Decisionmaking Required of Article III Courts*, 98 Colum.L.Rev. 696 (1998), contends that § 2254(d)(1) would violate Article III if read to require habeas courts to defer to a state court decision that was erroneous when rendered. In the authors' view, Article III requires that a federal court given jurisdiction by Congress be able, *inter alia*, (1) to decide federal questions "based on the whole supreme law"—an obligation that extends to reviewing de novo all "mixed" questions of law (*i.e.,* application of

---

[6]   Another example may be found in the harmless error context. In Brown v. Davenport, 596 U.S. 118 (2022), the Court held, 6–3, that where a state court has reviewed a petitioner's constitutional claim and found the alleged error to be harmless, a federal habeas court reviewing the state court's decision may not grant relief unless it finds both that the error in question was not harmless under the test adopted in Brecht v. Abrahamson, 507 U.S. 619 (1993), and that the habeas petitioner satisfies § 2254(d). (For discussion of Brecht, see p. 1551, *supra*.)

[7]   With AEDPA dramatically limiting the opportunities for relief available to habeas petitioners, some scholars have called upon the Supreme Court to take more criminal appeals on direct review. See, *e.g.*, Vázquez, note 2, *supra*. Some jurists, meanwhile, have lamented that the standards governing most habeas cases are statutory, as opposed to judge-made, with the former far more difficult to adjust as circumstances warrant. See Fletcher, *Symposium Introduction*, 107 Calif.L.Rev. 999 (2019).

In the absence of expanded direct review by the Court of state criminal convictions, AEDPA's inflexible deferential standards of review give state courts the last word on most questions of federal constitutional law that arise in state criminal cases.

legal principles to the facts) but not questions of historical fact—and (2) to make its judgment remedially effectual. On this view, the majority's interpretation of § 2254(d)(1) in Terry Williams is unconstitutional. The majority, of course, implicitly rejects any such constitutional objection.

Scheidegger, *Habeas Corpus, Relitigation, and the Legislative Power*, 98 Colum.L.Rev. 888 (1998), notes some tensions between Liebman & Ryan's approach and, *inter alia*, (1) the decision in Teague; (2) the qualified immunity doctrine in constitutional tort actions, which precludes damage awards when an officer acted unconstitutionally but did not violate "clearly established law"; (3) the Court's occasional practice of limiting a grant of certiorari to particular issues, effectively deferring entirely to the state court's determination of other issues; and (4) the res judicata doctrine, which limits the power of federal courts to relitigate constitutional questions that state courts may have decided incorrectly.[8]

Do limitations on the judicial power exercised on collateral review stand on a different constitutional footing from similar limitations on direct review? *Cf.* Steiker, *Habeas Exceptionalism*, 78 Tex.L.Rev. 1703 (2000). Do self-imposed limitations on judicial power like those in Teague stand on a different footing from limitations on judicial review imposed by Congress? See Note, *Powers of Congress and the Court Regarding the Availability and Scope of Review*, 114 Harv.L.Rev. 1551 (2001). *Cf.* United States v. Klein, 80 U.S. (13 Wall.) 128 (1871), p. 434, *supra*; Dickerson v. United States, 530 U.S. 428 (2000) (holding that Miranda rule was constitutionally based and could not be overruled by legislative act). In one early assessment of § 2254(d), Judge Easterbrook rejected a Suspension Clause challenge and concluded that § 2254(d)(1) "does no more than regulate relief." Lindh v. Murphy, 96 F.3d 856 (7th Cir.1996) (en banc).[9] Is that right?

(5) Section 2254(d) and Summary State Court Decisions. In Harrington v. Richter, 562 U.S. 86 (2011), the Supreme Court considered the application of § 2254(d) to summary state court decisions that deny federal constitutional claims on the merits without explanation. After Richter's conviction became final on direct review, he petitioned directly to the California Supreme Court for a state writ of habeas corpus. That court denied the petition in a one sentence summary order. When Richter's federal

---

[8]   On occasion, the Supreme Court has also limited its review of state court judgments to determining whether the state court identified the correct constitutional standard and whether in light of the evidence its application of that standard "was within the realm of permissible judgment." See, *e.g.*, Container Corp. of America v. Franchise Tax Bd., 463 U.S. 159 (1983).

[9]   Judge Easterbrook's majority opinion continued: "Regulating relief is a far cry from limiting the interpretive power of the courts * * *. Every day, courts decline to disturb judgments that they *know* are wrong." Dissenting, Judge Ripple contended that any deference required under § 2254(d)(1) is problematic because that would mean that "the federal court is free to have its own opinion of what federal law requires, but it must grant or deny the writ on the basis of another non-federal tribunal's view. Federal courts, however, must not merely expound on the cases before them; they must decide them."

For separate discussion of whether § 2254(d) is unconstitutional insofar as it requires determination of the relevant constitutional law by reference only to Supreme Court decisions rather than to all federal law, see Caminker, *Allocating the Judicial Power in a "Unified Judiciary"*, 78 Tex.L.Rev. 1513 (2000); Jackson, *Introduction: Congressional Control of Jurisdiction and the Future of the Federal Courts—Opposition, Agreement, and Hierarchy*, 86 Geo.L.J. 2445, 2470 (1998).

habeas corpus case reached the Supreme Court, it ruled, without dissent, that the California Supreme Court's order was an adjudication on the merits within the meaning of § 2254(d). Justice Kennedy's opinion stressed that if § 2254(d) applied only when the state court provided a statement of reasons, state judiciaries could be prevented from concentrating resources on cases where opinions are most needed. He noted that the California Supreme Court disposes of nearly 10,000 cases annually, including more than 3,400 original habeas petitions. Proceeding to apply § 2254(d), the Court said that a habeas court must determine what arguments or theories could have supported the state court's decision, and then ask whether fair-minded jurists could disagree about whether those arguments or theories are inconsistent with the holding in a prior Supreme Court decision.

In Johnson v. Williams, 568 U.S. 289 (2013), the Court extended Harrington. In Williams, the defendant had argued on appeal that the trial court's discharge of a particular juror violated both a California statute and the Sixth Amendment right to jury trial. In the course of rejecting the defendant's claims, the state appellate court's discussion never expressly stated that it was deciding the Sixth Amendment issue. On habeas review, the Court of Appeals held that § 2254(d) did not apply, deeming it "obvious" that the state appellate court had "overlooked or disregarded" the Sixth Amendment claim. The Supreme Court reversed. After noting that "Richter itself concerned a state-court order that did not address *any* of the defendant's claims," the Court said that there was "no reason why the Richter presumption should not also apply when a state-court opinion addresses some but not all of a defendant's claims." The Court noted several reasons why a state court may not expressly address one of many claims raised on appeal and refused to adopt an irrebuttable presumption that the state court must have rejected the federal claim on the merits.[10]

The Court returned to these questions in Wilson v. Sellers, 584 U.S. 122 (2018). After a Georgia trial court rejected Wilson's post-conviction challenge to the effectiveness of his counsel during the sentencing phase of his capital trial, the Georgia Supreme Court summarily denied his application for a certificate of probable cause to appeal. Writing for the Court, Justice Breyer concluded that in applying § 2254(d), which requires deferring to state court decisions "on the merits," a federal habeas court should " 'look through' the unexplained decision to the last related state court decision that does provide a relevant rationale," and "presume that the unexplained decision adopted the same reasoning." The Court also held, however, that this default proposition may be overcome where a party can demonstrate that the summary affirmance "relied or most likely did rely on different grounds than

---

[10]   Writing for the Court, Justice Alito suggested that when a petitioner seeks relief under both state and federal law, if the state standard is less protective than, or very different from, the federal standard, the presumption may be rebutted, either by the petitioner (in order to obtain de novo federal review) or by the state (in order to show that the claim was not decided on the merits at all and hence might have been forfeited). But § 2254(d) does not apply, he stressed, if the federal claim was rejected because of "sheer inadvertence."

Concurring in the judgment in Williams, Justice Scalia argued that the presumption should only be overcome by a showing, based on the text of the state court order (or when ambiguous, based on standard state practice) that the state court did not purport to decide the federal issue.

the lower state court's decision, such as alternative grounds for affirmance that were briefed or argued to the state supreme court or obvious in the record it reviewed."[11]

Dissenting for three Justices, Justice Gorsuch argued that the presumption adopted by the majority was at odds with the presumption applied in summary dispositions of federal court decisions, which posits that summary affirmances may be construed solely as approving of a lower court's judgment and not its reasoning. See Comptroller v. Wynne, 575 U.S. 542 (2015). Nonetheless, Justice Gorsuch concluded that regardless of which default rule controls, the majority's invitation to federal habeas courts in appropriate cases to review materials beyond the last reasoned state court decision opens the door to the rule governing the treatment of summary federal court decisions. Is Justice Gorsuch right, or is the majority's default presumption likely to govern in most cases given the amount of labor and potential speculation that could be involved where a federal habeas court tries to look behind state court judgments? And, in contrast to Justice Gorsuch's suggestion, can it be said that the majority's presumption, which enables state courts to clarify where their decisions do not conform with the last reasoned opinion, respects the state courts? *Cf.* Michigan v. Long, 463 U.S. 1032 (1983), p. 656, *supra.*

(6) When Must the Law Have Been Clearly Established? In Shoop v. Hill, 586 U.S. 45 (2019) (per curiam), the Court unanimously held that "clearly established law" for purposes of § 2254(d) does not encompass Supreme Court decisions rendered after the date on which the petitioner's conviction became final, while vacating a court of appeals decision granting habeas relief that "lean[ed] heavily" on such a decision.

Earlier, in Greene v. Fisher, 565 U.S. 34 (2011) (9–0), the Court ruled that "clearly established law," for purposes of § 2254(d), does not include Supreme Court decisions announced *after* the last decision on the merits in state court but *before* the defendant's conviction became final on direct review (when opportunity for Supreme Court review on direct has concluded). A petitioner's claim that relies on such decisions would not be "new" under (and therefore would not be barred by) Teague v. Lane, but in Greene, the Court stressed that the text of § 2254(d) focuses on the law in effect exclusively during state court proceedings.[12]

(7) The Different Standard Governing Review of State Post-Conviction Proceedings on Appeal. In the 2018 Term, a divided Court remanded for reconsideration a capital case on appeal from state post-conviction proceedings after having previously reversed the federal court of

---

[11] Justice Breyer drew support from the Court's earlier decision in Ylst v. Nunnemaker, 501 U.S. 797 (1991), p. 671, *supra,* holding that a federal habeas court should presume that where the last reasoned state court decision in a case determined that a federal claim had been procedurally defaulted, that reasoning similarly informed any summary affirmances by higher state courts.

[12] The Court said that the petitioner's predicament was one of his own creation because he could have sought certiorari in the U.S. Supreme Court—which surely would have granted the petition and vacated the state court's judgment—or could have filed a state post-conviction petition. Note, however, that defendants have no constitutional right to counsel before the U.S. Supreme Court or in state post-conviction proceedings.

appeals' grant of relief to the same petitioner based on similar claims. See Madison v. Alabama, 586 U.S. 265 (2019) ("Madison II"); see also Dunn v. Madison, 583 U.S. 10 (2018) (per curiam). Explaining the difference in outcomes with respect to the claims, which turned on the application of Ford v. Wainwright, 477 U.S. 399 (1986), and Panetti v. Quarterman, 551 U.S. 930 (2007), to a capital defendant suffering from dementia, the Court majority emphasized that in Madison II, "[b]ecause the case now comes to us on direct review of the state court's decision (rather than in a habeas proceeding), AEDPA's deferential standard no longer governs."

Perhaps at least in part because the review of state post-conviction proceedings on appeal is not subject to AEDPA's standards of review, recent Terms have witnessed an uptick in the number of cases that the Court has reviewed in this posture, notwithstanding earlier decisions stating that direct review of state post-conviction cases is disfavored.[13]

NOTE ON § 2254(d)(1) AND TEAGUE

(1) The Relationship of § 2254(d)(1) to Teague. Section 2254(d)(1) does not by its terms override the judge-made doctrine of Teague v. Lane and the two pose "distinct" inquiries. Horn v. Banks, 536 U.S. 266, 272 (2002) (per curiam). Ordinarily, however, § 2254(d)(1)'s limitation on review will be the key question, because that limitation is broader than the limitation established in Teague. But unlike Teague, § 2254(d)(1) applies only when a habeas claim was adjudicated in state court. Cases in which there was no state court adjudication will rarely go far in federal court: if state remedies remain, the petitioner will not have satisfied the exhaustion requirement, see pp. 1662–1665, *infra*, while if the petitioner failed properly to present the federal claim in the state courts, procedural default will ordinarily bar habeas review, see pp. 1631–1657, *infra*. But where there is neither a state court determination on the merits nor a procedural barrier to the exercise of habeas jurisdiction, the Teague doctrine applies. See Banks, *supra*.[1]

(2) A Threshold Issue? Justice O'Connor's opinion in Teague stated that "newness" is a threshold issue that must be resolved before a federal court may reach the constitutional merits. See p. 1581, *supra*. A parallel issue that arises under § 2254(d)(1) is whether its standard poses a threshold inquiry.

In Lockyer v. Andrade, 538 U.S. 63 (2003), p. 1601, *supra*, the Supreme Court rejected the assertion that federal habeas courts must first review the state court decision de novo before applying § 2254(d)'s standard of review, stating: "AEDPA does not require a federal habeas court to adopt any one methodology in deciding the only question that matters under § 2254(d)(1)— whether a state court decision is contrary to, or involved an unreasonable

---

[13] See Ahdout, *Direct Collateral Review*, 121 Colum.L.Rev. 159 (2021) (documenting the rise of Supreme Court review of state post-conviction cases and lauding that it "restores federal judicial primacy in developing constitutional law" in the criminal justice arena).

[1] Banks also held that "in addition to performing any analysis required by AEDPA, a federal court considering a habeas petition must conduct a threshold Teague analysis when the issue is properly raised by the state."

application of, clearly established federal law." Then, in Berghuis v. Thompkins, 560 U.S. 370 (2010), the Court reached the merits of a habeas claim and rejected it. It thereafter concluded that because "[t]he state court's decision rejecting Thompkins's Miranda claim was * * * correct under *de novo* review," it was "therefore necessarily reasonable under the more deferential AEDPA standard of review" (citing 28 U.S.C. § 2254(d)). Dissenting, Justice Sotomayor (joined by Justices Stevens, Ginsburg, and Breyer) disagreed with the Court's understanding of Miranda, and in addition complained that "[t]he broad rules the Court announces today are also troubling because they are unnecessary to decide this case, which is governed by the deferential standard of review set forth in the [AEDPA]."

Is there a systemic interest in having the Court resolve unsettled legal questions de novo in § 2254(d)(1) cases? For additional discussion, see pp. 1311–1328, *supra* (exploring qualified immunity doctrine).

(3) The Teague Exceptions and § 2254(d)(1). Unlike the Teague doctrine, the text of § 2254(d)(1) recognizes no exceptions. Suppose a state court "reasonably" decides that a petitioner's conduct is not constitutionally protected, but the Supreme Court later decides (in a different case) that the Constitution does protect the conduct in question. As the case fits Teague's first exception, Teague would not bar relief, but would § 2254(d)(1)?[2]

In Whorton v. Bockting, 549 U.S. 406 (2007), the Ninth Circuit had ruled that in enacting § 2254(d), Congress impliedly preserved Teague's two exceptions; a contrary interpretation, the Ninth Circuit suggested, would raise serious constitutional questions. The Supreme Court unanimously reversed the judgment, concluding that the new rule in question did not fall within Teague's second exception; the Court therefore had no need to decide whether § 2254(d) implicitly incorporates Teague's exceptions.[3] Subsequently, in the next principal case, Montgomery v. Louisiana, 577 U.S. 190 (2016), the Court held that the Constitution requires a *state* post-conviction court to grant relief based on new law that falls within Teague's first exception. How Montgomery intersects with § 2254(d) remains an open question.

(4) AEDPA and the Meaning of "Made Retroactively Applicable to Cases on Collateral Review." One puzzle under AEDPA involves the interaction of § 2254(d)(1) with other provisions added by the same Act. Some provisions of AEDPA, after setting forth procedural restrictions on the exercise of habeas jurisdiction, create exceptions to those restrictions when the petitioner relies on a new constitutional rule that the Supreme Court has "made" retroactive to cases on collateral review. See, *e.g.*, § 2244(b)(2)(A) (limits on successive petitions), p. 1609, *infra*; § 2254(e)(2)(a)(i) (availability of federal evidentiary hearings), p. 1629, *infra*. See also § 2244(d)(1)(C) (statute of limitations provision, requiring that the provision have been made retroactively applicable on collateral review without specifying that the Supreme Court itself must have done so), p. 1548, *supra*. But given that

---

[2]   Recall that in the nineteenth century, when post-conviction habeas relief was more limited, it embraced challenges to the constitutionality of the statute under which the petitioner was convicted. See Ex parte Siebold, 100 U.S. 371 (1879), p. 1556, *supra*.

[3]   See also Greene v. Fisher, 565 U.S. 34 (2011), p. 1606, *supra*.

§ 2254(d)(1) generally bars habeas courts from relying on new law, when (and how) will it be the case that the Supreme Court, or any federal habeas court, has made new law retroactive on habeas review? Might it be when a habeas case implicates the Teague exceptions—and then only on the assumption either that § 2254(d)(1) does not apply or that it implicitly recognizes the Teague exceptions?

The Court faced this question in Tyler v. Cain, 533 U.S. 656 (2001). After Tyler's federal habeas petition was denied, he filed a second petition, contending that the jury instruction in his case on proof beyond a reasonable doubt was substantively identical to one later invalidated in Cage v. Louisiana, 498 U.S. 39 (1990). Under § 2244(b)(2)(A), in order to raise this claim in a second federal habeas petition, Tyler had to demonstrate that the ruling in Cage had been "made retroactive to cases on collateral review by the Supreme Court."

The Court (per Justice Thomas) held that Tyler could not make that showing. The Court concluded that § 2244(b)(2)(A)'s requirement was not satisfied by the Court's later holding, in Sullivan v. Louisiana, 508 U.S. 275 (1993), that a "Cage error" is "structural" in the sense that it is not amenable to harmless error analysis and thus always invalidates a conviction.[4] Although the Court acknowledged that it could "make a rule retroactive over the course of two cases" without actually saying so through the logical implications of a "combination of holdings" that "dictate" the retroactivity of the new rule, it held that the Sullivan decision had not done so with respect to Cage by the time of Tyler's habeas petition.

Justice O'Connor joined the Court's opinion but added in a concurrence that, as to the first Teague exception, it "necessarily follows" from the very decision declaring the new rule that it has been "made" retroactive under Teague. She contrasted the (now eliminated) second exception, which, in her view, necessarily calls for separate a judgment regarding retroactivity.

Dissenting for four Justices, Justice Breyer argued that "[t]he Court made Cage retroactive" through the conjunction of Teague and Sullivan. He further complained that under the majority's approach, "the only way in which this Court can make a rule such as Cage's retroactive is to repeat its Sullivan reasoning in a case triggered by a prisoner's filing a first habeas petition * * * or in some other case that presents the issue in a posture that allows such language to have the status of a 'holding.' "[5]

---

[4]   Here, the Court held that structural error does not necessarily fall within the second Teague exception for bedrock procedural requirements. The Court subsequently eliminated the second exception to Teague in Edwards v. Vannoy, 593 U.S. 255 (2021), discussed at p. 1583, *supra*.

[5]   Note that even this route is made more difficult still by a subsequent decision interpreting the statute of limitations. In Dodd v. United States, 545 U.S. 353 (2005) (5–4), a § 2255 action brought by a petitioner in federal custody, the Court held that the one-year period from initial recognition by the Supreme Court of a new constitutional right, retroactively applicable to cases on collateral review, runs from the date on which the Supreme Court recognizes the new right, rather than the date on which the right is made retroactive. The language of § 2255(f) (governing timeliness of motions brought by those in federal custody) does not differ materially from that in § 2244(d)(1) (governing petitions brought by those in state custody).

INTRODUCTORY NOTE: RETROACTIVITY AND THE CONSTITUTIONAL OBLIGATIONS OF STATE AND FEDERAL COURTS IN COLLATERAL REVIEW PROCEEDINGS

In Montgomery v. Louisiana, below, the Court explored the retroactive application of new constitutional holdings in state court post-conviction proceedings. As indicated in the Note following the case, the decision likely bears significantly on federal habeas corpus proceedings, § 2254(d)(1), and the questions raised in Tyler v. Cain.

Montgomery v. Louisiana
577 U.S. 190 (2016).
Certiorari to the Supreme Court of Louisiana.

■ JUSTICE KENNEDY delivered the opinion of the Court.

This is another case in a series of decisions involving the sentencing of offenders who were juveniles when their crimes were committed. * * *

I

Petitioner is Henry Montgomery. In 1963, Montgomery killed Charles Hurt, a deputy sheriff in East Baton Rouge, Louisiana. Montgomery was 17 years old at the time of the crime. * * *

[After his first conviction and death sentence was reversed on appeal, Montgomery was retried and a jury found him "guilty without capital punishment." Under Louisiana law, Montgomery automatically received a life sentence without possibility of parole. At the time, therefore,] Montgomery had no opportunity to present mitigation evidence to justify a less severe sentence. That evidence might have included Montgomery's young age at the time of the crime; expert testimony regarding his limited capacity for foresight, self-discipline, and judgment; and his potential for rehabilitation. Montgomery, now 69 years old, has spent almost his entire life in prison.

Almost 50 years after Montgomery was first taken into custody, this Court decided Miller v. Alabama, 567 U.S. 460 (2012). Miller held that mandatory life without parole for juvenile homicide offenders violates the Eighth Amendment's prohibition on " 'cruel and unusual punishments.' " *Id.*, at 479. * * * Miller required that sentencing courts consider a child's "diminished culpability and heightened capacity for change" before condemning him or her to die in prison. Although Miller did not foreclose a sentencer's ability to impose life without parole on a juvenile, the Court explained that a lifetime in prison is a disproportionate sentence for all but the rarest of children, those whose crimes reflect " 'irreparable corruption.' " (quoting Roper v. Simmons, 543 U.S. 551, 573 (2005)).

After this Court issued its decision in Miller, Montgomery sought collateral review of his mandatory life-without parole sentence. [One form of collateral review available under Louisiana law "allows a prisoner to bring a collateral attack on his or her sentence by filing a motion to correct an illegal sentence." The relevant state statute provides that "[a]n illegal sentence may be corrected at any time by the court that imposed the sentence."]

Louisiana's collateral review courts will * * * consider a motion to correct an illegal sentence based on a decision of this Court holding that the Eighth Amendment to the Federal Constitution prohibits a punishment for a type of crime or a class of offenders. [Here, however, the trial court denied Montgomery's motion for collateral relief, holding that Miller was not retroactive on collateral review. The Louisiana Supreme Court then denied his application for a supervisory writ.]

II

[The Court first addressed the question whether it had jurisdiction to decide the case.]

[The argument against jurisdiction proceeds as follows:] [A] State is under no obligation to give a new rule of constitutional law retroactive effect in its own collateral review proceedings. As those proceedings are created by state law and under the State's plenary control * * *, it is for state courts to define applicable principles of retroactivity. * * *

If, however, the Constitution establishes a rule and requires that the rule have retroactive application, then a state court's refusal to give the rule retroactive effect is reviewable by this Court. Cf. Griffith v. Kentucky, 479 U.S. 314, 328 (1987) (holding that on direct review, a new constitutional rule must be applied retroactively "to all cases, state or federal"). States may not disregard a controlling, constitutional command in their own courts. See Martin v. Hunter's Lessee, 1 Wheat. 304, 340–341, 344 (1816). * * *

Justice O'Connor's plurality opinion in Teague v. Lane, 489 U.S. 288 (1989), set forth a framework for retroactivity in cases on federal collateral review. * * *

* * * [The argument against jurisdiction rests on the proposition that] Teague was an interpretation of the federal habeas statute, not a constitutional command; and so, the argument proceeds, Teague's retroactivity holding simply has no application in a State's own collateral review proceedings. * * *

* * * [But] Teague originated in a federal, not state, habeas proceeding; so it had no particular reason to discuss whether any part of its holding was required by the Constitution in addition to the federal habeas statute. * * *

* * * The Court now holds that when a new substantive rule of constitutional law controls the outcome of a case, the Constitution

requires state collateral review courts to give retroactive effect to that rule. Teague's conclusion establishing the retroactivity of new substantive rules is best understood as resting upon constitutional premises. That constitutional command is, like all federal law, binding on state courts. This holding is limited to Teague's first exception for substantive rules; the constitutional status of Teague's exception for watershed rules of procedure need not be addressed here.

* * * Justice Harlan defined substantive constitutional rules as "those that place, as a matter of constitutional interpretation, certain kinds of primary, private individual conduct beyond the power of the criminal law-making authority to proscribe." Mackey [v. United States, 401 U.S. 667,] 692 [(1971) (opinion concurring in judgments in part and dissenting in part)]. In Penry v. Lynaugh, decided four months after Teague, the Court recognized that "the first exception set forth in Teague should be understood to cover not only rules forbidding criminal punishment of certain primary conduct but also rules prohibiting a certain category of punishment for a class of defendants because of their status or offense." 492 U.S. 302, 330 (1989). Penry explained that Justice Harlan's first exception spoke "in terms of substantive categorical guarantees accorded by the Constitution, regardless of the procedures followed." *Id.*, at 329. Whether a new rule bars States from proscribing certain conduct or from inflicting a certain punishment, "[i]n both cases, the Constitution itself deprives the State of the power to impose a certain penalty." *Id.*, at 330.

Substantive rules, then, set forth categorical constitutional guarantees that place certain criminal laws and punishments altogether beyond the State's power to impose. It follows that when a State enforces a proscription or penalty barred by the Constitution, the resulting conviction or sentence is, by definition, unlawful. [Here, the Court contrasted procedural rules and observed that "a trial conducted under a procedure found to be unconstitutional in a later case does not, as a general matter, have the automatic consequence of invalidating a defendant's conviction or sentence."]

By holding that new substantive rules are, indeed, retroactive, Teague continued a long tradition of giving retroactive effect to constitutional rights that go beyond procedural guarantees. See Mackey, *supra*, at 692–693 (opinion of Harlan, J.) ("[T]he writ has historically been available for attacking convictions on [substantive] grounds"). Before Brown v. Allen, 344 U.S. 443 (1953), "federal courts would never consider the merits of a constitutional claim if the habeas petitioner had a fair opportunity to raise his arguments in the original proceeding." Desist v. United States, 394 U.S. 244, 261 (1969) (Harlan, J., dissenting). Even in the pre-1953 era of restricted federal habeas, however, an exception was made "when the habeas petitioner attacked the constitutionality of the state statute under which he had been convicted. Since, in this situation, the State had no power to proscribe the conduct for which the petitioner was imprisoned, it could not constitutionally insist that he remain in jail." *Id.*, at 261, n.2 (Harlan, J., dissenting). * * *

* * * It follows, as a general principle, that a court has no authority to leave in place a conviction or sentence that violates a substantive rule, regardless of whether the conviction or sentence became final before the rule was announced.

[The Court next conceded that the precedents "do not directly control the question the Court now answers for the first time," though they "have important bearing on the analysis necessary in this case."]

* * * There is no grandfather clause that permits States to enforce punishments the Constitution forbids. To conclude otherwise would undercut the Constitution's substantive guarantees. * * *

If a State may not constitutionally insist that a prisoner remain in jail on federal habeas review, it may not constitutionally insist on the same result in its own postconviction proceedings. Under the Supremacy Clause of the Constitution, state collateral review courts have no greater power than federal habeas courts to mandate that a prisoner continue to suffer punishment barred by the Constitution. If a state collateral proceeding is open to a claim controlled by federal law, the state court "has a duty to grant the relief that federal law requires." Yates v. Aiken, 484 U.S. 211, 218 (1988). * * *

As a final point, it must be noted that the retroactive application of substantive rules does not implicate a State's weighty interests in ensuring the finality of convictions and sentences. Teague warned against the intrusiveness of "*continually* forc[ing] the States to marshal resources in order to keep in prison defendants whose trials and appeals conformed to then-existing constitutional standards." 489 U.S., at 310. This concern has no application in the realm of substantive rules, for no resources marshaled by a State could preserve a conviction or sentence that the Constitution deprives the State of power to impose. See Mackey, 401 U.S., at 693 (opinion of Harlan, J.) ("There is little societal interest in permitting the criminal process to rest at a point where it ought properly never to repose"). * * *

III

* * * Miller announced a substantive rule that is retroactive in cases on collateral review.

The "foundation stone" for Miller's analysis was this Court's line of precedent holding certain punishments disproportionate when applied to juveniles. 567 U.S., at 470, n.4. Those cases include Graham v. Florida, [560 U.S. 48 (2010)], which held that the Eighth Amendment bars life without parole for juvenile nonhomicide offenders, and Roper v. Simmons, 543 U.S. 551, which held that the Eighth Amendment prohibits capital punishment for those under the age of 18 at the time of their crimes. * * *

[The Court observed that Miller "took as its starting premise the principle established in Roper and Graham that 'children are constitutionally different from adults for purposes of sentencing.'" It next noted that Miller "made clear that 'appropriate occasions for sentencing juveniles to this harshest possible penalty will be uncommon.'"]

Miller, then, did more than require a sentencer to consider a juvenile offender's youth before imposing life without parole; it established that the penological justifications for life without parole collapse in light of "the distinctive attributes of youth." [567 U.S.], at 472. Even if a court considers a child's age before sentencing him or her to a lifetime in prison, that sentence still violates the Eighth Amendment for a child whose crime reflects "'unfortunate yet transient immaturity.'" *Id.*, at 479 (quoting Roper, 543 U.S., at 573). * * * [Miller therefore] rendered life without parole an unconstitutional penalty for "a class of defendants because of their status"—that is, juvenile offenders whose crimes reflect the transient immaturity of youth. Penry, 492 U.S., at 330. As a result, Miller announced a substantive rule of constitutional law. Like other substantive rules, Miller is retroactive because it "'necessarily carr[ies] a significant risk that a defendant'"—here, the vast majority of juvenile offenders—"'faces a punishment that the law cannot impose upon him.'" Schriro v. Summerlin, 542 U.S. 348, 352 (2004) (quoting Bousley v. United States, 523 U.S. 614, 620 (1998)).

Louisiana nonetheless argues that Miller is procedural because it did not place any punishment beyond the State's power to impose; it instead required sentencing courts to take children's age into account before condemning them to die in prison. * * * Miller, it is true, did not bar a punishment for all juvenile offenders, as the Court did in Roper or Graham. Miller did bar life without parole, however, for all but the rarest of juvenile offenders, those whose crimes reflect permanent incorrigibility. For that reason, Miller is no less substantive than are Roper and Graham. * * *

To be sure, Miller's holding has a procedural component. * * * There are instances in which a substantive change in the law must be attended by a procedure that enables a prisoner to show that he falls within the category of persons whom the law may no longer punish. * * *

The procedure Miller prescribes is no different. * * *

[The Court next defended Miller's decision not to require trial courts to make findings of fact regarding a child's incorrigibility: "When a new substantive rule of constitutional law is established, this Court is careful to limit the scope of any attendant procedural requirement to avoid intruding more than necessary upon the States' sovereign administration of their criminal justice systems."]

Giving Miller retroactive effect, moreover, does not require States to relitigate sentences, let alone convictions, in every case where a juvenile offender received mandatory life without parole. A State may remedy a Miller violation by permitting juvenile homicide offenders to be considered for parole, rather than by resentencing them. See, *e.g.*, Wyo.Stat.Ann. § 6–10–301(c) (2013) (juvenile homicide offenders eligible for parole after 25 years). * * *

Extending parole eligibility to juvenile offenders does not impose an onerous burden on the States, nor does it disturb the finality of state convictions. Those prisoners who have shown an inability to reform will continue to serve life sentences. * * *

* * * In light of what this Court has said in Roper, Graham, and Miller about how children are constitutionally different from adults in their level of culpability, however, prisoners like Montgomery must be given the opportunity to show their crime did not reflect irreparable corruption; and, if it did not, their hope for some years of life outside prison walls must be restored.

The judgment of the Supreme Court of Louisiana is reversed, and the case is remanded for further proceedings not inconsistent with this opinion.

It is so ordered.

■ JUSTICE SCALIA, with whom JUSTICE THOMAS and JUSTICE ALITO join, dissenting.*

The Court has no jurisdiction to decide this case, and the decision it arrives at is wrong. I respectfully dissent.

I. Jurisdiction

* * * [A] majority of this Court, eager to reach the merits of this case, resolves the question of our jurisdiction by deciding that the Constitution *requires* state postconviction courts to adopt Teague's exception for so-called "substantive" new rules and to provide state-law remedies for the violations of those rules to prisoners whose sentences long ago became final. This conscription into federal service of state postconviction courts is nothing short of astonishing.

A

* * * Neither Teague nor its exceptions are constitutionally compelled. Unlike today's majority, the Teague-era Court understood that cases on collateral review are fundamentally different from those pending on direct review because of "considerations of finality in the judicial process." Shea v. Louisiana, 470 U.S. 51, 59–60 (1985). That line of finality demarcating the constitutionally required rule in Griffith from the habeas rule in Teague supplies the answer to the not-so-difficult question whether a state postconviction court must remedy the violation of a new substantive rule: No. A state court need only apply the law as it existed at the time a defendant's conviction and sentence became final.

---

* [Ed.] This dissent was Justice Scalia's final opinion.

See Griffith, *supra*, at 322. And once final, "a new rule cannot reopen a door already closed." James B. Beam Distilling Co. v. Georgia, 501 U.S. 529, 541 (1991) (opinion of Souter, J.). Any relief a prisoner might receive in a state court after finality is a matter of grace, not constitutional prescription.

B

* * * [T]he Supremacy Clause cannot possibly answer the question before us here. It only elicits another question: What federal law is supreme? Old or new? The majority's champion, Justice Harlan, said the old rules apply for federal habeas review of a state-court conviction: "[T]he habeas court need only apply the constitutional standards that prevailed at the time the original proceedings took place," Desist, 394 U.S., at 263 (dissenting opinion), for a state court cannot "toe the constitutional mark" that does not yet exist, Mackey, 401 U.S., at 687 (opinion of Harlan, J.). Following his analysis, we have clarified time and again—recently in Greene v. Fisher, 565 U.S. 34, 38–40 (2011)—that *federal* habeas courts are to review state-court decisions against the law and factual record that existed at the time the decisions were made. "Section 2254(d)(1) [of the federal habeas statute is written] in the past tense * * *. This backward-looking language requires an examination of the state-court decision at the time it was made." Cullen v. Pinholster, 563 U.S. 170, 181–182 (2011). * * *

* * * Until today, no federal court was *constitutionally obliged* to grant relief for the past violation of a newly announced substantive rule. Until today, it was Congress's prerogative to do away with Teague's exceptions altogether. Indeed, we had left unresolved the question whether Congress had already done that when it amended a section of the habeas corpus statute to add backward-looking language governing the review of state-court decisions [in] § 2254(d)(1); Greene, 565 U.S. at 39, n. A maxim shown to be more relevant to this case, by the analysis that the majority omitted, is this: The Supremacy Clause does not impose upon state courts a constitutional obligation it fails to impose upon federal courts.

C

All that remains to support the majority's conclusion is that all-purpose Latin canon: *ipse dixit*. The majority opines that because a substantive rule eliminates a State's power to proscribe certain conduct or impose a certain punishment, it has "the automatic consequence of invalidating a defendant's conviction or sentence." What provision of the Constitution could conceivably produce such a result? The Due Process Clause? It surely cannot be a denial of due process for a court to pronounce a final judgment which, though fully in accord with federal constitutional law at the time, fails to anticipate a change to be made by this Court half a century into the future. The Equal Protection Clause? Both statutory and (increasingly) constitutional laws change. If it were a denial of equal protection to hold an earlier defendant to a law more stringent than what exists today, it would also be a denial of equal protection to hold a later defendant to a law more stringent than what existed 50 years ago. No principle of equal protection requires the criminal law of all ages to be the same.

The majority grandly asserts that "[t]here is no grandfather clause that permits States to *enforce punishments the Constitution forbids.*" (emphasis added). Of course the italicized phrase begs the question. There most certainly is a grandfather clause—one we have called *finality*—which says that the Constitution does not require States to revise punishments that were lawful when they were imposed. * * *

The majority's imposition of Teague's first exception upon the States is all the worse because it does not adhere to that exception as initially conceived by Justice Harlan—an exception for rules that "place, as a matter of constitutional interpretation, certain kinds of primary, private individual *conduct* beyond the power of the criminal lawmaking authority to proscribe." Mackey, 401 U.S., at 692 (emphasis added). Rather, it endorses the exception as expanded by Penry. * * * [But t]he "evolving standards" test concedes that in 1969 the State had the power to punish Henry Montgomery as it did. * * *

II.   The Retroactivity of Miller

* * * Having distorted Teague, the majority simply proceeds to rewrite Miller.

* * * Miller stated, quite clearly * * *: "Our decision does not categorically bar a penalty for a class of offenders or type of crime—as, for example, we did in Roper or Graham. Instead, it mandates only that a sentencer *follow a certain process*—considering an offender's youth and attendant characteristics—before imposing a particular penalty." 567 U.S., at 483 (emphasis added).

* * * Under Miller, bear in mind, the inquiry is whether the inmate was seen to be incorrigible when he was sentenced—not whether he has proven corrigible and so can safely be paroled today. What silliness. (And how impossible in practice * * *.) * * *

* * * [O]ne of the justifications the Court gave for decreeing an end to the death penalty for murders (no matter how many) committed by a juvenile was that life without parole was a severe enough punishment. See Roper, 543 U.S., at 572. How could the majority—in an opinion written by the very author of Roper—now say *that* punishment is *also* unconstitutional? The Court expressly refused to say so in Miller, 567 U.S., at 479. So the Court refuses again today, but merely makes imposition of that severe sanction a practical impossibility. And then, in Godfather fashion, the majority makes state legislatures an offer they can't refuse: Avoid all the utterly impossible nonsense we have prescribed by simply "permitting juvenile homicide offenders to be considered for parole." Mission accomplished.

■ JUSTICE THOMAS, dissenting.

* * * We have jurisdiction under 28 U.S.C. § 1257 only if the Louisiana Supreme Court's decision implicates a federal right. * * *

I

* * *

A

No provision of the Constitution supports the Court's holding. The Court invokes only the Supremacy Clause, asserting that the Clause deprives state and federal postconviction courts alike of power to leave an unconstitutional sentence in place. But that leaves the question of what provision of the Constitution supplies that underlying prohibition.

The Supremacy Clause does not do so. That Clause merely supplies a rule of decision: *If* a federal constitutional right exists, that right supersedes any contrary provisions of state law. Accordingly, as we reaffirmed just last Term, the Supremacy Clause is no independent font of substantive rights. Armstrong v. Exceptional Child Center, Inc., 575 U.S. 320, 325 (2015).

[Justice Thomas then discussed other possible bases for the Court's decision. Article III, he wrote, "defines the scope of *federal* judicial power. It cannot compel *state* postconviction courts to apply new substantive rules retroactively." Turning to due process, Justice Thomas noted that "[q]uite possibly, ' "[d]ue process of law" was originally used as a shorthand expression for governmental proceedings according to the "law of the land" *as it existed at the time of those proceedings*' " (quoting In re Winship, 397 U.S. 358, 378 (Black, J., dissenting) (emphasis added)). As for equal protection, Justice Thomas observed that "under our precedents 'a classification neither involving fundamental rights nor proceeding along suspect lines . . . cannot run afoul of the Equal Protection Clause if there is a rational relationship between the disparity of treatment and some legitimate governmental purpose.' " He continued: "The disparity the Court eliminates today—between prisoners whose cases were on direct review when this Court announced a new substantive constitutional rule, and those whose convictions had already become final—is one we have long considered rational."]

B

The Court's new constitutional right also finds no basis in the history of state and federal postconviction proceedings. Throughout our history, postconviction relief for alleged constitutional defects in a conviction or sentence was available as a matter of legislative grace, not constitutional command.

The Constitution mentions habeas relief only in the Suspension Clause, which specifies that "[t]he Privilege of the Writ of *Habeas Corpus* shall not be suspended, unless when in Cases of Rebellion or Invasion the public Safety may require it." Art. I, § 9, cl. 2. But that Clause does not specify the scope of the writ. And the First Congress, in prescribing federal habeas jurisdiction in the 1789 Judiciary Act, understood its scope to reflect "the black-letter principle of the common law that the writ was simply not available at all to one convicted of crime by a court of competent jurisdiction." Bator, *Finality in Criminal Law and Federal Habeas Corpus for State Prisoners*, 76 Harv.L.Rev. 441, 466 (1963). Early cases echoed that understanding. *E.g.*, Ex parte Watkins, 3 Pet. 193, 202 (1830) ("An imprisonment under a judgment cannot be unlawful, unless that judgment be an absolute nullity; and it is not a nullity if the court has general jurisdiction of the subject, although it should be erroneous"). * * *

II

A

Not only does the Court's novel constitutional right lack any constitutional foundation; the reasoning the Court uses to construct this right lacks any logical stopping point. If, as the Court supposes, the Constitution bars courts from insisting that prisoners remain in prison when their convictions or sentences are later deemed unconstitutional, why can courts let stand a judgment that wrongly decided any constitutional question? * * *

B

There is one silver lining to today's ruling: States still have a way to mitigate its impact on their court systems. * * *

* * * Only when state courts have chosen to entertain a federal claim can the Supremacy Clause conceivably command a state court to apply federal law. As we explained last Term, private parties have no "constitutional . . . right to enforce federal laws against the States." Armstrong, 575 U.S., at 325. Instead, the Constitution leaves the initial choice to entertain federal claims up to state courts, which are "tribunals over which the government of the Union has no adequate control, and which may be closed to any claim asserted under a law of the United States." Osborn v. Bank of United States, 9 Wheat. 738, 821 (1824).

States therefore have a modest path to lessen the burdens that today's decision will inflict on their courts. States can stop entertaining claims alleging that this Court's Eighth Amendment decisions invalidated a sentence, and leave federal habeas courts to shoulder the burden of adjudicating such claims in the first instance. Whatever the desirability of that choice, it is one the Constitution allows States to make. * * *

NOTE ON MONTGOMERY V. LOUISIANA AND RETROACTIVITY IN STATE POST-CONVICTION AND FEDERAL COLLATERAL REVIEW

(1) The Montgomery Case and the Constitution. The Montgomery decision raises a number of complicated questions about the intersection of new law, retroactivity, and collateral review of "final" criminal convictions in both the state and federal courts. What is the basis for Montgomery's holding that "Teague's conclusion establishing the retroactivity of new substantive rules is best understood as resting upon constitutional premises" and, accordingly, that Miller must be applied retroactively to cases that would otherwise be considered final?[1] The Supremacy Clause? Due Process? Equal Protection? The Suspension Clause? Might the Eighth Amendment have some bearing on the retroactivity question? (Could one say that it violates the Eighth Amendment to continue to punish a person for constitutionally protected conduct? To carry out a constitutionally proscribed sentence?) How convincing are the arguments of Justices Scalia and Thomas that the Constitution contains no mandate to reopen final convictions? *Cf.* Harper v. Virginia Dept. of Taxation, 509 U.S. 86 (1993), and Reynoldsville Casket Co. v. Hyde, 514 U.S. 749 (1995), discussed at pp. 916–917, *supra*. How do (a) the Court's discussion of the role of the Supremacy Clause in Testa v. Katt, 330 U.S. 386 (1947), p. 586, *supra*, and Armstrong v. Exceptional Child Center, Inc., 575 U.S. 320 (2015), p. 1200, *supra*, along with (b) Justice Thomas's dissent in Haywood v. Drown, 556 U.S. 729 (2009), p. 593, *supra*, factor into the equation?

In Griffith v. Kentucky, 479 U.S. 314 (1987), p. 1580, *supra*, the Court relied on Justice Harlan's view of retroactivity for two propositions: (1) to " 'disregard current law in adjudicating cases' " still on direct review would be " 'quite simply an assertion that our constitutional function is not one of adjudication but in effect of legislation' " (quoting Mackey v. United States, 401 U.S. 667, 679 (1971) (Harlan, J., concurring in part and dissenting in part)); and (2) "selective application of new rules violates the principle of treating similarly situated defendants the same" (citing Desist v. United States, 394 U.S. 244, 258–59 (1969) (Harlan, J., dissenting in part)). Does this reasoning apply equally to cases like Montgomery that are no longer pending on direct review?[2]

(2) Substance v. Procedure. Despite having announced in Miller that the decision "does not categorically bar a penalty for a class of offenders or type of crime" but "mandates only that a sentencer follow a certain process," the Montgomery Court classified Miller's holding as substantive for Teague purposes. Is there a valid distinction to be drawn, as Justice Scalia suggests, between cases involving constitutionally protected conduct and cases involving sentences later deemed to be in violation of the Constitution? Relying on Teague's extension to cases like Penry v. Lynaugh, 492 U.S. 302 (1989), p. 1583, *supra*, the Montgomery Court reasoned that such a

---

[1]   Compare Danforth v. Minnesota, 552 U.S. 264, 278 (2008) (describing the Teague doctrine as "an exercise of th[e] Court's power to interpret the federal habeas statute").

[2]   In the wake of Montgomery, the Supreme Court held that its decision in Johnson v. United States, 576 U.S. 591 (2015), is a substantive decision that applies retroactively in federal criminal cases on collateral review. See Welch v. United States, 578 U.S. 120 (2016). In Welch, with Justice Kennedy once again writing for the majority, the Court held that Johnson had announced a new rule that "changed the substantive reach of the [federal criminal statute], altering 'the range of conduct or the class of persons that the [Act] punishes' " (quoting Schriro v. Summerlin, 542 U.S. 348, 353 (2004)). Because "[t]he residual clause is invalid under Johnson," the Court held, "it can no longer mandate or authorize any sentence." For further discussion of Welch, see pp. 1670–1672, *infra*.

distinction was unfounded. More generally, does Montgomery reveal the elusiveness of the distinction between substantive and procedural rules?

(3) Justice Thomas's Dissent and Its Implications. Before Montgomery could pursue federal habeas relief, he had to exhaust all available state remedies. Justice Thomas argues that states can simply eliminate post-conviction proceedings to avoid implementing the Court's decision in Miller.[3] Can his position be reconciled with the majority's apparent holding that the Constitution forbids a state from continuing to insist that one whose claim falls under Teague's first exception remain in jail? *Cf.* Case v. Nebraska, 381 U.S. 336 (1965); Haywood v. Drown, 556 U.S. 729 (2009), p. 593, *supra.* See also Martinez v. Ryan, 566 U.S. 1 (2012), p. 1647–1649, *infra.* If Justice Thomas is right, is Congress under an *obligation* to provide for collateral habeas review of Miller claims in federal court?

Professors Vázquez and Vladeck argue that post-Montgomery, state courts must provide post-conviction relief for petitioners seeking the benefit of new rules of substantive constitutional law where all avenues of direct review are foreclosed. See Vázquez & Vladeck, *The Constitutional Right to Collateral Post-Conviction Review,* 103 Va.L.Rev. 905 (2017). The authors argue that imposing such an obligation upon federal habeas courts would upend longstanding assumptions underlying Article III, including the Madisonian Compromise and the widely held view that "federal habeas corpus [is] constitutionally gratuitous as a means of postconviction review." Fallon & Meltzer, *New Law, Non-Retroactivity, and Constitutional Remedies,* 104 Harv.L.Rev. 1731, 1813 (1991). Nor do Vázquez and Vladeck read the Court's line of cases following from Testa v. Katt, 330 U.S. 386 (1947), p. 586, *supra,* as foreclosing the conclusion that state courts must be open in such cases. In their view, any limitation on state court jurisdiction to provide collateral relief to petitioners claiming the benefit of a new rule of substantive federal law "would be based, at bottom, on disagreement with the policies underlying the Constitution, as interpreted in Montgomery," and therefore would not constitute a "valid excuse" under Testa as applied in Haywood v. Drown, 556 U.S. 729 (2009), p. 593, *supra.*[4] This conclusion also follows, in the authors' view, under the Court's decision in General Oil Co. v. Crain, 209 U.S. 211 (1908), p. 1195, *supra,* which held that a state court's determination regarding its jurisdiction to award a potentially constitutionally required remedy is not an adequate and independent state ground precluding Supreme Court review of the decision. In support of their conclusion, the authors reject the proposition that closing state courts entirely to a particular class of claims based on state law necessarily will

---

    [3]   In a different case the same Term, Justice Alito posited that "[s]tates are under no obligation to permit collateral attacks on convictions that have become final, and if they allow such attacks, they are free to limit the circumstances in which claims may be relitigated." Foster v. Chatman, 578 U.S. 488, 520 (2016) (Alito, J., concurring in the judgment).

    [4]   Could one argue that state court resistance in this context would also be in tension with the policies underlying AEDPA and the Court's habeas jurisprudence insofar as both prioritize state court adjudication of federal rights in the first instance? Consider in this regard, *e.g.*, the exhaustion requirement, procedural default doctrine, and § 2254(d)(1)'s backward-looking and deferential standard of review.

justify the same jurisdictional limitation with respect to analogous federal claims.[5]

Professors Woolhandler and Collins dispute many of the premises on which Vázquez and Vladeck construct their argument, contending that evidence suggests that "the Framers did not contemplate compulsory state court jurisdiction over affirmative federal claims." Woolhandler & Collins, *State Jurisdictional Independence and Federal Supremacy*, 72 Fla.L.Rev. 73, 77 (2020). Viewing Haywood as inconsistent with this backdrop, the authors separately read Crain as a "modest" decision lending support to the proposition that any obligations upon state courts to afford constitutional remedies "tend to surface when lower federal court jurisdiction is disfavored or unavailable." It follows, on their view, that where federal courts are able to supply such remedies, arguments in favor of compelling state courts to do the same falter.[6]

What is left of the "valid excuse" doctrine under the interpretation of Testa and Haywood embraced by Vázquez and Vladeck, given that they reject the proposition that state legislatures could eliminate state post-conviction review?

(4) The Intersection of Montgomery, Teague, and AEDPA. Looking ahead, federal courts will have to determine the application of Montgomery to habeas proceedings in federal court. Consider two habeas petitioners: (a) one who, because of a failure to meet state procedural requirements, has lost the ability to raise, on direct review in state court, the Eighth Amendment claim later embraced in Miller, and (b) one who raised and thereby preserved the claim throughout direct proceedings before Miller. Would the two petitioners fare differently in federal habeas? Should they? With respect to the latter petitioner whose claim was presumably rejected on the merits by the state courts, does § 2254(d)(1) permit a federal habeas court to grant relief from a mandatory life sentence? Post-Montgomery, courts will have to wrestle with how Teague and Montgomery intersect with both habeas procedural default jurisprudence and § 2254(d)(1)'s "backward-looking language." Cullen v. Pinholster, 563 U.S. 170, 182 (2011).[7]

---

[5]   For elaboration on the ramifications of Montgomery for debates over the role of state courts as enforcers of federal rights, see Vladeck, *Constitutional Remedies in Federalism's Forgotten Shadow*, 107 Calif.L.Rev. 1043 (2019) (positing that "Montgomery may represent * * * the vindication of Professor Hart's famous conclusion about the centrality of state, rather than federal, courts to the protection of federal constitutional rights").

[6]   Responding in turn, Professors Vázquez and Vladeck argue that their account is more consistent with "[t]he default regime established by the Constitution," which "was one in which enforcement of federal law mainly depended on state courts." Vázquez & Vladeck, *Testa, Crain, and the Constitutional Right to Collateral Relief*, 72 Fla.L.Rev.F. 10, 13 (2021). They likewise contend that "the availability of a *constitutionally* required remedy should not depend on a congressional decision to confer jurisdiction on the lower federal courts." Finally, Vázquez and Vladeck emphasize the fact that the Court decided Ex parte Young, 209 U.S. 123 (1908), p. 1184, *supra*, the very same day as Crain. The availability of a Young action, they argue, strongly suggests Crain did not turn on the availability of federal remedies.

[7]   In Edwards v. Vannoy, 593 U.S. 255 (2021), pp. 1583–1585, *supra*, Justice Thomas, joined by Justice Gorsuch, concurred and argued that where § 2254(d) applies, there is no reason to do the Teague analysis. If a state court "reasonably relied" on then-existing federal law in "rejecting [a] claim," the Court's inquiry "beg[ins] and end[s] there—with § 2254(d)(1)'s plain text" that provides "relief 'shall not be granted.'" Justice Thomas added that "Congress' decision to create retroactivity exceptions to the statute of limitations and to the bar on second-or-

Consider also the litigant who has already pursued federal habeas relief on a prior occasion and must overcome the limits on successive petitions set forth in § 2244(b)(2). See pp. 1657–1662, *supra*. For the petitioner who has not previously presented the claim in federal habeas, does Montgomery, when combined with Miller, establish "a new rule of constitutional law, made retroactive to cases on collateral review by the Supreme Court that was previously unavailable" under § 2244(b)(2)(a)? For an argument that some court must be available to award relief where a petitioner seeks the benefit of a new rule of substantive constitutional law, see Vázquez & Vladeck, Paragraph (3), *supra*.

(5) Jurisdictional Infirmities and Montgomery. How, if at all, does the rationale of Montgomery v. Louisiana apply when the original court in which the state successfully prosecuted a criminal defendant lacked jurisdiction? In McGirt v. Oklahoma, 591 U.S. 894 (2020), the Supreme Court held that because a large swathe of Oklahoma constitutes land within the boundaries of Indian country as a matter of federal law, state courts lack jurisdiction to try crimes committed by Native Americans within that territory. (Only federal or tribal courts have jurisdiction in such cases.) Will petitions for habeas relief predicated upon McGirt fall within the first Teague exception?

(6) Retreat from Montgomery? In Jones v. Mississippi, 593 U.S. 98 (2021), the Supreme Court revisited Montgomery. Petitioner Jones had been convicted and sentenced to life without possibility of parole based on a homicide that he committed at the age of 15. On appeal from state post-conviction proceedings, he argued that after Miller and Montgomery, "a sentencer who imposes a life-without-parole sentence must *also* make a separate factual finding that the defendant is permanently incorrigible, or at least provide an on-the-record sentencing explanation with an implicit finding that the defendant is permanently incorrigible." The Court, 6–3, disagreed. Writing for the majority, Justice Kavanaugh noted that Miller had "mandated 'only that a sentence follow a certain process—considering an offender's youth and attendant characteristics—before imposing' a life-without-parole sentence" (quoting Miller, 567 U.S. at 483). Montgomery was clear, he added, that " 'a finding of fact regarding a child's incorrigibility . . . is not required' " (quoting Montgomery, 577 U.S. at 211). Miller "repeatedly described youth as a sentencing factor akin to a mitigating circumstance," like those considered in the death penalty context, which have traditionally not "require[d] the sentencer to make any particular factual finding regarding * * * mitigating circumstances." It followed, on the majority's view, that all Miller requires is that a sentencer "consider youth as a mitigating factor when deciding whether to impose a life-without-parole sentence." Nothing in Montgomery added anything "to Miller's requirements."

Justice Kavanaugh next addressed the fact that Montgomery classified the rule in Miller as substantive for retroactivity purposes. Although nowhere expressly saying that Montgomery erred in classifying the Miller rule as substantive, the majority left little doubt as to its views on the matter, stating: "[T]o the extent that Montgomery's application of the Teague

---

successive petitions but not for § 2254(d) is strong evidence that Teague" does not apply in cases governed by § 2254(d). For additional discussion of Teague and § 2254(d)(1), see p. 1601, *supra*.

standard is in tension with the Court's retroactivity precedents * * *, those * * * precedents—and not Montgomery—must guide the determination of whether rules other than Miller are substantive."[8] All the same, Justice Kavanaugh concluded by stating that "[t]oday's decision does not overrule Miller or Montgomery."[9]

Justice Thomas concurred in the judgment. In his view, the Miller rule was procedural and not watershed for purposes of Teague; Montgomery was wrong to conclude otherwise. But, he recognized, Montgomery labeled the Miller rule as substantive, which "creates problems for the majority in this case." Justice Thomas then observed that although Montgomery was not entirely consistent as to its reasoning, it did say that " 'Miller drew a line between children whose crimes reflect transient immaturity and those rare children whose crimes reflect irreparable corruption.' " Analogizing this "categorical exemption for certain offenders" to insanity or intellectual disability defenses, Justice Thomas argued that under Montgomery, "the 'legality' of Jones' sentence turns on whether his crime in fact 'reflect[s] permanent incorrigibility' " (quoting Montgomery, 577 U.S. at 205), a point that in turn warrants granting relief to Jones. But, he argued, the Court instead should "just acknowledge that Montgomery had no basis in law or the Constitution." Justice Thomas concluded that the Court had overruled Montgomery "in substance but not in name."

Justice Sotomayor, joined by Justices Breyer and Kagan, dissented and contended that the Court had "gut[ted]" Miller and Montgomery. She read Montgomery to establish that "[o]nly those rare few [whose crimes reflect irreparable corruption] are constitutionally eligible for LWOP under Miller." As such, she wrote, "before imposing a sentence of LWOP, a sentencer must actually 'make that judgment,' and make it correctly" (quoting Miller, 567 U.S. at 480). Justice Sotomayor also highlighted that Miller had drawn heavily on Roper and Graham, both of which had prohibited the application of certain sentences to classes of juvenile offenders, suggesting that Miller intended to accomplish the very same end. She continued, "[f]or Montgomery to make any sense * * *, Miller must have done more than mandate a certain procedure."[10] Finally, taking aim at the majority's statement that Montgomery is no longer sound precedent for purposes of determining whether a rule is procedural or substantive for retroactivity purposes, she observed: "How low this Court's respect for *stare decisis* has sunk."

Aren't Justices Thomas and Sotomayor correct that the Jones majority's reading of Miller and Montgomery is next to impossible to reconcile with

---

[8]   In addition, Justice Kavanaugh posited that a rule is procedural for Teague purposes "if it regulates " 'only the manner of determining the defendant's culpability" ' " (quoting Welch v. United States, 578 U.S. 120, 129 (2016) (quoting Schriro v. Summerlin, 542 U.S. 348, 353 (2004))).

[9]   The Court observed that "[b]y now, most offenders who could seek collateral review as a result of Montgomery have done so and, if eligible, have received new discretionary sentences under Miller."

[10]   In the dissent's view, if the majority's reading of Montgomery was correct (namely, that it only required discretionary consideration of youth generally but was still a substantive rule for Teague purposes), it followed that a host of earlier cases involving death penalty sentencing procedures (*e.g.*, those requiring consideration of certain mitigating factors) should also be classified as substantive for Teague purposes.

Montgomery's classification of the rule in Miller as substantive for Teague purposes? Or is the problem Montgomery itself? Jones suggests that had the Montgomery Court been clear that it was reading Miller to require a specific finding relating to incorrigibility (or had Miller itself been clear on the point), that would have made all the difference with respect to the retroactivity analysis and required granting Jones the relief he sought.

Only a few weeks after handing down Jones, in Edwards v. Vannoy, 593 U.S. 255 (2021), the Court, 6–3, eliminated Teague's second exception on the basis that it is "theoretical" and "not real." In so doing, the majority appeared to leave intact Teague's first exception, observing in a footnote that "a new *substantive* rule—for example, a rule that particular conduct cannot be criminalized—usually applies retroactively on federal collateral review."[11] Edwards therefore amplifies the importance of the distinction between procedural and substantive rules of decision for retroactivity purposes.

(7) The Role, if Any, of 28 U.S.C. § 2241. In Felker v. Turpin, 518 U.S. 651 (1996), the Court noted that a potential bypass of AEDPA's limitations on successive petitions may be found in the original writ. Several courts of appeals, moreover, have suggested that 28 U.S.C. § 2241, the modern descendant of the original provision for habeas jurisdiction in § 14 of the 1789 Judiciary Act, see p. 1465, *infra*, may serve as a proper vehicle for relief in certain cases where AEDPA otherwise appears to preclude it. Against this backdrop, if AEDPA is read to bar relief for a petitioner seeking the retroactive benefit of Miller or another substantive decision falling under Teague's first exception, one could argue that § 2241's broad language providing that a writ of habeas corpus "may be granted" where a petitioner "is in custody in violation of the Constitution or laws or treaties of the United States" would give a court a separate basis for awarding relief. The Court's recent decision in Jones v. Hendrix, 599 U.S. 465 (2023), however, held that those in *federal* custody with claims of legal innocence could not invoke § 2241 to bypass AEDPA's limitations on successive petitions. For additional discussion of Jones and the role, if any, of § 2241, see pp. 1676–1679, *infra*.

(8) Reopening Judgments Under Federal Rule of Civil Procedure 60(b). Federal Rule of Civil Procedure 60(b) permits a district court to reopen "a final judgment, order, or proceeding" for various reasons, including the discovery of new evidence that was previously unavailable and "any other reason that justifies relief." The Supreme Court has interpreted the rule to permit reopening a judgment on the basis of "extraordinary circumstances," noting that "[s]uch circumstances will rarely occur in the habeas context." Gonzalez v. Crosby, 545 U.S. 524, 535 (2005).

In Buck v. Davis, 580 U.S. 100 (2017), the Court nonetheless held, 6–2, that extraordinary circumstances justified reopening a 2006 judgment denying relief to a petitioner in state custody in what was then his first federal habeas petition. Petitioner Buck sought the benefit of the Court's decisions in Martinez v. Ryan, 566 U.S. 1 (2012), p. 1647, *infra*, and Trevino v. Thaler, 569 U.S. 413 (2013), p. 1649, *infra*, to excuse his failure to raise in

---

[11]   Justice Gorsuch, joined by Justice Thomas, concurred separately and appeared to question both Teague exceptions. For additional discussion, see pp. 1583–1585, *supra*.

state post-conviction proceedings a claim of ineffective assistance of counsel in his capital sentencing proceedings. The alleged ineffectiveness resulted from the decision of petitioner's own counsel to introduce an expert report and related testimony that characterized petitioner's race as a factor increasing his likelihood of future violence.

Writing for the Court, Chief Justice Roberts concluded that counsel's performance at his sentencing "fell outside the bounds of competent representation" and prejudiced the petitioner.[12] He then wrote that "extraordinary circumstances" may justify reopening a judgment where there is a " 'risk of injustice to the parties' " or a " 'risk of undermining the public's confidence in the judicial process' " from leaving a judgment intact (quoting Liljeberg v. Health Services Acquisition Corp., 486 U.S. 847, 864 (1988)). Deeming these factors present, the Court held that the district court abused its discretion in denying the Rule 60(b) motion. This conclusion followed from the State's confession of error in other cases in which it had relied upon the same expert and the possibility that "Buck may have been sentenced to death in part because of his race."

Buck v. Davis potentially opens a new avenue of relief for habeas petitioners seeking to rely on new law after the conclusion of federal habeas proceedings. Note, however, that Buck involved (1) the introduction of deeply objectionable and highly prejudicial expert testimony; (2) a confession of error by the State in related cases; and (3) waiver by the State of any Teague arguments relating to the new law on which petitioner sought to rely.

The Supreme Court again took up a Rule 60(b) motion brought to reopen federal habeas proceedings in Tharpe v. Sellers, 583 U.S. 33 (2018) (per curiam). The case involved evidence suggesting that race may have played a role in a juror's vote to convict and sentence petitioner Tharpe to death. As in Buck, the Court stressed "the unusual facts" of the case. But ultimately the Court remanded, acknowledging that the petitioner still "faces a high bar in showing that jurists of reason could disagree" with the district court's conclusion that under § 2254(e)(1) (discussed at pp. 1627–1628, *infra*), it should defer to the state court's rejection of the import of the relevant evidence. Deeming the Court's treatment of the case nothing more than "ceremonial handwringing," a dissent for three Justices written by Justice Thomas would have affirmed the district court's denial of relief. Although Tharpe reaffirms the Court's approval of using Rule 60(b) to reopen habeas proceedings (potentially opening a significant new avenue for challenging convictions in successive proceedings), the case's disposition suggests that such an avenue will be available only in extraordinary circumstances.

---

[12]   The Court also criticized the court of appeals for conflating the merits of petitioner's arguments with the decision whether to grant a certificate of appealability, an inquiry that asks " 'only if the District Court's decision was debatable' " (quoting Miller-El v. Cockrell, 537 U.S. 322, 327 (2003)), p. 1551, *supra*. The Court left open the question whether an appeal of the denial of a motion under Rule 60(b) requires a certificate of appealability.

NOTE ON RELITIGATING THE FACTS IN HABEAS CORPUS PROCEEDINGS

Although Brown v. Allen required de novo relitigation of issues of law (including so-called mixed questions—*i.e.*, application of legal principles to the facts)—it permitted, though it did not require, a habeas court to defer to state court factfindings.[1] And both Justice Reed's and Justice Frankfurter's opinions stated that a habeas court generally had discretion whether to hold an evidentiary hearing, being obliged to do so only if there were "unusual circumstances" (Reed) or a "vital flaw" (Frankfurter) in the state proceedings.

Over time, these flexible standards were modified by judicial decisions and statutory amendments that narrowed the power of federal courts both to reject state court factfindings and to hold evidentiary hearings. Then, in 1996, AEDPA included provisions further limiting the power of habeas courts to reject factual determinations made by the state courts.

A. Deference to State Court Factfindings

(1) The 1966 Amendment. A 1966 amendment, codified in former § 2254(d), began the shift from Brown's approach, which *permitted* deference to state court factfindings, to an approach *requiring* such deference. The amendment required a federal habeas court to presume that a state court's written determination of fact was correct, unless one of eight specified circumstances, relating generally to procedural defects in the state court proceeding, was present. If no exception applied, the petitioner had the burden of establishing by clear and convincing evidence that the state court's factual determination was erroneous.

(2) The AEDPA Amendments. In 1996, AEDPA replaced former § 2254(d) with two different provisions mandating deference to state court factfindings, neither of which included the limitations found in the earlier provision.

(a) Current § 2254(d) precludes habeas relief unless the federal court finds that a state court decision was either (i) contrary to or an unreasonable application of clearly established *law* (subsection (d)(1), the provision at issue in Terry Williams), or (ii) "based on an unreasonable determination of the *facts* in light of the evidence presented in the State court proceeding" (subsection (d)(2)) (emphasis added). Thus, today state court determinations, whether characterized as legal or factual, enjoy comparable deference from habeas courts.[2]

---

[1] Distinguishing questions of fact from mixed questions is anything but an exact science. See, *e.g.*, Thompson v. Keohane, 516 U.S. 99 (1995). Because the new § 2254(d) added by AEDPA requires deference to state court determinations, whether of law or fact, federal habeas courts no longer need to draw this distinction.

[2] Thus, it is the rare case in which a state court's determinations will be reversed. But, in Brumfield v. Cain, 576 U.S. 305 (2015), the Court rejected a state court's factual findings under § 2254(d)(2) as unreasonable. In the wake of Atkins v. Virginia, 536 U.S. 304 (2002), which held that application of the death penalty to persons with intellectual disabilities violates the Eighth Amendment, Brumfield sought a hearing in state court to prove his intellectual disability. Surveying the evidence presented during Brumfield's capital sentencing proceeding, the state court denied his request. Notwithstanding AEDPA's deferential standard, the Court,

(b)   Section 2254(e)(1) separately provides that "a determination of a factual issue made by a State court shall be presumed to be correct. The applicant shall have the burden of rebutting the presumption of correctness by clear and convincing evidence."

(c)   The relationship between §§ 2254(d)(2) and 2254(e)(1) is not entirely clear. The lower courts generally recite them together without suggesting that they differ.[3] Notably, however, neither § 2254(d)(2) nor § 2254(e)(1) includes any exception for findings resulting from state court determinations that were in some way procedurally defective.

(3) Determining What Facts the State Court Found. Not infrequently, a state court decision simply denies relief or otherwise makes no explicit finding on a factual issue relevant to a habeas claim. In LaVallee v. Delle Rose, 410 U.S. 690 (1973), the petitioner argued that a state court's decision that his confession was voluntary was not entitled to a presumption of correctness because the state court had made no finding as to the credibility of the petitioner's testimony that the confession had been coerced—and therefore had failed to resolve the merits of the factual dispute. The Court disagreed, ruling that the determination of voluntariness obviously, if implicitly, rested on a finding (to which the federal court must defer) that the petitioner's testimony was not credible. *Cf.* Harrington v. Richter, 562 U.S. 86 (2011), p. 1604, *supra* (holding that § 2254(d)(1) applies to summary state court decisions).

B.   The Availability of a Federal Evidentiary Hearing

(1) Pre-AEDPA Law and Practice. The power of federal courts to conduct evidentiary hearings, like that to override state court factfindings, has narrowed over time. In Townsend v. Sain, 372 U.S. 293 (1963), the Warren Court, after stating that "[i]t is the typical, not the rare, case in which constitutional claims turn upon the resolution of contested factual issues," spelled out six circumstances in which a defect in the state factfinding procedures made a federal hearing mandatory—without limiting the power to hold a hearing otherwise. Nonetheless, the percentage of habeas cases in which a hearing is conducted has always been low: after reaching 11% in the 1960s, by 1988 (even before AEDPA) it had declined to roughly 1%.[4]

5–4, concluded that the state court's denial of a hearing was unreasonable when held up against the evidence in the record. The majority emphasized that under the state's implementing standard for Atkins, Brumfield need only raise a reasonable doubt as to whether he had an intellectual disability in order to secure a full hearing on the issue. In dissent, Justice Thomas argued that the majority view was at odds with the Court's § 2254(d)(1) jurisprudence and even if § 2254(d)(2) proved the correct standard of review, Brumfield had failed to satisfy it.

[3]   For discussion of decisions that have found subtle differences between the provisions, see Marceau, *Deference and Doubt: The Interaction of AEDPA § 2254(d)(2) and (e)(1)*, 82 Tul.L.Rev. 385 (2007).

[4]   See Weisselberg, *Evidentiary Hearings in Federal Habeas Corpus Cases*, 1990 B.Y.U.L.Rev. 131, 165–68.

In Keeney v. Tamayo-Reyes, 504 U.S. 1 (1992), the Rehnquist Court shifted gears, forbidding federal courts from holding hearings unless strict criteria were satisfied.[5]

(2) Evidentiary Hearings and the 1996 Act. In 1996, AEDPA prescribed, for the first time, a statutory standard restricting federal court power to conduct evidentiary hearings. Section 2254(e)(2) precludes an evidentiary hearing when the petitioner "failed to develop the factual basis of a claim in State court proceedings" unless the petitioner shows that—

"(A) the claim relies on (i) a new rule of constitutional law, made retroactive to cases on collateral review by the Supreme Court, that was previously unavailable; or (ii) a factual predicate that could not have been previously discovered through the exercise of due diligence; and

"(B) the facts underlying the claim would be sufficient to establish by clear and convincing evidence that but for constitutional error, no reasonable factfinder would have found the applicant guilty of the underlying offense."

Would evidence that petitioner's conduct was constitutionally protected, or that a death sentence was constitutionally defective, establish that the petitioner did not commit *the underlying offense*, within the meaning of (B)? If not, is a habeas court barred from holding an evidentiary hearing on such a claim?

(3) The Meaning of "Failed to Develop." In Michael Williams v. Taylor, 529 U.S. 420 (2000), Justice Kennedy's opinion for a unanimous Court rejected the state's argument that non-development of the facts in state court was in itself enough to bar a federal evidentiary hearing. Section 2254(e)(2) applies only if the petitioner "failed to develop" the facts, and the Court posited that the word "fail" typically "connotes some omission, fault, or negligence on the part of the person who has failed to do something." Thus, "a failure to develop the factual basis of a claim is not established unless there is lack of diligence, or some greater fault, attributable to the prisoner or the prisoner's counsel."

The Court proceeded to find a lack of diligence as to one of the three claims asserted by Williams, but not as to the other two, both of which related to the questioning at voir dire. One prospective juror, when asked if she was related to any of the witnesses, failed to reveal that she had been married to a prosecution witness, and when asked if any of the lawyers involved had ever represented her, said nothing, although one of the prosecutors had done so in her divorce. The Court found that "[t]he trial record contains no evidence which would have put a reasonable attorney on notice that [the juror's] nonresponse was a deliberate omission of material information," and as a result, § 2254(e)(2) did not bar a hearing.

(4) Section 2254(d)(1) and Evidentiary Hearings. The Court sharply limited the significance of evidentiary hearings in Cullen v. Pinholster, 563

---

[5]   Borrowing from its procedural default doctrines, in Tamayo-Reyes, the Court held that an evidentiary hearing may be afforded only if the petitioner shows that (i) there was "cause and prejudice" for the failure to present the evidence in state court, or (ii) a "fundamental miscarriage of justice" would occur were relitigation foreclosed. (Those standards are discussed at pp. 1645–1655, *infra*; both have been given extremely narrow scope.)

U.S. 170 (2011), where it considered whether, when determining if § 2254(d)(1) bars habeas relief, the habeas court may consider evidence introduced in an evidentiary hearing permitted by § 2254(e)(2). Petitioner Pinholster claimed a denial of the effective assistance of counsel at his capital sentencing hearing, a claim rejected on the merits in state courts. In his federal habeas action, the district court held an evidentiary hearing and granted relief. Affirming, the Ninth Circuit, sitting en banc, ruled that a habeas court could consider evidence adduced in a federal evidentiary hearing permitted by § 2254(e)(2) when determining under § 2254(d)(1) whether the state court's rejection of a constitutional claim was contrary to, or an unreasonable application of, clearly established federal law.

The Supreme Court reversed. Justice Thomas's majority opinion reasoned that § 2254(d)(1)'s use of the past tense—in referring to a state court determination that "resulted" in a decision that was contrary to, or "involved" an unreasonable application of, clearly established law—required an examination of the record when the state court decision was made. In the Court's view, "[i]t would be strange to ask federal courts to analyze whether a state court's adjudication resulted in a decision that unreasonably applied federal law to facts not before the state court." Justice Thomas asserted that this approach did not render § 2254(e)(2) superfluous; that section's limits on the authority to conduct a hearing continue to have force where § 2254(d)(1) does not bar federal habeas relief.

Justice Sotomayor's dissent on the relationship between § 2254(d)(1) and § 2254(d)(2) stressed that evidentiary hearings are held in only 4 of every 1,000 non-capital cases and 9.5 of every 100 capital cases and that hearings are permitted by § 2254(e)(2) only when the petitioner had been diligent or where very restrictive requirements are satisfied. In these limited circumstances, she argued, consideration of new evidence does not upset the balance established by AEDPA. She further contested the majority's linguistic argument by noting that § 2254(d)(2) expressly requires district courts to base their review on the state court record. See 28 U.S.C. § 2254(d)(2) (precluding relief unless the state court adjudication "resulted in a decision that was based on an unreasonable determination of the facts in light of the evidence presented in the State court proceeding"). This direction, she argued, would be unnecessary if the use of the past tense in § 2254(d)(1), which makes no reference to the state court record, required the same result.[6]

After the Pinholster decision, how much remains of the federal evidentiary hearing? Indeed, under the majority's view, isn't the next logical

---

[6]   When § 2254(e)(2) permits a hearing, some courts of appeals had held (incorrectly, she declared) that § 2254(d)(1) simply does not apply; others had followed the approach of the Ninth Circuit, which permits consideration of new evidence adduced in a federal court hearing when assessing the reasonableness of the state court decision. No court of appeals, however, had followed the majority's approach, which, she said, has the potential to prevent diligent petitioners from introducing evidence in federal habeas proceedings where the state courts are closed to that petitioner.

Justice Alito's separate concurring opinion agreed with Justice Sotomayor's conclusion, although he would have read § 2254(e)(2) to preclude an evidentiary hearing unless the evidence was not and could not have been introduced in state court—a standard that he found the petitioner did not meet.

step to bar evidentiary hearings altogether until the habeas court has first determined that § 2254(d)(1) does not preclude relief? And the rare case in which § 2254(d)(1) is not a barrier to relief is likely to be one in which (a) the state court determination is plainly wrong on the merits (in which case no evidentiary hearing is likely to be necessary), or (b) no state court determination was rendered on the claim (in which case it is likely that the petitioner will run into a procedural bar for having failed to raise the claim in state court, a matter discussed immediately below).

(5) The Intersection of AEDPA's Limitations on Evidentiary Hearings and the All Writs Act. In Shoop v. Twyford, 596 U.S. 811 (2022), the Court reviewed a district court's decision to invoke the All Writs Act to order a petitioner transported to a medical facility for neurological testing that might lead to the development of new evidence supporting his habeas claim arguing that he suffers from neurological defects. The All Writs Act authorizes federal courts to "issue all writs necessary or appropriate in aid of their respective jurisdictions and agreeable to the usages and principles of law." 28 U.S.C. § 1651(a). Writing for five Justices, Chief Justice Roberts held that the district court's order improperly "circumvent[ed]" AEDPA's limitations on the admission and relevance of new evidence in collateral habeas proceedings. In the Court's view, "a writ seeking new evidence would not be 'necessary or appropriate in aid of' a federal habeas court's jurisdiction, as all orders issued under the All Writs Act must be, if it enables a prisoner to fish for unusable evidence * * *." Instead, the Court held the district court erred in ordering the transportation and testing because the petitioner "never argued that he could clear the bar in § 2254(e)(2) for expanding the state court record, or that the bar was somehow inapplicable."[7]

INTRODUCTORY NOTE ON FEDERAL HABEAS CORPUS AND STATE PROCEDURAL DEFAULT

(1) Introduction. Some habeas petitions include a claim that was not raised in state court at all or that was not raised in accordance with state procedural requirements. Typically, a state court will treat a procedural default—*i.e.*, a failure to have raised a claim in accordance with state procedural rules—as forfeiting a party's right to an adjudication on the merits. And so long as the state procedural ground is "adequate," it will bar Supreme Court review of the state court judgment. See Chap. V, Sec. 3(B), *supra*.

If the person convicted in state criminal proceedings then files a habeas corpus petition, ordinarily state remedies are no longer available; hence, there is no question of exhaustion of state remedies. The question, rather, is whether a procedural default that would preclude the Supreme Court from exercising appellate jurisdiction on direct review should also preclude the

---

[7]   The four dissenting Justices believed that the Court should not have reached the question.

exercise of federal habeas jurisdiction. In dealing with this question, the Supreme Court has shifted ground more than once. Two cases decided ten years apart—Daniels v. Allen, 344 U.S. 443 (1953), and Fay v. Noia, 372 U.S. 391 (1963)—took sharply different approaches to that question and provide the backdrop to the next principal case, Wainwright v. Sykes.

(2)   Daniels v. Allen. In Daniels v. Allen, a companion case to Brown v. Allen, 344 U.S. 443 (1953), p. 1558, *supra*, two defendants had been convicted and sentenced to death for murder. At trial, they raised federal claims (concerning jury discrimination and the introduction of coerced confessions) similar to those raised in Brown v. Allen. But the North Carolina Supreme Court refused to consider the merits of their appeals, because their lawyer had been tardy in serving the "statement of the case on appeal" on the prosecutor. According to Justice Frankfurter's dissent (which was unchallenged on this point), "if petitioners' lawyer had mailed his 'statement of the case on appeal' on the 60th day and the prosecutor's office had received it on the 61st day the law of North Carolina would clearly have been complied with, but because he delivered it by hand on the 61st day," it was untimely. In petitioners' federal habeas corpus action, Justice Reed's opinion for the Court ruled that the failure to have made timely service of the statement of the case on appeal precluded federal habeas review.

In dissent, Justice Black (joined by Justice Douglas) objected that the state supreme court's refusal to review the merits on state procedural grounds "is now held to cut off review in federal habeas corpus proceedings. But in the [cases of Brown and Speller, jointly decided in Brown v. Allen,] where the State Supreme Court did review the evidence, this Court has also reviewed it. I find it difficult to agree with the soundness of a philosophy which prompts this Court to grant a second review where the state has granted one but to deny any review at all where the state has granted none.

"* * * [T]he object of habeas corpus is to search records to prevent illegal imprisonments. * * * [I]t is never too late for courts in habeas corpus proceedings to look straight through procedural screens in order to prevent forfeiture of life or liberty in flagrant defiance of the Constitution. Perhaps there is no more exalted judicial function. I am willing to agree that it should not be exercised in cases like these except under special circumstances or in extraordinary situations. But I cannot join in any opinion that attempts to confine the Great Writ within rigid formalistic boundaries."[1]

(3)   Fay v. Noia. Ten years later, in Fay v. Noia, 372 U.S. 391 (1963), the Court rejected the Daniels rule and greatly expanded habeas review of defaulted claims. Noia had been convicted of a capital crime, but he avoided a death sentence. He then chose not to appeal. His subsequent motion for post-conviction relief in state court, asserting that his conviction was based

---

[1]   Justice Frankfurter's separate dissent (joined by Justices Black and Douglas) emphasized that because North Carolina did not have a fixed period for taking an appeal, the North Carolina courts had discretion to hear the appeal.

In a separate opinion in the same case, Justice Frankfurter wrote: "Normally rights under the Federal Constitution may be waived at the trial, and may likewise be waived by failure to assert such errors on appeal. * * * However, this does not touch one of those extraordinary cases in which a substantial claim goes to the very foundation of a proceeding * * *."

on a coerced confession, was denied because he had failed to appeal from his conviction. Meanwhile, Noia's two co-defendants, who had appealed from their convictions, eventually won relief on the ground that their confessions were coerced under extreme conditions. When Noia's federal habeas petition raising the coerced confession claim reached the Supreme Court, the Court held that his failure to have appealed his conviction did not preclude the exercise of federal habeas jurisdiction.

(a)   Writing for the Court, Justice Brennan rejected the contention that a procedural default that would block Supreme Court review of a state court's decision also bars the exercise of federal habeas corpus jurisdiction: "The fatal weakness of this contention is its failure to recognize that the adequate state-ground rule is a function of the limitations of *appellate* review. * * * [W]e have held that the adequate state-ground rule is a consequence of the Court's obligation to refrain from rendering advisory opinions or passing upon moot questions. * * * But while our appellate function is concerned only with the judgments or decrees of state courts, * * * [in habeas corpus cases t]he jurisdictional prerequisite is not the judgment of a state court but detention *simpliciter*. * * * Habeas lies to enforce the right of personal liberty; when that right is denied and a person confined, the federal court has the power to release him. Indeed, it has no other power; it cannot revise the state court judgment; it can act only on the body of the petitioner.

"To be sure, this may not be the entire answer to the contention that the adequate state-ground principle should apply to the federal courts on habeas corpus * * *. The [decision in Murdock v. City of Memphis, 87 U.S. 590 (1874), p. 636, *supra*, which held that the Supreme Court will not review state court decisions resting on an adequate state ground] may be supported not only by the factor of mootness, but in addition by certain characteristics of the federal system. * * * But the problem is crucially different from that posed in Murdock of the federal courts' deciding questions of substantive state law. In Noia's case the only relevant substantive law is federal—the Fourteenth Amendment. State law appears only in the procedural framework for adjudicating the substantive federal question. The paramount interest is federal. That is not to say that the States have not a substantial interest in exacting compliance with their procedural rules from criminal defendants asserting federal defenses. * * *

"* * * [I]f because of inadvertence or neglect [a prisoner] runs afoul of a state procedural requirement, and thereby forfeits his state remedies, appellate and collateral, as well as direct review thereof in this Court, those consequences should be sufficient to vindicate the State's valid interest in orderly procedure. Whatever residuum of state interest there may be under such circumstances is manifestly insufficient in the face of the federal policy * * * of affording an effective remedy for restraints contrary to the Constitution. * * *"

The Court did recognize that if a habeas petitioner, after consulting with competent counsel, intentionally relinquishes a known right (that is, "deliberately bypassed the orderly procedure of the state courts") "whether for strategic, tactical, or any other reasons * * *, then it is open to the federal court on habeas to deny him all relief if the state courts refused to entertain his federal claims on the merits * * *. * * * [T]he standard here put forth depends on the considered choice of the petitioner. A choice made by counsel not participated in by the petitioner does not automatically bar relief."

Although Noia's was one of the rare cases in which the defendant had in fact participated in a decision not to raise an issue in state court, the Court refused to find a deliberate bypass, stressing the "grisly choice" that Noia had faced—either forgoing an appeal from his conviction or running the risk that a successful appeal might lead to a death sentence on retrial.

(b)   Justice Harlan, joined by Justices Clark and Stewart, dissented, stressing that "[t]he adequate state ground doctrine * * * finds its source in basic constitutional principles," and asking whether a federal habeas court is "constitutionally more free than the Supreme Court on direct review to 'ignore' the adequate state ground, proceed to the federal question, and order the prisoner's release?

"The answer must be that it is not. Of course, as the majority states, a judgment is not a 'jurisdictional prerequisite' to a habeas corpus application, but that is wholly irrelevant. The point is that if the applicant is detained *pursuant* to a judgment, termination of the detention necessarily nullifies the judgment. * * *

"* * * [T]he Court exceeds its constitutional power if in fact the state ground relied upon to sustain the judgment of conviction is an adequate one. The effect of the approach adopted by the Court is, indeed, to do away with the adequate state ground rule entirely in every state case, involving a federal question, in which detention follows from a judgment."[2]

(4) Wainwright v. Sykes. In Wainwright v. Sykes, the Burger Court once again addressed the issue of procedural default.

Wainwright v. Sykes

433 U.S. 72 (1977).
Certiorari to the United States Court of Appeals for the Fifth Circuit.

■ MR. JUSTICE REHNQUIST delivered the opinion of the Court.

We granted certiorari to consider the availability of federal habeas corpus to review a state convict's claim that testimony was admitted at his trial in violation of his rights under Miranda v. Arizona, 384 U.S. 436 (1966), a claim which the Florida courts have previously refused to consider on the merits because of noncompliance with a state contemporaneous-objection rule. * * *

Respondent Sykes was convicted of third-degree murder after a jury trial * * *. He testified at trial that on the evening of January 8, 1972, he told his wife to summon the police because he had just shot Willie Gilbert.

---

[2]   For additional background on Fay v. Noia and the companion cases that made Noia's claims especially sympathetic, see Yackle, *The Story of Fay v. Noia: Another Case About Another Federalism*, in Federal Courts Stories (Jackson & Resnik eds. 2010), at 191.

Other evidence indicated that when the police arrived at respondent's trailer home, they found Gilbert dead of a shotgun wound, lying a few feet from the front porch. Shortly after their arrival, respondent came from across the road and volunteered that he had shot Gilbert, and a few minutes later respondent's wife approached the police and told them the same thing. Sykes was immediately arrested and taken to the police station.

Once there, it is conceded that he was read his Miranda rights * * *. He then made a statement, which was admitted into evidence at trial through the testimony of the two officers who heard it, to the effect that he had shot Gilbert * * *. There were several references during the trial to respondent's consumption of alcohol * * * and to his apparent state of intoxication * * *. At no time during the trial, however, was the admissibility of any of respondent's statements challenged by his counsel on the ground that respondent had not understood the Miranda warnings. * * *

[Respondent then] appealed his conviction, but apparently did not challenge the admissibility of the inculpatory statements. [He later filed a post-trial motion and state court petitions for habeas corpus, in which he,] apparently for the first time, challenged the statements made to police on grounds of involuntariness. In all of these efforts respondent was unsuccessful.

Having failed in the Florida courts, respondent initiated the present action under 28 U.S.C. § 2254, asserting the inadmissibility of his statements by reason of his lack of understanding of the Miranda warnings. * * *

The simple legal question before the Court calls for a construction of the language of 28 U.S.C. § 2254(a), which provides that the federal courts shall entertain an application for a writ of habeas corpus "in behalf of a person in custody pursuant to the judgment of a state court only on the ground that he is in custody in violation of the Constitution or laws or treaties of the United States." But, to put it mildly, we do not write on a clean slate in construing this statutory provision. * * *

* * * For more than a century since the [Act of 1867, which extended federal habeas corpus to persons held under state custody], this Court has grappled with the relationship between the classical common-law writ of habeas corpus and the remedy provided in 28 U.S.C. § 2254. * * * Where the habeas petitioner challenges a final judgment of conviction rendered by a state court, this Court has been called upon to decide [a host of questions, including]: * * * In what instances will an adequate and independent state ground bar consideration of otherwise cognizable federal issues on federal habeas review? * * *

As to the role of adequate and independent state grounds, it is a well-established principle of federalism that a state decision resting on an adequate foundation of state substantive law is immune from review in the federal courts. Fox Film Corp. v. Muller, 296 U.S. 207 (1935); Murdock v. Memphis, 20 Wall. 590 (1875). * * * The area of controversy which has developed has concerned the reviewability of federal claims which the state court has declined to pass on because [they were] not presented in the manner prescribed by its *procedural* rules. * * * The pertinent decisions marking the Court's somewhat tortuous efforts to deal with this problem are: Brown v. Allen, 344 U.S. 443 (1953); Fay v. Noia, [372 U.S. 391 (1963)]; Davis v. United States, 411 U.S. 233 (1973); and Francis v. Henderson, 425 U.S. 536 (1976).

[The Court here described the decisions in Daniels v. Allen and Fay v. Noia, noting that the Court in Noia effectively overruled Daniels.]

As a matter of comity but not of federal power, the Court [in Noia] acknowledged "a limited discretion in the federal judge to deny relief . . . to an applicant who had deliberately by-passed the orderly procedure of the state courts and in so doing has forfeited his state court remedies." [372 U.S.], at 438. In so stating, the Court made clear that the waiver must be knowing and actual * * *. Noting petitioner's "grisly choice" between acceptance of his life sentence and pursuit of an appeal which might culminate in a sentence of death, the Court concluded that there had been no deliberate bypass of the right to have the federal issues reviewed through a state appeal.

A decade later we decided Davis v. United States, *supra*, in which a federal prisoner's application under 28 U.S.C. § 2255 sought for the first time to challenge the makeup of the grand jury which indicted him. The Government contended that he was barred by the requirement of Fed. Rule Crim. Proc. 12(b)(2) providing that such challenges must be raised "by motion before trial." The Rule further provides that failure to so object constitutes a waiver of the objection, but that "the court for cause shown may grant relief from the waiver." We * * * held that this standard contained in the Rule, rather than the Fay v. Noia concept of waiver, should pertain in federal habeas as on direct review. Referring to previous constructions of Rule 12(b)(2), we concluded that review of the claim should be barred on habeas, as on direct appeal, absent a showing of cause for the noncompliance and some showing of actual prejudice resulting from the alleged constitutional violation.

Last Term, in Francis v. Henderson, *supra*, the rule of Davis was applied to the parallel case of a state procedural requirement that challenges to grand jury composition be raised before trial. * * * [T]he Court concluded that * * * " '[t]here is no reason to . . . give greater preclusive effect to procedural defaults by federal defendants than to similar defaults by state defendants.' " [425 U.S.] at 542, quoting Kaufman v. United States, 394 U.S. 217, 228 (1969). As applied to the federal petitions of state convicts, the Davis cause-and-prejudice standard was thus incorporated directly into the body of law governing the availability of federal habeas corpus review.

To the extent that the dicta of Fay v. Noia may be thought to have laid down an all-inclusive rule rendering state contemporaneous-objection rules ineffective to bar review of underlying federal claims in federal habeas proceedings—absent a "knowing waiver" or a "deliberate bypass" of the right to so object—its effect was limited by Francis, which applied a different rule and barred a habeas challenge to the makeup of a grand jury. * * *

We * * * conclude that Florida procedure did, consistently with the United States Constitution, require that respondent's confession be challenged at trial or not at all, and thus his failure to timely object to its admission amounted to an independent and adequate state procedural ground which would have prevented direct review here. We thus come to the crux of this case. Shall the rule of Francis v. Henderson, *supra*, barring federal habeas review absent a showing of "cause" and "prejudice" attendant to a state procedural waiver, be applied to a waived objection to the admission of a confession at trial? We answer that question in the affirmative.

* * * [The rule of Brown v. Allen, 344 U.S. 443 (1953), permitting federal courts to determine the constitutional challenges raised in a habeas petition, without being bound by the state court's determination of the merits,] is in no way changed by our holding today. Rather, we deal only with contentions of federal law which were *not* resolved on the merits in the state proceeding due to respondent's failure to raise them there as required by state procedure. We leave open for resolution in future decisions the precise definition of the "cause"-and-"prejudice" standard, and note here only that it is narrower than the standard set forth in dicta in Fay v. Noia, 372 U.S. 391 (1963), which would make federal habeas review generally available to state convicts absent a knowing and deliberate waiver of the federal constitutional contention. It is the sweeping language of Fay v. Noia, going far beyond the facts of the case eliciting it, which we today reject.[12]

The reasons for our rejection of it are several. The contemporaneous-objection rule itself is by no means peculiar to Florida, and deserves greater respect than Fay gives it, both for the fact that it is employed by a coordinate jurisdiction within the federal system and for the many interests which it serves in its own right. A contemporaneous objection enables the record to be made with respect to the constitutional claim

---

[12] We have no occasion today to consider the Fay rule as applied to the facts there confronting the Court. Whether the Francis rule should preclude federal habeas review of claims not made in accordance with state procedure where the criminal defendant has surrendered, other than for reasons of tactical advantage, the right to have all of his claims of trial error considered by a state appellate court, we leave for another day.

The Court in Fay stated its knowing-and-deliberate-waiver rule in language which applied not only to the waiver of the right to appeal, but to failures to raise individual substantive objections in the state trial. Then, with a single sentence in a footnote, the Court swept aside all decisions of this Court "to the extent that [they] may be read to suggest a standard of discretion in federal habeas corpus proceedings different from what we lay down today . . . ." 372 U.S., at 439 n.44. We do not choose to paint with a similarly broad brush here.

when the recollections of witnesses are freshest, not years later in a federal habeas proceeding. It enables the judge who observed the demeanor of those witnesses to make the factual determinations necessary for properly deciding the federal constitutional question. * * *

A contemporaneous-objection rule may lead to the exclusion of the evidence objected to, thereby making a major contribution to finality in criminal litigation. Without the evidence claimed to be vulnerable on federal constitutional grounds, the jury may acquit the defendant, and that will be the end of the case; or it may nonetheless convict the defendant, and he will have one less federal constitutional claim to assert in his federal habeas petition. If the state trial judge admits the evidence in question after a full hearing, the federal habeas court pursuant to the 1966 amendment to § 2254 will gain significant guidance from the state ruling in this regard.* Subtler considerations as well militate in favor of honoring a state contemporaneous-objection rule. An objection on the spot may force the prosecution to take a hard look at its whole card, and even if the prosecutor thinks that the state trial judge will admit the evidence he must contemplate the possibility of reversal by the state appellate courts or the ultimate issuance of a federal writ of habeas corpus based on the impropriety of the state court's rejection of the federal constitutional claim.

We think that the rule of Fay v. Noia, broadly stated, may encourage "sandbagging" on the part of defense lawyers, who may take their chances on a verdict of not guilty in a state trial court with the intent to raise their constitutional claims in a federal habeas court if their initial gamble does not pay off. The refusal of federal habeas courts to honor contemporaneous-objection rules may also make state courts themselves less stringent in their enforcement. Under the rule of Fay v. Noia, state appellate courts know that a federal constitutional issue raised for the first time in the proceeding before them may well be decided in any event by a federal *habeas* tribunal. Thus, their choice is between addressing the issue notwithstanding the petitioner's failure to timely object, or else face the prospect that the federal habeas court will decide the question without the benefit of their views.

The failure of the federal habeas courts generally to require compliance with a contemporaneous-objection rule tends to detract from the perception of the trial of a criminal case in state court as a decisive and portentous event. * * * To the greatest extent possible all issues which bear on [the accusation of crime] should be determined in this proceeding * * *. * * * Any procedural rule which encourages the result that those proceedings be as free of error as possible is thoroughly desirable, and the contemporaneous-objection rule surely falls within this classification.

---

*   [Ed.] The amendment in question required federal habeas courts ordinarily to presume state court factfindings to be correct.

* * * The "cause"-and-"prejudice" exception of the Francis rule will afford an adequate guarantee, we think, that the rule will not prevent a federal habeas court from adjudicating for the first time the federal constitutional claim of a defendant who in the absence of such an adjudication will be the victim of a miscarriage of justice. Whatever precise content may be given those terms by later cases, we feel confident in holding without further elaboration that they do not exist here. Respondent has advanced no explanation whatever for his failure to object at trial, and, as the proceeding unfolded, the trial judge is certainly not to be faulted for failing to question the admission of the confession himself. The other evidence of guilt presented at trial, moreover, was substantial to a degree that would negate any possibility of actual prejudice resulting to the respondent from the admission of his inculpatory statement.

We accordingly conclude that the judgment * * * must be reversed, and the cause remanded to the * * * District Court * * * with instructions to dismiss respondent's petition for a writ of habeas corpus.

It is so ordered.

■ MR. CHIEF JUSTICE BURGER, concurring.

* * * I write separately to emphasize one point * * *. In my view, the "deliberate bypass" standard enunciated in Fay v. Noia, 372 U.S. 391 (1963), was never designed for, and is inapplicable to, errors—even of constitutional dimension—alleged to have been committed during trial.

In Fay v. Noia, * * * the critical procedural decision—whether to take a criminal appeal—was entrusted to a convicted defendant. * * * [T]he role of the attorney was limited to giving advice and counsel. * * * Because * * * important rights hung in the balance of the *defendant's own decision*, the Court required that a waiver impairing such rights be a knowing and intelligent decision by the defendant himself. * * *

* * * In contrast, the claim in the case before us relates to events during the trial itself. * * * As a practical matter, a criminal defendant is rarely, if ever, in a position to decide, for example, whether certain testimony is hearsay and, if so, whether it implicates interests protected by the Confrontation Clause * * *.

Once counsel is appointed, the day-to-day conduct of the defense rests with the attorney. * * *[1] The trial process simply does not permit the type of frequent and protracted interruptions which would be necessary if it were required that clients give knowing and intelligent approval to each of the myriad tactical decisions as a trial proceeds. * * *

■ MR. JUSTICE STEVENS, concurring.

Although the Court's decision today may be read as a significant departure from the "deliberate bypass" standard announced in Fay v.

---

[1] Only such basic decisions as whether to plead guilty, waive a jury, or testify in one's own behalf are ultimately for the accused to make.

Noia, 372 U.S. 391, I am persuaded that the holding is consistent with the way other federal courts have actually been applying Fay.[1] The notion that a client must always consent to a tactical decision not to assert a constitutional objection to a proffer of evidence has always seemed unrealistic to me. Conversely, if the constitutional issue is sufficiently grave, even an express waiver by the defendant himself may sometimes be excused. Matters such as the competence of counsel, the procedural context in which the asserted waiver occurred, the character of the constitutional right at stake, and the overall fairness of the entire proceeding, may be more significant than the language of the test the Court purports to apply. I therefore believe the Court has wisely refrained from attempting to give precise content to its "cause"-and-"prejudice" exception to the rule of Francis v. Henderson, 425 U.S. 536.[4]

In this case I agree with the Court's holding that collateral attack on the state-court judgment should not be allowed. The record persuades me that competent trial counsel could well have made a deliberate decision not to object to the admission of the respondent's in-custody statement. That statement was consistent, in many respects, with the respondent's trial testimony. It even had some positive value, since it portrayed the respondent as having acted in response to provocation, which might have influenced the jury to return a verdict on a lesser charge. To the extent that it was damaging, the primary harm would have resulted from its effect in impeaching the trial testimony, but it would have been admissible for impeachment in any event. Counsel may well have preferred to have the statement admitted without objection when it was first offered rather than making an objection which, at best, could have been only temporarily successful.

Moreover, since the police fully complied with Miranda, the deterrent purpose of the Miranda rule is inapplicable to this case. Finally, there is clearly no basis for claiming that the trial violated any standard of fundamental fairness. Accordingly, no matter how the rule is phrased, this case is plainly not one in which a collateral attack should be allowed. I therefore join the opinion of the Court.

■ MR. JUSTICE WHITE, concurring in the judgment. * * *

■ MR. JUSTICE BRENNAN, with whom MR. JUSTICE MARSHALL joins, dissenting.

* * * [Today's decision leaves unanswered] the thorny question that must be recognized to be central to a realistic rationalization of this area of law: How should the federal habeas court treat a procedural default in

---

[1]   The suggestion in Fay that the decision must be made personally by the defendant has not fared well * * *. * * *

[4]   As Fay v. Noia makes clear, we are concerned here with a matter of equitable discretion rather than a question of statutory authority; and equity has always been characterized by its flexibility and regard for the necessities of each case.

a state court that is attributable purely and simply to the error or negligence of a defendant's trial counsel? * * *2 * * *

I

* * * If it could be assumed that a procedural default more often than not is the product of a defendant's conscious refusal to abide by the duly constituted, legitimate processes of the state courts, then I might agree that a regime of collateral review weighted in favor of a State's procedural rules would be warranted. Fay, however, recognized that such rarely is the case; and therein lies Fay's basic unwillingness to embrace a view of habeas jurisdiction that results in "an airtight system of [procedural] forfeitures." 372 U.S., at 432.

This, of course, is not to deny that there are times when the failure to heed a state procedural requirement stems from an intentional decision to avoid the presentation of constitutional claims to the state forum. * * * Indeed, the very purpose of [Fay's] bypass test is to detect and enforce such intentional procedural forfeitures of outstanding constitutionally based claims. * * *

But * * * Fay recognized that intentional, tactical forfeitures are not the norm upon which to build a rational system of federal habeas jurisdiction. In the ordinary case, litigants simply have no incentive to slight the state tribunal, since constitutional adjudication on the state and federal levels are not mutually exclusive. * * * [N]o rational lawyer would risk the "sandbagging" feared by the Court. * * *

II

* * * If the standard adopted today is later construed to require that the simple mistakes of attorneys are to be treated as binding forfeitures, it * * * would essentially leave it to the States, through the enactment of procedure and the certification of the competence of local attorneys, to determine whether a habeas applicant will be permitted the access to the federal forum that is guaranteed him by Congress.

* * * But federal review is not the full measure of Sykes' interest, for there is another of even greater immediacy: assuring that his constitutional claims can be addressed to *some* court. For the obvious consequence of barring Sykes from the federal courthouse is to insulate Florida's alleged constitutional violation from any and all judicial review because of a lawyer's mistake. From the standpoint of the habeas petitioner, it is a harsh rule indeed that denies him "any review at all where the state has granted none," Brown v. Allen, 344 U.S., at 552 (Black, J., dissenting)—particularly when he would have enjoyed both state and federal consideration had his attorney not erred. * * *

---

2   * * * This Court has never taken issue with the foundation principle established by Fay v. Noia—that [federal habeas courts] possess the *power* to look beyond a state procedural forfeiture in order to entertain the contention that a defendant's constitutional rights have been abridged. * * * Our disagreement, therefore, centers upon the standard that should govern a federal district court in the exercise of this power * * *. * * *

III

A regime of federal habeas corpus jurisdiction that permits the reopening of state procedural defaults does not invalidate any state procedural rule as such; Florida's courts remain entirely free * * * to deny any and all state rights and remedies to a defendant who fails to comply with applicable state procedure. The relevant inquiry is whether [the federal habeas courts should "impose additional sanctions for inadvertent noncompliance with state procedural requirements"]. * * *

Punishing a lawyer's unintentional errors by closing the federal courthouse door to his client is both a senseless and misdirected method of deterring the slighting of state rules. It is senseless because unplanned and unintentional action of any kind generally is not subject to deterrence; and, to the extent that it is hoped that a threatened sanction addressed to the defense will induce greater care and caution on the part of trial lawyers, * * * the potential loss of all valuable state remedies would be sufficient to this end. And it is a misdirected sanction because * * * the habeas applicant, as opposed to his lawyer, hardly is the proper recipient of such a penalty. Especially with fundamental constitutional rights at stake, no fictional relationship of principal-agent or the like can justify holding the criminal defendant accountable for the naked errors of his attorney. This is especially true when so many indigent defendants are without any realistic choice in selecting who ultimately represents them at trial. Indeed, if responsibility for error must be apportioned between the parties, it is the State, through its attorney's admissions and certification policies, that is more fairly held to blame for the fact that practicing lawyers too often are ill-prepared or ill-equipped to act carefully and knowledgeably when faced with decisions governed by state procedural requirements. * * *

IV

* * * [A]lthough some four years have passed since its introduction in Davis v. United States, 411 U.S. 233 (1973), the only thing clear about the Court's "cause"-and-"prejudice" standard is that it exhibits the notable tendency of keeping prisoners in jail without addressing their constitutional complaints. * * * Left unresolved is whether a habeas petitioner like Sykes can adequately discharge this burden by offering the commonplace and truthful explanation for his default: attorney ignorance or error beyond the client's control. The "prejudice" inquiry, meanwhile, appears to bear a strong resemblance to harmless-error doctrine. * * * [I]f this is what is meant by prejudice, respondent's constitutional contentions could be as quickly and easily disposed of in this regard by permitting federal courts to reach the merits of his complaint. * * *

One final consideration deserves mention. * * * [M]ost courts, this one included, traditionally have resisted any realistic inquiry into the competency of trial counsel. * * * [The conduct of a lawyer who unreasonably permits state procedural rules to bar the client's constitutional claims] may well fall below the level of competence that can fairly be expected of him. For almost 40 years it has been established that inadequacy of counsel undercuts the very competence and jurisdiction of the trial court and is always open to collateral review. Obviously, as a practical matter, a trial counsel cannot procedurally waive his own inadequacy. If the scope of habeas jurisdiction previously governed by Fay v. Noia is to be redefined so as to enforce the errors and neglect of lawyers with unnecessary and unjust rigor, the time may come when conscientious and fairminded federal and state courts * * * will have to reconsider whether they can continue to indulge the comfortable fiction that all lawyers are skilled or even competent craftsmen in representing the fundamental rights of their clients.

NOTE ON FEDERAL HABEAS CORPUS AND STATE COURT PROCEDURAL DEFAULT

A.   Introductory Questions

(1) The Relationship of Procedural Default to the Adequate State Ground Doctrine. What should be the relationship among the standards for forgiving procedural defaults applied by the state courts in the first instance, by the Supreme Court on direct review, and by federal habeas courts?

(a) A state procedural default that would not bar direct review by the Supreme Court (because the procedural ruling is not an "adequate" state ground) also does not bar federal habeas corpus review. See Lee v. Kemna, 534 U.S. 362 (2002). In addition, some defaults that would bar Supreme Court review on direct appeal do not bar habeas review—for example, where "cause and prejudice" can be shown. But, as is elaborated below, the standards applied in habeas for excusing state court defaults are so difficult for petitioners to satisfy that in practice the standards applied on direct and collateral review differ very little.

(b) In Noia, the Court stated that a habeas court's refusal to give effect to a state court forfeiture did not bar the state from enforcing the underlying procedural requirement. The regime thus created, the Court contended, had several advantages: (i) it minimized federal interference with the state courts; (ii) it adequately deterred violations of state procedural rules by permitting forfeiture of remedies in state court and on direct review; and (iii) under the deliberate bypass standard, it ensured virtually all criminal defendants an ultimate federal adjudication of their federal claims.[1] But as noted in Meltzer, *State Court Forfeitures of Federal Rights*, 99 Harv.L.Rev. 1128, 1150–58, 1190–1202 (1986), Noia placed considerable pressure on

---

[1]   Accord, Reitz, *Federal Habeas Corpus: Impact of an Abortive State Proceeding*, 74 Harv.L.Rev. 1315, 1347–48 (1961); Note, *Federal Habeas Corpus For State Prisoners: The Isolation Principle*, 39 N.Y.U.L.Rev. 78, 94 (1964). See also Brennan, *Federal Habeas Corpus and State Prisoners: An Exercise in Federalism*, 7 Utah L.Rev. 423 (1961).

states to excuse defaults that would ultimately be excused on habeas, a course that many states followed.[2]

(2) Procedural Default and the Adversary Process. The procedural default cases vividly highlight the intractable difficulties that arise when lawyers are responsible for compliance with state procedural rules but their mistakes jeopardize the constitutional rights of their clients. How should the costs of the inevitable errors be allocated between the state and defendants in criminal proceedings? Does the answer depend on whether Justice Rehnquist was correct, in Sykes, that broad excuse of procedural defaults creates a serious risk that defense lawyers will "sandbag" the prosecution? (How realistic is that risk?) Does it depend on the general quality of defense representation and on the strictness of constitutional standards of effective assistance of counsel? Note that under prevailing constitutional standards, many defaults resulting from lawyers' errors are not serious enough to constitute a violation of the defendant's Sixth Amendment rights.[3]

(3) Alternatives and the Role of Innocence. Should excuse of procedural default require a showing that the defaulted claim, if meritorious, would establish a reasonable probability that the petitioner was innocent of the crime on which custody is based? Jeffries & Stuntz, *Ineffective Assistance and Procedural Default in Federal Habeas Corpus*, 57 U.Chi.L.Rev. 679, 691–92 (1990), contends that if such a showing is made, procedural barriers to review should be swept aside so that a possibly innocent person can obtain federal review; absent such a showing, there is no reason to excuse a default. They argue that barring habeas review of defaulted claims that are unrelated to innocence sacrifices little: because state courts do not reach the merits of defaulted claims, habeas review cannot help ensure that state courts properly applied federal standards. How does the argument account for Justice Brennan's argument that habeas is about the legality of "detention simpliciter?"

(4) The Impact of Procedural Default. Studies prior to Sykes found that no more than 3% of *petitions* were denied on procedural default grounds.[4] One post-Sykes study found that at least one *claim* was barred by procedural default in 13% of non-capital cases and 42% of capital cases.[5]

---

[2]   Professor Meltzer argues that the doctrines that permit defendants to obtain direct or collateral federal review of federal claims, notwithstanding noncompliance with state procedural rules, should be characterized as rules of federal common law. As such, like other forms of federal common law, they should be binding on the states and require state courts to forgive any defaults that would not block federal review: "If the state's interest in imposing a forfeiture * * * is not sufficiently weighty to bar the Supreme Court or a federal habeas court from reviewing the federal issue, that interest is also not weighty enough to bar review of the federal issue in state court in the first instance." *Id.* 1189–90.

[3]   Kovarsky, *Delay in the Shadow of Death*, 95 N.Y.U.L.Rev. 1319 (2020), explains why in capital cases habeas petitioners often bring new claims once the state sets an execution date (often due to ripeness issues and lack of representation through much of the earlier process) and why consciously deferring ripe claims is irrational under current procedural default doctrine.

[4]   See Shapiro, *Federal Habeas Corpus: A Study in Massachusetts*, 87 Harv.L.Rev. 321, 346–47 (1973); Faust, Rubenstein & Yackle, *The Great Writ in Action: Empirical Light on the Federal Habeas Corpus Debate*, 18 N.Y.U.Rev.L. & Soc. Change 637, 692–93 (1991).

[5]   King, Cheesman & Ostrom, *Final Technical Report: Habeas Litigation in U.S. District Courts*, National Center for State Courts, Aug. 21, 2007, at 48. See also Flango, Habeas Corpus

B.   The Meaning of the Sykes Standard

(1) Introduction. Sykes left "cause and prejudice" to be defined in later cases.[6] The 1996 AEDPA amendments contain no general provision dealing with state court procedural defaults and therefore, with one small exception, leave in place the judge-made doctrines just described.[7]

A series of decisions has given "cause" a very restricted meaning, embracing only these categories: (a) reliance on a novel constitutional claim; (b) deficient performance by counsel that is serious enough to constitute ineffective assistance of counsel under the Sixth Amendment; and (c) the state's creation of an "external impediment" to presentation of the claim. A petitioner who can establish "cause" must also establish "prejudice" to gain the right to have a habeas court reach the merits.

The Court has also stated that a habeas court may hear a defaulted claim, even where cause and prejudice cannot be shown, in one other, narrowly defined circumstance—when the petitioner makes an adequate showing of "actual innocence."

(2) Cause 1: Novelty. In Reed v. Ross, 468 U.S. 1 (1984) (5–4), the Court, with Justice Brennan writing, held that "the cause requirement may be satisfied under certain circumstances" where petitioner seeks the benefit of a "novel" decision upholding a claim that counsel could not have anticipated during direct review. Specifically, Ross sought to benefit from In re Winship, 397 U.S. 358, 364 (1970), decided after his direct appeal was final. See *id.* 364 (holding that due process requires "proof beyond a reasonable doubt of every fact necessary to constitute the crime with which [a defendant] is charged").[8] The Court essentially closed off the narrow opening recognized in Ross five years later, when it held in Teague v. Lane, 489 U.S. 288 (1989), p. 1580, *supra*, that a habeas court could almost never entertain a petition (whether or not there had been a procedural default) based on "new law." A claim sufficiently novel to excuse a default will be barred by Teague, unless it fits within Teague's extraordinarily narrow first exception—and even then it may be barred by § 2254(d)(1), see pp. 1580–1585, 1587–1609, *supra*. Thus, novelty as cause is of little present significance.

(3) Cause 2: Ineffective Assistance of Counsel. In Murray v. Carrier, 477 U.S. 478 (1986), the Court recognized that "if [a] procedural default is the result of ineffective assistance of counsel [under the standard established in Strickland v. Washington, 466 U.S. 668 (1984)], the Sixth Amendment

---

in State and Federal Courts 67 (1994) (finding, after Sykes, that 6.2% of claims were dismissed on the basis of procedural default).

    [6]   On the evolution from Noia to Sykes, see Hill, *The Forfeiture of Constitutional Rights in Criminal Cases*, 78 Colum.L.Rev. 1050, 1051–62 (1978).

    [7]   AEDPA does have provisions that apply only in capital cases in states whose provision of counsel in state post-conviction proceedings satisfies statutorily specified standards. See, *e.g.*, §§ 2261, 2264, p. 1554, *supra*.

    [8]   In dissent, Justice Rehnquist questioned whether novelty should ever constitute cause, and added that in any event Ross's claim was not novel.

Two years earlier, the Court declined to excuse a state court default on the basis that, in view of the state courts' consistent rejection of similar claims, objection was futile: "Even a state court that has previously rejected a constitutional argument may decide, upon reflection, that the contention is valid." Engle v. Isaac, 456 U.S. 107, 130 (1982).

itself requires that responsibility for the default be imputed to the State * * *. Ineffective assistance of counsel, then, is cause for a procedural default." But, at the same time, the Court limited the window it had opened to relief. Carrier presented a case in which appellate counsel inadvertently failed to include in the brief on appeal one claim that was listed in the notice of appeal. In an opinion for five Justices, Justice O'Connor held that the state court procedural default barred federal habeas review of the claim, emphasizing that the "considerable costs" associated with habeas review "do not disappear when the default stems from counsel's ignorance or inadvertence rather than from a deliberate decision * * * to withhold a claim." These costs would increase, she argued, if the excuse of procedural defaults depended on whether they were unintentional, because "federal habeas courts would routinely be required to hold evidentiary hearings to determine what prompted counsel's failure to raise the claim in question." The Court thus held that a defendant who is "represented by counsel whose performance is not constitutionally ineffective" bears "the risk of attorney error that results in a procedural default."

By contrast, the Court has recognized that where a defendant is abandoned by counsel, the federal habeas petitioner should not bear the brunt of procedural defaults committed by counsel in state court.[9] Litigation of ineffectiveness—whether as cause or as a claim in itself—is full of pitfalls. The first time when such claims can effectively be raised is often state post-

---

[9]   Maples v. Thomas, 565 U.S. 266 (2012), presented just such a case. There, counsel of record abandoned an individual on death row. After a state trial court denied Maples's post-conviction petition, it sent notices to the two out-of-state lawyers who had been representing Maples. By then, however, the lawyers had left their former law firm, whose mailroom returned the unopened envelopes to the court stating that they could not be delivered at that address. The court clerk took no action in response. Local counsel also received a notice of the petition's denial but took no action, assuming that the out-of-state lawyers were responsible for the matter. No notice was sent to the petitioner, and no appeal was filed.

When petitioner's subsequent federal habeas corpus petition reached the Supreme Court, Justice Ginsburg, writing for the majority, posited that the general principle that a lawyer's negligence does not by itself constitute cause rests on the agency law ideal that a principal bears the risk of negligent conduct by one's agent. Here, by contrast, petitioner's attorneys had severed the agency relationship on whose existence that principle depends. And given local counsel's failure even to call the two out-of-state lawyers when the notice of the decision arrived, the Court concluded that at that time, he was not "serving as [petitioner's] agent 'in any meaningful sense of that word' " (quoting Holland v. Florida, 560 U.S. 631, 659 (2010) (opinion of Alito, J.)).

In dissent, Justice Scalia, joined by Justice Thomas, agreed that default "may be excused when it is attributable to abandonment by his attorney," but he contended that on the facts presented there had not been an abandonment.

The Court revisited the question of attorney abandonment in Christeson v. Roper, 574 U.S. 373 (2015) (per curiam), a capital case in which counsel appointed by the district court to represent a habeas petitioner failed to meet with their client and file a petition on his behalf within the one-year AEDPA filing deadline. Reversing the district court's refusal to grant petitioner's motion to substitute new counsel, the Court concluded that substitution served the "interests of justice." Petitioner's only chance to secure habeas review of his underlying claims was to prevail on an argument that appointed counsel's missteps warranted equitable tolling of the one-year filing deadline—an argument that the same appointed counsel unsurprisingly did not make. As Justice Alito noted in his dissent, however, even with new counsel, petitioner still had to satisfy the standard for equitable tolling, no easy task. See Holland v. Florida, 560 U.S. 631, 653 (2010) (holding that equitable tolling of AEDPA's one-year limitations period may be had only upon a showing of diligence and "extraordinary circumstances").

conviction proceedings,[10] where petitioners ordinarily lack counsel. Thus, petitioners in state post-conviction proceedings who proceed pro se—and even those few who obtain legal representation—often fail to advance a claim of ineffective assistance of trial counsel or fail to advance the claim in a way that complies with state time limits or other procedural requirements.

Apart from all the difficulties petitioners face in satisfying the limitations period, the exhaustion requirement, and state procedural rules generally, claims of ineffective assistance of counsel rarely succeed on the merits. Despite (or perhaps because of) the widespread shortcomings of criminal defense representation, defendants have generally had great difficulty in persuading courts that a lawyer's performance fell below the constitutional minimum and that any shortcoming was prejudicial.[11]

(4) Procedural Defaults in State Post-Conviction Proceedings Challenging the Effectiveness of Counsel. Coleman v. Thompson, 501 U.S. 722 (1991), addressed the effect of counsel's failure to file an appeal in state post-conviction proceedings. The Court held that the failure to appeal constituted a procedural default barring federal habeas review. In support of this conclusion, Coleman noted that the Court had never held there to be a right to counsel for state collateral proceedings.[12] Coleman also read Carrier as permitting ineffective assistance of counsel to serve as cause only where it rises to the level of a constitutional violation. In so holding, the Court observed that "[f]or Coleman to prevail * * *, there must be an exception to th[is] rule * * * in those cases where state collateral review is the first place a prisoner can present a challenge to his conviction. We need not answer this question broadly, however, for one state court has addressed Coleman's claims: the state habeas trial court."

(a) In Martinez v. Ryan, 566 U.S. 1 (2012), the Court faced the situation left unaddressed in Coleman. Arizona requires that ineffective assistance of counsel claims be litigated in state collateral proceedings rather than on direct review. During the pendency of Martinez's direct appeal, his lawyer commenced a state post-conviction proceeding but made no claim that Martinez's trial counsel had been ineffective, instead stating that she could not identify any colorable claim to raise on Martinez's behalf. Martinez did not respond to the trial court's invitation to raise any claims he felt his lawyer had overlooked, and the court then denied post-conviction relief. When a new lawyer launched a second state post-conviction proceeding,

---

[10]   Indeed, in Massaro v. United States, 538 U.S. 500 (2003), where a petitioner in federal custody filed a collateral attack, under 28 U.S.C. § 2255, asserting the ineffectiveness of his trial counsel, the Court unanimously rejected the government's argument that the failure of counsel on direct appeal to raise the ineffectiveness of trial counsel, even when that claim was based solely on the trial record, constituted a procedural default. The Court offered a variety of reasons why ineffectiveness claims are more appropriately litigated in collateral proceedings.

[11]   See, *e.g.*, Primus, *Structural Reform in Criminal Defense: Relocating Ineffective Assistance of Counsel Claims*, 92 Cornell L.Rev. 679, 682–88 (2007); Bright, *Counsel for the Poor: The Death Sentence Not for the Worst Crime but for the Worst Lawyer*, 103 Yale L.J. 1835, 1850–51 (1994); Green, *Lethal Fiction: The Meaning of "Counsel" in the Sixth Amendment*, 78 Iowa L.Rev. 433, 499–507 (1993).

[12]   See Ross v. Moffit, 417 U.S. 600 (1974) (holding that there is no Sixth Amendment right to counsel beyond a criminal defendant's first appeal); Douglas v. California, 372 U.S. 353 (1963) (holding State must appoint counsel on criminal defendant's first appeal).

alleging that Martinez's trial counsel had been ineffective, the court dismissed the claim on the basis of a state rule barring a claim that could have been raised in a prior state post-conviction proceeding. Martinez then filed a federal habeas corpus petition asserting the ineffectiveness of both his trial counsel and his counsel in the first state post-conviction proceeding.

The Supreme Court ruled, 7–2, that the lower federal courts had erred in ruling that Martinez had procedurally defaulted his underlying ineffectiveness of trial counsel claim. Although the Court recognized that regimes like Arizona's make it such that collateral review of ineffectiveness claims "is in many ways the equivalent of a prisoner's direct appeal," Justice Kennedy's majority opinion did not hold that the Sixth Amendment guarantees the assistance of counsel in state post-conviction proceedings that constitute the first opportunity for a defendant to allege the ineffectiveness of trial counsel.[13] Instead, the Court held in Martinez that "[i]nadequate assistance of counsel [in a state collateral proceeding that provides the first occasion at which the ineffectiveness of trial counsel may be litigated] may establish cause for a prisoner's procedural default of a claim of ineffective assistance at trial," thereby potentially excusing the default in state post-conviction proceedings of the underlying claim. Otherwise, the Court argued, no state court—and hence neither the Supreme Court on direct review nor a federal habeas court—could hear the claim.

The procedural default rules on habeas, Justice Kennedy noted, "are elaborated in the exercise of the Court's discretion" as "an equitable matter." He then drew on Sixth Amendment jurisprudence in ruling that cause can be established "in two circumstances. The first is where the state courts did not appoint counsel in the initial-review collateral proceeding for a claim of ineffective assistance at trial. The second is where appointed counsel in the initial-review collateral proceeding, where the claim should have been raised, was ineffective under the standards of Strickland v. Washington, 466 U.S. 668 (1984). To overcome the default, a prisoner must also demonstrate that the underlying ineffective-assistance-of-trial-counsel claim is a substantial one, which is to say that the prisoner must demonstrate that the claim has some merit."[14] The Court concluded by noting that "[a]n equitable ruling," by contrast to a constitutional mandate to appoint counsel in collateral review proceedings, "permits States a variety" of potential responses, including "elect[ing] between appointing counsel in initial-review collateral proceedings or not asserting a procedural default and raising a defense on the merits in federal habeas proceedings."

Justice Scalia's dissent (joined by Justice Thomas) objected that the Court's decision was no different in effect from the recognition of a constitutional right to counsel in this post-conviction setting. The Court, he claimed, may not have called into question the "*lawfulness*" of denying counsel in post-conviction proceedings, only its "*sanity*," for if counsel is

---

[13]   The Court also declined to revisit Coleman's holding.

[14]   AEDPA includes a provision, 28 U.S.C. § 2254(i), stating that "[t]he ineffectiveness * * * of counsel during Federal or State collateral post-conviction proceedings shall not be a ground for relief." The Court held that this provision did not bar relief, as recognizing ineffectiveness as "cause" to excuse a default differs from recognizing it as "a ground for relief."

denied, the state risks having to defend the adequacy of trial counsel in a federal habeas corpus proceeding many years later. (Might a state nonetheless rationally choose that option, given that some incarcerated persons will never file a federal habeas petition, while others will find their petitions blocked by other procedural rules limiting the exercise of habeas jurisdiction?)[15] Justice Scalia also accused the Court of giving insufficient weight to the value of finality and of ignoring the frequency with which claims of ineffective assistance of counsel can be made.[16]

(b) In his Martinez dissent, Justice Scalia objected that the Court's limitation of its holding to cases in which the state has barred litigation on direct appeal of the ineffectiveness of trial counsel "lacks any principled basis, and will not last." His prediction was realized the following Term in Trevino v. Thaler, 569 U.S. 413 (2013). There, the federal habeas petitioner set forth a claim of ineffective trial counsel that he had not raised either on direct review or in state post-conviction proceedings. Texas law did not bar the litigation of ineffective assistance of counsel claims on direct review, but the state courts had expressed a preference for litigating such claims in state collateral proceedings and had acknowledged that it was "virtually impossible for appellate counsel to adequately present an ineffective assistance [of trial counsel] claim."

In Trevino, the Court, with Justice Breyer writing for the majority, held, 5–4, that "where, as here, [a] state procedural framework, by reason of its design and operation, makes it highly unlikely in a typical case that a defendant will have a meaningful opportunity to raise a claim of ineffective assistance of trial counsel on direct appeal, our holding in Martinez applies." In a dissent joined by Justice Alito, Chief Justice Roberts objected that the narrow holding in Martinez, which he had joined, was being greatly expanded. He complained that the Court's opinion was unclear about "how meaningful is meaningful enough, how meaningfulness is to be measured, how unlikely highly unlikely is, * * * or what case qualifies as the 'typical' case." Justices Scalia and Thomas also dissented.

(c) In Martinez, the Court stressed that the right to effective assistance of *trial* counsel is a "bedrock principle" of the criminal adjudicative system. But what about the right to effective assistance of counsel in a criminal defendant's first appeal as of right? Should waiver in state post-conviction proceedings of an underlying claim of appellate counsel's ineffectiveness be excused in federal habeas proceedings? The Supreme Court took up this question in Davila v. Davis, 582 U.S. 521 (2017), answering it in the negative while holding that Martinez and Trevino should be limited to their particular circumstances.

---

[15] King, *Enforcing Effective Assistance After Martinez*, 122 Yale L.J. 2428 (2013), notes, *inter alia*, that state courts under fiscal constraints may refuse to appoint counsel in post-conviction cases, that when defendants plead guilty, courts increasingly accept waivers of the right to pursue post-conviction relief, and that even petitioners whose claims are resolved on the merits rarely prevail on ineffective assistance claims. For these and other reasons, she views the dissent's prediction that states will be forced to provide counsel in every case as "absurd."

[16] As Justice Scalia phrased it, "ineffective assistance of trial counsel is a monotonously standard claim on federal habeas," a point he followed by asking, "has a duly convicted defendant *ever* been effectively represented?"

Writing for a five-Justice majority, Justice Thomas stressed that "Martinez did not purport to displace Coleman as the general rule governing procedural default. Rather, it 'qualifie[d] Coleman by recognizing a narrow exception'" applying only to ineffective assistance of trial counsel claims and only where those claims "'must be raised in an initial-review collateral proceeding.'" Because Martinez and Trevino were focused on trial errors and because "[c]laims of ineffective assistance of appellate counsel" fail to "pose the same risk that a trial error—of any kind—will escape review altogether," the Court concluded that the default of claims by allegedly ineffective appellate counsel should not be excused. In support of this conclusion, the Court posited that "[i]f an unpreserved trial error was so obvious that appellate counsel was constitutionally required to raise it on appeal, then trial counsel likely provided ineffective assistance by failing to object to it in the first instance." In such circumstances, the Court noted, Martinez and Trevino would authorize excusing any default of claims relating to the trial counsels' ineffectiveness.[17]

Dissenting for four Justices, Justice Breyer emphasized that defendants in criminal proceedings have a constitutional right to effective assistance of counsel "at both trial and during an initial appeal" and that the Court's decisions have labeled effective assistance of appellate counsel—just like effective assistance of trial counsel—as "critically important." Turning to the majority's claims, Justice Breyer cited several scenarios in which the ineffectiveness of appellate counsel could result in underlying claims never being reviewed by any court, such as Brady claims that only become apparent after trial.[18]

Given that the Court has labeled both the effective assistance of trial *and* appellate counsel as critically important to a fair trial (and the Sixth Amendment guarantees constitutionally effective counsel at both stages), is there a principled distinction underlying the differing results in Martinez and Davila? After Davila, what, if any, avenues of relief remain for defaulted claims (including Brady claims) that were not available to a petitioner at the time of trial? To date, those circuits that have reached the question have declined to extend the reasoning of Martinez and Trevino to Brady claims discovered after trial.[19]

(d)   The Court further and dramatically curtailed the reach of Martinez and Trevino in Shinn v. Ramirez, 596 U.S. 366 (2022). Writing for a six-Justice majority, Justice Thomas addressed the question whether "the equitable rule announced in Martinez permits a federal court to dispense with § 2254(e)(2)'s narrow limits [on the holding of evidentiary hearings] because a prisoner's state postconviction counsel negligently failed to develop

---

[17]   As further support for declining to extend the Martinez line, Justice Thomas cited the likelihood that "[a]dopting petitioner's argument could flood the federal courts with defaulted claims of appellate ineffectiveness" and that such claims in turn "could serve as the gateway to federal review of a host of trial errors."

[18]   See Brady v. Maryland, 373 U.S. 83 (1963) (requiring disclosure of exculpatory evidence by the prosecution to the defense).

Justice Breyer also doubted that a different holding would open the floodgates with respect to the filing of new habeas petitions.

[19]   See, *e.g.*, Hunton v. Sinclair, 732 F.3d 1124 (9th Cir.2013).

the state-court record." Holding that Martinez does *not* displace AEDPA's "stringent" limitations in § 2254(e)(2), the Court concluded that even where the underlying claim alleges the ineffectiveness of trial counsel, defendants are bound by the actions taken by counsel in state post-conviction proceedings. Specifically, if post-conviction counsel "failed to develop the factual basis of a claim in State court proceedings"—including an ineffectiveness of trial counsel claim—then a federal court "shall not hold an evidentiary hearing on the claim" unless the petitioner satisfies one of the two limited exceptions set forth in § 2254(e)(2)(A).[20]

The habeas petitioners in Ramirez had argued that it made little sense to go from holding in Martinez that petitioners will not be deemed responsible for the failure of state post-conviction counsel to raise a claim of ineffectiveness of trial counsel to then hold the petitioner responsible for the same post-conviction counsel's failure to develop the record in state court supporting such a claim. But, Justice Thomas opined, this argument was foreclosed by Congress's enactment of § 2254(e)(2), which, he stated, "we have no authority to amend." The Court also emphasized the narrowness of the holding in Martinez along with that decision's prediction that it would not "put a significant strain on state resources" (quoting Martinez, 566 U.S. at 15). Permitting evidentiary hearings in the context of Martinez claims, Justice Thomas predicted, would do just that. Finally, Justice Thomas emphasized the state's interest in the finality of criminal convictions and worried that "broadly available habeas relief" may lead to sandbagging by petitioners who may hold certain claims back in state court, reserving them for federal habeas proceedings.

Justice Sotomayor, joined by Justices Breyer and Kagan, dissented. In her view, Ramirez "all but overrules" Martinez and Trevino, leaving a petitioner unable to vindicate the constitutional right to effective trial counsel, what the Court only ten years earlier in Martinez described as " 'a bedrock principle' that constitutes the very 'foundation for our adversary system' of criminal justice" (quoting Martinez, 566 U.S. at 12). Labeling the majority opinion as "perverse" and "illogical," the dissent disagreed that AEDPA required such an outcome. If, Justice Sotomayor wrote, "Martinez and Trevino establish that petitioners are not at fault for any failure to raise their claims in state court in these circumstances," it is only sensible to interpret AEDPA's § 2254(e)(2)'s "failed to develop" language as "incorporat[ing] a threshold requirement that the petitioner be at fault for not developing evidence." Such a conclusion, the dissent contended, is consistent with how the Court first interpreted § 2254(e)(2) in Michael Williams v. Taylor, where it noted that " 'a person is not at fault when his diligent efforts to perform an act are thwarted' by an external force" (quoting 529 U.S. at 432). In the dissent's view, "Martinez cases are among the rare ones in which attorney error constitutes such an external factor."

---

[20]   The Court referenced Michael Williams v. Taylor, 529 U.S. 420 (2000), p. 1629, *supra*, as defining "failed to develop" to encompass " 'lack of diligence, or some greater fault, attributable to the prisoner *or the prisoner's counsel*' " (quoting 529 U.S. at 432). For Ramirez, this conclusion essentially put an end to his claim that his trial counsel was ineffective because his post-conviction counsel did not present any ineffectiveness claim to the state courts nor create any associated record supporting such a claim.

Justice Sotomayor added, "AEDPA does not render state judgments unassailable, [it] strikes a balance between respecting state-court judgments and preserving the necessary and vital role federal courts play in 'guard[ing] against extreme malfunctions in the state criminal justice systems'" (quoting Harrington v. Richter, 562 U.S. 86, 102–03 (2011)). Concluding, she wrote, "[t]wo men whose trial attorneys did not provide even the bare minimum level of representation required by the Constitution may be executed because forces outside of their control prevented them from vindicating their constitutional right to counsel." This result, in the dissent's view, rendered the protections of the Sixth Amendment "illusory."

In states like Arizona, which require criminal defendants to bring claims of ineffective trial counsel in post-conviction proceedings in which they enjoy no Sixth Amendment right to counsel, Ramirez holds that federal habeas courts are bound by the state record developed by post-conviction counsel, whether they advanced a claim of ineffective trial counsel or not. (It is only those exceedingly rare situations falling within the exceptions to § 2254(e)(2) in which a hearing may be held in federal habeas proceedings.) Very often ineffective assistance claims turn on matters that trial counsel did not investigate with respect to the guilt and/or sentencing phase at trial and therefore failed to uncover and enter into the trial record. In such cases, the ability to introduce new evidence in federal habeas is often essential for petitioners effectively to advance their Strickland claims. If that is correct, what is left of Martinez and Trevino after Ramirez?[21] More generally, for someone who receives constitutionally deficient trial representation and then inadequate representation in subsequent state post-conviction proceedings, what is left of their underlying Sixth Amendment right to counsel under Ramirez's framework?

(5) Cause 3: External Impediment. Of the very few Supreme Court decisions that have found cause to exist, three involved "external impediments" created by the state.

(a) In Amadeo v. Zant, 486 U.S. 214 (1988), while the defendant's direct appeal was pending, an independent voting rights lawsuit uncovered a handwritten memorandum from the District Attorney's Office to the jury commissioners, listing figures for the number of Black jurors and women to be placed on master jury lists. The document's apparent purpose was to ensure that these groups were under-represented but not so much as to give rise to a prima facie case of discrimination. When the defendant asserted a jury discrimination claim for the first time on appeal, the Georgia Supreme Court rejected it as untimely. On federal habeas corpus, the Supreme Court found cause for the default because the basis for the claim was "reasonably

---

[21]　And if evidentiary matters are now controlled by § 2254(e)(2) regardless of whether an underlying claim qualifies for equitable exceptions to procedural default doctrine, what, if anything, is left of the Court's decision in McQuiggin v. Perkins, 569 U.S. 383 (2013), p. 1548, note 4, *supra* (applying equitable tolling to permit an untimely habeas claim of actual innocence based on new evidence)?

unknown" to the petitioner's lawyers as a result of "the 'objective factor' of 'some interference by officials.' "[22]

(b) The Court extended the "external impediment" concept in Strickler v. Greene, 527 U.S. 263 (1999). In his federal habeas petition, Strickler for the first time claimed that the government had not disclosed exculpatory information, in violation of the Due Process Clause. Justice Stevens's opinion for the Court on this point found cause to excuse Strickler's failure to obtain the information earlier where the prosecution had maintained at trial an "open file policy" toward discovery. In the Court's view, it was reasonable for Strickler's lawyers to rely on the government's "implicit representation that [exculpatory materials that the government was obliged to disclose] would be included in the open files tendered to defense counsel." Further, during state post-conviction proceedings, the state asserted that it had turned over all relevant material. These facts, Justice Stevens concluded, undercut any argument that Strickler or his counsel should have realized earlier that material was missing from those files.

(c) In Banks v. Dretke, 540 U.S. 668 (2004), the Court again addressed a case involving a claim that the prosecution had withheld exculpatory evidence. With Justice Ginsburg writing, the Court held that "[a] rule * * * declaring 'prosecutor may hide, defendant must seek,' is not tenable in a system constitutionally bound to accord defendants due process."

(6) Prejudice. The Sykes decision requires a petitioner to show cause *and* "prejudice," but the Supreme Court's subsequent decisions dealing with procedural default have not elaborated on just what constitutes a showing of prejudice.[23] The most pertinent statement came in United States v. Frady, 456 U.S. 152 (1982), a collateral post-conviction attack brought under 28 U.S.C. § 2255 by an individual in *federal* custody, but applying the same cause and prejudice standard. There, the Court said that to establish prejudice, the petitioner must show that errors at trial "worked to his *actual* and substantial disadvantage, infecting his entire trial with error of constitutional dimensions."[24]

(7) Actual Innocence. In Murray v. Carrier, Paragraph B(3), *supra*, the Court mentioned one circumstance, other than where "cause and prejudice"

---

[22] The Court read Amadeo narrowly in McCleskey v. Zant, 499 U.S. 467 (1991). In rejecting McCleskey's argument that the state's failure to turn over a document constituted cause for an earlier procedural default, the Court said: "This case differs from Amadeo in two crucial respects. First, there is no finding that the State concealed evidence. And second, * * * [any concealment that might have occurred] would not establish cause here because, in light of McCleskey's knowledge of the information in the document, any initial concealment would not have prevented him from raising the claim [in the earlier proceeding]."

[23] In two cases in which the Supreme Court has found cause—Reed v. Ross, Paragraph B(2), *supra*, and Amadeo v. Zant, Paragraph B(5)(a), *supra*—there was no dispute that prejudice was present. Two other cases both involved claims that the prosecution had unconstitutionally suppressed exculpatory evidence in violation of Brady v. Maryland, 373 U.S. 83 (1963). See Paragraph B(5)(b–c), *supra*. The more recent of them, Banks v. Dretke, Paragraph B(5)(c), *supra*, explained that in that situation, the meaning of prejudice essentially merges into the question whether the suppressed evidence "is 'material' for Brady purposes"—which in turn requires a " 'reasonable probability of a different result' " (quoting Kyles v. Whitley, 514 U.S. 419, 434 (1995)). In Martinez and Trevino, see Paragraph B(4), *supra*, as well as Maples, see p. 1646, note 9, *supra*, the Court did not reach the prejudice question.

[24] See generally Jeffries & Stuntz, Paragraph A(3), *supra*, at 684–85 & n.25.

are shown, in which a state court default could be excused: "in an extraordinary case, where a constitutional violation has probably resulted in the conviction of one who is actually innocent, a federal habeas court may grant the writ even in the absence of a showing of cause for the procedural default." Cases satisfying that approach have been rare in the lower courts, see Steiker, *Innocence and Federal Habeas*, 41 UCLA L.Rev. 303, 341 (1993), and it was more than twenty years before the Supreme Court recognized a case as satisfying that standard.[25] But in House v. Bell, 547 U.S. 518 (2006), the Court, dividing 5–3, ruled that the petitioner was entitled to litigate claims of ineffective assistance of counsel and failure to disclose exculpatory evidence that would otherwise have been foreclosed because of his procedural default in state court.

House's conviction of capital murder rested on circumstantial evidence, including testimony that a semen sample taken from the victim was consistent with House's semen and that blood stains on House's pants were consistent with the blood of the victim. In his federal habeas corpus proceeding, House presented new evidence (i) establishing that the semen was that of the victim's husband, (ii) suggesting that the victim's blood might have been spilled from autopsy samples onto House's pants before the pants were tested, and (iii) indicating that the victim's husband had a history of abuse as well as the opportunity to have caused his wife's death, and had told two people that he had accidentally done so.

The Supreme Court (per Justice Kennedy) ruled that House was entitled to relief if he could show that "it is more likely than not that no reasonable juror would have found [him] guilty beyond a reasonable doubt."[26] The Court concluded that House's was one of the "extraordinary" cases that meets this "demanding" standard: "Were House's challenge to the State's case limited to the questions he has raised about the blood and semen, the other evidence favoring the prosecution might well suffice to bar relief." But that evidence, together with the other testimony incriminating the victim's husband, made it more likely than not that no reasonable juror viewing all the evidence would lack reasonable doubt.

In dissent, Chief Justice Roberts (joined by Justices Scalia and Thomas) argued that the standard had not been met, objecting that the Court disregarded key findings of the district court: that the autopsy blood had

---

[25] In Dretke v. Haley, 541 U.S. 386 (2004), the Court declined to address whether the actual innocence exception to procedural default applies to constitutional claims challenging non-capital sentencing error and instead remanded a case in which the state conceded petitioner had been incorrectly sentenced to 16.5 years instead of the applicable maximum of two years. In so doing, the Court declared that "a federal court faced with allegations of actual innocence, whether of the sentence or of the crime charged, must first address all nondefaulted claims for comparable relief and other grounds for cause to excuse the procedural default."

[26] That standard was borrowed from Schlup v. Delo, 513 U.S. 298 (1995), dealing with whether a party could file a second or successive petition. In that context, the Court has discussed what it means to be "actually innocent" with respect to eligibility for the death penalty. See Sawyer v. Whitley, 505 U.S. 333 (1992), which requires proof "by clear and convincing evidence" that "no reasonable juror would find [the petitioner] eligible for the death penalty" under state law. Petitioners can meet this standard only by showing either that they are innocent of the crime itself or that no aggravating factor or "other condition of eligibility" for a capital sentence was present; the failure to have introduced mitigating evidence at sentencing does not satisfy this standard.

spilled after, not before, the blood stains on House's pants had been tested, and that two witnesses who said that the victim's husband had admitted to causing his wife's death were not credible. Adding that the evidence about semen had not been central to the prosecution's case at trial and that the jury had been told that the semen was just as likely to have come from the husband as from House, the Chief Justice concluded that "the evidence before us now is not substantially different from that considered by House's jury. I therefore find it more likely than not that in light of this new evidence, at least one juror, acting reasonably, would vote to convict House."

House put forward a distinct argument—that the new evidence supported not only his "gateway" claim (permitting the habeas court to reach otherwise defaulted constitutional claims) but also a freestanding claim of innocence that could itself be the substantive basis for relief under Herrera v. Collins, p. 1572, *supra*. All eight Justices hearing the case rejected the latter contention. Justice Kennedy noted that Herrera had indicated that *if* a freestanding claim of innocence can ever be the basis for habeas relief (a question he left open), the standard would be higher than the standard for establishing a "gateway" claim—and "given the closeness of the [gateway] question here," House had not established a freestanding claim of innocence.

Suppose that on remand the habeas court finds that the constitutional claims that House is now free to litigate lack merit. Wouldn't that leave the state free to execute House, despite the Supreme Court's having deemed it more likely than not that no reasonable juror could find him guilty beyond a reasonable doubt?

C.   The Extension of the Sykes Approach

(1) Introduction. In Sykes, the Court, declaring that it did "not choose to paint with a * * * broad brush" (footnote 12), left open whether the "cause and prejudice" standard, which it applied to a default at trial relating to a decision entrusted to the lawyer, governed other kinds of defaults. But over time, the approach in Sykes has been extended, through a series of smaller brush strokes, to cover virtually all state court procedural defaults.

(2) Defaults on Appeal: Murray v. Carrier. In Murray v. Carrier, Paragraph B(3), *supra*, where counsel, in appealing from the judgment of conviction, inadvertently failed to include one of several claims, the Court ruled that the cause and prejudice standard "should not vary depending on the timing of a procedural default or on the strength of an uncertain and difficult assessment of the relative magnitude of the benefits attributable to the state procedural rules that attach at each successive stage of the judicial process."

(3) Failure to Appeal: Coleman v. Thompson and the Overruling of Fay v. Noia. In Coleman v. Thompson, 501 U.S. 722, 749 (1991), the Court said that Fay v. Noia's deliberate bypass standard does not continue to apply "where a state prisoner has defaulted his entire appeal." In sweeping terms, the Court concluded that the Sykes regime governs all state court defaults.[27]

---

[27] Does Coleman rule out the possibility that as a matter of substantive constitutional law, some basic rights—including the right to appeal the conviction itself—cannot validly be waived except by the defendant personally? Note that in Coleman, the default occurred at a

(4) Discretionary State Appeals. In O'Sullivan v. Boerckel, 526 U.S. 838 (1999), the Court extended the Sykes regime to a defendant's failure to include claims in a petition seeking *discretionary* review before the Illinois Supreme Court, after the intermediate appellate court had affirmed his conviction. Most of Justice O'Connor's opinion was devoted to establishing that discretionary review was a state remedy that § 2254(c) requires a petitioner to exhaust. The Court added that because discretionary review was now time-barred, the petitioner had procedurally defaulted by not having raised the claims in question at the appropriate time.[28]

In the wake of O'Sullivan v. Boerckel, some lower courts have interpreted the Court's opinion as merely creating a default rule from which a state may opt out.[29]

(5) Procedural Default and Guilty Pleas. Most of the Court's procedural default decisions involve petitioners convicted after trial. For a case in which the Justices differed about the proper treatment of the failure of a person in *federal* custody to appeal from his conviction by *guilty plea*, see Bousley v. United States, 523 U.S. 614 (1998), pp. 1670–1671 & note 6, *infra*.

D. The Grounds of a State Court Decision, the Problem of Ambiguity, and Waiver by the State

(1) State Court Excuse of Procedural Default. If the state courts overlook a procedural default and decide the federal claim on the merits, a federal court on habeas may also reach the merits. See, *e.g.*, Warden v. Hayden, 387 U.S. 294, 297 n.3 (1967). (The Supreme Court follows a similar rule on direct review of state court decisions. See p. 711, *supra*.) But, the Court has made clear that a state's " 'procedural bar may count as an adequate and independent ground for denying a federal habeas petition even if the state court had discretion to reach the merits despite the default.' " Johnson v. Lee, 578 U.S. 605, 610 (2016) (per curiam) (quoting Walker v.

---

stage—appeal from denial of post-conviction relief—at which there is no right to counsel. Compare Roe v. Flores-Ortega, 528 U.S. 470 (2000), where the petitioner sought habeas relief on the ground that his lawyer's failure to consult him before deciding not appeal constituted ineffective assistance of counsel. Although the Justices varied in their formulations of when such a failure to consult violates the Sixth Amendment, all agreed it was a violation "in the vast majority of cases" and reiterated earlier holdings that counsel must appeal when so instructed by the client.

A divided Court extended the reasoning of Flores-Ortega in Garza v. Idaho, 586 U.S. 232 (2019), to hold that where an attorney fails to notice an appeal, despite express instructions from a defendant to do so, prejudice to the defendant under the Strickland standard is presumed, even where the defendant has signed an appeal waiver as part of a plea agreement.

[28] Note, however, the apparent dissonance between procedural default doctrine and exhaustion doctrine on whether a defendant must pursue state remedies that appear to be futile. Compare Engle v. Isaac, 456 U.S. 107 (1982), p. 1645, note 8, *supra* (failure to pursue an apparently futile remedy constitutes a procedural default), with the subsequent decision in Lynce v. Mathis, 519 U.S. 433 (1997), p. 1663, *infra* (no need to exhaust when the state supreme court had previously rejected similar claims in other cases).

[29] For decisions ruling that a state had opted out of the requirement that petitioners exhaust discretionary review before that state's highest court, see, *e.g.*, Swoopes v. Sublett, 196 F.3d 1008, 1010 (9th Cir.1999) (per curiam) (Arizona); Randolph v. Kemna, 276 F.3d 401, 404 (8th Cir.2002) (Missouri); Adams v. Holland, 330 F.3d 398, 402 (6th Cir.2003) (Tennessee); Lambert v. Blackwell, 387 F.3d 210, 233 (3d Cir.2004) (Pennsylvania); Ellis v. Raemisch, 872 F.3d 1064, 1077–82 (10th Cir.2017) (Colorado). For criticism of this approach, see Hills v. Washington, 441 F.3d 1374, 1378 (11th Cir.2006) (Carnes, J., concurring).

Martin, 562 U.S. 307, 311 (2011)). See also Beard v. Kindler, 558 U.S. 53 (2009), pp. 707–708, *supra*; *id.* 65 (Kennedy, J., concurring) (a state procedural ground will be treated as inadequate if there is a "purpose or pattern to evade constitutional guarantees").

(2) Ambiguous Decisions. Where it is unclear whether a state court rejected a defendant's federal constitutional claim on the merits or because the defendant had defaulted, relying on Michigan v. Long, 463 U.S. 1032 (1983), p. 656, *supra*, federal habeas courts have said that "a state court need do nothing more to preclude habeas review than it must do to preclude direct review." Harris v. Reed, 489 U.S. 255, 264 (1989). Subsequently, the Court has said this means "[i]n those cases in which it does not fairly appear that the state court rested its decision primarily on federal grounds, it is simply not true that the 'most reasonable explanation' is that the state judgment rested on federal grounds." Coleman v. Thompson, 501 U.S. 722 (1991), p. 671, *supra*. See also Ylst v. Nunnemaker, 501 U.S. 797 (1991), p. 671, *supra*. In considering the analogy to Supreme Court review via certiorari, is it relevant that a federal habeas court cannot vacate and remand to clarify an ambiguity?

(3) State Waiver of a Procedural Default Objection. In Trest v. Cain, 522 U.S. 87 (1997), the Court unanimously ruled that a procedural default does not deprive a federal habeas court of jurisdiction; rather, it is normally a defense that the state must raise. In Day v. McDonough, 547 U.S. 198, 206 (2006), the Court permitted a district court, "in appropriate circumstances," to raise a procedural default defense that the state neglected to raise due to a miscalculation on its part (there, a statute of limitations defense). But the Court later cautioned that "[a] court is not at liberty * * * to bypass, override, or excuse a State's deliberate waiver of a limitations defense." Wood v. Milyard, 566 U.S. 463, 466 (2012). Is it ironic that the procedural default doctrine is less sensitive to the plight of petitioners (who generally lack counsel) versus the state when it comes to possible forfeiture of arguments?

NOTE ON SUCCESSIVE AND ABUSIVE HABEAS PETITIONS

(1) Introduction. The preceding Note considered the consequences of a failure to properly raise a federal claim in *state court*. This Note considers the consequences of a failure to raise such a claim in a previous *federal habeas corpus petition*. Though not identical, the concerns in the two areas have important similarities, and the doctrinal evolution is broadly parallel: the Warren Court favored broad excuse of defaults, and subsequently, the Court sharply narrowed federal habeas review. Then, with respect to successive petitions, in 1996 Congress stepped in and further limited federal power, amidst concerns that individuals on death row were filing successive petitions (often at the eleventh hour) in order to delay their executions.

(2) The 1996 Amendments.

(a) The Standards Governing Second or Successive Petitions. As amended in 1996, § 2244(b)(1) requires dismissal (without exception) of any claim that was presented in a prior petition. In addition, § 2244(b)(2) requires dismissal of a claim not previously presented unless:

"(A) * * * the claim relies on a new rule of constitutional law, made retroactive to cases on collateral review by the Supreme Court, that was previously unavailable; or

"(B)(i)   the factual predicate for the claim could not have been discovered previously through the exercise of due diligence; and (ii) the facts underlying the claim, if proven and viewed in light of the evidence as a whole, would be sufficient to establish by clear and convincing evidence that, but for constitutional error, no reasonable factfinder would have found the applicant guilty of the underlying offense."

Note that § 2244(b)(2) combines various elements of procedural default doctrine in a way that narrows the basis for excuse. Thus, defaults in a prior federal proceeding, where a petitioner not under death sentence is unlikely to have had counsel, are harder to excuse than defaults in state court (where the defendant had a right to counsel at trial and on the first appeal).

(b) The Procedure for Filing a Second or Successive Petition. The 1996 amendments require a petitioner, before filing a successive petition in district court, to first file a motion in the court of appeals seeking authorization to file the petition in district court; the court of appeals is to act on the motion within 30 days, § 2244(b)(3)(D), and should grant the motion if the petition satisfies the criteria set forth in § 2244(b)(2). Without such authorization, a petitioner may not file a successive habeas petition in the district court.

Section 2244(b)(3)(E) provides that the grant or denial of authorization "by a court of appeals * * * shall not be appealable and shall not be the subject of a petition for rehearing or for a writ of certiorari." In Felker v. Turpin, 518 U.S. 651 (1996), p. 426, *supra*, the Court unanimously ruled that § 2244(b)(3)(E) did not preclude the petitioner whose request for authorization had been denied from filing a petition in the Supreme Court seeking an original writ of habeas corpus, but that the standards set forth in § 2244(b)(2) would inform the Court's decision whether to grant relief. The Court proceeded to conclude that neither of the petitioner's constitutional claims satisfied those standards, "let alone the requirement [in Sup.Ct.R. 20.4(a), governing original writs of habeas corpus,] that there be 'exceptional circumstances' justifying the issuance of the writ."[1]

(3) Unripe Claims and § 2244(b). If a claim was not ripe when a first habeas petition was filed, is a second petition containing the now ripe claim governed by the restrictions and authorization requirement of § 2244(b)? The Supreme Court has not charted a clear course on this question.

---

[1]   For discussion of Felker, see Tushnet, *"The King of France with Forty Thousand Men": Felker v. Turpin and the Supreme Court's Deliberative Processes*, 1996 Sup.Ct.Rev. 163. See also Kovarsky, *Original Habeas Redux*, 97 Va.L.Rev. 61, 90–94 (2011) (finding that more than half of petitioners seeking an original writ in the Supreme Court, including 80% of capital petitioners, are trying to avoid restrictions on successive petitions).

Two decisions have addressed the problem posed by claims brought by petitioners on death row that may be deemed premature if included in a first habeas petition that challenges the conviction or sentence. In Stewart v. Martinez-Villareal, 523 U.S. 637 (1998), a claim of incompetency disqualifying the petitioner from being eligible for execution was dismissed as premature when filed in a first petition. Then, after the other grounds for relief were denied, the petitioner, fearing § 2244(b) might foreclose a second petition raising the same claim, moved to re-open the earlier petition. The Court held that the petitioner had filed only one petition and that a district court should rule on each claim presented at the time it becomes ripe.

In Panetti v. Quarterman, 551 U.S. 930 (2007), the first petition of someone on death row did not include an incompetency claim; after that petition was denied and an execution date was set, the petitioner filed a second petition raising that claim. The Court, per Justice Kennedy, held that the phrase "second or successive" takes its meaning from case law, including decisions pre-dating the enactment of § 2244(b) in 1996. Stating that it was "hesitant to construe a statute, implemented to further the principles of comity, finality, and federalism, in a manner that would require unripe * * * claims to be raised as a mere formality, to the benefit of no party," the Court concluded that "[t]he statutory bar on 'second or successive' applications does not apply to [a claim that one is incompetent to be executed] brought in an application filed when the claim is first ripe."

In dissent, Justice Thomas, joined by the Chief Justice and Justices Scalia and Alito, argued that "second or successive" means "second or successive" and hence under § 2244(b), Panetti's second petition must be dismissed. He also relied on the unanimous per curiam decision in Burton v. Stewart, 549 U.S. 147 (2007). There, the petitioner's several convictions had been affirmed on direct review, but his sentence was vacated. After the trial court resentenced him, and while an appeal of the new sentence was pending, he filed a federal habeas petition challenging his convictions, which was denied. After the state court rejected his appeal from the new sentence, he filed a second petition in federal court, challenging the new sentence. The Supreme Court ruled that the second petition was barred for non-compliance with § 2244(b). In his Panetti dissent, Justice Thomas argued that Burton indicated that a petitioner is not excused from § 2244(b)'s limitations merely because the claim in a second petition would have been unripe if filed in the first petition. He concluded that the majority's decision "stands only for the proposition that [claims of incompetency to be executed] somehow deserve a special (and unjustified) exemption from the statute's plain import." The majority did not directly address the dissent's discussion of Burton. Isn't Justice Thomas correct that the two decisions are difficult to reconcile?

(4) Exhaustion and Successive Petitions. In Slack v. McDaniel, 529 U.S. 473 (2000), a habeas petition included some claims that had not yet been presented to the state courts. The "total exhaustion" doctrine, p. 1663, *infra*, prevents a federal court from entertaining a petition that includes both exhausted and unexhausted claims. Upon the petitioner's motion and without objection from the state, the district court dismissed the petition without prejudice; the order granted leave to refile after exhausting all state remedies. After exhaustion, Slack filed a new habeas corpus petition.[2] The Supreme Court held, 7–2, that the second petition was not successive, stressing that "the complete exhaustion rule is not to 'trap the unwary *pro se* prisoner' " (quoting Rose v. Lundy, 455 U.S. 509, 520 (1982)).[3]

(5) Reopening Judgments Under Federal Rules of Civil Procedure 59(e) and 60(b). In Banister v. Davis, 590 U.S. 504 (2020), the Supreme Court held that a motion under Federal Rule of Civil Procedure 59(e) "to alter or amend a judgment" does not qualify as a second or successive petition for purposes of 28 U.S.C. § 2244(b). Writing for a seven-Justice majority, Justice Kagan stressed the limited nature of Rule 59(e) motions. First, such motions must be filed within 28 days of entry of judgment, without possibility of extension, Fed. Rule Civ. Proc. 6(b)(2) (prohibiting extensions to Rule 59(e)'s deadline). Second, the Court has recognized that the Rule allows a district court " 'to rectify its own mistakes in the period immediately following' " its decision and that federal courts generally have invoked the rule "only" to "reconsider[ ] matters properly encompassed in a decision on the merits" (quoting White v. New Hampshire Dept. of Employment Security, 455 U.S. 445 (1982)). Thus, in reviewing Rule 59(e) motions, courts do not address new arguments or evidence that the moving party could have raised before the decision issued. Finally, the timely filing of a Rule 59(e) motion " 'suspends the finality of the original judgment' for purposes of an appeal" (quoting FCC v. League of Women Voters of Cal., 468 U.S. 364, 373, n.10 (1984)). Putting these factors together, the Court held that Rule 59(e) motions pertain to the same, original underlying judgment with respect to the habeas petitioner's first federal petition.

The Court also relied in part upon "historical habeas doctrine and practice" and AEDPA's purposes, which aim to limit " 'piecemeal litigation' " (quoting Panetti v. Quarterman, 551 U.S. 930 (2007)). Justice Kagan distinguished Gonzalez v. Crosby, 545 U.S. 524 (2005), in which the Court held that a motion filed under Federal Rule of Civil Procedure 60(b)[4] seeking "relie[f] from a final judgment" denying habeas relief counts as a second or successive habeas application for purposes of AEDPA where the motion " 'attacks the federal court's previous resolution of a claim on the merits.' " Holding that Rules 59(e) and 60(b) differ "in just about every way that matters to the inquiry" relating to successive petitions, the Banister Court distinguished Rule 60(b) motions as not governed by any strict time limits

---

[2]   Because Slack's second petition was filed in 1995, the Supreme Court noted that it was not governed by the 1996 amendments, "though we do not suggest the definition of second or successive would be different under [§ 2244(b), as amended in 1996]."

[3]   Addressing the state's concern that under the Court's ruling, a petitioner's new petition might contain still other unexhausted claims, "causing the process to repeat itself," the Court noted that states may limit multiple state post-conviction filings and federal courts may require, as a condition of dismissing the first petition, that any new filing contain only exhausted claims.

[4]   Rule 60(b) provides that a court may grant relief from a final judgment if a party can show "(1) mistake, inadvertence, surprise, or excusable neglect; (2) newly discovered evidence that, with reasonable diligence, could not have been discovered in time to move for a new trial under Rule 59(b); (3) fraud * * * misrepresentation, or misconduct by an opposing party; (4) the judgment is void; (5) the judgment has been satisfied, released, or discharged [or] reversed or vacated * * *; or (6) any other reason that justifies relief."

with respect to when they may be filed[5]; for giving rise to a separate appeal than an appeal from the original judgment; and for "attack[ing] an already completed judgment."[6]

The Court's decision in Gonzalez excepted Rule 60(b) motions that attack "some defect in the integrity of the federal habeas proceedings," such as a court's incorrect application of a statute of limitations. Although Gonzalez posited that such motions should only be permitted in "extraordinary circumstances" that "will rarely occur in the habeas context," the Court held, 6–2, in Buck v. Davis, 580 U.S. 100 (2017), that relief under Rule 60(b) was warranted. In Buck, the petitioner sought to reopen the judgment in his first federal habeas petition eight years after the fact based on the intervening Supreme Court decisions in in Martinez v. Ryan, 566 U.S. 1 (2012), p. 1647, *supra*, and Trevino v. Thaler, 569 U.S. 413 (2013), p. 1649, *supra*. Writing for the majority, Chief Justice Roberts emphasized the extraordinary circumstances of petitioner's claims, which suggested that "Buck may have been sentenced to death in part because of his race."[7] The Court suggested that it is appropriate to reopen a judgment under Rule 60(b) where there is a " 'risk of injustice to the parties' " or a " 'risk of undermining the public's confidence in the judicial process' " in leaving a judgment intact (quoting Liljeberg v. Health Services Acquisition Corp., 486 U.S. 847, 864 (1988)). In reaching its holding, the Buck Court did not discuss whether petitioner's Rule 60(b) motion was successive and emphasized that the State had waived any Teague arguments in the case.[8]

More recently, the Court has been far more rigid in enforcing AEDPA's limitations on the pursuit of second or successive motions in the context of filings by those in federal custody. See pp. 1676–1679, *infra* (discussing Jones v. Hendrix, 599 U.S. 465 (2023)).

(6) The Effect of the 1996 Act. Studies that predate both the judicial and legislative restrictions imposed in the 1990s found that anywhere from 13% to 54% of petitioners had filed one or more previous petitions.[9] One post-AEDPA study found that 41% of petitions contained four or more claims, compared to the 11–25% found in pre-AEDPA studies. That increase might be attributable in part to AEDPA's tightened restrictions on successive

---

[5] Federal Rule of Civil Procedure 60(c)(1) provides that Rule 60(b) motions should be filed within a "reasonable time."

[6] Banister is consistent with the Court's earlier decision in Magwood v. Patterson, 561 U.S. 320 (2010), where the Court held that if a petitioner secures relief resulting in a material change to the original judgment, such as an order requiring resentencing, the ensuing judgment is deemed "new" and any federal habeas petition that follows is not treated as second or successive.

[7] For additional discussion of Buck, see pp. 1625–1626, *supra*.

[8] See also Tharpe v. Sellers, 583 U.S. 33 (2018) (per curiam) (reversing and remanding the denial of a Rule 60(b) motion in another habeas case). For additional discussion, see p. 1626, *supra*.

[9] See Faust, Rubenstein & Yackle, *The Great Writ in Action: Empirical Light on the Federal Habeas Corpus Debate*, 18 N.Y.U.Rev.L. & Soc. Change 637, 687 (1991) (15–20%); Flango, Habeas Corpus in State and Federal Courts 37 (1994) (54%); Robinson, An Empirical Study of Federal Habeas Corpus Review of State Court Judgments 15 (1979) (31%); Shapiro, *Federal Habeas Corpus: A Study in Massachusetts*, 87 Harv.L.Rev. 321, 353–54 (1973) (13%).

petitions and in part to the change in the law that now permits a court to deny a habeas petition on the merits without first requiring exhaustion.[10]

NOTE ON EXHAUSTION OF STATE COURT REMEDIES[1]

(1) Origins. The requirement that those in state custody exhaust state court remedies before seeking federal habeas corpus relief derives from Ex parte Royall, 117 U.S. 241 (1886), where a petitioner detained in state custody for trial alleged that the state statute under which he was charged violated the federal Constitution. The Supreme Court affirmed the dismissal of his habeas petition, ruling that although the trial court had *power* to inquire into the allegation in advance of trial, it should exercise its discretion to permit the state court to resolve the question in the normal course of trial.[2]

In 1948, Congress codified aspects of the exhaustion rule in 28 U.S.C. § 2254. Subsequently, the Supreme Court raised doubts about whether judges may fashion non-statutory exceptions to the exhaustion requirement. See Duckworth v. Serrano, 454 U.S. 1, 4–5 (1981) (per curiam) (refusing to recognize an exception for "clear violations" of federal law).

(2) The Import of Exhaustion. In Rose v. Lundy, 455 U.S. 509 (1982), the Court said that the exhaustion requirement serves to "protect the state courts' role in the enforcement of federal law," to "prevent disruption of state judicial proceedings," and to " 'minimize friction between our federal and state systems of justice by allowing the State an initial opportunity to pass upon and correct alleged violations of prisoners' federal rights' " (quoting Duckworth v. Serrano, Paragraph (1), *supra*, at 3). The Court also observed that exhaustion helps to generate a complete factual record to aid federal review and that over time it may make state courts more familiar with and hospitable to federal claims.

(3) What Constitutes Exhaustion? A petitioner is required to exhaust only state remedies that remain available when the habeas petition is filed. If, for example, a petitioner did not appeal from a state court conviction and the time for doing so has expired, the exhaustion requirement (as distinguished from the procedural default doctrine) poses no barrier to habeas relief. Under § 2254(b), moreover, exhaustion is not required where

---

[10]   See King, Cheesman & Ostrom, *Final Technical Report: Habeas Litigation in U.S. District Courts, National Center for State Courts*, Aug. 21, 2007, at 57. See also Cheesman, Hanson & Ostrom, *A Tale of Two Laws: The U.S. Congress Confronts Habeas Corpus Petitions and Section 1983 Lawsuits*, 22 Law & Pol'y 89, 92, 105 (2000) (finding that despite AEDPA's many restrictions, habeas filings increased by 40% between 1996 and 1998, and suggesting that many persons in custody, rather than filing multiple challenges to a particular conviction, instead are serving long sentences for multiple convictions that they attack separately).

[1]   See generally Yackle, *The Exhaustion Doctrine in Federal Habeas Corpus: An Argument for a Return to First Principles*, 44 Ohio St.L.J. 393 (1983); Amsterdam, *Criminal Prosecutions Affecting Federally Guaranteed Civil Rights: Federal Removal and Habeas Corpus Jurisdiction to Abort State Court Trial*, 113 U.Pa.L.Rev. 793, 884–96 (1965).

[2]   Despite Royall's emphasis on "discretion," from early on the Supreme Court routinely reversed grants of the writ before exhaustion of state remedies. See, *e.g.*, New York v. Eno, 155 U.S. 89 (1894); Urquhart v. Brown, 205 U.S. 179 (1907); Duncan v. Henry, 513 U.S. 364 (1995) (per curiam).

a state remedy is "ineffective," which is true, the Court has ruled, where resort to the state courts would be clearly futile. See, *e.g.*, Lynce v. Mathis, 519 U.S. 433, 436 n.4 (1997) (excusing the failure to have raised an ex post facto challenge to a state statute that canceled early release credits, because the Florida Supreme Court had previously rejected such challenges and there was no reason to think the Florida courts would have changed course).[3]

Among other issues that have arisen in the administration of the exhaustion requirement are the following:

(a) Proper Presentation of the Federal Claim. Proper exhaustion requires presentation to the state courts of the *same* claim being raised on habeas. See Picard v. Connor, 404 U.S. 270, 276 (1971). And a mere claim of unconstitutionality in state court does not suffice; "ordinarily a state prisoner does not 'fairly present' a claim to a state court if that court must read beyond a petition or a brief (or a similar document) that does not alert it to the presence of a *federal* claim." Baldwin v. Reese, 541 U.S. 27, 32 (2004) (emphasis added).

(b) Which Remedies Must Be Exhausted? A petitioner ordinarily must exhaust state remedies available at trial and on appeal.[4] The Court has also stated that a criminal defendant whose conviction was affirmed by an intermediate court of appeals must exhaust discretionary review available in the state supreme court. See O'Sullivan v. Boerckel, 526 U.S. 838 (1999), p. 1656, *supra*. That individual need not seek certiorari before the U.S. Supreme Court, however, for § 2254(b)(1)(A) requires only that "the applicant has exhausted the remedies available in the courts of the State."

Although § 2254(c) states that an applicant must exhaust "any available procedure" under state law, Justice Reed's opinion in Brown v. Allen, p. 1558, *supra*, ruled that a petitioner who has properly presented a federal claim to the trial and appellate courts need not "ask the state for collateral relief, based on the same evidence and issues already decided by direct review." Nor must a petitioner resubmit the federal contention to the state courts because a change in their interpretation of federal law suggests that a second attempt would succeed. Francisco v. Gathright, 419 U.S. 59 (1974) (per curiam). Exhaustion of state post-conviction processes is required, however, when they are open to a claim not previously raised in state court; the most common example is a claim of ineffective assistance of counsel.

(4) "Mixed" Petitions and the Total Exhaustion Rule. Habeas petitions frequently include both exhausted and unexhausted claims. In Rose v. Lundy, 455 U.S. 509 (1982), the Court adopted a "total exhaustion" rule that requires dismissal of such "mixed" petitions.[5]

---

   [3] Note the apparent dissonance between procedural default doctrine and exhaustion doctrine on whether a defendant must pursue state remedies that appear to be futile. See p. 1656, note 28, *supra*.

   [4] In Pitchess v. Davis, 421 U.S. 482 (1975) (per curiam), the Court reaffirmed the holding of Ex parte Hawk, 321 U.S. 114 (1944), that application to state appellate courts for an extraordinary writ does not exhaust state remedies when the denial of that writ could not be taken as a decision on the merits and when normal channels of appellate review remain open.

   [5] That rule, Justice O'Connor argued for the Court, promotes the general purposes of exhaustion, eliminates any temptation for district courts to consider unexhausted claims, and

Some of the options for petitioners that Rose v. Lundy left open have become more hazardous because of provisions of the 1996 amendments. The petitioner may amend the petition to proceed with only the exhausted claims, but that course will generally forfeit the unexhausted claims, for even if the petitioner later exhausts remedies as to them, habeas review will ordinarily be barred by the statutory restrictions on second or successive petitions. Alternatively, the petitioner may dismiss the petition and return to state court to complete exhaustion, but in doing so may run afoul of the one-year limitations period; that period is tolled while state post-conviction proceedings are pending, but not during the pendency of federal proceedings nor when shuttling back and forth between federal and state courts. See generally Duncan v. Walker, 533 U.S. 167, 182 (2001) (Stevens, J., concurring in part and concurring in the judgment).

In Rhines v. Weber, 544 U.S. 269 (2005), the Court gave qualified approval to a third option, under which district courts stay mixed petitions pending exhaustion. Rhines, who had been sentenced to death, filed a timely habeas petition, but by the time the district court found that eight of his thirty-five claims were unexhausted, the limitations period had run. The district court held Rhines's petition in abeyance, conditioned upon his commencing state court proceedings within 60 days and returning to federal court within 60 days of completing exhaustion. When the case reached the Supreme Court, Justice O'Connor's majority opinion concluded that the district court's stay could undermine AEDPA's purposes of reducing delays in executing sentences (especially capital sentences) and encouraging litigants to exhaust all claims before filing in federal court. Accordingly, the Court held that the stay-and-abeyance procedure is appropriate only "when the district court determines there was good cause for the petitioner's failure to exhaust his claims first in state court." By contrast, the Court held, a district court would abuse its discretion by issuing a stay with respect to "plainly meritless" unexhausted claims. The Court added that to avoid delay, district courts should impose "reasonable time limits on a petitioner's trip to state court and back," and should not grant a stay "if a petitioner engages in abusive litigation tactics or intentional delay."[6]

(5) "Special Circumstances" Justifying Prompt Federal Intervention. Section 2254(b)(1)(B) excepts from the exhaustion requirement those situations in which "there is an absence of available State corrective process" or "circumstances exist that render such process ineffective to protect the rights of the applicant." In addition, the Court has recognized that certain circumstances may warrant earlier federal intervention.[7] See Justices of Boston Municipal Ct. v. Lydon, 466 U.S. 294

---

discourages piecemeal litigation in federal court. For criticism of Lundy, see Yackle, note 1, *supra*, at 424–40.

[6]   Concurring in part and concurring in the judgment, Justice Souter, joined by Justices Ginsburg and Breyer, would not have conditioned the availability of a stay on demonstration of good cause, particularly given the difficulties that tricky exhaustion issues pose for pro se petitioners. He would instead have denied a stay only upon a showing of "intentionally dilatory litigation tactics." In another concurring opinion, Justice Stevens (joined by Justices Ginsburg and Breyer) sounded similar views.

[7]   See also generally Amsterdam, note 1, *supra*, at 892–99.

(1984) (recognizing "the unique nature of the double jeopardy right," which "cannot be fully vindicated on appeal following final judgment, since in part the Double Jeopardy Clause protects 'against being twice put to *trial* for the same offense' "); Braden v. 30th Judicial Cir. Ct., 410 U.S. 484 (1973) (petitioner could seek relief premised on State's alleged denial of his right to a speedy trial; petitioner was trying "to enforce the Commonwealth's obligation to provide him with a state court forum").

(6) Waiver. The question whether a failure to exhaust always bars habeas review is now governed by two statutory provisions adopted in AEDPA in 1996. First, § 2254(b)(2) provides that the failure to exhaust does not bar a court from *denying* a petition on the merits. Second, § 2254(b)(3) confirms that the exhaustion requirement can be waived by the state, although only if there is an express waiver by counsel.

(7) The Exhaustion Requirement in Action. Older empirical studies suggested that failure to exhaust state remedies was a major obstacle to adjudication of habeas petitions on the merits.[8] One study post-dating AEDPA found that in 2003–2004, only 11% of non-capital petitions were dismissed on exhaustion grounds; the reduction may have resulted in part from the large number of petitions that, since the enactment of a limitations period in 1996, are now dismissed as time-barred.[9]

NOTE ON PROBLEMS OF CUSTODY AND REMEDY

(1) The Statutory Requirement of Custody. Echoing the common law, 28 U.S.C. § 2241(c) confers jurisdiction only when the petitioner is "in custody." Until the 1960s, courts interpreted the custody requirement strictly. See, *e.g.*, Wales v. Whitney, 114 U.S. 564 (1885) (naval officer's challenge to order confining him to city limits; no jurisdiction); Stallings v. Splain, 253 U.S. 339 (1920) (habeas will not lie if petitioner has been released on bail); Weber v. Squier, 315 U.S. 810 (1942) (habeas does not lie for petitioner released on parole).

(2) A Broadened Understanding of Custody. The Court's understanding of "custody" changed dramatically in Jones v. Cunningham, 371 U.S. 236 (1963), which held that a petitioner free on parole could obtain habeas review of the original criminal conviction.[1] The Court said that parole "imposes conditions which significantly confine and restrain [one's] freedom"—including the threat of re-imprisonment for parole violations, the obligation to report monthly to a parole officer, and the need for official

---

[8]   See, *e.g.*, Shapiro, *Federal Habeas Corpus: A Study in Massachusetts*, 87 Harv.L.Rev. 321, 356–61 (1973) (finding that more than half of the petitions filed from 1970–1972 were dismissed wholly or in part on exhaustion grounds in a study of Massachusetts habeas cases); Allen, Schachtman & Wilson, *Federal Habeas Corpus and Its Reform: An Empirical Analysis*, 13 Rutgers L.J. 675, 679, 695 (1982) (of 1,899 petitions filed in six district courts and one court of appeals between 1975 and 1977, finding that 37% were denied for failure to exhaust).

[9]   See King, Cheesman & Ostrom, *Final Technical Report: Habeas Litigation in U.S. District Courts, National Center for State Courts*, Aug. 21, 2007, at 47, 57.

[1]   For an inquiry into the reasons for expansion of the custody concept, see Yackle, *Explaining Habeas Corpus*, 60 N.Y.U.L.Rev. 991, 998–1010 (1985).

permission to travel, change residence, or drive an automobile. The opinion did not specify which of those constraints was essential to the finding of custody. But where all or most of these constraints accompany other forms of restraint (*e.g.*, probation[2] or release on a conditionally suspended sentence[3]), the lower courts have not hesitated since Jones to entertain applications for habeas corpus. See also Hensley v. Municipal Court, 411 U.S. 345 (1973) (petitioner who had exhausted all state remedies after having been sentenced to jail, but remained free on his own recognizance, awaiting execution of the sentence, was in custody).

Is Jones' relaxation of the custody requirement understandable when one conceives of habeas corpus as a means of ensuring federal review of state criminal convictions? With the scaling back of collateral federal habeas corpus witnessed in recent decades, does Jones' rule still make sense?

(3) Release from Custody. Maleng v. Cook, 490 U.S. 488, 492 (1989) (per curiam), rejected the argument that when a sentence has been fully served, a petitioner may challenge the conviction via habeas on the basis that civil disabilities still adhered or that the prior conviction could be used in another criminal case to enhance the sentence. See also Alaska v. Wright, 593 U.S. 152 (2021) (per curiam) (citing Maleng to hold a petitioner is not in custody under a state court judgment for purposes of § 2254 where that prior state conviction could serve as a predicate for a subsequent federal conviction).[4]

(4) The Nature of Relief: Release from Custody and the Rise and Fall of the Prematurity Rule. The correlative of the custody requirement is the notion that the only appropriate remedy is release from confinement. But in Peyton v. Rowe, 391 U.S. 54 (1968), the Court, overruling its decision in McNally v. Hill, 293 U.S. 131, 138 (1934), permitted a petitioner to challenge the validity of the second of two consecutive sentences while still serving the first.[5] Rejecting the view that the challenge was premature, the Court noted that if the first sentence is lengthy, it is impractical to wait to determine the validity of the second until the petitioner begins to serve it, when memories will have dimmed and witnesses may have disappeared.[6]

---

[2]   See, *e.g.*, Lawrence v. 48th Dist. Ct., 560 F.3d 475, 479–81 (6th Cir.2009).

[3]   See, *e.g.*, Sammons v. Rodgers, 785 F.2d 1343, 1345 (5th Cir.1986) & authorities cited.

For criticism of decisions holding that a sex offender subject to post-release registration and community notification requirements is not in custody, see Logan, *Federal Habeas in the Information Age*, 85 Minn.L.Rev. 147 (2000).

[4]   Maleng did not disturb the decision in Carafas v. LaVallee, 391 U.S. 234 (1968), that a petition filed while one is in custody does not automatically become moot following the expiration of the sentence and one's unconditional release. Thus, petitions filed one day before and one day after release are treated differently. See also Spencer v. Kemna, 523 U.S. 1 (1998); Lane v. Williams, 455 U.S. 624 (1982).

Maleng left open the question whether a court may consider a challenge to a prior conviction for which the petitioner is no longer in custody but which has been used to enhance the sentence that the petitioner is presently serving for a subsequent offense. The Court ruled in Lackawanna County Dist. Atty. v. Coss, 532 U.S. 394 (2001), subject to only the narrowest exceptions, a habeas court may not entertain such a petition.

[5]   In Walker v. Wainwright, 390 U.S. 335 (1968), the Court permitted attack on the validity of a sentence being served, even though another sentence awaited the petitioner.

[6]   The Court added that the prematurity rule prejudices petitioners who ultimately succeed, by forcing them to commence the second confinement before litigating its validity.

Garlotte v. Fordice, 515 U.S. 39 (1995) (7–2), was a case of Peyton in reverse: the petitioner, after completing a sentence for a drug offense, was serving a *consecutive* sentence for murder when he filed a habeas petition challenging the drug conviction. The warden argued that he was no longer in custody on the drug conviction, relying on Maleng v. Cook, Paragraph (3), *supra*. Rejecting the warden's contention, the Court ruled that the petitioner remained " 'in custody' under all of his sentences until all are served."

B. COLLATERAL ATTACK ON FEDERAL CONVICTIONS

NOTE ON 28 U.S.C. § 2255 AND ITS RELATIONSHIP TO FEDERAL HABEAS CORPUS

(1) The Enactment of § 2255. Before 1948, persons detained in federal custody after criminal convictions could file a habeas corpus petition only in the district in which they were being confined. That rule caused serious administrative problems. The few federal districts within whose territorial jurisdiction the major federal correctional facilities were located were inundated with petitions. Facially meritorious applications were often found wholly wanting after consulting the records of the sentencing court, but those records were not readily available to the habeas court. Venue also proved inconvenient when hearings had to be conducted far from the locale of the underlying events. See generally United States v. Hayman, 342 U.S. 205, 210–14 (1952).

To address these difficulties, in 1948 Congress enacted 28 U.S.C. § 2255,[1] which provides that in post-conviction review cases, persons in federal custody must file any motion for collateral relief in the court that entered the sentence. Entitled "Federal custody; remedies on motion attacking sentence," § 2255, like habeas corpus for persons in state custody, is available to attack convictions or sentences resulting in custody in violation of the federal Constitution or, in some cases, federal statutes or treaties. In Hayman, the Court stressed that § 2255 was not meant to "impinge upon prisoners' rights of collateral attack upon their convictions" but only "to minimize the difficulties encountered in habeas corpus hearings by affording the same rights in another and more convenient forum." In the twelve months ending September 30, 2020, the number of reported filings of

---

Petitioners have generally been permitted to mount attacks that, if successful, would shorten the total period of confinement but would not lead to immediate release. See, *e.g.*, Bostic v. Carlson, 884 F.2d 1267, 1269 (9th Cir.1989); Jensen v. Satran, 688 F.2d 76 (8th Cir.1982).

[1] A Judicial Conference Committee on Habeas Corpus Procedure drafted the provision. See Parker, *Limiting the Abuse of Habeas Corpus*, 8 F.R.D. 171 (1948). Along with the draft bill, the committee submitted a "Statement" describing the new motion as creating a "remedy [that] broadly covers all situations where the sentence is 'open to collateral attack.' As a remedy, it is intended to be as broad as habeas corpus." S.Rep. No. 80–1526, at 2 (1948) (Conf. Rep.).

such petitions totaled 2,709, as compared to 3,870 as of September 30, 2000, 1,413 as of June 30, 1980, and 980 as of June 30, 1960.[2]

This Note sketches the basic outlines of the § 2255 remedy, highlighting the ways in which it resembles, and differs from, collateral relief under § 2254 for those in state custody.

(2) The Exclusivity of § 2255. Although Congress, in enacting § 2255, did not repeal or limit the pre-existing grant of habeas corpus jurisdiction, § 2255 provides that a petition shall not be entertained unless the petitioner has first sought relief under § 2255 *and* "unless it also appears that the remedy by motion [under § 2255] is inadequate or ineffective to test the legality of his detention." 28 U.S.C. § 2255(e) (often referred to as § 2255's "savings clause"). In Hayman, the Supreme Court found no need to consider the petitioner's argument that § 2255 was an unconstitutional suspension of the writ, ruling that Hayman made no showing that the § 2255 remedy was inadequate, and that if he had, the statute would permit resort to the writ. Accord, Swain v. Pressley, 430 U.S. 372, 381 (1977), pp. 1475, 1577, *supra*.

Section 2255 applies only to persons "in custody under sentence of a court established by Act of Congress." It does not limit federal habeas corpus challenges to other kinds of federal detention—*e.g.*, that resulting from court martial proceedings, extradition, and immigration matters, as well as military detention of terrorists and civil commitment of the mentally ill.

(3) Proceedings Under § 2255. Unlike a habeas petition brought by one in state custody, a § 2255 motion is not a separate civil action but rather a continuation of the criminal proceeding. The motion will be opposed not by a prison warden but by the United States, which initiated the prosecution. Nonetheless, § 2255 motions are processed in much the same way as § 2254 petitions, and the Rules Governing § 2255 Proceedings in the United States District Courts are virtually identical to the parallel Rules Governing § 2254 Proceedings.[3] Rule 4 of the § 2255 Rules specifies that the motion shall be heard by the judge who presided at the original trial and sentencing (where possible)—although, as with petitions brought by those in state custody, § 2255 motions are often referred initially to magistrate judges.

(4) The Analogy to Brown v. Allen. In Kaufman v. United States, 394 U.S. 217 (1969), the Warren Court rejected the government's argument that the general approach of Brown v. Allen, permitting collateral attack on criminal convictions, was inapposite in § 2255 proceedings because federal petitioners, unlike their state counterparts, had already enjoyed the opportunity to litigate in a *federal* court. That opportunity, the Court said,

---

[2]   Annual Report of the Director of the Administrative Office of the United States Courts, Table C-3 (2020); Annual Report of the Director of the Administrative Office of the United States Courts, Table C-3 (2000); Annual Report of the Director of the Administrative Office of the United States Courts, Table C-3 (1980); Annual Report of the Director of the Administrative Office of the United States Courts, Table C-3 (1960). As with statistics reported at pp. 1552–1553, *supra*, the total numbers reflect the combination of denoted habeas petitions and death penalty matters initiated by those in federal custody.

[3]   For a catalogue of minor differences, see the Advisory Committee Notes to the § 2255 Rules, particularly the Note to Rule 1. Rule 12 of the § 2255 Rules (which has no counterpart in the § 2254 Rules) authorizes a district court to apply the criminal as well as the civil rules, as the court deems appropriate.

"is clearly not the sole justification for federal post-conviction relief; otherwise there would be no need to make such relief available to federal prisoners at all. The provision of federal collateral remedies rests more fundamentally upon a recognition that adequate protection of constitutional rights relating to the criminal trial process requires the continuing availability of a mechanism for relief." (The Court added, "[p]lainly the interest in finality is the same with regard to both federal and state prisoners.")

(5) Section 2255 in Practice. Despite Kaufman's assertion of an equivalence between those in state and federal custody, review under § 2255 is in practice considerably more restricted. Suppose that a defendant's constitutional challenge to a conviction was rejected on the merits at trial and on appeal. One in *state* custody can then seek a determination from a federal habeas court, which traditionally was not bound by the state court's determination (and, even after 1996, remains free to grant relief if it views the state court determination as unreasonable or directly in conflict with constitutional principles clearly established by the Supreme Court). But one in *federal* custody ordinarily will present a motion under § 2255 to the same judge who initially denied the claim, and who is likely to ask, "What's new?". If there was an appeal from the original conviction, the district judge in the § 2255 proceeding, even if not the original trial judge, would ordinarily be bound by a decision of the court of appeals rejecting the claim on direct appeal. Indeed, most circuits only permit a departure from circuit precedent by the en banc court of appeals; where that rule applies, only in the rare instance in which the en banc court, or the Supreme Court, reviews the denial of relief under § 2255 would a prior circuit decision not be binding.[4]

When, then, might one in federal custody obtain relief under § 2255?

(a) New Law. One situation is when legal standards have changed—for example, by virtue of a recent Supreme Court decision after the conviction became final. But although § 2255 contains no limitation on the scope of review similar to that added in 1996 by § 2254(d), the Supreme Court has applied its decision in Teague v. Lane, 489 U.S. 288 (1989), p. 1580, *supra*—which precludes habeas courts from considering claims brought by those in state custody based on new law in all but the most exceptional cases—to § 2255 proceedings.

The Court announced an important limit to the Teague doctrine in Bousley v. United States, 523 U.S. 614 (1998). Bousley, after pleading guilty to the federal crime of using a firearm during and in relation to a drug trafficking offense, had unsuccessfully appealed his sentence. Thereafter, the Supreme Court held in an unrelated case, Bailey v. United States, 516 U.S. 137 (1995), that "use" of a firearm requires not merely possession but "active employment" of the weapon—a narrower understanding of the elements of the crime than had been established at the plea allocution in Bousley's case. In a § 2255 motion, Bousley asserted the same claim that

---

[4]   In theory, the requirement that circuit precedent be followed may not apply when the panel in the § 2255 proceeding was also the panel on direct review. See 18B Wright, Miller & Cooper, Federal Practice and Procedure § 4478.

Bailey had upheld. On review, the Court, with Chief Justice Rehnquist writing, held that Bousley's motion stated a good due process claim that the guilty plea was not voluntary and intelligent. The Court stated that that claim was hardly new within the meaning of Teague, but then continued more broadly: "And because Teague by its terms applies only to procedural rules, we think it is inapplicable to the situation in which this Court decides the meaning of a criminal statute enacted by Congress."

"This distinction between substance and procedure is an important one in the habeas context. The Teague doctrine is founded on the notion that one of the 'principal functions of habeas corpus [is] "to assure that no man has been incarcerated under a procedure which creates an impermissibly large risk that the innocent will be convicted.'" Consequently, unless a new rule of criminal procedure is of such a nature that 'without [it] the likelihood of an accurate conviction is seriously diminished,' there is no reason to apply the rule retroactively on habeas review. By contrast, decisions of this Court holding that a substantive federal criminal statute does not reach certain conduct, like decisions placing conduct 'beyond the power of the criminal law-making authority to proscribe,' necessarily carry a significant risk that a defendant stands convicted of 'an act that the law does not make criminal'" (internal citations omitted).[5]

The Court next concluded that Bousley's failure to attack the voluntariness and intelligence of his plea in his initial appeal constituted a procedural default, at least where, as here, its resolution on appeal would not have required further factual development. But, the Court added that he might be able to demonstrate "actual innocence" so as to excuse the default, and it remanded the case to give him that opportunity.[6]

In Welch v. United States, 578 U.S. 120 (2016), the Court relied on Bousley to hold retroactive the rule of Johnson v. United States, 576 U.S. 591 (2015). The Johnson Court held that the residual clause of the Armed Career Criminal Act, 18 U.S.C. § 924(e)(2)(B)(ii), which provides for enhanced sentences in cases of possession of a firearm by a person convicted of a felony, was unconstitutionally vague in violation of due process.[7] After

---

[5]   The Court subsequently eliminated Teague's second category (applicable to new rules of criminal procedure) in Edwards v. Vannoy, 593 U.S. 255 (2021), see p. 1583, *supra*.

[6]   The Justices offered a range of views about whether there had been a procedural default and, if so, what effect it should have. Justice Scalia's dissent, joined by Justice Thomas, argued that a showing of actual innocence should not excuse a default in a guilty plea situation. Noting that most convictions are by guilty plea, Justice Scalia feared that the Court's ruling could produce a flood of collateral attacks. Justice Scalia also observed that pleas often are entered in exchange for dismissal of more serious charges.

Responding to Justice Scalia, the Court stressed that the government was free to introduce any admissible evidence of guilt, including evidence not presented at the plea colloquy, and added: "where the Government has forgone more serious charges in the course of plea bargaining, petitioner's showing of actual innocence must also extend to those charges."

What does this last statement mean? Surely if a petitioner is permitted to overturn a conviction, the government may re-open charges that had been dismissed as part of a plea agreement. But in order to establish his "actual innocence" of an offense whose elements he did not understand when he entered his plea, why must someone like Bousley be required to show that he was also innocent of other charges of which he was never convicted?

[7]   The Armed Career Criminal Act imposes a sentence enhancement of five years or more where a person previously convicted of a felony is found to possess a firearm and after three or more convictions for a "serious drug offense" or a "violent felony," the latter of which is defined

pleading guilty to one count of being a person convicted of a felony in possession of a firearm, Welch received an enhanced sentence under the Act based on three prior violent felony convictions. Throughout the proceedings that followed, Welch contended that one of his prior convictions fell outside the reach of the Act, rendering him ineligible for a sentence enhancement. After the district court rejected the argument in § 2255 proceedings, Welch applied to the Court of Appeals for a certificate of appealability, which the court denied. Shortly thereafter, the Supreme Court decided Johnson. Welch then sought certiorari review of the merits of his claim as well as the question whether Johnson announced a substantive rule that should apply retroactively to cases on collateral review.

Reaching only the latter question, the Court concluded that Johnson had announced a new rule for purposes of Teague. Writing for the majority, Justice Kennedy then turned to the question whether Johnson's rule "falls within one of the two categories that have retroactive effect under Teague." Relying on Schriro v. Summerlin, 542 U.S. 348, 353 (2004), and Montgomery v. Louisiana, 577 U.S. 190 (2016), p. 1610, *supra*, he concluded that it did. The Court had long indicated that a substantive rule under Teague " 'includes decisions that narrow the scope of a criminal statute by interpreting its terms' " (quoting Schriro, 542 U.S. at 351). Because of Johnson, the Act's residual clause "can no longer mandate or authorize any sentence." It followed, in the Court's view, that the decision in Johnson was substantive in nature.

Justice Kennedy explained that the Court's Teague jurisprudence determines "whether a new rule is substantive or procedural by considering the function of the rule," and does not turn on whether "the underlying constitutional guarantee [invoked by the petitioner] is characterized as procedural or substantive." Relying upon Bousley, Justice Kennedy also deemed it irrelevant to the Teague analysis that Congress retained power "to enact a new version of the residual clause that imposes the same punishment on the same persons for the same conduct, provided the new statute is precise enough to satisfy due process."

Justice Thomas dissented.[8] He complained that the majority had "erode[d] any meaningful limits on what a 'substantive' rule is" under Teague. Because "[t]he Government remains as free to enhance sentences for federal crimes based on the commission of previous violent felonies after Johnson as it was before," he argued, Johnson's rule should not be deemed

---

to encompass a range of circumstances, including in its so-called "residual clause" crimes involving "conduct that presents a serious potential risk of physical injury to another." 18 U.S.C. § 924(e)(2)(B). Johnson held that the "serious potential risk" residual language gave insufficient guidance as to the scope of its application.

[8]   As a threshold matter, Justice Thomas contended that the Court of Appeals correctly denied a certificate of appealability. The majority had reversed the Court of Appeals' denial of a certificate of appealability on the basis that "reasonable jurists at least could debate whether Welch is entitled to relief" under Johnson. Justice Thomas's dissent labeled the Court's conclusion "preposterous" given that Welch had sought the benefit of Johnson for the first time in an untimely motion for reconsideration of the Court of Appeals' prior denial of his application for a certificate. In Justice Thomas's view, the Court of Appeals could not be criticized for "denying Welch the opportunity to 'appeal' a claim that he failed to raise," which was based on "a decision that did not yet exist."

substantive under the Court's precedents. Bousley "applied only to new rules reinterpreting the text of federal criminal statutes in a way that narrows their reach." Johnson, by contrast, "announced only that there is no way in which to narrow the reach of the residual clause without running afoul of the Due Process Clause." Reading Johnson as substantive, he wrote, will mean that "if any decision has the effect of invalidating substantive provisions of a criminal statute," it will be treated as substantive, "no matter what the reason for the statute's invalidation."[9]

Does Justice Thomas successfully distinguish Bousley?

(b) New Evidence. Courts have long held that evidentiary issues ordinarily should be raised on direct appeal as opposed to in a § 2255 petition. See, *e.g.*, Williams v. United States, 365 F.2d 21, 22 (7th Cir.1966) (reliability of evidence is not appropriate for § 2255 review). Some cases suggest that § 2255 could reach claims based on new evidence that could not, with due diligence, have been discovered at trial, see, *e.g.*, Giacalone v. United States, 739 F.2d 40, 43 (2d Cir.1984) (stating that "new evidence" for purposes of § 2255 proceedings "is evidence that is discovered after the original hearing, and which could not, with due diligence of counsel, have been discovered sooner"), although it is difficult to find decisions granting relief on this basis.[10]

(c) No Previous Decision on the Merits. A § 2255 motion would not simply revisit ground already covered when it presents a claim not raised at trial or on direct review. The standards governing the effect of procedural defaults by those in state custody apply equally to those in federal custody,[11] however, and therefore in the situation posed, relief under § 2255 ordinarily will be foreclosed. See generally pp. 1631–1657, *supra*. But as with persons in state custody, some claims may appropriately be raised for the first time in § 2255 proceedings; the most important set of such claims are those alleging ineffective assistance of counsel. See Massaro v. United States, 538

---

[9]   More generally, Justice Thomas complained that the Court's Teague jurisprudence has moved well beyond the limited category of substantive claims Justice Harlan viewed as entitled to retroactive application. In support, Justice Thomas pointed to the extension of Teague's first exception to rules prohibiting certain punishments, see Penry v. Lynaugh, 492 U.S. 302 (1989); to those in federal custody challenging the reach of federal criminal statutes, as in Bousley; and to state post-conviction proceedings, see Montgomery v. Louisiana, 577 U.S. 190 (2016).

Is Justice Thomas's criticism on point here? See Mackey v. United States, 401 U.S. 667, 692 (1971) (Harlan, J., concurring in part and dissenting in part) (referring to rules that render "certain kinds of primary, private individual conduct beyond the power of the criminal law-making authority to proscribe"); see also p. 1580 (Paragraph (3)), *supra*. If so, is such an expansion of Justice Harlan's vision nonetheless warranted? For discussion of some of the complications when such claims are advanced, see Paragraph (8), *infra*.

[10]   In keeping with this idea, Congress provided in § 2255(h) that one of the bases for certifying a "second or successive motion" under § 2255 is where it is predicated upon "newly discovered evidence that, if proven and viewed in light of the evidence as a whole, would be sufficient to establish by clear and convincing evidence that no reasonable factfinder would have found the movant guilty of the offense."

[11]   See Bousley v. United States, Paragraph (5)(a), note 6, *supra*; Reed v. Farley, 512 U.S. 339, 354–55 (1994) (dictum); United States v. Frady, 456 U.S. 152 (1982). Whether or not one views those in state and federal custody as differently situated with respect to claims previously litigated, aren't the two classes similarly situated with respect to defaulted claims? For both, a refusal to excuse the default forfeits the claim altogether. See generally Meltzer, *State Court Forfeitures of Federal Rights*, 99 Harv.L.Rev. 1128, 1204–05 (1986).

U.S. 500 (2003), p. 1647, note 10, *supra* (unanimously rejecting the government's contention that the failure of counsel on direct appeal to raise the ineffectiveness of trial counsel, even when that claim was based solely on the trial record, constituted a procedural default).

(6) Nonconstitutional Claims. Like § 2254, § 2255 refers to sentences "imposed in violation of the Constitution *or laws* of the United States" (emphasis added). Federal prosecutions authorized by federal criminal statutes obviously involve federal nonconstitutional laws far more often than do state prosecutions; therefore, the reference to "laws" is far more significant in the § 2255 setting than in the § 2254 setting.

But not every claim alleging a violation of federal law provides the basis for collateral relief. In Hill v. United States, 368 U.S. 424 (1962), the Court held that § 2255 did not encompass a claim that the sentencing judge violated Rule 32(a) of the Criminal Rules by failing to ask whether the defendant (who was represented by counsel) had anything to say before sentence was imposed. The alleged error was "neither jurisdictional nor constitutional. It is not a fundamental defect which inherently results in a complete miscarriage of justice, nor an omission inconsistent with the rudimentary demands of fair procedure. It does not present 'exceptional circumstances where the need for the remedy afforded by the writ of *habeas corpus* is apparent' " (quoting Bowen v. Johnston, 306 U.S. 19, 27 (1939)).

The Court later relied upon Hill in holding that § 2255 also does not permit advancement of a claim of a purely "formal" violation of Fed.R.Crim.Proc. 11 (governing the taking of guilty pleas), see United States v. Timmreck, 441 U.S. 780 (1979), or a claim that in imposing a sentence, the judge had failed to foresee a change in parole regulations the effect of which was to delay the petitioner's release, see United States v. Addonizio, 442 U.S. 178, 186 (1979).[12]

But the Court did conclude that the statutory claim in Davis v. United States, 417 U.S. 333 (1974), satisfied the Hill test and therefore could provide the basis for relief. The Ninth Circuit had affirmed Davis's conviction for refusing to obey an order of induction into the armed forces, rejecting his claim that the federal regulation authorizing his induction for "delinquency" was invalid because it was promulgated without statutory authority. After a different Ninth Circuit panel, in an unrelated case, upheld the same claim that Davis had presented, Davis sought relief under § 2255.

Thus, Davis, like Bousley, Paragraph (5)(a), *supra*, sought relief because of a change in the interpretation of the scope of the criminal offense of which he was convicted. Unlike Bousley, Davis had gone to trial instead of pleading guilty, and therefore could not claim a due process violation in the submission of an involuntary or unintelligent plea. As a result, the Supreme Court treated Davis's claim as purely statutory. Concluding without discussion that the second panel's decision constituted "an intervening

---

[12]   Hill likewise has wielded some influence in the § 2254 context. See Reed v. Farley, 512 U.S. 339 (1994), p. 1547, note 1, *supra* (applying the Hill standard in a § 2254 proceeding and holding not cognizable a petitioner's claim that the state had violated an interstate compact, approved by Congress, which requires the trial of a person transferred from one state to another to commence within 120 days of the transfer).

change in the law,"[13] the Court ruled that Davis's claim that he had been convicted "for an act that the law does not make criminal" was sufficiently fundamental to fall within § 2255.

(7) Limitations on § 2255 Relief. Much of the doctrine governing habeas relief for those held in state custody has been imported into § 2255 proceedings.

(a) Exhaustion. Some doctrines found only in the statutory provisions governing the operation of § 2254 are also read into § 2255. Thus, although § 2255 does not mention exhaustion of remedies, the Advisory Committee Notes to the § 2255 Rules state that "courts have held that [a § 2255] motion is inappropriate if the movant is simultaneously appealing the [conviction]." (Recall that the exhaustion requirement was originally a judge-made doctrine. See pp. 1662–1665, *supra*.)

(b) Procedural default. Sometimes matters not expressly governed by statutory text under either § 2254 or § 2255 are treated similarly—as, for example, is the case with procedural defaults, see Paragraph (5)(c), *supra*.

(c) Statute-based. In 1996, AEDPA included a number of amendments to § 2255 that impose new restrictions on the availability of collateral relief and generally parallel AEDPA's restrictions with respect to those held in state custody. These include (i) a one-year statute of limitations for § 2255 motions, see § 2255(f), similar to § 2244(d)'s limitations period for petitioners in state custody, see p. 1548, *supra*,[14] and (ii) strict limits on the consideration of second or successive motions, see § 2255(h), similar to those governing petitioners in state custody under § 2244(b), see pp. 1657–1662, *supra*.[15]

---

[13]   Note that the only intervening "change in the law" resulted from a decision of another panel of the Ninth Circuit. Should collateral relitigation instead be permitted only when the asserted change in the law would be authoritative (*e.g.*, a ruling by the Supreme Court or by the court of appeals en banc)? What about a decision from another circuit? Compare the more limited language of § 2254(d)(1) (limiting the scope of relevant law to decisions of the Supreme Court of the United States).

[14]   Section 2255's limitations period, unlike that in § 2244, does not specify that a judgment becomes final on the date of "the conclusion of direct review or the expiration of the time for seeking such review." In Clay v. United States, 537 U.S. 522 (2003), the Court ruled unanimously that when a federal defendant whose conviction was affirmed on appeal does not petition for certiorari, the conviction becomes final when the time for filing a petition expired.

Under § 2255, as under § 2244, the one-year period runs from the latest of four dates, one of which is "the date on which the right asserted was initially recognized by the Supreme Court, if that right has been newly recognized by the Supreme Court and made retroactively applicable to cases on collateral review." In Dodd v. United States, 545 U.S. 353 (2005) (5–4), the Court held that the one-year period runs from the date on which the Supreme Court recognizes the new right, rather than the date on which the right is made retroactive in a subsequent proceeding. The Court recognized that when, as is often true and was true in Dodd's case, more than a year passes between the Supreme Court's recognition of a new right and it being made retroactively applicable, a petitioner will be unable to file a timely claim invoking the new right. It nonetheless held that the statutory language required such a result. In dissent, Justice Stevens (joined by Justices Souter, Ginsburg, and Breyer) refused to accept the view that Congress should be understood, "in the same provision, both to recognize a potential basis for habeas relief and also to make it highly probable that the statute of limitations would bar relief before the claim can be brought." Is that right?

[15]   Section 2255(h) requires that in order to proceed, any "second or successive motion must be certified" by "the appropriate court of appeals" to be predicated upon "newly discovered evidence that * * * would be sufficient to establish by clear and convincing evidence that no

In addition, AEDPA established time limits within which federal courts must decide § 2255 motions filed by petitioners under sentence of death: for the district courts, the earlier of 450 days after filing or 60 days after the date on which the case is submitted for decision, with one 30 day extension permitted; for the courts of appeals, 120 days after the reply brief is filed. 28 U.S.C. § 2266. (The parallel provisions for capital petitioners in state custody apply only if the state's provision of counsel in *state* post-conviction proceedings meets specified conditions. See pp. 1657–1662, *supra*.)[16]

(8) Problems Under the 1996 Act. The limitation on second or successive petitions for § 2255 petitioners largely tracks the similar limitation for state petitioners seeking habeas review, permitting successive § 2255 motions only where it rests on "a new rule of *constitutional* law, made retroactive * * * by the Supreme Court * * *" or is based on "newly discovered evidence" § 2255(h) (emphasis added). But Congress seems to have lost sight of the fact that petitioners in federal custody more often can raise federal *statutory* claims in their collateral attacks—notably in cases in which the federal criminal statute under which a petitioner was convicted has since been authoritatively interpreted more narrowly, as in Bailey and Bousley. See Paragraphs (5)(a) & (6), *supra*.

If a claim relying upon an authoritative change in the interpretation of a federal criminal offense that a petitioner was convicted for violating is foreclosed by § 2255's limits on successive petitions, the question arises whether the claim instead may be raised in a petition brought under § 2241. Recall that § 2255 contains a "savings clause," § 2255(e), under which review is foreclosed unless "the remedy by motion [under § 2255] is inadequate or ineffective to test the legality of [the petitioner's] detention." On the one hand, it cannot be that the restrictions on successive petitions make § 2255 "inadequate or ineffective" whenever a petitioner has already filed a § 2255 motion—for that would mean that any statutory restriction on § 2255 could be bypassed by filing under § 2241. On the other, if resort to § 2241 under the savings clause were precluded in such a case, a petitioner convicted of an offense that has been held not to exist would have no remedy.

---

reasonable factfinder would have found the movant guilty of the offense" or "a new rule of constitutional law, made retroactive to cases on collateral review by the Supreme Court, that was previously unavailable." Thus, § 2255 permits a successive petition based on newly discovered evidence without § 2244(b)(2)(B)(i)'s further requirement that "the factual predicate for the claim could not have been discovered previously through the exercise of due diligence."

With respect to second or successive motions that involve claims previously presented, some circuits have interpreted § 2255 to incorporate the restrictions on successive petitions found in §§ 2244(b)(1) & (2), despite the fact that those provisions are expressly limited to claims "presented in a second or successive habeas corpus application under section 2254." See, *e.g.*, In re Baptiste, 828 F.3d 1337 (11th Cir.2016) (per curiam); White v. United States, 371 F.3d 900 (7th Cir.2004) (same); but see Williams v. United States, 927 F.3d 427, 436 (6th Cir.2019) (holding otherwise). Some circuits have concluded that denials of certification under § 2255(h) to proceed with a successive petition may not be appealed, incorporating the standard of § 2244(b)(3)(E), which is not expressly limited to petitions filed under § 2254. See, *e.g.*, In re Graham, 714 F.3d 1181 (10th Cir.2013) (per curiam); Lykus v. Corsini, 565 F.3d 1 (1st Cir.2009) (en banc) (per curiam).

[16] A last change made by AEDPA is to extend to those detained in federal custody (whether or not under sentence of death) the rule, which before 1996 applied only to persons in state custody, that an appeal from a district court's denial of relief cannot be filed without having first obtained a certificate of appealability. See 28 U.S.C. § 2253, discussed at p. 1551, *supra*.

In Jones v. Hendrix, 599 U.S. 465 (2023), the Supreme Court finally addressed the intersection of § 2255(e) and § 2241. Jones had been convicted of unlawful possession of a firearm by a person convicted of a felony in violation of 18 U.S.C. § 922(g). After Jones filed his first § 2255 motion (which was unsuccessful), the Supreme Court decided Rehaif v. United States, 588 U.S. 225 (2019), holding that knowledge of the status that disqualifies an individual from owning a firearm is an element of § 922(g). Thereafter, Jones sought to file a § 2241 petition, arguing that he should benefit from the holding in Rehaif and that the limitations on successive § 2255 motions in § 2255(h) rendered § 2255 "inadequate or ineffective to test the legality of his detention" per the terms of the savings clause, § 2255(e).[17]

Writing for the Court, Justice Thomas disagreed. In the Court's view, the savings clause "does not permit a prisoner asserting an intervening change in statutory interpretation to circumvent AEDPA's restrictions on second or successive § 2255 motions by filing a § 2241 petition." Justice Thomas stressed the savings clause had long been understood to cover solely "unusual circumstances" such as where "it is impossible or impracticable for a prisoner to seek relief from the sentencing court," offering the example of a court that Congress has subsequently dissolved.[18] The "straightforward negative inference" of the two conditions set forth in § 2255(h) permitting successive petitions is that "a second or successive collateral attack on a federal sentence is not authorized unless one of" the conditions in § 2255(h) is satisfied. Relevant to the Court's reasoning was the fact that Congress expressly limited relief under § 2255(h) to application of "new rule[s] of constitutional law" and not "*nonconstitutional* law." "Any other reading" of the relevant provisions, Justice Thomas concluded, "would make AEDPA curiously self-defeating. It would mean that, by expressly excluding second or successive § 2255 motions based on nonconstitutional legal developments, Congress accomplished nothing in terms of actually limiting such claims."

The Court saw no constitutional concerns raised by its reading of the statute. There was no problem under the Suspension Clause because "[a]t the Founding, a sentence after conviction 'by a court of competent jurisdiction' was ' "*itself* sufficient cause" ' " for one's continued detention (quoting Brown v. Davenport, 596 U.S. 118, 128–29 (2022) (quoting in turn Ex parte Watkins, 28 U.S. (3 Pet.) 193, 202 (1830))). As for due process, Justice Thomas opined that it "does not guarantee a direct appeal" (citing McKane v. Durston, 153 U.S. 684, 687 (1894)), much less "the opportunity to have legal issues redetermined in successive collateral attacks on a final sentence." As for the Eighth Amendment, Justice Thomas posited that its

---

[17]   In the lead up to Jones, many (but not all) circuits had concluded that petitioners like Jones may resort to § 2241 in some circumstances, with some suggesting that any other conclusion would raise serious constitutional issues. See, *e.g.*, Triestman v. United States, 124 F.3d 361, 377 (2d Cir.1997); United States v. Tyler, 732 F.3d 241, 246 (3d Cir.2013); Brown v. Caraway, 719 F.3d 583, 586 (7th Cir.2013). But *cf.* Prost v. Anderson, 636 F.3d 578, 584, 593 (10th Cir.2011).

[18]   The Court added that the savings clause does not displace § 2241 in situations where a petitioner attacks their detention, as opposed to sentence, such as where "a prisoner * * * argue[s] that he is being detained in a place or manner not authorized by the sentence, that he has unlawfully been denied parole or good-time credits, or that an administrative sanction affecting the conditions of his detention is illegal."

text imposes limitations solely upon "the kinds of punishments governments may 'inflic[t]' " and does not offer a "freestanding entitlement to a second or successive round of postconviction review."

In adhering to a narrow view of the savings clause, the Court distinguished its holding in McQuiggin v. Perkins, 569 U.S. 383 (2013), p. 1548, note 4, *supra*, that a party could overcome AEDPA's statute of limitations based upon a colorable claim of "actual innocence." Justice Thomas reasoned that there is a difference between invoking equitable considerations to set aside the statute of limitations as opposed to displacing restrictions on second or successive motions, explaining:

"Statutes of limitations merely govern the *timeframe* for bringing a claim. AEDPA's second-or-successive restrictions, by contrast, 'constitute a modified res judicata rule,' Felker v. Turpin, 518 U. S. 651, 664 (1996), and thus embody Congress' judgment regarding the central policy question of postconviction remedies—the appropriate balance between finality and error correction. Insisting on a heightened standard of clarity in this context would effectively mean adopting a presumption against finality as a substantive value. We decline to do so."[19]

Justices Sotomayor and Kagan penned a joint dissent in which they decried the "disturbing results" of the Court's holding—namely, that "[a] prisoner who is actually innocent" will be "forever barred" from challenging his sentence because he previously did so before intervening caselaw "confirm[ed] his innocence." In their view, the savings clause should instead be read consistent with pre-AEDPA decisions holding that "federal prisoners can collaterally attack their convictions in successive petitions if they can make a colorable showing that they are innocent under an intervening decision of statutory construction" (citing Davis v. United States, 417 U.S. 333, 344–47 (1974), and McCleskey v. Zant, 499 U.S. 467, 493–95 (1991)).

Justice Jackson also dissented. She believed the Court's opinion misread both § 2255(e) and § 2255(h). In her view, the former should be read "to 'save' any claim that was available prior to § 2255(h)'s enactment where Congress has not expressed a clear intent to foreclose it," a category encompassing claims of legal innocence. Justice Jackson pointed to AEDPA's legislative history suggesting that Congress did not intend to preclude legal innocence claims brought in successive petitions. She further observed that Congress modeled § 2255(h) on AEDPA's provision governing successive petitions brought under § 2254, § 2244(b). But petitioners in state custody, she wrote, do not generally raise federal *statutory* claims. Thus, she noted, "it is plausible (and perhaps even likely) that Congress did not appreciate fully that the modeled-after language establishing a successive-petition bar did not capture the full scope of available claims for federal prisoners." Arguing for a clear statement rule before reading legislation to encroach upon a habeas court's equitable power to allow such a petition, Justice Jackson labeled the Court's interpretation "stingy" (relying on Ex parte Yerger, 75 U.S. (8 Wall.) 85, 95, 102 (1869), p. 419, *supra*, INS v. St. Cyr, 533

---

[19] Justice Thomas further rejected a clear statement rule calling for clearer evidence that Congress intended to foreclose such a "workaround."

U.S. 289, 298 (2001), p. 1471, *supra*, Demore v. Kim, 538 U.S. 510, 517 (2003), p. 467, note 3, *supra*, and Manning, *Textualism and the Equity of the Statute*, 101 Colum.L.Rev. 1, 121–22 (2001)).

Justice Jackson also argued in favor of application of the canon of constitutional avoidance. "There is a nonfrivolous argument that the Constitution's protection against 'cruel and unusual punishment' prohibits the incarceration of innocent individuals." She then stated, "[t]his is not to say that the Eighth Amendment creates a 'freestanding entitlement to a second or successive round of postconviction review'" (quoting the majority opinion). But, she wrote, Jones is seeking "a *single* meaningful opportunity to have a federal court consider his claim of legal innocence." Justice Jackson also suggested that legal innocence claims implicate the Suspension Clause because they call into question the validity of the jurisdiction of the convicting court. Concluding, she viewed the Court's decision as "creat[ing] an opening for Congress to step in and fix this problem."

Jones v. Hendrix marks yet another Supreme Court decision in recent Terms scaling back opportunities for post-conviction review while elevating the principle of finality. *Cf.* Friendly, *Is Innocence Irrelevant? Collateral Attack on Criminal Judgments*, 38 U.Chi.L.Rev. 142 (1970). It is, in this respect, in some tension with decisions from only a few Terms prior, such as Banister v. Davis, 590 U.S. 504 (2020), Buck v. Davis, 580 U.S. 100 (2017), and Tharpe v. Sellers, 583 U.S. 33 (2018) (per curiam), all of which permitted workarounds to AEDPA's preclusion of second or successive habeas petitions in extraordinary situations. (For discussion, see pp. 1625–1626, 1660–1661, *supra*.) See also Felker v. Turpin, 518 U.S. 651 (1996), p. 1658, *supra* (suggesting that a potential bypass of AEDPA's limitations on successive petitions may be found in the Court's original writ).

Similarly, Jones is in some tension with the Court's earlier decision in McQuiggin v. Perkins. Is Justice Thomas's distinction of that case convincing? Why should equitable tolling apply to permit an actual innocence claim to go forward in the face of a clear statute of limitations purporting to bar the claim while analogous equitable considerations not dictate that a legal innocence claim may be heard despite a statutory limitation on successive petitions? Is the relevant difference one between claims of actual versus legal innocence? And is it helpful or harmful to the petitioner's case that his claim of legal innocence parallels an analogous claim that Congress expressly permitted to go forward in a successive petition in § 2255(h)(2) (permitting successive § 2255 motion based on "a new rule of constitutional law")? Justice Thomas thought the express reference to new rules of constitutional law implied the *exclusion* of claims based on new *statutory* holdings, but could one argue that § 2255(h)(2) suggests that Congress was concerned as a general matter with permitting legal innocence claims to get around the bar on successive petitions and therefore all such claims—constitutional *and* statutory—should be permitted to go forward?

The Court's decision not to invoke the canon of constitutional avoidance in Jones is likewise in some tension with the Court's approach just seven years earlier in Montgomery v. Louisiana, 577 U.S. 190 (2016), p. 1610, *supra*, where it held the Constitution requires that a state post-conviction court be open to grant relief to a person detained by the state under a now-outdated understanding of constitutionally permissible punishments. In both Jones and Montgomery, the Court faced the argument that limitations on post-conviction availability precluded the relevant courts from awarding relief to the petitioner. In one (Montgomery), the Court held the Constitution required it. In another (Jones), the Court upheld the limitation and held there were no constitutional concerns implicated. Studying the cases together again raises the question whether the constitutional basis of an underlying claim (in Montgomery's case, an Eighth Amendment claim) as opposed to a claim over the proper interpretation of a federal statute (in Jones's case) should be treated differently.

In her Jones dissent, Justice Jackson argues that Congress could not have desired the result that follows under the Court's holding. In so doing, does she assign too little significance to the considerable changes and new hurdles imposed by AEDPA to both the § 2254 and § 2255 schemes? Or is she correct that Congress likely did not realize when it modeled § 2255(h) off of § 2244(b) that petitioners in federal custody will have additional legal innocence claims beyond those grounded in the Constitution? In all events, she calls upon Congress to step in and address the result in Jones. How likely is Congress to do so?

C. THE RELATIONSHIP BETWEEN HABEAS CORPUS AND SECTION 1983

INTRODUCTORY NOTE ON THE RELATIONSHIP BETWEEN HABEAS CORPUS AND SECTION 1983

(1) The Problem. Complex issues arise when a federal plaintiff seeks relief in an action under 42 U.S.C. § 1983 but—because the basis on which relief is sought could invalidate the plaintiff's criminal conviction or shorten the period of incarceration—the plaintiff might also have sought relief in a habeas corpus action. There are significant differences between the two causes of action, including available remedies and especially (but not exclusively) the requirement that before bringing a habeas action, the petitioner must have exhausted available state remedies. See pp. 1662–1665, *supra.*

The exhaustion requirement can have important effects on forum choice—in particular, on whether the federal plaintiff or petitioner can obtain a trial de novo of fact and law in federal court. In a § 1983 action, absent a prior state court judgment, the federal court would decide all relevant issues itself. In a habeas action, by contrast, the requirement that a petitioner first exhaust state remedies may generate a state court decision on the merits. The federal habeas regime has been treated as an exception to the command of 28 U.S.C. § 1738 (the Full Faith and Credit Statute), so that the state court decision would not have a preclusive effect in a habeas proceeding. See Allen v. McCurry, 449 U.S. 90 (1980) (holding nonetheless that issue preclusion may lie in a § 1983 action with respect to issues resolved in earlier state court proceedings unless "the party against whom an earlier court decision is asserted did not have a full and fair opportunity to litigate the claim or issue decided by the first court"). But, as explored earlier in this chapter, the state court decision is one to which habeas courts will nonetheless generally defer. Deference to factual findings has been common for decades, and since the enactment of AEDPA in 1996, the state court's determinations of law as well as fact are entitled to broad deference under 28 U.S.C. § 2254, often making the state court decision determinative of the outcome in federal court. See pp. 1627–1631, *supra.*

(2) The Preiser and Wolff Decisions. Preiser v. Rodriguez, 411 U.S. 475 (1973), was the first case affording the Supreme Court an opportunity to address the overlap of habeas corpus and § 1983. There, the majority held that a federal court could not entertain a § 1983 action in which plaintiffs incarcerated by a state sought the restoration of good-time credits—relief that, if granted, would result in immediate release. In the majority's view, the plaintiffs' claims "fell squarely within th[e] traditional scope of habeas corpus," for they went "directly to the constitutionality of [the] physical confinement itself and seek[ ] either immediate release from that confinement or the shortening of its duration." The Court then emphasized that "Congress has determined that habeas corpus is the appropriate remedy for state prisoners attacking the validity of the fact or length of their confinement, [a] specific determination [that] must override the general terms of § 1983." Such a rule, moreover, served the goal of "avoid[ing] the unnecessary friction between the federal and state court systems that would result if a lower federal court upset a state court conviction without first giving the state court system an opportunity to correct its own constitutional errors." It followed in the Court's view that habeas was the only available federal remedy in such a case. Justice Brennan, dissenting for himself and Justices Douglas and Marshall, argued that habeas should not be regarded as the exclusive remedy and hence exhaustion should not be required.

The limits of Preiser were tested in Wolff v. McDonnell, 418 U.S. 539 (1974), where plaintiffs incarcerated by the state brought § 1983 actions challenging the constitutionality of certain state disciplinary proceedings (which had resulted in loss of good-time credits), the state legal aid program, and the prison mail censorship system. The plaintiffs sought both damages and the restoration of good-time credits. The Court allowed the § 1983 action to proceed with respect to all claims save those seeking the restoration of good-time credits, which were foreclosed under Preiser.

Neither Preiser nor Wolff considered the question of the availability of a § 1983 action for damages when a determination in favor of the federal plaintiff would rest on grounds that would necessarily imply the invalidity of the plaintiff's underlying conviction or shorten the period of incarceration. The Court addressed that question in the following case.

Heck v. Humphrey

512 U.S. 477 (1994).

Certiorari to the United States Court of Appeals for the Seventh Circuit.

■ JUSTICE SCALIA delivered the opinion of the Court.

This case presents the question whether a state prisoner may challenge the constitutionality of his conviction in a suit for damages under 42 U.S.C. § 1983.

I

[While petitioner's appeal from his conviction in Indiana was pending, he filed a § 1983 action in federal court against prosecutorial and police officials.] The complaint alleged that respondents, acting under color of state law, had engaged in an "unlawful, unreasonable, and arbitrary investigation" leading to petitioner's arrest; "knowingly destroyed" evidence "which was exculpatory in nature and could have proved [petitioner's] innocence"; and caused "an illegal and unlawful voice identification procedure" to be used at petitioner's trial. The complaint sought, among other things, compensatory and punitive monetary damages. It did not ask for injunctive relief, and petitioner has not sought release from custody in this action.

The District Court dismissed the action without prejudice, because the issues it raised "directly implicate the legality of [petitioner's] confinement." While petitioner's appeal to the Seventh Circuit was pending, the Indiana Supreme Court upheld his conviction and sentence on direct appeal; his first petition for a writ of habeas corpus in Federal District Court was dismissed because it contained unexhausted claims; and his second federal habeas petition was denied, and the denial affirmed by the Seventh Circuit.

[Thereafter, the Seventh Circuit affirmed the dismissal of petitioner's § 1983 complaint.][2] Heck filed a petition for certiorari, which we granted.

II

This case lies at the intersection of the two most fertile sources of federal-court prisoner litigation—the Civil Rights Act of 1871, 42 U.S.C. § 1983, and the federal habeas corpus statute, 28 U.S.C. § 2254. Both of these provide access to a federal forum for claims of unconstitutional treatment at the hands of state officials, but they differ in their scope and operation. In general, exhaustion of state remedies "is *not* a prerequisite to an action under § 1983," Patsy v. Board of Regents of Fla., 457 U.S. 496, 501 (1982) (emphasis added), even an action by a state prisoner, *id.*,

---

[2]   Neither in his petition for certiorari nor in his principal brief on the merits did petitioner contest the description of his monetary claims (by both the District Court and the Court of Appeals) as challenging the legality of his conviction. * * * Petitioner [contended in his reply brief] that findings validating his damages claims would not invalidate his conviction. That argument comes too late. We did not take this case to review such a fact-bound issue, and we accept the characterization of the lower courts. * * *

at 509. The federal habeas corpus statute, by contrast, requires that state prisoners first seek redress in a state forum.

Preiser v. Rodriguez, 411 U.S. 475 (1973), considered the potential overlap between these two provisions, and held that habeas corpus is the exclusive remedy for a state prisoner who challenges the fact or duration of his confinement and seeks immediate or speedier release, even though such a claim may come within the literal terms of § 1983. We emphasize that Preiser did *not* create an exception to the "no exhaustion" rule of § 1983; it merely held that certain claims by state prisoners are not *cognizable* under that provision, and must be brought in habeas corpus proceedings, which do contain an exhaustion requirement.

This case is clearly not covered by the holding of Preiser, for petitioner seeks not immediate or speedier release, but monetary damages, as to which he could not "have sought and obtained fully effective relief through federal habeas corpus proceedings." *Id.*, at 488. In dictum, however, Preiser asserted that since a state prisoner seeking only damages "is attacking something other than the fact or length of . . . confinement, and . . . is seeking something other than immediate or more speedy release[,] . . . a damages action by a state prisoner could be brought under [§ 1983] in federal court without any requirement of prior exhaustion of state remedies." 411 U.S., at 494. That statement may not be true, however, when establishing the basis for the damages claim necessarily demonstrates the invalidity of the conviction. In that situation, the claimant *can* be said to be "attacking . . . the fact or length of . . . confinement," bringing the suit within the other dictum of Preiser: "Congress has determined that habeas corpus is the appropriate remedy for state prisoners attacking the validity of the fact or length of their confinement, and that specific determination must override the general terms of § 1983." *Id.*, at 490. In the last analysis, we think the dicta of Preiser to be an unreliable, if not an unintelligible, guide: that opinion had no cause to address, and did not carefully consider, the damages question before us today.

* * * [The Court also concluded that the question before it had not been resolved by Wolff v. McDonnell, 418 U.S. 539 (1974), discussed in Paragraph (2) of the Introductory Note preceding this case.]

Thus, the question posed by § 1983 damages claims that do call into question the lawfulness of conviction or confinement remains open. To answer that question correctly, we see no need to abandon * * * our teaching that § 1983 contains no exhaustion requirement beyond what Congress has provided. The issue with respect to monetary damages challenging conviction is not, it seems to us, exhaustion; but rather, the same as the issue was with respect to injunctive relief challenging conviction in Preiser: whether the claim is cognizable under § 1983 at all. We conclude that it is not. * * *

The common-law cause of action for malicious prosecution provides the closest analogy to claims of the type considered here because, unlike the related cause of action for false arrest or imprisonment, it permits damages for confinement imposed pursuant to legal process. * * *

One element that must be alleged and proved in a malicious prosecution action is termination of the prior criminal proceeding in favor of the accused. Prosser and Keeton [on Torts] 874 [(5th ed.1984)]. * * * "[T]o permit a convicted criminal defendant to proceed with a malicious prosecution claim would permit a collateral attack on the conviction through the vehicle of a civil suit." [8 S. Speiser, C. Krause, & A. Gans, American Law of Torts § 28:5, p. 24 (1991).][4] This Court has long expressed similar concerns for finality and consistency and has generally declined to expand opportunities for collateral attack. We think the hoary principle that civil tort actions are not appropriate vehicles for challenging the validity of outstanding criminal judgments applies to § 1983 damages actions that necessarily require the plaintiff to prove the unlawfulness of his conviction or confinement, just as it has always applied to actions for malicious prosecution.

We hold that, in order to recover damages for allegedly unconstitutional conviction or imprisonment, or for other harm caused by actions whose unlawfulness would render a conviction or sentence invalid, a § 1983 plaintiff must prove that the conviction or sentence has been reversed on direct appeal, expunged by executive order, declared invalid by a state tribunal authorized to make such determination, or called into question by a federal court's issuance of a writ of habeas corpus, 28 U.S.C. § 2254. A claim for damages bearing that relationship to a conviction or sentence that has *not* been so invalidated is not cognizable under § 1983. Thus, when a state prisoner seeks damages in a § 1983 suit, the district court must consider whether a judgment in favor of the plaintiff would necessarily imply the invalidity of his conviction or sentence; if it would, the complaint must be dismissed unless the plaintiff can demonstrate that the conviction or sentence has already been invalidated. But if the district court determines that the plaintiff's action, even if successful, will *not* demonstrate the invalidity of any outstanding criminal judgment against the plaintiff, the action should be allowed to proceed,[7] in the absence of some other bar to the suit.

---

4   * * * [E]ven if Justice Souter were correct in asserting that a prior conviction, although reversed, "dissolved [a] claim for malicious prosecution," [and we do not believe he is,] our analysis would be unaffected. It would simply demonstrate that *no* common-law action, *not even* malicious prosecution, would permit a criminal proceeding to be impugned in a tort action, *even after* the conviction had been reversed. That would, if anything, strengthen our belief that § 1983, which borrowed general tort principles, was not meant to permit such collateral attack.

7   For example, a suit for damages attributable to an allegedly unreasonable search may lie even if the challenged search produced evidence that was introduced in a state criminal trial resulting in the § 1983 plaintiff's still-outstanding conviction. Because of doctrines like independent source and inevitable discovery, and especially harmless error, such a § 1983 action, even if successful, would not *necessarily* imply that the plaintiff's conviction was unlawful. * * *

Respondents had urged us to adopt a rule that was in one respect broader than this: Exhaustion of state remedies should be required, they contended, not just when success in the § 1983 damages suit would necessarily show a conviction or sentence to be unlawful, but whenever "judgment in a § 1983 action would resolve a necessary element to a likely challenge to a conviction, even if the § 1983 court [need] not determine that the conviction is invalid." Such a broad sweep was needed, respondents contended, lest a judgment in a prisoner's favor in a federal-court § 1983 damages action claiming, for example, a Fourth Amendment violation, be given preclusive effect as to that subissue in a subsequent state-court postconviction proceeding. Preclusion might result, they asserted, if the State exercised sufficient control over the officials' defense in the § 1983 action. See Montana v. United States, 440 U.S. 147, 154 (1979). While we have no occasion to rule on the matter at this time, it is at least plain that preclusion will not necessarily be an automatic, or even a permissible, effect.[9]

In another respect, however, our holding sweeps more broadly than the approach respondents had urged. We do not engraft an exhaustion requirement upon § 1983, but rather deny the existence of a cause of action. Even a prisoner who has fully exhausted available state remedies has no cause of action under § 1983 unless and until the conviction or sentence is reversed, expunged, invalidated, or impugned by the grant of a writ of habeas corpus. * * *[10]

Applying these principles to the present action, * * * we find that the dismissal of the action was correct. * * *

■ JUSTICE THOMAS, concurring.

---

[9]   State courts are bound to apply federal rules in determining the preclusive effect of federal-court decisions on issues of federal law. See P. Bator, D. Meltzer, P. Mishkin, & D. Shapiro, Hart and Wechsler's The Federal Courts and the Federal System 1604 (3d ed.1988) ("It is clear that where the federal court decided a federal question, federal res judicata rules govern"). The federal rules on the subject of issue and claim preclusion, unlike those relating to exhaustion of state remedies, are "almost entirely judge-made." Hart & Wechsler's, *supra*, at 1598. And in developing them the courts can, and indeed should, be guided by the federal policies reflected in congressional enactments. * * * [The policy underlying the exhaustion requirement of § 2254 is] that state courts be given the first opportunity to review constitutional claims bearing upon state prisoners' release from custody.

[10]   Justice Souter also adopts the common-law principle that one cannot use the device of a civil tort action to challenge the validity of an outstanding criminal conviction, but thinks it necessary to abandon that principle in those cases (of which no real-life example comes to mind) involving former state prisoners who, because they are no longer in custody, cannot bring postconviction challenges. We think the principle barring collateral attacks—a longstanding and deeply rooted feature of both the common law and our own jurisprudence—is not rendered inapplicable by the fortuity that a convicted criminal is no longer incarcerated. Justice Souter opines that disallowing a damages suit for a former state prisoner framed by Ku Klux Klan–dominated state officials is "hard indeed to reconcile . . . with the purpose of § 1983." But if, as Justice Souter appears to suggest, the goal of our interpretive enterprise under § 1983 were to provide a remedy for all conceivable invasions of federal rights that freedmen may have suffered at the hands of officials of the former States of the Confederacy, the entire landscape of our § 1983 jurisprudence would look very different. We would not, for example, have adopted the rule that judicial officers have absolute immunity from liability for damages under § 1983, a rule that would prevent recovery by a former slave who had been tried and convicted before a corrupt state judge in league with the Ku Klux Klan.

* * * I write separately to note that it is we who have put § 1983 and the habeas statute on what Justice Souter appropriately terms a "collision course." It has long been recognized that we have expanded the prerogative writ of habeas corpus and § 1983 far beyond the limited scope either was originally intended to have. Expanding the two historic statutes brought them squarely into conflict in the context of suits by state prisoners, as we made clear in Preiser.

Given that the Court created the tension between the two statutes, it is proper for the Court to devise limitations aimed at ameliorating the conflict, provided that it does so in a principled fashion. Because the Court today limits the scope of § 1983 in a manner consistent both with the federalism concerns undergirding the explicit exhaustion requirement of the habeas statute, and with the state of the common law at the time § 1983 was enacted, I join the Court's opinion.

■ JUSTICE SOUTER, with whom JUSTICE BLACKMUN, JUSTICE STEVENS, and JUSTICE O'CONNOR join, concurring in the judgment.

* * * While I do not object to referring to the common law when resolving the question this case presents, I do not think that the existence of the tort of malicious prosecution alone provides the answer. Common-law tort rules can provide a "starting point for the inquiry under § 1983," Carey v. Piphus, 435 U.S. 247, 258 (1978), but we have relied on the common law in § 1983 cases only when doing so was thought to be consistent with ordinary rules of statutory construction * * *. At the same time, we have consistently refused to allow common-law analogies to displace statutory analysis, declining to import even well-settled common-law rules into § 1983 "if [the statute's] history or purpose counsel against applying [such rules] in § 1983 actions." Wyatt v. Cole, 504 U.S. 158, 164 (1992).

An examination of common-law sources arguably relevant in this case confirms the soundness of our hierarchy of principles for resolving questions concerning § 1983. * * * [A plaintiff in a malicious-prosecution action must prove both the absence of probable cause for the proceeding and malice. These requirements would mean that even a plaintiff whose] conviction was invalidated as unconstitutional (premised, for example, on a confession coerced by an interrogation-room beating) could not obtain damages for the unconstitutional conviction and ensuing confinement if [law enforcement officials] had probable cause to believe the plaintiff was guilty and intended to bring him to justice. * * *

Furthermore, * * * the Court overlooks a significant historical incongruity that calls into question the utility of the analogy to the tort of malicious prosecution insofar as it is used exclusively to determine the scope of § 1983: the damages sought in the type of § 1983 claim involved here, damages for unlawful conviction or postconviction confinement, were not available at all in an action for malicious prosecution at the time of § 1983's enactment. A defendant's conviction, under Reconstruction-era common law, dissolved his claim for malicious prosecution because the conviction was regarded as irrebuttable evidence that the prosecution never lacked probable cause. Thus the definition of "favorable termination" with which the framers of § 1983 were aware (if they were aware of any definition) included none of the events relevant to the type of § 1983 claim involved in this case ("revers[al] on direct appeal, expunge[ment] by executive order, [a] declar[ation] [of] invalid[ity] by a state tribunal authorized to make such determination, or [the] call[ing] into question by a federal court's issuance of a writ of habeas corpus") * * *. Indeed, relying on the tort of malicious prosecution to dictate the outcome of this case would logically drive one to the position, untenable as a matter of statutory interpretation (and, to be clear, disclaimed by the Court), that conviction of a crime wipes out a person's § 1983 claim for damages for unconstitutional conviction or postconviction confinement.

We are not, however, in any such strait, for our enquiry in this case may follow the interpretive methodology employed in Preiser v. Rodriguez. In Preiser, we read the "general" § 1983 statute in light of the "specific federal habeas corpus statute," which applies only to "person[s] in custody," 28 U.S.C. § 2254(a), and the habeas statute's policy, embodied in its exhaustion requirement, § 2254(b), that state courts be given the first opportunity to review constitutional claims bearing upon a state prisoner's release from custody. 411 U.S., at 489. Though in contrast to Preiser the state prisoner here seeks damages, not release from custody, the distinction makes no difference when the damages sought are for unconstitutional conviction or confinement. * * * Because allowing a state prisoner to proceed directly with a federal-court § 1983 attack on his conviction or sentence "would wholly frustrate explicit congressional intent" as declared in the habeas exhaustion requirement, Preiser, 411 U.S., at 489, the statutory scheme must be read as precluding such attacks. * * *

That leaves the question of how to implement what statutory analysis requires. It is at this point that the malicious-prosecution tort's favorable-termination requirement becomes helpful, not in dictating the elements of a § 1983 cause of action, but in suggesting a relatively simple way to avoid collisions at the intersection of habeas and § 1983. A state prisoner may seek federal-court § 1983 damages for unconstitutional conviction or confinement, but only if he has previously established the unlawfulness of his conviction or confinement, as on appeal or on habeas. This has the effect of requiring a state prisoner challenging the lawfulness of his confinement to follow habeas's rules before seeking § 1983 damages for unlawful confinement in federal court, and it is ultimately the Court's holding today. * * *

Th[e most] sensible way to read the [majority] opinion [is not to] needlessly place at risk the rights of those outside the intersection of § 1983 and the habeas statute, individuals not "in custody" for habeas purposes. If these individuals (people who were merely fined, for example, or who have completed short terms of imprisonment, probation, or parole, or who discover (through no fault of their own) a constitutional violation after full expiration of their sentences), like state prisoners, were required to show the prior invalidation of their convictions or sentences in order to obtain § 1983 damages for unconstitutional conviction or imprisonment, the result would be to deny any federal forum for claiming a deprivation of federal rights to those who cannot first obtain a favorable state ruling. The reason, of course, is that individuals not "in custody" cannot invoke federal habeas jurisdiction, the only statutory mechanism besides § 1983 by which individuals may sue state officials in federal court for violating federal rights. That would be an untoward result. * * *

NOTE ON THE PREISER-HECK DOCTRINE

In reading this Note, consider whether it is sensible to expect incarcerated persons, who are usually acting pro se, to navigate the complexities of the Preiser-Heck doctrine.

(1) Some Questions Raised by the Heck Decision. The Court's unanimous agreement on the result in Heck masked some difficult questions.

(a)   When is it sufficiently clear that upholding a damage claim under § 1983 would *necessarily* imply the invalidity of the plaintiff's conviction, thereby requiring resort to habeas corpus as the exclusive federal remedy? The Court stated in footnote 2 that it was no longer open to Heck to argue that his claim would not have such an effect, but had he been allowed to argue this point, should he have prevailed? May a plaintiff who is willing to stipulate that any relief would not impugn his conviction (or to waive any right to try to do so) obtain relief under § 1983?

In Skinner v. Switzer, 562 U.S. 521 (2011), the Court, 6–3, refused to extend Heck to a § 1983 case involving a claim seeking DNA testing of crime-scene evidence following the plaintiff's conviction in Texas. The Texas courts had held that Skinner did not qualify for DNA testing under a Texas law permitting such testing in certain circumstances. Claiming that the state's law denied him procedural due process, Skinner filed a federal court action under § 1983 seeking an order that the testing be performed. When the case reached the Supreme Court, it ruled that the action could be maintained under § 1983.

Writing for the majority, Justice Ginsburg held that it was crucial that "[s]uccess in [Skinner's] suit for DNA testing would not 'necessarily imply' the invalidity of his conviction" (quoting Heck). The test, she noted, might well prove inconclusive or even further incriminate him. Important as well in the Court's view was the fact that Skinner did "not challenge the adverse" state court decisions themselves but instead "target[ed] as unconstitutional the Texas statute [those courts] authoritatively construed." In no case, she observed, has the Court recognized habeas as the sole remedy—"or even an available one"—where the relief sought would not either terminate custody, reduce the level of custody, or accelerate release. And allowing such an action to be brought under § 1983 was not likely to result in a flood of litigation, because, among other things, the decision would not "spill over" to claims (under Brady v. Maryland, 373 U.S. 83 (1963)) that the prosecution had withheld exculpatory evidence to the prejudice of the defendant. Brady evidence is, she observed, "by definition, always favorable to the defendant and material to his guilt or punishment."[1]

Justice Thomas, joined by Justices Kennedy and Alito, dissented. Although accepting *arguendo* the majority's conclusion that the specific relief sought, if obtained, would not necessarily imply the invalidity of Skinner's conviction, Justice Thomas argued for an extension of the Preiser-Heck rule to "all constitutional challenges to procedures concerning the validity of a conviction." Failure to do so, he contended, would undermine federal-state comity as evidenced by the judicial and legislative restrictions that had in recent decades been imposed on the availability of the habeas remedy.

Skinner highlights the considerable tension between § 1983 and the habeas regime. On the one hand, isn't Justice Thomas correct that the due process claim in Skinner implicates, at least in part, his conviction? On the other hand, isn't there a problem in holding that the existence of the habeas remedy preempts other avenues of relief when the relief sought falls so far outside the core of the traditional habeas remedy that, as Justice Ginsburg noted, it is not even clear that habeas would lie?[2]

(b) If a person imprisoned by the state who is allowed to pursue a § 1983 claim relating to a prior conviction prevails on the merits, what is the res judicata effect of that determination in a later state post-conviction or federal habeas corpus proceeding? The question is not purely academic, since there are sure to be instances in which the issue determined has a bearing on the validity of the conviction, even though the determination does not *necessarily* imply its invalidity.

(c) What constitutes a favorable termination of prior proceedings? In Thompson v. Clark, 596 U.S. 36 (2022), the Court addressed the following questions in the context of a § 1983 claim brought to recover damages for alleged Fourth Amendment violations preceding charges that were subsequently dismissed before trial: "Does it suffice for a plaintiff to show that his criminal prosecution ended without a conviction? Or must the plaintiff also demonstrate that the prosecution ended with some affirmative indication of his innocence, such as an acquittal or a dismissal accompanied

---

[1] In light of the Court's decision two terms earlier in District Attorney's Office for Third Judicial Dist. v. Osborne, 557 U.S. 52 (2009) (5–4), it is unclear how significant the holding in Skinner is. Osborne suggested that it would be a rare case in which an incarcerated person could establish that a state's refusal of post-conviction DNA testing is a due process violation that can in turn undergird a § 1983 claim.

[2] A question left in the wake of Skinner was when the procedural due process claim based on a request for DNA testing accrues for purposes of calculating the statute of limitations under § 1983. In Reed v. Goertz, 598 U.S. 230 (2023), the Court held that when an incarcerated person advances DNA testing claims through the state courts, the clock on a § 1983 procedural due process claim begins to run only when the state litigation concludes. Such a rule recognizes that the state courts may cure any such "due process flaws," "thereby rendering a federal § 1983 suit unnecessary." Starting the clock earlier, the Court added, would lead to parallel litigation and "senseless duplication."

by a statement from the judge that the evidence was insufficient?" Writing for a six-Justice majority, Justice Kavanaugh embraced the former standard. Turning to American malicious prosecution tort law as of 1871, he concluded that the understanding at the time, which should inform today's interpretation of § 1983, "does not require the plaintiff to show that the criminal prosecution ended with some affirmative indication of innocence."

(d) Heck clearly bars a § 1983 damages action for a confession obtained by torture if a conviction that depended on that confession has not been invalidated on direct or collateral attack. But it remains unclear whether Heck bars a damages action for a constitutional violation that, under the harmless error doctrine, would not invalidate a conviction. (Even unconstitutionally obtained confessions can be harmless error.) A "harmless" constitutional error is likely (though not certain) to have been less egregious than one that is presumed or found to have affected the outcome. Is there a sound basis for a rule that may, as an empirical matter, be more permissive with respect to damages actions under § 1983 for *less serious* violations? (Note, however, that individual liability in damages for marginal violations may be precluded on the basis of qualified immunity.)

(e) Additional complications after Heck abound. Habeas corpus jurisdiction has been sharply limited by Supreme Court decisions and, in 1996, by congressional amendments via AEDPA to the habeas statutory scheme. Suppose a constitutional claim in a § 1983 action brought by one in custody based on a criminal conviction would not be cognizable in habeas corpus (for example, because the party failed to raise it in state court, or, alternatively, because the state court rejected it on the merits and that determination, though erroneous, was not unreasonable and thus under the 1996 amendments to 28 U.S.C. § 2254 could not provide a basis for relief). Is the party then left with no remedy whatsoever unless the state chooses to afford either a post-conviction remedy of its own or a damages action? Or can one escape Heck by arguing that a victory in a § 1983 action will not invalidate the prior conviction precisely because no court has jurisdiction under AEDPA to entertain a federal post-conviction attack?

(f) In Heck, does Justice Scalia adequately answer Justice Souter's argument that the majority's reasoning has no application to a state defendant who never was or no longer is in custody, because habeas corpus does not lie for such a defendant and thus § 1983 becomes the *only* form of available federal relief? Justice Scalia, in footnote 10, notes that in view of doctrines such as qualified or absolute official immunity, § 1983 is not a comprehensive remedy for all violations of federal law committed by state officers. But those doctrines are presumably based on a careful balancing of the interest in vindicating individual rights against the interest in not unduly undermining effective law enforcement. When the latter interest does not provide immunity from liability in damages, what factors might warrant denial of relief under § 1983?

In Spencer v. Kemna, 523 U.S. 1 (1998), it appeared that a majority of the Court agreed with Justice Souter. The case was a complicated one in which the Court held that a habeas petition was moot because the petitioner had been released. In a concurrence joined by three other Justices, Justice

Souter agreed that the case was moot while maintaining that the Heck decision did not bar a released person from bringing a § 1983 action based on the invalidity of his conviction. A fifth Justice (Justice Stevens in his dissent) agreed with Justice Souter on this point.

But six years later, in Muhammad v. Close, 540 U.S. 749, 752 n.2 (2004) (Paragraph (3)(a), *infra*), the Court indicated that it was still an open question whether the Heck doctrine applies to an action by a one whose sentence has been fully served or by a defendant who had been fined but not imprisoned. Citing Spencer, and the expression there by "[m]embers of the Court" of the view that "unavailability of habeas for other reasons may also dispense with the Heck requirement," the Court went on to state that "[t]his case is no occasion to settle the issue."

(2) The Application of Preiser-Heck to the Accrual of the Statute of Limitations. The Preiser-Heck rule has generated difficult questions in determining the proper accrual date for a § 1983 damages action that might affect the validity of a criminal conviction. In Heck, Justice Scalia wrote that it was "unnecessary for us to address the statute-of-limitations issue wrestled with by the Court of Appeals * * *. Under our analysis the statute of limitations poses no difficulty while the state challenges are being pursued, since the § 1983 claim has not yet arisen." 512 U.S. at 489. For his part, Justice Souter believed that his adoption of "[t]he favorable-termination requirement avoids [a host of] knotty statute-of-limitations problem[s] * * *." *Id.* 499 (Souter, J., concurring in the judgment).

McDonough v. Smith, 588 U.S. 109 (2019), involved similar claims as Heck with an important difference: McDonough had been acquitted at trial. In such circumstances, the Court held that Heck's reasoning dictated that the limitations period does not begin to run and the § 1983 cause of action does not accrue "to bring a fabricated-evidence challenge to criminal proceedings while those criminal proceedings are ongoing. Only once the criminal proceeding has ended in the defendant's favor, or a resulting conviction has been invalidated within the meaning of Heck, will the statute of limitations begin to run."[3]

Wallace v. Kato, 549 U.S. 384 (2007), presented more complicated questions. Petitioner Wallace had been convicted of murder, but the state courts ultimately concluded that he had been arrested without probable cause and that the unlawful arrest rendered his subsequent statements inadmissible. Some eight years after the arrest, the state dropped the relevant charges, and one year later, Wallace brought a § 1983 damages action, seeking, among other things, damages arising from the unlawful arrest. The defendants obtained summary judgment in the courts below on the basis that the action was time-barred.

In the Supreme Court, all the Justices agreed that the applicable statute of limitations (under relevant state law) was two years, that the question of when the cause of action accrued was a matter of federal law, and that the

---

[3]   Similar reasoning informed the Court's decision in Reed v. Goertz, 598 U.S. 230 (2023), holding the statute of limitations does not begin to run on procedural due process claims relating to DNA testing until state proceedings have concluded. See note 2, *supra*.

relevant accrual date (by analogy to the common law tort of false imprisonment) was the date when one's detention without legal process ended, "when, for example, he is bound over by a magistrate or arraigned on charges." That period had long since run before the suit was filed.

Wallace contended, however, that the normal accrual date for such an action was displaced because of the Preiser-Heck rule, under which the action could not accrue until the conviction was invalidated and the charges dropped. In an opinion by Justice Scalia, the majority held that the rule did not apply because at the time the statute of limitations began to run, "there was in existence no criminal conviction that the cause of action would impugn; indeed, there may not even have been an indictment." An extension of Heck to such facts would be "bizarre" and unnecessary: "If a plaintiff files a false-arrest claim before he has been convicted (or files any other claim related to rulings that will likely be made in a pending or anticipated criminal trial), it is within the power of the district court, and in accord with common practice, to stay the civil action until the criminal case or the likelihood of a criminal case is ended." The court may then proceed, or, if the plaintiff is ultimately convicted and the "stayed civil suit would impugn that conviction, Heck will require dismissal."[4]

Justice Stevens (joined by Justice Souter) concurred on the ground that Preiser-Heck was simply inapplicable to the case at bar because under Stone v. Powell, p. 1570, *supra*, success in a § 1983 suit based on an alleged Fourth Amendment violation cannot be used in a habeas proceeding to impugn a conviction. The majority responded that the Stone decision would not bar habeas if the state were to deny the habeas petitioner a full and fair hearing.[5]

Difficulties in applying the statute of limitations in the context of Heck-related issues are likely to persist. Does the Court's rationale in Wallace apply, for example, to a claim predicated upon a confession obtained by brutal means, the prosecution's knowing use of perjured testimony, or the prosecution's failure to disclose exculpatory evidence? Does the answer depend on whether the § 1983 plaintiff suffers any ascertainable harm prior to conviction? (The Court in Wallace did say that a cause of action accrues "when the wrongful act or omission results in damages.")

(3) The Application of Preiser-Heck in Other Contexts.

(a) **Prison Disciplinary Proceedings.** In Edwards v. Balisok, 520 U.S. 641 (1997), the Court unanimously extended the Heck rationale to § 1983 actions involving prison disciplinary proceedings. There, Balisok,

---

[4]   Suppose Wallace had filed suit a few days after his arrest, but upon his conviction the suit had been dismissed under Preiser-Heck, as this passage appears to require. If, eight years later but immediately after the conviction was set aside and the charges dropped, he had refiled, would the action be barred? If so, shouldn't the stay of the original § 1983 action be continued until all opportunities for invalidating the conviction have been exhausted?

[5]   Justice Stevens replied that since Stone would operate as a bar in almost all cases, the majority "lets the perfect become the enemy of the good." Justice Breyer (joined by Justice Ginsburg) dissented, arguing that when the possibility of a Preiser-Heck problem would justify a stay of the civil action, the principle of "equitable tolling" would be appropriate during the period when a filed civil action would be stayed. In response, the majority said that equitable tolling was a "rare remedy to be applied in unusual circumstances" and was not appropriate simply "to avoid the risk of concurrent litigation."

imprisoned by the state, had been found guilty of violating prison rules, and among the sanctions imposed was the loss of 30 days of good-time credit that he had previously earned. Alleging procedural due process violations, he brought a § 1983 action for damages and declaratory and injunctive relief, preserving the right to seek restoration of the good-time credit in an appropriate proceeding. The Court held that Preiser-Heck barred the action because certain allegations, if proved, would necessarily imply the invalidity of the deprivation of the good-time credit.

Note that the Court in Balisok made no explicit effort (as it had in Heck) to analogize the plaintiff's action to a common law claim for malicious prosecution or to any other common law action. Note also that the Balisok decision appears to enable a prison authority to avoid a § 1983 action by attaching a very small sentencing sanction to an otherwise non-custodial penalty. If so, does that bear on the soundness of the decision?

The Supreme Court distinguished Balisok in Muhammad v. Close, 540 U.S. 749 (2004). The case involved a § 1983 damages action brought by Muhammad, detained in a state institution, against a prison guard for injuries allegedly caused by the guard's efforts to retaliate for earlier proceedings filed by Muhammad against the guard.[6] In a per curiam decision, the Court held that the lower court's ruling barring Muhammad's § 1983 action under Preiser-Heck was flawed "as a matter of fact and as a matter of law." First, the Court held the factual error lay in the assumption that Muhammad had sought expungement of the misconduct ruling from his prison record. Second, the Court criticized the lower court for its legal error that subscribed to the view that Preiser-Heck "applies categorically" to all suits involving prison disciplinary proceedings. In this instance, no such bar applied because the federal magistrate judge had "found or assumed that [as a matter of state law,] no good-time credits were eliminated by the prehearing action Muhammad called in question."

(b) Challenges to the Validity of Parole Procedures. The Court further confined Preiser-Heck in Wilkinson v. Dotson, 544 U.S. 74 (2005). In a consolidated case involving two § 1983 actions, which together challenged the procedures by which the state assessed parole eligibility and suitability, one plaintiff challenged the validity of a parole officer's determination that he was not presently eligible for consideration for parole, and the other challenged the validity of a parole board determination that he was not suitable for parole. Both argued that the constitutional error consisted of the retroactive application of new, harsher guidelines, and each sought a parole hearing free from the alleged constitutional defect. In both cases, the lower district courts decided that the plaintiffs could seek relief only in habeas proceedings, but the Court of Appeals held the § 1983 actions could proceed. The Supreme Court affirmed the Court of Appeals, 8–1.

Writing for the Court, Justice Breyer summarized the prior holdings as focusing "on the need to ensure that state prisoners use only habeas corpus

---

[6]   As one result of the incidents complained of, Muhammad had been disciplined, and the discipline included detention, but Muhammad did not challenge that detention or the determination of misconduct on which it was based.

(or similar state) remedies when they seek to invalidate the duration of their confinement—either *directly* through an injunction compelling speedier release or *indirectly* through a judicial determination that necessarily implies the unlawfulness of the State's custody." Such cases, he observed, seek "core" habeas corpus relief. But here, neither plaintiff sought an injunction ordering immediate or speedier release, and a favorable judgment would not "necessarily imply" the invalidity of their convictions or sentences.

Concurring, Justice Scalia (joined by Justice Thomas) argued that under the circumstances, a habeas remedy should not lie at all because the relief sought "neither terminates custody, accelerates the future date of release from custody, nor reduces the level of custody." Thus, "a contrary holding would require us to broaden the scope of habeas relief beyond recognition." Dissenting, Justice Kennedy argued that Preiser-Heck should govern because "[c]hallenges to parole proceedings are cognizable in habeas."

Isn't Justice Scalia correct, at least as a matter of precedent and the traditional conception of habeas? Is there a case in which the Supreme Court has recognized habeas as an available remedy even though the relief sought would neither require immediate or accelerated release nor reduce the level of custody?[7]

    (c) Challenges to the Method of Execution. In Nelson v. Campbell, 541 U.S. 637 (2004), and Hill v. McDonough, 547 U.S. 573 (2006), the Court considered § 1983 actions challenging the constitutionality of a particular method of execution. (In both cases, a habeas petition probably would have been barred by 28 U.S.C. § 2244(b) as a successive petition.) The Court permitted both actions to go forward under § 1983, but since it was not clear in either case that a successful challenge would prevent the use of alternative methods of execution under existing state law, the Court has yet to confront a § 1983 cause of action under such circumstances. In dicta, however, the Court has suggested that such a claim should proceed exclusively in habeas. See Nelson, 541 U.S. at 647 (stating that a claim should proceed in habeas if granting relief "would *necessarily* prevent [the state] from carrying out its execution"); Nance v. Ward, 597 U.S. 159 (2022) (same).[8]

    (d) Challenges to Violations of Miranda. In Vega v. Tekoh, 597 U.S. 134 (2022), the Court held, 6–3, that "except in unusual circumstances, the 'exclusion of unwarned statements' should be 'a complete and sufficient remedy'" to any violation of Miranda v. Arizona, 384 U.S. 436 (1966). Thus, the Court held that no § 1983 claim could proceed based upon the introduction at trial of a confession extracted in violation of Miranda, even

---

    [7]   Is Justice Scalia's point undermined by the fact that a habeas court upholding a petitioner's claim may issue a conditional writ ordering the petitioner released unless a new proceeding (*e.g.*, a new trial or sentencing proceeding) is conducted? Perhaps not, since a federal court would probably lack authority to require release of the petitioner unless the constitutional defect is remedied.

    [8]   Nance held that a challenge to a particular method of execution (in that case, lethal injection) could proceed in § 1983 even though (unlike in Nelson and Hill) state law did not authorize any alternative method. This followed because the state remained free to amend its law to provide for an alternative means of carrying out the execution. Focusing on state law as it existed at the time, Justice Barrett dissented for four Justices and argued that the § 1983 action effectively sought to overturn a death sentence and therefore should proceed in habeas.

where the jury acquitted. It was of no moment that there was no conviction the § 1983 claim could call into question; in the Court's view, Heck's concern for conflicting litigation still applied and counseled pause. Any other rule would "requir[e] the federal court entertaining the § 1983 claim to pass judgment on legal and factual issues already settled in state court."

Writing for herself and Justices Breyer and Sotomayor, Justice Kagan dissented. She countered that the Court's reading of Miranda ignored Dickerson v. United States, 530 U.S. 428 (2000), which held "in no uncertain terms that Miranda is a 'constitutional rule.' " With that rule, Justice Kagan wrote, comes the "corresponding right" to exclusion of any confession obtained in violation of Miranda. Putting those things together, the dissent argued that "only one conclusion can follow—that Miranda's protections are a 'right[ ]' 'secured by the Constitution' " within the meaning of § 1983.

Given the jury's acquittal in the earlier prosecution, Vega v. Tekoh arguably extends the reach of Heck, while correspondingly cutting back the scope of § 1983. Are there other situations in which the Court might adopt the same approach in light of the potential for a § 1983 action to call upon a federal court to revisit legal and factual determinations reached in an earlier state court proceeding?

(e) Challenges to Conditions of Confinement. The Supreme Court has not resolved definitively whether challenges to conditions of confinement are appropriately brought via § 1983 or habeas. Preiser, however, suggested the former. See Preiser v. Rodriguez, 411 U.S. 475, 499, 500 (1973) (positing that generally the "proper remedy for a state prisoner who is making a constitutional challenge to the conditions of his prison life, but not to the fact or length of his custody" is an action under 42 U.S.C. § 1983, while leaving open "the appropriate limits of habeas corpus as an alternative remedy to a proper action under § 1983"); cf. Ziglar v. Abbasi, 582 U.S. 120, 144–45 (2017) (observing that the Court has "left open the question whether [parties] might be able to challenge their confinement conditions via a petition for a writ of habeas corpus").[9] The lower courts are divided on the question. See, e.g., Aamer v. Obama, 742 F.3d 1023 (D.C.Cir.2014) (noting that circuit precedent "establishes that one in custody may challenge the conditions of his confinement in a petition for habeas corpus," while recognizing lower courts are split in the issue). The matter took on new importance in the context of the global COVID-19 pandemic during which petitioners challenged prison and immigration detention conditions via habeas, sometimes with success.

---

[9]   Abbasi involved a Bivens lawsuit for damages brought against federal officials by individuals detained as part of the investigations into the 9/11 attacks. Writing for a 4–2 majority, Justice Kennedy held the plaintiffs could not proceed with their Bivens claims alleging abusive detention conditions, in part because other avenues of relief were available to them. "To address" their conditions of confinement, Justice Kennedy posited, "detainees may seek injunctive relief," but he left open what the appropriate avenue for such relief might be. The Court nonetheless held out "the habeas remedy" as "a faster and more direct route to relief than a suit for money damages" in such cases. In dissent, Justice Breyer highlighted that "[n]either a prospective injunction nor a writ of habeas corpus * * * will normally provide plaintiffs with redress for harms they have *already* suffered" and questioned the ability of incarcerated persons denied "access to most forms of communication with the outside world" (as the plaintiffs alleged they were) to pursue habeas proceedings while detained. Given the custody requirement for habeas jurisdiction, how effective would a habeas remedy be under the circumstances presented in cases like Abbasi?

See, *e.g.*, Hope v. Warden, 972 F.3d 310, 325 (3d Cir.2020) (petitioners' challenge to the constitutionality of their conditions of confinement during the pandemic was cognizable in habeas where they sought the remedy of outright release). Most recently, in Nance v. Ward, 597 U.S. 159 (2022), the Court described "the classic prisoner § 1983 suit" as "one challenging prison conditions—say, overcrowding or inadequate medical care . . . because [such suits] attack not the validity of a conviction or sentence, but only a way of implementing the sentence."

INDEX

References are to Pages